# DIRECTORY OF AMERICAN FIRMS OPERATING IN FOREIGN COUNTRIES

16th Edition

## VOLUME 2

Alphabetical Listing of American Corporations with Foreign Operations by Country (continued)

## El Salvador to Mauritius

Pages: 1383-2724

**UNIWORLD BUSINESS PUBLICATIONS, INC.**
257 Central Park West, Suite 10A
New York, NY 10024-4110
Tel: (212) 496-2448
Fax: (212) 769-0413
uniworldbp@aol.com
www.uniworldbp.com

| First Edition | 1954 |
| Second Edition | 1957 |
| Third Edition | 1959 |
| Fourth Edition | 1961 |
| Fifth Edition | 1964 |
| Sixth Edition | 1966 |
| Seventh Edition | 1969 |
| Eighth Edition | 1975 |
| Ninth Edition | 1979 |
| Tenth Edition | 1984 |
| Eleventh Edition | 1987 |
| Twelfth Edition | 1991 |
| Thirteenth Edition | 1994 |
| Fourteenth Edition | 1996 |
| Fifteenth Edition | 1999 |
| Sixteenth Edition | 2001 |

Copyright © 2001 by
Uniworld Business Publications, Inc.
257 Central Park West
New York, New York 10024
uniworldbp@aol.com
www.uniworldbp.com
ISBN: 0-8360-0045-5

Printed in the United States of America

# INTRODUCTION

**S**ince it was first published in 1955, *Directory of American Firms Operating in Foreign Countries* has been an authoritative source of information on American firms, which have branches, subsidiaries, or affiliates outside the United States. Designed to aid anyone interested in American business activities abroad, it is the only reference work of its kind. The directory has been used by public, university, business, government and special libraries, banks, accounting, brokerage and investment firms, manufacturers, transportation companies, advertising and personnel agencies, researchers, embassies and many governmental agencies dealing with commerce, trade and foreign relations.

The 16th edition contains 2,600 U.S. firms with nearly 35,000 branches, subsidiaries and affiliates in 190 countries.

## The Directory consists of three volumes

**Volume 1** - **Part One**: lists, in alphabetical order, American firms that have operations abroad. Each entry contains the company's U.S. address, telephone/fax, and principal product/service, and lists the foreign countries in which it has a branch, subsidiary, or affiliate. Some key personnel are noted, when provided: Chief Executive Officer (CEO), International Operations or Foreign Operations Officer (IO), and Human Resources Director (HR). These titles are meant to be generic and are assigned to the names given to us as the Chief Executive, the person in charge of International Operations and the senior Human Resources officer. Also the web site address, annual revenue and number of employees are included, when available.

**Volume 1** - **Part Two,** and **Volumes 2** and **3:** contain listings by country from Albania to Zimbabwe of the American firms' foreign operations. Each country listing includes, alphabetically, the name of the U.S. parent firm, address, telephone/fax, web site address, principal product/service, and the name and address of its branch, subsidiary, or affiliates in that country.

## U.S. Direct Investment Abroad

The overseas companies in this specialized listing are those in which American Firms have a substantial direct capital investment and which have been identified by the parent as a wholly or partially owned subsidiary, affiliate or branch. Franchises, representatives and non-commercial enterprises or institutions, such as hospitals, schools, etc., financed or operated by American philanthropic or religious organizations, are not included.

U.S. direct dollar investment in foreign countries has continued to increase by 12% for 1999, down from the 16% increase reported in 1998. The number of U.S. companies with foreign operations captured by our research has increased nearly 10% to over 2,600; however, the number of foreign subsidiaries, branches and affiliates of those U.S. companies has grown from 18,000 in our 14th edition (1996) to nearly 35,000 in this edition. These data and our empirical experience indicate significant consolidation, through merger and acquisition, mirroring the trend domestically.

### U.S. Direct Investment Abroad - Top Countries
### (Historical-cost basis in $ Billions)
### U.S. Bureau of Economic Analysis, 1999

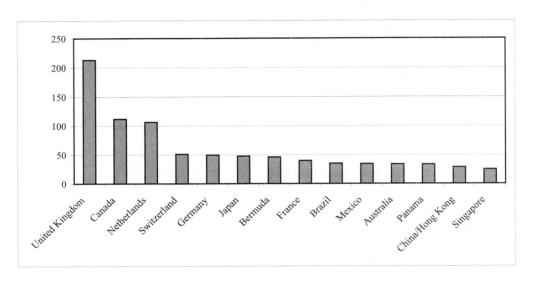

### U.S. Direct Investment Abroad - by Region
### (Historical-cost basis in $ Billions)
### U.S. Bureau of Economic Analysis, 1999

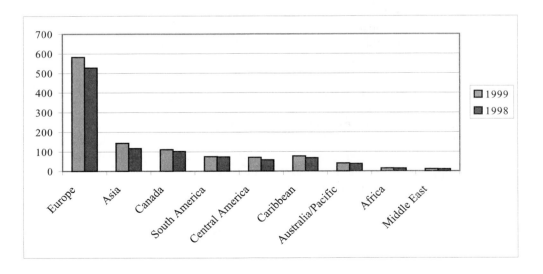

## Source and Accuracy of Listings

In preparing the 2001 - 16th edition, 500 new companies have been added, and over 300 firms which were dissolved, no longer maintain operations abroad or were acquired, have been deleted. The primary sources of information were questionnaires completed by the U.S. parent company, annual reports and other publications. Direct telephone and fax contact was used extensively for verification and clarification. Each firm in the previous edition was sent an announcement of the new revised edition, along with a printout of its former entry, and asked to provide current data. It was stated that if we did not receive a response from a firm, and there was no evidence that it had gone out of business, the previous entry would be carried forward to this edition.

The aim of this listing is to provide accurate, up-to-date listings. However, the Editor and Publisher cannot guarantee that the information received from a company or other source as the basis for an entry is correct. In addition, the designations and listings are not to be considered definitive as to legal status or the relationship between the American and the foreign firms.

As extensive as this compilation may be it does not claim to be all-inclusive. It contains only what has been disclosed to us. Also in a directory of this scope some inaccuracies are inevitable. It would be appreciated if the reader noting such would inform us so corrections can be made in future editions.

## Acknowledgments

Our sincere appreciation is extended to all company representatives who cooperated so generously in providing information for this directory, and to everyone who assisted in its preparation: Associate Editor Lynn Sherwood, Associate Publisher Debra Lipian, and Book Designer David Bornstein.

Barbara D. Fiorito, Editor
**Uniworld Business Publications, Inc**.

# Company Designations

| Abbreviation | Term | Country |
|---|---|---|
| AB | Aktiebolag | Sweden |
| AG | Aktiengesellschaft | Austria, Germany, Switzerland |
| AS | Anonim Sirketi | Turkey |
| A/S | Aktieselskab | Denmark |
| | Aksjeselskap | Norway |
| BV | Beslotene Vennootschap | Netherlands |
| CA | Compania Anonima | Venezuela |
| CIE | Compagnie | Belgium, France |
| CO/Co. | Company | Canada, England, U.S. |
| CORP/Corp. | Corporation | England, U.S. |
| GmbH | Gesellschaft mit beschrankter Haftung | Austria, Germany |
| INC/Inc. | Incorporated | Canada, England, U.S. |
| KG | Kommanditgesellschaft | Germany |
| KK | Kabushiki Kaisha | Japan |
| LTD/Ltd. | Limited | Canada, England, U.S. |
| MIJ | Maatschappij | Netherlands |
| NV | Naamloze Vennoostchap | Belgium, Netherlands |
| OY | Osakeyhtio | Finland |
| P/L | Proprietary Limited | Australia |
| PLC | Public Limited Company | England, Scotland |
| PT | Perusahaan Terbatas | Indonesia |
| SA | Sociedad Anonima | Argentina, Brazil, Colombia, Spain, Venezuela |
| | Societe Anonyme | Belgium, France, Switzerland |
| SARL | Societe Anonoyme a Responsabilite Limitee | Belgium, France, Switzerland |
| SPA | Societa per Azioni | Italy |
| Sp z o.o | Spolka Odpowiedzialnoscia | Poland |
| SPRL | Societe de Personnes a Responsabilite Limitee | Belgium |
| SRL | Societa a Responsabilita Limitata | Italy |

# Abbreviations Used in This Report

| | | | |
|---|---|---|---|
| A/C | Air Conditioning | EVP | Executive Vice President |
| Access | Accessories | Exch | Exchange |
| Adv | Advertising | Exec | Executive |
| Affil | Affiliate(d) | Exp | Export(er) |
| Agcy | Agent/Agency | Explor | Exploration |
| Agric | Agriculture | Fax | Facsimile |
| Apt | Apartment | Fin | Financial/Finance |
| Arch | Architect(ural) | Fl | Floor |
| Assur | Assurance | FO | Foreign Operation(s) Officer |
| Auto | Automotive | For | Foreign |
| Aux | Auxiliary | Frt | Freight |
| Av/Ave | Avenida/Avenue | Furn | Furniture |
| Bil | Billion | Fwdg | Forwarding |
| Bldg | Building | Gds | Goods |
| Blvd | Boulevard | Gen | General |
| Bus | Business | Hdqtrs/HQ | Headquarters |
| CEO | Chief Executive Officer | Hdwe | Hardware |
| Chem | Chemical | Hwy | Highway |
| Chmn | Chairman | Hos | Hospital |
| Cir | Circulation | HR | Human Resources Officer |
| Co | Company | Hydr | Hydraulic(s) |
| Col | Colonia | Imp | Import(er) |
| Com | Components | Inc | Incorporated |
| Coml | Commercial | Ind | Industrial/Industry |
| Commun | Communications | Inf | Information |
| Conslt | Consultant/Consulting | Ins | Insurance |
| Constr | Construction | Inspc | Inspect(ion) |
| Corp | Corporate/Corporation | Instru | Instrument |
| Cust | Customer | Intl | International |
| Dept | Department | Invest | Investment |
| Devel | Development | JV | Joint Venture |
| Diag | Diagnostic | Lab | Laboratory |
| Dir. | Director | Liq | Liquid |
| Dist | District | Ltd | Limited |
| Distr | Distributor/Distribution | Mach | Machine(ry) |
| Div | Division | Maint | Maintenance |
| Divers | Diversified | Mat | Material |
| Dom | Domestic | Mdse | Merchandise |
| Econ | Economics | Mdsng | Merchandising |
| Educ | Education | Meas | Measurement |
| Elec | Electric(al) | Med | Medical |
| Electr | Electronic(s) | Mfg | Manufacturing |
| Emp | Employee(s) | Mfr | Manufacture(r) |
| Eng | Engineer(ing) | Mgmt | Management |
| Envi | Environmental | Mgn | Managing |
| Equip | Equipment | Mgr. | Manager |

| | | | | |
|---|---|---|---|---|
| Mil | Million | Reins | Reinsurance |
| Mkt | Market | Rel | Relations |
| Mktg | Marketing | Rep | Representative |
| Mng Dir | Managing Director | Ret | Retail(er) |
| Mng Ptrn | Managing Partner | Rfg | Refining |
| Mng. | Managing | Ry | Railway |
| Nat | Natural | Sci | Scientific |
| NE | Northeast | SE | Southeast |
| No/N | North | Serv | Service(s) |
| NW | Northwest | So/S | South |
| Oper | Operation | Spec | Special(ty)/Specialized |
| Orgn | Organization(al) | St/Str | Street |
| Pass | Passenger | Sta | Station |
| Petrol | Petroleum | Ste | Suite |
| Pharm | Pharmaceutical(s) | Str | Strasse |
| Plt | Plant | Sub | Subsidiary |
| Prdt | Product(s) | Super | Supervision |
| Pres | President | Svce | Service(s) |
| Prin | Principal | SVP | Senior Vice President |
| Print | Printing | SW | Southwest |
| Proc | Process(ing) | Sys | System |
| Prod | Production | Tech | Technical/Technology |
| Prog | Programming | Tel | Telephone |
| Pte/Prt. | Private | Telecom | Telecommunications |
| Ptnr | Partner | Temp | Temperature |
| Pty | Proprietary | Trans | Transmission |
| Pub | Publisher/Publishing | Transp | Transport(ation) |
| R&D | Research & Development | TV | Television |
| Rd | Road | VP | Vice President |
| Recre | Recreation(al) | Whl | Wholesale(r) |
| Refrig | Refrigeration | Whse | Warehouse |
| Reg | Regional | | |

## Notes on Alphabetizing

Alphabetizing in this directory is by computer sort which places numerals before letters; and, among names, places special characters before numbers and letters in the following order: blanks, ampersands, plus signs, dashes, periods and slashes. For example, 3Z Co. precedes A Z Co., which precedes, in the following order, A&Z Co., A+Z Co., A-Z Co., AZ Co., A/Z Co., A1Z Co. and AZ Co.

Names such as The Jones Corp., Charles Jones Inc., and L.M. Jones & Co., are alphabetized conventionally: all will be found under J. Names that consist of initials only (e.g., LFM Co.) are in strict alphabetical order : Lewis., LFM Co., Lintz Inc.

While the custom in most countries is to place company designations (Co., Inc., etc.) at the end of the firm's name, that is not always the case. For example, Finland's "Oy" and Sweden's "AB" sometimes appear at the end and sometimes at the beginning of the company's name; in this directory they have been disregarded in alphabetizing. The reader is advised to check more than one location when looking for a firm whose listing might be affected by the company designation.

# Table of Contents – Volume 2

Alphabetical Listing of American Corporations with Foreign Operations by Country (continued):

**Publisher's Notes**...*Related Publications*

# El Salvador

## 3M

3M Center, St. Paul, MN, 55144-1000

Tel: (651) 733-1110      Fax: (651) 733-9973      www.mmm.com

*Mfr. diversified products for industry, health care, imaging, communications, transport, safety, consumer, etc.*

**3M El Salvador SA de CV,  Calle Chaporrastique 11, Urban. Industrial Santa Elena, Antiguo Cuzcatlan, La Liberdad El Salvador**

Tel: 503-278-3344   Fax: 503-278-3313

## AIR EXPRESS INTERNATIONAL CORPORATION

120 Tokeneke Road, PO Box 1231, Darien, CT, 06820

Tel: (203) 655-7900      Fax: (203) 655-5779      www.aeilogistics.com

*International air freight forwarder.*

**AEI de El Salvador, c/o Comar El Salvador, Calle y Col. Roma No. 240, San Salvador, El Salvador**
Tel: 503-223-6202   Fax: 503-223-0099

## AMERICAN & EFIRD, INC.

PO Box 507, Mt. Holly, NC, 28120

Tel: (704) 827-4311      Fax: (704) 822-6054      www.amefird.com

*Mfr. industrial sewing thread for worldwide industrial and consumer markets.*

**Hilos A&E De El Salvador,  Edificio D Kilometro 36,Carretera Panamericana A Santa Ana, San Salvador El Salvador**

## AMERICAN INTERNATIONAL GROUP INC. (AIG)

70 Pine Street, New York, NY, 10270

Tel: (212) 770-7000      Fax: (212) 509-9705      www.aig.com

*Worldwide insurance and financial services.*

**AIG, S.A.,  Calle Loma Linda 265, Col. San Benito, San Salvador El Salvador**

## ANC RENTAL CORP.

110 Southeast Sixth St., Ft. Lauderdale, FL, 33301

Tel: (954) 769-7000      Fax: (954) 769-7000      www.ancrental.com

*Engaged in car rental services, including National Car Rental and Alamo Rent A Car.*

**National Car Rental,  Centro Profesional Edif. Mena 1, Centro de Gobierno, San Salvador, El Salvador**

## AON CORPORATION

123 North Wacker Drive, Chicago, IL, 60606

Tel: (312) 701-3000      Fax: (312) 701-3100      www.aon.com

*Insurance brokers worldwide; underwrites accident and health insurance, specialty and professional insurance; and provides risk management consultation.*

**AON Worldwide / Auditores de Riesgos Internacionales,  Calle La Reforma y Av., San Salvador, El Salvador**

Tel: 503-223-7475   Fax: 503-298-4126   Contact: Guillermo Rovera- Paloma

## APPLERA CORPORATION

761 Main Avenue, Norwalk, CT, 06859-0001

Tel: (203) 762-1000     Fax: (203) 762-6000     www.applera.com

*Leading supplier of systems for life science research and related applications.*

**Coresa S.A., Ave. Izalco, Bloque 6 No. 40, San Salvador, El Salvador**

## AVON PRODUCTS INC.

1345 Avenue of the Americas, New York, NY, 10105-0196

Tel: (212) 282-5000     Fax: (212) 282-6049     www.avon.com

*Mfr./distributor beauty and related products, fashion jewelry, gifts and collectibles.*

**Productos Avon S.A., 15-1/2 Carretera al Puerto de la Libertad, Departamento de la Liberlad, San Salvador El Salvador**

Tel: 503-288-9511    Fax: 503-288-3952    Contact: Maribel de Campos, Sales Mgr.

## AVX CORPORATION

PO Box 867, Myrtle Beach, SC, 29578

Tel: (843) 448-9411     Fax: (843) 448-7139     www.avxcorp.com

*Mfr. multilayer ceramic capacitors.*

**AVX Industries, Apdto. Postal 1, Ilopango Calle Cajutepoque 4-2, Zona Franca, San Bartole San Salvador, El Salvador**

## BATES WORLDWIDE INC.

405 Lexington Ave., New York, NY, 10174

Tel: (212) 297-7000     Fax: (212) 986-0270     www.batesww.com

*Advertising, marketing, public relations and media consulting.*

**ANLE Publicidad, Corresponsal Bates, Av. La Capilla #331, Col. San Benito, El Salvador**

Tel: 503-289-1045    Fax: 503-289-1712    Contact: Luis Sanchez, Dir.

## LOUIS BERGER INTERNATIONAL INC.

100 Halsted Street, East Orange, NJ, 07019

Tel: (201) 678-1960     Fax: (201) 672-4284     www.louisberger.com

*Consulting engineers, engaged in architecture, environmental and advisory services.*

**Louis Berger International Inc., Av. 81 Norte y 9A, Calle Poniente Col. Escalon, San Salvador, El Salvador**

Tel: 503-263-3025    Fax: 503-263-3663

## BEST WESTERN INTERNATIONAL

6201 North 24th Place, Phoenix, AZ, 85106

Tel: (602) 957-4200     Fax: (602) 957-5740     www.bestwestern.com

*International hotel chain.*

**BW Siesta, Blvd. Los Proceres, San Salvador 01217, El Salvador**

Tel: 503-243-0377

## BRISTOL-MYERS SQUIBB COMPANY

345 Park Ave., New York, NY, 10154-0037

Tel: (212) 546-4000     Fax: (212) 546-4020     www.bms.com

*Pharmaceutical and food preparations, medical and surgical instruments.*

**Bristol-Myers Squibb, Ave. Olimpica 3765, Col. Escalon, San Salvador, El Salvador**

**Compania Bristol-Myers de Centro America, Col. Roma, Blvd Venezuela, Edif. Industrias, San Salvador, El Salvador**

## LEO BURNETT, DIV. B-COM 3 GROUP

35 West Wacker Drive, Chicago, IL, 60601

Tel: (312) 220-5959     Fax: (312) 220-6533     www.bcom3group.com

*Engaged in advertising, marketing, media buying and planning, and public relations.*

**Publicidad Diaz, S.A. de C.V., 67 Avenida Norte #120, Colonia Escalon, San Salvador, El Salvador**

## CITIGROUP, INC.

153 East 53rd Street, New York, NY, 10043

Tel: (212) 559-1000    Fax: (212) 559-3646    www.citigroup.com

*Provides insurance and financial services worldwide.*

**Citibank N.A., Alameda Dr. Manuel Enrique Araujo 3530, Km. 4 Edif. B, San Salvador, El Salvador**

Tel: 503-245-3011   Fax: 503-245-1842   Contact: Steven J. Puig

## THE COASTAL CORPORATION

Nine Greenway Plaza, Houston, TX, 77046-0995

Tel: (713) 877-1400    Fax: (713) 877-6752    www.coastalcorp.com

*Oil refining, natural gas, related services; independent power production.*

**Distribuidora Coastal, S.A. de C.V., San Salvador, El Salvador**

## COLGATE-PALMOLIVE COMPANY

300 Park Ave., New York, NY, 10022

Tel: (212) 310-2000    Fax: (212) 310-2919    www.colgate.com

*Mfr. pharmaceuticals, cosmetics, toiletries and detergents.*

**Colgate Palmolive (Central America) Inc., Km 9.5 Carretera Al Puerto la Libertad, San Salvador, El Salvador**

## COMMERCE GROUP CORPORATION

6001 N. 91st Street, Milwaukee, WI, 53225-1795

Tel: (414) 462-5310    Fax: (414) 462-5312    www.commercegroupcorp.com

*Gold mining.*

**Commerce/Sanseb Joint Venture, 6 Calle Poniente 208, San Miguel, El Salvador**

Tel: 503-660-1671   Fax: 503-661-6568   Contact: Luis A. Limay, Mgr.   Emp: 320

## CONTINENTAL AIRLINES INC.

2929 Allen Parkway, Ste. 2010, Houston, TX, 77019

Tel: (281) 834-5000    Fax: (281) 520-6329    www.continental.com

*International airline carrier.*

**Continental Airlines Inc., San Salvador, El Salvador**

## D'ARCY MASIUS BENTON & BOWLES INC. (DMB&B)

1675 Broadway, New York, NY, 10019

Tel: (212) 468-3622    Fax: (212) 468-2987    www.dmbb.com

*Full service international advertising and communications group.*

**Cronos/DMB&B, 75 Av. Norte 620, Col. Escalon, San Salvador, El Salvador**

Tel: 503-223-139   Fax: 503-279-2840

## DDB NEEDHAM WORLDWIDE INC.

437 Madison Ave., New York, NY, 10022

Tel: (212) 415-2000    Fax: (212) 415-3417    www.ddbn.com

*Advertising agency.*

**RCM DDB Needham, San Salvador, El Salvador**

## DHL WORLDWIDE EXPRESS

50 California Avenue, San Francisco, CA, 94111

Tel: (415) 677-6100    Fax: (415) 824-9700    www.dhl.com

*Worldwide air express carrier.*

**DHL Worldwide Express, 47 Av. Norte #104, San Salvador, El Salvador**

Tel: 503-2-790411

## DIONEX CORPORATION

1228 Titan Way, PO Box 3603, Sunnyvale, CA, 94086-3603

Tel: (408) 737-0700     Fax: (408) 730-9403     www.dionex.com

*Develop/mfr./market chromatography systems and related products.*

**Analitica Salvadorena, S.A. de C.V., Avenida Washington. No. 104, Colonia Libertad San Salvador, El Salvador**

## DOVER CORPORATION

280 Park Ave., New York, NY, 10017-1292

Tel: (212) 922-1640     Fax: (212) 922-1656     www.dovercorporation.com

*Holding company for varied industries; assembly and testing equipment, oil-well gear and other industrial products.*

**Distribuidora Yale, S.A. De C.V., 39 Av. Sur #540, Col. Flor Blanca, San Salvador, El Salvador**

Tel: 503-222-4817    Fax: 503-222-4850

## THE DOW CHEMICAL COMPANY

2030 Dow Center, Midland, MI, 48674

Tel: (517) 636-1000     Fax: (517) 636-3228     www.dow.com

*Mfr. chemicals, plastics, pharmaceuticals, agricultural products, consumer products.*

**Laboratorios Life de El Salvador SA, San Salvador, El Salvador**

## EAGLE GLOBAL LOGISTICS (EGL)

15350 Vickery Drive, Houston, TX, 77032

Tel: (281) 618-3100     Fax: (281) 618-3100     www.eaglegl.com

*Ocean/air freight forwarding, customs brokerage, packing and wholesale, logistics management and insurance.*

**Agencia Internacional de Carga Morales, 3A. Calle Oriente #226, Edif. Kury, San Salvador, El Salvador**

Tel: 503-2-221-415    Fax: 503-2-790-363

## ERNST & YOUNG, LLP

787 Seventh Ave., New York, NY, 10019

Tel: (212) 773-3000     Fax: (212) 773-6350     www.eyi.com

*Accounting and audit, tax and management consulting services.*

**Ernst & Young International, Attn: El Salvador Latin America Office, 200 S. Biscayne Blvd. #3900, Miami FL 33131**

Tel: 503-2-350-1459    Fax: 503-2-350-1301    Contact: Jaime Aycinena

## EXXON MOBIL CORPORATION

5959 Las Colinas Blvd., Irving, TX, 75039-2298

Tel: (972) 444-1000     Fax: (972) 444-1882     www.exxon.com

*Petroleum exploration, production, refining; mfr. petroleum and chemicals products; coal and minerals.*

**Exxon Mobil, Inc., San Salvador, El Salvador**

## FRITZ COMPANIES, INC.

706 Mission Street, Ste. 900, San Francisco, CA, 94103

Tel: (415) 904-8360     Fax: (415) 904-8661     www.fritz.com

*Integrated transportation, sourcing, distribution and customs brokerage services.*

**Fritz Companies Inc., San Salvador, El Salvador**

## H.B. FULLER COMPANY

1200 Willow Lake Blvd., Vadnais Heights, MN, 55110

Tel: (651) 236-5900        Fax: (651) 236-5898        www.hbfuller.com

*Mfr./distributor adhesives, sealants, coatings, paints, waxes, sanitation chemicals.*

**H.B. Fuller El Salvador, S.A. de C.V.,  Parque Industrial de Desarrollo, Km. 7 1/2 Antigua Carretera Panamericana, Soyapango, 1213 San Salvador, El Salvador**

Tel: 503-294-1933  Fax: 503-294-1910

**Kativo Industrial,  23 Ave. Sur Entre 12 y 14 Calle Ponientel, 1389 San Salvador, El Salvador**

Tel: 503-221-1466   Fax: 503-222-3263

## GARAN, INC.

350 Fifth Ave, New York, NY, 10118

Tel: (212) 563-2000        Fax: (212) 971-2250

*Designs, manufactures and markets apparel for men, women and children.*

**Garan de El Salvador,  San Salvador, El Salvador**

## THE GILLETTE COMPANY

Prudential Tower Building, Boston, MA, 02199

Tel: (617) 421-7000        Fax: (617) 421-7123        www.gillette.com

*Develop/mfr. personal care/use products: blades and razors, toiletries, cosmetics, stationery.*

**Gillette de El Salvador SA,  San Salvador, El Salvador**

## GRANT THORNTON INTERNATIONAL

800 One Prudential Plaza, 130 E. Randolph Drive, Chicago, IL, 60601-6050

Tel: (312) 856-0001        Fax: (312) 616-7052        www.grantthornton.com

*Accounting, audit, tax and management consulting services.*

**Grant Thornton, Castellanos Campos & Cia,  71 Av. Norte 346 Colonia Escalon, San Salvador El Salvador**

Contact: Jose Atilio Campos

## GREY GLOBAL GROUP

777 Third Ave., New York, NY, 10017

Tel: (212) 546-2000        Fax: (212) 546-1495        www.grey.com

*International advertising agency.*

**J.M. Creativos,  San Salvador, El Salvador**

## GRIFFITH LABORATORIES INC.

One Griffith Center, Alsip, IL, 60658

Tel: (708) 371-0900        Fax: (708) 597-3294        www.griffithlabs.com

*Mfr. industrial food ingredients and equipment.*

**Griffith Labs Inc.,  San Salvador, El Salvador**

Tel: 503-223-7575   Fax: 503-223-0398

## HOCKMAN-LEWIS LTD.

200 Executive Drive, Ste. 320, West Orange, NJ, 07052

Tel: (973) 325-3838        Fax: (973) 325-7974        www.hockman-lewis.com

*Export management.*

**Equigas de El Salvador SA,  Av. Altamira (Autopista Sur), Jardines de Montserrat, San Salvador, El Salvador**

## INTER-CONTINENTAL HOTELS

3 Ravina Drive, Suite 2900, Atlanta, GA, 30346-2149

Tel: (770) 604-2000       Fax: (770) 604-5403       www.interconti.com

*Worldwide hotel and resort accommodations.*

**Camino Real Inter-Continental San Salvador, Blvd. de Los Heroes & Ave. Sisimiles, San Salvador, El Salvador**

Tel: 503-260-1333   Fax: 503-260-5660

## J. WALTER THOMPSON COMPANY

466 Lexington Ave., New York, NY, 10017

Tel: (212) 210-7000       Fax: (212) 210-6944       www.jwt.com

*International advertising and marketing services.*

**APCU-Thompson, San Salvador, El Salvador**

## KENNAMETAL INC.

State Rte. 981, Latrobe, PA, 15650

Tel: (724) 539-5000       Fax: (724) 539-4710       www.kennametal.com

*Tools, hard carbide and tungsten alloys for metalworking industry.*

**Prometca, S.A. de C.V., 41 Av. Sur y Calle Colon No. 2143, Col. 3 de Mayo., San Salvador, El Salvador**

Tel: 503-245-4163   Fax: 503-223-3219

## KIMBERLY-CLARK CORPORATION

351 Phelps Drive, Irving, TX, 75038

Tel: (972) 281-1200       Fax: (972) 281-1435       www.kimberly-clark.com

*Mfr./sales/distribution of consumer tissue, household and personal care products.*

**Kimberly-Clark de Centro America SA, Sitio del Niño, El Salvador**

## KPMG INTERNATIONAL LLP

345 Park Avenue, New York, NY, 10022

Tel: (201) 307-7000       Fax: (201) 930-8617       www.kpmg.com

*Accounting and audit, tax and management consulting services.*

**KPMG Peat Marwick, Av. Olimpica 3324 y 3330, San Salvador, El Salvador**

Tel: 503-224-1351   Fax: 503-298-3354   Contact: Hector R. Figueroa, Sr. Ptnr.

## LANIER WORLDWIDE, INC.

2300 Parklake Drive, N.E., Atlanta, GA, 30345

Tel: (770) 496-9500       Fax: (770) 938-1020       www.lanier.com

*Specialize in digital copiers and multi-functional systems.*

**Lanier de El Salvador, S.A., Calle El Progreso No. 3114, Col. Avila, San Salvador, El Salvador**

Tel: 503-298-0944   Fax: 503-2452-429

## LEUCADIA NATIONAL CORPORATION

315 Park Ave. South, New York, NY, 10010

Tel: (212) 460-1900       Fax: (212) 598-4869

*Holding company: real estate, banking, insurance, equipment leasing, mfr. plastics, cable, sinks and cabinets.*

**Cia. de Alumbrado Electrico de San Salvador SA, Apartado 186, San Salvador, El Salvador**

## LOWE LINTAS & PARTNERS WORLDWIDE

One Dag Hammarskjold Plaza, New York, NY, 10017

Tel: (212) 605-8000       Fax: (212) 605-4705       www.interpublic.com

*Full-service, integrated marketing communications company/advertising agency.*

**Publicidad Ammirati Puris Lintas, Blvd. Del Hipodromo No. 42, Col. San Benito, San Salvador, El Salvador**

Tel: 503-243-2222   Fax: 5-3-243-3363   Contact: Juan Federico Salaverria

## MARRIOTT INTERNATIONAL INC.

10400 Fernwood Rd., Bethesda, MD, 20817

Tel: (301) 380-3000     Fax: (301) 380-5181     www.marriott.com

*Hotel services.*

**San Salvador Marriott Hotel, San Salvador , El Salvador**

Tel: 503-298-1433

## MARSH & McLENNAN COS INC.

1166 Ave. of the Americas, New York, NY, 10036-2774

Tel: (212) 345-5000     Fax: (212) 345-4808     www.marshmac.com

*Insurance agents/brokers, pension and investment management consulting services.*

**Consultores de Seguros S.A., Condominio Centro Roosevelt, Edif. C #34 - 55 A.S. #221 y Alameda Roosevelt, San Salvador, El Salvador**

Tel: 503-246-691   Fax: 503-241-247

**Servicios Y Asesorias S.A., 57 Av. Norte #201, San Salvador, El Salvador**

Tel: 503-260-5521   Fax: 503-260-5523   Contact: Carlos Iraheta

## McCANN-ERICKSON WORLDGROUP

750 Third Ave., New York, NY, 10017

Tel: (212) 984-3644     Fax: (212) 984-2629     www.mccann.com

*International advertising and marketing services.*

**McCann-Erickson Centroamericana (El Salvador) SA, Metrocentro Nivel 2, Aptdo. 1170, San Salvador, El Salvador**

## McCORMICK & COMPANY, INC.

18 Loveton Circle, Sparks, MD, 21152-6000

Tel: (410) 771-7301     Fax: (410) 527-8289     www.mccormick.com

*Manufactures, markets and distributes spices, seasonings, flavours and other specialty food products.*

**McCormick de Centro America, S.A. de C.V., Apartado Postal (01), 189 San Salvador, El Salvador**

Tel: 503-243-0122   Fax: 503-243-0735

## MYERS INTERNATIONAL INC.

1293 South Main Street, Akron, OH, 44301

Tel: (330) 253-5592     Fax: (330) 253-0035     www.myerstiresupply.com

*Mfr. tire retreading and maintenance equipment and supplies.*

**Myers De El Salvador, 4 ta Calle Poniente 2212, Colonia Flor Blanca, San Salvador, El Salvador**

Tel: 503-260-7636   Fax: 503-260-7176

## OGILVY PUBLIC RELATIONS WORLDWIDE

909 Third Ave., New York, NY, 10022

Tel: (212) 880-5201     Fax: (212) 697-8250     www.ogilvypr.com

*Engaged in public relations and communications.*

**Ogilvy Public Relations Worldwide, San Salvador, El Salvador**

## PAN-AMERICAN LIFE INSURANCE COMPANY

Pan American Life Center, PO Box 60219, New Orleans, LA, 70130-0219

Tel: (504) 566-1300     Fax: (504) 566-3600     www.palic.com

*Insurance services.*

**Pan-American Life Insurance Co., Condominio Torre Roble piso 10, Metrocentro, San Salvador, El Salvador**

Tel: 503-2-60-8899   Fax: 503-2-60-3340   Contact: Mario Hector Salazar   Emp: 72

## PERKIN ELMER, INC.

45 William Street, Wellesley, MA, 02481

Tel: (781) 237-5100      Fax: (781) 431-4255      www.perkinelmer.com

*Mfr. equipment and devices to detect explosives and bombs on airline carriers.*

**Coresa, Residencial San Luis, Av. Lincoln Block 6 #40, San Salvador, El Salvador**

## PHELPS DODGE CORPORATION

2600 North Central Ave., Phoenix, AZ, 85004-3089

Tel: (602) 234-8100      Fax: (602) 234-8337      www.phelpsdodge.com

*Copper, minerals, metals and special engineered products for transportation and electrical markets.*

**Conductores Electricos de Centro America SA (CONELCA), Aptdo. 283, San Salvador, El Salvador**

## PPL GLOBAL

11350 Random Hills Rd., Ste. 400, Fairfax, VA, 22030

Tel: (703) 293-2600      Fax: (703) 293-2659      www.pplresources.com

*Gas and electric.*

**Distribuidora de Electricidad del Sur S.A., San Salvador, El Salvador**

## PRICEWATERHOUSECOOPERS LLP

1301 Ave. of the Americas, New York, NY, 10019

Tel: (212) 596-7000      Fax: (212) 259-1301      www.pwcglobal.com

*Accounting and auditing, tax and management, and human resource consulting services.*

**PriceWaterhouseCoopers, Ct. Prof. Presidente, Av. La Revolucion y Calle, Circunvalacion, AP 695 San Salvador El Salvador**

Tel: 503-279-0745    Fax: 503-279-0751

## PROCTER & GAMBLE COMPANY

One Procter & Gamble Plaza, Cincinnati, OH, 45202

Tel: (513) 983-1100      Fax: (513) 562-4500      www.pg.com

*Personal care, food, laundry, cleaning and industry products.*

**Procter & Gamble, 35 Av. Notre y Prolongacion Calle Arce, #131 Col. Flor Blanca, San Salvador, El Salvador**

## RENA WARE DISTRIBUTORS INC.

PO Box 97050, Redmond, WA, 98073-9750

Tel: (425) 881-6171      Fax: (425) 882-7500      www.renaware.com

*Mfr. stainless steel cookware and water filtration products.*

**Distribuidores Rena Ware, S.A. de C.V., 1ra. Calle Poniente y 45 Avenida Norte, San Salvador, El Salvador**

## TEXACO INC.

2000 Westchester Ave., White Plains, NY, 10650

Tel: (914) 253-4000      Fax: (914) 253-7753      www.texaco.com

*Exploration/marketing crude oil, mfr. petro chemicals and products.*

**Texaco El Salvador, San Salvador, El Salvador**

## TRUE NORTH COMMUNICATIONS INC.

101 East Erie Street, Chicago, IL, 60611

Tel: (312) 425-6500      Fax: (312) 425-5010      www.truenorth.com

*Holding company, advertising agency.*

**Foote, Cone & Belding, 81 Av. Sur No. 206, Col. Escalon, San Salvador, El Salvador**

## UNITED AIRLINES INC.

1200 E. Algonquin Rd., Chicago, IL, 60007

Tel: (847) 700-4000     Fax: (847) 700-4081     www.ual.com

*Air transportation, passenger and freight services.*

**United Airlines, San Salvador, El Salvador**

## UNITED PARCEL SERVICE, INC.

55 Glenlake Parkway, NE, Atlanta, GA, 30328

Tel: (404) 828-6000     Fax: (404) 828-6593     www.ups.com

*International package-delivery service.*

**UPS / Courier Internacional S.A., Calle El Progreso No. 3139, Col. Roma, San Salvador, El Salvador**

Tel: 503-279-0934   Fax: 503-279-0936

## WACKENHUT CORPORATION

4200 Wackenhut Dr., Ste. 100, Palm Beach Gardens, FL, 33410

Tel: (561) 622-5656     Fax: (561) 691-6736     www.wackenhut.com

*Security systems and services.*

**Wackenhut de El Salvador SA de CV, Calle Loma Linda 327, Col. San Benito, San Salvador, El Salvador**

Tel: 503-298-6285   Fax: 503-298-6592

## WENDY'S INTERNATIONAL, INC.

428 West Dublin Granville Roads, Dublin, OH, 43017-0256

Tel: (614) 764-3100     Fax: (614) 764-3459     www.wendysintl.com

*Fast food restaurant chain.*

**Wendy's International, San Salvador, El Salvador**

## XEROX CORPORATION

800 Long Ridge Road, PO Box 1600, Stamford, CT, 06904

Tel: (203) 968-3000     Fax: (203) 968-4312     www.xerox.com

*Mfr. document processing equipment, systems and supplies.*

**Xerox de El Salvador S.A., Final Blvd. Santa Elena Y, Urban. Santa Elena, Edif. Xerox, San Salvador El Salvador**

Tel: 503-278-8000   Fax: 503-278-8686

## YOUNG & RUBICAM INC.

285 Madison Ave., New York, NY, 10017

Tel: (212) 210-3000     Fax: (212) 370-3796     www.yr.com

*Advertising, public relations, direct marketing and sales promotion, corporate and product ID management.*

**Lemisimun Publicidad, San Salvador, El Salvador**

# England, U.K.

**24/7 MEDIA, INC.**

1250 Broadway, New York, NY, 10001-3701

Tel: (212) 231-7100     Fax: (212) 760-1774     www.247media.com

*Provides global online advertising, sponsorships, e-commerce and direct marketing solutions to advertisers and Web publishers.*

**24/7 Media UK Ltd.,  Egyptian House - 170-173 Picadilly, London W1J 9EJ, UK**

Tel: 44-207-355-3223

**3COM CORPORATION**

5400 Bayfront Plaza, Santa Clara, CA, 95052-8145

Tel: (408) 326-5000     Fax: (408) 326-5001     www.3com.com

*Develop/mfr. computer networking products and systems.*

**3Com UK Ltd.,  Eaton Court, Maylands Avenue, Hemel Hempstead, Hertfordshire HP2 7DF, UK**

**3D LABS INC., LTD.**

480 Potrero Avenue, Sunnyvale, CA, 94086

Tel: (408) 530-4700     Fax: (408) 530-4701     www.3dlabs.com

*Produces 3D graphics accelerators chips for the PC computer platform.*

**3D Labs Ltd.,  Meadlake Place, Thorpe Lea Rd., Egham Surrey TW20 8HE UK**

Tel: 44-178-447-0555   Fax: 44-178-447-0699

**3D/INTERNATIONAL INC.**

1900 West Loop South, Ste. 400, Houston, TX, 77027

Tel: (713) 871-7000     Fax: (713) 871-7456     www.3di.com

*Engaged in design, management and environmental services.*

**3D/I-London,  London, UK**

**3dfx INTERACTIVE, INC.**

4435 Fortran Drive, San Jose, CA, 95134

Tel: (408) 935-4400     Fax: (408) 262-8874     www.3dfx.com

*Engaged in microchip, graphics, images and animation.*

**3dfx Interactive UK,  Meridian House, 2-4 The Grove, Slough Berkshire SL1 1QP, UK**

Tel: 44-1753-502-800   Fax: 44-1753-502-890

**THE 3DO COMPANY**

100 Cardinal Way, Ste. 425, Redwood City, CA, 94063

Tel: (650) 385-3000     Fax: (650) 385-3184     www.3do.com

*Mfr. entertainment software.*

**3DO UK Ltd.,  72 Hammersmith Road, London W14 8TH, UK**

Tel: 44-207-761-9300

**3M**

3M Center, St. Paul, MN, 55144-1000

Tel: (651) 733-1110     Fax: (651) 733-9973     www.mmm.com

*Mfr. diversified products for industry, health care, imaging, communications, transport, safety, consumer, etc.*

**3M United Kingdom PLC,  3M House, Market Place, PO Box 1, Bracknell Berkshire RG12 1JU  UK**

Tel: 44-990-360036   Contact: Wayne W. Brown

## A. B. DICK COMPANY

7400 Caldwell Avenue, Niles, IL, 60714-3806

Tel: (847) 779-1900 Fax: (847) 647-6940 www.abdick.com

*Mfr./sales automation systems.*

**A. B. Dick Itek Limited, 983 Great West Road, Brentford, Middlesex TW8 9DN, U.K.**

Tel: 44-181-568-9297 Fax: 44-181-847-0779

## AAF INTERNATIONAL (AMERICAN AIR FILTER)

215 Central Ave., PO Box 35690, Louisville, KY, 40232-5690

Tel: (502) 637-0011 Fax: (502) 637-0321 www.aafintl.com

*Mfr. air filtration/pollution control and noise control equipment.*

**AAF-Ltd., Bassington Lane, Cramlington, Northumberland NE23 8AF UK**

Tel: 44-1670-713477 Fax: 44-1670-714370

## AAR CORPORATION

One AAR Place, 1100 North Wood Dale Road, Wood Dale, IL, 60191

Tel: (630) 227-2000 Fax: (630) 227-2019 www.aarcorp.com

*Provides aviation repair and supply provisioning; aircraft sales and leasing.*

**AAR Allen Group International, Cardinal Point Newall Road, Hounslow, Middlesex TW6 2BP UK**

Tel: 44-181-759-4022 Fax: 44-181-897-9005 Contact: Jon Clark

**AAR Allen Group International, 35 Willow Lane, Mitcham, Surrey CR4 4UQ, UK**

Tel: 44-181-640-2225 Fax: 44-181-685-9247 Contact: Alex Vlielander

## ABBOTT LABORATORIES

One Abbott Park, Abbott Park, IL, 60064-3500

Tel: (847) 937-6100 Fax: (847) 937-1511 www.abbott.com

*Development/mfr./sale diversified health care products and services.*

**Abbott Laboratories Ltd., Norden Road, Maidenhead Berkshire, SL6 4XL, UK**

**Abbott Laboratories Ltd., Abbott House Norden Road, Maidenhead, Berkshire SL6 4XE, UK**

## ACADEMIC PRESS INC.

6277 Sea Harbor Drive, Orlando, FL, 32887

Tel: (407) 345-2000 Fax: (407) 345-8388 www.academicpress.com

*Publisher of educational and scientific books.*

**Academic Press Ltd., 24-28 Oval Rd., London NW1 7DX, UK**

Tel: 44-207-482-2893 Fax: 44-207-267-4752

## ACC CORPORATION

400 West Avenue, Rochester, NY, 14611

Tel: (716) 987-3000 Fax: (716) 987-3499 www.acccorp.com

*Long distance and telecommunications services.*

**ACC Telecom Ltd., 626 Chiswick High Rd., London W4 5RY, UK**

Tel: 44-181-400-4400 Fax: 44-181-400-4444 Contact: Ray Willshire, Mng. Dir. Emp: 425

## ACCLAIM ENTERTAINMENT, INC.

One Acclaim Plaza, Glen Cove, NY, 11542

Tel: (516) 656-5000 Fax: (516) 656-2040 www.acclaim.com

*Mfr. video games.*

**Acclaim Entertainment, Ltd., 112-120 Brompton Road, Knightsbridge London SW3 1JJ, UK**

Tel: 44-207-344-5000

**Acclaim Studioes Teeside, Ltd., Dunedin House Riverside Quay, Stockton-on-Tees, Cleveland TS17-6BJ U.K.**

**Acclaim Studios London, Ltd., Knolly's House 1st Fl, 17 Addiscombe Road, Croydon Surrey, England CRO 6SR U.K.**

## ACCO BRANDS, INC.

300 Tower Parkway, Lincoln, IL, 60069

Tel:  (847) 541-9500        Fax:  (847) 541-5750         www.acco.com

*Provides services in the office and computer markets and manufactures paper fasteners, clips, metal fasteners, binders and staplers.*

**ACCO Europe Plc,  Gatehouse Road, Aylesbury, Bucks HP 19 3DT, UK**

Tel: 44-1296-394833   Fax: 44-1296-483512

## ACCOUNTANTS ON CALL

Park 80 West, Plaza 2, 9th Fl., Saddle Brook, NJ, 07663

Tel:  (201) 843-0006        Fax:  (201) 843-4936         www.aocnet.com

*Full-service staffing and executive search firm specializing in accounting and financial personnel.*

**Accountants on Call,  Portland Tower, Portland St., Manchester M1 3LD UK**

Tel: 44-161-236-6866   Fax: 44-161-236-2053

**Accountants on Call,  31 A James St., Covent Garden WC2E 8PA, UK**

Tel: 44-207-140-9966   Fax: 44-207-379-4222

**Accountants on Call,  12/14 Devonshire Row, London EC2M 4RH, UK**

Tel: 44-207-247-3777   Fax: 44-207-377-1411

**Accountants on Call,  11 Sheen Rd., Richmond TW9 1AD, UK**

Tel: 44-181-332-1888   Fax: 44-181-332-0777

**Accountants on Call,  36 Park Row, Leeds LS1 5JL, UK**

Tel: 44-113-245-6145   Fax: 44-113-244-0023

**Accountants on Call,  93 Newman St., London, UK**

Tel: 44-207-491-7722   Fax: 44-207-491-7769

**Accountants on Call,  The Grange, 16 St. Peter St., St. Albans AL1 3NA UK**

Tel: 44-172-784-8482   Fax: 44-172-783-4151

## ACCURIDE INTERNATIONAL, INC.

12311 Shoemaker Ave., Santa Fe Springs, CA, 90670-4721

Tel:  (562) 903-0200        Fax:  (562) 903-0208         www.accuride.com

*Mfr. drawer slides.*

**Accuride,  Liliput Rd., Brackmills Industrial Estate, Northampton NN4 7AS, UK**

**Accuride International Inc.,  London, UK**

## ACE CONTROLS INC.

23435 Industrial Park Drive, Farmington Hills, MI, 48024

Tel:  (248) 476-0213        Fax:  (248) 276-2470         www.acecontrols.com

*Industry hydraulic shock absorbers, cylinders, valves and automation controls.*

**ACE Controls Intl.,  Belvedere, Newton-Le-Willows, Merseyside WA1 20JJ, UK**

Tel: 44-1925-227171   Fax: 44-1925-229323

## ACHESON COLLOIDS COMPANY

PO Box  611747, Port Huron, MI, 48061-1747

Tel:  (810) 984-5581        Fax:  (810) 984-1446         www.achesoncolloids.com

*Chemicals, chemical preparations, paints and lubricating oils.*

**Acheson Industries Ltd.,  Sun Life House - 85 Queens Road, Reading Berkshire RG1 4PT, UK**

Tel: 44-118-958-8844   Fax: 44-118-957-4897

## ACME UNITED CORPORATION

75 Kings Highway Cutoff, Fairfield, CT, 06430-5340

Tel: (203) 332-7330     Fax: (203) 576-0007     www.acmeunited.com

*Mfr. surgical and medical instruments, pharmaceutical supplies.*

**Acme United Limited, Surmanco Div.,  Unit 5 Manor Park Estate, Kettlebridge Road, Sheffield S9 3AJ, UK**

Tel: 44-114-564000   Fax: 44-114-564001

## ACTERNA CORPORATION

3 New England Executive Park, Burlington, MA, 01803

Tel: (781) 272-6100     Fax: (781) 272-2304     www.acterna.com

*Develop, manufacture and market communications test instruments, systems, software and services.*

**Acterna Corporation,  Billingshurst, West Sussex, UK**

**Acterna Corporation,  Crawley, West Sussex, UK**

**Acterna Corporation,  Newbury, Berkshire, UK**

**Acterna Corporation,  Waltham Cross, Hertfordshire, UK**

## ACTION INSTRUMENTS INC.

8601 Aero Drive, San Diego, CA, 92123

Tel: (619) 279-5726     Fax: (619) 279-6290     www.actionio.com

*Mfr. electronic instruments and industrial measurements computers.*

**Action Instruments Ltd.,  Dominion Way, Worthing West Sussex, BN14 8QL, UK**

Tel: 44-1-903-205-222   Fax: 44-1-903-203-767   Contact: David Morrice, Mgr.

## ACTIONPOINT, INC.

1299 Parkmoor Avenue, San Jose, CA, 95126

Tel: (408) 325-3800     Fax: (408) 325-3985     www.actionpoint.com

*Develops software for e-commerce.*

**ActionPoint UK,  Hanover House, Cross lanes, Buildford GU1 1UG, UK**

Tel: 44-1483-460500   Fax: 44-1483-460600

## ACTIVE VOICE CORPORATION

2901 Third Avenue, Ste. 500, Seattle, WA, 98121

Tel: (206) 441-4700     Fax: (206) 441-4784     www.activevoice.com

*Mfr. PC-based voice processing systems.*

**Active Voice UK,  Unit 8 Doncastle House, Doncastle Road Bracknell, Berkshire RG12 8PE, UK**

Tel: 44-1344-360-630   Fax: 44-1344-487-773

## ACTIVISION

3100 Ocean Park Boulevard, Santa Monica, CA, 90405

Tel: (310) 255-2000     Fax: (310) 255-2100     www.activision.com

*Development/mfr. entertainment software and video games.*

**Activision UK Ltd.,  Bemini House, 133 High St., Ylewsley West Drayton, Middlesex UB7 7QL UK**

Tel: 44-1895-456-7   Fax: 44-1895-456-709   Emp: 128

## ACTUATE CORPORATION

701 Gateway Boulevard South, San Francisco, CA, 94080

Tel: (650) 837-2000     Fax: (650) 827-1560     www.actuate.com

*Develops software.*

**Actuate UK Ltd.,  No. 1 The Arena, Downshire Way, Bracknell Berkshire RG12 1PU, UK**

Tel: 44-1344-316040   Fax: 44-1344-316001

## ACXIOM CORPORATION

301 Industrial Boulevard, Conway, AR, 72033-2000

Tel: (501) 336-1000     Fax: (501) 336-3919       www.acxiom.com

*Data warehouser, database manager, and other marketing information services.*

**Acxiom Limited, Counting House, 53 Tooley Street, London SE1 2QN, UK**

Tel: 44-207-526-5100   Fax: 44-207-526-5200

## ADAC LABORATORIES, INC.

540 Alder Drive, Milpitas, CA, 95035

Tel: (408) 321-9100     Fax: (408) 321-9536       www.adaclabs.com

*Mfr. cameras and equipment for nuclear medicine.*

**ADAC Laboratories UK, 3/4 Reycote Lane, Milton Common, Oxford OX9 2NP, UK**

Tel: 44-18-4427-8011

## ADAMS RITE MANUFACTURING COMPANY

260 Santa Fe Street, Pomona, CA, 91767

Tel: (909) 632-2300     Fax: (909) 632-3267       www.adamsrite.com

*Mfr. architectural hardware.*

**Adams Rite (Europe) Ltd., Unit 6 - Moreton Industrial Estate, London Rd., Swanley, Kent BR8 8TZ UK**

Tel: 44-1322-669211   Fax: 44-1322-613230

## ADAPTIVE BROADBAND INC.

1143 Borregas Avenue, Sunnyvale, CA, 94089-1306

Tel: (408) 732-4000     Fax: (408) 732-4244       www.adaptivebroadband.com

*Engaged in telecommunications and wireless broadband solutions.*

**Adaptive Broadband Inc. (European Hdqrts.), Westbrook Centre - Milton Road, Cambridge CB4 1YQ, UK**

## ADC TELECOMMUNICATIONS INC.

12501 Whitewater Drive, Minnetonka, MN, 55343

Tel: (612) 938-8080     Fax: (612) 946-3292       www.adc.com

*Mfr. telecommunications equipment.*

**ADC Europe, Unit 4 Beacontree Plaza, Gillette Way, Reading, RG2 OBS, UK**

Tel: 44-11-89-879-200   Fax: 44-11-89-314-388

## ADE CORPORATION

80 Wilson Way, Westwood, MA, 02090

Tel: (781) 467-3500     Fax: (781) 467-0500       www.ade.com

*Mfr. semiconductor wafers and computer disks.*

**ADE International, 10/11 Shenley Pavilions, Milton Keynes MK5 6LB, UK**

Tel: 44-1908-507799   Fax: 44-1908-503366

## ADEMCO INTERNATIONAL

1769 N.W. 79th Avenue, Miami, FL, 33126

Tel: (305) 477-5204     Fax: (305) 477-5404       www.ademcoint.com

*Mfr. security, fire and burglary systems and products.*

**ADEMCO Marketing, 12 The Paddock, Hambridge Rd., Newbury Berkshire RG14 5TQ UK**

## ADOBE SYSTEMS INCORPORATED

345 Park Avenue, San Jose, CA, 95110

Tel: (408) 536-6000     Fax: (408) 537-6000       www.adobe.com

*Engaged in print technology and distributor of Acrobat Reader.*

**Adobe Systems UK, Waterview House - 1 Roundwood Avenue, Stockley Park Uxbridge, Middlesex UB11 9AE, UK**

Tel: 44-208-606-4000

## ADVANCE PUBLICATIONS, INC.

950 Fingerboard Road, Staten Island, NY, 10305

Tel: (718) 981-1234    Fax: (718) 981-1415    www.advance.net

*Publishing company (Glamour, Vogue, GQ, Architectural Digest) and cable TV operations.*

**Advance Publications, Inc., London, UK**

## ADVANCED DIGITAL INFORMATION CORPORATION

11431 Willows Rd. NE, PO Box 97057, Redmond, WA, 98073

Tel: (425) 881-8004    Fax: (425) 881-2296    www.adic.com

*Mfr. computer storage systems.*

**Advanced Digital Information Corp., 115 Wharfedale Road, Winnersh Berkshire RG41 5RB, UK**

## ADVANCED FIBRE COMMUNICATIONS, INC.

1 Willow Brook Court, Petaluma, CA, 94954

Tel: (707) 794-7700    Fax: (707) 794-7777    www.fibre.com

*Engaged in voice and data network access devices.*

**Advanced Fibre Communications, 40 Thames Valley Park Drive, Reading Berkshire RG6 1PT, UK**
Tel: 44-118-963-7492

## ADVANCED MICRO DEVICES INC.

1 AMD Place, Sunnyvale, CA, 94086

Tel: (408) 732-2400    Fax: (408) 982-6164    www.amd.com

*Mfr. integrated circuits for communications and computation industry.*

**Advanced Micro Devices (UK), Intec Bldg. 4 - Wade Rd., Basingstoke, Hants RG2 41, UK**

## ADVANCED PRODUCTS COMPANY

33 Defco Park Road, North Haven, CT, 06473

Tel: (203) 239-3341    Fax: (203) 234-7233    www.advpro.com

*Mfr. Metallic and PTFE seals and gaskets.*

**Advanced Products (Seals & Gaskets) Ltd., Unit 25A - 1 Industrial Estate, Consett Durham DH8 6SR, UK**

## ADVENT SOFTWARE, INC.

301 Brannan Street, San Francisco, CA, 94107

Tel: (415) 543-7696    Fax: (415) 543-5070    www.advent.com

*Mfr. portfolio software.*

**Advent Europe Ltd., Berkeley Square House 2/F, 2 Berkeley Square, London W1Z 6EA, UK**
Tel: 44-20-7887-6021

## AEC INC.

801 AEC Drive, Wood Dale, IL, 60191

Tel: (630) 595-1060    Fax: (630) 595-8925    www.aecinternet.com

*Mfr./service auxiliary equipment for plastics industry.*

**Mannesmann Demag Hamilton Ltd., Sterling House, 20 Station Rd., Gerrads Cross, Buckinghamshire SL9 8EW, UK**

## AERO SYSTEMS ENGINEERING, INC.

358 E. Fillmore Ave., St. Paul, MN, 55107

Tel: (651) 227-7515    Fax: (651) 227-0519    www.aerosysengr.com

*Engaged in wind tunnel and jet engine testing and engineering.*

**Aero Systems Aviation Corp, 24 Sussex Rd., Haynards Heath, Sussex RH16 4FA UK**

## AKIN, GUMP, STRAUSS, HAUER & FELD LLP

1333 New Hampshire Ave., N.W., Washington, DC, 20036

Tel: (202) 877-4000      Fax: (202) 887-4288      www.akingump.com

*International law firm.*

**Akin Gump, Strauss, Hauer & Feld LLP, One Angel Court, London EC2R 7HJ, UK**

Tel: 44-207-796-9600   Fax: 44-207-796-9610

## ALADDIN INDUSTRIES INC.

703 Murfreesboro Road, Nashville, TN, 37210

Tel: (615) 748-3000      Fax: (615) 748-3070      www.aladdinindustries.com

*Mfr. vacuum insulated products, insulated food containers and servers.*

**Aladdin Industries Ltd., 6 Grovelands Business Center, Hemel Hempstead, Herts. HP2 7TE, UK**

## ALAMO RENT A CAR

110 Southeast 6th Street, Fort Lauderdale, FL, 33301

Tel: (954) 522-0000      Fax: (954) 220-0120      www.alamo.com

*Car rentals.*

**Alamo Rent A Car, London Central, 7-23 Bryanston St., Marble Arch, London UK**

## ALBANY INTERNATIONAL CORPORATION

PO Box 1907, Albany, NY, 12201

Tel: (518) 445-2200      Fax: (518) 445-2265      www.albint.com

*Mfr. broadwoven and engineered fabrics, plastic products, filtration media.*

**Albany Engineered Systems Europe Ltd., 2 Buckingham Ave., Trading Estate, Slough, Berkshire SL1 4NB UK**

**J.K. Industrial Fabrics, Roach Bank Mill, PO Box 28, Pimhole Rd., Bury, Lancashire BL9 7HA UK**

**James Kenyon & Son (PMC), Pilsworth Mill, PO Box 35, Bury, Lancashire BL9 8QE UK**

## ALBERTO-CULVER COMPANY

2525 Armitage Ave., Melrose Park, IL, 60160

Tel: (708) 450-3000      Fax: (708) 450-3354      www.alberto.com

*Mfr./marketing personal care and household brand products.*

**Alberto-Culver Co. (UK) Ltd., Lime Tree Way - Hampshire Business Park, Basingstoke Hampshire RG24 8WH, UK**

Tel: 44-1256-705000   Fax: 44-1256-705001

**Ogee Ltd., Unit 4 Area 10 Headley Park Ind. Estate, Headley Rd., Woodley nr. Reading, Berkshire RG5 4SW, UK**

## ALCOA INC.

Alcoa Center, 201 Isabella Street, Pittsburgh, PA, 15215-5858

Tel: (412) 553-4545      Fax: (412) 553-4498      www.alcoa.com

*World's leading producer of aluminum and alumina; mining, refining, smelting, fabricating and recycling.*

**Alcoa Extruded Products (UK) Ltd., Swansea UK**

**Alcoa Manufacturing (G.B.) Ltd., Swansea UK**

**Alcoa Systems (UK) Ltd., Stratford-on-Avon UK**

## ALCOA FUJIKURA LTD.

105 Westpark Drive, Brentwood, TN, 37027

Tel: (615) 370-2100      Fax: (615) 370-2180      www.alcoa-fujikura.com

*Mfr. optical groundwire, tube cable, fiber optic connectors and automotive wiring harnesses.*

**Alcoa Systems UK Ltd., Stratford-on-Avon, UK**

## ALCONE MARKETING GROUP

15 Whatney, Irvine, CA, 92618

Tel: (949) 770-4400    Fax: (949) 859-7493    www.alconemarketing.com

*Sales promotion and marketing services agencies.*

**Alcone Marketing Group, Alexander House Mere Park, Dedmere Road Marlow, Bucks SL71FX, UK**

Tel: 44-1628-477841   Fax: 44-1628-481179   Contact: Pat Readding, VP

## ALLEGHENY LUDLUM CORPORATION

1000 Six PPG Place, Pittsburgh, PA, 15222

Tel: (412) 394-2805    Fax: (412) 394-2800    www.alleghenyludlum.com

*Mfr. steel and alloys.*

**Allegheny Ludlum UK, Sheffield, UK**

Tel: 44-114-2720-081   Fax: 44-114-2731-637

## ALLEGHENY TECHNOLOGIES

1000 Six PPG Place, Pittsburgh, PA, 15222

Tel: (412) 394-2800    Fax: (412) 394-2805    www.alleghenytechnologies.com

*Diversified mfr. aviation and electronics, specialty metals, industrial and consumer products.*

**Allegheny Technologies, The Harlequin Centre, Southall Lane, Southall, London UB2 5NH, UK**

**Allvac Ltd., Atlas House, Attercliffe Road, Sheffield S4 7UY, UK**

**Titanium International Ltd., Keys House, Granby Avenue, Garrett Green, Birmingham B33 OSP, UK**

## ALLEGIANCE HEALTHCARE CORPORATION

1430 Waukegan Road, McGaw Park, IL, 60085

Tel: (847) 689-8410    Fax: (847) 578-4437    www.allegiance.net

*Manufactures and distributes medical, surgical, respiratory therapy and laboratory products.*

**Allegiance Healthcare Ltd., Wallingford Rd., Compton, RG 20 7QW UK**

Tel: 44-1635-206000   Fax: 44-1635-206028   Contact: Ian R. Hunter, Mgr.

## ALLEN TELECOM

25101 Chagrin Boulevard, Beachwood, OH, 44122-5619

Tel: (216) 765-5818    Fax: (216) 765-0410    www.allentele.com

*Mfr. communications equipment, automotive bodies and parts, electronic components.*

**Allen Telecom Ltd., 9 Cheapside, London EC2V 6AD, UK**

**FOREM U.K. Ltd., Unit D Castle Industrial Parkway, Pear Tree Lane, Newbury, Berkshire RG142EZ UK**

Tel: 44-163-556-9695   Fax: 44-163-556-9463

## ALLEN-BRADLEY COMPANY, INC.

1201 South Second Street, Milwaukee, WI, 53204

Tel: (414) 382-2000    Fax: (414) 382-4444    www.ab.com

*Mfr. electrical controls and information devices.*

**Allen-Bradley Applied Systems, Denbigh Rd., Bletchley, Milton Keynes MK1 1EP, UK**

**Allen-Bradley Industrial Automation Products, Pitfield, Kiln Farm, Milton Keynes MK11 3DR, UK**

**OSAI A-B Ltd., Allen-Bradley Motion Control Div., 2 Hatchpond Rd., Poole, Dorset BH17 7LQ, UK**

## ALLERGAN INC.

2525 Dupont Drive, PO Box 19534, Irvine, CA, 92713-9534

Tel: (714) 246-4500    Fax: (714) 246-6987    www.allergan.com

*Mfr. therapeutic eye care products, skin and neural care pharmaceuticals.*

**Allergan Ltd., Crown Centre, Coronation Road, Bucks HP 12 3SH, High Wycombe, UK**

Tel: 44-1494-444722   Fax: 44-1494-473593

## ALLIANCE CAPITAL MANAGEMENT HOLDING LP

1345 Ave. of the Americas, New York, NY, 10105

Tel: (212) 969-1000     Fax: (212) 969-2229     www.alliancecapital.com

*Engaged in fund management for large corporations.*

**Alliance Capital Limited, 1 Mayfair Place, London WIX 6JJ, UK**

Tel: 44-20-7470-0100

## ALLIANCE SEMICONDUCTOR CORPORATION

2675 Augustine Drive, Santa Clara, CA, 95054

Tel: (408) 855-4900     Fax: (408) 855-4999     www.alsc.com

*Mfr. semi-conductors and related chips.*

**Alliance Semiconductor European Hdqrts., Bldg. A Trinity Court, Wokingham Road, Bracknell Berkshire RG42 1PL, UK**

Tel: 44-1344-668031   Fax: 44-1344-668250

## ALLTEL CORPORATION

1 Allied Drive, Little Rock, AR, 72202

Tel: (501) 905-8000     Fax: (501) 905-6444     www.alltel.com

*Full range outsourcing services.*

**ALLTEL Systems Ltd., London, UK**

## ALPHA INDUSTRIES INC.

20 Sylvan Road, Woburn, MA, 01801

Tel: (781) 935-5150     Fax: (781) 824-4543     www.alphaind.com

*Mfr. electronic and microwave components.*

**Alpha Industries USA Ltd., 19-21 Chapel St., Marlow SL7 3HN, UK**

## ALPHA WIRE COMPANY

711 Lidgerwood Ave., Elizabeth, NJ, 07207

Tel: (908) 925-8000     Fax: (908) 925-6923     www.alphawire.com

*Mfr. wire, cable and tubing products.*

**Alpha Wire International, Sudbury Intl Business Ctr., Brooklands Close, Windmill Rd., Sunbury-on-Thames Middlesex TW16 7DX UK**

Tel: 44-1932-772422   Fax: 44-1932-772433   Contact: Evan Jarrell, Sales Mgr.   Emp: 5

## ALTERA CORPORATION

101 Innovation Drive, San Jose, CA, 95134

Tel: (408) 544-7000     Fax: (408) 544-8303     www.altera.com

*Mfr. high-density programmable chips for semi-conductor industry.*

**Altera UK Limited, Holmers Farm Way, High Wycombe, Buckinghamshire HP12 4XF, UK**

Tel: 44-1-494-602-000

## ALTHEIMER & GRAY

10 South Wacker Drive, Ste. 4000, Chicago, IL, 60606-7482

Tel: (312) 715-4000     Fax: (312) 715-4800     www.altheimer.com

*International law firm.*

**Altheimer & Gray, 7 Bishopsgate, London EC2N 3AR, UK**

Tel: 44-20-7786-5700   Fax: 44-20-7786-0000   Contact: Robert C. Bata

## ALZA CORPORATION

1900 Charleston Road, Mountain View, CA, 94039

Tel: (650) 564-5000     Fax: (650) 564-5121     www.alza.com

*Pharmaceutical firm engaged in drugs transmitted through the skin, including skin patches.*

**ALZA Limited UK, Cambridge, UK**

### AMAZON.COM, INC.

1200 12th Ave. South, Ste. 1200, Seattle, WA, 98144-2734

Tel: (206) 266-1000    Fax: (206) 266-4206    www.amazon.com

*Computer site that offers books, CDs, DVDS, videos, toys, tools, and electronics.*

**Amazon.Com UK,  1-9 The  Grove, Slough Berkshire SL1 QP, UK**

### AMBAC FINANCIAL GROUP

One State Street Plaza, New York, NY, 10004

Tel: (212) 668-0340    Fax: (212) 509-9109    www.ambac.com

*Reinsurance company.*

**Ambac Insurance UK Ltd.,  St. Helen's, One Undershaft, London EC3A 8JL, UK**

Tel: 44-207-444-7200   Fax: 44-207-444-7227   Contact: David Wallis, First VP

### AMCOL INTERNATIONAL CORPORATION

1500 West Shure Drive, Ste. 500, Arlington Heights, IL, 60004

Tel: (847) 394-8730    Fax: (847) 506-6199    www.amcol.com

*Mfr. specialty chemicals and environmental bentonite products.*

**Cetco Europe Ltd.,  Birch House, Scott Quays, Birkenhead, Merseyside L41 1FB UK**

Tel: 44-151-606-5900   Fax: 44-151-606-5963   Contact: Mike Lapinski, Mng. Dir.   Emp: 64

**Chemdal Ltd.,  East St., Birkenhead L41 1FG, UK**

Tel: 44-151-630-5299   Fax: 44-151-638-5312   Contact: Gary Castagna, Mng. Dir.   Emp: 155

**Volclay Ltd.,  Leonard House, Scotts Quays, Birkenhead, Merseyside L41 1FB, UK**

Tel: 44-151-638-0967   Fax: 44-151-638-7000   Contact: Peter Thorpe, Mng. Dir.   Emp: 100

### AMERADA HESS CORPORATION

1185 Avenue of the Americas, New York, NY, 10036

Tel: (212) 997-8500    Fax: (212) 536-8390    www.hess.com

*Crude oil and natural gas.*

**Amerada Hess Ltd.,  33 Grosvenor Place, London SW1X 7HY, UK**

### AMERICAN & EFIRD, INC.

PO Box 507, Mt. Holly, NC, 28120

Tel: (704) 827-4311    Fax: (704) 822-6054    www.amefird.com

*Mfr. industrial sewing thread for worldwide industrial and consumer markets.*

**A&E Thread (GB) Ltd.,  Bankside Mills, Chapelfield, Radcliffe Manchester M26 9JF, UK**

### AMERICAN AIRLINES INC.

4333 Amon Carter Boulevard, Ft. Worth, TX, 76155

Tel: (817) 963-1234    Fax: (817) 967-9641    www.amrcorp.com

*Air transport services.*

**American Airlines,  7 Albemarle St., London W1X 3AF, UK**

**American Airlines,  Rm. 6 Level 7, Manchester Airport, Cheshire M22 5PA, UK**

### AMERICAN AMICABLE LIFE INSURANCE COMPANY

PO Box 2549, Waco, TX, 76703

Tel: (254) 297-2777    Fax: (254) 297-2733    www.americanamicable.com

*Life, accident and health insurance.*

**American Amicable Life Insurance Co.,  London, UK**

### AMERICAN APPRAISAL ASSOCIATES INC.

411 E. Wisconsin Ave., Milwaukee, WI, 53202

Tel: (414) 271-7240    Fax: (414) 271-1041    www.american-appraisal.com

*Valuation consulting services.*

**American Appraisal (UK) Ltd.,  10 Gough Sq., London EC4A 3NJ, UK**

## AMERICAN AXLE & MANUFACTURING HOLDINGS, INC.

1840 Holbrook Ave., Detroit, MI, 48212

Tel: (313) 974-2000    Fax: (313) 974-3090    www.aam.com

*Mfr. axles, propeller shafts and chassis components.*

**Albion Automotive, Lancashire Enterprises Business Park, Centruion Way, Leyland Preston, PR5 1TZ, UK**

Contact: Michael D. Straney, VP Europe

**Farington Components Limited, Div. AAM, Farington Components Ltd., Golden Hill Lane, Leyland - Preston PR5 1UA, UK**

Contact: Michael D. Straney, VP Europe

## AMERICAN BUREAU OF SHIPPING

2 World Trade Center, 106th Fl., New York, NY, 10048

Tel: (212) 839-5000    Fax: (212) 839-5209    www.eagle.org

*Classification/certification of ships and offshore structures, development and technical assistance.*

**ABS Europe, ABS House, 1 Frying Pan Alley, London E1 7HR UK**

## AMERICAN ELECTRIC POWER COMPANY, INC.

1 Riverside Plaza, Columbus, OH, 43215-2373

Tel: (614) 223-1000    Fax: (614) 223-1823    www.aep.com

*Electric utility holding company.*

**CitiPower Services, Forest Gate - Brighton Road, Crawley West Sussex, RH11 9 BH, UK**

Tel: 44-1293-565888   Fax: 44-1293-657327

**Yourshire Electricity Group plc., Wetherby Road, Scarcroft, Leeds LS14 3HS, UK**

Tel: 44-113-289-2123

## AMERICAN EXPRESS COMPANY

American Express Tower, World Financial Center, New York, NY, 10285-4765

Tel: (212) 640-2000    Fax: (212) 619-9802    www.americanexpress.com

*Travel, travelers cheques, charge card and financial services.*

**Amex Services Europe Ltd., 78 Brompton Rd., Knightsbridge, London SW3 1ER UK**

Tel: 44-207-584-6482

## AMERICAN GREETINGS CORPORATION

One American Road, Cleveland, OH, 44144-2398

Tel: (216) 252-7300    Fax: (216) 252-6777    www.amgreetings.com

*Mfr./distributor greeting cards (American Greetings Forget Me Not and Gibson), gift wrappings, tags, seals, ribbons and party goods.*

**Carlton Cards Ltd., Mill St East, Dewsbury, W. Yorkshire WF12 9AW, UK**

**U.K. Greetings Ltd., London, UK**

## AMERICAN HOME PRODUCTS CORPORATION

Five Giralda Farms, Madison, NJ, 07940-0874

Tel: (973) 660-5000    Fax: (973) 660-6048    www.ahp.com

*Mfr. pharmaceutical, animal health care and crop protection products.*

**American Home Products Corporation, London, UK**

## AMERICAN INTERNATIONAL GROUP INC. (AIG)

70 Pine Street, New York, NY, 10270

Tel: (212) 770-7000    Fax: (212) 509-9705    www.aig.com

*Worldwide insurance and financial services.*

**AIG Europe, 120 Fenchurch Street, London EC3M 5 BP, UK**

**American Life Ins. Co., 55 Mark Lane, London EC3R 7NE, UK**

## AMERICAN LOCKER GROUP INC.

608 Allen Street, Jamestown, NY, 14701-3966

Tel: (716) 664-9600     Fax: (716) 483-2822     www.americanlocker.com

*Mfr. coin-operated locks and office furniture.*

**W.B. Bawn & Co., Ltd., Northern Way, Mildenhall Rd., Bury St. Edmunds, Suffolk IP32 6NH UK**

## AMERICAN MANAGEMENT SYSTEMS, INC.

4050 Legato Road, Fairfax, VA, 22033

Tel: (703) 267-8000     Fax: (703) 267-5073     www.amsinc.com

*Systems integration and consulting.*

**AMS Management Systems UK Ltd., 51-55 Gresham St. 2nd Fl., London EC2V 7HQ, UK**

Tel: 44-207-710-6600   Fax: 44-207-710-6700   Contact: David Ogram, Mng. Dir.   Emp: 240

## AMERICAN METER COMPANY

300 Welsh Road, Bldg. #1, Horsham, PA, 19044-2234

Tel: (215) 830-1800     Fax: (215) 830-1890     www.americanmeter.com

*Measure and control services for natural gas industry.*

**Intl. Gas Apparatus Ltd., Glebeland Rd., Yorktown Industrial Estate, Camberley, Surrey GU1 53X UK**

## AMERICAN OPTICAL LENS CO.

PO Box 8020, Southbridge, MA, 01550

Tel: (508) 764-5000     Fax: (508) 764-5010

*Mfr. ophthalmic lenses and frames, custom molded products, specialty lenses.*

**UK Optical Ltd., 76-77 Capitol Industrial Park, Capitol Way, London NW9 0EN, UK**

## AMERICAN PRECISION INDUSTRIES INC.

2777 Walden Ave., Buffalo, NY, 14225

Tel: (716) 684-9700     Fax: (716) 684-2129     www.apicorporate.com

*Mfr. heat transfer equipment, motion control devices, coils, capacitors, electro-mechanical clutches and brakes.*

**API Positran Ltd., Headlands Business Park, Salisbury Road, Ringwood Hampshire BH24 3PB UK**

Tel: 44-1425-46-3200   Fax: 44-1425-47-7755

## AMERICAN RE-INSURANCE COMPANY

555 College Road East, Princeton, NJ, 08543

Tel: (609) 243-4200     Fax: (609) 243-4257     www.amre.com

*Reinsurance.*

**American Re-Insurance Co. (UK) Ltd., 52/54 Grace Church St., London EC3V 0EH, UK**

## AMERICAN SAFETY RAZOR COMPANY

1 Razor Blade Lane, Verona, VA, 24482

Tel: (540) 248-8000     Fax: (540) 248-0522     www.asrco.com

*Mfr. private-label and branded shaving razors and blades and cotton swabs.*

**Personna International UK Ltd., Unite 11 Ratcher Wa, Crown Farm Ind. Estate, Forest Town Mansfield, Nottinghamshire NG19 OFS, U.K.**

## AMERICAN SOFTWARE, INC.

470 East Paces Ferry Road, NE, Atlanta, GA, 30305

Tel: (404) 261-4381     Fax: (404) 264-5514     www.amsoftware.com

*Mfr./sales of financial control software and systems.*

**American Software, St. Georges Business Centre, Locke King Road, Weybridge Surry KY13 OTS, U.K.**

Tel: 44-19-328-55554   Fax: 44-19-328-54563

## AMERICAN STANDARD INC.

One Centennial Avenue, Piscataway, NJ, 08855-6820

Tel: (732) 980-3000    Fax: (732) 980-6118    www.americanstandard.com

*Mfr. automotive, plumbing, heating, air conditioning products and medical diagnostics systems.*

**DiaSorin Ltd., Charles House - Toutley Road, Wokingham Berkshire RG 41 1QN, UK**

**Ideal Standard Ltd., PO Box 60, National Ave., Hull HU5 4JE, UK**

## AMERICAN TECHNICAL CERAMICS CORPORATION

17 Stepar Place, Huntington Station, NY, 11746

Tel: (631) 622-4700    Fax: (631) 622-4748    www.alceramics.com

*Mfr. ceramic porcelain capacitors and ceramic-based electronic products.*

**Phase Components Ltd., Unit 5 Genesis Centre Redkiln Way, Horsham, Sussex RH 13 5QH, UK**

Tel: 44-1403-241862  Fax: 44-1403-241858

## AMERICAN TOOL COMPANIES INC.

701 Woodlands Parkway, Vernon Hills, IL, 60061

Tel: (847) 478-1090    Fax: (847) 478-1091    www.americantool.com

*Mfr. hand tools, cutting tools and power tool accessories.*

**Record Tools, Ltd., Parkway Works, Sheffield S9 3BL, UK**

Tel: 44-114-244-9066   Fax: 44-114-256-1788

## AMES TEXTILE CORPORATION

710 Chelmsford Street, Lowell, MA, 01851

Tel: (978) 458-3321    Fax: (978) 441-9808    www.amestextile.com

*Mfr. textile products.*

**Ames Mills Victoria Mill, Church St., Westhoughton, Bolton, Lancaster BL5 3QP, UK**

## AMETEK INC.

37 N. Valley Road, PO Box 1764, Paoli, PA, 19301-0801

Tel: (610) 647-2121    Fax: (610) 296-3412    www.ametek.com

*Mfr. instruments, electric motors and engineered materials.*

**AMETEK Precision Instruments (UK) Ltd., 2 Queens Drive, Kings Norton Business Centre, Kings Norton, Birmingham B30 3HH UK**

Tel: 44-121-246-2260   Fax: 44-121-246-2270

**AMETEK Test and Calibration Instruments, LLOYD Instruments, 12 Barnes Wallis Rd., Segensworth East, Fareham Hampshire PO15 5TT UK**

Tel: 44-1489-574221   Fax: 44-1489-885118

## AMGEN INC.

One Amgen Center Drive, Thousand Oaks, CA, 91320-1799

Tel: (805) 447-1000    Fax: (805) 499-2694    www.amgen.com

*Biotechnology research and pharmaceruticals.*

**Amgen Limited, 240 Cambridge Science Park, Milton Road, Cambridge CB4 4WD, UK**

## AMPCO METAL, INC.

1745 S. 38th Street, PO Box 2004, Milwaukee, WI, 53201

Tel: (414) 645-3750    Fax: (414) 645-3225    www.ampcometal.com

*Mfr./distributor/sale cast and wrought copper-based alloys.*

**Ampco Metal Ltd., 17 Binns Close off Torington Ave., Coventry CV4 9TB, UK**

## AMPEX CORPORATION

500 Broadway, Redwood City, CA, 94063-3199

Tel: (650) 367-2011        Fax: (650) 367-4669        www.ampex.com

*Mfr. extremely high-performance digital data storage, data retrieval and image processing systems for a broad range of corporate scientific and government applications.*

**Ampex Great Britain Ltd., Ampex House Beechwood, Chineham Business Park, Chineham, Basingstoke RG24 8WA UK**

Tel: 44-1256-814410   Fax: 44-1256-814456   Contact: Chris Fitton   Emp: 15

## AMPHENOL CORPORATION

358 Hall Ave., Wallingford, CT, 06492-7530

Tel: (203) 265-8900        Fax: (203) 265-8793        www.amphenol.com

*Mfr. electrictronic interconnect penetrate systems and assemblies.*

**Amphenol Ltd., Thanet Way, Whitstable, Kent CT5 3JF, UK**

Tel: 44-1227-773-200

## AMSTED INDUSTRIES INC.

205 North Michigan Ave., Chicago, IL, 60601

Tel: (312) 645-1700        Fax: (312) 819-8523        www.amsted.com

*Privately-held, diversified manufacturer of products for the construction and building markets, general industry and the railroads.*

**Baltimore Aircoil Ltd., Princewood Rd., Earlstrees Industrial Estate, Corby Northants NN17-4AP UK**

Tel: 44-1536-200-312   Fax: 44-1536-265-793   Contact: Robert I. Macleod-Smith, Mng. Dir.   Emp: 100

## AMWAY CORPORATION

7575 Fulton Street East, Ada, MI, 49355-0001

Tel: (616) 787-6000        Fax: (616) 787-6177        www.amway.com

*Mfr./sale home care, personal care, nutrition and houseware products.*

**Amway (Europe) Ltd., Bank House, 171 Midsummer Blvd., Central Milton Keynes MK9 1ED, UK**

**Amway (UK) Ltd., Snowdon Dr., Winterhill, Milton Keynes MK6 1AR, UK**

## ANACOMP INC.

12365 Crosthwaite Circle, Poway, CA, 92064

Tel: (858) 679-9797        Fax: (858) 748-9482        www.anacomp.com

*Engaged in electronic information management services and products.*

**Anacomp Ltd., Mulberry Business Park, Fishponds Road, Wokingham, Berkshire RG41 2GY UK**

## ANADARKO PETROLEUM CORPORATION

17001 Northchase Drive, Houston, TX, 77060

Tel: (281) 875-1101        Fax: (281) 874-3316        www.anadarko.com

*Exploration, development, production and marketing of oil and gas.*

**Anadarko Petroleum Corp., PO Box 576 - 1 Harefield Road, Uxbridge Middlesex, London UB8 1YH, UK**

Tel: 44-1895-209-400   Fax: 44-1895-209-444

## ANADIGICS, INC.

35 Technology Drive, Warren, NJ, 07059

Tel: (908) 668-5000        Fax: (908) 668-5068        www.anadigics.com

*Mfr. radio-frequency, integrated circuits for wireless and fiber optic communications.*

**Anadigics UK Limited, Dimon Place, Riverside Way, Camberley Surrey GU15 3YF, UK**

Tel: 44-1276-63167

## ANALOG DEVICES INC.

1 Technology Way, Box 9106, Norwood, MA, 02062

Tel: (781) 329-4700      Fax: (781) 326-8703      www.analog.com

*Mfr. integrated circuits and related devices.*

**Analog Devices Ltd., Station Ave., Walton-on-Thames, Surrey KT12 1PF, UK**

## ANALOGIC CORPORATION

8 Centennial Drive, Peabody, MA, 01960

Tel: (978) 977-3000      Fax: (978) 977-6811      www.analogic.com

*Design/mfr. precision measure, signal processing and imaging equipment for medical, scientific, industry and communications.*

**Analogic Ltd., Ascot House, Doncastle Rd., Bracknell, Berkshire RG12 4PE UK**

**SKY Computers Ltd., Div. Analogic, Ascot House, Doncastle Rd., Bracknell, Berkshire RG12 4PE, UK**

## ANALYSTS INTERNATIONAL CORPORATION

3601 West 76th Street, Minneapolis, MN, 55435

Tel: (612) 835-5900      Fax: (612) 897-4555      www.analysts.com

*Provides computer software-related services, including systems analysis, design and programming.*

**Analysts International Corporation, Lincoln House The Paddocks, Cherry Hinton Road, Cambridge CB1 8DH, UK**

Tel: 44-1223-500055   Fax: 44-1223-576646

## ANAREN MICROWAVE INC.

6635 Kirkville Road, East Syracuse, NY, 13057

Tel: (315) 432-8909      Fax: (315) 432-9121      www.anaren.com

*Mfr./services microwave components.*

**Anaren Microwave Ltd., 12 Somerset House Suite 16 & 17, Hussar Court, Waterlooville, Hampshire PO7 7SG UK**

Tel: 44-1705-232392   Fax: 44-1705-254369

## ANC RENTAL CORP.

110 Southeast Sixth St., Ft. Lauderdale, FL, 33301

Tel: (954) 769-7000      Fax: (954) 769-7000      www.ancrental.com

*Engaged in car rental services, including National Car Rental and Alamo Rent A Car.*

**National Car Rental UK, Davis House, Wilton Rd., London SWI, UK**

## ANCHOR HOCKING CORPORATION

519 Pierce Ave., PO Box 600, Lancaster, OH, 43130-0600

Tel: (740) 687-2111      Fax: (740) 687-2543      www.anchorhocking.com

*Mfr. glassware and dinnerware plastic products.*

**Anchor Hocking Corp. UK, 271 High St., Berkhamsted, Herts. HP4 1AA, UK**

## ANDERSEN CONSULTING

100 S. Wacker Drive, Ste. 1059, Chicago, IL, 60606

Tel: (312) 693-0161      Fax: (312) 693-0507      www.ac.com

*Provides management and technology consulting services.*

**Andersen Consulting, 2 Arundel St., London WC2R 3LT, UK**

Tel: 44-207-438-5000   Fax: 44-207-831-1133

**Andersen Consulting, Riverside House, Riverside Walk, Windsor, Berkshire SL 4 1NA UK**

Tel: 44-1753-605-000   Fax: 44-1753-605-050

**Andersen Consulting, Kingsley Hall, 20 Bailey Lane, Manchester Airport, Manchester M90 4AN UK**

Tel: 44-161-435-5000   Fax: 44-161-435-5050

## ANDERSEN WORLDWIDE

33 West Monroe Street, Chicago, IL, 60603

Tel: (312) 580-0033     Fax: (312) 507-6748       www.arthurandersen.com

*Accounting and audit, tax and management consulting services.*

**Andersen Worldwide, Betjeman House, 104 Hills Rd., Cambridge CB2 1LH UK**

Tel: 44-1223-353906   Fax: 44-1223-366287

**Andersen Worldwide, One Victoria Square, Birmingham B1 1BD, UK**

Tel: 44-121-233-2101   Fax: 44-121-233-2954

**Andersen Worldwide, One City Square, Leeds LS1 2AL, UK**

Tel: 44-113-207-7000   Fax: 44-113-245-9240

**Andersen Worldwide, Broad Quay House, Broad Quay, Bristol BS1 4DJ UK**

Tel: 44-117-927-7436   Fax: 44-117-927-7507

**Andersen Worldwide, Fothergill House, 16 King St., Nottingham NG1 2AS UK**

Tel: 44-115-935-3900   Fax: 44-115-935-3949

**Andersen Worldwide, Pearl Assurance House, 7 New Bridge St., Newcastle-upon-Tyne NE1 8BQ UK**

Tel: 44-191-261-2481

**Andersen/Binder Hamlyn, Bank House, 9 Charlotte St., London EC4M 7BH UK**

Tel: 44-161-224-2121   Fax: 44-161-228-1421

**Andersen/Garretts, 1 Surrey St., London WC2R 2PS, UK**

Tel: 44-207-438-3000

**Binder Hamlyn, Bank House, 9 Charlotte St., Manchester M1 4EU UK**

**Garrett & Co., Abbots House, Abbey St., Reading Berkshire RG1 3BD UK**

## ANDREW CORPORATION

10500 West 153rd Street, Orland Park, IL, 60462

Tel: (708) 349-3300     Fax: (708) 349-5410       www.andrew.com

*Mfr. antenna systems, coaxial cable, electronic communications and network connectivity systems.*

**Andrew Ltd., Ilex Bldg., Mulberry Business Park, Fishponds Rd., Wokingham Berkshire RG41 2GY UK**

Tel: 44-118-977-6886   Fax: 44-118-979-4005

## ANDREWS & KURTH LLP

600 Travis Street, Ste. 4200, Houston, TX, 77002

Tel: (713) 220-4200     Fax: (713) 220-4285       www.andrewskurth.com

*International law firm.*

**Andrews & Kurth LLP, 2 Creed Court, 5-11 Ludgate Hill, London EC4M 7AA, UK**

## ANGELICA CORPORATION

424 South Woods Mill Road, Ste. 300, Chesterfield, MO, 63017-3406

Tel: (314) 854-3800     Fax: (314) 854-3890       www.angelica-corp.com

*Mfr. marketing and sales of uniforms.*

**Angelica Intl. Ltd., Ashton Rd., Golborne, Warrington WA3 3UL UK**

## ANHEUSER-BUSCH INTERNATIONAL INC.

One Busch Place, St. Louis, MO, 63118-1852

Tel: (314) 577-2000     Fax: (314) 577-2900       www.anheuser-busch.com

*Malt production, aluminum beverage containers, rice milling, real estate development, metalized and paper label printing, railcar repair and theme-park facilities.*

**Anheuser-Busch Europe Inc., Radgemore House, Henley-on-Thames, Oxon RG9 4NP, UK**

**Anheuser-Bush European Trade Ltd., London, UK**

**Stag Brewery, West London, UK**

## ANIXTER INTERNATIONAL INC..

4711 Golf Road, Skokie, IL, 60076

Tel: (847) 677-2600      Fax: (847) 677-8557      www.anixter.com

*Distributor wiring systems/products for voice, video, data and power applications.*

**Anixter Europe, 1 York Road, Uxbridge-Middlesex UR8 1RN, UK**

Tel: 44-1895-818181

**Anixter U.K., Howmoss Drive, Kirkhill Ind Est., Dyce Aberdeen AB 21 OGL, UK**

Tel: 44-121-472-2255   Fax: 44-122-472-2290

**Anixter U.K., Concourse House Ste 31, Dewsbury Road, Leeds LS 11 7DF UK**

**Anixter U.K., Saltley Trading Est. Unit 119, Saltley Birmingham, West Midlands B8 1BL, UK**

**Anixter U.K., 26 The Office Village-3rd Fl., Exchange Quay Salford, Manchester M5 3EQ, UK**

**Anixter U.K., Veritas House, 125 Finsbury Pavement, London EC2A 1NQ, UK**

Tel: 44-207-638-6380   Fax: 44-207-638-6387

## ANSELL HEALTHCARE, INC.

200 Schulz Drive, Red Bank, NJ, 07701

Tel: (732) 345-5400      Fax: (732) 219-5114      www.ansellhealthcare.com

*Mfr. industrial gloves, rubber and plastic products, protective clothing.*

**Ansell Healthcare UK, Ansell House - 119 Ewell Road, Surbiton Surrey KT6 6AL, UK**

Tel: 44-181-481-1800

## AOL TIME WARNER

75 Rockefeller Plaza, New York, NY, 10019

Tel: (212) 484-8000      Fax: (212) 275-3046      www.aoltimewarner.com

*Engaged in media and communications; provides internet services, communications, publishing and entertainment.*

**AOL Time Warner Ltd., London, UK**

**MacDonald & Co. (Publishers) Ltd., Greater London House, Hampstead Rd., London NW1 7 QX, UK**

**Time-Life International Ltd., Time & Life Bldg., New Bond St., London, UK**

## AON CORPORATION

123 North Wacker Drive, Chicago, IL, 60606

Tel: (312) 701-3000      Fax: (312) 701-3100      www.aon.com

*Insurance brokers worldwide; underwrites accident and health insurance, specialty and professional insurance; and provides risk management consultation.*

**AON Risk Services Ltd. - Head UK Office, Lloyds Chambers 1, Portsoken St., London E1 8DF, UK**

Tel: 44-207-680-4000   Fax: 44-207-601-4007   Contact: Nick Maher

## API MOTION INC.

45 Hazelwood Dr., Amherst, NY, 14228

Tel: (716) 691-9100      Fax: (716) 691-9181      www.apimotion.com

*Engaged in motion control solutions using motors and drives, motor gearheads, resolver and encoder feedback devices.*

**API Motion UK Ltd., Headlands Bus. Park, Salisbury Rd., Ringwood Hampshire BH24 3PB GB, UK**

## APL LIMITED

1111 Broadway, Oakland, CA, 94607

Tel: (510) 272-8000      Fax: (510) 272-7421      www.apt.com

*Provides container shipping and logistics services.*

**APL UK, Eagle Court, 9 Vine Street, Uxbridge Middlesex UB8 1QE, UK**

Tel: 44-1895-202600   Fax: 44-1895-202606

### APPLE COMPUTER, INC.

One Infinite Loop, Cupertino, CA, 95014

Tel: (408) 996-1010     Fax: (408) 974-2113     www.apple.com

*Personal computers, peripherals and software.*

**Apple Computer (UK) Ltd.,  Eastman Way, Helem, Hempstead, Herts. HP2 7HQ UK**

### APPLERA CORPORATION

761 Main Avenue, Norwalk, CT, 06859-0001

Tel: (203) 762-1000     Fax: (203) 762-6000     www.applera.com

*Leading supplier of systems for life science research and related applications.*

**Applied Biosystems UK,  7 Kingsland Grange, Woolston Warrington, Cheshire WA1 7SR, UK**

Tel: 44-1925-825-650

### APPLIED MATERIALS, INC.

3050  Bowers Ave., Santa Clara, CA, 95054-3299

Tel: (408) 727-5555     Fax: (408) 727-9943     www.appliedmaterials.com

*Supplies manufacturing systems and services to the semiconductor industry.*

**Applied Materials UK Ltd.,  European Technical Centre, Coble Dene Rd., Royal Quays, North Shields Tyne & Wear NE29 6AZ UK**

Tel: 44-191-293-6000   Fax: 44-191-293-6024

**Applied Materials, Ltd.,  Implant Division, Foundry Lane, Horsham, West Sussex RH13 5PY UK**

Tel: 44-1403-222345   Fax: 44-1403-222353

### APPLIED SYSTEMS INC.

200 Applied Pkwy., University Park, IL, 60466

Tel: (708) 534-5575     Fax: (708) 534-5943     www.appliedsystems.com

*Computer systems, peripherals and software.*

**Applied Systems,  Applied House, The Courtyard, Gorsey Lane, Coleshill, Birmingham B46 1JA UK**

Tel: 44-1675-463-033   Fax: 44-1675-464-734

### APPLIX, INC.

112 Turnpike Road, Westboro, MA, 01581

Tel: (508) 870-0300     Fax: (508) 366-4873     www.applix.com

*Engaged in business productivity application software.*

**APPLIX, Inc.,  48 Leicester Square, London WC2H 7LT, UK**

Tel: 44-207-968-4300

### APW, INC.

PO Box 325, Milwaukee, WI, 53201-0325

Tel: (262) 523-7600     Fax: (262) 523-7624     www.apw1.com

*Mfr. hi-pressure tools, vibration control products,  consumables, technical furniture and enclosures.*

**Vero Group,  Southampton, UK**

### AQUENT

711 Boylston Street, Boston, MA, 02116

Tel: (617) 535-5000     Fax: (617) 535-6001     www.aquent.com

*Engaged in temporary, specialized employment.*

**AQUENT,  Oxford Street - 3/F, Manchester M1 5JE, UK**

**AQUENT,  1 Bedford Street, London WC2E 9HD, UK**

## ARAMARK CORPORATION

1101 Market Street, Philadelphia, PA, 19107-2988

Tel: (215) 238-3000    Fax: (215) 238-3333    www.aramark.com

*Provides managed services for food, work and safety clothing, education, recreation and facilities*

**Aramark/UK, Aramark House, Honey End Lane, Tilehurst, Reading, Berkshire RG3 RQ1 UK**

Tel: 44-118-9596-761   Fax: 44-118-9580-039   Contact: William McCall, Mng. Dir.

## ARCH CHEMICALS

501 Merritt Seven, Norwalk, CT, 06856

Tel: (203) 229-2900    Fax: (203) 229-3213    www.archchemicals.com

*Mfr. specialty chemicals.*

**Hickson International, Div. Arch Chemicals, London, UK**

## ARCHER-DANIELS-MIDLAND COMPANY

4666 Faries Parkway, Decatur, IL, 62526

Tel: (217) 424-5200    Fax: (217) 424-6196    www.admworld.com

*Grain processing: flours, grains, oils and flax fibre.*

**British Arkady Co. Ltd., Old Trafford, Manchester M16 ONJ, UK**

## ARDENT SOFTWARE, INC.

50 Washington Street, Westboro, MA, 01581-1021

Tel: (508) 366-3888    Fax: (508) 366-3669    www.ardentsoftware.com

*Publisher of database and file management software.*

**Ardent Software, Inc., Aston Court, Kingsmead Business Park, London Rd., High Wycombe, HP11 1JU UK**

Tel: 44-1-494-684444   Fax: 44-1-494-684445

**Ardent Software, Inc., Engineering Power House, Davy Ave., Knowlhill, Milton Keynes, MK5 8HJ UK**

Tel: 44-1908-234990   Fax: 44-1908-234992

## ARIBA, INC.

1565 Charleston Rd., Mountain View, CA, 94043

Tel: (650) 930-6200    Fax: (650) 930-6300    www.ariba.com

*Mfr. software.*

**Ariba UK Ltd., 5 New Square, Bedfont Lakes Feltham, Middlesex TW14 H8A, UK**

Tel: 44-20-8751-6700

## ARMSTRONG HOLDINGS, INC.

2500 Columbia Avenue, Lancaster, PA, 17604-3001

Tel: (717) 397-0611    Fax: (717) 396-2787    www.armstrong.com

*Mfr. and marketing interior furnishings and specialty products for bldg, auto and textile industry.*

**Armstrong World Industries Ltd., Fleck Way Teesside Industrial Estate Thornaby, Stockton-on-Tees, Cleveland TS17 9JT UK**

Tel: 44-1642-760679

## ARNOLD & PORTER

555 12th Street, N.W., Washington, DC, 20004-1202

Tel: (202) 942-5000    Fax: (202) 942-5999    www.arnoldporter.com

*International law firm.*

**Arnold & Porter, 25 Buclersbury, London EC4NV BDA, UK**

Tel: 44-207-329-4329   Fax: 44-207-653-9829   Contact: James D. Dinnage

## ARO INTERNATIONAL CORPORATION

One Aro Center, Bryan, OH, 43506

Tel: (419) 636-4242    Fax: (419) 633-1674    www.aro.ingersoll-rand.com

*Mfr. fluid control products, including pumps, valves, cylinders, logic controls and air line components.*

**Aro Corp. (UK) Ltd., Walkers Rd., N. Moons Moat Industrial Park, Redditch, Worcs. B98 9HE UK**

## ARROW ELECTRONICS INC.

25 Hub Drive, Melville, NY, 11747

Tel: (516) 391-1300    Fax: (516) 391-1640    www.arrow.com

*Distributor of electronic components.*

**Arrow Alliance, St. Martins Business Centre, Cambridge Road, Bedford MK41 OLF, UK**

**Arrow Electronics (UK) Ltd., St. Martins Way, Cambridge Rd., Bedford MK4 20LF UK**

Tel: 44-1234-791-444   Fax: 44-1234-791-491   Contact: Harriet Green, Mng. Dir.

## ASG (ALLEN SYSTEMS GROUP)

1333 3rd Avenue South, Naples, FL, 33102

Tel: (941) 435-2200    Fax: (941) 263-3692    www.asg.com

*Mainframe computer software, specializing in OnMark 2000 software.*

**ASG UK, Ziggurat Grosvenor Road, St. Albans AL1 3HW, UK**

Tel: 44-1727-736-300

## ASHLAND OIL INC.

50 E. Rivercenter Blvd., Covington, KY, 41012-0391

Tel: (859) 815-3333    Fax: (859) 815-5053    www.ashland.com

*Petroleum exploration, refining and transportation; mfr. chemicals, oils and lubricants.*

**Ashland Chemical Ltd., Oldington Vale Industrial Estate, Kidderminster, Worcestershire QY11 7QP UK**

**Ashland Chemical Ltd.-Umenco Div., Heckmondwike, W. Yorkshire WF16 0PS, UK**

**Ashland International Ltd., 110 Jermyn Street, London SW1Y 6EE, UK**

Tel: 44-207-930-1040

**Ashland Oil Intl. Ltd., 58 James St., London SW1A 1PR, UK**

## ASHWORTH BROTHERS INC.

89 Globe Mills Ave., PO Box 670, Fall River, MA, 02722-0670

Tel: (508) 674-4693    Fax: (508) 675-9622    www.ashworth.com

*Mfr. of metal, plastic and hybrid process conveyor belting, engineering services and conveyor systems.*

**Ashworth Europe Ltd., Bldg. 19 First Ave., The Pensnett Estate, Kingswinford West Midlands DY6 7TR, UK**

Tel: 44-1384-355000

## ASPECT COMMUNICATIONS CORPORATION

1730 Fox Drive, San Jose, CA, 95131

Tel: (408) 325-2200    Fax: (408) 325-2260    www.aspect.com

*Mfr. software and related equipment.*

**Aspect UK, 11 The Parks, Haydock, Newton-Le Willows Merseyside WA12 OJQ, UK**

**Aspect UK, 2 The Square, Stockley Park, Uxbridge Middlesex UB11 1AD, UK**

Tel: 44-20-8589-1000

## ASPEN TECHNOLOGY, INC.

10 Canal Park, Cambridge, MA, 02141

Tel: (617) 949-1000    Fax: (617) 949-1030    www.aspentec.com

*Mfr. software for chemists and refineries.*

**AspenTech UK Ltd., 4 Churchgates - The Wilderness, Berkhamsted Herts HP4 2UB, UK**

**AspenTech UK Ltd., Waterway House - The Ham, Brentford Middlesex, UK**

## ASSOCIATED MERCHANDISING CORPORATION

500 Seventh Ave., 2nd Fl., New York, NY, 10018

Tel: (212) 819-6600   Fax: (212) 819-6701   www.theamc.com

*Retail service organization; apparel, shoes and accessories.*

**Associated Merchandising Corp., 32 Wigmore St., London W1H 0DB, UK**

## ASSOCIATED PRESS INC.

50 Rockefeller Plaza, New York, NY, 10020-1605

Tel: (212) 621-1500   Fax: (212) 621-5447   www.ap.com

*News gathering agency.*

**The Associated Press Ltd., 12 Norwich St., London EC4A 1BP, UK**

Tel: 44-207-353-1515

## ASSOCIATES FIRST CAPITAL CORPORATION

250 E. Carpenter Freeway, Irving, TX, 75062-2729

Tel: (972) 652-4000   Fax: (972) 652-7420   www.theassociates.com

*Diversified consumer and commercial finance organization which provides finance, leasing and related services.*

**Associates First Capital Corporation, London, UK**

## ASTEA INTERNATIONAL, INC.

455 Business Center Drive, Horsham, PA, 19044

Tel: (215) 682-2500   Fax: (215) 682-2515   www.astea.com

*Produces computer software that assists to automate and manage field service, sales and customer support operations.*

**Astea International Inc., TDS House, Terrace Rd. South, Binfield, Bracknell Berkshire RG42 4BH UK**

Tel: 44-1344-305501   Fax: 44-1344-305503

## ASTRONAUTICS CORPORATION OF AMERICA

PO Box 523, Milwaukee, WI, 53201-0523

Tel: (414) 447-8200   Fax: (414) 447-8231   www.astronautics.com

*Design/development/mfr. aircraft instruments, avionics, electronics systems, vehicle electronics and computer maintenance service.*

**Astronautics UK, 28 Tekels Ave., Camberley, Surrey UK**

## ASYST TECHNOLOGIES, INC.

48761 Kato Road, Fremont, CA, 94538

Tel: (510) 661-5000   Fax: (510) 661-5166   www.asyst.com

*Produces wafer handling equipment.*

**Asyst Technologies European Hdqrts., Shaw House - Pegler Way, Crawley W. Sussex R11 1AF, UK**

Tel: 44-1293-763016   Fax: 44-1293-763188

## AT HOME CORPORATION

450 Broadway Street, Redwood City, CA, 94063

Tel: (650) 556-5000   Fax: (650) 556-5100   www.excite.com

*Online computer internet service provider.*

**Excite, Inc., 23 Kingly Court, London W1R5LE, UK**

Tel: 44-207-447-1800   Fax: 44-207-447-1888

## AT&T BROADBAND, LLC

9197 South Peoria, Englewood, CO, 80112

Tel: (720) 875-5500   Fax: (720) 875-4984   www.broadband.att.com

*Provides broadband technology services; digital TV, digital telephone and high-speed cable internet services.*

**One 2 One, London, England**

**TeleWest, London, UK**

## AT&T CORPORATION

32 Avenue of the Americas, New York, NY, 10013-2412

Tel: (212) 387-5400     Fax: (212) 387-5695     www.att.com

*Telecommunications.*

**AT&T (UK) Ltd., Norfolk House, 31 St. James Sq., London SW1Y 4JR, UK**

## ATLANTIC MUTUAL COS

100 Wall St., New York, NY, 10005

Tel: (212) 943-1800     Fax: (212) 428-6566     www.atlanticmutual.com

*Engaged in insurance.*

**Whittington Ltd., London, UK**

Tel: 44-270-709-9991    Contact: Michael Walton

## ATLAS AIR, INC.

2000 Westchester Avenue, Purchase, NY, 10577-2543

Tel: (914) 701-8000     Fax: (914) 701-8001     www.atlasair.com

*Air cargo carrier.*

**Atlas Air UK, Heathrow Airport, London, UK**

Tel: 44-1784-266212   Fax: 44-1784-266219

## ATMEL CORPORATION

2325 Orchard Pkwy., San Jose, CA, 95131

Tel: (408) 441-0311     Fax: (408) 436-4200     www.atmel.com

*Design, manufacture and marketing of advanced semiconductors.*

**Atmel UK Ltd., Coliseum Business Centre, Riverside Way, Camberly Surrey GU15 3YL, UK**

Tel: 44-1276-686-677

## ATTACHMATE CORPORATION

3617 131st Ave. S.E., Bellevue, WA, 98006-1332

Tel: (425) 644-4010     Fax: (425) 747-9924     www.attachmate.com

*Mfr. connectivity software.*

**Attachmate International UK Ltd., Styal Road, Manchester, UK**

Tel: 44-161-490-8111   Fax: 44-161-49-8222

## AUDIO VISUAL SERVICES CORPORATION

16 West 61st Street, New York, NY, 10023

Tel: (212) 541-5300     Fax: (212) 541-5384     www.caribiner.com

*Plans and produces meetings, events, and media campaigns: creates film/video presentations; supports in-house communications and training programs: and supplies audio-visual equipment.*

**Audio Visual Services, 4 Buckingham Gate, London SW1E 6JP, UK**

Tel: 44-207-393-4950   Fax: 44-207-393-4951

**Audio Visual Services, 191 The Vale, Acton, London W3 7QS, UK**

Tel: 44-181-735-2000   Fax: 44-181-735-2020

## AUTODESK INC.

111 McInnis Parkway, San Rafael, CA, 94903

Tel: (415) 507-5000     Fax: (415) 507-6112     www.autodesk.com

*Develop/marketing/support computer-aided design, engineering, scientific and multimedia software products.*

**Autodesk Ltd., Cross Lanes, Guildford, Surrey GU1 1UK UK**

Tel: 44-1483-303-322   Fax: 44-1483-304-556

## AUTOMATIC DATA PROCESSING INC.

One ADP Blvd., Roseland, NJ, 07068

Tel: (973) 994-5000    Fax: (973) 994-5387    www.adp.com

*Data processing services.*

**ADP Network Services Ltd., ADP House, 2 Pine Trees Chertsey Lane, Staines, Surrey TW18 3DS UK**

Tel: 44-1784-429000   Fax: 44-1784-429010   Contact: Karen Burton

## AUTOMATIC SWITCH CO. (ASCO)

50-60 Hanover Rd., Florham Park, NJ, 07932

Tel: (973) 966-2000    Fax: (973) 966-2628    www.asco.com

*Mfr. solenoid valves, emergency power controls, pressure and temp. switches.*

**Asco (UK) Ltd., 2 Pit Hey Pl., West Pimbo, Skelmersdale, Lancastershire WN8 9PG UK**

Tel: 44-1695-724270   Fax: 44-1695-729477   Contact: T. Shepstone , P. Brannon, K. Preston

## AUTOSPLICE INC.

10121 Barnes Canyon Road, San Diego, CA, 92121

Tel: (858) 535-0077    Fax: (858) 535-0130    www.autosplice.com

*Mfr. electronic components.*

**Autosplice UK Ltd., Mill Studio Business Centre, Crane Mead, Ware Herfordshire SG12 9PY, UK**

Tel: 44-1920-444-222   Fax: 44-1920-444-228   Contact: Ged Bushnell

## AUTOTOTE CORPORATION

750 Lexington Avenue, 25th Fl., New York, Ny, 1022

Tel: (212) 754-2233    Fax: (212) 754-2372    www.autotote.com

*Mfr. video gaming machines and computerized pari-mutuel wagering systems used at racetracks.*

**Scientific Games International, Div. Autotote, 81 Kirkstall Road, Leeds L53 1LH, UK**

Tel: 44-113-204-5000   Fax: 44-113-204-5401

**Scientific Games International, Div. Autotote, Unit 2 Phoenix Way, Bradford BD4 8JP, UK**

**Scientific Games International, Div. Autotote, George Mann Road, Leeds LS10 1DJ, UK**

Tel: 44-113-385-5400   Fax: 44-113-385-5401

## AUTO-TROL TECHNOLOGY CORPORATION

12500 North Washington Street, Denver, CO, 80241-2400

Tel: (303) 452-4919    Fax: (303) 252-2249    www.auto-trol.com

*Develops, markets and integrates computer-based solutions for industrial companies and government agencies worldwide.*

**Centra Technology Ltd., The Technology Centre, Wolverhampton Science Park, Wolverhampton WV10 9RU, UK**

Tel: 44-1902-824282   Emp: 6

## AVERY DENNISON CORPORATION

150 N. Orange Grove Blvd., Pasadena, CA, 91103

Tel: (626) 304-2000    Fax: (626) 792-7312    www.averydennison.com

*Mfr. pressure-sensitive adhesives and materials, office products, labels, tags, retail systems, Carter's Ink and specialty chemicals.*

**Avery Intl. Adhesive Products Ltd., 48 West St., Marlow, Buckinghamshire SL7 2NB UK**

**Avery Label Systems Ltd., Gardener Rd., Maidenhead, Berkshire SL6 7PU UK**

**Dennison PLC, Merchant Drive, Indus Est Mead Hertford, Hert SG 137 AY, UK**

**Dennison Transoceanic Corp., Elvaco House, High St., Engham, Surrey TW20 9DN UK**

**Fasson UK Ltd., Eastman Way, Hemel Hempstead, Hampstead HP2 7HE UK**

## AVID TECHNOLOGY, INC.

1 Park West, Tewksbury, MA, 01876

Tel: (978) 640-6789     Fax: (978) 640-1366     www.avid.com

*Mfr. animation design software and digital and audio systems.*

**Avid Technology Europe Ltd., Westside Complex Pinewood Studios, Iver, Bucks SLO ONH, UK**

Tel: 44-175-365-5999   Fax: 44-175-365-4999

## AVMARK INC.

1600 Wilson Boulevard, Ste. 150, Arlington, VA, 22209

Tel: (703) 528-5610     Fax: (703) 528-3689     www.avmark.com

*Aviation consult, aircraft appraisal, aviation related publications.*

**Avmark International Ltd., 26 Eccleston Square, London SW1V 1NS, UK**

## AVNET INC.

2211 South 47th Street, Phoenix, AZ, 85034

Tel: (480) 643-2000     Fax: (480) 643-4670     www.avnet.com

*Distributor electronic components, computers and peripherals.*

**Avnet EMG Ltd., Avnet House, Rutherford Close, Meadway Stevenage Hertfordshire, SG1 2EF UK**

Tel: 44-1438-788500   Fax: 44-1438-788250

**BFI INEXSA Electronics Ltd., BFI-IBEXSA House, Burnt Ash Road, Quarry Wood Ind. Estate, Aylesford Kent ME20 7NA UK**

Tel: 44-1622-882-467   Fax: 44-1622-882-469

## AVON PRODUCTS INC.

1345 Avenue of the Americas, New York, NY, 10105-0196

Tel: (212) 282-5000     Fax: (212) 282-6049     www.avon.com

*Mfr./distributor beauty and related products, fashion jewelry, gifts and collectibles.*

**Avon Cosmetics Ltd., Earlstrees Rd., Corby NN17 4AZ, UK**

Tel: 44-845-60-50-400   Fax: 44-1536-402493   Contact: Peter Nicholls

## AVX CORPORATION

PO Box 867, Myrtle Beach, SC, 29578

Tel: (843) 448-9411     Fax: (843) 448-7139     www.avxcorp.com

*Mfr. multilayer ceramic capacitors.*

**AVX Ltd., Stafford House, Station Rd., Aldershot, Hants GU11 1BA UK**

## AXCIOM CORPORATION

1 Information Way, Little Rock, AR, 72203-8180

Tel: (501) 342-1000     Fax: (510) 342-3913     www.axciom.com

*Provides computer-based marketing information services.*

**Axciom UK Ltd., 60-68 St. Thomas St., London SE1 3QU, UK**

Tel: 44-20-7526-5100   Contact: David Victory

## AXENT TECHNOLOGIES, INC.

2400 Research Boulevard, Ste. 200, Rockville, MD, 20850

Tel: (301) 258-5043     Fax: (301) 330-5756     www.axent.com

*Designs and supplies security management software .*

**AXENT Technologies BV, International Headquarters, Apex House, 4A-10 West St., Epsom, Surrey KT 18 7RG UK**

Tel: 44-1372-729655   Fax: 44-1372-749965   Contact: Stephanie Bestley

## AZURIX CORPORATION

333 Clay Street, Ste. 1000, Houston, TX, 77002-7361

Tel: (713) 646-6001     Fax: (713) 345-5358     www.azurix.com

*Engaged in w water treatment and water dredging. (JV of Enron)*

**Azurix International Limited, Four Millbank, London SW1P 3ET, UK**

Tel: 44-20-7783-7763

**Azurix Services, Grosvenor House The Square, Lower Bristol Road, Bath BA2 3EZ, UK**

Tel: 44-1225-832-900

**Azurix Services Headquarters, Wessex House, Passage Street, Bristol BS2 0JQ, UK**

Tel: 44-117-929-0611

**Lurgi Invent Water Treatment Ltd., Dell Road Shawclogh Rochdale, OL 126 BZ Lancashire, UK**

## B&P PROCESS EQUIPMENT AND SYSTEMS LLC

1000 Hess Ave., Saginaw, MI, 48601

Tel: (517) 752-4121     Fax: (517) 757-1301     www.bpprocess.com

*Mfr. stand-alone machines and complete turnkey systems for food and chemicals processing.*

**Baker Perkins Holding Ltd., Petersborough, UK**

## BAE SYSTEMS, INC.

1601 Research Blvd., Rockville, MD, 20850

Tel: (301) 738-4000     Fax: (301) 738-4643     www.baesystems.com

*Engaged in aerospace, defense electronics and information systems.*

**BAE Systems, New Filton House, Filton Bristol, BS99 7AR, UK**

**BAE Systems, Grange Road, Christchurch, Dorset BH23 4JE, UK**

**BAE Systems Aerospace Training Solutions, Simjian House - Southmead Road, Filton Bristol, BS34 7RP, UK**

**BAE Systems Naval Support Systems, 2A Upper Borough Court, Upper Borough Walls, Bath BA1 1RG, UK**

**BAE Systems R&D, PO Box 5, Filton, Bristol BS34 7QW, UK**

Tel: 44-1-117-936-3400

**BAE Systems Submarine Combat Systems, Leanne House Avon Close, Granby Industrial Estate, Weymouth Dorset DT4 9UX, UK**

**Tracor Littelfuse (UK) Ltd., Crowther Dist. 3, Washington, Tyne & Wear NE38 OAB, UK**

## BAIN & COMPANY, INC.

Two Copley Place, Boston, MA, 02116

Tel: (617) 572-2000     Fax: (617) 572-2427     www.bain.com

*Strategic management consulting services.*

**Bain & Co. Inc. United Kingdom, 40 Strand, London WC2N 5HZ, UK**

Tel: 44-207-969-6000   Fax: 44-207-969-6666

## ROBERT W. BAIRD & CO.

PO Box 672, Milwaukee, WI, 53201

Tel: (414) 765-3500     Fax: (414) 765-3600     www.rwbaird.com

*Engaged in investment banking, serving individuals, corporations, municipalities and institutional investors.*

**Granville Baird, Aimtree House, 1 York Place, Leeds LD1 2DR, UK**

Tel: 44-113-280-3500   Fax: 44-113-280-3501   Contact: David Williamson

**Granville Baird, Cheshire House, 18-20 Booth Street, Manchester M2 4AN, UK**

Tel: 44-161-236-6600   Fax: 44-161-236-6650

**Granville Baird, Mint House, 77 Mansell Street, London E1 8AF, UK**

Tel: 44-20-7488-1212   Contact: Michael Proudlock

### BAKER & McKENZIE

130 East Randolph Drive, Ste. 2500, Chicago, IL, 60601

Tel: (312) 861-8000      Fax: (312) 861-2899      www.bakerinfo.com

*International legal services.*

**Baker & McKenzie,  100 New Bridge St., London EC4V 6JA, UK**

Tel: 44-207-919-1000   Fax: 44-207-919-1999

### BAKER BOTTS LLP

910 Louisiana Street, Ste. 3000, Houston, TX, 77002-4995

Tel: (713) 229-1234      Fax: (713) 229-1522      www.bakerbotts.com

*International law firm.*

**Baker Botts LLP,  45 Ludgate Hill, London EC4M 7JU, UK**

Tel: 44-207-778-1400   Contact: Jay T. Kolb,  Mng. Ptnr.

### MICHAEL BAKER CORPORATION

Airport Office Park, 420 Rouser Road, Bldg. 3
Coraopolis, PA 15108, Coraopolis, PA, 15108

Tel: (412) 269-6300      Fax: (412) 269-6097      www.mbakercorp.com

*Engineering and construction operations and technical services.*

**Baker/Overseas Technical Service (OTS) Ltd.,  104 College Rd. 1st Fl.,  Harrow, Middlesex HA1 1BQ, UK**

### BAKER HUGHES INCORPORATED

3900 Essex Lane, Ste. 1200, Houston, TX, 77027

Tel: (713) 439-8600      Fax: (713) 439-8699      www.bakerhughes.com

*Develop and apply technology to drill, complete and produce oil and natural gas wells; provide separation systems to petroleum, municipal, continuous process and mining industries.*

**Baker Hughes INTEQ,  Eastern Hemisphere Business Unit, Hammersley House 2nd Floor, 5/8 Warwick St., London  W2R 6JE  UK**

Tel: 44-207-544-8100  Fax: 44-207-544-8101

**Baker Hughes Process,  Swift House, Cosford Lane, Rugby Warwickshire CV21 1QN, UK**

Tel: 44-1788-555667

**Baker Hughes Process Syatems,  Swift House, Cosford Lane, Rugby Warwickshire CV21 1QN, UK**

Tel: 44-1788-534100   Fax: 44-1788-534101

**Baker Oil Tools (UK) Ltd.,  Eurocentre, North River Rd., Great Yarmouth Norfolk NR30 1TE, UK**

Tel: 44-1493-332212   Fax: 44-1493-852294

**Milchem Drilling Fluids,  East Quay, S. Denes Rd., Great Yarmouth Norfolk, UK**

### J.T. BAKER INC.

222 Red School Lane, Phillipsburg, NJ, 08865

Tel: (908) 859-2151      Fax: (908) 859-9318      www.jtbaker.com

*Mfr./sale/services lab and process chemicals.*

**J.T. Baker U.K.,  PO Box 9, Hayes Gate House, Hayes Middlesex UB4 0JD, UK**

### BAKER PETROLITE CORPORATION

3900 Essex Lane, Houston, TX, 77027

Tel: (713) 599-7400      Fax: (713) 599-7592      www.bakerhughes.com/bapt/

*Mfr. specialty chemical treating programs, performance-enhancing additives and related equipment and services.*

**Petrolite Ltd.,  Kirkby Bank Rd., Knowsley Industrial Park North, Liverpool L33 7SY, UK**

## BALDWIN TECHNOLOGY COMPANY, INC.

One Norwalk West, 40 Richards Ave., Norwalk, CT, 06854

Tel: (203) 838-7470　　Fax: (203) 852-7040　　www.baldwintech.com

*Mfr./services material handling, accessories, control and prepress equipment for print industry.*

**Baldwin (UK) Ltd., Unit 13 Apex Business Centre, Boscombe Rd., Dunstable, Bedfordshire LU5 4SB UK**

Tel: 44-1-582-477499　Fax: 44-1-582-478510　Contact: John S. Chapman, Mng. Dir.

## BALTEK CORPORATION

10 Fairway Court, PO Box 195, Northvale, NJ, 07647

Tel: (201) 767-1400　　Fax: (201) 387-6631　　www.baltek.com

*Light lumber.*

**Baltek Ltd., London, UK**

Tel: 44-181-688-4398

## BALTIMORE AIRCOIL CO., INC.

PO Box 7322, Baltimore, MD, 21227

Tel: (410) 799-6200　　Fax: (410) 799-6416　　www.baltimoreaircoil.com

*Mfr. evaporative heat transfer and ice thermal storage products.*

**Baltimore Aircoil Ltd., Princewood Rd., Earlstress Ind. Est., Corby, Northants NN17 2AP UK**

## BAND-IT IDEX CORPORATION

4799 Dahlia Street, Denver, CO, 80216

Tel: (303) 320-4555　　Fax: (303) 333-6549　　www.band-it-idex.com

*Mfr. pressure clamps.*

**Band-It Co. Ltd., Speedwell Industrial Estate, Staveley Chesterfield S43 3PF, UK**

## BANK OF AMERICA CORPORATION

555 California Street, San Francisco, CA, 94104

Tel: (415) 622-3530　　Fax: (415) 622-8467　　www.bankofamerica.com

*Financial services.*

**Bank of America Intl. Ltd., 1 Alie St., PO Box 407, London E1 8DE, UK**

Tel: 44-207-634-4402　Fax: 44-207-634-4707　Contact: Clive P. Adamson, SVP

## THE BANK OF NEW YORK

One Wall Street, New York, NY, 10286

Tel: (212) 495-1784　　Fax: (212) 495-2546　　www.bankofny.com

*Banking services.*

**The Bank of New York, One Canada Square, London E14 5AL, UK**

Tel: 44-207-322-6098　Fax: 44-207-322-6023

**The Bank of New York Capital Markets Ltd., 46 Berkeley Street, London W1X 6AA, UK**

Tel: 44-207-499-1234　Fax: 44-207-322-6030

## BANK ONE CORPORATION

One First National Plaza, Chicago, IL, 60670

Tel: (312) 732-4000　　Fax: (312) 732-3366　　www.fcnbd.com

*Provides financial products and services.*

**Bank One, NA, One Triton Square, London NW1 3FN, UK**

Tel: 44-207-388-3456　Fax: 44-207-388-4747　Contact: Pete B. McCarthy, Head of EMEA

## C. R. BARD, INC.

730 Central Ave., Murray Hill, NJ, 07974

Tel: (908) 277-8000　　Fax: (908) 277-8078　　www.crbard.com

*Mfr. health care products.*

**Bard Ltd., Forest House, Brighton Rd., Crawley, West Sussex RH11 9BP UK**

## BARNES GROUP INC.

123 Main Street, Bristol, CT, 06011-0489

Tel: (860) 583-7070    Fax: (860) 589-3507    www.barnesgroupinc.com

*Mfr. precision metal parts and industrial supplies for industrial markets.*

**Associated Spring SPEC Ltd.,  Evesham, UK**

**Bowman Distribution Europe,  Corsham, UK**

**Motalink & Bowman Systems UK,  Corsham, UK**

## BARRA, INC.

2100 Milvia Street, Berkeley, CA, 94704

Tel: (510) 548-5442    Fax: (510) 548-4374    www.barra.com

*Mfr. analytical software for private investors and portfolio managers.*

**BARRA International, Ltd.,  75 King William Street, London EC4N 7BE, UK**

Tel: 44-20-7283-2255   Fax: 44-20-7220-7555

## BARRINGER TECHNOLOGIES INC.

30 Technology Drive, Warren, NJ, 07059

Tel: (908) 222-9100    Fax: (908) 222-1557    www.barringer.com

*Provides advanced technology for security, law enforcement, including drug and explosive detectors.*

**Barringer Instruments UK Ltd.,  Unit 3 Lloyds Court Manor Royal, Crawley, West Sussex RH10 2QU UK**

Tel: 44-1293-433100   Fax: 44-1293-433200

## BARRY CONTROLS INC.

40 Guest Street, PO Box 9105, Brighton, MA, 02135-9105

Tel: (617) 787-1555    Fax: (617) 254-7381    www.barrymounts.com

*Mfr./sale vibration isolation mounting devices.*

**Barry Controls Europe,  Molesey Rd. Hersham, Walton-on-Thames, Surrey KT12 3PQ, UK**

**Barry Controls Ltd.,  Molesey Road Hersham, Walton-on-Thames, Surrey KT12 3PQ UK**

**Specialty Fasteners,  Unit D - Seymour Wharf , Steamer Quay Road, Totnes Devon, UK**

## R.G. BARRY CORPORATION

PO Box 129, Columbus, OH, 43216

Tel: (614) 864-6400    Fax: (614) 866-9787    www.rgbarry.com

*Mfr. slippers and footwear.*

**R. G. Barry International,  Ste. 3/5-6, Harbour Yard Chelsea Harbour, London SW 10 OXD UK**

Tel: 44-207-351-1322   Fax: 44-207-352-4068

## BARRY-WEHMILLER COMPANIES, INC.

8020 Forsyth Boulevard, Clayton, MO, 63105

Tel: (314) 862-8000    Fax: (314) 862-8858    www.barry-wehmiller.com

*Mfr. of packaging automation equipment for filling, closing, conveying, cartoning, shrink wrapping and case packing plus systems integration.*

**Barry-Wehmiller Europe Ltd.,  Roman Way, Thetford, Norfolk IP24 IXB, UK**

Tel: 44-1842-754-171   Fax: 44-1842-755-318   Contact: David Clark   Emp: 20

## BARTON INCORPORATED

55 East Monroe Street, Chicago, IL, 60603

Tel: (312) 346-9200    Fax: (312) 855-1220    www.bartoninc.com

*Mfr. bourbon and blended whiskey, Mexican beer (Corona Extra) and  German beer (St. Pauli Girl).*

**Barton Intl. Ltd.,  5th Fl. Sackville House, 40 Piccadilly, London W1V 9PA UK**

## BASE TEN SYSTEMS INC.

One Electronics Drive, Trenton, NJ, 08619

Tel: (609) 586-7010     Fax: (609) 586-1593     www.base10.com

*Mfr. proprietary control systems, flight test systems, communications products.*

**Base Ten Systems Ltd., Pilgrim's Well - 429 London Road, Camberley Surrey GU15-3HZ, UK**

## BATES WORLDWIDE INC.

405 Lexington Ave., New York, NY, 10174

Tel: (212) 297-7000     Fax: (212) 986-0270     www.batesww.com

*Advertising, marketing, public relations and media consulting.*

**Bates Communications, 121-141 Westbourne Terrace, London W2 5JR, UK**

Tel: 44-207-262-0708    Fax: 44-207-402-0020

**Bates Dorland, 121-141 Westbourne Terrace, London W2 5JR, UK**

Tel: 44-207-262-5077    Fax: 44-207-258-3757    Contact: G. Hinton, Chmn.

**Bates Healthcom, 141 Westbourne Terrace, London W1 6JR, UK**

Tel: 44-207-262-2141    Fax: 44-207-262-2208    Contact: Mike Lees, CEO

**Bates Interactive, 121-141 Westbourne Terrace, London W2 5JR, UK**

Tel: 44-207-724-7228    Fax: 44-207-724-3075    Contact: M. Crossman, Mng. Dir.

**The Decision Shop, Westbourne House, 14-16 Westbourn Grove, London W1 RRH UK**

Tel: 44-207-229-6699    Fax: 44-207-229-0606    Contact: Bernard Walsh, Mng. Dir.

## BATTELLE MEMORIAL INSTITUTE

505 King Ave., Columbus, OH, 43201-2693

Tel: (614) 424-6424     Fax: (614) 424-3260     www.battelle.org

*Develops new technologies, commercializes products, and provides solutions for industry and government.*

**Battelle Institute Ltd., 15 Hanover Sq., London W1R 9AJ, UK**

## BAUSCH & LOMB INC.

One Bausch & Lomb Place, Rochester, NY, 14604-2701

Tel: (716) 338-6000     Fax: (716) 338-6007     www.bausch.com

*Mfr. vision care products and accessories.*

**Bausch & Lomb U.K., Ltd., Bausch & Lomb House, 106-114 London Road, Kingston-Upon-Thames, Surrey KT2 6QJ, UK**

## BAXTER HEALTHCARE CORPORATION

One Baxter Parkway, Deerfield, IL, 60015

Tel: (847) 948-2000     Fax: (847) 948-3948     www.baxter.com

*Pharmaceutical preparations, surgical/medical instruments and cardiovascular products.*

**Baxter Healthcare Ltd., Wellington Business Park 31, Dukes Road Crowthorne, Berkshire RG45 6LS, UK**

Tel: 44-1344-75-9300

**Baxter Unicare, Cambridge Road, Harlow Essex CM20 2SG, UK**

Tel: 44-1279-641-111

## BDO SEIDMAN, LLP    BELGIUM

Two Prudential Plaza, 180 N. Stetson Ave., Ste. 2300, Chicago, IL, 60601

Tel: (312) 240-1236     Fax: (312) 240-3329     www.bdo.com

*International accounting and financial consulting firm.*

**BDO Stoy Hayward, 8 Baker St., London W1M 1DA ,UK**

Tel: 44-207-486-5888    Fax: 44-207-487-3686    Contact: Stephen P. Greene

## BEA SYSTEMS, INC.

2315 North First Street, St. Jose, CA, 95131

Tel: (408) 570-8000     Fax: (408) 570-8091     www.beasys.com

*Develops communications management software and provider of software consulting services.*

**BEA Systems Ltd., Windsor Court, Kingsmead Business Park, Frederick Place & London Rd., High Wycombe Buckinghamshire HP11 1JU UK**

Tel: 44-1494-559500   Fax: 44-1494-452202

## BEAR STEARNS & CO., INC.

245 Park Ave., New York, NY, 10167

Tel: (212) 272-2000     Fax: (212) 272-3092     www.bearstearns.com

*Investment banking, securities broker/dealer and investment advisory services.*

**Bear Stearns International Ltd., One Canada Sq., London E14 5AD, UK**

Tel: 44-207-516-6000   Fax: 44-207-516-6030

## BECHTEL GROUP INC.

50 Beale Street, PO Box 3965, San Francisco, CA, 94105-1895

Tel: (415) 768-1234     Fax: (415) 768-9038     www.bechtel.com

*General contractors in engineering and construction.*

**Bechtel Great Britain, Bechtel House, PO Box 739, 245 Hammersmith Rd., London W6 8DP UK**

Tel: 44-181-846-5111   Fax: 44-181-846-6940

**Bechtel Water, Chadwick House, Warrington Rd., Risley, Warrington WA3 6AE UK**

Tel: 44-192-585-7000   Fax: 44-192-585-7557

## BECKMAN COULTER, INC.

4300 N. Harbor Boulevard, Fullerton, CA, 92834

Tel: (714) 871-4848     Fax: (714) 773-8898     www.beckmancoulter.com

*Develop/mfr./marketing automated systems and supplies for biological analysis.*

**Beckman Coulter (U.K.) Limited, Oakley Court, Kingsmead Business Park, London Road, High Wycombe Buckinghamshire HP11 1JU, UK**

Tel: 44-1494-441181

## BELDEN, INC.

7701 Forsyth Blvd., Ste. 800, St. Louis, MO, 63015

Tel: (314) 854-8000     Fax: (314) 854-8001     www.belden.com

*Mfr. electronic wire and cable products.*

**Belden UK Ltd., 10 Watergate Row - Watergate Street, Chester, Cheshire CH1 2LD, UK**

## BELL & HOWELL COMPANY

5215 Old Orchard Road, Skokie, IL, 60077

Tel: (847) 470-7100     Fax: (847) 470-9625     www.bellhowell.com

*Diversified information products and services.*

**Bell & Howell Ltd., 33-35 Woodthorpe Rd., Ashford, Middlesex TW15 2RZ, UK**

**Bell & Howell Micromedia, Telford Rd., Bicester, Oxon OX6 OUP, UK**

## BELL MICROPRODUCTS INC.

1941 Ringwood Avenue, San Jose, CA, 95131

Tel: (408) 451-9400     Fax: (408) 451-1600     www.bellmicro.com

*Distributes semiconductor and computer products from manufacturers.*

**Bell Microproducts Inc., Cox Lane Chessington, Suttry KT9 1SJ, UK**

Tel: 44-20-8286-5000

## BELLSOUTH CORPORATION LATIN AMERICA

1155 Peachtree Street NE, Ste. 400, Atlanta, GA, 30367

Tel: (404) 249-4800     Fax: (404) 249-4880     www.bellsouth.com

*Mobile communications, telecommunications network systems.*

**Air Call Communications Ltd., Unit 6 Air Call Business Center, Colindeep Lane, Colindale London, UK**

## BEN & JERRY'S HOMEMADE INC.

30 Community Drive, South Burlington, VT, 05403-6828

Tel: (802) 651-9600     Fax: (802) 651-9647     www.benjerry.com

*Mfr. premium ice cream.*

**Ben & Jerry's International, London, UK**

## BENTLY NEVADA CORPORATION

1617 Water Street, PO Box 157, Minden, NV, 89423

Tel: (775) 782-3611     Fax: (775) 782-9259     www.bently.com

*Provides hardware, software, and services for machinery information and management systems.*

**Bently Nevada (UK) Ltd, 2 Kelvin Close, Science Park N., Birchwood, Warrington, Cheshire WA3 7PB UK**

## LOUIS BERGER INTERNATIONAL INC.

100 Halsted Street, East Orange, NJ, 07019

Tel: (201) 678-1960     Fax: (201) 672-4284     www.louisberger.com

*Consulting engineers, engaged in architecture, environmental and advisory services.*

**Louis Berger International Inc., Britannia House, 1 Glenthorne Road, Hammersmith London W 6OLH, UK**

Tel: 44-207-748-9898    Fax: 44-207-748-3880

## BERLITZ CROSS-CULTURAL TRAINING INC.

400 Alexander Park, Princeton, NJ, 08540

Tel: (609) 514-9650     Fax: (609) 514-9689     www.berlitz.com

*Consulting and management training services to bridge cultural gaps for international travelers as well as for business transferees and families.*

**Berlitz (U.K.) Limited, 9-13 Grosvenor St., London W1A 3BZ, UK**

**Berlitz (U.K.) Limited, 321 Oxford Street , London W1A 3BZ, UK**

## BERNARD HODES GROUP

555 Madison Ave., New York, NY, 10022

Tel: (212) 935-4000     Fax: (212) 755-7324     www.hodes.com

*Multinational recruitment agency.*

**MacMillan Bernard Hodes Group, Salisbury House - Bluecoats, Hertford SG14 1PU, UK**

## SANFORD C. BERNSTEIN & CO., LLC

767 Fifth Avenue, New York, NY, 10153

Tel: (212) 486-5800     Fax: (212) 756-4455     www.bernstein.com

*Engaged in investment management and research.*

**Sanford C. Bernstein & Co., Div. ACL Private Group, 99 Gresham Street, London EC2V 7NG, UK**

Tel: 44-20-7367-7300   Fax: 44-20-7367-7367    Contact: David Steyn, Mng. Dir.

## BEST WESTERN INTERNATIONAL

6201 North 24th Place, Phoenix, AZ, 85106

Tel: (602) 957-4200     Fax: (602) 957-5740     www.bestwestern.com

*International hotel chain.*

**Five Lake Hotel, Golf & Country Club, Colchester Rd., Essex, UK**

**Oatlands Park Hotel, Surrey, GB-Kt13 9HB, UK**

**BESTFOODS, INC.**

700 Sylvan Ave., International Plaza, Englewood Cliffs, NJ, 07632-9976

Tel: (201) 894-4000      Fax: (201) 894-2186      www.bestfoods.com

*Consumer foods products; corn refining.*

**Bestfoods UK Ltd.,  Claygate House, Esher, Surrey KT10 9PN, UK**

Tel: 44-1372-462-181  Fax: 44-1372-468-775   Contact: Richard Oppenheim, Mgr.

**BETSEY JOHNSON INC.**

498 Seventh Ave., 21st Fl., New York, NY, 10018

Tel: (212) 244-0843      Fax: (212) 244-0855

*Fashion clothing line.*

**Betsey Johnson Company,  106 Draycott Ave., London SW3 3AE, UK**

**BETZDEARBORN**

4636 Somerton Road, PO Box 3002, Trevose, PA, 19053-6783

Tel: (215) 953-2568      Fax: (215) 953-5524      www.betzdearborn.com

*Mfr. water/wastewater and process system treatment chemicals and services.*

**BetzDearborn Ltd.,  Foundry Lane, Widnes, Cheshire, WA8 8 UD UK**

**BICC GENERAL**

4 Tesseneer Drive, Highland Heights, KY, 41076

Tel: (606) 572-8000      Fax: (606) 572-8444      www.generalcable.com

*Mfr., marketing and distribution of copper, aluminum and fiber optic wire and cable products for the communications, energy and electrical markets.*

**BICC General,  Hall Lane - Prescot, Merseyside L34 5TG, UK**

**BINGHAM DANA LLP**

399 Park Avenue, New York, NY, 10022-4689

Tel: (212) 318-7700      Fax: (212) 752-5378      www.bingham.com

*International law firm.*

**Bingham Dana,  8-10 Mansion House Place, London EC49 8LB, UK**

Tel: 44-207-375-9770   Fax: 44-207-220-7431   Emp: 6

**BINNEY & SMITH INC.**

1100 Church Lane, PO Box 431, Easton, PA, 18044-0431

Tel: (610) 253-6271      Fax: (610) 250-5768      www.crayola.com

*Mfr. crayons, art supplies and craft kits.*

**Binney & Smith Ltd.,  Ampthill Rd., Bedford MK42 9RS, UK**

**BIOGEN, INC.**

14 Cambridge Center, Cambridge, MA, 02142

Tel: (617) 679-2000      Fax: (617) 679-2617      www.bigoten.com

*Engaged in medical research and development on autoimmune diseases.*

**Biogen Ltd.,  5D Roxborough Way Foundation Park, Maidenhead Berkshire SL6 2UD, UK**

Tel: 44-16-28-50-1000

**BIOMATRIX, INC.**

65 Railroad Ave., Ridgefield, NJ, 07657

Tel: (201) 945-9550      Fax: (201) 945-0363      www.biomatrix.com

*Mfr. hylan biological polymers for therapeutic medical and skin care products.*

**Biomatrix UK Ltd.,  Lamb House, Church Street, London W4 2PD, UK**

Tel: 44-181-956-2221  Fax: 44-181-956-2461   Contact: Martin Jordan, VP European Operations   Emp: 9

## BIO-RAD LABORATORIES INC.

1000 Alfred Nobel Drive, Hercules, CA, 94547

Tel: (510) 724-7000          Fax: (510) 724-3167          www.bio-rad.com

*Mfr. life science research products, clinical diagnostics, analytical instruments.*

**Bio-Rad Laboratories Ltd., Hemel Heampstead, UK**

## BIOWHITTAKER INC.

8830 Biggs Ford Road, Walkersville, MD, 21793

Tel: (301) 898-7025          Fax: (301) 845-6099          www.biowhittaker.com

*Mfr. cell culture products, endotoxin detection assays.*

**BioWhittaker UK Ltd., BioWhittaker House - 1 Ashville Way, Wokingham Berkshire RG41 2PL, UK**

Tel: 44-118-979-5234    Contact: David Guy

## BLACK & DECKER CORPORATION

701 E. Joppa Road, Towson, MD, 21286

Tel: (410) 716-3900          Fax: (410) 716-2933          www.blackanddecker.com

*Mfr. power tools and accessories, security hardware, small appliances, fasteners, information systems and services.*

**Black & Decker England, England Office, 701 East Joppa Road, Towson MD 21286**

## BLACK & VEATCH LLP

8400 Ward Pkwy., PO Box 8405, Kansas City, MO, 64114

Tel: (913) 339-2000          Fax: (913) 339-2934          www.bv.com

*Engineering, architectural and construction services.*

**Binnie Black & Veatch, c/o TW Utilities Engineering, Gainsboro/Blake House, Manor Farm Rd., Reading Berkshire RG2 0JN UK**

Tel: 44-118-923-6718    Fax: 44-118-923-6860    Contact: Stephen Beales, Div. Dir.

**Binnie Black & Veatch, Clifton Heights, Triangle West, Bristol BS8 1EJ UK**

Tel: 44-117-934-9896    Fax: 44-117-934-9897    Contact: Neil Bradley

**Binnie Black & Veatch, Grosvenor House, 69 London Rd., Redhill Surrey RH1 1LQ, UK**

Tel: 44-1737-774155    Fax: 44-1737-772767    Contact: Dave Still, EVP

**Binnie Black & Veatch, 25 Newgate St., Chester CH1 1DE, UK**

Tel: 44-1244-317044    Fax: 44-1244-347256    Contact: Richard Coackley

## BLACK BOX CORPORATION

1000 Park Dr., Lawrence, PA, 15055

Tel: (724) 746-5500          Fax: (724) 746-0746          www.blackbox.com

*Direct marketer and technical service provider of communications, networking and related computer connectivity products.*

**Black Box Catalogue Ltd., 15 Cradock Rd., Reading, Berkshire RG2 0JT UK**

Tel: 44-118-965-5000    Fax: 44-118-965-5050    Contact: Roger Croft, Gen. Mgr.

## BLACK CLAWSON COMPANY

405 Lexington Ave., 61st Fl., New York, NY, 10174

Tel: (212) 916-8000          Fax: (212) 916-8057          www.ligroup.com

*Paper and pulp mill machinery.*

**Black Clawson Intl. Ltd., 20/26 Wellesley Rd., Croydon, Surrey CR9 2BT, UK**

## H&R BLOCK, INC.

4400 Main Street, Kansas City, MO, 64111

Tel: (816) 753-6900          Fax: (816) 753-8628          www.hrblock.com

*Tax preparation services and software, financial products and services and mortgage loans.*

**H&R Block UK Ltd., 2 The Courtyard, London Rd., Horsham, West Sussex RH12 1AT, UK**

## BLOOMBERG L.P.

499 Park Ave., New York, NY, 10022

Tel: (212) 318-2000     Fax: (212) 940-1954     www.bloomberg.com

*Publishes magazines and provides TV, radio and newspaper wire services.*

**Bloomberg L.P., City Gate House, 39-45 Finsbury Square, London ECQA 1PQ, UK**

## BLOUNT INTERNATIONAL, INC

4520 Executive Park Dr., Montgomery, AL, 36116-1602

Tel: (334) 244-4000     Fax: (334) 271-8130     www.blount.com

*Mfr. cutting chain and equipment, timber harvest and handling equipment, sporting ammo, riding mowers.*

**Blount UK Ltd., 6 Station Dr., Bredon, Tewkesbury Gloucestershire GL20 7HQ, UK**

Tel: 44-1684-772736   Fax: 44-1684-773154   Contact: Simon Pears, Branch Mgr.

## BMC SOFTWARE, INC.

2101 City West Blvd., Houston, TX, 77042-2827

Tel: (713) 918-8800     Fax: (713) 918-8000     www.bmc.com

*Engaged in mainframe-related utilities software and services.*

**BMC Software Ltd., Assurance House, Vicarage Road, Egham Surrey TW20 9JY, UK**

## THE BOEING COMPANY

7755 East Marginal Way South, Seattle, WA, 98108

Tel: (206) 655-2121     Fax: (206) 655-6300     www.boeing.com.

*World's largest aerospace company; mfr. military and commercial aircraft, missiles and satellite launch vehicles.*

**Boeing Company, Heathrow Airport, London, UK**

## BOISE CASCADE CORPORATION

1111 West Jefferson Street, PO Box 50, Boise, ID, 83728-0001

Tel: (208) 384-6161     Fax: (208) 384-7189     www.bc.com

*Mfr./distributor paper and paper products, building products, office products.*

**Boise Cascade Office Products, Ltd., Doncaster, UK**

**Boise Cascade Office Products, Ltd., Bolton, UK**

**Boise Cascade Sales Ltd., 7C Hill Ave., Amersham, Buckinghamshire HP6 5BD, UK**

Tel: 44-149-443-4222   Fax: 44-149-443-1557   Contact: Kpjm Ramaer, Mng. Dir.

## BOOZ-ALLEN & HAMILTON INC.

8283 Greensboro Drive, McLean, VA, 22102

Tel: (703) 902-5000     Fax: (703) 902-3333     www.bah.com

*International management and technology consultants.*

**Booz, Allen & Hamilton Inc. Intl. (UK) Ltd., 7 Savoy Court, Strand, London WC2R 0EZ, UK**

Tel: 44-207-393-3333   Fax: 44-207-393-0025

## BORDEN INC.

180 East Broad Street, Columbus, OH, 43215-3799

Tel: (614) 225-4000     Fax: (614) 220-6453     www.bordenfamily.com

*Mfr. packaged foods, consumer adhesives, housewares and industrial chemicals.*

**Borden Chemical UK Ltd., Rownhams Rd., North Baddesley, Southampton S052 9ZB UK**

Tel: 44-1703-732-131   Fax: 44-1703-738-656

**Borden Foods International, Cedar House, Cedar Lane, Frimley, Surrey GU 16 5HY UK**

Tel: 44-1276-685-855

## BRISTOL BABCOCK INC.

1100 Buckingham Street, Watertown, CT, 06795

Tel: (203) 575-3000      Fax: (203) 575-3170      www.bristolbabcock.com

*Mfr. process control instruments and SCADA systems.*

**Bristol Babcock Ltd., Parsonage House, Parsonage Sq., Dorking Surrey RH4 1UP, UK**

## BRISTOL-MYERS SQUIBB COMPANY

345 Park Ave., New York, NY, 10154-0037

Tel: (212) 546-4000      Fax: (212) 546-4020      www.bms.com

*Pharmaceutical and food preparations, medical and surgical instruments.*

**Bristol-Myers Squibb - Reg. HQ/London, 141-149 Staines Rd., Hounslow, Middlesex UK**

**Bristol-Myers Squibb London, Swakeley House, Milton Rd., Ickenham, Uxbridge, London UK**

**C.V. Laboratories, Gordon House, Gordon Rd., Aldershot UK**

**ConvaTec Ltd., Harrington House, Milton Road, Ickenham Uxbridge UB 10 8 PU, UK**

**Matrix UK, 114 St. Martins Lane, London, WC 2N4AZ, UK**

**Zimmer, Ltd., Dunbeath Rd., Elgin Drive, Swindon Wiltshire, UK**

## BRK BRANDS/FIRST ALERT, INC.

3901 Liberty Street Road, Aurora, IL, 60504-8122

Tel: (630) 851-7330      Fax: (630) 851-1331      www.firstalert.com

*Mfr. smoke detectors, fire extinguishers, lights, timers and sensor systems.*

**BRK Brands Europe Ltd., Fountain House, Canal View Rd., Newbury, Berkshire, RG14 5XF UK**

## BROADCOM CORPORATION INTERNATIONAL

16215 Alton Parkway, PO Box 57013, Irvine, CA, 92618

Tel: (949) 450-8700      Fax: (949) 450-8710      www.broadcom.com

*Designs, develops and supplies integrated circuits and high density communication processors.*

**Broadcom Corporation, Fieldside Cottage - Fieldside, Thorpe Hesley, Rotherham, South Yorkshire S61 2RU, UK**

Tel: 44-114-2464832    Fax: 44-114-2464892    Contact: Julian M. Wood

## BROADVISION, INC.

585 Broadway, Redwood City, CA, 94063

Tel: (650) 261-5100      Fax: (650) 261-5900      www.broadvision.com

*Develops and delivers an integrated suite of packaged applications for personalized enterprise portals.*

**BroadVision UK, 100 Longwater Avenue - Green Park, Reading RG2 6GP, UK**

Tel: 44-118-920-7777

## BROBECK PHLEGER & HARRISON

Spear Street Tower, One Market St., San Francisco, CA, 94105

Tel: (415) 442-0900      Fax: (415) 442-1010      www.brobeck.com

*International law firm.*

**Brobeck Hale & Dorr International (JV), Alder Castle, 10 Noble Street, London EC2V7QJ, UK**

Tel: 44-20-7645-2400    Fax: 44-20-7645-2424    Contact: David A. Ayres, Mng. Prnt.

**Brobeck Hale & Dorr International (JV), 25 Milton Park, Oxford OX14 4SH, UK**

Tel: 44-1235-923-000    Fax: 44-1235-823-030    Contact: David A. Ayres, Mng. Prnt.

## BROOKS AUTOMATION, INC.

15 Elizabeth Drive, Chelmsford, MA, 01824

Tel: (978) 262-2400      Fax: (978) 262-2500      www.brooks.com

*Mfr. tool automation products.*

**Brooks Automation UK, 670 Eskdale Road, Winnersh Triangle, Wokingham RG41 5TS, UK**

Tel: 44-118-921-5600    Fax: 44-118-921-5660

Brooks Automation UK, Fairways Business Park - Unit 2, Deer Park Avenue, Livingston EH54 8AF, UK

Tel: 44-1506-449-000   Fax: 44-1506-449-001

## BROOKTROUT, INC.

410 First Avenue, Needham, MA, 02494

Tel: (781) 449-4100        Fax: (781) 449-9009        www.brooktroutinc.com

*Mfr. hardware and software products.*

Brooktrout Technology Europe, Stonebridge Street, Leatherhead, Surrey KT22 8BZ, UK

Tel: 44-1344-380280   Fax: 44-1372-379373

Brooktrout Technology Europe, Centennial Court - Easthampstead Road, Bracknell Berkshire RG12 1YQ, UK

Tel: 44-1344-380280   Fax: 44-1344-380288

## BROWN & WOOD LLP

One World Trade Center, 59th Fl., New York, NY, 10048

Tel: (212) 839-5300        Fax: (212) 839-5599        www.brownwoodlaw.com

*International law firm.*

Brown & Wood LLP, Princess Court, 7 Princess Street, London EC2R 8AQ, UK

Tel: 44-207-778-1800   Fax: 44-207-796-1807

## BROWN BROTHERS HARRIMAN & COMPANY

59 Wall Street, New York, NY, 10005

Tel: (212) 483-1818        Fax: (212) 493-8526        www.bbh.com

*Financial services.*

Brown Brothers Harriman Investor Services, Ltd., Garden House, 18 Finsbury Circus, London EC2M 7BP, UK

## BROWNING WINCHESTER

1 Browning Place, Morgan, UT, 84050

Tel: (801) 876-2711        Fax: (801) 876-3331        www.browning.com

*Sales/distribution of port firearms, fishing rods, etc.*

Browning Sports UK, Lda., Milton Park 37D, Milton 0X14 4RT Abingdon, Oxon UK

## BRUSH WELLMAN INC.

17876 St. Clair Ave., Cleveland, OH, 44110

Tel: (216) 486-4200        Fax: (216) 383-4091        www.brushwellman.com

*Mfr. beryllium, beryllium alloys and ceramics, specialty metal systems and precious metal products.*

Brush Wellman Ltd., 2405 Ely Rd., Theale Commercial. Est., Theale Reading RG7 4BQ, UK

Tel: 44-118-930-3733   Fax: 44-181-930-3635

## BTU INTERNATIONAL

23 Esquire Rd., North Billerica, MA, 01862

Tel: (508) 667-4111        Fax: (508) 667-9068        www.btu.com

*Mfr. of industrial furnaces.*

BTU Engineering Ltd., 14-15 Armstrong Mall, Southwood Summit Centre, Farnborough, Hants. GU14 0NR UK

## BUCK CONSULTANTS INC.

One Pennsylvania Plaza, New York, NY, 10119

Tel: (212) 330-1000        Fax: (212) 695-4184        www.buckconsultants.com

*Employee benefit, actuarial and compensation consulting services.*

Buck Paterson Consultants Ltd., 10 Buckingham Place, London SW1E 6HT, UK

## A. C. BUCKHORN INC.

55 West Techne Center Drive, Milford, OH, 45150

Tel: (513) 831-4402      Fax: (513) 831-5474      www.acbuckhorn.com

*Mfr. of reusable plastic packaging systems, plastic containers and pallets and project management services.*

**Buckhorn Ltd., Unit 6-8, Industrial Estate, Stanton Harcourt, Oxon OX8 1SL UK**

Tel: 44-1865-88310   Fax: 44-1865-882792   Contact: Neville Jarvis, Gen. Mgr.   Emp: 6

## BUCYRUS INTERNATIONAL, INC.

1100 Milwaukee Ave., PO Box 500, South Milwaukee, WI, 53172

Tel: (414) 768-4000      Fax: (414) 768-4474      www.bucyrus.com

*Mfr. of surface mining equipment, primarily walking draglines, electric mining shovels and blast hole drills.*

**Bucyrus-Europe Ltd., Becor House, Green Lane, Lincoln LN6 7DL, UK**

Tel: 44-15-22513421   Fax: 44-15-22544438   Contact: David Lee, Mng. Dir.

## BUDGET GROUP, INC.

125 Basin St., Ste. 210, Daytona Beach, FL, 32114

Tel: (904) 238-7035      Fax: (904) 238-7461      www.budgetrentacar.com

*Car and truck rental system.*

**Budget Rent A Car International, 41 Marlows, Hemel Hempstead, Herts HP1 1XL, UK**

Tel: 44-1442-276000   Fax: 44-1442-276000   Contact: Ron Norbut, VP, Mng. Dir.

## BULAB HOLDINGS INC.

1256 N. McLean Blvd, Memphis, TN, 38108

Tel: (901) 278-0330      Fax: (901) 276-5343      www.buckman.com

*Biological products; chemicals and chemical preparations.*

**Buckman Laboratories Ltd., Enterprise House, Manchester Science Park, Lloyd St. N., Manchester M15 6SE UK**

Tel: 44-161-226-1227   Fax: 44-161-227-9314

## BURLINGTON RESOURCES

5051 Westheimer, Ste. 1400, Houston, TX, 77056

Tel: (713) 624-9500      Fax: (713) 624-9555      www.br-inc.com

*Engaged in the exploration, development, production and marketing of crude oil and natural gas.*

**Burlington Resources, 1 Canada Square, Canary Wharf, London E14 5AA, UK**

Tel: 44-207-208-4646

## LEO BURNETT, DIV. B-COM 3 GROUP

35 West Wacker Drive, Chicago, IL, 60601

Tel: (312) 220-5959      Fax: (312) 220-6533      www.bcom3group.com

*Engaged in advertising, marketing, media buying and planning, and public relations.*

**Bartle Bogle Hegarty/Burnett, London, UK**

**Leo Burnett Company, London, UK**

## BURNS INTERNATIONAL SERVICES CORPORATION

200 S. Michigan Ave., Chicago, IL, 60604

Tel: (312) 322-8500      Fax: (312) 322-8398      www.burnsinternational.com

*Security services.*

**Burns International Security Services, 192 North Street, Bristol, BS3 1JF UK**

**Burns Intl. Security Services Ltd., 100 Warwick Rd., Ealing, London W5 5PT UK**

## BURSON-MARSTELLER

230 Park Ave., New York, NY, 10003-1566

Tel: (212) 614-4000      Fax: (212) 614-4262      www.bm.com

*Public relations/public affairs consultants.*

**Burson-Marsteller London, 24-28 Bloomsbury Way, London WC1A 2PX, UK**

Tel: 44-207-831-6262-   Fax: 44-207-430-1033   Emp: 160

**Burson-Marsteller Ltd., 24-28 Bloomsbury Way, London WC1A 2PX, UK**

Tel: 44-207-831-6262   Fax: 44-207-831-8138

## BUSH BOAKE ALLEN INC.

7 Mercedes Drive, Montvale, NJ, 07645

Tel: (201) 391-9870      Fax: (201) 391-0860      www.bushboakeallen.com

*Mfr. aroma chemicals for fragrances and flavor products for seasonings.*

**Bush Boake Allen, Dans Road, Widnes Cheshire WA8 0RF, UK**

Tel: 44-151-423-8000   Fax: 44-151-423-8010

**Bush Boake Allen Ltd., Stafford Works, Long Melford Sudbury, Suffolk CO10 7HU, UK**

Tel: 44-1787-314000   Fax: 44-1787-314130

**Bush Boake Allen Ltd., Blackhorse lane, Walthamstow, London E17 QP, UK**

Tel: 44-20-8523-6000   Fax: 44-29-8523-6011

**Bush Boake Allen Ltd., Colchester Road, Witham, Essex CM8 3BT, UK**

Tel: 44-1376-515140   Fax: 44-1376-511628

## BUTLER INTERNATIONAL

110 Summit Ave., Montvale, NJ, 07645

Tel: (201) 573-8000      Fax: (201) 573-9723      www.butlerintl.com

*Leading supplier of skilled technical personnel.*

**Butler International, King Mill Lane, South Nutfield, Redhill, Surrey RH15NE UK**

Tel: 44-1737-822000   Fax: 44-1737-823031   Contact: David Leyshon

**Butler International Executive Search, St. George's Business Centre, St. George's Square, Portsmouth, Hampshire PO1 3EZ UK**

Tel: 44-1705-819999   Fax: 44-1705-819990   Contact: Alex Rock, Dir.

**Butler Rail Services, 5th Fl. West Wing City Cloisters, 188-196 Old St., London ECIV 9AY UK**

Tel: 44-207-251-4234   Fax: 44-207-251-4449   Contact: Tony Godfrey

**Butler Services Group/Aerospace Services, Units D1, 2 & 3 Raylor Centre, James St., York Y013DW UK**

Tel: 44-1904-430233   Fax: 44-1904-430608   Contact: Dick Osguthorpe

## BUTTERICK COMPANY, INC.

161 Avenue of the Americas, New York, NY, 10013

Tel: (212) 620-2500      Fax: (212) 620-2746      www.butterick.com

*Prints sewing patterns and related magazines.*

**Butterick Fashion Marketing Ltd., New Lane, Havant, Hants. P09 2ND, UK**

## BWI KARTRIDG PAK

807 W. Kimberly Rd., PO Box 3848, Davenport, IA, 52808

Tel: (319) 391-1100      Fax: (319) 391-0017

*Meat packaging and aerosol filling equipment.*

**BWI plc, PO Box 95, Atlantic St., Altrincham WA145EW, Cheshire UK**

## C&D TECHNOLOGIES

1400 Union Meeting Road, Blue Bell, PA, 19422

Tel: (215) 619-2700      Fax: (215) 619-7840      www.cdtechno.com

*Mfr./produce electrical power storage and conversion products and industrial batteries.*

**C&D Technologies, Romsey Hampshire, UK**

## CABLE DESIGN TECHNOLOGIES CORPORATION

661 Andersen Drive, Plaza 7, Pittsburgh, PA, 15220

Tel: (412) 937-2300        Fax: (412) 937-9690        www.cdtc.com

*Mfr. computer connector copper, fiber optic and composite cables.*

**Raydex/CDT, Gladden Place, West Gillibrands Skelmersdale, Lancanshire WN8 9SX, UK**

Tel: 44-1695-733-061

## CABLETRON SYSTEMS, INC.

35 Industrial Way, PO Box 5005, Rochester, NH, 03866-5005

Tel: (603) 332-9400        Fax: (603) 337-3007        www.cabletron.com

*Develop/mfr./marketing/install/support local and wide area network connectivity hardware and software.*

**Cabletron System, Network House, Newbury Business Park, London Rd., Newbury, Berkshire RG13 2PZ UK**

## CABOT CORPORATION

75 State Street, Boston, MA, 02109-1807

Tel: (617) 345-0100        Fax: (617) 342-6103        www.cabot-corp.com

*Mfr. carbon blacks, plastics; oil and gas, information systems.*

**BOCMIN Metals Ltd. (Cabot Mineral Resources), Broadway Chambers, Hammersmith Broadway, London W67 AF UK**

**Cabot Alloys Europe (Engineered Products), Cabot House, William St., Windsor, Berkshire SL4 1BA, UK**

**Cabot Alloys UK Ltd. (HiTec Div.), Earlstrees Rd., Corby, Northants NN17 2AZ, UK**

**Cabot Europe Ltd., Cabot Plastics Europe (Energy), Silk House, 6 Park Green, Macclesfield, Cheshire SK11 7NA, UK**

**Cabot Plastics Division (Energy), Gate St., Dukinfield, Cheshire SK14 4RZ, UK**

**Cabot Safety Ltd. (E-A-R), First Ave., Poynton, Stockport, Cheshire SK12 1YJ, UK**

**Deloro Stellite (WearTec Div.), Stratton St. Margaret, Swindon, Wiltshire SN3 4QA, UK**

## CACI INTERNATIONAL INC.

1100 North Glebe Road, Arlington, VA, 22201

Tel: (703) 841-7800        Fax: (703) 841-7882        www.caci.com

*Provides simulation technology/software and designs factories, computer networks, and communications systems for military, electronic commerce digital document management, logistics and Y2K remediation.*

**CACI International, Inc., CACA House, Kensington Village - Avonmore Rd., London W14 8TS UK**

Tel: 44-207-602-6000

## CADILLAC PLASTIC & CHEMICAL COMPANY

2855 Coolidge Hwy, Ste. 300, Troy, MI, 48084-3217

Tel: (248) 205-3100        Fax: (248) 205-3187        www.cadillacplastic.com

*Distributor plastic basic shapes.*

**Cadillac Plastic Ltd., Rivermead Dr., Westlea, Swindon, Wittshire SN5 7YT UK**

## CADWALADER, WICKERSHAM & TAFT

100 Maiden Lane, New York, NY, 10038-4818

Tel: (212) 504-6000        Fax: (212) 504-6666        www.cadwalader.com

*International law firm.*

**Cadwalader, Wickersham & Taft, 55 Gracechurch St., London, EC3V 0EE UK**

Tel: 44-207-456-8500   Fax: 44-207-456-8600

## CALBIOCHEM-NOVABIOCHEM CORPORATION

PO Box 12087, La Jolla, CA, 92039

Tel: (619) 450-9600    Fax: (619) 452-3552    www.calbiochem.com

*Mfr. biochemicals, immunochemicals and reagents.*

**Calbiochem-Novabiochem UK Ltd., 3 Heathcoat Bldg., Highfields Science Park, University Blvd., Nottingham NG7 2QJ UK**

## CALGON CARBON CORPORATION

400 Calgon Carbon Drive, Pittsburgh, PA, 15230-0717

Tel: (412) 787-6700    Fax: (412) 787-4541    www.calgoncarbon.com

*Mfr. activated carbon, related systems and services.*

**Charcoal Cloth International Ltd., High Tech House Commerce Way, Arena Business Park, Houghton Le Spring Tyne & Wear, DH4 5PP UK**

**Chemviron Carbon Ltd., Number One Southlink, Oldham OL4 1DE, UK**

## CALIFORNIA CEDAR PRODUCTS COMPANY

PO Box 528, 400 Fresno Ave., Stockton, CA, 95201

Tel: (209) 944-5800    Fax: (209) 944-9072    www.duraflame.com

*Mfr. Duraframe-brand matches and fireplace logs, and incense-cedar products.*

**California Cedar Products Co., 12 Goodwin's Court St. Martin's Lane, London WC2N 4LL, UK**

## CALLAWAY GOLF COMPANY

2285 Rutherford Road, Carlsbad, CA, 92008

Tel: (760) 931-1771    Fax: (760) 931-8013    www.callawaygolf.com

*Mfr./sales of golf clubs.*

**Callaway Golf Europe Ltd., Barwell Business Park A-27, Leatherhead Road, Chessington Surrey KT9 2NY, UK**

Tel: 44-20-8391-0111    Fax: 44-20-8391-9399

## CALTEX CORPORATION

125 East John Carpenter Fwy., Irving, TX, 75062-2794

Tel: (972) 830-1000    Fax: (972) 830-1081    www.caltex.com

*Petroleum products.*

**Caltex Trading (UK) Ltd., Griffin House, 161 Hammersmith Rd., Hammersmith London W6 8B6, UK**

## CAMBREX CORPORATION

1 Meadowlands Plaza, East Rutherford, NJ, 07063

Tel: (201) 804-3000    Fax: (201) 804-9852    www.cambrex.com

*human health, animal health/agriculture and Mfr. biotechnology products and produce specialty chemicals.*

**Cambrex Corp. Seal Sands Chemicals, Inc., Seal Sands Rd., Seal Sands, Middlesbrough, TS2 1UB UK**

Tel: 44-1642-546546    Fax: 44-1642-546068

## CAMBRIDGE TECHNOLOGY PARTNERS, INC.

8 Cambridge Center, Cambridge, MA, 02142

Tel: (617) 374-9800    Fax: (617) 914-8300    www.ctp.com

*Engaged in e-commerce consultancy.*

**Cambridge Technology Partners, Inc., 18-24 Paradise Road, Richmond-upon-Thames, Surrey TW9 1SE, UK**

Tel: 44-20-8334-2700

**Cambridge Technology Partners, Inc., 71-75 Uxbridge Road, W5 5SL Ealing, UK**

Tel: 44-20-8338-500    Fax: 44-20-8338-5001

**Cambridge Technology Partners, Inc., Quay West Business Centre, Quay West, Trafford Wharf Road, Manchester M17 1PL, UK**

Tel: 44-161-872-2440    Fax: 44-161-872-2448

Cambridge Technology Partners, Inc., **27 Kings Road, Reading Berkshire RG1 3AR, UK**
Tel: 44-118-952-3600

## CAMPBELL SOUP COMPANY
Campbell Place, Camden, NJ, 08103-1799
Tel: (856) 342-4800      Fax: (856) 342-3878      www.campbellsoup.com
*Mfr. food products.*
**Campbell's UK Ltd., London, UK**

## CANBERRA-PACKARD INDUSTRIES
800 Research Parkway, Meriden, CT, 06450
Tel: (203) 238-2351      Fax: (203) 235-1347      www.canberra.com
*Mfr. instruments for nuclear research.*
**Canberra-Packard Ltd., Book House, 14 Station Rd., Pangbourne, Berkshire RG8 7DT UK**

## CANNY BOWEN INC.
521 Fifth Avenue, 19th Fl., New York, NY, 10175-1999
Tel: (212) 949-6611      Fax: (212) 949-5191      www.cannybowen.com
*Executive search firm.*
**Canny, Bowen & Associates Ltd., 14 Queen Anne's Gate, St. James Park SW1 9A8, UK**

## CAPITAL CONTROLS COMPANY, INC.
3000 Advance Lane, PO Box 211, Colmar, PA, 18915-0211
Tel: (215) 997-4000      Fax: (215) 997-4062      www.capitalcontrols.com
*Mfr./services water disinfecting products and systems.*
**Capital Controls Co. Ltd., Crown Quay Lane, Sittingbourne, Kent ME10 3JG, UK**
Tel: 44-121-722-6180

## THE CAPITAL GROUP COS INC.
333 South Hope Street, Los Angeles, CA, 90071
Tel: (213) 486-9200      Fax: (213) 486-9557      www.capgroup.com
*Investment management.*
**Capital International Ltd., 25 Bedford St., London WC2E 9HN, UK**

## CAPITAL ONE FINANCIAL CORPORATION
2980 Fairview Park Drive, Ste. 1300, Falls Church, VA, 22042-4525
Tel: (703) 205-1000      Fax: (703) 205-1090      www.capitalone.com
*Holding company for credit card companies.*
**Capital One Bank, 18 Hanover Square, London, W1R 9DA, UK**
Tel: 44-207-543-2900   Fax: 44-207-543-2955   Contact: Rob Habgood
**Capital One Services, Inc., Trent House, Station St., Nottingham, NG2 3HX, UK**
Tel: 44-115-843-3300   Fax: 44-115-843-3433   Contact: Rob Habgood

## CARAVAN TOURS INC.
401 North Michigan Ave., Chicago, IL, 60611
Tel: (312) 321-9800      Fax: (312) 321-9845      www.caravantours.com
*Tour operator.*
**Caravan Ltd., 59/65 Upper Ground, London SE1 9PQ, UK**

## CARBOLINE COMPANY
350 Hanley Industrial Court, St. Louis, MO, 63144
Tel: (314) 644-1000      Fax: (314) 644-4617      www.carboline.com
*Mfr. coatings and sealants.*
**StonCor UK Ltd., Torrington Avenue, Coventry, CV4 9TJ UK**
**Tremco Ltd., 86-88 Bestobell Rd., Slough, Berks SL1 4SZ, UK**

**CARGILL, INC.**

15407 McGinty Road West, Minnetonka, MN, 55440-5625

Tel: (612) 742-7575        Fax: (612) 742-7393        www.cargill.com

*Food products, feeds, animal products.*

**Cargill PLC,  Witham, St. Hughs, Lincoln LN6 9TN UK**

**CARLISLE COMPANIES INCORPORATED**

250 S. Clinton St., Ste. 201, Syracuse, NY, 13202-1258

Tel: (315) 474-2500        Fax: (315) 474-2008        www.carlisle.com

*Mfr. brakes, tires, wheels, turnkey systems.*

**Extract Technology Ltd.,  Bradley Junction Ind. Estate, Leeds Road, Huddersfield, West Yorkshire HD2 1UR, UK**

Tel: 44-1484-432727   Fax: 44-1484-432659

**CARLISLE SYNTEC SYSTEMS**

PO Box 7000, Carlisle, PA, 17013

Tel: (717) 245-7000        Fax: (717) 245-9107        www.carlislesyntec.com

*Mfr. elastomeric roofing and waterproofing systems.*

**Carlisle SynTec Systems UK,  Unit 24 The Nursery, Sutton Courtenay, Abingdon Oxon OX 14 4UA, UK**

Tel: 44-1-235-848-000   Fax: 44-1-235-848-727

**CARLSON COMPANIES, INC.**

Carlson Parkway, PO Box 59159, Minneapolis, MN, 55459

Tel: (612) 550-4520        Fax: (612) 550-4580        www.cmg.carlson.com

*Marketing services agency.*

**Aegis Carlson,  Aegis House - 42 New Street, Daventry NN11 4BU, UK**

**BBM Carlson,  220 Park Avenue, Aztec West Almondsbury, Bristol BS12 4SB, UK**

**Carlson Marketing Group,  116 Putney Bridge Road, London SW15 2NQ, UK**

**THE CARLYLE GROUP L.P.**

1001 Pennsylvania Avenue, NW, Washington, DC, 20004-2505

Tel: (202) 347-2626        Fax: (202) 347-1818        www.thecarlylegroup.com

*Global investor in defense contracts.*

**Carlyle London,  20 Berkeley Square, London W1X 6NB, UK**

Tel: 44-207-894-1200   Fax: 44-207-894-1600

**CARPENTER TECHNOLOGY CORPORATION**

101 W. Bern Street, PO Box 14662, Reading, PA, 19612-4662

Tel: (610) 208-2000        Fax: (610) 208-3214        www.cartech.com

*Mfr. specialty steels and structural ceramics for casting industrial.*

**Carpenter Technology (UK) Ltd.,  6 Royal House, 11 Market Pl., Redditch, Worcs. B98 8AA UK**

**Cartech Intl. Ltd.,  92c Bruneo Rd., Earlstrees Ind. Estate, Corby, Northants NN17 2JW UK**

**CARRIER CORPORATION**

One Carrier Place, Farmington, CT, 06034-4015

Tel: (860) 674-3000        Fax: (860) 679-3010        www.carrier.com

*Mfr./distributor/services A/C, heating and refrigeration equipment.*

**Carrier Distribution,  Biggin Hill, UK**

Tel: 44-1-959-5712   Fax: 44-1-959-570651

## CARTER-WALLACE INC.

1345 Ave. of the Americas, New York, NY, 10105

Tel: (212) 339-5000    Fax: (212) 339-5100    www.carterwallace.com

*Mfr. personal care products and pet products.*

**Carter-Wallace, Ltd., Wear Bay Rd., Folkestone Kent CT19 6PG, UK**

Tel: 44-1303-850-661    Fax: 44-1303-850-712

## CASCADE CORPORATION

2201 NE 201st Ave., Fairview, OR, 97024-9718

Tel: (503) 669-6300    Fax: (503) 669-6321    www.cascor.com

*Mfr. hydraulic forklift truck attachments.*

**Cascade (UK) Ltd., Bassington Industrial Estate, Cramlington New Town, Northumberland NE23 8AE, UK**

**Cascade Kenhar Products Ltd., Parkhouse Street Industrial Estate,Kelbrook Road, Openshaw Manchester M11 2DD, UK**

**Cascade Sheffield, 15 Orgreave Crescent, Dore House Industrial Estate, Handsworth, Sheffield S13 9 NQ, UK**

## CASE CORPORATION

700 State Street, Racine, WI, 53404

Tel: (414) 636-6011    Fax: (414) 636-0200    www.casecorp.com

*Mfr./sale agricultural and construction equipment.*

**Fermec Holdings Ltd., Barton Dock Rd., Stretford, Manchester, M32 0YH, UK**

Tel: 44-161-865-4400    Fax: 44-161-865-5427

**Gem Sprayers Ltd., Station Rd., North Hykeham, Lincoln LN6 9AA UK**

Tel: 44-1522-500909    Fax: 44-1522-500662

**J.I. Case Europe Ltd., Wheatley Hall Rd., Doncaster South Yorkshire DN2 4PG, UK**

Tel: 44-1302-73-3200    Fax: 44-1302-76-1038    Contact: Felicia Howell, Gen. Mgr.

## A.M. CASTLE & COMPANY

3400 N. Wolf Road, Franklin Park, IL, 60131

Tel: (784) 755-7111    Fax: (784) 455-7136    www.amcastle.com

*Metals distribution.*

**Castle Metals Europe, Blackburn, England UK**

**High Performance Alloys, Ltd., Manchester, UK**

## CAT PUMPS

1681 94th Lane NE, Minneapolis, MN, 55449-4324

Tel: (612) 780-5440    Fax: (612) 780-2958    www.catpumps.com

*Mfr./distributor pumps.*

**Cat Pumps UK Ltd., 1 Fleet Business Park, Sandy Lane, Church Crookham, Fleet, Hamps. GU13 0BF UK**

## CATAPULT COMMUNICATIONS CORPORATION

160 South Whisman Road, Mountain View, CA, 94041

Tel: (650) 960-1025    Fax: (650) 960-1029    www.catapult.com

*Mfr. test systems for telecommunications service providers.*

**Catapult Communications Corp., 1 Lansdowne Court, Bumpers Way, Chippenham, Wiltshire SN14 6RZ, UK**

**CATERPILLAR INC.**

100 NE Adams Street, Peoria, IL, 61629-6105

Tel: (309) 675-1000     Fax: (309) 675-1182     www.cat.com

*Mfr. earth/material-handling and construction machinery and equipment and engines.*

**Caterpillar Tractor Co. Ltd.,  Desford, Leicester LE9 9JT, UK**

Tel: 44-1455-82-6826

**C.B. RICHARD ELLIS**

533 South Fremont Ave., Los Angeles, CA, 90071-1712

Tel: (213) 613-3123     Fax: (213) 613-3535     www.cbrichardellis.com

*Commercial real estate services.*

**CB Hillier Parker Ltd.,  Cheshire House - 18/20 Booth St., Manchester, M2 4AN, UK**

Tel: 44-161-455-7666

**CB Hillier Parker Ltd.,  Berkeley Square House, Berkeley Square, London, W1X6AN UK**

Tel: 44-207-629-6699   Fax: 44-207-409-1476   Contact: Barry White, Co-Chmn.

**CB Hillier Parker Ltd.,  Berkeley Square House, London W1X 6BB, UK**

**CBS CORPORATION**

51 West 52 Street, New York, NY, 10019

Tel: (212) 975-4321     Fax: (212) 975-9387     www.cbs.com

*TV/radio broadcasting, mfr. electronic systems for industry/defense, financial and environmental services.*

**Ottermill Ltd.,  Ottery St. Mary, Devon, Essex 11 1AG, UK**

**Westinghouse Electronics & Control Co.,  Haden House, Argyle Way, Stevenage, Herts SG1 2AH, UK**

**CCH INCORPORATED**

2700 Lake Cook Road, Riverwoods, IL, 60015

Tel: (847) 267-7000     Fax: (800) 224-8299     www.cch.com

*Provides tax and business law information and software for accounting, legal, human resources, securities and health care professionals.*

**CCH Editions Ltd.,  Telford Rd., Bicester, Oxon OX6 0XD, UK**

**CCI/TRIAD**

804 Las Cimas Pkwy., Ste. 200, Austin, TX, 78746

Tel: (512) 328-2300     Fax: (512) 328-8209     www.cci-triad.com

*Information retrieval systems.*

**Tridex Systems Ltd.,  Orchard Court, Binely Business Park, Coventry, West Midlands, CV3 2TQ, UK**

Tel: 44-1203-636000   Fax: 44-1203-440049

**CCS INTERNATIONAL LTD**

360 Madison Ave., 6th Fl., New York, NY, 10017

Tel: (212) 557-3040     Fax: (212) 983-1278     www.spyzone.com

*Mfr. electronic security products.*

**CCS Counterspy Shop,  62 S. Audley St., London W1, UK**

**C-CUBE MICROSYSTEMS INC.**

1778 McCarthy Blvd., Milpitas, CA, 95035

Tel: (408) 490-8000     Fax: (408) 490-8132     www.c-cube.com

*Designs video compression chips.*

**C-Cube Microsystems Inc.,  1 Stoner House, London Road, Crawley West Sussex RH10 2LJ, UK**

Tel: 44-1293-651100   Fax: 44-1293-651119

## CDI CORPORATION

1717 Arch Street, 35th Fl., Philadelphia, PA, 19103

Tel: (215) 569-2200    Fax: (215) 569-1300    www.cdicorp.com

*Engineering, technical and temporary personnel services.*

**Anders Elite, Capital House, Houndwell Place, Southampton SO14 1HU, UK**

Contact: Paul Scott

**Anders Elite, 69 Old Broad Street, London EC2M 1NQ, UK**

Contact: Ray Shadforth

**Anders Glaser Wills, 15 London Road, Twickenham London TW1 3ST, UK**

Tel: 44-181-891-1144

**Anders Glaser Wills, Clifton Heights, Triangle West, Bristol BS8 1EJ, UK**

Tel: 44-117-922-1441

**Anders Glaser Wills, 24 Bennetts Hill, Birmingham B2 5QP, UK**

Tel: 44-121-643-5070

**Anders Glaser Wills Ltd., 4 Maddison Ct., Maddison St., Southampton S01 0BU, UK**

**CDI International Ltd., Michael House, 55/57 Chase Side, Southgate London N14 5BU, UK**

**Harvard Associates, 10 Kingfisher Court, Farnham Road, Slough, Berkshire SL2 1JF, UK**

**Humana International Group, London, UK**

Contact: Doug Bugie, Mng. Dir.

## CDM INTERNATIONAL INC.

50 Hampshire Street, Cambridge, MA, 02139

Tel: (617) 452-6000    Fax: (617) 452-8020    www.cdm.com

*Consulting engineers.*

**Sir Frederick Snow & Partners Ltd., Div. CDM, 235 Southwark Bridge Road, London SE1 0SZ, UK**

Tel: 44-207-378-6464   Fax: 44-207-378-0550

## CEILCOTE AIR POLLUTION CONTROL

14955 Sprague Road, Strongsville, OH, 44136

Tel: (440) 243-0700    Fax: (440) 234-3486    www.ceilcoteapc.com

*Mfr. corrosion-resistant material, air pollution control equipment, construction services.*

**Ceilcote UK Ltd., London Rd. S, Poynton, Stockport Cheshire SK12 1LH, UK**

## CENDANT CORPORATION

9 West 57th Street, New York, NY, 10019

Tel: (212) 413-1800    Fax: (212) 413-1918    www.cendant.com

*Membership-based, direct marketer offering shopping/travel/insurance and dining discount programs*

**National Car Parks (NCP), Heathrow Airport, London, UK**

## CENTERCORE INC.

2400 Sterling Ave., Elkhart, IN, 46516

Tel: (219) 293-0621    Fax: (219) 294-6176    www.centercore.com

*Design/mfr. modular office workstations.*

**CenterCore UK Ltd., 37 Harbour Exchange Square, London E14 9GE, UK**

## CENTEX CORPORATION

2728 N. Harwood, Dallas, TX, 75201-1516

Tel: (214) 981-5000    Fax: (214) 981-6859    www.centex.com

*Engaged in home building.*

**Centex International, London, UK**

## CENTIGRAM COMMUNICATIONS CORPORATION

91 East Tasman Drive, San Jose, CA, 95134

Tel: (408) 944-0250    Fax: (408) 428-3732    www.centigram.com

*Engaged in development of unified communications and messaging systems.*

**Centigram Europe Limited, Network House - Basing View, Basingstoke, Hampshire RG21 4HG, UK**

Tel: 44-1256-319600   Fax: 44-1256-319666

## CENTRAL NATIONAL-GOTTESMAN INC.

3 Manhattanville Road, Purchase, NY, 10577-2110

Tel: (914) 696-9000    Fax: (914) 696-1066

*Worldwide sales pulp and paper products.*

**Central National (UK) Ltd., The Pavillions, 1 Weston Rd., Kiln Lane, Epsom Surrey KT17 1JG, UK**

Tel: 44-1-372-739-966   Fax: 44-1-372-748-152   Contact: Michael Hobday

## CENTURA SOFTWARE CORPORATION

975 Island Drive, Redwood Shores, CA, 94065

Tel: (650) 596-3400    Fax: (650) 596-4900    www.centurasoft.com

*Mfr. software and database management tools*

**Centura Software Ltd., Field House Lane, Globe Park, Bucks SL7 1LW Marlow, UK**

Tel: 44-1628-47-8333

## CENTURY 21 REAL ESTATE CORPORATION

6 Sylvan Way, Parsippany, NJ, 07054-3826

Tel: (973) 496-5722    Fax: (973) 496-5527    www.century21.com

*Engaged in real estate.*

**Century 21 United Kingdom, Ltd., Brosnan House, Darkes Lane, Potters Bar Hertfordshire EN6 1BW, UK**

## CEPHALON, INC.

145 Brandywine Pkwy., West Chester, PA, 19380

Tel: (610) 344-0200    Fax: (610) 344-0065    www.cephalon.com

*Engaged in healthscience, research and development.*

**Cephalon UK Limited, 11/13 Frederick Sanger Road, Surrey Research Park, Guildord GU2 5YD, UK**

Tel: 44-1-48-345-3360   Fax: 44-1-48-345-3324   Contact: Mark Watling

## CERIDIAN CORPORATION

8100 34th Ave. South, Minneapolis, MN, 55425

Tel: (612) 853-8100    Fax: (612) 853-4068    www.ceridian.com

*Provides diversified information services.*

**Arbitron, Div. Ceridian Corp., Continental Research, 132-140 Goswell Rd., London EC1V 7 DP UK**

Tel: 44-207-490-5944

**Centrefile, 75 Leman St., London E1 8EX, UK**

Tel: 44-207-335-3000

## CH2M HILL INC.

6060 South Willow Drive, Greenwood Village, CO, 80111

Tel: (303) 771-0900    Fax: (303) 770-2616    www.ch2m.com

*Consulting engineers, planners, economists and scientists.*

**CH2M Hill, Mercury House,195 Knightsbridge, London UK, SW7 1RE, UK**

Tel: 44-207-591-4600   Fax: 44-207-591-4660

## CHADBOURNE & PARKE LLP

30 Rockefeller Plaza, New York, NY, 10112-0127

Tel: (212) 408-5100     Fax: (212) 541-5369     www.chadbourne.com

*International law firm.*

**Chadbourne & Parke, Regis House, 45 King William St., London EC4R 9AN, UK**

Tel: 44-207-337-8000   Fax: 44-207-337-8001   Contact: Nancy Persechino, Adm. Ptnr.

## CHASE H&Q

One Bush Street, San Francisco, CA, 94104

Tel: (415) 439-3000     Fax: (415) 439-3638     www.jpmhq.com

*Investment banking and venture capital services.*

**Chase H&Q, The Registry, Royal Mint Court, London EC3N 4EY, UK**

Tel: 44-207-488-2362

## CHATTEM INC.

1715 West 38th Street, Chattanooga, TN, 37409

Tel: (423) 821-4571     Fax: (423) 821-6132     www.chattem.com

*Mfr. health and beauty aids.*

**Chattem (UK) Ltd., Guerry House, Ringway Centre, Edison Rd., Basingstoke, Hampshire RG21 2YH UK**

## CHECK TECHNOLOGY CORPORATION

12500 Whitewater Drive, Minnetonka, MN, 55343-9420

Tel: (612) 939-9000     Fax: (612) 939-1151     www.checktechnology.com

*Mfr. computer-controlled check/coupon print systems.*

**Check Technology Limited, 3/4 Satellite Bus. Village, Fleming Way, Crawley, W. Sussex RH10 2NE UK**

## CHECKPOINT SYSTEMS, INC.

101 Wolf Drive, Thorofare, NJ, 08086

Tel: (856) 848-1800     Fax: (856) 848-0937     www.checkpointsystems.com

*Mfr. test, measurement and closed-circuit television systems.*

**Checkpoint Systems UK Ltd., Ash Industrial Estate Unit 13, Flex Meadow, Pinnacles West, Harlow Essex CM19 5TJ UK**

Tel: 44-1279-452233   Fax: 44-1279-452884   Contact: Steve Midani, Mng. Dir.

## CHEMINEER INC.

PO Box 1123, Dayton, OH, 45401-1123

Tel: (937) 454-3200     Fax: (937) 454-3379     www.chemineer.com

*Mfr. fluid agitators and static mixers for chemicals processing.*

**Chemineer Ltd., 7 Cranmer Rd., West Meadows, Derby DE2 6XT, UK**

## THE CHERRY CORPORATION

3600 Sunset Ave., PO Box 718, Waukegan, IL, 60087

Tel: (847) 662-9200     Fax: (847) 662-2990     www.cherrycorp.com

*Mfr. electrical switches, electronic keyboards, controls and displays.*

**Cherry Electrical Products Ltd., Coldharbour Lane, Harpenden, Hertfordshire AL5 4UN, UK**

Tel: 44-15-8276-3100   Fax: 44-15-8276-8883

## CHESAPEAKE CORPORATION

1021 E. Cary St., Richmond, VA, 23218

Tel: (804) 697-1000     Fax: (804) 697-1199     www.cskcorp.com

*Provides merchandising services and specialty packaging.*

**Field Group Plc., Misbourne House, Badminton Court, Old Amersham HP7 0DD, UK**

Tel: 44-1494-720200

## CHESTERTON BINSWANGER INTERNATIONAL

Two Logan Square, 4th Floor, Philadelphia, PA, 19103-2759

Tel: (215) 448-6000     Fax: (215) 448-6238     www.cbbi.com

*Real estate and related services.*

**Bingswanger Ltd., 22A The Ropewalk, Nottingham London NG1 5DT, UK**

**Chesterton Binswanger Intl., 54 Brook St., London W1A 2BU, UK**

Tel: 90-312-2862323

**Chesterton International plc, Minerva House East Parade, Leeds LS1 5PS, UK**

**Chesterton International plc, Swan House, 37/39 High Holborn, London WC1V 6AA, UK**

**Chesterton International plc, 1 Malvern House, Meridian Gate, 199 Marsh Wall, London E14 9YT, UK**

## CHEVRON CHEMICAL COMPANY

1301 McKinney Street, Houston, TX, 77010

Tel: (713) 754-2000     Fax: (713) 754-2016     www.chevron.com

*Mfr. petro chemicals.*

**Octel Associates, PO Box 17, Oil Sites Rd., Ellesmere Port, South Wirral L65 4HF, UK**

**The Associated Octel Co., PO Box 17, Oil Sites Rd., Ellesmere Port, South Wirral L65 4HF, UK**

## CHEVRON CORPORATION

575 Market Street, San Francisco, CA, 94105-2856

Tel: (415) 894-7700     Fax: (415) 894-2248     www.chevron.com

*Oil exploration, production and petroleum products.*

**Chevron U.K., Cheltenham, England, UK**

## CHICAGO BRIDGE & IRON COMPANY (CBI)

1501 North Division Street, Plainfield, IL, 60544

Tel: (815) 241-7546     Fax: (815) 439-6010     www.chicago-bridge.com

*Holding company: metal plate fabricating, construction, oil and gas drilling.*

**CBI Constructors, Ltd., Willowbank House - 97 Oxford Road, Uxbridge Middlesex UB8 1LU, UK**

## CHICAGO RAWHIDE INDUSTRIES (CRI)

735 Tollgate Road, Elgin, IL, 60123

Tel: (847) 742-7840     Fax: (847) 742-7845     www.chicago-rawhide.com

*Mfr. shaft and face seals.*

**CR Industrial Prdts. Ltd., Elmdon Trading Estate Unit 30, Bickenhill Lane, Marston Green, Birmingham B37 7HE UK**

## CHIEF INDUSTRIES INC.

PO Box 2078, 3942 West Old Highway 30, Grand Island, NE, 68802-2078

Tel: (308) 382-8820     Fax: (308) 381-7221     www.chiefind.com

*Mfr. grain bins, steel buildings, grain handling and drying equipment, elevator legs and components.*

**Chief Industries UK Ltd., Bentall Industrial Estates, Maldon, Essex CM9 6JA UK**

Tel: 44-1621-868944   Fax: 44-1621-868955

## CHIRON CORPORATION

4560 Horton Street, Emeryville, CA, 94608-2916

Tel: (510) 655-8730     Fax: (510) 655-9910     www.chiron.com

*Engaged in biotechnology; biopharmaceuticals, blood testing and vaccines.*

**Chiron Diagnostics, Chilton Industrial Estate, Sudbury, Suffolk CO10 6XD UK**

**Chiron Vision UK Ltd., 9 Prebendal Ct., Oxford Rd., Aylesbury, Buckinghamshire HP19 3EY UK**

## THE CHRISTIAN SCIENCE PUBLISHING SOCIETY

1 Norway Street, Boston, MA, 02115

Tel: (617) 450-2000     Fax: (617) 450-7575     www.christianscience.com

*Publishing company.*

**The Christian Science Monitor, 29 Chartfield Ave., London SW15 6HW, UK**

Tel: 44-181-780-5931    Contact: Alexander MacLeod    Emp: 1

## THE CHUBB CORPORATION

15 Mountain View Road, Warren, NJ, 07061-1615

Tel: (908) 580-2000     Fax: (908) 580-3606     www.chubb.com

*Holding company for property and casualty insurance.*

**Chubb Insurance Company of Europe, S.A., 52-54 Leadenhall Street, London EC3A 2BJ, UK**

Tel: 44-207-867-5555    Fax: 44-207-867-8687

**Chubb Insurance Company of Europe, SA, 8th Fl. 82 King St., Manchester M1 4WQ, UK**

Tel: 44-161-839-5624    Fax: 44-161-839-5625

**Chubb Insurance Company of Europe, SA, 6th Fl. Cornwall Court, 19 Cornwall St., Birmingham B3 2DT, UK**

Tel: 44-121-236-8803    Fax: 44-121-236-8994

**Chubb Insurance Company of Europe, SA, 106 Fenchurch St., London EC3M 5JB, UK**

Tel: 44-207-867-5555    Fax: 44-207-481-2256

**Chubb Insurance Company of Europe, SA, 4/6 Abbey Gardens, Rading, Berkshire RG1 3BA, UK**

Tel: 44-1734-510577    Fax: 44-1734-10505

**Lloyds of London/Chubb Insurance Company of Europe, SA, Lloyds Bldg., 1 Lime St., London EC3M 7HA, UK**

Tel: 44-207-867-555    Fax: 44-207-929-0166

## CHURCH & DWIGHT COMPANY, INC.

469 North Harrison Street, Princeton, NJ, 08543

Tel: (609) 683-5900     Fax: (609) 497-7269     www.churchdwight.com

*Specialty chemicals and consumer products.*

**Brotherton Specialty Products, Calder Vale Rd., Wakefield, West Yorkshire WF1 5PH, UK**

Tel: 44-1924-371-919    Contact: Roger Perry, Mng. Dir.

## CIGNA COMPANIES

One Liberty Place, Philadelphia, PA, 19192

Tel: (215) 761-1000     Fax: (215) 761-5511     www.cigna.com

*Insurance, invest, health care and other financial services.*

**CIGNA Insurance Co. of Europe SA/NV, Cigna House, 8 Lime St., London EC3M 7NA, UK**

**CIGNA Life Insurance Company of Europe S.A.-N.V., Tower House, 38 Trinity Square, London EC3N 4DJ, UK**

Tel: 44-207-200-2005    Fax: 44-207-200-2004    Contact: Philippa Dickson

**CIGNA Reinsurance Co. (UK) Ltd., Cigna House, 8 Lime St., London EC3M 7NA, UK**

**CIGNA Services UK Ltd., Cigna House, 8 Lime St., London EC3M 7NA, UK**

**CIGNA UK Holding Ltd., Cigna House, 8 Lime St., London EC3M 7NA, UK**

**CIGNA Unit Trust Managers Ltd., Crusader House, Reigate, Surrey RH2 8BL, UK**

**Crusader Managed Pension Funds Ltd., Crusader House, Reigate, Surrey RH2 8BL, UK**

**Crusader Staff Pension Investments Ltd., Crusader House, Reigate, Surrey RH2 8BL, UK**

**Ernest Linsdell Ltd., Commonwealth House, 1-19 New Oxford St., London WCIA 1NB UK**

**Esis Intl. Inc., Chesterfield House, 26-28 Fenchurch St., London EC3M 3DH, UK**

**Growth Property Management Co. Ltd., Crusader House, Reigate, Surrey RH2 8BL, UK**

**Insurance Co. of North America, Cigna House, 8 Lime St., London EC3M 7NA UK**

**Insurance Co. of North America (UK) Ltd., Cigna House, 8 Lime St., London EC3M 7NA UK**

Plough Investment Properties Ltd., Crusader House, Reigate, Surrey RH2 8BL, UK

## CINCINNATI MILACRON INC.

4701 Marburg Ave., Cincinnati, OH, 45209

Tel: (513) 841-8100    Fax: (513) 841-8919    www.cinbus.com

*Develop/mfr. technologies for metalworking and plastics processing industrial.*

Cincinnati Milacron Ltd., PO Box 505, Birmingham B4 0QU, UK

## CINCOM SYSTEMS INC.

55 Merchant Street, Cincinnati, OH, 45446

Tel: (513) 612-2300    Fax: (513) 481-8332    www.cincom.com

*Develop/distributor computer software.*

Cincom Systems Inc., Manchester, UK

Cincom Systems Inc., Maidenhead, UK

## CINERGY CORPORATION

139 East Fourth Street, Cincinnati, OH, 45202

Tel: (513) 421-9500    Fax: (513) 287-3171    www.cinergy.com

*Utility holding company - generates, transmits and distributes electricity and natural gas.*

Midlands Electricity Plc., London, England UK

## CISCO SYSTEMS, INC.

170 West Tasman Drive, San Jose, CA, 95134-1706

Tel: (408) 526-4000    Fax: (408) 526-4100    www.cisco.com

*Develop/mfr./market computer hardware and software networking systems.*

Cisco Systems, Eagle Court Concorde Business Park, Threapwood Road, Manchester M22 ORR, UK
Tel: 44-161-932-6270  Fax: 44-161-932-6333

Cisco Systems, 3/F, Old Broad Street, London EC 2 1HQ, UK
Tel: 44-207-496-3700  Fax: 44-207-496-3701

Cisco Systems Ltd., 3 The Square, Stockley Park, Uxbridge Middlesex, UK
Tel: 44-181-756-8000  Fax: 44-181-756-8099

## THE CIT GROUP

1211 Avenue of the Americas, New York, NY, 10036

Tel: (212) 536-1390    Fax: (212) 536-1912    www.citgroup.com

*Engaged in commercial finance.*

ERF Finance, Ltd., Div. CIT Grup, 7 Chantry Court - Forge Street, Crewe Cheshire CW1 2 DU, UK

Newcourt, Div. CIT Group, 80 Stokes Croft, Bristol BS1 3QW, UK

Newcourt, Div. CIT Group, Newcourt - 66 Buckingham Gate, London SW1E 6AU, UK

## CITIGROUP, INC.

153 East 53rd Street, New York, NY, 10043

Tel: (212) 559-1000    Fax: (212) 559-3646    www.citigroup.com

*Provides insurance and financial services worldwide.*

Citibank International plc., 65 Curzon St., London W1Y 7PE, UK
Tel: 44-207-355-4411   Contact: Tom Mulvihill, Mgr.

Citibank International plc., PO Box 200, Cottons Centre, Hay's Lane, London SE1 2 QT UK
Contact: Janet M. Allen, Mgr.

Citibank N.A., 332 Oxford Street, London W1N 9AA , UK

## CITRIX SYSTEMS, INC.

6400 NW 6th Way, Fort Lauderdale, FL, 33309

Tel: (954) 267-3000       Fax: (954) 267-9319       www.citrix.com

*Developer of computer software.*

**Citrix Systems UK Ltd., Buckingham Court, Kingsmead Business Park, London Rd., High Wycombe, Bucks HP11 1JU UK**

Tel: 44-1494-684900   Fax: 44-1494-684998

## CLARCOR INC.

2323 Sixth Street, PO Box 7007, Rockford, IL, 61125

Tel: (815) 962-8867       Fax: (815) 962-0417       www.clarcor.com

*Mfr. filtration products and consumer packaging products.*

**Baldwin Filters Ltd., Unit 2A Daimler Close, Royal Oak Industrial Estate, Daventry NN11 5QJ UK**

## CLAYTON INDUSTRIES

4213 N. Temple City Blvd., El Monte, CA, 91731

Tel: (626) 443-9381       Fax: (626) 442-1701       www.claytonindustries.com

*Mfr. steam generators, dynamometers and water treatment chemicals.*

**Clayton Thermal Products, 3 Tatton Court, Kingsland Grange, Woolston, Warrington Cheshire WA I 4RW, UK**

Tel: 44-1-925-823123  Fax: 44-1-925-817373

## CLEAR CHANNEL COMMUNICATIONS

200 East Basse Road, San Antonio, TX, 78209

Tel: (210) 822-2828       Fax: (210) 822-2299       www.clearchannel.com

*Programs and sells airtime for radio stations and owns and places outdoor advertising displays.*

**More Group, 33 Golden Square, London W1R 3PA, UK**

Tel: 44-207-287-6100  Fax: 44-20-287-9149

## CLEARY GOTTLIEB STEEN & HAMILTON

One Liberty Plaza, New York, NY, 10006

Tel: (212) 225-2000       Fax: (212) 225-3999       www.cgsh.com

*International law firm.*

**Cleary, Gottlieb, Steen & Hamilton, City Place House, 55 Basinghall St., London EC2V 5EH, UK**

## CLICK2LEARN.COM, INC.

110 110th Avenue NE, Bellevue, WA, 98004

Tel: (425) 462-0501       Fax: (425) 637-1504       www.click2learn.com

*Provides software and services for developing on-line educational programs.*

**Click2learn.Com Ltd., 225 Marsh Wall, Docklands E14 9FW, London UK**

Tel: 44-20-7517-4200   Fax: 44-20-7517-4201

## CLUBCORP, INC.

3030 LBJ Freeway, Ste. 700, Dallas, TX, 75234

Tel: (972) 243-6191       Fax: (972) 888-7700       www.clubcorp.com

*Operates golf courses and resorts.*

**Drift Golf Club, Surrey, UK**

## CMGI, INC.

100 Brickstone Square, Andover, MA, 01810

Tel: (978) 684-3600       Fax: (978) 684-3814       www.cmgi.com

*Holding company engaged in direct marketing and fulfillment and internet companies.*

**Flycast UK Limited, Berkeley Square House 2/F, Mayfair London W1X 6EA, UK**

## CNA FINANCIAL CORPORATION

CNA Plaza, Chicago, IL, 60685

Tel: (312) 822-5000      Fax: (312) 822-6419      www.cna.com

*Commercial property/casualty insurance policies.*

**CNA Insurance Company (Europe) Limited (CIE), London, UK**

**CNA/Marine Insurance Company, London, UK**

## COACH LEATHERWEAR COMPANY

516 West 34 Street, New York, NY, 10001

Tel: (212) 594-1850      Fax: (212) 594-1682      www.coach.com

*Mfr. and sales of high-quality leather products, including handbags and wallets.*

**The Coach Store, 8 Sloane Street, London SW1X 9LE, UK**

## THE COASTAL CORPORATION

Nine Greenway Plaza, Houston, TX, 77046-0995

Tel: (713) 877-1400      Fax: (713) 877-6752      www.coastalcorp.com

*Oil refining, natural gas, related services; independent power production.*

**Coastal Europe Ltd., London, UK**

## THE COCA-COLA COMPANY

PO Drawer 1734, Atlanta, GA, 30301

Tel: (404) 676-2121      Fax: (404) 676-6792      www.coca-cola.com

*Mfr./marketing/distributor soft drinks, syrups and concentrates, juice and juice-drink products.*

**Coca-Cola Beverages plc, One Queen Caroline Street, London W6 9HQ, UK**
Tel: 44-181-237-3000

**Coca-Cola Mid-East Ltd., Constitution House, 56 High St., Windsor Berkshire SL4 1JY, UK**
Contact: A.R.C. Allan

**Coca-Cola Northwest Europe, Pemberton House, 15 Wrights Lane, London W8 5SN UK**
Contact: John K. Sheppard

## COGNEX CORPORATION

1 Vision Drive, Natick, MA, 01760

Tel: (508) 650-3000      Fax: (508) 650-3333      www.cognex.com

*Mfr. machine vision systems.*

**Cognex Corporation Canada, Units 7-9 First Quarter, Blenheim Road, Epson
Surrey KT19 9QN, Canada**
Tel: 44-1372-726150    Fax: 44-1372-726276

**Cognex Corporation UK, Chancery House -199 Silbury Boulevard, Milton Keynes MK9 1JL, UK**
Tel: 44-1908-206000    Fax: 44-1908-392463

## COGNITRONICS CORPORATION

3 Corporate Drive, Danbury, CT, 06810-4130

Tel: (203) 830-3400      Fax: (203) 830-3405      www.cognitronics.com

*Mfr. telephone call processing products.*

**Dacon Electronics Plc., One Enterprise Way, Hemel Hempstead, Hertfordshire HP2 7YJ, UK**
Tel: 44-1442-233222  Fax: 44-1442-219653   Contact: Roy Strutt, Mng. Dir.

## COGNIZANT TECHNOLOGY SOLUTIONS CORPORATION

500 Glenpointe Centre West, Teaneck, NJ, 07666

Tel: (201) 801-0233      Fax: (201) 801-0243      www.cognizant.com

*Provides software development , application management, computer date corrections, and currency conversion.*

**Cognizant Technology Solutions, London, UK**

## COGSDILL TOOL PRODUCTS INC.

PO Box 7007, Camden, SC, 29020

Tel: (803) 438-4000    Fax: (803) 438-5263    www.cogsdill.com

*Mfr. precision metalworking tools.*

**Cogsdill-Nuneaton Ltd., Holbrook Industrial Estate, Sheffield, S19 5FR, UK**

**Cogsdill-Nuneaton Ltd., Tenlons Road, Nuneaton, UK**

Tel: 44-120-338-3792

## COHERENT INC.

5100 Patrick Henry Drive, PO Box 54980, Santa Clara, CA, 95056

Tel: (408) 764-4000    Fax: (408) 764-4800    www.cohr.com

*Mfr. lasers for science, industrial and medical.*

**Coherent (UK) Ltd., Cambridge Science Park, Milton Rd., Cambridge CB4 4FR, UK**

**Coherent Optics (Europe) Ltd., 28-35 Ashville Way, Whetstone, Leicester LE8 6NU, UK**

Tel: 44-1162-867-110

## COIN ACCEPTORS INC.

300 Hunter Ave., St. Louis, MO, 63124

Tel: (314) 725-0100    Fax: (314) 725-1243    www.coinco.com

*Coin mechanisms for vending machinery.*

**Coin Acceptors Europe Ltd, Coinco House - Imberhome Lane, East Grinstead, Sussex RH19 1QZ, UK**

Tel: 44-1342-315724  Fax: 44-1342-313850

## THE COLEMAN COMPANY, INC.

2111 E. 37th St., North, Wichita, KS, 67219

Tel: (316) 832-2700    Fax: (316) 832-2794    www.colemanoutdoors.com

*Mfr./distributor/sales camping and outdoor recreation products.*

**Coleman U.K. PLC, Gordano Gate Portishead, Bristol BS20 7GG, UK**

## COLGATE-PALMOLIVE COMPANY

300 Park Ave., New York, NY, 10022

Tel: (212) 310-2000    Fax: (212) 310-2919    www.colgate.com

*Mfr. pharmaceuticals, cosmetics, toiletries and detergents.*

**Colgate-Palmolive Ltd., Guilford Business Park, Middleton Rd., Guilford Surrey, UK**

## COLLAGEN TECHNOLOGIES, INC.

2500 Faber Place, Palo Alto, CA, 94303

Tel: (650) 856-0200    Fax: (650) 856-0533    www.cohensiontech.com

*Mfr. prod for repair/replacement of damaged human tissue.*

**Collagen UK Ltd., Longwich Rd., Princess Risborough, Buckinghamshire HP17 9RR UK**

## COMCAST CORPORATION

1500 Market St., Philadelphia, PA, 19102

Tel: (215) 665-1700    Fax: (215) 981-7790    www.comcast.com

*Provides cable and broadband services and QVC electronic retailing.*

**QVC England, South Boundary Road, Knowsley Industrial Park, Knowsley Liverpool, L70 2QA, UK**

**QVC England, Marco Polo House - Chelsea Bridge, 346 Queenstown Road, London SW8 4NQ, UK**

## COMDISCO INC.

6111 N. River Road, Rosemont, IL, 60018

Tel: (847) 698-3000    Fax: (847) 518-5440    www.comdisco.com

*Hi-tech asset and facility management and equipment leasing.*

**Comdisco United Kingdom, Ltd., Coventry, UK**

## COMMERCIAL INTERTECH CORPORATION

1775 Logan Ave., PO Box 239, Youngstown, OH, 44501-0239

Tel: (330) 746-8011      Fax: (330) 746-1148

*Mfr. hydraulic components, pre-engineered buildings and stamped metal products.*

**Commercial Hydraulics Keelavite Ltd., Tachbrook Park Dr., Tachbrook Park, Warwick CV34 6TU UK**

**Commercial Hydraulics Kontak Ltd., Belton Park, Londonthorpe Rd., Grantham, Lincolnshire NG31 9SJ UK**

## COMMUNICATIONS SYSTEMS INC.

213 S. Main Street, Hector, MN, 55342

Tel: (320) 848-6231      Fax: (320) 848-2702      www.commsystems.com

*Mfr. telecommunications equipment.*

**Austin Taylor Communications Ltd., Bethesda, Gwynedd LL57 3BX, UK**

Tel: 44-1248-600561   Contact: John Hudson   Emp: 150

## COMPAQ COMPUTER CORPORATION

20555 State Highway 249, PO Box 692000, Houston, TX, 77269-2000

Tel: (281) 370-0670      Fax: (281) 514-1740      www.compaq.com

*Develop/mfr. personal computers.*

**Compaq Computer Ltd., London, UK**

Tel: 44-141-270-4000   Fax: 44-1-41-270-4100

## COMPUTER ASSOCIATES INTERNATIONAL INC.

One Computer Associates Plaza, Islandia, NY, 11788

Tel: (516) 342-5224      Fax: (516) 342-5329      www.cai.com

*Integrated business software for enterprise computing and information management, application development, manufacturing, financial applications and professional services.*

**Computer Associates Plc, Computer Associates House, 183/187 Bath Rd., Slough, Berkshire SL-14AA UK**

Tel: 44-1753-577-733

## COMPUTER HORIZONS CORPORATION

49 Old Bloomfield Ave., Mountain Lakes, NJ, 07046-1495

Tel: (973) 299-4000      Fax: (973) 402-7988      www.computerhorizons.com

*Engaged in software development.*

**Computer Horizons ISG, 31 Beaufort Court, Admirals Way Waterside, South Quay London E14 9XL, UK**

Tel: 44-207-538-3388

## COMPUTER SCIENCES CORPORATION

2100 East Grand Ave., El Segundo, CA, 90245

Tel: (310) 615-0311      Fax: (310) 322-9768      www.csc.com

*Information technology services, management consulting, systems integration, outsourcing.*

**CSC Computer Sciences Ltd., 279 Farnborough Rd., Farnborough, Hampshire GU147LS, UK**

Contact: Ronald W. Mackintosh, Group Pres.

## COMPUWARE CORPORATION

31440 Northwestern Hwy., Farmington Hills, MI, 48334-2564

Tel: (248) 737-7300      Fax: (248) 737-7108      www.compuware.com

*Develop and market software for enterprise and e-commerce solutions.*

**Compuware Ltd., 163 Bath Road, Slough, Berkshire SL1 4AA, UK**

Tel: 44-1753-774-000   Fax: 44-1753-774-200

## COMSAT CORPORATION

6560 Rock Spring Drive, Bethesda, MD, 20817

Tel:  (301) 214-3200        Fax:  (301) 214-7100         www.comsat.com

*Provides global telecommunications services via satellite and develops advanced satellite networking technology.*

**COMSAT International,  BEL 278 - PO Box 289, Weybridge Surrey KT13 8WJ, UK**

## COMSHARE INC.

555 Briarwood Circle, Ste. 200, Ann Arbor, MI, 48108-3302

Tel:  (734) 994-4800        Fax:  (734) 994-5895         www.comshare.com

*Managerial application software.*

**Comshare Ltd.,  22 Chelsea Manor St., London SW3 5RL, UK**

## COMVERSE TECHNOLOGY, INC.

234 Crossways Park Drive, Woodbury, NY, 11797

Tel:  (516) 677-7200        Fax:  (516) 677-7355         www.comverse.com

*Mfr. telephone communication and recording systems.*

**Comverse Infosys UK, Ltd.,  Hertford Place Denham Way, Maple Cross, Rickmansworth Hertfordshire WD3 2XF UK**

Tel: 44-1923-717-432   Fax: 44-1923-717-311

**Loronix, Div. Comverse Infosys,  Unit 1B Intec 2 - Wade Road, Basingstoke Hants RG24 8NE, UK**

Tel: 44-12563-50711

## CONAGRA INC.

One ConAgra Drive, Omaha, NE, 68102-5001

Tel:  (402) 595-4000        Fax:  (402) 595-4707         www.conagra.com

*Prepared/frozen foods, grains, flour, animal feeds, agro chemicals, poultry, meat, dairy products, including Healthy Choice, Butterball and Hunt's.*

**ConAgra Inc.,  England, UK**

## CONCURRENT COMPUTER CORPORATION

4375 River Green Pkwy., Duluth, GA, 30096

Tel:  (678) 258-4000        Fax:  (678) 258-4300         www.ccur.com

*Mfr. computer systems and software.*

**Concurrent Computer Corporation Ltd.,  Concurrent House, Railway Terrace, Slough Berkshire SL2 5BY UK**

Tel: 44-1-753-216800   Fax: 44-1-753-571661

## CONDE NAST PUBLICATIONS INC.

350 Madison Ave., New York, NY, 10017

Tel:  (212) 880-8800        Fax:  (212) 880-8289         www.condenast.com

*Publishing company.*

**Conde Nast Publications UK,  Vogue House, Hanover Sq., London W1R 0AD, UK**

## CONEXANT SYSTEMS, INC.

4311 Jamboree Road, PO Box C, Newport Beach, CA, 92658-8902

Tel:  (949) 483-4600        Fax:  (949) 483-4078         www.conexant.com

*Provides semiconductor products for communications electronics.*

**Conexant Systems UK Ltd.,  Berkshire Court, Western Road Bracknell, Berkshire RG 12 1RE, UK**

Tel: 44-1344-486-444   Fax: 44-1344-486-555

## CONOCO INC.

PO Box 2197, 600 N. Dairy Ashford, Houston, TX, 77252

Tel:  (281) 293-1000        Fax:  (281) 293-1440         www.conoco.com

*Oil, gas, coal, chemicals and minerals.*

**Conch Methane Services Ltd.,  c/o Shell Intl. Gas Ltd., Shell Centre, London SE1 7NA, UK**

Conoco (UK) Ltd., South Denes Rd., Great Yarmouth, Norfolk NR30 3QD, UK

Conoco Ltd., Conoco House, 230 Blackfriars Rd., London SE1 8NR, UK

Conoco Ltd., Park House, 116 Park St., London WIY 4NN, UK

Continental Oil Holdings Ltd., 103/105 Wigmore St., London W1H OEL, UK

Humber Refinery, South Killingholme, South Humberside DN40 3DW, UK

Vinatex Ltd., New Lane, Havant, Hampshire P09 2NQ, UK

## CONSOLIDATED FREIGHTWAYS CORPORATION

175 Linfield Dr., Menlo Park, CA, 94025

Tel: (650) 326-1700        Fax: (650) 617-6700        www.cf.com

*Engaged in freight forwarding and logistics services.*

**Consolidated Freightways Corp., London, UK**

## CONSTELLATION BRANDS, INC.

300 Willowbrook Office Park, Fairport, NY, 14450

Tel: (716) 218-2169        Fax: (716) 218-6216        www.cbrands.com

*Distributes wines and spirits.*

**Matthew Clark plc, Whitchurch Lane, Bristol BS14 0JZ, UK**

Tel: 44-1275-836100    Contact: Peter Aikens, CEO

## CONSTRUCTION SPECIALTIES INC.

3 Werner Way, Lebanon, NJ, 08833

Tel: (908) 236-0800        Fax: (908) 236-0801        www.c-sgroup.com

*Mfr. architectural building products.*

**Construction Specialties (UK) Ltd., Conspec House, St. Andrews Way Ind. Estate, Bicester Rd., Aylesbur Buckinghamshire HP19 3AF UK**

Tel: 44-1-2963-99700   Fax: 44-1-2963-99444    Contact: Robert Adams, Mng. Dir.

## CONTICO INTERNATIONAL LLC

1101 Warson Road, St. Louis, MO, 63132

Tel: (314) 997-5900        Fax: (314) 997-1270        www.contico.com

*Mfr. plastic tool boxes, storage bins/shelves, parts organizers, sporting goods.*

**Contico Europe, Cardrew Way, Redruth TR15 1ST, UK**

Tel: 441-209-315-222

## CONTINENTAL AIRLINES INC.

2929 Allen Parkway, Ste. 2010, Houston, TX, 77019

Tel: (281) 834-5000        Fax: (281) 520-6329        www.continental.com

*International airline carrier.*

**Continental Airlines Inc., London, UK**

## CONVERGYS CORPORATION

201 E. 4th St., Cincinnati, OH, 45202

Tel: (513) 723-7000        Fax: (513) 421-8624        www.convergys.com

*Engaged in data bill processing, telemarketing and customer services representation for major corporations.*

**Convergys Corporation, 5 Bath Road, Slough, Berkshire SL1 3UA, UK**

Tel: 44-1753-727700

**Convergys Corporation, Baron House, Neville St., Newcastle NE1 5EA, UK**

Tel: 44-191-233-3000

## COOPER BUSSMANN

PO Box 14460, St. Louis, MO, 63178-4460

Tel: (636) 394-2877     Fax: (636) 527-1405     www.bussmann.com

*Mfr. and markets circuit protection products for the electrical, electronic, and automotive industries.*

**Bussmann UK Ltd., Burton-on-the-Wolds, Leicestershire LE12 5TH, UK**

Tel: 44 1509 882737   Fax: 44 1509 882786

## COOPER CAMERON CORPORATION

515 Post Oak Blvd., Ste.1200, Houston, TX, 77027

Tel: (713) 513-3300     Fax: (713) 513-3355     www.coopercameron.com

*Mfr. oil and gas industry equipment.*

**Cooper Cameron UK, 5 Mondial Way Harlington, Hayes, London UB3 5AR, UK**

Tel: 44-181-990-1800

**Cooper Cameron UK, Unit 1 and 2 Boundary Road, Harfrey's Industrial Estate, Great Yarmouth Norfolk, NR31 OLY, UK**

## THE COOPER COMPANIES, INC.

6140 Stoneridge Mall Road, Ste. 590, Pleasanton, CA, 94588

Tel: (925) 460-3600     Fax: (925) 460-3649     www.coopercos.com

*Mfr. contact lenses and gynecological instruments.*

**CooperVision UK Ltd., Hamble Hampshire, UK**

## COOPER INDUSTRIES INC.

6600 Travis Street, Ste. 5800, Houston, TX, 77002

Tel: (713) 209-8400     Fax: (713) 209-8995     www.cooperindustries.com

*Mfr./distributor electrical products, tools, hardware and automotive products, fuses and accessories for electronic applications and circuit boards.*

**Cooper (UK) Ltd. - Embray Contractors, Unit 5C Clay Flatts, Industrial Estate, Wokingham Cumbria CA14 3YD, UK**

Tel: 44-1900-970088   Fax: 44-1900-870099

**Cooper (UK) Ltd., Bussmann Division, Burton-on-the-Wolds, Leicestershire LE12 5TH, UK**

Tel: 44-1509-882737   Fax: 44-1509-882786

**Cooper Automotive Europe - Champion Spark Plug Division, Arrowebrook Rd., Upton Wirral, Merseyside L49 0UQ, UK**

Tel: 44-151-522-3000

**Cooper Menvier, Southam Road - Banbury ,Oxfordshire OX16 7RY, UK**

Tel: 44-1295-256363

## COOPER STANDARD AUTOMOTIVE

2401 South Gulley Road, Dearborn, MI, 48124

Tel: (313) 561-1100     Fax: (313) 561-6526     www.cooperstandard.com

*Mfr. molded and extruded rubber and plastic products for automotive and appliance industry, retread tire industry.*

**Cooper Standard Automotive, Dryden House, 1 St. Johns St., Huntingdon Cambs. PE18 6NU, UK**

Tel: 44-1480-423000   Fax: 44-1480-423111

## COOPER TIRE & RUBBER CO.

701 Lima Ave., Findlay, OH, 45840

Tel: (419) 423-1321     Fax: (419) 424-4108     www.coopertire.com

*Mfr. and marketing of tires and automotive products.*

**Cooper Avon Tyres Ltd., Bath Road, Melksham, Wiltshire SN12 8AA, UK**

Tel: 44-1225-703101   Fax: 44-1225-707880

## COOPER TURBOCOMPRESSOR

3101 Broadway, PO Box 209, Buffalo, NY, 14225-0209

Tel: (716) 896-6600    Fax: (716) 896-1233    www.turbocompressor.com

*Mfr. air and gas compressors.*

**Cooper Turbocompressor UK,  Cooper Cameron House, 5 Mondial Way, Middlesex UB35AR, UK**

Tel: 44-181-990-1950   Fax: 44-181-990-1955

## CORBIS CORPORATION

15395 SE 30th Place, Ste. 300, Bellevue, WA, 98007

Tel: (425) 641-4505    Fax: (425) 643-9740    www.corbis.com

*Provides digital photograph imagery to creative professionals in magazine, book and newspaper publishing, advertising and graphic design and Internet and new media publishing.*

**Corbin Corporation UK Ltd.,  4 Nile Street, London N19 RL, UK**

## CORDANT TECHNOLOGIES INC.

15 W. South Temple, Ste. 1600, Salt Lake City, UT, 84101-1532

Tel: (801) 933-4000    Fax: (801) 933-4014    www.cordanttech.com

*Mfr. solid rocket boosters for space shuttles and fasteners, rivets, and lock bolts for the transportation and construction industries.*

**Huck International Ltd.,  Unit C - Stafford Park 7, Telford Shropshire TF3-3BQ, UK**

**Huck International Mfr. Ctr.,  Telford Shropshire, UK**

Tel: 905-564-4825   Fax: 905-564-1963   Contact: Spencer C. Myer, Mgr.

## CORDIS CORPORATION

PO Box 25700, Miami, FL, 33102-5700

Tel: (305) 824-2000    Fax: (305) 824-2747    www.cordis.com

*Mfr. medical devices and systems.*

**Cordis Div., J&J Medical,  Coronation Road, South Ascot, Berkshire SL5 9EY, UK**

## CORNING INC.

One Riverfront Plaza, Corning, NY, 14831-0001

Tel: (607) 974-9000    Fax: (607) 974-8091    www.corning.com

*Mfr. glass and specialty materials, consumer products; communications, laboratory services.*

**Corning Communications Europe,  1 The Valley Centre, Gordon Road - High Wycombe, Buckingham HP13 6EQ, UK**

Contact: Sandy Lyons

**Corning Ltd.,  1 The Valley Centre, Gordon Road High Wycombe, Buckingham HP13 6EQ UK**

Tel: 44-1494-450589   Fax: 44-1494-450596

## CORRPRO COMPANIES, INC.

1090 Enterprise Drive, Medina, OH, 44256

Tel: (330) 725-6681    Fax: (330) 723-0244    www.corrpro.com

*Full-services corrosion engineering, cathodic protection.*

**Rohrback Cosasco Systems,  Strawberry Hill - Fishers Lane, Cold Ash Newbury, RG16 9NG UK**

Tel: 44-1635-202782   Fax: 44-1635-202582   Contact: Philip Large

**Wilson Walton Europe,  Adam St., Bowesfield Lane, Stockton-on-Tees Cleveland TS18 3HQ, UK**

Tel: 44-1642-614106   Fax: 44-1642-614100   Contact: John Chase and Mark Davies, Mgrs.

## COSMAIR INC.

575 Fifth Ave., New York, NY, 10017

Tel: (212) 818-1500    Fax: (212) 984-4776    www.cosmair.com

*Mfr. hair and skin care products.*

**Redken Laboratories Ltd.,  Precedent Dr., Milton Keynes MK13 8PF, UK**

## COSTCO WHOLESALE CORPORATION

999 Lake Dr., Issaquah, WA, 98027

Tel: (425) 313-8100    Fax: (425) 313-8103    www.costco.com

*Operates wholesale, membership warehouse stores.*

**Costco Wholesale Corp., Leathley Road, Hunslet, Leeds LS10-1PX, UK**

## COUDERT BROTHERS

1114 Ave. of the Americas, New York, NY, 10036-7794

Tel: (212) 626-4400    Fax: (212) 626-4120    www.coudert.com

*International law firm.*

**Coudert Brothers, 60 Cannon St., London EC4N 6JP, UK**

Tel: 44-207-248-3000    Fax: 44-207-248-3001

## COULTER PHARMACEUTICAL, INC.

600 Gateway Blvd., South San Francisco, CA, 94080

Tel: (650) 553-2000    Fax: (650) 553-2028    www.coulterpharm.com

*Mfr. blood analysis systems, flow cytometers, chemicals systems, scientific systems and reagents.*

**Coulter Electronics Ltd., Northwell Dr., Luton, Bedsforshire LU3 3RH UK**

## COVINGTON & BURLING

1201 Pennsylvania Ave., N.W., Washington, DC, 20004-2401

Tel: (202) 662-6000    Fax: (202) 662-6291    www.cov.com

*International law firm.*

**Covington & Burling, Leconfield House, Curzon St., London, UKW1 Y8S, UK**

Tel: 44-207-495-5655

## SG COWEN SECURITIES

1221 Avenue of the America, New York, NY, 10020

Tel: (212) 495-6000    Fax: (212) 380-8212    www.cowen.com

*Securities research, trading, broker/dealer services; investment banking and asset management.*

**Cowen Securities, One Angel Court, London EC2R 7HJ, UK**

Tel: 44-207-710-0900    Fax: 44-207-606-0289    Contact: Howard Dingley, Mgr.

## CRANE & CO., INC.

30 South Street, Dalton, MA, 01226

Tel: (413) 684-2600    Fax: (413) 684-4278    www.crane.com

*Mfr. fine cotton papers, currency paper for the U.S. Mint and high-performance battery separators.*

**SciMAT Limited, Dorcan 200, Murdock Road, Swindon SN3 5HY, UK**

Tel: 44-1793-511160    Fax: 44-1793-533352

## CRANE COMPANY

100 First Stamford Place, Stamford, CT, 06907

Tel: (203) 363-7300    Fax: (203) 363-7359    www.craneco.com

*Diversified mfr./distributor of engineered industrial products and the largest American distributor of doors, windows and millwork.*

**Crane Ltd., Audrey House, Ely Place, London EC1N 6SN, UK**

**UMC Industries Ltd., Dock Rd., Lytham, Lancshire FY8 5BD, UK**

## CRAVATH, SWAINE & MOORE

Worldwide Plaza, 825 Eighth Ave., New York, NY, 10019-7475

Tel: (212) 474-1000    Fax: (212) 474-3700    www.cravath.com

*International law firm.*

**Cravath, Swaine & Moore, 10th Fl. 33 King William St., London EC4R 9DU, UK**

Tel: 44-207-453-1000

**CRC PRESS LLC**

2000 NW Corporate Blvd., Boca Raton, FL, 33431

Tel: (561) 994-0555　　　Fax: (561) 997-0949　　　www.crcpress.com

*Publishing: science, technical and medical books and journals.*

**CRC Press UK, Pocock House, 235 Southwark Bridge Road,
London SE1 6LY, UK**

**CROMPTON CORPORATION**

Benson Road, Middlebury, CT, 06749

Tel: (203) 573-2000　　　Fax:　　　　　www.crompton-knowles.com

*Mfr. dyes, colors, flavors, fragrances, specialty chemicals and industrial products.*

**Baxenden Chemical Co. Ltd., Near Accrington, Lancashire BB5 2SL, UK**

**Crompton Corp. UK Ltd., Gorsey Lane, Widnes, Cheshire WA8 0HE, UK**

**Uniroyal Chemical Div., Uniroyal Ltd., First Ave., Trafford Park, Manchester M17 1DT, UK**

**Uniroyal Ltd., Monaco House, Bristol St., Birmingham B5 7AS, UK**

**Uniroyal Ltd., 62/64 Horseferry Rd., London, UK**

**CROSBY McKISSICK CORP.**

PO Box 3128, 2801 Dawson Rd., Tulsa, OK, 74101-3128

Tel: (918) 834-4611　　　Fax: (918) 832-0940　　　www.thecrosbygroup.com

*Mfr. machine tools, hardware, steel forgings.*

**Amdura Ltd., Euroway Blagrove Industrial Estate D-6/7, Swindon, Wilts. SN5 8YL UK**

**A.T. CROSS COMPANY**

One Albion Road, Lincoln, RI, 02865

Tel: (401) 333-1200　　　Fax: (401) 334-2861　　　www.cross.com

*Mfr. writing instruments, leads, erasers and ink refills.*

**A.T. Cross Ltd., Concorde House, Concorde St., Luton, Bedfordshire LU2 0JD UK**

Tel: 44-1582-422-793

**CROWELL & MORING**

1001 Pennsylvania Avenue, NW, Washington, DC, 20004-2595

Tel: (202) 624-2500　　　Fax: (202) 628-5116　　　www.crowellmoring.com

*International law firm.*

**Crowell & Moring, 180 Fleet St., London EC4A 2HD, UK**

Tel: 44-207-413-0011

**CROWN CASTLE INTERNATIONAL, INC.**

510 Bering Dr., Ste. 500, Houston, TX, 77057-1457

Tel: (713) 570-3000　　　Fax: (713) 570-3100　　　www.crowncomm.net

*Provides wireless communications and broadcast infrastructure services.*

**Crown Castle UK Limited, Warwick Technology Park, PO Box 98, Warwick CV34 6TN, UK**

**CROWN EQUIPMENT CORPORATION**

40 South Washington Street, New Bremen, OH, 45869

Tel: (419) 629-2311　　　Fax: (419) 629-2900　　　www.crownlift.com

*Mfr./sales/services forklift trucks, stackers.*

**Crown Lift Trucks Ltd., Fishponds Rd., Wokingham, Berkshire, UK**

**CRYOLIFE, INC.**

1655 Roberts Blvd. North West, Kennesaw, GA, 30144

Tel: (770) 419-3355        Fax: (770) 426-0031        www.cryolife.com

*Engaged in development of transplant organs and procedures.*

**CryoLife Europa, Ltd., Europa House Fareham Heights, Standard Way Fareham, Hampshire PO6 8XT, UK**

Tel: 44-1329-229800   Fax: 44-1329-229801

**CUBIC CORPORATION**

9333 Balboa Ave., PO Box 85587, San Diego, CA, 92123

Tel: (858) 277-6780        Fax: (858) 277-1878        www.cubic.com

*Automatic fare collection equipment, training systems.*

**Cubic Tiltman Langley, 177 Nutfield Rd., Merstham Surrey RHI 3HH, UK**

**Thorn Transit Systems International Ltd., Wooley Hole Rd., Wells Somerset BA5 1AA, UK**

Tel: 44-1749--670222  Fax: 44-1749-679363   Contact: Julian Slater, Mng. Dir.

**CULLIGAN WATER TECHNOLOGIES**

One Culligan Parkway, Northbrook, IL, 60062

Tel: (847) 205-6000        Fax: (847) 205-6030        www.culligan-man.com

*Water treatment products and services.*

**Culligan Intl. Co., Blenheim Rd., Cressex Industrial Estate, High Wycombe HP12 3RS, UK**

Tel: 44-1494-436484   Fax: 44-1494-523833

**CUMMINS ENGINE COMPANY, INC.**

500 Jackson Street, PO Box 3005, Columbus, IN, 47202-3005

Tel: (812) 377-5000        Fax: (812) 377-4937        www.cummins.com

*Mfr. diesel engines.*

**Cummins Engine Co. Ltd., 46-50 Coombe Rd., New Malden, Surrey KT3 4QL, UK**

**Holset Engineering Company Ltd., Huddersfield, UK**

**CURTIS, MALLET-PREVOST, COLT & MOSLE LLP**

101 Park Ave., 35th Floor, New York, NY, 10178

Tel: (212) 696-6000        Fax: (212) 697-1559        www.cm-p.com

*International law firm.*

**Curtis, Mallet-Prevost, Colt & Mosle LLP, Two Throgmorton Avenue, London, EC2N 2DL, UK**

Tel: 44-207-638-7957

**CURTISS-WRIGHT CORPORATION**

1200 Wall Street West, Lyndhurst, NJ, 07071-0635

Tel: (201) 896-8400        Fax: (201) 438-5680        www.curtisswright.com

*Mfr. precision components and systems, engineered services to aerospace, flow control and marine industry.*

**Metal Improvement Co. Inc., Ascot Drive, Derby DE2 8ST, UK**

**Metal Improvement Co. Inc., Ste. 2 Ivyholme, Station Rd., Heathfield, East Sussex TN21 8LD UK**

**Metal Improvement Co. Ltd., Navigation House, Hambridge Lane, Newbury, Berkshire RG14 5TU, UK**

**CUTLER-HAMMER, DIV. EATON CORP.**

173 Heatherdown Drive, Westerville, OH, 43082

Tel: (614) 882-3282        Fax: (614) 895-7111        www.cutlerhammer.com

*Mfr. electrical control products and power distribution equipment.*

**Cutler-Hammer Ltd., Mill Street, Ottery St. Mary, Devon EX11 1AG, UK**

Tel: 44-1404-812131   Fax: 44-1404-815471

**Cutler-Hammer Ltd., Carina - Sunrise Parkway, Linford Wood Milton Keynes, MK14 6NR, UK**

Tel: 44-1908-541600   Fax: 44-1908-660527

**CYBORG SYSTEMS INC.**

2 N. Riverside Plaza, Chicago, IL, 60606-0899

Tel: (312) 454-1865      Fax: (312) 454-0889      www.cyborg,com

*Develop/mfr. human resources, payroll and time/attendance software.*

**Cyborg Systems Ltd.,  Central Court, Knoll Rise, Orpington, Kent BR6 0JA UK**

Tel: 44-1-689-827011    Contact: David Stallion

**CYLINK CORPORATION**

3131 Jay Street, Santa Clara, CA, 95054

Tel: (408) 855-6000      Fax: (408) 855-6100      www.cyllink.com

*Develop and manufactures encryption software.*

**Cylink UK, Ltd.,  Intec Business Park Intec 4, Wade Road,
Basingstoke, Hants RG24 8NE, UK**

Tel: 44-1256-345-900

**CYPRESS SEMICONDUCTOR CORPORATION**

3901 N. First Street, San Jose, CA, 95134-1599

Tel: (408) 943-2600      Fax: (408) 943-2796      www.cypress.com

*Mfr. integrated circuits.*

**Cypress Semiconductor,  Gate House - Fretherne Road, Welwyn Garden City,
Herts AL8 6NS, UK**

Tel: 44-1-707-37-87-00   Fax: 44-1-707-37-87-37

**CYTEC INDUSTRIES, INC.**

5 Garret Mountain Plaza, West Paterson, NJ, 07424

Tel: (973) 357-3100      Fax: (973) 357-3054      www.cytec.com

*Mfr. specialty chemicals and materials,*

**Cytec Industries UK Ltd.,  Bowling Park Drive, Bradford BD4 7TT West Yorkshire, UK**

Tel: 44-1274-73-3891

**DALLAS SEMICONDUCTOR CORPORATION**

4401 South Beltway Parkway, Dallas, TX, 75244-3292

Tel: (972) 371-4000      Fax: (972) 371-4956      www.dalsemi.com

*Design/mfr. computer chips and chip-based subsystems.*

**Dallas Semiconductor,  11 Medway Close, Wokingham, Berkshire RG41 3TP, UK**

Tel: 44-121-782-2959   Fax: 44-121-782-2156   Contact: Terry Andrews, Reg. Sales Mgr.

**Dallas Semiconductor,  Unit 27 West Midland Freeport, Birmingham B26 3QD, UK**

Tel: 44-121-782-2959   Fax: 44-121-782-2156   Contact: Terry Andrews, Reg. Sales Mgr.

**DAMES & MOORE GROUP**

911 Wilshire Boulevard, Ste. 700, Los Angeles, CA, 90017

Tel: (213) 996-2200      Fax: (213) 996-2290      www.dames.com

*Engineering, environmental and construction management services.*

**Ashact Ltd.,  Bridge House, Station Approach, Great Missenden, Buckinghamshire HP18 9AZ UK**

**Dames & Moore,  5/F Blackfriar's House, St. Mary's Parsonage, Manchester M3 2JA, UK**

**Dames & Moore,  1/F Booth House, 15-17 Church St., Twickenham TW1 3NJ, UK**

**Dames & Moore,  The Clifton Dispensary, 13 Dowry Sq., Bristol BS8 4SL, UK**

**Food & Agriculture Intl. Ltd.,  1/F Booth House, 15-17 Church St., Twickenham TW1 3NJ, UK**

**O'Brien-Kreitzberg,  Artillery House 7th fl., Artillery Row, London SW1P R1T, UK**

## DANA CORPORATION

4500 Dorr Street, Toledo, OH, 43615

Tel: (419) 535-4500       Fax: (419) 535-4643       www.dana.com

*Mfr./sales of automotive, heavy truck, off-highway, fluid and mechanical power components and engine parts, filters and gaskets.*

**Dana Ltd./Dana Europe, Great Eastern House, Greenbridge Rd., Stratton St., Margaret Swindon UK**

**Dana Spicer Europe Ltd., 31 Lyveden Road, Brackmills Northampton, NN4 7ED, UK**

Tel: 44-01-6046-75005

**Spicer Europe, Electra Park- Electric Avenue, Witton B6 7DZ, UK**

**Spicer Off-Highway Axle Div., Abbey Road, Kirkstall Leeds, LS5 3NF, UK**

Tel: 44-113-258-4611

## DANIEL INDUSTRIES INC.

9753 Pine Lake Drive, PO Box 55435, Houston, TX, 77224

Tel: (713) 467-6000       Fax: (713) 827-3889       www.danielind.com

*Oil/gas equipment and systems; geophysical services.*

**Daniel International Ltd., Swinton Grange Malton, North Yorkshire Y017 0QR, UK**

Tel: 44-1653-600425   Fax: 44-1653-600425

## DANIEL MANN JOHNSON & MENDENHALL

3250 Wilshire Blvd., Los Angeles, CA, 90010

Tel: (213) 381-3663       Fax: (213) 383-3656       www.dmjm.com

*Architects and engineers.*

**DMJM Intl. Ltd., Brent House, 214 Kenton Rd., Harrow, Middlesex HA3 8BT UK**

## D'ARCY MASIUS BENTON & BOWLES INC. (DMB&B)

1675 Broadway, New York, NY, 10019

Tel: (212) 468-3622       Fax: (212) 468-2987       www.dmbb.com

*Full service international advertising and communications group.*

**DMB&B Europe, 2 St.James' Square, London SW1Y 4JN, UK**

**DMB&B Europe, 76 Oxford St., London W1A 1DT, UK**

## DATA DIMENSIONS, INC.

3535 Factoria Blvd., S.E., 3rd Fl., Bellevue, WA, 98006

Tel: (425) 688-1000       Fax: (425) 688-1099       www.data-dimensions.com

*Provides computer systems consulting services to adapt computerized systems for year 2000 problems, and other data processing services.*

**Data Dimensions, Inc., 1a Goodsons Mews, Wellington St., Thame Oxon OX9 3BX, UK**

Tel: 44-1844-219930   Fax: 44-1844-219938

## DATA GENERAL CORPORATION

4400 Computer Drive, Westboro, MA, 01580

Tel: (508) 898-5000       Fax: (508) 366-1319       www.dg.com

*Design, mfr. general purpose computer systems and peripheral products and services.*

**Data General Europe, Great West Road, Brentford Middlesex TW8 9AN, UK**

Tel: 44-181-58-6000

## DATA TRANSLATION INC.

100 Locke Drive, Marlborough, MA, 01752-1192

Tel: (508) 481-3700       Fax: (508) 481-8620       www.datx.com

*Mfr. peripheral boards for image and array processing micro-computers.*

**Data Translation Ltd., Unit 10, Plover House, Aviary Court Wade Road, Basingstoke Hants RG24 8PE, UK**

Tel: 44-1256-333330

## DATASCOPE CORPORATION

14 Phillips Pkwy., Montvale, NJ, 07645

Tel: (201) 391-8100    Fax: (201) 307-5400    www.datascope.com

*Mfr. medical devices.*

**Datascope Medical Co. Ltd., Lakeview Court Spitfire Close, Ermine Business Park, Huntingdon Cambs PE18 6XR, UK**

## DATAWARE TECHNOLOGIES INC.

1 Canal Park, Cambridge, MA, 02141

Tel: (617) 621-0820    Fax: (617) 577-2413    www.dataware.com

*Provides e-business solutions.*

**Data Technologies (UK) Ltd., Congress House, Lyon Rd., Harrow, Middlesex HA1 2EN UK**

**Data Technologies (UK) Ltd., Keaton House, Widewater Place, Harefield Middlesex UB9 6NS, UK**

## DAVIS POLK & WARDWELL

450 Lexington Ave., New York, NY, 10017

Tel: (212) 450-4000    Fax: (212) 450-4800    www.dpw.com

*International law firm.*

**Davis Polk & Wardwell, One Fredericks Place, London EC2R 8AB, UK**

Tel: 44-141-418-1300   Fax: 44-151-418-1400

## DAVOX CORPORATION

6 Technology Park Drive, Westford, MA, 01886

Tel: (978) 952-0200    Fax: (978) 952-0201    www.davox.com

*Mfr. call-center software for telephone operations.*

**Davox UK Ltd., Elvian House - Nixey Close, Slough, Berkshire SL1 1ND, UK**

Tel: 44-1753-756-700   Fax: 44-1753-756-701

## DAY RUNNER, INC.

15295 Alton Parkway, Irvine, CA, 92618

Tel: (714) 680-3500    Fax: (714) 680-0538    www.dayrunner.com

*Mfg./distribution of paper-based organizers.*

**Day Runner International Ltd., 2 Kings Hill Ave., Kings Hill, west Malling, Kent ME19 4TAQ, UK**

Tel: 44-1732-842828   Fax: 44-1732-849030   Contact: D. Blake

## DAYCO PRODUCTS INC.

PO Box 1004, Dayton, OH, 45401-1004

Tel: (937) 226-7000    Fax: (937) 226-4689    www.dayco.com

*Mfr. diversified auto, industrial and household products.*

**Dayco Rubber (UK) Ltd., St. James's House, Wellington Rd. North, Stockport SK4 2RH UK**

## DAYTON PROGRESS CORPORATION

500 Progress Road, Dayton, OH, 45449

Tel: (937) 859-5111    Fax: (937) 859-5353    www.daytonprogress.com

*Punches, dies and guide bushings.*

**Dayton Progress (UK) Ltd., G1 Holly Farm Business Park, Honiley Kenilworth, Warwickshire CV8 1NP UK**

## DDB NEEDHAM WORLDWIDE INC.

437 Madison Ave., New York, NY, 10022

Tel: (212) 415-2000    Fax: (212) 415-3417    www.ddbn.com

*Advertising agency.*

**BMP DDB Needham Worldwide Ltd., 12 Bishop's Bridge Rd., London W2 6AA, UK**

**Griffin Bacal, London UK**

## DEBEVOISE & PLIMPTON

919 Third Avenue, New York, NY, 10022

Tel: (212) 909-6000    Fax: (212) 909-6836    www.debevoise.com

*International law firm.*

**Debevoise & Plimpton,  The International Financial Centre, Old Broad St., London EC4M 7AA,UK**

Tel: 44-207-786-9000   Fax: 44-207-588-4180   Contact: David V. Smalley, Mng. Ptnr.   Emp: 22

## DECHERT PRICE & RHOADS

4000 Bell Atlantic Tower, 1717 Arch Street, Philadelphia, PA, 19103-2793

Tel: (215) 994-4000    Fax: (215) 994-2222    www.dechert.com

*International law firm.*

**Titmuss Sainer Dechert,  2 Sergeants  Inn, London EC4Y 1LT, UK**

Tel: 44-207-583-5353   Fax: 44-207-353-3683

## DECISION STRATEGIES FAIRFAX INTERNATIONAL

505 Park Avenue, 7th Fl., New York, NY, 10022

Tel: (212) 935-4040    Fax: (212) 935-4046    www.dsfx.com

*Provides discreet consulting, investigative, business intelligence and security services to corporations, financial and investment institutions, law firms and governments worldwide.*

**DSFX UK Ltd.,  31 Old Burlington Street - 2/F, London W1X 1LB, UK**

Tel: 44-207-734-5361   Fax: 44-207-734-5378

## DEERE & COMPANY

One John Deere Road, Moline, IL, 61265

Tel: (309) 765-8000    Fax: (309) 765-5772    www.deere.com

*Mfr./sale agricultural, construction, utility, forestry and lawn, grounds care equipment.*

**John Deere Ltd.,  Harby Road - UK-Langar, Nottingham NG13 9HT, UK**

Tel: 44-1949-860491   Fax: 44-1949-860490

## DELAVAN SPRAY TECHNOLOGIES

4115 Corporate Center Dr., Monroe, NC, 28110

Tel: (704) 291-3100    Fax: (704) 291-3101    www.delavan.com

*Mfr. spray nozzles for pumps and other fluid handling equipment.*

**Delavan Spray Technologies Ltd.,  Gorsey Lane, Widnes, Cheshire WA8 ORJ UK**

## DELL COMPUTER CORPORATION

One Dell Way, Round Rock, TX, 78682-2222

Tel: (512) 338-4400    Fax: (512) 728-3653    www.dell.com

*Direct marketer and supplier of computer systems.*

**Dell Computer,  Dell Plaza, Western Rd., Bracknell Berkshire RG12 IDX, UK**

Tel: 44-1344-748000   Fax: 44-1344-748008   Contact: Mika Sarhimaa, Pres. Dell Europe

**Dell Computer Corporation,  Milbanke House, Western Rd., Bracknell Berkshire RG12 1RW, UK**

Tel: 44-1344-860-4566   Fax: 44-1344-860-187   Contact: Adrian Weekes, Mng. Dir.

## DELOITTE TOUCHE TOHMATSU INTERNATIONAL

1633 Broadway, New York, NY, 10019

Tel: (212) 492-4000    Fax: (212) 392-4154    www.deloitte.com

*Accounting, audit, tax and management consulting services.*

**Braxton Associates,  90 Long Acre, London WC2E 9RA, UK**

**Deloitte & Touche,  Stonecutter Court, 1 Stonecutter St., London EC4A 4TR UK**

**Deloitte & Touche,  10-12 East Parade, Leeds LS1 2AJ, UK**

**DELTA AIR LINES INC.**

PO Box 20706, Atlanta, GA, 30320-6001

Tel: (404) 715-2600      Fax: (404) 715-5494      www.delta-air.com

*Major worldwide airline; international air transport services.*

**Delta Air Lines Inc., Manchester UK**

**Delta Air Lines Inc., London-Gatwick UK**

**Delta Air Lines Inc., Newcastle, UK**

**DELUXE CORPORATION**

3680 Victoria Street North, Shoreview, MN, 55126-2966

Tel: (612) 483-7111      Fax: (612) 481-4163      www.deluxe.com

*Leading U.S. check printer and provider of electronic payment services.*

**Deluxe Corporation, Nuffield Road Unit 1, Harrowbrook Estates, Hinckley, Leicestershire LE103DG UK**

**DENTSPLY INTERNATIONAL**

570 West College Ave., PO Box 872, York, PA, 17405-0872

Tel: (717) 845-7511      Fax: (717) 843-6357      www.dentsply.com

*Mfr. and distribution of dental supplies and equipment.*

**CMW Labs/Dentsply, Cornford Rd., Blackpool FY4 4QQ, UK**

**Dentsply AD Plastics, Clifton Rd., Marton, Blackpool FY4 4QF, UK**
Tel: 44-1253-765024

**Dentsply Ash Instruments, Pennycross Close, Beacon Park, Plymouth PL2 3NY, UK**
Tel: 44-1752-709751

**Dentsply Ceramco Ltd., Hamm Moor Lane, Addlestone, Weybridge Surrey KT15 2SE, UK**
Tel: 44-1932-856240

**Dentsply UK/Middle East/Africa, Hamm Moor Lane, Addlestone, Weybridge Surrey KT15 2SE, UK**
Tel: 44-1932-853422

**DETROIT DIESEL CORPORATION**

13400 Outer Drive West, Detroit, MI, 48239

Tel: (313) 592-5000      Fax: (313) 592-5058      www.detroitdiesel.com

*Mfr. diesel and aircraft engines, heavy-duty transmissions.*

**Mitchell Diesel Limited, Fulwood Road South, Sutton-IN-Ashfield, NHPS NG 17 2JZ, UK**
Tel: 44-16-2355-0550   Fax: 44-16-2355-1617

**DEWEY BALLANTINE LLP**

1301 Ave. of the Americas, New York, NY, 10019

Tel: (212) 259-8000      Fax: (212) 259-6333      www.deweyballantine.com

*International law firm.*

**Dewey Ballantine LLP, 1 Undershaft, London EC3A 8LP, UK**
Tel: 44-207-456-6000   Fax: 44-207-456-6001

**THE DEXTER CORPORATION**

1 Elm Street, Windsor Locks, CT, 06096

Tel: (860) 627-9051      Fax: (860) 627-7078      www.dexelec.com

*Mfr. polymer products, magnetic materials, biotechnology.*

**Dexter Magnetic Materials UK, Poyle 14 Unit 9, Newlands Dr., Colnbrook Slough Berkshire SL3 0DX, UK**

**The Dexter Corp., Stag Ind. Estate Unit 4C, Atlantic St., Altrincham Cheshire WA14 5DW, UK**

## DHL WORLDWIDE EXPRESS

50 California Avenue, San Francisco, CA, 94111

Tel: (415) 677-6100    Fax: (415) 824-9700    www.dhl.com

*Worldwide air express carrier.*

**DHL Worldwide Express, Orbital Park, 178-188 Great South West Rd., Hounslow Middlesex TW4 6JS, UK**

Tel: 44-181-818-8000  Fax: 44-181-818-8141

**DHL Worldwide Express, Hillblom House, 1 Dukes - Green Ave., Feltham Middlesex TW14 0LR, UK**

Tel: 44-181-831-5000   Fax: 44-181-831-5451

## DIAGNOSTIC PRODUCTS CORPORATION

5700 West 96th Street, Los Angeles, CA, 90045

Tel: (310) 645-8200    Fax: (310) 645-9999    www.dpcweb.com

*Mfr. diagnostic products.*

**Euro/DPC Ltd., Glyn Rhonwy, Llanberis Caernarfon, Gwynedd LL55 4EL, UK**

Tel: 44-1286-871-871  Fax: 44-1286-871-802

## DIAMOND CHAIN COMPANY

402 Kentucky Ave., Indianapolis, IN, 46225

Tel: (317) 638-6431    Fax: (317) 633-2243    www.diamondchain.com

*Mfr. roller chains.*

**Alremco Engineering/Diamond Chain (UK) Ltd., Unit 5 The Furlong, Berry Hill Industrial Estate, Droitwich, Worchester WR9 9AR UK**

Tel: 44-191-414-8822

## DIAMOND POWER INTERNATIONAL, INC.

PO Box 415, Lancaster, OH, 43130

Tel: (740) 687-6500    Fax: (740) 687-7430    www.diamondpower.com

*Mfg. boiler cleaning equipment and ash handling systems: sootblowers, controls, diagnostics systems, gauges, OEM parts, rebuilds and field service.*

**Diamond Power Site Services, Unit 5B - Heapham Road Industrial Estate, Gainsborough Lines, DN21 1XP, UK**

## DICTAPHONE CORPORATION

3191 Broadbridge Ave., Stratford, CT, 06497-2559

Tel: (203) 381-7000    Fax: (203) 381-7100    www.dictaphone.com

*Mfr./sale dictation, telephone answering and multi-channel voice communications recording systems.*

**Dictaphone International Ltd, Chalkhill Road, Hammersmith, London W6 8DN, UK**

Tel: 44-207-878-5000

## DIGITAL ORIGIN, INC.

460 East Middlefield Road, Mountainview, CA, 94043

Tel: (650) 404-6300    Fax: (650) 404-6200    www.digitalorigin.com

*Mfr. Digital Video (DV) software products.*

**Media 100 Ltd., 13 Westminster Ct., Hipley St., Old Woking, Surrey GU22 9LQ, UK**

## DIMON INCORPORATED

512 Bridge Street, PO Box 681, Danville, VA, 24543-0681

Tel: (804) 792-7511    Fax: (804) 791-0377    www.dimon.com

*One of world's largest importer and exporters of leaf tobacco.*

**DIMON International Services Limited, DIMON Place, Riverside Way Camberley, Surrey GU 15 3YF, UK**

Tel: 44-1276-404-600   Fax: 44-1276-404-700

**DIONEX CORPORATION**

1228 Titan Way, PO Box 3603, Sunnyvale, CA, 94086-3603

Tel: (408) 737-0700       Fax: (408) 730-9403       www.dionex.com

*Develop/mfr./market chromatography systems and related products.*

**Dionex (UK) Ltd.,  4 Albany Court, Camberley Surrey, GU15 2XA, UK**

**WALT DISNEY COMPANY**

500 South Buena Vista Street, Burbank, CA, 91521

Tel: (818) 560-1000       Fax: (818) 560-1930       www.disney.com

*Film/TV production, theme parks, resorts, publishing, recording and retail stores.*

**Walt Disney Productions Ltd.,  68 Pall Mall, London SW1Y 5EX, UK**

**DIXON TICONDEROGA COMPANY**

195 International Parkway, Heathrow, FL, 32746

Tel: (407) 829-9000       Fax: (407) 829-2574       www.dixonticonderoga.com

*Mfr./sales writing instruments, drawing and art supplies and office products*

**Dixon Wearever Ltd.,  36 Stapledon Rd., Peterboro PE2 OTD, UK**

**DMC STRATEX NETWORKS, INC.**

170 Rose Orchard Way, San Jose, CA, 95134

Tel: (408) 943-0777       Fax: (408) 944-1648       www.dmcstratexnetworks.com

*Designs, manufactures, and markets advanced wireless solutions for wireless broadband access.*

**DMC Stratex Networks,  Siskin Drive, Middlemarch Business Park, Coventry CV3 4JA, UK**

**DME COMPANY**

29111 Stephenson Highway, Madison Heights, MI, 48071

Tel: (248) 398-6000       Fax: (248) 544-5705       www.dmeco.com

*Basic tooling for plastic molding and die casting.*

**DME Europe UK,  Halifax Rd., Cressex Industrial Estate, High Wycombe, Bucks. HP12 3TN UK**

**DO ALL COMPANY**

254 North Laurel Ave., Des Plaines, IL, 60016

Tel: (847) 803-7380       Fax: (847) 699-7524       www.doall.com

*Distributors of machinery tools, metal cutting tools, instruments and industrial supplies for metalworking industry.*

**DoALL Company U.K., Ltd.,  Beldray Industrial Park Unit 9, Mount Pleasant, Bilston, West Midlands WV14 7NH UK**

Tel: 44-1902-404842   Fax: 44-1902-354303

**DOBOY PACKAGING MACHINERY INC.**

869 South Knowles Ave., New Richmond, WI, 54017-1797

Tel: (715) 246-6511       Fax: (715) 246-6539       www.doboy.com

*Mfr. packaging machinery.*

**Doboy UK,  Meteor Centre, Mansfield Rd., Derby DE2 4SY, UK**

**DOCUMENTUM, INC.**

6801 Koll Center Pkwy., Pleasanton, CA, 94566

Tel: (925) 600-6800       Fax: (925) 600-6850       www.documentum.com

*Mfr. content management software.*

**Documentum Software Europe Ltd,  5 Roundwood Avenue, Stockley Park, Uxbridge Middlesex UB11 1NZ, UK**

## DOLE FOOD COMPANY, INC.

31365 Oak Crest Drive, Westlake Village, CA, 91361

Tel: (818) 879-6600      Fax: (818) 879-6615      www.dole.com

*Produces/distributes fresh fruits and vegetables and canned juices and fruits.*

**Dole Food Company,  London, UK**

## DOMINICK & DOMINICK INC.

Financial Square, 32 Old Slip, New York, NY, 10005

Tel: (212) 558-8800      Fax: (212) 248-0592

*Investment brokers.*

**Dominick & Dominick Ltd.,  8 Little Trinity Lane, London EC4, UK**

## DONALDSON COMPANY, INC.

1400 West 94th Street, Minneapolis, MN, 55431

Tel: (612) 887-3131      Fax: (612) 887-3155      www.donaldson.com

*Mfr. filtration systems and replacement parts.*

**Donaldson Filter Components Ltd.,  65 Market St., Hednesford, Straffordshire WS12 5AD, UK**

Tel: 44-1543-425-515   Fax: 44-1543-879-136

## DONALDSON, LUFKIN & JENRETTE, INC.

277 Park Ave., New York, NY, 10172

Tel: (212) 892-3000      Fax: (212) 892-7272      www.dlj.com

*Investment banking, capital markets and financial services.*

**Donaldson, Lufkin & Jenrette Inc. Ltd.,  99 Bishopsgate, London EC2M 3XD, UK**

Tel: 44-207-655-7000   Emp: 800

**London Global Securities,  111 Old Broad Street, London, EC2N 1AP, UK**

Tel: 44 171-655-7815

**Pershing Ltd.,  3 Harbour Exchange Square, London, E14 9GD, UK**

Tel: 44-207-345-6000

## DONNA KARAN INTERNATIONAL INC.

550 Seventh  Ave., New York, NY, 10018

Tel: (212) 789-1500      Fax: (212) 921-3526      www.donnakaran.com

*Design/manufacture/sale men's, women's, and children's clothes.*

**Donna Karan International (DKNY),  London, England, UK**

## R.R. DONNELLEY & SONS COMPANY

77 West Wacker Drive, Chicago, IL, 60601-1696

Tel: (312) 326-8000      Fax: (312) 326-8543      www.rrdonnelley.com

*Commercial printing, allied communication services.*

**R. R. Donnelley (UK) Ltd.,  Donnelley House, 25 Worship St., London EC2A 2DX, UK**

Tel: 44-207-330-1690   Fax: 44-207-256-9133

**R. R. Donnelley Ltd. - Pindar,  513 Browells Lane, Feltham, Middlesex TW 13 7EQ, UK**

Tel: 44-181-890-8933

**R.R. Donnelley Ltd. York Division,  Boroughbridge Rd., York YO2 5SS, UK**

Tel: 44-190-479-8241

## DOREMUS & COMPANY, INC.

200 Varick Street, New York, NY, 10271

Tel: (212) 366-3000      Fax: (212) 366-3629      www.doremus.com

*Advertising and public relations.*

**Doremus & Co.,  5/11 Theobalds Rd., London WC14 8S8, UK**

Tel: 44-207-419-4000

## DORSEY & WHITNEY LLP

Pillsbury Center South, 220 S. Sixth Street, Minneapolis, MN, 55402

Tel: (612) 340-2600     Fax: (612) 340-2868     www.dorseylaw.com

*International law firm.*

**Dorsey & Whitney LLP,  Veritas House, 125 Finsbury Pavement, London ECZA INQ UK**

Tel: 44-207-588-0800  Fax: 44-207-588-0555   Contact: Peter E. Kohl, Mng. Ptnr.   Emp: 15

## DOUBLECLICK, INC.

450 West 33rd Street, New York, NY, 10001

Tel: (212) 683-0001     Fax: (212) 889-0062     www.doubleclick.net

*Engaged in online advertising.*

**Doubleclick, Ltd.,  204 Saint-Sacrement St. - Ste. 303, Montreal PQ H2Y 1W8, UK**

**Doubleclick, Ltd. (Media),  Cavendish House 3/F, 128/134 Cleveland Street, London W1P 5DN, UK**

Tel: 44-207-388-6565

## DOVER CORPORATION

280 Park Ave., New York, NY, 10017-1292

Tel: (212) 922-1640     Fax: (212) 922-1656     www.dovercorporation.com

*Holding company for varied industries; assembly and testing equipment, oil-well gear and other industrial products.*

**DEK Printing Machines Ltd.,  11 Albany Road, Granby Ind Est, Weymouth DT4 9TH UK**

## THE DOW CHEMICAL COMPANY

2030 Dow Center, Midland, MI, 48674

Tel: (517) 636-1000     Fax: (517) 636-3228     www.dow.com

*Mfr. chemicals, plastics, pharmaceuticals, agricultural products, consumer products.*

**Dow Chemical Co. Ltd.,  Meadow Bank, Bath Rd., Hounslow TW5 9QY, UK**

## DOW JONES & COMPANY, INC.

200 Liberty Street, New York, NY, 10281

Tel: (212) 416-2000     Fax: (212) 416-4348     www.dj.com

*Publishing and financial news services.*

**AP-Dow Jones,  76 Shoe Lane, London EC4 A3JB, UK**

## DRAFT WORLDWIDE

633 North St. Clair Street, Chicago, IL, 60611-3211

Tel: (312) 944-3500     Fax: (312) 944-3566     www.draftworldwide.com

*Full service international advertising agency, engaged in brand building, direct and promotional marketing.*

**LVB DraftWorldwide (Lovell Vass Boddey),  Worton Park, Cassington, Oxfordshire OX8 1EB, UK**

Tel: 44-1865-88-4444  Fax: 44-1865-88-4488

## DRAKE BEAM MORIN INC.

101 Huntington Ave., Boston, MA, 02199

Tel: (617) 375-9500     Fax: (617) 267-2011     www.dbm.com

*Human resource management consulting and training.*

**DBM UK,  5 Arlington St., St. James's, London SW1A 1RA, UK**

Tel: 44-207-955-8200   Fax: 44-207-955-8201

## DRESSER INSTRUMENT DIVISION

250 East Main Street, Stratford, CT, 06614-5145

Tel: (203) 378-8281     Fax: (203) 385-0357     www.dresserinstruments.com

*Mfr. pressure gauges and temperature instruments.*

**Dresser Europe SA,  187 Knightsbridge, London SW7 1RJ, UK**

**Dresser Industries UK,** East Gillibrands Skelmersdale, Lancashire WN8 9TU, UK

Tel: 44-1695-52600   Fax: 44-1695-52693

## DREVER COMPANY

PO Box 98, 380 Red Lion Road, Huntingdon, PA, 19006-0098

Tel: (215) 947-3400      Fax: (215) 947-7934      www.drever.com

*Mfr. industrial furnaces and heat processing equipment.*

**Drever U.K.,** Astor House 282 Lichfield Road, Sutton Coldfield, West Midlands B74 2UG, UK

Tel: 44-121-323-4994   Fax: 44-121-308-6336

## DRIVER-HARRIS COMPANY

308 Middlesex Street, Harrison, NJ, 07029

Tel: (973) 483-4802      Fax: (973) 483-4806

*Mfr. non-ferrous alloys.*

**Kestrel Cables Distribution Ltd.,** United A2, Baird Court, Park Farm North Industrial Estate, Wellingborough, Northants NN8 6QJ

Tel: 44-1933-402828   Fax: 44-1933-401832

**Kingston Cable Dist. Ltd.,** Unit 4C/4D, Amsterdam Rd., Sutton Fields, Kingston-upon-Hull UK

Tel: 44-1482-830367   Fax: 44-1482-830369

## DRS TECHNOLOGIES, INC.

5 Sylvan Way, Parsippany, NJ, 07054

Tel: (973) 898-1500      Fax: (973) 898-4730      www.drs.com

*Mfr. advanced products for military, aerospace and commercial applications.*

**DRS Hadland Ltd.,** Harrow Yard Akeman Street, Tring, Hertfordshire HP23 6AA, UK

Tel: 44-0-144-282-1500   Fax: 44-0-144-282-1599

**DRS Rugged Systems (Europe) Ltd.,** Cornbrash Park Bumpers Farm, Chippenham, Wiltshire SN14 6RA, UK

**DRS Rugged Systems (Europe) Ltd.,** Lynwood House The Trading Estate, Farnham, Surrey GU9 9NN, UK

Tel: 44-125-273-4488   Fax: 44-125-273-4466

## DST INNOVIS, INC.

11020 Sun Center Drive, Ranch Cordova, CA, 95670

Tel: (916) 636-4501      Fax: (916) 636-5750      www.dstinnovis.com

*Management/services software and hardware for cable TV, satellite and telecommunications industrial.*

**DST Innovis Limited,** Innovis House, 108 High Street - Crawley, West Sussex RH 10 1BB, UK

## E.I. DU PONT DE NEMOURS & COMPANY

1007 Market Street, Wilmington, DE, 19898

Tel: (302) 774-1000      Fax: (302) 774-7321      www.dupont.com

*Mfr./sale diversified chemicals, plastics, specialty products and fibers.*

**Du Pont (UK) Ltd.,** Du Pont House, 18 Bream's Bldgs., Fetter Lane, London EC4A 1HT UK

## DUFF & PHELPS CREDIT RATING CO.

55 East Monroe Street, Chicago, IL, 60603

Tel: (312) 368-3100      Fax: (312) 442-4121      www.dcrco.com

*Engaged in rating stocks and bonds, municipal securities and insurance company claims paying capabilities.*

**Duff & Phelps Credit Rating Co.,** Po Box 16777, St. Helens 1 Undershaft, London EC3 A8EE, UK

Tel: 44-207-417-7920   Fax: 44-207-417-7921

## DUKE ENERGY CORPORATION

422 South Church Street, Charlotte, NC, 28242

Tel: (704) 594-6200     Fax: (704) 382-3814     www.duke-energy.com

*Energy pipeliner, oil/gas exploration and production.*

**Duke Energy Internatinoal, 5 Park Place, London SW1A 1LP, UK**

Tel: 44-207-898-9006  Fax: 44-207-898-9261

**Texas Eastern North Sea Inc., Berkeley Square House, Berkeley Sq., London W1X 5LE, UK**

## THE DUN & BRADSTREET CORPORATION

1 Diamond Hill Road, Murray Hill, NJ, 07974

Tel: (908) 665-5000     Fax: (908) 665-5524     www.dnbcorp.com

*Provides corporate credit, marketing and accounts-receivable management services and publishes credit ratings and financial information.*

**D&B UK Ltd., Holmers Farm Way, High Wycombe, Bucks. HP12 4UL UK**

Tel: 44-1494-422000

**Dun & Bradstreet, Office 801 Holmers Farm Way, High Wycombe, Bucks HP12 4UL UK**

Tel: 44-1494-422000

## DUNHAM-BUSH INC.

175 South Street, West Hartford, CT, 06110

Tel: (860) 548-3780     Fax: (860) 548-1703     www.dunham-bush.com

*Provides innovative solutions for the heating, air conditioning and refrigeration segments.*

**Dunham-Bush Ltd., Fitzherbert Rd., Farlington, Portsmouth UK**

**Dunham-Bush UK, Havant, Hampshire, UK**

## DURACELL INTERNATIONAL INC.

8 Research Drive, Bethel, CT, 06801

Tel: (203) 796-4000     Fax: (203) 796-4745     www.duracell.com

*Mfr. batteries.*

**Duracell Batteries Ltd., Mallory House, Hazelwick Ave., Three Bridges Crawley, West Sussex RH10 1FQ UK**

## DYNEGY INC.

1000 Louisiana, Ste. 5800, Houston, TX, 77002

Tel: (713) 507-6400     Fax: (713) 507-3871     www.dynegy.com

*Holding company that transports and markets energy to local utilities and industrial businesses.*

**Dynegy U.K. Ltd., 1st Floor 4 Grosvenor Place, London SW1Z 7HJ, UK**

Tel: 44-207-591-6666  Fax: 44-207-591-6667  Contact: Gary Cardone, VP

## e TOYS INC.

12200 West Olympic Blvd., Los Angeles, CA, 90004

Tel: (310) 998-6000     Fax: (310) 998-6100     www.etoys.com

*On-line retailer of educational software.*

**eToys Europe, 10 St. Albans Street, London SW1Y 4SQ, UK**

**eToys Europe, Stirling Court - Unit A, South Marston SN3 4WD, UK**

## EAGLE GLOBAL LOGISTICS (EGL)

15350 Vickery Drive, Houston, TX, 77032

Tel: (281) 618-3100     Fax: (281) 618-3100     www.eaglegl.com

*Ocean/air freight forwarding, customs brokerage, packing and wholesale, logistics management and insurance.*

**Circle International Ltd., Cargo Administration Bldg. Rooms 1-4A, Cargo Terminal, Stansted Airport South, Stansted Essex CM24 8QW UK**

Tel: 44-1279-680-366  Fax: 44-1279-680-216

Circle International Ltd., 2 Rubastic Rd., Southall, Middlesex UB 2 5UP, UK

Tel: 44-181-843-9952   Fax: 44-181-571-6031

Circle International Ltd., Parker Ave. Building 1, Felixstow, Suffolk 1P118HF, UK

Tel: 44-1394-676-488   Fax: 44-1349-675-139

Circle International Ltd., Heywood Cargo Centre, Phoenix Close, Heywood Lancs OL10 1HJ UK

Tel: 44-1706-624-245   Fax: 44-1706-367-673

Circle International Ltd., 81 Witham, Hull HU9 1AT, UK

Tel: 44-1482-226-464   Fax: 44-1482-225-054

Circle International Ltd., Elmdon Trading Estate Unit 17, Bickenhill Lane, Birmingham B37 7HE, UK

Tel: 44-121-782-5561   Fax: 44-121-782-2623

Circle International Ltd., Batley Enterprise Centre Unit 18 & 19, 513 Bradford Rd., Batley West Yorkshire WF17 3JX, UK

Tel: 44-1924-470-730   Fax: 44-1924-470-787

Circle International Ltd., Concourse House, Lime St., Liverpool LI1 1NY, UK

Tel: 44-151-708-6666   Fax: 44-151-708-7836

Circle International Ltd., Bell Centre Unit 11, Newton Rd., Crawley Sussex RH10 2FZ, UK

Tel: 44-1293-544-851   Fax: 44-1293-562-716

Circle International Ltd., 40A Victoria Way, Charlton, London SE 7 7PS UK

Tel: 44-181-293-4000   Fax: 44-181-858-6143

Circle International Ltd., Bldg 301Unit 5 World Freight Terminal, Manchester Airport, Manchester M90 5FY UK

Tel: 44-161-436-4030   Fax: 44-161-437-8727

Circle International Ltd., Airport Freight Way, Freight Village, Newcastle Airport, Newcastle Upon Tyne NE13 8BU UK

Tel: 44-191-271-2337   Fax: 44-191-271-4093

Circle International Ltd., 2 Rubastic Rd., Southall, Middlesex UB2 5UP, UK

Tel: 44-181-843-9952   Fax: 44-181-574-4196

Circle International Ltd., 41 Barton Rd., Water Eaton Industrial Estate, Bletchely, Milton Keynes MK1 3EG UK

Tel: 44-1908-371-541   Fax: 44-1908-648-169

Circle International Ltd., 8 Willow Rd., Castle Donington, Derbyshire DE74 2NP, UK

Tel: 44-1332-850-111   Fax: 44-1332-811-164

United Intermodal Line, Luckyn Lane, Basildon, Essex SS14 3AX, UK

## EASTMAN & BEAUDINE INC.

One Ravinia Drive, Ste. 1110, Atlanta, GA, 30346-2103

Tel: (770) 039-0080       Fax: (770) 390-0875       www.beaudine.com

*Investments.*

Eastman & Beaudine Inc. (UK), DeWalden Court, 85 New Cavendish St., London W1M 7RA, UK

## EASTMAN CHEMICAL

100 North Eastman Road, Kingsport, TN, 37660

Tel: (423) 229-2000       Fax: (423) 229-1351       www.eastman.com

*Mfr. plastics, chemicals, fibers.*

Eastman Chemical Ectona Ltd., Siddick, Workington, Cumbria CA14 1LG UK

Tel: 44-190-060-9236  Fax: 44-190-060-9279

Eastman Chemical Ectona Ltd., Hunter House Industrial Estate, Brenda Rd., Hartlepool, Cleveland TS25 2BE UK

Tel: 44-1429-270084   Fax: 44-1429-222900

**Eastman Chemical European Technical Centre,** Acornfield Rd., Knowsley Industrial Park North, Kirkby, Merseyside, L33 7UT UK

Tel: 44-151-548-5100   Fax: 44-151-547-2002   Contact: Paul McBride, Mgr.

**Eastman Chemical Ltd.,** Brindley House, Corner Hall, Lawn Lane, Memel Hempstead, Herts., HP3 9YT UK

Tel: 44-144-224-1177   Fax: 44-144-224-1171   Contact: Frank Rescigno

**Eastman Chemical Ltd.,** Peboc Div., Industrial Estate, Llangefni, Anglesey, Gwynedd, LL77 7YQ UK

Tel: 44-1248-723-890   Fax: 44-1248-750-724

## EASTMAN KODAK COMPANY

343 State Street, Rochester, NY, 14650

Tel: (716) 724-4000      Fax: (716) 724-1089      www.kodak.com

*Develop/mfr. photo and chemicals products, information management/video/copier systems, fibers/plastics for various industry.*

**Eastman Chemical (UK) Ltd.,** Brindley House, Corner Hall & Lawn Lane, Hemel Hempstead Herts. HP1 3HQ UK

**Eastman Kodak Co.,** 245 Hammersmith Rd., London, W6 8PL UK

**Ectona Fibres Ltd.,** Siddick, Workington, Cumbria, CA14 1LG UK

**Kodak Ltd.,** Kodak House, Box 66 Station Rd., Hemel Hempstead Herts HP1 1JU, UK

**T.J. Kenyon & Co.,** CES Training Centre, Caxton Way, Stevenage Herts. SG1 2DJ UK

## EATON CORPORATION

Eaton Center, 1111 Superior Ave., Cleveland, OH, 44114-2584

Tel: (216) 523-5000      Fax: (216) 479-7068      www.eaton.com

*Advanced technical products for transportation and industrial markets.*

**Eaton Ltd.,** Eaton House, Staines Rd., Hounslow, Middlesex TW4 5DX UK

## ECHLIN INC.

100 Double Beach Road, Branford, CT, 06405

Tel: (203) 481-5751      Fax: (203) 481-6485      www.echlin.com

*Supplies commercial vehicle components and auto fluid handling systems for the used car market.*

**Echlin/Lucas Girling,** London, UK

## ECI TELECOM LTD.

12950 Worldgate Dr., Herndon, VA, 20170

Tel: (703) 456-3400      Fax: (703) 456-3410      www.ecitele.com

*Designs, develops, manufactures, markets and supports end-to-end digital telecommunications solutions.*

**ECI UK,** ISIS House Reading Road, Chineham Basingstoke, Hampshire RG24 8TW, UK

Tel: 44-1256-388000

## ECLIPSE INC.

1665 Elmwood Road, Rockford, IL, 61103

Tel: (815) 877-3031      Fax: (815) 877-3336      www.eclipse-inc.com

*Mfr. industrial process heating equipment and systems.*

**Eclipse Combustion Ltd.,** Wassage Way, Hampton Lovett Ind. Estate, Kidderminster Rd., Droitwich, Worcheshire WR9 0NX UK

## ECOLAB INC.

370 N. Wabasha Street, St. Paul, MN, 55102

Tel: (651) 293-2233      Fax: (651) 293-2379      www.ecolab.com

*Develop/mfr. premium cleaning, sanitizing and maintenance products and services for the hospitality, institutional, and residential markets.*

**Ecolab Ltd.,** London, UK

Tel: 44-1793-511221

## ECOWATER SYSTEMS INC.

PO Box 64420,1890 Woodlane Drive, St. Paul, MN, 55164-0420

Tel: (651) 739-5330    Fax: (651) 739-4547    www.ecowater.com

*Mfr. water treatment and purification products.*

**EcoWater Systems, Ltd., #1 Independent Bus. Pk. Mill Rd., Stokenchurch, Buckinghampshire HP14 3TP, UK**

Tel: 44-1-494-484000   Fax: 44-1-494-484396   Contact: Peter Marsh, Gen. Mgr.

## EDDIE BAUER INC.

PO Box 97000, Redmond, WA, 98073

Tel: (425) 882-6100    Fax: (425) 882-6383    www.eddiebauer.com

*Clothing retailer and mail order catalog company.*

**Eddie Bauer Inc.,  London, UK**

## EDELMAN PUBLIC RELATIONS WORLDWIDE

200 East Randolph Drive, 62nd Fl., Chicago, IL, 60601

Tel: (312) 240-3000    Fax: (312) 240-0596    www.edelman.com

*International independent public relations firm.*

**Edelman PR Worldwide,  Haymarket House, 28/29 Haymarket, London SW1Y 4SP, UK**

Tel: 44-207-344-1200   Fax: 44-207-344-1222   Contact: Tari Hibbitt, Mng. Dir.

## EDISON INTERNATIONAL

2244 Walnut Grove Avenue, PO Box 999, Rosemead, CA, 91770

Tel: (626) 302-2222    Fax: (626) 302-2517    www.edison.com

*Utility holding company.*

**Edison Mission Energy,  London, UK**

## J.D. EDWARDS & COMPANY

One Technology Way, Denver, CO, 80237

Tel: (303) 334-4000    Fax: (303) 334-4970    www.jdedwards.com

*Computer software products.*

**J. D. Edwards - London,  Colorado House, 300 Thames Valley Park Drive, Reading Berkshire RG6 1RD, UK**

Tel: 44-118-9091-700   Fax: 44-118-909-1699

## EFCO

1800 NE Broadway Ave., Des Moines, IA, 50316-0386

Tel: (515) 266-1141    Fax: (515) 266-7970    www.efco-usa.com

*Mfr. systems for concrete construction.*

**EFCO UK Ltd.,  22-28 Meadow Close, Ise Valley Ind. Estate, Wellingborough Northants NN8 4BH, UK**

## EG&G INC.

900 Clopper Road, Ste. 200, Gaithersburg, MD, 20878

Tel: (301) 840-3000    Fax: (301) 590-0502    www.egginc.com

*Diversified R/D, mfr. and services.*

**EG&G Astrophysics Research Ltd.,  Coronation Rd., Cressex Business Park, High Wycombe, Buckinghamshire HP12 3TP UK**

**EG&G Fiber Optics,  Sorbus House, Mulberry Business Park, Wokingham, Berkshire RG41 2GY UK**

**EG&G Ltd., Milton Keynes,  20 Vincent Ave., Crownhill Business Ctr., Crownhill, Milton Keynes MK8 0AB UK**

**EG&G Reticon,  34/35 Market Pl., Wokingham, Berkshire RG40 1AT UK**

**EG&G Sealol,  Coronation Rd., Cressex Business Park, High Wycombe, Buckinghamshire HP12 3TP UK**

**EL PASO ENERGY CORPORATION**

PO Box 2511, 1001 Louisiana, Houston, TX, 77252-2511

Tel:  (713) 420-2131        Fax:  (713) 420-4266        www.epenergy.com

*Energy and gas.*

**El Paso Energy International/Enfield Energy,  Enfield, North London UK**

**ELANTEC SEMICONDUCTOR, INC.**

675 Trade Zone Blvd., Milpitas, CA, 95035

Tel:  (408) 945-1323        Fax:  (408) 945-9305        www.elantec.com

*Mfr. of analog integrated circuits for electronic products.*

**Elantec Semiconductor, Inc., 3 Edward Ct., Wellington Road, Wokingham, UK
Berkshire RG40 2AN, UK**

Tel: 44-118-977-6020   Fax: 44-118-977-6080

**ELCOM INTERNATIONAL, INC.**

10 Oceana Way, Norwood, MA, 02062

Tel:  (781) 440-3333        Fax:  (781) 762-1540        www.elcominternational.com

*Mfr./sales PC products.*

**Elcom UK,  Avocet House - Aviary Court, Wade Road, Basingstoke, Hampshire RG24 8 PE, UK**

Tel: 44-1256-697-222   Fax: 44-1256-697-100

**Elcom UK,  349 Edinburgh Avenue, Slough Berkshire SL1 4TU, UK**

Tel: 44-1753-442-500

**Elcom UK,  Arrow Road North, Lakeside Redditch B98 8NN, UK**

Tel: 44-1527-66800   Fax: 44-1527-61818

**ELECTRO SCIENTIFIC INDUSTRIES, INC.**

13900 NW Science Park Drive, Portland, OR, 97229

Tel:  (503) 641-4141        Fax:  (503) 643-4873        www.esi.com

*Mfg. production and testing equipment used in manufacture of electronic components in pagers and cellular communication devices.*

**Electro Scientific Industries Ltd. - UK & Scandinavia,  6 Oak Court, Bretts Way, Crawley, West Sussex, RH10 2GB UK**

Tel: 44-1293-594005   Fax: 44-1293-594019   Contact: Peter Stamp

**ELECTRONIC ARTS INC.**

209 Redwood Shores Pkwy., Redwood City, CA, 94065

Tel:  (650) 628-1500        Fax:  (650) 628-1413        www.ea.com

*Distribution and sales of entertainment software.*

**Electronic Arts/Bullfrog Productions,  London, UK**

**ELECTRONIC DATA SYSTEMS CORPORATION (EDS)**

5400 Legacy Dr., Plano, TX, 75024

Tel:  (972) 605-6000        Fax:  (972) 605-2643        www.eds.com

*Provides professional services; management consulting, e.solutions, business process management and information solutions.*

**Electronic Data Systems Ltd.,  4 Roundwood Avenue, Stockley Park, Uxbridge Middlesex, UB11 1BQ UK**

**Telephone:
+44 (0)20 8 848 8989**

## ELECTRONICS FOR IMAGING, INC.

303 Velocity Way, Foster City, CA, 94404

Tel: (650) 357-3500        Fax: (650) 357-3907        www.efi.com

*Design/mfr. computer software and hardware for color desktop publishing.*

**Electronics for Imaging UK, Stonebridge House Padbury Oaks, Old Bath Road, Lomgford, Middlesex UB7 0EW, UK**

Tel: 44-181-476 7676

## ELECTRO-SCIENCE LABORATORIES, INC.

416 East Church Road, King of Prussia, PA, 19406

Tel: (610) 272-8000        Fax: (610) 272-6759        www.electroscience.com

*Mfr. advanced thick film materials for hybrid microcircuits and other electronic packaging and component applications.*

**ESL Agmet Ltd., 8 Commercial Road, Reading Berkshire, RG2 0QZ UK**

Tel: 44-118-987-3139

## EMC CORPORATION

35 Parkwood Drive, Hopkinton, MA, 01748-9103

Tel: (508) 435-1000        Fax: (508) 435-8884        www.emc.com

*Designs/supplies intelligent enterprise storage and retrieval technology for open systems, mainframes and midrange environments.*

**EMC Computer Systems (UK), Regents Park, Kingston Rd., Leatherhead Surrey KT22 7PY, UK**

Tel: 44-1372-360000

**EMC Computer Systems (UK), 7 The Parks, Newton le Willows, Merseyside Haydock WA12 0JQ, UK**

Tel: 44-1942-275514

**EMC Computer Systems (UK), Cobhan Gare, 34 Anyards Rd., Cogham Surrey KT11 2LA, UK**

Tel: 44-1932-868333

**EMC Computer Systems (UK), The Old Vicarage, Market Place, Castle Donington Derbyshire DE74 2JB, UK**

Tel: 44-1332-852809

**EMC Computer Systems (UK), Leigh Court, Abbotts Leigh, Bristol BS8 3RA, UK**

Tel: 44-127-537-5054

## EMCO WHEATON DTM, INC.

2501 Constant Comment Place, Louisville, KY, 40299

Tel: (502) 266-6677        Fax: (502) 266-6689        www.emcowheaton.com

*Design, development and manufacture of environmentally safe vapor and fluid transfer products for petroleum, petrochemical, chemical and industrial applications.*

**Emco Wheaton UK Ltd., Westwood, Margate, Kent CT9 4JR, UK**

## EMCOR GROUP

101 Merritt Seven, 7th Fl., Norwalk, CT, 06851

Tel: (203) 849-7800        Fax: (203) 849-7870        www.emcorgroup.com

*Engaged in specialty construction.*

**Emcor Group, London, UK**

## EMERSON & CUMING SPECIALTY POLYMERS

46 Manning Road, Bellerica, MA, 01821

Tel: (978) 436-9700        Fax: (978) 436-9701        www.emersoncuming.com

*Mfr. high performance encapsulants, adhesives and coatings for the automotive, telecommunications and electronic industries.*

**Emerson & Cuming UK, Windsor Court - Kingsmead Business Park, London Road, High Wycombe Bucks HP11 1JU, UK**

Tel: 44-1494-467-812

**EMERSON ELECTRIC COMPANY**

8000 W. Florissant Ave., PO Box 4100, St. Louis, MO, 63136

Tel: (314) 553-2000     Fax: (314) 553-3527     www.emersonelectric.com

*Electrical and electronic products, industrial components and systems, consumer, government and defense products.*

**Emerson Europe, 40 Portman Square, W1H 9FH London, UK**

Tel: 44-20-7-486-2755

**EMERY WORLDWIDE**

One Lagoon Drive, Ste. 400, Redwood City, CA, 94065

Tel: (650) 596-9600     Fax: (650) 596-7901     www.emeryworld.com

*Freight transport, global logistics and air cargo.*

**Emery Worldwide, Worldwide House, Unit 19 Airlinks Industrial Estate, Spitfire Way, Heston Middlesex T259NR UK**

Tel: 44-181-260-6000   Fax: 44-181-260-6030

**ENCAD, INC.**

6059 Cornerstone Court West, San Diego, CA, 92121

Tel: (858) 452-0882     Fax: (858) 452-5618     www.encad.com

*Mfr. large color printers for specialized graphics.*

**Encad Limited UK, Back Street, Wendover, Buckinghamshire HP22 6EB, UK**

Tel: 44-12-9662-2222

**ENCYCLOPAEDIA BRITANNICA INC.**

310 S. Michigan Ave., Chicago, IL, 60604

Tel: (312) 427-9700     Fax: (312) 294-2176     www.eb.com

*Publishing; books.*

**Encyclopaedia Britannica Intl. Ltd., Carew House, Station Approach, Wallington, Surrey SM6 0DA UK**

**ENERGIZER HOLDINGS, INC.**

800 Chouteau Avenue, St. Louis, MO, 63164

Tel: (314) 982-2970     Fax: (214) 982-2752     www.energizer.com

*Mfr. Eveready and Energizer brand batteries and lighting products.*

**Energizer UK, 93 Burleigh Gardens, Southgate London N14 5AQ, U.K.**

Tel: 44-181-82-8918   Fax: 44-181-882-8661

**ENERPAC**

P.O. Box 3241, Milwaukee, WI, 53201-3241

Tel: (414) 781-6600     Fax: (414) 781-1049     www.enerpac.com

*Mfr. hydraulic cylinders, pumps, valves, presses, tools, accessories and system components.*

**ENERPAC Ltd., Unit 3 Colemeadow Road, North Moons Moat, Redditch Worcester B98 9BP, UK**

**ENGELHARD CORPORATION**

101 Wood Ave. S., CN 770, Iselin, NJ, 08830

Tel: (732) 205-5000     Fax: (732) 632-9253     www.engelhard.com

*Mfr. pigments, additives, catalysts, chemicals, engineered materials.*

**Engelhard Clal UK, 28 Hatton Garden, London EC1 N8DB, UK**

Tel: 44-207-40-43100

**Engelhard-Clal UK, Davis Road, Chessington Surrey KT9 1TD, UK**

Tel: 44-181-974-3000

**Engelhard-Clal UK, West Midlands Freeport - Unit 22, Birmingham B26 3QD, UK**

Tel: 44-12-1782-4381

**Engelhard-Clal UK, Valley Road, Cinderford GL 14 2PB, UK**

Tel: 44-1594-822181

## ENRON CORPORATION

1400 Smith Street, Houston, TX, 77002-7369

Tel: (713) 853-6161     Fax: (713) 853-3129     www.enron.com

*Exploration, production, transportation and distribution of integrated natural gas and electricity.*

**Enron Direct, King Charles House, Park End Street, Oxford OX 1 1JD, UK**

Tel: 44-1865-202-545

**Enron Engineering Services, Crofton House, Crofton Road - Portrack Lane, Stockton on Tees, Cleveland TS18 2QZ, UK**

**Enron Europe, 25 Victoria St., London SW1H OEX, UK**

Tel: 44-207-316-5300    Contact: Mark Frevert, CEO

**Enron Europe, Four Millbank, Westminster, London SW1P 3ET, UK**

**Enron Europe Ltd., 40 Grosvenor Place, London SW1X 7EN, UK**

Tel: 44-20-7783-0000

**Enron Power Operations Ltd., Enron House - Merchants Wharf, Westpoint Road, Stockton on Tees, UK**

**Enron Teeside Ltd., PO Box 54, Wilton Middlesborough, Cleveland TS90 8JA, UK**

**Sutton Bridge Power Station, Sutton Bridge - Spaulding, Lincolnshire PE12 9TF, UK**

**Teesside Gas Processing Plant, Seal Sands Road, Middlesborough Cleveland, TS2 1UB, UK**

## EPICOR SOFTWARE CORPORATION

195 Technology Drive, Irvine, CA, 92618

Tel: (949) 585-4000     Fax: (949) 450-4419     www.epicor.com

*Mfr. software for e-business.*

**Epicor Birmingham UK, 2630 Kings Court, The Crescent Birmingham Business Park, Birmingham B37 7YE, UK**

Tel: 44-121-779-1122

**Epicor Birmingham UK, Cale Cross House - 5/F, 156 Pilgrim Street, Newcastle-Upon-Tyne NE1 6SU, UK**

Tel: 44-191-230-2020

**Epicor Birmingham UK, 1 The Arena, Downshire Way, Bracknell Berks RG12 1PU, UK**

Tel: 44-1344-468468

**Epicor Manchester UK, Trafalgar House - 110 Manchester Road, Altrincham, Cheshire WA14 1NU, UK**

Tel: 44-161-941-2727

## E-PRESENCE, INC.

120 Flanders Road, Westboro, MA, 01581

Tel: (508) 898-1000     Fax: (508) 898-1755     www.epresence.com

*Provides electronic business services.*

**e-Presence UK Ltd., No. 1 Poultry - 2/F, London EC2R 8JR, UK**

## EQUIFAX INC.

PO Box 4081, Atlanta, GA, 30302

Tel: (404) 885-8000     Fax: (404) 888-5452     www.equifax.com

*Provides information and knowledge-based solutions on consumers and businesses around the world.*

**Equifax Europe (UK) Ltd., Capital House, 25 Chapel St., London NW1 5DS UK**

**The Infocheck Group, Godmersham, Canterbury, UK**

**Transax PLC, Tricorn House, 51-53 Hagley Rd., Edgbaston, Birmingham B16 9DH, UK**

**UAPT-Infolink PLC, Capital House, 25 Chapel St., London NW1 5DS, UK**

## ERICO PRODUCTS INC.
34600 Solon Road, Cleveland, OH, 44139
Tel: (440) 248-0100      Fax: (440) 248-0723      www.erico.com
*Mfr. electric welding apparatus and hardware, metal stampings, specialty fasteners.*
**Erico Europa (UK) Ltd., 52 Milford Road, Reading, Berkshire RG1 8LJ, UK**
Tel: 44-118-958-8386

## ERIEZ MAGNETICS
PO Box 10652, Erie, PA, 16514
Tel: (814) 835-6000      Fax: (814) 838-4960      www.eriez.com
*Mfr. magnets, vibratory feeders, metal detectors, screeners/sizers, mining equipment, current separators.*
**Eriez Magnetics Europe Ltd., London, UK**
Tel: 44-29-208-68501    Contact: Andy Lewis, Dir.

## ERNST & YOUNG, LLP
787 Seventh Ave., New York, NY, 10019
Tel: (212) 773-3000      Fax: (212) 773-6350      www.eyi.com
*Accounting and audit, tax and management consulting services.*
**Ernst & Young, Cambridge House, 26 Tombland, Norwich NR3 1RH, UK**
**Ernst & Young, Wessex House, 19 Threefield Lane, Southampton SO14 3QB, UK**
**Ernst & Young, Talbot Chambers, 2-6 North Church St., Sheffield S1 2DH, UK**
**Ernst & Young, Silkhouse Court, Tithebarn St., Liverpool L2 2LE, UK**
**Ernst & Young, New Priestgate House, 57 Priestgate, Peterborough PE1 1JX,UK**
**Ernst & Young, City Gate, Toll House Hill, Nottingham NG1 5FY UK,**
**Ernst & Young, Apex Plaza, Reading RG1 1YE, UK**
**Ernst & Young, Old Town Court, 10-14 High St., Swindon SN1 3EP, UK**
**Ernst & Young, Rolls House, 7 Rolls Bldg. S, Fetter Lane, London EC4A 1NH UK**
Tel: 44-207-931-2587   Fax: 44-207-931-2504   Contact: Bill McHardy
**Ernst & Young, Commercial Union House, Albert Square, Manchester M2 6LP, UK**
**Ernst & Young, Norham House, 12 New Bridge St. West, Newcastle upon Tyne NE1 8AD, UK**
**Ernst & Young, 400 Capability Green, Luton LU1 3LU, UK**
**Ernst & Young, Queens Hose, Queen St., Ipswich 1P1 1SW, UK**
**Ernst & Young, PO Box 3, Lowgate House, Lowgate Hull HU1 1JJ, UK**
**Ernst & Young, PO Box 61, Cloth Hall Court, 1114 King St., Leeds LS1 2JN UK**
**Ernst & Young, Broadwalk House, Southernhay West, Exeter EX1 1LF, UK**
**Ernst & Young, Compass House, 80 Newmarket Rd., Cambridge CB5 8DZ, UK**
**Ernst & Young, One Colmore Row, Birmingham B3 2DB, UK**
**Ernst & Young, One Bridewell St., Bristol BS1 2AA, UK**
**Ernst & Young, Provincial House, 37 New Walk, Leicester LE1 6TU, UK**
**Ernst & Young, Becket House, 1 Lambeth Palace Rd., London SE1 7EU, UK**

## ESCO CORPORATION
2141 NW 25th Ave., Portland, OR, 97210
Tel: (503) 228-2141      Fax: (503) 778-6330      www.escocorp.com
*Mfr. equipment for mining, construction and forestry industries.*
**ESCO Corp., Guisborough, UK**

## ESCO ELECTRONICS CORPORATION
8888 Ladue Road, Ste. 200, St. Louis, MO, 63124-2090
Tel: (314) 213-7200      Fax: (314) 213-7250      www.escostl.com
*Electronic subassemblies and components.*
**Alvin Vehicles Ltd., England, UK**

## ESTERLINE TECHNOLOGIES

10800 NE 8th Street, Ste. 600, Bellevue, WA, 98004

Tel: (425) 453-9400      Fax: (425) 453-2916      www.esterline.com

*Mfr. equipment and instruments for industrial automation, precision measure, data acquisition.*

**Excellon UK, Dominion Way, Rustington, Littlehampton, West Sussex BN16 3HQ, UK**

Tel: 44-1903-858-000

## E-SYNC NETWORKS, INC.

35 Nutmeg Dr., Trumbull, CT, 06611

Tel: (203) 601-3000      Fax: (203) 601-3151      www.wiltek.com

*Provides managed business-to-business e-commerce applications and solutions for businesses and electronic messaging and integration software services.*

**Wiltek (UK) Ltd., 2 Apple Walk Kembrey Park, Swindon, Wiltshire SN2 6BL, UK**

Tel: 44-1-793-41-4141    Fax: 44-1-793-41-4142

## ETHYL CORPORATION

330 South 4th Street, PO Box 2189, Richmond, VA, 23219

Tel: (804) 788-5000      Fax: (804) 788-5688      www.ethyl.com

*Provide additive chemistry solutions to enhance the performance of petroleum products.*

**Ethyl Petroleum Additives Ltd., London Rd., Bracknell, Berkshire RG12 2UW UK**

## EURO RSCG WORLDWIDE

350 Hudson Street, New York, NY, 10014

Tel: (212) 886-2000      Fax: (212) 886-2016      www.eurorscg.com

*International advertising agency group.*

**Biss Lancaster, 69 Monmouth Street, London, UK**

## EXCEL COMMUNICATIONS, INC.

8750 N. Central Expwy., Ste. 2000, Dallas, TX, 75231

Tel: (214) 863-8000      Fax: (214) 863-8843      www.excel.com

*Long-distance telecommunications carrier.*

**ETI, Div. Excel Communications, Inc., Lincoln House, 137-143 Hammersmith Road, London W14 0QL, UK**

Tel: 44-20-7471-3440    Fax: 44-20-7471-3444

## EXCELLON AUTOMATION

24751 Crenshaw Boulevard, Torrance, CA, 90505

Tel: (310) 534-6300      Fax: (310) 534-6777      www.excellon.com

*PCB drilling and routing machines; optical inspection equipment.*

**Excellon Intl., Dominion Way, Rustington, Littlehampton, W. Sussex BN16 3HQ UK**

**Excellon UK, Dominion Way, Rustington, West Sussex BN163 HQ, UK**

Tel: 44-1-903-858000

## EXCELON INC.

25 Mall Road, Burlington, MA, 01803

Tel: (781) 674-5000      Fax: (781) 674-5010      www.exceloncorp.com

*Developer of object-oriented database management systems software.*

**eXcelon (UK) Limited, 1015 Arlington Business Park, Theale Reading Berkshire RG7 4SA, UK**

Tel: 44-118-930-1200

**eXcelon UK Ltd., 68 Lombard Street, London EC3V 9LJ, UK**

Tel: 44-207-868-1710    Fax: 44-207-868-1810

## EXE TECHNOLOGIES, INC.

8787 N. Stemmonds Fwy., Dallas, TX, 75247-3702

Tel: (214) 775-6000        Fax: (214) 775-0911        www.exe.com

*Provides a complete line of supply chain management execution software for WMS.*

**EXE Technologies, Inc. European Office, Ocean House, The Ring, Bracknell Berkshire RG 12 1AH, UK**

Tel: 44-1344-420144   Fax: 44-1344-41800

## EXIDE CORPORATION

645 Penn St., Reading, PA, 19601

Tel: (610) 378-0500        Fax: (610) 378-0824        www.exideworld.com

*Mfr. lead-acid automotive and industrial batteries.*

**Exide UK, Bolton, UK**

## EXPEDITORS INTERNATIONAL OF WASHINGTON INC.

1015 Third Avenue, 12th Fl., Seattle, WA, 98104-1182

Tel: (206) 674-3400        Fax: (206) 682-9777        www.expd.com

*Air/ocean freight forwarding, customs brokerage, international logistics solutions.*

**Expeditors International (UK) Ltd., Unit 5 The Heston Centre International Avenue, Southall Lane Heston Middlesex, TW5 9NJ UK**

## EXXON MOBIL CORPORATION

5959 Las Colinas Blvd., Irving, TX, 75039-2298

Tel: (972) 444-1000        Fax: (972) 444-1882        www.exxon.com

*Petroleum exploration, production, refining; mfr. petroleum and chemicals products; coal and minerals.*

**Exxon Mobil, Inc., 4600 Parkway, Whiteley Fareham, Hampshire PO15 7AP, UK**

Tel: 44-1489-884400

**Exxon Mobil, Inc., Esso House, Victoria St., London SW1E 5JW, UK**

**Exxon Mobil, Inc., Cadland Rd., Hardley, Hythe, Southampton, SO45 3NP UK**

**Exxon Mobil, Inc., Arundel Towers, Portland Terrace, Fawley, Southampton SO9 2GW UK**

## E-Z-EM INC.

717 Main Street, Westbury, NY, 11590

Tel: (516) 333-8230        Fax: (516) 333-8278        www.ezem.com

*World's leading supplier of barium contrast media for medical imaging and accessories.*

**E-Z-EM Ltd., 1230 High Rd., London N20 0LH, UK**

Tel: 44-181-446-9714   Fax: 44-181-446-9810   Contact: Ginette Camps-Walsh, Gen. Mgr.   Emp: 14

## FABREEKA INTERNATIONAL INC.

1023 Turnpike, PO Box 210, Stoughton, MA, 02072

Tel: (781) 341-3655        Fax: (781) 341-3983        www.fabreeka.com

*Mfr. vibration isolation materials; consulting and engineering services.*

**Fabreeka Intl. Inc., 8-12 Jubilee Way, Thackley Old Rd., Shipley, W. Yorkshire BD18 1QS UK**

Tel: 44-1274-531333   Fax: 44-1274-531717

## FACTSET RESEARCH SYSTEMS INC.

1 Greenwich Plaza, Greenwich, CT, 06830

Tel: (203) 863-1599        Fax: (203) 863-1501        www.factset.com

*Provides on-line financial information to financial professionals.*

**FactSet Limited, One Angel Court, London EC2R 7HJ, UK**

Tel: 44-207-606-0001

**FAEGRE & BENSON LLP**

2200 Norwest Center, 90 South Seventh Street, Minneapolis, MN, 55402-3901

Tel: (612) 336-3000   Fax: (612) 336-3026   www.faegre.com

*International law firm.*

**Faegre Benson Hobson Audley, 7 Pilgrim St., London EC4V 6LB, UK**

Tel: 44-207-450 4510   Fax: 44-20-7450-4544   Contact: Scott James, Ptnr.

**FAIR, ISAAC AND COMPANY, INC.**

200 Smith Ranch Road, San Rafael, CA, 94903

Tel: (415) 472-2211   Fax: (415) 492-5691   www.fairisaac.com

*Mfr. automated systems for credit and loan approvals.*

**Fair, Isaac and Co., Concorde House 2/F, Trinity Park, Birmingham B37 7ES, UK**

Tel: 44-121-781-4500

**FAIRCHILD PUBLICATIONS INC.**

7 West 34th Street, New York, NY, 10001

Tel: (212) 630-4000   Fax: (212) 630-3563   www.fairchildpub.com

*Magazine publishers: Women's Wear Daily, Supermarket News, Brand Marketing, Executive Technology, Footwear News, Salon News.*

**Fairchild Publications Inc., 20 Shorts Garden, London WC2H 9AU, UK**

Tel: 44-207-240-0420   Fax: 44-207-240-0290

**THE FALK CORPORATION**

3001 West Canal Street, PO Box 492,, Milwaukee, WI, 53208-4200

Tel: (414) 342-3131   Fax: (414) 937-4359   www.falkcorp.com

*Designers and manufacturers of power transmission equipment including gears, geared reducers and drives, couplings.*

**Falk Corp UK, 8 Brunel Gate, 8 Brunel Industrial Estate, Harworth Doncaster DN11 8QB, UK**

**FARR COMPANY**

2201 Park Place, El Segundo, CA, 90245

Tel: (310) 727-6300   Fax: (310) 643-9086   www.farrco.com

*Mfr. air and liquid filtration equipment.*

**Farr Europe - Farr Filtration Ltd., 272 Kings Rd., Tyseley, Birmingham B11 2AB, UK**

**FARREL CORPORATION**

25 Main Street, Ansonia, CT, 06401

Tel: (203) 736-5500   Fax: (203) 735-6267   www.farrel.com

*Mfr. polymer processing equipment.*

**Farrel Ltd., Queensway, Castleton, PO Box 27, Rochdale, Lancs. OL11 2PF UK**

**FAXON COMPANY, INC.**

15 Southwest Park, Westwood, MA, 02090

Tel: (781) 329-3350   Fax: (781) 329-9875   www.faxon.com

*Distributor books and periodicals.*

**RoweCom UK, Cannon House Folkestone, Kent CT19 5EE, UK**

**FEDDERS CORPORATION**

505 Martinsville Road, Liberty Corner, NJ, 07938-0813

Tel: (908) 604-8686   Fax: (908) 604-0715   www.fedders.com

*Mfr. room air conditioners, humidifiers and dehumidifiers.*

**Envirco Europe, Sub. Fedders, Reith Way West Portway Industrial Estate, Andover Hampshire SP 10 3 TY, UK**

Tel: 44-1264-364622   Contact: Peter Benn

## FEDERAL-MOGUL CORPORATION

26555 Northwestern Highway, PO Box 1966, Southfield, MI, 48034

Tel: (248) 354-7700        Fax: (248) 354-8983        www.federal-mogul.com

*Mfr./distributor precision parts for automobiles, trucks, farm and construction vehicles.*

**Federal-Mogul Holding UK Ltd., London, UK**

**Federal-Mogul Ltd., Neville Road - Bradford, West Yorkshire BD4 8TU, UK**

**Federal-Mogul Westwind Air Bearings Ltd., London, UK**

## FEDEX CORPORATION

942 South Shady Grove Rd., Memphis, TN, 38120

Tel: (901) 369-3600        Fax: (901) 395-2000        www.fdxcorp.com

*Package express delivery service.*

**Federal Express (UK) Ltd., 48-49 Westbrook Rd., Trafford Park, Manchester M17 1AY, UK**

Tel: 44-800-123-800

**Federal Express (UK) Ltd., 1A Girling Way, Feltham, Middlesex TW14 0PH, UK**

Tel: 44-800-123-800

## FEI CORPORATION

7451 N.W. Evergreen Pkwy., Hillsboro, OR, 97124-5830

Tel: (503) 640-7500        Fax: (503) 640-7509        www.feicompany.com

*Design and mfr. of charged particle beam systems serving the research, development and production needs of customers in semiconductor, data storage, and industry/institute markets.*

**Micrion Corporation (UK), The Aztec Centre, Aztec West Business Park, Almondsbury Bristol BS32 4TD, UK**

Tel: 44-468-172049   Fax: 44-1454-201885

## FERREX INTERNATIONAL INC.

26 Broadway, 26th Fl., New York, NY, 10004

Tel: (212) 509-7030        Fax: (212) 344-4728        www.ferrex.com

*Mfr./distributor of road maintenance machinery, welding and industrial equipment and supplies.*

**Ferrex Europe, 51 Downsview Drive, Wivelsfield Green - NR. Haywards Heath, Sussex RH 17 7 RN, UK**

Tel: 44-1-4444-71280   Fax: 44-1-4444-71073

## FERRO CORPORATION

1000 Lakeside Ave., Cleveland, OH, 44114-7000

Tel: (216) 641-8580        Fax: (216) 696-5784        www.ferro.com

*Mfr. Specialty chemicals, coatings, plastics, colors, refractories.*

**Ferro Ltd. Ceramic Division, Nile St., Burslem, Stoke-on-Tent, ST6 2BQ, UK**

Tel: 44-1782-824488   Fax: 44-1782-814238   Contact: Robert Latimer, Gen. Mgr.

**Ferro Ltd. Colour & Enamel Divisions, Ounsdale Rd., Wombourne, Wolverhampton WV5 8DA, UK**

Tel: 44-1902-324144   Fax: 44-1902-324265   Contact: Graham Rose, Mgr.

**Ferro Ltd. Plastics & Drynamels Divisions, Westgate, Aldridge, West Midlands, WS9 8YH, UK**

Tel: 44-1922-58300   Fax: 44-1922-52986   Contact: David Ankrett, Gen. Mgr.

## FERROFLUIDICS CORPORATION

40 Simon Street, Nashua, NH, 03061

Tel: (603) 883-9800        Fax: (603) 883-2308        www.ferrofluidics.com

*Mfr. rotary feedthrough designs, emission seals, automated crystal-growing systems, bearings, ferrofluids.*

**AP&T Ltd., Seacourt Tower, Fl 2, Botley, Oxford 0X2 0JJ, UK**

## FIDUCIARY TRUST COMPANY OF NY

2 World Trade Center, 94th Fl., New York, NY, 10048

Tel: (212) 466-4100     Fax: (212) 313-2662     www.ftc.com

*Banking services.*

**Fiduciary Trust (Intl.) SA, London, UK**

## FileNET CORPORATION

3565 Harbor Boulevard, Costa Mesa, CA, 92626

Tel: (714) 966-3400     Fax: (714) 966-3490     www.filenet.com

*Provides integrated document management (IDM) software and services for internet and client server-based imaging, workflow, cold and electronic document management solutions.*

**FileNET Ltd., One The Square, Stockley Park, Uxbridge, Middlesex UB11 1FN UK**

Tel: 44-181-867-6363   Fax: 44-181-867-6365   Contact: Lou Valdini, Mgr.

## FINANCIAL GUARANTY INSURANCE COMPANY

115 Broadway, New York, NY, 10006

Tel: (212) 312-3000     Fax: (212) 312-3093     www.fgic.com

*Engaged in insuring debt securities and investment, operation, and information services to state and local governments*

**Financial Guaranty Insurance Co. (London), 20 St. James's St., London SW1A 1ES, UK**

## FINNIGAN CORPORATION

355 River Oaks Parkway, San Jose, CA, 95134-1991

Tel: (408) 433-4800     Fax: (408) 433-4823     www.finnigan.com

*Mfr. mass spectrometers.*

**Finnigan Hypersil Division, Chadwick Road, Astmoor Runcorn, Cheshire WA7 1PR, UK**

**MassLab, Crewe Road, Manchester M23 9BE, UK**

## THE FINOVA GROUP, INC.

4800 N. Scottsdale Rd., Scottsdale, AZ, 85251-7623

Tel: (480) 636-4800     Fax: (480) 636-5726     www.finova.com

*Provides commercial financing and asset-based loans to businesses.*

**Finova Group UK, 11 Albemarle Street, London W1X 3HE, UK**

Contact: Robert Gordon

## FIRESTONE POLYMERS

381 W. Wilbeth Road, Akron, OH, 44301

Tel: (330) 379-7864     Fax: (330) 379-7875     www.firesyn.com

*Mfr. polymers; rubber, plastics and adhesives*

**Corrie Maccoll & Son, Ltd., New Loom House - 101 Backchurch Lane, London E1 1LU, UK**

Tel: 44-207-481-1516   Fax: 44-207-702-4168   Contact: Andy Hurley

## FIRST DATA CORPORATION

5660 New Northside Dr., Ste. 1400, Atlanta, GA, 30328

Tel: (770) 857-0001     Fax: (770) 857-0404     www.firstdatacorp.com

*Information and transaction processing services.*

**FDC Ltd., FDR House, Christopher Martin Rd., Basildon, Essex, S5149AA, UK**

Tel: 44-1-268-296-967   Contact: Joe Jackson, Mng. Dir.

## FISERV INC.

PO Box 979, 255 Fiserv Drive, Brookfield, WI, 53008-0979

Tel: (414) 879-5000     Fax: (414) 879-5013     www.fiserv.com

*Data processing products and services for the financial industry.*

**Fiserv Europe Ltd., 5 Roundwood Ave., Stockley Pk., Uxbridge, Middlesex, UB11 1AX UK**

## FISHER SCIENTIFIC INC.

1 Liberty Lane, Hampton, NH, 03842

Tel: (603) 929-5911     Fax: (603) 929-0222     www.fisher1.com

*Mfr. science instruments and apparatus, chemicals, reagents.*

**Fisher Scientific UK Ltd., Bishop Meadow Rd., Loughborough, Leicestershire LE11 5RG, UK**

Tel: 44-1509-231166  Fax: 44-1509-231893

**ORME Technologies, a division of Fisher Scientific UK Ltd., Whitbrook Way, Stakehill Industrial Park, Middleton, Manchester M24 2RH, UK**

Tel: 44-161-653-4589  Fax: 44-161-655-3011

## FISHER-ROSEMOUNT

8000 Maryland Ave., Ste. 500, Clayton, MO, 63105-4755

Tel: (314) 746-9900     Fax: (314) 746-9974     www.frco.com

*Mfr. industrial process control equipment.*

**Fisher Rosemount A/S, 6 Whitworth Rd., S.W. Ind. Estate, Peterlee Durham SR8 2LY, UK**

**Fisher-Rosemount, Claredon House, Clarendon Rd., Redhill Surrey RH 1 1FB UK**

Tel: 44-1737-767-600  Fax: 44-1737-769-166

**Fisher-Rosemount Ltd., Medway House, Knight Rd., Strood Rochester, Kent ME2 2EZ UK**

Contact: Dave Renfrey

**Fisher-Rosemount Ltd., Horsfield Way, Bredbury SK 6 2SU, UK**

## FLACK + KURTZ INC.

475 Fifth Ave., New York, NY, 10017

Tel: (212) 532-9600     Fax: (212) 689-7489     www.flackandkurtz.com

*Consulting engineers for building services, i.e.., HVAC, electrical, lighting, plumbing/hydraulics, life safety, fire protection and telecommunications.*

**Flack + Kurtz (UK) Inc., 143 Charing Cross Rd., London WC2H 0EE, UK**

Tel: 44-207-494-2441  Fax: 44-207-494-2401   Contact: David Stillman   Emp: 35

## C.B. FLEET COMPANY, INC.

4615 Murray Place, PO Box 11349, Lynchburg, VA, 24506

Tel: (804) 528-4000     Fax: (804) 847-4219     www.cbfleet.com

*Mfr. pharmaceutical, health and beauty aids.*

**E.C. De Witt & Company Ltd., Tudor Road - Manor Park, Runcorn Cheshire, WA7 ISZ, UK**

Tel: 44-1-928-579-029  Fax: 44-1-928-579-712

## FLEETBOSTON FINANCIAL CORPORATION

1 Federal Street, Boston, MA, 02110

Tel: (617) 346-4000     Fax: (617) 434-7547     www.fleet.com

*Banking and insurance services.*

**FleetBoston - London, Bank Boston House, 39 Victoria St., PO Box 155, London SW 1HOED UK**

Tel: 44-207-799-3333  Fax: 44-207-222-5649

**FleetBoston Capital Ltd., Bank Boston House, 39 Victoria St., PO Box 155, London SW 1HOED UK**

Tel: 44-207-732-9053  Fax: 44-207-932-9117

## FLEXTRONICS INC. INTERNATIONAL

2241 Lundy Ave., San Jose, CA, 95131-1822

Tel: (408) 428-1300     Fax: (408) 428-0420     www.flextronics.com

*Contract manufacturer for electronics industry.*

**Flextronics International, 17- 21 Bristol Road, Greenford, Middlesex UB6 8UP UK**

## FLINT INK CORPORATION

4600 Arrowhead Drive, Ann Arbor, MI, 48105

Tel: (734) 622-6000     Fax: (734) 622-6060     www.flintink.com

*Manufacturer of printing inks and pigments.*

**Flint Ink Europe, Stirling Rd. Industrial Estate, Dykehead Rd., Airdrie ML6 7UD, UK**

Tel: 44-1236-761220   Fax: 44-1236-766126   Contact: Jim Mahony, Pres. Europe

**Flint Ink Europe, PO Box 186, Old Heath Rd., Wolverhampton WV1 2RS, UK**

Tel: 44-1902-871028   Fax: 44-1902-457461   Contact: Jim Mahony, Pres. Europe

**Flint Ink Europe, Vauxhall Industrial Estate, Wrexham, Clwyd LL14 6 UH, Ruabon, UK**

Tel: 44-1978-823456   Fax: 44-1978-823331   Contact: Jim Mahony, Pres. Europe

**Flint Ink Europe, 5/6 Marketside, Albert Rd., St. Phillip's, Bristol BS2 OXJ, UK**

Tel: 44-207-9721181   Fax: 44-117-9710858   Contact: Jim Mahony, Pres. Europe

**Flint Ink Europe, 3-4 Prospect Drive, Britannia Enterprise Park, Litchfield's, Staffordshire WS14 9UX, UK**

Tel: 44-1543-414114   Fax: 4-1543-264489   Contact: Jim Mahony, Pres. Europe

**Flint Ink Europe, Willowyard Industrial Estate, Beith, Ayrshire K15 1LY, UK**

Tel: 44-1505-504681   Fax: 44-1505-504202   Contact: Jim Mahony, Pres. Europe

## FLIR SYSTEMS, INC.

16505 SW 72nd Ave., Portland, OR, 97224-1206

Tel: (503) 684-3731     Fax: (503) 684-5452     www.flir.com

*Designer, mfr., and marketer of imaging systems for aircraft, shipping, defense and environmental protection industries.*

**FLIR Systems International Ltd., 2 Kings Hill Ave., Kings Hill, West Malling, Kent, ME 19 4AQ UK**

Tel: 44-1732-220011   Fax: 44-1732-220014

## FLOWSERVE CORPORATION

222 W. Los Colinas Blvd., Irving, TX, 75039

Tel: (972) 443-6500     Fax: (972) 443-6858     www.flowserve.com

*Mfr. chemicals equipment, pumps, valves, filters, fans and heat exchangers.*

**Durco Process Equipment Ltd., 28 Heathfield, Stacey Bushes, Milton Keynes MK12 6HR, UK**

## FLOWSERVE FLUID SEALING DIVISION

222 Los Colinas Blvd., Ste. 1500, Irving, TX, 75039

Tel: (616) 381-2650     Fax: (616) 443-6800     www.flowserve.com

*Mfr. mechanical seals, compression packings and auxiliaries.*

**Durametallic UK, Unit 13B United Trading Estate, Old Trafford, Manchester M16 0RJ, UK**

## FLUKE CORPORATION

6920 Seaway Blvd. PO Box 9090, Everett, WA, 98203

Tel: (425) 347-6100     Fax: (425) 356-5116     www.fluke.com

*Mfr. handheld, electronic test tools for maintenance of electronic equipment.*

**Fluke (U.K.) Ltd., Colonial Way Watford, Hertfordshire WD2 4TT, UK**

Tel: 44-1923-216-405

## FLUOR CORPORATION

One Enterprise Drive, Aliso Viejo, CA, 92656-2606

Tel: (949) 349-2000     Fax: (949) 349-5271     www.flour.com

*Engineering and construction services.*

**Fluor Daniel International Ltd., 3 Shortlands, London W6 8DD, UK**

Tel: 44-181-222-7000   Fax: 44-181-222-7050

**Fluor Daniel Limited, Fluor Daniel House, Brownley Road, Sharston Manchester M224QF, UK**

Tel: 44-161-998-7777   Fax: 44-161-945-7402

**Fluor Daniel Ltd.,  Fluor Daniel Centre, Watchmoor Park, Riverside Way, Camberley Surrey GU15 3AQ UK**

Tel: 44-1276-62424    Fax: 44-1276-26762

## FM GLOBAL INC.

1301 Atwood Avenue, Johnston, RI, 02919

Tel: (401) 275-3000      Fax: (401) 275-3029      www.fmglobal.com

*Engaged in commercial and industrial property insurance and risk management, specializing in engineering-driven property protection.*

**FM Global,  1 Windsor Dials, Windsor, Berks SL4 1RS, UK**

Tel: 44-175-375-0000   Fax: 44-175-386-8700

**FM Insurance Co. Ltd.,  105 Victoria St., London SW1E 6QT, UK**

## FMC CORPORATION

200 E. Randolph Drive, Chicago, IL, 60601

Tel: (312) 861-6000      Fax: (312) 861-6141      www.fmc.com

*Produces chemicals and precious metals, mfr. machinery, equipment and systems for industrial, agricultural and government use.*

**FMC Corp. (UK) Ltd.,  Unit 3C Harcourt Way, Meridian Business Park, Leicester LE3 2WP, UK**

**FMC Corp. (UK) Ltd.,  Holt Rd., Fakenham, Norfolk NR21 8JH, UK**

**FMC Loading and Transfer Systems, c/o Smith Meter Inc.,  181 Farnham Road, Slough AL1 4XP, Berkshire UK**

**FMC Process Additives Div.,  Tenax Rd., Trafford Park, Manchester M17 1WT UK**

**Wellhead Technology Services Ltd.,  London, UK**

## FMC CORPORATION MATERIAL HANDLING EQUIPMENT

400 Highpoint Drive, Cahlfont, PA, 18914

Tel: (724) 479-4500      Fax: (215) 822-4553      www.fmcesg.com

*Mfr. bulk material handling and automation equipment.*

**FMC Material Handling,  Unit 3C Harcourt Way, Leicester LE3 2WP, UK**

## FMC JETWAY SYSTEMS

1805 W. 2550 South, PO Box 9368, Ogden, UT, 84401-3249

Tel: (801) 627-6600      Fax: (801) 629-3474      www.jetwaysystems.com

*Mfr. aircraft loading bridges and ground support equipment.*

**FMC APSD Europe,  Bldg. 391, Viscount Way, Heathrow Airport, Hounslow Middlesex TW6 2JD, UK**

Tel: 44-181-754-1544   Fax: 44-181-754-1545   Contact: Theo Miller, Regional Sales Mgr.

## FMR (FIDELITY INVESTMENTS)

82 Devonshire Street, Boston, MA, 02109

Tel: (617) 563-7000      Fax: (617) 476-6105      www.fidelity.com

*Diversified financial services company offering investment management, retirement, brokerage, and shareholder services directly to individuals and institutions and through financial intermediaries.*

**Fidelity InvestmentsLtd.,  Oakhill House - 130 Tonbridge Road, Hildenboroug Tonbridge, Kent TN11 9DZ, UK**

## FOOT LOCKER USA

112 West 34th Street, New York, NY, 10020

Tel: (212) 720-3700      Fax: (212) 553-2042      www.venatorgroup.com

*Mfr./sales shoes and sneakers.*

**Foot Locker International,  19 Bull St. Birmingham, B4 7AA, UK**

Tel: 44-121-2330396

**Foot Locker International,  52 Lakeside Centre,Thurrock RM16 1ZF, UK**

Tel: 44-1708-891232

Foot Locker International, 12 Palisades Shopping Centre, Birmingham B2 4XA, UK
Tel: 44-121-6325754

Foot Locker International, The Galleries, Unit G, 37 Broadmead, Bristol BS1 3EU UK
Tel: 44-117-9258132

Foot Locker International, Unit 43, The Pentagon Centre, Chatham, ME4 4HP UK
Tel: 44-1634-819112

Foot Locker International, 26 St. John's Rd., Clapham Junction, Clapham, SW11 1PW UK
Tel: 44-1717-7381286

## FORD MOTOR COMPANY

One American Road, Dearborn, MI, 48121
Tel: (313) 322-3000     Fax: (313) 322-9600     www.ford.com
*Mfr./sales motor vehicles.*
Ford Motor Co. Ltd., Eagle Way, Brentwood, Essex CM13 3BW, UK

## FOREST LABORATORIES INC.

909 Third Ave., 23rd Fl., New York, NY, 10022
Tel: (212) 421-7850     Fax: (212) 750-9152     www.frx.com
*Pharmaceuticals.*
Pharmax Limited, 5 Bourne Rd., Bexley, Kent DA5 1NX, UK
Tel: 44-1-322-550-550

## FORMICA CORPORATION

10155 Reading Road, Cincinnati, OH, 45241-4805
Tel: (513) 786-3400     Fax: (513) 786-3082     www.formica.com
*Mfr. decorative laminate, adhesives and solvents.*
Formica Limited, Coast Road - North Shields, Tyne & Wear NE 29 8RE, UK

## FORT JAMES CORPORATION

1650 Lake Cook Road, Deerfield, IL, 60015
Tel: (847) 317-5000     Fax: (847) 236-3755     www.fortjames.com
*Mfr. and markets consumer tissue products.*
Fort James Corporation, Harrow, UK
Fort James Corporation, London, UK

## FORTÉ SOFTWARE, INC.

1800 Harrison Street, Oakland, CA, 94612
Tel: (510) 869-3400     Fax: (510) 869-3480     www.forte.com
*Developer computer software applications.*
Forté Software Ltd., St. James' House, Oldbury, Bracknell, Berkshire RG12 8SA UK
Tel: 44-1344-482100   Fax: 44-1344-420905

## FORTEL INC.

46832 Lakeview Blvd., Fremont, CA, 94538-6543
Tel: (510) 440-9600     Fax: (510) 440-9696     www.fortel.com
*Mfr. e-business corporate software.*
FORTEL Ltd., Fountain House - Cleeve Road, Leatherhead, Surrey KT22 7LX, UK
Tel: 44-1372-378-899   Fax: 44-1372-378-845

**FORTUNE BRANDS**

200 Tower Parkway, Lincolnshire, IL, 60069

Tel: (847) 484-4400          Fax: (800) 310-5960          www.fortunebrands.com

*Mfr. diversified consumer products including Masterbrand, Acco office products, Jim Bean distillery products, Footjoy and Titleist golf products and Moen bath products.*

**Acco Europe,  The Lodge, Harmonsworth Lane, Harmonsworth, West Drayton Middlesex UB7 2LQ UK**

Tel: 44-181-759-4822

**L.B. FOSTER COMPANY**

415 Holiday Drive, Pittsburgh, PA, 15220

Tel: (412) 928-3400          Fax: (412) 928-7891          www.lbfoster.com

*Mfr./sales of steel pipe, railroad rail, highway products and accessories.*

**L.B. Foster Co., European Div.,  40 Charlwood Rd., Putney, London SW15, UK**

**FOSTER WHEELER CORPORATION**

Perryville Corporate Park, Clinton, NJ, 08809-4000

Tel: (908) 730-4000          Fax: (908) 730-4100          www.fwc.com

*Manufacturing, engineering and construction.*

**Foster Wheeler Energy Limited,  High Force Road - Riverside Park, Middlesbrough Cleveland, TS2 1RH, UK**

Tel: 44-1642-230600   Fax: 44-1642-241097   Contact: Simon Schmuck

**Foster Wheeler Lenergy Limited,  Shinfield Park, Berkshire RG2 9FW, UK**

Tel: 44-118-913-1234   Fax: 44-118-913-2333   Contact: Keith Batchelor

**Foster Wheeler Management Operations Limited,  Shinfield Park, Berkshire RG2 9FW, UK**

Tel: 44-118-913-1234   Fax: 44-118-913-2333   Contact: John Oakey

**Foster Wheeler Petroleum Development Limited,  Shinfield Park, Berkshire RG2 9FW, UK**

Tel: 44-118-913-1234   Fax: 44-118-913-2333   Contact: Don Harris, Mgr.

**FOUR WINDS INTERNATIONAL GROUP**

1500 SW First Ave., Ste. 850, Portland, OR, 97201-2013

Tel: (503) 241-2732          Fax: (503) 241-1829          www.vanlines.com.au

*Transportation of household goods and general cargo and third party logistics.*

**Four Winds UK Ltd.,  Wyvern Estate Unit 3, Beverley Way, New Malden Surrey KY3 4PH, UK**

Tel: 44-181-949-0900   Fax: 44-181-949-1300   Contact: Beverley McMahon, Gen. Mgr.   Emp: 120

**FRANK RUSSELL COMPANY**

909 A Street, Tacoma, WA, 98402

Tel: (253) 572-9500          Fax: (253) 591-3495          www.russell.com

*Investment management and asset strategy consulting.*

**Frank Russell Company Ltd.,  6 Cork St., London W1X 1PB, UK**

Tel: 44-207-287-2858  Fax: 44-207-414-0079   Contact: John Stannard, Mng. Dir. UK   Emp: 100

**Frank Russell Investments (UK) Ltd.,  12 Clifford St., London W1X 2FR, UK**

Tel: 44-207-287-2858  Fax: 44-207-495-5447   Contact: Alison Ramsdale, Director   Emp: 10

**FRANKLIN COVEY COMPANY**

2200 W. Parkway Blvd., Salt Lake City, UT, 84119-2331

Tel: (801) 975-1776          Fax: (801) 977-1431          www.franklincovey.com

*Provides productivity and time management products and seminars.*

**Franklin Covey U.K.,  Grant Thorton House, 46 West Bar Street, Banbury Oxfordshire OX16 9RZ, UK**

Tel: 44-1295-274100   Fax: 44-1295-274101

## THE FRANKLIN MINT

US Route 1, Franklin Center, PA, 19091

Tel: (610) 459-6000    Fax: (610) 459-6880    www.franklinmint.com

*Design/marketing collectibles and luxury items.*

**Franklin Mint Ltd., One South Quay Plaza, London E14 9WS, UK**

## FRANKLIN RESOURCES, INC.

777 Mariners Island Blvd., San Mateo, CA, 94404

Tel: (415) 312-2000    Fax: (415) 312-3655    www.frk.com

*Global and domestic investment advisory and portfolio management.*

**Templeton Investment Management Ltd., London, UK**

Tel: 44-131-469-4000   Fax: 44-131-228-4506

## FRIED, FRANK, HARRIS, SHRIVER & JACOBSON

One New York Plaza, New York, NY, 10004-1980

Tel: (212) 859-8000    Fax: (212) 859-4000    www.ffhsj.com

*International law firm.*

**Fried, Frank, Harris, Shriver & Jacobson, 4 Chiswell St., London EC1Y 4UP, UK**

Tel: 44-270-972-9600   Fax: 44-270-972-9602   Contact: Jerry Swirth, Ptnr.

## FRITO-LAY COMPANY

7701 Legacy Drive, Plano, TX, 75024

Tel: (972) 334-7000    Fax: (972) 334-2019    www.firtolay.com

*Mfr. snack food products.*

**Frito-Lay Holdings Ltd., London, UK**

**Walkers Smiths Snack Foods Ltd, London, UK**

## FRITZ COMPANIES, INC.

706 Mission Street, Ste. 900, San Francisco, CA, 94103

Tel: (415) 904-8360    Fax: (415) 904-8661    www.fritz.com

*Integrated transportation, sourcing, distribution and customs brokerage services.*

**Fritz Companies UK Ltd., Haslemere Heathrow Estate Unit 1, Silver Jubilee Way, Cranford Middlesex TW4 6NF, UK**

## FSI INTERNATIONAL INC.

322 Lake Hazeltine Drive, Chaska, MN, 55318

Tel: (612) 448-5440    Fax: (612) 448-2825    www.fsi-intl.com

*Manufacturing equipment for computer silicon wafers.*

**Metron Technology Ltd., 6-7 Grafton Way, Basingstoke, Hampshire RG22 6HY, UK**

Tel: 44-1273-513653   Fax: 44-1273-517449

## FULBRIGHT & JAWORSKI

1301 McKinney Street, Ste. 5100, Houston, TX, 77010

Tel: (713) 651-5151    Fax: (713) 651-5246    www.fulbright.com

*International law firm.*

**Fulbright & Jaworski, 2 St. Jane's Place, London SW1A 1NP, UK**

Tel: 44-207-629-1207   Fax: 44-207-493-8259

## H.B. FULLER COMPANY

1200 Willow Lake Blvd., Vadnais Heights, MN, 55110

Tel: (651) 236-5900    Fax: (651) 236-5898    www.hbfuller.com

*Mfr./distributor adhesives, sealants, coatings, paints, waxes, sanitation chemicals.*

**H.B. Fuller Coatings, Ltd., 95 Aston Church Road, Nechells, Birmingham B7 5RQ, UK**

Tel: 44-121-322-6900   Fax: 44-121-322-6901

**H.B. Fuller U.K. Limited, Moor Road Chesham, Buckinghamshire HP5 1SB, UK**

**H.B. Fuller U.K. Ltd.,  Amber Business Center, Greenhill Lane, Leabrooks Derbyshire DE55 4BR, UK**
Tel: 44-1773-608877    Fax: 44-1773-528070

**Linear Products, Ltd.,  95 Aston Church Road, Nechells Birmingham, B7 5RQ U.K.**

## FULTON BOILER WORKS INC.

3981 Jefferson Street, PO Box 257, Pulaski, NY, 13142

Tel:  (315) 298-5121         Fax:  (315) 298-6390         www.fulton.com

*Mfr. process heat transfer equipment, including steam and hot water boilers.*

**Fulton Boiler Works (GB) Ltd.,  Broomhill Rd., Brislington Trading Estate, Bristol BS4TU, UK**
Tel: 44-117-9723-322  Fax: 44-117-9723-358   Contact: Ian Davidson, Mng. Dir.   Emp: 50

## THE GAB ROBINS GROUP

Linden Plaza, 9 Campus Drive, Parsippany, NJ, 07054-4476

Tel:  (973) 993-3400         Fax:  (973) 993-9579         www.gabrobins.com

*Insurance adjustment.*

**Robins Davies Intl. (RDI),  107 Fenchurch St., London EC3M 5JB, UK**

## GAF CORPORATION

1361 Alps Road, Wayne, NJ, 07470

Tel:  (973) 628-3000         Fax:  (973) 628-3326         www.gaf.com

*Mfr. roofing and building materials.*

**GAF (Great Britain) Co. Ltd.,  Tilson Rd., Roundthorn, Wythenshawe, Manchester M23 9PH UK**
**.GAF Europe,  Rythe House, 12 Littleworth Rd., Esher Surrey KT10 9PD, UK**

## GAFFNEY CLINE & ASSOCIATES INC.

PO Box 796309, Dallas, TX, 75379

Tel:  (972) 733-1183         Fax:  (972) 380-0180         www.gaffney-cline.com

*Consultants to energy and mineral industrial.*

**Gaffney Cline & Assoc.,  Bentley Hall, Blacknest, Alton, Hampshire GU34 4PU UK**

## GALILEO INTERNATIONAL, INC.

9700 W. Higgins Rd., Ste. 400, Rosemont, IL, 600184796

Tel:  (847) 518-4000         Fax:  (847) 518-4085         www.galileo.com

*Operates computerized reservation systems (CRS).*

**Galileo Centre Europe,  2 Windsor Dials, Arthur Road, Windsor SL4 1RS, UK**
Tel: 44-1-753-498-500   Fax: 44-1-753-498-501

## GALVESTON-HOUSTON COMPANY.

4900 Woodway, PO Box 2207, Houston, TX, 77056

Tel:  (713) 966-2500         Fax:  (713) 966-2575         www.hensleyind.com

*Mfr. industrial equipment.*

**Bettis Actuators & Controls Ltd.,  Brunel Way, Fareham, Hantsford PO15 5SA, UK**

## GANNETT COMPANY, INC.

1100 Wilson Blvd., Arlington, VA, 22234

Tel:  (703) 284-6000         Fax:  (703) 364-0855         www.gannett.com

*Newspaper publishing and broadcasting company.*

**USA Today Intl.,  34-44 London Road, Morden Surrey SM4 5BR, UK**
Tel: 44-20-8640-8989

## THE GAP

1 Harrison Street, San Francisco, CA, 94105

Tel:  (650) 952-4400         Fax:  (650) 952-5884         www.gap.com

*Clothing store chain.*

**The Gap,  London, UK**

## GARDNER-DENVER INC.

1800 Gardner Expressway, Quincy, IL, 62301

Tel: (217) 222-5400     Fax: (217) 228-8247     www.gardnerdenver.com

*Mfr. portable air compressors and related drilling accessories.*

**Gardner Denver Limited, 51A Wycombe End - Beaconsfield, Bucks HP9 1LX, UK**

Tel: 44-1494-680560

**Gardner-Denver Ltd., Suite 3 - Parkway Business Centre 2, Princess Road, Manchester M14 7LU, UK**

Tel: 44-1612328986

## GARLOCK SEALING TECHNOLOGIES

1666 Division Street, Palmyra, NY, 14522

Tel: (315) 597-4811     Fax: (315) 597-3216     www.garlock-inc.com

*Mfr. of gaskets, packing, seals and expansion joints.*

**Garlock GB Ltd., Hambridge Rd., Newbury Berkshire RG14 5TG, UK**

Tel: 44-1635-38509    Contact: David Willis, Mng. Dir.

## GARTNER GROUP, INC.

56 Top Gallant Road, Stamford, CT, 06904-2212

Tel: (203) 316-1111     Fax: (203) 316-1100     www.gartner.com

*Information technology and research.*

**Gartner Group, Tamesis, The Glanty, Egham, TW20 9AW UK**

Tel: 44-1784-431611

## THE GATES RUBBER COMPANY

990 S. Broadway, PO Box 5887, Denver, CO, 80217-5887

Tel: (303) 744-1911     Fax: (303) 744-4000     www.gatesrubber.com

*Mfr. automotive and industrial belts and hoses.*

**Gates Rubber Company, Edinburgh Road, Dumfries DG1 1QA, UK**

## GATEWAY INC.

4545 Towne Centre Ct., San Diego, CA, 92121

Tel: (858) 799-3401     Fax: (858) 779-3459     www.gateway.com

*Computers manufacture, sales and services.*

**Gateway (UK) Ltd., 16 Kingfisher Ct., Hambridge Rd., Newbury, Berkshire RG14 5SJ UK**

## GATX CAPITAL CORPORATION

Four Embarcadero Center, Ste. 2200, San Francisco, CA, 94111

Tel: (415) 955-3200     Fax: (415) 955-3449     www.gatxcapital.com

*Lease and loan financing, residual guarantees.*

**GATX Asset Residual Management Plc., St. Andrew's House - West Street, Woking Surrey GU21 1EA, UK**

Tel: 44-1483-747133    Fax: 44-1483-727679

**Lombard Network Services Ltd., Lombard House - Waterfront Business Park, Elstree Road, Elstree Hertfordshire WD6 3BS, UK**

Tel: 44-181-236-7800    Fax: 44-181-236-7899

## GE CAPITAL FLEET SERVICES

3 Capital Drive, Eden Prairie, MN, 55344

Tel: (612) 828-1000     Fax: (612) 828-2010     www.gefleet.com

*Corporate vehicle leasing and services.*

**GE Capital Fleet Services, Old Hall Road - Sale, Cheshire M332G7, UK**

Tel: 44-870-444-9070

## GENCOR INDUSTRIES INC.

5201 N. Orange Blossom Trail, Orlando, FL, 32810

Tel: (407) 290-6000     Fax: (407) 578-0577     www.gencor.com

*Mfr. heat process systems, equipment, instrumentation and controls.*

**CPM Europe, Ltd.,  West March, Daventry, Northants NN11 4SA, UK**

Tel: 44-1327-70-4721   Fax: 44-1327-77-1831

**Gencor Acp, Ltd.,  Wharf Way, Glen Parva, Leicester LE2 9TF, UK**

Tel: 44-116-277-5555   Fax: 44-116-277-6563

**General Combusion Ltd.,  Brookers Road, Billinghurst, West Sussex, UK**

Tel: 44-1403-78-2091   Fax: 44-1403-78-2087

## GENERAL AUTOMATION INC.

17731 Mitchell North, Irvine, CA, 92614

Tel: (949) 250-4800     Fax: (949) 752-6772     www.genauto.com

*Mfr./sale/services computer hardware and software.*

**Edg Tech Systems Ltd.,  Banbury, UK**

**GA/Mentor Ltd.,  6 Albany Close, Bushey Heath, Herts. WD2 3SG, UK**

Contact: Bill Cotton

## GENERAL BINDING CORPORATION

One GBC Plaza, Northbrook, IL, 60062

Tel: (847) 272-3700     Fax: (847) 272-1369     www.gbc.com

*Engaged in the design, manufacture and distribution of branded office equipment, related supplies and thermal laminating films.*

**General Binding Co. Ltd.,  Rutherford Rd., Basingstoke, Hants RG24 0PD UK**

## GENERAL CABLE CORPORATION

4 Tesseneer Dr., Highland Heights, KY, 41076-9753

Tel: (859) 572-8000     Fax: (859) 572-8458     www.generalcable.com

*Mfr. aluminum, copper and fiber optic wire and cable products.*

**BICC General,  Hedgeley Road, Hebburn, Tyne and Wear NE31 1XR, UK**

Tel: 44-191-483-2244

## GENERAL DATACOMM INC.

1579 Straits Turnpike, PO Box 1299, Middlebury, CT, 06762-1299

Tel: (203) 574-1118     Fax: (203) 758-8507     www.gdc.com

*Mfr./sale/services transportation equipment for communications networks.*

**General DataComm Ltd.,  Molly Millar Lane, Wokingham, Berkshire RG11 2QF, UK**

## GENERAL DYNAMICS CORPORATION

3190 Fairview Park Drive, Falls Church, VA, 22042-4523

Tel: (703) 876-3000     Fax: (703) 876-3125     www.gendyn.com

*Mfr. aerospace equipment, submarines, strategic systems, armored vehicles, defense support systems.*

**Computing Devices Company Ltd.,  Churchfields Site Highfield Business Park, Sidney Little Rd., St. Leonards-On-Sea, East Sussex TN38 9UB UK**

Tel: 44-1424-853-481   Fax: 44-1424-798-575   Contact: Sir Donald Spiers, Chmn.

**Computing Devices Company Ltd.,  Castleham Site, Castleham Rd., St. Leonards-On-Sea, East Sussex TN38 9NJ UK**

Tel: 44-1424-853-481   Fax: 44-1424-851-520   Contact: Sir Donald Spiers, Chmn.

## GENERAL ELECTRIC CAPITAL CORPORATION

260 Long Ridge Road, Stamford, CT, 06927

Tel: (203) 357-4000        Fax: (203) 357-6489        www.gecapital.com

*Financial, property/casualty insurance, computer sales and trailer leasing services.*

**Employers Reinsurance Corp. (ERC), PO Box 309, Castle House, Castle Hill Ave., Folkestone Kent CT20 2TF UK**

Tel: 44-1303-221-111   Fax: 44-1303-851-408

**Employers Reinsurance Corp. (ERC), 7/8 Philpot Lane, London EC3M 8AA, UK**

Tel: 44-207-617-6800   Fax: 44-207-929-4204

**Employers Reinsurance Corp. (ERC), London Underwriting Centre Suite 11 2nd FL, 3 Minister Court, Mincing Lane London EC3R 7DD, UK**

Tel: 44-207-617-6800   Fax: 44-207-617-6860

## GENERAL ELECTRIC COMPANY

3135 Easton Turnpike, Fairfield, CT, 06431

Tel: (203) 373-2211        Fax: (203) 373-3131        www.ge.com

*Diversified manufacturing, technology and services.*

**GE Aircraft Engines, 3 Shortlands, Hammersmith London W6 8BX, UK**

Tel: 44-181-846-8738

**GE Appliances, Peterborough, UK**

Tel: 44-73-355-6061

**GE Appliances, 3 Shortlands, Hammersmith London W6 8BX, UK**

Tel: 44-181-846-8645

**GE FANUC Automation, Unit 1 Mill Square, Milton Keyes MK12 5BZ, UK**

Tel: 44-190-884-4041   Fax: 44-190-884-4001

**GE International, 3 Shortlands, Hammersmith, London W6 8BX, UK**

Tel: 44-181-741-9900

**GE/Nuovo Pignone, 25 Green St., London WIY 3FD, UK**

Tel: 44-207-493-8211   Fax: 44-207-629-5684

**International Wagon Services, Div. of GE Railcar, 3 Shortlands, Hammersmith, London W6 8BX, UK**

**NBC, Division of GE, 3 Shortlands, Hammersmith, London W6 8BX, UK**

Tel: 44-181-846-8704

## GENERAL INSTRUMENT CORPORATION

101 Tournament Road, Horsham, PA, 19044

Tel: (215) 674-4800        Fax: (215) 443-9554        www.gi.com

*Mfr. broadband communications and power rectifying components.*

**General Instrument (UK) Ltd., Imperium - Imperial Way, Reading Berkshire, RG2 OTD, UK**

Tel: 44-118-975-5555   Fax: 44-118-975-3933

## GENERAL MOTORS ACCEPTANCE CORPORATION

3044 W. Grand Blvd., Detroit, MI, 48202

Tel: (313) 556-5000        Fax: (313) 556-5108        www.gmac.com

*Automobile financing.*

**GMAC (UK) PLC, Oakland House, Talbot Rd., Old Trafford, Manchester M16 OPQ UK**

**GMAC (UK) PLC, Metropolitan House, 1 Hagley Rd., Five Ways, Edgbaston Birmingham B16 8TG UK**

**GMAC (UK) PLC, Aire House, Swingate, Leeds LS1 4AG, UK**

**GMAC (UK) PLC, Wesley House, 19 Chapel St., PO Box 11, Luton Beds. LU1 2SE UK**

**GMAC (UK) PLC, Kings House, Bond St., Bristol BS1 2AE, UK**

## GENERAL MOTORS CORPORATION

300 Renaissance Center, Detroit, MI, 48285

Tel: (313) 556-5000     Fax: (313) 556-5108     www.gm.com

*Mfr. full line vehicles, automotive electronics, commercial technologies, telecommunications, space, finance.*

**Delco Electronics Overseas Corp., Moorgate Rd., Kirkby, Liverpool L33 7XL, UK**

**Delco Products Overseas Corp., PO Box 4, High St. North, Dunstable LU6 1BQ, UK**

**General Motors Overseas Commercial Vehicle Corp., England, UK**

**Group Lotus PLC, Norwich, Norfolk NR14 8E2, UK**

**Saginaw Overseas Corp., 1/8 Capitol Way, London NW9 0EH, UK**

**Vauxhall Motors Ltd., PO Box 3, Kimpton Rd., Luton LU2 0SY, UK**

## GENERAL REINSURANCE CORPORATION

695 E. Main Street, Stamford, CT, 06904-2350

Tel: (203) 328-5000     Fax: (203) 328-6423     www.genre.com

*Reinsurance services worldwide.*

**General Re Europe Ltd. London, Corn Exchange, 55 Mark Lane, London EC3R 7NE, UK**

Tel: 44-207-426-6000   Fax: 44-207-426-6001   Contact: Berto Sciolla, VP

**General Re Europe Ltd. Manchester, 1 St. James Square 5th Fl., Manchester M2 6DN, UK**

Tel: 44-161-831-7555   Fax: 44-161-831-7700   Contact: Patricia A. Chandler, VP

**General Re Financial Services Ltd. - London, Broadgate Court, 199 Bishopgate, London EC2M 3TY, UK**

Tel: 44-207-448-4000   Fax: 44-207-448-4065

**The Cologne Reinsurance Company Ltd., Cologne House, 13 Haydon St., London EC3N 1DB, UK**

Tel: 44-207-481-1533   Fax: 44-207-480-6511   Contact: Brian Cragg, Mng. Dir.

**The Cologne Reinsurance Company Ltd., The Corn Exchange, 55 Mark Lane, London EC3R 7NE, UK**

Tel: 44-207-426-1846   Fax: 44-207-426-1898   Contact: Alex Cowley, Gen. Mgr.

## GENERAL SEMICONDUCTOR, INC.

10 Melville Park Road., Melville, NY, 11747

Tel: (631) 847-3000     Fax: (631) 847-3236     www.gensemi.com

*Mfr. of low- and medium-current power rectifiers and transient voltage suppressors.*

**General Semiconductor (UK) Ltd., The Grand Union Office Park, Packet Boat Lane, Cowley, Uxbridge UB8 2GH UK**

Tel: 44-1895-441445   Fax: 44-1895-441545

## GENERAL TIME CORPORATION

520 Guthridge Ct., Norcross, GA, 30092

Tel: (770) 447-5300     Fax: (770) 242-4009     www.westclox.com

*Mfr. clocks and watches.*

**General Time Europe, 8 Heathcote Industrial Estate, Warwick CV34 6TE, UK**

Tel: 44-1926-885-400   Fax: 44-1926-885-723

## GENICOM CORPORATION

14800 Conference Center Drive, Ste. 400, Chantilly, VA, 20151

Tel: (703) 802-9200     Fax: (703) 802-9039     www.genicom.com

*Supplier of network systems, service and printer solutions.*

**Genicom Limited, Armstrong Mall - Southwood, Farnborough, Hampshire GU14 0NR UK**

Tel: 44-1252-74-44-00

**Genicom Ltd., Armstrong Mall Southwood, Farnborough, Hampshire GU14 0NR UK**

Contact: Tony Hammell

## GENUITY, INC.

150 Cambridge Park Drive, Cambridge, MA, 02140

Tel: (617) 873-2000     Fax: (617) 873-2857     www.genuity.com

*R/D computer, communications, acoustics technologies and internetworking services.*

**Genuity, Inc., Regus House - Trinity Court, Wokingham Road Bracknell, Berkshire RG42 1PL, UK**

Tel: 44-1344-668419    Contact: Louise Pearl

## GENZYME CORPORATION

1 Kendall Square, Cambridge, MA, 02139-1562

Tel: (617) 252-7500     Fax: (617) 252-7600     www.genzyme.com

*Mfr. healthcare products for enzyme deficient diseases.*

**GBL Genzyme SA, 50 Gibson Drive, Kings Hill West Malling, Kent ME19 4HG, UK**

**Genzyme Ltd., 37 Hollands Road, Haverhill Suffolk CB98PU, UK**

Tel: 44-1440-703-522    Fax: 44-1440-707-783

## GEO LOGISTICS CORPORATION

1521 E. Dyer Rd., Santa Ana, CA, 92705

Tel: (714) 513-3000     Fax: (714) 513-3120     www.geo-logistics.com

*Freight forwarding, warehousing and distribution services, specializing in heavy cargo.*

**GeoLogistics Ltd., 117-120 Snargate Street, Dover Kent CT179EB, UK**

Tel: 44-1304-240242    Fax: 44-1304-240325

**GeoLogistics Ltd., Trafford Wharf Road, Trafford Park, Manchester M17 1EX, UK**

Tel: 44-161-872-4022    Fax: 44-161-876-6045

**GeoLogistics Ltd., Royal Court, 81 Tweedy Road, Bromley Kent BR1 1TW, UK**

**LEP Transport Ltd., Sunlight Wharf, Upper Thames Street, London EC4P 4AD, UK**

## GEONEX MARTEL, INC.

8950 Ninth Street North, St. Petersburg, FL, 33702-3044

Tel: (727) 578-0100     Fax: (727) 577-6946

*Geo-information services: mapping, resource interpretation, analysis, testing and data base management.*

**Geonex Corp., Barwell Business Ctr., Unit 7 Arthur St., Barwell, Leicestershire LE9 8GZ UK**

## GEOWORKS CORPORATION

960 Atlantic Avenue, Alameda, CA, 94501

Tel: (510) 614-1660     Fax: (510) 614-4250     www.geoworks.com

*Mfr. operating system software.*

**Geoworks Ltd. UK, London, UK**

Contact: Ken Norbury

## GETZ BROS & COMPANY, INC.

150 Post Street, Ste. 500, San Francisco, CA, 94108-4750

Tel: (415) 772-5500     Fax: (415) 772-5659     www.getz.com

*Diversified manufacturing, marketing and distribution services and travel services.*

**Getz Bros. & Co. Inc., 14 Queen Anne's Gate, St. James Park London SW1H 9A, UK**

Tel: 44-207-976-7701    Fax: 44-207-976-7265    Contact: Christopher Beale    Emp: 3

## GIBSON, DUNN & CRUTCHER LLP

333 S. Grand Ave., Los Angeles, CA, 90071

Tel: (213) 229-7000     Fax: (213) 229-7520     www.gdclaw.com

*International law firm.*

**Gibson, Dunn & Crutcher LLP, 30/35 Pall Mall, London SW1Y 5LP, UK**

Tel: 44-207-925-0440    Fax: 44-207-925-2465

**GIDDINGS & LEWIS INC.**

142 Doty Street, PO Box 590, Fond du Lac, WI, 54936-0590

Tel: (920) 921-9400      Fax: (920) 929-4522      www.giddings.com

*Mfr. machine tools, factory automation products and services.*

**Giddings & Lewis Cross Hüller,  Randles Rd., Knowsley Industrial Park South, Prescot, Merseyside L34 9EZ UK**

Tel: 44-151-546-2010   Fax: 44-151-547-2801   Contact: Alan Ruddock, Mng. Dir.

**GILEAD SCIENCES, INC.**

333 Lakeside Dr, Foster City, CA, 94404

Tel: (650) 574-3000      Fax: (650) 578-9264      www.gilead.com

*Engaged in healthcare research and development;  biotech treatments for viruses.*

**NeXstar Pharmaceuticals, Ltd.,  Granta Park Abington, Cambridge CB1 6GT UK**

Tel: 44-122-357-1400   Fax: 44-122-357-1444

**THE GILLETTE COMPANY**

Prudential Tower Building, Boston, MA, 02199

Tel: (617) 421-7000      Fax: (617) 421-7123      www.gillette.com

*Develop/mfr. personal care/use products: blades and razors, toiletries, cosmetics, stationery.*

**Braun (UK) Ltd.,  Sunbury-on-Thames, UK**

Contact: Roger Murphy, Gen. Mgr.

**Gillette Industries PLC,  Isleworth Middlesex, UK**

Contact: Roger Murphy, Gen. Mgr.

**Gillette Personal Care Ltd.,  Isleworth, UK**

Contact: Roger Murphy, Gen. Mgr.

**Gillette UK Ltd.,  Isleworth, UK**

Contact: Roger Murphy, Gen. Mgr.

**Jafra Cosmetics Intl. Ltd.,  Farnborough Hants., UK**

Contact: Roger Murphy, Gen. Mgr.

**Lidgate Intl. Ltd.,  Isleworth Middlesex, UK**

Contact: Roger Murphy, Gen. Mgr.

**Lustrasilk Intl. UK Ltd.,  Isleworth Middlesex, UK**

Contact: Roger Murphy, Gen. Mgr.

**Moorgate Industries Ltd.,  Isleworth Middlesex, UK**

Contact: Roger Murphy, Gen. Mgr.

**Nacet Co. Ltd.,  Isleworth Middlesex, UK**

Contact: Roger Murphy, Gen. Mgr.

**Oral-B Laboratories Dublin Inc.,  Aylesbury Buckinghamshire, UK**

Contact: Roger Murphy, Gen. Mgr.

**Oral-B Laboratories Intl. Ltd.,  Isleworth Middlesex, UK**

Contact: Roger Murphy, Gen. Mgr.

**Oral-B Laboratories Ltd.,  Aylesbury Buckinghamshire, UK**

Contact: Roger Murphy, Gen. Mgr.

**Oral-B Laboratories Newbridge Inc.,  Aylesbury Buckinghamshire, UK**

Contact: Roger Murphy, Gen. Mgr.

**Waterman Pens UK Ltd.,  Isleworth Middlesex, UK**

Contact: Roger Murphy, Gen. Mgr.

## GILSON INC.

3000 W. Beltline Hwy, PO Box 620027, Middleton, WI, 53562-0027

Tel: (608) 836-1551　　Fax: (608) 831-4451　　www.gilson.com

*Mfr. analytical/biomedical instruments.*

**Anachem Ltd., Anachem House - Charles Street, Luton Bedfordshire LU2-OEB, UK**

## GLEASON CORPORATION

1000 University Ave., Rochester, NY, 14692

Tel: (716) 473-1000　　Fax: (716) 461-4348　　www.gleasoncorp.com

*Mfr. gear making machine tools; tooling and services.*

**Gleason Works Ltd., 6B Derriford Business Park, Plymouth PL6 5QZ UK**

Tel: 44-1752-739661　Fax: 44-1752-724429

## GLENAYRE ELECTRONICS LTD.

5935 Carnegie Blvd.., Ste. 300, Charlotte, NC, 28209

Tel: (704) 553-0038　　Fax: (704) 553-7878　　www.glenayre.com

*Mfr. infrastructure components and pagers.*

**Glenayre Electronics (UK) Ltd., Challenge House Unit 22, Sherwood Drive, Bletchley Milton Keynes MK3 6JD, UK**

Tel: 44-1908-644-642　Fax: 44-1908-644-643

## GLOBAL MARINE INC.

777 North Eldridge, Houston, TX, 77079

Tel: (281) 496-8000　　Fax: (281) 531-1260　　www.glm.com

*Offshore contract drilling, turnkey drilling, oil and gas exploration and production.*

**Global Marine Inc., London UK**

## GLOBAL PAYMENT TECHNOLOGIES, INC.

20 East Sunrise Hwy., Ste. 291, Valley Stream, NY, 11581

Tel: (516) 256-1000　　Fax: (516) 256-1620　　www.gptx.com

*Mfr. validators for authenticating currency.*

**Global Payment Technologies, Ltd., 29 Park Royal Metro Centre, Britannia Way, London NW10 7PA, UK**

Tel: 44-20-8961-6116　Fax: 44-20-8961-6117

## GLOBAL SILVERHAWK

2190 Meridian Park Blvd., Ste G, Concord, CA, 94520

Tel: (925) 681-2889　　Fax: (925) 681-2755　　www.globalsilverhawk.com

*International moving and forwarding.*

**Global Silverhawk, 16 Perivale Ind. Park, Horsenden Lane S., Greenford Middlesex UB6 7RW, UK**

Contact: Helen Brabbs, Gen. Mgr.

## THE GOLDMAN SACHS GROUP

85 Broad Street, New York, NY, 10004

Tel: (212) 902-1000　　Fax: (212) 902-3000　　www.gs.com

*Investment bankers; securities broker dealers.*

**Goldman Sachs Group, Peterborough Court, 133 Fleet St., London EC4A 2BB, UK**

Tel: 44-207-774-1000

## THE GOODYEAR TIRE & RUBBER COMPANY

1144 East Market Street, Akron, OH, 44316

Tel: (330) 796-2121　　Fax: (330) 796-1817　　www.goodyear.com

*Mfr. tires, automotive belts and hose, conveyor belts, chemicals; oil pipeline transmission.*

**Goodyear Great Britain Ltd., Stafford Rd., Wolverhampton WV10 6D4, UK**

**GOSS GRAPHIC SYSTEMS INC.**

700 Oakmont Lane, Westmont, IL, 60559-5546

Tel: (630) 850-5600      Fax: (630) 850-6310      www.gossgraphic.com

*Mfr. web, off-site printing equipment.*

**Goss/Rockwell Graphic Systems Ltd., Central House, 3 Lampton Rd., Middlesex TW3 1HY UK**

**Goss/Rockwell Graphic Systems Ltd., Greenbank St., Preston, Lancs. PR1 7LA UK**

**GPU INTERNATIONAL, INC.**

300 Madison Ave., Morristown, NJ, 07962-1911

Tel: (973) 455-8200      Fax: (973) 455-8582      www.gpu.com

*Global electric energy company.*

**Midlands Electricity, Plc., Birmingham, UK**

**W. R. GRACE & COMPANY**

7500 Grace Drive, Columbia, MD, 21044

Tel: (410) 531-4000      Fax: (410) 531-4367      www.grace.com

*Mfr. specialty chemicals and materials: packaging, health care, catalysts, construction, water treatment/process.*

**Chomerics (UK) Ltd., Globe Park Ind. Estate Unit 8, First Avenue, Marlow, Bucks SL7 1YA UK**

**Grace Dearborn Ltd., Widnes, Cheshire WA8 8UD, UK**

**Servicised Ltd., 628 Ajax Avenue, Slough Berkshire SL1 4BH, UK**

Tel: 44-1753-69-2929   Fax: 44-1753-63-7702

**W.R. Grace Ltd., Clifton House, 1 Marston Rd., St. Neots Cambridgeshire PE19 2HN, UK**

Tel: 44-1480-224-000   Fax: 44-1480-244-066

**W.R. Grace Ltd., Northdale House, North Circular Rd., London NW10 7UH, UK**

**GRACO INC.**

4050 Olson Memorial Hwy, PO Box 1441, Minneapolis, MN, 55440-1441

Tel: (612) 623-6000      Fax: (612) 623-6777      www.graco.com

*Mfr. systems and equipment to service fluid handling systems and automotive equipment.*

**Graco UK, One Hovefield Ave., Burnt Mills B Industrial Estate, Basildon Essex SS 13 1ND UK**

Tel: 870-9090-510   Fax: 870-9090-505

**GRAHAM & JAMES LLP**

One Maritime Plaza, Ste. 300, San Francisco, CA, 94111-3404

Tel: (415) 954-0200      Fax: (415) 391-2493      www.gj.com

*International law firm.*

**Graham & James, London, UK**

**Graham & James, Carmelite, 50 Victoria Embarkment Blackfriars, London EC4Y 0DX, UK**

Tel: 44-207-353-1840   Fax: 44-207-353-1841   Contact: David M. Findlay

**GRANT THORNTON INTERNATIONAL**

800 One Prudential Plaza, 130 E. Randolph Drive, Chicago, IL, 60601-6050

Tel: (312) 856-0001      Fax: (312) 616-7052      www.grantthornton.com

*Accounting, audit, tax and management consulting services.*

**Grant Thornton, 18 Langton Place, Bury St. Edmunds, Suffolk IP33 1NE, UK**

Tel: 44-1284-701271   Fax: 44-1284-762760   Contact: Graham Shorter

**Grant Thornton, Heron House, Albert Square, Manchester M60 8GT, UK**

Tel: 44-161-834-5414   Fax: 44-161-832-6042   Contact: Graema Whittaker

**Grant Thornton, Kettering Pkwy., Kettering, Northants East Northampton NN15 6XR, UK**

Tel: 44-1536-310000   Fax: 44-1536-315400   Contact: Aidan O'Rourke

**Grant Thornton, 43 Queen Square, Bristol BS1 4QR, UK**

Tel: 44-117-936-8901   Fax: 44-117-926-5458   Contact: Roger C. Zair

**Grant Thornton International,** St John's Centre, 110 Albion Street, Leeds LS2 8LA UK

Tel: 44-113-246-0211    Contact: David Naylor

**Grant Thornton International,** Grant Thornton House, Melton St., Euston Square, London NW1 2EP UK

Tel: 44-207-383-5100    Fax: 44-207-728-2744    Contact: David C. McDonnell, Mgr.

**Grant Thornton International,** Grant Thornton House, Melton Street - Euston Square, London NW1 2EP, UK

Tel: 44-207-383 5100    Fax: 44-207-728-2744    Contact: Martin Goddard

## GREAT LAKES CHEMICAL CORPORATION

500 East 96th Street, Ste. 500, Indianapolis, IN, 46240

Tel: (317) 715-3000    Fax: (317) 715-3050    www.greatlakeschem.com

*Mfr. innovative specialty chemical solutions, including flame retardants and other polymer additives, water treatment chemicals, performance and fine chemicals, fire extinguishants.*

**Octel Associates & The Associated Octel Co. Ltd.,** PO Box 17, Oil Sites Rd., Ellesmere Port, South Wirral L65 4HF, UK

## GREENFIELD INDUSTRIES INC.

470 Old Evans Road, Evans, GA, 30809

Tel: (706) 863-7708    Fax: (706) 860-8559    www.greenfieldindustries.com

*Mfr. high-speed rotary cutting tools.*

**Cirbo Ltd. & RTW Ltd.,** 16 Normandy Way, Bodmin, Cornwall PL1 1EX UK

## GREY GLOBAL GROUP

777 Third Ave., New York, NY, 10017

Tel: (212) 546-2000    Fax: (212) 546-1495    www.grey.com

*International advertising agency.*

**Grey Communications Group,** 215-227 Great Portland St., London W1N 5HD, UK

**Grey Europe,** Wells Point, 79 Wells St., London W1P 3RE, UK

## GREYHOUND LINES INC.

PO Box 660362, Dallas, TX, 75266

Tel: (972) 789-7000    Fax: (972) 789-7330    www.greyhound.com

*Mfr. consumer products, transportation, consumer and financial services.*

**Greyhound Financial & Leasing Corp. AG,** 11 Albemarle St., London W1X 3HE, UK

**Greyhound Intl. Travel Inc.,** Sussex House, London Rd., East Grinstead, West Sussex RH19 1LD UK

## GRIFFITH LABORATORIES INC.

One Griffith Center, Alsip, IL, 60658

Tel: (708) 371-0900    Fax: (708) 597-3294    www.griffithlabs.com

*Mfr. industrial food ingredients and equipment.*

**Griffith Laboratories (UK) Ltd.,** Cotes Park Estate, Somercotes, Derby DE5 4NN UK

Tel: 44-1773-832-171    Fax: 44-1773-835-294

## GUARDIAN ELECTRIC MFG. COMPANY

1425 Lake Ave., Woodstock, IL, 60098

Tel: (815) 334-3600    Fax: (815) 337-0377    www.guardian-electric.com

*Mfr. industrial controls, electrical relays and switches.*

**Guardian International Sales,** Thrumsdorm House, Collafield, Littledean, Glos. GL14 3LG UK

## GUARDSMAN PRODUCTS/LILLY INDUSTRIES

4999 36th Street SE, PO Box 88010,, Grand Rapids, MI, 49512

Tel: (616) 940-2900    Fax: (616) 285-7870    www.lilly.com

*Mfr. custom industrial coatings, diversified consumer products.*

**Guardsman UK Ltd.,** 10 Blacklands Way, Abingdon Business Park, Abingdon, Oxfordshire OX14 1RD UK

**GUEST SUPPLY INC.**

4301 US Highway 1, PO Box 902, Monmouth Junction, NJ, 08852-0902

Tel: (609) 514-9696    Fax: (609) 514-2692    www.guestsupply.com

*Mfr. personal care and housekeeping products.*

**Guest Intl. (England) Ltd.,  4 Vulcan House, Calleva Park, Aldermaston, Berkshire RG7 4QW UK**

**GUILFORD MILLS INC.**

925 West Market Street,  PO Box 26969, Greensboro, NC, 27407

Tel: (336) 316-4000    Fax: (336) 316-4059    www.guilfordmills.com

*Mfr. textiles.*

**Guilford Europe Ltd.,  Cotes Park, Somercotes, Derbyshire DE55 4NJ UK**

Tel: 44-1773-607-401

**GULTON GRAPHIC INSTRUMENTS, INC.**

212 Durham Ave., Metuchen, NJ, 08840

Tel: (732) 548-6500    Fax: (732) 548-6781    www.gulton.com

*Electronic instruments, controls and communications equipment.*

**Gulton Graphic International,  The Hyde, Brighton BN2 4JU, UK**

**GUY CARPENTER & COMPANY, INC.**

Two World Trade Center, New York, NY, 10048

Tel: (212) 323-1000    Fax: (212) 313-4970    www.guycarp.com

*Engaged in global reinsurance and risk management.*

**Guy Carpenter & Company, Ltd.,  33 Aldgate High Street, London EC3N 1AQ, UK**

Tel: 44-207-357-1000   Fax: 44-207-357-1460

**Guy Carpenter & Company, Ltd.,  No. 1 The Marsh Centre, London E1 8DX, UK**

Tel: 44-207-357-1000   Fax: 44-207-357-2164

**Intermediary Systems Limited,  18 Mansell Street, London E1 8AA, UK**

Tel: 44-207-357-2312   Fax: 44-207-357-1460

**HAEMONETICS CORPORATION**

400 Wood Road, Braintree, MA, 02184-9114

Tel: (781) 848-7100    Fax: (781) 848-5106    www.haemonetics.com

*Mfr. automated blood processing systems and blood products.*

**Haemonetics U.K. Ltd.,  Beechwood House, Elmete Lane, Roundhay Leeds LS8 2LQ, UK**

Tel: 44-113-273-7711   Fax: 44-113-273-4055

**HAGGAR CORPORATION**

6113 Lemmon Avenue, Dallas, TX, 75209

Tel: (214) 352-8481    Fax: (214) 956-4367    www.haggarcorp.com

*Mfr. apparel.*

**Haggar Apparel Ltd.,  16-19 Eastcastle Street, London WIN 80B, UK**

Tel: 44-20-7636-5255   Contact: Karen Ames

**HALE AND DORR LLP**

60 State Street, Boston, MA, 02109

Tel: (617) 526-6000    Fax: (617) 526-5000    www.haledorr.com

*International law firm.*

**Brobeck Hale and Door International,  Hasilwood House, 60 Bishopsgate, London, EC2N 4AJ UK**

Tel: 44-207-638-6688   Fax: 44-207-638-5888   Contact: David M. Ayres

## HALLIBURTON COMPANY

500 North Akard Street, Ste. 3600, Dallas, TX, 75201-3391

Tel: (214) 978-2600   Fax: (214) 978-2685   www.halliburton.com

*Engaged in diversified energy services, engineering and construction.*

**Halliburton Ltd., Hill Park Court, Springfield Drive, Leatherhead KT 22 7NL, UK**

Tel: 44-181-544-5000   Fax: 44-181-544-6655

**Halliburton Ltd., South Denes Rd., Great Yarmouth Norfolk NR 30 3QF, UK**

Tel: 44-1493-330300   Fax: 44-1493-330302

**Halliburton Ltd., 2-18 Simpson Place, Nethermains, Kilwinning Ayshire KA 13 6PT, UK**

Tel: 44-1294-553-928   Fax: 44-1294-557-840

## HALLMARK CARDS INC.

2501 McGee Street, Kansas City, MO, 64108

Tel: (816) 274-5100   Fax: (816) 274-5061   www.hallmark.com

*Mfr. greeting cards and related products.*

**Hallmark Cards Ltd., Hallmark House, Station Rd., Henley-on-Thames, Oxfordshire RG9 1LQ UK**

Tel: 44-1491-578383

## HAMILTON SUNSTRAND

One Hamilton Rd., Windsor Locks, CT, 06096-1010

Tel: (860) 654-6000   Fax: (860) 654-3469   www.hamiltonsunstrandcorp.com

*Design/mfr. aerospace systems for commercial, regional, corporate and military aircraft.*

**Hamilton Sunstrand Corp., Wolverhampton, UK**

## HANDY & HARMAN

555 Theodore Fremd Ave., Rye, NY, 10580

Tel: (914) 921-5200   Fax: (914) 925-4496   www.handyha

*Precious and specialty metals for industry, refining, scrap metal; diversified industrial mfr.*

**Lucas-Milhaupt - Europe, Gunnels Wood Park, Stevenage, Herts. SG1 2BH, UK**

**Rigby Maryland (Stainless) Ltd., Crystal Works, Union Rd., Liversedge WF15 7JU, UK**

## M.A. HANNA COMPANY

200 Public Square, Ste. 36-5000, Cleveland, OH, 44114

Tel: (216) 589-4000   Fax: (216) 589-4200   www.mahanna.com

*Mfr. color and additive concentrates.*

**Victor International Plastics, Langley Road South, Salford Manchester M6 6SN, UK**

## HARBISON WALKER REFRACTORIES COMPANY

600 Grant Street, Pittsburgh, PA, 15219

Tel: (412) 562-6200   Fax: (412) 562-6331   www.hwr.com

*Mfr. refractories and lime.*

**Harbison Walker Refractories Ltd., Dock Rd. South, Bromborough, Wirral, Merseyside L62 4SP UK**

## HARBORLITE CORPORATION

PO Box 100, Vicksburg, MI, 49097

Tel: (616) 649-1352   Fax: (616) 649-3707   www.worldminerals.com

*Mining/process perlite filter media.*

**Harborlite UK Ltd., Livingston Rd., Hessle Hull, North Humberside HU13 0EG UK**

## HARCOURT GENERAL, INC.

27 Boylston St., Chestnut Hill, MA, 02467

Tel: (617) 232-8200   Fax: (617) 739-1395   www.harcourtgeneral.com

*Publisher of educational materials.*

**Harcourt General Ltd., Foortscray High St., Sidcup Kent DA 14 5HP, UK**

Tel: 44-181-300-3322   Fax: 44-181-309-0807

**Harcourt General Publishers International, 24-28 Oval Rd., London NW1 7DX, UK**

Tel: 44-207-424-4200    Fax: 44-207-482-2293

**W.B. Saunders Co. Ltd., 24-28 Oval Rd., London NW1 7DX, UK**

## HARLEY-DAVIDSON INTERNATIONAL

3700 West Juneau Ave., Milwaukee, WI, 53201

Tel: (414) 342-4680        Fax: (414) 343-4621        www.harleydavidson.com

*Mfr. motorcycles, recreational and commercial vehicles, parts and accessories.*

**Harley-Davidson U.K. Ltd., PO Box 27, Daventry, Northamptonshire NN11 5RW UK**

## HARMAN INTERNATIONAL INDUSTRIES, INC.

1101 Pennsylvania Ave. NW, Ste. 1010, Washington, DC, 20004

Tel: (202) 393-1101        Fax: (202) 393-3064        www.harman.com

*Mfr. audio and video equipment, loudspeakers and sound reinforcement equipment.*

**Harman UK Ltd., Unit 1B, Mill St., Slough, Berkshire S12 5DD, UK**

**Soundcraft Electronics Ltd., Cranborne House, Cranborne Ind. Estate, Cranborne Rd., Potters Bar Herts. EN6 3JN, UK**

## HARNISCHFEGER INDUSTRIES INC.

PO Box 554, Milwaukee, WI, 53201

Tel: (414) 797-6480        Fax: (414) 797-6573        www.harnischfeger.com

*Mfr. mining and material handling equipment, papermaking machinery and computer systems.*

**Beloit Walmsley Ltd., Crompton Way, Bolton, Lancashire BL1 8UL, UK**

## HARRIS CORPORATION

1025 West NASA Blvd., Melbourne, FL, 32919

Tel: (407) 727-9100        Fax: (407) 727-9344        www.harris.com

*Mfr. communications and information-handling equipment, including copying and fax systems.*

**Avnet PCC, Rutherford Close Mead Way, Stevenage SG1 2EF, UK**

Tel: 44-1438-788900

**Harris Corporation, Eskdale Road, Winnersh Wokingham, Berkshire RG41 5TS, UK**

Tel: 44-118-964-8000

**Harris Semiconductor, Riverside Way, Watchmoor Park, Camberley Surrey GU15 3YQ, UK**

Tel: 44-1276-686-886    Fax: 44-1276-682-323

## HARSCO CORPORATION

PO Box 8888, 350 Poplar Church Rd., Camp Hill, PA, 17001-8888

Tel: (717) 763-7064        Fax: (717) 763-6424        www.harsco.com

*Metal reclamation and mill services, infrastructure and construction and process industry products.*

**Nutter Engineering UK, Oxford St., Bilston, West Midlands WV14 7EG, UK**

**Permaquip, Giltway, Giltbrook, Nottingham NG16 2GQ, UK**

**Sherwood Div., Harsco (UK) Ltd., Giltway, Giltbrook, Nottingham NG16 2GQ, UK**

**Taylor-Wharton Cryogenics (UK), Oxford St., Bilston, West Midlands WV14 7EG, UK**

## HARSCO TRACK TECHNOLOGIES

2401 Edmund Road, Box 20, Cayce-West Colombia, SC, 29171

Tel: (803) 822-9160        Fax: (803) 822-8710        www.fairmonttamper.com

*Mfr./services railroad track maintenance-of-way equipment.*

**Harsco Track Technologies, Giltway, Giltbrook, Nottingham NG16 2GQ, UK**

Tel: 44-115-938-7000

## HARTFORD RE COMPANY

55 Farmington Ave., Ste. 800, Hartford, CT, 06105

Tel: (860) 520-2700        Fax: (860) 520-2726        www.thehartford.com

*Reinsurance.*

**Hartford Re Europe, London Underwriting Centre Suite 3 - 5/F, 3 Minister Court, Mincing Lane, London EC3R 7DD  UK**

Tel: 44-207-617-4400   Fax: 44-207-617-4422   Contact: John Daly, Gen. Mgr.

## HARVARD APPARATUS

84 October Hill Road, Holliston, MA, 01746

Tel: (508) 893-8999        Fax: (508) 429-5732        www.harvardapparatus.com

*Mfr./sales life science research products.*

**Harvard Apparatus, Ltd., Fircroft Way, Edenbridge, Kent TN8 6HE UK**

Tel: 44-1732-864001   Fax: 44-1732-863356   Contact: Hester Davies, Mng. Dir.

## HASBRO INDUSTRIES INC.

1027 Newport Ave., Pawtucket, RI, 02861

Tel: (401) 725-8697        Fax: (401) 727-5099        www.hasbro.com

*Mfr. toy products, including games and puzzles, dolls and plush products.*

**Europress, Div. Hasbro Interactive, Europe House Adlington Park, Macclesfield, SK10 4NP, UK**

Tel: 44-1625-855000

**Hasbro Europe, 2 Roundwood Ave., Scockley Park Uxbridge, Middlesex UB11 18Z UK**

Tel: 44-181-569-1234   Fax: 44-181-569-1133

**Wizards, Div. Hasbro Industries, 3/F - Nicholsons Walk, Maidenhead SL 6 1LD, UK**

Tel: 44-162-780-602

## HAUPPAUGE DIGITAL, INC.

91 Cabot Court, Hauppauge, NY, 11788

Tel: (631) 434-1600        Fax: (631) 434-3198        www.hauppauge.com

*Mfr. circuit boards.*

**Hauppauge Computer Works, Ltd., London, UK**

Tel: 44-207-378-1997   Fax: 44-207-357-9171

## HAYNES INTERNATIONAL INC.

1020 W. Park Ave., PO Box 9013, Kokomo, IN, 46904-9013

Tel: (765) 456-6000        Fax: (765) 456-6905        www.haynesintl.com

*Mfr. cobalt and nickel-base alloys for aerospace and chemicals industry.*

**Haynes International Ltd.., PO Box 10, Parkhouse St., Openshaw, Manchester M11 2ER UK**

Tel: 44-161-230-7777   Fax: 44-161-223-2412   Contact: P. L. Crawshaw, M.D.

## HAYSSEN, INC.

225 Spartangreen Blvd., Duncan, SC, 29334

Tel: (864) 486-4000        Fax: (864) 486-4333        www.barry-wehmiller.com

*Mfr. automatic packaging machinery.*

**Hayssen Europe Ltd., Fison Way, Thetford, Norfolk IP24 IHT, UK**

## HAYWARD INDUSTRIAL PRODUCTS INC.

900 Fairmount Avenue, Elizabeth, NJ, 07207

Tel: (908) 351-5400        Fax: (908) 351-7893        www.haywardindustrial.com

*Mfr. industrial strainers.*

**Hayward Industrial Products (UK) Ltd., Unit 2 Crowngate, Wyncolls Rd., Colchester, Essex CO4 4HT UK**

Tel: 44-1-206-854454   Fax: 44-1-206-851240

**HCA HEALTHCARE CORPORATION**

1 Park Plaza, Nashville, TN, 37203

Tel: (615) 344-9551      Fax: (615) 344-2266      www.columbia-hca.com

*Operates hospitals and surgery centers.*

**Harley Street Clinic, 35 Weymouth Street, London W1N 4BJ, UK**

**Portland Hospital, 209 Great Portland Street, London W1N 6AH, UK**

**Wellington Private Hospital, Wellington Place, London NW8 9LE, UK**

**HEALTHSOUTH CORPORATION**

One HealthSouth Parkway, Birmingham, AL, 35243

Tel: (205) 967-7116      Fax: (205) 969-4740      www.healthsouth.com

*Provider of comprehensive outpatient and rehabilitative healthcare services.*

**HealthSouth Diagnostic Center of Darlington, Hollyhurst Rd., Darlington, County Durham, DL3 6UA, UK**

Tel: 44-1325-3696   Fax: 44-1325-3617

**HealthSouth Diagnostic Center of Guilford, Egerton Rd., Guilford, Surrey GU2 5R6, UK**

Tel: 44-1483-3031   Fax: 44-1483-3046

**HealthSouth Diagnostic Center of Hertfordshire, Campus QE2 Hospitals Howlands, Welwyn Garden City, Hertfordshire AL7 4HQ UK**

Tel: 44-1707-3909   Fax: 44-1707-3919

**HealthSouth Diagnostic Center of Somerset, The Clinic Marsh Lane Huntworth Gate N. Bridgewater, Somerset TA6 62Q, UK**

Tel: 44-1278-4290   Fax: 44-1278-4458

**HealthSouth Diagnostic Center of York, Sir Peter Shepherd Bldg., Wigginton Rd., York 403 9YU UK**

Tel: 44-1904-6422   Fax: 44-1904-6422

**HEARME**

685 Clyde Avenue, Mountain View, CA, 94043

Tel: (650) 429-3900      Fax: (650) 429-3911      www.hearme.com

*Engaged in voice technology for Web sites.*

**HearMe UK, 54 Clarendon Road, Watford Herts, UK**

Tel: 44-1923-431660

**HECKETT MULTISERV**

PO Box 1071, Butler, PA, 16001-1071

Tel: (724) 283-5741      Fax: (724) 283-2410      www.harsco.com

*Metal reclamation and steel mill services.*

**Heckett MultiServ-East, Commonwealth House, 2 Chalkill Rd., London W6 8DW, UK**

**HEIDRICK & STRUGGLES INTERNATIONAL, INC.**

Sears Tower, 233 South Wacker Drive, Chicago, IL, 60606

Tel: (312) 496-1200      Fax: (312) 496-1290      www.heidrick.com

*Executive search firm.*

**Heidrick & Struggles Intl. Inc., 100 Picadilly, London W1V 9FN, UK**

Tel: 44-207-491-3124   Fax: 44-207-734-9581

**HEIL TRAILER INTERNATIONAL**

PO Box 181100, Chattanooga, TN, 37414

Tel: (423) 855-6386      Fax: (423) 855-3459      www.heiltrailer.com

*Mfr./sales of AP and SS tank trailers for liquid, powder, chemicals, asphalt and aircraft refuelers and modular bulk containers.*

**Thompson Carmichael Ltd., Great Bridge Rd., Bilston, West Midlands WV14 8NP, UK**

Tel: 44-1902-353-141   Fax: 44-1902-405-509   Contact: John Waite, Mng. Dir.

## HEIN-WERNER CORPORATION

2110 A Pewaukee Rd., PO Box 1606, Waukesha, WI, 53188

Tel: (262) 542-6611     Fax: (262) 542-7890     www.snapon.com

*Mfr. auto body repair equipment, engine rebuilding and brake repair equipment, hydraulic cylinders.*

**Blackhawk Automotive Ltd., Leacon Rd., Ashford, Kent TN23 2AU, UK**

## H.J. HEINZ COMPANY

600 Grant Street, Pittsburgh, PA, 15219

Tel: (412) 456-5700     Fax: (412) 456-6128     www.heinz.com

*Processed food products and nutritional services.*

**H.J. Heinz Central & Eastern Europe, Hayes Middlesex, UK**

**H.J. Heinz Co. Ltd., Hayes, Middlesex, UK**

**Magyar Foods Ltd., London, UK**

## HELLER FINANCIAL INC.

500 West Monroe Street, Chicago, IL, 60661

Tel: (312) 441-7000     Fax: (312) 441-7367     www.hellerfin.com

*Financial services.*

**NMB Heller Limited, 24 Bennetts Hill, Birmingham B2 5QP, UK**

**NMB Heller Limited, St. Christopher House - Wellington Rd., South Stockport, Cheshire SK2 6UA, UK**

## HENNINGSEN FOODS, INC.

5 International Drive, Rye Brook, NY, 10573

Tel: (914) 694-1000     Fax: (914) 935-0220     www.henningsenfoods.com

*Dehydrated egg, poultry and meat products.*

**Henningsen Foods Ltd., 168 Sloane St., London SW1, UK**

## HENRY SCHEIN, INC.

135 Duryea Rd., Melville, NY, 11747

Tel: (516) 843-5500     Fax: (516) 843-5658     www.henryschein.com

*Mfr. and supply dental equipment.*

**Henry Schein Procare, 25-27 Merrick Road, Southall Middlesex UB2 4AU, UK**

Tel: 44-181-235-5005

**Inter-Dental Equipment Ltd., Unit 9 Langley Park, North Street, Langley Mill Nottinghamshire, NG16 4BS UK**

Tel: 44-1773-714-141

**Zahn Dental Supplies Ltd., Unit 1E - South West Centre, 4 Anchor Road, Sheffield S8 OJR, UK**

Tel: 44-1142-551-213

## HERCULES INC.

Hercules Plaza, 1313 N. Market Street, Wilmington, DE, 19894-0001

Tel: (302) 594-5000     Fax: (302) 594-5400     www.herc.com

*Mfr. specialty chemicals, plastics, film and fibers, coatings, resins, food ingredients.*

**Hercules Chemicals Ltd., 31 London Rd., Reigate, Surrey RH2 9YA UK**

Tel: 44-1737-242434   Fax: 44-1737-224287   Contact: Charles Murray

## HERMAN MILLER INC.

855 East Main, Zeeland, MI, 49464

Tel: (616) 654-3000     Fax: (616) 654-5385     www.hermanmiller.com

*Mfr. office furnishings.*

**Geiger Brickel / Herman Miller, 48/50 St. John Street, London EC1M 4DT, UK**

**Herman Miller Ltd., The Bond, 180-182 Fazeley Street, Birmingham B5 5SE, UK**

**Herman Miller Ltd., Bath Road, Chippenham SN14 0AT, UK**

**Herman Miller Ltd.,** 149 Tottenham Court Road, London W1P 0JA, UK
Tel: 44-207-388-7331

## THE HERTZ CORPORATION

225 Brae Boulevard, Park Ridge, NJ, 07656-0713
Tel: (201) 307-2000      Fax: (201) 307-2644      www.hertz.com
*Worldwide headquarters office for car rental, car leasing and equipment rental.*
**Hertz Rental Car, London, UK**

## HEWITT ASSOCIATES LLC

100 Half Day Road, Lincolnshire, IL, 60069
Tel: (847) 295-5000      Fax: (847) 295-7634      www.hewitt.com
*Employee benefits consulting firm.*
**Hewitt Associates, Prospect House, Abbey View, St. Albans Hertfordshire AL1 2QU, UK**
Tel: 44-1727-88-8200

## HEWLETT-PACKARD COMPANY

3000 Hanover Street, Palo Alto, CA, 94304-1185
Tel: (650) 857-1501      Fax: (650) 857-5518      www.hp.com
*Mfr. computing, communications and measurement products and services.*
**Hewlett-Packard Ltd., Amen Corner/Cain Rd., Bracknell, Berkshire RG12 1HN, UK**

## HEXCEL CORPORATION

281 Tresser Blvd., Stamford, CT, 06901
Tel: (203) 969-0666      Fax: (203) 358-3977      www.hexcel.com
*Honeycomb core materials, specialty chemicals, resins and epoxies.*
**Hexcel UK, 31 Coope Green, Houghton, Preston, Lancashire PRS OUR, UK**

## HICKS, MUSE, TATE & FURST INC.

200 Crescent Court, Ste. 1600, Dallas, TX, 75201
Tel: (214) 740-7300      Fax: (214) 740-7313
*Institutional investment services.*
**Hillsdown Holdings plc, Hillsdown House, 32 Hampstead High St., London NW3 1QD, UK**

## HIGH VOLTAGE ENGINEERING COMPANY

401 Edgewater Place, Ste. 680, Wakefield, MA, 01880
Tel: (781) 224-1001      Fax: (781) 224-1011
*Holding company: industrial and scientific instruments.*
**Anacom Instruments Ltd., St. Peters Rd., Maidenhead SL6 7QA, UK**

## HIGHLANDS INSURANCE COMPANY

10370 Richmond Ave., Houston, TX, 77042-4123
Tel: (713) 952-9555      Fax: (713) 952-9977      www.highlandsinsurance.com
*Engaged in commercial property and casualty insurance.*
**Highlands Ins. Co. (UK) Ltd., 117 Fenchurch St., London EC3M 5EJ, UK**

## HILLENBRAND INDUSTRIES, INC.

700 State Route 46 East, Batesville, IN, 47006
Tel: (812) 934-7000      Fax: (812) 934-1963      www.hillenbrand.com
*Holding company: mfr. hospital beds, incubators and caskets.*
**Hill-Rom Company Ltd., 89 Station Road, Ampthill Bedford MK45 2RE, UK**
Tel: 44-1525-841-737    Contact: Bob Alexander
**Hill-Rom Ltd., Clinitron House, Ashby de la Zouch, Leicestershire LE65 1JG, UK**
Tel: 44-1530-411-000    Fax: 44-1530-411-555    Contact: Michael J. Clancy

## HILLERICH & BRADSBY COMPANY INC

800 West Main St., PO Box 35700, Louisville, KY, 40202

Tel: (502) 585-5226      Fax: (502) 585-1179      www.slugger.com

*Golf, baseball and softball equipment.*

**Hillerich & Bradsby Co. Ltd., Unit B4, Brookside Park, Middleton, Manchester M24 1GS, UK**

Tel: 44-161-6548881   Fax: 44-161-6536864

## HILTON HOTELS CORPORATION

9336 Civic Center Drive, Beverly Hills, CA, 90210

Tel: (310) 278-4321      Fax: (310) 205-7880      www.hiltonhotels.com

*International hotel chain: Hilton International, Vista Hotels and Hilton National Hotels.*

**London Gatwick Airport Hilton, Gatwick Airport, Crawley, West Sussex RH6 OLL, UK**

**London Kensington Hilton, 7th Fl. 179-199 Holland Park Ave., London W11 4UH, UK**

**The Langham Hilton London, 1 Portland Place, Regent St., London W1N 4JA, UK**

## HLW INTERNATIONAL, LLP

115 Fifth Ave., New York, NY, 10003

Tel: (212) 353-4600      Fax: (212) 353-4666      www.hlw.com

*Architecture, engineering, planning and interior design.*

**HLW International, LLP, London, UK**

## HNC SOFTWARE INC.

5930 Cornerstone Court West, San Diego, CA, 92121

Tel: (858) 546-8877      Fax: (858) 799-8006      www.hnc.com

*Mfr. software to manage and detect fraud.*

**HNC Software UK Ltd., 1 Northumberland Avenue, Trafalgar Square, London WC2N 5BW, UK**

Tel: 44-207-872-5526

## HOCKMAN-LEWIS LTD.

200 Executive Drive, Ste. 320, West Orange, NJ, 07052

Tel: (973) 325-3838      Fax: (973) 325-7974      www.hockman-lewis.com

*Export management.*

**Hockman UK Ltd., Saxon House, Downside, Sunbury on Thames, Middlesex TW16 6RX UK**

## HOGAN SYSTEMS INC.

5525 LBJ Freeway, Dallas, TX, 75240

Tel: (972) 386-0020      Fax: (972) 386-0315

*Sale/distribution integrated software.*

**Hogan Systems Europe, Hogan Business Centre, Church St. W, Woking, Surrey GU21 1DJ UK**

## HOLLINGSWORTH & VOSE COMPANY

112 Washington Street, East Walpole, MA, 02032

Tel: (508) 668-0295      Fax: (508) 668-3557      www.hollingsworth-vose.com

*Mfr. technical and industrial papers and non-woven fabrics.*

**Hollingsworth & Vose Air Filtration Limited, Waterford Bridge, Kentmere Cumbria, LA89JJ, UK**

**Hollingsworth & Vose Company, Ltd., Postlip Mills, Winchcombe Glos., GL54 5BB, UK**

Tel: 44-1242-602227   Fax: 44-1242-604099   Contact: Jean Paul Francois

## HOLME ROBERTS & OWEN LLP

1700 Lincoln Street, Ste. 4100, Denver, CO, 80203

Tel: (303) 861-7000      Fax: (303) 866-0200      www.hro.com

*International law firm.*

**Holme Roberts & Owen, Heathcoat House 3/F, 20 Saville Row, London W1X 1AE UK**

Tel: 44-207-494-5600   Fax: 44-20-7287-9344

**HOLOPHANE CORPORATION**

250 East Broad Street, #1400, Columbus, OH, 43215

Tel: (740) 345-9631     Fax: (740) 349-4426     www.holophane.com

*Mfr. industry, commercial, outdoor, roadway and emergency lighting fixtures; inverters, programmable controllers.*

**Holophane Europe Ltd., Box 36, Bond Ave., Bletchley, Milton Keynes MK1 1JG UK**

**HOME PRODUCTS INTERNATIONAL, INC.**

4501 W. 47th Street, Chicago, IL, 60632

Tel: (773) 890-1010     Fax: (773) 890-0523     www.hpii.com

*Mfr. plastic household products.*

**HPI Ltd./Selfix, The Aldyrich House, London, UK**

**HONEYWELL INTERNATIONAL INC.**

101 Columbia Road, Morristown, NJ, 07962

Tel: (973) 455-2000     Fax: (973) 455-4807     www.honeywell.com

*Develop/mfr. controls for home and building, industry, space and aviation.*

**Honeywell Ltd., Arlington Business Park, Bracknell, UK-Berkshire RG12 1EB UK**

Tel: 44-1344-656-000   Fax: 44-1344-656-240

**HONEYWELL-MEASUREX DMC CORPORATION**

PO Box 490, Gaithersburg, MD, 20884

Tel: (301) 948-2450     Fax: (301) 670-0506     www.measurex.com

*Mfr. quality and process control gauges.*

**Honeywell-Measurex DMC, UK, Unit 9 Tovil Green Business Park, Maidstone, Kent ME15 6TA, UK**

Tel: 44-1622-763124   Fax: 44-1622-763123   Contact: Gérald Goubau, Pres.

**HOOD SAILMAKERS INC.**

23 Johnny Cake Hill, Middletown, RI, 02842

Tel: (401) 849-9400     Fax: (401) 849-9700     www.hood-sails.com

*Mfr. furling genoas, jibs, easy stow mainsails, and spinnakers.*

**Hood Sailmakers Ltd., Bath Rd., Lymington, Hants. SO41 3RW UK**

**HORWATH INTERNATIONAL ASSOCIATION**

415 Madison Ave., New York, NY, 10017

Tel: (212) 838-5566     Fax: (212) 838-3636     www.horwath.com

*Public accountants and auditors.*

**Horwath Clark Whitehill, Queens House - 6/F, 2 Holly Road, Twickenham Middlesex, TW1 4EG UK**

**Horwath Consulting, 8 Baker St., London W1M 1DA, UK**

Contact: James H.F.Gemmell

**HOUGHTON INTERNATIONAL INC.**

PO Box 930, Madison & Van Buren Avenues, Valley Forge, PA, 19482-0930

Tel: (610) 666-4000     Fax: (610) 666-1376     www.houghtonintl.com

*Mfr. specialty chemicals, hydraulic fluids and lubricants.*

**Houghton Vaughan PLC, Legge St., Birmingham B4 7EU, UK**

Tel: 44-121-359-6100

**Houghton Vaughan PLC, Beacon Road Ashburton, Trafford Park, Manchester MI7 IAF, UK**

Tel: 44-161-872071

## HOUSEHOLD INTERNATIONAL INC.

2700 Sanders Road, Prospect Heights, IL, 60070

Tel: (847) 564-5000      Fax: (847) 205-7452      www.household.com

*Consumer finance and credit card services.*

**Hamilton Direct Bank,  North St., Winkfield, Windsor, Berkshire SL4 4TD UK**

Tel: 44-121-233-9100

## HOWMEDICA OSTEONICS, INC.

359 Veterans Blvd., Rutherford, NJ, 07070

Tel: (201) 507-7300      Fax: (201) 935-4873      www.howmedica.com

*Mfr. of maxillofacial products (orthopedic implants).*

**Howmedica International Ltd.,  London, UK**

Tel: 44-1784-444810

## HOWMET CORPORATION

475 Steamboat Road, PO Box 1960, Greenwich, CT, 06836-1960

Tel: (203) 661-4600      Fax: (203) 661-1134      www.howmet.com

*Mfr. precision investment castings, alloys, engineering and refurbishment for jet aircraft and industrial gas turbine (IGT) engine components.*

**Exeter Alloy,  Heron Road, Exeter, Devon EX2 7LL, UK**

Tel: 44-1392-429700   Fax: 44-1392-429702   Contact: Don Thompson

**Exeter Casting,  Kestrel Way, Exeter, Devon EX2 7LG, UK**

Tel: 44-1392-429700   Fax: 44-1392-429702   Contact: Greg Willis

## HQ GLOBAL WORKPLACES INC.

1155 Connecticut Ave. NW, Washington, DC, 20036

Tel: (202) 467-8500      Fax: (202) 467-8595      www.hq.com

*Provides office outsourcing, officing solutions, including internet access, telecommunications, meeting rooms, furnished offices and team rooms, state-of-the-art videoconferencing, and trained on-site administrative support teams -*

**HQ Global Workplaces,  33 St. James's Square, London SW1Y 4JS, UK**

**HQ Global Workplaces,  28 Grosvenor Street, London W1X 9FE, UK**

## HSB GROUP (HARTFORD STEAM BOILER INSPECTION & INSURANCE CO.)

One State Street, PO Box 5024, Hartford, CT, 06102-5024

Tel: (860) 722-1866      Fax: (860) 722-5770      www.hsb.com

*Provides commercial insurance and engineering consulting services.*

**HSB Engineering Insurance Ltd.,  Aldgate House, 33 Aldgate High St., London EC3N 1AH UK**

Tel: 44-207-265-6600   Fax: 44-207-247-3529

## HUBBARD ISA INC

PO Box 415, Walpole, NH, 03431

Tel: (603) 756-3311      Fax: (603) 756-9034      www.hubbard-isa.com

*Poultry breeding R&D, poultry foundation breeding stock.*

**British United Turkeys Ltd.,  Warren Hall, Broughton Nr. Chester CH4 0EW, UK**

Tel: 44-1244-661111   Fax: 44-1244-661105   Contact: Richard Hutchinson, Mgr.

## HUBBELL INCORPORATED

584 Derby Milford Road, Orange, CT, 06477

Tel: (203) 799-4100      Fax: (203) 799-4208      www.hubbell.com

*Electrical wiring components.*

**Hubbell Limited,  Woburn Road Industrial Estate, Kempston - Bedford MK42 7SH, UK**

Tel: 44-1234-855444   Fax: 44-1234-854008

## HUCK INTERNATIONAL INC.

3724 East Columbia Street, Tucson, AZ, 85714-3415

Tel: (520) 747-9898     Fax: (520) 750-7420     www.huck.com

*Designer and manufacturer of high-performance, proprietary fasteners and fastener installation systems.*

**Huck Intl. Ltd., Unit C Stafford Park 7, Telford, Shropshire TF3 3BQ UK**

## HUNKAR LABORATORIES INC.

7007 Valley Ave., Cincinnati, OH, 45244

Tel: (513) 272-1010     Fax: (513) 272-0013     www.hunkar.com

*Process equipment for plastics industry.*

**Hunkar UK Ltd., Royex House, Aldermanbury Sq., London EC2V 7LD UK**

## HUNT CORPORATION

2005 Market Street, Philadelphia, PA, 19103

Tel: (215) 656-0300     Fax: (215) 656-3700     www.hunt-corp.com

*Mfr. office, art and craft, and presentation products.*

**Hunt Europe Ltd., Chester Hall Lane, Basilton, Essex SS13 1ND UK**

## HUNTON & WILLIAMS

951 East Byrd Street, East Tower, Richmond, VA, 23219-4074

Tel: (804) 788-8200     Fax: (804) 788-8218     www.hunton.com

*International law firm.*

**Hunton & Williams Ltd., 61/63 St. John Street, London EC1M 4AN, UK**

Tel: 44-207-427-7850   Contact: Stephen J. Horvath III

## HUNTSMAN CORPORATION

500 Huntsman Way, Salt Lake City, UT, 84108

Tel: (801) 532-5200     Fax: (801) 536-1581     www.huntsman.com

*Mfr./sales specialty chemicals, industrial chemicals and petrochemicals.*

**Huntsman Polyurethanes, Hitchen Lane, Shepton Mallet, Somerset BA4 5TZ, UK**

Tel: 44-1749-343061   Contact: R. Bonsmann

**Huntsman Polyurethanes, PO Box 54, Middlesbrough, TS90 8JA, UK**

Tel: 44-1642-433498   Contact: B. Watson

**Huntsman Tioxide, Lincoln House, 137-143 Hammersmith Road, London W14 0QL, UK**

Tel: 44-207-3317777

**Huntsman Tioxide, Moody Lane, Grimsby, N.E. Lincolnshire DN31 2SW, UK**

**Huntsman Tioxide, Tees Road, Hartlepool TS25 2DD, UK**

**Huntsman Tioxide, Haverton Hill Road, Billingham, Stockton-on-Tees TS23 1PS, UK**

Tel: 44-1642-370300

## HYATT CORPORATION

200 West Madison Street, Chicago, IL, 60606

Tel: (312) 750-1234     Fax: (312) 750-8578     www.hyatt.com

*International hotel management.*

**Hyatt Carlton Tower, Cadogan Place, London SW1Z9PY, UK**

Tel: 44-207-235-1234   Fax: 44-207-858-7085

**Hyatt Regency Birmingham, 2 Bridge St., Birmingham B1 2JZ, UK**

Tel: 44-121-643-1234   Fax: 44-121-616-2323

**The Lowndes Hyatt, Lowndes St., London SW1X 9ES, UK**

Tel: 44-207-823-1234   Fax: 44-207-235-1154

## HYPERION SOLUTIONS CORPORATION

1344 Crossman Avenue, Sunnyvale, CA, 94089

Tel: (408) 744-9500      Fax: (408) 744-0400      www.hyperion.com

*Mfr. data analysis software tools.*

**Hyperion UK, Hyperion House, Old Bracknell Lane West, Bracknell Berkshire RG12 7DD, UK**

Tel: 44-1344-664-000    Fax: 44-1344-664-001

**Hyperion UK, Axis Centre Hogarth Business Park, Burlington lane, London W4 2TH, UK**

Tel: 44-20-8995-3631    Fax: 44-20-8995-3236

**Hyperion UK, Enterprise House, Greencourts Business Park, 333 Styal Road, Manchester M22 5HY, UK**

Tel: 44-161-498-2200    Fax: 44-161-498-2210

## i2 TECHNOLOGIES, INC.

11701 Luna Road, Dallas, TX, 75234

Tel: (214) 860-6106      Fax: (214) 860-6060      www.i2.com

*Mfr. business-to-business software.*

**i2 Technologies UK, Chineham Business Park, Basingstoke Hampshire RG24 8QY, UK**

Tel: 44-1256-705-500

**i2 Technologies UK, The Priory, Stomp Road Burnham, Berkshire SL1 7LL, UK**

Tel: 44-1628-601-200

## IBM CORPORATION

New Orchard Road, Armonk, NY, 10504

Tel: (914) 765-1900      Fax: (914) 765-7382      www.ibm.com

*Information products, technology and services.*

**IBM United Kingdom Holdings Ltd., PO Box 41, North Harbour Portsmouth, Hampshire PO6 3AU, UK**

Tel: 44-1705-482949    Fax: 44-1705-22114

## IBP INC.

PO Box 515, Dakota City, NE, 68731

Tel: (402) 494-2061      Fax: (402) 241-2068      www.ibpinc.com

*Produce beef and pork, hides and associated products, animal feeds, pharmaceuticals.*

**IBP Inc., 5 Devonhurst Place - Heathfield Terrace, Chiswick, London W4 4JD UK**

Tel: 44-181-742-2888    Fax: 44-181-742-2484    Contact: Paul Garnham

## ICC INDUSTRIES INC.

460 Park Ave., New York, NY, 10022

Tel: (212) 521-1700      Fax: (212) 521-1794      www.iccchem.com

*Manufacturing and trading of chemicals, plastics and pharmaceuticals.*

**Durham Plastic Ltd., 22 Coatham Ave., Aycliffe Industrial Estate, Aycliffe County Durham DL 5 6DB, UK**

Tel: 44-1325-300-437    Fax: 44-1325-318-173    Contact: Amiram Talmon

**Frutarom (UK) Ltd., Northbridge Rd., Berkhamsted Herts. HP4 1EF, UK**

Tel: 44-1442-876-611    Fax: 44-1442-876-204    Contact: Brian Watts

**ICC Chemicals (UK) Ltd., Northbridge Rd., Berkhamsted Hertfordshire HP 4 1EF, UK**

Tel: 44-1442-877-022    Fax: 44-1442-878-899    Contact: Michael Gaine

**Pipe U.K. Ld., Aycliffe Industrial Estate, Newton Aycliffe County Durham DL5 6DB, UK**

Tel: 44-1325-308-188    Fax: 44-1325-308-159    Contact: Amiran Talmon

## ICN PHARMACEUTICALS, INC.

3300 Hyland Ave., Costa Mesa, CA, 92626

Tel: (714) 545-0100    Fax: (714) 641-7268    www.icnpharm.com

*Mfr./distribute pharmaceuticals.*

**ICN Pharmaceuticals, Inc., Cedarwood, Chineham Business Park - Crockford Lane, Basingstoke RG24 8WD, Hampshire UK**

Tel: 44-125-670-7744

## ICORE INTERNATIONAL INC.

180 North Wolfe Road, Sunnyvale, CA, 94086

Tel: (408) 732-5400    Fax: (408) 720-8507    www.icoreintl.com

*Harness and conduit systems, battery connectors, etc.*

**Icore International Ltd, Leigh Road, Slough, Berkshire SC14BB, UK**

Tel: 44-1753-574134

## ICP

1815 West County Road 54, Tiffin, OH, 44883

Tel: (419) 447-6216    Fax: (419) 447-1878

*Magazines/directories for computer software marketing.*

**ICP Publishing Ltd., 37 Albert Embankment, London SE1 7TL, UK**

## IDENTIX INCORPORATED

510 North Pastoria Avenue, Sunnyvale, CA, 94085

Tel: (408) 731-2000    Fax: (408) 739-3308    www.identix.com

*Mfr. fingerprint verification systems.*

**Identix UK, Winton, Longmoor Lane, Mortimer Reading RG7 3RP, UK**

Tel: 44-118-933-1456    Fax: 44-118-933-1117

## IDEX CORPORATION

630 Dundee Road, Ste. 400, Northbrook, IL, 60062

Tel: (847) 498-7070    Fax: (847) 498-3940    www.idexcorp.com

*Mfr. industrial pumps, lubrication systems, metal fabrication equipment, bending and clamping devices.*

**Band-It Co. Ltd., Speedwell Industrial Estate, Staveley, Chesterfield S43 3PF, UK**

**Johnson Pump (UK) Limited, Highfield Industrial Estate, Edison Road - Eastbourne, East Sussex BN23 6PT, UK**

## IDG BOOKS WORLDWIDE INC.

919 E. Hillsdale Blvd., Foster City, CA, 94404

Tel: (650) 655-3000    Fax: (650) 655-3299    www.idgbooks.com

*Publisher of computer and self-help guidebooks, including "For Dummies" brand.*

**IDG Books Worldwide, London, UK**

Tel: 44-207-831-9252

## IDT CORPORATION

520 Broad Street, Newark, NJ, 07102

Tel: (973) 438-1000    Fax: (973) 438-4002    www.idt.net

*Engaged in domestic and international long distance telecommunications.*

**IDT Europe, 69-77 Paul Street, London EC2A 4NQ, UK**

Tel: 44-207-549-6000    Fax: 44-207-549-6001

## IHS (INFORMATION HANDLING SERVICES)

15 Inverness Way East, Englewood, CO, 80112

Tel: (303) 397-2300    Fax: (303) 397-2633    www.ihs.com

*Leading provider of technical engineering information.*

**Technical Indexes Ltd., Willoughby Rd., Bracknell, Berkshire RG12 4DW, UK**

## IKON OFFICE SOLUTIONS

70 Valley Stream Parkway, Malvern, PA, 19355

Tel: (610) 296-8000     Fax: (610) 408-7022     www.ikon.com

*Provider of office technology solutions.*

**Ikon Office Solutions, 30 Cowcross St., London EC1M 6DQ, UK**

Tel: 44-207-253-4545

**Ikon Office Solutions, Ullswater Crescent, Coulsdon, Surrey CR5 2EQ, UK**

Tel: 44-181-763-1010

## IKOS SYSTEMS, INC.

19050 Pruneridge Avenue, Cupertino, CA, 95014

Tel: (408) 255-4567     Fax: (408) 366-8699     www.ikos.com

*Mfr. hardware and software.*

**IKOS Systems, Inc., Stylus House - London Road, Bracknell Berkshire RG12 2UT, UK**

Tel: 44-1-344-306-565

## PERKINELMER ILC INC.

399 Java Drive, Sunnyvale, CA, 94089

Tel: (408) 745-7900     Fax: (408) 744-0829     www.perkinelmer.com

*Mfr. specialty lighting products for medical, industrial and scientific applications.*

**ILC Q-Arc, Ltd., Saxon Way, Bar Hill, Cambridge CB3 85L UK**

Tel: 44-195-478-2266    Fax: 44-195-478-2993    Contact: John Littlechild, Pres.    Emp: 100

## ILLINOIS TOOL WORKS (ITW)

3600 West Lake Ave., Glenview, IL, 60025-5811

Tel: (847) 724-7500     Fax: (847) 657-4268     www.itw.com

*Mfr. gears, tools, fasteners, sealants, plastic and metal components for industrial, medical, etc.*

**ITW Ltd., 470 Bath Rd., Cippenham, Slough Berkshire SL1 6BJ, UK**

## IMG (INTERNATIONAL MANAGEMENT GROUP)

1360 East Ninth Street, Ste. 100, Cleveland, OH, 44114

Tel: (216) 522-1200     Fax: (216) 522-1145     www.imgworld.com

*Manages athletes, sports academies and real estate facilities worldwide.*

**East Sussex National Golf Club, Little Horstead - Uckfield, East Sussex TN22 5ES, UK**

Tel: 44-4522-766-777    Fax: 49-4522-766-717

**European Golf Design, 75 Windsor Road, Chobham Surrey GU24 8LD, UK**

Tel: 44-1276-855-955    Fax: 44-1276-856-190

**IMG, Bentinck House, 3-8 Bolsover Street, London W1P 7HG, UK**

Tel: 44-207-486-8011    Fax: 44-207-487-3116

**IMG, Hogarth Business Park Level 5, Burlington Lane, Chiswick London W4 2TH, UK**

Tel: 44-208-233-5300    Fax: 44-208-233-5301

**IMG, TWI House - 23 Eyot Gardens, Hammersmith, London W6 9TR, UK**

Tel: 44-208-233-5400    Fax: 44-208-233-5801

**IMG London, Pier House, Strand On The Green, Chiswick London W4 3NN, UK**

Tel: 44-181-233-5000

**Media House IMG Artists, Lovell House. 610 Chiswick High Road, London W4 5RX, UK**

Tel: 44-208-233-5800    Fax: 44-208-233-5801

**The Wynyard Club, Wellington Drive, Wynyard Park, Billingham, TS22 5QJ UK**

Tel: 44-1-740-644-399    Fax: 44-1-740-644-599

**IMO INDUSTRIES, DIV. COLFAX INC.**

9211 Forest Hill Ave., Richmond, VA, 23235

Tel: (804) 560-4070        Fax: (804) 560-4076        www.imochain.com

*Mfr./support mechanical and electronic controls, chains and engineered power products.*

**IMO Industries (UK) Ltd., TransInstruments Div.,  Lennon Rd., Basingstoke, Hampshire RG22 4AW UK**

**Morse Controls Ltd.,  Christopher Martin Rd., Basildon, Essex SS14 3ES, UK**

**IMPAC GROUP, INC.**

1950 N. Ruby Street, Melrose Park, IL, 60160

Tel: (708) 344-9100        Fax: (708) 344-9113        www.klearfold.com

*Mfr. paper and plastic packaging for the entertainment and cosmetics industries.*

**Tinsley Robor Plc,  Drayton House, Drayton Chichester, West Sussex PQ20 6EW, UK**

Tel: 44-1243-774000   Fax: 44-1243-774567

**IMPCO TECHNOLOGIES, INC.**

16804 Gridley Place, Cerritos, CA, 90703

Tel: (562) 860-6666        Fax: (562) 809-1240        www.impco.ws

*Mfr. fuel control processors.*

**IMPCO Industrial Engine Systems Division,  3 Dands Drive, Middleton Cheney, Banbury, Oxon OX17 2NN, UK**

Tel: 44-1295-712196

**IMPCO-BERU Technologies Ltd.,  West Wellow, Romsey, Hampshire SO51 6DB, UK**

Tel: 44-1794-323-966   Fax: 44-1794-323-916

**IMR GLOBAL**

26750 US Highway. 19 North, Ste. 500, Clearwater, FL, 33761

Tel: (727) 797-7080        Fax: (727) 791-8152        www.imrglobal.com

*Provides application software, e-business and information technology solutions and outsourcing services to business.*

**IMR Intuitive Group Limited,  London, UK**

**IMR United Kingdom,  Link House, St. Mary's Way, Chesham, Buckinghamshire HP5 1HR UK**

Tel: 44-1-494-792792   Fax: 44-1-494-791059

**IMS HEALTH INCORPORATED**

200 Nyala Farms, Westport, CT, 06880

Tel: (203) 222-4200        Fax: (203) 222-4276        www.imshealth.com

*Provides sales management reports and prescription tracking reports for pharmaceutical and health-care companies.*

**IMS Health UK,  7 Harewood Avenue, London NW1 6JB, UK**

Tel: 44-20-7393-5888

**INCYTE GENOMICS, INC.**

3160 Porter Dr., Palo Alto, CA, 94304

Tel: (650) 855-0555        Fax: (650) 855-0572        www.incyte.com

*Engaged in development of genetic information for drug development.*

**Incyte Genomics Botanic UK,  100 Hills Road, Cambridge CB2 1FF, UK**

Tel: 44-1223-454-900

## INDUCTOTHERM CORPORATION

10 Indel Ave., PO Box 157, Rancocas, NJ, 08073-0157

Tel: (609) 267-9000     Fax: (609) 267-3537     www.inductotherm.com

*Mfr. induction melting furnaces, induction power supplies, charging and preheating systems, automatic pouring systems and computer control systems.*

**Inductotherm Europe Ltd., The Furlong, Droitwich, Worcestershire WR9 9AH UK**

Tel: 44-1905-79-5100    Contact: Graham E. Hawkins

## INDUSTRIAL ACOUSTICS COMPANY

1160 Commerce Ave., Bronx, NY, 10462

Tel: (718) 931-8000     Fax: (718) 863-1138     www.industrialacoustics.com

*Design/mfr. acoustic structures for sound conditioning and noise control.*

**Industrial Acoustics Co. Ltd., Walton House, Central Trading Estate, Staines, Middlesex UK**

## INFOGRAMES, INC.

417 Fifth Avenue, New York, NY, 10016

Tel: (212) 726-6500     Fax: (212) 679-3224     www.infogrames.com

*Mfr. video games.*

**Infogrames UK, 21 Castle Street, Castlefield Manchester M3 4SW, UK**

**Infogrames UK, Landmark House, Hammersmith Bridge Road, London W6 9DP, UK**

Tel: 44-181-222-9700

## INFONET SERVICES CORPORATION

2100 East Grand Ave., El Segundo, CA, 90245-1022

Tel: (310) 335-2600     Fax: (310) 335-4507     www.infonet.com

*Provider of Internet services and electronic messaging services.*

**Infonet UK, Ltd., Heathcoat House, 20 Saville Row, London W1X 1AE, UK**

Tel: 44-207-890-7500    Fax: 44-207-465-0453

## INFORMATION BUILDERS INC.

Two Penn Plaza, New York, NY, 10121-2898

Tel: (212) 736-4433     Fax: (212) 967-6406     www.ibi.com

*Develop/mfr./services computer software.*

**Information Builders (UK) Ltd., Station House, Harrow Rd., Wembley, Middlesex HA9 6DE UK**

## INFORMATION MANAGEMENT ASSOCIATES, INC.

One Corporate Drive, Ste. 414, Shelton, CT, 06484

Tel: (203) 925-6800     Fax: (203) 925-1170     www.ima-inc.com

*Sales/distribution of software for use by telephone call centers; consult, support and maintenance services.*

**IMA Software, Suite 6.04 Exchange Tower, One Harbour Exchange Square, London E14 9GB UK**

Tel: 44-207-512-1188

## INFORMATION RESOURCES, INC. (IRI)

150 N. Clinton St., Chicago, IL, 60661

Tel: (312) 726-1221     Fax: (312) 726-0360     www.infores.com

*Provides bar code scanner services for retail sales organizations; processes, analyzes and sells data from the huge database created from these services.*

**IRI InfoScan LTD., Eagle House, The Ring, Bracknell Berkshire RG12 1HB, UK**

Tel: 44-1344-746000    Fax: 44-1344-746001

## INFORMIX CORPORATION

4100 Bohannon Drive, Menlo Park, CA, 95025

Tel: (650) 926-6300    Fax: (650) 926-6593    www.informix.com

*Designs and produces database management software, connectivity interfaces and gateways, and other computer applications.*

**Informix Software Ltd., Broadgate Court, 199 Bishopsgate, London EC2M 3TY, UK**

Tel: 44-207-395-5900  Fax: 44-207-814-7368

**Informix Software, Ltd. Europe Hdqtrs., 6 New Square, Bedfont Lakes, Feltham Middlesex TW14 8HA, UK**

Tel: 44-181-818-1000

## INFOSPACE, INC.

601 108th Avenue, NE, Ste. 1200, Spokane, WA, 98004

Tel: (425) 201-6100    Fax: (425) 201-6163    www.infospace.com

*Provides internet content syndications, including web information on Yellow and White Pages Directories, maps, etc.*

**TDL InfoSpace UK Ltd., 1 Farnham Road, Guildford Surrey GU2 5RG, UK**

Tel: 44-1483-549013   Fax: 44-1483-549133

## INGERSOLL-RAND COMPANY

200 Chestnut Ridge Road, Woodcliff Lake, NJ, 07675

Tel: (201) 573-0123    Fax: (201) 573-3172    www.ingersoll-rand.com

*Mfr. compressors, rock drills, air tools, door hardware, ball bearings.*

**Ingersoll-Dresser Pumps (UK) Ltd., Queens Way, Team Valley Trading Estate, Gateshead Tyne & Wear NE11, UK**

**Ingersoll-Rand Holdings Ltd., 2 Chorley New Rd., Bolton, Lancashire BL6 6JN, UK**

Tel: 44-120-469-0690  Fax: 44-120-469-0388

**Ingersoll-Rand Sales Co. Ltd., PO Box 23, Southmoor Rd., Wythenshawe, Manchester M23 9LN UK**

## INGRAM MICRO INC.

PO Box 25125, 1600 E. St. Andrew Place, Santa Ana, CA, 92799

Tel: (714) 566-1000    Fax: (714) 566-7940    www.ingrammicro.com

*Engaged in wholesale distribution of microcomputer products.*

**Ingram Micro Inc., London, UK**

## INKTOMI CORPORATION

4100 East Third Avenue, Foster City, CA, 94404

Tel: (650) 653-2800    Fax: (650) 653-2801    www.iktomi.com

*Mfr. software to boost speeds of computer networks.*

**Inktomi Corporation, Aldwych House - 81 Aldwych, London WC2B 4HN, UK**

Tel: 44-207.430.5700

## INPRISE CORPORATION

100 Enterprise Way, Scotts Valley, CA, 95066

Tel: (831) 431-1000    Fax: (831) 431-4141    www.inprise.com

*Mfr. development software.*

**Inprise (UK) Ltd., 8 Pavilions, Ruscombe Business Park, Twyford Berkshire RG10 9NN, UK**

Tel: 44-118-932-0022

## INSTINET

875 Third Ave., New York, NY, 10022

Tel: (212) 310-9500    Fax: (212) 832-5183    www.instinet.com

*Online investment brokerage.*

**Instinet, London, UK**

## INSTRON CORPORATION

100 Royal Street, Canton, MA, 02021-1089

Tel: (781) 575-5000  Fax: (781) 575-5751  www.instron.com

*Mfr. material testing instruments.*

**Instron Ltd., Coronation Rd., High Wycombe, Buckinghamshire HP12 3SY, UK**

Tel: 44-1494-464646

## INSUL-8 CORPORATION

10102 F Street, Omaha, NE, 68127

Tel: (402) 339-9300  Fax: (402) 339-9627  www.insul-8.com

*Mfr. mobile electrification products; conductor bar and festoon equipment.*

**Insul-8 Ltd., One Michigan Ave., Salford M5 2GL, UK**

## INTEGRATED DEVICE TECHNOLOGY, INC.

2975 Stender Way, Santa Clara, CA, 95054

Tel: (408) 727-6116  Fax: (408) 492-8674  www.idt.com

*Mfr. high-performance semiconductors and modules.*

**Integrated Device Technology, Ltd., Prime House, Barnett Wood Lane, Leatherhead, Surrey KT22 7DE, UK**

Tel: 44-1372-363339  Fax: 44-1372-378851

## INTEGRATED SILICON SOLUTION, INC.

2231 Lawson Lane, Santa Clara, CA, 95054-3311

Tel: (408) 588-0800  Fax: (408) 588-0805  www.issiusa.com

*Mfr. high-speed memory chips and SRAMs.*

**Integrated Silicon Solution, Inc., Devon, UK**

Tel: 44-1803--840-110

## INTEL CORPORATION

Robert Noyce Bldg., 2200 Mission College Blvd., Santa Clara, CA, 95052-8119

Tel: (408) 765-8080  Fax: (408) 765-1739  www.intel.com

*Mfr. semiconductor, microprocessor and micro-communications components and systems.*

**Intel Corporation (UK) Ltd. (European Hdqtrs.), Pipers Way, Swindon SN3 1RJ, UK**

Tel: 44-1793-403-000

## INTELLI QUEST INFORMATION GROUP, INC.

1250 South Capital of Texas Hwy., Bldg. 1, Ste. 600, Austin, TX, 78746-6464

Tel: (512) 329-0808  Fax: (512) 329-0888  www.intelliquest.com

*Provides information-based services designed exclusively to help technology companies and Internet marketers.*

**IntelliQuest Information Group, Inc., Shand House, 14-20 Shand St., London SE1 2ES UK**

Tel: 44-207-357-9255  Fax: 44-207-403-1680

## INTELLIGROUP, INC.

499 Thornall Street, Edison, NJ, 08837

Tel: (732) 590-1600  Fax: (732) 362-2100  www.intelligroup.com

*Provides systems integration, customer software and Internet application development.*

**Intelligroup Europe Ltd., Del Monte House, London Road, Staines Middlesex TW18 4JD, UK**

Tel: 44-1784-41-2000

**INTER-CONTINENTAL HOTELS**

3 Ravina Drive, Suite 2900, Atlanta, GA, 30346-2149

Tel: (770) 604-2000     Fax: (770) 604-5403        www.interconti.com

*Worldwide hotel and resort accommodations.*

**Inter-Continental Hotels,  The Thameside Centre, Kew Bridge Road, Brentford Middlesex TW8 OEB, UK**

Tel: 44-181-847-3711   Fax: 44-181-569-9852

**May Fair Inter-Continental London,  Stratton St., London W1A 2AN, UK**

Tel: 44-207-629-7777   Fax: 44-207-629-1459

**INTERDEAN INTERCONEX,  INC**

55 Hunter Lane, Elmsford, NY, 10523-1317

Tel: (914) 347-6600     Fax: (914) 347-0129        www.interdeannterconex.com

*Freight forwarding.*

**Interconex Europe Ltd.,  Spilsby Rd., Harold Hill Ind. Estate, Romford, Essex RM3 8SB UK**

Tel: 44-1708-374-811   Fax: 44-1708-374-810   Contact: Tim Esposito

**INTERFACE, INC.**

2859 Paces Ferry Rd., Ste. 2000, Atlanta, GA, 30339

Tel: (770) 437-6800     Fax: (770) 803-6913        www.interfaceinc.com

*Mfr. commercial broadloom carpet, textile, chemicals, architectural products and access flooring systems.*

**Interface Europe,  Ashlyns Hall, Chesham Road, Berkhamstead, Hertfordshire HP4 2ST, UK**

Tel: 44-1442-285-000

**Interface Fabrics Ltd.,  Hopton Mills, Mirfield West Yorkshire, UK**

Tel: 44-1924-491666

**INTERGEN (INTERNATIONAL GENERATING CO., LTD.)**

One Bowdoin Square, 5th Fl., Boston, MA, 02114

Tel: (617) 747-1777     Fax: (617) 747-1778        www.intergen.com

*Global power and fuel asset development company; develops/owns/operates electric power plants and related distribution facilities.*

**InterGen (UK), Ltd.,  20 St. James's St., London SWIA IES, UK**

Tel: 44-207-543-3300   Fax: 44-207-839-0905

**INTERGRAPH CORPORATION**

One Madison Industrial Park, Huntsville, AL, 35894-0001

Tel: (256) 730-2000     Fax: (256) 730-7898        www.intergraph.com

*Develop/mfr. interactive computer graphic systems.*

**Intergraph (UK) Ltd.,  Delta Business Park, Great Western Way, Swindon Wiltshire SN5 7XP, UK**

Tel: 44-1793-619999   Fax: 44-1793-618508

**INTERMAGNETICS GENERAL CORPORATION**

450 Old Niskayuna Road, PO Box 461, Latham, NY, 12110-0461

Tel: (518) 782-1122     Fax: (518) 783-2601        www.igc.com

*Design/mfr. superconductive magnets, magnetic systems and conductors, cryogenic products, refrigerants.*

**APD Cryogenics,  5 Jupiter House, Calleva Industrial Park, Aldermaston, Berkshire RG7 8NN UK**

**Intermagnetics General (Europe) Ltd.,  PO Box 181, Oxford OX44 7AB, UK**

**INTERMEC TECHNOLOGIES CORPORATION**

6001 36th Ave. West, PO Box 4280, Everett, WA, 98203-9280

Tel: (425) 348-2600     Fax: (425) 355-9551        www.intermec.com

*Mfr./distributor automated data collection systems.*

**Intermec International,  Inc.,  Sovereign House, Vastern Road, Reading RG1 8BT, UK**

Tel: 44-118-987-9400   Fax: 44-118-987-9401

**Intermec Technologies UK Ltd., 2 Bennet Court - Bennet Road, Reading Berkshire, RG2 0QX, UK**
Tel: 44-118-923-0800    Fax: 44-118-923-0801

## INTERNAP NETWORK SERVICES CORPORATION
601 Union Street, Ste. 1000, Seattle, WA, 98101
Tel: (206) 441-8800      Fax: (206) 264-1833      www.internap.com
*Mfr. software for data routing.*
**InterNap Network Services Corp. UK, 42 Brook Street - Ste. 208, London W1Y 1YB, UK**
Contact: Martin Burvill, VP

## INTERNATIONAL CLOSEOUT EXCHANGE SYSTEMS INC.
220 W. 19th Street, Ste.1200, New York, NY, 10011
Tel: (212) 647-8901      Fax: (212) 647-8900      www.icesinc.com
*Online service listing off-price merchandise.*
**ICES (UK) Ltd., PO Box 2035, Manchester M60 3EX, UK**

## INTERNATIONAL COMPONENTS CORPORATION
420 N. May Street, Chicago, IL, 60622
Tel: (312) 829-2525      Fax: (312) 829-0213      www.icc-charge.com
*Mfr./sale/services portable DC battery chargers.*
**International Components Corp. (UK) Ltd., Kamone House, 63 St. Leonards Rd., Windsor, Bray, Berkshire SL4 3BX UK**

## INTERNATIONAL FLAVORS & FRAGRANCES INC.
521 West 57th Street, New York, NY, 10019-2960
Tel: (212) 765-5500      Fax: (212) 708-7132      www.iff.com
*Design/mfr. flavors, fragrances and aroma chemicals.*
**International Flavors & Fragrances, Ltd., Commonwealth House, Hammersmith Intl. Centre, London W6 8DN, UK**
Tel: 44-181-741-5771    Fax: 44-181-741-2566

## INTERNATIONAL LOTTERY & TOTALIZATOR SYSTEMS INC.
2131 Faraday Ave., Carlsbad, CA, 92008
Tel: (760) 931-4000      Fax: (760) 931-1789      www.ilts.com
*Mfr. fluid meters, counting devices; radio/TV and electronic stores.*
**Totalizator Systems (UK) Ltd., 241 Horton Rd., Yiewsley, West Drayton UB7 8HT, UK**

## INTERNATIONAL PAPER COMPANY
2 Manhattanville Road, Purchase, NY, 10577
Tel: (914) 397-1500      Fax: (914) 397-1596      www.ipaper.com
*Mfr./distributor container board, paper and wood products.*
**Anitec Image Ltd., 3&4 Suffolk Way, Drayton Rd., Abingdon-Oxon OX14 5JX, UK**
**Aussedat Rey Ltd., Hill House, McDonald Rd., Highgate Hill, London N19 SNA UK**
**Bergvik Sales Ltd., Glen House, Stag Place, Victoria, London SW1E 5AG UK**
**Boardcraft Ltd., Howard Rd., Eaton Socon, St. Neots, Huntingdon PE19 3ET UK**
**Forest Lines Agencies Ltd., 14A Orwell House, Ferry Lane, Felixstowe, Suffolk IP11 8QL UK**
**Horsell Graphic Industries, Howley Park Estate, Morley, Leeds LS27 0QT UK**
**Horsell PLC, Nepshaw Lane S., Gildersome, Morley, Leeds LS27 7JQ UK**
**Horsell Systems Ltd., Holt Court North, Aston Science Park, Birmingham B7 4AX UK**
**Iford-Anitec, 14-22 Tottenham St., London W1P 0AH, UK**
**Ilford Ltd., Town Lane, Mobberley, Knutsford, Cheshire WA16 7HA UK**
**International Paper Co. Ltd., 4/5 Grosvenor Pl., London SW1X 7HD, UK**
**Intl. Paper Cont., Road Three, Industrial Estate, Winsford, Cheshire CW7 3RJ UK**
**IP Property Co. Ltd., Road Three, Industrial Estate, Winsford, Cheshire CW7 3RJ UK**
**Masonite Co. Ltd., West Wing, Jason House, Kerry Hill, Horsforth, Leeds LS18 4JR, UK**

Polyrey Ltd., Mattey House, 128-136 High St., Edgware, Middlesex HA8 7EL, UK

Strathmore-Beckett Intl. Ltd., 165 Dukes Ride, Crowthorne, Berkshire RG11 6DR, UK

Veratec Ltd., 4/5 Grosvenor Pl., London SW1X 7HD, UK

Veratec Ltd., First Field Lane, Braunton, N. Devon EX33 1ER, UK

## INTERNATIONAL RECTIFIER CORPORATION

233 Kansas Street, El Segundo, CA, 90245

Tel: (310) 322-3331     Fax: (310) 322-3332     www.irf.com

*Mfr. power semiconductor components.*

International Rectifier (Great Britain) Ltd., Holland Rd., Hurst Green, Oxted, Surrey RH8 9BB UK

Tel: 44-1883-732020   Fax: 44-1883-733410

## INTERNATIONAL SPECIALTY PRODUCTS, INC.

1361 Alps Rd., Wayne, NJ, 07470

Tel: (877) 389-3083     Fax: (973) 628-4117     www.ispcorp.com

*Mfr. specialty chemical products.*

ISP (Great Britain) Co. Ltd., Tilson Road, Wythenshawe, Manchester M23 9PH, UK

Tel: 44-161-998-1122   Fax: 44-161-998-6218

ISP Europe, 40 Alan Turing Road, Surrey Research Park, Guilford Surrey, UK

Tel: 44-1483-407600   Fax: 44-1483-302175

## INTER-TEL INC.

7300 W. Boston Street, Chandler, AZ, 85226

Tel: (602) 961-9000     Fax: (602) 961-1370     www.inter-tel.com

*Design/mfr. business communications systems.*

Inter-Tel Equipment UK Ltd., 9 Enterprise Ct., Newton Close Park Farm, Wellingborough, Northants. NN8 3UX UK

## INTERVOICE INC.

17811 Waterview Pkwy., Dallas, TX, 75206

Tel: (972) 454-8000     Fax: (972) 454-8707     www.intervoice.com

*Mfr. voice automation systems and provides interactive information solutions.*

InterVoice-Brite Limited, Brite Court - Park Road, Gatley, Cheshire SK8 4HZ, UK

Tel: 44-161-495-1000   Fax: 44-161-495-1001

InterVoice-Brite Limited, Brannan House, 4 The Cambridge Business Park, Milton Road Cambridge, CB4 0WZ UK

Tel: 44-1223-423-366   Fax: 44-1223-425-554

## INTRALOX INC.

201 Laitram Lane, New Orleans, LA, 70123

Tel: (504) 733-0463     Fax: (504) 734-0063     www.intralox.com

*Mfr. plastic, modular conveyor belts and accessories.*

Intralox Ltd., 3rd Ave. Bldg. 69, Pensnett Trading Estate, Kingswinford, West Midlands DY6 7PP UK

## INTRUSION.COM, INC.

1101 East Arapaho Road, Richardson, TX, 75081

Tel: (972) 234-6400     Fax: (972) 234-1467     www.intrusion.com

*Mfr. security software.*

Intrusion.Com, Ltd., Ancells Court Ancells Business Park, Fleet, Hants GU 138UY, UK

## INTUIT INC.

2535 Garcia Avenue, Mountain View, CA, 94043

Tel: (650) 944-6000     Fax: (650) 944-3699     www.intuit.com

*Mfr. personal finance software.*

Intuit UK Ltd., PO Box 2093, Swindon SN5 8TR, UK

Tel: 44-1793-699500

## INVENTION SUBMISSION CORPORATION

217 Ninth Street, Pittsburgh, PA, 15222

Tel: (412) 288-1300    Fax: (412) 288-1354    www.inventionsubmission.com

*Inventor assistance services.*

**Invention Submission Corp., 50 New Bond St., London W1Y 9HA, UK**

## INVISION TECHNOLOGIES, INC.

7151 Gateway Blvd., Newark, CA, 94560

Tel: (510) 739-2400    Fax: (510) 739-6400    www.invision-tech.com

*Mfr. detection systems to scan carry-on bags.*

**Invision Technologies UK, Silkin House - 5-7 Bath Road, Heathrow Hounslow TW6 2AA, UK**

Tel: 44-208-754-9540    Fax: 44-208-754-9541

## IOMEGA CORPORATION

1821 West 4000 South, Roy, UT, 84067

Tel: (801) 778-4494    Fax: (801) 778-3450    www.iomega.com

*Mfr. data storage products.*

**Iomega, 7 Mt. Mews, High St., Hampton-on-Thames, Middlesex UK**

## IONICS INC.

65 Grove Street, Watertown, MA, 02172

Tel: (617) 926-2500    Fax: (617) 926-4304    www.ionics.com

*Mfr. desalination equipment.*

**Ionics UK Ltd., 16 Endeavour Way, London SW19 8UH, UK**

## IPSEN INDUSTRIES INC.

894 Ipsen Rd., Cherry Valley, IL, 61016

Tel: (815) 332-4941    Fax: (815) 332-7625    www.ipsen-intl.com

*Heat treating equipment.*

**Ipsen UK Ltd., UNIT 1A Nechlls Business Centre, 31 Bollman St., Nechlls, Birmingham B74RP UK**

Tel: 44-121-359-5959    Fax: 44-121-359-5995    Contact: Rob Neale, Mgr.

## THE IT GROUP, INC.

2790 Mosside Boulevard, Monroeville, PA, 15146-2792

Tel: (412) 372-7701    Fax: (412) 373-7135    www.theitgroup.com

*Engaged in environmental management; hazardous waste clean-up services.*

**IT Group UK, London, UK**

## ITT INDUSTRIES, INC.

4 West Red Oak Lane, White Plains, NY, 10604

Tel: (914) 641-2000    Fax: (914) 696-2950    www.ittind.com

*Mfr. pumps, systems and services to move and control water/fluids and produces connectors, switches, keypads and cabling used in computing, telecommunications, aerospace and industrial applications, as well as network services.*

**Jabsco (Marlow Pumps) UK, Thaxted Road, Saffron Walden Essex CB10 2UR, UK**

Tel: 44-1799-513893    Fax: 44-1799-513902

**Jabsco (UK), Bingley Road - Hoddesdon, Hertfordshire EN11, UK**

Tel: 44-1992-450145    Fax: 44-1992-467132

**Network Systems & Services/UK, Jays Close - Viables Estate, Hants RG22 4BW Basingstoke, UK**

Tel: 44-1256-3116    Fax: 44-1256-840556

## ITT-GOULDS PUMPS INC.

240 Fall Street, Seneca Falls, NY, 13148

Tel: (315) 568-2811    Fax: (315) 568-2418    www.gouldspumps.com

*Mfr. industrial and water systems pumps.*

**Chemquip Limited, High Peak Stockport, Cheshire SK23 6AR, UK**

**ITT Industries - Goulds Pumps, White Hart House, London Road, Blackwater Camberley, Surrey GU19 9AD UK**

Tel: 44-1276-600646

**Jabsco (Marlow Pumps) UK, Thaxted Road, Saffron Walden Essex CB10 2UR, UK**

Tel: 44-1799-513893    Fax: 44-1799-513902

**Plenty Mirrlees Pumps Ltd., Hambridge Road, Newbury, Berkshire RG14 5TR UK**

Tel: 44-1635-42363

## ITW DEVCON PLEXUS

30 Endicott Street, Danvers, MA, 01923

Tel: (978) 777-1100    Fax: (978) 774-0516    www.devcon-equip.com

*Mfr. filled epoxies, urethanes, adhesives and metal treatment products.*

**Devcon UK Ltd., Brunel Close, Park Farm Estate, Wellingborough, Northantshire UK**

Tel: 44-1-933-675299

## ITW RANSBURG FINISHING SYSTEMS

320 Phillips Ave., Toledo, OH, 43612

Tel: (419) 470-2000    Fax: (419) 470-2112    www.itwransburg.com

*Mfr. liquid electrostatic paint application equipment.*

**ITW Ransburg, Ringwood Rd., Bournemouth, Hants BH11 9LH UK**

**ITW Switches, Norway Rd., Portsmouth PO3 5HT, UK**

## IXL ENTERPRISES, INC.

1600 Peachtree Street NW, Atlanta, GA, 30309

Tel: (404) 279-1000    Fax: (404) 279-3801    www.ixl.com

*Provides on-line development services.*

**IXL UK, Elizabeth House, 39 York Road, London SE1 7NQ, UK**

Tel: 44-20-7071-6300    Fax: 44-20-7071-6666

## IXYS CORPORATION

3540 Bassett Street, Santa Clara, CA, 95054

Tel: (408) 982-0700    Fax: (408) 748-9788    www.ixys.com

*Mfr. semiconductors and modules.*

**IXYS Semiconductor, Providence House, Forest Road Binfield, Bracknell Berkshire RG12 5HP, UK**

Tel: 44-1344-482820

## J. WALTER THOMPSON COMPANY

466 Lexington Ave., New York, NY, 10017

Tel: (212) 210-7000    Fax: (212) 210-6944    www.jwt.com

*International advertising and marketing services.*

**J. Walter Thompson Co., London, UK**

## JACOBS ENGINEERING GROUP INC.

1111 S. Arroyo Parkway, Pasadena, CA, 91105

Tel: (626) 578-3500    Fax: (626) 578-6916    www.jacobs.com

*Engineering, design and consulting; construction and construction management; process plant maintenance.*

**Jacobs Engineering Ltd., England, UK**

Tel: 44-161-80-4088    Fax: 44-161-474-7745    Contact: T. Michael Tate, Dir.    Emp: 256

**Jacobs Engineering Ltd., Knollys House, 17 Addiscombe Rd., Croydon, Surrey CR0 6SR UK**

Tel: 44-181-688-4477　Fax: 44-181-649-9213　Contact: Richard J. Slater, VP Mng. Dir.　Emp: 184

## JAMESBURY CORPORATION

640 Lincoln Street, Box 15004, Worcester, MA, 01615-0004

Tel: (508) 852-0200　　Fax: (508) 852-8172　　www.jamesbury.com

*Mfr. valves and accessories.*

**Jamesbury Ltd., Rustington Trading Estate Unit A-1, Dominion Way, Rustington, W. Sussex BN16 3HQ UK**

## JCI JONES CHEMICALS, INC.

808 Sarasota Quay, Sarasota, FL, 34236

Tel: (941) 330-1537　　Fax: (941) 330-9657　　www.jcichem.com

*Repackager of chlorine and other chemicals used in water purification.*

**Jones Chemicals, Inc., London, UK**

Tel: 44-20-7407-2212

## JDA SOFTWARE GROUP, INC.

14400 N. 87th St., Scottsdale, AZ, 85260-3649

Tel: (480) 308-3000　　Fax: (480) 308-3001　　www.jda.com

*Developer of information management software for retail, merchandising, distribution and store management.*

**JDA International, Ltd., 4-6 Churchill Court, Hortons Way, Westerham Kent TN16 BT1, UK**

Tel: 44-1959-491-000　Fax: 44-1959-491-001

## JDS UNIPHASE CORPORATION

210 Baypoint Pkwy., San Jose, CA, 95134

Tel: (408) 434-1800　　Fax: (408) 954-0760　　www.jdsunph.com

*Mfr. advanced fiberoptic products for the cable television and telecommunications industries.*

**JDS Uniphase Ltd., Plymouth, UK**

Tel: 44-1993-700800　Contact: Tim Greaves, VP

**SIFAM Limited (SIFAM), London, UK**

## JETBORNE INC.

8361 NW 64th Street, Miami, FL, 33166

Tel: (305) 591-2999　　Fax: (305) 513-0050

*Aircraft sales, leasing, support.*

**Jetborne UK Ltd., Unit 12 Hampton Farm Ind. Estate, Hampton Rd. West, Hanworth, Middlesex TW13 6DH UK**

## JET-LUBE INC.

4849 Homestead, Ste. 200, Houston, TX, 77028

Tel: (713) 674-7617　　Fax: (713) 678-4604　　www.jetlube.com

*Mfr. anti-seize compounds, thread sealants, lubricants, greases.*

**Ilex Lubricants Ltd., Reform Rd., Maidenhead, Berkshire SL6 8BY UK**

Tel: 44-16286-31913　Fax: 44-1628-773138

## JLG INDUSTRIES INC.

One JLG Drive, McConnellsburg, PA, 17233-9533

Tel: (717) 485-5161　　Fax: (717) 485-6417　　www.jlg.com

*Mfr. aerial work platforms and vertical personnel lifts.*

**JLG Industries UK, 7 Mount Mews, High Street Hampton TW12 2SH, UK**

Tel: 44-208-213-5977　Fax: 44- 208-213-5976

**JLG Industries UK, Unit 12 Southside, Bredbury Park Industrial Estate, Bredbury Stockport SK6 2SP, UK**

Tel: 44-870-200-7700　Fax: 44-870-200-7711

## JOHN HANCOCK FINANCIAL SERVICES, INC.

John Hancock Place, Boston, MA, 02117

Tel: (617) 572-6000     Fax: (617) 572-9799     www.johnhancock.com

*Life insurance services.*

**Hancock International Private Equity Management, Ltd., 38 Trinity Sq., London, UK**

## JOHNS MANVILLE CORPORATION

717 17th Street, Denver, CO, 80202

Tel: (303) 978-2000     Fax: (303) 978-2318     www.jm.com

*Mfr. fiberglass insulation, roofing products and systems, fiberglass material and reinforcements, filtration mats.*

**Johns Manville International, Canada House, 272 Field End Rd., Ruislip, Middlesex HA4 9NA UK**

## JOHNSON & JOHNSON

One Johnson & Johnson Plaza, New Brunswick, NJ, 08933

Tel: (732) 524-0400     Fax: (732) 214-0334     www.jnj.com

*Mfr./distributor/R&D pharmaceutical, health care and cosmetic products.*

**Janssen-Cilag Ltd., PO Box 79, Saunderton, High Wycombe HP14 4HJ UK**

**Johnson & Johnson Ltd., Foundation Park, Roxborough Way, Maidenhead, Berkshire SL6 3UG UK**

**Johnson & Johnson Medical Ltd., Coronation Rd., Ascot, Berkshire 5L5 9EY UK**

**Johnson & Johnson Professional Products Ltd. (Europe), The Braccans, London Rd., Bracknell, Berkshire RG12 2AT UK**

**LifeScan U.K., PO Box 79, Saunderton, High Wycombe HP14 4HJ, UK**

**Ortho-Clinical Diagnostics, Enterprise House, Station Rd., Loudwater, High Wycombe Bucks HP10 9UF UK**

**Vistakon Europe, Bracknell, Berkshire RG12 2AT, UK**

## S C JOHNSON & SON INC.

1525 Howe St., Racine, WI, 53403

Tel: (414) 260-2000     Fax: (414) 260-2133     www.scjohnsonwax.com

*Home, auto, commercial and personal care products and specialty chemicals.*

**S.C. Johnson & Son Ltd., Frimley Green Rd., Frimley, Surrey GU16 5AJ, UK**

## JOHNSON CONTROLS INC.

5757 N. Green Bay Ave., PO Box 591, Milwaukee, WI, 53201-0591

Tel: (414) 228-1200     Fax: (414) 228-2077     www.johnsoncontrols.com

*Mfr. facility management and control systems and auto seating.*

**Johnson Control Systems Ltd., Convex House, Randall's Research Park, Leatherhead Surrey KT22 7TS, UK**

Tel: 44-1-372-376111   Fax: 44-1-372-361413   Contact: Andrew J. Schlidt, Mng. Dir.

## THE JOHNSON CORPORATION

805 Wood Street, Three Rivers, MI, 49093

Tel: (616) 278-1715     Fax: (616) 273-2230     www.joco.com

*Mfr. rotary joints and siphon systems.*

**Johnson Corp (JOCO) Ltd., Little Lane, Ilkley, West Yorkshire LS29 8HY, UK**

Tel: 44-1943-607550   Fax: 44-1943-609463

**Johnson Systems International, Ilkey, England, UK**

## JOHNSON OUTDOORS, INC.

1326 Willow Road, Sturtevant, WI, 53177

Tel: (414) 884-1500      Fax: (414) 884-1600      www.jwa.com

*Mfr. diving, fishing, boating and camping sports equipment.*

**Scubapro U.K. Ltd., Vickers Business Centre, Ste. 10, Priestly Rd., Basingstoke, Hampshire RG24 9NP UK**

Tel: 44-1256-812636    Fax: 44-1256-812646

**Uwatec U.K. Ltd., 172 Winchester Rd., Four Marks Alton, Hampshire GU34 5HZ, UK**

Tel: 44-420-561-412    Fax: 44-420-561-424

## JONES LANG LASALLE

101 East 52nd Street, New York, NY, 10022

Tel: (212) 688-8181      Fax: (212) 308-5199      www.jlw.com

*International marketing consultants, leasing agents and property management advisors.*

**Jones Lang Wootton, London, UK**

## JONES, DAY, REAVIS & POGUE

North Point, 901 Lakeside Ave., Cleveland, OH, 44114

Tel: (216) 586-3939      Fax: (216) 579-0212      www.jonesday.com

*International law firm.*

**Jones, Day, Reavis & Pogue, Bucklersbury House, 3 Queen Victoria St., London EC4N 8NA, UK**

Tel: 44-207-236-3939    Fax: 44-207-236-1113    Contact: Stephen E. Fiamma, Partner    Emp: 55

## JOY MINING AND MACHINERY

177 Thorn Hill Road, Warrendale, PA, 15086-7527

Tel: (724) 779-4500      Fax: (724) 779-4507

*Mfr. of underground mining equipment.*

**Joy Manufacturing Co. (UK) Ltd., Joy House, Bestwood Village, Nottingham NE6 8WP, UK**

## JUKI UNION SPECIAL CORPORATION

5 Haul Road, Wayne, NJ, 07470

Tel: (973) 633-7200      Fax: (973) 633-9629      www.unionspecial.com

*Mfr. sewing machines.*

**Union Special (UK) Ltd., 22 Mandervell Rd., Industrial Estate, Oadby Leicester LE2 5LQ, UK**

Tel: 44-116-271-3292    Fax: 44-116-271-9239

## JUPITER MEDIA METRIX INC.

21 Astor Place, New York, NY, 10003

Tel: (212) 780-6060      Fax: (212) 780-6075      www.jmm.com

*Engaged in research services to determine audience measurement.*

**Jupiter Media Metrix Inc., 32 Haymarket, Piccadilly, London SW1Y 4TP, UK**

Tel: 44-207-747-0500

## K-2, INC.

4900 South Eastern Ave., Los Angeles, CA, 90040

Tel: (323) 724-2800      Fax: (323) 724-8174      www.k2sports.com

*Mfr. sporting goods, recreational and industrial products.*

**Shakespeare, Div. K2, PO Box 1 - Broad Ground Road, Lakeside Redditch, GB Worchester B98 8NQ, UK**

Tel: 44-1527-510-570

**KAISER ENGINEERS INC.**

9300 Lee Highway, Fairfax, VA, 22031

Tel: (703) 934-3600     Fax: (703) 934-9740     www.icfkaiser.com

*Engineering, construction and consulting services.*

**Kaiser Engineers Ltd., Regal House, London Rd., Twickenham, Middlesex TW1 3QQ UK**

Tel: 44-181-892-4433

**KAMAN CORPORATION**

1332 Blue Hills Ave., Bloomfield, CT, 06002

Tel: (860) 243-7100     Fax: (860) 243-6365     www.kaman.com

*Mfr. aviation and aerospace products and services, musical instruments.*

**KMI Europe, Inc., London, UK**

**KAMDEN INTERNATIONAL SHIPPING INC.**

179-02 150th Avenue, Jamaica, NY, 11434

Tel: (718) 553-8181     Fax: (718) 244-0030     www.kamden.com

*Full service, international freight forwarder and customs broker.*

**Kamden Intl. Shipping Ltd., Unit 5 - Lawnhurst Trading Estate - Ashurst Drive, Cheadle Heath Stockport, Cheshire SK3 0SD, UK**

**Kamden Intl. Shipping Ltd., Kamden House - 673 Spur Road, North Feltham Trading Estate, Feltham Middlesex TW14 0SL, UK**

**KANEB SERVICES INC.**

2435 N. Central Expwy, 7th Fl., Richardson, TX, 75080

Tel: (972) 699-4000     Fax: (972) 699-4025     www.kaneb.com

*Specialized industry services: leak sealing, on-site machining, safety testing, fire protection, etc.*

**Furmanite PLC, Furman House, Shap Rd., Kendal, Cumbria LA9 6RU UK**

**KAPPLER PROTECTIVE APPAREL & FABRICS**

PO Box 218, 70 Grimes Drive, Guntersville, AL, 35976

Tel: (205) 505-4000     Fax: (205) 505-4004     www.kappler.com

*Mfr. of protective apparel and fabrics.*

**Kappler Europe Ltd., Kappler Close, Netherfield, Nottingham NG4 1PT UK**

Tel: 44-115-961-8182   Fax: 44-115-961-5676   Contact: Thomas Mankert, Mng. Dir.   Emp: 120

**KATY INDUSTRIES INC.**

6300 South Syracuse Way, Ste. 300, Englewood, CO, 80111

Tel: (303) 290-9300     Fax: (303) 290-9344     www.katyindustries.com

*Mfr. electronic and maintenance equipment for industrial and consumer markets.*

**Bach Simpson (UK) Ltd., Trenant Estate, Wadebridge, Cornwall PL27 6HD UK**

**Darwins Alloy Castings Co. Ltd., Sheffield Rd., Tinsley, Sheffield S9 1RL UK**

**LaBour Pump Co. Ltd., Denington Estate, Wellingborough, Northants NN8 2QL, UK**

**KAWNEER COMPANY, INC.**

555 Guthridge Court, Norcross, GA, 30092

Tel: (770) 449-5555     Fax: (770) 734-1570     www.kawneer.com

*Mfr. arch aluminum products for commercial construction.*

**Kawneer UK Ltd., Astmoor Rd., Astmoor, Runcorn, Cheshire WA7 1QQ UK**

**KAYDON CORPORATION**

315 E. Eisenhower Pkwy., Ste. 300, Ann Arbor, MI, 48108-3330

Tel: (734) 747-7025     Fax: (734) 747-6565     www.kaydon.com

*Design/mfr. custom engineered products: bearings, rings, seals, etc.*

**Cooper Roller Bearings Co. Ltd., Wisbech, Kings Lynn, Norfolk PE30 5JX UK**

**IDM Electronics Ltd., 30 Suttons Park Ave., Suttons Park Industrial Estate, Reading, Berkshire RG6 1AW UK**

## KEANE, INC.

10 City Square, Boston, MA, 02129

Tel: (617) 241-9200    Fax: (617) 241-9507    www.keane.com

*Provides information technology services.*

**Keane UK, 53-55 New Bond Street, London W1Y 9DG, UK**

Tel: 44-207-339-0000   Fax: 44-207-339-0001

**Keane UK, Lion House, Oscott Road, Wilton Birmingham B6 7UH, UK**

Tel: 44-121-356-8383   Fax: 44-121-356-0463

**Keane UK, Stonecourt, Siskin Drive, Coventry CV3 4FJ, UK**

Tel: 44-1203-514400   Fax: 44-1203-514491

## A.T. KEARNEY INC.

222 West Adams Street, Chicago, IL, 60606

Tel: (312) 648-0111    Fax: (312) 223-6200    www.atkearney.com

*Management consultants and executive search.*

**A. T. Kearney Inc. Ltd., Lansdowne House, Berkeley Square, London W2X 5DH, UK**

Tel: 44-207-468-8000

## KEER-McGEE CORPORATION

123 Robert S. Kerr Avenue, Oklahoma City, OK, 73102

Tel: (405) 270-1313    Fax: (405) 270-3029    www.kerr-mcgee.com

*Oil and gas exploration and production.*

**Kerr-McGee Resources Ltd., London, UK**

## KEITHLEY INSTRUMENTS INC.

28775 Aurora Road, Cleveland, OH, 44139

Tel: (440) 248-0400    Fax: (440) 248-6168    www.keithley.com

*Mfr. electronic test/measure instruments, PC-based data acquisition hardware/software.*

**Keithley Instruments Ltd., The Minister, 58 Portman Rd., Reading, Berks RG30 1EA UK**

## KELLOGG BROWN & ROOT INC.

PO Box 3, Houston, TX, 77001

Tel: (713) 676-3011    Fax: (713) 676-8695    www.halliburton.com

*Engaged in technology-based engineering and construction.*

**Kellogg Brown & Root, Hill Park Court, Springfield Drive, Leatherhead Surrey KT22 7NL, UK**

Tel: 44-181-544-5000   Fax: 44-181-544-4400   Contact: Roderick Kyle

**Kellogg Brown & Root, Kellogg Tower KT 08A, Greenford Road, Greenford Middlesex UB6 0JA, UK**

Tel: 44-20-8872-7000   Fax: 44-20-8872-7272

**Kellogg Brown & Root AOC, PO Box No. 8, ICI Acrylics - Cassel Works, New Road, BillinghamTS23 1PR UK**

**Kellogg Brown & Root Cardinal, Greenford Road, Greenford, London UB6 9AP UK**

**Kellogg Brown & Root Civil, M65 Contract 1 - Resident Engineers Office, Higher Stanworth Farm Bolton Road, Whithnell Chorley, PR6 8PB UK**

**Kellogg Brown & Root Civil, Churchgate House - 56 Oxford Street, Manchester M1 6EU, UK**

**Kellogg Brown & Root Ltd., Wessex House, Market St., Eastleigh Hants SO5 4FD, UK**

**Kellong Brown & Root Civil, Thorncroft Manor, Dorking Road, Leatherhead Surrey KT22 8JB, UK**

## KELLOGG COMPANY

One Kellogg Square, PO Box 3599, Battle Creek, MI, 49016-3599

Tel: (616) 961-2000    Fax: (616) 961-2871    www.kelloggs.com

*Mfr. ready-to-eat cereals and convenience foods.*

**Kellogg Co. of Great Britain Ltd., Attn: English Office, One Kellogg Square, PO Box 3599, Battle Creek MI 49016-3599**

**KELLY SERVICES, INC.**

999 W. Big Beaver Road, Troy, MI, 48084

Tel: (248) 362-4444      Fax: (248) 244-4154      www.kellyservices.com

*Temporary help placement.*

**Kelly Services (UK) Ltd., Roswell House, 100 Middlesex St., London E1 7HD UK**

Tel: 44-207-247-4494   Fax: 44-207-247-2570

**KEMLITE COMPANY, INC.**

PO Box 2429, Joliet, IL, 60434

Tel: (815) 467-8600      Fax: (815) 467-8666      www.kemlite.com

*Mfr. fiberglass reinforced plastic panels.*

**Kemlite Company, 25 Tower Quays, Birkenhead Wirral, Cheshire CH41 1BP, UK**

Tel: 44-151-650-0123   Fax: 44-151-650-0365

**KENDA SYSTEMS INC.**

One Stiles Road, Salem, NH, 03079

Tel: (603) 898-7884      Fax: (603) 898-3016      www.kenda.com

*Computer programming services.*

**Kenda Systems Ltd., Regency House, 6b Queen St., Godalming, Surrey GU7 1BD UK**

Tel: 44-1483-418-191

**KENDA Systems, Ltd., 1 Royal Exchange Avenue, London EC3V 3LT, UK**

Tel: 44-20-7464-4070

**Kenda Systems, Ltd., Lynnfield House - Church Street, Altrincham Cheshire WA14 4DZ, UK**

Tel: 44-161-926-9000

**THE KENDALL COMPANY (TYCO HEALTHCARE)**

15 Hampshire Street, Mansfield, MA, 02048

Tel: (508) 261-8000      Fax: (508) 261-8542      www.kendalhq,com

*Mfr. medical disposable products, home health care products and specialty adhesive products.*

**The Kendall Co. (UK) Ltd., 154 Fareham Rd., Gosport, Hampshire PO13 0AS, UK**

Tel: 44-1329-224-4114   Fax: 44-1329-224-4390

**KENNAMETAL INC.**

State Rte. 981, Latrobe, PA, 15650

Tel: (724) 539-5000      Fax: (724) 539-4710      www.kennametal.com

*Tools, hard carbide and tungsten alloys for metalworking industry.*

**Kennametal Hertel Ltd., Box 29, Kingswinford, West Midland DY6 7NP, UK**

Tel: 44-1384-401000   Fax: 44-1384-408015

**KENT-MOORE**

28635 Mound Road, Ste. 335, Warren, MI, 48092-3499

Tel: (810) 578-7289      Fax: (810) 578-7375      www.spx.com

*Mfr. service equipment for auto, construction, recreational, military and agricultural vehicles.*

**Kent-Moore UK Ltd., 86 Wharfdale Rd., Tyseley, Birmingham B11 2DD UK**

**KEPNER-TREGOE INC.**

PO Box 704, Princeton, NJ, 08542-0740

Tel: (609) 921-2806      Fax: (609) 497-0130      www.kepner-tregoe.com

*Management consulting; specializing in strategy formulation, problem solving, decision making, project management, and cost reduction.*

**Kepner-Tregor Ltd., 13-15 Victoria St., Windsor, Berkshire SL4 1HB UK**

Tel: 44-1753-856716   Fax: 44-1753-854929

## KERR-McGEE CORPORATION

PO Box 25861, Oklahoma City, OK, 73125

Tel: (405) 270-1313        Fax: (405) 270-3123        www.kerr-mcgee.com

*Engaged in oil and gas exploration and manufacture of inorganic chemicals.*

**KG and Kerr-McGee Resources (U.K.) Limited,  75 Davies St., Mayfair, London W1Y 1FA, UK**

## KIDDE-FENWAL, INC.

400 Main Street, Ashland, MA, 01721

Tel: (508) 881-2000        Fax: (508) 881-6729        www.kidde-fenwal.com

*Temperature controls, ignition systems, fire/smoke detection and suppression systems.*

**Fenwal Intl.,  Lyons House, 2A Station Rd., Frimley, Camberley Surrey GU16 5HP, UK**

## KILPATRICK STOCKTON LLP

1100 Peachtree Street, NE, Ste. 2800, Atlanta, GA, 30309-4530

Tel: (404) 815-6500        Fax: (404) 815-6555        www.kilstock.com

*International law firm.*

**Kilpatrick Stockton,  68 Pall Mall, London SW1Y 5ES, UK**

Tel: 44-207-321-0477    Fax: 44-207-930-9733

## KIMBALL INTERNATIONAL INC.

PO Box 460, Jasper, IN, 47549

Tel: (812) 482-1600        Fax: (812) 482-8804        www.kimball.com

*Mfr. office furniture and seating, pianos, wood veneers, plywood products.*

**Herrburger Brooks Ltd.,  Meadow Lane, Long Eaton, Nottingham NG10 2FG UK**

**Kimball Europe Ltd.,  21-27 Marylebone Lane, London W1M 5FG, UK**

## KIMBERLY-CLARK CORPORATION

351 Phelps Drive, Irving, TX, 75038

Tel: (972) 281-1200        Fax: (972) 281-1435        www.kimberly-clark.com

*Mfr./sales/distribution of consumer tissue, household and personal care products.*

**Kimberly-Clark Ltd.,  PO Box 152, Reigate, Surrey RH2 9ZP, UK**

## KINKO'S, INC.

255 W. Stanley Ave., Ventura, CA, 93002-8000

Tel: (805) 652-4000        Fax: (805) 652-4347        www.kinkos.com

*Kinko's operates a 24-hour-a-day, global chain of photocopy stores.*

**Kinko's,  326 High Holburn St., London WC1V 7DD, UK**

Tel: 44-207-539-2900    Fax: 44-207-539-2901

## KIRKLAND & ELLIS

200 East Randolph Drive, Chicago, IL, 60601

Tel: (312) 861-2000        Fax: (312) 861-2200        www.kirkland.com

*International law firm.*

**Kirkland & Ellis,  Old Broad St., London EC2N 1HQ, UK**

Tel: 44-207-816-8700    Fax: 44-207-816-8800    Contact: Samuel H. Hanbold, Ptnr.

## LESTER B. KNIGHT & ASSOCIATES INC.

549 West Randolph Street, Chicago, IL, 60661

Tel: (312) 346-2300        Fax: (312) 648-1085

*Architecture, engineering, planning, operations and management consulting.*

**Knight Wendling Consulting Ltd./KW Executive Search,  140 Park Lane, London W1Y 3AA, UK**

**KNIGHT TRADING GROUP, INC.**

525 Washington Blvd., Jersey City, NJ, 07310

Tel: (201) 222-9400    Fax: (201) 557-6853    www.knight-sec.com

*Engaged in securities trading.*

**Knight Securities International Ltd.,  London Stock Exchange Bldg., 2 Throgmorton Street, London EC2 N1TE, UK**

Tel: 44-207-997-1234   Fax: 44-207-997-7600   Contact: Walter F. Raquet, Chmn.

**KNIGHT-RIDDER INC.**

One Herald Plaza, Miami, FL, 33132

Tel: (305) 376-3800    Fax: (305) 376-3828    www.kri.com

*Newspaper publishing, business information services.*

**Knight-Ridder Financial/Europe,  KR House, 78 Fleet St., London EC4Y 1HY UK**

**KNOLL, INC.**

1235 Water Street, East Greenville, PA, 18041

Tel: (215) 679-7991    Fax: (215) 679-3904    www.knoll.com

*Mfr. and sale of office furnishings.*

**Form Intl Ltd.,  20 Saville Row, London W1X 1AE, UK**

**KNOWLES ELECTRONICS INC.**

1151 Maplewood Drive, Itasca, IL, 60131

Tel: (630) 250-5100    Fax: (630) 250-0575    www.knowleselectronics.com

*Microphones and loudspeakers.*

**Knowles Electronics Ltd.,  75 Victoria Rd., Burgess Hill, Sussex RH15 9LP UK**

**KOCH INDUSTRIES INC.**

4111 East 37th Street North, Wichita, KS, 67220-3203

Tel: (316) 828-5500    Fax: (316) 828-5950    www.kochind.com

*Oil, financial services, agriculture and Purina Mills animal feed.*

**Koch Metals Trading Limited,  7 George Yard Lombard St. - 7/F, London, EC3V 9DH, UK**

Tel: 44-207-648-6300   Fax: 44-20-7648-6301

**KODAK POLYCHROME GRAPHICS**

401 Merritt 7, Norwalk, CT, 06851

Tel: (203) 845-7000    Fax: (203) 845-7113    www.kodak.com

*Metal offset plates, coating specialties, graphic arts films.*

**Polychrome Corp Ltd.,  Sandown Rd., Watford, Herts WDZ 4XA, UK**

**THE KOHLER COMPANY**

444 Highland Drive, Kohler, WI, 53044

Tel: (920) 457-4441    Fax: (920) 459-1274    www.kohlerco.com

*Plumbing products, ceramic tile and stone, cabinetry, furniture, engines, generators, switch gear and hospitality.*

**Kohler Engines - Reg. Office,  Command House Unit 1, Elder Way & Waterside Drive, Langley Business Park, Langley Slough Berkshire SL3 6EP UK**

Tel: 44-1753-580-771   Fax: 44-1753-580-036

**Kohler Engines-United  Kingdom & Erie, J.H. Hancox Ltd., Alchester Rd., Portway, Birmingham B48 7JP UK**

Tel: 44-1564-824343   Fax: 44-1564-824073

**Kohler Power Systems International,  London, UK**

## KOHN PEDERSEN FOX ASSOCIATES PC

111 West 57th Street, New York, NY, 10019

Tel: (212) 977-6500     Fax: (212) 956-2526     www.kpf.com

*Architectural design.*

**Kohn Pedersen Fox Intl. PA, 13 Langley St., London WC2H 9JG, UK**

Tel: 44-207-836-6668

## KOLLMORGEN CORPORATION

1601 Trapelo Road, Waltham, MA, 02154

Tel: (781) 890-5655     Fax: (781) 890-7150     www.kollmorgen.com

*Mfr. high-performance electronic motion-control systems and design and supply advanced submarine periscopes, weapons directors, and military optics.*

**Kollmorgen (UK) Ltd., 219 Kings Rd., Reading, Berkshire, UK**

## KOPPERS INDUSTRIES INC.

Koppers Bldg, 436 Seventh Ave., Pittsburgh, PA, 15219-1800

Tel: (412) 227-2000     Fax: (412) 227-2333     www.koppers.com

*Construction materials and services; chemicals and building products.*

**Bitmac UK, England, UK**

## KORN/FERRY INTERNATIONAL

1800 Century Park East, Los Angeles, CA, 90067

Tel: (310) 843-4100     Fax: (310) 553-6452     www.kornferry.com

*Executive search; management consulting.*

**Korn/Ferry International Ltd., Regent Arcade House, 252 Regent St., London W1R 5DA, UK**

Tel: 44-207-312-3100   Fax: 44-207-312-3130

## KOSTER KEUNEN INC.

1021 Echo Lake Rd., Box 69, Watertown, CT, 06795-0069

Tel: (860) 945-3333     Fax: (860) 945-0330     www.kosterkeunen.com

*Mfr. waxes, beeswax, paraffin.*

**Captiva Chemicals, 2 Priors Close, Bray - Maidenhead Berkshire, SL6 2ER, UK**

Tel: 44-1-628-544540   Fax: 44-1-628-544541   Contact: Roy Clarkson

## KPMG INTERNATIONAL LLP

345 Park Avenue, New York, NY, 10022

Tel: (201) 307-7000     Fax: (201) 930-8617     www.kpmg.com

*Accounting and audit, tax and management consulting services.*

**KPMG, St. James' Square, Manchester M2 6DS, UK**

**KPMG EMA, Richmond House, 1 Rumford Place, Liverpool L3 9QY, UK**

**KPMG EMA, Richmond park House, 15 Pembroke Rd., Clifton Bristol BS8 3BG, UK**

**KPMG EMA, 110 The Quayside, Newcastle-upon-Tyne, NE1 3DX, UK**

**KPMG EMA, 8 Salisbury Square, London EC4V 8BB, UK**

Tel: 44-207-311-1000   Fax: 44-207-311-3311   Contact: Geoff R. Russell, Ptnr.

**KPMG EMA, 2 Cornwall St., Birmingham B3 2DL, UK**

**KPMG EMA, 37 Hills Rd., Cambridge CB2 1XL, UK**

**KPMG EMA, 1 Puddle Dock, Blackfriars, London EC4V 3PD, UK**

## KRAFT FOODS INTERNATIONAL, INC. ( DIV. PHILIP MORRIS COS.)

800 Westchester Ave., Rye Brook, NY, 10573-1301

Tel: (914) 335-2500     Fax: (914) 335-7144     www.kraftfoods.com

*Processor, distributor and manufacturer of food products.*

**Kraft Jacobs Suchard, St. Georges House, Bayshill Rd., Cheltenham GL 50 3AE UK**

## THE KROLL-O'GARA COMPANY

9113 Le Saint Drive, Fairfield, OH, 45014

Tel: (513) 874-2112     Fax: (513) 874-2558     www.kroll-ogara.com

*Security and consulting services and vehicles.*

**Kroll Associates UK Ltd., 25 Saville Row, London W1X 0AL, UK**

Tel: 44-207-396-0000   Fax: 44-207-396-9966

**O'Gara Satellite Networks, c/o Next Destination, Ltd, 25 The Claredon Centre, Salisbury Business Centre, Salisbury, Wiltshire SP1 2TJ, UK**

Tel: 44-1722-410800   Fax: 44-1722-410777   Contact: Mark White

## KRONOS INCORPORATED

400 Fifth Avenue, Waltham, MA, 02154

Tel: (781) 890-3232     Fax: (781) 890-8768     www.kronos.com

*Mfr. timekeeping systems software.*

**Kronos Systems Ltd., 2 Carey Road, Wokingham Berkshire RG 40 2NP, UK**

Tel: 44-118-978-9784   Fax: 44-118-978-2214

**Kronos Systems Ltd., Ten Pound Walk, Doncaster, South Yorkshire DN4 5HX, UK**

Tel: 44-130-232-3880   Fax: 44-1302-32-8883

## K-SWISS INC.

31248 Oak Crest Dr., Westlake Village, CA, 91361

Tel: (818) 706-5100     Fax: (818) 706-5390     www.k-swiss.com

*Mfr. casual and athletic shoes, socks and leisure apparel.*

**K-Swiss (UK) Ltd., Tannery House - 4 Middle Leigh Street, Somerset BA16 OLA , UK**

**44-145-844-6536**

Tel: 44-145-844-5502

## K-TEL INTERNATIONAL INC.

2605 Fernbrook Lane North, Plymouth, MN, 55447-4736

Tel: (612) 559-6800     Fax: (612) 559-6803     www.k-tel.com

*Sales and distribution of packaged consumer music entertainment and convenience products.*

**K-Tel Entertainment (UK) Ltd., Windmill Ct., 192 Windmill Lane, Greenford, Middlesex VB6 9DW UK**

## KULICKE & SOFFA INDUSTRIES INC.

2101 Blair Mill Road, Willow Grove, PA, 19090

Tel: (215) 784-6000     Fax: (215) 659-7588     www.kns.com

*Semiconductor assembly systems and services.*

**IMPS Ltd., Unit 4 - Apex Business Park, Diplocks Way Hailsham, East Sussex BN27 3JU, UK**

## THE KULJIAN CORPORATION

3700 Science Center, Philadelphia, PA, 19104

Tel: (215) 243-1900     Fax: (215) 243-1909

*Studies, design, engineering, construction management and site supervision.*

**Kuljian Corp., 500 Chesham House, 150 Regent St., London WIR 5FA, UK**

## KURT SALMON ASSOCIATES INC.

1355 Peachtree Street NE, Atlanta, GA, 30309

Tel: (404) 892-0321     Fax: (404) 898-9590     www.kurtsalmon.com

*Management consulting: consumer products, retailing.*

**Kurt Salmon Associates Ltd., Bruce Court, 25 Hale Rd., Altrincham WA14 2EY, UK**

## LADAS & PARRY

26 West 61st Street, New York, NY, 10023

Tel: (212) 708-1800     Fax: (212) 246-8959     www.ladasparry.com

*International law firm, engaged in the practice of intellectual property law.*

.

**Ladas & Parry,  High Holborn House, 52-54 High Holborn, WC1V 6RR London, UK**

Tel: 44-207-242-5566   Fax: 44-207-405-1908

## LANCER CORPORATION

6655 Lancer Blvd, San Antonio, TX, 78219

Tel: (210) 310-7000     Fax: (210) 310-7252     www.lancercorp.com

*Mfr. beverage dispensing equipment.*

**Lancer Corporation UK,  17 Bembridge Gardens, Ruislip Middlesex HA4 7ER, UK**

Tel: 44-189-567-2667   Fax: 44-189-563-7537

## LANDAUER INC.

2 Science Road, Glenwood, IL, 60425-1586

Tel: (708) 755-7000       Fax: (708) 755-7035     www.landauerinc.com

*Provider of radiation dosimetry services to hospitals, medical and dental offices, university and national laboratories, nuclear power plants and other industries.*

**Landauer Inc.,  12 North Oxford Business Centre, Lakesmere Close, Kidlington, Oxford OX5 1LG, UK**

Tel: 44-1-86-537-3008    Contact: Dr. T. Finnigan, Dir. European Operation

## LANDIS GARDNER

20 East Sixth Street, Waynesboro, PA, 17268-2050

Tel: (717) 762-2161       Fax: (717) 765-5143     www.landisgardner.com

*Mfr. precision cylindrical grinding machinery and double disc grinding.*

**Landis Lund Ltd.,  Cross Hills, Keighley, Yorkshire BD20 7SD, UK**

Contact: Roger Coverdale

## LANDOR ASSOCIATES

Klamath House, 1001 Front Street, San Francisco, CA, 94111-1424

Tel: (415) 955-1400       Fax: (415) 365-3190     www.landor.com

*International marketing consulting firm, focused on developing and maintaining brand identity.*

**Landor Associates,  18 Clerkenwell Green, London EC1R ODP, UK**

Tel: 44-207-880-8000    Fax: 44-207-880-8001    Contact: Richard Ford, Dir. Europe

## LANDS' END INC.

1 Lands' End Lane, Dodgeville, WI, 53595

Tel: (608) 935-9341       Fax: (608) 935-4260     www.landsend.com

*Clothing, home furnishings and mail order catalog company.*

**Lands' End U.K.,  Pillings Rd., Oakham, Rutland LE15 6N4, UK**

Tel: 44-1572-722-553   Fax: 44-1572-722-554   Contact: Steve Miles, Mng. Dir.   Emp: 400

## THE LANGER BIOMECHANICS GROUP, INC.

450 Commack Road, Deer Park, NY, 11729

Tel: (631) 667-1200       Fax: (631) 667-1203     www.langerbiomechanics.com

*Mfr. prescription foot orthotics and gait-related products.*

**The Langer Biomechanics Group, Inc. (U.K.) Ltd.,  The Green, Stoke-on-Trent ST10 1RL, UK**

Tel: 44-1538-755-861   Fax: 44-1538-755-862   Contact: Paul Barcroft

## LANIER WORLDWIDE, INC.

2300 Parklake Drive, N.E., Atlanta, GA, 30345
Tel: (770) 496-9500     Fax: (770) 938-1020     www.lanier.com
*Specialize in digital copiers and multi-functional systems.*
**Lanier United Kingdom Ltd., Eskdale Rd., Winnershire, Wokingham Berkshire RG 41 5TS, UK**
Tel: 44-181-969-9500   Fax: 44-181-927-2771
**Lanier United Kingdom Ltd., Kingmaker House, Station Rd., New Barnet Herts EN5 1NZ, UK**
Tel: 44-181-447-1001   Fax: 44-181-364-8646
**Lanier United Kingdom Ltd., Faraday Court Unit 1B, Faraday Road, Crawley, West Sussex RH10 2PX UK**
Tel: 44-1293-516-804   Fax: 44-1293-516-807
**Lanier United Kingdom Ltd., Renown House, Merchants Quay, Salford Quays, Manchester M5 255 UK**
Tel: 44-161-848-0110   Fax: 44-161-848-0220

## LATHAM & WATKINS

633 West 5th St., Ste. 4000,, Los Angeles, CA, 90071-2007
Tel: (213) 485-1234     Fax: (213) 891-8763     www.lw.com
*International law firm.*
**Latham & Watkins, One Angel Court, EC2R 7HJ London, UK**
Tel: 44-141-374-4444   Fax: 44-207-374-4460

## LATIN AMERICAN FINANCIAL PUBLICATIONS INC.

2121 Ponce de Leon Blvd., Ste. 1020, Coral Gables, FL, 33134
Tel: (305) 448-6593     Fax: (305) 448-0718     www.latinfinance.com
*Latin America business magazine.*
**Latin Finance, London, UK**
Tel: 44-181-579-4836   Fax: 44-181-579-5057   Contact: Robert Logan

## LAWSON MARDON WHEATON, INC.

1101 Wheaton Ave., Millville, NJ, 08332
Tel: (856) 825-1400     Fax: (856) 825-0146     www.algroupwheaton.com
*Engaged in pharmaceutical and cosmetic packaging, glass and plastic containers.*
**Fibrenyle, Ellough, Beccles Suffolk NR34 7TB, UK**
Tel: 44-1-502-71-400   Contact: David Taylor
**Fibrenyle, Brunel Way, Thetford Norfolk, IP24 5HA UK**
**Fibrenyle, Forest Works, Coxmoor Road, Sutton-in-Ashfield Notts, NG17 5LH, UK**
Tel: 44-1-623-512-012   Fax: 44-1-623-440-948
**Fibrenyle, 43-47 Barker Street, Norwich, Norfolk NR2 4TN, UK**
Tel: 44-1-603-660-841   Fax: 44-1-603-763-123
**Pharmaflex, 49 Colbourne Avenue, Nelson Park, Cramlington Northumberland NE23 9WD, UK**
Contact: John Roberts
**Rockware Plastics Ltd., Lower Ham Rd., Kingston KT2 5AE, UK**

## LAWTER INTERNATIONAL INC.

1 Terra Way, 8601 95th St., Pleasant Prairie, WI, 53158
Tel: (262) 947-7300     Fax: (262) 947-7328     www.lawter.com
*Resins, pigments and coatings.*
**Lawter Chemicals Ltd., Murdock Rd., Bicester, Oxon, UK**
Tel: 44-1-86-924-1212

## LA-Z-BOY INCORPORATED

1284 N. Telegraph Rd., Monroe, MI, 48162

Tel: (734) 242-1444      Fax: (734) 241-4422      www.lazboy.com

*Furniture gallery stores; upholstered furniture including chairs, sofas, reclining sofas, and modular seating groups.*

**Centurion Furniture PLC, Centurion Bldg., Lancashire Enterprises Business Park, Leyland, Lancashire PR5 3JW, UK**

Tel: 44-1772-450111   Fax: 44-1772-453511

## LE TOURNEAU COMPANY

PO Box 2307, Longview, TX, 75606

Tel: (903) 237-7000      Fax: (903) 267-7032

*Mfr. heavy construction and mining machinery equipment.*

**Le Tourneau Ltd., Blockwood-Hodge, Hunsbury, Hill Ave., Northampton NN4 9QT, UK**

## LEACH INTERNATIONAL, INC.

6900 Orangethorp Ave., Buena Park, CA, 90622-5032

Tel: (714) 739-0770      Fax: (714) 739-1713      www.leachintl.com

*Mfr. and design electrical switching and control devices for the aerospace and rail industries.*

**Leach International, 11 Westlinks - Tollgate Business Park, Chandlers Ford, Southampton Hampshire SO53 3TG, UK**

Tel: 44-2380-653535

## LEADINGSIDE, INC.

1 Canal Park, Cambridge, MA, 02141

Tel: (617) 577-2400      Fax: (617) 577-2413      www.leadingside.com

*Engaged in e-business services.*

**LeadingSide Ltd., Keaton House - Widewater Place, Harefield Middlesex UB9 6NS, UK**

Tel: 44-1895-827-200   Fax: 44-1895-827-222

## LEARNING TREE INTERNATIONAL, INC.

6053 West Century Blvd., Los Angeles, CA, 90045-0028

Tel: (310) 417-9700      Fax: (310) 417-8684      www.learningtree.com

*Information technology training services.*

**Learning Tree International Ltd. (UK), Mole Business Park, Leatherhead, Surrey KT22 7AD UK**

Tel: 44-1372-364600   Fax: 44-1372-364611   Contact: Staffan Windrup, Mng. Dir.   Emp: 109

## LEARONAL INC.

272 Buffalo Ave., Freeport, NY, 11520

Tel: (516) 868-8800      Fax: (516) 868-8824      www.learonal.com

*Specialty chemicals for the printed circuit board, semiconductor, connector and metal finishing industries.*

**LeaRonal UK Ltd., Ashbourne Rd., Buxton, Derbyshire SK17 9SS, UK**

Tel: 44-1298-71122   Fax: 44-1298-71124   Contact: Paul K. Smith, Mng. Dir.

## LeBOEUF, LAMB, GREENE & MacRAE LLP

125 West 55th Street, 12th Fl., New York, NY, 10019

Tel: (212) 424-8000      Fax: (212) 424-8500      www.llgm.com

*International law firm.*

**LeBoeuf, Lamb, Greene & MacRae LLP, No.1 Minster Court, Mincing Lane, London EC3R 7AA UK**

Tel: 44-207-459-5000   Fax: 44-207-459-5099

## LECROY CORPORATION

700 Chestnut Ridge Road, Chestnut Ridge, NY, 10977

Tel: (845) 425-2000     Fax: (845) 425-8967     www.lecroy.com

*Mfr. signal analyzers and electronic measurement systems.*

**LeCroy Ltd., 27 Blacklands Way, Abingdon Business Park, Abingdon Oxon OX14 1DY, UK**

Tel: 44-1235-536973

## LEGG MASON, INC.

100 Light St., Baltimore, MD, 21202

Tel: (410) 539-0000     Fax: (410) 539-4175     www.leggmason.com

*Financial services; securities brokerage and trading, investment management, institutional and individual clients, investment and commercial mortgage banking.*

**Legg Mason Wood Walker, London, UK**

## LEGGETT & PLATT, INC.

1 Leggett Road, Carthage, MO, 64836

Tel: (417) 358-8131     Fax: (417) 358-5840     www.leggett.com

*Mfr. components for bedding and furniture.*

**Gateway Textiles Ltd., Nottinghamshire, UK**

**John Pring & Son Limited, Elworth Wire Mills, Sandbach, Cheshire CW11 3JQ, UK**

Tel: 44-1270-763331   Fax: 44-1270-768279

## LEHMAN BROTHERS HOLDINGS INC.

Three World Financial Center, New York, NY, 10285

Tel: (212) 526-7000     Fax: (212) 526-3738     www.lehman.com

*Financial services, securities and merchant banking services.*

**Lehman Brothers - European Hdqtrs., One Broadgate, London EC2M 7HA, UK**

Tel: 44-207-601-0011   Fax: 44-207-260-3165

## LENNOX INDUSTRIES INC.

2100 Lake Park Blvd., Richardson, TX, 75080

Tel: (972) 497-5000     Fax: (214) 497-5299     www.davelennox.com

*Mfr. a/c products, gas heating products.*

**Lennox Industries Ltd., PO Box 174, Westgate Interchange, Northampton NN5 5AG, UK**

## LEVI STRAUSS & COMPANY

1155 Battery St., San Francisco, CA, 94111-1230

Tel: (415) 544-6000     Fax: (415) 501-3939     www.levistrauss.com

*Mfr./distributor casual wearing apparel.*

**Levi Strauss (UK) Ltd., Levi's House, Moulton Park, Northampton NN3 1QAG, UK**

Tel: 44-1604-790-436   Fax: 44-1604-790-400

## LEXMARK INTERNATIONAL

1 Lexmark Centre Dr., Lexington, KY, 40550

Tel: (606) 232-2000     Fax: (606) 232-1886     www.lexmark.com

*Develop, manufacture, supply of printing solutions and products, including laser, inkjet, and dot matrix printers.*

**Lexmark International Ltd., Westhorpe House, Little Marlow Road, Marlow Buckinghamshire, Sl7 3RQ, UK**

Tel: 44-8704-44-0044   Fax: 44-8704-44-0033

## LIBERTY MUTUAL GROUP

175 Berkeley Street, Boston, MA, 02117

Tel: (617) 357-9500      Fax: (617) 350-7648      www.libertymutual. com

*Provides workers' compensation insurance and operates physical rehabilitation centers and provides risk prevention management.*

**Liberty Mutual Insurance UK, One Minster Court 4/F, Mincing Lane, London EC3R 7YE, UK**

## LIFE TECHNOLOGIES INC.

9800 Medical Center Drive, Rockville, MD, 20850

Tel: (301) 840-8000      Fax: (301) 329-8635      www.lifetech.com

*Produces biotechnology research materials.*

**Life Technologies Ltd., 3 Fountain Drive, Inchinnan Business Park, Paisley UK**

## LIGHTBRIDGE, INC.

67 South Bedfore Street, Burlington, MA, 01803

Tel: (781) 359-4000      Fax: (781) 359-4500      www.lightbridge.com

*Engaged in consulting for telecom companies.*

**Lightbridge Technologies Ltd., Knyvett House - The Causeway, Staines, Middlesex TW18 3BA, UK**

Tel: 44-1784-898-551   Fax: 44-1784-898-553

## LIGHTNIN

135 Mt. Read Blvd., PO Box 1370, Rochester, NY, 14611

Tel: (716) 436-5550      Fax: (716) 436-5589      www.lightnin-mixers.com

*Mfr./sale/services industrial mixing machinery, aerators.*

**LIGHTNIN Mixers Ltd., London Road South, Poyndon Stockport, Cheshire SK12 1LH, UK**

Tel: 44-1625-87-6421

## ELI LILLY & COMPANY

Lilly Corporate Center, Indianapolis, IN, 46285

Tel: (317) 276-2000      Fax: (317) 277-6579      www.lilly.com

*Mfr. pharmaceuticals and animal health products.*

**Eli Lilly and Company Limited, Dextra Court Chapel Hill, Basingstoke Hampshire, RG21 5SY, UK**

**Eli Lilly and Company Limited, Fleming Road, Speke, Liverpool L24-9LN, UK**

**Eli Lilly and Company Limited, Earl Wood Manor, Windlesham Surrey GU20 6PH, UK**

**Eli Lilly Intl. Corp., Lilly House 40-42, 13 Hanover Square, London W1R 0PA, UK**

Tel: 44-207-409-4800   Fax: 44-207-409-4818   Contact: Gerhard N. Mayr, Pres. Intl.

## LILLY INDUSTRIES

200 W. 103rd St., Indianapolis, IN, 46290

Tel: (317) 814-8700      Fax: (317) 814-8880      www.lillyindustries.com

*Mfr. industrial coatings and specialty chemicals.*

**Lilly Industries UK Ltd., 152 Milton Park Abingdon, Oxfordshire OX14 4SD, UK**

Tel: 44-123-544-4700   Fax: 44-123-583-2975

## LIMITORQUE

PO Box 11318, 5114 Woodall Road, Lynchburg, VA, 24506

Tel: (804) 528-4400      Fax: (804) 845-9736      www.limitorque.com

*Mfr./marketing/services electric valve actuators.*

**Limitorque International, Trinity House Kennet Side, Newbury, Berkshire RG14 5EH, UK**

Tel: 44-1-635-46999   Fax: 44-1-635-36034

## LINCOLN ELECTRIC HOLDINGS

22801 St. Clair Ave., Cleveland, OH, 44117-1199

Tel: (216) 481-8100    Fax: (216) 486-8385    www.lincolnelectric.com

*Mfr. arc welding and welding related products, oxy-fuel and thermal cutting equipment and integral AC motors.*

**Lincoln Electric (UK) Ltd., 6th Fifth Drive, Attercliffe Sheffield S4 7UT, UK**

Tel: 44-114-249-3601   Fax: 44-114-249-3602   Contact: John Herold, Plant Mgr.

**Lincoln Electric (UK) Ltd., Mansfield Road, Aston Sheffield S26 2BS, UK**

Tel: 44-114-287-2401   Fax: 44-114-287-2582   Contact: Anthony Reid, Mng. Dir.

## LINCOLN FINANCIAL GROUP

1500 Market St., Ste. 3900, Philadelphia, PA, 19102-2112

Tel: (215) 448-1400    Fax: (215) 448-3962    www.lfg.com

*Provides annuities, life insurance, 401(k) plans, life-health reinsurance, mutual funds, institutional investment management and financial planning and advisory services.*

**Lincoln Financial Group UK, London, UK**

## LINEAR TECHNOLOGY CORPORATION

1630 McCarthy Blvd., Milpitas, CA, 95035

Tel: (408) 432-1900    Fax: (408) 434-6441    www.linear-tech.com

*Mfr. linear integrated circuit chips.*

**Linear Technology (UK) Ltd., The Coliseum Business Centre, Riverside Way, Camberley, Surrey GU15 3YL, UK**

Tel: 44-1276-677676   Fax: 44-1276-64851

## ARTHUR D. LITTLE, INC.

25 Acorn Park, Cambridge, MA, 02140-2390

Tel: (617) 498-5000    Fax: (617) 498-7200    www.adlittle.com

*Management, environmental, health and safety consulting; technical and product development.*

**Arthur D. Little Ltd., Berkeley Square House, Berkeley Square, London W1X 6EY UK**

Tel: 44-207-409-2277   Fax: 44-207-491-8983   Emp: 160

**Arthur D. Little Ltd., Windsor House, Cornwall Rd., Harrogate, North Yorkshire HG1 2PW UK**

Tel: 44-1423-567862   Fax: 44-1423-567873

**Arthur D. Little Ltd., Science Park, Milton Rd., Cambridge CB4 4DW UK**

Tel: 44-1223-420024   Fax: 44-1223-420021

## LITTON INDUSTRIES INC.

21240 Burbank Boulevard, Woodland Hills, CA, 91367

Tel: (818) 598-5000    Fax: (818) 598-3313    www.littoncorp.com

*Shipbuilding, electronics, and information technology.*

**Aero Products, 5/6 Victory Business Ctr., Fleming Way/Worton Rd., Isleworth, Middlesex TW7 6DB UK**

Tel: 44-181-847-2212   Fax: 44-181-568-0655

**Litton Marine Systems B.V., Burlington House, 118 Burlington Road, New Malden, Surrey KT3 4NR, UK**

Tel: 44-181-329-2000

**Litton Precision Products, 6 First Avenue, Marlow, Buckinghamshire SL7 1YA, UK**

Tel: 44-1628-486060

## LIZ CLAIBORNE INC.

1441 Broadway, 22nd Fl., New York, NY, 10018

Tel: (212) 354-4900    Fax: (212) 626-1800    www.lizclaiborne.com

*Apparel manufacturer.*

**Liz Claiborne Inc., Watford, UK**

## LOCKHEED MARTIN CORPORATION

6801 Rockledge Drive, Bethesda, MD, 20817

Tel: (301) 897-6000      Fax: (301) 897-6652      www.imco.com

*Design/mfr./management systems in fields of space, defense, energy, electronics and technical services.*

**CalComp Europe Ltd., 176 Lutto Road, Chatham Kent ME4 5BP, UK**

Tel: 44-1634-828385   Fax: 44-1634-828386

**Lockheed Martin IMS, 20 Maltby Street, London SE1 3PG, UK**

Tel: 44-207-252-1119   Fax: 44-207-252-1389

**Lockheed Martin Intl. Ltd., 2 Castle End Farm Business Park, Castle End Road, Ruscomb Reading Berkshire RG10 9XQ, UK**

Tel: 44-207-344-0500   Fax: 44-207-734-341474

**Lockheed Martin Intl. S.A., 8th Fl. Berkeley Square House 9-14, Berkeley Square London W1X 5LA, UK**

Tel: 44-207-412-0555   Fax: 44-207-412-0547

**Lockheed Martin Intl. S.A., Communications Centre London, Alliance House, 29/30 High Holborn, London WC1V 6AZ UK**

Tel: 44-207-405-2969   Fax: 44-207-413-8120   Contact: K. Khambatta, Mgr.

**Lockheed Martin UK Ltd., PO Box 41, North Harbour Portsmouth, Hampshire PO6 3AU, UK**

Tel: 44-1-705-563406   Fax: 44-1-705-214889

**MountainGate Data Systems UK Ltd., 20 Little Basing, PO Box 5064, Basingstoke Hants G24 8JA, UK**

Tel: 44-1256-464-767   Fax: 44-1256-59748   Contact: M. D. Phillips, Mgr.

## LOCTITE CORPORATION

1001 Trout Brook Crossing, Rocky Hill, CT, 06067-3910

Tel: (860) 571-5100      Fax: (860) 571-5465      www.loctite.com

*Mfr./sale industrial adhesives, sealants and coatings..*

**Loctite U.K. Ltd., Walchmead, Welwyn Garden City, Hertfordshire AL7 1JB, UK**

Tel: 44-1707-358800   Fax: 44-1707-358900

## LORAL SPACE & COMMUNICATIONS LTD.

600 Third Ave., New York, NY, 10016

Tel: (212) 697-1105      Fax: (212) 338-5662      www.loral.com

*Marketing coordination: defense electronics, communications systems.*

**Loral CyberStar, Pinewood Studios - Pinewood Road, Iver Buckinghamshire SLO ONH, UK**

**Loral Skynet, 9 Clifford Street, London W1X 1RB, UK**

Tel: 44-207-534-7950   Fax: 44-207-534-7999

## LORD CORPORATION

2000 West Grandview Blvd, Erie, PA, 16514

Tel: (814) 868-0924      Fax: (814) 486-4345      www.chemlok.com

*Adhesives, coatings, chemicals, film products.*

**Durham Chemicals Ltd., Birtley, Chester-le-St., Durham DH3 1QX UK**

**Hughson Chemicals Co, Stretford Motorway Estate, Barton Dock Rd., Stretford, Manchester M32 0ZH UK**

## LOWE LINTAS & PARTNERS WORLDWIDE

One Dag Hammarskjold Plaza, New York, NY, 10017

Tel: (212) 605-8000      Fax: (212) 605-4705      www.interpublic.com

*Full-service, integrated marketing communications company/advertising agency.*

**Ammirati Puris Lintas London, 25 SoHo Square, London SW1V 1PX0, UK**

Tel: 44-207-434-5000   Contact: James Allman, CEO

## LSI LOGIC CORPORATION

1551 McCarthy Blvd, Milpitas, CA, 95035

Tel: (408) 433-8000        Fax: (408) 954-3220        www.lsilogic.com

*Develop/mfr. semiconductors.*

**LSI Logic Europe PLC,  Greenwood House, London Road, Bracknell, Berkshire RE12 2UB, UK**

Tel: 44-1-1344-426544    Fax: 44-1-1344-481039

## LTX CORPORATION

LTX Park, University Ave., Westwood, MA, 02090

Tel: (617) 461-1000        Fax: (617) 326-4883        www.ltx.com

*Design/mfr. computer-controlled semiconductor test systems.*

**LTX (Europe) Ltd.,  Woking Business Park, Albert Dr., Woking Surrey GU21 5JY, UK**

## THE LUBRIZOL CORPORATION

29400 Lakeland Blvd., Wickliffe, OH, 44092-2298

Tel: (440) 943-4200        Fax: (440) 943-5337        www.lubrizol.com

*Mfr. chemicals additives for lubricants and fuels.*

**Lubrizol (UK) Ltd.,  Palm Court, 4 Heron Sq., Richmond-upon-Thames, Surrey TW9 1EW, UK**

Tel: 44-181-940-6060

**Lubrizol Great Britain Ltd.,  Hampshire, UK**

Tel: 44-1329-825-823

## LUCENT NPS (NETWORK CARE PROFESSIONAL SERVICES)

1213 Innsbruck Dr., Sunnyvale, CA, 94089

Tel: (408) 542-0100        Fax: (408) 542-0101        www.ins.com

*Provides computer network support, designs networking systems, manages equipment purchase performance and software solutions.*

**International Network Services UK, Ltd.,  14/18 Bell St..2/F, Maidenhead, Berkshire SL6 1BR, UK**

Tel: 44-1628-675919    Fax: 44-1628-675918

## LUCENT TECHNOLOGIES, INC.

600 Mountain Ave., Murray Hill, NJ, 07974-0636

Tel: (908) 582-3000        Fax: (908) 582-2576        www.lucent.com

*Design/mfr. wide range of public and private networks, communication systems and software, data networking systems, business telephone systems and microelectronics components.*

**Lucent Technologies - Network Systems,  Swindon Rd., Malmesbury, Wiltshire SN16 9NA, UK**

Tel: 44-1666-822-861    Fax: 44-1666-824-515    Contact: Sam Baxter, PR Mgr.

**Lucent Technologies Bus. Communications Systems,  Octel House, Ancells Road, Fleet Hampshire GU 13, UK**

**Lucent Technologies Bus. Communications Systems Bell Labs,  Northgate House, Staple Gardens, Winchester Hants S023 8SR, UK**

**Lucent Technologies Wireless Ltd.,  Greenways Business Park - Unit 7, Bellinger Close, Malmesbury Rd., Chippenham SN15 1BN, UK**

Tel: 44-1666-832-740    Fax: 44-1666-832-181

**Lucent Technologies/Bell Labs,  Europe House, The Southwood Crescent, Farnborough, Hants, GU14 0NR, UK**

Tel: 44-1252-391600    Fax: 44-1252-376966

**Lucent Technologies/Bell Labs,  Swindon Road, Malmesbury Wiltshire, SN16 9NA, UK**

**Lucent Technologies/Bell Labs Global Commercial Markets,  101 Wigmore Street- 1/F, London W1H 9AB, UK**

Tel: 44-207-647-8000

**Microelectronics Europe,  Microelectronics House, Kingswood Kings Ride, Ascot Berkshire SL5 8AD, UK**

**Network Systems,  101 Wedmore St., 2nd Fl., London WIH 9AB, UK**

## LYONDELL

3801 West Chester Pike, Newtown Square, PA, 19073-2387

Tel: (610) 359-2000    Fax: (610) 359-2722    www.arcochem.com

*Mfr. propylene oxide, a chemical used for flexible foam products, coatings/paints and solvents/inks.*

**ARCO Chemical Europe, Inc., ARCO Chemical House, Bridge Ave., Maidenhead, Berkshire SL6 1YP UK**

Tel: 44-1628-77-5000

## LYONDELL CHEMICAL COMPANY

1221 McKinney St., Houston, TX, 77010

Tel: (713) 652-7200    Fax: (713) 309-2074    www.lyondell.com

*Mfr. polymers and petrochemicals.*

**Lyondell Chemical European Hdqrts., Lyondell House - Bridge Avenue, Maidenhead Berkshire SL6 1 YP, UK**

Tel: 44-1626-77-5000

## M/A-COM INC.

1011 Pawtucket Boulevard, Lowell, MA, 01853-3295

Tel: (978) 442-5000    Fax: (978) 442-5354    www.macom.com

*Mfr. electronic components, semiconductor devices and communications equipment.*

**M/A-COM Ltd., Centennial Court, Easthampstead Road, Bracknell Berkshire RG12 1YQ, UK**

Tel: 44-1344-869595   Fax: 44-1344-300020

## MacANDREWS & FORBES GROUP INC.

35 East 62nd St., New York, NY, 10021

Tel: (212) 688-9000    Fax: (212) 572-8400

*Jewelry, watches, chocolate, cocoa and cosmetics.*

**MacAndrews & Forbes Co. Inc., Pembroke House, 44 Wellesley Rd., Croydon CR9 3QE, UK**

## MacDERMID INC.

245 Freight Street, Waterbury, CT, 06702-0671

Tel: (203) 575-5700    Fax: (203) 575-7900    www.macdermid.com

*Chemicals processing for metal industrial, plastics, electronics cleaners, strippers.*

**MacDermid G.B. Ltd., Stafford Park, 18 Telford, Shropshire TF3 3BN, UK**

Tel: 44-1952-290292   Fax: 44-1952-290375

## R.H. MACY & COMPANY INC.

151 West 34th Street, New York, NY, 10001

Tel: (212) 695-4400    Fax: (212) 643-1307    www.macys.com

*Department stores; importers.*

**R.H. Macy & Co. Inc., Elsley House, 24/30 Great Titchfield St., London WIP 8AO, UK**

## MAGNETEK

26 Century Blvd., Ste. 600, Nashville, TN, 37214

Tel: (615) 316-5100    Fax: (615) 316-5181    www.magnetek.com

*Mfr. fractional horsepower electric motors.*

**MagneTek Universal Electric Ltd., PO Box 8, Peatham Rd., Gainsborough, Lincolnshire DN21 1XU, UK**

## MAGNETROL INTERNATIONAL

5300 Belmont Road, Downers Grove, IL, 60515-4499

Tel: (630) 969-4000    Fax: (630) 969-9489    www.magnetrol.com

*Mfr. level and flow instrumentation.*

**Magnetrol International, Regent Business Centre, Jubilee Rd., Burgess Hill, W. Sussex RH15 9T1 UK**

Tel: 44-1444-871-313   Fax: 44-1444-871-317   Contact: Paul Sayers, Gen. Mgr.

## MAIL-WELL, INC.

23 Inverness Way East, Ste. 160, Englewood, CO, 80112-5713

Tel: (303) 790-8023     Fax: (303) 566-7466     www.mail-well.com

*Engaged in commercial printing of custom envelopes and labels for direct mail, billing and catalogs.*

**Mail-Well Label, Victoria House, Victoria Road, Eccleshill - Bradford, West Yorkshire BD2 2DD, UK**

**Mail-Well Label, Unit 4 City Estates, Corngreaves Road, Cardley Heath West Midlands B64 7EP, UK**

**Mail-Well Label, Bingswood Industrial Estate, Whaley Bridge, Stockport SK23 7SP, UK**

## MALLINCKRODT INC.

675 McDonnell Blvd., St. Louis, MO, 63134

Tel: (314) 654-2000     Fax: (314) 654-5380     www.mallinckrodt.com

*Distributes health care products and specialty pharmaceuticals.*

**Mallinckrodt UK Limited, 10 Talisman Business Centre, London Road Bicester Oxfordshire OX6 0JX, UK**

Tel: 44-1869-322700   Fax: 44-1869-321890

## THE MANITOWOC COMPANY, INC.

500 South 16th St., Manitowoc, WI, 54220

Tel: (920) 684-4410     Fax: (920) 683-8129     www.manitowoc.com

*Mfr. cranes, ice-making machinery and contract products; ship repair and conversion.*

**Manitowoc Europe Ltd., St. James Mill Rd., Northampton NN5 5JW, UK**

## MANPOWER INTERNATIONAL INC.

5301 N. Ironwood Rd., PO Box 2053, Milwaukee, WI, 53201-2053

Tel: (414) 961-1000     Fax: (414) 961-7081     www.manpower.com

*Temporary help, contract service, training and testing.*

**Manpower Plc. - International Hdqtrs., International House, 66 Chiltern St., London W1M 1PR, UK**

Tel: 44-207-224-6688  Fax: 44-207-224-5253

## MANUGISTICS INC.

2115 East Jefferson Street, Rockville, MD, 20852

Tel: (301) 984-5000     Fax: (301) 984-5094     www.manugistics.com

*Computer software development services.*

**Manugistics International Ltd., Royal Albert House, Sheet St., Windsor, Berkshire SL4 1BE, UK**

## MARATHON OIL COMPANY

5555 San Felipe Road, Houston, TX, 77056

Tel: (713) 629-6600     Fax: (713) 296-2952     www.marathon.com

*Oil and gas exploration.*

**Marathon Oil (UK) Ltd., Marathon House, 174 Marylebone Rd., London NW1 5AT, UK**

## MARCONI DATA SYSTEMS, INC.

1500 Mittel Blvd., Wood Dale, IL, 60191

Tel: (630) 860-7300     Fax: (630) 616-3657     www.videojet.com

*Mfr. computer peripherals and hardware, state-of-the-art industrial ink jet marking and coding products.*

**Marconi Data Systems, 153 Dixons Hill Road, Welham Green, Herts, AL9 7JE, UK**

Tel: 44-1707-275-844   Fax: 44-1707-272-492

## MARK IV INDUSTRIES INC.

501 John James Audubon Pkwy., PO Box 810, Amherst, NY, 14226-0810

Tel: (716) 689-4972     Fax: (716) 689-1529     www.mark-iv.com

*Mfr. of engineered systems and components utilizing mechanical and fluid power transmission, fluid transfer, and power systems and components.*

**Dayco Europe Ltd., The Washington Centre, Halesowen Rd., Dudley West Midlands DY2 9RE, UK**

Tel: 44-1384-245200   Fax: 44-1384-240222

**MARKEM CORPORATION**

150 Congress Street, Keene, NH, 03431

Tel: (603) 352-1130     Fax: (603) 357-1835     www.markem.com.

*Mfr./sales of industrial marking, print machinery and hot stamping foils.*

**Markem Systems Ltd., Astor Road & Eccles New Road, Salford Manchester M5 3DA, UK**

Tel: 44-161-789-5500    Fax: 44-161-707-5566

**Markem Systems, Ltd., Ladywell Trading Estate, Eccles Ne Rd., PO Box 3, Salford, Lancashire M5 2DA UK**

Tel: 44-161-789-5500    Fax: 44-161-707-5566

**MARKET FACTS INC.**

3040 Salt Creek Lane, Arlington Heights, IL, 60005

Tel: (847) 590-7000     Fax: (847) 590-7010     www.marketfacts.com

*Market research services.*

**Market Facts, Inc., Parker Tower 43-49, Parker Street, London WC2B 5PS, UK**

Tel: 44-207-430-6132    Contact: Virginia Weil

**MARLEY COOLING TOWER COMPANY**

7401 West 129th Street, Overland Park, KS, 66213

Tel: (913) 664-7400     Fax: (913) 664-7641     www.marleyct.com

*Cooling and heating towers and waste treatment systems.*

**Marley Davenport Ltd., Gregory's Bank, Worcester WR3 8AB, UK**

Tel: 44-1905-720-200    Fax: 44-1905-720-201

**MARRIOTT INTERNATIONAL INC.**

10400 Fernwood Rd., Bethesda, MD, 20817

Tel: (301) 380-3000     Fax: (301) 380-5181     www.marriott.com

*Hotel services.*

**Marriott Courtyard Milton Keynes, London Rd., Newport Pagnell, Buckinghamshire, Milton Keynes MK 16 0JA UK**

Tel: 44-1908-613688    Fax: 44-1908-617335

**Marriott Courtyard Northampton, Bedford Rd., Northampton NN4 7YF, UK**

Tel: 44-1604-622777    Fax: 44-1604-635454

**MARS INC.**

6885 Elm Street, McLean, VA, 22101-3810

Tel: (703) 821-4900     Fax: (703) 448-9678     www.mars.com

*Mfr. candy, snack foods, rice products and cat food.*

**Mars Ltd., Dundee Rd., Trading Estate, Slough, Buckinghamshire UK**

**MARSH & McLENNAN COS INC.**

1166 Ave. of the Americas, New York, NY, 10036-2774

Tel: (212) 345-5000     Fax: (212) 345-4808     www.marshmac.com

*Insurance agents/brokers, pension and investment management consulting services.*

**Global Risk Management Consultancy, Aldgate House, 33 Aldgate High St., London EC3N 1AQ, UK**

Tel: 44-207-945-7978    Fax: 44-207-945-7955

**J&H Marsh & McLennan Ltd., Aldgate House, 33 Aldgate High St., London EC3N 1AQ, UK**

Tel: 44-207-945-7700    Fax: 44-207-481-4277    Contact: Patrick Franklin-Adams

**J&H Marsh & McLennan UK Ltd., The Bowring Bldg., Tower Place, London EC3P 3BE, UK**

Tel: 44-207-357-1000    Fax: 44-207-929-2705    Contact: Dan Jones

**Sedgwick Group, Sackville House,143-152 Finchurch Street, London EC3N 6BN, UK**

Tel: 44-207-377-3456    Fax: 44-207-377-3199    Contact: R. White-Cooper, CEO

**William M. Mercer Fraser Ltd., Burwood House, 16 Caxton St., London SW1H 0QV, UK**

## MARSH BELLOFRAM

State Route 2, Box 305, Newell, WV, 26050

Tel: (304) 387-1200     Fax: (304) 387-1212     www.marshbellofram.com

*Distributor of pressure gauges, valves and transmitters.*

**Bellofram Europe, Crossgate Drive, Queens Drive Industrial Estate, Nottingham NG2 1LQ, UK**

Tel: 44-115-993-3303  Fax: 44-115-993-3301   Contact: Steve Clissold

## MASCO CORPORATION

21001 Van Born Road, Taylor, MI, 48180

Tel: (313) 274-7400     Fax: (313) 374-6666     www.masco.com

*Mfr. faucets, cabinets, locks and numerous home improvement, building and home furnishings products.*

**A&J Gummers, Birmingham, UK**

**Ametex UK Ltd., New England House, E. Riddlesden Bus. Park, Bradford Rd., Keighley W. Yorkshire BD20 5JH, UK**

**Avocet Hardware Plc, Brighton, UK**

**Berglen Group, Ltd., Waxford Business Park, Caxton Way, Watford Hertfordshire WD1 8ZF, UK**

Tel: 44-1923-690100

**Moore Group Ltd., Queen Mary House, Thorp Arch Trading Estate, Wetherby, West Yorkshire LS23 7BR UK**

Tel: 44-1937-842394

## MASONITE CORPORATION

One South Wacker Drive, Chicago, IL, 60606

Tel: (312) 750-0900     Fax: (312) 750-0958     www.masonite.com

*Mfr. hardboard, softboard and molded products.*

**Masonite Europe UK, Jason House Kerry Hill, Horseforth Leeds, LS18 4JR, UK**

Tel: 44-113-2587-689   Contact: Rogar Bruce

## MATTEL INC.

333 Continental Blvd., El Segundo, CA, 90245-5012

Tel: (310) 252-2000     Fax: (310) 252-2179     www.mattelmedia.com

*Mfr. toys, dolls, games, crafts and hobbies.*

**Fisher-Price Ltd., Fisher-Price House, Oaklands Park, Fishponds Rd., Wokingham RG11 2FD UK**

**Kiddicraft Ltd., 13 Bridge Rd., Southall UB2 4AG, UK**

**Mattel United Kingdom Ltd., Meridian West, Leicester LE3 2WJ, UK**

## MAXON CORPORATION

201 East 18th Street, Muncie, IN, 47302

Tel: (765) 284-3304     Fax: (765) 286-8394     www.maxoncorp.com

*Industry combustion equipment and valves.*

**Maxon Combustion Systems Ltd., Chantry House, High Street, B46 3BP Coleshil, UK**

Tel: 44-1675-464334  Fax: 44-1675-467285

## MAXTOR CORPORATION

510 Cottonwood Drive, Milpitas, CA, 95035-7403

Tel: (408) 432-1700     Fax: (408) 432-4510     www.maxtor.com

*Mfr. develops and markets hard disk drives for desktop computer systems.*

**Maxtor Europe Ltd., Herts, UK**

## MAXXAM INC.

5847 San Felipe, Ste. 2600, Houston, TX, 77057

Tel: (713) 975-7600     Fax: (713) 267-3701

*Holding company for aluminum and timber products and real estate industries.*

**MAXXAM Inc., England, UK**

## MAYER, BROWN & PLATT

190 S. LaSalle Street, Chicago, IL, 60603

Tel: (312) 782-0600      Fax: (312) 701-7711      www.mayerbrown.com

*International law firm.*

**Mayer, Brown & Platt, Bucklersbury House, 3 Queen Victoria St., London EC4N 8EL, UK**

Tel: 44-207-246-6200   Fax: 44-207-329-4465

## MAYTAG CORPORATION

403 West Fourth Street North, Newton, IA, 50208

Tel: (515) 792-8000      Fax: (515) 787-8376      www.maytagcorp.com

*Mfr./sales of large appliances, ovens, dishwashers, refrigerators and washing machines.*

**Maytag International, Hayes Gate House, 27 Uxbridge Rd., Middlesex, UB4 OJN, UK**

Tel: 44-181-569-3030

## MBIA INC.

113 King Street, Armonk, NY, 10504

Tel: (914) 273-4545      Fax: (914) 765-3299      www.mbia.com

*Provides investment and treasury management services and insurance for municipal bonds.*

**MBIA Insurance Corporation, 1 Great St. Helen's 2/F, London EC3A6HX, UK**

Tel: 44-20-7920-6363   Contact: Jack Caouette

## MBNA CORPORATION

1100 N. King Street, Wilmington, DE, 19801

Tel: (302) 453-9930      Fax: (302) 432-3614      www.mbna.com

*Credit card issuer dealing primarily with VISA and MasterCard, home equity loans and property and casualty insurance.*

**MBNA International Bank Ltd., London, UK**

**MBNA International Bank Ltd., Chester, UK**

## McCALL PATTERN COMPANY

11 Penn Plaza, New York, NY, 10001

Tel: (212) 465-6800      Fax: (212) 465-6831      www.mccallpattern.com

*Fashion patterns.*

**McCall Pattern Co., England, UK**

## McCANN-ERICKSON WORLDGROUP

750 Third Ave., New York, NY, 10017

Tel: (212) 984-3644      Fax: (212) 984-2629      www.mccann.com

*International advertising and marketing services.*

**McCann Direct, Haddon House, 2-4 Fitzroy Street, London W1A 1AT, UK**

**McCann-Erickson Advertising Ltd., McCann-Erickson House, 36 Howland Street, London W1A 1AT, UK**

**McCann-Erickson Network Ltd., 36 Howland Street, London W1A 1AT, UK**

**Salesdesk Ltd., Haddon House, 2-4 Fitzroy Street, London W1A 1AT, UK**

**The Harrison Agency, Haddon House, 2-4 Fitzroy Street, London W1A 1AT, UK**

## McCORMICK & COMPANY, INC.

18 Loveton Circle, Sparks, MD, 21152-6000

Tel: (410) 771-7301      Fax: (410) 527-8289      www.mccormick.com

*Manufactures, markets and distributes spices, seasonings, flavours and other specialty food products.*

**McCormick U.K. PLC, Thame Rd., Haddenham, Aylesbury, Buckinghamshire HP 17 8LB, UK**

## McDERMOTT INTERNATIONAL INC.

1450 Poydras Street, PO Box 60035, New Orleans, LA, 70160-0035

Tel: (504) 587-5400     Fax: (504) 587-6153     www.mcdermott.com

*Provides energy, engineering and construction services for industrial, utility, and hydrocarbon processing facilities, and to the offshore oil and natural gas industries.*

**J. Ray McDermott SA,  One Albemarle St., London W1X 3HF, UK**

## McDERMOTT WILL & EMERY

227 W. Monroe Street, Chicago, IL, 60606-5096

Tel: (312) 372-2000     Fax: (312) 984-7700     www.mwe.com

*International law firm.*

**McDermott, Will & Emery LLC,  7 Bishopsgate, London EC2N 3AQ, UK**

Tel: 44-207-577-6900   Fax: 44-207-577-6950   Contact: John Reynolds

## McDONALD'S CORPORATION

McDonald's Plaza, Oak Brook, IL, 60523

Tel: (630) 623-3000     Fax: (630) 623-7409     www.mcdonalds.com

*Fast food chain stores.*

**McDonald's Corp.,  London, UK**

## THE McGRAW-HILL COMPANIES

1221 Ave. of the Americas, New York, NY, 10020

Tel: (212) 512-2000     Fax: (212) 512-2703     www.mccgraw-hill.com

*Books, magazines, information systems, financial service, publishing and broadcast operations.*

**DRI Europe Ltd.,  Wimbledon Bridge House, 1 Hartfield Rd., Wimbledon SW19 3RU, UK**

**McGraw-Hill Book Co. UK Ltd., McG-H Intl. Training Systems,  Shoppenhangers Rd., Maidenhead, Berkshire SL6 2Q1, UK**

**McGraw-Hill Intl. Publications Co. Ltd.,  Wimbledon Bridge House, 1 Hartfield Rd., Wimbledon SW19 3RU, UK**

## McKINSEY & COMPANY

55 East 52nd Street, New York, NY, 10022

Tel: (212) 446-7000     Fax: (212) 446-8575     www.mckinsey.com

*Management and business consulting services.*

**McKinsey & Company,  London - BTO, 1 Jermyn St., London SW1Y 4UH UK**

Tel: 44-207-839-8040   Fax: 44-207-873-9777

**McKinsey & Company,  One Jermyn St., London SW1Y 4UH, UK**

Tel: 44-207-839-8040   Fax: 44-207-873-9777

## MCS SOFTWARE CORPORATION

815 Colorado Blvd., Los Angeles, CA, 90041

Tel: (323) 258-9111     Fax: (323) 259-3838     www.macsch.com

*Develop finite element analysis software used in the field of computer-aided engineering.*

**PDA Engineering,  Rowan House, Woodlands Business Village, Coronation Rd., Basingstoke, Hamps RG21 2IX UK**

**The MacNeal-Schwendler Co. Ltd.,  MSC House - Lyon Way, Frimley, Camberley, Surrey GU16 5ER UK**

**The MacNeal-Schwendler Co. Ltd.,  Magnetic House, 51 Waterfront Quay, Salford, Manchester M5 2XW UK**

## MEAD CORPORATION

Courthouse Plaza, NE, Dayton, OH, 45463

Tel: (937) 495-6323     Fax: (937) 461-2424     www.mead.com

*Mfr. paper, packaging, pulp, lumber and other wood products, school and office products; electronic publishing and distribution.*

**Mead Coated Board U.K. Ltd., Hartford House, Rickmansworth, Hertfordshire WD2 24B, UK**

Tel: 44-923-897272   Fax: 44-923-896880   Contact: Nick Croggs, Mng. Dir.

**Mead Packaging Ltd., 500 Woodward Ave., Yate, Bristol BS175YS, UK**

Tel: 44-1454-32-0000   Fax: 44-1454-32-0033   Contact: Ian Gatehouse, Mng. Dir.

## MECHANICAL DYNAMICS, INC.

2301 Commonwealth Blvd., Ann Arbor, MI, 48105

Tel: (734) 994-3800     Fax: (734) 994-6418     www.adams.com

*Mfr. Adams prototyping software to automotive industry.*

**Mechanical Dynamics International Ltd., 12 Clarendon Street, Warwickshire CV32 5ST, UK**

Tel: 441-926-420-230

## MEDAR INC.

24775 Crestview Court, Farmington Hills, MI, 48335-1563

Tel: (248) 477-3900     Fax: (248) 477-8897     www.medar.com

*Mfr. machine vision-based inspection systems and resistance welding controls for industry manufacturers.*

**Integral Vision Ltd., Unit 12 Railton Rd., Woburn Road Industrial Estate, Kempston, Bedford MK42 7PW UK**

## MEDEX ASSISTANCE CORPORATION

9515 Deereco Road, 4th Fl., Timonium, MD, 21093

Tel: (410) 453-6300     Fax: (410) 453-6301     www.medexassist.com

*Medical and travel related assistance service.*

**Medex Assistance (Europe) PLC, Norwood House, 9 Dyke Rd., Brighton, East Sussex BN1 3FE, UK**

## MEDIALINK WORLDWIDE INC.

708 Third Ave., New York, NY, 10017

Tel: (212) 682-8300     Fax: (212) 682-2370     www.medialink.com

*Produces and distributes video and news releases for corporate and institutional clients worldwide, and public relations services.*

**Medialink Worldwide Inc., 37/38 Golden Square, London W1R 3AA, UK**

Tel: 44-207-439-1774   Fax: 44-207-439-1378   Contact: Jim Gold

## MEDICUS GROUP INTERNATIONAL

1675 Broadway, New York, NY, 10019

Tel: (212) 468-3100     Fax: (212) 468-3222     www.medicusgroup.com

*Healthcare communications company engaged in professional advertising, sales promotion, global branding and launch planning.*

**Medicus UK London, 516 Wandsworth Road, London SW8 3JX, UK**

## MEDTRONIC INC.

7000 Central Ave., NE, Minneapolis, MN, 55432

Tel: (612) 574-4000     Fax: (612) 574-4879     www.medtronic.com

*Mfr./sale/service electrotherapeutic medical devices.*

**Medtronic Ltd., Sherbourne House, Suite One, Croxley Business Centre, Watford WD1 8YE, UK**

## MELLON FINANCIAL CORPORATION

One Mellon Bank Center, Pittsburgh, PA, 15258-0001

Tel: (412) 234-5000     Fax: (412) 236-1662     www.mellon.com

*Commercial and trade banking and foreign exchange.*

**Mellon Europe Ltd., Princess House, 1 Suffolk Lane, London EC4R 0AN, UK**

Tel: 44-207-623-0800

**Mellon London Branch, Princess House, 1 Suffolk Lane, London EC4R 0AN, UK**

**Newton Management Ltd., London, UK**

Tel: 44-207-323-9000    Contact: Stewart W. Newton

**Pareto Partners, 271 Regent St., London W1R 8PP, UK**

**Premier Administration Ltd., 5 Rayleigh Rd., Hutton, Brentwood, Essex CM13 1AA, UK**

Tel: 44-127-722-7300

## MEMC ELECTRONIC MATERIALS, INC.

501 Pearl Drive, St. Peters, MO, 63376

Tel: (636) 474-5500     Fax: (636) 474-5161     www.memc.com

*Mfg. and distribution of silicon wafers.*

**MEMC Electronic Materials (UK) Ltd., Witan Court, 272 Witan Gate West, Central Milton Keynes, Buckinghamshire MK9 1EJ UK**

Tel: 44-1908-398500   Fax: 44-1908-398508

## MEMOREX CORPORATION

10100 Pioneer Blvd., Ste. 110, Santa Fe Springs, CA, 90670

Tel: (562) 906-2800     Fax: (562) 906-2848     www.memorex.com

*Magnetic recording tapes, etc.*

**Memorex UK Ltd., Hounslow House, 730 London Rd., Hounslow Middlesex, UK**

**Memorex UK Ltd., 96-102 Church St., Staines, Middlesex, UK**

## MENTOR CORPORATION

201 Menton Drive, Santa Barbara, CA, 93111

Tel: (805) 879-6000     Fax: (805) 967-7108     www.mentorcorp.com

*Mfr. breast implants.*

**Mentor Medical Systems Ltd., U.K., The Woolpack - Church Street, Wantage Oxon OX12 8BL, UK**

Tel: 44-1235-768758

## MENTOR GRAPHICS/MICROTEC RESEARCH

8005 SW Boeckman Road, Wilsonville, OR, 97070-7777

Tel: (503) 685-7000     Fax: (503) 685-1202     www.mentorg.com

*Develop/mfr. software tools for embedded systems market.*

**Microtec Research Ltd., 8 Elmwood, Chineham Business Park, Basingstoke RG 24 8WG, UK**

## MERCER MANAGEMENT CONSULTING INC.

1166 Ave. of the Americas, New York, NY, 10036

Tel: (212) 345-3400     Fax: (212) 345-7414     www.mercermc.com

*Provides clients with counsel in such areas as corporate and business strategy and growth planning, org development, and market and operations enhancement.*

**Mercer Management, 1-3 Grosvenor Place, London SW1X 7HJ, UK**

## MERCK & COMPANY, INC.

One Merck Drive, PO Box 100, Whitehouse Station, NJ, 08889-0100

Tel: (908) 423-1000     Fax: (908) 423-2592     www.merck.com

*Pharmaceuticals, chemicals and biologicals.*

**Merck, Sharp & Dohme Ltd., Herford Rd., Hoddesdon Herts, Herts. EN11 9BU, UK**

## MERCURY INTERACTIVE CORPORATION

1325 Borregas Ave., Sunnyvale, CA, 94089

Tel: (408) 822-5200      Fax: (408) 822-5300      www.merc-int.com

*Mfr. computer software to decipher and eliminate "bugs" from systems.*

**Mercury Interactive (UK) Ltd., 16 Coliseum Business Centre, Riverside Way, Watchmoor Park - Camberley, Surrey GU 15 3YL UK**

Tel: 44-1276-808200   Fax: 44-1276-29134

## MERITOR AUTOMOTIVE, INC.

2135 West Maple Road, Troy, MI, 48084-7186

Tel: (248) 435-1000      Fax: (248) 435-1393      www.meritorauto.com

*Mfr./sales of light and heavy vehicle systems for trucks, cars and specialty vehicles.*

**Meritor Heavy Vehicle Systems Ltd., 75/76 Brindley Rd., Astmoor Industrial Estate, Runcorn, Cheshire WA7 1BR UK**

**Meritor Light Vehicle Systems (UK) Ltd.,, Birmingham, West Midlands UK**

## MERRILL LYNCH & COMPANY, INC.

World Financial Center, 250 Vesey Street, New York, NY, 10281-1332

Tel: (212) 449-1000      Fax: (212) 449-2892      www.ml.com

*Security brokers and dealers, investment and business services.*

**Mercury Asset Management Co., London, UK**

**Merrill Lynch Europe PLC, Ropemaker Place, 25 Ropemaker St., London EC2Y 9LY, UK**

**Merrill Lynch International, 20 Farringdon Rd., London EC1M 3NH, UK**

Tel: 44-207-772-1000

**Merrill Lynch International Bank, 33 Chester St., London SW1X 7XD, UK**

Tel: 44-207-628-1000   Fax: 44-207-867-4040

## METAL IMPROVEMENT COMPANY

10 Forest Ave., Paramus, NJ, 07652

Tel: (201) 843-7800      Fax: (201) 843-3460      www.metalimprovement.com

*Mfr. shot peening.*

**Metal Improvement Co., Ascot Dr., Derby DE2 8ST, UK**

**Metal Improvement Co., Hambridge Lane Unit 3, Newbury Berkshire, UK**

## METALLURG INC.

6 East 43rd Street, New York, NY, 10017

Tel: (212) 687-9470      Fax: (212) 697-2874      www.mettalurg.com

*Mfr. ferrous and nonferrous alloys and metals.*

**London & Scandinavian Metallurgical Co. Ltd., 45 Wimbledon Hill Rd., London SW19 7LZ, UK**

**Metallurg UK, Fullerton Road, Rotherham, South Yorkshire S60 1DL, UK**

## METHODE ELECTRONICS INC.

7401 W. Wilson Ave., Chicago, IL, 60656

Tel: (708) 867-6777      Fax: (708) 867-6999      www.methode.com

*Mfr. electronic components.*

**Methode Electronics Europe Ltd., 17 Bishop Street, Cherry Orchard, Shrewsbury Shropshire SY2 SHA, UK**

**Methode Electronics Europe Ltd., Vale of Leven Industrial Estate, Dumbarton G82 3PD, UK**

## METROPOLITAN LIFE INSURANCE COMPANY

1 Madison Ave., New York, NY, 10010-3603

Tel: (212) 578-3818     Fax: (212) 252-7294     www.metlife.com

*Insurance and retirement savings products and services.*

**Albany Life Assurance Co. Ltd., Metropolitain House, 3 Darkes Lane, Potters Bar Hertsford EN6 1AJ, UK**

Tel: 44-852-2973-4000   Fax: 44-852-2826-9189   Contact: Joseph Yau, CEO & Mng. Dir.

**GFM Intl. Investors Ltd., Orion House 11th floor, 5 Upper St. Martin's Lane, London WC2H 9EA, UK**

Tel: 44-207-957-9000   Fax: 44-207-957-9020   Contact: Ralph F. Verni, Chmn. & CEO

## METZLER/PAYDEN, LLC

333 South Grand Avenue, Los Angeles, CA, 90071

Tel: (213) 625-1900     Fax: (213) 617-3110     www.payden-rygel.com

*Engaged in financial and investment advisory services.*

**Payden and Rygel Global Ltd., London, UK**

## MICREL, INCORPORATED

1849 Fortune Drive, San Jose, CA, 95131

Tel: (408) 944-0800     Fax: (408) 944-0970     www.micrel.com

*Designer and mfr. of analog integrated circuits.*

**Micrel Europe, 21 Old Newtown Rd., Newbury RG14 7DP, UK**

Tel: 44-1635-524455   Fax: 44-1635-524466

## MICRO AGE, INC.

2400 South MicroAge Way, Tempe, AZ, 85282-1896

Tel: (480) 366-2000     Fax: (480) 966-7339     www.microage.com

*Computer systems integrator, software products and telecommunications equipment.*

**MicroAge EMEA Regional Headquarters, Unit 7, Argent Centre, Silverdale Road, Haye, Middlesex UB3 3BS, UK**

Tel: 44-181-587-3636   Fax: 44-181-587-3619

## MICRO TOUCH SYSTEMS, INC.

300 Griffin Brook Park Drive, Methuen, MA, 01844

Tel: (978) 659-9000     Fax: (978) 659-9100     www.microtouch.com

*Mfr. clear coatings for computer monitors.*

**MicroTouch Systems, Ltd., 163 Milton Park, Abingdon, Oxon OX14 4SD, UK**

Tel: 44-1235-444400   Fax: 44-1235-861603

## MICRO WAREHOUSE, INC.

535 Connecticut Ave., Norwalk, CT, 06854

Tel: (203) 899-4000     Fax: (203) 899-4203     www.warehouse.com

*Catalog computer sales.*

**Micro Warehouse Ltd., Horizon One Studio Way, Borehamwood, Herts WD6 6WH, UK**

Tel: 44-870-516-8674   Fax: 44-870-514-3338

## MICROCHIP TECHNOLOGY INCORPORATED

2355 West Chandler Boulevard, Chandler, AZ, 85224

Tel: (602) 786-7200     Fax: (602) 899-9210     www.microchip.com

*Mfr. electronic subassemblies and components.*

**AZ Microchip Technology Ltd., Microchip House, 505 Eskdale Rd., Wokingham, Berkshire RG41 5TU UK**

Tel: 44-118-921-5800   Fax: 44-118-921-5820

## MICROMERITICS INSTRUMENT CORPORATION

One Micromeritics Drive, Norcross, GA, 30093-1877

Tel: (770) 662-3620      Fax: (770) 662-3696      www.micromeritics.com

*Mfr. analytical instruments.*

**Micromeritics Ltd., Unit 2 Chestnut House, 178-182 High Street North, Dunstable Bedfordshire LU6 1AT, UK**

Tel: 44-1582-475248

## MICRON TECHNOLOGY, INC. (MTI)

8000 S. Federal Way, Boise, ID, 83707-0006

Tel: (208) 368-4000      Fax: (208) 368-4435      www.micron.com

*Mfr. random-access memory chips and semi-conductor memory components.*

**Micron Europe Limited, Micron House Wellington Business Park, Dukes Ride, Crowthorne Berkshire RG45 6LS, UK**

Tel: 44-1344-750750   Fax: 44-1344-750710

**Micron Europe Ltd., Orchard Court, 1 Warfield Road, Bracknell Berkshire RG12 2XJ, UK**

Tel: 44-1344-383-300

## MICROSOFT CORPORATION

One Microsoft Way, Redmond, WA, 98052-6399

Tel: (425) 882-8080      Fax: (425) 936-7329      www.microsoft.com

*Computer software, peripherals and services.*

**Microsoft United Kingdom Ltd., Microsoft Campus, Thames Valley Park, Reading RG6 1WG, UK**

Tel: 44-870-601-0100   Fax: 44-870-602-0100

## MIDAMERICAN ENERGY HOLDINGS

666 Grand Ave., Des Moines, IA, 50303

Tel: (515) 281-2900      Fax: (515) 281-2389      www.midamerican.com

*Geothermal power; generates, transmits, and distributes electricity.*

**MidAmerican Energy Holdings, Tyne, UK**

## MILACRON INC.

2090 Florence Ave., Cincinnati, OH, 45206

Tel: (513) 487-5000      Fax: (513) 487-5057      www.milacron.com

*Metalworking and plastics technologies.*

**Ferromatik Milacron (U.K.) Ltd., Carrwood Road, Chesterfield Trading Estate, GB Chesterfield/Derbyshire S41 9QB, UK**

Tel: 44-1246-260666   Fax: 44-1246-260474   Contact: David Lister

## MILBANK, TWEED, HADLEY & McCLOY LLP

1 Chase Manhattan Plaza, New York, NY, 10005-1413

Tel: (212) 530-5000      Fax: (212) 530-5219      www.milbank.com

*International law practice.*

**Milbank, Tweed, Hadley & McCloy, Dashwood House, 69 Old Brad St., EC2M 1QS, London, UK**

Tel: 44-207-448-3000   Fax: 44-207-448-3029

## MILGO-TIMEPLEX, INC.

1619 N. Harrison Pkwy., Bldg. D, Sunrise, FL, 33323

Tel: (954) 846-6434      Fax: (954) 846-3275      www.milgo.com

*Mfr. sale and services data communications equipment for network solutions.*

**Timeplex Ltd., Timeplex House, North Parkway, Leeds LS14 6PX, UK**

**Timeplex Ltd., 77 Boston Manor Rd., Brentford, Middlesex TW8 95W, UK**

## MILLER ELECTRIC MFG. COMPANY

PO Box 1079, 1636 W. Spencer, Appleton, WI, 54912-1079

Tel: (920) 734-9821     Fax: (920) 735-4125     www.millerwelds.com

*Mfr. arc welding machines.*

**ITW Welding Products, Unit B1 Deakins Business Park, Blackburn Road Egerton, Bolton BL7 9RP, UK**

Tel: 44-1204-593-493   Fax: 44-1204-598-066

## MILLIPORE CORPORATION

80 Ashby Road, PO Box 9125, Bedford, MA, 01730

Tel: (781) 533-6000     Fax: (781) 533-3110     www.millipore.com

*Mfr. flow and pressure measurement and control components; precision filters, hi-performance liquid chromatography instruments.*

**Millipore (UK) Ltd., The Boulevard, Blackmoor Lane, Watford Hertshire WD1 8YW, UK**

## MILTON ROY COMPANY

201 Ivyland Road, Ivylan, PA, 18974

Tel: (215) 441-0800     Fax: (215) 293-0468     www.miltonroy.com

*Mfr. medical and industry equipment and process control instruments.*

**Milton Roy UK Ltd., Oaklands Business Centre Wokingham Berks RG41 2FD, UK**

Tel: 44-11-89-77-10-66   Fax: 44-11-89-77-11-98   Contact: Martin Eagle

## MINOLTA QMS INC.

One Magnum Pass, Mobile, AL, 36618

Tel: (205) 633-4300     Fax: (205) 633-4866     www.qms.com

*Mfr. monochrome and color computer printers.*

**QMS UK Ltd., Old Bridge House - The Hythe, Staines Middlesex, TW18 3JF UK**

## MINTEQ INTERNATIONAL INC.

405 Lexington Ave., 19th Fl., New York, NY, 10174-1901

Tel: (212) 878-1800     Fax: (212) 878-1952     www.mineralstech.com

*Mfr./market specialty refractory and metallurgical products and application systems.*

**MINTEQ U.K. Ltd., Aldwarke Road, Rawmarsh, Rotherham, SouthYorkshire S65 3SR UK**

Tel: 44-1709-528-816   Fax: 44-1709-710-073   Contact: R. Brown, Mng. Dir.   Emp: 84

## MODEM MEDIA, INC.

230 East Avenue, Norwalk, CT, 06855

Tel: (203) 299-7000     Fax: (230) 299-7060     www.modemmedia.com

*Provides on-line marketing and consulting services.*

**Modem Media, Inc., 183 Eversholt Street, London NW1 1BU, UK**

Tel: 44-20-7874-9400   Fax: 44-20-7874-9555   Contact: Tim Sexton, Mng. Dir.

## MODINE MANUFACTURING COMPANY

1500 DeKoven Ave., Racine, WI, 53403

Tel: (262) 636-1200     Fax: (262) 636-1424     www.modine.com

*Mfr. heat-transfer products.*

**Modine Intl. Sales Ltd., Raines House, Denby Dale Rd., Wakefield West Yorkshire WF1 1HR, UK**

## MODIS PROFESSIONAL SERVICES, INC.

1 Independent Dr., Jacksonville, FL, 32202-5060

Tel: (904) 360-2000     Fax: (904) 360-2814     www.modispro.com

*Engaged in staffing for professional services and information technology.*

**Badenoch & Clark, 14 Waterloo Street, Birmingham EN B2STX, UK**

Tel: 44-181-686-6337

**Badenoch & Clark,** 16-18 New Bridge Street, London EC4V 6AU, UK
Tel: 44-207-583-0073    Fax: 44-207-353-3908

**Badenoch & Clark,** 16-18 New Bridge Street, London EC4V 6AU, UK
Tel: 44-207-583-0073    Fax: 44-207-353-3908

**Badenoch & Clark,** 520-522 Elder Gate, Milton Keynes, MK9 1LS, UK

**Badenoch & Clark,** 51-63 Dunsgate, Manchester, M3 2BW, UK

**Badenoch & Clark,** 26 Albion Square - 2/F, Leeds, EN LS1 6HX, UK
Tel: 44-113-231-4545    Fax: 44-113-231-4531

**Badenoch & Clark,** 16-18 Wellesley Road, Croyden EN CRO 2DD, UK
Tel: 44-181-686-6337

**Modis Solutions,** 130 City Road, London EC1V 2NW, UK
Tel: 44-207-426-8300

**Modis Solutions,** 25-26 Brenkley Way, Newcastle NE13 6DS, UK

**Modis Solutions,** 24030 King Street, Watford WD1 8BP, UK

# MOLEX INC.
2222 Wellington Court, Lisle, IL, 60532
Tel: (630) 969-4550    Fax: (630) 969-1352    www.molex.com
*Mfr. electronic, electrical and fiber optic interconnection products and systems, switches, application tooling.*
**Molex Inc.,** Molex House, Millennium Centre, Farnham Surrey GU9 7XX, UK

# MOLTECH POWER SYSTEMS
9062 South Rita Road, Tucson, AZ, 85747
Tel: (520) 799-7500    Fax: (520) 799-7501    www.moltechpower.com
*Provides rechargeable battery solutions for industry applications.*
**Moltech Power Systems Ltd.,** Unit 20 Loomer Road, Chesterton Newcastle Staffs, ST5 7LB, U.K.
Tel: 44-1782-566688  Fax: 44-1782-565910

# MONARCH MACHINE TOOL COMPANY
PO Box 668, 2600 Kettering Tower, Dayton, OH, 45423
Tel: (937) 910-9300    Fax: (937) 492-7958    www.monarchmt.com
*Mfr. metal cutting lathes, machining centers and coil processing equipment.*
**Dean Smith & Grace Ltd.,** PO Box 15, Worth Valley Works, Pitt St., Keighley West Yorkshire BD21 4PG UK
**Stamco UK Ltd.,** Bath House, Bath St., Walsall, West Midlands WS1 3BD UK

# MOODY'S INVESTOR SERVICES, INC.
99 Church St., New York, NY, 10007
Tel: (212) 553-1658    Fax: (212) 553-0462    www.moodys.com
*Publishes credit ratings*
**Moody's Investors Service Ltd.,** 2 Minister Court, Mincing Lane, London EC3R 7XB, UK
Tel: 44-20-7621-9068

# MOOG INC.
Jamison Road, East Aurora, NY, 14052-0018
Tel: (716) 652-2000    Fax: (716) 687-4471    www.moog.com
*Mfr. precision control components and systems.*
**Moog Controls Ltd.,** Ashchurch, Tewkesbury, Gloucester GL20 8NA, UK

## J. P. MORGAN CHASE & CO. INC.

World Headquarters, 270 Park Ave., New York, NY, 10017

Tel: (212) 270-6000     Fax: (212) 622-9030     www.jpmorganchase.com

*Provides integrated financial solutions for institutions and individuals worldwide, including asset management, investment banking and commercial banking.*

**J. P. Morgan Chase & Co., Chaseside, Bournemouth, Dorset BH7 7DB, UK**

**J. P. Morgan Chase & Co., 3 & 4th Fls. 68 Upper Thames St., London EC4V 3BJ, UK**

**J. P. Morgan Chase & Co., 125 London Wall, London EC2Y 5AJ, UK**

**J. P. Morgan Chase & Co., Colville House, 32 Curzon St., London W1Y 8AL, UK**

**J. P. Morgan Chase & Co., Chaseside, Bournemouth, Dorset BH7 7DB, UK**

**J. P. Morgan Chase & Co., Colville House, 32 Curzon St., London W1Y 8AL, UK**

**J. P. Morgan Chase & Co., Trinity Tower, 9 Thomas More St., London E1 9YT, UK**

**J. P. Morgan Chase & Co., Woolgate House, Coleman St., London EC2P 2HD, UK**

**J. P. Morgan Chase & Co., 80 Coleman St., London EC2R 5BJL, UK**

## MORGAN STANLEY DEAN WITTER & CO.

1585 Broadway, New York, NY, 10036

Tel: (212) 761-4000     Fax: (212) 761-0086     www.msdw.com

*Securities and commodities brokerage, investment banking, money management, personal trusts.*

**Morgan Stanley & Co. International Ltd., 25 Cabot Square, Canary Wharf, London E 14 4 QA, UK**

**Morgan Stanley Dean Witter, 1 Appold St., 6th fl., Broadgate 5, London EC2A 2AA, UK**

## MORGAN, LEWIS & BOCKIUS LLP

1701 Market St., Philadelphia, PA, 19103-6993

Tel: (215) 963-5000     Fax: (215) 963-5299     www.mlb.com

*International law firm.*

**Morgan, Lewis & Bockius LLP, 4 Carlton Gardens, Pall Mall, London SW1Y 5AA, UK**

Tel: 44-207-839-1677    Fax: 44-207-930-7961    Contact: Thomas J. Benz, Mng. Ptnr.    Emp: 52

## MORRISON & FOERSTER

425 Market Street, San Francisco, CA, 94105

Tel: (415) 268-7000     Fax: (415) 268-7522     www.mofo.com

*International law firm.*

**Morrison & Foerster, 21-26 Garlick Hill, London EC4V 2AU, UK**

## MOTOROLA, INC.

1303 East Algonquin Road, Schaumburg, IL, 60196

Tel: (847) 576-5000     Fax: (847) 538-5191     www.motorola.com

*Mfr. communications equipment, semiconductors and cellular phones.*

**Motorola Information Systems, York Stream House, Suite 6 - 2nd Fl. St. Ives Rd., Maidenhead Berkshire SL6 1RD, UK**

Tel: 44-1628-586100    Fax: 44-1628-586101

**Motorola Ltd., Taylors Rd., Stotfold, Hitchin Hertshire SG5 4AY, UK**

Tel: 44-1462-831111    Fax: 44-1462-835879

**Motorola Ltd. - European Research, Jays Close, Viables Industrial Estate, Basingstoke Hampshire RG22 4PD, UK**

Tel: 44-1256-358211    Fax: 44-1256-469838

## MPSI DATA METRIX INC.

4343 South 118 East Avenue, Tulsa, OK, 74146

Tel: (918) 877-6774     Fax: (918) 254-8764     www.mpsisys.com

*Computer software, information system services.*

**MPSI Systems Ltd., Castlemead Lower Castle Street, Bristol BS1 3AG, UK**

Tel: 44-117-917-5170    Fax: 44-117-917-5179

## MTI TECHNOLOGY CORPORATION

4905 East LaPalma Avenue, Anaheim, CA, 92807

Tel: (714) 970-0300     Fax: (714) 693-2202     www.mti.com

*Mfr. data storage systems software.*

**MTI Europe, Riverview House - Weyside Park, Catteshall Lane, Godalming GU7 1XE, UK**

Tel: 44-1483-520-200   Fax: 44-1483-520-222

## MTS SYSTEMS CORPORATION

1400 Technology Drive, Eden Prairie, MN, 55344-2290

Tel: (612) 937-4000     Fax: (612) 937-4515     www.mts.com

*Develop/mfr. mechanical testing and simulation products and services, industry measure and automation instrumentation.*

**MTS Systems Ltd., Tricorn House, Cainscross, Stroud, Glos. GL5 4LF UK**

## MUELLER INDUSTRIES, INC.

8285 Tournament Drive, Ste. 150, Memphis, TN, 38125

Tel: (901) 753-3200     Fax: (901) 753-3255

*Mfr. plumbing and heating products, refrigeration and A/C components, copper and copper alloy and metal forgings and extrusions.*

**Mueller Industries, Inc., London, UK**

## MULTEX.COM, INC.

100 Williams Street, 7th Fl., New York, Ny, 10038

Tel: (212) 607-2500     Fax: (212) 607-2510     www.multex.com

*Distributes financial information of corporations via the internet to professional investors.*

**Multex.com UK, 101 Finsbury Pavement, London EC2A 1RS, UK**

Tel: 44-20-7871-8888   Fax: 44-20-7871-8800

## MULTI GRAPHICS

431 Lakeview Court, Mt. Prospect, IL, 60056

Tel: (847) 375-1700     Fax: (847) 375-1810     www.multigraphics.com

*Mfr./sale/service printing and print prod equipment, mailroom/bindery systems, services and supplies for graphics industry.*

**Multi Graphics Intl. Inc., PO Box 17, Maylands Ave., Hemel Hempstead, Herts. HP2 7ET UK**

**Multi Graphics Intl. Inc., 2K Buckingham Ave., Slough, Berkshire SL1 4NA UK**

## MURPHY OIL CORPORATION

PO Box 7000, 200 Peach St., El Dorado, AR, 71731-7000

Tel: (870) 862-6411     Fax: (870) 862-9057     www.murphyoilcorp.com

*Crude oil, natural gas, mfr. petroleum products.*

**Murco Petroleum Ltd., Winston House, Dollis Park, Finchley, London N3 1HZ, UK**

**Murphy Petroleum Ltd., Winston House, Dollis Park, Finchley, London N3 1HZ, UK**

## NABISCO HOLDINGS, CORP.

7 Campus Drive, Parsippany, NJ, 07054

Tel: (973) 682-5000     Fax: (973) 503-2153     www.nabisco.com

*Mfr. consumer packaged food products and tobacco products.*

**Associated Biscuits Ltd., 7353 County Rd., Liverpool, Merseyside LP9 7BG, UK**

**Nabisco Brands (UK) Ltd., 121 Kings Rd., Reading, Berks RG1 3EF, UK**

**R.J. Reynolds Tobacco (UK) Ltd., 62 London Rd., Staines, Surrey TW18 4JE, UK**

**Smiths Foods, 121 Kings Rd., Reading, Berkshire RG1 3ES, UK**

## NAC REINSURANCE CORPORATION

70 Seaview Ave., Stamford, CT, 06902-6040

Tel: (203) 964-5200          Fax: (203) 964-0763          www.nacre.com

*Provides property and casualty reinsurance.*

**NAC Reinsurance International Ltd., New London House, 6 London St. 7th Fl., London EC3R 7LQ, UK**

Tel: 44-207-264-5100   Fax: 44-207-338-0160   Contact: Charles J. Catt, Mng. Dir.   Emp: 34

## NACCO INDUSTRIES INC.

5875 Landerbrook Drive, Mayfield Heights, OH, 44124

Tel: (440) 449-9600          Fax: (440) 449-9607

*Mfr. fork lifts, trucks, trailers, towing winches, personnel lifts and compaction equipment and small appliances*

**Hyster Europe Ltd., Berk House, Basing View, Basingstoke, Hants RG21 2HQ UK**

## NALCO CHEMICAL COMPANY

One Nalco Center, Naperville, IL, 60563-1198

Tel: (630) 305-1000          Fax: (630) 305-2900          www.nalco.com

*Chemicals for water and waste water treatment, oil products and refining, industry processes; water and energy management service.*

**Nalco Diversified Technologies, PO Box 11, Winnington Ave., Northwich, Cheshire CW 8 4D4 UK**
Tel: 44-1606-74480   Fax: 44-1606-79557

**Nalco Ltd., PO Box 11, Northwich, Cheshire CW8 4DX, UK**
Tel: 44-1606-74488   Fax: 44-1606-79557

**Nalco/Exxon Energy Chemicals, LP, PO Box 123, Fareham, Hampshire P015 7AR UK**
Tel: 44-1604-405-311   Fax: 44-1604-406-809

**Nalfleet Marine Chemicals, PO Box 11, Winnington Ave., Northwich, Cheshire CW 8 4D4 UK**
Tel: 44-1-606-721616   Fax: 44-1-606-783875

## THE NASH ENGINEERING COMPANY

3 Trefoil Drive, Trumbull, CT, 06611

Tel: (203) 459-3900          Fax: (203) 459-3511          www.nasheng.com

*Mfr. air and gas compressors, vacuum pumps.*

**Nash Europe Ltd., Road One, Industrial Estate, Winsford, Cheshire CW7 3PL, UK**

## NASHUA CORPORATION

11 Trafalgar Sq., 2nd Fl., Nashua, NH, 03061-2002

Tel: (603) 880-2323          Fax: (603) 880-5671          www.nashua.com

*Mfg. imaging supplies (printer cartridges, toners, developers), labels, and specialty coated papers.*

**Nashua Photo Ltd., Brunel Rd., Newton Abbot, Devon TQ12 4PB, UK**

## NATCO GROUP, INC.

2950 North Loop West, Houston, TX, 77092-8839

Tel: (713) 683-9292          Fax: (713) 683-6787          www.natcogroup.com

*Mfr./sale/service oil and gas products.*

**NATCO (UK) Ltd., Station House, Harrow Rd. Wembley, Middlesex HA9 6EN, UK**

## NATIONAL DATA CORPORATION

National Data Plaza, Atlanta, GA, 30329-2010

Tel: (404) 728-2000          Fax: (404) 728-2551          www.ndcorp.com

*Information systems and services for retail, healthcare, government and corporate markets.*

**NDC International Ltd., Crown House, 72 Hammersmith Rd., London W14 8YD, UK**

## NATIONAL FORGE COMPANY

Front Street, Rt. No 6, Irvine, PA, 16329

Tel: (814) 563-7522     Fax: (814) 563-9209     www.nationalforge.com

*Mfr. forged and cast steel.*

**Mitchell, Shackleton & Co. Ltd.,  Green Lane, Patricroft, Manchester M30 8AD, UK**

Tel: 44-161-789-2241

**North West Forgemasters Ltd.,  Hyde, Greater Manchester, UK**

## NATIONAL GYPSUM COMPANY

2001 Rexford Road, Charlotte, NC, 28211

Tel: (704) 365-7300     Fax: (704) 365-7276     www.national-gypsum.com

*Mfr. building products and services.*

**The Austin Co. of U.K. Ltd.,  London, UK**

## NATIONAL MACHINERY COMPANY

161 Greenfield St., Tiffin, OH, 44883-2471

Tel: (419) 447-5211     Fax: (419) 447-5299     www.nationalmachinery.com

*Mfr. high-speed metal parts forming machines.*

**National Machinery Company,  Birmingham, UK**

Tel: 44-0121-585-3072

## NATIONAL STARCH AND CHEMICAL COMPANY

10 Finderne Ave., Bridgewater, NJ, 08807-3300

Tel: (908) 685-5000     Fax: (908) 685-5005     www.nationalstarch.com

*Mfr. adhesives and sealants, resins and specialty chemicals, electronic materials and adhesives, food products, industry starch.*

**National Starch & Chemical,  Dexter Works Barge Dock, Goole, Yorkshire DN14 5TG, UK**

**National Starch & Chemical Holdings Ltd. European Hdqrts.,  Windsor Court, Kingsmead Business Park - London Road, High Wycombe Bucks HP11 1JU UK**

Tel: 44-1494-467-500

**National Starch & Chemical Ltd.,  Welton Rd., Braunston, Daventry, Northants NN11 7JL UK**

Tel: 44-1788-890248   Fax: 44-1788-891489

## NATIONAL-OILWELL, INC.

PO Box 4638, Houston, TX, 77210-4638

Tel: (713) 960-5100     Fax: (713) 960-5428     www.natoil.com

*Design, manufacture and sale of comprehensive systems and components used in oil and gas drilling and production.*

**National-Oilwell UK Ltd.,  South Gates Rd., Great Yarmouth, Norfolk UK**

Tel: 44-1493-856941   Fax: 44-1493-330039

**National-Oilwell UK Ltd.,  Cheadle Heath, Stockport, Cheshire SK3 0SA,  UK**

Tel: 44-161-428-0755   Fax: 44-161-491-3733

## NATIONAL-STANDARD COMPANY

1618 Terminal Road, Niles, MI, 49120

Tel: (616) 683-8100     Fax: (616) 683-6249     www.nationalstardard.com

*Mfr. wire, wire related products, machinery and medical products.*

**National-Standard Co. Ltd.,  Stourport on Severn, UK**

**National-Standard Co. Ltd.,  Stourport Rd., PO Box 23, Kidderminster, Worcestershire, UK**

**National-Standard Co. Ltd.,  Heslop, Halesfield Industrial Estate, Telford, Shropshire, UK**

## NATIONWIDE INSURANCE

One Nationwide Plaza, Columbus, OH, 43215-2220

Tel: (614) 249-7111     Fax: (614) 249-7705     www.nationwide.com

*Insurance services.*

**Gartmore Investment Management PLC, London, UK**

## NCR (NATIONAL CASH REGISTER)

1700 South Patterson Blvd., Dayton, OH, 45479

Tel: (937) 445-5000     Fax: (937) 445-7042     www.ncr.com

*Mfr. automated teller machines and high-performance stationary bar code scanners.*

**NCR Ltd., 206 Marylebone Rd., London, NW1 6LY UK**

Tel: 44-207-725-8689   Fax: 44-207-725-8755   Contact: Andy Morss, VP

## NEAC COMPRESSOR SERVICE USA, INC.

191 Howard Street, Franklin, PA, 16323

Tel: (814) 437-3711     Fax: (814) 432-3334     www.neacusa.com

*Mfr. air tools and equipment.*

**Chicago Pneumatic Tool Co. Ltd., PO Box 241, Mark Court, 37 Mark Rd., Hemel Hempstead Herts HP2 7RN UK**

## NETEGRITY, INC.

52 Second Avenue, Waltham, MA, 02154

Tel: (781) 890-1700     Fax: (781) 487-7791     www.netegrity.com

*Mfr. security software.*

**Netegrity UK, Regus House - 268 Bath Road, Slough Berkshire SL1 4DX, UK**

Tel: 44-1753-708-405   Fax: 44-1753-708-421

## NETLINKS PUBLISHING SOLUTIONS INC.

PO Box 13626, Sacramento, CA, 95853

Tel: (916) 929-9481     Fax: (916) 928-0414     www.sii.com

*Develop/marketing software for publishing and newspapers.*

**Netlinks Publishing Solutions, 44 Finchamstead Rd., Wokingham, Reading, Berkshire RG11 2NN, UK**

## NETMANAGE, INC.

10725 N. De Anza Blvd., Cupertino, CA, 95014

Tel: (408) 973-7171     Fax: (408) 257-6405     www.netmanage.com

*Develop/mfr. computer software applications and tools.*

**NetManage UK, Ltd., Lyon Court - 2/F, Walsworth Rd., Hitchin Hertfordshire SG4 9SX, UK**

Tel: 44-1462-775050   Fax: 44-1462-755055

## NETSCAPE COMMUNICATIONS

501 East Middlefield Road, Mountain View, CA, 94043

Tel: (650) 254-1900     Fax: (650) 528-4124     www.netscape.com

*Mfr./distribute Internet-based commercial and consumer software applications.*

**Netscape Communications Ltd., No. 4 Status Park, Nobel Drive, Hayes Middlesex UB 3 5EY, UK**

Tel: 44-181-564-5100   Fax: 44-181-564-5101

## NETWORK ASSOCIATES, INC.

3965 Freedom Circle, Santa Clara, CA, 95054

Tel: (408) 988-3832     Fax: (408) 970-9727     www.networkassociates.com

*Designs and produces network security and network management software and hardware.*

**Network Associates, 227 Bath Road, Slough, Berkshire SL1 5PP, UK**

Tel: 44-1753-217500  Fax: 44-1753-217520

**Network General UK Ltd., Alton House - Gatehouse Way, Buckinghamshire HP19 3XU, UK**

Tel: 44-1296-318700  Fax: 44-1296-318777

## NETWORK EQUIPMENT TECHNOLOGIES INC.

6500 Paseo Padre Pkwy., Freemont, CA, 94555

Tel: (510) 713-7300      Fax: (510) 574-4000      www.net.com

*Mfr./service networking products to info-intensive organizations.*

**NET Ltd., Manor Court, Manor Royal, Crawley, West Sussex RH10 2PY, UK**

## NEUTROGENA CORPORATION

5760 West 96th Street, Los Angeles, CA, 90045

Tel: (310) 642-1150      Fax: (310) 337-5564      www.neutrogena.com

*Mfr. facial cleansing, moisturizing products; body care, sun and hair care specialty products.*

**Neutrogena United Kingdom Ltd., Neutrogena House, Century Point, Halifax Rd., Cressex, High Wycombe HP12 3SL, UK**

## NEVILLE CHEMICAL COMPANY

2800 Neville Road, Pittsburgh, PA, 15225-1496

Tel: (412) 331-4200      Fax: (412) 777-4234

*Mfr. hydrocarbon resins.*

**Alliance Technical Products, Ltd. (JV), Gloucester, UK**

## NEW BRUNSWICK SCIENTIFIC COMPANY, INC.

44 Talmadge Road, Box 4005, Edison, NJ, 08818-4005

Tel: (732) 287-1200      Fax: (732) 287-4222      www.nbsc.com

*Mfr. research and production equipment for life sciences.*

**New Brunswick Scientific (UK) Ltd., 163 Dixons Hill Rd., North Mymms, Hatfield AL9 75E, UK**

Tel: 44-17072-75733    Fax: 41-17072-67859    Contact: Nick Vosper, Gen. Mgr.

## NEW HAMPSHIRE BALL BEARINGS INC. (NHBB)

Route 202 South, Peterborough, NH, 03458-0805

Tel: (603) 924-3311      Fax: (603) 924-6632      www.nhbb.com

*Mfr. bearings and bearing assemblies.*

**NHBB Europe, 1 Sterling Centre, Eastern Rd., Bracknell Berkshire RG12 2PW, UK**

## NEW YORK LIFE INSURANCE COMPANY

51 Madison Ave., New York, NY, 10010

Tel: (212) 576-7000      Fax: (212) 576-4291      www.newyorklife.com

*Insurance services.*

**New York Life Insurance Co. UK, London, UK**

## THE NEW YORK TIMES COMPANY

229 West 43rd Street, New York, NY, 10036-3959

Tel: (212) 556-1234      Fax: (212) 556-7389      www.nytimes.com

*Diversified media company including newspapers, magazines, television and radio stations, and electronic information and publishing.*

**International Herald Tribune (IHT), 40 Marsh Wall, London E14 9TP, UK**

Tel: 44-207-510-5700

**The New York Times London Bureau Ltd., 66 Burlingham Gate, London SW1E 64U, UK**

## NEWELL RUBBERMAID

29 East Stephenson Street, Freeport, IL, 61032-0943

Tel: (815) 235-4171      Fax: (815) 489-8212      www.newellco.com

*Mfr. hardware, housewares, and office products.*

**McKechnie, Plc., Leighswood Rd., Aldridge Walsall, West Midlands WS9 8DS UK**

Tel: 44-192-274-3887    Fax: 44-192-245-1045

**Newell Office Products of UK Inc., Unit 3, Clifton Rd., Shefford, Bedfordshire SG17 5AG UK**

## NEWSWEEK INTERNATIONAL INC.

251 West 57 Street, New York, NY, 10019

Tel: (212) 445-4000　　　Fax: (212) 445-4120　　　www.washpostco.com

*Engaged in magazine publishing.*

**Newsweek Inc.,  25 Upper Brook St., London, UK**

## NICHOLAS CRITELLI ASSOCIATES, P.C.

Ste. 500, 317 Sixth Ave., Des Moines, IA, 50309-4128

Tel: (515) 243-3122　　　Fax: (515) 243-3121　　　www.icclaw.com

*International law firm.*

**Nicholas Critelli Associates, P.C.,  11 Stone Buildings, Lincoln's Inn, London WC2A 3TG, UK**
Tel: 44-20-7404-5055

## NICOLET INSTRUMENT CORPORATION

5225 Verona Road, Madison, WI, 53711-4495

Tel: (608) 276-6100　　　Fax: (608) 276-6222　　　www.nicolet.com

*Mfr. infrared spectrometers and oscilloscopes and medical electro-diagnostic equipment.*

**Nicolet Instrument Ltd.,  Nicolet House, Budbrooke Road, Warwick CV34 5XH, UK**

## A .C. NIELSEN COMPANY

177 Broad Street, Stamford, CT, 06901

Tel: (203) 961-3000　　　Fax: (203) 961-3190　　　www.acnielsen.com

*Market and consumer research firm.*

**A. C.Nielsen Company Ltd.,  A.C.Nielsen House, London Road Headington, Oxford OX3 9RX UK**

## NIKE INC.

One Bowerman Drive, Beaverton, OR, 97005

Tel: (503) 671-6453　　　Fax: (503) 671-6300　　　www.nike.com

*Mfr. athletic footwear, equipment and apparel.*

**Nike United Kingdom Ltd.,  Dist. 4, Washington, Tyne & Wear NE38 7RN, UK**

## NORDSON CORPORATION

28601 Clemens Road, Westlake, OH, 44145-4551

Tel: (440) 892-1580　　　Fax: (440) 892-9507　　　www.nordson.com

*Mfr. industry application equipment, sealants and packaging machinery.*

**Nordson U.K. Ltd.,  Wenman Rd., Thame, Oxfordshire OX9 3XB, UK**
Tel: 44-1844-26-4500　　Fax: 44-1844-21-5358

**Nordson U.K. Ltd.,  Ashurst Dr., Cheadle Heath, Stockport Cheshire SK3 0RY, UK**
Tel: 44-161-495-4200　　Fax: 44-161-428-6716

## NORFOLK SOUTHERN CORPORATION

3 Commercial Place, Norfolk, VA, 23510-1291

Tel: (757) 629-2600　　　Fax: (757) 629-2798　　　www.nscorp.com

*Holding company: transportation, including Conrail.*

**North American Van Lines Ltd.,  15/16 Chestnut Way, Felthambrook Industrial Estate, Feltham, Middlesex TW13 7OP, UK**

## NORGREN

5400 S. Delaware Street., Littleton, CO, 80120-1663

Tel: (303) 794-2611　　　Fax: (303) 795-9487　　　www.usa.norgren.com

*Mfr. pneumatic filters, regulators, lubricators, valves, automation systems, dryers, push-in fittings.*

**IMI Norgren Ltd.,  PO Box 22, Eastern Ave., Lichfield, Staffordshire, WS13 6SB UK**
Tel: 44-1543-414333　　Fax: 44-1543-268052

## NORRISEAL CONTROLS

PO Box 40575, Houston, TX, 77240

Tel: (713) 466-3552      Fax: (713) 896-7386      www.norriseal.com

*Mfr. butterfly valves, fittings and plugs primarily for the oil and gas industries.*

**NF Technical Service Ltd., 4 Possil House, 23 Copse Hill, Wimbledon SW20 ONR, UK**

Tel: 44-181-8793859   Fax: 44-181-8797374

## NORTHERN TRUST CORPORATION

50 South LaSalle Street, Chicago, IL, 60675

Tel: (312) 630-6000      Fax: (312) 630-1512      www.ntrs.com

*Banking and financial services.*

**Northern Trust Corp. - London Branch, 155 Bishopsgate, London EC2M 3XS, UK**

## NORTON ABRASIVES COMPANY

1 New Bond Street, Worcester, MA, 01606

Tel: (508) 795-5000      Fax: (508) 795-5741      www.nortonabrasives.com

*Mfr. abrasives for industrial manufacturing.*

**Christensen Diamond Products (UK) Ltd., Govett Ave., Shepperton, Walton-on-Thames, Middlesex UK**

**Clipper Mfr. Co., Thurmaston Blvd., Barkby Rd., Leicester LE4 7JB UK**

**Norton Abrasives Ltd., Bridge Rd., East Welwyn Garden City, Herts, AL 7HZ, UK**

**Norton Chemical Process Products Ltd., King St., Fenton, Stoke-on-Trent ST4 3LY, UK**

**Norton Intl., Cartwright House, 39/43 Monument Hill, Weybridge, Surrey KT13 8RN, UK**

## NOVELL INC.

1800 S. Novell Place, Provo, UT, 84606

Tel: (801) 861-7000      Fax: (801) 861-5555      www.novell.com

*Develop/mfr. networking software and related equipment.*

**Digital Research (UK) Ltd., Oxford House, Oxford St., Newbury, Berkshire RG13 1JB UK**

**Novell (UK) Ltd., Sweetwell Rd., Bracknell, Berkshire RG12 1HH, UK**

## NOVELLUS SYSTEMS INC.

4000 North First Street, San Jose, CA, 95134

Tel: (408) 943-9700      Fax: (408) 943-3422      www.novellus.com

*Mfr. chemical vapor deposition (CVD), physical vapor deposition (PVD) and copper electrofill systems.*

**Novellus Systems Ltd., Bishops Weald House Unit 1EB, Albion Way, Horsham, West Sussex RH12 1AH UK**

Tel: 44-1403-265550   Fax: 44-1403-266554   Contact: David Avery, Pres.

## NOVO SYSTEMS CORPORATION

4061 Clipper Court, Fremont, CA, 94538-6540

Tel: (510) 360-8100      Fax: (510) 623-4484      www.novosystems.com

*Design/development/mfr./market logic and fault simulation acceleration products; system engineering services.*

**Zycad Ltd., Zycad House, London Rd., Bracknell, Berkshire RE12 2UT, UK**

## NRG ENERGY, INC.

1221 Nicollet Ave., Ste. 700, Minneapolis, MN, 55403

Tel: (612) 373-5300      Fax: (612) 373-5312      www.nrgenergy.com

*Electric power generation.*

**NRG Energy, Ltd., 54 St. James's Street, London SW1A 1JT, UK**

Tel: 44-207-409-1025   Fax: 44-207-409-1074

## NU SKIN ENTERPRISES, INC.

75 West Center St., Provo, UT, 84601

Tel: (801) 345-6100    Fax: (801) 345-5999    www.nuskin.com

*Develops and distributes premium-quality personal care and nutritional products.*

**NuSkin Europe UK,  Gomm Road, High Wycombe, Buckinghamshire HP13 7DL, UK**

## NUMATICS INC.

1450 North Milford Road, Highland, MI, 48357

Tel: (248) 887-4111    Fax: (248) 887-9190    www.numatics.com

*Mfr. control valves and manifolds.*

**Numatics Ltd.,  PO Box 18, 23/24 Acacia Close, Cherrycourt Way, Leighton Buzzard, Beds. LU7 7DJ, UK**

## NUS INFORMATION SERVICES, INC.

2650 McCormick Dr., Ste. 300, Clearwater, FL, 33759-1049

Tel: (727) 669-3000    Fax: (727) 669-3100    www.nus.com

*Provides case-based expert knowledge, bench-marking, trending, and operational services to the electric power and inventory industries.*

**National Utility Services Ltd.,  Carolyn House, Dingwall Rd., Croydon, Surrey CR9 3LX, UK**

## THE O'BRIEN & GERE COMPANIES

5000 Brittonfield Parkway, Syracuse, NY, 13221

Tel: (315) 437-6100    Fax: (315) 463-7554    www.obg.com

*Specializes in engineering, procurement and construction management of water/wastewater treatment facilities and provides specialized health and safety environmental advice to industry, commerce and government.*

**RMC Consultants Ltd.,  Abingdon, UK**

Tel: 44-123-553-8616   Contact: John Gebrian   Emp: 60

## OCCIDENTAL PETROLEUM CORPORATION

10889 Wilshire Blvd., Los Angeles, CA, 90024

Tel: (310) 208-8800    Fax: (310) 443-6690    www.oxy.com

*Petroleum and petroleum products, chemicals, plastics.*

**Occidental Intl. Oil Inc.,  16 Palace Street, London SW1 E5BQ, UK**

## OCEANEERING INTERNATIONAL INC.

11911 FM 529, Houston, TX, 77041

Tel: (713) 329-4500    Fax: (713) 329-4951    www.oceaneering.com

*Transportation equipment, underwater service to offshore oil and gas industry.*

**Solus Engineering and Inspection Services Ltd.,  10/11 Church House - St. Mary's Gate, 96 Church Street, Lancaster LA1 1TD UK**

**Solus Schall,  Matlock Green, Matlock, Derbyshire, DE4 3BX UK**

## OCTAGON SPORTS MARKETING

1114 Ave. of the Americas, New York, NY, 10036

Tel: (212) 888-8847    Fax: (212) 403-7098    www.octagon.com

*Engaged in sports and entertainment marketing.*

**Octagon Sports Marketing,  6 Eaton Gate, London, SW1W 9BJ, UK**

Tel: 44-207-881-8888   Fax: 44-20-7828-0887

## ODETICS INC.

1515 South Manchester Ave., Anaheim, CA, 92802-2907

Tel: (714) 774-5000    Fax: (714) 780-7857

*Design/mfr. digital data management products for mass data storage, communications and video security markets.*

**Odetics Europe Ltd.,  The Minster, 58 Portman, Reading Berkshire RG3 1EA, UK**

## C.M. OFFRAY & SON INC.

360 Rt. 24, Box 601, Chester, NJ, 07930-0601

Tel: (908) 879-4700    Fax: (908) 879-8588    www.offray.com

*Mfr. ribbons and narrow fabrics.*

**C.M. Offray & Son Ltd.,  Fir Tree Pl., Church Rd., Ashford, Middlesex TW15 2PH UK**

## OGILVY PUBLIC RELATIONS WORLDWIDE

909 Third Ave., New York, NY, 10022

Tel: (212) 880-5201    Fax: (212) 697-8250    www.ogilvypr.com

*Engaged in public relations and communications.*

**Ogilvy Public Relations Worldwide,  10 Cabot Square, Canary Wharf, London E14 4QB, UK**

Tel: 44-207-345-3000   Fax: 44-20-7345-6618   Contact: Donna Zurcher

## OHAUS CORPORATION

29 Hanover Road, PO Box 900, Florham Park, NJ, 07932-0900

Tel: (973) 377-9000    Fax: (973) 593-0359    www.ohaus.com

*Mfr. balances and scales for laboratories, industry and education.*

**Ohaus UK Ltd.,  64 Boston Road, Beaumont Leys, Leicester LE41AW, UK**

Tel: 44-116-234-507   Fax: 44-116-235-9256

## THE OHIO ART COMPANY

One Toy Street, Bryan, OH, 43506

Tel: (419) 636-3141    Fax: (419) 636-7614    www.world-of-toys.com

*Mfg./distribution toys; provides custom metal lithography and moulded plastic products to other companies.*

**The Ohio Art Company (European Office),  74 Warren Rise, Frimley Camberly, Surrey GU165 SW, UK**

Tel: 44-1276-675-501   Fax: 44-1276-675-451

## OIL STATES INDUSTRIES

7701 South Cooper Street, Arlington, TX, 76017

Tel: (817) 468-1400    Fax: (817) 468-6250    www.oilstates.com

*Mfr. drilling and production machinery and supplies for oil/gas production.*

**Oil States Industries Ltd.,  PO Box 18192, London EC2A 4WB, UK**

**Oil States MCS, Ltd.,  Bouthwood Road - Sowerby Woods, Barrow-in-Furness, Cumbria LA14 4HB, UK**

## OIL-DRI CORPORATION OF AMERICA

410 North Michigan Ave., Ste. 400, Chicago, IL, 60611-4213

Tel: (312) 321-1515    Fax: (312) 321-1271    www.oil-dri.com

*Developer, manufacturer and marketer of products for consumer, industrial and automotive, agricultural, sports fields and fluids purification markets and cat litter products.*

**Oil-Dri UK Ltd.,  c/o Consolidated Land Services, Humber Rd., South Killingsholme, Grimsby DN40 3DU, UK**

## THE OILGEAR COMPANY

2300 S. 51st Street, Milwaukee, WI, 53219

Tel: (414) 327-1700    Fax: (414) 327-0532    www.oilgear.com

*Mfr. hydraulic power transmission machinery.*

**Oilgear Toweler Ltd.,  Oaklands Rd., Leeds LS13 1LG, UK**

**Oilgear Towler Ltd.,  Shuttleworth Rd., Goldington, Bedford Bedshire MK41 0EP, UK**

## OLIN CORPORATION

501 Merritt Seven, Norwalk, CT, 06856-4500

Tel: (203) 750-3000    Fax: (203) 750-3292    www.olin.com

*Mfr. chemicals, metals, sporting ammunition and copper and copper alloy sheets.*

**Olin UK Ltd.,  Site 7 Kidderminster Rd., Cutnall Green, Droitwich, Worchestershire WR9 0NS UK**

## OMNICARE, INC.

100 E. River Center Blvd., Covington, KY, 41011

Tel: (859) 392-3300    Fax: (859) 392-3333    www.omnicare.com

*Provides pharmaceutical and nursing home services.*

**Omnicare Clinical Packaging, Chippenham, UK**

## OMNICOM GROUP

437 Madison Ave., New York, NY, 10022

Tel: (212) 415-3600    Fax: (212) 415-3530    www.omnicomgroup.com

*International network of advertising, marketing, direct mail, public relations and consulting services.*

**BHWG Media, 191 Old Marylebone Road, London NW1 5DW, UK**

**GGT Group, 82 Dean St., London, W1V 5AB, UK**

Tel: 44-207-437-0434  Fax: 44-207-836-6626  Contact: Michael E. Greenlees, Chmn.  Emp: 3,082

## ON ASSIGNMENT, INC.

26651 West Agoura Road, Calabasas, CA, 91302

Tel: (818) 878-7900    Fax: (818) 878-7930    www.assignment.net

*Temporary employment agency.*

**On Assignment UK Limited, Birmingham, Midlands, UK**

Tel: 44-121-224-5617

**On Assignment UK Limited, Cambridge, UK**

Tel: 44-1223-451-021

## ONAN CORPORATION

1400 73rd Ave. NE, Minneapolis, MN, 55432

Tel: (612) 574-5000    Fax: (612) 574-5298    www.onan.com

*Mfr. electric generators, controls and switchgears.*

**Onan Intl. Ltd., PO Box 29, 54 Broadway, Peterborough, Cambs. PE1 1QD, UK**

## ONEIDA LTD.

163-181 Kenwood Avenue, Oneida, NY, 13421-2899

Tel: (315) 361-3000    Fax: (315) 361-3658    www.oneida.com

*Mfr. stainless steel flatware, glassware, cookware and chine and plastic serving products.*

**Oneida Silversmiths Ltd., Elder Way, Waterside Drive, Langley Berkshire SL3 6EP, U.K.**

Tel: 44-1753-212500  Fax: 44-1753-543476

## ONESOURCE INFORMATION SERVICES, INC.

300 Baker Avenue, Concord, MA, 01742

Tel: (978) 318-4300    Fax: (978) 318-4690    www.onesource.com

*Provides business information services on line.*

**One Source Information Services, 7/F Block E Dukes Court, Duke Street, Woking Surrey GU21 5BH, UK**

Tel: 44-1483-241200  Fax: 44-1-1483-240007

## ONTRACK DATA INTERNATIONAL, INC.

9023 Columbine Rd., Eden Prairie, MN, 55347

Tel: (612) 937-1107    Fax: (612) 937-5815    www.ontrack.com

*Computer data evidence services company, rescuing lost or corrupted data, and software sales.*

**Ontrack Data International, Inc., The Pavillions, One Weston Road, Kiln Lane, Epsom Surrey KT17 1JG UK**

Tel: 44-1372-741999  Fax: 44-1372-741441

## ONYX SOFTWARE CORPORATION

3180 139th Avenue, SE, Bellevue, WA, 98005

Tel: (425) 451-8060     Fax: (425) 451-8277     www.onyx.com

*Mfr. customer relationship management software.*

**Onyx Software UK, Trinity Court, Wokingham Road, Bracknell Berkshire RG42 1 PL, UK**

Tel: 44-1344-322-000

## OPEN MARKET, INC.

1 Wayside Road, Burlington, MA, 01803

Tel: (781) 359-3000     Fax: (781) 359-8111     www.openmarket.com

*Mfr. catalog management software.*

**Open Market UK Ltd., Arundell House - One Farm Yard, Windsor Berkshire SL4 1QL, UK**

## OPRYLAND MUSIC GROUP

65 Music Square West, Nashville, TN, 37203

Tel: (615) 321-5000     Fax: (615) 327-0560     www.acuffrose.com

*Music publisher.*

**Acuff-Rose Music Ltd., 25 James St., London W1M 6AA, UK**

Tel: 44-207-486-2525    Fax: 44-207-486-2424    Contact: Tony Peters, Gen. Mgr.    Emp: 5

## ORACLE CORPORATION

500 Oracle Parkway, Redwood Shores, CA, 94065

Tel: (650) 506-7000     Fax: (650) 506-7200     www.oracle.com

*Develop/manufacture software.*

**Oracle Corp., Oracle Park, Bittams Lane, Guilford Rd., Chertsey, Surrey KT16 9RG, UK**

## ORIEL INSTRUMENTS CORPORATION

150 Long Beach Boulevard, Stratford, CT, 06615

Tel: (203) 377-8282     Fax: (203) 378-2457     www.oriel.com

*Mfr. optical goods.*

**L.O.T.-Oriel Ltd., 1 Mole Business Park, Leatherhead, Surrey KT22 7AU, UK**

Tel: 44-1-372-378822    Fax: 44-1-372-375353

## OSMONICS INC.

5951 Clearwater Drive, Minnetonka, MN, 55343-8995

Tel: (952) 933-2277     Fax: (952) 933-0141     www.osmonics.com

*Mfr. equipment, controls and components for the filtration and water-treatment industries.*

**Osmonics, Bristol, UK**

## OTIS ELEVATOR COMPANY

10 Farm Springs Road, Farmington, CT, 06032

Tel: (860) 676-6000     Fax: (860) 676-5111     www.otis.com

*Mfr. elevators and escalators.*

**Evans Lifts Ltd., Prospect Works, Abbey Lane, Leicester LE4 5QX, UK**

Contact: Adel Eissa

**Otis Elevator Co. UK, The Otis Bldg., 187 Twyford Abbey Road, London NW10 7DG, UK**

Tel: 44-208-955-3000

**Otis PLC, The Otis Bldg., 43/59 Clapham Rd., London SW9 OJZ, UK**

## OUTOKUMPU TECHNOLOGY, INC. , CARPCO DIV.

1310-1 Tradeport Drive, Jacksonville, FL, 32218

Tel: (904) 353-3681     Fax: (904) 353-8705     www.carpco.com

*Design/mfr. separation equipment for mining, recycling and research; testing and flowsheet design.*

**Outokumpu Technology Ltd.,**

**Carpco Division,  Unit B Marish Wharf, Langley Slough, Berkshire, SL3 6DA UK**

Tel: 44-1753-542200   Fax: 44-1753-542300

## OWENS-CORNING CORPORATION

One Owens Corning Pkwy., Toledo, OH, 43659

Tel: (419) 248-8000     Fax: (419) 248-8445     www.owenscorning.com

*Mfr. building materials systems and composites systems.*

**Owens Corning Insulation UK,  PO Box 10, Stafford Road, St. Helens WA10 3NS, UK**

## OWENS-ILLINOIS, INC.

One SeaGate, PO Box 1035, Toledo, OH, 43666

Tel: (419) 247-5000     Fax: (419) 247-2839     www.o-i.com

*Largest mfr. of glass containers in the US; plastic containers, compression-molded closures and dispensing systems.*

**United Glass Ltd.,  Porters Wood St.. Albans, Hertfordshire AL3 6NY, UK**

## PACCAR INC.

777 106th Ave. NE, Bellevue, WA, 98004

Tel: (425) 468-7400     Fax: (425) 468-8216     www.pacar.com

*Heavy duty dump trucks, military vehicles.*

**Leyland Trucks,  Farington, UK**

**PACCAR  International,  Moss Lane, Sandbach, Cheshire, CW11 9YW, UK**

Tel: 44-1271-763244   Fax: 44-1270-767788

## PACIFIC BELL

140 New Montgomery Street, San Francisco, CA, 94105

Tel: (415) 542-9000     Fax: (415) 543-7079     www.pacbell.com

*Telecommunications and information systems.*

**One-to-One Ltd.,  Scorpio House, 102 Syndey St., London SW3 6NL, UK**

## PACIFIC LIFE INSURANCE

700 Newport Center Dr., Newport Beach, CA, 92660

Tel: (949) 640-3011     Fax: (949) 640-3483     www.pacificlife.com

*Provides life and health insurance products, individual annuities and group employee benefits.*

**World-Wide Reassurance Company Limited,  Windsor, UK**

## PACIFIC SCIENTIFIC COMPANY

4301 Kishwaukee Street, PO Box 106, Rockford, IL, 61105-0106

Tel: (815) 226-3100     Fax: (815) 226-3148     www.pacsci.com

*Mfr. high performance motors and drives.*

**Pacific Scientific Ltd.,  Seven Centre, Bourne End, Buckinghamshire SL8 5YS, UK**

## PADCO INC.

1025 Thomas Jefferson Street NW, Ste. 170, Washington, DC, 20007-5209

Tel: (202) 337-2326     Fax: (202) 944-2350     www.padcoinc.com

*Provides governments and private clients with comprehensive policy, planning, financial, environmental, geo-information management (GIS), privatization and training services for urban and regional development.*

**PADCO Europe, Ltd.,  London, UK**

## PAINE WEBBER GROUP INC.

1285 Ave. of the Americas, New York, NY, 10019

Tel: (212) 713-2000     Fax: (212) 713-4889     www.painewebber.com

*Stock brokerage and investment services.*

**PaineWebber Intl. (UK) Ltd., One Finsbury Ave., London EC2M 2PA, UK**

Tel: 44-207-422-2000

## PALL CORPORATION

2200 Northern Boulevard, East Hills, NY, 11548-1289

Tel: (516) 484-5400     Fax: (516) 484-5228     www.pall.com

*Specialty materials and engineering; filters and related fluid clarification equipment.*

**Pall Europe Ltd., Europa House, Havant Street, Portsmouth P01 3PD, UK**

Tel: 44-705-30-3303    Fax: 441-705-30-2506

**Pall/Gelman Sciences Ltd., Brackmills Business Park, Caswell Road, Northampton NN4 7EZ, UK**

Tel: 44-1604-70-4704    Fax: 44-1604-70-4724

## PANAMETRICS

221 Crescent Street, Waltham, MA, 02154

Tel: (781) 899-2719     Fax: (781) 899-1552     www.panametrics.com

*Process/non-destructive test instrumentation.*

**Panametrics Ltd., Unit 2 Villiers Court, 40 Upper Mulgrave Rd., Cheam Surrey SM2 7AJ, UK**

Tel: 44-181-643-5150    Fax: 44-181-643-4225    Contact: Arthur Berry

**Panametrics NDT, Ltd., 12 Nightingale Close, Rotherham, South Yorkshire S60 2AB, UK**

Tel: 44-1709-836115    Fax: 44-1709-8355177

## PANDUIT CORPORATION

17301 Ridgeland Ave., Tinley Park, IL, 60477-0981

Tel: (708) 532-1800     Fax: (708) 532-1811     www.panduit.com

*Mfr. electrical/electronic wiring components.*

**Panduit Europe Ltd., West World, Westgate, London W5 1XP, UK**

Tel: 44-208-601-7200

## PAPA JOHN'S INTERNATIONAL, INC.

2002 Papa John's Blvd., Louisville, KY, 40299-2334

Tel: (502) 266-5200     Fax: (502) 266-2925     www.papajohns.com

*Retailer and pizza franchiser.*

**Papa John's International Inc., 56 Orsett Road, Grays, Essex RM17 5EH, UK**

Tel: 44-1-375-382-828

## PAPER CONVERTING MACHINE COMPANY

PO Box 19005, 2300 S. Ashland Ave., Green Bay, WI, 54307

Tel: (920) 494-5601     Fax: (920) 494-8865

*Paper converting machinery.*

**Paper Converting Machine Co. Ltd., Southway Dr., Plymouth, Devon, UK**

## PARADYNE NETWORKS, INC.

8545 126 Ave. North, Largo, FL, 33773

Tel: (727) 530-2000     Fax: (727) 530-2875     www.paradyne.com

*Engaged in data communications and high-speed network access solutions.*

**Paradyne Ltd., 225 Berwick Ave., Slough, Berkshire SL1 4QT, UK**

## PARAMETRIC TECHNOLOGY CORPORATION

128 Technology Drive, Waltham, MA, 02154

Tel: (781) 398-5000        Fax: (781) 398-5674        www.ptc.com

*Supplier of mechanical design automation and product data management software and services.*

**Parametric Technology (UK) Ltd., Fifth Avenue Plaza Block A, Queensway No., Team Valley Trading Estates, Gateshead Tyne & Wear NE11 0HF UK**

Tel: 44-191-491-5664    Fax: 44-191-491-4888

**Parametric Technology (UK) Ltd., The Courtyard, Alban Park, Unit V  Hatfield Road, St. Albans AL4 0LA UK**

Tel: 44-172-786-7577    Fax: 44-172-785-8314

**Parametric Technology (UK) Ltd., 20 Brindley Road Unit 5 1st Fl., Metropolitan House, Manchester M16 9HQ, UK**

Tel: 44-161-877-6447    Fax: 44-161-877-6435

**Parametric Technology (UK) Ltd., Argent Court, Sir William Lyons Road, Coventry CV4 7EZ, UK**

Tel: 44-120-341-7718    Fax: 44-120-369-0924

**Parametric Technology (UK) Ltd., Kings Hall St. Ives Business Park, Parsons Green, St. Ives Huntingson, Cambridge PE17 4WY UK**

Tel: 44-148-046-1791    Fax: 44-148-046-1792

**Parametric Technology (UK) Ltd., 190 Aztec West, Park Avenue, Almondsbury, Bristol BS 12 4TD, UK**

Tel: 44-145-461-3201    Fax: 44-145-461-4522

**Parametric Technology (UK) Ltd., One Fleetwood Park, Barley Way, Fleet Hampshire GU13 8UT, UK**

Tel: 44-125-281-7000    Fax: 44-125-280-0722

## PAREXEL INTERNATIONAL CORPORATION

195 West Street, Waltham, MA, 02154

Tel: (781) 487-9900        Fax: (781) 487-0525        www.parexel.com

*Provides contract medical, biotechnology, and pharmaceutical research and consulting services.*

**PAREXEL MMS Europe, Ltd., Wicker House, High St., Worthing, West Sussex BN11 1DJ UK**

Tel: 44-1903-205884    Fax: 44-1903-234862

## PARK ELECTROCHEMICAL CORPORATION

5 Dakota Drive, Lake Success, NY, 11042

Tel: (516) 354-4100        Fax: (516) 354-4128        www.parkelectrochemical.com

*Multi-layer laminate printed circuit materials, industry comps, plumbing hardware products.*

**New England Laminates (UK) Ltd., 1 Paddock Rd., W. Pimbo, Skelmersdale, Lancashire, UK**

## PARKER HANNIFIN CORPORATION

6035 Parkland Blvd., Cleveland, OH, 44124-4141

Tel: (216) 896-3000        Fax: (216) 896-4000        www.parker.com

*Mfr. motion-control products.*

**Fluid Connector Products/Parker Hannifin PLC, Haydock Park Road, Derby DE2 8JA, UK**

**Hydraulic Filtration Div./Parker Hannifin PLC, Peel Street, Morley, Leeds LS27 8EL, UK**

**Instrumentation Products Div./Parker Hannifin PLC, Riverside Road, Barnstaple, Devon EX31 1NP, UK**

**Parker Digiplan Ltd., 21-22 Balena Close, Poole, Dorset BH17 7DX, UK**

**Parker Hannifin Corp., Parker House, 55 Maylands Avenue, Hemel Hempstead, Hertshire HP2 4SJ UK**

**Parker Hannifin PLC, Barbados Way, Hellaby Industrial Estate, Hellaby Rotherham, South Yorkshire S66 8RX UK**

**Parker Hannifin PLC, Cylinder Div., 6 Greycaine Road, Watford, Hertshire WD2 4QA, UK**

**Parker Hannifin PLC., Pneumatic Div., Walkmill Lane, Bridgtown Cannock, Staffordshire WS1 3LR, UK**

**Seal Products/Parker Hannifin PLC, Abbott House, Primrose Hill, Kings Langley, Hertshire WD4 8HY UK**

**Seal Products/Parker Hannifin PLC/Chomerics Europe, Parkway, Globe Park, Marlow, Buckinghamshire SL7 1YB UK**

## PARSONS BRINCKERHOFF QUADE & DOUGLAS

One Penn Plaza, New York, NY, 10119-0061

Tel: (212) 465-5000      Fax: (212) 465-5096      www.pbworld.com

*Engineering consultants, planners and architects.*

**PB Kennedy & Donkin, 4 Roger Street, London WC1N 2JX, UK**

**PB Kennedy & Donkin, Westbrook Mills, Godalming, Surrey GU7 2AZ, UK**

**PB Kennedy & Donkin, 44/45 Calthorpe Road, Edgbaston, Birmingham B15 1TH, UK**

## THE PARSONS CORPORATION

100 West Walnut Street, Pasadena, CA, 91124

Tel: (626) 440-2000      Fax: (626) 440-2630      www.parsons.com

*Engineering and construction.*

**The Ralph M. Parsons Co. Ltd., Parsons House, Kew Bridge Rd., Brentford, Middlesex TW8 0EH, UK**

## PARSONS ENERGY & CHEMICALS GROUP INC.

2675 Morgantown Road, Reading, PA, 19607

Tel: (610) 855-2000      Fax: (610) 855-2186      www.parsons.com

*Provide full engineer-procurement-construction services, studies and project and construction management for utilities and independent power producers worldwide.*

**Parsons Energy & Chemicals Group Inc., Parsons House, Kew Bridge Rd., Brentford, Middlesex TW8 0EH, UK**

Tel: 44-181-742-5029    Fax: 44-181-560-3236    Contact: D. Tankosic, Office Head

## PARSONS ENGINEERING SCIENCE INC.

100 West Walnut Street, Pasadena, CA, 91124

Tel: (626) 440-2000      Fax: (626) 440-4919      www.parsons.com

*Environmental engineering.*

**Engineering Science Environmental Engineers, Parsons House, Kew Bridge Rd., Brentford, Middlesex TW8 0EH UK**

**Parsons Engineering Science Inc., Newporte House, Low Moor Rd., Doddington Rd., Lincoln LN6 3JY, UK**

## PARSONS TRANSPORTATION GROUP

1133 15th Street NW, 9th Fl., Washington, DC, 20005

Tel: (202) 775-3300      Fax: (202) 775-3422      www.parsons.com

*Consulting engineers.*

**De Leuw Cather Intl. Ltd., Parsons House, Kew Bridge Rd., Brentford, Middlesex TW8 0EH UK**

## PCA ELECTRONICS INC.

16799 Schoenborn Street, North Hills, CA, 91343

Tel: (818) 892-0761      Fax: (818) 894-5791      www.pca.com

*Mfr./sales of electronic equipment.*

**Dau Components, Bardham, West Sussex 70-74, Bardham Rd., PO Box 22 UK**

Tel: 44-2345-53031    Fax: 44-2435-53860

**Tekdata Ltd., Federation Rd., Burslem Stoke-on-Trent, UK**

Tel: 44-1782-577677    Fax: 44-1782--823881

## PEDDINGHAUS CORPORATION

300 North Washington Avenue, Bradley, IL, 60915

Tel: (815) 937-3800      Fax: (815) 937-4003      www.peddinghaus.com

*Mfr./distribute structure steel and plate-fabricating equipment.*

**Peddinghaus Corporation UK Ltd.,  Unit 6 Queensway Link Industrial Estate, Stafford Park 17, Talford TF3 3DN Shropshire UK**

Tel: 44-1952-200-377   Fax: 44-1952-292-877

## PENFORD CORPORATION

777 108th Ave. NE, Ste 2390, Bellevue, WA, 98004-5193

Tel: (425) 462-6000      Fax: (425) 462-2819      www.penx.com

*Mfr. food ingredients, nutritional supplements, spec. carbohydrate and synthetic polymer chemicals.*

**Edward Mendell Co.,  Lonsdale House, 7-11 High St., Reigate, Surrey RH2 9AA UK**

## PENNZOIL-QUAKER STATE COMPANY

PO Box 2967, Houston, TX, 77252-2967

Tel: (713) 546-4000      Fax: (713) 546-6589      www.pennzoil-quakerstate.com

*Produce/refine/market oil, natural gas, sulfur.*

**Pennzoil-Quaker State Ltd.,  Duckett's Wharf - South Street, Bishops Stortford, Hertfordshire CM23 3AR UK**

Tel: 44-1279-710-400   Fax: 44-1279-461-828

## PENSKE CORPORATION

13400 Outer Drive West, Detroit, MI, 48239

Tel: (313) 592-5000      Fax: (313) 592-5256      www.penske.com

*Diversified transportation company, design and manufacture engines and operate truck leasing facilities.*

**Penske Corporation,  England, UK**

## PENTON MEDIA

1100 Superior Ave., Cleveland, OH, 44114-2543

Tel: (216) 696-7000      Fax: (216) 696-7648      www.penton.com

*Publisher of industrial/trade magazines.*

**Air Transport World,  34A West Street, Marlow, Buckinghamshire SL7 2NB, UK**

Tel: 44-1628-477-775   Fax: 44-1628-481-111

**Meko, Ltd.,  134 Upper Chobham Road, Camberley, Surrey GU 15 1EJ, UK**

Tel: 44-1276-22677   Fax: 44-1276-64004

**New Hope International Media,  Brighton Media Center, Brighton, East Sussex BN1 1AL, UK**

Tel: 44-1273-384-282   Fax: 44-1273-384-285

**Penton Media Europe,  Penton House, 288-290 Worton Road, Isleworth, Middlesex TW7 6EL, UK**

Tel: 44-208-232-1600   Fax: 44-208-232-1650

**Streaming Media,  45 Whitechapel Road 3/F, London E1 1DU, UK**

Tel: 44-20-7375-7500   Fax: 44-20-7375-7511

## PEOPLESOFT INC.

4460 Hacienda Drive, Pleasanton, CA, 94588-8618

Tel: (925) 225-3000      Fax: (925) 694-4444      www.peoplesoft.com

*Mfr. applications to manage business operations across computer networks.*

**PeopleSoft UK,  Apex Plaza - Reading, Berkshire G+RG1 1AX, UK**

Tel: 44-118-952-2000   Fax: 44-181-952-2001

## PEPSiCO INC.

700 Anderson Hill Road, Purchase, NY, 10577-1444

Tel: (914) 253-2000      Fax: (914) 253-2070      www.pepsico.com

*Beverages and snack foods.*

**Crispflow Ltd.,  London, UK**

Frito-Lay Holdings Ltd., London, UK

PepsiCo Holdings Ltd., London, UK

PFI Agriculture Europe Ltd., London, UK

Walkers Smiths Snack Foods Ltd, London, England UK

## PERIPHONICS CORPORATION

4000 Veterans Highway, Bohemia, NY, 11716

Tel: (631) 468-9000      Fax: (631) 981-2689      www.periphonics.com

*Mfr. voice processing systems.*

Periphonics VPS Ltd., Albany Court, Albany Park, Camberley, Surrey GU15 2XA, UK

Tel: 44-1-276-692020

## PERKIN ELMER, INC.

45 William Street, Wellesley, MA, 02481

Tel: (781) 237-5100      Fax: (781) 431-4255      www.perkinelmer.com

*Mfr. equipment and devices to detect explosives and bombs on airline carriers.*

PerkinElmer Life Sciences, Mulberry Business park, Wokingham Berks RG41 2GY, UK

Tel: 44-118-977-3493

PerkinElmer Life Sciences, Saxon Way Bar Hill, Cambridge CB3 8SL, UK

## PEROT SYSTEMS CORPORATION

PO Box 809022, Dallas, TX, 75380

Tel: (972) 340-5000      Fax: (972) 455-4100      www.perotsystems.com

*Engaged in computer services technology.*

Perot Systems Corporation, English House, 14 St. George St., Mayfair, London UK

## PETERSON AMERICAN CORPORATION

21200 Telegraph Road, Southfield, MI, 48086-5059

Tel: (248) 799-5400      Fax: (248) 357-3176      www.pspring.com

*Mfr. springs and wire products, metal stampings.*

AP Spring, Reddings Lane, Tyseley, Birmingham B11 3HA, UK

Tel: 44-121-706-2236

Peterson Spring UK Ltd. - Heath Plant, Hewell Road, Redditch, Worchestershire B97 6AY, UK

Tel: 44-527-61952   Fax: 44-527-591660   Contact: Edward Roberts

## PFAUDLER, INC.

1000 West Ave., PO Box 23600, Rochester, NY, 14692-3600

Tel: (716) 235-1000      Fax: (716) 436-9644      www.pfaudler.com

*Mfr. glass lined reactors, storage vessels and reglassing services.*

Chemical Reactor Services Ltd., Bilston, UK

Tel: 44-1902-353-637   Fax: 44-1902-495-696

Chemical Reactor Services Ltd., Bolton, England UK

## PFIZER INC.

235 East 42nd Street, New York, NY, 10017-5755

Tel: (212) 573-2323      Fax: (212) 573-7851      www.pfizer.com

*Research-based, global health care company.*

Biomedical Sensors (Holdings) Ltd., London, UK

Biomedical Sensors Ltd., London, UK

Coty Ltd., London, UK

Feldene Ltd., London, UK

Invicta Pharmaceuticals Ltd., London, UK

Measurim Ltd., London, UK

Pfizer Group Ltd., London, UK

Pfizer Hospital Products Group Ltd., London, UK

Pfizer Hospital Products Group Pension Trustee Ltd., London, UK

Pfizer Hospital Products Inc., London, UK

Pfizer Ltd., London, UK

Pfizer Pension Trustees Ltd., London, UK

Richborough Pharmaceuticals Ltd., London, UK

Shiley Ltd., London, UK

TCP Ltd., London, UK

Unicliffe Ltd., London, UK

## PHARMACIA CORPORATION

100 Route 206 North, Peapack, NJ, 07977

Tel: (908) 901-8000      Fax: (908) 901-8379      www.pharmacia.com

*Mfr. pharmaceuticals, agricultural products, industry chemicals.*

Upjohn Intl. Ltd., Fleming Way, Crawley, Sussex RH10 2NJ, UK

Upjohn Ltd., PO Box No. 8, Fleming Way, Crawley Sussex, RH 10 2LZ UK

Upjohn Ltd., Davy Ave., Knowhill, Milton Keynes MK 5 8PH, UK

Upjohn Ltd., 23 Grosvenor Rd., St. Albans AL 1 3AW, UK

## PHARMACIA MONSANTO

800 N. Lindbergh Boulevard, St. Louis, MO, 63167

Tel: (314) 694-1000      Fax: (314) 694-7625      www.monsanto.com

*Life sciences company focusing on agriculture, nutrition, pharmaceuticals, health and wellness and sustainable development.*

Monsanto Co. Chemical Group, PO Box 53. Lane End Road, High Wycombe Bucks HP12 4HL, UK

## PHD INC.

9009 Clubridge Dr., PO Box 9070, Fort Wayne, IN, 46899

Tel: (219) 747-6151      Fax: (219) 747-6754      www.phdinc.com.

*Mfr. pneumatic and hydraulic products used in factory automation.*

PHD Ltd., 7 Eden Way, Pages Industrial Park, Leighton Buzzard, Bedfordshire LU7 8TP, UK

Tel: 44-1525-853-488    Fax: 44-1515-853-488

## PHELPS DODGE CORPORATION

2600 North Central Ave., Phoenix, AZ, 85004-3089

Tel: (602) 234-8100      Fax: (602) 234-8337      www.phelpsdodge.com

*Copper, minerals, metals and special engineered products for transportation and electrical markets.*

Columbian Chemicals Co., England, UK

## PHH VEHICLE MANAGEMENT SERVICES

307 International Circle, Hunt Valley, MD, 21030

Tel: (410) 771-3600      Fax: (410) 771-2841      www.phh.com

*Provides vehicle fleet management, corporate relocation, and mortgage banking services.*

PHH Vehicle Management Services, PHH Centre, Windmill Hill, Whitehall Way, Swindon,SN5 6PE, Wiltshire UK

Tel: 44-1793-887000

PHH Vehicle Management Services, Oakland House, Talbot Rd., Old Tafford, Manchester M16 0PQ UK

Tel: 44-1618-729571

## PHILIP SERVICES CORP. INDUSTRIAL GROUP

5151 San Felipe Street, #1600, Houston, TX, 77056-3609

Tel: (713) 623-8777 Fax: (713) 625-7085 www.philipinc.com

*Trucking, refuse systems, staffing and numerous industrial-oriented services.*

**Ferrous Bath Reclamation Co., Ltd., Ironchurch Road, Off St. Andrews Road, Avonmouth Bristol BS11 9BP, UK**

Tel: 44-117-982-6300 Fax: 44-117-938-1313 Contact: Phil Mumby

**Ferrous Philip Metals (Europe) Ltd., Seven Brethren Bank, Industrial Estate, Barnstaple Devon, UK**

Tel: 44-127-142-131 Fax: 44-127-142-669 Contact: Alec Heale

**Industrial Services Philip Services (Europe), Thornley House, Carrington Business Park, Manchester M31 4SG, UK**

Tel: 44-161-775-4488 Fax: 44-161-775-4407 Contact: Ralph Davies

**Philip Services (Europe) Ltd., 44 Davies St., London W1Y ILD, UK**

Tel: 44-207-518-0950 Fax: 44-207-518-0955 Contact: Ayman Gabarin, President

## PHILIPP BROTHERS CHEMICALS INC.

1 Parker Plaza, Fort Lee, NJ, 07029

Tel: (201) 944-6020 Fax: (201) 944-7916 www.philipp-brothers.com

*Mfr. industry and agricultural chemicals.*

**Ferro Metal & Chemical Corp., Crompton House, Aldwych WC2B 4JF, UK**

Tel: 44-118-959-1961

## PHILLIPS PETROLEUM COMPANY

Phillips Building, 411 S. Keeler Ave., Bartlesville, OK, 74004

Tel: (918) 661-6600 Fax: (918) 661-7636 www.phillips66.com

*Crude oil, natural gas, liquefied petroleum gas, gasoline and petro-chemicals.*

**Phillips Petroleum Co., Portland House, Stag Place, London SW1E 5DA, UK**

## PICTURETEL CORPORATION

100 Minuteman Road, Andover, MA, 01810

Tel: (978) 292-5000 Fax: (978) 292-3300 www.picturetel.com

*Mfr. video conferencing systems, network bridging and multiplexing products, system peripherals.*

**PictureTel International Corp., St. James Court, Wilderspool Causeway, Warrington WA4 6PS, UK**

Tel: 44-1925-633664 Fax: 44-1925-658878

**PictureTel UK Ltd., 270 Bath Rd., Slough, Berkshire, SL1 4DX UK**

Tel: 44-1753-723000 Fax: 44-1753-723010

## PIER 1 IMPORTS, INC.

301 Commerce St., Ste. 600, Fort Worth, TX, 76102

Tel: (817) 878-8000 Fax: (817) 252-8801 www.pier1.com

*Specialty retailer of imported decorative home furnishings.*

**Pier 1 Imports, Inc., 200 Tottenham Court Road, WIP OAD, UK**

Tel: 44-270-6377001

**Pier 1 Imports, Inc., 91-95 King's Road, Chelsea SW3 4PA, UK**

Tel: 44-270-351-7100

## PILLAR INDUSTRIES

21905 Gateway Road, Brookfield, WI, 53045

Tel: (262) 317-5300 Fax: (262) 317-5353 www.pillar.com

*Mfr. induction heating and melting equipment.*

**Pillar Europe, Unit 9 Spring Rise, Falconer Road, Haverhill Suffolk CB9 7HJ, UK**

## PINNACLE WORLDWIDE, INC.

1201 Marquette Ave., Ste. 300, Minneapolis, MN, 55403

Tel: (612) 338-2215     Fax: (612) 338-2572     www.pinnacleww.com

*International network of independent public relations firms.*

**Barclay Stratton,  Albert House, 27 Kelso Place, London W8 5QG, UK**

Tel: 44-20-7544-6000   Fax: 44-20-7544-6290

## PIONEER HI-BRED INTERNATIONAL INC.

400 Locust Street, Ste. 800, Des Moines, IA, 50309

Tel: (515) 248-4800     Fax: (515) 248-4999     www.pioneer.com

*Agricultural chemicals, farm supplies, biological products, research.*

**Pioneer Hi-Bred Northern Europe GmbH,  The Barn - Blisworth Hill Farm, Northampton Northants, Blisworth NN7 3DB, UK**

Tel: 44-1604-858008

## PIONEER-STANDARD ELECTRONICS, INC.

6065 Parkland Blvd., Cleveland, OH, 44124

Tel: (440) 720-8500     Fax: (440) 720-8501     www.pios.com

*Mfr./distribution of electronic parts for computers and networking equipment.*

**Eurodis Electron Plc.,  Reigate Hill House, Reigate, Surrey RH2 9NG, UK**

Tel: 44-1737-242-464

**Eurodis HB Electronics,  Lever Street, Bolton, Lancashire BL3 6BJ, UK**

Tel: 44-1204-555-000

## PITNEY BOWES INC.

1 Elmcroft Road, Stamford, CT, 06926-0700

Tel: (203) 356-5000     Fax: (203) 351-6835     www.pitneybowes.com

*Mfr. postage meters, mailroom equipment, copiers, bus supplies, bus services, facsimile systems and financial services.*

**Pitney Bowes Ltd.,  The Pinnacles, Harlow, Essex CM19 5BD, UK**

Tel: 44-1279-426-731   Fax: 44-1279-449-275   Contact: Malachy Smith, Mng. Dir.   Emp: 1,700

**Pitney Bowes Management Services Ltd.,  New City Court, 20 St. Thomas Street, London SE1 9RS, UK**

Tel: 44-207-962-1175

## PITTSTON BAX GROUP

16808 Armstrong Ave., PO Box 19571, Irvine, CA, 92623

Tel: (949) 752-4000     Fax: (949) 260-3182     www.baxworld.com

*Air freight forwarder.*

**BAX Global,  Burlington House, 30-38 Church St., Staines Middlesex TW18 4EP UK**

Tel: 44-1784-877000   Fax: 44-1784-877003

**BAX Global,  Unitair Centre, Great South West Rd., Feltham, Middlesex TW14 8NT UK**

Tel: 44-181-899-3000   Fax: 44-181-899-3112

## PLANET HOLLYWOOD INTERNATIONAL, INC.

8669 Commodity Circle, Orlando, FL, 32819

Tel: (407) 363-7827     Fax: (407) 363-4862     www.planethollywood.com

*Theme-dining restaurant chain and merchandise retail stores.*

**Planet Hollywood International, Inc.,  London, UK**

## PLANTRONICS

345 Encinal Street, Santa Cruz, CA, 95060

Tel: (831) 426-5858     Fax: (831) 425-5198     www.plantronics.com

*Mfr. communications equipment, electrical and electronic appliances and apparatus.*

**Plantronics Ltd., Interface Business Park, Bincknoll Lane, Wootton Bassett, Wiltshire SN4 8QQ UK**

Tel: 44-1793-848999   Fax: 44-1793-848853   Contact: Howard Shenton

## POLAROID CORPORATION

784 Memorial Dr., Cambridge, MA, 02139

Tel: (781) 386-2000     Fax: (781) 386-3924     www.polaroid.com

*Photographic equipment and supplies, optical products.*

**Polaroid (UK) Ltd., Ashley Rd., St. Albans, Herts, UK**

## POLICY MANAGEMENT SYSTEMS CORPORATION

One PMSC Center, Blythewood, SC, 29016

Tel: (803) 333-4000     Fax: (803) 333-5544     www.pmsc.com

*Computer software, insurance industry support services.*

**PMS Europe Ltd., Creative House, Broad Lane, Bracknell, Berkshire RE12 9GU, UK**

## R.L. POLK & COMPANY

26955 Northwestern Hwy., Southfield, MI, 48034

Tel: (248) 728-7111     Fax: (248) 393-2860     www.polk.com

*Directories and direct mail advertising.*

**Polk (Europe) Ltd., Millfield, Ashwells Rd., Brentwood, Essex CM15 9ST, UK**

**Portica Ltd., Addison Rd., Chilton Industrial Estate, Sudbury, Suffolk CO10 6YJ, UK**

**The Ultimate Perspective Management Consultancy (TUP), Gladstone Place, 36-38 Upper Marlborough Rd., St. Albans, Herts. AL1 3US, UK**

## POLO RALPH LAUREN CORPORATION

650 Madison Ave., New York, NY, 10022

Tel: (212) 318-7000     Fax: (212) 888-5780     www.poloralphlauren.com

*Designs and markets clothing, bath and bedding and operates Polo Ralph Lauren and Polo Sport stores.*

**Ralph Lauren, Ltd., 143 New Bond St., London W1Y 9FD, UK**

Tel: 44-207-493-4828   Contact: Sarah Manley, Mng. Dir.

## PORTA SYSTEMS CORPORATION

575 Underhill Boulevard, Syosset, NY, 11791

Tel: (516) 364-9300     Fax: (516) 682-4636     www.portasystems.com

*Design/mfr. products for the connection, protection, testing, administration and management of public and private telecommunications lines and networks.*

**Porta Systems Ltd., Royal Oak Way N., Royal Oak Ind. Est., Coventry NN1 15PQ, UK**

## PORTER PRECISION PRODUCTS COMPANY

2734 Banning Road, PO Box 538706, Cincinnati, OH, 45239

Tel: (513) 923-3777     Fax: (513) 923-1111     www.porterpunch.com

*Mfr. piercing punches and die supplies for metal stamping and tool/die industry.*

**Porter Precision Products Ltd., Masons Rd., Stratford-upon-Avon, Warwickshire CV37 9NF, UK**

## POTTERS INDUSTRIES INC.

PO Box 840, Valley Forge, PA, 19482-0840

Tel: (610) 651-4700     Fax: (610) 408-9724     www.pottersbeads.com

*Mfr. glass spheres for road marking and industry applications.*

**Potters Ballotini Ltd., Bury St. Edmunds, UK**

Tel: 44-1-284-715400

**Potters-Ballotini Ltd., Pontefract Rd., Barnsley, South Yorkshire S71 1HJ, UK**

## POWER TECHNOLOGIES INC. (PTI)

1482 Erie Blvd., PO Box 1058, Schenectady, NY, 12301

Tel: (518) 395-5000      Fax: (518) 346-2777      www.pti-us.com

*Power systems engineering, consulting, services and related control software; power quality hardware.*

**Power Technologies Ltd., Graham Bishop -Cranford Court, King Street Knutsford, WA16 8BW Cheshire UK**

## POWERWARE CORPORATION

8609 Six Forks Road, Raleigh, NC, 27615

Tel: (919) 870-3020      Fax: (919) 870-3100      www.powerware.com

*Mfr./services uninterruptible power supplies and related equipment.*

**Powerware Electronics Ltd., 221 Dover Rd., Slough, Berkshire, SL1 4RS, UK**

Tel: 44-1753-608-700   Fax: 44-1753-608-995

## PPG INDUSTRIES

One PPG Place, Pittsburgh, PA, 15272

Tel: (412) 434-3131      Fax: (412) 434-2190      www.ppg.com

*Mfr. coatings, flat glass, fiber glass, chemicals, coatings.*

**PPG Indusries (UK) Ltd., Fiber Glass, PO Box 132 Leigh Rd., Wigam EN2 4XZ, UK**

**PPG Industries (UK) Ltd., Coatings, PO Box 359, Rotton Park St., Birmingham B16 0AD, UK**

## PPL GLOBAL

11350 Random Hills Rd., Ste. 400, Fairfax, VA, 22030

Tel: (703) 293-2600      Fax: (703) 293-2659      www.pplresources.com

*Gas and electric.*

**Wester Power Distribution plc., London, UK**

**Western Power Distribution, Sub. PPL Global, Bristol, UK**

## PRC INC.

1500 PRC Drive, McLean, VA, 22102

Tel: (703) 556-1000      Fax: (703) 556-1174      www.prc.com

*Computer systems and services.*

**PRC, 6 First Ave., Globe Park, Marlow, Bucks UK**

## PRECISION VALVE & TRIM, INC.

PO Box 3091, 1923 Cloverland Avenue, Baton Rouge, LA, 70809

Tel: (225) 752-5600      Fax: (225) 752-5400      www.precisionvalve.com

*Mfr. aerosol valves.*

**Precision Valve UK Ltd., Unit C, Newcombe Way, Orton Southgate, Peterborough, Cambs PE2 0SF, UK**

## PREFORMED LINE PRODUCTS COMPANY

600 Beta Drive, PO Box 91129, Mayfield, OH, 44143

Tel: (440) 461-5200      Fax: (440) 442-8816      www.preformed.com

*Mfr. pole line hardware for electrical transmission lines; splice closures and related products for telecommunications.*

**Preformed Line Products (Great Britain) Ltd., Andover, Hants, UK**

## PREMARK INTERNATIONAL INC.

1717 Deerfield Road, Deerfield, IL, 60015

Tel: (847) 405-6000      Fax: (847) 405-6013      www.premarkintl.com

*Mfr. Hobart commercial food equipment, diversified consumer and commercial products, small appliances, and exercise equipment.*

**Dart Industries Ltd., 130 College Rd., Harrow, Middlesex HA1 1BQ UK**

## PREMIX INC.

PO Box 281, Rt. 20, Harmon Road, North Kingsville, OH, 44068-0281

Tel: (440) 224-2181     Fax: (440) 224-2766     www.premix.com

*Mfr. molded fiber glass, reinforced thermoset molding compounds and plastic parts.*

**Permali RP Ltd., 125 Bristol Rd., Gloucester GL 15TT, UK**

Tel: 44-1452-528-671   Fax: 44-1452-304-215   Contact: Mike Malloria, Mng. Dir   Emp: 104

## PRESTOLITE ELECTRIC INC.

2100 Commonwealth Blvd., Ste. 300, Ann Arbor, MI, 48105

Tel: (734) 913-6600     Fax: (734) 913-6656     www.prestolite.com

*Mfr. alternators, DC motors, relays, switches.*

**Prestolite Electric Ltd., Cleveland Rd., Leyland PR5 1XB, UK**

**Prestolite Electric Ltd., Larden Road - Acton, London W3 7RP, UK**

## PREVIO, INC.

12636 High Bluff Drive, 4th Fl., San Diego, CA, 92130

Tel: (858) 794-4300     Fax: (858) 794-4572     www.previo.com

*Engaged in corporate electronic business support.*

**Previo Europe Limited, High View House - Ste. 406, Charles Square, Bracknell Berkshire RG12 1DF, UK**

Tel: 44-1344-397-593   Fax: 44-1377-397-617`

## PRI AUTOMATION, INC.

805 Middlesex Turnpike, Billerica, MA, 01821-3986

Tel: (978) 663-8555     Fax: (978) 663-9755     www.pria.com

*Provides factory automation systems for silicon chip makers.*

**PRI Automation, Inc., 199 Silbury Boulevard, Central Milton Keynes, Buckinghamshire MK9 1JL, UK**

Tel: 44-1-908-247000   Fax: 44-1-908-247001

## PRICEWATERHOUSECOOPERS LLP

1301 Ave. of the Americas, New York, NY, 10019

Tel: (212) 596-7000     Fax: (212) 259-1301     www.pwcglobal.com

*Accounting and auditing, tax and management, and human resource consulting services.*

**PriceWaterhouseCoopers, The Quay, 30 Channel Way, Ocean Village Southampton, Hants SO14 3QG UK**

Tel: 44-1703-330077   Fax: 44-1703-223473

**PriceWaterhouseCoopers, York House, York Street, Manchester M2 4WS, UK**

Tel: 44-161-245-2000   Fax: 44-161-228-1429

**PriceWaterhouseCoopers, Docklands Island Quay, 161 Marsh Wall, London E14 9SQ, UK**

Tel: 44-207-939-3000   Fax: 44-207-538-5547

**PriceWaterhouseCoopers, Southwark Towers, 32 London Bridge Street, London SE1 9SY, UK**

Tel: 44-207-939-3000   Fax: 44-207-939-2526

**PriceWaterhouseCoopers, 31 Great George St., Bristol BS1 5QD, UK**

Tel: 44-117-929-1500   Fax: 44-117-929-0519

**PriceWaterhouseCoopers, Cornwall Court, 19 Cornwall Street, Birmingham B3 2DT, UK**

Tel: 44-121-200-3000   Fax: 44-121-200-2464

## PRIMARK CORPORATION

100 Winter Street, Ste. 4300-N, Waltham, MA, 02451

Tel: (781) 466-6611     Fax: (781) 890-6187     www.primark.com

*Provides financial and business information.*

**Primark Data Company, 58-64 City Road, London EC1Y 2AL, UK**

Tel: 44-207-250-3000

**Primark UK,  #1 Mark Square, London EC2A 4PR, UK**

Tel: 44-207-631-0757

## PRINTRONIX INC.

14600 Myford Road, Irvine, CA, 92606

Tel:  (714) 368-2300          Fax:  (714) 368-2600          www.printronix.com

*Mfr. computer printers.*

**Printronix UK,  Downmill Rd., Bracknell, Berkshire, RG12 1QS UK**

Tel: 44-1344-869666    Fax: 44-1344-360967

**Printronix UK,  Loddon Vale House, Hurricane Way, Woodley, Berkshire RG5 4UX, UK**

## PROCTER & GAMBLE COMPANY

One Procter & Gamble Plaza, Cincinnati, OH, 45202

Tel:  (513) 983-1100          Fax:  (513) 562-4500          www.pg.com

*Personal care, food, laundry, cleaning and industry products.*

**Procter & Gamble,  St. Nicholas Ave., PO Box 1EL Gosforth, Newcastle-upon-Tyne Tyne NE99 1EE, UK**

Tel: 44-191-279-2000

## PROCTER & GAMBLE PHARMACEUTICALS (P&GP)

17 Eaton Ave., Norwich, NY, 13815-1799

Tel:  (607) 335-2111          Fax:  (607) 335-2798          www.pg.com

*Develop/manufacture pharmaceuticals, chemicals and health products.*

**Eaton Laboratories,  Regent House, The Broadway, Wokingham, Surrey GU21 5AP UK**

## PRODUCTION GROUP INTERNATIONAL, INC.

2200 Wilson Blvd., Ste 200, Arlington, VA, 22201-3324

Tel:  (703) 528-8484          Fax:  (703) 528-1724          www.pgi.com

*Provides major corporations with promotional events, planning and travel services, trade shows and exhibitions.*

**Spearhead Exhibitions, Ltd.,  Ocean St., Kingston Rd., New Malden, Surrey KT3 3L2, UK**

Tel: 44-181-949-9222    Fax: 44-181-94-8186

## PROJECT SOFTWARE & DEVELOPMENT, INC.

100 Crosby Drive, Bedford, MA, 01730

Tel:  (781) 280-2000          Fax:  (781) 280-0207          www.mrosoftware.com

*Design/sales of enterprise asset maintenance software.*

**MRO Software,  88-100 Chertsey Road, Woking, Surrey GU2 15BJ, UK**

Tel: 44-1483-778-600

## PROVIDIAN FINANCIAL CORPORATION

201 Mission St., San Francisco, CA, 94105

Tel:  (415) 543-0404          Fax:  (415) 278-6028          www.providian.com

*Provides standard and premium credit cards to consumers.*

**Providian Financial Corporation,  Crawley, West Sussex, UK**

Contact: James V. Elliott, Pres.

## PSDI MAXIMO

100 Crosby Drive, Bedford, MA, 01730

Tel:  (781) 280-2000          Fax:  (781) 280-0200          www.psdi.com

*Develops, markets and provides maintenance management software systems.*

**PSDI (UK) Ltd.,  Unit 5 Woking Eight, Forsyth Rd., Woking Surrey GU21 5SB, UK**

Tel: 44-1-483-727000    Fax: 44-1-483-727979    Contact: Richard Konarek, Gen. Mgr.    Emp: 40

## PSI NET (PERFORMANCE SYSTEMS INTERNATIONAL INC.)

510 Huntmar Park Drive, Herndon, VA, 22170

Tel: (703) 904-4100    Fax: (703) 904-4200    www.psinet.com

*Internet service provider.*

**PSINet UK Ltd., Brook Mount Court Units A & B , Kirkwood Road, Cambridge CB4 2QH, UK**

Tel: 44-1-1223-577577  Fax: 44-1223-506577  Contact: Valerie Holt, VP & Mng. Dir.

## PUBLIC SERVICE ENTERPRISE GROUP (PSEG)

80 Park Plaza, Newark, NJ, 07101

Tel: (973) 430-7000    Fax: (973) 623-5389    www.pseg.com

*Electric and gas utility.*

**PSEG Global Ltd., 8 Bourdon Street, London W1X 9HX, UK**

Tel: 44-207-744-0100   Fax: 44-207-744-0177   Contact: Matthew McGrath

## PULSE ENGINEERING INC.

12220 World Trade Drive, PO 12235, San Diego, CA, 92112

Tel: (858) 674-8100    Fax: (858) 674-8262    www.pulseeng.com

*Engineer/mfr. OEM devices for local area network markets and major voice/data transmission systems.*

**Pulse Engineering UK, 1 & 2 Huxley Road, The Surrey Research Park, Guildford Surrey GU2 5RE, UK**

## PURE CARBON COMPANY

441 Hall Ave., Saint Marys, PA, 15857

Tel: (814) 781-1573    Fax: (814) 781-9262    www.mamat.com

*Mfr. carbon graphite and silicon carbide components.*

**Morganite Special Carbons, Hampshire, UK**

Contact: Dr. Rice

**Pure Industries Ltd., 12 & 13 Madeley Rd., North Moons Moat, Redditch, Worcestershire B98 9NB, UK**

## PURE FISHING

1900 18th Street, Spirit Lake, IA, 51360

Tel: (712) 336-1520    Fax: (712) 336-4183    www.purefishing.com

*Mfr. fishing rods, reels, lines and tackle, outdoor products, soft and hard baits.*

**Outdoor Technologies Group United Kingdom (OTG UK), Unit 5 Aston Way, Middlewich Motorway Estate, Middlewich Cheshire CW10 OHS, UK**

Tel: 44-1606-836-921   Fax: 44-1606-836-411   Contact: Robbie Brightwell, Mng. Dir.   Emp: 17

## PUTNAM INVESTMENTS

1 Post Office Square, Boston, MA, 02109

Tel: (617) 292-1000    Fax: (617) 292-1499    www.putnaminv.com

*Money management; mutual funds, annuities and retirement plans.*

**Putnam Advisory Co. Ltd., Pollen House, 10-12 Cork St., London, W1X 1PD, UK**

## QUAKER CHEMICAL CORPORATION

Elm & Lee Streets, Conshohocken, PA, 19428-0809

Tel: (610) 832-4000    Fax: (610) 832-8682    www.quakerchem.com

*Mfr. developer, producer, and marketer of custom-formulated chemical specialty products.*

**Quaker Chemical Ltd., Bath Rd., Woodchester, Stroud, Gloucestershire, UK**

Contact: John H. Powell

## THE QUAKER OATS COMPANY

Quaker Tower, 321 North Clark Street, Chicago, IL, 60610-4714

Tel: (312) 222-7111    Fax: (312) 222-8323    www.quakeroats.com

*Mfr. foods and beverages.*

**Quaker Oats Ltd., PO Box 24, Bridge Rd., Southall Middlesex UB2 4AG, UK**

## QUALCOMM INC.

5775 Morehouse Dr., San Diego, CA, 92121-1714

Tel: (858) 587-1121     Fax: (858) 658-2100     www.qualcomm.com

*Digital wireless telecommunications systems.*

**QUALCOMM UK,  Block B 2/F Spectrum Point, Farnborough Road, Farnborough, UK**

## QUANTUM

500 McCarthy Blvd., Milpitas, CA, 95035

Tel: (408) 894-4000     Fax: (408) 894-3218     www.quantum.com

*Mfr. computer peripherals.*

**Quantum Peripheral Products Ltd.,  10 Bracknell Beeches, Bracknell, Berkshire RG12 7BW, UK**

Tel: 44-1344-353510

## QUINTILES TRANSNATIONAL CORPORATION

4709 Creekstone Dr., Durham, NC, 27703

Tel: (919) 998-2000     Fax: (919) 998-9113     www.quintiles.com

*Mfr. pharmaceuticals.*

**G.D.R.U. Limited,  6 Newcomen Street, London SE1 1YR, UK**

**Medical Action Communications Ltd.,  Action International House, Crabtree Office Village, Eversley Way Thorpe Egham, Surrey TW20 8RY, UK**

## QWEST COMMUNICATIONS INTERNATIONAL INC.

1801 California Street, Ste. 5200, Denver, CO, 80202

Tel: (303) 896-2020     Fax: (303) 793-6654     www.uswest.com

*Tele-communications provider; integrated communications services.*

**Telewest, U.K.,  London, UK**

Tel: 44-207-333-8866   Fax: 44-207-333-8232

## R&B FALCON CORPORATION

901 Threadneedle, Ste. 200, Houston, TX, 77079

Tel: (281) 496-5000     Fax: (281) 496-4363     www.rbfalcon.com

*Offshore contract drilling.*

**R&B Falcon (UK) Ltd.,  Newfield House, Middleton Rd., Heysham LA3 3PP, UK**

## R. H. DONNELLY CORPORATION (RHD)

287 Bowman Ave., Purchase, NY, 10577

Tel: (914) 933-6800     Fax: (914) 933-6544     www.rhdonnelly.com

*Publish Yellow Pages and telephone directories and provide direct mail and merchandising services.*

**Thomson Directories Ltd.,  296 Farnborough Rd., Farnborough, Hants GU14 7NU, UK**

## RADISSON HOTELS INTERNATIONAL

Carlson Pkwy., PO Box 59159, Minneapolis, MN, 55459-8204

Tel: (612) 540-5526     Fax: (612) 449-3400     www.radisson.com

*Hotels and resorts.*

**Radisson Court Hotels,  Attn: British Office, Carlson Parkway, PO Box 59159, Minneapolis MN 55459-8204**

Tel: 44-207-589-2424   Fax: 44-207-225-2293

**Radisson Savoy Court Hotel,  Granville Place, London W1H OEH, UK**

Tel: 44-207-408-0130   Fax: 44-207-493-2070

## RAIN BIRD SPRINKLER MFG. CORPORATION

145 North Grand Ave., Glendora, CA, 91741-2469

Tel: (626) 963-9311      Fax: (626) 963-4287      www.rainbird.com

*World's largest manufacturer of lawn sprinklers and irrigation systems equipment.*

**Rain Bird in UK, Riddens Lanes, Plimpton Green, Lewes, East Sussex BN7 3BJ UK**

Tel: 44-1273-891326  Fax: 44-1273-891327   Contact: Victor Jamieson

## RAINBOW TECHNOLOGY INC.

50 Technology Dr., Irvine, CA, 92618

Tel: (949) 450-7300      Fax: (949) 450-7450      www.rainbow.com

*Mfr. computer related security products.*

**Rainbow Technologies Ltd., 4 The Forum, Hanworth Lane, Chertsey, Surrey KT16 9JX, UK**

## RAMSEY TECHNOLOGY INC.

501 90th Ave. NW, Coon Rapids, MN, 55433

Tel: (763) 783-2500      Fax: (763) 780-2525

*Mfr. in-motion weighing, inspection, monitoring and control equipment for the process industry.*

**Ramsey Process Controls Ltd., Unit A2 Swift Park, Old Leicester Rd., Rugby, Warwickshire CV21 1De, UK**

## RANCO INC.

8115 US Route 42 North, Plain City, OH, 43064

Tel: (614) 873-9000      Fax: (614) 873-3819      www.rancocontrols.com

*Mfr. controls for appliance, automotive, comfort, commercial and consumer markets.*

**Ranco Controls Ltd., Southway Dr., Southway, Plymouth PL6 6QT, UK**

## RAND McNALLY & COMPANY

8255 North Central Park Ave., Skokie, IL, 60076-2970

Tel: (847) 329-8100      Fax: (847) 673-0539      www.randmcnally.com

*Publishing, consumer software, information and retail.*

**De Agostini-Rand McNally, Griffin House, London UK**

## RAY & BERNDTSON, INC.

301 Commerce, Ste. 2300, Fort Worth, TX, 76102

Tel: (817) 334-0500      Fax: (817) 334-0779      www.prb.com

*Executive search, management audit and management consulting firm.*

**Ray & Berndtson, 11 Hanover Square, London W1R 9HD, UK**

Tel: 44-207-529-1111  Fax: 44-207-529-1000   Contact: Richard Boggis-Rolfe

## RAYCHEM CORPORATION

300 Constitution Dr., Menlo Park, CA, 94025-1164

Tel: (650) 361-3333      Fax: (650) 361-5579      www.raychem.com

*Develop/mfr./market materials science products for electronics, telecommunications and industry.*

**Raychem Ltd., Index House, St. George's Lane, London Rd., Ascot Berkshire SL5 7EU UK**

**Raychem Ltd., Faraday Rd., Dorcan Swindon, Wiltshire SN3 5HH, UK**

Tel: 44-1793-528-171  Fax: 44-1793-572-516

**Raychem Ltd., Cheney Manor Industrial Estates, Swindon, Wiltshire SN2 2QE, UK**

Tel: 44-1793-528-171  Fax: 44-1793-616-652

**Sigmaform (UK) Ltd., Slywell Rd., Park Farm Ind. Estates, Wellingborough, Northampshire NN8 3XD UK**

## RAYCHEM INTERCONNECT

300 Constitution Dr., Menlo Park, CA, 94025-1164

Tel: (650) 361-3333        Fax: (650) 361-2108        www.raychem.com

*Supplies interconnect products that seal, connect, protect and identify wire and cable harnesses and electronic components.*

**Raychem Interconnect, London, UK**

## RAYMOND JAMES FINANCIAL, INC.

880 Carillon Parkway, St. Petersburg, FL, 33716

Tel: (813) 573-3800        Fax: (813) 573-8244        www.rjf.com

*Financial services; securities brokerage, asset management, and investment banking services.*

**Raymond James & Associates - London,  Neptune House - 14 Finsbury Square, London EC2A 1BR, UK**

Tel: 44-207-696-6150    Fax: 44-207-696-6197    Contact: E. Rowe

## RAYONIER INC.

50 N. Laura St., 18-19 Fls., Jacksonville, FL, 32202

Tel: (904) 357-9100        Fax: (904) 357-9155        www.rayonier.com

*Chemicals cellulose, paper pulps, logs and lumber.*

**Rayonier Industries Ltd.,  17A Curson St., London W1, UK**

## RAYOVAC CORPORATION

601 Rayovac Drive, Madison, WI, 53711-2497

Tel: (608) 275-3340        Fax: (608) 275-4577        www.rayovac.com

*Mfr. batteries and lighting devices.*

**Rayovac Ltd.,  King St., Mainstone, Kent ME14 1BG, UK**

Tel: 441-622-676699

**Rayovac Micro Power Ltd., Stephenson Estate, Dist. 12, Washington, Tyne & Wear NE37 3HW, UK**

**Rayovac Vidor Ltd.,  Beaumont Way, Aycliffe Industrial Estate, County Durham DL5 6SN, UK**

## RAYTHEON COMPANY

141 Spring Street, Lexington, MA, 02173

Tel: (781) 862-6600        Fax: (781) 860-2172        www.raytheon.com

*Mfr. diversified electronics, appliances, aviation, energy and environmental products; publishing, industry and construction services.*

**Cosser Electronics Ltd.,  The Pinnacles, Elizabeth Way, Harlow Essex CM19 5BB, UK**

**Data Logic Ltd.,  The Pinnacles, Elizabeth Way, Harlow Essex CM19 5BB, UK**

**Electrical Installations Ltd.,  65 Vincent Sq., Westminster, London SW1P 2NX UK**

**Raytheon Europe Ltd.,  Queens House, Greenhill Way, Harrow Middlesex HA1 1YR, UK**

**Raytheon Marine,  Portsmouth, UK**

## RAZORFISH, INC.

107 Grand Street, 3rd Fl., New York, NY, 10013

Tel: (212) 966-5960        Fax: (212) 966-6915        www.razorfish.com

*Engaged in consulting and web services.*

**Razorfish UK,  2 East Poultry Avenue, Smithfield London EC1A 9 PT, UK**

Tel: 44-0207-549-4200

## READER'S DIGEST ASSOCIATION, INC.

Reader's Digest Rd., Pleasantville, NY, 10570

Tel: (914) 238-1000        Fax: (914) 238-4559        www.readersdigest.com

*Publisher of magazines and books and direct mail marketer.*

**Reader's Digest Association Ltd.,  25 Berkeley Square, London W1X 6AB, UK**

## RED WING SHOE COMPANY, INC.

314 Main Street, Red Wing, MN, 55066

Tel: (612) 388-8211     Fax: (612) 388-7415      www.redwingshoe.com

*Leather tanning and finishing; mfr. footwear, retail shoe stores.*

**Red Wing Europe, Ltd., 26 Upper Tachbrook St., London SW1V 1SW, UK**

Contact: Joseph Goggin, Pres.

## REEBOK INTERNATIONAL LTD.

100 Technology Center Drive, Stoughton, MA, 02072

Tel: (781) 401-5000     Fax: (781) 401-7402      www.reebok.com

*Mfr. athletic shoes including casual, dress golf and walking shoes.*

**Reebok Intl. Ltd., One The Square, Stockley Park, Uxbridge, Middlesex UB11 1DN, UK**

**Reebok United Kingdom, Moor Lane Mill, Lancaster LA1 1GF, UK**

## REED-HYCALOG INC.

6501 Navigation Blvd., PO Box 2119, Houston, TX, 77252

Tel: (713) 924-5200     Fax: (713) 924-5667      www.schlumberger.com

*Mfr. rock bits for oil and gas exploration.*

**Reed-Hycalog Tool Co., London, UK**

## REFAC

115 River Rd., Edgewater, NJ, 07020-1099

Tel: (201) 943-4400     Fax: (201) 943-7400      www.refac.com

*Consults to international technology transfer, foreign trade and power supplies firms for brand and trademarking licensing services..*

**REFAC, 175 Rivermead Ct., Ranelagh Gardens, London, SW6 3SF, UK**

Tel: 44-207-736-4909

## REFCO GROUP LTD.

111 West Jackson Blvd, Suite 1800, Chicago, IL, 60604

Tel: (312) 930-6500     Fax: (312) 930-6534      www.refco.com

*Commodity and security brokers engaged in the execution and clearing of futures and options and institutional asset management services.*

**Refco Futures Ltd., London, UK**

Tel: 44-207-755-32914    Contact: John Steptoe

## REFLEXITE TECHNOLOGY

120 Darling Drive, Avon, CT, 06001

Tel: (860) 676-7100     Fax: (860) 676-7199      www.reflexite.com

*Mfr. plastic film, sheet, materials and shapes, optical lenses.*

**Reflexite UK Ltd., 4420 Nash Court - John Smith Drive, Oxford Business Park South Cowley, Oxford OX4 2RU, UK**

Tel: 44-1865-396959   Fax: 44-1865-396960    Contact: Andrew McNeill

## REGAL-BELOIT CORPORATION

200 State Street, Beloit, WI, 53512-0298

Tel: (608) 364-8800     Fax: (608) 364-8818      www.regal-beloit.com

*Mfr. power transmission equipment, perishable cutting tools.*

**Marathon Electric-U.K., 6/F Thistleton Sales Ind. Estate, Market Overton, Oakham Rutland LE15 7PP, UK**

Tel: 44-1572-768206   Fax: 44-1572-768217

**Opperman Mastergear, Ltd., Hambridge Road, Newbury Berkshire RG145TS, UK**

Tel: 44-1635-811500   Fax: 44-1635-811501

## RELIANCE GROUP HOLDINGS, INC.

55 East 52nd Street, New York, NY, 10055

Tel: (212) 909-1100     Fax: (212) 909-1864     www.rgh.com

*Financial and insurance management services.*

**Reliance National Insurance Co. (Europe) Ltd.,  Reliance National House, 80 Leadenhall St., London EC3A 3DH, UK**

Tel: 44-207-283-7110   Fax: 44-207-929-7453   Contact: Carl Bach, Mng. Dir.

## RELIANT ENERGY, INC.

1111 Louisiana Street, Houston, TX, 77002

Tel: (713) 207-3000     Fax: (713) 207-0206     www.houind.com

*Provides gas and electric services.*

**Reliant Energy Trading & Marketing,  London, UK**

## REMEDY CORPORATION

1505 Salado Drive, Mountain View, CA, 94043-1110

Tel: (650) 903-5200     Fax: (650) 903-9001     www.remedy.com

*Developer and marketer of computer applications for the operations management market.*

**Remedy UK,  Greenwood House, 5 London Rd., Bracknell Berkshire RG12 2UB, UK**

Tel: 44-1344-866600   Fax: 44-1344-866601

## REMINGTON PRODUCTS COMPANY, L.L.C.

60 Main Street, Bridgeport, CT, 06604

Tel: (203) 367-4400     Fax: (203) 332-4848     www.remington-products.com

*Mfr. home appliances, electric shavers.*

**Remington Consumer Products Ltd.,  116 High St., Egham, Surrey TW 20 9HQ, UK**

Tel: 44-1784-434343   Fax: 44-1784-437919   Contact: Geoffrey L. Hoddinott, VP & Gen. Mgr.

## RENAISSANCE HOTELS AND RESORTS

10400 Fernwood Road, Bethesda, MD, 20817

Tel: (301) 380-3000     Fax: (301) 380-5181     www.renaissancehotels.com

*Hotel and resort chain.*

**Renaissance London Hotel,  Chancery Court, London, UK**

Tel: 44-6196-4960

## RENAISSANCE WORLDWIDE, INC.

52 Second Ave., Waltham, MA, 02451

Tel: (781) 290-3000     Fax: (781) 965-4807     www.rens.com

*Provides technology consulting, staffing services, corporate and systems strategies and software and hardware installation.*

**Renaissance Worldwide, Inc.,  Abbey Court, St. John's Road, TN4 9TQ, Turnbridge Wells, Kent, UK**

Tel: 44-189-151-3344   Fax: 44-189-251-4477

**Renaissance Worldwide, Inc.,  22 Grafton Street, W1X 3LD London, UK**

Tel: 44-207-290-3700   Fax: 44-207-290-3737

**Renaissance Worldwide, Inc.,  40 Holborn Viaduct, EC1N 2PB, London, UK**

Tel: 44-207-577-8000   Fax: 44-207-577-8001

**The Hunter Group,  11/12 Clifford Street, Clarendon House, W1X 1RB, London, UK**

Tel: 44-207-629-7629   Fax: 44-207-629-7621

## THE RENDON GROUP INC.

1875 Connecticut Ave., N.E., Washington, DC, 20009

Tel: (202) 745-4900     Fax: (202) 745-0215     www.rendon.com

*Public relations, print and video production, strategic communications.*

**TRG-UK,  PO Box 698, Titchfield House, 69-85 Tabernacle St., London EC2A 4RR UK**

## RESMED INC.

1440 Danielson Street, Poway, CA, 92064

Tel: (858) 746-2400     Fax: (858) 880-1618     www.resmed.com

*Mfr. sleep apnea aids, including nasal masks and accessories.*

**ResMed UK Limited, 67B Milton Park, Abingdon Oxon OX14 4RS, UK**

Tel: 44-1235-862-997   Fax: 44-1235-831-336

## REVLON INC.

625 Madison Ave., New York, NY, 10022

Tel: (212) 527-4000     Fax: (212) 527-4995     www.revlon.com

*Mfr. cosmetics, fragrances, toiletries and beauty care products.*

**Revlon Intl. Corp. Ltd., 86 Brook St., London, UK**

Contact: David Windeatt, Gen. Mgr.

## REXNORD CORPORATION

4701 West Greenfield Ave., Milwaukee, WI, 53214

Tel: (414) 643-3000     Fax: (414) 643-3078     www.rexnord.com

*Mfr. power transmission products.*

**Rexnord UK Ltd., Berkshire House, 252-256 Kings Rd., Reading Berkshire RG1 4HP, UK**

## RHEOMETRIC SCIENTIFIC INC.

1 Possumtown Road, Piscataway, NJ, 08854

Tel: (732) 560-8550     Fax: (732) 560-7451     www.rheosci.com

*Design/mfr. rheological instruments and systems.*

**Rheometric Scientific Ltd., Surrey Business Park, Weston Rd., Epsom, Surrey KT17 1JF, UK**

## RICE FOWLER

201 St. Charles Ave., 36th Fl., New Orleans, LA, 70170

Tel: (504) 523-2600     Fax: (504) 523-2705     www.ricefowler.com

*Law firm specializing in maritime, insurance, int'l, environmental, oil/gas, transportation, bankruptcy and reorganization.*

**Rice Fowler, Mitre House, 4th Fl., 12-14 Mitre St., London EC3A 5BU, UK**

Tel: 44-207-929-4222   Fax: 44-207-929-0043   Emp: 1

## RICH PRODUCTS CORPORATION

1150 Niagara St., Buffalo, NY, 14213

Tel: (716) 878-8000     Fax: (716) 878-8765     www.richs.com

*Mfr. non-dairy products.*

**Rich Products Ltd., Falstaff House, 33 Birmingham Rd., Stratford-upon-Avon, Warwickshire CV37 0AZ UK**

## RICHCO, INC.

5825 N. Tripp Ave., PO Box 804238, Chicago, IL, 60680

Tel: (773) 539-4060     Fax: (773) 539-6770     www.richco.com

*Mfr. plastic and metal parts for the electric, electronic, appliance, and fiber-optic industries.*

**Richco Plastic UK, Richco House, Springhead Enterprise Park
Springhead Road, Gravesend, Kent DA11 8HE, UK**

Tel: 44-1474-327527

## RIDGE TOOL COMPANY

400 Clark Street, Elyria, OH, 44035

Tel: (440) 323-5581     Fax: (440) 329-4853     www.ridgid.com

*Mfr. hand and power tools for working pipe, drain cleaning equipment, etc.*

**Ridge Tool Ltd., Royston Rd., Baldock Herts, UK**

## RIGHT MANAGEMENT CONSULTANTS, INC.

1818 Market Street, 14th Fl., Philadelphia, PA, 19103-3614

Tel: (215) 988-1588      Fax: (215) 988-9112      www.right.com

*Out placement and human resources consulting services.*

**Right Associates, Prospect House, 32 Sovereign St., Leeds. LS1 4BJ UK**

Tel: 44-532-425445

**Right Associates, Dammas Lane, Dammas House, Swindon, Wiltshire SN1 3EJ, UK**

Tel: 44-793-514660

**Right Associates, Ouseburn Bldg., Albion Row, East Quayside, Newcastle-upon-Tyne UK**

Tel: 44-191-265-0555

**Right Associates, Quay West Business Ctr., Trafford Wharf Rd., Manchester M17 1HH UK**

Tel: 44-161-877-7631

**Right Associates, Savannah House, 11-12 Charles II St., St. James's, London SW1Y 4QU UK**

Tel: 44-207-839-1001

## THE RITZ-CARLTON HOTEL COMPANY, L.L.C.

3414 Peachtree Road NE, Ste. 300, Atlanta, GA, 30326

Tel: (404) 237-5500      Fax: (404) 365-9643      www.ritzcarlton.com

*5-star hotel and restaurant chain.*

**The Ritz-Carlton Hotel Company, London, Bowater House West 8th Floor, 114 Knightsbridge, London, UK**

Tel: 44-207-581-4052

## RIVIANA FOODS INC.

2777 Allen Parkway, 15th Fl., Houston, TX, 77019

Tel: (713) 529-3251      Fax: (713) 529-1661      www.rivianafoods.com

*Process, market and distribute branded and private-label rice products.*

**Stevens & Brotherton Ltd., S&B House, 2 Vinson Close, Knoll Rise, Orpington, Kent BR6 0XG, UK**

## ROBBINS & MYERS INC.

1400 Kettering Tower, Dayton, OH, 45423-1400

Tel: (937) 222-2610      Fax: (937) 225-3355      www.robn.com

*Mfr. progressing cavity pumps, valves and agitators.*

**Robbins & Myers Ltd., London, UK**

## ROBERT HALF INTERNATIONAL INC.

2884 Sand Hill Road, Ste. 200, Menlo Park, CA, 94025

Tel: (650) 234-6000      Fax: (650) 234-6999      www.rhii.com

*World leader in personnel and specialized staffing services.*

**Robert Half Intl. Inc., 63 Temple Row, Birmingham B2 5LS, UK**

**Robert Half Intl. Inc., Walter House, 418 Strand, London WC2R 0PT, UK**

## ROBERTS-GORDON INC.

1250 William Street, PO Box 44, Buffalo, NY, 14240-0044

Tel: (716) 852-4400      Fax: (716) 852-0854      www.roberts-gordon.com

*Mfr. industry gas burners, industry space heaters, infrared radiant tube heaters.*

**Blackheat Ltd., 12 Cobham Rd., Ferndown Industrial Estate, Wimborne, Dorset BH21 7PS UK**

## C. H. ROBINSON WORLDWIDE, INC. (CHR)

8100 Mitchell Road, Eden Prairie, MN, 55344

Tel: (612) 937-8500      Fax: (612) 937-6714      www.chrobinson.com

*Global door-to-door freight forwarding services, including flexible transportation solutions and global logistics.*

**C. H. Robinson (CHR), London, UK**

Tel: 44-1817-548800

## ROBOTIC VISION SYSTEMS, INC.

5 Shawmut Road, Canton, MA, 02021

Tel: (781) 821-0830    Fax: (781) 828-9852    www.rvsi.com

*Mfr. machine vision-based systems for semiconductor industry.*

**RVSI UK, RVSI House - Claybrook Drive, Redditch Worcestershire B98 0FH, UK**

Tel: 44 1527 505000    Fax: 44 1527 505001

## ROCHESTER INSTRUMENT SYSTEMS INC.

255 North Union Street, Rochester, NY, 14605

Tel: (716) 263-7700    Fax: (716) 262-4777    www.rochester.com

*Mfr. transient recorders, microprocessor-based relays, calibrators, annunciators, and signal conditioners.*

**Rochester Instrument Systems Ltd., Maxim Rd., Crayford, Kent DA1 4BG, UK**

## ROCHESTER MIDLAND CORPORATION

PO Box 31515, 333 Hollenbeck St., Rochester, NY, 14603-1515

Tel: (716) 336-2200    Fax: (716) 467-4406    www.rochestermidland.com

*Mfr. specialty chemicals for industry cleaning and maintenance, water treatment and personal hygiene.*

**Rochester Midland UK, London, UK**

Tel: 44-1908-608088

## ROCKWELL INTERNATIONAL CORPORATION

777 East Wisconsin Ave., Ste. 1400, Milwaukee, WI, 53202

Tel: (414) 212-5200    Fax: (414) 212-5201    www.rockwell.com

*Products and service for aerospace and defense, automotive, electronics, graphics and automation industry.*

**Rockwell Automation Ltd., Rockwell House, Gateway, Crewe Cheshire CW1 6XN UK**

Tel: 44-1270-580-142    Fax: 44-1270-580-141

**Rockwell Automation Ltd. Dodge UK, Hortonwood 10 Ste. A4, Telford, Shropshire TF1 4ES UK**

Tel: 44-1952-604-222    Fax: 44-1952-677-383

**Rockwell Collins Passenger Systems, PO Box 7251, Tadley, Hampshire RG26 5XS UK**

Tel: 44-1256-883-743    Fax: 44-1256-883-783

**Rockwell Collins UK, 21 Suttons Business Park, Earley, Reading Berkshire, RG6 1LA, UK**

**Rockwell Elecronic Eommerce, Rockwell House, Caldecotte Lake Business Park, Milton Keynes MK7 8LE, UK**

**Rockwell Electronic Commerce Ltd., Howes Percival House, 252 Upper Third St., Central Milton Keynes, Buckinghamshire MK9 1DZ UK**

Tel: 44-1908-200-200    Fax: 44-1908-609-124

**Rockwell Semiconductor Systems Ltd., Spectrum Point, 279 Farnborough Rd., Farnborough, Hampshire GU14 7LS UK**

Tel: 44-1252-370-008    Fax: 44-1252-370-009

**Rockwell-Collins (UK) Ltd., 21 Suttons Business Park, Earley, Reading, Berkshire RG6 1LA, UK**

Tel: 44-118-926-111    Fax: 44-118-966-4016

## R.A. RODRIGUEZ, INC.

20 Seaview Boulevard, Garden City, NY, 11050

Tel: (516) 625-8080    Fax: (516) 621-2424    www.rodriguez-usa.com

*Distribution of ball and roller bearings, precision gears, mechanical systems and related products.*

**R. A. Rodriguez (UK) Ltd., 28 Campus Five, Letchworth Business Park, Letchworth, Herts SG6 2JF, UK**

Tel: 44-1462-670044    Fax: 44-1462-670880    Contact: Derrick Elliott, Mng. Dir.

## ROHM AND HAAS COMPANY

100 Independence Mall West, Philadelphia, PA, 19106

Tel: (215) 592-3000     Fax: (215) 592-3377     www.rohmhaas.com

*Mfr. industrial and agricultural chemicals, plastics.*

**Morton International Limited, 18 Chesford Grange, Woolston Warrington WA1 4RQ, UK**

**Morton International Ltd., Heckmondwike Road, Dewsbury Moore EF13 3NG, West Yorkshire UK**

**Rohm and Haas (UK) Limited, Tynesdie Works Ellison Street, Jarrow Tyne and Wear NE32 3DJ, UK**

**Rohm and Haas (UK) Ltd., Lennig House, 2 Mason's Ave., Croydon, Surrey CR9 3NB, UK**

Tel: 44-181-774-5300

**Shipley Europe Ltd., Herald Way, Coventry CV3 2RQ, UK**

Tel: 44-120-365-4400

**Shipley Ronal, High Peak Laboratories, Ashbourne Road, Buxton Derbyshire SK17 9SS, UK**

## ROPES & GRAY

1 International Pl., Boston, MA, 02110-2624

Tel: (617) 951-7000     Fax: (617) 951-7050     www.ropesgray.com

*International law firm.*

**Ropes & Gray UK, 12-14 Mitre Street, London EC3A 5BU, UK**

Tel: 44-207-283-3367   Fax: 44-207-283-5195

## ROSENBLUTH INTERNATIONAL

2401 Walnut Street, Philadelphia, PA, 19103-4390

Tel: (215) 977-4000     Fax: (215) 977-4028     www.rosenbluth.com

*Provides corporate business travel services.*

**Rosenbluth International Alliance (RIA), London, UK**

## ROWAN COMPANIES INC.

2800 Post Oak Boulevard, Houston, TX, 77056-6196

Tel: (713) 621-7800     Fax: (713) 960-7560     www.rowancompanies.com

*Contract drilling and air charter service.*

**British American Offshore Ltd., 43 Upper Grosvenor Sq., London W1X 9P6, UK**

## ROWE INTERNATIONAL INC.

1500 Union Ave., S.E., Grand Rapids, MI, 49507

Tel: (616) 243-3633     Fax: (616) 243-9414     www.roweinternational.com

*Vending machines, background music systems and jukeboxes; bill and coin changers.*

**Rowe (Europe) Ltd., St. Clare House - Holly Road, Hampton Hill, Middlesex TW12 1QQ, UK**

Tel: 44-208-941-4579   Fax: 44-208-941-7273

## T. ROWE PRICE ASSOCIATES, INC.

100 East Pratt Street, Baltimore, MD, 21202

Tel: (410) 345-2000     Fax: (410) 345-2394     www.troweprice.com

*Investment and portfolio asset management.*

**Rowe Price-Fleming International, London, UK**

## ROYAL APPLIANCE MFG. COMPANY

650 Alpha Drive, Cleveland, OH, 44143

Tel: (440) 449-6150     Fax: (440) 449-7806     www.royalappliance.com

*Mfr. vacuum cleaners.*

**J.A. Balch Ltd., Surrey House, 34 Eden St., Kingston-upon-Thames, Surrey KT1 1ER UK**

## RSA SECURITY INC.

36 Crosby Drive, Bedford, MA, 01730

Tel: (781) 687-7000 Fax: (781) 687-7010 www.rsasecurity.com

*Mfr. software and hardware security products.*

**RSA Security UK, RSA House, Western Road, Bracknell Berks RG12 1RT, UK**

Tel: 44-134-478-100 Fax: 44-134-478-1010

## RUDER FINN INC.

301 East 57th Street, New York, NY, 10022

Tel: (212) 593-6400 Fax: (212) 593-6397 www.ruderfinn.com

*Engaged in public relations service and broadcast communications.*

**Ruder Finn Complete Medical Communications Ltd., CMC House, Jordangate, Macclesfield, Cheshire SK10 1EW UK**

**Ruder Finn U.K., 19 Chelsea Wharf, Lots Rd., London SW10 0QJ, UK**

## RUSS BERRIE AND COMPANY, INC.

111 Bauer Drive, Oakland, NJ, 07436

Tel: (201) 337-9000 Fax: (201) 405-7355 www.russberrie.com

*Engaged in the design and sale of gift items, including stuffed animals and home décor items.*

**Russ Berrie UK Ltd., 40 Oriana Way, Nursling Industrial Estate, Southampton Hants SO16 0YU, UK**

Tel: 44-1703-747-747

## RUSSELL REYNOLDS ASSOCIATES INC.

200 Park Ave., New York, NY, 10166-0002

Tel: (212) 351-2000 Fax: (212) 370-0896 www.russreyn.com

*Executive recruiting services.*

**Russell Reynolds Associates Ltd., 24 St. James's Square, London SW1Y 4HZ, UK**

Tel: 44-207-839-7788 Fax: 44-207-839-9395 Contact: Jane Kingsley/Simon Hearn

## RVSI (ROBOTIC VISION SYSTEMS, INC.)

5 Shawmut Road, Canton, MA, 02021

Tel: (781) 821-0830 Fax: (781) 828-8942 www.rvsi.com

*Mfr. bar code scanners and data collection equipment.*

**Computer Identics Ltd., St. James' Ct., Bridgnorth Rd., Wollaston, Stourbridge West Midlands DY8 3QG UK**

## SAFETY-KLEEN CORPORATION

1301 Gervais Street, Columbia, SC, 29201

Tel: (803) 933-4200 Fax: (803) 933-4345 www.safety-kleen.com

*Solvent based parts cleaning service; sludge/solvent recycling service.*

**Safety-Kleen Parts Washer Svce. Ltd., Box 14, Worton Hall, Worton Rd., Isleworth, Hounslow Middlesex, UK**

## SALANS HERTZFELD HEILBRONN CHRISTY & VIENER

620 Fifth Avenue, New York, NY, 10020-2457

Tel: (212) 632-5500 Fax: (212) 632-5555 www.salans.com

*International law firm.*

**Salans Hertzfeld & Heilbronn HRK, Clements House, 14-18 Gresham Street, London EC2V 7NN, UK**

## SALOMON SMITH BARNEY HOLDINGS INC.

388 Greenwich Street, New York, NY, 10013

Tel: (212) 816-6000 Fax: (212) 816-8915 www.smithbarney.com

*Securities dealers and underwriters.*

**Salomon Smith Barney Holdings, One Angel Ct., London EC2, UK**

## SANDUSKY INTERNATIONAL

615 W. Market Street, PO Box 5012, Sandusky, OH, 44871-8012

Tel: (419) 626-5340     Fax: (419) 626-3339     www.sanduskyintl.com

*Mfr. roll shells for paper machines, centrifugal tubular products.*

**Sandusky Walmsley Limited,  Crompton Way , Bolton, Lancashire BL1 8UL, UK**

Tel: 44-1204-396060

## THE SANTA CRUZ OPERATION, INC.

400 Encinal Street, Santa Cruz, CA, 95060

Tel: (831) 425-7222     Fax: (831) 427-5448     www.sco.com

*Mfr. server software.*

**SCO Europe UK,  Croxley Business Park, Hatters Lane, Watford WD1 8YN, UK**

Tel: 44-192-816344

## SANTILLANA PUBLISHING USA

2105 N.W. 86th Ave., Miami, FL, 33122

Tel: (305) 591-9522     Fax: (305) 591-9145     www.insite-network.com/santillana

*Children and adult book publishing.*

**Santillana Publishing Co., Ltd.,  Suite 4 Little Gate House, St. Ebbe's St., Oxford OX1 1PS, UK**

## SAPHIRE INTERNATIONAL LTD.

3060 Main Street, Ste. 202, Stratford, CT, 06614

Tel: (203) 375-8668     Fax: (203) 375-1965     www.dataease.com

*Mfr. applications development software.*

**Sapphire International Ltd,  13-19 Curtain Road, London EC2A 3LU, UK**

Tel: 44-207-539-0800

**SupportEase,  Anchor House - Anchor Quay, Norwich NR3 3XP, UK**

## SAPIENT CORPORATION

1 Memorial Drive, Cambridge, MA, 02142

Tel: (617) 621-0200     Fax: (617) 621-1300     www.sapient.com

*Engaged in information technology and consulting services.*

**Sapient UK,  1 Bartholomew Lane, London EC2N 2AB, UK**

Tel: 44-207-786-4500   Fax: 44-207-786-4600

## SARA LEE CORPORATION

3 First National Plaza, Chicago, IL, 60602-4260

Tel: (312) 726-2600     Fax: (312) 558-4995     www.saralee.com

*Mfr./distributor food and consumer packaged goods, intimate apparel and knitwear.*

**KOSL UK,  Carnaby Industrial Estate, Bridlington, East Yorkshire YO15 3QY, UK**

**Pretty Polly Ltd.,  Unwin Rd., Sutton-in-Ashfield, Nottinghamshire NG17 4JJ, UK**

## SAS INSTITUTE INC.

SAS Campus Drive, Cary, NC, 27513

Tel: (919) 677-8000     Fax: (919) 677-4444     www.sas.com

*Mfr./distributes decision support software.*

**SAS Institute (United Kingdon) Ltd.,  Marlow, UK**

Tel: 44-16284-86933   Fax: 44-16284-83203

## W. B. SAUNDERS COMPANY

625 Walnut St., Ste. 300, Philadelphia, PA, 19106-3399

Tel: (215) 238-7800     Fax: (215) 238-7883     www.wbsaunders.com

*Develop medical educational software.*

**Churchill Livingstone, Robert Stevenson House, 1-3 Baxter's Place, Leith Walk, Edinburgh EH1 3AF UK**

Tel: 44-131-535-1022

**W.B. Saunders Co. Ltd., 24-28 Oval Rd., London NW1 7DX, UK**

Tel: 44-207-267-4466    Fax: 44-207-482-2293

## SAVAIR INC.

33200 Freeway Drive, St. Clair Shores, MI, 48082

Tel: (810) 296-7390     Fax: (810) 296-7305     www.savairinc.com

*Mfr. welding guns, air and hydraulic cylinders, clinch and pierce units.*

**Savair Ltd., Black Moor Rd., Ebb Lake Industrial Estate, Verwood Dorset BH21 6AX, UK**

## SBC COMMUNICATIONS INC.

175 East Houston, San Antonio, TX, 78205

Tel: (210) 821-4105     Fax: (210) 351-5034     www.sbc.com

*Engaged in telecommunications.*

**TeleWest, London, UK**

## SCANSOFT, INC.

9 Centennial Dr., Peabody, MA, 01960

Tel: (978) 977-2000     Fax: (978) 977-2436     www.scansoft.com

*Mfr. digital imaging software.*

**Ingram Micro, Garamonde Drive, Wymbush, Milton Keynes, Buckinghamshire MK 8 8DF UK**

Tel: 44-1908-60-422

## SCHENECTADY INTERNATIONAL INC.

PO Box 1046, Schenectady, NY, 12301

Tel: (518) 370-4200     Fax: (518) 382-8129     www.siigroup.com

*Mfr. electrical insulating varnishes, enamels, phenolic resins, alkylphenols.*

**Schenectady Europe Ltd., Four Ashes, Wolverhampton WV10 7BT, UK**

Tel: 44-1902-790-555    Fax: 44-1902-791-640    Contact: Geoffrey Harrison, Mng. Dir.

## SCHENKER INTERNATIONAL FORWARDERS INC.

150 Albany Ave., Freeport, NY, 11520

Tel: (516) 377-3000     Fax: (516) 377-3005     www.schenkerusa.com

*Freight forwarders.*

**Schenker International, 51-53 Hatton Garden, London EC1 N8QJ, UK**

Tel: 44-207-242-3344   Fax: 44-207-242-0395

**Schenker International, Newcastle Intl Airport, Freightway Woolsington, Newcastle upon Tyne NE 13 8 BH, UK**

Tel: 44-191-214-0593    Fax: 44-191-214-0591

## R. P. SCHERER CORPORATION

645 Martinsville Rd., Ste. 200, Baskin Ridge, NJ, 07920

Tel: (908) 580-1500     Fax: (908) 580-9220     www.rpscherer.com

*Mfr. pharmaceuticals; soft gelatin and two-piece hard shell capsules.*

**R.P. Scherer Ltd., Frankland Rd., Blagrove, Swindon Wilts. SN5 8YS, UK**

Tel: 44-1793-488411    Fax: 44-1793-613394    Contact: Dr. Alan Raymond, Reg. VP    Emp: 346

**R.P. Scherer UK, London, UK**

## SCHERING-PLOUGH CORPORATION

One Giralda Farms, Madison, NJ, 07940-1000

Tel: (973) 822-7000    Fax: (973) 822-7048    www.sch-plough.com

*Proprietary drug and cosmetic products.*

**Schering Plough, 204 St. John St., London EC1P 1DH, UK**

**Schering-Plough Animal Health, Breakspear Road South, Harefield Uxbridge, Middlesex UB 9 6LS UK**

## SCHLEGEL SYSTEMS

1555 Jefferson Road, PO Box 23197, Rochester, NY, 14692-3197

Tel: (716) 427-7200    Fax: (716) 427-9993    www.schlegel.com

*Mfr. engineered perimeter sealing systems for residential and commercial construction; fibers; rubber product.*

**Hertfordshire BTR Ltd., London Rd., Dunstable, Bedfordshire LU6 3DY UK**

**Schiegel (UK) Ltd., Beveridge Lane, Bardon Hill, Coalville Leicester LE6 2TA, UK**

## SCHLUMBERGER LIMITED

277 Park Avenue, New York, NY, 10021

Tel: (212) 350-9400    Fax: (212) 350-9564    www.schlumberger.com

*Engaged in oil and gas services, metering and payment systems, and produces semiconductor testing equipment and smart cards.*

**Schlumberger Cambridge Research, High Cross Madingley Road, Cambridge CB3 0EL, UK**
Tel: 44-1223-315576

**Schlumberger Cards & Services, 1 Kingsway, London, WC2B 6XH, UK**

**Schlumberger Ltd., Harfrey Road Unit 9c, Harfrey Ind. Estate, Great Yarmouth Norfolk NR31 OLS, UK**

## SCHOLASTIC CORPORATION

555 Broadway, New York, NY, 10012

Tel: (212) 343-6100    Fax: (212) 343-6934    www.scholastic.com

*Publishing/distribution educational and children's magazines, books, software.*

**Scholastic Ltd., Villiers House, Clarendon Ave., Leamington Spa, Warwickshire CV32 5PR, UK**
Tel: 44-1926-887799   Contact: David Kewley, Mgn. Dir.

## SCHRODER & COMPANY, INC.

787 Seventh Ave., New York, NY, 10019

Tel: (212) 492-6000    Fax: (212) 492-7029    www.wsdinc.com

*Engaged in investment banking, securities research, sales, trading and clearance and asset management.*

**Wertheim Securities Ltd., 12 Cheapside, London EC2 V6DS, UK**

## THE CHARLES SCHWAB CORPORATION

101 Montgomery Street, San Francisco, CA, 94104

Tel: (415) 627-7000    Fax: (415) 627-8840    www.schawb.com

*Financial services; discount brokerage, retirement accounts.*

**Charles Schwab, Ltd., 38 Bishopgate, Crosby Court, London EC2N 4AJ UK**
Tel: 44-207-786-7102   Fax: 44-207-786-7172

**Schwab Europe, Cannon House - 24 The Priory Queensway, Birmingham B4 6BS, UK**

## SCIENCE APPLICATIONS INTL. CORPORATION (SAIC)

10260 Campus Point Dr., San Diego, CA, 92121

Tel: (858) 826-6000    Fax: (858) 535-7589    www.saic.com

*Engaged in research and engineering.*

**SAIC Europe Ltd., 8/9 Stratton Street, London, W1J 8, UK**

**SAIC UK Ltd., Castle Park, Cambridge, CB3 O, UK**
Tel: 44-1223-518790

## SCIENTIFIC-ATLANTA, INC.

1 Technology Pkwy South, Norcross, GA, 30092-2967

Tel: (770) 903-5000      Fax: (770) 903-2967      www.sciatl.com

*A leading supplier of broadband communications systems, satellite-based video, voice and data communications networks and worldwide customer service and support.*

**Scientific-Atlanta (UK) Ltd., Home Park Estate, Kings Langley, Herts WO4 8LZ, UK**

Tel: 44-1923-266-133    Fax: 44-01923-269-018

## SCOTTS COMPANY

41 South High Street, Ste. 3500, Marysville, OH, 43215

Tel: (937) 644-0011      Fax: (937) 644-7244      www.scottscompany.com

*Leading U.S. maker of lawn and garden products.*

**Miracle Garden Care, London, UK**

**Scotts/Levington Horticulture Ltd., London, UK**

## SEAGATE TECHNOLOGY, INC.

920 Disc Dr., Scotts Valley, CA, 95066

Tel: (408) 438-6550      Fax: (408) 438-7205      www.seagate.com

*Develop computer technology, software and hardware.*

**Seagate Software Ltd., 107 King St., Maidenhead, Berkshire SL6 1DP, UK**

Tel: 44-1628-771-299   Fax: 44-1628-771-523

**Seagate Technology, Inc., Seagate House, Globe Park, Fieldhouse Lane, Marlow Buckinghamshire SL5 1LW, UK**

Tel: 44-1628-890366   Fax: 44-1628-890660   Contact: Brian Stanley, Dir.   Emp: 40

## SEALED AIR CORPORATION

Park 80 East, Saddle Brook, NJ, 07663

Tel: (201) 791-7600      Fax: (201) 703-4205      www.sealedair.com

*Mfr. protective and specialty packaging solutions for industrial, food and consumer products.*

**Sealed Air (FPD) Ltd., Stafford Park 9, Telford, Shropshire TF3 3BZ, UK**

Tel: 44-1-952-290471   Fax: 44-1-952-290950

**Sealed Air Ltd., Saxton Way, Melbourne, Royston, Hertfordshire SG8 6DN UK**

Tel: 44-1763-261900   Fax: 44-1-763-261234

**Sealed Air Ltd., Telford Way, Kettering, Northants NN16 8UN, UK**

Tel: 44-1536-315700   Fax: 44-1536-410576

## SEAQUIST PERFECT DISPENSING

1160 North Silver Lake Road, Cary, IL, 60013

Tel: (847) 639-2124      Fax: (847) 639-2142      www.seaquistperect.com

*Mfr. and sale of dispensing systems; lotion pumps and spray-through overcaps.*

**Perfect-Valois U.K. Ltd., Bletcheley, Milton Keynes, UK**

**Seaquist Perfect Dispensing U.K. Ltd., 11 Holdom Ave., Saxon Park Industriale Estate, Bletchley-Milton Keynes MK1 1QU, UK**

Tel: 44-1908-270462   Fax: 44-1908-270471   Contact: Chris Aworth   Emp: 10

## G.D. SEARLE & COMPANY

5200 Old Orchard Road, Skokie, IL, 60077

Tel: (847) 982-7000      Fax: (847) 470-1480      www.searlehealthnet.com

*Mfr. pharmaceuticals, health care, optical products and specialty chemicals.*

**Searle & Co. Ltd., PO Box 53, Lane End Rd., High Wycombe, Buckinghamshire HP12 4HL UK**

Tel: 44-1494-521124   Fax: 44-1494-447872

**Searle Pharmaceuticals, Whalton Rd., Morpeth, Northumberland NE61 3YA, UK**

Tel: 44-1671-514311   Fax: 44-1670-517112

## SECURE COMPUTING CORPORATION

One Almaden Blvd., Ste. 400, San Jose, CA, 95113

Tel: (408) 918-6100      Fax: (408) 918-6101      www.sctc.com

*Mfr. software.*

**Secure Computing UK Ltd., 9 Shaftesbury Court, Chalvey Park, Slough Berkshire SL1 2ER, UK**

Tel: 44-1753-826-000

## SEDGWICK, DETERT, MORAN & ARNOLD

One Embarcadero Center, 16th Fl., San Francisco, CA, 94111

Tel: (415) 781-7900      Fax: (415) 781-2635      www.sdma.com

*International law firm.*

**Sedgwick, Detert, Moran & Arnold, 5 Lloyds Avenue, London EC3N 3AE, UK**

Tel: 44-207-929-1829   Fax: 44-207-929-1808

## SEI INVESTMENTS COMPANY

1 Freedom Valley Drive, Oaks, PA, 19456-1100

Tel: (610) 676-1000      Fax: (610) 676-2995      www.seic.com

*Accounting, evaluation and financial automated systems and services.*

**SEI Investments, 6-7 Queen St., London, EC4N 1SP, UK**

## SEMTECH CORPORATION

652 Mitchell Road, PO Box 367, Newbury Park, CA, 91320

Tel: (805) 498-2111      Fax: (805) 498-3804      www.semtech.com

*Mfr. silicon rectifiers, rectifier assemblies, capacitors, switching regulators, AC/DC converters.*

**Acapella Ltd., Delta House, Chilworth Research Centre, Southampton SO16 7NS, UK**

Tel: 44-1703-769008   Fax: 44-1703-768612

## SENCO PRODUCTS INC.

8485 Broadwell Road, Cincinnati, OH, 45244

Tel: (513) 388-2000      Fax: (513) 388-2026      www.senco.com

*Mfr. industry nailers, staplers, fasteners and accessories.*

**Senco Pneumatics (UK) Ltd., 211 Europa Blvd., Westbrook, Warrington, Cheshire WA5 5TN, UK**

## SENSIENT TECHNOLOGIES CORPORATION

433 E. Michigan Street, Milwaukee, WI, 53202

Tel: (414) 271-6755      Fax: (414) 347-4783      www.sensient.com

*Mfr. food products and food ingredients.*

**Felton Worldwide Ltd., Castle Tower Works, Bilton Rd., Bletchley, Milton Keynes MK1 1HP UK**

## SENSORMATIC ELECTRONICS CORPORATION

951 Yamato Road, Boca Raton, FL, 33431-0700

Tel: (561) 989-7000      Fax: (561) 989-7774      www.sensormatic.com

*Electronic article surveillance equipment.*

**Sensormatic UK, Harefield Grove, Rickmansworth Road, Harefield Uxbridge, Middlesex UB9 6JY, UK**

Tel: 44-1895-873-000   Fax: 44-1895-873-920   Contact: Mark Clark

## SERVICE CORPORATION INTERNATIONAL

1929 Allen Parkway, Houston, TX, 77019

Tel: (713) 522-5141      Fax: (713) 525-5586      www.sci-corp.com

*Operates funeral homes, cemeteries and crematoriums and sells caskets, burial vaults and cremation receptacles.*

**Great Southern Group plc, London UK**

**Plantsbrook Group plc, London, UK**

## THE SERVICEMASTER COMPANY

One ServiceMaster Way, Downers Grove, IL, 60515-1700

Tel: (630) 271-1300      Fax: (630) 271-2710      www.svm.com

*Management service to health care, school and industry facilities; diversified residential and commercial services.*

**ServiceMaster Ltd.,  308 Melton Rd., Leicester LE4 7SL, UK**

## SFX ENTERTAINMENT, INC.

650 Madison Ave., 16th Fl., New York, NY, 10022

Tel: (212) 838-3100      Fax: (212) 750-6682      www.sfx.com

*Sports marketing, management and consulting.*

**SFX Sports Group UK,  14-15 Craven St., London WC2N 5AD, UK**

## SHAKESPEARE FISHING TACKLE GROUP

3801 Westmore Drive, Columbia, SC, 29223

Tel: (803) 754-7000      Fax: (803) 754-7342      www.shakespeare-fishing.com

*Mfr. fishing tackle.*

**Shakespeare Co. (UK),  Broad Ground Rd., Lakeside, Redditch, Worcestershire B98 8NQ, UK**

## SHARED MEDICAL SYSTEMS CORPORATION

51 Valley Stream Pkwy, Malvern, PA, 19355

Tel: (610) 219-6300      Fax: (610) 219-3124      www.smed.com

*Computer-based information processing for healthcare industry.*

**SMS Europe,  Deane House, Sarum Hill, Basingstoke, Hampstead RG21 1SR, UK**

## SHEAFFER PEN, INC.

301 Ave. H, Fort Madison, IA, 52627

Tel: (319) 372-3300      Fax: (319) 372-1263      www.sheaffer.com

*Mfr. writing instruments.*

**Sheaffer Pen (UK) Ltd.,  Maylands Avenue, Hemel Hempstead, Herts HP2 7ER UK**

Tel: 44-1442-233411    Fax: 44-01442-233022

## SHEARMAN & STERLING

599 Lexington Ave., New York, NY, 10022-6069

Tel: (212) 848-4000      Fax: (212) 848-7179      www.shearman.com

*Law firm engaged in general American and international financial and commercial practice.*

**Shearman & Sterling,  199 Bishopsgate 4th Fl., London EC2M 3TY, UK**

Tel: 44-207-920-9000    Fax: 44-207-920-9020    Contact: Pamela M. Gibson, Mng. Ptnr.

## SHERWIN-WILLIAMS CO., INC.

101 Prospect Ave., N.W., Cleveland, OH, 44115-1075

Tel: (216) 566-2000      Fax: (216) 566-2947      www.sherwin-williams.com

*Mfr. paint, wallcoverings and related products.*

**FSW Ltd.,  Wharfedale Rd., Bradford, W. Yorks. BD4 6SE UK**

**Lyons Technological Products Ltd.,  26 New St. Square, London, UK**

## SHIPLEY COMPANY, LLC

455 Forest Street, Marlborough, MA, 01752

Tel: (508) 481-7950      Fax: (508) 485-9113      www.shipley.com

*Supplier of materials and processes technology to the microelectronics and printed wiring board industries.*

**Shipley Europe Ltd.,  18 Chesford Grange Woolston, Warrington WA1 4RQ, UK**

**Shipley Europe Ltd.,  18 Chesford Grange, Woolston, Warrington WA1 4RQ, UK**

Tel: 44-1925-824105

**Shipley Europe Ltd.,  Herald Way, Coventry CV3 2RQ, UK**

Tel: 44-1203-654400    Fax: 44-1203-440331    Contact: R. Passmore, Pres., Euro. Group

## SHOOK, HARDY & BACON L.L.P.

1200 Main Street, Ste. 3100, Kansas City, MO, 64105-2118

Tel: (816) 474-6550        Fax: (816) 421-5547        www.shb.com

*International law firm.*

**Shook, Hardy & Bacon,  Manning House, 22 Carlisle Place, London SW1P 1JA, UK**

## SHOREWOOD PACKAGING CORPORATION

277 Park Ave., New York, NY, 10172-3000

Tel: (212) 371-1500        Fax: (212) 752-5610        www.shorepak.com

*Mfr. packaging for video/music industry and consumer products.*

**Shorewood Packaging Co. Ltd.,  36 Berwick St, London W1, UK**

## SHUTTS & BOWEN

1500 Miami Center, 201 Biscayne Boulevard, Miami, FL, 33131

Tel: (305) 358-6300        Fax: (305) 381-9982        www.shutts-law.com

*International law firm.*

**Shutts & Bowen,  48 Mount St., London W1Y 5RE, UK**

## SIDLEY & AUSTIN

Bank One Plaza 10 S. Dearborn, Chicago, IL, 60603

Tel: (312) 853-7000        Fax: (312) 853-7036        www.sidley.com

*International law firm.*

**Sidley & Austin,  One Threadneedle St., London EC2R 8AW, UK**

Tel: 44-207-360-3600   Fax: 44-207-626-7937   Contact: Graeme C. Harrower, Ptnr.

## SILICON GRAPHICS INC.

2011 N. Shoreline Blvd., Mountain View, CA, 94043-1389

Tel: (650) 960-1980        Fax: (650) 961-0595        www.sgi.com

*Design/mfr. special-effects computer graphic systems and software.*

**Silicon Graphics Ltd.,  Eagle Court, Concord Business Park, Threapwood Rd., Manchester M22 ORR UK**

Tel: 44-161-932-6000   Fax: 44-161-932-6001

**Silicon Graphics Ltd.,  Unit 9 Callendar Business Park, Callendar Rd., Falkirk FK 1 1XR, UK**

Tel: 44-1342-614-300   Fax: 44-1324-611-214

**Silicon Graphics Ltd.,  24 Chiswell St., London EC1Y 4TY, UK**

Tel: 44-207-614-5900   Fax: 44-207-614-5905

**Silicon Graphics Ltd.,  1530 Arlington Business Park, Theale, Reading RG7 4SB, UK**

Tel: 44-118-925-7500   Fax: 44-118-925-7569

**Silicon Graphics Ltd.,  Forum 1, Station Rd., Theale, Reading RG7 4RA UK**

Tel: 44-118-930-7778   Fax: 44-118-930-7823

**Silicon Studio London,  20 Soho Square, London W1V 5FD, UK**

Tel: 44-207-478-5000   Fax: 44-207-478-5001

## SILICON STORAGE TECHNOLOGY, INC.

1171 Sonora Court, Sunnyvale, CA, 94086

Tel: (408) 735-9110        Fax: (408) 735-9036        www.ssti.com

*Mfr./sale single power supply small ease-block flash memory components, and two-power supply MTP flash products.*

**Silicon Storage Technology Ltd.,  Terminal House, Station Approach, Shepperon, Middlesex, TW17 8AS UK**

Tel: 44-1932-221212   Fax: 44-1932-230567   Contact: Richard Sawers

## SILICON VALLEY GROUP, INC.

101 Metro Dr., Ste. 400, San Jose, CA, 95110

Tel: (408) 467-5870      Fax: (408) 467-5955      www.svg.com

*Manufacturer of automated wafer processing equipment for the worldwide semiconductor industry.*

**Thermco Semiconductor Equipment Ltd., Div. Silicon Valley, Daux Rd., Billingshurst, Sussex RH14 9SJ, UK**

## SIMON & SCHUSTER INC.

1230 Avenue of the Americas, New York, NY, 10020

Tel: (212) 698-7000      Fax: (212) 698-7007      www.simonandschuster.com

*Publishes and distributes hardcover and paperback books, audiobooks and software.*

**Prentice-Hall Intl. (UK) Ltd., 66 Wood Lane End, Hemel Hempstead, Herts. HP2 4RG, UK**

**Simon & Schuster Ltd., West Garden Pl., Kendal St., London W1 1AW, UK**

## SIMPLEX SOLUTIONS, INC.

521 Almanor Ave., Sunnyvale, CA, 94085

Tel: (408) 617-6100      Fax: (408) 774-0285      www.simplex.com

*Develops full-chip, multi-level IC extraction and analysis software.*

**Simplex UK, Innovations Centre - 68 Milton Park, Abingdon Oxfordshire OX14 4RX, UK**

Tel: 44-1235-863132

## SIMPLEX TIME RECORDER COMPANY

100 Simplex Dr., Westminster, MA, 01441

Tel: (978) 731-2500      Fax: (978) 731-7052      www.simplexnet.com

*Provides safety, fire detection, integrated security, communications, time and attendance and workforce management systems.*

**Simplex Europe, Greville House - Hatton Road, Feltham, Middlesex TW14 9PX, UK**

Tel: 44-20-8893-1333    Fax: 44-20-8893-1933

**Simplex Europe, 15 Harvard Court, Quay Business Centre Winwick Quay, Warrington WA2 8LT, UK**

Tel: 44-1925-234-959    Fax: 44-1925-243-221

## SIMPLICITY PATTERN COMPANY, INC.

2 Park Avenue, New York, NY, 10016

Tel: (212) 372-0500      Fax: (212) 372-0628      www.simplicity.com

*Dress patterns.*

**Simplicity Patterns Ltd., Metropolis House, 39-45 Tottenham Court Rd., London W1P 9RD, UK**

## SIMPSON THACHER & BARTLETT

425 Lexington Ave., New York, NY, 10017

Tel: (212) 455-2000      Fax: (212) 455-2502      www.simpsonthacher.com

*International law Firm.*

**Simpson Thacher & Bartlett, 99 Bishopsgate, London EC2M 3YH, UK**

Tel: 44-207-422-4000    Fax: 44-207-422-4022    Contact: Walter A. Looney, Jr., Ptnr.

## SKADDEN, ARPS, SLATE, MEAGHER & FLOM LLP

4 Times Square, New York, NY, 10036

Tel: (212) 735-3000      Fax: (212) 735-2000      www.sasmf.com

*American/International law practice.*

**Skadden, Arps, Slate, Meagher & Flom LLP, One Canada Square, Canary Wharf, London E14 5DS, UK**

Tel: 44-207-519-7000    Fax: 44-207-519-7070    Contact: Bruce M. Buck, Partner

## SKIDMORE OWINGS & MERRILL LLP

224 S. Michigan Ave., Ste. 1000, Chicago, IL, 60604-2707

Tel: (312) 554-9090     Fax: (312) 360-4545     www.som.com

*Engaged in architectural and engineering services.*

**SOM Inc., 46 Berkeley St., London W1X 6NT, UK**

Tel: 44-207-930-9700   Fax: 44-207-930-9108

## WILBUR SMITH ASSOCIATES

PO Box 92, Columbia, SC, 29202

Tel: (803) 758-4500     Fax: (803) 251-2064     www.wilbursmith.com

*Consulting engineers.*

**Wilbur Smith Associates Inc. Intl., Linen Hall 4/F, 162-168 Regent Street, London W1R 5TB, UK**

Tel: 44-207-663-9706   Fax: 44-207-306-3166   Contact: Jamie Wheway

## A.O. SMITH CORPORATION

11270 West Park Place, PO Box 23972, Milwaukee, WI, 53224

Tel: (414) 359-4000     Fax: (414) 359-4064     www.aosmith.com

*Auto and truck frames, motors, water heaters, storage/handling systems, plastics, railroad products.*

**A.O. Smith International Corporation, 1 Cheapside Court, Burckurst Rd., Ascot, LSL5 7RF UK**

Tel: 44-1344-874470   Fax: 44-1344-874480   Contact: Albert E. Medice, V.P. Europe

## SMURFIT-STONE CONTAINER CORPORATION

150 N. Michigan Ave., Chicago, IL, 60601-7568

Tel: (312) 346-6600     Fax: (312) 580-3486     www.smurfit-stone.net

*Mfr. paper and paper packaging.*

**Smurfit-Stone Container Corporation, Chesterfield, UK**

## SNAP-ON INCORPORATED

10801 Corporate Dr., Pleasant Prairie, WI, 53158-1603

Tel: (262) 656-5200     Fax: (262) 656-5577     www.snapon.com

*Mfr. auto maintenance, diagnostic and emission testing equipment, hand tools, hydraulic lifts and tire changers.*

**Suntester (UK) Ltd., Oldmedow Rd., Hardwick Estate, King's Lynn, Norfolk PE30 4JW, UK**

Tel: 44-1553-692422   Fax: 44-1553-691844   Contact: Michael Waldron, Mng. Dir.

## SONOCO PRODUCTS COMPANY

North Second Street, PO Box 160, Hartsville, SC, 29550

Tel: (843) 383-7000     Fax: (843) 383-7008     www.sonoco.com

*Mfr. packaging for consumer and industrial market and recycled paperboard.*

**Sonoco Capseals Liners, Greenock Rd., Trading Estate, Slough, Berkshire SL1 4QQ UK**

Tel: 44-1753-773000

**Sonoco Consumer Packaging Europe, Stokes St., Clayton, Manchester M11 4QX, UK**

Tel: 44-61-230-7000

**Sonoco Engraph Label, Land of Green Ginger House, Anlaby, Hull HU10 6RN, UK**

Tel: 44-1482-561166

**Sonoco Engraph Label, Hedgehog House, 2 Michigan Ave., Broadway Salford, UK**

Tel: 44-161-848-4800   Fax: 44-161-848-4830

**Sonoco Europe Board Mills, Holywell Green, Stainland Halifax, West Yorkshire HX4 9PY UK**

Tel: 44-1422-374741

**Sonoco Industrial Products, Station Rd., Milnrow, Lancashire OL16 4HQ, UK**

Tel: 44-1706-41661

**Sonoco Industrial Products, Tufthorne Ave., Cloeford, Gloucestershire GL16 8PP, UK**

Tel: 44-1594-833272

## SOTHEBY'S HOLDINGS, INC.

1334 York Avenue, New York, NY, 10021

Tel: (212) 606-7000      Fax: (212) 606-7027      www.sothebys.com

*Auction house specializing in fine art and jewelry.*

**Sotheby's Holdings, Inc., Summers Place, Billingshurst, West Sussex RH14 9AD, UK**

Tel: 44-1403-833-500    Fax: 44-1403-833-699    Contact: Timothy Wonnacott, Chmn.

**Sotheby's Holdings, Inc., 34-35 New Bond Street, London W1A2AA, UK**

Tel: 44-20-7293-5000    Fax: 44-20-7293-5989

## THE SOUTHERN COMPANY

270 Peachtree Street, N.W., Atlanta, GA, 30303

Tel: (404) 506-5000      Fax: (404) 506-0642      www.southernco.com

*Electric utility.*

**Southern Energy-Europe, 31 Curzon St., London, UK W147 7AE, UK**

Tel: 44-207-491-1116    Fax: 44-207-491-1588    Contact: Barney Rush, Pres.

**Southwestern Electricity, plc., 800 Park Ave., Aztec West, Almondsbury, Bristol, UK B512 4SE, UK**

Tel: 44-1454-201-101    Contact: Gale Klappa, Pres.

## SPALDING HOLDINGS CORPORATION

425 Meadow Street, Chicopee, MA, 01021

Tel: (413) 536-1200      Fax: (413) 536-1404      www.spalding.com

*Mfr. sports equipment and infant and juvenile furniture and accessories.*

**Spalding Sports (UK) Ltd., 16 Trafalgar Way, Ball Hill, Cambridge CB3 8SQ, UK**

## SPENCER STUART MANAGEMENT CONSULTANTS

401 North Michigan Ave., Ste. 3400, Chicago, IL, 60611

Tel: (312) 822-0080      Fax: (312) 822-0116      www.spencerstuart.com

*Executive recruitment firm.*

**Spencer Stuart & Associates Inc., 16 Connaught Place, London W2 2ED, UK**

Tel: 44-207-298-3333    Fax: 44-207-298-3388    Contact: Lorna Parker

**Spencer Stuart & Associates Inc., Gladstone House, Redvers Close, Lawnswood Park, Leeds London LS16 6QY UK**

Tel: 44-113-230-7774    Fax: 44-113-230-7775    Contact: Michael Holford

## SPERRY-SUN DRILLING

3000 North Sam Houston Pkwy. East, Houston, TX, 77032

Tel: (281) 871-5100      Fax: (281) 871-5742      www.sperry-sun.com

*Provides drilling services to the oil and gas drilling industry.*

**Sperry-Sun, Inc., Morton Peto Road, Gapton Hall Ind. Estate, Great Yarmouth, Norfolk NR31 0LT, UK**

**Sperry-Sun, Inc., Unit 4 Enterprise Way, Cheltenham Trade Park Arle Road, Cheltenham, Gloucestershire GL51 8LZ, UK**

## SPHERION CORPORATION

2050 Spectrum Boulevard, Fort Lauderdale, FL, 33309

Tel: (954) 938-7600      Fax: (954) 938-7666      www.spherion.com

*Provides temporary personnel placement and staffing.*

**Accountancy Additions, Hadleigh House, Guilford, UK**

Tel: 44-148-345-0278

**Interim Technology Consulting Group, Calthorpe House, Edgbaston, Birmingham UK**

Tel: 44-121-456-1020

**Interim Technology Consulting Group, Nordic House, Purley, Surrey UK**

Tel: 44-181-660-1177

**Michael Page Corporate Finance, 50 Cannon St., London EC4N 6JJ, UK**

Tel: 44-207-269-1866

**Michael Page Finance, Centurion House, St. Albans AL 1 1SA, UK**

Tel: 44-172-786-5813

**Michael Page Finance, 29 St. Augustine's Parade, Bristol BS1 4UL, UK**

Tel: 44-117-927-6509

**Sales Recruitment Specialits, Aquis House 6th Floor, Leeds LS1 5RU, UK**

Tel: 44-113-242-7444

## SPIROL INTERNATIONAL CORPORATION

30 Rock Ave., Danielson, CT, 06239

Tel: (860) 774-8571    Fax: (860) 774-0487    www.spirol.com

*Mfr. engineered fasteners, shims, automation equipment.*

**Spirol Automation UK, Valley Rd., Lye. Stourbridge, West Midlands, UK DY9 8JH**

Tel: 44-1384-893381   Fax: 44-1384-891059   Contact: David Waddington, Gen. Mgr.   Emp: 12

**Spirol Ind. Ltd., Princewood Rd., Corby, Northants. NN17 2ET, UK**

Tel: 44-1536-267634   Fax: 44-1536-203415   Contact: Jon Fennell, Mng. Dir.   Emp: 38

## SPRAYING SYSTEMS COMPANY

PO Box 7900, Wheaton, IL, 60189-7900

Tel: (630) 665-5000    Fax: (630) 260-0842    www.spray.com

*Designs and manufactures industrial spray nozzles.*

**Spraying Systems Limited, 4 Bourne Mill Industrial Estate, Guildford Road, Farnham Surrey GU9 9PS, UK**

## SPRINT INTERNATIONAL

World Headquarters, 2330 Shawnee Mission Parkway, Westwood, KS, 66205

Tel: (913) 624-3000    Fax: (913) 624-3281    www.sprint.com

*Telecommunications equipment and services.*

**Sprint International-Northern Europe, Rawdon House, Bond Close, Kingsland Business Park, Basingstoke Hampshire RG24 0PZ UK**

## SPS TECHNOLOGIES INC.

101 Greenwood Avenue, Ste. 470, Jenkintown, PA, 19046

Tel: (215) 517-2000    Fax: (215) 517-2032    www.spstech.com

*Mfr. aerospace and industry fasteners, tightening systems, magnetic materials, superalloys.*

**Chevron Aerospace Group Limited, Nottingham South Industrial Estate, Wilford Nottingham NG11 7EP, UK**

Tel: 44-115-936-5365   Fax: 44-115-936-5366

**SPS Technologies Ltd., 191 Barkby Road, Troon Industrial Area, Leicester LE4 9HX, UK**

**SPS Technologies Ltd., PO Box 38, Burnaby Rd., Coventry CV6 4AE, UK**

**Unbrako UK/SPS Technologies Ltd, Cranford Street, Smethwick, West Midlands B66 2TA, UK**

Tel: 44-121- 555 8855   Fax: 44-121-555 8866

## SPSS INC.

233 S. Wacker Dr., Chicago, IL, 60606

Tel: (312) 651-6000    Fax: (312) 329-3668    www.spss.com

*Mfr. statistical software.*

**SPSS UK Ltd., SPSS House, 5 London St., Chertsey, Surrey KT16 8AP, UK**

## SPX CORPORATION

700 Terrace Point Drive, PO Box 3301, Muskegon, MI, 49443-3301

Tel: (231) 724-5000    Fax: (231) 724-5720    www.spx.com

*Mfr. auto parts, special service tools, engine and drive-train parts.*

**Bear (UK) Ltd., Mercers Row, Cambridge CB5 8HY, UK**

Kent-Moore UK & Euroline, 86 Wharfdale Rd., Tyseley, Birmingham B11 2DD UK

Power Team UK, Unit 17E Number One Industrial Estate, Co. Durham DH8 65Y, UK

Robinair UK, c/o Kent-Moore UK, 86 Wharfdale Rd., Tyseley, Birmingham B11 2DD UK

SPX/Fenner Plc., Fenner Fluid Power Div., Yorkshire, UK

V.L. Churchill Ltd., PO Box 3, London Rd., Daventry, Northants NN11 4NF UK

## SQUIRE, SANDERS & DEMPSEY

127 Public Square, Key Tower, Ste. 4900, Cleveland, OH, 44114-1304

Tel: (216) 479-8500      Fax: (216) 479-8780      www.ssd.com

*International law firm.*

Squire, Sanders & Dempsey, Royex House, Aldermanbury Square, London EC2V 7HR, UK

Tel: 44-207-776-5200   Fax: 44-207-776-5233   Contact: Joseph P. Markoski

## SRI INTERNATIONAL

333 Ravenswood Ave., Menlo Park, CA, 94025-3493

Tel: (650) 859-2000      Fax: (650) 326-5512      www.sri.com

*Engaged in international consulting and research.*

Cambridge Computer Science Research Center, 23 Millers Yard - Mill Lane, Cambridge CB2 1RQ, UK

Tel: 44-1223-518234   Fax: 44-1223-517417

SRI Europe-London, Stanford House, 2 Manchester Square, London W1M 5RF, UK

## THE ST. PAUL COMPANIES, INC.

385 Washington Street, St. Paul, MN, 55102

Tel: (651) 310-7911      Fax: (651) 310-8294      www.stpaul.com

*Provides investment, insurance and reinsurance services.*

Ashley Palmer Ltd., 27 Leaden Hall St., London EC3A 1AA, UK

Tel: 44-207-488-0103   Fax: 44-207-481-4995

Camperdown UK Ltd., The St. Paul House, 23-27 Alie St., London E1 8DS, UK

Tel: 44-207-488-6321   Fax: 44-207-680-8903   Contact: Duncan Wilkinson, CEO

Cassidy Davis Underwriting Ltd., St. Helen's, 1 Undershaft, London EC3A 8JR UK

Tel: 44-207-623-1026   Fax: 44-207-623-5225   Contact: Tony Cassidy

Eagle Star Insurance Company Ltd., London Commercial Centre, 82-84 Fenchurch St., London EC3M 4ES, UK

Gravett & Tilling Ltd., 61 St. Mary Avenue 5th Floor, London EC3A 8AA, UK

Tel: 44-207-397-6800   Fax: 44-207-623-5718   Contact: John Tilling

St. Paul International Insurance Co. Ltd., 61-63 London Road, Redhill Surrey RH1 1N8, UK

Tel: 44-1737-787-787   Fax: 44-1737-787-172   Contact: Kent Urness, Pres. & CEO

St. Paul International Insurance Company Ltd., St. Paul House, 23-27 Alie St., London E1 8DS, UK

Tel: 44-207-488-6313   Fax: 44-207-488-6348

## STANDARD COMMERCIAL CORPORATION

2201 Miller Rd., PO Box 450, Wilson, NC, 27893

Tel: (919) 291-5507      Fax: (919) 237-1109      www.sccgroup.com

*Leaf tobacco dealers/processors and wool processors.*

Standard Commercial Ltd., Standard House - Weyside Park, Godalming GU7 1XE, Surrey UK

Standard Wool (UK) Limited, Carlton Buildings, Clifton Street, Bradford BD8 7DB, UK

## STANDARD MICROSYSTEMS CORPORATION

80 Arkay Drive, Hauppauge, NY, 11788

Tel: (631) 435-6000      Fax: (631) 273-5550      www.smsc.com

*Telecommunications systems.*

Insight MEMEC UK, Aylesbury, England

Tel: 44-1296-330061

## STANDEX INTERNATIONAL CORPORATION

6 Manor Parkway, Salem, NH, 03079

Tel: (603) 893-9701      Fax: (603) 893-7324      www.standex.com

*Mfr. diversified graphics, institutional, industry/electronic and consumer products.*

**Barbeque King, 16 Richfield Ave., Reading Berkshire RG1 8PB, UK**

Tel: 44-118-950-822   Fax: 44-118-959-1968   Contact: Stewart Greener, Mgr.

**James Burn Binders, Stanton Harcourt Rd., Ensham Oxford OX8 1JE, UK**

Tel: 44-1865-880-458   Fax: 44-1865-880-661   Contact: Mike Chapman

**James Burn International, Cannon Way, Barugh Green, Barnsley South Yorkshire S75 1JU, UK**

Tel: 44-1226-380-088   Fax: 44-1226-388-110   Contact: Clive Bromley, Mgr.

**James Burn International, Douglas Rd., Esher, Surrey KT10 8BD, UK**

Tel: 44-1372-466-801   Fax: 44-1372-469-422   Contact: David Baddaley, Mgr.

**Standex Electronics UK Ltd., 40 Morley Rd., Tonbridge, Kent TN9 1RA, UK**

Tel: 44-1732-771-023   Fax: 44-1732-770-122   Contact: John Hill, Mgr.

**Standex Holdings Ltd., Stanton Harcourt Rd., Eynsham Oxfordshire OX8 1JE, UK**

Tel: 44-1865-882-389   Fax: 44-1865-882-768   Contact: Mark Hampton, Mgr.

**Standex International Ltd., Unit 6 Cromwell Road, Trading Estate, Bredbury Stockport, Cheshire SK6 2RF UK**

Tel: 44-161-430-6815   Fax: 44-161-494-5696   Contact: George Fryer, Mgr.

## STANLEY BOSTITCH FASTENING SYSTEMS

815 Briggs Street, East Greenwich, RI, 02818

Tel: (401) 884-2500      Fax: (401) 885-6511      www.centerplex.net

*Mfr. stapling machines, stapling supplies, fastening systems and wire.*

**Stanley Bostitch UK, Station Road, Edenbridge, Kent, UK**

## THE STANLEY WORKS

1000 Stanley Drive, PO Box 7000, New Britain, CT, 06053

Tel: (860) 225-5111      Fax: (860) 827-3987      www.stanleyworks.com

*Mfr. hand tools and hardware.*

**Stanley Curtain Companions Ltd., Woodside, Sheffield S3 9PD, UK**

**Stanley Magic Door Ltd., 802 Oxford Ave., Slough, Berkshire SL1 4LN, UK**

**Stanley Power Tools Ltd., Nelson Way, Cramlington, Northumberland NE23 9JS, UK**

**Stanley Tools Ltd., Woodside, Sheffield S3 9PD, UK**

**Stanley Tools-Europe, Cory House, The Ring, Bracknell, Berkshire RG12 1AS UK**

## STAPLES, INC.

500 Staples Dr., Framingham, MA, 01702

Tel: (508) 253-3000      Fax: (508) 253-8989      www.staples.com

*Superstore for office supplies and equipment.*

**Staples, UK, Westfields, London Rd., High Wycombe, HP 11 1HA, UK**

Tel: 44-1494-474-990   Fax: 44-1494-474-194

## STAR TELECOMMUNICATIONS, INC.

223 East De La Guerra Street, Santa Barbara, CA, 93101

Tel: (805) 899-1962      Fax: (805) 899-2972      www.startel.com

*Provides long-distance telecommunications services.*

**Star Europe Ltd., Adelaide House, 626 Chiswick High Road - Level 3, London W4 5RY, UK**

Tel: 44-208-580-5150

## STARBUCKS COFFEE CORPORATION

PO Box 34067, Seattle, WA, 98124-1967

Tel: (206) 447-4127    Fax: (206) 682-7570    www.starbucks.com

*Coffee bean retail store and coffee bars.*

**Starbucks Coffee Corp.,  London, UK**

## STARWOOD HOTELS & RESORTS WORLDWIDE

777 Westchester Avenue, White Plains, NY, 10604

Tel: (914) 640-8100    Fax: (914) 640-8316    www.starwoodhotels.com

*Hotel operations including Sheraton, Westin, St. Regis, Four Points and Caesars.*

**Sheraton Sales Center,  The Kiln House, 210 New Kings Rd., London SW6 4NZ, UK**

## STATE STREET BANK & TRUST COMPANY

225 Franklin Street, Boston, MA, 02101

Tel: (617) 786-3000    Fax: (617) 654-3386    www.statestreet.com

*Banking and financial services.*

**Rexiter Capital Management Limited,  21 Saint James Square, London SWIY 4SS, UK**

**State Street Bank & Trust,  One Royal Exchange Steps, Royal Exchange, London EC3V 3LE, UK**

**State Street Fund Services,  One Canada Square, Canary Wharf, London E14 5AF, UK**

**State Street Global Advisors,  Almack House, 28 King St., London SW14 6QW, UK**

**State Street Global Advisors,  20 Saint James Square, London SWIY 4SS, UK**

## STEMCO INC.

PO Box 1989, Longview, TX, 75606

Tel: (903) 758-9981    Fax: (903) 232-3508    www.stemco.com

*Mfr. seals, hubcaps, hubodometers and locking nuts for heavy duty trucks, buses, trailers.*

**Garlock GB-Stemco Prdts.,  Hambridge Rd., Newbury, Berkshire RG14 5TG, UK**

Tel: 44-1635-38668   Fax: 44-1635-49586   Contact: Bob Bannister

## STERIS CORPORATION

5960 Heisley Road, Mentor, OH, 44060

Tel: (440) 354-2600    Fax: (440) 639-4459    www.steris.com

*Mfr. sterilization/infection control equipment, surgical tables, lighting systems for health, pharmaceutical and scientific industries.*

**Steris Corporation,  53 Church Rd., Ashford, Middlesex TW15 2TY UK**

## STIEFEL LABORATORIES INC.

255 Alhambra Circle, Ste. 1000, Coral Gables, FL, 33134

Tel: (305) 443-3807    Fax: (305) 443-3467    www.stiefel.com

*Mfr. pharmaceuticals, dermatological specialties.*

**Stiefel Laboratories Ltd.,  Holtsur Lane, Woodburn Green, High Wycombe, Buckinghamshire HP10 0AU, UK**

**Stiefel Laboratories Ltd.,  Whitebrook Park, 68 Lower Cookham Rd., Maidenhead, Berkshire SL6 8AL, UK**

## STOKES VACUUM INC.

5500 Tabor Road, Philadelphia, PA, 19120

Tel: (215) 831-5400    Fax: (215) 831-5420    www.stokesvacuum.com

*Vacuum pumps and components, vacuum dryers, oil-upgrading equipment and metallizers.*

**Stokes Vacuum, Div. Hick Hargreaves & Co. Ltd.,  Crook Street, Bolton Lancashire BL3 6DB, UK**

Tel: 44-120-452-3373   Fax: 44-120-439-5261   Contact: Vic Cheetham

## STONE & WEBSTER ENGINEERING CORPORATION

8545 United Plaza Blvd., Baton Rouge, LA, 02210-2288

Tel: (617) 589-5111     Fax: (617) 589-2156     www.shawgroup.com

*Engineering, construction, environmental and management services.*

**Stone & Webster Engineering Ltd., Stone & Webster House, 500 Elder Gate, Milton Keynes, Bucks MK9 1BA UK**

## STORAGE TECHNOLOGY CORPORATION

One Storagetech Dr., Louisville, CO, 80028-4377

Tel: (303) 673-5151     Fax: (303) 673-5019     www.stortek.com

*Mfr./market/service information, storage and retrieval systems.*

**StorageTek Holding Ltd., 6 Genesis Business Park, Albert Drive, Wokingham Surrey GU21 5RW, UK**

## STRUCTURAL DYNAMICS RESEARCH CORPORATION

2000 Eastman Dr., Milford, OH, 45150-2740

Tel: (513) 576-2400     Fax: (513) 576-2922     www.sdrc.com

*Developer of software used in Modeling testing, drafting and manufacturing.*

**SDRC UK Ltd., TRADA Business Campus, Stocking Lane, Hughenden Valley High Wycombe, Buckshire HP14 4ND UK**

Tel: 44-1494-564759   Fax: 44-1494-564772

## STRYKER CORPORATION

2725 Fairfield Rd., Kalamazoo, MI, 49002

Tel: (616) 385-2600     Fax: (616) 385-1062     www.strykercorp.com

*Mfr. surgical instruments and medical equipment.*

**Stryker Europe, London, UK**

## SUDLER & HENNESSEY

1633 Broadway, 25th Fl., New York, NY, 10019

Tel: (212) 969-5800     Fax: (212) 969-5996     www.sudler-hennessey.com

*Engaged in healthcare products advertising.*

**Sudler & Hennessey Ltd., Greater London House, Hampstead Rd., London NW1 7QP, UK**

Tel: 44-207-383-3316   Fax: 44-207-611-6423   Contact: Dr. Brian Kelly, Mng. Dir.

## SULLAIR CORPORATION

3700 E. Michigan Blvd., Bldg. 1-2, Michigan City, IN, 46360

Tel: (219) 879-5451     Fax: (219) 874-1273     www.sullair.com

*Mfr. high efficiency tandem compressors, vacuum systems, encapsulated compressors and air tools.*

**Sullair (UK) Ltd., 274 High St., Uxbridge, Middlesex UB8 ILQ, UK**

## SULLIVAN & CROMWELL

125 Broad Street, New York, NY, 10004-2498

Tel: (212) 558-4000     Fax: (212) 558-3588     www.sullcrom.com

*International law firm.*

**Sullivan & Cromwell, St. Olave's House, 9a Ironmonger Lane, London EC2V 8EY, UK**

## SUN HEALTHCARE GROUP, INC.

101 Sun Avenue, N.E., Albuquerque, NM, 87109

Tel: (505) 821-3355     Fax: (505) 858-4735     www.sunh.com

*Provides long-term and skilled nursing care.*

**Ashbourne PLC, London, England**

Contact: Elaine Farrall, Dir.

**Sunscript U.K., London, England**

## SUNGARD DATA SYSTEMS

1285 Drummers Lane, Wayne, PA, 19087

Tel: (610) 341-8700     Fax: (610) 341-8851     www.sungard.com

*Provides ASP solutions to the buyside investment management market.*

**SunGard Data Systems, 10-16 North Street, Carshalton, Surrey SM5 2HU, UK**

Tel: 44-181-669-5285   Contact: Norman Ireland, Pres.

**SunGard Data Systems, 33 St.. Mary Ave. - Exchequer Court, London EC3A 8AA, UK**

Tel: 44-20-7337-6000   Contact: Gavin Lavelle, Pres.

## SUNRISE MEDICAL INC.

2382 Faraday Ave., Ste. 200, Carlsbad, CA, 92008

Tel: (760) 930-1500     Fax: (760) 930-1580     www.sunrisemedical.com

*Designs, manufactures and markets rehabilitation products and assistive technology devices for people with disabilities, and patient care products used in nursing homes, hospitals and homecare settings.*

**Sunrise Medical Ltd., High Street Wollaston, West Midlands DY8 4PS, UK**

Tel: 44-1384-44-6688

## SUPERIOR GRAPHITE COMPANY

10 South Riverside Plaza, Chicago, IL, 60606

Tel: (312) 559-2999     Fax: (312) 559-9064     www.graphitesgc.com

*Mfr. natural and synthetic graphites, electrodes, lubricants, suspensions, carbide and carbon.*

**Superior Graphite Co., 4th Fl., Knightsbridge, 197 Knightsbridge, London, SW 7 1RB UK**

Tel: 44-207-973-8866   Fax: 44-207-581-5413

## SUPERIOR TUBE COMPANY

3900 Germantown Pike, Collegeville, PA, 19426

Tel: (610) 489-5200     Fax: (610) 489-5252     www.superiortube.com

*Mfr. precision, seamless tubes for automotive, medical, aerospace and nuclear industries.*

**Fine Tubes Limited, Estober Works, Plymouth PL6 7LJ, UK**

## SYBASE, INC.

6475 Christie Ave., Emeryville, CA, 94608

Tel: (510) 922-3500     Fax: (510) 922-3210     www.sybase.com

*Design/mfg/distribution of database management systems, software development tools, connectivity products, consulting and technical support services..*

**Sybase UK Ltd., Sybase Court, Crown Lane, Maidenhead, Berkshire SL6 8Q2 UK**

Tel: 44-1628-597100   Fax: 44-1628-597000

## SYBRON INTERNATIONAL CORPORATION

411 E. Wisconsin Ave., Milwaukee, WI, 53202

Tel: (414) 274-6600     Fax: (414) 274-6561     www.sybron.com

*Mfr. products for laboratories, professional orthodontic and dental markets.*

**Genevac Limited, Ipswich, England, UK**

**Kerr UK Ltd., 27 Coningsby Rd., Bretton, Peterborough, Cambridgeshire PE3 8SB UK**

**Nalge (UK) Ltd., Foxwood Ct., Rotherwas Industrial Estate, Hereford HR2 6JQ, UK**

## SYMANTEC CORPORATION

20330 Stevens Creek Blvd., Cupertino, CA, 95014-2132

Tel: (408) 253-9600     Fax: (408) 253-3968     www.symantec.com

*Designs and produces PC network security and network management software and hardware.*

**Symantec Ltd., St. Cloud's Gate, St. Cloud Way, Maidenhead, Berkshire SL6 8W UK**

Tel: 44-1628-59-2222   Fax: 44-1628-59-2393

## SYMBOL TECHNOLOGIES, INC.

One Symbol Plaza, Holtsville, NY, 11742-1300

Tel: (631) 738-2400     Fax: (631) 738-5990     www.symbol.com

*Mfr. Bar code-driven data management systems, wireless LAN's, and Portable Shopping System™.*

**Symbol Technologies Intl., Symbol Place, Winnersh Triangle, Berkshire, UK RG41 5TP**

Tel: 44-118-945-7000    Fax: 44-118-945-7500

## SYNOPSYS, INC.

700 East Middlefield Road, Mountain View, CA, 94043

Tel: (650) 962-5000     Fax: (650) 965-8637     www.synopsys.com

*Mfr. electronic design automation software.*

**Synopsys Europe, Imperium - Imperial Way, Worton Grange, Reading Berkshire RG2 0TD, UK**

Tel: 44-118-931-3822    Fax: 44-118-975-0081

## SYNTEGRA

4201 Lexington Ave., North Arden Hills, MN, 55126-6198

Tel: (651) 415-2999     Fax: (651) 415-4891     www.cdc.com

*Computer peripherals and hardware.*

**Syntegra Ltd., 3 Roundwood Ave., Stockley Park, Uxbridge Middlesex, London UB11 1AG, UK**

Tel: 44-181-867-6000   Fax: 44-181-569-2511

## SYSTEM SOFTWARE ASSOCIATES, INC.

500 W. Madison St., Ste. 3200, Chicago, IL, 60661

Tel: (312) 258-6000     Fax: (312) 474-7500     www.ssax.com

*Mfr. computer software.*

**System Software Associates, Frimley Business Park, Frimley, Cambeley, Surrey GU 16 55G, UK**

Tel: 44-1276-692-111   Fax: 4-1276-692-135

## SYSTEMAX INC.

22 Harbor Park Dr., Port Washington, NY, 11050

Tel: (516) 608-7000     Fax: (516) 608-7111     www.systemax.com

*Direct marketer of computers and related products to businesses.*

**Misco Computer Supplies UK, Faraday Close, Park Farm Industrial Estate, Wellingborough, Northants NN8 6XH, UK**

Tel: 44-1933-400-400

## TACONIC LTD.

PO Box 69, Coonbrook Rd., Petersburg, NY, 12138

Tel: (518) 658-3202     Fax: (518) 658-3204     www.taconic.com

*Mfr. teflon/silicone-coated fiberglass fabrics, tapes and belts; specialty tapes and circuit board substrates.*

**Taconic United Kingdom, 15 Brunel Close, Drayton Fields Industrial Estate, Daventry, Northants NN11 5RB UK**

Tel: 44-1327-304500   Fax: 44-1327-304501

## TANDY CORPORATION

100 Throckmorton Street, Fort Worth, TX, 76102

Tel: (817) 390-3700     Fax: (817) 415-2647     www.tandy.com

*Mfr. electronic and acoustic equipment; Radio Shack retail stores.*

**Memtek UK Div., 2 Ascot Rd., Bedfont, Feltham, Middlesex TW14 8QH, UK**

**Tandy Corp., Tameway Tower, Bridge St., Walsallow WS1 1LA, UK**

## TATE ACCESS FLOORS INC.

7510 Montevideo Road, PO Box 278, Jessup, MD, 20794-0278

Tel: (410) 799-4200     Fax: (410) 799-4250     www.tateaccessfloors.com

*Mfr. access floors for offices, equipment rooms, clean rooms and specialty applications.*

**Tate Access Floors Ltd., Carrier House, 1-9 Warwick Row, London SW1E 5ER, UK**

## TBWA CHIAT/DAY

488 Madison Avenue, 6th Floor, New York, NY, 10022

Tel: (212) 804-1000     Fax: (212) 804-1200     www.tbwachiat.com

*International full service advertising agency.*

**TBWA UK, London, UK**

## TC INDUSTRIES

3703 South Route 31, Crystal Lake, IL, 60012-1312

Tel: (815) 459-2400     Fax: (815) 459-3303     www.tcindustries.com

*Mfr./sales of fabricated metal products.*

**TC Industries of Europe Ltd., PO Box 2, Carlin How, Saltburn-by-the-Sea, Cleveland TS13 4EU, UK**

## THE TCW GROUP

865 S. Figueroa St., Ste. 1800, Los Angeles, CA, 90017

Tel: (213) 244-0000     Fax: (213) 244-0000     www.tcwgroup.com

*Engaged in managing pension and profit sharing funds, retirement/health and welfare funds, insurance company funds, endowments and foundations.*

**TCW Group, London, UK**

## TEAM INDUSTRIAL SERVICES, INC.

1019 S. Hood Street, Alvin, TX, 77511

Tel: (281) 331-6154     Fax: (281) 331-4107     www.teamindustrialservices.com

*Consulting, engineering and rental services.*

**Team Environmental Services Ltd., MacAuley Rd., Unit 1, Huddersfield, W. Yorks. HD2 2US, UK**

Tel: 44-1484-401900    Fax: 44-1484-401666

## TECH/OPS SEVCON INC.

40 North Ave., Burlington, MA, 01803

Tel: (718) 229-7896     Fax: (718) 229-8603     www.sevcon.com

*Design, manufacture, and marketing of microprocessor based control systems for battery powered vehicles.*

**Sevcon Ltd., Kingsway South, Gateshead, NE11 OQA, UK**

## TECHNITROL INC.

1210 Northbrook Drive, #385, Trevose, PA, 19053

Tel: (215) 355-2900     Fax: (215) 355-7397     www.technitrol.com

*Mfr. of electronic components, electrical contacts, and other parts/materials.*

**Lloyd Instruments Ltd., Whittle Ave., Segensworth West, Fareham, Hants. PO15 5SH UK**

## TECHNOLOGY SOLUTIONS COMPANY (TSC)

205 N. Michigan Ave., Ste. 1500, Chicago, IL, 60601

Tel: (312) 228-4500     Fax: (312) 228-4501     www.techsol.com

*Designs computer information systems and strategic business and management consulting for major corporations.*

**TSC Europe, Regina House, 5 Queen Street, London EC4N 1SP, UK**

Tel: 44-207-236-5000   Fax: 44-207-236-5001   Contact: Arthur Bird

## TECH-SYM CORPORATION

10500 Westoffice Drive, Ste. 200, Houston, TX, 77042-5391

Tel: (713) 785-7790     Fax: (713) 780-3524     www.tech-sym.com

*Designs, develops, and manufactures electronic systems and components used in diverse markets including communications, defense systems, and weather information systems.*

**Syntron Europe Ltd., Birchwood Way, Cotes Park Industrial Estate, Somercotes, Alfreton Derbyshire DE55 4QQ UK**

Tel: 44-1773-605078   Fax: 44-1773-41778

## TECUMSEH PRODUCTS COMPANY

100 E. Patterson Street, Tecumseh, MI, 49286-1899

Tel: (517) 423-8411     Fax: (517) 423-8526     www.tecumseh.com

*Mfr. of hermetic compressors for air conditioning and refrigeration products, gasoline engines and power train components for lawn and garden applications, and pumps.*

**Tecnamotor (UK) Ltd., 152/154 Commercial Rd., Staines, Middlesex TW18 2QP UK**

## TEKELEC

26580 West Agoura Road, Calabasas, CA, 91302

Tel: (818) 880-5656     Fax: (818) 880-6993     www.tekelec.com

*Mfr. telecommunications testing equipment.*

**Tekelec UK, London, UK**

Contact: David Colbeck

## TEKNIS CORPORATION

PO Box 3189, North Attleboro, MA, 02761

Tel: (508) 695-3591     Fax: (508) 699-6059     www.teknis.com

*Sale advanced technical products, fiber optics, materials for semiconductor mfr., security holographics*

**Teknis Ltd., Technology House, PO Box 12, Ilminster TA12 9YU, UK**

## TEKTRONIX INC.

14200 SW Karl Braun Dr., PO Box 500, Beaverton, OR, 97077

Tel: (503) 627-7111     Fax: (503) 627-2406     www.tek.com

*Mfr. test and measure, visual systems/color printing and communications/video and networking products.*

**Tektronix (UK) Ltd., Fourth Ave., Marlow London, Buckinghamshire SL7 1YD, UK**

Tel: 44-1628-403300  Fax: 44-1628-403301

**Tektronix UK Ltd, The Arena - Downshire Way, Bracknell Berkshire, RG12 1PU, UK**

Tel: 44-1344-392000  Fax: 44-1344-392001

## TELEFLEX INC.

630 W. Germantown Pike, Ste. 450, Plymouth Meeting, PA, 19462

Tel: (610) 834-6301     Fax: (610) 834-8307     www.teleflex.com

*Designs/mfr./market mechanical and electro-mechanical systems, measure systems.*

**Astraflex Limited, West Yorkshire, UK**

**Cetrek Ltd., Dorset, UK**

**Rüsch International, West Sussex, UK**

**Rüsch UK Ltd., Buckinghamshire, UK**

**Sermatech (UK) Limited, Lincoln, UK**

**Sermatech-Mal (UK), Dunnockshaw, UK**

**SermeTel (UK) Ltd., High Holborn Rd., Codner, Ripley, Derbyshire DE5 3NW, UK**

**TFX Marine International, Dorset, UK**

**United Parts Driver Control Systems (UK) Ltd., Birmingham, England, UK**

## TELEX COMMUNICATIONS INC.

12000 Portland Ave. South, Burnsville, MN, 55337

Tel: (952) 884-4051      Fax: (952) 884-0043        www.telexcommunications.com

*Mfr. communications, audio-visual and professional audio products.*

**Telex Communications (UK) Ltd.,  Viking House - Swallowdale Lane, Hemel Hempstead HP2 7HA, UK**

**Telex Communications (UK) Ltd.,  Premier Suites Exchange House, 494 Midsummer Blvd., Milton Keynes MK9 2EA, UK**

## TELLABS INC.

4951 Indiana Ave. 6303788800, Lisle, IL, 60532-1698

Tel: (630) 378-8800      Fax: (630) 679-3010        www.tellabs.com

*Design/mfr./service voice/data transport and network access systems.*

**Tellabs Coventry,  5 Ensign Business Center, Westwood Business Park, Westwood Way Coventry CV4 8JA, UK**

**Tellabs EMEA,  Abbey Place - 24-28 Easton Street, High Wycombe
Bucks HP11 1NT, UK**

**Tellabs Oxfordshire,  29 The Quadrant, Abingdon Science Park, Barton Lane Abingdon Oxfordshire OX14 3YS, UK**

**Tellabs UK Ltd.,  Eton Pl., 64 High St., Burnham, Buckinghamshire SL1 7J7, UK**

## TELXON CORPORATION

1000 Summitt Dr., Cincinnati, OH, 45150

Tel: (330) 664-1000      Fax: (330) 664-2220        www.telxon.com

*Develop/mfr. portable computer systems and related equipment.*

**Telxon Ltd.,  Old Orchard, High St., Poole, Dorset BH15 1AE, UK**

## TENNECO AUTOMOTIVE INC.

500 North Field Drive, Lake Forest, IL, 60045

Tel: (847) 482-5241      Fax: (847) 482-5295        www.tenneco-automotive.com

*Mfr. automotive parts, exhaust systems and service equipment.*

**Monroe Europe (UK) Ltd.,  Manor Lane, Shipton Rd., York YO3 6UA, UK**
Tel: 44-1904-659-833   Fax: 44-1904-623-159   Contact: Dave Westley, Mgr.   Emp: 554

**Tenneco-Walker (UK) Ltd.,  Liverpool Rd., Burnley, Lancashire BB12 6HJ, UK**
Tel: 44-1282-433-171   Fax: 44-1282-451-778   Contact: Ray Jenkins, Mgr.   Emp: 208

**Walker UK Ltd.,  Wharfdale Rd., Tyseley, Birmingham B11 2DF, UK**
Tel: 44-121-609-3001   Fax: 44-121-609-3049   Contact: Jeff Penny, Mgr.

## TENNECO PACKAGING CORPORATION OF AMERICA

1900 West Field Court, Lake Forest, IL, 60045

Tel: (847) 482-2000      Fax: (847) 482-2181        www.agplus.net/tenneco

*Mfr. custom packaging, aluminum and plastic molded fibre, corrugated containers.*

**Alcan Ekco Ltd.,  90 Asheridge Rd., Chesham, Buckinghamshire HP5 2QE, UK**

**Omni-Pac UK Ltd.,  Marine Parade, South Denes, Great Yarmouth, Norfolk NR30 3QH UK**

**Tenneco Packaging,  Bristol, UK**

## TERADYNE INC.

321 Harrison Ave., Boston, MA, 02118

Tel: (617) 482-2700      Fax: (617) 422-2910        www.teradyne.com

*Mfr. electronic test equipment and blackplane connection systems.*

**Teradyne Ltd.,  The Western Centre Units 4-5, Western Rd., Bracknell, Berkshire RG12 1RW, UK**
Tel: 44-1344-426899   Contact: Jeff Corrigan, Reg. Mgr

## TEREX CORPORATION

500 Post Road East, Ste. 320, Westport, CT, 06880

Tel: (203) 222-7170     Fax: (203) 222-7976     www.terex.com

*Mfr. lifting and earthmoving equipment.*

**Benford Limited,  The Cape - Warwick, Warwickshire CV34 5DR, UK**

Tel: 44-1926-493466  Fax: 44-1926-490985  Contact: Tony Gardner

**BL-Pegson ltd., Div. Terex,  Mammoth Street, Coalville Leicestershire LE676 3GN, UK**

Tel: 44-1530-518600

**Powerscreen Equipment Ltd.,  Cheltonian House, Portsmouth Road, Esher Surrey KT10 9AA, UK**

Tel: 44-1372-466-286  Fax: 44-1372-466-415

**Powerscreen EquipmentUK,  Portsmouth Road, Esher, Surrey KT10 9AA, UK**

**Powerscreen Ltd.,  Appleton Thorn Trading Estate, Appleton Thorn Warrington, Cheshire WA4 4SN, UK**

Tel: 44-1925-267-486

**Powerscreen Ltd.,  2 Sycamore Court, Birmingham Road, Allesley Coventry CV5 9BA, UK**

Tel: 44-1203-405-100

**Powerscreen Midlands Ltd.,  3 The Old Vicarage, Wardington Banbury, Oxfordshire OX17 1SA, UK**

Tel: 44-1295-758-717

**Powerscreen Southern Ltd.,  The Conifers, Filton Road, Hambrook Bristol BS16 1QG, UK**

Tel: 44-1179-579017

**Terex UK Limited,  Watford Village, Northants NN6 YXN, UK**

## TEXACO INC.

2000 Westchester Ave., White Plains, NY, 10650

Tel: (914) 253-4000     Fax: (914) 253-7753     www.texaco.com

*Exploration/marketing crude oil, mfr. petro chemicals and products.*

**Texaco North Sea UK Co.,  One Knightsbridge Green, London SW1X 7QJ, UK**

## TEXAS INSTRUMENTS INC.

8505 Forest Lane, Dallas, TX, 75243

Tel: (972) 995-3773     Fax: (972) 995-4360     www.ti.com

*Mfr. semiconductor devices, electronic electro-mechanical systems, instruments and controls.*

**Texas Instruments,  Manton Lane, Bedford MK41 7PA, UK**

**Texas Instruments,  Northampton, UK**

## TEXAS UTILITIES (TXU)

1601 Bryan St., Dallas, TX, 75201

Tel: (214) 812-4600     Fax: (214) 812-7077     www.txu.com

*Provides electric and natural gas services, energy trading, energy marketing and telecommunications.*

**Eastern Generation/TXU,  London, UK**

## TEXTRON INC.

40 Westminster Street, Providence, RI, 02903

Tel: (401) 421-2800     Fax: (401) 421-2878     www.textron.com

*Mfr. Aerospace (Bell Helicopter and Cessna Aircraft), industry and consumer products, fasteners and financial services.*

**Avco Group Ltd.,  Avco House, Castle St., Reading, Berkshire RG1 7DW UK**

**Avdel Textron Ltd.,  Mundells, Welwyn Garden City, Hertfordshire AL7 1EZ UK**

Tel: 44-1707-668-668  Fax: 44-1707-338-828  Contact: Frank Gulden, Acting Pres.

**Textron Automotive Co. Ltd., McCord Winn Div.,  Beech Lane, Derby Rd., Burton-on-Trent, Straffordshire, UK**

Tel: 44-128-350-9409  Fax: 44-128-353-8605  Contact: J. R. Langridge

**Textron Systems, Essex House, 141 Kings Rd., Brentwood, Essex CM 144 DT, UK**

Tel: 44-1277-229-192    Fax: 44-1277-228-745    Contact: John Dunk, Dir. European Sales/Mktg.

## THEGLOBE.COM, INC.

120 Broadway, 22nd Fl, New York, NY, 10271

Tel: (212) 894-3600       Fax: (212) 367-8588        www.theglobe.com

*Provides homepage-building.*

**Theglobe.com, Inc., London, UK**

## THERMADYNE HOLDINGS CORPORATION

101 South Hanley Road, Suite 300, St. Louis, MO, 63105

Tel: (314) 746-2197       Fax: (314) 746-2349        www.thermadyne.com

*Mfr. welding, cutting, and safety products.*

**Thermadyne Europe, Lancashire, UK**

Tel: 44-1257-261755

**Thermadyne Industries Ltd., Unitie, Deacon Estate, Forstal Rd., Aylesford Kent ME20 7SW, UK**

## THERMO ELECTRIC COOLING AMERICA (TECA)

109 North Fifth Street, Saddle Brook, NJ, 07662

Tel: (201) 843-5800       Fax: (201) 843-7144        www.thermoelectric.com

*Mfr. solid state cooling products, including air-conditioners, cold plates and liquid chillers.*

**Thermo Electric International, 17E Upper Field Rd., Dolphin Park, Eurolink, Sittingbourne Kent ME10 3UP UK**

## THERMO ELECTRON CORPORATION

81 Wyman Street, Waltham, MA, 02454-9046

Tel: (781) 622-1000       Fax: (781) 622-1207        www.thermo.com

*Develop/mfr./sale of process equipment &instruments for energy intensive and healthcare industries.*

**MicroPatent Europe, Div. Thermo Electron, 235 Southwark Bridge Road, London SE1 6LY, UK**

Tel: 44-20-7450-5105

**Nicolet Biomedical Ltd., Budbrooke Road, Warwick CV34 5XH, UK**

Tel: 44-1926-490888

**Thermo Electron Ltd., Woolborough Lane, Crawley, W. Sussex RH10 2AQ, UK**

**Winterburn Ltd., PO Box 6, Riverside Works, Woodhill Rd., Bury Lancashire BL8 1DF UK**

## THERMO ORION, INC.

500 Cummings Court, Beverly, MA, 01915

Tel: (978) 922-4400       Fax: (978) 922-6015        www.thermoorion.com

*Mfr. laboratory and industrial products, measure and display instruments.*

**Thermo Orion Europe, 12-16 Sedgeway Business Park, Witchford, Cambridgeshire CB6 2HY, UK**

Tel: 44-1353-666111    Fax: 44-1353-666001

## THERMON MANUFACTURING COMPANY

100 Thermon Drive, PO Box 609, San Marcos, TX, 78667-0609

Tel: (512) 396-5801       Fax: (512) 396-3627        www.thermon.com

*Mfr. steam and electric heat tracing systems, components and accessories.*

**Thermon (UK) Ltd., 18 Tower Rd., Glover West Trading Estate, District 11, Washington Tyne and Wear NE37 2SH UK**

## THETFORD CORPORATION

7101 Jackson Road, PO Box 1285, Ann Arbor, MI, 48106

Tel: (734) 769-6000       Fax: (734) 769-2023        www.thetford.com

*Mfr. sanitation products and chemicals.*

**Thetford Aqua Products Ltd., Centrovell Ind. Estate, Caldwell Rd., Nuneaton, Warwickshire CV11 4UD, UK**

## THOMAS & BETTS CORPORATION

8155 T&B Blvd., Memphis, TN, 38125

Tel: (901) 252-5000    Fax: (901) 685-1988    www.tnb.com

*Mfr. elect/electronic connectors and accessories.*

**Thomas & Betts International, European Centre, Third Ave., Globe Park, Marlow Buckinghamshire SL7 1YF UK**

## THOMAS INDUSTRIES INC.

4360 Brownsboro Road, Ste. 300, Louisville, KY, 40232

Tel: (502) 893-4600    Fax: (502) 893-4685    www.thomasind.com

*Mfr. lighting fixtures and specialty pumps and compressors for global OEM applications.*

**ASF Thomas Limited, Unit 2 Alton Business Ctr., Omega Park, Alton, Hampshire GU34 2YU UK**

Tel: 44-1420-54-41-84   Fax: 44-1420-54-41-83   Contact: Warren Beese, Mng. Dir.

## THOMAS TECHNOLOGY SOLUTIONS, INC.

One Progress Drive, Horsham, PA, 19044

Tel: (215) 643-5000    Fax: (215) 682-5300    www.reedtech.com

*Provides custom solutions and services to help companies effectively create, manage, and publish information via multiple media.*

**RTIS International House, One St. Katharine's Way, London E19UN, UK**

Tel: 44-207-369-1618   Fax: 44-207-464-1412   Contact: Peter Camilleri, Gen. Mgr.

## TIDELAND SIGNAL CORPORATION

4310 Directors Row, PO Box 52430, Houston, TX, 77052-2430

Tel: (713) 681-6101    Fax: (713) 681-6233    www.tidelandsignal.com

*Mfr./sale aids to marine navigation.*

**Tideland Signal Ltd., 15-19 Trowers Way, Redhill, Surrey RH1 2LH, UK**

Tel: 44-1737-768-711   Fax: 44-1737-768-192   Contact: Roger Brown, Mng. Dir.

## TIFFANY & COMPANY

727 Fifth Ave., New York, NY, 10022

Tel: (212) 755-8000    Fax: (212) 605-4465    www.tiffany.com

*Mfr./retail fine jewelry, silverware, china, crystal, leather goods, etc.*

**Tiffany & Co.- Harrod's, Knightsbridge London SW1X 7XL, UK**

Tel: 44-207-893-8503

**Tiffany & Co. Ltd., 25 Old Bond St., London W1X 3AA, UK**

Tel: 44-207-409-2790

## THE TIMBERLAND COMPANY

200 Domain Drive, Stratham, NH, 03885

Tel: (603) 772-9500    Fax: (603) 773-1640    www.timberland.com

*Design/mfr. footwear, apparel and accessories for men and women.*

**Timberland UK Ltd., River Park Ave., Staines, Middlesex TW18 3EN, UK**

## TIMET CORPORATION

1999 Broadway, Suite 4300, Denver, CO, 80202

Tel: (303) 296-5600    Fax: (303) 296-5650    www.timet.com

*Non-ferrous drawing and rolling, coal and other minerals, metals service centers.*

**TIMET United Kingdom Ltd., 17 Woodford Trade Estate, Southend Rd., Woodford Green, Essex IG8 8HF, UK**

## TIMKEN SUPER PRECISION (MPB)

7 Optical Ave., Keene, NH, 03431-0547

Tel: (603) 352-0310     Fax: (603) 355-4553     www.timken.com

*Mfr./sales/distribution bearings, tape guides and systems for missiles, etc.*

**Timken Aerospace UK Ltd., PO Box 667 Upper Villiers Street, Wolverhampton, West Midlands WV2 4UH, UK**

Tel: 44-1902-773300   Fax: 44-1902-771448

## THE TIMKEN COMPANY

1835 Dueber Ave. SW, PO Box 6927, Canton, OH, 44706-2798

Tel: (330) 438-3000     Fax: (330) 471-4118     www.timken.com

*Mfr. tapered roller bearings and quality alloy steels.*

**British Timken, Main Rd., Duston, Northampton NN5 6UL, UK**

## TITAN INDUSTRIAL CORPORATION

555 Madison Ave., 10th Floor, New York, NY, 10022

Tel: (212) 421-6700     Fax: (212) 421-6708

*Import and export steel products.*

**Titan Industrial Ltd., Camelot House, 76 Brompton Rd., London SW3, UK**

## TJX COMPANIES INC.

770 Cochituate Road, Framingham, MA, 01701

Tel: (508) 390-1000     Fax: (508) 390-2828     www.tjx.com

*Retail stores, catalog and mail order houses.*

**T. J. Maxx, Edward Hyde Bldg., 38 Clarendon Rd., Watford, Hertfershire WD1 1TX UK**

Tel: 44-1-92-347-5700

## TMP WORLDWIDE, INC.

622 Third Ave., New York, NY, 10017

Tel: (212) 351-7000     Fax: (212) 658-0540     www.tmpw.com

*#1 Yellow Pages agency and a leader in the recruitment and interactive advertising fields.*

**TMP Worldwide, Cardinal House, 39-40 Albemarie Street, London W1X 4ND, UK**

Tel: 44-207-872-1500

**TMP Worldwide, 47 London Road, St. Albans, Hertfordshire AL1 1LJ, UK**

**TMP Worldwide, Lilly House - 2/F, London W1R 9HD, UK**

**TMP Worldwide, 15 Station Road, Reading, Berkshire RG1 1LG, UK**

**TMP Worldwide eResourcing, 20 Soho Square, London W1V 5FD, UK**

## TODD-AO DVD CORPORATION

6601 Romaine Street, Hollywood, CA, 90038

Tel: (323) 962-5304     Fax: (323) 466-2327     www.todd-ao.com

*Provides post-production and distribution services for TV and film production companies, including sound services and visual effects.*

**Todd-AO UK, 13 Hawley Crescent, London, NW1 8NP, UK**

Tel: 44-207-884-7900   Contact: Graham Hall, Mng. Dir.

## TOKHEIM CORPORATION

PO Box 360, 10501 Corporate Drive, Fort Wayne, IN, 46845

Tel: (219) 470-4600     Fax: (219) 482-2677     www.tokheim.com

*Engaged in design, manufacture and service of electronic and mechanical petroleum marketing systems.*

**Tokheim UK Ltd., Unit 4 Cliveden Office Village, Lancaster Road High Wycombe, Buckinghamshire HP12 3YZ, UK**

## THE TOPPS COMPANY, INC.

1 Whitehall Street, New York, NY, 10004-2108

Tel: (212) 376-0300     Fax: (212) 376-0573     www.topps.com

*Mfr. entertainment products, principally collectible trading cards, confections, sticker collections, and comic books.*

**Topps (UK) Ltd., 18 Vincent Ave., Crownhill, Milton Keynes MK8 0AW UK**

Tel: 44-1908-800100    Fax: 44-1908-800200

## THE TORO COMPANY

8111 Lyndale Ave. South, Minneapolis, MN, 55420

Tel: (612) 888-8801     Fax: (612) 887-8258     www.toro.com

*Mfr. lawn and turf maintenance products and snow removal equipment.*

**Toro Wheel Horse UK, Unit 7 Heron Ind. Estate, Basingstoke Rd., Spencers Wood, Reading Berkshire UK**

## TOTES ISOTONER CORPORATION

9655 International Blvd., PO Box 465658, Cincinnati, OH, 45246

Tel: (513) 682-8200     Fax: (513) 682-8602     www.totes.com

*Mfr. rubber and plastic footwear, slippers, umbrellas.*

**Totes UK Limited, London, UK**

## TOWERS PERRIN

335 Madison Ave., New York, NY, 10017-4605

Tel: (212) 309-3400     Fax: (212) 309-0975     www.towers.com

*Management consulting services.*

**Kinsley Lord, Towers, Perrin, 10 Picadilly Circus, London W1V OAE, UK**

Tel: 44-207-379-4000    Fax: 44-207-806-6401

**Tillinghast Towers Perrin, Verulam Point, Station Way, St. Albans, Hertfordshire AL1 5HE UK**

Tel: 44-172-784-6161    Fax: 44-17-278-48869

**Tillinghast Towers Perrin, Castlewood House, 77-91 New Oxford St., London WC1A 1PX, UK**

Tel: 44-207-379-4411    Fax: 44-207-379-7478

**Tillinghast Towers Perrin, Lambourn Square, 2500 First Ave., Newbury Business Park, Newbury, Berkshire RG14 2PZ UK**

Tel: 44-163-555-0200    Fax: 44-163-541-322

## TOYS R US INC.

461 From Road, Paramus, NJ, 07652

Tel: (201) 262-7800     Fax: (201) 845-0973     www.toysrus.com

*Retail stores: toys and games, sporting goods, computer software, books, records.*

**Toys R Us Holdings PLC, Kenvon Dr., Forbury Ind. Estate, Reading, Berks RG1 3DH, UK**

## TRAMMELL CROW COMPANY

2200 Ross Ave., Ste. 3700, Dallas, TX, 75201

Tel: (214) 979-6100     Fax: (214) 979-6326     www.trammellcrow.com

*Commercial real estate company providing brokerage, property management, development, construction and retail services.*

**Trammell Crow Savills (TCS), 36 Gervis Road , Bournemouth Dorset BH1 3EF, UK**

Tel: 44-120-2314-151    Fax: 44-120-2214-181    Contact: Richard Buckley

**Trammell Crow Savills (TCS), 20 Grosvenor Hill, Berkeley Square, London W1X 0HQ, UK**

Tel: 44-207-4099-959    Fax: 44-207-4953-773    Contact: Edward Lyons, Pres. & CEO

## THE TRANE COMPANY

3600 Pammel Creek Road, La Crosse, WI, 54601

Tel: (608) 787-2000      Fax: (608) 787-4990      www.trane.com

*Mfr./distributor/service A/C systems and equipment.*

**Trane (UK) Ltd., 218 Rothbury Terrace, Heaton, Newcastle-upon-Tyne NE6 5DF, UK**

**Trane (UK) Ltd., Enterprise Trading Estate, Guinness Rd., Trafford Park, Manchester MI7 1SD UK**

**Trane (UK) Ltd., 60 Lenton Blvd., Nottingham N67 2EN, UK**

**Trane (UK) Ltd., Howard House, 55 Marsh Lane, Hampton-in-Arden, Solihull B92 0AJ, UK**

**Trane (UK) Ltd., Centenary House, 205 New John St. W., Hockley Birmingham B19 3TZ, UK**

**Trane (UK) Ltd., 162 Windmill Rd. W., Sunbury-on-Thames, Middlesex TW16 7HB, UK**

**Trane Central Africa, 1st Floor Unit 3 Priory Court, Tuscan Way, Camberly, Surrey GU15 3YX UK**

## TRANS WORLD AIRLINES INC.

515 North Sixth Street, St. Louis, MO, 63101

Tel: (314) 589-3000      Fax: (314) 589-3129      www.twa.com

*Air transport services.*

**Trans World Airlines Inc., 7 Regent St., London SW1Y 4LR, UK**

Tel: 44-207-345-333333

## TRANTER PHE, INC.

PO Box 2289, Wichita Falls, TX, 76306

Tel: (940) 723-7125      Fax: (706) 723-1131      www.tranter.com

*Mfr. heat exchangers.*

**SWEP Ltd., Chobham Ridges, The Maultway, Camberley, Surrey GU15 1QE, UK**

Tel: 44-1276-64221    Fax: 44-1276-64344

**SWEP Ltd., Lygon Ct., Hereward Rise, Halesowen, West Midlands B62 8AN, UK**

Tel: 44-121-550-7176    Fax: 44-121-550-7160

**SWEP Ltd., Hillgate Business Centre, Swallow St., Stockport SKI 3AU, UK**

Tel: 44-161-476-6915    Fax: 44-161-476-6916

## TREMCO INC.

3735 Green Road, Beachwood, OH, 44122-5718

Tel: (216) 292-5000      Fax: (216) 292-5041      www.tremcoroofing.com

*Mfr. protective coatings and sealants for building, maintenance and construction.*

**Tremco Ltd., 88 Bestobell Rd., Slough, Berkshire SL1 4SZ, UK**

Tel: 44-1753-691696    Contact: John Newens

## TRIBUNE COMPANY

435 North Michigan Ave., Chicago, IL, 60611

Tel: (312) 222-9100      Fax: (312) 222-9100      www.tribune.com

*Media company engaged in television and radio broadcasting, publishing and interactive.*

**TM/TribunePublishers Ltd., Lynton House, 7-12 Tavistock Sq., London WC1H 9LB, UK**

## TRICO PRODUCTS CORPORATION

817 Washington Street, Buffalo, NY, 14203

Tel: (716) 852-5700      Fax: (716) 853-6242      www.tricoproducts.com

*Mfr. windshield wiper systems and components.*

**Trico Folberth Ltd., Great West Rd., Brentford, Middlesex, UK**

## TRICON GLOBAL RESTAURANTS INC.

1441 Gardner Lane, Louisville, KY, 40213

Tel: (502) 874-1000      Fax: (502) 874-8315      www.triconglobal.com

*Owns and operates KFC, Taco Bell and Pizza Hut restaurant food chains.*

**Kentucky Fried Chicken (GB) Ltd., London, UK**

**Pizza Hut (UK) Ltd.,** London, UK

**Pizza Hut Intl (England) Ltd.,** London, UK

**Tricon Global, 32 Goldsworth Road, Working Surrey GU21 1JT, UK**

## TRIMBLE NAVIGATION LIMITED

645 N. Mary Ave., Sunnyvale, CA, 94086

Tel: (408) 481-8000     Fax: (408) 481-2000     www.trimble.com

*Design/mfr. electronic geographic instrumentation.*

**Trimble Navigation Europe Ltd., Trimble House, Meridian Office Park, Osborne Way, Hook, Hampshire RG27 9HX, UK**

Tel: 44-1256-746   Fax: 44-1256-760-148

## TRION INC.

101 McNeil Road, PO Box 760, Sanford, NC, 27331-0760

Tel: (919) 775-2201     Fax: (919) 774-8771     www.trioninc.com

*Mfr. commercial and residential air cleaners and humidifiers.*

**Trion Ltd., Reith Way, West Portway Industrial Estate, Andover, Hampshire SP1 03TY, UK**

Tel: 44-1264-364622   Fax: 44-1264-350983

## TRITON ENERGY LIMITED

6688 N. Central Expressway, Ste. 1400, Dallas, TX, 75206-3925

Tel: (214) 691-5200     Fax: (214) 691-0340     www.tritonenergy.com

*Provider of oil and gas services to the energy industry.*

**Triton Europe PLC, 38 Saville Row, London W1X 1AG, UK**

## TROPICANA PRODUCTS, INC.

1001 13th Avenue East, Bradenton, FL, 34208

Tel: (941) 747-4461     Fax: (941) 665-5330     www.tropicana.com

*Marketer and producer of branded juices, including Tropicana, Dole, Looza and Copella.*

**Copella Fruit Juices Ltd., Hill Farm Boxford Sudbury, Suffolk, C010 5 NY, UK**

**Tropicana U.K., Dorset House Regent Park, Leatherhead, Surrey KT 22 7PL, UK**

## TRUE NORTH COMMUNICATIONS INC.

101 East Erie Street, Chicago, IL, 60611

Tel: (312) 425-6500     Fax: (312) 425-5010     www.truenorth.com

*Holding company, advertising agency.*

**FCB Direct, 110 St. Martin's Lane, London WC2N 4DY, UK**

**FCB International, 110 St. Martin's Lane, London WC2N 4DY, UK**

## TruServ CORPORATION

8600 West Bryn Mawr, Chicago, IL, 60631-3505

Tel: (773) 695-5000     Fax: (773) 695-6541     www.truserv.com

*Dealer-owned, independent, hardware store cooperative.*

**TruServ Corporation, London, UK**

## TRW INC.

1900 Richmond Road, Cleveland, OH, 44124-3760

Tel: (216) 291-7000     Fax: (216) 291-7932     www.trw.com

*Electric and energy-related products, automotive and aerospace products, tools and fasteners.*

**British Pleuger Submersible Pumps Ltd., Station Rd., Coleshill Birmingham B46 1JH, UK**

**Cam Gears Ltd., 45 Wilbury Way, Hitchin, Hertfordshire SG4 OUT, UK**

**Hydrosteer, Arundel Rd., Luton, Bedfordshire UK**

**Nelson Stud Welding Div. Carr Fastener Co. Ltd., Bessell Lane, Stapleford, Nottingham NG9 7BX, UK**

**TRW, 46 Park Street, London W1Y 4DJ, UK**

Tel: 44-207-647-0610

TRW,  Hitchin Plant, 45 Wilbury Way, Hitchin Hertfordshire SG4 0TO, UK

TRW,  Clevedon Plant, Kenn Rd., Clevedon Avon BS21 GL5, UK

TRW Clifford Ltd.,  DuPont House 101, Vaughan Way, Leicester LE1 4SA, UK

TRW Datacom Intl.,  Park House, 191 London Rd., Isleworth Middlesex TW7 5BQ, UK

TRW Mission Ltd.,  Berkeley Sq. House, Berkeley Sq., London W1X 6JE, UK

TRW Reda, Div. TRW Mission Ltd.,  Ste. 8 Westminster Palace Gardens, 1/7 Artillery Row, London SW1, UK

TRW Spares,  Furnace Rd., Likeston, Derbyshire DE7 5EP, UK

United-Carr Supplies Ltd.,  112 Station Rd., Likeston, Derbyshire DE7 5LF, UK

Ventek Ltd.,  Station House, Harrow Rd., Wembley Middlesex HA9 6ER, UK

## THE TURNER CORPORATION

901 Main St., Ste. 4900, Dallas, TX, 75202

Tel: (214) 915-9600      Fax: (214) 915-9700      www.turnerconstruction.com

*Engaged in general construction and construction management.*

Turner Steiner International SA,  London, UK

## TUSCARORA INCORPORATED

800 Fifth Avenue, New Brighton, PA, 15066

Tel: (724) 843-8200      Fax: (724) 847-2140      www.tuscarora.com

*Mfr. custom molded, foam plastic.*

Tuscarora Limited UK,  33 Stannary Street, London SE11 4AA, UK

Tel: 44-207-735-8848

Tuscarora Limited UK,  Firth Road, Houstoun Industrial Estate, Livingston West Lothian EH54 5DJ, UK

Tel: 44-1506-434201

Tuscarora Limited UK,  Cornhill Close, Lodge Farm Industrial Estate, Northampton NN5 7UB, UK

Tel: 44-1604-759543

## TW METALS INC.

2211 Tubeway Ave., Los Angeles, CA, 90040

Tel: (213) 728-9101      Fax: (213) 728-5310      www.twmetals.com

*Distributor pipe, tube, valves, fittings and flanges.*

Components Ltd.,  Folkes Road - Hayes Trading Estate, Lye Stourbridge, West Midlands DY9 8RG, UK

Philip Cornes & Company Ltd.,  Lanner Building Clews Road, Redditch, Worcestershire B98 7ST, UK

## U.S. BANCORP PIPER JAFFRAY

222 South Ninth Street, Minneapolis, MN, 55402-3804

Tel: (612) 342-6000      Fax: (612) 342-1040      www.piperjaffray.com

*Investment Banking and securities brokerage services.*

U.S. Bancorp Piper Jaffray,  76 Cannon St., London EC4N 6AE, UK

Tel: 44-207-489-9902    Fax: 44-207-489-1128    Contact: B. Omlie, VP & D. Lingafelter, Mng. Dir.    Emp: 4

## U.S. OFFICE PRODUCTS COMPANY

1025 Thomas Jefferson St., NW, Ste. 600E, Washington, DC, 20007

Tel: (202) 339-6700      Fax: (202) 339-6720      www.usop.com

*Sales and distribution of educational products, office supplies and office related services.*

Dudley Stationery Limtied,  London, UK

**U.S. SAFETY**

8101 Lenexa Drive, Lenexa, KS, 66214

Tel: (913) 599-5555      Fax: (800) 252-5002      www.ussafety.com

*Design/development/mfr. personal protection equipment.*

**Parmelee Ltd., Middlemore Lane W., Redhouse Industrial Estate, Aldridge, Walsall WS9 8DZ, UK**

**UNIFI INC.**

7201 West Friendly Ave., Greensboro, NC, 27410-6237

Tel: (336) 294-4410      Fax: (336) 316-5422      www.unifi-inc.com

*Yarn spinning mills, throwing/winding mills.*

**Unifi Intl. Service Inc., St. Philipcourt Yard, Coleshill, Birmingham, W. Mids. B46 3AD, UK**

**UNION CARBIDE CORPORATION**

39 Old Ridgebury Road, Danbury, CT, 06817

Tel: (203) 794-2000      Fax: (203) 794-6269      www.unioncarbide.com

*Mfr. industrial chemicals, plastics and resins.*

**Union Carbide (UK) Ltd., 95 High St., Rickmansworth, Hertshire WD3 1RB, UK**

**UNIQUE BALANCE**

2225 Kerper Blvd., Dubuque, IA, 52001

Tel: (319) 583-9776      Fax: (319) 583-5281

*Mfr./sale of building hardware and sash balances.*

**Pomeroy Inc. (UK), Unit 5 Brookvale Estate, Brookvale Rd., Ulitton Birmingham B67 7AQ, UK**

Tel: 44-121-344-7833   Fax: 44-121-344-7834   Contact: Tom Ryder

**UNISTAR AIR CARGO, INC.**

500 East Thorndale Ave., Suite F, Wood Dale, IL, 60190

Tel: (630) 616-3900      Fax: (630) 616-3960      www.unistaraircargo.com

*Package distribution company offering air freight transportation options.*

**UniStar Air Cargo United Kingdom Agent, c/o Atlas Air , Atlas House, Central Way Feltham Middlesex, TW 14 OUU, UK**

Tel: 44-181-448-2749

**UNISYS CORPORATION.**

PO Box 500, Union Meeting Road, Blue Bell, PA, 19424

Tel: (215) 986-4011      Fax: (215) 986-6850      www.unisys.com

*Mfr./marketing/servicing electronic information systems.*

**BMX Information Systems UK Ltd., 31 Brentfield, Stonebridge Park, London NW10 8LS UK**

**Sperry Ireland Ltd., 31 Brentfield, Stonebridge Park, London NW10 8LS, UK**

**Sperry Rand Ltd., 31 Brentfield, Stonebridge Park, London NW10 8LS, UK**

**Unisys Europe-Africa Ltd., Bakers Court, Bakers Road, Uxbridge UB8 1RG, UK**

**Unisys Ltd., 31 Brentfield, Stonebridge Park, London NW10 8LS, UK**

**UNITED AIRLINES INC.**

1200 E. Algonquin Rd., Chicago, IL, 60007

Tel: (847) 700-4000      Fax: (847) 700-4081      www.ual.com

*Air transportation, passenger and freight services.*

**United Airlines, 718 Conduit St., London W1, UK**

**UNITED ASSET MANAGEMENT CORPORATION**

One International Place, 44th Fl., Boston, MA, 02110

Tel: (617) 330-8900      Fax: (617) 330-1133      www.uam.com

*Investment management services.*

**Alpha Global Fixed Income Managers, Clutha House, 10 Story's Gate, London, SW 1 P 3AY, UK**

**Murray Johnstone Ltd., Birmingham, UK**
Contact: John Graham, Dir.

## UNITED ELECTRIC CONTROLS COMPANY
PO Box 9143, Watertown, MA, 02172-9143
Tel: (617) 926-1000      Fax: (617) 926-4354      www.ueonline.com
*Mfr./sale electro-mechanical and electronic controls and recorders.*
**United Electric Controls UK, Sulby House, North St., Sudbury Suffolk CO10 6RE, UK**

## UNITED PARCEL SERVICE, INC.
55 Glenlake Parkway, NE, Atlanta, GA, 30328
Tel: (404) 828-6000      Fax: (404) 828-6593      www.ups.com
*International package-delivery service.*
**UPS Ltd. -Head Office, UPS House, Forest Rd., Feltham, Middlesex TW13 7DY UK**
Tel: 44-345-877-877

## UNITED PRESS INTERNATIONAL
1510 H Street NW, Washington, DC, 20005
Tel: (202) 898-8000      Fax: (202) 898-8057      www.upi.com
*Collection and distributor of news, newspictures, financial data.*
**United Press Intl., 8 Bouverie St., London EC4Y 8BB, UK**

## UNITED STATES SURGICAL CORPORATION
150 Glover Ave., Norwalk, CT, 06856
Tel: (203) 845-1000      Fax: (203) 847-0635      www.ussurg.com
*Mfr./development/market surgical staplers, laparoscopic instruments and sutures.*
**Auto Suture Co. UK, Attn: British Office, U.S. Surgical, 150 Glover Avenue, Norwalk CT 06856**
**Auto Suture UK Ltd., Attn: British Office, U.S. Surgical, 150 Glover Avenue, Norwalk CT 06856**

## UNITED TECHNOLOGIES CORPORATION
One Financial Plaza, Hartford, CT, 06103
Tel: (860) 728-7000      Fax: (860) 728-7979      www.utc.com
*Mfr. aircraft engines, elevators, A/C, auto equipment, space and military electronic and rocket propulsion systems. Products include Pratt and Whitney, Otis elevators, Carrier heating and air conditioning and Sikorsky helicopters.*
**Caricor Ltd., Knightsbridge House, 197 Knightsbridge, London SW7 1RB UK**
**Otis Elevator Co. Ltd., Otis Building, 43/59 Clapham Rd., London SW9 0JZ, UK**
**Porvair Ltd., Estuary Rd., Kings Lynn, Norfolk PE30 2HS, UK**

## UNITRODE CORPORATION
7 Continental Blvd., Merrimack, NH, 03054
Tel: (603) 424-2410      Fax: (603) 429-8771      www.unitrode.com
*Mfr. electronic components (analog/linear and mixed-signal).*
**Unitrode UK Ltd., 6 Cresswell Park, Blackheath, London SE3 9RD, UK**
Tel: 44-181-318-1431   Fax: 44-181-318-2549   Contact: David Wells, Dir.   Emp: 4

## UNIVERSAL CORPORATION
1501 N. Hamilton Street, Richmond, VA, 23230
Tel: (804) 359-9311      Fax: (804) 254-3582      www.universalcorp.com
*Holding company for tobacco and commodities.*
**Universal Leaf (UK) Ltd., 25 Coombs Rd., Kingston-upon-Thames, Surrey KT2 7AB, UK**
**Universal Leaf Services Ltd., 2 Alric Ave., London SW3, UK**

## UNIVERSAL INSTRUMENTS

90 Bevier Street, S. Dock, Binghamton, NY, 13904

Tel: (607) 779-7522　　Fax: (607) 779-7971　　www.uic.com

*Mfr./sales of instruments for electronic circuit assembly.*

**Universal Instruments Electronics Ltd., Redhill, Surrey, UK**

Tel: 44-1737-77911　Fax: 44-1737-779710

## UNIVERSAL WEATHER & AVIATION INC.

8787 Tallyho Road, Houston, TX, 77061

Tel: (713) 944-1622　　Fax: (713) 943-4650　　www.univ-wea.com

*Provides service management, and worldwide weather and communications to the corporate aviation community.*

**Universal Aviation (UK) Ltd., Stansted Airport Bldg. 56D, Stansted, Essex CM24 1QH, UK**

Tel: 44-1279-680-349　Fax: 44-1279-680-372

## UNOCAL CORPORATION

2141 Rosecrans Ave., Ste. 4000, El Segundo, CA, 90245

Tel: (310) 726-7600　　Fax: (310) 726-7817　　www.unocal.com

*Engaged in oil and gas exploration and production.*

**Unocal (UK) Ltd., 32 Cadbury Rd., Sunbury on Thames, Middlesex TW16 7LU, UK**

## UNOVA INC.

21900 Burbank Blvd., Woodland Hills, CA, 91367-7418

Tel: (818) 992-3000　　Fax: (818) 992-2848　　www.unova.com

*Automated data collection, mobile computing and manufacturing systems.*

**Unova Inc., London, UK**

## UNUMPROVIDENT

2211 Congress Street, Portland, ME, 04122

Tel: (207) 770-2211　　Fax: (207) 770-4510　　www.unum.com

*Disability and special risk insurance.*

**UNUM Life Insurance Co. Ltd., Hamilton House, 1 Temple Avenue, Victoria Embankment, London EC4Y 0HA, UK**

Tel: 44-1-306-887766　Fax: 44-1-306-887504　Contact: Martyn Field, Mng. Dir.

**UNUM Limited U.K., Milton Court, Dorking, Surrey RH4 3LZ, UK**

Tel: 44-1-306-887766　Fax: 44-1-306-887504　Contact: Martyn Field, Mng. Dir.

**UNUM Limited UK, Swan House - 37/39 High Holborn, London WC1 V6AA, UK**

## UOP LLC.

25 East Algonquin Road, Des Plaines, IL, 60017

Tel: (847) 391-2000　　Fax: (847) 391-2253　　www.uop.com

*Engaged in developing and commercializing technology for license to the oil refining, petrochemical and gas processing industries.*

**UOP (UK) Ltd., Weedon Rd., Industrial Estate, Northampton, UK**

**UOP Ltd., 'Liongate' Ladymead, Guildford, Surrey GU1 1AT, UK**

Tel: 44-1483-304-848　Fax: 44-1483-304-863

## UPRIGHT INC.

1775 Park Street, Selma, CA, 93662

Tel: (209) 891-5200　　Fax: (209) 896-9012　　www.upright.com

*Mfr. aerial work platforms and telescopic handlers.*

**UpRight UK Ltd., Telford, UK**

## URBAN OUTFITTERS INC.

1809 Walnut St., Philadelphia, PA, 19103

Tel: (215) 564-2313      Fax: (215) 568-1549      www.urbanoutfitters.com

*Retail stores for young adults.*

**Urban Outfitters, Inc.,  36-38 Kensington High St., London, UK**

Tel: 44-207-761-1001

## UROPLASTY INC.

2718 Summer Street NE, Minneapolis, MN, 55413-2820

Tel: (612) 378-1180      Fax: (612) 378-2027      www.uroplasty.com

*Mfr. urology products.*

**Bioplasty Ltd.,  Unit 3 Woodside Business Park, Whitley Wood Lane, Reading, Berkshire RG2 8LW UK**

## URS CORPORATION

100 California Street, Ste. 500, San Francisco, CA, 94111-4529

Tel: (415) 774-2700      Fax: (415) 398-1904      www.urscorp.com

*Provides planning, design and construction management services, pollution control and hazardous waste management.*

**URS (Dames & Moore),  London, UK**

## URSCHEL LABORATORIES INC.

2503 Calumet Ave., PO Box 2200, Valparaiso, IN, 46384-2200

Tel: (219) 464-4811      Fax: (219) 462-3879      www.urschel.com

*Design/mfr. precision food processing equipment.*

**Urschel Intl. Ltd.,  6 Groby Trading Estate, Leicester LE6 0FH, UK**

## USAA

9800 Fredericksburg Road, San Antonio, TX, 78288-3533

Tel: (210) 498-2211      Fax: (210) 498-9940      www.usaa.com

*Provides financial services, life, property and casualty insurance and consumer sales services primarily to military and U.S. government personnel and their families.*

**USAA,  London, UK**

## USFILTER WALLACE & TIERNAN

1901 West Garden Road, Vineland, NJ, 08360

Tel: (609) 507-9000      Fax: (609) 507-4125      www.usfwt.com

*Mfr. disinfections and chemical feed equipment.*

**USFilter Wallace & Tiernan Limited,  Priory Works, Tonbridge, Kent TN11 0QL, UK**

Tel: 44-732-771777   Fax: 44-732-771800

## UTILICORP UNITED INC.

PO Box 13287, Kansas City, MO, 64199-3287

Tel: (816) 421-6600      Fax: (816) 472-6281      www.utilicorp.com

*Electric and gas utility.*

**United Gas Ltd.,  London UK**

## UTILX CORPORATION

22820 Russell Rd., PO Box 97009, Kent, WA, 98064-9709

Tel: (253) 395-0200      Fax: (253) 395-1040      www.utilx.com

*Mfr. utility construction machinery and guided boring systems and provides cable restoration services.*

**FlowMole Ltd.,  33 Maylan Rd., Earlstrees Industrial Estate, Corby, Northamptonshire NN17 4DR UK**

Tel: 44-1536-400141   Fax: 44-1536-400142   Contact: Robert Bailey, Mng. Dir   Emp: 25

## UUNET

22001 Loudoun County Pkwy., Ashburn, VA, 20147

Tel: (703) 206-5600    Fax: (703) 206-5601    www.uu.net

*World's largest Internet service provider; World Wide Web hosting services, security products and consulting services to businesses, professionals, and on-line service providers.*

**UUNET UK, 332 Science Park, Milton Rd., Cambridge CB 4 4BZ, UK**

Tel: 44-1223 250100   Fax: 44-1223-2500335   Contact: Richard Keyes, Acting Mng. Dir.   Emp: 400

**UUNET UK, Internet House, 332 Science Park, Cambridge CB4 0BZ, UK**

## VALENITE INC

31751 Research Park Dr., Madison Heights, MI, 48071-9636

Tel: (248) 589-1000    Fax: (248) 597-4820    www.valenite.com

*Cemented carbide, high speed steel, ceramic and diamond cutting tool products, etc.*

**Valenite-Modco (UK) Ltd., Unit 12 Alston Dr., Bradwell Abbey Industrial Estate, Milton Keynes MK13 9HA, UK**

## VALHI INC.

5430 LBJ Freeway, Ste. 1700, Dallas, TX, 75240

Tel: (972) 233-1700    Fax: (972) 448-1445

*Mfr. titanium products and computer office components.*

**Kronos UK Ltd., Winslow Cheshire, UK**

## VALSPAR CORPORATION

1101 South Third Street, Minneapolis, MN, 55415-1259

Tel: (612) 332-7371    Fax: (612) 375-7723    www.valspar.com

*Produce paint, varnish and allied products.*

**Valspar Inc., London UK**

## VANTON PUMP & EQUIPMENT CORPORATION

201 Sweetland Ave., Hillside, NJ, 07205

Tel: (908) 688-4216    Fax: (908) 686-9314    www.vanton.com

*Mfr. non-metallic rotary, horizontal and vertical pumps and accessories for corrosive, abrasive and chemically pure fluids.*

**Vanton Pumps Ltd., 26 Sandown Crescent, Unit 6 Radnor Industrial Estate, Congleton, Cheshire CW12 4XL, UK**

Tel: 44-12602-77040   Fax: 44-12602-280605   Contact: Shaun Manley, CEO   Emp: 15

## VAPOR CORPORATION

6420 West Howard Street, Niles, IL, 60714-3395

Tel: (847) 967-8300    Fax: (847) 965-9874    www.vapordoors.com

*Mfr. bus and rail transit automatic door systems, railcar/locomotive relays and contractors, vehicle ID systems.*

**Vapor UK, 28 Springdale Ct., Mickleover Derby, Derby DE3 5SW, UK**

Tel: 44-1332-518788   Fax: 44-1332-519071   Contact: Anthony J. Walsh

**Vapor UK, 2nd Avenue Centrum 100, Burton on Trent, Staffordshire DE14 2WF, UK**

Tel: 44-1283-743300   Fax: 44-1283-743333

## VARIAN MEDICAL SYSTEMS, INC.

3050 Hansen Way, Palo Alto, CA, 94304-100

Tel: (650) 493-4000    Fax: (650) 424-5358    www.varian.com

*Mfr. microwave tubes and devices, analytical instruments, semiconductor process and medical equipment, vacuum systems.*

**Varian Medical Systems, 28 Manor Rd., Walton-on-Thames, Surrey KT12 2QF, UK**

**Varian Medical Systems -TEM Limited, Gatwick Road, Crawley, West Sussex RH10 2RG, UK**

Tel: 44-1293-601-272   Fax: 44-1293-534-570

## VEECO INSTRUMENTS INC.

Terminal Drive, Plainview, NY, 11803

Tel: (516) 349-8300     Fax: (516) 349-9079     www.veeco.com

*Mfr. surface profiler, atomic force microscopes, leak and plating thickness detectors and semiconductor products.*

**Veeco Instruments Ltd., Unit 8 Colne Way Court, Colne Way, Watford, Herts WD2 4NE, UK**

Tel: 44-1923-210044    Fax: 44-1923-235130

## VELCRO USA INC.

406 Brown Avenue, Manchester, NH, 03108

Tel: (603) 669-4892     Fax: (603) 669-9271     www.velcro.com

*Mfr./sales of velcro brand hook and loop fasteners, plastic buckles and metal hardware and cable control straps.*

**Velcro Limited, 1 Aston Way, Middlewich Industrial Estate, Middlewich Cheshire CW10 0HS, UK**

Tel: 44-1606-738806

## VELSICOL CHEMICAL CORPORATION

10400 West Higgins Road, Ste. 600, Rosemont, IL, 60018-3728

Tel: (847) 298-9000     Fax: (847) 298-9014     www.velsicol.com

*Produces high performance specialty chemicals based on benzoic acid and cyclo pentadiene.*

**Velsicol Chemical Ltd., 8 Cedarwood, Chineham Business Park, Basingstoke, Hampshire RE24 8WD, UK**

Tel: 44-1256-464649    Fax: 44-1256-817744    Contact: David Frederick, Exec. Mng. Dir.

## VERITAS DGC INC.

3701 Kirby Drive, Houston, TX, 77096

Tel: (713) 512-8300     Fax: (713) 512-8701     www.veritasdgc.com

*Geophysical services.*

**Veritas DGC Ltd., Crompton Way, Manor Royal Estate, Crawley, West Sussex RH 10 2QR UK**

Tel: 44-1293-44300    Fax: 44-1293-443010

## VERITY, INC.

894 Ross Drive, Sunnyvale, CA, 94089

Tel: (408) 541-1500     Fax: (408) 541-1600     www.verity.com

*Mfr. software to simplify management of information.*

**Verity UK Ltd., The Pavilions - Kiln Park Business Ctr., Kiln Lane, Epsom KT17 1JG, UK**

Tel: 44-1372-74 70 76

## VERIZON

1095 Ave. of the Americas, New York, NY, 10036

Tel: (212) 395-2121     Fax: (212) 395-1285     www.verizon.com

*Telecommunications.*

**Cable & Wireless Communications, London, UK**

## VERIZON COMMUNICATIONS INC.

1255 Corporate Drive, Irving, TX, 75038

Tel: (972) 507-5000     Fax: (972) 507-5002     www.gte.com

*Engaged in wireline and wireless communications.*

**Cable & Wireless Plc & NTL, London, UK**

**FLAG Telecom Holdings Limited, 103 Mount Street, London W1Y 5HE, UK**

Contact: Andres B. Bande

**VERMEER MANUFACTURING COMPANY**

PO Box 200, Pella, IA, 50219-0200

Tel: (515) 628-3141    Fax: (515) 621-7730    www.vermeer.com.

*Mfr. agricultural and construction equipment.*

**B-Trac Equipment Ltd., 45-51 Rixon Road, Wellingborough, Northants NN8 4BA, UK**

Tel: 44-1-933-274400    Fax: 44-1-933-274403    Contact: Martin Wright

**VIACOM INC.**

1515 Broadway, 28th Fl., New York, NY, 10036-5794

Tel: (212) 258-6000    Fax: (212) 258-6358    www.viacom.com

*Communications, publishing and entertainment.*

**Prentice Hall Intl. (UK) Ltd., 66 Wood Lane End, Hemel Hempstead, Herts. HP2 4RG, UK**

**Viacom Intl. Ltd., 40 Conduit St., London W1R 9FB, UK**

**VIAD CORPORATION**

1850 North Central Ave., Phoenix, AZ, 85077

Tel: (602) 207-4000    Fax: (602) 207-5900    www.viad.com

*Provides convention, exhibit design and production services.*

**SDD Exhibitions, Div. Exhibitgroup/Giltspur, Marlborough House, Marlborough Road, Sheffield, UK**

Contact: Charles J. Corsentino, Pres.

**VICON INDUSTRIES INC.**

89 Arkay Dr., Hauppauge, NY, 11788

Tel: (631) 952-2288    Fax: (631) 951-2288    www.vicon-cctv.com

*Engaged in design, engineering and production of high quality video systems and equipment.*

**Vicon Industies (UK) Ltd., Brunel Way, Fareham, Hampshire PO15 5TX, UK**

**VICOR CORPORATION**

23 Frontage Road, Andover, MA, 01810

Tel: (978) 470-2900    Fax: (978) 749-3536    www.vicr.com

*Designs, manufactures, and markets modular power components and complete configurable and custom power systems.*

**Vicor UK, Coliseum Business Centre, Riverside Way, Camberley Surrey GU15 3YL, UK**

Tel: 44-1276-678222

**VIDEO DISPLAY CORPORATION**

1868 Tucker Industrial Road, Tucker, GA, 30084

Tel: (770) 938-2080    Fax: (770) 493-3903    www.videodisplay.com

*Mfr./rebuild/distribute video display components.*

**Video Display Europe, Ltd., 7 Arden Business Centre, Alcester Warkshire B49 6HW, UK**

Tel: 44-1789-766664    Fax: 44-1789-764234

**THE VIKING CORPORATION**

210 N. Industrial Park Rd., Hastings, MI, 49058

Tel: (616) 945-9501    Fax: (616) 945-9599    www.vikingcorp.com

*Mfr. fire extinguishing equipment.*

**Lansdale Viking Limited, Churchtown, Belton Doncaster, South Yorkshire DN9 1PB, UK**

Tel: 44-1427 875999    Fax: 44-1427 875998

**VIKING ELECTRONICS**

1531 Industrial St., Hudson, WI, 54016

Tel: (715) 386-8861    Fax: (715) 386-4344    www.vikingelectronics.com

*Mfr./sales of electronic interconnect systems.*

**Viking Connectors (UK) Ltd., Chatsworth House, Portland Close, Dunstable, Beds. LU5 4AW, UK**

## VIKING OFFICE PRODUCTS

950 West 190th Street, Torrance, CA, 90502

Tel: (310) 225-4500    Fax: (310) 324-2396    www.vikingop.com

*International direct marketer of office products, computer supplies, business furniture and stationery.*

**Viking Direct, Ltd., Bersom Industrial Park, Tolwell Rd., Leicester LE4 1BR, UK**

Tel: 44-112-340404   Fax: 44-1162-364042   Contact: Keithr Cain, Mgr.   Emp: 840

## VINSON & ELKINS LP

2300 First City Tower, 1001 Fannin, Houston, TX, 77002-6760

Tel: (713) 758-2222    Fax: (713) 758-2346    www.vinson-elkins.com

*International law firm.*

**Vinson & Elkins LP, 45 King William Street, London EC4R 9AN, UK**

Tel: 44-20-7618-6000    Contact: Douglas B. Glass

## VISHAY INTERTECHNOLOGY INC.

63 Lincoln Hwy., Malvern, PA, 19355

Tel: (610) 644-1300    Fax: (610) 296-0657    www.vishay.com

*Mfr. resistors, strain gages, capacitors, inductors, printed circuit boards.*

**Measurements Group UK Ltd., Stroudley Rd., Basingstoke RG24 0FW, UK**

**Vishay Components (UK) Ltd., Ayton Rd., Wymondham, Norfold NR18 0RA, UK**

**Vishay Components (UK) Ltd., Pallion Industrial Estate, Sunderland SR4 6SU, UK**

Tel: 44-191-514-4155

## VISHAY VITRAMON INC.

PO Box 544, Bridgeport, CT, 06601

Tel: (203) 268-6261    Fax: (203) 261-4446    www.vitramon.com

*Ceramic capacitors.*

**Vitramon Ltd., Wycombe Lane, Wooburn Green, Bucks, UK**

## VITAL SIGNS, INC.

20 Campus Road, Totowa, NJ, 07512

Tel: (973) 790-1330    Fax: (973) 790-3307    www.vital-signs.com

*Mfr. disposable medical products for critical care procedures.*

**Vital Signs Ltd., Bath Avon, UK**

## VIVITAR CORPORATION

1280 Rancho Conejo Blvd, Newbury Park, CA, 91320

Tel: (805) 498-7008    Fax: (805) 498-5086    www.vivitar.com

*Mfr. photographic equipment, electronic supplies.*

**Vivitar UK Ltd., Vivitar House, Ashfield Trading Estate, Nuffield Wy., Abington, Oxon OX14 1RP, UK**

## VIZACOM INC.

300 Frank W. Burr Blvd., 7th Fl., Teaneck, NJ, 07666

Tel: (201) 928-1001    Fax: (201) 928-1003    www.vizacom.com

*Mfr. graphics applications software.*

**Serif Europe Ltd., Unit 12 Wilford Industrial Estate, Nottingham NG11 7EP, UK**

Tel: 44-115-914-2000

## VOLT INFORMATION SCIENCES, INC.

1221 Ave. of the Americas, 47th Fl., New York, NY, 10020-1579

Tel: (212) 704-2400    Fax: (212) 704-2417    www.volt.com

*Staffing services and telecommunication services.*

**Gatton Volt Computing Group, Gatton Place - St. Matthews Road, Redhill Surrey, RH1 1TA, UK**

**Gatton Volt Computing Group, Artillery House, 11-19 Artillery Row, London SW1P 1RT, UK**

Volt Autologic Ltd., Alban Park, Hatfield Rd., St. Albans, Herts AL4 0JJ, UK

Volt Management Corp. Technical Services, 150 Minories, London EC3N 1LS, UK

Tel: 44-1712-642246

VoltDelta Europe Ltd., Dolphin House, Windmill Rd., Sunbury on Thames, Middlesex TW 16 7HT UK

Tel: 44-1932-75555

## VTEL (VIDEOTELECOM CORPORATION )

108 Wild Basin Road, Austin, TX, 78746

Tel: (512) 314-2700      Fax: (512) 314-2792      www.vtel.com

*Design/mfr. long-distance interactive video communications products.*

VTEL Europe Ltd., The Atrium Court, Apex Plaza, Reading RG1 1AX, UK

Tel: 44-118-955-3200

## WACHOVIA CORPORATION

100 North Main Street, PO Box, Winston-Salem, NC, 27150

Tel: (336) 770-5000      Fax: (336) 770-5931      www.wachovia.com

*Engaged in commercial and retail banking services.*

Wachovia Bank of North Carolina, 7 Albemarle St., London W1X 3HF, UK

## WACKENHUT CORPORATION

4200 Wackenhut Dr., Ste. 100, Palm Beach Gardens, FL, 33410

Tel: (561) 622-5656      Fax: (561) 691-6736      www.wackenhut.com

*Security systems and services.*

Wackenhut UK Ltd. (WUK), 875 Sidcup Rd., New Etham, London SE9 3PP, UK

Tel: 44-181-850-4647  Fax: 44-181-850-0612

## WAHL CLIPPER CORPORATION

2902 N. Locust Street, Sterling, IL, 61081

Tel: (815) 625-6525      Fax: (815) 625-1193      www.wahlclipper.com

*Mfr. hair clippers, beard and mustache trimmers, shavers, pet clippers and soldering irons.*

Wahl Europe Ltd., Herne Bay Trade Park, Sea St., Herne Bay, Kent CT6 8SZ, UK

## WALBRO CORPORATION, TI GROUP AUTOMOTIVE

6242 Garfield Ave., Cass City, MI, 48726-1325

Tel: (517) 872-2131      Fax: (517) 872-3090      www.walbro.com

*Mfr. motor vehicle accessories and parts, automotive fluid carrying systems.*

TI Group Automotive Systems, Tenth Avenue, Deeside Industrial Park, Deeside Flintshire CH5 2UA, UK

## WALKER INTERACTIVE SYSTEMS, INC.

303 Second St., Marathon Plaza 3 N., San Francisco, CA, 94107

Tel: (415) 495-8811      Fax: (415) 957-1711      www.walker.com.

*Provider of premier financial software solutions for large and medium-size enterprises.*

Walker Interactive Systems Pty Ltd., The Gatehouse, Gatehouse Way, Aylesbury Buckinghamshire HP19 3DL, UK

Tel: 44-1296-432951  Fax: 44-1296-398964  Contact: Paul Lord, Sr. VP    Emp: 125

## WAL-MART STORES INC.

702 SW 8th Street, Bentonville, AR, 72716-8611

Tel: (501) 273-4000      Fax: (501) 273-1917      www.wal-mart.com

*Retailer.*

ASDA Group Limited, ASDA House - Southbank, Great Wilson St. Leeds, LS11 5AD UK

Tel: 44-113-243-5435  Fax: 44-113-241-8666  Contact: Allan L. Leighton, CEO

## WARNACO INC.

90 Park Ave., New York, NY, 10016

Tel: (212) 661-1300　　Fax: (212) 687-0480　　www.warnaco.com

*Mfr./sales intimate apparel and men's and women's sportswear.*

**Warner's (UK) Ltd., Blenheim Ind. Park., Dabell Ave., Nottingham NG6 8WA, UK**

**Warner's (UK) Ltd., Montague Row, Baker St., London W1H 1AB, UK**

## WARNER BROS INTERNATIONAL TELEVISION

4000 Warner Boulevard, Bldg.170, 3rd Fl., Burbank, CA, 91522

Tel: (818) 954-6000　　Fax: (818) 977-4040　　www.wbitv.com

*Distributor TV programming and theatrical features.*

**Warner Bros. Intl. Television, 135 Wardour St., London W1V 4AP, UK**

Tel: 44-207-494-3710　Fax: 44-207-465-4207　Contact: John Berger, VP

## WARNER ELECTRIC BRAKE & CLUTCH COMPANY

449 Gardner St., South Beloit, IL, 61080

Tel: (815) 389-3771　　Fax: (815) 389-2582　　www.warnernet.com

*Global supplier of Power Transmission and Motion Control Solution Systems; automotive, industry brakes, and clutches.*

**Warner Electric, Div. Dana Ltd., St. Helen Aukland, Bishop Auckland, Co. Durham DL14 9AA, UK**

Tel: 44-1388-45-8877

## WARNER-JENKINSON COMPANY, INC.

2526 Baldwin Street, St. Louis, MO, 63106

Tel: (314) 889-7600　　Fax: (314) 658-7305

*Mfr. synthetic and natural colors for food, drugs and cosmetics.*

**Warner-Jenkinson Europe Ltd., Oldmedow Rd., Hardwick Industrial Estate, King's Lynn, Norfolk PE30 4JJ, UK**

## WARRANTECH CORPORATION

300 Atlantic Street, Stamford, CT, 06901

Tel: (203) 975-1100　　Fax: (203) 975-1148　　www.warrantech.com

*Engaged in third party insurance in administering service warranties for manufacturers.*

**Warrantech UK Limited, London, UK**

## WASHINGTON GROUP INTERNATIONAL, INC.

720 Park Blvd., PO Box 73, Boise, ID, 83729

Tel: (208) 386-5000　　Fax: (208) 386-7186　　www.wgint.com

*Engaged in engineering and construction.*

**Morrison Knudsen Limited, Spencer House Unit 93, Dewhurst Road, Birchwood, Warrington Cheshire WA3 7PG, UK**

Tel: 44-1925-854500　Fax: 44-1925-854599

**Washington Group International, Inc., C.I. Tower - St. Georges Square, High Street New Malden, Surrey UK**

Tel: 44-20-8336-5100

## THE WASHINGTON POST COMPANY

1150 15th St. NW, Washington, DC, 20071

Tel: (202) 334-6000　　Fax: (202) 334-4536　　www.washpostco.com

*Engaged in magazine publishing, cable and television broadcasting, educational services and the Internet.*

**International Herald Tribune, 40 Marsh Wall, London E14 9TP, UK**

Tel: 44-207-510-5700

## WASSERSTEIN PERELLA & CO., INC.

31 West 52nd Street, New York, NY, 10019

Tel:  (212) 969-2700        Fax:  (212) 969-7969        www.wassersteinperella.com

*Engaged in international investment banking and financial services.*

**Wasserstein Perella & Co., Ltd.,  3 Burlington Garden, London W1X 1LE, UK**

Tel: 44-207-446-8000   Fax: 44-207-494-2053

## WASTE MANAGEMENT, INC.

1001 Fannin Street, Ste. 4000, Houston, TX, 77002

Tel:  (713) 512-6200        Fax:  (713) 512-6299        www.wastemanagement.com

*Environmental services and disposal company; collection, processing, transfer and disposal facilities.*

**UK Waste Management Ltd.,  Gate House Castle Estate, Turnpike Rd., High Wycombe, Buckinghamshire HP12 3NR UK**

**Waste Management Intl. PLC,  3 Shortlands, Hammersmith International Centre, London W6 8RX, UK**

Tel: 44-181-563-7000   Fax: 44-181-563-6300   Contact: Bill Johnson, Pres.

## WATERBURY FARREL TECHNOLOGIES

60 Fieldstone Court, Cheshire, CT, 06410

Tel:  (203) 272-3271        Fax:  (203) 271-0487        www.anker-holth.com

*Machine tools and metal working machinery.*

**Waterbury Farrel Ltd.,  Station Tower Block, Station Sq., Coventry CV1 2GF, UK**

## WATERS CORPORATION

34 Maple Street, Milford, MA, 01757

Tel:  (508) 478-2000        Fax:  (508) 872-1990        www.waters.com

*Mfr./distribute liquid chromatographic instruments and test and measurement equipment.*

**Waters (UK) Ltd.,  Millipore House, 11-15 Peterborough Rd., Harrow, Middlesex HA1 2YH, UK**

**Waters (UK) Ltd.,  Millipore House, Abbey Rd., London NW10 7SP, UK**

**Waters Associates Ltd.,  324 Chester Rd., Hartford, Northwich, Cheshire CW8 2AH, UK**

## WATLOW ELECTRIC MFG. COMPANY

12001 Lackland Rd., St. Louis, MO, 63146-4039

Tel:  (314) 878-4600        Fax:  (314) 434-1020        www.watlow.com

*Mfr. electrical heating units, electronic controls, thermocouple wire, metal-sheathed cable, infrared sensors.*

**Watlow Ltd.,  Robey Close, Linby Industrial Estate, Linby Nottingham NG15 8AA, UK**

Tel: 44-115-964-0777   Fax: 44-14-115-964-0071

## WATSON WYATT & COMPANY HOLDINGS

6707 Democracy Blvd., Ste. 800, Bethesda, MD, 20817

Tel:  (301) 581-4600        Fax:  (301) 581-4937        www.watsonwyatt.com

*Creates compensation and benefits programs for major corporations.*

**Watson Wyatt & Co.,  21 Tothill Street, London SW1H 9LL, UK**

Tel: 44-207-222-8033   Fax: 44-207-222-9182   Contact: Babloo Ramamurthy

## WATTS INDUSTRIES, INC.

815 Chestnut Street, North Andover, MA, 01845-6098

Tel:  (978) 688-1811        Fax:  (978) 688-5841        www.wattsind.com

*Designs/mfr./sales of industry valves and safety control products.*

**Watts UK Limited,  St. Richards Road, Evesham, Worcestershire WR11 6XJ, UK**

## WD-40 COMPANY

1061 Cudahy Place, San Diego, CA, 92110-3998

Tel: (619) 275-1400    Fax: (619) 275-5823    www.wd40.com

*Mfr. branded multiple-purpose lubrication, protection and general maintenance products.*

**WD-40 Company Ltd. (UK),  PO Box 440, Brick Close, Kiln Farm, Milton Keynes MK11 3LF UK**

## WEATHERFORD INTERNATIONAL, INC.

5 Post Oak Blvd, Ste. 1760, Houston, TX, 77227-3415

Tel: (713) 287-8400    Fax: (713) 963-9785    www.weatherford.com

*Oilfield services, products and equipment; mfr. marine cranes for oil and gas industry.*

**Weatherford Intl. Inc.,  Harfreys Road Harfreys Industrial Estate Great Yarmouth NR31 0LS, Norfolk UK**

Tel: 44-1-493-657516   Fax: 44-1-493-653925

## JERVIS B. WEBB COMPANY

34375 W.Twelve Mile Rd., Farmington Hills, MI, 48331

Tel: (248) 553-1220    Fax: (248) 553-1237    www.jervisbwebb.com

*Mfr. integrators of material handling systems.*

**Jervis B. Webb Co. Ltd.,  Dawson Rd., Mount Farm, Milton Keynes MK1 1QY UK**

## WEBER-STEPHEN PRODUCTS COMPANY

200 E. Daniels Road, Palatine, IL, 60067-6266

Tel: (847) 934-5700    Fax: (847) 934-0291    www.weberbq.com

*Mfr./sales Weber cooking systems and barbeque and gas grills.*

**Erin Gardena/Weber-Stephen, U.K. Ltd., Astonia House, Baldock, Herts. SG7 6UK, UK**

Tel: 44-1462-89-6989   Fax: 44-1462-89-3598

## WEDCO INC.

PO Box 397, Bloomsbury, NJ, 08804

Tel: (908) 479-4181    Fax: (908) 479-6622    www.icoinc.com

*Plastics grinding and related services, machinery and equipment for plastics industry.*

**WEDCO Technology UK Ltd.,  Sandars Rd., Heapham Rd. Ind. Estate, Gainsborough, Lincolnshire DN21 1RZ, UK**

Tel: 44-1427-811401   Fax: 44-1427-811360   Contact: Stuart Grant, Mng. Dir.

## WEIGHT WATCHERS INTERNATIONAL, INC.

175 Crossways Park Dr., Woodbury, NY, 11797

Tel: (516) 390-1400    Fax: (516) 390-1763    www.weightwatchers.com

*Weight loss programs.*

**Weight Watchers (UK) Ltd,  Kidwells Park House, Kidwells Park Drive, Maidenhead Berks SL6 8YT, UK**

## WEIL, GOTSHAL & MANGES LLP

767 Fifth Ave., New York, NY, 10153

Tel: (212) 310-8000    Fax: (212) 310-8007    www.weil.com

*International law firm.*

**Weil, Gotshal & Manges LLP,  One South Place, London EC2M 2WG, UK**

Tel: 44-207-903-1000   Fax: 44-207-903-0990   Contact: Erica L. Handling, Ptnr.

## WELCH ALLYN DCD INC.

4341 State Street Road, Skaneateles Falls, NY, 13153

Tel: (315) 685-4100    Fax: (315) 685-4091    www.welchallyn.com

*Mfr. bar code data collection systems.*

**CEL Instruments, Ltd.,  35-37 Bury Mead Road, Hitchin, Hertz SG5 1RT, UK**

**Hand Held Products, Ltd.,  Dallam Court Dallam Lane, Warrington, Cheshire WA2 7LT, UK**

Tel: 44-1925-240055

**Welch Allyn U.K. Ltd.,  Aston Abbotts, Buckinghamshire HP22 4ND, UK**

## WELLS LAMONT INDUSTRY GROUP

7525 N. Oak Park Ave., Niles, IL, 60714

Tel:  (847) 647-1231       Fax:  (847) 647-0755       www.wellslamontindustry.com

*Mfr. industrial protective work gloves and industrial rainwear.*

**Manabo Ltd.,  North Yorkshire, UK**

Contact: Richard Shaw

## WENDY'S INTERNATIONAL, INC.

428 West Dublin Granville Roads, Dublin, OH, 43017-0256

Tel:  (614) 764-3100       Fax:  (614) 764-3459       www.wendysintl.com

*Fast food restaurant chain.*

**Wendy's International,  London, UK**

## WESCO INTERNATIONAL INC.

Four Station Square, Ste. 700, Pittsburgh, PA, 15219

Tel:  (412) 454-2200       Fax:  (412) 454-2505       www.wescodist.com

*Mfr.electronic equipment and parts.*

**Wesco International,  Knyvett House, The Causeway, Staines TW18 3BA England UK**

Tel: 44-1784-898-641   Fax: 44-1784-898-305

## WEST PHARMACEUTICAL SERVICES

101 Gordon Drive, PO Box 645, Lionville, PA, 19341-0645

Tel:  (610) 594-2900       Fax:  (610) 594-3014       www.westpharma.com

*Mfr. products for filling, sealing, dispensing and delivering needs of health care and consumer products markets.*

**The West Company (UK) Ltd.,  Bucklers Lane, Holmbush, St. Austell, Cornwall PL25 3JL UK**

Tel: 44-1726-63563   Fax: 44-1726-61992

**The West Company (UK) Ltd.,  Cooksland Industrial Estate, Bodwin, Cornwall PL 31 2PZ, UK**

Tel: 44-120-873-211   Fax: 44-120-877-792

**The West Company (UK) Ltd.,  Nottingham, UK**

## WEST POINT STEVENS INC.

507 West 10th Street, PO Box 71, West Point, GA, 31833

Tel:  (706) 645-4000       Fax:  (706) 645-4121       www.westpointstevens.com

*Industry household and apparel fabrics and bed and bath products.*

**West Point Stevens Inc.,  Todmorden, UK**

**West Point Stevens Inc.,  Berkhanstead UK**

## WESTAFF SERVICES, INC.

301 Lennon Lane, Walnut Creek, CA, 94598-2453

Tel:  (925) 930-5300       Fax:  (925) 934-5489       www.westaff.com

*Secretarial and clerical temporary service.*

**Western Temporary Services Ltd.,  46/50 Southgate St., Gloucester GL1 2DR, UK**

## WESTERN DIGITAL CORPORATION

8105 Irvine Center Drive, Irvine, CA, 92718

Tel:  (949) 932-5000       Fax:  (949) 932-6629       www.westerndigital.com

*Mfr. hard disk drives, video graphics boards, VLSI.*

**Western Digital UK Ltd.,  Fairmount House, Bull Hill, Leatherhead, Surrey, UK**

## WESTERN GEOPHYSICAL, INC.

10205 Westheimer, Houston, TX, 77251-1407

Tel: (713) 972-4000     Fax: (713) 952-9837     www.bakerhughes.com

*Provides comprehensive seismic services for oil and gas exploration, field development, and reservoir monitoring.*

**E & P Services, 455 London Rd., Isleworth, Middlesex TW7 5AB, UK**

Tel: 44-181-560-3160   Fax: 44-181-231-7045   Contact: Orval Brannan, Pres.

**Entec Energy Consultants, Ltd., NLA Tower 15th Floor, 12-16 Addiscombe Rd., Croydon, Surrey CR9 2DR UK**

Tel: 44-181-680-1737   Fax: 44-181-688-6056   Contact: Elio Poggiagliolmi, Gen. Mgr.

**Western Atlas Logging Services, Marine Park, Gapton Hall Industrial Estate, Great Yarmouth, Norfolk NR31 0NL UK**

Tel: 44-1493-442-200   Fax: 44-1493-442-378   Contact: Duncan Lee, Ops. Mgr.

**Western Geophysical, Manton Lane, Bedford MK41 7PA, UK**

Tel: 44-1234-224-500   Fax: 44-1234-224-159   Contact: David Todhunter, Mgr.

**Western Geophysical, 455 London Road, Isleworth, Middlesex TW7 5AA, UK**

Tel: 44-20-8560-3160   Fax: 44-20-8560-3160

**Western Geophysical, 455 London Rd., Isleworth, Middlesex TW7 5AB, UK**

Tel: 44-181-560-3160   Fax: 44-181-847-3131   Contact: W.S. Schrom, SVP

## WESTERN RESOURCES, INC.

818 Kansas Ave., Topeka, KS, 66612

Tel: (785) 575-6300     Fax: (785) 575-1796     www.wstnres.com

*Engaged in security monitoring, natural gas and electricity.*

**Protection One Europe, London, UK**

## WESTERN UNION FINANCIAL SERVICES

6200 South Quebec St., Englewood, CO, 80111

Tel: (303) 488-8000     Fax: (303) 488-8705     www.westernunion.com

*Financial and messaging service.*

**Londis Western Union, Londis 4-8, Mont Fort Place, Wimbledon, UK**

Tel: 44-181-741-3639

**Temple Fortune News, 11 Hallfwelle Parade, Finchley Rd., London, UK**

## WEYERHAEUSER COMPANY

33663 Weyerhaeuser Way South, Federal Way, WA, 98003

Tel: (253) 924-2345     Fax: (253) 924-2685     www.weyerhaeuser.com

*Wood and wood fiber products.*

**Weyerhaeuser (UK) Ltd., 3 Curfew Yare Thames St., Windsor, Berkshire SL4 1SN, UK**

## WHIRLPOOL CORPORATION

2000 N. M-63, Benton Harbor, MI, 49022-2692

Tel: (616) 923-5000     Fax: (616) 923-5443     www.whirlpoolcorp.com

*Mfr./market home appliances: Whirlpool, Roper, KitchenAid, Estate, and Inglis.*

**Whirlpool (UK) Ltd., 209 Purley Way, Croydon, Surrey CR9 4RY UK**

## WHITE & CASE LLP

1155 Ave. of the Americas, New York, NY, 10036-2767

Tel: (212) 819-8200     Fax: (212) 354-8113     www.whitecase.com

*International law firm.*

**White & Case LLP, 7-11 Moorgate, London EC2R 6HH, UK**

Tel: 44-207-726-6361   Fax: 44-207-726-8558   Contact: Peter D. Finlay

**WHITE ELECTRONIC DESIGNS**

3601 East University Drive, Phoenix, AZ, 85034

Tel: (602) 437-1520      Fax: (602) 437-1731      www.whitemicro.com

*Mfr. of high density memory modules and micro processor MCMs; state of the art micro-electronics devices.*

**White Electronic Designs Ltd., 64 Dene Rd., Wylam, Northumberland NE 41 8HB, UK**

Tel: 44-1661-853777  Fax: 44-1661-854111   Contact: Ian Robinson, Mgr.

**WHITEHALL-ROBINS INC.**

1407 Cummings Drive, PO Box 26609, Richmond, VA, 23261-6609

Tel: (804) 257-2000      Fax: (804) 257-2120      www.ahp.com

*Mfr. ethical pharmaceuticals and consumer healthcare products.*

**Whitehall-Robins Co. Ltd., Gatwick Rd., West Sussex, UK**

**WHITTMAN-HART & USWEB/CKS**

311 S. Wacker Drive, Ste. 3500, Chicago, IL, 60606-6621

Tel: (312) 922-9200      Fax: (312) 913-3020      www.uswebcks.com

*Internet professional services firm; design and implementation services for multimedia marketing programs.*

**USWeb/CKS UK, 3 Shortlands, London, W6 8DA UK**

Tel: 44-181-741-8999  Fax: 44-181-741-9413

**WHX CORPORATION**

110 East 59th St., New York, NY, 10022

Tel: (212) 355-5200      Fax: (212) 355-5336      www.handyharman.com

*Mfr. flat-rolled steel and associated metal products.*

**Lucas-Milhaupt Europe, Div. Handy & Harman, 24-26 Boulton Road, Stevenage, Hertfordshire SG1 4QX, UK**

Tel: 44-1438-750087   Fax: 44-1438-750098

**Rigby-Maryland Ltd., Div. Handy & Harmon, Crystal Works - Union Road, Liversedge, West Yorkshire WF15 7JT, UK**

Tel: 44-1924-407083   Fax: 44-1924-400071

**JOHN WILEY & SONS INC.**

605 Third Ave., New York, NY, 10158-0012

Tel: (212) 850-6000      Fax: (212) 850-6088      www.wiley.com

*Develops, publishes, and sells products in print and electronic media for the educational, professional, scientific, technical, medical, and consumer markets*

**Wiley Europe Ltd., Baffins Lane, Chichester, West Sussex P019 IUD, UK**

Tel: 44-1-243-779777   Fax: 44-1-243-775-878   Contact: John Jarvis, SVP

**WILLAMETTE INDUSTRIES, INC.**

1300 SW Fifth Ave., Ste. 3800, Portland, OR, 97201

Tel: (503) 227-5581      Fax: (503) 273-5603      www.wii.com

*Mfr./sales and distribution of paper and wood products.*

**Willamette Europe Ltd., Maitland House 10/F, Warrior Square, Southend-on-Sea, Essex SS1 2JY, UK**

Tel: 44-1702-619044

**WILLIAM MORRIS AGENCY INC.**

One William Morris Place, Beverly Hills, CA, 90212

Tel: (310) 859-4000      Fax: (310) 859-4462      www.wma.com

*Book, theatre, music, film, television and commercials agency.*

**William Morris Agency (UK) Ltd., 52/53 Poland Street, London W1F 7LX, UK**

Tel: 44-207-534-6800   Fax: 44-207-534-6900

## T.D. WILLIAMSON INC.

PO Box 2299, Tulsa, OK, 74101

Tel: (918) 254-9400      Fax: (918) 254-9474      www.tdwilliamson.com

*Mfr. equipment and provide service for pipeline maintenance.*

**T.D. Williamson (UK) Ltd., Faraday Rd., Dorcan Way, Swindon Wiltshire SN3 5HF, UK**

## WILLKIE FARR & GALLAGHER

787 Seventh Avenue, New York, NY, 10019-6099

Tel: (212) 821-8000      Fax: (212) 821-8111      www.willkie.com

*International law firm.*

**Willkie Farr & Gallagher, 35 Wilson St., London EC2M 2SJ, UK**

Tel: 44-207-696-5454

## WILMER, CUTLER & PICKERING

2445 M Street, N.W., Washington, DC, 20037-1420

Tel: (202) 663-6000      Fax: (202) 663-6363      www.wilmer.com

*International law firm.*

**Wilmer, Cutler & Pickering, 4 Carlton Gardens, London SW1Y 5AA, UK**

## WILSON, ELSER, MOSKOWITZ, EDELMAN & DICKER LLP

150 East 42nd St., New York, NY, 10017

Tel: (212) 490-3000      Fax: (212) 490-3038      www.wemed.com

*International law firm.*

**Wilson, Elser, Moskowitz, Edelman & Dicker, 141 Fenchurch St., London EC3M 6BL, UK**

## A. WIMPFHEIMER & BRO., INC.

22 Bayview Ave., PO Box 472, Stonington, CT, 06378

Tel: (860) 535-1050      Fax: (860) 535-4398      www.wimpvel.com

*Mfr. of fine velvets, velveteens and corduroy.*

**Denholme Velvets Ltd., Halifax Road, Denholme, Bradford BD13 4EZ, UK**

Tel: 44-1274-832185

## WIND RIVER SYSTEMS, INC.

500 Wind River Way, Alameda, CA, 94501

Tel: (510) 748-4100      Fax: (510) 749-2010      www.isi.com

*Develops and markets computer software products and services.*

**Wind River Systems UK, Unit 5 - 2/F - Ashted Lock Way, Aston Science Park, Birmingham B7 4AZ UK**

Tel: 44-121-359-0999   Fax: 44-121-628-1889

## WINTHROP, STIMSON, PUTNAM & ROBERTS

One Battery Park Plaza, 31st Fl., New York, NY, 10004-1490

Tel: (212) 858-1000      Fax: (212) 858-1500      www.winstim.com

*International law firm.*

**Winthrop, Stimson, Putnam & Roberts, 54 Lombard Street, London EC3V 9DH, UK**

Tel: 44-207-648-9200   Fax: 44-207-283-1656

## WIREMOLD COMPANY INC.

60 Woodlawn Street, West Hartford, CT, 06110

Tel: (860) 233-6251      Fax: (860) 523-3699      www.wiremold.com

*Mfr. noncurrent-carrying wiring devices.*

**Arena Cable Management, West Bromwich, UK**

**Davis International, Ltd., Salamandre plc, London, UK**

**Electrunk Ltd., London, UK**

**Walsall Cable Management, Ltd., West Midlands, UK**

## WIT SOUNDVIEW GROUP, INC.

826 Broadway, 6th Fl., New York, NY, 10003

Tel: (212) 253-4400    Fax: (212) 253-4428    www.witsoundview.com

*Internet-based investment bank.*

**Wit Soundview Group Ltd., 120 Old Broad Street, London EC2 N1AR, UK**

## WOODWARD GOVERNOR COMPANY

5001 N. Second Street, PO Box 7001, Rockford, IL, 61125-7001

Tel: (815) 877-7441    Fax: (815) 639-6033    www.woodward.com

*Mfr./service speed control devices and systems for aircraft turbines, industrial engines and turbines.*

**Woodward Governor (UK) Ltd., 350 Basingstoke Rd., Reading, Berkshire RG2 0NY, UK**

Tel: 44-118-975-2727   Fax: 44-118-975-1599   Contact: Tony Murphy   Emp: 165

## WORLD COURIER INC.

1313 Fourth Ave., New Hyde Park, NY, 11041

Tel: (516) 354-2600    Fax: (516) 354-2644    www.worldcourier.com

*International courier service.*

**World Courier (UK) Ltd., Faulkner House, Faulkner St., Manchester M14DU, UK**

**World Courier (UK) Ltd., 10-14 Bedford St., Covent Garden, London, UK**

## WORLD MINERALS INC.

130 Castilian Drive, Santa Barbara, CA, 93117

Tel: (805) 562-0200    Fax: (805) 562-0298    www.worldminerals.com

*Mfr. premium quality diatomite and perlite products.*

**World Minerals Ltd., Livingston Rd., Hessle Hull, North Humberside HU13 0EG, UK**

## WORLDCOM, INC.

500 Clinton Center Drive, Clinton, MS, 39060

Tel: (601) 360-8600    Fax: (601) 360-8616    www.wcom.com

*Telecommunications company serving local, long distance and Internet customers domestically and internationally.*

**WorldCom International, 14 Grays Inn Road, London WC1X 8HN, UK**

## WORLDXCHANGE COMMUNICATIONS

9999 Willow Creek Road, San Diego, CA, 92131

Tel: (858) 547-4933    Fax: (800) 995-4502    www.worldxchange.com

*Provides international, long distance telecommunications services worldwide.*

**WorldxChange Communications, 626 Chiswick High Rd., London W4 5RY, UK**

Tel: 44-181-400-4400   Fax: 44-181-400-4444   Emp: 425

## WORTHINGTON INDUSTRIES, INC.

1205 Dearborn Dr., Columbus, OH, 43085

Tel: (614) 438-3210    Fax: (614) 438-7948    www.worthingtonindustries.com

*Mfr. flat-rolled steel.*

**Worthington Armstrong UK Ltd., Unit 401 Princes Way Central, Team Valley Trading Estate, Gateshead NE 11 OTU, UK**

Tel: 44-191-48-0606

## WRIGHT LINE INC.

160 Gold Star Blvd., Worcester, MA, 01606

Tel: (508) 852-4300    Fax: (508) 853-8904    www.wrightline.com

*Mfr. filing systems.*

**Datafile Ltd., 8D Cosgrove Way, Luton, Bedfordshire LU1 1XL, UK**

## WM WRIGLEY JR. COMPANY

410 N. Michigan Ave., Chicago, IL, 60611-4287

Tel: (312) 644-2121    Fax: (312) 644-0353    www.wrigley.com

*Mfr. chewing gum.*

**The Wrigley Company Ltd., Eastover, Plymouth, Devon PL6 7PR, UK**

## WWF PAPER CORPORATION

Two Bala Plaza, 2nd Fl., Bala Cynwyd, PA, 19004

Tel: (610) 667-9210    Fax: (610) 667-1663    www.wwfpaper.com

*Wholesale of fine papers.*

**WWF Paper Sales UK Ltd., Claire House, Bridge St., Leatherhead, Surrey KT22 8HY, UK**

Tel: 44-1372-376133   Fax: 44-1372-374456   Contact: Roger Spikesman, Mng. Dir.

## WYETH-AYERST INTERNATIONAL INC.

150 Radnot-Chester Road, St. Davids, PA, 19087

Tel: (610) 902-4100    Fax: (610) 989-4586    www.ahp.com/wyeth

*Antibiotics and pharmaceutical products.*

**John Wyeth & Brother, Ltd., Huntercombe Lane South, Taplow Maidenhead Berks SL6 OPH, UK**

Tel: 44-1628-604-377

## WYNN OIL COMPANY

1050 West Fifth Street, Azusa, CA, 91702-9510

Tel: (626) 334-0231    Fax: (626) 334-1456    www.wynnoil.com

*Mfr. of specialty chemicals, equipment and related service programs for automotive and industrial markets.*

**Wynn Oil Co. (UK) Ltd., Thames Court, 2 Richfield Ave., Reading, Berkshire RG1 8EQ, UK**

Tel: 44-118-950-4090   Fax: 44-118-950-4001   Contact: David Sussex, Gen. Mgr.   Emp: 12

## WYNN'S PRECISION INC.

104 Hartman Drive, Lebanon, TN, 37087

Tel: (615) 444-0191    Fax: (615) 444-4072    www.wynns.com

*Mfr. rings, seals and custom molded rubber products.*

**Wynn's Precision Seals (UK) Ltd., 459 London Rd., 24676 Camberley, Surrey GU15 3JA, UK**

## WYSE TECHNOLOGY INC.

3471 North First Street, San Jose, CA, 95134

Tel: (408) 473-1200    Fax: (408) 473-2080    www.wyse.com

*Mfr. computer network terminals.*

**Wyse Technology, 1 The Pavilions, Ruscombe Park, Twyford Berks RG10 9NN, UK**

Tel: 44-118-934-2200   Fax: 44-118-934-0749

## X CEL ENERGY INC. (XEL)

414 Nicollet Mall, Minneapolis, MN, 55401

Tel: (612) 215-4559    Fax: (612) 215-4535    www.excelenergy.com

*Electric and natural gas utility.*

**Yorkshire Electricity Group Plc. (XEL), Wetherby Road, Scarcroft Leeds, LS14 3HS, UK**

Tel: 44-11-289-2123

**Yorkshire Electricity Group Plc. (XEL), 200 Clough Road, Hull HU5 1SN, UK**

Tel: 44-345-413-356

## XEROX CORPORATION

800 Long Ridge Road, PO Box 1600, Stamford, CT, 06904

Tel: (203) 968-3000    Fax: (203) 968-4312    www.xerox.com

*Mfr. document processing equipment, systems and supplies.*

**Xerox (UK) Ltd., Bridge House, Uxbridge, Middlesex UB8 1HS, UK**

Tel: 44-800-454-19   Fax: 44-1895-843-665

**Xerox (UK) Ltd., 438 Midsummer Blvd., Central Milton Keynes, Milton Keynes MK9 2DZ, UK**
Tel: 44-1908-692-444    Fax: 44-1908-609--225

**Xerox (UK) Ltd., Parkway, Marlow, Buckinghamshire SL7 1YL, UK**

## XILINX INC.

2100 Logic Drive, San Jose, CA, 95124-3400

Tel: (408) 559-7778    Fax: (408) 559-7114    www.xilinx.com

*Programmable logic and related development systems software.*

**Xilinx Ltd., Benchmark House, 203 Brooklands Rd., Weybridge, Surrey KT 13 ORH UK**
Tel: 44-1932-349401

## XIRCOM, INC.

2300 Corporate Center Drive, Thousand Oaks, CA, 91320

Tel: (805) 376-9300    Fax: (805) 376-9311    www.xircom.com

*Mfr. PC card network adapters and modems.*

**Xircom UK Limited, Worting House, Basingstoke, Hampshire RG23 8PY, UK**
Tel: 44-1256-332-552

## XTRA CORPORATION

1807 Park 270 Dr., Ste. 400, St. Louis, MO, 63146-4020

Tel: (314) 579-9320    Fax: (314) 579-0299    www.xtracorp.com

*Holding company: leasing.*

**XTRA (UK) Leasing Ltd., Wilson's Corner, 1-5 Ingrave Rd., Bretwood, Essex CN15 8TB, UK**

**XTRA International, London, UK**

## YAHOO! INC.

3420 Central Expressway, Santa Clara, CA, 95051

Tel: (408) 731-3300    Fax: (408) 731-3301    www.yahoo-inc.com

*Internet media company providing specialized content, free electronic mail and community offerings and commerce.*

**Yahoo! UK Ltd., 80/81 St. Martin's Lane, London WC2N 4AA, UK**
Tel: 44-207-664-0400  Fax: 44-207-664-0401   Contact: Fabiola Arredondo

## YELLOW CORPORATION

10990 Roe Ave., PO Box 7270, Overland Park, KS, 66207

Tel: (913) 696-6100    Fax: (913) 696-6116    www.yellowcorp.com

*Commodity transportation.*

**Frans Maas (UK) Ltd., Link House - Tower Lane, Eastleigh Hampshire S05 5NZ, UK**

## YORK INTERNATIONAL CORPORATION

631 South Richland Ave., York, PA, 17403

Tel: (717) 771-7890    Fax: (717) 771-6212    www.york.com

*Mfr. heating, ventilating, air conditioning and refrigeration equipment.*

**York Intl. Ltd., Gardiners Lane S., Basildon, Essex SS14 3HE, UK**

**York U.K., Unit 17 Garonor Way, Royal Portbury, Bristol BS20 9XE, UK**
Tel: 44-1275-375713

## YOUNG & RUBICAM INC.

285 Madison Ave., New York, NY, 10017

Tel: (212) 210-3000    Fax: (212) 370-3796    www.yr.com

*Advertising, public relations, direct marketing and sales promotion, corporate and product ID management.*

**Young & Rubicam Holdings Ltd. (European HQ), Greater London House, Hampstead Rd., London NW1 7QP, UK**
Tel: 44-207-387-9366  Fax: 44-207-611-6570

## YSI INC.

1725 Brannum Lane, PO Box 279, Yellow Springs, OH, 45387

Tel: (937) 767-7241    Fax: (937) 767-9353    www.ysi.com

*Mfr. analyzers, measure instruments and electrical components.*

**YSI Ltd., Lynchford House, Lynchford Lane, Farnborough, Hampshire GU14 6LT, UK**

## ZEDTEC COMBUSTION SYSTEMS, INC.

3901 Washington Rd., Ste. 203, McMurray, PA, 15317

Tel: (724) 942-3408    Fax: (724) 942-4747    www.zedtec.com

*Mfr./sale/service combustion equipment for industrial furnaces in glass, forging heat treating, and aluminum industries.*

**Dyson/Hotwork, Bretton St., Saville Town Dewsbury, West Yorkshire WF129DB, UK**

Tel: 44-724-942-3408    Fax: 44-724-942-4747    Contact: Dr. John Laming

## ZIEBART INTERNATIONAL CORPORATION

1290 East Maple Road, Troy, MI, 48083

Tel: (248) 588-4100    Fax: (248) 588-0718    www.ziebart.com

*Automotive aftermarket services.*

**Ziebart (EC) Ltd., PO Box 377, Eastbourne, East Sussex BN22 9QF, UK**

## JOHN ZINK COMPANY

PO Box 21220, Tulsa, OK, 74121-1220

Tel: (918) 234-1800    Fax: (918) 234-2700    www.johnzink.com

*Mfr. flare systems, thermal oxidizers, vapor recovery systems, process heater burners.*

**John Zink Co. Ltd., High Common, 77 Woodside Rd., Amersham, Buckinghamshire HP6 6AA UK**

**John Zink UK, London, UK**

Tel: 44-1932-769838    Contact: Doug Harckham

## ZITEL CORPORATION

47211 Bayside Pkwy., Fremont, CA, 94538-6517

Tel: (510) 440-9600    Fax: (510) 440-9696    www.zitel.com

*Mfr. computer peripherals and software.*

**Datametrics Systems, Ltd., Fountain House, Cleeve Rd., Leatherhead Surrey KT22 7LX, UK**

Contact: Reginald H.W. Webb

**Zitel International Corporation, 16 Thatcham Business Village, Colthrop Way, Thatcham RG19-4LW, Berkshire, UK**

## ZOLL MEDICAL CORPORATION

32 Second Avenue, Burlington, MA, 01803

Tel: (781) 229-0020    Fax: (781) 272-5578    www.zoll.com

*Mfr. electrical resuscitation devices and equipment.*

**ZOLL Medical UK Ltd., Unit 13 - Empress Business Centre, 380 Chester Road, Old Trafford Manchester M16 9EB, UK**

Tel: 44-161-877-2883

## ZOOM TELEPHONICS, INC.

207 South Street, Boston, MA, 02111

Tel: (617) 423-1072    Fax: (617) 338-5015    www.zoomtel.com

*Mfr. fax modems.*

**Hayes, Div. Zoom Telephonics, 430 Frimley Business Park, Frimley Camberley, Surrey GU16 5SG, UK**

Tel: 44-870-720-0060    Fax: 44-870-720-0040

# Estonia

## AMERICAN INTERNATIONAL GROUP INC. (AIG)

70 Pine Street, New York, NY, 10270

Tel: (212) 770-7000     Fax: (212) 509-9705     www.aig.com

*Worldwide insurance and financial services.*

**Seesam International Ins. Co.,  Vambota 6, EE0001 Tallin, Estonia**

## ANDERSEN WORLDWIDE

33 West Monroe Street, Chicago, IL, 60603

Tel: (312) 580-0033     Fax: (312) 507-6748     www.arthurandersen.com

*Accounting and audit, tax and management consulting services.*

**Andersen Estonia AS,  Parnu mnt. 21, EE-0001 Tallinn, Estonia**

Tel: 372-6-266-466

## APPLERA CORPORATION

761 Main Avenue, Norwalk, CT, 06859-0001

Tel: (203) 762-1000     Fax: (203) 762-6000     www.applera.com

*Leading supplier of systems for life science research and related applications.*

**Applied Biosystems,  Kreutzwaldi 1, 51014 Tartu, Estonia**

## AVNET INC.

2211 South 47th Street, Phoenix, AZ, 85034

Tel: (480) 643-2000     Fax: (480) 643-4670     www.avnet.com

*Distributor electronic components, computers and peripherals.*

**Avnet Baltronic,  Akadeemia tee 21F, EE-0026 Tallinn, Estonia**

Tel: 372-639-7000   Fax: 372-639-7009

## BATES WORLDWIDE INC.

405 Lexington Ave., New York, NY, 10174

Tel: (212) 297-7000     Fax: (212) 986-0270     www.batesww.com

*Advertising, marketing, public relations and media consulting.*

**Bates Estonia,  Ala 6, EE-3600 Parnu, Estonia**

Tel: 372-44-78555   Fax: 372-44-78555   Contact: R. Elsler, CEI

**Bates Estonia Tallin,  Endina 69, Tallinn EE-006, Estonia**

Tel: 372-6-105-800   Fax: 372-6-015-800   Contact: R. Vaga

## BRISTOL-MYERS SQUIBB COMPANY

345 Park Ave., New York, NY, 10154-0037

Tel: (212) 546-4000     Fax: (212) 546-4020     www.bms.com

*Pharmaceutical and food preparations, medical and surgical instruments.*

**BMS Estonia,  Sepise 18, Tallinn 11415, Estonia**

Tel: 372-6401-1301

## LEO BURNETT, DIV. B-COM 3 GROUP

35 West Wacker Drive, Chicago, IL, 60601

Tel: (312) 220-5959     Fax: (312) 220-6533     www.bcom3group.com

*Engaged in advertising, marketing, media buying and planning, and public relations.*

**Kontuur - Leo Burnett,  Tallinn, Estonia**

## THE COASTAL CORPORATION

Nine Greenway Plaza, Houston, TX, 77046-0995

Tel: (713) 877-1400      Fax: (713) 877-6752      www.coastalcorp.com

*Oil refining, natural gas, related services; independent power production.*

**Coastal Baltica Marketing Company Ltd.,   Tallinn, Estonia**

## DDB NEEDHAM WORLDWIDE INC.

437 Madison Ave., New York, NY, 10022

Tel: (212) 415-2000      Fax: (212) 415-3417      www.ddbn.com

*Advertising agency.*

**Brand Sellers DDb Estonia,   Tallinn, Estonia**

## DELOITTE TOUCHE TOHMATSU INTERNATIONAL

1633 Broadway, New York, NY, 10019

Tel: (212) 492-4000      Fax: (212) 392-4154      www.deloitte.com

*Accounting, audit, tax and management consulting services.*

**Deloitte & Touche,   Suur-Karja 21, EE-0001 Tallinn, Estonia**

## DHL WORLDWIDE EXPRESS

50 California Avenue, San Francisco, CA, 94111

Tel: (415) 677-6100      Fax: (415) 824-9700      www.dhl.com

*Worldwide air express carrier.*

**DHL Worldwide Express,   5 Joe St., Tallinn, EE-0001, Estonia**

Tel: 372-6-261083

## DIAGNOSTIC PRODUCTS CORPORATION

5700 West 96th Street, Los Angeles, CA, 90045

Tel: (310) 645-8200      Fax: (310) 645-9999      www.dpcweb.com

*Mfr. diagnostic products.*

**DPC Baltic OÜ,   Pirita Tee 26B, 10127 Tallinn, Estonia**

Tel: 372-627-93-44    Fax: 372-627-93-45

## DRAKE BEAM MORIN INC.

101 Huntington Ave., Boston, MA, 02199

Tel: (617) 375-9500      Fax: (617) 267-2011      www.dbm.com

*Human resource management consulting and training.*

**DBM c/o MPS Mainor AS,   1 Kuhlbarsi St., Tallin EE-0001, Estonia**

Tel: 372-620-7561    Fax: 372-620-7562

## ERNST & YOUNG, LLP

787 Seventh Ave., New York, NY, 10019

Tel: (212) 773-3000      Fax: (212) 773-6350      www.eyi.com

*Accounting and audit, tax and management consulting services.*

**Ernst & Young Eesti AS,   Tallinn Business Ctr., Harju St. 6 Ste. 510, EE-0001 Tallinn, Estonia**

Tel: 372-6-310613    Fax: 372-6-310611    Contact: Kari Bjork

## FORT JAMES CORPORATION

1650 Lake Cook Road, Deerfield, IL, 60015

Tel: (847) 317-5000      Fax: (847) 236-3755      www.fortjames.com

*Mfr. and markets consumer tissue products.*

**Fort James Corporation,   Tallinn, Estonia**

## GETZ BROS & COMPANY, INC.

150 Post Street, Ste. 500, San Francisco, CA, 94108-4750

Tel: (415) 772-5500      Fax: (415) 772-5659      www.getz.com

*Diversified manufacturing, marketing and distribution services and travel services.*

**Getz Estonia Ltd., 26 Ringtee St., Tartu, Estonia**

Tel: 372-7-471531   Fax: 372-7-471853   Contact: Hanno Hansson

## GREY GLOBAL GROUP

777 Third Ave., New York, NY, 10017

Tel: (212) 546-2000      Fax: (212) 546-1495      www.grey.com

*International advertising agency.*

**Inorek Marketing, Tallinn, Estonia**

## JUKI UNION SPECIAL CORPORATION

5 Haul Road, Wayne, NJ, 07470

Tel: (973) 633-7200      Fax: (973) 633-9629      www.unionspecial.com

*Mfr. sewing machines.*

**Pavel Ltd. Estonia, Liimi 3A, EE-0006 Tallinn, Estonia**

## KPMG INTERNATIONAL LLP

345 Park Avenue, New York, NY, 10022

Tel: (201) 307-7000      Fax: (201) 930-8617      www.kpmg.com

*Accounting and audit, tax and management consulting services.*

**KPMG Estonia, Ahtri 10A, Tallinn EE-0001, Estonia**

Tel: 372-6-268700   Fax: 372-6-268777   Contact: Andres Root, Sr. Ptnr.

## LECROY CORPORATION

700 Chestnut Ridge Road, Chestnut Ridge, NY, 10977

Tel: (845) 425-2000      Fax: (845) 425-8967      www.lecroy.com

*Mfr. signal analyzers and electronic measurement systems.*

**LeCroy S.A., Estroonika Ou, Akadeemiatee 21 F/F101, EE-0016 Tallin, Estonia**

Tel: 372-654-2721

## ELI LILLY & COMPANY

Lilly Corporate Center, Indianapolis, IN, 46285

Tel: (317) 276-2000      Fax: (317) 277-6579      www.lilly.com

*Mfr. pharmaceuticals and animal health products.*

**Eli Lilly (Suisse) S.A., Roosikrantsi 10A-15, EE-0001 Tallinn, Estonia**

Tel: 372-2-44-29-28   Fax: 372-2-44-29-28

## LOCTITE CORPORATION

1001 Trout Brook Crossing, Rocky Hill, CT, 06067-3910

Tel: (860) 571-5100      Fax: (860) 571-5465      www.loctite.com

*Mfr./sale industrial adhesives, sealants and coatings..*

**Loctite Roees Handelsges.m.b.H., Estonia & Baltic States, Riia 132, EE-2400 Tartu, Estonia**

Tel: 372-7-380365   Fax: 372-7-390171

## McCANN-ERICKSON WORLDGROUP

750 Third Ave., New York, NY, 10017

Tel: (212) 984-3644      Fax: (212) 984-2629      www.mccann.com

*International advertising and marketing services.*

**Division McCann-Erickson Tallinn, Tallinn, Estonia**

## McDONALD'S CORPORATION

McDonald's Plaza, Oak Brook, IL, 60523

Tel: (630) 623-3000     Fax: (630) 623-7409       www.mcdonalds.com

*Fast food chain stores.*

**McDonald's Corp., Tallinn, Estonia**

## A .C. NIELSEN COMPANY

177 Broad Street, Stamford, CT, 06901

Tel: (203) 961-3000     Fax: (203) 961-3190       www.acnielsen.com

*Market and consumer research firm.*

**A.C. Nielsen Eesti, Narva mnt., 13a Tallinn, 10151 Estonia**

## NRG ENERGY, INC.

1221 Nicollet Ave., Ste. 700, Minneapolis, MN, 55403

Tel: (612) 373-5300     Fax: (612) 373-5312       www.nrgenergy.com

*Electric power generation.*

**NRGenerating International B.V., Muurivahe 41 - 2/F, 10140 Tallinn, Estonia**

Tel: 372-6-311-553    Fax: 372-6-311-554

## OWENS-ILLINOIS, INC.

One SeaGate, PO Box 1035, Toledo, OH, 43666

Tel: (419) 247-5000     Fax: (419) 247-2839       www.o-i.com

*Largest mfr. of glass containers in the US; plastic containers, compression-molded closures and dispensing systems.*

**A/S Jarvakandi Klaas, Tehaste 7, 79101 Jarvakandi, Estonia**

Tel: 372-48-77285

## PITTSTON BAX GROUP

16808 Armstrong Ave., PO Box 19571, Irvine, CA, 92623

Tel: (949) 752-4000     Fax: (949) 260-3182       www.baxworld.com

*Air freight forwarder.*

**Vim Agency Ltd., Lennujaama 2 Tee 2, EE-0011 Tallinn, Estonia**

Tel: 372-6-388331    Fax: 372-6-388-332

## PRICEWATERHOUSECOOPERS LLP

1301 Ave. of the Americas, New York, NY, 10019

Tel: (212) 596-7000     Fax: (212) 259-1301       www.pwcglobal.com

*Accounting and auditing, tax and management, and human resource consulting services.*

**PriceWaterhouseCoopers, Narva mnt 9A, EE-0001 Tallinn, Estonia**

Tel: 372-6-302-222    Fax: 372-6-302-220

## PROCTER & GAMBLE COMPANY

One Procter & Gamble Plaza, Cincinnati, OH, 45202

Tel: (513) 983-1100     Fax: (513) 562-4500       www.pg.com

*Personal care, food, laundry, cleaning and industry products.*

**Procter & Gamble, Peterburi tee 63, EE-0014 Tallinn, Estonia**

Tel: 372-8-2-800-3000

## UNITED PARCEL SERVICE, INC.

55 Glenlake Parkway, NE, Atlanta, GA, 30328

Tel: (404) 828-6000     Fax: (404) 828-6593       www.ups.com

*International package-delivery service.*

**UPS Estonia - Head Office, 1 Nafta Str, EE-0001 Tallinn, Estonia**

Tel: 372-6-419090

## VELSICOL CHEMICAL CORPORATION

10400 West Higgins Road, Ste. 600, Rosemont, IL, 60018-3728

Tel: (847) 298-9000    Fax: (847) 298-9014    www.velsicol.com

*Produces high performance specialty chemicals based on benzoic acid and cyclo pentadiene.*

**Velsicol Eesti, Parnu mnt. 16, Tuba 9, EE-001 Tallinn, Estonia**

Tel: 372-6-314276   Fax: 372-6-314278   Contact: A. Nathan Scott, Mng. Dir.

## WEIGHT WATCHERS INTERNATIONAL, INC.

175 Crossways Park Dr., Woodbury, NY, 11797

Tel: (516) 390-1400    Fax: (516) 390-1763    www.weightwatchers.com

*Weight loss programs.*

**Weight Watchers Estonia, Forelli 12-203, 10621 Tallinn, Estonia**

## WHIRLPOOL CORPORATION

2000 N. M-63, Benton Harbor, MI, 49022-2692

Tel: (616) 923-5000    Fax: (616) 923-5443    www.whirlpoolcorp.com

*Mfr./market home appliances: Whirlpool, Roper, KitchenAid, Estate, and Inglis.*

**Whirlpool Eesti, Ehitajate tee 110, 12618 Tallinn, Estonia**

## YELLOW CORPORATION

10990 Roe Ave., PO Box 7270, Overland Park, KS, 66207

Tel: (913) 696-6100    Fax: (913) 696-6116    www.yellowcorp.com

*Commodity transportation.*

**Frans Maas Expeditie B.V., Donker Duyvisweg 70, 3316 BL Dordrecht, Estonia**

Tel: 31-78-6520-200

# Ethiopia

## AIR EXPRESS INTERNATIONAL CORPORATION

120 Tokeneke Road, PO Box 1231, Darien, CT, 06820

Tel: (203) 655-7900     Fax: (203) 655-5779     www.aeilogistics.com

*International air freight forwarder.*

**AEI/PanAfric Global p.l.c.,  Tsigie Marian Bldg. 2nd Fl., Churchill Ave., Addis Ababa, Ethiopia**

Tel: 251-1-516-250   Fax: 251-1-612-766

## LOUIS BERGER INTERNATIONAL INC.

100 Halsted Street, East Orange, NJ, 07019

Tel: (201) 678-1960     Fax: (201) 672-4284     www.louisberger.com

*Consulting engineers, engaged in architecture, environmental and advisory services.*

**Louis Berger International Inc.,  PO Box 11880, Woreda 17 Kebele 20, Addis Ababa, Ethiopia**

Tel: 251-1-183457   Fax: 251-1-615220

## CROWN CORK & SEAL COMPANY,  INC.

One Crown Way, Philadelphia, PA, 19154-4599

Tel: (215) 698-5100     Fax: (215) 698-5201     www.crowncork.com

*Mfr. metal and plastic packaging, including steel and aluminum cans for food, beverage and household products.*

**Crown Cork & Can Mfr. Industries SC,  PO Box 5501, Addis Ababa, Ethiopia**

## DHL WORLDWIDE EXPRESS

50 California Avenue, San Francisco, CA, 94111

Tel: (415) 677-6100     Fax: (415) 824-9700     www.dhl.com

*Worldwide air express carrier.*

**DHL Worldwide Express,  Off Bole Rd., PO Box 40850, Addis Ababa, Ethiopia**

Tel: 251-1-614281

## HORWATH INTERNATIONAL ASSOCIATION

415 Madison Ave., New York, NY, 10017

Tel: (212) 838-5566     Fax: (212) 838-3636     www.horwath.com

*Public accountants and auditors.*

**Bocresion Haile & Co.,  PO Box 825, Addis Ababa, Ethiopia**

## IBM CORPORATION

New Orchard Road, Armonk, NY, 10504

Tel: (914) 765-1900     Fax: (914) 765-7382     www.ibm.com

*Information products, technology and services.*

**IBM World Trade Corp.,  PO Box 3533, Addis Ababa, Ethiopia**

## LOCKHEED MARTIN CORPORATION

6801 Rockledge Drive, Bethesda, MD, 20817

Tel: (301) 897-6000     Fax: (301) 897-6652     www.imco.com

*Design/mfr./management systems in fields of space, defense, energy, electronics and technical services.*

**Lockheed Martin Aeronautical Systems,  PO Box 1755, Addis Ababa, Ethiopia**

Contact: E. Cunningham, Rep.

## McCANN-ERICKSON WORLDGROUP

750 Third Ave., New York, NY, 10017

Tel: (212) 984-3644     Fax: (212) 984-2629     www.mccann.com

*International advertising and marketing services.*

**Lion McCann,  Addis Ababa, Ethiopia**

## PIONEER HI-BRED INTERNATIONAL INC.

400 Locust Street, Ste. 800, Des Moines, IA, 50309

Tel: (515) 248-4800     Fax: (515) 248-4999     www.pioneer.com

*Agricultural chemicals, farm supplies, biological products, research.*

**Pioneer Hi-Bred Seeds Inc.,  PO Box 1134, Addis Ababa, Ethiopia**

## SCHENKER INTERNATIONAL FORWARDERS INC.

150 Albany Ave., Freeport, NY, 11520

Tel: (516) 377-3000     Fax: (516) 377-3005     www.schenkerusa.com

*Freight forwarders.*

**Shenkkor Ethiopia,  Bole-Amce Rd., PO Box 3700, Addis Ababa, Ethiopia**

Tel: 251-1-611-422   Fax: 251-1-611-392

## STARWOOD HOTELS & RESORTS WORLDWIDE

777 Westchester Avenue, White Plains, NY, 10604

Tel: (914) 640-8100     Fax: (914) 640-8316     www.starwoodhotels.com

*Hotel operations including Sheraton, Westin, St. Regis, Four Points and Caesars.*

**Sheraton Addis Ababa,  Addis Ababa, Ethiopia**

## WESTERN GEOPHYSICAL, INC.

10205 Westheimer, Houston, TX, 77251-1407

Tel: (713) 972-4000     Fax: (713) 952-9837     www.bakerhughes.com

*Provides comprehensive seismic services for oil and gas exploration, field development, and reservoir monitoring.*

**Western Geophysical,  Higher 17 Kebele 20, House #2583, Addis Ababa, Ethiopia**

## XEROX CORPORATION

800 Long Ridge Road, PO Box 1600, Stamford, CT, 06904

Tel: (203) 968-3000     Fax: (203) 968-4312     www.xerox.com

*Mfr. document processing equipment, systems and supplies.*

**M&M Trans-Africa Trading Plc,  PO Box 669, Addis Ababa, Ethiopia**

Tel: 251-1-510-433

# Fiji

**3M**

3M Center, St. Paul, MN, 55144-1000

Tel: (651) 733-1110      Fax: (651) 733-9973      www.mmm.com

*Mfr. diversified products for industry, health care, imaging, communications, transport, safety, consumer, etc.*

**3M Australia Pty. Ltd.,  PO Box 1121, Suva, Fiji**

Tel: 67-9-30-4604

**AIR EXPRESS INTERNATIONAL CORPORATION**

120 Tokeneke Road, PO Box 1231, Darien, CT, 06820

Tel: (203) 655-7900      Fax: (203) 655-5779      www.aeilogistics.com

*International air freight forwarder.*

**AEI (Fiji) P/L.,  Unit 12 ATS Cargo Building, Nadi, Fiji**

Tel: 67-9-72-0538    Fax: 67-9-72-0484

**ANDERSEN WORLDWIDE**

33 West Monroe Street, Chicago, IL, 60603

Tel: (312) 580-0033      Fax: (312) 507-6748      www.arthurandersen.com

*Accounting and audit, tax and management consulting services.*

**Andersen Worldwide,  Level 6 - LICL House, Butt St., PO Box 855 GPO, Suva Fiji**

**AON CORPORATION**

123 North Wacker Drive, Chicago, IL, 60606

Tel: (312) 701-3000      Fax: (312) 701-3100      www.aon.com

*Insurance brokers worldwide; underwrites accident and health insurance, specialty and professional insurance; and provides risk management consultation.*

**AON Risk Services (Fiji) Ltd.,  8th Fl. FNPF Place Victoria Parade, Suva, Fiji**

Tel: 67-9-31-3177    Fax: 67-9-31-3373    Contact: Paul S. Dunk

**BDO SEIDMAN, LLP    BELGIUM**

Two Prudential Plaza, 180 N. Stetson Ave., Ste. 2300, Chicago, IL, 60601

Tel: (312) 240-1236      Fax: (312) 240-3329      www.bdo.com

*International accounting and financial consulting firm.*

**BDO Zarin, Ali,  PO Box 2475, Government Buildings 8/F, Dominion House - Thompson St., Suva Fiji**

Tel: 67-9-31-4044    Fax: 67-9-30-2188    Contact: Nur Bano Ali

**DELOITTE TOUCHE TOHMATSU INTERNATIONAL**

1633 Broadway, New York, NY, 10019

Tel: (212) 492-4000      Fax: (212) 392-4154      www.deloitte.com

*Accounting, audit, tax and management consulting services.*

**Vishnu Prasad & Company,  PO Box 1396, Pacific House, Butt St., Suva Fiji**

**DHL WORLDWIDE EXPRESS**

50 California Avenue, San Francisco, CA, 94111

Tel: (415) 677-6100      Fax: (415) 824-9700      www.dhl.com

*Worldwide air express carrier.*

**DHL Worldwide Express,  10 Holland St., Toorak, Box 13036, Suva Fiji**

Tel: 67-9-31-3166

## EAGLE GLOBAL LOGISTICS (EGL)

15350 Vickery Drive, Houston, TX, 77032

Tel: (281) 618-3100    Fax: (281) 618-3100    www.eaglegl.com

*Ocean/air freight forwarding, customs brokerage, packing and wholesale, logistics management and insurance.*

**Gibson Freight International (Fiji) Ltd., Office No. 125 CAAF Cargo Bldg., PO Box 9907, Nadi Airport, Fiji**

Tel: 67-9-72-0333   Fax: 67-9-72-0306

## ERNST & YOUNG, LLP

787 Seventh Ave., New York, NY, 10019

Tel: (212) 773-3000    Fax: (212) 773-6350    www.eyi.com

*Accounting and audit, tax and management consulting services.*

**Ernst & Young, GPO Box 1359, Suva, Fiji**

Tel: 67-9-30-2142   Fax: 67-9-30-0612   Contact: Francis Chung

## FRITZ COMPANIES, INC.

706 Mission Street, Ste. 900, San Francisco, CA, 94103

Tel: (415) 904-8360    Fax: (415) 904-8661    www.fritz.com

*Integrated transportation, sourcing, distribution and customs brokerage services.*

**Fritz Companies Inc., Suva, Fiji**

## KOPPERS INDUSTRIES INC.

Koppers Bldg, 436 Seventh Ave., Pittsburgh, PA, 15219-1800

Tel: (412) 227-2000    Fax: (412) 227-2333    www.koppers.com

*Construction materials and services; chemicals and building products.*

**Koppers-Hickson Timber, PO Box 4735, Lautoka, Fiji Islands**

## KPMG INTERNATIONAL LLP

345 Park Avenue, New York, NY, 10022

Tel: (201) 307-7000    Fax: (201) 930-8617    www.kpmg.com

*Accounting and audit, tax and management consulting services.*

**KPMG Peat Marwick, 2nd Fl. Meghji Arjun Bldg., 157 Vitogo Parade, Lautoka Fiji**

**KPMG Peat Marwick, Level 5 ANZ House, 25 Victoria Parade, Suva Fiji**

Tel: 67-9-30-1155   Fax: 67-9-30-1312   Contact: Brian J. Murphy, Sr. Ptnr.

## MARSH & McLENNAN COS INC.

1166 Ave. of the Americas, New York, NY, 10036-2774

Tel: (212) 345-5000    Fax: (212) 345-4808    www.marshmac.com

*Insurance agents/brokers, pension and investment management consulting services.*

**J&H Marsh & McLennan Ltd., Fifth Fl. - Civic House, Victoria Parade, Suva, Fiji**

Tel: 67-9-31-2799   Fax: 67-9-30-0737   Contact: Paul Wilkins

**J&H Marsh & McLennan Ltd., 117 Vitogo Parade, Second Fl., Lautoka, Fiji**

Tel: 67-9-66-2687   Fax: 67-9-66-1422   Contact: Paul Wilkins

## McDONALD'S CORPORATION

McDonald's Plaza, Oak Brook, IL, 60523

Tel: (630) 623-3000    Fax: (630) 623-7409    www.mcdonalds.com

*Fast food chain stores.*

**McDonald's Corp., Suva, Fiji**

## PACIFIC CENTURY FINANCIAL CORPORATION

130 Merchant Street, Honolulu, HI, 96813

Tel: (808) 643-3888        Fax: (808) 537-8440        www.boh.com

*Engaged in commercial and consumer banking services.*

**Pacific Century Financial,  15 Naviti Street, PO Box 6286, Lautoka, Fiji**

## PRICEWATERHOUSECOOPERS LLP

1301 Ave. of the Americas, New York, NY, 10019

Tel: (212) 596-7000        Fax: (212) 259-1301        www.pwcglobal.com

*Accounting and auditing, tax and management, and human resource consulting services.*

**PriceWaterhouseCoopers,  Dominion House 6th Floor, Thomson Street, PO Box 156, Suva Fiji**

Tel: 67-9-31-3955   Fax: 67-9-30-0981

**PriceWaterhouseCoopers,  131 Vitogo Parade, PO Box 514, Lautoka, Fiji**

Tel: 67-9-66-1055   Fax: 67-9-66-4671

## THE ST. PAUL COMPANIES, INC.

385 Washington Street, St. Paul, MN, 55102

Tel: (651) 310-7911        Fax: (651) 310-8294        www.stpaul.com

*Provides investment, insurance and reinsurance services.*

**QBE Insurance (Fiji) Ltd.,  Queensland Insurance Centre, PO Box 101, Victoria Parade, Suva Fiji**

## STARWOOD HOTELS & RESORTS WORLDWIDE

777 Westchester Avenue, White Plains, NY, 10604

Tel: (914) 640-8100        Fax: (914) 640-8316        www.starwoodhotels.com

*Hotel operations including Sheraton, Westin, St. Regis, Four Points and Caesars.*

**Sheraton Fiji Resort,  Denarau Beach, Nadi, Fiji**

Tel: 67-9-75-0777   Fax: 679-750-818

# Finland

### 24/7 MEDIA, INC.
1250 Broadway, New York, NY, 10001-3701

Tel: (212) 231-7100    Fax: (212) 760-1774    www.247media.com

*Provides global online advertising, sponsorships, e-commerce and direct marketing solutions to advertisers and Web publishers.*

**24/7 Media Suomi,  Bulevardi 13 A 9, FIN-00120 Helsinki, Finland**

Tel: 358-9-540-7870

### 3COM CORPORATION
5400 Bayfront Plaza, Santa Clara, CA, 95052-8145

Tel: (408) 326-5000    Fax: (408) 326-5001    www.3com.com

*Develop/mfr. computer networking products and systems.*

**3 Com Nordic,  Tekniikantie 12, FIN-02150 Espoo, Finland**

Tel: 358-435-42067

### 3M
3M Center, St. Paul, MN, 55144-1000

Tel: (651) 733-1110    Fax: (651) 733-9973    www.mmm.com

*Mfr. diversified products for industry, health care, imaging, communications, transport, safety, consumer, etc.*

**Suomen 3M OY,  PO Box 26, Sinimaentie 6, FIN-02630 Espoo Finland**

Tel: 358-9-52521    Fax: 358-9-520-664

### ABBOTT LABORATORIES
One Abbott Park, Abbott Park, IL, 60064-3500

Tel: (847) 937-6100    Fax: (847) 937-1511    www.abbott.com

*Development/mfr./sale diversified health care products and services.*

**Abbott Oyj,  Pihatorma 1A, FIN-02240 ESPOO, Finland**

### AGCO CORPORATION
4205 River Green Parkway, Duluth, GA, 30096-2568

Tel: (770) 813-9200    Fax: (770) 813-6038    www.agcocorp.com

*Mfr. farm equipment and machinery.*

**OY Agrolux AB,  Teollisuuskata 1B, PO Box 185, SF 00511 Helsinki, Finland**

### AGILENT TECHNOLOGIES, INC.
395 Page Mill Road, PO Box 10395, Palo Alto, CA, 94303

Tel: (650) 752-5000    Fax: (650) 752-5633    www.agilent.com

*Mfr. communications components.*

**Agilent Technologies Oy,  Piispankalliontie 17, SF-02200 Espoo, Finland**

### AIR EXPRESS INTERNATIONAL CORPORATION
120 Tokeneke Road, PO Box 1231, Darien, CT, 06820

Tel: (203) 655-7900    Fax: (203) 655-5779    www.aeilogistics.com

*International air freight forwarder.*

**AEI Finland Oy,  Koivuhaankuja 1A, FIN-01531 Vantaa 53 Helsinki, Finland**

Tel: 358-9-825-4610    Fax: 358-9-825-46157

## ALBANY INTERNATIONAL CORPORATION

PO Box 1907, Albany, NY, 12201

Tel: (518) 445-2200     Fax: (518) 445-2265     www.albint.com

*Mfr. broadwoven and engineered fabrics, plastic products, filtration media.*

**Fennofelt AB Oy, BVO Silantie 10, FIN-00390 Helsinki, Finland**

## ALTERA CORPORATION

101 Innovation Drive, San Jose, CA, 95134

Tel: (408) 544-7000     Fax: (408) 544-8303     www.altera.com

*Mfr. high-density programmable chips for semi-conductor industry.*

**Altera Oy, Metsaneidonkuja 8, FIN-02130 Espoo, Finland**

Tel: 358-9-43078216

## AMERICAN EXPRESS COMPANY

American Express Tower, World Financial Center, New York, NY, 10285-4765

Tel: (212) 640-2000     Fax: (212) 619-9802     www.americanexpress.com

*Travel, travelers cheques, charge card and financial services.*

**Amex Services Finland Oy, Finland**

Tel: 358-9-628788

## AMERICAN INTERNATIONAL GROUP INC. (AIG)

70 Pine Street, New York, NY, 10270

Tel: (212) 770-7000     Fax: (212) 509-9705     www.aig.com

*Worldwide insurance and financial services.*

**AIG Europe S.A., Unioninkatu 15, FIN-00130 Helsinki, Finland**

## ANC RENTAL CORP.

110 Southeast Sixth St., Ft. Lauderdale, FL, 33301

Tel: (954) 769-7000     Fax: (954) 769-7000     www.ancrental.com

*Engaged in car rental services, including National Car Rental and Alamo Rent A Car.*

**National Car Rental Systems Inc., Mariankatu 27, Helsinki, Finland**

## ANDERSEN CONSULTING

100 S. Wacker Drive, Ste. 1059, Chicago, IL, 60606

Tel: (312) 693-0161     Fax: (312) 693-0507     www.ac.com

*Provides management and technology consulting services.*

**Andersen Consulting, Kansakoulukuja 1A, FIN-00100 Helsinki, Finland**

Tel: 358-9-348-100   Fax: 358-9-693-633-50

## ANDERSEN WORLDWIDE

33 West Monroe Street, Chicago, IL, 60603

Tel: (312) 580-0033     Fax: (312) 507-6748     www.arthurandersen.com

*Accounting and audit, tax and management consulting services.*

**Andersen Kihlman Oy, Kansakoulukuja 1 A, FIN-00100 Helsinki, Finland**

Tel: 358-0-693-631

**Andersen Kihlman Oy, Takojankatu 1, FIN-33540 Tampere, Finland**

**Arthur Andersen Kihlman Oy, Rautatienkatu 19, FIN-15110 Lahti, Finland**

Tel: 358-18-752-1880

**Arthur Andersen Oy, Takojankatu 1, FIN-33540 Tampere, Finland**

Tel: 358-31-253-7700

**Tilintarkastusosakeyhtio Soinio & Co., Veist "m"naukio 1-3, FIN-20100 Turku, Finland**

Tel: 358-21-281-36816

## AON CORPORATION

123 North Wacker Drive, Chicago, IL, 60606

Tel: (312) 701-3000    Fax: (312) 701-3100    www.aon.com

*Insurance brokers worldwide; underwrites accident and health insurance, specialty and professional insurance; and provides risk management consultation.*

**AON Finland OY, Arkadiankatu 23, FIN-00100 Helsinki, Finland**

Tel: 358-9-434-2050   Fax: 358-9-434-20540   Contact: Ilkka Jaakkola

## APPLERA CORPORATION

761 Main Avenue, Norwalk, CT, 06859-0001

Tel: (203) 762-1000    Fax: (203) 762-6000    www.applera.com

*Leading supplier of systems for life science research and related applications.*

**Applied Biosystems, Metsanneidonkuja 8, FIN-02130 Espoo, Finland**

## APW, INC.

PO Box 325, Milwaukee, WI, 53201-0325

Tel: (262) 523-7600    Fax: (262) 523-7624    www.apw1.com

*Mfr. hi-pressure tools, vibration control products, consumables, technical furniture and enclosures.*

**APW Electronics, Puistotie 1, FIN-02760 Espoo, Finland**

## ARMSTRONG HOLDINGS, INC.

2500 Columbia Avenue, Lancaster, PA, 17604-3001

Tel: (717) 397-0611    Fax: (717) 396-2787    www.armstrong.com

*Mfr. and marketing interior furnishings and specialty products for bldg, auto and textile industry.*

**Armstrong Floor Products Europe, Panimokatu IG, SF 00580 Helsinki, Finland**

Tel: 358-9-701-1511   Fax: 358-9-701-1744

## ARROW ELECTRONICS INC.

25 Hub Drive, Melville, NY, 11747

Tel: (516) 391-1300    Fax: (516) 391-1640    www.arrow.com

*Distributor of electronic components.*

**Arrow Finland, Tykistokatu 2B, FIN-20520 Turku, Finland**

**Arrow Northern Europe, Hankasuontie 3, FIN-00390 Helsinki, Finland**

## ATMEL CORPORATION

2325 Orchard Pkwy., San Jose, CA, 95131

Tel: (408) 441-0311    Fax: (408) 436-4200    www.atmel.com

*Design, manufacture and marketing of advanced semiconductors.*

**Atmel Oy, Kappelitie 6B, FIN-02200 Espoo, Finland**

Tel: 358-9-4520-820

## AVERY DENNISON CORPORATION

150 N. Orange Grove Blvd., Pasadena, CA, 91103

Tel: (626) 304-2000    Fax: (626) 792-7312    www.averydennison.com

*Mfr. pressure-sensitive adhesives and materials, office products, labels, tags, retail systems, Carter's Ink and specialty chemicals.*

**Fasson Tarra Oy, Box 217, FIN-02101 Espoo, Finland**

Tel: 358-9-455-8233   Fax: 358-9-455-8501

## AVID TECHNOLOGY, INC.

1 Park West, Tewksbury, MA, 01876

Tel: (978) 640-6789    Fax: (978) 640-1366    www.avid.com

*Mfr. animation design software and digital and audio systems.*

**Radio KATU, Palkkatilankatu 1-3, FIN-00240 Helsinki, Finland**

Fax: 358-9-2290-1620

## AVNET INC.

2211 South 47th Street, Phoenix, AZ, 85034

Tel: (480) 643-2000     Fax: (480) 643-4670     www.avnet.com

*Distributor electronic components, computers and peripherals.*

**Avnet Nortec OY, Italahdenkatua 18A, PL159, FIN-002111 Helsinki, Finland**

Tel: 358-096-13181    Fax: 358-096-92326

## AVON PRODUCTS INC.

1345 Avenue of the Americas, New York, NY, 10105-0196

Tel: (212) 282-5000     Fax: (212) 282-6049     www.avon.com

*Mfr./distributor beauty and related products, fashion jewelry, gifts and collectibles.*

**A-Cosmetics Oy, Kutomotie 18, FIN-00380 Helsinki, Finland**

Tel: 358-9-561-1510    Fax: 35-80-561-1615    Contact: Ismo Jarvinen

## C. R. BARD, INC.

730 Central Ave., Murray Hill, NJ, 07974

Tel: (908) 277-8000     Fax: (908) 277-8078     www.crbard.com

*Mfr. health care products.*

**Bard Medical Systems Oy, PL 25, 00731 Helsinki, Finland**

## BATES WORLDWIDE INC.

405 Lexington Ave., New York, NY, 10174

Tel: (212) 297-7000     Fax: (212) 986-0270     www.batesww.com

*Advertising, marketing, public relations and media consulting.*

**Bates Helsinki Oy, Simonkaju 8, FIN-00100 Helsinki, Finland**

Tel: 358-9-134431    Fax: 358-9-685-2446    Contact: Karl Koskinen, CEO

**Bates Media, 141 Finland, Simonkatu 8, FIN-00100, Helsinki, Finland**

Tel: 358-9-1344-344    Fax: 358-9-1344-3299    Contact: P. Ajanto, Dir.

## BAXTER HEALTHCARE CORPORATION

One Baxter Parkway, Deerfield, IL, 60015

Tel: (847) 948-2000     Fax: (847) 948-3948     www.baxter.com

*Pharmaceutical preparations, surgical/medical instruments and cardiovascular products.*

**Baxter Oy, Myyrmaentie 2 C 47, PO Box 46, FIN-01601 Vantaa, Finland**

## BBDO WORLDWIDE

1285 Ave. of the Americas, New York, NY, 10019

Tel: (212) 459-5000     Fax: (212) 459-6645     www.bbdo.com

*Multinational group of advertising agencies.*

**BBDO Helsinki, Helsinki, Finland**

## BDO SEIDMAN, LLP    BELGIUM

Two Prudential Plaza, 180 N. Stetson Ave., Ste. 2300, Chicago, IL, 60601

Tel: (312) 240-1236     Fax: (312) 240-3329     www.bdo.com

*International accounting and financial consulting firm.*

**BDO Finland OY, PL 166, Tukholmankatu 2, FIN-00251 Helsinki, Finland**

Tel: 358-9-478-0812    Fax: 358-9-477-2521    Contact: Andre Kumlander

## BEA SYSTEMS, INC.

2315 North First Street, St. Jose, CA, 95131

Tel: (408) 570-8000     Fax: (408) 570-8091     www.beasys.com

*Develops communications management software and provider of software consulting services.*

**BEA Systems Oy, Westenintie 1, FIN-02160 Espoo, Finland**

Tel: 358-9-502-4440    Fax: 358-9-502-44430

## BEST WESTERN INTERNATIONAL

6201 North 24th Place, Phoenix, AZ, 85106

Tel: (602) 957-4200    Fax: (602) 957-5740    www.bestwestern.com

*International hotel chain.*

**Seaside Hotel, FIN 00180 Helsinki, Finland**

## BESTFOODS, INC.

700 Sylvan Ave., International Plaza, Englewood Cliffs, NJ, 07632-9976

Tel: (201) 894-4000    Fax: (201) 894-2186    www.bestfoods.com

*Consumer foods products; corn refining.*

**CPC Foods Oy, Ahventie 4A, FIN-02170 ESPOO, Finland**

Tel: 358-9-423-622    Fax: 358-9-452-44-66    Contact: Sakari Tolvanen, Mgr.

## BETZDEARBORN

4636 Somerton Road, PO Box 3002, Trevose, PA, 19053-6783

Tel: (215) 953-2568    Fax: (215) 953-5524    www.betzdearborn.com

*Mfr. water/wastewater and process system treatment chemicals and services.*

**BetzDearborn OY, Tarmontie 6, FIN-15860 Hollola, Finland**

## SAMUEL BINGHAM COMPANY

127 East Lake Street, Ste. 300, Bloomingdale, IL, 60108

Tel: (630) 924-9250    Fax: (630) 924-0469    www.binghamrollers.com

*Print and industrial rollers and inks.*

**Stowe-Woodward Finland OY, PO Box 7, FIN-04261 Kerava 6, Finland**

## BIOGEN, INC.

14 Cambridge Center, Cambridge, MA, 02142

Tel: (617) 679-2000    Fax: (617) 679-2617    www.bigoten.com

*Engaged in medical research and development on autoimmune diseases.*

**Biogen Finland Oy, Pakkalankuja 6, SF-0150 Vantaa, Finland**

Tel: 358-9-77-43-700

## BLACK & DECKER CORPORATION

701 E. Joppa Road, Towson, MD, 21286

Tel: (410) 716-3900    Fax: (410) 716-2933    www.blackanddecker.com

*Mfr. power tools and accessories, security hardware, small appliances, fasteners, information systems and services.*

**Black & Decker Finland, Attn: Finland Office, 701 East Joppa Road, Towson MD 21286**

## BMC SOFTWARE, INC.

2101 City West Blvd., Houston, TX, 77042-2827

Tel: (713) 918-8800    Fax: (713) 918-8000    www.bmc.com

*Engaged in mainframe-related utilities software and services.*

**BMC Software, Lars Sonckin kaari 10, FIN-02600 Espoo, Finland**

## THE BOSTON CONSULTING GROUP

Exchange Place, 31st Fl., Boston, MA, 02109

Tel: (617) 973-1200    Fax: (617) 973-1339    www.bcg.com

*Management consulting company.*

**The Boston Consulting Group, Keskuskatu 1A 4th Fl., FIN-00100 Helsinki, Finland**

Tel: 358-9-228-661

## BOWNE & COMPANY, INC.

345 Hudson Street, New York, NY, 10014

Tel: (212) 924-5500     Fax: (212) 229-3420     www.bowne.com

*Financial printing and foreign language translation, localization (software), internet design and maintenance and facilities management.*

**Bowne International,  Sepänkatu 14, FIN-40720 Jyväskylä, Finland**

Tel: 358-14-334-8050   Fax: 358-14-334-8099

## BOYDEN CONSULTING CORPORATION

364 Elwood Ave., Hawthorne, NY, 10502

Tel: (914) 747-0093     Fax: (914) 980-6147     www.boyden.com

*International executive search firm.*

**Boyden Associates Ltd.,  Etelaranta 4 B 10, FIN-00130 Helsinki, Finland**

Tel: 358-9-6226-860

## BOZELL GROUP

40 West 23rd Street, New York, NY, 10010

Tel: (212) 727-5000     Fax: (212) 645-9173     www.bozell.com

*Advertising, marketing, public relations and media consulting.*

**Kauppaminos Bozell Oy,  Etelaesplanadi 22A, FIN-00130 Helsinki, Finland**

Tel: 358-9-478-200   Fax: 358-9-478-20400   Contact: Vesa-Pekka Leskinen, Mng. Dir.

## BRANSON ULTRASONICS CORPORATION

41 Eagle Road, Danbury, CT, 06813-1961

Tel: (203) 796-0400     Fax: (203) 796-2285     www.branson-plasticsjoin.com

*Mfr. plastics assembly equipment, ultrasonic cleaning equipment.*

**Oy Telko AB,  PO Box 50, Hitsaanjankatu 9, Helsinki 10, Finland**

Tel: 358-9-615-500   Fax: 358-9-780-064

## BRISTOL-MYERS SQUIBB COMPANY

345 Park Ave., New York, NY, 10154-0037

Tel: (212) 546-4000     Fax: (212) 546-4020     www.bms.com

*Pharmaceutical and food preparations, medical and surgical instruments.*

**ConvaTec, Div. Bristol-Myers Squibb,  Fredrikssgatan 33B, FIN-00120 Helsinki 12, Finland**

**Oriola Oy,  PO Box 8, Oriontie 5, SF-02101 Espoo, Finland**

## CAMBREX CORPORATION

1 Meadowlands Plaza, East Rutherford, NJ, 07063

Tel: (201) 804-3000     Fax: (201) 804-9852     www.cambrex.com

*human health, animal health/agriculture and Mfr. biotechnology products and produce specialty chemicals.*

**Timi H B Johansson Fima,  Havsstrñmmen 13, SF-02320 ESPOO, Finland**

## CARRIER CORPORATION

One Carrier Place, Farmington, CT, 06034-4015

Tel: (860) 674-3000     Fax: (860) 679-3010     www.carrier.com

*Mfr./distributor/services A/C, heating and refrigeration equipment.*

**Carrier OY,  Linnavourentie 28A, FIN-00950 Helsinki, Finland**

Tel: 358-0-613-131   Fax: 358-0-613-13500

## CASCADE CORPORATION

2201 NE 201st Ave., Fairview, OR, 97024-9718

Tel: (503) 669-6300     Fax: (503) 669-6321     www.cascor.com

*Mfr. hydraulic forklift truck attachments.*

**Cascade Finland,  Albert Petreliuksenkatu 3, FIN-01370 Vantaa, Finland**

## THE CHERRY CORPORATION

3600 Sunset Ave., PO Box 718, Waukegan, IL, 60087

Tel: (847) 662-9200 Fax: (847) 662-2990 www.cherrycorp.com

*Mfr. electrical switches, electronic keyboards, controls and displays.*

**RepiComp OY, PO Box 36, FIN-00641 Helsinki, Finland**

Tel: 358-9-75276650

## CHESTERTON BINSWANGER INTERNATIONAL

Two Logan Square, 4th Floor, Philadelphia, PA, 19103-2759

Tel: (215) 448-6000 Fax: (215) 448-6238 www.cbbi.com

*Real estate and related services.*

**Blumenauer Immobilien, Sateen Kaari 3A 26, FIN-02100 Helsinki, Finland**

## CINCINNATI INCORPORATED

PO Box 11111, Cincinnati, OH, 45211

Tel: (513) 367-7100 Fax: (513) 367-7552 www.e-ci.com

*Mfr. metal fabricating equipment.*

**OY Gronblom AB, PO Box 81, Helsinki, FIN-00811 Finland**

Tel: 358-9-755-81 Fax: 358-9-780-715

## CISCO SYSTEMS, INC.

170 West Tasman Drive, San Jose, CA, 95134-1706

Tel: (408) 526-4000 Fax: (408) 526-4100 www.cisco.com

*Develop/mfr./market computer hardware and software networking systems.*

**Cisco Systems Finland, Jaakonkatu 2, FIN-01620 Vantaa, Finland**

Tel: 358-9-878061 Fax: 358-9-5305-6775

## CITIGROUP, INC.

153 East 53rd Street, New York, NY, 10043

Tel: (212) 559-1000 Fax: (212) 559-3646 www.citigroup.com

*Provides insurance and financial services worldwide.*

**Citibank N.A., Aleksanterinkatu 48A, PO Box 980, FIN-00101 Helsinki, Finland**

Contact: Stephen L. Dwyre, Mgr.

## CLEAR CHANNEL COMMUNICATIONS

200 East Basse Road, San Antonio, TX, 78209

Tel: (210) 822-2828 Fax: (210) 822-2299 www.clearchannel.com

*Programs and sells airtime for radio stations and owns and places outdoor advertising displays.*

**More Group, PO Box 23, Helsinki FIN-00721, Finland**

Tel: 358-9-8567-2700

## COHERENT INC.

5100 Patrick Henry Drive, PO Box 54980, Santa Clara, CA, 95056

Tel: (408) 764-4000 Fax: (408) 764-4800 www.cohr.com

*Mfr. lasers for science, industrial and medical.*

**Coherent Tutcore Ltd., Korkeakoulunkatu 52, POB 48, FIN-33721 Tampere, Finland**

Tel: 358-3-357-1400 Fax: 358-3-318-4544

## COMPAQ COMPUTER CORPORATION

20555 State Highway 249, PO Box 692000, Houston, TX, 77269-2000

Tel: (281) 370-0670 Fax: (281) 514-1740 www.compaq.com

*Develop/mfr. personal computers.*

**Compaq Computer OY, Keilaranta 1, FIN-02150 Espoo, Finland**

Tel: 358-0-6155-599 Fax: 358-0-6155-9898

## COMPUTER ASSOCIATES INTERNATIONAL INC.

One Computer Associates Plaza, Islandia, NY, 11788

Tel: (516) 342-5224      Fax: (516) 342-5329      www.cai.com

*Integrated business software for enterprise computing and information management, application development, manufacturing, financial applications and professional services.*

**Computer Associates Finland OY, Italahdenkatu 15-17, FIN-00210 Helsinki, Finland**

Tel: 358-9-34-8484

## COMPUWARE CORPORATION

31440 Northwestern Hwy., Farmington Hills, MI, 48334-2564

Tel: (248) 737-7300      Fax: (248) 737-7108      www.compuware.com

*Develop and market software for enterprise and e-commerce solutions.*

**Compuware Nordic, PO Box 38 - Sornaisten Rantatie 23, FIN-00501 Helsinki, Finland**

Tel: 358-9-5842-4040

## CORDIS CORPORATION

PO Box 25700, Miami, FL, 33102-5700

Tel: (305) 824-2000      Fax: (305) 824-2747      www.cordis.com

*Mfr. medical devices and systems.*

**Cordis Denmark, Metsänneidonkuja 8, FIN- 02130 Espoo, Finland**

## CSX CORPORATION

901 East Cary Street, Richmond, VA, 23860

Tel: (804) 782-1400      Fax: (804) 782-6747      www.csx.com

*Provides freight delivery and contract logistics services.*

**Hamina Multimodal Terminals, Gerhardinväylä 7, FIN-49600 Hamina, Finland**

Tel: 358-5-230-6140    Fax: 358-5-230-6119

## CYPRESS SEMICONDUCTOR CORPORATION

3901 N. First Street, San Jose, CA, 95134-1599

Tel: (408) 943-2600      Fax: (408) 943-2796      www.cypress.com

*Mfr. integrated circuits.*

**Cypress Semiconductor, Lehdokkitie 2B, Vantaa FIN-1300, Finland**

Tel: 358-98511471    Fax: 358-98511482

## D'ARCY MASIUS BENTON & BOWLES INC. (DMB&B)

1675 Broadway, New York, NY, 10019

Tel: (212) 468-3622      Fax: (212) 468-2987      www.dmbb.com

*Full service international advertising and communications group.*

**IMP Finland, Arkadiankatu 4C, FIN-00100 Helsinki, Finland**

## DATA GENERAL CORPORATION

4400 Computer Drive, Westboro, MA, 01580

Tel: (508) 898-5000      Fax: (508) 366-1319      www.dg.com

*Design, mfr. general purpose computer systems and peripheral products and services.*

**Data General Oy, Nihtisillantie 3D, FIN-02631 Espoo, Finland**

## DDB NEEDHAM WORLDWIDE INC.

437 Madison Ave., New York, NY, 10022

Tel: (212) 415-2000      Fax: (212) 415-3417      www.ddbn.com

*Advertising agency.*

**DDB Worldwide Helsinki, Helsinki, Finland**

## DELOITTE TOUCHE TOHMATSU INTERNATIONAL

1633 Broadway, New York, NY, 10019

Tel: (212) 492-4000    Fax: (212) 392-4154    www.deloitte.com

*Accounting, audit, tax and management consulting services.*

**Tuokko Deloitte & Touche Oy,  PO Box 94, Munkkiniemen puistotie 25, FIN-00330 Helsinki, Finland**

## DELTA AIR LINES INC.

PO Box 20706, Atlanta, GA, 30320-6001

Tel: (404) 715-2600    Fax: (404) 715-5494    www.delta-air.com

*Major worldwide airline; international air transport services.*

**Delta Air Lines Inc.,  Helsinki, Finland**

## DHL WORLDWIDE EXPRESS

50 California Avenue, San Francisco, CA, 94111

Tel: (415) 677-6100    Fax: (415) 824-9700    www.dhl.com

*Worldwide air express carrier.*

**DHL Worldwide Express,  Valimotie 7, FIN-01510 Vantaa, Finland**

Tel: 358-9-777991

## DIAGNOSTIC PRODUCTS CORPORATION

5700 West 96th Street, Los Angeles, CA, 90045

Tel: (310) 645-8200    Fax: (310) 645-9999    www.dpcweb.com

*Mfr. diagnostic products.*

**DPC Finland O,  Itäkatu 1-5 D 223, FIN-00930 Helsinki, Finland**

Tel: 358-9-3434-960    Fax: 358-9-3434-9696

## DIAMOND POWER INTERNATIONAL, INC.

PO Box 415, Lancaster, OH, 43130

Tel: (740) 687-6500    Fax: (740) 687-7430    www.diamondpower.com

*Mfg. boiler cleaning equipment and ash handling systems: sootblowers, controls, diagnostics systems, gauges, OEM parts, rebuilds and field service.*

**Diamond Power Finland OY,  PO Box 33, FIN-00701 Helsinki, Finland**

Tel: 358-9-3508850    Fax: 358-9-3508850

## DIONEX CORPORATION

1228 Titan Way, PO Box 3603, Sunnyvale, CA, 94086-3603

Tel: (408) 737-0700    Fax: (408) 730-9403    www.dionex.com

*Develop/mfr./market chromatography systems and related products.*

**Oriola-Oy Prolab,  PO Box 8, FIN-02101 Espoo, Finland**

## DOUBLECLICK, INC.

450 West 33rd Street, New York, NY, 10001

Tel: (212) 683-0001    Fax: (212) 889-0062    www.doubleclick.net

*Engaged in online advertising.*

**Doubleclick, Ltd.,  Kalevankatu 30, 7 Krs FIN-00100 Helsinki, Finland**

## THE DOW CHEMICAL COMPANY

2030 Dow Center, Midland, MI, 48674

Tel: (517) 636-1000    Fax: (517) 636-3228    www.dow.com

*Mfr. chemicals, plastics, pharmaceuticals, agricultural products, consumer products.*

**Dow Suomi Oy,  Palokankaantie 1, 49460 Hamina, Finland**

## DRAFT WORLDWIDE

633 North St. Clair Street, Chicago, IL, 60611-3211

Tel: (312) 944-3500     Fax: (312) 944-3566     www.draftworldwide.com

*Full service international advertising agency, engaged in brand building, direct and promotional marketing.*

**LAB Advertising Oy,  Perameihenkatu 12E, FIN-00150 Helsinki, Finland**

Tel: 358-9-622-635-20   Fax: 358-9-622-635-69

## DRAKE BEAM MORIN INC.

101 Huntington Ave., Boston, MA, 02199

Tel: (617) 375-9500     Fax: (617) 267-2011     www.dbm.com

*Human resource management consulting and training.*

**DBM Outplacement Scandinavia Oy,  Sarkiniementie 7, FIN-00210 Helsinki, Finland**

Tel: 358-9-4300-0502   Fax: 358-9-4300-0301

## E.I. DU PONT DE NEMOURS & COMPANY

1007 Market Street, Wilmington, DE, 19898

Tel: (302) 774-1000     Fax: (302) 774-7321     www.dupont.com

*Mfr./sale diversified chemicals, plastics, specialty products and fibers.*

**Suomen Du Pont Oy,  Helsinki, Finland**

## THE DUN & BRADSTREET CORPORATION

1 Diamond Hill Road, Murray Hill, NJ, 07974

Tel: (908) 665-5000     Fax: (908) 665-5524     www.dnbcorp.com

*Provides corporate credit, marketing and accounts-receivable management services and publishes credit ratings and financial information.*

**Dun & Bradstreet Finland,  Sinimaentie 14C, Espoo, Finland**

## EAGLE GLOBAL LOGISTICS (EGL)

15350 Vickery Drive, Houston, TX, 77032

Tel: (281) 618-3100     Fax: (281) 618-3100     www.eaglegl.com

*Ocean/air freight forwarding, customs brokerage, packing and wholesale, logistics management and insurance.*

**Oy Victor EK AB,  Siipitie 10, PO Box 15, FIN-01531 Vantaa, Finland**

Tel: 358-826-133   Fax: 358-870-1482

## EASTMAN KODAK COMPANY

343 State Street, Rochester, NY, 14650

Tel: (716) 724-4000     Fax: (716) 724-1089     www.kodak.com

*Develop/mfr. photo and chemicals products, information management/video/copier systems, fibers/plastics for various industry.*

**Kodak Oy,  PO Box 19, FIN-01511 Vantaa 51, Finland**

## ECOLAB INC.

370 N. Wabasha Street, St. Paul, MN, 55102

Tel: (651) 293-2233     Fax: (651) 293-2379     www.ecolab.com

*Develop/mfr. premium cleaning, sanitizing and maintenance products and services for the hospitality, institutional, and residential markets.*

**Ecolab Ltd.,  Finland**

Tel: 358-396-551

## J.D. EDWARDS & COMPANY

One Technology Way, Denver, CO, 80237

Tel: (303) 334-4000     Fax: (303) 334-4970     www.jdedwards.com

*Computer software products.*

**Major Blue Company,  Vanhaistentie 1, FIN-00420 Helsinki, Finland**

Tel: 358-530-531   Fax: 358-530-53300

## EG&G INC.

900 Clopper Road, Ste. 200, Gaithersburg, MD, 20878

Tel: (301) 840-3000     Fax: (301) 590-0502     www.egginc.com

*Diversified R/D, mfr. and services.*

**Wallac OY,  Mustionkatu 6, PO Box 10, FIN-20101 Turku, Finland**

## ELECTRONIC DATA SYSTEMS CORPORATION (EDS)

5400 Legacy Dr., Plano, TX, 75024

Tel: (972) 605-6000     Fax: (972) 605-2643     www.eds.com

*Provides professional services; management consulting, e.solutions, business process management and information solutions.*

**EDS Finland Oy,  Metsänneidonkuja 12, FIN-02130 Espoo, Finland**

Tel: 358 9 4242 41    Contact: Kaj Green

## EMC CORPORATION

35 Parkwood Drive, Hopkinton, MA, 01748-9103

Tel: (508) 435-1000     Fax: (508) 435-8884     www.emc.com

*Designs/supplies intelligent enterprise storage and retrieval technology for open systems, mainframes and midrange environments.*

**EMC Computer-Systems Oy,  Rauduntie 1, FIN-02130 Espoo, Finland**

## EMERY WORLDWIDE

One Lagoon Drive, Ste. 400, Redwood City, CA, 94065

Tel: (650) 596-9600     Fax: (650) 596-7901     www.emeryworld.com

*Freight transport, global logistics and air cargo.*

**Emery Worldlwide,  Raissitie 6, FIN-O1510 Vantaa-Helsinki, Finland**

## ENGELHARD CORPORATION

101 Wood Ave. S., CN 770, Iselin, NJ, 08830

Tel: (732) 205-5000     Fax: (732) 632-9253     www.engelhard.com

*Mfr. pigments, additives, catalysts, chemicals, engineered materials.*

**Engelhard-Clal Finland,  Teollisuuskatu 16, PO Box 22, 20520 Turku, Finland**

Tel: 358-82-23-75-648    Fax: 358-82-23-78-368

## ENRON CORPORATION

1400 Smith Street, Houston, TX, 77002-7369

Tel: (713) 853-6161     Fax: (713) 853-3129     www.enron.com

*Exploration, production, transportation and distribution of integrated natural gas and electricity.*

**Enron International Finland,  Kasarmikatu 28A3, Helsinki FIN 00130 Finland**

Tel: 35-896815-7555

## ERNST & YOUNG, LLP

787 Seventh Ave., New York, NY, 10019

Tel: (212) 773-3000     Fax: (212) 773-6350     www.eyi.com

*Accounting and audit, tax and management consulting services.*

**Tilintarkastajien Oy/Oy Ernst & Young Ab,  Kaivokatu 8, FIN-00100 Helsinki, Finland**

Tel: 358-0-1727-7406   Fax: 358-0-6221323    Contact: Tuula Helaniemi

## EURO RSCG WORLDWIDE

350 Hudson Street, New York, NY, 10014

Tel: (212) 886-2000     Fax: (212) 886-2016     www.eurorscg.com

*International advertising agency group.*

**VPV EURO RSCG,  Ruoholahdenkatu 26, Helsinki, Finland**

## EXPEDITORS INTERNATIONAL OF WASHINGTON INC.

1015 Third Avenue, 12th Fl., Seattle, WA, 98104-1182

Tel: (206) 674-3400        Fax: (206) 682-9777        www.expd.com

*Air/ocean freight forwarding, customs brokerage, international logistics solutions.*

**Expeditors Finland Oy, Kuriiritie 15, FIN-01511 Vantaa, Finland**

Tel: 358-9-870-1580    Fax: 358-9-870-1500

## FISHER-ROSEMOUNT

8000 Maryland Ave., Ste. 500, Clayton, MO, 63105-4755

Tel: (314) 746-9900        Fax: (314) 746-9974        www.frco.com

*Mfr. industrial process control equipment.*

**Oy Valmet-Rolsemount AG, Lentokentankatu 11, FIN-33900 Tampere, Finland**

**Oy Valmet-Rolsemount AG, Sinimaentie 10B, FIN-02630 Espoo, Finland**

## FLEXTRONICS INC. INTERNATIONAL

2241 Lundy Ave., San Jose, CA, 95131-1822

Tel: (408) 428-1300        Fax: (408) 428-0420        www.flextronics.com

*Contract manufacturer for electronics industry.*

**Kyrel Ems Oy, Box 23, FIN-39201 Kyröskoski, Finland**

Tel: 358-205-345

## FLUKE CORPORATION

6920 Seaway Blvd. PO Box 9090, Everett, WA, 98203

Tel: (425) 347-6100        Fax: (425) 356-5116        www.fluke.com

*Mfr. handheld, electronic test tools for maintenance of electronic equipment.*

**Fluke Finland Oy, Halsuantie 4 - 3. krs, Kannelmaki PL 53, FIN-00421 Helsinki, Finland**

Tel: 358-9-530-8680    Fax: 358-9-530-86830

## FORD MOTOR COMPANY

One American Road, Dearborn, MI, 48121

Tel: (313) 322-3000        Fax: (313) 322-9600        www.ford.com

*Mfr./sales motor vehicles.*

**Oy Ford AB, Henry Fordin Katu 6, FIN-00101 Helsinki, Finland**

## FORT JAMES CORPORATION

1650 Lake Cook Road, Deerfield, IL, 60015

Tel: (847) 317-5000        Fax: (847) 236-3755        www.fortjames.com

*Mfr. and markets consumer tissue products.*

**Fort James Corporation, Ikaalinen, Finland**

## FOSTER WHEELER CORPORATION

Perryville Corporate Park, Clinton, NJ, 08809-4000

Tel: (908) 730-4000        Fax: (908) 730-4100        www.fwc.com

*Manufacturing, engineering and construction.*

**Foster Wheeler Energia Oy, PO Box 201, FIN-78201 Varkaus, Relanderinkatua 2, Finland**

Tel: 358-10-39311    Fax: 358-393-3309

**Foster Wheeler Energia Oy, Varkaus Office - PO Box 21, FIN-78201 Varkaus, Relanderinkatua 2 Finland**

Tel: 358-10-39311    Fax: 358-10-393-7689

**Foster Wheeler Energia Oy, PO Box 45, FIN-00441 Helsinki, Sentnerikuja 2, Finland**

Tel: 358-10-39311    Fax: 358-10-393-6199

**Foster Wheeler Energia Oy, PO Box 15, FIN-20781 Kaarina, Lautakunnankatu 6, Finland**

Tel: 358-10-39311    Fax: 358-10-393-6300

Foster Wheeler Energia Oy, PO Box 66, FIN-48601 Karhula, Finland
Tel: 358-10-39311   Fax: 358-393-3309

Foster Wheeler Energia Oy, PO Box 6, FIN-45201 Kouvola, Finland
Tel: 358-10-39311   Fax: 358-393-3309

## FRITZ COMPANIES, INC.

706 Mission Street, Ste. 900, San Francisco, CA, 94103

Tel: (415) 904-8360   Fax: (415) 904-8661   www.fritz.com

*Integrated transportation, sourcing, distribution and customs brokerage services.*

Fritz Companies Inc., Helsinki, Finland

## GARDNER-DENVER INC.

1800 Gardner Expressway, Quincy, IL, 62301

Tel: (217) 222-5400   Fax: (217) 228-8247   www.gardnerdenver.com

*Mfr. portable air compressors and related drilling accessories.*

Gardner Denver OY, Etu-Hankkionkatu 9, FIN-33700 Tampere, Finland
Tel: 358-205-44141

## GENERAL MOTORS ACCEPTANCE CORPORATION

3044 W. Grand Blvd., Detroit, MI, 48202

Tel: (313) 556-5000   Fax: (313) 556-5108   www.gmac.com

*Automobile financing.*

GMAC Rahoitus Oy, Kutojantie 8, FIN-02630 Espoo, Finland

## GENERAL MOTORS CORPORATION

300 Renaissance Center, Detroit, MI, 48285

Tel: (313) 556-5000   Fax: (313) 556-5108   www.gm.com

*Mfr. full line vehicles, automotive electronics, commercial technologies, telecommunications, space, finance.*

Suomen General Motors Oy, Kutojantje 8, FIN-02630 Espoo, Finland

## GETZ BROS & COMPANY, INC.

150 Post Street, Ste. 500, San Francisco, CA, 94108-4750

Tel: (415) 772-5500   Fax: (415) 772-5659   www.getz.com

*Diversified manufacturing, marketing and distribution services and travel services.*

Getz Bros. & Co. (Finland) Oy, FIN-15141 Lahti, Finland
Tel: 358-3-752-5182   Fax: 358-3-752-5192   Contact: N. Suti, Gen. Mgr.   Emp: 1

## THE GILLETTE COMPANY

Prudential Tower Building, Boston, MA, 02199

Tel: (617) 421-7000   Fax: (617) 421-7123   www.gillette.com

*Develop/mfr. personal care/use products: blades and razors, toiletries, cosmetics, stationery.*

Braun Finland Oy, Helsinki, Finland

Oy Gillette Finland AB, Helsinki, Finland

## GILSON INC.

3000 W. Beltline Hwy, PO Box 620027, Middleton, WI, 53562-0027

Tel: (608) 836-1551   Fax: (608) 831-4451   www.gilson.com

*Mfr. analytical/biomedical instruments.*

Norlab Oy, PO Box 44, 01721 Vantaa Hameenkylan Kartano FIN-01721 Vantaa, Finland

## GIW INDUSTRIES, INC.

5000 Wrightsboro Rd., Grovetown, GA, 30813

Tel: (706) 863-1011   Fax: (706) 860-5897   www.giwindustries.com

*Mfr. slurry pumps.*

Oy Mercantile-KSB AB, PO Box 129, Helsinki, Finland

## GLEASON CORPORATION

1000 University Ave., Rochester, NY, 14692

Tel: (716) 473-1000      Fax: (716) 461-4348      www.gleasoncorp.com

*Mfr. gear making machine tools; tooling and services.*

**Machinery Oy, Ansatie 5, Vantaa, FIN-01740 Finland**

## GRACO INC.

4050 Olson Memorial Hwy, PO Box 1441, Minneapolis, MN, 55440-1441

Tel: (612) 623-6000      Fax: (612) 623-6777      www.graco.com

*Mfr. systems and equipment to service fluid handling systems and automotive equipment.*

**Lastentarvike Oy, Sarkatie 3, FIN-01720 Vantaa, Finland**

Tel: 358-9-852-05-100   Fax: 358-9-852-05-426   Contact: Tukku Myynti

## GREY GLOBAL GROUP

777 Third Ave., New York, NY, 10017

Tel: (212) 546-2000      Fax: (212) 546-1495      www.grey.com

*International advertising agency.*

**AS & Grey, Annankatu 28, FIN-00100 Helsinki, Finland**

**Creator Grey, Eerikinkatu 28, FIN-00180 Helsinki, Finland**

## HARNISCHFEGER INDUSTRIES INC.

PO Box 554, Milwaukee, WI, 53201

Tel: (414) 797-6480      Fax: (414) 797-6573      www.harnischfeger.com

*Mfr. mining and material handling equipment, papermaking machinery and computer systems.*

**Beloit Corp., Valtameri Oy, Pakilantic 61, FIN-00660 Helsinki, Finland**

## HEIDRICK & STRUGGLES INTERNATIONAL, INC.

Sears Tower, 233 South Wacker Drive, Chicago, IL, 60606

Tel: (312) 496-1200      Fax: (312) 496-1290      www.heidrick.com

*Executive search firm.*

**Heidrick & Struggles Intl. Inc., Erottajankatu 9A, FIN-00130 Helsinki, Finland**

Tel: 358-9-612-2130   Fax: 358-9-612-21340

## HERCULES INC.

Hercules Plaza, 1313 N. Market Street, Wilmington, DE, 19894-0001

Tel: (302) 594-5000      Fax: (302) 594-5400      www.herc.com

*Mfr. specialty chemicals, plastics, film and fibers, coatings, resins, food ingredients.*

**Hercules ChemicalsLtd., Tampere, Finland**

**Oy Hercules AB, Mannerheimintie 14A, FIN-00100 Helsinki, Finland**

## HEWLETT-PACKARD COMPANY

3000 Hanover Street, Palo Alto, CA, 94304-1185

Tel: (650) 857-1501      Fax: (650) 857-5518      www.hp.com

*Mfr. computing, communications and measurement products and services.*

**Hewlett-Packard Oy, Piispankalliontie 17, FIN-02200 Espoo, Finland**

Tel: 358-9-88-721

## HONEYWELL INTERNATIONAL INC.

101 Columbia Road, Morristown, NJ, 07962

Tel: (973) 455-2000      Fax: (973) 455-4807      www.honeywell.com

*Develop/mfr. controls for home and building, industry, space and aviation.*

**Honeywell OYJ, Ruukintie 8, FIN-02320 Espoo 32, Finland**

Tel: 358-9-3480101   Fax: 358-9-348-01234

## HOUGHTON INTERNATIONAL INC.

PO Box 930, Madison & Van Buren Avenues, Valley Forge, PA, 19482-0930

Tel: (610) 666-4000     Fax: (610) 666-1376     www.houghtonintl.com

*Mfr. specialty chemicals, hydraulic fluids and lubricants.*

**Teknoma Oy, PO Box 150, FIN-00211 Helsinki, Finland**

Tel: 358-9-681021

## HOWMEDICA OSTEONICS, INC.

359 Veterans Blvd., Rutherford, NJ, 07070

Tel: (201) 507-7300     Fax: (201) 935-4873     www.howmedica.com

*Mfr. of maxillofacial products (orthopedic implants).*

**Howmedica Finland, Helsinki, Finland**

Tel: 358-9773-2277

## J.M. HUBER CORPORATION

333 Thornall Street, Edison, NJ, 08818

Tel: (732) 549-8600     Fax: (732) 549-2239     www.huber.com

*Crude oil, gas, carbon black, kaolin clay, rubber and paper pigments, timber and minerals.*

**J.M. Huber, Hamina, Finland**

## HYPERION SOLUTIONS CORPORATION

1344 Crossman Avenue, Sunnyvale, CA, 94089

Tel: (408) 744-9500     Fax: (408) 744-0400     www.hyperion.com

*Mfr. data analysis software tools.*

**Hyperion Finland, Westendintie 1-A, FIN-02160 Espoo, Finland**

Tel: 358-9-439-20500

## i2 TECHNOLOGIES, INC.

11701 Luna Road, Dallas, TX, 75234

Tel: (214) 860-6106     Fax: (214) 860-6060     www.i2.com

*Mfr. business-to-business software.*

**i2 Technologies Finland, Eskolantie 1, Helsinki FIN-00720, Finland**

## IBM CORPORATION

New Orchard Road, Armonk, NY, 10504

Tel: (914) 765-1900     Fax: (914) 765-7382     www.ibm.com

*Information products, technology and services.*

**IBM Oy, IBM Nordic Information Center, PL 265 FIN-00101, Helsinki Finland**

Tel: 358-9-4591   Fax: 358-9-459-4442

## INFONET SERVICES CORPORATION

2100 East Grand Ave., El Segundo, CA, 90245-1022

Tel: (310) 335-2600     Fax: (310) 335-4507     www.infonet.com

*Provider of Internet services and electronic messaging services.*

**Oy Infonet Finland Ltd., Elimanenkatu 20 - 1st Floor, FIN-00510 Helsinki, Finland**

Tel: 358-2040-3737   Fax: 358-2040-3736

## INGRAM MICRO INC.

PO Box 25125, 1600 E. St. Andrew Place, Santa Ana, CA, 92799

Tel: (714) 566-1000     Fax: (714) 566-7940     www.ingrammicro.com

*Engaged in wholesale distribution of microcomputer products.*

**Ingram Micro Oy, Vapaalantie 8, FIN-01650 Vantaa, Finland**

### INTEGRATED DEVICE TECHNOLOGY, INC.

2975 Stender Way, Santa Clara, CA, 95054

Tel: (408) 727-6116    Fax: (408) 492-8674    www.idt.com

*Mfr. high-performance semiconductors and modules.*

**Integrated Device Technology, AB, Innopoli, Tekniikantie 12, Espoo FIN-02150, Finland**

Tel: 358-9-2517 3044    Fax: 358-9-2517 3045

### INTER-CONTINENTAL HOTELS

3 Ravina Drive, Suite 2900, Atlanta, GA, 30346-2149

Tel: (770) 604-2000    Fax: (770) 604-5403    www.interconti.com

*Worldwide hotel and resort accommodations.*

**Strand Inter-Continental Helsinki, John Stenbergin Ranta 4, FIN-00530 Helsinki, Finland**

Tel: 358-9-39-351    Fax: 358-9-393-5255

### INTERGRAPH CORPORATION

One Madison Industrial Park, Huntsville, AL, 35894-0001

Tel: (256) 730-2000    Fax: (256) 730-7898    www.intergraph.com

*Develop/mfr. interactive computer graphic systems.*

**Intergraph (Finland) OY, Kutojantie 11, FIN-02630 Espoo, Finland**

Tel: 358-9-80-4641    Fax: 358-9-80-464333

### INTERMEC TECHNOLOGIES CORPORATION

6001 36th Ave. West, PO Box 4280, Everett, WA, 98203-9280

Tel: (425) 348-2600    Fax: (425) 355-9551    www.intermec.com

*Mfr./distributor automated data collection systems.*

**Intermec Technologies OY, Valkjärventie 1, FIN-02130 Espoo, Finland**

Tel: 358-9-523721    Fax: 358-9-529224

### INTERNATIONAL PAPER COMPANY

2 Manhattanville Road, Purchase, NY, 10577

Tel: (914) 397-1500    Fax: (914) 397-1596    www.ipaper.com

*Mfr./distributor container board, paper and wood products.*

**Horsell Graafinen Oy, Rilhimietientie 4, FIN-01720 Vantaa, Finland**

### INTERNATIONAL RECTIFIER CORPORATION

233 Kansas Street, El Segundo, CA, 90245

Tel: (310) 322-3331    Fax: (310) 322-3332    www.irf.com

*Mfr. power semiconductor components.*

**International Rectifier - Finland, Mikkelankallio 3, FIN-02770 Espoo, Finland**

Tel: 358-859-9155    Fax: 358-9-859-91560

### ITT-GOULDS PUMPS INC.

240 Fall Street, Seneca Falls, NY, 13148

Tel: (315) 568-2811    Fax: (315) 568-2418    www.gouldspumps.com

*Mfr. industrial and water systems pumps.*

**Mäntän Pumppauspalvelu OY, Voimankatu 3, FIN-35820 Mänttä, Finland**

Tel: 358-3-4748-136    Fax: 358-3-4748-135

### J. WALTER THOMPSON COMPANY

466 Lexington Ave., New York, NY, 10017

Tel: (212) 210-7000    Fax: (212) 210-6944    www.jwt.com

*International advertising and marketing services.*

**Thompson-Interplan, Helsinki, Finland**

## JUKI UNION SPECIAL CORPORATION

5 Haul Road, Wayne, NJ, 07470

Tel: (973) 633-7200     Fax: (973) 633-9629     www.unionspecial.com

*Mfr. sewing machines.*

**Pavel Ltd. Finland,  Melkonkatu 16B, SF 00210 Helsinki, Finland**

## A.T. KEARNEY INC.

222 West Adams Street, Chicago, IL, 60606

Tel: (312) 648-0111     Fax: (312) 223-6200     www.atkearney.com

*Management consultants and executive search.*

**A. T. Kearney Oy,  Metsanneidonkuja 10, PO Box 34, FIN-02131 Espoo, Finland**

Tel: 358-9-751-7100

## KELLOGG COMPANY

One Kellogg Square, PO Box 3599, Battle Creek, MI, 49016-3599

Tel: (616) 961-2000     Fax: (616) 961-2871     www.kelloggs.com

*Mfr. ready-to-eat cereals and convenience foods.*

**Kellogg Finland,  Attn: Finland Office, One Kellogg Square, PO Box 3599, Battle Creek MI 49016-3599**

## KENNAMETAL INC.

State Rte. 981, Latrobe, PA, 15650

Tel: (724) 539-5000     Fax: (724) 539-4710     www.kennametal.com

*Tools, hard carbide and tungsten alloys for metalworking industry.*

**Hertek OY,  FIN-05840 Hyvinkdd, Finland**

Tel: 358-14-483050   Fax: 358-14-3053

## KEPNER-TREGOE INC.

PO Box 704, Princeton, NJ, 08542-0740

Tel: (609) 921-2806     Fax: (609) 497-0130     www.kepner-tregoe.com

*Management consulting; specializing in strategy formulation, problem solving, decision making, project management, and cost reduction.*

**Oy Rastor AB,  Wavulinintie 3, FIN-00210 Helsinki, Finland**

## KIMBERLY-CLARK CORPORATION

351 Phelps Drive, Irving, TX, 75038

Tel: (972) 281-1200     Fax: (972) 281-1435     www.kimberly-clark.com

*Mfr./sales/distribution of consumer tissue, household and personal care products.*

**Kimberly-Clark Corp.,  Helsinki, Finland**

## LESTER B. KNIGHT & ASSOCIATES INC.

549 West Randolph Street, Chicago, IL, 60661

Tel: (312) 346-2300     Fax: (312) 648-1085

*Architecture, engineering, planning, operations and management consulting.*

**Knight Wendling Kupair Ltd.,  Martinkatu 3, PO Box 16, FIN-01621 Vantaa, Finland**

## KORN/FERRY INTERNATIONAL

1800 Century Park East, Los Angeles, CA, 90067

Tel: (310) 843-4100     Fax: (310) 553-6452     www.kornferry.com

*Executive search; management consulting.*

**Korn/Ferry International,  Helsinki, Finland**

Tel: 358-9-61-22-560   Fax: 358-9-61-22-5656

## KPMG INTERNATIONAL LLP

345 Park Avenue, New York, NY, 10022

Tel: (201) 307-7000     Fax: (201) 930-8617     www.kpmg.com

*Accounting and audit, tax and management consulting services.*

**KPMG Management Consultants OY, Kalcoankatu 3A, Helsinki, Finland**

**KPMG Wideri Oy Ab, Mannerheimintie 20 B, FIN-00100 Helsinki, Finland**

Tel: 358-9-693931    Fax: 358-9-693-9399    Contact: Hannu Niilekselä, Ptnr.

## K-TEL INTERNATIONAL INC.

2605 Fernbrook Lane North, Plymouth, MN, 55447-4736

Tel: (612) 559-6800     Fax: (612) 559-6803     www.k-tel.com

*Sales and distribution of packaged consumer music entertainment and convenience products.*

**K-Tel Intl. (Finland) Oy, Saynaslahdentie 18, FIN-00560 Helsinki, Finland**

## LEVI STRAUSS & COMPANY

1155 Battery St., San Francisco, CA, 94111-1230

Tel: (415) 544-6000     Fax: (415) 501-3939     www.levistrauss.com

*Mfr./distributor casual wearing apparel.*

**Suomen Levi Strauss OY, Kaisaniemenkatu 3 B 25, FIN-00100 Helsinki, Finland**

Tel: 358-962-5955    Fax: 358-962-4452

## LEXMARK INTERNATIONAL

1 Lexmark Centre Dr., Lexington, KY, 40550

Tel: (606) 232-2000     Fax: (606) 232-1886     www.lexmark.com

*Develop, manufacture, supply of printing solutions and products, including laser, inkjet, and dot matrix printers.*

**Lexmark Finland, Piispantilankuja 6, FIN-022400 Espoo, Finland**

## ELI LILLY & COMPANY

Lilly Corporate Center, Indianapolis, IN, 46285

Tel: (317) 276-2000     Fax: (317) 277-6579     www.lilly.com

*Mfr. pharmaceuticals and animal health products.*

**Oy Eli Lilly Finland, Rajatorpantie 41C 3rd Fl., FIN-01640 Vantaa, Finland**

Tel: 358-9-854-5250    Fax: 358-9-854-2515

## LOCTITE CORPORATION

1001 Trout Brook Crossing, Rocky Hill, CT, 06067-3910

Tel: (860) 571-5100     Fax: (860) 571-5465     www.loctite.com

*Mfr./sale industrial adhesives, sealants and coatings..*

**Loctite Finland OY, Ralssitie 6, FIN-01510 Vantaa, Finland**

Tel: 358-9-8254-1120    Contact: Jari Jalava, Bus. Mgr.

## LOWE LINTAS & PARTNERS WORLDWIDE

One Dag Hammarskjold Plaza, New York, NY, 10017

Tel: (212) 605-8000     Fax: (212) 605-4705     www.interpublic.com

*Full-service, integrated marketing communications company/advertising agency.*

**Ammirati Puris Lintas Finland, Pormestarinrinne 5, FIN-00161 Helsinki, Finland**

Tel: 358-9-476-19400    Fax: 358-9-476-19429    Contact: Ismo Ojanen, Mng. Dir.

## THE LUBRIZOL CORPORATION

29400 Lakeland Blvd., Wickliffe, OH, 44092-2298

Tel: (440) 943-4200     Fax: (440) 943-5337     www.lubrizol.com

*Mfr. chemicals additives for lubricants and fuels.*

**Lubrizol Finland, Helsinki, Finland**

Tel: 358-9-7001-7221

### M/A-COM INC.

1011 Pawtucket Boulevard, Lowell, MA, 01853-3295

Tel: (978) 442-5000     Fax: (978) 442-5354     www.macom.com

*Mfr. electronic components, semiconductor devices and communications equipment.*

**M/A-COM Ltd., Konalantie 47C, PO Box 100, FIN-00390 Helsinki, Finland**

Tel: 3589-5123-420    Fax: 3589-5123-4250

### MARK IV INDUSTRIES INC.

501 John James Audubon Pkwy., PO Box 810, Amherst, NY, 14226-0810

Tel: (716) 689-4972     Fax: (716) 689-1529     www.mark-iv.com

*Mfr. of engineered systems and components utilizing mechanical and fluid power transmission, fluid transfer, and power systems and components.*

**M-Filter/Mark IV Automotive, PL 12, FIN-88601 Haapavesi, Finland**

Tel: 358-8-452-232    Fax: 358-8-451-795

### McCANN-ERICKSON WORLDGROUP

750 Third Ave., New York, NY, 10017

Tel: (212) 984-3644     Fax: (212) 984-2629     www.mccann.com

*International advertising and marketing services.*

**Oy Liikemainonta-McCann AB, Keskuskatu 57, FIN-00100 Helsinki, Finland**

**Womena Oy, Yrjonkatu 29A, FIN-00100 Helsinki, Finland**

### McDONALD'S CORPORATION

McDonald's Plaza, Oak Brook, IL, 60523

Tel: (630) 623-3000     Fax: (630) 623-7409     www.mcdonalds.com

*Fast food chain stores.*

**McDonald's Corp., Finland**

### McKINSEY & COMPANY

55 East 52nd Street, New York, NY, 10022

Tel: (212) 446-7000     Fax: (212) 446-8575     www.mckinsey.com

*Management and business consulting services.*

**McKinsey & Company, Mannerheimintie 14 B, FIN-00100 Helsinki, Finland**

Tel: 358-9-615-7100    Fax: 358-9-615-71200

### MECHANICAL DYNAMICS, INC.

2301 Commonwealth Blvd., Ann Arbor, MI, 48105

Tel: (734) 994-3800     Fax: (734) 994-6418     www.adams.com

*Mfr. Adams prototyping software to automotive industry.*

**MBS Models Oy, Nihtisalontie 6 A1,FIN- 02630 Espoo, Finland**

Tel: 358-9-43-926555    Fax: 358-9-43-926556

### MEMOREX CORPORATION

10100 Pioneer Blvd., Ste. 110, Santa Fe Springs, CA, 90670

Tel: (562) 906-2800     Fax: (562) 906-2848     www.memorex.com

*Magnetic recording tapes, etc.*

**Oy Memorex AB, Hopeatie 1B, PO Box 3, FIN-00400 Helsinki, Finland**

### MERCK & COMPANY, INC.

One Merck Drive, PO Box 100, Whitehouse Station, NJ, 08889-0100

Tel: (908) 423-1000     Fax: (908) 423-2592     www.merck.com

*Pharmaceuticals, chemicals and biologicals.*

**Suomen MSD Oy, Maapallonkuja 1, FIN-02210 Espoo, Finland**

## MICROSOFT CORPORATION

One Microsoft Way, Redmond, WA, 98052-6399

Tel: (425) 882-8080      Fax: (425) 936-7329      www.microsoft.com

*Computer software, peripherals and services.*

**Microsoft Finland OY, Jaakonkatu 2, FIN-01620 Vantaa, Suomi, Finland**

Tel: 358-9-0525-501    Fax: 358-9-0878-8778

## MILACRON INC.

2090 Florence Ave., Cincinnati, OH, 45206

Tel: (513) 487-5000      Fax: (513) 487-5057      www.milacron.com

*Metalworking and plastics technologies.*

**Tresmeka Oy, PO Box 14, FIN-00371 Helsinki, Finland**

Tel: 358-9-4764500    Fax: 358-9-4764525    Contact: Marcus Töttermann

## MILLIPORE CORPORATION

80 Ashby Road, PO Box 9125, Bedford, MA, 01730

Tel: (781) 533-6000      Fax: (781) 533-3110      www.millipore.com

*Mfr. flow and pressure measurement and control components; precision filters, hi-performance liquid chromatography instruments.*

**Millipore Oy, Ruukinkuja 1, FIN-02320 Espoo 32, Finland**

## MOLEX INC.

2222 Wellington Court, Lisle, IL, 60532

Tel: (630) 969-4550      Fax: (630) 969-1352      www.molex.com

*Mfr. electronic, electrical and fiber optic interconnection products and systems, switches, application tooling.*

**Molex Finland, Lämmittäjänkatu 4, SF-00810 Helsinki, Finland**

## MOOG INC.

Jamison Road, East Aurora, NY, 14052-0018

Tel: (716) 652-2000      Fax: (716) 687-4471      www.moog.com

*Mfr. precision control components and systems.*

**Moog Finland, Tekniikanti 4, FIN-02150 Espoo, Finland**

## J. P. MORGAN CHASE & CO. INC.

World Headquarters, 270 Park Ave., New York, NY, 10017

Tel: (212) 270-6000      Fax: (212) 622-9030      www.jpmorganchase.com

*Provides integrated financial solutions for institutions and individuals worldwide, including asset management, investment banking and commercial banking.*

**J. P. Morgan Chase & Co., PO Box 50, Kaivokatu 10A, FIN-00100 Helsinki, Finland**

## MOTOROLA, INC.

1303 East Algonquin Road, Schaumburg, IL, 60196

Tel: (847) 576-5000      Fax: (847) 538-5191      www.motorola.com

*Mfr. communications equipment, semiconductors and cellular phones.*

**Motorola Finland AB, Hopeatie 2, FIN-00440 Helsinki, Finland**

Tel: 358-9-6866-880    Fax: 358-9-676-287

## NALCO CHEMICAL COMPANY

One Nalco Center, Naperville, IL, 60563-1198

Tel: (630) 305-1000      Fax: (630) 305-2900      www.nalco.com

*Chemicals for water and waste water treatment, oil products and refining, industry processes; water and energy management service.*

**Suomen Nalco Oy, Mikonkatu 8 A 9 KRS, FIN-00100 Helsinki, Finland**

Tel: 358-9-4354-3360    Fax: 358-9-4354-3367

## NATIONAL STARCH AND CHEMICAL COMPANY

10 Finderne Ave., Bridgewater, NJ, 08807-3300

Tel: (908) 685-5000     Fax: (908) 685-5005     www.nationalstarch.com

*Mfr. adhesives and sealants, resins and specialty chemicals, electronic materials and adhesives, food products, industry starch.*

**National Starch & Chemical AB, Pihatorma 1 A, FIN-02240 Espoo Helsinki, Finland**

Tel: 358-9-2709-5436   Fax: 358-9-2709-5437

## NETWORK ASSOCIATES, INC.

3965 Freedom Circle, Santa Clara, CA, 95054

Tel: (408) 988-3832     Fax: (408) 970-9727     www.networkassociates.com

*Designs and produces network security and network management software and hardware.*

**Network Associates Oy, Mikonkatu 9 - 5/F, FIN-00100 Helsinki, Finland**

Tel: 358-9-527-070   Fax: 358-9-5270-7100

## A .C. NIELSEN COMPANY

177 Broad Street, Stamford, CT, 06901

Tel: (203) 961-3000     Fax: (203) 961-3190     www.acnielsen.com

*Market and consumer research firm.*

**Marketindex OY, Tietajantie 14, FIN-021 30 Espoo, Finland**

## NORDSON CORPORATION

28601 Clemens Road, Westlake, OH, 44145-4551

Tel: (440) 892-1580     Fax: (440) 892-9507     www.nordson.com

*Mfr. industry application equipment, sealants and packaging machinery.*

**Nordson Finland Oy, Pihkatie 4, FIN-00410 Helsinki, Finland**

Tel: 358-9-530-8080   Fax: 358-9-530-80850

## OM GROUP, INC. (OMG)

3800 Terminal Tower, Cleveland, OH, 44113-2203

Tel: (216) 781-0083     Fax: (216) 781-0902     www.omgi.com

*Producer and marketer of metal-based specialty chemicals.*

**OM Group, Inc., Kokkola, Finland**

## ORACLE CORPORATION

500 Oracle Parkway, Redwood Shores, CA, 94065

Tel: (650) 506-7000     Fax: (650) 506-7200     www.oracle.com

*Develop/manufacture software.*

**Oracle Finland, Piispanportti 10, PO Box 47, FIN-02200 Espoo, Finland**

## OSMOSE INTERNATIONAL INC.

980 Ellicott Street, Buffalo, NY, 14209

Tel: (716) 882-5905     Fax: (716) 882-5139     www.osmose.com

*Mfr. wood preservatives; maintenance and inspection utility poles, railroad track and marine piling.*

**Injecta Osmose A/S, PL 72, 00131 Helsinki, Finland**

Tel: 46-0-431-54766

## OTIS ELEVATOR COMPANY

10 Farm Springs Road, Farmington, CT, 06032

Tel: (860) 676-6000     Fax: (860) 676-5111     www.otis.com

*Mfr. elevators and escalators.*

**Otis Oy, Vesimyllynkatu 3, PO Box 473, FIN-33310 Tampere, Finland**

## OUTOKUMPU TECHNOLOGY, INC. , CARPCO DIV.

1310-1 Tradeport Drive, Jacksonville, FL, 32218

Tel: (904) 353-3681     Fax: (904) 353-8705     www.carpco.com

*Design/mfr. separation equipment for mining, recycling and research; testing and flowsheet design.*

**Outokumpu Mintec Oy, Riihitontuntie 7C, PO Box 84, FIN-02201 Espoo, Finland**

Tel: 358-9-4211    Fax: 358-9-421-3156

## OWENS-ILLINOIS, INC.

One SeaGate, PO Box 1035, Toledo, OH, 43666

Tel: (419) 247-5000     Fax: (419) 247-2839     www.o-i.com

*Largest mfr. of glass containers in the US; plastic containers, compression-molded closures and dispensing systems.*

**Karbulan Lasi Oy, PL 18, FIN-48601 Karhula, Finland**

Tel: 358-5-224-2711    Fax: 358-5-224-2700

## PANAMETRICS

221 Crescent Street, Waltham, MA, 02154

Tel: (781) 899-2719     Fax: (781) 899-1552     www.panametrics.com

*Process/non-destructive test instrumentation.*

**Orion Corporation, Ltd./Medion, Nilsiankatu 10-14, FIN-00510 Helsinki, Finland**

Tel: 358-9-39371   Fax: 358-9-7018398    Contact: Ken Enberg

## PARAMETRIC TECHNOLOGY CORPORATION

128 Technology Drive, Waltham, MA, 02154

Tel: (781) 398-5000     Fax: (781) 398-5674     www.ptc.com

*Supplier of mechanical design automation and product data management software and services.*

**Parametric Technology (Findland) Oy, Piispantilankuja 4, FIN-02240 Espoo, Finland**

Tel: 358-9-8870-650   Fax: 358-9-8870-6525

## PARKER HANNIFIN CORPORATION

6035 Parkland Blvd., Cleveland, OH, 44124-4141

Tel: (216) 896-3000     Fax: (216) 896-4000     www.parker.com

*Mfr. motion-control products.*

**Oy Parker Hannifin (Finland), Tuupakantie 8-10 B, FIN-01740 Vantaa, Finland**

**Parker Hannifin OY, Finn-Filter Div., FIN-31700 Urjala AS, Finland**

## PENFORD CORPORATION

777 108th Ave. NE, Ste 2390, Bellevue, WA, 98004-5193

Tel: (425) 462-6000     Fax: (425) 462-2819     www.penx.com

*Mfr. food ingredients, nutritional supplements, spec. carbohydrate and synthetic polymer chemicals.*

**Edward Mendell Co., Maitotie 4, FIN-15560 Nastola, Finland**

## PERKIN ELMER, INC.

45 William Street, Wellesley, MA, 02481

Tel: (781) 237-5100     Fax: (781) 431-4255     www.perkinelmer.com

*Mfr. equipment and devices to detect explosives and bombs on airline carriers.*

**PerkinElmer Life Sciences, PO Box 10, FIN-20101 Turku, Finland**

## PFIZER INC.

235 East 42nd Street, New York, NY, 10017-5755

Tel: (212) 573-2323     Fax: (212) 573-7851     www.pfizer.com

*Research-based, global health care company.*

**Pfizer Oy, Tapiontori, Tapiola, Keskustorni 3rd Fl, FIN-02100 Espoo 1Q, Finland**

## PHARMACIA CORPORATION

100 Route 206 North, Peapack, NJ, 07977

Tel: (908) 901-8000      Fax: (908) 901-8379      www.pharmacia.com

*Mfr. pharmaceuticals, agricultural products, industry chemicals.*

**Pharmacia & Upjohn,  Rajatorpantie 41C, FIN-01640 Vantaa, Finland**

## PITNEY BOWES INC.

1 Elmcroft Road, Stamford, CT, 06926-0700

Tel: (203) 356-5000      Fax: (203) 351-6835      www.pitneybowes.com

*Mfr. postage meters, mailroom equipment, copiers, bus supplies, bus services, facsimile systems and financial services.*

**Pitney Bowes Oy,  PL 109, FIN-00211 Helsinki 21, Finland**

Tel: 358-0-692-5600   Fax: 358-0-692-6227   Contact: Kari Jantti, Mng. Dir.   Emp: 45

## PLANET HOLLYWOOD INTERNATIONAL, INC.

8669 Commodity Circle, Orlando, FL, 32819

Tel: (407) 363-7827      Fax: (407) 363-4862      www.planethollywood.com

*Theme-dining restaurant chain and merchandise retail stores.*

**Planet Hollywood International, Inc.,  Helsinki, Finland**

## POWERWARE CORPORATION

8609 Six Forks Road, Raleigh, NC, 27615

Tel: (919) 870-3020      Fax: (919) 870-3100      www.powerware.com

*Mfr./services uninterruptible power supplies and related equipment.*

**Powerware Electronics Oy,  Koskelontie 13, FIN-02920 Espoo, Finland**

Tel: 358-9-452-661   Fax: 358-9-452-66568

## PRICEWATERHOUSECOOPERS LLP

1301 Ave. of the Americas, New York, NY, 10019

Tel: (212) 596-7000      Fax: (212) 259-1301      www.pwcglobal.com

*Accounting and auditing, tax and management, and human resource consulting services.*

**PriceWaterhouseCoopers,  Kehrasaari B, FIN-33200 Tampere, Finland**

Tel: 358-31-242-8656   Fax: 358-31-2122-987

**PriceWaterhouseCoopers,  Vattuniemenranta 2, FIN-000210 Helsinki, Finland**

Tel: 358-0-673-011   Fax: 358-0-674-118

## PROCTER & GAMBLE COMPANY

One Procter & Gamble Plaza, Cincinnati, OH, 45202

Tel: (513) 983-1100      Fax: (513) 562-4500      www.pg.com

*Personal care, food, laundry, cleaning and industry products.*

**Procter & Gamble Nordic,  Pl 173 - lars Sonckin Kaari 10, FIN-02601 Espoo, Finland**

**Procter & Gamble Oy,  Kuluttajapalvelu Pl 73, FIN-00701 Helsinki, Finland**

Tel: 358-9-203-25525

## QUINTILES TRANSNATIONAL CORPORATION

4709 Creekstone Dr., Durham, NC, 27703

Tel: (919) 998-2000      Fax: (919) 998-9113      www.quintiles.com

*Mfr. pharmaceuticals.*

**Quintiles OY,  Tapiola Spektri Pilotti Building 3F, ValkjSrventie 2 Espoo, SF-02130 Finland**

## QWEST COMMUNICATIONS INTERNATIONAL INC.

1801 California Street, Ste. 5200, Denver, CO, 80202

Tel: (303) 896-2020      Fax: (303) 793-6654      www.uswest.com

*Tele-communications provider; integrated communications services.*

**KPNQwest (JV),  Helsinki, Finland**

## RADISSON HOTELS INTERNATIONAL
Carlson Pkwy., PO Box 59159, Minneapolis, MN, 55459-8204

Tel: (612) 540-5526      Fax: (612) 449-3400      www.radisson.com

*Hotels and resorts.*

**Radisson SAS Royal Hotel Helsinki,  Runeberginkatu 1, FIN-00100 Helsinki, Finland**

Tel: 358-9-69-580   Fax: 358-9-69-587100

## RAY & BERNDTSON, INC.
301 Commerce, Ste. 2300, Fort Worth, TX, 76102

Tel: (817) 334-0500      Fax: (817) 334-0779      www.prb.com

*Executive search, management audit and management consulting firm.*

**Ray & Berndtson,  Bulevardi 5A, FIN-00120 Helsinki, Finland**

Tel: 358-0-607300   Fax: 358-0-6801390   Contact: Finn Wardi, Mng. Ptnr.

## RAYCHEM CORPORATION
300 Constitution Dr., Menlo Park, CA, 94025-1164

Tel: (650) 361-3333      Fax: (650) 361-5579      www.raychem.com

*Develop/mfr./market materials science products for electronics, telecommunications and industry.*

**Raychem Oy,  Tiilitie 10, FIN-01720 Vantaa, Finland**

## RAZORFISH, INC.
107 Grand Street, 3rd Fl., New York, NY, 10013

Tel: (212) 966-5960      Fax: (212) 966-6915      www.razorfish.com

*Engaged in consulting and web services.*

**Razorfish Finland,  Lapuankatu 4, Helsinki FIN-00100, Finland**

Tel: 358-9-41580800

## READER'S DIGEST ASSOCIATION, INC.
Reader's Digest Rd., Pleasantville, NY, 10570

Tel: (914) 238-1000      Fax: (914) 238-4559      www.readersdigest.com

*Publisher of magazines and books and direct mail marketer.*

**Reader's Digest AB Oy Valitut Palat,  Sentnerikuja 5, FIN-00440 Helsinki, Finland**

## RICHCO, INC.
5825 N. Tripp Ave., PO Box 804238, Chicago, IL, 60680

Tel: (773) 539-4060      Fax: (773) 539-6770      www.richco.com

*Mfr. plastic and metal parts for the electric, electronic, appliance, and fiber-optic industries.*

**Richco Finland,  Riihltontuntle 2, FIN - 02200 Espoo, Finland**

Tel: 35-89-412-9170

## SANMINA CORPORATION
2700 North First Street, San Jose, CA, 95134

Tel: (408) 964-3500      Fax: (408) 964-3799      www.sanmina.com

*Mfr. electronic components, including multi-layered printed circuit boards, backplanes, cables, and complete systems.*

**Sanmina Corporation,  Teollisuuskatu 1, PO Box 60, Aanckoski FIN-44100, Finland**

Tel: 358-14-348-800   Fax: 358-14-348-8120

## SAPHIRE INTERNATIONAL LTD.
3060 Main Street, Ste. 202, Stratford, CT, 06614

Tel: (203) 375-8668      Fax: (203) 375-1965      www.dataease.com

*Mfr. applications development software.*

**West Soft A/B,  Hellerupvej 76, FIN-2900 Vantaa, Finland**

## SAS INSTITUTE INC.

SAS Campus Drive, Cary, NC, 27513

Tel: (919) 677-8000      Fax: (919) 677-4444      www.sas.com

*Mfr./distributes decision support software.*

**SAS Institute (Finland) Ltd., Espoo, Finland**

Tel: 358-9-5255-71   Fax: 358-9-5255-7200

## SCHENKER INTERNATIONAL FORWARDERS INC.

150 Albany Ave., Freeport, NY, 11520

Tel: (516) 377-3000      Fax: (516) 377-3005      www.schenkerusa.com

*Freight forwarders.*

**Schenker Kaukokiito Oy, Manttaalitie 7, PO Box 76, FIN-01530 Vantaa, Finland**

Tel: 358-9-7561-1   Fax: 358-9-7561-425

## SCI SYSTEMS INC.

2101 W. Clinton Avenue, Huntsville, AL, 35807

Tel: (256) 882-4800      Fax: (256) 882-4804      www.sci.com

*R/D and mfr. electronics systems for commerce, industry, aerospace, etc.*

**SCI Systems Finland, Johdinkuja 5, FIN-90630, Oulu Finland**

Tel: 358-8-5788-000

## SEALED AIR CORPORATION

Park 80 East, Saddle Brook, NJ, 07663

Tel: (201) 791-7600      Fax: (201) 703-4205      www.sealedair.com

*Mfr. protective and specialty packaging solutions for industrial, food and consumer products.*

**Sealed Air Oy, Kaavakuja 3, FIN-36220 Kangasala, Finland**

Tel: 358-3-379-2510   Fax: 358-3-379-2508

## G.D. SEARLE & COMPANY

5200 Old Orchard Road, Skokie, IL, 60077

Tel: (847) 982-7000      Fax: (847) 470-1480      www.searlehealthnet.com

*Mfr. pharmaceuticals, health care, optical products and specialty chemicals.*

**Searle, UCB Pharma oy Finland, Maistraatinportti 2, FIN-00240 Helsinka, Finland**

Tel: 358-0-1594-3040   Fax: 358-0-278-6828

## THE SERVICEMASTER COMPANY

One ServiceMaster Way, Downers Grove, IL, 60515-1700

Tel: (630) 271-1300      Fax: (630) 271-2710      www.svm.com

*Management service to health care, school and industry facilities; diversified residential and commercial services.*

**ServiceMaster, Helsinki, Finland**

## SOTHEBY'S HOLDINGS, INC.

1334 York Avenue, New York, NY, 10021

Tel: (212) 606-7000      Fax: (212) 606-7027      www.sothebys.com

*Auction house specializing in fine art and jewelry.*

**Sotheby's Holdings, Inc., Bernhardinkatu 1B, FIN-00130 Helsinki, Finland**

Tel: 358-962-21558   Contact: Claire Svartstrom

## THE ST. PAUL COMPANIES, INC.

385 Washington Street, St. Paul, MN, 55102

Tel: (651) 310-7911      Fax: (651) 310-8294      www.stpaul.com

*Provides investment, insurance and reinsurance services.*

**Enterprise Fennia Mutual Insurance Company, Asemamiehenkatu 3, FIN-00520 Helsinki, Finland**

## THE STANLEY WORKS

1000 Stanley Drive, PO Box 7000, New Britain, CT, 06053

Tel: (860) 225-5111　　　Fax: (860) 827-3987　　　www.stanleyworks.com

*Mfr. hand tools and hardware.*

**Suomen Stanley Oy, PO Box 71, FIN-00381 Helsinki, Finland**

## STERIS CORPORATION

5960 Heisley Road, Mentor, OH, 44060

Tel: (440) 354-2600　　　Fax: (440) 639-4459　　　www.steris.com

*Mfr. sterilization/infection control equipment, surgical tables, lighting systems for health, pharmaceutical and scientific industries.*

**Steris Corporation, Teollisuustie 2, FIN-04300 Tuusula, Finland**

**Steris Corporation, Tuusula (Helsinki), Finland**

## STORAGE TECHNOLOGY CORPORATION

One Storagetech Dr., Louisville, CO, 80028-4377

Tel: (303) 673-5151　　　Fax: (303) 673-5019　　　www.stortek.com

*Mfr./market/service information, storage and retrieval systems.*

**Storage Tek OY, Sinikalliontie 10, FIN-02630 Helsinki, Finland**

## STOWE WOODWARD MOUNT HOPE

333 Turnpike Rd., Southborough, MA, 01772

Tel: (508) 460-9600　　　Fax: (508) 481-5392　　　www.mounthope.com

*Mfr. roll covering and bowed roll technologies for the web handling industries.*

**Stowe Woodward Finland Oy, Box 7, 04261 Kerava, Finland**

## SUN MICROSYSTEMS, INC.

901 San Antonio Road, Palo Alto, CA, 94303

Tel: (650) 960-1300　　　Fax: (650) 856-2114　　　www.sun.com

*Computer peripherals and programming services.*

**Sun Microsystems Oy, Niittymaentie 9, FIN-02200 Espoo, Finland**

## SYBASE, INC.

6475 Christie Ave., Emeryville, CA, 94608

Tel: (510) 922-3500　　　Fax: (510) 922-3210　　　www.sybase.com

*Design/mfg/distribution of database management systems, software development tools, connectivity products, consulting and technical support services..*

**Sybase Finland OY, Jaakonkatu 2, FIN-01620 Vantaa, Finland**
Tel: 358-9-7250-2200　Fax: 358-9-7250-2201

## SYMBOL TECHNOLOGIES, INC.

One Symbol Plaza, Holtsville, NY, 11742-1300

Tel: (631) 738-2400　　　Fax: (631) 738-5990　　　www.symbol.com

*Mfr. Bar code-driven data management systems, wireless LAN's, and Portable Shopping System™.*

**Symbol Technologies Finland, Kaupintie 8A , Helsinki, Finland**
Tel: 358-9-5407-580

## SYNOPSYS, INC.

700 East Middlefield Road, Mountain View, CA, 94043

Tel: (650) 962-5000　　　Fax: (650) 965-8637　　　www.synopsys.com

*Mfr. electronic design automation software.*

**Synopsys Oy, Lars Sonckin Kaari 10, FIN-02600 Espoo, Finland**
Tel: 358-9-5406-4500　Fax: 358-9-5406-4519

## SYSTEM SOFTWARE ASSOCIATES, INC.

500 W. Madison St., Ste. 3200, Chicago, IL, 60661

Tel: (312) 258-6000　　Fax: (312) 474-7500　　www.ssax.com

*Mfr. computer software.*

**System Software Associates, Helsinki, Finland**

## TBWA CHIAT/DAY

488 Madison Avenue, 6th Floor, New York, NY, 10022

Tel: (212) 804-1000　　Fax: (212) 804-1200　　www.tbwachiat.com

*International full service advertising agency.*

**Paltemaa Huttunen Santala, Helsinki, Finland**

## TEKTRONIX INC.

14200 SW Karl Braun Dr., PO Box 500, Beaverton, OR, 97077

Tel: (503) 627-7111　　Fax: (503) 627-2406　　www.tek.com

*Mfr. test and measure, visual systems/color printing and communications/video and networking products.*

**Tektronix Oy, Piispantilankuja 2, FIN-02240 Espoo Helsinki, Finland**

Tel: 358-9-4783-400　Fax: 358-9-4783-4200

## TELLABS INC.

4951 Indiana Ave. 6303788800, Lisle, IL, 60532-1698

Tel: (630) 378-8800　　Fax: (630) 679-3010　　www.tellabs.com

*Design/mfr./service voice/data transport and network access systems.*

**Tellabs Espoo, Sinikalliontie 7, FIN-02630 Espoo, Finland**

## TEXAS INSTRUMENTS INC.

8505 Forest Lane, Dallas, TX, 75243

Tel: (972) 995-3773　　Fax: (972) 995-4360　　www.ti.com

*Mfr. semiconductor devices, electronic electro-mechanical systems, instruments and controls.*

**Texas Instruments, Helsinki, Finland**

## UNISYS CORPORATION.

PO Box 500, Union Meeting Road, Blue Bell, PA, 19424

Tel: (215) 986-4011　　Fax: (215) 986-6850　　www.unisys.com

*Mfr./marketing/servicing electronic information systems.*

**Unisys Oy, Niittijkatu 8, FIN-02201 Espoo, Finland**

## UNITED PARCEL SERVICE, INC.

55 Glenlake Parkway, NE, Atlanta, GA, 30328

Tel: (404) 828-6000　　Fax: (404) 828-6593　　www.ups.com

*International package-delivery service.*

**UPS Finland Oy - Head Office, Valimotle 22, FIN-01510 Vantaa, Finland**

Tel: 358-90-613-2477　Fax: 358-90-870-2267

## UNIVERSAL INSTRUMENTS

90 Bevier Street, S. Dock, Binghamton, NY, 13904

Tel: (607) 779-7522　　Fax: (607) 779-7971　　www.uic.com

*Mfr./sales of instruments for electronic circuit assembly.*

**Lucatron Oy, Espoo, Finland**

Tel: 358-0-9887-0610

**UUNET**

22001 Loudoun County Pkwy., Ashburn, VA, 20147

Tel: (703) 206-5600    Fax: (703) 206-5601    www.uu.net

*World's largest Internet service provider; World Wide Web hosting services, security products and consulting services to businesses, professionals, and on-line service providers.*

**UUNET Finland Oy, Metsänneidonkuja 10, FIN-02130 Espoo, Finland**

**THE VIKING CORPORATION**

210 N. Industrial Park Rd., Hastings, MI, 49058

Tel: (616) 945-9501    Fax: (616) 945-9599    www.vikingcorp.com

*Mfr. fire extinguishing equipment.*

**Viking Norhan AB, Meripuistotie 5/5 FIN - 0020, Helsinki, Finland**

**WASTE MANAGEMENT, INC.**

1001 Fannin Street, Ste. 4000, Houston, TX, 77002

Tel: (713) 512-6200    Fax: (713) 512-6299    www.wastemanagement.com

*Environmental services and disposal company; collection, processing, transfer and disposal facilities.*

**Waste Management Ymparistopalvelut Oy, Valimotie 33, FIN-01510 Vantaa, Finland**

**WATERS CORPORATION**

34 Maple Street, Milford, MA, 01757

Tel: (508) 478-2000    Fax: (508) 872-1990    www.waters.com

*Mfr./distribute liquid chromatographic instruments and test and measurement equipment.*

**Waters Associates, Helsinki, Finland**

**WEIGHT WATCHERS INTERNATIONAL, INC.**

175 Crossways Park Dr., Woodbury, NY, 11797

Tel: (516) 390-1400    Fax: (516) 390-1763    www.weightwatchers.com

*Weight loss programs.*

**Weight Watchers International, Painonvartijat, Vattuniemenkatu 19, 00210 Helsinki, Finland**

**WHITE & CASE LLP**

1155 Ave. of the Americas, New York, NY, 10036-2767

Tel: (212) 819-8200    Fax: (212) 354-8113    www.whitecase.com

*International law firm.*

**Asianajotoimisto White & Case Oy, Eteläranta 14, FIN-0010 Helsinki, Finland**

Tel: 358-9-228641    Fax: 358-9-22864-228    Contact: Petri Y.J. Haussila

**WIND RIVER SYSTEMS, INC.**

500 Wind River Way, Alameda, CA, 94501

Tel: (510) 748-4100    Fax: (510) 749-2010    www.isi.com

*Develops and markets computer software products and services.*

**Wind River, AB, PO Box 120, FIN-01301 Vanta, Finland**

Tel: 358-40-546-1469    Fax: 358-9-871-0405

**WONDERWARE CORPORATION**

100 Technology Dr., Irvine, CA, 92618

Tel: (949) 727-3200    Fax: (949) 727-3270    www.wonderware.com

*Mfr. industrial strength applications software and services.*

**Klinkmann Automation Oy, Helsinki, Finland**

Tel: 358-9-5404940

## WM WRIGLEY JR. COMPANY

410 N. Michigan Ave., Chicago, IL, 60611-4287

Tel: (312) 644-2121     Fax: (312) 644-0353     www.wrigley.com

*Mfr. chewing gum.*

**Oy Wrigley Scandinavia AB, IL Poisvagen 9, FIN-20740 Abo, Finland**

## XEROX CORPORATION

800 Long Ridge Road, PO Box 1600, Stamford, CT, 06904

Tel: (203) 968-3000     Fax: (203) 968-4312     www.xerox.com

*Mfr. document processing equipment, systems and supplies.*

**Xerox OY, PL 5, FIN-02601 Espoo Helsinki, Finland**

Tel: 358-9-887-0010     Fax: 358-9-0204 68599

## YELLOW CORPORATION

10990 Roe Ave., PO Box 7270, Overland Park, KS, 66207

Tel: (913) 696-6100     Fax: (913) 696-6116     www.yellowcorp.com

*Commodity transportation.*

**Frans Maas Finland Oy, Tyopajakatu 10B, PO Box 5, FIN-00501 Helsinki Finland**

## YOUNG & RUBICAM INC.

285 Madison Ave., New York, NY, 10017

Tel: (212) 210-3000     Fax: (212) 370-3796     www.yr.com

*Advertising, public relations, direct marketing and sales promotion, corporate and product ID management.*

**Young & Rubicam Inc., Helsinki, Finland**

# France

## 24/7 MEDIA, INC.
1250 Broadway, New York, NY, 10001-3701
Tel: (212) 231-7100     Fax: (212) 760-1774     www.247media.com
*Provides global online advertising, sponsorships, e-commerce and direct marketing solutions to advertisers and Web publishers.*
**24/7 Media France,  20 rue Cambon, F-75001 Paris, France**
Tel: 33-1-55-047-247

## 3COM CORPORATION
5400 Bayfront Plaza, Santa Clara, CA, 95052-8145
Tel: (408) 326-5000     Fax: (408) 326-5001     www.3com.com
*Develop/mfr. computer networking products and systems.*
**3Com France,  Les Conquerants, 1 Ave. de l'Atlantique, Boite Postale 965 - Les Ulis, F-91976 Courtaboeuf Cedex, France**
Tel: 33-1-69-86-6800    Fax: 33-1-69-07-1154
**3Com France,  Tour Kupka A, 18, rue Hoche, F-92980 Paris La Defense, France**
Tel: 33-1-41-97-4600    Fax: 33-1-49-07-0343

## 3dfx INTERACTIVE, INC.
4435 Fortran Drive, San Jose, CA, 95134
Tel: (408) 935-4400     Fax: (408) 262-8874     www.3dfx.com
*Engaged in microchip, graphics, images and animation.*
**3dfx Interactive France,  32 rue de Cambrai, F-75019 Paris, France**
Tel: 33-1-4036-6717    Fax: 33-1-4036-5938

## 3M
3M Center, St. Paul, MN, 55144-1000
Tel: (651) 733-1110     Fax: (651) 733-9973     www.mmm.com
*Mfr. diversified products for industry, health care, imaging, communications, transport, safety, consumer, etc.*
**3M France,  Blvd. de L'Oise, F-95006 Cergy Pontoise Cedex, France**
Contact: Stig G. Eriksson

## AAF INTERNATIONAL (AMERICAN AIR FILTER)
215 Central Ave., PO Box 35690, Louisville, KY, 40232-5690
Tel: (502) 637-0011     Fax: (502) 637-0321     www.aafintl.com
*Mfr. air filtration/pollution control and noise control equipment.*
**AAF-SA,  42 rue Fortuny, F-75017 Paris, France**
Tel: 33-1-44-29-9330

## AAR CORPORATION
One AAR Place, 1100 North Wood Dale Road, Wood Dale, IL, 60191
Tel: (630) 227-2000     Fax: (630) 227-2019     www.aarcorp.com
*Provides aviation repair and supply provisioning; aircraft sales and leasing.*
**AAR Allen Group International,  112 rue de Paris, F-92110 Boulogne, France**
Tel: 33-1-46-04-2211   Fax: 33-1-46-04-7015   Contact: Jean-Philippe Schumacher

## ABBOTT LABORATORIES

One Abbott Park, Abbott Park, IL, 60064-3500

Tel: (847) 937-6100    Fax: (847) 937-1511    www.abbott.com

*Development/mfr./sale diversified health care products and services.*

**Abbott France S.A., 12 rue de la Couture, F-94518 Rungis Cedex, France**

## ACADEMIC PRESS INC.

6277 Sea Harbor Drive, Orlando, FL, 32887

Tel: (407) 345-2000    Fax: (407) 345-8388    www.academicpress.com

*Publisher of educational and scientific books.*

**Academic Press, 92 Ave. de General de Gaulle, F-78600 Maisons-Lafitte, France**

Tel: 33-1-39-12-2929   Fax: 33-1-39-12-4745   Contact: David Charles, Mgr.

## ACCLAIM ENTERTAINMENT, INC.

One Acclaim Plaza, Glen Cove, NY, 11542

Tel: (516) 656-5000    Fax: (516) 656-2040    www.acclaim.com

*Mfr. video games.*

**Acclaim Entertainment SA, 67 rue de Courcelles, F-75008 Paris, France**

Tel: 33-1-56-21-3100   Fax: 33-1-48-88-9494

## ACCO BRANDS, INC.

300 Tower Parkway, Lincoln, IL, 60069

Tel: (847) 541-9500    Fax: (847) 541-5750    www.acco.com

*Provides services in the office and computer markets and manufactures paper fasteners, clips, metal fasteners, binders and staplers.*

**ACCO France SARL, Entrepot Nord, 11-35 Zone d'Ativite, F-93150 DuPont-Yblon, France**

## ACHESON COLLOIDS COMPANY

PO Box  611747, Port Huron, MI, 48061-1747

Tel: (810) 984-5581    Fax: (810) 984-1446    www.achesoncolloids.com

*Chemicals, chemical preparations, paints and lubricating oils.*

**Acheson France S.A., Z.I. Ouest rue Georges Besse, B.P. 68 - F-67152 Erstein, Cedex France**

Tel: 33-3-88-59-0123   Fax: 33-3-88-59-0100

## ACT MANUFACTURING, INC.

2 Cabot Road, Hudson, MA, 01749

Tel: (978) 567-4000    Fax: (978) 568-1904    www.actmfg.com

*Mfr. printed circuit boards.*

**ACT Manufacturing France, 34 rue du Nid de Pie, BP 428, F-9004 Angers Cedex 01, France**

Tel: 241-736-000   Fax: 241-737-480

## ACTERNA CORPORATION

3 New England Executive Park, Burlington, MA, 01803

Tel: (781) 272-6100    Fax: (781) 272-2304    www.acterna.com

*Develop, manufacture and market communications test instruments, systems, software and services.*

**Acterna Corporation, Saint Quentin en Yvelines, Guyancourt Cedes, France**

**Acterna Corporation, F-91961 Les Ulis Cedex, France**

**Acterna Corporation, Saint-Cloud, France**

## ACTION INSTRUMENTS INC.

8601 Aero Drive, San Diego, CA, 92123

Tel: (619) 279-5726    Fax: (619) 279-6290    www.actionio.com

*Mfr. electronic instruments and industrial measurements computers.*

**Action Instruments SA, 9 ave. du Canada, Parc Hightec, Les Ulis Cedex, France**

## ACTIVE VOICE CORPORATION

2901 Third Avenue, Ste. 500, Seattle, WA, 98121

Tel: (206) 441-4700        Fax: (206) 441-4784        www.activevoice.com

*Mfr. PC-based voice processing systems.*

**Active Voice France, AEI Business Center, 20-22 rue Louis Armand, F-75015 Paris, France**

Tel: 33-1-44-25 26 38   Fax: 33-1-44-25 26 00   Contact: Robert Pijselman

## ACTUATE CORPORATION

701 Gateway Boulevard South, San Francisco, CA, 94080

Tel: (650) 837-2000        Fax: (650) 827-1560        www.actuate.com

*Develops software.*

**Actuate France, 85 Avenue Pierre Grenier, F-92100 Boulogne, France**

## ACXIOM CORPORATION

301 Industrial Boulevard, Conway, AR, 72033-2000

Tel: (501) 336-1000        Fax: (501) 336-3919        www.acxiom.com

*Data warehouser, database manager, and other marketing information services.*

**Acxiom France, Le Pyramide, 36 Avenue Pierre Brosselette, F-92247 Malakoff Cedex France**

Tel: 33-1-46-57-0808

## ADAC LABORATORIES, INC.

540 Alder Drive, Milpitas, CA, 95035

Tel: (408) 321-9100        Fax: (408) 321-9536        www.adaclabs.com

*Mfr. cameras and equipment for nuclear medicine.*

**ADAC Laboratories SARL, 19 Avenue De Norvege, Courtaboefuf Cedex F-91953, France**

Tel: 33-16-092-0649

## ADOBE SYSTEMS INCORPORATED

345 Park Avenue, San Jose, CA, 95110

Tel: (408) 536-6000        Fax: (408) 537-6000        www.adobe.com

*Engaged in print technology and distributor of Acrobat Reader.*

**Adobe Systems France EURL, Immeuble Atria, 2 rue du Centre, 93885 Noisy-le-Grande, Cedex France**

## ADVANCE PUBLICATIONS, INC.

950 Fingerboard Road, Staten Island, NY, 10305

Tel: (718) 981-1234        Fax: (718) 981-1415        www.advance.net

*Publishing company (Glamour, Vogue, GQ, Architectural Digest) and cable TV operations.*

**Advance Publications, Inc., Paris, France**

## ADVANCED DIGITAL INFORMATION CORPORATION

11431 Willows Rd. NE, PO Box 97057, Redmond, WA, 98073

Tel: (425) 881-8004        Fax: (425) 881-2296        www.adic.com

*Mfr. computer storage systems.*

**Advanced Digital Information Corp., ZAC des Basses Auges, 1 rue Alfred de Vigny,F- 78112 Fourqueux, France**

Tel: 33.1.30.87.53.00

## ADVANCED FIBRE COMMUNICATIONS, INC.

1 Willow Brook Court, Petaluma, CA, 94954

Tel: (707) 794-7700        Fax: (707) 794-7777        www.fibre.com

*Engaged in voice and data network access devices.*

**Advanced Fibre Communications, 54-56 Avenue Hoche, F-75008 Paris, France**

Tel: 33-1-5660-5223   Fax: 33-1-5660-5558

## ADVANCED PRODUCTS COMPANY

33 Defco Park Road, North Haven, CT, 06473

Tel: (203) 239-3341     Fax: (203) 234-7233     www.advpro.com

*Mfr. Metallic and PTFE seals and gaskets.*

**Advanced Products SARL,  8 Place de l'Eglise, F-78360 Montesson, France**

## AERO SYSTEMS ENGINEERING, INC.

358 E. Fillmore Ave., St. Paul, MN, 55107

Tel: (651) 227-7515     Fax: (651) 227-0519     www.aerosysengr.com

*Engaged in wind tunnel and jet engine testing and engineering.*

**Aero Systems Aviation c/o M. Louis Casagrande,  278 rue des Bois Moissy, Vaux LePenil, Cedex F-77530 France**

Tel: 33-1-6068-7637   Fax: 33-1-606-6435

## THE AEROQUIP GROUP

3000 Strayer, PO Box 50, Maumee, OH, 43537

Tel: (419) 867-2200     Fax: (419) 867-2390     www.aeroquip.com

*Mfr. industrial, automotive, aerospace and defense products.*

**Aeroquip Corporation,  14 rue Du Morvan, Silic 507, F-94623 Rungis Cedex, France**

Tel: 33-1-46-86-2230

**Aeroquip Corporation,  22 rue Michael Faraday, AI de la Vrillonnerie, BP 349, F-38183 Chambray-Les-Tours, Cedex France**

Tel: 33-2-4748-4950   Fax: 33-2-4748-4900

## AGILENT TECHNOLOGIES, INC.

395 Page Mill Road, PO Box 10395, Palo Alto, CA, 94303

Tel: (650) 752-5000     Fax: (650) 752-5633     www.agilent.com

*Mfr. communications components.*

**Agilent Technologies France,  Z.A. de Courtaboeuf, 1 Avenue du Canada, F-91947 Les Ulis Cedex, France**

Tel: 33-1-6982-6090

## AGRIBRANDS INTERNATIONAL, INC.

9811 South Forty Drive, St. Louis, MO, 63124

Tel: (314) 812-0500     Fax: (314) 812-0400     www.agribrands.com

*Produces animal feeds and nutritional products for cattle, poultry, horses and fish.*

**Agribrands Europe France,  Zone Ind. BP 100, F-49160 Longue-Jumelles, France**

Tel: 33-2-41-53-0060   Fax: 33-2-41-53-56-85

## AIR EXPRESS INTERNATIONAL CORPORATION

120 Tokeneke Road, PO Box 1231, Darien, CT, 06820

Tel: (203) 655-7900     Fax: (203) 655-5779     www.aeilogistics.com

*International air freight forwarder.*

**AEI France - Distribution Center,  Fret 5 Sogaris Porte 7, 1 rue de Pre, Bat 3317, F-95707 Roissy Cedex France**

Tel: 33-1-49-19-6826   Fax: 33-1-48-62-8982

**AEI France - Reg. Hdqtrs.,  Roissytech 1 rue du Pre, Bat 3317 B.P. 10406, F-95707 Roissy Cedex, France**

Tel: 33-1-49-19-6830   Fax: 33-1-48-62-4994

**Air Express International,  59810 Aeroport de Lille, Lesquin, France**

## AIR PRODUCTS AND CHEMICALS, INC.

7201 Hamilton Boulevard, Allentown, PA, 18195-1501

Tel: (610) 481-4911        Fax: (610) 481-5900        www.airproducts.com

*Mfr. industry gases and related equipment, specialty chemicals, environmental/energy systems.*

**Air Products & Chemicals Inc., Tour Pleyel, Centre Paris, F-93521 Ste. Denis Cedex 01, France**

## AIR SEA PACKING

40-35 22nd Street, Long Island City, NY, 11101

Tel: (718) 937-6800        Fax: (718) 937-9646        www.airseapacking.com

*Air and sea freight.*

**Air Sea Packing Group Limited, 22-24 rue St. Just, F-93135 Noisy-Le-Sec Cedex, France**

Tel: 33-1-4846-8142   Fax: 33-1-4846-0333    Contact: Mark Drasar

## AIRBORNE FREIGHT CORPORATION

3101 Western Ave., PO Box 662, Seattle, WA, 98121

Tel: (206) 285-4600        Fax: (206) 281-1444        www.airborne.com

*Air transport services.*

**Airborne Express, Aeroport Zone De Fret, F-59817 Lesquin, France**

Tel: 33-3-20-879239   Fax: 33-3-20-879242

## AKAMAI TECHNOLOGIES, INC.

500 Technology Square, Cambridge, MA, 02139

Tel: (617) 250-3000        Fax: (617) 250-3001        www.akamai.com

*Develops routing technologies for websites.*

**Akamai Technologies France, 7 Avenue Georges Pompidou, 92593 Levallois Peret Cedex, France**

Tel: 33-1-4748-2218   Fax: 33-1-4748-2577

## ALADDIN INDUSTRIES INC.

703 Murfreesboro Road, Nashville, TN, 37210

Tel: (615) 748-3000        Fax: (615) 748-3070        www.aladdinindustries.com

*Mfr. vacuum insulated products, insulated food containers and servers.*

**Aladdin Industries SA, 5 rue de la Crois Martre, F-91120 Palaiseau, France**

## ALBANY INTERNATIONAL CORPORATION

PO Box 1907, Albany, NY, 12201

Tel: (518) 445-2200        Fax: (518) 445-2265        www.albint.com

*Mfr. broadwoven and engineered fabrics, plastic products, filtration media.*

**Postillion SA, F-24600 Riberac (Dordogne), France**

**Postillion SA, 6 rue Royale, F-77300 Fontainebleau, France**

## ALBERTO-CULVER COMPANY

2525 Armitage Ave., Melrose Park, IL, 60160

Tel: (708) 450-3000        Fax: (708) 450-3354        www.alberto.com

*Mfr./marketing personal care and household brand products.*

**Indola SA, 54 rue de Paradis, F-75010 Paris, France**

## ALCOA INC.

Alcoa Center, 201 Isabella Street, Pittsburgh, PA, 15215-5858

Tel: (412) 553-4545        Fax: (412) 553-4498        www.alcoa.com

*World's leading producer of aluminum and alumina; mining, refining, smelting, fabricating and recycling.*

**Kawneer France S.A., Lezat-sur-Leze, France**

**Z.I. Molina La Chazotte, rue de L'Avenir/B.P. 105, F-42003 Saint Etienne, Cedex 1 France**

## ALIGN-RITE INTERNATIONAL, INC.

2428 Ontario Street, Burbank, CA, 91504

Tel: (818) 843-7220    Fax: (818) 566-3042    www.align-rite.com

*Mfr. photomasks.*

**Align-Rite Europa, Paris Service Center, Paris, France**

Tel: 33-1-6012-6850    Contact: Patrick Leroux, Dir.

## ALLEGHENY LUDLUM CORPORATION

1000 Six PPG Place, Pittsburgh, PA, 15222

Tel: (412) 394-2805    Fax: (412) 394-2800    www.alleghenyludlum.com

*Mfr. steel and alloys.*

**Allegheny Ludlum, Paris, France**

Tel: 33-1-55-66-88-88    Fax: 33-6-07-54-25-13

## ALLEGHENY TECHNOLOGIES

1000 Six PPG Place, Pittsburgh, PA, 15222

Tel: (412) 394-2800    Fax: (412) 394-2805    www.alleghenytechnologies.com

*Diversified mfr. aviation and electronics, specialty metals, industrial and consumer products.*

**Allegheny Technologies, L'Arche du Parc, 738 rue Yves Kerman, F-92658 Boulogne-Billancourt Cedex, France**

**Allvac Ltd., Div. de Stellram S.A., 111 Avenue Francois Arago, F-92003 Nanterre, France**

**Titanium Industries, Inc., ZAI Des Bruveres, Av JP Tibaud, 78 190 Trappes, France**

## ALLEGIANCE HEALTHCARE CORPORATION

1430 Waukegan Road, McGaw Park, IL, 60085

Tel: (847) 689-8410    Fax: (847) 578-4437    www.allegiance.net

*Manufactures and distributes medical, surgical, respiratory therapy and laboratory products.*

**Allegiance Santé S.A., 6 Ave. Louis Pasteur, F-78311 Maurepas Cedex Paris, France**

Tel: 33-1-34-61-5050    Fax: 33-1-34-61-5141    Contact: Alain Pernin, Dir. Mktg.

## ALLEN TELECOM

25101 Chagrin Boulevard, Beachwood, OH, 44122-5619

Tel: (216) 765-5818    Fax: (216) 765-0410    www.allentele.com

*Mfr. communications equipment, automotive bodies and parts, electronic components.*

**FOREM France, Z.I. Des Ebisoires, Ferme des Ebisoires, F-78370 Plasir, France**

Tel: 33-1-30-79-1530    Fax: 33-1-30-55-5537    Contact: Jacky Thomas

**TELIA S.A., 46 Allee de Megevie, F-31170 Gradignan, France**

Tel: 33-5-56-89-5619    Fax: 33-5-56-89-5344

## ALLEN-BRADLEY COMPANY, INC.

1201 South Second Street, Milwaukee, WI, 53204

Tel: (414) 382-2000    Fax: (414) 382-4444    www.ab.com

*Mfr. electrical controls and information devices.*

**Allen-Bradley Servovision SA, 36 ave. de l'Europe, F-78140 Velizy-Villacoublay, France**

## ALLERGAN INC.

2525 Dupont Drive, PO Box 19534, Irvine, CA, 92713-9534

Tel: (714) 246-4500    Fax: (714) 246-6987    www.allergan.com

*Mfr. therapeutic eye care products, skin and neural care pharmaceuticals.*

**Allergan France, S.A., B.P. 442, 06251 Mougins Cedex, France**

Tel: 33-492-92-4400    Fax: 33-492-92-4410

## ALPHARMA INC.

One Executive Drive, 4th Fl., Fort Lee, NJ, 07024

Tel: (201) 947-7774     Fax: (201) 947-4879     www.alpharma.com

*Development/manufacture specialty human pharmaceuticals and animal health products.*

**Alpharma AS, Silic 411, 3 Impasse de la Noisette, F-91374 Verrieres le Buisson, Cedex France**

Tel: 33-1-6953-4050   Fax: 33-1-6953-4051   Contact: Alain Richard, Mgr.

## AMAZON.COM, INC.

1200 12th Ave. South, Ste. 1200, Seattle, WA, 98144-2734

Tel: (206) 266-1000     Fax: (206) 266-4206     www.amazon.com

*Computer site that offers books, CDs, DVDS, videos, toys, tools, and electronics.*

**Amazon.Com France, Paris, France**

## AMBAC FINANCIAL GROUP

One State Street Plaza, New York, NY, 10004

Tel: (212) 668-0340     Fax: (212) 509-9109     www.ambac.com

*Reinsurance company.*

**MBIA Assurance S.A., Citicenter, 19, le Parvia, F-92073 Paris LaDéfense Cedex 37, France**

Tel: 33-1-46-93-93   Contact: Manuel Chevalier, VP

## AMERICAN AIRLINES INC.

4333 Amon Carter Boulevard, Ft. Worth, TX, 76155

Tel: (817) 963-1234     Fax: (817) 967-9641     www.amrcorp.com

*Air transport services.*

**American Airlines Inc., 82 ave. Marceau, F-75008 Paris, France**

## ABC, INC.

77 West 66th Street, New York, NY, 10023

Tel: (212) 456-7777     Fax: (212) 456-6384     www.abc.com

*Radio/TV production and broadcasting.*

**ABC News, 22 ave. d'Eyleu, F-75116 Paris, France**

## AMERICAN EXPRESS COMPANY

American Express Tower, World Financial Center, New York, NY, 10285-4765

Tel: (212) 640-2000     Fax: (212) 619-9802     www.americanexpress.com

*Travel, travelers cheques, charge card and financial services.*

**American Express Carte France SA, 11 rue Scribe, F-75009 Paris, France**

Tel: 33-1-47-77-7707

## AMERICAN HOME PRODUCTS CORPORATION

Five Giralda Farms, Madison, NJ, 07940-0874

Tel: (973) 660-5000     Fax: (973) 660-6048     www.ahp.com

*Mfr. pharmaceutical, animal health care and crop protection products.*

**American Home Products Corporation, Paris, France**

## AMERICAN INTERNATIONAL GROUP INC. (AIG)

70 Pine Street, New York, NY, 10270

Tel: (212) 770-7000     Fax: (212) 509-9705     www.aig.com

*Worldwide insurance and financial services.*

**AIG Europe France, S.A., 20/22 Ru de Clichy, Paris F-75009 France**

## AMERICAN MANAGEMENT SYSTEMS, INC.

4050 Legato Road, Fairfax, VA, 22033

Tel: (703) 267-8000    Fax: (703) 267-5073    www.amsinc.com

*Systems integration and consulting.*

**AMS c/o Telecom Development,  85 rue des Trois Fontanot, F-94004 Nanterre, France**

Tel: 33-1-55-17-45-19   Fax: 33-1-55-17-49-93

## AMERICAN OPTICAL LENS CO.

PO Box 8020, Southbridge, MA, 01550

Tel: (508) 764-5000    Fax: (508) 764-5010

*Mfr. ophthalmic lenses and frames, custom molded products, specialty lenses.*

**AO Ouest Optique,  rue Augustin Fresnel, Z.I. de la Guenaudiere, F-35304 Fougeres, France**

## AMERICAN SOFTWARE, INC.

470 East Paces Ferry Road, NE, Atlanta, GA, 30305

Tel: (404) 261-4381    Fax: (404) 264-5514    www.amsoftware.com

*Mfr./sales of financial control software and systems.*

**American Software Tour Litwin,  10/10 bis rue Jean-Jaures, F-92807 Puteaux Ledex, Paris, France**

Tel: 33-1-4907-8555   Fax: 33-1-4907-8506

## AMERICAN STANDARD INC.

One Centennial Avenue, Piscataway, NJ, 08855-6820

Tel: (732) 980-3000    Fax: (732) 980-6118    www.americanstandard.com

*Mfr. automotive, plumbing, heating, air conditioning products and medical diagnostics systems.*

**DiaSorin S.A.,  Parc De Haute Technologie, 11 rue Georges Besse Bat 4, F-92160 Antony France**

Tel: 33-1-55-590422  Fax: 33-1-55-590440

**International Unitary Products Société Trane,  1 rue des Ameriques, B.P. 6 F-88191 Golbey Cedex, France**

Tel: 33-3-29-31-7300

## AMERON INTERNATIONAL CORPORATION

245 South Los Robles Ave., Pasadena, CA, 91109-7007

Tel: (626) 683-4000    Fax: (626) 683-4060    www.ameron.com

*Mfr. steel pipe systems, concrete products, traffic and lighting poles, protective coatings.*

**Tubolining SA,  BP 43, F-13367 Marseille Cedex 11, France**

## AMES TEXTILE CORPORATION

710 Chelmsford Street, Lowell, MA, 01851

Tel: (978) 458-3321    Fax: (978) 441-9808    www.amestextile.com

*Mfr. textile products.*

**Ames France,  3 Chemin Departemental, Fallieres, St. Nabord, F-88200 Remiremont, France**

## AMETEK INC.

37 N. Valley Road, PO Box 1764, Paoli, PA, 19301-0801

Tel: (610) 647-2121    Fax: (610) 296-3412    www.ametek.com

*Mfr. instruments, electric motors and engineered materials.*

**AMETEK Precision Instruments France SARL,  3 Ave. des Coudriers, Z.A. de l'Observatoire, F-78180 Montigny Le Bretonneux, France**

Tel: 33-1-30-64-8970   Fax: 33-1-30-64-8979

## AMGEN INC.

One Amgen Center Drive, Thousand Oaks, CA, 91320-1799

Tel: (805) 447-1000    Fax: (805) 499-2694    www.amgen.com

*Biotechnology research and pharmaceruticals.*

**Amgen, S.A.,  192 Avenue Charles de Gaulle, F-92523 Neuilly-sur-Seine Cedex, France**

## AMKOR TECHNOLOGY, INC.

1345 Enterprise Dr., West Chester, PA, 19380

Tel: (610) 431-9600      Fax: (610) 431-1988      www.amkor.com

*Microchip technology engaged in semiconductor packaging and test services.*

**Amkor Technology S.A.R.L., BP 99 - 13 Chemin du Levant, Ferney-Voltaire F-01210, France**

Tel: 33-4-50-40-9797

## AMPCO METAL, INC.

1745 S. 38th Street, PO Box 2004, Milwaukee, WI, 53201

Tel: (414) 645-3750      Fax: (414) 645-3225      www.ampcometal.com

*Mfr./distributor/sale cast and wrought copper-based alloys.*

**Ampco Metal SA, rue Claude Bernard, BP 22, F-78311 Maurepas Cedex, France**

## AMPEX CORPORATION

500 Broadway, Redwood City, CA, 94063-3199

Tel: (650) 367-2011      Fax: (650) 367-4669      www.ampex.com

*Mfr. extremely high-performance digital data storage, data retrieval and image processing systems for a broad range of corporate scientific and government applications.*

**Ampex SARL, Courcellor 1, 2 rue Curnonsky, F-75017 Paris, France**

## AMPHENOL CORPORATION

358 Hall Ave., Wallingford, CT, 06492-7530

Tel: (203) 265-8900      Fax: (203) 265-8793      www.amphenol.com

*Mfr. electrictronic interconnect penetrate systems and assemblies.*

**Amphenol Automotive France, Immeuble Newton C - 7 Mail B, Thimonnier, F-77185 Lognes France**

Tel: 33-1-16462-7676

## AMSTED INDUSTRIES INC.

205 North Michigan Ave., Chicago, IL, 60601

Tel: (312) 645-1700      Fax: (312) 819-8523      www.amsted.com

*Privately-held, diversified manufacturer of products for the construction and building markets, general industry and the railroads.*

**Keystone Industries, Acieries De Ploermel, BP 103, F-56804 Ploermel France**

Tel: 33-2-97-73-2470

## AMWAY CORPORATION

7575 Fulton Street East, Ada, MI, 49355-0001

Tel: (616) 787-6000      Fax: (616) 787-6177      www.amway.com

*Mfr./sale home care, personal care, nutrition and houseware products.*

**Amway France, 14 Ave. Francois Sommer, BP 140, F-92185 Antony Cedex, France**

## ANACOMP INC.

12365 Crosthwaite Circle, Poway, CA, 92064

Tel: (858) 679-9797      Fax: (858) 748-9482      www.anacomp.com

*Engaged in electronic information management services and products.*

**Anacomp SARL, 72-74 Quai de la Loire, F-75019 Paris, France**

## ANALOG DEVICES INC.

1 Technology Way, Box 9106, Norwood, MA, 02062

Tel: (781) 329-4700      Fax: (781) 326-8703      www.analog.com

*Mfr. integrated circuits and related devices.*

**Analog Devices SA, 3 rue Georges Besse, F-92160 Antony, France**

## ANC RENTAL CORP.

110 Southeast Sixth St., Ft. Lauderdale, FL, 33301

Tel: (954) 769-7000    Fax: (954) 769-7000    www.ancrental.com

*Engaged in car rental services, including National Car Rental and Alamo Rent A Car.*

**National Car Rental Systems Inc., BP 212, Clamart Cedex, France**

**National Car Rental Systems Inc., 13 rue Sainte Catherine, Abbeville, France**

## ANDERSEN CONSULTING

100 S. Wacker Drive, Ste. 1059, Chicago, IL, 60606

Tel: (312) 693-0161    Fax: (312) 693-0507    www.ac.com

*Provides management and technology consulting services.*

**Andersen Consulting, Tour Crédit Lyonnais, 129 rue Servient, F-69431 Lyon Cédex 03, France**

Tel: 33-4-78-63-7272   Fax: 33-4-78-95-37277

**Andersen Consulting, 55 Ave. George V, F-75379 Paris Cédex 08, France**

Tel: 33-1-53-23-5323   Fax: 33-1-53-23-5555

**Andersen Consulting, Technology Park, Les Genêts, 449 route de Crêtes, F-06560 Sophia Antipolis France**

Tel: 33-4-92-94-6700   Fax: 33-4-92-94-6799

## ANDERSEN WORLDWIDE

33 West Monroe Street, Chicago, IL, 60603

Tel: (312) 580-0033    Fax: (312) 507-6748    www.arthurandersen.com

*Accounting and audit, tax and management consulting services.*

**Andersen Consulting, 129 rue Servient, F-69431 Lyon cedex 03, France**

Tel: 33-78-63-7400

**Barbier Frinault & Associes, Tour Europe, 20 Place des Halles, F-67000 Strasbourg France**

Tel: 33-88-37-5930

**Barbier Frinault & Associes, 129 rue Servient, F-69431 Lyon cedex 03, France**

Tel: 33-78-63-7200

**S.G. Archibald/ Andersen Worldwide, Tour Gan, F-92082 Paris La Defense cedex, France**

Tel: 33-1-42-91-0700

## ANDREW CORPORATION

10500 West 153rd Street, Orland Park, IL, 60462

Tel: (708) 349-3300    Fax: (708) 349-5410    www.andrew.com

*Mfr. antenna systems, coaxial cable, electronic communications and network connectivity systems.*

**Andrew SARL, 320 rue Helene Boucher, Z.I. Centre, F-78531 Buc Cedex France**

Tel: 33-1-39-24-1470   Fax: 33-1-39-56-5137

## ANIXTER INTERNATIONAL INC..

4711 Golf Road, Skokie, IL, 60076

Tel: (847) 677-2600    Fax: (847) 677-8557    www.anixter.com

*Distributor wiring systems/products for voice, video, data and power applications.*

**Anixter France, ZAC Paris Nord 2, BP 50008, 69 rue de la Belle Etoile, F-95945 Roissy Cedex, France**

**Anixter France, Z. I. Mi-Plaine BP, 9 rue Jean Rostand, F-69744 Lyon Genas Cedex, France**

Tel: 33-4-78-90-0505   Fax: 33-4-78-40-6155

## ANSELL HEALTHCARE, INC.

200 Schulz Drive, Red Bank, NJ, 07701

Tel: (732) 345-5400    Fax: (732) 219-5114    www.ansellhealthcare.com

*Mfr. industrial gloves, rubber and plastic products, protective clothing.*

**Ansell Healthcare S.A., 9 Chaussée Jules César, B.P. 238, Osny F-95523 Cergy Pontoise, Cedex France**

Tel: 33-1-3424 5252

## AOL TIME WARNER

75 Rockefeller Plaza, New York, NY, 10019

Tel: (212) 484-8000      Fax: (212) 275-3046      www.aoltimewarner.com

*Engaged in media and communications; provides internet services, communications, publishing and entertainment.*

**AOL Time Warner France,  Paris, France**

**Time-Life International SA,  17 ave. Matignon, F-75008 Paris, France**

## AON CORPORATION

123 North Wacker Drive, Chicago, IL, 60606

Tel: (312) 701-3000      Fax: (312) 701-3100      www.aon.com

*Insurance brokers worldwide; underwrites accident and health insurance, specialty and professional insurance; and provides risk management consultation.*

**AON France,  7-9 rue Belgrand, F-92309 Levallois Perret Cedex, Paris, France**

Tel: 33-1-47-56-6060    Fax: 33-1-47-30-9420    Contact: Bruno Valette

## API MOTION INC.

45 Hazelwood Dr., Amherst, NY, 14228

Tel: (716) 691-9100      Fax: (716) 691-9181      www.apimotion.com

*Engaged in motion control solutions using motors and drives, motor gearheads, resolver and encoder feedback devices.*

**API Motion France SA,  2 rue Louis Pergaud, Maisons Alfort, Cedex F-94706, France**

## APPLE COMPUTER, INC.

One Infinite Loop, Cupertino, CA, 95014

Tel: (408) 996-1010      Fax: (408) 974-2113      www.apple.com

*Personal computers, peripherals and software.*

**Apple Computer France SARL,  BP 131, ave. de l'Oceanie, Z.I. de Courtaboeuf, F-91944 Les Ulis, France**

## APPLERA CORPORATION

761 Main Avenue, Norwalk, CT, 06859-0001

Tel: (203) 762-1000      Fax: (203) 762-6000      www.applera.com

*Leading supplier of systems for life science research and related applications.*

**Applied Biosystems,  BP 96, F-91943 Courtaboeuf, Cedex France**

## APPLIED MATERIALS, INC.

3050  Bowers Ave., Santa Clara, CA, 95054-3299

Tel: (408) 727-5555      Fax: (408) 727-9943      www.appliedmaterials.com

*Supplies manufacturing systems and services to the semiconductor industry.*

**Applied Materials France S.A.R.L.,  Parc de la Julienne, Batiment E or F, F-91830 Le Coudray-Montceaux, France**

Tel: 33-1-69-90-6100    Fax: 33-1-69-90-4045

## APPLIED SCIENCE AND TECHNOLOGY, INC.

35 Cabot Road, Woburn, MA, 01801

Tel: (781) 933-5560      Fax: (781) 933-0750      www.astex.com

*Mfr. specialized components for semiconductor manufacturing systems.*

**AsTex France,  Bat 5 Parc Club du Golf B, 13856 Aix en Provence Cedex 3, France**

Tel: 33-4-4297-5170    Fax: 33-4-4297-5179

## APPLIX, INC.

112 Turnpike Road, Westboro, MA, 01581

Tel: (508) 870-0300     Fax: (508) 366-4873     www.applix.com

*Engaged in business productivity application software.*

**APPLIX, Inc., 22 rue Colbert, F-78885 Saint Quentin en Yvelines, France**

Tel: 33-1-3064-7879   Fax: 33-1-3064-5435

## APW, INC.

PO Box 325, Milwaukee, WI, 53201-0325

Tel: (262) 523-7600     Fax: (262) 523-7624     www.apw1.com

*Mfr. hi-pressure tools, vibration control products, consumables, technical furniture and enclosures.*

**Norelem, Parc d'Activites du Moulin de Massy, 1 rue du Saule Trapu, BP 205, F-91882 Massy Cedex France**

**Power-Packer France SA, Parc d'Activites du Moulin de Massy, 5 rue du Saule Trapu, BP 232, F-91882 Massy Cedex France**

## AQUENT

711 Boylston Street, Boston, MA, 02116

Tel: (617) 535-5000     Fax: (617) 535-6001     www.aquent.com

*Engaged in temporary, specialized employment.*

**AQUENT, 94 rue Saint Lazare, F-75009 Paris, France**

## ARBOR ACRES FARM INC.

439 Marlborough Road, Glastonbury, CT, 06033

Tel: (860) 633-4681     Fax: (860) 633-2433

*Producers of male and female broiler breeders, commercial egg layers.*

**Grelier, Saint Laurent de la Plaine, France**

## ARDENT SOFTWARE, INC.

50 Washington Street, Westboro, MA, 01581-1021

Tel: (508) 366-3888     Fax: (508) 366-3669     www.ardentsoftware.com

*Publisher of database and file management software.*

**Ardent Software S.A., Les Renardieres B, F-92901 La Defense Cedex, France**

Tel: 33-1-49-04-6565   Fax: 33-1-49-04-6550

## ARIBA, INC.

1565 Charleston Rd., Mountain View, CA, 94043

Tel: (650) 930-6200     Fax: (650) 930-6300     www.ariba.com

*Mfr. software.*

**Ariba France SARL, 23 rue Balzac,F- 75008 Paris, France**

## ARMSTRONG HOLDINGS, INC.

2500 Columbia Avenue, Lancaster, PA, 17604-3001

Tel: (717) 397-0611     Fax: (717) 396-2787     www.armstrong.com

*Mfr. and marketing interior furnishings and specialty products for bldg, auto and textile industry.*

**Armstrong Floor Products Europe Sarl, Centre Atria, 58 Boulevard Carnot, F-62000 Arras France**

Tel: 33-3-21-13050

## ARROW ELECTRONICS INC.

25 Hub Drive, Melville, NY, 11747

Tel: (516) 391-1300     Fax: (516) 391-1640     www.arrow.com

*Distributor of electronic components.*

**Arrow Elecronique S.A.-Multicoposanta, Siege Socia, 73/79 rue des Solets - Silic 585, F-95\4663 Rungis, Cedex France**

**Arrow Electronique, 78-79 rue des Solets, Silic 585, F-94663 Rungis Cedex, France**

Tel: 33-1-49-49-78   Fax: 33-1-46-86-7551   Contact: Philippe Djeddah, VP Marketing

Arrow/CCI Elecronique,  Siege Social, 12 alee de la Vierge, Silic 57 F-94653 Rungis, Cedex France

## ARROW INTERNATIONAL, INC.

2400 Bernville Rd., Reading, PA, 19605

Tel: (610) 378-0131      Fax: (610) 374-5360      www.arrowintl.com

*Develop, manufacture, and marketing of medical devices.*

Arrow France S.A.,  Atlantic Parc Les Pyramides, 11 Route de Pitoys, P.A. de Maignon, F-64600 Anglet Cedex France

Tel: 33-5-59-313490    Fax: 33-5-59-313491    Contact: Patrick Schall

## ASG (ALLEN SYSTEMS GROUP)

1333 3rd Avenue South, Naples, FL, 33102

Tel: (941) 435-2200      Fax: (941) 263-3692      www.asg.com

*Mainframe computer software, specializing in OnMark 2000 software.*

ASG France,  6 Place de l'Iris, 92095 Paris La Défense Cedex, France

Tel: 33-1-41-02-8585

## ASHLAND OIL INC.

50 E. Rivercenter Blvd., Covington, KY, 41012-0391

Tel: (859) 815-3333      Fax: (859) 815-5053      www.ashland.com

*Petroleum exploration, refining and transportation; mfr. chemicals, oils and lubricants.*

Ashland-Avebene SA,  136 ave. Gilbert de Voisins, F-78670 Villennes-sur-Seine, France

## ASPECT COMMUNICATIONS CORPORATION

1730 Fox Drive, San Jose, CA, 95131

Tel: (408) 325-2200      Fax: (408) 325-2260      www.aspect.com

*Mfr. software and related equipment.*

Aspect France,  Immeuble Le Carillion, 5 Esplanade Charles de Gaulle, F-92000 Nanterre, France

Tel: 33-1-5551-2100

## ASPEN TECHNOLOGY, INC.

10 Canal Park, Cambridge, MA, 02141

Tel: (617) 949-1000      Fax: (617) 949-1030      www.aspentec.com

*Mfr. software for chemists and refineries.*

AspenTech Europe SA,  130 rue de Silly, F-2100 Boulogne, France

Tel: 33-1-4712-4772    Fax: 33-1-4712-4774

## ASSOCIATED MERCHANDISING CORPORATION

500 Seventh Ave., 2nd Fl., New York, NY, 10018

Tel: (212) 819-6600      Fax: (212) 819-6701      www.theamc.com

*Retail service organization; apparel, shoes and accessories.*

Associated Merchandising Corp.,  14 rue de Castiglione, F-75001 Paris, France

## ASSOCIATED PRESS INC.

50 Rockefeller Plaza, New York, NY, 10020-1605

Tel: (212) 621-1500      Fax: (212) 621-5447      www.ap.com

*News gathering agency.*

The Associated Press,  Paris, France

Tel: 33-1-43-59-8876

## ASSOCIATES FIRST CAPITAL CORPORATION

250 E. Carpenter Freeway, Irving, TX, 75062-2729

Tel: (972) 652-4000      Fax: (972) 652-7420      www.theassociates.com

*Diversified consumer and commercial finance organization which provides finance, leasing and related services.*

Associates First Capital,  Paris, France

## ASTEA INTERNATIONAL, INC.

455 Business Center Drive, Horsham, PA, 19044

Tel: (215) 682-2500    Fax: (215) 682-2515    www.astea.com

*Produces computer software that assists to automate and manage field service, sales and customer support operations.*

**Astea France, Tour Aurore, 18 Place des Reflets, F-92975 Paris La Defense, France**

Tel: 33-1-47-786337   Fax: 33-1-47-786339

## AT HOME CORPORATION

450 Broadway Street, Redwood City, CA, 94063

Tel: (650) 556-5000    Fax: (650) 556-5100    www.excite.com

*Online computer internet service provider.*

**Excite, Inc., Paris, France**

## ATMEL CORPORATION

2325 Orchard Pkwy., San Jose, CA, 95131

Tel: (408) 441-0311    Fax: (408) 436-4200    www.atmel.com

*Design, manufacture and marketing of advanced semiconductors.*

**Atmel Rousset, Zone Industrielle, F-13106 Rousset Cedex, France**

Tel: 33-4-4253-6000

## ATTACHMATE CORPORATION

3617 131st Ave. S.E., Bellevue, WA, 98006-1332

Tel: (425) 644-4010    Fax: (425) 747-9924    www.attachmate.com

*Mfr. connectivity software.*

**Attachmate Sales France, 62 bis Ave. Andre Morizet, F-92643 Boulogne-Billancourt, Cedex France**

Tel: 33-1-46-04-1010   Fax: 33-1-49-09-0559

## AUTODESK INC.

111 McInnis Parkway, San Rafael, CA, 94903

Tel: (415) 507-5000    Fax: (415) 507-6112    www.autodesk.com

*Develop/marketing/support computer-aided design, engineering, scientific and multimedia software products.*

**Autodesk SARL, Batiment Les Ellipses 3/5, Ave. du Chemin de Presles, F-94410 Saint-Maurice, France**

Tel: 33-1-45-11-5000   Fax: 33-1-45-11-5001

## AUTOMATIC DATA PROCESSING INC.

One ADP Blvd., Roseland, NJ, 07068

Tel: (973) 994-5000    Fax: (973) 994-5387    www.adp.com

*Data processing services.*

**ADP Europe, 148 rue Anatole France, F-92688 Levallois Perret Cedex Paris, France**

Tel: 33-1-55-63-5027   Fax: 33-1-55-63-5079   Contact: Jenny Defaix

## AUTOMATIC SWITCH CO. (ASCO)

50-60 Hanover Rd., Florham Park, NJ, 07932

Tel: (973) 966-2000    Fax: (973) 966-2628    www.asco.com

*Mfr. solenoid valves, emergency power controls, pressure and temp. switches.*

**Asco/Jouco, France, 32 ave. Albert 1er, BP 312, F-92506 Ruycil Malmaison, France**

Tel: 33-1-47-14-3200   Fax: 33-1-47-14-3064   Contact: Pascal Lamonerie

## AUTOSPLICE INC.

10121 Barnes Canyon Road, San Diego, CA, 92121

Tel: (858) 535-0077        Fax: (858) 535-0130        www.autosplice.com

*Mfr. electronic components.*

**Autosplice France,  71 Boulevard Eugene Reguillon, F-69100 Villeurbonne, France**

Tel: 33-4-7884-3939    Contact: Yvon Dussurget

## AUTOTOTE CORPORATION

750 Lexington Avenue, 25th Fl., New York, Ny, 1022

Tel: (212) 754-2233        Fax: (212) 754-2372        www.autotote.com

*Mfr. video gaming machines and computerized pari-mutuel wagering systems used at racetracks.*

**Scientific Games International, Div. Autotote,  5-7 rue Salomon de Rothschild, 92150 Suresnes, France**

Tel: 33-141-44-3980    Fax: 33-141-44-3949

## AVERY DENNISON CORPORATION

150 N. Orange Grove Blvd., Pasadena, CA, 91103

Tel: (626) 304-2000        Fax: (626) 792-7312        www.averydennison.com

*Mfr. pressure-sensitive adhesives and materials, office products, labels, tags, retail systems, Carter's Ink and specialty chemicals.*

**Avery Dennison,  Immeuble La Panoramique, 5 Ave. de Verdun, F-94204 Irvy sur Siene Cedex, France**

Tel: 33-1-45-215780    Fax: 33-1-45-215799

**Doret SA,  8 rue Montgolfier, F-93115 Rosny-sous-Bois, France**

**Fasson France SARL,  Champ-sur-Drac, F-38560 Jarrie, France**

## AVID TECHNOLOGY, INC.

1 Park West, Tewksbury, MA, 01876

Tel: (978) 640-6789        Fax: (978) 640-1366        www.avid.com

*Mfr. animation design software and digital and audio systems.*

**Avid Technology SARL,  44 Avenue Georges Pompidou, F-92300 Levallois Perret, France**

Fax: 33-1-4757-1527

## AVNET INC.

2211 South 47th Street, Phoenix, AZ, 85034

Tel: (480) 643-2000        Fax: (480) 643-4670        www.avnet.com

*Distributor electronic components, computers and peripherals.*

**Avnet CK Electronique,  31 Blvd. Pre Pommier, ZA du Champfleuri, F-38300 Bourgouin-Jallieu, France**

Tel: 33-4744-38045    Fax: 33-47-4286911

**Avnet EMG France SA,  79 rue Pierre-Semard, F-92322 Chatillon Cedex, France**

Tel: 33-1-4965-2700    Fax: 33-1-5495-2769

**BFI-IBEXSA Electronique,  1 rue Lavoisier-ZI, F-91430 Igny, France**

Tel: 33-169-337427    Fax: 33-169-337470

## AVON PRODUCTS INC.

1345 Avenue of the Americas, New York, NY, 10105-0196

Tel: (212) 282-5000        Fax: (212) 282-6049        www.avon.com

*Mfr./distributor beauty and related products, fashion jewelry, gifts and collectibles.*

**Avon SA,  Chemin d'Uny, F-60290 Rantigny, France**

Tel: 33-11-69-1400    Fax: 33-44-69-1750    Contact: Pierre Decroux, Sales Mgr.

## AVX CORPORATION

PO Box 867, Myrtle Beach, SC, 29578

Tel: (843) 448-9411        Fax: (843) 448-7139        www.avxcorp.com

*Mfr. multilayer ceramic capacitors.*

**AVX SA,  Chemin de la Poudiere, BP 287, F-76120 Grand Quevilly Rouen, France**

## AXCIOM CORPORATION

1 Information Way, Little Rock, AR, 72203-8180

Tel: (501) 342-1000     Fax: (510) 342-3913     www.axciom.com

*Provides computer-based marketing information services.*

**Axciom Corporation, Paris, France**

## AXENT TECHNOLOGIES, INC.

2400 Research Boulevard, Ste. 200, Rockville, MD, 20850

Tel: (301) 258-5043     Fax: (301) 330-5756     www.axent.com

*Designs and supplies security management software .*

**AXENT Technologies S.A., 35 rue de Montjean, F-94266 Fresnes Cedex, France**

Tel: 33-1-49-84-8575   Fax: 33-1-49-84-8586   Contact: Jean-Charles Barbou

## AZON CORPORATION

2204 Ravine Road, Kalamazoo, MI, 49004-3506

Tel: (616) 385-5942     Fax: (616) 385-5937     www.azonintl.com

*Designs and manufactures special multi-component chemical metering, mixing and dispensing machines.*

**Azon FK&E France Ltd., 3 rue 6200, Compiegne, France**

## BAE SYSTEMS, INC.

1601 Research Blvd., Rockville, MD, 20850

Tel: (301) 738-4000     Fax: (301) 738-4643     www.baesystems.com

*Engaged in aerospace, defense electronics and information systems.*

**CTA International, 7 Route de Guerry, F-18023 Bourges Cedex, France**

Tel: 33-2-4821-9375

## BAIN & COMPANY, INC.

Two Copley Place, Boston, MA, 02116

Tel: (617) 572-2000     Fax: (617) 572-2427     www.bain.com

*Strategic management consulting services.*

**Bain & Compagnie, Snc., 21 blvd de la Madeleine, F-75001 Paris, France**

Tel: 33-1-44-55-7575   Fax: 33-1-44-55-7600

## ROBERT W. BAIRD & CO.

PO Box 672, Milwaukee, WI, 53201

Tel: (414) 765-3500     Fax: (414) 765-3600     www.rwbaird.com

*Engaged in investment banking, serving individuals, corporations, municipalities and institutional investors.*

**Granville Baird, 16 Avenue Hoehe, F-75008 Paris, France**

Tel: 33-1-4076-0401   Fax: 33-1-4076-0402   Contact: Jacques Paquin

## BAKER & McKENZIE

130 East Randolph Drive, Ste. 2500, Chicago, IL, 60601

Tel: (312) 861-8000     Fax: (312) 861-2899     www.bakerinfo.com

*International legal services.*

**Baker & McKenzie, 32 Ave. Kleber, F-75116 Paris, France**

Tel: 33-1-44-17-5300   Fax: 33-1-44-17-4575

## BAKER HUGHES INCORPORATED

3900 Essex Lane, Ste. 1200, Houston, TX, 77027

Tel: (713) 439-8600     Fax: (713) 439-8699     www.bakerhughes.com

*Develop and apply technology to drill, complete and produce oil and natural gas wells; provide separation systems to petroleum, municipal, continuous process and mining industries.*

**Baker Hughes International Ltd., Ave. Thimonnier, Zone Induspal, F- 64140 Lons France**

**Baker Oil Tools S.A., Ave. Thimonier, Z.I. Lons, F-64143 Pau Billere Cedex, France**

Tel: 33-5-59-32-8725   Fax: 33-5-59-62-3200

**Milchem France SARL, 201 Bureaux de la Colline, F-92213 St. Cloud, Paris, France**

## BAKER PETROLITE CORPORATION

3900 Essex Lane, Houston, TX, 77027

Tel: (713) 599-7400      Fax: (713) 599-7592      www.bakerhughes.com/bapt/

*Mfr. specialty chemical treating programs, performance-enhancing additives and related equipment and services.*

**Luzzatto & Figlio (France) SA, 10 ave. Percier, F-75008 Paris, France**

**Petrolite France SA, 10 ave. Percier, F-75008 Paris, France**

## BALDWIN TECHNOLOGY COMPANY, INC.

One Norwalk West, 40 Richards Ave., Norwalk, CT, 06854

Tel: (203) 838-7470      Fax: (203) 852-7040      www.baldwintech.com

*Mfr./services material handling, accessories, control and prepress equipment for print industry.*

**Baldwin France Sarl, 20 Ave. de Bergoide, F-60550 Verneuil en Halatta, France**

Tel: 33-3-42-50-681    Fax: 33-3-44-25-11640    Contact: Alain Fouque, Mng. Dir.

## BALTEK CORPORATION

10 Fairway Court, PO Box 195, Northvale, NJ, 07647

Tel: (201) 767-1400      Fax: (201) 387-6631      www.baltek.com

*Light lumber.*

**Baltek SA, 61 rue de La Fontaine, 75016 Paris, France**

Tel: 33-1-46-47-5850    Fax: 33-1-46-47-6658

## BANK OF AMERICA CORPORATION

555 California Street, San Francisco, CA, 94104

Tel: (415) 622-3530      Fax: (415) 622-8467      www.bankofamerica.com

*Financial services.*

**Bank of America NT & SA, 43-37 ave. de la Grande Armee, F-75782 Paris Cedex 16, France**

Tel: 33-1-45-02-6800    Fax: 33-1-45-01-7789    Contact: Christian Bartholin, SVP

## THE BANK OF NEW YORK

One Wall Street, New York, NY, 10286

Tel: (212) 495-1784      Fax: (212) 495-2546      www.bankofny.com

*Banking services.*

**The Bank of New York, 13-15 Boulevard de la Madeleine, F-75001 Paris, France**

Tel: 33-1-42-46-2625    Fax: 33-1-42-47-0236

## C. R. BARD, INC.

730 Central Ave., Murray Hill, NJ, 07974

Tel: (908) 277-8000      Fax: (908) 277-8078      www.crbard.com

*Mfr. health care products.*

**Laboratoires Bard SA, rue des Charmes, BP 145, F-78190 Trappes, France**

## BARNES GROUP INC.

123 Main Street, Bristol, CT, 06011-0489

Tel: (860) 583-7070      Fax: (860) 589-3507      www.barnesgroupinc.com

*Mfr. precision metal parts and industrial supplies for industrial markets.*

**Associated Spring Ressorts SPEC, Montigny, France**

**Autoliaisons & LeSysteme Bowman, Voisins Le Bretonneux, France**

**Bowman Distribution France Sa, Voisins Le Bretonneux, France**

## BARRINGER TECHNOLOGIES INC.

30 Technology Drive, Warren, NJ, 07059

Tel: (908) 222-9100      Fax: (908) 222-1557      www.barringer.com

*Provides advanced technology for security, law enforcement, including drug and explosive detectors.*

**Barringer Europe, SARL,  4 rue Du Te, F-95724 Roissy Cedex, France**

Tel: 33-1-48-62-5492  Fax: 33-1-48-62-5496

## BARRY CONTROLS INC.

40 Guest Street, PO Box 9105, Brighton, MA, 02135-9105

Tel: (617) 787-1555      Fax: (617) 254-7381      www.barrymounts.com

*Mfr./sale vibration isolation mounting devices.*

**Barry Controls Aerospace (European Service),  Zone d'Aviation d'Affaires Bat 41, Toulouse  F-31700, France**

## R.G. BARRY CORPORATION

PO Box 129, Columbus, OH, 43216

Tel: (614) 864-6400      Fax: (614) 866-9787      www.rgbarry.com

*Mfr. slippers and footwear.*

**Fargeot et Cie SA,  Route de Limoges, Thiviers F-24800, France**

Tel: 33-55-352-2486  Fax: 33-55-352-2649

**R.G Barry Paris,  31 Square Saint Charles, Paris F-75012 France**

Tel: 33-14-468-8808  Fax: 33-14-307-3849

## BASE TEN SYSTEMS INC.

One Electronics Drive, Trenton, NJ, 08619

Tel: (609) 586-7010      Fax: (609) 586-1593      www.base10.com

*Mfr. proprietary control systems, flight test systems, communications products.*

**Base Ten Systems Ltd.,  Espace Fauriel,  35 rue Ponchardier, 42100 Saint-Etienne, France**

## BATES WORLDWIDE INC.

405 Lexington Ave., New York, NY, 10174

Tel: (212) 297-7000      Fax: (212) 986-0270      www.batesww.com

*Advertising, marketing, public relations and media consulting.*

**Bates 141 France,  4 rue Sentou, F-92150 Sureenes, France**

Tel: 33-1-41-38-9350  Fax: 33-1-41-38-9351   Contact: Patrick Geindre, Chmn.

**Bates France,  11 rue Galvani, F 75838 Paris Cedex 17, France**

Tel: 33-1-44-09-5959  Fax: 33-1-45-74-0806   Contact: Violaine Sanson-Tricard, CEO

## BAUSCH & LOMB INC.

One Bausch & Lomb Place, Rochester, NY, 14604-2701

Tel: (716) 338-6000      Fax: (716) 338-6007      www.bausch.com

*Mfr. vision care products and accessories.*

**Bausch & Lomb France SA,  Route de Levis Saint No, 78320 Le Mesnil, St. Denis France**

## BAXTER HEALTHCARE CORPORATION

One Baxter Parkway, Deerfield, IL, 60015

Tel: (847) 948-2000      Fax: (847) 948-3948      www.baxter.com

*Pharmaceutical preparations, surgical/medical instruments and cardiovascular products.*

**Baxter SA,  Etaille, F-36400 La Chatre, France**

## BBDO WORLDWIDE

1285 Ave. of the Americas, New York, NY, 10019

Tel: (212) 459-5000      Fax: (212) 459-6645      www.bbdo.com

*Multinational group of advertising agencies.*

**La Compagnie/BBDO,  Issy-les-Moulineaux, France**

## BDO SEIDMAN, LLP   BELGIUM

Two Prudential Plaza, 180 N. Stetson Ave., Ste. 2300, Chicago, IL, 60601

Tel: (312) 240-1236      Fax: (312) 240-3329      www.bdo.com

*International accounting and financial consulting firm.*

**BDO Gendrot, 25 Quai Carnot, F-92210 Paris-Saint-Cloud, France**

Tel: 33-1-41-12-1314    Fax: 33-1-47-71-1700    Contact: Guy Gendrot

## BEA SYSTEMS, INC.

2315 North First Street, St. Jose, CA, 95131

Tel: (408) 570-8000      Fax: (408) 570-8091      www.beasys.com

*Develops communications management software and provider of software consulting services.*

**BEA Systems S.A., Tour Manhattan 6 - Place de l'Iris, F-92095 Paris La Defense Cedex, France**

Tel: 33-1-41-45-7000    Fax: 33-1-41-45-7099

## BEAR STEARNS & CO., INC.

245 Park Ave., New York, NY, 10167

Tel: (212) 272-2000      Fax: (212) 272-3092      www.bearstearns.com

*Investment banking, securities broker/dealer and investment advisory services.*

**Bear Stearns Finance, S.A., 21-25 rue de Balzac 8th Fl., F-75406 Paris, Cedex 08, France**

Tel: 33-1-42-99-6060    Fax: 33-1-42-99-6050

## BEARIUM METALS CORPORATION

4106 South Creek Road, Chattanooga, TN, 37406

Tel: (423) 622-9991      Fax: (423) 622-9991      www.bearium.com

*Bearium metal alloys.*

**Fonderies de Nogent, 91 rue Carnot Nogent sur Oise, BP 57, F-60105 Creil Cedex, France**

## BECHTEL GROUP INC.

50 Beale Street, PO Box 3965, San Francisco, CA, 94105-1895

Tel: (415) 768-1234      Fax: (415) 768-9038      www.bechtel.com

*General contractors in engineering and construction.*

**Bechtel International Corp., Centre Bassano, 38 rue de Bassano, F-75008 Paris, France**

Tel: 33-1-47-20-5304    Fax: 33-1-47-20-5506

## BECKMAN COULTER, INC.

4300 N. Harbor Boulevard, Fullerton, CA, 92834

Tel: (714) 871-4848      Fax: (714) 773-8898      www.beckmancoulter.com

*Develop/mfr./marketing automated systems and supplies for biological analysis.*

**Beckman Coulter France S.A., Paris Nord II, 33 rue des Vanesses, BP 50359 Villepinte F-95942 Roissy Cedex, France**

Tel: 33-1-49-90-9000

## BECTON DICKINSON AND COMPANY

One Becton Drive, Franklin Lakes, NJ, 07417-1880

Tel: (201) 847-6800      Fax: (201) 847-6475      www.bd.com

*Mfr./sale medical supplies, devices and diagnostic systems.*

**Becton Dickinson European Divisions, 5 Chemin des Sources BP 37, F-38241 Meylan, France**

**Becton Dickinson Pharmaceutical Systems, 11 rue Aristide Berges BP 4, F-38800 Pont de Claix, France**

## BELDEN, INC.

7701 Forsyth Blvd., Ste. 800, St. Louis, MO, 63015

Tel: (314) 854-8000      Fax: (314) 854-8001      www.belden.com

*Mfr. electronic wire and cable products.*

**Belden Electronics S.a.r.l., Immeuble le Cesar, 20 Place Louis Pradel, Lyon 69001 France**

## BELL & HOWELL COMPANY

5215 Old Orchard Road, Skokie, IL, 60077

Tel: (847) 470-7100     Fax: (847) 470-9625     www.bellhowell.com

*Diversified information products and services.*

**Bell & Howell France SA, 32/34 rue Fernand-Pelloutier, F-92110 Clichy, France**

## BELL SPORTS INC.

6350 San Ignacio Ave., San Jose, CA, 95119

Tel: (408) 574-3400     Fax: (408) 224-9129     www.bellsports.com

*Mfr. bicycle and automotive racing helmets and accessories.*

**Euro-Bell SA, Z.I. du Gatling, rue Mathieu Vallat, F-42230 St. Etienne, France**

## BELLSOUTH CORPORATION LATIN AMERICA

1155 Peachtree Street NE, Ste. 400, Atlanta, GA, 30367

Tel: (404) 249-4800     Fax: (404) 249-4880     www.bellsouth.com

*Mobile communications, telecommunications network systems.*

**Datech SA, 1 rue Marconi, Technopole Metz 2000, F-57070 Metz, France**

## BEN & JERRY'S HOMEMADE INC.

30 Community Drive, South Burlington, VT, 05403-6828

Tel: (802) 651-9600     Fax: (802) 651-9647     www.benjerry.com

*Mfr. premium ice cream.*

**Ben & Jerry's International, Paris, France**

## BENTLY NEVADA CORPORATION

1617 Water Street, PO Box 157, Minden, NV, 89423

Tel: (775) 782-3611     Fax: (775) 782-9259     www.bently.com

*Provides hardware, software, and services for machinery information and management systems.*

**Bently Nevada France SARL, 30 ave. de l'Amiral Lemonnier, F-78160 Marly-le-Roi, France**

## LOUIS BERGER INTERNATIONAL INC.

100 Halsted Street, East Orange, NJ, 07019

Tel: (201) 678-1960     Fax: (201) 672-4284     www.louisberger.com

*Consulting engineers, engaged in architecture, environmental and advisory services.*

**Louis Berger SARL, 71 rue Fondary, F-75015 Paris, France**

Tel: 33-1-45-78-3939   Fax: 33-1-45-77-7469

## BERLITZ CROSS-CULTURAL TRAINING INC.

400 Alexander Park, Princeton, NJ, 08540

Tel: (609) 514-9650     Fax: (609) 514-9689     www.berlitz.com

*Consulting and management training services to bridge cultural gaps for international travelers as well as for business transferees and families.*

**Berlitz France S.A.S., 15 rue Louis Le Grand, Paris F-75002, France**

## BERNARD HODES GROUP

555 Madison Ave., New York, NY, 10022

Tel: (212) 935-4000     Fax: (212) 755-7324     www.hodes.com

*Multinational recruitment agency.*

**Bernard Hodes Group, 40 Boulevard Henri Sellier, 92150 Suresnes, France**

## BEST WESTERN INTERNATIONAL

6201 North 24th Place, Phoenix, AZ, 85106

Tel: (602) 957-4200     Fax: (602) 957-5740     www.bestwestern.com

*International hotel chain.*

**Beau Manoir Hotel, 6 rue de l'arcade, F-75008, Paris, France**

**Grand Hotel Francais,  12 rue du Temple, F-33000 Bordeaux, France**

Tel: 33-5-56-481035

## BESTFOODS, INC.

700 Sylvan Ave., International Plaza, Englewood Cliffs, NJ, 07632-9976

Tel: (201) 894-4000     Fax: (201) 894-2186     www.bestfoods.com

*Consumer foods products; corn refining.*

**CPC France SA,  379 ave. du General de Gaulle, F-92140 Clamart, France**

Tel: 33-1-40-94-5252   Fax: 33-1-40-94-5200   Contact: Olivier Desforges, Mgr.

## BETZDEARBORN

4636 Somerton Road, PO Box 3002, Trevose, PA, 19053-6783

Tel: (215) 953-2568     Fax: (215) 953-5524     www.betzdearborn.com

*Mfr. water/wastewater and process system treatment chemicals and services.*

**BetzDearborn S.A.,  B.P. 43, F-77312 Marne-la-Vallee Cedex 02, France**

## BIJUR LUBRICATING CORPORATION

50 Kocher Dr., Bennington, VT, 05201-1994

Tel: (802) 447-2174     Fax: (802) 447-1365     www.bijur.com

*Design/mfr. pumps.*

**Bijur Products Inc.,  BP 50, Z.I. de Courtaboeuf, F-91942 Orsay Les Ulis Cedex, France**

Tel: 33-1-69-29-85-85  Fax: 33-1-69-07-76-27  Contact: John Pearce, Mgr. Dir.   Emp: 47

## BINNEY & SMITH INC.

1100 Church Lane, PO Box 431, Easton, PA, 18044-0431

Tel: (610) 253-6271     Fax: (610) 250-5768     www.crayola.com

*Mfr. crayons, art supplies and craft kits.*

**Binney & Smith Ltd.,  Succursale Francaise, 1 rue de la Mairie, F-60130 Saint-Remy-en-l'Eau, France**

## BIOGEN, INC.

14 Cambridge Center, Cambridge, MA, 02142

Tel: (617) 679-2000     Fax: (617) 679-2617     www.bigoten.com

*Engaged in medical research and development on autoimmune diseases.*

**Biogen Europe,  55 Avenue des Champs Pierreux, F-92012 Nanterre Cedex, France**

Tel: 33-1-41-37-95-95  Fax: 33-1-40-97-00-53

**Biogen France,  Le Capitole, 55 Avenue des Champs Pierreux, F-92012 Nanterre Cedex, France**

Tel: 33-1-41-37-95-95

## BIOMATRIX, INC.

65 Railroad Ave., Ridgefield, NJ, 07657

Tel: (201) 945-9550     Fax: (201) 945-0363     www.biomatrix.com

*Mfr. hylan biological polymers for therapeutic medical and skin care products.*

**Biomatrix France SARL,  75 rue La Fayette, F-75009 Paris, France**

Tel: 33-1-47-64-6016  Fax: 33-1-47-64-6023  Contact: Francois Bailleul, MD, VP   Emp: 5

## BIO-RAD LABORATORIES INC.

1000 Alfred Nobel Drive, Hercules, CA, 94547

Tel: (510) 724-7000     Fax: (510) 724-3167     www.bio-rad.com

*Mfr. life science research products, clinical diagnostics, analytical instruments.*

**Bio-Rad Laboratories,  Paris, France**

## BISSELL INC.

2345 Walker Road, NW, Grand Rapids, MI, 49504

Tel: (616) 453-4451     Fax: (616) 453-1383     www.bissell.com

*Mfr. home care products.*

**Bissell SA,  27 Av. Ampere, Z.I. de Villemilan Wissous, France**

### BLACK & DECKER CORPORATION

701 E. Joppa Road, Towson, MD, 21286

Tel: (410) 716-3900     Fax: (410) 716-2933     www.blackanddecker.com

*Mfr. power tools and accessories, security hardware, small appliances, fasteners, information systems and services.*

**Black & Decker Servitech, 140 Ave. de la Republique, Bordeaux, France**

Tel: 33-5-56-24-3838   Fax: 33-5-56-51-4471

### BLACK BOX CORPORATION

1000 Park Dr., Lawrence, PA, 15055

Tel: (724) 746-5500     Fax: (724) 746-0746     www.blackbox.com

*Direct marketer and technical service provider of communications, networking and related computer connectivity products.*

**Black Box France, 18 rue de L'Esterel, Silic 571, F-94653 Rungis Cedex, France**

Tel: 33-1-45-60-6700   Fax: 33-1-45-60-6747   Contact: Norbest Prommdt, Gen. Mgr.

### BLACK CLAWSON COMPANY

405 Lexington Ave., 61st Fl., New York, NY, 10174

Tel: (212) 916-8000     Fax: (212) 916-8057     www.ligroup.com

*Paper and pulp mill machinery.*

**Black Clawson France, 30 ave. Pierre Curie, BP 9, F-33270 Floirac Bordeaux, France**

### BLOOM ENGINEERING CO., INC.

5460 Horning Rd., Pittsburgh, PA, 15236

Tel: (412) 653-3500     Fax: (412) 653-2253     www.bloomeng.com

*Mfr. custom engineered burners and combustion systems.*

**Bloom Engineering (Europa) GmbH, 8 rue du Marechal Juin, F-95210 Saint Gratien, France**

Tel: 33-1-34-05-10-00   Fax: 33-1-34-05-10-01

### BMC SOFTWARE, INC.

2101 City West Blvd., Houston, TX, 77042-2827

Tel: (713) 918-8800     Fax: (713) 918-8000     www.bmc.com

*Engaged in mainframe-related utilities software and services.*

**BMC Software, Immeuble Danica , 21 avenue Georges Pompidou, F-69486 Lyon Cedex 03, France**

**BMC Software, 24 rue Salomon de Rothschild, 92150 Suresnes, France**

### BOART LONGYEAR COMPANY

2340 West 1700 South, Salt Lake City, UT, 84104

Tel: (801) 972-6430     Fax: (801) 977-3372     www.boartlongyear.com

*Mfr. diamond drills, concrete cutting equipment and drill services.*

**Longyear France, BP 1, 78191 Trappes Cedex, France**

### THE BOEING COMPANY

7755 East Marginal Way South, Seattle, WA, 98108

Tel: (206) 655-2121     Fax: (206) 655-6300     www.boeing.com.

*World's largest aerospace company; mfr. military and commercial aircraft, missiles and satellite launch vehicles.*

**Boeing Company, Paris, France**

### BOISE CASCADE CORPORATION

1111 West Jefferson Street, PO Box 50, Boise, ID, 83728-0001

Tel: (208) 384-6161     Fax: (208) 384-7189     www.bc.com

*Mfr./distributor paper and paper products, building products, office products.*

**Boise Cascade Office Products, Ltd., Paris, France**

## BOOZ-ALLEN & HAMILTON INC.

8283 Greensboro Drive, McLean, VA, 22102

Tel: (703) 902-5000        Fax: (703) 902-3333        www.bah.com

*International management and technology consultants.*

**Booz Allen Hamilton France, 112 Ave. Kleber, F-75116 Paris Cedex 16, France**

Tel: 33-1-44-34-3131   Fax: 33-1-44-34-3000

## BORDEN INC.

180 East Broad Street, Columbus, OH, 43215-3799

Tel: (614) 225-4000        Fax: (614) 220-6453        www.bordenfamily.com

*Mfr. packaged foods, consumer adhesives, housewares and industrial chemicals.*

**Borden Chemie, S.A., 3 et 5 rue Barbet, F-76250 Deville-Les-Rouen, France**

Tel: 33-23-282-7100   Fax: 33-23-575-4760

## BOSE CORPORATION

The Mountain, Framingham, MA, 01701-9168

Tel: (508) 879-7330        Fax: (508) 766-7543        www.bose.com

*Mfr. quality audio equipment/speakers.*

**BOSE SA, 6 rue St. Vincent, F-78100 Saint Germain en Laye, France**

Tel: 33-1-30616363

## THE BOSTON CONSULTING GROUP

Exchange Place, 31st Fl., Boston, MA, 02109

Tel: (617) 973-1200        Fax: (617) 973-1339        www.bcg.com

*Management consulting company.*

**The Boston Consulting Group, 4 rue d'Aguesseau, F-75008 Paris, France**

Tel: 33-1-40-17-1010

## BOSTON SCIENTIFIC CORPORATION

One Scientific Place, Natick, MA, 01760-1537

Tel: (508) 650-8000        Fax: (508) 650-8923        www.bsci.com

*Mfr./distributes medical devices for use in minimally invasive surgeries.*

**Antheor SNC, Site d'Activities Economiques de Chalembert, 4 rue Monge, F-86130 Juanay Clan, France**

Tel: 33-5-49-62-3838   Fax: 33-5-49-62-8484

**Boston Scientific International (European Hdqtrs.), Immeuble Vision Defense, 91 blvd National, F-92250 LaGarenne Colombes Cedex, Paris, France**

Tel: 33-1-46-49-6600   Fax: 33-1-46-49-6699

**Boston Scientific, S.A., Par de l'Observatoire, Batiment B, 4 Ave. des Trois Peoples, F-78180 Montigny-Le-Bratonneux, France**

Tel: 33-1-30-12-1649   Fax: 33-1-30-96-6010

## BOURNS INC.

1200 Columbia Avenue, Riverside, CA, 92507

Tel: (909) 781-5500        Fax: (909) 781-5006        www.bourns.com

*Mfr. resistive components and networks, precision potentiometers, panel controls, switches, transducers and surge protectors..*

**Bourns Ohmic SA, 21/23 rue des Ardennes, F-75019 Paris, France**

## BOWNE & COMPANY, INC.
345 Hudson Street, New York, NY, 10014

Tel: (212) 924-5500 Fax: (212) 229-3420 www.bowne.com

*Financial printing and foreign language translation, localization (software), internet design and maintenance and facilities management.*

**Bowne International, 3 rue Nationale, F-9100 Boulogne, France**

Tel: 33-1-47-61-4800 Fax: 33-1-47-61-1971

**Bowne International, 5 rue Royale, 3rd Fl., F-75008 Paris, France**

Tel: 33-1-44-94-3280 Fax: 33-1-44-94-3295 Contact: Antoine Antaki, Dir.

## BOYDEN CONSULTING CORPORATION
364 Elwood Ave., Hawthorne, NY, 10502

Tel: (914) 747-0093 Fax: (914) 980-6147 www.boyden.com

*International executive search firm.*

**Boyden Associates Ltd. - Search, 1 Rond-Point des Champs-Elysees, F-75008 Paris, France**

Tel: 33-1-44-13-6700

**Boyden International SARL Consulting, 38 rue Vauthier, F-92774 Boulogne Cedex, France**

Tel: 33-1-46-99-1818

## BOZELL GROUP
40 West 23rd Street, New York, NY, 10010

Tel: (212) 727-5000 Fax: (212) 645-9173 www.bozell.com

*Advertising, marketing, public relations and media consulting.*

**Bozell France/Bozell Marketing/TN Media, 20 rue de L'Eglise 36, F-92522 Neuilly sur Seine, France**

Tel: 33-1-41-92-1515 Fax: 33-1-41-92-1500 Contact: Brian Tucker, CEO

**Bozell Terre Lune, 20 rue de L'Eglise 36, F-92522 Neuilly sur Seine, France**

Tel: 33-1-41-92-1520 Fax: 33-1-41-92-1500 Contact: Serge Hugon, Mng. Dir.

## BRADY CORPORATION
6555 W. Good Hope Road, Milwaukee, WI, 53223

Tel: (414) 358-6600 Fax: (414) 358-6600 www.whbrady.com

*Mfr. industrial ID for wire marking, circuit boards; facility ID, signage, printing systems and software.*

**Signals S.A., Rond Point de la Republique, Z.I. de la Rochelle, F-17187 Perigny Cedex, France**

**W.H. Brady SARL, 2 Place Marcel Rebuffat, BP 362, Parc de Villejust, F-91959 Les Ulis Cedex France**

Tel: 33-1-69-31-9100 Fax: 33-1-69-31-1068 Contact: Max Squires, Country Sales/Mktg Dir.

## BRANSON ULTRASONICS CORPORATION
41 Eagle Road, Danbury, CT, 06813-1961

Tel: (203) 796-0400 Fax: (203) 796-2285 www.branson-plasticsjoin.com

*Mfr. plastics assembly equipment, ultrasonic cleaning equipment.*

**Branson Ultrasons (KBSA), 1-3 rue des Pyrenees, Silic 404, F-94573 Rungis Cedex, France**

Tel: 33-4-50-43-96-50 Fax: 33-4-50-43-96-60

## BRIGGS & STRATTON CORPORATION
12301 W. Wirth St., Wauwatosa, WI, 53222

Tel: (414) 259-5333 Fax: (414) 259-9594 www.briggesandstratton.com

*Mfr. air cooled, gasoline engines.*

**Briggs & Stratton France, Attn: French Office, PO Box 72, Milwaukee WI 53201**

## BRIGHTPOINT, INC.

6402 Corporate Dr., Indianapolis, IN, 46278

Tel: (317) 297-6100    Fax: (317) 297-6114    www.brightpoint.com

*Mfr./distribution of mobile phones.*

**Brightpoint France, 14 rue Davoust, 93698 Pantin Cedex, France**

Tel: 33-1-4810-1600  Fax: 33-1-4810-1699

## BRINK'S INC.

Thorndal Circle, Darien, CT, 06820

Tel: (203) 662-7800    Fax: (203) 662-7968    www.brinks.com

*Security transportation.*

**Brink's France, 61 rue Hautpoul, F-75019 Paris, France**

## BRISTOL BABCOCK INC.

1100 Buckingham Street, Watertown, CT, 06795

Tel: (203) 575-3000    Fax: (203) 575-3170    www.bristolbabcock.com

*Mfr. process control instruments and SCADA systems.*

**Bristol Babcock SA, Z.I. des Petits Pres, Route de Balagny, BP 129, F-60251 Mouy Cedex, France**

## BRISTOL-MYERS SQUIBB COMPANY

345 Park Ave., New York, NY, 10154-0037

Tel: (212) 546-4000    Fax: (212) 546-4020    www.bms.com

*Pharmaceutical and food preparations, medical and surgical instruments.*

**Bristol-Myers S.A., rue de la Maison Rouge, Le Mandinet, F-77185 Lognes, France**

**Bristol-Myers Squibb - Reg. Hdqtrs. - Africa/Paris, Quartier La Grande Arche, F-92057 Cedex 24, France**

**ConvaTec France, Tour Generale, F-92088 Cedex 22 Paris, France**

**Laboratires Guieu Franceia Ltd., Z.I. de la Barogne, rue des 22 Arpents, F-77230 Lognes, France**

**Laboratoires ConvaTec, La Grande Arche Nord, F-92044 La Defense, Paris Cedex France**

**Mead Johnson S.A., 33 Ave. du Marechal, de Lattre de Tassign, France**

**SOFCA, rue des Longes, F-28232 Epernon, France**

**UPSA - France, Av. du Dr. Bru, F-47400 Tonneins, France**

**UPSA France Bon-Encontre, Z.I. Laville, F-47240 Bon-Encontre, France**

**Zimmer S.A. (Rungis), 62 rue des Gemeaux, Silic 582, F-94663 Rungis Cedex, France**

## BROADVISION, INC.

585 Broadway, Redwood City, CA, 94063

Tel: (650) 261-5100    Fax: (650) 261-5900    www.broadvision.com

*Develops and delivers an integrated suite of packaged applications for personalized enterprise portals.*

**BroadVision France, 155 rue Anatole, Levallois-Perret F-92300, France**

Tel: 33-1-4748-8000

## BROWN BROTHERS HARRIMAN & COMPANY

59 Wall Street, New York, NY, 10005

Tel: (212) 483-1818    Fax: (212) 493-8526    www.bbh.com

*Financial services.*

**Brown Harriman Corp., 12-14 Rond Point des Champs Elysees, F-75008 Paris, France**

## BROWN SHOE COMPANY, INC.

8300 Maryland Avenue, St. Louis, MO, 63105

Tel: (314) 854-4000    Fax: (314) 854-4274    www.brownshoe.com

*Markets branded and private label footwear, including Dr. Scholl's, Air Step and Buster Brown.*

**Pagoda Intl. SARL, 6 rue St. Vincent, F-78100 St-Germain-en-Laye, France**

## BROWNING WINCHESTER

1 Browning Place, Morgan, UT, 84050

Tel: (801) 876-2711    Fax: (801) 876-3331    www.browning.com

*Sales/distribution of port firearms, fishing rods, etc.*

**Browning Sports France, S.A., 18 rue Salvatore Allende, Z.I. Molina-la-Chazotte, F-42350 La Taludiere, France**

## LEO BURNETT, DIV. B-COM 3 GROUP

35 West Wacker Drive, Chicago, IL, 60601

Tel: (312) 220-5959    Fax: (312) 220-6533    www.bcom3group.com

*Engaged in advertising, marketing, media buying and planning, and public relations.*

**Black Pencil SARL, 14 rue Alexandre Parodi, F-75010 Paris, France**

**Bordelais, Lemeunier & Leo Burnett, 185 ave. Charles de Gaulle, F-92521 Neuilly-sur-Seine, France**

## BURSON-MARSTELLER

230 Park Ave., New York, NY, 10003-1566

Tel: (212) 614-4000    Fax: (212) 614-4262    www.bm.com

*Public relations/public affairs consultants.*

**Burson-Marsteller Paris, 6 rue Escudier, F-92772 Boulogre Billancourt Cedex, France**

Tel: 33-1-41-86-76-76   Fax: 31-1-86-76-00   Emp: 42

## BUSH BOAKE ALLEN INC.

7 Mercedes Drive, Montvale, NJ, 07645

Tel: (201) 391-9870    Fax: (201) 391-0860    www.bushboakeallen.com

*Mfr. aroma chemicals for fragrances and flavor products for seasonings.*

**Bush Boake Allen Deutschland GmbH, Immeuble Avant Seine, 14 Quai de Dion Bouton, F-92806 Puteaux Cedex, France**

Tel: 33-1-4138-8000   Fax: 33-1-4104-3880

## BUTLER AUTOMATIC, INC.

41 Leona Drive, Middleborough, MA, 02346

Tel: (508) 923-0544    Fax: (508) 923-0885    www.butlerautomatic.com

*Mfr. web splicing equipment.*

**Butler Automatica Inc., St. Pierre, France**

## BUTTERICK COMPANY, INC.

161 Avenue of the Americas, New York, NY, 10013

Tel: (212) 620-2500    Fax: (212) 620-2746    www.butterick.com

*Prints sewing patterns and related magazines.*

**Vogue Pattern Service, 44 rue la Boetie, F-75008 Paris, France**

## CABOT CORPORATION

75 State Street, Boston, MA, 02109-1807

Tel: (617) 345-0100    Fax: (617) 342-6103    www.cabot-corp.com

*Mfr. carbon blacks, plastics; oil and gas, information systems.*

**Berylco-Cabot Metaux Speciaux (Cabot Berylco Div.), BP 17, F-44220 Coueron, France**

**Berylco-Cabot Metaux Speciaux (Cabot Berylco Div.), 76-78 Champs Elyses, F-75008 Paris, France**

**Berylco-Cabot Metaux Speciaux, Div. Plastiques, 6 ave. Charles de Gaulle, F-78150 Le Chesnay Paris, France**

## CACI INTERNATIONAL INC.

1100 North Glebe Road, Arlington, VA, 22201

Tel: (703) 841-7800    Fax: (703) 841-7882    www.caci.com

*Provides simulation technology/software and designs factories, computer networks, and communications systems for military, electronic commerce digital document management, logistics and Y2K remediation.*

**CACI International, Inc., Paris, France**

## CAHILL GORDON & REINDEL

80 Pine Street, New York, NY, 10005

Tel: (212) 701-3000     Fax: (212) 269-5420     www.cahill.com

*International law firm.*

**Cahill, Gordon & Reindel,  Paris, France**

## CALGON CARBON CORPORATION

400 Calgon Carbon Drive, Pittsburgh, PA, 15230-0717

Tel: (412) 787-6700     Fax: (412) 787-4541     www.calgoncarbon.com

*Mfr. activated carbon, related systems and services.*

**Chemviron Carbon,  Immeuble "Expansion", 9-11 rue Georges Enesco, F-94008 Creteil Cedex, France**

## CALVIN KLEIN, INC.

205 West 39th Street, 4th Fl., New York, NY, 10018

Tel: (212) 719-2600     Fax: (212) 768-8922     www.calvinklein.com

*Mfr. of high quality clothing and accessories*

**Calvin Klein Ltd.,  Paris, France**

## CAMBREX CORPORATION

1 Meadowlands Plaza, East Rutherford, NJ, 07063

Tel: (201) 804-3000     Fax: (201) 804-9852     www.cambrex.com

*human health, animal health/agriculture and Mfr. biotechnology products and produce specialty chemicals.*

**Francochim,  129 Chemin des Cr»tes, F-31120 Foyrans, France**

## CAMBRIDGE TECHNOLOGY PARTNERS, INC.

8 Cambridge Center, Cambridge, MA, 02142

Tel: (617) 374-9800     Fax: (617) 914-8300     www.ctp.com

*Engaged in e-commerce consultancy.*

**Cambridge Technology Partners, Inc.,  60 rue de Monceau, FR-75008, France**
Tel: 33-1-5659-5400    Fax: 33-1-5669-5499

## CAMPBELL SOUP COMPANY

Campbell Place, Camden, NJ, 08103-1799

Tel: (856) 342-4800     Fax: (856) 342-3878     www.campbellsoup.com

*Mfr. food products.*

**Societe Francaise des Biscuits Delacre SA,  Paris, France**

## CANBERRA-PACKARD INDUSTRIES

800 Research Parkway, Meriden, CT, 06450

Tel: (203) 238-2351     Fax: (203) 235-1347     www.canberra.com

*Mfr. instruments for nuclear research.*

**Canberra Electronique SARL,  Z.I. de Savigny-le-Temple, rue de l'Etain, BP 15, F-77541 Savigny-le-Temple, France**

**Packard Instrument SA,  4 a 10 rue de la Grosse Pierre, F-94533 Rungis, France**

## CARBOLINE COMPANY

350 Hanley Industrial Court, St. Louis, MO, 63144

Tel: (314) 644-1000     Fax: (314) 644-4617     www.carboline.com

*Mfr. coatings and sealants.*

**StonCor Europe South,  14 allee Emile Reynaud Bat. H, F-77200 Torcy, France**
Tel: 33-1-600-64419    Fax: 33-1-600-51460

## CARGILL, INC.

15407 McGinty Road West, Minnetonka, MN, 55440-5625

Tel: (612) 742-7575     Fax: (612) 742-7393     www.cargill.com

*Food products, feeds, animal products.*

**Compagnie Cargill SA, BP 215, F-78108 St. Germain-en-laye Cedex Paris, France**

## CARLISLE SYNTEC SYSTEMS

PO Box 7000, Carlisle, PA, 17013

Tel: (717) 245-7000     Fax: (717) 245-9107     www.carlislesyntec.com

*Mfr. elastomeric roofing and waterproofing systems.*

**Carlisle SynTec Systems France SARL, Parc Club du Moulin a Vent, 33 ave. du Docteur G. Levy, F-69693 Vennissieux Cedex, France**

## CARLSON COMPANIES, INC.

Carlson Parkway, PO Box 59159, Minneapolis, MN, 55459

Tel: (612) 550-4520     Fax: (612) 550-4580     www.cmg.carlson.com

*Marketing services agency.*

**Issy-Les-Moullineaux IPC Groupe, 2 rue Maurice Hartmann, F-92137 Issy-les-Moulineaux, France**
Tel: 33-1-40-95-2600

## THE CARLYLE GROUP L.P.

1001 Pennsylvania Avenue, NW, Washington, DC, 20004-2505

Tel: (202) 347-2626     Fax: (202) 347-1818     www.thecarlylegroup.com

*Global investor in defense contracts.*

**Carlyle Europe, 112 ave. Kelber, F-75116 Paris, France**
Tel: 33-1-53-703520

## CARPENTER TECHNOLOGY CORPORATION

101 W. Bern Street, PO Box 14662, Reading, PA, 19612-4662

Tel: (610) 208-2000     Fax: (610) 208-3214     www.cartech.com

*Mfr. specialty steels and structural ceramics for casting industrial.*

**Carpenter Technology (France) SARL, 77 ave. Fernand Auberger, F-03700 Bellerive-sur-Allier, France**

## CARRIER CORPORATION

One Carrier Place, Farmington, CT, 06034-4015

Tel: (860) 674-3000     Fax: (860) 679-3010     www.carrier.com

*Mfr./distributor/services A/C, heating and refrigeration equipment.*

**Carrier ETO Ltd., Tour Franklin, Defense 8, F-92042 Paris La Defense Cedex, France**
**Carrier SA, Montluel, France**
Tel: 33-72-25-2121   Fax: 33-72-25-2248

## CARTER-WALLACE INC.

1345 Ave. of the Americas, New York, NY, 10105

Tel: (212) 339-5000     Fax: (212) 339-5100     www.carterwallace.com

*Mfr. personal care products and pet products.*

**Laboratoires Fumouze, 110-114 rue Victor Hugo BP 314, F-92303 Levallois Perret Cedex, France**
Tel: 33-14-968-4100   Fax: 33-14-968-4140

## CASCADE CORPORATION

2201 NE 201st Ave., Fairview, OR, 97024-9718

Tel: (503) 669-6300     Fax: (503) 669-6321     www.cascor.com

*Mfr. hydraulic forklift truck attachments.*

**Cascade (France) SARL, 11 rue Jean Charcot, Zone Industrielle Sud, F-91421 Morangis, Cedex, France**
**Mecalev S.A., Les Fontaines Douces, F-58260 La Machine, France**

## CASE CORPORATION

700 State Street, Racine, WI, 53404

Tel: (414) 636-6011      Fax: (414) 636-0200        www.casecorp.com

*Mfr./sale agricultural and construction equipment.*

**Case Europe, 18 Place des Nympheas, Z1 Paris Nord II, F-95915 Roissy CDG Cedex, France**

Tel: 33-1-49-90-2300   Fax: 33-1-49-90-2587   Contact: Leopold Plattner, Pres. Eur/Africa/ME

**Case France S.A., 71 av. Georges Hannart, B.P. 109, F-59964 Croix Cedex, France**

Tel: 33-2066-3900   Fax: 33-2066-3902

**Case France S.A., Clos Saint Jean, BP 37, F-52102 St. Dizier, France**
**ce**

Tel: 33-2556-7900   Fax: 33-2505-2896

**Case France, S.A., 28 route de Bailly, Tracy-le-Mont, F-60170 Ribecourt, France**

Tel: 33-4475-5151   Fax: 33-4475-5100

**Case France, S.A., 17 rue des Tournelles, F-60803 Crepy-en-Valois Cedex, France**

Tel: 33-4494-3200   Fax: 33-4487-6869

**Case Poclain SA, av. Georges Bataille, F-60670 Le Plessis-Belleville Cedex, France**

## CATAPULT COMMUNICATIONS CORPORATION

160 South Whisman Road, Mountain View, CA, 94041

Tel: (650) 960-1025      Fax: (650) 960-1029       www.catapult.com

*Mfr. test systems for telecommunications service providers.*

**Catapult Communications Corp., Centre d'Entreprises CGIA , 5-7 rue Marcelin Berthelot F-92762 Antony Cedex, France**

Tel: 33-1-55-59-5591

## CATERPILLAR INC.

100 NE Adams Street, Peoria, IL, 61629-6105

Tel: (309) 675-1000      Fax: (309) 675-1182       www.cat.com

*Mfr. earth/material-handling and construction machinery and equipment and engines.*

**Caterpillar Holding (France) S.A.R.L., 40-48 ave. Leon Blum, F-38100 Grenoble, France**

**F.G. Wilson S.A., Paris, France**

## C.B. RICHARD ELLIS

533 South Fremont Ave., Los Angeles, CA, 90071-1712

Tel: (213) 613-3123      Fax: (213) 613-3535       www.cbrichardellis.com

*Commercial real estate services.*

**CB Richard Ellis SA, 28/32 Avenue Victor Hugo, F-75116 Paris, France**

## CCI/TRIAD

804 Las Cimas Pkwy., Ste. 200, Austin, TX, 78746

Tel: (512) 328-2300      Fax: (512) 328-8209       www.cci-triad.com

*Information retrieval systems.*

**Triad Systems France, rue des Commeres, F-78310 Coignieres, France**

Tel: 33-1-30-490607   Fax: 33-1-30-490209

## CENTRAL NATIONAL-GOTTESMAN INC.

3 Manhattanville Road, Purchase, NY, 10577-2110

Tel: (914) 696-9000      Fax: (914) 696-1066

*Worldwide sales pulp and paper products.*

**Central National France, S.A.R.L., 21 rue Auber, F-75009 Paris Cedex, France**

Tel: 33-1-47-42-2415   Fax: 33-1-47-42-2429   Contact: Bogdan Pohl

## CENTURY 21 REAL ESTATE CORPORATION

6 Sylvan Way, Parsippany, NJ, 07054-3826

Tel: (973) 496-5722    Fax: (973) 496-5527    www.century21.com

*Engaged in real estate.*

**Century 21 France, S.A., rue des Cevennes Batiment 4, Petite Montagne Sud, F-91017 Evry Cedex Lisses, France**

Tel: 33-1-69-11-1221    Contact: Frank Cluck, Gen. Mgr.

## CEPHALON, INC.

145 Brandywine Pkwy., West Chester, PA, 19380

Tel: (610) 344-0200    Fax: (610) 344-0065    www.cephalon.com

*Engaged in healthscience, research and development.*

**Cephalon France, 14 rue Albert Einstein, Champs Sur Marne F-77420, France**

Tel: 33-1-64-61-0505    Fax: 33-1-64-61-0500    Contact: Christian Lebreton

## CHASE H&Q

One Bush Street, San Francisco, CA, 94104

Tel: (415) 439-3000    Fax: (415) 439-3638    www.jpmhq.com

*Investment banking and venture capital services.*

**Chase H&Q Euromarkets SA, 42 rue Washington, Immeuble Friedland, F-75408 Paris Cedex 08, France**

Tel: 33-1-56-59-82-00    Fax: 33-1-56-59-82-19

## CHECK TECHNOLOGY CORPORATION

12500 Whitewater Drive, Minnetonka, MN, 55343-9420

Tel: (612) 939-9000    Fax: (612) 939-1151    www.checktechnology.com

*Mfr. computer-controlled check/coupon print systems.*

**Check Technology France S.A., 8-10 rue du bois Sauvage, F-91055, Evry Cedex France**

## CHECKPOINT SYSTEMS, INC.

101 Wolf Drive, Thorofare, NJ, 08086

Tel: (856) 848-1800    Fax: (856) 848-0937    www.checkpointsystems.com

*Mfr. test, measurement and closed-circuit television systems.*

**Checkpoint Systems France SARL, 3 bd. Des Bouvets, F-92022 Nanterre Cedex, France**

Tel: 33-1-55-69-6111    Fax: 33-1-55-69-6118    Contact: Gerald Valle, Mng. Dir.

## THE CHERRY CORPORATION

3600 Sunset Ave., PO Box 718, Waukegan, IL, 60087

Tel: (847) 662-9200    Fax: (847) 662-2990    www.cherrycorp.com

*Mfr. electrical switches, electronic keyboards, controls and displays.*

**Cherry SARL, 1 ave. des Violettes, F-94384 Bonneuil Cedex, France**

Tel: 33-1-437-72951    Fax: 33-1-437-72084

## CHESTERTON BINSWANGER INTERNATIONAL

Two Logan Square, 4th Floor, Philadelphia, PA, 19103-2759

Tel: (215) 448-6000    Fax: (215) 448-6238    www.cbbi.com

*Real estate and related services.*

**Chesterton Blumenauer Binswanger, c/o GVI, 11 Parc Ariane, blvd. des Chines, F-78280 Gyancourt, France**

## CHEVRON CHEMICAL COMPANY

1301 McKinney Street, Houston, TX, 77010

Tel: (713) 754-2000    Fax: (713) 754-2016    www.chevron.com

*Mfr. petro chemicals.*

**Chevron Chemical SA, 47 rue de Villiers, F-92527 Neuilly-sur-Seine, France**

## CHIEF INDUSTRIES INC.

PO Box 2078, 3942 West Old Highway 30, Grand Island, NE, 68802-2078

Tel: (308) 382-8820      Fax: (308) 381-7221      www.chiefind.com

*Mfr. grain bins, steel buildings, grain handling and drying equipment, elevator legs and components.*

**Phenix-Rousies Industries, S.A., Rousies, France**

Tel: 33-3-27-69-4242    Fax: 33-3-27-64-9585

## CHIRON CORPORATION

4560 Horton Street, Emeryville, CA, 94608-2916

Tel: (510) 655-8730      Fax: (510) 655-9910      www.chiron.com

*Engaged in biotechnology; biopharmaceuticals, blood testing and vaccines.*

**Chriron France, 10 rue Chevreul, F-92150 Suresnes, France**

## THE CHRISTIAN SCIENCE PUBLISHING SOCIETY

1 Norway Street, Boston, MA, 02115

Tel: (617) 450-2000      Fax: (617) 450-7575      www.christianscience.com

*Publishing company.*

**The Christian Science Monitor, 4 rue de Casablanca, F-75015 Paris, France**

Tel: 33-1-43-31-2290    Contact: Peter Ford    Emp: 1

## THE CHUBB CORPORATION

15 Mountain View Road, Warren, NJ, 07061-1615

Tel: (908) 580-2000      Fax: (908) 580-3606      www.chubb.com

*Holding company for property and casualty insurance.*

**Chubb Insurance Co. of Europe, SA, 9 rue Conde, F-33000 Bordeaux, France**

Tel: 33-5-5600-1257    Fax: 33-5-56-44-2351

**Chubb Insurance Company of Europe, S.A., 5 bd Vincent Gache BP 36204, F-44262 Nantes Cedex 02 France**

Tel: 33-2-40-41-7378    Fax: 33-2-40-41-7388

**Chubb Insurance Company of Europe, S.A., 298 Bd Clemenceau, 59700 Marcq en Baroeul, France**

Tel: 33-3-20-818506    Fax: 33-3-20-89-2373

**Chubb Insurance Company of Europe, S.A., 16 Avenue de Matignon, Paris 75008 France**

Tel: 33-1-45-61-7300    Fax: 33-1-45-61-9851

**Chubb Insurance Company of Europe, S.A., 14 Parc Club de Gold, 13856 Aix en Provence, Cedex 03 France**

Tel: 33-4-42-163525    Fax: 33-4-42-163526

**Chubb Insurance Company of Europe, SA, Le Forum Part Dieu 29, rue Maurice Flandin, F-69444 Lyon Cedex 03, France**

Tel: 33-72-34-5204    Fax: 33-72-33-6098

## CIGNA COMPANIES

One Liberty Place, Philadelphia, PA, 19192

Tel: (215) 761-1000      Fax: (215) 761-5511      www.cigna.com

*Insurance, invest, health care and other financial services.*

**CIGNA France Compagnie d'Assurances, 5 rue de Turin, F-75008 Paris, France**

**CIGNA I, 5 rue de Turin, F-75008 Paris, France**

**CIGNA Insurance Co. of Europe SA/NV, 17 rue Ballu, F-75008 Paris, France**

**CIGNA Life Insurance Copany of Europe S.A.-N.V., Le Colisee-8 Ave. de l'Arche, 92419 Courbevoi Cedex, Paris France**

Tel: 33-1-559`-4545

**Esis Intl. Inc., 5 rue Kleber, F-93100 Montreuil-sous-Bois, France**

**La Nouvelle SA, 14 rue Ballu, F-75009 Paris, France**

### CINCINNATI INCORPORATED

PO Box 11111, Cincinnati, OH, 45211

Tel: (513) 367-7100    Fax: (513) 367-7552    www.e-ci.com

*Mfr. metal fabricating equipment.*

**O.G.R., 20 rue De La Liberte, Gonesse F-95500, France**

Tel: 33-1-39-87-0816   Fax: 33-1-39-85-2616

### CINCINNATI MILACRON INC.

4701 Marburg Ave., Cincinnati, OH, 45209

Tel: (513) 841-8100    Fax: (513) 841-8919    www.cinbus.com

*Develop/mfr. technologies for metalworking and plastics processing industrial.*

**Cincinnati Milacron SA, Andrezieux, France**

### CINCOM SYSTEMS INC.

55 Merchant Street, Cincinnati, OH, 45446

Tel: (513) 612-2300    Fax: (513) 481-8332    www.cincom.com

*Develop/distributor computer software.*

**Cincom Systems France, Paris, France**

### CIRCON ACMI

300 Stillwater Ave., PO Box 1971, Stamford, CT, 06904-1971

Tel: (203) 357-8300    Fax: (203) 328-8789    www.circoncorp.com

*Mfr./sale/services medical and surgical endoscopes, instruments and video systems.*

**Circon France, Paris, France**

Tel: 33-1-691-12150

### CISCO SYSTEMS, INC.

170 West Tasman Drive, San Jose, CA, 95134-1706

Tel: (408) 526-4000    Fax: (408) 526-4100    www.cisco.com

*Develop/mfr./market computer hardware and software networking systems.*

**Cisco Systems Europe, s.a.r.l., Parc Evolic - Batiment L1/L2, 16 Ave. du Quebec, BP 706 - Villebon, F-91961Courtaboeuf Cedex France**

Tel: 33-1-6918-6100   Fax: 33-1-6928-8326

### THE CIT GROUP

1211 Avenue of the Americas, New York, NY, 10036

Tel: (212) 536-1390    Fax: (212) 536-1912    www.citgroup.com

*Engaged in commercial finance.*

**Newcourt SNC, Le Patio de Rueil, 104 Avenue Albert 1ER, F-92500 Rueil Malmaison Paris, France**

Tel: 33-147-529500

### CITIGROUP, INC.

153 East 53rd Street, New York, NY, 10043

Tel: (212) 559-1000    Fax: (212) 559-3646    www.citigroup.com

*Provides insurance and financial services worldwide.*

**Citibank N.A., Paris, France**

Contact: Claude Jouven

### CITRIX SYSTEMS, INC.

6400 NW 6th Way, Fort Lauderdale, FL, 33309

Tel: (954) 267-3000    Fax: (954) 267-9319    www.citrix.com

*Developer of computer software.*

**Citrix Systems SARL, 84 Ave. du General Leclerc, F-92100 Boulogne-Billancourt, France**

Tel: 33-1-55-60-1070   Fax: 33-1-55-60-1071

## CLAYTON INDUSTRIES

4213 N. Temple City Blvd., El Monte, CA, 91731

Tel: (626) 443-9381     Fax: (626) 442-1701     www.claytonindustries.com

*Mfr. steam generators, dynamometers and water treatment chemicals.*

**Clayton de France, S.A.R.L.,  CE No. 1433, 2 rue Du Ventoux, Z.I. Petite Montagne, F-91019 Evry Cedex, France**

Tel: 33-1-60-77-02-50    Fax: 33-1-60-77-01-11

## CLEAR CHANNEL COMMUNICATIONS

200 East Basse Road, San Antonio, TX, 78209

Tel: (210) 822-2828     Fax: (210) 822-2299     www.clearchannel.com

*Programs and sells airtime for radio stations and owns and places outdoor advertising displays.*

**Dauphin Advertising,  21 Boulevard de la Madeleine, F-75001 Paris, France**

Tel: 33-1-40-82-8282    Contact: Claude Duval

## CLEARY GOTTLIEB STEEN & HAMILTON

One Liberty Plaza, New York, NY, 10006

Tel: (212) 225-2000     Fax: (212) 225-3999     www.cgsh.com

*International law firm.*

**Cleary, Gottlieb, Steen, & Hamilton,  41 ave. de Friedland, F-75008 Paris, France**

## CNA FINANCIAL CORPORATION

CNA Plaza, Chicago, IL, 60685

Tel: (312) 822-5000     Fax: (312) 822-6419     www.cna.com

*Commercial property/casualty insurance policies.*

**CNA Insurance Company (Europe) Limited (CIE),  Paris, France**

## COACH LEATHERWEAR COMPANY

516 West 34 Street, New York, NY, 10001

Tel: (212) 594-1850     Fax: (212) 594-1682     www.coach.com

*Mfr. and sales of high-quality leather products, including handbags and wallets.*

**Coach at Boutique ALMA,  1 rue Henri Rivière, F-78200 Mantes-La-Jolie, France**

## THE COCA-COLA COMPANY

PO Drawer 1734, Atlanta, GA, 30301

Tel: (404) 676-2121     Fax: (404) 676-6792     www.coca-cola.com

*Mfr./marketing/distributor soft drinks, syrups and concentrates, juice and juice-drink products.*

**Coca-Cola France,  Paris, France**

## COGNEX CORPORATION

1 Vision Drive, Natick, MA, 01760

Tel: (508) 650-3000     Fax: (508) 650-3333     www.cognex.com

*Mfr. machine vision systems.*

**Cognex Corporation France,  Immeuble le Patio, 104 Avenue Albert 1er, F- 92563 Rueil Malmaison Cedex, France**

Tel: 33-1-4777-1550    Fax: 33-1-4777-1555

## COHERENT INC.

5100 Patrick Henry Drive, PO Box 54980, Santa Clara, CA, 95056

Tel: (408) 764-4000     Fax: (408) 764-4800     www.cohr.com

*Mfr. lasers for science, industrial and medical.*

**Coherent SA,  Domaine Technologique de Saclay, Batiment Azur, 4 rue Rene Razel,  F-91892 Orsay Cedex France**

## COIN ACCEPTORS INC.

300 Hunter Ave., St. Louis, MO, 63124

Tel: (314) 725-0100     Fax: (314) 725-1243     www.coinco.com

*Coin mechanisms for vending machinery.*

**Coin Acceptors Sarl, 1-3 Avenue Georges Clemenceau, F-93421 Villepinte, Cedex France**

Tel: 33-01-56-48-05-05    Fax: 33-01-56-48-05-06

## THE COLEMAN COMPANY, INC.

2111 E. 37th St., North, Wichita, KS, 67219

Tel: (316) 832-2700     Fax: (316) 832-2794     www.colemanoutdoors.com

*Mfr./distributor/sales camping and outdoor recreation products.*

**Coleman/ Campingaz Europe Head Office, BP 55 - Route de Brignais, F-69563 Saint-Genis Laval Cedex, France**

## COLGATE-PALMOLIVE COMPANY

300 Park Ave., New York, NY, 10022

Tel: (212) 310-2000     Fax: (212) 310-2919     www.colgate.com

*Mfr. pharmaceuticals, cosmetics, toiletries and detergents.*

**Colgate Palmolive, 55 Blvd. de la Mission Marchand, F-92401 Courbevoie, France**

## COMDISCO INC.

6111 N. River Road, Rosemont, IL, 60018

Tel: (847) 698-3000     Fax: (847) 518-5440     www.comdisco.com

*Hi-tech asset and facility management and equipment leasing.*

**Comdisco France, 42 rue Pre Gaudry, Batiment 6, F-69007 Lyon France**

Tel: 33-4-72-763360

**Comdisco France SA, Centre d'Affaires Le Louvre, 2 Place du Palais Royal, F-75044 Paris Cedex 1, France**

## COMMERCIAL INTERTECH CORPORATION

1775 Logan Ave., PO Box 239, Youngstown, OH, 44501-0239

Tel: (330) 746-8011     Fax: (330) 746-1148

*Mfr. hydraulic components, pre-engineered buildings and stamped metal products.*

**Commercial Hydraulics Astron SARL, BP 73, 20 rue Pierre Mendes-France - TORCY, F-77202 Marne LaVallee Cedex 01, France**

## COMPAQ COMPUTER CORPORATION

20555 State Highway 249, PO Box 692000, Houston, TX, 77269-2000

Tel: (281) 370-0670     Fax: (281) 514-1740     www.compaq.com

*Develop/mfr. personal computers.*

**Compaq Computer S.A.R.L., 5 allee Gustave Eiffell, F-92442 Issy-les-Moulineaux Cedex, France**

Tel: 33-1-4133-4100    Fax: 33-1-4133-4400

## COMPUTER ASSOCIATES INTERNATIONAL INC.

One Computer Associates Plaza, Islandia, NY, 11788

Tel: (516) 342-5224     Fax: (516) 342-5329     www.cai.com

*Integrated business software for enterprise computing and information management, application development, manufacturing, financial applications and professional services.*

**Computer Associates SA, 14 Ave. Francois Arago, F-92003 Nanterre Cedex, France**

Tel: 33-1-40-97-5050

## COMPUTER SCIENCES CORPORATION

2100 East Grand Ave., El Segundo, CA, 90245

Tel: (310) 615-0311      Fax: (310) 322-9768      www.csc.com

*Information technology services, management consulting, systems integration, outsourcing.*

**CSC Computer Sciences SA - French Division,  Boulogne-Billancourt Cedex, France**

Contact: Claude Czechowski, Pres.

## COMPUWARE CORPORATION

31440 Northwestern Hwy., Farmington Hills, MI, 48334-2564

Tel: (248) 737-7300      Fax: (248) 737-7108      www.compuware.com

*Develop and market software for enterprise and e-commerce solutions.*

**Compuware Sarl,  1 Avenue de la Cristallerie, F-92310 Sevres, France**

Tel: 33-1-4114-2000    Fax: 33-1-4623-8889

## COMSHARE INC.

555 Briarwood Circle, Ste. 200, Ann Arbor, MI, 48108-3302

Tel: (734) 994-4800      Fax: (734) 994-5895      www.comshare.com

*Managerial application software.*

**Comshare SA,  73 blvd Haussmann, F-75008 Paris, France**

## COMVERSE TECHNOLOGY, INC.

234 Crossways Park Drive, Woodbury, NY, 11797

Tel: (516) 677-7200      Fax: (516) 677-7355      www.comverse.com

*Mfr. telephone communication and recording systems.*

**Comverse Infosys France,  54-56 Ave du General Leclerc, F-92100 Boulogne, Billancourt, France**

Tel: 33-155-384-750    Fax: 33-155-384-755

## CONAGRA INC.

One ConAgra Drive, Omaha, NE, 68102-5001

Tel: (402) 595-4000      Fax: (402) 595-4707      www.conagra.com

*Prepared/frozen foods, grains, flour, animal feeds, agro chemicals, poultry, meat, dairy products, including Healthy Choice, Butterball and Hunt's.*

**Gelazur SA (JV),  Les Portes De L'Arenas Gate: C 455, Promenade Des Anglais, B.P. 291, F-06205 Nice Cedex 3, France**

## CONCURRENT COMPUTER CORPORATION

4375 River Green Pkwy., Duluth, GA, 30096

Tel: (678) 258-4000      Fax: (678) 258-4300      www.ccur.com

*Mfr. computer systems and software.*

**Concurrent Computer France, S.A.,  Square Franklin - Montigny Le Bretonneux, BP 308, F-78054 St. Quentin En Yvelines Cedex, France**

Tel: 33-13-085-3700    Fax: 33-13-460-3753

## CONDE NAST PUBLICATIONS INC.

350 Madison Ave., New York, NY, 10017

Tel: (212) 880-8800      Fax: (212) 880-8289      www.condenast.com

*Publishing company.*

**Les Editions Conde Nast SA,  4 Place de Palais Bourbon, F-75007 Paris, France**

## CONEXANT SYSTEMS, INC.

4311 Jamboree Road, PO Box C, Newport Beach, CA, 92658-8902

Tel: (949) 483-4600      Fax: (949) 483-4078      www.conexant.com

*Provides semiconductor products for communications electronics.*

**Conexant Systems France S.A.S.,  Les Taissounieres B1, 1680 Route des Dolines BP 283, F-06905 Sophia Antipolis Cedex France**

Tel: 33-4-9300-3335    Fax: 33-4-9300-3303

**Conexant Systems France S.A.S., Immeuble Le Franklin, 34 Ave Franklin Roosevelt BP92, F-92159 Suresnes Cedex France**

Tel: 33-1-4144-3650    Fax: 33-1-4144-3690

## CONOCO INC.

PO Box 2197, 600 N. Dairy Ashford, Houston, TX, 77252

Tel: (281) 293-1000       Fax: (281) 293-1440       www.conoco.com

*Oil, gas, coal, chemicals and minerals.*

**Continental Oil Co. of Niger,  17 ave. Matignon, F-75008 Paris, France**

## CONSTRUCTION SPECIALTIES INC.

3 Werner Way, Lebanon, NJ, 08833

Tel: (908) 236-0800       Fax: (908) 236-0801       www.c-sgroup.com

*Mfr. architectural building products.*

**Construction Specialties Steel,  1 rue de la Cressonniere, F-27950 St. Marcel, France**

Tel: 33-2-32648400    Contact: Philippe Luguet, Mng. Dir.

## CONTINENTAL AIRLINES INC.

2929 Allen Parkway, Ste. 2010, Houston, TX, 77019

Tel: (281) 834-5000       Fax: (281) 520-6329       www.continental.com

*International airline carrier.*

**Continental Airlines Inc.,  Paris, France**

## CONVERGYS CORPORATION

201 E. 4th St., Cincinnati, OH, 45202

Tel: (513) 723-7000       Fax: (513) 421-8624       www.convergys.com

*Engaged in data bill processing, telemarketing and customer services representation for major corporations.*

**Convergys Corporation,  153 Avenue d'Italie, Paris F-75013, France**

## COOPER CAMERON CORPORATION

515 Post Oak Blvd., Ste.1200, Houston, TX, 77027

Tel: (713) 513-3300       Fax: (713) 513-3355       www.coopercameron.com

*Mfr. oil and gas industry equipment.*

**Cooper Cameron France,  19 bis, Blvd. d'Argenson, F-92200 Neuilly-Sur-Seine, Paris France**

**Cooper Cameron France,  Plaine Saint-Pierre, CS 620, F-34535 Beziers Cedex, France**

## COOPER INDUSTRIES INC.

6600 Travis Street, Ste. 5800, Houston, TX, 77002

Tel: (713) 209-8400       Fax: (713) 209-8995       www.cooperindustries.com

*Mfr./distributor electrical products, tools, hardware and automotive products, fuses and accessories for electronic applications and circuit boards.*

**Cooper Hand Tools,  Bonneuil, France**

## COOPER STANDARD AUTOMOTIVE

2401 South Gulley Road, Dearborn, MI, 48124

Tel: (313) 561-1100       Fax: (313) 561-6526       www.cooperstandard.com

*Mfr. molded and extruded rubber and plastic products for automotive and appliance industry, retread tire industry.*

**Cooper Standard Automotive,  5 rue Auguste Desgenetais, F-76210 Bolbec, France**

Tel: 33-2-3539-5999    Fax: 33-2-274-3538-4011

**Cooper Standard Automotive,  9 rue Lois Rameau PBS, F-95871 Bezins, France**

Tel: 33-1-34-23-3737    Fax: 33-1-39-47-1235

**Cooper Standard Automotive,  Route des Eaux BP63, F-35503 Vitre Cedex, France**

Tel: 33-2-9975-8740    Fax: 33-2-9975-8749

**Cooper Standard Automotive,  1 rue Fond Valee, F-76170 Lillebonne, France**

Tel: 33-2-3284-1600    Fax: 33-2-3538-1147

## CORDANT TECHNOLOGIES INC.

15 W. South Temple, Ste. 1600, Salt Lake City, UT, 84101-1532

Tel: (801) 933-4000     Fax: (801) 933-4014     www.cordanttech.com

*Mfr. solid rocket boosters for space shuttles and fasteners, rivets, and lock bolts for the transportation and construction industries.*

**Huck S.A., Clos D'Asseville BP4, F-95450 US, France**

Tel: 33-1-3027-9510   Contact: Rene Belin, VP

## CORDIS CORPORATION

PO Box 25700, Miami, FL, 33102-5700

Tel: (305) 824-2000     Fax: (305) 824-2747     www.cordis.com

*Mfr. medical devices and systems.*

**Cordis S.A., rue Camille Desmoulins 1, TSA 71001, F-92787 Issy-les-Moulineaux, France**

## CORNING INC.

One Riverfront Plaza, Corning, NY, 14831-0001

Tel: (607) 974-9000     Fax: (607) 974-8091     www.corning.com

*Mfr. glass and specialty materials, consumer products; communications, laboratory services.*

**Corning S.A., B.P. No. 3, F-77167 Bagneaux-Sur-Loing, France**

Tel: 33-1-6445-4000   Fax: 33-1-6445-4379

**Corning S.A., B.P. 61, 44 Avenue de Valvins, F-77211 Avon Cedex France**

Tel: 33-1-6469-7521   Fax: 33-1-6422-8437

## CORRPRO COMPANIES, INC.

1090 Enterprise Drive, Medina, OH, 44256

Tel: (330) 725-6681     Fax: (330) 723-0244     www.corrpro.com

*Full-services corrosion engineering, cathodic protection.*

**Corrpro Lyon, 16 Chemin des Pivolles, F-69150 Decines, France**

Tel: 33-4-72-149494   Fax: 33-4-78-265174

## COTY INC.

1325 Avenue of the Americas, New York, NY, 10019

Tel: (212) 479-4300     Fax: (212) 479-4399     www.coty.com

*Fragrance, cosmetics and beauty treatments.*

**Coty Div. de Pfizer France, 86 rue de Paris, F-91101 Orsay Cedex 7, France**

## COUDERT BROTHERS

1114 Ave. of the Americas, New York, NY, 10036-7794

Tel: (212) 626-4400     Fax: (212) 626-4120     www.coudert.com

*International law firm.*

**Coudert Freres, 52 Ave. des Champs-Elysees, F-75008 Paris, France**

Tel: 33-1-53-83-6000   Fax: 33-1-53-83-6060   Contact: Jacques Buhart, Ptnr.

## COULTER PHARMACEUTICAL, INC.

600 Gateway Blvd., South San Francisco, CA, 94080

Tel: (650) 553-2000     Fax: (650) 553-2028     www.coulterpharm.com

*Mfr. blood analysis systems, flow cytometers, chemicals systems, scientific systems and reagents.*

**Coultronics France SA, 29 ave Georges Pompidou, F-95580 Margency, France**

## SG COWEN SECURITIES

1221 Avenue of the America, New York, NY, 10020

Tel: (212) 495-6000     Fax: (212) 380-8212     www.cowen.com

*Securities research, trading, broker/dealer services; investment banking and asset management.*

**Cowen Securities, 368-370 rue St. Honores 4etage, F-75001 Paris, France**

Tel: 33-1-42-44-1740   Fax: 33-1-42-44-1745   Contact: Patrick Halbers, Mgr.

## CROMPTON CORPORATION

Benson Road, Middlebury, CT, 06749

Tel: (203) 573-2000     Fax:                    www.crompton-knowles.com

*Mfr. dyes, colors, flavors, fragrances, specialty chemicals and industrial products.*

**Crompton Chemical SA,  10 rue Cambacere, F-75008 Paris, France**

**Crompton SA,  Les Algorithmas-Thales, Saint Aubin, F-91197 Gif sur Yvette Cedex, France**

## A.T. CROSS COMPANY

One Albion Road, Lincoln, RI, 02865

Tel: (401) 333-1200     Fax: (401) 334-2861     www.cross.com

*Mfr. writing instruments, leads, erasers and ink refills.*

**A.T. Cross France,  12 bis rue Keppler, F-75016 Paris, France**

Tel: 33-1-5367-3130

## CROWN CORK & SEAL COMPANY,  INC.

One Crown Way, Philadelphia, PA, 19154-4599

Tel: (215) 698-5100     Fax: (215) 698-5201     www.crowncork.com

*Mfr. metal and plastic packaging, including steel and aluminum cans for food, beverage and household products.*

**Crown Cork,  Le Colisee 1, rue Fructidor, F-75830 Paris Cedex 17 France**

Tel: 33-1-49-18-4000

**Emballages Couronne SA, Crown Cork Co. France,  BP 1, F-91170 Viry Chatillon, France**

## CROWN EQUIPMENT CORPORATION

40 South Washington Street, New Bremen, OH, 45869

Tel: (419) 629-2311     Fax: (419) 629-2900     www.crownlift.com

*Mfr./sales/services forklift trucks, stackers.*

**Crown Manutention SNC,  9 rue Ampere, BP 107, F-95500 Gonesse, France**

## CULLIGAN WATER TECHNOLOGIES

One Culligan Parkway, Northbrook, IL, 60062

Tel: (847) 205-6000     Fax: (847) 205-6030     www.culligan-man.com

*Water treatment products and services.*

**Culligan France SA,  4 ave. du President Kennedy, F-78340 Les Clayes sous Bois Yvelines, France**

Tel: 33-1-30-55-8055   Fax: 33-1-30-55-5623

## CUMMINS ENGINE COMPANY, INC.

500 Jackson Street, PO Box 3005, Columbus, IN, 47202-3005

Tel: (812) 377-5000     Fax: (812) 377-4937     www.cummins.com

*Mfr. diesel engines.*

**Cummins Diesel SA,  91 quai Emile Cormerais, ZI de la Loire, F-44800 Saint Herblain France**

**Cummins Diesel Sales & Service /S,  Hovedvejen 233B, F-08300 Rethel, France**

**Cummins Diesel Sales Corp.,  39 rue Ampere, Z.I., F-69680 Chassieu, France**

## CURTIS, MALLET-PREVOST, COLT & MOSLE LLP

101 Park Ave., 35th Floor, New York, NY, 10178

Tel: (212) 696-6000     Fax: (212) 697-1559     www.cm-p.com

*International law firm.*

**Curtis, Mallet-Prevost, Colt & Mosle LLP,  15 rue d'Astorg, F-75008 Paris, France**

Tel: 33-1-42-66-39-10

## CURTISS-WRIGHT CORPORATION

1200 Wall Street West, Lyndhurst, NJ, 07071-0635

Tel: (201) 896-8400          Fax: (201) 438-5680          www.curtisswright.com

*Mfr. precision components and systems, engineered services to aerospace, flow control and marine industry.*

**Metal Improvement Co. Inc., Zone Industrielle de St. Etienne, rue de Cazenave, F-64100 Bayonne, France**

**Metal Improvement Co. Inc., Zone Industrielle d'Amilly, F-45200 Montargis, France**

## CYPRESS SEMICONDUCTOR CORPORATION

3901 N. First Street, San Jose, CA, 95134-1599

Tel: (408) 943-2600          Fax: (408) 943-2796          www.cypress.com

*Mfr. integrated circuits.*

**Cypress Semiconductor, Za De Courtaboeuf, 6 Avenue Des Andes, Miniparc Bat No 8, Les Ulis Cedex F-91952, France**

Tel: 33-1-692-988-90   Fax: 33-1-690-755-71

## CYTEC INDUSTRIES, INC.

5 Garret Mountain Plaza, West Paterson, NJ, 07424

Tel: (973) 357-3100          Fax: (973) 357-3054          www.cytec.com

*Mfr. specialty chemicals and materials,*

**Cytec Industries S.A.R.L., 1 Place des Etats-Unis, Immeuble Liege Silic 256,F- 94568 Rungis-Cedex, France**

Tel: 33-1-41-80-17-00

## DALLAS SEMICONDUCTOR CORPORATION

4401 South Beltway Parkway, Dallas, TX, 75244-3292

Tel: (972) 371-4000          Fax: (972) 371-4956          www.dalsemi.com

*Design/mfr. computer chips and chip-based subsystems.*

**Dallas Semiconductor, 3 La Garene Dulet, F-33610 Canejan, France**

Tel: 33-5-56-89-6820   Fax: 33-5-56-89-6588   Contact: Yves Le Bras, Reg. Sales Mgr.

**Dallas Semiconductor, 192 ave de General de Gaulle, F-92140 Clamart, France**

Tel: 33-1-46-30-3026   Fax: 33-1-46-30-3061   Contact: Frederic Martin, Dist.Sales.Mgr.

## DAMES & MOORE GROUP

911 Wilshire Boulevard, Ste. 700, Los Angeles, CA, 90017

Tel: (213) 996-2200          Fax: (213) 996-2290          www.dames.com

*Engineering, environmental and construction management services.*

**Dames & Moore, 2 rue de Marly-le-Roi, F-78150 Le Chesnay, France**

## DANA CORPORATION

4500 Dorr Street, Toledo, OH, 43615

Tel: (419) 535-4500          Fax: (419) 535-4643          www.dana.com

*Mfr./sales of automotive, heavy truck, off-highway, fluid and mechanical power components and engine parts, filters and gaskets.*

**Dana Corporation France, 2 Chemin Notre Dame de la Ronde, F-28100 Dreux France**

**Dana Corporation France, 33/35 Ave. Charles Edouard Jeannerel, Le Technoparc F-78306 Poissy, France**

**Floquet Monopole, 53 blvd Robespierre BP31, F-78301 Poissy Cedex, France**

**Perfect Circle, Div. Dana, Le Technoparc, 1 rue Gustave Eiffel, F-78306 Poissy Cedex France**

**Spicer France, 11 rue George Mangin, F-69400 Villefrance sur Saone, France**

**Warner & Turco, Route de Spay BP 313, F-72007 Le Mans Cedex, France**

## D'ARCY MASIUS BENTON & BOWLES INC. (DMB&B)

1675 Broadway, New York, NY, 10019

Tel: (212) 468-3622     Fax: (212) 468-2987     www.dmbb.com

*Full service international advertising and communications group.*

**DMB&B Europe,  10 blvd du Parc, F-92521 Neuilly Cedex, France**

## DATA GENERAL CORPORATION

4400 Computer Drive, Westboro, MA, 01580

Tel: (508) 898-5000     Fax: (508) 366-1319     www.dg.com

*Design, mfr. general purpose computer systems and peripheral products and services.*

**Data General France,  Batiment Energy IV BP-29, 34 Avenue de L'Europe, F-78147 Velizy Villacoublay, Cedex France**

Tel: 33-1-3926-8054   Fax: 33-1-3925-8282

## DATA RESEARCH ASSOCIATES, INC. (DRA)

1276 North Warson Road, St. Louis, MO, 63132

Tel: (314) 432-1100     Fax: (314) 993-8927     www.dra.com

*Systems integrator for libraries and information providers.*

**MultiLIS Europe S.A.,  231 rue de la Fontaine, F-94134 Fontenay-sous-Bois Cedex, France**

Tel: 33-1-48-7-1000   Fax: 33-1-48-76-5888

## DATASCOPE CORPORATION

14 Phillips Pkwy., Montvale, NJ, 07645

Tel: (201) 391-8100     Fax: (201) 307-5400     www.datascope.com

*Mfr. medical devices.*

**Datascope France SARL,  Z.I Athelia 1, F-13705 La Ciotat, Cedex France**

**InterVascular SARL,  Paris, France**

## DATAWARE TECHNOLOGIES INC.

1 Canal Park, Cambridge, MA, 02141

Tel: (617) 621-0820     Fax: (617) 577-2413     www.dataware.com

*Provides e-business solutions.*

**Dataware Technologies France SARL,  168 Ave. Jean-Jaures, F-92120 Montrouge, France**

## DAVIS POLK & WARDWELL

450 Lexington Ave., New York, NY, 10017

Tel: (212) 450-4000     Fax: (212) 450-4800     www.dpw.com

*International law firm.*

**Davis Polk & Wardwell,  15, Matignon, F-75088 Paris, France**

Tel: 33-1-56-59-3600   Fax: 33-1-56-59-3690

## DAYCO PRODUCTS INC.

PO Box 1004, Dayton, OH, 45401-1004

Tel: (937) 226-7000     Fax: (937) 226-4689     www.dayco.com

*Mfr. diversified auto, industrial and household products.*

**Dayco,  Paris, France**

## DAYTON PROGRESS CORPORATION

500 Progress Road, Dayton, OH, 45449

Tel: (937) 859-5111     Fax: (937) 859-5353     www.daytonprogress.com

*Punches, dies and guide bushings.*

**MJ Industries,  93 Avenue de l'Epinette, BP 128  Zone Industrielle, F-77107 Meaux Cedex France**

## DDB NEEDHAM WORLDWIDE INC.

437 Madison Ave., New York, NY, 10022

Tel: (212) 415-2000  Fax: (212) 415-3417  www.ddbn.com

*Advertising agency.*

**DDB Needham Worldwide SA, 12/14 rue Mederic, F-75849 Paris Cedex 17, France**

## DEBEVOISE & PLIMPTON

919 Third Avenue, New York, NY, 10022

Tel: (212) 909-6000  Fax: (212) 909-6836  www.debevoise.com

*International law firm.*

**Debevoise & Plimpton, 21 Ave. George V, F-75008 Paris, France**

Tel: 33-1-40-73-1212  Fax: 33-1-47-20-5082  Contact: James A. Kiernan, III, Mng. Ptnr.  Emp: 36

## DECHERT PRICE & RHOADS

4000 Bell Atlantic Tower, 1717 Arch Street, Philadelphia, PA, 19103-2793

Tel: (215) 994-4000  Fax: (215) 994-2222  www.dechert.com

*International law firm.*

**Dechert Price & Rhoads, 55 Ave. Kleber, F-75116 Paris, France**

Tel: 33-1-53-65-0500  Fax: 33-1-53-65-0505

## DEERE & COMPANY

One John Deere Road, Moline, IL, 61265

Tel: (309) 765-8000  Fax: (309) 765-5772  www.deere.com

*Mfr./sale agricultural, construction, utility, forestry and lawn, grounds care equipment.*

**John Deere France, rue du Paradis, Ormes BP 219, F-45144 St. Jean de la Ruelle, Cedex France**

Tel: 33-238-72-3000  Fax: 33-238-74-8665

## DELL COMPUTER CORPORATION

One Dell Way, Round Rock, TX, 78682-2222

Tel: (512) 338-4400  Fax: (512) 728-3653  www.dell.com

*Direct marketer and supplier of computer systems.*

**Dell Computer, 1068 rue de la Vielle Poste BP 9646, F-34054 Montepellier Cedex 1, France**

Tel: 33-4-67-06-6000  Fax: 33-4-67-06-6001  Contact: Marie Eve Schauber, Mng. Dir.

**Dell France/Putenux La Defense, 12-12 Bis rue Jean Jaures, Immeuble Plein Jour, F-92800 Puteaux la Defense, France**

Tel: 33-1-47-62-6900  Fax: 33-1-47-62-6871  Contact: Marie Eve Schauber, Mng. Dir.

## DELOITTE TOUCHE TOHMATSU INTERNATIONAL

1633 Broadway, New York, NY, 10019

Tel: (212) 492-4000  Fax: (212) 392-4154  www.deloitte.com

*Accounting, audit, tax and management consulting services.*

**Deloitte & Touche, "Paek Ave.," 81 Blvd. se Stalingrad, F-69100 Villeurbanne, France**

**Deloitte Touche Tohmatsu, 185 ave Charles de Gaulle, F-92200 Neuilly sur Seine Cedex, France**

## DELTA AIR LINES INC.

PO Box 20706, Atlanta, GA, 30320-6001

Tel: (404) 715-2600  Fax: (404) 715-5494  www.delta-air.com

*Major worldwide airline; international air transport services.*

**Delta Air Lines Inc., Nice, France**

**Delta Air Lines Inc., Paris-De Gaulle, France**

## DENTSPLY INTERNATIONAL

570 West College Ave., PO Box 872, York, PA, 17405-0872

Tel: (717) 845-7511      Fax: (717) 843-6357      www.dentsply.com

*Mfr. and distribution of dental supplies and equipment.*

**De Trey Dentsply SA,  72 rue de General-Leclerc, F-92270 Bois-Colombes, France**

**Dentsply France,  17 rue Michael Farady, F-78180 Montigny-le-Bretonneux, France**

Tel: 33-1-30-14-7777

**Dentsply Laboratoire SPAD,  14D rue Pierre de Coubertin, Paro de Mirande BP 242, F-21007 Dijon Cedex, France**

Tel: 33-3-80-68-4848

**Dentsply SIMFRA,  21 rue de Maurbeuge, F-75009 Paris, France**

Tel: 33-1-48-78-0898

## THE DEUTSCH COMPANY

2444 Wilshire Blvd, Santa Monica, CA, 90403

Tel: (310) 453-0055      Fax: (310) 453-6467

*Electronic components.*

**Compagne Deutsch,  10 rue Lionelterray, F-92500 Rueil Malmaison, France**

## THE DEXTER CORPORATION

1 Elm Street, Windsor Locks, CT, 06096

Tel: (860) 627-9051      Fax: (860) 627-7078      www.dexelec.com

*Mfr. polymer products, magnetic materials, biotechnology.*

**Dexter SA,  14 rue Chanay BP 51, F-71700 Tournus, France**

**The Dexter GmbH,  40 rue des Envierges, F-75020 Paris, France**

## DHL WORLDWIDE EXPRESS

50 California Avenue, San Francisco, CA, 94111

Tel: (415) 677-6100      Fax: (415) 824-9700      www.dhl.com

*Worldwide air express carrier.*

**DHL Worldwide Express,  ZI. Paris Nord II, 241 rue de la Belle Etoile BP 50252, F-95957 Roissy, France**

Tel: 33-1-48-17-6600

## DIAGNOSTIC PRODUCTS CORPORATION

5700 West 96th Street, Los Angeles, CA, 90045

Tel: (310) 645-8200      Fax: (310) 645-9999      www.dpcweb.com

*Mfr. diagnostic products.*

**Dade Behring S.A.,  19-29 rue du Capitaine Guynemer, F-92081 Paris La Defense, France**

Tel: 33-1-4291-2166   Fax: 33-1-4291-2367

**DPC France, SAS,  90 Boulevard National, F-92257 La Garenne-Colombes Cedex, France**

Tel: 33-1-55-66-86-00   Fax: 33-1-55-66-86-66

## DIGITAL ORIGIN, INC.

460 East Middlefield Road, Mountainview, CA, 94043

Tel: (650) 404-6300      Fax: (650) 404-6200      www.digitalorigin.com

*Mfr. Digital Video (DV) software products.*

**Media 100 SA,  BP 422 - Bureau 300, World Trade Ctr. 2 CNIT, 2 Place de la Defense, F-92053 Paris, France**

## DIONEX CORPORATION

1228 Titan Way, PO Box 3603, Sunnyvale, CA, 94086-3603

Tel: (408) 737-0700     Fax: (408) 730-9403     www.dionex.com

*Develop/mfr./market chromatography systems and related products.*

**Dionex - Bureau France Sud, 1210 rue Ampere, Z.I. Les Milles, F-13851 Aix en Provence Cedex 03, France**

**Dionex SA, 98 rue Albert Calmette, BPN 47, F-78354 Jouy en Josas Cedex, France**

## WALT DISNEY COMPANY

500 South Buena Vista Street, Burbank, CA, 91521

Tel: (818) 560-1000     Fax: (818) 560-1930     www.disney.com

*Film/TV production, theme parks, resorts, publishing, recording and retail stores.*

**Walt Disney Productions (France) SA, 52 ave. des Champs-Elysees, F-75008 Paris, France**

## DME COMPANY

29111 Stephenson Highway, Madison Heights, MI, 48071

Tel: (248) 398-6000     Fax: (248) 544-5705     www.dmeco.com

*Basic tooling for plastic molding and die casting.*

**DME France SARL, Blvd. Foch 10, F-93800 Epinay sur Seine, France**

## DOCUMENTUM, INC.

6801 Koll Center Pkwy., Pleasanton, CA, 94566

Tel: (925) 600-6800     Fax: (925) 600-6850     www.documentum.com

*Mfr. content management software.*

**Documentum International Inc., 696 rue Yves Kermen, F-92658 Boulogne Billancourt, Cedex France**

## DONALDSON COMPANY, INC.

1400 West 94th Street, Minneapolis, MN, 55431

Tel: (612) 887-3131     Fax: (612) 887-3155     www.donaldson.com

*Mfr. filtration systems and replacement parts.*

**Donaldson France, S.A., 4 Bis rue Maryse Bastie, F-69500 Bron, France**

**Tecnov Donaldson, S.A., Z-1 La Campagne, F-50420 Domjean, France**

## DONALDSON, LUFKIN & JENRETTE, INC.

277 Park Ave., New York, NY, 10172

Tel: (212) 892-3000     Fax: (212) 892-7272     www.dlj.com

*Investment banking, capital markets and financial services.*

**Donaldson, Lufkin & Jenrette Inc., 21-25 rue Balzac, F-75406 Paris Cedex 08, France**

Tel: 33-1-53-75-8500

## R.R. DONNELLEY & SONS COMPANY

77 West Wacker Drive, Chicago, IL, 60601-1696

Tel: (312) 326-8000     Fax: (312) 326-8543     www.rrdonnelley.com

*Commercial printing, allied communication services.*

**R. R. Donnelley Financial, 23 rue Cambon - 4th Fl., F-75001 Paris, France**

Tel: 33-1-5345-1900

**R. R. Donnelley France S.A., 86 rue Regnault, F-75013 Paris, France**

Tel: 33-1-42-16-6380

## DONNELLY CORPORATION

49 W. 3rd St., Holland, MI, 49423-2813

Tel: (616) 786-7000     Fax: (616) 786-6034     www.donnelly.com

*Mfr. fabricated, molded and coated glass products for the automotive and electronics industries.*

**Donnelly Hohe Paris Sarl, 26 Avenue des Champs Pierreux, F-92022 Nanterre Cedex, France**

Tel: 33-3-25-84-3434   Fax: 33-3-25-84-3843   Contact: Mark Guiheneuf, Mgr.

## DOUBLECLICK, INC.

450 West 33rd Street, New York, NY, 10001

Tel: (212) 683-0001 Fax: (212) 889-0062 www.doubleclick.net

*Engaged in online advertising.*

**Doubleclick, Ltd., 16-18 rue Rivay 2/F, F-92300 Levallois-Perret, France**

Tel: 33-1-49-6683-83

## THE DOW CHEMICAL COMPANY

2030 Dow Center, Midland, MI, 48674

Tel: (517) 636-1000 Fax: (517) 636-3228 www.dow.com

*Mfr. chemicals, plastics, pharmaceuticals, agricultural products, consumer products.*

**Dow France S.A., 8 Route de Herrlisheim, F-67410 Drusenheim, France**

## DRAFT WORLDWIDE

633 North St. Clair Street, Chicago, IL, 60611-3211

Tel: (312) 944-3500 Fax: (312) 944-3566 www.draftworldwide.com

*Full service international advertising agency, engaged in brand building, direct and promotional marketing.*

**DDW Santé, 3 blvd Paul Emile Victor, Ill de la Jalle, F-92528 Neuilly-sur-Seine Cedex, France**

Tel: 33-1-47-47-7915 Fax: 33-1-47-47-7865 Contact: Loke Robert, Mng. Dir.

**DraftWorldwide SA, 76 rue Thiers, F-92100 Boulogne, France**

Tel: 33-1-47-61-8410 Fax: 33-1-47-61-8411 Contact: Jean-Paul Dupey, Pres. Europe

## DRAKE BEAM MORIN INC.

101 Huntington Ave., Boston, MA, 02199

Tel: (617) 375-9500 Fax: (617) 267-2011 www.dbm.com

*Human resource management consulting and training.*

**DBM France, 44 rue Jeanne d'Arc, F-76000 Rouen, France**

Tel: 33-23-571-8005 Fax: 33-23-571-7927

**DBM France, 17 a 21 rue de Faubourg St. Honore, F-75008 Paris, France**

Tel: 33-1-44-515280 Fax: 33-1-44-515282

## DRESSER INSTRUMENT DIVISION

250 East Main Street, Stratford, CT, 06614-5145

Tel: (203) 378-8281 Fax: (203) 385-0357 www.dresserinstruments.com

*Mfr. pressure gauges and temperature instruments.*

**Dresser Europe GmbH, 74 rue d'Arceuil, F-94578, Silic 265 France**

Tel: 33-1-49-79-22-59 Fax: 33-1-46-86-25-24

**Dresser Products Industriels, 5 rue d'Antony, F-94150 Val-de-Marne, France**

## DRESSER-RAND COMPANY

10077 Grogans Mill Road, Ste. 500, The Woodlands, TX, 77380

Tel: (281) 363-7650 Fax: (281) 363-7654 www.dresser-rand.com

*Provides energy conversion solutions.*

**Dresser-Rand S.A., 32 Boulevard Winston Churchill, Cedex 7013 LeHavre F-76080, France**

Tel: 33-235-255225

## E.I. DU PONT DE NEMOURS & COMPANY

1007 Market Street, Wilmington, DE, 19898

Tel: (302) 774-1000 Fax: (302) 774-7321 www.dupont.com

*Mfr./sale diversified chemicals, plastics, specialty products and fibers.*

**Du Pont de Nemours (France) SA, Paris, France**

## THE DUN & BRADSTREET CORPORATION

1 Diamond Hill Road, Murray Hill, NJ, 07974

Tel: (908) 665-5000          Fax: (908) 665-5524          www.dnbcorp.com

*Provides corporate credit, marketing and accounts-receivable management services and publishes credit ratings and financial information.*

**Dun & Bradstreet France S.A., 345 Ave. Georges Clémenceau, Immeuble Défense Bergères, F-92882 Nanterre CTC Cedex 9, France**

Tel: 33-1-40-77-0707

**S&W, Boie Postale 15 05 Lyon, 4 Quai Jean-Moulin, F-6924 Lyon Cedex 01, France**

Tel: 33-1-41-35-1700

## EAGLE GLOBAL LOGISTICS (EGL)

15350 Vickery Drive, Houston, TX, 77032

Tel: (281) 618-3100          Fax: (281) 618-3100          www.eaglegl.com

*Ocean/air freight forwarding, customs brokerage, packing and wholesale, logistics management and insurance.*

**Harper Logistics International, Gateway Department Zone De Fret, Bat 288 - 1 Etag. Bur 1210, Orly Fret 690, F-94394 Orly France**

Tel: 33-1-49-75-3266   Fax: 33-1-49-75-3286

**Harper Logistics International, Zone De Fret, F-31703 Blagnac Cedex, France**

Tel: 33-61-719-696   Fax: 33-61-304-511

**Harper Logistics International, Zone De Fret 4 - Roissytech, 4 rue Du Cercle, B.P. 10169, F-95702 Roissy CDG Cedex France**

Tel: 33-1-48-62-4322   Fax: 33-1-48-62-0704

**Harper Logistics International, Zone De Fret, Satolas Aeroport, F-69125 Lyon, France**

Tel: 33-72-227-990   Fax: 33-71-227-982

**Harper Logistics International, Aulnat Airport, Clermont Ferrand, F-63510 Aulnat, France**

Tel: 33-736-27160   Fax: 33-736-27159

## EASTMAN & BEAUDINE INC.

One Ravinia Drive, Ste. 1110, Atlanta, GA, 30346-2103

Tel: (770) 039-0080          Fax: (770) 390-0875          www.beaudine.com

*Investments.*

**Eastman & Beaudine Inc., 3 rue de Penthievre, F-75008 Paris, France**

## EASTMAN CHEMICAL

100 North Eastman Road, Kingsport, TN, 37660

Tel: (423) 229-2000          Fax: (423) 229-1351          www.eastman.com

*Mfr. plastics, chemicals, fibers.*

**Eastman Chemical B.V., 65 rue de Bercy, F-75012 Paris, France**

Tel: 33-1-44-67-8899   Fax: 33-1-44-67-8888   Contact: Yves Hamon

## EASTMAN KODAK COMPANY

343 State Street, Rochester, NY, 14650

Tel: (716) 724-4000          Fax: (716) 724-1089          www.kodak.com

*Develop/mfr. photo and chemicals products, information management/video/copier systems, fibers/plastics for various industry.*

**Eastman Kodak Chemical Intl. SA, 1 Allee du 1er Mai, F-77423 Mame-laVallee, Cedex France**

**Kodak Industrie, Usine de fabrication, Route de Demigny, F-71102 Chalon-sur-Saone, France**

**Kodak Pathe, 8-26 rue Villiot, F-75594 Paris Cedex 12, France**

**Laboratoires et Services Kodak, Europarc, 1 rue Le Corbusier - F-94400 Creteil, France**

### EATON CORPORATION

Eaton Center, 1111 Superior Ave., Cleveland, OH, 44114-2584

Tel: (216) 523-5000     Fax: (216) 479-7068     www.eaton.com

*Advanced technical products for transportation and industrial markets.*

**Eaton SA,  Zone Industrial de Brais, Saint Nazaire, Loire Atlantique, France**

### ECI TELECOM LTD.

12950 Worldgate Dr., Herndon, VA, 20170

Tel: (703) 456-3400     Fax: (703) 456-3410     www.ecitele.com

*Designs, develops, manufactures, markets and supports end-to-end digital telecommunications solutions.*

**ECI Telecom,  Espace Velizy "Le Nungesser", 13 Avenue Morane Saulnier, F-78140 Velizy France**

Tel: 33-1-34-63-0480

### ECOLAB INC.

370 N. Wabasha Street, St. Paul, MN, 55102

Tel: (651) 293-2233     Fax: (651) 293-2379     www.ecolab.com

*Develop/mfr. premium cleaning, sanitizing and maintenance products and services for the hospitality, institutional, and residential markets.*

**Ecolab Ltd.,  Paris, France**

Tel: 33-1-40-93-93-94

### EDELMAN PUBLIC RELATIONS WORLDWIDE

200 East Randolph Drive, 62nd Fl., Chicago, IL, 60601

Tel: (312) 240-3000     Fax: (312) 240-0596     www.edelman.com

*International independent public relations firm.*

**Edelman PR Worldwide,  54 rue Monceau, F-75008 Paris, France**

Tel: 33-1-56-69-7500   Fax: 33-1-56-69-7575   Contact: Remy Ossard, Pres. Europe

### J.D. EDWARDS & COMPANY

One Technology Way, Denver, CO, 80237

Tel: (303) 334-4000     Fax: (303) 334-4970     www.jdedwards.com

*Computer software products.*

**J. D. Edwards France,  Focal, le 6 eme Ave., 75 cours Albert Thomas, F-69447 Lyon Cedex, France**

Tel: 33-4-72-13-16-16   Fax: 33-4-72-34-55-38

**J. D. Edwards France,  Sydec, 6 rue Thomas Mann, F-67200 Strasbourg, France**

Tel: 33-88-27-94-94   Fax: 33-88-27-94-85

**J. D. Edwards France,  Unilog, 9 Blvd. Gouvion St. Cyr, F-45849 Paris Cedex 17, France**

Tel: 33-1-40-68-4000   Fax: 33-1-40-68-4020

**J. D. Edwards France,  Progicentre, 8 Place Jean Monnet BP 4543, F-45045 Orleans, France**

Tel: 33-2-38-72-63-64   Fax: 33-2-38-72-00-88

**J. D. Edwards France,  104 bis rue de Reuilly, F-75012 Paris, France**

Tel: 33-1-44-74-2000   Fax: 33-1-4474-2020

**J. D. Edwards France, Eurexpert Conseil,  Tour Manhattan, La Defense 2, 5-6 place de l'iris, F-92095 Paris France**

Tel: 33-1-46-93-75-00   Fax: 33-1-47-76-20-33

### EG&G INC.

900 Clopper Road, Ste. 200, Gaithersburg, MD, 20878

Tel: (301) 840-3000     Fax: (301) 590-0502     www.egginc.com

*Diversified R/D, mfr. and services.*

**EG&G Berthold,  62 ave. Foch, F-92250 la Garenne Colombes, France**

**EG&G Instruments Div.,  1 rue du Gevaudan, CE 1734, ZI Petite Montagne Sud, F-91047 Evry Cedex, France**

**EG&G Sealol Callisto,  18 Ter rue des Osiers, BP 54, Coignieres, F-78311 Maurepas Cedex, France**

**ELANCO ANIMAL HEALTH**

500 East 96th Street, Ste. 125, Indianapolis, IN, 46240

Tel: (317) 276-3000    Fax: (317) 276-6116    www.elanco.com

*Antibiotics and fine chemicals.*

**Elanco Animal Health, 203 Bureaux de la Colline, 92-213 Saint-Cloud, France**

**ELECTRO SCIENTIFIC INDUSTRIES, INC.**

13900 NW Science Park Drive, Portland, OR, 97229

Tel: (503) 641-4141    Fax: (503) 643-4873    www.esi.com

*Mfg. production and testing equipment used in manufacture of electronic components in pagers and cellular communication devices.*

**Electro Scientific Industries SARL, Cite Descartes, 1 allee Lorentz, F-77420 Champs-sur-Marne, France**

Tel: 33-1-64-61-0011    Fax: 33-1-64-61-0016    Contact: Christian Saulnier

**ELECTROGLAS INC.**

6042 Silver Creek Valley Road, San Jose, CA, 95138

Tel: (408) 528-3000    Fax: (408) 528-3542    www.electroglas.com

*Mfr. semi-conductor test equipment, automatic wafer probers.*

**Electroglas Intl. Inc., 13 Chemin du Levant, F-01210 Ferney Voltaire, France**

**ELECTRONIC DATA SYSTEMS CORPORATION (EDS)**

5400 Legacy Dr., Plano, TX, 75024

Tel: (972) 605-6000    Fax: (972) 605-2643    www.eds.com

*Provides professional services; management consulting, e.solutions, business process management and information solutions.*

**EDS France, 4 Avenue Pablo Picasso, F-92024 Nanterre, France**

Tel: 33-1-4729-6402

**ELECTRONICS FOR IMAGING, INC.**

303 Velocity Way, Foster City, CA, 94404

Tel: (650) 357-3500    Fax: (650) 357-3907    www.efi.com

*Design/mfr. computer software and hardware for color desktop publishing.*

**EFI France, Immeuble Atria, 5 Place des Marseilles, F-94227 Charenton-le-Pont Cedex, France**

Tel: 33-1-4179 0000

**ELECTRO-SCIENCE LABORATORIES, INC.**

416 East Church Road, King of Prussia, PA, 19406

Tel: (610) 272-8000    Fax: (610) 272-6759    www.electroscience.com

*Mfr. advanced thick film materials for hybrid microcircuits and other electronic packaging and component applications.*

**ESL (SNC), 7 rue de l'Avenir, F-92360 Meudon-la-Foret, France**

**EMC CORPORATION**

35 Parkwood Drive, Hopkinton, MA, 01748-9103

Tel: (508) 435-1000    Fax: (508) 435-8884    www.emc.com

*Designs/supplies intelligent enterprise storage and retrieval technology for open systems, mainframes and midrange environments.*

**EMC Aquitaine Midi + Pyrenes S.A., Aeropole 1, 5 Ave. Albert Durand, F-31700 Blaqnac Toulouse, France**

Tel: 33-5-61-16-4-01

**EMC Computer Systems France S.A., 6 Mail de l'Europe, La Celle, F-78170 St. Cloud, France**

Tel: 33-1-30-82-5100

EMC Computer Systems France S.A., Immeuble Le Discover 84, blvd Vivier Merle, F-69485 Lyon Cedex 09, France

Tel: 33-4-78-14-1320

EMC Computer Systems France S.A., 3 rue du Parc, Immeuble Tourmaline, Oberhausbergen, F-67205 Strasbourge France

Tel: 33-3-88-56-0083

EMC Computer Systems France S.A., 3 Ave. Pierre et Marie Curie, F-59260 Lezennes Lille, France

Tel: 33-3-20-71-4012

## EMCO WHEATON DTM, INC.

2501 Constant Comment Place, Louisville, KY, 40299

Tel: (502) 266-6677      Fax: (502) 266-6689      www.emcowheaton.com

*Design, development and manufacture of environmentally safe vapor and fluid transfer products for petroleum, petrochemical, chemical and industrial applications.*

Emco Wheaton SA, rue Paul Appell, Parc Moderne d'Enterprises, St. Quen l'Aumone, France

## EMERSON & CUMING SPECIALTY POLYMERS

46 Manning Road, Bellerica, MA, 01821

Tel: (978) 436-9700      Fax: (978) 436-9701      www.emersoncuming.com

*Mfr. high performance encapsulants, adhesives and coatings for the automotive, telecommunications and electronic industries.*

Emerson & Cuming France, Zone Industrielle Nord B.P. 438, F-69655 Villefranche Cedex, France

Tel: 33-4-74-02-3960

## EMERY WORLDWIDE

One Lagoon Drive, Ste. 400, Redwood City, CA, 94065

Tel: (650) 596-9600      Fax: (650) 596-7901      www.emeryworld.com

*Freight transport, global logistics and air cargo.*

Emery Worldwide, (Fret 2) 3 rue du Trait-D'Union, BP 10408, F-95707 Roissy Airport Cedex, France

## ENCAD, INC.

6059 Cornerstone Court West, San Diego, CA, 92121

Tel: (858) 452-0882      Fax: (858) 452-5618      www.encad.com

*Mfr. large color printers for specialized graphics.*

Encad Europe SA, 84/88 Blvd. de la Mission Marchand, F-92400 Courbevoie, France

Tel: 33-1-4199-9230

## ENCYCLOPAEDIA BRITANNICA INC.

310 S. Michigan Ave., Chicago, IL, 60604

Tel: (312) 427-9700      Fax: (312) 294-2176      www.eb.com

*Publishing; books.*

Encyclopaedia Britannica, Immeuble Le Montcalm, 2 rue du Pont-Colbert, F-78023 Versailles Cedex, France

Encyclopedia Universalis, 10 rue Vercingetorix, F-75680 Paris Cedex 14, France

## ENERGIZER HOLDINGS, INC.

800 Chouteau Avenue, St. Louis, MO, 63164

Tel: (314) 982-2970      Fax: (214) 982-2752      www.energizer.com

*Mfr. Eveready and Energizer brand batteries and lighting products.*

Ralston Energy Systems, rue 5 Emile Pathe, F-78403 Chatou, France

Tel: 33-1-3480-1703    Fax: 33-1-3480-1800

## ENERPAC

P.O. Box 3241, Milwaukee, WI, 53201-3241

Tel: (414) 781-6600          Fax: (414) 781-1049          www.enerpac.com

*Mfr. hydraulic cylinders, pumps, valves, presses, tools, accessories and system components.*

**ENERPAC S. A., BP 200, Parc d'Activities du Moulin de Massy, 1 rue du Saule Trapu, F-91882 Massy Cedex, France**

## ENGELHARD CORPORATION

101 Wood Ave. S., CN 770, Iselin, NJ, 08830

Tel: (732) 205-5000          Fax: (732) 632-9253          www.engelhard.com

*Mfr. pigments, additives, catalysts, chemicals, engineered materials.*

**Engelhard Corporation, 96 rue Saint-Charles, F-75015 Paris, France**

**Engelhard SA, 4 rue de Beaubourg, F-75004 Paris, France**

## EQUIFAX INC.

PO Box 4081, Atlanta, GA, 30302

Tel: (404) 885-8000          Fax: (404) 888-5452          www.equifax.com

*Provides information and knowledge-based solutions on consumers and businesses around the world.*

**TechniCob SA, 42 rue Poussin, F-75016 Paris, France**

## ERICO PRODUCTS INC.

34600 Solon Road, Cleveland, OH, 44139

Tel: (440) 248-0100          Fax: (440) 248-0723          www.erico.com

*Mfr. electric welding apparatus and hardware, metal stampings, specialty fasteners.*

**Erico France SARL, BP 31, rue Benoit Fourneyron, One Industrielle Sud, F-42160 Andrezieux-Boutheon, France**

Tel: 33-4-7736-5656

## ERNST & YOUNG, LLP

787 Seventh Ave., New York, NY, 10019

Tel: (212) 773-3000          Fax: (212) 773-6350          www.eyi.com

*Accounting and audit, tax and management consulting services.*

**HSD Ernst & Young - Societe d'Avocates, Tour Manhattan, Cedex 21, F-92095 Paris La Defense 2, France**

Tel: 33-1-46-93-6795   Fax: 33-1-47-67-0106   Contact: Jack Anderson

## ESCO CORPORATION

2141 NW 25th Ave., Portland, OR, 97210

Tel: (503) 228-2141          Fax: (503) 778-6330          www.escocorp.com

*Mfr. equipment for mining, construction and forestry industries.*

**ESCO Corp., Lyon, France**

**ESCO SA, BP 229, F-69803 Saint-Priest Cedex, France**

## ESCO ELECTRONICS CORPORATION

8888 Ladue Road, Ste. 200, St. Louis, MO, 63124-2090

Tel: (314) 213-7200          Fax: (314) 213-7250          www.escostl.com

*Electronic subassemblies and components.*

**Filtertek S.A., Div. Esco Electronics, ZA du Prè de la Dame Jeanne, BP 11, F-60128 Plailly France**

## ESTERLINE TECHNOLOGIES

10800 NE 8th Street, Ste. 600, Bellevue, WA, 98004

Tel: (425) 453-9400          Fax: (425) 453-2916          www.esterline.com

*Mfr. equipment and instruments for industrial automation, precision measure, data acquisition.*

**Auxitrol Technologies S.A., Bureaux de la Colline, F-92213 Saint-Cloud Cedex, France**

Tel: 33-149-116-565

## ETEC SYSTEMS, INC.

26460 Corporate Ave., Hayward, CA, 94545

Tel: (510) 783-9210      Fax: (510) 887-2870      www.etec.com

*Mfr. of photolithography equipment used in semiconductor manufacturing.*

**Etec Systems Europe, Parc de la Sainte-Victoire, G-13590 Meyreuil, France**

Tel: 33-4-42-12-5646   Fax: 33-4-42-58-6860

## ETHYL CORPORATION

330 South 4th Street, PO Box 2189, Richmond, VA, 23219

Tel: (804) 788-5000      Fax: (804) 788-5688      www.ethyl.com

*Provide additive chemistry solutions to enhance the performance of petroleum products.*

**Succursale d'Ethyl Europe SA, Tour Anjou, 33 Quai de Dion-Bouton,F- 92800 Puteaux-Cedex, France**

Tel: 33-1-46939180   Fax: 33-1-47788717

## EURO RSCG WORLDWIDE

350 Hudson Street, New York, NY, 10014

Tel: (212) 886-2000      Fax: (212) 886-2016      www.eurorscg.com

*International advertising agency group.*

**Ailleurs Exactement, 38 bis rue du Fer a Moulin, Paris, France**

## EXCELLON AUTOMATION

24751 Crenshaw Boulevard, Torrance, CA, 90505

Tel: (310) 534-6300      Fax: (310) 534-6777      www.excellon.com

*PCB drilling and routing machines; optical inspection equipment.*

**Excellon France S.A.R.L., CE 1728, 91047 Evry Cedex, France**

Tel: 49-6074-3000

## EXIDE CORPORATION

645 Penn St., Reading, PA, 19601

Tel: (610) 378-0500      Fax: (610) 378-0824      www.exideworld.com

*Mfr. lead-acid automotive and industrial batteries.*

**Exide France, Nanterre, France**

## EXXON MOBIL CORPORATION

5959 Las Colinas Blvd., Irving, TX, 75039-2298

Tel: (972) 444-1000      Fax: (972) 444-1882      www.exxon.com

*Petroleum exploration, production, refining; mfr. petroleum and chemicals products; coal and minerals.*

**Exxon Mobil Raffinage SAF, Raffinerie de Fos, Route de Guigonnet, F-13270 Fos-sur-mer, France**

**Exxon Mobil, Inc., B.P. 138, F-76330 Notre-Dame de Gravenchon, France**

**Exxon Mobil, Inc., 31 Place des Corolles, Courbevoie, France**

**Exxon Mobil, Inc., Chemin de Vermelles, BP No. 19, F-62440 Harnes, France**

**Exxon Mobil, Inc., 2 rue des Martinets, F-92500 Reveil Malmaison, France**

Tel: 33-1-4710-6000   Fax: 33-1-470-5511

## FAIR, ISAAC AND COMPANY, INC.

200 Smith Ranch Road, San Rafael, CA, 94903

Tel: (415) 472-2211      Fax: (415) 492-5691      www.fairisaac.com

*Mfr. automated systems for credit and loan approvals.*

**Fair, Isaac and Co., Atria 21 Avenue Edouard Beling, F-92566 Rueil-Malmaison Cedex, France**

Tel: 33-1-4196-8080   Fax: 33-1-4708-2808

## FAIRCHILD PUBLICATIONS INC.

7 West 34th Street, New York, NY, 10001

Tel:  (212) 630-4000      Fax:  (212) 630-3563      www.fairchildpub.com

*Magazine publishers: Women's Wear Daily, Supermarket News, Brand Marketing, Executive Technology, Footwear News, Salon News.*

**Fairchild Publications,  9 rue Royale, F-75008 Paris, France**

Tel: 33-1-44-51-1300

## FAXON COMPANY, INC.

15 Southwest Park, Westwood, MA, 02090

Tel:  (781) 329-3350      Fax:  (781) 329-9875      www.faxon.com

*Distributor books and periodicals.*

**RoweCom France,  rue de la Prairie, Villebon sur Yvette F-91121, Palaiseau Cedex, France**

## FEDERAL-MOGUL CORPORATION

26555 Northwestern Highway, PO Box 1966, Southfield, MI, 48034

Tel:  (248) 354-7700      Fax:  (248) 354-8983      www.federal-mogul.com

*Mfr./distributor precision parts for automobiles, trucks, farm and construction vehicles.*

**Federal Mogul SA,  Fontenary-Soux-Boix, France**

## FEDEX CORPORATION

942 South Shady Grove Rd., Memphis, TN, 38120

Tel:  (901) 369-3600      Fax:  (901) 395-2000      www.fdxcorp.com

*Package express delivery service.*

**Federal Express (France) SARL,  44/46 ave. du 8 Mai 1945, F-92390 Villeneuve la Garenne, France**

Tel: 800-123 800

## FERRO CORPORATION

1000 Lakeside Ave., Cleveland, OH, 44114-7000

Tel:  (216) 641-8580      Fax:  (216) 696-5784      www.ferro.com

*Mfr. Specialty chemicals, coatings, plastics, colors, refractories.*

**Eurostar SA,  Zone Industrielle, rue de la Ferme St. Ladre BP 2, F-95470 Fosses, France**

Tel: 33-1-34-47-4700   Fax: 33-1-34-68-5840

**Ferro Chemicals SA,  Etang de la Gafette BP 28, G-13521 Port-de-Bouc Cedex, France**

Tel: 33-42-40-7300   Fax: 33-42-40-7333   Contact: John Mcllwraith, Mng. Dir.

**Ferro France S.A.R.L.,  43 rue Jeanne d'Arc, F-52115 Saint Dizier, France**

Tel: 33-25-073333   Fax: 33-25-563606   Contact: J. Bonnal, Gen. Mgr.

## FileNET CORPORATION

3565 Harbor Boulevard, Costa Mesa, CA, 92626

Tel:  (714) 966-3400      Fax:  (714) 966-3490      www.filenet.com

*Provides integrated document management (IDM) software and services for internet and client server-based imaging, workflow, cold and electronic document management solutions.*

**FileNET France,  Velizy Plus, Batiment C, 1 bis rue du Petit-Clamart, F-78140 Velizy, France**

Tel: 33-1-40-83-0606   Fax: 33-1-40-94-9170

## FINANCIAL GUARANTY INSURANCE COMPANY

115 Broadway, New York, NY, 10006

Tel:  (212) 312-3000      Fax:  (212) 312-3093      www.fgic.com

*Engaged in insuring debt securities and investment, operation, and information services to state and local governments*

**Financial Guaranty Insurance Co. (Paris),  107 rue St.-Lazare, F-75009, Paris, France**

## FINNIGAN CORPORATION

355 River Oaks Parkway, San Jose, CA, 95134-1991

Tel: (408) 433-4800     Fax: (408) 433-4823     www.finnigan.com

*Mfr. mass spectrometers.*

**Automass Products,  98 ter Boulevard Heloise, F-95814 Argenteuil Cedex, France**

**Cedex, France**

## FISHER SCIENTIFIC INC.

1 Liberty Lane, Hampton, NH, 03842

Tel: (603) 929-5911     Fax: (603) 929-0222     www.fisher1.com

*Mfr. science instruments and apparatus, chemicals, reagents.*

**Fisher Scientific - S.A.,  12 rue Gay Lussac, ZAC Clé de Saint Pierre BP2, F-78996 Elancourt, Cedex, France**

Tel: 33-1-30-13-2400   Fax: 33-1-30-13-2424

## FISHER-ROSEMOUNT

8000 Maryland Ave., Ste. 500, Clayton, MO, 63105-4755

Tel: (314) 746-9900     Fax: (314) 746-9974     www.frco.com

*Mfr. industrial process control equipment.*

**Fisher-Rosemount, S.A.,  19 Parc Blub de Gold, F-13856 Aix en Provence, France**

**Fisher-Rosemount, S.A.,  1 rue Edison ZAC due Chêne, F-69500 Bron, France**

**Fisher-Rosemount, S.A.,  rue Paul Baudry BP 10, F-68700 Cernay, France**

**Fisher-Rosemount, S.A.,  La Grande Campagne Nord, rue Claude Bernard, F-76330 Notre Dame de Gravenchon (Le Havre), France**

## C.B. FLEET COMPANY, INC.

4615 Murray Place, PO Box 11349, Lynchburg, VA, 24506

Tel: (804) 528-4000     Fax: (804) 847-4219     www.cbfleet.com

*Mfr. pharmaceutical, health and beauty aids.*

**DeWitt International S.A.,  50 ave. du President Wilson, LaPlaine, F-93214 St. Denis, France**

## FLEETBOSTON FINANCIAL CORPORATION

1 Federal Street, Boston, MA, 02110

Tel: (617) 346-4000     Fax: (617) 434-7547     www.fleet.com

*Banking and insurance services.*

**FleetBoston S.A. - Paris,  104 Ave. des Champs-Elyseés, F-75008 Paris, France**

Tel: 33-1-40-76-7500   Fax: 33-1-40-76-7595

## FLEXTRONICS INC. INTERNATIONAL

2241 Lundy Ave., San Jose, CA, 95131-1822

Tel: (408) 428-1300     Fax: (408) 428-0420     www.flextronics.com

*Contract manufacturer for electronics industry.*

**Flextronics International France S.A,  2 rue Lavoisier,  Z.I. Moncel-Les-Luneville, F-54300 Lunéville, France**

Tel: 33-383-761-616

## FLOWSERVE CORPORATION

222 W. Los Colinas Blvd., Irving, TX, 75039

Tel: (972) 443-6500     Fax: (972) 443-6858     www.flowserve.com

*Mfr. chemicals equipment, pumps, valves, filters, fans and heat exchangers.*

**Durco France SARL,  51 rue Tremiere, Village d'Enterprises, Quartier du Triolo, F-59650 Villeneuve d'Asaq, France**

Contact: Lille, Their

## FLUKE CORPORATION

6920 Seaway Blvd. PO Box 9090, Everett, WA, 98203

Tel: (425) 347-6100     Fax: (425) 356-5116     www.fluke.com

*Mfr. handheld, electronic test tools for maintenance of electronic equipment.*

**Fluke France, 94 a 106 rue Blaise Pascal, ZI des Mardelles - BP 71, F-93602 Aulnay Sous Bois, Cedex France**

Tel: 33-1-48-17-3737   Fax: 33-48-17-3730

**Fluke France, 94 a 106 rue Blaise, Pascal ZL des Mardelles - BP 71, F-93602 Aulnay Sous Bois, Cedex France**

## FM GLOBAL INC.

1301 Atwood Avenue, Johnston, RI, 02919

Tel: (401) 275-3000     Fax: (401) 275-3029     www.fmglobal.com

*Engaged in commercial and industrial property insurance and risk management, specializing in engineering-driven property protection.*

**FM Insurance Company, Ltd., Tour Europlaza, Défense 4, F-92927 Paris La Défense Cedex, France**

Tel: 33-1-46-93-9700

## FMC CORPORATION

200 E. Randolph Drive, Chicago, IL, 60601

Tel: (312) 861-6000     Fax: (312) 861-6141     www.fmc.com

*Produces chemicals and precious metals, mfr. machinery, equipment and systems for industrial, agricultural and government use.*

**FMC Europe S.A., Route de Clerimois BP 705, 89107 Sens Cedex, France**

Tel: 33-86-958770   Fax: 33-86-646-552

**FMC Smith Meter Inc., ALMA Ingenierie SA, 47 rue Paris, Boissy St. Leger, F-94470 France**

**Gelager SARL, Paris, France**

## FMC CORPORATION MATERIAL HANDLING EQUIPMENT

400 Highpoint Drive, Cahlfont, PA, 18914

Tel: (724) 479-4500     Fax: (215) 822-4553     www.fmcesg.com

*Mfr. bulk material handling and automation equipment.*

**FMC Europe S.A., Route des Clerimois BP 705, F-89107 Sens Cedex, France**

**FMC Material Handling, 17 rue Joel le Theule BP 229, F-78051 St. Quentin Yvelines Cedex, France**

Tel: 33-1-3060-9990   Fax: 33-1-3057-2307

## FMR (FIDELITY INVESTMENTS)

82 Devonshire Street, Boston, MA, 02109

Tel: (617) 563-7000     Fax: (617) 476-6105     www.fidelity.com

*Diversified financial services company offering investment management, retirement, brokerage, and shareholder services directly to individuals and institutions and through financial intermediaries.*

**Fidelity Investments SAS, 17 Ave. George V, F-75008 Paris, France**

Tel: 33-1-53-67-5566

## FOOT LOCKER USA

112 West 34th Street, New York, NY, 10020

Tel: (212) 720-3700     Fax: (212) 553-2042     www.venatorgroup.com

*Mfr./sales shoes and sneakers.*

**Foot Locker International, C.C. Cite De L'Europe, Calais, F-62231, France**

Tel: 33-3-21-36-3726

**Foot Locker International, 22 Ave. du Giniral Leclerc, Paris, F-75014, France**

Tel: 33-1-40-44-9901

Foot Locker International, C.C. Lille Grand Place, F-59000 Lille, France
Tel: 33-3-20-13-9595

Foot Locker International, 20 Blvd Alexandre Lii, F-59140 Dunkerque, France
Tel: 33-3-28-65-1223

Foot Locker International, Centre Commercial Euralille, F-59777 Euralille, France
Tel: 33-3-20-13-1542

Foot Locker International, C.C. Villeneuve 2, Case Nr 47, F-59658 Villeneuve D'Ascq, France
Tel: 33-3-20-47-0136

## FORD MOTOR COMPANY

One American Road, Dearborn, MI, 48121

Tel: (313) 322-3000     Fax: (313) 322-9600     www.ford.com

*Mfr./sales motor vehicles.*

Ford France SA, 344 ave. Napoleon Bonaparte, BP 307, F-92506 Rueil Malmaison Cedex, France

## FORMICA CORPORATION

10155 Reading Road, Cincinnati, OH, 45241-4805

Tel: (513) 786-3400     Fax: (513) 786-3082     www.formica.com

*Mfr. decorative laminate, adhesives and solvents.*

Formica SA, BP 19, 77313 Marne La Vallee, Cedex 2 France

## FORRESTER RESEARCH, INC.

400 Technology Square, Cambridge, MA, 02139

Tel: (617) 497-7090     Fax: (617) 868-0577     www.forrester.com

*Provides clients an analysis of the effect of changing technologies on their operations.*

Altis, Cinseil en Management, 40-42 quai du Point de Jour, F-92659 Boulogne-Billancourt Cedex, France

Tel: 33-1-41-41-4578   Fax: 33-1-41-41-4500   Contact: Marc Jeton, Mgr.

## FORT JAMES CORPORATION

1650 Lake Cook Road, Deerfield, IL, 60015

Tel: (847) 317-5000     Fax: (847) 236-3755     www.fortjames.com

*Mfr. and markets consumer tissue products.*

Fort James Corporation, Kunheim, France

Fort James Corporation, Courbevoie, France

Fort James Corporation, Gien and Hondouville, France

## FORTÉ SOFTWARE, INC.

1800 Harrison Street, Oakland, CA, 94612

Tel: (510) 869-3400     Fax: (510) 869-3480     www.forte.com

*Developer computer software applications.*

Forté Software France, 159 Ave. Charles de Gaulle, F-92200 Neuilly sur Seine, France
Tel: 33-1-41-43-0180   Fax: 33-1-41-43-0189

## FOSTER WHEELER CORPORATION

Perryville Corporate Park, Clinton, NJ, 08809-4000

Tel: (908) 730-4000     Fax: (908) 730-4100     www.fwc.com

*Manufacturing, engineering and construction.*

Foster Wheeler France SA, BP 114-Z.I. de la Grande Campagne Nord, rue Branly-F-76330 N.D. de Gravenchon, France

Tel: 33-2-3539-5900   Fax: 33-2-3538-3128   Contact: R. Herpin, Mgr.

Foster Wheeler France SA, 31 rue des Bourdonnais, F-75021 Paris Cedex 1, France

Foster Wheeler France SA, 92 quai de Bercy, F-75597 Paris Cedex 12, France

Tel: 33-1-4346-4000   Fax: 33-1-4346-4700   Contact: G. Bonadies, Pres. & CEO

**Foster Wheeler France SA, Bâtiment Pythagore-Les Algorithmes, Parc d'Innovation-rue Jean Sapidus, F-67400 Illkirch-Graffenstaden, France**

Tel: 33-3-8840-8300　　Fax: 33-3-8867-8202　　Contact: P. Muller, Mgr.

**Foster Wheeler France SA, Clairiere de l'Anjoly - Bât. D, Ave. de l'Europe - F-13127 Vitrolles, France**

Tel: 33-4-4275-1100　　Fax: 33-4-4289-9154　　Contact: A. Combier, Mgr

## FRANK RUSSELL COMPANY

909 A Street, Tacoma, WA, 98402

Tel: (253) 572-9500　　　　Fax: (253) 591-3495　　　　www.russell.com

*Investment management and asset strategy consulting.*

**Frank Russell Company S.A., 6 rue Christophe Colomb, F-75008 Paris, France**

Tel: 33-1-53-57-4020　　Fax: 33-1-53-57-4021　　Contact: Frédéric Jolly, Mng. Dir.　　Emp: 7

## THE FRANKLIN MINT

US Route 1, Franklin Center, PA, 19091

Tel: (610) 459-6000　　　　Fax: (610) 459-6880　　　　www.franklinmint.com

*Design/marketing collectibles and luxury items.*

**Le Medaillier Franklin SA, 4 ave. de l'Escouvrier, F-95207 Sarcelles, France**

## FRANKLIN RESOURCES, INC.

777 Mariners Island Blvd., San Mateo, CA, 94404

Tel: (415) 312-2000　　　　Fax: (415) 312-3655　　　　www.frk.com

*Global and domestic investment advisory and portfolio management.*

**Templeton Global Strategic Services, S.A., 16 Ave. George V, F-75008 Paris, France**

Tel: 33-1-40-73-8600　　Fax: 33-1-40-73-8610

## FRIED, FRANK, HARRIS, SHRIVER & JACOBSON

One New York Plaza, New York, NY, 10004-1980

Tel: (212) 859-8000　　　　Fax: (212) 859-4000　　　　www.ffhsj.com

*International law firm.*

**Fried, Frank, Harris, Shriver & Jacobson, 7 rue Royale, F-75008 Paris, France**

Tel: 33-1-40-17-0404　　Fax: 33-1-40-17-0830　　Contact: Eric Cafritz, Ptnr.

## FRITZ COMPANIES, INC.

706 Mission Street, Ste. 900, San Francisco, CA, 94103

Tel: (415) 904-8360　　　　Fax: (415) 904-8661　　　　www.fritz.com

*Integrated transportation, sourcing, distribution and customs brokerage services.*

**Fritz Companies Inc., Le Harve, France**

## FSI INTERNATIONAL INC.

322 Lake Hazeltine Drive, Chaska, MN, 55318

Tel: (612) 448-5440　　　　Fax: (612) 448-2825　　　　www.fsi-intl.com

*Manufacturing equipment for computer silicon wafers.*

**Metron Technology France, Z.I. de la Mariniere, Bondoufle, 6 rue Bernard Palissy, F-91912 Evry Cedex 9, France**

**Metron Technology France, Immeuble le Grenat, 3 Avenue Doyen Louis Weil, F-38024 Grenoble Cedex 1, France**

## H.B. FULLER COMPANY

1200 Willow Lake Blvd., Vadnais Heights, MN, 55110

Tel: (651) 236-5900　　　　Fax: (651) 236-5898　　　　www.hbfuller.com

*Mfr./distributor adhesives, sealants, coatings, paints, waxes, sanitation chemicals.*

**EFTEC S.A., 131 blvd. Carnot, F-78110 Le Vesinet, France**

Tel: 33-1-34-80-0667　　Fax: 33-1-39-76-4826

**H.B. Fuller France, Zone Industrielle BP 12, F-76580 Le Trait, France**

Tel: 33-235-059221　　Fax: 33-235-373678

## GAF CORPORATION

1361 Alps Road, Wayne, NJ, 07470

Tel: (973) 628-3000     Fax: (973) 628-3326     www.gaf.com

*Mfr. roofing and building materials.*

**GAF (France) SA,  BP 50007, F-95945 Roissy Charles de Gaulle Cedex, France**

## GALVESTON-HOUSTON COMPANY.

4900 Woodway, PO Box 2207, Houston, TX, 77056

Tel: (713) 966-2500     Fax: (713) 966-2575     www.hensleyind.com

*Mfr. industrial equipment.*

**Compagnie Auxiliarie Industrielle,  57-59 rue Etienne-Marcel, F-93100 Montreuil, France**

## THE GAP

1 Harrison Street, San Francisco, CA, 94105

Tel: (650) 952-4400     Fax: (650) 952-5884     www.gap.com

*Clothing store chain.*

**The Gap,  Paris, France**

## GARDNER-DENVER INC.

1800 Gardner Expressway, Quincy, IL, 62301

Tel: (217) 222-5400     Fax: (217) 228-8247     www.gardnerdenver.com

*Mfr. portable air compressors and related drilling accessories.*

**Gardner-Denver S.A.,  3 rue Charles, Francois Daubigny F-95870, Bezons France**

Tel: 33-1-34344120

## GARLOCK SEALING TECHNOLOGIES

1666 Division Street, Palmyra, NY, 14522

Tel: (315) 597-4811     Fax: (315) 597-3216     www.garlock-inc.com

*Mfr. of gaskets, packing, seals and expansion joints.*

**Cefilac,  90 rue de la Roche du Geai, F-42029 St. Etienne, Cedex, France**

Contact: Bruno Lagree

## GaSONICS INTERNATIONAL CORPORATION

404 East Plumeria Drive, San Jose, CA, 95134

Tel: (408) 570-7000     Fax: (408) 570-7612     www.gasonics.com

*Mfr. gas-based dry cleaning systems for semi-conductor production equipment.*

**GaSonics International,  3 rue Jacques Prevert, 94880 Noiseau, France**

Tel: 33-1-4590-10-98  Fax: 33-1-4590-15-41

## THE GATES RUBBER COMPANY

990 S. Broadway, PO Box 5887, Denver, CO, 80217-5887

Tel: (303) 744-1911     Fax: (303) 744-4000     www.gatesrubber.com

*Mfr. automotive and industrial belts and hoses.*

**Gates SA,  rue des Grands Pres, BP 19, F-58026 Nevers Cedex, France**

## GATEWAY INC.

4545 Towne Centre Ct., San Diego, CA, 92121

Tel: (858) 799-3401     Fax: (858) 779-3459     www.gateway.com

*Computers manufacture, sales and services.*

**Gateway France,  63 Boulevard Haussman, F-75008 Paris, France**

**Gateway France,  Centre Commercial, Avenue du Général de Gaulle Entrée n° 7 - Unit 134, F-93110 Rosny, France**

## GATX CAPITAL CORPORATION

Four Embarcadero Center, Ste. 2200, San Francisco, CA, 94111

Tel: (415) 955-3200     Fax: (415) 955-3449     www.gatxcapital.com

*Lease and loan financing, residual guarantees.*

**GATX International Ltd., Centreda 1, Avenue Didier Daurat F-31700 Blagnac, France**

Tel: 33-561-77-39-40   Fax: 33-561-16-72-44   Contact: Mike D. Sanders

## GE CAPITAL FLEET SERVICES

3 Capital Drive, Eden Prairie, MN, 55344

Tel: (612) 828-1000     Fax: (612) 828-2010     www.gefleet.com

*Corporate vehicle leasing and services.*

**GE Capital Fleet Services, rue le Corbusier 41, 94046 Creteil, Cedex France**

Tel: 33-1-4956-5000

## GENCOR INDUSTRIES INC.

5201 N. Orange Blossom Trail, Orlando, FL, 32810

Tel: (407) 290-6000     Fax: (407) 578-0577     www.gencor.com

*Mfr. heat process systems, equipment, instrumentation and controls.*

**CPM Europe, S.A., BP 35, 34 Avenue Albert 1, F-92502 Rueil Malmaison, France**

Tel: 33-1-479-92999   Fax: 33-1-475-18411

## GENERAL BINDING CORPORATION

One GBC Plaza, Northbrook, IL, 60062

Tel: (847) 272-3700     Fax: (847) 272-1369     www.gbc.com

*Engaged in the design, manufacture and distribution of branded office equipment, related supplies and thermal laminating films.*

**GBC France, 44 rue Maurice de Broglie, Z.A.C. Les Mardelles, F-93602 Aulnay sous Bois Cedex, France**

## GENERAL DATACOMM INC.

1579 Straits Turnpike, PO Box 1299, Middlebury, CT, 06762-1299

Tel: (203) 574-1118     Fax: (203) 758-8507     www.gdc.com

*Mfr./sale/services transportation equipment for communications networks.*

**General DataComm SARL, 14 rue Jules Saulnier, Parc du Colombier, BP 221, F-93200 St. Denis, France**

## GENERAL ELECTRIC CAPITAL CORPORATION

260 Long Ridge Road, Stamford, CT, 06927

Tel: (203) 357-4000     Fax: (203) 357-6489     www.gecapital.com

*Financial, property/casualty insurance, computer sales and trailer leasing services.*

**Employers Reinsurance Corp. (ERC), 107 rue St. Lazare, F-75009 Paris, France**

Tel: 33-1-55-07-1400   Fax: 33-1-5507-1402

## GENERAL ELECTRIC COMPANY

3135 Easton Turnpike, Fairfield, CT, 06431

Tel: (203) 373-2211     Fax: (203) 373-3131     www.ge.com

*Diversified manufacturing, technology and services.*

**GE Aircraft Engines, F-77750 Moissy Cramayel Villaroche, France**

Tel: 33-6-212-2100

**GE Capital Services GENSTAR Container, 30 rue D'Orleans, Paris, France**

Tel: 33-1-47-45-0951

**GE FANUC Automation, 45 rue du Bois Chaland, F-91029 Evry Cedex, France**

Tel: 33-1-69-89-7020   Fax: 33-1-69-89-7049

**General Electric France, 18 rue Horace Vernet, F-92136 Issy Les Moulineaux, France**

Tel: 33-1-40-93-3336

GEPC Export Department,  Route de Guise, BP 642, F-02322 St. Quentin Cedex, France

Tel: 33-3-23-50-7035    Fax: 33-3-23-50-7088

Nuovo Pignone,  19 Ave. de l'Opera, F-75001 Paris, France

Tel: 33-1-43-16-1496    Fax: 33-1-43-16-1499

## GENERAL INSTRUMENT CORPORATION

101 Tournament Road, Horsham, PA, 19044

Tel: (215) 674-4800      Fax: (215) 443-9554      www.gi.com

*Mfr. broadband communications and power rectifying components.*

General Instrument SAS, France,  Espace Europeen de l'Entreprise, Batiment C Avenue de l'Europe B.P. 17, F-67305 Schiltigheim Cedex France

Tel: 33-390-20-06-30

## GENERAL MOTORS ACCEPTANCE CORPORATION

3044 W. Grand Blvd., Detroit, MI, 48202

Tel: (313) 556-5000      Fax: (313) 556-5108      www.gmac.com

*Automobile financing.*

Banque de Credit General Motors,  Tour Manhattan, F-92095 Paris Cedex 21, France

Banque de Credit GM,  BP 354, F-33694 Merignac Cedex, France

Banque de Credit GM,  Tour Credit Lyonnais, 129 rue Servient, F-69431 Lyon 03, France

## GENERAL MOTORS CORPORATION

300 Renaissance Center, Detroit, MI, 48285

Tel: (313) 556-5000      Fax: (313) 556-5108      www.gm.com

*Mfr. full line vehicles, automotive electronics, commercial technologies, telecommunications, space, finance.*

Delco Remy Div. GM,  BP 819, F-57208 Sarreguemines, France

Harrison Radiator Div. GM,  BP 14, Zone Industrielle, F-08350 Donchery, France

Hydra-matic Div. GM,  BP 33, F-67026 Strasbourg Cedex, France

## GENERAL REINSURANCE CORPORATION

695 E. Main Street, Stamford, CT, 06904-2350

Tel: (203) 328-5000      Fax: (203) 328-6423      www.genre.com

*Reinsurance services worldwide.*

General Re Europe Ltd. - Paris,  119-121 Ave. des Champs Elysees, F-75008 Paris, France

Tel: 33-1-53-67-76-76    Fax: 33-1-40-70-91-60    Contact: Emmanuel Brouquier, VP

La Kölnische Rück S.A.,  121 Ave. des Champs-Elysées, F-75008 Paris, France

Tel: 33-1-5367-7676    Fax: 33-1-4070-9160    Contact: Bertrand Gautheron, Mng. Dir.

## GENERAL SEMICONDUCTOR, INC.

10 Melville Park Road., Melville, NY, 11747

Tel: (631) 847-3000      Fax: (631) 847-3236      www.gensemi.com

*Mfr. of low- and medium-current power rectifiers and transient voltage suppressors.*

General Semiconductor  France,  2 rue Louis Pergaud, F-94706 Maisons Alfort Cedex, France

Fax: 00331417931 99

Jean

Tel: 33-1-41-793190    Fax: 33-1-417-93199    Contact: Jean-Jacque Meli

## GENETICS INSTITUTE INC.

150 Cambridge Park Drive, Cambridge, MA, 02140

Tel: (617) 876-1170      Fax: (617) 876-0388

*Develop/commercialize biopharmaceutical therapeutic products.*

Genetics Institute of Europe BV,  8 rue de la Michodiere, F-75002 Paris, France

## GENICOM CORPORATION

14800 Conference Center Drive, Ste. 400, Chantilly, VA, 20151

Tel: (703) 802-9200　　　Fax: (703) 802-9039　　　www.genicom.com

*Supplier of network systems, service and printer solutions.*

**Genicom France SA, 17 avenue du Garigliano, ZAC les Gâtines F-91600 Savigny Sur Orge, France**

Tel: 33-1-69-542317　　Contact: Michel Fargier

## GENUITY, INC.

150 Cambridge Park Drive, Cambridge, MA, 02140

Tel: (617) 873-2000　　　Fax: (617) 873-2857　　　www.genuity.com

*R/D computer, communications, acoustics technologies and internetworking services.*

**Genuity, Inc., 54 Avenue Hoche, F-75008 Paris, France**

Tel: 33-1-5660 5273　　Contact: Michel Azoulay

## GENZYME CORPORATION

1 Kendall Square, Cambridge, MA, 02139-1562

Tel: (617) 252-7500　　　Fax: (617) 252-7600　　　www.genzyme.com

*Mfr. healthcare products for enzyme deficient diseases.*

**Genzyme SA, 9 Chaussee Jules Cesar, Batiment 2 BP 225 OsnyF- 95523, Cergy-Pointoise Cedex, France**

Tel: 33-1-34-22-9570　　Fax: 33-1-30-3-9919

## GIBSON, DUNN & CRUTCHER LLP

333 S. Grand Ave., Los Angeles, CA, 90071

Tel: (213) 229-7000　　　Fax: (213) 229-7520　　　www.gdclaw.com

*International law firm.*

**Gibson, Dunn & Crutcher LLP, 166 rue du Faubourg Saint Honore, F-75008 Paris, France**

Tel: 33-1-56-43-1300　　Fax: 33-1-56-43-1333

## GILEAD SCIENCES, INC.

333 Lakeside Dr, Foster City, CA, 94404

Tel: (650) 574-3000　　　Fax: (650) 578-9264　　　www.gilead.com

*Engaged in healthcare research and development; biotech treatments for viruses.*

**NeXstar Pharaceutique, 39 rue Godot de Mauroy, F-75009 Paris, France**

Tel: 33-1-4268-3450　　Fax: 33-1-4266-2605

## THE GILLETTE COMPANY

Prudential Tower Building, Boston, MA, 02199

Tel: (617) 421-7000　　　Fax: (617) 421-7123　　　www.gillette.com

*Develop/mfr. personal care/use products: blades and razors, toiletries, cosmetics, stationery.*

**Braun France SA, Clichy/Paris, France**

Contact: Alain Calviera, Gen. Mgr.

**Gillette France SA, Annecy, France**

Contact: Alain Calviera, Gen. Mgr.

**Oral-B Laboratories SA, Saint Herblain, France**

Contact: Alain Calviera, Gen. Mgr.

**Silk-Epil SA, La Farlede/Toulon, France**

Contact: Alain Calviera, Gen. Mgr.

**Societe de Participations Financieres Gillette, Annecy Cedex, France**

Contact: Alain Calviera, Gen. Mgr.

**Societe Francaise d'Appareillages et d'Instrument de Mesure, Caluire Cedex, France**

Contact: Alain Calviera, Gen. Mgr.

**Waterman SA, Paris, France**
Contact: Alain Calviera, Gen. Mgr.

## GILSON INC.

3000 W. Beltline Hwy, PO Box 620027, Middleton, WI, 53562-0027

Tel: (608) 836-1551          Fax: (608) 831-4451          www.gilson.com

*Mfr. analytical/biomedical instruments.*

**Gilson Medical Electronics France SA, 72 rue Gambetta, F-95400 Villiers-le-Bel, France**

**Gilson S.A., BP 45, 19 Avenue des Entrepreneurs, F- 95400 Villiers Le Bel, France**

## P.H. GLATFELTER COMPANY

96 South George St., Ste. 500, York, PA, 17401

Tel: (717) 225-4711          Fax: (717) 225-6834          www.glatfelter.com

*Mfr. engineered and specialty printing papers.*

**Glatfelter Ltd., Paris, France**

## GLEASON CORPORATION

1000 University Ave., Rochester, NY, 14692

Tel: (716) 473-1000          Fax: (716) 461-4348          www.gleasoncorp.com

*Mfr. gear making machine tools; tooling and services.*

**Gleason France, Paris Nord II, BP 60070 22 Avenue des Nation, Roissy CDG Cedex, F-95972 France**
Tel: 33-1-49389000   Fax: 33-1-49389009

## GODIVA CHOCOLATIER INC.

355 Lexington Ave., New York, NY, 10017

Tel: (212) 984-5900          Fax: (212) 984-5901          www.godiva.com

*Mfr. chocolate candy, Biscotti dipping cookies and after-dinner coffees.*

**Godiva Chocolatier, Inc., Paris, France**

## THE GOLDMAN SACHS GROUP

85 Broad Street, New York, NY, 10004

Tel: (212) 902-1000          Fax: (212) 902-3000          www.gs.com

*Investment bankers; securities broker dealers.*

**Goldman Sachs Group, 2 rue de Thann, F-75017 Paris, France**
Tel: 33-1-42-12-1000

## BF GOODRICH

2550 West Tyvola Road, Charlotte, NC, 28217

Tel: (704) 423-7000          Fax: (704) 423-7100          www.bfgoodrich.com

*Engaged in aerospace systems and services, performance materials and engineered industrial products.*

**Cefilac, S.A., 90 rue de la Roche du Geai, F-42029 Saint Etienne, Cedex 1 France**
Tel: 33-4-7743-5100

## THE GOODYEAR TIRE & RUBBER COMPANY

1144 East Market Street, Akron, OH, 44316

Tel: (330) 796-2121          Fax: (330) 796-1817          www.goodyear.com

*Mfr. tires, automotive belts and hose, conveyor belts, chemicals; oil pipeline transmission.*

**Cie. Francaise Goodyear SA, BP 310, F-92506 Rueil-Malmaison Cedex, France**

## GOSS GRAPHIC SYSTEMS INC.

700 Oakmont Lane, Westmont, IL, 60559-5546

Tel: (630) 850-5600          Fax: (630) 850-6310          www.gossgraphic.com

*Mfr. web, off-site printing equipment.*

**Goss/Rockwell Systems Graphique Nantes SA, Tour Gan, F-92082 Paris Cedex 13, France**

## W. R. GRACE & COMPANY
7500 Grace Drive, Columbia, MD, 21044

Tel: (410) 531-4000      Fax: (410) 531-4367      www.grace.com

*Mfr. specialty chemicals and materials: packaging, health care, catalysts, construction, water treatment/process.*

**Grace SARL, BP 136, F-67603 Selestat Cedex, France**

**Rollin SA, BP 70, F-68702 Cernay Cedex, France**

**W.R. Grace S.A.S., 33 Route de Gallardon, F-28234 Epernon Cedex, France**

Tel: 33-2-37-18-8600   Fax: 33-2-37-18-8686

## GRACO INC.
4050 Olson Memorial Hwy, PO Box 1441, Minneapolis, MN, 55440-1441

Tel: (612) 623-6000      Fax: (612) 623-6777      www.graco.com

*Mfr. systems and equipment to service fluid handling systems and automotive equipment.*

**Graco Puericulture, 155 Av. Jean Jaures, F-93531 Aubervilliers Cedex, France**

Tel: 33-1-48-1179-24   Fax: 33-1-48-1179-24

## GRANT THORNTON INTERNATIONAL
800 One Prudential Plaza, 130 E. Randolph Drive, Chicago, IL, 60601-6050

Tel: (312) 856-0001      Fax: (312) 616-7052      www.grantthornton.com

*Accounting, audit, tax and management consulting services.*

**Grant Thornton France Exco France, 7 rue de Madrid, F-75008 Paris, France**

Tel: 33-1-44-70-3000   Fax: 33-1-42-93-3216   Contact: André Zagouri

**Grant Thornton France Exco France, 64 rue Francois Marceau, B.P. 208, F-33021 Bordeaux Cedex, France**

Tel: 33-56-42-4344   Fax: 33-56-42-4380   Contact: Bernard Junières

**Grant Thornton France Exco France, 156 blvd Delbecque, B.P. 99, F-59502 Douai Cedex Douai, France**

Tel: 33-27-94-3000   Fax: 33-27-94-3001   Contact: Erik Voituriez

**Grant Thornton France Exco France, 46 bis rue des Hauts-Paves, B.P. 289, F-44010 Nantes Cedex 01, France**

Tel: 33-40-20-2122   Fax: 33-40-08-0430   Contact: Michel Piau

**Grant Thornton France Exco France, 37 Ave. de la Foret Noire, BP 21/R1, F-67001 Strasbourg Cedex, France**

Tel: 33-88-61-0802   Fax: 33-88-60-6710   Contact: Philippe Ley

## GREAT LAKES CHEMICAL CORPORATION
500 East 96th Street, Ste. 500, Indianapolis, IN, 46240

Tel: (317) 715-3000      Fax: (317) 715-3050      www.greatlakeschem.com

*Mfr. innovative specialty chemical solutions, including flame retardants and other polymer additives, water treatment chemicals, performance and fine chemicals, fire extinguishants.*

**Great Lakes Chemical France SA, Paris, France**

## GREY GLOBAL GROUP
777 Third Ave., New York, NY, 10017

Tel: (212) 546-2000      Fax: (212) 546-1495      www.grey.com

*International advertising agency.*

**Grey Communications Group, 63 bis rue de Sevres, F-92514 Boulogne-Billancourt Cedex, France**

## GRIFFITH LABORATORIES INC.

One Griffith Center, Alsip, IL, 60658

Tel: (708) 371-0900     Fax: (708) 597-3294     www.griffithlabs.com

*Mfr. industrial food ingredients and equipment.*

**Griffith Labs Inc., Paris, France**

Tel: 33-1-46-43-9393    Fax: 33-1-46-43-9394

## GUIDANT CORPORATION

111 Monument Circle, 29th Fl., Indianapolis, IN, 46204

Tel: (317) 971-2000     Fax: (317) 971-2040     www.guidant.com

*Mfr. cardiovascular therapeutic devices.*

**Guidant France S.A., 9 rue d'Estienne d'Orves, F-92504 rueil Malmaison, France**

Tel: 33-1-4714-4014

## GUY CARPENTER & COMPANY, INC.

Two World Trade Center, New York, NY, 10048

Tel: (212) 323-1000     Fax: (212) 313-4970     www.guycarp.com

*Engaged in global reinsurance and risk management.*

**Guy Carpenter & Company, S.A., 47-53 rue Raspail, 92594 Levallois-Perret Cedex, France**

Tel: 33-1-56-76-400    Fax: 33-1-41-27-9303

## HAEMONETICS CORPORATION

400 Wood Road, Braintree, MA, 02184-9114

Tel: (781) 848-7100     Fax: (781) 848-5106     www.haemonetics.com

*Mfr. automated blood processing systems and blood products.*

**Haemonetics France SARL, 46 bis rue Pierre Curie , Z.l. Les Gatines -F-78370, Plaisir, France**

**Haemonetics Germany**

Tel: 33-1-308-141-41    Fax: 33-1-308-141-30

## HALLIBURTON COMPANY

500 North Akard Street, Ste. 3600, Dallas, TX, 75201-3391

Tel: (214) 978-2600     Fax: (214) 978-2685     www.halliburton.com

*Engaged in diversified energy services, engineering and construction.*

**Halliburton Ltd., BP 209, F-64142 Billere Cedex, France**

Tel: 33-59-32-1446    Fax: 33-59-62-1862

**Halliburton Ltd., Le Florestan, 2 blvd Vauban, F-78180 Montigney-Le-Bretonneux, St. Quentin-En-Yvelines France**

Tel: 33-1-30-43-9898    Fax: 33-1-30-43-5662

**Halliburton Ltd., rue de la foret, Zone Industriel Espinay Sous, F-91860 Epinay Sous Senart, France**

Tel: 33-1-69-438135    Fax: 33-1-60-464038

## HALLMARK CARDS INC.

2501 McGee Street, Kansas City, MO, 64108

Tel: (816) 274-5100     Fax: (816) 274-5061     www.hallmark.com

*Mfr. greeting cards and related products.*

**Hallmark Group France, S.A., rue Eiffel, ZAC de Mercieres, F-60200 Compiegne, France**

Tel: 33-3-44-51-5151

## HAMILTON SUNSTRAND

One Hamilton Rd., Windsor Locks, CT, 06096-1010

Tel: (860) 654-6000     Fax: (860) 654-3469     www.hamiltonsunstrandcorp.com

*Design/mfr. aerospace systems for commercial, regional, corporate and military aircraft.*

**Hamilton Sunstrand Corp., Zone Industrial Dijon Sud, B.P. 30, F-21604 Longvic Cedex, France**

Tel: 33-3-80-38-33-01   Fax: 33-3-80-38-33-91

## M.A. HANNA COMPANY

200 Public Square, Ste. 36-5000, Cleveland, OH, 44114

Tel: (216) 589-4000     Fax: (216) 589-4200     www.mahanna.com

*Mfr. color and additive concentrates.*

**Synthecolor, 7 rue des Oziers, Z.I. du Vert Galant, F-95310 Saint Ouen L'Aumone, France**

**Z.I Molina La Chazotte, rue de L'Avenir/BP 105, F-42003 Saint Etienne, Cedex 1 France**

## HARBORLITE CORPORATION

PO Box 100, Vicksburg, MI, 49097

Tel: (616) 649-1352     Fax: (616) 649-3707     www.worldminerals.com

*Mining/process perlite filter media.*

**Harborlite France, 9 rue de Colonel de Rochebrune, BP 240, F-92504 Rueil-Malmaison Cedex, France**

## HARMAN INTERNATIONAL INDUSTRIES, INC.

1101 Pennsylvania Ave. NW, Ste. 1010, Washington, DC, 20004

Tel: (202) 393-1101     Fax: (202) 393-3064     www.harman.com

*Mfr. audio and video equipment, loudspeakers and sound reinforcement equipment.*

**Audax SA, 2 Route de Tours, F-72500 Chateau du Loir, France**

**Harman France SA, Peripole 243, 33 ave. du Marechal de Lattre de Tassigny, F-94127 Fontenay sous Bois Cedex, France**

## HARNISCHFEGER INDUSTRIES INC.

PO Box 554, Milwaukee, WI, 53201

Tel: (414) 797-6480     Fax: (414) 797-6573     www.harnischfeger.com

*Mfr. mining and material handling equipment, papermaking machinery and computer systems.*

**Beloit Papermachines SA, Creusot Loire, 15 rue Pasquier, F-75383 Paris, France**

## HARRIS CALORIFIC COMPANY

2345 Murphy Boulevard, Gainesville, GA, 30501

Tel: (770) 536-8801     Fax: (770) 536-0544     www.harriscal.com

*Mfr./sales of gas welding and cutting equipment.*

**Harris France SARL, Div. Lincoln Electric, Avenue Franklin Roosevelt, BP 214, F-76121 Grand-Quevilly Cedex, France**

## HARRIS CORPORATION

1025 West NASA Blvd., Melbourne, FL, 32919

Tel: (407) 727-9100     Fax: (407) 727-9344     www.harris.com

*Mfr. communications and information-handling equipment, including copying and fax systems.*

**Harris Semiconducteurs, 2-4 Ave. de l'Europe, F-78941 Velizy Cedex, France**

Tel: 33-1-34-65-4080   Fax: 33-1-34-65-0978

## HARTFORD RE COMPANY

55 Farmington Ave., Ste. 800, Hartford, CT, 06105

Tel: (860) 520-2700     Fax: (860) 520-2726     www.thehartford.com

*Reinsurance.*

**HartRe Company, Square Edouard VII, 26 boulevard des Capucines, 6me Etage F-75009 Paris, France**

Tel: 33-15-818-3030   Fax: 33-14-456-0939   Contact: François Lanoote

## HARVARD APPARATUS

84 October Hill Road, Holliston, MA, 01746

Tel: (508) 893-8999     Fax: (508) 429-5732     www.harvardapparatus.com

*Mfr./sales life science research products.*

**Harvard Apparatus SARL,  6 Ave. des Andes, Miniparc-Bat. 8, F-91952 Les Ulis Cedex, France**

Tel: 33-1-64-46-0085   Fax: 33-1-64-46-9438   Contact: Hester Davies, Mng. Dir.

## HASBRO INDUSTRIES INC.

1027 Newport Ave., Pawtucket, RI, 02861

Tel: (401) 725-8697     Fax: (401) 727-5099     www.hasbro.com

*Mfr. toy products, including games and puzzles, dolls and plush products.*

**Wizards, Div. Hasbro Industries,  2 rue du Nouveau Bercy, F-94220 Charenton Le Pont, Paris France**

Tel: 33-1-4396-3565

## HAUPPAUGE DIGITAL, INC.

91 Cabot Court, Hauppauge, NY, 11788

Tel: (631) 434-1600     Fax: (631) 434-3198     www.hauppauge.com

*Mfr. circuit boards.*

**Hauppauge Computer Works, Ltd.,  91 Avenue Kleber, Paris, France**

Tel: 33-156-265-121

## HAYNES INTERNATIONAL INC.

1020 W. Park Ave., PO Box 9013, Kokomo, IN, 46904-9013

Tel: (765) 456-6000     Fax: (765) 456-6905     www.haynesintl.com

*Mfr. cobalt and nickel-base alloys for aerospace and chemicals industry.*

**Haynes International, S.A.R.L.,  Boite Postale 9535, F-95061 Cergy Pontoise Cedex, France**

Tel: 33-1-34-48-3100   Fax: 33-1-30-37-8022

## HEIDRICK & STRUGGLES INTERNATIONAL, INC.

Sears Tower, 233 South Wacker Drive, Chicago, IL, 60606

Tel: (312) 496-1200     Fax: (312) 496-1290     www.heidrick.com

*Executive search firm.*

**Heidrick & Struggles Intl. Inc.,  112 Ave. Kleber, F-75784 Paris Cedex 18, France**

Tel: 33-1-44-34-1700   Fax: 33-1-44-34-1717

## HEIN-WERNER CORPORATION

2110 A Pewaukee Rd., PO Box 1606, Waukesha, WI, 53188

Tel: (262) 542-6611     Fax: (262) 542-7890     www.snapon.com

*Mfr. auto body repair equipment, engine rebuilding and brake repair equipment, hydraulic cylinders.*

**Blackhawk SA,  Centre Eurofret, rue du Rheinfeld, F-67100 Strasbourg, France**

## H.J. HEINZ COMPANY

600 Grant Street, Pittsburgh, PA, 15219

Tel: (412) 456-5700     Fax: (412) 456-6128     www.heinz.com

*Processed food products and nutritional services.*

**Ets. Paul Paulet,  Douarnenez, France**

**H.J. Heinz SARL,  Paris, France**

## HELLER FINANCIAL INC.

500 West Monroe Street, Chicago, IL, 60661

Tel: (312) 441-7000     Fax: (312) 441-7367     www.hellerfin.com

*Financial services.*

**Factofrance Heller,  Tour Facto - Cedex 88, F-92988 Paris la Défense, France**

## HENRY SCHEIN, INC.

135 Duryea Rd., Melville, NY, 11747

Tel: (516) 843-5500    Fax: (516) 843-5658    www.henryschein.com

*Mfr. and supply dental equipment.*

**Henry Schein France SA, Immeuble Activille, 4 rue de Charenton, F-94140 Alfortville Cedex, France**

Tel: 33-1-41-79-6565

## HERCULES INC.

Hercules Plaza, 1313 N. Market Street, Wilmington, DE, 19894-0001

Tel: (302) 594-5000    Fax: (302) 594-5400    www.herc.com

*Mfr. specialty chemicals, plastics, film and fibers, coatings, resins, food ingredients.*

**Hercules Chemical Ltd., Aklizay, France**

**Hercules France SA, 3 rue Eugene et Armaud Peugeot, F-92508 Rueil-Malmaison Cedex, France**

Tel: 33-1-47-10-2400   Fax: 33-1-47-08-5075   Contact: Christian Tavaux

## HERMAN MILLER INC.

855 East Main, Zeeland, MI, 49464

Tel: (616) 654-3000    Fax: (616) 654-5385    www.hermanmiller.com

*Mfr. office furnishings.*

**Herman Miller et Cie, Immeuble Tivoli, 257 av Georges Clémenceau, Nanterre Cedex F-92000, France**

Tel: 33-1-5517-6262   Fax: 33-1-5517-6260

## THE HERTZ CORPORATION

225 Brae Boulevard, Park Ridge, NJ, 07656-0713

Tel: (201) 307-2000    Fax: (201) 307-2644    www.hertz.com

*Worldwide headquarters office for car rental, car leasing and equipment rental.*

**Hertz Rental Car, Paris, France**

## HEWITT ASSOCIATES LLC

100 Half Day Road, Lincolnshire, IL, 60069

Tel: (847) 295-5000    Fax: (847) 295-7634    www.hewitt.com

*Employee benefits consulting firm.*

**Hewitt Associates, 20 Ave. André Malraux, F-92309 Levallois-Perret Cedex Paris, France**

Tel: 33-1-47-59-3939

## HEWLETT-PACKARD COMPANY

3000 Hanover Street, Palo Alto, CA, 94304-1185

Tel: (650) 857-1501    Fax: (650) 857-5518    www.hp.com

*Mfr. computing, communications and measurement products and services.*

**Hewlett-Packard France, Parc d'Activite du Bois Briard, 2 ave.du Lac, F-91040 Evry Cedex, France**

## HEXCEL CORPORATION

281 Tresser Blvd., Stamford, CT, 06901

Tel: (203) 969-0666    Fax: (203) 358-3977    www.hexcel.com

*Honeycomb core materials, specialty chemicals, resins and epoxies.*

**Hexcel France, Z.I. des Bethunes, rue de l'Equerre, F-95311 Saint Quen l'Aumone, France**

## HILLENBRAND INDUSTRIES, INC.

700 State Route 46 East, Batesville, IN, 47006

Tel: (812) 934-7000    Fax: (812) 934-1963    www.hillenbrand.com

*Holding company: mfr. hospital beds, incubators and caskets.*

**Hill-Rom Ltd., PB 14 ZI du Talhouet, F-56330 Pluvigner, France**

Tel: 33-297-509275   Fax: 33-297-509202   Contact: Pascal Pouligny

## HILTON HOTELS CORPORATION

9336 Civic Center Drive, Beverly Hills, CA, 90210

Tel: (310) 278-4321     Fax: (310) 205-7880     www.hiltonhotels.com

*International hotel chain: Hilton International, Vista Hotels and Hilton National Hotels.*

**Hilton International Hotels,  18 Ave. de Suffren, F-75740 Paris Cedex 15, France**

**Noga Hilton Cannes,  50 blvd de la Croisette, F-06414 Cannes Cedex, France**

**Paris Hilton,  18 Ave. de Suffren, F-75740 Paris Cedex 15, France**

## HOLIDAY INN (BASS RESORTS) WORLDWIDE, INC.

3 Ravinia Drive, Ste. 2900, Atlanta, GA, 30346-2149

Tel: (770) 604-2000     Fax: (770) 604-5403     www.holidayinn.com

*Hotels, restaurants and casinos.*

**Holiday Inn France,  110 rue Jean Joures, 59810 Lesquin Paris, France**

**Holiday Inn France,  69 Blvd. Victor, F-75015 Port de Versailles, Paris, France**

**Holiday Inn France,  4 ave. Charles Lindberg, Orly Airport, F-94656 Rungis Paris, France**

## HOLOGIC, INC.

35 Crosby Drive, Bedford, MA, 01730

Tel: (781) 999-7300     Fax: (781) 280-0669     www.hologic.com

*Mfr. x-ray systems to measure bone density.*

**Hologic France,  35 rue du Saule Trapu, 91882 Massy, France**

Tel: 33-1-6013-3938   Fax: 33-1-6913-3441

## HONEYWELL INTERNATIONAL INC.

101 Columbia Road, Morristown, NJ, 07962

Tel: (973) 455-2000     Fax: (973) 455-4807     www.honeywell.com

*Develop/mfr. controls for home and building, industry, space and aviation.*

**Honeywell SA,  Parc Technologique de St. Aubin, Route de l'Orme (CD 128), F-91190 Saint Aubin, France**

Tel: 33-1-6919-8000   Fax: 33-1-6019-8181

## HONEYWELL-MEASUREX DMC CORPORATION

PO Box 490, Gaithersburg, MD, 20884

Tel: (301) 948-2450     Fax: (301) 670-0506     www.measurex.com

*Mfr. quality and process control gauges.*

**Honeywell-Measurex DMC France,  1 Parc de Diane, F-78350 Jouy en Josas, France**

Tel: 33-1-39-56-5326   Fax: 33-1-39-56-5305   Contact: Jacques Rouet, Area Sales Mgr.

## HORWATH INTERNATIONAL ASSOCIATION

415 Madison Ave., New York, NY, 10017

Tel: (212) 838-5566     Fax: (212) 838-3636     www.horwath.com

*Public accountants and auditors.*

**Horwath France,  12 rue de Madrid, F-75008 Paris, France**

## HOUGHTON INTERNATIONAL INC.

PO Box 930, Madison & Van Buren Avenues, Valley Forge, PA, 19482-0930

Tel: (610) 666-4000     Fax: (610) 666-1376     www.houghtonintl.com

*Mfr. specialty chemicals, hydraulic fluids and lubricants.*

**Produtec Houghton SA,  259 rue Benoit-Mulsant, ZAC Nord Est BP 41, F-69652 Villefranche Cedex, France**

Tel: 33-4-74-65-6500

## HOWMEDICA OSTEONICS, INC.

359 Veterans Blvd., Rutherford, NJ, 07070

Tel: (201) 507-7300     Fax: (201) 935-4873     www.howmedica.com

*Mfr. of maxillofacial products (orthopedic implants).*

**Howmedica France,  Lyon, France**

Tel: 33-4-78-78-6060

## HOWMET CORPORATION

475 Steamboat Road, PO Box 1960, Greenwich, CT, 06836-1960

Tel: (203) 661-4600     Fax: (203) 661-1134     www.howmet.com

*Mfr. precision investment castings, alloys, engineering and refurbishment for jet aircraft and industrial gas turbine (IGT) engine components.*

**Burgundy Casting,  26 rue de Pologne, F-71201 Le Creusot, Cedex France**

Tel: 33-3-85-77-6600   Fax: 33-2-43-01-3413   Contact: Mike Hanrahan   Emp: 250

**Evron Casting,  Immeuble le Pereire, 6-8 Avenue Salvador Allerde, F- 93804 Epinay Sur Seine, Cedex France**

Fax: 33-1-49-40-1594    Contact: Bernard Poissonnier

**Gennevilliers Casting,  68 A 78 rue du Moulin de Cage, F-92300 Gennevilliers, France**

Tel: 33-1-40-85-3600   Contact: Terry Zuk

**Normandy Casting,  Z.A.C. des Grandes Pres., F-14160 Dives sur Mer, France**

Tel: 33-2-31-28-2930   Fax: 33-2-31-24-5866   Contact: Jean Castillon

## HQ GLOBAL WORKPLACES INC.

1155 Connecticut Ave. NW, Washington, DC, 20036

Tel: (202) 467-8500     Fax: (202) 467-8595     www.hq.com

*Provides office outsourcing, officing solutions, including internet access, telecommunications, meeting rooms, furnished offices and team rooms, state-of-the-art videoconferencing, and trained on-site administrative support teams -*

**HQ Global Workplaces,  10 Place Vendôme, Paris 75001, France**

Tel: 33-1-53-45-5454

## J.M. HUBER CORPORATION

333 Thornall Street, Edison, NJ, 08818

Tel: (732) 549-8600     Fax: (732) 549-2239     www.huber.com

*Crude oil, gas, carbon black, kaolin clay, rubber and paper pigments, timber and minerals.*

**J.M. Huber,  Clairefontaine, France**

## HUCK INTERNATIONAL INC.

3724 East Columbia Street, Tucson, AZ, 85714-3415

Tel: (520) 747-9898     Fax: (520) 750-7420     www.huck.com

*Designer and manufacturer of high-performance, proprietary fasteners and fastener installation systems.*

**Huck SA,  Clos d'Asseville, BP 4, F-95450 US, France**

## HUGHES HUBBARD & REED LLP

One Battery Park Plaza, New York, NY, 10004-1482

Tel: (212) 837-6000     Fax: (212) 422-4726     www.hugheshubbard.com

*International law firm.*

**Hughes, Hubbard & Reed LLP,  47 ave. Georges Mandel, F-75116 Paris, France**

Tel: 33-1-44-05-8000   Fax: 33-1-45-53-1504

## HUNTSMAN CORPORATION

500 Huntsman Way, Salt Lake City, UT, 84108

Tel: (801) 532-5200     Fax: (801) 536-1581     www.huntsman.com

*Mfr./sales specialty chemicals, industrial chemicals and petrochemicals.*

**Huntsman Tioxide,  Boite Postale 89, 1 rue des Garennes,  F-62102 Calais Cedex, France**

## HYATT CORPORATION

200 West Madison Street, Chicago, IL, 60606

Tel: (312) 750-1234     Fax: (312) 750-8578        www.hyatt.com

*International hotel management.*

**Hyatt Regency Paris Madeleine Hotel, 24 blvd Malesherbes, F-75008 Paris, France**

Tel: 33-1-55-27-1234   Fax: 33-1-55-27-1235

**Hyatt Regency/Charles de Gaulle Hotel, 351 Ave. du Bois de la Pie, BP 40048, Paris Nord II, F-95912 Roissy Cédex CDG Cédex, France**

Tel: 33-1-48-17-1234   Fax: 33-1-48-17-1717

## HYPERION SOLUTIONS CORPORATION

1344 Crossman Avenue, Sunnyvale, CA, 94089

Tel: (408) 744-9500     Fax: (408) 744-0400        www.hyperion.com

*Mfr. data analysis software tools.*

**Hyperion France, L'Albert 1er, 65 Avenue de Colmar, F-92507 Rueil Malmaison, France**

Tel: 33-1-55-940120

## i2 TECHNOLOGIES, INC.

11701 Luna Road, Dallas, TX, 75234

Tel: (214) 860-6106     Fax: (214) 860-6060        www.i2.com

*Mfr. business-to-business software.*

**i2 Technologies France, 90 Boulevard National 2/F, LaGarenne-Colombes F-92250, France**

## IBM CORPORATION

New Orchard Road, Armonk, NY, 10504

Tel: (914) 765-1900     Fax: (914) 765-7382        www.ibm.com

*Information products, technology and services.*

**IBM France, Centre de Relations Clientsa, BP 51, F-45802 Saint Jean de Braye, France**

Tel: 33-8-01-835426   Fax: 33-8-01-329426

## ICC INDUSTRIES INC.

460 Park Ave., New York, NY, 10022

Tel: (212) 521-1700     Fax: (212) 521-1794        www.iccchem.com

*Manufacturing and trading of chemicals, plastics and pharmaceuticals.*

**Frutarom (UK) Ltd., Acticlub Bat A. rue Des Champs, Z.I. De La Pilaerie, F-59650 Villeneuve D'Ascq, France**

Tel: 33-3-20-89-7020   Fax: 33-3-20-89-7400   Contact: Olivier Reiss

## ICN PHARMACEUTICALS, INC.

3300 Hyland Ave., Costa Mesa, CA, 92626

Tel: (714) 545-0100     Fax: (714) 641-7268        www.icnpharm.com

*Mfr./distribute pharmaceuticals.*

**ICN Pharmaceuticals, Inc., Parc Club D'Orsay, 4 rue Jean Rostand, F-91893 Orsay Cedex, France**

Tel: 33-1-60-19-37-37   Fax: 33-1-60-19-34-60

## ICORE INTERNATIONAL INC.

180 North Wolfe Road, Sunnyvale, CA, 94086

Tel: (408) 732-5400     Fax: (408) 720-8507        www.icoreintl.com

*Harness and conduit systems, battery connectors, etc.*

**Icore International France, 29 rue Franqois de Tessan, F-77330 Ozoir la Ferriere, France**

Tel: 33-1-6440-0110

## IDT CORPORATION

520 Broad Street, Newark, NJ, 07102

Tel: (973) 438-1000    Fax: (973) 438-4002    www.idt.net

*Engaged in domestic and international long distance telecommunications.*

**IDT France, 163-165 Avenue Charles de Gaulle, F-92200 Neuilly sur Seine, France**

Tel: 33-1-4715-6966   Fax: 33-1-4715-6977

## IKON OFFICE SOLUTIONS

70 Valley Stream Parkway, Malvern, PA, 19355

Tel: (610) 296-8000    Fax: (610) 408-7022    www.ikon.com

*Provider of office technology solutions.*

**Ikon - Axion Group, Villeneuve, France**

Contact: Huub Van Den Boogaard

## IKOS SYSTEMS, INC.

19050 Pruneridge Avenue, Cupertino, CA, 95014

Tel: (408) 255-4567    Fax: (408) 366-8699    www.ikos.com

*Mfr. hardware and software.*

**IKOS Systems, Inc., 6 Avenue des Andes, Les Ulis,F- 91952 Courtaboeuf Cedex France**

Tel: 33-1-60-92-36-90

## ILLINOIS TOOL WORKS (ITW)

3600 West Lake Ave., Glenview, IL, 60025-5811

Tel: (847) 724-7500    Fax: (847) 657-4268    www.itw.com

*Mfr. gears, tools, fasteners, sealants, plastic and metal components for industrial, medical, etc.*

**ITW de France, 305 Chaussee Jules Cesar, F-95250 Beauchamp, France**

**ITW de France, 20 rue Fizeau, F-75015 Paris, France**

## IMG (INTERNATIONAL MANAGEMENT GROUP)

1360 East Ninth Street, Ste. 100, Cleveland, OH, 44114

Tel: (216) 522-1200    Fax: (216) 522-1145    www.imgworld.com

*Manages athletes, sports academies and real estate facilities worldwide.*

**Golf Club France, Gold de Montpellier-Massane BP83, Baillargues F-34670, France**

Tel: 33-4-6791-2537   Fax: 33-4-6791-2530

**IMG, 54 Avenue Marceau, Paris F-75008, France**

Tel: 33-1-4431-4431   Fax: 33-1-4431-4432

**IMG Models, 16 Avenue de L'Opera, Paris F-75001, France**

Tel: 33-1-5535-1200   Fax: 33-1-5535-1201

**Racing Club de Strasbourg-Football, Stade de la Meinau, 12 rue de 'Extenwoerth, Strasbourg F-67100, France**

Tel: 33-3-8844-5500   Fax: 33-3-8844-55011

## IMO INDUSTRIES, DIV. COLFAX INC.

9211 Forest Hill Ave., Richmond, VA, 23235

Tel: (804) 560-4070    Fax: (804) 560-4076    www.imochain.com

*Mfr./support mechanical and electronic controls, chains and engineered power products.*

**IMO Industries SARL, Techniparc, 3 ave. Boole, F-91240 St. Michel sur Orge, France**

**Morse Controls SARL, 3 ave. Rene Villemer, Z.A. du Thillay, F-95500 Le Thillay, France**

## IMPCO TECHNOLOGIES, INC.

16804 Gridley Place, Cerritos, CA, 90703

Tel: (562) 860-6666    Fax: (562) 809-1240    www.impco.ws

*Mfr. fuel control processors.*

**IMPCO-BERU Technologies Sarl, 8 rue Jean Rostand, BP 364, F-69746 Genas, France**

Tel: 33-472-795-990   Fax: 33-472-795-991

## IMR GLOBAL

26750 US Highway. 19 North, Ste. 500, Clearwater, FL, 33761

Tel: (727) 797-7080    Fax: (727) 791-8152    www.imrglobal.com

*Provides application software, e-business and information technology solutions and outsourcing services to business.*

**IMR France, 20 ave de l'Opera, F-75001 Paris, France**

Tel: 33-1-52-45-6700   Fax: 33-1-42-61-0678

## INDUCTOTHERM CORPORATION

10 Indel Ave., PO Box 157, Rancocas, NJ, 08073-0157

Tel: (609) 267-9000    Fax: (609) 267-3537    www.inductotherm.com

*Mfr. induction melting furnaces, induction power supplies, charging and preheating systems, automatic pouring systems and computer control systems.*

**Inductothermie SA, 6-10 Quai de Seine, F-93200 St. Denis, France**

Tel: 33-1-48-13-1080   Contact: Jean Lovens

## INFOGRAMES, INC.

417 Fifth Avenue, New York, NY, 10016

Tel: (212) 726-6500    Fax: (212) 679-3224    www.infogrames.com

*Mfr. video games.*

**Infogrames France, Les Coteaux de Saône 13-15, rue des Draperies, 69450 Saint Cyr au Mont d'Or, France**

## INFONET SERVICES CORPORATION

2100 East Grand Ave., El Segundo, CA, 90245-1022

Tel: (310) 335-2600    Fax: (310) 335-4507    www.infonet.com

*Provider of Internet services and electronic messaging services.*

**Infonet France SA, 6 rue Jean Haures, F-92807 Puteaux Cedex, France**

Tel: 33-1-46-92-2660   Fax: 33-1-46-92-0276

## INFORMATION BUILDERS INC.

Two Penn Plaza, New York, NY, 10121-2898

Tel: (212) 736-4433    Fax: (212) 967-6406    www.ibi.com

*Develop/mfr./services computer software.*

**Information Builders France SA, 78 Blvd. de la Republique, F-92100 Boulogne-Billancourt, France**

## INFORMATION RESOURCES, INC. (IRI)

150 N. Clinton St., Chicago, IL, 60661

Tel: (312) 726-1221    Fax: (312) 726-0360    www.infores.com

*Provides bar code scanner services for retail sales organizations; processes, analyzes and sells data from the huge database created from these services.*

**IRI Secodip, 4 rue Andre-Derain BP-49, F-78240 Chambourcy, France**

Tel: 33-1-30-74-8282   Fax: 33-1-30-65-0945

## INFORMIX CORPORATION

4100 Bohannon Drive, Menlo Park, CA, 95025

Tel: (650) 926-6300     Fax: (650) 926-6593     www.informix.com

*Designs and produces database management software, connectivity interfaces and gateways, and other computer applications.*

**Informix Software SARL,  La Grande Arche, F-92044 Paris la Defense Cedex 41, France**

Tel: 33-1-46-96-3636

## INGERSOLL-RAND COMPANY

200 Chestnut Ridge Road, Woodcliff Lake, NJ, 07675

Tel: (201) 573-0123     Fax: (201) 573-3172     www.ingersoll-rand.com

*Mfr. compressors, rock drills, air tools, door hardware, ball bearings.*

**Compagnie Ingersoll-Rand,  5-7 Ave. Albert Einstein, F-78192 Trappes Cedex, France**

Tel: 33-1-30-50-6110    Fax: 33-1-30-69-0327

**Ingersoll-Dresser Pompes,  7230 Arnage rue d'Angers, Arnage, France**

**Ingersoll-Rand Equipements de Production,  111 ave. Roger Salengro, F-59450 Sin le Noble, France**

**I-R Montabert,  203 route de Grenoble BP 671, F-69805 Saint-Priest Cedex, France**

**Torrington CEMC,  34 ave. Albert 1er BP 35, F-92502 Rueil Malmaison Cedex, France**

## INGRAM MICRO INC.

PO Box 25125, 1600 E. St. Andrew Place, Santa Ana, CA, 92799

Tel: (714) 566-1000     Fax: (714) 566-7940     www.ingrammicro.com

*Engaged in wholesale distribution of microcomputer products.*

**Ingram Micro Inc.,  Carrefour de l'Europe, BP 221, F-59812 Lesquin Cedex, France**

## INKTOMI CORPORATION

4100 East Third Avenue, Foster City, CA, 94404

Tel: (650) 653-2800     Fax: (650) 653-2801     www.iktomi.com

*Mfr. software to boost speeds of computer networks.*

**Inktomi Corporation,  54-56 Avenue Hoche, F-75008 Paris, France**

Tel: 33-1-56-60-5060    Fax: 33-1-56-60-5061

## INPRISE CORPORATION

100 Enterprise Way, Scotts Valley, CA, 95066

Tel: (831) 431-1000     Fax: (831) 431-4141     www.inprise.com

*Mfr. development software.*

**Inprise France,  100 terrasse Boeldieu,  Tour Franklin, La défense 8 F-92042 Cedex, France**

Tel: 33-1-55-23-5500

## INSTINET

875 Third Ave., New York, NY, 10022

Tel: (212) 310-9500     Fax: (212) 832-5183     www.instinet.com

*Online investment brokerage.*

**Instinet,  Paris, France**

## INSTRON CORPORATION

100 Royal Street, Canton, MA, 02021-1089

Tel: (781) 575-5000     Fax: (781) 575-5751     www.instron.com

*Mfr. material testing instruments.*

**Instron SA,  11 Parc Club Ariane, F-78284 Guyancourt Cedex, France**

Tel: 33-1-3057-2353

## INSUL-8 CORPORATION

10102 F Street, Omaha, NE, 68127

Tel: (402) 339-9300     Fax: (402) 339-9627     www.insul-8.com

*Mfr. mobile electrification products; conductor bar and festoon equipment.*

**Delachaux S.A., Paris, France**

**Railtech, Div. Delachaux S.A., ZI du Bas Pré, F-59590 Raismes, France**

## INTEGRATED DEVICE TECHNOLOGY, INC.

2975 Stender Way, Santa Clara, CA, 95054

Tel: (408) 727-6116     Fax: (408) 492-8674     www.idt.com

*Mfr. high-performance semiconductors and modules.*

**Integrated Device Technology, Inc., 18 rue Saarinen, Bat Dublin Silic 215, Rungis Cedex F-94518, France**

Tel: 33-1-41-80-85-00     Fax: 33-1-41-80-85-10

## INTEL CORPORATION

Robert Noyce Bldg., 2200 Mission College Blvd., Santa Clara, CA, 95052-8119

Tel: (408) 765-8080     Fax: (408) 765-1739     www.intel.com

*Mfr. semiconductor, microprocessor and micro-communications components and systems.*

**Intel Semiconductor (France) S.A., Paris, France**

Tel: 33-1-45-71-7171

## INTER PARFUMS, INC.

551 Fifth Avenue, New York, NY, 10176

Tel: (212) 983-2640     Fax: (212) 983-4197     www.jeanphilippe.com

*Engaged in the marketing and sales of brand name perfumes.*

**Inter Parfums, S.A., 4 Rond Point, Des Champs-Elysees, F-75008 Paris, France**

## INTER-CONTINENTAL HOTELS

3 Ravina Drive, Suite 2900, Atlanta, GA, 30346-2149

Tel: (770) 604-2000     Fax: (770) 604-5403     www.interconti.com

*Worldwide hotel and resort accommodations.*

**Carlton Inter-Continental Cannes, 58 La Croisette, BP 155, F-06406 Cannes Cedex, France**
Tel: 33-493-064006

**Inter-Continental Hotels, 5 Place de l'Opera, F-75009 Paris, France**
Tel: 33-1-42-68-1380     Fax: 33-1-42-68-1531

## INTERGRAPH CORPORATION

One Madison Industrial Park, Huntsville, AL, 35894-0001

Tel: (256) 730-2000     Fax: (256) 730-7898     www.intergraph.com

*Develop/mfr. interactive computer graphic systems.*

**Intergraph (France) S.A., 95-101 rue Des Solets - Silic 578, F-94653 Rungis Cedex, France**
Tel: 33-1-45-6-03000     Fax: 33-1-45-60-4885

**Intergraph (France) S.A. - Bureau de Cherbourg, Immeuble Cherbourg Helios, 120 rue Roger Glinel B.P. 19, F-50460 Querqueville, France**
Tel: 33-233-080120     Fax: 33-233-080082

**Intergraph Nantes, Centre D'Affaires Nantais, 5 blvd Vincent Gauche, F-36204 Nantes Cedex 2, France**
Tel: 33-240-417335     Fax: 33-240-353091

**Intergraph Public Safety (France) S.A., 14 Parc Club Du Golf, F-13856 Aix-En-Provence Cedex 3, France**
Tel: 33-44-2163587     Fax: 33-44-2163509

## INTERMAGNETICS GENERAL CORPORATION

450 Old Niskayuna Road, PO Box 461, Latham, NY, 12110-0461

Tel: (518) 782-1122     Fax: (518) 783-2601     www.igc.com

*Design/mfr. superconductive magnets, magnetic systems and conductors, cryogenic products, refrigerants.*

**Alsthom-Intermagnetics SA,  3 ave. de Trois Chenes, F-90018 Belfort Cedex, France**

## INTERMEC TECHNOLOGIES CORPORATION

6001 36th Ave. West, PO Box 4280, Everett, WA, 98203-9280

Tel: (425) 348-2600     Fax: (425) 355-9551     www.intermec.com

*Mfr./distributor automated data collection systems.*

**Intermec Technologies SA,  Immeuble "Le Newton", 23 Ave. de l'Europe, F-78402 Chatau, France**

Tel: 33-1-30-15-2535    Fax: 33-1-34-80-1433

## INTERNATIONAL FLAVORS & FRAGRANCES INC.

521 West 57th Street, New York, NY, 10019-2960

Tel: (212) 765-5500     Fax: (212) 708-7132     www.iff.com

*Design/mfr. flavors, fragrances and aroma chemicals.*

**International Flavors & Fragrances,  47 rue Victor Hugo, F-92270 Bois-Colombes, France**

Tel: 33-1-4649-6060   Fax: 33-1-4781-8573

**International Flavors & Fragrances,  Boulevard de Beauregard - B.P.5, F-21601 Longvic-Dijon, France**

Tel: 33-3-8073-7878   Fax: 33-3-8073-7899

## INTERNATIONAL PAPER COMPANY

2 Manhattanville Road, Purchase, NY, 10577

Tel: (914) 397-1500     Fax: (914) 397-1596     www.ipaper.com

*Mfr./distributor container board, paper and wood products.*

**Aussedat Rey SA,  Parc Ariane, 5/7 boulevard des Chenes,F-78284 Guyancourt Cedex, France**

Tel: 33-1-40-83-4478

**Comptoir des Bois de Brive,  Chemin du Bois-de-Tulle, La Pigeonnie, F-19100 Brive, France**

**Copadip,  115 ave. du President Wilson, F-93212 La Plaine St. Denis Cedex, France**

**Corimex SA,  1 rue du Petit Clamart, BP 5, F-78141 Velizy Villacoublay, France**

**Europapier SA,  Route de Piscop, BP 35, F-95350 St. Brice sous Foret, France**

**Horsell Industries Graphiques,  Peripole 208, F-94127 Fontenay sous Bois, France**

**Ilford-Anitec SA,  BP 336, Chemin de la Fouillouse, F-69802 Saint-Priest, France**

**International Container/Bergvik SARL,  25 rue Michel Salles, F-92210 St. Cloud, France**

Tel: 33-1-4771-1218

**International Paper Cellulose,  36 ave. Hoche, F-75008 Paris, France**

**Iridium,  1 rue du Petit Clamart, F-78141 Velizy Villacoublay, France**

**Papeteries de France,  8a 24 rue du Cheval Blanc, BP 198, F-93501 Pantin Cedex, France**

**Papeteries de Lancey,  1 rue du Petit Clamart, F-78141 Velizy Villacoublay, France**

**Papeteries J. Rezard,  21-23 blvd de la Muette, F-95140 Garges-les-Gonesse, France**

**Polyrey,  1 rue du Petit Clamart, BP 79, F-78143 Velizy Villacoublay, France**

**Promafor,  Chemin du Bois-de-Tulle, La Pigeonnie, F-19100 Brive, France**

**Societe de Reboisement,  Chemin du Bois-de-Tulle, F-19100 La Pigeonnie Brive, France**

**Societe Immo des Papeteries de France,  1 rue du Petit Clamart, BP 5, Velizy Villacoublay, France**

**Societe Moderne d'Emballage,  25 rue Michel Salles, F-92210 St. Cloud, France**

**Societe Normande de Carton Ondule,  BP 3, F-61400 St. Langis les Montagne, France**

**Sofar,  25 rue Colonel Dumont, BP 481, F-38016 Grenoble Cedex, France**

## INTERNATIONAL RECTIFIER CORPORATION

233 Kansas Street, El Segundo, CA, 90245

Tel: (310) 322-3331    Fax: (310) 322-3332    www.irf.com

*Mfr. power semiconductor components.*

**International Rectifier - France, 32 rue des Processions, BP 61, F-91241 St. Michel sur Orge Cedex, France**

Tel: 33-16-449-5959   Fax: 33-16-449-5969

## INTERNATIONAL SPECIALTY PRODUCTS, INC.

1361 Alps Rd., Wayne, NJ, 07470

Tel: (877) 389-3083    Fax: (973) 628-4117    www.ispcorp.com

*Mfr. specialty chemical products.*

**ISP (France) SA, ZAC Paris Nord II, BP 50007, F-95945 Roissy CDG Cédex, France**

Tel: 33-1-49-9058   Fax: 33-1-49-9058

## INTERVOICE INC.

17811 Waterview Pkwy., Dallas, TX, 75206

Tel: (972) 454-8000    Fax: (972) 454-8707    www.intervoice.com

*Mfr. voice automation systems and provides interactive information solutions.*

**InterVoice-Brite Limited, Tour CIT, 3 rue de l'Arrivée, F-75749 Paris, Cedex 15 France**

## INTRUSION.COM, INC.

1101 East Arapaho Road, Richardson, TX, 75081

Tel: (972) 234-6400    Fax: (972) 234-1467    www.intrusion.com

*Mfr. security software.*

**Intrusion.Com, SARL, 115 Avenue De Paris, 94160 Saint-Mande, France**

## INVACARE CORPORATION

One Invacare Way, Elyria, OH, 44036

Tel: (440) 329-6000    Fax: (440) 366-6568    www.invacare.com

*Mfr. home medical equipment, wheelchairs, respiratory care products, home care aids.*

**Invacare Poirier SA, Les Roches, F-37230 Fondettes, France**

Tel: 33-2-47-62-6491   Fax: 33-2-47-62-6488

## IOMEGA CORPORATION

1821 West 4000 South, Roy, UT, 84067

Tel: (801) 778-4494    Fax: (801) 778-3450    www.iomega.com

*Mfr. data storage products.*

**Iomega, 70 ave. du General de Gaulle, F-94022 Creteil Cedex, France**

## IONICS INC.

65 Grove Street, Watertown, MA, 02172

Tel: (617) 926-2500    Fax: (617) 926-4304    www.ionics.com

*Mfr. desalination equipment.*

**Eau et Industrie, 121 ave. du 8 Mai 1945, F-94170 Le Perreux, France**

**Ionics Europe, Paris, France**

## IRRIDELCO INTERNATIONAL CORPORATION

440 Sylvan Ave., Englewood Cliffs, NJ, 07632

Tel: (201) 569-3030    Fax: (201) 569-9237    www.irridelco.com

*Mfr./distributor of the most comprehensive lines of mechanical and micro irrigation; pumps and irrigation systems.*

**IDC France, Chemin d'Antonelle, F-13090 Aix En Provence, France**

Tel: 33-442-92-1247   Fax: 33-442-92-1678   Contact: Jerome Lamy

## ITT INDUSTRIES, INC.

4 West Red Oak Lane, White Plains, NY, 10604

Tel: (914) 641-2000     Fax: (914) 696-2950     www.ittind.com

*Mfr. pumps, systems and services to move and control water/fluids and produces connectors, switches, keypads and cabling used in computing, telecommunications, aerospace and industrial applications, as well as network services.*

**Cannon/Switch Products, 2 Avenue Des Sablons Bouillants, F-77109 Meaux Cedex, France**

Tel: 33-1-6024-515

**KONI France, B.P. no. 9, 06271 Villeneuve-Loubet Cedex France**

Tel: 33-4-9320-9070

## ITT-GOULDS PUMPS INC.

240 Fall Street, Seneca Falls, NY, 13148

Tel: (315) 568-2811     Fax: (315) 568-2418     www.gouldspumps.com

*Mfr. industrial and water systems pumps.*

**ITT Richter France SA, 22/24 rue Lavoisier, Nanterre F-920000, France**

Tel: 33-1-41-3-6400   Fax: 33-1-41-3-6401

## ITW DEVCON PLEXUS

30 Endicott Street, Danvers, MA, 01923

Tel: (978) 777-1100     Fax: (978) 774-0516     www.devcon-equip.com

*Mfr. filled epoxies, urethanes, adhesives and metal treatment products.*

**Devcon France SARL, 22 rue Paul Langevin, F-75002 Herblay, France**

## ITW RANSBURG FINISHING SYSTEMS

320 Phillips Ave., Toledo, OH, 43612

Tel: (419) 470-2000     Fax: (419) 470-2112     www.itwransburg.com

*Mfr. liquid electrostatic paint application equipment.*

**ITW Surfaces & Finitions, 163 a 171 ave. des Aureats, BP 1453, F-26014 Valence, France**

## J. WALTER THOMPSON COMPANY

466 Lexington Ave., New York, NY, 10017

Tel: (212) 210-7000     Fax: (212) 210-6944     www.jwt.com

*International advertising and marketing services.*

**J. Walter Thompson Co., Paris, France**

## JACOBS ENGINEERING GROUP INC.

1111 S. Arroyo Parkway, Pasadena, CA, 91105

Tel: (626) 578-3500     Fax: (626) 578-6916     www.jacobs.com

*Engineering, design and consulting; construction and construction management; process plant maintenance.*

**3S, Le Charlemayne, 132 Cours Charlemayne, F-69002 Lyon, Cedex, France**

Tel: 33-4-72-77-1050   Fax: 33-4-72-77-1051   Contact: Cyrille Bernal, Mgr.

**3S/Serete, Le Stratége, BP 2746, F-31312 Labége Cedex, Labége, France**

Tel: 33-5-61-29-9238   Fax: 33-4-61-39-9240

**3S/Serete, 26 rue du Chateau Des Rentiers, F-75013, Paris, France**

Tel: 33-1-45-70-50-87   Fax: 33-1-45-86-09-02   Contact: Jean Levy, Chmn. & CEO

**3S/Serete, La Triade, 167 Ave. de la Somme, BP 368, F-33694 Merignac Cedex, Bordeaux, France**

Tel: 33-5-56-47-7923   Fax: 33-5-56-47-7927   Contact: Jacques Coutou, Mgr.

**3S/Serete, Z.A. Les Andenges, F-25420 Bart, Sochoux, France**

Tel: 33-3-81-90-41-72   Fax: 33-3-81-90-41-01   Contact: Bruno Leprince, Mgr.   Emp: 5

**Prosys, 20 rue de Chateau Des Rentiers, F-75013, Paris, France**

Tel: 33-1-45-70-57-12   Fax: 33-1-45-83-65-13   Contact: Jean Levy, Chmn. & CEO

**Serete Constructions, 86 rue Regnault, F-75640 Paris Cedex 13, France**

Tel: 33-1-45-70-5000   Fax: 33-1-45-70-5299   Contact: Pierre Larapldic, Chmn. & CEO

Serete Est,  23 Ollée Glück, BP 2331, F-68069 Hulhouse Cedex, France

Tel: 33-3-89-32-01-21   Fax: 33-3-89-42-30-48   Contact: Jacques Clerc, Mgr.

Serete Gestion & Industries,  18 rue Regnault, F-75640 Paris Cedex 13, France

Tel: 33-1-45-70-5000   Fax: 33-1-45-70-5024   Contact: Sylvie Biscorra, Mgr.

Serete Midi-Pryénees,  Le Stratége, BP 2746, F-31312 Labége Cedex, France

Tel: 33-5-61-39-0506   Fax: 33-4-61-39-2575

Serete Sud-Est,  Le Charlemayne, 140 Cours Charlemayne, F-69286 Lyon Cedex, France

Tel: 33-4-72-77-1050   Fax: 33-4-72-77-1051   Contact: Bernard Nicol, Mgr.

Serete Sud-Ouest,  La Triade, 167 Ave. de la Somme, BP 368, F-33694 Merignac Cedex, Bordeaux, France

Tel: 33-5-56-13-1616   Fax: 33-5-56-34-1064   Contact: Jean-Claude Berthelst, Mgr.   Emp: 20

## JDA SOFTWARE GROUP, INC.

14400 N. 87th St., Scottsdale, AZ, 85260-3649

Tel: (480) 308-3000      Fax: (480) 308-3001      www.jda.com

*Developer of information management software for retail, merchandising, distribution and store management.*

JDA Software SA,  70 Boulevard de Courcelles, F-75017 Paris, France

Tel: 33-1-156-792-700   Fax: 33-1-47-645-050

## JOHNSON & JOHNSON

One Johnson & Johnson Plaza, New Brunswick, NJ, 08933

Tel: (732) 524-0400      Fax: (732) 214-0334      www.jnj.com

*Mfr./distributor/R&D pharmaceutical, health care and cosmetic products.*

DePuy France,  Villeurbanne, France

Ethicon SA/Ethicon Endo-Surgery SA,  Issy-Les-Moulineaux, France

Janssen-Cilag SA,  Issy-Les-Moulineaux, France

Johnson & Johnson Medical SARL,  Issy-Les-Moulineaux, France

Johnson & Johnson SA,  Issy-Les-Moulineaux, France

Johnson & Johnson Sante SA,  Paris, France

LifeScan SA,  Issy-Les-Moulineaux, France

Neutrogena France,  Issy-Les-Moulineaux, France

Ortho-Clinical Diagnostics SA,  Issy-Les-Moulineaux, France

RoC SA,  Issy-Les-Moulineaux, France

## S C JOHNSON & SON INC.

1525 Howe St., Racine, WI, 53403

Tel: (414) 260-2000      Fax: (414) 260-2133      www.scjohnsonwax.com

*Home, auto, commercial and personal care products and specialty chemicals.*

La Johnson Francaise S.A.,  B.P. 606, F-95004 Cergy Paris, France

## JOHNSON CONTROLS INC.

5757 N. Green Bay Ave., PO Box 591, Milwaukee, WI, 53201-0591

Tel: (414) 228-1200      Fax: (414) 228-2077      www.johnsoncontrols.com

*Mfr. facility management and control systems and auto seating.*

Johnson Control France SARL,  357 rue d'Estiennes d'Orves, F-92700 Colombes, France

Tel: 33-1-46-13-1600   Fax: 33-1-42-42- 4261   Contact: Bruno Nicholas

## THE JOHNSON CORPORATION

805 Wood Street, Three Rivers, MI, 49093

Tel: (616) 278-1715      Fax: (616) 273-2230      www.joco.com

*Mfr. rotary joints and siphon systems.*

Johnson France,  Sartrouville, France

Tel: 33-1-61043010

## JOHNSON OUTDOORS, INC.

1326 Willow Road, Sturtevant, WI, 53177

Tel: (414) 884-1500     Fax: (414) 884-1600     www.jwa.com

*Mfr. diving, fishing, boating and camping sports equipment.*

**Mitchell Sports SA, 396 rue de la Precision, F-74970 Marignier, France**

Tel: 33-4-50-967716   Fax: 33-4-50-340521

**Scubapro France S.A., Nova Antipolis, Les Terriers Nord, 175 Allee Belle Vue, F-06600 Antibes, France**

Tel: 33-4-92-913-030   Fax: 33-4-92-913-031

## JONES LANG LASALLE

101 East 52nd Street, New York, NY, 10022

Tel: (212) 688-8181     Fax: (212) 308-5199     www.jlw.com

*International marketing consultants, leasing agents and property management advisors.*

**Jones Lang Wootton, France**

## JONES, DAY, REAVIS & POGUE

North Point, 901 Lakeside Ave., Cleveland, OH, 44114

Tel: (216) 586-3939     Fax: (216) 579-0212     www.jonesday.com

*International law firm.*

**Jones, Day, Reavis & Pogue, 120 rue du Faubourg Saint-Honore, F-75008 Cedex Paris, France**

Tel: 33-1-44-71-3939   Fax: 33-1-49-24-0471   Contact: Wesley R. Johnson, Jr., Ptnr.   Emp: 59

## JUKI UNION SPECIAL CORPORATION

5 Haul Road, Wayne, NJ, 07470

Tel: (973) 633-7200     Fax: (973) 633-9629     www.unionspecial.com

*Mfr. sewing machines.*

**Union Special France SA, 33 rue Jean Jaures BP 455, F-59814 Lesquin Cedex, France**

Tel: 33-3-20-86-2003   Fax: 33-3-20-86-2118   Contact: E. Salu, Mng.

## KAPPLER PROTECTIVE APPAREL & FABRICS

PO Box 218, 70 Grimes Drive, Guntersville, AL, 35976

Tel: (205) 505-4000     Fax: (205) 505-4004     www.kappler.com

*Mfr. of protective apparel and fabrics.*

**Kappler France, rue de la Chanterie BP 03, F-49180 St. Barthelemy-d'Anjou Cedex, France**

Tel: 33-2-41-93-44-8   Fax: 33-2-41-37-1605   Contact: Serge Denis, Mng. Dir.   Emp: 10

## KATY INDUSTRIES INC.

6300 South Syracuse Way, Ste. 300, Englewood, CO, 80111

Tel: (303) 290-9300     Fax: (303) 290-9344     www.katyindustries.com

*Mfr. electronic and maintenance equipment for industrial and consumer markets.*

**Sofema, 206 rue de Fontenay, F-94300 Vincennes, France**

**Sofema SARL, 4 rue du Marechal Joffre, F-67240 Bischwiller, France**

## KAUFMAN & BROAD HOME CORPORATION

10990 Wilshire Blvd., Los Angeles, CA, 90024

Tel: (310) 231-4000     Fax: (310) 231-4222     www.kaufmanandbroad.com

*Housing construction and financing.*

**Kaufman & Broad France, 44 rue de Washington, F-75408 Paris, France**

Tel: 33-1-45-61-7000   Contact: Guy Nafilyan

## KAWNEER COMPANY, INC.

555 Guthridge Court, Norcross, GA, 30092

Tel: (770) 449-5555     Fax: (770) 734-1570     www.kawneer.com

*Mfr. arch aluminum products for commercial construction.*

**Kawneer France SA, rue de la Garenne, Zone Industrielle, BP 24, F-34740 Vendargues, France**

## A.T. KEARNEY INC.

222 West Adams Street, Chicago, IL, 60606

Tel: (312) 648-0111     Fax: (312) 223-6200     www.atkearney.com

*Management consultants and executive search.*

**A. T. Kearney Executive Search, 48 rue Jacques Dulud, F-92200 Neuilly-sur-Seine, France**
Tel: 33-141-92-1092

**A. T. Kearney Management Consultants S.A.S., 8-10 rue Victor Noir, F-92521 Neuilly-sur-Seine Cedex, France**
Tel: 33-1-41-92-1111

## KEITHLEY INSTRUMENTS INC.

28775 Aurora Road, Cleveland, OH, 44139

Tel: (440) 248-0400     Fax: (440) 248-6168     www.keithley.com

*Mfr. electronic test/measure instruments, PC-based data acquisition hardware/software.*

**Keithley Instruments SARL, 3 allee de Garays, BP 60, F-91122 Palaiseau Cedex, France**

## KELLOGG BROWN & ROOT INC.

PO Box 3, Houston, TX, 77001

Tel: (713) 676-3011     Fax: (713) 676-8695     www.halliburton.com

*Engaged in technology-based engineering and construction.*

**Kellogg Brown & Root, La Defense 6, Paris Cedex 92973, France**

## KELLOGG COMPANY

One Kellogg Square, PO Box 3599, Battle Creek, MI, 49016-3599

Tel: (616) 961-2000     Fax: (616) 961-2871     www.kelloggs.com

*Mfr. ready-to-eat cereals and convenience foods.*

**Kellogg Products, Attn: French Office, One Kellogg Square, PO Box 3599, Battle Creek MI 49016-3599**

## KELLY SERVICES, INC.

999 W. Big Beaver Road, Troy, MI, 48084

Tel: (248) 362-4444     Fax: (248) 244-4154     www.kellyservices.com

*Temporary help placement.*

**Societe Services Kelly (HQ), 73 blvd. Haussmann, F-75008 Paris, France**
Tel: 33-1-44-94-6-64   Fax: 33-1-44-94-6465

## THE KENDALL COMPANY (TYCO HEALTHCARE)

15 Hampshire Street, Mansfield, MA, 02048

Tel: (508) 261-8000     Fax: (508) 261-8542     www.kendalhq,com

*Mfr. medical disposable products, home health care products and specialty adhesive products.*

**Kendall France SA, 15 rue Marcelin Berthelot, F-92167 Antony Cedex, France**
Tel: 33-1-46-74-7980   Fax: 33-1-423-70920

## KENNAMETAL INC.

State Rte. 981, Latrobe, PA, 15650

Tel: (724) 539-5000     Fax: (724) 539-4710     www.kennametal.com

*Tools, hard carbide and tungsten alloys for metalworking industry.*

**Kennametal Hertel France SA, POBox 201, F-91007 Evry Cedex, France**
Tel: 33-1-69-77-8383   Fax: 33-1-69-77-8390

## KEPNER-TREGOE INC.

PO Box 704, Princeton, NJ, 08542-0740

Tel: (609) 921-2806    Fax: (609) 497-0130    www.kepner-tregoe.com

*Management consulting; specializing in strategy formulation, problem solving, decision making, project management, and cost reduction.*

**Kepner-Tregoe France SARL,  91 rue du Faubourg St. Honore, F-75370 Paris Cedex 8, France**

Tel: 33-1-4471-3605   Fax: 33-1-4471-3572

## KIMBERLY-CLARK CORPORATION

351 Phelps Drive, Irving, TX, 75038

Tel: (972) 281-1200    Fax: (972) 281-1435    www.kimberly-clark.com

*Mfr./sales/distribution of consumer tissue, household and personal care products.*

**Kimberly-Clark Industries SA,  Orleans, France**

**LTR Industries SA,  Villey-Saint-Etienne, France**

**Paperterie de Mauduit SA,  Kerisole Quimperle, France**

**Papeterie de Malaucene SA,  F-84340 Malaucene, France**

**Sopalin,  Bureaux de la Colline, F-92213 Saint Cloud, France**

## LESTER B. KNIGHT & ASSOCIATES INC.

549 West Randolph Street, Chicago, IL, 60661

Tel: (312) 346-2300    Fax: (312) 648-1085

*Architecture, engineering, planning, operations and management consulting.*

**Knight Wendling SARL,  15 ave. Victor-Hugo, F-75116 Paris, France**

## KNOLL, INC.

1235 Water Street, East Greenville, PA, 18041

Tel: (215) 679-7991    Fax: (215) 679-3904    www.knoll.com

*Mfr. and sale of office furnishings.*

**Knoll International,  268 Blvd. Saint Germain, F-75007 Paris, France**

## KOCH INDUSTRIES INC.

4111 East 37th Street North, Wichita, KS, 67220-3203

Tel: (316) 828-5500    Fax: (316) 828-5950    www.kochind.com

*Oil, financial services, agriculture and Purina Mills animal feed.*

**Koch International S.A.R.L., John Zink Div.,  3 rue de La Haye, Roissy Charles de Gaulle, 95731 France**

Tel: 33-1-4816-4871   Fax: 33-1-4816-4857

## KOCH-GLITSCH, INC.

PO Box 8127, Wichita, KS, 67208

Tel: (316) 828-5110    Fax: (316) 828-5950    www.koch-ind.com

*Mfr./services mass transfer/chemicals separation equipment, process engineering.*

**Koch-Glitsch France,  Chemin des Moines, BP 76, F-13632 Arles Cedex, France**

Tel: 33-4-90-18-4800   Fax: 33-4-90-18-4807   Contact: Ian Shepherd

## THE KOHLER COMPANY

444 Highland Drive, Kohler, WI, 53044

Tel: (920) 457-4441    Fax: (920) 459-1274    www.kohlerco.com

*Plumbing products, ceramic tile and stone, cabinetry, furniture, engines, generators, switch gear and hospitality.*

**Dupont Sanitaire Chauffage, S.A.,  France**

**Holdiam S.A.,  Paris, France**

**Jacob Delafon/Neomediam,  Paris, France**

## KOLLMORGEN CORPORATION

1601 Trapelo Road, Waltham, MA, 02154

Tel: (781) 890-5655 Fax: (781) 890-7150 www.kollmorgen.com

*Mfr. high-performance electronic motion-control systems and design and supply advanced submarine periscopes, weapons directors, and military optics.*

**SA Artus, Chemin du Champ des Martyrs, BP 9, F-49240 Avrille, France**

## KORN/FERRY INTERNATIONAL

1800 Century Park East, Los Angeles, CA, 90067

Tel: (310) 843-4100 Fax: (310) 553-6452 www.kornferry.com

*Executive search; management consulting.*

**Korn/Ferry International SA, 166 rue du Faubourg Saint-Honore, F-75008 Paris, France**

Tel: 33-1-45-61-6660 Fax: 33-1-45-63-5667

## KPMG INTERNATIONAL LLP

345 Park Avenue, New York, NY, 10022

Tel: (201) 307-7000 Fax: (201) 930-8617 www.kpmg.com

*Accounting and audit, tax and management consulting services.*

**Fidal Paris et International, 47 rue de Villiers, F-92200 Neuilly sur Seine, France**

Tel: 33-1-46-39-40 Fax: 33-1-47-59-0078 Contact: Jean-Francis Blouet, Ptnr.

**Fiduciaire de France, Les Hauts de Villiers, 2 bis, rue de Villiers, F-92309 Paris, France**

**Fiduciaire Juridique et Fiscale de France, Le Montesquicu, Av. du Pr., F-33704 Bordeaux, France**

**KPMG Audit, 47 rue de Villiers, F-92200 Neuilly sur Seine, France**

Tel: 33-1-46-39-4444 Fax: 33-1-47-58-7138 Contact: Jean Delsol, Ptnr.

**KPMG Audit Equipe Interregionale d'Audit, 574 rue de Chantabord, F-73000 Lyon, France**

**KPMG Corporate Finance, Tour Framatome, 1 Place de la Coupole, F-92084 Paris/La Défense, France**

Tel: 33-1-47-96-6760 Fax: 33-1-47-96-6750 Contact: Dominique Lecendreux, Ptnr.

**KPMG Peat Marwick, Tour Framatome, 1 Place de la Coupole, F-92084 Paris/La Défense, France**

Tel: 33-1-47-93-2000 Fax: 33-1-47-96-2058 Contact: Patrick Laredo, Ptnr.

**KPMG Peat Marwick, 53 Ave. Montaigne, F-75008 Paris, France**

Tel: 33-1-45-63-1540 Fax: 33-1-45-61-0925 Contact: Curtis H. Behrent, Ptnr.

## THE KROLL-O'GARA COMPANY

9113 Le Saint Drive, Fairfield, OH, 45014

Tel: (513) 874-2112 Fax: (513) 874-2558 www.kroll-ogara.com

*Security and consulting services and vehicles.*

**Kroll Associates, 153 rue de Courcelles, F-75017 Paris, France**

Tel: 33-1-42-67-3500 Fax: 33-1-42-67-7100

**Labbe, S.A., Z.I. rue d'Armor B.P. 414, F-22404 Lamballe Cedex, France**

Tel: 33-2-96-50-1280 Fax: 33-2-96-34-7265 Contact: Jean-Philippe Tible

## KULICKE & SOFFA INDUSTRIES INC.

2101 Blair Mill Road, Willow Grove, PA, 19090

Tel: (215) 784-6000 Fax: (215) 659-7588 www.kns.com

*Semiconductor assembly systems and services.*

**Caleo, 421 rue Helene Boucher; F-78532 Buc Cedex, France**

## LA ROCHE INDUSTRIES INC.

1100 Johnson Ferry Road, NE, Atlanta, GA, 30342

Tel: (404) 851-0300 Fax: (404) 851-0421 www.larocheind.com

*Produce and distribute organic and inorganic chemicals.*

**Chlor Alp Plant/LaRoche, Pont-de-Claix, France**

Emp: 225

## LANDOR ASSOCIATES

Klamath House, 1001 Front Street, San Francisco, CA, 94111-1424

Tel: (415) 955-1400     Fax: (415) 365-3190     www.landor.com

*International marketing consulting firm, focused on developing and maintaining brand identity.*

**Landor Associates, 44 rue des Petites Ecuries, F-75010 Paris, France**

Tel: 33-1-53-34-3100   Fax: 33-1-53-34-3101   Contact: Jean-Louis Dumeu, Mng. Dir.

## LANIER WORLDWIDE, INC.

2300 Parklake Drive, N.E., Atlanta, GA, 30345

Tel: (770) 496-9500     Fax: (770) 938-1020     www.lanier.com

*Specialize in digital copiers and multi-functional systems.*

**Lanier France S.A.,  Bâtiment le Cérame, 47 ave des Genottes, F-95802 Cergy Pontoise, France**

Tel: 33-1-47-67-7676   Fax: 33-1-47-67-7600

## LAWSON MARDON WHEATON, INC.

1101 Wheaton Ave., Millville, NJ, 08332

Tel: (856) 825-1400     Fax: (856) 825-0146     www.algroupwheaton.com

*Engaged in pharmaceutical and cosmetic packaging, glass and plastic containers.*

**Boxal,  Route de Romans, F-38270 Beaurepaire, France**

Contact: Marc Bettinger

**Charmettes,  10 Avenue Raspail, B.P. 372, F-94103 Saint-Maur Cedex, France**

Tel: 33-1-45-11-4000   Contact: Jean-Paul Soulier

**Wheaton France,  6-10 rue Troyon, 92316 Sèvres Cedex, France**

Tel: 33-1-46-23-61-33   Contact: Stéphanie Scalabre

## LEACH INTERNATIONAL, INC.

6900 Orangethorp Ave., Buena Park, CA, 90622-5032

Tel: (714) 739-0770     Fax: (714) 739-1713     www.leachintl.com

*Mfr. and design electrical switching and control devices for the aerospace and rail industries.*

**Leach International S.A.,  2 rue Goethe, F-57430 Sarralbe, France**

Tel: 33-3-87-97-9897

## LEARNING TREE INTERNATIONAL, INC.

6053 West Century Blvd., Los Angeles, CA, 90045-0028

Tel: (310) 417-9700     Fax: (310) 417-8684     www.learningtree.com

*Information technology training services.*

**Learning Tree International SA (France),  Espace Clichy, 68, rue Villenueve, F-92110 Clichy Cedex, France**

Tel: 33-1-49-68-5308   Fax: 33-1-49-68-5374   Contact: Yann Houdent, Gen. Mgr.   Emp: 35

## LEARONAL INC.

272 Buffalo Ave., Freeport, NY, 11520

Tel: (516) 868-8800     Fax: (516) 868-8824     www.learonal.com

*Specialty chemicals for the printed circuit board, semiconductor, connector and metal finishing industries.*

**LeaRonal France,  3 rue Sigmund Freud, BP 55, F-69511 Vaulx-en-Velin Lyon, France**

Tel: 33-4-78-80-0832   Fax: 33-4-72-04-3778   Contact: Alain Menard, Mng. Dir.

## G. LEBLANC CORPORATION

7001 Leblanc Blvd., PO Box 1415, Kenosha, WI, 53141-1415

Tel: (414) 658-1644     Fax: (414) 658-2824     www.gleblanc.com

*Mfr./sale/services musical wind instruments.*

**Leblanc France SA,  13 rue Georges-LeBlanc, BP 42, F-27750 La Couture Boussey, France**

## LeBOEUF, LAMB, GREENE & MacRAE LLP

125 West 55th Street, 12th Fl., New York, NY, 10019

Tel: (212) 424-8000      Fax: (212) 424-8500      www.llgm.com

*International law firm.*

**LeBoeuf, Lamb, Greene & MacRae LLP, 130 rue du Faubourg, F-75008 Saint-Honore Paris, France**

Tel: 33-1-5393-7700   Fax: 33-1-4256-0806

## LECROY CORPORATION

700 Chestnut Ridge Road, Chestnut Ridge, NY, 10977

Tel: (845) 425-2000      Fax: (845) 425-8967      www.lecroy.com

*Mfr. signal analyzers and electronic measurement systems.*

**LeCroy S.A., 1 Avenue de l'Atlantique, LP 903 - Les Ulis, F-91976 Couraboeuf, France**

Tel: 33-1-69-188320

## LEGG MASON, INC.

100 Light St., Baltimore, MD, 21202

Tel: (410) 539-0000      Fax: (410) 539-4175      www.leggmason.com

*Financial services; securities brokerage and trading, investment management, institutional and individual clients, investment and commercial mortgage banking.*

**Legg Mason Wood Walker, Paris, France**

## LEHMAN BROTHERS HOLDINGS INC.

Three World Financial Center, New York, NY, 10285

Tel: (212) 526-7000      Fax: (212) 526-3738      www.lehman.com

*Financial services, securities and merchant banking services.*

**Lehman Brothers, 21 rue Balzac, F-75008 Paris, France**

Tel: 33-1-5389-3000

## LEVI STRAUSS & COMPANY

1155 Battery St., San Francisco, CA, 94111-1230

Tel: (415) 544-6000      Fax: (415) 501-3939      www.levistrauss.com

*Mfr./distributor casual wearing apparel.*

**Levi Strauss Continental, 6 ave. du Pacifique, BP115 Z.A., F-91944 Courtaboeuf Les Ulis, France**

Tel: 33-1-69-86-8998   Fax: 33-1-64-46-5478

## LEXMARK INTERNATIONAL

1 Lexmark Centre Dr., Lexington, KY, 40550

Tel: (606) 232-2000      Fax: (606) 232-1886      www.lexmark.com

*Develop, manufacture, supply of printing solutions and products, including laser, inkjet, and dot matrix printers.*

**Lexmark International S.N.C., Immeuble Newton - La Défense 5, 9 place des Vosges, F-92924 Paris Cedex France**

Tel: 33-1-46-67-4000

## LIFE TECHNOLOGIES INC.

9800 Medical Center Drive, Rockville, MD, 20850

Tel: (301) 840-8000      Fax: (301) 329-8635      www.lifetech.com

*Produces biotechnology research materials.*

**Life Technologies SARL, BP 96, Cergy Pontoise F-95613, France**

## ELI LILLY & COMPANY

Lilly Corporate Center, Indianapolis, IN, 46285

Tel: (317) 276-2000      Fax: (317) 277-6579      www.lilly.com

*Mfr. pharmaceuticals and animal health products.*

**Lilly France, rue du Colonel Lilly, F-6760 Fegersheim, France**

Tel: 33-3-38-64-4000   Fax: 33-3-38-64-4022

**Lilly France SA, 203 Bureaux de la Colline, F-92213 Saint-Cloud, France**
Tel: 33-1-49-11-3434    Fax: 33-1-46-02-2767

## LIMITORQUE

PO Box 11318, 5114 Woodall Road, Lynchburg, VA, 24506
Tel: (804) 528-4400      Fax: (804) 845-9736      www.limitorque.com
*Mfr./marketing/services electric valve actuators.*

**Limitorque France, Alpha Forum Etoile, 2 rue Troyon, F-75017 Paris France**
Tel: 33-1-4055-4640   Fax: 33-1-4068-7962

## LINCOLN ELECTRIC HOLDINGS

22801 St. Clair Ave., Cleveland, OH, 44117-1199
Tel: (216) 481-8100      Fax: (216) 486-8385      www.lincolnelectric.com
*Mfr. arc welding and welding related products, oxy-fuel and thermal cutting equipment and integral AC motors.*

**Lincoln Electric International, 2 blvd Albert 1 ER, F-94130 Nogent Sur Marne, Paris, France**
Tel: 33-1-43-24-6015   Fax: 33-1-43-24-6017   Contact: Jean Mazingue

**The Lincoln Electric Company France SA, Ave. Franklin Roosevelt BP214, F-76120 LeGrand Quevilly, France**
Tel: 33-2-32-11-4040   Fax: 33-2-32-1104011

## LINEAR TECHNOLOGY CORPORATION

1630 McCarthy Blvd., Milpitas, CA, 95035
Tel: (408) 432-1900      Fax: (408) 434-6441      www.linear-tech.com
*Mfr. linear integrated circuit chips.*

**Linear Technology S.A.R.L., Immeuble "Le Quartz", 58 Chemin De La Justice, 92290 Chatenay Malabry, France**
Tel: 33-1-41079555   Fax: 33-1-46314613

## ARTHUR D. LITTLE, INC.

25 Acorn Park, Cambridge, MA, 02140-2390
Tel: (617) 498-5000      Fax: (617) 498-7200      www.adlittle.com
*Management, environmental, health and safety consulting; technical and product development.*

**Arthur D. Little International, Inc., 50 Ave. Théophile Gautier, F-75016 Paris, France**
Tel: 33-1-55-74-2900   Fax: 33-1-55-74-2800

## LITTON INDUSTRIES INC.

21240 Burbank Boulevard, Woodland Hills, CA, 91367
Tel: (818) 598-5000      Fax: (818) 598-3313      www.littoncorp.com
*Shipbuilding, electronics, and information technology.*

**Litton Marine Systems S.a.r.l, Z.A. Mouretiane Port Activites, 467 Chemin du Littoral - Lot 221 F-13016, Marseille, France**
Tel: 33-4-91-699-002

**Litton Precision Products International, 58 rue Pottier, F-78150 Le Chesnay, France**

## LOCKHEED MARTIN CORPORATION

6801 Rockledge Drive, Bethesda, MD, 20817
Tel: (301) 897-6000      Fax: (301) 897-6652      www.imco.com
*Design/mfr./management systems in fields of space, defense, energy, electronics and technical services.*

**CalComp S.A., Le Clemenceau, 205 Ave. Georges, F-92000 Nanterre Hermes, France**
Tel: 33-1-47-29-5500   Fax: 33-1-47-29-1372

**Lockheed Martin International, 4 rue de Penthievre, F-75008 Paris, France**
Tel: 33-1-42-65-3981   Contact: G. Cass, VP

## LOCTITE CORPORATION

1001 Trout Brook Crossing, Rocky Hill, CT, 06067-3910

Tel: (860) 571-5100      Fax: (860) 571-5465      www.loctite.com

*Mfr./sale industrial adhesives, sealants and coatings..*

**France G.I.E., 10 Ave. Eugene Gazeau, BP 90, F-60304 Senlis Cedex, France**

Tel: 33-3-44-21-6600   Fax: 33-3-44-60-9257   Contact: Cedric Berthod, Bus. Mgr.

## LORAL SPACE & COMMUNICATIONS LTD.

600 Third Ave., New York, NY, 10016

Tel: (212) 697-1105      Fax: (212) 338-5662      www.loral.com

*Marketing coordination: defense electronics, communications systems.*

**Loral CyberStar, 90 avenue des Champs-Elysees,F- 75 008 Paris, France**

Tel: 33-156-43-5072

## LOTUS DEVELOPMENT CORPORATION

55 Cambridge Pkwy., Cambridge, MA, 02142

Tel: (617) 577-8500      Fax: (617) 693-1779      www.lotus.com

*Mrs. business software.*

**Immeuble Lotus France, La Defense 6, 35-41 rue du Capitaine Guynemer, F-92925 Paris La Defense Cedex, France**

## LOUIS ALLIS COMPANY

2498 State Highway 160, Warrior, AL, 35180

Tel: (205) 297-2100      Fax: (205) 647-2755      www.louisallis.com

*Electric motors, adjustable speed drives, generators and compressors.*

**Litton/Allis Precision Products International Inc., 58 rue Pottier, F-78150 Le Chesney, France**

## LOWE LINTAS & PARTNERS WORLDWIDE

One Dag Hammarskjold Plaza, New York, NY, 10017

Tel: (212) 605-8000      Fax: (212) 605-4705      www.interpublic.com

*Full-service, integrated marketing communications company/advertising agency.*

**Ammirati Puris Lintas France Group, 22 Quai de la Megisserie, F-75046 Paris Cedex 1, France**

Tel: 33-1-55-25-5525  Fax: 33-1-55-25-5555   Contact: Malcolm Hunter, Dir.

**Initiative Media, 115 rue du Bac B.P. 397.07, F-75327 Paris Cedex 07, France**

Tel: 33-1-42-84-4141   Fax: 33-1-42-84-4141   Contact: Marie-Jose Forissier, Chmn.

**MacLaren Lintas, 21 rue Faidherbe, F-75011 Paris, France**

Tel: 33-1-55-25-5727  Fax: 33-1-55-25-5747   Contact: Raynald Duplessy

## LSI LOGIC CORPORATION

1551 McCarthy Blvd, Milpitas, CA, 95035

Tel: (408) 433-8000      Fax: (408) 954-3220      www.lsilogic.com

*Develop/mfr. semiconductors.*

**LSI Logic S.A., 53 bis Ave. de l'europe, B.P. 139, F-78148 Velizzy-Villacoublay Cedex Paris, France**

Tel: 33-1-34-63-1313   Fax: 33-1-34-63-1319

## LTX CORPORATION

LTX Park, University Ave., Westwood, MA, 02090

Tel: (617) 461-1000      Fax: (617) 326-4883      www.ltx.com

*Design/mfr. computer-controlled semiconductor test systems.*

**LTX France SA, 50 Boulevard Rabelais, F-94100 Saint-Maur, France**

Tel: 33-14-889-5240   Fax: 33-14-889-5375

## THE LUBRIZOL CORPORATION

29400 Lakeland Blvd., Wickliffe, OH, 44092-2298

Tel: (440) 943-4200    Fax: (440) 943-5337    www.lubrizol.com

*Mfr. chemicals additives for lubricants and fuels.*

**Lubrizol France SA,  Tour Europe, F-92400 Courbevoie Paris Cedex 7, France**

Tel: 33-1-41-25-1300

## LUCENT TECHNOLOGIES, INC.

600 Mountain Ave., Murray Hill, NJ, 07974-0636

Tel: (908) 582-3000    Fax: (908) 582-2576    www.lucent.com

*Design/mfr. wide range of public and private networks, communication systems and software, data networking systems, business telephone systems and microelectronics components.*

**TRT Lucent Technologies,  49 rue de la Rebublique BP 26, F-76250 Deville-les -Rouen, France**

Tel: 33-2-32-10-7000   Fax: 33-2-32-10-7010   Contact: Henri-Alain Rault, Location Head

**TRT Lucent Technologies,  16 Ave. Descartes, F-92352 Le Plessis, Robinson Cedex, France**

Tel: 33-1-41-28-7000   Fax: 33-1-46-30-6224   Contact: Christelle Pollet, PR Mgr.

## LYDALL INC.

1 Colonial Road, PO Box 151, Manchester, CT, 06040

Tel: (860) 646-1233    Fax: (860) 646-4917    www.lydall.com

*Mfr. converted paper products, paperboard, non-woven specialty media.*

**Axohm Axohm SA,  Saint-Rivalain, F-56310 Melrand, France**

Tel: 33-2-9728-5300   Fax: 33-2-9739-5890

## LYONDELL

3801 West Chester Pike, Newtown Square, PA, 19073-2387

Tel: (610) 359-2000    Fax: (610) 359-2722    www.arcochem.com

*Mfr. propylene oxide, a chemical used for flexible foam products, coatings/paints and solvents/inks.*

**ARCO Chemical Products Europe, Inc.,  Technical Ctr., Z.I. du Pre Sarrazin, Boite Postale No. 34, Villers Saint Paul F-60870 Rieux France**

Tel: 33-4429-6300   Fax: 33-471-76322

**ARCO Chimie France SNC,  12-14 Rond-Point des Champs Elysees, F-75008 Paris, France**

Tel: 33-1-5353-1606   Fax: 33-1-5353-1607

**ARCO Chimie France, SNC,  BP 201, F-12775 Fos-sur-Mer Cedex, France**

Tel: 33-42-47-5100

## LYONDELL CHEMICAL COMPANY

1221 McKinney St., Houston, TX, 77010

Tel: (713) 652-7200    Fax: (713) 309-2074    www.lyondell.com

*Mfr. polymers and petrochemicals.*

**Lyondell Chemical Products Europe, Inc.,  Z.I. du Pre Sarrazin, Boite Postale No. 34, F-60870 Villers Saint Paul, France**

Tel: 33-04-42-47-5100

**Lyondell Chemical Products Europe, Inc.,  BP 201, 13775 Fos-Sur-Mer Cedex, France**

Tel: 33-04-42-47-5100

## M/A-COM INC.

1011 Pawtucket Boulevard, Lowell, MA, 01853-3295

Tel: (978) 442-5000    Fax: (978) 442-5354    www.macom.com

*Mfr. electronic components, semiconductor devices and communications equipment.*

**M/A-COM France S.A.,  29 Chaussee Jules Cesar, F-95300 Pontoise, France**

Tel: 33-1-34208888   Fax: 33-1-34208232

## MacDERMID INC.

245 Freight Street, Waterbury, CT, 06702-0671

Tel: (203) 575-5700     Fax: (203) 575-7900     www.macdermid.com

*Chemicals processing for metal industrial, plastics, electronics cleaners, strippers.*

**MacDermid France SA, rue de la Closerie, Z.I. du Clos aux Pois, C.E. 4831, F-91048 Evry Cedex, France**

Tel: 33-1-60-86-1427   Fax: 33-1-60-86-1876

## R.H. MACY & COMPANY INC.

151 West 34th Street, New York, NY, 10001

Tel: (212) 695-4400     Fax: (212) 643-1307     www.macys.com

*Department stores; importers.*

**R.H. Macy & Co. Inc., 35 rue de Ponthieu, F-75008 Paris, France**

## MAGNETROL INTERNATIONAL

5300 Belmont Road, Downers Grove, IL, 60515-4499

Tel: (630) 969-4000     Fax: (630) 969-9489     www.magnetrol.com

*Mfr. level and flow instrumentation.*

**Magnetrol International, 11 rue Albert Einstein, Espace Descartes, F-77420 Champs-sur-Marne, France**

Tel: 33-1-64-68-5828   Fax: 33-1-64-68-5827   Contact: Alain Demaitre, Sales Mgr.

## MALLINCKRODT INC.

675 McDonnell Blvd., St. Louis, MO, 63134

Tel: (314) 654-2000     Fax: (314) 654-5380     www.mallinckrodt.com

*Distributes health care products and specialty pharmaceuticals.*

**Mallinckrodt France SARL, Parc d'Affaires Technopolis, 3 avenue du Canada, Les Ulis, F-91975 Courtaboeuf Cedex France**

Tel: 33-16-9821400   Fax: 33-16-9821500

## MANPOWER INTERNATIONAL INC.

5301 N. Ironwood Rd., PO Box 2053, Milwaukee, WI, 53201-2053

Tel: (414) 961-1000     Fax: (414) 961-7081     www.manpower.com

*Temporary help, contract service, training and testing.*

**Manpower France SARL, 9 rue Jacques Bingen, F-75017 Paris, France**

Tel: 33-1-44-15-4040   Fax: 33-1-47-63-1077

## MARCONI DATA SYSTEMS, INC.

1500 Mittel Blvd., Wood Dale, IL, 60191

Tel: (630) 860-7300     Fax: (630) 616-3657     www.videojet.com

*Mfr. computer peripherals and hardware, state-of-the-art industrial ink jet marking and coding products.*

**Marconi Data Systems, Parc Gutenberg, 7 vole la Cardon BP n 81, F-91126 Palaiseau Cedex, France**

Tel: 33-1-69-19-7000   Fax: 33-1-69-32-0145

## MARK IV INDUSTRIES INC.

501 John James Audubon Pkwy., PO Box 810, Amherst, NY, 14226-0810

Tel: (716) 689-4972     Fax: (716) 689-1529     www.mark-iv.com

*Mfr. of engineered systems and components utilizing mechanical and fluid power transmission, fluid transfer, and power systems and components.*

**Dayco Europe SARL, Roissypole le Dome, 1 rue de la Haye BP 10909, F-95731 Roissy CDG Cedex, France**

Tel: 33-1-48-62-9351   Fax: 33-1-48-62-9352

**Mark IV Systemes Moteurs S.A., 1 rue Charles Edouard Jeanneret, F-78306 Poissy Cedex, France**

Tel: 33-1-3922-3423   Fax: 33-13911-3040

**Mark IV Systemes Moteurs S.A., Z.Z. des Grands Pres., F-68370 Orbey, France**
Tel: 33-329590-8806   Fax: 33-32950-8817

**Mark IV Systemes Moteurs S.A., 11 blvd d'Anvaux, F-36000 Chageauroux, France**
Tel: 33-25408-5959   Fax: 33-25434-6130

# MARKEM CORPORATION
150 Congress Street, Keene, NH, 03431
Tel: (603) 352-1130      Fax: (603) 357-1835      www.markem.com.
*Mfr./sales of industrial marking, print machinery and hot stamping foils.*

**Markem France SA, 23 rue Auguste Perret, Z.A.C. de Petites, F-94808 Bruyeres Villejuif Cedex, France**
Tel: 33-1-43-90-1100   Fax: 33-1-46-78-4763

# MARLEY COOLING TOWER COMPANY
7401 West 129th Street, Overland Park, KS, 66213
Tel: (913) 664-7400      Fax: (913) 664-7641      www.marleyct.com
*Cooling and heating towers and waste treatment systems.*

**Marley Cooling Tower (France), Polyparc 540 allee des Hetres, F-69760 Limonest, France**
Tel: 33-4-7252-1700   Contact: Pierre-Yves Gerard

# MARRIOTT INTERNATIONAL INC.
10400 Fernwood Rd., Bethesda, MD, 20817
Tel: (301) 380-3000      Fax: (301) 380-5181      www.marriott.com
*Hotel services.*

**Marriott Courtyard Neuilly, 58 blvd Victor Hugo, F-92200 Neuilly, France**
Tel: 33-155-636-465   Fax: 33-155-636-465

**Paris Marriott Hotel, Champs Elysees, Paris, France**

# MARSH & McLENNAN COS INC.
1166 Ave. of the Americas, New York, NY, 10036-2774
Tel: (212) 345-5000      Fax: (212) 345-4808      www.marshmac.com
*Insurance agents/brokers, pension and investment management consulting services.*

**J&H Marsh & McLennan Global Broking Paris, 32 rue Lafitte, F-75009 Paris, France**
Tel: 33-4-783-2071   Fax: 33-4-783-2070   Contact: Mohanned Dahbi

# MASTERCARD INTERNATIONAL INC.
200 Purchase Street, Purchase, NY, 10577
Tel: (914) 249-2000      Fax: (914) 249-5475      www.mastercard.com
*Provides financial payment systems globally.*

**MasterCard International Inc., Middle East/Africa Region, Tour Maine Montpaarnasse, 33 Ave. de Maine, F-75755 Paris Cedex 15, France**

# MATTEL INC.
333 Continental Blvd., El Segundo, CA, 90245-5012
Tel: (310) 252-2000      Fax: (310) 252-2179      www.mattelmedia.com
*Mfr. toys, dolls, games, crafts and hobbies.*

**Fisher-Price SA, rue de Gradoux, F-45800 St. Jean de Braye, France**

**Mattel France SA, 64-68 ave. de la Victoire, F-94310 Orly, France**

# MAURICE PINCOFFS COMPANY, INC.
2040 North Loop West, Suite 200, Houston, TX, 77018
Tel: (713) 681-5461      Fax: (713) 681-8521      www.pincoffs.com
*International marketing and distribution.*

**Maurice Pincoffs Paris, 27-29 ave. de Saint Mande, F-75012 Paris, France**

## MAXON CORPORATION

201 East 18th Street, Muncie, IN, 47302

Tel: (765) 284-3304     Fax: (765) 286-8394     www.maxoncorp.com

*Industry combustion equipment and valves.*

**Maxon S.A.R.L., 2 Avenue du Parc Le Campus, F-95033 Cergy Pontoise, Cedex Paris France**

Tel: 33-1-34-20-1080   Fax: 33-1-34-20-1088

## MAXTOR CORPORATION

510 Cottonwood Drive, Milpitas, CA, 95035-7403

Tel: (408) 432-1700     Fax: (408) 432-4510     www.maxtor.com

*Mfr. develops and markets hard disk drives for desktop computer systems.*

**Maxtor Europe S.A.R.L., 18 rue Saarinen, Silic 242, F-94568 Rungis Cedex, France**

Tel: 33-1-41-80-0860   Fax: 33-1-46-86-4048

## MAYER, BROWN & PLATT

190 S. LaSalle Street, Chicago, IL, 60603

Tel: (312) 782-0600     Fax: (312) 701-7711     www.mayerbrown.com

*International law firm.*

**Lambert & Lee, 13 Avenue Hoche, F-75008 Paris, France**

Tel: 33-1-5353-4343

## MAYFRAN INTERNATIONAL, INC.

PO Box 43038, Cleveland, OH, 44143

Tel: (440) 461-4100     Fax: (440) 461-5565     www.mayfran.com

*Mfr. conveying systems, filtration equipment and separators that facilitate material handling and coolant recovery for automobile manufacturers and machine tool builders.*

**Mayfran France, Centre D'Affairs, 93153 LeBlanc Mesnil, PO Box 45 Paris-Nord, France**

Tel: 33-1-48-65-7800   Fax: 33-1-48-67-7629

## MBIA INC.

113 King Street, Armonk, NY, 10504

Tel: (914) 273-4545     Fax: (914) 765-3299     www.mbia.com

*Provides investment and treasury management services and insurance for municipal bonds.*

**MBIA Assurance, S.A., 112 Avenue Kléber, Paris F-75116, France**


**Deborah Zurkow**

Tel: 33-1-53-70-4343

## McCANN-ERICKSON WORLDGROUP

750 Third Ave., New York, NY, 10017

Tel: (212) 984-3644     Fax: (212) 984-2629     www.mccann.com

*International advertising and marketing services.*

**Joannis Schneider Conseil SA, 2 rue Voltaire, F-92309 Levallois Perret Cedex, France**

**McCann Erickson SA, rue de Villiere, F-92309 Levallois Perret Cedex, France**

## McDONALD'S CORPORATION

McDonald's Plaza, Oak Brook, IL, 60523

Tel: (630) 623-3000     Fax: (630) 623-7409     www.mcdonalds.com

*Fast food chain stores.*

**McDonald's Corp., Paris, France**

## McKINSEY & COMPANY

55 East 52nd Street, New York, NY, 10022

Tel: (212) 446-7000      Fax: (212) 446-8575        www.mckinsey.com

*Management and business consulting services.*

**McKinsey & Company,  79 avenue des Champs-Elysées, F-75008 Paris, France**

Tel: 33-1-40-69-1400   Fax: 33-1-40-69-9393

## MCS SOFTWARE CORPORATION

815 Colorado Blvd., Los Angeles, CA, 90041

Tel: (323) 258-9111      Fax: (323) 259-3838        www.macsch.com

*Develop finite element analysis software used in the field of computer-aided engineering.*

**MacNeal-Schwendler France,  Immeuble "L'Europeen", 98 allee des Champs Elysees, F-91042 Evry Cedex, France**

**MSC Partner Relations Europe,  13 Square Alfred de Musset, F-78960 Voisins le Bretonneux, France**

**PDA Engineering SARL,  BP 314, F-78054 St. Quentin Yvelines Cedex, France**

## MEAD CORPORATION

Courthouse Plaza, NE, Dayton, OH, 45463

Tel: (937) 495-6323      Fax: (937) 461-2424        www.mead.com

*Mfr. paper, packaging, pulp, lumber and other wood products, school and office products; electronic publishing and distribution.*

**Mead Europe Engineering SARL,  B. P. 15, Z.1. LaMartinerie, F-36130 Deals, France**

Tel: 33-54-291-800   Fax: 33-54-224-100   Contact: Gerard Louret, Gen. Mgr.

**Mead Packaging Europe SARL,  B.P. 131, Saifee du Bourbonnais, F-78312 Maurepas Cedex, France**

Tel: 33-1-30-51-6168   Fax: 33-1-30-51-1627   Contact: O. Iacobelli, Gen. Mgr.

**Mead-Emballage SA,  Blvd. d'Anvaux, Zone Industrielle, BP 205, Chateauroux, France**

## MECHANICAL DYNAMICS, INC.

2301 Commonwealth Blvd., Ann Arbor, MI, 48105

Tel: (734) 994-3800      Fax: (734) 994-6418        www.adams.com

*Mfr. Adams prototyping software to automotive industry.*

**Mechanical Dynamics Sarl,  58 rue Pottier, F-7815 LeChesnay, France**

Tel: 33-1-3966-040

## MEDICUS GROUP INTERNATIONAL

1675 Broadway, New York, NY, 10019

Tel: (212) 468-3100      Fax: (212) 468-3222        www.medicusgroup.com

*Healthcare communications company engaged in professional advertising, sales promotion, global branding and launch planning.*

**Medicus 1 Team SA,  8 rue Bellini, F-75016 Paris Cedex 16, France**

Tel: 33-1-53-65-6333   Contact: Dr. Jean-Marc Menat

## MEDTRONIC INC.

7000 Central Ave., NE, Minneapolis, MN, 55432

Tel: (612) 574-4000      Fax: (612) 574-4879        www.medtronic.com

*Mfr./sale/service electrotherapeutic medical devices.*

**Medtronic France SA,  Zone Industrielle Sud, Route d'Anor, F-59610 Fourmies, France**

## MEMC ELECTRONIC MATERIALS, INC.

501 Pearl Drive, St. Peters, MO, 63376

Tel: (636) 474-5500      Fax: (636) 474-5161        www.memc.com

*Mfg. and distribution of silicon wafers.*

**MEMC Huls France S.A.,  Tour Horizon, 52 quai de Dion Bouton, F-92806 Puteaux Cedex, France**

Tel: 33-1-46-93-2305   Fax: 33-1-40-90-9281

## MEMOREX CORPORATION

10100 Pioneer Blvd., Ste. 110, Santa Fe Springs, CA, 90670

Tel: (562) 906-2800    Fax: (562) 906-2848    www.memorex.com

*Magnetic recording tapes, etc.*

**Memorex SA, 25 Blvd. de I'Amiral Bruix, F-75016 Paris, France**

## MENTOR CORPORATION

201 Menton Drive, Santa Barbara, CA, 93111

Tel: (805) 879-6000    Fax: (805) 967-7108    www.mentorcorp.com

*Mfr. breast implants.*

**Mentor Medical Systems France, S.A., 171 Avenue George Clemenceau, Bldg. D F-92024 Nanterre, France**

Tel: 33-1-147-21-3366

## MENTOR GRAPHICS/MICROTEC RESEARCH

8005 SW Boeckman Road, Wilsonville, OR, 97070-7777

Tel: (503) 685-7000    Fax: (503) 685-1202    www.mentorg.com

*Develop/mfr. software tools for embedded systems market.*

**Microtec Research SA, Le Sesame, 8 rue Germain Soufflot, F-78180 Montigny le Bretonneux, France**

## MERCER MANAGEMENT CONSULTING INC.

1166 Ave. of the Americas, New York, NY, 10036

Tel: (212) 345-3400    Fax: (212) 345-7414    www.mercermc.com

*Provides clients with counsel in such areas as corporate and business strategy and growth planning, org development, and market and operations enhancement.*

**Mercer Management, 69 rue de Monceau, F-75008 Paris, France**

**Mercer Management Consulting, 28 avenue Victor Hugo, 75 116 Paris, France**

## MERCK & COMPANY, INC.

One Merck Drive, PO Box 100, Whitehouse Station, NJ, 08889-0100

Tel: (908) 423-1000    Fax: (908) 423-2592    www.merck.com

*Pharmaceuticals, chemicals and biologicals.*

**Merck, Sharp & Dohme / Chibret, 3 ave. Hoche, F-75008 Paris, France**

## MERCURY INTERACTIVE CORPORATION

1325 Borregas Ave., Sunnyvale, CA, 94089

Tel: (408) 822-5200    Fax: (408) 822-5300    www.merc-int.com

*Mfr. computer software to decipher and eliminate "bugs" from systems.*

**Mercury Interactive France SARL, Ibis rue du Petit Clamart, Bâtiment E, F-78140 Vélizy, France**

Tel: 33-1-40-83-6868  Fax: 33-1-40-83-6850

## MERITOR AUTOMOTIVE, INC.

2135 West Maple Road, Troy, MI, 48084-7186

Tel: (248) 435-1000    Fax: (248) 435-1393    www.meritorauto.com

*Mfr./sales of light and heavy vehicle systems for trucks, cars and specialty vehicles.*

**Meritor Heavy Vehicle Systems SA, rue Anatole France, F-70300 Luxeuil, France**

**Meritor Heavy Vehicle Systems SARL, Chassey-les-Scey, F-70170 Port-sur-Saone, France**

**Meritor Light Vehicle Systems Electric Motors, Esson, France**

## MERRILL LYNCH & COMPANY, INC.

World Financial Center, 250 Vesey Street, New York, NY, 10281-1332

Tel: (212) 449-1000    Fax: (212) 449-2892    www.ml.com

*Security brokers and dealers, investment and business services.*

**Merrill Lynch Capital Markets France, S.A., 96 Ave. Kleber, F-75761 Paris Cedex 16, France**

Tel: 33-1-53-65-5555  Fax: 33-1-53-65-5600

**Merrill Lynch France,  96 Ave. d'Iena, F-75783 Paris Cedex 16, France**

Tel: 33-1-40-69-1500    Fax: 33-1-47-20-2238

## MESTEK, INC.

260 North Elm St., Westfield, MA, 01085

Tel: (413) 568-9571        Fax: (413) 568-2969        www.mestek.com

*Mfr. air diffusers, grilles and related equipment for air conditioning, heating and ventilation.*

**Anemotherm SA,  4749 rue Jean Bleuzen, F-92170 Vanves, France**

## METAL IMPROVEMENT COMPANY

10 Forest Ave., Paramus, NJ, 07652

Tel: (201) 843-7800        Fax: (201) 843-3460        www.metalimprovement.com

*Mfr. shot peening.*

**Metal Improvement Co.,  Z.I. de St. Etienne, rue de Cazenave, F-64100 Bayonne, France**

**Metal Improvement Co. France,  Zone Industrielle d'Amilly, F-45200 Montargis, France**

## M-I

PO Box 48242, Houston, TX, 77242-2842

Tel: (713) 739-0222        Fax: (713) 308-9503        www.midf.com

*Drilling fluids.*

**M-I Drilling Fluids Intl B.V.,  Zone Induspal Avenue Joliot Curie, BP 205 Lons, 64142 Billere Cedex, France**

Tel: 33-559923551    Fax: 33-559923556

## MICRO TOUCH SYSTEMS, INC.

300 Griffin Brook Park Drive, Methuen, MA, 01844

Tel: (978) 659-9000        Fax: (978) 659-9100        www.microtouch.com

*Mfr. clear coatings for computer monitors.*

**MicroTouch Systems SARL,  Europarc de Créteil, 19 rue Le Corbusier,F- 94042 Créteil Cedex, France**

Tel: 33-1-4513-9030

## MICRO WAREHOUSE, INC.

535 Connecticut Ave., Norwalk, CT, 06854

Tel: (203) 899-4000        Fax: (203) 899-4203        www.warehouse.com

*Catalog computer sales.*

**Inmac,  125 Avenue du Bois de la Pie, Roissy-en-France F-95921 Roissy Cedex, France**

## MICROCHIP TECHNOLOGY INCORPORATED

2355 West Chandler Boulevard, Chandler, AZ, 85224

Tel: (602) 786-7200        Fax: (602) 899-9210        www.microchip.com

*Mfr. electronic subassemblies and components.*

**AZ Microchip Technology SARL,  Zone Industrielle de la Bonde, 2 rue Du Buisson aux Fraises, F-91300 Massy, France**

Tel: 33-1-69-53-6320    Fax: 33-1-69-30-9079

**LeadREP,  99 route de Versailles, F-91160 Champlain, France**

Tel: 33-1-69-79-9350    Fax: 33-1-69-79-9359

## MICROMERITICS INSTRUMENT CORPORATION

One Micromeritics Drive, Norcross, GA, 30093-1877

Tel: (770) 662-3620        Fax: (770) 662-3696        www.micromeritics.com

*Mfr. analytical instruments.*

**Micromeritics France SA,  181 rue Henri Bessemer, F-60100 Creil, France**

Tel: 33-3-4464-6080

## MICROSOFT CORPORATION

One Microsoft Way, Redmond, WA, 98052-6399

Tel: (425) 882-8080     Fax: (425) 936-7329     www.microsoft.com

*Computer software, peripherals and services.*

**Microsoft Europe (European HQ),  Tour Pacific, F-92977 Paris La Defense Cedex 77, France**

Tel: 33-1-46-35-1010   Fax: 33-1-46-35-1030

**Microsoft France SARL,  18 ave. du Quebec, Zone de Courteboeuf, F-91957 Les Ulis Cedex, France**

Tel: 33-1-69-29-1111   Fax: 33-1-64-46-0660

## MILACRON INC.

2090 Florence Ave., Cincinnati, OH, 45206

Tel: (513) 487-5000     Fax: (513) 487-5057     www.milacron.com

*Metalworking and plastics technologies.*

**Ferromatik Milacron S.A.,  BP 173, rue Marie Curie, F-F-78313 Maurepas Cédex, France**

Tel: 33-1-34821800   Fax: 33-1-30660469

## MILLENNIUM CHEMICALS INC.

230 Half Mile Rd., Red Bank, NJ, 07701

Tel: (732) 933-5000     Fax: (732) 933-5240     www.millenniumchem.com

*Mfr. specialty chemicals that for paints, perfumes, and flavorings.*

**Millennium Chemicals,  85 Avenue Victor Hugo, F-92563 rueil Malmaison Cedex, France**

Tel: 33-1-55-47-2250   Fax: 33-1-55-47-2251

## MILTON ROY COMPANY

201 Ivyland Road, Ivylan, PA, 18974

Tel: (215) 441-0800     Fax: (215) 293-0468     www.miltonroy.com

*Mfr. medical and industry equipment and process control instruments.*

**DOSAPRO-Milton Roy SA,  10 Grande rue, F-27360 Pont St. Pierre, France**

Tel: 33-232-68-3000   Fax: 33-232-68-3093

**Robin Industries,  10 rue du bois Gasseau - BP 94, F-77212 Avon Cedex, France**

**33-1-64-23-74-02**

Tel: 33-1-60-74-95-20

## MINE SAFETY APPLIANCES COMPANY

121 Gamma Drive, PO Box 426, Pittsburgh, PA, 15230

Tel: (412) 967-3000     Fax: (412) 967-3452     www.msa.net

*Safety equipment, industry filters.*

**MSA de France,  13 rue de la Guivernone, BP 617, F-95004 Cergy Pontoise Cedex, France**

## MINOLTA QMS INC.

One Magnum Pass, Mobile, AL, 36618

Tel: (205) 633-4300     Fax: (205) 633-4866     www.qms.com

*Mfr. monochrome and color computer printers.*

**QMS France,  1 bis rue du petit Clamart BP 17, F-78142 Vélizy Cedex, France**

## MODEM MEDIA, INC.

230 East Avenue, Norwalk, CT, 06855

Tel: (203) 299-7000     Fax: (230) 299-7060     www.modemmedia.com

*Provides on-line marketing and consulting services.*

**Modem Media Paris,  11 rue Mogador, Paris F-75009, France**

Tel: 33-1-42-818282   Contact: Carol Gué, Mng. Dir

## MODINE MANUFACTURING COMPANY

1500 DeKoven Ave., Racine, WI, 53403

Tel: (262) 636-1200    Fax: (262) 636-1424    www.modine.com

*Mfr. heat-transfer products.*

**Modine Intl., 131-135 Blvd. Carnot, Bureau 441, F-78110 Le Vesinet, France**

## MOLEX INC.

2222 Wellington Court, Lisle, IL, 60532

Tel: (630) 969-4550    Fax: (630) 969-1352    www.molex.com

*Mfr. electronic, electrical and fiber optic interconnection products and systems, switches, application tooling.*

**Molex France, 18 Parc Burospace, F-91571 Bièvres Cédex, France**

## MOLTECH POWER SYSTEMS

9062 South Rita Road, Tucson, AZ, 85747

Tel: (520) 799-7500    Fax: (520) 799-7501    www.moltechpower.com

*Provides rechargeable battery solutions for industry applications.*

**Moltech Power Systems Nordic AB, Immeuble Apollo, 48 Cours Blaise Pascal, F-91004 Evry Cedex France**

Tel: 33-1-60871680    Fax: 33-1-60871681

## MONSANTO SEED CORP.

3100 Sycamore Road, DeKalb, IL, 60115-9600

Tel: (815) 758-3461    Fax: (815) 758-3711    www.dekalb.com

*Develop/produce hybrid corn, sorghum, sunflower seed, varietal soybeans, alfalfa.*

**R.A.G.T. Societe Anonyme, Ave. Saint Pierre, Site de Bourran - B.P. 31, F-12033 Rodez Cedex 9, France**

Tel: 33-5-65-73-4100    Fax: 33-5-65-73-4198    Contact: Alain Fabre, Chmn. & Gen. Mgr.

**SocKalb, G.I.E., Siege Social: 18 rue de Seguret Saincric, F-12033 Rodez Cedex 9, France**

Tel: 33-5-65 73 41 00    Fax: 33-5-65 73 41 98    Contact: Daniel Segonds, President

## MOODY'S INVESTOR SERVICES, INC.

99 Church St., New York, NY, 10007

Tel: (212) 553-1658    Fax: (212) 553-0462    www.moodys.com

*Publishes credit ratings*

**Moody's France S.A., Services aux Investisseurs, 4 rue Auber, F-75009 Paris, France**

Tel: 33-1-53-30-10-20

## MOOG INC.

Jamison Road, East Aurora, NY, 14052-0018

Tel: (716) 652-2000    Fax: (716) 687-4471    www.moog.com

*Mfr. precision control components and systems.*

**Moog SARL, 38 rue du Morvan, Silic 417, F-94573 Rungis, France**

## J. P. MORGAN CHASE & CO. INC.

World Headquarters, 270 Park Ave., New York, NY, 10017

Tel: (212) 270-6000    Fax: (212) 622-9030    www.jpmorganchase.com

*Provides integrated financial solutions for institutions and individuals worldwide, including asset management, investment banking and commercial banking.*

**J. P. Morgan Chase & Co., Washington Plaza, 42 rue Washington, F-75008 Paris, France**

Tel: 33-1-53-77-1000    Fax: 33-1-53-77-1049

## MORGAN STANLEY DEAN WITTER & CO.

1585 Broadway, New York, NY, 10036

Tel: (212) 761-4000    Fax: (212) 761-0086    www.msdw.com

*Securities and commodities brokerage, investment banking, money management, personal trusts.*

**Morgan Stanley SA, 25 rue Balzac, F-75008 Paris, France**

## MOTOROLA, INC.

1303 East Algonquin Road, Schaumburg, IL, 60196

Tel: (847) 576-5000    Fax: (847) 538-5191    www.motorola.com

*Mfr. communications equipment, semiconductors and cellular phones.*

**Motorola AIEG SA, 1 blvd Victor, F-75015 Paris, France**

Tel: 33-1-53-78-1800   Fax: 33-1-53-78-1815

**Motorola Electronique Automobile SA, 8 Blvd. Charles Detriche, F-49015 Angers, France**

## MTI TECHNOLOGY CORPORATION

4905 East LaPalma Avenue, Anaheim, CA, 92807

Tel: (714) 970-0300    Fax: (714) 693-2202    www.mti.com

*Mfr. data storage systems software.*

**MTI France S.A., 7 Avenue des Pommerots, BP 25, F-78400 Chatou, France**

Tel: 33-1-3009-5200   Fax: 33-1-3009-5222

## MTS SYSTEMS CORPORATION

1400 Technology Drive, Eden Prairie, MN, 55344-2290

Tel: (612) 937-4000    Fax: (612) 937-4515    www.mts.com

*Develop/mfr. mechanical testing and simulation products and services, industry measure and automation instrumentation.*

**MTS France, 6 rue de Sainte Claire Deville, F-77185 Lognes, France**

## MULTI GRAPHICS

431 Lakeview Court, Mt. Prospect, IL, 60056

Tel: (847) 375-1700    Fax: (847) 375-1810    www.multigraphics.com

*Mfr./sale/service printing and print prod equipment, mailroom/bindery systems, services and supplies for graphics industry.*

**Multi Graphics Intl. SA, BP 307, 60 rue Berthelot, F-92402 Courbevoie Cedex, France**

## NABISCO HOLDINGS, CORP.

7 Campus Drive, Parsippany, NJ, 07054

Tel: (973) 682-5000    Fax: (973) 503-2153    www.nabisco.com

*Mfr. consumer packaged food products and tobacco products.*

**R.J. Reynolds Tobacco France, 36 rue de Naples, F-75008 Paris, France**

## NALCO CHEMICAL COMPANY

One Nalco Center, Naperville, IL, 60563-1198

Tel: (630) 305-1000    Fax: (630) 305-2900    www.nalco.com

*Chemicals for water and waste water treatment, oil products and refining, industry processes; water and energy management service.*

**Nalco France SARL, BP 179, rue Lavoisier, Z.I. de Coignieres-Maurepas, F-78313 Maurepas Cedex, France**

Tel: 33-1-34-82-1200   Fax: 33-1-30-62-6806

## NATIONAL MACHINERY COMPANY

161 Greenfield St., Tiffin, OH, 44883-2471

Tel: (419) 447-5211    Fax: (419) 447-5299    www.nationalmachinery.com

*Mfr. high-speed metal parts forming machines.*

**National Machinery Company, Paris, France**

Tel: 33-1-4378-4084

## NATIONAL SERVICE INDUSTRIES INC.

1420 Peachtree Street NE, Atlanta, GA, 30309

Tel: (404) 853-1000    Fax: (404) 853-1211    www.nationalservice.com

*Mfr. lighting equipment, specialty chemicals; textile rental.*

**Zep Europe, Paris, France**

## NATIONAL STARCH AND CHEMICAL COMPANY

10 Finderne Ave., Bridgewater, NJ, 08807-3300

Tel: (908) 685-5000    Fax: (908) 685-5005    www.nationalstarch.com

*Mfr. adhesives and sealants, resins and specialty chemicals, electronic materials and adhesives, food products, industry starch.*

**National Starch & Chemical SA, PB 438, 299 rue Grange Morin, F-69400 Villefranche-sur-Saône, France**

Tel: 33-4-74-02-3800    Fax: 33-4-74-02-3900

## NATIONAL-OILWELL, INC.

PO Box 4638, Houston, TX, 77210-4638

Tel: (713) 960-5100    Fax: (713) 960-5428    www.natoil.com

*Design, manufacture and sale of comprehensive systems and components used in oil and gas drilling and production.*

**National-Oilwell, 66 rue Cantgrel, F-75013Paris, France**

Tel: 33-1-44-24-2080    Fax: 33-1-44-24-0013

## NCR (NATIONAL CASH REGISTER)

1700 South Patterson Blvd., Dayton, OH, 45479

Tel: (937) 445-5000    Fax: (937) 445-7042    www.ncr.com

*Mfr. automated teller machines and high-performance stationary bar code scanners.*

**NCR Ltd., 1 Square John H. Patterson, F-91749 Massy Cedex, France**

Tel: 33-1-69-533573    Fax: 33-1-69-533545    Contact: Patrick Goasguen

## NETEGRITY, INC.

52 Second Avenue, Waltham, MA, 02154

Tel: (781) 890-1700    Fax: (781) 487-7791    www.netegrity.com

*Mfr. security software.*

**Netegrity France, CNIT Service Affaires, 2 Place de la Defense, BP 240, F-92053 Paris La Defense, France**

Tel: 33-1-4692-23-55

## NETLINKS PUBLISHING SOLUTIONS INC.

PO Box 13626, Sacramento, CA, 95853

Tel: (916) 929-9481    Fax: (916) 928-0414    www.sii.com

*Develop/marketing software for publishing and newspapers.*

**Netlinks Publishing Solutions, Paris, France**

## NETMANAGE, INC.

10725 N. De Anza Blvd., Cupertino, CA, 95014

Tel: (408) 973-7171    Fax: (408) 257-6405    www.netmanage.com

*Develop/mfr. computer software applications and tools.*

**NetManage SARL, 2 Blvd. De la Libération, F-93206 Saint-Denis Cedex, Paris, France**

Tel: 33-1-48-13-7550    Fax: 33-1-42-43-9944

## NETSCAPE COMMUNICATIONS

501 East Middlefield Road, Mountain View, CA, 94043

Tel: (650) 254-1900      Fax: (650) 528-4124      www.netscape.com

*Mfr./distribute Internet-based commercial and consumer software applications.*

**Netscape Communications Europe, 2 Place de la Defense, B.P. 370, F-92053 Paris La Defense, France**

Tel: 33-1-41-97-55-55  Fax: 33-1-41-97-55-00

**Netscape Communications Societe Anonyme, CNIT B.P. 370, 2 Place de la Defense, F-92053 Paris de la Defense, France**

Tel: 33-1-41-97-5500   Fax: 33-1-41-97-5500

## NETWORK ASSOCIATES, INC.

3965 Freedom Circle, Santa Clara, CA, 95054

Tel: (408) 988-3832      Fax: (408) 970-9727      www.networkassociates.com

*Designs and produces network security and network management software and hardware.*

**Network Associates, 50 rue de Londres, F-75008 Paris, France**

Tel: 33-1-44-90-8737   Fax: 33-1-45-22-7601

## NETWORK EQUIPMENT TECHNOLOGIES INC.

6500 Paseo Padre Pkwy., Freemont, CA, 94555

Tel: (510) 713-7300      Fax: (510) 574-4000      www.net.com

*Mfr./service networking products to info-intensive organizations.*

**NET SA, Z.I. Paris Nord II Parc des Reflets, 165 ave. de Bois de la Pie, BP 40041, F-95912 Poissy, France**

## NEUTROGENA CORPORATION

5760 West 96th Street, Los Angeles, CA, 90045

Tel: (310) 642-1150      Fax: (310) 337-5564      www.neutrogena.com

*Mfr. facial cleansing, moisturizing products; body care, sun and hair care specialty products.*

**Neutrogena (France), 5 rue de Logelbach, F-75017 Paris, France**

## NEVILLE CHEMICAL COMPANY

2800 Neville Road, Pittsburgh, PA, 15225-1496

Tel: (412) 331-4200      Fax: (412) 777-4234

*Mfr. hydrocarbon resins.*

**Les Derives Resiniques & Terpeniques (DRT) (JV), Dax Landes, France**

## NEW BRUNSWICK SCIENTIFIC COMPANY, INC.

44 Talmadge Road, Box 4005, Edison, NJ, 08818-4005

Tel: (732) 287-1200      Fax: (732) 287-4222      www.nbsc.com

*Mfr. research and production equipment for life sciences.*

**New Brunswick Scientific S.A.R.L., 15 Allées de Bellefontaine, F-31100 Toulouse, France**

Tel: 33-1-61-40-264706  Fax: 33-1-61-40-265423   Contact: Gerry Burgers, Gen. Mgr.

## THE NEW YORK TIMES COMPANY

229 West 43rd Street, New York, NY, 10036-3959

Tel: (212) 556-1234      Fax: (212) 556-7389      www.nytimes.com

*Diversified media company including newspapers, magazines, television and radio stations, and electronic information and publishing.*

**International Herald Tribune SA, 181 ave. Charles-de-Gaulle, F-92521 Neuilly-sur-Seine, France**

Tel: 33-1-41-43-9300   Contact: Peter C. Goldmark, Chmn. & CEO

## NEWELL RUBBERMAID

29 East Stephenson Street, Freeport, IL, 61032-0943

Tel: (815) 235-4171      Fax: (815) 489-8212      www.newellco.com

*Mfr. hardware, housewares, and office products.*

**Ateliers 28/Newell Rubbermaid, Tremblay Les Villages, France**

Reynolds S. A (JV),  Valence, France

## NEWPORT CORPORATION

1791 Deere Ave., PO Box 19607, Irvine, CA, 92606

Tel:  (949) 863-3144        Fax:  (949) 253-1800        www.newport.com

*Mfr./distributor precision components and systems for laser/optical technology, vibration/motion measure and control.*

**Newport/Micro-Controle,  P.A. de Saint-Guenault, 3 bis rue Jean Mermoz BP 189, F-91006 Evry Cedex, France**

Tel: 33-1-60-91-6868    Fax: 33-1-60-91-6869    Contact: Alain Danielo, VP European Ops.

## NEWSWEEK INTERNATIONAL INC.

251 West 57 Street, New York, NY, 10019

Tel:  (212) 445-4000        Fax:  (212) 445-4120        www.washpostco.com

*Engaged in magazine publishing.*

**Newsweek Inc.,  162 rue du Faubourg Saint Honore, F-75008 Paris, France**

## NHC CORPORATION

2727 Chemsearch Blvd., Irving, TX, 75062

Tel:  (972) 438-0211        Fax:  (972) 438-0707        www.nch.com

*Engaged in manufacturing.*

**National Chemsearch France,  Zone Industrielle, F-77160 Provins, France**

## NICOLET INSTRUMENT CORPORATION

5225 Verona Road, Madison, WI, 53711-4495

Tel:  (608) 276-6100        Fax:  (608) 276-6222        www.nicolet.com

*Mfr. infrared spectrometers and oscilloscopes and medical electro-diagnostic equipment.*

**Thermo Optek S.A.R.L.,  Zone d'Activites du Pas du Lac, 1 Square Franklin, 78180 Montigny le Bretonneux, France**

Tel: 33-1-3930-5300

## A .C. NIELSEN COMPANY

177 Broad Street, Stamford, CT, 06901

Tel:  (203) 961-3000        Fax:  (203) 961-3190        www.acnielsen.com

*Market and consumer research firm.*

**A.C. Nielsen SA,  44 Blvd. de Grenelle, F-75732 Paris, Cedex 15, France**

## NORDSON CORPORATION

28601 Clemens Road, Westlake, OH, 44145-4551

Tel:  (440) 892-1580        Fax:  (440) 892-9507        www.nordson.com

*Mfr. industry application equipment, sealants and packaging machinery.*

**Nordson France SA,  2 rue Niels Borh-l'Esplanade, Saint Thibault des Vignes, F-77462 Lagny sur Marre Cedex, France**

Tel: 33-1-64-12-1400    Fax: 33-1-64-121452

## NORGREN

5400 S. Delaware Street., Littleton, CO, 80120-1663

Tel:  (303) 794-2611        Fax:  (303) 795-9487        www.usa.norgren.com

*Mfr. pneumatic filters, regulators, lubricators, valves, automation systems, dryers, push-in fittings.*

**IMI Norgren SA,  Zone Industrielle de Noisiel 1, BP 22, F-77422 Marne la Vall, France**

Tel: 33-1-60-05-9212    Fax: 33-1-90-06-0852

## NORTON ABRASIVES COMPANY

1 New Bond Street, Worcester, MA, 01606

Tel: (508) 795-5000    Fax: (508) 795-5741    www.nortonabrasives.com

*Mfr. abrasives for industrial manufacturing.*

**Carbo Abrasifs, Zone Industrielle, 8 rue De La Taxe-BP 45, F-28111 Luce, Cedex France**
Tel: 33-237-916413   Fax: 33-237-342855

**Christensen Diamond Products Co., Place de la Gare, F-78320 St. Denis la Verriere, France**

**Norton Houard SA, 33 Route de Blois, F-37400 Amboise, France**

**Norton SA, 178 ave. Paul-Vaillant-Couturier, La Courneuve, France**

**Norton SA, rue de l'Ambassadeur, F-78702 Couflane Ste. Honorine, France**

## NOVELLUS SYSTEMS INC.

4000 North First Street, San Jose, CA, 95134

Tel: (408) 943-9700    Fax: (408) 943-3422    www.novellus.com

*Mfr. chemical vapor deposition (CVD), physical vapor deposition (PVD) and copper electrofill systems.*

**Novellus Systems SARL, 1488 Corniche de St. Ferreol, F-83510 Lorgues, France**
Tel: 33-4-946-76952   Fax: 33-4-946-76990

**Novellus Systems SARL, Parc de la Julienne Bat D 1 er etage, F-91830 LeCoudray-Montceaux, France**
Tel: 33-1-64-93-7070   Fax: 33-1-64-93-8787

## NOVO SYSTEMS CORPORATION

4061 Clipper Court, Fremont, CA, 94538-6540

Tel: (510) 360-8100    Fax: (510) 623-4484    www.novosystems.com

*Design/development/mfr./market logic and fault simulation acceleration products; system engineering services.*

**Zycad SARL, 69 rue d'Aguesseau, F-92100 Boulogne, France**

## NU SKIN ENTERPRISES, INC.

75 West Center St., Provo, UT, 84601

Tel: (801) 345-6100    Fax: (801) 345-5999    www.nuskin.com

*Develops and distributes premium-quality personal care and nutritional products.*

**NuSkin France, 90 Ave. des Champs Elysees, F-75008 Paris, France**

## NUS INFORMATION SERVICES, INC.

2650 McCormick Dr., Ste. 300, Clearwater, FL, 33759-1049

Tel: (727) 669-3000    Fax: (727) 669-3100    www.nus.com

*Provides case-based expert knowledge, bench-marking, trending, and operational services to the electric power and inventory industries.*

**National Utility Service France SA, Tour Fiat, Cedex 16, F-92084 Paris La Defense, France**

## NVF (NATIONAL VULCANIZED FIBRE) COMPANY

1166 Yorklyn Road, Yorklyn, DE, 19736

Tel: (302) 239-5281    Fax: (302) 239-4323    www.nvf.com

*Metal containers, steel products, laminated plastics and papers.*

**NVF Europe, F-69540 Irigny, France**

## OCLI, INC. (OPTICAL COATING LABORATORY, INC.)

2789 Northpoint Pkwy., Santa Rosa, CA, 95407-7397

Tel: (707) 545-6440    Fax: (707) 525-7410    www.ocli.com

*Mfr. thin film precision coated optical devices.*

**OCLI Optical Coating Lab EURL, Centre Vie, Batiment Le Tropic, Villejust, F-91969 Courtaboeuf Cedex, France**
Tel: 33-1-69-07-0761

**OFFICE DEPOT, INC.**

2200 Old Germantown Road, Delray Beach, FL, 33445

Tel: (561) 278-4800        Fax: (561) 265-4406        www.officedepot.com

*Discount office product retailer with warehouse-style superstores.*

**Office Depot France, 3 Chemin De La Croix Brisse, F-92160 Antony Z.A., Paris, France**

Tel: 33-1-46-11-7000    Fax: 33-1-46-11-7011

**Office Depot France, Z.I. Senia Nord, 7 rue Des Alouettes, F-94320 Thiais, France**

Tel: 33-1-17-32-525    Fax: 33-1-17-32-2526

**OGILVY PUBLIC RELATIONS WORLDWIDE**

909 Third Ave., New York, NY, 10022

Tel: (212) 880-5201        Fax: (212) 697-8250        www.ogilvypr.com

*Engaged in public relations and communications.*

**Ogilvy Public Relations Worldwide, 40 Avenue George V, 75008 Paris, France**

Tel: 33-1-5357 9200    Fax: 33-1-5357 9202    Contact: Nick May

**OHAUS CORPORATION**

29 Hanover Road, PO Box 900, Florham Park, NJ, 07932-0900

Tel: (973) 377-9000        Fax: (973) 593-0359        www.ohaus.com

*Mfr. balances and scales for laboratories, industry and education.*

**Ohaus SARL, 85 rue Joseph-Bertrand, BP 30, F-78220 Viroflay, France**

Tel: 33-1-3924-0193

**OIL STATES INDUSTRIES**

7701 South Cooper Street, Arlington, TX, 76017

Tel: (817) 468-1400        Fax: (817) 468-6250        www.oilstates.com

*Mfr. drilling and production machinery and supplies for oil/gas production.*

**Oil States Industries, Inc., Rep Office, 36 Bd des Oceans, 13275 Marseille Cedex 9, France**

Tel: 33-491-291-833

**THE OILGEAR COMPANY**

2300 S. 51st Street, Milwaukee, WI, 53219

Tel: (414) 327-1700        Fax: (414) 327-0532        www.oilgear.com

*Mfr. hydraulic power transmission machinery.*

**Oilgear Towler SA, Marne-la-Valee, ZI de Pariest, Alle des Freres Montgolfier, F-77183 Croissy-Beaubourg France**

**OLIN CORPORATION**

501 Merritt Seven, Norwalk, CT, 06856-4500

Tel: (203) 750-3000        Fax: (203) 750-3292        www.olin.com

*Mfr. chemicals, metals, sporting ammunition and copper and copper alloy sheets.*

**Olin SA-Hunt/Winchester, ZAC Paris Nord 11, 209 ave. des Nations BP 60019, F-95970 Charles de Galle Cedex, France**

**OM GROUP, INC. (OMG)**

3800 Terminal Tower, Cleveland, OH, 44113-2203

Tel: (216) 781-0083        Fax: (216) 781-0902        www.omgi.com

*Producer and marketer of metal-based specialty chemicals.*

**OM Group, Inc., Ezanville, France**

## OMNICOM GROUP

437 Madison Ave., New York, NY, 10022

Tel: (212) 415-3600    Fax: (212) 415-3530    www.omnicomgroup.com

*International network of advertising, marketing, direct mail, public relations and consulting services.*

**BDDP Worldwide, 162-164 rue de Billancourt, F-92100 Boulogne Paris, France**

Tel: 33-1-49-09-7010   Fax: 33-1-49-09-7633   Contact: Jean-marie Dru   Emp: 2,139

## ONTRACK DATA INTERNATIONAL, INC.

9023 Columbine Rd., Eden Prairie, MN, 55347

Tel: (612) 937-1107    Fax: (612) 937-5815    www.ontrack.com

*Computer data evidence services company, rescuing lost or corrupted data, and software sales.*

**Ontrack Data International, Inc., 2 impasse de la Noisette, F-91371 Verriéres-le-Buisson Cedex 413, France**

Tel: 33-1-4919-2263   Fax: 33-1-4919-2237

## ONYX SOFTWARE CORPORATION

3180 139th Avenue, SE, Bellevue, WA, 98005

Tel: (425) 451-8060    Fax: (425) 451-8277    www.onyx.com

*Mfr. customer relationship management software.*

**Onyx Software France, 2 rue Victor Griffuelhes, 92772 Boulogne Cedex, France**

Tel: 33-1-4694-7575

## OPEN MARKET, INC.

1 Wayside Road, Burlington, MA, 01803

Tel: (781) 359-3000    Fax: (781) 359-8111    www.openmarket.com

*Mfr. catalog management software.*

**Open Market France SARL, 120 avenue Charles de Gaulle, F-92200 Neuilly sur Seine, France**

Tel: 33-14640-3895

## ORACLE CORPORATION

500 Oracle Parkway, Redwood Shores, CA, 94065

Tel: (650) 506-7000    Fax: (650) 506-7200    www.oracle.com

*Develop/manufacture software.*

**Oracle France, 65 rue des Trois Fontanot, F-92732 Nanterre Cedex, France**

## ORIEL INSTRUMENTS CORPORATION

150 Long Beach Boulevard, Stratford, CT, 06615

Tel: (203) 377-8282    Fax: (203) 378-2457    www.oriel.com

*Mfr. optical goods.*

**L.O.T.-Oriel SARL, 9 ave. de Laponie, Z.A. de Courtaboeuf, F-91940 Les Ulis, France**

Tel: 33-1-60-92-1616   Fax: 33-1-60-92-1610

## OSMONICS INC.

5951 Clearwater Drive, Minnetonka, MN, 55343-8995

Tel: (952) 933-2277    Fax: (952) 933-0141    www.osmonics.com

*Mfr. equipment, controls and components for the filtration and water-treatment industries.*

**Osmonics, Le Mee Sur Seine (Paris), France**

## OTIS ELEVATOR COMPANY

10 Farm Springs Road, Farmington, CT, 06032

Tel: (860) 676-6000    Fax: (860) 676-5111    www.otis.com

*Mfr. elevators and escalators.*

**Otis Elevator Intl. Inc., 4 Place de La Defense, F-92974 Paris la Defense, France**

## OWENS-CORNING CORPORATION

One Owens Corning Pkwy., Toledo, OH, 43659

Tel: (419) 248-8000      Fax: (419) 248-8445      www.owenscorning.com

*Mfr. building materials systems and composites systems.*

**Owens Corning France, 68 Clos du Prieure Rozereuilles, F-57160 Moulins les Metz, France**

**Owens-Corning France SA, 21 rue des Pervenches, 31830 Plaisance du Touch, France**

Tel: 33-5-6186-9839

**Owens-Corning Isolation, 14 rue Ravelin, 10001 Troyes Cedex, France**

Tel: 33-325-74-0303

## PACCAR INC.

777 106th Ave. NE, Bellevue, WA, 98004

Tel: (425) 468-7400      Fax: (425) 468-8216      www.pacar.com

*Heavy duty dump trucks, military vehicles.*

**PACCAR International, BP 140 Les jardins de Farues, F-84130 LePontet, France**

Tel: 33-4-90-32-0621

## PACIFIC SCIENTIFIC COMPANY

4301 Kishwaukee Street, PO Box 106, Rockford, IL, 61105-0106

Tel: (815) 226-3100      Fax: (815) 226-3148      www.pacsci.com

*Mfr. high performance motors and drives.*

**Pacific Scientific SARL, 2 Allee des Garays, F-91124 Palaiseau, France**

## PALL CORPORATION

2200 Northern Boulevard, East Hills, NY, 11548-1289

Tel: (516) 484-5400      Fax: (516) 484-5228      www.pall.com

*Specialty materials and engineering; filters and related fluid clarification equipment.*

**Pall Filtration Industrielle, Div. De Pall France, 3 rue des Gaudines BP 5252, F-78175 St. Germain en Laye Cedex, France**

Tel: 33-1-30-61-3953   Fax: 33-1-30-61-3898

**Pall Gelman Sciences, Cite Descartes - 10 allee, Lorentz, F-77420 Champs sur Marne, France**

Tel: 33-1-6461-5252   Fax: 33-1-6461-5262

## PANALARM DIV. AMETEK

1725 Western Dr., West Chicago, IL, 60185

Tel: (630) 231-5900      Fax: (630) 231-4502      www.panalarm.com

*Mfr. electrical alarm systems, temp monitors, display systems, sensors.*

**AMETEK Precision Instruments France SARL, 3 Avenue des Coudriers, Z.A. de l'Observatoire, Montigny Le Bretonneux CampF- 78180, France**

Tel: 33-1-30-64-89-70

## PANAMETRICS

221 Crescent Street, Waltham, MA, 02154

Tel: (781) 899-2719      Fax: (781) 899-1552      www.panametrics.com

*Process/non-destructive test instrumentation.*

**Panametrics, S.A., 11 rue du Renard, F-92250 La Garenne Colombes, France**

Tel: 33-1-47-82-4281   Fax: 33-1-47-86-7490   Contact: Alan Chapas

**Sofranel, 59 rue Parmentier, F-78500 Sartrouville, France**

Tel: 33-1-39-13-8236   Fax: 33-1-39-13-1942

## PANDUIT CORPORATION

17301 Ridgeland Ave., Tinley Park, IL, 60477-0981

Tel: (708) 532-1800      Fax: (708) 532-1811      www.panduit.com

*Mfr. electrical/electronic wiring components.*

**Panduit SNC, 91 blvd. Alsace Lorraine, F-93110 Rosny sous Bois, France**

## PARADYNE NETWORKS, INC.

8545 126 Ave. North, Largo, FL, 33773

Tel: (727) 530-2000     Fax: (727) 530-2875     www.paradyne.com

*Engaged in data communications and high-speed network access solutions.*

**Paradyne France, Paris, France**

## PARAMETRIC TECHNOLOGY CORPORATION

128 Technology Drive, Waltham, MA, 02154

Tel: (781) 398-5000     Fax: (781) 398-5674     www.ptc.com

*Supplier of mechanical design automation and product data management software and services.*

**Parametric Technology S.A., Technopole Metz 2000 Cescom, 4 rue Marconi, F-57070 Metz Cedex, France**

Tel: 33-3-87-20-41-47   Fax: 33-3-87-20-41-48

**Parametric Technology S.A., Technorparc Du Griffon, 511 Route de la Seds, F-13746 Vitolles Cedex, France**

Tel: 33-4-42-40-53-80   Fax: 33-4-42-10-53-99

**Parametric Technology S.A., 13 rue des Granges Galand, BP 414, F-37554 Saint Avertin Cedex, France**

Tel: 33-2-47-80-31-35   Fax: 33-2-47-27-89-64

**Parametric Technology S.A., Aeropole 1, 5 Ave. Albert Durand, F-37160 Blagnac, France**

Tel: 33-5-61-31-62-61   Fax: 33-5-61-71-35-00

**Parametric Technology S.A., Parc Tertiaire Valparc, F-67205 Oberhausbergen, France**

Tel: 33-3-90-20-50-50   Fax: 33-3-88-56-32-44

**Parametric Technology S.A., Parc d'Activities de Limonest, 283 rue de l'Etang, F-69760 Linoest, France**

Tel: 33-4-78-66-41-80   Fax: 33-4-78-35-94-11

**Parametric Technology S.A., Parc Innolin, 3 rue du Golfe, F-33700 Merignac France**

Tel: 33-5-56-34-75-00   Fax: 33-5-56-34-74-12

**Parametric Technology S.A., Place Francois Mitterrand 01, Tour Credit Lyonnais, F-59777 Eura Lille, France**

Tel: 33-3-20-12-52-88   Fax: 33-3-20-12-52-87

**Parametric Technology S.A., Novapole 18, rue de la Tullerie, F-38170 Seyssinet, France**

Tel: 33-4-76-70-30-70   Fax: 33-4-76-70-30-96

**Parametric Technology S.A., 1 rue Charles Lindbergh, F-44340 Nantes Bouguenais, France**

Tel: 33-2-40-32-25-07   Fax: 32-2-40-04-10-80

**Parametric Technology S.A., Parc Curospace, Baitement 19, F-91573 Bievrex Cedex France**

Tel: 33-1-69-33-65-00   Fax: 33-1-69-33-65-65

**Parametric Technology S.A., Centre Atria, Ave. De L'Esperance, F-90000 Belfort France**

Tel: 33-3-88-56-93-50   Fax: 33-3-88-56-93-43

**Parametric Technology S.A., 1 Rond-Point Des Bruyeres N1, F-76300 Sottesville-Les-Rouen, France**

Tel: 33-2-32-81-97-00   Fax: 32-2-32-81-97-01

## PAREXEL INTERNATIONAL CORPORATION

195 West Street, Waltham, MA, 02154

Tel: (781) 487-9900     Fax: (781) 487-0525     www.parexel.com

*Provides contract medical, biotechnology, and pharmaceutical research and consulting services.*

**PAREXEL International, 124/126 rue de Provence, F-75008 Paris, France**

Tel: 33-1-44-90-3200   Fax: 33-1-44-90-3232

## PARK ELECTROCHEMICAL CORPORATION

5 Dakota Drive, Lake Success, NY, 11042

Tel: (516) 354-4100        Fax: (516) 354-4128        www.parkelectrochemical.com

*Multi-layer laminate printed circuit materials, industry comps, plumbing hardware products.*

**Nelco SA, Rte.de Beze, 213 Mirebeau sur Beze, France**

## PARKER HANNIFIN CORPORATION

6035 Parkland Blvd., Cleveland, OH, 44124-4141

Tel: (216) 896-3000        Fax: (216) 896-4000        www.parker.com

*Mfr. motion-control products.*

**Parker Hannifin Corp., Motion & Control/Parker Hannifin RAK, SA Centre Paris Pleyel, Tour Wuest, 153 Blvd. Anatole France, F-93521 St. Denis Cedex France**

**Parker Hannifin Corp./Parker Hannifin RAK SA, 8 rue Pierre Dechanet BP 229, F-25303 Pontarlier Cedex, France**

**Parker Hannifin Corp./Parker Hannifin RAK SA, Z.A.E. La Foret, F-74138 Contamine-sur-Arve, France**

**Parker Hannifin RAK SA, 17 rue des Buchillons, ZI du Mont-Blanc, BP 524 Ville-La-Grand, F-74112 Annemasse France**

**Parker Hennifin Corp., Telemecanique, rue Henri Becquerel, BP 3124, F-27031 Evreux Cedex France**

## PARTECH INTERNATIONAL

50 California Street, Ste. 3200, San Francisco, CA, 94111-4624

Tel: (415) 788-2929        Fax: (415) 788-6763        www.partechintl.com

*Invests in startup and growth companies in information technology, communications and healthcare.*

**Partech International, 42 Avenue Raymond Poincare, F-75116 Paris, France**

## PATAGONIA INC.

259 West Santa Clara Street, Ventura, CA, 93001

Tel: (805) 643-8616        Fax: (805) 653-6355        www.patagonia.com

*Outdoor clothing retail stores and mail-order catalogue company.*

**Patagonia, Inc., Paris, France**

## PAUL, WEISS, RIFKIND, WHARTON & GARRISON

1285 Ave. of the Americas, New York, NY, 10019-6064

Tel: (212) 373-3000        Fax: (212) 373-2268        www.paulweiss.com

*Law firm engaged in American and international law practice.*

**Paul, Weiss, Rifkind, Wharton & Garrison, 62 rue du Fauberb Saint-Honore, F-75008, Paris, France**
Tel: 33-1-53-43-1414   Fax: 33-1-53-43-0023

## PCA ELECTRONICS INC.

16799 Schoenborn Street, North Hills, CA, 91343

Tel: (818) 892-0761        Fax: (818) 894-5791        www.pca.com

*Mfr./sales of electronic equipment.*

**Secre Composants, 117 rue des Pre Martin, F-77348 Pontault Compault Cedex, France**
Tel: 33-1-60-18-2000   Fax: 33-1-60-18-2020

## THE PEELLE COMPANY

34 Central Ave., Hauppauge, NY, 11788-4734

Tel: (631) 231-6000        Fax: (631) 231-6059        www.peelledoor.com

*Mfr./sales/service elevator, fire and specially engineered doors.*

**Ascenseurs Fermetures, Rep. Peelle Company, 7 rue de la Croix Blanche, F-78618 Saint Leger en Yvelines, France**

## PEOPLESOFT INC.

4460 Hacienda Drive, Pleasanton, CA, 94588-8618

Tel: (925) 225-3000     Fax: (925) 694-4444     www.peoplesoft.com

*Mfr. applications to manage business operations across computer networks.*

**PeopleSoft France, S.A., 153 rue de Courcelles, F-75017 Paris Cedex, France**

Tel: 33-1-4429-5000   Fax: 33-1-4429-5001

## PEPSiCO INC.

700 Anderson Hill Road, Purchase, NY, 10577-1444

Tel: (914) 253-2000     Fax: (914) 253-2070     www.pepsico.com

*Beverages and snack foods.*

**PepsiCo de France SARL, Paris, France**

## PEROT SYSTEMS CORPORATION

PO Box 809022, Dallas, TX, 75380

Tel: (972) 340-5000     Fax: (972) 455-4100     www.perotsystems.com

*Engaged in computer services technology.*

**Perot Systems Corporation, Paris, France**

## PFIZER INC.

235 East 42nd Street, New York, NY, 10017-5755

Tel: (212) 573-2323     Fax: (212) 573-7851     www.pfizer.com

*Research-based, global health care company.*

**CAL Pfizer, Paris, France**

**Climo SA, Paris, France**

**Laboratoire Beral SA, Paris, France**

**Orsim SA, Paris, France**

**Pfizer Diagnostic Products SARL, Paris, France**

**Pfizer SA, Paris, France**

**SA Benoist Girard & Cie., Paris, France**

## PHARMACIA CORPORATION

100 Route 206 North, Peapack, NJ, 07977

Tel: (908) 901-8000     Fax: (908) 901-8379     www.pharmacia.com

*Mfr. pharmaceuticals, agricultural products, industry chemicals.*

**Laboratoires Upjohn SARL, Tour Franklin, F-92081 Paris Cedex 11, France**

## PHARMACIA MONSANTO

800 N. Lindbergh Boulevard, St. Louis, MO, 63167

Tel: (314) 694-1000     Fax: (314) 694-7625     www.monsanto.com

*Life sciences company focusing on agriculture, nutrition, pharmaceuticals, health and wellness and sustainable development.*

**Monsanto Co. Chemical Group, Division Agriculture, Europarc du Chene, 11 rue Pascal, 69673 Bron Cedex France**

**Monsanto France, Immeuble Elysees La Defense, 7 Place de Dome, F-92056 Paris La Defense Cedex, France**

Tel: 33-1-55-23-1201   Fax: 33-1-55-23-1212

## PHH VEHICLE MANAGEMENT SERVICES

307 International Circle, Hunt Valley, MD, 21030

Tel: (410) 771-3600     Fax: (410) 771-2841     www.phh.com

*Provides vehicle fleet management, corporate relocation, and mortgage banking services.*

**Arval Service Lease, 119-121 Grande rue, F-92318 Serves Cedex, Paris, France**

Tel: 33-1-41-14-1818

## PHILIPP BROTHERS CHEMICALS INC.

1 Parker Plaza, Fort Lee, NJ, 07029

Tel: (201) 944-6020        Fax: (201) 944-7916        www.philipp-brothers.com

*Mfr. industry and agricultural chemicals.*

**Phibrotec SA, 33 rue de la Baume, F-75008 Paris, France**

## PHILLIPS PETROLEUM COMPANY

Phillips Building, 411 S. Keeler Ave., Bartlesville, OK, 74004

Tel: (918) 661-6600        Fax: (918) 661-7636        www.phillips66.com

*Crude oil, natural gas, liquefied petroleum gas, gasoline and petro-chemicals.*

**Phillips Petroleum International France, 37 ave. d'Lena, F-75116 Paris, France**

## PICTURETEL CORPORATION

100 Minuteman Road, Andover, MA, 01810

Tel: (978) 292-5000        Fax: (978) 292-3300        www.picturetel.com

*Mfr. video conferencing systems, network bridging and multiplexing products, system peripherals.*

**PictureTel International Corp., 38 rue de Villiers, F-92532 Levallois Perret Cedex, France**

Tel: 33-1-41-49-5969   Fax: 33-1-41-49-5968

## PINNACLE WORLDWIDE, INC.

1201 Marquette Ave., Ste. 300, Minneapolis, MN, 55403

Tel: (612) 338-2215        Fax: (612) 338-2572        www.pinnacleww.com

*International network of independent public relations firms.*

**Self Images Relationes Publiques, 88 Avenue Kléber, F-75116 Paris, France**

## PIONEER HI-BRED INTERNATIONAL INC.

400 Locust Street, Ste. 800, Des Moines, IA, 50309

Tel: (515) 248-4800        Fax: (515) 248-4999        www.pioneer.com

*Agricultural chemicals, farm supplies, biological products, research.*

**Pioneer France Mais SA, 4 rue Paul Bernies, F-31200 Toulouse, France**

**Pioneer Genetique SARL Ltd., Chemin de l'Enseigure, F-31700 Blagnac, France**

## PIONEER-STANDARD ELECTRONICS, INC.

6065 Parkland Blvd., Cleveland, OH, 44124

Tel: (440) 720-8500        Fax: (440) 720-8501        www.pios.com

*Mfr./distribution of electronic parts for computers and networking equipment.*

**Eurodis Electronics France, 30 Ave de L'Epi D'Or, 94807 Villejuif Cedex, France**

## PITNEY BOWES INC.

1 Elmcroft Road, Stamford, CT, 06926-0700

Tel: (203) 356-5000        Fax: (203) 351-6835        www.pitneybowes.com

*Mfr. postage meters, mailroom equipment, copiers, bus supplies, bus services, facsimile systems and financial services.*

**Pitney Bowes Finance S.A., Espace Clichy Batiment Andromede, 82 rue de Villeneuve, F-92587 Clichy Cedex-Paris, France**

Tel: 33-143-94-9925

## PITTSTON BAX GROUP

16808 Armstrong Ave., PO Box 19571, Irvine, CA, 92623

Tel: (949) 752-4000        Fax: (949) 260-3182        www.baxworld.com

*Air freight forwarder.*

**BAX Global, rue des Deux Cedres, BP 10287, F-95704 Roissy Aeroport Cedex Paris, France**

Tel: 33-1-48-64-6363   Fax: 33-1-48-62-7715

## PITTWAY CORPORATION

200 South Wacker Drive, Chicago, IL, 60606

Tel: (312) 831-1070     Fax: (312) 831-0808     www.pittway.com

*Mfr. alarm and other controls.*

**ADEMCO France,  Parc Gutenberg 13, Voie La Cardon, PO F-91120 Palaiseau, France**

Tel: 33-1-6932-1090   Fax: 33-1-6932-1088

## PLANET HOLLYWOOD INTERNATIONAL, INC.

8669 Commodity Circle, Orlando, FL, 32819

Tel: (407) 363-7827     Fax: (407) 363-4862     www.planethollywood.com

*Theme-dining restaurant chain and merchandise retail stores.*

**Planet Hollywood International, Inc.,  Paris, France**

## PLANTRONICS

345 Encinal Street, Santa Cruz, CA, 95060

Tel: (831) 426-5858     Fax: (831) 425-5198     www.plantronics.com

*Mfr. communications equipment, electrical and electronic appliances and apparatus.*

**Plantronics France,  Parc Technologique "La Corvette", 142-176 Ave. de Stalingrad, F-92700 Colombes, France**

Tel: 33-1-46-49-8300   Fax: 33-1-46-49-8309   Contact: William Amoyal, Sales Mgr.

## PLAYTEX APPAREL INC.

700 Fairfield Ave., Stamford, CT, 06904

Tel: (203) 356-8000     Fax: (203) 356-8448     www.playtexbras.com

*Mfr. intimate apparel.*

**Playtex France,  BP 55, Zone Industrielle, F-38356 La Tour du Pin Cedex, France**

## POLARIS INDUSTRIES INC.

2100 Highway 55, Medina, MN, 55440

Tel: (612) 542-0500     Fax: (612) 542-0599     www.polarisindustries.com

*Mfr. snowmobiles and all-terrain recreational and utility vehicles.*

**Wintersnow,  2770 Avenue De Saint-Martin, F074190 Passy, France**

Tel: 33-4-5093-9614

## POLAROID CORPORATION

784 Memorial Dr., Cambridge, MA, 02139

Tel: (781) 386-2000     Fax: (781) 386-3924     www.polaroid.com

*Photographic equipment and supplies, optical products.*

**Polaroid (France) S.A.,  B.P. 7, 78996 Elancourt Cedex, France**

**Polaroid France SA,  57 rue de Villiers, F-92202 Neuilly, France**

## POTTERS INDUSTRIES INC.

PO Box 840, Valley Forge, PA, 19482-0840

Tel: (610) 651-4700     Fax: (610) 408-9724     www.pottersbeads.com

*Mfr. glass spheres for road marking and industry applications.*

**Potters-Ballotini SA,  Z.I. DuPont-Panay, 4 rue des Champs Elysees, F-03500 Saint-Pourcain-sur-Sioule, France**

## POWERWARE CORPORATION

8609 Six Forks Road, Raleigh, NC, 27615

Tel: (919) 870-3020     Fax: (919) 870-3100     www.powerware.com

*Mfr./services uninterruptible power supplies and related equipment.*

**Powerware Electronics SA,  2/4 rue Gustave Flourens, F-92150 Suresnes, France**

Tel: 33-1-42-04-9400   Fax: 33-1-42-04-4222

## PPG INDUSTRIES

One PPG Place, Pittsburgh, PA, 15272

Tel: (412) 434-3131     Fax: (412) 434-2190     www.ppg.com

*Mfr. coatings, flat glass, fiber glass, chemicals, coatings.*

**PPG Industries (France) SA, Immeuble SCOR, 1 ave. du President Wilson, F-92074 Paris La Defense Cedex, France**

**Sipsy Chimie Fine S.C.A., Route de Beaucouze, F-49240 Avrille, France**

## PRAXAIR, INC.

39 Old Ridgebury Road, Danbury, CT, 06810-5113

Tel: (203) 837-2000     Fax: (203) 837-2450     www.praxair.com

*Produces and distributes industrial and specialty gases.*

**Praxair S.A., 1-7 rue Traversiere, Silic 402, F-94573 Rungis Cedex, France**

Tel: 33-1-49-78-4500   Fax: 33-1-46-75-9461

## PRECISION CASTPARTS CORPORATION

4650 SW Macadam Ave., Ste. 440, Portland, OR, 97206

Tel: (503) 417-4800     Fax: (503) 417-4817     www.precast.com

*Mfr. metal castings.*

**Precision Castparts Corp. France SA, 64680 Ogeu Bains, France**

## PRECISION VALVE & TRIM, INC.

PO Box 3091, 1923 Cloverland Avenue, Baton Rouge, LA, 70809

Tel: (225) 752-5600     Fax: (225) 752-5400     www.precisionvalve.com

*Mfr. aerosol valves.*

**Valve Precision SARL, 3 rue de la Croix Martre, BP 38, F-91120 Palaiseau, France**

## PREMARK INTERNATIONAL INC.

1717 Deerfield Road, Deerfield, IL, 60015

Tel: (847) 405-6000     Fax: (847) 405-6013     www.premarkintl.com

*Mfr. Hobart commercial food equipment, diversified consumer and commercial products, small appliances, and exercise equipment.*

**Dart Europe SA, BP 327, F-37303 Joue-les-Tours Cedex, France**

## PRI AUTOMATION, INC.

805 Middlesex Turnpike, Billerica, MA, 01821-3986

Tel: (978) 663-8555     Fax: (978) 663-9755     www.pria.com

*Provides factory automation systems for silicon chip makers.*

**PRI Automation, European Headquarters, Les Jardins de Maupertuis, Bat. le Juparana, 7 Chemin de la Dhuy, F-38240 Meylan France**

Tel: 33-4-76-18-92-00   Fax: 33-4-76-18-91-98

## PRICEWATERHOUSECOOPERS LLP

1301 Ave. of the Americas, New York, NY, 10019

Tel: (212) 596-7000     Fax: (212) 259-1301     www.pwcglobal.com

*Accounting and auditing, tax and management, and human resource consulting services.*

**PriceWaterhouseCoopers, 1 allee Baco, BP 471, F-44015 Nantes Cedex, France**

Tel: 33-40-89-7373   Fax: 33-40-48-4544

**PriceWaterhouseCoopers, 1 rue de la Republique, F-69001 Lyon, France**

Tel: 33-78-27-5060   Fax: 33-7-78-27-5029

**PriceWaterhouseCoopers, 1 rue Daumier, F-13008 Marseille, France**

Tel: 33-91-37-2736   Fax: 33-91-81-2-55

**PriceWaterhouseCoopers, Tour AIG, 34 place des Corolles, F-92908 Paris La Defense 2 Cedex 105, France**

Tel: 33-1-41-26-1000   Fax: 33-1-41-26-4222

PriceWaterhouseCoopers, 1 Place Alfonse Jourdain, F-31000 Toulouse, France
Tel: 33-61-21-1871   Fax: 33-61-21-03-60

PriceWaterhouseCoopers, Le Sebastopol, 3 Quai Kleber, F-67055 Strausbourg Cedex, France
Tel: 33-88-22-2200   Fax: 33-88-75-6401

PriceWaterhouseCoopers, Parvis Sud de la Gare, 19 rue de Chatillon, F-35000 Rennes, France
Tel: 33-99-32-2100   Fax: 33-99-32-2032

PriceWaterhouseCoopers, 99 rue Nationale, F-59800 Lille, France
Tel: 33-20-12-5645   Fax: 33-20-12-5642

PriceWaterhouseCoopers, Parc de la Vatine, 20 rue Aron, F-76130 Mont Saint Aignan, France
Tel: 33-35-59-00-85   Fax: 33-35-59-9596

## PRIMARK CORPORATION

100 Winter Street, Ste. 4300-N, Waltham, MA, 02451
Tel: (781) 466-6611      Fax: (781) 890-6187      www.primark.com
*Provides financial and business information.*

Primark France S.A., 59-61 rue La Fayette, F-75009 Paris, France
Tel: 33-1-5332-3900

## PRINTRONIX INC.

14600 Myford Road, Irvine, CA, 92606
Tel: (714) 368-2300      Fax: (714) 368-2600      www.printronix.com
*Mfr. computer printers.*

Printronix France, 8 rue Parmentier, F-92800 Puteaux, France
Tel: 33-1-46-25-1900   Fax: 33-1-46-25-1919

## PROCTER & GAMBLE COMPANY

One Procter & Gamble Plaza, Cincinnati, OH, 45202
Tel: (513) 983-1100      Fax: (513) 562-4500      www.pg.com
*Personal care, food, laundry, cleaning and industry products.*

Procter & Gamble France, 96 ave. Charles de Gaulle, F-92201 Neuilly sur Seine, France
Tel: 33-1-40-88-5923

## PRODUCTION GROUP INTERNATIONAL, INC.

2200 Wilson Blvd., Ste 200, Arlington, VA, 22201-3324
Tel: (703) 528-8484      Fax: (703) 528-1724      www.pgi.com
*Provides major corporations with promotional events, planning and travel services, trade shows and exhibitions.*

PGI/Spearhead, 18 rue Germain Pilon, F-75018 Paris, Cedex France
Tel: 33-1-4258-04 01

## PROSKAUER ROSE LLP

1585 Broadway, New York, NY, 10036
Tel: (212) 969-3000      Fax: (212) 969-2900      www.proskauer.com
*International law firm.*

Dubarry Le Douarin & Veil, 9 rue Le Tasse, Trocadero, Paris, France
Proskauer Rose LLP, 9 rue Le Tasse, Trocadero, Paris, France
Contact: William Krisel

## PSDI MAXIMO

100 Crosby Drive, Bedford, MA, 01730
Tel: (781) 280-2000      Fax: (781) 280-0200      www.psdi.com
*Develops, markets and provides maintenance management software systems.*

PSDI France SARL, Immeuble ATRIA, 2 rue de Centre, F-93885 Noisy Le Grand Cedex, France
Tel: 33-1-48-15-5580   Fax: 33-1-48-15-5599   Contact: Pascal Robez, Gen. Mgr.   Emp: 12

**PSI NET (PERFORMANCE SYSTEMS INTERNATIONAL INC.)**

510 Huntmar Park Drive, Herndon, VA, 22170

Tel: (703) 904-4100        Fax: (703) 904-4200        www.psinet.com

*Internet service provider.*

**PSINet France S.A.R.L.,  8/10 rue Nieuport, F-78140 Vélizy, France**

Tel: 33-1-346-319-19    Fax: 33-1-346-319-48    Contact: Moos Bulder, Reg. VP

**PURE FISHING**

1900 18th Street, Spirit Lake, IA, 51360

Tel: (712) 336-1520        Fax: (712) 336-4183        www.purefishing.com

*Mfr. fishing rods, reels, lines and tackle, outdoor  products, soft and hard baits.*

**Johnson Outdoors Berkley,  Marignier, France**

**QUAKER CHEMICAL CORPORATION**

Elm & Lee Streets, Conshohocken, PA, 19428-0809

Tel: (610) 832-4000        Fax: (610) 832-8682        www.quakerchem.com

*Mfr. developer, producer, and marketer of custom-formulated chemical specialty products.*

**Quaker Chemical S.A,  21 ave. Nobel, F-92396 Villeneuve la Garenne Cedex, France**

Tel: 33-1-40.85.71.71    Contact: P. Peignoux

**THE QUAKER OATS COMPANY**

Quaker Tower, 321 North Clark Street, Chicago, IL, 60610-4714

Tel: (312) 222-7111        Fax: (312) 222-8323        www.quakeroats.com

*Mfr. foods and beverages.*

**Quaker Oats France,  40 Blvd. de Dunkerque, F-13002 Marseille, France**

**QUALCOMM INC.**

5775 Morehouse Dr., San Diego, CA, 92121-1714

Tel: (858) 587-1121        Fax: (858) 658-2100        www.qualcomm.com

*Digital wireless telecommunications systems.*

**QUALCOMM,  2000 Route des Lucioles - 3/F, Sophia Antipolis, 06560 Valbonne, France**

**QUINTILES TRANSNATIONAL CORPORATION**

4709 Creekstone Dr., Durham, NC, 27703

Tel: (919) 998-2000        Fax: (919) 998-9113        www.quintiles.com

*Mfr. pharmaceuticals.*

**Benefit International SNC,  3-5 rue Maurice Ravel Levallois-Perret, Cedex F-92594 France**

**Benefit International SNC,  3-5 rue Maurice Ravel Levallois-Perret, Cedex, F-92594 France**

**Innovex SARL,  1416 rue de la Vanne, Montrouge F-92120, France**

**Quintiles S.A.,  3-5 rue Maurice Ravel Levallois-Perret, Cedex F-92594, France**

**QWEST COMMUNICATIONS INTERNATIONAL INC.**

1801 California Street, Ste. 5200, Denver, CO, 80202

Tel: (303) 896-2020        Fax: (303) 793-6654        www.uswest.com

*Tele-communications provider; integrated communications services.*

**KPNQwest (JV),  Paris, France**

**RADISSON HOTELS INTERNATIONAL**

Carlson Pkwy., PO Box 59159, Minneapolis, MN, 55459-8204

Tel: (612) 540-5526        Fax: (612) 449-3400        www.radisson.com

*Hotels and resorts.*

**Radisson SAS Hotel,  223 Promenade des Anglais, F-06200 Nice, France**

Tel: 33-4-93-37-17-17    Fax: 33-4-93-71-21-71

## RAIN BIRD SPRINKLER MFG. CORPORATION

145 North Grand Ave., Glendora, CA, 91741-2469

Tel: (626) 963-9311     Fax: (626) 963-4287     www.rainbird.com

*World's largest manufacturer of lawn sprinklers and irrigation systems equipment.*

**Rain Bird Europe, 535 rue Georges Claude, BP 72000, F-13792 Aix-en Provence Cedex 3, France**

Tel: 33-4-42-24-4461   Fax: 33-4-42-24-2472

**Rain Bird France, 415 rue Louis Armand, BP 72000, F-13792 Aix-en Provence Cedex 3, France**

Tel: 33-4-42-24-4461   Fax: 33-4-42-24-2472   Contact: Eric Tortelier

## RAINBOW TECHNOLOGY INC.

50 Technology Dr., Irvine, CA, 92618

Tel: (949) 450-7300     Fax: (949) 450-7450     www.rainbow.com

*Mfr. computer related security products.*

**Microphar France, 122 ave. Charles de Gaulle, F-29522 Neuilly-sur-Seine Cedex, France**

## RALSTON PURINA COMPANY

Checkerboard Square, St. Louis, MO, 63164-0001

Tel: (314) 982-1000     Fax: (314) 982-1211     www.ralston.com

*Produces dog and cat food and animal feed.*

**Duquesne Purina SA, Place Charles de Gaulle, F-78180 Montigny le Bretonneux, France**

## RAMSEY TECHNOLOGY INC.

501 90th Ave. NW, Coon Rapids, MN, 55433

Tel: (763) 783-2500     Fax: (763) 780-2525

*Mfr. in-motion weighing, inspection, monitoring and control equipment for the process industry.*

**Ramsey Engineering, 63 Place du Commerce, F-78370 Plaisir, France**

## RANCO INC.

8115 US Route 42 North, Plain City, OH, 43064

Tel: (614) 873-9000     Fax: (614) 873-3819     www.rancocontrols.com

*Mfr. controls for appliance, automotive, comfort, commercial and consumer markets.*

**Ranco France SA, rue Senouque, ZAC, F-78530 Buc, France**

## RAY & BERNDTSON, INC.

301 Commerce, Ste. 2300, Fort Worth, TX, 76102

Tel: (817) 334-0500     Fax: (817) 334-0779     www.prb.com

*Executive search, management audit and management consulting firm.*

**Ray & Berndtson, 73 Champs Elysées, F-75008 Paris, France**

Tel: 33-1-53-77-2200   Fax: 33-1-53-77-2209   Contact: Xavier Alix, Mng. Ptnr.

## RAYCHEM CORPORATION

300 Constitution Dr., Menlo Park, CA, 94025-1164

Tel: (650) 361-3333     Fax: (650) 361-5579     www.raychem.com

*Develop/mfr./market materials science products for electronics, telecommunications and industry.*

**Raychem SA, 3 Cours Mirabeau, F-13100 Aix-En-Provence, France**

Tel: 33-1-34-20-2122   Fax: 33-1-30-37-1650

**Raynet France, 2 Blvd. du Moulin a Vent, F-9580 Cergy St. Christophe, France**

Tel: 33-1-34-20-2122   Fax: 33-1-34-24-0312

## RAYMOND JAMES FINANCIAL, INC.

880 Carillon Parkway, St. Petersburg, FL, 33716

Tel: (813) 573-3800     Fax: (813) 573-8244     www.rjf.com

*Financial services; securities brokerage, asset management, and investment banking services.*

**Raymond James International, 14 rue de Berri, F-75008 Paris, France**

Tel: 33-1-45-63-6345   Fax: 33-1-45-63-3047   Contact: E. Laussinotte

## RAYTHEON COMPANY

141 Spring Street, Lexington, MA, 02173

Tel: (781) 862-6600    Fax: (781) 860-2172    www.raytheon.com

*Mfr. diversified electronics, appliances, aviation, energy and environmental products; publishing, industry and construction services.*

**Raytheon, 326 Bureaux de la Colline, F-92213 Saint Cloud Cedex, France**

## READER'S DIGEST ASSOCIATION, INC.

Reader's Digest Rd., Pleasantville, NY, 10570

Tel: (914) 238-1000    Fax: (914) 238-4559    www.readersdigest.com

*Publisher of magazines and books and direct mail marketer.*

**Selection du Readers Digest SA, 1 a 7 ave. Louis Pasteur, F-92220 Bagneux, France**

## REALNETWORKS, INC.

2601 Elliott Avenue, Ste. 1000, Seattle, WA, 98121

Tel: (206) 674-2700    Fax: (206) 674-2699    www.realnetworks.com

*Mfr. software, including RealPlayer.*

**RealNetworks, Inc., 2 Place De La Defense BP, Puteaux F-92053, France**
Tel: 33-1-5517-4078

## REEBOK INTERNATIONAL LTD.

100 Technology Center Drive, Stoughton, MA, 02072

Tel: (781) 401-5000    Fax: (781) 401-7402    www.reebok.com

*Mfr. athletic shoes including casual, dress golf and walking shoes.*

**Reebok France SA, 184 rue Tabuteau, F-78532 Buc Cedex, France**

## REED-HYCALOG INC.

6501 Navigation Blvd., PO Box 2119, Houston, TX, 77252

Tel: (713) 924-5200    Fax: (713) 924-5667    www.schlumberger.com

*Mfr. rock bits for oil and gas exploration.*

**Reed-Hycalog Tool Co., c/o Rig Service, BP 119, Z.I. Lons, F-64143 Pau-Billere-Cedex, France**

## REFCO GROUP LTD.

111 West Jackson Blvd, Suite 1800, Chicago, IL, 60604

Tel: (312) 930-6500    Fax: (312) 930-6534    www.refco.com

*Commodity and security brokers engaged in the execution and clearing of futures and options and institutional asset management services.*

**Refco Futures Ltd., Paris, France**

## REFLEXITE TECHNOLOGY

120 Darling Drive, Avon, CT, 06001

Tel: (860) 676-7100    Fax: (860) 676-7199    www.reflexite.com

*Mfr. plastic film, sheet, materials and shapes, optical lenses.*

**Reflexite France, Espace Florentin, 71 Chemin Du Moulin Carron, Dardilly F-69570, France**
Tel: 33-472-191910   Fax: 33-478-645833

## RELIANCE STEEL & ALUMINUM COMPANY

2550 E. 25th St., Los Angeles, CA, 90058

Tel: (323) 582-2272    Fax: (323) 582-2801    www.rsac.com

*Provides customized metal processing services.*

**Valex Corporation, Div. Reliance Steel & Aluminum, 77 Sac St. Charles, F-13710 FUV EAU, France**
Tel: 33-4-4253-4641   Fax: 33-4-4253-4644   Contact: Daniel A. Mangan

## REMEDY CORPORATION

1505 Salado Drive, Mountain View, CA, 94043-1110

Tel: (650) 903-5200     Fax: (650) 903-9001     www.remedy.com

*Developer and marketer of computer applications for the operations management market.*

**Remedy SARL,  19 Boulevard Malesherbes, F-75008 Paris, France**

Tel: 33-1-42-99-9580   Fax: 33-1-42-99-9591

## REMINGTON PRODUCTS COMPANY, L.L.C.

60 Main Street, Bridgeport, CT, 06604

Tel: (203) 367-4400     Fax: (203) 332-4848     www.remington-products.com

*Mfr. home appliances, electric shavers.*

**Remington Products Co.,  65-75 Au Jean Mermoz, Batiment K, F-93120 La Courneuve, France**

Tel: 33-1-48-35-3450   Fax: 33-1-48-35-0562   Contact: Pierre Pichard, Gen. Mgr.

## RENAISSANCE HOTELS AND RESORTS

10400 Fernwood Road, Bethesda, MD, 20817

Tel: (301) 380-3000     Fax: (301) 380-5181     www.renaissancehotels.com

*Hotel and resort chain.*

**Renaissance Paris Hotel,  Le Defense, Paris, France**

Tel: 33-1-41-97-5050

## RENAISSANCE WORLDWIDE, INC.

52 Second Ave., Waltham, MA, 02451

Tel: (781) 290-3000     Fax: (781) 965-4807     www.rens.com

*Provides technology consulting, staffing services, corporate and systems strategies and software and hardware installation.*

**Exad Galons,  1 Rond Point Victor Hugo, F-92130 Issy-les-Mouleneaux, France**

Tel: 33-1-4190-1666   Fax: 33-1-4190-1650

## RESMED INC.

1440 Danielson Street, Poway, CA, 92064

Tel: (858) 746-2400     Fax: (858) 880-1618     www.resmed.com

*Mfr. sleep apnea aids, including nasal masks and accessories.*

**ResMed SA,  Parc de la Bandonnière, 2 rue Maurice Audibert,
69800 Saint-Priest, France**

Tel: 33-4-37-251-251   Fax: 33-4-37-251-260

## REVLON INC.

625 Madison Ave., New York, NY, 10022

Tel: (212) 527-4000     Fax: (212) 527-4995     www.revlon.com

*Mfr. cosmetics, fragrances, toiletries and beauty care products.*

**Revlon SA,  42 ave. Montaine, F-75008 Paris, France**

Contact: Philippe Perrin, Gen. Mgr.

## REXNORD CORPORATION

4701 West Greenfield Ave., Milwaukee, WI, 53214

Tel: (414) 643-3000     Fax: (414) 643-3078     www.rexnord.com

*Mfr. power transmission products.*

**Rexnord France SARL,  ZA les Petits Carreaux, 5 ave. des Marguerites, F-94380 Bonneuil sur Marne Cedex, France**

## RHEOMETRIC SCIENTIFIC INC.

1 Possumtown Road, Piscataway, NJ, 08854

Tel: (732) 560-8550     Fax: (732) 560-7451     www.rheosci.com

*Design/mfr. rheological instruments and systems.*

**Rheometric Scientific SARL,  7 rue Albert Einstein, F-77436 Marne la Vallee Cedex, France**

## RICHCO, INC.

5825 N. Tripp Ave., PO Box 804238, Chicago, IL, 60680

Tel: (773) 539-4060    Fax: (773) 539-6770    www.richco.com

*Mfr. plastic and metal parts for the electric, electronic, appliance, and fiber-optic industries.*

**Richco France, Z.A. La Croix des Hormes, F-69250 Montanay, France**

Tel: 33-4-72-08-7140

## RIDGE TOOL COMPANY

400 Clark Street, Elyria, OH, 44035

Tel: (440) 323-5581    Fax: (440) 329-4853    www.ridgid.com

*Mfr. hand and power tools for working pipe, drain cleaning equipment, etc.*

**Emerson Electric France SA, Div. Ridge Tool, Morangis, France**

## RIGHT MANAGEMENT CONSULTANTS, INC.

1818 Market Street, 14th Fl., Philadelphia, PA, 19103-3614

Tel: (215) 988-1588    Fax: (215) 988-9112    www.right.com

*Out placement and human resources consulting services.*

**Right Associates, L. M. & P., 18-20 rue Foureroy, F-75017 France
Paris, France**

Tel: 33-1-42-27-6300

**Right Associates - Conviction, 152 Ave. de Malakoff, F-75116 Paris, France**

Tel: 33-1-44-17-1888

## RMO INC.

650 West Colfax Ave., Denver, CO, 80204

Tel: (303) 534-8181    Fax: (303) 592-8209    www.rmotho.com

*Mfr. dental equipment and supplies.*

**RMO Europe, Parc d'Innovation, rue Geiler de Kaysersberg, F-67400 Illkirch-Graffenstaden, Strasbourg, France**

Tel: 33-3-88-40-6740    Fax: 33-3-88-67-9695

## ROBERT HALF INTERNATIONAL INC.

2884 Sand Hill Road, Ste. 200, Menlo Park, CA, 94025

Tel: (650) 234-6000    Fax: (650) 234-6999    www.rhii.com

*World leader in personnel and specialized staffing services.*

**Robert Half Intl. Inc., 15/17 rue Marsollier, F-75002 Paris, France**

Tel: 331-5504-1818

## C. H. ROBINSON WORLDWIDE, INC. (CHR)

8100 Mitchell Road, Eden Prairie, MN, 55344

Tel: (612) 937-8500    Fax: (612) 937-6714    www.chrobinson.com

*Global door-to-door freight forwarding services, including flexible transportation solutions and global logistics.*

**C. H. Robinson (CHR), Paris, France**

Tel: 33-1-48-16-13-80

## ROBOTIC VISION SYSTEMS, INC.

5 Shawmut Road, Canton, MA, 02021

Tel: (781) 821-0830    Fax: (781) 828-9852    www.rvsi.com

*Mfr. machine vision-based systems for semiconductor industry.*

**RVSI Europe S.A., Parc d'Activités des Bellevues, Immeuble Le Floride
Allée Rosa, Luxembourg BP 258 95615, Cergy Pontoise Cedex, France**

## ROCKWELL INTERNATIONAL CORPORATION

777 East Wisconsin Ave., Ste. 1400, Milwaukee, WI, 53202

Tel: (414) 212-5200 Fax: (414) 212-5201 www.rockwell.com

*Products and service for aerospace and defense, automotive, electronics, graphics and automation industry.*

**Rockwell Automation, 36 Avenue de L'Europe, F-78940 Velizy-Villacoublay, France**

Tel: 33-1-3067-7200

**Rockwell Automation - Dodge/Reliance, Z.A. les Romains BP 9024, 16 Route de la Salle, F-74990 Annecy, Cedex 9 France**

Tel: 33-4-5067-0201 Fax: 33-4-50-67-8041

**Rockwell Automation S.A., Siège et Direction Commerciale, 36 Ave. de l'Europe, F-78941 Vélizy Cedex, France**

Tel: 33-1-30-67-7200 Fax: 33-1-34-65-3233

**Rockwell Collins France, 6 avenue Didier Daurat BP 9, F-31701 Blagnac, Cedex France**

**Rockwell Semiconductor Systems S.A.S., Les Taissounières - B1, 1681 Route des Dolines, BP 283, F-06905 Sophia Antipolis Cedex, France**

Tel: 33-1-49-06-3980 Fax: 33-1-49-06-3990

**Rockwell-Collins France SA, Centre Commercial Belle Epine, Tour Europa, F-94532 Thiais, France**

Tel: 33-1-45-12-2350 Fax: 33-1-46-86-5401

## R.A. RODRIGUEZ, INC.

20 Seaview Boulevard, Garden City, NY, 11050

Tel: (516) 625-8080 Fax: (516) 621-2424 www.rodriguez-usa.com

*Distribution of ball and roller bearings, precision gears, mechanical systems and related products.*

**R. A. Rodriguez France, 12 rue George Clemenceau, F-78220 Viroflay, France**

Tel: 33-1-30-24-1333

## ROHM AND HAAS COMPANY

100 Independence Mall West, Philadelphia, PA, 19106

Tel: (215) 592-3000 Fax: (215) 592-3377 www.rohmhaas.com

*Mfr. industrial and agricultural chemicals, plastics.*

**Compagnie des Salins du Midi, 3 rue Sigmund Freud B.P. 55, F-69511 Vaulx-en-Velin, Lyon France**

**Compagnie des Salins du Midi, rue de la Saline, BP 73-F-40100 Dax, France**

**Compagnie des Salins du Midi, Exploitation Saliniere BP 1, F-13129 Salin-de-Giraud, France**

**Compagnie des Salins du Midi, Exploitation Saliniere, F-30220 Aigues-Mortes, France**

**Morton International, S.A., Le Pressoir Vert, Semoy, F-45400 Fleury LesAubrais, France**

**NorsoHaas, Site Atochem, Bat 201 - BP 20, F-60670 Villers Saint Paul, France**

**NorsoHaas, Vereuil en Halatte Plant, 10 Av. De Bergoide, F-60550 Verneuil en Halatte, France**

Tel: 33-3-44-61-7878

**Rohm and Haas France S.A., BP 48-F-02301 Chauny Cedex, France**

**Rohm and Haas France SA, 185 rue de Bercy, F-75579 Paris Cedex 12, France**

Tel: 33-1-40-02-5000

**Rohm and Haas France SA European Laboratories, 371 rue L.V. Beethoven, Sophia Antipolis, F-06565 Valbonne Cedex, France**

Tel: 33-193-95-5353

**Shipley, S.A., 2 rue Pierre Josse, Boite Postale 27, F-91071 Bondoufle Cedex, France**

Tel: 33-1-60-86-8182

**Usine Rohm and Haas France S.A., BP 27,F- 67630 Lauterbourg, France**

## RPM INC.

PO Box 777, 2628 Pearl Road, Medina, OH, 44258

Tel: (330) 273-5090     Fax: (330) 225-8743     www.rpminc.com

*Mfr. protective coatings and paints.*

**Rust-Oleum France S.A., B.P. 39, 95322 St. Leu la Foret Cedex, France**

Tel: 33-130-400044   Fax: 33-130-409980

## RUDER FINN INC.

301 East 57th Street, New York, NY, 10022

Tel: (212) 593-6400     Fax: (212) 593-6397     www.ruderfinn.com

*Engaged in public relations service and broadcast communications.*

**Ruder Finn France, 3 rue du Faubourg Saint Honore, F-75008 Paris, France**

## RUSSELL REYNOLDS ASSOCIATES INC.

200 Park Ave., New York, NY, 10166-0002

Tel: (212) 351-2000     Fax: (212) 370-0896     www.russreyn.com

*Executive recruiting services.*

**Russell Reynolds Associates Ltd., 7 Place Vendome, F-75001 Paris, France**

Tel: 33-1-49-26-1300   Fax: 33-1-42-60-0385   Contact: Brigette Lemercier-Saltiel

## RVSI (ROBOTIC VISION SYSTEMS, INC.)

5 Shawmut Road, Canton, MA, 02021

Tel: (781) 821-0830     Fax: (781) 828-8942     www.rvsi.com

*Mfr. bar code scanners and data collection equipment.*

**Computer Identics SA, 30 Chemin du Travers des Champs Guillaume, F-95240 Cormeilles en Parisis, France**

## SAFETY-KLEEN CORPORATION

1301 Gervais Street, Columbia, SC, 29201

Tel: (803) 933-4200     Fax: (803) 933-4345     www.safety-kleen.com

*Solvent based parts cleaning service; sludge/solvent recycling service.*

**Sopia/Safety-Kleen France, 12 rue de Tilsitt, F-75008 Paris, France**

## SALANS HERTZFELD HEILBRONN CHRISTY & VIENER

620 Fifth Avenue, New York, NY, 10020-2457

Tel: (212) 632-5500     Fax: (212) 632-5555     www.salans.com

*International law firm.*

**Salans Hertzfeld & Heilbronn, 9 rue Boissy d'Anglais, F-75008 Paris, France**

## SANMINA CORPORATION

2700 North First Street, San Jose, CA, 95134

Tel: (408) 964-3500     Fax: (408) 964-3799     www.sanmina.com

*Mfr. electronic components, including multi-layered printed circuit boards, backplanes, cables, and complete systems.*

**Sanmina Corporation France, rue des Fouleries, BP 69, Chateaudun F-28202 Cedex, France**

Tel: 33-2-3497-3500

## SAPHIRE INTERNATIONAL LTD.

3060 Main Street, Ste. 202, Stratford, CT, 06614

Tel: (203) 375-8668     Fax: (203) 375-1965     www.dataease.com

*Mfr. applications development software.*

**Microformatic, 2 rue Navoisaau, F-93100 Montreuil sous Bois, France**

## SARA LEE CORPORATION

3 First National Plaza, Chicago, IL, 60602-4260

Tel: (312) 726-2600      Fax: (312) 558-4995      www.saralee.com

*Mfr./distributor food and consumer packaged goods, intimate apparel and knitwear.*

**Brossard/Sara Lee,  Paris, France**

**Dim SA,  6 rue Marius Aufan, F-92300 Levallois-Perret Cedex, France**

**Sara Lee Personal Products,  28 rue Jacques Ibert, F-92300 Levallois-Perret Cedex, France**

## SAS INSTITUTE INC.

SAS Campus Drive, Cary, NC, 27513

Tel: (919) 677-8000      Fax: (919) 677-4444      www.sas.com

*Mfr./distributes decision support software.*

**SAS Institute (France) Ltd.,  Gregy-sur-Yerres, France**

Tel: 33-1-60-62-1111   Fax: 33-1-60-62-1199

## SBC COMMUNICATIONS INC.

175 East Houston, San Antonio, TX, 78205

Tel: (210) 821-4105      Fax: (210) 351-5034      www.sbc.com

*Engaged in telecommunications.*

**Cegetel,  1 place Carpeaux,F- 92915 Paris La Defense, France**

Tel: 33-1-7107-0707   Contact: Jean-Marie Messier, Chmn.

**Societe Francaise de Radiotelephone (SRF),  Paris, France**

## SCANSOFT, INC.

9 Centennial Dr., Peabody, MA, 01960

Tel: (978) 977-2000      Fax: (978) 977-2436      www.scansoft.com

*Mfr. digital imaging software.*

**Tech Data,  26 avenue Henri Barbusse,F-93012 Bobigny, France**

## SCHENECTADY INTERNATIONAL INC.

PO Box 1046, Schenectady, NY, 12301

Tel: (518) 370-4200      Fax: (518) 382-8129      www.siigroup.com

*Mfr. electrical insulating varnishes, enamels, phenolic resins, alkylphenols.*

**Schenectady Europe SA,  916 ave. George Washington, F-62404 Bethune, France**

Tel: 33-3-2157-3005   Fax: 33-3-2157-4301

## SCHENKER INTERNATIONAL FORWARDERS INC.

150 Albany Ave., Freeport, NY, 11520

Tel: (516) 377-3000      Fax: (516) 377-3005      www.schenkerusa.com

*Freight forwarders.*

**Jules Roy SA,  32 rue P. Brossolette Frankling Bldg., PO Box 263, F-76055 Le Havre Cedex, France**

Tel: 33-2-35-195470   Fax: 33-2-35-214409

**Jules Roy SA,  12 blvd Frederick Sauvage, PO Box 215, F-13014 Marseille Cedex 14, France**

Tel: 33-4-91-02-0400   Fax: 33-4-91-02-8952

## R. P. SCHERER CORPORATION

645 Martinsville Rd., Ste. 200, Baskin Ridge, NJ, 07920

Tel: (908) 580-1500      Fax: (908) 580-9220      www.rpscherer.com

*Mfr. pharmaceuticals; soft gelatin and two-piece hard shell capsules.*

**R.P. Scherer SA,  74, rue Principale, F-67930 Beinheim, France**

Tel: 33-3-88-633131   Fax: 33-3-88-862248   Contact: Denis Vannson, Gen. Mgr.   Emp: 150

## SCHERING-PLOUGH CORPORATION

One Giralda Farms, Madison, NJ, 07940-1000

Tel: (973) 822-7000        Fax: (973) 822-7048        www.sch-plough.com

*Proprietary drug and cosmetic products.*

**Schering Plough, 92 rue Baudin, F-92307 Levallois-Perret Cedex, France**

Tel: 33-1-41-96-3789    Contact: Daniel Pons

## SCHLEGEL SYSTEMS

1555 Jefferson Road, PO Box 23197, Rochester, NY, 14692-3197

Tel: (716) 427-7200        Fax: (716) 427-9993        www.schlegel.com

*Mfr. engineered perimeter sealing systems for residential and commercial construction; fibers; rubber product.*

**Etablissements Mesnel SA, 9-11 rue de la Riviere, F-78420 Carrieres-sur-Seine, France**

## SCHLUMBERGER LIMITED

277 Park Avenue, New York, NY, 10021

Tel: (212) 350-9400        Fax: (212) 350-9564        www.schlumberger.com

*Engaged in oil and gas services, metering and payment systems, and produces semiconductor testing equipment and smart cards.*

**Schlumberger Limited, 42 rue Saint-Dominique, 75007 Paris, France**

## SCHRODER & COMPANY, INC.

787 Seventh Ave., New York, NY, 10019

Tel: (212) 492-6000        Fax: (212) 492-7029        www.wsdinc.com

*Engaged in investment banking, securities research, sales, trading and clearance and asset management.*

**Wertheim & Cie. SA, 10 rue Duphot, F-75001 Paris, France**

## A. SCHULMAN INC.

3550 West Market Street, Akron, OH, 44333

Tel: (330) 666-3751        Fax: (330) 668-7204        www.aschulman.com

*Mfr./sale plastic resins and compounds.*

**A. Schulman Plastics SA, rue Alex Schuylman, F-08600 Givet, France**

**A. Schulman SA/Diffusion Plastique, Immeuble Dynasteur, 10/12 rue Andras Beck, F-92360 Meudon-la-Foret, Paris, France**

## SCI SYSTEMS INC.

2101 W. Clinton Avenue, Huntsville, AL, 35807

Tel: (256) 882-4800        Fax: (256) 882-4804        www.sci.com

*R/D and mfr. electronics systems for commerce, industry, aerospace, etc.*

**SCI Systems France, Zone Tech rue Hilaire Chardonnet, F-38042 Grenoble Cedex 9, France**

Tel: 33-4-7-620-3040

## SCIENCE APPLICATIONS INTL. CORPORATION (SAIC)

10260 Campus Point Dr., San Diego, CA, 92121

Tel: (858) 826-6000        Fax: (858) 535-7589        www.saic.com

*Engaged in research and engineering.*

**SAIC France, 2 Place De La Defense, Center 3 - Suite 209, Cit. - BP 464 Paris La Defense, F-92053 France**

Tel: 33-1410-20333

## SEAGATE TECHNOLOGY, INC.

920 Disc Dr., Scotts Valley, CA, 95066

Tel: (408) 438-6550        Fax: (408) 438-7205        www.seagate.com

*Develop computer technology, software and hardware.*

**Seagate Technology, Inc., 62 bis Ave. Andre Morizet, F-92643 Boulogne-Billancourt Cedex, France**

Tel: 33-1-41-86-1000   Fax: 33-1-48-25-2861   Contact: Jean-Louis Cazenave, Dir.   Emp: 40

## SEALED AIR CORPORATION

Park 80 East, Saddle Brook, NJ, 07663

Tel: (201) 791-7600     Fax: (201) 703-4205     www.sealedair.com

*Mfr. protective and specialty packaging solutions for industrial, food and consumer products.*

**Sealed Air S.A., 3 Ave. de la Mare, Z.A. des Béthunes, F-95310 Saint-Ouen-l´Aumone, France**

Tel: 33-1-34-32-5950   Fax: 33-1-34-64-6385

## SEAQUIST PERFECT DISPENSING

1160 North Silver Lake Road, Cary, IL, 60013

Tel: (847) 639-2124     Fax: (847) 639-2142     www.seaquistperect.com

*Mfr. and sale of dispensing systems; lotion pumps and spray-through overcaps.*

**General Plastics S.A., Meaux, France**

## G.D. SEARLE & COMPANY

5200 Old Orchard Road, Skokie, IL, 60077

Tel: (847) 982-7000     Fax: (847) 470-1480     www.searlehealthnet.com

*Mfr. pharmaceuticals, health care, optical products and specialty chemicals.*

**Searle, Division of Monsanto France S.A., 2 Ave. de Guesclin B.P. 285, F-27002 Evreux, France**

Tel: 33-32-29-5800   Fax: 33-32-33-1248

## SECURE COMPUTING CORPORATION

One Almaden Blvd., Ste. 400, San Jose, CA, 95113

Tel: (408) 918-6100     Fax: (408) 918-6101     www.sctc.com

*Mfr. software.*

**Secure Computing International Sarl, La Grande Arche, Paroi Nord, 14eme Etage Bureau 1410, F-92044 Paris la Defense, France**

Tel: 33-1-4090-3105

## SEDGWICK, DETERT, MORAN & ARNOLD

One Embarcadero Center, 16th Fl., San Francisco, CA, 94111

Tel: (415) 781-7900     Fax: (415) 781-2635     www.sdma.com

*International law firm.*

**Sedgwick, Detert, Moran & Arnold, 104 Avenue Kléber, F-75116 Paris, France**

Tel: 33-1-4704-5502   Fax: 33-1-4704-5502

## SELAS CORPORATION OF AMERICA

2034 S. Limekiln Pike, Dresher, PA, 19025

Tel: (215) 646-6600     Fax: (215) 646-3536     www.selas.com

*Mfr. heat treating equipment for metal, glass, ceramic and chemical industry.*

**Selas SA, 3/5 Place du Village, F-92632 Gennevilliers Cedex, France**

Contact: Christian Bailliart

## SEMTECH CORPORATION

652 Mitchell Road, PO Box 367, Newbury Park, CA, 91320

Tel: (805) 498-2111     Fax: (805) 498-3804     www.semtech.com

*Mfr. silicon rectifiers, rectifier assemblies, capacitors, switching regulators, AC/DC converters.*

**Semtech Ltd. France, 21 Ave. au Quebec, F-91951 Courtaboeuf Cedex, France**

Tel: 33-1-69-28-2200   Fax: 33-1-69-28-1298

## SENSIENT TECHNOLOGIES CORPORATION

433 E. Michigan Street, Milwaukee, WI, 53202

Tel: (414) 271-6755     Fax: (414) 347-4783     www.sensient.com

*Mfr. food products and food ingredients.*

**Les Colorants Wackherr, Paris, France**

## SENSORMATIC ELECTRONICS CORPORATION

951 Yamato Road, Boca Raton, FL, 33431-0700

Tel: (561) 989-7000    Fax: (561) 989-7774    www.sensormatic.com

*Electronic article surveillance equipment.*

**Sensormatic S.A.,  Parc de Haute Technologie 7, Rue Alexis de Tocqueville, F-92183 Antony Cedex, France**

Tel: 33-1-40-96-2400   Fax: 33-1-40-96-0003

## SEQUA CORPORATION

200 Park Ave., New York, NY, 10166

Tel: (212) 986-5500    Fax: (212) 370-1969    www.sequa.com

*Mfr. aerospace products and systems, machinery and metal coatings, spec chemicals, automotive products.*

**Materiels Equipements Graphiques,  32-34 rue des Malines, Z.I. Les Malines, Lisses-Evry, France**

## SERVICE CORPORATION INTERNATIONAL

1929 Allen Parkway, Houston, TX, 77019

Tel: (713) 522-5141    Fax: (713) 525-5586    www.sci-corp.com

*Operates funeral homes, cemeteries and crematoriums and sells caskets, burial vaults and cremation receptacles.*

**Pompes Funereraves Geneacuterales (PFG),  Paris, France**

## SFX ENTERTAINMENT, INC.

650 Madison Ave., 16th Fl., New York, NY, 10022

Tel: (212) 838-3100    Fax: (212) 750-6682    www.sfx.com

*Sports marketing, management and consulting.*

**SFX Sports Group Europe,  20 rue de Billancourt, F-92100 Boulogne, France**

## SHARED MEDICAL SYSTEMS CORPORATION

51 Valley Stream Pkwy, Malvern, PA, 19355

Tel: (610) 219-6300    Fax: (610) 219-3124    www.smed.com

*Computer-based information processing for healthcare industry.*

**SMS France,  Bâtiment 7 Mini Parc, Parc Euromédicine, Montpellier F-34198 Cedex 5, France**

Tel: 33-4-67-04-1143   Fax: 33-4-67-04-11-45

## SHEARMAN & STERLING

599 Lexington Ave., New York, NY, 10022-6069

Tel: (212) 848-4000    Fax: (212) 848-7179    www.shearman.com

*Law firm engaged in general American and international financial and commercial practice.*

**Shearman & Sterling,  114 Ave. des Champs-Elysées, F-75008 Paris, France**

Tel: 33-1-53-89-7000   Fax: 33-1-53-89-7070   Contact: Emmanuel Gaillard, Mng. Ptnr.

## SHELDAHL, INC.

1150 Sheldahl Rd., Northfield, MN, 55057-9444

Tel: (507) 663-8000    Fax: (507) 663-8545    www.sheldahl.com

*Mfr. electrical and electronic components and laminated plastic products/adhesive-based tapes and materials and adhesiveless Novaclad®.*

**CCI Eurolan/Sheldahl Europe,  71/78 rue Grand, F-92310 Sevres, France**

## SHELDON'S INC.

626 Center Street, Antigo, WI, 54409-2496

Tel: (715) 623-2382    Fax: (715) 623-3001    www.mepps.com

*Mfr. recreational fishing tackle.*

**MEPPS SA,  BP 09, F-06390 Contes, France**

## SHIPLEY COMPANY, LLC

455 Forest Street, Marlborough, MA, 01752

Tel: (508) 481-7950      Fax: (508) 485-9113      www.shipley.com

*Supplier of materials and processes technology to the microelectronics and printed wiring board industries.*

**Shipley S.A.S, 3 rue Sigmund Freud - B.P. 55, F-69511 Vaulx-en-Velin Lyon, France**

Tel: 33 4 7880 0832    Fax: 33 4 7204 3778

**Shipley SAS, La Tour de Lyon, 185 rue de Bercy, F-75579 Paris, Cedex 12 France**

Tel: 33-1-4002-5000    Fax: 33-1-4002-5008

## SIGNODE PACKAGING SYSTEMS

3610 West Lake Ave., Glenview, IL, 60025

Tel: (847) 724-6100      Fax: (847) 657-4392      www.signode.com

*Mfr. industrial tools and machinery for packaging and strapping.*

**Signode France SA, 35 rue de la Motte, F-93308 Aubervilliers Cedex, France**

## SILICON GRAPHICS INC.

2011 N. Shoreline Blvd., Mountain View, CA, 94043-1389

Tel: (650) 960-1980      Fax: (650) 961-0595      www.sgi.com

*Design/mfr. special-effects computer graphic systems and software.*

**Espace Performance, Batiment J Bronze, F-35769 Saint Grégoire Cedex, France**

Tel: 33-2-99-23-1280    Fax: 33-2-99-23-1895

**Siege Social, 21 rue Albert Calmette, F-78350 Jouy-en-Josas Paris, France**

Tel: 33-1-34-88-8000    Fax: 33-1-34-65-9619

## SIMPLEX SOLUTIONS, INC.

521 Almanor Ave., Sunnyvale, CA, 94085

Tel: (408) 617-6100      Fax: (408) 774-0285      www.simplex.com

*Develops full-chip, multi-level IC extraction and analysis software.*

**Simplex Grenoble, 29 Boulevard des Alpes, F-38246 Meylan Cedex, France**

**Simplex Voiron, ZA Le Parvis, F-38500 Voiron, France**

## SKADDEN, ARPS, SLATE, MEAGHER & FLOM LLP

4 Times Square, New York, NY, 10036

Tel: (212) 735-3000      Fax: (212) 735-2000      www.sasmf.com

*American/International law practice.*

**Skadden, Arps, Slate, Meagher & Flom LLP, 68 rue du Faubourg Saint-Honoré, F-75008 Paris, France**

Tel: 33-1-40-75-4444    Fax: 33-1-49-53-0999

## SMITH INTERNATIONAL, INC.

PO Box 60068, Houston, TX, 77205-0068

Tel: (713) 443-3370      Fax: (713) 233-5996      www.smith.com

*Mfr. drilling tools and equipment and provides related services for the drilling, completion and production sectors of the petroleum and mining industries.*

**Smith International France SARL, B.P. 217- Lons, F-64142 Billere (Pau), France**

Tel: 33-59-92-3550    Contact: Georges Italiano, District Mgr.

## SMITHFIELD FOODS, INC.

200 Commerce Street, Smithfield, VA, 23430

Tel: (757) 365-3000      Fax: (757) 365-3017      www.smithfieldhams.com

*Mfr. processed meats.*

**Societe Bretonne De Salaisons, BP 80359 Lampaul-Guimiliau, F-29403 Landivisiau Cedex, France**

Tel: 33-2-9868-6868    Fax: 33-3-9868-6899    Contact: Adrien Czaja, Mgr.

## SMURFIT-STONE CONTAINER CORPORATION

150 N. Michigan Ave., Chicago, IL, 60601-7568

Tel: (312) 346-6600     Fax: (312) 580-3486     www.smurfit-stone.net

*Mfr. paper and paper packaging.*

**Societe Emballages des Cevennes SA, F-30410 Molieres-sur-Ceze, France**

## SNAP-ON INCORPORATED

10801 Corporate Dr., Pleasant Prairie, WI, 53158-1603

Tel: (262) 656-5200     Fax: (262) 656-5577     www.snapon.com

*Mfr. auto maintenance, diagnostic and emission testing equipment, hand tools, hydraulic lifts and tire changers.*

**Snap-On Tools BV, ZI de la Petite, Montagne Sud, 13 allee du Dauphine, F-91008 Evry France**

## SOLECTRON CORPORATION

777 Gibraltar Drive, Milpitas, CA, 95035

Tel: (408) 957-8500     Fax: (408) 956-6075     www.solectron.com

*Provides contract manufacturing services to equipment manufacturers.*

**Solectron Corporation, Chemin Departmental 109E, Canajan BP 6, F-33611 Cestas Cedex, France**

Tel: 33-5-57-12-7575   Fax: 33-5-57-12-7813

## SONOCO PRODUCTS COMPANY

North Second Street, PO Box 160, Hartsville, SC, 29550

Tel: (843) 383-7000     Fax: (843) 383-7008     www.sonoco.com

*Mfr. packaging for consumer and industrial market and recycled paperboard.*

**European Development Center, BP 1, 16 Chemin des Amoureux, F-89140 Pont-sur-Yonne, France**

Tel: 33-3-86-672830

**Papeteries du Rhin - Lhomme S.A., BP 148, F-68313 Illzach Cedex, France**

Tel: 33-3-89-61-8584

**Sonoco Consumer Products, Ltd., Zone Industrielle de Lievin, rue Francois Jacob, F-62800 Lievin, France**

Tel: 33-2-1720033

**Sonoco Gunther SA, F-70800 Fontaine les Luxeuil, France**

**Sonoco Lhomme S.A., BP 27, 88 rue de Lille, F-59520 Marquette-Lez-Lille, France**

Tel: 33-3-20-14-9714   Fax: 33-3-20-13-1701

**Sonoco Lhomme S.A., BP 1, Route de Paris, F-89140 Pont-sur-Yonne, France**

Tel: 33-3-86-675000

**Sonoco Lhomme S.A., 60 rue Gabriel Péri, F-59320 Haubourdin, France**

Tel: 33-3-20-076040

**Sonoco Pages S.A., Lieu-dit 'Mandete', F-09200 St-Girons, France**

Tel: 33-5-61-66-2626

## SOTHEBY'S HOLDINGS, INC.

1334 York Avenue, New York, NY, 10021

Tel: (212) 606-7000     Fax: (212) 606-7027     www.sothebys.com

*Auction house specializing in fine art and jewelry.*

**Sotheby's Holdings, Inc., Galerie Charpentier, 76 rue du Faubourg Saint Honore, F-75008 Paris, France**

Tel: 33-1-5305-5380

## SPALDING HOLDINGS CORPORATION

425 Meadow Street, Chicopee, MA, 01021

Tel: (413) 536-1200     Fax: (413) 536-1404     www.spalding.com

*Mfr. sports equipment and infant and juvenile furniture and accessories.*

**Spalding Sports, Paris, France**

## SPARTECH CORPORATION

120 S. Central, Ste. 1700, Clayton, MO, 63105-1705

Tel: (314) 721-4242     Fax: (314) 721-1447     www.spartech.com

*Mfr./sales of engineered thermoplastic materials and polymeric compounds.*

**Spartech Polycom Canada, Donchery, France**

## SPECTRIAN CORPORATION

350 West Java Drive, Sunnyvale, CA, 94089

Tel: (408) 745-5400     Fax: (408) 541-0263     www.spectrian.com

*Mfr. linear power amplifiers.*

**Spectrian France, 22 rue Violet, F-75015 Paris Cedex, France**

Tel: 33-1-45-79-10-77   Fax: 33-1-45-79-10-77

## SPENCER STUART MANAGEMENT CONSULTANTS

401 North Michigan Ave., Ste. 3400, Chicago, IL, 60611

Tel: (312) 822-0080     Fax: (312) 822-0116     www.spencerstuart.com

*Executive recruitment firm.*

**Spencer Stuart & Associates Inc., 83 Ave. Marceau, F-75116 Paris, France**

Tel: 33-1-53-57-8123   Fax: 33-1-53-57-8100   Contact: Henri dePitray

## SPHERION CORPORATION

2050 Spectrum Boulevard, Fort Lauderdale, FL, 33309

Tel: (954) 938-7600     Fax: (954) 938-7666     www.spherion.com

*Provides temporary personnel placement and staffing.*

**Michael Page Finance, 159 Ave. Achille Peretti, F-92200 Neuilly-sur-Seine Paris, France**

Tel: 33-115-948-3480

## SPIROL INTERNATIONAL CORPORATION

30 Rock Ave., Danielson, CT, 06239

Tel: (860) 774-8571     Fax: (860) 774-0487     www.spirol.com

*Mfr. engineered fasteners, shims, automation equipment.*

**Prym-Spirol SA, 209 rue de Hocher de Lorzier, Parc d' Activities Centr' Alp, F-38430 Moirans, France**

Tel: 33-4-76-351300   Fax: 33-4-76-351301   Contact: Gerald Souillard, Sales Mgr.   Emp: 10

## SPRAYING SYSTEMS COMPANY

PO Box 7900, Wheaton, IL, 60189-7900

Tel: (630) 665-5000     Fax: (630) 260-0842     www.spray.com

*Designs and manufactures industrial spray nozzles.*

**Spraying Systems France, 77 Avenue Aristide Briand, F-94118 Arcueil Cedex, France**

## SPS TECHNOLOGIES INC.

101 Greenwood Avenue, Ste. 470, Jenkintown, PA, 19046

Tel: (215) 517-2000     Fax: (215) 517-2032     www.spstech.com

*Mfr. aerospace and industry fasteners, tightening systems, magnetic materials, superalloys.*

**SPS Technologies France, 46 Avenue Kleber F-92700, Colombes, France**

## SPX CORPORATION

700 Terrace Point Drive, PO Box 3301, Muskegon, MI, 49443-3301

Tel: (231) 724-5000     Fax: (231) 724-5720     www.spx.com

*Mfr. auto parts, special service tools, engine and drive-train parts.*

**Automotive Diagnostics Intl., Technoparc, 15 rue Charles Edouard Jeanneret, F-78306 Poissy Cedex, France**

**Bear Export Division, BP 42, F-67450 Mundolsheim, France**

**Bear France SA, rue du Chemin de Fer, Wisconsin Building, ZAC de Lampertheim, F-67450 Lampertheim France**

Robinair Europe, Technoparc, 15 rue Charles Edouard Jeanneret, F-78306 Poissy Cedex, France

Sealed Power Europe, c/o Sealed Power Technologies Pringy SA, F-74370 Pringy, France

## THE ST. PAUL COMPANIES, INC.

385 Washington Street, St. Paul, MN, 55102

Tel: (651) 310-7911    Fax: (651) 310-8294    www.stpaul.com

*Provides investment, insurance and reinsurance services.*

Les Mutuelles duMans Assurances, 16 rue de Londres, F-75009 Paris, France

St. Paul International Insurance Company Ltd., 103 blvd. Haussmann, F-75008 Paris, France

Tel: 33-1-43-12-3282   Fax: 33-1-42-66-705

## STANDARD COMMERCIAL CORPORATION

2201 Miller Rd., PO Box 450, Wilson, NC, 27893

Tel: (919) 291-5507    Fax: (919) 237-1109    www.sccgroup.com

*Leaf tobacco dealers/processors and wool processors.*

Standard Wool France SA, 157 rue de Roubaix, F-59336 Tourcoing, France

## STANDARD MICROSYSTEMS CORPORATION

80 Arkay Drive, Hauppauge, NY, 11788

Tel: (631) 435-6000    Fax: (631) 273-5550    www.smsc.com

*Telecommunications systems.*

Insight France, Rungis, France

Tel: 33-1-4180-2900   Fax: 33-1-4686-6763

## STANDEX INTERNATIONAL CORPORATION

6 Manor Parkway, Salem, NH, 03079

Tel: (603) 893-9701    Fax: (603) 893-7324    www.standex.com

*Mfr. diversified graphics, institutional, industry/electronic and consumer products.*

James Burn International SA, BP 134, 67 rue du Docteur Blaizot, F-61304 L'Aigle Cedex Orne, France

Tel: 33-233-842-150   Fax: 33-233-842-151   Contact: Guy Vatome, Mgr.

Mold-Tech S.A.R.L., Route Nationale 7, ZA Les Longues Raies, F-77310 Pringy, France

Tel: 33-1-60-65-7015   Fax: 33-1-60-65-6916   Contact: Patrick Cambier, Mgr.

## STANLEY BOSTITCH FASTENING SYSTEMS

815 Briggs Street, East Greenwich, RI, 02818

Tel: (401) 884-2500    Fax: (401) 885-6511    www.centerplex.net

*Mfr. stapling machines, stapling supplies, fastening systems and wire.*

SIMAX, Maxonchamp, F-88360 Rupt sur Moselle, France

Societe de Fabrications Bostitch SA, Maxonchamp, F-88360 Rupt sur Moselle, France

Stanley Bostitch France, BP 74, 112 ave. Charles de Gaulle, F-91423 Morangis Cedex, France

## THE STANLEY WORKS

1000 Stanley Drive, PO Box 7000, New Britain, CT, 06053

Tel: (860) 225-5111    Fax: (860) 827-3987    www.stanleyworks.com

*Mfr. hand tools and hardware.*

SICFO SA, Siege Social, F-67700 RCS Saverne, France

Stanley Works Ltd., 20 ave. Vladimir Komarov, F-98192 Trappes Cedex, France

Stanley-Mabo SA, BP 1579, F-25009 Besancon Cedex, France

## STA-RITE INDUSTRIES INC.

293 Wright Street, Delavan, WI, 53115

Tel: (262) 728-5551    Fax: (262) 728-7323    www.sta-rite.com

*Mfr. water pumps, filters and systems.*

**Nocchi Pompe Europe, 6 Ave. de la Gloriette, Z.I. Fontcouverte, F-84000 Avignon, France**

Emp: 7

## STARWOOD HOTELS & RESORTS WORLDWIDE

777 Westchester Avenue, White Plains, NY, 10604

Tel: (914) 640-8100    Fax: (914) 640-8316    www.starwoodhotels.com

*Hotel operations including Sheraton, Westin, St. Regis, Four Points and Caesars.*

**Sheraton Sales Center, 89 Blvd. Haussmann, F-75008 Paris, France**

## STATE STREET BANK & TRUST COMPANY

225 Franklin Street, Boston, MA, 02101

Tel: (617) 786-3000    Fax: (617) 654-3386    www.statestreet.com

*Banking and financial services.*

**State Street Bank & Trust, 56 Avenue Samuel Champlain, F-34000 Montpellier, France**

**State Street Banque SA, 21/25 rue Balzac, F-75008 Paris, France**

## STEELCASE INC.

901 44th Street SE, Grand Rapids, MI, 49508

Tel: (616) 247-2710    Fax: (616) 248-7010    www.steelcase.com

*Mfr. office, computer-support and systems furniture.*

**Steelcase Strafor SA, BP 6K, 56 rue Jean Giraudoux, F-67035 Strasbourg Cedex, France**

## STEINER CORPORATION

505 E. South Temple, Salt Lake City, UT, 84102

Tel: (801) 328-8831    Fax: (801) 363-5680

*Soap and towel dispensers.*

**Steiner Company, Paris, France**

## STEPAN COMPANY

22 West Frontage Road, Northfield, IL, 60093

Tel: (847) 446-7500    Fax: (847) 501-2443    www.stepan.com

*Mfr. basic intermediate chemicals.*

**Stepan Europe, BP 127, F-38340 Voreppe, France**

## STIEFEL LABORATORIES INC.

255 Alhambra Circle, Ste. 1000, Coral Gables, FL, 33134

Tel: (305) 443-3807    Fax: (305) 443-3467    www.stiefel.com

*Mfr. pharmaceuticals, dermatological specialties.*

**Laboratoires Stiefel SARL, Z.I. du Petit Nanterre, 15 rue des Grands Pres, F-92000 Nanterre, France**

## STOKES VACUUM INC.

5500 Tabor Road, Philadelphia, PA, 19120

Tel: (215) 831-5400    Fax: (215) 831-5420    www.stokesvacuum.com

*Vacuum pumps and components, vacuum dryers, oil-upgrading equipment and metallizers.*

**Stokes Vaccum, Div. de Ets George Hibon S.A., 38 blvd de Reims, F-59058 Roubaix Cedex, France**

Tel: 33-3-20-45-3902   Fax: 33-3-20-45-3997   Contact: R. Berroyer

## STORAGE TECHNOLOGY CORPORATION

One Storagetech Dr., Louisville, CO, 80028-4377

Tel: (303) 673-5151      Fax: (303) 673-5019      www.stortek.com

*Mfr./market/service information, storage and retrieval systems.*

**StorageTex European Ops S.A.,  1 Rond-Point du General, Eisenhower F-31106 Toulouse Cedex, France**

## STOWE WOODWARD MOUNT HOPE

333 Turnpike Rd., Southborough, MA, 01772

Tel: (508) 460-9600      Fax: (508) 481-5392      www.mounthope.com

*Mfr. roll covering and bowed roll technologies for the web handling industries.*

**Stowe Woodward France,  12 rue Jean Jaurés, F-69330 Meyzieu, France**

Tel: 33-4-72 5770

## STREAM INTERNATIONAL

85 Dan Road, Canton, MA, 02021

Tel: (781) 575-6800      Fax: (781) 575-6999      www.stream.com

*Provider of outsourced technical support for major computer industry companies.*

**Steam International Services Corp., 23 ave. Louis Brequet, BP 257, F-78147 Velizy, France**

Tel: 33-1-3067-1000    Fax: 3-1-3067-1005

## STRUCTURAL DYNAMICS RESEARCH CORPORATION

2000 Eastman Dr., Milford, OH, 45150-2740

Tel: (513) 576-2400      Fax: (513) 576-2922      www.sdrc.com

*Developer of software used in Modeling testing, drafting and manufacturing.*

**SDRC France, S.A. - Paris,  Immeuble Le Capitole, 55 Ave. des Champs-Pierreux, F-92012 Nanterre Cedex, France**

Tel: 33-1-46-95-9797   Fax: 33-1-46-95-9798

## SUDLER & HENNESSEY

1633 Broadway, 25th Fl., New York, NY, 10019

Tel: (212) 969-5800      Fax: (212) 969-5996      www.sudler-hennessey.com

*Engaged in healthcare products advertising.*

**S&H/Paragraphe,  79 bis, rue Dassault, F-92100 Boulogne Billancourt, Paris, France**

Tel: 33-1-46-10-5959   Fax: 33-1-46-10-5960   Contact: Catherine Verdieve

## SULLAIR CORPORATION

3700 E. Michigan Blvd., Bldg. 1-2, Michigan City, IN, 46360

Tel: (219) 879-5451      Fax: (219) 874-1273      www.sullair.com

*Mfr. high efficiency tandem compressors, vacuum systems, encapsulated compressors and air tools.*

**Sullair Europe SARL,  Zone des Granges BP 82, 42602 Montbrison, Cedex, France**

Tel: 33-4-77-96-8470

## SULLIVAN & CROMWELL

125 Broad Street, New York, NY, 10004-2498

Tel: (212) 558-4000      Fax: (212) 558-3588      www.sullcrom.com

*International law firm.*

**Sullivan & Cromwell,  8 Place Vendome, F-75001 Paris, France**

## SUN MICROSYSTEMS, INC.

901 San Antonio Road, Palo Alto, CA, 94303

Tel: (650) 960-1300      Fax: (650) 856-2114      www.sun.com

*Computer peripherals and programming services.*

**Sun Microsystems France S.A.,  13 Ave. Morane Saulnier - B.P. 53, F-78142 Velizy Cedex, France**

Tel: 33-5-90-6157

## SUNGARD DATA SYSTEMS

1285 Drummers Lane, Wayne, PA, 19087

Tel: (610) 341-8700     Fax: (610) 341-8851     www.sungard.com

*Provides ASP solutions to the buyside investment management market.*

**SunGard Data Systems, 173 Bureaux de la Colline, Batiment E, F-92213 Saint-Cloud Paris, France**

Tel: 33-1-49-11-3000   Contact: Bernard Hure

## SUNRISE MEDICAL INC.

2382 Faraday Ave., Ste. 200, Carlsbad, CA, 92008

Tel: (760) 930-1500     Fax: (760) 930-1580     www.sunrisemedical.com

*Designs, manufactures and markets rehabilitation products and assistive technology devices for people with disabilities, and patient care products used in nursing homes, hospitals and homecare settings.*

**Sunrise Medical SA, Rochecorbon, Z.l La Planche, 37210 Rochecorbon, France**

Tel: 33-247-88-5858

## SUPERIOR GRAPHITE COMPANY

10 South Riverside Plaza, Chicago, IL, 60606

Tel: (312) 559-2999     Fax: (312) 559-9064     www.graphitesgc.com

*Mfr. natural and synthetic graphites, electrodes, lubricants, suspensions, carbide and carbon.*

**Foseco-SMC, 12 Ave. Marie Ampere, Champs sur Marne F-77420, France**

## SYBASE, INC.

6475 Christie Ave., Emeryville, CA, 94608

Tel: (510) 922-3500     Fax: (510) 922-3210     www.sybase.com

*Design/mfg/distribution of database management systems, software development tools, connectivity products, consulting and technical support services..*

**Sybase France, 27 rue du Colonel Avia, F-75508 Paris Cedex 15, France**

Tel: 33-1-41-90-4190   Fax: 33-1-41-90-4200

## SYMANTEC CORPORATION

20330 Stevens Creek Blvd., Cupertino, CA, 95014-2132

Tel: (408) 253-9600     Fax: (408) 253-3968     www.symantec.com

*Designs and produces PC network security and network management software and hardware.*

**Symantec SARL, 31-35 rue Gambetta, F-92150 Suresnes, France**

Tel: 33-1-41-38-5700   Fax: 33-1-41-38-5729

## SYMBOL TECHNOLOGIES, INC.

One Symbol Plaza, Holtsville, NY, 11742-1300

Tel: (631) 738-2400     Fax: (631) 738-5990     www.symbol.com

*Mfr. Bar code-driven data management systems, wireless LAN's, and Portable Shopping System™.*

**Symbol Technologies France SA, Centre d'affaires d'Antony, 3 rue de la Renaissance, F-92184 Antony Cedex, France**

Tel: 33-1-40-96-5200   Fax: 33-1-40-96-5252

## SYNOPSYS, INC.

700 East Middlefield Road, Mountain View, CA, 94043

Tel: (650) 962-5000     Fax: (650) 965-8637     www.synopsys.com

*Mfr. electronic design automation software.*

**Synopsys SARL, 24 rue Saarinen Silic 217, F-94518 Rungis Cedex, France**

Tel: 33-1-4512-0606   Fax: 33-1-4512-0707

**SYNTEGRA**

4201 Lexington Ave., North Arden Hills, MN, 55126-6198

Tel: (651) 415-2999        Fax: (651) 415-4891        www.cdc.com

*Computer peripherals and hardware.*

**Syntegra France, Le Capitole, 55 Ave. des Champs Pierreux, F-92012 Nanterre Cedex Paris, France**

Tel: 33-1-41-37-8000    Fax: 33-1-41-37-8001

**SYSTEM SOFTWARE ASSOCIATES, INC.**

500 W. Madison St., Ste. 3200, Chicago, IL, 60661

Tel: (312) 258-6000        Fax: (312) 474-7500        www.ssax.com

*Mfr. computer software.*

**System Software Associates, Paris, France**

**SYSTEMAX INC.**

22 Harbor Park Dr., Port Washington, NY, 11050

Tel: (516) 608-7000        Fax: (516) 608-7111        www.systemax.com

*Direct marketer of computers and related products to businesses.*

**HCS Misco France, BP 69, 91371 Verrieres le Buisson Cedex, Paris, France**

Tel: 33-1-6993-2121

**TACONIC LTD.**

PO Box 69, Coonbrook Rd., Petersburg, NY, 12138

Tel: (518) 658-3202        Fax: (518) 658-3204        www.taconic.com

*Mfr. teflon/silicone-coated fiberglass fabrics, tapes and belts; specialty tapes and circuit board substrates.*

**Taconic France, Za Des Vernays, Leiu-Dit "Lecouarnet", F-74210 Doussard, France**

Tel: 33-450-443147    Fax: 33-450-448845

**TANDY CORPORATION**

100 Throckmorton Street, Fort Worth, TX, 76102

Tel: (817) 390-3700        Fax: (817) 415-2647        www.tandy.com

*Mfr. electronic and acoustic equipment; Radio Shack retail stores.*

**Tandy France SA, BP 147, Cergy Pointoise Cedex, France**

**TBWA CHIAT/DAY**

488 Madison Avenue, 6th Floor, New York, NY, 10022

Tel: (212) 804-1000        Fax: (212) 804-1200        www.tbwachiat.com

*International full service advertising agency.*

**TBWA, Paris, France**

**TEAM INDUSTRIAL SERVICES, INC.**

1019 S. Hood Street, Alvin, TX, 77511

Tel: (281) 331-6154        Fax: (281) 331-4107        www.teamindustrialservices.com

*Consulting, engineering and rental services.*

**Team Inc. Europe B.V., Paris, France**

Tel: 33-442-39-7438    Fax: 33-442-39-7422

**TECH DATA CORPORATION**

5350 Tech Data Drive, Clearwater, FL, 34620-3122

Tel: (727) 539-7429        Fax: (727) 538-7876        www.techdata.com

*Distributor of computer systems, software and related equipment.*

**Tech Data, 29 Av. Henri Barbusse, 390 Bobiny, Cedex, France**

## TECH/OPS SEVCON INC.

40 North Ave., Burlington, MA, 01803

Tel: (718) 229-7896     Fax: (718) 229-8603     www.sevcon.com

*Design, manufacture, and marketing of microprocessor based control systems for battery powered vehicles.*

**Sevcon SA, 12 rue Jean Poulmarch, F-95100 Argenteuil, France**

## TECHNITROL INC.

1210 Northbrook Drive, #385, Trevose, PA, 19053

Tel: (215) 355-2900     Fax: (215) 355-7397     www.technitrol.com

*Mfr. of electronic components, electrical contacts, and other parts/materials.*

**Technitrol Inc., Attn: France Office, 1210 Northbrook Drive Suite 285, Trevose PA 19053**

## TECHNOLOGY SOLUTIONS COMPANY (TSC)

205 N. Michigan Ave., Ste. 1500, Chicago, IL, 60601

Tel: (312) 228-4500     Fax: (312) 228-4501     www.techsol.com

*Designs computer information systems and strategic business and management consulting for major corporations.*

**TSC Europe, 19 Boulevard Malesherbes,F- 75008 Paris, France**

Tel: 33-1-55-27-3663   Fax: 33-1-55-27-3847   Contact: Philippe Villaeys

## TECUMSEH PRODUCTS COMPANY

100 E. Patterson Street, Tecumseh, MI, 49286-1899

Tel: (517) 423-8411     Fax: (517) 423-8526     www.tecumseh.com

*Mfr. of hermetic compressors for air conditioning and refrigeration products, gasoline engines and power train components for lawn and garden applications, and pumps.*

**L'Unite Hermetique, F-38290 La Verpilliere, France**

**TIGER Moteurs Industriels, 1A 3 rue d'Anjou, Z.A. des Bethunes-St. Oune l'Aumone, BP 9094, F-95073 Cergy Pontoise Cedex, France**

## TEKELEC

26580 West Agoura Road, Calabasas, CA, 91302

Tel: (818) 880-5656     Fax: (818) 880-6993     www.tekelec.com

*Mfr. telecommunications testing equipment.*

**Tekelec Europe, 5 rue Carle Vernet, F-92315 Sevres Cedex, France**

Tel: 33-1-46-23-25-63

## TEKNIS CORPORATION

PO Box 3189, North Attleboro, MA, 02761

Tel: (508) 695-3591     Fax: (508) 699-6059     www.teknis.com

*Sale advanced technical products, fiber optics, materials for semiconductor mfr., security holographics*

**Teknis France, 28 rue Georges Herbert, F-76250 De Ville les Rouen, France**

## TEKTRONIX INC.

14200 SW Karl Braun Dr., PO Box 500, Beaverton, OR, 97077

Tel: (503) 627-7111     Fax: (503) 627-2406     www.tek.com

*Mfr. test and measure, visual systems/color printing and communications/video and  networking products.*

**Tektronix S.A. France, Batiment Omega Tech 3, Ave. de Canada, BP13, F-91941 Courtaboeuf Les Ulis Cedex, France**

Tel: 33-1-69-86-8181   Fax: 33-1-69-07-0937

## TELEFLEX INC.

630 W. Germantown Pike, Ste. 450, Plymouth Meeting, PA, 19462

Tel: (610) 834-6301     Fax: (610) 834-8307     www.teleflex.com

*Designs/mfr./market mechanical and electro-mechanical systems, measure systems.*

**Asept Inmed S.A., Le Faget, France**

**Pilling Weck Europe, Le Faget, France**

Rüsch France S.A.R.L., Betschdorf, France

Sermatech Manufacturing Group, LaPacaudiere, France

TFX Marine European Sales Office, LaRochelle, France

United Parts France S.A., Cluses Cedex, France

## TELEX COMMUNICATIONS INC.

12000 Portland Ave. South, Burnsville, MN, 55337

Tel: (952) 884-4051    Fax: (952) 884-0043    www.telexcommunications.com

*Mfr. communications, audio-visual and professional audio products.*

EVI Audio France, S.A., Parc de Courcerin, Allee Lech Walesa, Lognes Marne La Vallee F-77185, France

## TELLABS INC.

4951 Indiana Ave. 6303788800, Lisle, IL, 60532-1698

Tel: (630) 378-8800    Fax: (630) 679-3010    www.tellabs.com

*Design/mfr./service voice/data transport and network access systems.*

Tellabs France, 6 Parc Club Ariane, Bâtiment Mercure, Boulevard des Chênes, F-78284 Guyancourt Cedex, France

## TELXON CORPORATION

1000 Summitt Dr., Cincinnati, OH, 45150

Tel: (330) 664-1000    Fax: (330) 664-2220    www.telxon.com

*Develop/mfr. portable computer systems and related equipment.*

Telxon France, BP 301, F-91958 Les Ulis Cedex A, France

## TENNECO AUTOMOTIVE INC.

500 North Field Drive, Lake Forest, IL, 60045

Tel: (847) 482-5241    Fax: (847) 482-5295    www.tenneco-automotive.com

*Mfr. automotive parts, exhaust systems and service equipment.*

Gillet Tubes Technologies S.A.R.L., Re des Fontangues, Zone Industrielle, B.P. 31, F-55400 Etain, France

Tel: 33-29-83-2250   Fax: 33-29-87-8900   Contact: Juergen Blum, Mgr.   Emp: 125

Monroe France, 7 Ave de Fief, F-95310 Saint Ouen L' Aumone, France

Walker France SA, BP 4149, La Croix des Landes, 53941 Saint-Bertheven, F-53500 Ernee, France

Tel: 33-2-43-59-1160   Fax: 33-2-43-59-1166   Contact: Daniel Bellanger, Mgr.   Emp: 627

## TENNECO PACKAGING CORPORATION OF AMERICA

1900 West Field Court, Lake Forest, IL, 60045

Tel: (847) 482-2000    Fax: (847) 482-2181    www.agplus.net/tenneco

*Mfr. custom packaging, aluminum and plastic molded fibre, corrugated containers.*

Omni-Pac SARL, 64 rue de Miromesnil, F-75008 Paris, France

Tenneco Packaging, Meyzieu, France

## TERADYNE INC.

321 Harrison Ave., Boston, MA, 02118

Tel: (617) 482-2700    Fax: (617) 422-2910    www.teradyne.com

*Mfr. electronic test equipment and blackplane connection systems.*

Teradyne SA, ZAC Kleber Batiment F, 165 blvd. de Valmy, F-92700 Colombes, France

## TEXACO INC.

2000 Westchester Ave., White Plains, NY, 10650

Tel: (914) 253-4000    Fax: (914) 253-7753    www.texaco.com

*Exploration/marketing crude oil, mfr. petro chemicals and products.*

Texaco France SA, 39 rue Cambon, F-75001 Paris, France

## TEXAS INSTRUMENTS INC.

8505 Forest Lane, Dallas, TX, 75243

Tel: (972) 995-3773 Fax: (972) 995-4360 www.ti.com

*Mfr. semiconductor devices, electronic electro-mechanical systems, instruments and controls.*

**Texas Instruments France, Velizy, France**

## TEXTRON INC.

40 Westminster Street, Providence, RI, 02903

Tel: (401) 421-2800 Fax: (401) 421-2878 www.textron.com

*Mfr. Aerospace (Bell Helicopter and Cessna Aircraft), industry and consumer products, fasteners and financial services.*

**Textron Industries S.A., 2 rue de Thann, F-75017, Paris, France**

Tel: 33-1-44-291-888 Fax: 33-1-44-29-1890 Contact: Henri Gagnaire, Gen. Dir.

## THERMADYNE HOLDINGS CORPORATION

101 South Hanley Road, Suite 300, St. Louis, MO, 63105

Tel: (314) 746-2197 Fax: (314) 746-2349 www.thermadyne.com

*Mfr. welding, cutting, and safety products.*

**Thermadyne France, Paris, France**

Tel: 33-1-69-63-3260

## THERMO ELECTRIC COOLING AMERICA (TECA)

109 North Fifth Street, Saddle Brook, NJ, 07662

Tel: (201) 843-5800 Fax: (201) 843-7144 www.thermoelectric.com

*Mfr. solid state cooling products, including air-conditioners, cold plates and liquid chillers.*

**Thermo Electric SA, 25 rue Pasteur, F-94456 Limeil Brevannes Cedex, France**

## THERMO ELECTRON CORPORATION

81 Wyman Street, Waltham, MA, 02454-9046

Tel: (781) 622-1000 Fax: (781) 622-1207 www.thermo.com

*Develop/mfr./sale of process equipment &instruments for energy intensive and healthcare industries.*

**Nicolet Biomedical SARL, 1 rue Blaise Pascal, Batiment C - B.P. 144, F-7816 Trappes Cedex, France**

## THERMON MANUFACTURING COMPANY

100 Thermon Drive, PO Box 609, San Marcos, TX, 78667-0609

Tel: (512) 396-5801 Fax: (512) 396-3627 www.thermon.com

*Mfr. steam and electric heat tracing systems, components and accessories.*

**Thermon France, 1 a 15 rue de Valmy, Lot #10, F-93100 Montreuil, France**

## THETFORD CORPORATION

7101 Jackson Road, PO Box 1285, Ann Arbor, MI, 48106

Tel: (734) 769-6000 Fax: (734) 769-2023 www.thetford.com

*Mfr. sanitation products and chemicals.*

**Thetford S.A.R.L., BP 204, 95614 Cergy Pontoise Cedex, France**

## THOMAS & BETTS CORPORATION

8155 T&B Blvd., Memphis, TN, 38125

Tel: (901) 252-5000 Fax: (901) 685-1988 www.tnb.com

*Mfr. elect/electronic connectors and accessories.*

**Thomas & Betts France, 57 Place de la Seine, Silic 120, F-94513 Rungis Cedex, France**

## THOMAS PUBLISHING COMPANY

5 Penn Plaza, New York, NY, 10007

Tel: (212) 695-0500 Fax: (212) 290-7362 www.thomaspublishing.com

*Publishing magazines and directories.*

**Editions Thomas/Elsevier SA, 128 rue Daguesseau, F-92100 Boulogne-Billancourt, France**

## TIDEWATER INC.

601 Poydras Street, Ste.1900, New Orleans, LA, 70130

Tel: (504) 568-1010      Fax: (504) 566-4582      www.tdw.com

*Marine service and equipment to companies engaged in exploration, development and production of oil, gas and minerals.*

**S.A.M.I. (Socite D'Affretement), SA,  35 rue Bergere, F-75009 Paris, France**

Tel: 33-1-44-83-68-68   Fax: 33-1-44-83-68-69

## THE TIMBERLAND COMPANY

200 Domain Drive, Stratham, NH, 03885

Tel: (603) 772-9500      Fax: (603) 773-1640      www.timberland.com

*Design/mfr. footwear, apparel and accessories for men and women.*

**Timberland SARL,  Space Antipolis Immeuble 9, 2323 Chemin de St. Bernard, F-06220 Vallauris, France**

## TIMET CORPORATION

1999 Broadway, Suite 4300, Denver, CO, 80202

Tel: (303) 296-5600      Fax: (303) 296-5650      www.timet.com

*Non-ferrous drawing and rolling, coal and other minerals, metals service centers.*

**TIMET France SARL,  2 Mall des Cerdiates, F-95000 Cergy, France**

## TIMEX CORPORATION

Park Road Extension, Middlebury, CT, 06762

Tel: (203) 573-5000      Fax: (203) 573-6901      www.timex.com

*Mfr. watches, clocks, timing instruments.*

**Usine Kelton,  1 rue Denis Papin, F-25011 Besancon, France**

## TIMKEN SUPER PRECISION (MPB)

7 Optical Ave., Keene, NH, 03431-0547

Tel: (603) 352-0310      Fax: (603) 355-4553      www.timken.com

*Mfr./sales/distribution bearings, tape guides and systems for missiles, etc.*

**Timken Super Precision,  Succersale France, 14 Bureau A101 Bis, rue de Mal Foch, F-77780 Bourron-Marlotte, France**

Tel: 33-1-644-59880

## THE TIMKEN COMPANY

1835 Dueber Ave. SW, PO Box 6927, Canton, OH, 44706-2798

Tel: (330) 438-3000      Fax: (330) 471-4118      www.timken.com

*Mfr. tapered roller bearings and quality alloy steels.*

**Timken France,  2 rue Timken, BP 89, F-68002 Colmar Cedex, France**

## TIW CORPORATION

12300 S. Main Street, PO Box 35729, Houston, TX, 77035

Tel: (713) 729-2110      Fax: (713) 728-4767      www.tiwtools.com

*Mfr. liner hanger equipment, production packers, safety and kelly valves.*

**TIW France,  Paris, France**

Tel: 33-1-30-50-12-16   Fax: 33-4-92-74-64-52

## TMP WORLDWIDE, INC.

622 Third Ave., New York, NY, 10017

Tel: (212) 351-7000      Fax: (212) 658-0540      www.tmpw.com

*#1 Yellow Pages agency and a leader in the recruitment and interactive advertising fields.*

**TMP Worldwide Advertising & Communications,  8 rue Duquesne, Lyon F-69006 France**

**TMP Worldwide Advertising & Communications,  3 Boulevard Bineau, Levallois Perret F-92594, France**

## TOKHEIM CORPORATION

PO Box 360, 10501 Corporate Drive, Fort Wayne, IN, 46845

Tel: (219) 470-4600    Fax: (219) 482-2677    www.tokheim.com

*Engaged in design, manufacture and service of electronic and mechanical petroleum marketing systems.*

**Tokheim Europe,  AC Paris Nord 2, B.P. 40027, F-95912 Roissy Cedex, Paris**

## TOPFLIGHT CORPORATION

277 Commerce Dr., Glen Rock, PA, 17327

Tel: (717) 227-5400    Fax: (717) 227-1415    www.topflight.com

*Commercial printing and service paper.*

**Topflight France,  Chatou Cedex, France**

## TOTES ISOTONER CORPORATION

9655 International Blvd., PO Box 465658, Cincinnati, OH, 45246

Tel: (513) 682-8200    Fax: (513) 682-8602    www.totes.com

*Mfr. rubber and plastic footwear, slippers, umbrellas.*

**Totes France,  Paris, France**

## TOWERS PERRIN

335 Madison Ave., New York, NY, 10017-4605

Tel: (212) 309-3400    Fax: (212) 309-0975    www.towers.com

*Management consulting services.*

**Cresap,  57 Blvd. de Montmorency, F-75016 Paris, France**

**Tillinghast Towers Perrin,  Tor Neptune, La Defense 1, 20 Place de Seine, F-92086 Paris la Defense Cedex, France**

Tel: 33-1-41-02-0202    Fax: 33-1-41-02-5454

**Tillinghast Towers Perrin,  Tor Neptune, La Defense 1, 20 Place de Seine, F-92086 Paris la Defense Cedex, France**

Tel: 33-1-41-02-0202    Fax: 33-1-41-02-5454

## TOYS R US INC.

461 From Road, Paramus, NJ, 07652

Tel: (201) 262-7800    Fax: (201) 845-0973    www.toysrus.com

*Retail stores: toys and games, sporting goods, computer software, books, records.*

**Toys R Us SARL,  2 rue Thomas Edison, Evry, F-91044 Essonne, France**

## THE TRANE COMPANY

3600 Pammel Creek Road, La Crosse, WI, 54601

Tel: (608) 787-2000    Fax: (608) 787-4990    www.trane.com

*Mfr./distributor/service A/C systems and equipment.*

**Societe Trane,  1 rue des Ameriques, BP 6, F-88191 Golbey Cedex, France**

**Societe Trane,  5 blvd. de la Grande Thumine, ZAC du Jas de Bouffan, F-13090 Aix-en-Provence, France**

**Societe Trane,  Direction Regionale Nord, 62 rue des Meuniers, F-92220 Bagneux, France**

**Societe Trane,  Direction Regionale Sud,  Allee de la Combe, F-69380 Lissieu, France**

## TRANS WORLD AIRLINES INC.

515 North Sixth Street, St. Louis, MO, 63101

Tel: (314) 589-3000    Fax: (314) 589-3129    www.twa.com

*Air transport services.*

**Trans World Airlines Inc.,  6 rue Christophe Colomb, F-75008 Paris, France**

Tel: 33-801-892-892

## TRANTER PHE, INC.

PO Box 2289, Wichita Falls, TX, 76306

Tel: (940) 723-7125     Fax: (706) 723-1131      www.tranter.com

*Mfr. heat exchangers.*

**SWEP France SA, 81 rue Auguste Renoir, ZI Croix Sant Marc, BP 135, F-93623 Aulnay-sous-Bois Cedex, France**

Tel: 33-1-48-19-8709    Fax: 33-1-48-69-3415

## TRIMBLE NAVIGATION LIMITED

645 N. Mary Ave., Sunnyvale, CA, 94086

Tel: (408) 481-8000     Fax: (408) 481-2000      www.trimble.com

*Design/mfr. electronic geographic instrumentation.*

**Trimble Navigation France S.A., Espace Enterprises du Haute-Blosne, 34 rue Frederic Le Guyader, F-35200 Rennes Saint-Jacques, France**

Tel: 33-2-99-26-3181    Fax: 33-2-99-26-3900

## TRITON ENERGY LIMITED

6688 N. Central Expressway, Ste. 1400, Dallas, TX, 75206-3925

Tel: (214) 691-5200     Fax: (214) 691-0340      www.tritonenergy.com

*Provider of oil and gas services to the energy industry.*

**Triton France SA, 109 rue du Faubourg St. Honore, F-75008 Paris, France**

## TROPICANA PRODUCTS, INC.

1001 13th Avenue East, Bradenton, FL, 34208

Tel: (941) 747-4461     Fax: (941) 665-5330      www.tropicana.com

*Marketer and producer of branded juices, including Tropicana, Dole, Looza and Copella.*

**Loóza Distribution France S.A., 67 rue de Margueri, F-60370 Hermes, France**

**Tropicana France, Continental Square Batiment Uranus, Place de Londeres, F-95727 Roissy, France**

## TRUE NORTH COMMUNICATIONS INC.

101 East Erie Street, Chicago, IL, 60611

Tel: (312) 425-6500     Fax: (312) 425-5010      www.truenorth.com

*Holding company, advertising agency.*

**Foote, Cone & Belding, 79-83 rue Baudin, F-92309 Levallois-Perret Paris Cedex, France**

## TruServ CORPORATION

8600 West Bryn Mawr, Chicago, IL, 60631-3505

Tel: (773) 695-5000     Fax: (773) 695-6541      www.truserv.com

*Dealer-owned, independent, hardware store cooperative.*

**TruServ Corporation, Paris, France**

## TRW INC.

1900 Richmond Road, Cleveland, OH, 44124-3760

Tel: (216) 291-7000     Fax: (216) 291-7932      www.trw.com

*Electric and energy-related products, automotive and aerospace products, tools and fasteners.*

**Gemmer France, 97 rue de Verdun, F-92151 Suresnes Seine, France**

**Le Thillot, Vosges, France**

**Societe de Mecanique de Pringy, 74 Pringy, Haute Savoie, France**

**Societe Hydro-Mecanique Pleuger, 21 rue de la Mouchetierre, ZI d'Ingres, F-45140 Saint Jean de la Ruelle Orleans, France**

**Societe Metallurgique G. Jeudy, 31 rue des Forges, F-67130 Schirmeck, France**

**TRW Composants Electroniques, ave. de la Jalle Re, F-33300 Bordeaux-Lac, France**

**TRW Mission Hydrosys. SA, Monceau Commerce Bldg., 38 rue de Lisbonne, F-75008 Paris, France**

## TW METALS INC.

2211 Tubeway Ave., Los Angeles, CA, 90040

Tel: (213) 728-9101    Fax: (213) 728-5310    www.twmetals.com

*Distributor pipe, tube, valves, fittings and flanges.*

**Philip Cornes Ltd.,  Boulevard Des Apprentis, F-44550 Montoir De Bretagne, Saint-Nazaire, France**

## UNION CARBIDE CORPORATION

39 Old Ridgebury Road, Danbury, CT, 06817

Tel: (203) 794-2000    Fax: (203) 794-6269    www.unioncarbide.com

*Mfr. industrial chemicals, plastics and resins.*

**Union Carbide Chemicals France SA,  4 Place des Etats-Unis, F-94518 Rungis, France**

## UNISTAR AIR CARGO, INC.

500 East Thorndale Ave., Suite F, Wood Dale, IL, 60190

Tel: (630) 616-3900    Fax: (630) 616-3960    www.unistaraircargo.com

*Package distribution company offering air freight transportation options.*

**UniStar Air Cargo France Agent,  c/o S.L.M.N. Air Services, 15 Avenue De L'Industrie, F-69960 Corbas (Lyon), France**

## UNISYS CORPORATION.

PO Box 500, Union Meeting Road, Blue Bell, PA, 19424

Tel: (215) 986-4011    Fax: (215) 986-6850    www.unisys.com

*Mfr./marketing/servicing electronic information systems.*

**Unisys France Sa,  La Palette Orange, Cergy, F-95015 Val d'Oise, France**

## UNITED AIRLINES INC.

1200 E. Algonquin Rd., Chicago, IL, 60007

Tel: (847) 700-4000    Fax: (847) 700-4081    www.ual.com

*Air transportation, passenger and freight services.*

**United Airlines,  40 rue Jean Jaures, F-93176 Bagnolet Cedex, France**

## UNITED PARCEL SERVICE, INC.

55 Glenlake Parkway, NE, Atlanta, GA, 30328

Tel: (404) 828-6000    Fax: (404) 828-6593    www.ups.com

*International package-delivery service.*

**Espaces Express UPS,  34 blvd. Malesherbes, F-75008 Paris, France**

Tel: 800-877-877

## UNITED STATES SURGICAL CORPORATION

150 Glover Ave., Norwalk, CT, 06856

Tel: (203) 845-1000    Fax: (203) 847-0635    www.ussurg.com

*Mfr./development/market surgical staplers, laparoscopic instruments and sutures.*

**ASE Partners SNC,  Attn: French Office, U.S. Surgical, 150 Glover Avenue, Norwalk CT 06856**

**Auto Suture Europe SA,  Attn: French Office, U.S. Surgical, 150 Glover Avenue, Norwalk CT 06856**

**Auto Suture European Services Center SA,  Attn: French Office, U.S. Surgical, 150 Glover Avenue, Norwalk CT 06856**

**Merlin Medical SA,  Attn: French Office, U.S. Surgical, 150 Glover Avenue, Norwalk CT 06856**

## UNITED TECHNOLOGIES CORPORATION

One Financial Plaza, Hartford, CT, 06103

Tel: (860) 728-7000    Fax: (860) 728-7979    www.utc.com

*Mfr. aircraft engines, elevators, A/C, auto equipment, space and military electronic and rocket propulsion systems.  Products include Pratt and Whitney, Otis elevators, Carrier heating and air conditioning and Sikorsky helicopters.*

**United Technologies Intl. Operations Inc.,  141 rue de Saussure, F-75017 Paris, France**

## UNIVERSAL INSTRUMENTS

90 Bevier Street, S. Dock, Binghamton, NY, 13904

Tel: (607) 779-7522     Fax: (607) 779-7971      www.uic.com

*Mfr./sales of instruments for electronic circuit assembly.*

**Universal Instruments SARL,  Gennevilliers, France**

Tel: 33-1-41-11-4123   Fax: 33-1-40-86-9954

## UNIVERSAL WEATHER & AVIATION INC.

8787 Tallyho Road, Houston, TX, 77061

Tel: (713) 944-1622     Fax: (713) 943-4650      www.univ-wea.com

*Provides service management, and worldwide weather and communications to the corporate aviation community.*

**Universal Aviation France SA,  Aeroport de Paris Bourget, Hangar 5 Bat 44, Le Bourget, F-93350 Seine St. Denis, France**

Tel: 33-1-4835-9638   Fax: 33-1-4835-8546   Contact: Sandrine Laroche-Jackson

## UNUMPROVIDENT

2211 Congress Street, Portland, ME, 04122

Tel: (207) 770-2211     Fax: (207) 770-4510      www.unum.com

*Disability and special risk insurance.*

**Unum France,  21/23 rue Renan F- 69007, Lyon, France**

Tel: 33-4-78-619797

## UOP LLC.

25 East Algonquin Road, Des Plaines, IL, 60017

Tel: (847) 391-2000     Fax: (847) 391-2253      www.uop.com

*Engaged in developing and commercializing technology for license to the oil refining, petrochemical and gas processing industries.*

**UOP France SARL,  24 rue Saarinen-SILIC 252, 94568 Rungis Cedex, France**

Tel: 33-1-41-80-1660   Fax: 33-1-41-80-1666

## URS CORPORATION

100 California Street, Ste. 500, San Francisco, CA, 94111-4529

Tel: (415) 774-2700     Fax: (415) 398-1904      www.urscorp.com

*Provides planning, design and construction management services, pollution control and hazardous waste management.*

**URS (Organisation et Surete Industrielles SA),  Aix-en-Provence, France**

Tel: 33-4-42-91-3933

## URSCHEL LABORATORIES INC.

2503 Calumet Ave., PO Box 2200, Valparaiso, IN, 46384-2200

Tel: (219) 464-4811     Fax: (219) 462-3879      www.urschel.com

*Design/mfr. precision food processing equipment.*

**Urschel Intl. Ltd.,  Orly Fret 747, F-94398 Orly Aerogare, Cedex, Succursale, France**

## US AIRWAYS GROUP, INC.

2345 Crystal Drive, Arlington, VA, 22227

Tel: (703) 872-7000     Fax: (703) 294-5096      www.usairways.com

*Commercial airline.*

**USAir Inc.,  Charles de Gaulle Airport, BP 20247, F-95712 Paris//Roisy, France**

**UUNET**

22001 Loudoun County Pkwy., Ashburn, VA, 20147

Tel: (703) 206-5600     Fax: (703) 206-5601     www.uu.net

*World's largest Internet service provider; World Wide Web hosting services, security products and consulting services to businesses, professionals, and on-line service providers.*

**UUNET France, 215 Avenue Georges, Clemenceau, Le Clemenceau 2, F-92000 Nanterre, France**

Tel: 33-1-56-38-22-00   Fax: 33-156-38-2201   Contact: Jerome Lecat

**VALENITE INC**

31751 Research Park Dr., Madison Heights, MI, 48071-9636

Tel: (248) 589-1000     Fax: (248) 597-4820     www.valenite.com

*Cemented carbide, high speed steel, ceramic and diamond cutting tool products, etc.*

**Valenite-Modco SARL, 5 blvd. Pierre Desgranges, Zone Industrielle Nord, F-42162 Andrezieux-Boutheon Cedex, France**

**VALHI INC.**

5430 LBJ Freeway, Ste. 1700, Dallas, TX, 75240

Tel: (972) 233-1700     Fax: (972) 448-1445

*Mfr. titanium products and computer office components.*

**Bentone-Sud SA, 11 ave. Morane Saulnier, F-78140 Yvelines, France**

**Societe Industrielle du Titane SA, 45 rue de Courcelles, F-75008 Paris, France**

**VALMONT INDUSTRIES INC.**

1 Valmont Plaza, Omaha, NE, 68154

Tel: (402) 963-1000     Fax: (402) 963-1199     www.valmont.com

*Mfr. irrigation systems, steel lighting, utility and communication poles.*

**Sermeto - Industrial Equipment Division, Les Rebrillons, F-03330 Creuzier-Le-Neuf, France**

Tel: 33-470-58-4740   Fax: 33-470-58-0022

**Valmont Sermeto-Charmeil, Les Martoulets-B.P.1, 03110 Charmeil, France**

Tel: 33-470-58-8686   Fax: 33-470-58-8687   Contact: Philippe Guidez

**Valmont Tubalco, Vallee de Couzon, F-42800 Rive-de-Gier, France**

Tel: 33-477-83-0010   Fax: 33-477-83-7425   Contact: Paul von Iseghem

**VALSPAR CORPORATION**

1101 South Third Street, Minneapolis, MN, 55415-1259

Tel: (612) 332-7371     Fax: (612) 375-7723     www.valspar.com

*Produce paint, varnish and allied products.*

**Valspar Inc., Paris, France**

**VARIAN MEDICAL SYSTEMS, INC.**

3050 Hansen Way, Palo Alto, CA, 94304-100

Tel: (650) 493-4000     Fax: (650) 424-5358     www.varian.com

*Mfr. microwave tubes and devices, analytical instruments, semiconductor process and medical equipment, vacuum systems.*

**Varian Medical France, C.A.A. Tolbiac-Massena C.E. 16, 5 rue Watt, F-75644 Paris Cedex 13, France**

**VARIAN SEMICONDUCTOR EQUIPMENT ASSOCIATES, INC.**

35 Dory Road, Gloucester, MA, 01930

Tel: (978) 281-2000     Fax: (978) 283-5391     www.vsea.com

*Mfr. ion implantation systems.*

**Varian Semiconductor Equipment Assocates, 7 Avenue des Tropiques, Z.A. Courtaboeuf BP 12, F-91941 Les Ulis Cedex, France**

Tel: 33-1-6986-3838

## VEECO INSTRUMENTS INC.

Terminal Drive, Plainview, NY, 11803

Tel: (516) 349-8300     Fax: (516) 349-9079      www.veeco.com

*Mfr. surface profiler, atomic force microscopes, leak and plating thickness detectors and semiconductor products.*

**Veeco S.A., 11 rue Maire Poussepin, Zi de la Gare, F-91412 Dourdan, France**

Tel: 33-1-64-59-3520    Fax: 33-1-64-59-7222

## VEEDER-ROOT COMPANY

125 Powder Forest Drive, PO Box 2003, Simsbury, CT, 06070-2003

Tel: (860) 651-2700     Fax: (860) 651-2704      www.veeder.com

*Mfr. of automatic tank gauging systems.*

**Veeder Root SARL, 8 Place de la Loire, Silic 422, F-94583 Rungis Cedex, France**

## VELCRO USA INC.

406 Brown Avenue, Manchester, NH, 03108

Tel: (603) 669-4892     Fax: (603) 669-9271      www.velcro.com

*Mfr./sales of velcro brand hook and loop fasteners, plastic buckles and metal hardware and cable control straps.*

**Systems de Fermeture S.A., Zone d'Activite Valnor - B.P.62, 21-23 rue Des Jeunes Chiens, F-95508 Le Thillay, France**

Tel: 33-1-39-88100    Fax: 33-1-39-889161

## VERITY, INC.

894 Ross Drive, Sunnyvale, CA, 94089

Tel: (408) 541-1500     Fax: (408) 541-1600      www.verity.com

*Mfr. software to simplify management of information.*

**Verity France, 14 Place Marie Jeanne Bassot,F-92593 Levallois Perret Cedex, France**

Tel: 33-1-4149-0450

## VERIZON COMMUNICATIONS INC.

1255 Corporate Drive, Irving, TX, 75038

Tel: (972) 507-5000     Fax: (972) 507-5002      www.gte.com

*Engaged in wireline and wireless communications.*

**GTE International Telecom Services, Barentin, France**

## VF CORPORATION

1047 North Park Road, Wyomissing, PA, 19610

Tel: (610) 378-1151     Fax: (610) 378-9371      www.vfc.com

*Mfr./marketing apparel including Lee and Wrangler jeans, Jansport backpacks and Healthtex.*

**VF Intimate Apparel, 65 ave. Kleber, F-75116 Paris, France**

## VIACOM INC.

1515 Broadway, 28th Fl., New York, NY, 10036-5794

Tel: (212) 258-6000     Fax: (212) 258-6358      www.viacom.com

*Communications, publishing and entertainment.*

**Films Paramount SA, 1 rue Meyerbeer, F-75009 Paris, France**

## VICOR CORPORATION

23 Frontage Road, Andover, MA, 01810

Tel: (978) 470-2900     Fax: (978) 749-3536      www.vicr.com

*Designs, manufactures, and markets modular power components and complete configurable and custom power systems.*

**Vicor France, 6 Parc Ariane, Immeuble "Le Mercure", F-78284 Guyancourt Cedex, France**

## THE VIKING CORPORATION

210 N. Industrial Park Rd., Hastings, MI, 49058

Tel: (616) 945-9501    Fax: (616) 945-9599    www.vikingcorp.com

*Mfr. fire extinguishing equipment.*

**Sprinkler Viking SARL, 43 Blvd. Chilperic, F-77500 Chelles, France**

## VIKING OFFICE PRODUCTS

950 West 190th Street, Torrance, CA, 90502

Tel: (310) 225-4500    Fax: (310) 324-2396    www.vikingop.com

*International direct marketer of office products, computer supplies, business furniture and stationery.*

**Viking Direct S.A.R.L., Z-1-Mitry-Campans, rue Mercier, F-77294 Mitry Mory Cedex, France**

Tel: 33-1-64-67-4747   Fax: 33-1-64-67-48-99   Contact: Bernard Pagneux, Mgr.   Emp: 427

## VISHAY INTERTECHNOLOGY INC.

63 Lincoln Hwy., Malvern, PA, 19355

Tel: (610) 644-1300    Fax: (610) 296-0657    www.vishay.com

*Mfr. resistors, strain gages, capacitors, inductors, printed circuit boards.*

**Aztronic Societe Nouvelle, Z.I. de Bellitourne, AZE, F-53200 Chateau-Gontier, France**

**Nicolitch, 1 ave. du Bois de L'Epine, BP 143, F-91005 Evry Cedex, France**

**Sfernice SA, 199 Blvd. de la Madeleine, BP 159, F-06003 Nice Cede, France**

**Sprague, 8 ave. du Danemark, F-37100 Tours, France**

**Vishay Geka/Sovcor, 11 Chemin de Ronde, BP 8, F-78110 Le Vesinet, France**

## VISHAY SILICONIX INC.

2201 Laurelwood Drive, Santa Clara, CA, 95054

Tel: (408) 988-8000    Fax: (408) 970-3950    www.vishay.com

*Semiconductor components.*

**Vishay Siliconix SARL, Centre Commercial de l'Echat, Place de l'Europe, F-94019 Creteil Cedex, France**

## VIVITAR CORPORATION

1280 Rancho Conejo Blvd, Newbury Park, CA, 91320

Tel: (805) 498-7008    Fax: (805) 498-5086    www.vivitar.com

*Mfr. photographic equipment, electronic supplies.*

**Vivitar France SA, 41-43 rue de Ville Neuve, Silic 197, F-94563 Rungis, France**

## VOLT INFORMATION SCIENCES, INC.

1221 Ave. of the Americas, 47th Fl., New York, NY, 10020-1579

Tel: (212) 704-2400    Fax: (212) 704-2417    www.volt.com

*Staffing services and telecommunication services.*

**Autologic Intl. Ltd., 26 rue Robert Witxhitz, F-94200 Ivy-Sur-Seine, Paris, France**

Tel: 33-1-45-21-6960   Fax: 33-1-46-71-5049

## VTEL (VIDEOTELECOM CORPORATION )

108 Wild Basin Road, Austin, TX, 78746

Tel: (512) 314-2700    Fax: (512) 314-2792    www.vtel.com

*Design/mfr. long-distance interactive video communications products.*

**VTEL France SA, 15 rue J.B. Berlier, F-75013 Paris, France**

Tel: 33-1-53-94-6161   Fax: 33-1-53-94-6171   Contact: Jean-Christophe Lenglart

## WABTEC CORPORATION

1001 Air Brake Ave., Wilmerding, PA, 15148

Tel: (412) 825-1000    Fax: (412) 825-1501    www.wabtec.com

*Mfr. equipment for locomotives, railway freight cars, and passenger transit vehicles*

**Railroad Friction Products Corporation, Wissenbourg, France**

## WACKENHUT CORPORATION

4200 Wackenhut Dr., Ste. 100, Palm Beach Gardens, FL, 33410

Tel: (561) 622-5656        Fax: (561) 691-6736        www.wackenhut.com

*Security systems and services.*

**Wackenhut France, 9-11 ave. Michelet, F-93400 Saint Ouen, Paris, France**

Tel: 33-1-49-48-7956    Fax: 33-1-40-10-1771

## WALBRO CORPORATION, TI GROUP AUTOMOTIVE

6242 Garfield Ave., Cass City, MI, 48726-1325

Tel: (517) 872-2131        Fax: (517) 872-3090        www.walbro.com

*Mfr. motor vehicle accessories and parts, automotive fluid carrying systems.*

**TI Group Automotive Systems, Boulevard de l'Industrie Z.I., F-37530 Nazelles-Negron, France**

Tel: 33-2-27-23-4000

**TI Group Automotive Systems, ZI Technoland, 25600 Brognard, France**

## WALL COLMONOY CORPORATION

30261 Stephenson Hwy., Madison Heights, MI, 48071

Tel: (248) 585-6400        Fax: (248) 585-7960        www.wallcolmonoy.com

*Mfr. hard-surfacing and brazing alloys, equipment and services.*

**Wall Colmonoy France, 9 rue des Aulnettes, F-95104 Argenteuil, France**

Tel: 33-1-30-25-9860    Fax: 33-1-30-25-9865    Contact: Gerard Caville    Emp: 12

## WARNACO INC.

90 Park Ave., New York, NY, 10016

Tel: (212) 661-1300        Fax: (212) 687-0480        www.warnaco.com

*Mfr./sales intimate apparel and men's and women's sportswear.*

**Warner's Aiglon SA, 66 rue du Faubourg St.-Honore, F-75008 Paris, France**

## WARNER BROS INTERNATIONAL TELEVISION

4000 Warner Boulevard, Bldg.170, 3rd Fl., Burbank, CA, 91522

Tel: (818) 954-6000        Fax: (818) 977-4040        www.wbitv.com

*Distributor TV programming and theatrical features.*

**Warner Bros. Intl. Television, 33 Ave. de Wagram, F-75057 Paris, France**

Tel: 33-1-55-37-5966    Fax: 33-1-55-37-5968    Contact: Michel Lecourt, VP

## WARNER ELECTRIC BRAKE & CLUTCH COMPANY

449 Gardner St., South Beloit, IL, 61080

Tel: (815) 389-3771        Fax: (815) 389-2582        www.warnernet.com

*Global supplier of Power Transmission and Motion Control Solution Systems; automotive, industry brakes, and clutches.*

**Warner & Tourco, Rte de Spay, BP 313, F-72700 Allonnes, France**

Tel: 33-243-43-6363    Fax: 33-243-6340

## WARNER-JENKINSON COMPANY, INC.

2526 Baldwin Street, St. Louis, MO, 63106

Tel: (314) 889-7600        Fax: (314) 658-7305

*Mfr. synthetic and natural colors for food, drugs and cosmetics.*

**Warner-Jenkinson France, 2 rue de la Montjoie, F-93212 La Plaine Saint-Denis Cedex, France**

## THE WASHINGTON POST COMPANY

1150 15th St. NW, Washington, DC, 20071

Tel: (202) 334-6000        Fax: (202) 334-4536        www.washpostco.com

*Engaged in magazine publishing, cable and television broadcasting, educational services and the Internet.*

**International Herald Tribune, 181 Avenue Charles-de-Gaulle, F-91521 Neuilly Cedex, France**

Tel: 33-1-41-43-9300

## WASSERSTEIN PERELLA & CO., INC.

31 West 52nd Street, New York, NY, 10019

Tel: (212) 969-2700     Fax: (212) 969-7969     www.wassersteinperella.com

*Engaged in international investment banking and financial services.*

**Wasserstein Perella & (France), Ltd., 10 rue de la Paix, F-72002 Paris Cedex, France**

Tel: 33-1-44-58-9115   Fax: 33-1-42-96-9115

## WATERS CORPORATION

34 Maple Street, Milford, MA, 01757

Tel: (508) 478-2000     Fax: (508) 872-1990     www.waters.com

*Mfr./distribute liquid chromatographic instruments and test and measurement equipment.*

**Waters SA, 6 rue Jean Pierre Timbaud, F-78180 Montigny le Bretonneux, France**

## WATLOW ELECTRIC MFG. COMPANY

12001 Lackland Rd., St. Louis, MO, 63146-4039

Tel: (314) 878-4600     Fax: (314) 434-1020     www.watlow.com

*Mfr. electrical heating units, electronic controls, thermocouple wire, metal-sheathed cable, infrared sensors.*

**Watlow France SARL, Immeuble Somag, 16 rue Ampere, F-95307 Cergy Pontoise Cedex , France**

Tel: 33-1-30-73-2425   Fax: 33-1-34-73-2875

## WATTS INDUSTRIES, INC.

815 Chestnut Street, North Andover, MA, 01845-6098

Tel: (978) 688-1811     Fax: (978) 688-5841     www.wattsind.com

*Designs/mfr./sales of industry valves and safety control products.*

**Etablissements Trubert SA, 6 ave. Gustave Eiffel, Gellainville BP 339, F-28630 Chartres Cedex, France**

**Watts-SFR, 13 rue Jean Jacques Rousseau, F-80390 Fressenneville, France**

## WEATHERFORD INTERNATIONAL, INC.

5 Post Oak Blvd, Ste. 1760, Houston, TX, 77227-3415

Tel: (713) 287-8400     Fax: (713) 963-9785     www.weatherford.com

*Oilfield services, products and equipment; mfr. marine cranes for oil and gas industry.*

**Weatherford SA, rue Marie Joliot Curie, Z.I. BP 130, F-64143 Lons Cedex, France**

Tel: 33-5-59-622664   Fax: 33-5-59-323197

## WEBER-STEPHEN PRODUCTS COMPANY

200 E. Daniels Road, Palatine, IL, 60067-6266

Tel: (847) 934-5700     Fax: (847) 934-0291     www.weberbq.com

*Mfr./sales Weber cooking systems and barbeque and gas grills.*

**Le Creuset/Weber-Stephen, rue Olivier Deguise, F-02230 Frenoy LeGrand, France**

Tel: 33-3-23-06-2222   Fax: 33-3-23-09-0662

## WEDCO INC.

PO Box 397, Bloomsbury, NJ, 08804

Tel: (908) 479-4181     Fax: (908) 479-6622     www.icoinc.com

*Plastics grinding and related services, machinery and equipment for plastics industry.*

**WEDCO France SA, 3 Route de la Grande-Paroisse, F-77130 Montereau, France**

Tel: 33-1-64-32-4467   Fax: 33-1-64-32-4467   Contact: Olivier Vilcot, Mng. Dir.

## WEIGHT WATCHERS INTERNATIONAL, INC.

175 Crossways Park Dr., Woodbury, NY, 11797

Tel: (516) 390-1400     Fax: (516) 390-1763     www.weightwatchers.com

*Weight loss programs.*

**Weight Watchers France, Le Florilege, 4 Allee de la Frasnerie, B.P. 64.F, F-748330 Fontenay-le-Fleury, France**

## WELCH ALLYN DCD INC.

4341 State Street Road, Skaneateles Falls, NY, 13153

Tel: (315) 685-4100      Fax: (315) 685-4091      www.welchallyn.com

*Mfr. bar code data collection systems.*

**Hand Held Products France,  50 rue Marcel Dassault, Boulougne-Billancourt F-92100, France**

Tel: 33-1-46-10-4111

## WEST PHARMACEUTICAL SERVICES

101 Gordon Drive, PO Box 645, Lionville, PA, 19341-0645

Tel: (610) 594-2900      Fax: (610) 594-3014      www.westpharma.com

*Mfr. products for filling, sealing, dispensing and delivering needs of health care and consumer products markets.*

**The West Company France S.A.,  Le Nouvion en Thierache, France**

**The West Company France S.A.,  ZA des Coteaux du Bel-Air, 29-31 blvd de la Paix, F-78100 Saint-Germain en Laye, France**

Tel: 33-1-39-21-5400   Fax: 33-1-34-51-365552

## WESTERN DIGITAL CORPORATION

8105 Irvine Center Drive, Irvine, CA, 92718

Tel: (949) 932-5000      Fax: (949) 932-6629      www.westerndigital.com

*Mfr. hard disk drives, video graphics boards, VLSI.*

**Western Digital Corp.,  Parc Club Orsay Universite, Batiment N, 3 rue Jean Rostand, Orsay Cedex, France**

## WESTERN GEOPHYSICAL, INC.

10205 Westheimer, Houston, TX, 77251-1407

Tel: (713) 972-4000      Fax: (713) 952-9837      www.bakerhughes.com

*Provides comprehensive seismic services for oil and gas exploration, field development, and reservoir monitoring.*

**Western Atlas Logging Services,  134 rue d'Assas, F-75006 Paris, France**

Tel: 33-1-55-42-9657   Fax: 33-1-55-42-9657   Contact: J.P. Amiard, Exec. Dir.

## WHIRLPOOL CORPORATION

2000 N. M-63, Benton Harbor, MI, 49022-2692

Tel: (616) 923-5000      Fax: (616) 923-5443      www.whirlpoolcorp.com

*Mfr./market home appliances: Whirlpool, Roper, KitchenAid, Estate, and Inglis.*

**Whirlpool Europe BV,  Amiens, France**

## WHITE & CASE LLP

1155 Ave. of the Americas, New York, NY, 10036-2767

Tel: (212) 819-8200      Fax: (212) 354-8113      www.whitecase.com

*International law firm.*

**White & Case LLP,  Avocates au Barreau de Paris, Toque Générale: J002, 11 blvd de la Madeleine, F-75001 Paris France**

Tel: 33-1-55-04-1515   Fax: 33-1-55-04-1516   Contact: Michael Hancock

## WHITEHALL-ROBINS INC.

1407 Cummings Drive, PO Box 26609, Richmond, VA, 23261-6609

Tel: (804) 257-2000      Fax: (804) 257-2120      www.ahp.com

*Mfr. ethical pharmaceuticals and consumer healthcare products.*

**Laboratoires Martinet,  222 Blvd. Pereire, F-75017 Paris, France**

## WHITTMAN-HART & USWEB/CKS

311 S. Wacker Drive, Ste. 3500, Chicago, IL, 60606-6621

Tel: (312) 922-9200     Fax: (312) 913-3020     www.uswebcks.com

*Internet professional services firm; design and implementation services for multimedia marketing programs.*

**USWeb/CKS France,  95 rue Marcel Dassault, F-92100 Boulogne Billancourt, France**

Tel: 33-1-46-94-9842   Contact: Robert T. Clarkson

## WILLAMETTE INDUSTRIES, INC.

1300 SW Fifth Ave., Ste. 3800, Portland, OR, 97201

Tel: (503) 227-5581     Fax: (503) 273-5603     www.wii.com

*Mfr./sales and distribution of paper and wood products.*

**Willamette Europe,  One Industrielle, B.P. 50, F-40110 Morcenx, Orcenx, France**

Tel: 33-5-58-82-5900   Fax: 33-5-58-07-9136

**Willamette Europe Darso SAS,  40260 Linxe, France**

## T.D. WILLIAMSON INC.

PO Box 2299, Tulsa, OK, 74101

Tel: (918) 254-9400     Fax: (918) 254-9474     www.tdwilliamson.com

*Mfr. equipment and provide service for pipeline maintenance.*

**T.D. Williamson,  ba 11, rue de L'Atome-BP 81, Zone Industriele F-67802, Bischheim Cedex,  France**

## WILLKIE FARR & GALLAGHER

787 Seventh Avenue, New York, NY, 10019-6099

Tel: (212) 821-8000     Fax: (212) 821-8111     www.willkie.com

*International law firm.*

**Willkie Farr & Gallagher,  21-23 rue de la Ville l'Evêque,F- 75008 Paris, France**

Tel: 33-1-5- 43-4500

## WILSON, ELSER, MOSKOWITZ, EDELMAN & DICKER LLP

150 East 42nd St., New York, NY, 10017

Tel: (212) 490-3000     Fax: (212) 490-3038     www.wemed.com

*International law firm.*

**Honig Buffat Mettetal,  Société D' Avocats, 21 rue Clément Marot, Paris F-75008, France**

## WIND RIVER SYSTEMS, INC.

500 Wind River Way, Alameda, CA, 94501

Tel: (510) 748-4100     Fax: (510) 749-2010     www.isi.com

*Develops and markets computer software products and services.*

**Wind River Systems S.A.R.L.,  19 Avenue de Norvège, Immeuble OSLO Bâtiment 3**
**Z.A. de Courtaboeuf 1, 91953 Les Ulis Cédex,**
**France**

Tel: 33-1-60-92-63-00   Fax: 33-1-60-92-63-15

## WINSTON & STRAWN

35 West Wacker Drive - Ste. 4200, Chicago, IL, 60601-9703

Tel: (312) 558-5600     Fax: (312) 558-5700     www.winston.com

*International law firm.*

**Winston & Strawn,  6 rue de Cirque, F-75008 Paris, France**

Tel: 33-1-42-25-1055   Contact: Paul Bishop, Ptnr.

## HARRY WINSTON INC.

718 Fifth Ave., New York, NY, 10019

Tel: (212) 245-2000       Fax:                    www.harry-winston.com

*Diamonds and lapidary work.*

**Harry Winston de New York SARL,  29 ave. Montaigne, F-75008 Paris, France**

Tel: 33-1-4720-0309

## WONDERWARE CORPORATION

100 Technology Dr., Irvine, CA, 92618

Tel: (949) 727-3200       Fax: (949) 727-3270       www.wonderware.com

*Mfr. industrial strength applications software and services.*

**Factory Systemes,  Marne la Vallee, France**

Tel: 33-164616868

## WOODHEAD INDUSTRIES INC.

Three Parkway North, Ste. 550, Deerfield, IL, 60015

Tel: (847) 236-9300       Fax: (847) 236-0503       www.woodhead.com

*Develop/mfr./sale/distributor elect/electronic, fiber optic and ergonomic special-function, non-commodity products.*

**Elitec S.A.,  Z.A.C. Des Cherisiers, 16 rue Louis Martin, F-77400 Thorigny-Sur-Marne, France**

## WORLD COURIER INC.

1313 Fourth Ave., New Hyde Park, NY, 11041

Tel: (516) 354-2600       Fax: (516) 354-2644       www.worldcourier.com

*International courier service.*

**World Courier France,  BP, F-10484 Roissy Paris, France**

## WORLD MINERALS INC.

130 Castilian Drive, Santa Barbara, CA, 93117

Tel: (805) 562-0200       Fax: (805) 562-0298       www.worldminerals.com

*Mfr. premium quality diatomite and perlite products.*

**World Minerals France SA,  257 avenue Georges Clemenceau, F-92745 Nanterre Cedex France**

Tel: 33-1-41-91-5711

## WORLDCOM, INC.

500 Clinton Center Drive, Clinton, MS, 39060

Tel: (601) 360-8600       Fax: (601) 360-8616       www.wcom.com

*Telecommunications company serving local, long distance and Internet customers domestically and internationally.*

**WorldCom International,  125 ave. des Champs-Elysees, F-75008 Paris, France**

## WORLDXCHANGE COMMUNICATIONS

9999 Willow Creek Road, San Diego, CA, 92131

Tel: (858) 547-4933       Fax: (800) 995-4502       www.worldxchange.com

*Provides international, long distance telecommunications services worldwide.*

**WorldxChange Communications S.A.,  Paris, France**

## WM WRIGLEY JR. COMPANY

410 N. Michigan Ave., Chicago, IL, 60611-4287

Tel: (312) 644-2121       Fax: (312) 644-0353       www.wrigley.com

*Mfr. chewing gum.*

**Wrigley France S.N.C.,  Zone Industrielle BP 29, F-68600 Neufbrisach Biesheim, France**

## WYETH-AYERST INTERNATIONAL INC.

150 Radnot-Chester Road, St. Davids, PA, 19087

Tel: (610) 902-4100     Fax: (610) 989-4586     www.ahp.com/wyeth

*Antibiotics and pharmaceutical products.*

**Wyeth-Lederle, Le Wilson 2, 80 Avenue du President Wilson Puteaux, F-92031 Paris Cedex France**

Tel: 33-1-4102-7102

## WYNN OIL COMPANY

1050 West Fifth Street, Azusa, CA, 91702-9510

Tel: (626) 334-0231     Fax: (626) 334-1456     www.wynnoil.com

*Mfr. of specialty chemicals, equipment and related service programs for automotive and industrial markets.*

**Wynn's Automotive France, 5 chemin de Lou Tribail, ZI de Toctoucau, BP 5, F-33610 Cestas, France**

Tel: 33-5-5-97-9899   Fax: 33-5-56-68-0008   Contact: Bernard-Lionel Poulard, Mng. Dir.   Emp: 87

**Wynn's France SA (Industrial), 11 ave. Dubonnet, F-92407 Courbevoie Cedex, France**

Tel: 33-1-49-04-0420   Fax: 33-1-47-89-9670   Contact: Bernard-Lionel Poulard, Mng. Dir.   Emp: 95

## WYSE TECHNOLOGY INC.

3471 North First Street, San Jose, CA, 95134

Tel: (408) 473-1200     Fax: (408) 473-2080     www.wyse.com

*Mfr. computer network terminals.*

**Wyse Technology, Immeuble Mercure, 6 Parc Club Arlane, F-78284 Guyancourt, Cedex France**

Tel: 33-1-3944-0044   Fax: 33-1-3452-0930

## XEROX CORPORATION

800 Long Ridge Road, PO Box 1600, Stamford, CT, 06904

Tel: (203) 968-3000     Fax: (203) 968-4312     www.xerox.com

*Mfr. document processing equipment, systems and supplies.*

**Xerox SA, 1 rue Celestin Freinet BP 2069, F-44201 Nantes Cedex 02, France**

Tel: 33-2-51-88-80-80   Fax: 33-2-51-88-80-00

**Xerox SA, 20 rue Garibaldi, F-69451 Lyon Cedex 06, France**

Tel: 33-4-72-69-22-69   Fax: 33-4-72-69-23-91

**Xerox SA, 90 chemin du Roy d'Espagne BP 171, F-13279 Marseille,Cedex 09, France**

Tel: 33-4-91-76-70-00   Fax: 33-4-91-76-60-10

**Xerox SA, 20 place des Halles, Tour Europe, F-67000 Strasbourg, France**

Tel: 33-3-88-25-48-00   Fax: 33-3-88-25-48-12

**Xerox SA, ZI La Pilaterie, F-59700 Marcq En Baroeul, France**

Tel: 33-3-20-66-7100   Fax: 33-3-20-66-7171

**Xerox SA, 7 rue Touzet, F-93586 St.-Ouen Cedex, France**

## XILINX INC.

2100 Logic Drive, San Jose, CA, 95124-3400

Tel: (408) 559-7778     Fax: (408) 559-7114     www.xilinx.com

*Programmable logic and related development systems software.*

**Xilinx SARL, Espace Jouy Technology, 21 rue Albert Calmette Bt. C, F-78353 Jouy En Josas Cedex, France**

## XIRCOM, INC.

2300 Corporate Center Drive, Thousand Oaks, CA, 91320

Tel: (805) 376-9300     Fax: (805) 376-9311     www.xircom.com

*Mfr. PC card network adapters and modems.*

**Xircom France SARL, 41 Bis Avenue de l'Europe, BP 264, F-78147 Velizy Cedex, France**

## XTRA CORPORATION

1807 Park 270 Dr., Ste. 400, St. Louis, MO, 63146-4020

Tel: (314) 579-9320     Fax: (314) 579-0299     www.xtracorp.com

*Holding company: leasing.*

**XTRA International,  Paris, France**

## YAHOO! INC.

3420 Central Expressway, Santa Clara, CA, 95051

Tel: (408) 731-3300     Fax: (408) 731-3301     www.yahoo-inc.com

*Internet media company providing specialized content, free electronic mail and community offerings and commerce.*

**Yahoo! Inc.,  14 Place Marie-Jeanne Bassot, F-92593 Levallois-Perret Cedex, Paris, France**

Tel: 33-1-46-39-5582   Fax: 33-1-46-39-0070

## YELLOW CORPORATION

10990 Roe Ave., PO Box 7270, Overland Park, KS, 66207

Tel: (913) 696-6100     Fax: (913) 696-6116     www.yellowcorp.com

*Commodity transportation.*

**Frans Maas Sud Transports Internationaux Snc,  Z.I. De Revoisson - rue Calmette, F- 69740 Genas, France**

**Frans Maas Sud Transports Internationaux Snc,  C.E.N. 116 Route du Bassin N.1, 92631 Gennevilliers, Cedex France**

## YORK INTERNATIONAL CORPORATION

631 South Richland Ave., York, PA, 17403

Tel: (717) 771-7890     Fax: (717) 771-6212     www.york.com

*Mfr. heating, ventilating, air conditioning and refrigeration equipment.*

**Le Froid Industriel-York SA,  BP 10, F-44471 Carquefou Nantes, France**

**York Neige-Nantes,  18 rue Gustave Eiffel B.P. 66, Ste. Luce sur Loire, F-44980 France**

Tel: 33-2-4018-4600   Fax: 33-2-5185-0193

## YOUNG & RUBICAM INC.

285 Madison Ave., New York, NY, 10017

Tel: (212) 210-3000     Fax: (212) 370-3796     www.yr.com

*Advertising, public relations, direct marketing and sales promotion, corporate and product ID management.*

**Young & Rubicam France SA,  23 allee Maillasson, BP 73, F-92105 Boulogne Cedex, France**

## JOHN ZINK COMPANY

PO Box 21220, Tulsa, OK, 74121-1220

Tel: (918) 234-1800     Fax: (918) 234-2700     www.johnzink.com

*Mfr. flare systems, thermal oxidizers, vapor recovery systems, process heater burners.*

**John Zink France,  Paris, France**

Contact: Jean Langjahr

## ZITEL CORPORATION

47211 Bayside Pkwy., Fremont, CA, 94538-6517

Tel: (510) 440-9600     Fax: (510) 440-9696     www.zitel.com

*Mfr. computer peripherals and software.*

**Zitel SARL,  130 rue Henri Barbesse, F-95100 Argenteuil, France**

Contact: Reginald H.W. Webb

# French Antilles

## AON CORPORATION

123 North Wacker Drive, Chicago, IL, 60606

Tel: (312) 701-3000    Fax: (312) 701-3100    www.aon.com

*Insurance brokers worldwide; underwrites accident and health insurance, specialty and professional insurance; and provides risk management consultation.*

**AON Worldwide / Wachter Assurances, rue Ferdinand Forest Z.I. Jarry, 97122 Baie Mahault, Guadeloupe**

Tel: 590-326-701   Fax: 590-326-686   Contact: M. Wachter

## BUTLER INTERNATIONAL

110 Summit Ave., Montvale, NJ, 07645

Tel: (201) 573-8000    Fax: (201) 573-9723    www.butlerintl.com

*Leading supplier of skilled technical personnel.*

**Sotrama, BP 802 Canal Alaric Ouest, Route Portuaire de L'Hydrobase, 97207 Fort-de-France, Martinique French Antilles**

Tel: 596-512-035   Fax: 596-516-017

## DHL WORLDWIDE EXPRESS

50 California Avenue, San Francisco, CA, 94111

Tel: (415) 677-6100    Fax: (415) 824-9700    www.dhl.com

*Worldwide air express carrier.*

**DHL Worldwide Express, z.I. Acajou-Californie, 97232 Le Lamentin, Martinique**

Tel: 596-504-141

## EAGLE GLOBAL LOGISTICS (EGL)

15350 Vickery Drive, Houston, TX, 77032

Tel: (281) 618-3100    Fax: (281) 618-3100    www.eaglegl.com

*Ocean/air freight forwarding, customs brokerage, packing and wholesale, logistics management and insurance.*

**Fort-de-France (Air) (FDF), Sotrama BP 802 - Canal Alaric Ouest, Route Portuaire de L'Hydrobase, 97207 Fort-de-France Martinique, French Antilles**

Tel: 596-512-035   Fax: 596-516-017

**Sogera (Air), Bat. Fret, Aeroport du Raizet, Pointe-a-Pitre, Guadeloupe French Antilles**

Tel: 590-830-708   Fax: 590-835-426

**Sogera (Ocean), rue H. Becquerel - Z.I. De Jarry, 97122 Baie-Bahault, Point-a-Pitre Guadeloupe, French Antilles**

Tel: 590-268-062   Fax: 590-268-519

## EXXON MOBIL CORPORATION

5959 Las Colinas Blvd., Irving, TX, 75039-2298

Tel: (972) 444-1000    Fax: (972) 444-1882    www.exxon.com

*Petroleum exploration, production, refining; mfr. petroleum and chemicals products; coal and minerals.*

**Exxon Mobil, Inc., Martinique, French Antilles**

## IBM CORPORATION

New Orchard Road, Armonk, NY, 10504

Tel: (914) 765-1900     Fax: (914) 765-7382     www.ibm.com

*Information products, technology and services.*

**IBM Martinique, Martinique, French Antilles**

Tel: 596-753-000   Fax: 596-753-261

## KPMG INTERNATIONAL LLP

345 Park Avenue, New York, NY, 10022

Tel: (201) 307-7000     Fax: (201) 930-8617     www.kpmg.com

*Accounting and audit, tax and management consulting services.*

**Fiduciaire de France, Immeuble SCI-BTB, Voie Principale Z.I. Jarry, 97122 Baie Mahault, Guadeloupe**

**Fiduciaire de France, Lotissement Acajou, Californie, 97232 Le Lamentin, Martinique**

# French Guiana

**EAGLE GLOBAL LOGISTICS (EGL)**

15350 Vickery Drive, Houston, TX, 77032

Tel: (281) 618-3100      Fax: (281) 618-3100      www.eaglegl.com

*Ocean/air freight forwarding, customs brokerage, packing and wholesale, logistics management and insurance.*

**Gondrand, Immeuble de Fret R4, Aeroport de Rochambeau, Matoury 97341, Ceyenne CAY French Guiana**

Tel: 594-357-836   Fax: 594-358-961

**IBM CORPORATION**

New Orchard Road, Armonk, NY, 10504

Tel: (914) 765-1900      Fax: (914) 765-7382      www.ibm.com

*Information products, technology and services.*

**IBM French Guiana, French Guiana**

Tel: 594-311-241   Fax: 594-305-609

# French Polynesia

**DHL WORLDWIDE EXPRESS**

50 California Avenue, San Francisco, CA, 94111

Tel: (415) 677-6100      Fax: (415) 824-9700      www.dhl.com

*Worldwide air express carrier.*

**DHL Worldwide Express, Boite Poste 6480 FAAA Tahiti, Papeete Tahiti, French Polynesia**

Tel: 689-830024

**KPMG INTERNATIONAL LLP**

345 Park Avenue, New York, NY, 10022

Tel: (201) 307-7000      Fax: (201) 930-8617      www.kpmg.com

*Accounting and audit, tax and management consulting services.*

**Fidupac S.A., Fare-Ute, Papeete, Tahiti**

Tel: 689-427542   Fax: 689-413297   Contact: Gilles Redon, Sr. Ptnr.

**PACIFIC CENTURY FINANCIAL CORPORATION**

130 Merchant Street, Honolulu, HI, 96813

Tel: (808) 643-3888      Fax: (808) 537-8440      www.boh.com

*Engaged in commercial and consumer banking services.*

**Pacific Century Financial, PO Box 1602, Papeete Tahiti, French Polynesia**

# Gabon

## AMERADA HESS CORPORATION

1185 Avenue of the Americas, New York, NY, 10036

Tel: (212) 997-8500        Fax: (212) 536-8390        www.hess.com

*Crude oil and natural gas.*

**Amerada Hess Production Gabon,  PO Box 20316, Libreville, Gabon**

## BAKER HUGHES INCORPORATED

3900 Essex Lane, Ste. 1200, Houston, TX, 77027

Tel: (713) 439-8600        Fax: (713) 439-8699        www.bakerhughes.com

*Develop and apply technology to drill, complete and produce oil and natural gas wells; provide separation systems to petroleum, municipal, continuous process and mining industries.*

**Baker Oil Tools,  PO Box 587, Port Gentil, Gabon**

Tel: 241-553612   Fax: 241-550928

## CITIGROUP, INC.

153 East 53rd Street, New York, NY, 10043

Tel: (212) 559-1000        Fax: (212) 559-3646        www.citigroup.com

*Provides insurance and financial services worldwide.*

**Citibank N.A.,  Blvd. Quaben & rue Kringer BP 3940, Libreville, Gabon**

Contact: Nuhad K. Saliba

## COOPER CAMERON CORPORATION

515 Post Oak Blvd., Ste.1200, Houston, TX, 77027

Tel: (713) 513-3300        Fax: (713) 513-3355        www.coopercameron.com

*Mfr. oil and gas industry equipment.*

**Cooper Cameron Gabon,  B.P. No. 869, Port Gentil, Gabon**

## DHL WORLDWIDE EXPRESS

50 California Avenue, San Francisco, CA, 94111

Tel: (415) 677-6100        Fax: (415) 824-9700        www.dhl.com

*Worldwide air express carrier.*

**DHL Worldwide Express,  rue Victor Schoelcher BP 6113, Libreville, Gabon**

Tel: 241-721170

## ERNST & YOUNG, LLP

787 Seventh Ave., New York, NY, 10019

Tel: (212) 773-3000        Fax: (212) 773-6350        www.eyi.com

*Accounting and audit, tax and management consulting services.*

**Ernst & Young,  Immeuble Sonagar, Ave. du Colonel Parant BP 1013, Libreville, Gabon**

Tel: 241-74-32-17   Fax: 241*72-64-94   Contact: Bernard Esteve

## FRITZ COMPANIES, INC.

706 Mission Street, Ste. 900, San Francisco, CA, 94103

Tel: (415) 904-8360        Fax: (415) 904-8661        www.fritz.com

*Integrated transportation, sourcing, distribution and customs brokerage services.*

**Fritz Companies Inc.,  Gabon**

## GENERAL ELECTRIC COMPANY

3135 Easton Turnpike, Fairfield, CT, 06431

Tel: (203) 373-2211        Fax: (203) 373-3131        www.ge.com

*Diversified manufacturing, technology and services.*

**GE Medical Systems Europe, BP 20320, Libreville, Gabon**

## GLOBAL MARINE INC.

777 North Eldridge, Houston, TX, 77079

Tel: (281) 496-8000        Fax: (281) 531-1260        www.glm.com

*Offshore contract drilling, turnkey drilling, oil and gas exploration and production.*

**Global Marine Inc., Port Gentil, Gabon**

## HALLIBURTON COMPANY

500 North Akard Street, Ste. 3600, Dallas, TX, 75201-3391

Tel: (214) 978-2600        Fax: (214) 978-2685        www.halliburton.com

*Engaged in diversified energy services, engineering and construction.*

**Halliburton S.A.S., Zone Industrielle Oprag, B.P. 917, Port Gentil
Gabon**

## HELMERICH & PAYNE INC.

21st Street and Utica, Tulsa, OK, 74114

Tel: (918) 742-5531        Fax: (918) 743-2671        www.hpinc.com

*Oil/gas exploration and drilling, real estate, mfr. gas odorants.*

**Helmerich & Payne (Gabon), Boite Postal 20381, Libreville, Gabon**

## INTER-CONTINENTAL HOTELS

3 Ravina Drive, Suite 2900, Atlanta, GA, 30346-2149

Tel: (770) 604-2000        Fax: (770) 604-5403        www.interconti.com

*Worldwide hotel and resort accommodations.*

**Leconi Palace Inter-Continental Franceville, PO Box 735, Franceville, Gabon**

Tel: 241-67-74-16   Fax: 241-67-74-19

## LEXMARK INTERNATIONAL

1 Lexmark Centre Dr., Lexington, KY, 40550

Tel: (606) 232-2000        Fax: (606) 232-1886        www.lexmark.com

*Develop, manufacture, supply of printing solutions and products, including laser, inkjet, and dot matrix printers.*

**Revendeur Lexmark, BP 1079, Libreville, Gabon**

Tel: 241-73-3988

## MARATHON OIL COMPANY

5555 San Felipe Road, Houston, TX, 77056

Tel: (713) 629-6600        Fax: (713) 296-2952        www.marathon.com

*Oil and gas exploration.*

**Marathon Oil Company, Port Gentil, Gabon**

## M-I

PO Box 48242, Houston, TX, 77242-2842

Tel: (713) 739-0222        Fax: (713) 308-9503        www.midf.com

*Drilling fluids.*

**IMCO SARL, Barge 106, Boite Postale 507, Port Gentil, Gabon**

## NABORS INDUSTRIES INC.

515 W. Greens Road, Ste. 1200, Houston, TX, 77067

Tel: (281) 874-0035    Fax: (281) 872-5205

*Oil and gas drilling, petrol products.*

**Nabors Drilling Co. Ltd., Gabon**

## OCCIDENTAL PETROLEUM CORPORATION

10889 Wilshire Blvd., Los Angeles, CA, 90024

Tel: (310) 208-8800    Fax: (310) 443-6690    www.oxy.com

*Petroleum and petroleum products, chemicals, plastics.*

**Occidental of Gabon Inc., Gabon**

## OCEANEERING INTERNATIONAL INC.

11911 FM 529, Houston, TX, 77041

Tel: (713) 329-4500    Fax: (713) 329-4951    www.oceaneering.com

*Transportation equipment, underwater service to offshore oil and gas industry.*

**Oceaneering International, Port Gentil, Gabon**

## PRICEWATERHOUSECOOPERS LLP

1301 Ave. of the Americas, New York, NY, 10019

Tel: (212) 596-7000    Fax: (212) 259-1301    www.pwcglobal.com

*Accounting and auditing, tax and management, and human resource consulting services.*

**PriceWaterhouseCoopers, BP 584 Port-Gentil, Gabon**

Tel: 241-55-33-24   Fax: 241-55-16-28

**PriceWaterhouseCoopers, rue Alfred-Marche, BP 2164, Libreville, Gabon**

Tel: 241-76-23-71   Fax: 241-74-43-25

## STARWOOD HOTELS & RESORTS WORLDWIDE

777 Westchester Avenue, White Plains, NY, 10604

Tel: (914) 640-8100    Fax: (914) 640-8316    www.starwoodhotels.com

*Hotel operations including Sheraton, Westin, St. Regis, Four Points and Caesars.*

**Sheraton Re-Ndama Hotel, Boite Postale 4064, Libreville, Gabon**

## TRITON ENERGY LIMITED

6688 N. Central Expressway, Ste. 1400, Dallas, TX, 75206-3925

Tel: (214) 691-5200    Fax: (214) 691-0340    www.tritonenergy.com

*Provider of oil and gas services to the energy industry.*

**Sasol/Triton Energy, Libreville, Gabon**

## TRUE NORTH COMMUNICATIONS INC.

101 East Erie Street, Chicago, IL, 60611

Tel: (312) 425-6500    Fax: (312) 425-5010    www.truenorth.com

*Holding company, advertising agency.*

**Edicom Advertising, BP 5007, Libreville, Gabon**

## WEATHERFORD INTERNATIONAL, INC.

5 Post Oak Blvd, Ste. 1760, Houston, TX, 77227-3415

Tel: (713) 287-8400    Fax: (713) 963-9785    www.weatherford.com

*Oilfield services, products and equipment; mfr. marine cranes for oil and gas industry.*

**Weatherford Intl., Boite Postale 654, Port Gentil, Gabon**

Tel: 241-56-0826   Fax: 241-56-0828

## XEROX CORPORATION

800 Long Ridge Road, PO Box 1600, Stamford, CT, 06904

Tel: (203) 968-3000      Fax: (203) 968-4312      www.xerox.com

*Mfr. document processing equipment, systems and supplies.*

**Electra Xerox, BP 613, Libreville, Gabon**

Tel: 241-761-502    Fax: 241-741-776

# Gambia

**DHL WORLDWIDE EXPRESS**

50 California Avenue, San Francisco, CA, 94111

Tel: (415) 677-6100      Fax: (415) 824-9700      www.dhl.com

*Worldwide air express carrier.*

**DHL Worldwide Express, 71 Hagan St., Banjul, Gambia**

Tel: 220-228414

**KPMG INTERNATIONAL LLP**

345 Park Avenue, New York, NY, 10022

Tel: (201) 307-7000      Fax: (201) 930-8617      www.kpmg.com

*Accounting and audit, tax and management consulting services.*

**KPMG Peat Marwick, Meridien Bank Bldg., 3/4 Buckle St., Banjul, Gambia**

**WACKENHUT CORPORATION**

4200 Wackenhut Dr., Ste. 100, Palm Beach Gardens, FL, 33410

Tel: (561) 622-5656      Fax: (561) 691-6736      www.wackenhut.com

*Security systems and services.*

**Wackenhut International Inc.-Gambia, PO Box 2506 SK, Serekunda, Gambia**

Tel: 220-46-3772    Fax: 220-46-0009

**XEROX CORPORATION**

800 Long Ridge Road, PO Box 1600, Stamford, CT, 06904

Tel: (203) 968-3000      Fax: (203) 968-4312      www.xerox.com

*Mfr. document processing equipment, systems and supplies.*

**Shyben Hadi & Sons, 3A Russell St., PO Box 184, Banjul, Gambia**

Tel: 220-21-226-659    Fax: 220-21-228-827

# Georgia

## THE AES CORPORATION
1001 North 19th Street, Arlington, VA, 22209
Tel: (703) 522-1315    Fax: (703) 528-4510      www.aesc.com
*Gas and electric utility.*
**AES Silk Road,  Tbilisi, Georgia**
Contact: Garry Levesley

## DHL WORLDWIDE EXPRESS
50 California Avenue, San Francisco, CA, 94111
Tel: (415) 677-6100    Fax: (415) 824-9700      www.dhl.com
*Worldwide air express carrier.*
**DHL Worldwide Express,  105, Tsereteli Ave., Tbilisi 380019, Georgia**
Tel: 995-8832-999568

## McCANN-ERICKSON WORLDGROUP
750 Third Ave., New York, NY, 10017
Tel: (212) 984-3644    Fax: (212) 984-2629      www.mccann.com
*International advertising and marketing services.*
**KEDI McCann-Erickson,  Tbilisi, Georgia**

## ORION MARINE CORPORATION
79 West Monroe Street, Ste. 1105, Chicago, IL, 60603
Tel: (312) 263-5153    Fax: (312) 263-4233      www.orion-marine.com
*Ocean transportation.*
**LTT Tbilisi,  Barmonov St. 1, Tbilisi 380008, Georgia**
Tel: 995-32-986545   Fax: 995-39-320215   Contact: Klaus Droege

## PALMS & COMPANY, INC. (U.S. FUR EXCHANGE)
515 Lake Street South, Bldg. #103, Kirkland, WA, 98033
Tel: (425) 828-6774    Fax: (425) 827-5528      www.peterpalms.com
*Fur auctioning, distribution and sale; investment banking.*
**Palms & Co. (Georgia) Inc.,  PO Box 25, Lutsk-23 City Volyn Region, Ukraine 262023**
Contact: Dr. Oleg Jourin

## WESTERN WIRELESS CORPORATION
3650 131st Avenue SE, Ste. 400, Bellevue, WA, 98006
Tel: (425) 586-8700    Fax: (425) 586-8666      www.wwireless.com
*Provides wireless communication services.*
**MagtiCom Gsm, Ltd., Div. Western Wireless International,  T'bilisi, Georgia**

# Germany

## 24/7 MEDIA, INC.

1250 Broadway, New York, NY, 10001-3701

Tel: (212) 231-7100    Fax: (212) 760-1774    www.247media.com

*Provides global online advertising, sponsorships, e-commerce and direct marketing solutions to advertisers and Web publishers.*

**24/7 Media Germany,  Gladbacher Strasse 6, D-40219 Duesseldorf, Germany**
Tel: 49-211-600-0111

**24/7 Media Germany,  AM Weingarten 25, D-60487 Frankfurt, Germany**
Tel: 49-69-90-59612

## 3COM CORPORATION

5400 Bayfront Plaza, Santa Clara, CA, 95052-8145

Tel: (408) 326-5000    Fax: (408) 326-5001    www.3com.com

*Develop/mfr. computer networking products and systems.*

**3Com Germany GmbH,  Office Unterfoehring, Muenchner Str. 12, D-85774 Unterföhring, Germany**
Tel: 49-89-992200    Fax: 49-89-9577-220

**3Com Germany GmbH,  Office Neuperlach Sued, Gustav-Heinemann-Ring 123, D-18739 Münich, Germany**
Tel: 49-89-627-320    Fax: 49-89-627-32-233

**3Com GmbH,  Kollaustrasse 95, D-22453 Hamburg, Germany**
Tel: 49-40-5549300    Fax: 49-40-553930-20

**3Com GmbH,  Gustav-Heinemann-Ring 123, D-81739 Münich, Germany**
Tel: 49-89-627-320    Fax: 49-89-627-32-233

**3Com GmbH,  Kaiserin-Augusta-Allee 111, D-10553 Berlin, Germany**
Tel: 49-30-3498790    Fax: 49-30-34987999

**3Com GmbH,  Gustav-Nachtigal-Strasse 5, D-65189 Wiesbaden, Germany**
Tel: 49-611-973-660    Fax: 49-611-97366-99

**3Com GmbH,  Muenchner Str. 12, D-85774 Unterfoehring, Germany**
Tel: 49-89-992-200    Fax: 49-89-9577-220

**3Com Project Office EG 11,  Deutsche Bank, Optima Haus, Koelner Str. 12, D-65760 Eschborn, Germany**
Tel: 49-69-910-68882    Fax: 49-69-910-68878

## 3dfx INTERACTIVE, INC.

4435 Fortran Drive, San Jose, CA, 95134

Tel: (408) 935-4400    Fax: (408) 262-8874    www.3dfx.com

*Engaged in microchip, graphics, images and animation.*

**3dfx Interactive GmbH,  Am Soldnermoos 17, 85399 Halibergmoos, Germany**
Tel: 49-89-607-69997    Fax: 49-89-607-69990

### 3M

3M Center, St. Paul, MN, 55144-1000

Tel: (651) 733-1110      Fax: (651) 733-9973      www.mmm.com

*Mfr. diversified products for industry, health care, imaging, communications, transport, safety, consumer, etc.*

**3M Deutschland GmbH,  Carl-Schurz-Strasse 1, D-41453 Neuss, Germany**

Tel: 49-2131-14-3000   Fax: 49-2131-14-3470   Contact: Reinhold Hiersemann

### AAF INTERNATIONAL (AMERICAN AIR FILTER)

215 Central Ave., PO Box 35690, Louisville, KY, 40232-5690

Tel: (502) 637-0011      Fax: (502) 637-0321      www.aafintl.com

*Mfr. air filtration/pollution control and noise control equipment.*

**AAF-Lufttechnik GmbH,  Postfach 130618, D-44316 Dortmund, Germany**

Tel: 49-231-921-0330   Fax: 49-231-921-03323

### ABBOTT LABORATORIES

One Abbott Park, Abbott Park, IL, 60064-3500

Tel: (847) 937-6100      Fax: (847) 937-1511      www.abbott.com

*Development/mfr./sale diversified health care products and services.*

**Deutsche Abbott GmbH,  Postfach 2103, D65011 Wiesbaden, Germany**

Tel: 49-6122-580

### ACADEMIC PRESS INC.

6277 Sea Harbor Drive, Orlando, FL, 32887

Tel: (407) 345-2000      Fax: (407) 345-8388      www.academicpress.com

*Publisher of educational and scientific books.*

**Academic Press,  Buchauerstrasse 9, D-88348 Allmannsweiler, Germany**

Tel: 49-7582-2464   Fax: 49-7582-2464   Contact: Gary Utterson, Mgr.

### ACC CORPORATION

400 West Avenue, Rochester, NY, 14611

Tel: (716) 987-3000      Fax: (716) 987-3499      www.acccorp.com

*Long distance and telecommunications services.*

**ACC TeleKommunikation GmbH,  Wilhelm-Marx-Haus, Heinrich-Heine-Allee 53, D-40213 Düsseldorf, Germany**

Tel: 49-211-8307-204   Fax: 49-211-8307-378   Contact: Wolfgang Weinschrod, Mng. Dir.   Emp: 40

### ACCLAIM ENTERTAINMENT, INC.

One Acclaim Plaza, Glen Cove, NY, 11542

Tel: (516) 656-5000      Fax: (516) 656-2040      www.acclaim.com

*Mfr. video games.*

**Acclaim Entertainment GmbH,  Leuchtenbergring 20, 81677 Munchen, Germany**

Tel: 49-89-4-12190

### ACCO BRANDS, INC.

300 Tower Parkway, Lincoln, IL, 60069

Tel: (847) 541-9500      Fax: (847) 541-5750      www.acco.com

*Provides services in the office and computer markets and manufactures paper fasteners, clips, metal fasteners, binders and staplers.*

**ACCO International GmbH,  Industrie Str. 25, Postfach 1146, D-6470 Budingen l, Germany**

### ACCURIDE INTERNATIONAL, INC.

12311 Shoemaker Ave., Santa Fe Springs, CA, 90670-4721

Tel: (562) 903-0200      Fax: (562) 903-0208      www.accuride.com

*Mfr. drawer slides.*

**Accuride,  Postfach 1464, D-65573 Diez Lahn, Germany**

Accuride International Inc., Münich, Germany

## ACE CONTROLS INC.

23435 Industrial Park Drive, Farmington Hills, MI, 48024

Tel: (248) 476-0213     Fax: (248) 276-2470     www.acecontrols.com

*Industry hydraulic shock absorbers, cylinders, valves and automation controls.*

**ACE Stossdampfer GmbH, Herzogstrasse 28, Postfach 3161, D-40764 Langenfeld Germany**

Tel: 49-2173-922610   Fax: 49-2173-922619

## ACHESON COLLOIDS COMPANY

PO Box 611747, Port Huron, MI, 48061-1747

Tel: (810) 984-5581     Fax: (810) 984-1446     www.achesoncolloids.com

*Chemicals, chemical preparations, paints and lubricating oils.*

**Acheson Industries Deutschland, Postfach 7, 89156 Dornstadt, Germany**

Tel: 49-7348-20010   Fax: 49-7348-200127

## ACME UNITED CORPORATION

75 Kings Highway Cutoff, Fairfield, CT, 06430-5340

Tel: (203) 332-7330     Fax: (203) 576-0007     www.acmeunited.com

*Mfr. surgical and medical instruments, pharmaceutical supplies.*

**Emil Schlemper, GmbH, PO Box 13 02 39, D-42680 Solingen, Germany**

Tel: 49-212-330011

## ACTERNA CORPORATION

3 New England Executive Park, Burlington, MA, 01803

Tel: (781) 272-6100     Fax: (781) 272-2304     www.acterna.com

*Develop, manufacture and market communications test instruments, systems, software and services.*

**Acterna Corporation, Denkendorf, Germany**

**Acterna Corporation, Friedrichsdorf, Germany**

## ACTION INSTRUMENTS INC.

8601 Aero Drive, San Diego, CA, 92123

Tel: (619) 279-5726     Fax: (619) 279-6290     www.actionio.com

*Mfr. electronic instruments and industrial measurements computers.*

**Action Industrie Computer GmbH, Voltastrasse 8, D-6072 Dreich, Germany**

## ACTIONPOINT, INC.

1299 Parkmoor Avenue, San Jose, CA, 95126

Tel: (408) 325-3800     Fax: (408) 325-3985     www.actionpoint.com

*Develops software for e-commerce.*

**ActionPoint GmbH, Nymphenburger Str. 136, 80636 Münich, Germany**

Tel: 49-89-189516

## ACTIVISION

3100 Ocean Park Boulevard, Santa Monica, CA, 90405

Tel: (310) 255-2000     Fax: (310) 255-2100     www.activision.com

*Development/mfr. entertainment software and video games.*

**Activision Germany, Auf der Haar 47, Postfach 1553, D-332245 Guterloh, Germany**

Tel: 49-5-241-480811   Fax: 49-5-241-480848   Emp: 11

## ACTUATE CORPORATION

701 Gateway Boulevard South, San Francisco, CA, 94080

Tel: (650) 837-2000     Fax: (650) 827-1560     www.actuate.com

*Develops software.*

**Actuate Germany GmbH, Lyoner Strasse 34, 60576 Frankfurt/Maim, Germany**

## ADAPTEC INC.

691 South Milpitas Boulevard, Milpitas, CA, 95035

Tel: (408) 945-8600     Fax: (408) 262-2533     www.adaptec.com

*Design/mfr./marketing hardware and software solutions.*

**Adaptec GmbH,  Munchner Strasse 17, D-85540 Haar, Germany**

## ADE CORPORATION

80 Wilson Way, Westwood, MA, 02090

Tel: (781) 467-3500     Fax: (781) 467-0500     www.ade.com

*Mfr. semiconductor wafers and computer disks.*

**ADE International GmbH,  Klausnerring 17, 85551 Kirschheim Heimstetten, Germany**

Tel: 49-89-909-9610   Fax: 49-89-909-96120

## ADEMCO INTERNATIONAL

1769 N.W. 79th Avenue, Miami, FL, 33126

Tel: (305) 477-5204     Fax: (305) 477-5404     www.ademcoint.com

*Mfr. security, fire and burglary systems and products.*

**ADEMCO Sicherheitseinrichtungen GmbH,  Postfach 4125, D-7302 Ostfildern 1, Germany**

## ADOBE SYSTEMS INCORPORATED

345 Park Avenue, San Jose, CA, 95110

Tel: (408) 536-6000     Fax: (408) 537-6000     www.adobe.com

*Engaged in print technology and distributor of Acrobat Reader.*

**Adobe Systems GmbH,  Ohmstraße 1, D-85716 Unterschleißheim, Germany**

## ADVANCED DIGITAL INFORMATION CORPORATION

11431 Willows Rd. NE, PO Box 97057, Redmond, WA, 98073

Tel: (425) 881-8004     Fax: (425) 881-2296     www.adic.com

*Mfr. computer storage systems.*

**ADIC/GRAU,  Eschenstrasse 3, D-89558 Böhmenkirch, Germany**

Tel: 49-7332-830

## ADVANCED MICRO DEVICES INC.

1 AMD Place, Sunnyvale, CA, 94086

Tel: (408) 732-2400     Fax: (408) 982-6164     www.amd.com

*Mfr. integrated circuits for communications and computation industry.*

**AMD Saxony Manufacturing GmbH,  Mailstop E02-HR, Postfach 110, 01330 Dresden, Germany**

Tel: 49-3-51-277-4444

## ADVANCED PRODUCTS COMPANY

33 Defco Park Road, North Haven, CT, 06473

Tel: (203) 239-3341     Fax: (203) 234-7233     www.advpro.com

*Mfr. Metallic and PTFE seals and gaskets.*

**Advanced Products,  Karl Arnold Strasse 63, D-5130 Geilenkirchen Gilrath, Germany**

## AERONAUTICAL INSTRUMENTS & RADIO COMPANY

234 Garibaldi Ave., Lodi, NJ, 07644

Tel: (973) 473-0034     Fax: (973) 473-8748

*Mfr. aeronautical instruments.*

**Elan GmbH,  Freudenber Str. 27, D-6200 Weisbaden Schienstien, Germany**

## THE AEROQUIP GROUP

3000 Strayer, PO Box 50, Maumee, OH, 43537

Tel: (419) 867-2200     Fax: (419) 867-2390     www.aeroquip.com

*Mfr. industrial, automotive, aerospace and defense products.*

**Aeroquip Group,  Carl-Benz-Strasse 9, D-82205 Gilching, Germany**

**Aeroquip-Vickers GmbH, PO Box 2060, D-76490 Baden-Baden, Germany**

Tel: 49-7221-682-0

## AEROTEK

6992 Columbia Gateway Dr., Bldg. D, Columbia, MD, 21046

Tel: (410) 540-7000    Fax: (410) 540-7099    www.aerotek.com

*Recruitment and placement services.*

**Aerotek, GW2, Ludwie-Erhaldt-Rin 94, 15827 Dahlewitz, Germany**

## AGCO CORPORATION

4205 River Green Parkway, Duluth, GA, 30096-2568

Tel: (770) 813-9200    Fax: (770) 813-6038    www.agcocorp.com

*Mfr. farm equipment and machinery.*

**AGCO GmbH & Co., Am Sande 20, 37213 Witzenhausen, Germany**

**AGCO GmbH & Co., Johann-Georg-Fendtstraße 4, D-87616 Marktoberdorf Germany**

Tel: 49-8342-770   Fax: 49-8342-77-220

## AGILENT TECHNOLOGIES, INC.

395 Page Mill Road, PO Box 10395, Palo Alto, CA, 94303

Tel: (650) 752-5000    Fax: (650) 752-5633    www.agilent.com

*Mfr. communications components.*

**Agilent Technologies GmbH, Bereich Halbleiter, Eschenstr. 5, 82024 Taufkirchen, Germany**

Tel: 49-89-6141-2300

## AIR EXPRESS INTERNATIONAL CORPORATION

120 Tokeneke Road, PO Box 1231, Darien, CT, 06820

Tel: (203) 655-7900    Fax: (203) 655-5779    www.aeilogistics.com

*International air freight forwarder.*

**AEI GmbH - Distribution Center, Frankfurter Str. 93, D-65479 Raunheim, Germany**

Tel: 49-6142-20060   Fax: 49-6142-200660

**AEI GmbH - Hdqtrs., Fasanenweg 4, D-65451 Kelsterbach Frankfurt, Germany**

Tel: 49-69-6107-7020   Fax: 49-69--6107-702390

## AIR PRODUCTS AND CHEMICALS, INC.

7201 Hamilton Boulevard, Allentown, PA, 18195-1501

Tel: (610) 481-4911    Fax: (610) 481-5900    www.airproducts.com

*Mfr. industry gases and related equipment, specialty chemicals, environmental/energy systems.*

**Air Products GmbH, Hauptverwaltung Hattingen, Huettenstrasse 50, D-4320 Hattingen Ruhr, Germany**

## AIRBORNE FREIGHT CORPORATION

3101 Western Ave., PO Box 662, Seattle, WA, 98121

Tel: (206) 285-4600    Fax: (206) 281-1444    www.airborne.com

*Air transport services.*

**RGW Express Airfreight GmbH, Postfach 750433, 60534 Frankfurt, Germany**

Tel: 49-6969-80080   Fax: 49-6969-800840

## AKAMAI TECHNOLOGIES, INC.

500 Technology Square, Cambridge, MA, 02139

Tel: (617) 250-3000    Fax: (617) 250-3001    www.akamai.com

*Develops routing technologies for websites.*

**Akamai Technologies EMEA, Heisenbergbogen 2, 85609 Dornach, Germany**

Tel: 49-89-9400-6101   Fax: 49-89-9400-6006

## ALAMO RENT A CAR

110 Southeast 6th Street, Fort Lauderdale, FL, 33301

Tel: (954) 522-0000        Fax: (954) 220-0120        www.alamo.com

*Car rentals.*

**Alamo Rent A Car, Frankfurt International Airport, Flughafen & Eschersheimer Landstr 115, Frankfurt, Germany**

## ALBANY INTERNATIONAL CORPORATION

PO Box 1907, Albany, NY, 12201

Tel: (518) 445-2200        Fax: (518) 445-2265        www.albint.com

*Mfr. broadwoven and engineered fabrics, plastic products, filtration media.*

**Filtra GmbH, Postfach 1640, Steinackerstr 20, D-7858 Weil Rhein, Germany**

**Filtra GmbH, Postfach 5, Filtrastr. 5, D-4730 Ahlen 5, Germany**

## ALCO CONTROLS, DIV. EMERSON ELECTRIC

PO Box 411400, St. Louis, MO, 63141

Tel: (314) 569-4500        Fax: (314) 567-2101        www.alcocontrols.com

*Mfr. air conditioning and refrigerator flow controls.*

**ALCO Controls, Div. Emerson Electric GmbH, Heerstr. 111 Postfach 1229, D-7050 Waiblingen, Germany**

Tel: 49-7151-5090

## ALCOA INC.

Alcoa Center, 201 Isabella Street, Pittsburgh, PA, 15215-5858

Tel: (412) 553-4545        Fax: (412) 553-4498        www.alcoa.com

*World's leading producer of aluminum and alumina; mining, refining, smelting, fabricating and recycling.*

**Alcoa Automotive Structures GmbH, Soest, Germany**

**Alcoa Chemie GmbH, Ludwigshafen, Germany**

**Alcoa Deutschland GmbH, Oldendorfer Strasse 9, D-49324 Melle, Germany**

Tel: 49-5422-94470    Contact: Reinhard Deipenwisch

**Alcoa Extrusions Hannover GmbH & Co. KG, Hannover, Germany**

**Michels GmbH & Co., KG, Herzebrock, Germany**

**Stribel GmbH, Frickenhausen, Germany**

## ALCOA FUJIKURA LTD.

105 Westpark Drive, Brentwood, TN, 37027

Tel: (615) 370-2100        Fax: (615) 370-2180        www.alcoa-fujikura.com

*Mfr. optical groundwire, tube cable, fiber optic connectors and automotive wiring harnesses.*

**Alcoa Fujikura Ltd., Dieselstrabe 64-72, D-33442 Herzebrock-Clarholz, Germany**

Tel: 49-5245-449-207    Fax: 49-5245-449-390    Contact: James Edwards, VP Europe

## ALIGN-RITE INTERNATIONAL, INC.

2428 Ontario Street, Burbank, CA, 91504

Tel: (818) 843-7220        Fax: (818) 566-3042        www.align-rite.com

*Mfr. photomasks.*

**Align-Rite GmbH, Theresienstrasse 2, 74025 Heilbronne, Germany**

Tel: 49-7131-672156

## ALLEGHENY LUDLUM CORPORATION

1000 Six PPG Place, Pittsburgh, PA, 15222

Tel: (412) 394-2805        Fax: (412) 394-2800        www.alleghenyludlum.com

*Mfr. steel and alloys.*

**Allegheny Rodney, Duesseldorf, Germany**

Tel: 49-211-513-560-0    Fax: 49-211-513-560-50

## ALLEGHENY TECHNOLOGIES

1000 Six PPG Place, Pittsburgh, PA, 15222

Tel: (412) 394-2800    Fax: (412) 394-2805    www.alleghenytechnologies.com

*Diversified mfr. aviation and electronics, specialty metals, industrial and consumer products.*

**Allegheny Rodney, Postfach 1326, Kleinbeckstasse 7 D-45549, Sprockhovel Germany**

Tel: 49-2324-97360

**Allegheny Technologies, Hagenauer Str. 42, D-65203 Wiesbaden, Germany**

**Allvac Ltd., Div. Teledyne GmbH, Sternstrasse 5, 40479 Dusseldorf, Germany**

**Titanium International GmbH, Tiefenbroicher Weg 35, 40472 Dusseldorf, Germany**

## ALLEGIANCE HEALTHCARE CORPORATION

1430 Waukegan Road, McGaw Park, IL, 60085

Tel: (847) 689-8410    Fax: (847) 578-4437    www.allegiance.net

*Manufactures and distributes medical, surgical, respiratory therapy and laboratory products.*

**Allegiance Deutschland GmbH, Edisonstrasse 3-4, Unterschleissheim, D-85716 Münich, Germany**

Tel: 49-89-31788    Fax: 49-89-31788-788    Contact: Josef Bernlochner, Mgr.

## ALLEN TELECOM

25101 Chagrin Boulevard, Beachwood, OH, 44122-5619

Tel: (216) 765-5818    Fax: (216) 765-0410    www.allentele.com

*Mfr. communications equipment, automotive bodies and parts, electronic components.*

**MIKOM GmbH, Industriering 10, D-86675 Buchdorf, Germany**

Tel: 49-9099-690    Fax: 49-9099-6931

**MIKOM GmbH, Am Seegraben 2, D-99099 Erfurt, Germany**

Tel: 49-361-4171-103    Fax: 49-361-4171-104

**MIKOM GmbH, Am Amezonenwerk 5, D-49205 Hasbergen, Germany**

Tel: 49-5405-92200    Fax: 49-5405-922010

## ALLENBERG COTTON COMPANY, INC.

PO Box 3254, Cordova, TN, 38018-3254

Tel: (901) 383-5000    Fax: (901) 383-5010

*Raw cotton.*

**Allenberg Baumwoll GmbH, Ostertorsteinweg 57a, D-2800 Bremen, Germany**

## ALLEN-BRADLEY COMPANY, INC.

1201 South Second Street, Milwaukee, WI, 53204

Tel: (414) 382-2000    Fax: (414) 382-4444    www.ab.com

*Mfr. electrical controls and information devices.*

**Allen-Bradley GmbH, Robert-Bosch Strasse 5, D-6072 Dreieich-Sprendlingen, Germany**

**Allen-Bradley GmbH, Duesselbergerstr. 15, D-5657 Haan 2 Gruiten, Germany**

## ALLERGAN INC.

2525 Dupont Drive, PO Box 19534, Irvine, CA, 92713-9534

Tel: (714) 246-4500    Fax: (714) 246-6987    www.allergan.com

*Mfr. therapeutic eye care products, skin and neural care pharmaceuticals.*

**Pharm-Allergan GmbH, Postfach 10 06 61, D-76260 Ettlingen, Germany**

Tel: 49-7243-5010    Fax: 49-7243-501-100

## THE ALLSTATE CORPORATION

Allstate Plaza, 2775 Sanders Road, Northbrook, IL, 60062-6127

Tel: (847) 402-5000    Fax: (847) 836-3998    www.allstate.com

*Personal property, auto and life insurance.*

**Allstate Direct AG, Postfach 140 165, 14301 Berlin, Germany**

## ALPHA INDUSTRIES INC.

20 Sylvan Road, Woburn, MA, 01801

Tel: (781) 935-5150      Fax: (781) 824-4543      www.alphaind.com

*Mfr. electronic and microwave components.*

**Alpha Industries GmbH,  Berenterstr. 20A, D-81927 Münich, Germany**

**Municom GmbH,  4 Fuchsgrube, Traunstein, Germany**

## ALTERA CORPORATION

101 Innovation Drive, San Jose, CA, 95134

Tel: (408) 544-7000      Fax: (408) 544-8303      www.altera.com

*Mfr. high-density programmable chips for semi-conductor industry.*

**Altera GmbH,  Max-Planck-Str. 5, D-85716 Unterschleissheim, Germany**

Tel: 49-89-32-18250

## AMAZON.COM, INC.

1200 12th Ave. South, Ste. 1200, Seattle, WA, 98144-2734

Tel: (206) 266-1000      Fax: (206) 266-4206      www.amazon.com

*Computer site that offers books, CDs, DVDS, videos, toys, tools, and electronics.*

**Amazon.Com GmbH,  Lilienthalstr. 2, 8399 Hallbergmoos b., Münich, Germany**

## AMERICAN AIRLINES INC.

4333 Amon Carter Boulevard, Ft. Worth, TX, 76155

Tel: (817) 963-1234      Fax: (817) 967-9641      www.amrcorp.com

*Air transport services.*

**American Airlines,  Terminal C/Rm. 2234, Flughafen, D-4000 Düsseldorf 30, Germany**

**American Airlines,  Airport Münich, Rm. 430, D-8000 Münich 87, Germany**

**American Airlines,  Monckebergstr. 31, D-2000 Hamburg 1, Germany**

## AMERICAN AMICABLE LIFE INSURANCE COMPANY

PO Box 2549, Waco, TX, 76703

Tel: (254) 297-2777      Fax: (254) 297-2733      www.americanamicable.com

*Life, accident and health insurance.*

**American Amicable Life Insurance Co.,  Münich, Germany**

## AMERICAN AXLE & MANUFACTURING HOLDINGS, INC.

1840 Holbrook Ave., Detroit, MI, 48212

Tel: (313) 974-2000      Fax: (313) 974-3090      www.aam.com

*Mfr. axles, propeller shafts and chassis components.*

**American Axle & Manufacturing, GmbH,  Pfarrer-Weiss-Weg 10, Ulm, Germany**

Contact: Ulrich Stockert, Dir.

## ABC, INC.

77 West 66th Street, New York, NY, 10023

Tel: (212) 456-7777      Fax: (212) 456-6384      www.abc.com

*Radio/TV production and broadcasting.*

**Overseas Media GmbH,  Schiller Str. 19-25, Frankfurt Main, Germany**

## AMERICAN BUSINESS PRODUCTS, INC.

2100 Riveredge Pkwy., Ste. 1200, Atlanta, GA, 30328

Tel: (770) 953-8300      Fax: (770) 952-2343      www.goabp.com

*Supplies printing, book printing, label production and extrusion coating for flexible packaging.*

**Curtis 1000 Europe GmbH (JV),  Rostocker Strasse 15, D-56561 Neuwied, Germany**

Contact: Ingo Hafner, Mng. Ptnr.

## AMERICAN EXPRESS COMPANY

American Express Tower, World Financial Center, New York, NY, 10285-4765

Tel: (212) 640-2000　　Fax: (212) 619-9802　　www.americanexpress.com

*Travel, travelers cheques, charge card and financial services.*

**ACS AllCard Service GmbH,　Münich, Germany**

## AMERICAN HOME PRODUCTS CORPORATION

Five Giralda Farms, Madison, NJ, 07940-0874

Tel: (973) 660-5000　　Fax: (973) 660-6048　　www.ahp.com

*Mfr. pharmaceutical, animal health care and crop protection products.*

**American Home Products Corporation,　Münich, Germany**

## AMERICAN INTERNATIONAL GROUP INC. (AIG)

70 Pine Street, New York, NY, 10270

Tel: (212) 770-7000　　Fax: (212) 509-9705　　www.aig.com

*Worldwide insurance and financial services.*

**AIG Europe S.A.,　Oberlendau 76-78, D-60323 Frankfurt, Germany**

## AMERICAN MANAGEMENT SYSTEMS, INC.

4050 Legato Road, Fairfax, VA, 22033

Tel: (703) 267-8000　　Fax: (703) 267-5073　　www.amsinc.com

*Systems integration and consulting.*

**AMS Management Systems Deutschland GmbH,　Querstrasse 8-10, D-60322 Frankfurt, Germany**
Tel: 49-69-95-51-11-0　Fax: 49-69-95-51-11-99　Contact: James W. Sheaffer, Mng. Dir.　Emp: 300

## AMERICAN PRECISION INDUSTRIES INC.

2777 Walden Ave., Buffalo, NY, 14225

Tel: (716) 684-9700　　Fax: (716) 684-2129　　www.apicorporate.com

*Mfr. heat transfer equipment, motion control devices, coils, capacitors, electro-mechanical clutches and brakes.*

**API Schmidt-Bretten / API Motion,　Pforzheimer Strasse 46, D-75015 Bretten, Germany**
Tel: 49-725-253101

## AMERICAN STANDARD INC.

One Centennial Avenue, Piscataway, NJ, 08855-6820

Tel: (732) 980-3000　　Fax: (732) 980-6118　　www.americanstandard.com

*Mfr. automotive, plumbing, heating, air conditioning products and medical diagnostics systems.*

**DiaSorin GmbH,　Heltofer Strasse 12, D-40472 Dusseldorf, Germany**
Tel: 49-211-47220　Fax: 49-211-472-2333

**Ideal Standard GmbH,　Euskirchenerstr. 80, Postfach 549, D-5300 Bonn, Germany**

## AMERICAN TECHNICAL CERAMICS CORPORATION

17 Stepar Place, Huntington Station, NY, 11746

Tel: (631) 622-4700　　Fax: (631) 622-4748　　www.alceramics.com

*Mfr. ceramic porcelain capacitors and ceramic-based electronic products.*

**American Tehcnical Ceramics,　Marienstrasse 5, D-85567 Grafing, Germany**
Tel: 49-80-92-851086　Fax: 49-80-92-851087

## AMERON INTERNATIONAL CORPORATION

245 South Los Robles Ave., Pasadena, CA, 91109-7007

Tel: (626) 683-4000　　Fax: (626) 683-4060　　www.ameron.com

*Mfr. steel pipe systems, concrete products, traffic and lighting poles, protective coatings.*

**Ameron BV,　Rheinstr. 21, D-6000 Frankfurt, Germany**

## AMETEK INC.

37 N. Valley Road, PO Box 1764, Paoli, PA, 19301-0801

Tel: (610) 647-2121     Fax: (610) 296-3412     www.ametek.com

*Mfr. instruments, electric motors and engineered materials.*

**AMETEK GmbH, Weilimdorfer Str. 47, D-70825 Korntal-Munchingen, Germany**

Tel: 49-611-98921-0   Fax: 49-611-98921-10

**AMETEK Italia S.r.l.,, Schleusingen, Jagerhausstrasse 5, D-98553 Schleusingen, Germany**

Tel: 49-36841240   Fax: 49-3684124220

## AMGEN INC.

One Amgen Center Drive, Thousand Oaks, CA, 91320-1799

Tel: (805) 447-1000     Fax: (805) 499-2694     www.amgen.com

*Biotechnology research and pharmaceruticals.*

**Amgen GmbH, Reisstrasse 25, D-80992 Münich, Germany**

## AMPEX CORPORATION

500 Broadway, Redwood City, CA, 94063-3199

Tel: (650) 367-2011     Fax: (650) 367-4669     www.ampex.com

*Mfr. extremely high-performance digital data storage, data retrieval and image processing systems for a broad range of corporate scientific and government applications.*

**Ampex Europa GmbH., Otto-Volger-Strasse 7C, D-65842 Sulzbach Taunus Frankfurt, Germany**

Tel: 49-6196-76520   Fax: 49-6196-76529   Contact: Willy Bjorklund   Emp: 13

## AMPHENOL CORPORATION

358 Hall Ave., Wallingford, CT, 06492-7530

Tel: (203) 265-8900     Fax: (203) 265-8793     www.amphenol.com

*Mfr. electrictronic interconnect penetrate systems and assemblies.*

**Amphenol-Tuchel Electronics, August-Haeusser-Strasse 10, D-74080 Heilbronn, Germany**

Tel: 49-7131-9290

## AMSTED INDUSTRIES INC.

205 North Michigan Ave., Chicago, IL, 60601

Tel: (312) 645-1700     Fax: (312) 819-8523     www.amsted.com

*Privately-held, diversified manufacturer of products for the construction and building markets, general industry and the railroads.*

**Keystone Industries, Karl George Bahntechnik, Rheinstrassee 15, D-57638 Neitersen Germany**

Tel: 49-2681-8080

## AMWAY CORPORATION

7575 Fulton Street East, Ada, MI, 49355-0001

Tel: (616) 787-6000     Fax: (616) 787-6177     www.amway.com

*Mfr./sale home care, personal care, nutrition and houseware products.*

**Amway GmbH, Benzstrasse 11A, D-8039 Puchheim, Germany**

## ANACOMP INC.

12365 Crosthwaite Circle, Poway, CA, 92064

Tel: (858) 679-9797     Fax: (858) 748-9482     www.anacomp.com

*Engaged in electronic information management services and products.*

**Anacomp GmbH, Abraham Lincoln Str. 28, D-6200 Wiesbaden, Germany**

## ANALOG DEVICES INC.

1 Technology Way, Box 9106, Norwood, MA, 02062

Tel: (781) 329-4700     Fax: (781) 326-8703     www.analog.com

*Mfr. integrated circuits and related devices.*

**Analog Devices GmbH, Edelsbergstrasse 8-10, D-8000 Münich, Germany**

## ANC RENTAL CORP.

110 Southeast Sixth St., Ft. Lauderdale, FL, 33301

Tel: (954) 769-7000     Fax: (954) 769-7000     www.ancrental.com

*Engaged in car rental services, including National Car Rental and Alamo Rent A Car.*

**National Car Rental GmbH, Franfurter Ring 243, D-8000 Münich 46, Germany**

## ANDERSEN CONSULTING

100 S. Wacker Drive, Ste. 1059, Chicago, IL, 60606

Tel: (312) 693-0161     Fax: (312) 693-0507     www.ac.com

*Provides management and technology consulting services.*

**Andersen Consulting, Otto-Volger-StraBe 15, D-65843 Sulzbach/Frankfurt, Germany**

Tel: 49-6196-5760   Fax: 49-6196-57-6710

## ANDERSEN WORLDWIDE

33 West Monroe Street, Chicago, IL, 60603

Tel: (312) 580-0033     Fax: (312) 507-6748     www.arthurandersen.com

*Accounting and audit, tax and management consulting services.*

**Arthur Andersen & Co., GmbH, Mergenthalerallee 10-12, Postfach 5323, D-65760 Eschborn Frankfurt German**

Tel: 49-6196-9960

## ANDREW CORPORATION

10500 West 153rd Street, Orland Park, IL, 60462

Tel: (708) 349-3300     Fax: (708) 349-5410     www.andrew.com

*Mfr. antenna systems, coaxial cable, electronic communications and network connectivity systems.*

**Andrew GmbH, Julius-Moserstrasse, 13, D-75179 Pforzheim, Germany**

Tel: 49-7231-140150   Fax: 49-7231-140151

**Andrew GmbH, Freischützstrasse 96, D-81927 München, Germany**

Tel: 49-89-99271-100   Fax: 49-89-99271-120

**Andrew GmbH Kommunikationssysteme, Daniel-Eckhardt-Strasse 3a, D-43356 Essen, Germany**

Tel: 49-201-836070   Fax: 49-201-8360720

## ANIXTER INTERNATIONAL INC..

4711 Golf Road, Skokie, IL, 60076

Tel: (847) 677-2600     Fax: (847) 677-8557     www.anixter.com

*Distributor wiring systems/products for voice, video, data and power applications.*

**Anixter Germany, Wittestrasse 30, Haus JVOG, 13509 Berlin Germany**

Tel: 49-30-435-6830

**Anixter Germany, Gottlieb-Daimler-Strasse 55, 71711 Murr bei Stuttgart, Germany**

Tel: 49-7144-26940   Fax: 49-7144-2694-111

## ANSELL HEALTHCARE, INC.

200 Schulz Drive, Red Bank, NJ, 07701

Tel: (732) 345-5400     Fax: (732) 219-5114     www.ansellhealthcare.com

*Mfr. industrial gloves, rubber and plastic products, protective clothing.*

**Ansell Healthcare Germany, Stahlgruberring 3, 81829 München, Germany**

Tel: 49-89-451180

## AOL TIME WARNER

75 Rockefeller Plaza, New York, NY, 10019

Tel: (212) 484-8000     Fax: (212) 275-3046     www.aoltimewarner.com

*Engaged in media and communications; provides internet services, communications, publishing and entertainment.*

**AOL Time Warner Bertelsmann AG (JV), Gütersloh, Germany**

**AOL Time Warner Germany, Münich, Germany**

Time-Life International GmbH, Akadamiestrasse 7, D-8000 Münich 40, Germany

## AON CORPORATION

123 North Wacker Drive, Chicago, IL, 60606

Tel: (312) 701-3000    Fax: (312) 701-3100    www.aon.com

*Insurance brokers worldwide; underwrites accident and health insurance, specialty and professional insurance; and provides risk management consultation.*

AON Deutschland GmbH, 180 Darmstädter Landstrasse, D-60598 Frankfurt, Germany

Tel: 49-69-686-0730   Fax: 49-69-686-07349   Contact: Klaus P. Obereigner

## API MOTION INC.

45 Hazelwood Dr., Amherst, NY, 14228

Tel: (716) 691-9100    Fax: (716) 691-9181    www.apimotion.com

*Engaged in motion control solutions using motors and drives, motor gearheads, resolver and encoder feedback devices.*

API Motion Deutschland GmbH, Gulichstrasse 12, D-75179 Pforzheim, Germany

## APPLE COMPUTER, INC.

One Infinite Loop, Cupertino, CA, 95014

Tel: (408) 996-1010    Fax: (408) 974-2113    www.apple.com

*Personal computers, peripherals and software.*

Apple Computers GmbH, Ingolstadterstr. 20, D-8000 Münich 45, Germany

## APPLERA CORPORATION

761 Main Avenue, Norwalk, CT, 06859-0001

Tel: (203) 762-1000    Fax: (203) 762-6000    www.applera.com

*Leading supplier of systems for life science research and related applications.*

Analytical Instruments, Askaniaweg 6, D-88662 Uberlingen, Germany

Applied Biosystems GmbH, Brunnenweg 13, 64331 Weiterstadt, Germany

Tel: 49-6150-1010

## APPLIED MATERIALS, INC.

3050 Bowers Ave., Santa Clara, CA, 95054-3299

Tel: (408) 727-5555    Fax: (408) 727-9943    www.appliedmaterials.com

*Supplies manufacturing systems and services to the semiconductor industry.*

Applied Materials G.m.b.H, Buchenstrasse 16b, D-01097 Dresden, Germany

Tel: 49-351-8002-30   Fax: 49-351-8002-310

Applied Materials G.m.b.H - Training Center, Gutenbergstrasse 25, D-85748 Garching-Hochbrck, Germany

Tel: 49-89-329-4830   Fax: 49-89-329-48310

## APPLIED SCIENCE AND TECHNOLOGY, INC.

35 Cabot Road, Woburn, MA, 01801

Tel: (781) 933-5560    Fax: (781) 933-0750    www.astex.com

*Mfr. specialized components for semiconductor manufacturing systems.*

AsTex GmbH, Gustav-Meyer-Allee 25, D-13355 Berlin, Germany

Tel: 49-30-464-0030   Fax: 49-30-464-00313

## APPLIX, INC.

112 Turnpike Road, Westboro, MA, 01581

Tel: (508) 870-0300    Fax: (508) 366-4873    www.applix.com

*Engaged in business productivity application software.*

APPLIX, Inc., Westendstraße 19, 60325 Frankfurt, Germany

Tel: 49-69-97546-447

APPLIX, Inc., Hildesheimer Straße 53, 30169 Hannover, Germany

Tel: 49-0511-807-1161

**APPLIX, Inc., Boschetsrieder Straße 67, 81379 Muenchen, Germany**
Tel: 49-89-7485-890    Fax: 49-89-7485-8920

### APW, INC.

PO Box 325, Milwaukee, WI, 53201-0325
Tel: (262) 523-7600      Fax: (262) 523-7624        www.apw1.com
*Mfr. hi-pressure tools, vibration control products, consumables, technical furniture and enclosures.*
**APW GmbH, Mundelheimer Weg 51, Postfach 30 01 13, D-40472 Düsseldorf, Germany**

### AQUENT

711 Boylston Street, Boston, MA, 02116
Tel: (617) 535-5000      Fax: (617) 535-6001        www.aquent.com
*Engaged in temporary, specialized employment.*
**AQUENT, Mullerstrasse 27, D-80469 Munchen, Germany**
**AQUENT, Hedderichstraße 104, D-60596 Frankfurt, Germany**
Tel: 49-69-603262

### ARAMARK CORPORATION

1101 Market Street, Philadelphia, PA, 19107-2988
Tel: (215) 238-3000      Fax: (215) 238-3333        www.aramark.com
*Provides managed services for food, work and safety clothing, education, recreation and facilities*
**Aramark/Germany, Martin-Behaim-Str. 6, D-63263 Neu Isenburg, Germany**
Tel: 49-6-102-745-220   Fax: 49-6-102-745-234   Contact: Udo Luerssen, Pres.

### ARDENT SOFTWARE, INC.

50 Washington Street, Westboro, MA, 01581-1021
Tel: (508) 366-3888      Fax: (508) 366-3669        www.ardentsoftware.com
*Publisher of database and file management software.*
**Ardent Software GmbH, Hagenauer Strasse 44, D-65203 Wiesbaden, Germany**
Tel: 49-611-1820207   Fax: 49-611-18249-10

### ARIBA, INC.

1565 Charleston Rd., Mountain View, CA, 94043
Tel: (650) 930-6200      Fax: (650) 930-6300        www.ariba.com
*Mfr. software.*
**Ariba Germany, Feringastrasse 6, Unterfoehring 85774 Münich, Germany**

### ARMSTRONG HOLDINGS, INC.

2500 Columbia Avenue, Lancaster, PA, 17604-3001
Tel: (717) 397-0611      Fax: (717) 396-2787        www.armstrong.com
*Mfr. and marketing interior furnishings and specialty products for bldg, auto and textile industry.*
**Armstrong Floor Products Europe GmbH, Robert Bosch Strasse 10, 48153 Munster, Germany**
Tel: 49-251-760-30

### ARO INTERNATIONAL CORPORATION

One Aro Center, Bryan, OH, 43506
Tel: (419) 636-4242      Fax: (419) 633-1674        www.aro.ingersoll-rand.com
*Mfr. fluid control products, including pumps, valves, cylinders, logic controls and air line components.*
**Aro GmbH, Kaiserswerther Str. 49-51, Postfach 1152, D-4030 Ratingen 1, Germany**

### ARROW ELECTRONICS INC.

25 Hub Drive, Melville, NY, 11747
Tel: (516) 391-1300      Fax: (516) 391-1640        www.arrow.com
*Distributor of electronic components.*
**Spoerle Electronic, Max-Planck-Strasse 1-3, D-63303 Dreiech, Germany**
Tel: 49-6103-30-40   Fax: 49-6103-30-45-25   Contact: Carlo Giersch, Chmn.

## ARROW INTERNATIONAL, INC.

2400 Bernville Rd., Reading, PA, 19605

Tel: (610) 378-0131      Fax: (610) 374-5360         www.arrowintl.com

*Develop, manufacture, and marketing of medical devices.*

**Arrow Deutschland GmbH, Justus-von-Liebig-Strasse 2, D-85435 Erding, Germany**

Tel: 49-8122-98200    Fax: 49-8122-40384    Contact: Klaus Holzer

## ARVIN MERITOR INC

2135 W. Maple Rd., Troy, Mi, 48084-7186

Tel: (248) 435-1000      Fax: (248) 435-1393         www.arvinmeritor.com

*Mfr. of automotive exhaust systems and ride control products, axles and power-steering pumps.*

**ArvinMeritor Exhaust Germany (Zeuna Stärker), Ufestrasse 6, D-57413 Finnentrop, Germany**

Tel: 49-2721-517-0   Fax: 49-2721-517-48    Contact: Andreas Schmitz, Engineer

## ASG (ALLEN SYSTEMS GROUP)

1333 3rd Avenue South, Naples, FL, 33102

Tel: (941) 435-2200      Fax: (941) 263-3692         www.asg.com

*Mainframe computer software, specializing in OnMark 2000 software.*

**ASG Central Europe, Grillparzerstrasse 18, 81675 München, Germany**

Tel: 49-89-45-716-300

**ASG Central Europe, Max-Planck-Straße 15a, 40699 Erkrath Düsseldorf, Germany**

Tel: 49-211-75658-0

## ASHLAND OIL INC.

50 E. Rivercenter Blvd., Covington, KY, 41012-0391

Tel: (859) 815-3333      Fax: (859) 815-5053         www.ashland.com

*Petroleum exploration, refining and transportation; mfr. chemicals, oils and lubricants.*

**Ashland-Suedchemie-Kernfest GmbH, Postfach 440, Reisholzstrasse 16, D-4010 Hilden, Germany**

## ASPECT COMMUNICATIONS CORPORATION

1730 Fox Drive, San Jose, CA, 95131

Tel: (408) 325-2200      Fax: (408) 325-2260         www.aspect.com

*Mfr. software and related equipment.*

**Aspect GmbH, Frankfurter Straße 233, 63263 Neu-Isenburg, Germany**

Tel: 49-6102-5670

## ASPEN TECHNOLOGY, INC.

10 Canal Park, Cambridge, MA, 02141

Tel: (617) 949-1000      Fax: (617) 949-1030         www.aspentec.com

*Mfr. software for chemists and refineries.*

**AspenTech Europe SA, Am Seestern 24, D-40547 Duesseldorf, Germany**

Tel: 49-211-596-787

## ASSOCIATED MERCHANDISING CORPORATION

500 Seventh Ave., 2nd Fl., New York, NY, 10018

Tel: (212) 819-6600      Fax: (212) 819-6701         www.theamc.com

*Retail service organization; apparel, shoes and accessories.*

**Associated Merchandising Corp., Bleichstrasse 2-4, D-6000 Frankfurt/Main 1, Germany**

## ASSOCIATED METALS & MINERALS CORP. (ASOMA)

3 North Corporate Park Drive, White Plains, NY, 10604

Tel: (914) 872-2640      Fax: (914) 251-1073         www.macsteel.com

*Metals and ores.*

**Rheinischer Erz-und Metallhandel GmbH, Untersachsenhausen 37, D-5000 Cologne, Germany**

## ASSOCIATED PRESS INC.

50 Rockefeller Plaza, New York, NY, 10020-1605

Tel: (212) 621-1500    Fax: (212) 621-5447    www.ap.com

*News gathering agency.*

**The Associated Press,  Berlin, Germany**

Tel: 49-30-399-9250

**The Associated Press GmbH,  Moselstr. 27, Frankfurt Main, Germany**

Tel: 49-69-272300

## AT HOME CORPORATION

450 Broadway Street, Redwood City, CA, 94063

Tel: (650) 556-5000    Fax: (650) 556-5100    www.excite.com

*Online computer internet service provider.*

**Excite, Inc.,  München, Germany**

## ATMEL CORPORATION

2325 Orchard Pkwy., San Jose, CA, 95131

Tel: (408) 441-0311    Fax: (408) 436-4200    www.atmel.com

*Design, manufacture and marketing of advanced semiconductors.*

**Atmel Gmbh,  Pulverstrasse 55, D-22880 Wedel, Germany**

Tel: 49-4103-93160

## ATTACHMATE CORPORATION

3617 131st Ave. S.E., Bellevue, WA, 98006-1332

Tel: (425) 644-4010    Fax: (425) 747-9924    www.attachmate.com

*Mfr. connectivity software.*

**Attachmate Germany GmbH,  Stefan-George-Ring 6, 81929 München, Germany**

Tel: 49-89-99-3510   Fax: 49-89-99-351-111

**Attachmate International Sales,  Schnackenburgallee 15, 22525 Hamburg, Germany**

Tel: 49-40-85-32660   Fax: 49-40-85-326632

**Attachmate International Sales,  Schimmelbuschstrasse 9, 40699 Erkrath-Hochdahl, Germany**

Tel: 49-21-04-93980   Fax: 49-21-04-939850

**Attachmate International Sales,  Untere Waldplatze 2, 70569 Stuttgart, Germany**

Tel: 49-711-67-9680   Fax: 49-711-67-96833

**Attachmate International Sales,  Lurgiallee 6-8, 60439 Frankfurt/Main, Germany**

Tel: 49-69-958210-0   Fax: 49-69-958210-20

## AUTODESK INC.

111 McInnis Parkway, San Rafael, CA, 94903

Tel: (415) 507-5000    Fax: (415) 507-6112    www.autodesk.com

*Develop/marketing/support computer-aided design, engineering, scientific and multimedia software products.*

**Autodesk GmbH,  Hansastrasse 28, D-8000 München 21, Germany**

Tel: 49-89-547690   Fax: 49-89-5769433

## AUTOMATIC DATA PROCESSING INC.

One ADP Blvd., Roseland, NJ, 07068

Tel: (973) 994-5000    Fax: (973) 994-5387    www.adp.com

*Data processing services.*

**ADP Autonom Computer GmbH,  Heddernheimer Landstrasse 144, D-60439 Frankfurt, Germany**

Tel: 49-69-58-040   Fax: 49-69-5804-241   Contact: Gabriele Bauer

## AUTOMATIC SWITCH CO. (ASCO)

50-60 Hanover Rd., Florham Park, NJ, 07932

Tel: (973) 966-2000      Fax: (973) 966-2628      www.asco.com

*Mfr. solenoid valves, emergency power controls, pressure and temp. switches.*

**Asco GmbH & Co.,  PO Box 101138, D-40831 Ratingen 1, Germany**

Tel: 49-2102-8501-0   Fax: 49-2102-850136   Contact: H. Hummel

## AUTOSPLICE INC.

10121 Barnes Canyon Road, San Diego, CA, 92121

Tel: (858) 535-0077      Fax: (858) 535-0130      www.autosplice.com

*Mfr. electronic components.*

**Autosplice Europe GmbH,  Waldstrasse 12, D-90579 Langenzenn Laubendorf, Germany**

Tel: 49-9102-9957-12   Fax: 49-9102-9957-19   Contact: Wolfgang Blust

## AUTOTOTE CORPORATION

750 Lexington Avenue, 25th Fl., New York, Ny, 1022

Tel: (212) 754-2233      Fax: (212) 754-2372      www.autotote.com

*Mfr. video gaming machines and computerized pari-mutuel wagering systems used at racetracks.*

**Scientific Games International, Div. Autotote,  Fischerried 33, D-82362 Weilheim, Germany**

Tel: 49-881-93940   Fax: 49-881-939415

## AUTO-TROL TECHNOLOGY CORPORATION

12500 North Washington Street, Denver, CO, 80241-2400

Tel: (303) 452-4919      Fax: (303) 252-2249      www.auto-trol.com

*Develops, markets and integrates computer-based solutions for industrial companies and government agencies worldwide.*

**Auto-Trol Technology GmbH,  Heltorfer Strasse 6, 40472 Düsseldorf, Germany**

Tel: 49-211-907-950   Emp: 3

## AVERSTAR

23 Fourth Ave., Burlington, MA, 01803-3303

Tel: (781) 221-6990      Fax: (781) 221-6991      www.averstar.com

*Software and systems engineering services.*

**Averstar,  Stuttgart, Germany**

## AVERY DENNISON CORPORATION

150 N. Orange Grove Blvd., Pasadena, CA, 91103

Tel: (626) 304-2000      Fax: (626) 792-7312      www.averydennison.com

*Mfr. pressure-sensitive adhesives and materials, office products, labels, tags, retail systems, Carter's Ink and specialty chemicals.*

**Avery Maschinen GmbH,  Kollaustrasse 105, D-2000 Hamburg, Germany**

**Fasson Handelsgesellschaft GmbH,  Alte Strasse 39, Dortmund, Germany**

## AVID TECHNOLOGY, INC.

1 Park West, Tewksbury, MA, 01876

Tel: (978) 640-6789      Fax: (978) 640-1366      www.avid.com

*Mfr. animation design software and digital and audio systems.*

**Avid Technology GmbH,  Isar Office Park, Am Soeldermoos, D-85399 Hallbergmoos, Germany**

Fax: 49-811-55-20999

## AVNET INC.

2211 South 47th Street, Phoenix, AZ, 85034

Tel: (480) 643-2000     Fax: (480) 643-4670     www.avnet.com

*Distributor electronic components, computers and peripherals.*

**Avnet EMG Gmbh, Wolfenbutteler Str. 33, D-81829 München, Germany**

Tel: 49-531-220-7330   Fax: 49-531-220-7335

**BFI IBEXSA Elektronik GmbH, Assar Gabrielssonstrasse 1B, D-61328 Steinberg, Germany**

Tel: 49-6074-40980   Fax: 49-6074-409810

## AVON PRODUCTS INC.

1345 Avenue of the Americas, New York, NY, 10105-0196

Tel: (212) 282-5000     Fax: (212) 282-6049     www.avon.com

*Mfr./distributor beauty and related products, fashion jewelry, gifts and collectibles.*

**Avon Cosmetics GmbH, Postfach 400140, D-8000 München 40, Germany**

Tel: 49-8165-720   Fax: 49-8165-721226   Contact: Walter Biel

## AXENT TECHNOLOGIES, INC.

2400 Research Boulevard, Ste. 200, Rockville, MD, 20850

Tel: (301) 258-5043     Fax: (301) 330-5756     www.axent.com

*Designs and supplies security management software .*

**AXENT Technologies GmbH, Arnulfstrasse 27, D-80335 München, Germany**

Tel: 49-89-5904-7103   Fax: 49-89-5904-7208   Contact: Travis Witteveen

## AZURIX CORPORATION

333 Clay Street, Ste. 1000, Houston, TX, 77002-7361

Tel: (713) 646-6001     Fax: (713) 345-5358     www.azurix.com

*Engaged in w water treatment and water dredging. (JV of Enron)*

**Lurgi Bamag GmbH, Wetzlarer Str. 136, D-35510 Butzbach, Germany**

## BADGER METER INC.

4545 W. Brown Deer Road, Milwaukee, WI, 53223-0099

Tel: (414) 355-0400     Fax: (414) 371-5956     www.badgermeter.com

*Mfr. liquid meters and controls.*

**Badger Meter Europe GmbH, Karlstrasse 11, D-72660 Beuren, Germany**

Tel: 49-7025-9208-0  Fax: 49-7025-9208-25   Contact: Hors Gras   Emp: 25

## BAE SYSTEMS, INC.

1601 Research Blvd., Rockville, MD, 20850

Tel: (301) 738-4000     Fax: (301) 738-4643     www.baesystems.com

*Engaged in aerospace, defense electronics and information systems.*

**BAE Systems, Heckler & Koch Postfach 1329, 78727 Oberndorf, Germany**

Tel: 49-7-423-7923790

## BAIN & COMPANY, INC.

Two Copley Place, Boston, MA, 02116

Tel: (617) 572-2000     Fax: (617) 572-2427     www.bain.com

*Strategic management consulting services.*

**Bain & Co. Germany Inc., Thomas-Wimmer-Ring 3, D-8000 München 22, Germany**

Tel: 49-89-290-110  Fax: 48-89-290-11-113

## ROBERT W. BAIRD & CO.

PO Box 672, Milwaukee, WI, 53201

Tel: (414) 765-3500     Fax: (414) 765-3600     www.rwbaird.com

*Engaged in investment banking, serving individuals, corporations, municipalities and institutional investors.*

**Granville Baird, Haus am Hafen, Steinhoeft 5-7, 20459 Hamburg, Germany**

Tel: 49-40-3748-0210    Contact: Wolfgang Alvano

## BAKER & McKENZIE

130 East Randolph Drive, Ste. 2500, Chicago, IL, 60601

Tel: (312) 861-8000     Fax: (312) 861-2899     www.bakerinfo.com

*International legal services.*

**Döser Amereller Noack / Baker & McKenzie, Palais am Lembachplatz, Ottostrasse 8, D-80333 München, Germany**

Tel: 49-89-552380    Fax: 49-89-55238-199    Contact: Walter R. Henle, Ptnr.

**Döser Amereller Noack / Baker & McKenzie, Friedrichstrasse 79-80, D-10117 Berlin, Germany**

Tel: 49-30-20387-600    Fax: 49-30-20387-699    Contact: Carl H. Andres, Ptnr.

**Döser Amereller Noack / Baker & McKenzie, Bethmannstrasse 50-54, D-60311 Frankfurt/Main, Germany**

Tel: 49-69-299080    Fax: 49-69-29908108    Contact: Horst Amereller, Ptnr.

## BAKER HUGHES INCORPORATED

3900 Essex Lane, Ste. 1200, Houston, TX, 77027

Tel: (713) 439-8600     Fax: (713) 439-8699     www.bakerhughes.com

*Develop and apply technology to drill, complete and produce oil and natural gas wells; provide separation systems to petroleum, municipal, continuous process and mining industries.*

**Baker Hughes Process, Dillenburger Str. 100, D-51105 Cologne, Germany**

Tel: 49-221-9856-0   Fax: 49-221-9856-202

**Baker Oil Tools GmbH, Christensenstrasse 1, D-29221 Celle, Germany**

Tel: 49-5141-2030   Fax: 49-5141-203626

## J.T. BAKER INC.

222 Red School Lane, Phillipsburg, NJ, 08865

Tel: (908) 859-2151     Fax: (908) 859-9318     www.jtbaker.com

*Mfr./sale/services lab and process chemicals.*

**Baker Chemikaliem, Postfach 1661, D-6080 Gross Gerau, Germany**

## BAKER PETROLITE CORPORATION

3900 Essex Lane, Houston, TX, 77027

Tel: (713) 599-7400     Fax: (713) 599-7592     www.bakerhughes.com/bapt/

*Mfr. specialty chemical treating programs, performance-enhancing additives and related equipment and services.*

**Petrolite GmbH, Kaiser Friedrich Promenade 59, Postfach 2031, D-6380 Bad Homburg 1, Germany**

## BAKER PROCESSING

PO Box 9103, South Walpole, MA, 02071

Tel: (508) 668-0400     Fax: (508) 668-6855     www.bakerhughes.com

*Mfr. of liquid solid separation equipment.*

**Bird Humboldt A.G., D-51057 Koln Wiersbergstrasse, Germany**

Tel: 49-221-822-7203    Fax: 49-221-822-6556    Contact: Wolfgang Eupper, Gen. Mgr.    Emp: 300

## BALDWIN TECHNOLOGY COMPANY, INC.

One Norwalk West, 40 Richards Ave., Norwalk, CT, 06854

Tel: (203) 838-7470      Fax: (203) 852-7040      www.baldwintech.com

*Mfr./services material handling, accessories, control and prepress equipment for print industry.*

**Baldwin Grafotec GmbH, Derchinger Strasse 137, D-86165 Augsburg, Germany**

Tel: 49-821-79420   Fax: 49-821-794222   Contact: Dr. Rolf Enders, Geschäftsführer

## BANK OF AMERICA CORPORATION

555 California Street, San Francisco, CA, 94104

Tel: (415) 622-3530      Fax: (415) 622-8467      www.bankofamerica.com

*Financial services.*

**Bank of America NT & SA, Ulmenstrasse 30, Postfach 110243, D-60325 Frankfurt, Germany**

Tel: 49-69-7100-1461   Fax: 49-69-7100-1261   Contact: Rudi Perkowsky, VP

## THE BANK OF NEW YORK

One Wall Street, New York, NY, 10286

Tel: (212) 495-1784      Fax: (212) 495-2546      www.bankofny.com

*Banking services.*

**The Bank of New York, Niedenau 61-63, Postfach 60077, D-60235 Frankfurt/Main 17, Germany**

Tel: 49-69-971510   Fax: 49-69-721798

## BANK ONE CORPORATION

One First National Plaza, Chicago, IL, 60670

Tel: (312) 732-4000      Fax: (312) 732-3366      www.fcnbd.com

*Provides financial products and services.*

**Bank One, NA, Hochstrasse 35-37, D-60313 Frankfurt/Main, Germany**

Tel: 49-69-299876-0   Fax: 49-69-299876-80   Contact: Volker Loeser, Br. Mgr.

## C. R. BARD, INC.

730 Central Ave., Murray Hill, NJ, 07974

Tel: (908) 277-8000      Fax: (908) 277-8078      www.crbard.com

*Mfr. health care products.*

**C.R. Bard GmbH, Siemenstrasse 1, D-8044 Unterschleissheim, Münich, Germany**

## BARRA, INC.

2100 Milvia Street, Berkeley, CA, 94704

Tel: (510) 548-5442      Fax: (510) 548-4374      www.barra.com

*Mfr. analytical software for private investors and portfolio managers.*

**BARRA International, Ltd., Goethestraße 5, D-60313 Frankfurt, Germany**

Tel: 49-69-28-1700

## BARRY CONTROLS INC.

40 Guest Street, PO Box 9105, Brighton, MA, 02135-9105

Tel: (617) 787-1555      Fax: (617) 254-7381      www.barrymounts.com

*Mfr./sale vibration isolation mounting devices.*

**Barry Controls Intl. GmbH, Karl Liebknecht Str. 30, Postfach 1137, D-65479 Raunheim, Germany**

## BASE TEN SYSTEMS INC.

One Electronics Drive, Trenton, NJ, 08619

Tel: (609) 586-7010      Fax: (609) 586-1593      www.base10.com

*Mfr. proprietary control systems, flight test systems, communications products.*

**Base Ten Systems Ltd., Ismaninger Str. 17-19, D-81675 Münich, Germany**

## BATES WORLDWIDE INC.

405 Lexington Ave., New York, NY, 10174

Tel: (212) 297-7000     Fax: (212) 986-0270     www.batesww.com

*Advertising, marketing, public relations and media consulting.*

**Bates Dialog Direkt Marketing, Hanauer Landstrasse 287-289, D-60314 Frankfurt, Germany**

Tel: 49-69-405-7203    Fax: 49-69-405-72359    Contact: Relner Blau, Dir.

**Bates Germany GmbH, Hanauer Landstrasse 287-289, D-60314 Frankfurt Main, Germany**

Tel: 49-69-405-7200    Fax: 49-69-405-72-359    Contact: Ulrich Voigel, CEO

## BATTELLE MEMORIAL INSTITUTE

505 King Ave., Columbus, OH, 43201-2693

Tel: (614) 424-6424     Fax: (614) 424-3260     www.battelle.org

*Develops new technologies, commercializes products, and provides solutions for industry and government.*

**Battelle Europe, Am Romerhof 35, D-6000 Frankfurt Main 90, Germany**

## BAUSCH & LOMB INC.

One Bausch & Lomb Place, Rochester, NY, 14604-2701

Tel: (716) 338-6000     Fax: (716) 338-6007     www.bausch.com

*Mfr. vision care products and accessories.*

**Bausch & Lomb GmbH (Vision Care), Max-Planck-Str. 6, 85609 Dornach, Germany**

**Dr. Mann Pharma Fabrik, GmbH, Brunsbuetteler Damm 165 - 173, 13581 Berlin, Germany**

**Dr. Winzer Pharma GmbH, Lizweg 7, 82140 Olching, Germany**

## BAXTER HEALTHCARE CORPORATION

One Baxter Parkway, Deerfield, IL, 60015

Tel: (847) 948-2000     Fax: (847) 948-3948     www.baxter.com

*Pharmaceutical preparations, surgical/medical instruments and cardiovascular products.*

**Baxter Deutschland GmbH, Edisonstrasse 3-4, D-85716 Unterschleissheim, Münich, Germany**

## BBDO WORLDWIDE

1285 Ave. of the Americas, New York, NY, 10019

Tel: (212) 459-5000     Fax: (212) 459-6645     www.bbdo.com

*Multinational group of advertising agencies.*

**BBDO Group Germany, Düsseldorf, Germany**

## BDO SEIDMAN, LLP    BELGIUM

Two Prudential Plaza, 180 N. Stetson Ave., Ste. 2300, Chicago, IL, 60601

Tel: (312) 240-1236     Fax: (312) 240-3329     www.bdo.com

*International accounting and financial consulting firm.*

**BDO Deutsche Warentreuhand Aktiengesellschaft, Grüneburgweg 12, D-60322 Frankfurt, Germany**

Tel: 49-69-95-9410    Fax: 49-69-55-4335    Contact: Dr. Hans-Joachim Jacob

## BEA SYSTEMS, INC.

2315 North First Street, St. Jose, CA, 95131

Tel: (408) 570-8000     Fax: (408) 570-8091     www.beasys.com

*Develops communications management software and provider of software consulting services.*

**BEA Systems Europe GmbH, Max-Planck-Strasse 5, D-85609 Aschheim-Dornach, Germany**

Tel: 49-89-945180    Fax: 49-89-945-18222

**BEA Systems Europe GmbH, Wilhelm-Theodor-Römheld-Strasse 14, Gebäude 14, D-55130 Mainz, Germany**

Tel: 49-6131-9211-05    Fax: 49-6131-9211-42

## BECHTEL GROUP INC.

50 Beale Street, PO Box 3965, San Francisco, CA, 94105-1895

Tel: (415) 768-1234    Fax: (415) 768-9038    www.bechtel.com

*General contractors in engineering and construction.*

**Bechtel (Deutschland) GmbH, Inselstr. 34, D-4000 Düsseldorf, Germany**

## BECKMAN COULTER, INC.

4300 N. Harbor Boulevard, Fullerton, CA, 92834

Tel: (714) 871-4848    Fax: (714) 773-8898    www.beckmancoulter.com

*Develop/mfr./marketing automated systems and supplies for biological analysis.*

**Beckman Coulter GmbH, Europark Fichtenhain B 13, 47807 Krefeld, Germany**

Tel: 49-21-51-3335

## BELDEN, INC.

7701 Forsyth Blvd., Ste. 800, St. Louis, MO, 63015

Tel: (314) 854-8000    Fax: (314) 854-8001    www.belden.com

*Mfr. electronic wire and cable products.*

**Belden-EIW GmbH & Co. KG, Postfach 13 40 Am Krebsgraben 1-3, 78048 Villingen-Schwenningen, Germany**

## BELLSOUTH CORPORATION LATIN AMERICA

1155 Peachtree Street NE, Ste. 400, Atlanta, GA, 30367

Tel: (404) 249-4800    Fax: (404) 249-4880    www.bellsouth.com

*Mobile communications, telecommunications network systems.*

**E-Plus Mobilfunk GmbH, E-Plus Platz 1, D-40468 Düsseldorf, Germany**

Tel: 49-211-4480

## BEMIS COMPANY, INC.

222 South 9th Street, Ste. 2300, Minneapolis, MN, 55402-4099

Tel: (612) 376-3000    Fax: (612) 376-3180    www.bemis.com

*Mfr. flexible packaging, specialty coated and graphics products.*

**Hayssen Europa GmbH, Postfach 3280, D-7500 Karlsruhe l, Germany**

## BENTLY NEVADA CORPORATION

1617 Water Street, PO Box 157, Minden, NV, 89423

Tel: (775) 782-3611    Fax: (775) 782-9259    www.bently.com

*Provides hardware, software, and services for machinery information and management systems.*

**Bently Nevada GmbH, Postfach 60, Hermannstr. 25, D-6078 Neu-Isenburg, Germany**

## BERLITZ CROSS-CULTURAL TRAINING INC.

400 Alexander Park, Princeton, NJ, 08540

Tel: (609) 514-9650    Fax: (609) 514-9689    www.berlitz.com

*Consulting and management training services to bridge cultural gaps for international travelers as well as for business transferees and families.*

**Berlitz Deutschland GmbH, Marienplatz 18/19, Münich 80331, Germany**

## BEST WESTERN INTERNATIONAL

6201 North 24th Place, Phoenix, AZ, 85106

Tel: (602) 957-4200    Fax: (602) 957-5740    www.bestwestern.com

*International hotel chain.*

**Hotel Domicil, Thomas-Mann-Strasse 24-26, D-53111 Bonn, Germany**

## BESTFOODS, INC.

700 Sylvan Ave., International Plaza, Englewood Cliffs, NJ, 07632-9976

Tel: (201) 894-4000       Fax: (201) 894-2186       www.bestfoods.com

*Consumer foods products; corn refining.*

**CPC Deutschland GmbH,  Knorrstrasse 1, D-74074 Heilbronn, Germany**

Tel: 49-7131-501-1   Fax: 49-7131-501-206   Contact: Manfred Lange, Mgr.

## BETZDEARBORN

4636 Somerton Road, PO Box 3002, Trevose, PA, 19053-6783

Tel: (215) 953-2568       Fax: (215) 953-5524       www.betzdearborn.com

*Mfr. water/wastewater and process system treatment chemicals and services.*

**BetzDearborn GmbH,  Siemensring 44, D-47877 Willich 1, Germany**

## BICC GENERAL

4 Tesseneer Drive, Highland Heights, KY, 41076

Tel: (606) 572-8000       Fax: (606) 572-8444       www.generalcable.com

*Mfr., marketing and distribution of copper, aluminum and fiber optic wire and cable products for the communications, energy and electrical markets.*

**BICC General,  Riedelstrasse 1, D-12347 Berlin, Germany**

## BIOGEN, INC.

14 Cambridge Center, Cambridge, MA, 02142

Tel: (617) 679-2000       Fax: (617) 679-2617       www.bigoten.com

*Engaged in medical research and development on autoimmune diseases.*

**Biogen GmbH,  Carl-Zeiss Ring 6, 85737 Ismaning, Germany**

Tel: 49-89-99-6170

## BIOMATRIX, INC.

65 Railroad Ave., Ridgefield, NJ, 07657

Tel: (201) 945-9550       Fax: (201) 945-0363       www.biomatrix.com

*Mfr. hylan biological polymers for therapeutic medical and skin care products.*

**Biomatix Germany GmbH,  Schleebrugenkamp 15, Munster 48159, Germany**

## BIO-RAD LABORATORIES INC.

1000 Alfred Nobel Drive, Hercules, CA, 94547

Tel: (510) 724-7000       Fax: (510) 724-3167       www.bio-rad.com

*Mfr. life science research products, clinical diagnostics, analytical instruments.*

**Bio-Rad Laboratories Inc.,  Düsseldorf, Germany**

## BLACK & DECKER CORPORATION

701 E. Joppa Road, Towson, MD, 21286

Tel: (410) 716-3900       Fax: (410) 716-2933       www.blackanddecker.com

*Mfr. power tools and accessories, security hardware, small appliances, fasteners, information systems and services.*

**Black & Decker Kundendienst,  Black & Decker-Strasse 40, D-65510 Idstein, Germany**

Tel: 49-6-126-212483   Fax: 49-6-126-212770

**DeWalt Kundendienst,  Richard-Klinger-Strasse, D-65510 Idstein, Germany**

Tel: 49-6-126-212483   Fax: 49-6-126-212770

**Zentral-Kundendienst ELU International,  Richard-Klinger-Strasse, D-65510 Idstein, Germany**

Tel: 49-6-126-212483   Fax: 49-6-126-212770

## BLACK & VEATCH LLP

8400 Ward Pkwy., PO Box 8405, Kansas City, MO, 64114

Tel: (913) 339-2000     Fax: (913) 339-2934     www.bv.com

*Engineering, architectural and construction services.*

**PROWA - Black & Veatch GmbH, Magdeburger Strasse 38, D-06112 Halle, Germany**

Tel: 49-345-2125-0   Fax: 49-345-2125-201   Contact: Klaus Klingel

## BLACK BOX CORPORATION

1000 Park Dr., Lawrence, PA, 15055

Tel: (724) 746-5500     Fax: (724) 746-0746     www.blackbox.com

*Direct marketer and technical service provider of communications, networking and related computer connectivity products.*

**Black Box Deutschland, Ludwigsforum, Ludwigstrasse 456, D-85399 Hallbergmoos, Germany**

Tel: 49-811-5541-0   Fax: 49-811-5541-499   Contact: Michael Balmforth, Gen. Mgr.

## BLOOM ENGINEERING CO., INC.

5460 Horning Rd., Pittsburgh, PA, 15236

Tel: (412) 653-3500     Fax: (412) 653-2253     www.bloomeng.com

*Mfr. custom engineered burners and combustion systems.*

**Bloom Engineering Company (Europa) GmbH, Büttgenbachstrasse 14, D-40549 Dusseldorf, Germany**

Tel: 49-211-500910   Fax: 49-211-501397

## BLOUNT INTERNATIONAL, INC

4520 Executive Park Dr., Montgomery, AL, 36116-1602

Tel: (334) 244-4000     Fax: (334) 271-8130     www.blount.com

*Mfr. cutting chain and equipment, timber harvest and handling equipment, sporting ammo, riding mowers.*

**Blount GmbH, Postfach 1146, Reinhardstrasse 23, D-71112 Gartringen, Germany**

Tel: 49-7034-92850   Fax: 49-7034-26754   Contact: Roland Stolz, Mgr.

## BMC INDUSTRIES INC.

One Meridian Crossings, Ste. 850, Minneapolis, MN, 55423

Tel: (612) 851-6000     Fax: (612) 851-6065     www.bmcind.com

*Design/mfr./marketing precision etched products, electroformed components, special printed circuits, ophthalmic devices.*

**BMC Europe GmbH, Renkenrunsstrasse 24-26, D-79379 Mullheim, Germany**

Tel: 49-7631-802-115   Fax: 49-7631-802-311   Contact: John Springer, Mng. Dir.   Emp: 300

## BMC SOFTWARE, INC.

2101 City West Blvd., Houston, TX, 77042-2827

Tel: (713) 918-8800     Fax: (713) 918-8000     www.bmc.com

*Engaged in mainframe-related utilities software and services.*

**BMC Software, Postfach 71 01 49, D-60491 Frankfurt, Germany**

**BMC Software, Amsinckstraße 57, 20097 Hamburg, Germany**

## BOART LONGYEAR COMPANY

2340 West 1700 South, Salt Lake City, UT, 84104

Tel: (801) 972-6430     Fax: (801) 977-3372     www.boartlongyear.com

*Mfr. diamond drills, concrete cutting equipment and drill services.*

**Longyear GmbH, Postfach 460, Grafftring 1, D-3100 Celle, Germany**

## THE BOEING COMPANY

7755 East Marginal Way South, Seattle, WA, 98108

Tel: (206) 655-2121     Fax: (206) 655-6300     www.boeing.com.

*World's largest aerospace company; mfr. military and commercial aircraft, missiles and satellite launch vehicles.*

**Boeing Berliner Flughafen GmbH, Geschaftsfuhrung, Postfach 51 01 43, 13361 Berlin Germany**

## BOISE CASCADE CORPORATION

1111 West Jefferson Street, PO Box 50, Boise, ID, 83728-0001

Tel: (208) 384-6161      Fax: (208) 384-7189      www.bc.com

*Mfr./distributor paper and paper products, building products, office products.*

**Boise Cascade Office Products, Ltd., Hamburg, Germany**

## BOOZ-ALLEN & HAMILTON INC.

8283 Greensboro Drive, McLean, VA, 22102

Tel: (703) 902-5000      Fax: (703) 902-3333      www.bah.com

*International management and technology consultants.*

**Booz Allen & Hamilton GmbH, Mainzer Landstrasse/16, D-60325 Frankfurt, Germany**

Tel: 49-69-971670    Fax: 49-69-97167-400

**Booz Allen & Hamilton GmbH, Lenbachplatz 3, D-80333 München, Germany**

Tel: 49-89-545250    Fax: 49-89-545-25500

**Booz, Allen & Hamilton Inc., Koenigsallee 106, D-40215 Düsseldorf, Germany**

Tel: 49-211-38900    Fax: 49-211-371002

## BORG-WARNER AUTOMOTIVE INC.

200 S. Michigan Ave., Chicago, IL, 60604

Tel: (312) 322-8500      Fax: (312) 461-0507      www.bwauto.com

*Mfr. automotive components; provider of security services.*

**Borg-Warner Automotive GmbH, Postfach 101360, D-69003 Heidelberg, Germany**

**Borg-Warner Automotive GmbH, Postfach 40, D-68767 Ketsch, Germany**

## BOSE CORPORATION

The Mountain, Framingham, MA, 01701-9168

Tel: (508) 879-7330      Fax: (508) 766-7543      www.bose.com

*Mfr. quality audio equipment/speakers.*

**BOSE GmbH, Max-Planck-Strasse 36, Postfach 1125, D-61381 Friedrichsdorf, Germany**

## THE BOSTON CONSULTING GROUP

Exchange Place, 31st Fl., Boston, MA, 02109

Tel: (617) 973-1200      Fax: (617) 973-1339      www.bcg.com

*Management consulting company.*

**The Boston Consulting Group, GmbH, Heinrich-Heine-Allee 1, D-40213 Düsseldorf, Germany**

Tel: 49-211-13830

**The Boston Consulting Group, GmbH, Chilehaus A, Fischertwiete 2, D-20095 Hamburg, Germany**

Tel: 49-40-301-82

**The Boston Consulting Group, GmbH, Westend-Carree, Gruneburgweg 18, D-60322 Frankfurt am Main, Germany**

Tel: 49-711-16-23-3

**The Boston Consulting Group, GmbH, Kronprinzstr. 28, D-70173 Stuttgart, Germany**

Tel: 49-69-9-15-02

**The Boston Consulting Group, GmbH, Sendlinger Str. 7, D-80331 München, Germany**

Tel: 49-89-23-17-40

## BOSTON SCIENTIFIC CORPORATION

One Scientific Place, Natick, MA, 01760-1537

Tel: (508) 650-8000      Fax: (508) 650-8923      www.bsci.com

*Mfr./distributes medical devices for use in minimally invasive surgeries.*

**Boston Scientific Medizintechnik GmbH, Christinenstrasse 2, D-40880 Ratigen, Germany**

Tel: 49-2102-489-3    Fax: 49-2102-489-439

## BOURNS INC.

1200 Columbia Avenue, Riverside, CA, 92507

Tel: (909) 781-5500    Fax: (909) 781-5006    www.bourns.com

*Mfr. resistive components and networks, precision potentiometers, panel controls, switches, transducers and surge protectors..*

**Bourns GmbH, Postfach 100644, Brietestrasse 2, D-7000 Stuttgart 10, Germany**

## BOWNE & COMPANY, INC.

345 Hudson Street, New York, NY, 10014

Tel: (212) 924-5500    Fax: (212) 229-3420    www.bowne.com

*Financial printing and foreign language translation, localization (software), internet design and maintenance and facilities management.*

**Bowne International, Bettinastrasse 30, D-60325 Frankfurt am Main, Germany**

Tel: 49-69-9714-760   Fax: 49-69-72-43-41   Contact: Matthew Gould, Mgr.

**Bowne International, Inselkammerstraße 11, D-82008 Unterhaching Münich, Germany**

Tel: 49-89-666-790   Fax: 49-89-666-79166

## BOYDEN CONSULTING CORPORATION

364 Elwood Ave., Hawthorne, NY, 10502

Tel: (914) 747-0093    Fax: (914) 980-6147    www.boyden.com

*International executive search firm.*

**Boyden Intl. GmbH, Kathaarina-Heinroth-Ufer 1, D-10787 Berlin, Germany**

Tel: 49-30-23-09090

**Boyden Intl. GmbH, Postfach 1724, Ferinandstr., D-61348 Bad Homburg-v.d.H, Germany**

Tel: 49-6172-180200

## BOZELL GROUP

40 West 23rd Street, New York, NY, 10010

Tel: (212) 727-5000    Fax: (212) 645-9173    www.bozell.com

*Advertising, marketing, public relations and media consulting.*

**Bozell Direct Friends, Werbesgentur fur Direct Marketing GmbH, Borsteler Chaussee 55, D-22453 Hamburg, Germany**

Tel: 49-40-514-320   Fax: 49-40-514-32200   Contact: Uwe H. Drescher, Chmn.

**Bozell Werbeaentur GmbH, Hansaallee 16, D-60322 Frankfurt am Main 1, Germany**

Tel: 49-69-1530-920   Fax: 49-69-1530-9215   Contact: Dietmar Steuer, Mng. Dir.

## BRADY CORPORATION

6555 W. Good Hope Road, Milwaukee, WI, 53223

Tel: (414) 358-6600    Fax: (414) 358-6600    www.whbrady.com

*Mfr. industrial ID for wire marking, circuit boards; facility ID, signage, printing systems and software.*

**W.H. Brady GmbH, Lagerstrasse 13, D-64807 Dieburg, Germany**

Tel: 49-6071-960-3  Fax: 49-6071-960-400  Contact: Christian Thomczek, Country Mgr.

## BRANSON ULTRASONICS CORPORATION

41 Eagle Road, Danbury, CT, 06813-1961

Tel: (203) 796-0400    Fax: (203) 796-2285    www.branson-plasticsjoin.com

*Mfr. plastics assembly equipment, ultrasonic cleaning equipment.*

**Branson Ultraschall Niederlassung der Emerson, Waldstrasse 53-55, D-63128 Dietzenbach-Steinberg, Germany**

Tel: 49-6074-4970   Fax: 49-6074-497499

**BRIGGS & STRATTON CORPORATION**

12301 W. Wirth St., Wauwatosa, WI, 53222

Tel: (414) 259-5333      Fax: (414) 259-9594      www.briggesandstratton.com

*Mfr. air cooled, gasoline engines.*

**Briggs & Stratton Deutschland GmbH,  Attn: German Office, PO Box 72, Milwaukee WI 53201**

**BRIGHTPOINT, INC.**

6402 Corporate Dr., Indianapolis, IN, 46278

Tel: (317) 297-6100      Fax: (317) 297-6114      www.brightpoint.com

*Mfr./distribution of mobile phones.*

**Brightpoint GmbH,  Hanns-Martin-Schleyer-Straße 9a-c, D-47877 Willich, Germany**

Tel: 49-2154-9390

**BRINK'S INC.**

Thorndal Circle, Darien, CT, 06820

Tel: (203) 662-7800      Fax: (203) 662-7968      www.brinks.com

*Security transportation.*

**Brink's Deutschland GmbH,  Insterburger Straße 7a, 60487 Frankfurt/Main, Germany**

**BRISTOL-MYERS SQUIBB COMPANY**

345 Park Ave., New York, NY, 10154-0037

Tel: (212) 546-4000      Fax: (212) 546-4020      www.bms.com

*Pharmaceutical and food preparations, medical and surgical instruments.*

**Bristol-Myers - Regensburg Plant,  Postfach 177, Donaustaufer Strasse 378, D-8400 Regensburg, Germany**

**ConvaTec Germany,  Volkartstrasse 83, D-8000 München 19, Germany**

**ConvaTech Vertriebs GmbH,  Ein Unter. der, Volkartstrasse 3, D-80636 München, Germany**

**S+G Implants GmbH,  Grapengieberstrasse 34, D-2400 Lubeck 1, Germany**

**Zimmer Chirurgie GmbH,  Waldstrasse 23, D-6057 Dietzenbach, Germany**

**BROOKS AUTOMATION, INC.**

15 Elizabeth Drive, Chelmsford, MA, 01824

Tel: (978) 262-2400      Fax: (978) 262-2500      www.brooks.com

*Mfr. tool automation products.*

**Brooks Automation GmbH,  Göschwitzer Strasse 25, D-07745 Jena, Germany**

Tel: 49-3641-65-4000    Fax: 49-3641-65-4444

**Brooks Automation GmbH,  Freisinger Strasse 32, D-85737 Ismaning, Germany**

Tel: 49-89-9621-026-0    Fax: 49-89-9621-026-99

**BROWNING WINCHESTER**

1 Browning Place, Morgan, UT, 84050

Tel: (801) 876-2711      Fax: (801) 876-3331      www.browning.com

*Sales/distribution of port firearms, fishing rods, etc.*

**Browning Sports GmbH,  Allscheidt 7, D-40883 Ratingen, Germany**

**BRUSH WELLMAN INC.**

17876 St. Clair Ave., Cleveland, OH, 44110

Tel: (216) 486-4200      Fax: (216) 383-4091      www.brushwellman.com

*Mfr. beryllium, beryllium alloys and ceramics, specialty metal systems and precious metal products.*

**Brush Wellman GmbH,  Motorstrasse 34, D-70499, Stuttgart, Germany**

Tel: 49-711-830-930    Fax: 49-711-833-822

## BUCKEYE TECHNOLOGIES, INC.

1001 Tillman St., Memphis, TN, 38108-0407

Tel: (901) 320-8100  Fax: (901) 320-8131  www.bkitech.com

*Mfr. specialty cellulose and absorbency products.*

**Buckeye Technologies GmbH, Glückstadt, Germany**

## BULAB HOLDINGS INC.

1256 N. McLean Blvd, Memphis, TN, 38108

Tel: (901) 278-0330  Fax: (901) 276-5343  www.buckman.com

*Biological products; chemicals and chemical preparations.*

**Buckman Laboratories GmbH, Marienbader Platz 22, D-61348 Bad Homburg v.d.H, Germany**

Tel: 49-6172-670059  Fax: 49-6172-22107

## LEO BURNETT, DIV. B-COM 3 GROUP

35 West Wacker Drive, Chicago, IL, 60601

Tel: (312) 220-5959  Fax: (312) 220-6533  www.bcom3group.com

*Engaged in advertising, marketing, media buying and planning, and public relations.*

**Kastner & Partner GmbH, Werbeagentur, Kennedyallee 94, D-6000 Frankfurt/Main 1, Germany**

**Michale Conrad & Leo Burnett GmbH, Feuerbachstrasse 26, D-6000 Frankfurt/Main 1, Germany**

## BURSON-MARSTELLER

230 Park Ave., New York, NY, 10003-1566

Tel: (212) 614-4000  Fax: (212) 614-4262  www.bm.com

*Public relations/public affairs consultants.*

**Burson-Marsteller GmbH, Untermainkai 20, D-60329 Frankfurt/Main, Germany**

Tel: 49-69-23-8090  Fax: 49-69-23-80944  Emp: 50

**Burson-Marsteller Hamburg, Hopensack 19, D-20457 Hamburg, Germany**

Tel: 49-40-32110  Fax: 49-40-3233-1199

## BUSH BOAKE ALLEN INC.

7 Mercedes Drive, Montvale, NJ, 07645

Tel: (201) 391-9870  Fax: (201) 391-0860  www.bushboakeallen.com

*Mfr. aroma chemicals for fragrances and flavor products for seasonings.*

**Bush Boake Allen Deutschland GmbH, Am Burgholz 17, D052372 Kreuzau-Stockheim, Germany**

Tel: 49-24-215-9260

## C&D TECHNOLOGIES

1400 Union Meeting Road, Blue Bell, PA, 19422

Tel: (215) 619-2700  Fax: (215) 619-7840  www.cdtechno.com

*Mfr./produce electrical power storage and conversion products and industrial batteries.*

**C&D Technologies, Münich, Germany**

## CABLE DESIGN TECHNOLOGIES CORPORATION

661 Andersen Drive, Plaza 7, Pittsburgh, PA, 15220

Tel: (412) 937-2300  Fax: (412) 937-9690  www.cdtc.com

*Mfr. computer connector copper, fiber optic and composite cables.*

**HEW CDT, Gewerbegebiet Klingsiepen 12, D-51688 Wipperfurth, Germany**

Tel: 49-2267-6830

## CABOT CORPORATION

75 State Street, Boston, MA, 02109-1807

Tel: (617) 345-0100  Fax: (617) 342-6103  www.cabot-corp.com

*Mfr. carbon blacks, plastics; oil and gas, information systems.*

**Cabot GmbH, Postfach 901120, Hanau 9, Germany**

**Deloro Stellite GmbH (Weartec Div.), Postfach 520, Carl-Spaeterstr. 11, D-5400 Koblenz, Germany**

**Deutssche Beryllium GmbH (Cabot Berylco Div.),  Postfach 1620, D-6370 Oberursel, Germany**

**Nickel Contor Deutschland GmbH (Hitec Div.),  Taunusanlage 21, D-6000 Frankfurt/Main 1, Germany**

## CACI INTERNATIONAL INC.

1100 North Glebe Road, Arlington, VA, 22201

Tel:  (703) 841-7800         Fax:  (703) 841-7882          www.caci.com

*Provides simulation technology/software and designs factories, computer networks, and communications systems for military, electronic commerce digital document management, logistics and Y2K remediation.*

**CACI International, Inc.,  Frankfurt am Main, Germany**

## CALBIOCHEM-NOVABIOCHEM CORPORATION

PO Box 12087, La Jolla, CA, 92039

Tel:  (619) 450-9600         Fax:  (619) 452-3552          www.calbiochem.com

*Mfr. biochemicals, immunochemicals and reagents.*

**Calbiochem-Novabiochem GmbH,  Postfach 1167, Lisztweg 1, D-6232 Bad Soden, Germany**

## CALGON CARBON CORPORATION

400 Calgon Carbon Drive, Pittsburgh, PA, 15230-0717

Tel:  (412) 787-6700         Fax:  (412) 787-4541          www.calgoncarbon.com

*Mfr. activated carbon, related systems and services.*

**Calgon Carbon GmbH,  Robert-Hoch-Strasse 5-7, D-6078 Neu-Isenburg, Germany**

## CAMBREX CORPORATION

1 Meadowlands Plaza, East Rutherford, NJ, 07063

Tel:  (201) 804-3000         Fax:  (201) 804-9852          www.cambrex.com

*human health, animal health/agriculture and Mfr. biotechnology products and produce specialty chemicals.*

**Cambrex GmbH,  Wettsteinstrasse 4, D-82024 Taufkirchen, Germany**

Tel: 49-89-612-00821    Fax: 49-86-612-00825

**Midas Pharmachemie GmbH,  Weingasse, 36-6535 Gau-Algesheim, Germany**

Tel: 49-61-329900

## CAMBRIDGE TECHNOLOGY PARTNERS, INC.

8 Cambridge Center, Cambridge, MA, 02142

Tel:  (617) 374-9800         Fax:  (617) 914-8300          www.ctp.com

*Engaged in e-commerce consultancy.*

**Cambridge Technology Partners, Inc.,  Zeil 79, D-60313 Frankfurt, Germany**

Tel: 49-69-2174-1500

**Cambridge Technology Partners, Inc.,  Rosenheimer Straße 141, D-81671 Munchen, Germany**

Tel: 49-89-20600-1500

## CAMPBELL SOUP COMPANY

Campbell Place, Camden, NJ, 08103-1799

Tel:  (856) 342-4800         Fax:  (856) 342-3878          www.campbellsoup.com

*Mfr. food products.*

**Campbell Grocery Products, GmbH,  Frankfurt/Main, Germany**

**Eugen Lacroix, GmbH,  Frankfurt/Main, Germany**

## CANBERRA-PACKARD INDUSTRIES

800 Research Parkway, Meriden, CT, 06450

Tel:  (203) 238-2351         Fax:  (203) 235-1347          www.canberra.com

*Mfr. instruments for nuclear research.*

**Canberra Elektronik GmbH,  D-6000 Frankfurt, Germany**

## CARBOLINE COMPANY

350 Hanley Industrial Court, St. Louis, MO, 63144

Tel: (314) 644-1000    Fax: (314) 644-4617    www.carboline.com

*Mfr. coatings and sealants.*

**StonCor Germany, Schumanstrabe 18, 52146 Wurlselen, Germany**

Tel: 49-2405-44-1148   Fax: 49-2405-44-1169

## CARGILL, INC.

15407 McGinty Road West, Minnetonka, MN, 55440-5625

Tel: (612) 742-7575    Fax: (612) 742-7393    www.cargill.com

*Food products, feeds, animal products.*

**Deutsche Cargill GmbH, Ruedekenstrasse 51/ Am Hafen, 38239 Salzgitter-Beddingen, Germany**

## CARLSON COMPANIES, INC.

Carlson Parkway, PO Box 59159, Minneapolis, MN, 55459

Tel: (612) 550-4520    Fax: (612) 550-4580    www.cmg.carlson.com

*Marketing services agency.*

**LPP Carlson, Kreuzberger Ring 64, 65205 Weisbaden, Germany**

Tel: 49- 611-778-470   Fax: 49-611-778-4766

## THE CARLYLE GROUP L.P.

1001 Pennsylvania Avenue, NW, Washington, DC, 20004-2505

Tel: (202) 347-2626    Fax: (202) 347-1818    www.thecarlyegroup.com

*Global investor in defense contracts.*

**Carlyle Europe, ResidenzstraBe 18, D-80333 Münich, Germany**

Tel: 49-89-29-19-580

## CARPENTER TECHNOLOGY CORPORATION

101 W. Bern Street, PO Box 14662, Reading, PA, 19612-4662

Tel: (610) 208-2000    Fax: (610) 208-3214    www.cartech.com

*Mfr. specialty steels and structural ceramics for casting industrial.*

**Carpenter Technology (Deutschland) GmbH, Waldenbucher Strasse 22, D-7032 Sindelfingen 1, Germany**

## CARRIER CORPORATION

One Carrier Place, Farmington, CT, 06034-4015

Tel: (860) 674-3000    Fax: (860) 679-3010    www.carrier.com

*Mfr./distributor/services A/C, heating and refrigeration equipment.*

**Carrier GmbH, Münich, Germany**

Tel: 49-89-321-540   Fax: 49-89-321-5410

## CASCADE CORPORATION

2201 NE 201st Ave., Fairview, OR, 97024-9718

Tel: (503) 669-6300    Fax: (503) 669-6321    www.cascor.com

*Mfr. hydraulic forklift truck attachments.*

**Cascade GmbH, Klosterhofweg 52, D-4050 Munchen Gladbach 3, Germany**

## CASE CORPORATION

700 State Street, Racine, WI, 53404

Tel: (414) 636-6011    Fax: (414) 636-0200    www.casecorp.com

*Mfr./sale agricultural and construction equipment.*

**Case Germany GmbH, Heinrich-Fuchs-Strasse 124, D-69126 Heidelberg, Germany**

Tel: 49-6221-318-600   Fax: 49-6221-318-680   Contact: Gunther Apfalter

**Case Harvesting Systems, Berghausstrasse 1 - Postfach 110, D-01841 Neustadt, Germany**

Tel: 49-3596-53-2405   Fax: 49-3506-53-2202   Contact: Herbert Wolf, Gen. Mgr.

## CAT PUMPS

1681 94th Lane NE, Minneapolis, MN, 55449-4324

Tel: (612) 780-5440     Fax: (612) 780-2958     www.catpumps.com

*Mfr./distributor pumps.*

**Cat Pumps Deutschland GmbH, Buchwiese 2, D-65510 Idstein, Germany**

## CATAPULT COMMUNICATIONS CORPORATION

160 South Whisman Road, Mountain View, CA, 94041

Tel: (650) 960-1025     Fax: (650) 960-1029     www.catapult.com

*Mfr. test systems for telecommunications service providers.*

**Catapult Communications Corp., Lechwiesenstrasse 56, D-86899 Landsberg/Lech, Germany**

## CATERPILLAR INC.

100 NE Adams Street, Peoria, IL, 61629-6105

Tel: (309) 675-1000     Fax: (309) 675-1182     www.cat.com

*Mfr. earth/material-handling and construction machinery and equipment and engines.*

**Caterpillar Holding Germany GmbH, Münich, Germany**

**Claas Caterpillar Europe GmbH & Co. KG, Unterschleissheim, Germany**

## C.B. RICHARD ELLIS

533 South Fremont Ave., Los Angeles, CA, 90071-1712

Tel: (213) 613-3123     Fax: (213) 613-3535     www.cbrichardellis.com

*Commercial real estate services.*

**CB Richard Ellis GmbH, Maximilianstrasse 27, 80539 Münich, Germany**

**CB Richard Ellis GmbH, Feuerbachstrasse 26/32, 60325 Frankfurt am Main, Germany**

## CBS CORPORATION

51 West 52 Street, New York, NY, 10019

Tel: (212) 975-4321     Fax: (212) 975-9387     www.cbs.com

*TV/radio broadcasting, mfr. electronic systems for industry/defense, financial and environmental services.*

**H. Maihak AG, Samperstr. 38, D-2000 Hamburg 60, Germany**

**Westinghouse Controlmatic GmbH, Postfach 560200, D-6000 Frankfurt 56, Germany**

## CCH INCORPORATED

2700 Lake Cook Road, Riverwoods, IL, 60015

Tel: (847) 267-7000     Fax: (800) 224-8299     www.cch.com

*Provides tax and business law information and software for accounting, legal, human resources, securities and health care professionals.*

**CCH Europe GmbH, Parkstrasse 71-73, D-65191 Wiesbaden, Germany**

## CDM INTERNATIONAL INC.

50 Hampshire Street, Cambridge, MA, 02139

Tel: (617) 452-6000     Fax: (617) 452-8020     www.cdm.com

*Consulting engineers.*

**Jessberger Partners GmbH, Am Umweltpark 5, D-44793 Bochum, Germany**
Tel: 49-234-78775-355

## CEILCOTE AIR POLLUTION CONTROL

14955 Sprague Road, Strongsville, OH, 44136

Tel: (440) 243-0700     Fax: (440) 234-3486     www.ceilcoteapc.com

*Mfr. corrosion-resistant material, air pollution control equipment, construction services.*

**Air-Cure GmbH, Ostendstrasse 1, Pfungstadt D-64319, Germany**
Tel: 49-6157-91-55-0

## CEPHALON, INC.

145 Brandywine Pkwy., West Chester, PA, 19380

Tel: (610) 344-0200     Fax: (610) 344-0065     www.cephalon.com

*Engaged in healthscience, research and development.*

**Cephalon Germany,  Hippmannstrasse 13, D-80639 Munchen, Germany**

Tel: 49-89-1709-4499   Fax: 49-89-1709-4495   Contact: Uwe Mascheck

## CHART INDUSTRIES, INC.

5885 Landerbrook Drive, Cleveland, OH, 44124

Tel: (440) 753-1490     Fax: (440) 753-1491     www.chart-ind.com

*Mfr. cryogenic storage and shipping containers and related industrial products.*

**Chart Europe GmbH,  Brosshauser Strasse 20, D-42697 Solingen, Germany**

Tel: 49-212-700-570   Fax: 49-212-700-577

## CHECKPOINT SYSTEMS, INC.

101 Wolf Drive, Thorofare, NJ, 08086

Tel: (856) 848-1800     Fax: (856) 848-0937     www.checkpointsystems.com

*Mfr. test, measurement and closed-circuit television systems.*

**Checkpoint Systems Deutschland GmbH,  Forumstrasse 2, D-41468 Neuss, Germany**

Tel: 49-2131-93190   Fax: 49-2131-33303   Contact: Volker Kalkowski, Mng. Dir.

## CHEMETALL OAKITE

50 Valley Road, Berkeley Heights, NJ, 07922-2798

Tel: (908) 464-6900     Fax: (908) 464-7914     www.oakite.com

*Mfr. chemical products for industry cleaning and metal treating.*

**Chemetall GmbH Group,  Frankfurt/Main, Germany**

## THE CHERRY CORPORATION

3600 Sunset Ave., PO Box 718, Waukegan, IL, 60087

Tel: (847) 662-9200     Fax: (847) 662-2990     www.cherrycorp.com

*Mfr. electrical switches, electronic keyboards, controls and displays.*

**Cherry GmbH,  Industriestrasse 19, 91275 Auerbach/Opf., Germany**

Tel: 49-96-43180   Fax: 49-96-4318406

**Cherry GmbH,  Cherrystraße, D-91275 Auerbach/Opf, Germany**

Tel: 49-96-43180   Fax: 49-96-4318262

## CHESTERTON BINSWANGER INTERNATIONAL

Two Logan Square, 4th Floor, Philadelphia, PA, 19103-2759

Tel: (215) 448-6000     Fax: (215) 448-6238     www.cbbi.com

*Real estate and related services.*

**Blumenauer Berlin,  Tauentzienstrasse 9-12, Europa-Centre, 10789 Berlin, Germany**

**Blumenauer Dresden,  Bertolt-Brecht-Allee 9, 01309 Dresden, Germany**

**Blumenauer Dusseldor,  Georg-Glock-Strasse 2, 40474 Dusseldorf, Germany**

**Blumenauer Hamburg,  Neuer Dovenhof, Brandstwiete, 120457 Hamburg,  Germany**

**Blumenauer Immobilien,  Mendelssohnstr. 85, D-60325 Frankfurt, Germany**

**Blumenauer Leipzig,  Thomasiusstrasse 21, 04109 Leipzig, Germany**

**Blumenauer Nuremberg,  Laufamholzstrasse 116, 90482 Nuremberg,  Germany**

## A.W. CHESTERTON COMPANY

225 Fallon Road, Stoneham, MA, 02180

Tel: (781) 438-7000     Fax: (781) 438-8971     www.chesterton.com

*Packing gaskets, sealing products systems, etc.*

**Chesterton International (Deutschland) GmbH,  Carl-Zeiss-Ring 9, 85737 Ismaning, Germany**

**Chesterton International (Deutschland) GmbH,  Trierer Str. 12, D-68309 Mannheim, Germany**

## CHEVRON CHEMICAL COMPANY

1301 McKinney Street, Houston, TX, 77010

Tel: (713) 754-2000      Fax: (713) 754-2016      www.chevron.com

*Mfr. petro chemicals.*

**Orogil KG, Mainzer Str. 172, Postfach 190369, D-6000 Frankfurt/Main, Germany**

## CHICAGO BRIDGE & IRON COMPANY (CBI)

1501 North Division Street, Plainfield, IL, 60544

Tel: (815) 241-7546      Fax: (815) 439-6010      www.chicago-bridge.com

*Holding company: metal plate fabricating, construction, oil and gas drilling.*

**CBI Industriestahlbau GmbH, D-4650 Gelsenkirchen, Germany**

## CHICAGO RAWHIDE INDUSTRIES (CRI)

735 Tollgate Road, Elgin, IL, 60123

Tel: (847) 742-7840      Fax: (847) 742-7845      www.chicago-rawhide.com

*Mfr. shaft and face seals.*

**CR Elastomere GmbH, Dusseldorf Str. 121, D-51379 Leverkusen-Opladen, Germany**

## CHIQUITA BRANDS INTERNATIONAL INC.

250 East Fifth Street, Cincinnati, OH, 45202

Tel: (513) 784-8000      Fax: (513) 784-8030      www.chiquita.com

*Sale and distribution of bananas, fresh fruits and processed foods.*

**Chiquita Brands International, Münich, Germany**

## CHIRON CORPORATION

4560 Horton Street, Emeryville, CA, 94608-2916

Tel: (510) 655-8730      Fax: (510) 655-9910      www.chiron.com

*Engaged in biotechnology; biopharmaceuticals, blood testing and vaccines.*

**Chiron Behring GmbH, Emil Von Behring Strasse 76, Marburg 35041, Germany**
Tel: 49-6421-393-264

## THE CHUBB CORPORATION

15 Mountain View Road, Warren, NJ, 07061-1615

Tel: (908) 580-2000      Fax: (908) 580-3606      www.chubb.com

*Holding company for property and casualty insurance.*

**Chubb Insurance Co. of Europe, SA, Martin-Luther-Platz 28, D-40212 Düsseldorf, Germany**
Tel: 49-211-8773-0   Fax: 49-211-8773-333

**Chubb Insurance Company of Europe, SA, Fleethof Stadthausbrueke 1-3, D-20355 Hamburg, Germany**
Tel: 49-36-98050   Fax: 49-36-980590

**Chubb Insurance Company of Europe, SA, Niederlassung Munchen, Josephspitalstrabe 15, D-80332 Munchen, Germany**
Tel: 49-89-54551-0   Fax: 49-89-54551-12

**Chubb Insurance Company of Europe, SA, Freiherr Von Stein Strasse II, D-60323 Frankfurt/Main Strasse II, Germany**
Tel: 49-69-97-12160   Fax: 49-69-97-122633

## CIGNA COMPANIES

One Liberty Place, Philadelphia, PA, 19192

Tel: (215) 761-1000      Fax: (215) 761-5511      www.cigna.com

*Insurance, invest, health care and other financial services.*

**CIGNA Insurance Co. of Europe SA/NV, Erlenstrasse 2-6, D-6000 Frankfurt/Main, Germany**

**Esis Intl. Inc., Erlenstrasse 2-6, D-6000 Frankfurt/Main, Germany**

Insurance Co. of North America,  Direktion Fuer Deutschland, Erlenstrasse 2-6, D-6000 Frankfurt/Main, Germany

## CINCINNATI MILACRON INC.

4701 Marburg Ave., Cincinnati, OH, 45209

Tel: (513) 841-8100      Fax: (513) 841-8919      www.cinbus.com

*Develop/mfr. technologies for metalworking and plastics processing industrial.*

Cincinnati Milacron GmbH,  Malterdingen, Germany

## CINCOM SYSTEMS INC.

55 Merchant Street, Cincinnati, OH, 45446

Tel: (513) 612-2300      Fax: (513) 481-8332      www.cincom.com

*Develop/distributor computer software.*

Cincom Systems Deutschland,  Am Kronberger Hang , D-65824 Schwalbach, Germany

Cincom Systems GmbH,  19 Im Hargarten, 54316 Pluwig, Germany

Cincom Systems GmbH,  Industriestrasse 3, 70565 Stuttgart, Germany

Cincom Systems Inc.,  Holsteiner Chaussee 303b,  D-22457 Hamburg, Germany

## CINEMARK USA INC.

3900 Dallas Pkwy., Ste. 500, Plano, TX, 75093

Tel: (972) 665-1000      Fax: (972) 665-1004      www.cinemark.com

*Operates multiplex cinemas.*

Cinemark,  Herne 13, Dusseldorf, Germany

## CISCO SYSTEMS, INC.

170 West Tasman Drive, San Jose, CA, 95134-1706

Tel: (408) 526-4000      Fax: (408) 526-4100      www.cisco.com

*Develop/mfr./market computer hardware and software networking systems.*

Cisco Systems GmbH,  Isar Buero Park, Lilienthalstrasse 9, D-85399 Hallbergmoos, Germany

Tel: 49-811-55430    Fax: 49-811-554310

## THE CIT GROUP

1211 Avenue of the Americas, New York, NY, 10036

Tel: (212) 536-1390      Fax: (212) 536-1912      www.citgroup.com

*Engaged in commercial finance.*

Newcourt, Div. CIT Group,  Alexanderstrasse 59, Frankfurt 60489, Germany

Tel: 49-69-247-840

## CITIGROUP, INC.

153 East 53rd Street, New York, NY, 10043

Tel: (212) 559-1000      Fax: (212) 559-3646      www.citigroup.com

*Provides insurance and financial services worldwide.*

Citibank Aktiengesellschaft,  Neue Mainzer Strasse 75, D-60311 Frankfurt, Germany

Contact: Willy P. Socquet

## CITRIX SYSTEMS, INC.

6400 NW 6th Way, Fort Lauderdale, FL, 33309

Tel: (954) 267-3000      Fax: (954) 267-9319      www.citrix.com

*Developer of computer software.*

Citrix GmbH (Europe HQ),  Am Soeldnermoos 17, D-85399 Hallbergmoos, Germany

Tel: 49-89-607687-10    Fax: 49-89-607687-11

## CLAYTON INDUSTRIES

4213 N. Temple City Blvd., El Monte, CA, 91731

Tel: (626) 443-9381      Fax: (626) 442-1701      www.claytonindustries.com

*Mfr. steam generators, dynamometers and water treatment chemicals.*

**Clayton Deutschland GmbH, Mevissenstrasse 64a, D-47803 Krefeld, Germany**

Tel: 49-2151-8775-0    Fax: 49-2151-8775-22

## CLEARY GOTTLIEB STEEN & HAMILTON

One Liberty Plaza, New York, NY, 10006

Tel: (212) 225-2000      Fax: (212) 225-3999      www.cgsh.com

*International law firm.*

**Cleary, Gottlieb, Steen & Hamilton, Ulmenstrasse 37-39, D-6000 Frankfurt/Main, Germany**

## CNA FINANCIAL CORPORATION

CNA Plaza, Chicago, IL, 60685

Tel: (312) 822-5000      Fax: (312) 822-6419      www.cna.com

*Commercial property/casualty insurance policies.*

**CNA Insurance Company (Europe) Limited (CIE), Münich, Germany**

## COACH LEATHERWEAR COMPANY

516 West 34 Street, New York, NY, 10001

Tel: (212) 594-1850      Fax: (212) 594-1682      www.coach.com

*Mfr. and sales of high-quality leather products, including handbags and wallets.*

**Coach at E.C. Trading, Burgmauer 12, D-50667 Cologne, Germany**

## THE COASTAL CORPORATION

Nine Greenway Plaza, Houston, TX, 77046-0995

Tel: (713) 877-1400      Fax: (713) 877-6752      www.coastalcorp.com

*Oil refining, natural gas, related services; independent power production.*

**Holborn Europa Raffinerie GmbH, Hamburg, Germany**

## THE COCA-COLA COMPANY

PO Drawer 1734, Atlanta, GA, 30301

Tel: (404) 676-2121      Fax: (404) 676-6792      www.coca-cola.com

*Mfr./marketing/distributor soft drinks, syrups and concentrates, juice and juice-drink products.*

**Coca-Cola Eastern Europe GmbH, Frankenstrasse 348, D-4300 Essen, Germany**

Contact: John P. Sechi

**Coca-Cola Erfrischungsgetränke AG, Münich, Germany**

Contact: John P. Sechi

## COGNEX CORPORATION

1 Vision Drive, Natick, MA, 01760

Tel: (508) 650-3000      Fax: (508) 650-3333      www.cognex.com

*Mfr. machine vision systems.*

**Cognex Corporation Germany, Greschbachstrasse 12, D-76229 Karlsruhe, Germany**

Tel: 49-721-96187-0    Fax: 49-721-61566-1

## COHERENT INC.

5100 Patrick Henry Drive, PO Box 54980, Santa Clara, CA, 95056

Tel: (408) 764-4000      Fax: (408) 764-4800      www.cohr.com

*Mfr. lasers for science, industrial and medical.*

**Coherent GmbH, Diesenstrasse 5-b, D-64807 Dieburg, Germany**

**Lambda Physik GmbH, Hans-Bockler-Strasse 12, D-37079 Gottingen, Germany**

## COHU, INC.

5755 Kearny Vill Road, San Diego, CA, 92123

Tel: (858) 541-5194 Fax: (858) 277-0221 www.cohu.com

*Mfr. semiconductor test handling systems.*

**Macrotron Systems, Ammerthalstrasse 7, D-95551 Kirchheim, Münich, Germany**

Tel: 49-89-45111-0 Fax: 49-89-45111-102

## COIN ACCEPTORS INC.

300 Hunter Ave., St. Louis, MO, 63124

Tel: (314) 725-0100 Fax: (314) 725-1243 www.coinco.com

*Coin mechanisms for vending machinery.*

**Coin Acceptors GmbH, Siemensring 44D,47877 Willich, Germany**

Tel: 49-2154-205000 Fax: 49-12154-205002

## THE COLEMAN COMPANY, INC.

2111 E. 37th St., North, Wichita, KS, 67219

Tel: (316) 832-2700 Fax: (316) 832-2794 www.colemanoutdoors.com

*Mfr./distributor/sales camping and outdoor recreation products.*

**Coleman Deutschland GmbH, Ezetilstr., D-6303 Hungen 3, Germany**

## COLGATE-PALMOLIVE COMPANY

300 Park Ave., New York, NY, 10022

Tel: (212) 310-2000 Fax: (212) 310-2919 www.colgate.com

*Mfr. pharmaceuticals, cosmetics, toiletries and detergents.*

**Colgate-Palmolive GmbH, Liebigstr. 2-20, D-22113 Hamburg, Germany**

## COMCAST CORPORATION

1500 Market St., Philadelphia, PA, 19102

Tel: (215) 665-1700 Fax: (215) 981-7790 www.comcast.com

*Provides cable and broadband services and QVC electronic retailing.*

**QVC Deutschland GmbH, Kaistrasse 7-9, 40221 Dusseldorf, Germany**

Tel: 49-211-300-0 Fax: 49--211-3007-100

## COMDISCO INC.

6111 N. River Road, Rosemont, IL, 60018

Tel: (847) 698-3000 Fax: (847) 518-5440 www.comdisco.com

*Hi-tech asset and facility management and equipment leasing.*

**Comdisco Deutschland GmbH, Dusseldorf, Germany**

## COMMERCIAL INTERTECH CORPORATION

1775 Logan Ave., PO Box 239, Youngstown, OH, 44501-0239

Tel: (330) 746-8011 Fax: (330) 746-1148

*Mfr. hydraulic components, pre-engineered buildings and stamped metal products.*

**Commercial Intertech GmbH, Wilh. Theod. Romheld Str. 30, D-6500 Mainz, Germany**

**Hydraulik Rochlitz GmbH, Poststrasse 3, D-09290 Rochlitz, Germany**

**Sachsenhydraulik GmbH, Neefestrasse 96, Postfach 58, D-09116 Chemnitz, Germany**

## COMPAQ COMPUTER CORPORATION

20555 State Highway 249, PO Box 692000, Houston, TX, 77269-2000

Tel: (281) 370-0670 Fax: (281) 514-1740 www.compaq.com

*Develop/mfr. personal computers.*

**Compaq Computer EMES EmbH, PO Box 810244, D-81902 Münich, Germany**

Tel: 49-89-99330 Fax: 49-48-910-1705

**Compaq Computer GmbH, Einsteinring 30, D-85609 Dornach, Germany**

Tel: 49-89-99330 Fax: 49-89-9933-1158

## COMPUTER ASSOCIATES INTERNATIONAL INC.

One Computer Associates Plaza, Islandia, NY, 11788

Tel: (516) 342-5224       Fax: (516) 342-5329       www.cai.com

*Integrated business software for enterprise computing and information management, application development, manufacturing, financial applications and professional services.*

**Computer Associates GmbH, Hauptverwaltung, Marienburgstrasse 35, D-64297 Darmstadt, Germany**

Tel: 49-6151-4-9490

## COMPUTER SCIENCES CORPORATION

2100 East Grand Ave., El Segundo, CA, 90245

Tel: (310) 615-0311       Fax: (310) 322-9768       www.csc.com

*Information technology services, management consulting, systems integration, outsourcing.*

**CSC Computer Sciences GmbH -Plöenzke, Kiedrich/Rheingau, Germany**

Contact: Klaus C. Plöenzke, CEO

## COMPUWARE CORPORATION

31440 Northwestern Hwy., Farmington Hills, MI, 48334-2564

Tel: (248) 737-7300       Fax: (248) 737-7108       www.compuware.com

*Develop and market software for enterprise and e-commerce solutions.*

**Compuware GmbH, Niederkasseler Lohweg 20, 40547 Dusseldorf, Germany**

Tel: 49-211-5303-0

## COMSHARE INC.

555 Briarwood Circle, Ste. 200, Ann Arbor, MI, 48108-3302

Tel: (734) 994-4800       Fax: (734) 994-5895       www.comshare.com

*Managerial application software.*

**Comshare GmbH, Comshare Haus, Waltherstrasse 78, D-5000 Cologne 80, Germany**

## COMVERSE TECHNOLOGY, INC.

234 Crossways Park Drive, Woodbury, NY, 11797

Tel: (516) 677-7200       Fax: (516) 677-7355       www.comverse.com

*Mfr. telephone communication and recording systems.*

**Comverse Infosys GmbH, Am Storrenacker 2, D-76139 Karlsruhe, Germany**

Tel: 49-721-625-310    Fax: 49-721-625-3119

## CONAGRA INC.

One ConAgra Drive, Omaha, NE, 68102-5001

Tel: (402) 595-4000       Fax: (402) 595-4707       www.conagra.com

*Prepared/frozen foods, grains, flour, animal feeds, agro chemicals, poultry, meat, dairy products, including Healthy Choice, Butterball and Hunt's.*

**ConAgra Inc., München, Germany**

## CONCURRENT COMPUTER CORPORATION

4375 River Green Pkwy., Duluth, GA, 30096

Tel: (678) 258-4000       Fax: (678) 258-4300       www.ccur.com

*Mfr. computer systems and software.*

**Concurrent Computer Corporation GmbH, Schunannstrasse 7, D-64287 Darmstadt, Germany**

Tel: 49-6151-712069    Fax: 49-6151-7111267

**Concurrent Computer Corporation GmbH, Scheibenhardter Strasse 10, D-76275 Ettlingen/Ettlingenweir, Germany**

Tel: 49-7243-90922

**Concurrent Computer Corporation GmbH, Kampstrasse 53, D-52525 Heinsberg, Germany**

Tel: 49-161-323-1097

**Concurrent Computer Corporation GmbH, Lena-Christ Strasse 46, Martinsried, D-82152 Planegg, Münich, Germany**
Tel: 49-89-856-030    Fax: 49-89-856-03150

## CONEXANT SYSTEMS, INC.

4311 Jamboree Road, PO Box C, Newport Beach, CA, 92658-8902
Tel: (949) 483-4600        Fax: (949) 483-4078        www.conexant.com
*Provides semiconductor products for communications electronics.*
**Conexant Systems Germany GmbH, Paul-Gerhardt-Allee 50A, Munchen 81245, Germany**
Tel: 49-89-829-13220    Fax: 49-89-834-2734

## CONOCO INC.

PO Box 2197, 600 N. Dairy Ashford, Houston, TX, 77252
Tel: (281) 293-1000        Fax: (281) 293-1440        www.conoco.com
*Oil, gas, coal, chemicals and minerals.*
**CONDEA Petrochemie GmbH, Fritz-Staiger-Str., Postfach 2212, Brunsbuettel, Germany**
**Conoco Mineraloel GmbH, Hudtwalckerstr. 2-8, D-2000 Hamburg 39, Germany**

## CONTINENTAL AIRLINES INC.

2929 Allen Parkway, Ste. 2010, Houston, TX, 77019
Tel: (281) 834-5000        Fax: (281) 520-6329        www.continental.com
*International airline carrier.*
**Continental Airlines Inc., Münich, Germany**

## THE COOPER COMPANIES, INC.

6140 Stoneridge Mall Road, Ste. 590, Pleasanton, CA, 94588
Tel: (925) 460-3600        Fax: (925) 460-3649        www.coopercos.com
*Mfr. contact lenses and gynecological instruments.*
**CooperSurgical Leisegang Medical GmbH, Berlin, Germany**

## COOPER INDUSTRIES INC.

6600 Travis Street, Ste. 5800, Houston, TX, 77002
Tel: (713) 209-8400        Fax: (713) 209-8995        www.cooperindustries.com
*Mfr./distributor electrical products, tools, hardware and automotive products, fuses and accessories for electronic applications and circuit boards.*
**Apparatebau Hundsbach GmbH, Baden-Baden, Germany**
**CEAG Sicherheilslechnik GmbH, Senator-Schwartz-Reng 26, 59494 Soest, Germany**
Tel: 49-2921-690
**CEAG Sicherheitstechnik GmbH, Münich, Germany**
Tel: 49-29-21690    Fax: 49-29-2169-630
**Cooper Hand Tools Div., Besigheim, Germany**
**Cooper Power Tools Div., Westhausen, Germany**
**Metronix Elektronik GmbH, Braunschweig, Germany**

## COOPER TURBOCOMPRESSOR

3101 Broadway, PO Box 209, Buffalo, NY, 14225-0209
Tel: (716) 896-6600        Fax: (716) 896-1233        www.turbocompressor.com
*Mfr. air and gas compressors.*
**Cooper Turbocompressor GmbH, Heinrichstrasse 169, Dusseldorf D-40239 Germany**
Tel: 49-211-613051    Fax: 49-211-614718

## CORDIS CORPORATION

PO Box 25700, Miami, FL, 33102-5700
Tel: (305) 824-2000        Fax: (305) 824-2747        www.cordis.com
*Mfr. medical devices and systems.*
**Cordis Germany, Rheinische Strasse 2, 42781 Haan, Germany**

## CORNING INC.

One Riverfront Plaza, Corning, NY, 14831-0001

Tel: (607) 974-9000     Fax: (607) 974-8091       www.corning.com

*Mfr. glass and specialty materials, consumer products; communications, laboratory services.*

**Corning International GmbH, Abraham-Lincoln-Strasse 30, D-65189 Wiesbaden, Germany**

Tel: 49-611-7366-100    Fax: 49-611-7366-143

## COSMAIR INC.

575 Fifth Ave., New York, NY, 10017

Tel: (212) 818-1500     Fax: (212) 984-4776       www.cosmair.com

*Mfr. hair and skin care products.*

**Redken Laboratories GmbH, Friesstr. 15, D-6000 Frankfurt 60, Germany**

## COUDERT BROTHERS

1114 Ave. of the Americas, New York, NY, 10036-7794

Tel: (212) 626-4400     Fax: (212) 626-4120       www.coudert.com

*International law firm.*

**Coudert Brothers, Markgrafenstrasse 36, Am Gendarmenmarkt, D-10117 Berlin, Germany**

Tel: 49-30-202-2990    Fax: 49-30-202-29929    Contact: Dr. Karl H. Pilny

## COULTER PHARMACEUTICAL, INC.

600 Gateway Blvd., South San Francisco, CA, 94080

Tel: (650) 553-2000     Fax: (650) 553-2028       www.coulterpharm.com

*Mfr. blood analysis systems, flow cytometers, chemicals systems, scientific systems and reagents.*

**Coulter Electronics GmbH, Europark Fichtenhain B-13, Postfach 547, D-4150 Krefeld 1, Germany**

## CRANE COMPANY

100 First Stamford Place, Stamford, CT, 06907

Tel: (203) 363-7300     Fax: (203) 363-7359       www.craneco.com

*Diversified mfr./distributor of engineered industrial products and the largest American distributor of doors, windows and millwork.*

**National Rejectors Inc. GmbH, Zum Fruchthof 6, D-2150 Buxtehude, Germany**

## CRITICARE SYSTEMS INC.

20925 Crossroads Circle, Waukesha, WI, 53186

Tel: (262) 798-8282     Fax: (262) 798-8491       www.csiusa.com

*Develop/mfr. diagnostic and therapeutic products and patient monitoring systems..*

**Criticare Systems Inc. Europe, Gotzenmuhlweg 66, D-6380 Bad Homburg, Germany**

**Medlog GmbH, Gotzenmuhlweg 66, D-6380 Bad Homburg, Germany**

## CROMPTON CORPORATION

Benson Road, Middlebury, CT, 06749

Tel: (203) 573-2000     Fax:               www.crompton-knowles.com

*Mfr. dyes, colors, flavors, fragrances, specialty chemicals and industrial products.*

**Crompton GmbH, Grueneburgweg 16-18, D-6000 Frankfurt/Main 1, Germany**

**Crompton GmbH, Postfach 1540, IC Regionalvertrieb, Ernst Schering Str. 14, D-4709 Bergkamen 1, Germany**

**Crompton Polymers & Resins BV, Postfach 1160, Max-Wolf-Strasse 7, Industriegebiet West, D-6497 Steinau an der Strasse, Germany**

**Uniroyal GmbH, Huttenstr. 44, Aachen l, Germany**

## A.T. CROSS COMPANY

One Albion Road, Lincoln, RI, 02865

Tel: (401) 333-1200　　Fax: (401) 334-2861　　www.cross.com

*Mfr. writing instruments, leads, erasers and ink refills.*

**A.T. Cross GmbH, Rheinallee 189, Postfach 1220, D-55120 Mainz, Germany**

Tel: 49-6131-626010

## CROWN CORK & SEAL COMPANY, INC.

One Crown Way, Philadelphia, PA, 19154-4599

Tel: (215) 698-5100　　Fax: (215) 698-5201　　www.crowncork.com

*Mfr. metal and plastic packaging, including steel and aluminum cans for food, beverage and household products.*

**Bender-Werke GmbH, Postfach 245, D-6710 Frankenthal Pfalz, Germany**

## CROWN EQUIPMENT CORPORATION

40 South Washington Street, New Bremen, OH, 45869

Tel: (419) 629-2311　　Fax: (419) 629-2900　　www.crownlift.com

*Mfr./sales/services forklift trucks, stackers.*

**Crown Gabelstapler GmbH, Kronstadterstr. 11, D-8000 München 80, Germany**

## CSX CORPORATION

901 East Cary Street, Richmond, VA, 23860

Tel: (804) 782-1400　　Fax: (804) 782-6747　　www.csx.com

*Provides freight delivery and contract logistics services.*

**Container Terminal Germersheim (CTG), Wörthstrasse 13, 76726 Germersheim, Germany**

Tel: 49-7274-70825　Fax: 49-7274-70840

## CULLIGAN WATER TECHNOLOGIES

One Culligan Parkway, Northbrook, IL, 60062

Tel: (847) 205-6000　　Fax: (847) 205-6030　　www.culligan-man.com

*Water treatment products and services.*

**Culligan Deutschland GmbH, Jagerhofstrasse 3, D-40880 Ratingen, Germany**

Tel: 49-2102-40740　Fax: 49-2102-443960

## CUMMINS ENGINE COMPANY, INC.

500 Jackson Street, PO Box 3005, Columbus, IN, 47202-3005

Tel: (812) 377-5000　　Fax: (812) 377-4937　　www.cummins.com

*Mfr. diesel engines.*

**Cummins Diesel Deutschland GmbH, Postfach 1134, D-6080 Grob-Gerau, Germany**

**Cummins Diesel Deutschland GmbH, Odenwaldstrasse 23, 64521 Grob-Gerau, Germany**

## CURTIS, MALLET-PREVOST, COLT & MOSLE LLP

101 Park Ave., 35th Floor, New York, NY, 10178

Tel: (212) 696-6000　　Fax: (212) 697-1559　　www.cm-p.com

*International law firm.*

**Curtis, Mallet-Prevost, Colt & Mosle LLP, Staufenstrasse 42, 60323 Frankfurt Am Main, Germany**

Tel: 49-69-971-442-0

## CURTISS-WRIGHT CORPORATION

1200 Wall Street West, Lyndhurst, NJ, 07071-0635

Tel: (201) 896-8400　　Fax: (201) 438-5680　　www.curtisswright.com

*Mfr. precision components and systems, engineered services to aerospace, flow control and marine industry.*

**Metal Improvement Co. Inc., Otto-Hahn-Strasse 3, Postfach 1708, D-4750 Unna, Germany**

**Metal Improvement Co. Inc., Bahnstrasse 19, Postfach 2164, D-5657 Haan-Gruiten, Germany**

## CUTLER-HAMMER, DIV. EATON CORP.

173 Heatherdown Drive, Westerville, OH, 43082

Tel: (614) 882-3282      Fax: (614) 895-7111      www.cutlerhammer.com

*Mfr. electrical control products and power distribution equipment.*

**Eaton GmbH (Cutler-Hammer), Oranienpassage 1, D-57258 Freudenberg, Germany**

Tel: 49-2734-46-63-0   Fax: 49-2734-4-76-05

## CYLINK CORPORATION

3131 Jay Street, Santa Clara, CA, 95054

Tel: (408) 855-6000      Fax: (408) 855-6100      www.cyllink.com

*Develop and manufactures encryption software.*

**Algorithmic Research GmbH, Siemenstrasse 100, D-63755 Alzenau, Germany**

Tel: 49-6023-948560   Fax: 49-6023-948589

## CYPRESS SEMICONDUCTOR CORPORATION

3901 N. First Street, San Jose, CA, 95134-1599

Tel: (408) 943-2600      Fax: (408) 943-2796      www.cypress.com

*Mfr. integrated circuits.*

**Cypress Semiconductor, Muenchener Str. 15A, Zorneding 85604, Germany**

Tel: 49-8106-2448-0   Fax: 49-8106-2008-7

## CYTEC INDUSTRIES, INC.

5 Garret Mountain Plaza, West Paterson, NJ, 07424

Tel: (973) 357-3100      Fax: (973) 357-3054      www.cytec.com

*Mfr. specialty chemicals and materials,*

**Cytec Industries B.V., Hermann-Klammt Str. 3, 41460 Neuss, Germany**

Tel: 49-2131-9524-0

## DALLAS SEMICONDUCTOR CORPORATION

4401 South Beltway Parkway, Dallas, TX, 75244-3292

Tel: (972) 371-4000      Fax: (972) 371-4956      www.dalsemi.com

*Design/mfr. computer chips and chip-based subsystems.*

**Dallas Semiconductor, Am Soldnermoos 17, D-85399 Hallbergmoos, Germany**

Tel: 49-811-600960   Fax: 49-811-6009620   Contact: David Thomas, Area Sales Mgr.

## LEO A. DALY

8600 Indian Hills Drive, Omaha, NE, 68114

Tel: (402) 391-8111      Fax: (402) 391-8564      www.leoadaly.com

*Planning, arch, engineering and interior design services.*

**Leo A. Daly GmbH, Luisenstrasse 44, 10117 Berlin, Germany**

Tel: 49-30-262-2058   Fax: 49-30-262-2600   Contact: Peter Crone    Emp: 2

## DAMES & MOORE GROUP

911 Wilshire Boulevard, Ste. 700, Los Angeles, CA, 90017

Tel: (213) 996-2200      Fax: (213) 996-2290      www.dames.com

*Engineering, environmental and construction management services.*

**Dames & Moore, Leberstrasse 37, D-10829 Berlin, Germany**

**Dames & Moore, Frintroper Strasse 53, D-45355 Essen, Germany**

**Dames & Moore, Goernestrasse 32, D-20249 Hamburg, Germany**

**Dames & Moore, Hoechster Strasse 92, D-65835 Liederbach/Ts., Germany**

## DANA CORPORATION

4500 Dorr Street, Toledo, OH, 43615

Tel: (419) 535-4500      Fax: (419) 535-4643      www.dana.com

*Mfr./sales of automotive, heavy truck, off-highway, fluid and mechanical power components and engine parts, filters and gaskets.*

**ATV Antriebstechnik Vertriers Gmbh,  Benzstrasse 1, D-7448 Wolfschlugen, Germany**

**Erwin Hengstler Hydraulik GmbH,  Postfach 1220, Schaetzlestrasse 2-8, D-7613 Hausach, Germany**

**Perfect Circle, Div. Dana,  Hannoversche Strasse, Barginhausen D-30890, Germany**

**Stieber Fiormstrag GmbH,  Dieselstrasse 14, D-8046 Garching, Germany**

**Thermoplast + Apparatebau GmbH,  Postfach 1220, Black u. Decker-Str. 25, 65510 Idstein/Taunus Germany**

**Victor Rinz Dichtungs GmbH,  Reinzstrasse 3-7, Postfach 1909 D-89229, Neu-Ulm Germany**

Tel: 49-731-70460   Fax: 49-731-719089

**Warner Electric GmbH,  Postfach 2008, D-7440 Nurtingen, Germany**

**Weatherhead GmbH,  Dieselstrasse 14, D-8046 Garching, Germany**

## DANAHER CORPORATION

1250 24th St. NW, Ste. 800, Washington, DC, 20037

Tel: (202) 828-0850      Fax: (202) 828-0860      www.danaher.com

*Mfr. tools and controls.*

**Danaher GmbH,  Willstaetterstr. 11, Dusseldorf D-40649, Germany**

**Danaher GmbH,  Koningsweg 10, Berlin D-14163, Germany**

Tel: 49-30809-860   Contact: Dr. Bruno Lang

**Danaher GmbH,  Uhlandstrasse 49, Aldingen D-78554, Germany**

## DANIEL INDUSTRIES INC.

9753 Pine Lake Drive, PO Box 55435, Houston, TX, 77224

Tel: (713) 467-6000      Fax: (713) 827-3889      www.danielind.com

*Oil/gas equipment and systems; geophysical services.*

**Daniel Messtechnik,  Gartenstraße 2/12, D-1591 Potsdam, Germany**

Tel: 49-331-76-10   Fax: 49-331-76-14-01

## D'ARCY MASIUS BENTON & BOWLES INC. (DMB&B)

1675 Broadway, New York, NY, 10019

Tel: (212) 468-3622      Fax: (212) 468-2987      www.dmbb.com

*Full service international advertising and communications group.*

**DMB&B Europe,  Karlplatz 21, D-4000 Düsseldorf 1, Germany**

**Dorger Dialog,  Kaufmannshaus, Bleichenbruecke 10, D-2000 Hamburg 36, Germany**

## DATA GENERAL CORPORATION

4400 Computer Drive, Westboro, MA, 01580

Tel: (508) 898-5000      Fax: (508) 366-1319      www.dg.com

*Design, mfr. general purpose computer systems and peripheral products and services.*

**Data General GmbH,  Am Kronberger Hang 3, D-62854 Schwalbach/TS, Germany**

**Data General GmbH,  Hammfelddamm 6, D-41460 Neuss, Germany**

## DATA I/O CORPORATION

PO Box 97046, 10525 Willows Road, NE, Redmond, WA, 98073-9746

Tel: (425) 881-6444      Fax: (425) 882-1043      www.dataio.com

*Mfr. computer testing devices.*

**Data I/O Germany,  Münich, Germany**

Tel: 49-8-985-8580

## DATA TRANSLATION INC.

100 Locke Drive, Marlborough, MA, 01752-1192

Tel: (508) 481-3700      Fax: (508) 481-8620      www.datx.com

*Mfr. peripheral boards for image and array processing micro-computers.*

**Data Translation GmbH, Im Weilerlen 10, D-74321 Bietigheim-Bissingen, Germany**

Tel: 49-7142-95310

## DATASCOPE CORPORATION

14 Phillips Pkwy., Montvale, NJ, 07645

Tel: (201) 391-8100      Fax: (201) 307-5400      www.datascope.com

*Mfr. medical devices.*

**Datascope GmbH, Zeppelinstrasse 2-, D-64625 Bensheim, Germany**

## DATAWARE TECHNOLOGIES INC.

1 Canal Park, Cambridge, MA, 02141

Tel: (617) 621-0820      Fax: (617) 577-2413      www.dataware.com

*Provides e-business solutions.*

**Dataware Technologies GmbH, Barthstrasse 24, D-80339 Münich, Germany**

## DAVIS POLK & WARDWELL

450 Lexington Ave., New York, NY, 10017

Tel: (212) 450-4000      Fax: (212) 450-4800      www.dpw.com

*International law firm.*

**Davis Polk & Wardwell, MesseTurm, D-60308 Frankfurt am Main, Germany**

Tel: 49-69-9757030    Fax: 49-69-747744

## DAVOX CORPORATION

6 Technology Park Drive, Westford, MA, 01886

Tel: (978) 952-0200      Fax: (978) 952-0201      www.davox.com

*Mfr. call-center software for telephone operations.*

**Davox GmbH, Hayn Parc 11, An der Trift 65, 63303 Dreieich BRD, Germany**

Tel: 49-6103-90230

## DAYCO PRODUCTS INC.

PO Box 1004, Dayton, OH, 45401-1004

Tel: (937) 226-7000      Fax: (937) 226-4689      www.dayco.com

*Mfr. diversified auto, industrial and household products.*

**Dayco Corp. GmbH, Daimlerstr. 6, Postfach 36, D-7401 Pliezhausen 1, Germany**

## DAYTON PROGRESS CORPORATION

500 Progress Road, Dayton, OH, 45449

Tel: (937) 859-5111      Fax: (937) 859-5353      www.daytonprogress.com

*Punches, dies and guide bushings.*

**Schneider Stanznormalien GmbH, Im Heidegraben 8 Postfach 1165, 61401 Oberursel, Germany**

## DDB NEEDHAM WORLDWIDE INC.

437 Madison Ave., New York, NY, 10022

Tel: (212) 415-2000      Fax: (212) 415-3417      www.ddbn.com

*Advertising agency.*

**DDB GmbH, Streitfeldstrasse 19, D-8000 Münich 80, Germany**

**DDB GmbH, Postfach 1065, Osterholzallee 76, D-7140 Ludwigsburg, Germany**

**DDB GmbH, Schadowstrasse 48/50, D-4000 Düsseldorf 1, Germany**

**Heye & Partner GmbH, Mittelweg 17, D-2000 Hamburg 13, Germany**

**Heye & Partner GmbH, Ottobrunner Strasse 28, Unteraching, D-8025 Münich, Germany**

## DEERE & COMPANY

One John Deere Road, Moline, IL, 61265

Tel: (309) 765-8000 Fax: (309) 765-5772 www.deere.com

*Mfr./sale agricultural, construction, utility, forestry and lawn, grounds care equipment.*

**John Deere Internatinal GmbH, Steubenstrasse 36-42, D-68163 Mannheim, Germany**

Tel: 49-621-829-01 Fax: 49-621-829-8427

## DELL COMPUTER CORPORATION

One Dell Way, Round Rock, TX, 78682-2222

Tel: (512) 338-4400 Fax: (512) 728-3653 www.dell.com

*Direct marketer and supplier of computer systems.*

**Dell Computer GmbH, Monzastrasse 4, D-63225 Langen, Germany**

Tel: 49-6103-971-0 Fax: 49-6103-971-701 Contact: Hans-Jurgen Mammitesch, Mng. Dir.

## DELOITTE TOUCHE TOHMATSU INTERNATIONAL

1633 Broadway, New York, NY, 10019

Tel: (212) 492-4000 Fax: (212) 392-4154 www.deloitte.com

*Accounting, audit, tax and management consulting services.*

**Deloitte & Touche GmbH, Schumannstrase 27, D-60325 Frankfurt/Main, Germany**

## DELTA AIR LINES INC.

PO Box 20706, Atlanta, GA, 30320-6001

Tel: (404) 715-2600 Fax: (404) 715-5494 www.delta-air.com

*Major worldwide airline; international air transport services.*

**Delta Air Lines Inc., Frankfurt, Germany**

## DENTSPLY INTERNATIONAL

570 West College Ave., PO Box 872, York, PA, 17405-0872

Tel: (717) 845-7511 Fax: (717) 843-6357 www.dentsply.com

*Mfr. and distribution of dental supplies and equipment.*

**Denstsply GmbH, Postfach 101074, Eisenbahntrasse 180, D-63303 Dreieich, Germany**

Tel: 49-6103-6070

**Dentsply Gendex, Albert-Einstein - Ring 13, D-22761 Hamburg, Germany**

Tel: 49-4089-96880

**Dentsply GmbH, Postfach 5346, DeTrey Strasse 1, D-78467 Konstanz 12, Germany**

Tel: 49-7531-5830

## DETROIT DIESEL CORPORATION

13400 Outer Drive West, Detroit, MI, 48239

Tel: (313) 592-5000 Fax: (313) 592-5058 www.detroitdiesel.com

*Mfr. diesel and aircraft engines, heavy-duty transmissions.*

**Diesel Und Getriebe Service, Wernher Von Braun Strasse 11, 6500 Mainz-Hechtsheim, Germany**

Tel: 49-61-315-8070 Fax: 49-61-315-80714

## THE DEUTSCH COMPANY

2444 Wilshire Blvd, Santa Monica, CA, 90403

Tel: (310) 453-0055 Fax: (310) 453-6467

*Electronic components.*

**Deutsch-Amerikanische Asphalt-Produkte GmbH, Huhnerposten 14, D-2000 Hamburg 1, Germany**

## THE DEXTER CORPORATION

1 Elm Street, Windsor Locks, CT, 06096

Tel: (860) 627-9051 Fax: (860) 627-7078 www.dexelec.com

*Mfr. polymer products, magnetic materials, biotechnology.*

**Dexter Aerospace Materials, Knorrstrasse 83a, W8 München 40, Germany**

**Dexter Automotive Materials,  Im Knollen 3, D-69231 Rauemberg, Germany**

**Dexter Magnetic Materials GmbH,  Lilienthal Strasse 5, D-8036 Garching, Germany**

**Life Technologies GmbH,  Postfach 1212, Dieselstrasse 5, D-7514 Eggenstein, Germany**

**The Dexter GmbH Ltd.,  Lilienthal Str. 5, D-8046 Garching, Germany**

## DHL WORLDWIDE EXPRESS

50 California Avenue, San Francisco, CA, 94111

Tel:  (415) 677-6100        Fax:  (415) 824-9700        www.dhl.com

*Worldwide air express carrier.*

**DHL Worldwide Express,  Lyoner Strasse 20, D-60528 Frankfurt, Germany**

Tel: 49-69-66-904494

## DIAGNOSTIC PRODUCTS CORPORATION

5700 West 96th Street, Los Angeles, CA, 90045

Tel:  (310) 645-8200        Fax:  (310) 645-9999        www.dpcweb.com

*Mfr. diagnostic products.*

**DPC Biermann GmbH,  Hohe Strasse 4-8, D-61231 Bad Nauheim, Germany**

Tel: 49-6032-994-00   Fax: 49-6032-994-200

## THE DIAL CORPORATION

15501 North Dial Blvd., Scottsdale, AZ, 85260-1619

Tel:  (480) 754-3425        Fax:  (480) 754-1098        www.dialcorp.com

*Mfr. soaps, detergents, air fresheners, specialty personal care products and Armour Star canned meats.*

**Dial/Henkel LLC (JV),  Düsseldorf, Germany**

## DICTAPHONE CORPORATION

3191 Broadbridge Ave., Stratford, CT, 06497-2559

Tel:  (203) 381-7000        Fax:  (203) 381-7100        www.dictaphone.com

*Mfr./sale dictation, telephone answering and multi-channel voice communications recording systems.*

**Dictaphone Deutschland GmbH,  Bad-Homburg, Germany**

Tel: 49-6172-682682

## DIEBOLD INC.

5995 Mayfair Road, North Canton, OH, 44720-8077

Tel:  (330) 490-4000        Fax:  (330) 490-3794        www.diebold.com

*Mfr. automated banking systems; security services for banking industrial and related fields.*

**Diebold Germany GmbH,  Zur Falkenburg 84, 484 32 Rheine, Germany**

Tel: 49-2572-2881   Fax: 49-2572-151208

## DIGITAL ORIGIN, INC.

460 East Middlefield Road, Mountainview, CA, 94043

Tel:  (650) 404-6300        Fax:  (650) 404-6200        www.digitalorigin.com

*Mfr. Digital Video (DV) software products.*

**Media 100 GmbH,  Hallbergmoos, Germany**

## DIMON INCORPORATED

512 Bridge Street, PO Box 681, Danville, VA, 24543-0681

Tel:  (804) 792-7511        Fax:  (804) 791-0377        www.dimon.com

*One of world's largest importer and exporters of leaf tobacco.*

**DIMON Rotag A.G.,  PO Box 10 01 02, D-76231 Karlsruhe, Germany**

Tel: 49-721-509-010   Fax: 49-721-509-0111

## DIONEX CORPORATION

1228 Titan Way, PO Box 3603, Sunnyvale, CA, 94086-3603

Tel: (408) 737-0700    Fax: (408) 730-9403    www.dionex.com

*Develop/mfr./market chromatography systems and related products.*

**Dionex GmbH,  Am Woertzgarten 10, D-65510 Idstein, Germany**

## WALT DISNEY COMPANY

500 South Buena Vista Street, Burbank, CA, 91521

Tel: (818) 560-1000    Fax: (818) 560-1930    www.disney.com

*Film/TV production, theme parks, resorts, publishing, recording and retail stores.*

**Walt Disney Production (Germany) GmbH,  Savignystr 76, D-6000 Frankfurt/Main, Germany**

## DMC STRATEX NETWORKS, INC.

170 Rose Orchard Way, San Jose, CA, 95134

Tel: (408) 943-0777    Fax: (408) 944-1648    www.dmcstratexnetworks.com

*Designs, manufactures, and markets advanced wireless solutions for wireless broadband access.*

**DMC Stratex Networks,  Gute Anger 3, 85356 Freising, Germany**

Tel: 49-8161-9927-0

## DME COMPANY

29111 Stephenson Highway, Madison Heights, MI, 48071

Tel: (248) 398-6000    Fax: (248) 544-5705    www.dmeco.com

*Basic tooling for plastic molding and die casting.*

**DME Germany,  D-7106 Neuenstadt am Kocher, Germany**

## DO ALL COMPANY

254 North Laurel Ave., Des Plaines, IL, 60016

Tel: (847) 803-7380    Fax: (847) 699-7524    www.doall.com

*Distributors of machinery tools, metal cutting tools, instruments and industrial supplies for metalworking industry.*

**DoALL GmbH,  Kleberstrasse 5, D-4020 Mettmann, Germany**

## DOBOY PACKAGING MACHINERY INC.

869 South Knowles Ave., New Richmond, WI, 54017-1797

Tel: (715) 246-6511    Fax: (715) 246-6539    www.doboy.com

*Mfr. packaging machinery.*

**Doboy Verpackungsmaschinen GmbH,  Bendemannstrasse 11, D-4000 Düsseldorf 1, Germany**

## DOCUMENTUM, INC.

6801 Koll Center Pkwy., Pleasanton, CA, 94566

Tel: (925) 600-6800    Fax: (925) 600-6850    www.documentum.com

*Mfr. content management software.*

**Documentum International Inc.,  Erlenhof Park, Unterhaching, Inselkammerstrasse 2, 82008 Unterhaching, Germany**

## DOLE FOOD COMPANY, INC.

31365 Oak Crest Drive, Westlake Village, CA, 91361

Tel: (818) 879-6600    Fax: (818) 879-6615    www.dole.com

*Produces/distributes fresh fruits and vegetables and canned juices and fruits.*

**Dole Food Company,  Münich, Germany**

## DOMINICK & DOMINICK INC.

Financial Square, 32 Old Slip, New York, NY, 10005

Tel: (212) 558-8800    Fax: (212) 248-0592

*Investment brokers.*

**Dominick & Dominick GmbH,  Westendstr. 24, D-6000 Frankfurt Main, Germany**

## DONALDSON COMPANY, INC.

1400 West 94th Street, Minneapolis, MN, 55431

Tel: (612) 887-3131      Fax: (612) 887-3155      www.donaldson.com

*Mfr. filtration systems and replacement parts.*

**Donaldson Gesellschaft m.b.H., Postfach 1251, D-48233 Dülmen, Germany**

## DONNA KARAN INTERNATIONAL INC.

550 Seventh Ave., New York, NY, 10018

Tel: (212) 789-1500      Fax: (212) 921-3526      www.donnakaran.com

*Design/manufacture/sale men's, women's, and children's clothes.*

**Donna Karan International (DKNY), Berlin, Germany**

## R.R. DONNELLEY & SONS COMPANY

77 West Wacker Drive, Chicago, IL, 60601-1696

Tel: (312) 326-8000      Fax: (312) 326-8543      www.rrdonnelley.com

*Commercial printing, allied communication services.*

**R. R. Donnelley Deutschland GmbH, Bockenheimer Landstrasse 39 (5th Fl.), D-60325 Frankfurt am Main, Germany**

Tel: 49-69-1708-8300   Fax: 49-69-1708-8143

## DONNELLY CORPORATION

49 W. 3rd St., Holland, MI, 49423-2813

Tel: (616) 786-7000      Fax: (616) 786-6034      www.donnelly.com

*Mfr. fabricated, molded and coated glass products for the automotive and electronics industries.*

**Donnelly Hohe GmbH & Co. KG / Mirror Systems, Industriestrasse 10-16, D97904, Dorfprozelten, Germany**

**Hohe GmbH & Co. KG, Hauptstrasse 36, D-97903 Collenberg, Germany**

Tel: 49-93-768-0   Fax: 49-93-768-1133   Contact: Hans Huber, CEO

## DOUBLECLICK, INC.

450 West 33rd Street, New York, NY, 10001

Tel: (212) 683-0001      Fax: (212) 889-0062      www.doubleclick.net

*Engaged in online advertising.*

**Doubleclick GmbH, Koelner Strasse 10, 65760 Eshborn, Germany**

Tel: 49-6196-400-870

**Doubleclick GmbH, Phoenixhof, Ruhrstrasse 11a, 22761 Hamburg, Germany**

Tel: 49-408-53570

**Doubleclick GmbH, Scheinerstrasse 7, 81679 Munchen, Germany**

**Doubleclick GmbH, Kolner Strasse 17, 40211 Dusseldorf, Germany**

## DOVER CORPORATION

280 Park Ave., New York, NY, 10017-1292

Tel: (212) 922-1640      Fax: (212) 922-1656      www.dovercorporation.com

*Holding company for varied industries; assembly and testing equipment, oil-well gear and other industrial products.*

**European Lift Engineering, Schleswigstrabe 3 GMB, D-30853 Langenhagen, Germany**

Tel: 49-511-972420   Fax: 49-511-9723730

## THE DOW CHEMICAL COMPANY

2030 Dow Center, Midland, MI, 48674

Tel: (517) 636-1000      Fax: (517) 636-3228      www.dow.com

*Mfr. chemicals, plastics, pharmaceuticals, agricultural products, consumer products.*

**Dow Chemical GmbH, Grunerstr. 46, D-4000 Düsseldorf 1, Germany**

**Dow Chemical GmbH, Gansheidestr. 55, D-7000 Stuttgart 1, Germany**

**Dow Chemical GmbH, Briennerstrasse 44, D-8000 München 2, Germany**

Dow Chemical GmbH, Werk Stade Butzenflether Sand, D-2160 Stade-Butzfletz, Germany

Dow Chemical GmbH, Kommandantendeich 8, D-2160 Stade, Germany

Dow Chemical GmbH, Winterhunder Weg 29/31, D-2000 Hamburg 76, Germany

Dow Chemical GmbH, Wiesenhuttenstr. 18, D-6000 Frankfurt/Main, Germany

Dow Deutschland Inc., Werk Rheinmünster, Industriestr. 1, D-77836 Rheinmünster, Germany

## DRAFT WORLDWIDE

633 North St. Clair Street, Chicago, IL, 60611-3211

Tel: (312) 944-3500     Fax: (312) 944-3566     www.draftworldwide.com

*Full service international advertising agency, engaged in brand building, direct and promotional marketing.*

**DraftWorldwide GmbH, Wandsbeker Zollstrasse 15, 22041 Hamburg, Germany**

Tel: 49-40-6891-35-85   Fax: 49-40-6891-35-87

**Mailpool, TheresienstraBe 10, D-04129 Leipzig, Germany**

Tel: 49-34-9120-833   Fax: 49-341-9120-847   Contact: Christina Dorn, Supervisor

**Mailpool, Birkenwaldstrasse 200, D-70191 Stuttgart, Germany**

Tel: 49-7-11-257-3050   Fax: 49-7-11-257-9240   Contact: E. Wolff, Co-Mng. Dir.

**Peter Reincke/DraftWorldwide, Mühlstrasse 98a, 63741 Aschaffenburg, Germany**

Tel: 49-6021-4024-0   Fax: 49-6021-4024-13   Contact: Peter Richard Reincke

## DRAKE BEAM MORIN INC.

101 Huntington Ave., Boston, MA, 02199

Tel: (617) 375-9500     Fax: (617) 267-2011     www.dbm.com

*Human resource management consulting and training.*

**DBM Deutschland Hdqtrs., v. Rundstedt & Partner GmbH, Konigsalle 70, D-40212 Düsseldorf, Germany**

Tel: 49-211-83-9612   Fax: 49-211-13-4322

## DRESSER INSTRUMENT DIVISION

250 East Main Street, Stratford, CT, 06614-5145

Tel: (203) 378-8281     Fax: (203) 385-0357     www.dresserinstruments.com

*Mfr. pressure gauges and temperature instruments.*

**Dresser Europe GmbH, Postfach 11 20, Max-Planck-Strasse 1, D-52499 Baesweiler, Germany**

Tel: 49-2401-8080   Fax: 49-2401-7027

## DRESSER-RAND COMPANY

10077 Grogans Mill Road, Ste. 500, The Woodlands, TX, 77380

Tel: (281) 363-7650     Fax: (281) 363-7654     www.dresser-rand.com

*Provides energy conversion solutions.*

**Dresser-Rand GmbH, Postfach 101629, 46016 Oberhausen, Germany**

## DRG INTERNATIONAL INC.

PO Box 1188, 1162 Highway 22 East, Mountainside, NJ, 07092

Tel: (908) 233-2075     Fax: (908) 233-0758     www.drgintl.com

*Mfr./sale/service medical devices, diagnostic kits, clinical equipment.*

**DRG Instruments GmbH, Frankfurter Strasse 59, D-35037 Marburg, Germany**

Tel: 49-6421-17-000   Fax: 49-6421-921-100   Contact: Wilhelm Saenger, Mng. Dir.

## DRS TECHNOLOGIES, INC.

5 Sylvan Way, Parsippany, NJ, 07054

Tel: (973) 898-1500     Fax: (973) 898-4730     www.drs.com

*Mfr. advanced products for military, aerospace and commercial applications.*

**DRS Hadland GmbH, Implerstraße 89, D-81371 Münich, Germany**

## E.I. DU PONT DE NEMOURS & COMPANY

1007 Market Street, Wilmington, DE, 19898

Tel: (302) 774-1000        Fax: (302) 774-7321        www.dupont.com

*Mfr./sale diversified chemicals, plastics, specialty products and fibers.*

**Du Pont de Nemours (Deutschland) GmbH, Hans-Bocklerstr. 33, D-4000 Düsseldorf Nord, Germany**

## THE DUN & BRADSTREET CORPORATION

1 Diamond Hill Road, Murray Hill, NJ, 07974

Tel: (908) 665-5000        Fax: (908) 665-5524        www.dnbcorp.com

*Provides corporate credit, marketing and accounts-receivable management services and publishes credit ratings and financial information.*

**D&B Schimmelpfeng GmbH, Hahnstrasse 31-35, D-60528 Frankfurt/Main, Germany**

Tel: 49-69-663030

## DUNHAM-BUSH INC.

175 South Street, West Hartford, CT, 06110

Tel: (860) 548-3780        Fax: (860) 548-1703        www.dunham-bush.com

*Provides innovative solutions for the heating, air conditioning and refrigeration segments.*

**Dunham-Bush GmbH, Wiesenstr. 5, D-6140 Bensheim 1, Germany**

## DUO FASTENER CORPORATION

2400 Galvin Dr., Elgin, IL, 60123

Tel: (847) 783-5500        Fax: (847) 669-7301        www.duo-fast.com

*Staplers, tackers and nailers.*

**Duo-Fast Europe GmbH, Ruhrstr. 49, D-4041 Norf, Germany**

**Vessfoff & Co., Duo-Fast GmbH, D-5757 Wickède, Germany**

## DYN CORPORATION

11710 Plaza America Drive, Reston, VA, 20190

Tel: (703) 261-5000        Fax: (703) 261-5090        www.dyncorp.com

*Diversified technical services.*

**ITS Intl. Service, Schiersteiner Str. 52, Lindsey Air Station, D-6200 Wiesbaden, Germany**

## EAGLE GLOBAL LOGISTICS (EGL)

15350 Vickery Drive, Houston, TX, 77032

Tel: (281) 618-3100        Fax: (281) 618-3100        www.eaglegl.com

*Ocean/air freight forwarding, customs brokerage, packing and wholesale, logistics management and insurance.*

**Circle Freight International, Flughafen, Franchtgebaude 1st Fl., D-13405 Berlin  Germany**

Tel: 49-30-410-13397    Fax: 49-30-413-5659

**Circle Freight International Speditionsgesellschaft MbH, Am Suedpark 10, D-65241Kelsterbach, Germany**

Tel: 49-6107-750-980    Fax: 49-6107-790-945

**Circle Freight International Speditionsgesellschaft MbH, Flughafen, Frachtgebaude, D-70629 Stuttgart Germany**

Tel: 49-711-798-013    Fax: 49-711-795-644

**Circle Freight International Speditionsgesellschaft MbH, Cadolto Geb., Flughfenstrasse 100, D-90411 Nuernberg, Germany**

Tel: 49-911-356-9300    Fax: 49-911-365-9301

**Circle Freight International Speditionsgesellschaft MbH, Flughafen Muenchen, Air Cargo Ctr., Modul F - 3rd Fl.- Rm. 327-331, D-85356 Münich, Germany**

Tel: 49-89-975-9437-0    Fax: 49-89-975-9437-6

**Circle Freight International Speditionsgesellschaft MbH, Flughafen Fuhlsbuettel, Frachtgebaeude 150, Room 2010-2113, D-22335 Hamburg Germany**

Tel: 49-40-507-5200-1    Fax: 49-40-506-564

**Circle Freight International Speditionsgesellschaft mbH, Langer Kornweg 19-23, Alfa Haus - 3rd Fl., D-65451 Kelsterbach, Germany**

Tel: 49-6107-750-924  Fax: 49-6107-907-318

**Circle Freight International Speditionsgesellschaft MbH, Flughafenstrasse, Frachtgebaude, D-01109 Dresden, Germany**

Tel: 49-351-881-4830  Fax: 49-351-881-4831

**Circle Freight International Speditionsgesellschaft mbH, Frachthalle 2 - Room 185-186, D-51147 Cologne, Germany**

Tel: 49-2203-402-174  Fax: 49-2203-402-238

**Circle Freight International Speditionsgesellschaft MbH, Aeropark Ratingen-West, Broichhofstrasse 5, D-40880 Ratingen, Germany**

Tel: 49-2102-474-077  Fax: 49-2101-471-204

**Max Grunhut Circle Freight International, Billhorner Deich 96, D-20539 Hamburg, Germany**

Tel: 49-40-788-700  Fax: 49-40-788-70111

**Max Grunhut, Circle Freight International, Martinistrasse 33, D-28195 Bremen, Germany**

Tel: 49-421-366-90  Fax: 49-421-366-9666

**Max Grunhut, Circle Freight International, C. T. Nordhafen, Gate House 3, D-27568 Bremerhaven, Germany**

Tel: 49-471-400-97  Fax: 49-471-412-055

## EASTMAN CHEMICAL

100 North Eastman Road, Kingsport, TN, 37660

Tel: (423) 229-2000  Fax: (423) 229-1351  www.eastman.com

*Mfr. plastics, chemicals, fibers.*

**Eastman Chemical B.V., Zweigniederlassung Koln, Charlottenstrasse 61, D-51149 Koln, Germany**

Tel: 49-2203-1705-24  Fax: 49-2203-1705-0  Contact: Norbert Uecker, Mgr.

## EASTMAN KODAK COMPANY

343 State Street, Rochester, NY, 14650

Tel: (716) 724-4000  Fax: (716) 724-1089  www.kodak.com

*Develop/mfr. photo and chemicals products, information management/video/copier systems, fibers/plastics for various industry.*

**Eastman Chemical Intl. AG, Xantenerstr. 105, D-5000 Cologne 60, Germany**

**Kodak AG, Postfach 60 03 45, Hedelfinger Strasse, D-7000 Stuttgart 60, Germany**

## EATON CORPORATION

Eaton Center, 1111 Superior Ave., Cleveland, OH, 44114-2584

Tel: (216) 523-5000  Fax: (216) 479-7068  www.eaton.com

*Advanced technical products for transportation and industrial markets.*

**Eaton GmbH, Am Lindenkamp 31, D-5620 Velbert Rheinland, Germany**

## EBSCO INDUSTRIES

PO Box 1943, Birmingham, AL, 35201

Tel: (205) 991-6600  Fax: (205) 995-1586  www.ebscoind.com

*Engaged in information management services, journal and periodical subscription services, fishing lure manufacturing, custom printing, loose-leaf binder manufacturing and specialty office and computer furniture sales and distribution.*

**EBSCO Subscription Services, Bodenstedtstrasse 6, D-6200 Wiesbaden, Germany**

## ECHLIN INC.

100 Double Beach Road, Branford, CT, 06405

Tel: (203) 481-5751  Fax: (203) 481-6485  www.echlin.com

*Supplies commercial vehicle components and auto fluid handling systems for the used car market.*

**FAG Kugelfischer, Münich, Germany**

## ECI TELECOM LTD.

12950 Worldgate Dr., Herndon, VA, 20170

Tel: (703) 456-3400      Fax: (703) 456-3410        www.ecitele.com

*Designs, develops, manufactures, markets and supports end-to-end digital telecommunications solutions.*

**ECI Telecom GmbH, In der Au 27 61440 Oberursel, Germany**

Tel: 49-6171-6209-0    Fax: 49-6171-6209-88

## ECOLAB INC.

370 N. Wabasha Street, St. Paul, MN, 55102

Tel: (651) 293-2233      Fax: (651) 293-2379        www.ecolab.com

*Develop/mfr. premium cleaning, sanitizing and maintenance products and services for the hospitality, institutional, and residential markets.*

**Henkel-Ecolab (JV), IDR Gebaude, Reisholzer Werftrasse 42, D-4000 Düsseldorf, Germany**

Tel: 49-211-9893-101

## ECOLOGY AND ENVIRONMENT INC.

368 Pleasant View Drive, Lancaster, NY, 14086-1397

Tel: (716) 684-8060      Fax: (716) 684-0844        www.ecolen.com

*Environmental, scientific and engineering consulting.*

**E&E Umwelt Baratung GmbH, Chemnitzer Strassse 13, Postfach 7, D-09222 Gruna, Germany**

## EDDIE BAUER INC.

PO Box 97000, Redmond, WA, 98073

Tel: (425) 882-6100      Fax: (425) 882-6383        www.eddiebauer.com

*Clothing retailer and mail order catalog company.*

**Eddie Bauer Inc., Münich, Germany**

## EDELMAN PUBLIC RELATIONS WORLDWIDE

200 East Randolph Drive, 62nd Fl., Chicago, IL, 60601

Tel: (312) 240-3000      Fax: (312) 240-0596        www.edelman.com

*International independent public relations firm.*

**Edelman PR Worldwide, Bettinastrasse 64, D-60325 Frankfurt am Main 1, Germany**

Tel: 49-69-75-61-990    Fax: 49-69-75-61-9910    Contact: Eduard Weber-Bemnet, Mng. Dir.

## J.D. EDWARDS & COMPANY

One Technology Way, Denver, CO, 80237

Tel: (303) 334-4000      Fax: (303) 334-4970        www.jdedwards.com

*Computer software products.*

**J. D. Edwards - Germany, Monzastrasse 2B, D-63885 Langen, Germany**

Tel: 49-6103-7620    Fax: 49-6103-762299

**J. D. Edwards - Germany, Osterbekstrasse 90b, D-22083 Hamburg, Germany**

Tel: 49-40-27814-5    Fax: 49-40-27814-799

## EFCO

1800 NE Broadway Ave., Des Moines, IA, 50316-0386

Tel: (515) 266-1141      Fax: (515) 266-7970        www.efco-usa.com

*Mfr. systems for concrete construction.*

**EFCO Schalungsbau GmbH, Bahnhofstrasse 1, D-82402 Seeshaupt, Germany**

## EG&G INC.

900 Clopper Road, Ste. 200, Gaithersburg, MD, 20878

Tel: (301) 840-3000      Fax: (301) 590-0502        www.egginc.com

*Diversified R/D, mfr. and services.*

**EG&G Berthold, Calmbacher Strasse 22, Postfach 100163, D-75323 Bad Wildbad, Germany**

**EG&G GmbH Reticon, Hohenlindener Str. 12, D-81677 Münich, Germany**

EG&G GmbH/Instrument Div., Hohenlindener Str. 12, D-81677 Münich, Germany

EG&G GmbH/Sealol Euroseals, Weher Koeppel 6, D-65013 Wiesbaden, Germany

EG&G Heimann Optoelectronics GmbH, Weher Koeppel 6, D-65199 Wiesbaden, Germany

## ELANCO ANIMAL HEALTH

500 East 96th Street, Ste. 125, Indianapolis, IN, 46240

Tel: (317) 276-3000     Fax: (317) 276-6116     www.elanco.com

*Antibiotics and fine chemicals.*

**Elanco Animal Health, Teichweg 3, 35396 Giessen, Germany**

## ELECTRIC FURNACE COMPANY

435 Wilson Street, Salem, OH, 44460

Tel: (330) 332-4661     Fax: (330) 332-1853     www.electricfurnace.com

*Mfr./design heat treating furnaces for metals industrial.*

**Electric Furnace (Germany)**
**GmbH, Lohstätte 4 - Postfach 1327, D-47513 Kleve, Germany**

Tel: 49-2821-77590

## ELECTRO SCIENTIFIC INDUSTRIES, INC.

13900 NW Science Park Drive, Portland, OR, 97229

Tel: (503) 641-4141     Fax: (503) 643-4873     www.esi.com

*Mfg. production and testing equipment used in manufacture of electronic components in pagers and cellular communication devices.*

**Electro Scientific Industries GmbH, Riesstrasse 17, D-80992 Munchen 50, Germany**

Tel: 49-89-149-0070   Fax: 49-89-149-00720   Contact: Robert Meisenbacher

## ELECTROGLAS INC.

6042 Silver Creek Valley Road, San Jose, CA, 95138

Tel: (408) 528-3000     Fax: (408) 528-3542     www.electroglas.com

*Mfr. semi-conductor test equipment, automatic wafer probers.*

**Electroglas GmbH, Carl-Zeiss Strasse 5, D-85748 Garching, Germany**

## ELECTRONIC ARTS INC.

209 Redwood Shores Pkwy., Redwood City, CA, 94065

Tel: (650) 628-1500     Fax: (650) 628-1413     www.ea.com

*Distribution and sales of entertainment software.*

**Electronic Arts/Kingsoft, Münich, Germany**

## ELECTRONIC DATA SYSTEMS CORPORATION (EDS)

5400 Legacy Dr., Plano, TX, 75024

Tel: (972) 605-6000     Fax: (972) 605-2643     www.eds.com

*Provides professional services; management consulting, e.solutions, business process management and information solutions.*

**EDS Germany, Eisenstrasse 56, 65428 Ruesselsheim, Hesse**
**Germany**

Tel: 49-6142-80-3507

## ELECTRONICS FOR IMAGING, INC.

303 Velocity Way, Foster City, CA, 94404

Tel: (650) 357-3500     Fax: (650) 357-3907     www.efi.com

*Design/mfr. computer software and hardware for color desktop publishing.*

**EFI GmbH, Luegallee 18, D-40545 Düesseldorf, Germany**

Tel: 49-211-576841

**EFI GmbH, Kaiserwerther Strasse 115, D-40880 Ratingen**
**Düesseldorf, Germany**

Tel: 49 2102-74540

## ELECTRO-SCIENCE LABORATORIES, INC.

416 East Church Road, King of Prussia, PA, 19406

Tel: (610) 272-8000     Fax: (610) 272-6759     www.electroscience.com

*Mfr. advanced thick film materials for hybrid microcircuits and other electronic packaging and component applications.*

**ESL Deutschland, Sendinger Tor Platz 8, D-8000 München 2, Germany**

## EMC CORPORATION

35 Parkwood Drive, Hopkinton, MA, 01748-9103

Tel: (508) 435-1000     Fax: (508) 435-8884     www.emc.com

*Designs/supplies intelligent enterprise storage and retrieval technology for open systems, mainframes and midrange environments.*

**EMC Computer Systems Deutschland GmbH, Suedwestpark 92, D-90449 Neurnberg, Germany**

Tel: 49-911-688698-0

**EMC Computer Systems Deutschland GmbH, Boeblinger Strabe 29, D-71229 Leonberg Stuttgartt, Germany**

Tel: 49-7152-979340

**EMC Computer Systems Deutschland GmbH, Auguste-Victoria-Allee 4, D-13403 Berlin, Germany**

Tel: 49-30-417071-0

**EMC Computer Systems Deutschland GmbH, Stefan-George-Ring 6, D-81929 München, Germany**

Tel: 49-89-930960-0

**EMC Computer Systems Deutschland GmbH, Hammfelddamm 6, D-41460 Neuss Düsseldorf, Germany**

Tel: 49-2131-9191-0

**EMC Computer Systems Deutschland GmbH, Messerschmittstrasse 4, D-80992 München, Germany**

Tel: 49-89-143132-0

**EMC Computer Systems Deutschland GmbH, Osterbekstrabe 906, D-22083 Hamburg, Germany**

Tel: 49-40-271315-00

**EMC Computer Systems Deutschland GmbH, Schwalbach/TS, D-65824 Frankfurt, Germany**

Tel: 49-6196-4728-0

## EMCO WHEATON DTM, INC.

2501 Constant Comment Place, Louisville, KY, 40299

Tel: (502) 266-6677     Fax: (502) 266-6689     www.emcowheaton.com

*Design, development and manufacture of environmentally safe vapor and fluid transfer products for petroleum, petrochemical, chemical and industrial applications.*

**EMCO Wheaton GmbH, Emcostr. 2-4, Postfach 25 35 75, Kerchhain 1, Germany**

## EMERSON & CUMING SPECIALTY POLYMERS

46 Manning Road, Bellerica, MA, 01821

Tel: (978) 436-9700     Fax: (978) 436-9701     www.emersoncuming.com

*Mfr. high performance encapsulants, adhesives and coatings for the automotive, telecommunications and electronic industries.*

**Emerson & Cuming GmbH, Emil-von-Behring-Strasse 2, D-60439 Frankfurt Main, Germany**

## EMERY WORLDWIDE

One Lagoon Drive, Ste. 400, Redwood City, CA, 94065

Tel: (650) 596-9600     Fax: (650) 596-7901     www.emeryworld.com

*Freight transport, global logistics and air cargo.*

**Emery Worldwide, Langer Komweg 8, D-65451 Kelsterbach Frankfurt Main, Germany**

## ENCAD, INC.

6059 Cornerstone Court West, San Diego, CA, 92121

Tel: (858) 452-0882     Fax: (858) 452-5618       www.encad.com

*Mfr. large color printers for specialized graphics.*

**Encad Europe SA, Alte Landstrasse 21, D-85521 Ottobrunn, Germany**

Tel: 49-89-6603-903

## ENCYCLOPAEDIA BRITANNICA INC.

310 S. Michigan Ave., Chicago, IL, 60604

Tel: (312) 427-9700     Fax: (312) 294-2176       www.eb.com

*Publishing; books.*

**Encyclopaedia Britannica (Germany) Ltd., Hildebrandtstrasse 4, D-40215 Dusseldorf, Germany**

## ENERGIZER HOLDINGS, INC.

800 Chouteau Avenue, St. Louis, MO, 63164

Tel: (314) 982-2970     Fax: (214) 982-2752       www.energizer.com

*Mfr. Eveready and Energizer brand batteries and lighting products.*

**Ralston Energy Systems, Max Planck Strasse 30, PO Box 3243, 40699 Erkrath-Dusseldorf, Germany**

Tel: 49-11-2002109   Fax: 49-211-20020

## ENERPAC

P.O. Box 3241, Milwaukee, WI, 53201-3241

Tel: (414) 781-6600     Fax: (414) 781-1049       www.enerpac.com

*Mfr. hydraulic cylinders, pumps, valves, presses, tools, accessories and system components.*

**ENERPAC**
**Applied Power GmbH, PO Box 300113, D-40401 Düsseldorf, Germany**

## ENGELHARD CORPORATION

101 Wood Ave. S., CN 770, Iselin, NJ, 08830

Tel: (732) 205-5000     Fax: (732) 632-9253       www.engelhard.com

*Mfr. pigments, additives, catalysts, chemicals, engineered materials.*

**Engelhard-Clal Germany, Lise-Meitner Strasse 7, D-63303 Dreieich, Germany**

Tel: 49-61-03-93450

## ENRON CORPORATION

1400 Smith Street, Houston, TX, 77002-7369

Tel: (713) 853-6161     Fax: (713) 853-3129       www.enron.com

*Exploration, production, transportation and distribution of integrated natural gas and electricity.*

**Enron Energie GmbH, Brosenstrasse 2-4, 60313 Frankfurt, Germany**

Tel: 49-69-1330-80

**Tacke Windenergie GmbH, Holsterfeld 5A, Salzbergen 48499, Germany**

Tel: 49-597-197-0871

## EPICOR SOFTWARE CORPORATION

195 Technology Drive, Irvine, CA, 92618

Tel: (949) 585-4000     Fax: (949) 450-4419       www.epicor.com

*Mfr. software for e-business.*

**Epicor Deutschland GmbH, Gutenbergstrasse 5, D-85716 Unterschießheim, Münich, Germany**

Tel: 49-89-317060

## E-PRESENCE, INC.

120 Flanders Road, Westboro, MA, 01581

Tel: (508) 898-1000      Fax: (508) 898-1755      www.epresence.com

*Provides electronic business services.*

**e-Presence Germany, Kapellenstr. 10, 85622 Feldkirchen, Germany**

Tel: 49-89-990-2240

## ERICO PRODUCTS INC.

34600 Solon Road, Cleveland, OH, 44139

Tel: (440) 248-0100      Fax: (440) 248-0723      www.erico.com

*Mfr. electric welding apparatus and hardware, metal stampings, specialty fasteners.*

**Erico Elektrotechnische, Spezialfabrik GmbH, Postfach Steinalben, D-66851 Schwanenmuehle, Germany**

Tel: 49-63-079-1810

## ERNST & YOUNG, LLP

787 Seventh Ave., New York, NY, 10019

Tel: (212) 773-3000      Fax: (212) 773-6350      www.eyi.com

*Accounting and audit, tax and management consulting services.*

**Ernst & Young GmbH, Eschersheimer Landstrasse 14, D-60322 Frankfurt am Main, Germany**

Tel: 49-69-152-08-01   Fax: 49-69-152-08-550   Contact: Karin Skiba

## ESCO CORPORATION

2141 NW 25th Ave., Portland, OR, 97210

Tel: (503) 228-2141      Fax: (503) 778-6330      www.escocorp.com

*Mfr. equipment for mining, construction and forestry industries.*

**ESCO Corp., Moenchengladbach, Germany**

## ESCO ELECTRONICS CORPORATION

8888 Ladue Road, Ste. 200, St. Louis, MO, 63124-2090

Tel: (314) 213-7200      Fax: (314) 213-7250      www.escostl.com

*Electronic subassemblies and components.*

**Esco Electronics Corp., Münich, Germany**

## ESTERLINE TECHNOLOGIES

10800 NE 8th Street, Ste. 600, Bellevue, WA, 98004

Tel: (425) 453-9400      Fax: (425) 453-2916      www.esterline.com

*Mfr. equipment and instruments for industrial automation, precision measure, data acquisition.*

**Excellon Europe GmbH, Juston-von-Liebig-Str. 19, D-6057 Dietzenbach, Germany**

Tel: 49-6074-3000

## ETEC SYSTEMS, INC.

26460 Corporate Ave., Hayward, CA, 94545

Tel: (510) 783-9210      Fax: (510) 887-2870      www.etec.com

*Mfr. of photolithography equipment used in semiconductor manufacturing.*

**Etec EBT and Etec GmbH, Philip-Hauck-Str. 6, D-85622 Feldkirchen, Germany**

Tel: 49-89-90507-210   Fax: 49-89-90507-170

## ETHYL CORPORATION

330 South 4th Street, PO Box 2189, Richmond, VA, 23219

Tel: (804) 788-5000      Fax: (804) 788-5688      www.ethyl.com

*Provide additive chemistry solutions to enhance the performance of petroleum products.*

**Ethyl Mineraloel-Additives GmbH, Oberstrasse 14b, D-20144 Hamburg, Germany**

Tel: 49-40-42-92-90-0

## EURO RSCG WORLDWIDE

350 Hudson Street, New York, NY, 10014

Tel: (212) 886-2000      Fax: (212) 886-2016      www.eurorscg.com

*International advertising agency group.*

**ABC Berlin,  Kurfuerstendamm 66, Berlin, Germany**

## EXCELLON AUTOMATION

24751 Crenshaw Boulevard, Torrance, CA, 90505

Tel: (310) 534-6300      Fax: (310) 534-6777      www.excellon.com

*PCB drilling and routing machines; optical inspection equipment.*

**Excellon Europa GmbH,  PO Box 1328, 36113 Dietzenbach, Germany**

Tel: 49-6074-3000

## EXCELON INC.

25 Mall Road, Burlington, MA, 01803

Tel: (781) 674-5000      Fax: (781) 674-5010      www.exceloncorp.com

*Developer of object-oriented database management systems software.*

**eXcelon Deutschland GmbH,  Kreuzberger Ring 64, 65205 Wiesbaden. Germany**

Tel: 49-611-977190    Fax: 49-611-977-1919

## EXIDE CORPORATION

645 Penn St., Reading, PA, 19601

Tel: (610) 378-0500      Fax: (610) 378-0824      www.exideworld.com

*Mfr. lead-acid automotive and industrial batteries.*

**Exide Germany,  Budingen, Germany**

## EXPEDITORS INTERNATIONAL OF WASHINGTON INC.

1015 Third Avenue, 12th Fl., Seattle, WA, 98104-1182

Tel: (206) 674-3400      Fax: (206) 682-9777      www.expd.com

*Air/ocean freight forwarding, customs brokerage, international logistics solutions.*

**Expeditors International GmbH - Frankfurt,  Langer Kornweg 27-29, D-65451 Kelsterbach, Germany**

Tel: 49-6107-7990    Fax: 49-6107-63179

## EXXON MOBIL CORPORATION

5959 Las Colinas Blvd., Irving, TX, 75039-2298

Tel: (972) 444-1000      Fax: (972) 444-1882      www.exxon.com

*Petroleum exploration, production, refining; mfr. petroleum and chemicals products; coal and minerals.*

**Brigitta Erdgas GmbH,  Katstadtring 2, D-2000 Hamburg 60, Germany**

**Exxon Mobil, Inc.,  Kapstadtring 2, D-2000 Hamburg 60, Germany**

**Exxon Mobil, Inc.,  Neusser Landstrasse 16, D-50735 Koln, Germany**

Tel: 49-221-770-31

**Exxon Mobil, Inc.,  Neusser Landestrasse 16, D-50735 Köln, Germany**

Tel: 49-221-77031    Fax: 49-221-770-3320

**Exxon Mobil, Inc.,  Postfach 10 03 55, D-85003 Ingolstadt, Germany**

## FABREEKA INTERNATIONAL INC.

1023 Turnpike, PO Box 210, Stoughton, MA, 02072

Tel: (781) 341-3655      Fax: (781) 341-3983      www.fabreeka.com

*Mfr. vibration isolation materials; consulting and engineering services.*

**Fabreeka Deutschland GmbH,  Postfach 103, D-64570 Buttelborn, Germany**

Tel: 49-6152-9597-0    Fax: 49-6152-9597-40

## FACTSET RESEARCH SYSTEMS INC.

1 Greenwich Plaza, Greenwich, CT, 06830

Tel: (203) 863-1599      Fax: (203) 863-1501      www.factset.com

*Provides on-line financial information to financial professionals.*

**FactSet Limited, Trianon-Gebaeude 7/F, Mainzer Landstrasse 16, Frankfurt 60323, Germany**

Tel: 49-69-97168-200

## FAEGRE & BENSON LLP

2200 Norwest Center, 90 South Seventh Street, Minneapolis, MN, 55402-3901

Tel: (612) 336-3000      Fax: (612) 336-3026      www.faegre.com

*International law firm.*

**Faegre & Benson LLP, Wiesenau 1, D-60323 Frankfurt Am Main, Germany**

Tel: 49-69-971-227-0   Fax: 49-69-971-227-70   Contact: Philip B. Haleen, Ptnr.

## FAIR, ISAAC AND COMPANY, INC.

200 Smith Ranch Road, San Rafael, CA, 94903

Tel: (415) 472-2211      Fax: (415) 492-5691      www.fairisaac.com

*Mfr. automated systems for credit and loan approvals.*

**Fair, Isaac and Co., Berliner Strasse 207-211, D-65205 Wiesbaden, Germany**

Tel: 49-611-97850

## FAIRCHILD AEROSPACE CORPORATION

10823 NE Entrance Rd., San Antonio, TX, 78216

Tel: (210) 824-9421      Fax: (210) 824-9476      www.faidor.com

*Mfr. turboprop aircraft.*

**Fairchild Dornier, PO Box 1103, Airfield Oberpfassenhofen, D-8230 Wessling, Germany**

Tel: 49-8153-300

## FARREL CORPORATION

25 Main Street, Ansonia, CT, 06401

Tel: (203) 736-5500      Fax: (203) 735-6267      www.farrel.com

*Mfr. polymer processing equipment.*

**Farrel-Rockstedt GmbH, Haupstrasse 1, D-5481 Schalkenbach, Germany**

## FEDERAL-MOGUL CORPORATION

26555 Northwestern Highway, PO Box 1966, Southfield, MI, 48034

Tel: (248) 354-7700      Fax: (248) 354-8983      www.federal-mogul.com

*Mfr./distributor precision parts for automobiles, trucks, farm and construction vehicles.*

**Federal-Mogul GmbH, Otto-Hahn-Strausse 26-28, D-65520 Bad Camberg, Germany**

**F-M Motorentiele Holding GmbH, Münich, Germany**

**Glyco AG, Münich, Germany**

**Glyco Antriebstechnik GmbH, Münich, Germany**

**Glyco KG, Münich, Germany**

## FEDEX CORPORATION

942 South Shady Grove Rd., Memphis, TN, 38120

Tel: (901) 369-3600      Fax: (901) 395-2000      www.fdxcorp.com

*Package express delivery service.*

**Federal Express (Deutschland) GmbH, Wanheimer Str. 61, D-4000 Düsseldorf 30, Germany**

Tel: 800-1230800

**Federal Express (Deutschland) GmbH, Kleiner Kornweg 6-24, D-6092 Kezsterbach, Germany**

Tel: 800-1230800

**Federal Express (Deutschland) GmbH, Flughafen, Gebaude 192, D-2000 Hamburg 63, Germany**

Tel: 800-1230800

**Federal Express (Deutschland) GmbH, Stahlgruberring 32, D-8000 Münich 82, Germany**
Tel: 800-1230800

## FEI CORPORATION

7451 N.W. Evergreen Pkwy., Hillsboro, OR, 97124-5830

Tel: (503) 640-7500     Fax: (503) 640-7509     www.feicompany.com

*Design and mfr. of charged particle beam systems serving the research, development and production needs of customers in semiconductor, data storage, and industry/institute markets.*

**FEI Deutschland GmbH, Kirchenstrasse 2, D-85622 Feldkirchen, Germany**
Tel: 45-561-9983611

## FERRO CORPORATION

1000 Lakeside Ave., Cleveland, OH, 44114-7000

Tel: (216) 641-8580     Fax: (216) 696-5784     www.ferro.com

*Mfr. Specialty chemicals, coatings, plastics, colors, refractories.*

**Ferro GmbH, Electro Materials Division, Obere Vorstadt 16, D-71063 Sindelfingen, Germany**
Tel: 49-7031-809003   Fax: 49-7031-809694

**Ferro GmbH, Postfach 1032, Langenbergstrasse 10, D-67657 Kaiserslautern, Germany**
Tel: 49-631-41640   Fax: 49-631-4164-147   Contact: C.L. Kolff

**Ferro GmbH Enamel Lab, Amt Schwarzenberg, Robert-Koch Strasse 16a, D-9430 Schwarzenberg, Germany**
Tel: 49-3774-22066   Fax: 49-3774-25567

**Ferro Plastics GmbH, Osningstrasse 12, D-33605 Bielefeld, Germany**
Tel: 49-521-25084   Fax: 49-521-25086

**Ruhr Pulverlack GmbH, Zur Alten Ruhr 4, D-59755 Arnsberg, Germany**
Tel: 49-2932-62990   Fax: 49-2932-629936   Contact: Gunter Jung, Dir.

## FERROFLUIDICS CORPORATION

40 Simon Street, Nashua, NH, 03061

Tel: (603) 883-9800     Fax: (603) 883-2308     www.ferrofluidics.com

*Mfr. rotary feedthrough designs, emission seals, automated crystal-growing systems, bearings, ferrofluids.*

**AP&T GmbH, Hohes Gestade 14, D-72622 Nurtingen, Germany**

## FIBERMARK, INC.

161 Wellington Rd., Brattleboro, VT, 05302

Tel: (802) 257-0365     Fax: (802) 257-5900     www.fibermark.com

*Mfr. specialty fiber-based materials, including insulating printed circuit boards, air filters, vacuum cleaner bags and tape substrates.*

**FiberMark Gessner and Filter Media, GmbH, Otto Von Steinbeis-Strasse 14b , D-83052 Bruckmühl, Germany**
Tel: 49-8062-703-0

**FiberMark Lahnstein GmbH, Auf Brühl 15-27, 56112 Lahnstein, Germany**
Tel: 49-2621-177-0

## FileNET CORPORATION

3565 Harbor Boulevard, Costa Mesa, CA, 92626

Tel: (714) 966-3400     Fax: (714) 966-3490     www.filenet.com

*Provides integrated document management (IDM) software and services for internet and client server-based imaging, workflow, cold and electronic document management solutions.*

**FileNET GmbH, Dietrich-Bonhoeffer-Strasse 4, D-61380 Bad Homburg v.d.H, Germany**
Tel: 49-6172-963-0   Fax: 49-6172-963-478

## FINNIGAN CORPORATION

355 River Oaks Parkway, San Jose, CA, 95134-1991

Tel: (408) 433-4800     Fax: (408) 433-4823     www.finnigan.com

*Mfr. mass spectrometers.*

**Finnigan MAT GmbH, Barkhausenstrasse 2, Bremen D-28197, Germany**

## FIRESTONE POLYMERS

381 W. Wilbeth Road, Akron, OH, 44301

Tel: (330) 379-7864     Fax: (330) 379-7875     www.firesyn.com

*Mfr. polymers; rubber, plastics and adhesives*

**Gratenau & Hesselbacher Chemie KG, PO Box 10 24 25, D20017 Hamburg, Germany**

Tel: 49-40-32-1011   Fax: 49-40-33-6623   Contact: Stephan Löhden

## FISCHER IMAGING CORPORATION

12300 North Grant Street, Denver, CO, 80241

Tel: (303) 452-6800     Fax: (303) 452-4335     www.fischerimaging.com

*Mfr. x-ray equipment.*

**Fischer Imaging Europe A/S, Hummelsbuetteler Steindamm 78 A, D-22851 Norderstedt, Germany**

## FISHER SCIENTIFIC INC.

1 Liberty Lane, Hampton, NH, 03842

Tel: (603) 929-5911     Fax: (603) 929-0222     www.fisher1.com

*Mfr. science instruments and apparatus, chemicals, reagents.*

**Fisher Scientific GmbH, Binnerheide 33, D-58239 Schwerte, Germany**

Tel: 49-2304-9325   Fax: 49-2304-932-950

**Fisher Scientific GmbH, Liebigstrasse 16, D-61130 Nidderau, Germany**

Tel: 49-6187-20190   Fax: 49-6187-201949

## FISHER-ROSEMOUNT

8000 Maryland Ave., Ste. 500, Clayton, MO, 63105-4755

Tel: (314) 746-9900     Fax: (314) 746-9974     www.frco.com

*Mfr. industrial process control equipment.*

**Fisher Gulde, Reiherstieg 6, D-21217 Seevetal, Germany**

**Fisher-Guulde, Mannheimer Str. 63, D-67071 Ludwigshafen, Germany**

**Fisher-Rosemount, Argelsrieder Feld 7 POB 1227, D-82234 Wessling, Germany**

**Fisher-Rosemount, Rheinische Str. 2, D-42781 Haan, Germany**

## FLEETBOSTON FINANCIAL CORPORATION

1 Federal Street, Boston, MA, 02110

Tel: (617) 346-4000     Fax: (617) 434-7547     www.fleet.com

*Banking and insurance services.*

**FleetBoston Frankfurt, Postfach 17 05 38, D-60069 Frankfurt, Germany**

Tel: 49-69-97265-0   Fax: 49-69-721162

## FLEXTRONICS INC. INTERNATIONAL

2241 Lundy Ave., San Jose, CA, 95131-1822

Tel: (408) 428-1300     Fax: (408) 428-0420     www.flextronics.com

*Contract manufacturer for electronics industry.*

**Flextronics International Germany GmbH, Heinz-Nixdorf-Ring 1, D-33106 Paderborn, Germany**

## FLOW INTERNATIONAL CORPORATION

23500 64th Ave. S., PO Box 97040, Kent, WA, 98064-9740

Tel: (253) 872-4900     Fax: (253) 813-3285     www.flowcorp.com

*Mfr. high-pressure water jet cutting/cleaning equipment, powered scaffolding; concrete cleaning/removal.*

**Flow Europe GmbH, Daimlerweg 6, D-6100 Darmstadt, Germany**

## FLOWSERVE CORPORATION

222 W. Los Colinas Blvd., Irving, TX, 75039

Tel: (972) 443-6500     Fax: (972) 443-6858     www.flowserve.com

*Mfr. chemicals equipment, pumps, valves, filters, fans and heat exchangers.*

**Durco GmbH/Atomac, Postfach 1162, von-Braun-Strasse 19a, D-4422 Ahaus, Germany**

## FLOWSERVE FLUID SEALING DIVISION

222 Los Colinas Blvd., Ste. 1500, Irving, TX, 75039

Tel: (616) 381-2650     Fax: (616) 443-6800     www.flowserve.com

*Mfr. mechanical seals, compression packings and auxiliaries.*

**Durametallic Europe GmbH, Blumenstr. 10, Postfach 201108, D-6072 Drieich 2, Germany**

## FLUKE CORPORATION

6920 Seaway Blvd. PO Box 9090, Everett, WA, 98203

Tel: (425) 347-6100     Fax: (425) 356-5116     www.fluke.com

*Mfr. handheld, electronic test tools for maintenance of electronic equipment.*

**Fluke Deutschland GmbH, Heinrich-Hertz-Str.11, 34123 Kassel, Germany**

## FLUOR CORPORATION

One Enterprise Drive, Aliso Viejo, CA, 92656-2606

Tel: (949) 349-2000     Fax: (949) 349-5271     www.flour.com

*Engineering and construction services.*

**Fluor Daniel GmbH, Buero Leipzig, Ellenburger Strasse 15a, D-7050 Leipzig, Germany**

## FM GLOBAL INC.

1301 Atwood Avenue, Johnston, RI, 02919

Tel: (401) 275-3000     Fax: (401) 275-3029     www.fmglobal.com

*Engaged in commercial and industrial property insurance and risk management, specializing in engineering-driven property protection.*

**FM Germany, Eschersheimer Landstrasse 55, 60322 Frankfurt am Main, Germany**

## FMC CORPORATION

200 E. Randolph Drive, Chicago, IL, 60601

Tel: (312) 861-6000     Fax: (312) 861-6141     www.fmc.com

*Produces chemicals and precious metals, mfr. machinery, equipment and systems for industrial, agricultural and government use.*

**FMC Smith Meter/Mess Und Foerdertechnik, Weidenbaumsweg 91A, D-21035 Hamburg, Germany**

**Smith Meter GmbH, PO Box 1164, 25470 Ellerbek, Germany**

Tel: 49-4101-3040

## FMR (FIDELITY INVESTMENTS)

82 Devonshire Street, Boston, MA, 02109

Tel: (617) 563-7000     Fax: (617) 476-6105     www.fidelity.com

*Diversified financial services company offering investment management, retirement, brokerage, and shareholder services directly to individuals and institutions and through financial intermediaries.*

**Fidelity International Ltd., Frankfort, Germany**

## FOOT LOCKER USA

112 West 34th Street, New York, NY, 10020

Tel: (212) 720-3700     Fax: (212) 553-2042     www.venatorgroup.com

*Mfr./sales shoes and sneakers.*

**Foot Locker International, Q 1-3, D-68161Mannheim, Germany**

Tel: 49-621-14334

**Foot Locker International, Ludwigstrasse 20, D-64283 Darmstadt, Germany**

Tel: 49-6151-28862

Foot Locker International, Kaiserstrasse 1-3, D-97070 Wurzburg, Germany
Tel: 49-931-17077

Foot Locker International, Hauptstrasse 63, D-69117 Heidelberg, Germany
Tel: 49-6221-21344

Foot Locker International, Wilhelm Leuscnerstrasse 1, D-67547 Worms, Germany
Tel: 49-6241-23391

Foot Locker International, Spitalstrasse, 18-20, D-97421 Schweinfurt, Germany
Tel: 49-9721-24681

## FORD MOTOR COMPANY

One American Road, Dearborn, MI, 48121

Tel: (313) 322-3000     Fax: (313) 322-9600     www.ford.com

*Mfr./sales motor vehicles.*

Ford-Werke AG, Werke Koeln-Niehl, Henry Ford Str., Postfach 604002, D-5000 Cologne 60, Germany

## FOREST OIL CORPORATION

1600 Broadway, Ste. 2200, Denver, CO, 80202

Tel: (303) 812-1400     Fax: (303) 812-1602     www.forestoil.com

*Crude oil and natural gas.*

Forest Oil Germany, c/o Forest Oil Corp., 1600 Broadway Suite 2200, Denver CO 80202

## FORMICA CORPORATION

10155 Reading Road, Cincinnati, OH, 45241-4805

Tel: (513) 786-3400     Fax: (513) 786-3082     www.formica.com

*Mfr. decorative laminate, adhesives and solvents.*

Formica Vertriebs GmbH, Belgische Allee 9, 53842 Troisdorf, Germany

## FORTÉ SOFTWARE, INC.

1800 Harrison Street, Oakland, CA, 94612

Tel: (510) 869-3400     Fax: (510) 869-3480     www.forte.com

*Developer computer software applications.*

Forté Software GmbH, Bundeskanzlerplatz 2-10, Bonn-Center HI XIII, D-53113 Bonn, Germany
Tel: 49-228-914-990   Fax: 49-228-914-9990

## FOSTER WHEELER CORPORATION

Perryville Corporate Park, Clinton, NJ, 08809-4000

Tel: (908) 730-4000     Fax: (908) 730-4100     www.fwc.com

*Manufacturing, engineering and construction.*

Foster Wheeler Energi GmbH, Hohenstaufenstrasse 4, D-40547 Düsseldorf, Germany
Tel: 49-211-559-0551   Fax: 49-211-559-0553

## FOUR WINDS INTERNATIONAL GROUP

1500 SW First Ave., Ste. 850, Portland, OR, 97201-2013

Tel: (503) 241-2732     Fax: (503) 241-1829     www.vanlines.com.au

*Transportation of household goods and general cargo and third party logistics.*

Four Winds International Germany, In den Wiesen 31, D-53227, Bonn, Germany
Tel: 49-228-973-8543   Fax: 49-228-429--8659   Contact: Dirk Ellerman, Gen. Mgr. Operations   Emp: 200

## FRANKLIN ELECTRIC COMPANY, INC.

400 East Spring Street, Bluffton, IN, 46714-3798

Tel: (219) 824-2900     Fax: (219) 824-2909     www.fele.com

*Mfr./distribute electric motors, submersible motors and controls.*

Franklin Electric Europa GmbH, Rudolf-Diesel-Straße 20, D-54516 Wittlich, Germany
Tel: 49-6571-105-0   Fax: 49-6571-105-520

### THE FRANKLIN MINT

US Route 1, Franklin Center, PA, 19091

Tel: (610) 459-6000    Fax: (610) 459-6880    www.franklinmint.com

*Design/marketing collectibles and luxury items.*

**Franklin Mint GmbH,  Im Taubental 5, D-41468 Neuss bei Düsseldorf, Germany**

### FRANKLIN RESOURCES, INC.

777 Mariners Island Blvd., San Mateo, CA, 94404

Tel: (415) 312-2000    Fax: (415) 312-3655    www.frk.com

*Global and domestic investment advisory and portfolio management.*

**Templeton Global Strategic Services (Deutschland) GmbH,  Taunusanlage 11, D-60329 Frankfurt, Germany**

Tel: 49-1-80-232-4632   Fax: 49-69-272-23120

### FRITZ COMPANIES, INC.

706 Mission Street, Ste. 900, San Francisco, CA, 94103

Tel: (415) 904-8360    Fax: (415) 904-8661    www.fritz.com

*Integrated transportation, sourcing, distribution and customs brokerage services.*

**Fritz Companies Inc.,  Berlin, Germany**

### FSI INTERNATIONAL INC.

322 Lake Hazeltine Drive, Chaska, MN, 55318

Tel: (612) 448-5440    Fax: (612) 448-2825    www.fsi-intl.com

*Manufacturing equipment for computer silicon wafers.*

**Metron Technology GmbH,  PO Box 1243, D-85606 Aschheim, Germany**

### H.B. FULLER COMPANY

1200 Willow Lake Blvd., Vadnais Heights, MN, 55110

Tel: (651) 236-5900    Fax: (651) 236-5898    www.hbfuller.com

*Mfr./distributor adhesives, sealants, coatings, paints, waxes, sanitation chemicals.*

**H.B. Fuller Europe - Group Office,  Salzbrücker Strasse 1-4, D-21335 Lüeneburg, Germany**
Tel: 49-4131-705296   Fax: 49-4131-705299

**H.B. Fuller GmbH,  An der Roten Bleiche 2-3, D-21335, Lüeneburg, Germany**
Tel: 49-4131-705360   Fax: 49-4131-705227

**H.B. Fuller, GmbH,  Postfach 83 04 52, 81704, München Germany**

### GAF CORPORATION

1361 Alps Road, Wayne, NJ, 07470

Tel: (973) 628-3000    Fax: (973) 628-3326    www.gaf.com

*Mfr. roofing and building materials.*

**GAF (Deutschland) GmbH,  Postfach 1380, D-5020 Frechen, Germany**

### THE GAP

1 Harrison Street, San Francisco, CA, 94105

Tel: (650) 952-4400    Fax: (650) 952-5884    www.gap.com

*Clothing store chain.*

**The Gap,  München, Germany**

### GARDNER-DENVER INC.

1800 Gardner Expressway, Quincy, IL, 62301

Tel: (217) 222-5400    Fax: (217) 228-8247    www.gardnerdenver.com

*Mfr. portable air compressors and related drilling accessories.*

**Gardner Denver Wittig GmbH,  Johann-Sutter-Straße 6+8, D-79650 Schopfheim, Germany**
Tel: 49-7622-394-0

## GARLOCK SEALING TECHNOLOGIES

1666 Division Street, Palmyra, NY, 14522

Tel: (315) 597-4811     Fax: (315) 597-3216     www.garlock-inc.com

*Mfr. of gaskets, packing, seals and expansion joints.*

**Garlock GmbH, Postfach 210464, D-41430 Neuss, Germany**

Tel: 49-2131-3490   Fax: 49-2131-349-222   Contact: Harold Poppke, Mng. Dir.

## GaSONICS INTERNATIONAL CORPORATION

404 East Plumeria Drive, San Jose, CA, 95134

Tel: (408) 570-7000     Fax: (408) 570-7612     www.gasonics.com

*Mfr. gas-based dry cleaning systems for semi-conductor production equipment.*

**GaSonics International, Postfach 1109, 86938 Schondorf, Germany**

Tel: 49-8192-999969   Fax: 49-8192-999954

## THE GATES RUBBER COMPANY

990 S. Broadway, PO Box 5887, Denver, CO, 80217-5887

Tel: (303) 744-1911     Fax: (303) 744-4000     www.gatesrubber.com

*Mfr. automotive and industrial belts and hoses.*

**Gates GmbH, Postfach 1428, D-52015 Aachen 1, Germany**

## GATEWAY INC.

4545 Towne Centre Ct., San Diego, CA, 92121

Tel: (858) 799-3401     Fax: (858) 779-3459     www.gateway.com

*Computers manufacture, sales and services.*

**Gateway Deutschland GmbH, Hoechstrasse 94, D-65835 Leiderbach, Germany**

## GATX CAPITAL CORPORATION

Four Embarcadero Center, Ste. 2200, San Francisco, CA, 94111

Tel: (415) 955-3200     Fax: (415) 955-3449     www.gatxcapital.com

*Lease and loan financing, residual guarantees.*

**GATX Financial Services GmbH, Wilhelm-Leuscher Strasse 7BR, 60329 Frankfurt, Germany**

**49.69.238.583**

Tel: 49-69-238-5210    Contact: Michael Stahl, VP

## GENCORP INC.

Hwy. 50 and Aerojet Rd., Ranchero Cordova, CA, 95853

Tel: (916) 355-4000     Fax: (916) 355-2459     www.gencorp.com

*Mfr. aerospace/defense and automotive products.*

**Henniges Vehicle Sealing Div., Nienburger Strasse 46, D-31547 Rehburg-Luccum, Germany**

## GENERAL BINDING CORPORATION

One GBC Plaza, Northbrook, IL, 60062

Tel: (847) 272-3700     Fax: (847) 272-1369     www.gbc.com

*Engaged in the design, manufacture and distribution of branded office equipment, related supplies and thermal laminating films.*

**GBC Deutschland GmbH, Rather Str. 28, D-4000 Düsseldorf 30, Germany**

**GBC Deutschland GmbH, Boschstr. 1, D-8901 Konigsbrunn, Germany**

## GENERAL DYNAMICS CORPORATION

3190 Fairview Park Drive, Falls Church, VA, 22042-4523

Tel: (703) 876-3000     Fax: (703) 876-3125     www.gendyn.com

*Mfr. aerospace equipment, submarines, strategic systems, armored vehicles, defense support systems.*

**General Dynamics Intl. Corp., Buerohaus Am Stadtpark, Koblenzer Str. 99, Bad Godesbert, D-5300 Bonn 1, Germany**

## GENERAL ELECTRIC CAPITAL CORPORATION

260 Long Ridge Road, Stamford, CT, 06927

Tel: (203) 357-4000     Fax: (203) 357-6489     www.gecapital.com

*Financial, property/casualty insurance, computer sales and trailer leasing services.*

**Employers Reinsurance Corp. (ERC),  SchloB-Rahe-StraBe 15, D-520-7 Aachen, Germany**

Tel: 49-241-93690   Fax: 49--241-9369-205

**Employers Reinsurance Corp. (ERC),  Maria-Theresia-StraBe 35, D-81675 München, Germany**

Tel: 49-89-92280   Fax: 49-89-9228-395

## GENERAL ELECTRIC COMPANY

3135 Easton Turnpike, Fairfield, CT, 06431

Tel: (203) 373-2211     Fax: (203) 373-3131     www.ge.com

*Diversified manufacturing, technology and services.*

**GE Capital Services GENSTAR container,  Grosser Burstah 2000 11, Hamburg, Germany**

Tel: 49-40-378-9030

**GE FANUC Automation,  Bernhauser Strasse 22, D-73765 Neuhausen A.D.F., Germany**

Tel: 49-71-5818-7400   Fax: 49-71-5818-7400

**General Electric Deutschland,  Praunhimer Landdstrasse 50, D-60488 Frankfurt am Main, Germany**

Tel: 49-69-9760-7348   Fax: 49-69-7682-091   Contact: Arno Bohn, Pres.

**GEPC Germany,  Buechekstrasse 63, D-53227 Bonn, Germany**

Tel: 49-22-844-543   Fax: 49-22-844-5468

**Nuovo Pignone,  Rennbahnstrasse 72-74, D-60528 Frankfurt am Main, Germany**

Tel: 49-6-9678-7021   Fax: 49-6-967-1988

## GENERAL INSTRUMENT CORPORATION

101 Tournament Road, Horsham, PA, 19044

Tel: (215) 674-4800     Fax: (215) 443-9554     www.gi.com

*Mfr. broadband communications and power rectifying components.*

**Fuba Communications Systems GmbH,  Bodenburger Straße 25/26, D-31162 Bad Salzdetfurth, Germany**

Tel: 49-50-63-89-215   Fax: 33-390-20-06-31

## GENERAL MOTORS ACCEPTANCE CORPORATION

3044 W. Grand Blvd., Detroit, MI, 48202

Tel: (313) 556-5000     Fax: (313) 556-5108     www.gmac.com

*Automobile financing.*

**Opel Bank GmbH,  Am Fernmeldeamt 15, Postfach 102817, D-4300 Essen, Germany**

**Opel Bank GmbH,  Postfach 4666, Herschelstrasse 32, Hanover 1, Germany**

**Opel Bank GmbH,  IHZ Friedrichstr., D-1086 Berlin, Germany**

**Opel Bank GmbH,  Grosse Bleichen 21, Postfach 304050, D-2000 Hamburg, Germany**

**Opel Bank GmbH,  Postfach 103643, D-7000 Stuttgart 10, Germany**

**Opel Bank GmbH,  Stahlstrasse 34, D-6090 Russelsheim, Germany**

**Opel Bank GmbH,  Prielmayerstrasse 1, Postfach 201826, D-8000 Münich, Germany**

## GENERAL MOTORS CORPORATION

300 Renaissance Center, Detroit, MI, 48285

Tel: (313) 556-5000     Fax: (313) 556-5108     www.gm.com

*Mfr. full line vehicles, automotive electronics, commercial technologies, telecommunications, space, finance.*

**Adam Opel AG,  D-6090 Russelsheim, Germany**

Contact: Robert W. Hendry, Chmn.

**Unicables SA,  c/o Kabelwerke Reinshagen GmbH, Reinshagenstr. 1, D-5600 Wuppertal 21, Germany**

## GENERAL REINSURANCE CORPORATION

695 E. Main Street, Stamford, CT, 06904-2350

Tel: (203) 328-5000     Fax: (203) 328-6423     www.genre.com

*Reinsurance services worldwide.*

**Die Kölnische Rück., Postfach 10 22 44, D-50462 Köln, Germany**

Tel: 49-221-97380    Fax: 49-221-9738494    Contact: Dr. Peter Lütke-Bornefeld, Mng. Dir.

**General Re Europe Ltd. - Cologne, Niederlassung Deutschland, 5th Fl. Sedanstrasse 8, D-50668 Cologne, Germany**

Tel: 49-221-9738-160    Fax: 49-221-9738-1619    Contact: Andreas Kessler, VP

## GENERAL SEMICONDUCTOR, INC.

10 Melville Park Road., Melville, NY, 11747

Tel: (631) 847-3000     Fax: (631) 847-3236     www.gensemi.com

*Mfr. of low- and medium-current power rectifiers and transient voltage suppressors.*

**General Semiconductor Deutschland GmbH, Albert-Schweitzer Strasse 64, D-81735 München, Germany**

Tel: 49-89-679790    Fax: 49-89-67979-100    Contact: Theo Heithorn

## GENICOM CORPORATION

14800 Conference Center Drive, Ste. 400, Chantilly, VA, 20151

Tel: (703) 802-9200     Fax: (703) 802-9039     www.genicom.com

*Supplier of network systems, service and printer solutions.*

**Genicom GmbH, Industriestr. 4, D-65779 Kelkheim/Ts, Germany**

Contact: Dirk De Waegeneire

## GENUITY, INC.

150 Cambridge Park Drive, Cambridge, MA, 02140

Tel: (617) 873-2000     Fax: (617) 873-2857     www.genuity.com

*R/D computer, communications, acoustics technologies and internetworking services.*

**Genuity, Mergnthalerallee, 79081 Topas 2, 65760, Frankfurt/Eschborn, Germany**

Tel:
49-6196-9588913    Contact: Iris Korzilius

## GENZYME CORPORATION

1 Kendall Square, Cambridge, MA, 02139-1562

Tel: (617) 252-7500     Fax: (617) 252-7600     www.genzyme.com

*Mfr. healthcare products for enzyme deficient diseases.*

**Genzyme Virotech GmbH, Loewenplatz 5,D-65428 Ruesselsheim, Germany**

Tel: 49-6142-6909-0    Fax: 49-6142-82621

## GEO LOGISTICS CORPORATION

1521 E. Dyer Rd., Santa Ana, CA, 92705

Tel: (714) 513-3000     Fax: (714) 513-3120     www.geo-logistics.com

*Freight forwarding, warehousing and distribution services, specializing in heavy cargo.*

**GeoLogisics GmbH, PO Box 12 07, D-88322 Aulendorf, Germany**

Tel: 49-7525-9219-0    Fax: 49-7525-490

**GeoLogisics GmbH, PO Box 13 05 50, D-40555 Dusseldorf, Germany**

Tel: 49-211-9-9520    Fax: 49-211-995-2199

### GILEAD SCIENCES, INC.

333 Lakeside Dr, Foster City, CA, 94404

Tel: (650) 574-3000    Fax: (650) 578-9264    www.gilead.com

*Engaged in healthcare research and development; biotech treatments for viruses.*

**NeXstar Pharmaceuticals GmbH, Fraunhoferstrasse 22, 82152 Martinsried/Münich, Germany**

Tel: 49-89-899-8900   Fax: 49-89-899-89090

### THE GILLETTE COMPANY

Prudential Tower Building, Boston, MA, 02199

Tel: (617) 421-7000    Fax: (617) 421-7123    www.gillette.com

*Develop/mfr. personal care/use products: blades and razors, toiletries, cosmetics, stationery.*

**Braun AB, Kronberg/Ts., Germany**

**Braun de Mexico GmbH, Kronberg/Ts., Germany**

**Braun do Brasil GmbH, Kronberg/Ts., Germany**

**Consul GmbH, Kronberg/Ts., Germany**

Contact: Norbert Koll, Gen. Mgr.

**Gillette Beteiligungs GmbH, Berlin, Germany**

Contact: Norbert Koll, Gen. Mgr.

**Gillette Continental Trading GmbH, Florsheim, Germany**

Contact: Norbert Koll, Gen. Mgr.

**Gillette Deutschland GmbH & Co., Berlin, Germany**

Contact: Norbert Koll, Gen. Mgr.

**Gillette Verwaltungs GmbH, Berlin, Germany**

Contact: Norbert Koll, Gen. Mgr.

**Helit Innovative Buroproduckte GmbH, Kierspe, Germany**

Contact: Norbert Koll, Gen. Mgr.

**Jafra Cosmetics GmbH, Münich, Germany**

Contact: Norbert Koll, Gen. Mgr.

**Oral-B Laboratories GmbH, Frankfurt/Main, Germany**

Contact: Norbert Koll, Gen. Mgr.

**WEBA Betriebsrenten-Verwaltungs GmbH, Kronberg/Taunus, Germany**

Contact: Norbert Koll, Gen. Mgr.

### GILSON INC.

3000 W. Beltline Hwy, PO Box 620027, Middleton, WI, 53562-0027

Tel: (608) 836-1551    Fax: (608) 831-4451    www.gilson.com

*Mfr. analytical/biomedical instruments.*

**Abimed Analysen-Technik Gmbh, Raiffeisenstr. 3, 40764 Langenfeld, Germany**

### GIW INDUSTRIES, INC.

5000 Wrightsboro Rd., Grovetown, GA, 30813

Tel: (706) 863-1011    Fax: (706) 860-5897    www.giwindustries.com

*Mfr. slurry pumps.*

**KSB Service GmbH, Leunawerk II Bau 3024, Leuna 06236, Germany**

### P.H. GLATFELTER COMPANY

96 South George St., Ste. 500, York, PA, 17401

Tel: (717) 225-4711    Fax: (717) 225-6834    www.glatfelter.com

*Mfr. engineered and specialty printing papers.*

**Glatfelter Ltd., Münich, Germany**

## GLEASON CORPORATION

1000 University Ave., Rochester, NY, 14692

Tel: (716) 473-1000     Fax: (716) 461-4348     www.gleasoncorp.com

*Mfr. gear making machine tools; tooling and services.*

**Gleason-Hurth, Maschinen und Werkzeuge GmbH, Moosacher Str. 36, D-80809 Münich, Germany**

Tel: 49-89-354010   Fax: 49-89-35401-643

**Gleason-Pfauter**
**Maschinenfabrik GmbH, Daimlerstr 14, D-71634 Ludwigsburg, Germany**

**Gleason-Pfauter/Maschinenfabrik GmbH, Daimlerstrasse 14, D-71636 Luwigsburg, Germany**

Tel: 49-7141-4040   Fax: 49-7141-404500

## GLOBAL SILVERHAWK

2190 Meridian Park Blvd., Ste G, Concord, CA, 94520

Tel: (925) 681-2889     Fax: (925) 681-2755     www.globalsilverhawk.com

*International moving and forwarding.*

**Global Silverhawk, Auf Dem Dransdorferberg 64, D-53121 Bonn, Germany**

Tel: 49-228-66-40-11   Contact: Jurgen Thielen, Gen. Mgr.

**Global Silverhawk, Opelstrasse 30, D-6082 Moerfelden, Germany**

Tel: 49-6105-92520   Contact: William Gibbon, Gen. Mgr.

## THE GOLDMAN SACHS GROUP

85 Broad Street, New York, NY, 10004

Tel: (212) 902-1000     Fax: (212) 902-3000     www.gs.com

*Investment bankers; securities broker dealers.*

**Goldman Sachs Group, MesseTurm, Friedrich-Ebert-Anlage 49, D-60308 Frankfurt am Main, Germany**

Tel: 49-69-7532-1000

## THE GOODYEAR TIRE & RUBBER COMPANY

1144 East Market Street, Akron, OH, 44316

Tel: (330) 796-2121     Fax: (330) 796-1817     www.goodyear.com

*Mfr. tires, automotive belts and hose, conveyor belts, chemicals; oil pipeline transmission.*

**Deutsche Goodyear GmbH, Xantener Str. 105, Postfach 100508, D-5000 Cologne 60, Germany**

**Gummiwerke Fulda GmbH, Kuenzellerstr. 59/61, D-6400 Fulda, Germany**

## W. L. GORE & ASSOCIATES, INC.

555 Paper Mill Road, Newark, DE, 19711

Tel: (302) 738-4880     Fax: (302) 738-7710     www.gorefabrics.com

*Mfr. electronic, industrial filtration, medical and fabric products.*

**W. L. Gore & Associates GmbH, Hermann-Oberth-Strasse 22, D-85640 Putzbrunn, Germany**

Tel: 49-89-4612-0

## GOSS GRAPHIC SYSTEMS INC.

700 Oakmont Lane, Westmont, IL, 60559-5546

Tel: (630) 850-5600     Fax: (630) 850-6310     www.gossgraphic.com

*Mfr. web, off-site printing equipment.*

**Goss/Rockwell Graphic Systems Ltd., Grenzstr 30, Postfach 1268, D-6053 Obertshavsen, Germany**

## W. R. GRACE & COMPANY

7500 Grace Drive, Columbia, MD, 21044

Tel: (410) 531-4000     Fax: (410) 531-4367     www.grace.com

*Mfr. specialty chemicals and materials: packaging, health care, catalysts, construction, water treatment/process.*

**Grace GmbH, In der Hollerhecke 1, D-67547 Worms, Germany**

Tel: 49-6241-4030   Fax: 49-6241-403211

**Grace GmbH, Erlengang 31, D-22844 Norderstedt, Germany**

Tel: 49-40-526010   Fax: 49-40-52601-511

## GRACO INC.

4050 Olson Memorial Hwy, PO Box 1441, Minneapolis, MN, 55440-1441

Tel: (612) 623-6000       Fax: (612) 623-6777       www.graco.com

*Mfr. systems and equipment to service fluid handling systems and automotive equipment.*

**Graco GmbH, Moselstrasse 19, D-41464 Neuss, Germany**

## GRAHAM & JAMES LLP

One Maritime Plaza, Ste. 300, San Francisco, CA, 94111-3404

Tel: (415) 954-0200       Fax: (415) 391-2493       www.gj.com

*International law firm.*

**Graham & James/Haarmann Hemmelradt & Partners, Frankfurt, Germany**

**Graham & James/Haarmann Hemmelradt & Partners, Düsseldorf, Germany**

**Graham & James/Haarmann Hemmelradt & Partners, Berlin, Germany**

**Graham & James/Haarmann Hemmelradt & Partners, Münich, Germany**

**Graham & James/Haarmann Hemmelradt & Partners, Leipzig, Germany**

**Graham & James/Kau Rechtsanwalte, Immermannstrasse 11, D-40210 Düsseldorf, Germany**

Tel: 49-211-355-9190   Fax: 49-211-355-91919   Contact: Wolfgang Kau

## GRANT THORNTON INTERNATIONAL

800 One Prudential Plaza, 130 E. Randolph Drive, Chicago, IL, 60601-6050

Tel: (312) 856-0001       Fax: (312) 616-7052       www.grantthornton.com

*Accounting, audit, tax and management consulting services.*

**Grant Thornton GmbH, RitterstraBe 2a, Bechsteinhaus, D-10969 Berlin, Germany**

Tel: 49-30-61-69-0412   Fax: 49-30-61-69-0499   Contact: Norbert Jost

**Grant Thornton GmbH, Warburgstrasse 50, D-20354 Hamburg, Germany**

Tel: 49-40-415-22280   Fax: 49-40-415-22111   Contact: Dr Wolfgang Wawrzinek

## GREAT LAKES CHEMICAL CORPORATION

500 East 96th Street, Ste. 500, Indianapolis, IN, 46240

Tel: (317) 715-3000       Fax: (317) 715-3050       www.greatlakeschem.com

*Mfr. innovative specialty chemical solutions, including flame retardants and other polymer additives, water treatment chemicals, performance and fine chemicals, fire extinguishants.*

**Bayrol Chemische Fabrik GmbH, Münich, Germany**

**Chemische Werke LOWI Beteiligungs GmbH & Co., Waldkraiburg, Germany**

## GREENFIELD INDUSTRIES INC.

470 Old Evans Road, Evans, GA, 30809

Tel: (706) 863-7708       Fax: (706) 860-8559       www.greenfieldindustries.com

*Mfr. high-speed rotary cutting tools.*

**Kemmer Europe, Hartmetall Feinwerkzeuge Hangendeinbacherstrasse 4, D-73527 Schwabisch Gmund, Germany**

## GREG MANNING AUCTIONS, INC.

775 Passaic Avenue, West Caldwell, NJ, 07006

Tel: (973) 882-0004       Fax: (973) 882-3499       www.gregmanning.com

*Specialty auction house; dealing primarily in stamps.*

**GMAI Europe, Feldbergstrasse 57, D-61440 Oberursel, Germany**

## GREY GLOBAL GROUP

777 Third Ave., New York, NY, 10017

Tel: (212) 546-2000       Fax: (212) 546-1495       www.grey.com

*International advertising agency.*

**Grey Europe, Schanzenstrasse 82, D-40549 Düsseldorf, Germany**

Grey Gruppe Deutschland, Corneliusstrasse 168-24, D-40215 Düsseldorf, Germany

## GRIFFITH LABORATORIES INC.

One Griffith Center, Alsip, IL, 60658

Tel: (708) 371-0900     Fax: (708) 597-3294     www.griffithlabs.com

*Mfr. industrial food ingredients and equipment.*

**Griffith Labs Inc., Heidelberg, Germany**

Tel: 49-6221-301-027   Fax: 49-6221-302-484

## GRIFFON CORPORATION

100 Jericho Quadrangle, Jericho, NY, 11753

Tel: (516) 938-5544     Fax: (516) 938-5564     www.griffoncorp.com

*Mfr. residential and industrial garage doors and related products and services for the home building and replacement markets.*

**Böhme Verpackungsfolien GmbH & Co, Dombühl, Germany**

Contact: Ulrich W. Böhme

## GUARDIAN ELECTRIC MFG. COMPANY

1425 Lake Ave., Woodstock, IL, 60098

Tel: (815) 334-3600     Fax: (815) 337-0377     www.guardian-electric.com

*Mfr. industrial controls, electrical relays and switches.*

**Franz Kreuzer, Stuttgart, Germany**

## GUIDANT CORPORATION

111 Monument Circle, 29th Fl., Indianapolis, IN, 46204

Tel: (317) 971-2000     Fax: (317) 971-2040     www.guidant.com

*Mfr. cardiovascular therapeutic devices.*

**Guidant B.V. & Co. Medizintechnik KG, Wingertschecke 6, 35392 Giessen, Germany**

Tel: 49-641-922-210

## GULTON GRAPHIC INSTRUMENTS, INC.

212 Durham Ave., Metuchen, NJ, 08840

Tel: (732) 548-6500     Fax: (732) 548-6781     www.gulton.com

*Electronic instruments, controls and communications equipment.*

**Electro Voice Div., Unternehmenbereich der Gulton GmbH, Laerchenstr. 99, Postfach 831164, D-6230 Frankfurt/Main 80, Germany**

## GUY CARPENTER & COMPANY, INC.

Two World Trade Center, New York, NY, 10048

Tel: (212) 323-1000     Fax: (212) 313-4970     www.guycarp.com

*Engaged in global reinsurance and risk management.*

**Guy Carpenter & Company, GmbH, Brienner Strasse 14, 80333 Münich, Germany**

Tel: 49-89-26-6030   Fax: 49-89-286-6033

## HACH COMPANY

PO Box 389, 5600 Lindbergh Drive, Loveland, CO, 80539-0389

Tel: (970) 669-3050     Fax: (970) 669-2932     www.hach.com

*Mfr./distributor water analysis and organic instruments, test kits and chemicals.*

**Hach Company,, c/o Dr. Bruno Lange, Willstätterstr. 11, D-40549 Düsseldorf, Germany**

Tel: 49-211-52-880   Fax: 49-211-52-88231

## HADCO CORPORATION

8C Industrial Way, Salem, NH, 03079

Tel: (603) 898-8000     Fax: (603) 893-0025     www.hadco.com

*Mfr. electronic interconnect products.*

**Hadco Corporation, Marienweg 2, D-98617 Meiningen, Germany**

## HAEMONETICS CORPORATION

400 Wood Road, Braintree, MA, 02184-9114

Tel: (781) 848-7100     Fax: (781) 848-5106     www.haemonetics.com

*Mfr. automated blood processing systems and blood products.*

**Haemonetics Germany GmbH,  Rohrauerstrasse 72, 81477 Münich, Germany**

Tel: 49-89-785-8070    Fax: 49-89-780-9779

## HALLIBURTON COMPANY

500 North Akard Street, Ste. 3600, Dallas, TX, 75201-3391

Tel:  (214) 978-2600     Fax:  (214) 978-2685     www.halliburton.com

*Engaged in diversified energy services, engineering and construction.*

**Halliburton GmbH,  Postfach 1248, D-49361 Vechta, Germany**

Tel: 49-4441-93930   Fax: 49-4441-939333

**Halliburton GmbH,  Postfach 3250, D-29227 Celle, Germany**

Tel: 49-5141-9990   Fax: 49-5141-999390

## HAMILTON SUNSTRAND

One Hamilton Rd., Windsor Locks, CT, 06096-1010

Tel:  (860) 654-6000     Fax:  (860) 654-3469     www.hamiltonsunstrandcorp.com

*Design/mfr. aerospace systems for commercial, regional, corporate and military aircraft.*

**Hamilton Sunstrand Corp.,  Frankfurt, Germany**

## M.A. HANNA COMPANY

200 Public Square, Ste. 36-5000, Cleveland, OH, 44114

Tel:  (216) 589-4000     Fax:  (216) 589-4200     www.mahanna.com

*Mfr. color and additive concentrates.*

**M.A. Hanna GmbH,  Adolf-Dambach Str .2-4, 76571 Gaggenau, Germany**

**M.A. Hanna GmbH,  Oldendorfer Strasse 9, D-49324 Elle, Germany**

Contact: Reinhard Deipenwisch

## HARLEY-DAVIDSON INTERNATIONAL

3700 West Juneau Ave., Milwaukee, WI, 53201

Tel:  (414) 342-4680     Fax:  (414) 343-4621     www.harleydavidson.com

*Mfr. motorcycles, recreational and commercial vehicles, parts and accessories.*

**Harley-Davidson GmbH,  7 Industriestrasse, D-6096 Raunheim, Germany**

## HARMAN  INTERNATIONAL INDUSTRIES, INC.

1101 Pennsylvania Ave. NW, Ste. 1010, Washington, DC, 20004

Tel:  (202) 393-1101     Fax:  (202) 393-3064     www.harman.com

*Mfr. audio and video equipment, loudspeakers and sound reinforcement equipment.*

**Harman Deutschland GmbH,  Hunderstrasse 1, D-7100 Heilbronn, Germany**

## HARNISCHFEGER INDUSTRIES INC.

PO Box 554, Milwaukee, WI, 53201

Tel:  (414) 797-6480     Fax:  (414) 797-6573     www.harnischfeger.com

*Mfr. mining and material handling equipment, papermaking machinery and computer systems.*

**Beloit Lenox GmbH,  Zellerstrasse 13, D-73271 Holzmaden, Germany**

**Harnischfeger GmbH,  Postfach 710411, D-6000 Frankfurt/Main, Germany**

**Rader International,  Am Konigshof 3, D-8400 Regensburg, Germany**

## HARRIS CALORIFIC COMPANY

2345 Murphy Boulevard, Gainesville, GA, 30501

Tel:  (770) 536-8801     Fax:  (770) 536-0544     www.harriscal.com

*Mfr./sales of gas welding and cutting equipment.*

**Harris Calorific Deutschland GmbH,  586 Iserlohn, Masteweg 7, Germany**

## HARRIS CORPORATION

1025 West NASA Blvd., Melbourne, FL, 32919

Tel: (407) 727-9100     Fax: (407) 727-9344     www.harris.com

*Mfr. communications and information-handling equipment, including copying and fax systems.*

**Harris Semiconductors, Richard-Reitzner-Allee 4, D-85540 Haar, Germany**

Tel: 49-89-462-63-0   Fax: 49-89-462-63-133

**Harris Semiconductors, Kolumbusstrasse 35/1, D-71063 Sindelfingen, Germany**

Tel: 49-7031-8-69-40   Fax: 49-7031-87-38-49

## HARSCO CORPORATION

PO Box 8888, 350 Poplar Church Rd., Camp Hill, PA, 17001-8888

Tel: (717) 763-7064     Fax: (717) 763-6424     www.harsco.com

*Metal reclamation and mill services, infrastructure and construction and process industry products.*

**Harsco GmbH, Postfach 1565, D-25805 Husum, Germany**

**Harsco GmbH, Postfach 30 03005, D-4600 Dortmund 30, Germany**

## HARTFORD RE COMPANY

55 Farmington Ave., Ste. 800, Hartford, CT, 06105

Tel: (860) 520-2700     Fax: (860) 520-2726     www.thehartford.com

*Reinsurance.*

**HartRe Company, Mauerkircherstrasse 8, D-81679 Münich, Germany**

Tel: 49-89-998-4030   Fax: 49-89-998-4033   Contact: Chris Genillard, Gen. Mgr.

## HARVARD APPARATUS

84 October Hill Road, Holliston, MA, 01746

Tel: (508) 893-8999     Fax: (508) 429-5732     www.harvardapparatus.com

*Mfr./sales life science research products.*

**Hugo Sachs Elektronik - Harvard Apparatus GmbH, Gruenstrasse 1, D-79232 March Hugstetten, Germany**

Tel: 49-7665-92-00-0   Fax: 49-7665-92-00-90

## HASBRO INDUSTRIES INC.

1027 Newport Ave., Pawtucket, RI, 02861

Tel: (401) 725-8697     Fax: (401) 727-5099     www.hasbro.com

*Mfr. toy products, including games and puzzles, dolls and plush products.*

**Hasbro Deutschland GmbH, Max-Planck-Straße 10, D-63128 Dietzenbach, Germany**

## HAYES LEMMERZ INTERNATIONAL

15300 Centennial Dr., Northville, MI, 48167

Tel: (734) 737-5000     Fax: (734) 737-2003     www.hayes-lemmerz.com

*Mfr. steel and aluminum car wheels.*

**Hayes Lemmerz System Service, Friedrich-List-Strasse 6, Ind. Area Hansalinie, 28309 Bremen, Germany**

Tel: 49-421-458-760

**Hayes Lemmerz System Service, Margot-Kalinke-Strasse 9, Münich 80939 Germany**

**Hayes Lemmerz Werke GmbH, Postfach 11 20, D-53621 Konigswinter, Germany**

## HEIDRICK & STRUGGLES INTERNATIONAL, INC.

Sears Tower, 233 South Wacker Drive, Chicago, IL, 60606

Tel: (312) 496-1200     Fax: (312) 496-1290     www.heidrick.com

*Executive search firm.*

**Heidrick & Struggles • Mülder & Partner, Airport Ctr. 1, Hugo-Eckerner-Ring, D-60549 Frankfurt, Germany**

Tel: 49-69-69-70020   Fax: 49-69-69-700299

**Heidrick & Struggles Mülder & Partner, Theresienstraße 29, 01097 Dresden, Germany**

## HEIN-WERNER CORPORATION

2110 A Pewaukee Rd., PO Box 1606, Waukesha, WI, 53188

Tel: (262) 542-6611       Fax: (262) 542-7890       www.snapon.com

*Mfr. auto body repair equipment, engine rebuilding and brake repair equipment, hydraulic cylinders.*

**Blackhawk GmbH,  Postfach 2064, Karlstrasse 1, D-7640 Kehl, Germany**

## H.J. HEINZ COMPANY

600 Grant Street, Pittsburgh, PA, 15219

Tel: (412) 456-5700       Fax: (412) 456-6128       www.heinz.com

*Processed food products and nutritional services.*

**H.J. Heinz GmbH,  Cologne, Germany**

## HELLER FINANCIAL INC.

500 West Monroe Street, Chicago, IL, 60661

Tel: (312) 441-7000       Fax: (312) 441-7367       www.hellerfin.com

*Financial services.*

**Heller Bank A.G.,  Weberstraße 21, 55130 Mainz, Germany**

## HENRY SCHEIN, INC.

135 Duryea Rd., Melville, NY, 11747

Tel: (516) 843-5500       Fax: (516) 843-5658       www.henryschein.com

*Mfr. and supply dental equipment.*

**Henry Schein Dentina,  Max-Stromeyer-Strasse 170 C-D, 78467 Konstanz, Germany**

Tel: 49-7531-992100

## HERCULES INC.

Hercules Plaza, 1313 N. Market Street, Wilmington, DE, 19894-0001

Tel: (302) 594-5000       Fax: (302) 594-5400       www.herc.com

*Mfr. specialty chemicals, plastics, film and fibers, coatings, resins, food ingredients.*

**Hercules Chemicals Ltd.,  Germany**

**Hercules GmbH,  Curslacker Neur Diech 66, D-2050 Hamburg 80, Germany**

**Pomosin AG,  Von-Herwath-Strasse, D-2443 Grossenbrode, Germany**

## HERMAN MILLER INC.

855 East Main, Zeeland, MI, 49464

Tel: (616) 654-3000       Fax: (616) 654-5385       www.hermanmiller.com

*Mfr. office furnishings.*

**Herman Miller Deutschland,  Kaiserswerther Str. 85, 40878 Ratingen, Germany**

## HERSHEY FOODS CORPORATION

100 Crystal A Drive, Hershey, PA, 17033

Tel: (717) 534-6799       Fax: (717) 534-6760       www.hersheys.com

*Mfr. chocolate, food and confectionery products.*

**Gubor Schokoladenfabrik GbmH,  Neuenburger Strasse, D-79373 Mullheim Schwarzwald, Germany**

## HEWITT ASSOCIATES LLC

100 Half Day Road, Lincolnshire, IL, 60069

Tel: (847) 295-5000       Fax: (847) 295-7634       www.hewitt.com

*Employee benefits consulting firm.*

**Hewitt Associates GmbH,  Hagenauer Strasse 42, D-65203 Wiesbaden, Germany**

Tel: 49-611-928830

## HEWLETT-PACKARD COMPANY

3000 Hanover Street, Palo Alto, CA, 94304-1185

Tel: (650) 857-1501     Fax: (650) 857-5518     www.hp.com

*Mfr. computing, communications and measurement products and services.*

**Hewlett-Packard GmbH, Herrenberger Strasse 130, D-71034 Boebligen, Germany**

## HILLENBRAND INDUSTRIES, INC.

700 State Route 46 East, Batesville, IN, 47006

Tel: (812) 934-7000     Fax: (812) 934-1963     www.hillenbrand.com

*Holding company: mfr. hospital beds, incubators and caskets.*

**Hill-Rom GmbH, Kurhessen Strasse 11, D-64546 Morfelden, Germany**

Tel: 49-6105-932-100   Fax: 49-6105-932-102

## HILTON HOTELS CORPORATION

9336 Civic Center Drive, Beverly Hills, CA, 90210

Tel: (310) 278-4321     Fax: (310) 205-7880     www.hiltonhotels.com

*International hotel chain: Hilton International, Vista Hotels and Hilton National Hotels.*

**Hilton International Hotels, Kaiserstrasse 47, D-60329 Frankfurt/Main, Germany**

**Hilton International Hotels, Georg Glock Strasse 20, D-40474 Düsseldorf, Germany**

**Munich City Hilton, Rosenheimer Strasse 15, D-81667 Münich, Germany**

## HOLIDAY INN (BASS RESORTS) WORLDWIDE, INC.

3 Ravinia Drive, Ste. 2900, Atlanta, GA, 30346-2149

Tel: (770) 604-2000     Fax: (770) 604-5403     www.holidayinn.com

*Hotels, restaurants and casinos.*

**Holiday Inn Munich, Leapoldstr. 200, D-8000 Münich 40, Germany**

**Holiday Inn Munich, Schleissheimerstr. 188, D-8000 Münich 40, Germany**

**Holiday Inn Stuttgart-Munchingen, Siemensstr 50, D-7015 Stuttgart/Munchingen, Germany**

**Holiday Inn Stuttgart-Sindelfingen, Schwertstr. 65, D-7032 Sindelfingen 3, Germany**

**Holiday Inn Trier, Zurmaienerstr. 164, D-5500 Trier, Germany**

**Holiday Inn Viernheim-Mannheim, Bgm Neffstr. 12, D-6806 Viemheim, Germany**

**Holiday Inn Wolfsburg, Rathausstr. 1, D-3180 Wolfsburg 1, Germany**

## HOLLINGSWORTH & VOSE COMPANY

112 Washington Street, East Walpole, MA, 02032

Tel: (508) 668-0295     Fax: (508) 668-3557     www.hollingsworth-vose.com

*Mfr. technical and industrial papers and non-woven fabrics.*

**Hollingsworth & Vose Europe NV, Norsk-Data Strasse 1, D-61352 Bad Homburg, Germany**

## HONEYWELL INTERNATIONAL INC.

101 Columbia Road, Morristown, NJ, 07962

Tel: (973) 455-2000     Fax: (973) 455-4807     www.honeywell.com

*Develop/mfr. controls for home and building, industry, space and aviation.*

**Honeywell AG, Kaiserleistrasse 39, D-63067 Offenbach, Germany**

Tel: 49-69-806-40   Fax: 49-69-818620

## HONEYWELL-MEASUREX DMC CORPORATION

PO Box 490, Gaithersburg, MD, 20884

Tel: (301) 948-2450     Fax: (301) 670-0506     www.measurex.com

*Mfr. quality and process control gauges.*

**DMC Mess & Regeltechnik GmbH, Postfach 3169, D-64712 Michelstadt, Germany**

Tel: 49-6061-615   Fax: 49-6061-72838   Contact: Peter Krings, Director

## HORWATH INTERNATIONAL ASSOCIATION

415 Madison Ave., New York, NY, 10017

Tel: (212) 838-5566    Fax: (212) 838-3636    www.horwath.com

*Public accountants and auditors.*

**AWT-Allgemeine, Wirtschattreuhand GmbH,  Leonhard-Mall-Bogen, D-8000 Münich 70, Germany**

**Dr. Lipfert GmbH,  Berner Strasse 49, D-6000 Frankfurt/Main 56, Germany**

**Dr. Lipfert GmbH,  Postfach 103023, Alexanderstr. 12, D-7000 Stuttgart 1, Germany**

**Horwath & Gelbert GmbH,  Berner Strasse 49, D-6000 Frankfurt/Main 56, Germany**

**RWT Reutlinger Wirtschaftstreuhand GmbH,  Charlottenstrasse 45-51, 72764 Reutlingen, Germany**

Tel: 49-7121-489-226

## HOUGHTON INTERNATIONAL INC.

PO Box 930, Madison & Van Buren Avenues, Valley Forge, PA, 19482-0930

Tel: (610) 666-4000    Fax: (610) 666-1376    www.houghtonintl.com

*Mfr. specialty chemicals, hydraulic fluids and lubricants.*

**Houghton Deutschland GmbH,  Robert-Koch-Str., 6 D-65479 Raunheim/Main, Germany**

Tel: 49-61-42-9430

**Houghton Durferrit GmbH Thermotechnik,  PO Box 1853, D-63406 Hanau, Germany**

Tel: 49-6181-59-426

**Houghton Lubricor GmbH,  Werkstrasse 26, 52076 Aachen, Germany**

Tel: 49-2408-1406-0

## HOWMEDICA OSTEONICS, INC.

359 Veterans Blvd., Rutherford, NJ, 07070

Tel: (201) 507-7300    Fax: (201) 935-4873    www.howmedica.com

*Mfr. of maxillofacial products (orthopedic implants).*

**Howmedica Germany GmbH,  Eastern Europe: Kiel, Germany**

Tel: 49-4348-7020

**Howmedica International Inc.,  Richard-Wagner-Str. 27, D-5000 Cologne 1, Germany**

## HQ GLOBAL WORKPLACES INC.

1155 Connecticut Ave. NW, Washington, DC, 20036

Tel: (202) 467-8500    Fax: (202) 467-8595    www.hq.com

*Provides office outsourcing, officing solutions, including internet access, telecommunications, meeting rooms, furnished offices and team rooms, state-of-the-art videoconferencing, and trained on-site administrative support teams -*

**HQ Global Workplaces,  Arabellapark Center, Weltenburger Strasse 70, Münich 81677, Germany**

Tel: 49-89-92-40-4290

## HUCK INTERNATIONAL INC.

3724 East Columbia Street, Tucson, AZ, 85714-3415

Tel: (520) 747-9898    Fax: (520) 750-7420    www.huck.com

*Designer and manufacturer of high-performance, proprietary fasteners and fastener installation systems.*

**Huck Intl. GmbH & Co.,  An der Unteren Sose 26, D-37520 Osterode/Harz, Germany**

## HUNT CORPORATION

2005 Market Street, Philadelphia, PA, 19103

Tel: (215) 656-0300    Fax: (215) 656-3700    www.hunt-corp.com

*Mfr. office, art and craft, and presentation products.*

**Ademco-Seal GmbH,  Ulrichstrasse 15B, D-7014 Kornwestheim, Germany**

## HUNTSMAN CORPORATION

500 Huntsman Way, Salt Lake City, UT, 84108

Tel: (801) 532-5200      Fax: (801) 536-1581      www.huntsman.com

*Mfr./sales specialty chemicals, industrial chemicals and petrochemicals.*

**Huntsman Polyurethanes GmbH,  Land-Au 30, D-94454 Deggendorf, Germany**

Tel: 49-991-27040   Contact: R. Oertel

**Huntsman Tioxide Europe GmbH,  Am Brüll 17, D40878 Ratingen, Germany**

## HYATT CORPORATION

200 West Madison Street, Chicago, IL, 60606

Tel: (312) 750-1234      Fax: (312) 750-8578      www.hyatt.com

*International hotel management.*

**Grand Hyatt Berlin Hotel,  Marlene-Dietrich Platz 2, D-10785 Berlin, Germany**

Tel: 49-30-2553-1234   Fax: 49-30-2553-1235

**Hyatt Regency Cologne Hotel,  Kennedy-Ufer 2A, D-50679 Cologne Deutz, Germany**

Tel: 49-221-828-1234   Fax: 49-221-828-1370

**Hyatt Regency Mainz Hotel,  Malakoff-Terrasse 1, D-55116 Mainz, Germany**

Tel: 49-6131-73-1234   Fax: 49-6131-73-1235

## HYPERION SOLUTIONS CORPORATION

1344 Crossman Avenue, Sunnyvale, CA, 94089

Tel: (408) 744-9500      Fax: (408) 744-0400      www.hyperion.com

*Mfr. data analysis software tools.*

**Hauptniederlassung Frankfurt,  Platz der Einheit 1, 60327 Frankfurt/Main, Germany**

Tel: 49-69-505050

**Niederlassung Duesseldorf,  Heinrich-Heine-Allee 53, 40213 Duesseldorf, Germany**

**Niederlassung Germany,  Muenchner Strasse 16, 85774 Unterfoehring, Germany**

**Niederlassung Germany,  Fritz-Elsas-Strasse 38, 70174 Stuttgart, Germany**

**Niederlassung Germany,  Zuerich Haus, Domstrasse 17, 20095 Hamburg, Germany**

## i2 TECHNOLOGIES, INC.

11701 Luna Road, Dallas, TX, 75234

Tel: (214) 860-6106      Fax: (214) 860-6060      www.i2.com

*Mfr. business-to-business software.*

**i2 Technologies Germany,  Richard-Reitzner-Allee 8, D-85540 Haar by Münich, Germany**

## IBM CORPORATION

New Orchard Road, Armonk, NY, 10504

Tel: (914) 765-1900      Fax: (914) 765-7382      www.ibm.com

*Information products, technology and services.*

**IBM Deutschland Direct GmbH,  Am Fichtenberg 1, D-71083 Herrenberg, Germany**

Tel: 49-7032-152720   Fax: 49-7032-153777

## ICN PHARMACEUTICALS, INC.

3300 Hyland Ave., Costa Mesa, CA, 92626

Tel: (714) 545-0100      Fax: (714) 641-7268      www.icnpharm.com

*Mfr./distribute pharmaceuticals.*

**ICN Biomedicals,  Thüringer Straße 15, D-37269 Eschwege, Germany**

Tel: 49-5651-921-0

## ICORE INTERNATIONAL INC.

180 North Wolfe Road, Sunnyvale, CA, 94086

Tel: (408) 732-5400   Fax: (408) 720-8507   www.icoreintl.com

*Harness and conduit systems, battery connectors, etc.*

**Icore International GmbH., Hohestrasse 31-33, 61348 Bad Homburg, Germany**

Tel: 49-6172-67730

## IDT CORPORATION

520 Broad Street, Newark, NJ, 07102

Tel: (973) 438-1000   Fax: (973) 438-4002   www.idt.net

*Engaged in domestic and international long distance telecommunications.*

**IDT Germany GmbH, Gruneburgweg 12, 60322 Frankfurt, Germany**

Tel: 49-69-548-100

## IKON OFFICE SOLUTIONS

70 Valley Stream Parkway, Malvern, PA, 19355

Tel: (610) 296-8000   Fax: (610) 408-7022   www.ikon.com

*Provider of office technology solutions.*

**Ikon Office Solutions, Berner Str. 34, D-60437 Frankfurt, Germany**

Tel: 49-69-952010-0

**Ikon Office Solutions, Kreuzberger Ring26, D-65205 Wiesbaden, Germany**

Tel: 49-611-714522

**Ikon Office Solutions, Buttnerstr 13, D-30165 Hannover, Germany**

Tel: 49-511-358840

## ILLINOIS TOOL WORKS (ITW)

3600 West Lake Ave., Glenview, IL, 60025-5811

Tel: (847) 724-7500   Fax: (847) 657-4268   www.itw.com

*Mfr. gears, tools, fasteners, sealants, plastic and metal components for industrial, medical, etc.*

**ITW-Ateco GmbH, Stormannstr. 43, Norderstedt, Germany**

## IMATION CORPORATION

One Imation Place, Oakdale, MN, 55128

Tel: (612) 704-4000   Fax: (612) 704-3444   www.imation.com

*Dry laser-imaging film systems.*

**Imation GmbH, Hilden, Germany**

Tel: 49-2103-9830

## IMG (INTERNATIONAL MANAGEMENT GROUP)

1360 East Ninth Street, Ste. 100, Cleveland, OH, 44114

Tel: (216) 522-1200   Fax: (216) 522-1145   www.imgworld.com

*Manages athletes, sports academies and real estate facilities worldwide.*

**IMG GmbH, Magdalenenstrasse 7, Hamburg 20148, Germany**

Tel: 49-4041-40040   Fax: 49-4041-400420

**Nick Bollettieri Tennis Academy, Pachter Roland Mank, Am Golfplaz 1, Bad Saarow, Germany**

Tel: 49-33631-63-700   Fax: 49-33631-63-710

**Sporting Club Berlin, International Tennis Center, Am Golfplatz 1, Bad Saarow, Berlin 155526, Germany**

Tel: 49-33-631-37000   Fax: 49-33-631-63710

**Sportpark Buhl IMG, Hagenichstraße 10, Buhl 77815, Germany**

Tel: 49-7223-940-8630   Fax: 49-7223-940-8613

## IMO INDUSTRIES, DIV. COLFAX INC.

9211 Forest Hill Ave., Richmond, VA, 23235

Tel: (804) 560-4070     Fax: (804) 560-4076     www.imochain.com

*Mfr./support mechanical and electronic controls, chains and engineered power products.*

**IMO Industries GmbH, Dorn-Assenheimer Strasse 27, D-61201 Reichelsheim, Germany**

**IMO Industries GmbH, Morse Teleflex, Hoeseler Strasse 40, D-42579 Heiligenhaus, Germany**

**IMO-Pumpen, Hamelner Strasse 52, Postfach 1228, D-32678 Barntrup, Germany**

## IMPCO TECHNOLOGIES, INC.

16804 Gridley Place, Cerritos, CA, 90703

Tel: (562) 860-6666     Fax: (562) 809-1240     www.impco.ws

*Mfr. fuel control processors.*

**IMPCO-BERU Technologies GmbH, Perchstätten 16, 35428 Langgöns, Germany**

Tel: 49-6403-911-330    Fax: 49-6403-911-335

## IMS HEALTH INCORPORATED

200 Nyala Farms, Westport, CT, 06880

Tel: (203) 222-4200     Fax: (203) 222-4276     www.imshealth.com

*Provides sales management reports and prescription tracking reports for pharmaceutical and health-care companies.*

**IMS Health GmbH & Co., Hahnstrasse 30-32, Frankfurt/Maim 60528, Germany**

Tel: 69-66-0401    Fax: 69-66-04299

## INDUCTOTHERM CORPORATION

10 Indel Ave., PO Box 157, Rancocas, NJ, 08073-0157

Tel: (609) 267-9000     Fax: (609) 267-3537     www.inductotherm.com

*Mfr. induction melting furnaces, induction power supplies, charging and preheating systems, automatic pouring systems and computer control systems.*

**Inductotherm Deutschland GmbH, Haupstrasse 7, D-5107 Simmerath, Germany**

Tel: 49-2473-8002    Contact: Helmuth Ronig

## INDUSTRIAL ACOUSTICS COMPANY

1160 Commerce Ave., Bronx, NY, 10462

Tel: (718) 931-8000     Fax: (718) 863-1138     www.industrialacoustics.com

*Design/mfr. acoustic structures for sound conditioning and noise control.*

**Industrial Acoustics GmbH, Sohlweg 24, D-4055 Niederkruchten, Germany**

## INFOGRAMES, INC.

417 Fifth Avenue, New York, NY, 10016

Tel: (212) 726-6500     Fax: (212) 679-3224     www.infogrames.com

*Mfr. video games.*

**Infogrames Germany, Robert Bosch Strasse 18, 63303 Dreieich Sprendlingen, Germany**

## INFONET SERVICES CORPORATION

2100 East Grand Ave., El Segundo, CA, 90245-1022

Tel: (310) 335-2600     Fax: (310) 335-4507     www.infonet.com

*Provider of Internet services and electronic messaging services.*

**Infonet Network Services Deutschland GmbH, Lyonerstrase 14, D-60494 Frankfurt am Main, Germany**

Tel: 49-69-665-220    Fax: 49-69-666-4566

## INFORMATION BUILDERS INC.

Two Penn Plaza, New York, NY, 10121-2898

Tel: (212) 736-4433     Fax: (212) 967-6406     www.ibi.com

*Develop/mfr./services computer software.*

**Information Builders Deutschland GmbH, Leopoldstrasse 236-238, D-80807 Münich, Germany**

## INFORMATION MANAGEMENT ASSOCIATES, INC.

One Corporate Drive, Ste. 414, Shelton, CT, 06484

Tel: (203) 925-6800    Fax: (203) 925-1170    www.ima-inc.com

*Sales/distribution of software for use by telephone call centers; consult, support and maintenance services.*

**IMA Software GmbH, Im Atricom Box A5, Lyoner Strasse 15, D-60528 Frankfurt, Germany**

Tel: 49-696-657-7380

## INFORMATION RESOURCES, INC. (IRI)

150 N. Clinton St., Chicago, IL, 60661

Tel: (312) 726-1221    Fax: (312) 726-0360    www.infores.com

*Provides bar code scanner services for retail sales organizations; processes, analyzes and sells data from the huge database created from these services.*

**GfK Panel Services, Nordwestring 101, Postfach 2854, D-90319 Nurenberg 90, Germany**

Tel: 49-911-395-3202    Fax: 49-911-395-4013

## INFORMIX CORPORATION

4100 Bohannon Drive, Menlo Park, CA, 95025

Tel: (650) 926-6300    Fax: (650) 926-6593    www.informix.com

*Designs and produces database management software, connectivity interfaces and gateways, and other computer applications.*

**Informix Software GmbH, Geschaeftsstelle Frankfurt, Mergenthaler Alle 77, D-65760 Eschborn/Taunus Frankfurt, Germany**

Tel: 49-6196-401600

## INGERSOLL INTERNATIONAL INC.

707 Fulton Ave., Rockford, IL, 61103

Tel: (815) 987-6000    Fax: (815) 987-6725    www.ingersoll.com

*Automated production systems.*

**Ingersoll Funkenerosionstechnik, Daimlerstrasse 22, D-57299 Burbach, Germany**

Tel: 49-2736-493-225    Fax: 49-2736-493-810

**Ingersoll Naxos, Pittlerstrasse 6, D-63225 Langen, Germany**

Tel: 49-6105-755-0    Fax: 49-6103-755-412

**Ingersoll Werkzeuge, Daimlerstrasse 22, D 57299, Burbach, Germany**

Tel: 49-2736-493-01    Fax: 49-2736-493-244

**Waldrich Coburg, Postfach 3253, 96450 Coburg, Germany**

Tel: 49-9561-651    Fax: 49-9561-60500

**Waldrich Siegen, Daimlerstrasse 24, D-57299 Burbach, Germany**


**München, Germany**

Tel: 49-2736-493-02    Fax: 49-2736-493-706

## INGERSOLL-RAND COMPANY

200 Chestnut Ridge Road, Woodcliff Lake, NJ, 07675

Tel: (201) 573-0123    Fax: (201) 573-3172    www.ingersoll-rand.com

*Mfr. compressors, rock drills, air tools, door hardware, ball bearings.*

**G. Klemm Bohrtechnik GmbH, Wintersohler Str. 5, D-57489 Drolshagen-Wenkhausen, Germany**

**Ingersoll-Rand GmbH, Gwerbeallee 17, D-45478 Mulheim/Ruhr, Germany**

Tel: 49-208-99940    Fax: 49-208-9994-486

**Ingersoll-Rank Waterjet Cutting Systems, European HQ, Auf der Laukert II, D-61231 Bad Nauheim, Germany**

**Ingersol-Rand ABG, Kuhbruckenstrasse 18, Postfach 10133, D-31785 Hameln, Germany**

**Pleuger Worthington GmbH, Friedrich-Ebert Damm 105, D-2000 Hamburg 70, Germany**

Torrington Nadellagher GmbH,  Werkstrasse 5, Postfach 1263/1264, D-33788 Halle Westfalen, Germany

## INGRAM MICRO INC.

PO Box 25125, 1600 E. St. Andrew Place, Santa Ana, CA, 92799

Tel:  (714) 566-1000       Fax:  (714) 566-7940       www.ingrammicro.com

*Engaged in wholesale distribution of microcomputer products.*

**Ingram Micro Inc.,  München, Germany**

## INKTOMI CORPORATION

4100 East Third Avenue, Foster City, CA, 94404

Tel:  (650) 653-2800       Fax:  (650) 653-2801       www.iktomi.com

*Mfr. software to boost speeds of computer networks.*

**Inktomi Corporation,  Maximilianstr. 35a, D-80539 Munchen, Germany**
Tel: 49-89-24218-109

**Inktomi Corporation,  Platz der Einheit 1, 60327 Frankfurt, Germany**
Tel: 49-69-97503-119

## INSTINET

875 Third Ave., New York, NY, 10022

Tel:  (212) 310-9500       Fax:  (212) 832-5183       www.instinet.com

*Online investment brokerage.*

**Instinet,  Germany**

## INSTRON CORPORATION

100 Royal Street, Canton, MA, 02021-1089

Tel:  (781) 575-5000       Fax:  (781) 575-5751       www.instron.com

*Mfr. material testing instruments.*

**Instron Schenck Testing Systems GmbH,  Landwehrstrasse 65,  D-64293 Darmstadt, Germany**
Tel: 49-6151-32-47-00

## INTEGRATED SILICON SOLUTION, INC.

2231 Lawson Lane, Santa Clara, CA, 95054-3311

Tel:  (408) 588-0800       Fax:  (408) 588-0805       www.issiusa.com

*Mfr. high-speed memory chips and SRAMs.*

**Integrated Silicon Solution, Inc.,  Planegg Germany**
Tel: 49-89-899-30193    Fax: 49-89-899-0399

## INTEL CORPORATION

Robert Noyce Bldg., 2200 Mission College Blvd., Santa Clara, CA, 95052-8119

Tel:  (408) 765-8080       Fax:  (408) 765-1739       www.intel.com

*Mfr. semiconductor, microprocessor and micro-communications components and systems.*

**Intel Semiconductor GmbH,  Seidl 27, D-8200 München, Germany**
Tel: 49-89-99143-0

## INTER-CONTINENTAL HOTELS

3 Ravina Drive, Suite 2900, Atlanta, GA, 30346-2149

Tel:  (770) 604-2000       Fax:  (770) 604-5403       www.interconti.com

*Worldwide hotel and resort accommodations.*

**Forum Hotel Berlin,  Alexanderplatz, D-10178 Berlin, Germany**
Tel: 49-30-2389    Fax: 49-30-2389-4305

**Hotel Inter-Continental Leipzig,  Gerberstrasse 15, D-04105 Leipzig, Germany**
Tel: 49-341-988-0    Fax: 49-341-988-1229

**Inter-Continental Hotels,  Moselstrasse 4, D-60329 Frankfurt am Main, Germany**
Tel: 49-69-27-40140    Fax: 49-69-23-0255

## INTERGRAPH CORPORATION

One Madison Industrial Park, Huntsville, AL, 35894-0001

Tel: (256) 730-2000    Fax: (256) 730-7898    www.intergraph.com

*Develop/mfr. interactive computer graphic systems.*

**Intergraph (Deutschland) GmbH,  München, Germany**

Tel: 49-40-278500   Fax: 49-40-273360

**Intergraph (Deutschland) GmbH,  Robert-Bosch-Strasse 5, Dreieich-Sprendlingen, D-63303 Frankfurt, Germany**

Tel: 49-610-33770   Fax: 49-610-337-7100

**Intergraph (Deutschland) GmbH,  Zettachring 4, Stuttgart, Germany**

Tel: 49-7-117253500   Fax: 49-7-117288913

**Intergraph (Deutschland) GmbH,  Reuterstrasse 161, D-53113 Bonn, Germany**

Tel: 49-228-9140956   Fax: 49-228-9140957

**Intergraph (Deutschland) GmbH,  Alt-Moabit 96b, D-10559 Berlin, Germany**

Tel: 49-3-03999120   Fax: 49-3-03919427

**Intergraph (Deutschland) GmbH,  Paul-Thomas-Strasse 58, D-40599 Düsseldorf, Germany**

Tel: 49-211-97460   Fax: 49-211-9746150

## INTERMEC TECHNOLOGIES CORPORATION

6001 36th Ave. West, PO Box 4280, Everett, WA, 98203-9280

Tel: (425) 348-2600    Fax: (425) 355-9551    www.intermec.com

*Mfr./distributor automated data collection systems.*

**Intermec Technologies GmbH,  Schiess-Strasse 44a, D-40549 Düsseldorf, Germany**

Tel: 49-211-536010   Fax: 49-211-5360150

## INTERNATIONAL COMPONENTS CORPORATION

420 N. May Street, Chicago, IL, 60622

Tel: (312) 829-2525    Fax: (312) 829-0213    www.icc-charge.com

*Mfr./sale/services portable DC battery chargers.*

**International Components GmbH (ICG),  Kleinreuther Weg 120, D-90425 Nuremberg, Germany**

## INTERNATIONAL FLAVORS & FRAGRANCES INC.

521 West 57th Street, New York, NY, 10019-2960

Tel: (212) 765-5500    Fax: (212) 708-7132    www.iff.com

*Design/mfr. flavors, fragrances and aroma chemicals.*

**International Flavors & Fragrances GmbH,  Postfach 302789, D-2000 Hamburg 36, Germany**

Tel: 49-40-355358-0   Fax: 49-40-355358-23

**International Flavors & Fragrances GmbH,  Emmerich/Rheim, Germany**

## INTERNATIONAL PAPER COMPANY

2 Manhattanville Road, Purchase, NY, 10577

Tel: (914) 397-1500    Fax: (914) 397-1596    www.ipaper.com

*Mfr./distributor container board, paper and wood products.*

**Anitec Image (Deutschland) GmbH,  Bachemer Landstrasse 29, Postfach 40 01 51, D-5000 Cologne 40, Germany**

**Aussedat Rey Deutschland GmbH,  Volmerswerther Strasse 20, D-4000 Düsseldorf 1, Germany**

**Bergvik Chemie GmbH,  Bahrenfelder Str. 244, D-2000 Hamburg 50, Germany**

**Freundorfer GmbH,  Steinerstrasse 11, Postfach 70 06 60, D-8000 München 70, Germany**

**Hammerhill Paper GmbH,  Duisburger Landstrasse 25, D-4000 Düsseldorf 31, Germany**

**Ilford Photo GmbH,  An der Gohrsmuhle, D-5060 Bergisch Gladbach 2, Germany**

**Joost & Preuss GbmH,  Rodingsmarkt 14, D-2000 Hamburg 11, Germany**

**Zanders Feinpapiere AG,  An der Gohrsmuhle, D-5060 Bergisch Gladbach 2, Germany**

## INTERNATIONAL RECTIFIER CORPORATION

233 Kansas Street, El Segundo, CA, 90245

Tel: (310) 322-3331     Fax: (310) 322-3332     www.irf.com

*Mfr. power semiconductor components.*

**International Rectifier - Germany, Saalburgstrasse 157, D-61350 Bad Homburg, Germany**

Tel: 49-6172-96590   Fax: 49-6172-965933

## INTERNATIONAL SPECIALTY PRODUCTS, INC.

1361 Alps Rd., Wayne, NJ, 07470

Tel: (877) 389-3083     Fax: (973) 628-4117     www.ispcorp.com

*Mfr. specialty chemical products.*

**ISP Global Technologies Deutschland GmbH, Emil Hofman-Strasse 1 a, D-50996 Cologne-Rodenkirchen, Germany**

Tel: 49-2236-96490   Fax: 49-2236-9649

## INTERVOICE INC.

17811 Waterview Pkwy., Dallas, TX, 75206

Tel: (972) 454-8000     Fax: (972) 454-8707     www.intervoice.com

*Mfr. voice automation systems and provides interactive information solutions.*

**InterVoice-Brite GmbH, Bleichstrasse 1-3, 65183 Wiesbaden, Germany**

Tel: 49-611-18444-0   Fax: 49-611-18444-44

## INTRALOX INC.

201 Laitram Lane, New Orleans, LA, 70123

Tel: (504) 733-0463     Fax: (504) 734-0063     www.intralox.com

*Mfr. plastic, modular conveyor belts and accessories.*

**Intralox GmbH, Heinrich-Hertz Str. 44, D-4006 Erkrath-Unterfeldhaus, Germany**

## INTRUSION.COM, INC.

1101 East Arapaho Road, Richardson, TX, 75081

Tel: (972) 234-6400     Fax: (972) 234-1467     www.intrusion.com

*Mfr. security software.*

**Intrusion.Com, GmbH, Erfurter Strasse 29, D-85386 Eching, Germany**

## INVACARE CORPORATION

One Invacare Way, Elyria, OH, 44036

Tel: (440) 329-6000     Fax: (440) 366-6568     www.invacare.com

*Mfr. home medical equipment, wheelchairs, respiratory care products, home care aids.*

**Invacare Deutschland GmbH, Dehmer Strasse 66, D-32549 Bad Oeynhausen, Germany**

Tel: 49-5731-7540   Fax: 49-5731-754-111

## IOMEGA CORPORATION

1821 West 4000 South, Roy, UT, 84067

Tel: (801) 778-4494     Fax: (801) 778-3450     www.iomega.com

*Mfr. data storage products.*

**Iomega, Konigsallee 60/F, D-4000 Düsseldorf 1, Germany**

## IPSEN INDUSTRIES INC.

894 Ipsen Rd., Cherry Valley, IL, 61016

Tel: (815) 332-4941     Fax: (815) 332-7625     www.ipsen-intl.com

*Heat treating equipment.*

**Ipsen International GmbH, PO Box 1447, D-47514 Kleve, Germany**

Tel: 49-2821-804-0   Fax: 49-2821-804-324

## IRIDIUM LLC

1575 "I" Street, NW, Washington, DC, 20005

Tel: (202) 408-3800     Fax: (202) 408-3801     www.iridium.com

*Consortium of companies sharing the construction and implementation of a global satellite communications system.*

**Iridium Communications Germany GmbH (ICG), Iridium North Europe Reg. HQ, Jagerhofstrasse 19-20, D-40479 Düsseldorf, Germany**

Tel: 49-211-4973-200   Fax: 49-211-4973-112   Contact: Thomas Loewenthal, Dir.

## IRRIDELCO INTERNATIONAL CORPORATION

440 Sylvan Ave., Englewood Cliffs, NJ, 07632

Tel: (201) 569-3030     Fax: (201) 569-9237     www.irridelco.com

*Mfr./distributor of the most comprehensive lines of mechanical and micro irrigation; pumps and irrigation systems.*

**Irrigation & Industrial Development Corp. GmbH, Niddastr 42-44, D-6000 Frankfurt, Germany**

## ITT INDUSTRIES, INC.

4 West Red Oak Lane, White Plains, NY, 10604

Tel: (914) 641-2000     Fax: (914) 696-2950     www.ittind.com

*Mfr. pumps, systems and services to move and control water/fluids and produces connectors, switches, keypads and cabling used in computing, telecommunications, aerospace and industrial applications, as well as network services.*

**ITT Industries- Fluid Handling Systems, Talhausstrasse 14, D-68766 Hockenheim, Germany**

Tel: 49-6205-2008-800   Fax: 49-6205-2008-850

**ITT Systems Intl. Corp., Bldg. 3113, Daenner Kaserne, Mannheimer Strasse, D-6750 Kaiserslautern, Germany**

**KONI Germany, Industriegebiet, 56424 Ebernhahn, Germany**

Tel: 49-2623-602-30

**Richter Chemie-Technik, Otto-Schott Strasse 2, D-47906 Kempen, Germany**

Tel: 49-2151-1460   Fax: 49-2152-146190

## ITT-GOULDS PUMPS INC.

240 Fall Street, Seneca Falls, NY, 13148

Tel: (315) 568-2811     Fax: (315) 568-2418     www.gouldspumps.com

*Mfr. industrial and water systems pumps.*

**Vogel Ochsner Pumpen GmbH, Yorckstraße 24, Düsseldorf D-40476, Germany**

Tel: 49-211-480206   Fax: 49-211-480208

## ITW DEVCON PLEXUS

30 Endicott Street, Danvers, MA, 01923

Tel: (978) 777-1100     Fax: (978) 774-0516     www.devcon-equip.com

*Mfr. filled epoxies, urethanes, adhesives and metal treatment products.*

**ITW Devcon GmbH, Siemansstr. 15, D-4030 Ratingen 4 Lantare, Germany**

Tel: 49-431-718830

## ITW RANSBURG FINISHING SYSTEMS

320 Phillips Ave., Toledo, OH, 43612

Tel: (419) 470-2000     Fax: (419) 470-2112     www.itwransburg.com

*Mfr. liquid electrostatic paint application equipment.*

**ITW Oberflaechentechnik GmbH, Justus-Von-Liebigstr 31, D-6057 Dietzenbach 1, Germany**

## IXYS CORPORATION

3540 Bassett Street, Santa Clara, CA, 95054

Tel: (408) 982-0700     Fax: (408) 748-9788     www.ixys.com

*Mfr. semiconductors and modules.*

**IXYS Semiconductor GmbH, Edisonstrasse 15, D-68623 Lampertheim, Germany**

## J. WALTER THOMPSON COMPANY

466 Lexington Ave., New York, NY, 10017

Tel: (212) 210-7000     Fax: (212) 210-6944     www.jwt.com

*International advertising and marketing services.*

**DSB&K Frakfurt, Frankfurt, Germany**

**J. Walter Thompson Co., Frankfurt, Germany**

## JAMESBURY CORPORATION

640 Lincoln Street, Box 15004, Worcester, MA, 01615-0004

Tel: (508) 852-0200     Fax: (508) 852-8172     www.jamesbury.com

*Mfr. valves and accessories.*

**Jamesbury GmbH, Tolnauer Str. 3, Postfach 104, D-7992 Tettnang Buergermoos, West Germany**

## JDA SOFTWARE GROUP, INC.

14400 N. 87th St., Scottsdale, AZ, 85260-3649

Tel: (480) 308-3000     Fax: (480) 308-3001     www.jda.com

*Developer of information management software for retail, merchandising, distribution and store management.*

**JDA Software GmbH, Garather Schlossallee 19, D-40595 Duesseldorf, Germany**

Tel: 49-6966-554-266    Fax: 49-6966-554-100

## JEUNIQUE BEAUTY FOR ALL SEASONS, INC.

19501 E. Walnut Dr., City of Industry, CA, 91748

Tel: (909) 598-8598     Fax: (909) 594-8258     www.jeunique.com

*Mfr./sale vitamins, food supplements, cosmetics and diet products.*

**Jeunique Beauty For All Seasons., Ginnheimer Strasse 24, D-65760 Eschborn, Germany**

## JLG INDUSTRIES INC.

One JLG Drive, McConnellsburg, PA, 17233-9533

Tel: (717) 485-5161     Fax: (717) 485-6417     www.jlg.com

*Mfr. aerial work platforms and vertical personnel lifts.*

**JLG Deutschland GmbH, Max Planck Strasse 21, D-27721 Ritterhude/Ihlpohl Bei Bremen, Germany**

Tel: 49-42-1693-5000    Fax: 49-42-1693-5035

## JOHNS MANVILLE CORPORATION

717 17th Street, Denver, CO, 80202

Tel: (303) 978-2000     Fax: (303) 978-2318     www.jm.com

*Mfr. fiberglass insulation, roofing products and systems, fiberglass material and reinforcements, filtration mats.*

**Johns Manville International, Postfach 1555, D-97865 Wertheim, Germany**

## JOHNSON & JOHNSON

One Johnson & Johnson Plaza, New Brunswick, NJ, 08933

Tel: (732) 524-0400     Fax: (732) 214-0334     www.jnj.com

*Mfr./distributor/R&D pharmaceutical, health care and cosmetic products.*

**DePuy Orthopädie GmbH, Sulzbach, Germany**

**Ethicon GmbH/Ethicon Endo-Surgery (Europe) GmbH, Robert-Kochstr. 15, D-2000 Norderstedt, Germany**

Jannsen-Cilag GmbH, Rosellen, Germany

Johnson & Johnson GmbH, Postfach 103161, D-40022 Düsseldorf, Germany

Johnson & Johnson Medical GmbH, Postfach 1364, D-22803 Norderstedt, Germany

LifeScan GmbH, D-69141 Neckargemund, Germany

Ortho-Clinical Diagnostics GmbH, Postfach 1340, D-69141 Neckargemund, Germany

Penaten GmbH, Postfach 1680, D-53588 Bad Honnef, Germany

## S C JOHNSON & SON INC.

1525 Howe St., Racine, WI, 53403

Tel: (414) 260-2000      Fax: (414) 260-2133      www.scjohnsonwax.com

*Home, auto, commercial and personal care products and specialty chemicals.*

S.C. Johnson & Son Ltd., Postfach 1100, Solingen, D-5657 Haan Rhld, Germany

## JOHNSON CONTROLS INC.

5757 N. Green Bay Ave., PO Box 591, Milwaukee, WI, 53201-0591

Tel: (414) 228-1200      Fax: (414) 228-2077      www.johnsoncontrols.com

*Mfr. facility management and control systems and auto seating.*

JCI Regelungstechnik GmbH, Industriesstrasse 20-30, Burcheid, Germany

Tel: 49-2174-65-110

JCI Regelungstechnik GmbH, Alderstrasse 1, D-45307 Essen, Germany

Tel: 49-201-55880   Fax: 49-201-5588280   Contact: Peter Pienker, Branch Mgr.

## THE JOHNSON CORPORATION

805 Wood Street, Three Rivers, MI, 49093

Tel: (616) 278-1715      Fax: (616) 273-2230      www.joco.com

*Mfr. rotary joints and siphon systems.*

Johnson Deutschland GmbH, Langendfeld, Germany

## JOHNSON OUTDOORS, INC.

1326 Willow Road, Sturtevant, WI, 53177

Tel: (414) 884-1500      Fax: (414) 884-1600      www.jwa.com

*Mfr. diving, fishing, boating and camping sports equipment.*

Jack Wolfskin, Ausrustung fur Draussen GmbH, Limburger Strasse 38-40, D-65510 Idstein/Ts., Germany

Tel: 49-6126-9540   Fax: 49-6126-954159

Scubapro Germany, Rheinvogtstrasse 17, D-79713 Bad Sackingen-Wallbach, Germany

Tel: 49-7761-92100   Fax: 49-7761-921030

Uwatec Instruments Deutschland, Tauchsportvertrieb GmbH, Murgralstrasse 28, D-79736 Rickenbach-Hottingen, Germany

Tel: 49-77-651043   Fax: 49-77-658548

## JONES LANG LASALLE

101 East 52nd Street, New York, NY, 10022

Tel: (212) 688-8181      Fax: (212) 308-5199      www.jlw.com

*International marketing consultants, leasing agents and property management advisors.*

Jones Lang Wootton, Germany

## JONES, DAY, REAVIS & POGUE

North Point, 901 Lakeside Ave., Cleveland, OH, 44114

Tel: (216) 586-3939      Fax: (216) 579-0212      www.jonesday.com

*International law firm.*

Jones, Day, Reavis & Pogue, 20/F - Hochhaus am Park, Grüneburgweg 102, D-60323 Frankfurt am Main, Germany

Tel: 49-69-9726-3939   Fax: 49-69-9726-3993   Contact: Karl G. Herold, Partner   Emp: 62

## JUKI UNION SPECIAL CORPORATION

5 Haul Road, Wayne, NJ, 07470

Tel: (973) 633-7200        Fax: (973) 633-9629        www.unionspecial.com

*Mfr. sewing machines.*

**Union Special GmbH,  Raiffeisenstrasse3, Po Box 1148, D-71696 Moglingen, Germany**

Tel: 49-7141-2470   Fax: 49-7141-247-100   Contact: A. Briegel, Mng.

## JUPITER MEDIA METRIX INC.

21 Astor Place, New York, NY, 10003

Tel: (212) 780-6060        Fax: (212) 780-6075        www.jmm.com

*Engaged in research services to determine audience measurement.*

**Jupiter Media Metrix Inc.,  Pilotystrasse 4, 80538 Münich, Germany**

Tel: 49-89-23035-315

## K-2, INC.

4900 South Eastern Ave., Los Angeles, CA, 90040

Tel: (323) 724-2800        Fax: (323) 724-8174        www.k2sports.com

*Mfr. sporting goods, recreational and industrial products.*

**K2 Sport and Mode GmbH,  Seeshaupter Strasse 60, D-8237 Penzberg, Germany**

Tel: 49-8856-9010

## KAPPLER PROTECTIVE APPAREL & FABRICS

PO Box 218, 70 Grimes Drive, Guntersville, AL, 35976

Tel: (205) 505-4000        Fax: (205) 505-4004        www.kappler.com

*Mfr. of protective apparel and fabrics.*

**Kappler Germany,  Mathias-Brüggeu-Strasse 144, D-50829 Köln, Germany**

Tel: 49-221-956-4820   Fax: 49-221-956-4828   Contact: Andreas Heine, Mng. Dir.   Emp: 20

## KATY INDUSTRIES INC.

6300 South Syracuse Way, Ste. 300, Englewood, CO, 80111

Tel: (303) 290-9300        Fax: (303) 290-9344        www.katyindustries.com

*Mfr. electronic and maintenance equipment for industrial and consumer markets.*

**Schon & Cie AG,  Im Gehornerwald 2, D-6780 Pirmasems 17, Germany**

## KAWNEER COMPANY, INC.

555 Guthridge Court, Norcross, GA, 30092

Tel: (770) 449-5555        Fax: (770) 734-1570        www.kawneer.com

*Mfr. arch aluminum products for commercial construction.*

**Kawneer Aluminium GmbH,  Erfstrasse 75, Postfach 20 07 45, D-41207 Monchengladbach 2, Germany**

## KAYSER-ROTH CORPORATION

4905 Koger Blvd., Greensboro, NC, 27407

Tel: (336) 852-2030        Fax: (336) 632-1921        www.nononsense.com

*Mfr. hosiery.*

**Arlington Socks,  Fabrikstr. 1, D-7860 Schopfheim, Germany**

## A.T. KEARNEY INC.

222 West Adams Street, Chicago, IL, 60606

Tel: (312) 648-0111        Fax: (312) 223-6200        www.atkearney.com

*Management consultants and executive search.*

**A. T. Kearney GmbH,  Am Festungsgraben 1, D-10117 Berlin, Germany**

Tel: 49-30-2202-260

**A. T. Kearney GmbH,  Am Hauptbahnhof 9, D-70173 Stuttgart, Germany**

Tel: 49-711-132550

**A. T. Kearney GmbH, Maximilianstrasse 40, D-80539 Münich, Germany**
Tel: 49-89-290-620

**A. T. Kearney GmbH, Jan-Wellem-Platz 3, D-40212 Düsseldorf, Germany**
Tel: 49-211-1377-0

**A. T. Kearney GmbH, Charlottenstrasse 57, D-10117 Berlin, Germany**
Tel: 49-30-202-260

## KEER-McGEE CORPORATION

123 Robert S. Kerr Avenue, Oklahoma City, OK, 73102

Tel: (405) 270-1313      Fax: (405) 270-3029      www.kerr-mcgee.com

*Oil and gas exploration and production.*

**Kerr-McGee Pigments GmbH & Co. KG, Münich, Germany**

## KEITHLEY INSTRUMENTS INC.

28775 Aurora Road, Cleveland, OH, 44139

Tel: (440) 248-0400      Fax: (440) 248-6168      www.keithley.com

*Mfr. electronic test/measure instruments, PC-based data acquisition hardware/software.*

**Keithley Instruments GmbH, Landsberger Str. 65, D-82110 Germering, Germany**

## KELLOGG BROWN & ROOT INC.

PO Box 3, Houston, TX, 77001

Tel: (713) 676-3011      Fax: (713) 676-8695      www.halliburton.com

*Engaged in technology-based engineering and construction.*

**Kellogg Brown & Root/Philip Morris (JV), Haberstrasse 10, Berlin 12057, Germany**

## KELLOGG COMPANY

One Kellogg Square, PO Box 3599, Battle Creek, MI, 49016-3599

Tel: (616) 961-2000      Fax: (616) 961-2871      www.kelloggs.com

*Mfr. ready-to-eat cereals and convenience foods.*

**Kellogg (Deutschland) GmbH, Attn: German Office, One Kellogg Square, PO Box 3599, Battle Creek MI 49016-3599**

## KELLY SERVICES, INC.

999 W. Big Beaver Road, Troy, MI, 48084

Tel: (248) 362-4444      Fax: (248) 244-4154      www.kellyservices.com

*Temporary help placement.*

**Kelly Services (Deutschland) GmbH, Ludwig-Erhard-Str. 37, 20459 Hamburg, Germany**
Tel: 49-40-31-77310   Fax: 49-40-317-3112

## KENDA SYSTEMS INC.

One Stiles Road, Salem, NH, 03079

Tel: (603) 898-7884      Fax: (603) 898-3016      www.kenda.com

*Computer programming services.*

**Kenda Systems GmbH, Am Seerten 24, 40547, Düsseldorf, Germany**
Tel: 49-211-596-789

## THE KENDALL COMPANY (TYCO HEALTHCARE)

15 Hampshire Street, Mansfield, MA, 02048

Tel: (508) 261-8000      Fax: (508) 261-8542      www.kendalhq.com

*Mfr. medical disposable products, home health care products and specialty adhesive products.*

**CDK Holding Deutschland GmbH, Postfach 1217, D-93328 Neustadt/Donau, Germany**
Tel: 49-951-60470   Fax: 49-951-68392

**CDK Holding Deutschland GmbH, Postfach 1217, D-9333 Neustadt/Donau, Germany**
Tel: 49-94-45-959-0   Fax: 49-94-45-959-155

OFA Bamberg, Postfach 1480, D-96005 Bamberg, Germany

Tel: 49-951-60470    Fax: 49-951-68392

## KENNAMETAL INC.

State Rte. 981, Latrobe, PA, 15650

Tel: (724) 539-5000    Fax: (724) 539-4710    www.kennametal.com

*Tools, hard carbide and tungsten alloys for metalworking industry.*

**Kennametal Hertel AG - European Hdqtrs., Werkzeuge + Hartstoffe, Postfach 1751, D-90707 Fürth, Germany**

Tel: 49-911-97350    Fax: 49-911-9735-388

**Kennametal Hertel GmbH, Max Planck Str. 13, Postfach 1347, D-61364 Friedrichsdorf, Germany**

Tel: 49-61-72-7370    Fax: 49-61-72-78490

## KENT-MOORE

28635 Mound Road, Ste. 335, Warren, MI, 48092-3499

Tel: (810) 578-7289    Fax: (810) 578-7375    www.spx.com

*Mfr. service equipment for auto, construction, recreational, military and agricultural vehicles.*

**Kent-Moore Deutschland GmbH, Postfach 1528, Alfred Nobel Strasse 12, D-6806 Viernheim, Germany**

## KEPNER-TREGOE INC.

PO Box 704, Princeton, NJ, 08542-0740

Tel: (609) 921-2806    Fax: (609) 497-0130    www.kepner-tregoe.com

*Management consulting; specializing in strategy formulation, problem solving, decision making, project management, and cost reduction.*

**Kepner-Tregoe GmbH, An der Alster 17, 20099 Hamburg, Germany**

Tel: 49-40-284075-0    Fax: 49-40-284075-28

## KERR-McGEE CORPORATION

PO Box 25861, Oklahoma City, OK, 73125

Tel: (405) 270-1313    Fax: (405) 270-3123    www.kerr-mcgee.com

*Engaged in oil and gas exploration and manufacture of inorganic chemicals.*

**Kerr-McGee Pigments GmbH & Co. KG, Münich, Germany**

## KIMBERLY-CLARK CORPORATION

351 Phelps Drive, Irving, TX, 75038

Tel: (972) 281-1200    Fax: (972) 281-1435    www.kimberly-clark.com

*Mfr./sales/distribution of consumer tissue, household and personal care products.*

**Kimberly-Clark GmbH, D-5400 Koblenz, Germany**

## KIRSCH

309 N. Prospect Street, Sturgis, MI, 49091-0370

Tel: (616) 659-5100    Fax: (616) 659-5614    www.kirsch.com

*Mfr. drapery hardware and accessories, wood shelving, woven wood shades, etc.*

**Sani-Kirsch Inc. & Co. KG, Bornbarch 8, D-22848 Norderstedt, Germany**

## LESTER B. KNIGHT & ASSOCIATES INC.

549 West Randolph Street, Chicago, IL, 60661

Tel: (312) 346-2300    Fax: (312) 648-1085

*Architecture, engineering, planning, operations and management consulting.*

**Knight Wendling Consulting GmbH/KW Executive Search, Lyoner Strasse 14, Postfach 71 05 17, D-60495 Frankfurt, Germany**

**Knight Wendling Executive Search/KW Consulting GmbH, Heinze Schmole Strasse 12, D-40227 Düsseldorf, Germany**

**Knight Wendling Gesellschaft Fur Unternehmensentwicklung mbH, Schubertstrasse 1, D-65189 Wiesbaden, Germany**

## KNOLL, INC.

1235 Water Street, East Greenville, PA, 18041

Tel: (215) 679-7991 Fax: (215) 679-3904 www.knoll.com

*Mfr. and sale of office furnishings.*

**Knoll International GmbH, Gottlieb-Dailer Strasse 37, D-7141 Murr, Germany**

## KNOWLES ELECTRONICS INC.

1151 Maplewood Drive, Itasca, IL, 60131

Tel: (630) 250-5100 Fax: (630) 250-0575 www.knowleselectronics.com

*Microphones and loudspeakers.*

**Ruf Electronics, GmbH, Bahnhofstrasse 26-28, D-85635 Höhenkirchen, Germany**

Tel: 49-8102-781-0 Fax: 49-8102-1859

## KOCH INDUSTRIES INC.

4111 East 37th Street North, Wichita, KS, 67220-3203

Tel: (316) 828-5500 Fax: (316) 828-5950 www.kochind.com

*Oil, financial services, agriculture and Purina Mills animal feed.*

**Koch-Glitsch GmbH, Membrane Systems Div., Neusser Strasse 33, 4000 Duesseldorf 1, Germany**

Tel: 49-211-901950 Fax: 49-211-305273

## KOCH-GLITSCH, INC.

PO Box 8127, Wichita, KS, 67208

Tel: (316) 828-5110 Fax: (316) 828-5950 www.koch-ind.com

*Mfr./services mass transfer/chemicals separation equipment, process engineering.*

**Koch-Glitsch GmbH, c/o IB&E, 1m Lucken 14, D-64673 Zweingenberg, Germany**

Tel: 49-6251-787903 Fax: 49-6251-787903

**Koch-Glitsch GmbH, Membrane Systems Div., Neusserstrasse, Nr. 33, D-4000 Düsseldorf 1, Germany**

Tel: 49-211-901950 Fax: 49-211-305273

## KODAK POLYCHROME GRAPHICS

401 Merritt 7, Norwalk, CT, 06851

Tel: (203) 845-7000 Fax: (203) 845-7113 www.kodak.com

*Metal offset plates, coating specialties, graphic arts films.*

**Polychrome GmbH, Seesenerstr. 11, D-3360 Osterrode, Germany**

## KOHN PEDERSEN FOX ASSOCIATES PC

111 West 57th Street, New York, NY, 10019

Tel: (212) 977-6500 Fax: (212) 956-2526 www.kpf.com

*Architectural design.*

**Kohn Pedersen Fox GmbH, Bulowstrasse 66, D-10783 Berlin, Germany**

## KOLLMORGEN CORPORATION

1601 Trapelo Road, Waltham, MA, 02154

Tel: (781) 890-5655 Fax: (781) 890-7150 www.kollmorgen.com

*Mfr. high-performance electronic motion-control systems and design and supply advanced submarine periscopes, weapons directors, and military optics.*

**Kollmorgen Seidel, Dusseldorf, Germany**

## KORN/FERRY INTERNATIONAL

1800 Century Park East, Los Angeles, CA, 90067

Tel: (310) 843-4100 Fax: (310) 553-6452 www.kornferry.com

*Executive search; management consulting.*

**Korn/Ferry International, Koenigsallee 64, D-40212 Düsseldorf, Germany**

Tel: 49-211-55-8650 Fax: 49-211-55-86555

**Korn/Ferry International GmbH,** Lyoner Strasse 15, Atricom, D-60528 Frankfurt/Main, Germany
Tel: 49-69-669-0170    Fax: 49-69-669-01766

## KPMG INTERNATIONAL LLP

345 Park Avenue, New York, NY, 10022
Tel: (201) 307-7000      Fax: (201) 930-8617       www.kpmg.com
*Accounting and audit, tax and management consulting services.*

**KPMG Deutsche Treuhand-Gesellschaft AG,** Barbarossplatz 1a, D-50674 Cologne, Germany
Tel: 49-221-207300   Fax: 49-221-207-3209   Contact: Axel Berger, Ptnr.

**KPMG Deutsche Treuhand-Gesellschaft AG,** Bahnofstrasse 30-32, D-65185 Wiesbaden, Germany

**KPMG Deutsche Treuhand-Gesellschaft AG,** HessbrDhlstrasse 21, D-70565 Stuttgart, Germany

**KPMG Deutsche Treuhand-Gesellschaft AG,** Spitalerhof, Kurze Mahren 1, D-20095 Hamburg, Germany

**KPMG Deutsche Treuhand-Gesellschaft AG,** Marie-Curie-Strasse 30, D-60439 Frankfurt/Mai, Germany

**KPMG Deutsche Treuhand-Gesellschaft AG,** Elektrastrasse 6, D-81925 Münich, Germany

**KPMG Deutsche Treuhand-Gesellschaft AG,** Am Bommeshof 35, D-40474 Düsseldorf, Germany

**KPMG Deutsche Treuhand-Gesellschaft AG,** Olof-Palme-Strasse 31, National Office, D-60439 Frankfurt/Main, Germany

**KPMG Deutsche Treuhand-Gesellschaft AG,** KurfDrstendamm 207-208, D-10719 Berlin, Germany

## THE KROLL-O'GARA COMPANY

9113 Le Saint Drive, Fairfield, OH, 45014
Tel: (513) 874-2112      Fax: (513) 874-2558       www.kroll-ogara.com
*Security and consulting services and vehicles.*

**Kroll Associates Frankfurt, Germany,** Bleidensstrasse 6, D-60311 Frankfurt Am Main, Germany
Tel: 49-69-299840    Fax: 49-69-29984-170

## K-TEL INTERNATIONAL INC.

2605 Fernbrook Lane North, Plymouth, MN, 55447-4736
Tel: (612) 559-6800      Fax: (612) 559-6803       www.k-tel.com
*Sales and distribution of packaged consumer music entertainment and convenience products.*

**Dominion Vertriebs GmbH,** Max Planck Strasse 34, D-6367 Karben 1, Germany

## KULICKE & SOFFA INDUSTRIES INC.

2101 Blair Mill Road, Willow Grove, PA, 19090
Tel: (215) 784-6000      Fax: (215) 659-7588       www.kns.com
*Semiconductor assembly systems and services.*

**Minitron Elektronik GmbH,** Ettinger Strasse 20, D-85057 Ingolstadt, Germany

**Simac Masic Europe,** Dientzenhofer Strasse 7; D-83098 Brannenburg, Germany

## KURT SALMON ASSOCIATES INC.

1355 Peachtree Street NE, Atlanta, GA, 30309
Tel: (404) 892-0321      Fax: (404) 898-9590       www.kurtsalmon.com
*Management consulting: consumer products, retailing.*

**Kurt Salmon Associates GmbH,** Rheindorfer Weg 13, D-40591 Düsseldorf, Germany

## L-3 COMMUNICATIONS HOLDINGS, INC.

600 Third Avenue, New York, NY, 10016
Tel: (212) 697-1111      Fax: (212) 490-0731       www.L-3com.com
*Design/mfr. high-tech communications systems, including specialized flight recorders.*

**L3 Communications GmbH,** Virtrieb, Neufeld Straße, D-24118 Kiel, Germany
Emp: 40

## LA ROCHE INDUSTRIES INC.

1100 Johnson Ferry Road, NE, Atlanta, GA, 30342

Tel: (404) 851-0300     Fax: (404) 851-0421     www.larocheind.com

*Produce and distribute organic and inorganic chemicals.*

**LaRoche Industries GmbH/LII Europe GmbH, Frankfurt-Höchst" Industrial Park, Frankfurt, Germany**

Emp: 360

## LADAS & PARRY

26 West 61st Street, New York, NY, 10023

Tel: (212) 708-1800     Fax: (212) 246-8959     www.ladasparry.com

*International law firm, engaged in the practice of intellectual property law.*

**Ladas & Parry, Altheimer ECK 2, D-80331 Münich, Germany**

Tel: 49-89-269077   Fax: 49-89-269040

## LAMSON & SESSIONS COMPANY

25701 Science Park Drive, Cleveland, OH, 44122

Tel: (216) 464-3400     Fax: (216) 464-1455     www.lamson-home.com

*Mfr. thermoplastic electrical conduit and related products; products for transportation equipment industry.*

**Lamson & Sessions GmbH, Postfach 5144, D-5970 Plettenberg 5, Germany**

## LANDOR ASSOCIATES

Klamath House, 1001 Front Street, San Francisco, CA, 94111-1424

Tel: (415) 955-1400     Fax: (415) 365-3190     www.landor.com

*International marketing consulting firm, focused on developing and maintaining brand identity.*

**Landor Associates, Pickhuben 6, Sandtorkaihof, D-20457 Hamburg, Germany**

Tel: 49-40-378-5670   Fax: 49-40-378-56718   Contact: Ulf-Bruen Drechsel, Mng. Dir.

## LANDS' END INC.

1 Lands' End Lane, Dodgeville, WI, 53595

Tel: (608) 935-9341     Fax: (608) 935-4260     www.landsend.com

*Clothing, home furnishings and mail order catalog company.*

**Lands' End GmbH, In Der Langwiese, D-66693 Mettlach, Germany**

Tel: 49-6864-971-0   Fax: 49-6864-921-111   Contact: Stephen Bechwar, Mng. Dir.   Emp: 100

## LANIER WORLDWIDE, INC.

2300 Parklake Drive, N.E., Atlanta, GA, 30345

Tel: (770) 496-9500     Fax: (770) 938-1020     www.lanier.com

*Specialize in digital copiers and multi-functional systems.*

**Lanier Deutschland GmbH, Pestalozzi Str. 5-8, D-1318 Berlin, Germany**

Tel: 49-30-486-37-625   Fax: 49-30-486-37-627

**Lanier Deutschland GmbH, Motorstrasse 4, D-70499 Stuttgart, Germany**

Tel: 49-711-83098-31   Fax: 49-711-83098-20

**Lanier Deutschland GmbH, Wendenstr. 309, D-20537 Hamburg, Germany**

Tel: 49-40-251-527-20   Fax: 49-40-251-527-15

**Lanier Deutschland GmbH, IM Taubental 6, D-41468 Neuss, Germany**

Tel: 49-2131-387-0   Fax: 49-2131-387-203

## LAWSON MARDON WHEATON, INC.

1101 Wheaton Ave., Millville, NJ, 08332

Tel: (856) 825-1400     Fax: (856) 825-0146     www.algroupwheaton.com

*Engaged in pharmaceutical and cosmetic packaging, glass and plastic containers.*

**Lawson Mardon Singen GmbH, Alusingen-Platz 1, D-78221 Singen, Germany**

## LAWTER INTERNATIONAL INC.

1 Terra Way, 8601 95th St., Pleasant Prairie, WI, 53158

Tel: (262) 947-7300　　　Fax: (262) 947-7328　　　www.lawter.com

*Resins, pigments and coatings.*

**Lawter Chemicals GmbH, Kolnerstrasse 114, 502226 Frechen, Germany**

Tel: 49-2234-120-52　Fax: 49-2234-583-44

## LEACH INTERNATIONAL, INC.

6900 Orangethorp Ave., Buena Park, CA, 90622-5032

Tel: (714) 739-0770　　　Fax: (714) 739-1713　　　www.leachintl.com

*Mfr. and design electrical switching and control devices for the aerospace and rail industries.*

**Leach International GmbH, Hoferstrasse 5, D-86720 Nordlingen, Germany**

Tel: 49-9081-800-0

## LEAR CORPORATION

21557 Telegraph Road, Southfield, MI, 48086-5008

Tel: (248) 746-1500　　　Fax: (248) 746-1722　　　www.lear.com

*Mfr. and distribute automotive materials and car seats.*

**Lear Corporation, Ebersburg, Germany**

**Lear Corporation (Keiper Car Seating Division), Bremen, Germany**

**Lear Corporation (Keiper Car Seating Division), Besigheim, Germany**

**Lear Corporation (Opel Division), Gustavsburg, Germany**

**Lear Corporation (Opel Division), Eisenbach, Germany**

## LEARONAL INC.

272 Buffalo Ave., Freeport, NY, 11520

Tel: (516) 868-8800　　　Fax: (516) 868-8824　　　www.learonal.com

*Specialty chemicals for the printed circuit board, semiconductor, connector and metal finishing industries.*

**LeaRonal GmbH, Gewerbestrasse 19, D-75217 Birkenfeld 2, Germany**

Tel: 49-70-82-79140　Fax: 49-70-82-20895　Contact: Karl-Hans Fuchs, Mng. Dir.

## LECROY CORPORATION

700 Chestnut Ridge Road, Chestnut Ridge, NY, 10977

Tel: (845) 425-2000　　　Fax: (845) 425-8967　　　www.lecroy.com

*Mfr. signal analyzers and electronic measurement systems.*

**LeCroy GmbH, Postfach 103767, D-69027 Heidelberg, Germany**

Tel: 49-6221-82700

## LEGGETT & PLATT, INC.

1 Leggett Road, Carthage, MO, 64836

Tel: (417) 358-8131　　　Fax: (417) 358-5840　　　www.leggett.com

*Mfr. components for bedding and furniture.*

**Spühl AG, Div. Leggett & Platt, St.Gallen, Grüntalstrasse 23, CH-9303 Wittenbach, Germany**

## LEHMAN BROTHERS HOLDINGS INC.

Three World Financial Center, New York, NY, 10285

Tel: (212) 526-7000　　　Fax: (212) 526-3738　　　www.lehman.com

*Financial services, securities and merchant banking services.*

**Lehman Brothers, Grueneburgweg #18, D-60322 Frankfurt, Germany**

Tel: 49-69-153070

## LEVI STRAUSS & COMPANY

1155 Battery St., San Francisco, CA, 94111-1230

Tel: (415) 544-6000    Fax: (415) 501-3939    www.levistrauss.com

*Mfr./distributor casual wearing apparel.*

**Levi Strauss Germany GmbH / Levi Strauss Alle,  Postfach 1451, Grosser Seligenstaedter Grund 10-12, D-6056 Heusenstamm, Germany**

Tel: 49-6104-6010   Fax: 49-6104-601350

## LEXMARK INTERNATIONAL

1 Lexmark Centre Dr., Lexington, KY, 40550

Tel: (606) 232-2000    Fax: (606) 232-1886    www.lexmark.com

*Develop, manufacture, supply of printing solutions and products, including laser, inkjet, and dot matrix printers.*

**Lexmark Deutschland, GmbH,  Postfach 1560, 63115 Dietzenbach, Germany**

## LHS GROUP INC.

6 Concourse Pkwy., Ste. 2700, Atlanta, GA, 30328

Tel: (770) 280-3000    Fax: (770) 280-3099    www.lhsgroup.com

*Provides multilingual software for telecommunications carriers.*

**LHS Specifications GmbH,  Otto-Hahn-StraBe 36, D-63303 Dreieich-Sprendlingen, Germany**

Tel: 49-6103-482-770   Fax: 49-6103-482-799

## LIFE TECHNOLOGIES INC.

9800 Medical Center Drive, Rockville, MD, 20850

Tel: (301) 840-8000    Fax: (301) 329-8635    www.lifetech.com

*Produces biotechnology research materials.*

**Life Technologies GmbH,  Technologiepark Karlsruhe, Emmy-Noether Strasse 10, Karlsruhe 76131, Germany**

## ELI LILLY & COMPANY

Lilly Corporate Center, Indianapolis, IN, 46285

Tel: (317) 276-2000    Fax: (317) 277-6579    www.lilly.com

*Mfr. pharmaceuticals and animal health products.*

**Beiersdorf-Lilly GmbH,  Wiesingerweg 25, 20253 Hamburg, Germany**

**Lilly Deutschland GmbH,  Teichweg 3, 35396 Giessen, Germany**

**Lilly Deutschland GmbH,  Saalburgstrasse 153, D-61350 Bad Homburg, Germany**

Tel: 49-6172-2730   Fax: 49-6172-273-283

## LILLY INDUSTRIES

200 W. 103rd St., Indianapolis, IN, 46290

Tel: (317) 814-8700    Fax: (317) 814-8880    www.lillyindustries.com

*Mfr. industrial coatings and specialty chemicals.*

**Lilly Industries GmbH,  Postfach 1126, D-8649 Wallenfels/Ofr, Germany**

Tel: 49-9262-533   Fax: 49-2403-709250

**Lilly Industries GmbH,  Friedenstrassen 40, 52249 Eschweiler, Germany**

Tel: 49-2403-7090   Fax: 49-2403-709250

## LINCOLN ELECTRIC HOLDINGS

22801 St. Clair Ave., Cleveland, OH, 44117-1199

Tel: (216) 481-8100    Fax: (216) 486-8385    www.lincolnelectric.com

*Mfr. arc welding and welding related products, oxy-fuel and thermal cutting equipment and integral AC motors.*

**Lincoln Smitweld GmbH,  Heinrich Hertz-Strasse 16, D-40699 Erkrath-Unterfeldhaus, Germany**

Tel: 49-211-92-550   Fax: 49-211-92-55179   Contact: Knut Pink, Mng. Ptnr.

**Uhrhan & Schwill GmbH, Max-Keith Strasse 39, D-45136 Essen, Germany**

Tel: 49-201-259-61  Fax: 49-201-256-538  Contact: Heinrich Schwill, Mng. Dir.

## LINCOLN INDUSTRIAL

1 Lincoln Way, St. Louis, MO, 63120

Tel: (314) 679-4200  Fax: (314) 424-5359  www.lincolnindustrial.com

*Lubrication equipment and materials dispensing equipment.*

**Lincoln GmbH, Heinrich-Hertz-Strasse, Postfach 1263, D-6909, Walldorf, Germany**

Tel: 49-6227-33-0

## LINEAR TECHNOLOGY CORPORATION

1630 McCarthy Blvd., Milpitas, CA, 95035

Tel: (408) 432-1900  Fax: (408) 434-6441  www.linear-tech.com

*Mfr. linear integrated circuit chips.*

**Linear Technology GmbH, Oskar-Messter-Str. 24, D-85737 Ismaning, Germany**

Tel: 49-89-9624550  Fax: 49-89-963147

## ARTHUR D. LITTLE, INC.

25 Acorn Park, Cambridge, MA, 02140-2390

Tel: (617) 498-5000  Fax: (617) 498-7200  www.adlittle.com

*Management, environmental, health and safety consulting; technical and product development.*

**Arthur D. Little International Inc., Delta Haus, Gustav-Stresemann-Ring 1, D-65189 Wiesbaden, Germany**

Tel: 49-611-71480  Fax: 49-611-7148-290

**Arthur D. Little International, Inc., Kurfurstendamm 66, D-10707 Berlin, Germany**

Tel: 49-30-885-9200  Fax: 49-30-885-92099

**Arthur D. Little International, Inc., Martin-Luther-Platz 26, D-40212 Düsseldorf, Germany**

Tel: 49-211-86090  Fax: 49-211-8609-599

**Arthur D. Little International, Inc., Leopoldstr. 11a, D-80802 Münich, Germany**

Tel: 49-89-381-9010  Fax: 49-89-381-90150

## LITTON INDUSTRIES INC.

21240 Burbank Boulevard, Woodland Hills, CA, 91367

Tel: (818) 598-5000  Fax: (818) 598-3313  www.littoncorp.com

*Shipbuilding, electronics, and information technology.*

**Litton Advanced Systems, Theaterplatz 3, 53177 Bonn, Germany**

Tel: 49-228-35-63-63

**Litton Precision Products Intl. Inc., Oberfoehringer Strasse 8, D-81679 Münich, Germany**

**VEAM Elektro-Anschulusstechnik GmbH, Postfach 1304, D-70774 Filderstadt, Stuttgart, Germany**

## LOCKHEED MARTIN CORPORATION

6801 Rockledge Drive, Bethesda, MD, 20817

Tel: (301) 897-6000  Fax: (301) 897-6652  www.imco.com

*Design/mfr./management systems in fields of space, defense, energy, electronics and technical services.*

**CalComp GmbH, Max Planckstrasse 25, D-6072 Dreieich, Germany**

**CalComp GmbH, Hansaallee, D-4000 Düsseldorf 11, Germany**

**CalComp GmbH, Nilolaus-Otto-Strasse 29, D-7022 Leinfelden-Echterdingen, Germany**

**CalComp GmbH, Elmshorner Strasse 7-11, D-2080 Pinneberg, Germany**

**CalComp GmbH, Hermann-Klammt-Strase, Postfach 10 03 02, D-41403 Neuss, Germany**

Contact: R. Winfried, VP

**Lockheed Martin GmbH, Arn Michaelshof 4/B, D-53177 Bonn, Germany**

Tel: 49-228-1620  Fax: 49-228-957-1611  Contact: Manfred Wiese, Dir

**Lockheed Martin Intl. GmbH, Turmstasse 10, D-53175 Bonn, Germany**

**Mountain Gate Data Systems GmbH, D-86633 Neuburg, Germany**

## LOCTITE CORPORATION

1001 Trout Brook Crossing, Rocky Hill, CT, 06067-3910

Tel: (860) 571-5100    Fax: (860) 571-5465    www.loctite.com

*Mfr./sale industrial adhesives, sealants and coatings..*

**Loctite Deutschland GmbH, Postfach 810580, D-81905 Münich, Germany**

Tel: 49-89-92680   Fax: 49-89-910-1978   Contact: Fritz Lohr, Bus. Mgr.

**Loctite Europe EEIG, Arabellastrasse 17, D-81925 Münich, Germany**

Tel: 49-89-92680   Fax: 49-89-910-1978

**Loctite Research & Development & Engineering Group., Gutenbergstrasse 3, D-85748 Garching-Hochbruck, Germany**

Tel: 49-89-32-08-0041   Fax: 49-89-32-08-0086

## LORAL SPACE & COMMUNICATIONS LTD.

600 Third Ave., New York, NY, 10016

Tel: (212) 697-1105    Fax: (212) 338-5662    www.loral.com

*Marketing coordination: defense electronics, communications systems.*

**Loral CyberStar, Bruesseler Str. 7, DE-30539 Hannover, Germany**

Tel: 49-511-87430

## LORD CORPORATION

2000 West Grandview Blvd, Erie, PA, 16514

Tel: (814) 868-0924    Fax: (814) 486-4345    www.chemlok.com

*Adhesives, coatings, chemicals, film products.*

**Agomet Klebstoffe, Postfach 602, D-6450 Hanau 1, Germany**

**Henkel KG, Postfach 1100, D-4000 Düsseldorf 1, Germany**

**pAr Oberflächenchemie GmbH, Hücklehoven-Baal, Germany**

## LOWE LINTAS & PARTNERS WORLDWIDE

One Dag Hammarskjold Plaza, New York, NY, 10017

Tel: (212) 605-8000    Fax: (212) 605-4705    www.interpublic.com

*Full-service, integrated marketing communications company/advertising agency.*

**Ammirati Puris Lintas Deutschland, Postfach 10 40, D-20027 Hamburg, Germany**

Tel: 49-40-414-410   Fax: 49-40-414-41580   Contact: Uwe Lang, Reg. Dir.

**Ammirati Puris Lintas Deutschland, Beethovenstrasse 71, D-60325 Frankfurt, Germany**

Tel: 49-69-977-5010   Fax: 49-69-977-501100   Contact: Thomas Brockmann, Mng. Dir.

**Baader, Lang, Behnken GmbH Germany, Van-der-Smissen-Strasse 2, D-22767 Hamburg, Germany**

Tel: 49-40-306-160   Contact: Thomas Witt

**Glockauer, Hellner, Partner GmbH, Admiralitatsstrasse 55, D-20459 Hamburg, Germany**

Tel: 49-40-3766-7601

**Interactive Marketing Partner, Stadthausbrücke 7, D-20355 Hamburg, Germany**

Tel: 49-40-378-860   Fax: 49-40-378-86133   Contact: Hendrick Dohmeyer

**Lintas Marketing Communications, Burchardstrasse 14, D-20095 Hamburg, Germany**

Tel: 49-40-3397-5523   Fax: 49-40-3397-5726   Contact: Dirk Glockauer

**Wüschner, Rohwer, Albrecht GmbH, Thomas-Wimmer-Ring 11, D-80539 München, Germany**

Tel: 49-89-2900-330   Fax: 49-89-2911-3313   Contact: Carsten Rohwer, Jt. Mng. Dir.

## LSI LOGIC CORPORATION

1551 McCarthy Blvd, Milpitas, CA, 95035

Tel: (408) 433-8000    Fax: (408) 954-3220    www.lsilogic.com

*Develop/mfr. semiconductors.*

**LSI Logic GmbH, Mittlerer Pfad 4, D-70499 Stuttgart, Germany**

Tel: 49-711-13-9690

**LSI Logic GmbH, Orleansstrasse 4, D-81669 München, Germany**

Tel: 49-89-458-330    Fax: 49-89-458-33108

## LTX CORPORATION

LTX Park, University Ave., Westwood, MA, 02090

Tel: (617) 461-1000     Fax: (617) 326-4883      www.ltx.com

*Design/mfr. computer-controlled semiconductor test systems.*

**LTX (Deutschland) GmbH, AM Hochacker 5, 85630 Grasbrunn Neukeferloh, Germany**

Tel: 49-89-4623550   Fax: 49-89-46235510

## THE LUBRIZOL CORPORATION

29400 Lakeland Blvd., Wickliffe, OH, 44092-2298

Tel: (440) 943-4200     Fax: (440) 943-5337      www.lubrizol.com

*Mfr. chemicals additives for lubricants and fuels.*

**Langer & Co. GmbH, Ritterhude, Germany**

Tel: 49-421-69-333

**Lubrizol Coatings Additives Company GmbH, Kurze Muehren 3, D-2000 Hamburg 1, Germany**

Tel: 49-40-32-32-820

## LUCENT TECHNOLOGIES, INC.

600 Mountain Ave., Murray Hill, NJ, 07974-0636

Tel: (908) 582-3000     Fax: (908) 582-2576      www.lucent.com

*Design/mfr. wide range of public and private networks, communication systems and software, data networking systems, business telephone systems and microelectronics components.*

**Lucent Technologies Network Systems, GmbH, Thiern-und-Taxis-Str. 10, D-90411 Nuernberg, Germany**

Tel: 49-228-917-77-62   Fax: 49-911-526-3890   Contact: Harald Kettenbach, PR Mgr.

**Optimay Lucent Technologies Int'l GmbH, Orleansstrasse 4, D-81669 München, Germany**

Tel: 49-89-45-91-83   Fax: 49-89-45-91-84-74   Contact: Sam Goodner, Pres. & CEO

## LYDALL INC.

1 Colonial Road, PO Box 151, Manchester, CT, 06040

Tel: (860) 646-1233     Fax: (860) 646-4917      www.lydall.com

*Mfr. converted paper products, paperboard, non-woven specialty media.*

**Lydall Gerhardi & Cie GmbH & Co., Ludenscheid, Germany**

## LYONDELL

3801 West Chester Pike, Newtown Square, PA, 19073-2387

Tel: (610) 359-2000     Fax: (610) 359-2722      www.arcochem.com

*Mfr. propylene oxide, a chemical used for flexible foam products, coatings/paints and solvents/inks.*

**ARCO Chemical GmbH, Kaiserswerthe Strasse 115, D-40880 Ratingen, Germany**

Tel: 49-2101-420-950   Fax: 49-2102-420-809

## M/A-COM INC.

1011 Pawtucket Boulevard, Lowell, MA, 01853-3295

Tel: (978) 442-5000     Fax: (978) 442-5354      www.macom.com

*Mfr. electronic components, semiconductor devices and communications equipment.*

**M/A-COM GmbH, Building 6408 - Room 686, Rupert-Mayer-Str. 44, D-81359 München, Germany**

Tel: 49-89-722-33990   Fax: 49-89-722-63567

## MacDERMID INC.

245 Freight Street, Waterbury, CT, 06702-0671

Tel: (203) 575-5700      Fax: (203) 575-7900      www.macdermid.com

*Chemicals processing for metal industrial, plastics, electronics cleaners, strippers.*

**MacDermid GmbH,  Industrial 37, D-76707 Hambrucken, Germany**

Tel: 49-7455-7171    Fax: 49-7455-9539

## MACKIE DESIGNS INC.

16220 Wood-Red Road, NE, Woodinville, WA, 98072

Tel: (425) 487-4333      Fax: (425) 487-4337      www.mackie.com

*Mfr. speakers, amplifiers, monitors and digital consoles.*

**Mackie Designs Deutschland GmbH,  Kuhlmannstraße 7, Emsdetten 48282, Germany**

Tel: 49-2572-960-4218    Fax: 49-2572-960-4210

## MAGNETROL INTERNATIONAL

5300 Belmont Road, Downers Grove, IL, 60515-4499

Tel: (630) 969-4000      Fax: (630) 969-9489      www.magnetrol.com

*Mfr. level and flow instrumentation.*

**Magnetrol International,  Schlossstrasse 76, D-51429 Bergisch Gladbach 1, Germany**

Tel: 49-2204-9536-0   Fax: 49-2204-9536-53    Contact: Dieter Greiner

## MALLINCKRODT INC.

675 McDonnell Blvd., St. Louis, MO, 63134

Tel: (314) 654-2000      Fax: (314) 654-5380      www.mallinckrodt.com

*Distributes health care products and specialty pharmaceuticals.*

**Mallinckrodt Medical GmbH,  Josef-Dietzgen-Straße 1-3, 53773 Hennef, Germany**

Tel: 49-22428870    Fax: 49-22426070

## MANPOWER INTERNATIONAL INC.

5301 N. Ironwood Rd.,  PO Box 2053, Milwaukee, WI, 53201-2053

Tel: (414) 961-1000      Fax: (414) 961-7081      www.manpower.com

*Temporary help, contract service, training and testing.*

**Manpower-Planen-Leisten GmbH,  Stiftstrasse 30, D-60313 Frankfurt/Main 1, Germany**

Tel: 49-69-299-8050    Fax: 49-69-296-582

## MARCONI DATA SYSTEMS, INC.

1500 Mittel Blvd., Wood Dale, IL, 60191

Tel: (630) 860-7300      Fax: (630) 616-3657      www.videojet.com

*Mfr. computer peripherals and hardware, state-of-the-art industrial ink jet marking and coding products.*

**Marconi Data Systems,  An der Meil 1, D-65555 Limburg, Germany**

Tel: 49-6431-9940    Fax: 49-6431-994-112

## MARK IV INDUSTRIES INC.

501 John James Audubon Pkwy., PO Box 810, Amherst, NY, 14226-0810

Tel: (716) 689-4972      Fax: (716) 689-1529      www.mark-iv.com

*Mfr. of engineered systems and components utilizing mechanical and fluid power transmission, fluid transfer, and power systems and components.*

**Dayco Europe GmbH,  Max-Born-Strasse 2-4, D-68519 Viernheim, Germany**

Tel: 49-6204-6060-0   Fax: 49-6204-6895

## MARKEM CORPORATION

150 Congress Street, Keene, NH, 03431

Tel: (603) 352-1130      Fax: (603) 357-1835      www.markem.com.

*Mfr./sales of industrial marking, print machinery and hot stamping foils.*

**Markem GmbH, Westpreussenstrasse 33, D-47809 Krefeld Linn Düsseldorf, Germany**

Tel: 49-2151-94-88-0   Fax: 49-2151-94-88-20

## MARLEY COOLING TOWER COMPANY

7401 West 129th Street, Overland Park, KS, 66213

Tel: (913) 664-7400      Fax: (913) 664-7641      www.marleyct.com

*Cooling and heating towers and waste treatment systems.*

**Marley Kuhllturm GmbH, PO Box 34 02 61, D-40441 Düsseldorf, Germany**

Tel: 49-203-997790   Fax: 49-203-741642

## MARRIOTT INTERNATIONAL INC.

10400 Fernwood Rd., Bethesda, MD, 20817

Tel: (301) 380-3000      Fax: (301) 380-5181      www.marriott.com

*Hotel services.*

**Bremen Marriott Hotel, Bremen, Germany**

**Frankfurt Marriott Hotel, Frankfurt, Germany**

**Hamburg Marriott Hotel and Golf Club, Hamburg, Germany**

**Marriott Courtyard Berlin-Koepenick, Grunanerstrassee 3-15, D-12557 Berlin, Germany**

Tel: 49-30-65479-0   Fax: 49-30-65479-555

**Marriott Courtyard Frankfurt Messe, Oeserstrasse 180, Frankfurt, D-65933 Hessen, Germany**

Tel: 49-69-3905-0   Fax: 49-69-3808218

## MARS INC.

6885 Elm Street, McLean, VA, 22101-3810

Tel: (703) 821-4900      Fax: (703) 448-9678      www.mars.com

*Mfr. candy, snack foods, rice products and cat food.*

**Mars Schokladenvertrieb GmbH, Worringerstr. 7-9, D-4000 Düsseldorf, Germany**

## MARSH & McLENNAN COS INC.

1166 Ave. of the Americas, New York, NY, 10036-2774

Tel: (212) 345-5000      Fax: (212) 345-4808      www.marshmac.com

*Insurance agents/brokers, pension and investment management consulting services.*

**Gradmann & Holler Group, Kasernenstrasse 69, D-40213 Düsseldorf, Germany**

Tel: 49-2-118-9870   Fax: 49-211-898-7369   Contact: Dr. Christian Doenecke

**Gradmann & Holler Group, Kerknerstrasse 50, D-70182 Stuttgart, Germany**

Tel: 49-7-112-3800   Fax: 49-7-112-380622   Contact: Dr. George Brauchle

**Gradmann & Holler Holding, Pacellistrasse 14, D-80333 Munchen, Germany**

Tel: 49-892-905-6620   Fax: 49-892-905-6619   Contact: Peter Hesse

**Gradmann & Holler Kiefhaber GmbH, Versicherungsmalder, Alt-Moabit 101 B, D-10559 Berlin, Germany**

Tel: 49-30-399-9450   Fax: 49-303-999-4519   Contact: Bernd Kaiser

**Gradmann & Holler Kiefhaber GmbH, Cremon 3, D-20457 Hamburg, Germany**

Tel: 49-40-37-6920   Fax: 49-40-3769-2622   Contact: Harald Sack

**Gradmann & Holler Kiefhaber GmbH, Herriotstrasse 3, D-60528 Frankfurt/Main, Germany**

Tel: 49-69-66760   Fax: 49-69-667-6522   Contact: Hans Theo Niklas

## MARY KAY COSMETICS INC.

16251 No. Dallas Pkwy, Dallas, TX, 75248

Tel: (972) 687-6300     Fax: (972) 687-1609     www.marykay.com

*Mfr. and sales cosmetics and toiletries.*

**Mary Kay Cosmetics GmbH, Fraunhoferstr. 10, D-8033 Münich Martinsried, Germany**

## MASCO CORPORATION

21001 Van Born Road, Taylor, MI, 48180

Tel: (313) 274-7400     Fax: (313) 374-6666     www.masco.com

*Mfr. faucets, cabinets, locks and numerous home improvement, building and home furnishings products.*

**Alfred Reinecke GmbH & Co., Koebbingser Muehle 2, D-58640 Iserlohn, Germany**

Tel: 49-2371-94900

**Alma Kuchen Aloys Meyer GmbH & Co., Von-Rontgen-StraBe 8-14, D-48683 Ahaus, Germany**

Tel: 49-2561-69465

**E. Missel GmbH, Hortensienweg 2/27, D-70374 Stuttgart, Germany**

Tel: 49-711-5308-106

**Gebhardt Ventilatoren GmbH & Co., 74638 Waldenburg, Gebhardstrasse, 19-25, PO Box 40, D-74636 Waldenburg, Germany**

Tel: 49-7942-1010

**Horst Breuer GmbH, Meerpfac 27-31, D-56566 Neuwied, Germany**

Tel: 49-2631-86-07-45

**Jung Pumpen GmbH & Co., Industriestr. 4-6 - Postfach 1341, D-4803 Steinhagen, Germany**

Tel: 49-5204-170

**SKS Gmbh & Co., KG, EisenbahnstraBe 2, D-47198 Duiburg Homburg, Germany**

Tel: 49-2066-20-040

## MATTEL INC.

333 Continental Blvd., El Segundo, CA, 90245-5012

Tel: (310) 252-2000     Fax: (310) 252-2179     www.mattelmedia.com

*Mfr. toys, dolls, games, crafts and hobbies.*

**Fisher-Price Spielwaren GmbH, Bruehler Str. 101, D-50389 Wesseling, Germany**

**Mattel GmbH, An der Trift 75, D-63303 Dreieich, Germany**

## MAXITROL COMPANY

23555 Telegraph Road, PO Box 2230, Southfield, MI, 48037-2230

Tel: (248) 356-1400     Fax: (248) 356-0829     www.maxitrol.com

*Mfr. gas pressure regulators, emergency shut-off valves, electronic temp controls.*

**Mertik Maxitrol GmbH, Industrie Strasse, D-4403 Senden, Germany**

Tel: 49-3947-400-0   Fax: 49-3947-400-200

## MAXON CORPORATION

201 East 18th Street, Muncie, IN, 47302

Tel: (765) 284-3304     Fax: (765) 286-8394     www.maxoncorp.com

*Industry combustion equipment and valves.*

**Maxon GmbH, Niederlassung Stuttgart, Gottlieb-Daimler-Strasse 1 71394 Kernen Stuttgart, Germany**

Tel: 49-7151-949040   Fax: 49-7151-949044

**Maxon GmbH, Steeler-Strasse 491, D-45276 Essen, Germany**

Tel: 49-201-85-1160   Fax: 49-201-851-1661

## MAXTOR CORPORATION

510 Cottonwood Drive, Milpitas, CA, 95035-7403

Tel: (408) 432-1700        Fax: (408) 432-4510        www.maxtor.com

*Mfr. develops and markets hard disk drives for desktop computer systems.*

**Maxtor Europe GmbH,  Max-von-Eyth-Str. 3, D-85737 Ismaning, Germany**

Tel: 49-89-962-4190    Fax: 49-89-968572

## MAYER, BROWN & PLATT

190 S. LaSalle Street, Chicago, IL, 60603

Tel: (312) 782-0600        Fax: (312) 701-7711        www.mayerbrown.com

*International law firm.*

**Mayer, Brown & Platt,  An Lyskirchen 14, D-50676 Cologne, Germany**

Tel: 49-221-921-5210    Fax: 49-221-921-5214    Contact: Kim D. Larsen, Mng. Ptnr.

## MAYFRAN INTERNATIONAL, INC.

PO Box 43038, Cleveland, OH, 44143

Tel: (440) 461-4100        Fax: (440) 461-5565        www.mayfran.com

*Mfr. conveying systems, filtration equipment and separators that facilitate material handling and coolant recovery for automobile manufacturers and machine tool builders.*

**Mayfran GmbH,  Postfach 230124, Alfredstr. 295, D-4300 Essen, Germany**

**May-Fran GmbH,  Fruehlingstr. 52, D-4300 Essen, Germany**

## McCANN-ERICKSON WORLDGROUP

750 Third Ave., New York, NY, 10017

Tel: (212) 984-3644        Fax: (212) 984-2629        www.mccann.com

*International advertising and marketing services.*

**McCann-Erickson Deutschland GmbH,  Postfach 101636, D-6000 Frankfurt/Main, Germany**

**McCann-Erickson Hamburg GmbH,  Neuerwall 41, Postfach 303640, D-2000 Hamburg 36, Germany**

## McDONALD'S CORPORATION

McDonald's Plaza, Oak Brook, IL, 60523

Tel: (630) 623-3000        Fax: (630) 623-7409        www.mcdonalds.com

*Fast food chain stores.*

**McDonald's Corp.,  Münich, Germany**

## THE McGRAW-HILL COMPANIES

1221 Ave. of the Americas, New York, NY, 10020

Tel: (212) 512-2000        Fax: (212) 512-2703        www.mccgraw-hill.com

*Books, magazines, information systems, financial service, publishing and broadcast operations.*

**McGraw-Hill Book Co. GmbH,  Lademannbogen 136, Postfach 630520, D-2000 Hamburg 63, Germany**

## McKINSEY & COMPANY

55 East 52nd Street, New York, NY, 10022

Tel: (212) 446-7000        Fax: (212) 446-8575        www.mckinsey.com

*Management and business consulting services.*

**McKinsey & Company,  Königsallee 60C, D-40027 Düsseldorf, Germany**

Tel: 49-211-13640    Fax: 49-211-1364-700

**McKinsey & Company,  Taunustor 2, D-60311 Frankfurt am Main, Germany**

Tel: 49-69-71620    Fax: 49-69-7162-700

**McKinsey & Company,  Birkenwaldstrasse 149, D-70191 Stuttgart, Germany**

Tel: 49-711-25535    Fax: 49-711-2553-700

**McKinsey & Company,  Am Sandtorkai 77, D-20457 Hamburg, Germany**

Tel: 49-40-3612-10    Fax: 49-40-3612-1700

McKinsey & Company, St.-Apern-Strasse 1, D-50667 Cologne, Germany
Tel: 49-221-20870   Fax: 49-221-2087-700

McKinsey & Company, Kurfürstendamm 185, D-10707 Berlin, Germany
Tel: 49-30-88-452-0   Fax: 49-30-88-452-700

McKinsey & Company, Prinzregentenstrasse 22, D-80538 Münich, Germany
Tel: 49-89-55940   Fax: 49-89-5594-700

McKinsey & Company -, Frankfurt - BTO, Taunustor 2, D-60311 Frankfurt am Main, Germany
Tel: 49-69-71620   Fax: 49-69-7162-700

## JOHN J McMULLEN ASSOCIATES INC. (JJMA)

4300 King Street, Alexandria, VA, 22302
Tel: (703) 418-0100      Fax: (703) 933-6774      www.jjma.com

*Engaged in marine engineering and naval architecture.*

John J. McMullen GmbH, Glockengiestr-Wall 20, D-2000 Hamburg 1, Germany

## MCS SOFTWARE CORPORATION

815 Colorado Blvd., Los Angeles, CA, 90041
Tel: (323) 258-9111      Fax: (323) 259-3838      www.macsch.com

*Develop finite element analysis software used in the field of computer-aided engineering.*

CAE Partner GmbH, Im Rudert 2, D-35043 Marburg-Cappel, Germany

MacNeal-Schwendler GmbH, Innsbrucker Ring 15, Postfach 801240, D-81612 Münich, Germany

MacNeal-Schwendler GmbH, Nenndorfer Strasse 51, D-30952 Ronnenberg, Germany

MacNeal-Schwendler GmbH, Carl-Zeiss-Strasse 2, D-63755 Alzenau, Germany

PDA Engineering Intl. GmbH, Frankfurter Ring 2124, D-8000 Münich 40, Germany

## MEAD CORPORATION

Courthouse Plaza, NE, Dayton, OH, 45463
Tel: (937) 495-6323      Fax: (937) 461-2424      www.mead.com

*Mfr. paper, packaging, pulp, lumber and other wood products, school and office products; electronic publishing and distribution.*

Mead Verpackung GmbH, Postfach 181329, D-5500 Trier, Germany
Tel: 49-651-96690   Fax: 49-651-9669124   Contact: Alo Buschkohl, Mgr.

## MECHANICAL DYNAMICS, INC.

2301 Commonwealth Blvd., Ann Arbor, MI, 48105
Tel: (734) 994-3800      Fax: (734) 994-6418      www.adams.com

*Mfr. Adams prototyping software to automotive industry.*

Ing. Buro Kik- Are Care, Rheingaustrasse 22, D-12161 Berlin, Germany
Tel: 49-30-8270-2776

Mechanical Dynamics GmbH, Mollenbachstrasse 23, D-71229 Loenberg, Germany
Tel: 49-7152-399800

Mechanical Dynamics GmbH, Joseph-Dollinger-Bogen 12, D-80807 Münich, Germany
Tel: 49-89-546-44622

Mechanical Dynamics GmbH, Universitatsstraße 51, D-35037 Marburg/Lahn, Germany
Tel: 49-6421-17070   Contact: Jurgen Fett, VP

## MEDTRONIC INC.

7000 Central Ave., NE, Minneapolis, MN, 55432
Tel: (612) 574-4000      Fax: (612) 574-4879      www.medtronic.com

*Mfr./sale/service electrotherapeutic medical devices.*

Medtronic GmbH, Am Seestern 24, D-40547 Düsseldorf, Germany

## MEMC ELECTRONIC MATERIALS, INC.

501 Pearl Drive, St. Peters, MO, 63376

Tel: (636) 474-5500      Fax: (636) 474-5161      www.memc.com

*Mfg. and distribution of silicon wafers.*

**MEMC Electronic Materials, Inc., Limeetrasse 111, D-81243 Münich, Germany**

Tel: 49-89-89-87666-30    Fax: 49-89-89-7666-40

## MEMOREX CORPORATION

10100 Pioneer Blvd., Ste. 110, Santa Fe Springs, CA, 90670

Tel: (562) 906-2800      Fax: (562) 906-2848      www.memorex.com

*Magnetic recording tapes, etc.*

**Memorex GmbH, Hauptverwaltung, Hahnstr. 41, D-6000 Frankfurt/Main 71, Germany**

## MENTOR CORPORATION

201 Menton Drive, Santa Barbara, CA, 93111

Tel: (805) 879-6000      Fax: (805) 967-7108      www.mentorcorp.com

*Mfr. breast implants.*

**Mentor Deutschland GmbH, Ludwigsforum**
**Ludwigstrasse 45/Haus C**
**D-85399 Hallbergmoos**

Tel: 49-8116-00500

## MENTOR GRAPHICS/MICROTEC RESEARCH

8005 SW Boeckman Road, Wilsonville, OR, 97070-7777

Tel: (503) 685-7000      Fax: (503) 685-1202      www.mentorg.com

*Develop/mfr. software tools for embedded systems market.*

**Microtec Research GmbH, Haidgraben 1c, D-85521 Ottobrunn/Münich, Germany**

## MERCER MANAGEMENT CONSULTING INC.

1166 Ave. of the Americas, New York, NY, 10036

Tel: (212) 345-3400      Fax: (212) 345-7414      www.mercermc.com

*Provides clients with counsel in such areas as corporate and business strategy and growth planning, org development, and market and operations enhancement.*

**Mercer Management Consulting GmbH`, Stefan-George-Ring 2, D-81929 Münich, Germany**

## MERCK & COMPANY, INC.

One Merck Drive, PO Box 100, Whitehouse Station, NJ, 08889-0100

Tel: (908) 423-1000      Fax: (908) 423-2592      www.merck.com

*Pharmaceuticals, chemicals and biologicals.*

**Merck, Sharp & Dohme GmbH, Lindenplatz 1, D-85540 Haar, Germany**

## MERCURY INTERACTIVE CORPORATION

1325 Borregas Ave., Sunnyvale, CA, 94089

Tel: (408) 822-5200      Fax: (408) 822-5300      www.merc-int.com

*Mfr. computer software to decipher and eliminate "bugs" from systems.*

**Mercury Interactive GmbH, Geschäfsstelle Frankfurt, Seligenstädter Grund 9, D-63150 Heusenstamm, Germany**

Tel: 49-89-613767-0   Fax: 49-89-613767-60

**Mercury Interactive GmbH, Inselkammerstrasse 1, D-82008 Unterhaching bei München, Germany**

Tel: 49-89-613767-0   Fax: 49-89-613767-60

## MERITOR AUTOMOTIVE, INC.

2135 West Maple Road, Troy, MI, 48084-7186

Tel: (248) 435-1000      Fax: (248) 435-1393      www.meritorauto.com

*Mfr./sales of light and heavy vehicle systems for trucks, cars and specialty vehicles.*

**Meritor Automotive GmbH, Frankfurt Main, Germany**

## MERRILL LYNCH & COMPANY, INC.

World Financial Center, 250 Vesey Street, New York, NY, 10281-1332

Tel: (212) 449-1000  Fax: (212) 449-2892  www.ml.com

*Security brokers and dealers, investment and business services.*

**Merrill Lynch Bank AG, Neue Mainzerstrasse 75, D-6000 Frankfurt, Germany**

Tel: 49-69-2994

**Merrill Lynch International Bank, Ulmenstrasse 30, D-60325 Frankfurt am Main 1, Germany**

Tel: 49-69-97117  Fax: 49-69-971172-47

**Merrill Lynch International Bank, Moehlstrasse 2, D-81675 Münich, Germany**

Tel: 49-89-41305

## MESTEK, INC.

260 North Elm St., Westfield, MA, 01085

Tel: (413) 568-9571  Fax: (413) 568-2969  www.mestek.com

*Mfr. air diffusers, grilles and related equipment for air conditioning, heating and ventilation.*

**Anemostat Raumlufttechnik, Grafenmuhlenweg 19, D-5000 Cologne 80, Germany**

## METAL IMPROVEMENT COMPANY

10 Forest Ave., Paramus, NJ, 07652

Tel: (201) 843-7800  Fax: (201) 843-3460  www.metalimprovement.com

*Mfr. shot peening.*

**Metal Improvement Co. Inc., Otto-Hahne-Str. 3, D-4750 Unna, Germany**

## METALLURG INC.

6 East 43rd Street, New York, NY, 10017

Tel: (212) 687-9470  Fax: (212) 697-2874  www.mettalurg.com

*Mfr. ferrous and nonferrous alloys and metals.*

**Elektrowerk Weisweiler GmbH, Postfach 7209, D-5180 Eschweiler, Germany**

**Gesellschaft fur Elektrometallurgie mbH, Postfach 3520, D-4000 Düsseldorf 1, Germany**

**GfE GmbH, Höfener Straße 45, D-90431 Nürnberg, Germany**

## METZLER/PAYDEN, LLC

333 South Grand Avenue, Los Angeles, CA, 90071

Tel: (213) 625-1900  Fax: (213) 617-3110  www.payden-rygel.com

*Engaged in financial and investment advisory services.*

**Metzler Bank (JV), Frankfurt, Germany**

## M-I

PO Box 48242, Houston, TX, 77242-2842

Tel: (713) 739-0222  Fax: (713) 308-9503  www.midf.com

*Drilling fluids.*

**M-I Drilling Fluids Intl. B.V., Grafftring 5-7, 29227 Celle, Germany**

Tel: 49-5141-98410  Fax: 49-5141-84064

## MICRO TOUCH SYSTEMS, INC.

300 Griffin Brook Park Drive, Methuen, MA, 01844

Tel: (978) 659-9000  Fax: (978) 659-9100  www.microtouch.com

*Mfr. clear coatings for computer monitors.*

**MicroTouch Systems GmbH, Schiess-Str. 55, 40549 Düsseldorf, Germany**

Tel: 49-211-59907-0

## MICRO WAREHOUSE, INC.

535 Connecticut Ave., Norwalk, CT, 06854

Tel: (203) 899-4000        Fax: (203) 899-4203        www.warehouse.com

*Catalog computer sales.*

**Micro Warehouse GmbH, Postfach 108, 55247 Mainz-Kastel, Germany**

## MICROCHIP TECHNOLOGY INCORPORATED

2355 West Chandler Boulevard, Chandler, AZ, 85224

Tel: (602) 786-7200        Fax: (602) 899-9210        www.microchip.com

*Mfr. electronic subassemblies and components.*

**AZ Microchip Technology GmbH, Gustav-Heinemann Ring 125, D-81739 München, Germany**
Tel: 49-89-627-1440    Fax: 49-89-627-1444

## MICROMERITICS INSTRUMENT CORPORATION

One Micromeritics Drive, Norcross, GA, 30093-1877

Tel: (770) 662-3620        Fax: (770) 662-3696        www.micromeritics.com

*Mfr. analytical instruments.*

**Micromeritics GmbH, Erftstrasse 54, D-41238 Möchengladbach, Germany**
Tel: 49-2166-98708-0

## MICRON TECHNOLOGY, INC. (MTI)

8000 S. Federal Way, Boise, ID, 83707-0006

Tel: (208) 368-4000        Fax: (208) 368-4435        www.micron.com

*Mfr. random-access memory chips and semi-conductor memory components.*

**Micron Semiconductor GmbH, Sternstrasse 20, D-85609 Aschheim, Germany**
Tel: 49-89-904-8720    Fax: 49-89-904-87250

## MICROSOFT CORPORATION

One Microsoft Way, Redmond, WA, 98052-6399

Tel: (425) 882-8080        Fax: (425) 936-7329        www.microsoft.com

*Computer software, peripherals and services.*

**Microsoft Eastern Europe, Edisonstrasse 1, D-8044 Unterschleissheim, München, Germany**
**Microsoft Germany GmbH, Edisonstrasse 1, D-85716 Unterschleissheim, München, Germany**
Tel: 49-89-31760    Fax: 49-89-3176-1000

## MILACRON INC.

2090 Florence Ave., Cincinnati, OH, 45206

Tel: (513) 487-5000        Fax: (513) 487-5057        www.milacron.com

*Metalworking and plastics technologies.*

**Ferromatik Milacron Maschinenbau GmbH, Riegelerstr. 4, D 79364 Malterdingen, Germany**
Tel: 49-7644-78-0

## MILLENNIUM CHEMICALS INC.

230 Half Mile Rd., Red Bank, NJ, 07701

Tel: (732) 933-5000        Fax: (732) 933-5240        www.millenniumchem.com

*Mfr. specialty chemicals that for paints, perfumes, and flavorings.*

**Millennium Chemicals, Neuer Markt 1, 42781 Haan, Germany**
Tel: 49-2119-93010

## MINE SAFETY APPLIANCES COMPANY

121 Gamma Drive, PO Box 426, Pittsburgh, PA, 15230

Tel: (412) 967-3000        Fax: (412) 967-3452        www.msa.net

*Safety equipment, industry filters.*

**Auergesellschaft GmbH, Thiemannstr. 1-11, Postfach 440208, D-1000 Berlin 44, Germany**
**MSA Europe, Thiemannstr. 1-11, Postfach 440208, D-1000 Berlin 44, Germany**

## MINOLTA QMS INC.

One Magnum Pass, Mobile, AL, 36618

Tel: (205) 633-4300     Fax: (205) 633-4866     www.qms.com

*Mfr. monochrome and color computer printers.*

**QMS GmbH,  Gustav-Heinemann-Ring 212, D-81739 München, Germany**

## MINTEQ INTERNATIONAL INC.

405 Lexington Ave., 19th Fl., New York, NY, 10174-1901

Tel: (212) 878-1800     Fax: (212) 878-1952     www.mineralstech.com

*Mfr./market specialty refractory and metallurgical products and application systems.*

**MINTEQ International GmbH,  Kuhstrabe 23-25, D-47051 Duisburg, Germany**

Tel: 49-203-2-86480    Fax: 49-203-2-864848    Contact: David Rosenberg/Christian Wasmuht, Mgrs. Emp: 23

## MODEM MEDIA, INC.

230 East Avenue, Norwalk, CT, 06855

Tel: (203) 299-7000     Fax: (230) 299-7060     www.modemmedia.com

*Provides on-line marketing and consulting services.*

**Modem Media Mex,  Isartalstrasse 49, 80469 Münich, Germany**

Tel: 49-89-7461660    Contact: Juergen Funk, Mng. Dir.

## MODINE MANUFACTURING COMPANY

1500 DeKoven Ave., Racine, WI, 53403

Tel: (262) 636-1200     Fax: (262) 636-1424     www.modine.com

*Mfr. heat-transfer products.*

**Modine GmbH,  Burgsteinfurter Damm, D-4445 Neuenkirchen, Germany**

**Modine GmbH,  Efeustrasse 10, D-8000 Münich 21, Germany**

**Modine Manufacturing Co.,  Bernhause, Germany**

## MOLEX INC.

2222 Wellington Court, Lisle, IL, 60532

Tel: (630) 969-4550     Fax: (630) 969-1352     www.molex.com

*Mfr. electronic, electrical and fiber optic interconnection products and systems, switches, application tooling.*

**Molex Services GmbH,  Felix-Wankel-Strasse 11, D-74078 Heilbronn-Biberach, Germany**

Tel: 49-7066-95550    Fax: 49-7066-9555-29

## MOLTECH POWER SYSTEMS

9062 South Rita Road, Tucson, AZ, 85747

Tel: (520) 799-7500     Fax: (520) 799-7501     www.moltechpower.com

*Provides rechargeable battery solutions for industry applications.*

**Moltech Power Systems Ltd.,  Opelstrasse 2, D-64546 Moerfelden Walldorf, Germany**

Tel: 49-6105-912610    Fax: 49-6105-24449

## MONARCH MACHINE TOOL COMPANY

PO Box 668, 2600 Kettering Tower, Dayton, OH, 45423

Tel: (937) 910-9300     Fax: (937) 492-7958     www.monarchmt.com

*Mfr. metal cutting lathes, machining centers and coil processing equipment.*

**Monarch Werkzeugmaschinen GmbH,  Berliner Str. 13, Postfach 1140, D-6944 Hemsbach, Germany**

## MOODY'S INVESTOR SERVICES, INC.

99 Church St., New York, NY, 10007

Tel: (212) 553-1658     Fax: (212) 553-0462     www.moodys.com

*Publishes credit ratings*

**Moody's Deutschland GmbH, Taunusanlage 11, D-60329 Frankfurt, Germany**

Tel: 49-69-2-42-84-0

## MOOG INC.

Jamison Road, East Aurora, NY, 14052-0018

Tel: (716) 652-2000     Fax: (716) 687-4471     www.moog.com

*Mfr. precision control components and systems.*

**Moog GmbH, Hanns Klemmstr. 28, D-7030 Boblingen, Germany**

## J. P. MORGAN CHASE & CO. INC.

World Headquarters, 270 Park Ave., New York, NY, 10017

Tel: (212) 270-6000     Fax: (212) 622-9030     www.jpmorganchase.com

*Provides integrated financial solutions for institutions and individuals worldwide, including asset management, investment banking and commercial banking.*

**J. P. Morgan Chase & Co., Munzgasse 2, D-01067 Dresden, Germany**

**J. P. Morgan Chase & Co., Ulmenstrasse 30, D-60325 Frankfurt am Main, Germany**

**J. P. Morgan Chase & Co., Unter den Linden 12, D-10117 Berlin, Germany**

Tel: 49-30-2039-450   Fax: 49-30-2039-4510

**J. P. Morgan Chase & Co., Grueneburgweg 2, D-60322 Frankfurt am Main, Germany**

Tel: 49-69-7158-2500   Fax: 49-69-7158-2209

**J. P. Morgan Chase & Co., GlockengieBerwall 26, D-20095 Hamburg, Germany**

## MORGAN STANLEY DEAN WITTER & CO.

1585 Broadway, New York, NY, 10036

Tel: (212) 761-4000     Fax: (212) 761-0086     www.msdw.com

*Securities and commodities brokerage, investment banking, money management, personal trusts.*

**Morgan Stanley Bank AG, Rahmhofstrasse 2-4, D-60313 Frankfurt, Germany**

## MORGAN, LEWIS & BOCKIUS LLP

1701 Market St., Philadelphia, PA, 19103-6993

Tel: (215) 963-5000     Fax: (215) 963-5299     www.mlb.com

*International law firm.*

**Morgan, Lewis & Bockius LLP, Guiollettstrabe 54 (5th Fl), D-60325 Frankfurt am Main, Germany**

Tel: 49-69-714-0070   Fax: 49-69-714-007-10    Contact: Robert V. Daly, Mng. Ptnr.    Emp: 29

## MOTOROLA, INC.

1303 East Algonquin Road, Schaumburg, IL, 60196

Tel: (847) 576-5000     Fax: (847) 538-5191     www.motorola.com

*Mfr. communications equipment, semiconductors and cellular phones.*

**Motorola GmbH, Heinrich-Hertz-Strasse 1, D-65232 Taunusstein, Germany**

Tel: 49-6128-700   Fax: 49-6128-72920

## MTI TECHNOLOGY CORPORATION

4905 East LaPalma Avenue, Anaheim, CA, 92807

Tel: (714) 970-0300     Fax: (714) 693-2202     www.mti.com

*Mfr. data storage systems software.*

**MTI Technology GmbH, Orleansstrasse 4, 81669 Münich, Germany**

Tel: 49-89-4587-570   Fax: 49-89-4587-5750

**MTI Technology GmbH, Otto-Von-Guericke-Ring 15, 652 Wiesbaden, Germany**

Tel: 49-61-229950   Fax: 49-61-2299-5100

## MTS SYSTEMS CORPORATION

1400 Technology Drive, Eden Prairie, MN, 55344-2290

Tel: (612) 937-4000    Fax: (612) 937-4515    www.mts.com

*Develop/mfr. mechanical testing and simulation products and services, industry measure and automation instrumentation.*

**MTS Sensors Technologie GmbH & Co. KG,  Postfach 8130, D-5880 Ludenscheid, Germany**

**MTS Systems GmbH,  Potsdamer Str. 23/24, D-1000 Berlin 37, Germany**

**MTS Systems GmbH,  Erchanbertstrasse 8, 81929 Münich, Germany**

Contact: Eckehard Werner

## MULTI GRAPHICS

431 Lakeview Court, Mt. Prospect, IL, 60056

Tel: (847) 375-1700    Fax: (847) 375-1810    www.multigraphics.com

*Mfr./sale/service printing and print prod equipment, mailroom/bindery systems, services and supplies for graphics industry.*

**Multi Graphics GmbH,  Robert-Bosch-Str. 18, Postfach 10-20-08, D-6072 Dreieich B. Frankfurt Main, Germany**

## NABISCO HOLDINGS, CORP.

7 Campus Drive, Parsippany, NJ, 07054

Tel: (973) 682-5000    Fax: (973) 503-2153    www.nabisco.com

*Mfr. consumer packaged food products and tobacco products.*

**R.J. Reynolds Tobacco GmbH,  Bernerstrasse 107, D-6000 Frankfurt, Germany**

**Star Cooperation GmbH,  Maria-Ablass-Platz 15, D-5000 Cologne, Germany**

## NALCO CHEMICAL COMPANY

One Nalco Center, Naperville, IL, 60563-1198

Tel: (630) 305-1000    Fax: (630) 305-2900    www.nalco.com

*Chemicals for water and waste water treatment, oil products and refining, industry processes; water and energy management service.*

**Deutsche Nalco Chemie GmbH,  Postfach 970110, D-6000 Frankfurt Main 90, Germany**

Tel: 49-69-793-40   Fax: 49-69-793-4295

## NAMCO CONTROLS CORPORATION

760 Beta Dr., Bldg. E-F, Mayfield Village, OH, 44143

Tel: (440) 460-1360    Fax: (440) 460-3800    www.namcocontrols.com

*Mfr. sensors, switches and encoders.*

**Namco GmbH,  Mittelfeld 10, D-2209 Hezhorn, Germany**

## THE NASH ENGINEERING COMPANY

3 Trefoil Drive, Trumbull, CT, 06611

Tel: (203) 459-3900    Fax: (203) 459-3511    www.nasheng.com

*Mfr. air and gas compressors, vacuum pumps.*

**Nash Pumpen GmbH,  Hohemarkstrasse 15, Postfach 1729, D-6370 Overursel, Germany**

## NATIONAL DATA CORPORATION

National Data Plaza, Atlanta, GA, 30329-2010

Tel: (404) 728-2000    Fax: (404) 728-2551    www.ndcorp.com

*Information systems and services for retail, healthcare, government and corporate markets.*

**NDC International Ltd.,  Mainzer Landstr. 97, D-6000 Frankfurt Main, Germany**

## NATIONAL MACHINERY COMPANY

161 Greenfield St., Tiffin, OH, 44883-2471

Tel: (419) 447-5211        Fax: (419) 447-5299        www.nationalmachinery.com

*Mfr. high-speed metal parts forming machines.*

**National Machinery Europe GmbH, Klingenhofstrabe 5, D-90411 Nürnberg, Germany**

Tel: 49-911-519.0

## NATIONAL SEMICONDUCTOR CORPORATION

2900 Semiconductor Dr., PO Box 58090, Santa Clara, CA, 95052-8090

Tel: (408) 721-5000        Fax: (408) 739-9803        www.national.com

*Engaged in producing computer-on-a-chip solutions for the information highway.*

**National Semiconductor, Livry-Gargon Str. 10, D-82256 Fuerstenfeldbruck, Germany**

Tel: 49-8141-35-0   Fax: 49-8141-351-506   Contact: Roland Anderson, VP & Gen. Mgr.   Emp: 300

## NATIONAL STARCH AND CHEMICAL COMPANY

10 Finderne Ave., Bridgewater, NJ, 08807-3300

Tel: (908) 685-5000        Fax: (908) 685-5005        www.nationalstarch.com

*Mfr. adhesives and sealants, resins and specialty chemicals, electronic materials and adhesives, food products, industry starch.*

**National Starch & Chemical GmbH, Postfach 17 01 63, D-67418 Neustadt Weinstrasse, Germany**

Tel: 49-6327-3820   Fax: 49-6327-382-259

## NATIONAL-STANDARD COMPANY

1618 Terminal Road, Niles, MI, 49120

Tel: (616) 683-8100        Fax: (616) 683-6249        www.nationalstardard.com

*Mfr. wire, wire related products, machinery and medical products.*

**Herbert GmbH/National-Standard, Hunfield, Germany**

## NATIONWIDE INSURANCE

One Nationwide Plaza, Columbus, OH, 43215-2220

Tel: (614) 249-7111        Fax: (614) 249-7705        www.nationwide.com

*Insurance services.*

**Neckura Versicherungs AG, Oberstedter Str. 14, Postfach 1480, D-6370 Oberursel/Ts. 1, Germany**

## NCR (NATIONAL CASH REGISTER)

1700 South Patterson Blvd., Dayton, OH, 45479

Tel: (937) 445-5000        Fax: (937) 445-7042        www.ncr.com

*Mfr. automated teller machines and high-performance stationary bar code scanners.*

**NCR GmbH, Ulmer Strasse 160, D-86135 Augsburg, Germany**

Tel: 49-821-405-8030   Fax: 49-821-405-8013   Contact: Walter Muecke, Dir.

## NEAC COMPRESSOR SERVICE USA, INC.

191 Howard Street, Franklin, PA, 16323

Tel: (814) 437-3711        Fax: (814) 432-3334        www.neacusa.com

*Mfr. air tools and equipment.*

**Chicago Pneumatic-Germany, Postfach 120251, Hagenauer Strasse 47, D-6200 Wiesbaden 12, Germany**

## NETEGRITY, INC.

52 Second Avenue, Waltham, MA, 02154

Tel: (781) 890-1700        Fax: (781) 487-7791        www.netegrity.com

*Mfr. security software.*

**Netegrity GmbH, Atricom Box 5A, Lyoner Straße 15, Frankfurt D-60528, Germany**

Tel: 49-69-6-65-770

## NETLINKS PUBLISHING SOLUTIONS INC.

PO Box 13626, Sacramento, CA, 95853

Tel: (916) 929-9481     Fax: (916) 928-0414     www.sii.com

*Develop/marketing software for publishing and newspapers.*

**Netlinks Publishing Solutions,  Münich, Germany**

## NETMANAGE, INC.

10725 N. De Anza Blvd., Cupertino, CA, 95014

Tel: (408) 973-7171     Fax: (408) 257-6405     www.netmanage.com

*Develop/mfr. computer software applications and tools.*

**NetManage Software GmbH,  Niederlassung München, Grünwalder Weg 13a, D-82008 Unterhaching, Germany**

Tel: 49-89-614-543-21   Fax: 49-89-614-543-43

## NETSCAPE COMMUNICATIONS

501 East Middlefield Road, Mountain View, CA, 94043

Tel: (650) 254-1900     Fax: (650) 528-4124     www.netscape.com

*Mfr./distribute Internet-based commercial and consumer software applications.*

**Netscape Communications GMBH,  Airport Office Park Münich, Am Söldnermoos 6, D-85399 Hallbergmoos, Germany**

Tel: 49-811-5537-000   Fax: 49-811-5537-100

## NETWORK ASSOCIATES, INC.

3965 Freedom Circle, Santa Clara, CA, 95054

Tel: (408) 988-3832     Fax: (408) 970-9727     www.networkassociates.com

*Designs and produces network security and network management software and hardware.*

**Network Associates GmbH,  Ohmstrasse 1, 85716 Unterschleissheim, Germany**

Tel: 49-89-3707-0   Fax: 49-89-3707-1199

**Network Associates GmbH,  Luisenweg 40, 20537 Hamburg Germany**

Tel: 49-40-2531-0   Fax: 49-40-2531-2829

## NEUTROGENA CORPORATION

5760 West 96th Street, Los Angeles, CA, 90045

Tel: (310) 642-1150     Fax: (310) 337-5564     www.neutrogena.com

*Mfr. facial cleansing, moisturizing products; body care, sun and hair care specialty products.*

**Neutrogena (Germany),  Postfach 1216, Rheydter Str. 1-3, D-4052 Korschenbroich, Germany**

## NEW BRUNSWICK SCIENTIFIC COMPANY, INC.

44 Talmadge Road, Box 4005, Edison, NJ, 08818-4005

Tel: (732) 287-1200     Fax: (732) 287-4222     www.nbsc.com

*Mfr. research and production equipment for life sciences.*

**New Brunswick Scientific GmbH,  In der Au 14, D-72622 Nürtingen, Germany**

Tel: 49-7022-932490  Fax: 49-7022-932486   Contact: Gerry Burgers, Gen. Mgr.

## THE NEW YORK TIMES COMPANY

229 West 43rd Street, New York, NY, 10036-3959

Tel: (212) 556-1234     Fax: (212) 556-7389     www.nytimes.com

*Diversified media company including newspapers, magazines, television and radio stations, and electronic information and publishing.*

**International Herald Tribune (IHT),  Friedrichstrasse 15, 60323 Frankfurt/Main, Germany**

Tel: 49-69-97-12-5000

## NEWELL RUBBERMAID

29 East Stephenson Street, Freeport, IL, 61032-0943

Tel: (815) 235-4171      Fax: (815) 489-8212         www.newellco.com

*Mfr. hardware, housewares, and office products.*

**Gardinia Groujp,  Isny, Germany**

**Rotring Group,  Hamburg, Germany**

## NEWPORT CORPORATION

1791 Deere Ave., PO Box 19607, Irvine, CA, 92606

Tel: (949) 863-3144      Fax: (949) 253-1800         www.newport.com

*Mfr./distributor precision components and systems for laser/optical technology, vibration/motion measure and control.*

**Newport GmbH,  Holzhofalle 19, D-64295 Darmstadt, Germany**

Tel: 49-6151-36210   Fax: 49-6151-362150

## NICOLET INSTRUMENT CORPORATION

5225 Verona Road, Madison, WI, 53711-4495

Tel: (608) 276-6100      Fax: (608) 276-6222         www.nicolet.com

*Mfr. infrared spectrometers and oscilloscopes and medical electro-diagnostic equipment.*

**Nicolet Instrument GmbH,  Senefelderstr. 162, D-63069 Offenbach Main, Germany**

Tel: 49-69-98408-0   Fax: 49-69-98408-122

## A .C. NIELSEN COMPANY

177 Broad Street, Stamford, CT, 06901

Tel: (203) 961-3000      Fax: (203) 961-3190         www.acnielsen.com

*Market and consumer research firm.*

**A.C. Nielsen GmbH,  Ludwig-Landmann-Strasse 405, D-6000 Frankfurt Main 90, Germany**

## NORDSON CORPORATION

28601 Clemens Road, Westlake, OH, 44145-4551

Tel: (440) 892-1580      Fax: (440) 892-9507         www.nordson.com

*Mfr. industry application equipment, sealants and packaging machinery.*

**Nordson Deutschland GbmH,  Postfach 3234, Heinrich-Hertz-Strasse 42, D-40699 Erkrath 1, Germany**

Tel: 49-211-92050   Fax: 49-211-254652

**Nordson Engineering GmbH,  Postfach 2165, Lilienthalstrasse 6, D-21337 Luneburg, Germany**

Tel: 49-4131-8940   Fax: 49-4131-894-149

## NORGREN

5400 S. Delaware Street., Littleton, CO, 80120-1663

Tel: (303) 794-2611      Fax: (303) 795-9487         www.usa.norgren.com

*Mfr. pneumatic filters, regulators, lubricators, valves, automation systems, dryers, push-in fittings.*

**IMI Norgren GmbH,  Postfach 1120, Bruckstrasse 93, D-46519 Alpern/ Niederrhein, Germany**

Tel: 49-28-02-490   Fax: 49-28-02-49356

## NORTON ABRASIVES COMPANY

1 New Bond Street, Worcester, MA, 01606

Tel: (508) 795-5000      Fax: (508) 795-5741         www.nortonabrasives.com

*Mfr. abrasives for industrial manufacturing.*

**Christensen Diamond Products GmbH,  Postfach 309, Heerstr. 61, D-3100 Braunschweiger, Germany**

**Norton GmbH,  Vorgebirgsstr. 10, D-5047 Wesseling, Germany**

## NOVELLUS SYSTEMS INC.

4000 North First Street, San Jose, CA, 95134

Tel: (408) 943-9700     Fax: (408) 943-3422     www.novellus.com

*Mfr. chemical vapor deposition (CVD), physical vapor deposition (PVD) and copper electrofill systems.*

**Novellus Systems GmbH, Manfred Von Ardenne, Ring 20 01099, Dresden, Germany**

Tel: 49-351-89252-10   Fax: 49-351-89252-20

**Novellus Systems GmbH, Ingolstaedter Strasse 22 , 80807 Münich, Germany**

Tel: 49-893-50152-0   Fax: 49-89-350-152-99

## NOVO SYSTEMS CORPORATION

4061 Clipper Court, Fremont, CA, 94538-6540

Tel: (510) 360-8100     Fax: (510) 623-4484     www.novosystems.com

*Design/development/mfr./market logic and fault simulation acceleration products; system engineering services.*

**Zycad GmbH, Bahnhofplatz 4A, D-8013 Haar, Germany**

## NRG ENERGY, INC.

1221 Nicollet Ave., Ste. 700, Minneapolis, MN, 55403

Tel: (612) 373-5300     Fax: (612) 373-5312     www.nrgenergy.com

*Electric power generation.*

**NRG Energy Development GmbH, Friedrichstrasse 50, 10117 Berlin, Germany**

Tel: 49-30-20-65-9219   Fax: 49-30-20-65-9330

## NU SKIN ENTERPRISES, INC.

75 West Center St., Provo, UT, 84601

Tel: (801) 345-6100     Fax: (801) 345-5999     www.nuskin.com

*Develops and distributes premium-quality personal care and nutritional products.*

**NuSkin Germany GmbH, Ginnheimer Strasse 4, 65760 Eschborn, Germany**

## NUMATICS INC.

1450 North Milford Road, Highland, MI, 48357

Tel: (248) 887-4111     Fax: (248) 887-9190     www.numatics.com

*Mfr. control valves and manifolds.*

**Numatics GmbH, Otto von Guericke Str. 13, D-5205 St. Augustin 3, Germany**

Tel: 49-2241-3160-0   Fax: 49-2241-316040

## NUS INFORMATION SERVICES, INC.

2650 McCormick Dr., Ste. 300, Clearwater, FL, 33759-1049

Tel: (727) 669-3000     Fax: (727) 669-3100     www.nus.com

*Provides case-based expert knowledge, bench-marking, trending, and operational services to the electric power and inventory industries.*

**NUS Deutschland GmbH, Berliner Allee 52, D-4000 Düsseldorf 1, Germany**

## OCCIDENTAL PETROLEUM CORPORATION

10889 Wilshire Blvd., Los Angeles, CA, 90024

Tel: (310) 208-8800     Fax: (310) 443-6690     www.oxy.com

*Petroleum and petroleum products, chemicals, plastics.*

**Kleinholz Mineraloel GmbH, Huysenallee 66-68, Postfach 856, D-4300 Essen, Germany**

**Mineraloel KG, Jungfernstieg 51, D-2000 Hamburg 36, Germany**

**Occidental Oil GmbH, Graf-Adolf-Str. 73, D-4000 Düsseldorf, Germany**

## OCLI, INC. (OPTICAL COATING LABORATORY, INC.)

2789 Northpoint Pkwy., Santa Rosa, CA, 95407-7397

Tel: (707) 545-6440          Fax: (707) 525-7410          www.ocli.com

*Mfr. thin film precision coated optical devices.*

**OCLI Germany,  Alte Heerstrasse 14, D-38644 Goslar, Germany**

Tel: 49-5321-3590

**OCLI Optical Coating Laboratory GmbH,  Tilsiter Strasse 12, D-64354 Reinheim, Germany**

Tel: 49-6162-93210

## OGDEN ENVIRONMENTAL & ENERGY SERVICES COMPANY

4455 Brookfield Corporate Dr., Suite 100, Chantilly, VA, 20151

Tel: (703) 488-3700          Fax: (703) 488-3701          www.ogden.com

*Environmental and energy consulting services for commercial clients and government agencies.*

**IEAL Energie & Umwelt Consult GmbH,  Lieberman Strasse 76, D-13088 Berlin, Germany**

**IEAL. Energie Consult GmbH,  Konigswintererstrasse 272, D-53327 Bonn, Germany**

**Ogden Umwelt und Energie Systeme GmbH,  Niederlassung Wurzburg, Am Sonnenhof 16, D-97076 Wurzburg, Germany**

## OGILVY PUBLIC RELATIONS WORLDWIDE

909 Third Ave., New York, NY, 10022

Tel: (212) 880-5201          Fax: (212) 697-8250          www.ogilvypr.com

*Engaged in public relations and communications.*

**Ogilvy Healthcare,  Burgplatz 21-22, D-40213 Düsseldorf, Germany**

Tel: 49-211-1367-0   Contact: Maria Unland

**Ogilvy Healthcare,  Geleitsstrasse 25, D-60599 Frankfurt, Germany**

Tel: 49-69 609101-0   Contact: Sabine Kreusch

## OHAUS CORPORATION

29 Hanover Road, PO Box 900, Florham Park, NJ, 07932-0900

Tel: (973) 377-9000          Fax: (973) 593-0359          www.ohaus.com

*Mfr. balances and scales for laboratories, industry and education.*

**Ohaus Germany GmbH,  An der Johanneskirche 6, D-35390 Giessen, Germany**

Tel: 49-641-71023

## THE OILGEAR COMPANY

2300 S. 51st Street, Milwaukee, WI, 53219

Tel: (414) 327-1700          Fax: (414) 327-0532          www.oilgear.com

*Mfr. hydraulic power transmission machinery.*

**Oilgear Towler GmbH,  Im Gotthelf 8, D-65795 Hattersheim, Germany**

## OLIN CORPORATION

501 Merritt Seven, Norwalk, CT, 06856-4500

Tel: (203) 750-3000          Fax: (203) 750-3292          www.olin.com

*Mfr. chemicals, metals, sporting ammunition and copper and copper alloy sheets.*

**Olin Chemicals GmbH,  Ander Hoffnung 125, 40885 Ratingen, Germany**

Tel: 49-2102-77-110

## OM GROUP, INC. (OMG)

3800 Terminal Tower, Cleveland, OH, 44113-2203

Tel: (216) 781-0083          Fax: (216) 781-0902          www.omgi.com

*Producer and marketer of metal-based specialty chemicals.*

**OMG Europe GmbH,  Düsseldorf, Germany**

## OMNICARE, INC.

100 E. River Center Blvd., Covington, KY, 41011

Tel: (859) 392-3300    Fax: (859) 392-3333    www.omnicare.com

*Provides pharmaceutical and nursing home services.*

**IFNS (Institut Fur Numerische Statistik), Cologne, Germany**

Contact: Dr. Wolfgang Haase

## ONTRACK DATA INTERNATIONAL, INC.

9023 Columbine Rd., Eden Prairie, MN, 55347

Tel: (612) 937-1107    Fax: (612) 937-5815    www.ontrack.com

*Computer data evidence services company, rescuing lost or corrupted data, and software sales.*

**Ontrack Data International, Inc., Hanns-Klemm-Straße 5, D-71034 Böblingen, Germany**

Tel: 49-7031-644-150   Fax: 49-7031-644-100

## ONYX SOFTWARE CORPORATION

3180 139th Avenue, SE, Bellevue, WA, 98005

Tel: (425) 451-8060    Fax: (425) 451-8277    www.onyx.com

*Mfr. customer relationship management software.*

**Onyx Software Germany, Franziskaner Strasse 38, 81669 München, Germany**

## OPEN MARKET, INC.

1 Wayside Road, Burlington, MA, 01803

Tel: (781) 359-3000    Fax: (781) 359-8111    www.openmarket.com

*Mfr. catalog management software.*

**Open Market GmbH, Hessenring 119, D-61348 Bad Homburg, Germany**

## OPRYLAND MUSIC GROUP

65 Music Square West, Nashville, TN, 37203

Tel: (615) 321-5000    Fax: (615) 327-0560    www.acuffrose.com

*Music publisher.*

**Acuff-Rose Musikveriage, GmbH, c/o Warner Chappell Music, GMBH Marstallstr. 8, D-80539 München, Germany**

Tel: 49-89-29069-0   Fax: 49-89-29069-100

## ORACLE CORPORATION

500 Oracle Parkway, Redwood Shores, CA, 94065

Tel: (650) 506-7000    Fax: (650) 506-7200    www.oracle.com

*Develop/manufacture software.*

**Oracle Deutschland GmbH, Hauptverwaltung, Hanover Strasse 87, D-8000 München 50, Germany**

## ORC MACRO INTERNATIONAL INC.

11785 Beltsville Dr., Calverton, MD, 20705-3119

Tel: (301) 572-0200    Fax: (301) 572-0999    www.macroint.com

*Engaged in research and evaluation, training, consulting and information technology.*

**Macro Internatinoal Inc., Im Brohl 16, 614 Kronberg/Ts., Germany**

Tel: 49-61-7395-0862   Fax: 49-61-7395-0863   Contact: Douglas Ziurys, Mng. Dir.

## ORIEL INSTRUMENTS CORPORATION

150 Long Beach Boulevard, Stratford, CT, 06615

Tel: (203) 377-8282    Fax: (203) 378-2457    www.oriel.com

*Mfr. optical goods.*

**L.O.T.-Oriel GmbH & CO KG, Im Tiefen See 58, D-64293 Darmstadt, Germany**

Tel: 49-6151-88-060

## OSMONICS INC.

5951 Clearwater Drive, Minnetonka, MN, 55343-8995

Tel: (952) 933-2277      Fax: (952) 933-0141      www.osmonics.com

*Mfr. equipment, controls and components for the filtration and water-treatment industries.*

**Osmonics GmbH, Düsseldorf, Germany**

## OSRAM SYLVANIA CHEMICALS INC.

100 Endicott Street, Danvers, MA, 01923

Tel: (978) 777-1900      Fax: (978) 750-2152      www.osramsylvania.com

*Lighting applications.*

**Osram Sylvania Chemicals, Münich, Germany**

## OTIS ELEVATOR COMPANY

10 Farm Springs Road, Farmington, CT, 06032

Tel: (860) 676-6000      Fax: (860) 676-5111      www.otis.com

*Mfr. elevators and escalators.*

**Otis Escalator GmbH, Industriestrasse 2, D-31655 Stadthagen, Germany**

**Otis GmbH, Otisstrasse 33, D-13507 Berlin, Germany**

## OWENS-CORNING CORPORATION

One Owens Corning Pkwy., Toledo, OH, 43659

Tel: (419) 248-8000      Fax: (419) 248-8445      www.owenscorning.com

*Mfr. building materials systems and composites systems.*

**Deutsche Owens-Corning Glasswool GmbH, Idsteiner Strasse 82, D-65232 Taunusstein-Neuhof, Germany**

**Owens-Corning Fiberglas Deutschland GmbH, Königsberger Ring 82, D-30559 Hannover, Germany**

## PACIFIC ARCHITECTS & ENGINEERS INC.

888 South Figueroa Street, 17th Fl., Los Angeles, CA, 90017

Tel: (213) 481-2311      Fax: (213) 481-7189      www.pae.com

*Technical engineering services.*

**PAE GmbH Planning & Construction, Kurhessen Strasse 1, D-64546 Moerfelden-Walldorf, Germany**

Tel: 49-6105-91110   Fax: 49-6105-33069   Contact: John D. Pawulak, Mgr.   Emp: 10

## PALL CORPORATION

2200 Northern Boulevard, East Hills, NY, 11548-1289

Tel: (516) 484-5400      Fax: (516) 484-5228      www.pall.com

*Specialty materials and engineering; filters and related fluid clarification equipment.*

**Pall Filtrationstechnik GmbH, Philipp-Reis Strasse 6, D-63303 Frankfurt, Germany**

Tel: 49-6-103-3070   Fax: 49-6-103-34037

**Pall Gelman Sciences, Arheilger Weg 6, D-64380 Robdorf, Germany**

Tel: 49-6-154-60220   Fax: 49-6-154-602260

**Pall Rochem, Stenzelring 14A, D-2102 Hamburg 93, Germany**

Tel: 49-4-75-27940   Fax: 49-4-75-279434

## PANALARM DIV. AMETEK

1725 Western Dr., West Chicago, IL, 60185

Tel: (630) 231-5900      Fax: (630) 231-4502      www.panalarm.com

*Mfr. electrical alarm systems, temp monitors, display systems, sensors.*

**AMETEK Precision Instruments Europe GmbH, Rudolf-Diesel-Strasse 16, Meerbusch Camp D-40670, Germany**

Tel: 49-2159-9136-0   Fax: 49-2159-9136-39

## PANAMETRICS

221 Crescent Street, Waltham, MA, 02154

Tel: (781) 899-2719     Fax: (781) 899-1552     www.panametrics.com

*Process/non-destructive test instrumentation.*

**Panametrics Gmbh, Analysen-und Prüftechnik, Rudolf-Diesel-Strabe 1, D-65719 Hofheim, Germany**

Tel: 49-6122-8090   Fax: 49-6122-8147   Contact: Hans-Juergen Boeger

## PANDUIT CORPORATION

17301 Ridgeland Ave., Tinley Park, IL, 60477-0981

Tel: (708) 532-1800     Fax: (708) 532-1811     www.panduit.com

*Mfr. electrical/electronic wiring components.*

**Panduit GmbH, Steinmuehlstr. 14, D-61352 Bad Homburg, Germany**

## PARAMETRIC TECHNOLOGY CORPORATION

128 Technology Drive, Waltham, MA, 02154

Tel: (781) 398-5000     Fax: (781) 398-5674     www.ptc.com

*Supplier of mechanical design automation and product data management software and services.*

**Parametric Technology GmbH, Parkallee 117, D-28209 Breman, Germany**

Tel: 49-421-3475-619   Fax: 49-421-3499-827

**Parametric Technology GmbH, Paulinenstasse 94, D-88046 Griedrichshafen, Germany**

Tel: 49-7541-3811-0   Fax: 49-7541-3811-15

**Parametric Technology GmbH, Sachsenfeld 4 (4th Fl.), D-20097 Hamburg, Germany**

Tel: 49-40-23505-666   Fax: 49-40-235085-665

**Parametric Technology GmbH, Geschastsstelle Hannover, Hildesheimer Stasse 53, D-30169 Kassel, Germany**

Tel: 49-511-8071-130   Fax: 49-511-8071-132

**Parametric Technology GmbH, Wilhemshoher Allee 239, D-34121 Kassel, Germany**

Tel: 49-561-935-3134   Fax: 49-561-935-3100

**Parametric Technology GmbH, Simemensstasse 9, D-63263 Neu-Isenburg, Germany**

Tel: 49-6102-782-5   Fax: 49-6102-782-666

**Parametric Technology GmbH, Salomonstasse 17, D-04129 Leipzig, Germany**

Tel: 49-341-994-0360   Fax: 49-341-994-0361

**Parametric Technology GmbH, Kaiserswerter Strasse 115, D-40882 Ratingen, Germany**

Tel: 49-2102-742-60   Fax: 49-2102-742-6666

**Parametric Technology GmbH, In deu Spoeck 6, D-77656 Offenburg, Germany**

Tel: 49-781-6102   Fax: 49-781-61229

**Parametric Technology GmbH, Edisonstasse 8, D-85716 Unteerschlessheim, Germany**

Tel: 49-89-32106-0   Fax: 49-89-32106-150

**Parametric Technology GmbH, Geschaegtsstelle Nuremberg, Kleinreuther Weg 120, D-90425 Nuremburg , Germany**

Tel: 49-911-3651-126   Fax: 49-911-3651-131

**Parametric Technology GmbH, Zettachring 2, D-70567 Stuttgart, Germany**

Tel: 49-711-7287-265   Fax: 49-711-7280-396

**Parametric Technology GmbH, Rudower Stasse 90/94, D-12351 Berlin, Germany**

Tel: 49-30-60008-319   Fax: 49-30-60008-619

**Parametric Technology GmbH, Otto-Brenner Strasse 207-209, D-33604 Bielefeld, Germany**

Tel: 49-52-19276-131   Fax: 49-52-19276-132

**Parametric Technology GmbH, In den Dauen 6, D-53117 Bonn, Germany**

Tel: 49-22-8555-1240   Fax: 49-22-8555-110

## PAREXEL INTERNATIONAL CORPORATION

195 West Street, Waltham, MA, 02154

Tel: (781) 487-9900     Fax: (781) 487-0525     www.parexel.com

*Provides contract medical, biotechnology, and pharmaceutical research and consulting services.*

**PAREXEL International, Klinikum Westend Haus 18, Spandauer Damm 130, D-14050 Berlin, Germany**

Tel: 49-30-306850   Fax: 49-30-30685-299

**PAREXEL International, Schleussnerstr. 90, D-63263 Neu-Isenburg, Germany**

Tel: 49-6102-71620   Fax: 49-6102-716222

**PAREXEL LOGOS, Kartauserstrasse 47, D-79102 Freiburg, Germany**

Tel: 49-761-282800   Fax: 49-761-34086

## PARKER ABEX NWL CORPORATION

2222 Palmer Ave., Kalamazoo, MI, 49001

Tel: (616) 384-3400     Fax: (616) 384-3623     www.parkerhannifin.com

*Mfr. aerospace and automotive friction materials and equipment.*

**Abex GmbH-Aerohydraul, Lorenz-Schott-Str. 9, D-6503 Mainz Kastel, Germany**

## PARKER HANNIFIN CORPORATION

6035 Parkland Blvd., Cleveland, OH, 44124-4141

Tel: (216) 896-3000     Fax: (216) 896-4000     www.parker.com

*Mfr. motion-control products.*

**Hauser Elektronik GmbH, Postfach 1720, D-77607 Offenburg, Germany**

**Parker GmbH Fluid Verbindungsteile, Postfach 1120, Freiherr-vom-Stein-Strasse, D-35325 Mucke, Germany**

**Parker Hannefin GmbH, Automotive & Refrigeration Group, Postfach 1120, D-35322 Mucke, Germany**

**Parker Hannifin Corp., Polyflex Div. Europe, An der Tuckbleiche 4, D-68623 Lampertheim Huttenfeld, Germany**

**Parker Hannifin Corp., Seal Products/Parker Praedifa GmbH, Praezisions-Dichtungen, Postfach 40, Stuifenstrasse 55, D-74385 Pleidelsheim Germany**

**Parker Hannifin GmbH, Romerweg 13, D-78727 Oberndorf am Neckar, Germany**

**Parker Hannifin GmbH, Heimchenweg 8, D-65929 Frankfurt/Main, Germany**

**Parker Hannifin GmbH, Johann-Strauss-Strasse 51, D-70794 Filderstadt, Germany**

**Parker Hannifin GmbH, Ermeto Div., Am Metallwerk 9, D-33659 Bielefeld, Germany**

**Parker Hannifin NMF GmbH, Delmenhorster Str. 10, D-50735 Cologne, Germany**

**Parker Hannifin NMF GmbH, Hydraulic Control Div., Gutenbergstrasse 36, D-41564 Kaarst, Germany**

**Parker Hannifin Schrader Bellows GmbH, Heidestr. 71, D-42549 Velbert, Germany**

**Parker Praedifa GmbH, Postfach 1641, D-74306 Beitigheim-Bissingen, Germany**

## PATAGONIA INC.

259 West Santa Clara Street, Ventura, CA, 93001

Tel: (805) 643-8616     Fax: (805) 653-6355     www.patagonia.com

*Outdoor clothing retail stores and mail-order catalogue company.*

**Patagonia, Inc., Münich, Germany**

## PEDDINGHAUS CORPORATION

300 North Washington Avenue, Bradley, IL, 60915

Tel: (815) 937-3800     Fax: (815) 937-4003     www.peddinghaus.com

*Mfr./distribute structure steel and plate-fabricating equipment.*

**Peddinghaus Anlagen Und Maschinen GmbH (PAM), Hasslinghauser Strasse 150, D-58285 Geelsberg, Germany**

Tel: 49-2332-9126-25   Fax: 49-2332-9126-28

## PENSKE CORPORATION

13400 Outer Drive West, Detroit, MI, 48239

Tel: (313) 592-5000      Fax: (313) 592-5256      www.penske.com

*Diversified transportation company, design and manufacture engines and operate truck leasing facilities.*

**Penske Corporation, Münich, Germany**

## PENTAIR, INC.

1500 County Road, B2 West, St. Paul, MN, 55113-3105

Tel: (612) 636-7920      Fax: (612) 636-5508      www.pentair.com

*Diversified manufacturer operating in electrical and electronic enclosures, professional tools/equipment and water products.*

**Lincoln GmbH, Heinrich-Hertz Strasse, Postfach 1263, D-6909 Walldorf, Germany**

## PEOPLESOFT INC.

4460 Hacienda Drive, Pleasanton, CA, 94588-8618

Tel: (925) 225-3000      Fax: (925) 694-4444      www.peoplesoft.com

*Mfr. applications to manage business operations across computer networks.*

**PeopleSoft GmbH, Haus 13i-3-OG, Postfach 39, Friedrich-Ebert-Straße, D-51429 Bergisch Gladbach Germany**

Tel: 49-2204-84-2980

## PEPSiCO INC.

700 Anderson Hill Road, Purchase, NY, 10577-1444

Tel: (914) 253-2000      Fax: (914) 253-2070      www.pepsico.com

*Beverages and snack foods.*

**Florida Intl. Fruchsaftgetraenke GmbH, Münich, Germany**

**PepsiCo GmbH, Münich, Germany**

## PERIPHONICS CORPORATION

4000 Veterans Highway, Bohemia, NY, 11716

Tel: (631) 468-9000      Fax: (631) 981-2689      www.periphonics.com

*Mfr. voice processing systems.*

**Periphonics VPS Ltd., Martin-Behaim Strasse 12, D-63263 Neu-Isenburg, Germany**

Tel: 49-6102-74190

## PERKIN ELMER, INC.

45 William Street, Wellesley, MA, 02481

Tel: (781) 237-5100      Fax: (781) 431-4255      www.perkinelmer.com

*Mfr. equipment and devices to detect explosives and bombs on airline carriers.*

**PerkinElmer Life Sciences, Wenzel-Jaksch-Str. 31, D-65199 Wiesbaden, Germany**

## PEROT SYSTEMS CORPORATION

PO Box 809022, Dallas, TX, 75380

Tel: (972) 340-5000      Fax: (972) 455-4100      www.perotsystems.com

*Engaged in computer services technology.*

**Perot Systems Corporation, Frankfort, Germany**

## PFAUDLER, INC.

1000 West Ave., PO Box 23600, Rochester, NY, 14692-3600

Tel: (716) 235-1000      Fax: (716) 436-9644      www.pfaudler.com

*Mfr. glass lined reactors, storage vessels and reglassing services.*

**Pfaudler-Werke GmbH, Postfach 1780, Pfaudler Strasse, D-6830 Schwetzingen, Germany**

Tel: 49-620-2850   Fax: 49-620-222-412

## PFIZER INC.

235 East 42nd Street, New York, NY, 10017-5755

Tel: (212) 573-2323        Fax: (212) 573-7851        www.pfizer.com

*Research-based, global health care company.*

**C.H. Buer GmbH,  Münich, Germany**

**Forster & Hug KG,  Münich, Germany**

**Heinrich Mack Nachf. Gmbh & Co. KG,  Buro Karlsruhe, Pfizerstraße 1, 76139 Karlsruhe, Germany**

**Hilekes GmbH,  Münich, Germany**

**Leibinger GmbH,  Freiburg, Germany**

**Pfizer GmbH,  Heinrich-Mack-Straße 35, 89257 Illertissen, Germany**

Tel: 49-28-02-2000

**Pfizer Holding und Verwaltungs GmbH,  Pfizerstraße 1, 76139 Karlsruhe, Germany**

**Taylor Kosmetic GmbH,  Pfizerstraße 1, 76139 Karlstruhe, Germany**

## PHARMACIA CORPORATION

100 Route 206 North, Peapack, NJ, 07977

Tel: (908) 901-8000        Fax: (908) 901-8379        www.pharmacia.com

*Mfr. pharmaceuticals, agricultural products, industry chemicals.*

**Upjohn PharmaciGmbH,  AM Wolfsmantel 46, D-91058 Erlangen, Germany**

## PHARMACIA MONSANTO

800 N. Lindbergh Boulevard, St. Louis, MO, 63167

Tel: (314) 694-1000        Fax: (314) 694-7625        www.monsanto.com

*Life sciences company focusing on agriculture, nutrition, pharmaceuticals, health and wellness and sustainable development.*

**Monsanto Co. Chemical Group,  Inmmermannstr 3, D -40210 Dusseldorf, Germany**

## PHD INC.

9009 Clubridge Dr., PO Box 9070, Fort Wayne, IN, 46899

Tel: (219) 747-6151        Fax: (219) 747-6754        www.phdinc.com.

*Mfr. pneumatic and hydraulic products used in factory automation.*

**PHD GmbH,  Arnold-Sommerfeld, D-52499 Baesweiler, Germany**

Tel: 49-2401-805-230    Fax: 49-2401-805-232

## PHELPS DODGE CORPORATION

2600 North Central Ave., Phoenix, AZ, 85004-3089

Tel: (602) 234-8100        Fax: (602) 234-8337        www.phelpsdodge.com

*Copper, minerals, metals and special engineered products for transportation and electrical markets.*

**Columbian Carbon Deutschland GmbH,  Antwerpenstrasse 1, D-2103 Hamburg 95, Germany**

**Columbian Chemicals GmbH,  Hannover, Germany**

## PHH VEHICLE MANAGEMENT SERVICES

307 International Circle, Hunt Valley, MD, 21030

Tel: (410) 771-3600        Fax: (410) 771-2841        www.phh.com

*Provides vehicle fleet management, corporate relocation, and mortgage banking services.*

**PHH Vehicle Management Services,  Stäblistrasse 8, D-81477 Münich, Germany**

Tel: 49-89-780440

## PHILIP SERVICES CORP. INDUSTRIAL GROUP

5151 San Felipe Street, #1600, Houston, TX, 77056-3609

Tel: (713) 623-8777        Fax: (713) 625-7085        www.philipinc.com

*Trucking, refuse systems, staffing and numerous industrial-oriented services.*

**Industrial Services Philip Services (Europe),  Landshuterstrasse 56, D-84130 Dingolfing, Germany**

Tel: 49-87-31-72-5100    Fax: 49-87-31-72-5864    Contact: Gernot Waltenstorfer

**PHILIPP BROTHERS CHEMICALS INC.**

1 Parker Plaza, Fort Lee, NJ, 07029

Tel: (201) 944-6020    Fax: (201) 944-7916    www.philipp-brothers.com

*Mfr. industry and agricultural chemicals.*

**Ferro Metal & Chemical Corp., Münich, Germany**

Tel: 44-118-959-1961

**PHILLIPS PETROLEUM COMPANY**

Phillips Building, 411 S. Keeler Ave., Bartlesville, OK, 74004

Tel: (918) 661-6600    Fax: (918) 661-7636    www.phillips66.com

*Crude oil, natural gas, liquefied petroleum gas, gasoline and petro-chemicals.*

**Phillips Petroleum International GmbH, Ulmenstr. 37, D-6000 Frankfurt/Main, Germany**

**PICTURETEL CORPORATION**

100 Minuteman Road, Andover, MA, 01810

Tel: (978) 292-5000    Fax: (978) 292-3300    www.picturetel.com

*Mfr. video conferencing systems, network bridging and multiplexing products, system peripherals.*

**PictureTel GmbH, Messeturm - Box 23, D-60208 Frankfurt am Main, Germany**

Tel: 49-69-975-44503  Fax: 49-69-975-44928

**PictureTel GmbH, Büropark Oktavian, Feringstrasse 6, D-85774 Münich-Unterfohring, Germany**

Tel: 49-89-992-110  Fax: 49-89-992-11200

**PictureTel GmbH, Demo Center Düsseldorf, Wilhelm-Marx-Haus, Heinrich-Heine-Allee 53, D-40213 Düsseldorf Germany**

Tel: 49-211-8307205  Fax: 49-211-8308370

**PIERCE & STEVENS CORPORATION**

710 Ohio Street, Buffalo, NY, 14203

Tel: (716) 856-4910    Fax: (716) 856-0942    www.dualite-spheres.com

*Mfr. coatings, adhesives and specialty chemical for packaging and graphic arts..*

**Lehmann & Voss & Co., Alsteruler 19, 20354 Hamburg, Germany**

**PINNACLE SYSTEMS**

280 North Bernardo Ave., Mountain View, CA, 94043

Tel: (650) 526-1600    Fax: (650) 526-1601    www.pinnaclesys.com

*Designs, manufactures, markets and supports a wide range of high-quality digital solutions that enable businesses and consumers to create, store, distribute and view video programs.*

**Pinnacle Systems GmbH, Frankfurter Str. 3, Braunschweig, D-38122, Germany**

Tel: 49-531-2183-0

**PIONEER HI-BRED INTERNATIONAL INC.**

400 Locust Street, Ste. 800, Des Moines, IA, 50309

Tel: (515) 248-4800    Fax: (515) 248-4999    www.pioneer.com

*Agricultural chemicals, farm supplies, biological products, research.*

**Pioneer Hi-Bred Northern Europe GmbH, Apensener Str. 198 PO Box 1464, D-2150 Buxtehude, Germany**

**PIONEER-STANDARD ELECTRONICS, INC.**

6065 Parkland Blvd., Cleveland, OH, 44124

Tel: (440) 720-8500    Fax: (440) 720-8501    www.pios.com

*Mfr./distribution of electronic parts for computers and networking equipment.*

**Eurodis Enatechnik, Pascalkehre 1, 24551 Quickborn, Germany**

## PITNEY BOWES INC.

1 Elmcroft Road, Stamford, CT, 06926-0700

Tel: (203) 356-5000     Fax: (203) 351-6835       www.pitneybowes.com

*Mfr. postage meters, mailroom equipment, copiers, bus supplies, bus services, facsimile systems and financial services.*

**Pitney Bowes Deutschland GmbH, Tiergartenstrasse 7, D-64636 Happenheim, Germany**

Tel: 49-6252-7080   Fax: 49-6252-708-206   Contact: Klaus Karl, Mng. Dir.   Emp: 600

## PITTSTON BAX GROUP

16808 Armstrong Ave., PO Box 19571, Irvine, CA, 92623

Tel: (949) 752-4000     Fax: (949) 260-3182       www.baxworld.com

*Air freight forwarder.*

**BAX Global, c/o Wendschlag & Pohl, Frachthalle Tegel Airport, D-1000 Berlin 51, Germany**

## PLANET HOLLYWOOD INTERNATIONAL, INC.

8669 Commodity Circle, Orlando, FL, 32819

Tel: (407) 363-7827     Fax: (407) 363-4862       www.planethollywood.com

*Theme-dining restaurant chain and merchandise retail stores.*

**Planet Hollywood International, Inc., Berlin, Germany**

**Planet Hollywood International, Inc., Promenade 1, Centro, D-46047 Oberhausen Nord Rhein Westjalen, Germany**

## PLANTRONICS

345 Encinal Street, Santa Cruz, CA, 95060

Tel: (831) 426-5858     Fax: (831) 425-5198       www.plantronics.com

*Mfr. communications equipment, electrical and electronic appliances and apparatus.*

**Plantronics GmbH, Postfach 7101, D-50342 Hurth, Germany**

Tel: 49-2233-932340   Fax: 49-2233-373274

## POLARIS INDUSTRIES INC.

2100 Highway 55, Medina, MN, 55440

Tel: (612) 542-0500     Fax: (612) 542-0599       www.polarisindustries.com

*Mfr. snowmobiles and all-terrain recreational and utility vehicles.*

**Taubenreuther GmbH, Postfach 2008, Kulmbach 95326, Germany**

Tel: 49-922-195-6222

## POLAROID CORPORATION

784 Memorial Dr., Cambridge, MA, 02139

Tel: (781) 386-2000     Fax: (781) 386-3924       www.polaroid.com

*Photographic equipment and supplies, optical products.*

**Polaroid GmbH, Koenigslacherstr. 15-21, D-6000 Frankfurt-Niederrad 1, Germany**

## POLICY MANAGEMENT SYSTEMS CORPORATION

One PMSC Center, Blythewood, SC, 29016

Tel: (803) 333-4000     Fax: (803) 333-5544       www.pmsc.com

*Computer software, insurance industry support services.*

**PMS Germany GmbH, Hulchrather Str. 15, D-50670 Cologne, Germany**

## R.L. POLK & COMPANY

26955 Northwestern Hwy., Southfield, MI, 48034

Tel: (248) 728-7111     Fax: (248) 393-2860       www.polk.com

*Directories and direct mail advertising.*

**Portica GmbH, Von-Galen Str. 35, D-4152 Kempen 1, Germany**

## PORTER PRECISION PRODUCTS COMPANY

2734 Banning Road, PO Box 538706, Cincinnati, OH, 45239

Tel: (513) 923-3777     Fax: (513) 923-1111     www.porterpunch.com

*Mfr. piercing punches and die supplies for metal stamping and tool/die industry.*

**Porter Intl. GmbH,  Am Gewerbepark 23, D-6108 Gros-Umstadt, Germany**

## POTTERS INDUSTRIES INC.

PO Box 840, Valley Forge, PA, 19482-0840

Tel: (610) 651-4700     Fax: (610) 408-9724     www.pottersbeads.com

*Mfr. glass spheres for road marking and industry applications.*

**Potters-Ballotini,  Benderstrasse 8, D-40625 Düsseldorf, Germany**

**Potters-Ballotini GmbH,  Morschheimerstr. 9, Postfach 1226, D-67292 Kirchheimbolanden, Germany**

## POWERWARE CORPORATION

8609 Six Forks Road, Raleigh, NC, 27615

Tel: (919) 870-3020     Fax: (919) 870-3100     www.powerware.com

*Mfr./services uninterruptible power supplies and related equipment.*

**Powerware Electronics GmbH,  Bem Alten Bahnhof 1, D-76530 Baden Baden, Germany**

Tel: 49-7221-9388-0   Fax: 49-7221-9388-33

## PPG INDUSTRIES

One PPG Place, Pittsburgh, PA, 15272

Tel: (412) 434-3131     Fax: (412) 434-2190     www.ppg.com

*Mfr. coatings, flat glass, fiber glass, chemicals, coatings.*

**PPG Industries Lacke GmbH,  Stackenbergstrasse 34, D-42329 Wuppertal, Germany**

**PPG Industries Lackfabrik GmbH,  Werner-Siemensstrasse 1, D-76356 Weingarten, Germany**

## PRAXAIR, INC.

39 Old Ridgebury Road, Danbury, CT, 06810-5113

Tel: (203) 837-2000     Fax: (203) 837-2450     www.praxair.com

*Produces and distributes industrial and specialty gases.*

**Praxair GmbH,  Justus-von-Liebig Strasse 2, D-64580 Biebesheim/Rhein, Germany**

Tel: 49-6258-8980   Fax: 49-6258-89850

## PRC INC.

1500 PRC Drive, McLean, VA, 22102

Tel: (703) 556-1000     Fax: (703) 556-1174     www.prc.com

*Computer systems and services.*

**PRC GmbH,  Oberfoehringer Strasse 8, D-81679 Münich, Germany**

## PRECISION VALVE & TRIM, INC.

PO Box 3091, 1923 Cloverland Avenue, Baton Rouge, LA, 70809

Tel: (225) 752-5600     Fax: (225) 752-5400     www.precisionvalve.com

*Mfr. aerosol valves.*

**Deutsche Prazisions Ventil GmbH,  Schulstr. 33, D-6234 Battersheim Main, Germany**

## PREMARK INTERNATIONAL INC.

1717 Deerfield Road, Deerfield, IL, 60015

Tel: (847) 405-6000     Fax: (847) 405-6013     www.premarkintl.com

*Mfr. Hobart commercial food equipment, diversified consumer and commercial products, small appliances, and exercise equipment.*

**Premark GmbH,  Praunheimer Landstrasse 70, Postfach 93-01-20, D-6000 Frankfurt/Main 93, Germany**

## PRI AUTOMATION, INC.

805 Middlesex Turnpike, Billerica, MA, 01821-3986

Tel: (978) 663-8555    Fax: (978) 663-9755    www.pria.com

*Provides factory automation systems for silicon chip makers.*

**PRI Automation, OEM Systems,  Robert-Bosch Strasse 29A, D-88131 Lindau, Germany**

Tel: 49-83-8297-7227    Fax: 49-83-8297-7228

## PRICEWATERHOUSECOOPERS LLP

1301 Ave. of the Americas, New York, NY, 10019

Tel: (212) 596-7000    Fax: (212) 259-1301    www.pwcglobal.com

*Accounting and auditing, tax and management, and human resource consulting services.*

**PriceWaterhouseCoopers,  Mozartstrasse 1, Postfach 405, D-04004 Leipzig, Germany**

Tel: 49-341-2135-6   Fax: 49-341-2135-777

**PriceWaterhouseCoopers,  An der Muhle 3, D-13507 Berlin, Germany**

Tel: 49-30-43902-0   Fax: 49-30-43902-999

**PriceWaterhouseCoopers,  Ostra-Allee 25, Postfach 12 03 11, D-01004  Dresden, Germany**

Tel: 49-351-4860260   Fax: 49-351-4860245

**PriceWaterhouseCoopers,  Graf-Recke-Strasse 82, Postfach 17 02 64, D-40083 Düsseldorf, Germany**

Tel: 49-211-9615-01   Fax: 49-211-9615-700

**PriceWaterhouseCoopers,  ABC-Strasse 45, Postfach 30 40 69, D-20313 Hamburg, Germany**

Tel: 49-40-3-55-56-0   Fax: 49-40-3-55-56-123

**PriceWaterhouseCoopers,  Arnulfstrasse 25, Postfach 20 16 42, D-80016 Münich, Germany**

Tel: 49-89-55-14-80   Fax: 49-89-55-14-8-222

**PriceWaterhouseCoopers,  Heilbronner Strasse 190, Postfach 10 38 53, D-70033 Stuttgart, Germany**

Tel: 49-711-1652-0   Fax: 49-711-1652-222

**PriceWaterhouseCoopers,  Gervinusstrasse 15, D-60322 Frankfurt am Main, Germany**

Tel: 49-69-15204-600   Fax: 49-69-15204-666

## PRIMARK CORPORATION

100 Winter Street, Ste. 4300-N, Waltham, MA, 02451

Tel: (781) 466-6611    Fax: (781) 890-6187    www.primark.com

*Provides financial and business information.*

**Primark Germany GmbH,  Mainzer Landstrasse 16, Trianonhaus D-60325, Frankfurt, Germany**

Tel: 49-69-71-405-0

## PRINTRONIX INC.

14600 Myford Road, Irvine, CA, 92606

Tel: (714) 368-2300    Fax: (714) 368-2600    www.printronix.com

*Mfr. computer printers.*

**Printronix GmbH,  Goethering 56, D-63067 Offenbach, Germany**

Tel: 49-69-829-7060   Fax: 49-69-829-70622

## PROCTER & GAMBLE COMPANY

One Procter & Gamble Plaza, Cincinnati, OH, 45202

Tel: (513) 983-1100    Fax: (513) 562-4500    www.pg.com

*Personal care, food, laundry, cleaning and industry products.*

**Procter & Gamble GmbH,  Sulzbacherstr. 40, D-65824 Schwalbach/Ts., Germany**

## PSDI MAXIMO

100 Crosby Drive, Bedford, MA, 01730

Tel: (781) 280-2000    Fax: (781) 280-0200    www.psdi.com

*Develops, markets and provides maintenance management software systems.*

**PSDI Deutschland GmbH,  Stadionstrasse 6, 70771 Leinfelden-Echterdingen (Stuttgart) Germany**

Tel: 49-231-9798-245   Fax: 49-231-9798-111   Contact: Frank Geisler, Gen. Mgr.   Emp: 13

## PSI NET (PERFORMANCE SYSTEMS INTERNATIONAL INC.)

510 Huntmar Park Drive, Herndon, VA, 22170

Tel: (703) 904-4100    Fax: (703) 904-4200    www.psinet.com

*Internet service provider.*

**Interactive Network GmbH (INX), Hardenbergplatz 2, D-10623 Berlin, Germany**

Tel: 49-30-254-310    Fax: 49-30-254-31299    Contact: Moos Bulder, Reg. VP

**PSINet Germany GmbH, Carl-Zeiss-Ring 21, D-85737 Ismaning, Germany**

Tel: 49-89-96-28-70    Fax: 49-89-9620-94-25    Contact: Moos Bulder, Reg. VP

## QUALCOMM INC.

5775 Morehouse Dr., San Diego, CA, 92121-1714

Tel: (858) 587-1121    Fax: (858) 658-2100    www.qualcomm.com

*Digital wireless telecommunications systems.*

**QUALCOMM Germany, Münich Airport Business Center, Soeldnermoos 17 Entrance B - 4/F, Hallbergmoos 85399, Germany**

## QUALITROL CORPORATION

1385 Fairport Road, Fairport, NY, 14450

Tel: (716) 586-1515    Fax: (716) 377-0220    www.qualitrolcorp.com

*Mfr. gauges and thermometers.*

**Qualitrol GmbH, Industriestr., Postfach 1170, D-6222 Geisenheim, Germany**

## QUANTUM

500 McCarthy Blvd., Milpitas, CA, 95035

Tel: (408) 894-4000    Fax: (408) 894-3218    www.quantum.com

*Mfr. computer peripherals.*

**Quantum GmbH, Berner Strasse 28, Frankfurt D-60437, Germany**

Tel: 49-69-950767-91

## QUINTILES TRANSNATIONAL CORPORATION

4709 Creekstone Dr., Durham, NC, 27703

Tel: (919) 998-2000    Fax: (919) 998-9113    www.quintiles.com

*Mfr. pharmaceuticals.*

**Innovex (Biodesign) GmbH, Quintiles Phase I Services Obere Hardtstr. 8-16, Freiburg D-79114, Germany**

**Quintiles GmbH, Schleussnerstrasse 42, Neu-Isenburg D-63236, Germany**

## QWEST COMMUNICATIONS INTERNATIONAL INC.

1801 California Street, Ste. 5200, Denver, CO, 80202

Tel: (303) 896-2020    Fax: (303) 793-6654    www.uswest.com

*Tele-communications provider; integrated communications services.*

**KPNQwest (JV), Frankfurt, Germany**

## RADISSON HOTELS INTERNATIONAL

Carlson Pkwy., PO Box 59159, Minneapolis, MN, 55459-8204

Tel: (612) 540-5526    Fax: (612) 449-3400    www.radisson.com

*Hotels and resorts.*

**Radisson Hotels Intl., Attn: German Office, Carlson Parkway, PO Box 59159, Minneapolis MN 55459-8204**

**Radisson SAS Hotel, Karl-Liebknecht-Strasse 5, D-10178 Berlin, Germany**

Tel: 49-30-23-82-8    Fax: 49-30-23-82-7590

## RAIN BIRD SPRINKLER MFG. CORPORATION

145 North Grand Ave., Glendora, CA, 91741-2469

Tel: (626) 963-9311      Fax: (626) 963-4287      www.rainbird.com

*World's largest manufacturer of lawn sprinklers and irrigation systems equipment.*

**Rain Bird Deutschland, Siedlerstrasse 46, D-71126 Gäufelden-Nebringen, Germany**

Tel: 49-7032-99010    Fax: 49-7032-99010    Contact: Rolf Kruger

## RAINBOW TECHNOLOGY INC.

50 Technology Dr., Irvine, CA, 92618

Tel: (949) 450-7300      Fax: (949) 450-7450      www.rainbow.com

*Mfr. computer related security products.*

**IBV Informatik AG, Lerzenstr. 27, CH-8953 Dietikon, Schweiz**

**IBV Informatik GmbH, Fabrikstr. 5, D-79539 Lörrach, Germany**

**Rainbow Technologies GmbH, Oskar-Messter-Strasse 16, D-8045 Ismaning, Germany**

## RAMSEY TECHNOLOGY INC.

501 90th Ave. NW, Coon Rapids, MN, 55433

Tel: (763) 783-2500      Fax: (763) 780-2525

*Mfr. in-motion weighing, inspection, monitoring and control equipment for the process industry.*

**Ramsey Engineering GmbH, Max-Eyth-Str. 45, D-4200 Oberhausen 11, Germany**

## RANCO INC.

8115 US Route 42 North, Plain City, OH, 43064

Tel: (614) 873-9000      Fax: (614) 873-3819      www.rancocontrols.com

*Mfr. controls for appliance, automotive, comfort, commercial and consumer markets.*

**Deutsche Ranco GmbH, Am Neven Rheinhaven 4, Postfach 2009, D-6720 Speyer, Germany**

## RAY & BERNDTSON, INC.

301 Commerce, Ste. 2300, Fort Worth, TX, 76102

Tel: (817) 334-0500      Fax: (817) 334-0779      www.prb.com

*Executive search, management audit and management consulting firm.*

**Ray & Berndtson, Olof-Palme-StraBe 35, D-60393 Frankfurt, Germany**

Tel: 49-69-95777-01    Fax: 49-69-95777-901    Contact: Theo Gehlen, Mng. Ptnr.

## RAY BURNER COMPANY

401 Parr Boulevard, Richmond, CA, 94801

Tel: (510) 236-4972      Fax: (510) 236-4083      www.rayburner.com

*Mfr. gas and oil burners, controls, oil pump sets, boilers.*

**Ray Oel-u. Gasbrenner GmbH, Schloss-Str. 92, Postfach 2931, D-7000 Stuttgart 1, Germany**

## RAYCHEM CORPORATION

300 Constitution Dr., Menlo Park, CA, 94025-1164

Tel: (650) 361-3333      Fax: (650) 361-5579      www.raychem.com

*Develop/mfr./market materials science products for electronics, telecommunications and industry.*

**Raychem GmbH, Haidgraben 6, Ottobrun (Münich), Germany**

Tel: 49-89-608-90    Fax: 49-89-609-6345

**Raynet Germany, Clemens-August Strasse 16-18, D-5300 Bonn 1, Germany**

**Sigmaform GmbH, Neckarave 25, D-7148 Hochberg, Germany**

**Walter Rose GmbH, Profilstrasse 6-8, D-5800 Hagen 1, Germany**

## RAYMOND JAMES FINANCIAL, INC.

880 Carillon Parkway, St. Petersburg, FL, 33716

Tel: (813) 573-3800     Fax: (813) 573-8244     www.rjf.com

*Financial services; securities brokerage, asset management, and investment banking services.*

**Raymond James Deutschland, Lange Str. 8, 70173 Stuttgart, Germany**

Tel: 49-711-222-9740   Fax: 49-711-227-0999   Contact: F. Reissland

**Raymond James Deutschland Gmbh & Co. KG, Moerser Strasse 100, D-40667 Meerbusch, Germany**

Tel: 49-213-293-070   Fax: 49-213-293-0714

## RAYTECH CORPORATION

Four Corporate Drive, Ste. 295, Shelton, CT, 06484

Tel: (203) 925-8000     Fax: (203) 925-8088     www.raytech.com

*Mfr. friction components and products for automotive and construction industry.*

**Raybestos Industrie- Produkte GmbH, Industriestrasse 7, D-54497 Morbach, Germany**

## RAYTHEON COMPANY

141 Spring Street, Lexington, MA, 02173

Tel: (781) 862-6600     Fax: (781) 860-2172     www.raytheon.com

*Mfr. diversified electronics, appliances, aviation, energy and environmental products; publishing, industry and construction services.*

**Raytheon Marine, Kiel, Germany**

## RAZORFISH, INC.

107 Grand Street, 3rd Fl., New York, NY, 10013

Tel: (212) 966-5960     Fax: (212) 966-6915     www.razorfish.com

*Engaged in consulting and web services.*

**Razorfish GmbH, Gutshof Menterschwaige, Menterschweigstrasse 4, 81545 Munchen, Germany**

Tel: 49-89-64-2000

**Razorfish GmbH, Solmsstrasse 8, 60486 Frankfurt, Germany**

Tel: 49-69-9726580

## READER'S DIGEST ASSOCIATION, INC.

Reader's Digest Rd., Pleasantville, NY, 10570

Tel: (914) 238-1000     Fax: (914) 238-4559     www.readersdigest.com

*Publisher of magazines and books and direct mail marketer.*

**Reader's Digest Verlag Das Beste GmbH, Augustenstr. 1, D-7000 Stuttgart 1, Germany**

## REEBOK INTERNATIONAL LTD.

100 Technology Center Drive, Stoughton, MA, 02072

Tel: (781) 401-5000     Fax: (781) 401-7402     www.reebok.com

*Mfr. athletic shoes including casual, dress golf and walking shoes.*

**Reebok Deutschland GmbH, Keltenring 14, D-82039 Oberhaching, Germany**

## REFCO GROUP LTD.

111 West Jackson Blvd, Suite 1800, Chicago, IL, 60604

Tel: (312) 930-6500     Fax: (312) 930-6534     www.refco.com

*Commodity and security brokers engaged in the execution and clearing of futures and options and institutional asset management services.*

**Refco Futures Ltd., Hamburg, Germany**

## REFLEXITE TECHNOLOGY

120 Darling Drive, Avon, CT, 06001

Tel: (860) 676-7100      Fax: (860) 676-7199      www.reflexite.com

*Mfr. plastic film, sheet, materials and shapes, optical lenses.*

**Fresnel Optics, GmbH,  Flurstedter Marktweg 13, 99510 Apolda,Germany**

Tel: 49-3644-50110   Fax: 49-3644-501150   Contact: Olivier Bulcourt, Mgr.

## REGAL-BELOIT CORPORATION

200 State Street, Beloit, WI, 53512-0298

Tel: (608) 364-8800      Fax: (608) 364-8818      www.regal-beloit.com

*Mfr. power transmission equipment, perishable cutting tools.*

**Mastergear GmbH,  Postfach 1216, D-61260 Neu-Anspach, Germany**

Tel: 49-6081-94300   Fax: 49-6081-943030

## REGENT SPORTS CORPORATION

PO Box 11357, Hauppauge, NY, 11788

Tel: (516) 234-2800      Fax: (516) 234-2948      www.regent-halex.com

*Mfr. sporting goods equipment, including Spalding, MacGregor, Regent and Halex.*

**Regent Sports GmbH Germany,  Pfarrweg 1, D-8035 Gauting, Germany**

## RELIANCE GROUP HOLDINGS, INC.

55 East 52nd Street, New York, NY, 10055

Tel: (212) 909-1100      Fax: (212) 909-1864      www.rgh.com

*Financial and insurance management services.*

**Reliance National Insurance Co. (Europe) Ltd.,  Niederlassung München, Ottostrasse 5, D-80333 München, Germany**

Tel: 49-89-550-8956   Fax: 49-89-550-8956

**Reliance National Insurance Co. (Europe) Ltd.,  Direktion für Deutschland, Kaiser-Wilhelm-Ring 50, D-50672 Köln, Germany**

Tel: 49-221-912-7670   Fax: 49-221-912-7676

## RELIANT ENERGY, INC.

1111 Louisiana Street, Houston, TX, 77002

Tel: (713) 207-3000      Fax: (713) 207-0206      www.houind.com

*Provides gas and electric services.*

**Reliant Energy Trading & Marketing,  Frankfurt, Germany**

## REMEDY CORPORATION

1505 Salado Drive, Mountain View, CA, 94043-1110

Tel: (650) 903-5200      Fax: (650) 903-9001      www.remedy.com

*Developer and marketer of computer applications for the operations management market.*

**Remedy GmbH,  Eurohaus Lyoner Str. 26, D-60528 Frankfurt, Germany**

Tel: 49-69-677-33160   Fax: 49-69-677-33333

## REMINGTON ARMS COMPANY, INC.

870 Remington Drive, PO Box 700, Madison, NC, 27025

Tel: (336) 548-8700      Fax: (336) 548-7801      www.remington.com

*Mfr. sporting firearms and ammunition.*

**Remington Arms GmbH,  Postfach 3266, Wurzburg, Germany**

## REMINGTON PRODUCTS COMPANY, L.L.C.

60 Main Street, Bridgeport, CT, 06604

Tel: (203) 367-4400     Fax: (203) 332-4848     www.remington-products.com

*Mfr. home appliances, electric shavers.*

**Remington Products GmbH, Niederlassung Deutschland, Siemensstrasse 7, D-8849 Riedlingen, Germany**

Tel: 49-7371-9325-0

## RENAISSANCE HOTELS AND RESORTS

10400 Fernwood Road, Bethesda, MD, 20817

Tel: (301) 380-3000     Fax: (301) 380-5181     www.renaissancehotels.com

*Hotel and resort chain.*

**Renaissance Hamburg Hotel, Hamburg, Germany**

Tel: 49-40-349-180

**Renaissance Hotel, Chemnitz, Germany**

Tel: 49-221-203-40

## RENAISSANCE WORLDWIDE, INC.

52 Second Ave., Waltham, MA, 02451

Tel: (781) 290-3000     Fax: (781) 965-4807     www.rens.com

*Provides technology consulting, staffing services, corporate and systems strategies and software and hardware installation.*

**The Hunter Group, Fellnerstrasse 729, D-60322 Frankfurt, Germany**

Tel: 49-69-959-6500

**The Hunter Group, Josef-Jagerhuber-Strasse 11, D-8222319 Starnberg, Germany**

Tel: 49-8151-90-570   Fax: 49-8151-90-5799

## RESMED INC.

1440 Danielson Street, Poway, CA, 92064

Tel: (858) 746-2400     Fax: (858) 880-1618     www.resmed.com

*Mfr. sleep apnea aids, including nasal masks and accessories.*

**ResMed GmbH & Co. KG, Rudolfstraße 10, D-41068 Mönchengladbach, Germany**

Tel: 49-2161-3521

## REVELL/MONOGRAM

8601 Waukegan Rd., Morton Grove, IL, 60053

Tel: (847) 966-3500     Fax: (847) 767-5857     www.revell-monogram.com

*Mfr. plastic hobby kits.*

**Revell AG, Henschelstr. 20-30, D-4980 Buende 1, Germany**

## REVLON INC.

625 Madison Ave., New York, NY, 10022

Tel: (212) 527-4000     Fax: (212) 527-4995     www.revlon.com

*Mfr. cosmetics, fragrances, toiletries and beauty care products.*

**Deutsche Revlon GmbH, Tiefenbroicher Weg 15, D-4000 Düsseldorf, Germany**

## REXNORD CORPORATION

4701 West Greenfield Ave., Milwaukee, WI, 53214

Tel: (414) 643-3000     Fax: (414) 643-3078     www.rexnord.com

*Mfr. power transmission products.*

**Rexnord Antriebstechnik GmbH, Ueberwasserstr. 64, D-44147 Dortmund 1, Germany**

**Rexnord Kette GmbH & Co. KG, Postfach 120, D-57501 Betzdorf, Germany**

## REYNOLDS METALS COMPANY, DIV. ALCOA

6601 West Broad St., Richmond, VA, 23230

Tel: (804) 281-2000      Fax: (804) 281-3602      www.rmc.com

*Mfr. aluminum for flexible packaging products for food service and pharmaceutical industries and aluminum doors.*

**Reynolds Metals Company (JV), Hamburg, Germany**

## RHEOMETRIC SCIENTIFIC INC.

1 Possumtown Road, Piscataway, NJ, 08854

Tel: (732) 560-8550      Fax: (732) 560-7451      www.rheosci.com

*Design/mfr. rheological instruments and systems.*

**Rheometric Scientific GmbH, Schwanheimer Strasse 144a, D-64625 Bensheim, Germany**

## RICHCO, INC.

5825 N. Tripp Ave., PO Box 804238, Chicago, IL, 60680

Tel: (773) 539-4060      Fax: (773) 539-6770      www.richco.com

*Mfr. plastic and metal parts for the electric, electronic, appliance, and fiber-optic industries.*

**Richco Plastic Deutschland GmbH, Breslauer Weg 31, 82358 Geretsfried #2, Germany**

Tel: 49-8171-43280

## RIDGE TOOL COMPANY

400 Clark Street, Elyria, OH, 44035

Tel: (440) 323-5581      Fax: (440) 329-4853      www.ridgid.com

*Mfr. hand and power tools for working pipe, drain cleaning equipment, etc.*

**Ridge Tool GmbH, Limburg, Lahn, Germany**

## RIGHT MANAGEMENT CONSULTANTS, INC.

1818 Market Street, 14th Fl., Philadelphia, PA, 19103-3614

Tel: (215) 988-1588      Fax: (215) 988-9112      www.right.com

*Out placement and human resources consulting services.*

**Right Associates, Senefelderstr. 166, D-6050 Offenbach Frankfurt, Germany**

## THE RITZ-CARLTON HOTEL COMPANY, L.L.C.

3414 Peachtree Road NE, Ste. 300, Atlanta, GA, 30326

Tel: (404) 237-5500      Fax: (404) 365-9643      www.ritzcarlton.com

*5-star hotel and restaurant chain.*

**The Ritz-Carlton Hotel Company, Westendstrasse 19, D-60325 Frankfurt/Main, Germany**

Tel: 49-69-975-46224

## C. H. ROBINSON WORLDWIDE, INC. (CHR)

8100 Mitchell Road, Eden Prairie, MN, 55344

Tel: (612) 937-8500      Fax: (612) 937-6714      www.chrobinson.com

*Global door-to-door freight forwarding services, including flexible transportation solutions and global logistics.*

**C. H. Robinson (CHR), Augsburg, Germany**

## ROBOTIC VISION SYSTEMS, INC.

5 Shawmut Road, Canton, MA, 02021

Tel: (781) 821-0830      Fax: (781) 828-9852      www.rvsi.com

*Mfr. machine vision-based systems for semiconductor industry.*

**RVSI Europe (Central) GmbH, Industriestrasse 20, 61381 Friedrichsdorf, Germany**

Tel: 49 617 228 50

## ROCKWELL INTERNATIONAL CORPORATION

777 East Wisconsin Ave., Ste. 1400, Milwaukee, WI, 53202

Tel: (414) 212-5200     Fax: (414) 212-5201     www.rockwell.com

*Products and service for aerospace and defense, automotive, electronics, graphics and automation industry.*

**Rockwell Automation - Allen-Bradley, Dusselberger Str. 15, 41781 Haan-Gruiten, Germany**

Tel: 49-2104-9600

**Rockwell Automation - Dodge/Reliance GmbH, Brühlstraße 22, D-72834 Eltzal-Dallau, Germany**

Tel: 49-6261-9410    Fax: 49-6261-941122

**Rockwell Automation -Dodge Europe, Industriering Ost 66, D-47906 Kempen, Germany**

Tel: 49-2152-205570    Fax: 49-2152-22055720

**Rockwell Collins Deutschland, Borsigstrase 6, D-63150 Heusenstam, Germany**

Tel: 49-6104-93680

**Rockwell Semiconductor Systems, Paul-Gerhardt-Allee 50 A, D-81245 München, Germany**

Tel: 49-89-829-1320    Fax: 49-89-834-2734

**Rockwell-Collins Deutschland, Boschstrasse 6, , D-33150 Heusenstamm, Germany**

Tel: 49-6104-93680    Fax: 49-6104-15673

## R.A. RODRIGUEZ, INC.

20 Seaview Boulevard, Garden City, NY, 11050

Tel: (516) 625-8080     Fax: (516) 621-2424     www.rodriguez-usa.com

*Distribution of ball and roller bearings, precision gears, mechanical systems and related products.*

**R. A. Rodriguez GmbH, rue De Wattrelos 17, D-52249 Eschweiler, Germany**

Tel: 49-2403-7800    Fax: 49-2403-78050    Contact: Gunther Schulz, Mng. Dir.

## ROHM AND HAAS COMPANY

100 Independence Mall West, Philadelphia, PA, 19106

Tel: (215) 592-3000     Fax: (215) 592-3377     www.rohmhaas.com

*Mfr. industrial and agricultural chemicals, plastics.*

**Morton International GmbH, Beim Struckenberge 11, D-2823 Bremen, Germany**

Tel: 49-541-91410

**Morton International GmbH, Hefenrignstrasse 1, D-49090 Osnabruck, Germany**

**Morton International GmbH, Reinhard-Reichnow-Strasse 4, D-8618 Strullendorf, Germany**

**Rohm and Haas (Deutschland) GmbH, Postfach 940322, D-60461 Frankfurt/Main, Germany**

Tel: 49-69-78996-0

**Shipley GmbH, Wolf-Hirt-Str. 12, PO Box 507, D-73706 Esslingen, Germany**

Tel: 49-711-931-320

## RONALD E. LAIS, INC.

136 South Imperial Highway, Anaheim, CA, 92807-3943

Tel: (714) 998-6633     Fax: (714) 937-1791     www.laislaw.com

*International law firm.*

**Ronald E. Lais, Inc., Knorrstrasse 85, D-80807 Münich, Germany**

Tel: 49-89-62-4080    Fax: 49-89-62-408-444

## ROYAL APPLIANCE MFG. COMPANY

650 Alpha Drive, Cleveland, OH, 44143

Tel: (440) 449-6150     Fax: (440) 449-7806     www.royalappliance.com

*Mfr. vacuum cleaners.*

**Royal Appliances Mfg. GmbH, Weisshausstrasse 21, D-5000 Cologne 41, Germany**

## RUSSELL REYNOLDS ASSOCIATES INC.

200 Park Ave., New York, NY, 10166-0002

Tel: (212) 351-2000     Fax: (212) 370-0896     www.russreyn.com

*Executive recruiting services.*

**Russell Reynolds Associates Inc., Heilwigstraße 33, D-20249 Hamburg, Germany**

Tel: 49-40-4806610   Fax: 49-40-480661-40   Contact: Harald Grosser

**Russell Reynolds Associates Inc., Messe Turm, Ludwig-Erhard-Anlage, D-60308 Frankfurt/Main, Germany**

Tel: 49-69-7560900   Fax: 49-69-756090-11   Contact: Harald Grosser

## RVSI (ROBOTIC VISION SYSTEMS, INC.)

5 Shawmut Road, Canton, MA, 02021

Tel: (781) 821-0830     Fax: (781) 828-8942     www.rvsi.com

*Mfr. bar code scanners and data collection equipment.*

**Computer Identics GmbH, Otto-Hahn-Str. 40, D-61381 Friedrichsdorf-Koeppern, Germany**

## RYDER SYSTEM, INC.

3600 NW 82nd Ave., Miami, FL, 33166

Tel: (305) 500-3726     Fax: (305) 500-4129     www.ryder.com

*Integrated logistics, full-service truck leasing, truck rental and public transportation services.*

**Ryder Deutschland, Parsevalstrasse 9A, D-40468 Düsseldorf, Germany**

Tel: 49-211-472-100   Fax: 49-211-472-1099

## SAFETY-KLEEN CORPORATION

1301 Gervais Street, Columbia, SC, 29201

Tel: (803) 933-4200     Fax: (803) 933-4345     www.safety-kleen.com

*Solvent based parts cleaning service; sludge/solvent recycling service.*

**Safety-Kleen GmbH Reinigungstechnik, Auf dem Huls 16, D-4020 Mettmann 1, Germany**

## SAPHIRE INTERNATIONAL LTD.

3060 Main Street, Ste. 202, Stratford, CT, 06614

Tel: (203) 375-8668     Fax: (203) 375-1965     www.dataease.com

*Mfr. applications development software.*

**Markt & Technik Verlag AG, Hans Pinsel Str. 2, D-8013 Haar bei Munchen, Germany**

## SAPIENT CORPORATION

1 Memorial Drive, Cambridge, MA, 02142

Tel: (617) 621-0200     Fax: (617) 621-1300     www.sapient.com

*Engaged in information technology and consulting services.*

**Sapient Dusseldorf, Furstenwall 65, 40219 Dusseldorf, Germany**

Tel: 49-211-60-116

**Sapient GmbH, Schaefflerhof, Maffeistrasse 3, D-80333 Münich, Germany**

Tel: 49-89-255-58853

## SAS INSTITUTE INC.

SAS Campus Drive, Cary, NC, 27513

Tel: (919) 677-8000     Fax: (919) 677-4444     www.sas.com

*Mfr./distributes decision support software.*

**SAS Institute GmbH (European Hdqtrs.), Neuenheimer Landstrasse 28-30, PO Box 10 53 40, D-69043 Heidelberg, Germany**

Tel: 49-6221-4160   Fax: 49-6221-474850

## SCHENECTADY INTERNATIONAL INC.

PO Box 1046, Schenectady, NY, 12301

Tel: (518) 370-4200     Fax: (518) 382-8129     www.siigroup.com

*Mfr. electrical insulating varnishes, enamels, phenolic resins, alkylphenols.*

**Schenectady Europe GmbH, Grossmannstrasse 105, D-20539 Hamburg, Germany**

Tel: 49-40-78-946   Fax: 49-40-78-946-276

## SCHENKER INTERNATIONAL FORWARDERS INC.

150 Albany Ave., Freeport, NY, 11520

Tel: (516) 377-3000     Fax: (516) 377-3005     www.schenkerusa.com

*Freight forwarders.*

**Schenker International Deutschland GmbH, PO Box 42 01 65, D-30855 Hannover, Germany**

Tel: 49-511-7408560   Fax: 49-511-740-85639

**Schenker International Deutschland GmbH, Cargo Term. A+B4 Etage, PO Box 23 19 44, D-85356 München, Germany**

Tel: 49-89-97-5900   Fax: 49-89-97-590090

**Schenker International Deutschland GmbH, Ruhrorter Strasse 9-21, PO Box 10 26 64, D-68219 Mannheim, Germany**

Tel: 49-621-8046-785   Fax: 49-621-8046-666

**Schenker International Deutschland GmbH, PO Box 11 03 13, D-20457 Hamburg, Germany**

Tel: 49-40-36135   Fax: 49-40-36135-216

## R. P. SCHERER CORPORATION

645 Martinsville Rd., Ste. 200, Baskin Ridge, NJ, 07920

Tel: (908) 580-1500     Fax: (908) 580-9220     www.rpscherer.com

*Mfr. pharmaceuticals; soft gelatin and two-piece hard shell capsules.*

**R.P. Scherer GmbH, Postfach 1243, D-69402 Eberbach/Baden, Germany**

Tel: 49-6271-8402   Fax: 49-6271-842700   Contact: Dr. Gunter Blankenhorn, Gen. Mgr.   Emp: 1,000

## SCHERING-PLOUGH CORPORATION

One Giralda Farms, Madison, NJ, 07940-1000

Tel: (973) 822-7000     Fax: (973) 822-7048     www.sch-plough.com

*Proprietary drug and cosmetic products.*

**Essex Tierarznei Ndl der Essex Pharma GmbH, Dr. Christian Wirth Thomas, Dehler Str. 27 D81737, München Germany**

Tel: 49-89-62731-430

## SCHLEGEL SYSTEMS

1555 Jefferson Road, PO Box 23197, Rochester, NY, 14692-3197

Tel: (716) 427-7200     Fax: (716) 427-9993     www.schlegel.com

*Mfr. engineered perimeter sealing systems for residential and commercial construction; fibers; rubber product.*

**Schlegel GmbH, Bredowstrasse 33, D-2000 Hamburg 74, Germany**

## SCHLUMBERGER LIMITED

277 Park Avenue, New York, NY, 10021

Tel: (212) 350-9400     Fax: (212) 350-9564     www.schlumberger.com

*Engaged in oil and gas services, metering and payment systems, and produces semiconductor testing equipment and smart cards.*

**Messerchmidt Apparate GmbH, Haenseatenstrasse 1, Postfach 1348, 30834 Langenhagen, Germany**

**Schlumberger Cards & Systems GmbH, Gutenbergstr. 2-4, D-85737 Ismaning, Germany**

**Schlumberger Systems GmbH, Hanhnstr. 70, 60528 Frankfurt, Germany**

Tel: 49-69-668042-0   Fax: 49-69-668042-42

## A. SCHULMAN INC.
3550 West Market Street, Akron, OH, 44333

Tel: (330) 666-3751        Fax: (330) 668-7204        www.aschulman.com

*Mfr./sale plastic resins and compounds.*

**A. Schulman GmbH, Huttenstr. 211, D-50170 Kerpen Sindorf, Germany**

## SCIENCE APPLICATIONS INTL. CORPORATION (SAIC)
10260 Campus Point Dr., San Diego, CA, 92121

Tel: (858) 826-6000        Fax: (858) 535-7589        www.saic.com

*Engaged in research and engineering.*

**SAIC C/O Detesystem GmbH, Hahnstrasse 43D, Frankfurt D-605, Germany**

Tel: 49-69-665313490

## SEAGATE TECHNOLOGY, INC.
920 Disc Dr., Scotts Valley, CA, 95066

Tel: (408) 438-6550        Fax: (408) 438-7205        www.seagate.com

*Develop computer technology, software and hardware.*

**Seagate Technology GmbH, Messerschmittstrasse 4, D-80992 Münich, Germany**

Tel: 49-89-14305000  Fax: 49-89-14305100   Contact: Hans-Dieter Blaser, VP    Emp: 25

## SEALED AIR CORPORATION
Park 80 East, Saddle Brook, NJ, 07663

Tel: (201) 791-7600        Fax: (201) 703-4205        www.sealedair.com

*Mfr. protective and specialty packaging solutions for industrial, food and consumer products.*

**Sealed Air GmbH, Max-Planck Strasse 15, D-61381 Friedrichsdorf, Germany**

Tel: 49-6172-760635   Fax: 49-6172-760637

## SEAQUIST PERFECT DISPENSING
1160 North Silver Lake Road, Cary, IL, 60013

Tel: (847) 639-2124        Fax: (847) 639-2142        www.seaquistperect.com

*Mfr. and sale of dispensing systems; lotion pumps and spray-through overcaps.*

**Ing. Erich Pfeiffer GmbH, Radolfzell, Germany**

**Seaquist Perfect Dispensing GmbH, Postfach 130265, 4-`3`2 Dortmund (Wickede), Germany**

Tel: 49-231-92-400   Fax: 49-231-21-1752   Contact: Jacques Blanie    Emp: 250

## G.D. SEARLE & COMPANY
5200 Old Orchard Road, Skokie, IL, 60077

Tel: (847) 982-7000        Fax: (847) 470-1480        www.searlehealthnet.com

*Mfr. pharmaceuticals, health care, optical products and specialty chemicals.*

**Heumann Pharma GmbH & Co., Nürnberger Str. 12, 90537 Feucht, Germany**

Tel: 49-9128-404-0   Fax: 49-9128-404-581

**Searle East Europe & Candarel, Frankfurter Strasse 181, D-6078 Neu-Isenberg, Germany**

## SECURE COMPUTING CORPORATION
One Almaden Blvd., Ste. 400, San Jose, CA, 95113

Tel: (408) 918-6100        Fax: (408) 918-6101        www.sctc.com

*Mfr. software.*

**Secure Computing GmbH, Luise-Kiesselbach-Platz 35, D-81377 Münich, Germany**

Tel: 49-89-71-04-6100

## SELAS CORPORATION OF AMERICA
2034 S. Limekiln Pike, Dresher, PA, 19025

Tel: (215) 646-6600        Fax: (215) 646-3536        www.selas.com

*Mfr. heat treating equipment for metal, glass, ceramic and chemical industry.*

**Selas Waermetechnik GmbH, Christenenstrasse 2, D-40880 Ratingen, Germany**

## SEMTECH CORPORATION

652 Mitchell Road, PO Box 367, Newbury Park, CA, 91320

Tel: (805) 498-2111      Fax: (805) 498-3804      www.semtech.com

*Mfr. silicon rectifiers, rectifier assemblies, capacitors, switching regulators, AC/DC converters.*

**Semtech Ltd. Deutschland,  Weinstrasse 2, D-74172 Neckarsulum, Germany**

Tel: 49-7132-37780   Fax: 49-7132-37775

## SENCO PRODUCTS INC.

8485 Broadwell Road, Cincinnati, OH, 45244

Tel: (513) 388-2000      Fax: (513) 388-2026      www.senco.com

*Mfr. industry nailers, staplers, fasteners and accessories.*

**Deutsche Senco Industrie-Erzeugnisse GmbH & Co. KG,  Gelsenkirchenerstr. 27, Postfach 10 68 67, D-2800 Bremen 1, Germany**

## SENSORMATIC ELECTRONICS CORPORATION

951 Yamato Road, Boca Raton, FL, 33431-0700

Tel: (561) 989-7000      Fax: (561) 989-7774      www.sensormatic.com

*Electronic article surveillance equipment.*

**Sensormatic GmbH,  Am Schimmersfeld 7, D-40880 Ratingen, Germany**

Tel: 49-2102-431-303   Fax: 49-2102-431-341   Contact: Karl-Heinz Hollung

## THE SERVICEMASTER COMPANY

One ServiceMaster Way, Downers Grove, IL, 60515-1700

Tel: (630) 271-1300      Fax: (630) 271-2710      www.svm.com

*Management service to health care, school and industry facilities; diversified residential and commercial services.*

**ServiceMaster Operations-Germany GmbH,  Lange Strasse 33, D-7293 Pfalzgrafenweiler, Germany**

**Terminix,  Münich, Germany**

## SHAKESPEARE FISHING TACKLE GROUP

3801 Westmore Drive, Columbia, SC, 29223

Tel: (803) 754-7000      Fax: (803) 754-7342      www.shakespeare-fishing.com

*Mfr. fishing tackle.*

**Shakespeare Intl. GmbH,  Postfach 420 424, D-5000 Cologne 41, Germany**

## SHARED MEDICAL SYSTEMS CORPORATION

51 Valley Stream Pkwy, Malvern, PA, 19355

Tel: (610) 219-6300      Fax: (610) 219-3124      www.smed.com

*Computer-based information processing for healthcare industry.*

**SMS Dataplan,  Kilner Strasse 10B, D-6236 Eschborn/TS, Frankfurt, Germany**

## SHEARMAN & STERLING

599 Lexington Ave., New York, NY, 10022-6069

Tel: (212) 848-4000      Fax: (212) 848-7179      www.shearman.com

*Law firm engaged in general American and international financial and commercial practice.*

**Shearman & Sterling,  Bockenheimer Landstrasse 55, D-60325 Frankfurt/Main, Germany**

Tel: 49-69-971070   Fax: 49-69-97107-100   Contact: Georg F. Thoma, Mng. Ptnr.

**Shearman & Sterling,  Couvenstrasse 8, D-40211 Düsseldorf, Germany**

Tel: 49-211-178-880   Fax: 49-211-178-8888   Contact: Georg F. Thoma, Mng. Ptnr.

## SHIPLEY COMPANY, LLC

455 Forest Street, Marlborough, MA, 01752

Tel: (508) 481-7950     Fax: (508) 485-9113     www.shipley.com

*Supplier of materials and processes technology to the microelectronics and printed wiring board industries.*

**Shipley GmbH, Gewerbestrasse 19, D-75217 Birkenfeld, Germany**

Tel: 49-70-82-79140

## SHURE INCORPORATED

222 Hartrey Ave., Evanston, IL, 60202-3696

Tel: (847) 866-2200     Fax: (847) 866-2279     www.shure.com

*Mfr. microphones, teleconferencing systems, circuitry products.*

**Shure Europe GmbH, Münich, Germany**

Contact: Markus Winkler, Mng. Dir.

## SIGNODE PACKAGING SYSTEMS

3610 West Lake Ave., Glenview, IL, 60025

Tel: (847) 724-6100     Fax: (847) 657-4392     www.signode.com

*Mfr. industrial tools and machinery for packaging and strapping.*

**Signode Bernpak GmbH, Greul 1a, D-42897 Remscheid, Germany**

**Signode Pan-European Consumable Systems, Magusstrasse 18, D-46535 Dinslaken, Germany**

**Signode Pan-European Metals Systems, Magnustrasse 18, D-46535 Dinslaken, Germany**

**Signode System GmbH, Magnustrasse 18, D-46535 Dinslaken, Germany**

## SILICON GRAPHICS INC.

2011 N. Shoreline Blvd., Mountain View, CA, 94043-1389

Tel: (650) 960-1980     Fax: (650) 961-0595     www.sgi.com

*Design/mfr. special-effects computer graphic systems and software.*

**Silicon GmbH, Münich, Germany**

## SILICON VALLEY GROUP, INC.

101 Metro Dr., Ste. 400, San Jose, CA, 95110

Tel: (408) 467-5870     Fax: (408) 467-5955     www.svg.com

*Manufacturer of automated wafer processing equipment for the worldwide semiconductor industry.*

**Thermco Products GmbH, Div. Silicon Valley, Fraunhoferstr. 11A, D-8033 Martinsried, Germany**

## SIMPLICITY PATTERN COMPANY, INC.

2 Park Avenue, New York, NY, 10016

Tel: (212) 372-0500     Fax: (212) 372-0628     www.simplicity.com

*Dress patterns.*

**Simplicity Modeschnitt GmbH, Postfach 101664, D-5000 Cologne 1, Germany**

## J.R. SIMPLOT COMPANY, INC.

999 Main Street, Ste.1300, Boise, ID, 83702

Tel: (208) 336-2110     Fax: (208) 389-7515     www.simplot.com

*Fresh/frozen fruits and vegetables, animal feeds, fertilizers.*

**Simplot Europe GmbH & Co. KG, Kielsgrassen 6, Monheim, Germany**

## SKADDEN, ARPS, SLATE, MEAGHER & FLOM LLP

4 Times Square, New York, NY, 10036

Tel: (212) 735-3000     Fax: (212) 735-2000     www.sasmf.com

*American/International law practice.*

**Skadden, Arps, Slate, Meagher & Flom LLP, MesseTurm 27th Fl., D-60308 Frankfurt am Main, Germany**

Tel: 49-69-9757-3000    Fax: 49-69-9757-3050    Contact: Hilary S. Foulkes, Partner

## SL INDUSTRIES, INC.

520 Fellowship Road, Ste. A-114,, Mount Laurel, NJ, 08054

Tel: (609) 727-1500     Fax: (609) 727-1683     www.slindustries.com

*Mfr./design electronic protection and power fluctuation devices.*

**Elektro-Metall Export GmbH, Manchinger Str. 116, D-85053 Ingolstadt, Germany**

## SMITH INTERNATIONAL, INC.

PO Box 60068, Houston, TX, 77205-0068

Tel: (713) 443-3370     Fax: (713) 233-5996     www.smith.com

*Mfr. drilling tools and equipment and provides related services for the drilling, completion and production sectors of the petroleum and mining industries.*

**Smith International Deutschland GmbH, Grafftring 5-7, D-29227 Celle, Germany**

Tel: 49-514-801-243   Contact: Dietmar Muckstein, Area Mgr.

## SMURFIT-STONE CONTAINER CORPORATION

150 N. Michigan Ave., Chicago, IL, 60601-7568

Tel: (312) 346-6600     Fax: (312) 580-3486     www.smurfit-stone.net

*Mfr. paper and paper packaging.*

**Europa Carton AG, Spitalerstrasse 11, D-2000 Hamburg 1, Germany**

## SNAP-ON INCORPORATED

10801 Corporate Dr., Pleasant Prairie, WI, 53158-1603

Tel: (262) 656-5200     Fax: (262) 656-5577     www.snapon.com

*Mfr. auto maintenance, diagnostic and emission testing equipment, hand tools, hydraulic lifts and tire changers.*

**Sun Electric Deutschland GmbH, Postfach 100609, D-4020 Mettamann, Germany**

Tel: 49-2104-7990   Fax: 49-2104-799212   Contact: H. Laube, Mng. Dir.

## SOLECTRON CORPORATION

777 Gibraltar Drive, Milpitas, CA, 95035

Tel: (408) 957-8500     Fax: (408) 956-6075     www.solectron.com

*Provides contract manufacturing services to equipment manufacturers.*

**Force Computers, Inc., Prof. Messerschmitt Strasse 1, D-85579 Neubiberg Münich, Germany**

Tel: 49-89-608-140   Fax: 49-89-609-7793

**Solectron Corporation, Solectronstrasse 1, D-71083 Herrenberg, Germany**

Tel: 49-70-329-980   Fax: 49-70-329-98222

## SONOCO PRODUCTS COMPANY

North Second Street, PO Box 160, Hartsville, SC, 29550

Tel: (843) 383-7000     Fax: (843) 383-7008     www.sonoco.com

*Mfr. packaging for consumer and industrial market and recycled paperboard.*

**Sonoco Consumer Products GmbH, Nikolaus-Otostrasse, D-56727 Mayer-Oft, Germany**

Tel: 49-2651-4876

**Sonoco Deutschland GmbH, Lauda Plant, Tauberstrasse 36, D-97922 Lauda - Königshofen, Germany**

Tel: 49-9343-7017

**Sonoco Deutschland GmbH, Fennastrasse 94, D-48529 Nordhorn, Germany**

Tel: 49-5921-8831-0

**Sonoco Engraph Machine Division, Am Webrhabn, D-40211 Düsseldorf, Germany**

Tel: 49-211-35 68 68

**Sonoco IPD GmbH, Düren Plant, Math v.d. Drieschstrasse 2, D-52399 Merzenich Girbelsrath, Germany**

Tel: 49-2421-704-0

**Sonoco OPV Hülsen GmbH,** **Industriestrasse 6-9, Postfach 1154, D-77741 Neuried Altenheim, Germany**

Tel: 49-7807-990

**Sonoco Plastics GmbH,** **Lindestrasse 20, D-53842 Troisdorf, Germany**

Tel: 49-2241-48000

## SOTHEBY'S HOLDINGS, INC.

1334 York Avenue, New York, NY, 10021

Tel: (212) 606-7000        Fax: (212) 606-7027        www.sothebys.com

*Auction house specializing in fine art and jewelry.*

**Sotheby's Holdings, Inc.,** **Mendelssohnstrasse 66, D-60325 Frankfurt Main, Germany**

Tel: 49-69-7407-87    Contact: Nina Buhne

**Sotheby's Holdings, Inc.,** **Odeansplatz 16, D-80539 Münich, Germany**

Tel: 49-89-291-3151    Contact: Heinrich Graf von Spreti, Pres.

## THE SOUTHERN COMPANY

270 Peachtree Street, N.W., Atlanta, GA, 30303

Tel: (404) 506-5000        Fax: (404) 506-0642        www.southernco.com

*Electric utility.*

**Southern Energy, Inc.,** **3 Markgrafenstrasse, D-10117 Berlin, Germany**

Tel: 49-30-2092-4000    Fax: 49-30-2092-4200    Contact: Jason Harlan, Dir.

## SPALDING HOLDINGS CORPORATION

425 Meadow Street, Chicopee, MA, 01021

Tel: (413) 536-1200        Fax: (413) 536-1404        www.spalding.com

*Mfr. sports equipment and infant and juvenile furniture and accessories.*

**Spalding Sports,** **Münich, Germany**

## SPARKLER FILTERS INC.

PO Box 19, Conroe, TX, 77305-0019

Tel: (936) 756-4471        Fax: (936) 539-1165        www.sparklerfilters.com

*Mfr. liquid filtration systems.*

**Sparkler Filters Europe GmbH,** **Belvedered Allee 23C, D-99425 Weimar, Germany**

## SPENCER STUART MANAGEMENT CONSULTANTS

401 North Michigan Ave., Ste. 3400, Chicago, IL, 60611

Tel: (312) 822-0080        Fax: (312) 822-0116        www.spencerstuart.com

*Executive recruitment firm.*

**Spencer Stuart & Associates Inc.,** **Albstrasse 14, D-70597 Stuttgart, Germany**

Tel: 49-711-97682-0    Fax: 49-711-97682-82    Contact: Hermann Sendele

**Spencer Stuart & Associates Inc.,** **Konigsallee 82, D-40212 Düsseldorf, Germany**

Tel: 49-211-864070    Fax: 49-211-132975    Contact: Hermann Sendele

**Spencer Stuart & Associates Inc.,** **Prinzregentenstrasse 61, D-81675 Münich, Germany**

Tel: 49-89-455553-0    Fax: 49-89-455553-33    Contact: Hermann Sendele

## SPERRY-SUN DRILLING

3000 North Sam Houston Pkwy. East, Houston, TX, 77032

Tel: (281) 871-5100        Fax: (281) 871-5742        www.sperry-sun.com

*Provides drilling services to the oil and gas drilling industry.*

**Sperry-Sun c/o DB Stratabit GmbH,** **Hunaustrasse 7a, 29227 Celle, Westercelle, Germany**

## SPHERION CORPORATION

2050 Spectrum Boulevard, Fort Lauderdale, FL, 33309

Tel: (954) 938-7600    Fax: (954) 938-7666    www.spherion.com

*Provides temporary personnel placement and staffing.*

**Michael Page Finance,  Graf-Adolf-Strasse 70, D-40210 Düsseldorf, Germany**

Tel: 49-211-177-220

**Michael Page Finance,  Mainzer Landstrasse 39, D-60329 Frankfort, Germany**

Tel: 49-9-242-6180

## SPRAYING SYSTEMS COMPANY

PO Box 7900, Wheaton, IL, 60189-7900

Tel: (630) 665-5000    Fax: (630) 260-0842    www.spray.com

*Designs and manufactures industrial spray nozzles.*

**Feinbau Maschinen GmbH,  Postfach 1340, D-7065 Winterbach, Germany**

**Spraying Systems Deutschland,  Grossmoorring 9, D-2100 Hamburg 90, Germany**

## SPS TECHNOLOGIES INC.

101 Greenwood Avenue, Ste. 470, Jenkintown, PA, 19046

Tel: (215) 517-2000    Fax: (215) 517-2032    www.spstech.com

*Mfr. aerospace and industry fasteners, tightening systems, magnetic materials, superalloys.*

**Unbrako Schrauben GmbH,  Postfach 2180, Ernst-Sach-Str. 11, D-5400 Koblenz, Germany**

## SPSS INC.

233 S. Wacker Dr., Chicago, IL, 60606

Tel: (312) 651-6000    Fax: (312) 329-3668    www.spss.com

*Mfr. statistical software.*

**SPSS GmbH Software,  Steinsdorfstrasse 19, D-8000 München 22, Germany**

## SPX CORPORATION

700 Terrace Point Drive, PO Box 3301, Muskegon, MI, 49443-3301

Tel: (231) 724-5000    Fax: (231) 724-5720    www.spx.com

*Mfr. auto parts, special service tools, engine and drive-train parts.*

**Allen Motordiagnose Systeme/SPX Deutschland GmbH,  Dieselstrasse 10, D-63512 Hainburg, Germany**

**Bear Automobil Servicegerate,  Postfach 1108, D-77671 Kehl, Germany**

**Kent-Moore & Euroline,  Alfred Nobel Str. 12, Postfach 1528, D-68519 Viernheim, Germany**

**Lowener OTC Tool GbmH,  Industriestrasse 67, D-40764 Langenfegi, Germany**

**Sealed Power Europe,  Postfach 1355, D-3013 Barsinghausen, Germany**

**SPX Deutschland,  Alfred-Nobel-Strasse 12, Postfach 1528, D-68519 Viernheim, Germany**

## THE ST. PAUL COMPANIES, INC.

385 Washington Street, St. Paul, MN, 55102

Tel: (651) 310-7911    Fax: (651) 310-8294    www.stpaul.com

*Provides investment, insurance and reinsurance services.*

**St. Paul Deutschland,  Neue Weyerstrasse 6, D-50676 Cologne, Germany**

Tel: 49-221-92-44-70  Fax: 49-221-92-44-710   Contact: Bodo Sartorius, Mgr.

**Victoria Verischerung AG,  Victoriaplatz 1, D-40198 Düsseldorf, Germany**

## STANDARD COMMERCIAL CORPORATION

2201 Miller Rd., PO Box 450, Wilson, NC, 27893

Tel: (919) 291-5507    Fax: (919) 237-1109    www.sccgroup.com

*Leaf tobacco dealers/processors and wool processors.*

**Leafco Trading GmbH,  D-2000 Hamburg, Germany**

**Standard Wool GmbH,  Schwachhauser Heerstrasse 57, D-2800 Bremen, Germany**

Werkhof GmbH,  Brook 6, 20457 Hamburg, Germany

Werkhof GmbH,  An der Alster 18, D-2000 Hamburg 1, Germany

## STANDARD MICROSYSTEMS CORPORATION

80 Arkay Drive, Hauppauge, NY, 11788

Tel:  (631) 435-6000        Fax:  (631) 273-5550        www.smsc.com

*Telecommunications systems.*

Standard Microsystems GmbH,  Johanneskirchner Str. 100, 81927 Münich, Germany

Tel: 49-89-9592-990   Fax: 49-89-9592-9990

## STANDEX INTERNATIONAL CORPORATION

6 Manor Parkway, Salem, NH, 03079

Tel:  (603) 893-9701        Fax:  (603) 893-7324        www.standex.com

*Mfr. diversified graphics, institutional, industry/electronic and consumer products.*

James Burn International GbmH,  Postfach 540752, D-22507 Hamburg 54, Germany

Tel: 49-40-540-7013   Fax: 49-40-540-7090   Contact: Peter Timm, Mgr.

Roehlen Industries/Europe,  Postfach 130665, D-47758 Krefeld 1, Germany

Tel: 49-2151-37120   Fax: 49-2151-3712-58   Contact: Giorgio Mazza, Mgr.

Standex  International GmbH,  PO Box 130665, D-47758 Krefeld 1, Germany

Tel: 49-2151-37120   Fax: 49-2151-371258   Contact: Eckhard Roeder, Mgr.

Standex International GmbH, Mold-Tech Div. South,  Postfach 1444, D-74604 Oehringen, Germany

Tel: 49-7941-91700   Fax: 49-7941-9170-33

## STANLEY BOSTITCH FASTENING SYSTEMS

815 Briggs Street, East Greenwich, RI, 02818

Tel:  (401) 884-2500        Fax:  (401) 885-6511        www.centerplex.net

*Mfr. stapling machines, stapling supplies, fastening systems and wire.*

Stanley Bostitch GmbH,  Postfach 1349, Oststr. 26, D-2000 Norderstedt l Bez-Hamburg, Germany

## THE STANLEY WORKS

1000 Stanley Drive, PO Box 7000, New Britain, CT, 06053

Tel:  (860) 225-5111        Fax:  (860) 827-3987        www.stanleyworks.com

*Mfr. hand tools and hardware.*

Bostitch Germany GmbH,  Postfach 1349, Oststr. 26, D-2000 Norderstedt bei Hamburg, Germany

Stanley Hardware Inc.,  Postfach 100970, D-5620 Velbert, Germany

## STAPLES, INC.

500 Staples Dr., Framingham, MA, 01702

Tel:  (508) 253-3000        Fax:  (508) 253-8989        www.staples.com

*Superstore for office supplies and equipment.*

MAXI Papier,  Am Werder 1, D-21073 Hamburg, Germany

Tel: 49-40-76741-0   Fax: 49-40-76741-299

MAXI Papier Direct,  Warehouse Bldg., HalskestraBe 1, D-21465 Reinbek, Germany

Tel: 49-40-76741-278   Fax: 49-40-727-309-11

## STAR TELECOMMUNICATIONS, INC.

223 East De La Guerra Street, Santa Barbara, CA, 93101

Tel:  (805) 899-1962        Fax:  (805) 899-2972        www.startel.com

*Provides long-distance telecommunications services.*

Star Germany,  Voltastrasse 1a, 60486 Frankfurt am Main, Germany

Tel: 49-699-8240-0   Fax: 49-699-8240-100

### STA-RITE INDUSTRIES INC.

293 Wright Street, Delavan, WI, 53115

Tel: (262) 728-5551     Fax: (262) 728-7323         www.sta-rite.com

*Mfr. water pumps, filters and systems.*

**Sta-Rite Industries GmbH, Wiesenstr 6, D-64347 Griesheim, Germany**

Tel: 49-6155-8417-0   Fax: 49-6155-8417-99   Contact: Gert Van de Sand   Emp: 17

### STARWOOD HOTELS & RESORTS WORLDWIDE

777 Westchester Avenue, White Plains, NY, 10604

Tel: (914) 640-8100     Fax: (914) 640-8316         www.starwoodhotels.com

*Hotel operations including Sheraton, Westin, St. Regis, Four Points and Caesars.*

**Sheraton Sales Center, Ander Hauptwache 11, D-6000 Frankfurt/Main 1, Germany**

### STATE STREET BANK & TRUST COMPANY

225 Franklin Street, Boston, MA, 02101

Tel: (617) 786-3000     Fax: (617) 654-3386         www.statestreet.com

*Banking and financial services.*

**State Street Global GmbH, Brienner Strasse 59, 80333 Münich, Germany**

### STEINER CORPORATION

505 E. South Temple, Salt Lake City, UT, 84102

Tel: (801) 328-8831     Fax: (801) 363-5680

*Soap and towel dispensers.*

**Steiner Company, Münich, Germany**

### STEINWAY MUSICAL INSTRUMENTS, INC.

800 South St., Ste. 425, Waltham, MA, 02453

Tel: (718) 894-9770     Fax: (718) 894-9803         www.steinway.com

*Mfr./mktg. pianos.*

**Steinway & Sons Hamburg, Rindenburg 10, Postfach 54 07 48, D-22525 Hamburg 54, Germany**

Tel: 49-40-853-910   Fax: 49-40-853-91199   Contact: Thomas Kurrer, Mng. Dir.   Emp: 400

### STEPAN COMPANY

22 West Frontage Road, Northfield, IL, 60093

Tel: (847) 446-7500     Fax: (847) 501-2443         www.stepan.com

*Mfr. basic intermediate chemicals.*

**Stepan Germany, Wesseling, Germany**

### STIEFEL LABORATORIES INC.

255 Alhambra Circle, Ste. 1000, Coral Gables, FL, 33134

Tel: (305) 443-3807     Fax: (305) 443-3467         www.stiefel.com

*Mfr. pharmaceuticals, dermatological specialties.*

**Stiefel Laboratorium GmbH, Muhlheimer Strasse 231, D-63075 Offenbach/Main, Germany**

### STORAGE TECHNOLOGY CORPORATION

One Storagetech Dr., Louisville, CO, 80028-4377

Tel: (303) 673-5151     Fax: (303) 673-5019         www.stortek.com

*Mfr./market/service information, storage and retrieval systems.*

**Storage Technology GmbH, Bernerstrasse 35, D-6000 Frankfurt 56, Germany**

### STOWE WOODWARD MOUNT HOPE

333 Turnpike Rd., Southborough, MA, 01772

Tel: (508) 460-9600     Fax: (508) 481-5392         www.mounthope.com

*Mfr. roll covering and bowed roll technologies for the web handling industries.*

**Gummiwerke Becker AG, Robert-Koch Str. 3, Postfach 1126, D-7920 Heidenhein, Germany**

**Stowe Woodward AG, Hellweg 184-194, 33758 Schloß Holte, Germany**

Stowe Woodward AG,   Am Langen Graben 22, D-52353 Düren, Germany

## STREAM INTERNATIONAL

85 Dan Road, Canton, MA, 02021

Tel: (781) 575-6800      Fax: (781) 575-6999        www.stream.com

*Provider of outsourced technical support for major computer industry companies.*

Stream International GmbH,   Komturstrasse 18, 12099 Berlin, Germany

## STRUCTURAL DYNAMICS RESEARCH CORPORATION

2000 Eastman Dr., Milford, OH, 45150-2740

Tel: (513) 576-2400      Fax: (513) 576-2922        www.sdrc.com

*Developer of software used in Modeling testing, drafting and manufacturing.*

SDRC Software und Services GmbH,   Schoenhauser Allee 163a, D-10435 Berlin, Germany

Tel: 49-30-443-7140    Fax: 49-30-443-71499

## SUDLER & HENNESSEY

1633 Broadway, 25th Fl., New York, NY, 10019

Tel: (212) 969-5800      Fax: (212) 969-5996        www.sudler-hennessey.com

*Engaged in healthcare products advertising.*

Sudler & Hennessey GmbH,   Kleyerstrasse 25, D-60326 Frankfurt am Main, Germany

Tel: 49-69-75-06-03    Fax: 49-69-75-06-15-42    Contact: Thomas Schmidt-Breber, Mng. Dir.

## SULLIVAN & CROMWELL

125 Broad Street, New York, NY, 10004-2498

Tel: (212) 558-4000      Fax: (212) 558-3588        www.sullcrom.com

*International law firm.*

Sullivan & Cromwell,   Oberlindau 54-56, D-60323 Frankfurt am Main, Germany

## SUN HEALTHCARE GROUP, INC.

101 Sun Avenue, N.E., Albuquerque, NM, 87109

Tel: (505) 821-3355      Fax: (505) 858-4735        www.sunh.com

*Provides long-term and skilled nursing care.*

Heim-lan Unternehmensgruppe,   Münich, Germany

## SUN MICROSYSTEMS, INC.

901 San Antonio Road, Palo Alto, CA, 94303

Tel: (650) 960-1300      Fax: (650) 856-2114        www.sun.com

*Computer peripherals and programming services.*

Sun Microsystems,   Personalabteilung, Bretonischer Ring 3, Grasbrunn D-85630, Germany

## SUNBEAM CORPORATION

2381 Executive Center Dr., Boca Raton, FL, 33431

Tel: (561) 912-4100      Fax: (561) 912-4567        www.sunbeam.com

*Mfr. household and personal grooming appliances; Sunbeam, Mr. Coffee, First Alert, Mixmaster and Oster.*

Oster Intl. GmbH,   Schreberstrasse 18, D-6050 Offenbach/Main, Germany

## SUNGARD DATA SYSTEMS

1285 Drummers Lane, Wayne, PA, 19087

Tel: (610) 341-8700      Fax: (610) 341-8851        www.sungard.com

*Provides ASP solutions to the buyside investment management market.*

SunGard Data Systems,   Wilhelm-Leuschner-Strasse 14, D-60329 Frankfurt am Main, Germany

Tel: 49-69-2561440    Contact: George Zafirakis, Pres.

## SYBASE, INC.

6475 Christie Ave., Emeryville, CA, 94608

Tel: (510) 922-3500     Fax: (510) 922-3210     www.sybase.com

*Design/mfg/distribution of database management systems, software development tools, connectivity products, consulting and technical support services..*

**Sybase Germany GmbH, Mainzer Landstrasse 45/34 OG, D-62305 Frankfurt am Main, Germany**
Tel: 49-69-170820 Fax: 49-69-170-82111

**Sybase Germany GmbH, Heidenkampsweg 41, D-20097 Hamburg, Germany**
Tel: 49-4023-7809-0 Fax: 49-4023-7809-55

**Sybase Germany GmbH, Am Steestern 8, D-40547 Düsseldorf, Germany**
Tel: 49-2115-9760 Fax: 49-2115-9761-11

**Sybase Germany GmbH, Zettachring 2A, D-70567 Stuttgart, Germany**
Tel: 49-711-900-5220 Fax: 49-711-5222

**Sybase Germany GmbH, An der Trift 65, D-63303 Dreieich, Germany**
Tel: 49-6103-890500 Fax: 49-6103-890566

## SYBRON INTERNATIONAL CORPORATION

411 E. Wisconsin Ave., Milwaukee, WI, 53202

Tel: (414) 274-6600     Fax: (414) 274-6561     www.sybron.com

*Mfr. products for laboratories, professional orthodontic and dental markets.*

**Gerhard Menzel GmbH & Co. KG, Postfach 3157, D-38021 Braunschweig, Germany**

**Kerr GmbH, Listrasse 28, D-76185 Karlsruhe, Germany**

**Nunc GmbH, Postfach 12 05 43, D-65083 Wiesbaden, Germany**

**Ormco Dental GmbH & Co. KG, Hauptstrasse 102-a, D-88161 Lindenberg Allgau, Germany**

## SYMANTEC CORPORATION

20330 Stevens Creek Blvd., Cupertino, CA, 95014-2132

Tel: (408) 253-9600     Fax: (408) 253-3968     www.symantec.com

*Designs and produces PC network security and network management software and hardware.*

**Symantec (Deutschland) GmbH, Kaiserwerther Str. 115, D-40880 Ratingen, Germany**
Tel: 49-2102-74530 Fax: 49-2102-7452-922

## SYMBOL TECHNOLOGIES, INC.

One Symbol Plaza, Holtsville, NY, 11742-1300

Tel: (631) 738-2400     Fax: (631) 738-5990     www.symbol.com

*Mfr. Bar code-driven data management systems, wireless LAN's, and Portable Shopping System™.*

**Symbol Technologies Germany GmbH, Grabenstraße 5, D-40213, Düsseldorf, Germany**
Tel: 49-211-32-04-52 Fax: 49-211-32-04-70

**Symbol Technologies Germany GmbH, Gotensraße 12, D-20097, Hamburg, Germany**
Tel: 49-40-235-3990 Fax: 49-40-235-39999

**Symbol Technologies Germany GmbH, Waldstrasse 68, D-63128 Dietzenbach, Germany**
Tel: 49-60-74-490-20 Fax: 49-60-74-427-95

## SYNOPSYS, INC.

700 East Middlefield Road, Mountain View, CA, 94043

Tel: (650) 962-5000     Fax: (650) 965-8637     www.synopsys.com

*Mfr. electronic design automation software.*

**Synopsys GmbH, Süskindstraße 4, D-81929 München, Germany**
Tel: 49-89-993200

## SYNTEGRA

4201 Lexington Ave., North Arden Hills, MN, 55126-6198

Tel: (651) 415-2999        Fax: (651) 415-4891        www.cdc.com

*Computer peripherals and hardware.*

**Syntegra GmbH, Stressmannallee 30, D-60596 Frankfurt, Germany**

Tel: 49-69-630-5271    Fax: 49-69-630-5695

## SYSTEMAX INC.

22 Harbor Park Dr., Port Washington, NY, 11050

Tel: (516) 608-7000        Fax: (516) 608-7111        www.systemax.com

*Direct marketer of computers and related products to businesses.*

**Misco Germany Inc., Im Gefierth 14-16, 63303 Dreieich, Germany**

Tel: 49-6103-305305

## TANDY CORPORATION

100 Throckmorton Street, Fort Worth, TX, 76102

Tel: (817) 390-3700        Fax: (817) 415-2647        www.tandy.com

*Mfr. electronic and acoustic equipment; Radio Shack retail stores.*

**Memtek Co., Hahnstr. 41, D-6000 Frankfurt, Germany**

**Tandy Intl. Electronics, Christenenstr. 11, D-4030 Ratingen 2, Germany**

## TBWA CHIAT/DAY

488 Madison Avenue, 6th Floor, New York, NY, 10022

Tel: (212) 804-1000        Fax: (212) 804-1200        www.tbwachiat.com

*International full service advertising agency.*

**Planet Communications, Frankfurt, Germany**

**TBWA GmbH, Frankfurt, Germany**

## TECH DATA CORPORATION

5350 Tech Data Drive, Clearwater, FL, 34620-3122

Tel: (727) 539-7429        Fax: (727) 538-7876        www.techdata.com

*Distributor of computer systems, software and related equipment.*

**Macrotron, Münich, Germany**

## TECHNITROL INC.

1210 Northbrook Drive, #385, Trevose, PA, 19053

Tel: (215) 355-2900        Fax: (215) 355-7397        www.technitrol.com

*Mfr. of electronic components, electrical contacts, and other parts/materials.*

**Pulse Engineering - Electronic Components, Huchenfeld, Germany**

## TECHNOLOGY SOLUTIONS COMPANY (TSC)

205 N. Michigan Ave., Ste. 1500, Chicago, IL, 60601

Tel: (312) 228-4500        Fax: (312) 228-4501        www.techsol.com

*Designs computer information systems and strategic business and management consulting for major corporations.*

**TSC Europe, Vor den Siebenburgen 2, D-50676 Koln, Germany**

Tel: 49-221-93-1224    Fax: 49-221-93-122499    Contact: Robert Philipp

## TECH-SYM CORPORATION

10500 Westoffice Drive, Ste. 200, Houston, TX, 77042-5391

Tel: (713) 785-7790        Fax: (713) 780-3524        www.tech-sym.com

*Designs, develops, and manufactures electronic systems and components used in diverse markets including communications, defense systems, and weather information systems.*

**Telefunken Sendertechnik GmbH, Berlin-Moabit Sickingerstr. 20-28, D-10553 Berlin, Germany**

Tel: 49-30-3463-2535    Fax: 49-30-3463-2733    Contact: Jurgen Graaff, Mng. Dir.

## TECUMSEH PRODUCTS COMPANY

100 E. Patterson Street, Tecumseh, MI, 49286-1899

Tel: (517) 423-8411    Fax: (517) 423-8526    www.tecumseh.com

*Mfr. of hermetic compressors for air conditioning and refrigeration products, gasoline engines and power train components for lawn and garden applications, and pumps.*

**Tecnamotor Deutschland Vertrieb GmbH, Necklenbroicher Str. 52-54, D-4005 Meerbusch 1, Germany**

## TEKELEC

26580 West Agoura Road, Calabasas, CA, 91302

Tel: (818) 880-5656    Fax: (818) 880-6993    www.tekelec.com

*Mfr. telecommunications testing equipment.*

**Tekelec Europe GmbH, Kapuzinerstrasse 9, 80337 Münich, Germany**

Tel: 49-89-516-4100

## TEKNIS CORPORATION

PO Box 3189, North Attleboro, MA, 02761

Tel: (508) 695-3591    Fax: (508) 699-6059    www.teknis.com

*Sale advanced technical products, fiber optics, materials for semiconductor mfr., security holographics*

**Teknis Germany, Münich, Germany**

## TEKTRONIX INC.

14200 SW Karl Braun Dr., PO Box 500, Beaverton, OR, 97077

Tel: (503) 627-7111    Fax: (503) 627-2406    www.tek.com

*Mfr. test and measure, visual systems/color printing and communications/video and networking products.*

**Tektronix GmbH, Stolberger Str. 200, D-50933 Cologne, Germany**

Tel: 49-221-94770   Fax: 49-221-9477-200

## TELAIR INTERNATIONAL

1950 Williams Drive, Oxnard, CA, 93030

Tel: (805) 988-1902    Fax: (805) 983-2492

*Mfr./sale/service hot air and fuel valves, electro-mechanical actuators.*

**Telair International Services, GmbH, Karlsfeld, Germany**

## TELEFLEX INC.

630 W. Germantown Pike, Ste. 450, Plymouth Meeting, PA, 19462

Tel: (610) 834-6301    Fax: (610) 834-8307    www.teleflex.com

*Designs/mfr./market mechanical and electro-mechanical systems, measure systems.*

**Medical Service GmbH, Bad-Liebenzell, Germany**

**Pilling Weck GmbH, Karlstein am Main, Germany**

**Rüsch Care Vertriebs GmbH, Kernen, Germany**

**SermeTel Technical Services GmbH, Heiligenhaus, Germany**

**Telair International GmbH, Obere TiefenbachstraBe 8, 83734 Hausham, Germany**

Tel: 49-8026-3980   Fax: 49-8026-39830

**United Parts Driver Control Systems GmbH, Wiesbaden, Germany**

**Willy Rüsch AG, Willy-Rüsch-StraBe 4-10, 71394 Kernen, Germany**

Tel: 49-7151-406-0   Fax: 49-7151-406-130

## TELEX COMMUNICATIONS INC.

12000 Portland Ave. South, Burnsville, MN, 55337

Tel: (952) 884-4051    Fax: (952) 884-0043    www.telexcommunications.com

*Mfr. communications, audio-visual and professional audio products.*

**Telex EVI Audio GmbH, Hirschberger Ring 45, Straubing 94315, Germany**

## TELLABS INC.

4951 Indiana Ave. 6303788800, Lisle, IL, 60532-1698

Tel: (630) 378-8800     Fax: (630) 679-3010     www.tellabs.com

*Design/mfr./service voice/data transport and network access systems.*

**Tellabs Germany, Marsstr. 22, 80335 Münich, Germany**

## TELXON CORPORATION

1000 Summitt Dr., Cincinnati, OH, 45150

Tel: (330) 664-1000     Fax: (330) 664-2220     www.telxon.com

*Develop/mfr. portable computer systems and related equipment.*

**Telxon GmbH, Mergenthalerallee 77, D-65760 Eschborn, Germany**

## TENNANT COMPANY

701 North Lilac Drive, Minneapolis, MN, 55440

Tel: (612) 540-1208     Fax: (612) 540-1437     www.tennantco.com

*Mfr. industry floor maintenance sweepers and scrubbers and floor coatings.*

**Tennant GmbH & Co. KG, Weststrasse 22, Postfach 10 09 52, D-42809 Remscheid, Germany**
Tel: 49-2191-92810    Fax: 49-2191-928129

## TENNECO AUTOMOTIVE INC.

500 North Field Drive, Lake Forest, IL, 60045

Tel: (847) 482-5241     Fax: (847) 482-5295     www.tenneco-automotive.com

*Mfr. automotive parts, exhaust systems and service equipment.*

**Gillet Aggassysteme Zwickau GmbH, Postfach 862, Hilferdingste 8, D-08056 Zwickau, Germany**
Tel: 49-375-8250

**Monroe Auto Equipment GmbH, Herzog-Adolph-Strasse 4, D-6420 Konigstein/TS, Germany**

**Walker Deutschland GmbH, Waldgartenstrasse 4, D-68642 Buerstadt, Germany**
Tel: 49-6206-70255    Fax: 49-6206-70226    Contact: Horst Hermann, Mgr.

**Walker Gillet Europe GmbH, Luitpoldstrasse 83, Postfach 95, D-67477 Edenkoben, Germany**
Tel: 49-6323-470    Fax: 49-6323-47-2299    Contact: Lutz Kesselring, Mng. Dir.    Emp: 65

## TENNECO PACKAGING CORPORATION OF AMERICA

1900 West Field Court, Lake Forest, IL, 60045

Tel: (847) 482-2000     Fax: (847) 482-2181     www.agplus.net/tenneco

*Mfr. custom packaging, aluminum and plastic molded fibre, corrugated containers.*

**Omni-Pac Ekco GmbH, Friedensallee 23-25, D-2000 Hamburg 50, Germany**

**Omni-Pack GmbH, Am Tidehagen 5, Postfach 360, D-2887 Elsfeth/Weser, Germany**

**Tenneco Packaging, Bopfingen, Germany**

## TERADYNE INC.

321 Harrison Ave., Boston, MA, 02118

Tel: (617) 482-2700     Fax: (617) 422-2910     www.teradyne.com

*Mfr. electronic test equipment and blackplane connection systems.*

**Teradyne GmbH, Dingolfinger Strasse 2, D-81673 Münich, Germany**

**Zehntel GmbH, Paul-Gerhardt-Allee 50, D-81245 Münich, Germany**

## TEREX CORPORATION

500 Post Road East, Ste. 320, Westport, CT, 06880

Tel: (203) 222-7170     Fax: (203) 222-7976     www.terex.com

*Mfr. lifting and earthmoving equipment.*

**O&K Mining GmbH, Karl-Funke-Str. 36, 44149 Dortmund, Germany**
Tel: 49-0231-9223    Fax: 49-0231-922-5005

## TEXAS INSTRUMENTS INC.

8505 Forest Lane, Dallas, TX, 75243

Tel: (972) 995-3773     Fax: (972) 995-4360     www.ti.com

*Mfr. semiconductor devices, electronic electro-mechanical systems, instruments and controls.*

**Texas Instruments GmbH,  Haggertystrasse 1, D-8050 Freising, Germany**

**Texas Instruments GmbH,  Freising, Germany**

## TEXTRON INC.

40 Westminster Street, Providence, RI, 02903

Tel: (401) 421-2800     Fax: (401) 421-2878     www.textron.com

*Mfr. Aerospace (Bell Helicopter and Cessna Aircraft), industry and consumer products, fasteners and financial services.*

**Kautex Textron,  Hauptverwaltung, Postfach 30 07 63, D-53187, Bonn, Germany**

Tel: 49-228-4880   Fax: 49-228-488423   Contact: Dr. Wolfgang Theis

**Klauke Textron,  Auf Dem Knappe 46, PO Box 10 05 52, D-42805 Remscheid, Germany**

Tel: 49-2-191-9070   Fax: 49-2-191-907201   Contact: Karl-Gustav Diederichs, Mng. Dir.

**Sükosim Verbindungselemente,  Zeller Weg 25, D-7187 Schrozberg, Germany**

Tel: 49-7935-71-0   Fax: 49-7935-71-488

**Textron Fastening Systems, Germany - Friedr. Boexner GmbH,  Augustenthaler Strabbe 87, D-56567 Neuwied, Germany**

Tel: 49-2631-5010   Fax: 49-2631-501205   Contact: Horst Homuth, Gen. Mgr.

## THERMO ELECTRIC COOLING AMERICA (TECA)

109 North Fifth Street, Saddle Brook, NJ, 07662

Tel: (201) 843-5800     Fax: (201) 843-7144     www.thermoelectric.com

*Mfr. solid state cooling products, including air-conditioners, cold plates and liquid chillers.*

**Thermo Electric GmbH,  Postfach 900 406, Fuggerstrasse 34a, D-51114 Cologne, Germany**

## THERMO ELECTRON CORPORATION

81 Wyman Street, Waltham, MA, 02454-9046

Tel: (781) 622-1000     Fax: (781) 622-1207     www.thermo.com

*Develop/mfr./sale of process equipment &instruments for energy intensive and healthcare industries.*

**Jaeger Toennies, Div. Thermo Electron Corp.,  Leibnizstrasse 7, Hoechberg 9204, Germany**

Tel: 49-931-4972-0

**Nicolet Biomedical Germany,  Saalackerstrasse 8, 63801 Kleinostheim, Germany**

Tel: 49-6027-4698

**Van Hengel Instrumente GmbH,  Baiertalerstr. 24-26, D-6908 Wiesloch, Germany**

## THERMON MANUFACTURING COMPANY

100 Thermon Drive, PO Box 609, San Marcos, TX, 78667-0609

Tel: (512) 396-5801     Fax: (512) 396-3627     www.thermon.com

*Mfr. steam and electric heat tracing systems, components and accessories.*

**Thermon Deutschland,  Dillenburger Strasse 26, D-57299 Burbach, Germany**

## THETFORD CORPORATION

7101 Jackson Road, PO Box 1285, Ann Arbor, MI, 48106

Tel: (734) 769-6000     Fax: (734) 769-2023     www.thetford.com

*Mfr. sanitation products and chemicals.*

**Thetford GmbH,  Schallbruch 14, 42781 Haan, Germany**

## THOMAS & BETTS CORPORATION

8155 T&B Blvd., Memphis, TN, 38125

Tel: (901) 252-5000     Fax: (901) 685-1988     www.tnb.com

*Mfr. elect/electronic connectors and accessories.*

**Thomas & Betts GmbH,  Postfach 1274, Theodor-Heuss-Str. 7-9, D-6073 Egelsbach, Germany**

## THOMAS BUILT BUSES INC.

1408 Courtesy Road, PO Box 2450, High Point, NC, 27261

Tel: (336) 889-4871　　　Fax: (336) 889-2589　　　www.thomasbus.com

*Mfr. buses and bus chassis.*

**Freightliner, LLC (Daimler Chrysler AG), Stuttgart, Germany**

## THOMAS INDUSTRIES INC.

4360 Brownsboro Road, Ste. 300, Louisville, KY, 40232

Tel: (502) 893-4600　　　Fax: (502) 893-4685　　　www.thomasind.com

*Mfr. lighting fixtures and specialty pumps and compressors for global OEM applications.*

**ASF Thomas Industries GmbH, Postfach 1214, Luitpoldstrasse 28, D-8940 Memmingen, Germany**

**ASF Thomas Industries GmbH, Siemensstraße 4, Industriegebiet Nord, D-82178 Puchheim, Germany**

Contact: Peter Bissinger, VP

**ASF Thomas Industries GmbH, Hahnerbergerstrasse 173-185, Postfach 15 02 20, D-42349 12/Cronenberg, Germany**

## THOMAS PUBLISHING COMPANY

5 Penn Plaza, New York, NY, 10007

Tel: (212) 695-0500　　　Fax: (212) 290-7362　　　www.thomaspublishing.com

*Publishing magazines and directories.*

**Elsevier-Thomas Fachverlag, Postfach 1869, D-6500 Mainz, Germany**

## TIFFANY & COMPANY

727 Fifth Ave., New York, NY, 10022

Tel: (212) 755-8000　　　Fax: (212) 605-4465　　　www.tiffany.com

*Mfr./retail fine jewelry, silverware, china, crystal, leather goods, etc.*

**Tiffany & Co. Munich, Residenzstrasse 11, D-80333 Münich, Germany**

Tel: 49-89-29-00430

## THE TIMBERLAND COMPANY

200 Domain Drive, Stratham, NH, 03885

Tel: (603) 772-9500　　　Fax: (603) 773-1640　　　www.timberland.com

*Design/mfr. footwear, apparel and accessories for men and women.*

**Timberland World Trading GmbH, Rodelweg 7, D-82067 Ebenhausen, Germany**

## TIMET CORPORATION

1999 Broadway, Suite 4300, Denver, CO, 80202

Tel: (303) 296-5600　　　Fax: (303) 296-5650　　　www.timet.com

*Non-ferrous drawing and rolling, coal and other minerals, metals service centers.*

**Tisto GmbH, Dinnendahlstrasse 31, D-40235 Düsseldorf, Germany**

## TIMEX CORPORATION

Park Road Extension, Middlebury, CT, 06762

Tel: (203) 573-5000　　　Fax: (203) 573-6901　　　www.timex.com

*Mfr. watches, clocks, timing instruments.*

**Timex Corp., Wurmbergerstr. 125, D-7530 Pforzhelm, Germany**

## TIMKEN SUPER PRECISION (MPB)

7 Optical Ave., Keene, NH, 03431-0547

Tel: (603) 352-0310　　　Fax: (603) 355-4553　　　www.timken.com

*Mfr./sales/distribution bearings, tape guides and systems for missiles, etc.*

**Timken Super Precision, Obertorstrasse 3, D-97737 Gemunden, Germany**

Tel: 49-9351-3013

## TIW CORPORATION

12300 S. Main Street, PO Box 35729, Houston, TX, 77035

Tel: (713) 729-2110    Fax: (713) 728-4767    www.tiwtools.com

*Mfr. liner hanger equipment, production packers, safety and kelly valves.*

**TIW GmbH, Vogelberg 33a, D-3100 Celle, Germany**

Tel: 49-5141-81041

## TMP WORLDWIDE, INC.

622 Third Ave., New York, NY, 10017

Tel: (212) 351-7000    Fax: (212) 658-0540    www.tmpw.com

*#1 Yellow Pages agency and a leader in the recruitment and interactive advertising fields.*

**TMP Worldwide Advertising & Communications, Hohenstaufenstrasse 7, Wiesbaden D-65189, Germany**

## THE TORRINGTON COMPANY

59 Field St., PO Box 1008, Torrington, CT, 06790

Tel: (860) 626-2000    Fax: (860) 496-3625    www.torrington.com

*Mfr. precision bearings, motion control components and automotive steering assemblies.*

**Torrington Nadellager GmbH, Kuensebeck, Germany**

## TOWERS PERRIN

335 Madison Ave., New York, NY, 10017-4605

Tel: (212) 309-3400    Fax: (212) 309-0975    www.towers.com

*Management consulting services.*

**Tillinghast Towers Perrin, Im Trutz 55, D-60322 Frankfurt Main 1, Germany**

Tel: 49-69-153-09090    Fax: 49-69-153-09041

**Tillinghast Towers Perrin, Neue Wyerstrasse 6, D-50675 Cologne, Germany**

Tel: 49-221-921-2340    Fax: 49-221-921-23456

## TOYS R US INC.

461 From Road, Paramus, NJ, 07652

Tel: (201) 262-7800    Fax: (201) 845-0973    www.toysrus.com

*Retail stores: toys and games, sporting goods, computer software, books, records.*

**Toys R Us GmbH, Koehlstrasse 8, D-50827 Ossendorf, Germany**

## THE TRANE COMPANY

3600 Pammel Creek Road, La Crosse, WI, 54601

Tel: (608) 787-2000    Fax: (608) 787-4990    www.trane.com

*Mfr./distributor/service A/C systems and equipment.*

**H.W. Schmidt Klimakalte GmbH, Forststrasse 196A, D-70193 Stuttgart 1, Germany**

**Trane Klima Technisches Buero GmbH, Wilhelm-Spathstrasse 45D, D-90461 Nurnberg 40, Germany**

**Trane Klima und Kaeltetechnisches Buero GmbH, Lilienthal Strasse 6, D-82205 Münich Gilching, Germany**

**Trane Technisches Buero Dusseldorf GmbH, Am Kiekenbusch 15, D-47269 Duisburg 29, Germany**

**Trane Technisches Buero Frankfurt GmbH, Ohmstrasse 7, D-63477 Maintal 1, Germany**

**Trane Technisches Buero Hamburg GmbH, Fabriciusstrasse 15, D-22177 Hamburg 71, Germany**

## TRANS WORLD AIRLINES INC.

515 North Sixth Street, St. Louis, MO, 63101

Tel: (314) 589-3000    Fax: (314) 589-3129    www.twa.com

*Air transport services.*

**Trans World Airlines Inc., Hamburgealle 2-10, Frankfurt, Germany**

## TRANTER PHE, INC.

PO Box 2289, Wichita Falls, TX, 76306

Tel: (940) 723-7125        Fax: (706) 723-1131        www.tranter.com

*Mfr. heat exchangers.*

**SWEP Warmetauscher Deutschland AG, Kathe-Paulus-Strasse 9, Postfach 10 12 14, Daimlerring 29, D-31112 Hildesheim, Germany**

Tel: 49-5121-75200   Fax: 49-5121-54011

## TREIBACHER SCHLEIFMITTEL CORPORATION

2000 College Ave., Niagara Falls, NY, 14305

Tel: (716) 286-1234        Fax: (716) 286-1224        www.treibacher-schleifm.com

*Mfr. abrasives.*

**Treibacher Schleifmittel GmbH, Postf.1116, D-79719 Laufenburg, Germany**

## TRIBUNE COMPANY

435 North Michigan Ave., Chicago, IL, 60611

Tel: (312) 222-9100        Fax: (312) 222-9100        www.tribune.com

*Media company engaged in television and radio broadcasting, publishing and interactive.*

**Learning Intl. GmbH, Werfstrasse 20-22, D-40549 Düsseldorf, Germany**

## TRICO PRODUCTS CORPORATION

817 Washington Street, Buffalo, NY, 14203

Tel: (716) 852-5700        Fax: (716) 853-6242        www.tricoproducts.com

*Mfr. windshield wiper systems and components.*

**Trico Products Corp., Aachen, Germany**

## TRICON GLOBAL RESTAURANTS INC.

1441 Gardner Lane, Louisville, KY, 40213

Tel: (502) 874-1000        Fax: (502) 874-8315        www.triconglobal.com

*Owns and operates KFC, Taco Bell and Pizza Hut restaurant food chains.*

**Pizza Hut Restauration GmbH & Co., Münich, Germany**

## TRIMBLE NAVIGATION LIMITED

645 N. Mary Ave., Sunnyvale, CA, 94086

Tel: (408) 481-8000        Fax: (408) 481-2000        www.trimble.com

*Design/mfr. electronic geographic instrumentation.*

**Trimble Navigation Deutschland GmbH, Moselstrasse 27, D-63452 Hanau, Germany**

Tel: 49-6181-9002-0   Fax: 49-6181-9002-22

## TRION INC.

101 McNeil Road, PO Box 760, Sanford, NC, 27331-0760

Tel: (919) 775-2201        Fax: (919) 774-8771        www.trioninc.com

*Mfr. commercial and residential air cleaners and humidifiers.*

**Trion GmbH, Kapellenstrasse 95, D-5000 Cologne (Rondorf), Germany**

## TROPICANA PRODUCTS, INC.

1001 13th Avenue East, Bradenton, FL, 34208

Tel: (941) 747-4461        Fax: (941) 665-5330        www.tropicana.com

*Marketer and producer of branded juices, including Tropicana, Dole, Looza and Copella.*

**Tropicana Deutschland GmbH, Kackerstrasse 11, 52072 Aachen-Laurensberg, Germany**

## TRUE NORTH COMMUNICATIONS INC.

101 East Erie Street, Chicago, IL, 60611

Tel: (312) 425-6500        Fax: (312) 425-5010        www.truenorth.com

*Holding company, advertising agency.*

**APR/Wilkens, An der Alster 42, D-20099 Hamburg, Germany**

Baums, Mang & Zimmermann, Schirmerstrasse 76, D-4000 Düsseldorf 1, Germany

FCB Direct Europe, Hedderichstrasse 108-110, D-60596 Frankfurt, Germany

## TRW AUTOMOTIVE, INC.

4505 West 26 Mile Road, Washington, MI, 48094

Tel: (810) 786-7903     Fax: (810) 786-7888     www.trw.com

*Mfr. steering gears, power steering pumps, columns, linkage.*

TRW Automotive Europe, Industriestrasse 2-8, D--78315 Radolfzell, Germany

Tel: 49-7732-809-342   Fax: 49-7732-809-421

## TRW INC.

1900 Richmond Road, Cleveland, OH, 44124-3760

Tel: (216) 291-7000     Fax: (216) 291-7932     www.trw.com

*Electric and energy-related products, automotive and aerospace products, tools and fasteners.*

Repa Feinstanzwerk GmbH, D-7071 Lindach Ueber Schwaebisch Guend, Germany

Teves-Thompson GmbH, D-3013 Barsinghausen Hannover, Germany

TRW Carr Europe, Rennbahnstr. 72, D-6000 Frankfurt 71, Germany

Werner Messmer GmbH, Industriestrasse 2-8, D-7760 Radolfzell am Bodensee, Germany

## TUTOGEN MEDICAL, INC.

925 Allwood Road, Clifton, NJ, 07012

Tel: (973) 365-2799     Fax: (973) 365-1690     www.tutogen.com

*Engaged in sterilization of transplanted tissue for use in surgical procedures.*

Tutogen Medical GmbH, Industriestrasse 6, D-91077 Neunkirchen, Germany

Tel: 49-9134-9998   Fax: 49-9134-9988419

## W. S. TYLER INC.

8570 Tyler Road, Mentor, OH, 44060

Tel: (440) 974-1047     Fax: (440) 974-0921     www.wstyler.com

*Mfr. vibrating screens, lab equipment and related screening media, crushing equipment.*

Haver and Boecker GmbH, Robert-Bosch-StraBe 6, D-48153 Munster, Germany

Tel: 49-251-9793-0   Fax: 49-251-9793156

Haver and Boecker GmbH, Ennigerloher StraBe 64, D-59302 Oelde, Germany

Tel: 49-2522-30-0   Fax: 49-2522-30404

## UNION CARBIDE CORPORATION

39 Old Ridgebury Road, Danbury, CT, 06817

Tel: (203) 794-2000     Fax: (203) 794-6269     www.unioncarbide.com

*Mfr. industrial chemicals, plastics and resins.*

Union Carbide Deutschland GmbH, Morsenbroicher Weg 200, D-4000 Düsseldorf 30, Germany

## UNISYS CORPORATION.

PO Box 500, Union Meeting Road, Blue Bell, PA, 19424

Tel: (215) 986-4011     Fax: (215) 986-6850     www.unisys.com

*Mfr./marketing/servicing electronic information systems.*

Sperry Zentrallager Europe GmbH, Kleiner Kornweg 34-C, D-6092 Keisterbach, Germany

Unisys Deutschland GmbH, Am Unisys Park 1, D-6231 Sulzbach, Germany

## UNITED AIRLINES INC.

1200 E. Algonquin Rd., Chicago, IL, 60007

Tel: (847) 700-4000     Fax: (847) 700-4081     www.ual.com

*Air transportation, passenger and freight services.*

United Airlines, Munchenerstr. 7, D-6000 Frankfurt Main, Germany

## UNITED PARCEL SERVICE, INC.

55 Glenlake Parkway, NE, Atlanta, GA, 30328

Tel: (404) 828-6000      Fax: (404) 828-6593      www.ups.com

*International package-delivery service.*

**UPS Deutschland OHG, Droopweg 31, D-20537 Hamburg, Germany**

Fax: 49-2131-947-2233

## UNITED STATES SURGICAL CORPORATION

150 Glover Ave., Norwalk, CT, 06856

Tel: (203) 845-1000      Fax: (203) 847-0635      www.ussurg.com

*Mfr./development/market surgical staplers, laparoscopic instruments and sutures.*

**Auto Suture (Deutschland) GmbH, Attn: German Office, U.S. Surgical, 150 Glover Avenue, Norwalk CT 06856**

**USSC (Deutschland) GmbH, Attn: German Office, U. S. Surgical, 150 Glover Avenue, Norwalk CT 06856**

**USSC Medical GmbH, Attn: German Office, U. S. Surgical, 150 Glover Avenue, Norwalk CT 06856**

## UNITED TECHNOLOGIES CORPORATION

One Financial Plaza, Hartford, CT, 06103

Tel: (860) 728-7000      Fax: (860) 728-7979      www.utc.com

*Mfr. aircraft engines, elevators, A/C, auto equipment, space and military electronic and rocket propulsion systems. Products include Pratt and Whitney, Otis elevators, Carrier heating and air conditioning and Sikorsky helicopters.*

**Carrier GmbH, Vogelsbergstr. 3, D-6082 Moerfelden Walldorf, Germany**

**Carrier GmbH, Aarstr. 247, D-6204 Taunusstein 4, Germany**

**Carrier GmbH, Beckmesserstr. 4, D-8000 Münich 81, Germany**

**Flohr Otis GmbH, Wichmannstr. 5, D-1000 Berlin 30, Germany**

**Flohr Otis GmbH, Fichrstr. 1-10, D-1000 Borsigwalde Berlin 27, Germany**

**Flohr Otis GmbH, Industriestr. 2, D-3060 Stadthagen, Germany**

## UNITRODE CORPORATION

7 Continental Blvd., Merrimack, NH, 03054

Tel: (603) 424-2410      Fax: (603) 429-8771      www.unitrode.com

*Mfr. electronic components (analog/linear and mixed-signal).*

**Vectron GmbH, Postfach 29, D-8035 Stockdorf/Munchen, Germany**

Tel: 49-89-895180    Fax: 49-89-89518199    Emp: 4

## UNIVERSAL INSTRUMENTS

90 Bevier Street, S. Dock, Binghamton, NY, 13904

Tel: (607) 779-7522      Fax: (607) 779-7971      www.uic.com

*Mfr./sales of instruments for electronic circuit assembly.*

**Universal Instruments GmbH, Bad Vilbel, Germany**

Tel: 49-6101-8080    Fax: 49-6101-808-222

## UNOVA INC.

21900 Burbank Blvd., Woodland Hills, CA, 91367-7418

Tel: (818) 992-3000      Fax: (818) 992-2848      www.unova.com

*Automated data collection, mobile computing and manufacturing systems.*

**Unova Inc., Münich, Germany**

## UOP LLC.

25 East Algonquin Road, Des Plaines, IL, 60017

Tel: (847) 391-2000     Fax: (847) 391-2253     www.uop.com

*Engaged in developing and commercializing technology for license to the oil refining, petrochemical and gas processing industries.*

**Universal Matthey Products (Deutschland) GmbH, Steinhof 39, D-40699 Erkrath, Germany**

Tel: 49-211-24903-25   Fax: 49-211-249109

## URS CORPORATION

100 California Street, Ste. 500, San Francisco, CA, 94111-4529

Tel: (415) 774-2700     Fax: (415) 398-1904     www.urscorp.com

*Provides planning, design and construction management services, pollution control and hazardous waste management.*

**URS, Frankfurt, Germany**

## URSCHEL LABORATORIES INC.

2503 Calumet Ave., PO Box 2200, Valparaiso, IN, 46384-2200

Tel: (219) 464-4811     Fax: (219) 462-3879     www.urschel.com

*Design/mfr. precision food processing equipment.*

**Urschel Intl. Ltd., Dieselstr. 7, D-61239 Ober-Morlen, Germany**

## US AIRWAYS GROUP, INC.

2345 Crystal Drive, Arlington, VA, 22227

Tel: (703) 872-7000     Fax: (703) 294-5096     www.usairways.com

*Commercial airline.*

**USAir Inc., Rhein/Main Flughafen, Postfach 22, D-0549 Frankfurt, Germany**

## USAA

9800 Fredericksburg Road, San Antonio, TX, 78288-3533

Tel: (210) 498-2211     Fax: (210) 498-9940     www.usaa.com

*Provides financial services, life, property and casualty insurance and consumer sales services primarily to military and U.S. government personnel and their families.*

**USAA, Frankfurt, Germany**

## USFILTER WALLACE & TIERNAN

1901 West Garden Road, Vineland, NJ, 08360

Tel: (609) 507-9000     Fax: (609) 507-4125     www.usfwt.com

*Mfr. disinfections and chemical feed equipment.*

**USFilter Wallace & Tiernan GmbH, Auf der Weide 10, 89312 Gunzburg-Wasserburg, Germany**

Tel: 49-8221-9040

**USFilter Wallace & Tiernan GmbH, Postfach 1563, D-89305, Gunzburg, Germany**

Tel: 49-8221-9040   Fax: 49-8221-904203   Contact: Gunther Fuhrer

## USG CORPORATION

125 South Franklin Street, Chicago, IL, 60606-4678

Tel: (312) 606-4000     Fax: (312) 606-4093     www.usg.com

*Holding company for the building products industry.*

**Donn Products GmbH, Münich, Germany**

## UTILICORP UNITED INC.

PO Box 13287, Kansas City, MO, 64199-3287

Tel: (816) 421-6600     Fax: (816) 472-6281     www.utilicorp.com

*Electric and gas utility.*

**Utilicorp United, Münich, Germany**

## UTILX CORPORATION
22820 Russell Rd., PO Box 97009, Kent, WA, 98064-9709

Tel: (253) 395-0200        Fax: (253) 395-1040        www.utilx.com

*Mfr. utility construction machinery and guided boring systems and provides cable restoration services.*

**CableCURE, Hermannstrasse 20, D-31737 Rinteln, Germany**

Tel: 49-5751-918715

## UUNET
22001 Loudoun County Pkwy., Ashburn, VA, 20147

Tel: (703) 206-5600        Fax: (703) 206-5601        www.uu.net

*World's largest Internet service provider; World Wide Web hosting services, security products and consulting services to businesses, professionals, and on-line service providers.*

**UUNET Deutschland GmbH, Sebrathweg 20, D-44149 Dortmund, Germany**

Tel: 49-231-972-00  Fax: 49-231-972-1111   Contact: Karsten Lerenth

## VALENITE INC
31751 Research Park Dr., Madison Heights, MI, 48071-9636

Tel: (248) 589-1000        Fax: (248) 597-4820        www.valenite.com

*Cemented carbide, high speed steel, ceramic and diamond cutting tool products, etc.*

**Valenite-Modco GmbH, Carl-Benz Strasse, D-74876 Sinsheim, Germany**

## VALHI INC.
5430 LBJ Freeway, Ste. 1700, Dallas, TX, 75240

Tel: (972) 233-1700        Fax: (972) 448-1445

*Mfr. titanium products and computer office components.*

**Bentone-Chemie GmbH, Titanstrasse, D-2890 Niedrsachs, Germany**

**Kronos Titan GmbH, Postfach 100720, Leverkusen, Germany**

## VALMONT INDUSTRIES INC.
1 Valmont Plaza, Omaha, NE, 68154

Tel: (402) 963-1000        Fax: (402) 963-1199        www.valmont.com

*Mfr. irrigation systems, steel lighting, utility and communication poles.*

**Valmont Mastbau GmbH & Co KG, Paderborn 33106, Germany**

Tel: 49-5251-500400  Fax: 49-5251-5004045   Contact: Udo Ruesing

## VALSPAR CORPORATION
1101 South Third Street, Minneapolis, MN, 55415-1259

Tel: (612) 332-7371        Fax: (612) 375-7723        www.valspar.com

*Produce paint, varnish and allied products.*

**Valspar Inc., Münich, Germany**

## VARIAN MEDICAL SYSTEMS, INC.
3050 Hansen Way, Palo Alto, CA, 94304-100

Tel: (650) 493-4000        Fax: (650) 424-5358        www.varian.com

*Mfr. microwave tubes and devices, analytical instruments, semiconductor process and medical equipment, vacuum systems.*

**Varian GmbH, Postfach 11 14 45, D-64229 Darmstadt, Germany**

Tel: 49-6151-7030

## VARIAN SEMICONDUCTOR EQUIPMENT ASSOCIATES, INC.
35 Dory Road, Gloucester, MA, 01930

Tel: (978) 281-2000        Fax: (978) 283-5391        www.vsea.com

*Mfr. ion implantation systems.*

**Varian Semiconductor Equipment Associates, Carl-Zeiss-Ring 23, D-85737 Ismaning Münich, Germany**

Varian Semiconductor Equipment Assocates, Zettachring 2A, Postfach 81 06 49, 70567 Stuttgart, Germany

## VEECO INSTRUMENTS INC.

Terminal Drive, Plainview, NY, 11803

Tel: (516) 349-8300     Fax: (516) 349-9079     www.veeco.com

*Mfr. surface profiler, atomic force microscopes, leak and plating thickness detectors and semiconductor products.*

**Veeco GmbH, Wissenschaftliche Geraete, D-85716 Unterschleissheim Münich, Germany**

Tel: 49-89-317-8250   Fax: 49-89-317-3440

## VEEDER-ROOT COMPANY

125 Powder Forest Drive, PO Box 2003, Simsbury, CT, 06070-2003

Tel: (860) 651-2700     Fax: (860) 651-2704     www.veeder.com

*Mfr. of automatic tank gauging systems.*

**Veeder-Root GmbH, Postfach 1110, D-7303 Neuhausen Filder, Germany**

## VELCON FILTERS INC.

4525 Centennial Blvd., Colorado Springs, CO, 80919-3350

Tel: (719) 531-5855     Fax: (719) 531-5690     www.velcon.com

*Mfr. filtration and coalescing products for airports, terminals, refineries, bulk storage plants, and utility companies.*

**Warner Lewis Jr. Industrie-Filter GmbH, Fasanenweg 5, D-6092 Kelsterbach/Frankfurt/Main, Germany**

## VELCRO USA INC.

406 Brown Avenue, Manchester, NH, 03108

Tel: (603) 669-4892     Fax: (603) 669-9271     www.velcro.com

*Mfr./sales of velcro brand hook and loop fasteners, plastic buckles and metal hardware and cable control straps.*

**Velcro GmbH, 2 Seimens Strasse, D-74343 Sachsenheim, Germany**

Tel: 49-7147-9900   Fax: 49-7-7147-99011

## VERITY, INC.

894 Ross Drive, Sunnyvale, CA, 94089

Tel: (408) 541-1500     Fax: (408) 541-1600     www.verity.com

*Mfr. software to simplify management of information.*

**Verity Deutschland GmbH, Babenhäuser Straße 50, D-63762 Großostheim, Germany**

Tel: 49-6026-9710-0   Fax: 49-6026-971020

## VERIZON COMMUNICATIONS INC.

1255 Corporate Drive, Irving, TX, 75038

Tel: (972) 507-5000     Fax: (972) 507-5002     www.gte.com

*Engaged in wireline and wireless communications.*

**Hopt Electronic GmbH, Koenigsbergerstr. 12, D-7210 Rottweil, Germany**

**Richard Bosse & Co. GmbH, Reichenbergerstr. 78, D-1000 Berlin 36, Germany**

**Saba-Werke GmbH, Hermann-Scwer-Str., D-7730 Villingen Schwarzwald, Germany**

**Sylvania Lichtlechalk und Elektronik GmbH, Vahrenwalder Str. 205, Postfach 5327, D-3000 Hannover 1, Germany**

## VERTEX COMMUNICATIONS RSI

2600 North Longview Street, Kilgore, TX, 75662-6842

Tel: (903) 984-0555      Fax: (903) 984-1826      www.vertencomm.com

*High-tech holding company; microwave components, amplifiers, converters, terminal network workstations, voice, video and data applications.*

**Vertex Antennentechnik GmbH,  Baumstrasse 50, D-41798 Duisburg, Germany**

Tel: 49-206-620960    Fax: 49-206-6209611    Contact: Dr. Karl-Heinz Stenvers, Pres.

## VF CORPORATION

1047 North Park Road, Wyomissing, PA, 19610

Tel: (610) 378-1151      Fax: (610) 378-9371      www.vfc.com

*Mfr./marketing apparel including Lee and Wrangler jeans, Jansport backpacks and Healthtex.*

**H.I.S. Sportswear AG,  Münich, Germany**

## VIACOM INC.

1515 Broadway, 28th Fl., New York, NY, 10036-5794

Tel: (212) 258-6000      Fax: (212) 258-6358      www.viacom.com

*Communications, publishing and entertainment.*

**KirchGroup,  Münich, Germany**

## VIAD CORPORATION

1850 North Central Ave., Phoenix, AZ, 85077

Tel: (602) 207-4000      Fax: (602) 207-5900      www.viad.com

*Provides convention, exhibit design and production services.*

**Voblo Innenausbau GmbH,  Siemenstrasse 19, 42551 Velbert, Germany**

Tel: 49-2051-28110    Fax: 49-2051-281128

## VICOR CORPORATION

23 Frontage Road, Andover, MA, 01810

Tel: (978) 470-2900      Fax: (978) 749-3536      www.vicr.com

*Designs, manufactures, and markets modular power components and complete configurable and custom power systems.*

**Vicor Germany GmbH,  Adalperostraße 29, 85737 Ismaning, Germany**

## VIKING OFFICE PRODUCTS

950 West 190th Street, Torrance, CA, 90502

Tel: (310) 225-4500      Fax: (310) 324-2396      www.vikingop.com

*International direct marketer of office products, computer supplies, business furniture and stationery.*

**Viking Direkt, GmbH,  Industriehandelspark Nord, Babenhauser Strasse 50, D-63762 Gro Bostheim, Germany**

Tel: 49-6026-97340    Fax: 49-6026-973499    Contact: Rolf van Kaldekerken, Mgr.    Emp: 466

## VISHAY INTERTECHNOLOGY INC.

63 Lincoln Hwy., Malvern, PA, 19355

Tel: (610) 644-1300      Fax: (610) 296-0657      www.vishay.com

*Mfr. resistors, strain gages, capacitors, inductors, printed circuit boards.*

**Draloric Electronic GmbH,  Porschestrasse 18, D-8950 Kaufbeuren, Germany**

**Measurements Group GmbH,  Am Lochhamer Schlag 6, D-8032 Lochham, Münich, Germany**

**Roederstein GmbH,  Schillerstrasse 2, D-8300 Landshut, Germany**

**Vishay Electronic GmbH,  Geheimrat-Rosenthal-Str. 100, 95100 Postfach 1180, 95092 Selb, Germany**

Tel: 49-9287-710

## VISHAY SILICONIX INC.

2201 Laurelwood Drive, Santa Clara, CA, 95054

Tel: (408) 988-8000     Fax: (408) 970-3950     www.vishay.com

*Semiconductor components.*

**Vishay Siliconix GmbH, Postfach 1340, Johannesstr. 27, D-7024 Filderstadt, Germany**

## VISHAY VITRAMON INC.

PO Box 544, Bridgeport, CT, 06601

Tel: (203) 268-6261     Fax: (203) 261-4446     www.vitramon.com

*Ceramic capacitors.*

**Vitramon GmbH, Muhlbachstr. 7, Postfach 1420, D-7150 Backnang Waldrems, Germany**

## VITESSE SEMICONDUCTOR CORPORATION

741 Calle Plano, Camarillo, CA, 93012

Tel: (805) 388-3700     Fax: (805) 389-7188     www.vitesse.com

*Mfr. integrated circuits.*

**Vitesse Semiconductor, Altstadt 296, D-84036 Landshut, Germany**

Tel: 49-871-9663344   Fax: 49-871-9663343   Contact: Hermann Helmbold

**Vitesse Semiconductor GmbH, Zwoelferweg 2, 86 836 Lagerlechfeld, Germany**

Tel: 49-8232-78-626   Fax: 49-8232-78-627   Contact: Harald King

## VIVITAR CORPORATION

1280 Rancho Conejo Blvd, Newbury Park, CA, 91320

Tel: (805) 498-7008     Fax: (805) 498-5086     www.vivitar.com

*Mfr. photographic equipment, electronic supplies.*

**Vivitar Photo-Electronik GmbH, Vivitarstr. 7-9, Postfach 1564, D-6238 Hofheim/TS, Germany**

## VIZACOM INC.

300 Frank W. Burr Blvd., 7th Fl., Teaneck, NJ, 07666

Tel: (201) 928-1001     Fax: (201) 928-1003     www.vizacom.com

*Mfr. graphics applications software.*

**Serif GmbH, Ritterstrasse 20, 52072 Aachen, Germany**

Tel: 49-241-89-49-700

**SPC Serif Software Publishing GmbH, Erfurter Strasse 21, 85386 Echingen, Germany**

Tel: 49-896-139-4000

## VOLT INFORMATION SCIENCES, INC.

1221 Ave. of the Americas, 47th Fl., New York, NY, 10020-1579

Tel: (212) 704-2400     Fax: (212) 704-2417     www.volt.com

*Staffing services and telecommunication services.*

**Autologic Intl. Ltd., Frankfurter Strasse 63-69, D-65760, Eschborn, Germany**

Tel: 49-6196-481796   Fax: 49-6196-42389

## VTEL (VIDEOTELECOM CORPORATION )

108 Wild Basin Road, Austin, TX, 78746

Tel: (512) 314-2700     Fax: (512) 314-2792     www.vtel.com

*Design/mfr. long-distance interactive video communications products.*

**VTEL Deutschland GmbH, Industriestr. 18, 89423 Gundelfingen, Germany**

## WACKENHUT CORPORATION

4200 Wackenhut Dr., Ste. 100, Palm Beach Gardens, FL, 33410

Tel: (561) 622-5656     Fax: (561) 691-6736     www.wackenhut.com

*Security systems and services.*

**Wackenhut Central Europe GmbH, Tulpenhofstrasse 18, D-68067 Offenbach/Main, Germany**

Tel: 49-69-817025

## WAHL CLIPPER CORPORATION

2902 N. Locust Street, Sterling, IL, 61081

Tel: (815) 625-6525     Fax: (815) 625-1193     www.wahlclipper.com

*Mfr. hair clippers, beard and mustache trimmers, shavers, pet clippers and soldering irons.*

**Moser Elektrogeräte GmbH, Roggenbachweg 9, D-78089 Unterkirnach, Germany**

## WALBRO CORPORATION, TI GROUP AUTOMOTIVE

6242 Garfield Ave., Cass City, MI, 48726-1325

Tel: (517) 872-2131     Fax: (517) 872-3090     www.walbro.com

*Mfr. motor vehicle accessories and parts, automotive fluid carrying systems.*

**TI Group Automotive Systems, Heidelberg Engineering Centre, Dischingerstr 11, 69123 Heidelberg, Germany**

Tel: 49-6221-74910

**TI Group Automotive Systems, Lochfeldstr. 33, 76437 Rastatt, Germany**

## WAL-MART STORES INC.

702 SW 8th Street, Bentonville, AR, 72716-8611

Tel: (501) 273-4000     Fax: (501) 273-1917     www.wal-mart.com

*Retailer.*

**Wal-Mart Stores Inc. (Wertkauf), Münich, Germany**

## WALTER, CONSTON, ALEXANDER & GREEN, PC

90 Park Avenue, New York, NY, 10016-1387

Tel: (212) 210-9400     Fax: (212) 210-9444     www.wcag.com

*International law firm.*

**Walter, Conston, Alexander & Greene, PC, Brienner Strasse 11, D-80333 Münich, Germany**

## WARNACO INC.

90 Park Ave., New York, NY, 10016

Tel: (212) 661-1300     Fax: (212) 687-0480     www.warnaco.com

*Mfr./sales intimate apparel and men's and women's sportswear.*

**Warnaco, Münich, Germany**

## WARNER ELECTRIC BRAKE & CLUTCH COMPANY

449 Gardner St., South Beloit, IL, 61080

Tel: (815) 389-3771     Fax: (815) 389-2582     www.warnernet.com

*Global supplier of Power Transmission and Motion Control Solution Systems; automotive, industry brakes, and clutches.*

**Stieber GmbH, Hatschekstrasse 36, D-69126 Heidelberg, Germany**

Tel: 49-6221-30470    Fax: 49-6221-304717

**Warner Electric GmbH, Postfach 2008, D-72610 Nürtinger, Germany**

Tel: 49-7022-5040    Fax: 49-7022-55091

## WASHINGTON GROUP INTERNATIONAL, INC.

720 Park Blvd., PO Box 73, Boise, ID, 83729

Tel: (208) 386-5000     Fax: (208) 386-7186     www.wgint.com

*Engaged in engineering and construction.*

**Washington Group International, Inc., Wiesenstrasse 20, D-06727 Theissen, Germany**

Tel: 49-3441-684-611    Fax: 49-3441-684-415

**Washington Group International, Inc., Hagenauer Strasse 42, D-65203 Wiesbaden, Germany**

Tel: 49-611-18-2500    Fax: 49-611-18-85959

## THE WASHINGTON POST COMPANY

1150 15th St. NW, Washington, DC, 20071

Tel: (202) 334-6000 Fax: (202) 334-4536 www.washpostco.com

*Engaged in magazine publishing, cable and television broadcasting, educational services and the Internet,*

**International Herald Tribune, Friedrichstrasse 15, 60323 Frankfurt/Main, Germany**

Tel: 49-69-97-12-5020

## WASSERSTEIN PERELLA & CO., INC.

31 West 52nd Street, New York, NY, 10019

Tel: (212) 969-2700 Fax: (212) 969-7969 www.wassersteinperella.com

*Engaged in international investment banking and financial services.*

**Wasserstein Perella & Co. Deutschland GmbH, Rahmhofstrasse 2-4, D-60313, Frankfurt Au Main 1, Germany**

Tel: 49-69-25-25280 Fax: 49-69-23-0407

## WASTE MANAGEMENT, INC.

1001 Fannin Street, Ste. 4000, Houston, TX, 77002

Tel: (713) 512-6200 Fax: (713) 512-6299 www.wastemanagement.com

*Environmental services and disposal company; collection, processing, transfer and disposal facilities.*

**WMD Waste Management (Deutschland) GmbH, Im Teelbruch 134b, D-45219 Essen, Germany**

Contact: Wolfgang Otte, Mgr.

## WATER PIK TECHNOLOGIES, INC.

23 Corporate Plaza, Ste. 246, Newport Beach, CA, 92660

Tel: (949) 719-3700 Fax: (949) 719-6472 www.waterpik.com

*Mfr. oral hygiene appliances, shower massage equipment, water filtration products.*

**Water Pik GmbH, Hagenauer Str. 42-46, D-65203 Wiesbaden, Germany**

## WATERS CORPORATION

34 Maple Street, Milford, MA, 01757

Tel: (508) 478-2000 Fax: (508) 872-1990 www.waters.com

*Mfr./distribute liquid chromatographic instruments and test and measurement equipment.*

**Waters GmbH, Hauptstr. 71-79, D-6236 Eschborn, Germany**

**Waters GmbH, Siemensstr. 20, D-6078 Neu-Isenburg, Germany**

## WATLOW ELECTRIC MFG. COMPANY

12001 Lackland Rd., St. Louis, MO, 63146-4039

Tel: (314) 878-4600 Fax: (314) 434-1020 www.watlow.com

*Mfr. electrical heating units, electronic controls, thermocouple wire, metal-sheathed cable, infrared sensors.*

**Watlow Electric Mfg. Co. GmbH, Lauchwasenstr. 1, Postfach 1165, D-76709 Kronau, Germany**

Tel: 49-7253-9400-50 Fax: 49-7253-9400-99

## WATSON WYATT & COMPANY HOLDINGS

6707 Democracy Blvd., Ste. 800, Bethesda, MD, 20817

Tel: (301) 581-4600 Fax: (301) 581-4937 www.watsonwyatt.com

*Creates compensation and benefits programs for major corporations.*

**Watson Wyatt GmbH, Konigsallee 86, D-40212 Dusseldorf 1, Germany**

Tel: 49-211-8228-0 Fax: 49-211-8228-100 Contact: Thierry Hamon

## WATTS INDUSTRIES, INC.

815 Chestnut Street, North Andover, MA, 01845-6098

Tel: (978) 688-1811 Fax: (978) 688-5841 www.wattsind.com

*Designs/mfr./sales of industry valves and safety control products.*

**Watts MTR GmbH, Rudolf-Diesel-Strabe 5, Gewerbegebiet Ottmarsheim, D-74354 Besigheim, Germany**

## WEATHERFORD INTERNATIONAL, INC.

5 Post Oak Blvd, Ste. 1760, Houston, TX, 77227-3415

Tel: (713) 287-8400      Fax: (713) 963-9785      www.weatherford.com

*Oilfield services, products and equipment; mfr. marine cranes for oil and gas industry.*

**Weatherford Oil Tool GmbH, Hainhauser Weg 150, D-3012 Langenhagen 6, Germany**

Tel: 49-511-7702-300      Fax: 49-511-7705-333

## WEBER MARKING SYSTEMS INC.

711 West Algonquin Road, Arlington Heights, IL, 60005-4457

Tel: (847) 364-8500      Fax: (847) 364-8575      www.webermarking.com

*Mfr. label printing systems and custom labels.*

**Weber Marking Systems GmbH, Postfach/Box 0154, Honnefer Str. 41, D-53572 Unkel/Rhein, Germany**

## WEBER-STEPHEN PRODUCTS COMPANY

200 E. Daniels Road, Palatine, IL, 60067-6266

Tel: (847) 934-5700      Fax: (847) 934-0291      www.weberbq.com

*Mfr./sales Weber cooking systems and barbeque and gas grills.*

**Le Creuset/Weber-Stephen, Zeppelinstrasse 9, D-73274 Notzingen, Germany**

Tel: 49-7021-97-490      Fax: 49-7021-480-214

## WELCH ALLYN DCD INC.

4341 State Street Road, Skaneateles Falls, NY, 13153

Tel: (315) 685-4100      Fax: (315) 685-4091      www.welchallyn.com

*Mfr. bar code data collection systems.*

**Speidel & Keller GmbH & Co., Postfach 31, Zollerstrasse 2-4, 72417 Jungingen, Germany**

**Welch Allyn GmbH, Zollerstrasse 2-4, 72417 Jungingen, Germany**

Tel: 49-7477-92-71-0

## WELLMAN INC.

1040 Broad Street, Ste. 302, Shrewsbury, NJ, 07702

Tel: (732) 542-7300      Fax: (732) 542-9344      www.wellmanwlm.com

*Plastic recycler; mfr. polyester fibres and resins.*

**Wellman International GmbH, Alterhellweg 1111, D-4800 Dortmund 70, Germany**

Tel: 49-2-316-1181

## WEST PHARMACEUTICAL SERVICES

101 Gordon Drive, PO Box 645, Lionville, PA, 19341-0645

Tel: (610) 594-2900      Fax: (610) 594-3014      www.westpharma.com

*Mfr. products for filling, sealing, dispensing and delivering needs of health care and consumer products markets.*

**The West Company Deutschland GmbH & Co, KG, Stolberger Strasse 21-41, D-52249 Eschweiler, Germany**

Tel: 49-24-.3-7960      Fax: 49-24-03-796-110

**The West Company Deutschland GmbH & Co, KG, Leimberg 33, D-52222 Stolberg, Germany**

Tel: 49-24-03-7960      Fax: 49-24-02-796-777

## WESTERN DIGITAL CORPORATION

8105 Irvine Center Drive, Irvine, CA, 92718

Tel: (949) 932-5000      Fax: (949) 932-6629      www.westerndigital.com

*Mfr. hard disk drives, video graphics boards, VLSI.*

**Western Digital Deutschland, Samdorfer Str. 26, D-3000 Münich 80, Germany**

## WHIRLPOOL CORPORATION

2000 N. M-63, Benton Harbor, MI, 49022-2692

Tel: (616) 923-5000    Fax: (616) 923-5443    www.whirlpoolcorp.com

*Mfr./market home appliances: Whirlpool, Roper, KitchenAid, Estate, and Inglis.*

**Whirlpool Europe BV, Schorndorf, Germany**

## WHITEHALL-ROBINS INC.

1407 Cummings Drive, PO Box 26609, Richmond, VA, 23261-6609

Tel: (804) 257-2000    Fax: (804) 257-2120    www.ahp.com

*Mfr. ethical pharmaceuticals and consumer healthcare products.*

**Arzneimittel-Fabrik GmbH, Alpirsbach/Schwarzwald, Germany**

**Kytta-Werk Sauter GmbH, Alpirssbach/Schwarzwald, Germany**

## WHITTMAN-HART & USWEB/CKS

311 S. Wacker Drive, Ste. 3500, Chicago, IL, 60606-6621

Tel: (312) 922-9200    Fax: (312) 913-3020    www.uswebcks.com

*Internet professional services firm; design and implementation services for multimedia marketing programs.*

**USWeb/CKS Germany, Neumann Reichardt Str. 27-33, D-22041 Hamburg, Germany**

Tel: 49-40-657-33800    Contact: Robert T. Clarkson

## JOHN WILEY & SONS INC.

605 Third Ave., New York, NY, 10158-0012

Tel: (212) 850-6000    Fax: (212) 850-6088    www.wiley.com

*Develops, publishes, and sells products in print and electronic media for the educational, professional, scientific, technical, medical, and consumer markets*

**Wiley VCH Verlag GmbH, Pappelallee 3, D-69469 Weinheim, Germany**

Tel: 49-6201-6060    Fax: 49-6201-606328

## WILLKIE FARR & GALLAGHER

787 Seventh Avenue, New York, NY, 10019-6099

Tel: (212) 821-8000    Fax: (212) 821-8111    www.willkie.com

*International law firm.*

**Willkie Farr & Gallagher, Frankfurter Welle, An der Welle 4, D-60322 Frankfurt, Germany**

## WILMER, CUTLER & PICKERING

2445 M Street, N.W., Washington, DC, 20037-1420

Tel: (202) 663-6000    Fax: (202) 663-6363    www.wilmer.com

*International law firm.*

**Wilmer, Cutler & Pickering, Friedrichstrasse 95, D-10117 Berlin, Germany**

## WILSON, ELSER, MOSKOWITZ, EDELMAN & DICKER LLP

150 East 42nd St., New York, NY, 10017

Tel: (212) 490-3000    Fax: (212) 490-3038    www.wemed.com

*International law firm.*

**Bach, Langheid & Dallmayr (Wilson Elser affiliate), Maximiliansplatz 5, München 80333, Germany**

Tel: 49-8954-58-77-0    Contact: Dr. Reinhard Dallmayr

**Bach, Langheid & Dallmayr (Wilson Elser affiliate), Schutzenstrasse 4, Frankfurt/Main 60313, Germany**

Tel: 49-69-920-7400

**Bach, Langheid & Dallmayr (Wilson Elser affiliate), Wilhelm-Waldeyer-Strasse 14, Cologne 5093, Germany**

Tel: 49-221-944-0270

## WIND RIVER SYSTEMS, INC.

500 Wind River Way, Alameda, CA, 94501

Tel: (510) 748-4100     Fax: (510) 749-2010     www.isi.com

*Develops and markets computer software products and services.*

**Wind River Systems GmbH, Freisinger Straße 34, D-85737 Ismaning, Germany**

Tel: 49-89-962445-0

**Wind River Systems GmbH, Zettachring 4, 70567 Stuttgart, Germany**

Tel: 49-71-17-27-23-53-0

**Wind River Systems GmbH, Chilehaus A, Fischertwiete 2, D-20095 Hamburg, Germany**

Tel: 49-40-32005-202

## WONDERWARE CORPORATION

100 Technology Dr., Irvine, CA, 92618

Tel: (949) 727-3200     Fax: (949) 727-3270     www.wonderware.com

*Mfr. industrial strength applications software and services.*

**Wonderware GmbH, München, Germany**

Tel: 49-89-450558-0

## WOODHEAD INDUSTRIES INC.

Three Parkway North, Ste. 550, Deerfield, IL, 60015

Tel: (847) 236-9300     Fax: (847) 236-0503     www.woodhead.com

*Develop/mfr./sale/distributor elect/electronic, fiber optic and ergonomic special-function, non-commodity products.*

**H.F. Vogel GmbH, Elektrotechnische Fabrik, GewerbestraBe 60, 75015 Bretten-"G"Ishausen, Germany**

## WOODWARD GOVERNOR COMPANY

5001 N. Second Street, PO Box 7001, Rockford, IL, 61125-7001

Tel: (815) 877-7441     Fax: (815) 639-6033     www.woodward.com

*Mfr./service speed control devices and systems for aircraft turbines, industrial engines and turbines.*

**Woodward Governor Germany, GmbH, Frankenhaeuser Strasse 21a, D-06537 Kelbra, Germany**

Tel: 49-34651-3590    Fax: 49-34651-35999    Contact: Jacques van Oppen    Emp: 50

**Woodward Governor Germany, GmbH, Koethener Chaussee 46, D-06385 Aken Elbe, Germany**

Tel: 49-34909-8800    Fax: 49-34909-82049    Contact: Pieter Jan van Rijnbach    Emp: 50

## WORLDCOM, INC.

500 Clinton Center Drive, Clinton, MS, 39060

Tel: (601) 360-8600     Fax: (601) 360-8616     www.wcom.com

*Telecommunications company serving local, long distance and Internet customers domestically and internationally.*

**WorldCom International, Langstrasse 50, D-6450 Hanau, Germany**

## WORLDXCHANGE COMMUNICATIONS

9999 Willow Creek Road, San Diego, CA, 92131

Tel: (858) 547-4933     Fax: (800) 995-4502     www.worldxchange.com

*Provides international, long distance telecommunications services worldwide.*

**WorldxChange Communications GmbH, Wilhelm-Marx-Haus, Heinrich-Heine-Allee 53, D-40213 Düsseldorf, Germany**

Tel: 49-211-8307-204    Fax: 49-211-8307-378    Emp: 40

**WRIGHT LINE INC.**

160 Gold Star Blvd., Worcester, MA, 01606

Tel: (508) 852-4300     Fax: (508) 853-8904     www.wrightline.com

*Mfr. filing systems.*

**Wright Line GmbH, Waechtersbacherstr. 61, D-6000 Frankfurt/Main 61, Germany**

**WM WRIGLEY JR. COMPANY**

410 N. Michigan Ave., Chicago, IL, 60611-4287

Tel: (312) 644-2121     Fax: (312) 644-0353     www.wrigley.com

*Mfr. chewing gum.*

**Wrigley GmbH, Albrecht Duerer Str. 2, Postfach 1414, D-8025 Unterhaching, Germany**

**WYETH-AYERST INTERNATIONAL INC.**

150 Radnot-Chester Road, St. Davids, PA, 19087

Tel: (610) 902-4100     Fax: (610) 989-4586     www.ahp.com/wyeth

*Antibiotics and pharmaceutical products.*

**Wyeth-Pharma GmbH, Schleebruggenkamp 15, D-48159 Munster, Germany**

Tel: 49-251-2040

**WYNN OIL COMPANY**

1050 West Fifth Street, Azusa, CA, 91702-9510

Tel: (626) 334-0231     Fax: (626) 334-1456     www.wynnoil.com

*Mfr. of specialty chemicals, equipment and related service programs for automotive and industrial markets.*

**Wynn's Deutschland GmbH, Gothaer Str. 4, D-40880 Ratinger, Germany**

Tel: 49-2102-48-0300    Fax: 49-2102-48-0310

**WYSE TECHNOLOGY INC.**

3471 North First Street, San Jose, CA, 95134

Tel: (408) 473-1200     Fax: (408) 473-2080     www.wyse.com

*Mfr. computer network terminals.*

**Wyse Technology, Humboldt Park Haus 7, Humboldstrasse 10, D-85609 Aschheim/Dornach, Germany**

Tel: 49-89-460099

**XEROX CORPORATION**

800 Long Ridge Road, PO Box 1600, Stamford, CT, 06904

Tel: (203) 968-3000     Fax: (203) 968-4312     www.xerox.com

*Mfr. document processing equipment, systems and supplies.*

**Rank Xerox GmbH, Heesenetrasse 70, D-40549 Heerst Düsseldorf 11, Germany**

Tel: 49-211-9900    Fax: 49-211-9907832

**Rank Xerox GmbH, Emanuel-Leutze Strasse 20, D-40547 Lorick Düsseldorf 11, Germany**

Tel: 49-211-9900    Fax: 49-211-990-7832

**XILINX INC.**

2100 Logic Drive, San Jose, CA, 95124-3400

Tel: (408) 559-7778     Fax: (408) 559-7114     www.xilinx.com

*Programmable logic and related development systems software.*

**Xilinx GmbH, Dorfstrasse 1, D-85609 Ascheim Münich, Germany**

**XIRCOM, INC.**

2300 Corporate Center Drive, Thousand Oaks, CA, 91320

Tel: (805) 376-9300     Fax: (805) 376-9311     www.xircom.com

*Mfr. PC card network adapters and modems.*

**Xircom Europe GmbH, Am Soldnermoos 17, 85399 Hallbergmoos, Germany**

## XTRA CORPORATION

1807 Park 270 Dr., Ste. 400, St. Louis, MO, 63146-4020

Tel: (314) 579-9320　　　　Fax: (314) 579-0299　　　　www.xtracorp.com

*Holding company: leasing.*

**XTRA International, Bremen, Germany**

## YAHOO! INC.

3420 Central Expressway, Santa Clara, CA, 95051

Tel: (408) 731-3300　　　　Fax: (408) 731-3301　　　　www.yahoo-inc.com

*Internet media company providing specialized content, free electronic mail and community offerings and commerce.*

**Yahoo! Deutschland, Riesstraße 25, Haus C, D-80992 München, Germany**

Tel: 49-89-143-12576　　Fax: 49-89-143-12575

## YELLOW CORPORATION

10990 Roe Ave., PO Box 7270, Overland Park, KS, 66207

Tel: (913) 696-6100　　　　Fax: (913) 696-6116　　　　www.yellowcorp.com

*Commodity transportation.*

**FM Deutschland GmbH, Poststrase 58, 4143 Nettetal-Kaldenkirchen, Germany**

**FM Deutschland GmbH, Schollersheiderstrasse 2-4, 40822 Mettmann, Germany**

**FM Deutschland GmbH, Carl-Benz Strasse 9, 71634 Ludwigsburg, Germany**

## YORK INTERNATIONAL CORPORATION

631 South Richland Ave., York, PA, 17403

Tel: (717) 771-7890　　　　Fax: (717) 771-6212　　　　www.york.com

*Mfr. heating, ventilating, air conditioning and refrigeration equipment.*

**York International GmbH, Gottlieb Daimler Str. 6, Postfach 100465, Mannheim D-68165 Germany**

Tel: 49-621-468222

**York, Kalte und Klimatechnik GmbH, Postfach 100465, D-6800 Mannheim 1, Germany**

## YOUNG & RUBICAM INC.

285 Madison Ave., New York, NY, 10017

Tel: (212) 210-3000　　　　Fax: (212) 370-3796　　　　www.yr.com

*Advertising, public relations, direct marketing and sales promotion, corporate and product ID management.*

**Young & Rubicam GmbH Werbung, Postfach 4665, Bleichstr. 64, D-6000 Frankfurt/Main, Germany**

## JOHN ZINK COMPANY

PO Box 21220, Tulsa, OK, 74121-1220

Tel: (918) 234-1800　　　　Fax: (918) 234-2700　　　　www.johnzink.com

*Mfr. flare systems, thermal oxidizers, vapor recovery systems, process heater burners.*

**John Zink Frankfurt, Frankfurt, Germany**

Tel: 352-51899309　　Contact: Siegfried Scholz

## ZIPPERTUBING COMPANY

13000 S. Broadway, PO Box 61129, Los Angeles, CA, 90061

Tel: (310) 527-0488　　　　Fax: (310) 767-1714　　　　www.zippertubing.com

*Mfr. zip-on plastic tubing, wire markers, pipe insulation, EMI shielding.*

**Zipper-Technik GmbH, Wernher von Braun Strasse 3, D-63238 Neu Isenburg, Germany**

## ZOLL MEDICAL CORPORATION

32 Second Avenue, Burlington, MA, 01803

Tel: (781) 229-0020　　　　Fax: (781) 272-5578　　　　www.zoll.com

*Mfr. electrical resuscitation devices and equipment.*

**ZOLL Medical Deutschland, Schillingsrotter Str. 23, 50996 Cologne, Germany**

Tel: 49-22-139-89340

## ZOMAX INCORPORATED

5353 Nathan Lane, Plymouth, MN, 55442

Tel: (763) 553-9300    Fax: (763) 553-0826    www.zomax.com

*Mfr./sales CD-ROM's, digital video discs and cassettes.*

**Zomax Limited, Paul-Ehrlich-Str. 11-13, 63225 Langen, Germany**

Tel: 49-6103-9702-0   Fax: 49-6103-9702-11   Contact: Ben Vaske

## ZYGO CORPORATION

Laurel Brook Road, Middlefield, CT, 06455

Tel: (860) 347-8506    Fax: (860) 347-8372    www.zygo.com

*Mfr. high-precision, electro-optical measuring equipment.*

**Syncotec Neue Tech GmbH, Loherstrasse 4, D-35614 Asslar, Germany**

Tel: 49-644-188-889   Fax: 49-644-181-588

**ZygoLOT GmbH, Im Tiefen See 58, D-64293 Darmstadt, Germany**

Tel: 49-6151-88060   Fax: 49-6151-896667

# Ghana

## LOUIS BERGER INTERNATIONAL INC.

100 Halsted Street, East Orange, NJ, 07019

Tel: (201) 678-1960        Fax: (201) 672-4284        www.louisberger.com

*Consulting engineers, engaged in architecture, environmental and advisory services.*

**Louis Berger International Inc., Water Sector, Restructuring Secretariat, PO Box M43, Accra Ghana**

Tel: 233-21-764111    Fax: 233-21764111

## CIGNA COMPANIES

One Liberty Place, Philadelphia, PA, 19192

Tel: (215) 761-1000        Fax: (215) 761-5511        www.cigna.com

*Insurance, invest, health care and other financial services.*

**Crusader Co. (Ghana) Ltd., Samlotte House, Kwame Nkrumah Ave., Accra, Ghana**

## CMS ENERGY CORPORATION

330 Town Center Dr., Ste. 1100, Dearborn, MI, 48126

Tel: (313) 436-9200        Fax: (313) 436-9225        www.cmsenergy.com

*Independent power plant operator.*

**CMS Energy/Takoradi Power Co, Takoradi, Ghana**

## DELOITTE TOUCHE TOHMATSU INTERNATIONAL

1633 Broadway, New York, NY, 10019

Tel: (212) 492-4000        Fax: (212) 392-4154        www.deloitte.com

*Accounting, audit, tax and management consulting services.*

**Deloitte & Touche, 4 Liberation Rd., (PO Box 453), Accra, Ghana**

**Deloitte & Touche Consulting, 350 Nima Ave., North Ridge, Accra Ghana**

## DHL WORLDWIDE EXPRESS

50 California Avenue, San Francisco, CA, 94111

Tel: (415) 677-6100        Fax: (415) 824-9700        www.dhl.com

*Worldwide air express carrier.*

**DHL Worldwide Express, North Ridge Cresent, House C913/3, PO Box 207, Accra Ghana**

Tel: 233-21-221647

## EAGLE GLOBAL LOGISTICS (EGL)

15350 Vickery Drive, Houston, TX, 77032

Tel: (281) 618-3100        Fax: (281) 618-3100        www.eaglegl.com

*Ocean/air freight forwarding, customs brokerage, packing and wholesale, logistics management and insurance.*

**Walfred Services Ltd., No. 2 Cargo Village, Kotoka International Airport, PO Box 16774, Accra-North Ghana**

Tel: 233-21-772-667    Fax: 233-21-775-419

## ERNST & YOUNG, LLP

787 Seventh Ave., New York, NY, 10019

Tel: (212) 773-3000        Fax: (212) 773-6350        www.eyi.com

*Accounting and audit, tax and management consulting services.*

**Associates of Ernst & Young/ Owusu & Fiadjoe, PO Box 2239 Asylum Down, Accra, Ghana**

Tel: 233-21-227054    Fax: 233-21-234335    Contact: Kwame Nini Owusu

## GREY GLOBAL GROUP

777 Third Ave., New York, NY, 10017

Tel: (212) 546-2000    Fax: (212) 546-1495    www.grey.com

*International advertising agency.*

**Insight Advertising,  Accra, Ghana**

## H.J. HEINZ COMPANY

600 Grant Street, Pittsburgh, PA, 15219

Tel: (412) 456-5700    Fax: (412) 456-6128    www.heinz.com

*Processed food products and nutritional services.*

**Star-Kist Europe Inc.,  Tema, Ghana**

## J. WALTER THOMPSON COMPANY

466 Lexington Ave., New York, NY, 10017

Tel: (212) 210-7000    Fax: (212) 210-6944    www.jwt.com

*International advertising and marketing services.*

**Ghana Advertising & Marketing,  Accra, Ghana**

## S C JOHNSON & SON INC.

1525 Howe St., Racine, WI, 53403

Tel: (414) 260-2000    Fax: (414) 260-2133    www.scjohnsonwax.com

*Home, auto, commercial and personal care products and specialty chemicals.*

**S.C. Johnson & Son Ltd.,  PO Box C537, Cantonments, Accra, Ghana**

## KAISER ALUMINUM CORPORATION

5847 San Felipe, Ste. 2600, Houston, TX, 77057-3010

Tel: (713) 267-3777    Fax: (713) 267-3701    www.kaiseral.com

*Aluminum refining and manufacturing.*

**Volta Aluminum Company Ltd.,  Tema, Ghana**

## KPMG INTERNATIONAL LLP

345 Park Avenue, New York, NY, 10022

Tel: (201) 307-7000    Fax: (201) 930-8617    www.kpmg.com

*Accounting and audit, tax and management consulting services.*

**KPMG EMA,  Ivory Coast (Cote d'Ivoire), Ghana**

**KPMG EMA,  2nd Fl., Mobil House, Liberia Rd., Accra Ghana**

Tel: 233-21-664881   Fax: 233-21-667909   Contact: Albert N. Kotey, Sr. Ptnr.

## LOWE LINTAS & PARTNERS WORLDWIDE

One Dag Hammarskjold Plaza, New York, NY, 10017

Tel: (212) 605-8000    Fax: (212) 605-4705    www.interpublic.com

*Full-service, integrated marketing communications company/advertising agency.*

**Ammirati Puris Lintas Ghana,  Advantage House, Klanaa St., PO Box 1262, Accra Ghana**

Tel: 233-21-772-321   Fax: 233-21-772-498   Contact: Jake Obetsebi-Lamptey, Mng. Dir.

## MARS INC.

6885 Elm Street, McLean, VA, 22101-3810

Tel: (703) 821-4900    Fax: (703) 448-9678    www.mars.com

*Mfr. candy, snack foods, rice products and cat food.*

**Mars Ltd.,  Airport, PO Box M 109, Accra, Ghana**

## MAXXAM INC.

5847 San Felipe, Ste. 2600, Houston, TX, 77057

Tel: (713) 975-7600    Fax: (713) 267-3701

*Holding company for aluminum and timber products and real estate industries.*

**MAXXAM Inc.,  Ghana**

## McCANN-ERICKSON WORLDGROUP

750 Third Ave., New York, NY, 10017

Tel: (212) 984-3644      Fax: (212) 984-2629      www.mccann.com

*International advertising and marketing services.*

**STB&A, Accra, Ghana**

## PFIZER INC.

235 East 42nd Street, New York, NY, 10017-5755

Tel: (212) 573-2323      Fax: (212) 573-7851      www.pfizer.com

*Research-based, global health care company.*

**Pfizer Ltd., Ghana**

## PHILLIPS PETROLEUM COMPANY

Phillips Building, 411 S. Keeler Ave., Bartlesville, OK, 74004

Tel: (918) 661-6600      Fax: (918) 661-7636      www.phillips66.com

*Crude oil, natural gas, liquefied petroleum gas, gasoline and petro-chemicals.*

**Phillips Petroleum Co. (Ghana), Private Post Box, Central Post Office, Accra, Ghana**

## PRICEWATERHOUSECOOPERS LLP

1301 Ave. of the Americas, New York, NY, 10019

Tel: (212) 596-7000      Fax: (212) 259-1301      www.pwcglobal.com

*Accounting and auditing, tax and management, and human resource consulting services.*

**PriceWaterhouseCoopers, PO Box 16009, Airport, Accra, Ghana**

Tel: 233-21-772088   Fax: 233-21-772934

## THE ST. PAUL COMPANIES, INC.

385 Washington Street, St. Paul, MN, 55102

Tel: (651) 310-7911      Fax: (651) 310-8294      www.stpaul.com

*Provides investment, insurance and reinsurance services.*

**New India Assurance Co. (Ghana) Ltd., Queensway Building, D-619/4 Kimberley Ave., PO Box 138, Accra Ghana**

## UNITED PARCEL SERVICE, INC.

55 Glenlake Parkway, NE, Atlanta, GA, 30328

Tel: (404) 828-6000      Fax: (404) 828-6593      www.ups.com

*International package-delivery service.*

**UPS Ghana, Danquah Circle, PO Box C693, Cantonments Accra, Ghana**

Tel: 223-21-762509   Fax: 233-21-772487

## WACKENHUT CORPORATION

4200 Wackenhut Dr., Ste. 100, Palm Beach Gardens, FL, 33410

Tel: (561) 622-5656      Fax: (561) 691-6736      www.wackenhut.com

*Security systems and services.*

**Wackenhut Ghana Ltd., Belmont Place, E153/3 Gamel Abdul Nasser Ave., PO Box C2616, Cantonments, Accra, Ghana**

Tel: 233-21-224276   Fax: 233-21-220302

## XEROX CORPORATION

800 Long Ridge Road, PO Box 1600, Stamford, CT, 06904

Tel: (203) 968-3000      Fax: (203) 968-4312      www.xerox.com

*Mfr. document processing equipment, systems and supplies.*

**Interlink Communications, Ring Rd. Central, PO Box 15930, Accra, Ghana**

Tel: 233-21-226-659

# Gibraltar

**BDO SEIDMAN, LLP   BELGIUM**

Two Prudential Plaza, 180 N. Stetson Ave., Ste. 2300, Chicago, IL, 60601

Tel: (312) 240-1236      Fax: (312) 240-3329      www.bdo.com

*International accounting and financial consulting firm.*

**BDO Fidees,  PO Box 575, Ste. 2C Eurolife Building, 1 Corral Rd., Gibraltar**

Tel: 350-42686   Fax: 350-42701    Contact: Timothy J. Revill

**DELOITTE TOUCHE TOHMATSU INTERNATIONAL**

1633 Broadway, New York, NY, 10019

Tel: (212) 492-4000      Fax: (212) 392-4154      www.deloitte.com

*Accounting, audit, tax and management consulting services.*

**Deloitte & Touche,  Imossi House, PO Box 758, 1/5 Irish Town, Gibraltar**

**DHL WORLDWIDE EXPRESS**

50 California Avenue, San Francisco, CA, 94111

Tel: (415) 677-6100      Fax: (415) 824-9700      www.dhl.com

*Worldwide air express carrier.*

**DHL AI Couriers Ltd.,  11 Engineer Lane, PO Box 532, Gibraltar**

Tel: 350-73775   Fax: 350-74389

**ERNST & YOUNG, LLP**

787 Seventh Ave., New York, NY, 10019

Tel: (212) 773-3000      Fax: (212) 773-6350      www.eyi.com

*Accounting and audit, tax and management consulting services.*

**Ernst & Young,  Ste. 5 International House, Bell Lane, Gibraltar**

Tel: 350-79799  Fax: 350-75141   Contact: Kenneth A. Robinson

**GRANT THORNTON INTERNATIONAL**

800 One Prudential Plaza, 130 E. Randolph Drive, Chicago, IL, 60601-6050

Tel: (312) 856-0001      Fax: (312) 616-7052      www.grantthornton.com

*Accounting, audit, tax and management consulting services.*

**Grant Thornton International,  Suite 944, Europort Gibraltar, Gibraltar**

**KPMG INTERNATIONAL LLP**

345 Park Avenue, New York, NY, 10022

Tel: (201) 307-7000      Fax: (201) 930-8617      www.kpmg.com

*Accounting and audit, tax and management consulting services.*

**KPMG,  Regal House, Queensway, Gibraltar**

Tel: 350-74015   Fax: 350-74016   Contact: Francis A. Isola, Sr. Ptnr.

**PRICEWATERHOUSECOOPERS LLP**

1301 Ave. of the Americas, New York, NY, 10019

Tel: (212) 596-7000      Fax: (212) 259-1301      www.pwcglobal.com

*Accounting and auditing, tax and management, and human resource consulting services.*

**PriceWaterhouseCoopers,  PO Box 615, Europort, Gibraltar**

Tel: 350-41992   Fax: 350-41996

## VERIZON COMMUNICATIONS INC.

1255 Corporate Drive, Irving, TX, 75038

Tel: (972) 507-5000      Fax: (972) 507-5002      www.gte.com

*Engaged in wireline and wireless communications.*

**Gibraltar NYNEX Communications, Gibraltar**

## XEROX CORPORATION

800 Long Ridge Road, PO Box 1600, Stamford, CT, 06904

Tel: (203) 968-3000      Fax: (203) 968-4312      www.xerox.com

*Mfr. document processing equipment, systems and supplies.*

**Image Graphics Ltd., c/o Holiday Inn, 21/23 Governor's Parade, Gibraltar**

Tel: 350-76834    Fax: 350-71892

# Greece

**3M**

3M Center, St. Paul, MN, 55144-1000

Tel: (651) 733-1110     Fax: (651) 733-9973     www.mmm.com

*Mfr. diversified products for industry, health care, imaging, communications, transport, safety, consumer, etc.*

**3M Hellas Ltd.,  Kifissias 20, GR-151-25 Maroussi, Athens Greece**

Tel: 30-1-68-85-300   Fax: 30-1-68-43-281

**AAF INTERNATIONAL (AMERICAN AIR FILTER)**

215 Central Ave., PO Box 35690, Louisville, KY, 40232-5690

Tel: (502) 637-0011     Fax: (502) 637-0321     www.aafintl.com

*Mfr. air filtration/pollution control and noise control equipment.*

**AAF-Environmental Control Epe,  2 Papada Street, 11525 Athens, Greece**

**ABBOTT LABORATORIES**

One Abbott Park, Abbott Park, IL, 60064-3500

Tel: (847) 937-6100     Fax: (847) 937-1511     www.abbott.com

*Development/mfr./sale diversified health care products and services.*

**Abbott Laboratories Hellas S.A.,  512 Vouliagmenis AV, GR 17456 Alimos, Athens Greece**

**ACADEMIC PRESS INC.**

6277 Sea Harbor Drive, Orlando, FL, 32887

Tel: (407) 345-2000     Fax: (407) 345-8388     www.academicpress.com

*Publisher of educational and scientific books.*

**KC Enterprises,  15 Mavili St., GR-166-73 Voula, Athens, Greece**

Tel: 30-1-965-8244   Fax: 30-1-899-1873   Contact: Katia Zevelekakis

**AIR EXPRESS INTERNATIONAL CORPORATION**

120 Tokeneke Road, PO Box 1231, Darien, CT, 06820

Tel: (203) 655-7900     Fax: (203) 655-5779     www.aeilogistics.com

*International air freight forwarder.*

**AEI Hellas S.A.,  20 Satovriandou Str, PO Box 8518, GR-100-10 Athens Greece**

Tel: 30-1-524-6512   Fax: 30-1-524-6134

**ALAMO RENT A CAR**

110 Southeast 6th Street, Fort Lauderdale, FL, 33301

Tel: (954) 522-0000     Fax: (954) 220-0120     www.alamo.com

*Car rentals.*

**Alamo Rent A Car,  Athens Airport, East Terminal & 33 Syngrou Ave., Athens, Greece**

**AMERICAN BUREAU OF SHIPPING**

2 World Trade Center, 106th Fl., New York, NY, 10048

Tel: (212) 839-5000     Fax: (212) 839-5209     www.eagle.org

*Classification/certification of ships and offshore structures, development and technical assistance.*

**ABS Europe,  Akti Miaouli & Filellinon St. 1-3, PO Box 80139, GR-185-10 Pireaus, Greece**

## AMERICAN EXPRESS COMPANY

American Express Tower, World Financial Center, New York, NY, 10285-4765

Tel: (212) 640-2000      Fax: (212) 619-9802      www.americanexpress.com

*Travel, travelers cheques, charge card and financial services.*

**American Express Intl. AE, Athens, Greece**

## AMERICAN INTERNATIONAL GROUP INC. (AIG)

70 Pine Street, New York, NY, 10270

Tel: (212) 770-7000      Fax: (212) 509-9705      www.aig.com

*Worldwide insurance and financial services.*

**AILCO, 119, Kifissias Avenue, 151 24 Marcusi Athens, Greece**

## AMERICAN LOCKER GROUP INC.

608 Allen Street, Jamestown, NY, 14701-3966

Tel: (716) 664-9600      Fax: (716) 483-2822      www.americanlocker.com

*Mfr. coin-operated locks and office furniture.*

**Panos Thomadakis MTI, Athens, Greece**

Tel: 30-1-9959063

## ANC RENTAL CORP.

110 Southeast Sixth St., Ft. Lauderdale, FL, 33301

Tel: (954) 769-7000      Fax: (954) 769-7000      www.ancrental.com

*Engaged in car rental services, including National Car Rental and Alamo Rent A Car.*

**National Car Rental, 7 Stadium St., Athens, Greece**

## ANDERSEN CONSULTING

100 S. Wacker Drive, Ste. 1059, Chicago, IL, 60606

Tel: (312) 693-0161      Fax: (312) 693-0507      www.ac.com

*Provides management and technology consulting services.*

**Andersen Consulting, 24 Kifissias Ave., GR-152-31 Chalandri, Athens, Greece**

Tel: 30-1-6776-4004    Fax: 30-1-6776-405

## ANDERSEN WORLDWIDE

33 West Monroe Street, Chicago, IL, 60603

Tel: (312) 580-0033      Fax: (312) 507-6748      www.arthurandersen.com

*Accounting and audit, tax and management consulting services.*

**Arthur Andersen/ S. Pantzopoulos & Co., Syngrou Ave. 377, GR-175-64 Athens, Greece**

Tel: 30-1-9302-063

## ANIXTER INTERNATIONAL INC..

4711 Golf Road, Skokie, IL, 60076

Tel: (847) 677-2600      Fax: (847) 677-8557      www.anixter.com

*Distributor wiring systems/products for voice, video, data and power applications.*

**Anixter Greece Network Systems Ltd., 282 Messogion Ave, 15562 Holargos Athens, Greece**

Tel: 30-1-653-5073    Fax: 30-1-653-1509

## AON CORPORATION

123 North Wacker Drive, Chicago, IL, 60606

Tel: (312) 701-3000      Fax: (312) 701-3100      www.aon.com

*Insurance brokers worldwide; underwrites accident and health insurance, specialty and professional insurance; and provides risk management consultation.*

**Alexander Howden (Hellas) Ltd., 141 Filonos St. 6th Fl., Piraeus, Greece**

Tel: 30-1-429-4961    Fax: 30-1-429-4960    Contact: George Georgoulis

**AON Hellenic Bain Hogg SA, 262 Sygrou Ave. & 2 Filaretou St., GR-176-72 Athens, Greece**

Tel: 30-1-957-6111    Fax: 30-1-957-6116    Contact: Stavros C. Papagiannopoulos

## APPLERA CORPORATION

761 Main Avenue, Norwalk, CT, 06859-0001

Tel: (203) 762-1000     Fax: (203) 762-6000     www.applera.com

*Leading supplier of systems for life science research and related applications.*

**Analytical Instruments S.A., 9 Tzavella Strasse, GR-152 31 Chalandri, Athens, Greece**

## ARBOR ACRES FARM INC.

439 Marlborough Road, Glastonbury, CT, 06033

Tel: (860) 633-4681     Fax: (860) 633-2433

*Producers of male and female broiler breeders, commercial egg layers.*

**Hellenic Livestock Development, 28 Vas. Constandinou St., Athens, Greece**

## ARROW INTERNATIONAL, INC.

2400 Bernville Rd., Reading, PA, 19605

Tel: (610) 378-0131     Fax: (610) 374-5360     www.arrowintl.com

*Develop, manufacture, and marketing of medical devices.*

**Arrow Hellas A.E.E., Leoforos Kifissias 294 & Narvarinou, Halandri, GR-152-32 Athens, Greece**

Tel: 30-1-68-13024   Fax: 30-1-68-18145   Contact: Paula Kondopoulos

## ASSOCIATED MERCHANDISING CORPORATION

500 Seventh Ave., 2nd Fl., New York, NY, 10018

Tel: (212) 819-6600     Fax: (212) 819-6701     www.theamc.com

*Retail service organization; apparel, shoes and accessories.*

**Associated Merchandising Corp., 220 Messagion St., Holargos, GR-155-61 Athens, Greece**

## AT&T CORPORATION

32 Avenue of the Americas, New York, NY, 10013-2412

Tel: (212) 387-5400     Fax: (212) 387-5695     www.att.com

*Telecommunications.*

**AT&T (Greece) Ltd., 64 Kifissias Ave., GR-151-25 Maroussi Athens, Greece**

## BANK OF AMERICA CORPORATION

555 California Street, San Francisco, CA, 94104

Tel: (415) 622-3530     Fax: (415) 622-8467     www.bankofamerica.com

*Financial services.*

**Bank of America NT & SA, 39 Panepistimiou St., PO Box 3630, GR-105-64 Athens, Greece**

Tel: 30-1-325-1901   Fax: 30-1-323-1376   Contact: Leonidas Metaxas, VP

## BATES WORLDWIDE INC.

405 Lexington Ave., New York, NY, 10174

Tel: (212) 297-7000     Fax: (212) 986-0270     www.batesww.com

*Advertising, marketing, public relations and media consulting.*

**Bates Hellas, 11b Konitsis St., GR-151-25 Maroussi Athens, Greece**

Tel: 30-1-612-5520   Fax: 30-1-805-0138   Contact: Yannis Papagiannacopoulos, CEO

## BAUSCH & LOMB INC.

One Bausch & Lomb Place, Rochester, NY, 14604-2701

Tel: (716) 338-6000     Fax: (716) 338-6007     www.bausch.com

*Mfr. vision care products and accessories.*

**Bausch & Lomb Greece, 73 Apostolopou Street, Chalandri 15231, Athens Greece**

## BAXTER HEALTHCARE CORPORATION

One Baxter Parkway, Deerfield, IL, 60015

Tel: (847) 948-2000     Fax: (847) 948-3948     www.baxter.com

*Pharmaceutical preparations, surgical/medical instruments and cardiovascular products.*

**Baxter (Hellas) EPE, 67 Daskaroli St., & Gr. Lambraki St., GR-166-75 Flytada, Greece**

## BBDO WORLDWIDE

1285 Ave. of the Americas, New York, NY, 10019

Tel: (212) 459-5000      Fax: (212) 459-6645      www.bbdo.com

*Multinational group of advertising agencies.*

**BBDO Group, Athens, Greece**

## BDO SEIDMAN, LLP    BELGIUM

Two Prudential Plaza, 180 N. Stetson Ave., Ste. 2300, Chicago, IL, 60601

Tel: (312) 240-1236      Fax: (312) 240-3329      www.bdo.com

*International accounting and financial consulting firm.*

**BDO Kolokotronis & Co., 16 Metsovou St., GR-175-63 Paleo Firo, Athens, Greece**

Tel: 30-1-9317-117    Fax: 30-1-93-12-319    Contact: Loizos E. Kolokotronis

## BENTLY NEVADA CORPORATION

1617 Water Street, PO Box 157, Minden, NV, 89423

Tel: (775) 782-3611      Fax: (775) 782-9259      www.bently.com

*Provides hardware, software, and services for machinery information and management systems.*

**Tesims SA, PO Box 80285, GR-185-10 Piraeus, Greece**

## LOUIS BERGER INTERNATIONAL INC.

100 Halsted Street, East Orange, NJ, 07019

Tel: (201) 678-1960      Fax: (201) 672-4284      www.louisberger.com

*Consulting engineers, engaged in architecture, environmental and advisory services.*

**Mott Berger Joint Venture, 205 Alexander Ave. 3rd Fl., GR-115-23 Athens, Greece**

Tel: 30-1-641-7543    Fax: 30-1-641-7543

## BEST WESTERN INTERNATIONAL

6201 North 24th Place, Phoenix, AZ, 85106

Tel: (602) 957-4200      Fax: (602) 957-5740      www.bestwestern.com

*International hotel chain.*

**Hotel Europa, Ancient Olympia, Piloponnese, Greece**

## BESTFOODS, INC.

700 Sylvan Ave., International Plaza, Englewood Cliffs, NJ, 07632-9976

Tel: (201) 894-4000      Fax: (201) 894-2186      www.bestfoods.com

*Consumer foods products; corn refining.*

**Knorr Bestfoods Hellas A.B.E.E., Pigon 33, GR-145-64 Kifissias, Greece**

Tel: 30-1-620-6440    Fax: 30-1-807-1045    Contact: Chronis Drossinos, Mgr.

## BOYDEN CONSULTING CORPORATION

364 Elwood Ave., Hawthorne, NY, 10502

Tel: (914) 747-0093      Fax: (914) 980-6147      www.boyden.com

*International executive search firm.*

**Boyden Associates Ltd., 12 Kinitsis St., GR-151-25 Maroussi, Greece**

Tel: 30-1-6127-777

## BOZELL GROUP

40 West 23rd Street, New York, NY, 10010

Tel: (212) 727-5000      Fax: (212) 645-9173      www.bozell.com

*Advertising, marketing, public relations and media consulting.*

**Solid Advertising, Artemidos 3, Paradissos, Amarusius Athens, Greece**

Tel: 30-1-685-5000    Fax: 30-1-685-5009    Contact: Stavros Leoussis, Mng. Dir.

## BRISTOL-MYERS SQUIBB COMPANY

345 Park Ave., New York, NY, 10154-0037

Tel: (212) 546-4000     Fax: (212) 546-4020     www.bms.com

*Pharmaceutical and food preparations, medical and surgical instruments.*

**Bristol Hellas A.E.B.E., 11th KLM., Athens-Lamia National Rd., Athens, Greece**

**ConvaTec Greece, 22nd KLM National Rd., GR-114-51 Metamorfosi, Greece**

**ConvaTec, Div. Bristol-Myers Squibb, 357-359 Messoghion Ae. 152 31 Chalandri, Greece**

Tel: 30-1-6501-582

## LEO BURNETT, DIV. B-COM 3 GROUP

35 West Wacker Drive, Chicago, IL, 60601

Tel: (312) 220-5959     Fax: (312) 220-6533     www.bcom3group.com

*Engaged in advertising, marketing, media buying and planning, and public relations.*

**Leo Burnett Company, 371 Sygrou Ave., GR-175-64 Athens, Greece**

## CAMBREX CORPORATION

1 Meadowlands Plaza, East Rutherford, NJ, 07063

Tel: (201) 804-3000     Fax: (201) 804-9852     www.cambrex.com

*human health, animal health/agriculture and Mfr. biotechnology products and produce specialty chemicals.*

**Chemico-Technica Renos J. Sashpelis SA, 8 SP Donda Street, Athens, Greece**

Tel: 30-1-922-6391

## CARGILL, INC.

15407 McGinty Road West, Minnetonka, MN, 55440-5625

Tel: (612) 742-7575     Fax: (612) 742-7393     www.cargill.com

*Food products, feeds, animal products.*

**Diamandouros Brothers S.A., 5 Mimnermou and Rigillis Street, Athens, Greece**

## THE CHERRY CORPORATION

3600 Sunset Ave., PO Box 718, Waukegan, IL, 60087

Tel: (847) 662-9200     Fax: (847) 662-2990     www.cherrycorp.com

*Mfr. electrical switches, electronic keyboards, controls and displays.*

**G. Parpanelas & Co., Salaminos 10, GR-54625 Thessaloniki, Greece**

Tel: 30-31-51-8485   Fax: 30-31-51-7156

## CIGNA COMPANIES

One Liberty Place, Philadelphia, PA, 19192

Tel: (215) 761-1000     Fax: (215) 761-5511     www.cigna.com

*Insurance, invest, health care and other financial services.*

**CIGNA Insurance Co. (Hellas) SA, Phidippidou 2, Ampelokipi, GR-115-26 Athens, Greece**

**CIGNA Insurance Co. of Europe SA/NV, Apollo Tower 17/F, GR-115-23 Athens, Greece**

## CISCO SYSTEMS, INC.

170 West Tasman Drive, San Jose, CA, 95134-1706

Tel: (408) 526-4000     Fax: (408) 526-4100     www.cisco.com

*Develop/mfr./market computer hardware and software networking systems.*

**Cisco Systems Greece, Caravel Hotel Ste. 427, Vas. Alexandrou 2, Athens, Greece**

Tel: 30-1-7253-725   Fax: 30-1-7253-770

## CITIGROUP, INC.

153 East 53rd Street, New York, NY, 10043

Tel: (212) 559-1000     Fax: (212) 559-3646     www.citigroup.com

*Provides insurance and financial services worldwide.*

**Citibank N.A., 8 Othonos St., GR 105-57 Athens, Greece**

Contact: Efstratios-George A. Arapoglou

## THE COCA-COLA COMPANY

PO Drawer 1734, Atlanta, GA, 30301

Tel: (404) 676-2121　　　Fax: (404) 676-6792　　　www.coca-cola.com

*Mfr./marketing/distributor soft drinks, syrups and concentrates, juice and juice-drink products.*

**Coca-Cola Greece, Athens, Greece**

## COLGATE-PALMOLIVE COMPANY

300 Park Ave., New York, NY, 10022

Tel: (212) 310-2000　　　Fax: (212) 310-2919　　　www.colgate.com

*Mfr. pharmaceuticals, cosmetics, toiletries and detergents.*

**Colgate-Palmolive (Hellas) SA, 89 Athinon St., Piraeus, Greece**

## COMPUWARE CORPORATION

31440 Northwestern Hwy., Farmington Hills, MI, 48334-2564

Tel: (248) 737-7300　　　Fax: (248) 737-7108　　　www.compuware.com

*Develop and market software for enterprise and e-commerce solutions.*

**Compuware Corporation, 59 Valtetsio Street, 13231 Athens, Greece**

## CONCURRENT COMPUTER CORPORATION

4375 River Green Pkwy., Duluth, GA, 30096

Tel: (678) 258-4000　　　Fax: (678) 258-4300　　　www.ccur.com

*Mfr. computer systems and software.*

**Concurrent Hellas, 2 Vas Georgiou St., GR-151-22 Maroussi Athens, Greece**

Tel: 30-1-612-8935　Fax: 30-1-612-8934

## D'ARCY MASIUS BENTON & BOWLES INC. (DMB&B)

1675 Broadway, New York, NY, 10019

Tel: (212) 468-3622　　　Fax: (212) 468-2987　　　www.dmbb.com

*Full service international advertising and communications group.*

**International Marketing & Promotions, 8 Koumbari St., GR-106-74 Athens, Greece**

## DDB NEEDHAM WORLDWIDE INC.

437 Madison Ave., New York, NY, 10022

Tel: (212) 415-2000　　　Fax: (212) 415-3417　　　www.ddbn.com

*Advertising agency.*

**Olympic DDB SA, 124 Kifissias Ave., GR-115-26 Athens, Greece**

## DELOITTE TOUCHE TOHMATSU INTERNATIONAL

1633 Broadway, New York, NY, 10019

Tel: (212) 492-4000　　　Fax: (212) 392-4154　　　www.deloitte.com

*Accounting, audit, tax and management consulting services.*

**Deloitte & Touche Hadjipavlou Sofianos & Cambanis SA, 250-254 Kifissias Ave., GR-152 31 Halandri Athens, Greece**

## DELTA AIR LINES INC.

PO Box 20706, Atlanta, GA, 30320-6001

Tel: (404) 715-2600　　　Fax: (404) 715-5494　　　www.delta-air.com

*Major worldwide airline; international air transport services.*

**Delta Air Lines Inc., Athens, Greece**

## DHL WORLDWIDE EXPRESS

50 California Avenue, San Francisco, CA, 94111

Tel: (415) 677-6100　　　Fax: (415) 824-9700　　　www.dhl.com

*Worldwide air express carrier.*

**DHL Worldwide Express, Alimou 44 & Rome 17, GR-174-55 Alimos Athens, Greece**

Tel: 30-1-989-0000

## DIAGNOSTIC PRODUCTS CORPORATION

5700 West 96th Street, Los Angeles, CA, 90045

Tel: (310) 645-8200 Fax: (310) 645-9999 www.dpcweb.com

*Mfr. diagnostic products.*

**DPC N.Tsakiris S.A., Ionias Oreokastro, PO Box 238, 57008 Thessaloniki, Greece**

Tel: 30-31-783-891 Fax: 30-31-784-712

## DIMON INCORPORATED

512 Bridge Street, PO Box 681, Danville, VA, 24543-0681

Tel: (804) 792-7511 Fax: (804) 791-0377 www.dimon.com

*One of world's largest importer and exporters of leaf tobacco.*

**DIMON Hellas Tobacco S.A., 19 Thermaikou Street, PO Box 10319, GR 541 10 56430 Stavroupoli, Thessaloniki Greece**

## DIONEX CORPORATION

1228 Titan Way, PO Box 3603, Sunnyvale, CA, 94086-3603

Tel: (408) 737-0700 Fax: (408) 730-9403 www.dionex.com

*Develop/mfr./market chromatography systems and related products.*

**Hellamco, PO Box 65074, Psyhiko-Athens, 154.10, Greece**

## DMC STRATEX NETWORKS, INC.

170 Rose Orchard Way, San Jose, CA, 95134

Tel: (408) 943-0777 Fax: (408) 944-1648 www.dmcstratexnetworks.com

*Designs, manufactures, and markets advanced wireless solutions for wireless broadband access.*

**DMC Stratex Networks, 2 Eratoshenous Str., 116-35 Athens, Greece**

Tel: 30-1-752-2066

## DRAFT WORLDWIDE

633 North St. Clair Street, Chicago, IL, 60611-3211

Tel: (312) 944-3500 Fax: (312) 944-3566 www.draftworldwide.com

*Full service international advertising agency, engaged in brand building, direct and promotional marketing.*

**DraftWorldwide Hellas, 172 N. Plastera St., Agious Anargerous, Athens, Greece**

Tel: 30-1-269-0373 Fax: 30-1-269-1827 Contact: Chris Gaitanaria, CEO

## DRAKE BEAM MORIN INC.

101 Huntington Ave., Boston, MA, 02199

Tel: (617) 375-9500 Fax: (617) 267-2011 www.dbm.com

*Human resource management consulting and training.*

**DBM Greece, c/o S & S Consulting, Apollo Twr. Ste. 12B4, 64 Louise Reincourt St., GR-115-23 Athens, Greece**

Tel: 30-1-648-4235 Fax: 30-1-692-3452

## EAGLE GLOBAL LOGISTICS (EGL)

15350 Vickery Drive, Houston, TX, 77032

Tel: (281) 618-3100 Fax: (281) 618-3100 www.eaglegl.com

*Ocean/air freight forwarding, customs brokerage, packing and wholesale, logistics management and insurance.*

**All Cargo Company/Cargo Service Corporation, 7 Tantalou St., Thessaloniki, Greece**

Tel: 30-31-517-184 Fax: 30-31-532-174

**Circle Freight Intternational S.A., 226 Syngrou Ave., GR-176-72 Athens, Greece**

Tel: 30-1-958-1349 Fax: 30-1-952-1988

## EASTMAN KODAK COMPANY

343 State Street, Rochester, NY, 14650

Tel: (716) 724-4000     Fax: (716) 724-1089       www.kodak.com

*Develop/mfr. photo and chemicals products, information management/video/copier systems, fibers/plastics for various industry.*

**Kodak (Near East) Inc., PO Box 8253, GR-100-10 Athens, Greece**

## EATON CORPORATION

Eaton Center, 1111 Superior Ave., Cleveland, OH, 44114-2584

Tel: (216) 523-5000     Fax: (216) 479-7068       www.eaton.com

*Advanced technical products for transportation and industrial markets.*

**Eaton Intl. Inc., 6 Queen Frederikis St., Glyfada, Athens, Greece**

## ECOLAB INC.

370 N. Wabasha Street, St. Paul, MN, 55102

Tel: (651) 293-2233     Fax: (651) 293-2379       www.ecolab.com

*Develop/mfr. premium cleaning, sanitizing and maintenance products and services for the hospitality, institutional, and residential markets.*

**Ecolab Ltd., Athens, Greece**

Tel: 30-1-68-11010

## J.D. EDWARDS & COMPANY

One Technology Way, Denver, CO, 80237

Tel: (303) 334-4000     Fax: (303) 334-4970       www.jdedwards.com

*Computer software products.*

**Softecon, 25 Mavromateon Str. & Kotsika, GR-104 34 Athens, Greece**

Tel: 30-1-825-3803    Fax: 30-1-821-8249

## ELECTRONIC DATA SYSTEMS CORPORATION (EDS)

5400 Legacy Dr., Plano, TX, 75024

Tel: (972) 605-6000     Fax: (972) 605-2643       www.eds.com

*Provides professional services; management consulting, e.solutions, business process management and information solutions.*

**EDS Greece, Astronafton 2, GR-151 25 Maroussi, Athens Greece**

Tel: 30-1-680-1142

## ERNST & YOUNG, LLP

787 Seventh Ave., New York, NY, 10019

Tel: (212) 773-3000     Fax: (212) 773-6350       www.eyi.com

*Accounting and audit, tax and management consulting services.*

**Ernst & Young, 3-5 Ilisson St., GR-115 Athens, Greece**

Tel: 30-1-748-8610-20    Fax: 30-1-788-2044    Contact: Themis Lianopoulos

## EURO RSCG WORLDWIDE

350 Hudson Street, New York, NY, 10014

Tel: (212) 886-2000     Fax: (212) 886-2016       www.eurorscg.com

*International advertising agency group.*

**EURO RSCG, 4 Priynis Street, Nea Smyrni, Athens Greece**

## EXPEDITORS INTERNATIONAL OF WASHINGTON INC.

1015 Third Avenue, 12th Fl., Seattle, WA, 98104-1182

Tel: (206) 674-3400     Fax: (206) 682-9777       www.expd.com

*Air/ocean freight forwarding, customs brokerage, international logistics solutions.*

**Expeditors/Planair Ltd., Androutsou 4 St, GR-117-41 Athens, Greece**

## FEDERAL-MOGUL CORPORATION

26555 Northwestern Highway, PO Box 1966, Southfield, MI, 48034

Tel: (248) 354-7700　　Fax: (248) 354-8983　　www.federal-mogul.com

*Mfr./distributor precision parts for automobiles, trucks, farm and construction vehicles.*

**Federal-Mogul de Venezuela CA,　Athens, Greece**

## FERRO CORPORATION

1000 Lakeside Ave., Cleveland, OH, 44114-7000

Tel: (216) 641-8580　　Fax: (216) 696-5784　　www.ferro.com

*Mfr. Specialty chemicals, coatings, plastics, colors, refractories.*

**Ferro B.V.,　14. Makedonias Str., GR-151-24 Maroussi-Athens, Greece**

Tel: 30-1-8062486

## FISHER-ROSEMOUNT

8000 Maryland Ave., Ste. 500, Clayton, MO, 63105-4755

Tel: (314) 746-9900　　Fax: (314) 746-9974　　www.frco.com

*Mfr. industrial process control equipment.*

**TEVEX,　3, Xirogianni St., GR-157-73 Zografos Athens, Greece**

## FMC CORPORATION

200 E. Randolph Drive, Chicago, IL, 60601

Tel: (312) 861-6000　　Fax: (312) 861-6141　　www.fmc.com

*Produces chemicals and precious metals, mfr. machinery, equipment and systems for industrial, agricultural and government use.*

**FMC Smith Meter/Metron Ltd.,　23 Strat. Fragou Street, Elefsina, GR-19200 Greece**

Tel: 301-556-0193

## FORT JAMES CORPORATION

1650 Lake Cook Road, Deerfield, IL, 60015

Tel: (847) 317-5000　　Fax: (847) 236-3755　　www.fortjames.com

*Mfr. and markets consumer tissue products.*

**Fort James Corporation,　Athens, Greece**

**Fort James Corporation,　Patras, Greece**

## FRITZ COMPANIES, INC.

706 Mission Street, Ste. 900, San Francisco, CA, 94103

Tel: (415) 904-8360　　Fax: (415) 904-8661　　www.fritz.com

*Integrated transportation, sourcing, distribution and customs brokerage services.*

**Fritz Companies Inc.,　Athens, Greece**

## GENERAL DYNAMICS CORPORATION

3190 Fairview Park Drive, Falls Church, VA, 22042-4523

Tel: (703) 876-3000　　Fax: (703) 876-3125　　www.gendyn.com

*Mfr. aerospace equipment, submarines, strategic systems, armored vehicles, defense support systems.*

**Hellenic Business Development & Investment Co. SA,　32 Kifissias Ave., Marousi Athens, Greece**

## GENERAL ELECTRIC COMPANY

3135 Easton Turnpike, Fairfield, CT, 06431

Tel: (203) 373-2211　　Fax: (203) 373-3131　　www.ge.com

*Diversified manufacturing, technology and services.*

**General Electric Intl.,　Attn: Greek Office, 3135 Easton Turnpike, Fairfield CT 06431 USA**

Tel: 518-438-6500

## GENERAL MOTORS CORPORATION

300 Renaissance Center, Detroit, MI, 48285

Tel: (313) 556-5000      Fax: (313) 556-5108      www.gm.com

*Mfr. full line vehicles, automotive electronics, commercial technologies, telecommunications, space, finance.*

**General Motors Hellas ABEE, PO Box 61020, Amaroussion, GR-151-10 Athens, Greece**

## GENZYME CORPORATION

1 Kendall Square, Cambridge, MA, 02139-1562

Tel: (617) 252-7500      Fax: (617) 252-7600      www.genzyme.com

*Mfr. healthcare products for enzyme deficient diseases.*

**Jasonpharm & Co., Div. Genzyme Ltd., Ymittou 97, Athens 116 33, Greece**

Tel: 30-1-751-7608

## GILEAD SCIENCES, INC.

333 Lakeside Dr, Foster City, CA, 94404

Tel: (650) 574-3000      Fax: (650) 578-9264      www.gilead.com

*Engaged in healthcare research and development; biotech treatments for viruses.*

**NeXstar Pharmaceuticals, Inc., 602A Vouliagmenis Avenue, 16452 Argiroupolis, Athens, Greece**

Tel: 30-1-996-8758/    Fax: 30-1-996-8777

## THE GILLETTE COMPANY

Prudential Tower Building, Boston, MA, 02199

Tel: (617) 421-7000      Fax: (617) 421-7123      www.gillette.com

*Develop/mfr. personal care/use products: blades and razors, toiletries, cosmetics, stationery.*

**Gillette Greece, Athens, Greece**

Contact: Domenico Ottavis, Gen. Mgr.

## GILSON INC.

3000 W. Beltline Hwy, PO Box 620027, Middleton, WI, 53562-0027

Tel: (608) 836-1551      Fax: (608) 831-4451      www.gilson.com

*Mfr. analytical/biomedical instruments.*

**Meditec S.A., 29 Paradisou & Zagoras str., 151 25 Athens, Greece**

## THE GOODYEAR TIRE & RUBBER COMPANY

1144 East Market Street, Akron, OH, 44316

Tel: (330) 796-2121      Fax: (330) 796-1817      www.goodyear.com

*Mfr. tires, automotive belts and hose, conveyor belts, chemicals; oil pipeline transmission.*

**Goodyear Hellas SAIC, 94 Kifissou Ave., PO Box 41092, GR-122-10 Aibaleo Athens, Greece**

## W. R. GRACE & COMPANY

7500 Grace Drive, Columbia, MD, 21044

Tel: (410) 531-4000      Fax: (410) 531-4367      www.grace.com

*Mfr. specialty chemicals and materials: packaging, health care, catalysts, construction, water treatment/process.*

**Grace Hellas E.P.E., 20 Lagoumitzi St., GR-176-71 Kallitha Athens, Greece**

Tel: 30-1-9231-404    Fax: 30-1-9235-993

## GRANT THORNTON INTERNATIONAL

800 One Prudential Plaza, 130 E. Randolph Drive, Chicago, IL, 60601-6050

Tel: (312) 856-0001      Fax: (312) 616-7052      www.grantthornton.com

*Accounting, audit, tax and management consulting services.*

**Grant Thornton SA, 99 Pratinou & Nereidon Str., 116 34 Athens, Greece**

Tel: 30-172- 53315    Contact: Vassilis Kazas

### GREY GLOBAL GROUP

777 Third Ave., New York, NY, 10017

Tel: (212) 546-2000　　Fax: (212) 546-1495　　www.grey.com

*International advertising agency.*

**Grey Athens, 294 Syngrou Ave., GR-176-73 Kalithea Athens, Greece**

### HALLIBURTON COMPANY

500 North Akard Street, Ste. 3600, Dallas, TX, 75201-3391

Tel: (214) 978-2600　　Fax: (214) 978-2685　　www.halliburton.com

*Engaged in diversified energy services, engineering and construction.*

**Halliburton Ltd., PO Box 1525, GR-651-10 Kavala, Greece**

Tel: 30-51-831-842　Fax: 30-51-831-842

### HARRIS CORPORATION

1025 West NASA Blvd., Melbourne, FL, 32919

Tel: (407) 727-9100　　Fax: (407) 727-9344　　www.harris.com

*Mfr. communications and information-handling equipment, including copying and fax systems.*

**EBV Elektronik, Anaxagora St. 1, GR-177-78 Travros Athens, Greece**

Tel: 30-1-32-53-626　Fax: 30-1-32-16-063

### HASBRO INDUSTRIES INC.

1027 Newport Ave., Pawtucket, RI, 02861

Tel: (401) 725-8697　　Fax: (401) 727-5099　　www.hasbro.com

*Mfr. toy products, including games and puzzles, dolls and plush products.*

**Hasbro Industries, Athens, Greece**

### H.J. HEINZ COMPANY

600 Grant Street, Pittsburgh, PA, 15219

Tel: (412) 456-5700　　Fax: (412) 456-6128　　www.heinz.com

*Processed food products and nutritional services.*

**COPAIS SA, Athens, Greece**

### HEWLETT-PACKARD COMPANY

3000 Hanover Street, Palo Alto, CA, 94304-1185

Tel: (650) 857-1501　　Fax: (650) 857-5518　　www.hp.com

*Mfr. computing, communications and measurement products and services.*

**Hewlett-Packard Hellas, 62 Kifissias Ave., GR-151-25, Greece**

### HILTON HOTELS CORPORATION

9336 Civic Center Drive, Beverly Hills, CA, 90210

Tel: (310) 278-4321　　Fax: (310) 205-7880　　www.hiltonhotels.com

*International hotel chain: Hilton International, Vista Hotels and Hilton National Hotels.*

**Hilton International Hotels, 46 Vassilissis Sofias Ave., GR-115 28 Athens, Greece**

### HOLIDAY INN (BASS RESORTS) WORLDWIDE, INC.

3 Ravinia Drive, Ste. 2900, Atlanta, GA, 30346-2149

Tel: (770) 604-2000　　Fax: (770) 604-5403　　www.holidayinn.com

*Hotels, restaurants and casinos.*

**Holiday Inn Inc., Michalacopoulou 50, Ilissia, Athens, Greece**

### HONEYWELL INTERNATIONAL INC.

101 Columbia Road, Morristown, NJ, 07962

Tel: (973) 455-2000　　Fax: (973) 455-4807　　www.honeywell.com

*Develop/mfr. controls for home and building, industry, space and aviation.*

**Honeywell E.P.E., 313 Irakliou/Ave./1-3 Viotias Str., Neon Iraklion, Athens, Greece**

Tel: 30-1-284-8049　Fax: 30-1-284-8055

## HORWATH INTERNATIONAL ASSOCIATION

415 Madison Ave., New York, NY, 10017

Tel: (212) 838-5566      Fax: (212) 838-3636      www.horwath.com

*Public accountants and auditors.*

**Alexander, Young & Co., 5-7 Filellinon St., GR-185-36 Piraeus, Greece**

**Euroauditing S.A., 25 Stournari Street, 106.82 Athens, Greece**

Tel: 30-1-380-0082

## HOWMEDICA OSTEONICS, INC.

359 Veterans Blvd., Rutherford, NJ, 07070

Tel: (201) 507-7300      Fax: (201) 935-4873      www.howmedica.com

*Mfr. of maxillofacial products (orthopedic implants).*

**Howmedica Greece, Athens, Greece**

Tel: 30-1-330-4318

## IBM CORPORATION

New Orchard Road, Armonk, NY, 10504

Tel: (914) 765-1900      Fax: (914) 765-7382      www.ibm.com

*Information products, technology and services.*

**IBM Hellas S.A., 284 Kifissias Ave., GR-152-32 Halandri, Greece**

Tel: 30-1-688-1220    Fax: 30-1-680-1300

## INFONET SERVICES CORPORATION

2100 East Grand Ave., El Segundo, CA, 90245-1022

Tel: (310) 335-2600      Fax: (310) 335-4507      www.infonet.com

*Provider of Internet services and electronic messaging services.*

**Infonet Greece, 99, Kifissias Ave., GR-151-81 Marousi, Greece**

Tel: 30-1-611-53756    Fax: 30-1-806-4299

## INFORMATION RESOURCES, INC. (IRI)

150 N. Clinton St., Chicago, IL, 60661

Tel: (312) 726-1221      Fax: (312) 726-0360      www.infores.com

*Provides bar code scanner services for retail sales organizations; processes, analyzes and sells data from the huge database created from these services.*

**Information Resources Hellas, 133 Michalakopoulou St., GR-115-27 Athens, Greece**

Tel: 30-1-7488-241    Fax: 30-1-7488-240

## INTER-CONTINENTAL HOTELS

3 Ravina Drive, Suite 2900, Atlanta, GA, 30346-2149

Tel: (770) 604-2000      Fax: (770) 604-5403      www.interconti.com

*Worldwide hotel and resort accommodations.*

**Athenaeum Inter-Continental Athens, 89-93 Syngrou Ave., GR-117-45 Athens, Greece**

Tel: 30-1-920-6000    Fax: 30-1-924-3000

## INTERGRAPH CORPORATION

One Madison Industrial Park, Huntsville, AL, 35894-0001

Tel: (256) 730-2000      Fax: (256) 730-7898      www.intergraph.com

*Develop/mfr. interactive computer graphic systems.*

**Intergraph Hellas S.A, 237 Messogion Ave., GR-154-51 Neo Psychiko Athens, Greece**

Tel: 30-1-6729091    Fax: 30-1-6729094

## INTERMEC TECHNOLOGIES CORPORATION

6001 36th Ave. West, PO Box 4280, Everett, WA, 98203-9280

Tel: (425) 348-2600     Fax: (425) 355-9551     www.intermec.com

*Mfr./distributor automated data collection systems.*

**Intermec Hellas, 125 Michalakopoulou Ave., GR-115-27 Athens, Greece**

## ITT-GOULDS PUMPS INC.

240 Fall Street, Seneca Falls, NY, 13148

Tel: (315) 568-2811     Fax: (315) 568-2418     www.gouldspumps.com

*Mfr. industrial and water systems pumps.*

**Goulds Pumps - Athens, Achileos Kyrou 4 Neo Psychiko, Athens 11525, Greece**

## J. WALTER THOMPSON COMPANY

466 Lexington Ave., New York, NY, 10017

Tel: (212) 210-7000     Fax: (212) 210-6944     www.jwt.com

*International advertising and marketing services.*

**Spot Thompson Athens, Athens, Greece**

## JOHNSON & JOHNSON

One Johnson & Johnson Plaza, New Brunswick, NJ, 08933

Tel: (732) 524-0400     Fax: (732) 214-0334     www.jnj.com

*Mfr./distributor/R&D pharmaceutical, health care and cosmetic products.*

**Janssen-Cilag Pharmaceutical S.A.C.I., 246 Kifissias Ave., Halandri, Athens, Greece**

**Johnson & Johnson Hellas SA, PO Box 65069, GR-154-10 Psychico, Athens, Greece**

**Johnson & Johnson Medical Products SA, Athens, Greece**

## S C JOHNSON & SON INC.

1525 Howe St., Racine, WI, 53403

Tel: (414) 260-2000     Fax: (414) 260-2133     www.scjohnsonwax.com

*Home, auto, commercial and personal care products and specialty chemicals.*

**S.C. Johnson & Son (Hellas), 479 Messogion Ave., 153 Aghia Paraskevi, Athens, Greece**

## KENNAMETAL INC.

State Rte. 981, Latrobe, PA, 15650

Tel: (724) 539-5000     Fax: (724) 539-4710     www.kennametal.com

*Tools, hard carbide and tungsten alloys for metalworking industry.*

**Kennametal / D.Panayoditis - J. Tsatsis S.A., GR-183-46 Moschaton Athens, Greece**

Tel: 30-1-4810-81789   Fax: 30-1-3014-829673

## KORN/FERRY INTERNATIONAL

1800 Century Park East, Los Angeles, CA, 90067

Tel: (310) 843-4100     Fax: (310) 553-6452     www.kornferry.com

*Executive search; management consulting.*

**Korn/Ferry International, Athens, Greece**

Tel: 30-1-777-7718   Fax: 30-1-748-9511

## KPMG INTERNATIONAL LLP

345 Park Avenue, New York, NY, 10022

Tel: (201) 307-7000     Fax: (201) 930-8617     www.kpmg.com

*Accounting and audit, tax and management consulting services.*

**KPMG Peat Marwick Kyriacou, 3 Stratigou Tombra St., GR-153-42 Aghia Paraskevi, Greece**

Tel: 30-1-606-2100   Fax: 30-1-606-2111   Contact: Marios T. Kyriacou, Sr. Ptnr.

## LANIER WORLDWIDE, INC.

2300 Parklake Drive, N.E., Atlanta, GA, 30345

Tel: (770) 496-9500      Fax: (770) 938-1020      www.lanier.com

*Specialize in digital copiers and multi-functional systems.*

**Lanier Hellas AEBE, Eleon 29, GR-145-64 Kifissias Athens, Greece**

Tel: 30-1-807-8212    Fax: 30-1-807-8014

## LEVI STRAUSS & COMPANY

1155 Battery St., San Francisco, CA, 94111-1230

Tel: (415) 544-6000      Fax: (415) 501-3939      www.levistrauss.com

*Mfr./distributor casual wearing apparel.*

**Levi Strauss Hellas, AEBE, 11 Argonafton Street, GR-152-32 Halandri Athens, Greece**

Tel: 30-1-685-6350    Fax: 30-1-685-6271

## ELI LILLY & COMPANY

Lilly Corporate Center, Indianapolis, IN, 46285

Tel: (317) 276-2000      Fax: (317) 277-6579      www.lilly.com

*Mfr. pharmaceuticals and animal health products.*

**Pharmaserve-Lilly Saci, 15th KLM National Rd., Athens-Lamia, GR-145-64 Kifissias Athens, Greece**

Tel: 30-1-629-4600    Fax: 30-1-629-4610

## LOCKHEED MARTIN CORPORATION

6801 Rockledge Drive, Bethesda, MD, 20817

Tel: (301) 897-6000      Fax: (301) 897-6652      www.imco.com

*Design/mfr./management systems in fields of space, defense, energy, electronics and technical services.*

**Lockheed Martin International S.A., 9 Giannitson Street, Holargos, GR-155 62 Athens, Greece**

Tel: 30-1-654-7082    Fax: 30-1-653-6632    Contact: Alex K. Papadimitrious, Dir.

**Lockheed-Hellas S.A., 64 Kifissias Ave., 32 Maroussi, GR-151-25 Athens, Greece**

## LOWE LINTAS & PARTNERS WORLDWIDE

One Dag Hammarskjold Plaza, New York, NY, 10017

Tel: (212) 605-8000      Fax: (212) 605-4705      www.interpublic.com

*Full-service, integrated marketing communications company/advertising agency.*

**Ammirati Puris Lintas, Atrina Ctr., 32 Kifissias Ave., GR-151-25 Marcoussi Athens, Greece**

Tel: 30-1-684-5902    Fax: 30-1-684-5980    Contact: Vangelis Yannakos, Mng. Dir.

**Lintas Sprint, 22 Kifissias Ave., GR-151-25 Marcoussi Athens, Greece**

Tel: 30-1-6845-570    Fax: 30-1-6845-515    Contact: Dinos Lambrinopoulos

## THE LUBRIZOL CORPORATION

29400 Lakeland Blvd., Wickliffe, OH, 44092-2298

Tel: (440) 943-4200      Fax: (440) 943-5337      www.lubrizol.com

*Mfr. chemicals additives for lubricants and fuels.*

**Lubrizol Greece, Athens, Greece**

Tel: 30-1-933-5367

## LYRIC HIGH FIDELITY INC.

1221 Lexington Ave., New York, NY, 10028

Tel: (212) 535-5710      Fax:      www.lyricusa.com

*Electrical equipment.*

**Lyric High Fidelity Center (Athens), 52 Alexandras Ave., Athens, Greece**

## MARRIOTT INTERNATIONAL INC.

10400 Fernwood Rd., Bethesda, MD, 20817

Tel: (301) 380-3000     Fax: (301) 380-5181     www.marriott.com

*Hotel services.*

**Athlens Ledra Marriott Hotel,  Athens, Greece**

## MARSH & McLENNAN COS INC.

1166 Ave. of the Americas, New York, NY, 10036-2774

Tel: (212) 345-5000     Fax: (212) 345-4808     www.marshmac.com

*Insurance agents/brokers, pension and investment management consulting services.*

**Marsh & McLennan-Hellas LLC,  124 Kifissias Ave., Ambelokipi, GR-115-26 Athens, Greece**

Tel: 30-1-685-7575   Fax: 30-1-685-7573   Contact: Panayiotis Lisseos

## McCANN-ERICKSON WORLDGROUP

750 Third Ave., New York, NY, 10017

Tel: (212) 984-3644     Fax: (212) 984-2629     www.mccann.com

*International advertising and marketing services.*

**McCann-Erickson (Hellas) LLC,  7 Ventiri St., GR-115-28 Athens, Greece**

## McDONALD'S CORPORATION

McDonald's Plaza, Oak Brook, IL, 60523

Tel: (630) 623-3000     Fax: (630) 623-7409     www.mcdonalds.com

*Fast food chain stores.*

**McDonald's Corp.,  Athens, Greece**

## THE McGRAW-HILL COMPANIES

1221 Ave. of the Americas, New York, NY, 10020

Tel: (212) 512-2000     Fax: (212) 512-2703     www.mccgraw-hill.com

*Books, magazines, information systems, financial service, publishing and broadcast operations.*

**McGraw-Hll Hellas,  21A Patriarchou Gregoriou E. Str. 153 41 Ag. Paraskevi Athens, Greece**

## MECHANICAL DYNAMICS, INC.

2301 Commonwealth Blvd., Ann Arbor, MI, 48105

Tel: (734) 994-3800     Fax: (734) 994-6418     www.adams.com

*Mfr. Adams prototyping software to automotive industry.*

**Omega Vision 2000 s.a.,  Ravine 22, #1 Kolonaki, GR-115 21 Athens, Greece**

Tel: 30-1-725-2044

## MERCK & COMPANY, INC.

One Merck Drive, PO Box 100, Whitehouse Station, NJ, 08889-0100

Tel: (908) 423-1000     Fax: (908) 423-2592     www.merck.com

*Pharmaceuticals, chemicals and biologicals.*

**Merck, Sharp & Dohme Inc.,  Athens Tower, Messogion 2-4, Athens, Greece**

## MERRILL LYNCH & COMPANY, INC.

World Financial Center, 250 Vesey Street, New York, NY, 10281-1332

Tel: (212) 449-1000     Fax: (212) 449-2892     www.ml.com

*Security brokers and dealers, investment and business services.*

**Merrill Lynch, Pierce, Fenner & Smith Hellas LLC,  17 Valaorithous Street, GR-106-71 Athens, Greece**

Tel: 30-1-361-8916   Fax: 30-1-364-8046

## M-I

PO Box 48242, Houston, TX, 77242-2842

Tel: (713) 739-0222      Fax: (713) 308-9503      www.midf.com

*Drilling fluids.*

**MIOL Greece, PO Box 1291, Kavala, Greece 65110**

Tel: 30-51-223530    Fax: 30-51-837017

## MICROSOFT CORPORATION

One Microsoft Way, Redmond, WA, 98052-6399

Tel: (425) 882-8080      Fax: (425) 936-7329      www.microsoft.com

*Computer software, peripherals and services.*

**Microsoft Greece, 64 Kifissias Ave., Polis Centre, GR-151-25 Maroussi Athens, Greece**

Tel: 30-1-680-6775    Fax: 30-1-680-6780

## J. P. MORGAN CHASE & CO. INC.

World Headquarters, 270 Park Ave., New York, NY, 10017

Tel: (212) 270-6000      Fax: (212) 622-9030      www.jpmorganchase.com

*Provides integrated financial solutions for institutions and individuals worldwide, including asset management, investment banking and commercial banking.*

**J. P. Morgan Chase & Co., PO Box 89, 95 Akti Miaouli, GR-185-10 Piraeus, Greece**

Tel: 30-1-42-90-678    Fax: 30-1-42-90-693

**J. P. Morgan Chase & Co., 3 Korai St., PO Box3005, GR-102-10 Athens, Greece**

## MOTOROLA, INC.

1303 East Algonquin Road, Schaumburg, IL, 60196

Tel: (847) 576-5000      Fax: (847) 538-5191      www.motorola.com

*Mfr. communications equipment, semiconductors and cellular phones.*

**Motorola Greece, 22 Kifissias Ave., GR-151-25 Maroussi Athens, Greece**

Tel: 30-1-689-0898    Fax: 30-1-684-3079

## NABISCO HOLDINGS, CORP.

7 Campus Drive, Parsippany, NJ, 07054

Tel: (973) 682-5000      Fax: (973) 503-2153      www.nabisco.com

*Mfr. consumer packaged food products and tobacco products.*

**R.J. Reynolds Tobacco (Hellas) AEBE, 506 Athens Tower B, Athens 610, Greece**

## A .C. NIELSEN COMPANY

177 Broad Street, Stamford, CT, 06901

Tel: (203) 961-3000      Fax: (203) 961-3190      www.acnielsen.com

*Market and consumer research firm.*

**A.C. Nielsen Hellas Ltd., 196 Sygrou Ave., GR-176-71 Kallithea, Athens, Greece**

## NORDSON CORPORATION

28601 Clemens Road, Westlake, OH, 44145-4551

Tel: (440) 892-1580      Fax: (440) 892-9507      www.nordson.com

*Mfr. industry application equipment, sealants and packaging machinery.*

**Meltko S.A., 54 Korai Str., 18345 Moschato, Athens, Greece**

Tel: 30-1-940-7907

## OGILVY PUBLIC RELATIONS WORLDWIDE

909 Third Ave., New York, NY, 10022

Tel: (212) 880-5201      Fax: (212) 697-8250      www.ogilvypr.com

*Engaged in public relations and communications.*

**Stigma Communication Ltd./Ogilvy, 7 Granikou Street, 15125 Maroussi Athens, Greece**

Contact: Marina Leonidhopoulos

## OPTEK TECHNOLOGY, INC.

1215 West Crosby Road, Carrollton, TX, 75006

Tel: (972) 323-2200    Fax: (972) 323-2208    www.optekinc.com

*Mfr. standard and custom sensors utilizing infrared and magnetic devices.*

**Optrionics Yet, El. Venizelou 222, 175 63 Pal. Faliro, Athens Greece**

## OTIS ELEVATOR COMPANY

10 Farm Springs Road, Farmington, CT, 06032

Tel: (860) 676-6000    Fax: (860) 676-5111    www.otis.com

*Mfr. elevators and escalators.*

**C. Veremis Otis SA, 38 Bouboulinco St., GR-106-82 Athens, Greece**

## PANAMETRICS

221 Crescent Street, Waltham, MA, 02154

Tel: (781) 899-2719    Fax: (781) 899-1552    www.panametrics.com

*Process/non-destructive test instrumentation.*

**Meta Engineering, 54 Agias Marinis St., GR-151-27 Melissia Athens Hellas, Greece**

Tel: 30-1-613-0929   Fax: 30-1-613-1329

## PANDUIT CORPORATION

17301 Ridgeland Ave., Tinley Park, IL, 60477-0981

Tel: (708) 532-1800    Fax: (708) 532-1811    www.panduit.com

*Mfr. electrical/electronic wiring components.*

**Panduit Greece, 56 AG. Paraskevis St., Elliniko 16777, Greece**

Tel: 30-1-9931816

## PEPSiCO INC.

700 Anderson Hill Road, Purchase, NY, 10577-1444

Tel: (914) 253-2000    Fax: (914) 253-2070    www.pepsico.com

*Beverages and snack foods.*

**PepsiCo IVI SA, Athens, Greece**

## PFIZER INC.

235 East 42nd Street, New York, NY, 10017-5755

Tel: (212) 573-2323    Fax: (212) 573-7851    www.pfizer.com

*Research-based, global health care company.*

**Pfizer Hellas AE, Athens, Greece**

## PHARMACIA CORPORATION

100 Route 206 North, Peapack, NJ, 07977

Tel: (908) 901-8000    Fax: (908) 901-8379    www.pharmacia.com

*Mfr. pharmaceuticals, agricultural products, industry chemicals.*

**Pharmacia & Upjohn, 61-66 Marinou Antypas Str., GR-141 21 N. Irklio Athens, Greece**

## PHELPS DODGE CORPORATION

2600 North Central Ave., Phoenix, AZ, 85004-3089

Tel: (602) 234-8100    Fax: (602) 234-8337    www.phelpsdodge.com

*Copper, minerals, metals and special engineered products for transportation and electrical markets.*

**Viem Metal Works SA, 115 Kifissias Ave., GR-115-24 Athens, Greece**

## PINNACLE WORLDWIDE, INC.

1201 Marquette Ave., Ste. 300, Minneapolis, MN, 55403

Tel: (612) 338-2215    Fax: (612) 338-2572    www.pinnacleww.com

*International network of independent public relations firms.*

**Connective Communication Ltd., V. Sofias Ave. 5 Xenias Str., 11527 Athens, Greece**

# PIONEER HI-BRED INTERNATIONAL INC.

400 Locust Street, Ste. 800, Des Moines, IA, 50309

Tel: (515) 248-4800    Fax: (515) 248-4999    www.pioneer.com

*Agricultural chemicals, farm supplies, biological products, research.*

**Athens HellaSeed, 15 Fleming Street, Marousi Athens, Greece**

# PREMARK INTERNATIONAL INC.

1717 Deerfield Road, Deerfield, IL, 60015

Tel: (847) 405-6000    Fax: (847) 405-6013    www.premarkintl.com

*Mfr. Hobart commercial food equipment, diversified consumer and commercial products, small appliances, and exercise equipment.*

**Dart Hellas SAI, 4 Academias St., Athens, Greece**

# PRICEWATERHOUSECOOPERS LLP

1301 Ave. of the Americas, New York, NY, 10019

Tel: (212) 596-7000    Fax: (212) 259-1301    www.pwcglobal.com

*Accounting and auditing, tax and management, and human resource consulting services.*

**PriceWaterhouseCoopers, Europa Plaza 5th Fl., 330 El Venizelou (Thisseos) Ave., GR-176-75 Kallithea Athens, Greece**

Tel: 30-1-9308180    Fax: 30-1-9308182

# PROCTER & GAMBLE COMPANY

One Procter & Gamble Plaza, Cincinnati, OH, 45202

Tel: (513) 983-1100    Fax: (513) 562-4500    www.pg.com

*Personal care, food, laundry, cleaning and industry products.*

**Procter & Gamble Hellas SA, 165 Syngrou Ave., GR-171-21 N. Smyrni, Athens, Greece**

Tel: 30-1-939-4300

# PROCTER & GAMBLE PHARMACEUTICALS (P&GP)

17 Eaton Ave., Norwich, NY, 13815-1799

Tel: (607) 335-2111    Fax: (607) 335-2798    www.pg.com

*Develop/manufacture pharmaceuticals, chemicals and health products.*

**Eaton Laboratories (Hellas), 28 Kapodistriou St., Athens, Greece**

# QUINTILES TRANSNATIONAL CORPORATION

4709 Creekstone Dr., Durham, NC, 27703

Tel: (919) 998-2000    Fax: (919) 998-9113    www.quintiles.com

*Mfr. pharmaceuticals.*

**Quintiles Athens, Themistocleous 25, Maroussi 151 25 Athens, Greece**

# R&B FALCON CORPORATION

901 Threadneedle, Ste. 200, Houston, TX, 77079

Tel: (281) 496-5000    Fax: (281) 496-4363    www.rbfalcon.com

*Offshore contract drilling.*

**R&B Falcon International Energy Services B.V., 2 Filellinon Street, 65302 Kavala, Greece**

# ROHM AND HAAS COMPANY

100 Independence Mall West, Philadelphia, PA, 19106

Tel: (215) 592-3000    Fax: (215) 592-3377    www.rohmhaas.com

*Mfr. industrial and agricultural chemicals, plastics.*

**Rohm and Haas Greece Ltd., 9 Leontariou St., Alsoupolis, GR-142-35 Nea Ionia, Athens Greece**

Tel: 30-1-6843-780

## SCHENKER INTERNATIONAL FORWARDERS INC.

150 Albany Ave., Freeport, NY, 11520

Tel: (516) 377-3000      Fax: (516) 377-3005      www.schenkerusa.com

*Freight forwarders.*

**Schenker A.E., Zefyrou St., 12 Paleo Faliro, PO Box 77281, Athens Greece**

Tel: 30-1-950-2111   Fax: 30-1-930-1560

## SCHERING-PLOUGH CORPORATION

One Giralda Farms, Madison, NJ, 07940-1000

Tel: (973) 822-7000      Fax: (973) 822-7048      www.sch-plough.com

*Proprietary drug and cosmetic products.*

**Schering-Plough Veterinary S.A.,  63 Ag. Dimitriou str., 17455 Alimos, Athens Greece**

## G.D. SEARLE & COMPANY

5200 Old Orchard Road, Skokie, IL, 60077

Tel: (847) 982-7000      Fax: (847) 470-1480      www.searlehealthnet.com

*Mfr. pharmaceuticals, health care, optical products and specialty chemicals.*

**Serale Vianex, 38 Kifissias St., GR-151-25 Athens, Greece**

Tel: 30-1-958-8325   Fax: 30-1-958-5078

## SNAP-ON INCORPORATED

10801 Corporate Dr., Pleasant Prairie, WI, 53158-1603

Tel: (262) 656-5200      Fax: (262) 656-5577      www.snapon.com

*Mfr. auto maintenance, diagnostic and emission testing equipment, hand tools, hydraulic lifts and tire changers.*

**Snap-On Tools Intl. Ltd.,  PO Box 65033, GR-154-10 Psychico Athens, Greece**

## SOCOTAB LEAF TOBACCO COMPANY, INC.

706 Ellis Road, Durham, NC, 27703

Tel: (919) 596-4993      Fax: (919) 596-2902

*Tobacco dealer.*

**Socotab Leaf Tobacco Co.,  PO Box  10007, GR-541-10 Thessaloniki, Greece**

## SOLUTIA INC.

575 Maryville Center Dr, St. Louis, MO, 63141

Tel: (314) 674-1000      Fax: (314) 694-8686      www.solutia.com

*Mfr. specialty chemical based products.*

**Solutia Europe SA/NV,  Tatoiou 122 and Parthenonos St., 14671 Nea Erithrea, Athens Greece**

## SONOCO PRODUCTS COMPANY

North Second Street, PO Box 160, Hartsville, SC, 29550

Tel: (843) 383-7000      Fax: (843) 383-7008      www.sonoco.com

*Mfr. packaging for consumer and industrial market and recycled paperboard.*

**Evien (Office), 2-Vas. Georgion St., GR-546 40 Thessaloniki, Greece**

Tel: 30-31-84-1474

**Evien (Plant), PO Box 96, GR-570-08 Ionia Thessaloniki, Greece**

Tel: 30-31-78-0098

## SPRAYING SYSTEMS COMPANY

PO Box 7900, Wheaton, IL, 60189-7900

Tel: (630) 665-5000      Fax: (630) 260-0842      www.spray.com

*Designs and manufactures industrial spray nozzles.*

**Spraying Systems Hellas SA,  4 Tziraion Street, 117 42 Athens, Greece**

## THE ST. PAUL COMPANIES, INC.

385 Washington Street, St. Paul, MN, 55102

Tel: (651) 310-7911      Fax: (651) 310-8294      www.stpaul.com

*Provides investment, insurance and reinsurance services.*

**Olympic Victoria General Insurance Co., S.A., 21 Tsimiski, GR-546-24 Thessaloniki, Greece**

## STANDARD COMMERCIAL CORPORATION

2201 Miller Rd., PO Box 450, Wilson, NC, 27893

Tel: (919) 291-5507      Fax: (919) 237-1109      www.sccgroup.com

*Leaf tobacco dealers/processors and wool processors.*

**Exelka SA, 6 Km Simmachiki Odos, 57013 Paleokastro, Thessoloniki, Greece**

**Transhellenic Tobacco SA, Salonika, Greece**

## THE STANLEY WORKS

1000 Stanley Drive, PO Box 7000, New Britain, CT, 06053

Tel: (860) 225-5111      Fax: (860) 827-3987      www.stanleyworks.com

*Mfr. hand tools and hardware.*

**Stanley Works (Sales) Ltd., PO Box 18, Kallithea, Athens, Greece**

## STIEFEL LABORATORIES INC.

255 Alhambra Circle, Ste. 1000, Coral Gables, FL, 33134

Tel: (305) 443-3807      Fax: (305) 443-3467      www.stiefel.com

*Mfr. pharmaceuticals, dermatological specialties.*

**Stiefel Laboratories SA, PO Box 67247, GR-151-92 Melissia, Athens, Greece**

## TBWA CHIAT/DAY

488 Madison Avenue, 6th Floor, New York, NY, 10022

Tel: (212) 804-1000      Fax: (212) 804-1200      www.tbwachiat.com

*International full service advertising agency.*

**TBWA Producta, Athens, Greece**

## TEXACO INC.

2000 Westchester Ave., White Plains, NY, 10650

Tel: (914) 253-4000      Fax: (914) 253-7753      www.texaco.com

*Exploration/marketing crude oil, mfr. petro chemicals and products.*

**Texaco Greek Petroleum Co. SA, Katehaki, Athens, Greece**

## THE TRANE COMPANY

3600 Pammel Creek Road, La Crosse, WI, 54601

Tel: (608) 787-2000      Fax: (608) 787-4990      www.trane.com

*Mfr./distributor/service A/C systems and equipment.*

**Trane Hellas, 7 Zoodohou, Pigis 3, GR-152-31 Halandri Athens, Greece**

## TRANS WORLD AIRLINES INC.

515 North Sixth Street, St. Louis, MO, 63101

Tel: (314) 589-3000      Fax: (314) 589-3129      www.twa.com

*Air transport services.*

**Trans World Airlines Inc., 8 Xenophontos & Philellinon Sts., Athens, Greece**

Tel: 30-1-322-6451

## TRUE NORTH COMMUNICATIONS INC.

101 East Erie Street, Chicago, IL, 60611

Tel: (312) 425-6500      Fax: (312) 425-5010      www.truenorth.com

*Holding company, advertising agency.*

**Horizon Athens, City Plaza, 85 Vouliagmenis Ave., GR-166-74 Glyfada Athens, Greece**

## UNION CARBIDE CORPORATION
39 Old Ridgebury Road, Danbury, CT, 06817

Tel: (203) 794-2000      Fax: (203) 794-6269      www.unioncarbide.com

*Mfr. industrial chemicals, plastics and resins.*

**Union Carbide Middle East Ltd., PO Box Psyhico 65045, GR-154-10 Athens, Greece**

## UNITED PARCEL SERVICE, INC.
55 Glenlake Parkway, NE, Atlanta, GA, 30328

Tel: (404) 828-6000      Fax: (404) 828-6593      www.ups.com

*International package-delivery service.*

**UPS Greece Inc. - Head Office, 98a Alimou Ave., GR-164-52 Argiroupoli Athens, Greece**

Tel: 30-1-9966840

## UNITED TECHNOLOGIES CORPORATION
One Financial Plaza, Hartford, CT, 06103

Tel: (860) 728-7000      Fax: (860) 728-7979      www.utc.com

*Mfr. aircraft engines, elevators, A/C, auto equipment, space and military electronic and rocket propulsion systems. Products include Pratt and Whitney, Otis elevators, Carrier heating and air conditioning and Sikorsky helicopters.*

**Carrier Intl. Corp., 2-4 Mesogion St., Athens, Greece**

## UNIVERSAL CORPORATION
1501 N. Hamilton Street, Richmond, VA, 23230

Tel: (804) 359-9311      Fax: (804) 254-3582      www.universalcorp.com

*Holding company for tobacco and commodities.*

**Gretoba SA, PO Box 169, Thessaloniki, Greece**

## URS CORPORATION
100 California Street, Ste. 500, San Francisco, CA, 94111-4529

Tel: (415) 774-2700      Fax: (415) 398-1904      www.urscorp.com

*Provides planning, design and construction management services, pollution control and hazardous waste management.*

**URS (O'Brien Kreitzberg), Athens, Greece**

## UUNET
22001 Loudoun County Pkwy., Ashburn, VA, 20147

Tel: (703) 206-5600      Fax: (703) 206-5601      www.uu.net

*World's largest Internet service provider; World Wide Web hosting services, security products and consulting services to businesses, professionals, and on-line service providers.*

**UUNET Hellas, 90 Kifissias Avenue, 151 25 Marousi, Athens, Greece**

## VERIZON
1095 Ave. of the Americas, New York, NY, 10036

Tel: (212) 395-2121      Fax: (212) 395-1285      www.verizon.com

*Telecommunications.*

**STET Hellas Telecommunications S.A., 60 Kifissias Avenue Maroussi, 15125 Athens, Greece**

Tel: 30-1-618-6000   Fax: 30-1-610-6504   Contact: Roberto Rovera, CEO

## VERIZON COMMUNICATIONS INC.
1255 Corporate Drive, Irving, TX, 75038

Tel: (972) 507-5000      Fax: (972) 507-5002      www.gte.com

*Engaged in wireline and wireless communications.*

**STET Hellas Telecommunications, S.A., Athens, Greece**

Contact: Roberto Rovera

## THE VIKING CORPORATION

210 N. Industrial Park Rd., Hastings, MI, 49058

Tel: (616) 945-9501     Fax: (616) 945-9599     www.vikingcorp.com

*Mfr. fire extinguishing equipment.*

**Viking Greece, Karali 19 GR - 015669, Papagou Athens, Greece**

## WACKENHUT CORPORATION

4200 Wackenhut Dr., Ste. 100, Palm Beach Gardens, FL, 33410

Tel: (561) 622-5656     Fax: (561) 691-6736     www.wackenhut.com

*Security systems and services.*

**Wackenhut Security (Hellas) Ltd., 100 Kapodistriou St. GR-142-35 Alsoupolis, Athens, Greece**

Tel: 30-1-2714-870    Fax: 30-1-2714-500

## WENDY'S INTERNATIONAL, INC.

428 West Dublin Granville Roads, Dublin, OH, 43017-0256

Tel: (614) 764-3100     Fax: (614) 764-3459     www.wendysintl.com

*Fast food restaurant chain.*

**Wendy's International, Athens, Greece**

## WHIRLPOOL CORPORATION

2000 N. M-63, Benton Harbor, MI, 49022-2692

Tel: (616) 923-5000     Fax: (616) 923-5443     www.whirlpoolcorp.com

*Mfr./market home appliances: Whirlpool, Roper, KitchenAid, Estate, and Inglis.*

**Whirlpool Europe BV, Athens, Greece**

## WHITEHALL-ROBINS INC.

1407 Cummings Drive, PO Box 26609, Richmond, VA, 23261-6609

Tel: (804) 257-2000     Fax: (804) 257-2120     www.ahp.com

*Mfr. ethical pharmaceuticals and consumer healthcare products.*

**Whitehall-Robins Intl. Co., Athens, Greece**

## WORLD COURIER INC.

1313 Fourth Ave., New Hyde Park, NY, 11041

Tel: (516) 354-2600     Fax: (516) 354-2644     www.worldcourier.com

*International courier service.*

**World Courier Hellas, 27 Skoufa St., Athens, Greece**

## WYETH-AYERST INTERNATIONAL INC.

150 Radnot-Chester Road, St. Davids, PA, 19087

Tel: (610) 902-4100     Fax: (610) 989-4586     www.ahp.com/wyeth

*Antibiotics and pharmaceutical products.*

**Wyeth Hellas SA, Chrysostomou Smyrnis, 126 Kyprou Ave. Argyroupolis, Athens Greece**

Tel: 30-1-998-1600

## XEROX CORPORATION

800 Long Ridge Road, PO Box 1600, Stamford, CT, 06904

Tel: (203) 968-3000     Fax: (203) 968-4312     www.xerox.com

*Mfr. document processing equipment, systems and supplies.*

**Rank Xerox Greece SA, 127 Syngrou Ave., Kalithea, GR-117-45 Athens, Greece**

Tel: 30-1-931-1000    Fax: 30-1-931-1075

## YORK INTERNATIONAL CORPORATION

631 South Richland Ave., York, PA, 17403

Tel: (717) 771-7890     Fax: (717) 771-6212     www.york.com

*Mfr. heating, ventilating, air conditioning and refrigeration equipment.*

**York Hellas S.A., 62 Kifissias Avenue, Athens 11526, Greece**

## YOUNG & RUBICAM INC.

285 Madison Ave., New York, NY, 10017

Tel: (212) 210-3000     Fax: (212) 370-3796     www.yr.com

*Advertising, public relations, direct marketing and sales promotion, corporate and product ID management.*

**Geo Young & Rubicam Inc., Athens, Greece**

# Greenland

## DELOITTE TOUCHE TOHMATSU INTERNATIONAL

1633 Broadway, New York, NY, 10019

Tel: (212) 492-4000     Fax: (212) 392-4154     www.deloitte.com

*Accounting, audit, tax and management consulting services.*

**Deloitte & Touche, Skibshavnsvej 22, Postbox 20, DK-3900 Nuuk, Greenland**

## DHL WORLDWIDE EXPRESS

50 California Avenue, San Francisco, CA, 94111

Tel: (415) 677-6100     Fax: (415) 824-9700     www.dhl.com

*Worldwide air express carrier.*

**DHL Worldwide Express, CPH CO, Greenland**

Tel: 45-7013-1131

## POLARIS INDUSTRIES INC.

2100 Highway 55, Medina, MN, 55440

Tel: (612) 542-0500     Fax: (612) 542-0599     www.polarisindustries.com

*Mfr. snowmobiles and all-terrain recreational and utility vehicles.*

**Polaris Import Greenland, Po Box 142, Qivittoqarfik Nr. 17, Holsteinsborg 3911, Greenland**

Contact: Ole Andersen

# Grenada

## AON CORPORATION

123 North Wacker Drive, Chicago, IL, 60606

Tel: (312) 701-3000    Fax: (312) 701-3100    www.aon.com

*Insurance brokers worldwide; underwrites accident and health insurance, specialty and professional insurance; and provides risk management consultation.*

**AON Worldwide / L.H. Williams Marketing Agency Ltd.,  Gore St., PO Box 213, St. George's, Grenada**

Tel: 471-440-2179   Fax: 471-440-4187   Contact: L.H. Williams

## LOUIS BERGER INTERNATIONAL INC.

100 Halsted Street, East Orange, NJ, 07019

Tel: (201) 678-1960    Fax: (201) 672-4284    www.louisberger.com

*Consulting engineers, engaged in architecture, environmental and advisory services.*

**Louis Berger International Inc.,  PO Box 445, St. George's, Grenada**

Tel: 471-444-4687   Fax: 471-444-4822

## DHL WORLDWIDE EXPRESS

50 California Avenue, San Francisco, CA, 94111

Tel: (415) 677-6100    Fax: (415) 824-9700    www.dhl.com

*Worldwide air express carrier.*

**DHL Worldwide Express,  Carenage PO Box 188, St. George's, Grenada**

Tel: 599-542-952

## FRITZ COMPANIES, INC.

706 Mission Street, Ste. 900, San Francisco, CA, 94103

Tel: (415) 904-8360    Fax: (415) 904-8661    www.fritz.com

*Integrated transportation, sourcing, distribution and customs brokerage services.*

**Fritz Companies Inc.,  St. George's, Grenada**

## RENAISSANCE HOTELS AND RESORTS

10400 Fernwood Road, Bethesda, MD, 20817

Tel: (301) 380-3000    Fax: (301) 380-5181    www.renaissancehotels.com

*Hotel and resort chain.*

**Renaissance Grenada Resort,  St. George's, Grenada**

Tel: 809-221-2222

# Guam

## AON CORPORATION

123 North Wacker Drive, Chicago, IL, 60606

Tel: (312) 701-3000    Fax: (312) 701-3100    www.aon.com

*Insurance brokers worldwide; underwrites accident and health insurance, specialty and professional insurance; and provides risk management consultation.*

**AON Insurance Micronesia (Guam) Inc.,  Aon Building, Hengi Plaza, Tamuning Guam 96911**

Tel: 671-646-3681   Fax: 671-646-8084   Contact: Garry J. Curran

## BERGEN BRUNSWIG CORPORATION

4000 Metropolitan Drive, Orange, CA, 92868-3598

Tel: (714) 385-4000    Fax: (714) 385-1442    www.bergenbrunswig.com

*Wholesale pharmaceutical distributor supplying drugs and medical/surgical supplies to managed care facilities and hospitals.*

**Bergen Brunswig Corp.,  Tamuning, Guam**

## BRISTOL-MYERS SQUIBB COMPANY

345 Park Ave., New York, NY, 10154-0037

Tel: (212) 546-4000    Fax: (212) 546-4020    www.bms.com

*Pharmaceutical and food preparations, medical and surgical instruments.*

**Bristol-Myers (Guam),  PO Box 9007, Tamuning, Guam 96911**

## CITIGROUP, INC.

153 East 53rd Street, New York, NY, 10043

Tel: (212) 559-1000    Fax: (212) 559-3646    www.citigroup.com

*Provides insurance and financial services worldwide.*

**Citibank N.A.,  402 East Marine Drive, PO Box FF, Agana Guam 69632**

Tel: 671-475-4121   Contact: Renzo C. Viegas

## DELOITTE TOUCHE TOHMATSU INTERNATIONAL

1633 Broadway, New York, NY, 10019

Tel: (212) 492-4000    Fax: (212) 392-4154    www.deloitte.com

*Accounting, audit, tax and management consulting services.*

**Deloitte & Touche,  361 South Marine Drive, Tamuning, Guam 966911**

## DHL WORLDWIDE EXPRESS

50 California Avenue, San Francisco, CA, 94111

Tel: (415) 677-6100    Fax: (415) 824-9700    www.dhl.com

*Worldwide air express carrier.*

**DHL Worldwide Express,  c/o Republic Express, PO Box 497, Koror Palau Guam 96940**

Tel: 671-646-1765

## EA INTERNATIONAL, INC.

11019 McCormick Road, Hunt Valley, MD, 21031

Tel: (410) 584-7000    Fax: (410) 771-1625    www.eaest.com

*Environmental engineering and consulting, pollution control and water resources management.*

**EA International, Inc.,  PO Box 4355, Andersen AFB, Yigo, Guam 96929**

Tel: 671-366-5231   Fax: 671-366-3902   Contact: Joel L. Lazzeri, Installation Mgr.   Emp: 8

**EA International, Inc.,  PO Box 4355 AFBB, Yigo, Guam 96929-4355**

## EAGLE GLOBAL LOGISTICS (EGL)

15350 Vickery Drive, Houston, TX, 77032

Tel: (281) 618-3100   Fax: (281) 618-3100   www.eaglegl.com

*Ocean/air freight forwarding, customs brokerage, packing and wholesale, logistics management and insurance.*

**Westpac Freight (Guam),  Harmon Industrial Park, Harmon, Guam**

Tel: 671-649-6291   Fax: 671-649-6290

## ERNST & YOUNG, LLP

787 Seventh Ave., New York, NY, 10019

Tel: (212) 773-3000   Fax: (212) 773-6350   www.eyi.com

*Accounting and audit, tax and management consulting services.*

**Ernst & Young,  Orlean Pacific Plaza Ste. B 201, 865 South Marine Drive, Tamuning, Guam 96911**

Tel: 671-649-3700   Fax: 671-649-3920   Contact: Lance Kamigaki

## FRITZ COMPANIES, INC.

706 Mission Street, Ste. 900, San Francisco, CA, 94103

Tel: (415) 904-8360   Fax: (415) 904-8661   www.fritz.com

*Integrated transportation, sourcing, distribution and customs brokerage services.*

**Fritz Companies Inc.,  Tamuning, Guam**

## HILTON HOTELS CORPORATION

9336 Civic Center Drive, Beverly Hills, CA, 90210

Tel: (310) 278-4321   Fax: (310) 205-7880   www.hiltonhotels.com

*International hotel chain: Hilton International, Vista Hotels and Hilton National Hotels.*

**Guam Hilton,  Tumon Bay, PO Box 11199, Tamuning, Guam 96931**

## HYATT CORPORATION

200 West Madison Street, Chicago, IL, 60606

Tel: (312) 750-1234   Fax: (312) 750-8578   www.hyatt.com

*International hotel management.*

**Hyatt Regency Guam Resort,  1155 Pale San Vitores Rd., Tumon, Guam 96911**

Tel: 671-647-1234   Fax: 671-647-1235

## LOCKHEED MARTIN CORPORATION

6801 Rockledge Drive, Bethesda, MD, 20817

Tel: (301) 897-6000   Fax: (301) 897-6652   www.imco.com

*Design/mfr./management systems in fields of space, defense, energy, electronics and technical services.*

**Airport Group International, Inc.,  AB Wonpat Int'l Airport, PO Box 7418, Tamuning Guam 96931**

## MOTOROLA, INC.

1303 East Algonquin Road, Schaumburg, IL, 60196

Tel: (847) 576-5000   Fax: (847) 538-5191   www.motorola.com

*Mfr. communications equipment, semiconductors and cellular phones.*

**Motorola Guam,  215 Rojas No. 123, Harmon, Guam 96911**

Tel: 671-647-6140   Fax: 671-647-6130

## OUTBACK STEAKHOUSE, INC.

2202 N. Westshore Blvd. 5th Fl., Tampa, FL, 33607

Tel: (813) 282-1225   Fax: (813) 282-1209   www.outback.com

*Chain of casual dining steak restaurants.*

**Outback Steakhouse, Inc.,  1411 Pale San Vitores, Tamuning 96911, Guam**

Tel: 671-646-1543

## PLANET HOLLYWOOD INTERNATIONAL, INC.

8669 Commodity Circle, Orlando, FL, 32819

Tel: (407) 363-7827    Fax: (407) 363-4862    www.planethollywood.com

*Theme-dining restaurant chain and merchandise retail stores.*

**Planet Hollywood International, Inc., Tamuning, Guam**

## THE ST. PAUL COMPANIES, INC.

385 Washington Street, St. Paul, MN, 55102

Tel: (651) 310-7911    Fax: (651) 310-8294    www.stpaul.com

*Provides investment, insurance and reinsurance services.*

**Moylans Insurance Underwriters, Inc., 101 Agana Shopping Center, Agana, Guam**

# Guatemala

## 3M

3M Center, St. Paul, MN, 55144-1000

Tel: (651) 733-1110     Fax: (651) 733-9973     www.mmm.com

*Mfr. diversified products for industry, health care, imaging, communications, transport, safety, consumer, etc.*

**3M Guatemala SA, Km. 13 Calzada Roosevelt 12-33, Z.3 Mixco, Guatemala City, Guatemala**

Tel: 502-2-591-1236   Fax: 502-2-593-4177

## ABBOTT LABORATORIES

One Abbott Park, Abbott Park, IL, 60064-3500

Tel: (847) 937-6100     Fax: (847) 937-1511     www.abbott.com

*Development/mfr./sale diversified health care products and services.*

**Abbott Laboratories, S.A., Apartado Postal 37, 01901 Guatemala**

## AGRIBRANDS INTERNATIONAL, INC.

9811 South Forty Drive, St. Louis, MO, 63124

Tel: (314) 812-0500     Fax: (314) 812-0400     www.agribrands.com

*Produces animal feeds and nutritional products for cattle, poultry, horses and fish.*

**Agribrands Purina de Guatemala S.A., Calzada Aguilar Batres 52-34, Zone 11, 01011C.A, Guatemala**

Tel: 502-4-773832   Fax: 502-4-773535

## AIR EXPRESS INTERNATIONAL CORPORATION

120 Tokeneke Road, PO Box 1231, Darien, CT, 06820

Tel: (203) 655-7900     Fax: (203) 655-5779     www.aeilogistics.com

*International air freight forwarder.*

**AEI Guatemala, c/o Comar Guatemala, 24 Ave. 41-81 zona 12, Interior Almacendora Integrada, Guatemala City Guatemala**

Tel: 502-4743-3686   Fax: 502-4743-3697

## ALBERTO-CULVER COMPANY

2525 Armitage Ave., Melrose Park, IL, 60160

Tel: (708) 450-3000     Fax: (708) 450-3354     www.alberto.com

*Mfr./marketing personal care and household brand products.*

**Alberto-Culver de Guatemala SA, 10a Av. 18-67, Zona 11, Col. Mariscal, Guatemala City, Guatemala**

## AMERICAN & EFIRD, INC.

PO Box 507, Mt. Holly, NC, 28120

Tel: (704) 827-4311     Fax: (704) 822-6054     www.amefird.com

*Mfr. industrial sewing thread for worldwide industrial and consumer markets.*

**Hilos A&E de Guatemala, Lote 7-B Parque Industrial Zeta, La Union SA Zona Franca, Autopista A Amatitlan KM30 Guatemala**

## AMERICAN BILTRITE INC.

57 River Street, Wellesley Hills, MA, 02181

Tel: (781) 237-6655     Fax: (781) 237-6880     www.americanbiltriteinc.com

*Mfr. vinyl composition and rubber floor coverings and produces pressure sensitive tape and rubber matting.*

**American Biltrite Guatemala Ltd., Guatemala**

## AMERICAN INTERNATIONAL GROUP INC. (AIG)

70 Pine Street, New York, NY, 10270

Tel: (212) 770-7000     Fax: (212) 509-9705     www.aig.com

*Worldwide insurance and financial services.*

**La Compania de Seguros SA, 7 a Av.- 12-23 Zona 9, Edif. Elisa, Nivel 3, Guatamala City Guatamala**

## AMERICAN STANDARD INC.

One Centennial Avenue, Piscataway, NJ, 08855-6820

Tel: (732) 980-3000     Fax: (732) 980-6118     www.americanstandard.com

*Mfr. automotive, plumbing, heating, air conditioning products and medical diagnostics systems.*

**Industria Centroamericana de Sanitarios SA, Aptdo. 2553, Guatemala City, Guatemala**

## AMWAY CORPORATION

7575 Fulton Street East, Ada, MI, 49355-0001

Tel: (616) 787-6000     Fax: (616) 787-6177     www.amway.com

*Mfr./sale home care, personal care, nutrition and houseware products.*

**Amway de Guatemala SA, 7a Av. 6-69, Zona 9, Guatemala City, Guatemala**

## ANC RENTAL CORP.

110 Southeast Sixth St., Ft. Lauderdale, FL, 33301

Tel: (954) 769-7000     Fax: (954) 769-7000     www.ancrental.com

*Engaged in car rental services, including National Car Rental and Alamo Rent A Car.*

**National Car Rental, 14 Calle 1-42, Zona 10, Guatemala City, Guatemala**

## ANDERSEN WORLDWIDE

33 West Monroe Street, Chicago, IL, 60603

Tel: (312) 580-0033     Fax: (312) 507-6748     www.arthurandersen.com

*Accounting and audit, tax and management consulting services.*

**Andersen Worldwide, Diagonal 6 10-65, Zona10, Centro Gerencial Las Margaritas 50 Nivel, Guatemala City 01010 Guatemala**

Tel: 502-2-332-7939

## AON CORPORATION

123 North Wacker Drive, Chicago, IL, 60606

Tel: (312) 701-3000     Fax: (312) 701-3100     www.aon.com

*Insurance brokers worldwide; underwrites accident and health insurance, specialty and professional insurance; and provides risk management consultation.*

**AON Worldwide / AISFA (Agencia Independiente de Seg. y Fias), Av. Reforma 6, 64 Zona 9, Guatemala City, Guatemala**

Tel: 502-2-336-0921   Fax: 502-2-339-0929   Contact: Moises Cupersmith

## AVIS GROUP HOLDINGS, INC.

900 Old Country Road., Garden City, NY, 11530

Tel: (516) 222-3000     Fax: (516) 222-4381     www.avis.com

*Car rental services.*

**Avis Group Holdings Ltd.., 12 Calle 2-73, Zona 9, Guatemala City, Guatemala**

## AVON PRODUCTS INC.

1345 Avenue of the Americas, New York, NY, 10105-0196

Tel: (212) 282-5000     Fax: (212) 282-6049     www.avon.com

*Mfr./distributor beauty and related products, fashion jewelry, gifts and collectibles.*

**Avon Productos de Guatemala, Apartado Postal 3004-A, Guatemala City, Guatemala**

Tel: 502-5943-0600   Fax: 502-5943-0589   Contact: Estela Matamoros, Mgr.

### BATES WORLDWIDE INC.
405 Lexington Ave., New York, NY, 10174

Tel: (212) 297-7000    Fax: (212) 986-0270    www.batesww.com

*Advertising, marketing, public relations and media consulting.*

**PM&S Bates CentroAmerica,  4a Av. 15-70 Zona 10, Edif. Paladlum 10 nival, Of. 10, Guatemala City Guatemala**

Tel: 502-2-366-4384   Fax: 502-2-366-4391    Contact: Armando S. Esponda, Pres.

### BDO SEIDMAN, LLP   BELGIUM
Two Prudential Plaza, 180 N. Stetson Ave., Ste. 2300, Chicago, IL, 60601

Tel: (312) 240-1236    Fax: (312) 240-3329    www.bdo.com

*International accounting and financial consulting firm.*

**Platero Reyes y Asociados,  12 Calle 2-04 Zona 9, Edif. Plaza del Sol, 4º Nivel Of. 413, Guatemala City Guatemala**

Tel: 502-2-331-9744   Fax: 502-2-331-4217    Contact: Mauricio Platero

### BEST WESTERN INTERNATIONAL
6201 North 24th Place, Phoenix, AZ, 85106

Tel: (602) 957-4200    Fax: (602) 957-5740    www.bestwestern.com

*International hotel chain.*

**BW Royal Palace,  6 Av. 12-66 Zone 1, Guatemala City, Guatemala 01010**

Tel: 502-2325-125

### BESTFOODS, INC.
700 Sylvan Ave., International Plaza, Englewood Cliffs, NJ, 07632-9976

Tel: (201) 894-4000    Fax: (201) 894-2186    www.bestfoods.com

*Consumer foods products; corn refining.*

**Productos de Maiz y Alimentos, S.A.,  Aptdo. 1765, Guatemala City, Guatemala**

Tel: 502-2-477-5060   Fax: 502-2-477-5018    Contact: Haroldo Barillas, Mgr.

### BRISTOL-MYERS SQUIBB COMPANY
345 Park Ave., New York, NY, 10154-0037

Tel: (212) 546-4000    Fax: (212) 546-4020    www.bms.com

*Pharmaceutical and food preparations, medical and surgical instruments.*

**Compania Bristol-Myers de Centro America,  Blvd. Liberacion 5-55, Zona 9, Guatemala City, Guatemala**

### LEO BURNETT, DIV. B-COM 3 GROUP
35 West Wacker Drive, Chicago, IL, 60601

Tel: (312) 220-5959    Fax: (312) 220-6533    www.bcom3group.com

*Engaged in advertising, marketing, media buying and planning, and public relations.*

**Leo Burnett - Comunica,  5ta Av. 6-39, Zona 14, Col. El Campo, Guatemala City Guatemala**

### CARBOLINE COMPANY
350 Hanley Industrial Court, St. Louis, MO, 63144

Tel: (314) 644-1000    Fax: (314) 644-4617    www.carboline.com

*Mfr. coatings and sealants.*

**Sigma Quimica,  12 Calle 5-34, Zona 1, Guatemala, Guatemala**

### CARGILL, INC.
15407 McGinty Road West, Minnetonka, MN, 55440-5625

Tel: (612) 742-7575    Fax: (612) 742-7393    www.cargill.com

*Food products, feeds, animal products.*

**Hohenberg Bros. Ltd.,  Aptdo. 2857, Guatemala City, Guatemala**

## CATERPILLAR INC.

100 NE Adams Street, Peoria, IL, 61629-6105

Tel: (309) 675-1000      Fax: (309) 675-1182      www.cat.com

*Mfr. earth/material-handling and construction machinery and equipment and engines.*

**Caterpillar Energy Company, Guatemala**

## CHESTERTON BINSWANGER INTERNATIONAL

Two Logan Square, 4th Floor, Philadelphia, PA, 19103-2759

Tel: (215) 448-6000      Fax: (215) 448-6238      www.cbbi.com

*Real estate and related services.*

**Binswanger Guatemala, Ingenieros Valuadores, 7avenida 3-33 zona 9, of. 605 Guatemala City, Guatemala**

## CIGNA COMPANIES

One Liberty Place, Philadelphia, PA, 19192

Tel: (215) 761-1000      Fax: (215) 761-5511      www.cigna.com

*Insurance, invest, health care and other financial services.*

**Empresa Guatemalteco CIGNA de Seguros, S.A., 6a. Ave 20-25 Zona 10, Edi Plaza Maritima 100 Nivel, Guatemala City C.A. 01010**

## CITIGROUP, INC.

153 East 53rd Street, New York, NY, 10043

Tel: (212) 559-1000      Fax: (212) 559-3646      www.citigroup.com

*Provides insurance and financial services worldwide.*

**Citibank N.A., Ave. Reforma 15-45, Zona 10, Guatemala City, Guatemala**
Tel: 502-2-333-6574   Fax: 502-2-333-6860   Contact: Juan Miró, V.P.& Gen. Mgr.

## THE COCA-COLA COMPANY

PO Drawer 1734, Atlanta, GA, 30301

Tel: (404) 676-2121      Fax: (404) 676-6792      www.coca-cola.com

*Mfr./marketing/distributor soft drinks, syrups and concentrates, juice and juice-drink products.*

**Industria de Cafe, Guatemala**

## COLGATE-PALMOLIVE COMPANY

300 Park Ave., New York, NY, 10022

Tel: (212) 310-2000      Fax: (212) 310-2919      www.colgate.com

*Mfr. pharmaceuticals, cosmetics, toiletries and detergents.*

**Colgate-Palmolive (Central America) Inc., Av. del Ferrocarril 49-65, Zona 12, Guatemala City, Guatemala**

## COMSAT CORPORATION

6560 Rock Spring Drive, Bethesda, MD, 20817

Tel: (301) 214-3200      Fax: (301) 214-7100      www.comsat.com

*Provides global telecommunications services via satellite and develops advanced satellite networking technology.*

**COMSAT International, 6 Avenida 7-39, Zona 10 Edificio Las Brisas, 3er. Nivel Oficina 302, Guatemala City, Guatemala**

## CONTINENTAL AIRLINES INC.

2929 Allen Parkway, Ste. 2010, Houston, TX, 77019

Tel: (281) 834-5000      Fax: (281) 520-6329      www.continental.com

*International airline carrier.*

**Continental Airlines Inc., Guatemala**

## D'ARCY MASIUS BENTON & BOWLES INC. (DMB&B)

1675 Broadway, New York, NY, 10019

Tel: (212) 468-3622    Fax: (212) 468-2987    www.dmbb.com

*Full service international advertising and communications group.*

**DMBB Dos Puntos, 17 Av. 42-26, Zona 8, Guatemala City, Guatemala**

Tel: 502-471-8262   Fax: 502-472-5103   Contact: Estuardo Aguilar, Pres.

## DDB NEEDHAM WORLDWIDE INC.

437 Madison Ave., New York, NY, 10022

Tel: (212) 415-2000    Fax: (212) 415-3417    www.ddbn.com

*Advertising agency.*

**Publinac DDB, Guatemala City, Guatemala**

## DELOITTE TOUCHE TOHMATSU INTERNATIONAL

1633 Broadway, New York, NY, 10019

Tel: (212) 492-4000    Fax: (212) 392-4154    www.deloitte.com

*Accounting, audit, tax and management consulting services.*

**Lara & Coyoy, CPA, 7a. Av. 7-07, Zna 9, 4 Nivel, (Apartado Postal 646-A), Guatemala**

## DHL WORLDWIDE EXPRESS

50 California Avenue, San Francisco, CA, 94111

Tel: (415) 677-6100    Fax: (415) 824-9700    www.dhl.com

*Worldwide air express carrier.*

**DHL Worldwide Express, 7a. Av. 2-42, Zona 9, Guatemala City 01009, Guatemala**

Tel: 502-2-323023

## THE DIAL CORPORATION

15501 North Dial Blvd., Scottsdale, AZ, 85260-1619

Tel: (480) 754-3425    Fax: (480) 754-1098    www.dialcorp.com

*Mfr. soaps, detergents, air fresheners, specialty personal care products and Armour Star canned meats.*

**International Soap & Cosmetics (ISC), 10 Ave. 5-49 Zona 14, Guatemala City 01014, Guatemala**

Tel: 502-366-6880   Fax: 502-337-2537

## DIMON INCORPORATED

512 Bridge Street, PO Box 681, Danville, VA, 24543-0681

Tel: (804) 792-7511    Fax: (804) 791-0377    www.dimon.com

*One of world's largest importer and exporters of leaf tobacco.*

**DIMON Guatemala S.A., Km. 12.5 Carretera A Villa Canales, Boca del Monte Guatemala City, Guatemala**

## DOVER CORPORATION

280 Park Ave., New York, NY, 10017-1292

Tel: (212) 922-1640    Fax: (212) 922-1656    www.dovercorporation.com

*Holding company for varied industries; assembly and testing equipment, oil-well gear and other industrial products.*

**De Elevadores, S.A. - Eveva Compañia Internacional, 14 Ave. 15-01, Zona 12, Guatemala**

Tel: 502-473-0362   Fax: 502-473-1092

**Guatemale, C.A., 3a. Ave. 16-38, Zona 10, Guatemala**

Tel: 502-268-1315   Fax: 502-63-1745

## THE DOW CHEMICAL COMPANY

2030 Dow Center, Midland, MI, 48674

Tel: (517) 636-1000    Fax: (517) 636-3228    www.dow.com

*Mfr. chemicals, plastics, pharmaceuticals, agricultural products, consumer products.*

**Dow Quimica de Guatemala Ltda., Guatemala City, Guatemala**

## EAGLE GLOBAL LOGISTICS (EGL)

15350 Vickery Drive, Houston, TX, 77032

Tel: (281) 618-3100      Fax: (281) 618-3100      www.eaglegl.com

*Ocean/air freight forwarding, customs brokerage, packing and wholesale, logistics management and insurance.*

**Aerosistemas Agentes de Circle International,  Edif. Galerias Reforma, Av. Reforma 8-60, Zona 9 Of. 319, Guatemala City Guatemala**

Tel: 502-2-394-037   Fax: 502-2-394-039

## ECOLAB INC.

370 N. Wabasha Street, St. Paul, MN, 55102

Tel: (651) 293-2233      Fax: (651) 293-2379      www.ecolab.com

*Develop/mfr. premium cleaning, sanitizing and maintenance products and services for the hospitality, institutional, and residential markets.*

**Ecolab Ltd.,  Guatemala City, Guatemala**

Tel: 502-2-599-3697

## ENRON CORPORATION

1400 Smith Street, Houston, TX, 77002-7369

Tel: (713) 853-6161      Fax: (713) 853-3129      www.enron.com

*Exploration, production, transportation and distribution of integrated natural gas and electricity.*

**Puerto Quetzal Power Corp.,  Km 112 Carretera A Iztapa, Puerto Quetzal Escuintla, Guatemala, CA**

## ERNST & YOUNG, LLP

787 Seventh Ave., New York, NY, 10019

Tel: (212) 773-3000      Fax: (212) 773-6350      www.eyi.com

*Accounting and audit, tax and management consulting services.*

**Lizarralde, Ayestas, Asturias y Ramos Ernst & Young,  13 Calle 1-51, Zona 10, Guatemala, Guatemala**

Tel: 502-2-321-249   Fax: 502-2-315-687   Contact: Carlos Asturias

## FEDERAL-MOGUL CORPORATION

26555 Northwestern Highway, PO Box 1966, Southfield, MI, 48034

Tel: (248) 354-7700      Fax: (248) 354-8983      www.federal-mogul.com

*Mfr./distributor precision parts for automobiles, trucks, farm and construction vehicles.*

**Federal-Mogul de Guatemala SA,  Guatemala**

## FERRO CORPORATION

1000 Lakeside Ave., Cleveland, OH, 44114-7000

Tel: (216) 641-8580      Fax: (216) 696-5784      www.ferro.com

*Mfr. Specialty chemicals, coatings, plastics, colors, refractories.*

**J.C. Niemann (Rep),  Calle Mariscal Cruz 10-69, Zone 5, Guatemala City, Guatemala**

Tel: 502-2-315454   Contact: Juan Niemann

## FMC CORPORATION

200 E. Randolph Drive, Chicago, IL, 60601

Tel: (312) 861-6000      Fax: (312) 861-6141      www.fmc.com

*Produces chemicals and precious metals, mfr. machinery, equipment and systems for industrial, agricultural and government use.*

**FMC Guatemala SA,  Guatemala**

## FRITZ COMPANIES, INC.

706 Mission Street, Ste. 900, San Francisco, CA, 94103

Tel: (415) 904-8360      Fax: (415) 904-8661      www.fritz.com

*Integrated transportation, sourcing, distribution and customs brokerage services.*

**Fritz Companies Inc.,  Guatemala City, Guatemala**

## H.B. FULLER COMPANY

1200 Willow Lake Blvd., Vadnais Heights, MN, 55110

Tel: (651) 236-5900    Fax: (651) 236-5898    www.hbfuller.com

*Mfr./distributor adhesives, sealants, coatings, paints, waxes, sanitation chemicals.*

**Kativo de Guatemala SA, 2061 Guatemala City, Guatemala**

Tel: 502-2-477-4873    Fax: 502-2-477-5393

## THE GILLETTE COMPANY

Prudential Tower Building, Boston, MA, 02199

Tel: (617) 421-7000    Fax: (617) 421-7123    www.gillette.com

*Develop/mfr. personal care/use products: blades and razors, toiletries, cosmetics, stationery.*

**Gillette de Centro America SA, Guatemala, Guatemala**

**Jafra Cosmeticos de Guatemala SA, Guatemala, Guatemala**

## THE GOODYEAR TIRE & RUBBER COMPANY

1144 East Market Street, Akron, OH, 44316

Tel: (330) 796-2121    Fax: (330) 796-1817    www.goodyear.com

*Mfr. tires, automotive belts and hose, conveyor belts, chemicals; oil pipeline transmission.*

**Gran Industrial de Neumaticos Centroamericana SA, Aptdo. 1946, 50 Calle 23-70 Zona 12, Guatemala City 01012, Guatemala**

## GRANT THORNTON INTERNATIONAL

800 One Prudential Plaza, 130 E. Randolph Drive, Chicago, IL, 60601-6050

Tel: (312) 856-0001    Fax: (312) 616-7052    www.grantthornton.com

*Accounting, audit, tax and management consulting services.*

**Grant Thornton - Pineda Tezo Y Asociados, S.C., 15 Avda 15-81, Zona 13, Guatamala City, Guatamala**

Contact: Sergio L. Pineda

## GREY GLOBAL GROUP

777 Third Ave., New York, NY, 10017

Tel: (212) 546-2000    Fax: (212) 546-1495    www.grey.com

*International advertising agency.*

**Tobar & Conde Publicidad, Guatemala City, Guatemala**

## GRIFFITH LABORATORIES INC.

One Griffith Center, Alsip, IL, 60658

Tel: (708) 371-0900    Fax: (708) 597-3294    www.griffithlabs.com

*Mfr. industrial food ingredients and equipment.*

**Griffith Labs Inc., Guatemala City, Guatemala**

Tel: 502-2-223-8643    Fax: 502-2-234-0555

## GUILFORD MILLS INC.

925 West Market Street, PO Box 26969, Greensboro, NC, 27407

Tel: (336) 316-4000    Fax: (336) 316-4059    www.guilfordmills.com

*Mfr. textiles.*

**Guilford Mills, Inc., 2nd Avenida 10-37, Zona 10, Guatemala**

Tel: 502-261-0437    Fax: 502-261-0447    Contact: Venicio Savedra

## HALLIBURTON COMPANY

500 North Akard Street, Ste. 3600, Dallas, TX, 75201-3391

Tel: (214) 978-2600    Fax: (214) 978-2685    www.halliburton.com

*Engaged in diversified energy services, engineering and construction.*

**Halliburton Ltd., 2 a. Calle 15-96, Zonal 13, 01013 Ciudad de Guatemala, Guatemala**

Tel: 502-2-318-185    Fax: 502-2-325-096

## HOCKMAN-LEWIS LTD.

200 Executive Drive, Ste. 320, West Orange, NJ, 07052

Tel: (973) 325-3838    Fax: (973) 325-7974    www.hockman-lewis.com

*Export management.*

**Equigas de Guatemala SA,  41 Calle 8-69, Zona 8, Guatemala, Guatemala**

## HORWATH INTERNATIONAL ASSOCIATION

415 Madison Ave., New York, NY, 10017

Tel: (212) 838-5566    Fax: (212) 838-3636    www.horwath.com

*Public accountants and auditors.*

**Bocanegra, Cruz y Associados,  Ave Reforma 1-50 Zona 9, Edif. El Reformador Nivel 4, Guatemala City, Guatemala**

## HYATT CORPORATION

200 West Madison Street, Chicago, IL, 60606

Tel: (312) 750-1234    Fax: (312) 750-8578    www.hyatt.com

*International hotel management.*

**Hyatt Regency Guatemala Hotel,  Calzada Roosevelt, 22-43 Zona 11, Guatamala City, Guatemala**

Tel: 502-440-1234   Fax: 502-440-4050

## IBM CORPORATION

New Orchard Road, Armonk, NY, 10504

Tel: (914) 765-1900    Fax: (914) 765-7382    www.ibm.com

*Information products, technology and services.*

**IBM de Guatemala SA,  Guatemala City, Guatemala**

## IMATION CORPORATION

One Imation Place, Oakdale, MN, 55128

Tel: (612) 704-4000    Fax: (612) 704-3444    www.imation.com

*Dry laser-imaging film systems.*

**Imation de Guatemala, S.A.,  Calzada Roosevelt 22-43, Zona 11 Edificio Tikal Futura Torre Sol Nivel 7, Oficina 70 Guatemala, Guatemala**

## INFORMATION RESOURCES, INC. (IRI)

150 N. Clinton St., Chicago, IL, 60661

Tel: (312) 726-1221    Fax: (312) 726-0360    www.infores.com

*Provides bar code scanner services for retail sales organizations; processes, analyzes and sells data from the huge database created from these services.*

**Grupo de Servicios de Informacion, SA GSI/IRI,  Plaza GSI  5 Av. 6-39, Zona 14, Condominio Las Plazas, Guatemala City Guatemala**

Tel: 502-337-3751   Fax: 502-337-3744

## IRRIDELCO INTERNATIONAL CORPORATION

440 Sylvan Ave., Englewood Cliffs, NJ, 07632

Tel: (201) 569-3030    Fax: (201) 569-9237    www.irridelco.com

*Mfr./distributor of the most comprehensive lines of mechanical and micro irrigation; pumps and irrigation systems.*

**IDC Guatemala,  13 Calle B - 4-50, Zona 3, Guatemala**

Tel: 502-251-4354   Fax: 502-202-3274   Contact: Leonel Santa Cruz

## J. WALTER THOMPSON COMPANY

466 Lexington Ave., New York, NY, 10017

Tel: (212) 210-7000    Fax: (212) 210-6944    www.jwt.com

*International advertising and marketing services.*

**APCU-Thompson,  Guatemala City, Guatemala**

## JOHNSON & JOHNSON

One Johnson & Johnson Plaza, New Brunswick, NJ, 08933

Tel: (732) 524-0400      Fax: (732) 214-0334      www.jnj.com

*Mfr./distributor/R&D pharmaceutical, health care and cosmetic products.*

**Johnson & Johnson Guatemala SA, Aptdo. 2067, Guatemala City, Guatemala**

## KELLOGG COMPANY

One Kellogg Square, PO Box 3599, Battle Creek, MI, 49016-3599

Tel: (616) 961-2000      Fax: (616) 961-2871      www.kelloggs.com

*Mfr. ready-to-eat cereals and convenience foods.*

**Kellogg's de Centro America SA, Attn: Guatemalan Office, One Kellogg Square, PO Box 3599, Battle Creek MI 49016-3599**

## KOPPERS INDUSTRIES INC.

Koppers Bldg, 436 Seventh Ave., Pittsburgh, PA, 15219-1800

Tel: (412) 227-2000      Fax: (412) 227-2333      www.koppers.com

*Construction materials and services; chemicals and building products.*

**Impregnadora de Madera de Guatemala SA, 8a Calle 2-31, Zona l, Guatemala City, Guatemala**

## KPMG INTERNATIONAL LLP

345 Park Avenue, New York, NY, 10022

Tel: (201) 307-7000      Fax: (201) 930-8617      www.kpmg.com

*Accounting and audit, tax and management consulting services.*

**KPMG Aldana, Salazar, Garcia & Asociados, Centro Financiero Torre I, Nivel 16, 7a. Av. 5-10, Zona 4 Guatemala**

Tel: 502-334-2628    Fax: 502-331-5477    Contact: Arturo Aldana, Sr. Ptnr.

## LANIER WORLDWIDE, INC.

2300 Parklake Drive, N.E., Atlanta, GA, 30345

Tel: (770) 496-9500      Fax: (770) 938-1020      www.lanier.com

*Specialize in digital copiers and multi-functional systems.*

**Lanier de Guatemala, S.A., 5a. Av. 11-24 Zona 9, PO Box 885 A, Guatemala City, Guatemala**

Tel: 502-2-331-8083    Fax: 502-2-331-4770

## LOWE LINTAS & PARTNERS WORLDWIDE

One Dag Hammarskjold Plaza, New York, NY, 10017

Tel: (212) 605-8000      Fax: (212) 605-4705      www.interpublic.com

*Full-service, integrated marketing communications company/advertising agency.*

**Publicentro, 16 Calle 7-00, Zona 14, 01014 Guatemala**

Tel: 502-333-7420

**Publicentro, PO Box 2353, Guatemala City, Guatemala**

Tel: 502-2-333-7240    Fax: 502-2-368-3364    Contact: Florentino Fernandez

## MARRIOTT INTERNATIONAL INC.

10400 Fernwood Rd., Bethesda, MD, 20817

Tel: (301) 380-3000      Fax: (301) 380-5181      www.marriott.com

*Hotel services.*

**Guatemala City Marriott, Guatemala City, Guatemala**

Tel: 502-2-331-2070

## MARSH & McLENNAN COS INC.

1166 Ave. of the Americas, New York, NY, 10036-2774

Tel: (212) 345-5000      Fax: (212) 345-4808      www.marshmac.com

*Insurance agents/brokers, pension and investment management consulting services.*

**Consultores de Seguros S.A., 2 Avenuda 8-48, Zona 9, Edif. Profesional 2 Nivel, Guatemala City Guatemala 01009**

Tel: 502-2-239-2595   Fax: 502-2-239-2596

**Tecniseguros Cia. Ltda., Av. Reforma 9-00, zona 9, Edif. Plaza Panamericana 6o. nivel, Guatemala City, Guatemala**

Tel: 502-2-332-1555   Fax: 502-2-331-1917   Contact: Enrique Fernandez B.

## McCANN-ERICKSON WORLDGROUP

750 Third Ave., New York, NY, 10017

Tel: (212) 984-3644      Fax: (212) 984-2629      www.mccann.com

*International advertising and marketing services.*

**McCann-Erickson Centroamericana (Guatemala) SA, Aptdo. 390, 7a Av. 5-10 Zona 4, Centro Financiero Torre 11, Guatemala City Guatemala**

## MERLE NORMAN COSMETICS INC.

9130 Bellance Ave., Los Angeles, CA, 90045

Tel: (310) 641-3000      Fax: (310) 641-7144      www.merlenorman.com

*Mfr./sales/distribution of cosmetics.*

**Merle Norman Cosmetics, 1600 Calle 200, Zone 145, Central Guatemala**

## J. P. MORGAN CHASE & CO. INC.

World Headquarters, 270 Park Ave., New York, NY, 10017

Tel: (212) 270-6000      Fax: (212) 622-9030      www.jpmorganchase.com

*Provides integrated financial solutions for institutions and individuals worldwide, including asset management, investment banking and commercial banking.*

**J. P. Morgan Chase & Co., Aptdo. 40-F, Guatemala City, Guatemala**

## MYERS INTERNATIONAL INC.

1293 South Main Street, Akron, OH, 44301

Tel: (330) 253-5592      Fax: (330) 253-0035      www.myerstiresupply.com

*Mfr. tire retreading and maintenance equipment and supplies.*

**Orientadores Comerciales S.A., Myers De Guatemala, 3 ra Calle 5-49, Zona 9 Guatamala**

Tel: 502-360-0608   Fax: 502-360-0628

## NABISCO HOLDINGS, CORP.

7 Campus Drive, Parsippany, NJ, 07054

Tel: (973) 682-5000      Fax: (973) 503-2153      www.nabisco.com

*Mfr. consumer packaged food products and tobacco products.*

**Nabisco Royal, Inc. Salvavaidas de Guatemala SA, Km. 13.5 Carretera Roosevelt, 12 Av. 0-68, Zona 2, Guatemala City Guatemala**

## PAN-AMERICAN LIFE INSURANCE COMPANY

Pan American Life Center, PO Box 60219, New Orleans, LA, 70130-0219

Tel: (504) 566-1300      Fax: (504) 566-3600      www.palic.com

*Insurance services.*

**Compania de Seguros Panamericana SA, Edif. Plaza Panamericana, Av. Reforma 9-00, Zona 9, Guatemala City, Guatemala**

Tel: 502-2-332-5922   Fax: 502-2-331-5026   Contact: Salvador Ortega, VP & Gen. Mgr.   Emp: 95

## PAPA JOHN'S INTERNATIONAL, INC.

2002 Papa John's Blvd., Louisville, KY, 40299-2334

Tel: (502) 266-5200    Fax: (502) 266-2925    www.papajohns.com

*Retailer and pizza franchiser.*

**Papa John's International Inc., Anillo Periférico Zona 11, Centro Comercial Las Majadas Local 27, Cd. de Guatemala, Guatemala**

Tel: 502-474-2441

## PEPSiCO INC.

700 Anderson Hill Road, Purchase, NY, 10577-1444

Tel: (914) 253-2000    Fax: (914) 253-2070    www.pepsico.com

*Beverages and snack foods.*

**PepsiCo Interamericana de Guatemala SA, Guatemala**

## PHARMACIA CORPORATION

100 Route 206 North, Peapack, NJ, 07977

Tel: (908) 901-8000    Fax: (908) 901-8379    www.pharmacia.com

*Mfr. pharmaceuticals, agricultural products, industry chemicals.*

**Compania Farmaceutica Upjohn SA, Aptdo. 991, Guatemala City, Guatemala**

## PHELPS DODGE CORPORATION

2600 North Central Ave., Phoenix, AZ, 85004-3089

Tel: (602) 234-8100    Fax: (602) 234-8337    www.phelpsdodge.com

*Copper, minerals, metals and special engineered products for transportation and electrical markets.*

**Fabrica de Conductores Elecricos, Apartado Postal 2856, Guatemala City, Guatemala**

## PRICEWATERHOUSECOOPERS LLP

1301 Ave. of the Americas, New York, NY, 10019

Tel: (212) 596-7000    Fax: (212) 259-1301    www.pwcglobal.com

*Accounting and auditing, tax and management, and human resource consulting services.*

**PriceWaterhouseCoopers, Edif. Tivoli Plaza, 6a Calle 6-38, AP 868 Guatemala City 9, Guatemala**

Tel: 502-2-345080    Fax: 502-2-312819

## PROCTER & GAMBLE COMPANY

One Procter & Gamble Plaza, Cincinnati, OH, 45202

Tel: (513) 983-1100    Fax: (513) 562-4500    www.pg.com

*Personal care, food, laundry, cleaning and industry products.*

**Procter & Gamble, Diagonal 6 10-65 Nivel 16, Centro Gerencial Las Margaritas, Zona 10, 01010 Guatemala City Guatemala**

## RAYOVAC CORPORATION

601 Rayovac Drive, Madison, WI, 53711-2497

Tel: (608) 275-3340    Fax: (608) 275-4577    www.rayovac.com

*Mfr. batteries and lighting devices.*

**Rayovac Guatemala, Guatemala City, Guatemala**

## RIVIANA FOODS INC.

2777 Allen Parkway, 15th Fl., Houston, TX, 77019

Tel: (713) 529-3251    Fax: (713) 529-1661    www.rivianafoods.com

*Process, market and distribute branded and private-label rice products.*

**Alimentos Kern de Guatemala SA, Km. 6.5 Carretera al Atlantico, Zona 18, Guatemala City 01018, Guatemala**

## SCHENKER INTERNATIONAL FORWARDERS INC.

150 Albany Ave., Freeport, NY, 11520

Tel: (516) 377-3000     Fax: (516) 377-3005     www.schenkerusa.com

*Freight forwarders.*

**Schenker Internacional, SA,  5 Ave. 3-30 Zone 13, PO Box 1159, Guatemala City 01901, Guatemala**

Tel: 502-475-4260    Fax: 502-475-4259

## SEARS ROEBUCK & COMPANY

3333 Beverly Road, Hoffman Estates, IL, 60179

Tel: (847) 286-2500     Fax: (847) 286-1517     www.sears.com

*Diversified general merchandise.*

**Sears Roebuck SA,  Aptdo. 513, Guatemala City, Guatemala**

## SENSIENT TECHNOLOGIES CORPORATION

433 E. Michigan Street, Milwaukee, WI, 53202

Tel: (414) 271-6755     Fax: (414) 347-4783     www.sensient.com

*Mfr. food products and food ingredients.*

**Levaduras Universal,  Km. 16 Carretera Roosevelt, Guatemala City, Guatemala**

## STARWOOD HOTELS & RESORTS WORLDWIDE

777 Westchester Avenue, White Plains, NY, 10604

Tel: (914) 640-8100     Fax: (914) 640-8316     www.starwoodhotels.com

*Hotel operations including Sheraton, Westin, St. Regis, Four Points and Caesars.*

**Conquistador Sheraton Hotel,  Via 5 4-68, Zona 4, Guatemala City, Guatemala**

## TEXACO INC.

2000 Westchester Ave., White Plains, NY, 10650

Tel: (914) 253-4000     Fax: (914) 253-7753     www.texaco.com

*Exploration/marketing crude oil, mfr. petro chemicals and products.*

**Texaco Guatemala Inc.,  Av. Petapa 23-01, Zona 12, Guatemala City, Guatemala**

## TRUE NORTH COMMUNICATIONS INC.

101 East Erie Street, Chicago, IL, 60611

Tel: (312) 425-6500     Fax: (312) 425-5010     www.truenorth.com

*Holding company, advertising agency.*

**Foote, Cone & Belding,  Av. La Reforma 8-60 Zona 9, Edif. Galerias Reforma Torre 1, Guatemala City Guatemala**

## U.S. WHEAT ASSOCIATES

1620  I Street, NW, Washington, DC, 20006

Tel: (202) 463-0999     Fax: (202) 785-1052

*Market development for wheat products.*

**U.S. Wheat Associates Inc.,  15 Av. A 3-67, Zona 13, Guatemala City, Guatemala**

## UNION CARBIDE CORPORATION

39 Old Ridgebury Road, Danbury, CT, 06817

Tel: (203) 794-2000     Fax: (203) 794-6269     www.unioncarbide.com

*Mfr. industrial chemicals, plastics and resins.*

**Union Carbide Guatemala,  Guatemala City, Guatemala**

## UNITED AIRLINES INC.

1200 E. Algonquin Rd., Chicago, IL, 60007

Tel: (847) 700-4000     Fax: (847) 700-4081     www.ual.com

*Air transportation, passenger and freight services.*

**United Airlines,  Guatemala**

## UNITED PARCEL SERVICE, INC.

55 Glenlake Parkway, NE, Atlanta, GA, 30328

Tel: (404) 828-6000      Fax: (404) 828-6593      www.ups.com

*International package-delivery service.*

**UPS / Courier Internacional S.A., 12 Calle 5-53, Zona 10, Guatemala City, Guatemala**

Tel: 502-2-360-6470   Fax: 502-2-332-6607

## WACKENHUT CORPORATION

4200 Wackenhut Dr., Ste. 100, Palm Beach Gardens, FL, 33410

Tel: (561) 622-5656      Fax: (561) 691-6736      www.wackenhut.com

*Security systems and services.*

**Wackenhut de Guatemala SA (WAGSA), Calle 14 8-51, Zona 10, Barrio Santa Clara, Guatemala**

Tel: 502-2-335803   Fax: 502-2-634560

**Wackenhut Electronics S.A., 14 Calle 7-49, Zona 9, 2ndo Nivel Interior, Portal Belmont, Guatemala, C.A.**

Tel: 502-344834   Fax: 502-317553

## WENDY'S INTERNATIONAL, INC.

428 West Dublin Granville Roads, Dublin, OH, 43017-0256

Tel: (614) 764-3100      Fax: (614) 764-3459      www.wendysintl.com

*Fast food restaurant chain.*

**Wendy's International, Guatemala**

## WEST CHEMICAL PRODUCTS INC.

1000 Herrontown Road, Princeton, NJ, 08540

Tel: (609) 921-0501      Fax: (609) 924-4308

*Sanitary equipment and supplies.*

**West Chemical Products de Guatemala, 3a Calle 10-25, Zona 12, Guatemala City, Guatemala**

## WESTERN GEOPHYSICAL, INC.

10205 Westheimer, Houston, TX, 77251-1407

Tel: (713) 972-4000      Fax: (713) 952-9837      www.bakerhughes.com

*Provides comprehensive seismic services for oil and gas exploration, field development, and reservoir monitoring.*

**Western Geophysical, 15 Ave. A 14-15 Zone 10, Oakland, 01010 Guatemala City, Guatemala**

## WHITEHALL-ROBINS INC.

1407 Cummings Drive, PO Box 26609, Richmond, VA, 23261-6609

Tel: (804) 257-2000      Fax: (804) 257-2120      www.ahp.com

*Mfr. ethical pharmaceuticals and consumer healthcare products.*

**Industrial Santa Agape SA, Guatemala City, Guatemala**

## WORLD COURIER INC.

1313 Fourth Ave., New Hyde Park, NY, 11041

Tel: (516) 354-2600      Fax: (516) 354-2644      www.worldcourier.com

*International courier service.*

**World Courier Guatemala SA, Edif. el Triangulo, 7a Av. 6-53, Zona 4, Guatemala City, Guatemala**

## WORLDXCHANGE COMMUNICATIONS

9999 Willow Creek Road, San Diego, CA, 92131

Tel: (858) 547-4933      Fax: (800) 995-4502      www.worldxchange.com

*Provides international, long distance telecommunications services worldwide.*

**WorldxChange Communications S.A., Guatamala**

## XEROX CORPORATION

800 Long Ridge Road, PO Box 1600, Stamford, CT, 06904

Tel:  (203) 968-3000      Fax:  (203) 968-4312      www.xerox.com

*Mfr. document processing equipment, systems and supplies.*

**Xerox De Guatemala, S.A.,  Av. Hincapie 14-71, Zona 13, Ciudad De Guatemala, Guatemala 01013 Guatemala**

Tel: 502-2-334-4811    Fax: 501-2-334-4876

## YOUNG & RUBICAM INC.

285 Madison Ave., New York, NY, 10017

Tel:  (212) 210-3000      Fax:  (212) 370-3796      www.yr.com

*Advertising, public relations, direct marketing and sales promotion, corporate and product ID management.*

**Eco Young & Rubicam,  Guatemala City, Guatemala**

# Guinea

## AGCO CORPORATION

4205 River Green Parkway, Duluth, GA, 30096-2568

Tel: (770) 813-9200     Fax: (770) 813-6038     www.agcocorp.com

*Mfr. farm equipment and machinery.*

**Les Ateliets De Guiness, Div. Massey Ferguson, BP 658, Conakry, Guinea**

## ALCOA INC.

Alcoa Center, 201 Isabella Street, Pittsburgh, PA, 15215-5858

Tel: (412) 553-4545     Fax: (412) 553-4498     www.alcoa.com

*World's leading producer of aluminum and alumina; mining, refining, smelting, fabricating and recycling.*

**Halco (Mining), Inc., Sangaredi, Guinea**

## LOUIS BERGER INTERNATIONAL INC.

100 Halsted Street, East Orange, NJ, 07019

Tel: (201) 678-1960     Fax: (201) 672-4284     www.louisberger.com

*Consulting engineers, engaged in architecture, environmental and advisory services.*

**Louis Berger International Inc., Immeuble de M. Fofana, Quartier Camayenne, Boite Postale 383, Conakry Guinea**

Tel: 224-462023    Fax: 224-462023

## THE COCA-COLA COMPANY

PO Drawer 1734, Atlanta, GA, 30301

Tel: (404) 676-2121     Fax: (404) 676-6792     www.coca-cola.com

*Mfr./marketing/distributor soft drinks, syrups and concentrates, juice and juice-drink products.*

**BONAGUI, Guinea**

## DHL WORLDWIDE EXPRESS

50 California Avenue, San Francisco, CA, 94111

Tel: (415) 677-6100     Fax: (415) 824-9700     www.dhl.com

*Worldwide air express carrier.*

**DHL Worldwide Express, 4 blvd Ave. de la Republique, Conakry, Guinee, Guinea**

Tel: 224-411766

## ERNST & YOUNG, LLP

787 Seventh Ave., New York, NY, 10019

Tel: (212) 773-3000     Fax: (212) 773-6350     www.eyi.com

*Accounting and audit, tax and management consulting services.*

**FFA Ernst & Young, Immeuble SAADI, Ave. de la Republique, B.P. 1762, Conakry Guinea**

Tel: 224-41-28-31    Fax: 224-41-28-31

## XEROX CORPORATION

800 Long Ridge Road, PO Box 1600, Stamford, CT, 06904

Tel: (203) 968-3000     Fax: (203) 968-4312     www.xerox.com

*Mfr. document processing equipment, systems and supplies.*

**Xeroguinee, BP 114, Conakry, Guinea**

Tel: 224-414-774    Fax: 224-414-803

# Guyana

## AON CORPORATION

123 North Wacker Drive, Chicago, IL, 60606

Tel: (312) 701-3000     Fax: (312) 701-3100     www.aon.com

*Insurance brokers worldwide; underwrites accident and health insurance, specialty and professional insurance; and provides risk management consultation.*

**AON Worldwide / Insurance Brokers-Guyana Ltd., 125 Carmichael St. South Cummingsburg, PO Box 10750, Georgetown Guyana**

Tel: 592-2-67261   Fax: 592-2-53187   Contact: E.W. Adams

## COLGATE-PALMOLIVE COMPANY

300 Park Ave., New York, NY, 10022

Tel: (212) 310-2000     Fax: (212) 310-2919     www.colgate.com

*Mfr. pharmaceuticals, cosmetics, toiletries and detergents.*

**Colgate-Palmolive (Guyana) Ltd., R.1 Ruimveldt, Georgetown, Guyana**

## DELOITTE TOUCHE TOHMATSU INTERNATIONAL

1633 Broadway, New York, NY, 10019

Tel: (212) 492-4000     Fax: (212) 392-4154     www.deloitte.com

*Accounting, audit, tax and management consulting services.*

**Deloitte & Touche, 77 Brickdam, PO Box 10506, Stabroek Georgetown, Guyana**

## DHL WORLDWIDE EXPRESS

50 California Avenue, San Francisco, CA, 94111

Tel: (415) 677-6100     Fax: (415) 824-9700     www.dhl.com

*Worldwide air express carrier.*

**DHL Worldwide Express, 50 East Fifth Sreet, Alberttown, Georgetown, Guyana**

Tel: 592-4-2019

## ERNST & YOUNG, LLP

787 Seventh Ave., New York, NY, 10019

Tel: (212) 773-3000     Fax: (212) 773-6350     www.eyi.com

*Accounting and audit, tax and management consulting services.*

**Christopher L. Ram & Co., 157 C. Waterloo St., Georgetown, Guyana**

Tel: 592-2-74891   Fax: 592-2-54221   Contact: Christopher Ram

## IBM CORPORATION

New Orchard Road, Armonk, NY, 10504

Tel: (914) 765-1900     Fax: (914) 765-7382     www.ibm.com

*Information products, technology and services.*

**IBM Guyana, Guyana**

Tel: 592-826900   Fax: 592-826969

## KPMG INTERNATIONAL LLP

345 Park Avenue, New York, NY, 10022

Tel: (201) 307-7000     Fax: (201) 930-8617     www.kpmg.com

*Accounting and audit, tax and management consulting services.*

**KPMG EMA, 9, Church Path, Georgetown, Guyana**

Tel: 592-2-78825   Fax: 592-2-78824   Contact: Nizam Ali, Sr. Ptnr.

## PRICEWATERHOUSECOOPERS LLP

1301 Ave. of the Americas, New York, NY, 10019

Tel: (212) 596-7000     Fax: (212) 259-1301     www.pwcglobal.com

*Accounting and auditing, tax and management, and human resource consulting services.*

**PriceWaterhouseCoopers, 145 Crown Street, PO Box 10351, Georgetown 6, Guyana**

Tel: 592-2-62904   Fax: 592-2-53849

## TEXACO INC.

2000 Westchester Ave., White Plains, NY, 10650

Tel: (914) 253-4000     Fax: (914) 253-7753     www.texaco.com

*Exploration/marketing crude oil, mfr. petro chemicals and products.*

**Texaco West Indies Ltd., 45 Main St., Georgetown, Guyana**

# Haiti

## AIR EXPRESS INTERNATIONAL CORPORATION
120 Tokeneke Road, PO Box 1231, Darien, CT, 06820

Tel: (203) 655-7900     Fax: (203) 655-5779     www.aeilogistics.com

*International air freight forwarder.*

**AEI of Haiti,  International Airport of Maia Gate (PAP), Cargo Section, Port-au-Prince, Haiti**

Tel: 509-460102    Fax: 509-463522

## AMERICAN & EFIRD, INC.
PO Box 507, Mt. Holly, NC, 28120

Tel: (704) 827-4311     Fax: (704) 822-6054     www.amefird.com

*Mfr. industrial sewing thread for worldwide industrial and consumer markets.*

**American & Efird Haiti,  Batiments 1 Et 2, Complexe Industriel Des Nimes Route De l' Aeroport, Port-au-Prince Haiti**

**Port-au-Prince, Haiti**

## AMERICAN AIRLINES INC.
4333 Amon Carter Boulevard, Ft. Worth, TX, 76155

Tel: (817) 963-1234     Fax: (817) 967-9641     www.amrcorp.com

*Air transport services.*

**American Airlines,  Cite de l'Exposition, Francois Duvalier Intl. Airport, Port-au-Prince, Haiti**

## AMERICAN INTERNATIONAL GROUP INC. (AIG)
70 Pine Street, New York, NY, 10270

Tel: (212) 770-7000     Fax: (212) 509-9705     www.aig.com

*Worldwide insurance and financial services.*

**Compagnie d'Assurance d'Haiti SA,  158 rue de Centre, Port-au-Prince, Haiti**

## AON CORPORATION
123 North Wacker Drive, Chicago, IL, 60606

Tel: (312) 701-3000     Fax: (312) 701-3100     www.aon.com

*Insurance brokers worldwide; underwrites accident and health insurance, specialty and professional insurance; and provides risk management consultation.*

**AON Worldwide / Bain Hogg Insurance Brokers,  184, rue Pavee, Port-au-Prince, Haiti**

Tel: 809-567-7178  Fax: 809-541-9333   Contact: M.R. Redondo

## AVIS GROUP HOLDINGS, INC.
900 Old Country Road., Garden City, NY, 11530

Tel: (516) 222-3000     Fax: (516) 222-4381     www.avis.com

*Car rental services.*

**Avis Group Holdings Ltd..,  rue Mais Gate, Port-au-Prince, Haiti**

## CITIGROUP, INC.
153 East 53rd Street, New York, NY, 10043

Tel: (212) 559-1000     Fax: (212) 559-3646     www.citigroup.com

*Provides insurance and financial services worldwide.*

**Citibank N.A.,  242 Delmas Rd., PO Box 1688, Port-au-Prince, Haiti**

Contact: Gladys M. Coupet

## DHL WORLDWIDE EXPRESS

50 California Avenue, San Francisco, CA, 94111

Tel: (415) 677-6100     Fax: (415) 824-9700     www.dhl.com

*Worldwide air express carrier.*

**DHL Worldwide Express, 17 BIS. Route de L'Aeroport, Port au Prince, Haiti**

Tel: 509-464800

## EAGLE GLOBAL LOGISTICS (EGL)

15350 Vickery Drive, Houston, TX, 77032

Tel: (281) 618-3100     Fax: (281) 618-3100     www.eaglegl.com

*Ocean/air freight forwarding, customs brokerage, packing and wholesale, logistics management and insurance.*

**CM Brokerage Service, Hamaserco Bldg. Door No. 4, Airport Rd., PO Box 1795, Port-au-Prince Haiti**

Tel: 509-46-3253    Fax: 509-46-5540

## FRITZ COMPANIES, INC.

706 Mission Street, Ste. 900, San Francisco, CA, 94103

Tel: (415) 904-8360     Fax: (415) 904-8661     www.fritz.com

*Integrated transportation, sourcing, distribution and customs brokerage services.*

**Fritz Companies Inc., Port-au-Prince, Haiti**

## HOLIDAY INN (BASS RESORTS) WORLDWIDE, INC.

3 Ravinia Drive, Ste. 2900, Atlanta, GA, 30346-2149

Tel: (770) 604-2000     Fax: (770) 604-5403     www.holidayinn.com

*Hotels, restaurants and casinos.*

**Holiday Inn, rue Capois 10, B.P. 1429, Dwin, Port-au-Prince, Haiti**

## HORWATH INTERNATIONAL ASSOCIATION

415 Madison Ave., New York, NY, 10017

Tel: (212) 838-5566     Fax: (212) 838-3636     www.horwath.com

*Public accountants and auditors.*

**Turnier Laurent, 126 Angle rue des Miracles & Mgsr. Guilloux, Port-au-Prince, Haiti**

## KPMG INTERNATIONAL LLP

345 Park Avenue, New York, NY, 10022

Tel: (201) 307-7000     Fax: (201) 930-8617     www.kpmg.com

*Accounting and audit, tax and management consulting services.*

**KPMG Peat Marwick, 47, Route de l'Aeroport, Port-au-Prince, Haiti**

Tel: 509-464854   Fax: 509-460625    Contact: Mireille Mérové-Pierre, Sr. Ptnr.

## LUCKETT TOBACCOS INC.

222 South First Street, #403, Louisville, KY, 40202

Tel: (502) 561-0070     Fax: (502) 584-1650

*Wholesale tobacco, cigarette mfr. supplies and equipment.*

**Compagnie des Tabacs Comme Il Faut, B.P. 797, Port-au-Prince, Haiti**

## NORTON ABRASIVES COMPANY

1 New Bond Street, Worcester, MA, 01606

Tel: (508) 795-5000     Fax: (508) 795-5741     www.nortonabrasives.com

*Mfr. abrasives for industrial manufacturing.*

**Norton SA, Meu's Bldg., B.P. 652, Port-au-Prince, Haiti**

**TEXACO INC.**

2000 Westchester Ave., White Plains, NY, 10650

Tel: (914) 253-4000    Fax: (914) 253-7753    www.texaco.com

*Exploration/marketing crude oil, mfr. petro chemicals and products.*

**Texaco Caribbean Ltd., rue Roux, B.P. 867, Port-au-Prince, Haiti**

# Honduras

## AIR EXPRESS INTERNATIONAL CORPORATION

120 Tokeneke Road, PO Box 1231, Darien, CT, 06820

Tel: (203) 655-7900     Fax: (203) 655-5779     www.aeilogistics.com

*International air freight forwarder.*

**AEI of Honduras, c/o Cormar Honduras - Ave. Independencia, 8a Calle B - No. Q-6 Col. 15 de Setiembre, Comayaguela Tegucigalpa Honduras**

Tel: 504-2-342-612

## AMERICAN BILTRITE INC.

57 River Street, Wellesley Hills, MA, 02181

Tel: (781) 237-6655     Fax: (781) 237-6880     www.americanbiltriteinc.com

*Mfr. vinyl composition and rubber floor coverings and produces pressure sensitive tape and rubber matting.*

**Compania Hulera SA, Aptdo. 164, San Pedro Sula, Honduras**

## AMERICAN INTERNATIONAL GROUP INC. (AIG)

70 Pine Street, New York, NY, 10270

Tel: (212) 770-7000     Fax: (212) 509-9705     www.aig.com

*Worldwide insurance and financial services.*

**American Home Assurance Co., Edif Los Costanos, Blvd. Morazan, Tegucigalpa, Honduras**

## AON CORPORATION

123 North Wacker Drive, Chicago, IL, 60606

Tel: (312) 701-3000     Fax: (312) 701-3100     www.aon.com

*Insurance brokers worldwide; underwrites accident and health insurance, specialty and professional insurance; and provides risk management consultation.*

**AON Worldwide / Consultores y Corredores de Seguros, 6 Av. 2 y 3 Calles, N.O. Plaza G.M.C., San Pedro Sula, Honduras**

Tel: 504-552-2595   Fax: 504-550-9644   Contact: Rene Kattan

## APPLERA CORPORATION

761 Main Avenue, Norwalk, CT, 06859-0001

Tel: (203) 762-1000     Fax: (203) 762-6000     www.applera.com

*Leading supplier of systems for life science research and related applications.*

**Analytical Instruments, Ave. Colon, No. 523 Piso 2, Tegucigalpa, Honduras**

## AVON PRODUCTS INC.

1345 Avenue of the Americas, New York, NY, 10105-0196

Tel: (212) 282-5000     Fax: (212) 282-6049     www.avon.com

*Mfr./distributor beauty and related products, fashion jewelry, gifts and collectibles.*

**Productos Avon S.A., Apartado Postal "1763", San Pedro Sula, Honduras**

Tel: 504-52-6118   Fax: 504-57-3883   Contact: Napoleon Garcia, Div. Sales Mgr.

## LOUIS BERGER INTERNATIONAL INC.

100 Halsted Street, East Orange, NJ, 07019

Tel: (201) 678-1960     Fax: (201) 672-4284     www.louisberger.com

*Consulting engineers, engaged in architecture, environmental and advisory services.*

**Louis Berger International Inc., Unidad Coordinadoro-BID, Ed. Inatlantic, 2da Planta 2da Av., Entre Calle1y2, San Predo Sula Honduras**

## BEST WESTERN INTERNATIONAL

6201 North 24th Place, Phoenix, AZ, 85106

Tel: (602) 957-4200      Fax: (602) 957-5740      www.bestwestern.com

*International hotel chain.*

**Best Western International,  San Pedro Sula, Honduras**

**BW Posada Real Copan,  Km 164 Carr, San Pedro Sula, Copan Ruins, Honduras 23400**

Tel: 504-614-483

## BRISTOL-MYERS SQUIBB COMPANY

345 Park Ave., New York, NY, 10154-0037

Tel: (212) 546-4000      Fax: (212) 546-4020      www.bms.com

*Pharmaceutical and food preparations, medical and surgical instruments.*

**Compania Bristol-Myers de Centro America,  Col. John F. Kennedy, Tegucigalpa, Honduras**

## LEO BURNETT, DIV. B-COM 3 GROUP

35 West Wacker Drive, Chicago, IL, 60601

Tel: (312) 220-5959      Fax: (312) 220-6533      www.bcom3group.com

*Engaged in advertising, marketing, media buying and planning, and public relations.*

**Calderon Publicidad,  Tegucigalpa, Honduras**

## CALMAQUIP ENGINEERING CORPORATION

7240 N.W. 12th Street, Miami, FL, 33121

Tel: (305) 592-4510      Fax: (305) 593-9618      www.calmaquip.com

*Engineering*

**Calmaquip Ingenieros de Honduras SA,  Aptdo. 845, blvd Morazan 1518, Barrio de Guacerique, Comayaguela, Honduras**

## CARGILL, INC.

15407 McGinty Road West, Minnetonka, MN, 55440-5625

Tel: (612) 742-7575      Fax: (612) 742-7393      www.cargill.com

*Food products, feeds, animal products.*

**Alcon (Alimentos Concentrados Nacionales SA),  Aptdo. 283, San Pedro Sula, Bufalo, Cortes, Honduras**

## CHIQUITA BRANDS INTERNATIONAL INC.

250 East Fifth Street, Cincinnati, OH, 45202

Tel: (513) 784-8000      Fax: (513) 784-8030      www.chiquita.com

*Sale and distribution of bananas, fresh fruits and processed foods.*

**Tela Railroad Co.,  Aptdo. Aereo 30, San Pedro Sula, Honduras**

## CITIGROUP, INC.

153 East 53rd Street, New York, NY, 10043

Tel: (212) 559-1000      Fax: (212) 559-3646      www.citigroup.com

*Provides insurance and financial services worldwide.*

**Citibank N.A.,  Blvd. Suyapa, Tegucigalpa Francisco, Morazan 3434, Honduras**

Contact: Patricia Ferro

## COLGATE-PALMOLIVE COMPANY

300 Park Ave., New York, NY, 10022

Tel: (212) 310-2000      Fax: (212) 310-2919      www.colgate.com

*Mfr. pharmaceuticals, cosmetics, toiletries and detergents.*

**Colgate-Palmolive Inc.,  Dos Cuadros al Norte de Granitos, Terrazas Contiguo Honduprint, Tegucigalpa, Honduras**

## CONTINENTAL AIRLINES INC.

2929 Allen Parkway, Ste. 2010, Houston, TX, 77019

Tel: (281) 834-5000     Fax: (281) 520-6329     www.continental.com

*International airline carrier.*

**Continental Airlines Inc.,  Honduras**

## DDB NEEDHAM WORLDWIDE INC.

437 Madison Ave., New York, NY, 10022

Tel: (212) 415-2000     Fax: (212) 415-3417     www.ddbn.com

*Advertising agency.*

**Adcom/DDB Needham Worldwide,  San Pedro Sula, Honduras**

## DHL WORLDWIDE EXPRESS

50 California Avenue, San Francisco, CA, 94111

Tel: (415) 677-6100     Fax: (415) 824-9700     www.dhl.com

*Worldwide air express carrier.*

**DHL Worldwide Express,  Col. Palmira, Ave. Republica of Chile, Frente Of. Principal Banexpo, Tegucigalpa Honduras**

Tel: 504-39-4882

## DOLE FOOD COMPANY, INC.

31365 Oak Crest Drive, Westlake Village, CA, 91361

Tel: (818) 879-6600     Fax: (818) 879-6615     www.dole.com

*Produces/distributes fresh fruits and vegetables and canned juices and fruits.*

**Agropecuaria el Porvenir S.A. (Agropor,  Honduras**

## EAGLE GLOBAL LOGISTICS (EGL)

15350 Vickery Drive, Houston, TX, 77032

Tel: (281) 618-3100     Fax: (281) 618-3100     www.eaglegl.com

*Ocean/air freight forwarding, customs brokerage, packing and wholesale, logistics management and insurance.*

**Terminales de Cortes, S.A. de C.V.,  4a Calle - 4a Ave. N.O. #29, Edif. Bonilla Gastel #2 Barrio Guamilito, PO Box 298, San Pedro Sula Honduras**

Tel: 504-532-600   Fax: 504-577-000

**Terminales de Cortes, S.A. de C.V.,  2a Calle - 4a Ave., A #238 Col. Palmira, PO Box 988, Tegucigalpa Honduras**

Tel: 504-532-600   Fax: 504-577-000

## ECOLAB INC.

370 N. Wabasha Street, St. Paul, MN, 55102

Tel: (651) 293-2233     Fax: (651) 293-2379     www.ecolab.com

*Develop/mfr. premium cleaning, sanitizing and maintenance products and services for the hospitality, institutional, and residential markets.*

**Ecolab Ltd.,  Tegucigalpa, Honduras**

Tel: 504-553-4679

## ERNST & YOUNG, LLP

787 Seventh Ave., New York, NY, 10019

Tel: (212) 773-3000     Fax: (212) 773-6350     www.eyi.com

*Accounting and audit, tax and management consulting services.*

**Morales Palao William y Asociados,  Apdo. Postal 2232, San Pedro Sula, Honduras**

Tel: 504-31-3712   Fax: 504-313709   Contact: David O. Palo

## FRITZ COMPANIES, INC.

706 Mission Street, Ste. 900, San Francisco, CA, 94103

Tel: (415) 904-8360    Fax: (415) 904-8661    www.fritz.com

*Integrated transportation, sourcing, distribution and customs brokerage services.*

**Fritz Companies Inc., San Pedro de Sula**

## H.B. FULLER COMPANY

1200 Willow Lake Blvd., Vadnais Heights, MN, 55110

Tel: (651) 236-5900    Fax: (651) 236-5898    www.hbfuller.com

*Mfr./distributor adhesives, sealants, coatings, paints, waxes, sanitation chemicals.*

**H.B. Fuller Co., Kativo de Honduras, 193 San Pedro Sula, Honduras**

**H.B. Fuller Co., Kativo de Honduras, 454 Tegucigalpa, Honduras**

Tel: 504-32-2039   Fax: 504-32-0436

**H.B. Fuller Honduras, S.A., 1103 San Pedro Sula, Honduras**

Tel: 504-51-7914   Fax: 504-51-7510

## GARAN, INC.

350 Fifth Ave, New York, NY, 10118

Tel: (212) 563-2000    Fax: (212) 971-2250

*Designs, manufactures and markets apparel for men, women and children.*

**Garan de Honduras, Honduras**

## GREY GLOBAL GROUP

777 Third Ave., New York, NY, 10017

Tel: (212) 546-2000    Fax: (212) 546-1495    www.grey.com

*International advertising agency.*

**Talento Publicidad, Tegucigalpa, Honduras**

## GRIFFITH LABORATORIES INC.

One Griffith Center, Alsip, IL, 60658

Tel: (708) 371-0900    Fax: (708) 597-3294    www.griffithlabs.com

*Mfr. industrial food ingredients and equipment.*

**Griffith Labs Inc., San Pedro Sula, Honduras**

Tel: 504-52-2938   Fax: 504-52-7071

## HOLIDAY INN (BASS RESORTS) WORLDWIDE, INC.

3 Ravinia Drive, Ste. 2900, Atlanta, GA, 30346-2149

Tel: (770) 604-2000    Fax: (770) 604-5403    www.holidayinn.com

*Hotels, restaurants and casinos.*

**Holiday Inn, Calle Peatonal, Aptdo. 175, Tegucigalpa, Honduras**

## IBM CORPORATION

New Orchard Road, Armonk, NY, 10504

Tel: (914) 765-1900    Fax: (914) 765-7382    www.ibm.com

*Information products, technology and services.*

**IBM de Honduras SA, Tegucigalpa, Honduras**

## INTER-CONTINENTAL HOTELS

3 Ravina Drive, Suite 2900, Atlanta, GA, 30346-2149

Tel: (770) 604-2000    Fax: (770) 604-5403    www.interconti.com

*Worldwide hotel and resort accommodations.*

**Camino Real Inter-Continental San Pedro Sula, Col. Hernandez y Blvd. del Sur, Multiplaza Mall, San Pedro Sula, Honduras**

Tel: 504-50-5555   Fax: 504-50-6255

### J. WALTER THOMPSON COMPANY

466 Lexington Ave., New York, NY, 10017

Tel: (212) 210-7000    Fax: (212) 210-6944    www.jwt.com

*International advertising and marketing services.*

**APCU-Thompson, Tegucigalpa, Honduras**

### KIMBERLY-CLARK CORPORATION

351 Phelps Drive, Irving, TX, 75038

Tel: (972) 281-1200    Fax: (972) 281-1435    www.kimberly-clark.com

*Mfr./sales/distribution of consumer tissue, household and personal care products.*

**Kimberly-Clark Co. de Honduras SA de CV, San Pedro Sula, Honduras**

### KPMG INTERNATIONAL LLP

345 Park Avenue, New York, NY, 10022

Tel: (201) 307-7000    Fax: (201) 930-8617    www.kpmg.com

*Accounting and audit, tax and management consulting services.*

**KPMG Peat Marwick, Edif. Barnco Atlantida SA, 7 piso No. 703, la. Calle N.O. 3 a. Av., San Pedro Sula Honduras**

**KPMG Peat Marwick, Col. Palmire 2da Calle, 2da Av., Casa No. 417, Tegucigalpa, Honduras**

Tel: 504-32-2806    Fax: 504-32-5925    Contact: Armando Barnica, Sr. Ptnr.

### LOWE LINTAS & PARTNERS WORLDWIDE

One Dag Hammarskjold Plaza, New York, NY, 10017

Tel: (212) 605-8000    Fax: (212) 605-4705    www.interpublic.com

*Full-service, integrated marketing communications company/advertising agency.*

**Publicidad Comercial APL, Ave. Enrique Tierno Galvan, Col. Lomas del Guijarro 2949 Tegucigalpa Honduras**

Tel: 504-32-6743    Fax: 504-38-1585    Contact: Norma Alvarez

### MARSH & McLENNAN COS INC.

1166 Ave. of the Americas, New York, NY, 10036-2774

Tel: (212) 345-5000    Fax: (212) 345-4808    www.marshmac.com

*Insurance agents/brokers, pension and investment management consulting services.*

**Correduria Internacional de Seguros, Edif. Cruz-Heath, 3 Av. 6 Calle, Col. Alameda, 1876 Tegucigalpa, Honduras**

Tel: 504-32-2676    Fax: 504-39-3558

**Tecniseguros S. de R.L., Edif. Rivera & Cia. 3er piso, San Pedro Sula, Honduras**

Tel: 504-5-553-3069    Fax: 504-5-552-7418    Contact: Claudo Guell

### McCANN-ERICKSON WORLDGROUP

750 Third Ave., New York, NY, 10017

Tel: (212) 984-3644    Fax: (212) 984-2629    www.mccann.com

*International advertising and marketing services.*

**McCann-Erickson Centroamericana S de RL (Honduras), Edif. Banco Atlantida piso 8, Aptdo. 802, San Pedro Sula, Honduras**

### McDONALD'S CORPORATION

McDonald's Plaza, Oak Brook, IL, 60523

Tel: (630) 623-3000    Fax: (630) 623-7409    www.mcdonalds.com

*Fast food chain stores.*

**McDonald's Corp., Honduras**

## THE McGRAW-HILL COMPANIES

1221 Ave. of the Americas, New York, NY, 10020

Tel: (212) 512-2000     Fax: (212) 512-2703     www.mccgraw-hill.com

*Books, magazines, information systems, financial service, publishing and broadcast operations.*

**McGraw-Hill Honduras, Colonia Luis Landa, Cuarta Calle Case E-, Tegucigalpa, Honduras**

Tel: 504-322-475

## J. P. MORGAN CHASE & CO. INC.

World Headquarters, 270 Park Ave., New York, NY, 10017

Tel: (212) 270-6000     Fax: (212) 622-9030     www.jpmorganchase.com

*Provides integrated financial solutions for institutions and individuals worldwide, including asset management, investment banking and commercial banking.*

**J. P. Morgan Chase & Co., Aptdo. 57-C, 5a Calle y 7a. Av., San Pedro Sula, Honduras**

## PAN-AMERICAN LIFE INSURANCE COMPANY

Pan American Life Center, PO Box 60219, New Orleans, LA, 70130-0219

Tel: (504) 566-1300     Fax: (504) 566-3600     www.palic.com

*Insurance services.*

**Pan-American Life Insurance Co., Av. Republica de Chile 804, Edif. PALIC, Tegucigalpa, Honduras**

Tel: 504-232-8774   Fax: 504-232-3907   Contact: Alberto Agurcia   Emp: 105

## PERKIN ELMER, INC.

45 William Street, Wellesley, MA, 02481

Tel: (781) 237-5100     Fax: (781) 431-4255     www.perkinelmer.com

*Mfr. equipment and devices to detect explosives and bombs on airline carriers.*

**PerkinElmer Honduras, Avenida Colon Casa #523, 2do Piso Joyeria Handal, Frente a Bancasa Apdo. 5, Tegucigalpa, Honduras**

## PHELPS DODGE CORPORATION

2600 North Central Ave., Phoenix, AZ, 85004-3089

Tel: (602) 234-8100     Fax: (602) 234-8337     www.phelpsdodge.com

*Copper, minerals, metals and special engineered products for transportation and electrical markets.*

**Electro Conductores de Honduras SA de CV (ECOHSA), Aptdo. 3192, Tegucigalpa, Honduras**

## PRICEWATERHOUSECOOPERS LLP

1301 Ave. of the Americas, New York, NY, 10019

Tel: (212) 596-7000     Fax: (212) 259-1301     www.pwcglobal.com

*Accounting and auditing, tax and management, and human resource consulting services.*

**PriceWaterhouseCoopers, Col. Loma Linda Norte, Bloque F-3 Calle, Diagonal Gema No 1, Tegucigalpa Honduras**

Tel: 504-32-01-51   Fax: 504-31-19-06

**PriceWaterhouseCoopers, Edif. Banco Atlantida No 903, Apartado 563, San Pedro Sula, Honduras**

Tel: 504-53-3060   Fax: 504-52-6728

## RAYOVAC CORPORATION

601 Rayovac Drive, Madison, WI, 53711-2497

Tel: (608) 275-3340     Fax: (608) 275-4577     www.rayovac.com

*Mfr. batteries and lighting devices.*

**Rayovac Honduras, Comayaguella, Honduras**

## ROHM AND HAAS COMPANY

100 Independence Mall West, Philadelphia, PA, 19106

Tel: (215) 592-3000     Fax: (215) 592-3377     www.rohmhaas.com

*Mfr. industrial and agricultural chemicals, plastics.*

**Rocasa Honduras, Aptdo. 1854, San Pedro Sula, Honduras**

## SEARS ROEBUCK & COMPANY

3333 Beverly Road, Hoffman Estates, IL, 60179

Tel: (847) 286-2500    Fax: (847) 286-1517    www.sears.com

*Diversified general merchandise.*

**Sears Roebuck & Cia., Pasaje Valle, San Pedro Sula, Honduras**

## TRUE NORTH COMMUNICATIONS INC.

101 East Erie Street, Chicago, IL, 60611

Tel: (312) 425-6500    Fax: (312) 425-5010    www.truenorth.com

*Holding company, advertising agency.*

**Foote, Cone & Belding, Edif. Palmira 4th piso, Local C, Col. Palmira, Tegucigalpa D.C. Honduras**

## UNITED PARCEL SERVICE, INC.

55 Glenlake Parkway, NE, Atlanta, GA, 30328

Tel: (404) 828-6000    Fax: (404) 828-6593    www.ups.com

*International package-delivery service.*

**UPS / Courier Internacional S.A., Edif. Maya, Frente Hotel Maya, Primer piso, Local 4, Tegucigalpa Honduras**

Tel: 504-31-4-755   Fax: 504-31-1244

## WACKENHUT CORPORATION

4200 Wackenhut Dr., Ste. 100, Palm Beach Gardens, FL, 33410

Tel: (561) 622-5656    Fax: (561) 691-6736    www.wackenhut.com

*Security systems and services.*

**Seguridad Tecnica S.A. de C.V., Col. Miramontes, Av. Altiplano, Casa 1411, Tegucigalpa, Honduras**

Tel: 504-32-0778   Fax: 504-32-2926

**Wackenhut Honduras SA, Col. Miramontes, Av. Altiplano, Casa 1411, Tegucigalpa, Honduras**

Tel: 504-32-0778   Fax: 504-32-2926

## WARNACO INC.

90 Park Ave., New York, NY, 10016

Tel: (212) 661-1300    Fax: (212) 687-0480    www.warnaco.com

*Mfr./sales intimate apparel and men's and women's sportswear.*

**Warnaco, San Pedro Sula, Honduras**

## WENDY'S INTERNATIONAL, INC.

428 West Dublin Granville Roads, Dublin, OH, 43017-0256

Tel: (614) 764-3100    Fax: (614) 764-3459    www.wendysintl.com

*Fast food restaurant chain.*

**Wendy's International, Honduras**

## XEROX CORPORATION

800 Long Ridge Road, PO Box 1600, Stamford, CT, 06904

Tel: (203) 968-3000    Fax: (203) 968-4312    www.xerox.com

*Mfr. document processing equipment, systems and supplies.*

**Xerox De Honduras, S.A., Apt. Postal 897, Col. La Paloma No. 2401, Blvd. Morazan, Tegucigalpa D.C. Honduras**

Tel: 504-38-2211   Fax: 504-31-3689

## YOUNG & RUBICAM INC.

285 Madison Ave., New York, NY, 10017

Tel: (212) 210-3000    Fax: (212) 370-3796    www.yr.com

*Advertising, public relations, direct marketing and sales promotion, corporate and product ID management.*

**Delfos Publicidad, Teguicgalpa, Honduras**

# Hong Kong

## 3COM CORPORATION

5400 Bayfront Plaza, Santa Clara, CA, 95052-8145

Tel: (408) 326-5000     Fax: (408) 326-5001     www.3com.com

*Develop/mfr. computer networking products and systems.*

**3Com Asia Ltd. - Hong Kong, 23/F Li Po Chun Chambers, 189 Des Voeux Rd., Central Hong Kong PRC**

Tel: 852-2501-1111   Fax: 852-2537-1149

## 3D/INTERNATIONAL INC.

1900 West Loop South, Ste. 400, Houston, TX, 77027

Tel: (713) 871-7000     Fax: (713) 871-7456     www.3di.com

*Engaged in design, management and environmental services.*

**3D/I-Hong Kong, 17/F Malaysia Bldg., 50 Gloucester Rd., Wanchai, Hong Kong PRC**

## 3M

3M Center, St. Paul, MN, 55144-1000

Tel: (651) 733-1110     Fax: (651) 733-9973     www.mmm.com

*Mfr. diversified products for industry, health care, imaging, communications, transport, safety, consumer, etc.*

**3M Hong Kong Ltd., 5/F Victoria Ctr., 15 Watson Rd., Northpoint, Causeway Bay Hong Kong PRC**

Tel: 852-2806-6111  Fax: 852-5807-1308

## ABBOTT LABORATORIES

One Abbott Park, Abbott Park, IL, 60064-3500

Tel: (847) 937-6100     Fax: (847) 937-1511     www.abbott.com

*Development/mfr./sale diversified health care products and services.*

**Abbott Laboratories, Ltd., 20/F AIA Tower, 183 Electric Road, North Point Hong Kong PRC**

Tel: 852-2-566-8711

## ACTERNA CORPORATION

3 New England Executive Park, Burlington, MA, 01803

Tel: (781) 272-6100     Fax: (781) 272-2304     www.acterna.com

*Develop, manufacture and market communications test instruments, systems, software and services.*

**Acterna Corporation, Central, Hong Kong PRC**

## ACTION INSTRUMENTS INC.

8601 Aero Drive, San Diego, CA, 92123

Tel: (619) 279-5726     Fax: (619) 279-6290     www.actionio.com

*Mfr. electronic instruments and industrial measurements computers.*

**Action Instruments (China) Ltd., 24/F Unit D Gee Change Hong Centre, 65 Wong Chuk Hang Road, Hong Kong PRC**

## ACTIVE VOICE CORPORATION

2901 Third Avenue, Ste. 500, Seattle, WA, 98121

Tel: (206) 441-4700     Fax: (206) 441-4784     www.activevoice.com

*Mfr. PC-based voice processing systems.*

**Active Voice Hong Kong, Rm. 806 Tower 1 Harbour Centre, 1 Hok Cheung Street, Hung Hom Kowloon, Hong Kong PRC**

Tel: 852-2774-2986  Fax: 852-2334-8910

## ADEMCO INTERNATIONAL

1769 N.W. 79th Avenue, Miami, FL, 33126

Tel: (305) 477-5204     Fax: (305) 477-5404     www.ademcoint.com

*Mfr. security, fire and burglary systems and products.*

**ADEMCO (Hong Kong) Ltd., Flat A&B - 7/F CDW Bldg., 388 Castle Peak Rd., Tseun Wan N.T., Hong Kong PRC**

Tel: 852-2405-2323   Fax: 852-2415-3112

## THE AEROQUIP GROUP

3000 Strayer, PO Box 50, Maumee, OH, 43537

Tel: (419) 867-2200     Fax: (419) 867-2390     www.aeroquip.com

*Mfr. industrial, automotive, aerospace and defense products.*

**Aeroquip Corporation, Unit 6-9, 18/F Citimark, No. 28 Yuen Shun Circuit, Siu Lek Yuen, Shatin New Territory Hong Kong PRC**

Tel: 852-2637-7626   Fax: 852-2646-4163

## AETNA INC.

151 Farmington Avenue, Hartford, CT, 06156

Tel: (860) 273-0123     Fax: (860) 275-2677     www.aetna.com

*Managed health care, annuities, individual retirement and group pension services, and asset management products worldwide.*

**Aetna Hong Kong, Hong Kong PRC**

## AIR EXPRESS INTERNATIONAL CORPORATION

120 Tokeneke Road, PO Box 1231, Darien, CT, 06820

Tel: (203) 655-7900     Fax: (203) 655-5779     www.aeilogistics.com

*International air freight forwarder.*

**AEI (Hong Kong) Ltd., AEI Warehouse & Distribution Centre, Units 3-6 G/F Pacific Trade Centre, Kai Hing Rd., Kowloon Bay Hong Kong PRC**

Tel: 852-2750-2051   Fax: 852-2798-8246

**AEI (Hong Kong) Ltd., Room 28 1/F Pacific Trade Centre, 2 Kai Hing Rd., Kowloon Bay, Hong Kong PRC**

Tel: 852-2796-3668   Fax: 852-2796-6533

## AIR PRODUCTS AND CHEMICALS, INC.

7201 Hamilton Boulevard, Allentown, PA, 18195-1501

Tel: (610) 481-4911     Fax: (610) 481-5900     www.airproducts.com

*Mfr. industry gases and related equipment, specialty chemicals, environmental/energy systems.*

**Air Products Asia Inc., Room 1901, ETE Tower 838, 89 Queensway, Central, Hong Kong PRC**

Contact: Wayne A. Hinman, Pres.

## ALARON INC.

1026 Doris Road, PO Box 215287, Auburn Hills, MI, 48326

Tel: (248) 340-7500     Fax: (248) 340-7555     www.alaron.com

*Distributor of consumer electronic products.*

**Alaron Asia Ltd., Ste. 2007-8 Tower I, 33 Canton Rd. Tsim Sha Tsui, Kowloon, Hong Kong PRC**

Tel: 852-2375-7448   Fax: 852-2375-7445   Contact: H. K. Law   Emp: 15

## ALBERTO-CULVER COMPANY

2525 Armitage Ave., Melrose Park, IL, 60160

Tel: (708) 450-3000     Fax: (708) 450-3354     www.alberto.com

*Mfr./marketing personal care and household brand products.*

**Alberto-Culver (HK) Ltd., Rm. 110-111 Stanhope House, 738 King's Rd., Quarry Bay, Hong Kong PRC**

## ALCONE MARKETING GROUP

15 Whatney, Irvine, CA, 92618

Tel: (949) 770-4400      Fax: (949) 859-7493      www.alconemarketing.com

*Sales promotion and marketing services agencies.*

**Alcone Marketing Group, Unit 2113 Miramar Tower, 1-23 Kimberley Road, Tsimshatsui Kowloon, Hong Kong PRC**

Tel: 852-2311-4491   Fax: 852-2316-2937

## ALLEGHENY TECHNOLOGIES

1000 Six PPG Place, Pittsburgh, PA, 15222

Tel: (412) 394-2800      Fax: (412) 394-2805      www.alleghenytechnologies.com

*Diversified mfr. aviation and electronics, specialty metals, industrial and consumer products.*

**Allegheny Technologies, New World Centre (East Wing) #918, 24 Salisbury Rd., Tsim Sha Tsui, Hong Kong PRC**

## ALLEN TELECOM

25101 Chagrin Boulevard, Beachwood, OH, 44122-5619

Tel: (216) 765-5818      Fax: (216) 765-0410      www.allentele.com

*Mfr. communications equipment, automotive bodies and parts, electronic components.*

**Allen Telecom (Hong Kong) Ltd., Room 1603 Remington Ctr., 23 Hung To Rd., Kwun Tong, Kowloon Hong Kong PRC**

Tel: 852-2839-1844   Fax: 852-2839-4864   Contact: James Fong

**Orion Industries Ltd., East Tower Bldg., 41 Lockhart Rd., Wan Chai, Hong Kong PRC**

## ALLEN-BRADLEY COMPANY, INC.

1201 South Second Street, Milwaukee, WI, 53204

Tel: (414) 382-2000      Fax: (414) 382-4444      www.ab.com

*Mfr. electrical controls and information devices.*

**Allen-Bradley (Hong Kong) Ltd., Room 1006, Block B, Sea View Estate, 2-8 Watson Rd., Hong Kong PRC**

## ALLERGAN INC.

2525 Dupont Drive, PO Box 19534, Irvine, CA, 92713-9534

Tel: (714) 246-4500      Fax: (714) 246-6987      www.allergan.com

*Mfr. therapeutic eye care products, skin and neural care pharmaceuticals.*

**Allergan Asia Limited, Unit 3001, New Metroplaza-Tower 1, 223 Hing Fong Road, Kwai Chung NT, Hong Kong PRC**

Tel: 852-2480-3330   Fax: 852-2424-0213

## ALLTEL CORPORATION

1 Allied Drive, Little Rock, AR, 72202

Tel: (501) 905-8000      Fax: (501) 905-6444      www.alltel.com

*Full range outsourcing services.*

**ALLTEL Systems Ltd. Hong Kong, 3610 Syun Tak Centre, 200 Connaught Rd., Hong Kong PRC**

## ALPHA INDUSTRIES INC.

20 Sylvan Road, Woburn, MA, 01801

Tel: (781) 935-5150      Fax: (781) 824-4543      www.alphaind.com

*Mfr. electronic and microwave components.*

**Pangaea Hong Kong Ltd., 181 Johnston Road, Rm. 1810 Tai Yau Bldg., Wanchai Hong Kong PRC**

## ALTERA CORPORATION

101 Innovation Drive, San Jose, CA, 95134

Tel: (408) 544-7000     Fax: (408) 544-8303     www.altera.com

*Mfr. high-density programmable chips for semi-conductor industry.*

**Altera International, Ltd., Suites 908-920 Tower 1 Metroplaza, 223 Hing Fong Road, Kwai Fong New Territories, Hong Kong PRC**

## AMERICAN & EFIRD, INC.

PO Box 507, Mt. Holly, NC, 28120

Tel: (704) 827-4311     Fax: (704) 822-6054     www.amefird.com

*Mfr. industrial sewing thread for worldwide industrial and consumer markets.*

**American & Efird (HK) Ltd., Unit 1501 Tsuen Wan Ind. Centre 15/F, 220-248 Texaco Road, Tsuen Wan NT, Hong Kong PRC**

## AMERICAN AIRLINES INC.

4333 Amon Carter Boulevard, Ft. Worth, TX, 76155

Tel: (817) 963-1234     Fax: (817) 967-9641     www.amrcorp.com

*Air transport services.*

**American Airlines, Caxton House, 1 Duddell St., Hong Kong PRC**

## AMERICAN APPRAISAL ASSOCIATES INC.

411 E. Wisconsin Ave., Milwaukee, WI, 53202

Tel: (414) 271-7240     Fax: (414) 271-1041     www.american-appraisal.com

*Valuation consulting services.*

**American Appraisal Hong Kong Ltd., 2901 Central Plaza, 18 Harbour Rd., Wanchai, Hong Kong PRC**

## AMERICAN INTERNATIONAL GROUP INC. (AIG)

70 Pine Street, New York, NY, 10270

Tel: (212) 770-7000     Fax: (212) 509-9705     www.aig.com

*Worldwide insurance and financial services.*

**AIG International Inc., 2809-11 Ceitibank Tower, 3 Garden Road, Central Hong Kong PRC**

## AMERICAN LOCKER GROUP INC.

608 Allen Street, Jamestown, NY, 14701-3966

Tel: (716) 664-9600     Fax: (716) 483-2822     www.americanlocker.com

*Mfr. coin-operated locks and office furniture.*

**Titak Limited, Wanchai, Hong Kong PRC**
Tel: 852-2861-0720

## AMERICAN PRESIDENT LINES LTD.

1111 Broadway, Oakland, CA, 94607

Tel: (510) 272-8000     Fax: (510) 272-7941     www.apl.com

*Intermodal shipping services.*

**American President Lines Ltd., PO Box 98470, World Shipping Centre, 7 Canton Rd., Kowloon Hong Kong PRC**

## AMERICAN STANDARD INC.

One Centennial Avenue, Piscataway, NJ, 08855-6820

Tel: (732) 980-3000     Fax: (732) 980-6118     www.americanstandard.com

*Mfr. automotive, plumbing, heating, air conditioning products and medical diagnostics systems.*

**World Standard Ltd., 14-16F St. John's Bldg., 33 Garden Road, Central Hong Kong PRC**
Tel: 852-2971-3610

## AMGEN INC.

One Amgen Center Drive, Thousand Oaks, CA, 91320-1799

Tel: (805) 447-1000      Fax: (805) 499-2694      www.amgen.com

*Biotechnology research and pharmaceruticals.*

**Amgen Greater China, Ltd., Room 1501-4 15/F Dah Sing Financial Centre, 108 Gloucester Road, Wanchai, Hong Kong PRC**

## AMPEX CORPORATION

500 Broadway, Redwood City, CA, 94063-3199

Tel: (650) 367-2011      Fax: (650) 367-4669      www.ampex.com

*Mfr. extremely high-performance digital data storage, data retrieval and image processing systems for a broad range of corporate scientific and government applications.*

**Ampex Ferrotec Ltd., 603 Tai Nan West St., 6/F & 7/F, Kowloon, Hong Kong PRC**

**Ampex World Operations SA, 709-11 World Finance Ctr., Harbour City, Canton Rd., Tsim Sha Tsui, Hong Kong PRC**

## AMPHENOL CORPORATION

358 Hall Ave., Wallingford, CT, 06492-7530

Tel: (203) 265-8900      Fax: (203) 265-8793      www.amphenol.com

*Mfr. electrictronic interconnect penetrate systems and assemblies.*

**Amphenol East Asia Limited, 22/F Railway Plaza, 39 Chatham Road South, TST Kowloon Hong Kong PRC**

Tel: 852-2699-2663    Fax: 852-2688-0974

## AMWAY CORPORATION

7575 Fulton Street East, Ada, MI, 49355-0001

Tel: (616) 787-6000      Fax: (616) 787-6177      www.amway.com

*Mfr./sale home care, personal care, nutrition and houseware products.*

**Amway Intl. Inc., 26/F Citicorp Centre, 18 Whitfield Rd., Causeway Bay, Hong Kong PRC**

## ANDERSEN CONSULTING

100 S. Wacker Drive, Ste. 1059, Chicago, IL, 60606

Tel: (312) 693-0161      Fax: (312) 693-0507      www.ac.com

*Provides management and technology consulting services.*

**Andersen Consulting, Wing On Centre 23/F, 111 Connaught Rd. Central, Hong Kong PRC**

Tel: 852-2852-0388    Fax: 852-2850-8956

## ANDERSEN WORLDWIDE

33 West Monroe Street, Chicago, IL, 60603

Tel: (312) 580-0033      Fax: (312) 507-6748      www.arthurandersen.com

*Accounting and audit, tax and management consulting services.*

**Andersen Worldwide, Wing On Centre 25/F, 111 Connaught Rd. Central, GPO Box 3289, Hong Kong PRC**

Tel: 852-2852-0222

## ANDREA ELECTRONICS CORPORATION

45 Melville Park Road, Melville, NY, 11747

Tel: (631) 719-1800      Fax: (631) 719-1950      www.andreaelectronics.com

*Mfr. noise reduction electronic headsets, handsets and microphones.*

**Andrea ANC Manufacturing, Room 817 2/F Blk. B, Seaview Estate, 2-8 Watson Road, Hong Kong PRC**

## ANDREW CORPORATION

10500 West 153rd Street, Orland Park, IL, 60462

Tel: (708) 349-3300    Fax: (708) 349-5410    www.andrew.com

*Mfr. antenna systems, coaxial cable, electronic communications and network connectivity systems.*

**Andrew Hong Kong Ltd., Suite 1901 East Asia Aetna Tower, 308-320 Des Voeux Rd., Central Hong Kong PRC**

Tel: 852-2515-7500    Fax: 852-2515-7599

## AOL TIME WARNER

75 Rockefeller Plaza, New York, NY, 10019

Tel: (212) 484-8000    Fax: (212) 275-3046    www.aoltimewarner.com

*Engaged in media and communications; provides internet services, communications, publishing and entertainment.*

**AOL Time Warner Hong Kong, Hong Kong PRC**

## AON CORPORATION

123 North Wacker Drive, Chicago, IL, 60606

Tel: (312) 701-3000    Fax: (312) 701-3100    www.aon.com

*Insurance brokers worldwide; underwrites accident and health insurance, specialty and professional insurance; and provides risk management consultation.*

**AON Holdings Asia Ltd., 15/F Aon Insurance Tower, 3 Lockhart Rd., Wanchai, Hong Kong PRC**

Tel: 852-2861-6555    Fax: 852-2866-1926    Contact: Clive Bate

**AON Risk Services Hong Kong Ltd., 9/F Asian House 1, Wanchai, Hong Kong PRC**

Tel: 852-2862-4200    Fax: 852-2862-4200    Contact: Anthony Langridge

## APPLE COMPUTER, INC.

One Infinite Loop, Cupertino, CA, 95014

Tel: (408) 996-1010    Fax: (408) 974-2113    www.apple.com

*Personal computers, peripherals and software.*

**Apple Computer Intl. Ltd., 2401 NatWest Tower, Times Square, Causeway Bay, Hong Kong PRC**

Tel: 852-2506-8888    Fax: 852-2506-2833    Contact: Vincent Tai, Gen. Mgr.

## APPLERA CORPORATION

761 Main Avenue, Norwalk, CT, 06859-0001

Tel: (203) 762-1000    Fax: (203) 762-6000    www.applera.com

*Leading supplier of systems for life science research and related applications.*

**Analytical Instruments, Room 1112-13, New East Ocean Centre, 9 Science Museum Road, Tsim Sha Tsui East, Hong Kong PRC**

## APPLICA, INCORPORATED

5980 Miami Lakes Drive, Hialeah, FL, 33014

Tel: (305) 362-2611    Fax: (305) 364-0635    www.applicainc.com

*Mfr. and distributor of a broad range of household appliances for major retailers and appliance distributors.*

**Durable Electrical Metal Factory, Ltd., 1/F Efficiency House, 35 Tai Yau St., San Po Kong, Kowloon, Hong Kong PRC**

Contact: Lai Kin, Chmn.

## APW, INC.

PO Box 325, Milwaukee, WI, 53201-0325

Tel: (262) 523-7600    Fax: (262) 523-7624    www.apw1.com

*Mfr. hi-pressure tools, vibration control products, consumables, technical furniture and enclosures.*

**APW Products Hong Kong, 2304 & 2309 Wharf Cable Tower, 9 Hoi Shing Road, Tsuen Wan, Hong Kong PRC**

## ARCHER-DANIELS-MIDLAND COMPANY

4666 Faries Parkway, Decatur, IL, 62526

Tel: (217) 424-5200      Fax: (217) 424-6196        www.admworld.com

*Grain processing: flours, grains, oils and flax fibre.*

**ADM Asia Pacific, Ltd.,  Hong Kong PRC**

## ARIBA, INC.

1565 Charleston Rd., Mountain View, CA, 94043

Tel: (650) 930-6200      Fax: (650) 930-6300        www.ariba.com

*Mfr. software.*

**Ariba Hong Kong,  One Pacific Place 39/F, 88 Queensway, Hong Kong PRC**

## ARMSTRONG HOLDINGS, INC.

2500 Columbia Avenue, Lancaster, PA, 17604-3001

Tel: (717) 397-0611      Fax: (717) 396-2787        www.armstrong.com

*Mfr. and marketing interior furnishings and specialty products for bldg, auto and textile industry.*

**Armstrong World Industries (HK) Ltd.,  19/F Cindic Topwer, 128 Gloucester Road, Hong Kong PRC**

Tel: 852-2585-7800   Fax: 852-2598-7181

## ARROW COMPANY

48 West 38 St., 12th Fl., New York, NY, 10018

Tel: (212) 984-8900      Fax: (212) 984-8957        www.arrowshirts.com

*Men's apparel.*

**Bidermann Company, Ltd.,  Unit 305 Tower III, Enterprise Square, 9 Sheung Yuet Rd., Kowloon Bay Hong Kong PRC**

Tel: 852-279-52655   Fax: 852-275-48275

## ARROW ELECTRONICS INC.

25 Hub Drive, Melville, NY, 11747

Tel: (516) 391-1300      Fax: (516) 391-1640        www.arrow.com

*Distributor of electronic components.*

**Arrow Asia Pacific Ltd.,  20/F Tower Two Ever Gain Plaza, 88 Container Port Road, Kwai Chung Hong Kong PRC**

Tel: 852-2484-2484   Fax: 852-2484-2468    Contact: John Tam, Pres.

## ASG (ALLEN SYSTEMS GROUP)

1333 3rd Avenue South, Naples, FL, 33102

Tel: (941) 435-2200      Fax: (941) 263-3692        www.asg.com

*Mainframe computer software, specializing in OnMark 2000 software.*

**ASG Hong Kong,  Suite 1415-16, Sun Hung Kai Centre, 14th Floor30 Harbour Road, Wanchai, Hong Kong PRC**

## ASHLAND OIL INC.

50 E. Rivercenter Blvd., Covington, KY, 41012-0391

Tel: (859) 815-3333      Fax: (859) 815-5053        www.ashland.com

*Petroleum exploration, refining and transportation; mfr. chemicals, oils and lubricants.*

**Valvoline International Inc.,  12/F Jubilee Commercial Bldg., 42-46 Gloucester Rd., Wanchai, Hong Kong PRC**

## ASSOCIATED MERCHANDISING CORPORATION

500 Seventh Ave., 2nd Fl., New York, NY, 10018

Tel: (212) 819-6600      Fax: (212) 819-6701        www.theamc.com

*Retail service organization; apparel, shoes and accessories.*

**Associated Merchandising Corp.,  5/F West Wing Tsim Sha Tsui Centre, 66 Mody Rd., Kowloon, Hong Kong PRC**

## ASSOCIATED PRESS INC.

50 Rockefeller Plaza, New York, NY, 10020-1605

Tel: (212) 621-1500    Fax: (212) 621-5447    www.ap.com

*News gathering agency.*

**The Associated Press, Telecom House, 3 Gloucester Rd., Wan Chai, Hong Kong PRC**

Tel: 852-2802-4324

## ASSOCIATES FIRST CAPITAL CORPORATION

250 E. Carpenter Freeway, Irving, TX, 75062-2729

Tel: (972) 652-4000    Fax: (972) 652-7420    www.theassociates.com

*Diversified consumer and commercial finance organization which provides finance, leasing and related services.*

**Associates First Capital, Hong Kong PRC**

## AT&T CORPORATION

32 Avenue of the Americas, New York, NY, 10013-2412

Tel: (212) 387-5400    Fax: (212) 387-5695    www.att.com

*Telecommunications.*

**AT&T Asia Pacific Inc., Shell Tower 30/F, Times Square, 1 Matheson St., Causeway Bay Hong Kong PRC**

## ATMEL CORPORATION

2325 Orchard Pkwy., San Jose, CA, 95131

Tel: (408) 441-0311    Fax: (408) 436-4200    www.atmel.com

*Design, manufacture and marketing of advanced semiconductors.*

**Atmel Asia Ltd., Chinachem Golden Plaza, 77 Mody Road, Tsimhatsui East Kowloon, Hong Kong PRC**

Tel: 852-2721-9778

## ATTACHMATE CORPORATION

3617 131st Ave. S.E., Bellevue, WA, 98006-1332

Tel: (425) 644-4010    Fax: (425) 747-9924    www.attachmate.com

*Mfr. connectivity software.*

**Attachmate Hong Kong Ltd., Units 2701-3 27/F Vicwood Plaza, 199 Des Voeux Road, Central Hong Kong PRC**

Tel: 852-2572-8988    Fax: 852-2572-7497

## AUDIO VISUAL SERVICES CORPORATION

16 West 61st Street, New York, NY, 10023

Tel: (212) 541-5300    Fax: (212) 541-5384    www.caribiner.com

*Plans and produces meetings, events, and media campaigns: creates film/video presentations; supports in-house communications and training programs: and supplies audio-visual equipment.*

**Audio Visual Services, 15/F Kinwick Centre, 32 Hollywood Rd., Central Hong Kong PRC**

Tel: 852-2805-1767    Fax: 852-2805-1768

## AUTODESK INC.

111 McInnis Parkway, San Rafael, CA, 94903

Tel: (415) 507-5000    Fax: (415) 507-6112    www.autodesk.com

*Develop/marketing/support computer-aided design, engineering, scientific and multimedia software products.*

**Autodesk Far East Ltd., Units 414-416 4/F, Hong Kong Industrial Technology Centre, 72 Tat Chee Ave., Kowloon Tong Hong Kong PRC**

Tel: 852-2824-2338    Fax: 852-2824-3228

## AUTOMATIC SWITCH CO. (ASCO)

50-60 Hanover Rd., Florham Park, NJ, 07932

Tel: (973) 966-2000      Fax: (973) 966-2628      www.asco.com

*Mfr. solenoid valves, emergency power controls, pressure and temp. switches.*

**Asco Asia, Hong Kong, c/o Branson Ultrasonics Asia Pacific Co. Inc., 5A Pioneer Bldg., 213 Wai Yip St., Kwun Tong Kowloon Hong Kong PRC**

Tel: 852-2343-8580    Fax: 852-2790-1771    Contact: Tony Wong

## AUTOTOTE CORPORATION

750 Lexington Avenue, 25th Fl., New York, Ny, 1022

Tel: (212) 754-2233      Fax: (212) 754-2372      www.autotote.com

*Mfr. video gaming machines and computerized pari-mutuel wagering systems used at racetracks.*

**Scientific Games International, Div. Autotote, Inter-Continental 7/F, Plaza 94 Granville Road, Tsim Sha Tsui, Kowloon Hong Kong PRC**

Tel: 852-2723-7911    Fax: 852-2723-8711

## AVERY DENNISON CORPORATION

150 N. Orange Grove Blvd., Pasadena, CA, 91103

Tel: (626) 304-2000      Fax: (626) 792-7312      www.averydennison.com

*Mfr. pressure-sensitive adhesives and materials, office products, labels, tags, retail systems, Carter's Ink and specialty chemicals.*

**Dennison Trading Hong Kong Ltd., 1301-3 Lu Plaza, 2 Wing Yip Street, Kwun Tong Kowloon Hong Kong PRC**

Tel: 852-2802-9618    Fax: 852-2588-1344

**Soabar Systems (HK) Ltd., 16 Westland Rd., Quarry Bay, Hong Kong PRC**

## AVIS GROUP HOLDINGS, INC.

900 Old Country Road., Garden City, NY, 11530

Tel: (516) 222-3000      Fax: (516) 222-4381      www.avis.com

*Car rental services.*

**Avis Group Holdings Ltd.., Bonaventure House, 85-91 Leighton Rd., Causeway Bay, Hong Kong PRC**

## AVNET INC.

2211 South 47th Street, Phoenix, AZ, 85034

Tel: (480) 643-2000      Fax: (480) 643-4670      www.avnet.com

*Distributor electronic components, computers and peripherals.*

**Avnet WKK Components Ltd., 16/F Spectrum Tower, 53 Hung To Road, Kwun Tong, Kowloon, Hong Kong PRC**

Tel: 852-217-65388    Fax: 852-279-02182

## AVON PRODUCTS INC.

1345 Avenue of the Americas, New York, NY, 10105-0196

Tel: (212) 282-5000      Fax: (212) 282-6049      www.avon.com

*Mfr./distributor beauty and related products, fashion jewelry, gifts and collectibles.*

**Avon Cosmetics Hong Kong Ltd., 3601 Bond St., East Tower, Queensway, Hong Kong PRC**

Contact: Jose Ferreira, Pres. Asia-Pacific

## AVX CORPORATION

PO Box 867, Myrtle Beach, SC, 29578

Tel: (843) 448-9411      Fax: (843) 448-7139      www.avxcorp.com

*Mfr. multilayer ceramic capacitors.*

**AVX/Kyocera Asia Ltd., Hilder Centre 3/F, 2 Sung Ping St., Hunghom, Kowloon, Hong Kong PRC**

## BAIN & COMPANY, INC.

Two Copley Place, Boston, MA, 02116

Tel: (617) 572-2000     Fax: (617) 572-2427     www.bain.com

*Strategic management consulting services.*

**Bain & Company (Hong Kong), 10/F One Pacific Place, 88 Queensway, Hong Kong PRC**

Tel: 852-2978-8800   Fax: 852-2978-8801

## BAKER & McKENZIE

130 East Randolph Drive, Ste. 2500, Chicago, IL, 60601

Tel: (312) 861-8000     Fax: (312) 861-2899     www.bakerinfo.com

*International legal services.*

**Baker & McKenzie, 14/F Hutchison House, 10 Harcourt Rd., Hong Kong PRC**

Tel: 852-2846-1888   Fax: 852-2845-2476

## BAKER HUGHES INCORPORATED

3900 Essex Lane, Ste. 1200, Houston, TX, 77027

Tel: (713) 439-8600     Fax: (713) 439-8699     www.bakerhughes.com

*Develop and apply technology to drill, complete and produce oil and natural gas wells; provide separation systems to petroleum, municipal, continuous process and mining industries.*

**Baker Hughes Inc., c/o Star Business Centre, Ste. 1229 Satr House, 3 Salisbury Rd., TST Kowloon Hong Kong PRC**

Tel: 852-2314-4416   Fax: 852-2736-9631

## BALDWIN TECHNOLOGY COMPANY, INC.

One Norwalk West, 40 Richards Ave., Norwalk, CT, 06854

Tel: (203) 838-7470     Fax: (203) 852-7040     www.baldwintech.com

*Mfr./services material handling, accessories, control and prepress equipment for print industry.*

**Baldwin Asia Pacific Ltd., Unit A 26/F Seaview Plaza, 283 Shaukeiwan Rd., Hong Kong PRC**

Tel: 852-2811-2987   Fax: 852-2811-0641   Contact: Akira Hara, Pres.

**Baldwin Printing Controls Ltd., Unit A 26/F Seaview Plaza, 283 Shaukeiwan Rd., Hong Kong PRC**

Tel: 852-2811-2987   Fax: 852-2811-0641   Contact: Simon Li, Mgr.

## BALL CORPORATION

10 Longs Peak Drive, Broomfield, CO, 80021

Tel: (303) 469-3131     Fax: (303) 460-2127     www.ball.com

*Mfr. metal beverage and food containers, glass containers, aerospace systems and services.*

**Ball Asia Pacific Ltd., Hong Kong PRC**

## BANK OF AMERICA CORPORATION

555 California Street, San Francisco, CA, 94104

Tel: (415) 622-3530     Fax: (415) 622-8467     www.bankofamerica.com

*Financial services.*

**BA Asia Ltd., Bank of America Tower 14/F, 12 Harcourt Rd., GPO Box 799, Hong Kong PRC**

Tel: 852-2847-6467   Fax: 852-2847-6566   Contact: Frances Taylor

**Bank of America - Asia Region, Devon House 17/F, 979 King's Rd., Quarry Bay, Hong Kong PRC**

Tel: 852-2597-3888   Fax: 852-2597-3886   Contact: Robert P. Morrow III

**Bank of America NT & SA, Bank of America Tower 2/F, 12 Harcourt Rd., GPO Box 472, Hong Kong PRC**

Tel: 852-2847-5882   Fax: 852-2847-5200   Contact: D.H. Garschagen, EVP

## THE BANK OF NEW YORK

One Wall Street, New York, NY, 10286

Tel: (212) 495-1784      Fax: (212) 495-2546      www.bankofny.com

*Banking services.*

**The Bank of New York, New Henry House 7/F, 10 Ice House St., GPO Box 67, Hong Kong PRC**

Tel: 852-2840-9888   Fax: 852-2810-5279

**Wing Hang Bank Limited, 161 Queen's Road Central, Hong Kong PRC**

## BANK ONE CORPORATION

One First National Plaza, Chicago, IL, 60670

Tel: (312) 732-4000      Fax: (312) 732-3366      www.fcnbd.com

*Provides financial products and services.*

**Bank One, NA, 13/F Jardine House, 1 Connaught Place, Hong Kong PRC**

Tel: 852-2844-9222   Fax: 852-2844-9318   Contact: Richard L. Kolehmainen, Head of Office

## C. R. BARD, INC.

730 Central Ave., Murray Hill, NJ, 07974

Tel: (908) 277-8000      Fax: (908) 277-8078      www.crbard.com

*Mfr. health care products.*

**Bard International, Fleet House 901, 38 Gloucester Rd., Wanchai, Hong Kong PRC**

## BARRA, INC.

2100 Milvia Street, Berkeley, CA, 94704

Tel: (510) 548-5442      Fax: (510) 548-4374      www.barra.com

*Mfr. analytical software for private investors and portfolio managers.*

**BARRA International, Ltd., Unit C2 21/F United Centre, 95 Queensway, Hong Kong PRC**

Tel: 852-2521-3083

## BATES WORLDWIDE INC.

405 Lexington Ave., New York, NY, 10174

Tel: (212) 297-7000      Fax: (212) 986-0270      www.batesww.com

*Advertising, marketing, public relations and media consulting.*

**Bates 141 Hong Kong, 17/F The Lee Gardens, 33 Hysan Ave., Causeway Bay Hong Kong PRC**

Tel: 852-2103-6666   Fax: 852-2520-6660   Contact: Simon Holt, Dir.

**Bates Graffix Ltd., 4/F Golden Star Bldg., 11 Lockhart Rd., Wanchai Hong Kong PRC**

Tel: 852-2527-2766   Contact: S. Siu, Mgr.

**Bates Hong Kong, 18/F The Lee Gardens, 33 Hysan Ave., Causeway Bay Hong Kong PRC**

Tel: 852-2103-6666   Contact: Jeffrey Yu, CEO

## BAUSCH & LOMB INC.

One Bausch & Lomb Place, Rochester, NY, 14604-2701

Tel: (716) 338-6000      Fax: (716) 338-6007      www.bausch.com

*Mfr. vision care products and accessories.*

**Bausch & Lomb (Hong Kong) Ltd., Shaukeiwan, Hong Kong PRC**

**Bausch & Lomb Hong Kong, 26/F Cityplaza 1, Taikooshing, Hong Kong PRC**

## BAXTER HEALTHCARE CORPORATION

One Baxter Parkway, Deerfield, IL, 60015

Tel: (847) 948-2000      Fax: (847) 948-3948      www.baxter.com

*Pharmaceutical preparations, surgical/medical instruments and cardiovascular products.*

**Baxter Healthcare Ltd., Rm 2003-6 CRC Protective Tower, 38 Gloucester Road Wanchai, Hong Kong PRC**

Tel: 852-2-802-4535

**BBDO WORLDWIDE**

1285 Ave. of the Americas, New York, NY, 10019

Tel: (212) 459-5000　　Fax: (212) 459-6645　　www.bbdo.com

*Multinational group of advertising agencies.*

**BBDO Asia Pacific, Hong Kong PRC**

**BBDO Hong Kong, Hong Kong PRC**

**BDO SEIDMAN, LLP　BELGIUM**

Two Prudential Plaza, 180 N. Stetson Ave., Ste. 2300, Chicago, IL, 60601

Tel: (312) 240-1236　　Fax: (312) 240-3329　　www.bdo.com

*International accounting and financial consulting firm.*

**BDO Asia Pacific Reg. Office, 29/F Wing On Centre, 111 Connaught Road, Central Hong Kong PRC**

Tel: 852-2541-5041　Fax: 852-2815-0002　Contact: Floyd T, Chan, Reg. Dir.

**BDO China, 29/F Wing On Centre, 111 Connaught Road, Central Hong Kong PRC**

Tel: 852-2541-5041　Fax: 852-2815-0002　Contact: Jennifer Y. Yip

**BDO Mcabe Lo & Co., 29/F Wing On Centre, 111 Connaught Road, Central Hong Kong PRC**

Tel: 852-2541-5041　Fax: 852-2815-0002　Contact: Albert Au

**BEA SYSTEMS, INC.**

2315 North First Street, St. Jose, CA, 95131

Tel: (408) 570-8000　　Fax: (408) 570-8091　　www.beasys.com

*Develops communications management software and provider of software consulting services.*

**BEA Systems HK Ltd., 1505B 15/F Sino Plaza, 255-257 Gloucester Rd., Causeway Bay, Hong Kong PRC**

Tel: 852-2956-0306　Fax: 852-2956-0207

**BEAR STEARNS & CO., INC.**

245 Park Ave., New York, NY, 10167

Tel: (212) 272-2000　　Fax: (212) 272-3092　　www.bearstearns.com

*Investment banking, securities broker/dealer and investment advisory services.*

**Bear Stearns Asia Ltd., Citibank Tower, Citibank Plaza 26th Fl., 3 Garden Rd., Hong Kong PRC**

Tel: 852-2593-2700　Fax: 852-2593-2870

**BECHTEL GROUP INC.**

50 Beale Street, PO Box 3965, San Francisco, CA, 94105-1895

Tel: (415) 768-1234　　Fax: (415) 768-9038　　www.bechtel.com

*General contractors in engineering and construction.*

**Bechtel International Corp., 22/F Li Po Chun Chambers, 189 Des Voeux Rd., Central Hong Kong PRC**

Tel: 852-2970-7000　Fax: 852-2840-1272

**BECKMAN COULTER, INC.**

4300 N. Harbor Boulevard, Fullerton, CA, 92834

Tel: (714) 871-4848　　Fax: (714) 773-8898　　www.beckmancoulter.com

*Develop/mfr./marketing automated systems and supplies for biological analysis.*

**Beckman Coulter Hong Kong Ltd., Oxford House 12/F, 979 King's Road, TaiKoo Place, Hong Kong PRC**

Tel: 852-2814-7431

**BEL FUSE INC.**

198 Van Vorst Street, Jersey City, NJ, 07302

Tel: (201) 432-0463　　Fax: (201) 432-9542　　www.belfuse.com

*Mfr. electronic components for networking, fuses, delay lines, hybrids and magnetic products.*

**Bel Fuse Ltd., 8/F 8 Luk Hop St., San Po Kong, Kowloon, Hong Kong PRC**

## BELDEN, INC.

7701 Forsyth Blvd., Ste. 800, St. Louis, MO, 63015

Tel: (314) 854-8000    Fax: (314) 854-8001    www.belden.com

*Mfr. electronic wire and cable products.*

**Belden International, Inc.,  2/F Shui On Centre, 6-8 Harbour Road, Wanchai, Hong Kong PRC**

## BELLSOUTH CORPORATION LATIN AMERICA

1155 Peachtree Street NE, Ste. 400, Atlanta, GA, 30367

Tel: (404) 249-4800    Fax: (404) 249-4880    www.bellsouth.com

*Mobile communications, telecommunications network systems.*

**BellSouth Intl.,  Hong Kong PRC**

## LOUIS BERGER INTERNATIONAL INC.

100 Halsted Street, East Orange, NJ, 07019

Tel: (201) 678-1960    Fax: (201) 672-4284    www.louisberger.com

*Consulting engineers, engaged in architecture, environmental and advisory services.*

**Louis Berger Finance & Dev. Co., Ltd.,  GPO Box 8764, Central District, Hong Kong PRC**

Tel: 852-2523-6111   Fax: 852-2845-9584

## BERNARD HODES GROUP

555 Madison Ave., New York, NY, 10022

Tel: (212) 935-4000    Fax: (212) 755-7324    www.hodes.com

*Multinational recruitment agency.*

**Bernard Hodes Group (Hong Kong),  18/F Centre Point, 181-183 Gloucester Road, Hong Kong PRC**

## BESTFOODS, INC.

700 Sylvan Ave., International Plaza, Englewood Cliffs, NJ, 07632-9976

Tel: (201) 894-4000    Fax: (201) 894-2186    www.bestfoods.com

*Consumer foods products; corn refining.*

**Bestfoods Asia,  Ste. 1408 Cityplaza 4, 12 Taikoo Wan Rd., Taikoo Shing, Hong Kong PRC**

Tel: 852-2531-3600   Fax: 852-2845-2914   Contact: Heribert H. Grünert, Pres.

**CPC/AJI (Hong Kong) Ltd.,  6 Dai Fu St., Tai Po Industrial Estate, Tai Po New Territories, Hong Kong PRC**

Tel: 852-2664-2011   Fax: 852-2664-2845   Contact: Charles E. Lloyd, Dir.

## BETZDEARBORN

4636 Somerton Road, PO Box 3002, Trevose, PA, 19053-6783

Tel: (215) 953-2568    Fax: (215) 953-5524    www.betzdearborn.com

*Mfr. water/wastewater and process system treatment chemicals and services.*

**BetzDearborn China, Ltd.,  Unit 1501 Greenfield Tower, Concordia Plaza, 1 Science Museum Rd., Tsimshatsui East Kowloon Hong Kong PRC**

## BIOMATRIX, INC.

65 Railroad Ave., Ridgefield, NJ, 07657

Tel: (201) 945-9550    Fax: (201) 945-0363    www.biomatrix.com

*Mfr. hylan biological polymers for therapeutic medical and skin care products.*

**Biomatrix Ltd. (Hong Kong),  Room 1905 Queen's Place, 74 Queen's Rd., Central Hong Kong PRC**

Tel: 852-2810-1613   Fax: 852-2810-1667   Contact: Clifford Krause, Dir.

## BIO-RAD LABORATORIES INC.

1000 Alfred Nobel Drive, Hercules, CA, 94547

Tel: (510) 724-7000    Fax: (510) 724-3167    www.bio-rad.com

*Mfr. life science research products, clinical diagnostics, analytical instruments.*

**Bio-Rad Pacific (HK),  Hong Kong PRC**

## BLACK & VEATCH LLP

8400 Ward Pkwy., PO Box 8405, Kansas City, MO, 64114

Tel: (913) 339-2000     Fax: (913) 339-2934     www.bv.com

*Engineering, architectural and construction services.*

**Binnie Black & Veatch Hong Kong Ltd.,  New Town Tower 11/F, Pak Hok Ting St., Shatin NT, Hong Kong PRC**

Tel: 852-2601-1000   Fax: 852-2601-3988   Contact: Martin D. McMillan

## BLOOMBERG L.P.

499 Park Ave., New York, NY, 10022

Tel: (212) 318-2000     Fax: (212) 940-1954     www.bloomberg.com

*Publishes magazines and provides TV, radio and newspaper wire services.*

**Bloomberg L.P.,  Hong Kong PRC**

## BMC SOFTWARE, INC.

2101 City West Blvd., Houston, TX, 77042-2827

Tel: (713) 918-8800     Fax: (713) 918-8000     www.bmc.com

*Engaged in mainframe-related utilities software and services.*

**BMC Software,  Suite 5501 55/F Central Plaza - 18 Harbour Road, Wanchai, Hong Kong PRC**

## BONTEX INC.

One Bondex, Buena Vista, VA, 24416

Tel: (540) 261-2181     Fax: (540) 261-3784     www.bontex.com

*Engaged in development and distribution of advanced materials, systems for a broad range of applications.*

**Bontex Hong Kong,  Flat B3 Paterson Bldg., 7 Great George Street, Causeway Bay, Hong Kong PRC**

## BOOZ-ALLEN & HAMILTON INC.

8283 Greensboro Drive, McLean, VA, 22102

Tel: (703) 902-5000     Fax: (703) 902-3333     www.bah.com

*International management and technology consultants.*

**Booz Allen & Hamilton (HK) Ltd.,  6408 Central Plaza, 18 Harbour Rd., Hong Kong PRC**

Tel: 852-2845-0057   Fax: 852-2593-9663

## THE BOSTON CONSULTING GROUP

Exchange Place, 31st Fl., Boston, MA, 02109

Tel: (617) 973-1200     Fax: (617) 973-1339     www.bcg.com

*Management consulting company.*

**The Boston Consulting Group,  34/F Shell Tower, Times Square, Causeway Bay, Hong Kong PRC**

Tel: 852-2506-2111

## BOSTON SCIENTIFIC CORPORATION

One Scientific Place, Natick, MA, 01760-1537

Tel: (508) 650-8000     Fax: (508) 650-8923     www.bsci.com

*Mfr./distributes medical devices for use in minimally invasive surgeries.*

**Boston Scientific Hong Kong Ltd.,  Unit 1403, Kodak House II, 39 Healthy St. East, North Point, Hong Kong PRC**

Tel: 852-2563-1227   Fax: 852-2563-5276

## BOURNS INC.

1200 Columbia Avenue, Riverside, CA, 92507

Tel: (909) 781-5500     Fax: (909) 781-5006     www.bourns.com

*Mfr. resistive components and networks, precision potentiometers, panel controls, switches, transducers and surge protectors..*

**Bourns Asia Pacific Inc.,  Room 905 Tower 3, 33 Canton, Tsim Shat Sui, Kowloon, Hong Kong PRC**

## BOWNE & COMPANY, INC.

345 Hudson Street, New York, NY, 10014

Tel: (212) 924-5500        Fax: (212) 229-3420        www.bowne.com

*Financial printing and foreign language translation, localization (software), internet design and maintenance and facilities management.*

**Bowne International,  3402 Citibank Tower, Citibank Plaza, Central Hong Kong PRC**

Tel: 852-2526-0688    Fax: 852-2526-1200    Contact: Paul Dalton, Mng. Dir.

## BOYDEN CONSULTING CORPORATION

364 Elwood Ave., Hawthorne, NY, 10502

Tel: (914) 747-0093        Fax: (914) 980-6147        www.boyden.com

*International executive search firm.*

**Boyden Associates Ltd.,  1 on Hing Terrace 10th Fl., Wyndham St., Central Hong Kong PRC**

Tel: 852-2868-3882

## BOZELL GROUP

40 West 23rd Street, New York, NY, 10010

Tel: (212) 727-5000        Fax: (212) 645-9173        www.bozell.com

*Advertising, marketing, public relations and media consulting.*

**Bozell Hong Kong,  6/F Sino Plaza, 256 Gloucester Rd., Causeway Bay, Hong Kong PRC**

Tel: 852-2892-8698    Fax: 852-2892-8797    Contact: Gary Tse, Mgr.

**Bozell Tong Barnes PR,  Room 805B Sino Plaza, 256 Gloucester Rd., Causeway Bay, Hong Kong PRC**

Tel: 852-2575-0448    Fax: 852-2573-4823    Contact: Wendy Tong Barnes, Dir.

**Bozell Worldwide, Inc. (Asia Pacific),  6/F. Sino Plaza, 256 Gloucester Rd., Causeway Bay, Hong Kong PRC**

Tel: 852-2892-8678    Fax: 852-2892-8765    Contact: Roger Winter, CEO

**Grant Advertising,  Room 303 Sino Plaza, 256 Gloucester Rd., Causeway Bay, Hong Kong PRC**

Tel: 852-2893-7171    Fax: 852-2893-3799    Contact: Dionne Kung, Gen. Mgr.

## BRADY CORPORATION

6555 W. Good Hope Road, Milwaukee, WI, 53223

Tel: (414) 358-6600        Fax: (414) 358-6600        www.whbrady.com

*Mfr. industrial ID for wire marking, circuit boards; facility ID, signage, printing systems and software.*

**Brady Corporation S.E.A. Pte. Ltd.,  Unit 1803-04 - 18/F, CRE Centre, 889 Chenng Shawan Road, Kowloon, Hong Kong PRC**

Tel: 852-2370-2082    Fax: 852-2359-3164

## BRAND FARRAR BUXBAUM LLP

515 Flower Street, Ste. 3500, Los Angeles, CA, 90017-2201

Tel: (213) 228-0288        Fax: (213) 426-6222

*International law firm specializing in cross-border disputes and business transactions; intellectual property.*

**Brand Farrar Buxbaum LLP,  Ste. 1408-10 Shui On Centre, 6-8 Harbour Rd., Wanchai, Hong Kong PRC**

Tel: 852-2523-7001    Fax: 852-2845-0947    Contact: Messrs. Farrar & Buxbaum, Sr. Ptnrs

## BRANSON ULTRASONICS CORPORATION

41 Eagle Road, Danbury, CT, 06813-1961

Tel: (203) 796-0400        Fax: (203) 796-2285        www.branson-plasticsjoin.com

*Mfr. plastics assembly equipment, ultrasonic cleaning equipment.*

**Branson Ultrasonics (Asia Pacific) Co. Ltd.,  5/F Trinity Industrial Bldg., 10 Shing Yip St., Kwun Tong, Kowloon, Hong Kong PRC**

Tel: 852-2790-3393    Fax: 852-2341-2716

## BRISTOL-MYERS SQUIBB COMPANY

345 Park Ave., New York, NY, 10154-0037

Tel: (212) 546-4000     Fax: (212) 546-4020     www.bms.com

*Pharmaceutical and food preparations, medical and surgical instruments.*

**BMS (Hong Kong), 29 Wong Chuk Hang Rd., Aberdeen, Hong Kong PRC**

**Bristol-Myers Squibb - Reg. HQ/ Hong Kong, Vita Tower 8/F Block B, 29 Wong Chuk Hang Rd., Hong Kong PRC**

**ConvaTec Pacific, Unit D - 16/F Manulife Tower, 169 Electric Road, North Point Hong Kong PRC**

Tel: 852-2510-6500

## BROADVISION, INC.

585 Broadway, Redwood City, CA, 94063

Tel: (650) 261-5100     Fax: (650) 261-5900     www.broadvision.com

*Develops and delivers an integrated suite of packaged applications for personalized enterprise portals.*

**BroadVision Hong Kong, Room 6403 Central Plaza, 18 Harbour Road, Wanchai, Hong Kong PRC**

Tel: 852-2824-4238

## BROWN & WOOD LLP

One World Trade Center, 59th Fl., New York, NY, 10048

Tel: (212) 839-5300     Fax: (212) 839-5599     www.brownwoodlaw.com

*International law firm.*

**Brown & Wood, Bank Of China Tower, One Garden Rd., Central, Hong Kong PRC**

Tel: 852-2509-7888    Fax: 852-2509-3110

## BROWN GROUP, INC.

8300 Maryland Ave., St. Louis, MO, 63105

Tel: (314) 854-4000     Fax: (314) 854-4274     www.browngroup.com

*Footwear wholesaler and retailer, including Naturalizer brand.*

**Brown Group, Inc., Hong Kong PRC**

## BROWN SHOE COMPANY, INC.

8300 Maryland Avenue, St. Louis, MO, 63105

Tel: (314) 854-4000     Fax: (314) 854-4274     www.brownshoe.com

*Markets branded and private label footwear, including Dr. Scholl's, Air Step and Buster Brown.*

**Pagoda Intl. Footwear, 3/F Two Harbour Front, 22 Tak Fung St., The Harbourfront, Hung Hom, Kowloon, Hong Kong PRC**

## BUCK CONSULTANTS INC.

One Pennsylvania Plaza, New York, NY, 10119

Tel: (212) 330-1000     Fax: (212) 695-4184     www.buckconsultants.com

*Employee benefit, actuarial and compensation consulting services.*

**Buck Consultants, 32/F One Exchange Sq., 8 Connaught Place, Central, Hong Kong PRC**

## BULOVA CORPORATION

One Bulova Ave., Woodside, NY, 11377-7874

Tel: (718) 204-3300     Fax: (718) 204-3546     www.bulova.com

*Mfr. timepieces, watches and clocks, watch parts, batteries and precision defense products.*

**Bulova Watch Intl. Ltd., Unit 2-3 3/F Siu Wai Ind. Centre, 29-33 Wing Hong St., Cheung Sha Wan, Kowloon Hong Kong PRC**

## LEO BURNETT, DIV. B-COM 3 GROUP

35 West Wacker Drive, Chicago, IL, 60601

Tel: (312) 220-5959     Fax: (312) 220-6533     www.bcom3group.com

*Engaged in advertising, marketing, media buying and planning, and public relations.*

**Leo Burnett Ltd., 9/F Mount Parker House, 1111 King's Road, Quarry Bay, Hong Kong PRC**

## BURSON-MARSTELLER

230 Park Ave., New York, NY, 10003-1566

Tel: (212) 614-4000    Fax: (212) 614-4262    www.bm.com

*Public relations/public affairs consultants.*

**Burson-Marsteller (HK) Ltd., 14/F Stanhope House, 738 King's Rd., North Point, Hong Kong PRC**

Tel: 852-2880-0229   Fax: 852-2856-1101

## BUSH BOAKE ALLEN INC.

7 Mercedes Drive, Montvale, NJ, 07645

Tel: (201) 391-9870    Fax: (201) 391-0860    www.bushboakeallen.com

*Mfr. aroma chemicals for fragrances and flavor products for seasonings.*

**Bush Boake Allen, Units 1-3 17/F Regent Centre, Tower A - 63 Wo Yi Hop Road, Kwai Chung New Territories, Hong Kong PRC**

Tel: 852-2408-7170

## CADENCE DESIGN SYSTEMS, INC.

2655 Seely Ave., Bldg. 5, San Jose, CA, 95134

Tel: (408) 943-1234    Fax: (408) 943-0513    www.cadence.com

*Mfr. electronic design automation software.*

**Cadence Design Systems, Suites 03-07 Tower 2, The Gateway - 25 Canton Road Tsimshatsui, Kowloon, Hong Kong PRC**

Tel: 852-2377-7111

## CALLAWAY GOLF COMPANY

2285 Rutherford Road, Carlsbad, CA, 92008

Tel: (760) 931-1771    Fax: (760) 931-8013    www.callawaygolf.com

*Mfr./sales of golf clubs.*

**Callaway/Sportsmark Trading, Rm. 409-10 - Haiphong Mansion 4/F, 53-55 Haiphong Road, Tsim Sha Tsui, Kowloon Hong Kong PRC**

Tel: 852-272-13366   Fax:
852-272-13268

## CALTEX  CORPORATION

125 East John Carpenter Fwy., Irving, TX, 75062-2794

Tel: (972) 830-1000    Fax: (972) 830-1081    www.caltex.com

*Petroleum products.*

**Caltex Oil Hong Kong Ltd., GPO Box 147, Hong Kong, PRC**

## CALVIN KLEIN, INC.

205 West 39th Street, 4th Fl., New York, NY, 10018

Tel: (212) 719-2600    Fax: (212) 768-8922    www.calvinklein.com

*Mfr. of high quality clothing and accessories*

**Calvin Klein Ltd., Hong Kong PRC**

## CAMBREX CORPORATION

1 Meadowlands Plaza, East Rutherford, NJ, 07063

Tel: (201) 804-3000    Fax: (201) 804-9852    www.cambrex.com

*human health, animal health/agriculture and Mfr. biotechnology products and produce specialty chemicals.*

**Biesterfeld Asia Pacific Ltd., 1608 South Tower World Finance Center, Harbour City - Canton Road, TST Kowloon, Hong Kong PRC**

## CAMPBELL SOUP COMPANY

Campbell Place, Camden, NJ, 08103-1799

Tel: (856) 342-4800     Fax: (856) 342-3878     www.campbellsoup.com

*Mfr. food products.*

**Campbell Soup Asia Ltd.,  Hong Kong PRC**

Contact: Andrew Hughson, VP

## CAPITAL CONTROLS COMPANY, INC.

3000 Advance Lane, PO Box 211, Colmar, PA, 18915-0211

Tel: (215) 997-4000     Fax: (215) 997-4062     www.capitalcontrols.com

*Mfr./services water disinfecting products and systems.*

**Capital Controls Co. Ltd.,  Hong Kong**

## THE CAPITAL GROUP COS INC.

333 South Hope Street, Los Angeles, CA, 90071

Tel: (213) 486-9200     Fax: (213) 486-9557     www.capgroup.com

*Investment management.*

**Capital Research Company,  2601 One International Finance Centre, No. 1 Harbour View Street, Hong Kong PRC**

Tel: 852-2842-1000   Fax: 852-2810-6788

## CARGILL, INC.

15407 McGinty Road West, Minnetonka, MN, 55440-5625

Tel: (612) 742-7575     Fax: (612) 742-7393     www.cargill.com

*Food products, feeds, animal products.*

**Cargill Hong Kong Ltd.,  36/F One Pacific Place, 88 Queensway, Central, Hong Kong PRC**

## CARLISLE COMPANIES INCORPORATED

250 S. Clinton St., Ste. 201, Syracuse, NY, 13202-1258

Tel: (315) 474-2500     Fax: (315) 474-2008     www.carlisle.com

*Mfr. brakes, tires, wheels, turnkey systems.*

**Carlisle Companies Hong Kong,  1204-5 Great Eagle Centre, 23 Harbour Road, Wanchai, Hong Kong PRC**

Tel: 852-2511-5800   Contact: Kevin G. Forster

## CARLISLE SYNTEC SYSTEMS

PO Box 7000, Carlisle, PA, 17013

Tel: (717) 245-7000     Fax: (717) 245-9107     www.carlislesyntec.com

*Mfr. elastomeric roofing and waterproofing systems.*

**Carlisle Asia Pacific,  1204-5 Great Eagle Centre, 23 Harbour Road, Wanchai, Hong Kong PRC**

Tel: 852-2511-5800   Fax: 852-2824-4747

## THE CARLYLE GROUP L.P.

1001 Pennsylvania Avenue, NW, Washington, DC, 20004-2505

Tel: (202) 347-2626     Fax: (202) 347-1818     www.thecarlylegroup.com

*Global investor in defense contracts.*

**Carlyle Asia,  Asia Pacific Finance Tower - 32/F, 3 Garden Road, Hong Kong PRC**

Tel: 852-2878-7000   Fax: 852-2878-7007   Contact: John J. Ying, Mng. Dir

## CARRIER CORPORATION

One Carrier Place, Farmington, CT, 06034-4015

Tel: (860) 674-3000     Fax: (860) 679-3010     www.carrier.com

*Mfr./distributor/services A/C, heating and refrigeration equipment.*

**Carrier China Ltd.,  Shatin NT, Hong Kong PRC**

Tel: 852-2694-3111   Fax: 852-2691-2845

**Carrier Hong Kong Ktd.,** PO Box 260, Shatin Post Office, NT, Hong Kong PRC

**Carrier Transicold (HK) Ltd.,** King's Rd., Hong Kong PRC

## CATERPILLAR INC.

100 NE Adams Street, Peoria, IL, 61629-6105

Tel: (309) 675-1000  Fax: (309) 675-1182  www.cat.com

*Mfr. earth/material-handling and construction machinery and equipment and engines.*

**Caterpillar (HK) Ltd., c/o Caterpillar Far East Ltd., Sun Hung Kai Centre, 30 Harbour Rd., GPO 3069, Wanchai Hong Kong PRC**

**Caterpillar Far East Ltd., Sun Hung Kai Centre, 30 Harbour Rd., GPO 3069, Wanchai Hong Kong PRC**

## C.B. RICHARD ELLIS

533 South Fremont Ave., Los Angeles, CA, 90071-1712

Tel: (213) 613-3123  Fax: (213) 613-3535  www.cbrichardellis.com

*Commercial real estate services.*

**CB Richard Ellis Ltd., 32/F Bank of China Tower, 1 Garden Rd., Central Hong Kong PRC**

Tel: 852-2820-2800  Fax: 852-2810-0380  Contact: David Runciman, Chmn.

**CB Richard Ellis Ltd., Suite 3401 Central Plaza, 18 Harbour Rd., Wanchai, Hong Kong**

**CB Richard Ellis Ltd., 1130 Ocean Center, Harbour City Tsimshatsui, KW Kowloon, Hong Kong PRC**

## CCH INCORPORATED

2700 Lake Cook Road, Riverwoods, IL, 60015

Tel: (847) 267-7000  Fax: (800) 224-8299  www.cch.com

*Provides tax and business law information and software for accounting, legal, human resources, securities and health care professionals.*

**CCH Hong Kong Limited, Room 801-2 Luk Yu Building, 24-26 Stanley Street, Central Hong Kong, Hong Kong PRC**

Tel: 852-2526-7614  Fax: 852-2521-7874

## C-COR.NET CORP.

60 Decibel Road, State College, PA, 16801

Tel: (814) 238-2461  Fax: (814) 238-4065  www.c-cor.com

*Design/mfr. amplifiers, fiber optics electronic equipment for data and cable TV systems.*

**C-COR.net Hong Kong, 4/F Flat 4B 48 Crestmont Villa, Discovery Bay, Hong Kong PRC**

Tel: 852-2914-2705  Fax: 852-2914-2460  Contact: Howard Rupert, Mgr.

## C-CUBE MICROSYSTEMS INC.

1778 McCarthy Blvd., Milpitas, CA, 95035

Tel: (408) 490-8000  Fax: (408) 490-8132  www.c-cube.com

*Designs video compression chips.*

**C-Cube Microsystems Inc., Unit 301-302, Hong Kong Industrial Technology Centre, 72 Tat Chee Avenue, Kowloon Tong Kowloon, Hong Kong PRC**

Tel: 852 2192 1789

## CDM INTERNATIONAL INC.

50 Hampshire Street, Cambridge, MA, 02139

Tel: (617) 452-6000  Fax: (617) 452-8020  www.cdm.com

*Consulting engineers.*

**Camp Dresser & McKee Intl. Inc., 38/F Metroplaza Tower 1, 223 Hing Fong Rd., Kwai Fong, Hong Kong PRC**

## CENDANT CORPORATION

9 West 57th Street, New York, NY, 10019

Tel: (212) 413-1800  Fax: (212) 413-1918  www.cendant.com

*Membership-based, direct marketer offering shopping/travel/insurance and dining discount programs*

**Europe Tax Free Shopping, Pacific Leisure Group 10/F, Tung Ming Bldg., 40 Des Voeux Rd., Central Hong Kong PRC**

Tel: 852-2525-1365  Fax: 852-252-53290

## CENTIGRAM COMMUNICATIONS CORPORATION

91 East Tasman Drive, San Jose, CA, 95134

Tel: (408) 944-0250  Fax: (408) 428-3732  www.centigram.com

*Engaged in development of unified communications and messaging systems.*

**Centigram Asia Limited, Unit 316, Hong Kong Industrial Technology Centre, 72 Tat Chee Avenue, Kowloon, Hong Kong PRC**

## CENTRAL NATIONAL-GOTTESMAN INC.

3 Manhattanville Road, Purchase, NY, 10577-2110

Tel: (914) 696-9000  Fax: (914) 696-1066

*Worldwide sales pulp and paper products.*

**Central National Hong Kong Ltd., New Trend Centre Rm. 1504, 704 Prince Edward Rd. East, Sanpo Kong Kowloon, Hong Kong PRC**

Tel: 852-2398-7666  Fax: 852-2398-7570  Contact: Ian K. Y. Fung

## CENTURY 21 REAL ESTATE CORPORATION

6 Sylvan Way, Parsippany, NJ, 07054-3826

Tel: (973) 496-5722  Fax: (973) 496-5527  www.century21.com

*Engaged in real estate.*

**Century 21 Hong Kong, Ste. 1207 12/F Wing Shan Tower, 173 Des Voeux Rd., Central Hong Kong, Hong Kong PRC**

Tel: 852-2869-7221  Fax: 852-2522-8596

## CH2M HILL INC.

6060 South Willow Drive, Greenwood Village, CO, 80111

Tel: (303) 771-0900  Fax: (303) 770-2616  www.ch2m.com

*Consulting engineers, planners, economists and scientists.*

**CH2M Hill, Wanchai, Hong Kong PRC**

Tel: 852-2507-2203

## CHADBOURNE & PARKE LLP

30 Rockefeller Plaza, New York, NY, 10112-0127

Tel: (212) 408-5100  Fax: (212) 541-5369  www.chadbourne.com

*International law firm.*

**Chadbourne & Parke, Suite 2203 Tower I Lippo Centre, 89 Queensway, Hong Kong PRC**

Tel: 852-2842-5400  Fax: 852-2521-7527  Contact: N. Theodore Zink

## CHASE H&Q

One Bush Street, San Francisco, CA, 94104

Tel: (415) 439-3000  Fax: (415) 439-3638  www.jpmhq.com

*Investment banking and venture capital services.*

**Chase H&Q Asia Pacific (H.K.), Ltd., 1606 Asia Pacific Finance Tower, Citibank Plaza, 3 Garden Road, Central Hong Kong PRC**

Tel: 852-2868-4780

## THE CHERRY CORPORATION

3600 Sunset Ave., PO Box 718, Waukegan, IL, 60087

Tel: (847) 662-9200     Fax: (847) 662-2990     www.cherrycorp.com

*Mfr. electrical switches, electronic keyboards, controls and displays.*

**Cherasia Ltd., 14/F Block B, North Point Industrial Bldg., 499 Kings Rd., North Point, Hong Kong PRC**

Tel: 852-2565-6678    Fax: 852-2565-6827

## CHESTERTON BINSWANGER INTERNATIONAL

Two Logan Square, 4th Floor, Philadelphia, PA, 19103-2759

Tel: (215) 448-6000     Fax: (215) 448-6238     www.cbbi.com

*Real estate and related services.*

**Chesterton Petty Ltd., Jardine House 28/F, 1 Connaught Place, Central, Hong Kong PRC**

## THE CHUBB CORPORATION

15 Mountain View Road, Warren, NJ, 07061-1615

Tel: (908) 580-2000     Fax: (908) 580-3606     www.chubb.com

*Holding company for property and casualty insurance.*

**Federal Insurance Co., Rm. 1801-3 Harcourt House, 39 Gloucester Rd., Wanchai, Hong Kong PRC**

Tel: 852-2861-3668    Fax: 852-2861-2681

## CIGNA COMPANIES

One Liberty Place, Philadelphia, PA, 19192

Tel: (215) 761-1000     Fax: (215) 761-5511     www.cigna.com

*Insurance, invest, health care and other financial services.*

**CIGNA Property & Casualty Insurance Co., 29/F Office Tower, Convention Plaza, 1 Harbour Rd., Wanchai, Hong Kong PRC**

**CIGNA Worldwide Insurance Co., 16/F East Point Centre, 555 Hennessy Rd., Causeway Bay, Hong Kong PRC**

**Esis Intl. Inc., 5/F Edinburgh Tower, The Landmark, 15 Queen's Rd., Central, Hong Kong PRC**

**Insurance Co. of North America, 29/F Office Tower/Convention Plaza, Wanchai, 1 Harbour Rd., PO Box 703, Hong Kong PRC**

## CINCOM SYSTEMS INC.

55 Merchant Street, Cincinnati, OH, 45446

Tel: (513) 612-2300     Fax: (513) 481-8332     www.cincom.com

*Develop/distributor computer software.*

**Cincom Systems Asia, Hong Kong PRC**

**Cincom Systems Inc., Hong Kong PRC**

## CISCO SYSTEMS, INC.

170 West Tasman Drive, San Jose, CA, 95134-1706

Tel: (408) 526-4000     Fax: (408) 526-4100     www.cisco.com

*Develop/mfr./market computer hardware and software networking systems.*

**Cisco Systems Hong Kong, Ltd., Ste. 1009 Great Eagle Centre, 23 Harbour Rd., Wanchai, Hong Kong PRC**

Tel: 852-583-9110    Fax: 852-824-9528

## THE CIT GROUP

1211 Avenue of the Americas, New York, NY, 10036

Tel: (212) 536-1390     Fax: (212) 536-1912     www.citgroup.com

*Engaged in commercial finance.*

**Newcourt Credit, Div. CIT Grup, 20 Des Voeux Road, Rm. 1402 Takshing House, Central Hong Kong, Hong Kong PRC**

Tel: 852-2869-0790    Fax: 852-2537-1612

## CITIGROUP, INC.

153 East 53rd Street, New York, NY, 10043

Tel: (212) 559-1000      Fax: (212) 559-3646      www.citigroup.com

*Provides insurance and financial services worldwide.*

**Citibank N.A., 8/F Dorst House, Taikoo Place, 979 King's Rd., Quarry Bay Hong Kong PRC**

Tel: 852-2810-1961   Fax: 852-2860-0222   Contact: Stephen Long

## CLARCOR INC.

2323 Sixth Street, PO Box 7007, Rockford, IL, 61125

Tel: (815) 962-8867      Fax: (815) 962-0417      www.clarcor.com

*Mfr. filtration products and consumer packaging products.*

**Clarcor,  Flat 3 9/F Port Centre, 38 Chengtu Rd., Aberdeen, Hong Kong PRC**

## CLEARY GOTTLIEB STEEN & HAMILTON

One Liberty Plaza, New York, NY, 10006

Tel: (212) 225-2000      Fax: (212) 225-3999      www.cgsh.com

*International law firm.*

**Cleary, Gottlieb, Steen & Hamilton,  56/F Bank of China Tower, One Garden Rd., Hong Kong PRC**

## THE CLOROX COMPANY

1221 Broadway, PO Box 24305, Oakland, CA, 94623-1305

Tel: (510) 271-7000      Fax: (510) 832-1463      www.clorox.com

*Mfr. soap and detergents, and domestic consumer packaged products.*

**Clorox (Far East) Ltd.,  Hong Kong PRC**

## COACH LEATHERWEAR COMPANY

516 West 34 Street, New York, NY, 10001

Tel: (212) 594-1850      Fax: (212) 594-1682      www.coach.com

*Mfr. and sales of high-quality leather products, including handbags and wallets.*

**Coach Leatherwear Co.,  Landmark Boutique Shop G4 G/F, 5-17 Pedder Street, Central Hong Kong PRC**

## THE COCA-COLA COMPANY

PO Drawer 1734, Atlanta, GA, 30301

Tel: (404) 676-2121      Fax: (404) 676-6792      www.coca-cola.com

*Mfr./marketing/distributor soft drinks, syrups and concentrates, juice and juice-drink products.*

**Coca-Cola Central Pacific Ltd.,  GPO Box 916, Hong Kong, PRC**

**Swire Bottlers,  GPO Box 916, Hong Kong, PRC**

## COGNEX CORPORATION

1 Vision Drive, Natick, MA, 01760

Tel: (508) 650-3000      Fax: (508) 650-3333      www.cognex.com

*Mfr. machine vision systems.*

**Cognex Hong Kong,  Unit 3506 35/F. Tower 2,, Lippo Centre, 89 Queensway Admiralty, Hong Kong PRC**

Tel: 852-28019618   Fax: 852-28019617

## COHERENT INC.

5100 Patrick Henry Drive, PO Box 54980, Santa Clara, CA, 95056

Tel: (408) 764-4000      Fax: (408) 764-4800      www.cohr.com

*Mfr. lasers for science, industrial and medical.*

**Coherent Pacific,  Unit No. 1515-18 Level 15 Tower II, Grand Century Plaza, 193 Prince Edward Rd. West, Mongkok Kowloon Hong Kong PRC**

Tel: 852-2174-2800

## COLGATE-PALMOLIVE COMPANY

300 Park Ave., New York, NY, 10022

Tel: (212) 310-2000    Fax: (212) 310-2919    www.colgate.com

*Mfr. pharmaceuticals, cosmetics, toiletries and detergents.*

**Colgate-Palmolive Hong Kong Ltd., 11/F Caroline Centre, 28 Yun Ping Rd., Causeway Bay, Hong Kong PRC**

## COMMERCIAL METALS COMPANY (CMC)

PO Box 1046, Dallas, TX, 75221

Tel: (214) 689-4300    Fax: (214) 689-4320    www.commercialmetals.com

*Metal collecting/processing, steel mills and metal trading.*

**CMC Far East Ltd., Unit C, 128 Gloucester Rd., Hong Kong PRC**

## COMPAQ COMPUTER CORPORATION

20555 State Highway 249, PO Box 692000, Houston, TX, 77269-2000

Tel: (281) 370-0670    Fax: (281) 514-1740    www.compaq.com

*Develop/mfr. personal computers.*

**Compaq Computer Hong Kong Ltd., 27/F Windsor House, 311 Gloucester Rd., Causeway Bay, Hong Kong PRC**

Tel: 852-2867-1600    Fax: 852-2524-9533

## COMPUTER ASSOCIATES INTERNATIONAL INC.

One Computer Associates Plaza, Islandia, NY, 11788

Tel: (516) 342-5224    Fax: (516) 342-5329    www.cai.com

*Integrated business software for enterprise computing and information management, application development, manufacturing, financial applications and professional services.*

**Computer Associates Intl. Ltd., Suite 3008 30/F 12 Convention Plaza Office Tower, 1 Harbour Rd., Wanchai, Hong Kong PRC**

Tel: 852-2587-1388

## COMSAT CORPORATION

6560 Rock Spring Drive, Bethesda, MD, 20817

Tel: (301) 214-3200    Fax: (301) 214-7100    www.comsat.com

*Provides global telecommunications services via satellite and develops advanced satellite networking technology.*

**Tian Hang Tech.Services (HK) Ltd., Room 1907 Lippo House, Causeway Bay Plaza II, 463-483 Lockhart Road, Causeway Bay Hong Kong PRC**

## COMVERSE TECHNOLOGY, INC.

234 Crossways Park Drive, Woodbury, NY, 11797

Tel: (516) 677-7200    Fax: (516) 677-7355    www.comverse.com

*Mfr. telephone communication and recording systems.*

**Comverse Infosys Hong Kong, Room 1105 Emperor Centre, 288 Hennessy Road, Wanchai, Hong Kong PRC**

Tel: 852-2574-7192    Fax: 852-2904-7676

## CONAIR CORPORATION

1 Cummings Point Road, Stamford, CT, 06904

Tel: (203) 351-9000    Fax: (203) 351-9180    www.conair.com

*Mfr. personal care and household appliances.*

**Continental Conair Ltd., World Trade Tower II, Kwun Tong, Kowloon, Hong Kong PRC**

## CONCURRENT COMPUTER CORPORATION

4375 River Green Pkwy., Duluth, GA, 30096

Tel: (678) 258-4000    Fax: (678) 258-4300    www.ccur.com

*Mfr. computer systems and software.*

**Concurrent Computer Hong Kong Ltd., 1701 Stanhope House 17/F, 738 King's Rd., Quarry Bay, Hong Kong PRC**

Tel: 852-2-880-0802   Fax: 852-2-880-0664

## CONE MILLS CORPORATION

3101 N. Elm Street, PO Box 26540, Greensboro, NC, 27415-6540

Tel: (336) 379-6220    Fax: (336) 379-6287    www.cone.com

*Mfr. denims, flannels, chamois and other fabrics.*

**Burlton International Ltd., Rm. 1307 New Treasure Centre, 10 Ng Fong St., San Po Kong, Kowloon, Hong Kong PRC**

Tel: 852-2721-2213   Fax: 852-2723-1117   Contact: Benjamin Cheung

## CONEXANT SYSTEMS, INC.

4311 Jamboree Road, PO Box C, Newport Beach, CA, 92658-8902

Tel: (949) 483-4600    Fax: (949) 483-4078    www.conexant.com

*Provides semiconductor products for communications electronics.*

**Conexant Systems Asia Pacific Limited, Ste. 8-10 Harbour Centre - 13/F, 25 Harbour Road, Wanchai Hong Kong PRC**

Tel: 852-2-827-0181   Fax: 852-2-827-6488

## CONTIGROUP COMPANIES, INC.

277 Park Avenue, New York, NY, 10172

Tel: (212) 207-5100    Fax: (212) 207-2910    www.contigroup.com

*Engaged in cattle feed and pork/poultry producers.*

**Asian Industries Merchandising, United Centre 35/F, 95 Queensway, Hong Kong PRC**

Tel: 852-2823-6111   Fax: 852-2528-0797   Contact: Michael A. Hoer, SVP

## COPELAND CORPORATION

1675 West Campbell Road, Sidney, OH, 45365-0669

Tel: (937) 498-3011    Fax: (937) 498-3334    www.copeland-corp.com

*Producer of compressors and condensing units for commercial and residential air conditioning and refrigeration equipment.*

**Copeland Hong Kong, 10/F Pioneer Building, 213 Wai Yip Street, Kwun Tong Kowloon, Hong Kong PRC**

## CORNING INC.

One Riverfront Plaza, Corning, NY, 14831-0001

Tel: (607) 974-9000    Fax: (607) 974-8091    www.corning.com

*Mfr. glass and specialty materials, consumer products; communications, laboratory services.*

**Corning Hong Kong Ltd., Manulife Tower 34th Fl., 169 Electric Road, North Point, Hong Kong PRC**

Tel: 852-2807-2723   Fax: 852-2807-2152

## CORRPRO COMPANIES, INC.

1090 Enterprise Drive, Medina, OH, 44256

Tel: (330) 725-6681    Fax: (330) 723-0244    www.corrpro.com

*Full-services corrosion engineering, cathodic protection.*

**Corrpro Companies Far East Ltd., Room 1008 Block B, Sea View Estate, No. 2-8 Watson Rd., North Point, Hong Kong PRC**

Tel: 852-2541-6875   Fax: 852-2541-7543   Contact: Colin Man

## COUDERT BROTHERS

1114 Ave. of the Americas, New York, NY, 10036-7794

Tel: (212) 626-4400    Fax: (212) 626-4120    www.coudert.com

*International law firm.*

**Coudert Brothers, 25/F 9 Queen's Rd., Central, Hong Kong PRC**

Tel: 852-2218-9100   Fax: 852-2868-1417   Contact: Henry J. Uscinski, Ptnr.

## COULTER PHARMACEUTICAL, INC.

600 Gateway Blvd., South San Francisco, CA, 94080

Tel: (650) 553-2000    Fax: (650) 553-2028    www.coulterpharm.com

*Mfr. blood analysis systems, flow cytometers, chemicals systems, scientific systems and reagents.*

**Coulter Electronics HK Ltd., Unit B 13/F Gee Chang Hong Centre, 65 Wong Chuk Hang Rd., Hong Kong PRC**

## CRAVATH, SWAINE & MOORE

Worldwide Plaza, 825 Eighth Ave., New York, NY, 10019-7475

Tel: (212) 474-1000    Fax: (212) 474-3700    www.cravath.com

*International law firm.*

**Cravath, Swaine & Moore, Ste. 2609 Asia Pacific Finance Tower, Citibank Plaza, 3 Garden Rd., Central Hong Kong PRC**

Tel: 852-2509-7200

## CROMPTON CORPORATION

Benson Road, Middlebury, CT, 06749

Tel: (203) 573-2000    Fax: (203) 573-3077    www.uniroyalchemical.com

*Tires, tubes and other rubber products, chemicals, plastics and textiles.*

**Uniroyal Intl., 1008 Shell House, 26 Queen's Rd., Central, Hong Kong PRC**

## CSX CORPORATION

901 East Cary Street, Richmond, VA, 23860

Tel: (804) 782-1400    Fax: (804) 782-6747    www.csx.com

*Provides freight delivery and contract logistics services.*

**Hong Kong Orient Trucking, Ltd. (HOTL), Kowloon, Hong Kong PRC**

## CUBIC CORPORATION

9333 Balboa Ave., PO Box 85587, San Diego, CA, 92123

Tel: (858) 277-6780    Fax: (858) 277-1878    www.cubic.com

*Automatic fare collection equipment, training systems.*

**Cubic Transportation Far East Ltd., Units 1102-3 11/F, Tower Enterprise Square, 8 Sheny Yuet Rd., Kowloon Bay Hong Kong PRC**

Tel: 852-2331-7888   Fax: 852-2331-3182

## CUMMINS ENGINE COMPANY, INC.

500 Jackson Street, PO Box 3005, Columbus, IN, 47202-3005

Tel: (812) 377-5000    Fax: (812) 377-4937    www.cummins.com

*Mfr. diesel engines.*

**Cummins Engine H.K. Ltd., Unison Industrial Centre 2/F, 27-31 Au Pui Wan Street, Fo Tan Shatin N.T. Hong Kong PRC**

## CURTIS, MALLET-PREVOST, COLT & MOSLE LLP

101 Park Ave., 35th Floor, New York, NY, 10178

Tel: (212) 696-6000    Fax: (212) 697-1559    www.cm-p.com

*International law firm.*

**Curtis, Mallet-Prevost, Colt & Mosle LLP, 401 St. George's Bldg., 2 Ice House St., Central, Hong Kong PRC**

## CYPRESS SEMICONDUCTOR CORPORATION

3901 N. First Street, San Jose, CA, 95134-1599

Tel: (408) 943-2600     Fax: (408) 943-2796     www.cypress.com

*Mfr. integrated circuits.*

**Cypress Semiconductor, Unit 1307-08 Tower 1 Metroplaza, Hing Fong Road, N.T., Hong Kong PRC**

Tel: 852-2420-2568   Fax: 852-2427-0335

## LEO A. DALY

8600 Indian Hills Drive, Omaha, NE, 68114

Tel: (402) 391-8111     Fax: (402) 391-8564     www.leoadaly.com

*Planning, arch, engineering and interior design services.*

**Leo A. Daly Pacific Ltd., 10/F CNAC Bldg., 10 Queen's Rd., Central Hong Kong PRC**

Tel: 852-2567-4321  Fax: 852-2885-3507   Contact: Michael R. Fowlerll   Emp: 11

## DAMES & MOORE GROUP

911 Wilshire Boulevard, Ste. 700, Los Angeles, CA, 90017

Tel: (213) 996-2200     Fax: (213) 996-2290     www.dames.com

*Engineering, environmental and construction management services.*

**O'Brien-Kreitzberg, 1801 Yue Xiu Bldg., 160-174 Lockhart Rd., Wanchai, Hong Kong PRC**

## DANA CORPORATION

4500 Dorr Street, Toledo, OH, 43615

Tel: (419) 535-4500     Fax: (419) 535-4643     www.dana.com

*Mfr./sales of automotive, heavy truck, off-highway, fluid and mechanical power components and engine parts, filters and gaskets.*

**Shui Hing Manufacturing Co. Ltd., Block B. Marvel Ind. Bldg. 4/F, 17-23 Kwai Fung Crescent, Kwai Chung NT, Hong Kong PRC**

## D'ARCY MASIUS BENTON & BOWLES INC. (DMB&B)

1675 Broadway, New York, NY, 10019

Tel: (212) 468-3622     Fax: (212) 468-2987     www.dmbb.com

*Full service international advertising and communications group.*

**DMB&B Asia Pacific, 6/F Devon House, 979 King's Rd., Quarry Bay, Hong Kong PRC**

Tel: 852-2590-5888   Fax: 852-2856-9905   Contact: Alan Thompson, Mng. Dir.

## DATA GENERAL CORPORATION

4400 Computer Drive, Westboro, MA, 01580

Tel: (508) 898-5000     Fax: (508) 366-1319     www.dg.com

*Design, mfr. general purpose computer systems and peripheral products and services.*

**Data General HK Sales & Service Ltd., 5/F Wheelock House, 20 Pedder St., Hong Kong PRC**

**Data General Hong Kong Ltd., 1014 New World Office Bldg., 20 Salisbury, Rd., Tsim Sha Tsui, Kowloon, Hong Kong PRC**

## DATASCOPE CORPORATION

14 Phillips Pkwy., Montvale, NJ, 07645

Tel: (201) 391-8100     Fax: (201) 307-5400     www.datascope.com

*Mfr. medical devices.*

**Datascope Hong Kong, Billion Trade Centre 1801, 31 Hung To Road, Kwun Tong, Kowloon Hong Kong PRC**

## DAVIS POLK & WARDWELL

450 Lexington Ave., New York, NY, 10017

Tel: (212) 450-4000     Fax: (212) 450-4800     www.dpw.com

*International law firm.*

**Davis Polk & Wardwell, The Hong Kong Club Bldg., 3A Chater Rd., Hong Kong PRC**

Tel: 852-2533-3300  Fax: 852-2533-3388

## DAY RUNNER, INC.

15295 Alton Parkway, Irvine, CA, 92618

Tel: (714) 680-3500     Fax: (714) 680-0538     www.dayrunner.com

*Mfg./distribution of paper-based organizers.*

**Day Runner Hong Kong Ltd., Room 2509 Harbour Centre, 25 Harbour Rd., Wanchai, Hong Kong PRC**

Tel: 852-2583-9218   Fax: 852-2827-4333   Contact: Daniel Kwan

## DDB NEEDHAM WORLDWIDE INC.

437 Madison Ave., New York, NY, 10022

Tel: (212) 415-2000     Fax: (212) 415-3417     www.ddbn.com

*Advertising agency.*

**DDB Asia Pacific Ltd., 17/F Citicorp Centre, 18 Whitfield Rd., Causeway Bay, Hong Kong PRC**

## DEBEVOISE & PLIMPTON

919 Third Avenue, New York, NY, 10022

Tel: (212) 909-6000     Fax: (212) 909-6836     www.debevoise.com

*International law firm.*

**Debevoise & Plimpton, 13/F Entertainment Bldg., 30 Queen's Rd. Central, Hong Kong PRC**

Tel: 852-2810-7918   Fax: 852-2810-9828   Contact: Jeffrey S. Wood, Mng. Ptnr.   Emp: 12

## DECISION STRATEGIES FAIRFAX INTERNATIONAL

505 Park Avenue, 7th Fl., New York, NY, 10022

Tel: (212) 935-4040     Fax: (212) 935-4046     www.dsfx.com

*Provides discreet consulting, investigative, business intelligence and security services to corporations, financial and investment institutions, law firms and governments worldwide.*

**DSFX Hong Kong, Room 704 1 Lyndhurst Terrace, Central District Hong Kong, PRC**

**(011)**

Tel: 852-2522-1352   Fax: 852-2536-0469

## DELL COMPUTER CORPORATION

One Dell Way, Round Rock, TX, 78682-2222

Tel: (512) 338-4400     Fax: (512) 728-3653     www.dell.com

*Direct marketer and supplier of computer systems.*

**Dell Computer Asia Ltd., 1001 Stanhope House, 734-738 King's Rd., Quarry Bay, Hong Kong PRC**

Tel: 852-2508-0500   Fax: 852-2887-2040   Contact: Diane Chan, Gen. Mgr.

## DELOITTE TOUCHE TOHMATSU INTERNATIONAL

1633 Broadway, New York, NY, 10019

Tel: (212) 492-4000     Fax: (212) 392-4154     www.deloitte.com

*Accounting, audit, tax and management consulting services.*

**Deloitte Touche Tohmatsu, Wing on Centre 22/F, 111 Connaught Rd., Central Hong Kong PRC**

## DENTSPLY INTERNATIONAL

570 West College Ave., PO Box 872, York, PA, 17405-0872

Tel: (717) 845-7511     Fax: (717) 843-6357     www.dentsply.com

*Mfr. and distribution of dental supplies and equipment.*

**Dentsply Asia Inc., 23/F Gee Chang Hong Centre, 65 Wong Chuk Hang Rd., Aberdeen Hong Kong PRC**

Tel: 852-2870-0336

## DETROIT DIESEL CORPORATION

13400 Outer Drive West, Detroit, MI, 48239

Tel: (313) 592-5000    Fax: (313) 592-5058    www.detroitdiesel.com

*Mfr. diesel and aircraft engines, heavy-duty transmissions.*

**China Diesel Support Services,  Unit B 10/FL Alex Ind. Bldg., Cheung Sha Wan Kowloon, Hong Kong**

## DEWEY BALLANTINE LLP

1301 Ave. of the Americas, New York, NY, 10019

Tel: (212) 259-8000    Fax: (212) 259-6333    www.deweyballantine.com

*International law firm.*

**Dewey Ballantine LLP,  Ste. 3907 Asian Pacific Finance Tower, Citibank Plaza, 3 Garden Rd., Central Hong Kong PRC**

Tel: 852-2509-7000   Fax: 852-2509-70883

## THE DEXTER CORPORATION

1 Elm Street, Windsor Locks, CT, 06096

Tel: (860) 627-9051    Fax: (860) 627-7078    www.dexelec.com

*Mfr. polymer products, magnetic materials, biotechnology.*

**Dexter Asia Pacific Ltd., Ste. 1201 Tower 6 Ching Hong Kong City, 33 Canton Rd., Tsim Shu Tsui, Kowloon Hong Kong PRC**

**Dexter Specialty Chemicals HK Ltd.,  Albion Plaza #1201-4, 2-6 Granville Rd., TST, Hong Kong PRC**

**Life Technologies (Pacific) Ltd.,  Mappin House 12/F, 98 Texaco Rd., Tsuen Wan, NT Hong Kong PRC**

## DHL WORLDWIDE EXPRESS

50 California Avenue, San Francisco, CA, 94111

Tel: (415) 677-6100    Fax: (415) 824-9700    www.dhl.com

*Worldwide air express carrier.*

**DHL Worldwide Express,  13 Mok Cheong St., Tokwawan, Kowloon, Hong Kong PRC**

Tel: 852-2765-8111

## DICTAPHONE CORPORATION

3191 Broadbridge Ave., Stratford, CT, 06497-2559

Tel: (203) 381-7000    Fax: (203) 381-7100    www.dictaphone.com

*Mfr./sale dictation, telephone answering and multi-channel voice communications recording systems.*

**Dictaphone Hong Kong,  Hong Kong PRC**

Tel: 852-2709-1163

## DILLINGHAM CONSTRUCTION CORPORATION

5960 Inglewood Dr., Pleasanton, CA, 94588-8535

Tel: (925) 463-3300    Fax: (925) 463-1571    www.dillinghamconstruction.com

*Engaged in construction services for the commercial, industrial, and marine markets.*

**Dillingham Construction (HK) Ltd.,  904 Tower Two South Seas Centre, 75 Mody St., Tsim Sha Tsui East, Kowloon Hong Kong PRC**

## DIMON INCORPORATED

512 Bridge Street, PO Box 681, Danville, VA, 24543-0681

Tel: (804) 792-7511    Fax: (804) 791-0377    www.dimon.com

*One of world's largest importer and exporters of leaf tobacco.*

**Intabex International Limited,  Unit 1004 Technology Plaza, 29-35 Sha Tsui Road, Tsuen Wan N.T., Hong Kong PRC**

Tel: 852-2492-3868   Fax: 852-2417-2256

## DIONEX CORPORATION

1228 Titan Way, PO Box 3603, Sunnyvale, CA, 94086-3603

Tel: (408) 737-0700    Fax: (408) 730-9403    www.dionex.com

*Develop/mfr./market chromatography systems and related products.*

**Techcomp,  Rm. 505 Shui Hing Ctr., 13 Sheung Yuet Road, Kowloon Bay Kowloon, Hong Kong PRC**

## DME COMPANY

29111 Stephenson Highway, Madison Heights, MI, 48071

Tel: (248) 398-6000    Fax: (248) 544-5705    www.dmeco.com

*Basic tooling for plastic molding and die casting.*

**DME Ltd., Unit 4 G/F Po Lung Centre, 11 Wang Chiu Rd., Kowloon Bay, Kowloon, Hong Kong PRC**

## DONALDSON COMPANY, INC.

1400 West 94th Street, Minneapolis, MN, 55431

Tel: (612) 887-3131    Fax: (612) 887-3155    www.donaldson.com

*Mfr. filtration systems and replacement parts.*

**Donaldson Far East Ltd.,  United A & B & C 21/F CDW Bldg., 388 Castle Peak Rd., Tsuen Wan N.T., Hong Kong PRC**

Tel: 852-2402-2830   Fax: 852-2493-2928   Contact: Rolf Sobolik

## DONALDSON, LUFKIN & JENRETTE, INC.

277 Park Ave., New York, NY, 10172

Tel: (212) 892-3000    Fax: (212) 892-7272    www.dlj.com

*Investment banking, capital markets and financial services.*

**Donaldson, Lufkin & Jenrette, Inc.,  Two Exchange Square, 8 Connaught Place, Central Hong Kong, Hong Kong PRC**

Tel: 852-2501-3800

## R.R. DONNELLEY & SONS COMPANY

77 West Wacker Drive, Chicago, IL, 60601-1696

Tel: (312) 326-8000    Fax: (312) 326-8543    www.rrdonnelley.com

*Commercial printing, allied communication services.*

**R. R. Donnelley Financial (h.K.) Ltd.,  Asia Pacific Finance Tower Suite 805, Citibank Plaza, 3 Garden Rd., Central Hong Kong PRC**

Tel: 852-2522-3803

## DOREMUS & COMPANY, INC.

200 Varick Street, New York, NY, 10271

Tel: (212) 366-3000    Fax: (212) 366-3629    www.doremus.com

*Advertising and public relations.*

**Doremus & Co.,  Hong Kong, PRC**

## DORSEY & WHITNEY LLP

Pillsbury Center South, 220 S. Sixth Street, Minneapolis, MN, 55402

Tel: (612) 340-2600    Fax: (612) 340-2868    www.dorseylaw.com

*International law firm.*

**Dorsey & Whitney LLP,  Ste. 801, Citic Tower, No. 1 Tim Mei Ave., Central, Hong Kong PRC**

Tel: 852-2526-5000   Fax: 852-2524-3000   Contact: Zhao Zhang, Mng. Ptnr.   Emp: 6

## DOUBLECLICK, INC.

450 West 33rd Street, New York, NY, 10001

Tel: (212) 683-0001    Fax: (212) 889-0062    www.doubleclick.net

*Engaged in online advertising.*

**Doubleclick, Ltd.,  36/F CEF Life Tower, 248 Queen's Road East, Wanchai, Hong Kong PRC**

## THE DOW CHEMICAL COMPANY

2030 Dow Center, Midland, MI, 48674

Tel: (517) 636-1000    Fax: (517) 636-3228    www.dow.com

*Mfr. chemicals, plastics, pharmaceuticals, agricultural products, consumer products.*

**Dow Chemical Hong Kong Ltd., Gammon House, 12 Harbour Rd., PO Box 711, Hong Kong PRC**

## DOW JONES & COMPANY, INC.

200 Liberty Street, New York, NY, 10281

Tel: (212) 416-2000    Fax: (212) 416-4348    www.dj.com

*Publishing and financial news services.*

**Asian Wall Street Journal, GPO Box 9825, Hong Kong, PRC**

## DRAFT WORLDWIDE

633 North St. Clair Street, Chicago, IL, 60611-3211

Tel: (312) 944-3500    Fax: (312) 944-3566    www.draftworldwide.com

*Full service international advertising agency, engaged in brand building, direct and promotional marketing.*

**DraftWorldwide, 7/F Siu On Centre, 188 Lockhard Rd., Wanchai, Hong Kong PRC**

Tel: 852-2531-8828   Fax: 852-2824-4386   Contact: Ana Lee, Pres.

## DRAKE BEAM MORIN INC.

101 Huntington Ave., Boston, MA, 02199

Tel: (617) 375-9500    Fax: (617) 267-2011    www.dbm.com

*Human resource management consulting and training.*

**DBM Hong Kong, Printing House 16/F, 6 Duddell St., Central, Hong Kong PRC**

Tel: 852-2840-0838   Fax: 852-2877-3721

## DRESSER INSTRUMENT DIVISION

250 East Main Street, Stratford, CT, 06614-5145

Tel: (203) 378-8281    Fax: (203) 385-0357    www.dresserinstruments.com

*Mfr. pressure gauges and temperature instruments.*

**Dresser Trading Div., American Chamber of Commerce Building, 1030 Swire House, Hong Kong PRC**

## DST INNOVIS, INC.

11020 Sun Center Drive, Ranch Cordova, CA, 95670

Tel: (916) 636-4501    Fax: (916) 636-5750    www.dstinnovis.com

*Management/services software and hardware for cable TV, satellite and telecommunications industrial.*

**DST Innovis Limited, 19/F - Kinwick Centre, 3 Hollywood Road, Central Hong Kong PRC**

## E.I. DU PONT DE NEMOURS & COMPANY

1007 Market Street, Wilmington, DE, 19898

Tel: (302) 774-1000    Fax: (302) 774-7321    www.dupont.com

*Mfr./sale diversified chemicals, plastics, specialty products and fibers.*

**DuPont Far East Inc., 915 Prince's Bldg., 10 Chater Rd., Hong Kong PRC**

## DUFF & PHELPS CREDIT RATING CO.

55 East Monroe Street, Chicago, IL, 60603

Tel: (312) 368-3100    Fax: (312) 442-4121    www.dcrco.com

*Engaged in rating stocks and bonds, municipal securities and insurance company claims paying capabilities.*

**Duff & Phelps Credit Rating Co., 1702 Ruttonjee House, 11 Duddell Street, Central Hong Kong PRC**

Tel: 852-2901-0500   Fax: 852-2536-9276

## DURACELL INTERNATIONAL INC.

8 Research Drive, Bethel, CT, 06801

Tel: (203) 796-4000      Fax: (203) 796-4745      www.duracell.com

*Mfr. batteries.*

**Duracell Asia Ltd., 1602 World Finance Centre, South Tower, Harbour City, Canton Rd., Kowloon, Hong Kong PRC**

## EAGLE GLOBAL LOGISTICS (EGL)

15350 Vickery Drive, Houston, TX, 77032

Tel: (281) 618-3100      Fax: (281) 618-3100      www.eaglegl.com

*Ocean/air freight forwarding, customs brokerage, packing and wholesale, logistics management and insurance.*

**Circle International Ltd., Room 2004-5 Devon House, 979 King's Rd., Quarry Bay, Hong Kong PRC**

Tel: 852-2590-9822   Fax: 852-2590-9130

## EASTMAN CHEMICAL

100 North Eastman Road, Kingsport, TN, 37660

Tel: (423) 229-2000      Fax: (423) 229-1351      www.eastman.com

*Mfr. plastics, chemicals, fibers.*

**Eastman Chemical Hong Kong Ltd., 1-3 Wang Lok St., Yuen Long Industrial Estate, Yuen Long, New Territories, Hong Kong PRC**

Tel: 852-2473-7188   Fax: 852-2474-0913   Contact: J. Ron Hilderbrand, Mgr.

**Eastman Chemical Ltd., 1/F Kodak House 1, 321 Java Rd., North Point, Hong Kong PRC**

Tel: 852-2565-6330   Fax: 852-2880-9729   Contact: Bruce Chiu

## EASTMAN KODAK COMPANY

343 State Street, Rochester, NY, 14650

Tel: (716) 724-4000      Fax: (716) 724-1089      www.kodak.com

*Develop/mfr. photo and chemicals products, information management/video/copier systems, fibers/plastics for various industry.*

**Eastman Chemical Intl. Ltd., 1/F Kodak House, 321 Java Rd., North Point Hong Kong PRC**
**Eastman Kodak Asia-Pacific Ltd., 2/F Kodak House, 321 Java Rd., North Point Hong Kong PRC**

## ECI TELECOM LTD.

12950 Worldgate Dr., Herndon, VA, 20170

Tel: (703) 456-3400      Fax: (703) 456-3410      www.ecitele.com

*Designs, develops, manufactures, markets and supports end-to-end digital telecommunications solutions.*

**ECI Telecom (HK) Ltd., 3903 China Resources Building, 26 Harbour Road, Wanchai, Hong Kong PRC**

Tel: 852-2824-4128

## ECOLAB INC.

370 N. Wabasha Street, St. Paul, MN, 55102

Tel: (651) 293-2233      Fax: (651) 293-2379      www.ecolab.com

*Develop/mfr. premium cleaning, sanitizing and maintenance products and services for the hospitality, institutional, and residential markets.*

**Ecolab Ltd., Hong Kong PRC**

Tel: 852-2341-4202

## EDELMAN PUBLIC RELATIONS WORLDWIDE

200 East Randolph Drive, 62nd Fl., Chicago, IL, 60601

Tel: (312) 240-3000     Fax: (312) 240-0596     www.edelman.com

*International independent public relations firm.*

**Edelman PR Worldwide, Room 3701-2 37/F Windsor House, 311 Gloucester Rd., Causeway Bay, Hong Kong PRC**

Tel: 852-2804-1338   Fax: 852-2804-1301   Contact: Clara Shek, Gen. Mgr.

## J.D. EDWARDS & COMPANY

One Technology Way, Denver, CO, 80237

Tel: (303) 334-4000     Fax: (303) 334-4970     www.jdedwards.com

*Computer software products.*

**J. D. Edwards, Unit A 24/F Entertainment Bldg., 30 Queens Rd., Central, Hong Kong PRC**

Tel: 852-2844-7400   Fax: 852-2590-9618

**System-Pro Solutions Ltd., 8/F West Warwick House, Taiko Place, 979 King's Rd., Quarry Bay Hong Kong PRC**

Tel: 852-2844-7400   Fax: 852-2521-4782

## ELANCO ANIMAL HEALTH

500 East 96th Street, Ste. 125, Indianapolis, IN, 46240

Tel: (317) 276-3000     Fax: (317) 276-6116     www.elanco.com

*Antibiotics and fine chemicals.*

**Elanco Agricultural & Industrial Products, 1026-1030 Prince's Bldg., 10 Chater Rd., Hong Kong PRC**

## ELECTRO SCIENTIFIC INDUSTRIES, INC.

13900 NW Science Park Drive, Portland, OR, 97229

Tel: (503) 641-4141     Fax: (503) 643-4873     www.esi.com

*Mfg. production and testing equipment used in manufacture of electronic components in pagers and cellular communication devices.*

**Asia Industrial Technology Ltd. ECS - Test, Room 1318 Level 13 Tower 1, Grand Central Plaza, 138 Shatin Rural Committee Rd., Shatin NT Hong Kong PRC**

Tel: 852-2558-8110   Fax: 852-2558-8139   Contact: Jackie Wong

## ELECTROGLAS INC.

6042 Silver Creek Valley Road, San Jose, CA, 95138

Tel: (408) 528-3000     Fax: (408) 528-3542     www.electroglas.com

*Mfr. semi-conductor test equipment, automatic wafer probers.*

**Electroglas Intl. Inc., Room 1901 Park-In Comm. Ctr., 56 Dundas St., Kowloon, Hong Kong PRC**

## ELECTRONIC DATA SYSTEMS CORPORATION (EDS)

5400 Legacy Dr., Plano, TX, 75024

Tel: (972) 605-6000     Fax: (972) 605-2643     www.eds.com

*Provides professional services; management consulting, e.solutions, business process management and information solutions.*

**EDS Electronic Data Systems (HK) Ltd., 33/F Citibank Tower - Citibank Plaza, 3 Garden Road, Central Hong Kong PRC**

Tel: 852-2867-9888

## ELECTRONICS FOR IMAGING, INC.

303 Velocity Way, Foster City, CA, 94404

Tel: (650) 357-3500     Fax: (650) 357-3907     www.efi.com

*Design/mfr. computer software and hardware for color desktop publishing.*

**Electronics for Imaging, 28/F Soundwill Plaza, 38 Russell Street, Causeway Bay, Hong Kong PRC**

Tel: 852 2922 1668

## EMC CORPORATION

35 Parkwood Drive, Hopkinton, MA, 01748-9103

Tel: (508) 435-1000    Fax: (508) 435-8884    www.emc.com

*Designs/supplies intelligent enterprise storage and retrieval technology for open systems, mainframes and midrange environments.*

**EMC Computer Systems Hong Kong,  Room 1101-3 Cityplaza 4, Tiakoosing, Hong Kong PRC**

Tel: 852-2839-9600

## EMCOR GROUP

101 Merritt Seven, 7th Fl., Norwalk, CT, 06851

Tel: (203) 849-7800    Fax: (203) 849-7870    www.emcorgroup.com

*Engaged in specialty construction.*

**Emcor Group,  Hong Kong PRC**

## EMERSON RADIO CORPORATION

9 Entin Road, Parsippany, NJ, 07054

Tel: (973) 884-5800    Fax: (973) 428-2033    www.emersonradio.com

*Consumer electronics, radios, TV and VCR, tape recorders and players, computer products.*

**Emerson Radio HK Ltd.,  Suite 1009-1015 World Shopping Ctr., Harbor City, Phase 1, 7 Canton Rd., Kowloon, Hong Kong PRC**

## EMERY WORLDWIDE

One Lagoon Drive, Ste. 400, Redwood City, CA, 94065

Tel: (650) 596-9600    Fax: (650) 596-7901    www.emeryworld.com

*Freight transport, global logistics and air cargo.*

**Emery Worldwide,  Unit 9-15 15/F Kwong Sang Hong Centre, 151-153 Hoi Bun Rd., Swun Tong Kowloon, Hong Kong PRC**

Tel: 852-2796-3883

## ENCAD, INC.

6059 Cornerstone Court West, San Diego, CA, 92121

Tel: (858) 452-0882    Fax: (858) 452-5618    www.encad.com

*Mfr. large color printers for specialized graphics.*

**Encad Hong Kong,  Suite 1901-3 - Chinachem Leighton Plaza, 29 Leighton Road, Causeway Bay, Hong Kong PRC**

Tel: 852-2881-8969

## ENGELHARD CORPORATION

101 Wood Ave. S., CN 770, Iselin, NJ, 08830

Tel: (732) 205-5000    Fax: (732) 632-9253    www.engelhard.com

*Mfr. pigments, additives, catalysts, chemicals, engineered materials.*

**Engelhard Corporation,  Room 1001-2 Yuenfoong Centre, 150-160 Castle Peak Rd., Yuen Long NT, Hong Kong PRC**

**Engelhard-Clal Hong Kong,  21 Ma Tau Wei Road, 6/F, Blk. B2, Hunghom, Kowloon Hong Kong PRC**

Tel: 852-2365-0301

## EPICOR SOFTWARE CORPORATION

195 Technology Drive, Irvine, CA, 92618

Tel: (949) 585-4000    Fax: (949) 450-4419    www.epicor.com

*Mfr. software for e-business.*

**Epicor Hong Kong,  10 Cityplaza One, 1111 King's Road, Taikoo Shing, Hong Kong PRC**

## ERICO PRODUCTS INC.

34600 Solon Road, Cleveland, OH, 44139

Tel: (440) 248-0100     Fax: (440) 248-0723     www.erico.com

*Mfr. electric welding apparatus and hardware, metal stampings, specialty fasteners.*

**Erico Products Hong Kong, 2/F Block A Po Yip Building, 62-70 Texaco Road, Tsuen Wan, New Territories Hong Kong PRC**

Tel: 852-2764-8808

## ERNST & YOUNG, LLP

787 Seventh Ave., New York, NY, 10019

Tel: (212) 773-3000     Fax: (212) 773-6350     www.eyi.com

*Accounting and audit, tax and management consulting services.*

**Ernst & Young, 17/F Hutchison, 10 Harcourt Rd., Central, Hong Kong PRC**

Tel: 852-2585-2642   Fax: 852-2827-9523   Contact: Jason Felton

## ESS TECHNOLOGY, INC.

48401 Fremont Blvd., Fremont, CA, 94538

Tel: (510) 492-1088     Fax: (510) 492-1098     www.esstech.com

*Mfr. audio chips.*

**ESS Technology, Inc., Unit 1 18/F Westley Square, 48 Hoi Yuen Road, Kwun Tong Kowloon, Hong Kong PRC**

Tel: 852-2418-0860   Fax: 852-2619-0053

## EURO RSCG WORLDWIDE

350 Hudson Street, New York, NY, 10014

Tel: (212) 886-2000     Fax: (212) 886-2016     www.eurorscg.com

*International advertising agency group.*

**EURO RSCG Partnership, 21/F Devon House, Taikoo Place, 979 King's Road, Quarry Bay Hong Kong PRC**

## EXCELLON AUTOMATION

24751 Crenshaw Boulevard, Torrance, CA, 90505

Tel: (310) 534-6300     Fax: (310) 534-6777     www.excellon.com

*PCB drilling and routing machines; optical inspection equipment.*

**Wong's Kong King Intl.Ltd., 11/F. WKK Building - 418A Kwun Tong Road, Kowloon Hong Kong PRC**

Tel: 852-2357-8888

## EXE TECHNOLOGIES, INC.

8787 N. Stemmonds Fwy., Dallas, TX, 75247-3702

Tel: (214) 775-6000     Fax: (214) 775-0911     www.exe.com

*Provides a complete line of supply chain management execution software for WMS.*

**EXE Technologies, Inc. Hong Kong, Rm. 805 8/F BOC Credit Card Centre, 68 Connaught Rd. West, Hong Kong PRC**

Tel: 852-2804-1881   Fax: 852-2849-8916

## EXPEDITORS INTERNATIONAL OF WASHINGTON INC.

1015 Third Avenue, 12th Fl., Seattle, WA, 98104-1182

Tel: (206) 674-3400     Fax: (206) 682-9777     www.expd.com

*Air/ocean freight forwarding, customs brokerage, international logistics solutions.*

**EI Freight (HK) Ltd., 201 South Seas Centre, Tower 2 - 75 Mody Rd., Tsim Sha Tsui East, Kowloon Hong Kong PRC**

Tel: 852-2739-2399   Fax: 852-2721-9734

## EXXON MOBIL CORPORATION

5959 Las Colinas Blvd., Irving, TX, 75039-2298

Tel: (972) 444-1000    Fax: (972) 444-1882    www.exxon.com

*Petroleum exploration, production, refining; mfr. petroleum and chemicals products; coal and minerals.*

**Exxon Mobil, Inc., St. George's Bldg., 2 Ice House St., Hong Kong PRC**

**Exxon Mobil, Inc., 18 Harbour Road, Central Plaza 22/F, Wanchai Hong Kong PRC**

## FACTSET RESEARCH SYSTEMS INC.

1 Greenwich Plaza, Greenwich, CT, 06830

Tel: (203) 863-1599    Fax: (203) 863-1501    www.factset.com

*Provides on-line financial information to financial professionals.*

**FactSet Limited, Bank of China Tower Level 25, One Garden Road, Central, Hong Kong PRC**

Tel: 852-2251-1833

## FEDERAL-MOGUL CORPORATION

26555 Northwestern Highway, PO Box 1966, Southfield, MI, 48034

Tel: (248) 354-7700    Fax: (248) 354-8983    www.federal-mogul.com

*Mfr./distributor precision parts for automobiles, trucks, farm and construction vehicles.*

**Federal-Mogul World Trade Hong Kong Ltd., Kwai Chung, Hong Kong PRC**

## FEDEX CORPORATION

942 South Shady Grove Rd., Memphis, TN, 38120

Tel: (901) 369-3600    Fax: (901) 395-2000    www.fdxcorp.com

*Package express delivery service.*

**Federal Express (HK) Ltd., 100 Sung Wong Toi Rd., Tokwawan, Kowloon, Hong Kong PRC**

Tel: 852-273-03333

## FEI CORPORATION

7451 N.W. Evergreen Pkwy., Hillsboro, OR, 97124-5830

Tel: (503) 640-7500    Fax: (503) 640-7509    www.feicompany.com

*Design and mfr. of charged particle beam systems serving the research, development and production needs of customers in semiconductor, data storage, and industry/institute markets.*

**FEI Hong Kong Company Ltd., Room 2604 Greenfield Tower, Concordia Plaza 1 Science Museum Road, TST East, Hong Kong PRC**

## FERRO CORPORATION

1000 Lakeside Ave., Cleveland, OH, 44114-7000

Tel: (216) 641-8580    Fax: (216) 696-5784    www.ferro.com

*Mfr. Specialty chemicals, coatings, plastics, colors, refractories.*

**Ferro Far East Ltd., PO Box 98436, Tsim Sha Tsui, Kowloon, Hong Kong PRC**

Tel: 852-2724-6193  Fax: 852-2724-6837   Contact: Ronald L. Klassen, Mng. Dir.

## FIDUCIARY TRUST COMPANY OF NY

2 World Trade Center, 94th Fl., New York, NY, 10048

Tel: (212) 466-4100    Fax: (212) 313-2662    www.ftc.com

*Banking services.*

**Fiduciary Trust (Intl.) SA, Hong Kong PRC**

## FileNET CORPORATION

3565 Harbor Boulevard, Costa Mesa, CA, 92626

Tel: (714) 966-3400    Fax: (714) 966-3490    www.filenet.com

*Provides integrated document management (IDM) software and services for internet and client server-based imaging, workflow, cold and electronic document management solutions.*

**FileNET Hong Kong Ltd., Unit 3206-7 32/F Shui On Centre, 8 Harbour Rd., Wanchai, Hong Kong PRC**

Tel: 852-2563-5822   Fax: 852-2811-5631

## FISHER-ROSEMOUNT

8000 Maryland Ave., Ste. 500, Clayton, MO, 63105-4755

Tel: (314) 746-9900  Fax: (314) 746-9974  www.frco.com

*Mfr. industrial process control equipment.*

**Fisher-Rosemount Pty. Ltd., Unit 2302 - 23/F Malaysia Bldg., 50 Gloucester Rd., Wanchai Hong Kong PRC**

Tel: 852-2802-9368  Fax: 852-2827-8670  Contact: Andrew Ho, Mgr.

**Loftyman Engineering Ltd., Unit B - 7/F Seabright Plaza, Shell St., North Point Hong Kong PRC**

Tel: 852-2571-1681  Fax: 852-2887-7750

## FLACK + KURTZ INC.

475 Fifth Ave., New York, NY, 10017

Tel: (212) 532-9600  Fax: (212) 689-7489  www.flackandkurtz.com

*Consulting engineers for building services, i.e.., HVAC, electrical, lighting, plumbing/hydraulics, life safety, fire protection and telecommunications.*

**Flack + Kurtz Asia, Ltd., Asian House 19/F, 1 Hennesy Rd., Wanchai, Hong Kong PRC**

Tel: 852-2893-3316  Fax: 852-2838-2708  Contact: Henry DiGregorio  Emp: 6

## FLEETBOSTON FINANCIAL CORPORATION

1 Federal Street, Boston, MA, 02110

Tel: (617) 346-4000  Fax: (617) 434-7547  www.fleet.com

*Banking and insurance services.*

**FleetBoston - Hong Kong, Jardine House, 1 Connaught Place Sts. 801-809, Central Hong Kong PRC**

Tel: 852-2526-4361  Fax: 852-2845-9222

## FLEXTRONICS INC. INTERNATIONAL

2241 Lundy Ave., San Jose, CA, 95131-1822

Tel: (408) 428-1300  Fax: (408) 428-0420  www.flextronics.com

*Contract manufacturer for electronics industry.*

**Flextronics Hong Kong Ltd., Wo Kee Hong Bldg., 585-609 Castle Peak Rd., Kwai Chung, Hong Kong PRC**

## FMC CORPORATION

200 E. Randolph Drive, Chicago, IL, 60601

Tel: (312) 861-6000  Fax: (312) 861-6141  www.fmc.com

*Produces chemicals and precious metals, mfr. machinery, equipment and systems for industrial, agricultural and government use.*

**FMC Asia Pacific Inc., Caroline Centre 12/F, 28 Yun Ping Rd., Causeway Bay, Hong Kong PRC**

**FMC Hong Kong Ltd., Hong Kong PRC**

**Friendship Minerals & Chemicals Ltd., Hong Kong PRC**

## FMC JETWAY SYSTEMS

1805 W. 2550 South, PO Box 9368, Ogden, UT, 84401-3249

Tel: (801) 627-6600  Fax: (801) 629-3474  www.jetwaysystems.com

*Mfr. aircraft loading bridges and ground support equipment.*

**FMC-Asia-Pacific, 12/F Caroline Centre, 28 Yun Ping Rd., Causeway Bay, Hong Kong PRC**

Tel: 852-2839-6600  Fax: 852-2576-3770  Contact: Jenny K. Lawton, North Asia Sales Mgr.

## FMR (FIDELITY INVESTMENTS)

82 Devonshire Street, Boston, MA, 02109

Tel: (617) 563-7000    Fax: (617) 476-6105    www.fidelity.com

*Diversified financial services company offering investment management, retirement, brokerage, and shareholder services directly to individuals and institutions and through financial intermediaries.*

**Fidelity Investments Management (HK) Ltd., PO Box 92053 Tsim Sha Tsui Post Office, Kowloon, Hong Kong PRC**

Tel: 852-2629-2626    Fax: 852-2956-2346

## FORTUNE BRANDS

200 Tower Parkway, Lincolnshire, IL, 60069

Tel: (847) 484-4400    Fax: (800) 310-5960    www.fortunebrands.com

*Mfr. diversified consumer products including Masterbrand, Acco office products, Jim Bean distillery products, Footjoy and Titleist golf products and Moen bath products.*

**Fortune Brands International Corporation, Ste. 4003 The Lee Gardens, 33 Hysan Avenue, Causeway Bay, Hong Kong PRC**

Tel: 852-2506-0660    Fax: 852-2506-0671

**Moen International Inc., 33 Hysan Avenue - Ste. 4003, Causeway Bay, Hong Kong PRC**

Tel: 852-2506-0670    Fax: 852-2506-0672

## FOUR WINDS INTERNATIONAL GROUP

1500 SW First Ave., Ste. 850, Portland, OR, 97201-2013

Tel: (503) 241-2732    Fax: (503) 241-1829    www.vanlines.com.au

*Transportation of household goods and general cargo and third party logistics.*

**Four Winds Removal Ltd., 5/F Len Shing Ind. Bldg., 4 A Kung Ngam Village Road, Shaukeiwan, Hong Kong PRC**

Tel: 852-2885-9666    Fax: 852-2567-7594    Contact: Christopher Wilkinson, Gen. Mgr.    Emp: 65

## FRANKLIN COVEY COMPANY

2200 W. Parkway Blvd., Salt Lake City, UT, 84119-2331

Tel: (801) 975-1776    Fax: (801) 977-1431    www.franklincovey.com

*Provides productivity and time management products and seminars.*

**Franklin Covey Taiwan, 7F-3 No. 9 1/F Admiralty Center Tower 1, 18 Harcourt Road, Hong Kong PRC**

Tel: 886-2731-7115    Fax: 886-2711-5285

## THE FRANKLIN MINT

US Route 1, Franklin Center, PA, 19091

Tel: (610) 459-6000    Fax: (610) 459-6880    www.franklinmint.com

*Design/marketing collectibles and luxury items.*

**Franklin Mint Ltd., Unit 5-7 19/F Tower III Enterprise Square, 9 Sheung Yuet Road, Kowloon Bay, Hong Kong PRC**

## FRANKLIN RESOURCES, INC.

777 Mariners Island Blvd., San Mateo, CA, 94404

Tel: (415) 312-2000    Fax: (415) 312-3655    www.frk.com

*Global and domestic investment advisory and portfolio management.*

**Templeton Asset Management Ltd., Hong Kong Branch Office, Shui On Centre 2701, 6-8 Harbour Rd., Wan Chai, Hong Kong PRC**

Tel: 852-2877-7733    Fax: 852-2877-5401

**Templeton Franklin Investment Services (Asia) Ltd., Shui On Centre 2701, 6-8 Harbour Rd., Wan Chai, Hong Kong PRC**

Tel: 852-2877-7733    Fax: 852-2877-5401

## FRITZ COMPANIES, INC.

706 Mission Street, Ste. 900, San Francisco, CA, 94103

Tel: (415) 904-8360     Fax: (415) 904-8661     www.fritz.com

*Integrated transportation, sourcing, distribution and customs brokerage services.*

**Fritz Air Freight (HK) Ltd., 3/F Goodwin "A", Sunshine Kowloon Bay Cargo Centre, 59 Tai Yip St., Kowloon Hong Kong PRC**

**Fritz Companies Asian Hdqtrs., Suite 906-10 Tai Building, 49 Austin Road, Tsim Sha Tsui, Kowloon Hong Kong PRC**

**Fritz Transportation Intl. (HK) Ltd., 9/F Tai Building, 49 Austin Road, Tsim Sha Tsui, Kowloon, Hong Kong PRC**

## FSI INTERNATIONAL INC.

322 Lake Hazeltine Drive, Chaska, MN, 55318

Tel: (612) 448-5440     Fax: (612) 448-2825     www.fsi-intl.com

*Manufacturing equipment for computer silicon wafers.*

**Metron Technology Ltd., Unit E 5/F - China Overseas Building, 139 Hennessy Road, Wanchai, Hong Kong PRC**

## FULBRIGHT & JAWORSKI

1301 McKinney Street, Ste. 5100, Houston, TX, 77010

Tel: (713) 651-5151     Fax: (713) 651-5246     www.fulbright.com

*International law firm.*

**Fulbright & Jaworski, The Hong Kong Club Bldg. 19/F, 3A Chater Rd., Central Hong Kong PRC**

Tel: 852-2523-3200   Fax: 852-2523-3255

## H.B. FULLER COMPANY

1200 Willow Lake Blvd., Vadnais Heights, MN, 55110

Tel: (651) 236-5900     Fax: (651) 236-5898     www.hbfuller.com

*Mfr./distributor adhesives, sealants, coatings, paints, waxes, sanitation chemicals.*

**H.B. Fuller International Inc., Asia/Pacific Area Office, Suite 2605 26/F Sino Plaza, 255-257 Glouchester Rd., Causeway Bay Hong Kong PRC**

Tel: 852-2832-9622   Fax: 852-2892-1680

## GALILEO INTERNATIONAL, INC.

9700 W. Higgins Rd., Ste. 400, Rosemont, IL, 600184796

Tel: (847) 518-4000     Fax: (847) 518-4085     www.galileo.com

*Operates computerized reservation systems (CRS).*

**Galileo International Asia, Vicwood Plaza - 33/F, 199 Des Voeux Road Central, Hong Kong PRC**

Tel: 852-2821-2288   Fax: 852-2821-2299

## LEWIS GALOOB TOYS INC.

500 Forbes Blvd., S. San Francisco, CA, 94080

Tel: (650) 952-1678     Fax: (650) 583-4996     www.galoob.com

*Mfr. toys, games, dolls.*

**Galco International Toys NV, 701-8 South Tower, World Finance Centre, 17 Canton Rd., Kowloon, Hong Kong PRC**

## THE GATES RUBBER COMPANY

990 S. Broadway, PO Box 5887, Denver, CO, 80217-5887

Tel: (303) 744-1911     Fax: (303) 744-4000     www.gatesrubber.com

*Mfr. automotive and industrial belts and hoses.*

**GNAPCO Pte. Ltd., Duke Wellington House 7/F, 14-24 Wellington StreetCentral Hong Kong, Hong Kong PRC**

Tel: 852-2525-1306   Fax: 852-2810-4289

## GATX CAPITAL CORPORATION

Four Embarcadero Center, Ste. 2200, San Francisco, CA, 94111

Tel: (415) 955-3200      Fax: (415) 955-3449      www.gatxcapital.com

*Lease and loan financing, residual guarantees.*

**GATX Leasing Hong Kong Ltd., Ste. 2705 2 Pacific Place, 88 Wueensway, Hong Kong PRC**

## GEMSTAR-TV GUIDE INTERNATIONAL, INC.

135 North Los Robles Avenue, Ste. 800, Pasadena, CA, 91101

Tel: (626) 792-5700      Fax: (626) 792-0257      www.gemstar.com

*Mfr. technology for VCR programming.*

**Gemstar Asia, Man Lok Centre - 23 Man Lok Street, Hung Hom Kowloon, Hong Kong PRC**

Tel: 852-2766-8445    Fax: 852-2363-3942

## GENERAL DATACOMM INC.

1579 Straits Turnpike, PO Box 1299, Middlebury, CT, 06762-1299

Tel: (203) 574-1118      Fax: (203) 758-8507      www.gdc.com

*Mfr./sale/services transportation equipment for communications networks.*

**General DataComm Intl., 803 Century Square, 1-13 D'Aguilar St., Central, Hong Kong PRC**

## GENERAL ELECTRIC CAPITAL CORPORATION

260 Long Ridge Road, Stamford, CT, 06927

Tel: (203) 357-4000      Fax: (203) 357-6489      www.gecapital.com

*Financial, property/casualty insurance, computer sales and trailer leasing services.*

**Employers Reinsurance Corp. (ERC), Ste. 2807-8 Citibank Tower, Citibank Plaza, 3 Garden Rd., Hong Kong PRC**

Tel: 852-2509-6888

## GENERAL ELECTRIC COMPANY

3135 Easton Turnpike, Fairfield, CT, 06431

Tel: (203) 373-2211      Fax: (203) 373-3131      www.ge.com

*Diversified manufacturing, technology and services.*

**GE Capital Global Projects, The Lee Gardens, 15-16F, Central Hong Kong PRC**

Tel: 852-2100-6717    Fax: 852-2100-8198

**GE International, The Lee Gardens, 15/F, Central Hong Kong**

Tel: 852-2100-8382    Fax: 852-2100-6688

**GE Silicones Hong Kong, 25 Canton Road, Tsimshatsui, Kowloon Hong Kong PRC**

Tel: 852-2629-0888    Fax: 852-2629-0803

**GE/AEG, Room 3009-11, Chaiwan, Hong Kong PRC**

Tel: 852-2426-6288    Fax: 852-2426-1874

**General Electric Co., Attn: Hong Kong PRC Office, 3135 Easton Turnpike, Fairfield CT 06431 USA**

Tel: 518-438-6500

**NBC, NBC Asia Ltd., 15/F 8 Commercial Tower, Chaiwan, Hong Kong PRC**

Tel: 852-2965-6800    Fax: 852-2965-6882

## GENERAL INSTRUMENT CORPORATION

101 Tournament Road, Horsham, PA, 19044

Tel: (215) 674-4800      Fax: (215) 443-9554      www.gi.com

*Mfr. broadband communications and power rectifying components.*

**General Instrument (Hong Kong) Ltd., Room 1017- China Chem Golden Plaza, 77 Mody Road Tsimshatsui East, Kowloon Hong Kong PRC**

Tel: 852-2587-1163    Fax: 852-2587-1093

## GENERAL REINSURANCE CORPORATION

695 E. Main Street, Stamford, CT, 06904-2350

Tel: (203) 328-5000     Fax: (203) 328-6423     www.genre.com

*Reinsurance services worldwide.*

**Cologne Reinsurance Company plc., 68/F Central Plaza, 18 Harbour Rd., Wanchai, Hong Kong PRC**

Tel: 852-2598-2388   Fax: 852-2598-2398   Contact: Jackie Y.C. Chun, Gen. Mgr.

**General Re Financial Products Ltd. - Hong Kong, Central Plaza 68/F, 18 Harbour Rd., Wanchai, Hong Kong PRC**

Tel: 852-2598-2488   Fax: 852-2598-2408   Contact: James Kao

## GENERAL SEMICONDUCTOR, INC.

10 Melville Park Road., Melville, NY, 11747

Tel: (631) 847-3000     Fax: (631) 847-3236     www.gensemi.com

*Mfr. of low- and medium-current power rectifiers and transient voltage suppressors.*

**General Semiconductor Hong Kong Ltd., Room 404 4/F Empire Centre, 68 Mody Rd., Kowloon, Hong Kong PRC**

Tel: 852-2369-8892   Fax: 852-2369-5730   Contact: Robert Wang

## GENERAL TIME CORPORATION

520 Guthridge Ct., Norcross, GA, 30092

Tel: (770) 447-5300     Fax: (770) 242-4009     www.westclox.com

*Mfr. clocks and watches.*

**General Time Asia, Room 1522 15/F Leighton Centre, 77 Leighton Road, Causeway Bay Hong Kong PRC**

Tel: 852-2-889-1303   Fax: 852-2-889-0331

## GEO LOGISTICS CORPORATION

1521 E. Dyer Rd., Santa Ana, CA, 92705

Tel: (714) 513-3000     Fax: (714) 513-3120     www.geo-logistics.com

*Freight forwarding, warehousing and distribution services, specializing in heavy cargo.*

**GeoLogistics Ltd., 93 Kwai Fuk Road 20th Floor, Kwai Chung, New Territories, Hong Kong PRC**

Tel: 852-2211-8998   Fax: 852-23-2877

**GeoLogistics Ltd., G57 Airfreight Forwarding Center, Chek Lap Kok, Hong Kong PRC**

Tel: 852-2237-1469   Fax: 852-22-37-1483

## GERBER PRODUCTS COMPANY

445 State Street, Fremont, MI, 49413-0001

Tel: (616) 928-2000     Fax: (616) 928-2723     www.gerber.com

*Mfr./distributor baby food and related products.*

**Gerber Baby Products Intl. Ltd., 1312 Hang Lung Ctr., 2-20 Paterson St., Causeway Bay, Hong Kong PRC**

## GETZ BROS & COMPANY, INC.

150 Post Street, Ste. 500, San Francisco, CA, 94108-4750

Tel: (415) 772-5500     Fax: (415) 772-5659     www.getz.com

*Diversified manufacturing, marketing and distribution services and travel services.*

**Asia Cardiovascular Products, 8/F Wyler Center, 200 Tai Lin Pai Rd., Kwai Chung NT, Hong Kong PRC**

Tel: 852-2484-9759   Fax: 852-2484-9616   Contact: Paul Rieff, President   Emp: 10

**Getz Bros. & Co. (Hong Kong) Ltd., 8/F Wyler Centre, 200 Tai Lin Pai Rd., Kwai Chung New Territories, Hong Kong PRC**

Tel: 852-2429-1292   Fax: 852-2480-4691   Contact: Stephen Lee, Gen. Mgr.   Emp: 135

**Getz Bros. & Co. Inc., 12/F Baskerville House, 22 Ice House St., Central, Hong Kong PRC**

## THE GILLETTE COMPANY

Prudential Tower Building, Boston, MA, 02199

Tel: (617) 421-7000     Fax: (617) 421-7123     www.gillette.com

*Develop/mfr. personal care/use products: blades and razors, toiletries, cosmetics, stationery.*

**Colton Trading Co. Ltd., Hong Kong PRC**

Contact: William Yeoh, Gen. Mgr.

**Gillette (Hong Kong) Ltd., North Point, Hong Kong PRC**

Contact: Ying Meng Lai, Mgr.

**Gillette Far East Trading Ltd., Hong Kong PRC**

Contact: Ying Meng Lai, Mgr.

## GILSON INC.

3000 W. Beltline Hwy, PO Box 620027, Middleton, WI, 53562-0027

Tel: (608) 836-1551     Fax: (608) 831-4451     www.gilson.com

*Mfr. analytical/biomedical instruments.*

**World Ways, 172-176 Wing Lok Street, 2/Fl.Winfull Commercial Bldg., Hong Kong PRC**

## GIW INDUSTRIES, INC.

5000 Wrightsboro Rd., Grovetown, GA, 30813

Tel: (706) 863-1011     Fax: (706) 860-5897     www.giwindustries.com

*Mfr. slurry pumps.*

**KSB Jebsen China Ltd., 24/F Caroline Centre, 28 Yun Ping Rd., Hong Kong PRC**

## GLENAYRE ELECTRONICS LTD.

5935 Carnegie Blvd.., Ste. 300, Charlotte, NC, 28209

Tel: (704) 553-0038     Fax: (704) 553-7878     www.glenayre.com

*Mfr. infrastructure components and pagers.*

**Glenayre Electronics (Hong Kong) Ltd., Units 2104-2105 Chow Tai Fook Centre, 580A Nathan Rd., Kowloon, Hong Kong PRC**

Tel: 852-2838-3236   Fax: 852-2838-3231

## GLOBAL SILVERHAWK

2190 Meridian Park Blvd., Ste G, Concord, CA, 94520

Tel: (925) 681-2889     Fax: (925) 681-2755     www.globalsilverhawk.com

*International moving and forwarding.*

**Global Silverhawk, 18B Cheung Lee Industrial Bldg., 9 Cheung Lee St., Chai Wan, Hong Kong PRC**

Tel: 852-2898-9200   Contact: Rich Sells, Gen. Mgr.

## THE GOLDMAN SACHS GROUP

85 Broad Street, New York, NY, 10004

Tel: (212) 902-1000     Fax: (212) 902-3000     www.gs.com

*Investment bankers; securities broker dealers.*

**Goldman Sachs Group, Asia Pacific Finance Tower, Citibank Plaza 37/F, 3 Garden Road, Central Hong Kong PRC**

Tel: 852-2978-1000

## W. L. GORE & ASSOCIATES, INC.

555 Paper Mill Road, Newark, DE, 19711

Tel: (302) 738-4880     Fax: (302) 738-7710     www.gorefabrics.com

*Mfr. electronic, industrial filtration, medical and fabric products.*

**W. L. Gore & Associates Ltd., Hong Kong PRC**

## W. R. GRACE & COMPANY

7500 Grace Drive, Columbia, MD, 21044

Tel: (410) 531-4000    Fax: (410) 531-4367    www.grace.com

*Mfr. specialty chemicals and materials: packaging, health care, catalysts, construction, water treatment/process.*

**W.R. Grace (Hong Kong) Ltd., Devon House 20/F, 979 King's Rd., Quarry Bay, Hong Kong PRC**

Tel: 852-2590-2828    Fax: 852-2811-2661

## GRACO INC.

4050 Olson Memorial Hwy, PO Box 1441, Minneapolis, MN, 55440-1441

Tel: (612) 623-6000    Fax: (612) 623-6777    www.graco.com

*Mfr. systems and equipment to service fluid handling systems and automotive equipment.*

**Graco Hong Kong, 21-08 Well Fung Industrial Ctr., 57-76 Ta Chuen Ping St., Kwai Chung, New Territory, Hong Kong PRC**

Tel: 852-2395-3189    Fax: 852-2392-0837

## GRAHAM & JAMES LLP

One Maritime Plaza, Ste. 300, San Francisco, CA, 94111-3404

Tel: (415) 954-0200    Fax: (415) 391-2493    www.gj.com

*International law firm.*

**Deacons Graham & James, 3-6/F Alexandra House, Hong Kong, PRC**

Tel: 852-2825-9211    Fax: 852-2810-0431    Contact: Mark Roberts

## GRANT THORNTON INTERNATIONAL

800 One Prudential Plaza, 130 E. Randolph Drive, Chicago, IL, 60601-6050

Tel: (312) 856-0001    Fax: (312) 616-7052    www.grantthornton.com

*Accounting, audit, tax and management consulting services.*

**Grant Thornton Byrne, Lippo Centre Lippo Tower 40/F, 89 Queensway, Hong Kong PRC**

Tel: 852-2840-1188    Fax: 852-2840-0789    Contact: Kevin O'Shaughnessy

**Grant Thornton International, 37th Fl. Wu Chung House, 213 Queen's Rd. East, Wanchai, Hong Kong PRC**

Tel: 852-2838-0099    Fax: 852-2838-0211    Contact: Gabriel R. Azedo

**PCS International, 803 Regent Centre, 88 Queen's Rd., Central, Hong Kong PRC**

## GREAT LAKES CHEMICAL CORPORATION

500 East 96th Street, Ste. 500, Indianapolis, IN, 46240

Tel: (317) 715-3000    Fax: (317) 715-3050    www.greatlakeschem.com

*Mfr. innovative specialty chemical solutions, including flame retardants and other polymer additives, water treatment chemicals, performance and fine chemicals, fire extinguishants.*

**Great Lakes Chemical Far East Ltd., Hong Kong PRC**

## GREENFIELD INDUSTRIES INC.

470 Old Evans Road, Evans, GA, 30809

Tel: (706) 863-7708    Fax: (706) 860-8559    www.greenfieldindustries.com

*Mfr. high-speed rotary cutting tools.*

**Rogers Tool Works Inc., 1903 Shiu Lam Bldg., 23 Luard Rd., Wan Chai, Hong Kong PRC**

## GREY GLOBAL GROUP

777 Third Ave., New York, NY, 10017

Tel: (212) 546-2000    Fax: (212) 546-1495    www.grey.com

*International advertising agency.*

**Grey Hong Kong, Manulife Tower 34/F, 169 Electric Rd., North Point, Hong Kong PRC**

## GRIFFITH LABORATORIES INC.

One Griffith Center, Alsip, IL, 60658

Tel: (708) 371-0900  Fax: (708) 597-3294  www.griffithlabs.com

*Mfr. industrial food ingredients and equipment.*

**Griffith Laboratories Ltd., 8/F Supreme Industrial Bldg., 15 Shan Mei St., Fo-Tan Shatin New Territories, Hong Kong PRC**

Tel: 852-2688-6119  Fax: 852-2688-6126

## GTE DIRECTORIES CORPORATION

2200 West Airfield Drive, DFW Airport, TX, 75261-9810

Tel: (972) 453-7000  Fax: (972) 453-7573  www.gte.com

*Publishing telephone directories.*

**GTE Directories (HK) Ltd., 22-/F Fortress Tower, 250 Kings Rd., North Point, Hong Kong PRC**

## GUIDANT CORPORATION

111 Monument Circle, 29th Fl., Indianapolis, IN, 46204

Tel: (317) 971-2000  Fax: (317) 971-2040  www.guidant.com

*Mfr. cardiovascular therapeutic devices.*

**Guidant Hong Kong, CRC Protective Tower Ste. 2201, 38 Gloucester Road, Wanchai, Hong Kong PRC**

Tel: 852-2827-2338  Fax: 852-2593-2222

## GUILFORD MILLS INC.

925 West Market Street, PO Box 26969, Greensboro, NC, 27407

Tel: (336) 316-4000  Fax: (336) 316-4059  www.guilfordmills.com

*Mfr. textiles.*

**Guilford Mills, Inc., Unit 702 7F, Lippo Sun Plaza, #28 Canton Road, Tsimshatsui, Kowloon, Hong Kong PRC**

Tel: 852-2730-9922  Fax: 852-2376-5922  Contact: Matthew Tsang

## GUY CARPENTER & COMPANY, INC.

Two World Trade Center, New York, NY, 10048

Tel: (212) 323-1000  Fax: (212) 313-4970  www.guycarp.com

*Engaged in global reinsurance and risk management.*

**Guy Carpenter & Company Limited, Miramar Tower Ste. 2118, 1-23 Kimberly Road Tsimshatsui, Kowloon Hong Kong PRC**

Tel: 852-2582-3500  Fax: 852-2827-5551

## HAEMONETICS CORPORATION

400 Wood Road, Braintree, MA, 02184-9114

Tel: (781) 848-7100  Fax: (781) 848-5106  www.haemonetics.com

*Mfr. automated blood processing systems and blood products.*

**Haemonetics Hong Kong Ltd., Ste. 1314 13/F Two Pacific Place, 88 Queensway, Hong Kong PRC**

Tel: 852-2868-9218  Fax: 852-2801-4380

## HALLMARK CARDS INC.

2501 McGee Street, Kansas City, MO, 64108

Tel: (816) 274-5100  Fax: (816) 274-5061  www.hallmark.com

*Mfr. greeting cards and related products.*

**Hallmark Cards Asia Ltd., Rm. 1501 Stanhope House, 734-738 King's Rd., Quarry Bay, Hong Kong PRC**

Tel: 852-2811-8551

## HANDY & HARMAN

555 Theodore Fremd Ave., Rye, NY, 10580

Tel: (914) 921-5200    Fax: (914) 925-4496    www.handyha

*Precious and specialty metals for industry, refining, scrap metal; diversified industrial mfr.*

**Handy & Harman (HK) Ltd., 6/F King Fook Bldg., 30-32 Des Voeux Rd., Central, Hong Kong PRC**

## HARCOURT GENERAL, INC.

27 Boylston St., Chestnut Hill, MA, 02467

Tel: (617) 232-8200    Fax: (617) 739-1395    www.harcourtgeneral.com

*Publisher of educational materials.*

**Harcourt General Asia Pte.Ltd., Rm. 803 8/F 331 Cheung Sha Wan Rd., Kowloon, Hong Kong PRC**

Tel: 852-8108-6882   Fax: 852-2861-3956   Contact: Joe Lam, Mgr.

## HARRIS CORPORATION

1025 West NASA Blvd., Melbourne, FL, 32919

Tel: (407) 727-9100    Fax: (407) 727-9344    www.harris.com

*Mfr. communications and information-handling equipment, including copying and fax systems.*

**Harris Semiconductor China Ltd., Unit 1801-2 18/F, 83 Austin Road, Tsimshatsui, Kowloon, Hong Kong PRC**

Tel: 852-2723-6339   Fax: 852-2724-4369

## HARTFORD RE COMPANY

55 Farmington Ave., Ste. 800, Hartford, CT, 06105

Tel: (860) 520-2700    Fax: (860) 520-2726    www.thehartford.com

*Reinsurance.*

**Hartford Re Company, Unit 3304-06 World Trade Centre, 280 Gloucester Road, Causeway Bay, Hong Kong PRC**

Tel: 852-2840-5100   Fax: 852-2840-1980   Contact: Daniel Stau, Gen. Mgr.

## HARTMARX CORPORATION

101 North Wacker Drive, Chicago, IL, 60606

Tel: (312) 372-6300    Fax: (312) 444-2710    www.hartmarx.com

*Mfr./licensing men's and women's apparel.*

**Hartmarx Far East, Unit 809 8/F Tower 2, Cheung Sha Wan Rd., Kowloon, Hong Kong PRC**

## HEIDRICK & STRUGGLES INTERNATIONAL, INC.

Sears Tower, 233 South Wacker Drive, Chicago, IL, 60606

Tel: (312) 496-1200    Fax: (312) 496-1290    www.heidrick.com

*Executive search firm.*

**Heidrick & Struggles Intl. Inc., The Bank of China Tower, One Garden Rd. - 54/F, Central, Hong Kong PRC**

Tel: 852-2802-8887   Fax: 852-2519-8411

## HELLER FINANCIAL INC.

500 West Monroe Street, Chicago, IL, 60661

Tel: (312) 441-7000    Fax: (312) 441-7367    www.hellerfin.com

*Financial services.*

**East Asia Heller Limited, Ste. 901-903 Central Plaza, 18 Harbour Road, Wanchai, Hong Kong PRC**

Tel: 852-2586-0000

## HELLER, EHRMAN, WHITE & McAULIFFE

333 Bush Street, Ste. 3000, San Francisco, CA, 94104-2878

Tel: (415) 772-6000      Fax: (415) 772-6268      www.hewm.com

*International law Firm.*

**Heller, Ehrman, White & McAuliffe, 1902A 19/F Tower Two Lippo Centre, 89 Queenway, Hong Kong PRC**

Tel: 852-2526-6381   Fax: 852-2810-6242

## HERCULES INC.

Hercules Plaza, 1313 N. Market Street, Wilmington, DE, 19894-0001

Tel: (302) 594-5000      Fax: (302) 594-5400      www.herc.com

*Mfr. specialty chemicals, plastics, film and fibers, coatings, resins, food ingredients.*

**Hercochem (HK) Ltd., 11/F Tower 3, China Hong Kong City, 33 Canton Rd., Tsim Sha Tsui, Kowloon, Hong Kong PRC**

Tel: 852-2527-2638

**Hercules Asia Pacific/Hercules China Ltd., 1907-8 Harcourt House, 39 Gloucester Rd., Wanchai, Hong Kong PRC**

Tel: 852-2527-2638   Fax: 852-2528-1598

## HEWITT ASSOCIATES LLC

100 Half Day Road, Lincolnshire, IL, 60069

Tel: (847) 295-5000      Fax: (847) 295-7634      www.hewitt.com

*Employee benefits consulting firm.*

**Hewitt Associates, Suite 2601-05 Shell Tower Times Square, 1 Matheson St., Causeway Bay, Hong Kong PRC**

Tel: 852-2877-8600

## HEWLETT-PACKARD COMPANY

3000 Hanover Street, Palo Alto, CA, 94304-1185

Tel: (650) 857-1501      Fax: (650) 857-5518      www.hp.com

*Mfr. computing, communications and measurement products and services.*

**Hewlett-Packard Hong Kong Ltd. Hdqtrs.- Asia Pacific, 19/F Cityplaza One, 1111 King's Road, Taikoo Shing, Hong Kong PRC**

Tel: 852-2-599-7777

## HILTON HOTELS CORPORATION

9336 Civic Center Drive, Beverly Hills, CA, 90210

Tel: (310) 278-4321      Fax: (310) 205-7880      www.hiltonhotels.com

*International hotel chain: Hilton International, Vista Hotels and Hilton National Hotels.*

**Hilton International Company, Rm. 2102 Lippo Tower Lippo Centre, 89 Queensway, Admiralty, Hong Kong PRC**

## HOLIDAY INN (BASS RESORTS) WORLDWIDE, INC.

3 Ravinia Drive, Ste. 2900, Atlanta, GA, 30346-2149

Tel: (770) 604-2000      Fax: (770) 604-5403      www.holidayinn.com

*Hotels, restaurants and casinos.*

**Holiday Inn Hong Kong, PO Box 95555, 50 Nathan Rd., Hong Kong PRC**

## HONEYWELL INTERNATIONAL INC.

101 Columbia Road, Morristown, NJ, 07962

Tel: (973) 455-2000      Fax: (973) 455-4807      www.honeywell.com

*Develop/mfr. controls for home and building, industry, space and aviation.*

**Honeywell Ltd., New Bright Bldg. 5/F, 11 Sheung Yuet Rd., Kowloon Bay - Hong Kong PRC**

Tel: 852-2331-9133   Fax: 852-2331-9998

## HORWATH INTERNATIONAL ASSOCIATION

415 Madison Ave., New York, NY, 10017

Tel: (212) 838-5566     Fax: (212) 838-3636     www.horwath.com

*Public accountants and auditors.*

**Horwath Asia Pacific,  Bank of America Tower 6/F, 12 Harcourt Rd., Central Hong Kong PRC**

Contact: Alan Johnson

## HOUGHTON INTERNATIONAL INC.

PO Box 930, Madison & Van Buren Avenues, Valley Forge, PA, 19482-0930

Tel: (610) 666-4000     Fax: (610) 666-1376     www.houghtonintl.com

*Mfr. specialty chemicals, hydraulic fluids and lubricants.*

**Houghton Oils & Chemicals (Far East) Co. Ltd.,  Unit B 16/F - Full Win Commercial Ctr., 573 Nathan Road, Kowloon, Hong Kong PRC**

Tel: 852-2770-8211

## HOWMEDICA OSTEONICS, INC.

359 Veterans Blvd., Rutherford, NJ, 07070

Tel: (201) 507-7300     Fax: (201) 935-4873     www.howmedica.com

*Mfr. of maxillofacial products (orthopedic implants).*

**Hong Kong Surgical Products Ltd.,  Hong Kong PRC**

Tel: 852-2527-9974

## HSB GROUP (HARTFORD STEAM BOILER INSPECTION & INSURANCE CO.)

One State Street, PO Box 5024, Hartford, CT, 06102-5024

Tel: (860) 722-1866     Fax: (860) 722-5770     www.hsb.com

*Provides commercial insurance and engineering consulting services.*

**Hartford Steam Boiler,  2705 Universal Trade Centre, 3 Arbuthnot Rd., Central Hong Kong PRC**

## HUBBELL INCORPORATED

584 Derby Milford Road, Orange, CT, 06477

Tel: (203) 799-4100     Fax: (203) 799-4208     www.hubbell.com

*Electrical wiring components.*

**Harvey Hubbell S.E. Asia Pte. Ltd.,  Room 112 I/F Sun House, 90 Connaught Road, Central Hong Kong PRC**

Tel: 852-2534-0812   Fax: 852-2851-8146

## HUNTON & WILLIAMS

951 East Byrd Street, East Tower, Richmond, VA, 23219-4074

Tel: (804) 788-8200     Fax: (804) 788-8218     www.hunton.com

*International law firm.*

**Hunton & Williams,  23/F CITIC Tower, 1 Tim Mei Ave., Central Hong Kong PRC**

Tel: 852-2841-9100   Fax: 852-2841-9191   Contact: Edward B. Koehler, Mng. Ptnr.   Emp: 16

## HYATT CORPORATION

200 West Madison Street, Chicago, IL, 60606

Tel: (312) 750-1234     Fax: (312) 750-8578     www.hyatt.com

*International hotel management.*

**Hyatt Regency Hong Kong,  67 Nathan Rd., Kowloon, Hong Kong PRC**

Tel: 852-2311-1234   Fax: 852-2739-8701

## HYPERION SOLUTIONS CORPORATION

1344 Crossman Avenue, Sunnyvale, CA, 94089

Tel: (408) 744-9500    Fax: (408) 744-0400    www.hyperion.com

*Mfr. data analysis software tools.*

**Niederlassung Hong Kong, 18 Harbour Road 32/F, Wanchai, Hong Kong PRC**

Tel: 852-2598-7900   Fax: 852-2914-2972

## i2 TECHNOLOGIES, INC.

11701 Luna Road, Dallas, TX, 75234

Tel: (214) 860-6106    Fax: (214) 860-6060    www.i2.com

*Mfr. business-to-business software.*

**i2 Technologies Hong Kong, Bank of America Tower 8/F, 12 Harcourt Road, Central Hong Kong PRC**

Tel: 852-2584-6201

## IBM CORPORATION

New Orchard Road, Armonk, NY, 10504

Tel: (914) 765-1900    Fax: (914) 765-7382    www.ibm.com

*Information products, technology and services.*

**IBM Hong Kong/Southeast Asia, 10/F Hong Kong Telecom Tower, Taikoo Place, 979 King's Road, Quarry Bay Hong Kong PRC**

Tel: 852-2825-6222   Fax: 852-2810-0210

## ICC INDUSTRIES INC.

460 Park Ave., New York, NY, 10022

Tel: (212) 521-1700    Fax: (212) 521-1794    www.iccchem.com

*Manufacturing and trading of chemicals, plastics and pharmaceuticals.*

**ICC (Hong Kong) Ltd., Rm. #1110 West Wing New World Office Bldg., 20 Salisbury Rd., Tsimshatsui East Kowloon, Hong Kong PRC**

Tel: 852-2366-1678   Fax: 852-2367-1377   Contact: Helen Ho So-King

## IMG (INTERNATIONAL MANAGEMENT GROUP)

1360 East Ninth Street, Ste. 100, Cleveland, OH, 44114

Tel: (216) 522-1200    Fax: (216) 522-1145    www.imgworld.com

*Manages athletes, sports academies and real estate facilities worldwide.*

**IMG, Sunning Plaza 12/F, 10 Hysan Avenue, Causeway Bay, Hong Kong PRC**

Tel: 852-2-894-0288   Fax: 852-2-882-2557

## IMPERIAL TOY CORPORATION

2060 East Seventh Street, Los Angeles, CA, 90021

Tel: (213) 489-2100    Fax: (213) 489-4467    www.imperialtoy.com

*Mfr. plastic toys and novelties.*

**Fred Kort Intl. Ltd., 501-2 Peninsula Centre 67, Mody Rd., Tsim Shu Tsui East, Kowloon, Hong Kong PRC**

## INACOM CORPORATION

2001 Westside Parkway, Ste. 260, Alpharetta, GA, 30004

Tel: (770) 643-2419    Fax: (770) 993-6375    www.inacom.com

*Provider of technology management products and services; reselling microcomputer systems, work stations and networking and telecommunications equipment.*

**System-Pro, 17/F Tower of Millennium City, 388 Kwun Tong Road, Kowloon Hong Kong PRC**

## INDUSTRIAL ACOUSTICS COMPANY

1160 Commerce Ave., Bronx, NY, 10462

Tel: (718) 931-8000    Fax: (718) 863-1138    www.industrialacoustics.com

*Design/mfr. acoustic structures for sound conditioning and noise control.*

**Industrial Acoustics Co. (HK) Ltd., 15/F Honour Industrial Centre, Unit 12, 6 Sun Yip St., Chai Wan, Hong Kong PRC**

## INFONET SERVICES CORPORATION

2100 East Grand Ave., El Segundo, CA, 90245-1022

Tel: (310) 335-2600    Fax: (310) 335-4507    www.infonet.com

*Provider of Internet services and electronic messaging services.*

**Infonet Hong Kong, Telcom Services - Infonet Section, 31/F Hong Kong Telecom Tower, Taikoo Place 979 King's Road, Quarry Bay Hong Kong PRC**

Tel: 852-2883-6383   Fax: 852-2962-5359

## INFORMIX CORPORATION

4100 Bohannon Drive, Menlo Park, CA, 95025

Tel: (650) 926-6300    Fax: (650) 926-6593    www.informix.com

*Designs and produces database management software, connectivity interfaces and gateways, and other computer applications.*

**Informix Software (China), Co. Ltd., 28-01 Central Plaza, 18 Harbour Road, Wanchai, Hong Kong PRC**

Tel: 852-2824-0981

## INGERSOLL-RAND COMPANY

200 Chestnut Ridge Road, Woodcliff Lake, NJ, 07675

Tel: (201) 573-0123    Fax: (201) 573-3172    www.ingersoll-rand.com

*Mfr. compressors, rock drills, air tools, door hardware, ball bearings.*

**Ingersoll-Rand Asia Pacific Inc., Ste. 1201-3 12/F Central Plaza, 18 Harbour Rd., Wanchai, Hong Kong PRC**

Tel: 852-2527-0183   Fax: 852-2824-2589

## INGRAM MICRO INC.

PO Box 25125, 1600 E. St. Andrew Place, Santa Ana, CA, 92799

Tel: (714) 566-1000    Fax: (714) 566-7940    www.ingrammicro.com

*Engaged in wholesale distribution of microcomputer products.*

**Ingram Micro Hong Kong, 17/F Seaview Centre, 139 Hoi Bun Road, Kwun Tong Kowloon, Hong Kong PRC**

## INSTINET

875 Third Ave., New York, NY, 10022

Tel: (212) 310-9500    Fax: (212) 832-5183    www.instinet.com

*Online investment brokerage.*

**Instinet, Hong Kong PRC**

## INTEGRATED SILICON SOLUTION, INC.

2231 Lawson Lane, Santa Clara, CA, 95054-3311

Tel: (408) 588-0800    Fax: (408) 588-0805    www.issiusa.com

*Mfr. high-speed memory chips and SRAMs.*

**Integrated Silicon Solution, Inc., Hong Kong PRC**

Tel: 852-2319-2212   Fax: 852-2768-8704

## INTEL CORPORATION

Robert Noyce Bldg., 2200 Mission College Blvd., Santa Clara, CA, 95052-8119

Tel: (408) 765-8080      Fax: (408) 765-1739      www.intel.com

*Mfr. semiconductor, microprocessor and micro-communications components and systems.*

**Intel Semiconductor Ltd., 32/F Two Pacific Place, 88 Queensway, Central Hong Kong PRC**

Tel: 852-2844-4555

## INTELLIGROUP, INC.

499 Thornall Street, Edison, NJ, 08837

Tel: (732) 590-1600      Fax: (732) 362-2100      www.intelligroup.com

*Provides systems integration, customer software and Internet application development.*

**Intelligroup Hong Kong Ltd., Wing On Centre 25/F, 111 Connaught Road Central Hong Kong PRC**

Contact: Madhukar Joshi

## INTER-CONTINENTAL HOTELS

3 Ravina Drive, Suite 2900, Atlanta, GA, 30346-2149

Tel: (770) 604-2000      Fax: (770) 604-5403      www.interconti.com

*Worldwide hotel and resort accommodations.*

**Inter-Continental Hotels, Unit 4701 Central Plaza, 18 Harbour Road, Wanchai, Hong Kong PRC**

Tel: 852-2827-1010    Fax: 852-2827-0505

## INTERDEAN INTERCONEX, INC

55 Hunter Lane, Elmsford, NY, 10523-1317

Tel: (914) 347-6600      Fax: (914) 347-0129      www.interdeannterconex.com

*Freight forwarding.*

**Interconex Far East Ltd., Units 2612-2624 Level 26, Metroplaza Tower, 223 Hing Fong Rd., Kwai Chung NT Hong Kong PRC**

Tel: 852-2480-3122    Fax: 852-2428-2881    Contact: Phil Hamill, Mgr.

## INTERGEN (INTERNATIONAL GENERATING CO., LTD.)

One Bowdoin Square, 5th Fl., Boston, MA, 02114

Tel: (617) 747-1777      Fax: (617) 747-1778      www.intergen.com

*Global power and fuel asset development company; develops/owns/operates electric power plants and related distribution facilities.*

**InterGen (HK) Limited, Tower One Lippo Centre 41/F, 89 Queensway, Hong Kong PRC**

Tel: 852-2912-8200    Fax: 852-2537-6400

## INTERGRAPH CORPORATION

One Madison Industrial Park, Huntsville, AL, 35894-0001

Tel: (256) 730-2000      Fax: (256) 730-7898      www.intergraph.com

*Develop/mfr. interactive computer graphic systems.*

**Intergraph Asia Pacific Ltd., Tai Yau Building Rooms 901-910, 181 Johnston Road, Wanchai, Hong Kong PRC**

Tel: 852-2-8933621    Fax: 852-2572-9787

**Intergraph Hong Kong Ltd., Units 401-4 4/F 72 Tat Chee Ave., Hong Kong Industrial Technology Centre, Kowloon, Hong Kong PRC**

Tel: 852-2593-1600    Fax: 852-2802-0781

## INTERMEC TECHNOLOGIES CORPORATION

6001 36th Ave. West, PO Box 4280, Everett, WA, 98203-9280

Tel: (425) 348-2600      Fax: (425) 355-9551      www.intermec.com

*Mfr./distributor automated data collection systems.*

**Hang Ching Co., Room 2514 Hong Kong Plaza, 186-92 Connaught Road West, Hong Kong PRC**

Intermec Technologies Corporation, 26-12 Shell Tower - Times Square, 1 Matheson Street, Causeway Bay Hong Kong PRC

Tel: 852-2574-9777   Fax: 852-2574-9725

## INTERNATIONAL CLOSEOUT EXCHANGE SYSTEMS INC.

220 W. 19th Street, Ste.1200, New York, NY, 10011

Tel: (212) 647-8901      Fax: (212) 647-8900      www.icesinc.com

*Online service listing off-price merchandise.*

**ICES/Prelic Ltd.,  New Treasure Ctr. #2807, 10 Ng Fong St, San Po Kong, Kowloon, Hong Kong PRC**

## INTERNATIONAL COMPONENTS CORPORATION

420 N. May Street, Chicago, IL, 60622

Tel: (312) 829-2525      Fax: (312) 829-0213      www.icc-charge.com

*Mfr./sale/services portable DC battery chargers.*

**Fabricators Intl. Ltd.,  11/F Safety Godown Industrial Bldg., 56 Ka Yip St., Chai Wan, Hong Kong PRC**

## INTERNATIONAL FLAVORS & FRAGRANCES INC.

521 West 57th Street, New York, NY, 10019-2960

Tel: (212) 765-5500      Fax: (212) 708-7132      www.iff.com

*Design/mfr. flavors, fragrances and aroma chemicals.*

**International Flavors & Fragrances Far East Ltd.,  11/F Watson Centre, 18-2 Kung Yip St., Kwai Chung, N.T., Kowloon, Hong Kong PRC**

## INTERNATIONAL PAPER COMPANY

2 Manhattanville Road, Purchase, NY, 10577

Tel: (914) 397-1500      Fax: (914) 397-1596      www.ipaper.com

*Mfr./distributor container board, paper and wood products.*

**International Paper Co. (Far East) Ltd.,  1008 Bank of America Tower, 12 Harcourt Rd., Hong Kong PRC**

**Veratec Nonwoven (Asia) Ltd.,  Suite 2112-2113 21/F Shui On Centre, 6-8 Harbour Rd., Hong Kong PRC**

## INTERNATIONAL RECTIFIER CORPORATION

233 Kansas Street, El Segundo, CA, 90245

Tel: (310) 322-3331      Fax: (310) 322-3332      www.irf.com

*Mfr. power semiconductor components.*

**International Rectifier - Hong Kong,  Unit 2210-2212 22/F, Paul Y Centre, Hong Kong PRC**

Tel: 852-2803-738   Fax: 852-2540-5835

## INTERNATIONAL SPECIALTY PRODUCTS, INC.

1361 Alps Rd., Wayne, NJ, 07470

Tel: (877) 389-3083      Fax: (973) 628-4117      www.ispcorp.com

*Mfr. specialty chemical products.*

**ISP (Hong Kong) Ltd.,  Ste. 1102 Ming An Plaza, No. 8 Sunning Road, Causeay Bay, Hong Kong PRC**

Tel: 852-2881-6108   Fax: 852-2895-1250

## THE IT GROUP, INC.

2790 Mosside Boulevard, Monroeville, PA, 15146-2792

Tel: (412) 372-7701      Fax: (412) 373-7135      www.theitgroup.com

*Engaged in environmental management; hazardous waste clean-up services.*

**IT Group Hong Kong,  Hong Kong PRC**

## J. WALTER THOMPSON COMPANY

466 Lexington Ave., New York, NY, 10017

Tel: (212) 210-7000      Fax: (212) 210-6944      www.jwt.com

*International advertising and marketing services.*

**J. Walter Thompson Co.,  Wanchai, Hong Kong PRC**

## JDA SOFTWARE GROUP, INC.

14400 N. 87th St., Scottsdale, AZ, 85260-3649

Tel: (480) 308-3000      Fax: (480) 308-3001      www.jda.com

*Developer of information management software for retail, merchandising, distribution and store management.*

**JDA Software Group,  28/F - 38 Russell Street, Causeway Bay Hong Kong, PRC**

Tel: 852-2106-1116   Fax: 852-2900-1195

## JLG INDUSTRIES INC.

One JLG Drive, McConnellsburg, PA, 17233-9533

Tel: (717) 485-5161      Fax: (717) 485-6417      www.jlg.com

*Mfr. aerial work platforms and vertical personnel lifts.*

**JLG Equipment Services Ltd.,  Rm.  No. 7 Level 11 - Landmark North 39, Lung Sum Avenue, Sheung Shui N.T., Hong Kong PRC**

Tel: 852-2639-5783   Fax: 852-2639-5797

## JOHNSON & JOHNSON

One Johnson & Johnson Plaza, New Brunswick, NJ, 08933

Tel: (732) 524-0400      Fax: (732) 214-0334      www.jnj.com

*Mfr./distributor/R&D pharmaceutical, health care and cosmetic products.*

**Janssen-Cilag Ltd.,  GPO 9733, Hong Kong PRC**

**Johnson & Johnson (Hong Kong) Ltd.,  GPO 9733, Hong Kong PRC**

**Johnson & Johnson Medical Hong Kong Ltd.,  GPO 9733, Hong Kong, PRC**

## S C JOHNSON & SON INC.

1525 Howe St., Racine, WI, 53403

Tel: (414) 260-2000      Fax: (414) 260-2133      www.scjohnsonwax.com

*Home, auto, commercial and personal care products and specialty chemicals.*

**S.C. Johnson Ltd.,  20/F OTB Bldg., 160 Gloucester Rd., Wanchai, Hong Kong PRC**

## JOHNSON CONTROLS INC.

5757 N. Green Bay Ave., PO Box 591, Milwaukee, WI, 53201-0591

Tel: (414) 228-1200      Fax: (414) 228-2077      www.johnsoncontrols.com

*Mfr. facility management and control systems and auto seating.*

**Johnson Controls Hong Kong Ltd.,  15/F Devon House #1501 Taikoo Place, 979 King's Rd., Quarry Bay, Hong Kong PRC**

Tel: 852-2590-0012   Fax: 852-2516-5648    Contact: Wing-On Yau, Branch Mgr.

## JOHNSON OUTDOORS, INC.

1326 Willow Road, Sturtevant, WI, 53177

Tel: (414) 884-1500      Fax: (414) 884-1600      www.jwa.com

*Mfr. diving, fishing, boating and camping sports equipment.*

**Scubapro Asia/Pacific,  1208 Block A M.P. Industrial Centre, 18 Ka Yip St., Chai Wan, Hong Kong PRC**

Tel: 852-2556-7338   Fax: 852-2898-9872

## JONES APPAREL GROUP INC.

250 Rittenhouse Circle, Bristol, PA, 19007

Tel: (215) 785-4000     Fax: (215) 785-1795     www.jny.com

*Designs and markets a broad range of women's career sportswear, suits, and dresses, casual sportswear and jeanswear.*

**Jones Intl. Ltd., Cheung Sha Wan Plaza Tower 1, 833 Cheung Sha Wan, Kowloon, Hong Kong PRC**

## JONES LANG LASALLE

101 East 52nd Street, New York, NY, 10022

Tel: (212) 688-8181     Fax: (212) 308-5199     www.jlw.com

*International marketing consultants, leasing agents and property management advisors.*

**Jones Lang Wootton, Hong Kong PRC**

## JONES, DAY, REAVIS & POGUE

North Point, 901 Lakeside Ave., Cleveland, OH, 44114

Tel: (216) 586-3939     Fax: (216) 579-0212     www.jonesday.com

*International law firm.*

**Jones, Day, Reavis & Pogue, 29/F Entertainment Bldg., 30 Queen's Rd., Central, Hong Kong PRC**

Tel: 852-2526-6895   Fax: 852-2868-5871   Contact: W. Anthony Stewart, Ptnr.   Emp: 14

## JUKI UNION SPECIAL CORPORATION

5 Haul Road, Wayne, NJ, 07470

Tel: (973) 633-7200     Fax: (973) 633-9629     www.unionspecial.com

*Mfr. sewing machines.*

**Union Special Far East Ltd., 223 Hing Fong Rd., Kwai Fong NT, Hong Kong PRC**

## KAISER ENGINEERS INC.

9300 Lee Highway, Fairfax, VA, 22031

Tel: (703) 934-3600     Fax: (703) 934-9740     www.icfkaiser.com

*Engineering, construction and consulting services.*

**Kaiser Engineers, Quarry Bay, Hong Kong PRC**

Tel: 852-2911-1233

## KAYE, SCHOLER, FIERMAN, HAYS & HANDLER, LLP

425 Park Ave., New York, NY, 10022-3598

Tel: (212) 836-8000     Fax: (212) 836-8689     www.kayescholer.com

*American and international law practice.*

**Kaye, Scholer, Fierman, Hays & Handler, LLP, Suite 2006-2010, One International Finance Centre, No. 1 Harbour View Street, Central Hong Kong PRC**

Tel: 852-2845-8989   Fax: 852-2845-3682

## A.T. KEARNEY INC.

222 West Adams Street, Chicago, IL, 60606

Tel: (312) 648-0111     Fax: (312) 223-6200     www.atkearney.com

*Management consultants and executive search.*

**A. T. Kearney (Hong Kong) Ltd., Level 31 One Pacofic Place, 88 Queensway, Hong Kong PRC**

Tel: 852-2501-1400

## KELLEY DRYE & WARREN LLP

101 Park Ave., New York, NY, 10178

Tel: (212) 808-7800     Fax: (212) 808-7898     www.kelleydrye.com

*International law firm.*

**Kelley Drye & Warren LLP, Suite 509-10 Tower Two Lippo Centre, 89 Queensway, Hong Kong PRC**

Tel: 852-2869-0821   Fax: 852-2869-0049

## KELLWOOD COMPANY

600 Kellwood Pkwy., Chesterfield, MO, 63017

Tel: (314) 576-3100     Fax:  (314) 576-3434     www.kellwood.com

*Mfr./marketing/sale primarily women's apparel and recreational camping products.*

**Smart Shirts Ltd., 55 King Yip St., Kwun Tong, Kowloon, Hong Kong PRC**

Tel: 852-279-75111   Fax: 852-234-32715   Contact: Jesse C. P. Zee, Mng. Dir

## KENNAMETAL INC.

State Rte. 981, Latrobe, PA, 15650

Tel: (724) 539-5000     Fax:  (724) 539-4710     www.kennametal.com

*Tools, hard carbide and tungsten alloys for metalworking industry.*

**Kennametal Hardpoint Hong Kong Ltd.,  Room C 9/F V Ga Bldg., 532-532A Castle Peak Rd., Kowloon, Hong Kong PRC**

Tel: 852-2314-9209   Fax: 852-2314-9207

## KIMBERLY-CLARK CORPORATION

351 Phelps Drive, Irving, TX, 75038

Tel: (972) 281-1200     Fax:  (972) 281-1435     www.kimberly-clark.com

*Mfr./sales/distribution of consumer tissue, household and personal care products.*

**Kimberly-Clark (Hong Kong) Ltd.,  Hong Kong PRC**

## KNIGHT-RIDDER INC.

One Herald Plaza, Miami, FL, 33132

Tel: (305) 376-3800     Fax:  (305) 376-3828     www.kri.com

*Newspaper publishing, business information services.*

**Knight-Ridder Financial/Asia,  Citibank Tower 501-4, Citibank Plaza, 3 Garden Rd., Central, Hong Kong PRC**

## KNOLL, INC.

1235 Water Street, East Greenville, PA, 18041

Tel: (215) 679-7991     Fax:  (215) 679-3904     www.knoll.com

*Mfr. and sale of office furnishings.*

**Knoll International, Inc. c/o Comer Co., Ltd.,  902 The Lee Gardens, 33 Hysan Avenue, Hong Kong PRC**

**85 22 895-6385**

Tel: 85-22-881-8734

## THE KOHLER COMPANY

444 Highland Drive, Kohler, WI, 53044

Tel: (920) 457-4441     Fax:  (920) 459-1274     www.kohlerco.com

*Plumbing products, ceramic tile and stone, cabinetry, furniture, engines, generators, switch gear and hospitality.*

**The Kohler Company Far East,  1110B Tower 2, China Hong Kong City, 33 Canton Rd., Kowloon, Hong Kong PRC**

Tel: 852-2730-2383   Fax: 852-2730-2318   Contact: George Tam, Sr. Area Mgr.

## KORN/FERRY INTERNATIONAL

1800 Century Park East, Los Angeles, CA, 90067

Tel: (310) 843-4100     Fax:  (310) 553-6452     www.kornferry.com

*Executive search; management consulting.*

**Korn/Ferry International (HK) Ltd.,  808 Gloucester Tower, The Landmark Central, Hong Kong PRC**

Tel: 852-2521-5457   Fax: 852-2810-1632

**KOSTER KEUNEN INC.**

1021 Echo Lake Rd., Box 69, Watertown, CT, 06795-0069

Tel: (860) 945-3333     Fax: (860) 945-0330     www.kosterkeunen.com

*Mfr. waxes, beeswax, paraffin.*

**Manhoko Limited, EW International Tower - 16/F, 120/124 Texaco Road, Tsuen Wan, New Territories Hong Kong PRC**

Tel: 852-2392-4231   Fax: 852-2789-1650

**KPMG INTERNATIONAL LLP**

345 Park Avenue, New York, NY, 10022

Tel: (201) 307-7000     Fax: (201) 930-8617     www.kpmg.com

*Accounting and audit, tax and management consulting services.*

**KPMG Peat Marwick, 8/F Prince's Bldg., 10 Chater Rd., Hong Kong PRC**

Tel: 852-2522-60   Fax: 852-2845-2588   Contact: Marvin K.T. Cheung, Sr. Ptnr.

**KRAFT FOODS INTERNATIONAL, INC. ( DIV. PHILIP MORRIS COS.)**

800 Westchester Ave., Rye Brook, NY, 10573-1301

Tel: (914) 335-2500     Fax: (914) 335-7144     www.kraftfoods.com

*Processor, distributor and manufacturer of food products.*

**Kraft Foods Asia/Pacific, One Pacific Place 15/F, 88 Queensway, Hong Kong PRC**

**KRAS CORPORATION**

2 Old Mill Lane, Media, PA, 19063

Tel: (215) 736-0981     Fax: (215) 736-8953

*Mfr. precision tools and machinery for electronic and plastics industrial.*

**Kras Asia Ltd., 78 Hung To Rd., Kwun Tong, Kowloon, Hong Kong PRC**

**THE KROLL-O'GARA COMPANY**

9113 Le Saint Drive, Fairfield, OH, 45014

Tel: (513) 874-2112     Fax: (513) 874-2558     www.kroll-ogara.com

*Security and consulting services and vehicles.*

**Kroll Associates (Asia) Ltd., Room 906/911 9/F Mount Parker House, 1111 King's Rd., Taikoo Shing, Hong Kong PRC**

Tel: 852-2884-7788   Fax: 852-2568-8505

**KULICKE & SOFFA INDUSTRIES INC.**

2101 Blair Mill Road, Willow Grove, PA, 19090

Tel: (215) 784-6000     Fax: (215) 659-7588     www.kns.com

*Semiconductor assembly systems and services.*

**Kulicke & Soffa (Asia) Ltd., 21/F Yen Sheng Centre, 64 Hoi Yen Rd., Kwun Tong, Kowloon, Hong Kong PRC**

Tel: 852-2955-3668   Fax: 852-2955-3666   Contact: Randy Wan, Sales Dir.

**THE KULJIAN CORPORATION**

3700 Science Center, Philadelphia, PA, 19104

Tel: (215) 243-1900     Fax: (215) 243-1909

*Studies, design, engineering, construction management and site supervision.*

**Development Consultants Intl., 9/F Hyde Ctr., 223 Gloucester Rd., Hong Kong PRC**

**KURT SALMON ASSOCIATES INC.**

1355 Peachtree Street NE, Atlanta, GA, 30309

Tel: (404) 892-0321     Fax: (404) 898-9590     www.kurtsalmon.com

*Management consulting: consumer products, retailing.*

**Kurt Salmon Associates Inc., Units 2101-2 21/F, 83 Austin Rd., Kowloon, Hong Kong PRC**

## LANDOR ASSOCIATES

Klamath House, 1001 Front Street, San Francisco, CA, 94111-1424

Tel: (415) 955-1400      Fax: (415) 365-3190      www.landor.com

*International marketing consulting firm, focused on developing and maintaining brand identity.*

**Landor Hong Kong, Kinwick Centre 17/F, 32 Hollywood Road, Central Hong Kong PRC**

Tel: 852-2851-8173   Fax: 852-2544-9199   Contact: Michael Ip,

## LATHAM & WATKINS

633 West 5th St., Ste. 4000,, Los Angeles, CA, 90071-2007

Tel: (213) 485-1234      Fax: (213) 891-8763      www.lw.com

*International law firm.*

**Latham & Watkins, Ste. 2205A, 22/F, No. 9 Queen's Rd., Central Hong Kong PRC**

Tel: 852-2522-7886   Fax: 852-2522-7006

## LEARNING TREE INTERNATIONAL, INC.

6053 West Century Blvd., Los Angeles, CA, 90045-0028

Tel: (310) 417-9700      Fax: (310) 417-8684      www.learningtree.com

*Information technology training services.*

**Learning Tree International Ltd. (Hong Kong), Ste. No. 5 16/F Queen's Place, 74 Queen's Rd. Central, Hong Kong PRC**

Tel: 852-2111-7700   Fax: 852-2530-2902   Contact: James Webb   Emp: 3

## LEARONAL INC.

272 Buffalo Ave., Freeport, NY, 11520

Tel: (516) 868-8800      Fax: (516) 868-8824      www.learonal.com

*Specialty chemicals for the printed circuit board, semiconductor, connector and metal finishing industries.*

**LeaRonal SE Asia Ltd., LeaRonal Asia Technology Centre, 15 On Lok Mun St. On Lok Tseun Fanling, N.T., Hong Kong PRC**

Tel: 852-2680-6888   Fax: 852-2680-6333   Contact: Luther Wong, Mng. Dir.

## LECROY CORPORATION

700 Chestnut Ridge Road, Chestnut Ridge, NY, 10977

Tel: (845) 425-2000      Fax: (845) 425-8967      www.lecroy.com

*Mfr. signal analyzers and electronic measurement systems.*

**LeCroy Corporation, Units 1503 Causeway Bay Plaza, Phase 2 - 463-483 Lockhart Road, Causeway Bay, Hong Kong PRC**

Tel: 852-2834-5630

## LEHMAN BROTHERS HOLDINGS INC.

Three World Financial Center, New York, NY, 10285

Tel: (212) 526-7000      Fax: (212) 526-3738      www.lehman.com

*Financial services, securities and merchant banking services.*

**Lehman Brothers, One Pacific Place Level 38-39, 88 Queensway, Hong Kong PRC**

Tel: 852-2869-3000

## LEVI STRAUSS & COMPANY

1155 Battery St., San Francisco, CA, 94111-1230

Tel: (415) 544-6000      Fax: (415) 501-3939      www.levistrauss.com

*Mfr./distributor casual wearing apparel.*

**Levi Strauss (Far East) Ltd., Unit A & B 10/F CDW Building, 388 Castle Peak Road, Tseun Wan New Territories, Hong Kong PRC**

Tel: 852-2412-8088   Fax: 852-2402-3067

## LEXMARK INTERNATIONAL

1 Lexmark Centre Dr., Lexington, KY, 40550

Tel: (606) 232-2000    Fax: (606) 232-1886    www.lexmark.com

*Develop, manufacture, supply of printing solutions and products, including laser, inkjet, and dot matrix printers.*

**Lexmark International (China) Limited, Rm. 3301 - Hong Kong Telecom Tower, TaiKoo Place - 979 King's Road, Quarry Bay Hong Kong PRC**

Tel: 852-2866-8900    Fax: 852-2866-8911

## LHS GROUP INC.

6 Concourse Pkwy., Ste. 2700, Atlanta, GA, 30328

Tel: (770) 280-3000    Fax: (770) 280-3099    www.lhsgroup.com

*Provides multilingual software for telecommunications carriers.*

**LHS Asia, Hong Kong Business Center, 4/F Dina House Ruttonjee Center, 11 Duddett Street Central, Hong Kong PRC**

Tel: 852-253-283-55    Fax: 852-281-002-35

## LIBERTY MUTUAL GROUP

175 Berkeley Street, Boston, MA, 02117

Tel: (617) 357-9500    Fax: (617) 350-7648    www.libertymutual. com

*Provides workers' compensation insurance and operates physical rehabilitation centers and provides risk prevention management.*

**Liberty International (H.K.) Ltd., 25 Westlands Road, Quarry Bay 504-5 DCH Commercial Center, Hong Kong PRC**

## LIFE TECHNOLOGIES INC.

9800 Medical Center Drive, Rockville, MD, 20850

Tel: (301) 840-8000    Fax: (301) 329-8635    www.lifetech.com

*Produces biotechnology research materials.*

**Life Technologies Pacific, 12/F Concord Technology Centre, 98 Texaco Road, Tsuen Wan, New Territories, Hong Kong PRC**

## ELI LILLY & COMPANY

Lilly Corporate Center, Indianapolis, IN, 46285

Tel: (317) 276-2000    Fax: (317) 277-6579    www.lilly.com

*Mfr. pharmaceuticals and animal health products.*

**Eli Lilly Asia, Inc., 3/F. Hua Fu Commercial Bldg., 111 Queen's Rd. West, Hong Kong PRC**

Tel: 852-2572-0160    Fax: 852-2572-7893

## LINEAR TECHNOLOGY CORPORATION

1630 McCarthy Blvd., Milpitas, CA, 95035

Tel: (408) 432-1900    Fax: (408) 434-6441    www.linear-tech.com

*Mfr. linear integrated circuit chips.*

**Linear Technology Corporation Ltd., Unit 2109 - Metroplaza Tower 2, 223 Hing Fong Road, Kwai Fong, N.T., Hong Kong PRC**

Tel: 852-2428-0303    Fax: 852-2348-0885

## ARTHUR D. LITTLE, INC.

25 Acorn Park, Cambridge, MA, 02140-2390

Tel: (617) 498-5000    Fax: (617) 498-7200    www.adlittle.com

*Management, environmental, health and safety consulting; technical and product development.*

**Arthur D. Little - Asia Pacific, Inc.Inc., Bank of America Tower 7/F, 12 Harcourt Rd., Central, Hong Kong PRC**

Tel: 852-2845-6221    Fax: 852-2845-5271

## LITTON INDUSTRIES INC.

21240 Burbank Boulevard, Woodland Hills, CA, 91367

Tel: (818) 598-5000      Fax: (818) 598-3313      www.littoncorp.com

*Shipbuilding, electronics, and information technology.*

**Litton Marine Systems, 14C Sun House, 181 Des Voeux Road, Central Hong Kong PRC**

Tel: 852-2581-9122

## LoBUE ASSOCIATES, INC.

1771 East Flamingo Road, Ste. 219A, Las Vegas, NV, 89119

Tel: (702) 989-6940      Fax: (702) 433-4021      www.lobue.com

*Management consulting services for financial services industry.*

**LoBue Associates Inc., 1133 Central Bldg., 1 Pedder St., GPO Box 11308, Central, Hong Kong PRC**

Tel: 852-841-7758   Fax: 852-810-1868

## LOCKHEED MARTIN CORPORATION

6801 Rockledge Drive, Bethesda, MD, 20817

Tel: (301) 897-6000      Fax: (301) 897-6652      www.imco.com

*Design/mfr./management systems in fields of space, defense, energy, electronics and technical services.*

**CalComp Asia Pacific Ltd., Sts. 701-704 7/F Chinachem Exchange Square, 1 Hoi Wan Street, Quarry Bay, Hong Kong PRC**

**Lockheed Martin International, Ltd., Three Exchange Square Rms.1004-1006, Central, Hong Kong PRC**

Contact: B. Miller

**Lockheed Martin International, Ltd., c/o Cathay Pacific Airways Ltd., Engineering Dept. Kai Tak Airport, Hong Kong PRC**

**Lockheed Martin International, Ltd., Rm. 1904 Wing On Centre, 111 Connaught Road, Central, Hong Kong PRC**

Contact: L. Fung, Mgr.

**Lockheed Martin Intl. Ltd., Two Pacific Place #1907, 88 Queensway, Hong Kong PRC**

## LOCTITE CORPORATION

1001 Trout Brook Crossing, Rocky Hill, CT, 06067-3910

Tel: (860) 571-5100      Fax: (860) 571-5465      www.loctite.com

*Mfr./sale industrial adhesives, sealants and coatings..*

**Loctite (Asia) Ltd & Loctite (Pacific Region HQ), 18/F Island Place Tower, 510 King's Road, North Point, Hong Kong PRC**

Tel: 852-2802-9998   Fax: 852-2802-9995   Contact: Bee Ng

## LORAL SPACE & COMMUNICATIONS LTD.

600 Third Ave., New York, NY, 10016

Tel: (212) 697-1105      Fax: (212) 338-5662      www.loral.com

*Marketing coordination: defense electronics, communications systems.*

**Loral CyberStar Asia-Pacific, Central Plaza 35/F, 18 Harbour Road, Wan Chai, Hong Kong PRC**

## LOWE LINTAS & PARTNERS WORLDWIDE

One Dag Hammarskjold Plaza, New York, NY, 10017

Tel: (212) 605-8000      Fax: (212) 605-4705      www.interpublic.com

*Full-service, integrated marketing communications company/advertising agency.*

**Ammirati Puris Lintas, 23/F Chinachem Exchange Square, No. 1 Hoi Wan St., Quarry Bay, Hong Kong PRC**

Tel: 852-2960-8688   Fax: 852-2960-1606   Contact: Sanford Kornberg, Dir.

## LSI LOGIC CORPORATION

1551 McCarthy Blvd, Milpitas, CA, 95035

Tel: (408) 433-8000     Fax: (408) 954-3220     www.lsilogic.com

*Develop/mfr. semiconductors.*

**LSI Logic Hong Kong Ltd., 7/F Southeast Industrial Building, 611-619 Castle Peak Road, Tsuen Wan N.T., Hong Kong PRC**

## LUCENT NPS (NETWORK CARE PROFESSIONAL SERVICES)

1213 Innsbruck Dr., Sunnyvale, CA, 94089

Tel: (408) 542-0100     Fax: (408) 542-0101     www.ins.com

*Provides computer network support, designs networking systems, manages equipment purchase performance and software solutions.*

**Lucent NetworkCare, 29/F Shell Tower Times Square, 1 Matheson St, Causeway Bay, Hong Kong PRC**

## LUCENT TECHNOLOGIES, INC.

600 Mountain Ave., Murray Hill, NJ, 07974-0636

Tel: (908) 582-3000     Fax: (908) 582-2576     www.lucent.com

*Design/mfr. wide range of public and private networks, communication systems and software, data networking systems, business telephone systems and microelectronics components.*

**Lucent Technologies Asia/Pacific (HK) Ltd., 29/F Shell Tower, Times Square, 1 Mathenson Street, Causeway Bay Hong Kong PRC**

Tel: 852-2506-8000   Fax: 852-2506-9621   Contact: Jonnie Oden, PR Mgr.

## LYONDELL

3801 West Chester Pike, Newtown Square, PA, 19073-2387

Tel: (610) 359-2000     Fax: (610) 359-2722     www.arcochem.com

*Mfr. propylene oxide, a chemical used for flexible foam products, coatings/paints and solvents/inks.*

**ARCO Chemical Asia Pacific, Ltd., 41/F The Lee Gardens, 33 Hysan Ave., Causeway Bay, Hong Kong PRC**

Tel: 852-2822-2668   Fax: 852-2840-1690

## LYONDELL CHEMICAL COMPANY

1221 McKinney St., Houston, TX, 77010

Tel: (713) 652-7200     Fax: (713) 309-2074     www.lyondell.com

*Mfr. polymers and petrochemicals.*

**Lyondell Asia Pacific, Ltd., The Lee Gardens 41/F, 33 Hysan Avenue, Causeway Bay, Hong Kong PRC**

Tel: 852-2-822-2668

## M/A-COM INC.

1011 Pawtucket Boulevard, Lowell, MA, 01853-3295

Tel: (978) 442-5000     Fax: (978) 442-5354     www.macom.com

*Mfr. electronic components, semiconductor devices and communications equipment.*

**Gentech Industries Ltd., 21/F Unit A CNT Tower, No. 338 Hennessey Road, Wanchai, Hong Kong PRC**

Tel: 852-2521-4567   Fax: 852-2845-1847

**M/A-COM, 601 N. Mur-Len Suite 21B, Wanchai, Hong Kong PRC**

Tel: 852-2521-4567

**Welllink Communications, Ltd., Unit 602 Westlands Centre, 20 Westlands Road, Quarry Bay, Hong Kong PRC**

Tel: 852-2884-4128   Fax: 852-2885-0113

## MacDERMID INC.

245 Freight Street, Waterbury, CT, 06702-0671

Tel: (203) 575-5700    Fax: (203) 575-7900    www.macdermid.com

*Chemicals processing for metal industrial, plastics, electronics cleaners, strippers.*

**MacDermid Asian Ltd./ MacDermid Hong Kong, Ltd., 9/F Block A&B, Tai Ping Industrial Park, 51 Ting Kok Road, Tao Po New Territories Hong Kong PRC**

Tel: 852-2667-8283    Fax: 852-2667-5063

**MacDermid Hong Kong Ltd., 10/F Block C/D, 2-12 Au Pui Wan St., Fo Tan Sha Tin, New Territories Hong Kong PRC**

## R.H. MACY & COMPANY INC.

151 West 34th Street, New York, NY, 10001

Tel: (212) 695-4400    Fax: (212) 643-1307    www.macys.com

*Department stores; importers.*

**R.H. Macy & Co. Inc., 922-924 Ocean Centre, Canton Rd., Kowloon, Hong Kong PRC**

## MALLINCKRODT INC.

675 McDonnell Blvd., St. Louis, MO, 63134

Tel: (314) 654-2000    Fax: (314) 654-5380    www.mallinckrodt.com

*Distributes health care products and specialty pharmaceuticals.*

**Mallinckrodt Hong Kong, Ltd., Evergo House - Rm. 1602, 38 Gloucester Road, Wanchai, Hong Kong PRC**

Tel: 852-2529-0363

## MANPOWER INTERNATIONAL INC.

5301 N. Ironwood Rd., PO Box 2053, Milwaukee, WI, 53201-2053

Tel: (414) 961-1000    Fax: (414) 961-7081    www.manpower.com

*Temporary help, contract service, training and testing.*

**Manpower Hong Kong Ltd., Prince's Building Suite 1216 (12/F), Central, Hong Kong PRC**

Tel: 852-28-68-2328    Fax: 852-281-06473

## MARKET FACTS INC.

3040 Salt Creek Lane, Arlington Heights, IL, 60005

Tel: (847) 590-7000    Fax: (847) 590-7010    www.marketfacts.com

*Market research services.*

**AMI - Asia Market Intelligence, 9/F Leighton Centre, 77 Leighton Road, Causeway Bay, Hong Kong PRC**

Tel: 852-2281-5388    Fax: 852-2281-5918

## MARRIOTT INTERNATIONAL INC.

10400 Fernwood Rd., Bethesda, MD, 20817

Tel: (301) 380-3000    Fax: (301) 380-5181    www.marriott.com

*Hotel services.*

**JW Marriott Hotel, Hong Kong PRC**

Tel: 852-2525-9966

## MARSH & McLENNAN COS INC.

1166 Ave. of the Americas, New York, NY, 10036-2774

Tel: (212) 345-5000    Fax: (212) 345-4808    www.marshmac.com

*Insurance agents/brokers, pension and investment management consulting services.*

**J&H Marsh & McLennan Consulting (Far East) Ltd., 805B-808 Empire Centre, 68 Mody Rd., Tsimshatsui, Kowloon, Hong Kong PRC**

Tel: 852-2301-7000    Fax: 852-2576-6419    Contact: Sidney Ku

**J&H Marsh & McLennan Ltd.,  Ste. 2118 21/F Miramar Tower 1-23, Kimberley Rd., Tsimshatsui, Kowloon Hong Kong PRC**

Tel: 852-2301-7000    Fax: 852-2576-3340    Contact: Sidney Ku

## MASCO CORPORATION

21001 Van Born Road, Taylor, MI, 48180

Tel: (313) 274-7400        Fax: (313) 374-6666        www.masco.com

*Mfr. faucets, cabinets, locks and numerous home improvement, building and home furnishings products.*

**Maitland-Smith Ltd.,  4-5/F Wyler Centre, 210 Tai Lin Pai Rd., Kwai Chung, NT, Hong Kong PRC**

**Universal Furniture Ltd.,  3/F Yo To Sang Bldg., 37 Queens Rd., Central, Hong Kong PRC**

## MASS MUTUAL LIFE INSURANCE COMPANY

1295 State St., Springfield, MA, 01111

Tel: (413) 788-8411        Fax: (413) 744-6005        www.massmutual.com

*Individual insurance,  personal accident insurance,  credit and group life insurance.*

**MassMutual Asia,  Mass Mutual Tower 12/F, 38 Gloucester Road, Hong Kong PRC**

Tel: 852-2919-9000    Fax: 852-2576-6756

## MASTERCARD INTERNATIONAL INC.

200 Purchase Street, Purchase, NY, 10577

Tel: (914) 249-2000        Fax: (914) 249-5475        www.mastercard.com

*Provides financial payment systems globally.*

**MasterCard International Inc.,  Suite 1401-1404 14/F Dah Sing Financial Ctr, 108 Gloucester Road, Wanchai, Hong Kong PRC**

## MATTEL INC.

333 Continental Blvd., El Segundo, CA, 90245-5012

Tel: (310) 252-2000        Fax: (310) 252-2179        www.mattelmedia.com

*Mfr. toys, dolls, games, crafts and hobbies.*

**Arco Toys Ltd.,  World Finance Ctr. South Tower, 17-19 Canton Rd., Kowloon, Hong Kong PRC**

**Fisher-Price (Hong Kong) Ltd.,  92 Grandville Rd., Tsim Sha Tsui, Kowloon, Hong Kong PRC**

**Mattel (HK) Ltd.,  Len Shing Ind. Bldg. 4, Ah Kung Ngam Village Rd., Shau Kei Wan, Hong Kong PRC**

**Pacific American Buying Service Ltd.,  Seaview Estate, 8 Watson's Rd., North Point, Hong Kong PRC**

## MAXTOR CORPORATION

510 Cottonwood Drive, Milpitas, CA, 95035-7403

Tel: (408) 432-1700        Fax: (408) 432-4510        www.maxtor.com

*Mfr. develops and markets hard disk drives for desktop computer systems.*

**Maxtor Asia Pacific Ltd.,  Sun Hung Kai Center Room 802-807, 30 Harbour Road, Wanchai, Hong Kong PRC**

Tel: 852-2585-4500

## McCANN-ERICKSON WORLDGROUP

750 Third Ave., New York, NY, 10017

Tel: (212) 984-3644        Fax: (212) 984-2629        www.mccann.com

*International advertising and marketing services.*

**McCann-Erickson (H.K.) Ltd.,  1/F Sunning Plaza, 10 Hysan Avenue, Hong Kong PRC**

## McDONALD'S CORPORATION

McDonald's Plaza, Oak Brook, IL, 60523

Tel: (630) 623-3000        Fax: (630) 623-7409        www.mcdonalds.com

*Fast food chain stores.*

**McDonald's Corp.,  Hong Kong PRC**

## THE McGRAW-HILL COMPANIES

1221 Ave. of the Americas, New York, NY, 10020

Tel: (212) 512-2000      Fax: (212) 512-2703      www.mccgraw-hill.com

*Books, magazines, information systems, financial service, publishing and broadcast operations.*

**McGraw-Hill Intl Enterprises, Inc.,  Ste. 2309-10 One Hung To Road, Kwun Tong, Kowloon Hong Kong PRC**

Tel: 852-2730-6640

## McKINSEY & COMPANY

55 East 52nd Street, New York, NY, 10022

Tel: (212) 446-7000      Fax: (212) 446-8575      www.mckinsey.com

*Management and business consulting services.*

**McKinsey & Company, 31/F Asia Pacific Finance Tower, Citibank Plaza, 3 Garden Rd., Hong Kong PRC**

Tel: 852-2868-1188    Fax: 852-2845-9985

## MEAD CORPORATION

Courthouse Plaza, NE, Dayton, OH, 45463

Tel: (937) 495-6323      Fax: (937) 461-2424      www.mead.com

*Mfr. paper, packaging, pulp, lumber and other wood products, school and office products; electronic publishing and distribution.*

**Mead Packaging International Inc.,  Room 1508 Tungwah Mansion, 199-203 Hennessy Rd., Wan Chai, Hong Kong PRC**

Tel: 852-2838-3226   Fax: 852-2836-3159   Contact: C. Y. Chan, Mgr.

## MECHANICAL DYNAMICS, INC.

2301 Commonwealth Blvd., Ann Arbor, MI, 48105

Tel: (734) 994-3800      Fax: (734) 994-6418      www.adams.com

*Mfr. Adams prototyping software to automotive industry.*

**IMAG Industries, Inc.,  Rm. 406 Wing On Plaza, 62 Mody Rd. Tsimshatsui E. Kowloon, Hong Kong PRC**

## MELLON FINANCIAL CORPORATION

One Mellon Bank Center, Pittsburgh, PA, 15258-0001

Tel: (412) 234-5000      Fax: (412) 236-1662      www.mellon.com

*Commercial and trade banking and foreign exchange.*

**Mellon Asia Ltd.,  Citibank Tower #3202, 3 Garden Rd., Central, Hong Kong PRC**

## THE MENTHOLATUM COMPANY, INC.

707 Sterling Drive, Orchard Park, NY, 14127-1587

Tel: (716) 677-2500      Fax: (716) 674-3696      www.mentholatum.com

*Mfr./distributor proprietary medicines, drugs, OTC's.*

**Mentholatum (Asia Pacific) Ltd.,  1616-21 Tower 1, Grand Central Plaza, 138 Shatin Rural Committee Road, Shatin N.T. Hong Kong PRC**

Tel: 852-2699-0078   Fax: 852-2694-7636

## MERCER MANAGEMENT CONSULTING INC.

1166 Ave. of the Americas, New York, NY, 10036

Tel: (212) 345-3400      Fax: (212) 345-7414      www.mercermc.com

*Provides clients with counsel in such areas as corporate and business strategy and growth planning, org development, and market and operations enhancement.*

**Mercer Management Consulting,  32nd Floor NatWest Tower, Times Square, One Matheson Street, Causeway Bay, Hong Kong PRC**

## MERCK & COMPANY, INC.

One Merck Drive, PO Box 100, Whitehouse Station, NJ, 08889-0100

Tel: (908) 423-1000      Fax: (908) 423-2592      www.merck.com

*Pharmaceuticals, chemicals and biologicals.*

**Merck, Sharp & Dohme (Asia) Ltd., 1401 Guardian House, 3201 Kwan Road, Hong Kong PRC**

## MERRILL LYNCH & COMPANY, INC.

World Financial Center, 250 Vesey Street, New York, NY, 10281-1332

Tel: (212) 449-1000      Fax: (212) 449-2892      www.ml.com

*Security brokers and dealers, investment and business services.*

**Merrill Lynch International, 18/F Asia Pacific Finance Tower, 3 Garden Road, Central, Hong Kong PRC**

Tel: 852-536-3888   Fax: 852-2536-3789

## METROPOLITAN LIFE INSURANCE COMPANY

1 Madison Ave., New York, NY, 10010-3603

Tel: (212) 578-3818      Fax: (212) 252-7294      www.metlife.com

*Insurance and retirement savings products and services.*

**Metropolitan Life Insurance Co. of Hong Kong Ltd., Bank of East Asia Building 11/F, 10 Des Voeux Road, Central, Hong Kong PRC**

## MICRO AGE, INC.

2400 South MicroAge Way, Tempe, AZ, 85282-1896

Tel: (480) 366-2000      Fax: (480) 966-7339      www.microage.com

*Computer systems integrator, software products and telecommunications equipment.*

**Hercules Data Comm, Hong Kong PRC**

## MICRO TOUCH SYSTEMS, INC.

300 Griffin Brook Park Drive, Methuen, MA, 01844

Tel: (978) 659-9000      Fax: (978) 659-9100      www.microtouch.com

*Mfr. clear coatings for computer monitors.*

**MicroTouch Systems, Limited, Unit 1 26/F Westly Square, 48 Hoi Yuen Road, Kwun Tong Kowloon, Hong Kong PRC**

Tel: 852-2333-6138

## MICROCHIP TECHNOLOGY INCORPORATED

2355 West Chandler Boulevard, Chandler, AZ, 85224

Tel: (602) 786-7200      Fax: (602) 899-9210      www.microchip.com

*Mfr. electronic subassemblies and components.*

**Microchip Asia Pacific Hdqtrs., Rm 3801B, Tower Two Metroplaza, Dwai Fong N.T., Hong Kong PRC**

Tel: 852-2401-1200   Fax: 852-2401-3431

## MICROSEMI CORPORATION

2830 South Fairview St., Santa Ana, CA, 92704

Tel: (714) 979-8220      Fax: (714) 557-5989      www.microsemi.com

*Design, manufacture and market analog, mixed-signal and discrete semiconductors.*

**Microsemi (H.K.) Ltd., 5-7/F Meeco Industrial Bldg., 53-55 Au Pui Wan St., Fotan, New Territories, Hong Kong PRC**

Tel: 852-2692-1202

## MICROSOFT CORPORATION

One Microsoft Way, Redmond, WA, 98052-6399

Tel: (425) 882-8080    Fax: (425) 936-7329    www.microsoft.com

*Computer software, peripherals and services.*

**Microsoft Hong Kong, 20/F City Plaza 3, 12 Taikoo Wan Rd., Quarry Bay, Hong Kong PRC**

Tel: 852-2804-4200  Fax: 852-2560-2217

## MILBANK, TWEED, HADLEY & McCLOY LLP

1 Chase Manhattan Plaza, New York, NY, 10005-1413

Tel: (212) 530-5000    Fax: (212) 530-5219    www.milbank.com

*International law practice.*

**Milbank, Tweed, Hadley & McCloy, 3007 Alexandra House, 16 Chater Rd., Central Hong Kong PRC**

Tel: 852-2971-4888  Fax: 852-2840-0792

## MILLENNIUM CHEMICALS INC.

230 Half Mile Rd., Red Bank, NJ, 07701

Tel: (732) 933-5000    Fax: (732) 933-5240    www.millenniumchem.com

*Mfr. specialty chemicals that for paints, perfumes, and flavorings.*

**Millennium Chemicals, China Hong Kong Tower 22/F, 8-12 Hennessy Road, Wanchai Hong Kong PRC**

Tel: 852-2528-4667

## MINOLTA QMS INC.

One Magnum Pass, Mobile, AL, 36618

Tel: (205) 633-4300    Fax: (205) 633-4866    www.qms.com

*Mfr. monochrome and color computer printers.*

**QMS AsiaPacific, Flat J-11 Grenville House, 1-3 Magazine Gap Rd., Hong Kong PRC**

## MODEM MEDIA, INC.

230 East Avenue, Norwalk, CT, 06855

Tel: (203) 299-7000    Fax: (230) 299-7060    www.modemmedia.com

*Provides on-line marketing and consulting services.*

**Modem Media Hong Kong, 2604-05 Sio Plaza - Ste. 2601, 256 Gloucester Road, Causeway Bay, Hong Kong PRC**

Tel: 852-2923-5777  Fax: 852-2891-2210  Contact: Eve Chu, Mng. Dir.

## MOEN INC.

25300 Al Moen Drive, North Olmstead, OH, 44070

Tel: (440) 962-2000    Fax: (440) 962-2089    www.moen.com

*Mfr. faucets, plumbing and bath accessories.*

**Moen Hong Kong, Rooms 5001-06 - Hopewell Centre, 183 Queen's Rd. East, Wanchai Hong Kong PRC**

## MOLEX INC.

2222 Wellington Court, Lisle, IL, 60532

Tel: (630) 969-4550    Fax: (630) 969-1352    www.molex.com

*Mfr. electronic, electrical and fiber optic interconnection products and systems, switches, application tooling.*

**Molex Hong Kong/China Ltd., 2/F. Block A Shatin Industrial Center, 5-7 Yuen Shun Circuit, Siu Lek Yuen, Shatin Hong Kong PRC**

Tel: 852-2637-3111  Fax: 852-2637-5990

## MOLTECH POWER SYSTEMS

9062 South Rita Road, Tucson, AZ, 85747

Tel: (520) 799-7500     Fax: (520) 799-7501     www.moltechpower.com

*Provides rechargeable battery solutions for industry applications.*

**Moltech Power Systems Ltd.,  Units 4-9 11/F, Worldwide Industrial Centre, 43-47 Shan Mei St, Fotan Shatin Hong Kong PRC**

Tel: 852-2601-2839   Fax: 852-2693-3793

## MOODY'S INVESTOR SERVICES, INC.

99 Church St., New York, NY, 10007

Tel: (212) 553-1658     Fax: (212) 553-0462     www.moodys.com

*Publishes credit ratings*

**Moody's Asia Pacific, Ltd.,  Central Tower 15/F, 22-28 Queens Rd., Central, Hong Kong PRC**

Tel: 852-2509-0200

**Moody's Asia-Pacfic Ltd.,  Room 2510-2514, International Finance Centre Tower One, One Harbour Street View Central, Hong Kong**
**852-2509-0200**

Tel: 852-2509-0200

## MOOG INC.

Jamison Road, East Aurora, NY, 14052-0018

Tel: (716) 652-2000     Fax: (716) 687-4471     www.moog.com

*Mfr. precision control components and systems.*

**Moog Controls Hong Kong Ltd.,  Unit 2915-6 29/F Tower 1 Metroplaza, 223 Hing Fong Rd., Kwaichung, Hong Kong PRC**

## J. P. MORGAN CHASE & CO. INC.

World Headquarters, 270 Park Ave., New York, NY, 10017

Tel: (212) 270-6000     Fax: (212) 622-9030     www.jpmorganchase.com

*Provides integrated financial solutions for institutions and individuals worldwide, including asset management, investment banking and commercial banking.*

**J. P. Morgan Chase & Co.,  G/F China Life Insurance Bldg., 313-317B Hennessy Rd., Hong Kong PRC**

**J. P. Morgan Chase & Co.,  15-22/F Chase Manhattan Tower, Shatin, Hong Kong PRC**

Tel: 852-2685-5111   Fax: 852-2685-5099

**J. P. Morgan Chase & Co.,  Alexander House, 6 Ice House St., Central, Hong Kong PRC**

**J. P. Morgan Chase & Co.,  40/F One Exchange Square, Connaught Place, Hong Kong PRC**

Tel: 852-2841-6008   Fax: 852-2841-4396

**J. P. Morgan Chase & Co.,  39/F One Exchange Square, Connaught Place, Hong Kong PRC**

Tel: 852-2843-1234   Fax: 852-2841-4396

**J. P. Morgan Chase & Co.,  G/F Shanghai Industrial Investment Bldg., 48-62 Hennessy Rd., Wanchai, Hong Kong PRC**

**J. P. Morgan Chase & Co.,  720 Nathan Rd., Mongkok, Kowloon, Hong Kong PRC**

**J. P. Morgan Chase & Co.,  G/F Shop 30-33 Silvercord Centre, 30 Canton Rd., Tsim Sha Tsui, Kowloon Hong Kong PRC**

## MORGAN STANLEY DEAN WITTER & CO.

1585 Broadway, New York, NY, 10036

Tel: (212) 761-4000     Fax: (212) 761-0086     www.msdw.com

*Securities and commodities brokerage, investment banking, money management, personal trusts.*

**Morgan Stanley Asia Ltd.,  31/F 3 Exchange Place, Hong Kong, PRC**

**Morgan Stanley Dean Witter (Hong Kong),  3408 Edinburg Tower, 15 Queen's Rd. Central, Hong Kong PRC**

## MORRISON & FOERSTER

425 Market Street, San Francisco, CA, 94105

Tel: (415) 268-7000     Fax: (415) 268-7522     www.mofo.com

*International law firm.*

**Morrison & Foerster, Entertainment Bldg. 23/F, 30 Queen's Rd. Central, Hong Kong PRC**

## MOTOROLA, INC.

1303 East Algonquin Road, Schaumburg, IL, 60196

Tel: (847) 576-5000     Fax: (847) 538-5191     www.motorola.com

*Mfr. communications equipment, semiconductors and cellular phones.*

**Motorola Asia Pacific Ltd., NatWest Tower, Times Square, 1 Matheson St., Causway Bay, Hong Kong PRC**

Tel: 852-2599-2800   Fax: 852-2506-2454

**Motorola Semiconductors HK Ltd., 7/F Profit Industrial Bldg., 1-15 Kwai Fund Crescent, Kwai Chung New Territories, Hong Kong PRC**

Tel: 852-2480-8333   Fax: 852-2419-2896

## MTS SYSTEMS CORPORATION

1400 Technology Drive, Eden Prairie, MN, 55344-2290

Tel: (612) 937-4000     Fax: (612) 937-4515     www.mts.com

*Develop/mfr. mechanical testing and simulation products and services, industry measure and automation instrumentation.*

**MTS Systems (Hong Kong) Ltd., Beverley Commercial Center Suite 831, 87-105 Chatham Rd. South, Tsim-Sha-Tsui, Hong Kong**

## MULTEX.COM, INC.

100 Williams Street, 7th Fl., New York, Ny, 10038

Tel: (212) 607-2500     Fax: (212) 607-2510     www.multex.com

*Distributes financial information of corporations via the internet to professional investors.*

**Multex.com Asia, 1 Wellington Road, Silver Fortune Plaza 21/F, Central, Hong Kong PRC**

Tel: 852-2810-0039   Fax: 852-2810-0939

## NABISCO HOLDINGS, CORP.

7 Campus Drive, Parsippany, NJ, 07054

Tel: (973) 682-5000     Fax: (973) 503-2153     www.nabisco.com

*Mfr. consumer packaged food products and tobacco products.*

**Nabisco China Ltd., Sun Hung Kai Ctr. 7/F, Wan Chai 1015, Hong Kong PRC**

**R.J. Reynolds Tobacco Co. (Hong Kong) Ltd., 30 Harbour Rd., Sun Hung Kai Ctr., Wan Chai 1015, Hong Kong PRC**

**RJR Industries Hong Kong Ltd., 8 Connaught Rd., Hong Kong, PRC**

## NALCO CHEMICAL COMPANY

One Nalco Center, Naperville, IL, 60563-1198

Tel: (630) 305-1000     Fax: (630) 305-2900     www.nalco.com

*Chemicals for water and waste water treatment, oil products and refining, industry processes; water and energy management service.*

**Nalco Chemical (HK) Ltd., 1806 Tower 6, China Hong Kong City, 33 Canton Rd., Kowloon, Hong Kong PRC**

Tel: 852-2736-3033   Fax: 852-2736-1317

## NATIONAL MACHINERY COMPANY

161 Greenfield St., Tiffin, OH, 44883-2471

Tel: (419) 447-5211     Fax: (419) 447-5299     www.nationalmachinery.com

*Mfr. high-speed metal parts forming machines.*

**National Machinery Company,  Hong Kong PRC**

Tel: 852-2597-5044

## NATIONAL SEMICONDUCTOR CORPORATION

2900 Semiconductor Dr.,  PO Box 58090, Santa Clara, CA, 95052-8090

Tel: (408) 721-5000     Fax: (408) 739-9803     www.national.com

*Engaged in producing computer-on-a-chip solutions for the information highway.*

**National Semiconductor HK Ltd.,  Suite 2501 Mirai Tower, 1-23 Kimberly Rd., Tsim shatsui Kowloon, Hong Kong PRC**

Tel: 852-2737-1654   Fax: 852-2736-9960   Contact: Martin Kidgell, Regional VP

## NATIONAL STARCH AND CHEMICAL COMPANY

10 Finderne Ave., Bridgewater, NJ, 08807-3300

Tel: (908) 685-5000     Fax: (908) 685-5005     www.nationalstarch.com

*Mfr. adhesives and sealants, resins and specialty chemicals, electronic materials and adhesives, food products, industry starch.*

**National Starch & Chemical Ltd.,  Suite 513-4 5/F Tower 1, Cheung Sha Wan Plaza, 833 Cheung Sha Wan Rd., Kowloon Hong Kong PRC**

Tel: 852-2745-7799   Fax: 852-2745-7063

## NCR (NATIONAL CASH REGISTER)

1700 South Patterson Blvd., Dayton, OH, 45479

Tel: (937) 445-5000     Fax: (937) 445-7042     www.ncr.com

*Mfr. automated teller machines and high-performance stationary bar code scanners.*

**NCR Asia Ltd.,  25/F Office Tower, Convention Plaza, 1 Harbour Rd., Wanchai, Hong Kong PRC**

Tel: 852-2859-6067   Fax: 852-2517-1381   Contact: Jolene Wong, Mgr.

## NETSCAPE COMMUNICATIONS

501 East Middlefield Road, Mountain View, CA, 94043

Tel: (650) 254-1900     Fax: (650) 528-4124     www.netscape.com

*Mfr./distribute Internet-based commercial and consumer software applications.*

**Netscape Communications Ltd. (Hong Kong),  NatWest Tower Room 3202-3, Times Square, 1 Matheson St., Causeway Bay Hong Kong PRC**

Tel: 852-2506-2882   Fax: 852-2506-2068

## NETWORK ASSOCIATES, INC.

3965 Freedom Circle, Santa Clara, CA, 95054

Tel: (408) 988-3832     Fax: (408) 970-9727     www.networkassociates.com

*Designs and produces network security and network management software and hardware.*

**Network Associates,  Plaza 2000 14/F, 2-4 Russell Street, Causeway Bay, Hong KongPRC**

Tel: 852-2892-9500   Fax: 852-2832-9530

## NEW YORK LIFE INSURANCE COMPANY

51 Madison Ave., New York, NY, 10010

Tel: (212) 576-7000     Fax: (212) 576-4291     www.newyorklife.com

*Insurance services.*

**New York Life Insurance Co. of Hong Kong,  Hong Kong PRC**

## THE NEW YORK TIMES COMPANY

229 West 43rd Street, New York, NY, 10036-3959

Tel: (212) 556-1234    Fax: (212) 556-7389    www.nytimes.com

*Diversified media company including newspapers, magazines, television and radio stations, and electronic information and publishing.*

**International Herald Tribune (IHT), 1201 K.Wah Centre, 191 Java Road, North Point, Hong Kong PRC**

Tel: 852-2922-1188

## NEWSWEEK INTERNATIONAL INC.

251 West 57 Street, New York, NY, 10019

Tel: (212) 445-4000    Fax: (212) 445-4120    www.washpostco.com

*Engaged in magazine publishing.*

**Newsweek, 2007 Realty Bldg., 71 Des Voeux Rd., Hong Kong PRC**

## NHC CORPORATION

2727 Chemsearch Blvd., Irving, TX, 75062

Tel: (972) 438-0211    Fax: (972) 438-0707    www.nch.com

*Engaged in manufacturing.*

**Natl. Chemsearch Corp. Hong Kong Ltd., 75/F 31 Ng Fong St., San Po Kong, Kowloon, Hong Kong PRC**

## NIBCO INC.

1516 Middlebury St., PO Box 1167, Elkhart, IN, 46515-1167

Tel: (219) 295-3000    Fax: (219) 295-3307    www.nibco.com

*Mfr. fluid handling products for residential, commercial, industrial and fire protection markets.*

**NIBCO Pacific (Flow Controls) Ltd., Unit A 16/F - Empireland Bldg., 81-85 Lockhart Rd., Wanchai, Hong Kong PRC**

Tel: 852-2512-8398    Fax: 852-2570-9428

## A .C. NIELSEN COMPANY

177 Broad Street, Stamford, CT, 06901

Tel: (203) 961-3000    Fax: (203) 961-3190    www.acnielsen.com

*Market and consumer research firm.*

**A.C. Nielsen, 2/F Warwick House East Wing, Taikoo Place 979 King's Road, Quarry Bay Hong Kong PRC**

Tel: 852-2563-9688

## NIKE INC.

One Bowerman Drive, Beaverton, OR, 97005

Tel: (503) 671-6453    Fax: (503) 671-6300    www.nike.com

*Mfr. athletic footwear, equipment and apparel.*

**Nike Hong Kong, The Gateway 26/F Tower 1, 25 Canton Road, Tsimshatsui, Kowloon Hong Kong PRC**

## NORDSON CORPORATION

28601 Clemens Road, Westlake, OH, 44145-4551

Tel: (440) 892-1580    Fax: (440) 892-9507    www.nordson.com

*Mfr. industry application equipment, sealants and packaging machinery.*

**Nordson Application Equipment Inc., Topsail Plaza Room 708, No. 11 On Sum St., Siu Lek Yuen, Shatin N.T. Hong Kong PRC**

Tel: 852-2687-2828    Fax: 852-2687-4748

**NORGREN**

5400 S. Delaware Street., Littleton, CO, 80120-1663

Tel: (303) 794-2611      Fax: (303) 795-9487      www.usa.norgren.com

*Mfr. pneumatic filters, regulators, lubricators, valves, automation systems, dryers, push-in fittings.*

**IMI Norgren Ltd., 14/F Hale Weal Industrial Bldg., 22-28 Tai Chung Rd., Tseun Wan, Hong Kong PRC**

Tel: 852-2492-7608   Fax: 852-2498-5878

**NORTEK INC.**

50 Kennedy Plaza, Providence, RI, 02903

Tel: (401) 751-1600      Fax: (401) 751-4610      www.nortek-inc.com

*Mfr. residential and commercial building products.*

**Linear HK Mfg. Ltd., 19/F Honour Industrial Centre, 6 Sun Yip St., Chai Wan, Hong Kong PRC**

**NORTON ABRASIVES COMPANY**

1 New Bond Street, Worcester, MA, 01606

Tel: (508) 795-5000      Fax: (508) 795-5741      www.nortonabrasives.com

*Mfr. abrasives for industrial manufacturing.*

**Norton International, Inc, 1001 Trans Asia Centre, 18 Kin Hong Street, Kwai Chung N.T., Hong Kong PRC**

Tel: 852-2589-3589   Fax: 852-2547-4848

**NUS INFORMATION SERVICES, INC.**

2650 McCormick Dr., Ste. 300, Clearwater, FL, 33759-1049

Tel: (727) 669-3000      Fax: (727) 669-3100      www.nus.com

*Provides case-based expert knowledge, bench-marking, trending, and operational services to the electric power and inventory industries.*

**NUS Far East Ltd., Yu Yuet Lai Bldg. 10/F, 43 Wyndham St., Central, Hong Kong PRC**

**OCLI, INC. (OPTICAL COATING LABORATORY, INC.)**

2789 Northpoint Pkwy., Santa Rosa, CA, 95407-7397

Tel: (707) 545-6440      Fax: (707) 525-7410      www.ocli.com

*Mfr. thin film precision coated optical devices.*

**Opton Ltd., Suite 1106 - Shatin Galleria, 18-24 Shan Mei Street, Fo Tan, Shatin Nt, Hong Kong PRC**

Tel: 852-2687-2350   Fax: 852-2687-6529

**S&T Enterprises Ltd. (Rep Office), Room 404 Block B,f - Sea View Estate, 2-8 Watson Road, North Point Hong Kong PRC**

**OGDEN CORPORATION**

Two Penn Plaza, New York, NY, 10121

Tel: (212) 868-6000      Fax: (212) 868-5714      www.ogdencorp.com

*Engaged in power generation.*

**Ogden Corporation, Entertainment Bldg. Ste. 24B, 30 Queens Road, Central, Hong Kong PRC**

Tel: 852-280-17474

**OGILVY PUBLIC RELATIONS WORLDWIDE**

909 Third Ave., New York, NY, 10022

Tel: (212) 880-5201      Fax: (212) 697-8250      www.ogilvypr.com

*Engaged in public relations and communications.*

**Ogilvy Public Relations Worldwide, Mount Parker House 7/F, Taikoo Shing, Hong Kong PRC**

**Ogilvy Public Relations Worldwide, The Center - 99 Queen's Road, Central Hong Kong PRC**

Tel: 852-2567-4461   Fax: 852-2885-3227   Contact: Debby Cheung

## OLIN CORPORATION

501 Merritt Seven, Norwalk, CT, 06856-4500

Tel: (203) 750-3000     Fax: (203) 750-3292     www.olin.com

*Mfr. chemicals, metals, sporting ammunition and copper and copper alloy sheets.*

**Olin Industrial (HK) Ltd., 1111 Peninsula Centre, 67 Mody Road, Tsim Sha Tsui East, Kowloon Hong Kong PRC**

Tel: 852-2366-8303   Fax: 852-2367-1309

## OMNICOM GROUP

437 Madison Ave., New York, NY, 10022

Tel: (212) 415-3600     Fax: (212) 415-3530     www.omnicomgroup.com

*International network of advertising, marketing, direct mail, public relations and consulting services.*

**BBDO Asia Pacific, 38/F, Dorset House, Taikoo Place - 979 King's Road, Quarry Bay Hong Kong PRC**

## ONYX SOFTWARE CORPORATION

3180 139th Avenue, SE, Bellevue, WA, 98005

Tel: (425) 451-8060     Fax: (425) 451-8277     www.onyx.com

*Mfr. customer relationship management software.*

**Onyx Software Hong Kong, Harcourt House #1010, 39 Gloucester Road, Wanchai, Hong Kong PRC**

Tel: 852-2868-2727

## ORACLE CORPORATION

500 Oracle Parkway, Redwood Shores, CA, 94065

Tel: (650) 506-7000     Fax: (650) 506-7200     www.oracle.com

*Develop/manufacture software.*

**Oracle Hong Kong, Hong Kong PRC**

## OSMONICS INC.

5951 Clearwater Drive, Minnetonka, MN, 55343-8995

Tel: (952) 933-2277     Fax: (952) 933-0141     www.osmonics.com

*Mfr. equipment, controls and components for the filtration and water-treatment industries.*

**Osmonics Asia/Pacific Ltd., Suite F 15/F Cameron Plaza, 23-25A Cameron Rd., Kowloon TST Hong Kong PRC**

## OSRAM SYLVANIA CHEMICALS INC.

100 Endicott Street, Danvers, MA, 01923

Tel: (978) 777-1900     Fax: (978) 750-2152     www.osramsylvania.com

*Lighting applications.*

**Osram Sylvania Chemicals, Hong Kong PRC**

## OTIS ELEVATOR COMPANY

10 Farm Springs Road, Farmington, CT, 06032

Tel: (860) 676-6000     Fax: (860) 676-5111     www.otis.com

*Mfr. elevators and escalators.*

**Otis Elevator Co., 5/F Luk Kwok Centre, 72 Gloucester Rd., Wanchai, Hong Kong PRC**

**Otis Elevator Co. (HK) Ltd., GPO Box 82, Hong Kong, PRC**

## OUTBACK STEAKHOUSE, INC.

2202 N. Westshore Blvd. 5th Fl., Tampa, FL, 33607

Tel: (813) 282-1225     Fax: (813) 282-1209     www.outback.com

*Chain of casual dining steak restaurants.*

**Outback Steakhouse, Inc., 398 Castle Peak Road - Level 2, Tsuen Wan NT, Hong Kong PRC**

Tel: 852-2940-0682

## OUTBOARD MARINE CORPORATION

100 Sea Horse Drive, Waukegan, IL, 60085

Tel: (847) 689-6200    Fax: (847) 689-5555    www.omc-online.com

*Mfr./market marine engines, boats and accessories.*

**OMC Asia (Hong Kong), 35-47 Sing Yi Rd., Sing Yi Island, Hong Kong PRC**

## PACIFIC CENTURY FINANCIAL CORPORATION

130 Merchant Street, Honolulu, HI, 96813

Tel: (808) 643-3888    Fax: (808) 537-8440    www.boh.com

*Engaged in commercial and consumer banking services.*

**Pacific Century Financial Corporation, 6201 Central Plaza, 18 Harbour Road, Wan Chai, Hong Kong**
Tel: 852-2588-9488

## PAINE WEBBER GROUP INC.

1285 Ave. of the Americas, New York, NY, 10019

Tel: (212) 713-2000    Fax: (212) 713-4889    www.painewebber.com

*Stock brokerage and investment services.*

**PaineWebber Intl., Ste. 3204-05 Citibank Tower, Citibank Plaza, 3 Garden Rd., Hong Kong PRC**
Tel: 852-2842-0600

## PALL CORPORATION

2200 Northern Boulevard, East Hills, NY, 11548-1289

Tel: (516) 484-5400    Fax: (516) 484-5228    www.pall.com

*Specialty materials and engineering; filters and related fluid clarification equipment.*

**Pall Asia International Ltd., Room 2806-7 Shu on Centre, 6-8 Harbour Road, Wanchai, Hong Kong PRC**
Tel: 852-2583-9610    Fax: 852-2511-5773

## PANDUIT CORPORATION

17301 Ridgeland Ave., Tinley Park, IL, 60477-0981

Tel: (708) 532-1800    Fax: (708) 532-1811    www.panduit.com

*Mfr. electrical/electronic wiring components.*

**Panduit Hong Kong, Suite 3310, 33rd Floor, The Gateway Tower 1, 25 Canton Road, Tsimshatsui, Kowloon Hong Kong PRC**

## PARADYNE NETWORKS, INC.

8545 126 Ave. North, Largo, FL, 33773

Tel: (727) 530-2000    Fax: (727) 530-2875    www.paradyne.com

*Engaged in data communications and high-speed network access solutions.*

**Paradyne Far East Corp., Room 901 Wing On Centre, 111 Connaught Rd., Central, Hong Kong PRC**

## PARAMETRIC TECHNOLOGY CORPORATION

128 Technology Drive, Waltham, MA, 02154

Tel: (781) 398-5000    Fax: (781) 398-5674    www.ptc.com

*Supplier of mechanical design automation and product data management software and services.*

**Parametric Tecnology (Hong Kong) Ltd., 37/F Suite 3703-4 Central Plaza, 18 Harbour Road, Wanchai, Hong Kong PRC**
Tel: 852-2802-8982    Fax: 852-2587-9095

## PARKER HANNIFIN CORPORATION

6035 Parkland Blvd., Cleveland, OH, 44124-4141

Tel: (216) 896-3000    Fax: (216) 896-4000    www.parker.com

*Mfr. motion-control products.*

**Parker Hannifin Hong Kong Ltd., Hong Kong Worsted Mills Ind. Bldg. #2104, 31-39 Wo Tong Tsui St., Kwai Chung NT Hong Kong PRC**

## PARSONS BRINCKERHOFF QUADE & DOUGLAS

One Penn Plaza, New York, NY, 10119-0061

Tel: (212) 465-5000      Fax: (212) 465-5096        www.pbworld.com

*Engineering consultants, planners and architects.*

**PB Kennedy & Donkin Transportation Limited, Suite 602-4 New Town Tower, 10-18 Pak Hok Ting Street, Sha Tin New Territories, Hong Kong PRC**

## PAUL, WEISS, RIFKIND, WHARTON & GARRISON

1285 Ave. of the Americas, New York, NY, 10019-6064

Tel: (212) 373-3000      Fax: (212) 373-2268        www.paulweiss.com

*Law firm engaged in American and international law practice.*

**Paul, Weiss, Rifkind, Wharton & Garrison, 13/F Hong Kong Club Bldg., 3A Chater Rd., Central Hong Kong PRC**

Tel: 852-2536-9933    Fax: 852-2536-9622

## PCA ELECTRONICS INC.

16799 Schoenborn Street, North Hills, CA, 91343

Tel: (818) 892-0761      Fax: (818) 894-5791        www.pca.com

*Mfr./sales of electronic equipment.*

**HPC Ltd., 26 Wong Chuk, Hang Road 1/F, Aberdeen, Hong Kong PRC**

Tel: 852-2580-1878    Fax: 852-2870-2663

## J.C. PENNEY COMPANY, INC.

6501 Legacy Drive, Plano, TX, 75024-3698

Tel: (972) 431-1000      Fax: (972) 431-1977        www.jcpenney.com

*Markets family apparel, shoes, home furnishings, jewelry, and offers credit cards.*

**J. C. Penney Purchasing Corp., 617 Peninsula Centre, 67 Mody Rd., Tsim Sha Tsui E., Kowloon, Hong Kong PRC**

## PENTON MEDIA

1100 Superior Ave., Cleveland, OH, 44114-2543

Tel: (216) 696-7000      Fax: (216) 696-7648        www.penton.com

*Publisher of industrial/trade magazines.*

**Penton Media Asia Ltd., 7/f, 9 Des Vouex Road West, Hong Kong PRC**

Tel: 852-2975-9051    Fax: 852-2857-6144

## PEOPLESOFT INC.

4460 Hacienda Drive, Pleasanton, CA, 94588-8618

Tel: (925) 225-3000      Fax: (925) 694-4444        www.peoplesoft.com

*Mfr. applications to manage business operations across computer networks.*

**PeopleSoft Hong Kong Ltd., 8/F-12 Harcourt Road, Central Hong Kong PRC**

Tel: 85-2-258-46180

## PERIPHONICS CORPORATION

4000 Veterans Highway, Bohemia, NY, 11716

Tel: (631) 468-9000      Fax: (631) 981-2689        www.periphonics.com

*Mfr. voice processing systems.*

**Periphonics Corp., Hong Kong PRC**

Tel: 852-2506-1001

## PERKIN ELMER, INC.

45 William Street, Wellesley, MA, 02481

Tel: (781) 237-5100     Fax: (781) 431-4255     www.perkinelmer.com

*Mfr. equipment and devices to detect explosives and bombs on airline carriers.*

**PerkinElmer Hong Kong, Room 1409 Kodak House II, 39 Healthy Street East, North Point, Hong Kong PRC**

Tel: 852-2590-0238

## PHARMACIA CORPORATION

100 Route 206 North, Peapack, NJ, 07977

Tel: (908) 901-8000     Fax: (908) 901-8379     www.pharmacia.com

*Mfr. pharmaceuticals, agricultural products, industry chemicals.*

**Pharmacia & Upjohn Asia Ltd., Rm.1101-3 Allied Kajima Building, 138 Gloucester Road, Wanchai, Hong Kong PRC**

## PHARMACIA MONSANTO

800 N. Lindbergh Boulevard, St. Louis, MO, 63167

Tel: (314) 694-1000     Fax: (314) 694-7625     www.monsanto.com

*Life sciences company focusing on agriculture, nutrition, pharmaceuticals, health and wellness and sustainable development.*

**Monsanto Far East Ltd., 2F City Plaza 3, 14 Taikoo Wan Road, Hong Kong PRC**

Tel: 852-2831-9121

## PHELPS DODGE CORPORATION

2600 North Central Ave., Phoenix, AZ, 85004-3089

Tel: (602) 234-8100     Fax: (602) 234-8337     www.phelpsdodge.com

*Copper, minerals, metals and special engineered products for transportation and electrical markets.*

**Phelps Dodge Intl. Corp., Hong Kong PRC**

## PHILIP MORRIS COMPANIES, INC.

120 Park Ave., New York, NY, 10017--559

Tel: (917) 663-5000     Fax: (917) 663-2167     www.philipmorris.com

*Mfr. cigarettes, food products, beer.*

**Philip Morris Asia Inc., Two Pacific Place 23/F, 88 Queensway, Hong Kong PRC**

## PHILLIPS PETROLEUM COMPANY

Phillips Building, 411 S. Keeler Ave., Bartlesville, OK, 74004

Tel: (918) 661-6600     Fax: (918) 661-7636     www.phillips66.com

*Crude oil, natural gas, liquefied petroleum gas, gasoline and petro-chemicals.*

**Phillips Petroleum Co. Asia, 9/F Citibank Tower, 8 Queen's Rd., Central, Hong Kong PRC**

**Phillips Petroleum Intl. Inc., 501 Cosmopolitan Bldg., 10 Stanley St., Hong Kong PRC**

## PICTURETEL CORPORATION

100 Minuteman Road, Andover, MA, 01810

Tel: (978) 292-5000     Fax: (978) 292-3300     www.picturetel.com

*Mfr. video conferencing systems, network bridging and multiplexing products, system peripherals.*

**PictureTel Intl. Corp. Hong Kong, Room 3401 Citibank Plaza, Citibank Tower, 3 Garden Road, Central Hong Kong PRC**

Tel: 852-2821-4700   Fax: 852-2821-4800

## PILLSBURY MADISON & SUTRO LLP

50 Fremont Street, San Francisco, CA, 94105

Tel: (415) 983-1000     Fax: (415) 983-1200     www.pillsburylaw.com

*International law firm.*

**Pillsbury Madison & Sutro LLP, 6/F Asia Pacific Finance Tower, Citibank Plaza, 3 Garden Road, Central Hong Kong PRC**

## PIONEER-STANDARD ELECTRONICS, INC.

6065 Parkland Blvd., Cleveland, OH, 44124

Tel: (440) 720-8500     Fax: (440) 720-8501     www.pios.com

*Mfr./distribution of electronic parts for computers and networking equipment.*

**WPI International,  Commercial Center Rm. 809, Tower B 37-39, Ma Tau Wai Road, Humghom Kowloon, Hong Kong PRC**

Tel: 852-2365-4860

## PITNEY BOWES INC.

1 Elmcroft Road, Stamford, CT, 06926-0700

Tel: (203) 356-5000     Fax: (203) 351-6835     www.pitneybowes.com

*Mfr. postage meters, mailroom equipment, copiers, bus supplies, bus services, facsimile systems and financial services.*

**Pitney Bowes Asian Operations,  10/F Beverly House, 93-107 Lockhart Rd., Wanchai, Hong Kong PRC**

Tel: 852-2528-9011   Fax: 852-2527-4077   Contact: Henri Ho, VP Asian Operations   Emp: 100

**Pitney Bowes Hong Kong Inc.,  21/F Beverly House, 93-107 Lockhart Road, Wanchai Hong Kong PRC**

## PITTSTON BAX GROUP

16808 Armstrong Ave., PO Box 19571, Irvine, CA, 92623

Tel: (949) 752-4000     Fax: (949) 260-3182     www.baxworld.com

*Air freight forwarder.*

**BAX Global,  2/F Sunhing Chekiang Godown, 8 Sze Shan St., Yau Tong, Kowloon Hong Kong PRC**

Tel: 852-2379-9280   Fax: 852-2379-9289

## PITTWAY CORPORATION

200 South Wacker Drive, Chicago, IL, 60606

Tel: (312) 831-1070     Fax: (312) 831-0808     www.pittway.com

*Mfr. alarm and other controls.*

**ADEMCO Asia Pacific Ltd.,  Flat A 16/F CDW Building, 388 Castle Peak Road, Tsuen Wan N.T., Hong Kong PRC**

Tel: 852-2405-2323   Fax: 852-2415-3112

## PLAINS COTTON COOPERATIVE ASSOCIATES

3301 East 50th Street, Lubbock, TX, 79404

Tel: (806) 763-8011     Fax: (806) 762-7333     www.pcca.com

*Merchandisers of raw cotton to domestic and foreign textile mills.*

**Amerasia Intl. Ltd.,  4/F Solar House, 26 Des Voeux Rd., Central, Hong Kong PRC**

## PLANET HOLLYWOOD INTERNATIONAL, INC.

8669 Commodity Circle, Orlando, FL, 32819

Tel: (407) 363-7827     Fax: (407) 363-4862     www.planethollywood.com

*Theme-dining restaurant chain and merchandise retail stores.*

**Planet Hollywood International, Inc.,  Kowloon, Hong Kong PRC**

## POLAROID CORPORATION

784 Memorial Dr., Cambridge, MA, 02139

Tel: (781) 386-2000     Fax: (781) 386-3924     www.polaroid.com

*Photographic equipment and supplies, optical products.*

**Polaroid Far East Ltd.,  10/F Block B, Watson's Estate, 8 Watson Rd., North Point, Hong Kong PRC**

## PPG INDUSTRIES

One PPG Place, Pittsburgh, PA, 15272

Tel: (412) 434-3131     Fax: (412) 434-2190     www.ppg.com

*Mfr. coatings, flat glass, fiber glass, chemicals, coatings.*

**PPG Industries International Inc.,  Cityplaza One Suite 1010-1015, 111 King's Rd., Taikoo Shing, Hong Kong PRC**

## PREMARK INTERNATIONAL INC.

1717 Deerfield Road, Deerfield, IL, 60015

Tel: (847) 405-6000     Fax: (847) 405-6013     www.premarkintl.com

*Mfr. Hobart commercial food equipment, diversified consumer and commercial products, small appliances, and exercise equipment.*

**Dart Industries Hong Kong Ltd., G-12 Kornhill Plaza North, Kornhill Rd., Quarry Bay, Hong Kong PRC**

## PRICEWATERHOUSECOOPERS LLP

1301 Ave. of the Americas, New York, NY, 10019

Tel: (212) 596-7000     Fax: (212) 259-1301     www.pwcglobal.com

*Accounting and auditing, tax and management, and human resource consulting services.*

**PriceWaterhouseCoopers, Prince's Building 22/F, GPO Box 690, Hong Kong PRC**

Tel: 852-2826-2111   Fax: 852-2810-9888   Contact: Augustine YY Lo

## THE PRINCIPAL FINANCIAL GROUP

711 High Street, Des Moines, IA, 50392-9950

Tel: (515) 248-8288     Fax: (515) 248-8049     www.principal.com

*Insurance and investment services.*

**Principal Insurance Company (Hong Kong) Ltd., Unit 1001-3 Central Plaza, 18 Harbour Rd., Wanchai, Hong Kong PRC**

Tel: 852-2827-1628   Fax: 852-2827-1618   Contact: Rex Auyeung, Mgr.

**Principal International Asia, Ltd., Unit 1001-3 Central Plaza, 18 Harbour Rd., Wanchai, Hong Kong PRC**

Tel: 852-2827-1628   Fax: 852-2827-1618   Contact: Christopher Reddy, Mktg. Dir.

## PROJECT SOFTWARE & DEVELOPMENT, INC.

100 Crosby Drive, Bedford, MA, 01730

Tel: (781) 280-2000     Fax: (781) 280-0207     www.mrosoftware.com

*Design/sales of enterprise asset maintenance software.*

**MRO Software, 25 Westlands Road - Ste. 503, Quarry Bay, Hong Kong PRC**

Tel: 852-2565-3500

## PRUDENTIAL INSURANCE COMPANY OF AMERICA

751 Broad Street, Newark, NJ, 07102-3777

Tel: (973) 802-6000     Fax: (973) 802-2804     www.prudential.com

*Sale of life insurance and provides financial services.*

**Prudential Reinsurance Co. (USA), 2906 Windsor Houser, 311 Gloucester Rd., Causeway Bay, Hong Kong PRC**

## PSDI MAXIMO

100 Crosby Drive, Bedford, MA, 01730

Tel: (781) 280-2000     Fax: (781) 280-0200     www.psdi.com

*Develops, markets and provides maintenance management software systems.*

**PSDI Hong Kong, Suite 503 DCH Commercial Bldg., 5 Westlands Road, Quarry Bay, Hong Kong PRC**

Tel: 852-2530-8812   Fax: 852-2530-8142   Contact: Andrew Moore, Gen. Mgr.   Emp: 1

## PSI NET (PERFORMANCE SYSTEMS INTERNATIONAL INC.)

510 Huntmar Park Drive, Herndon, VA, 22170

Tel: (703) 904-4100     Fax: (703) 904-4200     www.psinet.com

*Internet service provider.*

**Linkage Online Limited, 69-71 King Yip Street, Kwun Tong, Kowloon, Hong Kong PRC**

Tel: 852-23-31-81-23   Fax: 852-27-95-12-62   Contact: Chi H. Kwan, SVP, Asia

## PUBLIC SERVICE ENTERPRISE GROUP (PSEG)

80 Park Plaza, Newark, NJ, 07101

Tel: (973) 430-7000     Fax: (973) 623-5389     www.pseg.com

*Electric and gas utility.*

**Meiya Power Company, Room 1701-6 Harbour Centre, 25 Harbour Road, Wanchai, Hong Kong PRC**

Tel: 852-2593-3222   Fax: 852-2519-0313   Contact: Colin S. Tam

## PULSE ENGINEERING INC.

12220 World Trade Drive, PO 12235, San Diego, CA, 92112

Tel: (858) 674-8100     Fax: (858) 674-8262     www.pulseeng.com

*Engineer/mfr. OEM devices for local area network markets and major voice/data transmission systems.*

**Pulse Engineering Inc., Wo Kee Hong Bldg., 585-609 Castle Peak Rd., Kwai Chung, NT, Hong Kong PRC**

## QUAKER CHEMICAL CORPORATION

Elm & Lee Streets, Conshohocken, PA, 19428-0809

Tel: (610) 832-4000     Fax: (610) 832-8682     www.quakerchem.com

*Mfr. developer, producer, and marketer of custom-formulated chemical specialty products.*

**Quaker Chemical Ltd., East Asia Aetna Tower 26/F, 308 Des Voeux Rd., Central, Hong Kong PRC**

Tel: 852-2854-3311   Contact: Daniel S. Ma, Mng. Dir.

## QUANTUM

500 McCarthy Blvd., Milpitas, CA, 95035

Tel: (408) 894-4000     Fax: (408) 894-3218     www.quantum.com

*Mfr. computer peripherals.*

**Quantum Hong Kong Ltd., Great Eagle Centre 32/F, 23 Harbour Rd., Wanchai, Hong Kong PRC**

Tel: 852-2519-8606

## QUINTILES TRANSNATIONAL CORPORATION

4709 Creekstone Dr., Durham, NC, 27703

Tel: (919) 998-2000     Fax: (919) 998-9113     www.quintiles.com

*Mfr. pharmaceuticals.*

**Quintiles Hong Kong Limited, Room No. 1602 Ming An Plaza Phase II, 8 Sunning Road, Causeway Bay, Hong Kong PC**

## RAY & BERNDTSON, INC.

301 Commerce, Ste. 2300, Fort Worth, TX, 76102

Tel: (817) 334-0500     Fax: (817) 334-0779     www.prb.com

*Executive search, management audit and management consulting firm.*

**Ray & Berndtson, Allied Capital Resources Bldg. 8/F, 32-28 Ice House St., Central Hong Kong PRC**

Tel: 852-522-4118   Fax: 852-877-2418   Contact: David S. Seabrook, Mng. Ptnr.

## RAYCHEM CORPORATION

300 Constitution Dr., Menlo Park, CA, 94025-1164

Tel: (650) 361-3333     Fax: (650) 361-5579     www.raychem.com

*Develop/mfr./market materials science products for electronics, telecommunications and industry.*

**Raychem Hong Kong Ltd., Unit 601 South Tower, World Finance Centre, Harbour City, Kowloon Hong Kong PRC**

## RAYOVAC CORPORATION

601 Rayovac Drive, Madison, WI, 53711-2497

Tel: (608) 275-3340     Fax: (608) 275-4577     www.rayovac.com

*Mfr. batteries and lighting devices.*

**Rayovac Far East Corp, Room 720-723, Hollywood Plaza, 610 Nathan Rd., Mongkok, Kowloon, Hong Kong PRC**

## READER'S DIGEST ASSOCIATION, INC.

Reader's Digest Rd., Pleasantville, NY, 10570

Tel: (914) 238-1000     Fax: (914) 238-4559     www.readersdigest.com

*Publisher of magazines and books and direct mail marketer.*

**Reader's Digest Assn. Far East Ltd., 3A Kung Ngam Village Rd., Shaukiwan, Hong Kong PRC**

## REDBACK NETWORKS, INC.

1195 Borregas Avenue, Sunnyvale, CA, 94089

Tel: (408) 571-5200     Fax: (408) 541-0570     www.redbacknetworks.com

*Mfr. equipment for high-speed internet connections.*

**Redback Networks Hong Kong, Shun Tak Centre, 168-200 Connaught Road, Central Hong Kong PRC**

Tel: 852-9861-1873   Fax: 852-2291-4219

## REEBOK INTERNATIONAL LTD.

100 Technology Center Drive, Stoughton, MA, 02072

Tel: (781) 401-5000     Fax: (781) 401-7402     www.reebok.com

*Mfr. athletic shoes including casual, dress golf and walking shoes.*

**Reebok Intl. Asia-Pacific, Gitic Centre 17/F, 24-32 Queen's Rd. E., Wanchai, Hong Kong PRC**

## RELIANCE GROUP HOLDINGS, INC.

55 East 52nd Street, New York, NY, 10055

Tel: (212) 909-1100     Fax: (212) 909-1864     www.rgh.com

*Financial and insurance management services.*

**Reliance National (Asia) Ltd., Suite 2106-7 Lippo House, Causeway Bay Plaza 2, 463 Lockhart Rd., Causeway Bay, Hong Kong PRC**

Tel: 852-2892-2179   Fax: 852-3833-5694   Contact: Christopher J. Cron, Dir.

**The Hong Kong Chinese Insurance Company, Ltd., 24/F Lippo House Causeway Bay Plaza 2, 463 Lockhart Rd., Causeway Bay, Hong Kong PRC**

Tel: 852-2572-5488   Fax: 852-2672-5007   Contact: Paul Ng, Mgr.

## REMEDY CORPORATION

1505 Salado Drive, Mountain View, CA, 94043-1110

Tel: (650) 903-5200     Fax: (650) 903-9001     www.remedy.com

*Developer and marketer of computer applications for the operations management market.*

**Remedy Hong Kong, Bank of America Tower - 8/F,12 Harcourt Road, Central Hong Kong**

## RENA WARE DISTRIBUTORS INC.

PO Box 97050, Redmond, WA, 98073-9750

Tel: (425) 881-6171     Fax: (425) 882-7500     www.renaware.com

*Mfr. stainless steel cookware and water filtration products.*

**Rena Ware Limited, Room 1902 C.C. Wu Bldg., 302-308 Hennessy Road, Wanchai, Hong Kong PRC**

## RENAISSANCE HOTELS AND RESORTS

10400 Fernwood Road, Bethesda, MD, 20817

Tel: (301) 380-3000     Fax: (301) 380-5181     www.renaissancehotels.com

*Hotel and resort chain.*

**Renaissance Harbour View Hong Kong, Hong Kong PRC**

Tel: 852-2375-1133

## RENAISSANCE WORLDWIDE, INC.

52 Second Ave., Waltham, MA, 02451

Tel: (781) 290-3000        Fax: (781) 965-4807        www.rens.com

*Provides technology consulting, staffing services, corporate and systems strategies and software and hardware installation.*

**Renaissance Worldwide, Inc., 80 Gloucester Road 19/F, Wanchai, Hong Kong PRC**

Tel: 852-2-511-2831   Fax: 852-2-519-9503

## RESPIRONICS INC.

1501 Ardmore Blvd., Pittsburgh, PA, 15221-4401

Tel: (412) 731-2100        Fax: (412) 473-5011        www.respironics.com

*Design/mfr. patient ventilation medical products.*

**Respironics HK Ltd., 38 Hung To Rd., Kwun Tong, Kowloon, Hong Kong PRC**

Tel: 852-23-434218

## REVLON INC.

625 Madison Ave., New York, NY, 10022

Tel: (212) 527-4000        Fax: (212) 527-4995        www.revlon.com

*Mfr. cosmetics, fragrances, toiletries and beauty care products.*

**Revlon Hong Kong Ltd., 7/F 64-66 To Kwa Wan Rd., Kowloon, Hong Kong PRC**

Contact: Patrick Lee, Gen. Mgr.

## REXALL SUNDOWN INC.

6111 Broken Sound Parkway NW, Boca Raton, FL, 33487

Tel: (561) 241-9400        Fax: (561) 995-0197        www.rexallsundown.com

*Vitamins, nutritional supplements and diet and weight management products.*

**Rexall Sundown Inc., Hong Kong PRC**

## RICH PRODUCTS CORPORATION

1150 Niagara St., Buffalo, NY, 14213

Tel: (716) 878-8000        Fax: (716) 878-8765        www.richs.com

*Mfr. non-dairy products.*

**Rich Products Corp., Room 702A Euro Trade Centre, 13-14 Connaught Rd., Central, Hong Kong PRC**

## RIDGE TOOL COMPANY

400 Clark Street, Elyria, OH, 44035

Tel: (440) 323-5581        Fax: (440) 329-4853        www.ridgid.com

*Mfr. hand and power tools for working pipe, drain cleaning equipment, etc.*

**Ridge Tool Hong Kong, c/o Emerson Electric Asia Ltd., 3904 Central Plaza, 18 Harbour Rd., Wanchai, Hong Kong PRC**

Tel: 852-2802-9223   Fax: 852-2857-9433

## RIDGEVIEW, INC. (WOOLRICH)

2101 N. Main St., Newton, NC, 28658

Tel: (828) 464-2972        Fax: (828) 465-3198        www.woolrich.com

*Mfr. fabrics and apparel.*

**Woolkong Ltd., Po Lung Centre #907-8, Kowloon, Hong Kong PRC**

## THE RITZ-CARLTON HOTEL COMPANY, L.L.C.

3414 Peachtree Road NE, Ste. 300, Atlanta, GA, 30326

Tel: (404) 237-5500        Fax: (404) 365-9643        www.ritzcarlton.com

*5-star hotel and restaurant chain.*

**The Ritz-Carlton Hong Kong, 3 Connaught Rd., Central, Hong Kong PRC**

Tel: 852-2877-6666

## ROCKWELL INTERNATIONAL CORPORATION

777 East Wisconsin Ave., Ste. 1400, Milwaukee, WI, 53202

Tel: (414) 212-5200     Fax: (414) 212-5201     www.rockwell.com

*Products and service for aerospace and defense, automotive, electronics, graphics and automation industry.*

**Rockwell Automation Asia Pacific, 27/F Citicorp Centre, 18 Whitfield Road, Causeway Bay Hong Kong PRC**

**Rockwell Automation Asia Pacific Ltd., Room 1410 14/F, World Trade Tower II, 123 Hoi Bun Rd. Kwun Tong, Kowloon, Hong Kong PRC**

Tel: 852-2515-435  Fax: 852-2510-9436

**Rockwell Automation/Allen-Bradley (Hong Kong) Ltd., Room 1006 Block B, Seaview Estate, 2-8 Watson Rd., Hong Kong PRC**

**Rockwell Intl. (Asia Pacific) Ltd., Suite 1306-10 Harbour Centre, 25 Harbour Rd., Wanchai, Hong Kong PRC**

Tel: 852-2827-0181  Fax: 852-2827-6488

## ROHM AND HAAS COMPANY

100 Independence Mall West, Philadelphia, PA, 19106

Tel: (215) 592-3000     Fax: (215) 592-3377     www.rohmhaas.com

*Mfr. industrial and agricultural chemicals, plastics.*

**Rohm and Haas Hong Kong Ltd., Unit A 17/F On Hin Bldg., No.1 On Hing Terrace, Central Hong Kong PRC**

Tel: 852-2868-1383

**Shipley Chemicals (Hong Kong). Ltd., Unit 1301 New Town Tower, 10-18 Pak Hok Ting St., Shantin, N.T. Hong Kong PRC**

Tel: 852-2694-0661

## T. ROWE PRICE ASSOCIATES, INC.

100 East Pratt Street, Baltimore, MD, 21202

Tel: (410) 345-2000     Fax: (410) 345-2394     www.troweprice.com

*Investment and portfolio asset management.*

**Rowe Price-Fleming International, Hong Kong PRC**

## RUSSELL REYNOLDS ASSOCIATES INC.

200 Park Ave., New York, NY, 10166-0002

Tel: (212) 351-2000     Fax: (212) 370-0896     www.russreyn.com

*Executive recruiting services.*

**Russell Reynolds Associates Inc., 3801-4 Edinburgh Tower, 15 Queen's Rd. Central, The Landmark, Hong Kong PRC**

Tel: 852-2523-9123  Fax: 852-284-59044  Contact: Raymond C.P. Tang

## S2i CORPORATION

Three Church Circle, Ste. 207, Annapolis, MD, 21401

Tel: (410) 315-7995     Fax: (410) 315-8882     www.s2isecurity.com

*Provides worldwide security, strategic intelligence and business information services.*

**S2i Corporation, Hong Kong PRC**

Contact: Dave Bresett, VP Int'l.

## SALOMON SMITH BARNEY HOLDINGS INC.

388 Greenwich Street, New York, NY, 10013

Tel: (212) 816-6000     Fax: (212) 816-8915     www.smithbarney.com

*Securities dealers and underwriters.*

**Salomon Smith Barney Holdings, 2907 Alexandra House, 15-20 Chater Rd., Hong Kong PRC**

## SAPHIRE INTERNATIONAL LTD.

3060 Main Street, Ste. 202, Stratford, CT, 06614

Tel: (203) 375-8668      Fax: (203) 375-1965      www.dataease.com

*Mfr. applications development software.*

**Great Code Systems, 2204 Yung Wai Commercial, 109-111 Gloucester Rd., Wanchai, Hong Kong PRC**

## SAS INSTITUTE INC.

SAS Campus Drive, Cary, NC, 27513

Tel: (919) 677-8000      Fax: (919) 677-4444      www.sas.com

*Mfr./distributes decision support software.*

**SAS Institute (China) Ltd., Talkoo Shing, Hong Kong PRC**

Tel: 852-2568-4280    Fax: 852-2-568-7218

## SCHENKER INTERNATIONAL FORWARDERS INC.

150 Albany Ave., Freeport, NY, 11520

Tel: (516) 377-3000      Fax: (516) 377-3005      www.schenkerusa.com

*Freight forwarders.*

**Schenker (H.K.) Ltd., China Resources Bldg. Suite 3801-5, 26 Harbour Rd., PO Box 6611, Wanchai Hong Kong PRC**

Tel: 852-2585-9688    Fax: 852-2827-5363

## SCHERING-PLOUGH CORPORATION

One Giralda Farms, Madison, NJ, 07940-1000

Tel: (973) 822-7000      Fax: (973) 822-7048      www.sch-plough.com

*Proprietary drug and cosmetic products.*

**Plough Consumer Products (Asia) Ltd., 304 Watsons Estate B, 6 Watson Rd., Hong Kong PRC**

## SCHOLASTIC CORPORATION

555 Broadway, New York, NY, 10012

Tel: (212) 343-6100      Fax: (212) 343-6934      www.scholastic.com

*Publishing/distribution educational and children's magazines, books, software.*

**Scholastic Hong Kong Ltd., Tung Sung Hing Commercial Ctr., 20-22 Granville Rd., Kowloon, Hong Kong PRC**

Tel: 852-2722-6161    Contact: Linda H. Warfel, Reg. Dir.

## THE CHARLES SCHWAB CORPORATION

101 Montgomery Street, San Francisco, CA, 94104

Tel: (415) 627-7000      Fax: (415) 627-8840      www.schawb.com

*Financial services; discount brokerage, retirement accounts.*

**Schwab Hong Kong, 3301- Two Exchange Square, Central Hong Kong, PRC Hong Kong**

## SCIENTIFIC-ATLANTA, INC.

1 Technology Pkwy South, Norcross, GA, 30092-2967

Tel: (770) 903-5000      Fax: (770) 903-2967      www.sciatl.com

*A leading supplier of broadband communications systems, satellite-based video, voice and data communications networks and worldwide customer service and support.*

**Scientific-Atlanta (HK) Ltd., Ste. 56 & 57 5/F New Henry House, 10 Ice House St., Central Hong Kong PRC**

Tel: 852-2522-5059    Fax: 852-2522-5624

## SDI TECHNOLOGIES

1299 Main St., Rahway, NJ, 07065

Tel: (732) 574-9000     Fax: (732) 574-3797     www.sdidirect.com

*Mfr. clock radios and electronic products.*

**SDI Technologies, Hong Kong PRC**

**SDI Technologies, Kowloon Centre, 29-43 Ashley Rd., Kowloon, Hong Kong PRC**

## SEAGATE TECHNOLOGY, INC.

920 Disc Dr., Scotts Valley, CA, 95066

Tel: (408) 438-6550     Fax: (408) 438-7205     www.seagate.com

*Develop computer technology, software and hardware.*

**Seagate Technology, Rm. 1001 Energy Plaza, 92 Granville Rd., Tsim Sha Tsui East, Kowloon Hong Kong PRC**

Tel: 852-2368-9918   Fax: 852-2368-7173   Contact: Chia Hyaw Seong, Dir.   Emp: 10

## SEALED AIR CORPORATION

Park 80 East, Saddle Brook, NJ, 07663

Tel: (201) 791-7600     Fax: (201) 703-4205     www.sealedair.com

*Mfr. protective and specialty packaging solutions for industrial, food and consumer products.*

**Sealed Air (Far East) Ltd., 9/F Wing Kwai Ind. Bldg., 2-8 Wang Wo Tsai St., Tsuen Wan NT, Hong Kong PRC**

Tel: 852-2407-3367   Fax: 852-2407-3385

## G.D. SEARLE & COMPANY

5200 Old Orchard Road, Skokie, IL, 60077

Tel: (847) 982-7000     Fax: (847) 470-1480     www.searlehealthnet.com

*Mfr. pharmaceuticals, health care, optical products and specialty chemicals.*

**Searle Hong Kong, Unit 3106 Level 31 Metro Plaza Tower II, 223 Hing Fong Rd., Kai Chung, N.T. Hong Kong PRC**

Tel: 852-423-0923   Fax: 852-423-1169

## SEI INVESTMENTS COMPANY

1 Freedom Valley Drive, Oaks, PA, 19456-1100

Tel: (610) 676-1000     Fax: (610) 676-2995     www.seic.com

*Accounting, evaluation and financial automated systems and services.*

**SEI Investments, 1201 Chinachem Leighton Plaza, 29 Leighton Rd., Causeway Bay, Hong Kong PRC**

Tel: 852-2575-4772   Fax: 852-2575-3772   Contact: Vincent W. Chu, Mng. Dir.

## SEMTECH CORPORATION

652 Mitchell Road, PO Box 367, Newbury Park, CA, 91320

Tel: (805) 498-2111     Fax: (805) 498-3804     www.semtech.com

*Mfr. silicon rectifiers, rectifier assemblies, capacitors, switching regulators, AC/DC converters.*

**Dragon Technology Distribution Co., Ltd., Rm. 903 Landmark North, Sheung Shui N.T., Hong Kong PRC**

Tel: 852-2303-0711   Fax: 852-2317-7522

## THE SERVICEMASTER COMPANY

One ServiceMaster Way, Downers Grove, IL, 60515-1700

Tel: (630) 271-1300     Fax: (630) 271-2710     www.svm.com

*Management service to health care, school and industry facilities; diversified residential and commercial services.*

**ServiceMaster Hong Kong, Hong Kong PRC**

## SHAKESPEARE FISHING TACKLE GROUP

3801 Westmore Drive, Columbia, SC, 29223

Tel: (803) 754-7000       Fax: (803) 754-7342       www.shakespeare-fishing.com

*Mfr. fishing tackle.*

**Shakespeare Hong Kong Ltd.,  175 Hoi Bun Rd., Jwun Tong, Kowloon, Hong Kong PRC**

## SHAW INDUSTRIES, INC.

616 E. Walnut Ave., Dalton, GA, 30720

Tel: (706) 278-3812       Fax: (706) 275-3735       www.shawinc.com

*Mfr. carpet.*

**Shaw Industries, Inc.,  Hong Kong PRC**

## SHEARMAN & STERLING

599 Lexington Ave., New York, NY, 10022-6069

Tel: (212) 848-4000       Fax: (212) 848-7179       www.shearman.com

*Law firm engaged in general American and international financial and commercial practice.*

**Shearman & Sterling,  Standard Chartered Bank Bldg., 4 Des Voeux Rd. Central, Hong Kong PRC**

Tel: 852-2978-8000   Fax: 852-2978-8099   Contact: Edward L. Turner III, Mng. Ptnr.

## SHIPLEY COMPANY, LLC

455 Forest Street, Marlborough, MA, 01752

Tel: (508) 481-7950       Fax: (508) 485-9113       www.shipley.com

*Supplier of materials and processes technology to the microelectronics and printed wiring board industries.*

**Shipley Asia, Ltd.,  15 On Lok Mun Street, On Lok Tsuen, Fanling N.T. Hong Kong PRC**

Tel: 852-2680-16888   Fax: 852-2680-06333

**Shipley Chemicals Ltd.,  Unit 1303, New Town Tower, 10-18 Pok Hok Ting St., Shatin, NT, Hong Kong PRC**

Tel: 852-2694-0661   Fax: 852-2694-0939   Contact: R. Leung

## SHURE INCORPORATED

222 Hartrey Ave., Evanston, IL, 60202-3696

Tel: (847) 866-2200       Fax: (847) 866-2279       www.shure.com

*Mfr. microphones, teleconferencing systems, circuitry products.*

**Shure Asia Limited,  Unit 701 7th Floor Top Glory Tower, 26 2 Gloucester Road, Causeway Bay, Hong Kong PRC**

Tel: 852-2893-4290   Fax: 852-2893-4055   Contact: Tom Anderson

## SIGNODE PACKAGING SYSTEMS

3610 West Lake Ave., Glenview, IL, 60025

Tel: (847) 724-6100       Fax: (847) 657-4392       www.signode.com

*Mfr. industrial tools and machinery for packaging and strapping.*

**Signode Hong Kong Ltd.,  Unit B 9/F Kin Yip Factory Bldg., 9 Cheung Yee St., Kowloon, Hong Kong PRC**

## SILICON GRAPHICS INC.

2011 N. Shoreline Blvd., Mountain View, CA, 94043-1389

Tel: (650) 960-1980       Fax: (650) 961-0595       www.sgi.com

*Design/mfr. special-effects computer graphic systems and software.*

**Silicon Graphics Ltd.,  Rooms 513-522 5/F, Hong Kong Industrial Tech Centre, 72 Tat Chee Ave., Kowloon Hong Kong PRC**

Tel: 852-2784-3111   Fax: 852-2778-9100

## SILICON VALLEY GROUP, INC.

101 Metro Dr., Ste. 400, San Jose, CA, 95110

Tel: (408) 467-5870     Fax: (408) 467-5955     www.svg.com

*Manufacturer of automated wafer processing equipment for the worldwide semiconductor industry.*

**Thermco Systems (Far East) Ltd., Div. Silicon Valley,  Wilson House, 19-27 Wyndham St., Hong Kong PRC**

## THE SIMCO COMPANY, INC.

1178 Bordeaux Dr., Sunnyvale, CA, 94089

Tel: (408) 734-9750     Fax: (408) 734-9754     www.simco.com

*Provides electronics and commercial calibration services.*

**Simco Company c/o CO Packaging Corp( HK) Ltd.,  4/F Din Wai Industrial Bldg., 13 On Chuen St., On Lok Tsuen, Fanling New Territories, Hong Kong PRC**

Tel: 852-2785-2230   Fax: 852-2947-5770

## SIMPLEX TIME RECORDER COMPANY

100 Simplex Dr., Westminster, MA, 01441

Tel: (978) 731-2500     Fax: (978) 731-7052     www.simplexnet.com

*Provides safety, fire detection, integrated security, communications, time and attendance and workforce management systems.*

**Simplex Asia Limited,  Units 1101-2 Stelux House, 698 Prince Edward Road East, San Po Kong Kowloon, Hong Kong PRC**

## SIMPSON THACHER & BARTLETT

425 Lexington Ave., New York, NY, 10017

Tel: (212) 455-2000     Fax: (212) 455-2502     www.simpsonthacher.com

*International law Firm.*

**Simpson Thacher & Bartlett,  Asia Pacific Tower 32/F, 3 Garden Rd., Central Hong Kong PRC**

Tel: 852-2514-7600   Fax: 852-2869-7694   Contact: John E. Riley, Ptnr.

## SKADDEN, ARPS, SLATE, MEAGHER & FLOM LLP

4 Times Square, New York, NY, 10036

Tel: (212) 735-3000     Fax: (212) 735-2000     www.sasmf.com

*American/International law practice.*

**Skadden, Arps, Slate, Meagher & Flom LLP,  30/F Tower Two Lippo Centre, 89 Queensway, Central, Hong Kong PRC**

Tel: 852-2820-0700   Fax: 852-2820-0727   Contact: Robert C. Hinkley, Partner

## SKIDMORE OWINGS & MERRILL LLP

224 S. Michigan Ave., Ste. 1000, Chicago, IL, 60604-2707

Tel: (312) 554-9090     Fax: (312) 360-4545     www.som.com

*Engaged in architectural and engineering services.*

**SOM Inc.,  Trium Pacific Place 4606, 88 Queensway, Hong Kong PRC**

Tel: 852-2877-4606   Fax: 852-2810-6056

## SKYTEL COMMUNICATIONS, INC.

PO Box 2469, Jackson, MS, 39225

Tel: (601) 944-1300     Fax: (601) 944-3900     www.skytel.com

*Provides wireless messaging services, radio paging services and systems implementation.*

**SkyTel Services Ltd.,  Hong Kong PRC**

## WILBUR SMITH ASSOCIATES

PO Box 92, Columbia, SC, 29202

Tel: (803) 758-4500     Fax: (803) 251-2064     www.wilbursmith.com

*Consulting engineers.*

**Wilbur Smith Associates Inc., Unit 803-6 8/F - Two Harbourfront, 22 Tak Fung Street, Hung Hom Kowloon Hong Kong, PRC**

Tel: 852-2359-5738   Fax: 852-2385-7215   Contact: Chang Tai Tseng

## SOLUTIA INC.

575 Maryville Center Dr, St. Louis, MO, 63141

Tel: (314) 674-1000     Fax: (314) 694-8686     www.solutia.com

*Mfr. specialty chemical based products.*

**Solutia Hong Kong Limited, 18 Harbour Road, Unit 1706 Central Plaza, Wanchai Hong Kong PRC**

Tel: 852-28283232

## SONOCO PRODUCTS COMPANY

North Second Street, PO Box 160, Hartsville, SC, 29550

Tel: (843) 383-7000     Fax: (843) 383-7008     www.sonoco.com

*Mfr. packaging for consumer and industrial market and recycled paperboard.*

**Sonoco Asia Recycling Ltd., Two Pacific Place Suite 1101, 88 Queensway, Hong Kong PRC**

Tel: 852-2514-4300   Fax: 852-2869-6201

## SOTHEBY'S HOLDINGS, INC.

1334 York Avenue, New York, NY, 10021

Tel: (212) 606-7000     Fax: (212) 606-7027     www.sothebys.com

*Auction house specializing in fine art and jewelry.*

**Sotheby's Holdings, Inc., 4-4A Des Boeux Road Central 5/F, Hong Kong PRC**

Tel: 852-2524-8121   Fax: 852-1810-6238   Contact: Carlton C. Rochell, Jr.

## THE SOUTHERN COMPANY

270 Peachtree Street, N.W., Atlanta, GA, 30303

Tel: (404) 506-5000     Fax: (404) 506-0642     www.southernco.com

*Electric utility.*

**Consolidated Electric Power Asia (Cepa), 18/F Hong Kong Telecom Tower, 979 King's Rd., Quarry Bay, Hong Kong PRC**

Tel: 852-2179-3333   Fax: 852-2179-3334   Contact: Raymond D. Hill, Mng. Dir.

## SPENCER STUART MANAGEMENT CONSULTANTS

401 North Michigan Ave., Ste. 3400, Chicago, IL, 60611

Tel: (312) 822-0080     Fax: (312) 822-0116     www.spencerstuart.com

*Executive recruitment firm.*

**Spencer Stuart & Associates Inc., 17/F Bank of East Asia Bldg., 10 Des Voeux Rd. Central, Hong Kong PRC**

Tel: 852-2521-8373   Fax: 852-2810-5246   Contact: Martin Tang

## SPHERION CORPORATION

2050 Spectrum Boulevard, Fort Lauderdale, FL, 33309

Tel: (954) 938-7600     Fax: (954) 938-7666     www.spherion.com

*Provides temporary personnel placement and staffing.*

**Michael Page Finance, One Pacific Place Suite 601, Hong Kong, PRC**

Tel: 852-2530-2000

**Michael Page Sales & Marketing, One Pacific Place Suite 601, Hong Kong, PRC**

Tel: 852-2918-1333

## SPRINGS INDUSTRIES INC.

205 N. White Street, PO Box 70, Fort Mill, SC, 29715

Tel: (803) 547-1500    Fax: (803) 547-1772    www.springs.com

*Mfr. and sales of home furnishings, finished fabrics and industry textiles.*

**Springs Asia, 202 Wing on Plaza, 62 Mody Rd., TST-East, Kowloon Hong Kong PRC**

Tel: 852-2722-7671  Fax: 852-2722-1259   Contact: T. Arimitsu

## SPRINT INTERNATIONAL

World Headquarters, 2330 Shawnee Mission Parkway, Westwood, KS, 66205

Tel: (913) 624-3000    Fax: (913) 624-3281    www.sprint.com

*Telecommunications equipment and services.*

**Sprint International, Two Pacific Place #1212, 88 Queensway, Hong Kong PRC**

## SQUIRE, SANDERS & DEMPSEY

127 Public Square, Key Tower, Ste. 4900, Cleveland, OH, 44114-1304

Tel: (216) 479-8500    Fax: (216) 479-8780    www.ssd.com

*International law firm.*

**Squire, Sanders & Dempsey, Ste. 1101 St. George's Bldg., 2 Ice House Street, Hong Kong PRC**

Tel: 852-2509-9732  Fax: 852-2509-9772   Contact: James S. Tsang

## THE ST. PAUL COMPANIES, INC.

385 Washington Street, St. Paul, MN, 55102

Tel: (651) 310-7911    Fax: (651) 310-8294    www.stpaul.com

*Provides investment, insurance and reinsurance services.*

**QBE Insurance Hong Kong Ltd., Allied Kajima Building 16th Floor, 138 Gloucester Road, Wanchai, Hong Kong PRC**

## THE STANLEY WORKS

1000 Stanley Drive, PO Box 7000, New Britain, CT, 06053

Tel: (860) 225-5111    Fax: (860) 827-3987    www.stanleyworks.com

*Mfr. hand tools and hardware.*

**The Stanley Works Hong Kong Ltd., 1433 Central Bldg., Pedder St., Hong Kong PRC**

## STARWOOD HOTELS & RESORTS WORLDWIDE

777 Westchester Avenue, White Plains, NY, 10604

Tel: (914) 640-8100    Fax: (914) 640-8316    www.starwoodhotels.com

*Hotel operations including Sheraton, Westin, St. Regis, Four Points and Caesars.*

**Sheraton Hong Kong Hotel & Towers, 20 Nathan Rd., Kowloon, Hong Kong PRC**

Tel: 852-2369-1111  Fax: 852-2739-8707

## STATE STREET BANK & TRUST COMPANY

225 Franklin Street, Boston, MA, 02101

Tel: (617) 786-3000    Fax: (617) 654-3386    www.statestreet.com

*Banking and financial services.*

**State Street Trust (HK) Ltd., Two Exchange Square 32/F, 8 Connaught Place, Central, Hong Kong PRC**

Tel: 852-2103-0275   Contact: Raymond Hood

## STEPAN COMPANY

22 West Frontage Road, Northfield, IL, 60093

Tel: (847) 446-7500    Fax: (847) 501-2443    www.stepan.com

*Mfr. basic intermediate chemicals.*

**Stepan, House 15, 63 Deep Water Bay Rd., Deep Water Bay, Hong Kong PRC**

**STERIS CORPORATION**

5960 Heisley Road, Mentor, OH, 44060

Tel: (440) 354-2600     Fax: (440) 639-4459     www.steris.com

*Mfr. sterilization/infection control equipment, surgical tables, lighting systems for health, pharmaceutical and scientific industries.*

**Steris Corporation, 34D Manulife Tower, 169 Electric Rd., North Point, Hong Kong PRC**

**STIEFEL LABORATORIES INC.**

255 Alhambra Circle, Ste. 1000, Coral Gables, FL, 33134

Tel: (305) 443-3807     Fax: (305) 443-3467     www.stiefel.com

*Mfr. pharmaceuticals, dermatological specialties.*

**Stiefel Laboratories Limited, 601B Tower 2 Cheung Sha Wan Plaza, 833 Cheung Sha Wan Road, Kowloon, Hong Kong PRC**

**STOKES VACUUM INC.**

5500 Tabor Road, Philadelphia, PA, 19120

Tel: (215) 831-5400     Fax: (215) 831-5420     www.stokesvacuum.com

*Vacuum pumps and components, vacuum dryers, oil-upgrading equipment and metallizers.*

**Stokes Vacuum Inc., Hanaflex Sales, Hong Kong PRC**

Contact: E. Chan

**SULLIVAN & CROMWELL**

125 Broad Street, New York, NY, 10004-2498

Tel: (212) 558-4000     Fax: (212) 558-3588     www.sullcrom.com

*International law firm.*

**Sullivan & Cromwell, Nine Queen's Rd. 28/F, Central, Hong Kong PRC**

**SUMMIT INDUSTRIAL CORPORATION**

600 Third Ave., New York, NY, 10016

Tel: (212) 490-1100     Fax: (212) 949-6328

*Pharmaceuticals, agricultural and chemical products.*

**Summit Asia Ltd., 505 Watson's Estate, Hong Kong, PRC**

**SUN MICROSYSTEMS, INC.**

901 San Antonio Road, Palo Alto, CA, 94303

Tel: (650) 960-1300     Fax: (650) 856-2114     www.sun.com

*Computer peripherals and programming services.*

**Sun Microsystems, 22/F Shui on Center, 8 Harbour Road, Wanchai, Hong Kong PRC**

**SUNBEAM CORPORATION**

2381 Executive Center Dr., Boca Raton, FL, 33431

Tel: (561) 912-4100     Fax: (561) 912-4567     www.sunbeam.com

*Mfr. household and personal grooming appliances; Sunbeam, Mr. Coffee, First Alert, Mixmaster and Oster.*

**Orient Fair Development Ltd., Rm.1018 - 21-33 Tai Lin Pai Rd., Kwai Chung, N.T. Hong Kong PRC**

**SUNKIST GROWERS INC.**

14130 Riverside Drive, Van Nuys, CA, 91423

Tel: (818) 986-4800     Fax: (818) 379-7405     www.sunkist.com

*Citrus marketing cooperative; fruits and vegetables.*

**Sunkist c/o Reliance Commercial Enterprises HK Ltd., Rm. 705 7/F Central Plaza, 18 Harbor Rd., 1 Wan Chai, Hong Kong PRC**

Tel: 852-2525-2236

## SYBASE, INC.

6475 Christie Ave., Emeryville, CA, 94608

Tel: (510) 922-3500     Fax: (510) 922-3210     www.sybase.com

*Design/mfg/distribution of database management systems, software development tools, connectivity products, consulting and technical support services..*

**Sybase Hong Kong Ltd., 33rd Floor Natwest Tower, Times Square, I Matheson St., Causeway Bay Hong Kong PRC**

Tel: 852-2506-8900   Fax: 852-2506-6050

## SYBRON INTERNATIONAL CORPORATION

411 E. Wisconsin Ave., Milwaukee, WI, 53202

Tel: (414) 274-6600     Fax: (414) 274-6561     www.sybron.com

*Mfr. products for laboratories, professional orthodontic and dental markets.*

**Erie-Watala Glass Co. Ltd., Unit 401-405, World Wide Industrial Centre, 43-47 Shan Mei St., Fo Tan, Shatin, Hong Kong PRC**

## SYMANTEC CORPORATION

20330 Stevens Creek Blvd., Cupertino, CA, 95014-2132

Tel: (408) 253-9600     Fax: (408) 253-3968     www.symantec.com

*Designs and produces PC network security and network management software and hardware.*

**Symantec Ltd., Unit 1101-1102 Onfem Tower, No. 29 Wyndham St., Central Hong Kong PRC**

Tel: 852-2528-6206   Fax: 852-2861-3420

## SYNOPSYS, INC.

700 East Middlefield Road, Mountain View, CA, 94043

Tel: (650) 962-5000     Fax: (650) 965-8637     www.synopsys.com

*Mfr. electronic design automation software.*

**Synopsys Hong Kong, Radio City 15/F, 505 Hennessy Rd., Causeway Bay, Hong Kong PRC**

Tel: 852-2369-8156

## TANDY CORPORATION

100 Throckmorton Street, Fort Worth, TX, 76102

Tel: (817) 390-3700     Fax: (817) 415-2647     www.tandy.com

*Mfr. electronic and acoustic equipment; Radio Shack retail stores.*

**A & A International (YICHI-HK) Ltd., 1406-1411 World Commerce Centre, Harbour City, Phase 1, Kowloon, Hong Kong PRC**

## TBWA CHIAT/DAY

488 Madison Avenue, 6th Floor, New York, NY, 10022

Tel: (212) 804-1000     Fax: (212) 804-1200     www.tbwachiat.com

*International full service advertising agency.*

**TBWA Lee Davis, Hong Kong PRC**

**TBWA Thompson, Hong Kong PRC**

## THE TCW GROUP

865 S. Figueroa St., Ste. 1800, Los Angeles, CA, 90017

Tel: (213) 244-0000     Fax: (213) 244-0000     www.tcwgroup.com

*Engaged in managing pension and profit sharing funds, retirement/health and welfare funds, insurance company funds, endowments and foundations.*

**TCW Group, Hong Kong PRC**

## TEKTRONIX INC.

14200 SW Karl Braun Dr., PO Box 500, Beaverton, OR, 97077

Tel: (503) 627-7111    Fax: (503) 627-2406    www.tek.com

*Mfr. test and measure, visual systems/color printing and communications/video and networking products.*

**Tektronix Hong Kong Ltd.,  65/F The Lee Gardens, 3 Hysan Ave., Causeay Bay, Hong Kong PRC**

Tel: 852-2585-6688   Fax: 852-2598-6260

## TELEX COMMUNICATIONS INC.

12000 Portland Ave. South, Burnsville, MN, 55337

Tel: (952) 884-4051    Fax: (952) 884-0043    www.telexcommunications.com

*Mfr. communications, audio-visual and professional audio products.*

**EVI Audio (Hong Kong) Ltd.,  Unit E/F 21F Luk Hop Industrial Bldg., 8 Luk Hop Street, San Po Kong, Kowloon Hong Kong PRC**

## TELLABS INC.

4951 Indiana Ave. 6303788800, Lisle, IL, 60532-1698

Tel: (630) 378-8800    Fax: (630) 679-3010    www.tellabs.com

*Design/mfr./service voice/data transport and network access systems.*

**Tellabs Ltd.,  Suite 1702-4, 1111 King's Road, Taikoo Shing, Hong Kong PRC**

## TERADYNE INC.

321 Harrison Ave., Boston, MA, 02118

Tel: (617) 482-2700    Fax: (617) 422-2910    www.teradyne.com

*Mfr. electronic test equipment and blackplane connection systems.*

**Teradyne (Hong Kong) Ltd.,  33 Canton Rd. #1018, Kowloon, Hong Kong PRC**

## TERAYON COMMUNICATION SYSTEMS, INC..

2952 Bunker Hill Lane, Santa Clara, CA, 95054

Tel: (408) 727-4400    Fax: (408) 727-6205    www.terayon.com

*Mfr. cable modem systems.*

**Terayon Communication Systems Hong Kong,  Suite 2604-06 - The Gateway, 25 Canton Road, Kowloon, Hong Kong PRC**

Tel: 852 2111 5988   Contact: Andrew A. Bigbee

## TEXACO INC.

2000 Westchester Ave., White Plains, NY, 10650

Tel: (914) 253-4000    Fax: (914) 253-7753    www.texaco.com

*Exploration/marketing crude oil, mfr. petro chemicals and products.*

**Texaco Hong Kong Ltd.,  2005 American Intl. Tower, 16-18 Queen's Rd., Central, Hong Kong PRC**

## TEXAS INSTRUMENTS INC.

8505 Forest Lane, Dallas, TX, 75243

Tel: (972) 995-3773    Fax: (972) 995-4360    www.ti.com

*Mfr. semiconductor devices, electronic electro-mechanical systems, instruments and controls.*

**Texas Instruments Hong Kong,  Hong Kong PRC**

Tel: 800-96-1111-800-800-

## TEXTRON INC.

40 Westminster Street, Providence, RI, 02903

Tel: (401) 421-2800    Fax: (401) 421-2878    www.textron.com

*Mfr. Aerospace (Bell Helicopter and Cessna Aircraft), industry and consumer products, fasteners and financial services.*

**Avco Financial Services (Asia) Ltd.,  8/F Sunning Plaza, 10 Hysan Ave., Causeway Bay, Hong Kong PRC**

Tel: 852-2504-1332   Fax: 852-2504-1332   Contact: Gordon F. Burnett, Mng. Dir.

## THERMADYNE HOLDINGS CORPORATION

101 South Hanley Road, Suite 300, St. Louis, MO, 63105

Tel: (314) 746-2197     Fax: (314) 746-2349     www.thermadyne.com

*Mfr. welding, cutting, and safety products.*

**Thermadyne Hong Kong,  Hong Kong PRC**

Tel: 852-2791-9404

## THERMO ORION, INC.

500 Cummings Court, Beverly, MA, 01915

Tel: (978) 922-4400     Fax: (978) 922-6015     www.thermoorion.com

*Mfr. laboratory and industrial products, measure and display instruments.*

**Orion Research Far East Inc.,  Federal Bldg. #904, 369 Lockhart Rd., Wanchai, Hong Kong PRC**

Tel: 852-283-60981    Fax: 852-283-45160

## THERM-O-DISC, INC.

1320 S. Main Street, Mansfield, OH, 44907-0538

Tel: (419) 525-8500     Fax: (419) 525-8282     www.thermodisc.com

*Mfr. thermostats, controls, sensor and thermal cutoffs, switches.*

**Therm-O-Disc,  3904 Central Plaza, 18 Harbour Rd., Wanchai, Hong Kong PRC**

## THOMAS INDUSTRIES INC.

4360 Brownsboro Road, Ste. 300, Louisville, KY, 40232

Tel: (502) 893-4600     Fax: (502) 893-4685     www.thomasind.com

*Mfr. lighting fixtures and specialty pumps and compressors for global OEM applications.*

**T.I. Asia Pacific Ltd.,  Units 1-5 25/F Metropole Square, No. 2 On Yiu Street, Siu Lek Yuen, Shatin New Territories, Hong Kong PRC**

Tel: 852-2690-3502    Fax: 852-2792-4598

## THOMAS PUBLISHING COMPANY

5 Penn Plaza, New York, NY, 10007

Tel: (212) 695-0500     Fax: (212) 290-7362     www.thomaspublishing.com

*Publishing magazines and directories.*

**Interasia Publications Ltd.,  200 Lockhart Rd., Victoria, Hong Kong PRC**

## TIFFANY & COMPANY

727 Fifth Ave., New York, NY, 10022

Tel: (212) 755-8000     Fax: (212) 605-4465     www.tiffany.com

*Mfr./retail fine jewelry, silverware, china, crystal, leather goods, etc.*

**Tiffany & Co. Hong Kong,  The Peninsula Hotel, Shop E1, G/F Salisbury Rd., Hong Kong PRC**

Tel: 852-2722-7691

**Tiffany & Co. Hong Kong,  The Landmark Shop 17 G/F, Pedder St., Central Hong Kong PRC**

Tel: 852-2845-9853

## TOMMY HILFIGER CORPORATION

25 West 39th St., New York, NY, 10018

Tel: (212) 840-8888     Fax: (212) 302-8718     www.tommy.com

*Clothing manufacturer and chain stores. (JV with Tommy Hilfiger Corp., Hong Kong)*

**Tommy Hilfiger Corp.,  6/F Precious Industrial Centre, 18 Cheung Yue St., Cheung Sha Wan, Kowloon, Hong Kong PRC**

Tel: 852-2745-7798    Fax: 852-2312-1368    Contact: Silas K. F. Chou, Co-Chmn.

## TOOTSIE ROLL INDUSTRIES INC.

7401 S. Cicero Ave., Chicago, IL, 60629

Tel: (773) 838-3400       Fax: (773) 838-3534       www.tootsie.com

*Mfr. candies and chocolate products.*

**Tootsie Roll Worldwide Ltd., Room 1501 Eight Plaza, 8 Sunning Rd., Causeway Bay, Hong Kong PRC**

## TOSCO CORPORATION

72 Cummings Point Rd., Stamford, CT, 06902

Tel: (203) 977-1000       Fax: (203) 964-3187       www.tosco.com

*Engaged in oil refining and marketing and operates service stations and convenience stores.*

**Circle K Ltd., CNT Group Bldg. 10/F, 822 Lai Chi Kok Road, Lai Chi Kok, Hong Kong PRC**

Contact: Richard Yeung, CEO

## TOTES ISOTONER CORPORATION

9655 International Blvd., PO Box 465658, Cincinnati, OH, 45246

Tel: (513) 682-8200       Fax: (513) 682-8602       www.totes.com

*Mfr. rubber and plastic footwear, slippers, umbrellas.*

**Totes Asia, Hong Kong PRC**

## TOWERS PERRIN

335 Madison Ave., New York, NY, 10017-4605

Tel: (212) 309-3400       Fax: (212) 309-0975       www.towers.com

*Management consulting services.*

**Tillinghast Towers Perrin, Central Plaza Ste. 3001-2, 18 Harbour Rd., Wanchai, Hong Kong PRC**
Tel: 852-2593-4588   Fax: 852-2868-1517

**Tillinghast Towers Perrin, Central Plaza, Ste. 3001-2, 18 Harbour Rd., Wanchai, Hong Kong PRC**
Tel: 852-2593-4588   Fax: 852-2868-1517

## TOYS R US INC.

461 From Road, Paramus, NJ, 07652

Tel: (201) 262-7800       Fax: (201) 845-0973       www.toysrus.com

*Retail stores: toys and games, sporting goods, computer software, books, records.*

**Toys R Us Lifung Ltd., Yen Sheng Centre 11/F, 64 Hoi Yuen Rd., Kwun Tong, Kowloon, Hong Kong PRC**

## THE TRANE COMPANY

3600 Pammel Creek Road, La Crosse, WI, 54601

Tel: (608) 787-2000       Fax: (608) 787-4990       www.trane.com

*Mfr./distributor/service A/C systems and equipment.*

**Jardine Trane Air Conditioning, Jardine Engineering House 15/F, 260 King's Rd., North Point, Hong Kong PRC**

**Trane Asia Pacific (Reg. HQ), St. John's Bldg. 16/F, 33 Garden Rd., Hong Kong PRC**

## TRICON GLOBAL RESTAURANTS INC.

1441 Gardner Lane, Louisville, KY, 40213

Tel: (502) 874-1000       Fax: (502) 874-8315       www.triconglobal.com

*Owns and operates KFC, Taco Bell and Pizza Hut restaurant food chains.*

**Tricon Global Greater China, 33 Hysin Avenue - Rm. 1602, Causeway Bay, Hong Kong PRC**
Tel: 852-2834-8330   Fax: 852-2831-1879

## TRIDENT MICROSYSTEMS, INC.

2450 Walsh Avenue, Santa Clara, CA, 95051

Tel: (408) 496-1085     Fax: (408) 496-6858     www.tridentmicro.com

*Mfr. computer components.*

**Trident Microsystems Far East Ltd., Tower III 18/F Enterprise Square, 9 Sheung Yuet Road, Kowloon Bay, Kowloon, Hong Kong PRC**

## TROPICANA PRODUCTS, INC.

1001 13th Avenue East, Bradenton, FL, 34208

Tel: (941) 747-4461     Fax: (941) 665-5330     www.tropicana.com

*Marketer and producer of branded juices, including Tropicana, Dole, Looza and Copella.*

**Tropicana Beverages Greater China Limited, 1111 King's Road Ste 1203-6, Taikoo Shing, Hong Kong PRC**

Tel: 852-2121-8200   Fax: 852-2121-8201

## TRUE NORTH COMMUNICATIONS INC.

101 East Erie Street, Chicago, IL, 60611

Tel: (312) 425-6500     Fax: (312) 425-5010     www.truenorth.com

*Holding company, advertising agency.*

**FCB Asia-Pacific Reg. Office, 2/F Harbour Centre, 25 Harbour Rd., Wanchai, Hong Kong PRC**

**Foote, Cone & Belding, 2/F Harbour Centre, 25 Harbour Rd., Wanchai, Hong Kong PRC**

**Foote, Cone & Belding Ltd., 2309 Sun Hung Kai Centre, 30 Harbour Rd., Hong Kong PRC**

## TYCO PRESCHOOL INC.

200 Fifth Ave., New York, NY, 10010

Tel: (212) 620-8200     Fax: (212) 807-7183     www.mattel.com

*Distributor infant and preschool toys.*

**Tyco Preschool Ltd., World Shipping Ctr., 7 Canton Rd., Tsim Shat Sui, Kowloon, Hong Kong PRC**

## TYSON FOODS INC.

2210 W. Oaklawn Dr., Springdale, AR, 72762-6999

Tel: (501) 290-4000     Fax: (501) 290-4061     www.tyson.com

*Production/mfr./distributor poultry, beef, pork and seafood products.*

**Tyson Hong Kong, Rm. 3204-5 32/F Great Eagle Centre, 23 Harbour Rd., Wanchai, Hong Kong PRC**

Tel: 852-2878-1038   Fax: 852-2537-8316   Contact: Kenneth Shum, Regional Director   Emp: 21

## UNION CARBIDE CORPORATION

39 Old Ridgebury Road, Danbury, CT, 06817

Tel: (203) 794-2000     Fax: (203) 794-6269     www.unioncarbide.com

*Mfr. industrial chemicals, plastics and resins.*

**Union Carbide Asia Ltd., Metroplaza Tower 1 26/F Rm. 2612-2624, 223 High Fong Rd., Kwai Fong NT, Hong Kong PRC**

## UNISYS CORPORATION.

PO Box 500, Union Meeting Road, Blue Bell, PA, 19424

Tel: (215) 986-4011     Fax: (215) 986-6850     www.unisys.com

*Mfr./marketing/servicing electronic information systems.*

**Unisys Asia Ltd., Sun Hung Kai Centre, 30 Harbour Rd., Wanchai 1015, Hong Kong PRC**

**Unisys Hong Kong Ltd., 30 Harbour Rd., Sun Hung Kai Centre, Wan Chai 1015, Hong Kong PRC**

## UNITED AIRLINES INC.

1200 E. Algonquin Rd., Chicago, IL, 60007

Tel: (847) 700-4000     Fax: (847) 700-4081     www.ual.com

*Air transportation, passenger and freight services.*

**United Airlines, Hong Kong PRC**

## UNITED PARCEL SERVICE, INC.

55 Glenlake Parkway, NE, Atlanta, GA, 30328

Tel: (404) 828-6000      Fax: (404) 828-6593      www.ups.com

*International package-delivery service.*

**UPS Parcel Delivery Service Ltd., Ste. 602-610 North Tower, World Finance Centre, Harbour City Tsimshatsui, Kowloon Hong Kong PRC**

Tel: 852-2735-3535   Fax: 852-2738-5071

## UNITRODE CORPORATION

7 Continental Blvd., Merrimack, NH, 03054

Tel: (603) 424-2410      Fax: (603) 429-8771      www.unitrode.com

*Mfr. electronic components (analog/linear and mixed-signal).*

**Unitrode Electronics Asia Ltd., Suite 526 West Wing, New World Office Building, 20 Salisbury Road, Kowloon Hong Kong PRC**

Tel: 852-2722-1101   Fax: 852-2369-7596   Contact: Wilkie Wong, Dir.   Emp: 2

## UNIVERSAL CORPORATION

1501 N. Hamilton Street, Richmond, VA, 23230

Tel: (804) 359-9311      Fax: (804) 254-3582      www.universalcorp.com

*Holding company for tobacco and commodities.*

**Universal Leaf Far-East Ltd., 1435 Central Bldg., Queens Rd., Central, Hong Kong PRC**

## UNIVERSAL INSTRUMENTS

90 Bevier Street, S. Dock, Binghamton, NY, 13904

Tel: (607) 779-7522      Fax: (607) 779-7971      www.uic.com

*Mfr./sales of instruments for electronic circuit assembly.*

**Universal Instruments Ltd., Tsimshatsui, Kowloon, Hong Kong PRC**

Tel: 852-2723-2800   Fax: 852-2739-2698

## UOP LLC.

25 East Algonquin Road, Des Plaines, IL, 60017

Tel: (847) 391-2000      Fax: (847) 391-2253      www.uop.com

*Engaged in developing and commercializing technology for license to the oil refining, petrochemical and gas processing industries.*

**Norplex Pacific Div. UOP Hong Kong Ltd., Kowloon, Hong Kong PRC**

## UUNET

22001 Loudoun County Pkwy., Ashburn, VA, 20147

Tel: (703) 206-5600      Fax: (703) 206-5601      www.uu.net

*World's largest Internet service provider; World Wide Web hosting services, security products and consulting services to businesses, professionals, and on-line service providers.*

**UUNET Hong Kong, 18 Harbour Road, Suite 3601 Central Plaza, Wanchai, Hong Kong PRC**

## VARIAN MEDICAL SYSTEMS, INC.

3050 Hansen Way, Palo Alto, CA, 94304-100

Tel: (650) 493-4000      Fax: (650) 424-5358      www.varian.com

*Mfr. microwave tubes and devices, analytical instruments, semiconductor process and medical equipment, vacuum systems.*

**Varian Medical Systems Pacific, Inc., Room 1018-20 - Tower A, Mandarin Plaza 14 Science Museum Rd., Tsimshatsui East Kowloon, Hong Kong PRC**

## VARIAN SEMICONDUCTOR EQUIPMENT ASSOCIATES, INC.

35 Dory Road, Gloucester, MA, 01930

Tel: (978) 281-2000     Fax: (978) 283-5391     www.vsea.com

*Mfr. ion implantation systems.*

**Varian Semiconductor Equipment Assocates, Room 1018-20 Tower A, Mandarin Plaza, 14 Science Museum Road, Tsimshatsui East Kowloon, Hong Kong PRC**

Tel: 852-2724-2836

## VEECO INSTRUMENTS INC.

Terminal Drive, Plainview, NY, 11803

Tel: (516) 349-8300     Fax: (516) 349-9079     www.veeco.com

*Mfr. surface profiler, atomic force microscopes, leak and plating thickness detectors and semiconductor products.*

**Veeco Hong Kong Support Center, Ste. 2207-9 Peregrine Tower, Lippo Ctr., Admiralty, Hong Kong PRC**

Tel: 852-2530-8863   Fax: 852-2530-8123

## VELCRO USA INC.

406 Brown Avenue, Manchester, NH, 03108

Tel: (603) 669-4892     Fax: (603) 669-9271     www.velcro.com

*Mfr./sales of velcro brand hook and loop fasteners, plastic buckles and metal hardware and cable control straps.*

**Velcro Hong Kong Ltd., Rm.1103A Seaview Estate Blk. B, 2-8 Watson Road North Point, Hong Kong PRC**

Tel: 852-2570-3698   Fax: 852-2807-0285

## VERIZON COMMUNICATIONS INC.

1255 Corporate Drive, Irving, TX, 75038

Tel: (972) 507-5000     Fax: (972) 507-5002     www.gte.com

*Engaged in wireline and wireless communications.*

**GTE Intl. Ltd., 11/F Gammon House, 12 Harbour Rd., Hong Kong PRC**

**GTE Sylvania Far East Ltd., 10 Ng Fong St., San Po Kong, Kowloon, Hong Kong PRC**

## VF CORPORATION

1047 North Park Road, Wyomissing, PA, 19610

Tel: (610) 378-1151     Fax: (610) 378-9371     www.vfc.com

*Mfr./marketing apparel including Lee and Wrangler jeans, Jansport backpacks and Healthtex.*

**VF Asia/Pacific Ltd., Flat B, Kader Bldg. 10/F, 22 Kai Cheung Rd., Kowloon Bay, Kowloon, Hong Kong PRC**

## THE VIKING CORPORATION

210 N. Industrial Park Rd., Hastings, MI, 49058

Tel: (616) 945-9501     Fax: (616) 945-9599     www.vikingcorp.com

*Mfr. fire extinguishing equipment.*

**Viking Holding (HK) Limited, Room 905A New Kowloon Plaza, 38 Tai Kok Tsui Road, Tai Kok Tsui Kowloon, Hong Kong PRC**

Tel: 852-2391-1078

## VISHAY SILICONIX INC.

2201 Laurelwood Drive, Santa Clara, CA, 95054

Tel: (408) 988-8000     Fax: (408) 970-3950     www.vishay.com

*Semiconductor components.*

**Vishay Siliconix Hong Kong Ltd., 5-6-7/F Liven House, 61-63 King Yip St., Kowloon, Hong Kong PRC**

## VITAL SIGNS, INC.

20 Campus Road, Totowa, NJ, 07512

Tel: (973) 790-1330        Fax: (973) 790-3307        www.vital-signs.com

*Mfr. disposable medical products for critical care procedures.*

**Vital Signs Hong Kong Ltd.,  Hong Kong PRC**

## VIVITAR CORPORATION

1280 Rancho Conejo Blvd, Newbury Park, CA, 91320

Tel: (805) 498-7008        Fax: (805) 498-5086        www.vivitar.com

*Mfr. photographic equipment, electronic supplies.*

**Vivitar Hong Kong,  Hong Kong PRC**

## WACKENHUT CORPORATION

4200 Wackenhut Dr., Ste. 100, Palm Beach Gardens, FL, 33410

Tel: (561) 622-5656        Fax: (561) 691-6736        www.wackenhut.com

*Security systems and services.*

**Wackenhut Security (HK) Ltd.,  1404A Argyle Centre 1, 688 Nathan Rd., Kowloon, Hong Kong PRC**
Tel: 852-2390-3456   Fax: 852-2789-8311

## WARNER ELECTRIC BRAKE & CLUTCH COMPANY

449 Gardner St., South Beloit, IL, 61080

Tel: (815) 389-3771        Fax: (815) 389-2582        www.warnernet.com

*Global supplier of Power Transmission and Motion Control Solution Systems; automotive, industry brakes, and clutches.*

**Dana Asia c/o Shui Hing Mfg. Co. Ltd.,  Block B Marvel Industrial Building 4/F, 17 Kwai Fung Crescent, Hong Kong PRC**
Tel: 852-2422-0057   Fax: 852-2480-4450

## WARNER-JENKINSON COMPANY, INC.

2526 Baldwin Street, St. Louis, MO, 63106

Tel: (314) 889-7600        Fax: (314) 658-7305

*Mfr. synthetic and natural colors for food, drugs and cosmetics.*

**Warner-Jenkinson Hong Kong,  Mappin House 10/F, 98 Texaco Rd., Tsuen Wan, NT, Hong Kong PRC**

## THE WASHINGTON POST COMPANY

1150 15th St. NW, Washington, DC, 20071

Tel: (202) 334-6000        Fax: (202) 334-4536        www.washpostco.com

*Engaged in magazine publishing, cable and television broadcasting, educational services and the Internet,*

**International Herald Tribune,  1201 K. Wah Centre, 191 Java Road, North Point, Hong Kong PRC**

## WASTE MANAGEMENT, INC.

1001 Fannin Street, Ste. 4000, Houston, TX, 77002

Tel: (713) 512-6200        Fax: (713) 512-6299        www.wastemanagement.com

*Environmental services and disposal company; collection, processing, transfer and disposal facilities.*

**Pacific Waste Management Ltd.,  Room 4114-19 Sun Hung Kai Center, 30 Harbour Rd., Wanchai, Hong Kong PRC**

## TD WATERHOUSE GROUP

100 Wall Street, New York, NY, 10005

Tel: (212) 806-3500        Fax: (212) 361-6656        www.tdwaterhousegroup.com

*Engaged in online brokerage.*

**TD Waterhouse Group, Inc.,  Suite 3413-3422 - Two Pacific Place, 88 Queensway, Hong Kong PRC**
Tel: 852-2801-1112

## WATSON WYATT & COMPANY HOLDINGS

6707 Democracy Blvd., Ste. 800, Bethesda, MD, 20817

Tel: (301) 581-4600      Fax: (301) 581-4937      www.watsonwyatt.com

*Creates compensation and benefits programs for major corporations.*

**Watson Wyatt & Co., 27/F Sun Hung Kai Center, 30 Harbour Rd., Hong Kong PRC**

Tel: 852-2827-8833  Fax: 852-2827-8899   Contact: Paula DeLisle

## WEATHERFORD INTERNATIONAL, INC.

5 Post Oak Blvd, Ste. 1760, Houston, TX, 77227-3415

Tel: (713) 287-8400      Fax: (713) 963-9785      www.weatherford.com

*Oilfield services, products and equipment; mfr. marine cranes for oil and gas industry.*

**Weatherford Intl., 2803 Admiralty Centre, Tower 1, 18 Harcourt Rd., Hong Kong PRC**

## WEIGHT WATCHERS INTERNATIONAL, INC.

175 Crossways Park Dr., Woodbury, NY, 11797

Tel: (516) 390-1400      Fax: (516) 390-1763      www.weightwatchers.com

*Weight loss programs.*

**Weight Watchers Hong Kong, c/o Union Church, 22a Kennedy Road, Mid-Levels, Hong Kong PRC**

## WELCH ALLYN DCD INC.

4341 State Street Road, Skaneateles Falls, NY, 13153

Tel: (315) 685-4100      Fax: (315) 685-4091      www.welchallyn.com

*Mfr. bar code data collection systems.*

**Hand Held Products Asia/Pacific, Tung Sun Commercial Ctr. - Rm 1002, 194-200 Lockhart Road, Wanchai, Hong Kong**

Tel: 852-2511-3050

## WELLS FARGO & COMPANY

PO Box 63710, 420 Montgomery St., San Francisco, CA, 94163

Tel: (415) 396-0855      Fax: (415) 788-7404      www.wellsfargo.com

*Mortgage and general banking and financial services.*

**Wells Fargo HSBC Trade Bank, GPO Box 64 - 1 Queen's Road, Central Hong Kong, Hong Kong PRC**

Tel: 852-2822-1111   Contact: David Eldon

## WESTERN DIGITAL CORPORATION

8105 Irvine Center Drive, Irvine, CA, 92718

Tel: (949) 932-5000      Fax: (949) 932-6629      www.westerndigital.com

*Mfr. hard disk drives, video graphics boards, VLSI.*

**Western Digital Hong Kong, 807-809 Tower 3, 33 Canton Rd., Tsim Shat Sui, Hong Kong PRC**

## WESTVACO CORPORATION

299 Park Ave., New York, NY, 10171

Tel: (212) 688-5000      Fax: (212) 318-5055      www.westvaco.com

*Mfr. paper, packaging, chemicals.*

**Westvaco Hong Kong Ltd., Bank of America Tower 3705, 12 Harcourt Rd., Central, Hong Kong PRC**

## WEYERHAEUSER COMPANY

33663 Weyerhaeuser Way South, Federal Way, WA, 98003

Tel: (253) 924-2345      Fax: (253) 924-2685      www.weyerhaeuser.com

*Wood and wood fiber products.*

**Weyerhaeuser Far East Ltd., GPO Box 3818, Hong Kong, PRC**

## WHIRLPOOL CORPORATION

2000 N. M-63, Benton Harbor, MI, 49022-2692

Tel: (616) 923-5000      Fax: (616) 923-5443      www.whirlpoolcorp.com

*Mfr./market home appliances: Whirlpool, Roper, KitchenAid, Estate, and Inglis.*

**Whirlpool Asia Appliance Group, 16/F Paliburg Plaza, 68 Yee Wo St., Causeway Bay Hong Kong PRC**

## WHITE & CASE LLP

1155 Ave. of the Americas, New York, NY, 10036-2767

Tel: (212) 819-8200      Fax: (212) 354-8113      www.whitecase.com

*International law firm.*

**White & Case Solicitors, 9/F Glouster Tower, The Landmark, 11 Pedder St., Hong Kong PRC**

Tel: 852-2822-8700   Fax: 852-2845-9070   Contact: George K. Crozer

## W. A. WHITNEY COMPANY

650 Race Street, PO Box 1206, Rockford, IL, 61105-1206

Tel: (815) 964-6771      Fax: (815) 964-3175      www.wawhitney.com

*Mfr. hydraulic punch/plasma cutting metal fabricating equipment.*

**W.A. Whitney Esterline Technologies Ltd., 2502-3 Railway Plaza, 39 Chatham Rd. S., T.S.T., Kowloon, Hong Kong PRC**

Tel: 852-2311-9339

## WILBUR-ELLIS COMPANY

PO Box 7454, San Francisco, CA, 94120

Tel: (415) 772-4000      Fax: (415) 772-4011      www.wilburellis.com

*Marketing, distribution, formulation of agricultural products and industrial specialty chemicals and raw materials.*

**Connell Bros. Co. (HK) Ltd., 601 Stanhope House, 738 King's Rd., North Point, Hong Kong PRC**

## WINTHROP, STIMSON, PUTNAM & ROBERTS

One Battery Park Plaza, 31st Fl., New York, NY, 10004-1490

Tel: (212) 858-1000      Fax: (212) 858-1500      www.winstim.com

*International law firm.*

**Winthrop, Stimson, Putnam & Roberts, 2505 Asia Pacific Finance Tower, Citibank Plaza, 3 Garden Rd., Central Hong Kong PRC**

Tel: 852-2530-3400   Fax: 852-2530-3355

## WONDERWARE CORPORATION

100 Technology Dr., Irvine, CA, 92618

Tel: (949) 727-3200      Fax: (949) 727-3270      www.wonderware.com

*Mfr. industrial strength applications software and services.*

**Tecoford, Ltd., Tsuen Wan, N.T., Hong Kong PRC**

Tel: 852-36024458

## WORLD COURIER INC.

1313 Fourth Ave., New Hyde Park, NY, 11041

Tel: (516) 354-2600      Fax: (516) 354-2644      www.worldcourier.com

*International courier service.*

**World Courier Hong Kong, 404 Air Cargo Terminal Office Bldg., Kaitak Intl. Airport, Hong Kong PRC**

## WORLD MINERALS INC.

130 Castilian Drive, Santa Barbara, CA, 93117

Tel: (805) 562-0200    Fax: (805) 562-0298    www.worldminerals.com

*Mfr. premium quality diatomite and perlite products.*

**World Minerals Hong Kong,  Ste. 3715 Sun Hung Kai Ctr. 37/F, 30 Harbour Rd., Wanchai, Hong Kong PRC**

## WORLDCOM, INC.

500 Clinton Center Drive, Clinton, MS, 39060

Tel: (601) 360-8600    Fax: (601) 360-8616    www.wcom.com

*Telecommunications company serving local, long distance and Internet customers domestically and internationally.*

**WorldCom International,  10/F Sino Faovour Centre, 1 Yip Street, Chai Wan, Hong Kong PRC**

Tel: 852-2110-8899  Fax: 852-2505-0308   Contact: Fred Moss, Reg. Ops. Mgr.

**WorldCom International,  24/F Central Tower, 28 Queen's Road, Central, Hong Kong PRC**

Tel: 852-2110-8800  Fax: 852-2521-6933   Contact: Magdala Hoi, Gen. Mgr.

## WM WRIGLEY JR. COMPANY

410 N. Michigan Ave., Chicago, IL, 60611-4287

Tel: (312) 644-2121    Fax: (312) 644-0353    www.wrigley.com

*Mfr. chewing gum.*

**The Wrigley Co. (HK) Ltd.,  186-191 Connaught Rd. West, Hong Kong, PRC**

## WYETH-AYERST INTERNATIONAL INC.

150 Radnot-Chester Road, St. Davids, PA, 19087

Tel: (610) 902-4100    Fax: (610) 989-4586    www.ahp.com/wyeth

*Antibiotics and pharmaceutical products.*

**Wyeth (Hong Kong) Ltd.,  25/Shell Tower - Times Square, 1 Matheson Street Causeway Bay, Hong Kong PRC**

## XEROX CORPORATION

800 Long Ridge Road, PO Box 1600, Stamford, CT, 06904

Tel: (203) 968-3000    Fax: (203) 968-4312    www.xerox.com

*Mfr. document processing equipment, systems and supplies.*

**Xerox (China) Ltd..,  1308 Harcourt House 39, Glouster Rd. Manchai, Hong Kong PRC**

Tel: 852-2861-5333

## XILINX INC.

2100 Logic Drive, San Jose, CA, 95124-3400

Tel: (408) 559-7778    Fax: (408) 559-7114    www.xilinx.com

*Programmable logic and related development systems software.*

**Xilinx Asia Pacific,  Unit No. 4312 Tower 2 Metroplaza, Hing Fong Rd., Kwai Fong NT, Hong Kong PRC**

Tel: 852-2424-5200

## XIRCOM, INC.

2300 Corporate Center Drive, Thousand Oaks, CA, 91320

Tel: (805) 376-9300    Fax: (805) 376-9311    www.xircom.com

*Mfr. PC card network adapters and modems.*

**Xircom Asia Limited,  Central Building 11/F, 1 Pedder Street, Central Hong Kong PRC**

Tel: 852-2841-7813

## XTRA CORPORATION

1807 Park 270 Dr., Ste. 400, St. Louis, MO, 63146-4020

Tel: (314) 579-9320       Fax: (314) 579-0299       www.xtracorp.com

*Holding company: leasing.*

**XTRA International, Centre Point 20/F, 185 Gloucester Rd., Wanchai, Hong Kong PRC**

**XTRA International, Hong Kong PRC**

## YAHOO! INC.

3420 Central Expressway, Santa Clara, CA, 95051

Tel: (408) 731-3300       Fax: (408) 731-3301       www.yahoo-inc.com

*Internet media company providing specialized content, free electronic mail and community offerings and commerce.*

**Yahoo! Inc., Hong Kong PRC**

## YORK INTERNATIONAL CORPORATION

631 South Richland Ave., York, PA, 17403

Tel: (717) 771-7890       Fax: (717) 771-6212       www.york.com

*Mfr. heating, ventilating, air conditioning and refrigeration equipment.*

**York Air Conditioning & Refrig. Inc., Unit 5A, Sime Darby Ind. Centre, 420-424 Kwun Tong Rd., Kowloon, Hong Kong PRC**

**York International Corporation, Unit 1008 10/F Tower II, 123 Hoi Bun Road Kwun Tong, Kowloon Hong Kong PRC**

Tel: 852-2331-9286   Fax: 852-2331-9840

## YOUNG & RUBICAM INC.

285 Madison Ave., New York, NY, 10017

Tel: (212) 210-3000       Fax: (212) 370-3796       www.yr.com

*Advertising, public relations, direct marketing and sales promotion, corporate and product ID management.*

**Dentsu Young & Rubicam Brand Communications, Suite 418 Mount Parker House, 1111 King's Rd., Hong Kong PRC**

Tel: 852-2884-6668   Fax: 852-2885-3208

## YSI INC.

1725 Brannum Lane, PO Box 279, Yellow Springs, OH, 45387

Tel: (937) 767-7241       Fax: (937) 767-9353       www.ysi.com

*Mfr. analyzers, measure instruments and electrical components.*

**YSI Hong Kong, Hong Kong PRC**

# Hungary

## 3COM CORPORATION

5400 Bayfront Plaza, Santa Clara, CA, 95052-8145

Tel: (408) 326-5000      Fax: (408) 326-5001      www.3com.com

*Develop/mfr. computer networking products and systems.*

**3Com Magyarorszag,  Lajos utca 48-66, H-1036 Budapest, Hungary**

Tel: 36-1-250-83-41    Fax: 36-1-250-83-47

## 3M

3M Center, St. Paul, MN, 55144-1000

Tel: (651) 733-1110      Fax: (651) 733-9973      www.mmm.com

*Mfr. diversified products for industry, health care, imaging, communications, transport, safety, consumer, etc.*

**3M Hungaria Kft.,  Vaci ut 110, H-1133 Budapest, Hungary**

Tel: 36-1-270-7777   Fax: 36-1-267-1803

## ABBOTT LABORATORIES

One Abbott Park, Abbott Park, IL, 60064-3500

Tel: (847) 937-6100      Fax: (847) 937-1511      www.abbott.com

*Development/mfr./sale diversified health care products and services.*

**Abbott Laboratories Ltd.,  Varosligeti Fasor 47-49, H-1071 Budapest, Hungary**

## THE AES CORPORATION

1001 North 19th Street, Arlington, VA, 22209

Tel: (703) 522-1315      Fax: (703) 528-4510      www.aesc.com

*Gas and electric utility.*

**AES Borsod,  Budapest, Hungary**

## AGRIBRANDS INTERNATIONAL, INC.

9811 South Forty Drive, St. Louis, MO, 63124

Tel: (314) 812-0500      Fax: (314) 812-0400      www.agribrands.com

*Produces animal feeds and nutritional products for cattle, poultry, horses and fish.*

**Agribrands Europe,  Moszkva ter 9, H-1024 Budapest, Hungary**

Tel: 36-1-212-5035   Fax: 36-1-212-5763

## AIR EXPRESS INTERNATIONAL CORPORATION

120 Tokeneke Road, PO Box 1231, Darien, CT, 06820

Tel: (203) 655-7900      Fax: (203) 655-5779      www.aeilogistics.com

*International air freight forwarder.*

**AEI,  c/o Cargoplan Ferihegy Terminal 1 LR1, Air Cargo Terminal 1, LR1 Air Cargo Terminal, H-1675 Budapest Hungary**

Tel: 36-1-296-6756   Fax: 36-1-296-8621

## ALCOA INC.

Alcoa Center, 201 Isabella Street, Pittsburgh, PA, 15215-5858

Tel: (412) 553-4545      Fax: (412) 553-4498      www.alcoa.com

*World's leading producer of aluminum and alumina; mining, refining, smelting, fabricating and recycling.*

**AFL/Michels GmbH,  Enying, Hungary**

**AFL/Stribel GmbH,  Mor, Hungary**

**Alcoa-Köföém KFT,  Székesfehérvöár, Hungary**

CSI Hungary Mfg. and Trading, L.L.C., Székesfehérvöár, Hungary

## AMERICAN & EFIRD, INC.

PO Box 507, Mt. Holly, NC, 28120

Tel: (704) 827-4311    Fax: (704) 822-6054    www.amefird.com

*Mfr. industrial sewing thread for worldwide industrial and consumer markets.*

R Corp Budapest Ltd., 1085 Budapest, Jozsef Krt 29, II EM 201206 Budapest Hungary

## AMERICAN APPRAISAL ASSOCIATES INC.

411 E. Wisconsin Ave., Milwaukee, WI, 53202

Tel: (414) 271-7240    Fax: (414) 271-1041    www.american-appraisal.com

*Valuation consulting services.*

American Appraisal Hungary Co. Ltd., Ganz u. 16, 3/F #304, Pf. 18 (1277), H-1027 Budapest II, Hungary

## AMERICAN EXPRESS COMPANY

American Express Tower, World Financial Center, New York, NY, 10285-4765

Tel: (212) 640-2000    Fax: (212) 619-9802    www.americanexpress.com

*Travel, travelers cheques, charge card and financial services.*

American Express Hungary Kft., Budapest, Hungary

## AMERICAN INTERNATIONAL GROUP INC. (AIG)

70 Pine Street, New York, NY, 10270

Tel: (212) 770-7000    Fax: (212) 509-9705    www.aig.com

*Worldwide insurance and financial services.*

AIG Hungary, Szigelvari Utca 7, 1083 Budapest, Hungary

## AMWAY CORPORATION

7575 Fulton Street East, Ada, MI, 49355-0001

Tel: (616) 787-6000    Fax: (616) 787-6177    www.amway.com

*Mfr./sale home care, personal care, nutrition and houseware products.*

Amway Hungaria Marketing Kft., Kalvaria ter 7, H-1089 Budapest, Hungary

## ANDERSEN CONSULTING

100 S. Wacker Drive, Ste. 1059, Chicago, IL, 60606

Tel: (312) 693-0161    Fax: (312) 693-0507    www.ac.com

*Provides management and technology consulting services.*

Andersen Consulting, East-West Business Ctr., Rákóczi ú 1-3, H-1088 Budapest, Hungary
Tel: 36-1-266-7707   Fax: 36-1-266-7709

## ANDERSEN WORLDWIDE

33 West Monroe Street, Chicago, IL, 60603

Tel: (312) 580-0033    Fax: (312) 507-6748    www.arthurandersen.com

*Accounting and audit, tax and management consulting services.*

Andersen Worldwide, East-West Business Ctr., Rakoczi u. 1-3 , H-1088 Budapest, Hungary
Tel: 36-1-266-9744

## ANIXTER INTERNATIONAL INC..

4711 Golf Road, Skokie, IL, 60076

Tel: (847) 677-2600    Fax: (847) 677-8557    www.anixter.com

*Distributor wiring systems/products for voice, video, data and power applications.*

Anixter Hungary, Terra Park D8, Budaors - 2040, Hungary

## AON CORPORATION

123 North Wacker Drive, Chicago, IL, 60606

Tel: (312) 701-3000    Fax: (312) 701-3100    www.aon.com

*Insurance brokers worldwide; underwrites accident and health insurance, specialty and professional insurance; and provides risk management consultation.*

**AON Hungary Ltd.,  Pest Ctr., H-1071 Budapest, Hungary**

Tel: 36-1-351-7644   Fax: 36-1-351-7649   Contact: George Csik

## APPLERA CORPORATION

761 Main Avenue, Norwalk, CT, 06859-0001

Tel: (203) 762-1000    Fax: (203) 762-6000    www.applera.com

*Leading supplier of systems for life science research and related applications.*

**Analytical Instruments,  Szegedi ut 35-37, H-1135 Budapest, Hungary**

## ARENT FOX KINTNER PLOTKIN & KAHN, PLC

1050 Connecticut Ave., N.W., Washington, DC, 20036-5339

Tel: (202) 857-6000    Fax: (202) 857-6395    www.arentfox.com

*International law firm.*

**Arent Fox Kintner Plotkin & Kahn, PLLC,  Nagymezo Ut 44, H-1065 Budapest, Hungary**

## ARROW ELECTRONICS INC.

25 Hub Drive, Melville, NY, 11747

Tel: (516) 391-1300    Fax: (516) 391-1640    www.arrow.com

*Distributor of electronic components.*

**Spoerle Electronic Budapest,  Vaci ut 45, 1134 Budapest, Hungary**

## AT&T BROADBAND, LLC

9197 South Peoria, Englewood, CO, 80112

Tel: (720) 875-5500    Fax: (720) 875-4984    www.broadband.att.com

*Provides broadband technology services; digital TV, digital telephone and high-speed cable internet services.*

**Westel 450/900,  Budapest, Hungary**

## AUTODESK INC.

111 McInnis Parkway, San Rafael, CA, 94903

Tel: (415) 507-5000    Fax: (415) 507-6112    www.autodesk.com

*Develop/marketing/support computer-aided design, engineering, scientific and multimedia software products.*

**Autodesk Ltd.,  Arpad Ctr., Arboc u.6., H-1134 Budapest  Hungary**

Tel: 36-1-359-9882   Fax: 36-1-359-9884

## AUTOMATIC SWITCH CO. (ASCO)

50-60 Hanover Rd., Florham Park, NJ, 07932

Tel: (973) 966-2000    Fax: (973) 966-2628    www.asco.com

*Mfr. solenoid valves, emergency power controls, pressure and temp. switches.*

**Asco Magnesszelep Kft.,  Mikovinyi S. U. 2-4, H-1037 Budapest, Hungary**

Tel: 36-1-387-4811   Fax: 36-1-250-2383   Contact: L. Malmos

## AVERY DENNISON CORPORATION

150 N. Orange Grove Blvd., Pasadena, CA, 91103

Tel: (626) 304-2000    Fax: (626) 792-7312    www.averydennison.com

*Mfr. pressure-sensitive adhesives and materials, office products, labels, tags, retail systems, Carter's Ink and specialty chemicals.*

**Dennison/WW Office Products,  Mogyorodi ut 32, H-1149 Budapest, Hungary**

Tel: 36-1-252-7864   Fax: 36-1-383-2394

**AVNET INC.**

2211 South 47th Street, Phoenix, AZ, 85034

Tel: (480) 643-2000    Fax: (480) 643-4670    www.avnet.com

*Distributor electronic components, computers and peripherals.*

**Avnet Elektronika KFT,  Taboz u. 6, H-1037 Budapest, Hungary**

Tel: 36-1436-7210   Fax: 36-1250-7647

**AVON PRODUCTS INC.**

1345 Avenue of the Americas, New York, NY, 10105-0196

Tel: (212) 282-5000    Fax: (212) 282-6049    www.avon.com

*Mfr./distributor beauty and related products, fashion jewelry, gifts and collectibles.*

**Avon Cosmetics Hungary KFT,  Kosma u.4, H-1108 Budapest, Hungary**

Tel: 36-1-262-5555   Fax: 36-1-262-3374   Contact: Erika Nagy

**AZON CORPORATION**

2204 Ravine Road, Kalamazoo, MI, 49004-3506

Tel: (616) 385-5942    Fax: (616) 385-5937    www.azonintl.com

*Designs and manufactures special multi-component chemical metering, mixing and dispensing machines.*

**Azon Hungary Ltd.,  Azon Repro Centre, Belgrad, rpk, 1315, H1056 Budapest, Hungary**

**BAKER & McKENZIE**

130 East Randolph Drive, Ste. 2500, Chicago, IL, 60601

Tel: (312) 861-8000    Fax: (312) 861-2899    www.bakerinfo.com

*International legal services.*

**Baker & McKenzie,  Andrassy-ut 125, H-1062 Budapest, Hungary**

Tel: 36-1- 251-5777   Fax: 36-1- 342-0513

**BATES WORLDWIDE INC.**

405 Lexington Ave., New York, NY, 10174

Tel: (212) 297-7000    Fax: (212) 986-0270    www.batesww.com

*Advertising, marketing, public relations and media consulting.*

**Bates Saatchi & Saatchi Advertising,  Alvinci ut 16, H-1022 Budapest, Hungary**

Tel: 36-1-212-4039   Fax: 36-1-212-5506   Contact: Neil Hardwick, Dir.

**BAXTER HEALTHCARE CORPORATION**

One Baxter Parkway, Deerfield, IL, 60015

Tel: (847) 948-2000    Fax: (847) 948-3948    www.baxter.com

*Pharmaceutical preparations, surgical/medical instruments and cardiovascular products.*

**Baxter Kft.,  Dozsa Gy. u.44, H-1076 Budapest, Hungary**

**BBDO WORLDWIDE**

1285 Ave. of the Americas, New York, NY, 10019

Tel: (212) 459-5000    Fax: (212) 459-6645    www.bbdo.com

*Multinational group of advertising agencies.*

**BBDO Budapest,  Budapest, Hungary**

**BDO SEIDMAN, LLP    BELGIUM**

Two Prudential Plaza, 180 N. Stetson Ave., Ste. 2300, Chicago, IL, 60601

Tel: (312) 240-1236    Fax: (312) 240-3329    www.bdo.com

*International accounting and financial consulting firm.*

**BDO Kontroll KFT,  Belgrád rkp 13-15, H-1056 Budapest, Hungary**

Tel: 36-1-266-6445   Fax: 36-1-266-6438   Contact: Zaltán Gerendy

## BECKMAN COULTER, INC.

4300 N. Harbor Boulevard, Fullerton, CA, 92834

Tel: (714) 871-4848     Fax: (714) 773-8898     www.beckmancoulter.com

*Develop/mfr./marketing automated systems and supplies for biological analysis.*

**Diagon Kft. (Diagnostics), 1325 Ujpest 1. Pf. 41, Baross u. 52, 1047 Budapest Hungary**

## BELDEN, INC.

7701 Forsyth Blvd., Ste. 800, St. Louis, MO, 63015

Tel: (314) 854-8000     Fax: (314) 854-8001     www.belden.com

*Mfr. electronic wire and cable products.*

**Belden-Dunákabel, Hengermalom Straße 43, 1116 Budapest, Hungary**

## LOUIS BERGER INTERNATIONAL INC.

100 Halsted Street, East Orange, NJ, 07019

Tel: (201) 678-1960     Fax: (201) 672-4284     www.louisberger.com

*Consulting engineers, engaged in architecture, environmental and advisory services.*

**Louis Berger SA, Batthyany u. 46 II./4, H-1015 Budapest, Hungary**

Tel: 36-1-214-1281   Fax: 36-1-214-1281

## BEST WESTERN INTERNATIONAL

6201 North 24th Place, Phoenix, AZ, 85106

Tel: (602) 957-4200     Fax: (602) 957-5740     www.bestwestern.com

*International hotel chain.*

**Grand Hotel Hungaria, Budapest, Hungary**

## BESTFOODS, INC.

700 Sylvan Ave., International Plaza, Englewood Cliffs, NJ, 07632-9976

Tel: (201) 894-4000     Fax: (201) 894-2186     www.bestfoods.com

*Consumer foods products; corn refining.*

**Bestfoods Hungary Ltd., Szabadsag ut. 117, H-2040 Budapest, Hungary**

Tel: 36-23-507-153   Fax: 36-23-507-142   Contact: Jitte de Jong, Mgr.

## BMC INDUSTRIES INC.

One Meridian Crossings, Ste. 850, Minneapolis, MN, 55423

Tel: (612) 851-6000     Fax: (612) 851-6065     www.bmcind.com

*Design/mfr./marketing precision etched products, electroformed components, special printed circuits, ophthalmic devices.*

**BMC Hungary, Tauaszmezo U-6, H-2800 Tatabanya, Hungary**

Tel: 36-34-512-242   Fax: 36-34-512-267   Contact: John Springer   Emp: 250

## THE BOSTON CONSULTING GROUP

Exchange Place, 31st Fl., Boston, MA, 02109

Tel: (617) 973-1200     Fax: (617) 973-1339     www.bcg.com

*Management consulting company.*

**The Boston Consulting Group, Madach Trade Center, Madach Imre Ut. 13-14, H-1075 Budapest, Hungary**

Tel: 36-1-328-5020

## BOZELL GROUP

40 West 23rd Street, New York, NY, 10010

Tel: (212) 727-5000     Fax: (212) 645-9173     www.bozell.com

*Advertising, marketing, public relations and media consulting.*

**Bozell Hungary, Kft, Dereglye u. 5/B, H-1036 Budapest, Hungary**

Tel: 36-1-367-3747   Fax: 36-1-387-7696   Contact: Martin Hoffman, Mng. Dir.

## BRISTOL-MYERS SQUIBB COMPANY

345 Park Ave., New York, NY, 10154-0037

Tel: (212) 546-4000      Fax: (212) 546-4020      www.bms.com

*Pharmaceutical and food preparations, medical and surgical instruments.*

**ConvaTec KFT Budapest,  Kis Buda Ctr. Irodahaz, Frankel Leo U 30-34, H-1023 Budapest, Hungary**

**Pharmavit, Div. Bristol-Myers Squibb,  Veresegyhaz, Levai utca 5, 2112 Hungary**

## LEO BURNETT, DIV. B-COM 3 GROUP

35 West Wacker Drive, Chicago, IL, 60601

Tel: (312) 220-5959      Fax: (312) 220-6533      www.bcom3group.com

*Engaged in advertising, marketing, media buying and planning, and public relations.*

**Leo Burnett Budapest, Ltd.,  Budapest, Hungary**

## BURSON-MARSTELLER

230 Park Ave., New York, NY, 10003-1566

Tel: (212) 614-4000      Fax: (212) 614-4262      www.bm.com

*Public relations/public affairs consultants.*

**Golden Burson-Marsteller,  Lajos u. 46-66 Fifth Fl., H-1036 Budapest, Hungary**

Tel: 36-1-250-8560    Fax: 36-1-250-8535

## CATERPILLAR INC.

100 NE Adams Street, Peoria, IL, 61629-6105

Tel: (309) 675-1000      Fax: (309) 675-1182      www.cat.com

*Mfr. earth/material-handling and construction machinery and equipment and engines.*

**Caterpillar Hungary Component Mfg. Co. (COSA) (JV),  Godollo, Hungary**

## C.B. RICHARD ELLIS

533 South Fremont Ave., Los Angeles, CA, 90071-1712

Tel: (213) 613-3123      Fax: (213) 613-3535      www.cbrichardellis.com

*Commercial real estate services.*

**CB Richard Ellis Kft,  Lajos utca 48-66, 1036 Budapest, Hungary**

## CH2M HILL INC.

6060 South Willow Drive, Greenwood Village, CO, 80111

Tel: (303) 771-0900      Fax: (303) 770-2616      www.ch2m.com

*Consulting engineers, planners, economists and scientists.*

**CH2M Hill,  Budapest, Hungary**

Tel: 36-1-214-8303

## CHECKPOINT SYSTEMS, INC.

101 Wolf Drive, Thorofare, NJ, 08086

Tel: (856) 848-1800      Fax: (856) 848-0937      www.checkpointsystems.com

*Mfr. test, measurement and closed-circuit television systems.*

**Checkpoint Systems Hungary Kft.,  Dembinzky ul., H-1115 Budapest, Hungary**

Tel: 36-1-3050-100    Fax: 36-1-3050-101    Contact: Gabor Kekesi, Gen. Mgr.

## CHESTERTON BINSWANGER INTERNATIONAL

Two Logan Square, 4th Floor, Philadelphia, PA, 19103-2759

Tel: (215) 448-6000      Fax: (215) 448-6238      www.cbbi.com

*Real estate and related services.*

**Blumenauer Immobilien,  Varosmajor u. 41, H-1122 Budapest, Hungary**

**Chesterdon International plc.,  1082 Budapest Futo, Utca 52, Hungary**

## A.W. CHESTERTON COMPANY

225 Fallon Road, Stoneham, MA, 02180

Tel: (781) 438-7000     Fax: (781) 438-8971     www.chesterton.com

*Packing gaskets, sealing products systems, etc.*

**Chesterton Hungary Kft., Gödölloi ut 115, H-2146 Mogyorod, Hungary**

## CISCO SYSTEMS, INC.

170 West Tasman Drive, San Jose, CA, 95134-1706

Tel: (408) 526-4000     Fax: (408) 526-4100     www.cisco.com

*Develop/mfr./market computer hardware and software networking systems.*

**Cisco Systems Hungary, Cisco Systems Magyarorszag KFT., Vaci utca 81, H-1056 Budapest, Hungary**

Tel: 36-1-235-1100   Fax: 36-1-235-1111

## THE CIT GROUP

1211 Avenue of the Americas, New York, NY, 10036

Tel: (212) 536-1390     Fax: (212) 536-1912     www.citgroup.com

*Engaged in commercial finance.*

**Newcourt, Div. CIT Group, Zazlos u. 18, Budapest 1443, Hungary**

Tel: 36-1223-1202

## CITIGROUP, INC.

153 East 53rd Street, New York, NY, 10043

Tel: (212) 559-1000     Fax: (212) 559-3646     www.citigroup.com

*Provides insurance and financial services worldwide.*

**Citibank N.A., Citibank Tower, Bank Ctr., Szabadsag ter 7, H-1052 Budapest Hungary**

Contact: Richard D. Jackson

## CNA FINANCIAL CORPORATION

CNA Plaza, Chicago, IL, 60685

Tel: (312) 822-5000     Fax: (312) 822-6419     www.cna.com

*Commercial property/casualty insurance policies.*

**CNA Hungary, Budapest, Hungary**

## THE COASTAL CORPORATION

Nine Greenway Plaza, Houston, TX, 77046-0995

Tel: (713) 877-1400     Fax: (713) 877-6752     www.coastalcorp.com

*Oil refining, natural gas, related services; independent power production.*

**Coastal Hungary Ltd., Budapest, Hungary**

## THE COLEMAN COMPANY, INC.

2111 E. 37th St., North, Wichita, KS, 67219

Tel: (316) 832-2700     Fax: (316) 832-2794     www.colemanoutdoors.com

*Mfr./distributor/sales camping and outdoor recreation products.*

**Camping Gaz Hungaria, Dugonics UTCA 11, H-1043 Budapest, Hungary**

## COMPAQ COMPUTER CORPORATION

20555 State Highway 249, PO Box 692000, Houston, TX, 77269-2000

Tel: (281) 370-0670     Fax: (281) 514-1740     www.compaq.com

*Develop/mfr. personal computers.*

**Compaq Computer Kft., Királyhágo tér 8-9, H-1126 Budapest, Hungary**

Tel: 36-1-201-8776   Fax: 36-1-201-9696

## COUDERT BROTHERS

1114 Ave. of the Americas, New York, NY, 10036-7794

Tel: (212) 626-4400    Fax: (212) 626-4120    www.coudert.com

*International law firm.*

**Coudert Brothers Associated Office,, Nagy É Trócsányi Ügyrédi Iroda, Pálya u. 9, H-1012 Budapest, Hungary**

Tel: 36-1-212-0444   Fax: 36-1-212-0443

## D'ARCY MASIUS BENTON & BOWLES INC. (DMB&B)

1675 Broadway, New York, NY, 10019

Tel: (212) 468-3622    Fax: (212) 468-2987    www.dmbb.com

*Full service international advertising and communications group.*

**DMB&B Europe, Iranyl Utca 1, 11em 3, H-1056 Budapest, Hungary**

## DDB NEEDHAM WORLDWIDE INC.

437 Madison Ave., New York, NY, 10022

Tel: (212) 415-2000    Fax: (212) 415-3417    www.ddbn.com

*Advertising agency.*

**DDB/Hungary, Budapest, Hungary**

## DEBEVOISE & PLIMPTON

919 Third Avenue, New York, NY, 10022

Tel: (212) 909-6000    Fax: (212) 909-6836    www.debevoise.com

*International law firm.*

**Debevoise & Plimpton, Revay, Köz 2 III/I, H-1065 Budapest, Hungary**

Tel: 36-1-312-8067   Fax: 36-1-332-7995   Contact: Eva Tamasi, Office Mgr.   Emp: 4

## DELOITTE TOUCHE TOHMATSU INTERNATIONAL

1633 Broadway, New York, NY, 10019

Tel: (212) 492-4000    Fax: (212) 392-4154    www.deloitte.com

*Accounting, audit, tax and management consulting services.*

**Deloitte & Touche, Varmegye u. 3-5, H-1052 Budapest, Hungary**

## DEWEY BALLANTINE LLP

1301 Ave. of the Americas, New York, NY, 10019

Tel: (212) 259-8000    Fax: (212) 259-6333    www.deweyballantine.com

*International law firm.*

**Dewey Ballantine LLP, Andrassy ut 60, H-1062 Budapest, Hungary**

Tel: 36-1-374-2660   Fax: 36-1-374-2661

## DHL WORLDWIDE EXPRESS

50 California Avenue, San Francisco, CA, 94111

Tel: (415) 677-6100    Fax: (415) 824-9700    www.dhl.com

*Worldwide air express carrier.*

**DHL Worldwide Express, Rakoczi Ut 1-3, H-1088 Budapest, Hungary**

Tel: 36-1-266-7777

## DIAGNOSTIC PRODUCTS CORPORATION

5700 West 96th Street, Los Angeles, CA, 90045

Tel: (310) 645-8200    Fax: (310) 645-9999    www.dpcweb.com

*Mfr. diagnostic products.*

**Diatron Ltd., Pomázi út 15, H-1037 Budapest, Hungary**

Tel: 36-1-436-0640   Fax: 36-1-436-0649

## DIONEX CORPORATION

1228 Titan Way, PO Box 3603, Sunnyvale, CA, 94086-3603

Tel: (408) 737-0700    Fax: (408) 730-9403    www.dionex.com

*Develop/mfr./market chromatography systems and related products.*

**Chrompack,  CP-Analitika Kft, Telepes u. 113-115 a/1., H-1147 Budapest, Hungary**

## THE DUN & BRADSTREET CORPORATION

1 Diamond Hill Road, Murray Hill, NJ, 07974

Tel: (908) 665-5000    Fax: (908) 665-5524    www.dnbcorp.com

*Provides corporate credit, marketing and accounts-receivable management services and publishes credit ratings and financial information.*

**Dun & Bradstreet Hungaria Kft.,  Varmegye u.3-5, H 1052 Budapest, Hungary**

Tel: 36-1-267-4190

## EAGLE GLOBAL LOGISTICS (EGL)

15350 Vickery Drive, Houston, TX, 77032

Tel: (281) 618-3100    Fax: (281) 618-3100    www.eaglegl.com

*Ocean/air freight forwarding, customs brokerage, packing and wholesale, logistics management and insurance.*

**Pannon Air Cargo,  Ferihegyi Airport Term 1, H-1185 Budapest, Hungary**

Tel: 36-1-157-8086   Fax: 36-1-157-7487

## EASTMAN CHEMICAL

100 North Eastman Road, Kingsport, TN, 37660

Tel: (423) 229-2000    Fax: (423) 229-1351    www.eastman.com

*Mfr. plastics, chemicals, fibers.*

**Eastman Chemical B.V.,  Buda Busines Ctr. Off. 601, Kapas u. 11-15/601, H-1027 Budapest, Hungary**

Tel: 36-1-202-4615   Fax: 36-1-202-4642   Contact: Laszlo Siroki

## EASTMAN KODAK COMPANY

343 State Street, Rochester, NY, 14650

Tel: (716) 724-4000    Fax: (716) 724-1089    www.kodak.com

*Develop/mfr. photo and chemicals products, information management/video/copier systems, fibers/plastics for various industry.*

**Kodak Kft. Hungary,  Tartsay Vilmos u. 14 3.em, H-1126 Budapest XII, Hungary**

## ECOLAB INC.

370 N. Wabasha Street, St. Paul, MN, 55102

Tel: (651) 293-2233    Fax: (651) 293-2379    www.ecolab.com

*Develop/mfr. premium cleaning, sanitizing and maintenance products and services for the hospitality, institutional, and residential markets.*

**Ecolab Ltd.,  Bucharest, Hungary**

Tel: 36-1-372-5555

## ECOLOGY AND ENVIRONMENT INC.

368 Pleasant View Drive, Lancaster, NY, 14086-1397

Tel: (716) 684-8060    Fax: (716) 684-0844    www.ecolen.com

*Environmental, scientific and engineering consulting.*

**E&E Budapest Environmental Ltd.,  Toboz u. 19, H-1037 Budapest, Hungary**

## J.D. EDWARDS & COMPANY

One Technology Way, Denver, CO, 80237

Tel: (303) 334-4000    Fax: (303) 334-4970    www.jdedwards.com

*Computer software products.*

**Synergon Informatika Rt.,  Vaci ut 168/A, H-1138 Budapest, Hungary**

Tel: 36-1-270-5120   Fax: 36-1-270-5132

## EL PASO ENERGY CORPORATION

PO Box 2511, 1001 Louisiana, Houston, TX, 77252-2511

Tel: (713) 420-2131      Fax: (713) 420-4266      www.epenergy.com

*Energy and gas.*

**El Paso Energy Hungary,  Dunaujvaros, Hungary**

## ELECTRONIC DATA SYSTEMS CORPORATION (EDS)

5400 Legacy Dr., Plano, TX, 75024

Tel: (972) 605-6000      Fax: (972) 605-2643      www.eds.com

*Provides professional services; management consulting, e.solutions, business process management and information solutions.*

**EDS Hungary Kft.,  Egressy út 20, Budapest 1149, Hungary**

Tel: 36-1-221-5258    Contact: Attila Ritter

## EMERY WORLDWIDE

One Lagoon Drive, Ste. 400, Redwood City, CA, 94065

Tel: (650) 596-9600      Fax: (650) 596-7901      www.emeryworld.com

*Freight transport, global logistics and air cargo.*

**Emery Worldwide (Hungary), KFT.,  Terminal 1 LRI Cargo Bldg. 1st Fl., H-1675 Budapest-Ferihegy Airport, Hungary**

## ENRON CORPORATION

1400 Smith Street, Houston, TX, 77002-7369

Tel: (713) 853-6161      Fax: (713) 853-3129      www.enron.com

*Exploration, production, transportation and distribution of integrated natural gas and electricity.*

**Energovill,  Raday Ut 42-44, Budapest 1092 Hungary**

Tel: 36-1-456-4300

## ERICO PRODUCTS INC.

34600 Solon Road, Cleveland, OH, 44139

Tel: (440) 248-0100      Fax: (440) 248-0723      www.erico.com

*Mfr. electric welding apparatus and hardware, metal stampings, specialty fasteners.*

**Erico Products Hungary,  Ceglédi út 1-3, 1107 Budapest, Hungary**

Tel: 36-1-4313-464

## ERNST & YOUNG, LLP

787 Seventh Ave., New York, NY, 10019

Tel: (212) 773-3000      Fax: (212) 773-6350      www.eyi.com

*Accounting and audit, tax and management consulting services.*

**Ernst & Young Kft,  Hermina ut 17, H-1146 Budapest, Hungary**

Tel: 36-1-252-8333    Fax: 36-1-251-8778    Contact: Csaba Repassy

## EURO RSCG WORLDWIDE

350 Hudson Street, New York, NY, 10014

Tel: (212) 886-2000      Fax: (212) 886-2016      www.eurorscg.com

*International advertising agency group.*

**EURO RSCG Budapest,  1023 Daru utca 2/b, Budapest, Hungary**

## EXXON MOBIL CORPORATION

5959 Las Colinas Blvd., Irving, TX, 75039-2298

Tel: (972) 444-1000      Fax: (972) 444-1882      www.exxon.com

*Petroleum exploration, production, refining; mfr. petroleum and chemicals products; coal and minerals.*

**Exxon Mobil, Inc.,  Budapest, Hungary**

## FISHER-ROSEMOUNT

8000 Maryland Ave., Ste. 500, Clayton, MO, 63105-4755

Tel: (314) 746-9900    Fax: (314) 746-9974    www.frco.com

*Mfr. industrial process control equipment.*

**Fisher-Rosemount FKT,  Erzebet Kiralyne utja, 1/c, H-1146 Budapest, Hungary**

## FLEXTRONICS INC. INTERNATIONAL

2241 Lundy Ave., San Jose, CA, 95131-1822

Tel: (408) 428-1300    Fax: (408) 428-0420    www.flextronics.com

*Contract manufacturer for electronics industry.*

**Flextronics International,  8999 Zalalövö, Újmajor út 2, Zalalövö, Hungary**

Tel: 36-92-572-500

## FRITZ COMPANIES, INC.

706 Mission Street, Ste. 900, San Francisco, CA, 94103

Tel: (415) 904-8360    Fax: (415) 904-8661    www.fritz.com

*Integrated transportation, sourcing, distribution and customs brokerage services.*

**Fritz Companies Inc.,  Budapest, Hungary**

## GENERAL ELECTRIC COMPANY

3135 Easton Turnpike, Fairfield, CT, 06431

Tel: (203) 373-2211    Fax: (203) 373-3131    www.ge.com

*Diversified manufacturing, technology and services.*

**General Electric Co.,  Attn: Hungry Office, 3135 Easton Turnpike,  Fairfield CT 06431 USA**

Tel: 518-438-6500

## GENERAL MOTORS ACCEPTANCE CORPORATION

3044 W. Grand Blvd., Detroit, MI, 48202

Tel: (313) 556-5000    Fax: (313) 556-5108    www.gmac.com

*Automobile financing.*

**GMAC Hungary Financial Services Ltd.,  Marvany utca 17, H-1012 Budapest, Hungary**

## GENERAL MOTORS CORPORATION

300 Renaissance Center, Detroit, MI, 48285

Tel: (313) 556-5000    Fax: (313) 556-5108    www.gm.com

*Mfr. full line vehicles, automotive electronics, commercial technologies, telecommunications, space, finance.*

**AC Bakony,  Verszprem, Hungary**

## GETZ BROS & COMPANY, INC.

150 Post Street, Ste. 500, San Francisco, CA, 94108-4750

Tel: (415) 772-5500    Fax: (415) 772-5659    www.getz.com

*Diversified manufacturing, marketing and distribution services and travel services.*

**Getz Bros. & Co. Inc.,  PO Box 136, H-1431 Budapest, Hungary**

**Getz Intl. Travel,  Nephadsereg u.5, H-1055 Budapest, Hungary**

**Intercooperation Co. Ltd.,  H-1158 Budapest Kesmark, Hungary**

Tel: 36-1-416-0374   Fax: 36-1-413-3218   Contact: Lazlo Csiszar   Emp: 350

## THE GILLETTE COMPANY

Prudential Tower Building, Boston, MA, 02199

Tel: (617) 421-7000    Fax: (617) 421-7123    www.gillette.com

*Develop/mfr. personal care/use products: blades and razors, toiletries, cosmetics, stationery.*

**Jafra Cosmetics Hungaria Partnership,  Budapest, Hungary**

## GILSON INC.

3000 W. Beltline Hwy, PO Box 620027, Middleton, WI, 53562-0027

Tel: (608) 836-1551    Fax: (608) 831-4451    www.gilson.com

*Mfr. analytical/biomedical instruments.*

**Allegro Ltd., Szent Laszlo U. 95, H-1135 Budapest, Hungary**

## GRANT THORNTON INTERNATIONAL

800 One Prudential Plaza, 130 E. Randolph Drive, Chicago, IL, 60601-6050

Tel: (312) 856-0001    Fax: (312) 616-7052    www.grantthornton.com

*Accounting, audit, tax and management consulting services.*

**Grant Thornton Consulting Kft., Vamhaz krt 13, H-1093 Budapest, Hungary**

Tel: 36-1-455-2000    Contact: Dr. Dipl. Oec. Anna Kuti

## GREAT LAKES CHEMICAL CORPORATION

500 East 96th Street, Ste. 500, Indianapolis, IN, 46240

Tel: (317) 715-3000    Fax: (317) 715-3050    www.greatlakeschem.com

*Mfr. innovative specialty chemical solutions, including flame retardants and other polymer additives, water treatment chemicals, performance and fine chemicals, fire extinguishants.*

**Chemol RT, Budapest, Hungary**

## GREY GLOBAL GROUP

777 Third Ave., New York, NY, 10017

Tel: (212) 546-2000    Fax: (212) 546-1495    www.grey.com

*International advertising agency.*

**Grey Budapest, Belgrad rkp 26 II em, BP 1395 Pf. 431, H-1056 Budapest, Hungary**

## GTE DIRECTORIES CORPORATION

2200 West Airfield Drive, DFW Airport, TX, 75261-9810

Tel: (972) 453-7000    Fax: (972) 453-7573    www.gte.com

*Publishing telephone directories.*

**Dominion Directory Co., Budapest, Hungary**

## GUARDIAN INDUSTRIES CORPORATION

2300 Harmon Road, Auburn Hills, MI, 48326-1714

Tel: (248) 340-1800    Fax: (248) 340-9988    www.guardian.com

*Mfr. and fabricate flat glass products and insulation materials.*

**Hunguard Float Glass Co., Csorvasi U .31, Oroshaza, Hungary**

Tel: 36-68-411366    Fax: 36-68-411390

## HARRIS CORPORATION

1025 West NASA Blvd., Melbourne, FL, 32919

Tel: (407) 727-9100    Fax: (407) 727-9344    www.harris.com

*Mfr. communications and information-handling equipment, including copying and fax systems.*

**Avnet EMG, setron Electronika Kft., Toboz u.6., H-1037 Budapest, Hungary**

Tel: 36-1-250-4618    Fax: 36-1-250-7646

## H.J. HEINZ COMPANY

600 Grant Street, Pittsburgh, PA, 15219

Tel: (412) 456-5700    Fax: (412) 456-6128    www.heinz.com

*Processed food products and nutritional services.*

**Magyar Foods Ltd., Kecskemet, Hungary**

## HEWITT ASSOCIATES LLC

100 Half Day Road, Lincolnshire, IL, 60069

Tel: (847) 295-5000    Fax: (847) 295-7634    www.hewitt.com

*Employee benefits consulting firm.*

**Hewitt Associates, Bajcsy-Zsilinszky út 57., 1065 Budapest, Hungary**

Tel: 361-475-6020

## HEWLETT-PACKARD COMPANY

3000 Hanover Street, Palo Alto, CA, 94304-1185

Tel: (650) 857-1501    Fax: (650) 857-5518    www.hp.com

*Mfr. computing, communications and measurement products and services.*

**Hewlett-Packard Magyarorszag Kft., Erzebet kiralyne utja 1/c 11th/12th fl., H-1146 Budapest, Hungary**

## HILTON HOTELS CORPORATION

9336 Civic Center Drive, Beverly Hills, CA, 90210

Tel: (310) 278-4321    Fax: (310) 205-7880    www.hiltonhotels.com

*International hotel chain: Hilton International, Vista Hotels and Hilton National Hotels.*

**Hilton International Hotels, Hess András tèr 1-3, H-1014 Budapest, Hungary**

## HONEYWELL INTERNATIONAL INC.

101 Columbia Road, Morristown, NJ, 07962

Tel: (973) 455-2000    Fax: (973) 455-4807    www.honeywell.com

*Develop/mfr. controls for home and building, industry, space and aviation.*

**Honeywell Kft., Gogol u. 13, H-1133 Budapest, Hungary**

Tel: 36-1-451-4300   Fax: 36-1-451-4343

## HORWATH INTERNATIONAL ASSOCIATION

415 Madison Ave., New York, NY, 10017

Tel: (212) 838-5566    Fax: (212) 838-3636    www.horwath.com

*Public accountants and auditors.*

**Horwath Consulting Hungary, Paulay Ede u.13, H-1061 Budapest, Hungary**

**SALDO Penzugyi Szervezoe ee, Tanaacsado Vaallalat Bartok Beela Ut120-122, Budapest, Hungary**

## HYATT CORPORATION

200 West Madison Street, Chicago, IL, 60606

Tel: (312) 750-1234    Fax: (312) 750-8578    www.hyatt.com

*International hotel management.*

**Atrium Hyatt Budapest Hotel, Roosevelt Tér 2, H-1051 Budapest, Hungary**

Tel: 36-1-266-1234   Fax: 36-1-266-9101

## IBM CORPORATION

New Orchard Road, Armonk, NY, 10504

Tel: (914) 765-1900    Fax: (914) 765-7382    www.ibm.com

*Information products, technology and services.*

**IBM Hungary Ltd., Menesi ut. 22, H-1118 Budapest, Hungary**

Tel: 36-1-372-1111   Fax: 36-1-372-1199

## ICC INDUSTRIES INC.

460 Park Ave., New York, NY, 10022

Tel: (212) 521-1700    Fax: (212) 521-1794    www.iccchem.com

*Manufacturing and trading of chemicals, plastics and pharmaceuticals.*

**ICC Chemol Kft., Vaci Ut. 19, Budapest H-1134, Hungary**

Tel: 36-1-238-9200   Fax: 36-1-238-9210

## ICN PHARMACEUTICALS, INC.

3300 Hyland Ave., Costa Mesa, CA, 92626

Tel: (714) 545-0100       Fax: (714) 641-7268       www.icnpharm.com

*Mfr./distribute pharmaceuticals.*

**ICN Pharmaceuticals, Inc., Czararka u. 82-84, H-1025 Budapest II District, Hungary Hungary**

Tel: 36-1-345-5900

## IMG (INTERNATIONAL MANAGEMENT GROUP)

1360 East Ninth Street, Ste. 100, Cleveland, OH, 44114

Tel: (216) 522-1200       Fax: (216) 522-1145       www.imgworld.com

*Manages athletes, sports academies and real estate facilities worldwide.*

**IMG Hungary, Andrassy ut. 97, Budapest 1062, Hungary**

Tel: 36-1-352-2406    Fax: 36-1-352-2410

## INFONET SERVICES CORPORATION

2100 East Grand Ave., El Segundo, CA, 90245-1022

Tel: (310) 335-2600       Fax: (310) 335-4507       www.infonet.com

*Provider of Internet services and electronic messaging services.*

**Infonet Hungary, Naphegy ter.8, H-1016 Budapest, Hungary**

Tel: 36-1-1202-6246    Fax: 36-1-375-8064

## INPRISE CORPORATION

100 Enterprise Way, Scotts Valley, CA, 95066

Tel: (831) 431-1000       Fax: (831) 431-4141       www.inprise.com

*Mfr. development software.*

**Inprise Hungary, Hungaria krt. 79-81, Budapest H-1143, Hungary**

Tel: 36-1-252-8145    Fax: 36-1-252-8773    Contact: Jozsef Hizo

## INTER-CONTINENTAL HOTELS

3 Ravina Drive, Suite 2900, Atlanta, GA, 30346-2149

Tel: (770) 604-2000       Fax: (770) 604-5403       www.interconti.com

*Worldwide hotel and resort accommodations.*

**Hotel Inter-Continental Budapest, Budapest V, Apaczal Csere J.U. 12-14, H-1368 Budapest, Hungary**

Tel: 36-1-32-6333    Fax: 36-1-327-6357

## INTERGRAPH CORPORATION

One Madison Industrial Park, Huntsville, AL, 35894-0001

Tel: (256) 730-2000       Fax: (256) 730-7898       www.intergraph.com

*Develop/mfr. interactive computer graphic systems.*

**Intergraph Hungary Ltd., Istenhegyi Ut. 40/A, H-1126 Budapest, Hungary**

Tel: 36-1-2142007    Fax: 36-1-2149588

## INTERMEC TECHNOLOGIES CORPORATION

6001 36th Ave. West, PO Box 4280, Everett, WA, 98203-9280

Tel: (425) 348-2600       Fax: (425) 355-9551       www.intermec.com

*Mfr./distributor automated data collection systems.*

**Videoton Holding Informatike, Vallalat, PO Box 314, H-8002 Szekesfenervar, Hungary**

## INTERNATIONAL FLAVORS & FRAGRANCES INC.

521 West 57th Street, New York, NY, 10019-2960

Tel: (212) 765-5500       Fax: (212) 708-7132       www.iff.com

*Design/mfr. flavors, fragrances and aroma chemicals.*

**International Flavors & Fragrances, Budapest, Hungary**

**INTERNATIONAL SPECIALTY PRODUCTS, INC.**

1361 Alps Rd., Wayne, NJ, 07470

Tel: (877) 389-3083    Fax: (973) 628-4117    www.ispcorp.com

*Mfr. specialty chemical products.*

**ISP Hungaria, Kenese u.8. 11, H-1113 Budapest XI, Hungary**

Tel: 36-1-385-8288   Fax: 36-1-466-2550

**J. WALTER THOMPSON COMPANY**

466 Lexington Ave., New York, NY, 10017

Tel: (212) 210-7000    Fax: (212) 210-6944    www.jwt.com

*International advertising and marketing services.*

**Partners/J. Walter Thompson Co., Budapest, Hungary**

**JABIL CIRCUIT, INC.**

10560 Ninth St. North, St. Petersburg, FL, 33716

Tel: (727) 557-9749    Fax: (727) 579-8529    www.jabil.com

*Mfr. printed circuit boards, electronic components and systems.*

**Jabil Circuit Hungary, 3580 Tiszaujvaros, Huszar Andor ut 1, Tiszaujvarosi Ipari Park, (Budapest) Hungary**

Tel: 36-49-54-8500

**JOHNSON & JOHNSON**

One Johnson & Johnson Plaza, New Brunswick, NJ, 08933

Tel: (732) 524-0400    Fax: (732) 214-0334    www.jnj.com

*Mfr./distributor/R&D pharmaceutical, health care and cosmetic products.*

**Johnson & Johnson Kft., Hun u.2., 1135 Budapest, Hungary**

**S C JOHNSON & SON INC.**

1525 Howe St., Racine, WI, 53403

Tel: (414) 260-2000    Fax: (414) 260-2133    www.scjohnsonwax.com

*Home, auto, commercial and personal care products and specialty chemicals.*

**S.C. Johnson Kft., Hungary-1124 Budapest, Apor Vilmos ter 6, H-1016 Budapest, Hungary**

**JOHNSON CONTROLS INC.**

5757 N. Green Bay Ave., PO Box 591, Milwaukee, WI, 53201-0591

Tel: (414) 228-1200    Fax: (414) 228-2077    www.johnsoncontrols.com

*Mfr. facility management and control systems and auto seating.*

**Johnson Controls International Kft., Fertö u I/D, H-1107 Budapest, Hungary**

Tel: 36-1-263-3033   Fax: 36-30-263-1317   Contact: Istvan Dombovari, Branch Mgr.

**JONES LANG LASALLE**

101 East 52nd Street, New York, NY, 10022

Tel: (212) 688-8181    Fax: (212) 308-5199    www.jlw.com

*International marketing consultants, leasing agents and property management advisors.*

**Jones Lang Wootton, Budapest, Hungary**

**KAISER ENGINEERS INC.**

9300 Lee Highway, Fairfax, VA, 22031

Tel: (703) 934-3600    Fax: (703) 934-9740    www.icfkaiser.com

*Engineering, construction and consulting services.*

**Kaiser Engineers, Budapest, Hungary**

Tel: 36-1-1060-697

## KENNAMETAL INC.

State Rte. 981, Latrobe, PA, 15650

Tel: (724) 539-5000     Fax: (724) 539-4710     www.kennametal.com

*Tools, hard carbide and tungsten alloys for metalworking industry.*

**Hardt Gepforgalmazo Bt.,  Serhaz U. 3, H-4027 Debrecen, Hungary**

Tel: 36-52-431060    Fax: 36-52-431060

## KIMBERLY-CLARK CORPORATION

351 Phelps Drive, Irving, TX, 75038

Tel: (972) 281-1200     Fax: (972) 281-1435     www.kimberly-clark.com

*Mfr./sales/distribution of consumer tissue, household and personal care products.*

**Kimberly-Clark Corp.,  Budapest, Hungary**

## LESTER B. KNIGHT & ASSOCIATES INC.

549 West Randolph Street, Chicago, IL, 60661

Tel: (312) 346-2300     Fax: (312) 648-1085

*Architecture, engineering, planning, operations and management consulting.*

**Knight Wendling Consulting Ktt,  Teleki Blanka u 15-17, H-1142 Budapest, XIV, Hungary**

## KNOWLES ELECTRONICS INC.

1151 Maplewood Drive, Itasca, IL, 60131

Tel: (630) 250-5100     Fax: (630) 250-0575     www.knowleselectronics.com

*Microphones and loudspeakers.*

**Ruf Electronics Kft.,  Harsfa utca, 8400 Ajka, Hungary**

## KORN/FERRY INTERNATIONAL

1800 Century Park East, Los Angeles, CA, 90067

Tel: (310) 843-4100     Fax: (310) 553-6452     www.kornferry.com

*Executive search; management consulting.*

**Korn/Ferry International,  Chazar Andras U.9, H-1146 Budapest, Hungary**

Tel: 36-1-352-0027    Fax: 36-1-352-0026

## KPMG INTERNATIONAL LLP

345 Park Avenue, New York, NY, 10022

Tel: (201) 307-7000     Fax: (201) 930-8617     www.kpmg.com

*Accounting and audit, tax and management consulting services.*

**KPMG Hungária KFT,  XIII Váci út 99, H-1139 Budapest, Hungary**

Tel: 36-1-270-7100    Fax: 36-1-270-7101    Contact: Michael Kevehazi, Sr. Ptnr.

## LANCER CORPORATION

6655 Lancer Blvd, San Antonio, TX, 78219

Tel: (210) 310-7000     Fax: (210) 310-7252     www.lancercorp.com

*Mfr. beverage dispensing equipment.*

**Lancer Hungary,  Isaszegi út 67, H-2100 Gödöllõ, Hungary**

Tel: 36-28-417-179    Fax: 36-28416-881

## LEVI STRAUSS & COMPANY

1155 Battery St., San Francisco, CA, 94111-1230

Tel: (415) 544-6000     Fax: (415) 501-3939     www.levistrauss.com

*Mfr./distributor casual wearing apparel.*

**Levi Strauss Trading Kft.,  Rakoczi Str. 42, Emke Bldg., H-1072 Budapest, Hungary**

Tel: 36-1-327-7600    Fax: 36-1-267-9937

## ELI LILLY & COMPANY

Lilly Corporate Center, Indianapolis, IN, 46285

Tel: (317) 276-2000    Fax: (317) 277-6579    www.lilly.com

*Mfr. pharmaceuticals and animal health products.*

**Lilly Hungaria KFT,  Madach I.U 13-14 (7th Fl.), H-1075 Budapest, Hungary**

Tel: 36-1-328-5100   Fax: 36-1-328-5101

## LOCKHEED MARTIN CORPORATION

6801 Rockledge Drive, Bethesda, MD, 20817

Tel: (301) 897-6000    Fax: (301) 897-6652    www.imco.com

*Design/mfr./management systems in fields of space, defense, energy, electronics and technical services.*

**Aeroplex of Central Europe, Ltd.,  Ferihegy International Airport, Technical Base Gate oDo Bldg. A 3rd Fl., H-1185 Budapest, Hungary**

Tel: 36-1-157-7007   Fax: 36-1-167-6787

**Aeroplex of Central Europe, Ltd.,  PO Box 186, H-1675 Budapest, Hungary**

## LOCTITE CORPORATION

1001 Trout Brook Crossing, Rocky Hill, CT, 06067-3910

Tel: (860) 571-5100    Fax: (860) 571-5465    www.loctite.com

*Mfr./sale industrial adhesives, sealants and coatings..*

**Loctite Hungary Ltd.,  Tarogato ut 2-4, H-1021 Budapest, Hungary**

Tel: 36-1-274-2458   Fax: 36-1-176-2737

## LOWE LINTAS & PARTNERS WORLDWIDE

One Dag Hammarskjold Plaza, New York, NY, 10017

Tel: (212) 605-8000    Fax: (212) 605-4705    www.interpublic.com

*Full-service, integrated marketing communications company/advertising agency.*

**Ammirati Puris Lintas Hungary,  Emke Bldg., Rakoczi ut 42, H-1072 Budapest, Hungary**

Tel: 36-1-268-1320   Fax: 36-1-26801320   Contact: Pierre-Emmanuel Marie, Mng. Dir.

## LUCENT TECHNOLOGIES, INC.

600 Mountain Ave., Murray Hill, NJ, 07974-0636

Tel: (908) 582-3000    Fax: (908) 582-2576    www.lucent.com

*Design/mfr. wide range of public and private networks, communication systems and software, data networking systems, business telephone systems and microelectronics components.*

**Lucent Technologies Hungary Ltd.,  Vaci ut 168, H-1138 Budapest, Hungary**

Tel: 36-1-270-9500

## M/A-COM INC.

1011 Pawtucket Boulevard, Lowell, MA, 01853-3295

Tel: (978) 442-5000    Fax: (978) 442-5354    www.macom.com

*Mfr. electronic components, semiconductor devices and communications equipment.*

**Tavkozlest Innovations Co.,  Ungvar U-6466, H-1142 Budapest, Hungary**

## MAGNETEK

26 Century Blvd., Ste. 600, Nashville, TN, 37214

Tel: (615) 316-5100    Fax: (615) 316-5181    www.magnetek.com

*Mfr. fractional horsepower electric motors.*

**MagneTek Power,  Pomaz, Hungary**

## MANPOWER INTERNATIONAL INC.

5301 N. Ironwood Rd., PO Box 2053, Milwaukee, WI, 53201-2053

Tel: (414) 961-1000      Fax: (414) 961-7081      www.manpower.com

*Temporary help, contract service, training and testing.*

**Manpower, Hungaria KFT, H-1146 Budapest, Hungary**

Tel: 36-1-252-1578   Fax: 36-1-251-7014

## MARRIOTT INTERNATIONAL INC.

10400 Fernwood Rd., Bethesda, MD, 20817

Tel: (301) 380-3000      Fax: (301) 380-5181      www.marriott.com

*Hotel services.*

**Budapest Marriott Hotel, Budapest, Hungary**

## MARSH & McLENNAN COS INC.

1166 Ave. of the Americas, New York, NY, 10036-2774

Tel: (212) 345-5000      Fax: (212) 345-4808      www.marshmac.com

*Insurance agents/brokers, pension and investment management consulting services.*

**J&H Marsh & McLennan Budapest Kft., Vaci ut. 110, H-1133 Budapest, Hungary**

Tel: 36-1-465-4200   Fax: 36-1-465-4280   Contact: Jozef Klinger

## McCANN-ERICKSON WORLDGROUP

750 Third Ave., New York, NY, 10017

Tel: (212) 984-3644      Fax: (212) 984-2629      www.mccann.com

*International advertising and marketing services.*

**McCann-Erickson Budapest, Budakeszi UT 55, H-1021 Budapest 2, Hungary**

## McDONALD'S CORPORATION

McDonald's Plaza, Oak Brook, IL, 60523

Tel: (630) 623-3000      Fax: (630) 623-7409      www.mcdonalds.com

*Fast food chain stores.*

**McDonald's Corp., Budapest, Hungary**

## McKINSEY & COMPANY

55 East 52nd Street, New York, NY, 10022

Tel: (212) 446-7000      Fax: (212) 446-8575      www.mckinsey.com

*Management and business consulting services.*

**McKinsey & Company, Alexander Court, Nagysandor Jozsef u.6.,H-1054 Budapest, Hungary**

Tel: 36-1-248-2000   Fax: 36-1-248-2001

## MECHANICAL DYNAMICS, INC.

2301 Commonwealth Blvd., Ann Arbor, MI, 48105

Tel: (734) 994-3800      Fax: (734) 994-6418      www.adams.com

*Mfr. Adams prototyping software to automotive industry.*

**Tarok Mernokiroda BT, Karinthy F ut. 44 IX. e., H-1111 Budapest, Hungary**

Tel: 36-1-165-4377   Fax: 36-1-165-4495

## MICRO AGE, INC.

2400 South MicroAge Way, Tempe, AZ, 85282-1896

Tel: (480) 366-2000      Fax: (480) 966-7339      www.microage.com

*Computer systems integrator, software products and telecommunications equipment.*

**MicroAge, Inc., Budapest, Hungary**

## MICROSOFT CORPORATION

One Microsoft Way, Redmond, WA, 98052-6399

Tel: (425) 882-8080      Fax: (425) 936-7329      www.microsoft.com

*Computer software, peripherals and services.*

**Microsoft Hungary Kft,  Madach Imre 13-14, H-1075 Budapest, Hungary**

Tel: 36-1-268-1668    Fax: 36-1-268-1558

## MODINE MANUFACTURING COMPANY

1500 DeKoven Ave., Racine, WI, 53403

Tel: (262) 636-1200      Fax: (262) 636-1424      www.modine.com

*Mfr. heat-transfer products.*

**Modine Manufacturing Co.,  Mezőkövesd, Hungary**

## MOTOROLA, INC.

1303 East Algonquin Road, Schaumburg, IL, 60196

Tel: (847) 576-5000      Fax: (847) 538-5191      www.motorola.com

*Mfr. communications equipment, semiconductors and cellular phones.*

**Motorola Hungary,  Lajos UT. 48-66, Bii Fl., H-1036 Budapest, Hungary**

Tel: 36-1-250-8329    Fax: 36-1-250-8328

## NABISCO HOLDINGS, CORP.

7 Campus Drive, Parsippany, NJ, 07054

Tel: (973) 682-5000      Fax: (973) 503-2153      www.nabisco.com

*Mfr. consumer packaged food products and tobacco products.*

**Satoraljaujhely Dohanygyar,  Budapest, Hungary**

## NATIONAL STARCH AND CHEMICAL COMPANY

10 Finderne Ave., Bridgewater, NJ, 08807-3300

Tel: (908) 685-5000      Fax: (908) 685-5005      www.nationalstarch.com

*Mfr. adhesives and sealants, resins and specialty chemicals, electronic materials and adhesives, food products, industry starch.*

**National Starch & Chemical Ltd.,  Batthyany Utca. 28-11-8, H-1195 Budapest, Hungary**

Tel: 36-1-282-2226    Fax: 36-1-281-2954

## A .C. NIELSEN COMPANY

177 Broad Street, Stamford, CT, 06901

Tel: (203) 961-3000      Fax: (203) 961-3190      www.acnielsen.com

*Market and consumer research firm.*

**Nielsen Marketing Research Kft.,  Nyat Utca 32, 4/F, H-1075 Budapest, Hungary**

## NORDSON CORPORATION

28601 Clemens Road, Westlake, OH, 44145-4551

Tel: (440) 892-1580      Fax: (440) 892-9507      www.nordson.com

*Mfr. industry application equipment, sealants and packaging machinery.*

**Spett GmbH,  Postyen u.13, 1141 Budapest, Hungary**

Tel: 36-1-222-1951

## NORGREN

5400 S. Delaware Street., Littleton, CO, 80120-1663

Tel: (303) 794-2611      Fax: (303) 795-9487      www.usa.norgren.com

*Mfr. pneumatic filters, regulators, lubricators, valves, automation systems, dryers, push-in fittings.*

**IMI Norgren Kft,  Bathory utca 130, H-1196 Budapest, Hungary**

Tel: 36-1-2811-182    Fax: 36-1-2823-788

## OFFICE DEPOT, INC.

2200 Old Germantown Road, Delray Beach, FL, 33445

Tel: (561) 278-4800     Fax: (561) 265-4406     www.officedepot.com

*Discount office product retailer with warehouse-style superstores.*

**Elso Iroda Superstore Kft., Polus Center, Szentmihalyi UT.131, H-1152 Budapest, Hungary**

Tel: 36-1-419-4151   Fax: 36-1-461-419-4220   Contact: Istvan Miholec, Gen. Mgr.

## OHAUS CORPORATION

29 Hanover Road, PO Box 900, Florham Park, NJ, 07932-0900

Tel: (973) 377-9000     Fax: (973) 593-0359     www.ohaus.com

*Mfr. balances and scales for laboratories, industry and education.*

**Ohaus, Hatarhalom u 4, 1173 Budapest, Hungary**

## ORC MACRO INTERNATIONAL INC.

11785 Beltsville Dr., Calverton, MD, 20705-3119

Tel: (301) 572-0200     Fax: (301) 572-0999     www.macroint.com

*Engaged in research and evaluation, training, consulting and information technology.*

**TQ Center, Batthyany Ter 23, H-9022 Gyor, Hungary**

## OTIS ELEVATOR COMPANY

10 Farm Springs Road, Farmington, CT, 06032

Tel: (860) 676-6000     Fax: (860) 676-5111     www.otis.com

*Mfr. elevators and escalators.*

**Otis Felvono Kft., Hustzi ut 34, H-1033 Budapest, Hungary**

## OWENS-ILLINOIS, INC.

One SeaGate, PO Box 1035, Toledo, OH, 43666

Tel: (419) 247-5000     Fax: (419) 247-2839     www.o-i.com

*Largest mfr. of glass containers in the US; plastic containers, compression-molded closures and dispensing systems.*

**Continental PET Technologies, Inc., Gyor, Hungary**

**Oroshaza Glass Manufacturing and Trading, Kft., Oroshaza, Hungary**

## PAREXEL INTERNATIONAL CORPORATION

195 West Street, Waltham, MA, 02154

Tel: (781) 487-9900     Fax: (781) 487-0525     www.parexel.com

*Provides contract medical, biotechnology, and pharmaceutical research and consulting services.*

**PAREXEL International, Pest Ctr., Peterdy Utca 15, H-1071 Budapest, Hungary**

Tel: 36-1-351-7659

## PFIZER INC.

235 East 42nd Street, New York, NY, 10017-5755

Tel: (212) 573-2323     Fax: (212) 573-7851     www.pfizer.com

*Research-based, global health care company.*

**Pfizer Biogal LLC, Budapest, Hungary**

## PHARMACIA CORPORATION

100 Route 206 North, Peapack, NJ, 07977

Tel: (908) 901-8000     Fax: (908) 901-8379     www.pharmacia.com

*Mfr. pharmaceuticals, agricultural products, industry chemicals.*

**Pharmacia & Upjohn, Istenhegyi ut 18, H-1126 Budapest, Hungary**

## PHARMACIA MONSANTO

800 N. Lindbergh Boulevard, St. Louis, MO, 63167

Tel: (314) 694-1000     Fax: (314) 694-7625     www.monsanto.com

*Life sciences company focusing on agriculture, nutrition, pharmaceuticals, health and wellness and sustainable development.*

**Monsanto Co. Chemical Group,  Verhalm Utca 12-16, 1023 Budapest, Hungary**

Tel: 36-1-345-0671

## PHELPS DODGE CORPORATION

2600 North Central Ave., Phoenix, AZ, 85004-3089

Tel: (602) 234-8100     Fax: (602) 234-8337     www.phelpsdodge.com

*Copper, minerals, metals and special engineered products for transportation and electrical markets.*

**Columbian Chemicals Co.,  Budapest, Hungary**

**Columbian Tiszai Carbon,  Tiszuajvaros, Hungary**

## PIONEER HI-BRED INTERNATIONAL INC.

400 Locust Street, Ste. 800, Des Moines, IA, 50309

Tel: (515) 248-4800     Fax: (515) 248-4999     www.pioneer.com

*Agricultural chemicals, farm supplies, biological products, research.*

**Pioneer Hi-Bred,  Lajos Utca 48-66, H-1036 Budapest, Hungary**

## PIONEER-STANDARD ELECTRONICS, INC.

6065 Parkland Blvd., Cleveland, OH, 44124

Tel: (440) 720-8500     Fax: (440) 720-8501     www.pios.com

*Mfr./distribution of electronic parts for computers and networking equipment.*

**Eurodis Microdis Electronics Kft.,  Vaci ut 19, H-1134 Budapest, Hungary**

## PRICEWATERHOUSECOOPERS LLP

1301 Ave. of the Americas, New York, NY, 10019

Tel: (212) 596-7000     Fax: (212) 259-1301     www.pwcglobal.com

*Accounting and auditing, tax and management, and human resource consulting services.*

**PriceWaterhouseCoopers,  Rumbach Center, Rumbach Sebestyen utca 21, H-1075 Budapest, Hungary**

Tel: 36-1-269-6910   Fax: 36-1-269-6936

## PROCTER & GAMBLE COMPANY

One Procter & Gamble Plaza, Cincinnati, OH, 45202

Tel: (513) 983-1100     Fax: (513) 562-4500     www.pg.com

*Personal care, food, laundry, cleaning and industry products.*

**Procter & Gamble KTT,  Pf.243, H-1391 Budapest 62., Hungary**

Tel: 36-1-451-1100   Fax: 36-1-451-1391

## PSI NET (PERFORMANCE SYSTEMS INTERNATIONAL INC.)

510 Huntmar Park Drive, Herndon, VA, 22170

Tel: (703) 904-4100     Fax: (703) 904-4200     www.psinet.com

*Internet service provider.*

**PSINet Hungary,  Budapest, Hungary**

## QWEST COMMUNICATIONS INTERNATIONAL INC.

1801 California Street, Ste. 5200, Denver, CO, 80202

Tel: (303) 896-2020     Fax: (303) 793-6654     www.uswest.com

*Tele-communications provider; integrated communications services.*

**Kablekom,  Budapest, Hungary**

Tel: 36-1-165-2466   Fax: 36-1-181-2377

## RADISSON HOTELS INTERNATIONAL

Carlson Pkwy., PO Box 59159, Minneapolis, MN, 55459-8204

Tel: (612) 540-5526          Fax: (612) 449-3400          www.radisson.com

*Hotels and resorts.*

**Radisson Beke Hotel, Terez Korut 43, H-1067 Budapest, Hungary**

**Radisson SAS Beke Hotel, Terez Korut 43, H-1067 Budapest, Hungary**

Tel: 36-1-30-11600    Fax: 36-1-30-11615

## RALSTON PURINA COMPANY

Checkerboard Square, St. Louis, MO, 63164-0001

Tel: (314) 982-1000          Fax: (314) 982-1211          www.ralston.com

*Produces dog and cat food and animal feed.*

**Purina Hage Ltd., Moszkva ter 9, H-1024 Budapest, Hungary**

## RAY & BERNDTSON, INC.

301 Commerce, Ste. 2300, Fort Worth, TX, 76102

Tel: (817) 334-0500          Fax: (817) 334-0779          www.prb.com

*Executive search, management audit and management consulting firm.*

**Ray & Berndtson, Rakoczi ut 42, H-1072 Budapest, Hungary**

Tel: 36-1-327-4598    Fax: 36-1-267-9100    Contact: Joachim Zyla, Mng. Ptnr.

## SAPHIRE INTERNATIONAL LTD.

3060 Main Street, Ste. 202, Stratford, CT, 06614

Tel: (203) 375-8668          Fax: (203) 375-1965          www.dataease.com

*Mfr. applications development software.*

**VT-Soft Kft., Vorosvari Ut 103-105, H-1033 Budapest, Hungary**

## SARA LEE CORPORATION

3 First National Plaza, Chicago, IL, 60602-4260

Tel: (312) 726-2600          Fax: (312) 558-4995          www.saralee.com

*Mfr./distributor food and consumer packaged goods, intimate apparel and knitwear.*

**Compack Douwe Egberts Rt., Landler Jeno u. 23-25, H-1078 Budapest, Hungary**

## SAS INSTITUTE INC.

SAS Campus Drive, Cary, NC, 27513

Tel: (919) 677-8000          Fax: (919) 677-4444          www.sas.com

*Mfr./distributes decision support software.*

**SAS Institute (Hungary) Ltd., Budapest, Hungary**

Tel: 36-1-202-6247    Fax: 36-1-202-5847

## SCANSOFT, INC.

9 Centennial Dr., Peabody, MA, 01960

Tel: (978) 977-2000          Fax: (978) 977-2436          www.scansoft.com

*Mfr. digital imaging software.*

**ScanSoft Hungary Corp., Budapest, Hungary**

Contact: Akos Reszler

## SCHLUMBERGER LIMITED

277 Park Avenue, New York, NY, 10021

Tel: (212) 350-9400          Fax: (212) 350-9564          www.schlumberger.com

*Engaged in oil and gas services, metering and payment systems, and produces semiconductor testing equipment and smart cards.*

**Schlumberger Measurements, Rezső u. 5-7, 1089 Budapest, Hungary**

## SCI SYSTEMS INC.

2101 W. Clinton Avenue, Huntsville, AL, 35807

Tel: (256) 882-4800    Fax: (256) 882-4804    www.sci.com

*R/D and mfr. electronics systems for commerce, industry, aerospace, etc.*

**SCI Systems Hungary, 2800 Tatabanya, Kota Jozsef utca, Hungary**

Tel: 36-34-515-600

## SHARED MEDICAL SYSTEMS CORPORATION

51 Valley Stream Pkwy, Malvern, PA, 19355

Tel: (610) 219-6300    Fax: (610) 219-3124    www.smed.com

*Computer-based information processing for healthcare industry.*

**SMS Hungary (SMS Magyarország kft.), Hungária krt.162, H-1146 Budapest, Hungary**

Tel: 36-1-2527345

## SHEARMAN & STERLING

599 Lexington Ave., New York, NY, 10022-6069

Tel: (212) 848-4000    Fax: (212) 848-7179    www.shearman.com

*Law firm engaged in general American and international financial and commercial practice.*

**Shearman & Sterling, Szerb Utca 17-19, H-1056 Budapest, Hungary**

## SIEGMUND AND ASSOCIATES, INC.

49 Pavilion Avenue, Providence, RI, 02905

Tel: (401) 785-2600    Fax: (401) 785-3110    www.siegmundgroup.com

*Engaged in civil engineering services, including design of infrastructure elements, water supply and wastewater collection systems and transportation projects.*

**Marlett Kft., 1084 Budapest, Nagyfuvaros u. 6, Hungary**

Tel: 36-1-314-0082    Fax: 36-1-314-0082    Contact: Tibor Bekenyi

**NOVIA Ltd., 3535 Miskolc, Rakoczi u.11, Hungary**

Tel: 36-46-327-924    Fax: 36-46-411-764

## SILICON GRAPHICS INC.

2011 N. Shoreline Blvd., Mountain View, CA, 94043-1389

Tel: (650) 960-1980    Fax: (650) 961-0595    www.sgi.com

*Design/mfr. special-effects computer graphic systems and software.*

**Silicon Graphics, Budapest, Hungary**

## SPENCER STUART MANAGEMENT CONSULTANTS

401 North Michigan Ave., Ste. 3400, Chicago, IL, 60611

Tel: (312) 822-0080    Fax: (312) 822-0116    www.spencerstuart.com

*Executive recruitment firm.*

**Spencer Stuart & Associates Inc., Riado U. 12, H-1026 Budapest, Hungary**

Tel: 36-1-200-0850    Fax: 36-1-394-1097    Contact: Richard Kohlmann

## SPRAYING SYSTEMS COMPANY

PO Box 7900, Wheaton, IL, 60189-7900

Tel: (630) 665-5000    Fax: (630) 260-0842    www.spray.com

*Designs and manufactures industrial spray nozzles.*

**Spraying Systems GmbH, Lova u. 10.ll. Em.3, H-9028 Gyor, Hungary**

## SQUIRE, SANDERS & DEMPSEY

127 Public Square, Key Tower, Ste. 4900, Cleveland, OH, 44114-1304

Tel: (216) 479-8500    Fax: (216) 479-8780    www.ssd.com

*International law firm.*

**Squire, Sanders & Dempsey, Andrassy ut. 64, H-1062 Budapest, Hungary**

Tel: 36-1-312-7654    Fax: 36-1-312-7682    Contact: Blaise Pasztory

## THE ST. PAUL COMPANIES, INC.

385 Washington Street, St. Paul, MN, 55102

Tel: (651) 310-7911   Fax: (651) 310-8294   www.stpaul.com

*Provides investment, insurance and reinsurance services.*

**ÁB-Aegon Általanos Biztosito Rt.,  Üllöi únit 1, H-1091 Budapest, Hungary**

## SUN MICROSYSTEMS, INC.

901 San Antonio Road, Palo Alto, CA, 94303

Tel: (650) 960-1300   Fax: (650) 856-2114   www.sun.com

*Computer peripherals and programming services.*

**Sun Microsystems Magyarorszag Kft.,  Kapa's u 11-15, H-1027 Budapest, Hungary**

## SUPERIOR INDUSTRIES INTERNATIONAL, INC.

7800 Woodley Ave., Van Nuys, CA, 91406-1788

Tel: (818) 781-4973   Fax: (818) 780-5631   www.superiorindustries.com

*Designs and manufactures motor vehicle parts and accessories for sale to original equipment mfrs. (OEMs) and the automotive aftermarket.*

**SUOFTEC,  Tatabanya, Hungary**

## SYBRON INTERNATIONAL CORPORATION

411 E. Wisconsin Ave., Milwaukee, WI, 53202

Tel: (414) 274-6600   Fax: (414) 274-6561   www.sybron.com

*Mfr. products for laboratories, professional orthodontic and dental markets.*

**Erie Scientific Hungary Kft.,  Koerberki u. 36, 1502 Budapest Pf. 56, H-1112 Budapest, Hungary**

## TBWA CHIAT/DAY

488 Madison Avenue, 6th Floor, New York, NY, 10022

Tel: (212) 804-1000   Fax: (212) 804-1200   www.tbwachiat.com

*International full service advertising agency.*

**Fokusz TBWA,  Budapest, Hungary**

## TELLABS INC.

4951 Indiana Ave. 6303788800, Lisle, IL, 60532-1698

Tel: (630) 378-8800   Fax: (630) 679-3010   www.tellabs.com

*Design/mfr./service voice/data transport and network access systems.*

**Tellabs Hungary,  EMKE Building, Rakoczi Ut. 42, Budapest H-1072, Hungary**

## TENNECO PACKAGING CORPORATION OF AMERICA

1900 West Field Court, Lake Forest, IL, 60045

Tel: (847) 482-2000   Fax: (847) 482-2181   www.agplus.net/tenneco

*Mfr. custom packaging, aluminum and plastic molded fibre, corrugated containers.*

**PCA Budafok Ltd.,  Gyar u15, H-1222 Budapest, Hungary**

## TEXAS INSTRUMENTS INC.

8505 Forest Lane, Dallas, TX, 75243

Tel: (972) 995-3773   Fax: (972) 995-4360   www.ti.com

*Mfr. semiconductor devices, electronic electro-mechanical systems, instruments and controls.*

**Texas Instruments,  Budapest, Hungary**

## THETFORD CORPORATION

7101 Jackson Road, PO Box 1285, Ann Arbor, MI, 48106

Tel: (734) 769-6000   Fax: (734) 769-2023   www.thetford.com

*Mfr. sanitation products and chemicals.*

**Thetford Hungary (Rep),  Bartók Béla út 138, 1224 Budapest, Hungary**

## THE TRANE COMPANY

3600 Pammel Creek Road, La Crosse, WI, 54601

Tel: (608) 787-2000    Fax: (608) 787-4990    www.trane.com

*Mfr./distributor/service A/C systems and equipment.*

**Trane Hungaria Kft., Rubin Center Office N-305, Dayka Gabor u. 3, H-118 Budapest, Hungary**

## TREDEGAR CORPORATION

1100 Boulders Pkwy., Richmond, VA, 23225

Tel: (804) 330-1000    Fax: (804) 330-1177    www.tredegar.com

*Mfr. plastics and aluminum products; energy (oil and gas).*

**Tredegar Film Products BV, Budapest, Hungary**

## TRUE NORTH COMMUNICATIONS INC.

101 East Erie Street, Chicago, IL, 60611

Tel: (312) 425-6500    Fax: (312) 425-5010    www.truenorth.com

*Holding company, advertising agency.*

**Foote, Cone & Belding Kft., Seregely u. 11, H-1034 Budapest, Hungary**

## UNITED PARCEL SERVICE, INC.

55 Glenlake Parkway, NE, Atlanta, GA, 30328

Tel: (404) 828-6000    Fax: (404) 828-6593    www.ups.com

*International package-delivery service.*

**UPS Hungary Ltd., Kozma utca 4, H-1108 Budapest, Hungary**

Tel: 36-1-262-0000

## UUNET

22001 Loudoun County Pkwy., Ashburn, VA, 20147

Tel: (703) 206-5600    Fax: (703) 206-5601    www.uu.net

*World's largest Internet service provider; World Wide Web hosting services, security products and consulting services to businesses, professionals, and on-line service providers.*

**UUNET Magyarország, Bank Center City Bank Tower, 1054 Budapest, Hungary**

## VERIZON COMMUNICATIONS INC.

1255 Corporate Drive, Irving, TX, 75038

Tel: (972) 507-5000    Fax: (972) 507-5002    www.gte.com

*Engaged in wireline and wireless communications.*

**GTE Yellow Pages Publishing Hungary Kft., Budapest, Hungary**

## VISHAY INTERTECHNOLOGY INC.

63 Lincoln Hwy., Malvern, PA, 19355

Tel: (610) 644-1300    Fax: (610) 296-0657    www.vishay.com

*Mfr. resistors, strain gages, capacitors, inductors, printed circuit boards.*

**Vishay Electronic, Foti ut. 56., 1047 Budapest, Hungary**

Tel: 36-1-233-2236    Fax: 36-1-233-2263

## WAHL CLIPPER CORPORATION

2902 N. Locust Street, Sterling, IL, 61081

Tel: (815) 625-6525    Fax: (815) 625-1193    www.wahlclipper.com

*Mfr. hair clippers, beard and mustache trimmers, shavers, pet clippers and soldering irons.*

**Kuno Moser Kft., Mosonmagyaróvár, Hungary**

## WALBRO CORPORATION, TI GROUP AUTOMOTIVE

6242 Garfield Ave., Cass City, MI, 48726-1325

Tel: (517) 872-2131      Fax: (517) 872-3090      www.walbro.com

*Mfr. motor vehicle accessories and parts, automotive fluid carrying systems.*

**TI Group Automotive Systems, Ipari ut 1, H-5123 Jaszarokszallas, Postafiok 18, Hungary**

Tel: 36-57-531-800

## WEIL, GOTSHAL & MANGES LLP

767 Fifth Ave., New York, NY, 10153

Tel: (212) 310-8000      Fax: (212) 310-8007      www.weil.com

*International law firm.*

**Weil, Gotshal & Manges LLP, Bank Centre, Granite Tower, H-1944 Budapest, Hungary**

Tel: 36-1-302-9100    Fax: 36-1-302-9110    Contact: George Gluck, Ptnr.

## WENDY'S INTERNATIONAL, INC.

428 West Dublin Granville Roads, Dublin, OH, 43017-0256

Tel: (614) 764-3100      Fax: (614) 764-3459      www.wendysintl.com

*Fast food restaurant chain.*

**Wendy's International, Budapest, Hungary**

## WHIRLPOOL CORPORATION

2000 N. M-63, Benton Harbor, MI, 49022-2692

Tel: (616) 923-5000      Fax: (616) 923-5443      www.whirlpoolcorp.com

*Mfr./market home appliances: Whirlpool, Roper, KitchenAid, Estate, and Inglis.*

**Whirlpool Europe B.V., Budapest, Hungary**

## WHITE & CASE LLP

1155 Ave. of the Americas, New York, NY, 10036-2767

Tel: (212) 819-8200      Fax: (212) 354-8113      www.whitecase.com

*International law firm.*

**White & Case LLP, Süba Ctr., Nagymezo utca 44, H-1065 Budapest, Hungary**

Tel: 36-1-269-0550    Fax: 36-1-269-1199    Contact: Duncan G. Calder III

## WM WRIGLEY JR. COMPANY

410 N. Michigan Ave., Chicago, IL, 60611-4287

Tel: (312) 644-2121      Fax: (312) 644-0353      www.wrigley.com

*Mfr. chewing gum.*

**Wrigley Hungaria, KFT., Budapest, Hungary**

## YELLOW CORPORATION

10990 Roe Ave., PO Box 7270, Overland Park, KS, 66207

Tel: (913) 696-6100      Fax: (913) 696-6116      www.yellowcorp.com

*Commodity transportation.*

**FM Hungaria Kft., Akadaly u. 15, H-1183 Budapest, Hungary**

## YORK INTERNATIONAL CORPORATION

631 South Richland Ave., York, PA, 17403

Tel: (717) 771-7890      Fax: (717) 771-6212      www.york.com

*Mfr. heating, ventilating, air conditioning and refrigeration equipment.*

**York International Kft., York Magyaroszag, Vaci ut 206, Budapest H-1138 Hungary**

Tel: 36-1-465-7060

**YOUNG & RUBICAM INC.**
285 Madison Ave., New York, NY, 10017
Tel: (212) 210-3000    Fax: (212) 370-3796    www.yr.com
*Advertising, public relations, direct marketing and sales promotion, corporate and product ID management.*
**Young & Rubicam Hungary,  Budapest, Hungary**

# Iceland

## ABBOTT LABORATORIES

One Abbott Park, Abbott Park, IL, 60064-3500

Tel: (847) 937-6100     Fax: (847) 937-1511     www.abbott.com

*Development/mfr./sale diversified health care products and services.*

**Pharmaco HF,  Horgatuni 2, PO Box 200, 210 Gardabaer, Iceland**

Tel: 354-565-8111

## AIR EXPRESS INTERNATIONAL CORPORATION

120 Tokeneke Road, PO Box 1231, Darien, CT, 06820

Tel: (203) 655-7900     Fax: (203) 655-5779     www.aeilogistics.com

*International air freight forwarder.*

**AEI Iceland,  Hotabakki V/Holtaveg, 104 Reykjavik, Iceland**

Tel: 354-569-8050   Fax: 354-569-8001

## BDO SEIDMAN, LLP    BELGIUM

Two Prudential Plaza, 180 N. Stetson Ave., Ste. 2300, Chicago, IL, 60601

Tel: (312) 240-1236     Fax: (312) 240-3329     www.bdo.com

*International accounting and financial consulting firm.*

**BDO SamEnd ehf,  Ármúli 10, 108 Reykjavik, Iceland**

Tel: 354-568-7210   Fax: 354-568-8352   Contact: Sigurður B. Amporsson

## BOZELL GROUP

40 West 23rd Street, New York, NY, 10010

Tel: (212) 727-5000     Fax: (212) 645-9173     www.bozell.com

*Advertising, marketing, public relations and media consulting.*

**YDDA Advertising Agency,  Grjotagota 7, 101 Reykjavik, Iceland**

Tel: 354-562-2992   Fax: 354-551-7829   Contact: Hallur Baldursson, Mng. Dir.

## BRISTOL-MYERS SQUIBB COMPANY

345 Park Ave., New York, NY, 10154-0037

Tel: (212) 546-4000     Fax: (212) 546-4020     www.bms.com

*Pharmaceutical and food preparations, medical and surgical instruments.*

**Pharmaco, Div. Bristol-Myers Squibb,  Postholf 200, Horgatuni 2 - PO Box 200, IS-212 Gardabaer, Iceland**

Tel: 354-56-58-111

## DELOITTE TOUCHE TOHMATSU INTERNATIONAL

1633 Broadway, New York, NY, 10019

Tel: (212) 492-4000     Fax: (212) 392-4154     www.deloitte.com

*Accounting, audit, tax and management consulting services.*

**Deloitte & Touche,  Armula 40, PO Box 8736, 108 Reykjavik, Iceland**

## DHL WORLDWIDE EXPRESS

50 California Avenue, San Francisco, CA, 94111

Tel: (415) 677-6100     Fax: (415) 824-9700     www.dhl.com

*Worldwide air express carrier.*

**DHL Worldwide Express,  Faxafen 9, 108 Reykjavik, Iceland**

Tel: 354-535-1100   Fax: 354-535-1111

## ERNST & YOUNG, LLP

787 Seventh Ave., New York, NY, 10019

Tel: (212) 773-3000    Fax: (212) 773-6350    www.eyi.com

*Accounting and audit, tax and management consulting services.*

**Endurskodun & Radgjof HF/Ernst & Young International,  Skeifan 11 A, PO Box 8693, 108 Reykjavik, Iceland**

Tel: 354-568-55-11    Fax: 568-96-95-85    Contact: Erna Bryndis Halldorsdottir

## GILSON INC.

3000 W. Beltline Hwy, PO Box 620027, Middleton, WI, 53562-0027

Tel: (608) 836-1551    Fax: (608) 831-4451    www.gilson.com

*Mfr. analytical/biomedical instruments.*

**Groco Hf,  PO Box 83-64, Sudurlandsbraut 6, 128 Reykjavik, Iceland**

## GRANT THORNTON INTERNATIONAL

800 One Prudential Plaza, 130 E. Randolph Drive, Chicago, IL, 60601-6050

Tel: (312) 856-0001    Fax: (312) 616-7052    www.grantthornton.com

*Accounting, audit, tax and management consulting services.*

**Thema ehf., endurskodunarstofa,  Sudurlandsbraut 20, 108 Reykjavik, Iceland**

Contact:
Olafur Sigurdsson

## HENRY SCHEIN, INC.

135 Duryea Rd., Melville, NY, 11747

Tel: (516) 843-5500    Fax: (516) 843-5658    www.henryschein.com

*Mfr. and supply dental equipment.*

**Henry Schein Fides Inc.,  Laufasgata 9, 600 Akureyri, Iceland**

Tel: 35-446-11129

## IBM CORPORATION

New Orchard Road, Armonk, NY, 10504

Tel: (914) 765-1900    Fax: (914) 765-7382    www.ibm.com

*Information products, technology and services.*

**IBM Iceland,  Nyherji, Skaftahlid 24, 105 Reykjavik, Iceland**

Tel: 354-5697-700

## INTERMEC TECHNOLOGIES CORPORATION

6001 36th Ave. West, PO Box 4280, Everett, WA, 98203-9280

Tel: (425) 348-2600    Fax: (425) 355-9551    www.intermec.com

*Mfr./distributor automated data collection systems.*

**Intermec Iceland,  Bildshofda 12, PO Box 8589, 128 Reykjavik, Iceland**

## INTERNATIONAL GAME TECHNOLOGY INC.

9295 Prototype Drive, Reno, NV, 89511

Tel: (702) 448-0100    Fax: (702) 448-1488    www.igtonline.com

*Mfr. slot machines, video gaming machines and gaming terminals.*

**IGT Iceland, Ltd.,  Iceland**
**c/o Deloitte & Touche**
**Armula 40, 108 Reykjavic**
**Iceland**

Tel: 354-588-7622    Fax: 354-588-7632

## KPMG INTERNATIONAL LLP

345 Park Avenue, New York, NY, 10022

Tel: (201) 307-7000    Fax: (201) 930-8617    www.kpmg.com

*Accounting and audit, tax and management consulting services.*

**KPMG Endurskodun hf., Vegmuli 3, 108 Reykjavik, Iceland**

Tel: 354-533-5555   Fax: 354-533-5550   Contact: Tryggvi Jonsson, Ptnr.

## PAPA JOHN'S INTERNATIONAL, INC.

2002 Papa John's Blvd., Louisville, KY, 40299-2334

Tel: (502) 266-5200    Fax: (502) 266-2925    www.papajohns.com

*Retailer and pizza franchiser.*

**Papa John's International Inc., Grensasvegur 3, 108 Reykjavik, Iceland**

Tel: 354-567-8678

## SCHENKER INTERNATIONAL FORWARDERS INC.

150 Albany Ave., Freeport, NY, 11520

Tel: (516) 377-3000    Fax: (516) 377-3005    www.schenkerusa.com

*Freight forwarders.*

**BM Transport HF, Holtabakka v/Holtaveg, PO Box 904, Reykjavik, Iceland**

Tel: 354-588-9977   Fax: 354-588-9949

## SCIENCE APPLICATIONS INTL. CORPORATION (SAIC)

10260 Campus Point Dr., San Diego, CA, 92121

Tel: (858) 826-6000    Fax: (858) 535-7589    www.saic.com

*Engaged in research and engineering.*

**US Naval Hosp Keflavik/Chcs, SAIC/J Falconieri, Keflavikurflugvollur, Keflavik 235 Iceland**

Tel: 354-425-3380   Fax: 354-425-3203

## THE ST. PAUL COMPANIES, INC.

385 Washington Street, St. Paul, MN, 55102

Tel: (651) 310-7911    Fax: (651) 310-8294    www.stpaul.com

*Provides investment, insurance and reinsurance services.*

**Sjova-Almennar tryggingar hg, Kringlan 5, PO Box 5300, 103 Reykjavik, Iceland**

## WESTERN WIRELESS CORPORATION

3650 131st Avenue SE, Ste. 400, Bellevue, WA, 98006

Tel: (425) 586-8700    Fax: (425) 586-8666    www.wwireless.com

*Provides wireless communication services.*

**TAL, Ltd., Div. Western Wireless, 28 Sidumuli, Reykjavik, Iceland**

## WORLD MINERALS INC.

130 Castilian Drive, Santa Barbara, CA, 93117

Tel: (805) 562-0200    Fax: (805) 562-0298    www.worldminerals.com

*Mfr. premium quality diatomite and perlite products.*

**World Minerals Iceland, PO Box 70, Iceland**

Tel: 354-464-1288   Fax: 354-464-1041

# India

## 3COM CORPORATION

5400 Bayfront Plaza, Santa Clara, CA, 95052-8145

Tel: (408) 326-5000     Fax: (408) 326-5001     www.3com.com

*Develop/mfr. computer networking products and systems.*

**3Com Asia Ltd. - India, Ste. 702 7th Fl. International Trade Tower, Nehru Place, New Delhi 110 019 India**

Tel: 91-11-644-3974   Fax: 91-11-623-6509

## 3M

3M Center, St. Paul, MN, 55144-1000

Tel: (651) 733-1110     Fax: (651) 733-9973     www.mmm.com

*Mfr. diversified products for industry, health care, imaging, communications, transport, safety, consumer, etc.*

**Birla 3M Ltd., Jubilee Bldg., 45 Museum Rd., Bangalore 560 025 India**

Tel: 91-80-5588881   Fax: 91-80-5585612

## AAF INTERNATIONAL (AMERICAN AIR FILTER)

215 Central Ave., PO Box 35690, Louisville, KY, 40232-5690

Tel: (502) 637-0011     Fax: (502) 637-0321     www.aafintl.com

*Mfr. air filtration/pollution control and noise control equipment.*

**Kirloskar AAF Ltd., No. 11, Niton Compound, Palace Rd., Bangalore 560 052, India**

Tel: 91-80-220-0226   Fax: 91-80-228-1212

## ABBOTT LABORATORIES

One Abbott Park, Abbott Park, IL, 60064-3500

Tel: (847) 937-6100     Fax: (847) 937-1511     www.abbott.com

*Development/mfr./sale diversified health care products and services.*

**Abbott Laboratories, Ltd., PO Box 1334, Bombay 400 001, India**

Tel: 91-22-272159

## AIR EXPRESS INTERNATIONAL CORPORATION

120 Tokeneke Road, PO Box 1231, Darien, CT, 06820

Tel: (203) 655-7900     Fax: (203) 655-5779     www.aeilogistics.com

*International air freight forwarder.*

**AEI - India, c/o Lemuir Air Express - Head Office, 12 K. Dubash Marg, Fort Bombay Mumbai 400 023, India**

Tel: 91-22-284-4420   Fax: 91-22-204-0806

## AIRGAS, INC.

259 N. Radnor Chester Rd., Ste. 100, Radnor, PA, 19087-5283

Tel: (610) 687-5253     Fax: (610) 687-1052     www.airgas.com

*Engaged in distribution of specialty, industrial, and medical gases.*

**Airgas Management India Pvt. Ltd., Raheja Vihar Evening Star A-303, 119 Tungwa Chandivali Farm Rd., Powai Bombay 400072, India**

Contact: Neil Amber

**Bhoruka Gases Ltd., Whitefield Road, Mahadevapura, Bangalore 560-048, India**

Tel: 91-80-851-0288   Fax: 91-80-851-0365   Contact: M. Gururaj

**Superior Air Products Ltd.,  B1/J-3 Extension Mohan Co-Op Industrial Estate, Mathura Road, Badarpur 110044 New Delhi, India**

Tel: 91-11-694-8725   Fax: 91-11-694-2505   Contact: Ashok Chandra

## ALCOA INC.

Alcoa Center, 201 Isabella Street, Pittsburgh, PA, 15215-5858

Tel: (412) 553-4545       Fax: (412) 553-4498       www.alcoa.com

*World's leading producer of aluminum and alumina; mining, refining, smelting, fabricating and recycling.*

**Alcoa-ACC Industrial Chemicals Ltd.,  Falta, India**

## ALLEGHENY LUDLUM CORPORATION

1000 Six PPG Place, Pittsburgh, PA, 15222

Tel: (412) 394-2805       Fax: (412) 394-2800       www.alleghenyludlum.com

*Mfr. steel and alloys.*

**Allegheny Ludlum,  India**

Tel: 91-22-283-6366   Fax: 91-22-283-7288

## ALLEN TELECOM

25101 Chagrin Boulevard, Beachwood, OH, 44122-5619

Tel: (216) 765-5818       Fax: (216) 765-0410       www.allentele.com

*Mfr. communications equipment, automotive bodies and parts, electronic components.*

**Allen Telecom Inc. - India Liaison Office,  B-256 Ground Fl., Chittaranjan Park, New Delhi 110 019, India**

Tel: 91-11-643-5517   Fax: 91-11-646-8998   Contact: Rajiv Gupta

## ALLEN-BRADLEY COMPANY, INC.

1201 South Second Street, Milwaukee, WI, 53204

Tel: (414) 382-2000       Fax: (414) 382-4444       www.ab.com

*Mfr. electrical controls and information devices.*

**Allen-Bradley India Ltd.,  C-11 Industrial Area, Site 4, Sahibabad, Dist. Ghaziabad 201 010, India**

## ALLERGAN INC.

2525 Dupont Drive, PO Box 19534, Irvine, CA, 92713-9534

Tel: (714) 246-4500       Fax: (714) 246-6987       www.allergan.com

*Mfr. therapeutic eye care products, skin and neural care pharmaceuticals.*

**Alergan India Limited,  North Block Rear Wing-9th Fl., Manipal Centre 47 Dickenson Rd., Bangalore-560 042, India**

Tel: 91-80-555-0476   Fax: 91-80-555-0474

## ALLIANCE CAPITAL MANAGEMENT HOLDING LP

1345 Ave. of the Americas, New York, NY, 10105

Tel: (212) 969-1000       Fax: (212) 969-2229       www.alliancecapital.com

*Engaged in fund management for large corporations.*

**Alliance Capital Management,  Indage House, 82 Dr. Annie Besant Road, Worli Mumbai 400-018, India**

Tel: 91-22-497-8000

## ALLIANCE SEMICONDUCTOR CORPORATION

2675 Augustine Drive, Santa Clara, CA, 95054

Tel: (408) 855-4900       Fax: (408) 855-4999       www.alsc.com

*Mfr. semi-conductors and related chips.*

**Alliance India,  39 Langford Road, Bangalore 560025, India**

Tel: 91-80-224-6452   Fax: 91-80-224-6453

## ALLTEL CORPORATION

1 Allied Drive, Little Rock, AR, 72202

Tel: (501) 905-8000    Fax: (501) 905-6444    www.alltel.com

*Full range outsourcing services.*

**ALLTEL Systems Ltd., India**

## ALPHA INDUSTRIES INC.

20 Sylvan Road, Woburn, MA, 01801

Tel: (781) 935-5150    Fax: (781) 824-4543    www.alphaind.com

*Mfr. electronic and microwave components.*

**Aarjay International Pvt. Ltd., 167 1 Main II Cross, Domuir II Stage, Bangalore 560071 India**

## AMERICAN LOCKER GROUP INC.

608 Allen Street, Jamestown, NY, 14701-3966

Tel: (716) 664-9600    Fax: (716) 483-2822    www.americanlocker.com

*Mfr. coin-operated locks and office furniture.*

**Barnhardt International (India) Ltd., Chennai (Madras) 6000034, India**

Tel: 91-44-8272732

## AMPHENOL CORPORATION

358 Hall Ave., Wallingford, CT, 06492-7530

Tel: (203) 265-8900    Fax: (203) 265-8793    www.amphenol.com

*Mfr. electrictronic interconnect penetrate systems and assemblies.*

**Amphetronix Ltd., 105 Bhosari Ind. Area, Pune 411 026, India**

Tel: 91-20-790-363    Fax: 91-20-790-581

## ANALOG DEVICES INC.

1 Technology Way, Box 9106, Norwood, MA, 02062

Tel: (781) 329-4700    Fax: (781) 326-8703    www.analog.com

*Mfr. integrated circuits and related devices.*

**Analog Devices Asian Sales Inc., 1A Church St., Bangalore 560 001, India**

## ANDERSEN CONSULTING

100 S. Wacker Drive, Ste. 1059, Chicago, IL, 60606

Tel: (312) 693-0161    Fax: (312) 693-0507    www.ac.com

*Provides management and technology consulting services.*

**Andersen Consulting, 17th Fl. Express Towers, Nariman Point, Mumbai 400 021, India**

Tel: 91-22-282-5000    Fax: 91-22-2282-6000

## ANDERSEN WORLDWIDE

33 West Monroe Street, Chicago, IL, 60603

Tel: (312) 580-0033    Fax: (312) 507-6748    www.arthurandersen.com

*Accounting and audit, tax and management consulting services.*

**Andersen Worldwide, 66 Maker Towers F, Cuffe Parade, PO Box 16093 Colaba, Mumbai 400 005 India**

Tel: 91-22-218-2929

**Andersen Worldwide, 11th Fl. - Du Parc Trinity, 17 M.G. Rd., Bangalore 560 001 India**

Tel: 91-80-559-6262

**Andersen Worldwide, 426 World Trade Ctr., Barakhamba Lane, New Delhi 110 001 India**

## AON CORPORATION

123 North Wacker Drive, Chicago, IL, 60606

Tel: (312) 701-3000    Fax: (312) 701-3100    www.aon.com

*Insurance brokers worldwide; underwrites accident and health insurance, specialty and professional insurance; and provides risk management consultation.*

**AON Worldwide / Global Insurance Services Pvt. Ltd., Gresham Assurance House 4th Fl., Sir P.M. Rd., Mumbai 400 001, India**

Tel: 91-22-266-1387  Fax: 91-22-266-3649    Contact: Prabhat Thakker

## APPLE COMPUTER, INC.

One Infinite Loop, Cupertino, CA, 95014

Tel: (408) 996-1010    Fax: (408) 974-2113    www.apple.com

*Personal computers, peripherals and software.*

**Apple Computer International Inc., 5/F Du Parc Trinity, 17 MG Rd., Bangalore 560 001, India**

Tel: 91-80-555-0575  Fax: 91-80-555-0660  Contact: Samit Roy, Gen. Mgr.

## APPLERA CORPORATION

761 Main Avenue, Norwalk, CT, 06859-0001

Tel: (203) 762-1000    Fax: (203) 762-6000    www.applera.com

*Leading supplier of systems for life science research and related applications.*

**Labindia Instruments, Vaitalik USO Road, A-8 Qutab Institutional Area, New Delhi 110067, India**

## ARBOR ACRES FARM INC.

439 Marlborough Road, Glastonbury, CT, 06033

Tel: (860) 633-4681    Fax: (860) 633-2433

*Producers of male and female broiler breeders, commercial egg layers.*

**Arbor Acres Farm India Ltd., PO Box 73, Raipur Rd., Dehra Dun, Uttar Pradesh 248 001, India**

**Getz Bros. & Co., 2 Brabourne Rd., Mumbai 400 001, India**

## ARGO INTERNATIONAL CORPORATION

140 Franklin Street, New York, NY, 10013

Tel: (212) 431-1700    Fax: (212) 431-2206    www.argointl.com

*Distributor electrical spare parts.*

**Argo International India, Judges Colony 1/F, R.T. Nagar, Bangalore India**

## ARIBA, INC.

1565 Charleston Rd., Mountain View, CA, 94043

Tel: (650) 930-6200    Fax: (650) 930-6300    www.ariba.com

*Mfr. software.*

**Ariba India, DBS Business Centre 25, Cunningham Road, Bangalore 560 052, India**

## ARMSTRONG HOLDINGS, INC.

2500 Columbia Avenue, Lancaster, PA, 17604-3001

Tel: (717) 397-0611    Fax: (717) 396-2787    www.armstrong.com

*Mfr. and marketing interior furnishings and specialty products for bldg, auto and textile industry.*

**Inarco Ltd., Armstrong House, 2 Pokhran Road, Thane 400601 Bombay, India**

Tel: 91-22-536-2903  Fax: 91-22-534-8448

## ARROW ELECTRONICS INC.

25 Hub Drive, Melville, NY, 11747

Tel: (516) 391-1300    Fax: (516) 391-1640    www.arrow.com

*Distributor of electronic components.*

**Arrow Elecronics India Ltd., 34/4 Meanee Ave. Tank Road, Bangalore 560042 India**

**Arrow Elecronics India Ltd., Shere-E-Punjab Co-op, Mahakali Caves Road, Andheri E, Bombay 400093 India**

### ARVIN MERITOR INC

2135 W. Maple Rd., Troy, Mi, 48084-7186

Tel: (248) 435-1000    Fax: (248) 435-1393    www.arvinmeritor.com

*Mfr. of automotive exhaust systems and ride control products, axles and power-steering pumps.*

**Arvin Exhaust India Private Limited (JV),  Jakarta, India**

### ASSOCIATED MERCHANDISING CORPORATION

500 Seventh Ave., 2nd Fl., New York, NY, 10018

Tel: (212) 819-6600    Fax: (212) 819-6701    www.theamc.com

*Retail service organization; apparel, shoes and accessories.*

**Associated Merchandising Corp., 2/F World Trade Tower, Barakhamba Rd., New Delhi 110 001, India**

**Associated Merchandising Corp., 220 Backbay Reclamation, Nariman Point, Mumbai 400 021, India**

### ASSOCIATED PRESS INC.

50 Rockefeller Plaza, New York, NY, 10020-1605

Tel: (212) 621-1500    Fax: (212) 621-5447    www.ap.com

*News gathering agency.*

**The Associated Press,  New Delhi, India**

Tel: 91-11-462-8506

### ASSOCIATES FIRST CAPITAL CORPORATION

250 E. Carpenter Freeway, Irving, TX, 75062-2729

Tel: (972) 652-4000    Fax: (972) 652-7420    www.theassociates.com

*Diversified consumer and commercial finance organization which provides finance, leasing and related services.*

**Associates India, Sub. Associates First Capital Corp,  1 Raheja Chancery, 133 Brigade Road, Bangalore 560025, India**

### AT&T BROADBAND, LLC

9197 South Peoria, Englewood, CO, 80112

Tel: (720) 875-5500    Fax: (720) 875-4984    www.broadband.att.com

*Provides broadband technology services; digital TV, digital telephone and high-speed cable internet services.*

**BPL/US West Cellular Ltd.,  Delhi, India**

### AUTODESK INC.

111 McInnis Parkway, San Rafael, CA, 94903

Tel: (415) 507-5000    Fax: (415) 507-6112    www.autodesk.com

*Develop/marketing/support computer-aided design, engineering, scientific and multimedia software products.*

**Autodesk, SAARC,  206 Raheja Plaza, 17 Commissariat Rd., Shoolay Tank Bed Area, Bangalore 560 025 India**

Tel: 91-80-556-4939   Fax: 91-80-556-4897

### AUTOMATIC SWITCH CO. (ASCO)

50-60 Hanover Rd., Florham Park, NJ, 07932

Tel: (973) 966-2000    Fax: (973) 966-2628    www.asco.com

*Mfr. solenoid valves, emergency power controls, pressure and temp. switches.*

**Asco (India) Ltd.,  147 Karapakkan Village, Madras 600 096, India**

Tel: 91-44-496-0455  Fax: 91-44--496-0114  Contact: M. N. Radhakrishnan

## AVERY DENNISON CORPORATION

150 N. Orange Grove Blvd., Pasadena, CA, 91103

Tel: (626) 304-2000    Fax: (626) 792-7312    www.averydennison.com

*Mfr. pressure-sensitive adhesives and materials, office products, labels, tags, retail systems, Carter's Ink and specialty chemicals.*

**APG Avery Dennison India, Narsinghpur Ind Area, Six Kilometre Stone, Delhi Jaipur Highway, Dist. Gurgaon 122001, Haryana New Delhi, India**

Tel: 91-124-371-602  Fax: 91-124-371-601

## AVON PRODUCTS INC.

1345 Avenue of the Americas, New York, NY, 10105-0196

Tel: (212) 282-5000    Fax: (212) 282-6049    www.avon.com

*Mfr./distributor beauty and related products, fashion jewelry, gifts and collectibles.*

**Avon Beauty Products India Pvt. Ltd., M38 Commercial Complex, Greater Kailash II, New Delhi 110 048 India**

Tel: 91-11-623-3920  Fax: 91-11-623-3923   Contact: Mansoor Abdullah, VP

## BANDAG INCORPORATED

2905 North Highway 61, Muscatine, IA, 52761

Tel: (319) 262-1400    Fax: (319) 262-1252    www.bandag.com

*Mfr./sale retread tires.*

**Indag Rubber Ltd., New Delhi, India**

## BANK OF AMERICA CORPORATION

555 California Street, San Francisco, CA, 94104

Tel: (415) 622-3530    Fax: (415) 622-8467    www.bankofamerica.com

*Financial services.*

**Bank of America NT & SA, DCM Bldg. 6/F, 15 Barakhamba Rd., New Delhi 110 001, India**

Tel: 91-11-371-5565  Fax: 91-11-371-5554   Contact: Ambi Venkateswaran, SVP

## THE BANK OF NEW YORK

One Wall Street, New York, NY, 10286

Tel: (212) 495-1784    Fax: (212) 495-2546    www.bankofny.com

*Banking services.*

**The Bank of New York, Express Towers 13th Fl., Nariman Point, Mumbai 400 021, India**

Tel: 91-22-202-2936  Fax: 91-22-204-4941

## C. R. BARD, INC.

730 Central Ave., Murray Hill, NJ, 07974

Tel: (908) 277-8000    Fax: (908) 277-8078    www.crbard.com

*Mfr. health care products.*

**Bard International, 53 Free Press House, 215 Nariman Point, Mumbai 400 021, India**

## BATES WORLDWIDE INC.

405 Lexington Ave., New York, NY, 10174

Tel: (212) 297-7000    Fax: (212) 986-0270    www.batesww.com

*Advertising, marketing, public relations and media consulting.*

**Bates Clarion Bangalore, Ganash Towers, 111 Infantry Rd., Bangalore 560 001, India**

Tel: 91-80-559-9925  Fax: 91-80-559-5727

**Bates Clarion Corporate, Merchant Chambers, New Marine Lines, Mumbai (Bombay) 400 020 India**

Tel: 91-22-203-9702   Contact: K. Khalap, CEO

**Bates Clarion Corporate, 55B Mirza Ghalib St., Calcutta 700 016, India**

Tel: 91-33-295-270  Fax: 91-33-249-5290   Contact: Sudipio Sarkar, Chmn.

**Bates Clarion Delhi, Milap Naketan, Bahadurshah Zalar Marg, Delhi 110 002 India**

Tel: 91-11-331-9908  Fax: 91-11-331-9682   Contact: S. Sinha, SVP

## BAUSCH & LOMB INC.

One Bausch & Lomb Place, Rochester, NY, 14604-2701

Tel: (716) 338-6000    Fax: (716) 338-6007    www.bausch.com

*Mfr. vision care products and accessories.*

**Bausch & Lomb India, Ltd.,  Piccadilly Place 3/F, Capt. Gaur Marg Srinivaspuri, Okhla New Delhi 110065, India**

## BAXTER HEALTHCARE CORPORATION

One Baxter Parkway, Deerfield, IL, 60015

Tel: (847) 948-2000    Fax: (847) 948-3948    www.baxter.com

*Pharmaceutical preparations, surgical/medical instruments and cardiovascular products.*

**Baxter India Pvt. Ltd.,  Baxter House E-2 Udyog Nagar, Rohtak Road, New Delhi 110041 India**

Tel: 91-11-518-7970

## BBDO WORLDWIDE

1285 Ave. of the Americas, New York, NY, 10019

Tel: (212) 459-5000    Fax: (212) 459-6645    www.bbdo.com

*Multinational group of advertising agencies.*

**R K Swamy/BBDO,  Madras, India**

## BDO SEIDMAN, LLP    BELGIUM

Two Prudential Plaza, 180 N. Stetson Ave., Ste. 2300, Chicago, IL, 60601

Tel: (312) 240-1236    Fax: (312) 240-3329    www.bdo.com

*International accounting and financial consulting firm.*

**Lodha & Co.,  14 Government Place East, Calcutta 69, India**

Tel: 91-33-248-7102    Fax: 91-33-248-6960    Contact: Rajendra S. Lodha

## BECHTEL GROUP INC.

50 Beale Street, PO Box 3965, San Francisco, CA, 94105-1895

Tel: (415) 768-1234    Fax: (415) 768-9038    www.bechtel.com

*General contractors in engineering and construction.*

**Bechtel International Corp.,  249 A Udyog Vihar Phase IV, Haryana, Gurgaon 122 015, India**

Tel: 91-124-343-107    Fax: 91-124-343-110

## BELLSOUTH CORPORATION LATIN AMERICA

1155 Peachtree Street NE, Ste. 400, Atlanta, GA, 30367

Tel: (404) 249-4800    Fax: (404) 249-4880    www.bellsouth.com

*Mobile communications, telecommunications network systems.*

**SkyCell Communications,  Paramount Plaza, No. 22 Mahatma Gandhi Road, Nungambakkam, Madras 600 034 India**

Tel: 91-44-822-4595    Fax: 91-44-855-4503

**TBL,  7th Fl. Mercantile House, 15 Kasturba Gandhi Marg, New Delhi 110 001, India**

Tel: 91-11-371-7207    Fax: 91-11-371-7214

## BENTLY NEVADA CORPORATION

1617 Water Street, PO Box 157, Minden, NV, 89423

Tel: (775) 782-3611    Fax: (775) 782-9259    www.bently.com

*Provides hardware, software, and services for machinery information and management systems.*

**Sherman Intl. Pvt. Ltd.,  Himalaya House H-88, 23 Kasturba Gandhi Marg., New Delhi 110 001, India**

**Sherman Intl. Pvt. Ltd.,  711 Maker Chamber V, 221 Nariman Pt., Mumbai 400 021, India**

## LOUIS BERGER INTERNATIONAL INC.

100 Halsted Street, East Orange, NJ, 07019

Tel: (201) 678-1960     Fax: (201) 672-4284     www.louisberger.com

*Consulting engineers, engaged in architecture, environmental and advisory services.*

**Louis Berger International Inc., 1/F KUIDP, 38/1 Coles Road, Cross Frazer Town, Bangalore 560 005 India**

Tel: 91-80-563-866   Fax: 91-80-563-867

**Louis Berger International Inc., M-122 Greater Kailash Part-1, New Delhi 110 048, India**

## BEST WESTERN INTERNATIONAL

6201 North 24th Place, Phoenix, AZ, 85106

Tel: (602) 957-4200     Fax: (602) 957-5740     www.bestwestern.com

*International hotel chain.*

**Surya Hotel, New Friends Colony, New Delhi 110 065, India**

## BESTFOODS, INC.

700 Sylvan Ave., International Plaza, Englewood Cliffs, NJ, 07632-9976

Tel: (201) 894-4000     Fax: (201) 894-2186     www.bestfoods.com

*Consumer foods products; corn refining.*

**Corn Products Co. (India) Ltd., Shree Niwas House, M. Somani Marg, PO Box 994, Mumbai 400 001 India**

Tel: 91-22-207-2321   Fax: 91-22-207-6180   Contact: Salil Punoose, Chrm

**Corn Products Co. (India) Ltd., PO Box 994, Mumbai 400 001, India**

Tel: 91-22-207-2321   Fax: 91-22-207-6180   Contact: Salil Punoose, Chmn.

## BETZDEARBORN

4636 Somerton Road, PO Box 3002, Trevose, PA, 19053-6783

Tel: (215) 953-2568     Fax: (215) 953-5524     www.betzdearborn.com

*Mfr. water/wastewater and process system treatment chemicals and services.*

**BetzDearborn India Pvt. Ltd., 5th Fl. Vayudhooth-Chambers, 15/16 Mahatma Gandhi Rd., Bangalore 560 001, India**

## BLACK & VEATCH LLP

8400 Ward Pkwy., PO Box 8405, Kansas City, MO, 64114

Tel: (913) 339-2000     Fax: (913) 339-2934     www.bv.com

*Engineering, architectural and construction services.*

**Black & Veatch India, Ltd., 1006 Bhikaji Cama Place 10th Fl., Bhikaji Cama Bhawan, New Delhi 110 066, India**

Tel: 91-11-616-7375   Fax: 91-11-616-7250   Contact: Pradeep Jain, Dir.

## BLACK CLAWSON COMPANY

405 Lexington Ave., 61st Fl., New York, NY, 10174

Tel: (212) 916-8000     Fax: (212) 916-8057     www.ligroup.com

*Paper and pulp mill machinery.*

**Black Clawson India Engineers Pvt. Ltd., 38/3 Mount Rd., Madras 600 006, India**

## THE BLACKSTONE GROUP INC.

360 North Michigan Ave., Chicago, IL, 60601

Tel: (312) 419-0400     Fax: (312) 419-8419     www.bgglobal.com

*Marketing research, business consulting, engineering design and software.*

**Blackstone Market Facts, G/3 - Heera House 1st Road, Khar (West), Mumbai 400 052 India**

**Blackstone Market Facts, 201 Arunkiran Residency, Gagan Vihar Colony Begumpet, Hyderabad 560 016, India**

**Blackstone Market Facts, 2/F 6/J Keyatala Road, Calcutta 700 029, India**

Blackstone Market Facts, D-109, LBR Complex - 1/F, 1 Main Road, Anna Nagar (East) Chennai 600 102, India

Blackstone Market Facts, 315 Ground, Indira Nagar 1st stage, Bangalore 38 India

The Blackstone Group of India, F-14 Upper Ground Fl., East of Kailash, New Delhi 110 065, India
Tel: 91-11-622-162525   Fax: 91-11-622-1191

The Blackstone Group of India, AA 25 Anna Nagar, Madras 600 040, India
Tel: 91-44-6442976   Fax: 91-44-644-2983

The Blackstone Group of India, 68/A, First Fl., Kunj Society, Alkapuri, Baroda 390 005, India
Tel: 91-265-339563   Fax: 91-265-339583

## BLOOM ENGINEERING CO., INC.

5460 Horning Rd., Pittsburgh, PA, 15236

Tel: (412) 653-3500     Fax: (412) 653-2253     www.bloomeng.com

*Mfr. custom engineered burners and combustion systems.*

Thermax Ltd., Burner Development Group, Chinchwad, Pune 411 019 India
Tel: 91-212-770436   Fax: 91-212-774640

## BOOZ-ALLEN & HAMILTON INC.

8283 Greensboro Drive, McLean, VA, 22102

Tel: (703) 902-5000     Fax: (703) 902-3333     www.bah.com

*International management and technology consultants.*

Booz Allen & Hamilton (India) Ltd. Co. KG, Bajaj Bhavan 2nd Fl., Nariman Point, Mumbai 400 021, India
Tel: 91-22-282-8286   Fax: 91-22-282-8330

## THE BOSTON CONSULTING GROUP

Exchange Place, 31st Fl., Boston, MA, 02109

Tel: (617) 973-1200     Fax: (617) 973-1339     www.bcg.com

*Management consulting company.*

The Boston Consulting Group Pte. Ltd., 55/56 Free Press House, 215 Free Press Journal Marg, Nariman Point, Mumbai 400 021 India
Tel: 91-22-283-7451

## BOYDEN CONSULTING CORPORATION

364 Elwood Ave., Hawthorne, NY, 10502

Tel: (914) 747-0093     Fax: (914) 980-6147     www.boyden.com

*International executive search firm.*

Boyden Associates Ltd., 23 Gold Fields Plaza, 45 Sassoon Rd., Pune 411 001, India
Tel: 91-212-639-264

Boyden Associates Ltd., Hug 'S' S-24-25 2nd Fl., 80 Feet Main Rd., Koramangala, Bangalore 560 0995 India
Tel: 91-80-553-5825

Boyden Associates Ltd., 2-11 Phoenix Mills Compound, Senapati Bapat Mang, Lower Parel, Mumbai 400 013 India
Tel: 91-22-494-3521

## BOZELL GROUP

40 West 23rd Street, New York, NY, 10010

Tel: (212) 727-5000     Fax: (212) 645-9173     www.bozell.com

*Advertising, marketing, public relations and media consulting.*

MAA Communications Bozell, Hdqtrs., MAA House, 6 Service Rd. I Stage, Domlur Layout, Bangalore 560 071 India
Tel: 91-80-556-8910   Fax: 91-80-554-3891   Contact: Bunty Peerbhoy, Mng. Dir.

**MAA Communications Bozell, Ltd.,** 3rd Fl. David Sasoon Bldg., 143 Mahatma Gandhi Rd., Mumbai 400 023 India

Tel: 91-22-267-7374   Fax: 91-22-267-7547   Contact: Ram Kumar Seshu, EVP

**MAA Communications Bozell, Ltd. (Chennai),** 79 C P Ramaswamy Rd., Alawarpet, Chennai 600 018, India

Tel: 91-44-499-1353   Fax: 91-44-499-2035   Contact: Amrita Chugh

**MAA Communications Bozell, Ltd. (Cochin),** Door No. 41/615, Ground Fl., Krishnaswamy Rd., Cochin 682 035, India

Tel: 91-484-354-609   Fax: 91-484-354-614   Contact: P. Ravindranath, Mgr.

**MAA Communications Bozell, Ltd. (Coimbatore),** 4th Fl. 'Vyshnax', 95-A Race Course, Coimbatore 641 018, India

Tel: 91-422-211-183   Fax: 91-422-317-479   Contact: P. Ramskrishnan, Mgr.

**MAA Communications Bozell, Ltd. (Delhi),** K-77 Lajpat Nagar II, New Delhi 110 024, India

Tel: 91-11-691-4640   Fax: 91-11-691-4670   Contact: Shankar Narayan J. Alva, EVP

**MAA Communications Bozell, Ltd. (Pune),** 3015/8 Sri Nidhi Chambers, MHT Bldg. 4th Fl., Senapathi Bapat Rd., Pune 411 016 India

Tel: 91-212-353-632   Contact: Vishwas Shrikhande, Mgr.

## BRANSON ULTRASONICS CORPORATION

41 Eagle Road, Danbury, CT, 06813-1961

Tel:  (203) 796-0400      Fax:  (203) 796-2285      www.branson-plasticsjoin.com

*Mfr. plastics assembly equipment, ultrasonic cleaning equipment.*

**Branson Ultrasonics,** PO Box 6840, Santa Cruz East, Mumbai 400 055, India

Tel: 91-22-850-5570   Fax: 91-22-850-8681

## BRISTOL-MYERS SQUIBB COMPANY

345 Park Ave., New York, NY, 10154-0037

Tel:  (212) 546-4000      Fax:  (212) 546-4020      www.bms.com

*Pharmaceutical and food preparations, medical and surgical instruments.*

**ConvaTec, Div. Bristol-Myers Squibb,** Marol Naka, Sir MV Road, Andheri, East Bombay 400059 India

Tel: 91-22-852-2629

## BROADVISION, INC.

585 Broadway, Redwood City, CA, 94063

Tel:  (650) 261-5100      Fax:  (650) 261-5900      www.broadvision.com

*Develops and delivers an integrated suite of packaged applications for personalized enterprise portals.*

**BroadVision India**
**c/o DBS Corporate Club,** Raheja Chambers, 213 Nariman Point, Mumbai 400 021, India

## BRY-AIR INC.

10793 Street, Rt. 37 West, Sunbury, OH, 43074

Tel:  (740) 965-2974      Fax:  (740) 965-5470      www.bry-air.thomasregister.com

*Mfr. industrial dehumidifiers/auxiliary equipment for plastics industrial.*

**Bry-Air Asia Pvt. Ltd.,** 20 Rajpur Road, Delhi 110-054, India

Tel: 91-11-291-2800   Fax: 91-11-291-5127

## BUCYRUS INTERNATIONAL, INC.

1100 Milwaukee Ave., PO Box 500, South Milwaukee, WI, 53172

Tel:  (414) 768-4000      Fax:  (414) 768-4474      www.bucyrus.com

*Mfr. of surface mining equipment, primarily walking draglines, electric mining shovels and blast hole drills.*

**Bacyrus India Pvt. Ltd.,** B-1 Marble Arch, 9 Prithvi Raj Rd., New Delhi 110 011, India

Tel: 91-11-462-5572   Fax: 91-11-462-5561   Contact: David Lee, Mng. Dir.

## BUDGET GROUP, INC.

125 Basin St., Ste. 210, Daytona Beach, FL, 32114

Tel: (904) 238-7035     Fax: (904) 238-7461     www.budgetrentacar.com

*Car and truck rental system.*

**Budget Rent A Car,  G-3 Arunachal, Barakginba, Read, New Delhi India**

Tel: 91-11-3318600

## LEO BURNETT, DIV. B-COM 3 GROUP

35 West Wacker Drive, Chicago, IL, 60601

Tel: (312) 220-5959     Fax: (312) 220-6533     www.bcom3group.com

*Engaged in advertising, marketing, media buying and planning, and public relations.*

**Chiatra Leo Burnett,  Mumbai, India**

## BURSON-MARSTELLER

230 Park Ave., New York, NY, 10003-1566

Tel: (212) 614-4000     Fax: (212) 614-4262     www.bm.com

*Public relations/public affairs consultants.*

**Burson-Marsteller Rogers Pereira Communications Pvt. Ltd.,  Whitehall, 143 A.K.Marg. Kemp's Corner, Mumbai 400 036, India**

Tel: 91-22-363-0398  Fax: 91-22-364-3597

**Burson-Marsteller Rogers Pereira Communications Pvt. Ltd.,  306 NILGIRI, 9 Barakhamba Rd., New Delhi 110 001, India**

Tel: 91-11-335-4821  Fax: 91-11-335-4871   Emp: 35

## BUSH BOAKE ALLEN INC.

7 Mercedes Drive, Montvale, NJ, 07645

Tel: (201) 391-9870     Fax: (201) 391-0860     www.bushboakeallen.com

*Mfr. aroma chemicals for fragrances and flavor products for seasonings.*

**Bush Boake Allen,  F-93 Green Park, New Delhi 110 016, India**

Tel: 91-11-685-4754

**Bush Boake Allen,  1/5 Seven Wells Street, St. Thomas Mount, Chennai 6000016, India**

Tel: 91-44-234-1131   Fax: 91-44-234-6017

## CADENCE DESIGN SYSTEMS, INC.

2655 Seely Ave., Bldg. 5, San Jose, CA, 95134

Tel: (408) 943-1234     Fax: (408) 943-0513     www.cadence.com

*Mfr. electronic design automation software.*

**Cadence Design Systems (India) PVT Ltd.,  Prestige Center Point 201 - 7 Edward Road, Bangalore 560 052, India**

Tel: 91-80-2283651   Fax: 91-80-2283654

## CAMBREX CORPORATION

1 Meadowlands Plaza, East Rutherford, NJ, 07063

Tel: (201) 804-3000     Fax: (201) 804-9852     www.cambrex.com

*human health, animal health/agriculture and Mfr. biotechnology products and produce specialty chemicals.*

**Cambrex India,  316 Vardhaman Chambers, Sector - 17 Vashi, New Bombay 0 400 705, India**

Tel: 91-22-767-1472   Fax: 91-22-768-7204

**Osmic India,  124-B Sanjeeva, Reedy Nagar, Hyderabad 500 038 India**

## CAMBRIDGE TECHNOLOGY PARTNERS, INC.

8 Cambridge Center, Cambridge, MA, 02142

Tel: (617) 374-9800     Fax: (617) 914-8300     www.ctp.com

*Engaged in e-commerce consultancy.*

**Cambridge Technology Partners, Inc.,  Prestiget Meridian II - 14/F, 30/31 MG Road, Bangalore 560 001, India**

Tel: 91-80-558-3023   Fax: 91-80-558-1425

## CAPITAL CONTROLS COMPANY, INC.

3000 Advance Lane, PO Box 211, Colmar, PA, 18915-0211

Tel: (215) 997-4000     Fax: (215) 997-4062     www.capitalcontrols.com

*Mfr./services water disinfecting products and systems.*

**Capital Controls India Pvt. Ltd.,  Mumbai, India**

## CARBOLINE COMPANY

350 Hanley Industrial Court, St. Louis, MO, 63144

Tel: (314) 644-1000     Fax: (314) 644-4617     www.carboline.com

*Mfr. coatings and sealants.*

**CDC Carboline (India) Pvt. Ltd.,  162 A Greams Rd., Tamil Nadu, Madras 600 006, India**

## CARLSON COMPANIES, INC.

Carlson Parkway, PO Box 59159, Minneapolis, MN, 55459

Tel: (612) 550-4520     Fax: (612) 550-4580     www.cmg.carlson.com

*Marketing services agency.*

**Direm Marketing Services Pvt. Ltd.,  83-C Dr E Moses Road, Worli Mumbai 400 018, India**

Tel: 91- 22-495-4944   Fax: 91- 22-493-5575

## CARPENTER TECHNOLOGY CORPORATION

101 W. Bern Street,  PO Box 14662, Reading, PA, 19612-4662

Tel: (610) 208-2000     Fax: (610) 208-3214     www.cartech.com

*Mfr. specialty steels and structural ceramics for casting industrial.*

**Kalyani Carpenter Special Steels Ltd. (JV),  Pune, India**

## CARRIER CORPORATION

One Carrier Place, Farmington, CT, 06034-4015

Tel: (860) 674-3000     Fax: (860) 679-3010     www.carrier.com

*Mfr./distributor/services A/C, heating and refrigeration equipment.*

**Carrier Aircon Ltd.,  Narsingpur, Kherki dhaula Post, Gurgaon Haryana 120 01, India**

Tel: 91-124-323231   Fax: 91-124-323241

## CASE CORPORATION

700 State Street, Racine, WI, 53404

Tel: (414) 636-6011     Fax: (414) 636-0200     www.casecorp.com

*Mfr./sale agricultural and construction equipment.*

**Case India Limited,  103 Askoka Estate, 24 Barakhamba Road, New Delhi 110001 India**

Tel: 91-11-373-1589   Fax: 91-11-335-2306

**New Holland Tractors Pvt. Ltd.,  210 Okhla Industrial Area III, 110 020 New Delhi India**

Tel: 91-11-693-220-07

## CATERPILLAR INC.

100 NE Adams Street, Peoria, IL, 61629-6105

Tel: (309) 675-1000     Fax: (309) 675-1182     www.cat.com

*Mfr. earth/material-handling and construction machinery and equipment and engines.*

**Hindustan Powerplus Ltd.,  Saki-Vihar Rd., Powai, Mumbai 400 072, India**

## C.B. RICHARD ELLIS

533 South Fremont Ave., Los Angeles, CA, 90071-1712

Tel: (213) 613-3123 Fax: (213) 613-3535 www.cbrichardellis.com

*Commercial real estate services.*

**CB Richard Ellis Ltd., 2H Gee Emerald, 151 Village Road, Nungambakkam, Chennai 600 034 India**

**CB Richard Ellis Ltd., 113C Mittal Tower, Nariman Point, Mumbai 400 021, India**

**CB Richard Ellis Ltd., 207 Embassy Square, 148 Infantry Rd., Bangalore 560 001 India**

**CB Richard Ellis Ltd., 1/F E-1 Connaught Place, New Delhi 110 001, India**

## CDM INTERNATIONAL INC.

50 Hampshire Street, Cambridge, MA, 02139

Tel: (617) 452-6000 Fax: (617) 452-8020 www.cdm.com

*Consulting engineers.*

**CDM Camp Dresser & McKee International Inc., 1M Prince Arcade, 22A Cathedral Road, Channai 600 086, India**

Tel: 91-44-827-3755

## CENDANT CORPORATION

9 West 57th Street, New York, NY, 10019

Tel: (212) 413-1800 Fax: (212) 413-1918 www.cendant.com

*Membership-based, direct marketer offering shopping/travel/insurance and dining discount programs*

**Delhi Express Travels, Private Ltd., P-13 Connaught Circus, New Delhi 110 001, India**

Tel: 91-11-3365952 Fax: 91-11-3363718

## CENTIGRAM COMMUNICATIONS CORPORATION

91 East Tasman Drive, San Jose, CA, 95134

Tel: (408) 944-0250 Fax: (408) 428-3732 www.centigram.com

*Engaged in development of unified communications and messaging systems.*

**Centigram Asia Limited, 50/9 1/F, Tolstoy Lan Janpath, New Delhi 110 001, India**

Tel: 91-11-373-8573

## THE CHEMITHON CORPORATION

5430 West Marginal Way Southwest, Seattle, WA, 98106

Tel: (206) 937-9954 Fax: (206) 932-3786 www.chemithon.com.

*Mfr./services chemicals process equipment for detergent, specialty chemicals and power generation industries.*

**Chemithon Engineers (P) Ltd., 317 Maker V, 221 Nariman Point, Mumbai 400 021, India**

## CHEMTEX INTERNATIONAL INC.

1979 Eastwood Rd., Wilmington, NC, 28403

Tel: (910) 509-4400 Fax: (910) 509-4567 www.chemtex.com

*Mfr. fibers and petrochemicals; engineering, procurement, construction, construction management.*

**Chemtex Consultants Ltd., First Fl. B-1 Tower Corporate Block, Golden Enclave, Airport Rd., Bangalore 560 017 India**

Tel: 91-80-526-5627 Fax: 91-80-526 9659

**Chemtex Engineering of India Ltd., B-3/51 1/F, Safdarjung Enclave, New Delhi 110-029, India**

Tel: 91-11-616-2441 Fax: 91-11-616-1226

**Chemtex Engineering of India Ltd., Chemtex House, Main Street Sector 12, Hiranandani Gardens, Powai Mumbai 400 076 India**

Tel: 91-22-570-4491 Fax: 91-22-570-1998 Contact: R. K. Dasgupta, Pres.

## THE CHERRY CORPORATION

3600 Sunset Ave., PO Box 718, Waukegan, IL, 60087

Tel: (847) 662-9200      Fax: (847) 662-2990      www.cherrycorp.com

*Mfr. electrical switches, electronic keyboards, controls and displays.*

**TVS Cherry Pvt. Ltd., 205 Madhava Building, Bandra-Kurla Complex, Bandra East IND-Bombay 400 051, India**

Tel: 91-22-6452582   Fax: 91-22-6452582

## CHESTERTON BINSWANGER INTERNATIONAL

Two Logan Square, 4th Floor, Philadelphia, PA, 19103-2759

Tel: (215) 448-6000      Fax: (215) 448-6238      www.cbbi.com

*Real estate and related services.*

**Chesterton Meghraj Property Consultants Pvt. Ltd., 1109-10 Ashoka Estate, Barakhamba Road, Connaught Place, New Delhi 110001, India**

## CHICAGO RAWHIDE INDUSTRIES (CRI)

735 Tollgate Road, Elgin, IL, 60123

Tel: (847) 742-7840      Fax: (847) 742-7845      www.chicago-rawhide.com

*Mfr. shaft and face seals.*

**CR Seals India Pvt. Ltd., Apsara House 1/F, S.V. Road, Santacruz West Mumbai 400 054, India**

Tel: 91-22-600-1489   Fax: 91-22-600-1541

## THE CHUBB CORPORATION

15 Mountain View Road, Warren, NJ, 07061-1615

Tel: (908) 580-2000      Fax: (908) 580-3606      www.chubb.com

*Holding company for property and casualty insurance.*

**Federal Insurance Company/Chubb Group, Ste. 323 Hyatt Regency Delhi, Bhikaiji Cama Place, Ring Rd., New Delhi 110 066 India**

Tel: 91-11-619-6754   Fax: 91-11-616-5110

## CIGNA COMPANIES

One Liberty Place, Philadelphia, PA, 19192

Tel: (215) 761-1000      Fax: (215) 761-5511      www.cigna.com

*Insurance, invest, health care and other financial services.*

**CIGNA HealthCare Management Company Pvt. Limited, Ste. 301-305 Prestige Terminus II, No. 22 Airport Exit Road, Bangalore 560017 India**

Tel: 91-80-527-8398   Fax: 91-80-527-8402

## CINCINNATI INCORPORATED

PO Box 11111, Cincinnati, OH, 45211

Tel: (513) 367-7100      Fax: (513) 367-7552      www.e-ci.com

*Mfr. metal fabricating equipment.*

**Heatly & Gresham India, Ltd., E-47/4, Okhla Industrial Area Phase II, New Delhi, India**

Tel: 91-11-683-6293   Fax: 91-11-6847-171

## CINCOM SYSTEMS INC.

55 Merchant Street, Cincinnati, OH, 45446

Tel: (513) 612-2300      Fax: (513) 481-8332      www.cincom.com

*Develop/distributor computer software.*

**Cincom Systems India Inc., 914-915 Arunachal Bldg., 19 Barakhamba Road, New Delhi 110001, India**

## CISCO SYSTEMS, INC.

170 West Tasman Drive, San Jose, CA, 95134-1706

Tel: (408) 526-4000    Fax: (408) 526-4100    www.cisco.com

*Develop/mfr./market computer hardware and software networking systems.*

**Cisco Systems (HK) Ltd.,  New Delhi Office, M-6 GK II Market, New Delhi 110 048, India**

Tel: 91-11-623-3201    Fax: 91-11-623-3207

## CITIGROUP, INC.

153 East 53rd Street, New York, NY, 10043

Tel: (212) 559-1000    Fax: (212) 559-3646    www.citigroup.com

*Provides insurance and financial services worldwide.*

**Citibank N.A.,  Sakhar Bhavan 10th Fl., 230 Backbay Reclamation, Nairman Point, Bombay 400-021 India**

Contact: David P. Conner

## CLEAR CHANNEL COMMUNICATIONS

200 East Basse Road, San Antonio, TX, 78209

Tel: (210) 822-2828    Fax: (210) 822-2299    www.clearchannel.com

*Programs and sells airtime for radio stations and owns and places outdoor advertising displays.*

**More Group,  Maker Chambers 3 - 6/F Nariman Point, Mumbai 400 021, India**

Tel: 91-22-287-5141    Fax: 91-22-284-5763    Contact: Sandy Nandwani, Mgr.

## THE COCA-COLA COMPANY

PO Drawer 1734, Atlanta, GA, 30301

Tel: (404) 676-2121    Fax: (404) 676-6792    www.coca-cola.com

*Mfr./marketing/distributor soft drinks, syrups and concentrates, juice and juice-drink products.*

**Coca-Cola Ltd.,  India**

Contact: Donald W. Short

## COGNIZANT TECHNOLOGY SOLUTIONS CORPORATION

500 Glenpointe Centre West, Teaneck, NJ, 07666

Tel: (201) 801-0233    Fax: (201) 801-0243    www.cognizant.com

*Provides software development , application management, computer date corrections, and currency conversion.*

**Cognizant Technology Solutions,  Calcutta, India**

## COLGATE-PALMOLIVE COMPANY

300 Park Ave., New York, NY, 10022

Tel: (212) 310-2000    Fax: (212) 310-2919    www.colgate.com

*Mfr. pharmaceuticals, cosmetics, toiletries and detergents.*

**Colgate Palmolive (India) Pvt. Ltd.,  Steelcrete House, 3 Dinshaw Vacha Rd., Mumbai 400 020, India**

## COMPAQ COMPUTER CORPORATION

20555 State Highway 249, PO Box 692000, Houston, TX, 77269-2000

Tel: (281) 370-0670    Fax: (281) 514-1740    www.compaq.com

*Develop/mfr. personal computers.*

**Compaq Computer Asia Pte. Ltd.,  6th Fl. Du Parc Trinity, 17 Mahatma Gandhi Rd., Bangalore 560 001, India**

Tel: 91-80-559-6023    Fax: 91-80-559-6025

## COMPUTER ASSOCIATES INTERNATIONAL INC.

One Computer Associates Plaza, Islandia, NY, 11788

Tel: (516) 342-5224        Fax: (516) 342-5329        www.cai.com

*Integrated business software for enterprise computing and information management, application development, manufacturing, financial applications and professional services.*

**Computer Associates Pte. Ltd., 511/512 Merchant Chambers, 98A Hill Rd., Bandra West Mumbai 400 050 India**

Tel: 91-22-643-4681

## COMPUWARE CORPORATION

31440 Northwestern Hwy., Farmington Hills, MI, 48334-2564

Tel: (248) 737-7300        Fax: (248) 737-7108        www.compuware.com

*Develop and market software for enterprise and e-commerce solutions.*

**IMR Global Ltd., 38/1 Naganathapure, Aingasandra Post, Bangalore 560058, India**

## COMSAT CORPORATION

6560 Rock Spring Drive, Bethesda, MD, 20817

Tel: (301) 214-3200        Fax: (301) 214-7100        www.comsat.com

*Provides global telecommunications services via satellite and develops advanced satellite networking technology.*

**COMSAT International, Ste. 915 9/F Krishna Building, 224 AJC Bose Road, Calcutta 700 017 India**

**COMSAT International, The Estate - 8th Floor, 121 Dickinson Road, Bangalore 560 025, India**

**COMSAT International, D 222/24 TTC Industrial Area MIDC, Nerul Village Shirvane, Navi Mumbai - 400 706 India**

## CONAGRA INC.

One ConAgra Drive, Omaha, NE, 68102-5001

Tel: (402) 595-4000        Fax: (402) 595-4707        www.conagra.com

*Prepared/frozen foods, grains, flour, animal feeds, agro chemicals, poultry, meat, dairy products, including Healthy Choice, Butterball and Hunt's.*

**ConAgra Inc., Nepal, India**

## CONEXANT SYSTEMS, INC.

4311 Jamboree Road, PO Box C, Newport Beach, CA, 92658-8902

Tel: (949) 483-4600        Fax: (949) 483-4078        www.conexant.com

*Provides semiconductor products for communications electronics.*

**Conexant Systems Worldwide, Inc., 47 Community Centre, Friends Colony, New Delhi 110 065 India**

Tel: 91-11-692-4780   Fax: 91-11-692-4712

## COOPER BUSSMANN

PO Box 14460, St. Louis, MO, 63178-4460

Tel: (636) 394-2877        Fax: (636) 527-1405        www.bussmann.com

*Mfr. and markets circuit protection products for the electrical, electronic, and automotive industries.*

**Bussmann India, White House Unit #5 - 2/F, 23-29 St. Marks Road, Bangalore 560 001, India**

Tel: 91 80 227 0893   Fax: 91 80 224 0124

## COOPER INDUSTRIES INC.

6600 Travis Street, Ste. 5800, Houston, TX, 77002

Tel: (713) 209-8400        Fax: (713) 209-8995        www.cooperindustries.com

*Mfr./distributor electrical products, tools, hardware and automotive products, fuses and accessories for electronic applications and circuit boards.*

**Bussmann India, Div. Cooper Industries, 2nd Fl. Unit # 5 White House, 23-29 St. Marks Rd., Bangalore 560 001 India**

Tel: 91-80-227-0893   Fax: 91-80-224-0124

## COOPER STANDARD AUTOMOTIVE

2401 South Gulley Road, Dearborn, MI, 48124

Tel: (313) 561-1100     Fax: (313) 561-6526     www.cooperstandard.com

*Mfr. molded and extruded rubber and plastic products for automotive and appliance industry, retread tire industry.*

**Cooper Standard Automotive, 3 Bishen Udhyog Premises, Opp. Raja Industrial Estate, P.K. Road, Mulung W Mumbai 400 080 India**

Tel: 91-22-564-5313   Fax: 91-22-564-2577

## CORNING INC.

One Riverfront Plaza, Corning, NY, 14831-0001

Tel: (607) 974-9000     Fax: (607) 974-8091     www.corning.com

*Mfr. glass and specialty materials, consumer products; communications, laboratory services.*

**Corning India, World Trade Tower - 3rd Fl., Barakhamba Lane, New Delhi 110 001 India**

Tel: 91-11-332-7391   Fax: 91-11-372-1520

## CORRPRO COMPANIES, INC.

1090 Enterprise Drive, Medina, OH, 44256

Tel: (330) 725-6681     Fax: (330) 723-0244     www.corrpro.com

*Full-services corrosion engineering, cathodic protection.*

**Corrpro Companies India, Flat No. 51 - Charkop Happy Home C.H.S., Plot No. 210 - Road No. RDP-5 Sector 4, Charkop Kandivli (West) Mumbai 400067, India**

Tel: 91-22-8690343  Fax: 91-22-8690343   Contact: Madhav Joshi

## CUMMINS ENGINE COMPANY, INC.

500 Jackson Street, PO Box 3005, Columbus, IN, 47202-3005

Tel: (812) 377-5000     Fax: (812) 377-4937     www.cummins.com

*Mfr. diesel engines.*

**Kirldskar Cummins Ltd., Kothrun, Pune 411 029, India**

## CYBEREX INC.

7171 Industrial Park Boulevard, Mentor, OH, 44060

Tel: (440) 946-1783     Fax: (440) 946-5963     www.cyberex.com

*Mfr. uninterruptible power systems, line voltage regulators, static switches, power line filters.*

**Cyberex Intl. Services, Delhi, India**

## CYLINK CORPORATION

3131 Jay Street, Santa Clara, CA, 95054

Tel: (408) 855-6000     Fax: (408) 855-6100     www.cyllink.com

*Develop and manufactures encryption software.*

**Cylink India, A27/4 DLF Quatab Enclave-I, Gurgoan-12202, India**

Tel: 91-124 6346-14   Contact: Mash Khan

## CYPRESS SEMICONDUCTOR CORPORATION

3901 N. First Street, San Jose, CA, 95134-1599

Tel: (408) 943-2600     Fax: (408) 943-2796     www.cypress.com

*Mfr. integrated circuits.*

**Cypress Semiconductor, Sharda Towers 1/F, 56 Nandiurg Road, Benson Town Bangalore 560046, India**

Tel: 91-80-3530132   Fax: 91-80-3438679

## DANA CORPORATION

4500 Dorr Street, Toledo, OH, 43615

Tel: (419) 535-4500          Fax: (419) 535-4643          www.dana.com

*Mfr./sales of automotive, heavy truck, off-highway, fluid and mechanical power components and engine parts, filters and gaskets.*

**Perfect Circle Victor Limited,  20 Midc Estate, Satpur Nasik 422 007, India**

**Perfect Circle Victor Ltd.,  Magnet House, Narottan Mararjee Mrg, Ballard Estate, Bombay 400 038 India**

**Spicer India,  29 Milestone Pune-Nasik Hwy., Kuruli Khed, Pune 410501 India**

Tel: 91-212-798713

## D'ARCY MASIUS BENTON & BOWLES INC. (DMB&B)

1675 Broadway, New York, NY, 10019

Tel: (212) 468-3622          Fax: (212) 468-2987          www.dmbb.com

*Full service international advertising and communications group.*

**Enterprise Advertising Pvt. Ltd.,  4/F Pharma Search House, BG Kher Rd., Worli Mumbai 400 081, India**

## DDB NEEDHAM WORLDWIDE INC.

437 Madison Ave., New York, NY, 10022

Tel: (212) 415-2000          Fax: (212) 415-3417          www.ddbn.com

*Advertising agency.*

**Mudra Communications(DDB),  Ahmedabad, India**

## DELL COMPUTER CORPORATION

One Dell Way, Round Rock, TX, 78682-2222

Tel: (512) 338-4400          Fax: (512) 728-3653          www.dell.com

*Direct marketer and supplier of computer systems.*

**Dell Asia Pacific Sdn.,  India Liaison Office, 1 & 11 Fl. J. S. Towers, Brigade Rd., Bangalore 560 001 India**

Tel: 91-80-565842   Fax: 91-80-5544738   Contact: Naren Ayyar, Gen. Mgr.

## DELOITTE TOUCHE TOHMATSU INTERNATIONAL

1633 Broadway, New York, NY, 10019

Tel: (212) 492-4000          Fax: (212) 392-4154          www.deloitte.com

*Accounting, audit, tax and management consulting services.*

**C.C. Chokshi & Company,  Mafalal House, Backbay Reclamation, Mumbai Bombay 400 020, India**

**Deloitte Haskins & Sells,  2/2A Ho Chi Minh Sarani, Calcutta 700 071, India**

**Deloitte Haskins & Sells,  Jehangir Wadia Bldg. 3rd Fl., 51 Mahatma Gandhi Rd., Mumbai Bombay 400 023, India**

**Fraser & Company,  169 North Usman Rd., T Nagar, Madras 600 017, India**

## DELTA AIR LINES INC.

PO Box 20706, Atlanta, GA, 30320-6001

Tel: (404) 715-2600          Fax: (404) 715-5494          www.delta-air.com

*Major worldwide airline; international air transport services.*

**Delta Air Lines Inc.,  Mumbai, India**

## DELUXE CORPORATION

3680 Victoria Street North, Shoreview, MN, 55126-2966

Tel: (612) 483-7111          Fax: (612) 481-4163          www.deluxe.com

*Leading U.S. check printer and provider of electronic payment services.*

**HCL Deluxe Corp.,  A-10-11, Sector III, Noida 201 301 UP, India**

Tel: 91-11-9154-3256   Fax: 91-11-9154-0775

### DENTSPLY INTERNATIONAL

570 West College Ave., PO Box 872, York, PA, 17405-0872

Tel: (717) 845-7511     Fax: (717) 843-6357     www.dentsply.com

*Mfr. and distribution of dental supplies and equipment.*

**Dentsply India, 7th Main Fourth Cross, HAL 11nd Stage, Indiranagar Bangalore 560 008, India**
Tel: 91-80-526-2735

**Dentsply India, Flat #201 Tej Mahan Apartments, J.B.Nagar, Andheri East, Mumbai 400 059 India**
Tel: 91-22-820-3285

**Dentsply India, D-21 Saket, New Delhi 110 017, India**
Tel: 91-11-696-1714

**Dentsply India Plant, Plot #294 Udyog Vihar, Phase II, Gurgaon 122 016 Haryana, India**
Tel: 91-124-345-333

### DHL WORLDWIDE EXPRESS

50 California Avenue, San Francisco, CA, 94111

Tel: (415) 677-6100     Fax: (415) 824-9700     www.dhl.com

*Worldwide air express carrier.*

**DHL Worldwide Express, Lok Bharati Complex, Marol Maroshi Rd., Andheri East, Mumbai 400 059 India**
Tel: 91-22-851-5151

### DIAMOND CHAIN COMPANY

402 Kentucky Ave., Indianapolis, IN, 46225

Tel: (317) 638-6431     Fax: (317) 633-2243     www.diamondchain.com

*Mfr. roller chains.*

**T.I. Diamond Chain Ltd., 11/12 North Beach Rd., Madras 600 001, India**

### DIEBOLD INC.

5995 Mayfair Road, North Canton, OH, 44720-8077

Tel: (330) 490-4000     Fax: (330) 490-3794     www.diebold.com

*Mfr. automated banking systems; security services for banking industrial and related fields.*

**Diebold HMA, No. 1 - 2/F Ceebros Centre, 45 Montieth Road, Egmore Chennai 600 008 India**
Tel: 91-44-855-3139

### DIMON INCORPORATED

512 Bridge Street, PO Box 681, Danville, VA, 24543-0681

Tel: (804) 792-7511     Fax: (804) 791-0377     www.dimon.com

*One of world's largest importer and exporters of leaf tobacco.*

**DIMON International Services Limited, Door 3-30-15 - Ring Road, Guntur 522006, Andhra Pradesh, India**
Tel: 91-863-351-187   Fax: 91-863-350-199

### DIONEX CORPORATION

1228 Titan Way, PO Box 3603, Sunnyvale, CA, 94086-3603

Tel: (408) 737-0700     Fax: (408) 730-9403     www.dionex.com

*Develop/mfr./market chromatography systems and related products.*

**Indtech Analytical, K-227 Ansa Industrial Estate, Saki-Vihar Road, Saki-Naka, Bombay 400 072, India**
Tel: 91-22-852-4809

## DMC STRATEX NETWORKS, INC.

170 Rose Orchard Way, San Jose, CA, 95134

Tel: (408) 943-0777    Fax: (408) 944-1648    www.dmcstratexnetworks.com

*Designs, manufactures, and markets advanced wireless solutions for wireless broadband access.*

**DMC Stratex Networks, 1/F - 114 Jor Bagh, New Delhi 110 003, India**

Tel: 91-11-465-2860

## DONALDSON COMPANY, INC.

1400 West 94th Street, Minneapolis, MN, 55431

Tel: (612) 887-3131    Fax: (612) 887-3155    www.donaldson.com

*Mfr. filtration systems and replacement parts.*

**D. I. Filter Systems Pvt. Ltd., C-94 - 1st Fl. Shivalik (Near Malviya Nagar), New Delhi 110 017, India**

## DONALDSON, LUFKIN & JENRETTE, INC.

277 Park Ave., New York, NY, 10172

Tel: (212) 892-3000    Fax: (212) 892-7272    www.dlj.com

*Investment banking, capital markets and financial services.*

**Donaldson, Lufkin & Jenrette, Inc., 405 Prestige Centre Point, 7 Edward Rd., Bangalore 560 052, India**

Tel: 91-80-225-1924

## R.R. DONNELLEY & SONS COMPANY

77 West Wacker Drive, Chicago, IL, 60601-1696

Tel: (312) 326-8000    Fax: (312) 326-8543    www.rrdonnelley.com

*Commercial printing, allied communication services.*

**R. R. Donnelley Financial, c/o Tata Donnelley Ltd., Birya House, Prin Naiman St., Fort Mumbai 400 001 India**

Tel: 91-22-265-5737

**Tata Donnelley Ltd., 414 Veer Savarkar Marg, Prabhadevi, Mumbai 400 025, India**

Tel: 91-22-768-2430

## THE DOW CHEMICAL COMPANY

2030 Dow Center, Midland, MI, 48674

Tel: (517) 636-1000    Fax: (517) 636-3228    www.dow.com

*Mfr. chemicals, plastics, pharmaceuticals, agricultural products, consumer products.*

**Dow Chemical NV, PO Box 109, New Delhi 110 001, India**

**IDL Chemicals Ltd., Kukatpally, Sanatnagar (I.E.), PO Box, Hyderabad 500 018, India**

**Polychem Ltd., 7 Jamshedji Tata Rd., Churchgate Reclamation, Mumbai 400 020, India**

## DRAFT WORLDWIDE

633 North St. Clair Street, Chicago, IL, 60611-3211

Tel: (312) 944-3500    Fax: (312) 944-3566    www.draftworldwide.com

*Full service international advertising agency, engaged in brand building, direct and promotional marketing.*

**Corvo DraftWorldwide PVT Ltd., 52-57 Grants Bldg. 1st Fl., 19A Arthur Bunder Rd., Colaba Mumbai 400 005, India**

Tel: 91-22-285-2208    Fax: 91-22-285-2289

**DraftWorldwide, H-28 Basement Masjid Moth., Greater Kailash-II, New Delhi 110 048, India**

Tel: 91-11-641-4632    Fax: 91-11-621-6964

## DRESSER-RAND COMPANY

10077 Grogans Mill Road, Ste. 500, The Woodlands, TX, 77380

Tel: (281) 363-7650      Fax: (281) 363-7654      www.dresser-rand.com

*Provides energy conversion solutions.*

**Dresser-Rand India Pvt. Ltd., Rhone-Poulenc House - 2/F, S K Ahire Marg, Prabhadevi PO Box 9123, Mumbai-400 025 India**

Tel: 91-22-460-8600

## DUFF & PHELPS CREDIT RATING CO.

55 East Monroe Street, Chicago, IL, 60603

Tel: (312) 368-3100      Fax: (312) 442-4121      www.dcrco.com

*Engaged in rating stocks and bonds, municipal securities and insurance company claims paying capabilities.*

**Duff & Phelps Credit Rating India Private Ltd., N214 - North Block - Ideal Plaza, 11/1 Sarat Bose Road, Calcutta 700 020 India**

Tel: 91-33-240-7608    Fax: 91-33-280-6505

**Duff & Phelps Credit Rating India Private Ltd., 64 Atlanta, Nariman Point, Mumbai 400 021 India**

Tel: 91-22-282-88720

**Duff & Phelps Credit Rating India Private Ltd., Akshaya Plaza 14/F, 55/56 Aditanar Salai, Chennai 600 002, India**

Tel: 91-44-859-4602

## EAGLE GLOBAL LOGISTICS (EGL)

15350 Vickery Drive, Houston, TX, 77032

Tel: (281) 618-3100      Fax: (281) 618-3100      www.eaglegl.com

*Ocean/air freight forwarding, customs brokerage, packing and wholesale, logistics management and insurance.*

**Circle Freight International (India) Pvt. Ltd., Flat #1215/1216 12th Fl., Ansal Towers, 38 Nehru Place, New Delhi 110 018 India**

Tel: 91-11-646-6330    Fax: 91-11-646-5698

**Circle Freight International (India) Pvt. Ltd., 309 MPJ Chambers 3rd Fl., Wakadewadi, Bombay-Pune Rd., Pune 411 003 India**

Tel: 91-212-312-637    Fax: 91-212-313-264

**Circle Freight International (India) Pvt. Ltd., 2-A First Fl. Wellingdon Estate, 24 Commander In Chief Rd., Madras 600 015, India**

Tel: 91-44-827-8767    Fax: 91-44-825-1604

**Circle Freight International (India) Pvt. Ltd., SCP Towers 1st Fl., Model School Junction, Thampanoor, Trivandrum 695 001 India**

Tel: 91-471-659-31    Fax: 91-471-659-31

**Circle Freight International (India) Pvt. Ltd., 24/1592 Subramaniam Rd. 1st Fl., Wet Island, Cochin 682 003, India**

Tel: 91-484-666-453    Fax: 91-484-667-677

**Circle Freight International (India) Pvt. Ltd., 1-10-72/2B, Cheekoti Gardens, Begumpet, Hyderabad 500 016 India**

Tel: 91-842-811-346    Fax: 91-842-811-346

**Circle Freight International (India) Pvt. Ltd., Cheran Towers 81/10 2nd Fl., 78 Arts College Rd., Coimbatore 641 0118, India**

Tel: 91-422-213-864    Fax: 91-422-213-864

**Circle Freight International (India) Pvt. Ltd., 6F Everest Bldg. 6th Fl., 46C Jawaharl Nehru Rd., Calcutta 700 071, India**

Tel: 91-33-242-2033    Fax: 91-33-242-2529

**Circle Freight International (India) Pvt. Ltd., 1/B Vaspujya Chambers, Ashram Rd., Ahmedabad 380 014, India**

Tel: 91-79-447-158    Fax: 91-272-655-8744

Circle Freight International (India) Pvt. Ltd., 315 Siddarth Complex, R.C. Dutt Rd., Alakapuri, Baroda 390 005 India

Tel: 91-265-322-838    Fax: 91-265-339-336

Circle Freight International (India) Pvt. Ltd., 38-80 Feet Rd., Hall III Stage, Bangalore 560 075, India

Tel: 91-80-528-9202    Fax: 91-812-528-1796

Circle Freight Intl. (India) Pvt. Ltd., Atlanta Tower 4th Fl. Sahar Rd., Sahar Bombay Mumbai 400 099, India

Tel: 91-22-837-5724    Fax: 91-22-836-7488

## EASTMAN CHEMICAL

100 North Eastman Road, Kingsport, TN, 37660

Tel: (423) 229-2000        Fax: (423) 229-1351        www.eastman.com

*Mfr. plastics, chemicals, fibers.*

Eastman Chemical Ltd., 1301 Raheja Centre, Nariman Point, Mumbai 400 021, India

Tel: 91-22-287-6568    Fax: 91-22-284-3220    Contact: Harish Davey

## EASTMAN KODAK COMPANY

343 State Street, Rochester, NY, 14650

Tel: (716) 724-4000        Fax: (716) 724-1089        www.kodak.com

*Develop/mfr. photo and chemicals products, information management/video/copier systems, fibers/plastics for various industry.*

India Photographic Co. Ltd., Kodak House, Dr. Dadabhai Naoroji Rd., PO Box 343, Mumbai 400 001, India

## J.D. EDWARDS & COMPANY

One Technology Way, Denver, CO, 80237

Tel: (303) 334-4000        Fax: (303) 334-4970        www.jdedwards.com

*Computer software products.*

Systime Computer Systems Ltd., Steepz, Andheri (E), Mumbai 400 096, India

Tel: 91-22-832-0051    Fax: 91-22-836-4126

## EDWARDS SYSTEM TECHNOLOGY

90 Fieldston Court, Cheshire, CT, 06410

Tel: (203) 699-3000        Fax: (203) 699-3031        www.est.net

*Mfr. fire safety equipment, signaling systems.*

EST India, House Number 771 - Sector 15, Part II, Gurgaon
Haryana 122001, India

Tel: 91-124-301742

## EG&G INC.

900 Clopper Road, Ste. 200, Gaithersburg, MD, 20878

Tel: (301) 840-3000        Fax: (301) 590-0502        www.egginc.com

*Diversified R/D, mfr. and services.*

EG&G Sealol Hindustan Ltd., Survey 212/2, Sholapur Rd., Hadapsar, Pune 411 028, India

EG&G Sealol Hindustan Ltd., Bhupati Chambers 4/F, 13 Mathew Rd., Opera House, Mumbai 400 004, India

## ELECTRONIC DATA SYSTEMS CORPORATION (EDS)

5400 Legacy Dr., Plano, TX, 75024

Tel: (972) 605-6000        Fax: (972) 605-2643        www.eds.com

*Provides professional services; management consulting, e.solutions, business process management and information solutions.*

Electronic Data Systems (India) Pvt. Ltd., Ground Floor DLF Plaza Tower, DLF City Phase - 1 Gurgaon 122 002, Haryana India

Contact: Ram Seshadri

## EMERSON ELECTRIC COMPANY

8000 W. Florissant Ave., PO Box 4100, St. Louis, MO, 63136

Tel: (314) 553-2000 Fax: (314) 553-3527 www.emersonelectric.com

*Electrical and electronic products, industrial components and systems, consumer, government and defense products.*

**Emerson Electric Co., 1108 Maker Chambers V, Nariman Point, Bombay 400 002 India**

Tel: 91-22-285-2808

**Emerson Electric Company, 406 Metro House, 7 Mangaldas Road, Pune 411-001 India**

Tel: 91-20-639-590

## ENERPAC

P.O. Box 3241, Milwaukee, WI, 53201-3241

Tel: (414) 781-6600 Fax: (414) 781-1049 www.enerpac.com

*Mfr. hydraulic cylinders, pumps, valves, presses, tools, accessories and system components.*

**EMERPAC Pvt Ltd., Plot No. A-571 - MIDC TTC Industrial Area, Mahape-400 701, Navi Mumbai, India**

## ENGELHARD CORPORATION

101 Wood Ave. S., CN 770, Iselin, NJ, 08830

Tel: (732) 205-5000 Fax: (732) 632-9253 www.engelhard.com

*Mfr. pigments, additives, catalysts, chemicals, engineered materials.*

**Engelhard Environmental Systems (India) Ltd., Maramalai, Nagar, India**

## ENRON CORPORATION

1400 Smith Street, Houston, TX, 77002-7369

Tel: (713) 853-6161 Fax: (713) 853-3129 www.enron.com

*Exploration, production, transportation and distribution of integrated natural gas and electricity.*

**Dabhol Power Company, 517-518 Meridian West Tower, Raisina Rd., New Delhi 110 001, India**

Tel: 91-11-335-4182

**Dabhol Power Company, 611 Midas Sahar Plaza, Mathurdas Vassanji Road, Andheri (East) Mumbai 400 059, India**

**Enron India Pvt Ltd., 15/F - Nariman Point, Mumbai 400 021, India**

## ERIEZ MAGNETICS

PO Box 10652, Erie, PA, 16514

Tel: (814) 835-6000 Fax: (814) 838-4960 www.eriez.com

*Mfr. magnets, vibratory feeders, metal detectors, screeners/sizers, mining equipment, current separators.*

**Eriez MBI India Limited (EMIL), Whitefield, Bangalore, India**

Tel: 91-80-845-5381 Fax: 91-80-845-5380 Contact: Vinod Kochat

## ERNST & YOUNG, LLP

787 Seventh Ave., New York, NY, 10019

Tel: (212) 773-3000 Fax: (212) 773-6350 www.eyi.com

*Accounting and audit, tax and management consulting services.*

**S.R.Batliboi & Company, Himalaya House 7th Fl., 23 Kasturba Gandhi Marg, New Delhi 110 001, India**

Tel: 91-11-371-4387 Fax: 91-11-331-4802 Contact: Kashi Nath Memani

## ETHYL CORPORATION

330 South 4th Street, PO Box 2189, Richmond, VA, 23219

Tel: (804) 788-5000 Fax: (804) 788-5688 www.ethyl.com

*Provide additive chemistry solutions to enhance the performance of petroleum products.*

**Ethyl Corporation (India), G1 Sangeet Plaza - Marol Maroshi Road, Andheri-East Mumbai 77060, India**

Tel: 91-22-8597415 Fax: 91-22-8597417

## EURO RSCG WORLDWIDE

350 Hudson Street, New York, NY, 10014

Tel: (212) 886-2000    Fax: (212) 886-2016    www.eurorscg.com

*International advertising agency group.*

**EURO RSCG, PO Box 23937, The Pyramid Centre #307, Umm Hurair Road (Zabeel Road) Dubai, India**

## EXCELLON AUTOMATION

24751 Crenshaw Boulevard, Torrance, CA, 90505

Tel: (310) 534-6300    Fax: (310) 534-6777    www.excellon.com

*PCB drilling and routing machines; optical inspection equipment.*

**Max Atotech Ltd., 66 KM Stone NH 8 - Delhi Jaipur Highway, Sidhrawali Village Gurgaon -123 413 Haryana, India**

Tel: 91-1283-2115

## EXPEDITORS INTERNATIONAL OF WASHINGTON INC.

1015 Third Avenue, 12th Fl., Seattle, WA, 98104-1182

Tel: (206) 674-3400    Fax: (206) 682-9777    www.expd.com

*Air/ocean freight forwarding, customs brokerage, international logistics solutions.*

**Expeditors International (India) Pvt. Ltd., Salzburg Square 2/F, 107 Harrington Road, Chetpet Chennai, 600 031 India**

Tel: 91-44-8237647    Fax: 91-44-8238691

**Expeditors International Service Center, Khasta 411, 50B Sainik Farms, Village Khirki Tehsil-Mehrauli, New Delhi 110 062 India**

## EXXON MOBIL CORPORATION

5959 Las Colinas Blvd., Irving, TX, 75039-2298

Tel: (972) 444-1000    Fax: (972) 444-1882    www.exxon.com

*Petroleum exploration, production, refining; mfr. petroleum and chemicals products; coal and minerals.*

**Exxon Mobil, Inc., Plot No. 5 - Road No. 8, Export Promo Ind. Park, Whitefield Bangalore 560-06 India**

**Exxon Mobil, Inc., 92 Marker Chambers VI, 220 Backbay Reclamation, Nariman Point, Mumbai 400021 India**

## FIRESTONE POLYMERS

381 W. Wilbeth Road, Akron, OH, 44301

Tel: (330) 379-7864    Fax: (330) 379-7875    www.firesyn.com

*Mfr. polymers; rubber, plastics and adhesives*

**Empire Chemicals, 414 Senapati Bapat Marg., Lower Parel, Mumbai 400 013, India**

Tel: 91-22-496-4203    Fax: 91-22-493-1150    Contact: Niraj Shah

## FISHER-ROSEMOUNT

8000 Maryland Ave., Ste. 500, Clayton, MO, 63105-4755

Tel: (314) 746-9900    Fax: (314) 746-9974    www.frco.com

*Mfr. industrial process control equipment.*

**Fisher-Xomox Sanmar Ltd., 147 Karapakkam Village, Madras 600 096, India**

Tel: 91-44-492-5455    Fax: 91-44-492-6114

## FLEETBOSTON FINANCIAL CORPORATION

1 Federal Street, Boston, MA, 02110

Tel: (617) 346-4000    Fax: (617) 434-7547    www.fleet.com

*Banking and insurance services.*

**FleetBoston - Bombay, 1114-1115 Maker Chambers 11th Fl., Nariman Point, Mumbai 400-021, India**

Tel: 91-22-202-1141    Fax: 91-22-282-6108

## FLOWSERVE CORPORATION

222 W. Los Colinas Blvd., Irving, TX, 75039

Tel: (972) 443-6500 Fax: (972) 443-6858 www.flowserve.com

*Mfr. chemicals equipment, pumps, valves, filters, fans and heat exchangers.*

**Virgo Engineers Limited, J/517 MIDC Industrial Area, Off Telco Road, Bhosari Pune 411 026, India**

## FLOWSERVE FLUID SEALING DIVISION

222 Los Colinas Blvd., Ste. 1500, Irving, TX, 75039

Tel: (616) 381-2650 Fax: (616) 443-6800 www.flowserve.com

*Mfr. mechanical seals, compression packings and auxiliaries.*

**Durametallic India Ltd., 147 Karapakkam Village, Mahabalipuram Rd., Sholinganallur, PO Box, Madras 600 096, India**

## FLUOR CORPORATION

One Enterprise Drive, Aliso Viejo, CA, 92656-2606

Tel: (949) 349-2000 Fax: (949) 349-5271 www.flour.com

*Engineering and construction services.*

**Fluor Daniel India Private Limited, Block 4B Corporate Park, DLF Qutab Enclave Phase III, Gurgaon Haryana 122 002, India**

Tel: 91-124-358011 Fax: 91-124-358020

## FOSTER WHEELER CORPORATION

Perryville Corporate Park, Clinton, NJ, 08809-4000

Tel: (908) 730-4000 Fax: (908) 730-4100 www.fwc.com

*Manufacturing, engineering and construction.*

**Foster Wheeler India Pvt. Ltd., Prakash Presidium 1/F, 110 Mahatma Gandhi Road, Nungambakkam, Chennai 600 034 India**

Tel: 91-44-822-7341 Fax: 91-44-822-7340

## FRANKLIN COVEY COMPANY

2200 W. Parkway Blvd., Salt Lake City, UT, 84119-2331

Tel: (801) 975-1776 Fax: (801) 977-1431 www.franklincovey.com

*Provides productivity and time management products and seminars.*

**Leadership Resources Pte., 301-B Eden -3, Hiranandani Gardens, Powai Mumbai 40076, India**

Tel: 91-22-570-0005 Fax: 91-22-570-1383

## FRANKLIN RESOURCES, INC.

777 Mariners Island Blvd., San Mateo, CA, 94404

Tel: (415) 312-2000 Fax: (415) 312-3655 www.frk.com

*Global and domestic investment advisory and portfolio management.*

**Templeton Asset Management (India) Pvt. Ltd., Mumbai, India**

## FRITZ COMPANIES, INC.

706 Mission Street, Ste. 900, San Francisco, CA, 94103

Tel: (415) 904-8360 Fax: (415) 904-8661 www.fritz.com

*Integrated transportation, sourcing, distribution and customs brokerage services.*

**Fritz Companies Inc., Bangalore, India**

## FSI INTERNATIONAL INC.

322 Lake Hazeltine Drive, Chaska, MN, 55318

Tel: (612) 448-5440 Fax: (612) 448-2825 www.fsi-intl.com

*Manufacturing equipment for computer silicon wafers.*

**Fabteq, Div. FSI, No. 100 4th Cross, 2nd Block, Koramangala, Bangalore 560 034, India**

## THE GATES RUBBER COMPANY

990 S. Broadway, PO Box 5887, Denver, CO, 80217-5887

Tel: (303) 744-1911        Fax: (303) 744-4000        www.gatesrubber.com

*Mfr. automotive and industrial belts and hoses.*

**Gates Rubber India, Chandigarh Ambala Highway, District of Patiala 140501 Punjab, India**

Tel: 91-172-543599   Fax: 91-172-780-970

## GENERAL BINDING CORPORATION

One GBC Plaza, Northbrook, IL, 60062

Tel: (847) 272-3700        Fax: (847) 272-1369        www.gbc.com

*Engaged in the design, manufacture and distribution of branded office equipment, related supplies and thermal laminating films.*

**GBC Hi-Tech (India) Ltd., A-216 Okhla Industrial Area Phase I, New Delhi 100 020, India**

## GENERAL ELECTRIC COMPANY

3135 Easton Turnpike, Fairfield, CT, 06431

Tel: (203) 373-2211        Fax: (203) 373-3131        www.ge.com

*Diversified manufacturing, technology and services.*

**GE Automation, 10 Haddows Rd., Madras 600 006, India**

Tel: 91-44-826-7741   Fax: 91-44-825-7340

**GE FANUC Automation, AIFACS Bldg., New Delhi 110 001, India**

Tel: 91-11-335-5880   Fax: 91-11-335-5969

**General Electric Co., AIFACS Bldg., New Delhi 110 001, India**

Tel: 518-438-6500 USA   Contact: Scott Bayman, Pres.

**GETSCO, AIFACS Bldg., New Delhi 110 001, India**

Tel: 91-11-335-5800   Fax: 91-11-335-5955

## GENERAL INSTRUMENT CORPORATION

101 Tournament Road, Horsham, PA, 19044

Tel: (215) 674-4800        Fax: (215) 443-9554        www.gi.com

*Mfr. broadband communications and power rectifying components.*

**GI India Private Limited, 517-520 Prestige Centre Point, 7 Edward Road, Bangalore 560 052 India**

Tel: 91-80-225-7313   Fax: 91-80-228-5805

## GEO LOGISTICS CORPORATION

1521 E. Dyer Rd., Santa Ana, CA, 92705

Tel: (714) 513-3000        Fax: (714) 513-3120        www.geo-logistics.com

*Freight forwarding, warehousing and distribution services, specializing in heavy cargo.*

**GeoLogistics Ltd., 303 (1st Fl) Ashok Terrace, 100 Feet Rd, Indiranagar I stage, Bangalore 560 038 India**

Tel: 91-80-527-4724   Fax: 91-80-527-4725

**GeoLogistics Ltd., 2/F Chitrakoot Building 230A, AJC Bose Rd., Calcutta 700 020, India**

Tel: 91-33-240-2140   Fax: 91-33-240-2140

**GeoLogistics Ltd., Navkar Chambers Wing A 5th Floor, Andheri-Kurla Road, Andheri (E), Mumbai 400 059 India**

Tel: 91-22-859-6640   Fax: 91-22-859-7510

## GETZ BROS & COMPANY, INC.

150 Post Street, Ste. 500, San Francisco, CA, 94108-4750

Tel: (415) 772-5500        Fax: (415) 772-5659        www.getz.com

*Diversified manufacturing, marketing and distribution services and travel services.*

**Muller & Phipps (India) Ltd., Queen's Mansion, Amrit Keshav Naik Marg, Fort Mumbai 400 001, India**

Tel: 91-22-204-2544   Fax: 91-22-207-1097   Contact: U. Dhupelia   Emp: 35

## THE GILLETTE COMPANY

Prudential Tower Building, Boston, MA, 02199

Tel: (617) 421-7000     Fax: (617) 421-7123     www.gillette.com

*Develop/mfr. personal care/use products: blades and razors, toiletries, cosmetics, stationery.*

**Indian Shaving Products Ltd., Rajasthan, India**

## GILSON INC.

3000 W. Beltline Hwy, PO Box 620027, Middleton, WI, 53562-0027

Tel: (608) 836-1551     Fax: (608) 831-4451     www.gilson.com

*Mfr. analytical/biomedical instruments.*

**ASR Instruments, 1/F Baba Chambers, 73 Richmond Road, Bangalore 560 025, India**

## GIW INDUSTRIES, INC.

5000 Wrightsboro Rd., Grovetown, GA, 30813

Tel: (706) 863-1011     Fax: (706) 860-5897     www.giwindustries.com

*Mfr. slurry pumps.*

**KSB Pumps Limited, Bombay-Pune Road, Pune 411018, India**

## GLEASON CORPORATION

1000 University Ave., Rochester, NY, 14692

Tel: (716) 473-1000     Fax: (716) 461-4348     www.gleasoncorp.com

*Mfr. gear making machine tools; tooling and services.*

**Gleason Works (India) Pvt. Ltd., Plot No. 37, Doddenakundi Industrial Area, Whitefield Rd., Mahadevapura Bangalore 560 048, India**

Tel: 91-80-851-6177   Fax: 91-80-851-6178

## GLENAYRE ELECTRONICS LTD.

5935 Carnegie Blvd.., Ste. 300, Charlotte, NC, 28209

Tel: (704) 553-0038     Fax: (704) 553-7878     www.glenayre.com

*Mfr. infrastructure components and pagers.*

**Glenayre Electronics India Pvt. Ltd., c/o Continental Business Center, Flat No. 912, International Trade Tower, New Delhi 110 019, India**

Tel: 91-11-623-3635   Fax: 91-11-628-6173

## THE GOODYEAR TIRE & RUBBER COMPANY

1144 East Market Street, Akron, OH, 44316

Tel: (330) 796-2121     Fax: (330) 796-1817     www.goodyear.com

*Mfr. tires, automotive belts and hose, conveyor belts, chemicals; oil pipeline transmission.*

**Goodyear India Ltd., 3/F Godreg Bhavan, Mathura Rd., New Delhi 110 065, India**

## W. R. GRACE & COMPANY

7500 Grace Drive, Columbia, MD, 21044

Tel: (410) 531-4000     Fax: (410) 531-4367     www.grace.com

*Mfr. specialty chemicals and materials: packaging, health care, catalysts, construction, water treatment/process.*

**W.R. Grace & Co. (India), Suite 420 - 3A Cross - 3rd Block, 16th Main Koramangala, Bangalore 560 034, India**

Tel: 91-80-552-0316   Fax: 91-80-553-4500

## GRANT THORNTON INTERNATIONAL

800 One Prudential Plaza, 130 E. Randolph Drive, Chicago, IL, 60601-6050

Tel: (312) 856-0001     Fax: (312) 616-7052     www.grantthornton.com

*Accounting, audit, tax and management consulting services.*

**K.S. Aiyar & Co., East & West Bldg., 49-55 Mumbai Samachar Marg, Mumbai 400 023, India**

## GREFCO MINERALS, INC.

23705 Crenshaw Blvd., Ste. 101, Torrance, CA, 90505

Tel:  (310) 517-0700      Fax:  (310) 517-0794      www.grefco.com

*Mfr. diatomite and perlite products, and exclusive distributor of Dicaflock cellulose fibers.*

**Amoi Dicalite Ltd.,  Behind Haldervas Octroi Naka, Raknial Rd., Ahmedahad 380 023, India**

## GREY GLOBAL GROUP

777 Third Ave., New York, NY, 10017

Tel:  (212) 546-2000      Fax:  (212) 546-1495      www.grey.com

*International advertising agency.*

**Trikaya Grey,  Phoenix Estate Block 2-D, 3rd fl. 462 Tulsi Pipe Road, Mumbai 400 013 India**

## GUARDIAN INDUSTRIES CORPORATION

2300 Harmon Road, Auburn Hills, MI, 48326-1714

Tel:  (248) 340-1800      Fax:  (248) 340-9988      www.guardian.com

*Mfr. and fabricate flat glass products and insulation materials.*

**Gujarat Guardian Limited,  State Highway 13 - Village Kondh, Taluka Valia Dist. of Bharuch, Gujarat, PIN 393 011 India**

Tel: 91-2643-75106   Fax: 91-2643-75105

## HALLIBURTON COMPANY

500 North Akard Street, Ste. 3600, Dallas, TX, 75201-3391

Tel:  (214) 978-2600      Fax:  (214) 978-2685      www.halliburton.com

*Engaged in diversified energy services, engineering and construction.*

**Halliburton Ltd.,  Gintanjali Tubes Compound, 1/1 Poonamallee High Rd., Nerkundram Madras 600 107, India**

Tel: 91-44-487-1345   Fax: 91-44-487-1346

## HARCOURT GENERAL, INC.

27 Boylston St., Chestnut Hill, MA, 02467

Tel:  (617) 232-8200      Fax:  (617) 739-1395      www.harcourtgeneral.com

*Publisher of educational materials.*

**Harcourt General Asia Pte.Ltd.,  27 M-Block Market, Great Kailash II, New Delhi 110 048, India**

Tel: 91-11-646-4550   Fax: 91-11-647-5065   Contact: Sanjay Banerjee, Mgr.

## HARRIS CORPORATION

1025 West NASA Blvd., Melbourne, FL, 32919

Tel:  (407) 727-9100      Fax:  (407) 727-9344      www.harris.com

*Mfr. communications and information-handling equipment, including copying and fax systems.*

**Intersil Pvt. Ltd.,  Plot 54 SEEPZ, Marol Industrial Area, Anderi (E), Mumbai 400 096 India**

Tel: 91-22-832-3097   Fax: 91-22-836-6682

## HEIDRICK & STRUGGLES INTERNATIONAL, INC.

Sears Tower, 233 South Wacker Drive, Chicago, IL, 60606

Tel:  (312) 496-1200      Fax:  (312) 496-1290      www.heidrick.com

*Executive search firm.*

**Heidrick & Struggles Intl. Inc.,  505 International Trade Tower - Nehru Place, New Delhi 110019, India**

## H.J. HEINZ COMPANY

600 Grant Street, Pittsburgh, PA, 15219

Tel:  (412) 456-5700      Fax:  (412) 456-6128      www.heinz.com

*Processed food products and nutritional services.*

**Heinz India Pvt. Ltd.,  Mumbai, India**

## HERCULES INC.

Hercules Plaza, 1313 N. Market Street, Wilmington, DE, 19894-0001

Tel: (302) 594-5000     Fax: (302) 594-5400     www.herc.com

*Mfr. specialty chemicals, plastics, film and fibers, coatings, resins, food ingredients.*

**Herdillia Chemicals Ltd., Air India Bldg., Post Bag 9962, Nariman Point, Mumbai 400 021, India**

## HEWITT ASSOCIATES LLC

100 Half Day Road, Lincolnshire, IL, 60069

Tel: (847) 295-5000     Fax: (847) 295-7634     www.hewitt.com

*Employee benefits consulting firm.*

**Nobel & Hewitt, Getta Building Ground Floor, Dr. Pandita Ramaabai Road, Gamdevi Mumbai 400 007, India**

Tel: 91-22-369-7676

**Nobel & Hewitt, Ste. 810-81 Wing B 8th Fl. Mittal Tower, 6 M.G. Road, Bangalore 560 001, India**

Tel: 91-80-559-4592

**Nobel & Hewitt, Z-1 First Floor, Hauz Khas, New Delhi 110 016, India**

Tel: 91-11-686-1594    Fax: 91-11-651-5501

## HEWLETT-PACKARD COMPANY

3000 Hanover Street, Palo Alto, CA, 94304-1185

Tel: (650) 857-1501     Fax: (650) 857-5518     www.hp.com

*Mfr. computing, communications and measurement products and services.*

**Hewlett-Packard India Ltd., Paharpur Business Centre, 21 Nehru Place, New Delhi 110 019, India**

## HOLIDAY INN (BASS RESORTS) WORLDWIDE, INC.

3 Ravinia Drive, Ste. 2900, Atlanta, GA, 30346-2149

Tel: (770) 604-2000     Fax: (770) 604-5403     www.holidayinn.com

*Hotels, restaurants and casinos.*

**Holiday Inn Inc., Juhu Beach, Mumbai 400 049, India**

**Holiday Inn Inc. - India, Fatehabab Rd., Taj Ganj, Agra, India**

## HOLLINGSWORTH & VOSE COMPANY

112 Washington Street, East Walpole, MA, 02032

Tel: (508) 668-0295     Fax: (508) 668-3557     www.hollingsworth-vose.com

*Mfr. technical and industrial papers and non-woven fabrics.*

**H&V India Liaison Office, Summer Garden, Flat No. 5 South Main Road, Koregaon Park, Pune 411 001 India**

## HONEYWELL INTERNATIONAL INC.

101 Columbia Road, Morristown, NJ, 07962

Tel: (973) 455-2000     Fax: (973) 455-4807     www.honeywell.com

*Develop/mfr. controls for home and building, industry, space and aviation.*

**Honeywell Europe Inc., 403/404 "Madhava", Bandra Kurla Complex, Bundra East, Bombay, India**

Tel: 91-22-204-5827    Fax: 91-22-640-9513

**Tata Honeywell Ltd., 55-1 - 8&89 Hadapsar, Industrial Estate, Pune 411 013 India**

Tel: 91-212-670-445    Fax: 91-212-672-205

## HORWATH INTERNATIONAL ASSOCIATION

415 Madison Ave., New York, NY, 10017

Tel: (212) 838-5566     Fax: (212) 838-3636     www.horwath.com

*Public accountants and auditors.*

**N.M. Raiji Co., Universal Insurance Bldg., Pherozeshaha Mehta Rd., Mumbai 400 001, India**

**P.K. Chopra & Co., N Block, Mumbai Life Bldg., Connaught Place, New Delhi 110 001, India**

## HOUGHTON INTERNATIONAL INC.

PO Box 930, Madison & Van Buren Avenues, Valley Forge, PA, 19482-0930

Tel: (610) 666-4000      Fax: (610) 666-1376      www.houghtonintl.com

*Mfr. specialty chemicals, hydraulic fluids and lubricants.*

**Houghton Hardcastle India Ltd., Brabourne Stadium, 87 Veer Nariman Rd., Mumbai 400 020, India**

## HOWMEDICA OSTEONICS, INC.

359 Veterans Blvd., Rutherford, NJ, 07070

Tel: (201) 507-7300      Fax: (201) 935-4873      www.howmedica.com

*Mfr. of maxillofacial products (orthopedic implants).*

**Howmedica India, Mumbai, India**

Tel: 91-22-6783-432

## J.M. HUBER CORPORATION

333 Thornall Street, Edison, NJ, 08818

Tel: (732) 549-8600      Fax: (732) 549-2239      www.huber.com

*Crude oil, gas, carbon black, kaolin clay, rubber and paper pigments, timber and minerals.*

**J.M. Huber, Mumbai, India**

## HUNTSMAN CORPORATION

500 Huntsman Way, Salt Lake City, UT, 84108

Tel: (801) 532-5200      Fax: (801) 536-1581      www.huntsman.com

*Mfr./sales specialty chemicals, industrial chemicals and petrochemicals.*

**ICI India Limited C/O Huntsman Polyurethanes, Thane Belapur Road, PO Box 87, Thane Maharashtra 400 601, India**

Tel: 91-22-761-9835    Contact: A. Khetan

## i2 TECHNOLOGIES, INC.

11701 Luna Road, Dallas, TX, 75234

Tel: (214) 860-6106      Fax: (214) 860-6060      www.i2.com

*Mfr. business-to-business software.*

**i2 Technologies India Pvt. Ltd., No. 1 Primrose Road, Bangalore 560025, India**

## IBM CORPORATION

New Orchard Road, Armonk, NY, 10504

Tel: (914) 765-1900      Fax: (914) 765-7382      www.ibm.com

*Information products, technology and services.*

**IBM Global Services India Ltd., TISL Tower Golden Enclave, Airport Road, Bangalore 560 017 India**

Tel: 91-80-526-7117    Fax: 91-80-527-7991

## ICC INDUSTRIES INC.

460 Park Ave., New York, NY, 10022

Tel: (212) 521-1700      Fax: (212) 521-1794      www.iccchem.com

*Manufacturing and trading of chemicals, plastics and pharmaceuticals.*

**Lexicon Chemicals, Manorama, Lt. Dilip Gupte Road, Mahim Mumbai 400 016, India**

Tel: 91-22-445-7984    Fax: 91-22-446-3844

## IKOS SYSTEMS, INC.

19050 Pruneridge Avenue, Cupertino, CA, 95014

Tel: (408) 255-4567      Fax: (408) 366-8699      www.ikos.com

*Mfr. hardware and software.*

**IKOS India Private Limited, A-4 Sector 10, Noida UP 201301, India**

Tel: 91-118-4551466    Fax: 91-118-4538259

## IMG (INTERNATIONAL MANAGEMENT GROUP)

1360 East Ninth Street, Ste. 100, Cleveland, OH, 44114

Tel: (216) 522-1200    Fax: (216) 522-1145    www.imgworld.com

*Manages athletes, sports academies and real estate facilities worldwide.*

**IMG, 268 Masjid Moth - 4/F, Uday Park, New Delhi, 100 049 India**

Tel: 91-11-625-5864    Fax: 91-11-625-8583

**IMG, Unit 15 Upper Phoenix Centre, The Phoenix Mills Compound, 462 Senapati Bapat Marg, Lower Parel, Mumbai, 400 013 India**

Tel: 91-22-498-3811    Fax: 91-22-491-8621

## IMR GLOBAL

26750 US Highway. 19 North, Ste. 500, Clearwater, FL, 33761

Tel: (727) 797-7080    Fax: (727) 791-8152    www.imrglobal.com

*Provides application software, e-business and information technology solutions and outsourcing services to business.*

**IMR Bangalore, Bldg. 38/1, Naganthapura, Singasandra Post, Bangalore 560 058, India**

Tel: 91-80-852-1224    Fax: 91-80-852-1268

**IMR Mumbai, Plot 22, Seepz, Andheri (East), Mumbai 400 096, India**

Tel: 91-22-829-1421    Fax: 91-22-829-1818

## INACOM CORPORATION

2001 Westside Parkway, Ste. 260, Alpharetta, GA, 30004

Tel: (770) 643-2419    Fax: (770) 993-6375    www.inacom.com

*Provider of technology management products and services; reselling microcomputer systems, work stations and networking and telecommunications equipment.*

**CMS Computers Ltd., 201 Arcadai, Nariman Point, Mumbai 400021 India**

## INDUCTOTHERM CORPORATION

10 Indel Ave., PO Box 157, Rancocas, NJ, 08073-0157

Tel: (609) 267-9000    Fax: (609) 267-3537    www.inductotherm.com

*Mfr. induction melting furnaces, induction power supplies, charging and preheating systems, automatic pouring systems and computer control systems.*

**Inductotherm (India) Ltd., Ambli-Bopal Rd., Bopal, Ahmedabad 380 054, India**

Tel: 91-2717-31961    Contact: Bharat Sheth

## INFORMATION RESOURCES, INC. (IRI)

150 N. Clinton St., Chicago, IL, 60661

Tel: (312) 726-1221    Fax: (312) 726-0360    www.infores.com

*Provides bar code scanner services for retail sales organizations; processes, analyzes and sells data from the huge database created from these services.*

**Operations Research Group, 222 A.J.C. Bose Rd. 3rd Fl., Calcutta 700 017, India**

Tel: 91-33-240-48441    Fax: 91-33-240-6908

## INFORMIX CORPORATION

4100 Bohannon Drive, Menlo Park, CA, 95025

Tel: (650) 926-6300    Fax: (650) 926-6593    www.informix.com

*Designs and produces database management software, connectivity interfaces and gateways, and other computer applications.*

**Informix International Inc., c/o DBS Corporate Club, Raheja Chambers, 213 Nariman Point, Mumbai 400 021 India**

Tel: 91-22-829-0402    Fax: 91-22-829-0330

## INGERSOLL-RAND COMPANY

200 Chestnut Ridge Road, Woodcliff Lake, NJ, 07675

Tel: (201) 573-0123    Fax: (201) 573-3172    www.ingersoll-rand.com

*Mfr. compressors, rock drills, air tools, door hardware, ball bearings.*

**Ingersoll-Rand (India) Ltd., Rhone-Poulenc House, S.K. Ahire Marg., PO Box 9138, Mumbai 400 025 India**

Tel: 91-22-4936765   Fax: 91-22-4950516

**Ingersoll-Rand India, 22/29 GIDC Estate, Naroda, Ahmedabad 382 330, India**

## INGRAM MICRO INC.

PO Box 25125, 1600 E. St. Andrew Place, Santa Ana, CA, 92799

Tel: (714) 566-1000    Fax: (714) 566-7940    www.ingrammicro.com

*Engaged in wholesale distribution of microcomputer products.*

**Ingram Micro India Ltd., MF 7 Cipet Hostel Road, Thiru-Vi-Ka Nagar, Ekkatuthangal Chennai 600 097, India**

## INTER-CONTINENTAL HOTELS

3 Ravina Drive, Suite 2900, Atlanta, GA, 30346-2149

Tel: (770) 604-2000    Fax: (770) 604-5403    www.interconti.com

*Worldwide hotel and resort accommodations.*

**Taj Palace Inter-Continental New Delhi, 2 Sardar Patel Marg, Diplomatic Enclave, New Delhi 110 021, India**

Tel: 91-11-611-0202   Fax: 91-11-611-0808

## INTERGRAPH CORPORATION

One Madison Industrial Park, Huntsville, AL, 35894-0001

Tel: (256) 730-2000    Fax: (256) 730-7898    www.intergraph.com

*Develop/mfr. interactive computer graphic systems.*

**Intergraph (India) Pvt. Ltd., 1-8-446 & 447 Begumpet, Hyderabad, Andhra Pradesh 500 016 India**

Tel: 91-40-815378   Fax: 91-40-815379

## INTERNATIONAL COMPONENTS CORPORATION

420 N. May Street, Chicago, IL, 60622

Tel: (312) 829-2525    Fax: (312) 829-0213    www.icc-charge.com

*Mfr./sale/services portable DC battery chargers.*

**International Components Corp. (India) Ltd., 3-A Kodambakkam High Rd., Nungambakkam, Madras 600 034, India**

## INTERNATIONAL FLAVORS & FRAGRANCES INC.

521 West 57th Street, New York, NY, 10019-2960

Tel: (212) 765-5500    Fax: (212) 708-7132    www.iff.com

*Design/mfr. flavors, fragrances and aroma chemicals.*

**International Flavors & Fragrances, Pinnacle Chambers 6/F, Mathurdas Vassanji Road, Andheri East - Mumbai 400 093, India**

Tel: 91-22-822-5787   Fax: 91-22-824-4045

## INTERNATIONAL RECTIFIER CORPORATION

233 Kansas Street, El Segundo, CA, 90245

Tel: (310) 322-3331    Fax: (310) 322-3332    www.irf.com

*Mfr. power semiconductor components.*

**International Rectifier - India, c/o Semiconductor Electronics Ltd., S.D.F. #23, Seepz Post Office, Andheri East, Mumbai 400 096, India**

Tel: 91-22-829-1055   Fax: 91-22-829-0473

## INTERNATIONAL SPECIALTY PRODUCTS, INC.

1361 Alps Rd., Wayne, NJ, 07470

Tel: (877) 389-3083      Fax: (973) 628-4117      www.ispcorp.com

*Mfr. specialty chemical products.*

**ISP International Inc., C-211 Floral Deck Plaza, Opp: Seepz M.I.D.C. Andheri (East), Mumbai 400 093, India**

Tel: 91-22-837-0472   Fax: 91-22-837-0449

## IRIDIUM LLC

1575 "I" Street, NW, Washington, DC, 20005

Tel: (202) 408-3800      Fax: (202) 408-3801      www.iridium.com

*Consortium of companies sharing the construction and implementation of a global satellite communications system.*

**Iridium India Telecom Ltd. (South Asia Reg. HQ), 2nd Fl. c/8 St. No 22 M.I.D.C., Marol Andheri East Mumbai 400 093, India**

Tel: 91-22-821-4248   Fax: 91-22-821-4248   Contact: Moosa Raza, Chmn.

## J. WALTER THOMPSON COMPANY

466 Lexington Ave., New York, NY, 10017

Tel: (212) 210-7000      Fax: (212) 210-6944      www.jwt.com

*International advertising and marketing services.*

**Contract Advertising(JWT), Mumbai, India**

**Hindustan Thompson Associates, Mumbai, India**

## JACOBS ENGINEERING GROUP INC.

1111 S. Arroyo Parkway, Pasadena, CA, 91105

Tel: (626) 578-3500      Fax: (626) 578-6916      www.jacobs.com

*Engineering, design and consulting; construction and construction management; process plant maintenance.*

**Humphreys & Glasgow Consultants, H&G House, Sector II, Plot No. 12, DBD Belapur, Mumbai 400 614, India**

Tel: 91-22-757-3046   Fax: 91-22-757-3049

**Humphreys & Glasgow Consultants, 242 Okhla Industrial Estate, Phase-III, New Delhi, India 110 020**

Tel: 91-11-631-1584   Fax: 91-11-631-1767   Contact: S. N. Deshponde, Dir.

**Humphreys & Glasgow Consultants, Corporate Hdqrts., Gammon House, Scrarker Marq, Prabhadevi, Mumbei 400 025, India**

Tel: 91-22-430-2481   Fax: 91-22-422-2494   Contact: Dr. Arun N. Bravid, Dir.

**Humphreys & Glasgow Consultants Ltd., 2nd Fl. No. 3 Dacres Lane, West Bengal, Calcutta 708 069, India**

Tel: 91-33-221-4967   Fax: 91-33-221-4969   Contact: S. K. Sengupta, Mgr.   Emp: 54

**Humphreys & Glasgow Consultants Ltd., Natubhai Centre 11 Fl., Race Course, Gotri Rd., Vadodara, India 390 007**

Tel: 91-265-339-638   Fax: 91-265-341-522   Contact: S. N. Deshpande, Dir.   Emp: 43

## JLG INDUSTRIES INC.

One JLG Drive, McConnellsburg, PA, 17233-9533

Tel: (717) 485-5161      Fax: (717) 485-6417      www.jlg.com

*Mfr. aerial work platforms and vertical personnel lifts.*

**JLG Industries, G-62 Saket, New Delhi 110 017, India**

Tel: 91-11652-5507   Fax: 91-11652-5751

## JOHNSON & JOHNSON

One Johnson & Johnson Plaza, New Brunswick, NJ, 08933

Tel: (732) 524-0400      Fax: (732) 214-0334      www.jnj.com

*Mfr./distributor/R&D pharmaceutical, health care and cosmetic products.*

**Janssen-Cilag Pharmaceutica, Mumbai, India**

Johnson & Johnson Ltd., **30 Forjett St., Post Box 9301, Mumbai 400 036, India**

**Johnson & Johnson Professional, Mumbai, India**

## S C JOHNSON & SON INC.

1525 Howe St., Racine, WI, 53403

Tel: (414) 260-2000      Fax: (414) 260-2133      www.scjohnsonwax.com

*Home, auto, commercial and personal care products and specialty chemicals.*

**Lever-Johnson Pvt Ltd., Muttha Chambers IV Fl., Senapati Bapat Marg, Pune 411 016, India**

## JOHNSON CONTROLS INC.

5757 N. Green Bay Ave., PO Box 591, Milwaukee, WI, 53201-0591

Tel: (414) 228-1200      Fax: (414) 228-2077      www.johnsoncontrols.com

*Mfr. facility management and control systems and auto seating.*

**Johnson Controls / India, RV House, B-37 Veera Desai Rd., Off Link Rd., Andheri West Mumbai 400 053 India**

Tel: 91-22-6261734   Fax: 91-22-6261801   Contact: Karkal Pramoda, Br. Mgr.

## JONES, DAY, REAVIS & POGUE

North Point, 901 Lakeside Ave., Cleveland, OH, 44114

Tel: (216) 586-3939      Fax: (216) 579-0212      www.jonesday.com

*International law firm.*

**Pathak & Associates, 13th Fl. Dr. Gopal Das Bhavan, 28 Barakhamba Rd., New Delhi 110 001, India**

Tel: 91-11-373-8793   Fax: 91-11-335-3761   Contact: Jai S. Pathak, Res. Partner   Emp: 10

## JUKI UNION SPECIAL CORPORATION

5 Haul Road, Wayne, NJ, 07470

Tel: (973) 633-7200      Fax: (973) 633-9629      www.unionspecial.com

*Mfr. sewing machines.*

**JUKI Machineries India Pvt. Ltd., A-215/B Okhla Industrial Area Phase-1, New Delhi 110020, India**

Tel: 91-80-224-0957   Fax: 91-80-221-2442

**JUKI Machineries India Pvt. Ltd., 1st Fl. Fazal Manor, No. 89, Richmond Rd., Bangalore 560 025, India**

Tel: 91-80-224-0957   Fax: 91-80-221-2442

## A.T. KEARNEY INC.

222 West Adams Street, Chicago, IL, 60606

Tel: (312) 648-0111      Fax: (312) 223-6200      www.atkearney.com

*Management consultants and executive search.*

**A. T. Kearney Ltd., Taj Mahal Business Centre, One Mansingh Rd. Ste. 1001, New Delhi 110 011 India**

Tel: 91-11-301-6162

## THE KENDALL COMPANY (TYCO HEALTHCARE)

15 Hampshire Street, Mansfield, MA, 02048

Tel: (508) 261-8000      Fax: (508) 261-8542      www.kendalhq.com

*Mfr. medical disposable products, home health care products and specialty adhesive products.*

**Kendall South Asia, #22 Mirza Hyuder Ali Khan St., Royapettah, Madras 600 014, India**

Tel: 91-44-854-4981   Fax: 91-44-854-4981

## KENNAMETAL INC.

State Rte. 981, Latrobe, PA, 15650

Tel: (724) 539-5000      Fax: (724) 539-4710      www.kennametal.com

*Tools, hard carbide and tungsten alloys for metalworking industry.*

**Birla Kennametal Ltd., B-15/4 MIDC Industrial Area, Waluj, Aurangabad 431 133, India**

Tel: 91-240-554300   Fax: 91-240-554302

**Drillco Hertel Ltd., Motwani Chambers, 1187/59 J.M. Rd., Shivaji Nagar Pune 411 005, India**
Tel: 91-212-325-8292    Fax: 91-212-323225

## KIMBERLY-CLARK CORPORATION

351 Phelps Drive, Irving, TX, 75038

Tel: (972) 281-1200        Fax: (972) 281-1435        www.kimberly-clark.com

*Mfr./sales/distribution of consumer tissue, household and personal care products.*

**Kimberly-Clark Corp., India**

## KIRKWOOD INDUSTRIES INC.

4855 W. 130th Street, Cleveland, OH, 44135-5182

Tel: (216) 267-6200        Fax: (216) 362-3804        www.kirkwood-ind.com

*Mfr. electrical components, commutators, mica insulation, slip rings and carbon brushes.*

**Sahney Kirkwood Ltd., 27 Kirol, Vidyavihar West, PO Box 9222, Mumbai 400 086, India**

## KOCH-GLITSCH, INC.

PO Box 8127, Wichita, KS, 67208

Tel: (316) 828-5110        Fax: (316) 828-5950        www.koch-ind.com

*Mfr./services mass transfer/chemicals separation equipment, process engineering.*

**Glitsch Process India Ltd., 102 Swatsik Chambers, Sion-Trombay Road, Mumbai 400 071 India**
Tel: 91-22-5230509

## KOLLMORGEN CORPORATION

1601 Trapelo Road, Waltham, MA, 02154

Tel: (781) 890-5655        Fax: (781) 890-7150        www.kollmorgen.com

*Mfr. high-performance electronic motion-control systems and design and supply advanced submarine periscopes, weapons directors, and military optics.*

**Kollmorgen Tandon India, Mumbai (Bombay), India**

## KORN/FERRY INTERNATIONAL

1800 Century Park East, Los Angeles, CA, 90067

Tel: (310) 843-4100        Fax: (310) 553-6452        www.kornferry.com

*Executive search; management consulting.*

**Korn/Ferry International, New Delhi, India**
Tel: 91-11-652-2455    Fax: 91-11-652-2458

## KPMG INTERNATIONAL LLP

345 Park Avenue, New York, NY, 10022

Tel: (201) 307-7000        Fax: (201) 930-8617        www.kpmg.com

*Accounting and audit, tax and management consulting services.*

**KPMG, 2A Century Plaza, Fl. 2 560, Anna Salai, Madras 600 018, India**

**KPMG, The Metropolitan, West Wing Fl. 3, Bandra-Kurla Complex(E-Block), Mumbai 400 051 India**
Tel: 91-22-643-8110   Fax: 91-22-645-6930   Contact: Sridar A. Iyengar, Ptnr.

**KPMG, World Trade Centre, Central 11th Fl., #5&6 Cuffe Parade, Mumbai 400 005, India**

**KPMG, 5th Fl. Shariff Chambers 14, Cunningham Rd., Bangalore 560 052, India**

**KPMG Barat S. Raut & Co., 511 World Trade Centre, Barbar Rd., New Delhi 110 001, India**
Tel: 91-11-3355-1222   Fax: 91-11-332-3632   Contact: Rajesh Jain, Ptnr.

## THE KROLL-O'GARA COMPANY

9113 Le Saint Drive, Fairfield, OH, 45014

Tel: (513) 874-2112        Fax: (513) 874-2558        www.kroll-ogara.com

*Security and consulting services and vehicles.*

**Kroll Associates (Asia) Ltd. (India Liasion Office), 208 Barakhamba Rd., New Delhi 110 001, India**
Tel: 91-11-373-6355   Fax: 91-11-373-6356

## THE KULJIAN CORPORATION

3700 Science Center, Philadelphia, PA, 19104

Tel: (215) 243-1900        Fax: (215) 243-1909

*Studies, design, engineering, construction management and site supervision.*

**Development Consultants Pvt. Ltd., Hamed Bldg., 193 Anna Salai, Madras 600 006, India**

**Development Consultants Pvt. Ltd., 24-B Park St., Calcutta 700 016, India**

**The Kuljian Corp. India Pvt. Ltd., 307-309 Sahyog, 58 Nehru Place, New Delhi 110 019, India**

## LANCER CORPORATION

6655 Lancer Blvd, San Antonio, TX, 78219

Tel: (210) 310-7000        Fax: (210) 310-7252        www.lancercorp.com

*Mfr. beverage dispensing equipment.*

**Lancer India, Dr. Annie Besant Road, Worli Mumbai 400-018, India**

Tel: 91-22-283-0862

## LANDOR ASSOCIATES

Klamath House, 1001 Front Street, San Francisco, CA, 94111-1424

Tel: (415) 955-1400        Fax: (415) 365-3190        www.landor.com

*International marketing consulting firm, focused on developing and maintaining brand identity.*

**Landor Associates, c/o SNR Associates, D5 Hari Chambers, 3/F RB Centre 58-64 S.B. Road, Fort Bombay 400 023 India**

Tel: 91-22-266-2339   Fax: 91-22-265-4763   Contact: Swapnesh Patel

## LAWSON MARDON WHEATON, INC.

1101 Wheaton Ave., Millville, NJ, 08332

Tel: (856) 825-1400        Fax: (856) 825-0146        www.algroupwheaton.com

*Engaged in pharmaceutical and cosmetic packaging, glass and plastic containers.*

**Vazir Glass Works Ltd., M. Vasenji Rd., Mumbai 400 059, India**

## LE TOURNEAU COMPANY

PO Box 2307, Longview, TX, 75606

Tel: (903) 237-7000        Fax: (903) 267-7032

*Mfr. heavy construction and mining machinery equipment.*

**General Marketing & Mfg. Co. Ltd., Birla Bldg. 14/F, 9/I R. N. Mukherjee Rd, Calcutta 700 001, India**

## LEAR CORPORATION

21557 Telegraph Road, Southfield, MI, 48086-5008

Tel: (248) 746-1500        Fax: (248) 746-1722        www.lear.com

*Mfr. and distribute automotive materials and car seats.*

**Lear Corporation (Opel Division), Halol, India**

## LEHMAN BROTHERS HOLDINGS INC.

Three World Financial Center, New York, NY, 10285

Tel: (212) 526-7000        Fax: (212) 526-3738        www.lehman.com

*Financial services, securities and merchant banking services.*

**Lehman Brothers, Dr. Gopal Das Bhavan Bldg., 28 Barakhamba Road 15th Fl., New Delhi 110 001, India**

Tel: 91-11-373-6559

## LEXMARK INTERNATIONAL

1 Lexmark Centre Dr., Lexington, KY, 40550

Tel: (606) 232-2000     Fax: (606) 232-1886     www.lexmark.com

*Develop, manufacture, supply of printing solutions and products, including laser, inkjet, and dot matrix printers.*

**Lexmark Representative Office, Room 207 Apeejay Business Centre, Haddows Road, Chennai 600 006 India**

Tel: 91-44-822-4949   Fax: 91-44-826-2447

## LIFE TECHNOLOGIES INC.

9800 Medical Center Drive, Rockville, MD, 20850

Tel: (301) 840-8000     Fax: (301) 329-8635     www.lifetech.com

*Produces biotechnology research materials.*

**GIBCO BRL India Pvt. Ltd., 4/F G H Gopala Tower, 25 Rajendra Place, New Delhi 110008, India**

## ELI LILLY & COMPANY

Lilly Corporate Center, Indianapolis, IN, 46285

Tel: (317) 276-2000     Fax: (317) 277-6579     www.lilly.com

*Mfr. pharmaceuticals and animal health products.*

**Eli Lilly Ranbaxy JV, 8 Balaji Estate, Guru Ravi Dass Marg. Kalkaji, New Delhi 110 019, India**

Tel: 91-11-621-0084   Fax: 91-11-621-0075

## LINCOLN ELECTRIC HOLDINGS

22801 St. Clair Ave., Cleveland, OH, 44117-1199

Tel: (216) 481-8100     Fax: (216) 486-8385     www.lincolnelectric.com

*Mfr. arc welding and welding related products, oxy-fuel and thermal cutting equipment and integral AC motors.*

**The Lincoln Electric Company, India, 309 Solaris-II Third Fl., Saki Vihar Road, OPP. L&T Powai Gate No. 6, Andheri East Mumbai 400 072, India**

Tel: 91-22-851-4290   Fax: 91-22-852-4260   Contact: G. Gurushankar, Mng. Dir.

## ARTHUR D. LITTLE, INC.

25 Acorn Park, Cambridge, MA, 02140-2390

Tel: (617) 498-5000     Fax: (617) 498-7200     www.adlittle.com

*Management, environmental, health and safety consulting; technical and product development.*

**Arthur D. Little India Inc., Shelleys Estate, 30 P.J. Ramchandani Marg, Mumbai 400 039, India**

## LOCKHEED MARTIN CORPORATION

6801 Rockledge Drive, Bethesda, MD, 20817

Tel: (301) 897-6000     Fax: (301) 897-6652     www.imco.com

*Design/mfr./management systems in fields of space, defense, energy, electronics and technical services.*

**Lockheed Martin Global, Inc., Rm. 1462 Maurya Sheraton Diplomatic Enclave, New Delhi 110 021 India**

Tel: 91-11-302-3273   Fax: 91-11-302-3275   Contact: Jaggi B. Malhotra

**Lockheed Martin Intl. Ltd., 9 Jor Bagh 1st Fl., New Delhi 110 003, India**

Tel: 91-11-464-1915   Fax: 91-11-464-1916   Contact: J. Malhotra, VP

## LOCTITE CORPORATION

1001 Trout Brook Crossing, Rocky Hill, CT, 06067-3910

Tel: (860) 571-5100     Fax: (860) 571-5465     www.loctite.com

*Mfr./sale industrial adhesives, sealants and coatings..*

**Loctite India Pvt. Ltd., 28 Spencer Road, Fraser Town, Bangalore 560 005, India**

Tel: 91-80-557-9851   Fax: 91-80-557-9852   Contact: V. Srinivas, Gen. Mgr.

## LORAL SPACE & COMMUNICATIONS LTD.

600 Third Ave., New York, NY, 10016

Tel: (212) 697-1105     Fax: (212) 338-5662     www.loral.com

*Marketing coordination: defense electronics, communications systems.*

**Loral CyberStar, 203-204 Prestige Meridian 1, MG Road, Bangalore 560001, India**

Tel: 91-80-509-5858   Fax: 91-80-509-5857

## LOWE LINTAS & PARTNERS WORLDWIDE

One Dag Hammarskjold Plaza, New York, NY, 10017

Tel: (212) 605-8000     Fax: (212) 605-4705     www.interpublic.com

*Full-service, integrated marketing communications company/advertising agency.*

**Ammirati Puris Lintas, Shaki Towers III - 4/F, 766 Anna Salai, Madras 600 002, India**

Tel: 91-44-852-3471   Fax: 91-44-852-3410   Contact: Ashish Bhasin

**Ammirati Puris Lintas, Shivprasad Complex 5/F, 114 MG Rd., Bangalore 560 001, India**

Tel: 91-80-559-4377   Fax: 91-80-558-6679   Contact: Fali Vakeel, Gen. Mgr.

**Ammirati Puris Lintas, 801 Mohandev, 14 Tolstoy Marg, New Delhi 110 001, India**

Tel: 91-11-335-2261   Fax: 91-11-371-2852   Contact: Preet K. S. Bedi, Gen. Mgr.

**Ammirati Puris Lintas, Lintas House, 67/D Baliygunge Circular Rd., Calcutta 700 019, India**

Tel: 91-33-247-8392   Fax: 91-33-240-3814   Contact: Phashant Sanwal

**Ammirati Puris Lintas India, Express Towers, Nariman Point, PO Box 758, Mumbai 400 021 India**

Tel: 91-22-202-1577   Fax: 91-22-204-3136   Contact: Prem Mehta, CEO

**Karishma Advertising Ltd., Nimal 16/F, Nariman Point, Mumbai 400 021, India**

Tel: 91-22-285-4590   Fax: 91-22-285-4598   Contact: Raj Gupta

**Lintas Ltd., The Phoenix Complex, Senapati Bapat Marg. Lower Parel, Mumbai 400 013, India**

Tel: 91-22-493-5377   Fax: 91-22-495-0130   Contact: Ajay Chandwani

**Market Links, Express Towers, Nariman Point, PO Box 758, Mumbai 400 021 India**

Tel: 91-22-202-1577   Fax: 91-22-204-3136   Contact: Ratan Jalan

**Pathfinders India, 5/F Manek Mahal, Veer Nariman Rd., Churchgate, Mumbai 400 020 India**

Tel: 91-22-202-1552   Fax: 91-22-283-6505   Contact: Anand Varedarajan

## THE LUBRIZOL CORPORATION

29400 Lakeland Blvd., Wickliffe, OH, 44092-2298

Tel: (440) 943-4200     Fax: (440) 943-5337     www.lubrizol.com

*Mfr. chemicals additives for lubricants and fuels.*

**Lubrizol India Ltd., Leo House, 4/F, 88-C Old Prabhadevi Rd., Mumbai 400 025, India**

Tel: 91-22-430-0672

## LUCENT TECHNOLOGIES, INC.

600 Mountain Ave., Murray Hill, NJ, 07974-0636

Tel: (908) 582-3000     Fax: (908) 582-2576     www.lucent.com

*Design/mfr. wide range of public and private networks, communication systems and software, data networking systems, business telephone systems and microelectronics components.*

**Lucent Finolex Fiber Optic Cables, Ltd., Plot No. 344, Village Urse, Taluka Maval, Dist. Pune India**

Tel: 91-212-1423711   Fax: 91-212-1423762   Contact: Subrata Paul, Location Head

**Lucent Technologies India Pvt. Ltd., Dr. Gopal Dass Bhawan 3rd Floor, 28 Barakhamba Road, New Delhi 110 001, India**

Tel: 91-11-335-3233   Fax: 91-11-335-3198   Contact: Ragini Maheshwari, PR Mgr.

## M/A-COM INC.

1011 Pawtucket Boulevard, Lowell, MA, 01853-3295

Tel: (978) 442-5000     Fax: (978) 442-5354     www.macom.com

*Mfr. electronic components, semiconductor devices and communications equipment.*

**AMP India Pvt. Ltd., Maruthi Industrial Estate - Hoody Rajapalya, Whitefield Main Road, Mahadevapura Post Bangalore 560 048, India**

Tel: 91-80-841-0200   Fax: 91-80-841-0210

## MARK IV INDUSTRIES INC.

501 John James Audubon Pkwy., PO Box 810, Amherst, NY, 14226-0810

Tel: (716) 689-4972     Fax: (716) 689-1529     www.mark-iv.com

*Mfr. of engineered systems and components utilizing mechanical and fluid power transmission, fluid transfer, and power systems and components.*

**Purolator India Ltd. J.V. Mark IV Auto, Sarojini Nagar, New Dehli 110 023, India**

Tel: 91-11-688-5137   Fax: 91-11-688-5225

## MARKET FACTS INC.

3040 Salt Creek Lane, Arlington Heights, IL, 60005

Tel: (847) 590-7000     Fax: (847) 590-7010     www.marketfacts.com

*Market research services.*

**Blackstone Market Facts India Pvt. Ltd., Hotel Avion, Opp Domestic Airport, Nehru Road, Vile Parle (E), Mumbai 400 057, India**

## MARLEY COOLING TOWER COMPANY

7401 West 129th Street, Overland Park, KS, 66213

Tel: (913) 664-7400     Fax: (913) 664-7641     www.marleyct.com

*Cooling and heating towers and waste treatment systems.*

**Marley Cooling Tower Co., India Liaison Office, 1067/017 Prestige Centre Point, No. 7 Edward Road, Bangalore 560 052 India**

Tel: 91-80-228-5357   Fax: 91-80-228-4694

## MASTERCARD INTERNATIONAL INC.

200 Purchase Street, Purchase, NY, 10577

Tel: (914) 249-2000     Fax: (914) 249-5475     www.mastercard.com

*Provides financial payment systems globally.*

**MasterCard International Inc., 12 Upper Ground Floor, Antriksh Bhawan, Kasturba Gandhi Marg, New Delhi 110 001 India**

## MAYFRAN INTERNATIONAL, INC.

PO Box 43038, Cleveland, OH, 44143

Tel: (440) 461-4100     Fax: (440) 461-5565     www.mayfran.com

*Mfr. conveying systems, filtration equipment and separators that facilitate material handling and coolant recovery for automobile manufacturers and machine tool builders.*

**Miven Mayfran, PO Box 59, Karwar Road, Hubli-580 024, India**

Tel: 91-836-303246   Fax: 91-836-303265

## McCANN-ERICKSON WORLDGROUP

750 Third Ave., New York, NY, 10017

Tel: (212) 984-3644     Fax: (212) 984-2629     www.mccann.com

*International advertising and marketing services.*

**Tara Sinha McCann-Erickson Pvt. Ltd., 15 Green Park Ext., New Delhi 110 016, India**

## McDERMOTT INTERNATIONAL INC.

1450 Poydras Street, PO Box 60035, New Orleans, LA, 70160-0035

Tel: (504) 587-5400        Fax: (504) 587-6153        www.mcdermott.com

*Provides energy, engineering and construction services for industrial, utility, and hydrocarbon processing facilities, and to the offshore oil and natural gas industries.*

**Thermax Babcock & Wilcox, LTD., Sagar Complex, Mumbai Pune Rd., Near Nasik Phata, Kasarwadi, Pune 411 034 India**

Tel: 91-21-279-5745   Fax: 91-21-279-5533   Contact: Jack Treier, Mng. Dir.

## McDONALD'S CORPORATION

McDonald's Plaza, Oak Brook, IL, 60523

Tel: (630) 623-3000        Fax: (630) 623-7409        www.mcdonalds.com

*Fast food chain stores.*

**McDonald's Corp., India**

## THE McGRAW-HILL COMPANIES

1221 Ave. of the Americas, New York, NY, 10020

Tel: (212) 512-2000        Fax: (212) 512-2703        www.mccgraw-hill.com

*Books, magazines, information systems, financial service, publishing and broadcast operations.*

**Tata McGraw Hill Publishing Co. Ltd., 12/4 Asaf Ali Rd., New Delhi 110 002, India**

**Tata McGraw-Hill Publishing Co. Ltd., No. 7 West Patel Nagar, New Delhi 110 008, India**

Tel: 91-11-573-2841

## McKINSEY & COMPANY

55 East 52nd Street, New York, NY, 10022

Tel: (212) 446-7000        Fax: (212) 446-8575        www.mckinsey.com

*Management and business consulting services.*

**McKinsey & Company, Express Towers, 21st Fl., Nariman Point, Mumbai 400 021, India**

Tel: 91-22-285-5532   Fax: 91-22-285-5531

**McKinsey & Company, TAJ Palace Hotel, 2 Sardar Patel Marg, Diplomatic Enclave, New Delhi 110 021, India**

Tel: 91-11-302-3580   Fax: 91-11-687-3227

## MECHANICAL DYNAMICS, INC.

2301 Commonwealth Blvd., Ann Arbor, MI, 48105

Tel: (734) 994-3800        Fax: (734) 994-6418        www.adams.com

*Mfr. Adams prototyping software to automotive industry.*

**EDS Technlogies Pvt. Ltd., 153 II Cross, Promenade Road Frazier Town, Bangalore 560 005 India**

Tel: 91-80551-4338

**Mechanical Dynamics India, W19 Greater Kailash II, New Delhi 110048, India**

Tel: 91-11628-6596

**NIIt Ltd., NIIT House, C-125 Okhla Phase-I, New Delhi 110 020 India**

## THE MENTHOLATUM COMPANY, INC.

707 Sterling Drive, Orchard Park, NY, 14127-1587

Tel: (716) 677-2500        Fax: (716) 674-3696        www.mentholatum.com

*Mfr./distributor proprietary medicines, drugs, OTC's.*

**Mentholatum Pharmaceuticals India Pvt. Ltd., Sion-Trombay Road, Deonar, Mumbai 400 088, India**

Tel: 91-22-558-5037   Fax: 91-22-588-5054   Contact: Anil Nadkarni

## MERCK & COMPANY, INC.

One Merck Drive, PO Box 100, Whitehouse Station, NJ, 08889-0100

Tel: (908) 423-1000        Fax: (908) 423-2592        www.merck.com

*Pharmaceuticals, chemicals and biologicals.*

**Merck, Sharp & Dohme of India Ltd., New India Centre, 17 Cooperage, Mumbai 400 039, India**

## MERITOR AUTOMOTIVE, INC.

2135 West Maple Road, Troy, MI, 48084-7186

Tel: (248) 435-1000     Fax: (248) 435-1393     www.meritorauto.com

*Mfr./sales of light and heavy vehicle systems for trucks, cars and specialty vehicles.*

**Meritor Light Vehicle Systems Ltd., Bangalore, India**

## MERRILL LYNCH & COMPANY, INC.

World Financial Center, 250 Vesey Street, New York, NY, 10281-1332

Tel: (212) 449-1000     Fax: (212) 449-2892     www.ml.com

*Security brokers and dealers, investment and business services.*

**DSP Financial Consultants Ltd., Tulsiani Chambers West Wing, 212 Backbay Reclamation, Mumbai 400 021, India**

Tel: 91-22-285-3801   Fax: 91-22-287-5191

**DSP Securities, Cahnder Maklu 10/F, Nariman Road, Mumbai 400 021, India**

Tel: 91-22-288-2550   Fax: 91-22-287-2093

## METROPOLITAN LIFE INSURANCE COMPANY

1 Madison Ave., New York, NY, 10010-3603

Tel: (212) 578-3818     Fax: (212) 252-7294     www.metlife.com

*Insurance and retirement savings products and services.*

**MetLife India Limited, Brigade Seshamahal, No. 5 Vani Vilas Road, Basavanagudi, Bangalore 560 004 India**

Tel: 91-80-667-8617

## M-I

PO Box 48242, Houston, TX, 77242-2842

Tel: (713) 739-0222     Fax: (713) 308-9503     www.midf.com

*Drilling fluids.*

**IONA, Flat #31, Moulana Azad Road, Juhu Koliwada, Mumbai 400 049 India**

Tel: 91-22-660-1763

## MICRO ABRASIVES CORPORATION

720 Southampton Rd., Westfield, MA, 01086-0669

Tel: (413) 562-3641     Fax: (413) 562-7409     www.microgrit.com

*Precision abrasive powders and slurries.*

**Micro Abrasives (India) Ltd., 65 Jor Bagh, New Delhi 110 003, India**

## MICROCHIP TECHNOLOGY INCORPORATED

2355 West Chandler Boulevard, Chandler, AZ, 85224

Tel: (602) 786-7200     Fax: (602) 899-9210     www.microchip.com

*Mfr. electronic subassemblies and components.*

**Microchip Technology, Inc., No. 6 Legacy, Convent Road, Bangalore 560 025, India**

Tel: 91-80-229-0061   Fax: 91-80-229-0062

## MICROSEMI CORPORATION

2830 South Fairview St., Santa Ana, CA, 92704

Tel: (714) 979-8220     Fax: (714) 557-5989     www.microsemi.com

*Design, manufacture and market analog, mixed-signal and discrete semiconductors.*

**Microsemi Corp. India, Bombay, India**

Tel: 91-22-8291210

## MICROSOFT CORPORATION

One Microsoft Way, Redmond, WA, 98052-6399

Tel: (425) 882-8080      Fax: (425) 936-7329      www.microsoft.com

*Computer software, peripherals and services.*

**Microsoft Corporation (India) Pvt. Ltd., Peharpur Business Centre, 21 Nehru Place, New Delhi 110 019, India**

Tel: 91-11-646-0694   Fax: 91-11-647-4714

## MILACRON INC.

2090 Florence Ave., Cincinnati, OH, 45206

Tel: (513) 487-5000      Fax: (513) 487-5057      www.milacron.com

*Metalworking and plastics technologies.*

**Milacron Inc. Private Ltd., Factory: Plot No. 14/16, Phase-I, GIDC Vatva Ahmedabad 382 445, India**

Tel: 91-79-5830112   Fax: 91-79-5830125   Contact: Mahendra N. Patel

## MILLER ELECTRIC MFG. COMPANY

PO Box 1079, 1636 W. Spencer, Appleton, WI, 54912-1079

Tel: (920) 734-9821      Fax: (920) 735-4125      www.millerwelds.com

*Mfr. arc welding machines.*

**ITW Welding Products, H-No: 1-2-365/26, 2/A R.K. Mutt Road, Domalguda, Hyderabad-500029 Andhra Pradesh, India**

Tel: 91-40-760-4541   Fax: 91-40-374-0191

## MILLIPORE CORPORATION

80 Ashby Road, PO Box 9125, Bedford, MA, 01730

Tel: (781) 533-6000      Fax: (781) 533-3110      www.millipore.com

*Mfr. flow and pressure measurement and control components; precision filters, hi-performance liquid chromatography instruments.*

**Millipore (India) Pvt. Ltd., 50A 2nd Phase Ring Rd., Peenya, Bangalore 560 058, India**

## MILTON ROY COMPANY

201 Ivyland Road, Ivylan, PA, 18974

Tel: (215) 441-0800      Fax: (215) 293-0468      www.miltonroy.com

*Mfr. medical and industry equipment and process control instruments.*

**Milton Roy Asia, 4 Rajarajan St., Visaiakshi Nagar Ekkaduthangal, Madras 600 097, India**

Tel: 91-44-234-4200   Fax: 91-44-234-6294   Contact: Dr. G. Nallakrishnan

## MINE SAFETY APPLIANCES COMPANY

121 Gamma Drive, PO Box 426, Pittsburgh, PA, 15230

Tel: (412) 967-3000      Fax: (412) 967-3452      www.msa.net

*Safety equipment, industry filters.*

**Mine Safety Appliances Ltd., P-25 Transport Depot Rd., Calcutta 700 088, India**

## MOLEX INC.

2222 Wellington Court, Lisle, IL, 60532

Tel: (630) 969-4550      Fax: (630) 969-1352      www.molex.com

*Mfr. electronic, electrical and fiber optic interconnection products and systems, switches, application tooling.*

**Molex (India) Ltd., Plot No. 6(A) Sada Industrial Area, Kadugodi Bangalore 560 067, India**

Tel: 91-80-845-2911   Fax: 91-80-845-2922

## MOOG INC.

Jamison Road, East Aurora, NY, 14052-0018

Tel: (716) 652-2000      Fax: (716) 687-4471      www.moog.com

*Mfr. precision control components and systems.*

**Moog Controls (India) Pvt. Ltd., Plot 1-2-3 Electric City, Bangalore, India**

## J. P. MORGAN CHASE & CO. INC.

World Headquarters, 270 Park Ave., New York, NY, 10017

Tel: (212) 270-6000     Fax: (212) 622-9030     www.jpmorganchase.com

*Provides integrated financial solutions for institutions and individuals worldwide, including asset management, investment banking and commercial banking.*

**J. P. Morgan Chase & Co.,  Maker Chambers VI - 7/F, Nariman Point, Mumbai 400 021, India**

Tel: 91-22-285-5666   Fax: 91-2-202-7772

## MORGAN STANLEY DEAN WITTER & CO.

1585 Broadway, New York, NY, 10036

Tel: (212) 761-4000     Fax: (212) 761-0086     www.msdw.com

*Securities and commodities brokerage, investment banking, money management, personal trusts.*

**Morgan Stanley Asset Managemen/India PVT Ltd.,  4th Fl., Charanjit Rai Marg, Mumbai, 400 001, India**

## MOTOROLA, INC.

1303 East Algonquin Road, Schaumburg, IL, 60196

Tel: (847) 576-5000     Fax: (847) 538-5191     www.motorola.com

*Mfr. communications equipment, semiconductors and cellular phones.*

**Motorola Singapore Pte. Ltd.,  Meridien Commercial Towers 8th Fl., Windson Place, New Delhi 110 001, India**

Tel: 91-11-371-0080   Fax: 91-11-371-8086

## NALCO CHEMICAL COMPANY

One Nalco Center, Naperville, IL, 60563-1198

Tel: (630) 305-1000     Fax: (630) 305-2900     www.nalco.com

*Chemicals for water and waste water treatment, oil products and refining, industry processes; water and energy management service.*

**Nalco Chemicals India Ltd.,  Ste. 6, 20-A Park St., Calcutta 700 016, India**

Tel: 91-33-249-4883   Fax: 91-33-249-3999

## NATIONAL MACHINERY COMPANY

161 Greenfield St., Tiffin, OH, 44883-2471

Tel: (419) 447-5211     Fax: (419) 447-5299     www.nationalmachinery.com

*Mfr. high-speed metal parts forming machines.*

**National Machinery Company,  New Delhi, India**

Tel: 91-11-686-7282

**National Machinery Company,  Calcutta, India**

Tel: 91-33-220-4621

## NATIONAL-STANDARD COMPANY

1618 Terminal Road, Niles, MI, 49120

Tel: (616) 683-8100     Fax: (616) 683-6249     www.nationalstardard.com

*Mfr. wire, wire related products, machinery and medical products.*

**National-Standard Duncan Ltd.,  19/F Commerce Centre 1, Cuffe Parade, Mumbai 400 005, India**

## NEAC COMPRESSOR SERVICE USA, INC.

191 Howard Street, Franklin, PA, 16323

Tel: (814) 437-3711     Fax: (814) 432-3334     www.neacusa.com

*Mfr. air tools and equipment.*

**Chicago Pneumatic (India) Ltd.,  PO Box 7761, 201/302 L.B. Shastri Marg, Mulund, Mumbai 400 080, India**

## NORDSON CORPORATION

28601 Clemens Road, Westlake, OH, 44145-4551

Tel: (440) 892-1580    Fax: (440) 892-9507    www.nordson.com

*Mfr. industry application equipment, sealants and packaging machinery.*

**Nordson Corp. South Asia Reg. Office, #3 Ground Fl., Maya Apartments, Rd. #15, Chembur Mumbai 400 071 India**

Tel: 91-22-528-4800   Fax: 91-22-528-1334

**Nordson India Pvt. Ltd. (Hdqtrs.), 143-A Bommasandra, Industrial Area, Bangalore 562 158, India**

Tel: 91-8110-34915   Fax: 91-8110-34920

**Nordson India Pvt. Ltd. New Delhi Branch, B-4 Greater Kailash Enclave Part II, New Delhi 110 048, India**

Tel: 91-11-628-7581

## NORGREN

5400 S. Delaware Street., Littleton, CO, 80120-1663

Tel: (303) 794-2611    Fax: (303) 795-9487    www.usa.norgren.com

*Mfr. pneumatic filters, regulators, lubricators, valves, automation systems, dryers, push-in fittings.*

**Shavo Norgren India Pvt. Ltd., 78 Mittal Chambers, Nariman Point, Mumbai 400 021, India**

## NORTON ABRASIVES COMPANY

1 New Bond Street, Worcester, MA, 01606

Tel: (508) 795-5000    Fax: (508) 795-5741    www.nortonabrasives.com

*Mfr. abrasives for industrial manufacturing.*

**Grindwell Norton Ltd., Devanahalli Rd., off Old Madras Rd., Bangalore, India**

**Grindwell Norton Ltd., Army & Navy Bldg., 148 Mahatma Gandhi Rd., Mumbai 400 023, India**

## OCCIDENTAL PETROLEUM CORPORATION

10889 Wilshire Blvd., Los Angeles, CA, 90024

Tel: (310) 208-8800    Fax: (310) 443-6690    www.oxy.com

*Petroleum and petroleum products, chemicals, plastics.*

**Intl. Ore & Fertilizer India Pvt. Ltd., 5/F 71 Nehru Place, Guru Angad Bhavan, New Delhi 110 019, India**

## OCEANEERING INTERNATIONAL INC.

11911 FM 529, Houston, TX, 77041

Tel: (713) 329-4500    Fax: (713) 329-4951    www.oceaneering.com

*Transportation equipment, underwater service to offshore oil and gas industry.*

**Oceaneering International, Mumbai, India**

## OGILVY PUBLIC RELATIONS WORLDWIDE

909 Third Ave., New York, NY, 10022

Tel: (212) 880-5201    Fax: (212) 697-8250    www.ogilvypr.com

*Engaged in public relations and communications.*

**Ogilvy Public Relations Worldwide, Mahavir House, Basheer Bagh Cross Roads, Hyderabad 500 029, India**

Tel: 91-40-322-7316   Contact: Bhavani Giddu

**Ogilvy Public Relations Worldwide, 139/140 Marshalls Road - 3/F, Egmore Chennai 600008, India**

Tel: 91-44-852-9471   Contact: Arup Kavan

**Ogilvy Public Relations Worldwide, Kamala Mills Compound, Senapati Bapat Marg Lower Parel, Mumbai 400 013, India**

Tel: 91-22-491-3914   Contact: Mahnaz Curmally

**Ogilvy Public Relations Worldwide, Motijug House - 1 Auckland Place, Calcutta 700017 India**

Tel: 91-33-281-0658   Fax: 91-33-247-1663   Contact: Simky Barua

**Ogilvy Public Relations Worldwide,** Mahalaxmi Chambers - 2/F, 29 Mahatma Gandhi Road, **Bangalore 560001, India**

Tel: 91-80-506-5046   Fax: 91-80-506-5049   Contact: Mahnaz Curmally

## THE OILGEAR COMPANY

2300 S. 51st Street, Milwaukee, WI, 53219

Tel: (414) 327-1700   Fax: (414) 327-0532   www.oilgear.com

*Mfr. hydraulic power transmission machinery.*

**Oilgear Pvt. Ltd.,** Harman House #482, 80 Feet Rd., Ganganagar, Bangalore 560 032 India

**Oilgear Towler Polyhydron Pvt. Ltd.,** Plot #4 R.S. #680/2, Belgaum Mfrs. Co-op Industrial Estate **Ltd., Udyambag Belgaum 590 008, India**

## ORACLE CORPORATION

500 Oracle Parkway, Redwood Shores, CA, 94065

Tel: (650) 506-7000   Fax: (650) 506-7200   www.oracle.com

*Develop/manufacture software.*

**Oracle India,** Bangalore, India

## OTIS ELEVATOR COMPANY

10 Farm Springs Road, Farmington, CT, 06032

Tel: (860) 676-6000   Fax: (860) 676-5111   www.otis.com

*Mfr. elevators and escalators.*

**Otis Elevator Co. (India) Ltd.,** Gateway Bldg., Apollo Bunder, Mumbai 400 039, India

**Otis Elevator Co. (India) Ltd.,** Akurli Rd., Kandivli East, Mumbai 400 101, India

## OWENS-CORNING CORPORATION

One Owens Corning Pkwy., Toledo, OH, 43659

Tel: (419) 248-8000   Fax: (419) 248-8445   www.owenscorning.com

*Mfr. building materials systems and composites systems.*

**Owens Corning Building Materials Systems,** 10/1-B Graphite India Road, Hoodi Village, KR Puram **Hobli, Bangalore 560 048, India**

Tel: 91-80-852-4380

**Owens Corning India,** 301-10 Sahar Plaza Complex, Bonanza MV Road, Andheri East, Mumbai **(Bombay) 400 059, India**

Tel: 91-22-839-8250   Contact: Rajeev Moudgil

## OWENS-ILLINOIS, INC.

One SeaGate, PO Box 1035, Toledo, OH, 43666

Tel: (419) 247-5000   Fax: (419) 247-2839   www.o-i.com

*Largest mfr. of glass containers in the US; plastic containers, compression-molded closures and dispensing systems.*

**Owens-Brockway (India) Ltd.,** New Delhi, India

## PALL CORPORATION

2200 Northern Boulevard, East Hills, NY, 11548-1289

Tel: (516) 484-5400   Fax: (516) 484-5228   www.pall.com

*Specialty materials and engineering; filters and related fluid clarification equipment.*

**Pall Pharmalab Filtration PVT, Ltd.,** Star Metal Compoundm, LBS Marg, Vikhoroli, Bombay 400 **083 India**

Tel: 91-22-5783-368   Fax: 91-22-5785-329

## PANDUIT CORPORATION

17301 Ridgeland Ave., Tinley Park, IL, 60477-0981

Tel: (708) 532-1800   Fax: (708) 532-1811   www.panduit.com

*Mfr. electrical/electronic wiring components.*

**Panduit Asia Pacific Pte. Ltd. Bombay,** 203 - J.B. Nagar Andheri (E), Bombay 400 059, India

## PARAMETRIC TECHNOLOGY CORPORATION

128 Technology Drive, Waltham, MA, 02154

Tel: (781) 398-5000    Fax: (781) 398-5674    www.ptc.com

*Supplier of mechanical design automation and product data management software and services.*

**Parametric Technology India, Office # 506-509, Pahparpur Business Center, 21 Nehru Place, New Delhi 110 019 India**

Tel: 91-11-647-4701   Fax: 91-11-647-4718

**Parametric Technology India, DBS Corporate Club, 26 Cunningham Road, Bangalore 560 052, India**

Tel: 91-80-226-7272   Fax: 91-80-228-1092

**Parametric Technology India Pvt. Ltd., #402 A.N. Chambers, Guru Nanak Road, Bandra Bombay 400 050, India**

Tel: 91-22-645-4427   Fax: 91-22-645-4428

**Parametric Technology India Pvt. Ltd., TCI Business Center, 170 Dhole Patil Road, Pune 411 001, India**

Tel: 91-212-625156   Fax: 91-212-625156

**Parametric Technology India Pvt. Ltd., DBS Corporate Services, 31A Catheral Garden Road, Madras 600 034, India**

Tel: 91-44-822-2008x302   Fax: 91-44-825-7258

## PARKER ABEX NWL CORPORATION

2222 Palmer Ave., Kalamazoo, MI, 49001

Tel: (616) 384-3400    Fax: (616) 384-3623    www.parkerhannifin.com

*Mfr. aerospace and automotive friction materials and equipment.*

**Sundaram-Abex Ltd., 130 Mount Rd., Madras 600 060, India**

## PCS DATA CONVERSION

238 Main Street, Cambridge, MA, 02142

Tel: (617) 354-7424    Fax: (617) 876-4711

*Software consulting and contract programming services.*

**Patni Computer Systems Ltd., 303/304 Regent Chambers, Nariman Point, Mumbai 400 021, India**

## J.C. PENNEY COMPANY, INC.

6501 Legacy Drive, Plano, TX, 75024-3698

Tel: (972) 431-1000    Fax: (972) 431-1977    www.jcpenney.com

*Markets family apparel, shoes, home furnishings, jewelry, and offers credit cards.*

**J. C. Penney Purchasing Corp., 139/T Juhu Rd., Santacruz W., Mumbai 400 049, India**

## PEOPLESOFT INC.

4460 Hacienda Drive, Pleasanton, CA, 94588-8618

Tel: (925) 225-3000    Fax: (925) 694-4444    www.peoplesoft.com

*Mfr. applications to manage business operations across computer networks.*

**PeopleSoft India Pvt. Ltd., 26 Cunningham Road, Bangalore 560 052, India**

## PEPSiCO INC.

700 Anderson Hill Road, Purchase, NY, 10577-1444

Tel: (914) 253-2000    Fax: (914) 253-2070    www.pepsico.com

*Beverages and snack foods.*

**PepsiCo Ltd., India**

## PFAUDLER, INC.

1000 West Ave., PO Box 23600, Rochester, NY, 14692-3600

Tel: (716) 235-1000    Fax: (716) 436-9644    www.pfaudler.com

*Mfr. glass lined reactors, storage vessels and reglassing services.*

**GMM Pfaudler, Karamsad, India**

Tel: 91-26-923-0416   Fax: 91-26-924-6467

GMM Pfaulder, Churchgate House, 32-34 Veer Nariman Rd., Fort Bombay 400 001, India

## PFIZER INC.

235 East 42nd Street, New York, NY, 10017-5755

Tel: (212) 573-2323     Fax: (212) 573-7851     www.pfizer.com

*Research-based, global health care company.*

**Duchem Laboratories Ltd., Madras, India**

**Dumex Ltd., Madras, India**

**Pfizer Ltd., Madras, India**

## PHARMACIA CORPORATION

100 Route 206 North, Peapack, NJ, 07977

Tel: (908) 901-8000     Fax: (908) 901-8379     www.pharmacia.com

*Mfr. pharmaceuticals, agricultural products, industry chemicals.*

**Pharmacia & Upjohn, 100 Feet Road Office 4008, HAL II Stage, Indiranagar Bangalore 560 008, India**

## PHARMACIA MONSANTO

800 N. Lindbergh Boulevard, St. Louis, MO, 63167

Tel: (314) 694-1000     Fax: (314) 694-7625     www.monsanto.com

*Life sciences company focusing on agriculture, nutrition, pharmaceuticals, health and wellness and sustainable development.*

**Monsanto (India) Ltd., Ahura Centre 5/F, 96 Mahakali Caves Road, Andheri (East) Mumbai 400 093, India**

## PHELPS DODGE CORPORATION

2600 North Central Ave., Phoenix, AZ, 85004-3089

Tel: (602) 234-8100     Fax: (602) 234-8337     www.phelpsdodge.com

*Copper, minerals, metals and special engineered products for transportation and electrical markets.*

**Asian Cables Ltd., Great Mahal, 463 Dr. Annie Senant Road, Worit Mumbai 400 025, India**

## PHILLIPS PETROLEUM COMPANY

Phillips Building, 411 S. Keeler Ave., Bartlesville, OK, 74004

Tel: (918) 661-6600     Fax: (918) 661-7636     www.phillips66.com

*Crude oil, natural gas, liquefied petroleum gas, gasoline and petro-chemicals.*

**Cochin Refineries Ltd., Post Bag 2, PO Ambalamugal, Ernakulam Dist., Kerala 632 302, India**

**Gujarat Carbon Ltd., Harikripa, Alkapuri, Baroda, Gujarat 390 005, India**

**Phillips Carbon Black Ltd., Duncan House, 31 Netaji Subhas Rd., Calcutta 700 001, India**

**Phillips Petroleum Intl. Corp., 1-A Vandhana Blvd., 11 Tolstov Marg, New Delhi 110 001, India**

## PILLAR INDUSTRIES

21905 Gateway Road, Brookfield, WI, 53045

Tel: (262) 317-5300     Fax: (262) 317-5353     www.pillar.com

*Mfr. induction heating and melting equipment.*

**Pillar Induction (India) Pvt. Ltd., 2nd Avenue Block A-13, Anna Nagar, Madras 600 102, India**

## PIONEER HI-BRED INTERNATIONAL INC.

400 Locust Street, Ste. 800, Des Moines, IA, 50309

Tel: (515) 248-4800     Fax: (515) 248-4999     www.pioneer.com

*Agricultural chemicals, farm supplies, biological products, research.*

**Pioneer Hi-Bred, 401/402 Suneja Towers, District Centre II, Janakpuri 110 058, India**

## PITTSTON BAX GROUP

16808 Armstrong Ave., PO Box 19571, Irvine, CA, 92623

Tel: (949) 752-4000        Fax: (949) 260-3182        www.baxworld.com

*Air freight forwarder.*

**BAX Global - Reg. Office, 4G & H/4th Fl. Hansalaya Bldg., 15 Barakhamba Rd., New Delhi 110 001, India**

Tel: 91-11-331-3972   Fax: 91-11-332-9665

**BAX Global India Pvt. Ltd., 2nd Fl. Perstige Terminus 1, Airport Exit Rd., Konena Agrahara, Bangalore 560 017 India**

Tel: 91-80-526-8646   Fax: 91-80-527-3384

## PRAXAIR, INC.

39 Old Ridgebury Road, Danbury, CT, 06810-5113

Tel: (203) 837-2000        Fax: (203) 837-2450        www.praxair.com

*Produces and distributes industrial and specialty gases.*

**Praxair India Pvt., Ltd., Praxair House, No.8 Ulsoor Rd., Bangalore 560 042, India**

Tel: 91-80-555-9841   Fax: 91-80-559-5925

## PRECISION VALVE & TRIM, INC.

PO Box 3091, 1923 Cloverland Avenue, Baton Rouge, LA, 70809

Tel: (225) 752-5600        Fax: (225) 752-5400        www.precisionvalve.com

*Mfr. aerosol valves.*

**Precision Valve (India) Pvt. Ltd., 228 Pragti (TODI) Ind. Estate, N.M. Joshi Marg, Lower Parel, Mumbai 400 011, India**

## PRICEWATERHOUSECOOPERS LLP

1301 Ave. of the Americas, New York, NY, 10019

Tel: (212) 596-7000        Fax: (212) 259-1301        www.pwcglobal.com

*Accounting and auditing, tax and management, and human resource consulting services.*

**PriceWaterhouseCoopers, B-102 Himalaya House, 23 Kasturba Gandhi Marg, PO Box 466, New Delhi 110 001 India**

Tel: 91-11-3319856   Fax: 91-11-3323183

**PriceWaterhouseCoopers, Suite No. B (3rd Fl), 20-A Park St., Calcutta 700 016, India**

Tel: 91-33-2494680   Fax: 91-33-2434980

**PriceWaterhouseCoopers, 610 Anna Salai, PO Box 743, Madras 600 006, India**

Tel: 91-44-827-1597   Fax: 91-44-8260787

**PriceWaterhouseCoopers, 305-307 Century Arcade, 8/3 Narangi Baug Road, Off. Boat Club Road, Pune 411 001 India**

Tel: 91-212-663271

**PriceWaterhouseCoopers, B3/1 Gillander House, Netaji Subhas Road, PO Box 2238, Calcutta 700 001 India**

Tel: 91-33-2209001   Fax: 91-33-2202420

**PriceWaterhouseCoopers, 1002/1107 Raheja Chambers, Nariman Point, Mumbai 400 021, India**

Tel: 91-22-2835190   Fax: 91-22-2045592

**PriceWaterhouseCoopers, St. Patrick's Business Complex, 21 Museum Road, PO Box 2544, Bangalore 560 025 India**

Tel: 91-80-558-7239   Fax: 91-80-558-8751

## PRIMARK CORPORATION

100 Winter Street, Ste. 4300-N, Waltham, MA, 02451

Tel: (781) 466-6611        Fax: (781) 890-6187        www.primark.com

*Provides financial and business information.*

**Primark India Private Ltd., No. 93/A 4th 'B' Cross Industrial Layout, Koramangala V Block, Bangalore 560 095, India**

## PROCTER & GAMBLE COMPANY

One Procter & Gamble Plaza, Cincinnati, OH, 45202

Tel: (513) 983-1100      Fax: (513) 562-4500      www.pg.com

*Personal care, food, laundry, cleaning and industry products.*

**Procter & Gamble Hygiene & Health Care Ltd., Tiecicon House, Dr. E. Moses Road, Mumbai 400 011 Bombay India**

## PSDI MAXIMO

100 Crosby Drive, Bedford, MA, 01730

Tel: (781) 280-2000      Fax: (781) 280-0200      www.psdi.com

*Develops, markets and provides maintenance management software systems.*

**PSDI India, 401 World Trade Ctr., Hilton Complex, Barbar Rd., New Delhi, 110 001, India**

Tel: 91-11-331-9424   Fax: 91-11-331-9436   Contact: Anil Bakshi, Gen. Mgr.   Emp: 3

## PUBLIC SERVICE ENTERPRISE GROUP (PSEG)

80 Park Plaza, Newark, NJ, 07101

Tel: (973) 430-7000      Fax: (973) 623-5389      www.pseg.com

*Electric and gas utility.*

**PSEG India Inc., Prakash Presidium II Floor, 110 Mahatma Gandhi Road, Nungambakkam, Chennai 600034, India**

Tel: 91-44-821-0100   Fax: 91-44-822-3166   Contact: B. Vanchi

## QUAKER CHEMICAL CORPORATION

Elm & Lee Streets, Conshohocken, PA, 19428-0809

Tel: (610) 832-4000      Fax: (610) 832-8682      www.quakerchem.com

*Mfr. developer, producer, and marketer of custom-formulated chemical specialty products.*

**Quaker Chemical India Ltd. (JV), 7B Pretoria St., Calcutta 700 071, India**

Tel: 91-33-282-5414   Contact: G. Kumar Sachdev, Mng. Dir.

## QUALCOMM INC.

5775 Morehouse Dr., San Diego, CA, 92121-1714

Tel: (858) 587-1121      Fax: (858) 658-2100      www.qualcomm.com

*Digital wireless telecommunications systems.*

**QUALCOMM India, DBS Corporate Centre 1/F, World Trade Tower Rms.15-16, Barakhamba Lane, New Delhi 110 001, India**

## QUINTILES TRANSNATIONAL CORPORATION

4709 Creekstone Dr., Durham, NC, 27703

Tel: (919) 998-2000      Fax: (919) 998-9113      www.quintiles.com

*Mfr. pharmaceuticals.*

**Quintiles Spectral Limited, 3 Ashoknagar Bungalows Behind Sundarvan, Satellite Road, Ahmedabad 380 015, India**

## QWEST COMMUNICATIONS INTERNATIONAL INC.

1801 California Street, Ste. 5200, Denver, CO, 80202

Tel: (303) 896-2020      Fax: (303) 793-6654      www.uswest.com

*Tele-communications provider; integrated communications services.*

**BPL/USW - India, Maharashtra, India**

Tel: 91-11-301-0101x1110   Fax: 91-11-302-3153

## R&B FALCON CORPORATION

901 Threadneedle, Ste. 200, Houston, TX, 77079

Tel: (281) 496-5000      Fax: (281) 496-4363      www.rbfalcon.com

*Offshore contract drilling.*

**R&B Falcon Exploration Co., Bhavani Mansions 2/F, #3 4th Lane, Nungambakkam High Rd., Madras 600 034 India**

R&B Falcon Exploration Co., Ashok Hall 2/F, S.V. Rd., Vile Parle (W), Mumbai 400 056 India

## RADISSON HOTELS INTERNATIONAL

Carlson Pkwy., PO Box 59159, Minneapolis, MN, 55459-8204

Tel: (612) 540-5526    Fax: (612) 449-3400    www.radisson.com

*Hotels and resorts.*

**Radisson Hotel Delhi, National Highway 8, New Delhi 110 037, India**

Tel: 91-11-613-7373  Fax: 91-11-689-8540

**Radisson Hotel St. Thomas Mount, Chennai, 355C GST Rd., St. Thomas Mount, Chennai 600 016, India**

Tel: 91-44-4322382  Fax: 91-44-4323380

## RAY & BERNDTSON, INC.

301 Commerce, Ste. 2300, Fort Worth, TX, 76102

Tel: (817) 334-0500    Fax: (817) 334-0779    www.prb.com

*Executive search, management audit and management consulting firm.*

**Ray & Berndtson, 208 Richmond Tower, 12 Richmond Rd., Bangalore 560, India**

Tel: 91-80-227-8296  Fax: 91-80-227-8297   Contact: Charence Lobo, Mng. Ptnr.

**Ray & Berndtson, 606 Prabhadevi Estate, Veer Savakar Marg, Prabhadevi, Mumbai 400 025 India**

Tel: 91-22-437-7272  Fax: 91-22-436-2644   Contact: Mari & Clarence Lobo, Mng. Prtns.

## RAYCHEM CORPORATION

300 Constitution Dr., Menlo Park, CA, 94025-1164

Tel: (650) 361-3333    Fax: (650) 361-5579    www.raychem.com

*Develop/mfr./market materials science products for electronics, telecommunications and industry.*

**Raychem Ltd., 2-C Jubilee Bldg., 45 Museum Rd., Bangalore 560 001, India**

**Raychem Technologies Pvt Ltd., Ceat Mahal Annexe, 463 Dr. Annie Basant Rd., Mumbai 400 025, India**

## RAYMOND JAMES FINANCIAL, INC.

880 Carillon Parkway, St. Petersburg, FL, 33716

Tel: (813) 573-3800    Fax: (813) 573-8244    www.rjf.com

*Financial services; securities brokerage, asset management, and investment banking services.*

**ASK-Raymond James Securities India Ltd., Bandbox House (Rear 2/F), 254-D Dr. Annie Besant Road, Worli Mumbai 400 025, India**

Tel: 91-22-498-5670  Fax: 91-22-5665

## RAYTHEON COMPANY

141 Spring Street, Lexington, MA, 02173

Tel: (781) 862-6600    Fax: (781) 860-2172    www.raytheon.com

*Mfr. diversified electronics, appliances, aviation, energy and environmental products; publishing, industry and construction services.*

**Raytheon International, New Delhi, India**

## REEBOK INTERNATIONAL LTD.

100 Technology Center Drive, Stoughton, MA, 02072

Tel: (781) 401-5000    Fax: (781) 401-7402    www.reebok.com

*Mfr. athletic shoes including casual, dress golf and walking shoes.*

**Planet Reebok, 6/D Brigade Road, Bangalore 56001, India**

## REFCO GROUP LTD.

111 West Jackson Blvd, Suite 1800, Chicago, IL, 60604

Tel: (312) 930-6500    Fax: (312) 930-6534    www.refco.com

*Commodity and security brokers engaged in the execution and clearing of futures and options and institutional asset management services.*

**Refco-Sify Securities India Pvt. Ltd. (JV), Mumbai, India**

## RELIANT ENERGY, INC.

1111 Louisiana Street, Houston, TX, 77002

Tel: (713) 207-3000    Fax: (713) 207-0206    www.houind.com

*Provides gas and electric services.*

**Rain Calcining Limited, India**

## RENAISSANCE HOTELS AND RESORTS

10400 Fernwood Road, Bethesda, MD, 20817

Tel: (301) 380-3000    Fax: (301) 380-5181    www.renaissancehotels.com

*Hotel and resort chain.*

**Renaissance Goa Resort, Goa, India**

Tel: 91-834-74-5208

## RENAISSANCE WORLDWIDE, INC.

52 Second Ave., Waltham, MA, 02451

Tel: (781) 290-3000    Fax: (781) 965-4807    www.rens.com

*Provides technology consulting, staffing services, corporate and systems strategies and software and hardware installation.*

**Renaissance Worldwide, Inc., 703 Nirman Kendra, Bombay 400 011, India**

Tel: 91-22-498-0308   Fax: 91-22-498-0108

## ROBBINS & MYERS INC.

1400 Kettering Tower, Dayton, OH, 45423-1400

Tel: (937) 222-2610    Fax: (937) 225-3355    www.robn.com

*Mfr. progressing cavity pumps, valves and agitators.*

**Robbins & Myers India, New Delhi, India**

## ROCKWELL INTERNATIONAL CORPORATION

777 East Wisconsin Ave., Ste. 1400, Milwaukee, WI, 53202

Tel: (414) 212-5200    Fax: (414) 212-5201    www.rockwell.com

*Products and service for aerospace and defense, automotive, electronics, graphics and automation industry.*

**Rockwell Automation, 131 Industrial Area, Patparganj Delhi 110 092, India**

Tel: 91-11-214-5605

**Rockwell Automation/Allen-Bradley India Ltd., C-8&9 Minoo Minar, Veera Desai Rd., Andheri West, Mumbai 400 053, India**

Tel: 91-22-67-0400   Fax: 91-22-626-7127

**Rockwell International Overseas Corp., A-5 Kailash Colony, New Delhi 110 048, India**

Tel: 91-11-621-5374   Fax: 91-11-647-5138

**Rockwell Intl. (Asia Pacific) Ltd., C-11 Site IV Industrial Area, Dist. Ghaziabad, Sahibabad 201 010, India**

Tel: 91-575-771113   Fax: 91-575-770822

**Rockwell Semiconductor Systems, Capital Trust House, 47 Community Centre, Friends Colony, New Delhi 110 065 India**

Tel: 91-11-692-4780   Fax: 91-11-647-5138

## ROHM AND HAAS COMPANY

100 Independence Mall West, Philadelphia, PA, 19106

Tel: (215) 592-3000    Fax: (215) 592-3377    www.rohmhaas.com

*Mfr. industrial and agricultural chemicals, plastics.*

**Rohm and Haas (India) Pvt. Ltd., 114 Jorgagh, New Delhi 110 003, India**

Tel: 91-11-464-7682

**Rohm and Haas (India) Pvt. Ltd., Maks Commercial Centre, A/14 Veera Industrial Estate, Off Veera Desai Rd., Andheri West Mumbai 400 053 India**

## RONALD E. LAIS, INC.

136 South Imperial Highway, Anaheim, CA, 92807-3943

Tel: (714) 998-6633     Fax: (714) 937-1791     www.laislaw.com

*International law firm.*

**Ronald E. Lais, Inc.,  1230 Sector D, Pocket 1, Vasant Kung, New Delhi, India**

Tel: 91-11-6899515

## RYERSON TULL

2621 W. 15th Place, Chicago, IL, 60608

Tel: (773) 762-2121     Fax: (773) 762-0179     www.ryersontull.com

*Engaged in metal distribution.*

**Ryerson Tull (JV),  India**

## SAPIENT CORPORATION

1 Memorial Drive, Cambridge, MA, 02142

Tel: (617) 621-0200     Fax: (617) 621-1300     www.sapient.com

*Engaged in information technology and consulting services.*

**Sapient Corporation Private Limited,  Videocon Tower 12/F, Jhandewalan Extension, Rani Jhansi Marg, New Delhi 110 055, India**

## SAS INSTITUTE INC.

SAS Campus Drive, Cary, NC, 27513

Tel: (919) 677-8000     Fax: (919) 677-4444     www.sas.com

*Mfr./distributes decision support software.*

**SAS Institute (India) Ltd.,  Mumbaj, India**

Tel: 91-22-288-5101   Fax: 91-22-288-1476

## SCHENECTADY INTERNATIONAL INC.

PO Box 1046, Schenectady, NY, 12301

Tel: (518) 370-4200     Fax: (518) 382-8129     www.siigroup.com

*Mfr. electrical insulating varnishes, enamels, phenolic resins, alkylphenols.*

**Schenectady (Beck) India,  Beck House, Damle Path - Law College Road,  Pune 411 004 India**

Tel: 91-20-543-8540   Fax: 91-20-543-9048   Contact: Manu Tandon

**Schenectady India Ltd.,  195 Nariman Point, Mumbai 400 021, India**

**Schenectady Specialities Asia Ltd. (JV),  Janki Niwas N.C., Kelkar Road - Dadar, Mumbai 400 028 India**

Tel: 91-22-430-1454

## SCHENKER INTERNATIONAL FORWARDERS INC.

150 Albany Ave., Freeport, NY, 11520

Tel: (516) 377-3000     Fax: (516) 377-3005     www.schenkerusa.com

*Freight forwarders.*

**Schenker International Pvt Ltd.,  MKM Chambers 5th Fl., 154-155 Kodambakkam High Rd., Nungambakkam Madras 600-034 , India**

Tel: 91-44-823-1187   Fax: 91-44-823-0995

**Schenker International Pvt Ltd.,  22 Community Center, Basant Lok Vasant Vihar, New Delhi 110 057, India**

Tel: 91-80-823-4151   Fax: 91-22-835-5137

## SCHERING-PLOUGH CORPORATION

One Giralda Farms, Madison, NJ, 07940-1000

Tel: (973) 822-7000     Fax: (973) 822-7048     www.sch-plough.com

*Proprietary drug and cosmetic products.*

**C. E. Fulford (India) Pvt. Ltd.,  Oxford House, Apollo Bunder, Mumbai 400 039, India**

## SCHLUMBERGER LIMITED

277 Park Avenue, New York, NY, 10021

Tel: (212) 350-9400     Fax: (212) 350-9564     www.schlumberger.com

*Engaged in oil and gas services, metering and payment systems, and produces semiconductor testing equipment and smart cards.*

**Schlumberger India, 12-13/F - Mohan Dev Building, Tolstoy Marg, New Delhi-110001 India**

## SCHOLASTIC CORPORATION

555 Broadway, New York, NY, 10012

Tel: (212) 343-6100     Fax: (212) 343-6934     www.scholastic.com

*Publishing/distribution educational and children's magazines, books, software.*

**Scholastic India Pvt. Ltd., 29 Udyog Vihar, Phase-1, Gurgaon 122 016, Haryana, India**

Tel: 91-124-346-824     Contact: Arvind Kumar, Mng. Dir.

## SEALED AIR CORPORATION

Park 80 East, Saddle Brook, NJ, 07663

Tel: (201) 791-7600     Fax: (201) 703-4205     www.sealedair.com

*Mfr. protective and specialty packaging solutions for industrial, food and consumer products.*

**Sealed Air (Singapore) Pte. Ltd., 4/1 (122) Chord Rd., Industrial Suburb, Rajajinagar, Bangalore 560 010 India**

Tel: 91-80-3432528     Fax: 91-80-3432528

## G.D. SEARLE & COMPANY

5200 Old Orchard Road, Skokie, IL, 60077

Tel: (847) 982-7000     Fax: (847) 470-1480     www.searlehealthnet.com

*Mfr. pharmaceuticals, health care, optical products and specialty chemicals.*

**Searle (India) Ltd., Ralli House, 21 Damodardas Sukhadvala Marg, PO Box 233, Mumbai 400 001 India**

## SHIPLEY COMPANY, LLC

455 Forest Street, Marlborough, MA, 01752

Tel: (508) 481-7950     Fax: (508) 485-9113     www.shipley.com

*Supplier of materials and processes technology to the microelectronics and printed wiring board industries.*

**LeaRonal India, 114 Ansal Bhawan, 16 KG Marg , New Delhi 110001, India**

Tel: 91-11-3711123     Fax: 91-11-3713141

## SIGNODE PACKAGING SYSTEMS

3610 West Lake Ave., Glenview, IL, 60025

Tel: (847) 724-6100     Fax: (847) 657-4392     www.signode.com

*Mfr. industrial tools and machinery for packaging and strapping.*

**Signode India Ltd., Lulla Centre, 5 S.P. Rd., Begumpet, Hyderabad 500 016, India**

## SIMON & SCHUSTER INC.

1230 Avenue of the Americas, New York, NY, 10020

Tel: (212) 698-7000     Fax: (212) 698-7007     www.simonandschuster.com

*Publishes and distributes hardcover and paperback books, audiobooks and software.*

**Prentice Hall of India Pvt. Ltd., 14-97 Connaught Circus, New Delhi 110 001, India**

## WILBUR SMITH ASSOCIATES

PO Box 92, Columbia, SC, 29202

Tel: (803) 758-4500     Fax: (803) 251-2064     www.wilbursmith.com

*Consulting engineers.*

**Wilbur Smith Associates Inc., 505 Keshava - Bandra-Kurla Complex, Bandra (East) Mumbai 400 051 India**

Tel: 91-22-644-1599     Fax: 91-22-644-1347     Contact: Rajendra K. Mehta

## SOLUTIA INC.

575 Maryville Center Dr, St. Louis, MO, 63141

Tel: (314) 674-1000    Fax: (314) 694-8686    www.solutia.com

*Mfr. specialty chemical based products.*

**Solutia Chemical India Private Ltd., PO Box No. 7034, New Delhi 110 002, India**

Tel: 91-11-327-7651

**Solutia Chemical India Private Ltd., 205-207,'Midas' Sahar Plaza Complex, Andheri-Kurla Road, Andheri (East) Mumbai 400059, India**

Tel: 91-22-830-2860

## SPERRY-SUN DRILLING

3000 North Sam Houston Pkwy. East, Houston, TX, 77032

Tel: (281) 871-5100    Fax: (281) 871-5742    www.sperry-sun.com

*Provides drilling services to the oil and gas drilling industry.*

**Sperry-Sun, Inc., Sanghi Oxygen Compound, Mahakali Caves Road, Andheri (East) Mumbai 400 049, India**

## SPS TECHNOLOGIES INC.

101 Greenwood Avenue, Ste. 470, Jenkintown, PA, 19046

Tel: (215) 517-2000    Fax: (215) 517-2032    www.spstech.com

*Mfr. aerospace and industry fasteners, tightening systems, magnetic materials, superalloys.*

**Avitrade SPS Technologies, G02 #10 Haudin Road, Ussoor, Bangalore 560042, India**

Contact: Lt. Col. Ashok K. Soti

**Precision Fasteners Ltd., New India Centre, 17 Cooperage Rd., Marahashtra, Mumbai 400 039, India**

## SPSS INC.

233 S. Wacker Dr., Chicago, IL, 60606

Tel: (312) 651-6000    Fax: (312) 329-3668    www.spss.com

*Mfr. statistical software.*

**SPSS UK Ltd., Ashok Hotel #223, 50B Chanakyapuri, New Delhi 110 021, India**

## THE ST. PAUL COMPANIES, INC.

385 Washington Street, St. Paul, MN, 55102

Tel: (651) 310-7911    Fax: (651) 310-8294    www.stpaul.com

*Provides investment, insurance and reinsurance services.*

**The New India Assurance Company Ltd., 87 Mahatma Gandhi Road, Fort Mumbai 400 001, India**

## STANDARD COMMERCIAL CORPORATION

2201 Miller Rd., PO Box 450, Wilson, NC, 27893

Tel: (919) 291-5507    Fax: (919) 237-1109    www.sccgroup.com

*Leaf tobacco dealers/processors and wool processors.*

**Trans-Continental Tobacco, PO Box 400, Guntur 522007, Andhra Pradesh, South India**

## STA-RITE INDUSTRIES INC.

293 Wright Street, Delavan, WI, 53115

Tel: (262) 728-5551    Fax: (262) 728-7323    www.sta-rite.com

*Mfr. water pumps, filters and systems.*

**Chansuba Pumps Ltd., 125 Rajaji Road, Rannagar, Coimbatore 641 009, India**

## STARWOOD HOTELS & RESORTS WORLDWIDE

777 Westchester Avenue, White Plains, NY, 10604

Tel: (914) 640-8100    Fax: (914) 640-8316    www.starwoodhotels.com

*Hotel operations including Sheraton, Westin, St. Regis, Four Points and Caesars.*

**Chola Sheraton, 10 Cathedral Rd., Madras 600 086, India**

**Maurya Sheraton Hotel & Towers, Diplomatic Enclave, Sardar Patel Marg 110 021, India**

Mughal Sheraton, Fatehabad Rd., Agra 282 001, India

## STOKES VACUUM INC.

5500 Tabor Road, Philadelphia, PA, 19120

Tel: (215) 831-5400     Fax: (215) 831-5420     www.stokesvacuum.com

*Vacuum pumps and components, vacuum dryers, oil-upgrading equipment and metallizers.*

Lawrence & Mayo, 11Government Place, Calcutta, India

Tel: 91-33-248-1818   Fax: 9133--248-0068   Contact: Suman Kundu

## STRUCTURAL DYNAMICS RESEARCH CORPORATION

2000 Eastman Dr., Milford, OH, 45150-2740

Tel: (513) 576-2400     Fax: (513) 576-2922     www.sdrc.com

*Developer of software used in Modeling testing, drafting and manufacturing.*

SDRC Ltd. _ India Liasion Office, Block 4B 8th Fl. DLF Corporate Park, Qutab Enclave Phase-3, Guragaon Haryana New Delhi 122 002, India

Tel: 91-124-357971   Fax: 91-124-357970

## SYBASE, INC.

6475 Christie Ave., Emeryville, CA, 94608

Tel: (510) 922-3500     Fax: (510) 922-3210     www.sybase.com

*Design/mfg/distribution of database management systems, software development tools, connectivity products, consulting and technical support services..*

Sybase India Ltd. (Liason Office), 302 (3rd Fl.) Embassy Square, 148 Infantry Rd., Bangalore 560 001, India

Tel: 91-80-228-3850   Fax: 91-20-228-3851

## SYMBOL TECHNOLOGIES, INC.

One Symbol Plaza, Holtsville, NY, 11742-1300

Tel: (631) 738-2400     Fax: (631) 738-5990     www.symbol.com

*Mfr. Bar code-driven data management systems, wireless LAN's, and Portable Shopping System™.*

Symbol Technologies of India, A-29 Ghamshyam Industrial Estate, Veera Desai Road Andheri W, Bombay 400053, India

Tel: 91-22-623-7152

## SYNOPSYS, INC.

700 East Middlefield Road, Mountain View, CA, 94043

Tel: (650) 962-5000     Fax: (650) 965-8637     www.synopsys.com

*Mfr. electronic design automation software.*

Synopsys, 3rd A Cross, 18 Main 6th Block, Koramangala Bangalore 560 095, India

Tel: 91-80-552-2201

## THE TCW GROUP

865 S. Figueroa St., Ste. 1800, Los Angeles, CA, 90017

Tel: (213) 244-0000     Fax: (213) 244-0000     www.tcwgroup.com

*Engaged in managing pension and profit sharing funds, retirement/health and welfare funds, insurance company funds, endowments and foundations.*

TCW Group (JV), Bangalore, India

## TEKTRONIX INC.

14200 SW Karl Braun Dr., PO Box 500, Beaverton, OR, 97077

Tel: (503) 627-7111     Fax: (503) 627-2406     www.tek.com

*Mfr. test and measure, visual systems/color printing and communications/video and networking products.*

Tektronix (India) Ltd., Tek Tower, Hayes Rd., Bangalore 560 025, India

Tel: 91-80-227-5577   Fax: 91-80-227-5588

## TELEFLEX INC.

630 W. Germantown Pike, Ste. 450, Plymouth Meeting, PA, 19462

Tel: (610) 834-6301        Fax: (610) 834-8307        www.teleflex.com

*Designs/mfr./market mechanical and electro-mechanical systems, measure systems.*

**Rusch AVT Medical Limited,  Chennai, India**

## TELLABS INC.

4951 Indiana Ave. 6303788800, Lisle, IL, 60532-1698

Tel: (630) 378-8800        Fax: (630) 679-3010        www.tellabs.com

*Design/mfr./service voice/data transport and network access systems.*

**Tellabs Bangalore,  No. 45 Race Course Road 6/F, Bangalore 560001, India**

**Tellabs New Delhi,  U-1 Green Park, New Delhi 110016, India**

## TENNECO AUTOMOTIVE INC.

500 North Field Drive, Lake Forest, IL, 60045

Tel: (847) 482-5241        Fax: (847) 482-5295        www.tenneco-automotive.com

*Mfr. automotive parts, exhaust systems and service equipment.*

**Monroe,  c/o Renowned Auto Products Mfs, Ltd., Hosur, India**

Tel: 91-4344-76413   Fax: 91-4344-76414   Contact: K.A. Padmanabhan, Mgr.   Emp: 125

**Monroe,  c/o Hydraulics Ltd., 38A+B, Morrison St., Alandur, Madras 600 016, India**

Tel: 91-44-234-1942   Fax: 91-44-234-3690   Contact: N.N. Neelakantan, Mgr.   Emp: 389

**Monroe Hydraulics, Ltd.,  No. B80 Pipdic Industrial Estate, Mettupalayan Pondicherry 605 009, India**

Tel: 91-413-71348   Fax: 91-413-71739   Contact: T. Krishnamurthy, Mgr.   Emp: 162

## TETRA TECH, INC.

670 N. Rosemead Blvd., Pasadena, CA, 91107

Tel: (626) 351-4664        Fax: (626) 351-1188        www.tetratech.com

*Environmental engineering and consulting services.*

**Tetra Tech - India,  Plot No. 5, Sector 27C, Mathura Rd., Faridabad 121 003 India**

Tel: 91-129-27-2490   Fax: 91-129-27-0201   Contact: Dr. N. Sriram

## TEXAS INSTRUMENTS INC.

8505 Forest Lane, Dallas, TX, 75243

Tel: (972) 995-3773        Fax: (972) 995-4360        www.ti.com

*Mfr. semiconductor devices, electronic electro-mechanical systems, instruments and controls.*

**Texas Instruments India,  Delhi, India**

Tel: 91-17-800-800-1450

## THERMO ORION, INC.

500 Cummings Court, Beverly, MA, 01915

Tel: (978) 922-4400        Fax: (978) 922-6015        www.thermoorion.com

*Mfr. laboratory and industrial products, measure and display instruments.*

**Thermo Orion India,  105 Ashoka Apartments 1/F, Ranjit Nagar Commercial Complex, New Dehli 110008, India**

Tel: 91-11-5705775

## THERMON MANUFACTURING COMPANY

100 Thermon Drive, PO Box 609, San Marcos, TX, 78667-0609

Tel: (512) 396-5801        Fax: (512) 396-3627        www.thermon.com

*Mfr. steam and electric heat tracing systems, components and accessories.*

**Thermon Heat Tracers Ltd.,  Thermon Bhavan, GAT No. 566 & 570/1, Koregaon Bhima Taluka: Shirur, Pune 412 207 India**

**THE TORRINGTON COMPANY**

59 Field St., PO Box 1008, Torrington, CT, 06790

Tel: (860) 626-2000    Fax: (860) 496-3625    www.torrington.com

*Mfr. precision bearings, motion control components and automotive steering assemblies.*

**NRB Torrington Pvt. Ltd.,  New Delhi, India**

**THE TRANE COMPANY**

3600 Pammel Creek Road, La Crosse, WI, 54601

Tel: (608) 787-2000    Fax: (608) 787-4990    www.trane.com

*Mfr./distributor/service A/C systems and equipment.*

**Trane India Ltd.,  604 Dalamal House, 206 Jamnal Bajaj Rd., Nariman Point Mumbai 400 021, India**

**TRICO PRODUCTS CORPORATION**

817 Washington Street, Buffalo, NY, 14203

Tel: (716) 852-5700    Fax: (716) 853-6242    www.tricoproducts.com

*Mfr. windshield wiper systems and components.*

**Trico Products Corp.,  Lucknow, India**

**TRUE NORTH COMMUNICATIONS INC.**

101 East Erie Street, Chicago, IL, 60611

Tel: (312) 425-6500    Fax: (312) 425-5010    www.truenorth.com

*Holding company, advertising agency.*

**FCB Direct,  Haines Rd. Property 81, Dr. E. Moses Rd., Worli Mumbai 400 018, India**

**FCB-Ulka Advertising Ltd.,  Haines Rd. Property 81, Dr. E. Moses Rd., Worli, Mumbai 400 018, India**

**FCB-Ulka Advertising Ltd.,  811 Padma Tower 1, 5 Rajendra Place, New Delhi 110 008, India**

**FCB-Ulka Advertising Ltd.,  Nirmal 4th Fl., Nariman Point, Mumbai 400 021, India**

**FCB-Ulka Advertising Ltd.,  52 Chikoti Gardens, Begumpet, Hyderabad 500 016 India**

**FCB-Ulka Advertising Ltd.,  Vallamatam Estate 2nd Fl., MG Rd., Ravipuram Cochin 682 015, India**

**FCB-Ulka Advertising Ltd.,  22 Rajasekaran St., Mylapore, Chennai 600 004, India**

**FCB-Ulka Advertising Ltd.,  1/2 Lord Sinha Rd., Calcutta 700 071, India**

**FCB-Ulka Advertising Ltd.,  1103 Barton Centre, 84 M.G. Rd., Bangalore - 560 001 India**

**U.S. WHEAT ASSOCIATES**

1620 I Street, NW, Washington, DC, 20006

Tel: (202) 463-0999    Fax: (202) 785-1052

*Market development for wheat products.*

**U.S. Wheat Associates Inc.,  902 New Delhi House, 27 Barakhamba Rd., New Delhi 110 001, India**

**UNITED PARCEL SERVICE, INC.**

55 Glenlake Parkway, NE, Atlanta, GA, 30328

Tel: (404) 828-6000    Fax: (404) 828-6593    www.ups.com

*International package-delivery service.*

**UPS - Elbee Services Ltd.,  S.M. House, 11 Sahakar Rd., Vile Parle East, Mumbai 400 057 India**

Tel: 91-22-859-2200

**UNIVERSAL INSTRUMENTS**

90 Bevier Street, S. Dock, Binghamton, NY, 13904

Tel: (607) 779-7522    Fax: (607) 779-7971    www.uic.com

*Mfr./sales of instruments for electronic circuit assembly.*

**International Marketing Corporation,  Bangalore, India**

Tel: 91-80-223-7147    Fax: 91-80-223-147

**International Marketing Corporation,  Mumbai, India**

Tel: 91-22-269-7253    Fax: 91-22-269-1096

International Marketing Corporation, New Delhi, India

Tel: 91-11-623-5523    Fax: 91-11-623-5523

## UOP LLC.

25 East Algonquin Road, Des Plaines, IL, 60017

Tel: (847) 391-2000        Fax: (847) 391-2253        www.uop.com

*Engaged in developing and commercializing technology for license to the oil refining, petrochemical and gas processing industries.*

**UOP India Pvt. Ltd./UOP Asia Ltd., Industrial Park, Sector-36, Pace City II Gurgaon-122004 Haryana, India**

Tel: 91-124-373288-91    Fax: 91-124-373283-84

## VARIAN MEDICAL SYSTEMS, INC.

3050 Hansen Way, Palo Alto, CA, 94304-100

Tel: (650) 493-4000        Fax: (650) 424-5358        www.varian.com

*Mfr. microwave tubes and devices, analytical instruments, semiconductor process and medical equipment, vacuum systems.*

**Varian Intl. AG, 7 Community Centre, Basant Lok, Vasant Vihar, New Delhi 110 057, India**

## VERIZON

1095 Ave. of the Americas, New York, NY, 10036

Tel: (212) 395-2121        Fax: (212) 395-1285        www.verizon.com

*Telecommunications.*

**Reliance Telecom, New Delhi, India**

## VERIZON COMMUNICATIONS INC.

1255 Corporate Drive, Irving, TX, 75038

Tel: (972) 507-5000        Fax: (972) 507-5002        www.gte.com

*Engaged in wireline and wireless communications.*

**Reliance Telecom, Gujarat, India**

## WABTEC CORPORATION

1001 Air Brake Ave., Wilmerding, PA, 15148

Tel: (412) 825-1000        Fax: (412) 825-1501        www.wabtec.com

*Mfr. equipment for locomotives, railway freight cars, and passenger transit vehicles*

**Pioneer Friction Products, Calcutta, India**

## WACKENHUT CORPORATION

4200 Wackenhut Dr., Ste. 100, Palm Beach Gardens, FL, 33410

Tel: (561) 622-5656        Fax: (561) 691-6736        www.wackenhut.com

*Security systems and services.*

**Wackenhut & Lancers (India) Pvt. Ltd., B6/4 Commercial Complex, Safarjung Enclave, New Delhi 110 029, India**

Tel: 91-11-617-4562    Fax: 91-11-618-7462

## WALBRO CORPORATION, TI GROUP AUTOMOTIVE

6242 Garfield Ave., Cass City, MI, 48726-1325

Tel: (517) 872-2131        Fax: (517) 872-3090        www.walbro.com

*Mfr. motor vehicle accessories and parts, automotive fluid carrying systems.*

**TI Group Automotive Systems, 2 GIDC Estate - Makarpura, PO Box 70, Baroda 390-010 Gujarat, India**

## WARNER ELECTRIC BRAKE & CLUTCH COMPANY

449 Gardner St., South Beloit, IL, 61080

Tel: (815) 389-3771     Fax: (815) 389-2582     www.warnernet.com

*Global supplier of Power Transmission and Motion Control Solution Systems; automotive, industry brakes, and clutches.*

**Stieber Precision Ltd., B. 48 M.I.D.C., Ind-Satara 415 004, India**

Tel: 91-216-244454   Fax: 91-216-244204

## WATSON WYATT & COMPANY HOLDINGS

6707 Democracy Blvd., Ste. 800, Bethesda, MD, 20817

Tel: (301) 581-4600     Fax: (301) 581-4937     www.watsonwyatt.com

*Creates compensation and benefits programs for major corporations.*

**Watson Wyatt India Pvt. Ltd., Gokul Arcade 'B' 2nd Fl., Subash Road, Vile Parle (E) Mumbai 400057, India**

Tel: 91-22-823-4412   Fax: 91-22-823-4410   Contact: Ivan Mathias

**Watson Wyatt India Pvt. Ltd., 209 Meghdott Building, 94 Nehru Place, New Delhi 110 019, India**

Tel: 91-11-622-9174   Fax: 91-11-622-9784   Contact: Ivan Mathias

## WEATHERFORD INTERNATIONAL, INC.

5 Post Oak Blvd, Ste. 1760, Houston, TX, 77227-3415

Tel: (713) 287-8400     Fax: (713) 963-9785     www.weatherford.com

*Oilfield services, products and equipment; mfr. marine cranes for oil and gas industry.*

**Oilfield Eqmt. & Services Pvt. Ltd., Vaswani Mansions, Dinshaw Vachha Rd., Mumbai 400 020, India**

Tel: 91-22-820-3279   Fax: 91-22-822-2803

## JERVIS B. WEBB COMPANY

34375 W.Twelve Mile Rd., Farmington Hills, MI, 48331

Tel: (248) 553-1220     Fax: (248) 553-1237     www.jervisbwebb.com

*Mfr. integrators of material handling systems.*

**Webb India Ltd., Khaleel Plaza, 32/1 RV Rd., Basavanagudi, Bangalore 560 004, India**

## WEST PHARMACEUTICAL SERVICES

101 Gordon Drive, PO Box 645, Lionville, PA, 19341-0645

Tel: (610) 594-2900     Fax: (610) 594-3014     www.westpharma.com

*Mfr. products for filling, sealing, dispensing and delivering needs of health care and consumer products markets.*

**The West Company, Mumbai, India**

Tel: 91-22-620-6042

## WHIRLPOOL CORPORATION

2000 N. M-63, Benton Harbor, MI, 49022-2692

Tel: (616) 923-5000     Fax: (616) 923-5443     www.whirlpoolcorp.com

*Mfr./market home appliances: Whirlpool, Roper, KitchenAid, Estate, and Inglis.*

**TVS Whirlpool Ltd., Madras, India**

Emp: 5,700

**Whirlpool Asia Manufacturing, New Delhi, India**

## WHITE & CASE LLP

1155 Ave. of the Americas, New York, NY, 10036-2767

Tel: (212) 819-8200     Fax: (212) 354-8113     www.whitecase.com

*International law firm.*

**White & Case LLP, Nirmal Building 17th Fl., Nariman Point, Mumbai 400 021, India**

Tel: 91-22-282-6300   Fax: 91-22-282-6305   Contact: Raj Pande, Ptnr.

## WIND RIVER SYSTEMS, INC.

500 Wind River Way, Alameda, CA, 94501

Tel: (510) 748-4100      Fax: (510) 749-2010      www.isi.com

*Develops and markets computer software products and services.*

**Wind River Systems, Inc., U & I Business Centre, F-41 South Extension Part-I, New Delhi 110 049, India**

Tel: 91-11-464-9421   Fax: 91-11-462-3305   Contact: Sanjay Raina

**Wind River Systems, Inc., 4/1 Millers Road, High Grounds, Bangalore 560052, India**

Tel: 91-80-2283920   Contact: Ajit Edlabadkar

## WOODWARD GOVERNOR COMPANY

5001 N. Second Street, PO Box 7001, Rockford, IL, 61125-7001

Tel: (815) 877-7441      Fax: (815) 639-6033      www.woodward.com

*Mfr./service speed control devices and systems for aircraft turbines, industrial engines and turbines.*

**Woodward Governor India Pvt. Ltd., 23/6 Mathura Rd., Ballabgarh, Haryana 121 004, India**

Tel: 91-129-232-8040   Fax: 91-129-230-418   Contact: Ken Axelson   Emp: 50

## WM WRIGLEY JR. COMPANY

410 N. Michigan Ave., Chicago, IL, 60611-4287

Tel: (312) 644-2121      Fax: (312) 644-0353      www.wrigley.com

*Mfr. chewing gum.*

**Wrigley India Pvt. Ltd., Bangalore, India**

## WYETH-AYERST INTERNATIONAL INC.

150 Radnot-Chester Road, St. Davids, PA, 19087

Tel: (610) 902-4100      Fax: (610) 989-4586      www.ahp.com/wyeth

*Antibiotics and pharmaceutical products.*

**Wyeth-Lederle Limited, Magnet House Narottam Morarjee Marg, Ballard Estate, Mumbai 400-038, India**

Tel: 91-22-261-6991

**Wyeth-Lederle Limited, Nyloc House 254-D2, Dr. Annie Besant Rd., Mumbai 400-025 India**

Tel: 91-22-493-5211

## XEROX CORPORATION

800 Long Ridge Road, PO Box 1600, Stamford, CT, 06904

Tel: (203) 968-3000      Fax: (203) 968-4312      www.xerox.com

*Mfr. document processing equipment, systems and supplies.*

**Modi Xerox Ltd., 98 Nahru Place Ground Fl., New Delhi 110 019, India**

Tel: 91-11-643-4544   Fax: 91-11-644-4652

**Xerox Corp., Modipur (Bareilly Rd.), Rampur, India**

## XTRA CORPORATION

1807 Park 270 Dr., Ste. 400, St. Louis, MO, 63146-4020

Tel: (314) 579-9320      Fax: (314) 579-0299      www.xtracorp.com

*Holding company: leasing.*

**XTRA International, Mumbai, India**

## YORK INTERNATIONAL CORPORATION

631 South Richland Ave., York, PA, 17403

Tel: (717) 771-7890      Fax: (717) 771-6212      www.york.com

*Mfr. heating, ventilating, air conditioning and refrigeration equipment.*

**York Air Conditioning & Refrigeration, Inc., Greater Kallash II, New Delhi 110001, India**

Tel: 91-11-623-5246   Fax: 91-11-623-5246

**YOUNG & RUBICAM INC.**

285 Madison Ave., New York, NY, 10017

Tel: (212) 210-3000       Fax: (212) 370-3796        www.yr.com

*Advertising, public relations, direct marketing and sales promotion, corporate and product ID management.*

**DY&R/Rediffusion/Bombay,  Prabhadevi Mumbai, India**

# Indonesia

## 3COM CORPORATION

5400 Bayfront Plaza, Santa Clara, CA, 95052-8145

Tel: (408) 326-5000     Fax: (408) 326-5001     www.3com.com

*Develop/mfr. computer networking products and systems.*

**3Com Asia Ltd. - Indonesia, Level 7 Wisma 46 KOTA BNI, JL. Jend. Sudirman Kav. 1, Jakarta 10220 Indonesia**

Tel: 62-21-572-2088  Fax: 62-21-572-2089

## 3M

3M Center, St. Paul, MN, 55144-1000

Tel: (651) 733-1110     Fax: (651) 733-9973     www.mmm.com

*Mfr. diversified products for industry, health care, imaging, communications, transport, safety, consumer, etc.*

**PT 3M Indonesia, PO Box 6712/JKSRB, Jakarta 12067, Indonesia**

Tel: 62-21-883-46059   Fax: 62-21-883-46108

## ABBOTT LABORATORIES

One Abbott Park, Abbott Park, IL, 60064-3500

Tel: (847) 937-6100     Fax: (847) 937-1511     www.abbott.com

*Development/mfr./sale diversified health care products and services.*

**P.T. Abbott Indonesia, Jl. Raya Jakarta-Bogor Km. 37, Cimanggis Desa Sukamaju Bogor, Indonesia**

## AETNA INC.

151 Farmington Avenue, Hartford, CT, 06156

Tel: (860) 273-0123     Fax: (860) 275-2677     www.aetna.com

*Managed health care, annuities, individual retirement and group pension services, and asset management products worldwide.*

**Aetna Life Indonesia, Jakarta, Indonesia**

## AIR EXPRESS INTERNATIONAL CORPORATION

120 Tokeneke Road, PO Box 1231, Darien, CT, 06820

Tel: (203) 655-7900     Fax: (203) 655-5779     www.aeilogistics.com

*International air freight forwarder.*

**AEI Liaison Office - P.T. Angkutan Expressindo International, Jl. Ir H Juanda III/26 A-B, Jakarta Pusat - 10120, Indonesia**

Tel: 62-21-380-1239   Fax: 62-21-384-6700

## AIRBORNE FREIGHT CORPORATION

3101 Western Ave., PO Box 662, Seattle, WA, 98121

Tel: (206) 285-4600     Fax: (206) 281-1444     www.airborne.com

*Air transport services.*

**Airborne Express, Jl. Wijayai No 2a, Jakarta Selatan 12170, Indonesia**

Tel: 62-21-723-3364   Fax: 62-21-723-3368

## AMERICAN INTERNATIONAL GROUP INC. (AIG)

70 Pine Street, New York, NY, 10270

Tel: (212) 770-7000     Fax: (212) 509-9705     www.aig.com

*Worldwide insurance and financial services.*

**P.T. Asuransi AIU Indonesia, Jl.K.H. Hasyin Ashari 35, Jakarta 10130, Indonesia**

## AMWAY CORPORATION

7575 Fulton Street East, Ada, MI, 49355-0001

Tel: (616) 787-6000    Fax: (616) 787-6177    www.amway.com

*Mfr./sale home care, personal care, nutrition and houseware products.*

**PT Jasa Manajemen Amway, Wisma SSK, Jl. Daan Mogot KM 11, Jakarta Barat, Indonesia**

## ANDERSEN CONSULTING

100 S. Wacker Drive, Ste. 1059, Chicago, IL, 60606

Tel: (312) 693-0161    Fax: (312) 693-0507    www.ac.com

*Provides management and technology consulting services.*

**Andersen Consulting, Wisma 46 - Kota BNI 18th Fl., Jl. Jend. Sudirman Kav. 1, Jakarta 10220, Indonesia**

Tel: 62-21-574-6575   Fax: 62-21-574-6576

## ANDERSEN WORLDWIDE

33 West Monroe Street, Chicago, IL, 60603

Tel: (312) 580-0033    Fax: (312) 507-6748    www.arthurandersen.com

*Accounting and audit, tax and management consulting services.*

**Drs. Gunawan, Prijohandojo, Utomo & Co., Wisma Batamindo Level D3, Jl. Rasamala No. 1, Muka Kuning Batam 29433, Indonesia**

Tel: 62-778-611163

**Kautor Akuntan Publik, Prasetio, Utomo & Co., Wisma 46 Kota BNI, Jl. Jend. Sudirman Kav. 1, PO Box 2134, Jakarta 10001 Indonesia**

Tel: 62-21-575-7999

**Prasetio, Utomo & Co., Jl. Imam Bonjol No. 16A, PO Box 1994, Medan 20001, Indonesia**

Tel: 62-61-326075

**Prasetio, Utomo & Co., Jl. Raya Dr. Sutomo No. 77, PO Box 1172, Surabaya 60264, Indonesia**

Tel: 62-31-574471

**Prasetio, Utomo & Co., Jl. Sulanjana No. 4, PO Box 1339, Badung 40013, Indonesia**

Tel: 62-22-420-4464

## ANDREW CORPORATION

10500 West 153rd Street, Orland Park, IL, 60462

Tel: (708) 349-3300    Fax: (708) 349-5410    www.andrew.com

*Mfr. antenna systems, coaxial cable, electronic communications and network connectivity systems.*

**Andrew Jakarta Office, Benchmark, The Ascot Jakarta No. 2, Jl. Kebon Kacang Raya, Jakarta 10230 Indonesia**

Tel: 62-21-318-5821   Fax: 62-21-318-5820

## AON CORPORATION

123 North Wacker Drive, Chicago, IL, 60606

Tel: (312) 701-3000    Fax: (312) 701-3100    www.aon.com

*Insurance brokers worldwide; underwrites accident and health insurance, specialty and professional insurance; and provides risk management consultation.*

**P.T. Aon Lippo Indonesia, Menara Sudirman, Lantai 3 and 5 Jl. Jend. Sudirman KAV. 60, Jakarta 12190, Indonesia**

Tel: 62-21-522-0123   Fax: 62-21-522-0111   Contact: Junaedy Ganie

## APPLERA CORPORATION

761 Main Avenue, Norwalk, CT, 06859-0001

Tel: (203) 762-1000    Fax: (203) 762-6000    www.applera.com

*Leading supplier of systems for life science research and related applications.*

**PT Laborindo Savaria, Ruko Permata - Kevayoran Plaza - BN 11, Jl. Jiban No. 2, Kebayoran Lama, Jakarta 12220, Indonesia**

## ARBOR ACRES FARM INC.

439 Marlborough Road, Glastonbury, CT, 06033

Tel:  (860) 633-4681        Fax:  (860) 633-2433

*Producers of male and female broiler breeders, commercial egg layers.*

**PT Charoen Pokhpand Indonesia Animal Feedmill Co. Ltd.,  PO Box 83/JKT, Jakarta Kota, Indonesia**

## AT&T BROADBAND, LLC

9197 South Peoria, Englewood, CO, 80112

Tel:  (720) 875-5500        Fax:  (720) 875-4984        www.broadband.att.com

*Provides broadband technology services; digital TV, digital telephone and high-speed cable internet services.*

**AriaWest,  Jakarta, Indonesia**

## AUTODESK INC.

111 McInnis Parkway, San Rafael, CA, 94903

Tel:  (415) 507-5000        Fax:  (415) 507-6112        www.autodesk.com

*Develop/marketing/support computer-aided design, engineering, scientific and multimedia software products.*

**Autodesk Asia Pte. Ltd.,  c/o Servcorp, Level 43 Wisma 46, Jln. Jenderal Sudirman Kav. 1, Jakarta Selatan 10220, Indonesia**

## AUTOMATIC SWITCH CO. (ASCO)

50-60 Hanover Rd., Florham Park, NJ, 07932

Tel:  (973) 966-2000        Fax:  (973) 966-2628        www.asco.com

*Mfr. solenoid valves, emergency power controls, pressure and temp. switches.*

**Asco Asia, Indonesia,  c/o Emerson Electric South Asia, Jl. Cikini II No. 4, Jakarta 10330, Indonesia**
Tel: 62-21-315-6134   Fax: 62-21-314-0861   Contact: Djohan Gunawan

## AVERY DENNISON CORPORATION

150 N. Orange Grove Blvd., Pasadena, CA, 91103

Tel:  (626) 304-2000        Fax:  (626) 792-7312        www.averydennison.com

*Mfr. pressure-sensitive adhesives and materials, office products, labels, tags, retail systems, Carter's Ink and specialty chemicals.*

**Avery Dennison Asia Pacific Group,  Blk V-81D JI Jababeka V, Cikarang Ind Estate-Jababeka, Bekasi 17550 West Java Indonesia**
Tel: 62-21-893-6033   Fax: 62-21-93-6031

## AVIS GROUP HOLDINGS, INC.

900 Old Country Road., Garden City, NY, 11530

Tel:  (516) 222-3000        Fax:  (516) 222-4381        www.avis.com

*Car rental services.*

**Avis Group Holdings Ltd..,  Jl. Diponegoro 25, Jakarta, Indonesia**

## AVON PRODUCTS INC.

1345 Avenue of the Americas, New York, NY, 10105-0196

Tel:  (212) 282-5000        Fax:  (212) 282-6049        www.avon.com

*Mfr./distributor beauty and related products, fashion jewelry, gifts and collectibles.*

**P.T. Avon Indonesia,  Bldg. 208, Cilandak Commercial Estate, Cilandak Djakarta 12560, Indonesia**
Tel: 62-21-780-1200   Fax: 62-21-780-1712   Contact: Agung Sardjono, Mgr.

## BAKER & McKENZIE

130 East Randolph Drive, Ste. 2500, Chicago, IL, 60601

Tel: (312) 861-8000   Fax: (312) 861-2899   www.bakerinfo.com

*International legal services.*

**B & M Consultants, Jakarta Stock Exchange Bldg. Tower II 21/F, Sudirman Central Business District, Jl. Jend. Sudirman Kav. 52-53, Jakarta 12190 Indonesia**

Tel: 62-21-515-5090   Fax: 62-21-515-4840

## BAKER HUGHES INCORPORATED

3900 Essex Lane, Ste. 1200, Houston, TX, 77027

Tel: (713) 439-8600   Fax: (713) 439-8699   www.bakerhughes.com

*Develop and apply technology to drill, complete and produce oil and natural gas wells; provide separation systems to petroleum, municipal, continuous process and mining industries.*

**Baker Oil Tools, c/o PT DWI Sentana Prima, JL Mulawarman KM 16, Balikpapan East Kalimantan 76115, Indonesia**

Tel: 62-542-64391   Fax: 62-542-65068

**Baker Oil Tools, c/o PT Imeco Inter Sarana, JL Ampera Raya Kav. 10 4th Fl., Cilandak Jakarta 12550, Indonesia**

Tel: 62-21-780-5432   Fax: 62-21-780885

**PT Milchem Indonesia, D-5 Setiabudi Bldg., Jl. H.R. Rasuna Said 62, Kuningan, Jakarta Selatan Indonesia**

## BAKER PETROLITE CORPORATION

3900 Essex Lane, Houston, TX, 77027

Tel: (713) 599-7400   Fax: (713) 599-7592   www.bakerhughes.com/bapt/

*Mfr. specialty chemical treating programs, performance-enhancing additives and related equipment and services.*

**PT Petrolite Indonesia Pratama, Batu Ampar, Pulua Batam, Indonesia**

## BANK OF AMERICA CORPORATION

555 California Street, San Francisco, CA, 94104

Tel: (415) 622-3530   Fax: (415) 622-8467   www.bankofamerica.com

*Financial services.*

**Bank of America NT & SA, 22/F Jakarta Stock Exchange Bldg., Jl. Jend. Sudirman Kav. 52-53, Jakarta 12190, Indonesia**

Tel: 62-21-515-1392   Fax: 62-21-515-1407   Contact: K.C. Gan, SVP

## THE BANK OF NEW YORK

One Wall Street, New York, NY, 10286

Tel: (212) 495-1784   Fax: (212) 495-2546   www.bankofny.com

*Banking services.*

**The Bank of New York, Mashi Plaza, #18-09 Jl. Jend. Sudirman Kav. 25, Jakarta 12920, Indonesia**

Tel: 62-21-526-7806

## BARRY CONTROLS INC.

40 Guest Street, PO Box 9105, Brighton, MA, 02135-9105

Tel: (617) 787-1555   Fax: (617) 254-7381   www.barrymounts.com

*Mfr./sale vibration isolation mounting devices.*

**Androjaya Satryatama p.t., 2/F - Jl. Rajawali Barat No. 61, Bandung 40184 West Java, Indonesia**

## BATES WORLDWIDE INC.

405 Lexington Ave., New York, NY, 10174

Tel: (212) 297-7000      Fax: (212) 986-0270      www.batesww.com

*Advertising, marketing, public relations and media consulting.*

**Bates 141 Indonesia, Jl. Iskandarsyah Raya No. 97, Blok M. Jakarta 12160, Indonesia**

Tel: 62-21-723-2383   Fax: 62-21-723-2407   Contact: Linda Rustram

**Bates Indonesia, Jl. Iskandarsyah Raya No. 97, Blok M. Jakarta 12160, Indonesia**

Tel: 62-21-723-2383   Fax: 62-21-723-2407   Contact: Geoff Seebeck, CEO

## BBDO WORLDWIDE

1285 Ave. of the Americas, New York, NY, 10019

Tel: (212) 459-5000      Fax: (212) 459-6645      www.bbdo.com

*Multinational group of advertising agencies.*

**BBDO (Malaysia), Kuala Lumpur, Indonesia**

## BDO SEIDMAN, LLP    BELGIUM

Two Prudential Plaza, 180 N. Stetson Ave., Ste. 2300, Chicago, IL, 60601

Tel: (312) 240-1236      Fax: (312) 240-3329      www.bdo.com

*International accounting and financial consulting firm.*

**RB Tanubrata & Rekan, Bukit duri Permai Estate Blok 8/1, Jl. Jatinegara Barat 54E, Jakarta 13320, Indonesia**

Tel: 62-21-819-9189   Fax: 62-21-819-9949   Contact: Richard B. Tanubrata

## BECHTEL GROUP INC.

50 Beale Street, PO Box 3965, San Francisco, CA, 94105-1895

Tel: (415) 768-1234      Fax: (415) 768-9038      www.bechtel.com

*General contractors in engineering and construction.*

**Bechtel Inc., Bursa Efek Jakarta Bldg. 11th Fl., Jl.Jend. Sudirman Kav. 52, Jakarta 12190, Indonesia**

Tel: 62-21-515-7000   Fax: 62-21-515-3477

**Pacific Bechtel Corp., Jl. Menteng Raya 8, PO Box 467, Jakarta, Indonesia**

## LOUIS BERGER INTERNATIONAL INC.

100 Halsted Street, East Orange, NJ, 07019

Tel: (201) 678-1960      Fax: (201) 672-4284      www.louisberger.com

*Consulting engineers, engaged in architecture, environmental and advisory services.*

**Louis Berger International Inc., PO Box 4312, Kelurahan Mampang, Jakarta 12043, Indonesia**

Tel: 62-21-720-5774   Fax: 62-21-720-5775

**Louis Berger International Inc., Kabupaten Road Master Training Plan, Haery I Building Lt.2, Jl.Kemanh Selatan #151, Kebayoran Baru Jakarta Selatan Indonesia**

Tel: 62-21-789-1923   Fax: 62-21-789-1925

**Louis Berger International Inc., PO Box 195, Jl. Moh. Yamin #11, Maumere Flores, Nusa Tenggara Timur 86111, Indonesia**

## BEST WESTERN INTERNATIONAL

6201 North 24th Place, Phoenix, AZ, 85106

Tel: (602) 957-4200      Fax: (602) 957-5740      www.bestwestern.com

*International hotel chain.*

**Asean International, Jl. H. Adama Malik No. 5, 20114 Sumatera, Indonesia**

## BESTFOODS, INC.

700 Sylvan Ave., International Plaza, Englewood Cliffs, NJ, 07632-9976

Tel: (201) 894-4000      Fax: (201) 894-2186      www.bestfoods.com

*Consumer foods products; corn refining.*

**P.T. Knorr Indonesia, Jl. Pakubuwono VI No. 84, Kebayoran Baru, Jakarta 12120, Indonesia**

Tel: 62-21-725-2283   Fax: 62-21-725-4755   Contact: Peter N. M. Smith, Pres.

## BETZDEARBORN

4636 Somerton Road, PO Box 3002, Trevose, PA, 19053-6783

Tel: (215) 953-2568     Fax: (215) 953-5524     www.betzdearborn.com

*Mfr. water/wastewater and process system treatment chemicals and services.*

**PT BetzDearborn Persada, Gedung Bank Bali 6th Fl., Jl. Jend. Sudirman Kav 27, Jakarta 12920, Indonesia**

## SAMUEL BINGHAM COMPANY

127 East Lake Street, Ste. 300, Bloomingdale, IL, 60108

Tel: (630) 924-9250     Fax: (630) 924-0469     www.binghamrollers.com

*Print and industrial rollers and inks.*

**PT Kahardjaja, PO Box 2189, Jakarta, Indonesia**

## BLACK & VEATCH LLP

8400 Ward Pkwy., PO Box 8405, Kansas City, MO, 64114

Tel: (913) 339-2000     Fax: (913) 339-2934     www.bv.com

*Engineering, architectural and construction services.*

**Binnie Black & Veatch, Kemang Business Centre 2/F Building II, Jl. Kemang Raya No. 2, Kemang Jakarta Selatan 12730, Indonesia**

Tel: 62-21-572-2380   Fax: 62-21-572-2371   Contact: Ted Burgess

**Black & Veatch International, Menara Batavia 29/F, Jl. K.H. Mas Mansyur Kav. 126, Jakarta Pusat 10220, Indonesia**

Tel: 62-21-572-2380   Fax: 62-21-572-2385   Contact: John M. Gustke

## BMC SOFTWARE, INC.

2101 City West Blvd., Houston, TX, 77042-2827

Tel: (713) 918-8800     Fax: (713) 918-8000     www.bmc.com

*Engaged in mainframe-related utilities software and services.*

**BMC Software Ltd., Wisma GKBI Ste. 3901, Jl. Jend. Sudirman No. 28, Jakarta 10210, Indonesia**

Tel: 62-21-5799-8131   Fax: 62-21-5799-8080

## BOOZ-ALLEN & HAMILTON INC.

8283 Greensboro Drive, McLean, VA, 22102

Tel: (703) 902-5000     Fax: (703) 902-3333     www.bah.com

*International management and technology consultants.*

**PT Booz Allen & Hamilton Indonesia, 25th Fl. Wisma Danamon Aetna Tower, Jl. Jend. Sudirman Kav. 45-46, Jakarta 12930, Indonesia**

Tel: 62-21-577-0077   Fax: 62-21-577-1760

## THE BOSTON CONSULTING GROUP

Exchange Place, 31st Fl., Boston, MA, 02109

Tel: (617) 973-1200     Fax: (617) 973-1339     www.bcg.com

*Management consulting company.*

**The Boston Consulting Group, Level 11 Mashill Tower, J1. Jend. Sudirman Kav. 25, Jakarta Selantan 12920, Indonesia**

Tel: 62-21-526-7775

## BOWNE & COMPANY, INC.

345 Hudson Street, New York, NY, 10014

Tel: (212) 924-5500     Fax: (212) 229-3420     www.bowne.com

*Financial printing and foreign language translation, localization (software), internet design and maintenance and facilities management.*

**Bowne International, Jakarta Stock Exch. Bldg., 23/F Ste.2302, Jl.Jend Sudirman, Jakarta 12190 Indonesia**

Tel: 62-21-515-3210   Fax: 62-21-515-3211   Contact: Chui Peng Au, Mgr.

## BOYDEN CONSULTING CORPORATION

364 Elwood Ave., Hawthorne, NY, 10502

Tel: (914) 747-0093    Fax: (914) 980-6147    www.boyden.com

*International executive search firm.*

**Boyden Associates Ltd., Wisma Bank Dharmala #1801 B, Jl. Jend. Sudirman Kav. 28, Jakarta 12910, Indonesia**

Tel: 62-21-522-9652

## BOZELL GROUP

40 West 23rd Street, New York, NY, 10010

Tel: (212) 727-5000    Fax: (212) 645-9173    www.bozell.com

*Advertising, marketing, public relations and media consulting.*

**PT Dian Mentari Pratama Bozell, Jl. Permuda No. 715, Jakarta Timur, Indonesia**

Tel: 62-21-471-3738   Fax: 62-21-471-3739   Contact: Maria Indriani, Pres.

## BRISTOL-MYERS SQUIBB COMPANY

345 Park Ave., New York, NY, 10154-0037

Tel: (212) 546-4000    Fax: (212) 546-4020    www.bms.com

*Pharmaceutical and food preparations, medical and surgical instruments.*

**BMS (Indonesia), Tamara Cntra 10th Fl., Jl Jend. Sudirman Kav 24, Indonesia**

**ConvaTec Indonesia, c/o PT Enseval, 4/F - Jl. Jetjen, Suprapto, Jakarta Indonesia**

Tel: 62-21-424-3908

## BROWN GROUP, INC.

8300 Maryland Ave., St. Louis, MO, 63105

Tel: (314) 854-4000    Fax: (314) 854-4274    www.browngroup.com

*Footwear wholesaler and retailer, including Naturalizer brand.*

**Brown Group, Inc., Jakarta, Indonesia**

## BROWN SHOE COMPANY, INC.

8300 Maryland Avenue, St. Louis, MO, 63105

Tel: (314) 854-4000    Fax: (314) 854-4274    www.brownshoe.com

*Markets branded and private label footwear, including Dr. Scholl's, Air Step and Buster Brown.*

**Brown Shoe International, Jakarta, Indonesia**

## LEO BURNETT, DIV. B-COM 3 GROUP

35 West Wacker Drive, Chicago, IL, 60601

Tel: (312) 220-5959    Fax: (312) 220-6533    www.bcom3group.com

*Engaged in advertising, marketing, media buying and planning, and public relations.*

**Kreasindo Advertising & Marketing Consultants, Jakarta, Indonesia**

## BURSON-MARSTELLER

230 Park Ave., New York, NY, 10003-1566

Tel: (212) 614-4000    Fax: (212) 614-4262    www.bm.com

*Public relations/public affairs consultants.*

**Burson-Marsteller Jakarta, PT Binamitra Indocipta 16th Fl., Mid Plaza 2 Bldg., Jl. Jend. Sudirman KAV 10-11, Jakarta 10220 Indonesia**

Tel: 62-21-573-9646   Fax: 62-21-573-9647

## BUTLER INTERNATIONAL

110 Summit Ave., Montvale, NJ, 07645

Tel: (201) 573-8000    Fax: (201) 573-9723    www.butlerintl.com

*Leading supplier of skilled technical personnel.*

**Butler International, Jakarta, Indonesia**

## CALTEX CORPORATION

125 East John Carpenter Fwy., Irving, TX, 75062-2794

Tel: (972) 830-1000     Fax: (972) 830-1081     www.caltex.com

*Petroleum products.*

**P. T. Caltex Pacific Indonesia, Jakarta, Indonesia**

## CARBOLINE COMPANY

350 Hanley Industrial Court, St. Louis, MO, 63144

Tel: (314) 644-1000     Fax: (314) 644-4617     www.carboline.com

*Mfr. coatings and sealants.*

**PT Pacific Paint, Jl. Gunung Sahari XI/291, Jakarta 10720, Indonesia**

**PT Tirtajaya Segara, Jl. Hayam Wuruk 3T, PO Box 4228, Jakarta 10120, Indonesia**

## CARGILL, INC.

15407 McGinty Road West, Minnetonka, MN, 55440-5625

Tel: (612) 742-7575     Fax: (612) 742-7393     www.cargill.com

*Food products, feeds, animal products.*

**Cargill Indonesia, PO Box 4345, Jakarta 1001, Indonesia**

## CATERPILLAR INC.

100 NE Adams Street, Peoria, IL, 61629-6105

Tel: (309) 675-1000     Fax: (309) 675-1182     www.cat.com

*Mfr. earth/material-handling and construction machinery and equipment and engines.*

**P. T. Solar Services Indonesia, Jakarta, Indonesia**

## C.B. RICHARD ELLIS

533 South Fremont Ave., Los Angeles, CA, 90071-1712

Tel: (213) 613-3123     Fax: (213) 613-3535     www.cbrichardellis.com

*Commercial real estate services.*

**PT Urbana Daya Perkasa, 7/FJalan Jenderal Sadirman Kav 27, Jakarta 12920, Indonesia**

## CENTRAL NATIONAL-GOTTESMAN INC.

3 Manhattanville Road, Purchase, NY, 10577-2110

Tel: (914) 696-9000     Fax: (914) 696-1066

*Worldwide sales pulp and paper products.*

**PT Intersentral Nugraha, Wijaya Graha Centre Block H-18, Jl. Wijaya II Kebayron Baru, Jakarta 12160, Indonesia**

Tel: 62-21-725-4144   Fax: 62-21-725-7274   Contact: Benny Pranata

## CENTURY 21 REAL ESTATE CORPORATION

6 Sylvan Way, Parsippany, NJ, 07054-3826

Tel: (973) 496-5722     Fax: (973) 496-5527     www.century21.com

*Engaged in real estate.*

**Century 21 Indonesia, Gedung Mall Ciputra Lantai P1, Jl. Arteri S. Parman, Grogol Jakarta 11470, Indonesia**

Tel: 62-21-566-2121

## CHAMPION INTERNATIONAL CORPORATION

One Champion Plaza, Stamford, CT, 06921

Tel: (203) 358-7000     Fax: (203) 358-2975     www.championinternational.com

*Manufacture/sales of pulp and paper.*

**APRIL/Champion International, Indonesia**

## CHEMTEX INTERNATIONAL INC.

1979 Eastwood Rd., Wilmington, NC, 28403

Tel: (910) 509-4400        Fax: (910) 509-4567        www.chemtex.com

*Mfr. fibers and petrochemicals; engineering, procurement, construction, construction management.*

**Chemtex International Inc., Jakarta, Indonesia**

## CHESTERTON BINSWANGER INTERNATIONAL

Two Logan Square, 4th Floor, Philadelphia, PA, 19103-2759

Tel: (215) 448-6000        Fax: (215) 448-6238        www.cbbi.com

*Real estate and related services.*

**Pt. Chesterton Nusantara, Chase Plaza level 3, Jl. Jend. Sudirman Kav. 21, Jakarta 12910, Indonesia**

## CHEVRON CORPORATION

575 Market Street, San Francisco, CA, 94105-2856

Tel: (415) 894-7700        Fax: (415) 894-2248        www.chevron.com

*Oil exploration, production and petroleum products.*

**Caltex Pacific Indonesia PT, Jl. Thamrin, PO Box 158, Jakarta, Indonesia**

## CHICAGO BRIDGE & IRON COMPANY (CBI)

1501 North Division Street, Plainfield, IL, 60544

Tel: (815) 241-7546        Fax: (815) 439-6010        www.chicago-bridge.com

*Holding company: metal plate fabricating, construction, oil and gas drilling.*

**PT CBI Indonesia, PO Box 6924, Jakarta 12069, Indonesia**

## CIGNA COMPANIES

One Liberty Place, Philadelphia, PA, 19192

Tel: (215) 761-1000        Fax: (215) 761-5511        www.cigna.com

*Insurance, invest, health care and other financial services.*

**PT Asuransi Cigna Indonesia, The Landmark Centre 9/F-#901, Jl. Jen Sudirman Kav. 70-A, Jakarta 12910, Indonesia**

**PT Asuransi Niaga CIGNA Life, Menara Kadin Indonesia 15th Fl., JI. HR. Rasuna Said, Blk X-5 Kav. 02-03, Jakarta 12950 Indonesia**

Tel: 62-21-250-5313   Fax: 62-21-250-5310   Contact: Steve Novkov

## CINCOM SYSTEMS INC.

55 Merchant Street, Cincinnati, OH, 45446

Tel: (513) 612-2300        Fax: (513) 481-8332        www.cincom.com

*Develop/distributor computer software.*

**Cincom PT Mitra Integrasi, Wisma Metropolitan I - 6/F, Jalan Jend. Sudirman Kav. 29-31, Jakarta 12920 Indonesia**

## CISCO SYSTEMS, INC.

170 West Tasman Drive, San Jose, CA, 95134-1706

Tel: (408) 526-4000        Fax: (408) 526-4100        www.cisco.com

*Develop/mfr./market computer hardware and software networking systems.*

**Cisco Systems (HK), Indonesia, Level 12A Menara BCD, Jl. Jend. Sudirman Kav. 26, Jakarta 12920, Indonesia**

Tel: 62-21-250-6533   Fax: 62-21-250-6532

## CITIGROUP, INC.

153 East 53rd Street, New York, NY, 10043

Tel: (212) 559-1000        Fax: (212) 559-3646        www.citigroup.com

*Provides insurance and financial services worldwide.*

**Citibank N.A., Landmark Centre 5th Fl., Jl. Jend Sudriman No 1, Jakarta 12910, Indonesia**

Contact: Pijush Gupta

## THE COASTAL CORPORATION

Nine Greenway Plaza, Houston, TX, 77046-0995

Tel: (713) 877-1400      Fax: (713) 877-6752      www.coastalcorp.com

*Oil refining, natural gas, related services; independent power production.*

**Coastal Indonesia Bangko Ltd., Sumatra, Indonesia**

## THE COCA-COLA COMPANY

PO Drawer 1734, Atlanta, GA, 30301

Tel: (404) 676-2121      Fax: (404) 676-6792      www.coca-cola.com

*Mfr./marketing/distributor soft drinks, syrups and concentrates, juice and juice-drink products.*

**Jakarta Coca-Cola Bottler, Jakarta, Indonesia**

## COMPUTER ASSOCIATES INTERNATIONAL INC.

One Computer Associates Plaza, Islandia, NY, 11788

Tel: (516) 342-5224      Fax: (516) 342-5329      www.cai.com

*Integrated business software for enterprise computing and information management, application development, manufacturing, financial applications and professional services.*

**Computer Associates Indonesia, Wisma 46 Kota BNI -Level 34-05/06, Jl. Jend Sudirman Kav. 1, Jakarta 10220, Indonesia**

Tel: 62-21-251-5030

## CONOCO INC.

PO Box 2197, 600 N. Dairy Ashford, Houston, TX, 77252

Tel: (281) 293-1000      Fax: (281) 293-1440      www.conoco.com

*Oil, gas, coal, chemicals and minerals.*

**Conoco Irian Jaya Co., PO Box 367, Jakarta, Indonesia**

**Continental Oil Co./ Pertamina, Five Pillars Office Park, Jl. Let. Jen. M.T. Haryono 58, Jakarta, Indonesia**

## CORE LABORATORIES

6315 Windfern, Houston, TX, 77040

Tel: (713) 328-2673      Fax: (713) 328-2150      www.corelab.com

*Petroleum testing/analysis, analytical chemicals, laboratory and octane analysis instrumentation.*

**PT Corlab Indonesia, Bldg. 303 Cilandak Commercial Estate, JL Cilandak KKO, Jakarta Selantan 12560, Indonesia**

## CORRPRO COMPANIES, INC.

1090 Enterprise Drive, Medina, OH, 44256

Tel: (330) 725-6681      Fax: (330) 723-0244      www.corrpro.com

*Full-services corrosion engineering, cathodic protection.*

**P. T. Wilson Walton Indonesia, Jl. Haji Agus Salim No. 128, Menteng, Jakarta 10310 Indonesia**

Tel: 62-21-392-8989   Fax: 62-21-392-8990   Contact: Wawan Junaedi

## COUDERT BROTHERS

1114 Ave. of the Americas, New York, NY, 10036-7794

Tel: (212) 626-4400      Fax: (212) 626-4120      www.coudert.com

*International law firm.*

**Coudert Brothers Indonesian Practice, CB Indonesia 16th Fl. Central Plaza, Jl. Jend. Sudirman Kav. 47, Jakarta 12930, Indonesia**

Tel: 62-21-525-1985   Fax: 62-21-525-0734   Contact: Michael S. Horn, Ptnr.

## CROWLEY MARITIME CORPORATION

155 Grand Ave., Oakland, CA, 94612

Tel: (510) 251-7500     Fax: (510) 251-7788     www.crowley.com

*Engaged in marine transportation and logistics.*

**PT Patra Drilling Contractor, Jl. Banka Raya 59, PO Box 12730, Jakarta Selatan, Indonesia**

## CROWN CORK & SEAL COMPANY, INC.

One Crown Way, Philadelphia, PA, 19154-4599

Tel: (215) 698-5100     Fax: (215) 698-5201     www.crowncork.com

*Mfr. metal and plastic packaging, including steel and aluminum cans for food, beverage and household products.*

**PT Crown Cork & Seal Indonesia, PO Box 3420/JKT, Jakarta, Indonesia**

## DAMES & MOORE GROUP

911 Wilshire Boulevard, Ste. 700, Los Angeles, CA, 90017

Tel: (213) 996-2200     Fax: (213) 996-2290     www.dames.com

*Engineering, environmental and construction management services.*

**PT Environment Nusa Geotechnica, Jl. Tebet Barat IV #33, Jakarta 12810, Indonesia**

## DANA CORPORATION

4500 Dorr Street, Toledo, OH, 43615

Tel: (419) 535-4500     Fax: (419) 535-4643     www.dana.com

*Mfr./sales of automotive, heavy truck, off-highway, fluid and mechanical power components and engine parts, filters and gaskets.*

**P.T International Ganda Perdana, Jl. Pegangsaan Dua, Blok A1 Km. 1-6, Pulogadung Jakarta, Indonesia**

Tel: 62-21-460-2755     Fax: 62-21-460-2765

## D'ARCY MASIUS BENTON & BOWLES INC. (DMB&B)

1675 Broadway, New York, NY, 10019

Tel: (212) 468-3622     Fax: (212) 468-2987     www.dmbb.com

*Full service international advertising and communications group.*

**DMB&B Asia Pacific, Jl. Buncit Raya Penaten 28, Pasar Minggu, Jakarta 12510, Indonesia**

## DELOITTE TOUCHE TOHMATSU INTERNATIONAL

1633 Broadway, New York, NY, 10019

Tel: (212) 492-4000     Fax: (212) 392-4154     www.deloitte.com

*Accounting, audit, tax and management consulting services.*

**Hans Tuanakotta & Mustofa, Wisma Antara Bldg. 12th Fl., Jl. Medan Merdeka Selatan No. 17, Jakarta 10110, Indonesia**

## DETROIT DIESEL CORPORATION

13400 Outer Drive West, Detroit, MI, 48239

Tel: (313) 592-5000     Fax: (313) 592-5058     www.detroitdiesel.com

*Mfr. diesel and aircraft engines, heavy-duty transmissions.*

**PT Mabua Detroit Diesel, Bldg #109 Cilandak Comm EST, Jakarta 12560, Indonesia**

## DHL WORLDWIDE EXPRESS

50 California Avenue, San Francisco, CA, 94111

Tel: (415) 677-6100     Fax: (415) 824-9700     www.dhl.com

*Worldwide air express carrier.*

**DHL Worldwide Express, Jakarta, Indonesia**

Tel: 62-21-830-6677

## DIMON INCORPORATED

512 Bridge Street, PO Box 681, Danville, VA, 24543-0681

Tel: (804) 792-7511     Fax: (804) 791-0377     www.dimon.com

*One of world's largest importer and exporters of leaf tobacco.*

**DIMON Indonesia, Ruko Surya Inti Permata II, JL H.R. Muhammad Blok B-12B, Surabaya, Indonesia**

Tel: 62-31-734-3485    Fax: 62-31-734-3486

## DIONEX CORPORATION

1228 Titan Way, PO Box 3603, Sunnyvale, CA, 94086-3603

Tel: (408) 737-0700     Fax: (408) 730-9403     www.dionex.com

*Develop/mfr./market chromatography systems and related products.*

**Omega Indonesia, The Garden Center #04-0, Cilandak Commercial Estate, Cilandak Jakarta 12560, Indonesia**

## DMC STRATEX NETWORKS, INC.

170 Rose Orchard Way, San Jose, CA, 95134

Tel: (408) 943-0777     Fax: (408) 944-1648     www.dmcstratexnetworks.com

*Designs, manufactures, and markets advanced wireless solutions for wireless broadband access.*

**DMC Stratex Networks, Masindo, Perkantoran Hijau Arkadia, Block A - 5/F, J1. Letjen T.B. Simatupang No. 88, Jakarta 12520, Indonesia**

## DONALDSON COMPANY, INC.

1400 West 94th Street, Minneapolis, MN, 55431

Tel: (612) 887-3131     Fax: (612) 887-3155     www.donaldson.com

*Mfr. filtration systems and replacement parts.*

**PT Panata Jaya Mandiri, Jl Pluit Selatan No. 1A, Jakarta 14440, Indonesia**

## DOVER CORPORATION

280 Park Ave., New York, NY, 10017-1292

Tel: (212) 922-1640     Fax: (212) 922-1656     www.dovercorporation.com

*Holding company for varied industries; assembly and testing equipment, oil-well gear and other industrial products.*

**Pt. Karya Intertek Kencana, Jl. Daan Mogot 35 D-E, Jakarta 11470, Indonesia**

Tel: 62-21-566-5115    Fax: 62-21-568-2084

## THE DOW CHEMICAL COMPANY

2030 Dow Center, Midland, MI, 48674

Tel: (517) 636-1000     Fax: (517) 636-3228     www.dow.com

*Mfr. chemicals, plastics, pharmaceuticals, agricultural products, consumer products.*

**Pacific Chemicals Indonesia PT, Jl. M.H. Thamrin 59, Jakarta, Indonesia**

## DUFF & PHELPS CREDIT RATING CO.

55 East Monroe Street, Chicago, IL, 60603

Tel: (312) 368-3100     Fax: (312) 442-4121     www.dcrco.com

*Engaged in rating stocks and bonds, municipal securities and insurance company claims paying capabilities.*

**P.T. Kasnic Fuf & Phelps Credit Rating Indonesia, Menara Rawajali -11/F, Kawasan Mega Kuningan, Jl. Mega Kuningan Lot #5.1, Jakarta Indonesia 12950**

Tel: 62-21-576-1431    Fax: 62-21-576-1432

## EAGLE GLOBAL LOGISTICS (EGL)

15350 Vickery Drive, Houston, TX, 77032

Tel: (281) 618-3100     Fax: (281) 618-3100       www.eaglegl.com

*Ocean/air freight forwarding, customs brokerage, packing and wholesale, logistics management and insurance.*

**Harper Freight International, PT Hartapersada Interfreight 4th Fl., Ayu Mas Bldg., Jl Kwitang aya 24, Jakarta 10150 Indonesia**

Tel: 62-21-390-3033    Fax: 62-21-390-3031

## EASTMAN CHEMICAL

100 North Eastman Road, Kingsport, TN, 37660

Tel: (423) 229-2000     Fax: (423) 229-1351       www.eastman.com

*Mfr. plastics, chemicals, fibers.*

**Eastman Chemical Ltd., 9th Fl.- S. Widjojo Centre, Jl. Jend. Sudirman 71, Jakarta 12190, Indonesia**

Tel: 62-21-522-3102    Fax: 62-21-522-3101    Contact: Chen Yeow Wai

## ECOLAB INC.

370 N. Wabasha Street, St. Paul, MN, 55102

Tel: (651) 293-2233     Fax: (651) 293-2379       www.ecolab.com

*Develop/mfr. premium cleaning, sanitizing and maintenance products and services for the hospitality, institutional, and residential markets.*

**Ecolab Ltd., Jakarta, Indonesia**

Tel: 62-21-570-7557

## EDISON INTERNATIONAL

2244 Walnut Grove Avenue, PO Box 999, Rosemead, CA, 91770

Tel: (626) 302-2222     Fax: (626) 302-2517       www.edison.com

*Utility holding company.*

**Edison Mission Energy, Jakarta, Indonesia**

## J.D. EDWARDS & COMPANY

One Technology Way, Denver, CO, 80237

Tel: (303) 334-4000     Fax: (303) 334-4970       www.jdedwards.com

*Computer software products.*

**PT Infotech Global Distribusi, Mashill Tower 14th Floor, Jl. Jend Sundirman Kav. 125, Jakarta 12920, Indonesia**

Tel: 62-21-522-9828    Fax: 62-21-522-5538

## EL PASO ENERGY CORPORATION

PO Box 2511, 1001 Louisiana, Houston, TX, 77252-2511

Tel: (713) 420-2131     Fax: (713) 420-4266       www.epenergy.com

*Energy and gas.*

**El Paso Energy International, Sulawesi, Indonesia**

## ELECTRONIC DATA SYSTEMS CORPORATION (EDS)

5400 Legacy Dr., Plano, TX, 75024

Tel: (972) 605-6000     Fax: (972) 605-2643       www.eds.com

*Provides professional services; management consulting, e.solutions, business process management and information solutions.*

**PT Electronic Data Systems Indonesia, Stock Exchange Bldg. - Tower 2 Level 14, Jl. Jenderal Sudirman Kav. 52-53, Jakarta 12190 Indonesia**

## EMERSON ELECTRIC COMPANY

8000 W. Florissant Ave., PO Box 4100, St. Louis, MO, 63136

Tel: (314) 553-2000    Fax: (314) 553-3527    www.emersonelectric.com

*Electrical and electronic products, industrial components and systems, consumer, government and defense products.*

**Emerson Electric Pte. Ltd., Wisma Danamon Aetna Life - 19/F, Jl. Jend. Sudirman Kav. 45-46, Jakarta 12930 Indonesia**

## ENRON CORPORATION

1400 Smith Street, Houston, TX, 77002-7369

Tel: (713) 853-6161    Fax: (713) 853-3129    www.enron.com

*Exploration, production, transportation and distribution of integrated natural gas and electricity.*

**Enron International, 19/FJakarta Stock Exch. Bldg., Jl.Jend Sudirman KAV. 52-63, Jakarta 12910, Indonesia**

Tel: 62-21-515-0744

## ERICO PRODUCTS INC.

34600 Solon Road, Cleveland, OH, 44139

Tel: (440) 248-0100    Fax: (440) 248-0723    www.erico.com

*Mfr. electric welding apparatus and hardware, metal stampings, specialty fasteners.*

**Erico Products Inc., Danamon Aetna Life - 19/F, Jalan Jend Sudirman -Kav. 45-46, Jakarta 12930 Indonesia**

Tel: 62-21-575-0941

## ERNST & YOUNG, LLP

787 Seventh Ave., New York, NY, 10019

Tel: (212) 773-3000    Fax: (212) 773-6350    www.eyi.com

*Accounting and audit, tax and management consulting services.*

**Kantor Akuntan/Drs, Santoso Harsokusumo & Rekan, PO Box 2333, Jakarta 10001, Indonesia**

Tel: 62-21-522-0358   Fax: 62-21-520-1136   Contact: Jaja Zakaria

## EURO RSCG WORLDWIDE

350 Hudson Street, New York, NY, 10014

Tel: (212) 886-2000    Fax: (212) 886-2016    www.eurorscg.com

*International advertising agency group.*

**AdWork! EURO RSCG Partnership, Jl. Guntur 48, Jakarta, Indonesia**

## EXE TECHNOLOGIES, INC.

8787 N. Stemmonds Fwy., Dallas, TX, 75247-3702

Tel: (214) 775-6000    Fax: (214) 775-0911    www.exe.com

*Provides a complete line of supply chain management execution software for WMS.*

**EXE Technologies, Inc. Indonesia, c/o PT. Belmanda Lestari, Wijaya Grand Centre Blok C-17-18, Jakarta 12160, Indonesia**

Tel: 62-21-724-6212   Fax: 62-21-720-6625

## EXPEDITORS INTERNATIONAL OF WASHINGTON INC.

1015 Third Avenue, 12th Fl., Seattle, WA, 98104-1182

Tel: (206) 674-3400    Fax: (206) 682-9777    www.expd.com

*Air/ocean freight forwarding, customs brokerage, international logistics solutions.*

**Expeditors Cargo Management Systems, c/o Pt. Segara Pacific, Maju Jl. Muara Karang Raya 163-165, Jakarta Utara 14450, Indonesia**

Tel: 62-21-660-3301   Fax: 62-21-661-0474

**Expeditors/PT Lancar Utama Tatanusa, Jl. Let. Jend. Soeprato 86A-B, Jakarta 10540, Indonesia**

Tel: 62-21-421-2328   Fax: 62-21-421-4431

## EXXON MOBIL CORPORATION

5959 Las Colinas Blvd., Irving, TX, 75039-2298

Tel: (972) 444-1000      Fax: (972) 444-1882      www.exxon.com

*Petroleum exploration, production, refining; mfr. petroleum and chemicals products; coal and minerals.*

**Exxon Mobil, Inc., Jl. H.R. Rasuna Said, Sampoerna Plaza, Jakarta, Indonesia**

## FERRO CORPORATION

1000 Lakeside Ave., Cleveland, OH, 44114-7000

Tel: (216) 641-8580      Fax: (216) 696-5784      www.ferro.com

*Mfr. Specialty chemicals, coatings, plastics, colors, refractories.*

**P.T. Chandra Silamas Company, Jl. Intan No. 70, Cilandak Barat, Cilandak Jakarta, Selatan 12430 Indonesia**

Tel: 62-21-750-8426   Fax: 62-21-750-3524   Contact: W.M.W. Silalahi

**P.T. Ferro Mas Dinamika, Jl. Raya Cikarang, Ds. Pasir Sari Kp. Tegal Gede, Kec. Lemah Abang, Cibarusah - Bekasi Indonesia**

Tel: 62-82-136920   Fax: 62-82-136580   Contact: Victor B. Buenconsejo, Mng. Dir.

## FISHER-ROSEMOUNT

8000 Maryland Ave., Ste. 500, Clayton, MO, 63105-4755

Tel: (314) 746-9900      Fax: (314) 746-9974      www.frco.com

*Mfr. industrial process control equipment.*

**P.T. Control Systems, Jl. Ampera Raya No. 10 - 3rd Fl., Cilandak, Jakarta Selatan 12560, Indonesia**

Tel: 62-21-780-7881   Fax: 62-21-780-7879

## FLEETBOSTON FINANCIAL CORPORATION

1 Federal Street, Boston, MA, 02110

Tel: (617) 346-4000      Fax: (617) 434-7547      www.fleet.com

*Banking and insurance services.*

**FleetBoston - Jakarta, S. Widjojo Centre 10th Fl., Jl. Jend, Sudirman 71, Jakarta 12190 Indonesia**

Tel: 62-21-252-4111   Fax: 62-21-252-4113

## FLUOR CORPORATION

One Enterprise Drive, Aliso Viejo, CA, 92656-2606

Tel: (949) 349-2000      Fax: (949) 349-5271      www.flour.com

*Engineering and construction services.*

**Fluor Daniel Eastern Inc., Plaza 89 Suite 1101, PO Box 4569, Jakarta 12045, Indonesia**

Tel: 62-21-520-5663   Fax: 62-21-522-2745

## FMC CORPORATION

200 E. Randolph Drive, Chicago, IL, 60601

Tel: (312) 861-6000      Fax: (312) 861-6141      www.fmc.com

*Produces chemicals and precious metals, mfr. machinery, equipment and systems for industrial, agricultural and government use.*

**FMC Smith Meter Inc., Gedung Samudru Indonesia 5/F, Letjen S. Parman KAV 5, Jakarta 11480 Indonesia**

## FOSTER WHEELER CORPORATION

Perryville Corporate Park, Clinton, NJ, 08809-4000

Tel: (908) 730-4000      Fax: (908) 730-4100      www.fwc.com

*Manufacturing, engineering and construction.*

**Foster Wheeler Intercontinental Corporation, Graha Simatupang Menara, Jl. Simatupang Kav. 38, Jakarta 12540 Indonesia**

Tel: 62-21-782-9416

## FRANKLIN COVEY COMPANY

2200 W. Parkway Blvd., Salt Lake City, UT, 84119-2331

Tel: (801) 975-1776    Fax: (801) 977-1431    www.franklincovey.com

*Provides productivity and time management products and seminars.*

**Franklin Covey Indonesia,  Jl. Bendungan Jatiluhur 56, Bendungan Hilir, Jakarta 10210, Indonesia**

Tel: 62-21-572-0761  Fax: 62-21-572-0762

## FREEPORT-McMoRAN COPPER & GOLD INC.

1615 Poydras Street, New Orleans, LA, 70112

Tel: (504) 582-4000    Fax: (504) 582-4899    www.fcx.com

*Natural resources exploration and processing.*

**P.T. Smelting (Gresik),  Plaza 89 - 6/F S-602, Jl. H. R. Rasuna Said Kav. X-7 No. 6, Jakarta 12940 Indonesia**

Tel: 62-21-522-9616  Fax: 62-21-522-9615

**PT Freeport Indonesia Co.,  Plaza 89 - 5/F, Jl. H.R. Rasuna Said Kav. X-7 No. 6, Jakarta 12940, Indonesia**

Tel: 62-21-522-5666  Fax: 62-21-526-1874

**PT-FI IRIAN JAYA (Papua),  Tembagapura - Timika, Kuala Kencana, Indonesia**

## FRITZ COMPANIES, INC.

706 Mission Street, Ste. 900, San Francisco, CA, 94103

Tel: (415) 904-8360    Fax: (415) 904-8661    www.fritz.com

*Integrated transportation, sourcing, distribution and customs brokerage services.*

**PT Fritz Ritra Intl. Transportation,  Ritra Bldg. 3/F, J. Warung Buncit Raya 6, Jakarta 12740, Indonesia**

## H.B. FULLER COMPANY

1200 Willow Lake Blvd., Vadnais Heights, MN, 55110

Tel: (651) 236-5900    Fax: (651) 236-5898    www.hbfuller.com

*Mfr./distributor adhesives, sealants, coatings, paints, waxes, sanitation chemicals.*

**H.B. Fuller Company,  Wisma Bisnis Indonesia 10th Floor, Jl. Let. Jend. S. Parman Kav. 12, Jakarta 11480, Indonesia**

Tel: 62-21-530-7232  Fax: 62-21-530-7235

## GENERAL ELECTRIC COMPANY

3135 Easton Turnpike, Fairfield, CT, 06431

Tel: (203) 373-2211    Fax: (203) 373-3131    www.ge.com

*Diversified manufacturing, technology and services.*

**GE FANUC Automation,  c/o PT GE Lighting Indonesia Jln., Rungkut Industri IV/2, Surabaya 60289, Indonesia**

Tel: 62-31-849-5465  Fax: 62-31-849-5462

**GE International,  Menara Batavia 5th Fl., Jl. KH Mas Mansyur Kav. 126, Jakarta 10220, Indonesia**

Tel: 62-21-574-7123

**GEPS Global Power Generation,  Menara Batagvia 5th Fl., Jl. KH Mas Mansyur Kav. 126, Jakarta 10220, Indonesia**

Tel: 62-21-574-7123

## THE GILLETTE COMPANY

Prudential Tower Building, Boston, MA, 02199

Tel: (617) 421-7000    Fax: (617) 421-7123    www.gillette.com

*Develop/mfr. personal care/use products: blades and razors, toiletries, cosmetics, stationery.*

**PT Gillette Indonesia,  Jakarta, Indonesia**

## GILSON INC.

3000 W. Beltline Hwy, PO Box 620027, Middleton, WI, 53562-0027

Tel: (608) 836-1551      Fax: (608) 831-4451      www.gilson.com

*Mfr. analytical/biomedical instruments.*

**PT Siberhegindo Teknik,  Gedung Gajah  - Unit AJ, Jl. Dr. Saharjo Raya No. 11 Tebet, Jakarta 12810 Indonesia**

## GLOBAL MARINE INC.

777 North Eldridge, Houston, TX, 77079

Tel: (281) 496-8000      Fax: (281) 531-1260      www.glm.com

*Offshore contract drilling, turnkey drilling, oil and gas exploration and production.*

**Global Marine Inc.,  Jakarta, Indonesia**

## GLOBAL SILVERHAWK

2190 Meridian Park Blvd., Ste G, Concord, CA, 94520

Tel: (925) 681-2889      Fax: (925) 681-2755      www.globalsilverhawk.com

*International moving and forwarding.*

**Global Silverhawk,  Mampang Plaza First Fl., Jl. Mampang Prapatan Raya No.100, Jakarta 12760, Indonesia**

Tel: 62-21-800-4966    Contact: Jeff Offutt, Gen. Mgr.

## THE GOODYEAR TIRE & RUBBER COMPANY

1144 East Market Street, Akron, OH, 44316

Tel: (330) 796-2121      Fax: (330) 796-1817      www.goodyear.com

*Mfr. tires, automotive belts and hose, conveyor belts, chemicals; oil pipeline transmission.*

**PT Goodyear Indonesia,  PO Box 5, Jl. Pemuda 27, Bogor West Java 16161, Indonesia**

## W. R. GRACE & COMPANY

7500 Grace Drive, Columbia, MD, 21044

Tel: (410) 531-4000      Fax: (410) 531-4367      www.grace.com

*Mfr. specialty chemicals and materials: packaging, health care, catalysts, construction, water treatment/process.*

**P.T. Grace Specialty Chemicals Indonesia,  Cikarang Industrial Estate, Kav C-32, Cikarang Bekasi 17530, Indonesia**

Tel: 62-21-893-4260    Fax: 62-21-893-4315

## GRAHAM & JAMES LLP

One Maritime Plaza,  Ste. 300, San Francisco, CA, 94111-3404

Tel: (415) 954-0200      Fax: (415) 391-2493      www.gj.com

*International law firm.*

**Hannafiah Soeharto Ponggawa,  Jakarta, Indonesia**

**PT DGJ Consultants Indonesia,  Plaza Exim 24th Fl., Jl. Gatot Soebroto Kav. 36-38, Jakarta 12190 Indonesia**

Tel: 62-21-526-3475    Fax: 62-21-522-3476    Contact: John Biddle

## GREY GLOBAL GROUP

777 Third Ave., New York, NY, 10017

Tel: (212) 546-2000      Fax: (212) 546-1495      www.grey.com

*International advertising agency.*

**Rama & Grey Advertising,  J. Sultan Hasanuddin 72, Jakarta 12160, Indonesia**

## GTE DIRECTORIES CORPORATION

2200 West Airfield Drive, DFW Airport, TX, 75261-9810

Tel: (972) 453-7000      Fax: (972) 453-7573      www.gte.com

*Publishing telephone directories.*

**PT Elnusa Yellow Pages,  77-81 Jl. R.S. Fatmawati, Jakarta 12150, Indonesia**

### HARRIS CORPORATION
1025 West NASA Blvd., Melbourne, FL, 32919

Tel: (407) 727-9100    Fax: (407) 727-9344    www.harris.com

*Mfr. communications and information-handling equipment, including copying and fax systems.*

**P. T. Silicontama Jaya, Jl. A.M. Sangaji No. 15 B4, Jakarta Pusat, Indonesia**

Tel: 62-21-345-4050   Fax: 62-21-345-4427

### H.J. HEINZ COMPANY
600 Grant Street, Pittsburgh, PA, 15219

Tel: (412) 456-5700    Fax: (412) 456-6128    www.heinz.com

*Processed food products and nutritional services.*

**Heinz ABC Indonesia, Jakarta, Indonesia**

Contact: Kogan Mandala, Pres.

### HERCULES INC.
Hercules Plaza, 1313 N. Market Street, Wilmington, DE, 19894-0001

Tel: (302) 594-5000    Fax: (302) 594-5400    www.herc.com

*Mfr. specialty chemicals, plastics, film and fibers, coatings, resins, food ingredients.*

**Hercules Chemicals, Pandan, Indonesia**

### HEWITT ASSOCIATES LLC
100 Half Day Road, Lincolnshire, IL, 60069

Tel: (847) 295-5000    Fax: (847) 295-7634    www.hewitt.com

*Employee benefits consulting firm.*

**PT Hewitt Konsultan Indonesia, Suite 34-09 Level 34 Wisma BNI 46, Jl. Jend. Sudirman Kav. 1, Jakarta, Indonesia**

### HILTON HOTELS CORPORATION
9336 Civic Center Drive, Beverly Hills, CA, 90210

Tel: (310) 278-4321    Fax: (310) 205-7880    www.hiltonhotels.com

*International hotel chain: Hilton International, Vista Hotels and Hilton National Hotels.*

**Hilton International Company, PO Box 3315, Jl Jend Gatot Subroto, Senayan, Jakarta 10002, Indonesia**

### HONEYWELL INTERNATIONAL INC.
101 Columbia Road, Morristown, NJ, 07962

Tel: (973) 455-2000    Fax: (973) 455-4807    www.honeywell.com

*Develop/mfr. controls for home and building, industry, space and aviation.*

**PT Honeywell Indonesia, Wisma Budi 4th Fl.-Ste. 405, J.I.H.R. Rasuna Said Kav. C-6, Jakarta 12940, Indonesia**

Tel: 62-21-521-3330   Fax: 62-21-521-3735

### HORWATH INTERNATIONAL ASSOCIATION
415 Madison Ave., New York, NY, 10017

Tel: (212) 838-5566    Fax: (212) 838-3636    www.horwath.com

*Public accountants and auditors.*

**Drs. Pamintori & Rekan, Wisma Sejahtera #1C, #1E Jl.Let. Jend.S.Parman Kav.75, Jakarta Barat 11410, Indonesia**

### HOWMEDICA OSTEONICS, INC.
359 Veterans Blvd., Rutherford, NJ, 07070

Tel: (201) 507-7300    Fax: (201) 935-4873    www.howmedica.com

*Mfr. of maxillofacial products (orthopedic implants).*

**Howmedica Indionesia - Atra Widiya Agung, Jakarta, Indonesia**

Tel: 62-21-750-7707

## HQ GLOBAL WORKPLACES INC.

1155 Connecticut Ave. NW, Washington, DC, 20036

Tel: (202) 467-8500　　　Fax: (202) 467-8595　　　www.hq.com

*Provides office outsourcing, officing solutions, including internet access, telecommunications, meeting rooms, furnished offices and team rooms, state-of-the-art videoconferencing, and trained on-site administrative support teams -*

**HQ Global Workplaces, Ariobimo Central 4/F, Blok X-2 No. 5, Jakarta 12950, Indonesia**

Tel: 62-21-252-5725

## HUGHES ELECTRONICS CORPORATION

200 N. Sepulveda Blvd., PO Box 956, El Segundo, CA, 90245-0956

Tel: (310) 662-9821　　　Fax: (310) 647-6213　　　www.hughes.com

*Provides digital television entertainment, satellite services, and satellite-based private business networks.*

**Hughes Space, Mid Plaza II Building 22nd Floor, Jl. Jend. Sudirman Kav 10-11, Jakarta Pusat 10220, Indonesia**

Tel: 62-21-573-4161　　Fax: 62-21-573-4162

## HYATT CORPORATION

200 West Madison Street, Chicago, IL, 60606

Tel: (312) 750-1234　　　Fax: (312) 750-8578　　　www.hyatt.com

*International hotel management.*

**Grand Hyatt Bali Resort, PO Box 53, Nusa Dua, Bali, Indonesia**

Tel: 62-361-77-1234　　Fax: 62-361-772038

**Grand Hyatt Jakarta Hotel, Jl. M.H. Thamrin, Jakarta 10230, Indonesia**

Tel: 62-21-290-1234　　Fax: 62-21-334-321

**Hyatt Regency Yogyakarta, Jl. Palagan Tentara Pelajar, Yogyakarta 55581, Indonesia**

Tel: 62-274-869-123　　Fax: 62-274-869-588

## IBM CORPORATION

New Orchard Road, Armonk, NY, 10504

Tel: (914) 765-1900　　　Fax: (914) 765-7382　　　www.ibm.com

*Information products, technology and services.*

**IBM Indonesia PT, 5 Jim H. Thamrin, Jakarta, Indonesia**

**IBM World Trade Corp., Landmark Center One 31th Floor, Jl. Jend. Sudiman No.1, Jakarta 12910, Indonesia**

Tel: 62-21-251-2922　　Fax: 62-21-251-2933

## IMG (INTERNATIONAL MANAGEMENT GROUP)

1360 East Ninth Street, Ste. 100, Cleveland, OH, 44114

Tel: (216) 522-1200　　　Fax: (216) 522-1145　　　www.imgworld.com

*Manages athletes, sports academies and real estate facilities worldwide.*

**IMG Senayan Golf Club, Plaza Lippo 10/F, Jalen Jend. Sudtman Kav. 25, Jakarta 12920, Indonesia**

Tel: 62-21-526-8038　　Fax: 62-21-526-80339

## INFONET SERVICES CORPORATION

2100 East Grand Ave., El Segundo, CA, 90245-1022

Tel: (310) 335-2600　　　Fax: (310) 335-4507　　　www.infonet.com

*Provider of Internet services and electronic messaging services.*

**Infonet Indonesia, WITEL IV- GRHA CITRA CARAKA Lantai III, Jl. Gatot Subroto No. 52, Jakarta 12710 Indonesia**

Tel: 62-21-521-2996　　Fax: 62-21-522-2296

## INTER-CONTINENTAL HOTELS

3 Ravina Drive, Suite 2900, Atlanta, GA, 30346-2149

Tel: (770) 604-2000 Fax: (770) 604-5403 www.interconti.com

*Worldwide hotel and resort accommodations.*

**Borobudur Inter-Continental Jakarta, Jl. Lapangan Banteng Selatan, PO Box 1329, Jakarta, Indonesia**

Tel: 62-21-380-5555 Fax: 62-21-380-9595

## INTERGRAPH CORPORATION

One Madison Industrial Park, Huntsville, AL, 35894-0001

Tel: (256) 730-2000 Fax: (256) 730-7898 www.intergraph.com

*Develop/mfr. interactive computer graphic systems.*

**PT Indograf Teknotama, Menara Mulia 24th Fl. Ste. 2407, Jl. Jenderal Gatot Subroto Kavs 9-11, Jakarta 12930, Indonesia**

Tel: 62-21-5257488 Fax: 62-21-5204064

## INTERNATIONAL FLAVORS & FRAGRANCES INC.

521 West 57th Street, New York, NY, 10019-2960

Tel: (212) 765-5500 Fax: (212) 708-7132 www.iff.com

*Design/mfr. flavors, fragrances and aroma chemicals.*

**Essence Indonesia PT, Jl. Oto Iskandardinata 74, PO Box 3008/DKT, Jakarta, Indonesia**

## INTERNATIONAL SPECIALTY PRODUCTS, INC.

1361 Alps Rd., Wayne, NJ, 07470

Tel: (877) 389-3083 Fax: (973) 628-4117 www.ispcorp.com

*Mfr. specialty chemical products.*

**ISP (Singapore) Pte. Ltd., Indonesia Representative Office, Wisma Bisnis Indonesia 8th Fl., Jl. Let. Jend. S. Parman Kav 12, Jakarta 11480 Indonesia**

Tel: 62-21-530-7181 Fax: 62-21-530-7183

## J. WALTER THOMPSON COMPANY

466 Lexington Ave., New York, NY, 10017

Tel: (212) 210-7000 Fax: (212) 210-6944 www.jwt.com

*International advertising and marketing services.*

**AdForce/JWT, Jakarta, Indonesia**

## JOHN HANCOCK FINANCIAL SERVICES, INC.

John Hancock Place, Boston, MA, 02117

Tel: (617) 572-6000 Fax: (617) 572-9799 www.johnhancock.com

*Life insurance services.*

**P.T. Asuransi Jiwa Bumiputera John Hancock, Jakarta, Indonesia**

## JOHNSON & JOHNSON

One Johnson & Johnson Plaza, New Brunswick, NJ, 08933

Tel: (732) 524-0400 Fax: (732) 214-0334 www.jnj.com

*Mfr./distributor/R&D pharmaceutical, health care and cosmetic products.*

**Janssen-Cilag Pharmaceutica, Jakarta, Indonesia**

**PT Johnson & Johnson Indonesia, PO Box 3200, Jakarta, Indonesia**

## S C JOHNSON & SON INC.

1525 Howe St., Racine, WI, 53403

Tel: (414) 260-2000 Fax: (414) 260-2133 www.scjohnsonwax.com

*Home, auto, commercial and personal care products and specialty chemicals.*

**PT S.C. Johnson & Son Indonesia Ltd., PO Box 1345/JAT, Jakarta Timur, Indonesia**

## THE JOHNSON CORPORATION

805 Wood Street, Three Rivers, MI, 49093

Tel: (616) 278-1715        Fax: (616) 273-2230        www.joco.com

*Mfr. rotary joints and siphon systems.*

**Johnson Corporation Asia Pacific Pty. Ltd., Tangerang, West Java, Indonesia**

**Johnson Corporation Asia Pacific Pty. Ltd., Surabaya, East Java, Indonesia**

Tel: 62-31-7407950

## JOHNSON OUTDOORS, INC.

1326 Willow Road, Sturtevant, WI, 53177

Tel: (414) 884-1500        Fax: (414) 884-1600        www.jwa.com

*Mfr. diving, fishing, boating and camping sports equipment.*

**P.T. Uwatec Batam, Lot 258 Jl Kenanga, BIP, Muka Kuning, Batam 29433, Indonesia**

Tel: 62-778-611694   Fax: 62-778-611693

## JONES LANG LASALLE

101 East 52nd Street, New York, NY, 10022

Tel: (212) 688-8181        Fax: (212) 308-5199        www.jlw.com

*International marketing consultants, leasing agents and property management advisors.*

**Jones Lang Wootton, Indonesia**

## JUKI UNION SPECIAL CORPORATION

5 Haul Road, Wayne, NJ, 07470

Tel: (973) 633-7200        Fax: (973) 633-9629        www.unionspecial.com

*Mfr. sewing machines.*

**JUKI Singapore Ptd., Wisma Abadi 2nd Fl., C-3 Jl Kyaj Caringin No. 29-31, Jakarta 10160, Indonesia**

Tel: 62-21-384-8768   Fax: 62-21-386-5449

## A.T. KEARNEY INC.

222 West Adams Street, Chicago, IL, 60606

Tel: (312) 648-0111        Fax: (312) 223-6200        www.atkearney.com

*Management consultants and executive search.*

**A. T. Kearney, Sudirman Central Business District 18/F, Jl. Jend. Sudirman Kav. 52-53, Jakarta 12190 Indonesia**

Tel: 62-21-523-9130   Fax: 62-21-523-9193

## KELLOGG BROWN & ROOT INC.

PO Box 3, Houston, TX, 77001

Tel: (713) 676-3011        Fax: (713) 676-8695        www.halliburton.com

*Engaged in technology-based engineering and construction.*

**Kellogg Brown & Root, Bldgs.106/107 Cilandak Commercial Estate, Jl. Cilandak KKO, Jakarta Selantan 12560, Indonesia**

Tel: 62-21-780-1100

**Kellogg Brown & Root, Ratu Plaza Office Tower 10/F, Jl Jend Budirman 9, Jakarta 10270 Indonesia**

## KENNAMETAL INC.

State Rte. 981, Latrobe, PA, 15650

Tel: (724) 539-5000        Fax: (724) 539-4710        www.kennametal.com

*Tools, hard carbide and tungsten alloys for metalworking industry.*

**C.V. MultiTeknik, Gajkah Mada Tower 19th Fl. Ste. 1909, Jln. Gajah Mada 9-26, Jakarta 10130, Indonesia**

Tel: 62-21-6339151   Fax: 62-21-600-9150

**P.T. Germantara Toolindo Sistema, Jl. Permuda 44, Jakarta 13220, Indonesia**

Tel: 62-21489-3952   Fax: 62-21-471-3628

## KIMBERLY-CLARK CORPORATION

351 Phelps Drive, Irving, TX, 75038

Tel: (972) 281-1200 Fax: (972) 281-1435 www.kimberly-clark.com

*Mfr./sales/distribution of consumer tissue, household and personal care products.*

**PT Kimsari Paper Indonesia, Medan, Indonesia**

## KOCH INDUSTRIES INC.

4111 East 37th Street North, Wichita, KS, 67220-3203

Tel: (316) 828-5500 Fax: (316) 828-5950 www.kochind.com

*Oil, financial services, agriculture and Purina Mills animal feed.*

**Koch Membrane Systems, Inc., Jakarta Barat, Indonesia**

Tel: 62-21-584-6202

## KPMG INTERNATIONAL LLP

345 Park Avenue, New York, NY, 10022

Tel: (201) 307-7000 Fax: (201) 930-8617 www.kpmg.com

*Accounting and audit, tax and management consulting services.*

**Hanadi Sudjendro & Rekan, Jl Palang Merah 40, PO Box 506, Medan 20111, Indonesia**

**Hanadi Sudjendro & Rekan, Jl Ir H Juanda 49, Bandung, Indonesia**

**Hanadi Sudjendro & Rekan, 301 A Batam Industrial Park, Muka Kuning, Batam, Indonesia**

**Hanadi Sudjendro & Rekan, Wisma BII 7th Fl., Jl Pemuda 60-70, Surabaya 60271, Indonesia**

**PT Sudjendro Soesanto Management Consultants, Wisma Dharmala Sakti, Jl. Jend. Sudirman 32, Jakarta 10220, Indonesia**

Tel: 62-21-570-6111 Fax: 62-21-573-3003 Contact: Kanaka Puradiredja, Ptnr.

## LANDOR ASSOCIATES

Klamath House, 1001 Front Street, San Francisco, CA, 94111-1424

Tel: (415) 955-1400 Fax: (415) 365-3190 www.landor.com

*International marketing consulting firm, focused on developing and maintaining brand identity.*

**Landor Associates, Menara Estro 3/F, Tanah Abang 3 No. 31, Jakarta 10160, Indonesia**

Tel: 62-21-3483-0458 Fax: 62-21-3483-0459 Contact: Daniel Surya

## LEHMAN BROTHERS HOLDINGS INC.

Three World Financial Center, New York, NY, 10285

Tel: (212) 526-7000 Fax: (212) 526-3738 www.lehman.com

*Financial services, securities and merchant banking services.*

**Lehman Brothers, Bapindo Plaza Tower 2 (19/F), Jl. Jend Sudirman, Kav 54-55, Jakarta 12190 Indonesia**

Tel: 62-21-521-0715

## ELI LILLY & COMPANY

Lilly Corporate Center, Indianapolis, IN, 46285

Tel: (317) 276-2000 Fax: (317) 277-6579 www.lilly.com

*Mfr. pharmaceuticals and animal health products.*

**P.T. Tempo Scan Pacific, Bina Mulia II 7th Fl., Jl. H.R. Said Kav 11, Rasuna Jakarta 12950, Indonesia**

Tel: 62-21-520-1919 Fax: 62-21-520-1194

## LINCOLN ELECTRIC HOLDINGS

22801 St. Clair Ave., Cleveland, OH, 44117-1199

Tel: (216) 481-8100     Fax: (216) 486-8385     www.lincolnelectric.com

*Mfr. arc welding and welding related products, oxy-fuel and thermal cutting equipment and integral AC motors.*

**PT Lincoln Austenite Indonesia,  Bekasi International Industrial Estate, Block C-10 No 12A, Lippo Cikarang Bekasis 17550, Indonesia**

Tel: 62-21-8990-7629   Fax: 62-21-8990-76309   Contact: Dyonisius Soeprihandono, Plant Mgr.

**The Lincoln Electric Company, Indonesia,  Persona Bahari Apt. Blok Jade No. 26-D, Jl. Mangga Dua Abdad, Mangga Dua Jakarta Pusat 10730, Indonesia**

Tel: 62-21-612-9358   Fax: 62-21-612-9358   Contact: Richard Lane, Mgr.

## LOCKHEED MARTIN CORPORATION

6801 Rockledge Drive, Bethesda, MD, 20817

Tel: (301) 897-6000     Fax: (301) 897-6652     www.imco.com

*Design/mfr./management systems in fields of space, defense, energy, electronics and technical services.*

**Aircraft Systems International,  Bandung, Indonesia**

Tel: 62-22-2500303   Fax: 62-22-613935

**Lockheed Martin Global, Inc.,  Wisma Danamon Aetna 14/F, Jl. Jend Sudirman Kav. 45-46, Jakarta 12930 Indonesia**

Tel: 62-21-738-7533   Fax: 62-21-738-8861

## LOWE LINTAS & PARTNERS WORLDWIDE

One Dag Hammarskjold Plaza, New York, NY, 10017

Tel: (212) 605-8000     Fax: (212) 605-4705     www.interpublic.com

*Full-service, integrated marketing communications company/advertising agency.*

**Ammirati Puris Lintas Indonesia,  Lintas House J1, Sultan Hasanuddin No. 47-49-51 4-6 Fls., Jakarta 12160 Indonesia**

Tel: 62-21-725-4849   Fax: 62-21-725-4850   Contact: Eleanor S. Modesto, Mng. Dir.

## THE LUBRIZOL CORPORATION

29400 Lakeland Blvd., Wickliffe, OH, 44092-2298

Tel: (440) 943-4200     Fax: (440) 943-5337     www.lubrizol.com

*Mfr. chemicals additives for lubricants and fuels.*

**Lubrizol Indonesia,  Jakarta, Indonesia**

## LUCENT TECHNOLOGIES, INC.

600 Mountain Ave., Murray Hill, NJ, 07974-0636

Tel: (908) 582-3000     Fax: (908) 582-2576     www.lucent.com

*Design/mfr. wide range of public and private networks, communication systems and software, data networking systems, business telephone systems and microelectronics components.*

**P.T. Lucent Technologies Network Systems,  Wisma Danamon Aetna Life, 7th Floor JL. Jend. Sudiriman Kav 45-60, Jakarta 12930,  Indonesia**

Tel: 62-21-577-1677   Fax: 62-21-577-1676   Contact: Jonnie Oden, PR Mgr.

**P.T. Lucent Technologies Network Systems,  MM2100 Industrial Town Block B-3, Cibitung Bekasi 17520, Indonesia**

Tel: 62-21-898-0840   Fax: 62-21-8978-0808   Contact: Jonnie Oden, PR Mgr.

## LYONDELL

3801 West Chester Pike, Newtown Square, PA, 19073-2387

Tel: (610) 359-2000     Fax: (610) 359-2722     www.arcochem.com

*Mfr. propylene oxide, a chemical used for flexible foam products, coatings/paints and solvents/inks.*

**P.T. ARCO Chemical,  J1 Raya Anyer KM. 121, Tanjung Leneng, Ciwandan, Cilegon 42447 Indonesia**

Tel: 62-254-601-122

P.T. ARCO Chemical Indonesia, Ste. 1106 11th Fl. Plaza 89, J1 H.R. Rasuna Said Kav X-7 No. 6, Jakarta 12940, Indonesia

Tel: 62-21-252-0824   Fax: 62-21-252-0791

## MARATHON OIL COMPANY

5555 San Felipe Road, Houston, TX, 77056

Tel: (713) 629-6600     Fax: (713) 296-2952      www.marathon.com

*Oil and gas exploration.*

**Marathon Petroleum Indonesia Ltd.,  Jl. H.R. Rasuna Said, Kav. B-10, Lippo Life Bldg., Jakarta, Indonesia**

## MARLEY COOLING TOWER COMPANY

7401 West 129th Street, Overland Park, KS, 66213

Tel: (913) 664-7400     Fax: (913) 664-7641      www.marleyct.com

*Cooling and heating towers and waste treatment systems.*

**P. T. Tasan Megah, Rep. Office,  Komplek Grogol Permai Blok A 20-21, Jl. Prof. Dr. Latumeten, Jakarta Barat 11460, Indonesia**

## MARSH & McLENNAN COS INC.

1166 Ave. of the Americas, New York, NY, 10036-2774

Tel: (212) 345-5000     Fax: (212) 345-4808      www.marshmac.com

*Insurance agents/brokers, pension and investment management consulting services.*

**P.T. Peranas Agung,  Multika Bldg., JlN Mampang Prapatan Raya 71-73 Ste. 303, Jakarta 12790, Indonesia**

Tel: 62-21-797-5201   Fax: 62-21-797-5202   Contact: Adri G. Sinaulan

## MATTEL INC.

333 Continental Blvd., El Segundo, CA, 90245-5012

Tel: (310) 252-2000     Fax: (310) 252-2179      www.mattelmedia.com

*Mfr. toys, dolls, games, crafts and hobbies.*

**Mattel,  Jakarta, Indonesia**

## McCANN-ERICKSON WORLDGROUP

750 Third Ave., New York, NY, 10017

Tel: (212) 984-3644     Fax: (212) 984-2629      www.mccann.com

*International advertising and marketing services.*

**Grafik McCann-Erickson,  Jl. Riau 17, Jakarta, Indonesia**

## McDERMOTT INTERNATIONAL INC.

1450 Poydras Street, PO Box 60035, New Orleans, LA, 70160-0035

Tel: (504) 587-5400     Fax: (504) 587-6153      www.mcdermott.com

*Provides energy, engineering and construction services for industrial, utility, and hydrocarbon processing facilities, and to the offshore oil and natural gas industries.*

**P.T. Babcock & Wilcox,  Wisma Tugu II 4th Fl., PO Box 737/JKTM 12701, Jl. H.R. Rasuna said Kav. C 7-9, Kuningan, Jakarta 12940 Indonesia**

Tel: 62-21-520-8630   Fax: 62-21-520-8631   Contact: Nick Carter, Mgr.

## McDONALD'S CORPORATION

McDonald's Plaza, Oak Brook, IL, 60523

Tel: (630) 623-3000     Fax: (630) 623-7409      www.mcdonalds.com

*Fast food chain stores.*

**McDonald's Corp.,  Jakarta, Indonesia**

## THE McGRAW-HILL COMPANIES

1221 Ave. of the Americas, New York, NY, 10020

Tel: (212) 512-2000      Fax: (212) 512-2703      www.mccgraw-hill.com

*Books, magazines, information systems, financial service, publishing and broadcast operations.*

**McGraw-Hill Grand Boutique Centre, Block D 65JI Mangga Due Raya, Jakarta 11430, Indonesia**

## McKINSEY & COMPANY

55 East 52nd Street, New York, NY, 10022

Tel: (212) 446-7000      Fax: (212) 446-8575      www.mckinsey.com

*Management and business consulting services.*

**McKinsey & Company, MidPlaza 2 Bldg. Lt. 19, Jl. Jend. Sudirman Kav. 10-11, Jakarta 10220, Indonesia**

Tel: 62-21-573-5950   Fax: 62-21-573-5951

## THE MENTHOLATUM COMPANY, INC.

707 Sterling Drive, Orchard Park, NY, 14127-1587

Tel: (716) 677-2500      Fax: (716) 674-3696      www.mentholatum.com

*Mfr./distributor proprietary medicines, drugs, OTC's.*

**P.T. Rohto Laboratories Indonesia, JL. Tanah Abang 11/37, Jakarta 10160, Indonesia**

Tel: 62-21-350-897981   Fax: 62-21-386-1847

## MERRILL LYNCH & COMPANY, INC.

World Financial Center, 250 Vesey Street, New York, NY, 10281-1332

Tel: (212) 449-1000      Fax: (212) 449-2892      www.ml.com

*Security brokers and dealers, investment and business services.*

**P.T. Merrill Lynch Indonesia, 18th Fl. Jakarta Stock Exchange Bldg., Jl Jend. Sudirman Kav 52-53, Jakarta 12190, Indonesia**

Tel: 62-21-515-0888   Fax: 62-21-515-8819

## METROPOLITAN LIFE INSURANCE COMPANY

1 Madison Ave., New York, NY, 10010-3603

Tel: (212) 578-3818      Fax: (212) 252-7294      www.metlife.com

*Insurance and retirement savings products and services.*

**PT Metlife Sejahtera, Menara Mulia 3rd Floor, Jl. Jend. gatot Subroto Kav. 9, Jakarta Selatan 12930, Indonesia**

Tel: 62-21-527-7608   Fax: 62-21-527-7620   Contact: Leonard Logan, Pres. & Dir.

## M-I

PO Box 48242, Houston, TX, 77242-2842

Tel: (713) 739-0222      Fax: (713) 308-9503      www.midf.com

*Drilling fluids.*

**IMCO Services Indonesia PT, Setiabudi Bldg. 1, H.R. Rasuma Said 62, PO Box 3033, Jakarta Indonesia**

**PT M-I Indonesia, Jakarta, Indonesia**
**Annex Building, 2nd Floor**
**JL Ampera Raya Kav 9-10**
**Jakarta 12550, Indonesia**

Tel: 62-21-780-6578

## MICROSOFT CORPORATION

One Microsoft Way, Redmond, WA, 98052-6399

Tel: (425) 882-8080      Fax: (425) 936-7329      www.microsoft.com

*Computer software, peripherals and services.*

**Microsoft Indonesia P.T., 17th Floor Plaza Chase, Jl. Jend. Sudirman, Kav 21, Jakarta 12920, Indonesia**

Tel: 62-21-520-8111   Fax: 61-21-520-8122

## MILBANK, TWEED, HADLEY & McCLOY LLP

1 Chase Manhattan Plaza, New York, NY, 10005-1413

Tel: (212) 530-5000    Fax: (212) 530-5219    www.milbank.com

*International law practice.*

**Makarim & Taira S., 17th Fl., Summitmas Tower, Jl. Jend. Sudirman 61, Jakarta, Indonesia**

Tel: 62-21-252-1272   Fax: 62-21-252-2751

## J. P. MORGAN CHASE & CO. INC.

World Headquarters, 270 Park Ave., New York, NY, 10017

Tel: (212) 270-6000    Fax: (212) 622-9030    www.jpmorganchase.com

*Provides integrated financial solutions for institutions and individuals worldwide, including asset management, investment banking and commercial banking.*

**J. P. Morgan Chase & Co., 4/F Chase Plaza, Jl. Jend Sudirman Kav. 21, Jakarta 12920, Indonesia**

Tel: 62-21-571-0088   Fax: 62-21-570-3690

## MORGAN, LEWIS & BOCKIUS LLP

1701 Market St., Philadelphia, PA, 19103-6993

Tel: (215) 963-5000    Fax: (215) 963-5299    www.mlb.com

*International law firm.*

**P.T. Morgan, Lewis & Bockius Indonesia, Plaza Bapindo Tower II 21st Fl., Jl. Jend. Sudirman Kav 54-55, Jakarta 12190, Indonesia**

Tel: 62-21-526-7420   Fax: 62-21-526-7430   Contact: Mark A. Nelson, Mng. Ptnr.   Emp: 7

## MOTOROLA, INC.

1303 East Algonquin Road, Schaumburg, IL, 60196

Tel: (847) 576-5000    Fax: (847) 538-5191    www.motorola.com

*Mfr. communications equipment, semiconductors and cellular phones.*

**PT. Motorola Indonesia, BRI II. Ste. 3001, Jl. Jend. Sudirman Kav. 44-46, Jakarta 10210, Indonesia**

Tel: 62-21-251-3050   Fax: 62-21-571-3646

## NALCO CHEMICAL COMPANY

One Nalco Center, Naperville, IL, 60563-1198

Tel: (630) 305-1000    Fax: (630) 305-2900    www.nalco.com

*Chemicals for water and waste water treatment, oil products and refining, industry processes; water and energy management service.*

**PT Nalco Perkasa, c/o P.T. Astenia-Napan, Wisma Indocement, Jl. Jend Sudirman Kav. 70-71, Jakarta 12910 Indonesia**

Tel: 62-21-573-2188   Fax: 62-21-573-1870

## NATIONAL STARCH AND CHEMICAL COMPANY

10 Finderne Ave., Bridgewater, NJ, 08807-3300

Tel: (908) 685-5000    Fax: (908) 685-5005    www.nationalstarch.com

*Mfr. adhesives and sealants, resins and specialty chemicals, electronic materials and adhesives, food products, industry starch.*

**National Starch & Chemical, 26 Jl. Rembang Industri Raya, PIER Pasuruan, East Java 67152, Indonesia**

Tel: 62-34-374-4060   Fax: 62-34-374-4059

## NEW YORK LIFE INSURANCE COMPANY

51 Madison Ave., New York, NY, 10010

Tel: (212) 576-7000    Fax: (212) 576-4291    www.newyorklife.com

*Insurance services.*

**New York Life Insurance Co. Indonesia, Jakarta, Indonesia**

## NEWMONT MINING CORPORATION

1700 Lincoln Street, Denver, CO, 80203

Tel: (303) 863-7414        Fax: (303) 837-5837        www.newmont.corp

*Gold mining.*

**PT Newmont Minahasa Raya & Nusa Tenggara, Atria Square 14th Fl., Jl. Jend. Sudirman Kav. 33A, Jakarta 10220, Indonesia**

## NORTON ABRASIVES COMPANY

1 New Bond Street, Worcester, MA, 01606

Tel: (508) 795-5000        Fax: (508) 795-5741        www.nortonabrasives.com

*Mfr. abrasives for industrial manufacturing.*

**PT Norton Hamplas Industries, Surabaya, Indonesia**

## OCCIDENTAL PETROLEUM CORPORATION

10889 Wilshire Blvd., Los Angeles, CA, 90024

Tel: (310) 208-8800        Fax: (310) 443-6690        www.oxy.com

*Petroleum and petroleum products, chemicals, plastics.*

**Occidental of Indonesia Inc, Indonesia**

## OCEANEERING INTERNATIONAL INC.

11911 FM 529, Houston, TX, 77041

Tel: (713) 329-4500        Fax: (713) 329-4951        www.oceaneering.com

*Transportation equipment, underwater service to offshore oil and gas industry.*

**P.T. Calmarine, Imeco Building 10 - 1/F, Jl. Ampera Raya 9-10, Cilandak Jakarta 12550, Indonesia**

**P.T. Calmarine, Jalan Jendral Sudirman RT ll No. 237, Markoni, Balikpapan East Kalimantan, Indonesia**

**P.T. Calmarine, Miramar Utama Complex, Jalan M Taher Handil II, Muara Jawa, Samarinda Indonesia**

## OGILVY PUBLIC RELATIONS WORLDWIDE

909 Third Ave., New York, NY, 10022

Tel: (212) 880-5201        Fax: (212) 697-8250        www.ogilvypr.com

*Engaged in public relations and communications.*

**Ogilvy Public Relations Worldwide, Bapindo Plaza - Menara 1, Lantai 25 Jalan Jendral Sudirman Kav. 54-55, Jakarta 12190 Indonesia**

Tel: 62-21-526-6261    Contact: Ong Hock Chuan

## ORACLE CORPORATION

500 Oracle Parkway, Redwood Shores, CA, 94065

Tel: (650) 506-7000        Fax: (650) 506-7200        www.oracle.com

*Develop/manufacture software.*

**Oracle Indonesia, Jakarta, Indonesia**

## OSMONICS INC.

5951 Clearwater Drive, Minnetonka, MN, 55343-8995

Tel: (952) 933-2277        Fax: (952) 933-0141        www.osmonics.com

*Mfr. equipment, controls and components for the filtration and water-treatment industries.*

**Osmonics Indonesia, c/o PT Sembada Perdana Insan, Jl. Taman Tanah Abang 111 #19, Jakarta 10160, Indonesia**

## OTIS ELEVATOR COMPANY

10 Farm Springs Road, Farmington, CT, 06032

Tel: (860) 676-6000        Fax: (860) 676-5111        www.otis.com

*Mfr. elevators and escalators.*

**P.T. Citas Otis Elevator, Jl. Sultan Hasanuddin 56, Jakarta 12160, Indonesia**

### OWENS-ILLINOIS, INC.

One SeaGate, PO Box 1035, Toledo, OH, 43666

Tel: (419) 247-5000    Fax: (419) 247-2839    www.o-i.com

*Largest mfr. of glass containers in the US; plastic containers, compression-molded closures and dispensing systems.*

**PT Kangar Consolidated Industries, Jakarta, Indonesia**

### PACCAR INC.

777 106th Ave. NE, Bellevue, WA, 98004

Tel: (425) 468-7400    Fax: (425) 468-8216    www.pacar.com

*Heavy duty dump trucks, military vehicles.*

**PACCAR International, Jl. Zamrud VII, Block E-45, Permata Hijau Jakarta, Indonesia**

Tel: 62-21-535-5801   Fax: 62-21-535-5801

**PACCAR International/PT nited Tractors TBK, 2/F - Jl. Raya Bekasi Km. 22, Jakarta 3910 Indonesia**

Tel: 62-21-460-3932

### PACIFIC ARCHITECTS & ENGINEERS INC.

888 South Figueroa Street, 17th Fl., Los Angeles, CA, 90017

Tel: (213) 481-2311    Fax: (213) 481-7189    www.pae.com

*Technical engineering services.*

**P.T. Paranda Ekaysa, Papan Sejahtera Building 6th Fl., Jl. H.R. Rasuna Said Kav. C-1, Kuningan Jakarta, Indonesia**

Tel: 62-21-252-6188   Fax: 62-21-520-7724   Contact: Herman Sudjono, Pres. & Dir.

### PANDUIT CORPORATION

17301 Ridgeland Ave., Tinley Park, IL, 60477-0981

Tel: (708) 532-1800    Fax: (708) 532-1811    www.panduit.com

*Mfr. electrical/electronic wiring components.*

**Wisma Danamon Aetna Life, Jalan Jendral Ste. 29, Surdirman Kav. 45-46, Jakarta 12930, Indonesia**

### PARAMETRIC TECHNOLOGY CORPORATION

128 Technology Drive, Waltham, MA, 02154

Tel: (781) 398-5000    Fax: (781) 398-5674    www.ptc.com

*Supplier of mechanical design automation and product data management software and services.*

**Parametric Technology Indonesia, Wisma Danamon Aetna Life 19th Fl., JI. Jend. Sudirman Kav. 45-46, Jakarta 12930, Indonesia**

Tel: 62-21-575-0909   Fax: 62-21-575-0916

### PARKER DRILLING COMPANY

8 East Third Street, Tulsa, OK, 74103-3637

Tel: (918) 585-8221    Fax: (918) 585-1058    www.parkerdrilling.com

*Provides land contract drilling services to firms in the oil and gas industry.*

**Parker Drilling Co. of Indonesia-PT Dati, Jl. Sultan Hasanuddin 28, Kebayoran Bara, Jakarta 12160, Indonesia**

**Parker Drilling Co. of Indonesia-PT Sebina, Griya Ampera Bldg., Jl. Ampera Raya 18, Kemang Jakarta, Indonesia**

### PARSONS ENGINEERING SCIENCE INC.

100 West Walnut Street, Pasadena, CA, 91124

Tel: (626) 440-2000    Fax: (626) 440-4919    www.parsons.com

*Environmental engineering.*

**Parsons Engineering Science Inc., Jl Prapen Indah II/F2, Surabaya 60299, Indonesia**

## PARSONS TRANSPORTATION GROUP

1133 15th Street NW, 9th Fl., Washington, DC, 20005

Tel: (202) 775-3300          Fax: (202) 775-3422          www.parsons.com

*Consulting engineers.*

**De Leuw Cather Intl. Ltd., PO Box 36, Ujung Berung, Bandung West Java, Indonesia**

## PERKIN ELMER, INC.

45 William Street, Wellesley, MA, 02481

Tel: (781) 237-5100          Fax: (781) 431-4255          www.perkinelmer.com

*Mfr. equipment and devices to detect explosives and bombs on airline carriers.*

**PerkinElmer Life Sciences, Blok 207 Lantai 2, Jalan Beringin Kawasan, Industri Batamindo, Muka Kuning-Batam 29433, Indonesia**

Tel: 62-778-611084

## PFIZER INC.

235 East 42nd Street, New York, NY, 10017-5755

Tel: (212) 573-2323          Fax: (212) 573-7851          www.pfizer.com

*Research-based, global health care company.*

**Pfizer International, Indonesia**

## PHARMACIA CORPORATION

100 Route 206 North, Peapack, NJ, 07977

Tel: (908) 901-8000          Fax: (908) 901-8379          www.pharmacia.com

*Mfr. pharmaceuticals, agricultural products, industry chemicals.*

**PT Upjohn Indonesia, Menera Mulia Suite 2201, Jl. Jend Gatot Subroto Kav 9-11, Jakarta 12930, Indonesia**

## PHARMACIA MONSANTO

800 N. Lindbergh Boulevard, St. Louis, MO, 63167

Tel: (314) 694-1000          Fax: (314) 694-7625          www.monsanto.com

*Life sciences company focusing on agriculture, nutrition, pharmaceuticals, health and wellness and sustainable development.*

**Monsanto Co. Chemical Group, P T Monagro Kimia Permata Plaza 9/F, JI M H Thamrin 57 Jakarta 10077, Indonesia**

## PHILLIPS PETROLEUM COMPANY

Phillips Building, 411 S. Keeler Ave., Bartlesville, OK, 74004

Tel: (918) 661-6600          Fax: (918) 661-7636          www.phillips66.com

*Crude oil, natural gas, liquefied petroleum gas, gasoline and petro-chemicals.*

**Phillips Petroleum Co. Indonesia, Jl. Melawai Raya No. 16, Keb. Baru, Jakarta, Indonesia**

## PIONEER HI-BRED INTERNATIONAL INC.

400 Locust Street, Ste. 800, Des Moines, IA, 50309

Tel: (515) 248-4800          Fax: (515) 248-4999          www.pioneer.com

*Agricultural chemicals, farm supplies, biological products, research.*

**PT Pioneer Hibrida Indonesia, Jl. Imam Bonjol 80 - 8/F, Jakarta 10310, Indonesia**

## PLANET HOLLYWOOD INTERNATIONAL, INC.

8669 Commodity Circle, Orlando, FL, 32819

Tel: (407) 363-7827          Fax: (407) 363-4862          www.planethollywood.com

*Theme-dining restaurant chain and merchandise retail stores.*

**Planet Hollywood International, Inc., Jakarta, Indonesia**

## PRICEWATERHOUSECOOPERS LLP

1301 Ave. of the Americas, New York, NY, 10019

Tel: (212) 596-7000    Fax: (212) 259-1301    www.pwcglobal.com

*Accounting and auditing, tax and management, and human resource consulting services.*

**PriceWaterhouseCoopers, Price Waterhouse Center, Jl. HR Rasuna Said Kav. C-3, PO Box 2169/2473, Jakarta 10001, Indonesia**

Tel: 62-21-521-2941  Fax: 62-21-521-2950

## THE PRINCIPAL FINANCIAL GROUP

711 High Street, Des Moines, IA, 50392-9950

Tel: (515) 248-8288    Fax: (515) 248-8049    www.principal.com

*Insurance and investment services.*

**Dana Pensiun Lembaga Keuangan (DPLK), Jl. Tanah Abang II No. 15, Jakarta 10160, Indonesia**

Tel: 62-21-344-0238  Fax: 62-21-344-3191  Contact: Wartini Johan

**PT. Asuransi Jiwa Principal Egalita, Jl. Tanah Abang II No. 15, Jakarta 10160, Indonesia**

Tel: 62-21-344-0238  Fax: 62-21-344-0216  Contact: Doug Rasmussen, Mng. Dir.

## PROCTER & GAMBLE COMPANY

One Procter & Gamble Plaza, Cincinnati, OH, 45202

Tel: (513) 983-1100    Fax: (513) 562-4500    www.pg.com

*Personal care, food, laundry, cleaning and industry products.*

**PT Procter & Gamble Indonesia, Tifa Building 8th Fl., Jl. Kuningan Barat 26, Jakarta 12710, Indonesia**

## QWEST COMMUNICATIONS INTERNATIONAL INC.

1801 California Street, Ste. 5200, Denver, CO, 80202

Tel: (303) 896-2020    Fax: (303) 793-6654    www.uswest.com

*Tele-communications provider; integrated communications services.*

**Ariawest International, Jakarta, Indonesia**

Tel: 62-21-7398-222  Fax: 62-21-7243-371  Contact: Lawrence Tjandra, PR Mgr.

## R&B FALCON CORPORATION

901 Threadneedle, Ste. 200, Houston, TX, 77079

Tel: (281) 496-5000    Fax: (281) 496-4363    www.rbfalcon.com

*Offshore contract drilling.*

**R&B Falcon Exploration Co., Jl. Pupuk 44, Balikpapan, East Kalimantan 76114, Indonesia**

**R&B Falcon Exploration Co., c/o PT Bosara Mulia Tifa Bldg. #706, Jl. Kuningan Barat 26, Jakarta, Indonesia**

## RADISSON HOTELS INTERNATIONAL

Carlson Pkwy., PO Box 59159, Minneapolis, MN, 55459-8204

Tel: (612) 540-5526    Fax: (612) 449-3400    www.radisson.com

*Hotels and resorts.*

**Radisson Jakarta, Jl. Peconongan 72, Jakarta 10120, Indonesia**

Tel: 62-21-35-000-77  Fax: 62-21-35-000-55

## RAYTHEON COMPANY

141 Spring Street, Lexington, MA, 02173

Tel: (781) 862-6600    Fax: (781) 860-2172    www.raytheon.com

*Mfr. diversified electronics, appliances, aviation, energy and environmental products; publishing, industry and construction services.*

**Raytheon International, Jakarta, Indonesia**

## THE RENDON GROUP INC.

1875 Connecticut Ave., N.E., Washington, DC, 20009

Tel: (202) 745-4900      Fax: (202) 745-0215      www.rendon.com

*Public relations, print and video production, strategic communications.*

**PT TRG, Plaza 89 (4th fl.) Suite 407, Jl. H.R. Rasuna Said 4-7, Jakarta 12940, Indonesia**

## THE RITZ-CARLTON HOTEL COMPANY, L.L.C.

3414 Peachtree Road NE, Ste. 300, Atlanta, GA, 30326

Tel: (404) 237-5500      Fax: (404) 365-9643      www.ritzcarlton.com

*5-star hotel and restaurant chain.*

**The Ritz-Carlton Bali, Jl. Karang Mas Sejahtera, Jimbaran Bali 80364, Indonesia**

Tel: 62-361-702-222

## THE ROCKPORT COMPANY

220 Donald J. Lynch Blvd., Marlboro, MA, 01752

Tel: (508) 485-2090      Fax: (508) 480-0012      www.rockport.com

*Mfr./import dress and casual footwear.*

**Rockport Indonesia, Jl, Kapten Tendean 1 - 4/F, Jakarta 12710, Indonesia**

Emp: 21

## ROCKWELL INTERNATIONAL CORPORATION

777 East Wisconsin Ave., Ste. 1400, Milwaukee, WI, 53202

Tel: (414) 212-5200      Fax: (414) 212-5201      www.rockwell.com

*Products and service for aerospace and defense, automotive, electronics, graphics and automation industry.*

**Rockwell Automation Southeast Asia Pte. Ltd., Ste. 2301 Gedung BRI II 23rd Fl., Jl. Jend. Sudirman Kav 44-46, Jakarta 10210, Indonesia**

Tel: 62-21-571-906   Fax: 61-21-571-9065

## ROHM AND HAAS COMPANY

100 Independence Mall West, Philadelphia, PA, 19106

Tel: (215) 592-3000      Fax: (215) 592-3377      www.rohmhaas.com

*Mfr. industrial and agricultural chemicals, plastics.*

**PT Rohm and Haas Indonesia, Cilegon Plant Krakatau Industrial Estate, Kavling M-2 Jl. Raya Anyer, Cilegon 42401, Indonesia**

Tel: 62-254-380631

**Rohm and Haas Asia Inc., Jakarta Office, Summitas I 20th Fl., Jl. Jend. Sudirman Kav 61-62, Jakarta 12069, Indonesia**

Tel: 62-21-252-0535

## ROWAN COMPANIES INC.

2800 Post Oak Boulevard, Houston, TX, 77056-6196

Tel: (713) 621-7800      Fax: (713) 960-7560      www.rowancompanies.com

*Contract drilling and air charter service.*

**Rowan Intl. Inc., Jl. Letjen M.T. Haryono 58, Pancoran, Jakarta, Indonesia**

## SARA LEE CORPORATION

3 First National Plaza, Chicago, IL, 60602-4260

Tel: (312) 726-2600      Fax: (312) 558-4995      www.saralee.com

*Mfr./distributor food and consumer packaged goods, intimate apparel and knitwear.*

**House of Sara Lee, Jakarta, Indonesia**

**SAS INSTITUTE INC.**

SAS Campus Drive, Cary, NC, 27513

Tel: (919) 677-8000    Fax: (919) 677-4444    www.sas.com

*Mfr./distributes decision support software.*

**SAS Institute (Indonesia) Pte., Jakarta Pusat, Indonesia**

Tel: 62-21-3901761   Fax: 62-21-3902582

**SCHERING-PLOUGH CORPORATION**

One Giralda Farms, Madison, NJ, 07940-1000

Tel: (973) 822-7000    Fax: (973) 822-7048    www.sch-plough.com

*Proprietary drug and cosmetic products.*

**P.T. Pimaimas Citra, Po Box 2981/JKT, Jakarta 12810, Indonesia**

**SCHLUMBERGER LIMITED**

277 Park Avenue, New York, NY, 10021

Tel: (212) 350-9400    Fax: (212) 350-9564    www.schlumberger.com

*Engaged in oil and gas services, metering and payment systems, and produces semiconductor testing equipment and smart cards.*

**Schlumberger Ltd., PT Mecoindo, Sentra Mulia 16/F, Ste. 1603 Jl. HR Rasuna Said Kav. X-6, Jakarta 12940, Indonesia**

**Schlumberger Ltd., 214 Melawai Raya 18, Keb. Baru, Indonesia**

**SCIENCE APPLICATIONS INTL. CORPORATION (SAIC)**

10260 Campus Point Dr., San Diego, CA, 92121

Tel: (858) 826-6000    Fax: (858) 535-7589    www.saic.com

*Engaged in research and engineering.*

**SAIC C/O BP Expl. Oper. Co. Ltd., Kuningan Plaza South - Ste. 401, J1 H. R. Rasuna Said Kav C 11-14, Jakarta 12940, Indonesia**

Tel: 62-21-5201515   Contact: J. Espinosa

**SEAGATE TECHNOLOGY, INC.**

920 Disc Dr., Scotts Valley, CA, 95066

Tel: (408) 438-6550    Fax: (408) 438-7205    www.seagate.com

*Develop computer technology, software and hardware.*

**Seagate Technology, Lot 19 Batamindo Industrial Park, Muka Kuning, Batam Island, Indonesia**

Tel: 62-778-61564   Fax: 62-778-611942   Contact: Hamzah Bin Sulong, Dir.   Emp: 700

**G.D. SEARLE & COMPANY**

5200 Old Orchard Road, Skokie, IL, 60077

Tel: (847) 982-7000    Fax: (847) 470-1480    www.searlehealthnet.com

*Mfr. pharmaceuticals, health care, optical products and specialty chemicals.*

**Searle, Division of P.T. Soho Industri Pharmasi, Jl. Pulo Gadung No. 6, Jakarta 13920, Indonesia**

Tel: 62-21-461-0421   Fax: 62-21-461-0474

**THE SERVICEMASTER COMPANY**

One ServiceMaster Way, Downers Grove, IL, 60515-1700

Tel: (630) 271-1300    Fax: (630) 271-2710    www.svm.com

*Management service to health care, school and industry facilities; diversified residential and commercial services.*

**Terminix, Jarkata, Indonesia**

## SILICON GRAPHICS INC.

2011 N. Shoreline Blvd., Mountain View, CA, 94043-1389

Tel: (650) 960-1980      Fax: (650) 961-0595      www.sgi.com

*Design/mfr. special-effects computer graphic systems and software.*

**Silicon Graphics Pte. Ltd. Indonesia, Level 27 Wisma Danamon Aetna Life Tower II, Jl. Jend Sudirman Kav 45-46, Jakarta 12930, Indonesia**

Tel: 62-21-251-2828   Fax: 62-21-251-0868   Contact: Rene Widjaja, Mgr.

## SONOCO PRODUCTS COMPANY

North Second Street, PO Box 160, Hartsville, SC, 29550

Tel: (843) 383-7000      Fax: (843) 383-7008      www.sonoco.com

*Mfr. packaging for consumer and industrial market and recycled paperboard.*

**PT Tritunggal Sejahtera (Factory), Jl. Raya Cicadas Km 9 Gunung Putri Bogor, PO Box 18 Citeureup, Bogor Jawa Barat West Java, Indonesia**

Tel: 62-21-867-0417   Fax: 62-21-867-2927

**PT Tritunggal Sejahtera (Office), Jakarta Stock Exchange Bldg. Ste. 1709, Jl. Jend. Sudirman Kav 52-53, Jakarta 12190, Indonesia**

Tel: 62-21-515-0830   Fax: 62-21-515-0831

## SOTHEBY'S HOLDINGS, INC.

1334 York Avenue, New York, NY, 10021

Tel: (212) 606-7000      Fax: (212) 606-7027      www.sothebys.com

*Auction house specializing in fine art and jewelry.*

**Sotheby's Holdings, Inc., 31 Gatot Subroto, Kav. 21, Jakarta 12930, Indonesia**

## SPERRY-SUN DRILLING

3000 North Sam Houston Pkwy. East, Houston, TX, 77032

Tel: (281) 871-5100      Fax: (281) 871-5742      www.sperry-sun.com

*Provides drilling services to the oil and gas drilling industry.*

**P.T. Indokor Sperry-Sun, Jl. Letjen S. Parman, RT 04 RW 01 No. 41, Balikpapan Tengah, East Kalimantan, Indonesia**

Tel: 62-21-780-1100

## SPS TECHNOLOGIES INC.

101 Greenwood Avenue, Ste. 470, Jenkintown, PA, 19046

Tel: (215) 517-2000      Fax: (215) 517-2032      www.spstech.com

*Mfr. aerospace and industry fasteners, tightening systems, magnetic materials, superalloys.*

**Triple Mandiri Sentosa SPS, 14A Jalan Rawa Kemiri, Kebayoran Lama, Jakarta 12220, Indonesia**

Contact: Grace Santosa

## THE ST. PAUL COMPANIES, INC.

385 Washington Street, St. Paul, MN, 55102

Tel: (651) 310-7911      Fax: (651) 310-8294      www.stpaul.com

*Provides investment, insurance and reinsurance services.*

**PT Asuransi Central Asia, Komplek Duta Merlin Blok A No. 4-5, Jl. Gajah Mada No. 3-5, Jakarta 10130, Indonesia**

## STARWOOD HOTELS & RESORTS WORLDWIDE

777 Westchester Avenue, White Plains, NY, 10604

Tel: (914) 640-8100      Fax: (914) 640-8316      www.starwoodhotels.com

*Hotel operations including Sheraton, Westin, St. Regis, Four Points and Caesars.*

**Sheraton Bandara, Bandara Soekarno-Hatta Jakarta, 19110 PO Box 1198, Jakarta 19100, Indonesia**

Tel: 62-21-559-7777   Fax: 62-21-559-7700

**STEINER CORPORATION**

505 E. South Temple, Salt Lake City, UT, 84102

Tel: (801) 328-8831     Fax: (801) 363-5680

*Soap and towel dispensers.*

**Steiner Company, Jakarta, Indonesia**

**STIEFEL LABORATORIES INC.**

255 Alhambra Circle, Ste. 1000, Coral Gables, FL, 33134

Tel: (305) 443-3807     Fax: (305) 443-3467     www.stiefel.com

*Mfr. pharmaceuticals, dermatological specialties.*

**Stiefel Laboratories Limited, Graha Darya-Varia 3/F, Jl. Melawai Raya No. 93, Kebayoran Baru, Jakarta 12130, Indonesia**

**STONE & WEBSTER ENGINEERING CORPORATION**

8545 United Plaza Blvd., Baton Rouge, LA, 02210-2288

Tel: (617) 589-5111     Fax: (617) 589-2156     www.shawgroup.com

*Engineering, construction, environmental and management services.*

**Stone & Webster Canada Ltd., Central Plaza Bldg. 16/F, 47 Jl. Jend. Sudirman, Jakarta 12190, Indonesia**

**SUNBEAM CORPORATION**

2381 Executive Center Dr., Boca Raton, FL, 33431

Tel: (561) 912-4100     Fax: (561) 912-4567     www.sunbeam.com

*Mfr. household and personal grooming appliances; Sunbeam, Mr. Coffee, First Alert, Mixmaster and Oster.*

**Pt. Pelita Unggul Pratama, Permata Building 3/F, Jalan Ciputat Raya No. 30, Tanah Kusir, Jakarta Selatan 12240 Indonesia**

**SYBASE, INC.**

6475 Christie Ave., Emeryville, CA, 94608

Tel: (510) 922-3500     Fax: (510) 922-3210     www.sybase.com

*Design/mfg/distribution of database management systems, software development tools, connectivity products, consulting and technical support services..*

**PT Sybase Informatindo Indonesia, Menara 2 Plaza Bapindo 23rd Fl., Jl. Jend. Sudirman Kav. 54-55, Jakarta 12190, Indonesia**

Tel: 62-21-526-6520   Fax: 62-21-526-6523

**THE TCW GROUP**

865 S. Figueroa St., Ste. 1800, Los Angeles, CA, 90017

Tel: (213) 244-0000     Fax: (213) 244-0000     www.tcwgroup.com

*Engaged in managing pension and profit sharing funds, retirement/health and welfare funds, insurance company funds, endowments and foundations.*

**TCW Group (JV), Jakarta, Indonesia**

**TEKTRONIX INC.**

14200 SW Karl Braun Dr., PO Box 500, Beaverton, OR, 97077

Tel: (503) 627-7111     Fax: (503) 627-2406     www.tek.com

*Mfr. test and measure, visual systems/color printing and communications/video and networking products.*

**P.T. Cosmotec Sarana Elektronika Indonesia, Jl. Jembatan Dua, Komplek Ruko Harmoni Mas Blok A-15, Jakarta Utara 14450, Indonesia**

Tel: 62-21-667-0011   Fax: 62-21-667-0020

## TETRA TECH, INC.

670 N. Rosemead Blvd., Pasadena, CA, 91107

Tel: (626) 351-4664       Fax: (626) 351-1188       www.tetratech.com

*Environmental engineering and consulting services.*

**Tetra Tech - Indonesia,  First City Complex Blok 2 Nos. 30-32, PO Box 160 Batam Centre, Batam 29400, Indonesia**

Tel: 62-778-462-049   Fax: 62-778-462-127   Contact: Shannon B. Lumbanotobing

## TEXACO INC.

2000 Westchester Ave., White Plains, NY, 10650

Tel: (914) 253-4000       Fax: (914) 253-7753       www.texaco.com

*Exploration/marketing crude oil, mfr. petro chemicals and products.*

**PT Caltex Pacific Indonesia,  Jl. Kebon Sirih 52, Jakarta, Java, Indonesia**

## TEXAS INSTRUMENTS INC.

8505 Forest Lane, Dallas, TX, 75243

Tel: (972) 995-3773       Fax: (972) 995-4360       www.ti.com

*Mfr. semiconductor devices, electronic electro-mechanical systems, instruments and controls.*

**Texas Instruments Indonesia,  Jakarta, Indonesia**

Tel: 801-10-800-800-1450

## THERMADYNE HOLDINGS CORPORATION

101 South Hanley Road, Suite 300, St. Louis, MO, 63105

Tel: (314) 746-2197       Fax: (314) 746-2349       www.thermadyne.com

*Mfr. welding, cutting, and safety products.*

**Thermadyne Indonesia,  Jakarta, Indonesia**

Tel: 62-21-425-6243

## TIDEWATER INC.

601 Poydras Street, Ste.1900, New Orleans, LA, 70130

Tel: (504) 568-1010       Fax: (504) 566-4582       www.tdw.com

*Marine service and equipment to companies engaged in exploration, development and production of oil, gas and minerals.*

**Tidewater Marine International, Inc.,  Jalan Tegal Parang Utara 32, Tegal Parang Jakarta Selatan 12790, Indonesia**

Tel: 62-21-7993637   Fax: 62-21-7982330

## TOSCO CORPORATION

72 Cummings Point Rd., Stamford, CT, 06902

Tel: (203) 977-1000       Fax: (203) 964-3187       www.tosco.com

*Engaged in oil refining and marketing and operates service stations and convenience stores.*

**Circle K Indonesia,  JL Raya Jatinegara Barat No 124, Jakarta 13320, Indonesia**

Tel: 62-21-856-4437   Contact: Yogi Dewanto, Pres.

## THE TRANE COMPANY

3600 Pammel Creek Road, La Crosse, WI, 54601

Tel: (608) 787-2000       Fax: (608) 787-4990       www.trane.com

*Mfr./distributor/service A/C systems and equipment.*

**PT Tatasol Pratama,  Jl. Abdul Muis 24-26, Jakarta Pusat 10160, Indonesia**

**PT Tatasol USI Pratama,  42-44 Jl. Kayoon, Surabaya 60270, Indonesia**

### TRANSOCEAN SEDCO FOREX INC.

PO Box 2765, Houston, TX, 77252-2765

Tel: (713) 871-7500    Fax: (713) 850-3834    www.deepwater.com

*Engaged in oil and gas offshore drilling.*

**Sonat Offshore Drilling, PT Unimas Motor Wasta 3F Wisma Metropolitan, Jl. Jend. Sudirman Kav. 24, Jakarta 12920, Indonesia**

### TRUE NORTH COMMUNICATIONS INC.

101 East Erie Street, Chicago, IL, 60611

Tel: (312) 425-6500    Fax: (312) 425-5010    www.truenorth.com

*Holding company, advertising agency.*

**FCB/Advis, J1. Proklamasi No. 49, Jakarta 10320, Indonesia**

### U.S. OFFICE PRODUCTS COMPANY

1025 Thomas Jefferson St., NW, Ste. 600E, Washington, DC, 20007

Tel: (202) 339-6700    Fax: (202) 339-6720    www.usop.com

*Sales and distribution of educational products, office supplies and office related services.*

**MBE (Mail Boxes Etc.), Pt. Prima Meridiana, Komp. Duta Merlin Blok B No. 3, Jl. Gajah Mada 3-5, Jakarta Pusat Indonesia**

Tel: 62-21-634-0225    Fax: 62-21-633-4661

**MBE (Mail Boxes Etc.), Jelan Kelapa Hybrida Raya, Blok QJ 9/30, Kelapa Gading Permai, Jakarta 14240 Indonesia**

Tel: 62-21-451-6190    Fax: 62-21-451-5596

**MBE (Mail Boxes Etc.), Jl. Ampera Raya #2, Cilandak, Jakarta Selatan, Indonesia**

Tel: 62-21-782-1734    Fax: 62-21-780-2558

### UNION CARBIDE CORPORATION

39 Old Ridgebury Road, Danbury, CT, 06817

Tel: (203) 794-2000    Fax: (203) 794-6269    www.unioncarbide.com

*Mfr. industrial chemicals, plastics and resins.*

**PT Union Carbide Indonesia, Wisma Metropolitan II, Jl. Jend. Sudiman, PO Box 2677, Jakarta 12920 Indonesia**

### UNITED PARCEL SERVICE, INC.

55 Glenlake Parkway, NE, Atlanta, GA, 30328

Tel: (404) 828-6000    Fax: (404) 828-6593    www.ups.com

*International package-delivery service.*

**UPS - Pt. Cardig Citra Primajasa, Halim Perdanakusuma Airport, Jakarta 13610, Indonesia**

Tel: 62-21-800-7066    Fax: 62-21-809-1934

### UNOCAL CORPORATION

2141 Rosecrans Ave., Ste. 4000, El Segundo, CA, 90245

Tel: (310) 726-7600    Fax: (310) 726-7817    www.unocal.com

*Engaged in oil and gas exploration and production.*

**Unocal Makassar, Ltd., Jakarta, Indonesia**

### UOP LLC.

25 East Algonquin Road, Des Plaines, IL, 60017

Tel: (847) 391-2000    Fax: (847) 391-2253    www.uop.com

*Engaged in developing and commercializing technology for license to the oil refining, petrochemical and gas processing industries.*

**UOP Processes International, Inc., Wisma Rajawali 15/F, Jalan Jendral Sudirman, Kav 34, Jakarta 10220, Indonesia**

Tel: 62-21-573-6368    Fax: 62-21-573-8532

## URS CORPORATION

100 California Street, Ste. 500, San Francisco, CA, 94111-4529

Tel: (415) 774-2700      Fax: (415) 398-1904      www.urscorp.com

*Provides planning, design and construction management services, pollution control and hazardous waste management.*

**URS, Jakarta, Indonesia**

## VERITAS DGC INC.

3701 Kirby Drive, Houston, TX, 77096

Tel: (713) 512-8300      Fax: (713) 512-8701      www.veritasdgc.com

*Geophysical services.*

**Veritas DGC Mega Pratama, Graha Paramita 6/F, Jalan Denpasar Blok D-Kuningan, Jakarta 12940, Indonesia**

Tel: 62-21-252-2240    Contact: Andrew Cochran

## VERIZON

1095 Ave. of the Americas, New York, NY, 10036

Tel: (212) 395-2121      Fax: (212) 395-1285      www.verizon.com

*Telecommunications.*

**Excelcomindo, Jakarta, Indonesia**

## VERIZON COMMUNICATIONS INC.

1255 Corporate Drive, Irving, TX, 75038

Tel: (972) 507-5000      Fax: (972) 507-5002      www.gte.com

*Engaged in wireline and wireless communications.*

**Excelcomindo/PT Telekomindo (JV), Jakarta, Indonesia**

Contact: Yaya Winarno Junardy

## WAL-MART STORES INC.

702 SW 8th Street, Bentonville, AR, 72716-8611

Tel: (501) 273-4000      Fax: (501) 273-1917      www.wal-mart.com

*Retailer.*

**Wal-Mart Stores Inc., Jakarta, Indonesia**

## WASTE MANAGEMENT, INC.

1001 Fannin Street, Ste. 4000, Houston, TX, 77002

Tel: (713) 512-6200      Fax: (713) 512-6299      www.wastemanagement.com

*Environmental services and disposal company; collection, processing, transfer and disposal facilities.*

**PT Waste management Indonesia, Jl Raya Narogong Desa Nambo, PO Box 18 Cileungsi, Bogor 16820 Indonesia**

Contact: Nizar Mansur, Mgr.

**PT Waste Management Indonesia, Bimantara Building 17th Floor, Jl. Kebon Sirih, Kav. 17-19, Jakarta 10304 Indonesia**

## WATSON WYATT & COMPANY HOLDINGS

6707 Democracy Blvd., Ste. 800, Bethesda, MD, 20817

Tel: (301) 581-4600      Fax: (301) 581-4937      www.watsonwyatt.com

*Creates compensation and benefits programs for major corporations.*

**Watson Wyatt & Co., Setiabudi 2 Building Suite 507A, Jl H.R.Rasuna Said, Jakarta 12920, Indonesia**

Tel: 62-21-525-3926   Fax: 62-21-520-7467   Contact: Lilis Halim

## WEATHERFORD INTERNATIONAL, INC.

5 Post Oak Blvd, Ste. 1760, Houston, TX, 77227-3415

Tel: (713) 287-8400        Fax: (713) 963-9785        www.weatherford.com

*Oilfield services, products and equipment; mfr. marine cranes for oil and gas industry.*

**Weatherford Oil Tool Pte. Ltd.,  Cilandak Commercial Estate Unit 105 Raya, Cilandak KKO, Jakarta 12560, Indonesia**

Tel: 62-21-780-7801    Fax: 62-21-780-7796

## WENDY'S INTERNATIONAL, INC.

428 West Dublin Granville Roads, Dublin, OH, 43017-0256

Tel: (614) 764-3100        Fax: (614) 764-3459        www.wendysintl.com

*Fast food restaurant chain.*

**Wendy's International,  Jakarta, Indonesia**

## WESTERN GEOPHYSICAL, INC.

10205 Westheimer, Houston, TX, 77251-1407

Tel: (713) 972-4000        Fax: (713) 952-9837        www.bakerhughes.com

*Provides comprehensive seismic services for oil and gas exploration, field development, and reservoir monitoring.*

**Western Atlas Logging Services,  Bldg.404W Cilandak Commercial Estate 1427, Jl. Cilandak KKO, Jakarta 12560, Indonesia**

Tel: 62-21-780-1420   Fax: 62-21-780-0790   Contact: Steve Ellison, Dist. Mgr.

**Western Geophysical,  c/o PT Talanavindo, JL Sultan Iskandar Muda No. F-25, Kebayoran Lama, Jakarta 12240 Indonesia**

Tel: 62-21-739-5290   Fax: 62-21-720-6219   Contact: E. Ferris, Mgr.

## WHITE & CASE LLP

1155 Ave. of the Americas, New York, NY, 10036-2767

Tel: (212) 819-8200        Fax: (212) 354-8113        www.whitecase.com

*International law firm.*

**PT WCI Konsultan,  Wisma Danamon Aetna Life 27th Fl., Jl. Jend. Sudirman Kav. 45-46, Jakarta 12930, Indonesia**

Tel: 62-21-577-1527   Fax: 62-21-577-1535   Contact: Wendell C. Maddrey

## WILBUR-ELLIS COMPANY

PO Box 7454, San Francisco, CA, 94120

Tel: (415) 772-4000        Fax: (415) 772-4011        www.wilburellis.com

*Marketing, distribution, formulation of agricultural products and industrial specialty chemicals and raw materials.*

**Connell Bros. Co. Ltd.,  Lippo Centre 504, Jl. Gatot Subroto Kav. 35-36, Jakarta 12950, Indonesia**

## WYETH-AYERST INTERNATIONAL INC.

150 Radnot-Chester Road, St. Davids, PA, 19087

Tel: (610) 902-4100        Fax: (610) 989-4586        www.ahp.com/wyeth

*Antibiotics and pharmaceutical products.*

**AHP Overseas Ltd.,  Plaza Lippo 12th Floor, J1 Jend Sudirman Kav 25, Jakarta 12920 Indonesia**

Tel: 62-21-526-7985

## XEROX CORPORATION

800 Long Ridge Road, PO Box 1600, Stamford, CT, 06904

Tel: (203) 968-3000        Fax: (203) 968-4312        www.xerox.com

*Mfr. document processing equipment, systems and supplies.*

**PT Astra Graphia,  Jl Kramat Raya 43, Jakarta 10450, Indonesia**

Tel: 62-21-3909190  Fax: 62-21-3909181

**YORK INTERNATIONAL CORPORATION**

631 South Richland Ave., York, PA, 17403

Tel: (717) 771-7890     Fax: (717) 771-6212     www.york.com

*Mfr. heating, ventilating, air conditioning and refrigeration equipment.*

**York Air Conditioning & Refrigeration, Inc., Jalan Kyai Caringin No. 2B, Jakarta, Indonesia**

Tel: 62-21-385-9227

**YOUNG & RUBICAM INC.**

285 Madison Ave., New York, NY, 10017

Tel: (212) 210-3000     Fax: (212) 370-3796     www.yr.com

*Advertising, public relations, direct marketing and sales promotion, corporate and product ID management.*

**PT Dentsu Young & Rubicam Pte. Ltd., Jakarta, Indonesia**

# Iran

**DHL WORLDWIDE EXPRESS**

50 California Avenue, San Francisco, CA, 94111

Tel: (415) 677-6100      Fax: (415) 824-9700      www.dhl.com

*Worldwide air express carrier.*

**DHL Worldwide Express, No. 353 Dr. Beheshti Ave., Tehran 15166, Iran**

Tel: 98-21-871-7985

**GENERAL ELECTRIC COMPANY**

3135 Easton Turnpike, Fairfield, CT, 06431

Tel: (203) 373-2211      Fax: (203) 373-3131      www.ge.com

*Diversified manufacturing, technology and services.*

**GE Appliances, 1137 Vali Asr Ave. 6th Floor, Tehran 15119, Iran**

Tel: 98-21-801-6329

**GE International, 1137 Vali Asr Ave. 6th Floor, Tehran 15119, Iran**

Tel: 98-21-801-6708   Fax: 98-21-801-6965

**Nuovo Pignone, Mirzaye Shirazi Ave. 225, Tehran, Iran**

Tel: 98-21-872-5084   Fax: 98-21-872-5083

**KPMG INTERNATIONAL LLP**

345 Park Avenue, New York, NY, 10022

Tel: (201) 307-7000      Fax: (201) 930-8617      www.kpmg.com

*Accounting and audit, tax and management consulting services.*

**Bayat Rayan, 227 Ave. Iranshahr, 15847 Tehran, Iran**

Tel: 98-21-882-6684   Fax: 98-21-837927   Contact: M. Bayat, Sr. Ptnr.

**PANAMETRICS**

221 Crescent Street, Waltham, MA, 02154

Tel: (781) 899-2719      Fax: (781) 899-1552      www.panametrics.com

*Process/non-destructive test instrumentation.*

**Kavosh Azmoon Company, 141 Kheradmand Shomali 3rd Fl., Tehran, Iran**

Tel: 98-21-835954   Fax: 98-21-837535

**SCHENKER INTERNATIONAL FORWARDERS INC.**

150 Albany Ave., Freeport, NY, 11520

Tel: (516) 377-3000      Fax: (516) 377-3005      www.schenkerusa.com

*Freight forwarders.*

**Delta Bar Co. Ltd., PO Box 15745-181, Teheran 15745, Iran**

Tel: 98-21-882-0118   Fax: 98-21-882-0183

**XEROX CORPORATION**

800 Long Ridge Road, PO Box 1600, Stamford, CT, 06904

Tel: (203) 968-3000      Fax: (203) 968-4312      www.xerox.com

*Mfr. document processing equipment, systems and supplies.*

**Balli Group, 19 Kalantari St., Qarani Ave., POBox 15815-3445, Tehran Iran**

# Ireland

## 3COM CORPORATION

5400 Bayfront Plaza, Santa Clara, CA, 95052-8145

Tel: (408) 326-5000      Fax: (408) 326-5001      www.3com.com

*Develop/mfr. computer networking products and systems.*

**3Com Ireland,  Ballycoolin Business Park, Blanchardstown, Dublin 15, Ireland**

## 3dfx INTERACTIVE, INC.

4435 Fortran Drive, San Jose, CA, 95134

Tel: (408) 935-4400      Fax: (408) 262-8874      www.3dfx.com

*Engaged in microchip, graphics, images and animation.*

**3dfx Interactive UK,  Voodoo House Weaver's Court, Belfast BT12 5LA, UK**

## 3M

3M Center, St. Paul, MN, 55144-1000

Tel: (651) 733-1110      Fax: (651) 733-9973      www.mmm.com

*Mfr. diversified products for industry, health care, imaging, communications, transport, safety, consumer, etc.*

**3M Ireland Ltd.,  3M House, Adelphi Centre, Upper George St., Dun Laoghaire Dublin Ireland**
Tel: 353-280-3555   Fax: 353-280-3555   Contact: Wayne W. Brown

## ABBOTT LABORATORIES

One Abbott Park, Abbott Park, IL, 60064-3500

Tel: (847) 937-6100      Fax: (847) 937-1511      www.abbott.com

*Development/mfr./sale diversified health care products and services.*

**Abbott Laboratories Ltd.,  Finisklin Industrial Estate, Sligo, Ireland**
Tel: 353-71-71708

## ACCO BRANDS, INC.

300 Tower Parkway, Lincoln, IL, 60069

Tel: (847) 541-9500      Fax: (847) 541-5750      www.acco.com

*Provides services in the office and computer markets and manufactures paper fasteners, clips, metal fasteners, binders and staplers.*

**ACCO-Rexel Ltd.,  c/o ACCO England - Gatehouse Road, Aylesbury, Bucks HP 19 3DT, UK**

## ACT MANUFACTURING, INC.

2 Cabot Road, Hudson, MA, 01749

Tel: (978) 567-4000      Fax: (978) 568-1904      www.actmfg.com

*Mfr. printed circuit boards.*

**ACT Manufacturing Ireland,  Citywest Business Campus - Unit 2008, Naas Road, Dublin 24, Ireland**
Tel: 353-1-403-5200   Fax: 353-1-403-5299

## ACTERNA CORPORATION

3 New England Executive Park, Burlington, MA, 01803

Tel: (781) 272-6100      Fax: (781) 272-2304      www.acterna.com

*Develop, manufacture and market communications test instruments, systems, software and services.*

**Acterna Corporation,  County Meath, Ireland**

## AIR EXPRESS INTERNATIONAL CORPORATION

120 Tokeneke Road, PO Box 1231, Darien, CT, 06820

Tel: (203) 655-7900    Fax: (203) 655-5779    www.aeilogistics.com

*International air freight forwarder.*

**AEI (Ireland) Ltd., Furry Park, Santry, Dublin 9 Ireland**

Tel: 353-1-816-1000    Fax: 353-1-844-5833

## AIR PRODUCTS AND CHEMICALS, INC.

7201 Hamilton Boulevard, Allentown, PA, 18195-1501

Tel: (610) 481-4911    Fax: (610) 481-5900    www.airproducts.com

*Mfr. industry gases and related equipment, specialty chemicals, environmental/energy systems.*

**Air Products Ireland Ltd., Unit 950 Western Industrial Estate 2, Killeen Rd., Naasroad, Dublin, Ireland**

## ALAMO RENT A CAR

110 Southeast 6th Street, Fort Lauderdale, FL, 33301

Tel: (954) 522-0000    Fax: (954) 220-0120    www.alamo.com

*Car rentals.*

**Alamo Rent A Car, Cork, Dublin & Shannon International Airports, Arrivals Hall, Ireland**

## ALCOA INC.

Alcoa Center, 201 Isabella Street, Pittsburgh, PA, 15215-5858

Tel: (412) 553-4545    Fax: (412) 553-4498    www.alcoa.com

*World's leading producer of aluminum and alumina; mining, refining, smelting, fabricating and recycling.*

**AFL Ireland Ltd., Dundalk, Ireland**

## ALCOA FUJIKURA LTD.

105 Westpark Drive, Brentwood, TN, 37027

Tel: (615) 370-2100    Fax: (615) 370-2180    www.alcoa-fujikura.com

*Mfr. optical groundwire, tube cable, fiber optic connectors and automotive wiring harnesses.*

**Alcoa Fujikura Ireland Ltd., Dundalk, Ireland**

## ALLERGAN INC.

2525 Dupont Drive, PO Box 19534, Irvine, CA, 92713-9534

Tel: (714) 246-4500    Fax: (714) 246-6987    www.allergan.com

*Mfr. therapeutic eye care products, skin and neural care pharmaceuticals.*

**Allergan Ireland Ltd., Sweepstakes Centre, Ballsbridge, Dublin 4 Ireland**

Tel: 353-1-614-2000    Fax: 353-1-614-2099

## AMERICAN EXPRESS COMPANY

American Express Tower, World Financial Center, New York, NY, 10285-4765

Tel: (212) 640-2000    Fax: (212) 619-9802    www.americanexpress.com

*Travel, travelers cheques, charge card and financial services.*

**American Express Ireland Ltd., Dublin, Ireland**

## AMERICAN HOME PRODUCTS CORPORATION

Five Giralda Farms, Madison, NJ, 07940-0874

Tel: (973) 660-5000    Fax: (973) 660-6048    www.ahp.com

*Mfr. pharmaceutical, animal health care and crop protection products.*

**American Home Products Corporation, Dublin, Ireland**

## AMERICAN INTERNATIONAL GROUP INC. (AIG)

70 Pine Street, New York, NY, 10270

Tel: (212) 770-7000    Fax: (212) 509-9705    www.aig.com

*Worldwide insurance and financial services.*

**AIG Europe Ltd., AIG House, Merrion Road, Dublin 4, Ireland**

## AMES TRUE TEMPER CORPORATION

465 Railroad Ave., PO Box 8859, Camp Hill, PA, 17011-8859

Tel: (717) 737-1500    Fax: (717) 730-2550    www.amest.com

*Mfr. hand and edge tools, farm and garden tools, wheelbarrows.*

**Ames True Temper, White's Cross, County Cork, Ireland**

Tel: 353-21-302433   Fax: 353-21-304621

## ANALOG DEVICES INC.

1 Technology Way, Box 9106, Norwood, MA, 02062

Tel: (781) 329-4700    Fax: (781) 326-8703    www.analog.com

*Mfr. integrated circuits and related devices.*

**Analog Devices BV, Bay F-1, Raheen Industrial Estate, Limerick, Ireland**

## ANC RENTAL CORP.

110 Southeast Sixth St., Ft. Lauderdale, FL, 33301

Tel: (954) 769-7000    Fax: (954) 769-7000    www.ancrental.com

*Engaged in car rental services, including National Car Rental and Alamo Rent A Car.*

**National Car Rental, Baggott St. Bridge, Dublin 4, Ireland**

## ANDERSEN CONSULTING

100 S. Wacker Drive, Ste. 1059, Chicago, IL, 60606

Tel: (312) 693-0161    Fax: (312) 693-0507    www.ac.com

*Provides management and technology consulting services.*

**Andersen Consulting, Andersen House, Harbourwater Place, Dublin 1, Ireland**

Tel: 353-1-670-1000   Fax: 353-1-670-1010

## ANDERSEN WORLDWIDE

33 West Monroe Street, Chicago, IL, 60603

Tel: (312) 580-0033    Fax: (312) 507-6748    www.arthurandersen.com

*Accounting and audit, tax and management consulting services.*

**Arthur Andersen & Co., Andersen House, Int'l Financial Service Centre, Dublin 1, Ireland**

Tel: 353-1-670-1000

## ANIXTER INTERNATIONAL INC..

4711 Golf Road, Skokie, IL, 60076

Tel: (847) 677-2600    Fax: (847) 677-8557    www.anixter.com

*Distributor wiring systems/products for voice, video, data and power applications.*

**Anixter Ireland, Westlink Ind. Estate/Unit16, Kylemore Road, Dublin 10 Ireland**

Tel: 353-1-6244-68

**Anixter Northern Ireland, Lisburn Enterprise Centre Unit 270, Ballinderry Road, Lisburn County Antrim, Northern Ireland**

Tel: 353-1-846-634777   Fax: 353-1-846-634888

## AON CORPORATION

123 North Wacker Drive, Chicago, IL, 60606

Tel: (312) 701-3000    Fax: (312) 701-3100    www.aon.com

*Insurance brokers worldwide; underwrites accident and health insurance, specialty and professional insurance; and provides risk management consultation.*

**AON Alexander, Haddington Court, Haddington Rd., Dublin 4, Ireland**

Tel: 353-1-605-9400   Fax: 353-1-660-5831   Contact: Ken D. Reid

**AON MacDonald Boland, 9 Lr. Cecil St., Limerick, Ireland**

Tel: 353-61-417633   Fax: 353-61-310726   Contact: Ken D. Reid

## APPLE COMPUTER, INC.

One Infinite Loop, Cupertino, CA, 95014

Tel: (408) 996-1010      Fax: (408) 974-2113      www.apple.com

*Personal computers, peripherals and software.*

**Apple Computer Ltd.,  Holly Hill Ind. Estate, Holly Hill, Cork, Ireland**

## APPLIED MATERIALS, INC.

3050  Bowers Ave., Santa Clara, CA, 95054-3299

Tel: (408) 727-5555      Fax: (408) 727-9943      www.appliedmaterials.com

*Supplies manufacturing systems and services to the semiconductor industry.*

**Applied Materials, Ireland,  14 Collinstown Industrial Park, Leixlip County Kildare IR2, Ireland**

Tel: 353-1-606-6305    Fax: 353-1-606-8006

## APW, INC.

PO Box 325, Milwaukee, WI, 53201-0325

Tel: (262) 523-7600      Fax: (262) 523-7624      www.apw1.com

*Mfr. hi-pressure tools, vibration control products,  consumables, technical furniture and enclosures.*

**APW Custom Systems,  Ballybrit Industrial Estate, Galway, Ireland**

## AQUENT

711 Boylston Street, Boston, MA, 02116

Tel: (617) 535-5000      Fax: (617) 535-6001      www.aquent.com

*Engaged in temporary, specialized employment.*

**AQUENT,  Lower Fitzwilliam Street, Dublin 2, Ireland**

## ARBOR ACRES FARM INC.

439 Marlborough Road, Glastonbury, CT, 06033

Tel:  (860) 633-4681      Fax:  (860) 633-2433

*Producers of male and female broiler breeders, commercial egg layers.*

**Arbor Acres Ireland,  Walshestown, Mullingar, Westmeath, Ireland**

## ARROW ELECTRONICS INC.

25 Hub Drive, Melville, NY, 11747

Tel:  (516) 391-1300      Fax:  (516) 391-1640      www.arrow.com

*Distributor of electronic components.*

**Arrow Dublin,  37A Barrow Road, Dublin Industrial Estate, Glasnevin Dublin 11, Ireland**

Tel: 353-1-830-7522

## AT&T CORPORATION

32 Avenue of the Americas, New York, NY, 10013-2412

Tel:  (212) 387-5400      Fax:  (212) 387-5695      www.att.com

*Telecommunications.*

**AT&T Ireland,  Corke Abbey, Bray, Dublin, Ireland**

## ATTACHMATE CORPORATION

3617 131st Ave. S.E., Bellevue, WA, 98006-1332

Tel: (425) 644-4010      Fax: (425) 747-9924      www.attachmate.com

*Mfr. connectivity software.*

**Attachmate Ireland,  Bay 4 AD, Shannon Industrial Estate, Shannon County Clare, Ireland**

Tel: 353-61-474-666    Fax: 353-61-472-733

## AUTODESK INC.

111 McInnis Parkway, San Rafael, CA, 94903

Tel:  (415) 507-5000        Fax:  (415) 507-6112        www.autodesk.com

*Develop/marketing/support computer-aided design, engineering, scientific and multimedia software products.*

**Autodesk Ireland ltd.,  East Point Business Park, Alfie Byrne Road, Clontarf IRL-Dublin 3, Ireland**

Tel: 353-1-805-4400   Fax: 353-1-805-4401

## AVERY DENNISON CORPORATION

150 N. Orange Grove Blvd., Pasadena, CA, 91103

Tel:  (626) 304-2000        Fax:  (626) 792-7312        www.averydennison.com

*Mfr. pressure-sensitive adhesives and materials, office products, labels, tags, retail systems, Carter's Ink and specialty chemicals.*

**Fasson Ireland Ltd.,  Unit 5 Ballymount Bus. Park, Dublin 12, Ireland**

Tel: 353-1-456-9733   Fax: 353-1-456-9742

## AVID TECHNOLOGY, INC.

1 Park West, Tewksbury, MA, 01876

Tel:  (978) 640-6789        Fax:  (978) 640-1366        www.avid.com

*Mfr. animation design software and digital and audio systems.*

**Avid Technology BV,  Carmanhall Road - Unit 38, Sandyford Industrial Estate, Dublin 18, Ireland**

Tel: 353-1-207-8200   Fax: 353-1-295-0079

## AVNET INC.

2211 South 47th Street, Phoenix, AZ, 85034

Tel:  (480) 643-2000        Fax:  (480) 643-4670        www.avnet.com

*Distributor electronic components, computers and peripherals.*

**Avnet EMG,  Swords Business Park, Unit 7, Swords County, Dublin, Ireland**

Tel: 353-1-890-1000   Fax: 353-1-890-1010

## AVON PRODUCTS INC.

1345 Avenue of the Americas, New York, NY, 10105-0196

Tel:  (212) 282-5000        Fax:  (212) 282-6049        www.avon.com

*Mfr./distributor beauty and related products, fashion jewelry, gifts and collectibles.*

**Arlington Ltd.,  Cooltedexry, Port Arlington, County Laois, Ireland**

## BALDWIN TECHNOLOGY COMPANY, INC.

One Norwalk West, 40 Richards Ave., Norwalk, CT, 06854

Tel:  (203) 838-7470        Fax:  (203) 852-7040        www.baldwintech.com

*Mfr./services material handling, accessories, control and prepress equipment for print industry.*

**Graphics Financing Ireland Ltd.(Baldwin Europe Consolidated),  Altoste, Ireland**

## BANK OF AMERICA CORPORATION

555 California Street, San Francisco, CA, 94104

Tel:  (415) 622-3530        Fax:  (415) 622-8467        www.bankofamerica.com

*Financial services.*

**Bank of America NT & SA,  Russell Ct., St. Stephen's Green, Dublin 2, Ireland**

Tel: 353-1-407-2100   Fax: 353-1-407-2199   Contact: Adrian E. Wrafter, VP

## THE BANK OF NEW YORK

One Wall Street, New York, NY, 10286

Tel:  (212) 495-1784        Fax:  (212) 495-2546        www.bankofny.com

*Banking services.*

**AIB/BNY Fund Management (Ireland) Ltd.,  AIB International Centre, Dublin 1, Ireland**

Tel: 353-1-670-1158   Fax: 353-1-670-1168

## BANTA CORPORATION

River Place, 225 Main St., Menasha, WI, 54952-8003

Tel: (920) 751-7777     Fax: (920) 751-7790     www.banta.com

*Provides printing, electronic media and packaging services.*

**Banta Global Turnkey Group, Raheen Industrial Estate, Raheen Limerick, Ireland**

Tel: 353-61-303888

**Banta Global Turnkey Group, Hollyhill Industrial Estate, Hollyhill Cork, Ireland**

Tel: 353-21-397515

**Banta Global Turnkey Group, Woodford Business Park, Santry, Dublin 17, Ireland**

Tel: 353-1-816-3400

## C. R. BARD, INC.

730 Central Ave., Murray Hill, NJ, 07974

Tel: (908) 277-8000     Fax: (908) 277-8078     www.crbard.com

*Mfr. health care products.*

**C.R. Bard Ireland Ltd., Parkmore Industrial Estate, Galway, Ireland**

## BATES WORLDWIDE INC.

405 Lexington Ave., New York, NY, 10174

Tel: (212) 297-7000     Fax: (212) 986-0270     www.batesww.com

*Advertising, marketing, public relations and media consulting.*

**Bates Healthcom, 9 Upper Pembroke St., Dublin 1, Ireland**

Tel: 353-1-676-0221   Fax: 353-1-676-5201   Contact: Joe Clancy, CEO

**Bates Ireland, 9 Upper Pembroke St., Dublin 2, Ireland**

Tel: 353-1-676-0221   Fax: 353-1-676-5201   Contact: Joe Clancy, CEO

## BAXTER HEALTHCARE CORPORATION

One Baxter Parkway, Deerfield, IL, 60015

Tel: (847) 948-2000     Fax: (847) 948-3948     www.baxter.com

*Pharmaceutical preparations, surgical/medical instruments and cardiovascular products.*

**Baxter Healthcare Ltd., Unit 7, Deansgrange Ind. Estate, Blackrock, Co. Dublin, Ireland**

## BDO SEIDMAN, LLP    BELGIUM

Two Prudential Plaza, 180 N. Stetson Ave., Ste. 2300, Chicago, IL, 60601

Tel: (312) 240-1236     Fax: (312) 240-3329     www.bdo.com

*International accounting and financial consulting firm.*

**BDO Simpson Xavier, Simpson Xavier Court, Merchants Quay, Dublin 8, Ireland**

Tel: 353-1-617-0100   Fax: 353-1-679-0111   Contact: Liam Dowdall

## BEAR STEARNS & CO., INC.

245 Park Ave., New York, NY, 10167

Tel: (212) 272-2000     Fax: (212) 272-3092     www.bearstearns.com

*Investment banking, securities broker/dealer and investment advisory services.*

**Bear Stearns Bank plc, Blk 8 Harcourt Center - Fl. 3, Charlotte Way, Dublin 2, Ireland**

Tel: 353-1-402-6200   Fax: 353-1-402-6222

## BECKMAN COULTER, INC.

4300 N. Harbor Boulevard, Fullerton, CA, 92834

Tel: (714) 871-4848     Fax: (714) 773-8898     www.beckmancoulter.com

*Develop/mfr./marketing automated systems and supplies for biological analysis.*

**Labplan (Bioresearch), Allenwood Enterprise Park, Naas, Kildare Ireland**

## BERLITZ CROSS-CULTURAL TRAINING INC.

400 Alexander Park, Princeton, NJ, 08540

Tel: (609) 514-9650        Fax: (609) 514-9689        www.berlitz.com

*Consulting and management training services to bridge cultural gaps for international travelers as well as for business transferees and families.*

**Berlitz Language Centre, 3 West Pier Business Campus, County Dublin, Dun Laoghaire, Ireland**

## BEST WESTERN INTERNATIONAL

6201 North 24th Place, Phoenix, AZ, 85106

Tel: (602) 957-4200        Fax: (602) 957-5740        www.bestwestern.com

*International hotel chain.*

**Howth Lodge Hotel, Dublin, Ireland**

## BESTFOODS, INC.

700 Sylvan Ave., International Plaza, Englewood Cliffs, NJ, 07632-9976

Tel: (201) 894-4000        Fax: (201) 894-2186        www.bestfoods.com

*Consumer foods products; corn refining.*

**Knorr Bestfoods Ltd., Goldenbridge, Inchicore, Dublin 12, Ireland**

Tel: 353-1-455-7638   Fax: 353-1-455-3292   Contact: Richard Oppenheim, Mgr.

## BETZDEARBORN

4636 Somerton Road, PO Box 3002, Trevose, PA, 19053-6783

Tel: (215) 953-2568        Fax: (215) 953-5524        www.betzdearborn.com

*Mfr. water/wastewater and process system treatment chemicals and services.*

**BetzDearborn Ireland Ltd., 34 Greenmount Office Park, Harolds Cross Bridge, Dublin 6W, Ireland**

## BIJUR LUBRICATING CORPORATION

50 Kocher Dr., Bennington, VT, 05201-1994

Tel: (802) 447-2174        Fax: (802) 447-1365        www.bijur.com

*Design/mfr. pumps.*

**Bijur Ireland Ltd., Gort Rd., Ennis, County Clare, Ireland**

Tel: 353-65-21543   Fax: 353-65-20327   Contact: Martin Egan, Operations Mgr.   Emp: 80

## BISSELL INC.

2345 Walker Road, NW, Grand Rapids, MI, 49504

Tel: (616) 453-4451        Fax: (616) 453-1383        www.bissell.com

*Mfr. home care products.*

**Bissell Ireland, Donroe Rd., County Louth, Drogheda, Ireland**

Tel: 353-41-36491

## BLACK & VEATCH LLP

8400 Ward Pkwy., PO Box 8405, Kansas City, MO, 64114

Tel: (913) 339-2000        Fax: (913) 339-2934        www.bv.com

*Engineering, architectural and construction services.*

**Paterson Candy Ltd., Fitzwilliam Business Centre, 26/27 Upper Pembroke St., Dublin 2, Ireland**

Tel: 353-1-662-0448   Fax: 353-1-662-0365   Contact: John Devlin

## BORDEN INC.

180 East Broad Street, Columbus, OH, 43215-3799

Tel: (614) 225-4000        Fax: (614) 220-6453        www.bordenfamily.com

*Mfr. packaged foods, consumer adhesives, housewares and industrial chemicals.*

**Borden Foods Ireland, Athy, County Kildare, Ireland**

Tel: 353-507-31211

## BOSE CORPORATION

The Mountain, Framingham, MA, 01701-9168

Tel: (508) 879-7330     Fax: (508) 766-7543     www.bose.com

*Mfr. quality audio equipment/speakers.*

**BOSE Ireland,  Castleblayney Rd., Carrickmacross, County Monaghan, Ireland**

## BOSTON SCIENTIFIC CORPORATION

One Scientific Place, Natick, MA, 01760-1537

Tel: (508) 650-8000     Fax: (508) 650-8923     www.bsci.com

*Mfr./distributes medical devices for use in minimally invasive surgeries.*

**Boston Scientific Ireland Ltd.,  Ballybrit Business Park, Galway, Ireland**

Tel: 353-91-756300    Fax: 353-91-757398

## BOURNS INC.

1200 Columbia Avenue, Riverside, CA, 92507

Tel: (909) 781-5500     Fax: (909) 781-5006     www.bourns.com

*Mfr. resistive components and networks, precision potentiometers, panel controls, switches, transducers and surge protectors..*

**Bourns Electronics (Ireland),  Mahon Industrial Estate, Blackrock, Cork, Ireland**

## BOWNE & COMPANY, INC.

345 Hudson Street, New York, NY, 10014

Tel: (212) 924-5500     Fax: (212) 229-3420     www.bowne.com

*Financial printing and foreign language translation, localization (software), internet design and maintenance and facilities management.*

**Bowne International,  65/66 Lower Mount Street, Dublin 2, Ireland**

Tel: 353-1-614-6300   Fax: 353-1-614-6333

## BRIGHTPOINT, INC.

6402 Corporate Dr., Indianapolis, IN, 46278

Tel: (317) 297-6100     Fax: (317) 297-6114     www.brightpoint.com

*Mfr./distribution of mobile phones.*

**Brightpoint Ireland Ltd.,  Unit 6 Oak Court, Western Business Park, Dublin 12, Ireland**

Tel: 353-1-460-3300   Fax: 353-1-460-3330

## BRINK'S INC.

Thorndal Circle, Darien, CT, 06820

Tel: (203) 662-7800     Fax: (203) 662-7968     www.brinks.com

*Security transportation.*

**Brink's Allied Limited,  Dublin, Ireland**

## BRISTOL-MYERS SQUIBB COMPANY

345 Park Ave., New York, NY, 10154-0037

Tel: (212) 546-4000     Fax: (212) 546-4020     www.bms.com

*Pharmaceutical and food preparations, medical and surgical instruments.*

**ConvaTec Ireland (Eire),  2 St. John's Court, Santry, Dublin 9, Eire, Ireland**

**Irish Plant - Linson, Ltd.,  Swords,County Dublin, Ireland**

## BROWN-FORMAN CORPORATION

PO Box 1080, 850 Dixie Hwy., Louisville, KY, 40201-1080

Tel: (502) 585-1100     Fax: (502) 774-7876     www.brown-forman.com

*Mfr./distributor distilled spirits, wine, china, crystal, silverware and luggage.*

**Clintock Ltd.,  Fox & Geese, Robinhood Rd., Clondalkin Dublin 22, Ireland**

## BUCKEYE TECHNOLOGIES, INC.

1001 Tillman St., Memphis, TN, 38108-0407

Tel: (901) 320-8100      Fax: (901) 320-8131      www.bkitech.com

*Mfr. specialty cellulose and absorbency products.*

**Buckeye Technologies UK, Cork, Ireland**

## BUDGET GROUP, INC.

125 Basin St., Ste. 210, Daytona Beach, FL, 32114

Tel: (904) 238-7035      Fax: (904) 238-7461      www.budgetrentacar.com

*Car and truck rental system.*

**Budget Rent A Car, Ferry Port, 151 Lower Drumcondra Rd., Dublin, Ireland**
Tel: 353-1-837-9611

**Budget Rent A Car, Galway Airport, Ireland**
Tel: 353-91--566-376

**Budget Rent A Car, International Hotel, Kenmare St., Killarney, Ireland**
Tel: 353-64-34341

**Budget Rent A Car, Cork Airport, Cork, Ireland**

## LEO BURNETT, DIV. B-COM 3 GROUP

35 West Wacker Drive, Chicago, IL, 60601

Tel: (312) 220-5959      Fax: (312) 220-6533      www.bcom3group.com

*Engaged in advertising, marketing, media buying and planning, and public relations.*

**Young Advertising, Dublin, Ireland**

## BURNS INTERNATIONAL SERVICES CORPORATION

200 S. Michigan Ave., Chicago, IL, 60604

Tel: (312) 322-8500      Fax: (312) 322-8398      www.burnsinternational.com

*Security services.*

**Burns International Security Services, Phibsboro Tower 3/F, Phibsboro Dublin, 7 Ireland**

## BUSH BOAKE ALLEN INC.

7 Mercedes Drive, Montvale, NJ, 07645

Tel: (201) 391-9870      Fax: (201) 391-0860      www.bushboakeallen.com

*Mfr. aroma chemicals for fragrances and flavor products for seasonings.*

**Bush Boake Allen Ltd., Bracetown Office Park, Clonee, Country Meath, Ireland**
Tel: 353-1-825-1211

## C&D TECHNOLOGIES

1400 Union Meeting Road, Blue Bell, PA, 19422

Tel: (215) 619-2700      Fax: (215) 619-7840      www.cdtechno.com

*Mfr./produce electrical power storage and conversion products and industrial batteries.*

**C&D Technologies, Shannon, Ireland**

## CAMBREX CORPORATION

1 Meadowlands Plaza, East Rutherford, NJ, 07063

Tel: (201) 804-3000      Fax: (201) 804-9852      www.cambrex.com

*human health, animal health/agriculture and Mfr. biotechnology products and produce specialty chemicals.*

**Irotec Laboratories Limited, Little Island, Cork, Ireland**
**Irotec Laboratories Limited, Little Island, Cork, Ireland**

## CAMBRIDGE TECHNOLOGY PARTNERS, INC.

8 Cambridge Center, Cambridge, MA, 02142

Tel: (617) 374-9800 Fax: (617) 914-8300 www.ctp.com

*Engaged in e-commerce consultancy.*

**Cambridge Technology Partners, Inc., 118-119 Lower Baggot Street, Dublin 2, Ireland**

Tel: 353-1-607-9000 Fax: 353-1-607-9001

## CATERPILLAR INC.

100 NE Adams Street, Peoria, IL, 61629-6105

Tel: (309) 675-1000 Fax: (309) 675-1182 www.cat.com

*Mfr. earth/material-handling and construction machinery and equipment and engines.*

**Caterpillar International Finance plc., Wicklow, Ireland**

**Servtech Ltd., Dublin, Ireland**

## CBS CORPORATION

51 West 52 Street, New York, NY, 10019

Tel: (212) 975-4321 Fax: (212) 975-9387 www.cbs.com

*TV/radio broadcasting, mfr. electronic systems for industry/defense, financial and environmental services.*

**Thermo King Europe, Monivea Rd., Mervue, Galway, Ireland**

## CCI/TRIAD

804 Las Cimas Pkwy., Ste. 200, Austin, TX, 78746

Tel: (512) 328-2300 Fax: (512) 328-8209 www.cci-triad.com

*Information retrieval systems.*

**Tridex Systems Ireland Ltd., Longforg Office, Templemichael, Ballinalee Rd., Longford, Co Longford, Ireland**

Tel: 353-43-41857 Fax: 353-43-41858

## CDI CORPORATION

1717 Arch Street, 35th Fl., Philadelphia, PA, 19103

Tel: (215) 569-2200 Fax: (215) 569-1300 www.cdicorp.com

*Engineering, technical and temporary personnel services.*

**Anders Elite, 63 Lower Mount Street, Dublin, Ireland**

## CH2M HILL INC.

6060 South Willow Drive, Greenwood Village, CO, 80111

Tel: (303) 771-0900 Fax: (303) 770-2616 www.ch2m.com

*Consulting engineers, planners, economists and scientists.*

**CH2M Hill, High Street, Tallaght, Dublin 24, Ireland**

## CHEMFAB CORPORATION

701 Daniel Webster Hwy., PO Box 1137, Merrimack, NH, 03054

Tel: (603) 424-9000 Fax: (603) 424-9028 www.chemfab.com

*Mfr. advanced polymer materials.*

**Chemfab Europe, Fergus Lodge, Clonroad Bridge Ennis, County Clare, Ireland**

Tel: 353-65-20988 Fax: 353-65-20993

## THE CHUBB CORPORATION

15 Mountain View Road, Warren, NJ, 07061-1615

Tel: (908) 580-2000 Fax: (908) 580-3606 www.chubb.com

*Holding company for property and casualty insurance.*

**Chubb Insurance Co. of Europe, SA, 50 Dawson St., Dublin 2, Ireland**

Tel: 353-1-670-7070 Fax: 353-1-670-7271

## CISCO SYSTEMS, INC.

170 West Tasman Drive, San Jose, CA, 95134-1706

Tel: (408) 526-4000    Fax: (408) 526-4100    www.cisco.com

*Develop/mfr./market computer hardware and software networking systems.*

**Cisco Systems, Dunluce House, Eastpoint, Dublin 3 Ireland**

Tel: 353-1-819-2700   Fax: 353-1-819-2701

**Cisco Systems Ltd., Europa House 4th Fl., Harcourt St., Dublin 2, Ireland**

Tel: 353-1-475-4244   Fax: 353-1-475-4778

## CITIGROUP, INC.

153 East 53rd Street, New York, NY, 10043

Tel: (212) 559-1000    Fax: (212) 559-3646    www.citigroup.com

*Provides insurance and financial services worldwide.*

**Citibank N.A., IFSC House, Custom House Quay, Dublin 1, Ireland**

Contact: Aidan M. Brady, Mgr.

## CLEAR CHANNEL COMMUNICATIONS

200 East Basse Road, San Antonio, TX, 78209

Tel: (210) 822-2828    Fax: (210) 822-2299    www.clearchannel.com

*Programs and sells airtime for radio stations and owns and places outdoor advertising displays.*

**More Group, Beech House, Beech Hill Road - Donnybrook, Dublin 4, Ireland**

Tel: 353-1-478-4500   Fax: 353-1-478-4582   Contact: Terry Buckley, Mgr.

## CNA FINANCIAL CORPORATION

CNA Plaza, Chicago, IL, 60685

Tel: (312) 822-5000    Fax: (312) 822-6419    www.cna.com

*Commercial property/casualty insurance policies.*

**Galway Insurance Company, Galway, Ireland**

## COLGATE-PALMOLIVE COMPANY

300 Park Ave., New York, NY, 10022

Tel: (212) 310-2000    Fax: (212) 310-2919    www.colgate.com

*Mfr. pharmaceuticals, cosmetics, toiletries and detergents.*

**Colgate-Palmolive Ireland Ltd., Unit C Airport Industrial Estate, Swords Rd., Santry Dublin 9, Ireland**

## COMPAQ COMPUTER CORPORATION

20555 State Highway 249, PO Box 692000, Houston, TX, 77269-2000

Tel: (281) 370-0670    Fax: (281) 514-1740    www.compaq.com

*Develop/mfr. personal computers.*

**Compaq EMEA Service Center, 6-7 Blackrock Business Park, Carysfort Ave., Blackrock, County Dublin, Ireland**

Tel: 353-1-214-1000   Fax: 353-1-214-1001

## COMPUTER ASSOCIATES INTERNATIONAL INC.

One Computer Associates Plaza, Islandia, NY, 11788

Tel: (516) 342-5224    Fax: (516) 342-5329    www.cai.com

*Integrated business software for enterprise computing and information management, application development, manufacturing, financial applications and professional services.*

**Computer Associates Plc, Europa House 2nd Fl., Harcourt St., Dublin 2 IRE 18, Ireland**

Tel: 353-1-478-0800

## CONCURRENT COMPUTER CORPORATION

4375 River Green Pkwy., Duluth, GA, 30096

Tel: (678) 258-4000　　Fax: (678) 258-4300　　www.ccur.com

*Mfr. computer systems and software.*

**Concurrent Computers (Ireland) Ltd., 30 Green Mount Office Park, Harolds Cross, Dublin 6, Ireland**

## CONOCO INC.

PO Box 2197, 600 N. Dairy Ashford, Houston, TX, 77252

Tel: (281) 293-1000　　Fax: (281) 293-1440　　www.conoco.com

*Oil, gas, coal, chemicals and minerals.*

**Conoco Ireland Ltd., Conoco House, Deansgrange, Blackrock, Dublin, Ireland**

## COOPER CAMERON CORPORATION

515 Post Oak Blvd., Ste.1200, Houston, TX, 77027

Tel: (713) 513-3300　　Fax: (713) 513-3355　　www.coopercameron.com

*Mfr. oil and gas industry equipment.*

**Cooper Cameron Ireland, Aghafad, Longford, Ireland**

Tel: 353-43-45301

## COOPER INDUSTRIES INC.

6600 Travis Street, Ste. 5800, Houston, TX, 77002

Tel: (713) 209-8400　　Fax: (713) 209-8995　　www.cooperindustries.com

*Mfr./distributor electrical products, tools, hardware and automotive products, fuses and accessories for electronic applications and circuit boards.*

**Cooper Automotive, Naas Kildare, Ireland**

## A.T. CROSS COMPANY

One Albion Road, Lincoln, RI, 02865

Tel: (401) 333-1200　　Fax: (401) 334-2861　　www.cross.com

*Mfr. writing instruments, leads, erasers and ink refills.*

**A.T. Cross Ltd., One Cleaghmore, Ballinasloe, County Galway, Ireland**

Tel: 353-905-31400

## CROWN CORK & SEAL COMPANY, INC.

One Crown Way, Philadelphia, PA, 19154-4599

Tel: (215) 698-5100　　Fax: (215) 698-5201　　www.crowncork.com

*Mfr. metal and plastic packaging, including steel and aluminum cans for food, beverage and household products.*

**The Irish Crown Cork Co. Ltd., Church Field Industrial Estate, Cork, Ireland**

## CROWN EQUIPMENT CORPORATION

40 South Washington Street, New Bremen, OH, 45869

Tel: (419) 629-2311　　Fax: (419) 629-2900　　www.crownlift.com

*Mfr./sales/services forklift trucks, stackers.*

**Crown Equipment, Galway, Ireland**

## DAMES & MOORE GROUP

911 Wilshire Boulevard, Ste. 700, Los Angeles, CA, 90017

Tel: (213) 996-2200　　Fax: (213) 996-2290　　www.dames.com

*Engineering, environmental and construction management services.*

**Dames & Moore, 2214 Richmond Business Campus, North Brunswick St., Dublin 7, Ireland**

**D'ARCY MASIUS BENTON & BOWLES INC. (DMB&B)**

1675 Broadway, New York, NY, 10019

Tel: (212) 468-3622      Fax: (212) 468-2987      www.dmbb.com

*Full service international advertising and communications group.*

**DMB&B Europe, Stephens House, 7/8 Upper Mount St., Dublin 2, Ireland**

**DATA GENERAL CORPORATION**

4400 Computer Drive, Westboro, MA, 01580

Tel: (508) 898-5000      Fax: (508) 366-1319      www.dg.com

*Design, mfr. general purpose computer systems and peripheral products and services.*

**Data General Ireland Ltd., Haddington Court, Haddington Rd., Dublin 4, Ireland**

**Data General Ireland Ltd., Avoca Court, Temple Road, Blackrock Dublin, Ireland**

**Data General Ireland Ltd., 9 Wellington Park, Belfast BT9 6DJ, Ireland**

**DDB NEEDHAM WORLDWIDE INC.**

437 Madison Ave., New York, NY, 10022

Tel: (212) 415-2000      Fax: (212) 415-3417      www.ddbn.com

*Advertising agency.*

**Peter Owens DDB Worldwide, Dublin, Ireland**

**DELL COMPUTER CORPORATION**

One Dell Way, Round Rock, TX, 78682-2222

Tel: (512) 338-4400      Fax: (512) 728-3653      www.dell.com

*Direct marketer and supplier of computer systems.*

**Dell Computer Corporation, Bogdall Rd., Bray County, Wickow, Ireland**

Tel: 353-1-286-0500   Fax: 353-1-286-2020   Contact: Philip Van Houtte, Mng. Dir.

**Dell Products Europe BV, Raheen Industrial Estate, Limerick, Ireland**

Tel: 353-61-304091   Fax: 353-61-304090   Contact: Phil Hubble, Mng. Dir.

**DELOITTE TOUCHE TOHMATSU INTERNATIONAL**

1633 Broadway, New York, NY, 10019

Tel: (212) 492-4000      Fax: (212) 392-4154      www.deloitte.com

*Accounting, audit, tax and management consulting services.*

**Deloitte & Touche, Deloitte & Touche House, Earlsfort Terrace, Dublin 2, Ireland**

**Deloitte & Touche, 25 Stephen St., Sligo, Ireland**

**DELTA AIR LINES INC.**

PO Box 20706, Atlanta, GA, 30320-6001

Tel: (404) 715-2600      Fax: (404) 715-5494      www.delta-air.com

*Major worldwide airline; international air transport services.*

**Delta Air Lines Inc., Dublin, Ireland**

**DeMATTEIS CONSTRUCTION CORPORATION**

820 Elmont Road, Elmont, NY, 11003

Tel: (516) 285-5500      Fax: (516) 285-6950

*Real estate development and construction services.*

**DeMatteis Ireland Ltd., 21 Fitzwilliam Place, Dublin 2, Ireland**

Tel: 353-1-662-1188   Fax: 353-1-662-1191   Contact: Fergus J. Rainey, Mng. Dir.

**DHL WORLDWIDE EXPRESS**

50 California Avenue, San Francisco, CA, 94111

Tel: (415) 677-6100      Fax: (415) 824-9700      www.dhl.com

*Worldwide air express carrier.*

**DHL Worldwide Express, Dublin Airport Col., Dublin, Ireland**

Tel: 353-1-844-4111

## DICTAPHONE CORPORATION

3191 Broadbridge Ave., Stratford, CT, 06497-2559

Tel: (203) 381-7000     Fax: (203) 381-7100     www.dictaphone.com

*Mfr./sale dictation, telephone answering and multi-channel voice communications recording systems.*

**Dictaphone Company Ltd,  Dublin, Ireland**

Tel: 353-1-282-5222

## R.R. DONNELLEY & SONS COMPANY

77 West Wacker Drive, Chicago, IL, 60601-1696

Tel: (312) 326-8000     Fax: (312) 326-8543     www.rrdonnelley.com

*Commercial printing, allied communication services.*

**Irish Printers (Holdings) Ltd.,  Clonshaugh Industrial Estate, Clonshaugh, Dublin 17, Ireland**

## DONNELLY CORPORATION

49 W. 3rd St., Holland, MI, 49423-2813

Tel: (616) 786-7000     Fax: (616) 786-6034     www.donnelly.com

*Mfr. fabricated, molded and coated glass products for the automotive and electronics industries.*

**Donnelly Electronics Ireland,  IDA Industrial Estate, Ballinalee Road, Longford, Ireland**

Tel: 353-45-897101    Fax: 353-45-897157    Contact: David Watson, Mgr.

**Donnelly Mirrors Limited/Mirror Systems,  County Kildare, Naas, Ireland**

Tel: 353-725-5350    Contact: David Watson

## DOUBLECLICK, INC.

450 West 33rd Street, New York, NY, 10001

Tel: (212) 683-0001     Fax: (212) 889-0062     www.doubleclick.net

*Engaged in online advertising.*

**Doubleclick, Ltd.,  The Riverside Centre , 8-11 Sir John Rogersons Quay, Dublin 2, Ireland**

## DRAKE BEAM MORIN INC.

101 Huntington Ave., Boston, MA, 02199

Tel: (617) 375-9500     Fax: (617) 267-2011     www.dbm.com

*Human resource management consulting and training.*

**DBM Ireland,  3 Argos House, Greenmount Office Park, Dublin 6W, Ireland**

Tel: 353-1-4533-591    Fax: 353-1-4533-640

## DRIVER-HARRIS COMPANY

308 Middlesex Street, Harrison, NJ, 07029

Tel: (973) 483-4802     Fax: (973) 483-4806

*Mfr. non-ferrous alloys.*

**Irish Driver-Harris Co. Ltd.,  5A Ballymount Trading Estate, Lower Ballymount Rd., Walkinstown, Dublin 12, Ireland**

Tel: 353-1-450-6935    Fax: 353-1-450-6330    Contact: Jim Kinsella

**Irish Driver-Harris Co. Ltd.,  John St., New Ross, Wexford, Ireland**

Tel: 353-51-21405    Fax: 353-51-22983    Contact: A. J. Hartford

## E.I. DU PONT DE NEMOURS & COMPANY

1007 Market Street, Wilmington, DE, 19898

Tel: (302) 774-1000     Fax: (302) 774-7321     www.dupont.com

*Mfr./sale diversified chemicals, plastics, specialty products and fibers.*

**Conoco Ireland Ltd.,  Dublin, Ireland**

## THE DUN & BRADSTREET CORPORATION

1 Diamond Hill Road, Murray Hill, NJ, 07974

Tel: (908) 665-5000    Fax: (908) 665-5524    www.dnbcorp.com

*Provides corporate credit, marketing and accounts-receivable management services and publishes credit ratings and financial information.*

**Dun & Bradstreet Ireland Ltd., Holbrook House, Holles St., Dublin 2, Ireland**

Tel: 353-1-764-230

## EAGLE GLOBAL LOGISTICS (EGL)

15350 Vickery Drive, Houston, TX, 77032

Tel: (281) 618-3100    Fax: (281) 618-3100    www.eaglegl.com

*Ocean/air freight forwarding, customs brokerage, packing and wholesale, logistics management and insurance.*

**Reindear Freight International, Smithstown Ind. Est., County Clare, Shannon, Ireland**

Tel: 353-61-362766    Fax: 353-61-362-732

**Reindear Freight International, John F. Kennedy Rd., Naas Rd., Dublin 12, Ireland**

Tel: 353-1-450-9444    Fax: 353-1-450-9468

**Reindear Freight International, Cargo Terminal, Dublin Airport, Dublin, Ireland**

Tel: 353-1-844-5171    Fax: 353-1-842-7882

**Reindear Freight International, 4/5 Citylink Park, Forge Hill, Cork, Ireland**

Tel: 353-21-965-422    Fax: 353-21-314-140

## EASTMAN KODAK COMPANY

343 State Street, Rochester, NY, 14650

Tel: (716) 724-4000    Fax: (716) 724-1089    www.kodak.com

*Develop/mfr. photo and chemicals products, information management/video/copier systems, fibers/plastics for various industry.*

**Kodak Ireland Ltd., Kodak House, Pottery Rd., Dun Laoghaire County Dublin, Ireland**

## ECOLAB INC.

370 N. Wabasha Street, St. Paul, MN, 55102

Tel: (651) 293-2233    Fax: (651) 293-2379    www.ecolab.com

*Develop/mfr. premium cleaning, sanitizing and maintenance products and services for the hospitality, institutional, and residential markets.*

**Ecolab Ltd., Dublin, Ireland**

Tel: 353-1-286-8225

## ECOLOGY AND ENVIRONMENT INC.

368 Pleasant View Drive, Lancaster, NY, 14086-1397

Tel: (716) 684-8060    Fax: (716) 684-0844    www.ecolen.com

*Environmental, scientific and engineering consulting.*

**Ecology and Environment Ltd., Poulgorm, Maryboto 4,11, Douglas, Cork, Ireland**

## EDELMAN PUBLIC RELATIONS WORLDWIDE

200 East Randolph Drive, 62nd Fl., Chicago, IL, 60601

Tel: (312) 240-3000    Fax: (312) 240-0596    www.edelman.com

*International independent public relations firm.*

**Edelman PR Worldwide, Huguenot House 5th Fl., 35/38 Stephens Green, Dublin 2, Ireland**

Tel: 353-1-678-9333    Fax: 353-1-661-4408    Contact: John Mahony, Mng. Dir.

### J.D. EDWARDS & COMPANY

One Technology Way, Denver, CO, 80237

Tel: (303) 334-4000     Fax: (303) 334-4970     www.jdedwards.com

*Computer software products.*

**Software Resources, 7 South Leinster Street, Dublin, Ireland**

Tel: 353-1-678-9299     Fax: 353-1-678-9544

### EFCO

1800 NE Broadway Ave., Des Moines, IA, 50316-0386

Tel: (515) 266-1141     Fax: (515) 266-7970     www.efco-usa.com

*Mfr. systems for concrete construction.*

**EFCO, 2B Crofton Ct., Naas, Co. Kildare, Ireland**

### EG&G INC.

900 Clopper Road, Ste. 200, Gaithersburg, MD, 20878

Tel: (301) 840-3000     Fax: (301) 590-0502     www.egginc.com

*Diversified R/D, mfr. and services.*

**EG&G Intl./Sealol Div., Shannon Free Airport, County Clare, Ireland**

**EG&G Ireland/Instruments Div., Blanchardstown Industrial Park, Blanchardstown, Dublin 15, Ireland**

### ELECTRONIC DATA SYSTEMS CORPORATION (EDS)

5400 Legacy Dr., Plano, TX, 75024

Tel: (972) 605-6000     Fax: (972) 605-2643     www.eds.com

*Provides professional services; management consulting, e.solutions, business process management and information solutions.*

**EDS Ireland Ltd., Treasury Building, Lower Grand Canal Street, Dublin 2 Ireland**

Tel: 353-1-703-9000

### EMC CORPORATION

35 Parkwood Drive, Hopkinton, MA, 01748-9103

Tel: (508) 435-1000     Fax: (508) 435-8884     www.emc.com

*Designs/supplies intelligent enterprise storage and retrieval technology for open systems, mainframes and midrange environments.*

**EMC Computer Systems Ireland, Castlecourt Ctr., Castleknock, Dublin 15, Ireland**

Tel: 353-1-475-4172

### ENERGIZER HOLDINGS, INC.

800 Chouteau Avenue, St. Louis, MO, 63164

Tel: (314) 982-2970     Fax: (214) 982-2752     www.energizer.com

*Mfr. Eveready and Energizer brand batteries and lighting products.*

**Eveready Ltd., PO Box 373A, 17 Portobello Harbour, Dublin 8 Ireland**

Tel: 353-1-478-3764     Fax: 353-1-475-2327

### EPICOR SOFTWARE CORPORATION

195 Technology Drive, Irvine, CA, 92618

Tel: (949) 585-4000     Fax: (949) 450-4419     www.epicor.com

*Mfr. software for e-business.*

**Epicor Ireland, Park House - North Circular Road, Dublin 7, Ireland**

Tel: 353-1-868-1250     Fax: 353-1-868-1255

### ERNST & YOUNG, LLP

787 Seventh Ave., New York, NY, 10019

Tel: (212) 773-3000     Fax: (212) 773-6350     www.eyi.com

*Accounting and audit, tax and management consulting services.*

**Ernst & Young (Ireland), Kiltartan House, Fosters St., Galway, Ireland**

**Ernst & Young (Ireland), Barrington House, Barrington St., Limerick, Ireland**

**Ernst & Young (Ireland), Annaville House, Newtown, Waterford, Ireland**

**Ernst & Young (Ireland), Ernst & Young Bldg., Harcourt Centre, Harcourt St., Dublin 2 Ireland**

Tel: 353-1-4750555   Fax: 353-1-4750555   Contact: Jim Ryan

**Ernst & Young (Ireland), Stapleton House, 89 South Mall, Cork, Ireland**

## ESCO ELECTRONICS CORPORATION

8888 Ladue Road, Ste. 200, St. Louis, MO, 63124-2090

Tel:  (314) 213-7200        Fax:  (314) 213-7250        www.escostl.com

*Electronic subassemblies and components.*

**Filtertek, B.V., Newcastle West, County Limerick, Ireland**

## EXPEDITORS INTERNATIONAL OF WASHINGTON INC.

1015 Third Avenue, 12th Fl., Seattle, WA, 98104-1182

Tel:  (206) 674-3400        Fax:  (206) 682-9777        www.expd.com

*Air/ocean freight forwarding, customs brokerage, international logistics solutions.*

**Expeditors Sea Sky Limited, Units 1-3 University Hall Industrial Park, Sarsfield Road, Doughcloyne County Cork, Ireland**

Tel: 353-21-346111   Fax: 353-21-346112

**Expeditors Sea Sky Limited, Unit 9, Boeing Road Airways Industrial Estate, Cloghran Dublin 17, Ireland**

Tel: 353-1-816-1800

## E-Z-EM INC.

717 Main Street, Westbury, NY, 11590

Tel:  (516) 333-8230        Fax:  (516) 333-8278        www.ezem.com

*World's leading supplier of barium contrast media for medical imaging and accessories.*

**AngioDynamics Ltd., Enniscorthy, County Wexford, Ireland**

## FileNET CORPORATION

3565 Harbor Boulevard, Costa Mesa, CA, 92626

Tel:  (714) 966-3400        Fax:  (714) 966-3490        www.filenet.com

*Provides integrated document management (IDM) software and services for internet and client server-based imaging, workflow, cold and electronic document management solutions.*

**FileNET Co. Ltd., FileNet House, Blk. W, East Point Business Park, Faiview, Dublin 3, Ireland**

Tel: 353-1-819-0100

## FLEXTRONICS INC. INTERNATIONAL

2241 Lundy Ave., San Jose, CA, 95131-1822

Tel:  (408) 428-1300        Fax:  (408) 428-0420        www.flextronics.com

*Contract manufacturer for electronics industry.*

**Flextronics International, Kilbarry Industrial Park, Dublin Hill, Cork, Ireland**

Tel: 353-21-300-530

**Flextronics International, National Technology Park, Plassey Limerick, Ireland**

## FLINT INK CORPORATION

4600 Arrowhead Drive, Ann Arbor, MI, 48105

Tel:  (734) 622-6000        Fax:  (734) 622-6060        www.flintink.com

*Manufacturer of printing inks and pigments.*

**Flint Ink Europe, Dunsinea Works, Ashtown, Dublin 15, Ireland**

Tel: 353-1-838-7300   Fax: 353-1-838-7382   Contact: Jim Mahony, Pres. Europe

## FLOWSERVE CORPORATION

222 W. Los Colinas Blvd., Irving, TX, 75039

Tel: (972) 443-6500    Fax: (972) 443-6858    www.flowserve.com

*Mfr. chemicals equipment, pumps, valves, filters, fans and heat exchangers.*

**Durco Ireland,  Shannon Town Ctr. #2, Shannon, County Clare, Ireland**

## FMC CORPORATION

200 E. Randolph Drive, Chicago, IL, 60601

Tel: (312) 861-6000    Fax: (312) 861-6141    www.fmc.com

*Produces chemicals and precious metals, mfr. machinery, equipment and systems for industrial, agricultural and government use.*

**FMC Smith Meter Inc./Flow Management Ltd.,  6 Turnpike Business Park, Ballymount, Dublin 2 Ireland**

## FORD MOTOR COMPANY

One American Road, Dearborn, MI, 48121

Tel: (313) 322-3000    Fax: (313) 322-9600    www.ford.com

*Mfr./sales motor vehicles.*

**Ford Motor Co.,  Marina, Cork, Ireland**

## FOREST LABORATORIES INC.

909 Third Ave., 23rd Fl., New York, NY, 10022

Tel: (212) 421-7850    Fax: (212) 750-9152    www.frx.com

*Pharmaceuticals.*

**Forest Laboratories Ireland Limited,  Clonshaugh Industrial Estate, Dublin 17, Ireland**
Tel: 353-1-8670477

**Tosara Products Limited,  Baldoyle Industrial Estate, Grange Road, Dublin 13  Ireland**

## FORMICA CORPORATION

10155 Reading Road, Cincinnati, OH, 45241-4805

Tel: (513) 786-3400    Fax: (513) 786-3082    www.formica.com

*Mfr. decorative laminate, adhesives and solvents.*

**Formica Ireland,  Block B - Arran Court, Arran Quay, Dublin 7 Ireland**

## FRANKLIN COVEY COMPANY

2200 W. Parkway Blvd., Salt Lake City, UT, 84119-2331

Tel: (801) 975-1776    Fax: (801) 977-1431    www.franklincovey.com

*Provides productivity and time management products and seminars.*

**Franklin Covey Ireland,  5 Argyle Street, Donybrook, Dublin 4, Ireland**
Tel: 353-1-668-1422    Fax: 353-1-668-1459

## FRITZ COMPANIES, INC.

706 Mission Street, Ste. 900, San Francisco, CA, 94103

Tel: (415) 904-8360    Fax: (415) 904-8661    www.fritz.com

*Integrated transportation, sourcing, distribution and customs brokerage services.*

**Fritz Companies Inc.,  Cork, Ireland**

## GATEWAY INC.

4545 Towne Centre Ct., San Diego, CA, 92121

Tel: (858) 799-3401    Fax: (858) 779-3459    www.gateway.com

*Computers manufacture, sales and services.*

**Gateway Ireland,  Clonshaugh Industrial Estate, Dublin 17, Ireland**

## GENCOR INDUSTRIES INC.

5201 N. Orange Blossom Trail, Orlando, FL, 32810

Tel: (407) 290-6000     Fax: (407) 578-0577     www.gencor.com

*Mfr. heat process systems, equipment, instrumentation and controls.*

**CPM Europe, Ltd., Industrial Estate, Whitemill, Wexford, Ireland**

Tel: 353-532-3633   Fax: 353-532-4646

## GENCORP INC.

Hwy. 50 and Aerojet Rd., Ranchero Cordova, CA, 95853

Tel: (916) 355-4000     Fax: (916) 355-2459     www.gencorp.com

*Mfr. aerospace/defense and automotive products.*

**Henniges Vehicle Sealing Div., Crossmolina Rd., Ballina, County Mayo, Ireland**

**Penn Racquet Sports Co (Ireland), Lynn Rd., Mullingar, County Westmeath, Ireland**

## GENERAL ELECTRIC CAPITAL CORPORATION

260 Long Ridge Road, Stamford, CT, 06927

Tel: (203) 357-4000     Fax: (203) 357-6489     www.gecapital.com

*Financial, property/casualty insurance, computer sales and trailer leasing services.*

**Employers Reinsurance Corp. (ERC), International House, International Financial Services Centre, Dublin 1, Ireland**

Tel: 353-1-60-54-200   Fax: 353-1-60-54-250

## GENERAL ELECTRIC COMPANY

3135 Easton Turnpike, Fairfield, CT, 06431

Tel: (203) 373-2211     Fax: (203) 373-3131     www.ge.com

*Diversified manufacturing, technology and services.*

**General Electric Co., Attn: Ireland Office, 3135 Easton Turnpike, Fairfield CT 06431 USA**

Tel: 518-438-6500

## GENERAL MOTORS CORPORATION

300 Renaissance Center, Detroit, MI, 48285

Tel: (313) 556-5000     Fax: (313) 556-5108     www.gm.com

*Mfr. full line vehicles, automotive electronics, commercial technologies, telecommunications, space, finance.*

**General Motors Distribution Ireland Ltd., Belgard Rd., Tallaght, Dublin, Ireland**

**Packard Electric Ireland Ltd., Airton Rd., Tallaght, Dublin, Ireland**

## GENERAL REINSURANCE CORPORATION

695 E. Main Street, Stamford, CT, 06904-2350

Tel: (203) 328-5000     Fax: (203) 328-6423     www.genre.com

*Reinsurance services worldwide.*

**Cologne Reinsurance Company (Dublin) Ltd., 1 George's Dock, I.F.S.C., Dublin 1, Ireland**

Tel: 353-1-670-2060   Fax: 353-1-670-2066   Contact: John B. Houldsworth, Mgr.

## GENERAL SEMICONDUCTOR, INC.

10 Melville Park Road., Melville, NY, 11747

Tel: (631) 847-3000     Fax: (631) 847-3236     www.gensemi.com

*Mfr. of low- and medium-current power rectifiers and transient voltage suppressors.*

**General Semiconductor - Ireland, Manufacturing Facility - Macroom, County Cork, Ireland**

Emp: 750

## GILEAD SCIENCES, INC.

333 Lakeside Dr, Foster City, CA, 94404

Tel: (650) 574-3000     Fax: (650) 578-9264     www.gilead.com

*Engaged in healthcare research and development; biotech treatments for viruses.*

**NeXstar Pharmaceuticals, Ltd.,  Unit 13 Stillorgan Industrial Park, Blackrock County Dublin, Ireland**

Tel: 353-1-295-2729   Fax: 353-1-295-2449

## THE GILLETTE COMPANY

Prudential Tower Building, Boston, MA, 02199

Tel: (617) 421-7000     Fax: (617) 421-7123     www.gillette.com

*Develop/mfr. personal care/use products: blades and razors, toiletries, cosmetics, stationery.*

**Braun Ireland Ltd.,  Carlow, Ireland**

**Gillette Ireland Ltd.,  Carlow, Ireland**

Contact: Roger Murphy, Gen. Mgr.

**Jafra Cosmetics Intl. Ltd.,  Foxrock Dublin, Ireland**

Contact: Roger Murphy, Gen. Mgr.

**Rethgil Properties Ltd.,  Dublin, Ireland**

Contact: Roger Murphy, Gen. Mgr.

## THE GORMAN-RUPP COMPANY

PO Box 1217, 305 Bowman St., Mansfield, OH, 44901

Tel: (419) 755-1011     Fax: (419) 755-1266     www.gormanrupp.com

*Mfr. pumps and related equipment, waste water and environmental equipment.*

**Gorman-Rupp Ireland,  Dublin, Ireland**

## GOW-MAC INSTRUMENT COMPANY

277 Broadhead Rd., Bethlehem, PA, 18017

Tel: (610) 954-9000     Fax: (610) 954-0599     www.gow-mac.com

*Mfr. analytical instruments*

**GOW-MAC Instrument Co. Ireland,  Bay K 14a, Industrial Estate, Shannon County Clare, Ireland**

Tel: 353-61-471632   Fax: 353-61-471042

## W. R. GRACE & COMPANY

7500 Grace Drive, Columbia, MD, 21044

Tel: (410) 531-4000     Fax: (410) 531-4367     www.grace.com

*Mfr. specialty chemicals and materials: packaging, health care, catalysts, construction, water treatment/process.*

**Grace Construction Products,  Unit 200 Holly Road, Western Industrial Estate, Naas Road, Dublin 12, Ireland**

Tel: 353-1-456-960   Fax: 353-1-4569-604

## GRANT THORNTON INTERNATIONAL

800 One Prudential Plaza, 130 E. Randolph Drive, Chicago, IL, 60601-6050

Tel: (312) 856-0001     Fax: (312) 616-7052     www.grantthornton.com

*Accounting, audit, tax and management consulting services.*

**Grant Thornton International,  Ashford House, Tara St., Dublin 2, Ireland**

Tel: 353-1-671-4677   Fax: 353-1-671-7209   Contact: James Murphy

## GREY GLOBAL GROUP

777 Third Ave., New York, NY, 10017

Tel: (212) 546-2000     Fax: (212) 546-1495     www.grey.com

*International advertising agency.*

**Campbell Grey & Associates,  6 Adelaide Ct., Adelaide Road, Dublin 2, Ireland**

## GRIFFITH LABORATORIES INC.

One Griffith Center, Alsip, IL, 60658

Tel: (708) 371-0900     Fax: (708) 597-3294     www.griffithlabs.com

*Mfr. industrial food ingredients and equipment.*

**Griffith Labs Ltd., Dublin, Ireland**

Tel: 353-1-493-6000   Fax: 353-1-493-6151

## GUY CARPENTER & COMPANY, INC.

Two World Trade Center, New York, NY, 10048

Tel: (212) 323-1000     Fax: (212) 313-4970     www.guycarp.com

*Engaged in global reinsurance and risk management.*

**Guy Carpenter & Company, Ltd., 25-28 Adelaide Road - 5th Floor, Dublin 2, Ireland**

Tel: 353-1605-3000   Fax: 353-1605-3010

## HADCO CORPORATION

8C Industrial Way, Salem, NH, 03079

Tel: (603) 898-8000     Fax: (603) 893-0025     www.hadco.com

*Mfr. electronic interconnect products.*

**Hadco Corporation, Rosse Center - Holland Road, National Technological Park, Limerick, Ireland**

## HAMILTON SUNSTRAND

One Hamilton Rd., Windsor Locks, CT, 06096-1010

Tel: (860) 654-6000     Fax: (860) 654-3469     www.hamiltonsunstrandcorp.com

*Design/mfr. aerospace systems for commercial, regional, corporate and military aircraft.*

**Hamilton Sunstrand Corp., Shannon, Ireland**

## HARRIS CALORIFIC COMPANY

2345 Murphy Boulevard, Gainesville, GA, 30501

Tel: (770) 536-8801     Fax: (770) 536-0544     www.harriscal.com

*Mfr./sales of gas welding and cutting equipment.*

**Harris Calorific Ireland,, Harris House, Charvey Lane, Rathnew, Wicklow, Ireland**

## H.J. HEINZ COMPANY

600 Grant Street, Pittsburgh, PA, 15219

Tel: (412) 456-5700     Fax: (412) 456-6128     www.heinz.com

*Processed food products and nutritional services.*

**Custom Foods Ltd., Dundalk, Ireland**

**H.J. Heinz Co. (Ireland) Ltd., Dublin, Ireland**

## HENRY SCHEIN, INC.

135 Duryea Rd., Melville, NY, 11747

Tel: (516) 843-5500     Fax: (516) 843-5658     www.henryschein.com

*Mfr. and supply dental equipment.*

**Henry Schein Ireland Ltd., Unit 61A - Longmile Centre, Longmile Road, Dublin 12 Ireland**

## THE HERTZ CORPORATION

225 Brae Boulevard, Park Ridge, NJ, 07656-0713

Tel: (201) 307-2000     Fax: (201) 307-2644     www.hertz.com

*Worldwide headquarters office for car rental, car leasing and equipment rental.*

**Hertz Rental Car, Dublin, Ireland**

## HEWITT ASSOCIATES LLC

100 Half Day Road, Lincolnshire, IL, 60069

Tel: (847) 295-5000    Fax: (847) 295-7634    www.hewitt.com

*Employee benefits consulting firm.*

**Hewitt Associates, Iveagh Court, 6 Harcourt Rd., Dublin 2, Ireland**

Tel: 353-1-418-9130

## HEWLETT-PACKARD COMPANY

3000 Hanover Street, Palo Alto, CA, 94304-1185

Tel: (650) 857-1501    Fax: (650) 857-5518    www.hp.com

*Mfr. computing, communications and measurement products and services.*

**Hewlett-Packard Ireland Ltd., Hewlett-Packard House, Stradbrook Rd., Black Rock, County Dublin, Ireland**

## HIGH VOLTAGE ENGINEERING COMPANY

401 Edgewater Place, Ste. 680, Wakefield, MA, 01880

Tel: (781) 224-1001    Fax: (781) 224-1011

*Holding company: industrial and scientific instruments.*

**HIVEC-Ireland, Rathealy Rd., Fermoy, Co. Cork, Ireland**

## HOOD SAILMAKERS INC.

23 Johnny Cake Hill, Middletown, RI, 02842

Tel: (401) 849-9400    Fax: (401) 849-9700    www.hood-sails.com

*Mfr. furling genoas, jibs, easy stow mainsails, and spinnakers.*

**Hood Textiles Ltd., McCurtain Hill, Clonakilty, County Cork, Ireland**

## HORWATH INTERNATIONAL ASSOCIATION

415 Madison Ave., New York, NY, 10017

Tel: (212) 838-5566    Fax: (212) 838-3636    www.horwath.com

*Public accountants and auditors.*

**Simpson Xavier, 4 Michael St., Limerick, Ireland**

**Simpson Xavier, Simpson Xavier Court, Merchants Quay, Dublin 8, Ireland**

## HOSKINS MFG. COMPANY

10776 Hall Road, PO Box 218, Hamburg, MI, 48139-0218

Tel: (810) 231-1900    Fax: (810) 231-4311    www.hoskinsmfgco.com

*Formulates and manufactures base metal thermocouple alloys; supplied as coils, spools, pack pails, or straight lengths.*

**Hoskins Alloys Intl., Kildare Enterprise Centre, Melitta Rd., Kildare Town, Co. Kildare, Ireland**

## HOUGHTON INTERNATIONAL INC.

PO Box 930, Madison & Van Buren Avenues, Valley Forge, PA, 19482-0930

Tel: (610) 666-4000    Fax: (610) 666-1376    www.houghtonintl.com

*Mfr. specialty chemicals, hydraulic fluids and lubricants.*

**Houghton Oils & Chemicals (Ireland) Ltd., Dunboyne Industrial Park, Dunboyne, County Meath, Ireland**

## HOWMEDICA OSTEONICS, INC.

359 Veterans Blvd., Rutherford, NJ, 07070

Tel: (201) 507-7300    Fax: (201) 935-4873    www.howmedica.com

*Mfr. of maxillofacial products (orthopedic implants).*

**Howmedica Ireland, Limerick, Ireland**

Tel: 353-61-471866

## HUNT SCREW & MFG. COMPANY

4117 North Kilpatrick Ave., Chicago, IL, 60641

Tel: (773) 283-6900      Fax: (773) 283-6068      www.huntscrew.com

*Machine parts and components.*

**Hunt Associates Ltd., Leislip, Kildare, Ireland**

## HYPERION SOLUTIONS CORPORATION

1344 Crossman Avenue, Sunnyvale, CA, 94089

Tel: (408) 744-9500      Fax: (408) 744-0400      www.hyperion.com

*Mfr. data analysis software tools.*

**Niederlassung Ireland, Regus Business Centre Block C, The Sweep Stakes Balls Bridge, Dublin 4, Ireland**

Tel: 35-31-631-9096

## IBM CORPORATION

New Orchard Road, Armonk, NY, 10504

Tel: (914) 765-1900      Fax: (914) 765-7382      www.ibm.com

*Information products, technology and services.*

**IBM Ireland Ltd., 2 Burlington Rd., Ballsbrige, Dublin 4, Ireland**

Tel: 353-1-660-3744    Fax: 353-1-850-401601

## IBP INC.

PO Box 515, Dakota City, NE, 68731

Tel: (402) 494-2061      Fax: (402) 241-2068      www.ibpinc.com

*Produce beef and pork, hides and associated products, animal feeds, pharmaceuticals.*

**Foodbrands America, Inc., Naas, County Kildare, Ireland**

## IDEX CORPORATION

630 Dundee Road, Ste. 400, Northbrook, IL, 60062

Tel: (847) 498-7070      Fax: (847) 498-3940      www.idexcorp.com

*Mfr. industrial pumps, lubrication systems, metal fabrication equipment, bending and clamping devices.*

**Viking Pump (Europe) Ltd., R-79 Shannon Industrial Estate, Shannon, County Clare, Ireland**

## ILLINOIS TOOL WORKS (ITW)

3600 West Lake Ave., Glenview, IL, 60025-5811

Tel: (847) 724-7500      Fax: (847) 657-4268      www.itw.com

*Mfr. gears, tools, fasteners, sealants, plastic and metal components for industrial, medical, etc.*

**Devcon Corp., Dublin, Ireland**

**ITW Hi-Cone Ltd., Mallow, Ireland**

## IMG (INTERNATIONAL MANAGEMENT GROUP)

1360 East Ninth Street, Ste. 100, Cleveland, OH, 44114

Tel: (216) 522-1200      Fax: (216) 522-1145      www.imgworld.com

*Manages athletes, sports academies and real estate facilities worldwide.*

**IMG, 5 Clare Street, Dublin 2, Ireland**

Tel: 353-1-661-7420    Fax: 353-1-661-7425

## INACOM CORPORATION

2001 Westside Parkway, Ste. 260, Alpharetta, GA, 30004

Tel: (770) 643-2419      Fax: (770) 993-6375      www.inacom.com

*Provider of technology management products and services; reselling microcomputer systems, work stations and networking and telecommunications equipment.*

**Bull CARA Group, 27 Willsborough Industrial Estate, Clonshaugh, Dublin 17 Ireland**

## INFONET SERVICES CORPORATION

2100 East Grand Ave., El Segundo, CA, 90245-1022

Tel: (310) 335-2600  Fax: (310) 335-4507  www.infonet.com

*Provider of Internet services and electronic messaging services.*

**Infonet Ireland, Alexandra House, Earlsfort Centre, Earlsfort Terrace Dublin 2 Ireland**

Tel: 353-1-602-4999  Fax: 353-1-676-8745

## INFORMIX CORPORATION

4100 Bohannon Drive, Menlo Park, CA, 95025

Tel: (650) 926-6300  Fax: (650) 926-6593  www.informix.com

*Designs and produces database management software, connectivity interfaces and gateways, and other computer applications.*

**Informix Europe Software Center, Westgate Business Park No. 4, Ballymount Road, Dublin 24, Ireland**

Tel: 353-1-405-1000

## INGERSOLL-RAND COMPANY

200 Chestnut Ridge Road, Woodcliff Lake, NJ, 07675

Tel: (201) 573-0123  Fax: (201) 573-3172  www.ingersoll-rand.com

*Mfr. compressors, rock drills, air tools, door hardware, ball bearings.*

**CPM Europe Ltd., Whitemill Industrial Estate, Wexford, Ireland**

**Ingersoll-Rand Co. Ireland Ltd., John F. Kennedy Dr., Bluebell, Dublin 12, Ireland**

## INTERGRAPH CORPORATION

One Madison Industrial Park, Huntsville, AL, 35894-0001

Tel: (256) 730-2000  Fax: (256) 730-7898  www.intergraph.com

*Develop/mfr. interactive computer graphic systems.*

**Intergraph Ireland Ltd., Stradbrook House, Stradbrook Rd., Blackrock Dublin, Ireland**

Tel: 353-1-2801366  Fax: 353-1-2801116

## INTERMEC TECHNOLOGIES CORPORATION

6001 36th Ave. West, PO Box 4280, Everett, WA, 98203-9280

Tel: (425) 348-2600  Fax: (425) 355-9551  www.intermec.com

*Mfr./distributor automated data collection systems.*

**Intermec Ireland Ltd., 19-20 York Road, Dunlaoire, County Dublin, Ireland**

## INTERNATIONAL FLAVORS & FRAGRANCES INC.

521 West 57th Street, New York, NY, 10019-2960

Tel: (212) 765-5500  Fax: (212) 708-7132  www.iff.com

*Design/mfr. flavors, fragrances and aroma chemicals.*

**International Flavors & Fragrances, Industrial Estate - Donore Road, Drogheda County. Louth, Ireland**

Tel: 353-41-983-1031  Fax: 353-41-983-5119

## IONICS INC.

65 Grove Street, Watertown, MA, 02172

Tel: (617) 926-2500  Fax: (617) 926-4304  www.ionics.com

*Mfr. desalination equipment.*

**Ionics Ireland, Ballybane Galway, Ireland**

## ITT-GOULDS PUMPS INC.

240 Fall Street, Seneca Falls, NY, 13148

Tel: (315) 568-2811  Fax: (315) 568-2418  www.gouldspumps.com

*Mfr. industrial and water systems pumps.*

**ESI Technologies Limited, Crawford Commercial Park, Bishop Street, Cork, Ireland**

## ITW DEVCON PLEXUS

30 Endicott Street, Danvers, MA, 01923

Tel: (978) 777-1100      Fax: (978) 774-0516      www.devcon-equip.com

*Mfr. filled epoxies, urethanes, adhesives and metal treatment products.*

**Devcon Ltd., Shannon Ind. Estate, Shannon Free Airport, County Clare, Ireland**

## J. WALTER THOMPSON COMPANY

466 Lexington Ave., New York, NY, 10017

Tel: (212) 210-7000      Fax: (212) 210-6944      www.jwt.com

*International advertising and marketing services.*

**DDFH&B Advertising(JWT), Dublin, Ireland**

## JACOBS ENGINEERING GROUP INC.

1111 S. Arroyo Parkway, Pasadena, CA, 91105

Tel: (626) 578-3500      Fax: (626) 578-6916      www.jacobs.com

*Engineering, design and consulting; construction and construction management; process plant maintenance.*

**Jacobs Engineering Inc., Merrion House, Merrion Rd., Dublin 4, Ireland**

Tel: 353-1-269-5666   Fax: 353-1-269-5497   Contact: James R. Thomas, Dir.   Emp: 214

**Jacobs Engineering Inc., Mahon Industrial Estate, Blackrock, County Cork, Ireland**

Tel: 353-21-515-777   Fax: 353-21-358-977   Contact: Thomas G. Concannon, Mgr.   Emp: 233

## JOHN HANCOCK FINANCIAL SERVICES, INC.

John Hancock Place, Boston, MA, 02117

Tel: (617) 572-6000      Fax: (617) 572-9799      www.johnhancock.com

*Life insurance services.*

**John Hancock Advisors International (Ireland) Ltd., Dublin, Ireland**

## JOHNSON & JOHNSON

One Johnson & Johnson Plaza, New Brunswick, NJ, 08933

Tel: (732) 524-0400      Fax: (732) 214-0334      www.jnj.com

*Mfr./distributor/R&D pharmaceutical, health care and cosmetic products.*

**Janssen-Cilag Pharmaceutical Ltd., Little Island, Cork, Ireland**

**Johnson & Johnson (Ireland) Ltd., Belgard Rd., IRL Tallaght, Dublin 24, Ireland**

Tel: 353-1-4621089   Fax: 353-1-4510954

**Vistakon, Limerick, Ireland**

## S C JOHNSON & SON INC.

1525 Howe St., Racine, WI, 53403

Tel: (414) 260-2000      Fax: (414) 260-2133      www.scjohnsonwax.com

*Home, auto, commercial and personal care products and specialty chemicals.*

**S.C. Johnson & Son Ltd., Robinhood Industrial Estate, Clon Dalkin Co., Dublin, Ireland**

## JONES LANG LASALLE

101 East 52nd Street, New York, NY, 10022

Tel: (212) 688-8181      Fax: (212) 308-5199      www.jlw.com

*International marketing consultants, leasing agents and property management advisors.*

**Jones Lang Wootton, Dublin, Ireland**

## KELLOGG COMPANY

One Kellogg Square, PO Box 3599, Battle Creek, MI, 49016-3599

Tel: (616) 961-2000      Fax: (616) 961-2871      www.kelloggs.com

*Mfr. ready-to-eat cereals and convenience foods.*

**Kellogg Co. of Ireland Ltd., Attn: Ireland Office, One Kellogg Square, PO Box 3599, Battle Creek MI 49016-3599**

## KELLY SERVICES, INC.

999 W. Big Beaver Road, Troy, MI, 48084

Tel: (248) 362-4444    Fax: (248) 244-4154    www.kellyservices.com

*Temporary help placement.*

**Kelly Services (Ireland) Ltd.,  21-22 Grafton, Dublin 2, Ireland**

Tel: 353-1-679-3111   Fax: 353-1-677-3048

## KEPNER-TREGOE INC.

PO Box 704, Princeton, NJ, 08542-0740

Tel: (609) 921-2806    Fax: (609) 497-0130    www.kepner-tregoe.com

*Management consulting; specializing in strategy formulation, problem solving, decision making, project management, and cost reduction.*

**Kepner-Tregoe Ireland,  Orania House - 97 St. Stephen's Green, Dublin 2, Ireland**

Tel: 353-1-283-4030   Fax: 353-1-283-6230

## KEY TRONIC CORPORATION

4424 N. Sullivan Rd., PO Box 14687, Spokane, WA, 99214-0687

Tel: (509) 928-8000    Fax: (509) 927-5555    www.keytronic.com

*Mfr. computer keyboards and peripherals.*

**Key Tronic Corporation Europe,  Finnabair Industrial Park, Dundalk County Louth, Ireland**

Tel: 353-4238-100   Fax: 353-4238-309   Contact: Tony McVeigh

## KIMBERLY-CLARK CORPORATION

351 Phelps Drive, Irving, TX, 75038

Tel: (972) 281-1200    Fax: (972) 281-1435    www.kimberly-clark.com

*Mfr./sales/distribution of consumer tissue, household and personal care products.*

**Kimberly-Clark Corp.,  Dublin, Ireland**

## KOLLMORGEN CORPORATION

1601 Trapelo Road, Waltham, MA, 02154

Tel: (781) 890-5655    Fax: (781) 890-7150    www.kollmorgen.com

*Mfr. high-performance electronic motion-control systems and design and supply advanced submarine periscopes, weapons directors, and military optics.*

**Kollmorgan (Ireland) Ltd.,  Gort Rd., Ennis, County Clare, Ireland**

## KPMG INTERNATIONAL LLP

345 Park Avenue, New York, NY, 10022

Tel: (201) 307-7000    Fax: (201) 930-8617    www.kpmg.com

*Accounting and audit, tax and management consulting services.*

**KPMG,  One Stokes Place, St. Stephen's Green, Dublin, Ireland**

Tel: 353-1-708-1000   Fax: 353-1-708-1122   Contact: Jerome Kennedy, Sr. Ptnr.

## K-TEL INTERNATIONAL INC.

2605 Fernbrook Lane North, Plymouth, MN, 55447-4736

Tel: (612) 559-6800    Fax: (612) 559-6803    www.k-tel.com

*Sales and distribution of packaged consumer music entertainment and convenience products.*

**K-Tel Ireland Ltd.,  30/32 Sir John Rogersons Quay, Dublin 2, Ireland**

## KWIK LOK CORPORATION

PO Box 9548, Yakima, WA, 98909

Tel: (509) 248-4770    Fax: (509) 457-6531    www.kwiklok.com

*Mfr. bag closing machinery.*

**Kwik Lok Ireland,  Bay 72 Industrial Estate - Shannon Airport, Shannon, Ireland**

Tel: 353-6147-1193   Fax: 353-6147-2683

## LAWTER INTERNATIONAL INC.

1 Terra Way, 8601 95th St., Pleasant Prairie, WI, 53158

Tel: (262) 947-7300        Fax: (262) 947-7328        www.lawter.com

*Resins, pigments and coatings.*

**Lawter Products BV, Grannagh, Waterford, Ireland**

Tel: 353-51-876616   Fax: 353-51-879399

## LEVI STRAUSS & COMPANY

1155 Battery St., San Francisco, CA, 94111-1230

Tel: (415) 544-6000        Fax: (415) 501-3939        www.levistrauss.com

*Mfr./distributor casual wearing apparel.*

**Levi Strauss Ireland, Airton Rd., Tallaght, Dublin 24, Ireland**

Tel: 353-1-4517-622   Fax: 353-1-4519-911

## LIBERTY MUTUAL GROUP

175 Berkeley Street, Boston, MA, 02117

Tel: (617) 357-9500        Fax: (617) 350-7648        www.libertymutual. com

*Provides workers' compensation insurance and operates physical rehabilitation centers and provides risk prevention management.*

**Liberty Underwriters, 35-38 St. Stephen's Green, Huguenot House, Dublin 2, Ireland**

## ELI LILLY & COMPANY

Lilly Corporate Center, Indianapolis, IN, 46285

Tel: (317) 276-2000        Fax: (317) 277-6579        www.lilly.com

*Mfr. pharmaceuticals and animal health products.*

**Eli Lilly and Company Ireland Ltd., 44 Fitzwilliam Place, Dublin 2, Ireland**

Tel: 353-21-661-4377

## LILLY INDUSTRIES

200 W. 103rd St., Indianapolis, IN, 46290

Tel: (317) 814-8700        Fax: (317) 814-8880        www.lillyindustries.com

*Mfr. industrial coatings and specialty chemicals.*

**Lilly Industries Ireland, Willowfield Road, Ballinamore, County Leitrim, Ireland**

Tel: 353-78-45077   Fax: 353-78-45078

## LOCKHEED MARTIN CORPORATION

6801 Rockledge Drive, Bethesda, MD, 20817

Tel: (301) 897-6000        Fax: (301) 897-6652        www.imco.com

*Design/mfr./management systems in fields of space, defense, energy, electronics and technical services.*

**MountainGate Data Systems International, St. Joseph's Road, Portumna, County Galway, Ireland**

Contact: W. Burke, Gen. Mgr.

## LOCTITE CORPORATION

1001 Trout Brook Crossing, Rocky Hill, CT, 06067-3910

Tel: (860) 571-5100        Fax: (860) 571-5465        www.loctite.com

*Mfr./sale industrial adhesives, sealants and coatings..*

**Loctite (Ireland) Ltd., Manufacturing Facility, Tallaght Business Park, Whitestown Tallaght, Dublin 24 Ireland**

Tel: 353-1-451-9466   Fax: 353-1-451-9464

## LOUISIANA-PACIFIC CORPORATION

111 S.W. Fifth Ave., Portland, OR, 97204-3601

Tel: (503) 221-0800     Fax: (503) 796-0204     www.lpcorp.com

*Mfr. lumber and building products.*

**Louisiana-Pacific Coillte Ireland Ltd., Belview Port Rd., Waterford, Ireland**

Tel: 353-51-51233

## LUCENT TECHNOLOGIES, INC.

600 Mountain Ave., Murray Hill, NJ, 07974-0636

Tel: (908) 582-3000     Fax: (908) 582-2576     www.lucent.com

*Design/mfr. wide range of public and private networks, communication systems and software, data networking systems, business telephone systems and microelectronics components.*

**Bell Labs Network Products, Cork Abbey, Bray County, County Wicklow, Ireland**

Tel: 353-1-2882-333   Fax: 353-1-2822-864   Contact: Sam Baxter, PR Mgr.

**Lucent/Bell Labs, Lucent House, Ste. Stephens Green, Dublin 2, Ireland**

## R.H. MACY & COMPANY INC.

151 West 34th Street, New York, NY, 10001

Tel: (212) 695-4400     Fax: (212) 643-1307     www.macys.com

*Department stores; importers.*

**R.H. Macy & Co. Inc., 51 Wellington Rd., Dublin 4, Ireland**

**R.H. Macy & Co. Inc., Ballsbridge, Dublin 4, Ireland**

## MAIDENFORM WORLDWIDE INC.

154 Avenue E, Bayonne, NJ, 07002

Tel: (201) 436-9200     Fax: (201) 436-9009     www.maidenform.com

*Mfr. intimate apparel.*

**Maidenform Intl. Ltd., Shannon Industrial Estate, Shannon, Co. Clare, Ireland**

## MANPOWER INTERNATIONAL INC.

5301 N. Ironwood Rd., PO Box 2053, Milwaukee, WI, 53201-2053

Tel: (414) 961-1000     Fax: (414) 961-7081     www.manpower.com

*Temporary help, contract service, training and testing.*

**Manpower Ireland Ltd., 54 Grafton Street, Dublin 2, Ireland**

Tel: 44-1353-1677-7321

## MARATHON OIL COMPANY

5555 San Felipe Road, Houston, TX, 77056

Tel: (713) 629-6600     Fax: (713) 296-2952     www.marathon.com

*Oil and gas exploration.*

**Marathon Petroleum Ireland Ltd., Mahon Industrial Estate, Blackrock, Cork, Ireland**

## MARCONI DATA SYSTEMS, INC.

1500 Mittel Blvd., Wood Dale, IL, 60191

Tel: (630) 860-7300     Fax: (630) 616-3657     www.videojet.com

*Mfr. computer peripherals and hardware, state-of-the-art industrial ink jet marking and coding products.*

**Marconi Data Systems, Unit 1, Chestnut Rd., Western Industrial Estate, Dublin 12, Ireland**

Tel: 353-1-450-2833   Fax: 353-1-450-2941

## MARSH & McLENNAN COS INC.

1166 Ave. of the Americas, New York, NY, 10036-2774

Tel: (212) 345-5000     Fax: (212) 345-4808     www.marshmac.com

*Insurance agents/brokers, pension and investment management consulting services.*

**J&H Marsh & McLennan Ireland Ltd., Crescent House, Upper Hartstonge St., Limerick, Ireland**

Tel: 353-61-319155   Fax: 353-61-317598   Contact: David Bermington

**J&H Marsh & McLennan Ireland Ltd.,  10-11 South Leinster St, Dublin 2, Ireland**
Tel: 353-1-618-2720   Fax: 353-1-678-5839   Contact: David Caird

**J&H Marsh & McLennan Ireland Ltd.,  12 South Mall, Cork, Ireland**
Tel: 353-21-27-6743   Fax: 353-21-27-2555   Contact: Gerard O'Donovn

**J&H Marsh & McLennan Management Services (Dublin) Ltd.,  Level 2 Treasury Bldg., Lr Grand Canal St., Dublin 2, Ireland**
Tel: 353-1-676-2748   Fax: 353-1-678-9636   Contact: Ian J. Clancy

## MASONITE CORPORATION

One South Wacker Drive, Chicago, IL, 60606
Tel: (312) 750-0900      Fax: (312) 750-0958      www.masonite.com
*Mfr. hardboard, softboard and molded products.*

**Masonite Europe,  Segrave House, 19/29 Earlsfort Terrace, Dublin 2, Ireland**
Contact: Claire Devine

**Masonite Ireland,  Dublin Rd., ICA Industrial Estate, Carrick-on-Shannon, Co. Leitrim, Ireland**

## MAXTOR CORPORATION

510 Cottonwood Drive, Milpitas, CA, 95035-7403
Tel: (408) 432-1700      Fax: (408) 432-4510      www.maxtor.com
*Mfr. develops and markets hard disk drives for desktop computer systems.*

**Maxtor Ireland Ltd.,  Bray County Wicklow, Ireland**

## McCANN-ERICKSON WORLDGROUP

750 Third Ave., New York, NY, 10017
Tel: (212) 984-3644      Fax: (212) 984-2629      www.mccann.com
*International advertising and marketing services.*

**McCann-Erickson (Ireland),  Dublin, Ireland**

## McDONALD'S CORPORATION

McDonald's Plaza, Oak Brook, IL, 60523
Tel: (630) 623-3000      Fax: (630) 623-7409      www.mcdonalds.com
*Fast food chain stores.*

**McDonald's Corp.,  Tralee, Ireland**

## McKINSEY & COMPANY

55 East 52nd Street, New York, NY, 10022
Tel: (212) 446-7000      Fax: (212) 446-8575      www.mckinsey.com
*Management and business consulting services.*

**McKinsey & Company,  Canada House, 65-68 St. Stephen's Green, Dublin 2, Ireland**
Tel: 353-1-478-5500   Fax: 353-1-478-5512

## MELLON FINANCIAL CORPORATION

One Mellon Bank Center, Pittsburgh, PA, 15258-0001
Tel: (412) 234-5000      Fax: (412) 236-1662      www.mellon.com
*Commercial and trade banking and foreign exchange.*

**Mellon Fund Administration,  Dublin, Ireland**
**Premier Financial Services (Ireland) Ltd.,  20-22 Lower Hatch St., Dublin 2, Ireland**
Tel: 353-1-790-5000

## MEMOREX CORPORATION

10100 Pioneer Blvd., Ste. 110, Santa Fe Springs, CA, 90670
Tel: (562) 906-2800      Fax: (562) 906-2848      www.memorex.com
*Magnetic recording tapes, etc.*

**Memorex Ireland Ltd.,  Kestral House, Clanwilliam House, Clanwilliam Place, Lower Mount St., Dublin 2, Ireland**

## MERITOR AUTOMOTIVE, INC.

2135 West Maple Road, Troy, MI, 48084-7186

Tel: (248) 435-1000      Fax: (248) 435-1393      www.meritorauto.com

*Mfr./sales of light and heavy vehicle systems for trucks, cars and specialty vehicles.*

**Meritor Heavy Vehicle Systems Ltd., Kildare, Ireland**

## MERRILL LYNCH & COMPANY, INC.

World Financial Center, 250 Vesey Street, New York, NY, 10281-1332

Tel: (212) 449-1000      Fax: (212) 449-2892      www.ml.com

*Security brokers and dealers, investment and business services.*

**Merrill Lynch & Co. Ltd., 69 St. Stephen's Street, Dublin 2, Ireland**

**Merrill Lynch Capital Markets Bank, Treasury Building, Lower Grand Canal Street, Dublin 2, Ireland**

Tel: 353-1-605-8500   Fax: 353-1-605-8510

## METHODE ELECTRONICS INC.

7401 W. Wilson Ave., Chicago, IL, 60656

Tel: (708) 867-6777      Fax: (708) 867-6999      www.methode.com

*Mfr. electronic components.*

**Methode Electronics Ireland Ltd, Annacotty Industrial Estate, Annacotty, County Limerick, Ireland**

Tel: 353-61-330-013   Contact: Michael O'Donnell

## MICROSEMI CORPORATION

2830 South Fairview St., Santa Ana, CA, 92704

Tel: (714) 979-8220      Fax: (714) 557-5989      www.microsemi.com

*Design, manufacture and market analog, mixed-signal and discrete semiconductors.*

**Microsemi Corp. Ireland, Gort Rd., Ennis, Co. Clare, Ireland**

Tel: 353-65-68-40044

## MICROSOFT CORPORATION

One Microsoft Way, Redmond, WA, 98052-6399

Tel: (425) 882-8080      Fax: (425) 936-7329      www.microsoft.com

*Computer software, peripherals and services.*

**Microsoft Ireland Operations Ltd., Blackthorn Rd., Sandyford Ind. Estates, Dublin 18, Ireland**

## MILACRON INC.

2090 Florence Ave., Cincinnati, OH, 45206

Tel: (513) 487-5000      Fax: (513) 487-5057      www.milacron.com

*Metalworking and plastics technologies.*

**Plas-Tech Equipment Limited, 83 New Muirhevna Dublin Road, Dundalk County Louth, Ireland**

Tel: 353-42-9330900   Fax: 353-42-9326466   Contact: Bernhard Gründemann

## MILTON ROY COMPANY

201 Ivyland Road, Ivylan, PA, 18974

Tel: (215) 441-0800      Fax: (215) 293-0468      www.miltonroy.com

*Mfr. medical and industry equipment and process control instruments.*

**LDC-Shannon, Shannon Industrial Estate, Bldg. 89, Clare, Ireland**

## MINTEQ INTERNATIONAL INC.

405 Lexington Ave., 19th Fl., New York, NY, 10174-1901

Tel: (212) 878-1800      Fax: (212) 878-1952      www.mineralstech.com

*Mfr./market specialty refractory and metallurgical products and application systems.*

**MINTEQ Europe Ltd., Box 105, Tivoli Industrial Estate, Cork, Ireland**

Tel: 353-21-503-241   Fax: 353-21-506-352   Contact: David Rosenberg, VP   Emp: 45

## MOLEX INC.

2222 Wellington Court, Lisle, IL, 60532

Tel: (630) 969-4550        Fax: (630) 969-1352        www.molex.com

*Mfr. electronic, electrical and fiber optic interconnection products and systems, switches, application tooling.*

**Molex Inc., 62 Pembroke Road, Dublin 4, Ireland**

## MOOG INC.

Jamison Road, East Aurora, NY, 14052-0018

Tel: (716) 652-2000        Fax: (716) 687-4471        www.moog.com

*Mfr. precision control components and systems.*

**Moog Ltd. (Ireland), Ringeskiddy, County Cork, Ireland**

Tel: 353-21-4519000

## J. P. MORGAN CHASE & CO. INC.

World Headquarters, 270 Park Ave., New York, NY, 10017

Tel: (212) 270-6000        Fax: (212) 622-9030        www.jpmorganchase.com

*Provides integrated financial solutions for institutions and individuals worldwide, including asset management, investment banking and commercial banking.*

**J. P. Morgan Chase & Co., Chase Manhattan House, International Financial Services Centre, Dublin 1, Ireland**

Tel: 353-1-612-3000    Fax: 353-1-612-3123

## MOTOROLA, INC.

1303 East Algonquin Road, Schaumburg, IL, 60196

Tel: (847) 576-5000        Fax: (847) 538-5191        www.motorola.com

*Mfr. communications equipment, semiconductors and cellular phones.*

**Motorola Ireland Ltd., LMPS Bldg., Newtown Park, Holybanks, County Dublin Ireland**

Tel: 353-1-840-8866    Fax: 353-1-840-0920

## MTI TECHNOLOGY CORPORATION

4905 East LaPalma Avenue, Anaheim, CA, 92807

Tel: (714) 970-0300        Fax: (714) 693-2202        www.mti.com

*Mfr. data storage systems software.*

**MTI Technology Ireland, Blanchardstown Corporate Park #5, Ballycoolin, Dublin 15, Ireland**

Tel: 353-1-885-0500    Fax: 353-1-885-0555

## NCR (NATIONAL CASH REGISTER)

1700 South Patterson Blvd., Dayton, OH, 45479

Tel: (937) 445-5000        Fax: (937) 445-7042        www.ncr.com

*Mfr. automated teller machines and high-performance stationary bar code scanners.*

**NCR, Dublin, Ireland**

## NETSCAPE COMMUNICATIONS

501 East Middlefield Road, Mountain View, CA, 94043

Tel: (650) 254-1900        Fax: (650) 528-4124        www.netscape.com

*Mfr./distribute Internet-based commercial and consumer software applications.*

**Netscape Communications Ireland Ltd.., Logic Drive, Citywest Business Campus, Saggart, Dublin Ireland**

Tel: 353-1-403-5000    Fax: 353-1-403-5001

### NEWAY MANUFACTURING INC.

1013 N. Shiawassee Street, PO Box 188, Corunna, MI, 48817-0188

Tel: (517) 743-3458     Fax: (517) 743-5764     www.newaymfg.com

*Mfr. valve and valve seat reconditioning tools and equipment.*

**Neway Manufacturing Ltd., Unit 2 IDA Cluster Devel., Spollanstown Tullamore, County Offaly, Ireland**

### A .C. NIELSEN COMPANY

177 Broad Street, Stamford, CT, 06901

Tel: (203) 961-3000     Fax: (203) 961-3190     www.acnielsen.com

*Market and consumer research firm.*

**A.C. Nielsen of Ireland Ltd., 36 Merrion Sq., Dublin 2, Ireland**

### NORGREN

5400 S. Delaware Street., Littleton, CO, 80120-1663

Tel: (303) 794-2611     Fax: (303) 795-9487     www.usa.norgren.com

*Mfr. pneumatic filters, regulators, lubricators, valves, automation systems, dryers, push-in fittings.*

**IMI Norgren Ltd., 137 Slaney Close, Dublin Industrial Estate, Glasnevin, Dublin 11, Ireland**
Tel: 353-1-830-0288   Fax: 353-1-830-0082

### NORTHERN TRUST CORPORATION

50 South LaSalle Street, Chicago, IL, 60675

Tel: (312) 630-6000     Fax: (312) 630-1512     www.ntrs.com

*Banking and financial services.*

**Northern Trust Fund Managers (Ireland) Ltd., Lifetime House, Fourth Fl., Earlsfort Centre, Earlsfort Terrace, Dublin 2, Ireland**

### NORTHROP GRUMMAN CORPORATION

1840 Century Park East, Los Angeles, CA, 90067-2199

Tel: (310) 553-6262     Fax: (310) 201-3023     www.northgrum.com

*Advanced technology for aircraft, electronics, and technical support services.*

**Wescan Europe Ltd., Blanchardstown Industrial Park, Blanchardstown, Dublin 15, Ireland**
Tel: 353-1-820-0322   Fax: 353-1-820-0388

### NORTON ABRASIVES COMPANY

1 New Bond Street, Worcester, MA, 01606

Tel: (508) 795-5000     Fax: (508) 795-5741     www.nortonabrasives.com

*Mfr. abrasives for industrial manufacturing.*

**Drill Tools Ireland Ltd., Shannon Industrial Estate, Shannon, County Clare, Ireland**

### NOVELLUS SYSTEMS INC.

4000 North First Street, San Jose, CA, 95134

Tel: (408) 943-9700     Fax: (408) 943-3422     www.novellus.com

*Mfr. chemical vapor deposition (CVD), physical vapor deposition (PVD) and copper electrofill systems.*

**Novellus Systems Ireland Ltd., IR4-1-10, Colinstown Industrial Park - Leixlip, County Kildare, Ireland**
Tel: 353-1-606-5247   Fax: 353-1-606-5180

### C.M. OFFRAY & SON INC.

360 Rt. 24, Box 601, Chester, NJ, 07930-0601

Tel: (908) 879-4700     Fax: (908) 879-8588     www.offray.com

*Mfr. ribbons and narrow fabrics.*

**Offray Ribbon Ltd., Ashbury Rd., Roscrea, County Tipperary, Ireland**

## OGILVY PUBLIC RELATIONS WORLDWIDE

909 Third Ave., New York, NY, 10022

Tel: (212) 880-5201     Fax: (212) 697-8250      www.ogilvypr.com

*Engaged in public relations and communications.*

**Wilson Hartnell PR/Ogilvy, 14 Leeson Park, Dublin 6, Ireland**

Tel: 353-1-496-0244   Fax: 353-1-497-5163    Contact: Mary Finan

## OTIS ELEVATOR COMPANY

10 Farm Springs Road, Farmington, CT, 06032

Tel: (860) 676-6000     Fax: (860) 676-5111      www.otis.com

*Mfr. elevators and escalators.*

**Otis Elevator Co. UK, Naas Road Business Park Unit 21, Muirfield Drive, Dublin 12, Ireland**

## PACIFIC SCIENTIFIC COMPANY

4301 Kishwaukee Street, PO Box 106, Rockford, IL, 61105-0106

Tel: (815) 226-3100     Fax: (815) 226-3148      www.pacsci.com

*Mfr. high performance motors and drives.*

**Pacific Scientific Ltd., Ennis, Ireland**

## PALL CORPORATION

2200 Northern Boulevard, East Hills, NY, 11548-1289

Tel: (516) 484-5400     Fax: (516) 484-5228      www.pall.com

*Specialty materials and engineering; filters and related fluid clarification equipment.*

**Pall Gelman Sciences, 24 Kill Avenue, Dun Laoire, Dublin, Ireland**

Tel: 353-1-284-6177   Fax: 353-1-280-7739

**Pall Ireland (Div. Pall Netherlands), Rosanna Road, Tipperary Town, County Tipperary, Ireland**

Tel: 353-62-82600   Fax: 353-62-82680

## PANAMETRICS

221 Crescent Street, Waltham, MA, 02154

Tel: (781) 899-2719     Fax: (781) 899-1552      www.panametrics.com

*Process/non-destructive test instrumentation.*

**Panametrics Ltd., Bay 148 Shannon Airport, Shannon, Co. Claire, Ireland**

Tel: 353-61-471377   Fax: 353-61-471359    Contact: Jim Gibson

## PARAMETRIC TECHNOLOGY CORPORATION

128 Technology Drive, Waltham, MA, 02154

Tel: (781) 398-5000     Fax: (781) 398-5674      www.ptc.com

*Supplier of mechanical design automation and product data management software and services.*

**Parametric Technology (IRL) Ltd., Regus House, Hartcourt Centre, Hartcourt Road, Dublin 2 Ireland**

Tel: 353-1-4029575   Fax: 353-1-4029568

## PARSONS BRINCKERHOFF QUADE & DOUGLAS

One Penn Plaza, New York, NY, 10119-0061

Tel: (212) 465-5000     Fax: (212) 465-5096      www.pbworld.com

*Engineering consultants, planners and architects.*

**PB Kennedy & Donkin, 12 Lower Hatch Street, Dublin 2, Ireland**

## PATAGONIA INC.

259 West Santa Clara Street, Ventura, CA, 93001

Tel: (805) 643-8616     Fax: (805) 653-6355      www.patagonia.com

*Outdoor clothing retail stores and mail-order catalogue company.*

**Patagonia, Inc., Dublin, Ireland**

## PEPSiCO INC.
700 Anderson Hill Road, Purchase, NY, 10577-1444

Tel: (914) 253-2000    Fax: (914) 253-2070    www.pepsico.com

*Beverages and snack foods.*

**PepsiCo (Ireland) Ltd., Dublin, Ireland**

**PepsiCo Mfg. (Ireland), Little Island, Cork, Ireland**

Tel: 353-21-353921  Fax: 353-21-353926   Contact: Frank O'Mahony

**Seven-Up Ireland Ltd., Dublin, Ireland**

**The Concentrate Mfg. Co. of Ireland, Dublin, Ireland**

## PFIZER INC.
235 East 42nd Street, New York, NY, 10017-5755

Tel: (212) 573-2323    Fax: (212) 573-7851    www.pfizer.com

*Research-based, global health care company.*

**NAMIC Eireann BV, Tullamore, Ireland**

**Pfizer Ireland Ltd., Dublin, Ireland**

**Pfizer Pharmaceutical Production, Ringaskiddy, Ireland**

## PHARMACIA CORPORATION
100 Route 206 North, Peapack, NJ, 07977

Tel: (908) 901-8000    Fax: (908) 901-8379    www.pharmacia.com

*Mfr. pharmaceuticals, agricultural products, industry chemicals.*

**Pharmacia & Upjohn, Boeing Rd., Airways Industrial Estate, Cloghram Dublin 17, Ireland**

**Pharmacia & Upjohn, Letterkenny Ltd., High Road, Letterkenny County Donegal, Ireland**

**Pharmacia & Upjohn/aeleo Ltd., Little Island, Cork, Ireland**

## PHH VEHICLE MANAGEMENT SERVICES
307 International Circle, Hunt Valley, MD, 21030

Tel: (410) 771-3600    Fax: (410) 771-2841    www.phh.com

*Provides vehicle fleet management, corporate relocation, and mortgage banking services.*

**PHH Vehicle Management Services, Merchants House, 27-30A Merchants Quay, Dublin 8, Ireland**

Tel: 353-1-671-0022

## PHILLIPS PETROLEUM COMPANY
Phillips Building, 411 S. Keeler Ave., Bartlesville, OK, 74004

Tel: (918) 661-6600    Fax: (918) 661-7636    www.phillips66.com

*Crude oil, natural gas, liquefied petroleum gas, gasoline and petro-chemicals.*

**O'Brien Plastics Ltd., Bishopstown, Cork, Ireland**

**Star Plastics Co. Ltd., Ballyconnell, Cavan, Ireland**

## PITNEY BOWES INC.
1 Elmcroft Road, Stamford, CT, 06926-0700

Tel: (203) 356-5000    Fax: (203) 351-6835    www.pitneybowes.com

*Mfr. postage meters, mailroom equipment, copiers, bus supplies, bus services, facsimile systems and financial services.*

**Pitney Bowes Ireland Ltd., Unit 4 Parkmore Industrial Estate, Long Mile Road, Dublin 12 Ireland**

Tel: 353-1-4502-252   Fax: 3531-4505-493

## PITTSTON BAX GROUP
16808 Armstrong Ave., PO Box 19571, Irvine, CA, 92623

Tel: (949) 752-4000    Fax: (949) 260-3182    www.baxworld.com

*Air freight forwarder.*

**BAX Global, No. 29 The Mall, Waterford, Ireland**

Tel: 353-51-858238

**BAX Global,  Unit 6-7 Franksfield Rd. Industrial Estate, Franksfield Rd., Cork Ireland**

Tel: 353-21-319222    Fax: 353-21-319233

**BAX Global,  Smithstown, Shannon Country, Clare, Ireland**

Tel: 353-61-363200

**BAX Global,  Unit 16 Airways Industrial Estate, Dublin 17, Ireland**

Tel: 353-1-862-1044    Fax: 353-1-862-0134

## PNC FINANCIAL SERVICES GROUP

249 Fifth Ave., Pittsburgh, PA, 15222

Tel:  (412) 762-2000        Fax:  (412) 762-7829         www.pncbank.com

*Engaged in financial and asset management.*

**PFPC International (Dublin) Ltd.,  Abbey Court Block C, Irish Life Centre, Lower Abbey Street, Dublin 1 Ireland**

Tel: 353-1-790-3500    Contact: Fergus McKeon

## PPG INDUSTRIES

One PPG Place, Pittsburgh, PA, 15272

Tel:  (412) 434-3131        Fax:  (412) 434-2190        www.ppg.com

*Mfr. coatings, flat glass, fiber glass, chemicals, coatings.*

**Transitions Optical Ltd.,  IDA Industrial Estate, Dunmore Rd., Tuam, County Golway, Ireland**

## PRICEWATERHOUSECOOPERS LLP

1301 Ave. of the Americas, New York, NY, 10019

Tel:  (212) 596-7000        Fax:  (212) 259-1301         www.pwcglobal.com

*Accounting and auditing, tax and management, and human resource consulting services.*

**PriceWaterhouseCoopers,  Gardner House, Wilton Place, Dublin 2, Ireland**

Tel: 353-1-6626000    Fax: 353-1-6626200

**PriceWaterhouseCoopers,  Gardner House, Bank Place, Limerick, Ireland**

Tel: 353-61-416644    Fax: 353-61-416331

**PriceWaterhouseCoopers,  Gardner House, 1 South Mall, Cork, Ireland**

Tel: 353-21-276631    Fax: 353-21-276630

## PRIMARK CORPORATION

100 Winter Street, Ste. 4300-N, Waltham, MA, 02451

Tel:  (781) 466-6611        Fax:  (781) 890-6187         www.primark.com

*Provides financial and business information.*

**Primark Worldscope Ireland,  Unit K7B Shannon Free Zone, Shannon County Clare, Ireland**

Tel: 353-61-475-435

## PROCTER & GAMBLE COMPANY

One Procter & Gamble Plaza, Cincinnati, OH, 45202

Tel:  (513) 983-1100        Fax:  (513) 562-4500         www.pg.com

*Personal care, food, laundry, cleaning and industry products.*

**Procter & Gamble .,  Nenagh, Ireland**

## QUINTILES TRANSNATIONAL CORPORATION

4709 Creekstone Dr., Durham, NC, 27703

Tel:  (919) 998-2000        Fax:  (919) 998-9113         www.quintiles.com

*Mfr. pharmaceuticals.*

**Innovex Ireland,  Quintiles Building East, Point Business Park, Fairview Dublin 3, Ireland**

## RAYCHEM CORPORATION

300 Constitution Dr., Menlo Park, CA, 94025-1164

Tel: (650) 361-3333     Fax: (650) 361-5579     www.raychem.com

*Develop/mfr./market materials science products for electronics, telecommunications and industry.*

**Raychem International Ltd., 100/104 Industrial Estate, Shannon, Ireland**

## RAYONIER INC.

50 N. Laura St., 18-19 Fls., Jacksonville, FL, 32202

Tel: (904) 357-9100     Fax: (904) 357-9155     www.rayonier.com

*Chemicals cellulose, paper pulps, logs and lumber.*

**Rayonier Ireland, Dublin, Ireland**

## RAYTHEON COMPANY

141 Spring Street, Lexington, MA, 02173

Tel: (781) 862-6600     Fax: (781) 860-2172     www.raytheon.com

*Mfr. diversified electronics, appliances, aviation, energy and environmental products; publishing, industry and construction services.*

**Raytheon Systems Limited (RSL), Londonderry, Northern Ireland**

## REFLEXITE TECHNOLOGY

120 Darling Drive, Avon, CT, 06001

Tel: (860) 676-7100     Fax: (860) 676-7199     www.reflexite.com

*Mfr. plastic film, sheet, materials and shapes, optical lenses.*

**Reflexite Ireland Ltd., Unit 4, Industrial Estate - Cork Road, Waterford, Ireland**

Tel: 353-51-358132   Fax: 353-51-35825   Contact: Declan Cunningham

## REMEDY CORPORATION

1505 Salado Drive, Mountain View, CA, 94043-1110

Tel: (650) 903-5200     Fax: (650) 903-9001     www.remedy.com

*Developer and marketer of computer applications for the operations management market.*

**Remedy Ireland, c/o Sentinel Investments Ltd. Shannon Airport House - 2/F, County Clare Ireland**

## REMINGTON PRODUCTS COMPANY, L.L.C.

60 Main Street, Bridgeport, CT, 06604

Tel: (203) 367-4400     Fax: (203) 332-4848     www.remington-products.com

*Mfr. home appliances, electric shavers.*

**Remington Consumer Products Limited, Unit 7C Riverview Bus Park, New Magnor Road - Clondalkin, Dublin 12 Ireland**

Tel: 353-4604711

## REVLON INC.

625 Madison Ave., New York, NY, 10022

Tel: (212) 527-4000     Fax: (212) 527-4995     www.revlon.com

*Mfr. cosmetics, fragrances, toiletries and beauty care products.*

**Hydrocurve Ltd., Ireland**

**Reheis Chemical Ltd., Ireland**

**Revlon Ireland, Harmonstown Rd., Artane, Dublin 5, Ireland**

**Technicon Ireland Ltd., Ireland**

## RIDGE TOOL COMPANY

400 Clark Street, Elyria, OH, 44035

Tel: (440) 323-5581     Fax: (440) 329-4853     www.ridgid.com

*Mfr. hand and power tools for working pipe, drain cleaning equipment, etc.*

**The Ridge Tool Co., Div. of Emerson Electric Ireland Ltd., Cork, Ireland**

## ROCHESTER MIDLAND CORPORATION

PO Box 31515, 333 Hollenbeck St., Rochester, NY, 14603-1515

Tel: (716) 336-2200        Fax: (716) 467-4406        www.rochestermidland.com

*Mfr. specialty chemicals for industry cleaning and maintenance, water treatment and personal hygiene.*

**Rochester Midland Ireland, Raheens East, Ringaskiddy, Cork, Ireland**

Tel: 353-21-378689

## ROCKWELL INTERNATIONAL CORPORATION

777 East Wisconsin Ave., Ste. 1400, Milwaukee, WI, 53202

Tel: (414) 212-5200        Fax: (414) 212-5201        www.rockwell.com

*Products and service for aerospace and defense, automotive, electronics, graphics and automation industry.*

**Rockwell Automation (Ireland) Ltd., Naas Rd. Industrial Park, Dublin 12, Ireland**

Tel: 353-1-450-8164    Fax: 353-1-456-5474

## SANMINA CORPORATION

2700 North First Street, San Jose, CA, 95134

Tel: (408) 964-3500        Fax: (408) 964-3799        www.sanmina.com

*Mfr. electronic components, including multi-layered printed circuit boards, backplanes, cables, and complete systems.*

**Sanmina Corporation, Blanchardstown Industrial Park, Dublin 15, Ireland**

Tel: 353-1-802-5400    Fax: 353-1-882-2365

## SARA LEE CORPORATION

3 First National Plaza, Chicago, IL, 60602-4260

Tel: (312) 726-2600        Fax: (312) 558-4995        www.saralee.com

*Mfr./distributor food and consumer packaged goods, intimate apparel and knitwear.*

**Pretty Polly Ltd., Park Rd., Killarney County Kerry, Ireland**

## SCANSOFT, INC.

9 Centennial Dr., Peabody, MA, 01960

Tel: (978) 977-2000        Fax: (978) 977-2436        www.scansoft.com

*Mfr. digital imaging software.*

**MicroWareHouse, Unit 25 Western Parkway Business Centre, Ballymount Road, Dublin 12, Ireland**

## SCHENKER INTERNATIONAL FORWARDERS INC.

150 Albany Ave., Freeport, NY, 11520

Tel: (516) 377-3000        Fax: (516) 377-3005        www.schenkerusa.com

*Freight forwarders.*

**Inter Continental Cargo Ltd, Unit 3B Santry Industrial Estate, Santry, Dublin, Ireland**

Tel: 353-1-842-9955    Fax: 353-1-842-9708

## SCHERING-PLOUGH CORPORATION

One Giralda Farms, Madison, NJ, 07940-1000

Tel: (973) 822-7000        Fax: (973) 822-7048        www.sch-plough.com

*Proprietary drug and cosmetic products.*

**Schering-Plough Ireland AG, 4 Dartmouth Square, Dublin 6, Ireland**

Tel: 353-1-668-8566

## SCHLEGEL SYSTEMS

1555 Jefferson Road, PO Box 23197, Rochester, NY, 14692-3197

Tel: (716) 427-7200        Fax: (716) 427-9993        www.schlegel.com

*Mfr. engineered perimeter sealing systems for residential and commercial construction; fibers; rubber product.*

**Schlegel Ireland Ltd., Dublin Rd., Loughrea, Co. Galway, Ireland**

## SCHOLASTIC CORPORATION

555 Broadway, New York, NY, 10012

Tel: (212) 343-6100     Fax: (212) 343-6934     www.scholastic.com

*Publishing/distribution educational and children's magazines, books, software.*

**School Book Fairs Ltd., Dublin, Ireland**

## SCI SYSTEMS INC.

2101 W. Clinton Avenue, Huntsville, AL, 35807

Tel: (256) 882-4800     Fax: (256) 882-4804     www.sci.com

*R/D and mfr. electronics systems for commerce, industry, aerospace, etc.*

**SCI Ireland Ltd., Rathealy Road, Fermon Cork, Ireland**

## SEAGATE TECHNOLOGY, INC.

920 Disc Dr., Scotts Valley, CA, 95066

Tel: (408) 438-6550     Fax: (408) 438-7205     www.seagate.com

*Develop computer technology, software and hardware.*

**Seagate Technology, Victoria Cross, Cork, Ireland**

Tel: 353-21-856-620   Fax: 353-21-347-180   Contact: Kevin O'Dwyer, Mgr.   Emp: 10

## SEAQUIST PERFECT DISPENSING

1160 North Silver Lake Road, Cary, IL, 60013

Tel: (847) 639-2124     Fax: (847) 639-2142     www.seaquistperect.com

*Mfr. and sale of dispensing systems; lotion pumps and spray-through overcaps.*

**Caideil MP Teoranta, Tourmakeady, County Mayo, Ireland**

## G.D. SEARLE & COMPANY

5200 Old Orchard Road, Skokie, IL, 60077

Tel: (847) 982-7000     Fax: (847) 470-1480     www.searlehealthnet.com

*Mfr. pharmaceuticals, health care, optical products and specialty chemicals.*

**Serale & Company Ltd., Bray Industrial Estate Pinewood Close Bray, County Wicklow, Ireland**

Tel: 353-1-286-7412   Fax: 353-1-282-5894

## SENSORMATIC ELECTRONICS CORPORATION

951 Yamato Road, Boca Raton, FL, 33431-0700

Tel: (561) 989-7000     Fax: (561) 989-7774     www.sensormatic.com

*Electronic article surveillance equipment.*

**Sensormatic Electronics Corporation, Melbourne Road, Bishopstown, County Cork, Ireland**

Tel: 353-21-801000   Fax: 353-21-801050

## SERVICE CORPORATION INTERNATIONAL

1929 Allen Parkway, Houston, TX, 77019

Tel: (713) 522-5141     Fax: (713) 525-5586     www.sci-corp.com

*Operates funeral homes, cemeteries and crematoriums and sells caskets, burial vaults and cremation receptacles.*

**SCI Ireland, Dublin, Ireland**

## THE SERVICEMASTER COMPANY

One ServiceMaster Way, Downers Grove, IL, 60515-1700

Tel: (630) 271-1300     Fax: (630) 271-2710     www.svm.com

*Management service to health care, school and industry facilities; diversified residential and commercial services.*

**Merry Maids, Dublin, Ireland**

**ServiceMaster, Dublin, Ireland**

## SHARED MEDICAL SYSTEMS CORPORATION

51 Valley Stream Pkwy, Malvern, PA, 19355

Tel: (610) 219-6300    Fax: (610) 219-3124    www.smed.com

*Computer-based information processing for healthcare industry.*

**SMS Ireland, SMS House, St. John's Business Centre, Swords Rd., Santry, Dublin, Ireland**

## A.O. SMITH CORPORATION

11270 West Park Place, PO Box 23972, Milwaukee, WI, 53224

Tel: (414) 359-4000    Fax: (414) 359-4064    www.aosmith.com

*Auto and truck frames, motors, water heaters, storage/handling systems, plastics, railroad products.*

**A.O. Smith Electric Motors (Ireland) Ltd., Boghall Rd., Bray, Wicklow, Ireland**

Tel: 353-12-868-234    Fax: 353-12-868-237    Contact: Edward Smythe, Gen. Mgr.

## SMURFIT-STONE CONTAINER CORPORATION

150 N. Michigan Ave., Chicago, IL, 60601-7568

Tel: (312) 346-6600    Fax: (312) 580-3486    www.smurfit-stone.net

*Mfr. paper and paper packaging.*

**Smurfit-Stone Container Corporation, Dublin, Ireland**

## SNAP-TITE INC.

2930 W. 22nd Street, Erie, PA, 16506-2302

Tel: (814) 838-5700    Fax: (814) 838-6382    www.snap-tite.com

*Develop/mfr. laboratory, scientific and research instrumentation.*

**Snap-Tite Europe B.V., Industrial Estate, Whitemill-Wesford, Ireland**

Tel: 353-534-1566

## SOFTWARE SPECTRUM, INC.

2140 Merritt Drive, Garland, TX, 75041

Tel: (972) 840-6600    Fax: (972) 864-7878    www.softwarespectrum.com

*Engaged in software resale.*

**Software Spectrum Ireland, Merrion House, Merrion Road, Dublin 4, Ireland**

Tel: 353-1-260-1788

## SOLECTRON CORPORATION

777 Gibraltar Drive, Milpitas, CA, 95035

Tel: (408) 957-8500    Fax: (408) 956-6075    www.solectron.com

*Provides contract manufacturing services to equipment manufacturers.*

**Solectron Corporation, Clonshaugh Industrial Estate, Dublin 17, Ireland**

Tel: 353-1-8484222    Fax: 353-1-8484900

## SOTHEBY'S HOLDINGS, INC.

1334 York Avenue, New York, NY, 10021

Tel: (212) 606-7000    Fax: (212) 606-7027    www.sothebys.com

*Auction house specializing in fine art and jewelry.*

**Sotheby's Holdings, Inc., The Estate Office, Grey Abbey Newtownards, County Down BT22 2QA, Ireland**

**Sotheby's Holdings, Inc., 16 Molesworth Street, Dublin 2, Ireland**

Tel: 353-1-671-1786

## SPS TECHNOLOGIES INC.

101 Greenwood Avenue, Ste. 470, Jenkintown, PA, 19046

Tel: (215) 517-2000    Fax: (215) 517-2032    www.spstech.com

*Mfr. aerospace and industry fasteners, tightening systems, magnetic materials, superalloys.*

**Unbrako SPS Ltd., Shannon Industrial Estate, Shannon County Clare, Ireland**

Tel: 353-61-716500    Fax: 353-61-716584

## THE ST. PAUL COMPANIES, INC.

385 Washington Street, St. Paul, MN, 55102

Tel: (651) 310-7911    Fax: (651) 310-8294    www.stpaul.com

*Provides investment, insurance and reinsurance services.*

**Hibernian Insurance Company Ltd., Hibernian House, Haddington Road, Dublin 4, Ireland**

**St. Paul International Insurance Company Ltd., Longphort House, Earlsfort Centre, Lower Leeson St., Dublin 2 Ireland**

Tel: 353-1-609-5600   Fax: 353-1-662-4945   Contact: Pala Hodson

## STANDEX INTERNATIONAL CORPORATION

6 Manor Parkway, Salem, NH, 03079

Tel: (603) 893-9701    Fax: (603) 893-7324    www.standex.com

*Mfr. diversified graphics, institutional, industry/electronic and consumer products.*

**Standex (Ireland) Ltd., Acragar Road, Mountmellick, County Laois, Ireland**

Tel: 353-502-24350   Fax: 353-502-24744   Contact: Patrick McCormack, Mgr.

## STATE STREET BANK & TRUST COMPANY

225 Franklin Street, Boston, MA, 02101

Tel: (617) 786-3000    Fax: (617) 654-3386    www.statestreet.com

*Banking and financial services.*

**Bank of Ireland Securities, New Century House, International Financial Services Centre, Mayor Street Lower Dublin 1, Ireland**

## STIEFEL LABORATORIES INC.

255 Alhambra Circle, Ste. 1000, Coral Gables, FL, 33134

Tel: (305) 443-3807    Fax: (305) 443-3467    www.stiefel.com

*Mfr. pharmaceuticals, dermatological specialties.*

**Stiefel Laboratories Ltd., 15/16 Stillorgan Industrial Park, Blackrock, Co. Dublin, Ireland**

**Stiefel Laboratories Ltd., Finisklin Industrial Estate, Sligo, Ireland**

## SUMMIT TECHNOLOGY INC.

21 Hickory Drive, Waltham, MA, 02154

Tel: (781) 890-1234    Fax: (781) 890-0313    www.sum-tech.com

*Leading developer, manufacturer and marketer of ophthalmic laser systems and related products.*

**Summit Technology Ireland, Model Farm Rd., Cork Business & Technology Centre, Cork, Ireland**

## SUN MICROSYSTEMS, INC.

901 San Antonio Road, Palo Alto, CA, 94303

Tel: (650) 960-1300    Fax: (650) 856-2114    www.sun.com

*Computer peripherals and programming services.*

**Sun Microsystems, Hamilton House, East Point Business Park, Dublin 3, Ireland**

## SYBASE, INC.

6475 Christie Ave., Emeryville, CA, 94608

Tel: (510) 922-3500    Fax: (510) 922-3210    www.sybase.com

*Design/mfg/distribution of database management systems, software development tools, connectivity products, consulting and technical support services..*

**Sybase Products Ltd., 7 Inns Court Winetavern St., Dublin 8, Ireland**

Tel: 353-1-677-6777   Fax: 353-1-677-6614

## SYMANTEC CORPORATION

20330 Stevens Creek Blvd., Cupertino, CA, 95014-2132

Tel: (408) 253-9600    Fax: (408) 253-3968    www.symantec.com

*Designs and produces PC network security and network management software and hardware.*

**Symantec Ltd. Ireland, Ballycoolin Business Park, Blanchardstown, Dublin 15, Ireland**

Tel: 353-1-820-5060   Fax: 353-1-820-4055

## SYNOPSYS, INC.

700 East Middlefield Road, Mountain View, CA, 94043

Tel: (650) 962-5000      Fax: (650) 965-8637      www.synopsys.com

*Mfr. electronic design automation software.*

**Synopsys International Limited,  Unit 4B-1 - Blanchardstown Corporate Park, Blanchardstown Dublin 15, Ireland**

Tel: 353-1-808-9180

## TACONIC LTD.

PO Box 69, Coonbrook Rd., Petersburg, NY, 12138

Tel: (518) 658-3202      Fax: (518) 658-3204      www.taconic.com

*Mfr. teflon/silicone-coated fiberglass fabrics, tapes and belts; specialty tapes and circuit board substrates.*

**Taconic International, Ltd.,  Lynn Industrial Park, Mullingar, County Westmeath, Ireland**

Tel: 353-44-40477   Fax: 353-44-44369

## TECHNITROL INC.

1210 Northbrook Drive, #385, Trevose, PA, 19053

Tel: (215) 355-2900      Fax: (215) 355-7397      www.technitrol.com

*Mfr. of electronic components, electrical contacts, and other parts/materials.*

**Pulse Engineering - Electronic Components,  Tuam, Ireland**

## TELEFLEX INC.

630 W. Germantown Pike, Ste. 450, Plymouth Meeting, PA, 19462

Tel: (610) 834-6301      Fax: (610) 834-8307      www.teleflex.com

*Designs/mfr./market mechanical and electro-mechanical systems, measure systems.*

**Rüsch Manufacturing (UK) Ltd.,  Lurgan, County Armagh, Northern Ireland**

## TELLABS INC.

4951 Indiana Ave. 6303788800, Lisle, IL, 60532-1698

Tel: (630) 378-8800      Fax: (630) 679-3010      www.tellabs.com

*Design/mfr./service voice/data transport and network access systems.*

**Tellabs Drogheda,  Donore Industrial Site - Droghed, County Louth, Ireland**

**Tellabs Sandyford,  Unit 1B - Bracken Business Park, Sandyford Industrial Estate, Sandyford Dublin, Ireland**

## TERADYNE INC.

321 Harrison Ave., Boston, MA, 02118

Tel: (617) 482-2700      Fax: (617) 422-2910      www.teradyne.com

*Mfr. electronic test equipment and blackplane connection systems.*

**Teradyne Connection Systems (TCS),  Snugboro Industrial Park, Blanchardstown, Dublin 15, Ireland**

Tel: 353-1-820-2299   Fax: 353-1-820-3586

## TEREX CORPORATION

500 Post Road East, Ste. 320, Westport, CT, 06880

Tel: (203) 222-7170      Fax: (203) 222-7976      www.terex.com

*Mfr. lifting and earthmoving equipment.*

**Powerscreen Ireland Ltd.,  No. 4 - 90 Main Street, Portlaoise, County Laoise, Ireland**

Tel: 353-502-22978

**Powerscreen Ltd.,  Lower Main Street, Kilbeggan, County Westmeath, Ireland**

Tel: 353-506-32178

## TEXACO INC.

2000 Westchester Ave., White Plains, NY, 10650

Tel: (914) 253-4000     Fax: (914) 253-7753     www.texaco.com

*Exploration/marketing crude oil, mfr. petro chemicals and products.*

**Texaco Ireland Ltd., Texaco House, Ballsbridge, Dublin 4, Ireland**

**Texoil, Exham House, Douglas Cork, Ireland**

## TEXAS INSTRUMENTS INC.

8505 Forest Lane, Dallas, TX, 75243

Tel: (972) 995-3773     Fax: (972) 995-4360     www.ti.com

*Mfr. semiconductor devices, electronic electro-mechanical systems, instruments and controls.*

**Texas Instruments Ltd., Dublin, Ireland**

## THERM-O-DISC, INC.

1320 S. Main Street, Mansfield, OH, 44907-0538

Tel: (419) 525-8500     Fax: (419) 525-8282     www.thermodisc.com

*Mfr. thermostats, controls, sensor and thermal cutoffs, switches.*

**Therm-O-Disc, Raheen Estate, Limerick, Ireland**

## TJX COMPANIES INC.

770 Cochituate Road, Framingham, MA, 01701

Tel: (508) 390-1000     Fax: (508) 390-2828     www.tjx.com

*Retail stores, catalog and mail order houses.*

**T. J. Maxx, Dublin, Ireland**

## TMP WORLDWIDE, INC.

622 Third Ave., New York, NY, 10017

Tel: (212) 351-7000     Fax: (212) 658-0540     www.tmpw.com

*#1 Yellow Pages agency and a leader in the recruitment and interactive advertising fields.*

**TMP Worldwide, 10 Lower Mount Street - 2/F, Dublin 2, Ireland**

**TMP Worldwide Advertising & Communications, 15 D Gilford Road Sandymount, Dubin 4, Ireland**

## TOKHEIM CORPORATION

PO Box 360, 10501 Corporate Drive, Fort Wayne, IN, 46845

Tel: (219) 470-4600     Fax: (219) 482-2677     www.tokheim.com

*Engaged in design, manufacture and service of electronic and mechanical petroleum marketing systems.*

**Tokheim Ireland, Western Parkway, Ballymount Road, Dublin 12, Ireland**

Tel: 353-1-4500575   Fax: 353-1-4500597

## THE TOPPS COMPANY, INC.

1 Whitehall Street, New York, NY, 10004-2108

Tel: (212) 376-0300     Fax: (212) 376-0573     www.topps.com

*Mfr. entertainment products, principally collectible trading cards, confections, sticker collections, and comic books.*

**Topps Ireland Ltd., Innishmore, Ballincollig, County Cork, Ireland**

Tel: 353-21-871005   Fax: 353-21-870512

## THE TRANE COMPANY

3600 Pammel Creek Road, La Crosse, WI, 54601

Tel: (608) 787-2000     Fax: (608) 787-4990     www.trane.com

*Mfr./distributor/service A/C systems and equipment.*

**Trane (UK) Ltd., 8 The Mall, Lucan, Co. Dublin, Ireland**

**UNIFI INC.**

7201 West Friendly Ave., Greensboro, NC, 27410-6237

Tel: (336) 294-4410    Fax: (336) 316-5422    www.unifi-inc.com

*Yarn spinning mills, throwing/winding mills.*

**Unifi Textured Yarns Europe Ltd., Ballyraine, Letterkenny, Donegal, Ireland**

**UNITED PARCEL SERVICE, INC.**

55 Glenlake Parkway, NE, Atlanta, GA, 30328

Tel: (404) 828-6000    Fax: (404) 828-6593    www.ups.com

*International package-delivery service.*

**UPS Ireland Ltd., Unit 134 Slaney Close, Dublin Industrial Estate, Glasnevin, Dublin 11 Ireland**

Tel: 800-575757

**UNITED STATES SURGICAL CORPORATION**

150 Glover Ave., Norwalk, CT, 06856

Tel: (203) 845-1000    Fax: (203) 847-0635    www.ussurg.com

*Mfr./development/market surgical staplers, laparoscopic instruments and sutures.*

**U.S. Surgical Corp (Ireland) Ltd., Attn: Ireland Office, U.S. Surgical, 150 Glover Avenue, Norwalk CT 06856**

**UNIVERSAL INSTRUMENTS**

90 Bevier Street, S. Dock, Binghamton, NY, 13904

Tel: (607) 779-7522    Fax: (607) 779-7971    www.uic.com

*Mfr./sales of instruments for electronic circuit assembly.*

**Universal Instruments Elecronics Ltd., Dublin, Ireland**

Tel: 353-1-492-3766   Fax: 353-1-492-3766

**UOP LLC.**

25 East Algonquin Road, Des Plaines, IL, 60017

Tel: (847) 391-2000    Fax: (847) 391-2253    www.uop.com

*Engaged in developing and commercializing technology for license to the oil refining, petrochemical and gas processing industries.*

**UOP Johnson Well Screens (Ireland) Ltd., Leixlip, Ireland**

**UPRIGHT INC.**

1775 Park Street, Selma, CA, 93662

Tel: (209) 891-5200    Fax: (209) 896-9012    www.upright.com

*Mfr. aerial work platforms and telescopic handlers.*

**UpRight Ireland Ltd., Industrial Estate, Pottery Rd., Dun Laoire, Dublin, Ireland**

**URS CORPORATION**

100 California Street, Ste. 500, San Francisco, CA, 94111-4529

Tel: (415) 774-2700    Fax: (415) 398-1904    www.urscorp.com

*Provides planning, design and construction management services, pollution control and hazardous waste management.*

**URS (Dames & Moore), Dublin, Ireland**

Tel: 353-1-475-4422

**UUNET**

22001 Loudoun County Pkwy., Ashburn, VA, 20147

Tel: (703) 206-5600    Fax: (703) 206-5601    www.uu.net

*World's largest Internet service provider; World Wide Web hosting services, security products and consulting services to businesses, professionals, and on-line service providers.*

**UUNET Ireland, Erne Street, Dublin 2, Ireland**

## VIKING OFFICE PRODUCTS

950 West 190th Street, Torrance, CA, 90502

Tel: (310) 225-4500 Fax: (310) 324-2396 www.vikingop.com

*International direct marketer of office products, computer supplies, business furniture and stationery.*

**Viking Direct, Ltd., Unit 1, John F. Kennedy Park, Kileen Rd., Dublin 12, Ireland**

Tel: 353-1-450-9007 Fax: 353-1-456-7740 Contact: Keith Cain, Mgr. Emp: 67

## WARNACO INC.

90 Park Ave., New York, NY, 10016

Tel: (212) 661-1300 Fax: (212) 687-0480 www.warnaco.com

*Mfr./sales intimate apparel and men's and women's sportswear.*

**Warnaco, Dublin, Ireland**

## WASHINGTON GROUP INTERNATIONAL, INC.

720 Park Blvd., PO Box 73, Boise, ID, 83729

Tel: (208) 386-5000 Fax: (208) 386-7186 www.wgint.com

*Engaged in engineering and construction.*

**Washington Group International, Inc., 12 South Mall, Cork, Ireland**

Tel: 353-21-906800 Fax: 353-21-906801

## WATSON WYATT & COMPANY HOLDINGS

6707 Democracy Blvd., Ste. 800, Bethesda, MD, 20817

Tel: (301) 581-4600 Fax: (301) 581-4937 www.watsonwyatt.com

*Creates compensation and benefits programs for major corporations.*

**Watson Wyatt & Co., 65/66 Lower Mount Street 1st Fl., Dublin 2, Ireland**

Tel: 353-1-661-6448 Fax: 353-1-676-0818 Contact: Paul Kelly

## WELCH ALLYN DCD INC.

4341 State Street Road, Skaneateles Falls, NY, 13153

Tel: (315) 685-4100 Fax: (315) 685-4091 www.welchallyn.com

*Mfr. bar code data collection systems.*

**Welch Allyn Ireland Ltd., Kells Road, Navan, County Meath, Ireland**

Tel: 353-46-79060

**Welch Allyn Ltd. (Data Collection Division), 21 Sandyford Office Park, Sandyford, Dublin 18 Ireland**

## WELLMAN INC.

1040 Broad Street, Ste. 302, Shrewsbury, NJ, 07702

Tel: (732) 542-7300 Fax: (732) 542-9344 www.wellmanwlm.com

*Plastic recycler; mfr. polyester fibres and resins.*

**Wellman International Ltd., Mullagh, Kells, Meath, Ireland**

## WESTERN WIRELESS CORPORATION

3650 131st Avenue SE, Ste. 400, Bellevue, WA, 98006

Tel: (425) 586-8700 Fax: (425) 586-8666 www.wwireless.com

*Provides wireless communication services.*

**Meteor Mobile Communications Ltd., 4030 Kingswood Avenue, Citywest Business Park Naas Road, Dublin 24, Ireland**

## WHIRLPOOL CORPORATION

2000 N. M-63, Benton Harbor, MI, 49022-2692

Tel: (616) 923-5000 Fax: (616) 923-5443 www.whirlpoolcorp.com

*Mfr./market home appliances: Whirlpool, Roper, KitchenAid, Estate, and Inglis.*

**Whirlpool Europe B.V., Dublin, Ireland**

## WILLAMETTE INDUSTRIES, INC.

1300 SW Fifth Ave., Ste. 3800, Portland, OR, 97201

Tel: (503) 227-5581     Fax: (503) 273-5603     www.wii.com

*Mfr./sales and distribution of paper and wood products.*

**Willamette Europe, Redmondstown, Clonmel, County Tipperrary, Ireland**

Tel: 353-52-21166   Fax: 353-52-21815   Contact: Rory Kirwan, Mng. Dir.   Emp: 200

## HARRY WINSTON INC.

718 Fifth Ave., New York, NY, 10019

Tel: (212) 245-2000     Fax:     www.harry-winston.com

*Diamonds and lapidary work.*

**Harry Winston Irish Rough Diamonds Ltd., Hermitage, Ennis, Clare, Ireland**

## WORLDCOM, INC.

500 Clinton Center Drive, Clinton, MS, 39060

Tel: (601) 360-8600     Fax: (601) 360-8616     www.wcom.com

*Telecommunications company serving local, long distance and Internet customers domestically and internationally.*

**WorldCom International, MCI WorldCom House, Ballybrit Business Park, Galway, Irealnd**

**WorldCom International, Embassy House, Ballsbridge, Dublin 4, Ireland**

**WorldCom International, Versyss Building, Mahon Industrial Estate, Blackrock County Cork, Ireland**

**WorldCom International, International Business Centre, National Technological Park, Limerick, Ireland**

## WYETH-AYERST INTERNATIONAL INC.

150 Radnot-Chester Road, St. Davids, PA, 19087

Tel: (610) 902-4100     Fax: (610) 989-4586     www.ahp.com/wyeth

*Antibiotics and pharmaceutical products.*

**Wyeth Nutritionals Ireland, Askeaton, County Limerick, Ireland**

Tel: 353-61-392-168

**Wyeth-Medica Ireland, Little Connell, Newbridge, County Kildare, Ireland**

Tel: 353-45-434 -333

## XEROX CORPORATION

800 Long Ridge Road, PO Box 1600, Stamford, CT, 06904

Tel: (203) 968-3000     Fax: (203) 968-4312     www.xerox.com

*Mfr. document processing equipment, systems and supplies.*

**Xerox Ltd., Glasnevin Industrial Estate, Finglas Rd., Dublin 11, Ireland**

Tel: 353-1-661-6322   Fax: 353-1-806-2581

## XILINX INC.

2100 Logic Drive, San Jose, CA, 95124-3400

Tel: (408) 559-7778     Fax: (408) 559-7114     www.xilinx.com

*Programmable logic and related development systems software.*

**Xilinx Ireland, 1 Logic Dr., Citywest Business Campus, Saggart County, Dublin Ireland**

Tel: 353-1-464-0311

## YAHOO! INC.

3420 Central Expressway, Santa Clara, CA, 95051

Tel: (408) 731-3300     Fax: (408) 731-3301     www.yahoo-inc.com

*Internet media company providing specialized content, free electronic mail and community offerings and commerce.*

**Yahoo! Inc., Ireland -c/o 80/81 St. Martin's Lane, London WC2N 4AA, UK**

## YELLOW CORPORATION

10990 Roe Ave., PO Box 7270, Overland Park, KS, 66207

Tel: (913) 696-6100     Fax: (913) 696-6116     www.yellowcorp.com

*Commodity transportation.*

**Frans Maas Ireland Ltd., Swords Business Park, Swords, County Dublin Ireland**

**Frans Maas Ireland ltd., Newmarket on Fergus, Shannon, Count Cuare Ireland**

## YORK INTERNATIONAL CORPORATION

631 South Richland Ave., York, PA, 17403

Tel: (717) 771-7890     Fax: (717) 771-6212     www.york.com

*Mfr. heating, ventilating, air conditioning and refrigeration equipment.*

**York Ireland, Unit 2004/3 City West Business Campus, Naas Road, Dublin 22 Ireland**

Tel: 353-1-466-0177

**York Ireland, Unit 19, University Hale Ind. Estate, Sarsfield Road, Wilton Cork, Ireland**

Tel: 353-21-346-580

## ZOMAX INCORPORATED

5353 Nathan Lane, Plymouth, MN, 55442

Tel: (763) 553-9300     Fax: (763) 553-0826     www.zomax.com

*Mfr./sales CD-ROM's, digital video discs and cassettes.*

**Zomax Limited, Carrisbrook House - 6/F, 122 Pembroke Road, Ballsbridge Dublin 4, Ireland**

Tel: 353-1-405-6350   Fax: 353-1-457-7675   Contact: Patrice Dowling

**Zomax Limited, Unit 1 Cloverhill Industrial Estate, Clondalkin Dublin 22, Ireland**

Tel: 353-1-405-6350   Fax: 353-1-457-7675   Contact: Patrice Dowling

# Isle of Man

## AON CORPORATION

123 North Wacker Drive, Chicago, IL, 60606

Tel: (312) 701-3000    Fax: (312) 701-3100    www.aon.com

*Insurance brokers worldwide; underwrites accident and health insurance, specialty and professional insurance; and provides risk management consultation.*

**AON Insurance Managers (Isle of Man) Ltd., Post Office Chambers, Douglas IM1 12EA, UK**

Tel: 44-1634-689-400   Fax: 44-1624-673-242   Contact: Geoll Hunk

**AON Risk Services Ltd., 28 Athol St., Douglas 1M1 1QE, UK**

Tel: 44-1624-673-325   Fax: 44-1624-623-664   Contact: Mike Henthorn

## BDO SEIDMAN, LLP    BELGIUM

Two Prudential Plaza, 180 N. Stetson Ave., Ste. 2300, Chicago, IL, 60601

Tel: (312) 240-1236    Fax: (312) 240-3329    www.bdo.com

*International accounting and financial consulting firm.*

**BDO Binder, Ragnall House, 18 Peel Road, Douglas IM1 4LZ, UK**

Tel: 44-1624-620711   Fax: 44-1624-672446   Contact: John D. Clarke

## DHL WORLDWIDE EXPRESS

50 California Avenue, San Francisco, CA, 94111

Tel: (415) 677-6100    Fax: (415) 824-9700    www.dhl.com

*Worldwide air express carrier.*

**DHL Worldwide Express, Island Express, Unit 27 Spring Valley Industrial Estate, Bradden IM2 2QT UK**

Tel: 44-1624-661122   Fax: 44-1624-661394

## ERNST & YOUNG, LLP

787 Seventh Ave., New York, NY, 10019

Tel: (212) 773-3000    Fax: (212) 773-6350    www.eyi.com

*Accounting and audit, tax and management consulting services.*

**Ernst & Young, Derby Housem Athol St., Douglas,UK**

Tel: 44-1624-626661   Fax: 44-1624-626375   Contact: Larry A. Kearns

## ICC INDUSTRIES INC.

460 Park Ave., New York, NY, 10022

Tel: (212) 521-1700    Fax: (212) 521-1794    www.iccchem.com

*Manufacturing and trading of chemicals, plastics and pharmaceuticals.*

**Dover Chemical Ltd., 1 Athol St., Douglas 1M1 1LD, UK**

Tel: 44-1624-626-573   Fax: 44-1624-616-350   Contact: Dwain Colvin

## KPMG INTERNATIONAL LLP

345 Park Avenue, New York, NY, 10022

Tel: (201) 307-7000    Fax: (201) 930-8617    www.kpmg.com

*Accounting and audit, tax and management consulting services.*

**KPMG Peat Marwick, Heritage Court, 41 Athol Street, Douglas 1M99 1HN, UK**

Tel: 44-1624-681000   Fax: 44-1624-681098   Contact: Peter F. Pell-Hiley, Sr. Ptnr.

## MERRILL LYNCH & COMPANY, INC.

World Financial Center, 250 Vesey Street, New York, NY, 10281-1332

Tel: (212) 449-1000      Fax: (212) 449-2892      www.ml.com

*Security brokers and dealers, investment and business services.*

**Merrill Lynch International - Trust Services, Atlantic House, Circular Road, Douglas 1M1 1QW, UK**

Tel: 44-1624-688600   Fax: 44-1624-688601

## PRICEWATERHOUSECOOPERS LLP

1301 Ave. of the Americas, New York, NY, 10019

Tel: (212) 596-7000      Fax: (212) 259-1301      www.pwcglobal.com

*Accounting and auditing, tax and management, and human resource consulting services.*

**PriceWaterhouseCoopers, 1-3 Upper Church St., Douglas, Isle of Man, UK**

Tel: 44-1624-662550   Fax: 44-1624-673113

# Israel

## 3COM CORPORATION

5400 Bayfront Plaza, Santa Clara, CA, 95052-8145

Tel: (408) 326-5000      Fax: (408) 326-5001      www.3com.com

*Develop/mfr. computer networking products and systems.*

**3Com Israel, 1-3 (A) Nirim St., Beit Hasapanut, Tel-Aviv 67060 Israel**

Tel: 972-3-636-1720   Fax: 972-3-636-1733

## 3M

3M Center, St. Paul, MN, 55144-1000

Tel: (651) 733-1110      Fax: (651) 733-9973      www.mmm.com

*Mfr. diversified products for industry, health care, imaging, communications, transport, safety, consumer, etc.*

**3M Israel Ltd.,  c/o Monarch Consulting Co., 91 Medinat Hayehudim St., PO Box 2042, Herzilya-Pituah 46120 Israel**

Tel: 972-9-561-490   Fax: 972-9-561676

## ABBOTT LABORATORIES

One Abbott Park, Abbott Park, IL, 60064-3500

Tel: (847) 937-6100      Fax: (847) 937-1511      www.abbott.com

*Development/mfr./sale diversified health care products and services.*

**Abbott Pharmaceuticals ProMedico Ltd.,  PO Box 29031, Tel Aviv 61292, Israel**

## ADAMS RITE MANUFACTURING COMPANY

260 Santa Fe Street, Pomona, CA, 91767

Tel: (909) 632-2300      Fax: (909) 632-3267      www.adamsrite.com

*Mfr. architectural hardware.*

**A. Samuel Ltd.,  72 Nachlat Binyamin St. Box 990, Tel Aviv 61009, Israel**

Tel: 972-3-517-7072   Fax: 972-3-516-1298

## ADE CORPORATION

80 Wilson Way, Westwood, MA, 02090

Tel: (781) 467-3500      Fax: (781) 467-0500      www.ade.com

*Mfr. semiconductor wafers and computer disks.*

**G-Electronics,  3 Tefutsot Israel Street, Industrial Center, Givatayim 53583, Israel**

Tel: 972-35-14333   Fax: 972-35-13958

## AEROMARITIME, INC.

4115 Pleasant Valley Drive, Chantilly, VA, 22021

Tel: (703) 631-3111      Fax: (703) 631-3144      www.aeromar.com

*Military electronics.*

**Elul Technologies Ltd.,  35 Shaul Hamelech Blvd., Tel Aviv, Israel**

## AGILENT TECHNOLOGIES, INC.

395 Page Mill Road, PO Box 10395, Palo Alto, CA, 94303

Tel: (650) 752-5000      Fax: (650) 752-5633      www.agilent.com

*Mfr. communications components.*

**Agilent Technologies Israel Ltd.,  2 Hashlosh Street, Building B3,  IL-Tel Aviv 67060, Israel**

## AIR EXPRESS INTERNATIONAL CORPORATION

120 Tokeneke Road, PO Box 1231, Darien, CT, 06820

Tel: (203) 655-7900     Fax: (203) 655-5779     www.aeilogistics.com

*International air freight forwarder.*

**AEI c/o Flying Cargo Logistics Services, 79 Hayarok St.- Bldg. 121, Kanot Industrial Park, Maar Israel**

Tel: 972-8-869-2430   Fax: 972-8-869-2429

**Air Express Int., c/o Flying Cargo Ltd., 11 Hachilazon St., Ramat-Gan Tel Aviv 52522 , Israel**

Tel: 972-3-576-3939   Fax: 972-3-575-9123

## ALLEGHENY TECHNOLOGIES

1000 Six PPG Place, Pittsburgh, PA, 15222

Tel: (412) 394-2800     Fax: (412) 394-2805     www.alleghenytechnologies.com

*Diversified mfr. aviation and electronics, specialty metals, industrial and consumer products.*

**Allegheny Technologies, America House, 35 Shaul Hamelech Blvd., Tel Aviv 64927, Israel**

**Composite Ltd., 12 Ha-Gat Street - #27, Rishon Le Ziyyon 75498, Israel**

## ALPHA WIRE COMPANY

711 Lidgerwood Ave., Elizabeth, NJ, 07207

Tel: (908) 925-8000     Fax: (908) 925-6923     www.alphawire.com

*Mfr. wire, cable and tubing products.*

**Alexander Schneider Ltd./D. Danino, 16 Haim Hazaz Street, PO Box 18055, Tel Aviv 61180 Israel**

Tel: 972-3647-3331   Fax: 972-3647-4114   Contact: David Danino

## AMERICAN LOCKER GROUP INC.

608 Allen Street, Jamestown, NY, 14701-3966

Tel: (716) 664-9600     Fax: (716) 483-2822     www.americanlocker.com

*Mfr. coin-operated locks and office furniture.*

**Safe Locker Secure Storage Systems, Ness-Zioni-Israel**

Tel: 972-8-9403288

## AMERICAN SAFETY RAZOR COMPANY

1 Razor Blade Lane, Verona, VA, 24482

Tel: (540) 248-8000     Fax: (540) 248-0522     www.asrco.com

*Mfr. private-label and branded shaving razors and blades and cotton swabs.*

**Personna Israel, 1 Derech Hachativot Stret, Upper Nazareth 17000, Israel**

## ANALOG DEVICES INC.

1 Technology Way, Box 9106, Norwood, MA, 02062

Tel: (781) 329-4700     Fax: (781) 326-8703     www.analog.com

*Mfr. integrated circuits and related devices.*

**Analog Devices (Israel) Ltd., Giron Ctr., 3-5 Jabolinsky St., Raananna Central 43363, Israel**

## ANC RENTAL CORP.

110 Southeast Sixth St., Ft. Lauderdale, FL, 33301

Tel: (954) 769-7000     Fax: (954) 769-7000     www.ancrental.com

*Engaged in car rental services, including National Car Rental and Alamo Rent A Car.*

**National Car Rental System, Box 26113, Tel Aviv, Israel**

## ANDERSEN WORLDWIDE

33 West Monroe Street, Chicago, IL, 60603

Tel: (312) 580-0033     Fax: (312) 507-6748     www.arthurandersen.com

*Accounting and audit, tax and management consulting services.*

**Luboshitz, Kasierer & Co., 9, Achad Ha'am St., Shalom Tower, PO Box 29452, Tel-Aviv 61293 Israel**

Tel: 972-3-511-8222

## ANDREA ELECTRONICS CORPORATION

45 Melville Park Road, Melville, NY, 11747

Tel: (631) 719-1800     Fax: (631) 719-1950     www.andreaelectronics.com

*Mfr. noise reduction electronic headsets, handsets and microphones.*

**Lamar Signal Processing, Ltd., PO Box 273, Yoqneam Ilit 20692, Israel**

## APPLIED MATERIALS, INC.

3050 Bowers Ave., Santa Clara, CA, 95054-3299

Tel: (408) 727-5555     Fax: (408) 727-9943     www.appliedmaterials.com

*Supplies manufacturing systems and services to the semiconductor industry.*

**Applied Materials Israel, Ltd., SB Industry Campus Har Hotzvim, 5 Kiryat-Mada St. (Luz Bldg.), PO Box 45141, Jerusalem 91450 Israel**

Tel: 972-2-58-70750   Fax: 972-2-58-70757

**Applied Materials, Ltd., Atidim Industrial Park Bldg. 2, PO Box 58152, Tel Aviv 61581, Israel**

Tel: 972-3-645-0201   Fax: 972-3-645-0280

## ASSOCIATED MERCHANDISING CORPORATION

500 Seventh Ave., 2nd Fl., New York, NY, 10018

Tel: (212) 819-6600     Fax: (212) 819-6701     www.theamc.com

*Retail service organization; apparel, shoes and accessories.*

**Associated Merchandising Corp., Migdalel Vaiv Bldg. 6th Fl., 48A Petach Tikva Rd.,Tel Aviv 66184, Israel**

## ASTEA INTERNATIONAL, INC.

455 Business Center Drive, Horsham, PA, 19044

Tel: (215) 682-2500     Fax: (215) 682-2515     www.astea.com

*Produces computer software that assists to automate and manage field service, sales and customer support operations.*

**Astea-Israel Ltd., PO Box 7, Industrial Park Tefen, Migdal, Tefen 24959, Israel**

Tel: 972-4-987-2519   Fax: 972-4-987-2031

## ASTRONAUTICS CORPORATION OF AMERICA

PO Box 523, Milwaukee, WI, 53201-0523

Tel: (414) 447-8200     Fax: (414) 447-8231     www.astronautics.com

*Design/development/mfr. aircraft instruments, avionics, electronics systems, vehicle electronics and computer maintenance service.*

**Astronautics C.A. Ltd., 23 Hayarkon St., PO Box 882, Bnei-Brak, Israel**

## AUTODESK INC.

111 McInnis Parkway, San Rafael, CA, 94903

Tel: (415) 507-5000     Fax: (415) 507-6112     www.autodesk.com

*Develop/marketing/support computer-aided design, engineering, scientific and multimedia software products.*

**Audodesk Israel Ltd., 11 Galgalei Haplada St., PO Box 12590, Herzliya 46733, Israel**

Tel: 972-9-950-4610   Fax: 972-9-950-3726

## AVX CORPORATION

PO Box 867, Myrtle Beach, SC, 29578

Tel: (843) 448-9411     Fax: (843) 448-7139     www.avxcorp.com

*Mfr. multilayer ceramic capacitors.*

**AVX Israel Ltd., PO Box 3108, Jerusalem 91030, Israel**

## BARNWELL INDUSTRIES INC.

1100 Alakea Street, Ste. 2900, Honolulu, HI, 96813-2833

Tel: (808) 531-8400     Fax: (808) 531-7181     www.brninc.con

*Holding company: exploration/development gas and oil, drill water systems, farming/marketing papayas.*

**Barnwell of Israel Ltd., PO Box 3005, Tel Aviv 61030, Israel**

## BARRY CONTROLS INC.

40 Guest Street, PO Box 9105, Brighton, MA, 02135-9105

Tel: (617) 787-1555     Fax: (617) 254-7381     www.barrymounts.com

*Mfr./sale vibration isolation mounting devices.*

**Mono Electronics Ltd., PO Box 8198, New Industrial Zone, Netanya 422943 Israel**

## BATES WORLDWIDE INC.

405 Lexington Ave., New York, NY, 10174

Tel: (212) 297-7000     Fax: (212) 986-0270     www.batesww.com

*Advertising, marketing, public relations and media consulting.*

**Bates Baumann Ber Rivney, Century Tower, 124 Iben Gaviroi St., Tel-Aviv 62038, Israel**

Tel: 972-3-520-2826   Fax: 972-3-527-9096   Contact: Yoran Baumann, Pres.

## BBDO WORLDWIDE

1285 Ave. of the Americas, New York, NY, 10019

Tel: (212) 459-5000     Fax: (212) 459-6645     www.bbdo.com

*Multinational group of advertising agencies.*

**Gitam BBDO, Ramat-Gan, Israel**

## BDO SEIDMAN, LLP   BELGIUM

Two Prudential Plaza, 180 N. Stetson Ave., Ste. 2300, Chicago, IL, 60601

Tel: (312) 240-1236     Fax: (312) 240-3329     www.bdo.com

*International accounting and financial consulting firm.*

**BDO Almgor & Company, Silver House 12th Floor, 7 Habba Hillel Rd., Ramat Gan 52134, Israel**

Tel: 972-3-576-0606   Fax: 972-3-575-4671   Contact: Yali Sheffi

## BELLSOUTH CORPORATION LATIN AMERICA

1155 Peachtree Street NE, Ste. 400, Atlanta, GA, 30367

Tel: (404) 249-4800     Fax: (404) 249-4880     www.bellsouth.com

*Mobile communications, telecommunications network systems.*

**Cellcom, 2001 Merkazim Building, 29 Maskit Street, Herzliya Pituach 46733, Israel**

Tel: 972-9-959-9599

## BEN & JERRY'S HOMEMADE INC.

30 Community Drive, South Burlington, VT, 05403-6828

Tel: (802) 651-9600     Fax: (802) 651-9647     www.benjerry.com

*Mfr. premium ice cream.*

**Ben & Jerry's International, Jerusalem, Israel**

**Ben & Jerry's International, 1 Hameisav St., Yavne 70600, Israel**

Tel: 972-8-943-7474   Fax: 972-8-943-7475

**Ben & Jerry's International, Yavne, Israel**

## BEST WESTERN INTERNATIONAL

6201 North 24th Place, Phoenix, AZ, 85106

Tel: (602) 957-4200     Fax: (602) 957-5740     www.bestwestern.com

*International hotel chain.*

**Nof Hotel, 101 Hanassi Ave., Haifa, Israel**

## BESTFOODS, INC.

700 Sylvan Ave., International Plaza, Englewood Cliffs, NJ, 07632-9976

Tel: (201) 894-4000      Fax: (201) 894-2186      www.bestfoods.com

*Consumer foods products; corn refining.*

**Israel Edible Products Ltd. (TAMI), 91 Medinat Hayehudim Str., Herzelia Pituach 46766, Israel**

Tel: 972-9-959-2855   Fax: 972-9-959-2863   Contact: Ron Guttmann, Mgr.

## SAMUEL BINGHAM COMPANY

127 East Lake Street, Ste. 300, Bloomingdale, IL, 60108

Tel: (630) 924-9250      Fax: (630) 924-0469      www.binghamrollers.com

*Print and industrial rollers and inks.*

**Haglil Ltd., PO Box 862, Ashdod 77107, Israel**

## BIO-RAD LABORATORIES INC.

1000 Alfred Nobel Drive, Hercules, CA, 94547

Tel: (510) 724-7000      Fax: (510) 724-3167      www.bio-rad.com

*Mfr. life science research products, clinical diagnostics, analytical instruments.*

**Bio-Rad Laboratories Inc., Rehovot, Israel**

## BIO-TECHNOLOGY GENERAL CORP.

70 Wood Avenue South, Iselin, NJ, 08830

Tel: (732) 632-8800      Fax: (732) 632-8844

*Engaged in research, development and marketing of genetically engineered pharmaceuticals.*

**BTG Israel Ltd. (Bio-Technology General Ltd.), Kiryat Weizmann, Rehovot 76326, Israel**

Contact: Zvi Ben-Hetz, VP Operations

## BMC SOFTWARE, INC.

2101 City West Blvd., Houston, TX, 77042-2827

Tel: (713) 918-8800      Fax: (713) 918-8000      www.bmc.com

*Engaged in mainframe-related utilities software and services.*

**BMC Software, ATIDIM Bldg. 7, PO Box 58168, Tel Aviv 61581, Israel**

## BOZELL GROUP

40 West 23rd Street, New York, NY, 10010

Tel: (212) 727-5000      Fax: (212) 645-9173      www.bozell.com

*Advertising, marketing, public relations and media consulting.*

**Dahaf Group, 2-Ben-TZVI Blvd., Jaffa, Tel-Aviv 68181, Israel**

Tel: 972-3-512-7788   Fax: 972-3-683-5413   Contact: Oren Zurabin, Gen.Mgr./CEO

## BRANSON ULTRASONICS CORPORATION

41 Eagle Road, Danbury, CT, 06813-1961

Tel: (203) 796-0400      Fax: (203) 796-2285      www.branson-plasticsjoin.com

*Mfr. plastics assembly equipment, ultrasonic cleaning equipment.*

**Elina Ltd., PO Box 11439, Bet-Dagan 58001, Israel**

Tel: 972-3-559-0337   Fax: 972-3-556-0952

## BRINK'S INC.

Thorndal Circle, Darien, CT, 06820

Tel: (203) 662-7800      Fax: (203) 662-7968      www.brinks.com

*Security transportation.*

**Brink's Israel Ltd., Migdal Shalom Mayer Bldg., 9 Ahad-Haam St., PO Box 29785, Tel Aviv, Israel**

## BRISTOL-MYERS SQUIBB COMPANY

345 Park Ave., New York, NY, 10154-0037

Tel: (212) 546-4000     Fax: (212) 546-4020     www.bms.com

*Pharmaceutical and food preparations, medical and surgical instruments.*

**Bristol-Myer Squibb - Israel - Habinim, Pharmabest Beith Habonim, 2 Habonim St., Ramat Gan 52462, Israel**

**Philtel Ltd., 14 Shenkar str. Kiryat Arie, 49513 PO Box 3918, Petach Tikva 49130, Israel**

## BUDGET GROUP, INC.

125 Basin St., Ste. 210, Daytona Beach, FL, 32114

Tel: (904) 238-7035     Fax: (904) 238-7461     www.budgetrentacar.com

*Car and truck rental system.*

**Budget Rent A Car, 46 Hahistadrut Blvd., Check Post, Haifa, Israel**

Tel: 972-4-842-4004

**Budget Rent A Car, 8 King David St., Jerusalem, Israel**

Tel: 972-2-624=8991

**Budget Rent A Car, Rival St 34, Tel Aviv at Ben Gurion Airport, Israel**

Tel: 972-3-688-5777

## LEO BURNETT, DIV. B-COM 3 GROUP

35 West Wacker Drive, Chicago, IL, 60601

Tel: (312) 220-5959     Fax: (312) 220-6533     www.bcom3group.com

*Engaged in advertising, marketing, media buying and planning, and public relations.*

**Reuveni Pridan Adertising, Tel Aviv, Israel**

## CAMBREX CORPORATION

1 Meadowlands Plaza, East Rutherford, NJ, 07063

Tel: (201) 804-3000     Fax: (201) 804-9852     www.cambrex.com

*human health, animal health/agriculture and Mfr. biotechnology products and produce specialty chemicals.*

**Dexmor Ltd., PO Box 13141, Tel Aviv 61131, Israel**

Tel: 972-3-498503

## CENTURY 21 REAL ESTATE CORPORATION

6 Sylvan Way, Parsippany, NJ, 07054-3826

Tel: (973) 496-5722     Fax: (973) 496-5527     www.century21.com

*Engaged in real estate.*

**Century 21 Israel, Ltd., 20 Ben Gurion St. City Gate 1, Herzelia, Israel**

Tel: 972-9-957-7222   Fax: 972-9-957-7221

## CHECKPOINT SYSTEMS, INC.

101 Wolf Drive, Thorofare, NJ, 08086

Tel: (856) 848-1800     Fax: (856) 848-0937     www.checkpointsystems.com

*Mfr. test, measurement and closed-circuit television systems.*

**Checkpoint Systems Israel, PO Box 8301, 8 Ha'argaman St., New Industrial Zone K. Nordau, Netanya 42504, Israel**

Tel: 972-9-885-3332   Fax: 972-9-885-3155   Contact: Israel Elran

## THE CHERRY CORPORATION

3600 Sunset Ave., PO Box 718, Waukegan, IL, 60087

Tel: (847) 662-9200     Fax: (847) 662-2990     www.cherrycorp.com

*Mfr. electrical switches, electronic keyboards, controls and displays.*

**Astragal Ltd., 3 Hashikma Street, PO Box 906, IL-Tel Aviv 61008, Israel**

Tel: 972-3-5591660   Fax: 972-3-5592340

## CHESTERTON BINSWANGER INTERNATIONAL

Two Logan Square, 4th Floor, Philadelphia, PA, 19103-2759

Tel: (215) 448-6000    Fax: (215) 448-6238    www.cbbi.com

*Real estate and related services.*

**PIB Poalim Investments Binswanger,  2 Habarzel Street - 3/F, Tel Aviv, Israel**

## THE CHRISTIAN SCIENCE PUBLISHING SOCIETY

1 Norway Street, Boston, MA, 02115

Tel: (617) 450-2000    Fax: (617) 450-7575    www.christianscience.com

*Publishing company.*

**The Christian Science Monitor Publication,  Beit Agron, Box 3, 37 Hillel St., Jerusalem 93503, Israel**

## CIGNA COMPANIES

One Liberty Place, Philadelphia, PA, 19192

Tel: (215) 761-1000    Fax: (215) 761-5511    www.cigna.com

*Insurance, invest, health care and other financial services.*

**CIGNA Insurance Co.,  c/o Tocatly & Sons, Migdal Shalom Mayer, PO Box 1025, Tel Aviv, Israel**

**CIGNA Insurance Co. of Europe SA/NV (Securitas Ins. Ltd.),  38 Rothschild Bldg., PO Box 1791, Tel Aviv, Israel**

## CINCINNATI INCORPORATED

PO Box 11111, Cincinnati, OH, 45211

Tel: (513) 367-7100    Fax: (513) 367-7552    www.e-ci.com

*Mfr. metal fabricating equipment.*

**Josef Rosenthaler Co. Ltd.,  PO Box 791, Haifa 31007, Israel**

Tel: 972-4-852-2676   Fax: 972-4-85-8824

## CISCO SYSTEMS, INC.

170 West Tasman Drive, San Jose, CA, 95134-1706

Tel: (408) 526-4000    Fax: (408) 526-4100    www.cisco.com

*Develop/mfr./market computer hardware and software networking systems.*

**Cisco Systems Israel,  3 Hayezira St., Natanya 42160, Israel**

Tel: 972-9-863-2000   Fax: 972-9-658518

## CITIGROUP, INC.

153 East 53rd Street, New York, NY, 10043

Tel: (212) 559-1000    Fax: (212) 559-3646    www.citigroup.com

*Provides insurance and financial services worldwide.*

**Citibank N.A.,  76 Rothschild Blvd., Beit Mozes 7th Fl., Tel Aviv 65785, Israel**

Tel: 972-3-566-5567   Fax: 972-3-566-5565   Contact: Ron Braverman

## THE COCA-COLA COMPANY

PO Drawer 1734, Atlanta, GA, 30301

Tel: (404) 676-2121    Fax: (404) 676-6792    www.coca-cola.com

*Mfr./marketing/distributor soft drinks, syrups and concentrates, juice and juice-drink products.*

**Coca-Cola Bottlers Israel,  Israel Office c/o Zamberly Place, 107/111 Peascod St., Windsor Berks SL4 1PE UK**

## COMPUTER ASSOCIATES INTERNATIONAL INC.

One Computer Associates Plaza, Islandia, NY, 11788

Tel: (516) 342-5224    Fax: (516) 342-5329    www.cai.com

*Integrated business software for enterprise computing and information management, application development, manufacturing, financial applications and professional services.*

**Computer Associates Israel Ltd.,  Deborah Hanevia St., Neva Sharet, Atidim, PO Box 58160, Tel Aviv 61580 Israel**

Tel: 972-3-648-1120

## COMPUWARE CORPORATION
31440 Northwestern Hwy., Farmington Hills, MI, 48334-2564
Tel: (248) 737-7300    Fax: (248) 737-7108    www.compuware.com
*Develop and market software for enterprise and e-commerce solutions.*
**Formula Technologies Ltd.,  3 Ha'galim Avenue, PO Box 2062, Herzeliah 46120, Israel**
Tel: 972-9-959-8889

## COMVERSE TECHNOLOGY, INC.
234 Crossways Park Drive, Woodbury, NY, 11797
Tel: (516) 677-7200    Fax: (516) 677-7355    www.comverse.com
*Mfr. telephone communication and recording systems.*
**Comverse Infosys Ltd.,  23 Habarzel Street, Tel-Aviv 69710, Israel**
Tel: 972-3-766-5888   Fax: 972-3-766-5889

## CONEXANT SYSTEMS, INC.
4311 Jamboree Road, PO Box C, Newport Beach, CA, 92658-8902
Tel: (949) 483-4600    Fax: (949) 483-4078    www.conexant.com
*Provides semiconductor products for communications electronics.*
**Conexant Systems Israel Ltd.,  11 Galgalei Ha Plada Street, PO Box 12660, Herzlia 46733 Israel**
Tel: 972-9-952-4000   Fax: 972-9-957-3732

## CONVERGYS CORPORATION
201 E. 4th St., Cincinnati, OH, 45202
Tel: (513) 723-7000    Fax: (513) 421-8624    www.convergys.com
*Engaged in data bill processing, telemarketing and customer services representation for major corporations.*
**Convergys Corporation,  8 Maskit Street, Herzlia 46766, Israel**
Tel: 311-5360-6060

## COPELAND CORPORATION
1675 West Campbell Road, Sidney, OH, 45365-0669
Tel: (937) 498-3011    Fax: (937) 498-3334    www.copeland-corp.com
*Producer of compressors and condensing units for commercial and residential air conditioning and refrigeration equipment.*
**Scharf/Copeland Israel,  25 Hamerkava Street, Holon 58851, Israel**
Tel: 972-3-5595239   Fax: 972-3-5595243

## CROMPTON CORPORATION
Benson Road, Middlebury, CT, 06749
Tel: (203) 573-2000    Fax:    www.crompton-knowles.com
*Mfr. dyes, colors, flavors, fragrances, specialty chemicals and industrial products.*
**Crompton Chemical Ltd.,  PO Box 975, Haifa 31000, Israel**

## CYLINK CORPORATION
3131 Jay Street, Santa Clara, CA, 95054
Tel: (408) 855-6000    Fax: (408) 855-6100    www.cyllink.com
*Develop and manufactures encryption software.*
**Cylink Israel/Algorithmic Research,  10 Nevatim Street, Kiryat Matalon, Petach Tikva 49561, Israel**
Tel: 972- 3-927-9500   Fax: 972- 3-923-0864

## CYPRESS SEMICONDUCTOR CORPORATION
3901 N. First Street, San Jose, CA, 95134-1599
Tel: (408) 943-2600    Fax: (408) 943-2796    www.cypress.com
*Mfr. integrated circuits.*
**Cypress Semiconductor,  Pakris 2, Rehovot 76703, Israel**
Tel: 972-894-664-06   Fax: 972-894-664-05

## D'ARCY MASIUS BENTON & BOWLES INC. (DMB&B)

1675 Broadway, New York, NY, 10019

Tel: (212) 468-3622     Fax: (212) 468-2987     www.dmbb.com

*Full service international advertising and communications group.*

**DMB&B Mid East-Africa,  76 Rothschild Avenue, Tel Aviv 65785, Israel**

## DATA GENERAL CORPORATION

4400 Computer Drive, Westboro, MA, 01580

Tel: (508) 898-5000     Fax: (508) 366-1319     www.dg.com

*Design, mfr. general purpose computer systems and peripheral products and services.*

**Data General Israel Bet-Harel,  3 Abba Hillel Silver Street, 52522 Ramat Gan/Tel Aviv, Israel**

Tel: 972-3-754-1114

## DATA SYSTEMS & SOFTWARE INC.

200 Rte. 17, Mahwah, NJ, 07430

Tel: (201) 529-2026     Fax: (201) 529-3163     www.dssiinc.com

*Engaged in technology software consulting and development.*

**DSI Decision Systems Israel Ltd.,  11 Ben Gurion Street, Giv'at Shmuel 54017, Israel**

Tel: 972-3-531-3333   Fax: 972-3-531-3322   Contact: Yacov Kaufman, VP

## DDB NEEDHAM WORLDWIDE INC.

437 Madison Ave., New York, NY, 10022

Tel: (212) 415-2000     Fax: (212) 415-3417     www.ddbn.com

*Advertising agency.*

**Linial Huss DDB,  Tel Aviv, Israel**

## DELOITTE TOUCHE TOHMATSU INTERNATIONAL

1633 Broadway, New York, NY, 10019

Tel: (212) 492-4000     Fax: (212) 392-4154     www.deloitte.com

*Accounting, audit, tax and management consulting services.*

**Igal Brightman & Co.,  New Clal Ctr., 42 Agrippas St., Jerusalem 94301, Israel**

**Igal Brightman & Co.,  PO Box 16593, Tel Aviv 61164, Israel**

**Igal Brightman & Co.,  PO Box 5648, Haifa 31055, Israel**

## DHL WORLDWIDE EXPRESS

50 California Avenue, San Francisco, CA, 94111

Tel: (415) 677-6100     Fax: (415) 824-9700     www.dhl.com

*Worldwide air express carrier.*

**DHL Worldwide Express,  5 Hapardes St., Azur 58001, Israel**

Tel: 972-3-557-3850

## DIONEX CORPORATION

1228 Titan Way, PO Box 3603, Sunnyvale, CA, 94086-3603

Tel: (408) 737-0700     Fax: (408) 730-9403     www.dionex.com

*Develop/mfr./market chromatography systems and related products.*

**Manbar Tech,  17a Lazarov Street, PO Box 797, Rishon Le-Zion 75106, Israel**

## DME COMPANY

29111 Stephenson Highway, Madison Heights, MI, 48071

Tel: (248) 398-6000     Fax: (248) 544-5705     www.dmeco.com

*Basic tooling for plastic molding and die casting.*

**R.M. Industrial Services Ltd.,  27 Schocken St., Tel Aviv 66532, Israel**

## R.R. DONNELLEY & SONS COMPANY

77 West Wacker Drive, Chicago, IL, 60601-1696

Tel: (312) 326-8000    Fax: (312) 326-8543    www.rrdonnelley.com

*Commercial printing, allied communication services.*

**R. R. Donnelley Financial, Elnit Financial Printing Ltd., Sharbat House, 4 Kaufman St., Tel Aviv 68012 Israel**

Tel: 972-3-510-7818

## DRAFT WORLDWIDE

633 North St. Clair Street, Chicago, IL, 60611-3211

Tel: (312) 944-3500    Fax: (312) 944-3566    www.draftworldwide.com

*Full service international advertising agency, engaged in brand building, direct and promotional marketing.*

**DraftWorldwide, PO Box 16419, Jerusalem 91163, Israel**

Tel: 972-2-656-3008  Fax: 972-2-585-5851   Contact: Douglas Greener, Co-Mng. Dir.

**MediawiSe - DraftWorldwide, c/o Greener - 16/5 Gdud Hermesh Street, 97545 Jerusalem, Israel**

Tel: 972-2-656-3008   Fax: 972-2-585-5851

## DRAKE BEAM MORIN INC.

101 Huntington Ave., Boston, MA, 02199

Tel: (617) 375-9500    Fax: (617) 267-2011    www.dbm.com

*Human resource management consulting and training.*

**DBM Israel, 18 Hashoftim St., POB 3643, Ramat Hasharon 47134, Israel**

## THE DUN & BRADSTREET CORPORATION

1 Diamond Hill Road, Murray Hill, NJ, 07974

Tel: (908) 665-5000    Fax: (908) 665-5524    www.dnbcorp.com

*Provides corporate credit, marketing and accounts-receivable management services and publishes credit ratings and financial information.*

**Dun & Bradstreet (Israel) Ltd., 27 Hamered St., Fl. C-2, Tel Aviv 68125, Israel**

Tel: 972-3-510-3355

## EAGLE GLOBAL LOGISTICS (EGL)

15350 Vickery Drive, Houston, TX, 77032

Tel: (281) 618-3100    Fax: (281) 618-3100    www.eaglegl.com

*Ocean/air freight forwarding, customs brokerage, packing and wholesale, logistics management and insurance.*

**Tel Aviv (TLV), Albany Agents & Fowarders, 19 Hatzfira St., Tel Aviv 67779, Israel**

Tel: 972-3-537-6022   Fax: 972-3-537-6025

## EASTMAN CHEMICAL

100 North Eastman Road, Kingsport, TN, 37660

Tel: (423) 229-2000    Fax: (423) 229-1351    www.eastman.com

*Mfr. plastics, chemicals, fibers.*

**Eastman Chemical B.V., PO Box 11304, Yuhud 56450, Israel**

Tel: 972-3-632-0741  Fax: 972-3-632-0740   Contact: Wolf Lobato

## EATON CORPORATION

Eaton Center, 1111 Superior Ave., Cleveland, OH, 44114-2584

Tel: (216) 523-5000    Fax: (216) 479-7068    www.eaton.com

*Advanced technical products for transportation and industrial markets.*

**Automotive Equipment Ltd., 74 Petach Tikva Rd., PO Box 20205, Tel Aviv, Israel**

## ECI TELECOM LTD.

12950 Worldgate Dr., Herndon, VA, 20170

Tel: (703) 456-3400      Fax: (703) 456-3410      www.ecitele.com

*Designs, develops, manufactures, markets and supports end-to-end digital telecommunications solutions.*

**ECI Telecom Ltd., 30 Hasivim Street, Petah Tikva 49133, Israel**

Tel: 972-3-926-6555

**ECI Telecom Ltd., 43 Hasivim Street, Petah Tikva 49517, Israel**

Tel: 972-3-926-6663   Fax: 972-3-926-6452

**ECTel Ltd., 18 Hasivim Street, Petah Tikva 49130, Israel**

Tel: 972-3-926-3080   Fax: 972-3-926-3088

## ELECTRO SCIENTIFIC INDUSTRIES, INC.

13900 NW Science Park Drive, Portland, OR, 97229

Tel: (503) 641-4141      Fax: (503) 643-4873      www.esi.com

*Mfg. production and testing equipment used in manufacture of electronic components in pagers and cellular communication devices.*

**EMMTECH Advanced Packaging Group (Rep), PO Box 221, Gedera 70700, Israel**

Tel: 972-8-859-4361

## ELECTRONIC DATA SYSTEMS CORPORATION (EDS)

5400 Legacy Dr., Plano, TX, 75024

Tel: (972) 605-6000      Fax: (972) 605-2643      www.eds.com

*Provides professional services; management consulting, e.solutions, business process management and information solutions.*

**EDS Israel, Ackerstein House, 103 Medinat Hayehudim, Herzliya 46766 Israel**

Tel: 972-9970-8100

## EMC CORPORATION

35 Parkwood Drive, Hopkinton, MA, 01748-9103

Tel: (508) 435-1000      Fax: (508) 435-8884      www.emc.com

*Designs/supplies intelligent enterprise storage and retrieval technology for open systems, mainframes and midrange environments.*

**EMC Computer Systems Israel, Atidim Industrial Park Bldg. 7, PO Box 58061, Tel Aviv 61280, Israel**

Tel: 972-3-645-4220

## EPSTEIN ISI COM CORP.

600 W. Fulton Street, Chicago, IL, 60606-1199

Tel: (312) 454-9100      Fax: (312) 559-1217      www.epstein-isi.com

*Engineering and construction.*

**A. Epstein & Sons (UK) Ltd., 3 Nirim St., PO Box 9084, Tel Aviv 61090, Israel**

Tel: 972-3-636-1636

## ERNST & YOUNG, LLP

787 Seventh Ave., New York, NY, 10019

Tel: (212) 773-3000      Fax: (212) 773-6350      www.eyi.com

*Accounting and audit, tax and management consulting services.*

**Kost Levary and Forer, Certified Public Accountants, 2 Kremenstski St., Tel-Aviv 67899, Israel**

Tel: 972-3-623-2501   Fax: 972-3-562-2555   Contact: Itshak Forer

## EURO RSCG WORLDWIDE

350 Hudson Street, New York, NY, 10014

Tel: (212) 886-2000      Fax: (212) 886-2016      www.eurorscg.com

*International advertising agency group.*

**EURO RSCG Zarfatti Sternschuss Zamir, 12 Yad Harutzim Street, Tel Aviv, Israel**

## EXCELLON AUTOMATION

24751 Crenshaw Boulevard, Torrance, CA, 90505

Tel: (310) 534-6300     Fax: (310) 534-6777     www.excellon.com

*PCB drilling and routing machines; optical inspection equipment.*

**E&M Engineering Ltd., 5 Jabotinsky Street, PO Box 3191, Ramaat-Gan 52520, Israel**

Tel: 972-3-751-2929

## FRITZ COMPANIES, INC.

706 Mission Street, Ste. 900, San Francisco, CA, 94103

Tel: (415) 904-8360     Fax: (415) 904-8661     www.fritz.com

*Integrated transportation, sourcing, distribution and customs brokerage services.*

**Fritz Companies Israel Ltd., 34 Beit Hillel St., Tel Aviv 67017, Israel**

## FSI INTERNATIONAL INC.

322 Lake Hazeltine Drive, Chaska, MN, 55318

Tel: (612) 448-5440     Fax: (612) 448-2825     www.fsi-intl.com

*Manufacturing equipment for computer silicon wafers.*

**Metron Technology Ltd., 10 Haharootsim Street, K. Nordau New Industrial Area, PO Box 8226, Netanya 82293, Israel**

## GaSONICS INTERNATIONAL CORPORATION

404 East Plumeria Drive, San Jose, CA, 95134

Tel: (408) 570-7000     Fax: (408) 570-7612     www.gasonics.com

*Mfr. gas-based dry cleaning systems for semi-conductor production equipment.*

**GaSonics International, 2 Pekeris St., Tamar Industrial Park, Rehovot 76702, Israel**

Tel: 972-8-948-4666   Fax: 972-8-948-4660

## GENERAL DYNAMICS CORPORATION

3190 Fairview Park Drive, Falls Church, VA, 22042-4523

Tel: (703) 876-3000     Fax: (703) 876-3125     www.gendyn.com

*Mfr. aerospace equipment, submarines, strategic systems, armored vehicles, defense support systems.*

**General Dynamics Corp., Attn: Israel Office, Embassy of the USA/Israel, Peace Marble, APO New York 09672-0008**

## GENERAL ELECTRIC COMPANY

3135 Easton Turnpike, Fairfield, CT, 06431

Tel: (203) 373-2211     Fax: (203) 373-3131     www.ge.com

*Diversified manufacturing, technology and services.*

**General Electric Co. - General Engineers, 1 Maskit St., Herzliya 46105, Israel**

Tel: 972-9-959-2233   Fax: 972-9-955-5122

## GENZYME CORPORATION

1 Kendall Square, Cambridge, MA, 02139-1562

Tel: (617) 252-7500     Fax: (617) 252-7600     www.genzyme.com

*Mfr. healthcare products for enzyme deficient diseases.*

**Genzyme Israel Ltd.., Beit-Hapaamon, Hataas Street 20, Kfar-Saba-Industrial Zone 44111, Israel**

Tel: 972-9-7-666640   Fax: 92-9-7-666631

## GLEASON CORPORATION

1000 University Ave., Rochester, NY, 14692

Tel: (716) 473-1000     Fax: (716) 461-4348     www.gleasoncorp.com

*Mfr. gear making machine tools; tooling and services.*

**Josef Rosenthaler Co. Ltd., 17 Neemanim Street, PO Box 791, Haifa 31007 Israel**

Tel: 97-248-522-676   Fax: 97-248-528-824

**GREY GLOBAL GROUP**

777 Third Ave., New York, NY, 10017

Tel: (212) 546-2000      Fax: (212) 546-1495      www.grey.com

*International advertising agency.*

**Warshavsky Freilich Dover,  Tel Aviv, Israel**

**GRIFFITH LABORATORIES INC.**

One Griffith Center, Alsip, IL, 60658

Tel: (708) 371-0900      Fax: (708) 597-3294      www.griffithlabs.com

*Mfr. industrial food ingredients and equipment.*

**Griffith/Ein-Bar,  Kibbutz Einat, Israel**

Tel: 972-3-938-5167    Fax: 972-3-938-5176

**GUARDIAN ELECTRIC MFG. COMPANY**

1425 Lake Ave., Woodstock, IL, 60098

Tel: (815) 334-3600      Fax: (815) 337-0377      www.guardian-electric.com

*Mfr. industrial controls, electrical relays and switches.*

**Giveon Agencies Ltd.,  Tel Aviv, Israel**

**HARRIS CORPORATION**

1025 West NASA Blvd., Melbourne, FL, 32919

Tel: (407) 727-9100      Fax: (407) 727-9344      www.harris.com

*Mfr. communications and information-handling equipment, including copying and fax systems.*

**Aviv Electronics,  PO Box 2433, 43100 Ra'anana, Israel**

Tel: 972-9-748-3232    Fax: 972-9741-6510

**HEIDRICK & STRUGGLES INTERNATIONAL, INC.**

Sears Tower, 233 South Wacker Drive, Chicago, IL, 60606

Tel: (312) 496-1200      Fax: (312) 496-1290      www.heidrick.com

*Executive search firm.*

**Heidrick & Struggles Intl. Inc.,  3 Hayezira Street, SH.A.P House, Ramat-Gan, Israel**

Tel: 972-3-613-7210

**HENRY SCHEIN, INC.**

135 Duryea Rd., Melville, NY, 11747

Tel: (516) 843-5500      Fax: (516) 843-5658      www.henryschein.com

*Mfr. and supply dental equipment.*

**Henry Schein Israel,  Beit Hashinhav, Beit Hadfuss 12, Givat Shaul Jerusalem 95483, Israel**

Tel: 972-2-651-0701

**HILTON HOTELS CORPORATION**

9336 Civic Center Drive, Beverly Hills, CA, 90210

Tel: (310) 278-4321      Fax: (310) 205-7880      www.hiltonhotels.com

*International hotel chain: Hilton International, Vista Hotels and Hilton National Hotels.*

**Tel Aviv Hilton,  Independence Park, Tel Aviv 63405, Israel**

**HOLLAND & KNIGHT**

400 North Ashley Dr., Ste. 2300,, Tampa, FL, 33602

Tel: (813) 227-8500      Fax: (813) 229-0134      www.hklaw.com

*International law firm.*

**Holland & Knight,  Tel Aviv, Israel**

## HORWATH INTERNATIONAL ASSOCIATION

415 Madison Ave., New York, NY, 10017

Tel: (212) 838-5566        Fax: (212) 838-3636        www.horwath.com

*Public accountants and auditors.*

**Horwath, Bawly, Millner & Co.,  PO Box 50025, 27 Hamered Street, Tel Aviv 68125, Israel**

**Horwath, Bawly, Millner & Co.,  PO Box 33777, 5 Habankim Street, Haifa 31337, Israel**

## HOUGHTON INTERNATIONAL INC.

PO Box 930, Madison & Van Buren Avenues, Valley Forge, PA, 19482-0930

Tel: (610) 666-4000        Fax: (610) 666-1376        www.houghtonintl.com

*Mfr. specialty chemicals, hydraulic fluids and lubricants.*

**Delkol Ltd.,  PO Box 31, Lod 71100, Israel**

## IBM CORPORATION

New Orchard Road, Armonk, NY, 10504

Tel: (914) 765-1900        Fax: (914) 765-7382        www.ibm.com

*Information products, technology and services.*

**IBM Israel Ltd.,  IBM House, 2 Weizmann Street, PO Box 33666, Tel Aviv 61336, Israel**

Tel: 972-3-697-8500   Fax: 972-3-695-9985

## ICC INDUSTRIES INC.

460 Park Ave., New York, NY, 10022

Tel: (212) 521-1700        Fax: (212) 521-1794        www.iccchem.com

*Manufacturing and trading of chemicals, plastics and pharmaceuticals.*

**ICC (Israel) Chemicals Ltd.,  135 Dizengoff St., Tel Aviv 56461, Israel**

Tel: 972-3-522-5072   Fax: 972-3-524-9265   Contact: Yaakov Aviram

## INFOGRAMES, INC.

417 Fifth Avenue, New York, NY, 10016

Tel: (212) 726-6500        Fax: (212) 679-3224        www.infogrames.com

*Mfr. video games.*

**Infogrames Israel,  21 Atir Yeda Street, PO Box 2358,  Kefar Saba 44641, Israel**

Tel: 972-9-7679777

## INFONET SERVICES CORPORATION

2100 East Grand Ave., El Segundo, CA, 90245-1022

Tel: (310) 335-2600        Fax: (310) 335-4507        www.infonet.com

*Provider of Internet services and electronic messaging services.*

**Infonet Israel, Ltd.,  9 Hasivim Street, PO Box 7106, Petach-Tikva 49170, Israel**

Tel: 972-3-921-3663   Fax: 972-3-921-3665

## INTEL CORPORATION

Robert Noyce Bldg., 2200 Mission College Blvd., Santa Clara, CA, 95052-8119

Tel: (408) 765-8080        Fax: (408) 765-1739        www.intel.com

*Mfr. semiconductor, microprocessor and micro-communications components and systems.*

**Intel Semiconductor (Israel), Ltd.,  Tel Aviv, Israel**

Tel: 972-2-589-7111

## INTER-CONTINENTAL HOTELS

3 Ravina Drive, Suite 2900, Atlanta, GA, 30346-2149

Tel: (770) 604-2000        Fax: (770) 604-5403        www.interconti.com

*Worldwide hotel and resort accommodations.*

**Inter-Continental Hotels, 5 Yoni Netanyahu Street, Tel Aviv 60250, Israel**

Tel: 972-3-538-8444   Fax: 972-3-533-5986

## INTERGRAPH CORPORATION

One Madison Industrial Park, Huntsville, AL, 35894-0001

Tel: (256) 730-2000     Fax: (256) 730-7898     www.intergraph.com

*Develop/mfr. interactive computer graphic systems.*

**Intergraph Israel, 20 Galgaley Haplada Industrial Area, PO Box 708, Herzlia 46106, Israel**

Tel: 972-9-954-3101    Fax: 972-9-954-3972

## INTERMEC TECHNOLOGIES CORPORATION

6001 36th Ave. West, PO Box 4280, Everett, WA, 98203-9280

Tel: (425) 348-2600     Fax: (425) 355-9551     www.intermec.com

*Mfr./distributor automated data collection systems.*

**Intermec Bar Code Ltd., Bnei Moshe Street, PO Box 8161, Ramat-Gan 52181, Israel**

Tel: 972-3-926-9666    Fax: 972-3-924-7666

## INTERNATIONAL FLAVORS & FRAGRANCES INC.

521 West 57th Street, New York, NY, 10019-2960

Tel: (212) 765-5500     Fax: (212) 708-7132     www.iff.com

*Design/mfr. flavors, fragrances and aroma chemicals.*

**International Flavors & Fragrances, 4 Ha Taas Street. Ramat-Gan 52512, Israel**

Tel: 972-3-6138454    Fax: 972-3-6136644

## INTERNATIONAL PAPER COMPANY

2 Manhattanville Road, Purchase, NY, 10577

Tel: (914) 397-1500     Fax: (914) 397-1596     www.ipaper.com

*Mfr./distributor container board, paper and wood products.*

**International Paper USA Ltd., Starco Bldg., PO Box 34056, Haifa, Israel**

## IONICS INC.

65 Grove Street, Watertown, MA, 02172

Tel: (617) 926-2500     Fax: (617) 926-4304     www.ionics.com

*Mfr. desalination equipment.*

**Ionics Environmental, Herzlia, Israel**

Tel: 972-9-9509650

## ISM FASTENING SYSTEMS CORPORATION

PO Box 629, Butler, PA, 16003

Tel: (800) 378-3430     Fax: (800) 827-4762     www.ismsys.com

*Mfr. industrial stapling machines and supplies.*

**Packaging & Printing Systems (Dvikol) Ltd., 53 Petach Tikva Rd., PO Box 20122, Tel Aviv, Israel**

## IVC INDUSTRIES, INC.

500 Halls Mill Road, Freehold, NJ, 07728

Tel: (732) 308-3000     Fax: (732) 308-9793     www.ivcinc.com

*Mfr./distributor vitamins and dietary supplements.*

**IVC Industries, Inc., 32 Hazohar, Tel Aviv, Israel**

## J. WALTER THOMPSON COMPANY

466 Lexington Ave., New York, NY, 10017

Tel: (212) 210-7000     Fax: (212) 210-6944     www.jwt.com

*International advertising and marketing services.*

**Tamir Cohen, Tel Aviv, Israel**

## JOHNSON & JOHNSON

One Johnson & Johnson Plaza, New Brunswick, NJ, 08933

Tel: (732) 524-0400　　Fax: (732) 214-0334　　www.jnj.com

*Mfr./distributor/R&D pharmaceutical, health care and cosmetic products.*

**Biosense Europe, Haifa, Israel**

**Janssen-Cilag, Kibbutz Shefayim, 60990 Israel**

Tel: 972-9-9591109　Fax: 972-9-9503002

## JONES LANG LASALLE

101 East 52nd Street, New York, NY, 10022

Tel: (212) 688-8181　　Fax: (212) 308-5199　　www.jlw.com

*International marketing consultants, leasing agents and property management advisors.*

**Jones Lang Wootton, Israel**

## KIMBERLY-CLARK CORPORATION

351 Phelps Drive, Irving, TX, 75038

Tel: (972) 281-1200　　Fax: (972) 281-1435　　www.kimberly-clark.com

*Mfr./sales/distribution of consumer tissue, household and personal care products.*

**Hogla-Kimberly, Tel Aviv, Israel**

Contact: Avi Brener, General Manager

**Kimberly-Clark Corp., Hadera, Israel**

**Kimberly-Clark Corporation, Afula, Israel**

## KOCH-GLITSCH, INC.

PO Box 8127, Wichita, KS, 67208

Tel: (316) 828-5110　　Fax: (316) 828-5950　　www.koch-ind.com

*Mfr./services mass transfer/chemicals separation equipment, process engineering.*

**Koch-Glitsch, Inc., 17 Modin St., PO Box 6111, Bnei Brak, Israel**

## KOLLMORGEN CORPORATION

1601 Trapelo Road, Waltham, MA, 02154

Tel: (781) 890-5655　　Fax: (781) 890-7150　　www.kollmorgen.com

*Mfr. high-performance electronic motion-control systems and design and supply advanced submarine periscopes, weapons directors, and military optics.*

**Servotronix Ltd., Petach Tikva, Israel**

## KPMG INTERNATIONAL LLP

345 Park Avenue, New York, NY, 10022

Tel: (201) 307-7000　　Fax: (201) 930-8617　　www.kpmg.com

*Accounting and audit, tax and management consulting services.*

**KPMG Braude Bavly, 33 Jaffa Rd., Jerusalem 91002, Israel**

**KPMG Braude Bavly, 65 Ha'atzmaut Rd., Haifa 31338, Israel**

**KPMG Braude Bavly, 29 Hamered St., Tel-Aviv 68125, Israel**

Tel: 972-3-51408　Fax: 972-3-510-1918　Contact: Itzahk Rotman, Sr. Ptnr.

## KULICKE & SOFFA INDUSTRIES INC.

2101 Blair Mill Road, Willow Grove, PA, 19090

Tel: (215) 784-6000　　Fax: (215) 659-7588　　www.kns.com

*Semiconductor assembly systems and services.*

**Kulicke & Soffa (Israel) Ltd., Advanced Technology Center, PO Box 875, Haifa 31008, Israel**

Tel: 972-4-854-5222　Fax: 972-4-855-0007　Contact: Avner Hermoni, VP & Mng. Dir.

**Micro-Swiss Ltd., PO Box 90, Yokneam Elite 20692, Israel**

Tel: 972-4-993-9444　Fax: 972-4-959-1234

**Ortec Marketing Equipment & Supply Ltd.l, 11 Hasadna Street, Raanana 43650, Israel**

## LEHMAN BROTHERS HOLDINGS INC.

Three World Financial Center, New York, NY, 10285

Tel: (212) 526-7000      Fax: (212) 526-3738      www.lehman.com

*Financial services, securities and merchant banking services.*

**Lehman Brothers, Asia House, 4 Weizmann Street (4/F), Tel Aviv, Israel**

Tel: 972-3-696-6122

## ELI LILLY & COMPANY

Lilly Corporate Center, Indianapolis, IN, 46285

Tel: (317) 276-2000      Fax: (317) 277-6579      www.lilly.com

*Mfr. pharmaceuticals and animal health products.*

**Eli Lilly Israel LTC, 4 Kaufman St., Bet Sharbaat, Tel Aviv 68012, Israel**

Tel: 972-3-510-0840    Fax: 942-3-516-2643

## LOCKHEED MARTIN CORPORATION

6801 Rockledge Drive, Bethesda, MD, 20817

Tel: (301) 897-6000      Fax: (301) 897-6652      www.imco.com

*Design/mfr./management systems in fields of space, defense, energy, electronics and technical services.*

**Lockheed Fort Worth Intl. Corp., Technical Pubs, Peace Marble, Pitah Tikva, Israel**

Tel: 972-3-934-7629    Fax: 972-3-390-1326

**Lockheed Fort Worth Intl. Corp., Beit Ackerstein, 103 Medinat Hayehudim, Herzliya Pituach 46766, Israel**

Tel: 972-9-580621    Fax: 972-9-581189

**Lockheed Fort Worth Intl. Corp., L.R.O. Cyclone, Carmiel, Israel**

Tel: 972-967-058    Fax: 972-4-967-057

**Lockheed Martin International S.A., Asia House, 4 Weizman Street, Tel Aviv, Israel**

Tel: 972-3-695-8343    Fax: 972-3-695-9627

**Lockheed Martin Technical Operations, Beit-Eliahu, Tel Aviv 64077, Israel**

Tel: 972-3-430040    Fax: 972-3-695-2059

## LOWE LINTAS & PARTNERS WORLDWIDE

One Dag Hammarskjold Plaza, New York, NY, 10017

Tel: (212) 605-8000      Fax: (212) 605-4705      www.interpublic.com

*Full-service, integrated marketing communications company/advertising agency.*

**Weinberg Karasso & Shamir, 157 Ygal Alon St., Tel-Aviv 67443, Israel**

Tel: 972-3-691-8556    Fax: 972-3-695-1626    Contact: Yuval Shamir

## LSI LOGIC CORPORATION

1551 McCarthy Blvd, Milpitas, CA, 95035

Tel: (408) 433-8000      Fax: (408) 954-3220      www.lsilogic.com

*Develop/mfr. semiconductors.*

**LSI Logic Ramat Hashron, 40 Sokolov Street, PO Box 1311, Ramat Hashron 47235, Israel**

Tel: 972-3-5-480480    Fax: 972-3-5-403747

## LTX CORPORATION

LTX Park, University Ave., Westwood, MA, 02090

Tel: (617) 461-1000      Fax: (617) 326-4883      www.ltx.com

*Design/mfr. computer-controlled semiconductor test systems.*

**LTX Israel Ltd., Saharov 17 Rishon Lezion, PO Box 5053, 75105 Israel**

Tel: 972-50-3368-92    Fax: 972-3-5598606

## LUCENT TECHNOLOGIES, INC.

600 Mountain Ave., Murray Hill, NJ, 07974-0636

Tel: (908) 582-3000      Fax: (908) 582-2576      www.lucent.com

*Design/mfr. wide range of public and private networks, communication systems and software, data networking systems, business telephone systems and microelectronics components.*

**WaveAccess Ltd.,  Re'anana, Israel**

## M/A-COM INC.

1011 Pawtucket Boulevard, Lowell, MA, 01853-3295

Tel: (978) 442-5000      Fax: (978) 442-5354      www.macom.com

*Mfr. electronic components, semiconductor devices and communications equipment.*

**M/A-COM Iscom Ltd.,  Twin Towers II Rm. 911, 35 Zabotinski Road, Ramat Gan 525117, Israel**

Tel: 972-3-7518421   Fax: 972-3-7510498

## MacDERMID INC.

245 Freight Street, Waterbury, CT, 06702-0671

Tel: (203) 575-5700      Fax: (203) 575-7900      www.macdermid.com

*Chemicals processing for metal industrial, plastics, electronics cleaners, strippers.*

**MacDermid Israel Ltd.,  PO Box 13011, Tel Aviv 61130, Israel**

## R.H. MACY & COMPANY INC.

151 West 34th Street, New York, NY, 10001

Tel: (212) 695-4400      Fax: (212) 643-1307      www.macys.com

*Department stores; importers.*

**R.H. Macy & Co. Inc.,  America House, 35 Shaul Hamelech Blvd., Tel Aviv, Israel**

## MANPOWER INTERNATIONAL INC.

5301 N. Ironwood Rd.,  PO Box 2053, Milwaukee, WI, 53201-2053

Tel: (414) 961-1000      Fax: (414) 961-7081      www.manpower.com

*Temporary help, contract service, training and testing.*

**Manpower Israel Ltd.,  90-92 Yigal Alon Street, Tel Aviv 67891, Israel**

Tel: 972-3-563-9999   Fax: 972-3-562-5702

## MARRIOTT INTERNATIONAL INC.

10400 Fernwood Rd., Bethesda, MD, 20817

Tel: (301) 380-3000      Fax: (301) 380-5181      www.marriott.com

*Hotel services.*

**Nazareth Marriott Hotel,  Nazareth, Israel**

Tel: 972-2-628-4724

## MARSH & McLENNAN COS INC.

1166 Ave. of the Americas, New York, NY, 10036-2774

Tel: (212) 345-5000      Fax: (212) 345-4808      www.marshmac.com

*Insurance agents/brokers, pension and investment management consulting services.*

**Lowenthal Sagiv Ben-Zur Ltd.,  12 Yad Harutzim St., Tel Aviv 67778, Israel**

Tel: 972-3-638-3030   Fax: 972-3-639-2866   Contact: Elhanan Lowenthal

## McCANN-ERICKSON WORLDGROUP

750 Third Ave., New York, NY, 10017

Tel: (212) 984-3644      Fax: (212) 984-2629      www.mccann.com

*International advertising and marketing services.*

**Kesher Barel & Associates,  Tel Aviv, Israel**

## MCS SOFTWARE CORPORATION
815 Colorado Blvd., Los Angeles, CA, 90041

Tel: (323) 258-9111        Fax: (323) 259-3838        www.macsch.com

*Develop finite element analysis software used in the field of computer-aided engineering.*

**MSC/EMAS European Product Marketing, PO Box 998, 29a Jerusalem Blvd., Kiriat Yam 29011, Israel**

## MECHANICAL DYNAMICS, INC.
2301 Commonwealth Blvd., Ann Arbor, MI, 48105

Tel: (734) 994-3800        Fax: (734) 994-6418        www.adams.com

*Mfr. Adams prototyping software to automotive industry.*

**Matrix Engineering Ltd., PO Box 3021 Even Yeuda, 40500 Israel**

Tel: 972-9-899-9862

## MERCURY INTERACTIVE CORPORATION
1325 Borregas Ave., Sunnyvale, CA, 94089

Tel: (408) 822-5200        Fax: (408) 822-5300        www.merc-int.com

*Mfr. computer software to decipher and eliminate "bugs" from systems.*

**Mercury Interactive (Israel) Ltd., 19 Shabazi St., PO Box 170, Or-ehuda 60218, Israel**

Tel: 972-3-538-8888    Fax: 972-3-533-1617

## MICROSOFT CORPORATION
One Microsoft Way, Redmond, WA, 98052-6399

Tel: (425) 882-8080        Fax: (425) 936-7329        www.microsoft.com

*Computer software, peripherals and services.*

**Microsoft Israel Ltd., Business Park, 6 Maskit Street, Inddustrial Area, Herzelia Pituach Israel**

Tel: 972-9-525-353    Fax: 972-9-525-333

## MILACRON INC.
2090 Florence Ave., Cincinnati, OH, 45206

Tel: (513) 487-5000        Fax: (513) 487-5057        www.milacron.com

*Metalworking and plastics technologies.*

**Azur Technology and Marketing Ltd., PO Box 248, Moshav Bazra, IL-60944 Israel**

Tel: 972-9-7443111    Fax: 972-9-7440338    Contact: Pablo Yanovsky

## MOLEX INC.
2222 Wellington Court, Lisle, IL, 60532

Tel: (630) 969-4550        Fax: (630) 969-1352        www.molex.com

*Mfr. electronic, electrical and fiber optic interconnection products and systems, switches, application tooling.*

**Telsys Ltd., Div. Molex, Atidim Bldg 3, Dvora Hanevia Str. Neve Sharet, Tel Aviv 61431, Israel**

## MOTOROLA, INC.
1303 East Algonquin Road, Schaumburg, IL, 60196

Tel: (847) 576-5000        Fax: (847) 538-5191        www.motorola.com

*Mfr. communications equipment, semiconductors and cellular phones.*

**Motorola Israel Ltd., 3 Kremenetski St., PO Box 25016, Tel Aviv 67899, Israel**

Tel: 972-3-565-8888    Fax: 972-3-562-4925

## NETMANAGE, INC.
10725 N. De Anza Blvd., Cupertino, CA, 95014

Tel: (408) 973-7171        Fax: (408) 257-6405        www.netmanage.com

*Develop/mfr. computer software applications and tools.*

**NetManage Ltd., Matam-Advanced Tech Ctr., Bldg. 9m, Haifa 31905, Israel**

Tel: 972-4-855-0234    Fax: 972-4-855-0122

## NOVELLUS SYSTEMS INC.

4000 North First Street, San Jose, CA, 95134

Tel: (408) 943-9700    Fax: (408) 943-3422    www.novellus.com

*Mfr. chemical vapor deposition (CVD), physical vapor deposition (PVD) and copper electrofill systems.*

**Novellus Systems Israel Ltd., Zohar Tal #11, Herzlia Petuach 56741, Israel**

Tel: 972-9-957-1951    Fax: 972-9-957-1951

## OFFICE DEPOT, INC.

2200 Old Germantown Road, Delray Beach, FL, 33445

Tel: (561) 278-4800    Fax: (561) 265-4406    www.officedepot.com

*Discount office product retailer with warehouse-style superstores.*

**Office Depot Israel Ltd., Ha'Haroshet, Atar Hutzot-Hamifratz, PO Box 12007, Haifa 26119 Israel**

Tel: 972-4-842-0290  Fax: 972-4-842-0380

**Office Depot Israel Ltd., 76 Yigal St. Alon St., PO Box 9048, Tel-Aviv 67067 Israel**

Tel: 972-3-565-4416  Fax: 972-3-561-7877

**Office Depot Israel Ltd. - Corporate Office, 11 Ben-Gurion Rd., B'nei-Brak 51260, Israel**

Tel: 972-3-617-6431  Fax: 972-3-578-8199  Contact: Zach Fishbein, Pres.

## PANAMETRICS

221 Crescent Street, Waltham, MA, 02154

Tel: (781) 899-2719    Fax: (781) 899-1552    www.panametrics.com

*Process/non-destructive test instrumentation.*

**Dectal Advanced Technologies, PO Box 8043, 19 Ben Gurion St., Ramat-Gan 52180, Israel**

Tel: 972-3-5795001  Fax: 972-3-5795003

## PARAMETRIC TECHNOLOGY CORPORATION

128 Technology Drive, Waltham, MA, 02154

Tel: (781) 398-5000    Fax: (781) 398-5674    www.ptc.com

*Supplier of mechanical design automation and product data management software and services.*

**Parametric Technology Israel, 37 Havazelet Hasharon Street, Beit Noy, Herzlia 46641, Israel**

Tel: 972-9-958-9004  Fax: 972-9-958-9003

**Parametric Technology Israel Ltd., MATAM, Bllgd 23, Haifa 31905, Israel**

Tel: 972-4-855-0035  Fax: 972-4-855-0036

## PAREXEL INTERNATIONAL CORPORATION

195 West Street, Waltham, MA, 02154

Tel: (781) 487-9900    Fax: (781) 487-0525    www.parexel.com

*Provides contract medical, biotechnology, and pharmaceutical research and consulting services.*

**PAREXEL Lansal Ltd., Herzelia Business Park, 6 Maskit St. Bldg. B 2nd Fl., Herzelia, Israel**

Tel: 972-9-941-5411  Fax: 972-9-951-5313

## PCA ELECTRONICS INC.

16799 Schoenborn Street, North Hills, CA, 91343

Tel: (818) 892-0761    Fax: (818) 894-5791    www.pca.com

*Mfr./sales of electronic equipment.*

**Trust Electronics, PO Box 2115, Savion 56500, Israel**

Tel: 972-3-3-534-5026  Fax: 972-3-535-1468

## PLANET HOLLYWOOD INTERNATIONAL, INC.

8669 Commodity Circle, Orlando, FL, 32819

Tel: (407) 363-7827    Fax: (407) 363-4862    www.planethollywood.com

*Theme-dining restaurant chain and merchandise retail stores.*

**Planet Hollywood International, Inc., Tel Aviv, Israel**

## POLARIS INDUSTRIES INC.
2100 Highway 55, Medina, MN, 55440

Tel: (612) 542-0500      Fax: (612) 542-0599      www.polarisindustries.com

*Mfr. snowmobiles and all-terrain recreational and utility vehicles.*

**Polaris Machinery Importers, PO Box 304 Industrial Area, Ashkelon 78102, Israel**

Tel: 972-7-675-0734   Fax: 972-7-675-1181

## PRAXAIR, INC.
39 Old Ridgebury Road, Danbury, CT, 06810-5113

Tel: (203) 837-2000      Fax: (203) 837-2450      www.praxair.com

*Produces and distributes industrial and specialty gases.*

**Maxima Air Separation Center Ltd., Silver House, 7 Abba Hillel Rd., IL-Ramat-Gan 52522, Israel**

Tel: 972-3-575-5130   Fax: 972-3-575-5120

## PRICEWATERHOUSECOOPERS LLP
1301 Ave. of the Americas, New York, NY, 10019

Tel: (212) 596-7000      Fax: (212) 259-1301      www.pwcglobal.com

*Accounting and auditing, tax and management, and human resource consulting services.*

**PriceWaterhouseCoopers, PO Box 240, Tirat HaCarmel Haifa 39101, Israel**

Tel: 972-4-857-9888   Fax: 972-4-857-9857

**PriceWaterhouseCoopers, PO Box 609, Tel Aviv 61006, Israel**

Tel: 972-3-517-44-44   Fax: 972-3-517-44-40

**PriceWaterhouseCoopers, PO Box 212, Jerusalem 91001, Israel**

Tel: 972-2-253291   Fax: 972-2-353292

## QUALCOMM INC.
5775 Morehouse Dr., San Diego, CA, 92121-1714

Tel: (858) 587-1121      Fax: (858) 658-2100      www.qualcomm.com

*Digital wireless telecommunications systems.*

**QUALCOMM Israel, Omega Center 4/F, Nahum Het Street, Tyrat Hacarmel, Haifa 31905 Israel**

Tel: 972-4-850-6506

## QUINTILES TRANSNATIONAL CORPORATION
4709 Creekstone Dr., Durham, NC, 27703

Tel: (919) 998-2000      Fax: (919) 998-9113      www.quintiles.com

*Mfr. pharmaceuticals.*

**Quintiles Israel Ltd., Kibutz Shefayim 60990, Tel Aviv, Israel**

## RADISSON HOTELS INTERNATIONAL
Carlson Pkwy., PO Box 59159, Minneapolis, MN, 55459-8204

Tel: (612) 540-5526      Fax: (612) 449-3400      www.radisson.com

*Hotels and resorts.*

**Colony's Beach Resort, Attn: Israel Office, Carlson Parkway, PO Box 59159, Minneapolis MN 55459-8204**

**Colony's Mandarin Resort, Attn: Israel Office, Carlson Parkway, PO Box 59159, Minneapolis MN 55459-8204**

## RENAISSANCE HOTELS AND RESORTS
10400 Fernwood Road, Bethesda, MD, 20817

Tel: (301) 380-3000      Fax: (301) 380-5181      www.renaissancehotels.com

*Hotel and resort chain.*

**Renaissance Jerusalem Hotel, Jerusalem, Israel**

Tel: 972-2-6528111

## REVLON INC.

625 Madison Ave., New York, NY, 10022

Tel: (212) 527-4000      Fax: (212) 527-4995      www.revlon.com

*Mfr. cosmetics, fragrances, toiletries and beauty care products.*

**Revlon (Israel) Ltd., Industrial Zone, PO Box 131, Ashdod, Israel**

Contact: Moshe Vidam, Gen. Mgr.

## ROBERT HALF INTERNATIONAL INC.

2884 Sand Hill Road, Ste. 200, Menlo Park, CA, 94025

Tel: (650) 234-6000      Fax: (650) 234-6999      www.rhii.com

*World leader in personnel and specialized staffing services.*

**Robert Half Intl. Inc., Hatachana 4, Jerusalem, Israel**

## ROCKWELL INTERNATIONAL CORPORATION

777 East Wisconsin Ave., Ste. 1400, Milwaukee, WI, 53202

Tel: (414) 212-5200      Fax: (414) 212-5201      www.rockwell.com

*Products and service for aerospace and defense, automotive, electronics, graphics and automation industry.*

**Rockwell Semiconductor Systems (Israel) Ltd., 11 Galgaley Haplada St., PO Box 12660, Herzlia 46733, Israel**

Tel: 972-9-9524-000   Fax: 972-9-9573-732

## SBC COMMUNICATIONS INC.

175 East Houston, San Antonio, TX, 78205

Tel: (210) 821-4105      Fax: (210) 351-5034      www.sbc.com

*Engaged in telecommunications.*

**Amdocs Ltd., Tel Aviv, Israel**

**Aurec Group, Tel Aviv, Israel**

## SIGMA-ALDRICH CORPORATION

3050 Spruce Street, St. Louis, MO, 63103

Tel: (314) 771-5765      Fax: (314) 771-5757      www.sigma-aldrich.com

*Chemicals and biochemicals, aluminum and structural steel components.*

**Makor Chemical Ltd., PO Box 25469, Jerusalem 91060, Israel**

**Sigma Israel Chemical Ltd., PO Box 37673, Tel Aviv, Israel**

## SIKORSKY AIRCRAFT CORPORATION

6900 Main Street, PO Box 9729, Stratford, CT, 06615-9129

Tel: (203) 386-4000      Fax: (203) 386-4000      www.sikorsky.com

*Design and manufacture of advanced helicopters for commercial, industrial and military uses.*

**SIKORSKY AIRCRAFT CORP., Tel Aviv, Israel**

## SILICON GRAPHICS INC.

2011 N. Shoreline Blvd., Mountain View, CA, 94043-1389

Tel: (650) 960-1980      Fax: (650) 961-0595      www.sgi.com

*Design/mfr. special-effects computer graphic systems and software.*

**Silicon Graphics Israel, Dori Building, Hamenofim Street 1, PO Box 2010, Herzlya 46120 Israel**

Tel: 972-9-970-6666   Fax: 972-9-954-7779

## SLANT/FIN CORPORATION

100 Forest Drive at East Hills, Greenvale, NY, 11548

Tel: (516) 484-2600      Fax: (516) 484-2694

*Mfr. heating and A/C systems and components.*

**Slant/Fin Hidron Ltd., 7 Ben Zion St., Tel Aviv 61322, Israel**

## SOTHEBY'S HOLDINGS, INC.

1334 York Avenue, New York, NY, 10021

Tel: (212) 606-7000      Fax: (212) 606-7027      www.sothebys.com

*Auction house specializing in fine art and jewelry.*

**Sotheby's Holdings, Inc.,  46 Rothschild Boulevard, Tel Aviv 66883, Israel**

Tel: 972-3-560-1666   Fax: 972-3-560-8111   Contact: Rivka Saker

## STARWOOD HOTELS & RESORTS WORLDWIDE

777 Westchester Avenue, White Plains, NY, 10604

Tel: (914) 640-8100      Fax: (914) 640-8316      www.starwoodhotels.com

*Hotel operations including Sheraton, Westin, St. Regis, Four Points and Caesars.*

**Sheraton Jerusalem Plaza,  47 King George St., Jerusalem 91076, Israel**

**Tel Aviv Sheraton Hotel & Towers,  115 Hayarkon St., Tel Aviv 61034, Israel**

Tel: 972-3-521-1111   Fax: 972-3-523-3322

## STOKES VACUUM INC.

5500 Tabor Road, Philadelphia, PA, 19120

Tel: (215) 831-5400      Fax: (215) 831-5420      www.stokesvacuum.com

*Vacuum pumps and components, vacuum dryers, oil-upgrading equipment and metallizers.*

**VST Israel,  PO Box 4137, Petach-Tikva 49130, Israel**

Tel: 972-3-924-7710   Fax: 972-3-924-7711   Contact: Angel Hershako

## SUN MICROSYSTEMS, INC.

901 San Antonio Road, Palo Alto, CA, 94303

Tel: (650) 960-1300      Fax: (650) 856-2114      www.sun.com

*Computer peripherals and programming services.*

**Sun Microsystems,  Sun Israel Development Center, 10 Ha Sadnaot Herzliya Pituach 46733, Israel**

## SUPERIOR TELE COM INC.

1790 Broadway, 15th Fl., New York, NY, 10019-1412

Tel: (212) 757-3333      Fax: (212) 757-3423      www.superior essex.com

*Mfr. copper wire and cable.*

**Superior TeleCom Inc.,  Tel Aviv, Israel**

Tel: 972-4-846-6222   Fax: 972-4-846-6286

## SYNOPSYS, INC.

700 East Middlefield Road, Mountain View, CA, 94043

Tel: (650) 962-5000      Fax: (650) 965-8637      www.synopsys.com

*Mfr. electronic design automation software.*

**Synopsys Israel,  Herzelia Business Park, 4 Maskit Street - Bldg. C, Box 12323, Herzelia 46733, Israel**

Tel: 972-9-951-13771   Fax: 972-9-951-13772

## TBWA CHIAT/DAY

488 Madison Avenue, 6th Floor, New York, NY, 10022

Tel: (212) 804-1000      Fax: (212) 804-1200      www.tbwachiat.com

*International full service advertising agency.*

**Yehoshua TBWA,  Tel Aviv, Israel**

## TEKTRONIX INC.

14200 SW Karl Braun Dr., PO Box 500, Beaverton, OR, 97077

Tel: (503) 627-7111      Fax: (503) 627-2406      www.tek.com

*Mfr. test and measure, visual systems/color printing and communications/video and  networking products.*

**Eastronics Ltd.,  11 Rozanis St. Tel Branch, PO Box 39300, Tel Aviv 61392, Israel**

Tel: 972-3-645-8777   Fax: 972-3-645-8666

## TERAYON COMMUNICATION SYSTEMS, INC..

2952 Bunker Hill Lane, Santa Clara, CA, 95054

Tel: (408) 727-4400     Fax: (408) 727-6205     www.terayon.com

*Mfr. cable modem systems.*

**Terayon Communication Systems, 132 Petah Tikva Road, Tel Aviv 67021, Israel**

Tel: 972-3645-8500   Fax: 972-3645-8517

## TIMKEN SUPER PRECISION (MPB)

7 Optical Ave., Keene, NH, 03431-0547

Tel: (603) 352-0310     Fax: (603) 355-4553     www.timken.com

*Mfr./sales/distribution bearings, tape guides and systems for missiles, etc.*

**RDT Components Ltd.,  PO Box 58013, 61580 Tel Aviv, Israel**

Tel: 972-3645-0707

## TRANS WORLD AIRLINES INC.

515 North Sixth Street, St. Louis, MO, 63101

Tel: (314) 589-3000     Fax: (314) 589-3129     www.twa.com

*Air transport services.*

**Trans World Airlines Inc., 74-76 Hayarkon St., Tel Aviv 63432, Israel**

Tel: 972-3-517-1212

**Trans World Airlines Inc.,  City Tower Bldg., 34 Ben Yehuda St., Jerusalem, Israel**

## UNITED PARCEL SERVICE, INC.

55 Glenlake Parkway, NE, Atlanta, GA, 30328

Tel: (404) 828-6000     Fax: (404) 828-6593     www.ups.com

*International package-delivery service.*

**UPS Israel, 21 Bar Kochva St., Industrial zone, Bnei Brak 51260, Israel**

Tel: 972-3-577-0101   Fax: 972-3-618-4048

## UNIVERSAL INSTRUMENTS

90 Bevier Street, S. Dock, Binghamton, NY, 13904

Tel: (607) 779-7522     Fax: (607) 779-7971     www.uic.com

*Mfr./sales of instruments for electronic circuit assembly.*

**E&M Engineering (Y.G.R.) Ltd.,  Iramat-Gan, Israel**

Tel: 972-3-751-2929   Fax: 972-3-751-3201

## THE VIKING CORPORATION

210 N. Industrial Park Rd., Hastings, MI, 49058

Tel: (616) 945-9501     Fax: (616) 945-9599     www.vikingcorp.com

*Mfr. fire extinguishing equipment.*

**H.R.R. Marketing & Distribution Limited,  6 Rozanski Street New Ind., Zone IL-75706 Rishon Le Zion, Israel**

## VISHAY INTERTECHNOLOGY INC.

63 Lincoln Hwy., Malvern, PA, 19355

Tel: (610) 644-1300     Fax: (610) 296-0657     www.vishay.com

*Mfr. resistors, strain gages, capacitors, inductors, printed circuit boards.*

**Dale Israel Electronics Ltd.,  Industrial Park, PO Box 87, Dimona 86100, Israel**

**Vishay Israel Ltd.,  2 Haofan St., Holon 58125, Israel**

## VISHAY SILICONIX INC.

2201 Laurelwood Drive, Santa Clara, CA, 95054

Tel: (408) 988-8000     Fax: (408) 970-3950     www.vishay.com

*Semiconductor components.*

**Talviton Electronics Ltd.,  9 Biltmore St., PO Box 21104, Tel Aviv, Israel**

## VOLT INFORMATION SCIENCES, INC.

1221 Ave. of the Americas, 47th Fl., New York, NY, 10020-1579

Tel: (212) 704-2400      Fax: (212) 704-2417      www.volt.com

*Staffing services and telecommunication services.*

**Volt Autologic Ltd., 6 Ahallay St., Ramat Gan 52522, Israel**

## WARNER BROS INTERNATIONAL TELEVISION

4000 Warner Boulevard, Bldg.170, 3rd Fl., Burbank, CA, 91522

Tel: (818) 954-6000      Fax: (818) 977-4040      www.wbitv.com

*Distributor TV programming and theatrical features.*

**Warner Bros. International Television, Attn: Israel Office, 135 Wardour St., London W1V 4AP, UK**

Tel: 44-207-494-3710    Fax: 44-207-465-4207    Contact: Richard Milnes, VP Israel

## WASTE MANAGEMENT, INC.

1001 Fannin Street, Ste. 4000, Houston, TX, 77002

Tel: (713) 512-6200      Fax: (713) 512-6299      www.wastemanagement.com

*Environmental services and disposal company; collection, processing, transfer and disposal facilities.*

**Waste Management Israel Ltd., 3 Daniel Frish Street, Tel Aviv 64731, Israel**

## WIND RIVER SYSTEMS, INC.

500 Wind River Way, Alameda, CA, 94501

Tel: (510) 748-4100      Fax: (510) 749-2010      www.isi.com

*Develops and markets computer software products and services.*

**Wind River Systems Israel, Corex Building - 10 Zarchin St., PO Box 2535, Raanana, 43663 Israel**

Tel: 972-9-741-9561    Fax: 972-9-746-0867

## WOLFE AXELROD WEINBERGER

420 Lexington Ave., New York, NY, 10170

Tel: (212) 370-4500      Fax: (212) 370-4505      www.wolfeaxelrod.com

*Financial public relations, investor relations.*

**Wolfe Axelrod Associates, c/o Stephen J. Kohn, 42 Brenner St., Ranana, Israel**

## WM WRIGLEY JR. COMPANY

410 N. Michigan Ave., Chicago, IL, 60611-4287

Tel: (312) 644-2121      Fax: (312) 644-0353      www.wrigley.com

*Mfr. chewing gum.*

**Wrigley Israel Ltd., Herzeliya-Pituach, Israel**

## XEROX CORPORATION

800 Long Ridge Road, PO Box 1600, Stamford, CT, 06904

Tel: (203) 968-3000      Fax: (203) 968-4312      www.xerox.com

*Mfr. document processing equipment, systems and supplies.*

**ELDAF Ltd., 10 Kehilat Venezia St., Neot Afeka, Tel Aviv, Israel**

Tel: 972-3-645 6350    Fax: 972-3-647 4364

## ZYGO CORPORATION

Laurel Brook Road, Middlefield, CT, 06455

Tel: (860) 347-8506      Fax: (860) 347-8372      www.zygo.com

*Mfr. high-precision, electro-optical measuring equipment.*

**Lahat Technologies Ltd., Teradion Ind. Zone, 20179 D.N. Misgav, Israel**

# Italy

### 24/7 MEDIA, INC.
1250 Broadway, New York, NY, 10001-3701
Tel: (212) 231-7100     Fax: (212) 760-1774     www.247media.com
*Provides global online advertising, sponsorships, e-commerce and direct marketing solutions to advertisers and Web publishers.*
**24/7 Media Italia, Via San Maurilio 16, 20123 Milan, Italy**
Tel: 39-02-8699-7060

### 3M
3M Center, St. Paul, MN, 55144-1000
Tel: (651) 733-1110     Fax: (651) 733-9973     www.mmm.com
*Mfr. diversified products for industry, health care, imaging, communications, transport, safety, consumer, etc.*
**3M Italia SpA, Via San Bovio 3, I-20090 Segrate Milan, Italy**
Tel: 39-01-67-802145   Fax: 39-02-7035-2007   Contact: James B. Stake

### AAF INTERNATIONAL (AMERICAN AIR FILTER)
215 Central Ave., PO Box 35690, Louisville, KY, 40232-5690
Tel: (502) 637-0011     Fax: (502) 637-0321     www.aafintl.com
*Mfr. air filtration/pollution control and noise control equipment.*
**McQuay Italia SpA, Via Valassina 24, 20159 Milan, Italy**
Tel: 39-2-607-0251

### ABBOTT LABORATORIES
One Abbott Park, Abbott Park, IL, 60064-3500
Tel: (847) 937-6100     Fax: (847) 937-1511     www.abbott.com
*Development/mfr./sale diversified health care products and services.*
**Abbott SpA, Via Mar della Cina 262, 00144 Rome, Italy**
Tel: 39-6-529911

### ACADEMIC PRESS INC.
6277 Sea Harbor Drive, Orlando, FL, 32887
Tel: (407) 345-2000     Fax: (407) 345-8388     www.academicpress.com
*Publisher of educational and scientific books.*
**Academic Press, Via Dignano 13 int. 8, I-35135 Padova, Italy**
Tel: 39-049-612-229   Fax: 39-0335-637-7568   Contact: Rosanna Ramacciotti

### ACTERNA CORPORATION
3 New England Executive Park, Burlington, MA, 01803
Tel: (781) 272-6100     Fax: (781) 272-2304     www.acterna.com
*Develop, manufacture and market communications test instruments, systems, software and services.*
**Acterna Corporation, Rome, Italy**

### ADAC LABORATORIES, INC.
540 Alder Drive, Milpitas, CA, 95035
Tel: (408) 321-9100     Fax: (408) 321-9536     www.adaclabs.com
*Mfr. cameras and equipment for nuclear medicine.*
**ADAC Laboratories SRL, Via Torquato Tasso, 2920099 Sesto San Gioavanni, Italy**

## ADEMCO INTERNATIONAL

1769 N.W. 79th Avenue, Miami, FL, 33126

Tel: (305) 477-5204     Fax: (305) 477-5404     www.ademcoint.com

*Mfr. security, fire and burglary systems and products.*

**ADEMCO Italia SpA,  Via Cristoforo Colombo 1, I-20090 Corsico Milan, Italy**

Tel: 39-02-458-0750   Fax: 39-02-458-0762

## ADOBE SYSTEMS INCORPORATED

345 Park Avenue, San Jose, CA, 95110

Tel: (408) 536-6000     Fax: (408) 537-6000     www.adobe.com

*Engaged in print technology and distributor of Acrobat Reader.*

**Adobe Systems Italia Srl,  Viale Colleoni, 5 Centro Direzionale, Palazzo Taurus A3, 20041 Agrate Brianza, Milan, Italy**

## ADVANCED DIGITAL INFORMATION CORPORATION

11431 Willows Rd. NE, PO Box 97057, Redmond, WA, 98073

Tel: (425) 881-8004     Fax: (425) 881-2296     www.adic.com

*Mfr. computer storage systems.*

**Advanced Digital Information Corp.,  Viale Fulvio Testi 11, 20092 Cinisello B. Milan, Italy**

## AEP INDUSTRIES, INC.

125 Phillips Avenue, South Hackensack, NJ, 07606-1546

Tel: (201) 641-6600     Fax: (201) 807-2490     www.aepinc.com

*Mfr. plastic packaging film products.*

**Termofilm SrL,  Turate, Italy**

## THE AEROQUIP GROUP

3000 Strayer, PO Box 50, Maumee, OH, 43537

Tel: (419) 867-2200     Fax: (419) 867-2390     www.aeroquip.com

*Mfr. industrial, automotive, aerospace and defense products.*

**Aeroquip Corporation,  Dir e Stabilimento, Via Piave 24/26, 20016 Pero Italy**

Tel: 390-2-330-10185

## AGCO CORPORATION

4205 River Green Parkway, Duluth, GA, 30096-2568

Tel: (770) 813-9200     Fax: (770) 813-6038     www.agcocorp.com

*Mfr. farm equipment and machinery.*

**Agrinova SNC,  Via Strade per Porzano 9, 25025 Manerbio BS, Italy**

Tel: 39-30-993-8823

**Massey Ferguson Distribution. Div. AGCO,  Via Matteotti 7, 42042 Fabbrico, Reggio Emilia, Italy**

Tel: 39-522-665-951

## AGILENT TECHNOLOGIES, INC.

395 Page Mill Road, PO Box 10395, Palo Alto, CA, 94303

Tel: (650) 752-5000     Fax: (650) 752-5633     www.agilent.com

*Mfr. communications components.*

**Agilent Technologies Italy S.p.A,  Via Giuseppe Di Vittorio 9, I-20063 Cernusco S/N (MI), Italy**

Tel: 32-2-92-121

## AGRIBRANDS INTERNATIONAL, INC.

9811 South Forty Drive, St. Louis, MO, 63124

Tel: (314) 812-0500    Fax: (314) 812-0400    www.agribrands.com

*Produces animal feeds and nutritional products for cattle, poultry, horses and fish.*

**Agribrands Europe Italia S.p.A., Centro Direzionale Green Off., Via Dei Tulipani - 1 Palazzo A, 20090 Peve Emanuele, Italy**

Tel: 39-2-90460-1  Fax: 39-2-9078-2747

## AIR EXPRESS INTERNATIONAL CORPORATION

120 Tokeneke Road, PO Box 1231, Darien, CT, 06820

Tel: (203) 655-7900    Fax: (203) 655-5779    www.aeilogistics.com

*International air freight forwarder.*

**AEI Italy S.p.A., c/o Coimexco S.p.A., Alitalia Cargo Bldg. - Rm. 219, Aeroporto Leonardo da Vinci, Rome Italy**

**AEI Italy S.p.A. - Head Office, Via E. Montale 14/24, I-20090 Novegro di Segrate Milan, Italy**

Tel: 39-02-75271  Fax: 39-02-7527-454

## AIRBORNE FREIGHT CORPORATION

3101 Western Ave., PO Box 662, Seattle, WA, 98121

Tel: (206) 285-4600    Fax: (206) 281-1444    www.airborne.com

*Air transport services.*

**Airborne Express, Via Novegro 3, 20090 Novegro Di Segrate, Milan Italy**

Tel: 39-55-435666  Fax: 39-55-435701

## ALBANY INTERNATIONAL CORPORATION

PO Box 1907, Albany, NY, 12201

Tel: (518) 445-2200    Fax: (518) 445-2265    www.albint.com

*Mfr. broadwoven and engineered fabrics, plastic products, filtration media.*

**Albany Intl. Italiana SpA, Viale Lombardi 68, I-20010 Inveruno, Italy**

## ALBERTO-CULVER COMPANY

2525 Armitage Ave., Melrose Park, IL, 60160

Tel: (708) 450-3000    Fax: (708) 450-3354    www.alberto.com

*Mfr./marketing personal care and household brand products.*

**Alberto-Culver Products SRL, Viale Brenta 18, I--20139 Milan, Italy**

## ALCOA INC.

Alcoa Center, 201 Isabella Street, Pittsburgh, PA, 15215-5858

Tel: (412) 553-4545    Fax: (412) 553-4498    www.alcoa.com

*World's leading producer of aluminum and alumina; mining, refining, smelting, fabricating and recycling.*

**Alcoa Italia S.p.A, Milan, Italy**

Contact: Giuseppe Toia, Mng. Dir.

## ALCOA FUJIKURA LTD.

105 Westpark Drive, Brentwood, TN, 37027

Tel: (615) 370-2100    Fax: (615) 370-2180    www.alcoa-fujikura.com

*Mfr. optical groundwire, tube cable, fiber optic connectors and automotive wiring harnesses.*

**Alcoa Italia S.p.A., Modena, Italy**

## ALLEGHENY TECHNOLOGIES

1000 Six PPG Place, Pittsburgh, PA, 15222

Tel: (412) 394-2800    Fax: (412) 394-2805    www.alleghenytechnologies.com

*Diversified mfr. aviation and electronics, specialty metals, industrial and consumer products.*

**Allegheny Technologies, Corso de Porta Romana 2, I-20122 Milan, Italy**

## ALLEGIANCE HEALTHCARE CORPORATION

1430 Waukegan Road, McGaw Park, IL, 60085

Tel: (847) 689-8410      Fax: (847) 578-4437      www.allegiance.net

*Manufactures and distributes medical, surgical, respiratory therapy and laboratory products.*

**Allegiance Medica srl, Viale Tiziano 25, I- 00196 Rome, Italy**

Tel: 39-06-32-4911   Fax: 39-06-32-491204   Contact: Sandro Lombardi, Business Dir.

## ALLEN TELECOM

25101 Chagrin Boulevard, Beachwood, OH, 44122-5619

Tel: (216) 765-5818      Fax: (216) 765-0410      www.allentele.com

*Mfr. communications equipment, automotive bodies and parts, electronic components.*

**FOREM S.p.A., via Archimede North 22/24, I-20041 Agrate Brianza Milan, Italy**

Tel: 39-039-60541   Fax: 39-039-605-4450

**TEKMAR Sistemi s.r.l., via De Crescenzi, 40, I-48018 Faenza, Italy**

Tel: 39-054-620401   Fax: 39-054-668-2768

## ALLEN-BRADLEY COMPANY, INC.

1201 South Second Street, Milwaukee, WI, 53204

Tel: (414) 382-2000      Fax: (414) 382-4444      www.ab.com

*Mfr. electrical controls and information devices.*

**Allen-Bradley Italia SRL, Via Tortona 33, I-20144 Milan, Italy**

**Nuova OSAI SRL, Allen-Bradley Motion Control Div., Stradale Torino 603, I-10015 Ivrea, Italy**

## ALLERGAN INC.

2525 Dupont Drive, PO Box 19534, Irvine, CA, 92713-9534

Tel: (714) 246-4500      Fax: (714) 246-6987      www.allergan.com

*Mfr. therapeutic eye care products, skin and neural care pharmaceuticals.*

**Allergan S.p.A., Via Salvatore Quasimodo, N. 134/138, 00144 Rome, Italy**

Tel: 39-6-509561   Fax: 39-6-50956410

## ALTERA CORPORATION

101 Innovation Drive, San Jose, CA, 95134

Tel: (408) 544-7000      Fax: (408) 544-8303      www.altera.com

*Mfr. high-density programmable chips for semi-conductor industry.*

**Altera Italia S.R.L., Corso Lombardia 75, Autoporto Pescarito, 10099 San Mauro Torinese (Torino), Italy**

Tel: 39-11-223-8588

## AMERICAN & EFIRD, INC.

PO Box 507, Mt. Holly, NC, 28120

Tel: (704) 827-4311      Fax: (704) 822-6054      www.amefird.com

*Mfr. industrial sewing thread for worldwide industrial and consumer markets.*

**American & Efird (Italia) S.p.A, Via Salicchi 758, 55100 Acquacalda Lucca, Italy**

## AMERICAN AIRLINES INC.

4333 Amon Carter Boulevard, Ft. Worth, TX, 76155

Tel: (817) 963-1234      Fax: (817) 967-9641      www.amrcorp.com

*Air transport services.*

**American Airlines Inc., Via Sicilia 50, I-00187 Rome, Italy**

## AMERICAN APPRAISAL ASSOCIATES INC.

411 E. Wisconsin Ave., Milwaukee, WI, 53202

Tel: (414) 271-7240     Fax: (414) 271-1041     www.american-appraisal.com

*Valuation consulting services.*

**American Appraisal Italia SRL, Centro Direzionale Colleoni, Viale Colleoni 21, Edif. Pegaso 1, I-20041 Agrate Milan, Italy**

## AMERICAN EXPRESS COMPANY

American Express Tower, World Financial Center, New York, NY, 10285-4765

Tel: (212) 640-2000     Fax: (212) 619-9802     www.americanexpress.com

*Travel, travelers cheques, charge card and financial services.*

**American Express Co. SpA, Rome, Italy**

**American Express Factoring Ltda., Milan, Italy**

## AMERICAN HOME PRODUCTS CORPORATION

Five Giralda Farms, Madison, NJ, 07940-0874

Tel: (973) 660-5000     Fax: (973) 660-6048     www.ahp.com

*Mfr. pharmaceutical, animal health care and crop protection products.*

**American Home Products Corporation, Milan, Italy**

## AMERICAN INTERNATIONAL GROUP INC. (AIG)

70 Pine Street, New York, NY, 10270

Tel: (212) 770-7000     Fax: (212) 509-9705     www.aig.com

*Worldwide insurance and financial services.*

**AIG Europe S.A., Via Valcava 6, 20155 Milan, Italy**

## AMERICAN MANAGEMENT SYSTEMS, INC.

4050 Legato Road, Fairfax, VA, 22033

Tel: (703) 267-8000     Fax: (703) 267-5073     www.amsinc.com

*Systems integration and consulting.*

**AMS Management Systems Italia, SPA, Via Pontaccio 10, I-20121 Milan, Italy**
Tel: 39-02-7202-3697   Fax: 39-02-7202-3756

## AMERICAN SOFTWARE, INC.

470 East Paces Ferry Road, NE, Atlanta, GA, 30305

Tel: (404) 261-4381     Fax: (404) 264-5514     www.amsoftware.com

*Mfr./sales of financial control software and systems.*

**Information Technology Italia, 20089 Assago (MI) Strada 4, Palazzo Q7, Milanfiori Italy**
Tel: 39-2-5750-1440   Fax: 39-2-5750-1461

## AMERICAN STANDARD INC.

One Centennial Avenue, Piscataway, NJ, 08855-6820

Tel: (732) 980-3000     Fax: (732) 980-6118     www.americanstandard.com

*Mfr. automotive, plumbing, heating, air conditioning products and medical diagnostics systems.*

**DiaSorin s.r.l., Via Crescentino, 1340 Saluggia VC, Italy**
Tel: 390-161-487-087   Fax: 390-161-487-396

**WABCO Compagnia Italiana Segnali SpA, Via Volvera 51, I-10045 Piossasco Turin, Italy**

**WABCO SpA, Via Pier Carlo Boggio 20, I-10138 Turin, Italy**

## AMERICAN UNIFORM COMPANY

PO Box 2130, Cleveland, TN, 37311

Tel: (423) 476-6561     Fax: (423) 559-3855

*Mfr. work clothing and uniforms.*

**Amuco Italiana SpA, Via Pina Odardine 29, I-83100 Avellino, Italy**

## AMETEK INC.

37 N. Valley Road, PO Box 1764, Paoli, PA, 19301-0801

Tel: (610) 647-2121　　Fax: (610) 296-3412　　www.ametek.com

*Mfr. instruments, electric motors and engineered materials.*

**AMETEK Italia S.r.l., Vacuum Products,　Via De Gasperi 18/A, Ripalta Cremasca I-26010, Italy**

Tel: 39-0373-2101　Fax: 39-0373-268200

**AMETEK Italia Srl,　Via de Barzi, Robecco Sul Naviglio, I-20087 Milan, Italy**

Tel: 39-02-94-6931　Fax: 39-02-94-71179

## AMGEN INC.

One Amgen Center Drive, Thousand Oaks, CA, 91320-1799

Tel: (805) 447-1000　　Fax: (805) 499-2694　　www.amgen.com

*Biotechnology research and pharmaceruticals.*

**Amgen S.p.A.,　Via Vitruvio 38, I-20124 Milan, Italy**

## AMPACET CORPORATION

660 White Plains Road, Tarrytown, NY, 10591-5130

Tel: (914) 631-6600　　Fax: (914) 631-7197　　www.ampacet.com

*Mfr. color and additive concentrates for the plastics industry.*

**Ampacet Bergamo,　Via G. Verdi 36, I-24060 Telgate, Italy**

Tel: 39-01-3544-92211　Fax: 39-01-3583-0371

## AMPEX CORPORATION

500 Broadway, Redwood City, CA, 94063-3199

Tel: (650) 367-2011　　Fax: (650) 367-4669　　www.ampex.com

*Mfr. extremely high-performance digital data storage, data retrieval and image processing systems for a broad range of corporate scientific and government applications.*

**Ampex Italiana SpA,　Via Cristoforo Colombo 40, I-20090 Trezzano sul Naviglio Milan, Italy**

## AMPHENOL CORPORATION

358 Hall Ave., Wallingford, CT, 06492-7530

Tel: (203) 265-8900　　Fax: (203) 265-8793　　www.amphenol.com

*Mfr. electrictronic interconnect penetrate systems and assemblies.*

**Ampheno Italia, S.P.A.,　Galleria Ghandi 2/27, 20017 Mazzo di Rho, Milan Italy**

Tel: 39-02-9390-4192　Fax: 39-02-9390-1030

## AMSTED INDUSTRIES INC.

205 North Michigan Ave., Chicago, IL, 60601

Tel: (312) 645-1700　　Fax: (312) 819-8523　　www.amsted.com

*Privately-held, diversified manufacturer of products for the construction and building markets, general industry and the railroads.*

**Baltimore Aircoil Italia S.r.l.,　I-23030 Chiuro Sondrio, Italy**

Tel: 39-0342-482-882　Fax: 39-0342-83-022　Contact: Massimo Moltoni, Gen. Mgr.　Emp: 22

## AMWAY CORPORATION

7575 Fulton Street East, Ada, MI, 49355-0001

Tel: (616) 787-6000　　Fax: (616) 787-6177　　www.amway.com

*Mfr./sale home care, personal care, nutrition and houseware products.*

**Amway Italia SRL,　Via G. di Vittorio 10, I-20094 Corsico Milan, Italy**

## ANALOG DEVICES INC.

1 Technology Way, Box 9106, Norwood, MA, 02062

Tel: (781) 329-4700　　Fax: (781) 326-8703　　www.analog.com

*Mfr. integrated circuits and related devices.*

**Analog Devices SRL,　Via Galileo Galilei 2, I-20091 Bresso, Italy**

## ANDERSEN CONSULTING

100 S. Wacker Drive, Ste. 1059, Chicago, IL, 60606

Tel: (312) 693-0161    Fax: (312) 693-0507    www.ac.com

*Provides management and technology consulting services.*

**Andersen Consulting, Largo Donegani 2, I-20121 Milan, Italy**

Tel: 39-02-290381    Fax: 39-02-6598644

## ANDERSEN WORLDWIDE

33 West Monroe Street, Chicago, IL, 60603

Tel: (312) 580-0033    Fax: (312) 507-6748    www.arthurandersen.com

*Accounting and audit, tax and management consulting services.*

**Andersen Worldwide, Via Della Moscova 3, I-20121 Milan, Italy**

Tel: 39-02-290371

**Studio di Consulenza Legale e Tributaria, Largo Donegani 2, I-20121 Milan, Italy**

Tel: 39-02-62401

**Studio di Consulenza Legale e Tributaria, Via XX Settembre 1, I-00187 Rome, Italy**

Tel: 39-06-489901

**Studio di Consulenza Legale e Tributaria, Via M. D'Azeglio 19, I-40123 Bologna, Italy**

Tel: 39-051-237539

## ANDREW CORPORATION

10500 West 153rd Street, Orland Park, IL, 60462

Tel: (708) 349-3300    Fax: (708) 349-5410    www.andrew.com

*Mfr. antenna systems, coaxial cable, electronic communications and network connectivity systems.*

**Andrew SRL, Via Rombon 11, I-20134 Milan, Italy**

Tel: 39-02-215611    Fax: 39-02-215-0490

## ANHEUSER-BUSCH INTERNATIONAL INC.

One Busch Place, St. Louis, MO, 63118-1852

Tel: (314) 577-2000    Fax: (314) 577-2900    www.anheuser-busch.com

*Malt production, aluminum beverage containers, rice milling, real estate development, metalized and paper label printing, railcar repair and theme-park facilities.*

**S.P.A. Birra Peroni Industriale, Milan, Italy**

## ANIXTER INTERNATIONAL INC..

4711 Golf Road, Skokie, IL, 60076

Tel: (847) 677-2600    Fax: (847) 677-8557    www.anixter.com

*Distributor wiring systems/products for voice, video, data and power applications.*

**Anixter Italy, Via Della Grande Muraglia 284, 00144 Rome, Italy**

Tel: 39-06-526-201    Fax: 39-05-522-05-250

**Anixter Italy, Via Walter Tobagi 24, 20068 Peschiera Borromeo, Italy**

Tel: 39-02-54-7491    Fax: 39-02-55-301777

## AOL TIME WARNER

75 Rockefeller Plaza, New York, NY, 10019

Tel: (212) 484-8000    Fax: (212) 275-3046    www.aoltimewarner.com

*Engaged in media and communications; provides internet services, communications, publishing and entertainment.*

**Time-Life Intl. SARL, Via Turati 29, Milan, Italy**

## AON CORPORATION

123 North Wacker Drive, Chicago, IL, 60606

Tel: (312) 701-3000    Fax: (312) 701-3100    www.aon.com

*Insurance brokers worldwide; underwrites accident and health insurance, specialty and professional insurance; and provides risk management consultation.*

**AON Italia SpA, Piazza della Repubblica 32, Milan, Italy**

Tel: 39-02-678-481   Fax: 39-02-678-48200   Contact: Raffaele Bozzano

**Manzitti Howden Beck SpA, Via XX Settembre 33, Genoa, Italy**

Tel: 39-010-541-951   Fax: 39-010-582-825   Contact: Beppe Manzitti

## APPLE COMPUTER, INC.

One Infinite Loop, Cupertino, CA, 95014

Tel: (408) 996-1010    Fax: (408) 974-2113    www.apple.com

*Personal computers, peripherals and software.*

**Apple Computer SpA, Via Bovio 5, Zona Ind. di Mancasale, I-42100 Reggio Emilia, Italy**

## APPLERA CORPORATION

761 Main Avenue, Norwalk, CT, 06859-0001

Tel: (203) 762-1000    Fax: (203) 762-6000    www.applera.com

*Leading supplier of systems for life science research and related applications.*

**Applied Biosystems, Via Tiepolo 18, 20052 Monza (MI), Italy**

Tel: 39-0-39-838-9492

## APPLIED MATERIALS, INC.

3050 Bowers Ave., Santa Clara, CA, 95054-3299

Tel: (408) 727-5555    Fax: (408) 727-9943    www.appliedmaterials.com

*Supplies manufacturing systems and services to the semiconductor industry.*

**Applied Materials S.A.R.L., Centro Direaionale Colleoni, Viale Colleoni 15 - Palazzo Orione, I-20041 Agrate Brianza Milan, Italy**

Tel: 39-039-605-8111   Fax: 39-039-605-6446

## APW, INC.

PO Box 325, Milwaukee, WI, 53201-0325

Tel: (262) 523-7600    Fax: (262) 523-7624    www.apw1.com

*Mfr. hi-pressure tools, vibration control products, consumables, technical furniture and enclosures.*

**APW Enclosure Products, Corso Lombardia, 52 Regione Pescarito, 100099 S. Mauro, Torinese Italy**

**APW Italiana SpA, Via Canova 4, I-20094 Corsico Milan, Italy**

## ARBOR ACRES FARM INC.

439 Marlborough Road, Glastonbury, CT, 06033

Tel: (860) 633-4681    Fax: (860) 633-2433

*Producers of male and female broiler breeders, commercial egg layers.*

**Arbor Acres Italia SpA, Localita Mojentina, I-20070 San Rocco Al Porto Milan, Italy**

## ARGO INTERNATIONAL CORPORATION

140 Franklin Street, New York, NY, 10013

Tel: (212) 431-1700    Fax: (212) 431-2206    www.argointl.com

*Distributor electrical spare parts.*

**Argo International Europe Ltd., Viale Dei Mille 74, Florence, Italy**

**Argo International Italy, Via Bassa 33B, Scandicci Firenze 50018, Italy**

### ARIBA, INC.

1565 Charleston Rd., Mountain View, CA, 94043

Tel: (650) 930-6200      Fax: (650) 930-6300      www.ariba.com

*Mfr. software.*

**Ariba Italia,  Largo Richini 6, 20122 Milan, Italy**

### ARMSTRONG HOLDINGS, INC.

2500 Columbia Avenue, Lancaster, PA, 17604-3001

Tel: (717) 397-0611      Fax: (717) 396-2787      www.armstrong.com

*Mfr. and marketing interior furnishings and specialty products for bldg, auto and textile industry.*

**Armstrong World Industries Italia SRL,  Milan, Italy**

### ARROW ELECTRONICS INC.

25 Hub Drive, Melville, NY, 11747

Tel: (516) 391-1300      Fax: (516) 391-1640      www.arrow.com

*Distributor of electronic components.*

**Arrow Italia,  Via Collamarini 22, 40138 Bologna, Italy**

**Arrow Italia,  Corso Svizzera 185 bis, Centro Piero della Francesca, 10149 Torino, Italy**

**Arrow Italia,  Via A. da Noli 6, 50127 Firenze, Italy**

**Arrow Italia,  Via Bille 26, 63023 Ascoli Piceno, Italy**

**Arrow Italia,  Via A da Noli 6, 50127 Firenze, Italy**

**Arrow Italia,  Via Fulvio Testi 280, 20126 Milan, Italy**

**Arrow Italia,  Via Giunio Antonio Resti 63, 00143 Rome, Italy**

**Arrow Italia,  Via Crocillo 69, 80010 Naples, Italy**

**Arrow Italia,  Viale Delle Industrie 13, 35101 Padova, Italy**

**Silverstar,  Viale Fulvio Testi 280, I-20126 Milan, Italy**

Tel: 39-02-66-12-51   Fax: 39-02-66-10-42-79   Contact: Germano Fanelli, Mng. Dir.

### ASG (ALLEN SYSTEMS GROUP)

1333 3rd Avenue South, Naples, FL, 33102

Tel: (941) 435-2200      Fax: (941) 263-3692      www.asg.com

*Mainframe computer software, specializing in OnMark 2000 software.*

**ASG Italy,  Palazzo Pitagora, Centro Direzionale di Milano 3 City, Basiglio (MI) 20080, Italy**

Tel: 39-02-904-5001

### ASHLAND OIL INC.

50 E. Rivercenter Blvd., Covington, KY, 41012-0391

Tel: (859) 815-3333      Fax: (859) 815-5053      www.ashland.com

*Petroleum exploration, refining and transportation; mfr. chemicals, oils and lubricants.*

**Ashland Chemical Italiana SpA,  Via Giacomo Watt 42, I-20143 Milan, Italy**

### ASSOCIATED MERCHANDISING CORPORATION

500 Seventh Ave., 2nd Fl., New York, NY, 10018

Tel: (212) 819-6600      Fax: (212) 819-6701      www.theamc.com

*Retail service organization; apparel, shoes and accessories.*

**Amcrest Corp.,  Piazza della Republica 32, I-20124 Milan, Italy**

**Amcrest Corp.,  Via Guicciardini 13, I-50125 Florence, Italy**

### ASSOCIATED PRESS INC.

50 Rockefeller Plaza, New York, NY, 10020-1605

Tel: (212) 621-1500      Fax: (212) 621-5447      www.ap.com

*News gathering agency.*

**The Associated Press,  Piazza Grazioli 5, Rome, Italy**

Tel: 39-06-678-9936

## AT HOME CORPORATION

450 Broadway Street, Redwood City, CA, 94063

Tel: (650) 556-5000     Fax: (650) 556-5100     www.excite.com

*Online computer internet service provider.*

**Excite, Inc., Milan, Italy**

## AT&T CORPORATION

32 Avenue of the Americas, New York, NY, 10013-2412

Tel: (212) 387-5400     Fax: (212) 387-5695     www.att.com

*Telecommunications.*

**AT&T Italia SpA, 153 Via Cristoforo Colombo, I-00147 Rome, Italy**

## ATMEL CORPORATION

2325 Orchard Pkwy., San Jose, CA, 95131

Tel: (408) 441-0311     Fax: (408) 436-4200     www.atmel.com

*Design, manufacture and marketing of advanced semiconductors.*

**Atmel Italy, Uff di Milano Centro Dierzionale, Colleoni Palazzo Andromeda 3, Agrate Brianza 2004, Italy**

Tel: 39-39-605-6955   Fax: 39-39-605-6969

## ATTACHMATE CORPORATION

3617 131st Ave. S.E., Bellevue, WA, 98006-1332

Tel: (425) 644-4010     Fax: (425) 747-9924     www.attachmate.com

*Mfr. connectivity software.*

**Attachmate Italy, Via Vitruvio 38, 20124 Milan, Italy**

Tel: 39-02-671-3101   Fax: 39-02-669-1113

**Attachmate Italy, Via Cristoforo Colombo 440, 00145 Rome, Italy**

Tel: 39-06-542-3281   Fax: 39-06-540-8851

## AUTODESK INC.

111 McInnis Parkway, San Rafael, CA, 94903

Tel: (415) 507-5000     Fax: (415) 507-6112     www.autodesk.com

*Develop/marketing/support computer-aided design, engineering, scientific and multimedia software products.*

**Autodesk SpA, Milanofiori, Strada4 Palazzo A5, 1-20090 Milan, Italy**

Tel: 39-02-57-5511   Fax: 39-01-57-510-105

## AUTOMATIC DATA PROCESSING INC.

One ADP Blvd., Roseland, NJ, 07068

Tel: (973) 994-5000     Fax: (973) 994-5387     www.adp.com

*Data processing services.*

**ADP-GSI S.p.A., Via Natale Battaglia 8, I-20127 Milan, Italy**

Tel: 39-02-261651   Fax: 39-02-282-7639   Contact: Lina Gallo

## AUTOMATIC SWITCH CO. (ASCO)

50-60 Hanover Rd., Florham Park, NJ, 07932

Tel: (973) 966-2000     Fax: (973) 966-2628     www.asco.com

*Mfr. solenoid valves, emergency power controls, pressure and temp. switches.*

**Asco/Joucomatic S.P.A., Via Inverigo 14, I-20151 Milan, Italy**

Tel: 39-02-380411   Fax: 39-02-334-00409   Contact: D. Ferrari

## AUTOSPLICE INC.

10121 Barnes Canyon Road, San Diego, CA, 92121

Tel: (858) 535-0077　　Fax: (858) 535-0130　　www.autosplice.com

*Mfr. electronic components.*

**Autosplice Italia, Via Sicilia 19, I-20040, Carnate (MI) Italy**

Fax: 39-39-6705-30　Contact: Dr. Laura Camisasca

## AVERY DENNISON CORPORATION

150 N. Orange Grove Blvd., Pasadena, CA, 91103

Tel: (626) 304-2000　　Fax: (626) 792-7312　　www.averydennison.com

*Mfr. pressure-sensitive adhesives and materials, office products, labels, tags, retail systems, Carter's Ink and specialty chemicals.*

**Avery Dennison Italia SpA, Via Honduras 15, Pomezia, Italy**

Tel: 39-69-160-0311

**Fasson Italia SpA, Corso Italia 2, I-21040 Origgio Varese, Italy**

## AVID TECHNOLOGY, INC.

1 Park West, Tewksbury, MA, 01876

Tel: (978) 640-6789　　Fax: (978) 640-1366　　www.avid.com

*Mfr. animation design software and digital and audio systems.*

**Avid Technology Srl, Palazzo E-1, 20090-Assago-Milanofiori (MI), Milan, Italy**

Tel: 39-02-5778-971

## AVNET INC.

2211 South 47th Street, Phoenix, AZ, 85034

Tel: (480) 643-2000　　Fax: (480) 643-4670　　www.avnet.com

*Distributor electronic components, computers and peripherals.*

**Avnet EMG SRL Adelsy, Centro Direzionale, Via Novara 780, I-20153 Milan MI, Italy**

Tel: 39-238-1901　Fax: 39-238-2988

**BFI IBEXSA S.p.A., 18 Via Massena, Milan, Italy**

Tel: 39-233-100535　Fax: 39-233-611603

## AVON PRODUCTS INC.

1345 Avenue of the Americas, New York, NY, 10105-0196

Tel: (212) 282-5000　　Fax: (212) 282-6049　　www.avon.com

*Mfr./distributor beauty and related products, fashion jewelry, gifts and collectibles.*

**Avon Cosmetics SpA, Via XXV Aprile 15, I-22077 Olgiate Comasco Como, Italy**

Tel: 39-031-998111　Fax: 39-031-998312　Contact: Fabio Stillitano, Field Dir.

## BAIN & COMPANY, INC.

Two Copley Place, Boston, MA, 02116

Tel: (617) 572-2000　　Fax: (617) 572-2427　　www.bain.com

*Strategic management consulting services.*

**Bain, Cuneo e Associati, Via Lutezia 8, I-00198 Rome, Italy**

**Bain, Cuneo e Associati, Via Crocefisso 10/12, I-20122 Milan, Italy**

Tel: 39-02-582-881　Fax: 39-02-583-14070

## BAKER & McKENZIE

130 East Randolph Drive, Ste. 2500, Chicago, IL, 60601

Tel: (312) 861-8000　　Fax: (312) 861-2899　　www.bakerinfo.com

*International legal services.*

**Studio Avvocati Associati, Via degli Scipioni, 288, I-00192 Rome, Italy**

Tel: 39-06-3225162　Fax: 39-06-3203502

**Studio Legale de Libero Camilli Boniello Bartolo Di Garbo, 3 Piazza Meda, I-20121 Milan, Italy**

Tel: 39-02-76013921　Fax: 39-02-76008322

## BAKER HUGHES INCORPORATED

3900 Essex Lane, Ste. 1200, Houston, TX, 77027

Tel: (713) 439-8600      Fax: (713) 439-8699      www.bakerhughes.com

*Develop and apply technology to drill, complete and produce oil and natural gas wells; provide separation systems to petroleum, municipal, continuous process and mining industries.*

**Baker Oil Tools (Italia), SRL,  Via Monti 2, Zona Bassette, I-48101 Ravenna, Italy**

Tel: 39-054-445-6229    Fax: 39-054-445-4816

**Baker Oil Tools (Italia), SRL,  Via Monti 2 Zona Bassette, 48100 Ravenna, Italy**

Tel: 39-544-453-339

**Baker Oil Tools (Italia), SRL,  Strada Statale 602 Km 5 + 170, Santa Teresa, I-65010 Spoltore Pescara, Italy**

Tel: 39-085-497-1190    Fax: 39-085-497-1224

## BAKER PETROLITE CORPORATION

3900 Essex Lane, Houston, TX, 77027

Tel: (713) 599-7400      Fax: (713) 599-7592      www.bakerhughes.com/bapt/

*Mfr. specialty chemical treating programs, performance-enhancing additives and related equipment and services.*

**Petrolite Italiana SpA,  Via Sasari 86, I-95127 Catania, Italy**

## BALTIMORE AIRCOIL CO., INC.

PO Box 7322, Baltimore, MD, 21227

Tel: (410) 799-6200      Fax: (410) 799-6416      www.baltimoreaircoil.com

*Mfr. evaporative heat transfer and ice thermal storage products.*

**Baltimore Aircoil Italia s.r.l.,  23030 Chiuro (Sondrio), Italy**

## BANK OF AMERICA CORPORATION

555 California Street, San Francisco, CA, 94104

Tel: (415) 622-3530      Fax: (415) 622-8467      www.bankofamerica.com

*Financial services.*

**Bank of America - Southern Europe,  Corso Matteotti 10, I-20121 Milan, Italy**

Tel: 39-02-760-691  Fax: 39-02-760-69200   Contact: Pier Giorgio Rota Baldini, EVP

## THE BANK OF NEW YORK

One Wall Street, New York, NY, 10286

Tel: (212) 495-1784      Fax: (212) 495-2546      www.bankofny.com

*Banking services.*

**The Bank of New York,  Piazzale Cadorna 4, I-20123 Milan, Italy**

Tel: 39-02-720-10333    Fax: 39-02-720-10325

## C. R. BARD, INC.

730 Central Ave., Murray Hill, NJ, 07974

Tel: (908) 277-8000      Fax: (908) 277-8078      www.crbard.com

*Mfr. health care products.*

**Bard SpA,  Via Cina 444, I-00144 Rome, Italy**

## BARRY CONTROLS INC.

40 Guest Street, PO Box 9105, Brighton, MA, 02135-9105

Tel: (617) 787-1555      Fax: (617) 254-7381      www.barrymounts.com

*Mfr./sale vibration isolation mounting devices.*

**UVIT il Cingolo,  Via F Busoni, 20137 Milan, Italy**

## BATES WORLDWIDE INC.

405 Lexington Ave., New York, NY, 10174

Tel: (212) 297-7000     Fax: (212) 986-0270     www.batesww.com

*Advertising, marketing, public relations and media consulting.*

**Bates Italia, Via Paleocapa 7, I-20121 Milan, Italy**

Tel: 39-02-805-2283   Fax: 39-02-864-54305   Contact: Giordano Spagllardi, Mgr.

**Bates Italia, Via Panama 12, I-00195 Rome, Italy**

Tel: 39-06-844-0381   Fax: 39-06-853-55607   Contact: S. Pazzagli, Mgr.

**Bates Medical/Healthcom, Via Paleocapa 7, I-20121 Milan, Italy**

Tel: 39-02-72-2231   Fax: 39-02-72-010811   Contact: Leonardo Vinci, CEO

## BAXTER HEALTHCARE CORPORATION

One Baxter Parkway, Deerfield, IL, 60015

Tel: (847) 948-2000     Fax: (847) 948-3948     www.baxter.com

*Pharmaceutical preparations, surgical/medical instruments and cardiovascular products.*

**Baxter SpA, Viale Tiziano 25, I-00196 Rome, Italy**

**Laboratori Don Baxter SpA, Via Flavia 122, I-34146 Trieste, Italy**

## BBDO WORLDWIDE

1285 Ave. of the Americas, New York, NY, 10019

Tel: (212) 459-5000     Fax: (212) 459-6645     www.bbdo.com

*Multinational group of advertising agencies.*

**BBDO Italy, Milan, Italy**

## BDO SEIDMAN, LLP    BELGIUM

Two Prudential Plaza, 180 N. Stetson Ave., Ste. 2300, Chicago, IL, 60601

Tel: (312) 240-1236     Fax: (312) 240-3329     www.bdo.com

*International accounting and financial consulting firm.*

**Sala Scelsi, Farina BDO, Piazza del Liberty 4, I-20121 Milan, Italy**

Tel: 39-02-784563   Fax: 39-02-784567   Contact: Girogio Farina

## BEA SYSTEMS, INC.

2315 North First Street, St. Jose, CA, 95131

Tel: (408) 570-8000     Fax: (408) 570-8091     www.beasys.com

*Develops communications management software and provider of software consulting services.*

**BEA Systems Italia, Via Conservatorio 22, I-20122 Milan, Italy**

Tel: 39-02-772-9307   Fax: 39-02-772-940

## BECKMAN COULTER, INC.

4300 N. Harbor Boulevard, Fullerton, CA, 92834

Tel: (714) 871-4848     Fax: (714) 773-8898     www.beckmancoulter.com

*Develop/mfr./marketing automated systems and supplies for biological analysis.*

**Beckman-Analytical SpA, Centro Direzionale Lombardo, Palazzo F/1, Via Roma 108, I-20060 Cassina de Pecchi Milan, Italy**

## BELDEN, INC.

7701 Forsyth Blvd., Ste. 800, St. Louis, MO, 63015

Tel: (314) 854-8000     Fax: (314) 854-8001     www.belden.com

*Mfr. electronic wire and cable products.*

**Belden International Inc., Via Paracelso 26, Centro Direzionale Colleoni, Palazzo Cassiopea Ingr. 3, 20041 Agrate Brianza MI, Italy**

## BELL MICROPRODUCTS INC.

1941 Ringwood Avenue, San Jose, CA, 95131

Tel: (408) 451-9400     Fax: (408) 451-1600     www.bellmicro.com

*Distributes semiconductor and computer products from manufacturers.*

**Rorke Data, Div. Bell Microproducts, Via Angelo Carrara 210, 16147 Genova, Italy**

Tel: 39-10-373-3126

## BEST WESTERN INTERNATIONAL

6201 North 24th Place, Phoenix, AZ, 85106

Tel: (602) 957-4200     Fax: (602) 957-5740     www.bestwestern.com

*International hotel chain.*

**Hotel Syrene, Via Camerelle 51, Capri, Italy**

## BESTFOODS, INC.

700 Sylvan Ave., International Plaza, Englewood Cliffs, NJ, 07632-9976

Tel: (201) 894-4000     Fax: (201) 894-2186     www.bestfoods.com

*Consumer foods products; corn refining.*

**CPC Italia S.p.A.., Via G. Gozzano 14, I-20092 Cinisello Balsamo Milan, Italy**

Tel: 39-02-660-831   Fax: 39-02-660-15010   Contact: Claudio Rosso, Mgr.

## BETZDEARBORN

4636 Somerton Road, PO Box 3002, Trevose, PA, 19053-6783

Tel: (215) 953-2568     Fax: (215) 953-5524     www.betzdearborn.com

*Mfr. water/wastewater and process system treatment chemicals and services.*

**BetzDearborn S.p.A., Viale Gino Cervi 6, I-00139 Rome, Italy**

## BICC GENERAL

4 Tesseneer Drive, Highland Heights, KY, 41076

Tel: (606) 572-8000     Fax: (606) 572-8444     www.generalcable.com

*Mfr., marketing and distribution of copper, aluminum and fiber optic wire and cable products for the communications, energy and electrical markets.*

**BICC General, 16 Via Brescia, 10036 Settimo Torinese, Turin Italy**

## BIO-RAD LABORATORIES INC.

1000 Alfred Nobel Drive, Hercules, CA, 94547

Tel: (510) 724-7000     Fax: (510) 724-3167     www.bio-rad.com

*Mfr. life science research products, clinical diagnostics, analytical instruments.*

**Bio-Rad Laboratories SRL, Milan, Italy**

## BLACK & DECKER CORPORATION

701 E. Joppa Road, Towson, MD, 21286

Tel: (410) 716-3900     Fax: (410) 716-2933     www.blackanddecker.com

*Mfr. power tools and accessories, security hardware, small appliances, fasteners, information systems and services.*

**Black & Decker Italy, Attn: Italy Office, 701 East Joppa Road, Towson MD 21286**

## BLACK BOX CORPORATION

1000 Park Dr., Lawrence, PA, 15055

Tel: (724) 746-5500     Fax: (724) 746-0746     www.blackbox.com

*Direct marketer and technical service provider of communications, networking and related computer connectivity products.*

**Black Box Italia SpA, Viale Delle Industrie 11, I-20090 Vimodrone, Milan, Italy**

Tel: 39-02-2740-0815   Fax: 39-02-2740-0219   Contact: Giancarlo Mauri, Gen. Mgr.

### BLOOM ENGINEERING CO., INC.

5460 Horning Rd., Pittsburgh, PA, 15236

Tel: (412) 653-3500    Fax: (412) 653-2253    www.bloomeng.com

*Mfr. custom engineered burners and combustion systems.*

**Bloom Engineering (Europa) S.r.l., Via A. Cantore 30/B-7, 16149 Genova, Italy**

Tel: 390-10-466772    Fax: 390-10-6468473

### BMC SOFTWARE, INC.

2101 City West Blvd., Houston, TX, 77042-2827

Tel: (713) 918-8800    Fax: (713) 918-8000    www.bmc.com

*Engaged in mainframe-related utilities software and services.*

**BMC Software, Via M. Bianchini 51, 00142 Rome, Italy**

**BMC Software S.r.l., Via Ugo Bassi 8/A, 20159 Milan, Italy**

### THE BOEING COMPANY

7755 East Marginal Way South, Seattle, WA, 98108

Tel: (206) 655-2121    Fax: (206) 655-6300    www.boeing.com.

*World's largest aerospace company; mfr. military and commercial aircraft, missiles and satellite launch vehicles.*

**The Boeing Company, Rome, Italy**

### BOGUE ELECTRIC MFG. COMPANY

100 Pennsylvania Ave., Paterson, NJ, 07509

Tel: (973) 523-2200    Fax: (973) 278-8468    www.bogueelectric.com

*Electrical equipment, power supplies, battery chargers and micro projector controlled motors.*

**Hobart Intl., Rome, Italy**

**Tecnap, Via Zanotti Bianco, I-87100 Cosenza, Italy**

Tel: 39-0984-35091    Fax: 39-0984-31373    Contact: Enzo Farraro    Emp: 30

### BOISE CASCADE CORPORATION

1111 West Jefferson Street, PO Box 50, Boise, ID, 83728-0001

Tel: (208) 384-6161    Fax: (208) 384-7189    www.bc.com

*Mfr./distributor paper and paper products, building products, office products.*

**Carlos Proto Agencies, Rome, Italy**

Tel: 39-06-321-6565

### BONTEX INC.

One Bondex, Buena Vista, VA, 24416

Tel: (540) 261-2181    Fax: (540) 261-3784    www.bontex.com

*Engaged in development and distribution of advanced materials, systems for a broad range of applications.*

**Bontex Italia SRL, Via Francia N. 1, 37069 Villafranc, Italy**

Tel: 39-45 630 34 12    Fax: 39-0-630 35 88

### BOOZ-ALLEN & HAMILTON INC.

8283 Greensboro Drive, McLean, VA, 22102

Tel: (703) 902-5000    Fax: (703) 902-3333    www.bah.com

*International management and technology consultants.*

**Booz, Allen & Hamilton Italia Ltd., Via dei Bossi 4, I-20121 Milan, Italy**

Tel: 39-02-725091    Fax: 39-02-72-50-9400

## BORDEN INC.

180 East Broad Street, Columbus, OH, 43215-3799

Tel: (614) 225-4000      Fax: (614) 220-6453      www.bordenfamily.com

*Mfr. packaged foods, consumer adhesives, housewares and industrial chemicals.*

**Albadoro Spa, Corso Asti 18, I-12050 Guarene d'Alba CN, Italy**

Tel: 39-0173-362516

**Monder Aliment Spa, Via G. di Vittorio 5, I-20068 Peschiera Borromeo Milan, Italy**

Tel: 39-02-553-2536

## BORG-WARNER AUTOMOTIVE INC.

200 S. Michigan Ave., Chicago, IL, 60604

Tel: (312) 322-8500      Fax: (312) 461-0507      www.bwauto.com

*Mfr. automotive components; provider of security services.*

**Regina-Warner SpA, Via Monza 90, I-22052 Cernusco Lombardone, Italy**

## BOSE CORPORATION

The Mountain, Framingham, MA, 01701-9168

Tel: (508) 879-7330      Fax: (508) 766-7543      www.bose.com

*Mfr. quality audio equipment/speakers.*

**BOSE S.p.A, Via Della Magliana 876, 00148 Rome, Italy**

Tel: 39-066-567-0802

## THE BOSTON CONSULTING GROUP

Exchange Place, 31st Fl., Boston, MA, 02109

Tel: (617) 973-1200      Fax: (617) 973-1339      www.bcg.com

*Management consulting company.*

**The Boston Consulting Group, Via della Moscova 18, I-20121 Milan, Italy**

Tel: 39-02-65-5991

## BOSTON SCIENTIFIC CORPORATION

One Scientific Place, Natick, MA, 01760-1537

Tel: (508) 650-8000      Fax: (508) 650-8923      www.bsci.com

*Mfr./distributes medical devices for use in minimally invasive surgeries.*

**Boston Scientific SpA, World Trade Ctr. - 10th Fl., Via Dei Marini, I-16149 Genoa, Italy**

Tel: 39-010-60601    Fax: 39-010-6060200

**Boston Scientific SpA, Corso Mateotti 1, Scala A2nd piano, I-20121 Milan, Italy**

Tel: 39-02-783-890    Fax: 39-02-783-910

## BOWNE & COMPANY, INC.

345 Hudson Street, New York, NY, 10014

Tel: (212) 924-5500      Fax: (212) 229-3420      www.bowne.com

*Financial printing and foreign language translation, localization (software), internet design and maintenance and facilities management.*

**Bowne International, Via Senato 12, 20121 Milan, Italy**

Tel: 39-02-763623-09    Fax: 39-02-764097-27

## BOYDEN CONSULTING CORPORATION

364 Elwood Ave., Hawthorne, NY, 10502

Tel: (914) 747-0093      Fax: (914) 980-6147      www.boyden.com

*International executive search firm.*

**Boyden International. SRL, Via G. Carducci 32, I-20123 Milan, Italy**

Tel: 39-02-805-5352

**Boyden International. SRL, Via G.B. Martini 13, I-00198 Rome, Italy**

Tel: 39-06-841-3400

## BOZELL GROUP

40 West 23rd Street, New York, NY, 10010

Tel: (212) 727-5000      Fax: (212) 645-9173      www.bozell.com

*Advertising, marketing, public relations and media consulting.*

**Bozell Italia S.p.A., Corso Europa 2, I-20122 Milan, Italy**

Tel: 39-02-77411   Fax: 39-02-781263   Contact: Marco Vecchia, Pres.

## BRADY CORPORATION

6555 W. Good Hope Road, Milwaukee, WI, 53223

Tel: (414) 358-6600      Fax: (414) 358-6600      www.whbrady.com

*Mfr. industrial ID for wire marking, circuit boards; facility ID, signage, printing systems and software.*

**Brady Italia Srl, Via Lazzaroni 7, I-21047 Saronno, Italy**

Tel: 39-02-96-700-507   Fax: 39-02-96-703-644   Contact: Giancarlo Prosdotti, Gen. Mgr.

**Seton Italia Srl, Casella Postale 51, I-20037 Paderno Dugnano Milan, Italy**

Tel: 39-02-96-703-198   Fax: 39-02-96-703-644   Contact: Giancarlo Prosdotti, Gen. Mgr.

## BRANSON ULTRASONICS CORPORATION

41 Eagle Road, Danbury, CT, 06813-1961

Tel: (203) 796-0400      Fax: (203) 796-2285      www.branson-plasticsjoin.com

*Mfr. plastics assembly equipment, ultrasonic cleaning equipment.*

**Branson Ultrasuoni SpA, Via Dei Lavoratori 25, I-20092 Cinisello Balsamo Milan, Italy**

Tel: 39-02-660-10479   Fax: 39-02-660-10480

## BRINK'S INC.

Thorndal Circle, Darien, CT, 06820

Tel: (203) 662-7800      Fax: (203) 662-7968      www.brinks.com

*Security transportation.*

**Brink's Securmark SpA, Florence, Italy**

## BRISTOL-MYERS SQUIBB COMPANY

345 Park Ave., New York, NY, 10154-0037

Tel: (212) 546-4000      Fax: (212) 546-4020      www.bms.com

*Pharmaceutical and food preparations, medical and surgical instruments.*

**Bristol Italiana (SUD) S.p.A., Largo Carlo Salinari N. 18, I-00142 Rome, Italy**

**Clairol Italiana S.p.A., Via Boccaccio 15, I-20123 Milan, Italy**

**ConvaTec, Div. Bristol-Myers Squibb Co., Via Paolo di Dono 73, I-00143 Rome, Italy**

**Laboratori Guieu Italia, Via Lomellina 10, I-20133 Milan, Italy**

**Laboratori Guieu Italia, Via Robbio 35, I-26030 Confienza Pavia, Italy**

**Matrix Essentials Italia, S.p.A, Via Bruno Pontacorvo SNC, Via Tiburtina KM. 18700, I-00012 Guidonia Montecello Rome, Italy**

**Squibb S.p.A, Latina Plant, Vua del Murillo, Sermonet Latina, Italy**

**Squibb S.p.A., 50 Via Virgilio Maroso, 00142 Rome, Italy**

**UPSAMedica S.p.A., Via Agnello 18, I-20121 Milan, Italy**

**Zimmer S.r.L., Via Tolstoi #86, I-20098 San Giuliano Milanese, Italy**

## BROADVISION, INC.

585 Broadway, Redwood City, CA, 94063

Tel: (650) 261-5100      Fax: (650) 261-5900      www.broadvision.com

*Develops and delivers an integrated suite of packaged applications for personalized enterprise portals.*

**BroadVision Italy, Centro Direzionale Milanofiori, Strada 6 / Palazzo N2, Rozzano (Milan) 20089, Italy**

Tel: 39-02-89200539

## BROWN GROUP, INC.
8300 Maryland Ave., St. Louis, MO, 63105
Tel: (314) 854-4000    Fax: (314) 854-4274    www.browngroup.com
*Footwear wholesaler and retailer, including Naturalizer brand.*
**Brown Group, Inc.,  Milan, Italy**

## BROWN SHOE COMPANY, INC.
8300 Maryland Avenue, St. Louis, MO, 63105
Tel: (314) 854-4000    Fax: (314) 854-4274    www.brownshoe.com
*Markets branded and private label footwear, including Dr. Scholl's, Air Step and Buster Brown.*
**Pagoda Italia,  Via Garibaldi 8, I-50123 Florence, Italy**

## BROWNING WINCHESTER
1 Browning Place, Morgan, UT, 84050
Tel: (801) 876-2711    Fax: (801) 876-3331    www.browning.com
*Sales/distribution of port firearms, fishing rods, etc.*
**Browning Sports Italia, S.r.l.,  Via Enrico Mattei 8, I-25046 Cazzago S. Martino (Brescia), Italy**

## BULAB HOLDINGS INC.
1256 N. McLean Blvd, Memphis, TN, 38108
Tel: (901) 278-0330    Fax: (901) 276-5343    www.buckman.com
*Biological products; chemicals and chemical preparations.*
**Buckman Laboratories Italiana SRL,  Via Verdi 3, Zibido San Giacomo, I-20080 Milan, Italy**
Tel: 39-02-90003140   Fax: 39-02-26861240

## BUNGE LIMITED
50 Main St., Ste. 635, 6th Fl., White Plains, NY, 10606
Tel: (914) 684-2800    Fax: (914) 684-3499    www.bunge.com
*Engaged in agribusiness; oilseed and grain processing, fertilizer, wheat and corn milling, food ingredients, and commercial and branded food product markets.*
**Bunge International Trading,  Rome, Italy**

## LEO BURNETT, DIV. B-COM 3 GROUP
35 West Wacker Drive, Chicago, IL, 60601
Tel: (312) 220-5959    Fax: (312) 220-6533    www.bcom3group.com
*Engaged in advertising, marketing, media buying and planning, and public relations.*
**Leo Burnett Co. SRL,  Via Fatebenefratelli 14, I-20138 Milan, Italy**

## BURSON-MARSTELLER
230 Park Ave., New York, NY, 10003-1566
Tel: (212) 614-4000    Fax: (212) 614-4262    www.bm.com
*Public relations/public affairs consultants.*
**Burson-Marsteller S.r.l.,  Via Beatrice Cenci 7/a, I-00186 Rome, Italy**
Tel: 39-06-688-9631   Fax: 39-06-668-96368   Emp: 14
**Burson-Marsteller SRL,  Palazzo Recalcati Via Amedei 8, I-20123 Milan, Italy**
Tel: 39-02-721-431   Fax: 39-02-878-960   Emp: 50

## BUSH BOAKE ALLEN INC.
7 Mercedes Drive, Montvale, NJ, 07645
Tel: (201) 391-9870    Fax: (201) 391-0860    www.bushboakeallen.com
*Mfr. aroma chemicals for fragrances and flavor products for seasonings.*
**Bush Boake Allen Italia S.p.A.,  Via Cefalonia, Crystal Palace 70, 25124 Brescia, Italy**
Tel: 39-030-2219147

## BUTTERICK COMPANY, INC.

161 Avenue of the Americas, New York, NY, 10013

Tel: (212) 620-2500      Fax: (212) 620-2746      www.butterick.com

*Prints sewing patterns and related magazines.*

**Vla G.A. Boltraffio, Via Cola Montano 10, I-20159 Milan, Italy**

## CABLE DESIGN TECHNOLOGIES CORPORATION

661 Andersen Drive, Plaza 7, Pittsburgh, PA, 15220

Tel: (412) 937-2300      Fax: (412) 937-9690      www.cdtc.com

*Mfr. computer connector copper, fiber optic and composite cables.*

**Industria Tecnica/DCT, Via Bora 4, 48012 Bagnacavallo, Italy**

Tel: 39-0-545-60470

## CABOT CORPORATION

75 State Street, Boston, MA, 02109-1807

Tel: (617) 345-0100      Fax: (617) 342-6103      www.cabot-corp.com

*Mfr. carbon blacks, plastics; oil and gas, information systems.*

**Cabot Italiana SpA, Casella Postale 444, Via Senistra Canate Candiano, I-48100 Ravenna, Italy**

## CALVIN KLEIN, INC.

205 West 39th Street, 4th Fl., New York, NY, 10018

Tel: (212) 719-2600      Fax: (212) 768-8922      www.calvinklein.com

*Mfr. of high quality clothing and accessories*

**Calvin Klein Ltd., Milan, Italy**

## CAMBREX CORPORATION

1 Meadowlands Plaza, East Rutherford, NJ, 07063

Tel: (201) 804-3000      Fax: (201) 804-9852      www.cambrex.com

*human health, animal health/agriculture and Mfr. biotechnology products and produce specialty chemicals.*

**Bio Whittaker Italia s.r.l., 20155 Via D. Cucchiari 17, I-20155 Milan, Italy**

Tel: 39-02-33-105601   Fax: 39-02-33-105606

**Cambrex Corp. Profarmaco S.r.l., Via Cucchiari 17, I-20155 Milan, Italy**

Tel: 39-02-3310-5520   Fax: 39-02-3310-5730

**Profarmaco S.r.l., Via Cucchiari 17, 20155 Milan, Italy**

Tel: 39-02-3310-5520

## CAMBRIDGE TECHNOLOGY PARTNERS, INC.

8 Cambridge Center, Cambridge, MA, 02142

Tel: (617) 374-9800      Fax: (617) 914-8300      www.ctp.com

*Engaged in e-commerce consultancy.*

**Cambridge Technology Partners, Inc., Via Milanese 20, 20099 Sesto San Giovanni, Milan, Italy**

Tel: 39-02-2493-5221   Fax: 39-02-2493-5222

## CANBERRA-PACKARD INDUSTRIES

800 Research Parkway, Meriden, CT, 06450

Tel: (203) 238-2351      Fax: (203) 235-1347      www.canberra.com

*Mfr. instruments for nuclear research.*

**Canberra-Packard SRL, Via Vincenzo Monti 23, I-20016 Pero Milan, Italy**

**Canberra-Packard SRL, Via della Circonvallazione Nomentana 514, I-00162 Rome, Italy**

## CARBOLINE COMPANY

350 Hanley Industrial Court, St. Louis, MO, 63144

Tel: (314) 644-1000      Fax: (314) 644-4617      www.carboline.com

*Mfr. coatings and sealants.*

**APSA SpA, Via Pirelli 30, I-20124 Milan, Italy**

## CARGILL, INC.
15407 McGinty Road West, Minnetonka, MN, 55440-5625
Tel: (612) 742-7575    Fax: (612) 742-7393    www.cargill.com
*Food products, feeds, animal products.*
**Cargill Srl, Via Rombon 11, 20134 Milano, Italy**

## CARLSON COMPANIES, INC.
Carlson Parkway, PO Box 59159, Minneapolis, MN, 55459
Tel: (612) 550-4520    Fax: (612) 550-4580    www.cmg.carlson.com
*Marketing services agency.*
**SitCap, Via San Francesco da Paola, 10123 Torino, Italy**
Tel: 39-11-810-6511   Fax: 39-11-810-6565

## THE CARLYLE GROUP L.P.
1001 Pennsylvania Avenue, NW, Washington, DC, 20004-2505
Tel: (202) 347-2626    Fax: (202) 347-1818    www.thecarlylegroup.com
*Global investor in defense contracts.*
**CEP Advisors Srl, Via dell'Arcivescovado 1, I-20122 Milan, Italy**
Tel: 39-02-8901-2107   Fax: 39-02-8699-1301

## CARPENTER TECHNOLOGY CORPORATION
101 W. Bern Street, PO Box 14662, Reading, PA, 19612-4662
Tel: (610) 208-2000    Fax: (610) 208-3214    www.cartech.com
*Mfr. specialty steels and structural ceramics for casting industrial.*
**Carpenter Technology (Italy) SRL, Via Monte Rosa 60, I-20149 Milan, Italy**

## CARRIER CORPORATION
One Carrier Place, Farmington, CT, 06034-4015
Tel: (860) 674-3000    Fax: (860) 679-3010    www.carrier.com
*Mfr./distributor/services A/C, heating and refrigeration equipment.*
**Delchi Carrier SpA, Via Raffaello Sanzio 9, I-20058 Villasanta Milan, Italy**
Tel: 39-039-3636   Fax: 39-039-3636-252

## CARTER-WALLACE INC.
1345 Ave. of the Americas, New York, NY, 10105
Tel: (212) 339-5000    Fax: (212) 339-5100    www.carterwallace.com
*Mfr. personal care products and pet products.*
**S.P.A. Laboratori Bouty, Via Vanvitelli 4, I-20129 Milan, Italy**
Tel: 39-02-226-2891   Fax: 39-02-226-221-305
**S.P.A. Laboratori Bouty, Via Di Catallo 18, I-56100 Pisa Localita Compaldo, Italy**
Tel: 39-050-53-2457   Fax: 39-050-53-3284

## CASCADE CORPORATION
2201 NE 201st Ave., Fairview, OR, 97024-9718
Tel: (503) 669-6300    Fax: (503) 669-6321    www.cascor.com
*Mfr. hydraulic forklift truck attachments.*
**Assistance Italy Mecoil s.r.l., 59100 Prato, Via del Mandorlo 28, Italy**
**Nuova SAR s.r.l., 25080 Molinetto di Mazzano (Brescia) via L. Ariosto 7, Italy**

## CATERPILLAR INC.
100 NE Adams Street, Peoria, IL, 61629-6105
Tel: (309) 675-1000    Fax: (309) 675-1182    www.cat.com
*Mfr. earth/material-handling and construction machinery and equipment and engines.*
**Caterpillar, Inc., Milan, Italy**

### C.B. RICHARD ELLIS

533 South Fremont Ave., Los Angeles, CA, 90071-1712

Tel: (213) 613-3123      Fax: (213) 613-3535      www.cbrichardellis.com

*Commercial real estate services.*

**CB Richard Ellis SpA,  4 Via dei Giardini,  20121 Milan, Italy**

**CB Richard Ellis SpA,  18 Piazza Del Popolo, 00187 Rome, Italy**

### CENTRAL NATIONAL-GOTTESMAN INC.

3 Manhattanville Road, Purchase, NY, 10577-2110

Tel: (914) 696-9000      Fax: (914) 696-1066

*Worldwide sales pulp and paper products.*

**Central National Italia SRL,  Via Antonio da Recante 4, I-20124 Milan, Italy**

Tel: 39-02-670-3162   Fax: 39-02-670-2895   Contact: Manuel Polo

### CHECKPOINT SYSTEMS, INC.

101 Wolf Drive, Thorofare, NJ, 08086

Tel: (856) 848-1800      Fax: (856) 848-0937      www.checkpointsystems.com

*Mfr. test, measurement and closed-circuit television systems.*

**Checkpoint Systems Italia s.r.l.,  Via Senigallia 18/2, I-20161 Bruzzano Milano, Italy**

Tel: 39-2-6622-4097   Fax: 39-2-645-8136   Contact: Alfredo Maggi, Gen. Mgr.

### THE CHERRY CORPORATION

3600 Sunset Ave., PO Box 718, Waukegan, IL, 60087

Tel: (847) 662-9200      Fax: (847) 662-2990      www.cherrycorp.com

*Mfr. electrical switches, electronic keyboards, controls and displays.*

**Silverstar Ltd. S.p.A.,  280 Viale Fulvio Testi, 1-20126 Milan, Italy**

Tel: 39-2-661251   Fax: 39-2-66101359

### CHESTERTON BINSWANGER INTERNATIONAL

Two Logan Square, 4th Floor, Philadelphia, PA, 19103-2759

Tel: (215) 448-6000      Fax: (215) 448-6238      www.cbbi.com

*Real estate and related services.*

**Redilco SpA,  Via dell' Arcivescovado 1, I-20122 Milan, Italy**

**Redilco SpA,  Corte lambruschini, 8 C.so Buenos Aires, Genoa 16121, Italy**

**Redilco SpA,  115 Via XX Settembre, Bergamo 24100,  Italy**

### CHICAGO RAWHIDE INDUSTRIES (CRI)

735 Tollgate Road, Elgin, IL, 60123

Tel: (847) 742-7840      Fax: (847) 742-7845      www.chicago-rawhide.com

*Mfr. shaft and face seals.*

**RFT SpA,  41 Strada per Poirino, 1-14019 Villanova d'Asti, Italy**

### CHIQUITA BRANDS INTERNATIONAL INC.

250 East Fifth Street, Cincinnati, OH, 45202

Tel: (513) 784-8000      Fax: (513) 784-8030      www.chiquita.com

*Sale and distribution of bananas, fresh fruits and processed foods.*

**Chiquita Italia SpA,  Via Tempio del Ciela 3, I-00144 Rome, Italy**

### CHIRON CORPORATION

4560 Horton Street, Emeryville, CA, 94608-2916

Tel: (510) 655-8730      Fax: (510) 655-9910      www.chiron.com

*Engaged in biotechnology; biopharmaceuticals, blood testing and vaccines.*

**Chiron Biocine SpA,  Via Fiorentina 1, I-53100 Siena, Italy**

Tel: 39-57-724-3111   Fax: 39-57-724- 3085

## THE CHUBB CORPORATION

15 Mountain View Road, Warren, NJ, 07061-1615

Tel: (908) 580-2000    Fax: (908) 580-3606    www.chubb.com

*Holding company for property and casualty insurance.*

**Chubb Insurance Co. of Europe, SA,  Piazzetta Pattari 1, I-20122 Milan, Italy**
Tel: 39-01-806-7101  Fax: 39-02-805-7236

**Chubb Insurance Company of Europe, S..,  Via San Vitale 4, Bologna 40125, Italy**
Tel: 39-051-273-271  Fax: 39-051-227-453

**Chubb Insurance Company of Europe, S.A.,  Corso Milano 74, Padova 35139, Italy**
Tel: 39-049-872-6033  Fax: 39-049-871-0206

## CIGNA COMPANIES

One Liberty Place, Philadelphia, PA, 19192

Tel: (215) 761-1000    Fax: (215) 761-5511    www.cigna.com

*Insurance, invest, health care and other financial services.*

**CIGNA Insurance Co. of Europe SA/NV,  Viale Maresciallo Pilsudski 124, I-00197 Rome, Italy**
**CIGNA Italy-Societa A Responsabilita Limitada,  Viale Maresciallo Pilsudski 124, I-00197 Rome, Italy**
**Esis Intl. Inc.,  Via della Moscova 3, I-20120 Milan, Italy**

## CINCOM SYSTEMS INC.

55 Merchant Street, Cincinnati, OH, 45446

Tel: (513) 612-2300    Fax: (513) 481-8332    www.cincom.com

*Develop/distributor computer software.*

**Cincom Italia S.r.l.,  18 Via Botero, 10122 Torino, Italy**
**Cincom Italia S.r.l.,  1 Via San Clemente, 20122-Milan, Italy**

## CISCO SYSTEMS, INC.

170 West Tasman Drive, San Jose, CA, 95134-1706

Tel: (408) 526-4000    Fax: (408) 526-4100    www.cisco.com

*Develop/mfr./market computer hardware and software networking systems.*

**Cisco Systems Italy Srl,  Viale della Grande Muraglia 284, I-00114 Rome, Italy**
Tel: 39-06-527-9971  Fax: 39-06-5220-9952

**Cisco Systems Italy Srl,  Via Torri Bianche 7, Palazzo Faggio, I-20059 Vimercate Milan, Italy**
Tel: 39-039-62951  Fax: 39-039-6295-299

## THE CIT GROUP

1211 Avenue of the Americas, New York, NY, 10036

Tel: (212) 536-1390    Fax: (212) 536-1912    www.citgroup.com

*Engaged in commercial finance.*

**Newcourt, Div. CIT Group,  Via Alto Vannucci, Milan 13-20135, Italy**
Tel: 39-258-2031  Fax: 39-258-20380

## CITIGROUP, INC.

153 East 53rd Street, New York, NY, 10043

Tel: (212) 559-1000    Fax: (212) 559-3646    www.citigroup.com

*Provides insurance and financial services worldwide.*

**Citibank Finanziaria SpA,  Trade/Capital Markets 16, I-20121 Foro Buonaparte Milan, Italy**
Contact: Sergio Ungaro

### CLEAR CHANNEL COMMUNICATIONS
200 East Basse Road, San Antonio, TX, 78209

Tel: (210) 822-2828     Fax: (210) 822-2299     www.clearchannel.com

*Programs and sells airtime for radio stations and owns and places outdoor advertising displays.*

**AAFitalia,  Via Giulini 2, 20123 Milan, Italy**

Tel: 39-02-806651   Contact: Francesco Celentano, Mgr.

**Jolly Pubblicita Advertising,  Via B. Cellini 66, 35027 Noventa Padovana, Italy**

Tel: 39-0490625699   Contact: Francesco Celentano, Mgr.

### CLEARY GOTTLIEB STEEN & HAMILTON
One Liberty Plaza, New York, NY, 10006

Tel: (212) 225-2000     Fax: (212) 225-3999     www.cgsh.com

*International law firm.*

**Cleary, Gottlieb, Steen & Hamilton,  Rome, Italy**

### CNA FINANCIAL CORPORATION
CNA Plaza, Chicago, IL, 60685

Tel: (312) 822-5000     Fax: (312) 822-6419     www.cna.com

*Commercial property/casualty insurance policies.*

**CNA Insurance Company (Europe) Limited (CIE),  Corso Matteotti #22, I-20121 Milan, Italy**

### COACH LEATHERWEAR COMPANY
516 West 34 Street, New York, NY, 10001

Tel: (212) 594-1850     Fax: (212) 594-1682     www.coach.com

*Mfr. and sales of high-quality leather products, including handbags and wallets.*

**Coach at Mitsukoshi Rome,  Via Nazionale 259/Via Torino 29, 00184 Rome, Italy**

### THE COCA-COLA COMPANY
PO Drawer 1734, Atlanta, GA, 30301

Tel: (404) 676-2121     Fax: (404) 676-6792     www.coca-cola.com

*Mfr./marketing/distributor soft drinks, syrups and concentrates, juice and juice-drink products.*

**Coca-Cola Beverages plc,  Milan, Italy**

### COGNEX CORPORATION
1 Vision Drive, Natick, MA, 01760

Tel: (508) 650-3000     Fax: (508) 650-3333     www.cognex.com

*Mfr. machine vision systems.*

**Cognex Italy,  Via Gasparotto 1, 20124 Milan, Italy**

Tel: 39-02-6747-1200   Fax: 39-02-6747-1300

### THE COLEMAN COMPANY, INC.
2111 E. 37th St., North, Wichita, KS, 67219

Tel: (316) 832-2700     Fax: (316) 832-2794     www.colemanoutdoors.com

*Mfr./distributor/sales camping and outdoor recreation products.*

**Coleman SVB (Italy),  Via Canova 11, I-25010 Centenaro-Lonato Brescia, Italy**

### COLGATE-PALMOLIVE COMPANY
300 Park Ave., New York, NY, 10022

Tel: (212) 310-2000     Fax: (212) 310-2919     www.colgate.com

*Mfr. pharmaceuticals, cosmetics, toiletries and detergents.*

**Colgate-Palmolive SpA,  Via Georgione 59/63, I-00147 Rome, Italy**

## COMMERCIAL INTERTECH CORPORATION

1775 Logan Ave., PO Box 239, Youngstown, OH, 44501-0239

Tel: (330) 746-8011     Fax: (330) 746-1148

*Mfr. hydraulic components, pre-engineered buildings and stamped metal products.*

**Commercial Hydraulics SRL, Via dell' Agricoltura 1/A, I-37012 Bussolengo Verona, Italy**

## COMPAQ COMPUTER CORPORATION

20555 State Highway 249, PO Box 692000, Houston, TX, 77269-2000

Tel: (281) 370-0670     Fax: (281) 514-1740     www.compaq.com

*Develop/mfr. personal computers.*

**Compaq Computer S.p.A., Milanfiori - Strada 7 - Palazzo R, I-20089 Rozzano Milan, Italy**

Tel: 39-02-575901   Fax: 39-02-824-2015

## COMPUTER ASSOCIATES INTERNATIONAL INC.

One Computer Associates Plaza, Islandia, NY, 11788

Tel: (516) 342-5224     Fax: (516) 342-5329     www.cai.com

*Integrated business software for enterprise computing and information management, application development, manufacturing, financial applications and professional services.*

**Computer Associates S.p.A., Palazzo Leonardo da Vinci, Via Francisco Storza 3, I-20080 Basiglio Milan 3, Italy**

Tel: 39-01-90-4641

## COMPUWARE CORPORATION

31440 Northwestern Hwy., Farmington Hills, MI, 48334-2564

Tel: (248) 737-7300     Fax: (248) 737-7108     www.compuware.com

*Develop and market software for enterprise and e-commerce solutions.*

**Compuware S.p.A., Via Della Nocetta 109, Rome 00164, Italy**

Tel: 39-06-6613-001

## CONEXANT SYSTEMS, INC.

4311 Jamboree Road, PO Box C, Newport Beach, CA, 92658-8902

Tel: (949) 483-4600     Fax: (949) 483-4078     www.conexant.com

*Provides semiconductor products for communications electronics.*

**Conexant Systems Italia, Via G. DiVittorio 1, 20017 Mazzo Di Rho, Italy**

Tel: 39-02-9317-9911   Fax: 39-02-9317-9913

## CONOCO INC.

PO Box 2197, 600 N. Dairy Ashford, Houston, TX, 77252

Tel: (281) 293-1000     Fax: (281) 293-1440     www.conoco.com

*Oil, gas, coal, chemicals and minerals.*

**Conoco Idrocarburi SpA, Via Vittorio Veneto 116, I-00187 Rome, Italy**

**Continental Oil Co. of Italy, c/o Studio Dott. Rag. Sergio Pagani, Via G. Frua 24, I-20146 Milan, Italy**

## CONTINENTAL AIRLINES INC.

2929 Allen Parkway, Ste. 2010, Houston, TX, 77019

Tel: (281) 834-5000     Fax: (281) 520-6329     www.continental.com

*International airline carrier.*

**Continental Airlines Inc., Rome, Italy**

## CONVERGYS CORPORATION

201 E. 4th St., Cincinnati, OH, 45202

Tel: (513) 723-7000     Fax: (513) 421-8624     www.convergys.com

*Engaged in data bill processing, telemarketing and customer services representation for major corporations.*

**Convergys Corporation, Viale Fulvia Testi 280, 20100 Milan, Italy**

## COOPER INDUSTRIES INC.

6600 Travis Street, Ste. 5800, Houston, TX, 77002

Tel: (713) 209-8400    Fax: (713) 209-8995    www.cooperindustries.com

*Mfr./distributor electrical products, tools, hardware and automotive products, fuses and accessories for electronic applications and circuit boards.*

**Cooper Automotive, Capri, Italy**

**Kirsch Division, Milan, Italy**

## CORDIS CORPORATION

PO Box 25700, Miami, FL, 33102-5700

Tel: (305) 824-2000    Fax: (305) 824-2747    www.cordis.com

*Mfr. medical devices and systems.*

**Cordis Italia, Piazza Don Enrico Mapelli 1, 20099 Sesto San Giovanni, Italy**

## CORNING INC.

One Riverfront Plaza, Corning, NY, 14831-0001

Tel: (607) 974-9000    Fax: (607) 974-8091    www.corning.com

*Mfr. glass and specialty materials, consumer products; communications, laboratory services.*

**Corning International Italy, Via Cappelletti 1, I-20091 Bresso (Milan) Italy**

Tel: 39-2-66-50-5091    Fax: 39-2-66-50-5088

## COULTER PHARMACEUTICAL, INC.

600 Gateway Blvd., South San Francisco, CA, 94080

Tel: (650) 553-2000    Fax: (650) 553-2028    www.coulterpharm.com

*Mfr. blood analysis systems, flow cytometers, chemicals systems, scientific systems and reagents.*

**Coulter Scientific SpA, Viale Monza 338, I-20128 Milan, Italy**

## CROMPTON CORPORATION

Benson Road, Middlebury, CT, 06749

Tel: (203) 573-2000    Fax:    www.crompton-knowles.com

*Mfr. dyes, colors, flavors, fragrances, specialty chemicals and industrial products.*

**Crompton Chemical Italiana SRL, Via Vincenzo Monti 79/2, I-20145 Milan, Italy**

**CromptonItaliana SRL, Div. SITECH, Via Roccavecchia 9, I-27029 Vigevano, Italy**

**Uniroyal Chemica SpA, Viale XVIII Dicembre, Palazzo Rocco, Latina, Italy**

**Uniroyal Manull SpA, Zona Industriale Compolunga, I-63100 Ascoli Piceno, Italy**

**Uniroyal SpA, Via Volantari della Liberta 21, I-20010 Vittuone, Italy**

## A.T. CROSS COMPANY

One Albion Road, Lincoln, RI, 02865

Tel: (401) 333-1200    Fax: (401) 334-2861    www.cross.com

*Mfr. writing instruments, leads, erasers and ink refills.*

**A.T. Cross Italia S.r.l., Via R. Franchetti, 1, I-20124 Milan, Italy**

Tel: 39-02-636114

## CULLIGAN WATER TECHNOLOGIES

One Culligan Parkway, Northbrook, IL, 60062

Tel: (847) 205-6000    Fax: (847) 205-6030    www.culligan-man.com

*Water treatment products and services.*

**Culligan Italiana SpA, Via Gandolfi 6, I-40057 Cadriano di Granarolo, Emilia Bologna, Italy**

Tel: 39-051-601-7111    Fax: 39-051-601-7215

## CUMMINS ENGINE COMPANY, INC.

500 Jackson Street, PO Box 3005, Columbus, IN, 47202-3005

Tel: (812) 377-5000     Fax: (812) 377-4937     www.cummins.com

*Mfr. diesel engines.*

**Cummins Diesel Italia SpA, Piazza Locatelli 8, Zona Industriale, I-20098 San Guiliano Milan, Italy**

## CYPRESS SEMICONDUCTOR CORPORATION

3901 N. First Street, San Jose, CA, 95134-1599

Tel: (408) 943-2600     Fax: (408) 943-2796     www.cypress.com

*Mfr. integrated circuits.*

**Cypress Semiconductor, Centro Colleoni- Palazzo Liocorno, Via Paracelso 4-6 Piano Int 6 5/6, Agrate Brianza, Milan 20041, Italy**

Tel: 39-039-60-74-200    Fax: 39-039-60-74-222

## CYTEC INDUSTRIES, INC.

5 Garret Mountain Plaza, West Paterson, NJ, 07424

Tel: (973) 357-3100     Fax: (973) 357-3054     www.cytec.com

*Mfr. specialty chemicals and materials,*

**Cytec Industries Italia s.r.l., Via Sporting Mirasole 4, 20090 Noverasco Di Opera, Milan, Italy**

Tel: 39-2-576-06175

## DAMES & MOORE GROUP

911 Wilshire Boulevard, Ste. 700, Los Angeles, CA, 90017

Tel: (213) 996-2200     Fax: (213) 996-2290     www.dames.com

*Engineering, environmental and construction management services.*

**Dames & Moore, Via Caldera 21, I-20153 Milan, Italy**

## DANA CORPORATION

4500 Dorr Street, Toledo, OH, 43615

Tel: (419) 535-4500     Fax: (419) 535-4643     www.dana.com

*Mfr./sales of automotive, heavy truck, off-highway, fluid and mechanical power components and engine parts, filters and gaskets.*

**Ofira Italiano, Div. Dana, Via Eritrea 20F, Brescia 26126, Italy**

**Spicer Agricultural Axie Div., Via P Paoli 9/A, 1-22Ioo Como Co, Italy**

Tel: 39-31-523-515

**Spicer Italia, Via Prov. Lucchese 181, 50019 Sesto F. Ro. Firenze, Italy**

Tel: 39-55-341031

**Spicer Off-Highway Axle Div., Zona Industriale, 38062 Arco, Italy**

Tel: 39-4640-580-111

## D'ARCY MASIUS BENTON & BOWLES INC. (DMB&B)

1675 Broadway, New York, NY, 10019

Tel: (212) 468-3622     Fax: (212) 468-2987     www.dmbb.com

*Full service international advertising and communications group.*

**DMB&B Europe, Via Correggio 18, I-20149 Milan, Italy**

**DMB&B Europe, 24/a, 10121 Torino, Italy**

## DARDEN RESTAURANTS, INC.

5900 Lake Ellenor Drive, Orlando, FL, 32809

Tel: (407) 245-4000     Fax: (407) 245-5114     www.darden.com

*Operates casual dining, full-service restaurants, including Red Lobster and Olive Garden*

**Olive Garden Riserva di Fizzano, Tuscany, Italy**

## DATA GENERAL CORPORATION

4400 Computer Drive, Westboro, MA, 01580

Tel: (508) 898-5000     Fax: (508) 366-1319     www.dg.com

*Design, mfr. general purpose computer systems and peripheral products and services.*

**Data General S.R.L.,  Centro Dir San Felice, Via Rivoltana 13, 20090 Segrate Milan, Italy**

Tel: 39-02-753-961

## DATAWARE TECHNOLOGIES INC.

1 Canal Park, Cambridge, MA, 02141

Tel: (617) 621-0820     Fax: (617) 577-2413     www.dataware.com

*Provides e-business solutions.*

**Dataware Technologies SRL,  Via del Quirinale 26, I-00187 Rome, Italy**

## DDB NEEDHAM WORLDWIDE INC.

437 Madison Ave., New York, NY, 10022

Tel: (212) 415-2000     Fax: (212) 415-3417     www.ddbn.com

*Advertising agency.*

**Broucc/Verba DDB Needham SRL,  Galleria Passarella 2, I-20122 Milan, Italy**

**Verba DDB SRL,  Via Solari 11, I-20144 Milan, Italy**

## DECISION STRATEGIES FAIRFAX INTERNATIONAL

505 Park Avenue, 7th Fl., New York, NY, 10022

Tel: (212) 935-4040     Fax: (212) 935-4046     www.dsfx.com

*Provides discreet consulting, investigative, business intelligence and security services to corporations, financial and investment institutions, law firms and governments worldwide.*

**DSFX Italy,  Via Sacchi 4,  20121 Milan, Italy**

Tel: 39-02-8699-6834   Fax: 39-02-8909-7579

## DEERE & COMPANY

One John Deere Road, Moline, IL, 61265

Tel: (309) 765-8000     Fax: (309) 765-5772     www.deere.com

*Mfr./sale agricultural, construction, utility, forestry and lawn, grounds care equipment.*

**John Deere Italiana,  Casella Postale, I-20060 Vignate Milan, Italy**

Tel: 39-2-95458-1   Fax: 39-2-95604-82

## DELOITTE TOUCHE TOHMATSU INTERNATIONAL

1633 Broadway, New York, NY, 10019

Tel: (212) 492-4000     Fax: (212) 392-4154     www.deloitte.com

*Accounting, audit, tax and management consulting services.*

**Deloitte & Touche,  Palazzo Carducci, via Olona 2, I-20123 Milan, Italy**

**Deloitte & Touche Consulting,  Via Vittor Pisani 22, I-20124 Milan, Italy**

## DELTA AIR LINES INC.

PO Box 20706, Atlanta, GA, 30320-6001

Tel: (404) 715-2600     Fax: (404) 715-5494     www.delta-air.com

*Major worldwide airline; international air transport services.*

**Delta Air Lines Inc.,  Milan, Italy**

## DENTSPLY INTERNATIONAL

570 West College Ave., PO Box 872, York, PA, 17405-0872

Tel: (717) 845-7511     Fax: (717) 843-6357     www.dentsply.com

*Mfr. and distribution of dental supplies and equipment.*

**De Art SRL,  Via Rimini 22, I-20142 Milan, Italy**

**Dentsply Gendex,  via Capelli 12, I-20126 Milan, Italy**

Tel: 39-02-270-82600

**Dentsply Italia, via A. Cavaglieri 26, I-00173 Rome, Italy**
Tel: 39-06-723-3626

## DETROIT DIESEL CORPORATION

13400 Outer Drive West, Detroit, MI, 48239

Tel: (313) 592-5000      Fax: (313) 592-5058      www.detroitdiesel.com

*Mfr. diesel and aircraft engines, heavy-duty transmissions.*

**MDC-Detroit Diesel Italia SpA, Corso Aurelio Saffi 29/1-2, Genoa I-16128,Italy**
Tel: 39-1056-4979   Fax: 39-1053-2759

## THE DEXTER CORPORATION

1 Elm Street, Windsor Locks, CT, 06096

Tel: (860) 627-9051      Fax: (860) 627-7078      www.dexelec.com

*Mfr. polymer products, magnetic materials, biotechnology.*

**Dexter Aerospace Materials, Via Della Industrie 22, I-31020 San Zenone Degli Ezzeline Treviso, Italy**

**Lexter SA, Via Bellinzona 289, I-22100 Como Pontechiasso, Italy**

## DHL WORLDWIDE EXPRESS

50 California Avenue, San Francisco, CA, 94111

Tel: (415) 677-6100      Fax: (415) 824-9700      www.dhl.com

*Worldwide air express carrier.*

**DHL Worldwide Express, Viale Milanofiori, Palazzo U3 Strada 5, I-20089 Rozzano Milan, Italy**
Tel: 39-02-57571

## DIAGNOSTIC PRODUCTS CORPORATION

5700 West 96th Street, Los Angeles, CA, 90045

Tel: (310) 645-8200      Fax: (310) 645-9999      www.dpcweb.com

*Mfr. diagnostic products.*

**Medical Systems S.p.A., Via Rio Torbido N. 40, 16165 Struppa, Genoa, Italy**
Tel: 39-010-834-01   Fax: 39-010-808-007

## DIGITAL ORIGIN, INC.

460 East Middlefield Road, Mountainview, CA, 94043

Tel: (650) 404-6300      Fax: (650) 404-6200      www.digitalorigin.com

*Mfr. Digital Video (DV) software products.*

**Media 100 S.r.L, Brescia, Italy**

## DIMON INCORPORATED

512 Bridge Street, PO Box 681, Danville, VA, 24543-0681

Tel: (804) 792-7511      Fax: (804) 791-0377      www.dimon.com

*One of world's largest importer and exporters of leaf tobacco.*

**DIMON Italia S.r.l., 3 Via Nazioni Unite, 00046 Grottaferrata, Rome, Italy**
Tel: 390-6-9454-9033   Fax: 390-6-9454-7408

## DIONEX CORPORATION

1228 Titan Way, PO Box 3603, Sunnyvale, CA, 94086-3603

Tel: (408) 737-0700      Fax: (408) 730-9403      www.dionex.com

*Develop/mfr./market chromatography systems and related products.*

**Dionex S.r.l., Via della Maglianella 65R, 00166 Roma RM, Italy**

**Dionex S.r.l., 5 Via Tulipani, 20090 Pieve Emanuele Milan, Italy**

## WALT DISNEY COMPANY

500 South Buena Vista Street, Burbank, CA, 91521

Tel: (818) 560-1000     Fax: (818) 560-1930     www.disney.com

*Film/TV production, theme parks, resorts, publishing, recording and retail stores.*

**Creazioni Walt Disney SpAI, Via Hoepli 3, I-20121 Milan, Italy**

## DME COMPANY

29111 Stephenson Highway, Madison Heights, MI, 48071

Tel: (248) 398-6000     Fax: (248) 544-5705     www.dmeco.com

*Basic tooling for plastic molding and die casting.*

**COMAT-DME SpA, Via Desiderio 24, I-20131 Milan, Italy**

## DO ALL COMPANY

254 North Laurel Ave., Des Plaines, IL, 60016

Tel: (847) 803-7380     Fax: (847) 699-7524     www.doall.com

*Distributors of machinery tools, metal cutting tools, instruments and industrial supplies for metalworking industry.*

**DoALL Center, 5 Via L. Perosi, 1-20146 Milan, Italy**

Tel: 39-2-4236086   Fax: 39-2-48953828

## DONNELLY CORPORATION

49 W. 3rd St., Holland, MI, 49423-2813

Tel: (616) 786-7000     Fax: (616) 786-6034     www.donnelly.com

*Mfr. fabricated, molded and coated glass products for the automotive and electronics industries.*

**Donnelly Italy, Corso Orbassano 336, 10137 Torino, Italy**

## DOONEY & BOURKE

1 Regent Street, Norwalk, CT, 06855

Tel: (203) 853-7515     Fax: (203) 838-7754     www.dooney.com

*Mfr./sales/distribution of fine leather handbags, wallets, belts and accessories.*

**Dooney & Bourke, Rome, Italy**

## DOUBLECLICK, INC.

450 West 33rd Street, New York, NY, 10001

Tel: (212) 683-0001     Fax: (212) 889-0062     www.doubleclick.net

*Engaged in online advertising.*

**Doubleclick, Ltd., Piazza Bertarelli, 20122 Milan, Italy**

Tel: 39-02-855011-1

## DRAFT WORLDWIDE

633 North St. Clair Street, Chicago, IL, 60611-3211

Tel: (312) 944-3500     Fax: (312) 944-3566     www.draftworldwide.com

*Full service international advertising agency, engaged in brand building, direct and promotional marketing.*

**DraftWorldwide, Via Ariosto 23, I-20145 Milan, Italy**

Tel: 39-02-48-19-480   Fax: 39-02-48-19-836

## DRAKE BEAM MORIN INC.

101 Huntington Ave., Boston, MA, 02199

Tel: (617) 375-9500     Fax: (617) 267-2011     www.dbm.com

*Human resource management consulting and training.*

**DBM Italy, Via Anfiteatro 15, I-20121 Milan, Italy**

Tel: 39-02-86-2717   Fax: 39-02-72-00-4296

## DRESSER INSTRUMENT DIVISION

250 East Main Street, Stratford, CT, 06614-5145

Tel: (203) 378-8281      Fax: (203) 385-0357      www.dresserinstruments.com

*Mfr. pressure gauges and temperature instruments.*

**Dresser Energy Valve, Via Italo Betto 11, I-27058 Voghera, Italy**

Tel: 39-0383-6911   Fax: 39-0383-367-166   Contact: Salvatore Ruggeri, Pres.

## DREVER COMPANY

PO Box 98, 380 Red Lion Road, Huntingdon, PA, 19006-0098

Tel: (215) 947-3400      Fax: (215) 947-7934      www.drever.com

*Mfr. industrial furnaces and heat processing equipment.*

**Drever Italy, Ferre Milanofiori--Strada 6 Palazzo NI, 20089 Rozzano Milan, Italy**

## E.I. DU PONT DE NEMOURS & COMPANY

1007 Market Street, Wilmington, DE, 19898

Tel: (302) 774-1000      Fax: (302) 774-7321      www.dupont.com

*Mfr./sale diversified chemicals, plastics, specialty products and fibers.*

**Du Pont de Nemours Italiana SpA, Milan, Italy**

## DUFF & PHELPS CREDIT RATING CO.

55 East Monroe Street, Chicago, IL, 60603

Tel: (312) 368-3100      Fax: (312) 442-4121      www.dcrco.com

*Engaged in rating stocks and bonds, municipal securities and insurance company claims paying capabilities.*

**Societa Italiana Per Il Rating S.p.A., 20123 Milan Piazza Affari 6, Italy**

Tel: 39-2-862-214

## THE DUN & BRADSTREET CORPORATION

1 Diamond Hill Road, Murray Hill, NJ, 07974

Tel: (908) 665-5000      Fax: (908) 665-5524      www.dnbcorp.com

*Provides corporate credit, marketing and accounts-receivable management services and publishes credit ratings and financial information.*

**Dun & Bradstreet Kosmos S.p.A., 48 Via dei Valtorta, I-20127 Milan, Italy**

Tel: 39-02-284-551

## EAGLE GLOBAL LOGISTICS (EGL)

15350 Vickery Drive, Houston, TX, 77032

Tel: (281) 618-3100      Fax: (281) 618-3100      www.eaglegl.com

*Ocean/air freight forwarding, customs brokerage, packing and wholesale, logistics management and insurance.*

**Centro Servizi S.R.L., Via Darsena 7, I-56122 Pisa, Italy**

Tel: 39-050-502-522   Fax: 39-050-502-294

**Circle Freight International (Italia) SRL, Palazzina Spedizionieri, Aeroporto Caselle, Caselle Torinese, Italy**

Tel: 39-011-567-8151   Fax: 39-011-567-8153

**Circle Freight International (Italia) SRL, Via F. Righi, 52-Loc. Osmannoro, I-50019 Sesto Florento Florence, Italy**

Tel: 39-055-311062   Fax: 39-055-310-474

**Circle Freight International (Italia) SRL, Via J. F. Kennedy 3, Frazione Millepini, I-10090 Rodano Milan, Italy**

Tel: 39-02-953-2116-6   Fax: 39-01-953-2810-6

**Circle Freight International (Italia) SRL, Palazzina Spedizionieri, Aeroporto Malpensa, I-21010 Malpensa Milan, Italy**

Tel: 39-02-400-9933-5   Fax: 39-02-400-9939-6

**Circle Freight International (Italia) SRL,** Aeroporto Cristoforo Colombo, I-16154 Genoa, Italy
Tel: 39-010-650-8431 Fax: 39-010-651-6378

**Circle Freight International (Italia) SRL,** Cargo Bldg. AZ - Stamza 210, 00050 Fiumicino Aeroporto, I-00050 Rome, Italy
Tel: 39-06-652-9242 Fax: 39-06-652-9243

## EASTMAN CHEMICAL

100 North Eastman Road, Kingsport, TN, 37660
Tel: (423) 229-2000 Fax: (423) 229-1351 www.eastman.com
*Mfr. plastics, chemicals, fibers.*

**Eastman Chemical,** Via Rosellini 12, I-20124 Milan, Italy

## EASTMAN KODAK COMPANY

343 State Street, Rochester, NY, 14650
Tel: (716) 724-4000 Fax: (716) 724-1089 www.kodak.com
*Develop/mfr. photo and chemicals products, information management/video/copier systems, fibers/plastics for various industry.*

**Kodak SpA,** Casella Postale 11057, I-20110 Milan, Italy

## EATON CORPORATION

Eaton Center, 1111 Superior Ave., Cleveland, OH, 44114-2584
Tel: (216) 523-5000 Fax: (216) 479-7068 www.eaton.com
*Advanced technical products for transportation and industrial markets.*

**Eaton SpA,** Strada Lombardore, Km. 15.300, I-10040 Leini, Italy

## ECI TELECOM LTD.

12950 Worldgate Dr., Herndon, VA, 20170
Tel: (703) 456-3400 Fax: (703) 456-3410 www.ecitele.com
*Designs, develops, manufactures, markets and supports end-to-end digital telecommunications solutions.*

**ECI Telecom Italia,** Via Lima 41, 00198 Rome, Italy
Tel: 39-6-8449-8304 Fax: 39-6-8449-8332

## ECOLAB INC.

370 N. Wabasha Street, St. Paul, MN, 55102
Tel: (651) 293-2233 Fax: (651) 293-2379 www.ecolab.com
*Develop/mfr. premium cleaning, sanitizing and maintenance products and services for the hospitality, institutional, and residential markets.*

**Ecolab Ltd.,** Milan, Italy
Tel: 39-039-60501

## EDELMAN PUBLIC RELATIONS WORLDWIDE

200 East Randolph Drive, 62nd Fl., Chicago, IL, 60601
Tel: (312) 240-3000 Fax: (312) 240-0596 www.edelman.com
*International independent public relations firm.*

**Edelman PR Worldwide,** Via Telesio, 25, I-20145 Milan, Italy
Tel: 39-02-467141 Fax: 39-02-4671-4467 Contact: Rasanna D'antona, Mng. Dir.

## EDISON INTERNATIONAL

2244 Walnut Grove Avenue, PO Box 999, Rosemead, CA, 91770
Tel: (626) 302-2222 Fax: (626) 302-2517 www.edison.com
*Utility holding company.*

**Edison Mission Energy,** Milan, Italy

## J.D. EDWARDS & COMPANY

One Technology Way, Denver, CO, 80237

Tel: (303) 334-4000    Fax: (303) 334-4970    www.jdedwards.com

*Computer software products.*

**Consor, S.r.l., Via Plinio 11, I-20129 Milan, Italy**

Tel: 39-02-2940-5859   Fax: 39-02-2940-1800

**J. D. Edwards Segrate, Via Cassenese 224, Palazzo Tiziano, I-20090 Segrate Milan, Italy**

Tel: 39-02-26967-1   Fax: 39-02-26967-200

**Proxima Informatica Aziendale, Via P. Costa 2, I-48100 Ravenna, Italy**

Tel: 39-054-212-912   Fax: 39-054-421-2916

**Sirio Informatica, spa, Viale Fulvio Testi 126, I-20092 Cinisello Balsamo Milan, Italy**

Tel: 39-02-262-421   Fax: 39-02-425-5557

## EG&G INC.

900 Clopper Road, Ste. 200, Gaithersburg, MD, 20878

Tel: (301) 840-3000    Fax: (301) 590-0502    www.egginc.com

*Diversified R/D, mfr. and services.*

**EG&G SpA/Instruments Div., Via Bernardo Rucellai 23, I-20126 Milan, Italy**

**EG&G SpA/Sealol Div., Via Bernardo Rucellai 23, I-20126 Milan, Italy**

## ELANCO ANIMAL HEALTH

500 East 96th Street, Ste. 125, Indianapolis, IN, 46240

Tel: (317) 276-3000    Fax: (317) 276-6116    www.elanco.com

*Antibiotics and fine chemicals.*

**Elanco Animal Health, Caselle Postali 193-177, 50019 Sesto Fiorentino, Florence, Italy**

Tel: 39-55-42571

## ELECTRO SCIENTIFIC INDUSTRIES, INC.

13900 NW Science Park Drive, Portland, OR, 97229

Tel: (503) 641-4141    Fax: (503) 643-4873    www.esi.com

*Mfg. production and testing equipment used in manufacture of electronic components in pagers and cellular communication devices.*

**Factum Italia s.r.l., Trim, Via Lombardia 10, I-20064 Gorgonzola, Italy**

Tel: 39-02-9530-1791   Fax: 39-02-9530-1436   Contact: Roger Goldenberg

## ELECTRONIC DATA SYSTEMS CORPORATION (EDS)

5400 Legacy Dr., Plano, TX, 75024

Tel: (972) 605-6000    Fax: (972) 605-2643    www.eds.com

*Provides professional services; management consulting, e.solutions, business process management and information solutions.*

**EDS Italia Opel, Piazzale dell' Industria 40, 00144 Rome, Italy**

Tel: 39-06-5465-3303

## ELECTRONICS FOR IMAGING, INC.

303 Velocity Way, Foster City, CA, 94404

Tel: (650) 357-3500    Fax: (650) 357-3907    www.efi.com

*Design/mfr. computer software and hardware for color desktop publishing.*

**Electronics for Imaging, Centro Direzionale Milano Fiori, Strada 6 Palazzo E1, 20090 Assago (Milano), Italy**

Tel: 39 028 228 1219

## EMC CORPORATION

35 Parkwood Drive, Hopkinton, MA, 01748-9103

Tel: (508) 435-1000      Fax: (508) 435-8884      www.emc.com

*Designs/supplies intelligent enterprise storage and retrieval technology for open systems, mainframes and midrange environments.*

**EMC Computer Systems Italia SpA,  Corso Svizzera 185/Bis, I-10149 Torino, Italy**
Tel: 39-011-746527

**EMC Computer Systems Italia SpA,  Via Cefalonia 24, I-25125 Brescia, Italy**
Tel: 39-030-242-1791

**EMC Computer Systems Italia SpA,  Via A Saffi 15, I-40131 Bologna, Italy**
Tel: 39-051-522579

**EMC Computer Systems Italia SpA,  Via Savonarola 217, I-35153 Padova, Italy**
Tel: 39-049-823-5853

**EMC Computer Systems Italia SpA,  Piazza Marconi 25, I-00144 Rome, Italy**
Tel: 39-06-545041

**EMC Computer Systems Italia SpA,  Via Caldera 21, Palazzo D - Ala 3, I-20153 Milan, Italy**
Tel: 39-02-409081

## EMERSON & CUMING SPECIALTY POLYMERS

46 Manning Road, Bellerica, MA, 01821

Tel: (978) 436-9700      Fax: (978) 436-9701      www.emersoncuming.com

*Mfr. high performance encapsulants, adhesives and coatings for the automotive, telecommunications and electronic industries.*

**Emerson & Cuming Italia,  Via Roma 29, 20050 Mezzago (Milan), Italy**
Tel: 39-039-6092246

## EMERY WORLDWIDE

One Lagoon Drive, Ste. 400, Redwood City, CA, 94065

Tel: (650) 596-9600      Fax: (650) 596-7901      www.emeryworld.com

*Freight transport, global logistics and air cargo.*

**Emery Worldwide,  Off Airport Office (Linate), Via Degli Alpini 26, I-10900 Segrate Milan, Italy**

## ENCYCLOPAEDIA BRITANNICA INC.

310 S. Michigan Ave., Chicago, IL, 60604

Tel: (312) 427-9700      Fax: (312) 294-2176      www.eb.com

*Publishing; books.*

**Encyclopaedia Britannica (Italy) Ltd.,  Via Angelo Bargoni 28, I-00153 Rome, Italy**

## ENERGIZER HOLDINGS, INC.

800 Chouteau Avenue, St. Louis, MO, 63164

Tel: (314) 982-2970      Fax: (214) 982-2752      www.energizer.com

*Mfr. Eveready and Energizer brand batteries and lighting products.*

**Ralston Energy Systems S.p.A.,  Via di Vittorio 10, 20094 Corsico Milan, Italy**
Tel: 39-2-45-178-205   Fax: 39-2-45-178-1

## ENERPAC

P.O. Box 3241, Milwaukee, WI, 53201-3241

Tel: (414) 781-6600      Fax: (414) 781-1049      www.enerpac.com

*Mfr. hydraulic cylinders, pumps, valves, presses, tools, accessories and system components.*

**ENERPAC S.p.A.,  Via Canova 4, 20094 Corsico (Milan), Italy**

## ENGELHARD CORPORATION

101 Wood Ave. S., CN 770, Iselin, NJ, 08830

Tel: (732) 205-5000        Fax: (732) 632-9253        www.engelhard.com

*Mfr. pigments, additives, catalysts, chemicals, engineered materials.*

**Engelhard CLAL Italy, Via Ronchi 17, I-20134 Milan, Italy**

Tel: 39-226-4251    Fax: 39-221-57-167

**Engelhard-Clal Italy, 17 Via Ronchi, 20134 Milan, Italy**

**Engelhard-Clal Italy, 245 Via de Salone, I-00131 Rome, Italy**

Tel: 39-641-9921    Fax: 39-641992-338

## ENRON CORPORATION

1400 Smith Street, Houston, TX, 77002-7369

Tel: (713) 853-6161        Fax: (713) 853-3129        www.enron.com

*Exploration, production, transportation and distribution of integrated natural gas and electricity.*

**Enron International, Via Torina 2, 20123 Milan, Italy**

Tel: 39-02-725-464-00

**Sarlux, S.r.l., 8 Galleria De Cristoforis, 20122 Milan, Italy**

Tel: 39-02-773-7224

## ERICO PRODUCTS INC.

34600 Solon Road, Cleveland, OH, 44139

Tel: (440) 248-0100        Fax: (440) 248-0723        www.erico.com

*Mfr. electric welding apparatus and hardware, metal stampings, specialty fasteners.*

**Erico Italia SpA, Via Edison Nr. 50, 20019 Settimo Milan, Italy**

Tel: 39-2-3350-1178

## ERNST & YOUNG, LLP

787 Seventh Ave., New York, NY, 10019

Tel: (212) 773-3000        Fax: (212) 773-6350        www.eyi.com

*Accounting and audit, tax and management consulting services.*

**Studio Associato Legale Tributario, Via Cornaggia, 10, I-20123 Milan, Italy**

Tel: 39-02-8514204    Fax: 39-02-89010199    Contact: Fabio Greco

## EURO RSCG WORLDWIDE

350 Hudson Street, New York, NY, 10014

Tel: (212) 886-2000        Fax: (212) 886-2016        www.eurorscg.com

*International advertising agency group.*

**Agenpress, Via Filelfo 10, Milan, Italy**

**Equipe, Via Crocefisso 12, Milan, Italy**

**EURO RSCG Mezzano Costantini Mignani srl, Via Dante 7, Milan, Italy**

## EXCELLON AUTOMATION

24751 Crenshaw Boulevard, Torrance, CA, 90505

Tel: (310) 534-6300        Fax: (310) 534-6777        www.excellon.com

*PCB drilling and routing machines; optical inspection equipment.*

**Excellon Italia Srl., c/o Centre Direzionale Colleoni, Via Paracelso 16, Palazzo Andromeda 1, Piano 5 Interno 3, 20041 Agrate Brianza Italy**

## EXCELON INC.

25 Mall Road, Burlington, MA, 01803

Tel: (781) 674-5000        Fax: (781) 674-5010        www.exceloncorp.com

*Developer of object-oriented database management systems software.*

**eXcelon Software SRL, Via C. Esterle 9, 20132 Milan, Italy**

## EXIDE CORPORATION

645 Penn St., Reading, PA, 19601

Tel: (610) 378-0500     Fax: (610) 378-0824     www.exideworld.com

*Mfr. lead-acid automotive and industrial batteries.*

**Exide Italia, Romano, Italy**

## EXPEDITORS INTERNATIONAL OF WASHINGTON INC.

1015 Third Avenue, 12th Fl., Seattle, WA, 98104-1182

Tel: (206) 674-3400     Fax: (206) 682-9777     www.expd.com

*Air/ocean freight forwarding, customs brokerage, international logistics solutions.*

**Expeditors International Italia SRL, Via Leonardo da Vinci 13, I-20090 Segrate Milan, Italy**

Tel: 39-045-855-0433   Fax: 39-045-855-0450

## EXXON MOBIL CORPORATION

5959 Las Colinas Blvd., Irving, TX, 75039-2298

Tel: (972) 444-1000     Fax: (972) 444-1882     www.exxon.com

*Petroleum exploration, production, refining; mfr. petroleum and chemicals products; coal and minerals.*

**Exxon Mobil Italy, Stabilimento di Vado Ligure, Strada di Scorrimento 2 - CP 204, I-17047 Vado Ligure Savona, Italy**

**Exxon Mobil S.p.A., Via Vigevano 43, I-28069 San Martino di Trecate Novara, Italy**

**Exxon Mobil, Inc., Via Paleocapa 7, 20121 Milan, Italy**

Tel: 39-02-880-31

**Exxon Mobil, Inc., C.P. 101, I-96011 Augusta Siracusa, Italy**

**Exxon Mobil, Inc., Viale Castello della Magliana, I-00148 Rome, Italy**

## FAIR, ISAAC AND COMPANY, INC.

200 Smith Ranch Road, San Rafael, CA, 94903

Tel: (415) 472-2211     Fax: (415) 492-5691     www.fairisaac.com

*Mfr. automated systems for credit and loan approvals.*

**Fair, Isaac and Co., Via Dogana 3, 10123 Milan, Italy**

Tel: 39-02-86-7141

## FAIRCHILD PUBLICATIONS INC.

7 West 34th Street, New York, NY, 10001

Tel: (212) 630-4000     Fax: (212) 630-3563     www.fairchildpub.com

*Magazine publishers: Women's Wear Daily, Supermarket News, Brand Marketing, Executive Technology, Footwear News, Salon News.*

**Fairchild Publications, 2 Piazza Cavour, Milan 20121, Italy**

Tel: 39-02-76-00-50-78   Fax: 39-02-78-34-89

## FEDERAL-MOGUL CORPORATION

26555 Northwestern Highway, PO Box 1966, Southfield, MI, 48034

Tel: (248) 354-7700     Fax: (248) 354-8983     www.federal-mogul.com

*Mfr./distributor precision parts for automobiles, trucks, farm and construction vehicles.*

**Federal-Mogul SpA, Strada Valdellatorre KM 2 700,10091 Alpignano, Italy**

## FERRO CORPORATION

1000 Lakeside Ave., Cleveland, OH, 44114-7000

Tel: (216) 641-8580     Fax: (216) 696-5784     www.ferro.com

*Mfr. Specialty chemicals, coatings, plastics, colors, refractories.*

**Ecotech Italia SpA, Via Dell'Elettronica 15, I-28040 Verbania-Fondotoce, Italy**

Tel: 39-0323-586984   Fax: 39-0323-586977   Contact: Roberto Codecasa

**Ferro ICC Laboratory, Via Radici in Piano 312, I-41041 Casinalbo, Italy**

Tel: 39-059-559111   Fax: 39-059-462067

**Ferro SRL, Via Radici in Piano 312, I-41041 Casinalbo, Italy**

Tel: 39-059-1559111   Fax: 39-059-551109   Contact: P. Bencivenni, Gen. Mgr.

**Ferro SRL - Colour Division, Via Trentino, 9, I-41049 Sassuolo, Italy**

Tel: 39-053-6806912   Fax: 39-053-6811641

**Ferro SRL Cannara Plant, Localita' Isola, I-06033 Cannara, Italy**

Tel: 39-0742-3311   Fax: 39-0742-72144

## FileNET CORPORATION

3565 Harbor Boulevard, Costa Mesa, CA, 92626

Tel: (714) 966-3400       Fax: (714) 966-3490       www.filenet.com

*Provides integrated document management (IDM) software and services for internet and client server-based imaging, workflow, cold and electronic document management solutions.*

**FileNET Italy, Via Visconti di Modrone 33, I-20122 Milan, Italy**

Tel: 39-02-7733-051   Fax: 39-02-7729-40

## FINNIGAN CORPORATION

355 River Oaks Parkway, San Jose, CA, 95134-1991

Tel: (408) 433-4800       Fax: (408) 433-4823       www.finnigan.com

*Mfr. mass spectrometers.*

**CE Instruments Division, Strada Rivoltana, 20090 Rodano, Milan Italy**

## FISHER-ROSEMOUNT

8000 Maryland Ave., Ste. 500, Clayton, MO, 63105-4755

Tel: (314) 746-9900       Fax: (314) 746-9974       www.frco.com

*Mfr. industrial process control equipment.*

**Fisher-Rosemount s.r.l., Via Del Artiginato 8/12, I-20053 Muggio, Italy**

**Fisher-Rosemount s.r.l., Via Vittore Carpaccio 60, I-00147 Rome, Italy**

## FLEXTRONICS INC. INTERNATIONAL

2241 Lundy Ave., San Jose, CA, 95131-1822

Tel: (408) 428-1300       Fax: (408) 428-0420       www.flextronics.com

*Contract manufacturer for electronics industry.*

**Flextronics Design s.r.l., 27 Via Borgazzi, 20052 Milan, Italy**

Tel: 39-039-209-8610

## FLINT INK CORPORATION

4600 Arrowhead Drive, Ann Arbor, MI, 48105

Tel: (734) 622-6000       Fax: (734) 622-6060       www.flintink.com

*Manufacturer of printing inks and pigments.*

**Flint Ink Europe, Via Michelozzo da Forli 2/4i, I-10096 Pioltello Milana, Italy**

Tel: 39-02-921-60503   Fax: 39-02-9267309   Contact: Jim Mahony, Pres. Europe

## FLOWSERVE CORPORATION

222 W. Los Colinas Blvd., Irving, TX, 75039

Tel: (972) 443-6500       Fax: (972) 443-6858       www.flowserve.com

*Mfr. chemicals equipment, pumps, valves, filters, fans and heat exchangers.*

**Durco Europe SA, 3 Via Generale dalla Chiesa, I-24060 Costa Di Meggate, Italy**

## FLUKE CORPORATION

6920 Seaway Blvd. PO Box 9090, Everett, WA, 98203

Tel: (425) 347-6100       Fax: (425) 356-5116       www.fluke.com

*Mfr. handheld, electronic test tools for maintenance of electronic equipment.*

**Organizzazione Commerciale Fluke Italia S.r.l., Piazza A. Mancini 4, 00196 Rome, Italy**

Tel: 39-06-321-6391

**Organizzazione Commerciale Fluke Italia S.r.l., Viale delle Industrie 11, 20090 Vimodrone, Milan, Italy**

## FM GLOBAL INC.

1301 Atwood Avenue, Johnston, RI, 02919

Tel: (401) 275-3000     Fax: (401) 275-3029     www.fmglobal.com

*Engaged in commercial and industrial property insurance and risk management, specializing in engineering-driven property protection.*

**FM Global,  Factory Mutual International Italia SrL, Corso Unione Sovietica, 612/3/C 10135 Torino, Italy**

Tel: 39-011-39-76-011

## FMC CORPORATION

200 E. Randolph Drive, Chicago, IL, 60601

Tel: (312) 861-6000     Fax: (312) 861-6141     www.fmc.com

*Produces chemicals and precious metals, mfr. machinery, equipment and systems for industrial, agricultural and government use.*

**FMC Smith Meter Inc./Somefi S.P.A.,  Via Angera 16, Milan I-20125, Italy**

## FOOT LOCKER USA

112 West 34th Street, New York, NY, 10020

Tel: (212) 720-3700     Fax: (212) 553-2042     www.venatorgroup.com

*Mfr./sales shoes and sneakers.*

**Foot Locker International,  Via Crea 10, I-10095 Grugliasco Torino, Italy**

Tel: 39-011-7708646

**Foot Locker International,  Via Sestri 220, I-16039 Genoa, Italy**

Tel: 39-010-6049392

**Foot Locker International,  Via Aldo Moro 1, I-21100 Varese, Italy**

Tel: 39-02-831005

**Foot Locker International,  Via Xx Settembre 101/103/105r, I-16021 Genoa, Italy**

Tel: 39-010-586906

**Foot Locker International,  Via Rome 306, I-10121 Torino, Italy**

Tel: 39-011-537176

**Foot Locker International,  Via Martiri Della Liberta 33,  I-15100 Alessandria, Italy**

Tel: 39-01-31-254921

## FORD MOTOR COMPANY

One American Road, Dearborn, MI, 48121

Tel: (313) 322-3000     Fax: (313) 322-9600     www.ford.com

*Mfr./sales motor vehicles.*

**Ford Italiana SpA,  Viale Pasteur 8/10, Casella Postale 10058, I-00144 Rome, Italy**

## FOREST OIL CORPORATION

1600 Broadway, Ste. 2200, Denver, CO, 80202

Tel: (303) 812-1400     Fax: (303) 812-1602     www.forestoil.com

*Crude oil and natural gas.*

**Forest Oil Italy,  c/o Forest Oil Corp., 1600 Broadway Suite 2200, Denver CO 80202**

## FORMICA CORPORATION

10155 Reading Road, Cincinnati, OH, 45241-4805

Tel: (513) 786-3400     Fax: (513) 786-3082     www.formica.com

*Mfr. decorative laminate, adhesives and solvents.*

**Formica Italia Srl,  Via Sardegna 24 (M1), 20090 Pieve Emmanuele, Milan Italy**

## FORRESTER RESEARCH, INC.

400 Technology Square, Cambridge, MA, 02139

Tel: (617) 497-7090 Fax: (617) 868-0577 www.forrester.com

*Provides clients an analysis of the effect of changing technologies on their operations.*

**MATE Srl, Corso C. Colombo 10, I-20144 Milan, Italy**

Tel: 39-02-839-4414 Fax: 39-02-835-8747 Contact: Antonella Gerundino, Mgr.

## FORT JAMES CORPORATION

1650 Lake Cook Road, Deerfield, IL, 60015

Tel: (847) 317-5000 Fax: (847) 236-3755 www.fortjames.com

*Mfr. and markets consumer tissue products.*

**Fort James Corporation, Genova, Italy**

**Fort James Corporation, Joint ventures in Castelnuove, Cava dei Terreni and Potenza, Italy**

## FOSTER WHEELER CORPORATION

Perryville Corporate Park, Clinton, NJ, 08809-4000

Tel: (908) 730-4000 Fax: (908) 730-4100 www.fwc.com

*Manufacturing, engineering and construction.*

**Foster Wheeler Energia Italiana S.p.A, Via Sebastiano Caboto 1, I-20094 Corsico Milan, Italy**

Tel: 39-2-4486-1 Fax: 39-2-4486-3473

## FRANKLIN RESOURCES, INC.

777 Mariners Island Blvd., San Mateo, CA, 94404

Tel: (415) 312-2000 Fax: (415) 312-3655 www.frk.com

*Global and domestic investment advisory and portfolio management.*

**Templeton Italia SRL, Via Quintino Sella 4, I-20121 Milan, Italy**

Tel: 39-02-723021 Fax: 39-02-80-9394

## FRITZ COMPANIES, INC.

706 Mission Street, Ste. 900, San Francisco, CA, 94103

Tel: (415) 904-8360 Fax: (415) 904-8661 www.fritz.com

*Integrated transportation, sourcing, distribution and customs brokerage services.*

**Fritz Companies Inc., Florence, Italy**

## FSI INTERNATIONAL INC.

322 Lake Hazeltine Drive, Chaska, MN, 55318

Tel: (612) 448-5440 Fax: (612) 448-2825 www.fsi-intl.com

*Manufacturing equipment for computer silicon wafers.*

**Metron Technology (Italia) S.r.l., Via per Ornago, 20040 Bellusco Milan, Italy**

## H.B. FULLER COMPANY

1200 Willow Lake Blvd., Vadnais Heights, MN, 55110

Tel: (651) 236-5900 Fax: (651) 236-5898 www.hbfuller.com

*Mfr./distributor adhesives, sealants, coatings, paints, waxes, sanitation chemicals.*

**H.B. Fuller Italia s.r.l., S.S. 211 Della Lomellina, Km. 63.233, I-28071 Borgolavezzaro, Italy**

Tel: 39-0321-888-800 Fax: 39-0321-888-802

## GAF CORPORATION

1361 Alps Road, Wayne, NJ, 07470

Tel: (973) 628-3000 Fax: (973) 628-3326 www.gaf.com

*Mfr. roofing and building materials.*

**GAF ISP (Italia) SRL, Via Pipamonti 66, I-20141 Milan, Italy**

## GARTNER GROUP, INC.

56 Top Gallant Road, Stamford, CT, 06904-2212

Tel: (203) 316-1111    Fax: (203) 316-1100    www.gartner.com

*Information technology and research.*

**Gartner Group Italy,  Milan, Italy**

Tel: 39-02-482891    Fax: 39-02-48289389

## GaSONICS INTERNATIONAL CORPORATION

404 East Plumeria Drive, San Jose, CA, 95134

Tel: (408) 570-7000    Fax: (408) 570-7612    www.gasonics.com

*Mfr. gas-based dry cleaning systems for semi-conductor production equipment.*

**GaSonics International,  c/o Ponteggi Tubolari, Via 16 Strada 48-50, Piano D'Arci, 95121 Zona Industriale di Catania,
Italy**

Tel: 39-095-592-810    Fax: 39-095-592- 810

## GENERAL BINDING CORPORATION

One GBC Plaza, Northbrook, IL, 60062

Tel: (847) 272-3700    Fax: (847) 272-1369    www.gbc.com

*Engaged in the design, manufacture and distribution of branded office equipment, related supplies and thermal laminating films.*

**General Binding Corp. Italia SpA,  Viale Milanofiori Palazzo F10, I-20090 Assago Milan, italy**

Contact: Robert Baci

## GENERAL ELECTRIC CAPITAL CORPORATION

260 Long Ridge Road, Stamford, CT, 06927

Tel: (203) 357-4000    Fax: (203) 357-6489    www.gecapital.com

*Financial, property/casualty insurance, computer sales and trailer leasing services.*

**Employers Reinsurance Corp. (ERC),  Via Gasparotto 1, I-20124 Milan, Italy**

Tel: 39-02-66-711-260    Fax: 39-02-66-711-906

**Employers Reinsurance Corp. (ERC),  Via Ettore de Sonnaz 3, I-10121 Torino, Italy**

Tel: 39-011-56-12205    Fax: 39-011-56-12230

## GENERAL ELECTRIC COMPANY

3135 Easton Turnpike, Fairfield, CT, 06431

Tel: (203) 373-2211    Fax: (203) 373-3131    www.ge.com

*Diversified manufacturing, technology and services.*

**GE FANUC Automation,  Piazza Tirana 24/4B, I-20147 Milan, Italy**

Tel: 39-02-417176    Fax: 39-02-49669

**GE International,  Viale Farngosta 75, I-20142 Milan, Italy**

Tel: 39-02-8950-4755    Fax: 39-02-8953-1652

**General Electric Co.,  Attn: Italy Office, 3135 Easton Turnpike, Fairfield CT 06431**

Tel: 518-438-6500

**Nuovo Pignone,  2 Via Felice Matteucci, I-50127 Florence, Italy**

Tel: 39-055-423-2710    Fax: 39-055-423-2709

## GENERAL INSTRUMENT CORPORATION

101 Tournament Road, Horsham, PA, 19044

Tel: (215) 674-4800    Fax: (215) 443-9554    www.gi.com

*Mfr. broadband communications and power rectifying components.*

**General Instrument Italia SRL,  Via Cantu 11, I-20092 Cinisello Balsamo Milan, Italy**

## GENERAL MOTORS ACCEPTANCE CORPORATION

3044 W. Grand Blvd., Detroit, MI, 48202

Tel: (313) 556-5000 Fax: (313) 556-5108 www.gmac.com

*Automobile financing.*

**GMAC Italia SpA, Via Rivoltana 13, Milan San Felice, I-20090 Segrato, Italy**

**GMAC Italia SpA, Piazzale dell Industria 40, I-00144 Rome, Italy**

## GENERAL MOTORS CORPORATION

300 Renaissance Center, Detroit, MI, 48285

Tel: (313) 556-5000 Fax: (313) 556-5108 www.gm.com

*Mfr. full line vehicles, automotive electronics, commercial technologies, telecommunications, space, finance.*

**General Motors Italia SpA, Piazza dell' Industria, I-00144 Rome, Italy**

## GENERAL REINSURANCE CORPORATION

695 E. Main Street, Stamford, CT, 06904-2350

Tel: (203) 328-5000 Fax: (203) 328-6423 www.genre.com

*Reinsurance services worldwide.*

**General Re Europe Ltd. - Milan, Ufficio de Rappresentanza di Milan, Largo Augusto 7, I-20122 Milan, Italy**

Tel: 39-02-762-11852 Fax: 39-02-760-02667 Contact: Angelo Garbelli, VP

**La Kölnische Italia, Servzi Riassicurativi s.r.l., Largo Augusto 7, I-20122 Milan, Italy**

Tel: 39-02-762-1181 Fax: 39-02-7600-1577 Contact: Massimo Apolloni, Gen. Mgr.

## GENUITY, INC.

150 Cambridge Park Drive, Cambridge, MA, 02140

Tel: (617) 873-2000 Fax: (617) 873-2857 www.genuity.com

*R/D computer, communications, acoustics technologies and internetworking services.*

**Genuity Italia, Palazzo Tintoretto - Centro Milano Oltre, Via Cassanese 224 20090 Segrate, Milan Italy**

Tel: 39-02-2692-6142 Contact: Pia Boitano

## GENZYME CORPORATION

1 Kendall Square, Cambridge, MA, 02139-1562

Tel: (617) 252-7500 Fax: (617) 252-7600 www.genzyme.com

*Mfr. healthcare products for enzyme deficient diseases.*

**Genzyme SRL, Via Scaglia Est. 144, 1-41100 Modena, Italy**

Tel: 39-059-349811

## GILEAD SCIENCES, INC.

333 Lakeside Dr, Foster City, CA, 94404

Tel: (650) 574-3000 Fax: (650) 578-9264 www.gilead.com

*Engaged in healthcare research and development; biotech treatments for viruses.*

**NeXstar Pharmaceuticals, Via G. Frua 16, 20146 Milan, Italy**

Tel: 39-02-4802-1500 Fax: 39-02-4802-2578

## THE GILLETTE COMPANY

Prudential Tower Building, Boston, MA, 02199

Tel: (617) 421-7000 Fax: (617) 421-7123 www.gillette.com

*Develop/mfr. personal care/use products: blades and razors, toiletries, cosmetics, stationery.*

**Braun Italia SRL, Milan, Italy**

Contact: Domenico Ottavis, Gen. Mgr.

**Gillette Group Italy SpA, Milan, Italy**

Contact: Domenico Ottavis, Gen. Mgr.

**Jafra Cosmetics SpA, Saronno, Italy**

Contact: Domenico Ottavis, Gen. Mgr.

## GILSON INC.

3000 W. Beltline Hwy, PO Box 620027, Middleton, WI, 53562-0027

Tel: (608) 836-1551     Fax: (608) 831-4451     www.gilson.com

*Mfr. analytical/biomedical instruments.*

**Gilson Italia Srl., Via Alserio 5, 20159 Milan, Italy**

## GLEASON CORPORATION

1000 University Ave., Rochester, NY, 14692

Tel: (716) 473-1000     Fax: (716) 461-4348     www.gleasoncorp.com

*Mfr. gear making machine tools; tooling and services.*

**Gleason Milano, Via Caldera 21/B3, I-20153 Milan, Italy**

Tel: 39-024828571   Fax: 39-0248204698

## GLOBAL SILVERHAWK

2190 Meridian Park Blvd., Ste G, Concord, CA, 94520

Tel: (925) 681-2889     Fax: (925) 681-2755     www.globalsilverhawk.com

*International moving and forwarding.*

**Global Silverhawk, Via F. Iii Beltrami 61, I-20026 Novate Milanese Milan, Italy**

Tel: 39-2-356-0925   Contact: Gilberto Tumietto, Gen. Mgr.

## THE GOLDMAN SACHS GROUP

85 Broad Street, New York, NY, 10004

Tel: (212) 902-1000     Fax: (212) 902-3000     www.gs.com

*Investment bankers; securities broker dealers.*

**Goldman Sachs Group, Passaggio Centrale 2, I-20123 Milan, Italy**

Tel: 39-02-8022-1000

## THE GOODYEAR TIRE & RUBBER COMPANY

1144 East Market Street, Akron, OH, 44316

Tel: (330) 796-2121     Fax: (330) 796-1817     www.goodyear.com

*Mfr. tires, automotive belts and hose, conveyor belts, chemicals; oil pipeline transmission.*

**Goodyear Italiana SpA, Piazza G. Marconi 25, Casella Postale 10768, I-10100 Rome, Italy**

## W. R. GRACE & COMPANY

7500 Grace Drive, Columbia, MD, 21044

Tel: (410) 531-4000     Fax: (410) 531-4367     www.grace.com

*Mfr. specialty chemicals and materials: packaging, health care, catalysts, construction, water treatment/process.*

**Grace Italiana SpA, Voa Trento 7, 1-20017 Passirana di Rho Milan, Italy**

Tel: 39-02-935371   Fax: 39-02-93537-555

## GRACO INC.

4050 Olson Memorial Hwy, PO Box 1441, Minneapolis, MN, 55440-1441

Tel: (612) 623-6000     Fax: (612) 623-6777     www.graco.com

*Mfr. systems and equipment to service fluid handling systems and automotive equipment.*

**Graco SRL, Via Serra 22, I-40012 Lippo Calderarra di Reno Bologna, Italy**

## GRAHAM & JAMES LLP

One Maritime Plaza, Ste. 300, San Francisco, CA, 94111-3404

Tel: (415) 954-0200     Fax: (415) 391-2493     www.gj.com

*International law firm.*

**Graham & James LLP, Piazza San Babila 3, I-20122 Milan, Italy**

Tel: 39-02-777-21511   Fax: 39-02-777-21515   Contact: Gabriele Bernascone

## GRANT THORNTON INTERNATIONAL

800 One Prudential Plaza, 130 E. Randolph Drive, Chicago, IL, 60601-6050

Tel: (312) 856-0001     Fax: (312) 616-7052     www.grantthornton.com

*Accounting, audit, tax and management consulting services.*

**Grant Thornton Italia S.p.A., Via G. Zanellato 5, I-35121 Padova, Italy**

Tel: 39-049-870-3019   Fax: 39-049-870-2275   Contact: Beretta Giorgio

**Grant Thornton Italia S.p.A., Via Nizza 45, I-00198 Rome, Italy**

Tel: 39-06-854-0056   Fax: 39-06-855-7469

**Grant Thornton Italia S.p.A., Via Sparano 115, I-70121 Bari, Italy**

Tel: 39-080-587948   Fax: 39-080-521-4688

**Grant Thornton Italia S.p.A., Viale Brigate Partigiane 12, I-16129 Genoa, Italy**

Tel: 39-010-587948   Fax: 39-010-587948

**Grant Thornton Italia S.p.A., Via Santa Brigida 51, I-80133 Napoli, Italy**

Tel: 39-08-1552-9052   Fax: 39-08-1055-19055   Contact: Licio Duca

**Grant Thornton Italia S.p.A., Via Colli 20, I-10129 Torino, Italy**

Tel: 39-02-2561-1185   Fax: 39-011-561-1815

**Grant Thornton S.p.A., Largo Augusto 7, 20122 Milan, Italy**

Tel: 39-02-762970   Fax: 39-02-781498   Contact: Lorenzo Penca

## GREAT LAKES CHEMICAL CORPORATION

500 East 96th Street, Ste. 500, Indianapolis, IN, 46240

Tel: (317) 715-3000     Fax: (317) 715-3050     www.greatlakeschem.com

*Mfr. innovative specialty chemical solutions, including flame retardants and other polymer additives, water treatment chemicals, performance and fine chemicals, fire extinguishants.*

**Great Lakes Chemical Italia SRL, Milan, Italy**

## GREG MANNING AUCTIONS, INC.

775 Passaic Avenue, West Caldwell, NJ, 07006

Tel: (973) 882-0004     Fax: (973) 882-3499     www.gregmanning.com

*Specialty auction house; dealing primarily in stamps.*

**GMAI Europe, Via Privata Maria Teresa 11, I-20123 Milan, Italy**

## GREY GLOBAL GROUP

777 Third Ave., New York, NY, 10017

Tel: (212) 546-2000     Fax: (212) 546-1495     www.grey.com

*International advertising agency.*

**Milano & Grey, Via Bertani 6, I-20154 Milan, Italy**

## GRIFFITH LABORATORIES INC.

One Griffith Center, Alsip, IL, 60658

Tel: (708) 371-0900     Fax: (708) 597-3294     www.griffithlabs.com

*Mfr. industrial food ingredients and equipment.*

**Griffith Labs, Rome, Italy**

Tel: 39-06-3031-0632   Fax: 39-06-3031-0885

## GUARDIAN ELECTRIC MFG. COMPANY

1425 Lake Ave., Woodstock, IL, 60098

Tel: (815) 334-3600     Fax: (815) 337-0377     www.guardian-electric.com

*Mfr. industrial controls, electrical relays and switches.*

**Aerel S.R.L., Via Bolsena 27, 00191 Rome, Italy**

## GUY CARPENTER & COMPANY, INC.

Two World Trade Center, New York, NY, 10048

Tel: (212) 323-1000    Fax: (212) 313-4970    www.guycarp.com

*Engaged in global reinsurance and risk management.*

**Guy Carpenter & Company, S.r.l.,  Corso Magenta 2, 20123 Milan, Italy**

Tel: 39-02-8699-8075   Fax: 9-02-8699-7994

## HAEMONETICS CORPORATION

400 Wood Road, Braintree, MA, 02184-9114

Tel: (781) 848-7100    Fax: (781) 848-5106    www.haemonetics.com

*Mfr. automated blood processing systems and blood products.*

**Haemonetics Italia S.R.L.,  Via Donizetti 30, 20020 Lainate Milan, Italy**

Tel: 39-02-935-70113   Fax: 39-02-935-72132

## HALLIBURTON COMPANY

500 North Akard Street, Ste. 3600, Dallas, TX, 75201-3391

Tel: (214) 978-2600    Fax: (214) 978-2685    www.halliburton.com

*Engaged in diversified energy services, engineering and construction.*

**Halliburton Ltd.,  Zona Industriale Campoffero, Via Italo Betto 11, 2058 Vognera, Pavia Italy**

Tel: 39-0383-691557   Fax: 39-0383-640529

**Halliburton Ltd.,  CP 59, I-48023 Marina di Ravenna, Italy**

Tel: 39-054-453-0709   Fax: 39-054-453-1042

**Halliburton Ltd.,  Ufficio Postale Succursale 6, I-29110 Piacenza, Italy**

Tel: 39-052-3540401   Fax: 39-052-3593610

**Halliburton Ltd.,  Via Tolstoi 86, San Gluliano, I-10098 Milanese Milan, Italy**

Tel: 39-02-9849-1451   Fax: 39-02-9824-0488

**Halliburton Ltd.,  Via Elorina, Contrada Pantanelli, I-96100 Siracusa Sicily, Italy**

Tel: 39-093-146-3882   Fax: 39-093-146-3883

## HAMILTON SUNSTRAND

One Hamilton Rd., Windsor Locks, CT, 06096-1010

Tel: (860) 654-6000    Fax: (860) 654-3469    www.hamiltonsunstrandcorp.com

*Design/mfr. aerospace systems for commercial, regional, corporate and military aircraft.*

**Hamilton Sunstrand Corp.,  Torino, Italy**

## HARNISCHFEGER INDUSTRIES INC.

PO Box 554, Milwaukee, WI, 53201

Tel: (414) 797-6480    Fax: (414) 797-6573    www.harnischfeger.com

*Mfr. mining and material handling equipment, papermaking machinery and computer systems.*

**Beloit Italia SpA,  Via Martiri del XXI 76, I-10064 Pinerolo Turin, Italy**

## HARRIS CALORIFIC COMPANY

2345 Murphy Boulevard, Gainesville, GA, 30501

Tel: (770) 536-8801    Fax: (770) 536-0544    www.harriscal.com

*Mfr./sales of gas welding and cutting equipment.*

**Harris Europa SpA,  Via Nazionale 79, I-40065 Pianoro Bologna, Italy**

## HARRIS CORPORATION

1025 West NASA Blvd., Melbourne, FL, 32919

Tel: (407) 727-9100    Fax: (407) 727-9344    www.harris.com

*Mfr. communications and information-handling equipment, including copying and fax systems.*

**Harris Semiconductor,  Viale Fulvio Testi 126, I-20092 Cinisello Balsamo Milan, Italy**

Tel: 39-02-262-222131

## HARTFORD RE COMPANY

55 Farmington Ave., Ste. 800, Hartford, CT, 06105

Tel: (860) 520-2700      Fax: (860) 520-2726      www.thehartford.com

*Reinsurance.*

**HartRe Company, Via Soperga 2 - 6/F, Milan, Italy**

Tel: 39-02-673-34311    Fax: 39-02-673-34321

## HASBRO INDUSTRIES INC.

1027 Newport Ave., Pawtucket, RI, 02861

Tel: (401) 725-8697      Fax: (401) 727-5099      www.hasbro.com

*Mfr. toy products, including games and puzzles, dolls and plush products.*

**Hasbro Iberia, S.L., Poligono Industrial Sec. 13 - Calle 17, 46190 Ribarraja del Turia, Italy**

Tel: 96-271-9400

**Wizards, Div. Hasbro Industries, Via Giovanni da Udine 3, 20156 Milan, Italy**

Tel: 44-1628-780-530

## HAYES LEMMERZ INTERNATIONAL

15300 Centennial Dr., Northville, MI, 48167

Tel: (734) 737-5000      Fax: (734) 737-2003      www.hayes-lemmerz.com

*Mfr. steel and aluminum car wheels.*

**Hayes Lemmerz S.p.A., Via Cavour 26, 10060 Camiglione Fenile, Italy**

**Hayes Lemmerz S.p.A., Via Roma 200, 25020 Dello, Italy**

## HAYNES INTERNATIONAL INC.

1020 W. Park Ave., PO Box 9013, Kokomo, IN, 46904-9013

Tel: (765) 456-6000      Fax: (765) 456-6905      www.haynesintl.com

*Mfr. cobalt and nickel-base alloys for aerospace and chemicals industry.*

**Haynes International, S.R.L., Viale Brianza 8, 20127 Milan, Italy**

Tel: 39-2-2614-1331    Fax: 39-2-282-8273

## HEIDRICK & STRUGGLES INTERNATIONAL, INC.

Sears Tower, 233 South Wacker Drive, Chicago, IL, 60606

Tel: (312) 496-1200      Fax: (312) 496-1290      www.heidrick.com

*Executive search firm.*

**Heidrick & Struggles Intl. Inc., Via XXIV Maggio 43, 00187 Rome, Italy**

**Heidrick & Struggles Intl. Inc., Corso Venezia 16, I-20122 Milan, Italy**

Tel: 39-02-76-000-393    Fax: 39-02-76-000-801

## HEIN-WERNER CORPORATION

2110 A Pewaukee Rd., PO Box 1606, Waukesha, WI, 53188

Tel: (262) 542-6611      Fax: (262) 542-7890      www.snapon.com

*Mfr. auto body repair equipment, engine rebuilding and brake repair equipment, hydraulic cylinders.*

**Blackhawk Italia SRL, Via dell'Industria 5, I--37066 Sommacampagna Verona, Italy**

## H.J. HEINZ COMPANY

600 Grant Street, Pittsburgh, PA, 15219

Tel: (412) 456-5700      Fax: (412) 456-6128      www.heinz.com

*Processed food products and nutritional services.*

**AIAL (Arimpex SRL Industrie Alimentari), Commessaggio, Italy**

**Dega SRL, Mori, Italy**

**Heinz Italia SpA, Milan, Italy**

**PLADA SpA (Plasmon Dietetici Alimentari SpA), Milan, Italy**

## HERCULES INC.

Hercules Plaza, 1313 N. Market Street, Wilmington, DE, 19894-0001

Tel: (302) 594-5000      Fax: (302) 594-5400      www.herc.com

*Mfr. specialty chemicals, plastics, film and fibers, coatings, resins, food ingredients.*

**Hercules Italia SpA, Busnago, Italy**

**Hercules Italia SpA, Via Rosellini 2, I-20124 Milan, Italy**

## HERMAN MILLER INC.

855 East Main, Zeeland, MI, 49464

Tel: (616) 654-3000      Fax: (616) 654-5385      www.hermanmiller.com

*Mfr. office furnishings.*

**Herman Miller Italia, Via Gran Sasso 6, 20030 Lentate sul Seveso, Italy**

## HERSHEY FOODS CORPORATION

100 Crystal A Drive, Hershey, PA, 17033

Tel: (717) 534-6799      Fax: (717) 534-6760      www.hersheys.com

*Mfr. chocolate, food and confectionery products.*

**Sperlari SRL, Via Milan 16, I-26100 Cremona, Italy**

## HEWITT ASSOCIATES LLC

100 Half Day Road, Lincolnshire, IL, 60069

Tel: (847) 295-5000      Fax: (847) 295-7634      www.hewitt.com

*Employee benefits consulting firm.*

**Hewitt Associates, Via Alessandro Volta, 16 - Scala H, I-20093 Cologno Monzese Milan, Italy**

Tel: 39-02-254-0794

## HEWLETT-PACKARD COMPANY

3000 Hanover Street, Palo Alto, CA, 94304-1185

Tel: (650) 857-1501      Fax: (650) 857-5518      www.hp.com

*Mfr. computing, communications and measurement products and services.*

**Hewlett-Packard Italiana SpA, Via Giuseppe di Vittorio 9, I-20063 Cernusco sul Naviglio, Milan, Italy**

## HILLENBRAND INDUSTRIES, INC.

700 State Route 46 East, Batesville, IN, 47006

Tel: (812) 934-7000      Fax: (812) 934-1963      www.hillenbrand.com

*Holding company: mfr. hospital beds, incubators and caskets.*

**Hill-Rom SpA, Via Ambrosoli Nr. 6, 20090 Rodano Milan, Italy**

Tel: 39-02-950-541   Fax: 39-02-953-28578   Contact: Angelo Lugrini

## HILTON HOTELS CORPORATION

9336 Civic Center Drive, Beverly Hills, CA, 90210

Tel: (310) 278-4321      Fax: (310) 205-7880      www.hiltonhotels.com

*International hotel chain: Hilton International, Vista Hotels and Hilton National Hotels.*

**Hilton International Hotels, Via Galvani 12, I-20124 Milan, Italy**

## HOLIDAY INN (BASS RESORTS) WORLDWIDE, INC.

3 Ravinia Drive, Ste. 2900, Atlanta, GA, 30346-2149

Tel: (770) 604-2000      Fax: (770) 604-5403      www.holidayinn.com

*Hotels, restaurants and casinos.*

**Holiday Inn, Viale Castello della Magliana 65, I-10210 Parco Dei Medici Rome, Italy**

## HOLLINGSWORTH & VOSE COMPANY

112 Washington Street, East Walpole, MA, 02032

Tel: (508) 668-0295      Fax: (508) 668-3557      www.hollingsworth-vose.com

*Mfr. technical and industrial papers and non-woven fabrics.*

**Hollingsworth & Vose Company, SRL, Via Bodina 41, 12100 Cuneo, Italy**

## HONEYWELL INTERNATIONAL INC.

101 Columbia Road, Morristown, NJ, 07962

Tel: (973) 455-2000      Fax: (973) 455-4807      www.honeywell.com

*Develop/mfr. controls for home and building, industry, space and aviation.*

**Honeywell S.p.A., Via P. Gobetti - 2/b, I-20063 Cemusco sul Naviglio, Italy**

Tel: 39-02-921-461    Fax: 39-02-921-46888

## HORWATH INTERNATIONAL ASSOCIATION

415 Madison Ave., New York, NY, 10017

Tel: (212) 838-5566      Fax: (212) 838-3636      www.horwath.com

*Public accountants and auditors.*

**Horwath & Horwath Italia, Via Calabria 7, I-00187 Rome, Italy**

**Polandri Horwath, Piazza Navona 49, I-00186 Rome, Italy**

## HOUGHTON INTERNATIONAL INC.

PO Box 930, Madison & Van Buren Avenues, Valley Forge, PA, 19482-0930

Tel: (610) 666-4000      Fax: (610) 666-1376      www.houghtonintl.com

*Mfr. specialty chemicals, hydraulic fluids and lubricants.*

**Houghton Italia SpA, Casella Postale 6069, I-16100 Genoa, Italy**

Tel: 39-010-745-01-51

## HOWMEDICA OSTEONICS, INC.

359 Veterans Blvd., Rutherford, NJ, 07070

Tel: (201) 507-7300      Fax: (201) 935-4873      www.howmedica.com

*Mfr. of maxillofacial products (orthopedic implants).*

**Howmedica Italy, Rome, Italy**

Tel: 39-06-33182

## HOWMET CORPORATION

475 Steamboat Road, PO Box 1960, Greenwich, CT, 06836-1960

Tel: (203) 661-4600      Fax: (203) 661-1134      www.howmet.com

*Mfr. precision investment castings, alloys, engineering and refurbishment for jet aircraft and industrial gas turbine (IGT) engine components.*

**Ciral IT, Via P.G.A. Filippino 119, I-00144 Rome, Italy**

## HUNTSMAN CORPORATION

500 Huntsman Way, Salt Lake City, UT, 84108

Tel: (801) 532-5200      Fax: (801) 536-1581      www.huntsman.com

*Mfr./sales specialty chemicals, industrial chemicals and petrochemicals.*

**Huntsman Polyurethanes, Via Mazzini 58, I-21020 Ternate, Italy**

Tel: 39-332-941-111    Contact: A. Lettieri

**Tioxide Europe Srl, Stablimento di Scarlino, Contrada Casone CP113, 58022 Follonica, Italy**

Tel: 39-566-71111

## HYPERION SOLUTIONS CORPORATION

1344 Crossman Avenue, Sunnyvale, CA, 94089

Tel: (408) 744-9500      Fax: (408) 744-0400      www.hyperion.com

*Mfr. data analysis software tools.*

**Niederlassung Italy, Via Giorgione 18, 00147 Rome, Italy**

Tel: 39-06-542491    Fax: 39-06-5422-5821

**Niederlassung Italy, Via Margignoni 25, 20124 Milan, Italy**

Tel: 39-02-698131    Fax: 39-0-688-6567

### i2 TECHNOLOGIES, INC.

11701 Luna Road, Dallas, TX, 75234

Tel: (214) 860-6106     Fax: (214) 860-6060     www.i2.com

*Mfr. business-to-business software.*

**i2 Technologies Italy S.r.l.,  Via Albani 21 - 4/F, 4 Piano, Milan 20149, Italy**

### IBM CORPORATION

New Orchard Road, Armonk, NY, 10504

Tel: (914) 765-1900     Fax: (914) 765-7382     www.ibm.com

*Information products, technology and services.*

**IBM Italia SpA,  Via Lecco 61, I-20090 Vimercate Milan, Italy**

Tel: 39-039-600-7666   Fax: 39-039-600-7150

### ICC INDUSTRIES INC.

460 Park Ave., New York, NY, 10022

Tel: (212) 521-1700     Fax: (212) 521-1794     www.iccchem.com

*Manufacturing and trading of chemicals, plastics and pharmaceuticals.*

**ICC Talia S.R.L.,  Via G. Cardano 8, I-20124 Milan, Italy**

Tel: 39-02-670-1406   Fax: 39-02-670-0477   Contact: Francesco Minervino

### ICN PHARMACEUTICALS, INC.

3300 Hyland Ave., Costa Mesa, CA, 92626

Tel: (714) 545-0100     Fax: (714) 641-7268     www.icnpharm.com

*Mfr./distribute pharmaceuticals.*

**ICN Pharmaceuticals, Inc.,  Via Labor 23/25, 20090 Opera MI, Italy**

Tel: 39-2-57601041   Fax: 39-2-57601610

### ILLINOIS TOOL WORKS (ITW)

3600 West Lake Ave., Glenview, IL, 60025-5811

Tel: (847) 724-7500     Fax: (847) 657-4268     www.itw.com

*Mfr. gears, tools, fasteners, sealants, plastic and metal components for industrial, medical, etc.*

**ITW Fastex Italia SpA,  Turin, Italy**

### IMATION CORPORATION

One Imation Place, Oakdale, MN, 55128

Tel: (612) 704-4000     Fax: (612) 704-3444     www.imation.com

*Dry laser-imaging film systems.*

**Imation Corp.,  Milan, Italy**

### IMG (INTERNATIONAL MANAGEMENT GROUP)

1360 East Ninth Street, Ste. 100, Cleveland, OH, 44114

Tel: (216) 522-1200     Fax: (216) 522-1145     www.imgworld.com

*Manages athletes, sports academies and real estate facilities worldwide.*

**IMG Srl,  Viale Beatrice D'Este 1, Milan 20122, Italy**

Tel: 39-02-583-13364   Fax: 39-02-583-13095

### IMO INDUSTRIES, DIV. COLFAX INC.

9211 Forest Hill Ave., Richmond, VA, 23235

Tel: (804) 560-4070     Fax: (804) 560-4076     www.imochain.com

*Mfr./support mechanical and electronic controls, chains and engineered power products.*

**IMO Industries SRL, TransInstruments Div.,  Via Correggio 19, I-20149 Milan, Italy**

**Roltra-Morse SpA,  Via Albenga 9, I-10090 Cascine Vica Rivoli Turin, Italy**

## INFONET SERVICES CORPORATION

2100 East Grand Ave., El Segundo, CA, 90245-1022

Tel: (310) 335-2600        Fax: (310) 335-4507        www.infonet.com

*Provider of Internet services and electronic messaging services.*

**Infonet Italia, Via Rombon 11, I-20134 Milan, Italy**

Tel: 39-02-217131   Fax: 39-02-21713-203

## INFORMATION RESOURCES, INC. (IRI)

150 N. Clinton St., Chicago, IL, 60661

Tel: (312) 726-1221        Fax: (312) 726-0360        www.infores.com

*Provides bar code scanner services for retail sales organizations; processes, analyzes and sells data from the huge database created from these services.*

**IRI InfoScan, Viale Brenta 18, I-20139 Milan, Italy**

Tel: 39-02-525-79651   Fax: 39-02-569-5767

## INFORMIX CORPORATION

4100 Bohannon Drive, Menlo Park, CA, 95025

Tel: (650) 926-6300        Fax: (650) 926-6593        www.informix.com

*Designs and produces database management software, connectivity interfaces and gateways, and other computer applications.*

**Informix Software S.p.A., Via Donat Cattin 5, I-20063 Cernusco Sul Naviglio Milan, Italy**

Tel: 39-02-921451

## INGERSOLL-RAND COMPANY

200 Chestnut Ridge Road, Woodcliff Lake, NJ, 07675

Tel: (201) 573-0123        Fax: (201) 573-3172        www.ingersoll-rand.com

*Mfr. compressors, rock drills, air tools, door hardware, ball bearings.*

**Ingersoll-Rand Italiana SpA, Strada Prov. Cassamese 108, I-20060 Vignate Milan, Italy**

Tel: 39-02-95056-537   Fax: 39-02-9560194

**Worthington SpA, Via Rossini 90-92, I-20033 Desio Milan, Italy**

## INGRAM MICRO INC.

PO Box 25125, 1600 E. St. Andrew Place, Santa Ana, CA, 92799

Tel: (714) 566-1000        Fax: (714) 566-7940        www.ingrammicro.com

*Engaged in wholesale distribution of microcomputer products.*

**Ingram Micro Inc., Milan, Italy**

## INSTRON CORPORATION

100 Royal Street, Canton, MA, 02021-1089

Tel: (781) 575-5000        Fax: (781) 575-5751        www.instron.com

*Mfr. material testing instruments.*

**Instron Intl. Ltd., Via del Cignoli, Milan, Italy**

Tel: 39-2-380-00003

## INTEGRATED DEVICE TECHNOLOGY, INC.

2975 Stender Way, Santa Clara, CA, 95054

Tel: (408) 727-6116        Fax: (408) 492-8674        www.idt.com

*Mfr. high-performance semiconductors and modules.*

**Integrated Device Technology, Inc., Centro Direzionale Colleoni, Palazzo Astrolabio, Via Cardano 3, Agrate Brianza (MI) I-20041, Italy**

Tel: 39-39-6899987   Fax: 39-39-6899986

## INTEL CORPORATION

Robert Noyce Bldg., 2200 Mission College Blvd., Santa Clara, CA, 95052-8119

Tel: (408) 765-8080 Fax: (408) 765-1739 www.intel.com

*Mfr. semiconductor, microprocessor and micro-communications components and systems.*

**Intel Semiconductor (Italy) SpA, Milan, Italy**

Tel: 39-02-575-441

## INTER-CONTINENTAL HOTELS

3 Ravina Drive, Suite 2900, Atlanta, GA, 30346-2149

Tel: (770) 604-2000 Fax: (770) 604-5403 www.interconti.com

*Worldwide hotel and resort accommodations.*

**De La Ville Inter-Continental Roma, Via Sistina 6769, I-00018 Rome, Italy**

Tel: 39-06-67331 Fax: 39-06-678-4213

**Inter-Continental Hotels, Via Vittor Pisani 12, I-20124 Milan, Italy**

Tel: 39-02-669-2542

## INTERGRAPH CORPORATION

One Madison Industrial Park, Huntsville, AL, 35894-0001

Tel: (256) 730-2000 Fax: (256) 730-7898 www.intergraph.com

*Develop/mfr. interactive computer graphic systems.*

**Intergraph Italia LLC, Strada 7, Palazzo R, Milanofiori, I-20089 Rozzano Milan Italy**

Tel: 39-02-575451 Fax: 39-02-5751-2470

**Intergraph Rome, Via Dino Frescobaldi 7, Rome, Italy**

Tel: 39-06-8689-7200 Fax: 39-06-8689-7195

## INTERMEC TECHNOLOGIES CORPORATION

6001 36th Ave. West, PO Box 4280, Everett, WA, 98203-9280

Tel: (425) 348-2600 Fax: (425) 355-9551 www.intermec.com

*Mfr./distributor automated data collection systems.*

**Intermec Technologies S.r.l., Via Enrico Cialdini 37, I-20161 Milan, Italy**

Tel: 39-02-662-4051 Fax: 39-02-662-40558

## INTERNATIONAL FLAVORS & FRAGRANCES INC.

521 West 57th Street, New York, NY, 10019-2960

Tel: (212) 765-5500 Fax: (212) 708-7132 www.iff.com

*Design/mfr. flavors, fragrances and aroma chemicals.*

**International Flavors & Fragrances, Via Fratelli Cervi, I-20090 Trezzano sul Naviglio Milan, Italy**

## INTERNATIONAL PAPER COMPANY

2 Manhattanville Road, Purchase, NY, 10577

Tel: (914) 397-1500 Fax: (914) 397-1596 www.ipaper.com

*Mfr./distributor container board, paper and wood products.*

**Anitec Image Italia SRL, S.S. 233 Km. 20.5, I-21040 Origgio, Italy**

**Aussedat Rey Italia SRL, Viale Milanfiori, Palazzo F1, I-20090 Assago, Italy**

**Cartiera di Valtaggio SRL, Loc. Pian Maxina, I-15060 Voltaggio, Italy**

**Horsell Italia Industrie Grafiche SRL, Viale del Lavoro, I-37036 S. Martino Buon Albergo, Italy**

**Ilford Photo SpA, S.S. 233 Km. 20.5, I-21040 Origgio, Italy**

**International Paper Italia SpA, Via Omago 55, I-20040 Bellusco Milan, Italy.**

## INTERNATIONAL RECTIFIER CORPORATION

233 Kansas Street, El Segundo, CA, 90245

Tel: (310) 322-3331     Fax: (310) 322-3332     www.irf.com

*Mfr. power semiconductor components.*

**International Rectifier Corp. Italiana,  Via Privata Liguria 49, I-10071 Borgaro-Torino, Italy**

Tel: 39-011-451-0111   Fax: 39-011-4510-374

## INTERNATIONAL SPECIALTY PRODUCTS, INC.

1361 Alps Rd., Wayne, NJ, 07470

Tel: (877) 389-3083     Fax: (973) 628-4117     www.ispcorp.com

*Mfr. specialty chemical products.*

**ISP (Italia) Srl,  Via Ripaminti 66, I-20141 Milan, Italy**

Tel: 39-02-52-202-011   Fax: 39-02-52-202-0224

## INTERVOICE INC.

17811 Waterview Pkwy., Dallas, TX, 75206

Tel: (972) 454-8000     Fax: (972) 454-8707     www.intervoice.com

*Mfr. voice automation systems and provides interactive information solutions.*

**InterVoice-Brite SpA,  Via Flaminia 173, 00196 Rome, Italy**

Tel: 39-06-320-0450   Fax: 39-06-320-8467

## IONICS INC.

65 Grove Street, Watertown, MA, 02172

Tel: (617) 926-2500     Fax: (617) 926-4304     www.ionics.com

*Mfr. desalination equipment.*

**Ionics Italba,  Via Livraghi 1/B, I-21026 Milan, Italy**

## IRIDIUM LLC

1575 "I" Street, NW, Washington, DC, 20005

Tel: (202) 408-3800     Fax: (202) 408-3801     www.iridium.com

*Consortium of companies sharing the construction and implementation of a global satellite communications system.*

**Iridium South Europe Reg. HQ / Iridium Italia S.p.A.,  Via Leofreni 4, I-00131 Rome, Italy**

Tel: 39-6-417281   Fax: 39-6-4172-8296   Contact: Paolo Torresani, Chmn.

## THE IT GROUP, INC.

2790 Mosside Boulevard, Monroeville, PA, 15146-2792

Tel: (412) 372-7701     Fax: (412) 373-7135     www.theitgroup.com

*Engaged in environmental management; hazardous waste clean-up services.*

**IT Group Italy,  Milan, Italy**

## ITT INDUSTRIES, INC.

4 West Red Oak Lane, White Plains, NY, 10604

Tel: (914) 641-2000     Fax: (914) 696-2950     www.ittind.com

*Mfr. pumps, systems and services to move and control water/fluids and produces connectors, switches, keypads and cabling used in computing, telecommunications, aerospace and industrial applications, as well as network services.*

**ITT Automotive Italy S.p.A.,  Via San Maratino 87, Barge 12032 (CN) Italy**

Tel: 390-175-347228

**Lowara S.p.A.,  14 Via Dott Lombardi, 36075 Montecchio Maggiore Vicenza, Italy**

Tel: 39-444-70-7111   Fax: 39-444-492109

## J. WALTER THOMPSON COMPANY
466 Lexington Ave., New York, NY, 10017
Tel: (212) 210-7000     Fax: (212) 210-6944     www.jwt.com
*International advertising and marketing services.*
**J. Walter Thompson Italia, Milan, Italy**

## JABIL CIRCUIT, INC.
10560 Ninth St. North, St. Petersburg, FL, 33716
Tel: (727) 557-9749     Fax: (727) 579-8529     www.jabil.com
*Mfr. printed circuit boards, electronic components and systems.*
**Jabil Circuit Italia, Viale Europe 2, 24040 Stezzano, Bergamo Italy**
Tel: 39-035-4542-111

## JACOBS ENGINEERING GROUP INC.
1111 S. Arroyo Parkway, Pasadena, CA, 91105
Tel: (626) 578-3500     Fax: (626) 578-6916     www.jacobs.com
*Engineering, design and consulting; construction and construction management; process plant maintenance.*
**Serete Italia, Via Alessondro Volta No. 16, I-20093 Cologno Monzese Milan, Italy**
Tel: 39-02-250-981  Fax: 39-02-253-90-973  Contact: Alfredo Radeplia, Chmn. & CEO  Emp: 116

## JLG INDUSTRIES INC.
One JLG Drive, McConnellsburg, PA, 17233-9533
Tel: (717) 485-5161     Fax: (717) 485-6417     www.jlg.com
*Mfr. aerial work platforms and vertical personnel lifts.*
**JLG Industries (Italia) s.r.l., Via Po. 2.2, 20010 Pregnana Milanese, Milan Italy**
Tel: 39-02-935-95210  Fax: 39-02-935-95845

## JOHNSON & JOHNSON
One Johnson & Johnson Plaza, New Brunswick, NJ, 08933
Tel: (732) 524-0400     Fax: (732) 214-0334     www.jnj.com
*Mfr./distributor/R&D pharmaceutical, health care and cosmetic products.*
**DePuy Italy SRL, Milan, Italy**
**Ethicon SpA/ Ethicon Endo-Surgery SpA, Rome, Italy**
**Janssen-Cilag SpA, Milan, Italy**
**Johnson & Johnson SpA, Casella Postale 10742, I-00144 Rome, Italy**
**LifeScan SpA, Milan, Italy**
**Ortho-Clinical Diagnostics SpA, Casella Postale 17171, I-20170 Milan, Italy**

## S C JOHNSON & SON INC.
1525 Howe St., Racine, WI, 53403
Tel: (414) 260-2000     Fax: (414) 260-2133     www.scjohnsonwax.com
*Home, auto, commercial and personal care products and specialty chemicals.*
**S.C. Johnson & Son Ltd., Casella Postale 18, I-20020 Arese Milan, Italy**

## JOHNSON CONTROLS INC.
5757 N. Green Bay Ave., PO Box 591, Milwaukee, WI, 53201-0591
Tel: (414) 228-1200     Fax: (414) 228-2077     www.johnsoncontrols.com
*Mfr. facility management and control systems and auto seating.*
**Johnson Controls SpA, Via Monfalcone 15, I-20132 Milan, Italy**
Tel: 39-02-280421  Fax: 39-02-28042230  Contact: Giovanni Frangi, Branch Mgr.

## THE JOHNSON CORPORATION

805 Wood Street, Three Rivers, MI, 49093

Tel: (616) 278-1715     Fax: (616) 273-2230     www.joco.com

*Mfr. rotary joints and siphon systems.*

**Johnson Corporation Italia, S.r.l.,  Torino, Italy**

## JOHNSON OUTDOORS, INC.

1326 Willow Road, Sturtevant, WI, 53177

Tel: (414) 884-1500     Fax: (414) 884-1600     www.jwa.com

*Mfr. diving, fishing, boating and camping sports equipment.*

**Scubapro Italy s.r.l.,  Via Latino 21/C, I-16039 Sestri-Levante, Italy**

Tel: 39-0185-482321   Fax: 39-0185-459122

## JUKI UNION SPECIAL CORPORATION

5 Haul Road, Wayne, NJ, 07470

Tel: (973) 633-7200     Fax: (973) 633-9629     www.unionspecial.com

*Mfr. sewing machines.*

**Union Special Italia SpA,  Via Bergamo 4, I-20020 Lainate Milan, Italy**

Tel: 39-02-937-2142   Fax: 39-02-935-70164

## KAHLE ENGINEERING COMPANY

50 South Center Street, Bldg 1, Orange, NJ, 07050

Tel: (973) 678-2020     Fax: (973) 678-0326     www.kahleengineering.com

*Mfr. automatic assembly machinery, medical/industrial products.*

**Kahle SpA,  Via Artigiani 1, I-24043 Caravaggio, Italy**

Tel: 39-363-350351   Fax: 39-363-54458

## KAYDON CORPORATION

315 E. Eisenhower Pkwy., Ste. 300, Ann Arbor, MI, 48108-3330

Tel: (734) 747-7025     Fax: (734) 747-6565     www.kaydon.com

*Design/mfr. custom engineered products: bearings, rings, seals, etc.*

**Magi S.R.L,  Milan, Italy**

Tel: 39-02-551-94708

## A.T. KEARNEY INC.

222 West Adams Street, Chicago, IL, 60606

Tel: (312) 648-0111     Fax: (312) 223-6200     www.atkearney.com

*Management consultants and executive search.*

**A. T. Kearney SpA,  Corso Venezia 34/36, I-20121 Milan, Italy**

Tel: 39-02-76-2951

## KEITHLEY INSTRUMENTS INC.

28775 Aurora Road, Cleveland, OH, 44139

Tel: (440) 248-0400     Fax: (440) 248-6168     www.keithley.com

*Mfr. electronic test/measure instruments, PC-based data acquisition hardware/software.*

**Keithley Instruments SRL,  Viale S. Gimignano 38, I-20146 Milan, Italy**

## KELLOGG BROWN & ROOT INC.

PO Box 3, Houston, TX, 77001

Tel: (713) 676-3011     Fax: (713) 676-8695     www.halliburton.com

*Engaged in technology-based engineering and construction.*

**Kellogg Brown & Root/QGPC Project Italy,  c/o Snamprogetti, Viale Aleide De Gasperi 16, San Donata, Milano 20097 Italy**

## KELLOGG COMPANY

One Kellogg Square, PO Box 3599, Battle Creek, MI, 49016-3599

Tel: (616) 961-2000     Fax: (616) 961-2871     www.kelloggs.com

*Mfr. ready-to-eat cereals and convenience foods.*

**Kellogg Italia SpA,  Attn: Italian Office, One Kellogg Square, PO Box 3599, Battle Creek MI 49016-3599**

## KELLY SERVICES, INC.

999 W. Big Beaver Road, Troy, MI, 48084

Tel: (248) 362-4444     Fax: (248) 244-4154     www.kellyservices.com

*Temporary help placement.*

**Kelly Services Italia S.R.L.,  Corso Vittorio Emanuele II 30, I-20122 Milan, Italy**

Tel: 39-02-762-351   Fax: 39-02-762-3551

## THE KENDALL COMPANY (TYCO HEALTHCARE)

15 Hampshire Street, Mansfield, MA, 02048

Tel: (508) 261-8000     Fax: (508) 261-8542     www.kendalhq,com

*Mfr. medical disposable products, home health care products and specialty adhesive products.*

**Meditec-Kendall Italia,  Via Michelli 16, I-43056 San Polo di Torrile, Italy**

Tel: 39-052-1813-488   Fax: 39-052-1813-842

## KENNAMETAL INC.

State Rte. 981, Latrobe, PA, 15650

Tel: (724) 539-5000     Fax: (724) 539-4710     www.kennametal.com

*Tools, hard carbide and tungsten alloys for metalworking industry.*

**Kennametal Ca. Me. S. S.p.A.,  I-20141 Milan, Italy**

Tel: 39-02-8951-1508   Fax: 39-02-832-1456

**Kennametal Hertel S.p.A.,  Via Corrado 11 Salico 50, I-20141 Milan, Italy**

Tel: 39-02-895961   Fax: 39-02-500672

## KERR CORPORATION

1717 West Collins Ave., Orange, CA, 92867

Tel: (714) 516-7400     Fax: (714) 516-7648     www.sybrondental.com/kerr/

*Mfr. dental supplies, jewelry mfr. supplies and equipment.*

**Kerr Italia SpA,  Casella Postale 46, Via Passanti 140, I-84018 Scafati Salerno, Italy**

## KIMBERLY-CLARK CORPORATION

351 Phelps Drive, Irving, TX, 75038

Tel: (972) 281-1200     Fax: (972) 281-1435     www.kimberly-clark.com

*Mfr./sales/distribution of consumer tissue, household and personal care products.*

**Kimberly-Clark SpA,  Villanovetta, Italy**

## KIRSCH

309 N. Prospect Street, Sturgis, MI, 49091-0370

Tel: (616) 659-5100     Fax: (616) 659-5614     www.kirsch.com

*Mfr. drapery hardware and accessories, wood shelving, woven wood shades, etc.*

**Cooper Industries Italia,  Via Roma 108, Centro Direzional Lombardo, Palazo B/1, I-20060 Cassina de Pecchi Milan, Italy**

## KOCH-GLITSCH, INC.

PO Box 8127, Wichita, KS, 67208

Tel: (316) 828-5110     Fax: (316) 828-5950     www.koch-ind.com

*Mfr./services mass transfer/chemicals separation equipment, process engineering.*

**Koch-Glitsch International SpA,  Via Tonale 50, Casella Postale 19, I-24061 Albano S. Alessandro Bergamo, Italy**

Tel: 39-035-328611   Fax: 39-035-328600   Contact: Urban Monsch, Pres.

**Koch-Glitsch, SpA,** Casella Postale 13, I-24061 Albano S. Alessandro, Italy

## KOLLMORGEN CORPORATION

1601 Trapelo Road, Waltham, MA, 02154

Tel: (781) 890-5655     Fax: (781) 890-7150     www.kollmorgen.com

*Mfr. high-performance electronic motion-control systems and design and supply advanced submarine periscopes, weapons directors, and military optics.*

**Kollmorgen Calzoni,** Bologna, Italy

## KORN/FERRY INTERNATIONAL

1800 Century Park East, Los Angeles, CA, 90067

Tel: (310) 843-4100     Fax: (310) 553-6452     www.kornferry.com

*Executive search; management consulting.*

**Korn/Ferry International,** Sala dei Longobardi 2,I-20121 Milan, Italy

Tel: 39-02-806001   Fax: 39-02-80600-500

**Korn/Ferry International,** Via Nicolo Tartaglia 11, I-00197 Rome, Italy

Tel: 39-06-80-68-7090   Fax: 39-06-807-3380

## KPMG INTERNATIONAL LLP

345 Park Avenue, New York, NY, 10022

Tel: (201) 307-7000     Fax: (201) 930-8617     www.kpmg.com

*Accounting and audit, tax and management consulting services.*

**KPMG Consulting SpA,** Via Carlo Alberto 65, I-10123 Turin, Italy

**KPMG Fides Fiduciaria SpA,** Via Ettore Petrolini 2, I-00197 Rome, Italy

**KPMG SpA,** Via Abate Gemma 30, I-70121 Bari, Italy

**KPMG SpA,** Piazza della Repubblica 15, I-60121 Ancona, Italy

Tel: 39-07-12070-374   Fax: 39-07-12070-378   Contact: Stefano Bandini, Sr. Ptnr.

**KPMG SpA,** Via Vittor Pisani 25, I-20124 Milan, Italy

Tel: 39-02-67631   Fax: 39-02-6763-2445   Contact: Giorgio Loli, Ptnr.

**KPMG SpA,** Corsa Italia 2, I-50123 Florence, Italy

**KPMG SpA,** Viale Aldo Moro 64, I-40127 Bologna, Italy

**KPMG SpA,** Piazza Castelnuovo 12, I-90141 Palermo, Italy

**KPMG SpA,** Via G. Porzio, Edif. F.10, I-80143 Centro Direzionale Napoli, Italy

**KPMG SpA,** Piazza della Vittoria 10/7, Genoa, Italy

**Studio Associato,** Corso Cavour 39, I-37121 Verona, Italy

## THE KROLL-O'GARA COMPANY

9113 Le Saint Drive, Fairfield, OH, 45014

Tel: (513) 874-2112     Fax: (513) 874-2558     www.kroll-ogara.com

*Security and consulting services and vehicles.*

**Kroll-O'Gara,** Torino Facility, P. le Principessa Clotilde 8, I-20121 Milan, Italy

Tel: 39-0172-89434   Fax: 39-0172-89434

## KULICKE & SOFFA INDUSTRIES INC.

2101 Blair Mill Road, Willow Grove, PA, 19090

Tel: (215) 784-6000     Fax: (215) 659-7588     www.kns.com

*Semiconductor assembly systems and services.*

**Electron Mec, S.r.l.,** Via Negroli 51, 20133 Milan, Italy

## KURT SALMON ASSOCIATES INC.

1355 Peachtree Street NE, Atlanta, GA, 30309

Tel: (404) 892-0321     Fax: (404) 898-9590     www.kurtsalmon.com

*Management consulting: consumer products, retailing.*

**Kurt Salmon Associates SRL,** Via Sporting Mirasole 2, Noverasco di Opera, I-20090 Milan, Italy

## LANDOR ASSOCIATES

Klamath House, 1001 Front Street, San Francisco, CA, 94111-1424

Tel: (415) 955-1400     Fax: (415) 365-3190     www.landor.com

*International marketing consulting firm, focused on developing and maintaining brand identity.*

**Landor Associates, Piazza Eleonora Duse 2, I-20122 Milan, Italy**

Tel: 39-02-7601-2601   Fax: 39-02-7601-2596   Contact: Antonio Marazza

## LANIER WORLDWIDE, INC.

2300 Parklake Drive, N.E., Atlanta, GA, 30345

Tel: (770) 496-9500     Fax: (770) 938-1020     www.lanier.com

*Specialize in digital copiers and multi-functional systems.*

**Lanier Italia S.p.A., Via E. Vittorini 129, I-00144 Rome, Italy**

Tel: 39-06-501-4304   Fax: 39-06-501-7703

**Lanier Italia S.p.A., Via Cassanese 100, I-20090 Segrate Milan, Italy**

Tel: 39-02-216-041   Fax: 39-02-216-04444

**Lanier Italia S.p.A., Via Posillipo 203-Parco Ruffo, I-80122 Napoli, Italy**

Tel: 39-08-1575-1692   Fax: 39-08-1575-1917

## LAWTER INTERNATIONAL INC.

1 Terra Way, 8601 95th St., Pleasant Prairie, WI, 53158

Tel: (262) 947-7300     Fax: (262) 947-7328     www.lawter.com

*Resins, pigments and coatings.*

**Lawter International, Via A. Volta n 13, 20050 Mezzago (MI), Italy**

Tel: 39-039-602-0760   Fax: 39-039-602-0691

## LEAR CORPORATION

21557 Telegraph Road, Southfield, MI, 48086-5008

Tel: (248) 746-1500     Fax: (248) 746-1722     www.lear.com

*Mfr. and distribute automotive materials and car seats.*

**Lear Corporation, Torino, Italy**

## LEARONAL INC.

272 Buffalo Ave., Freeport, NY, 11520

Tel: (516) 868-8800     Fax: (516) 868-8824     www.learonal.com

*Specialty chemicals for the printed circuit board, semiconductor, connector and metal finishing industries.*

**Elga Ronal S.r.l., Via della Merlata 8, I-20014 Nerviano, Milan, Italy**

Tel: 39-0331-586947   Fax: 39-0331-580004   Contact: Calro Favini, Pres.

## LECROY CORPORATION

700 Chestnut Ridge Road, Chestnut Ridge, NY, 10977

Tel: (845) 425-2000     Fax: (845) 425-8967     www.lecroy.com

*Mfr. signal analyzers and electronic measurement systems.*

**LeCroy S.A., Centro Direzionale, Valecenter Office Via E Mattei, 1/102 I-30020 Marcon Venice, Italy**

## LEHMAN BROTHERS HOLDINGS INC.

Three World Financial Center, New York, NY, 10285

Tel: (212) 526-7000     Fax: (212) 526-3738     www.lehman.com

*Financial services, securities and merchant banking services.*

**Lehman Brothers, Piazza Del Carmine 4, I-20121 Milan, Italy**

Tel: 39-02-721581

## LEVI STRAUSS & COMPANY

1155 Battery St., San Francisco, CA, 94111-1230

Tel: (415) 544-6000     Fax: (415) 501-3939      www.levistrauss.com

*Mfr./distributor casual wearing apparel.*

**Levi Strauss Italia SpA, Corso Como Nr. 15, I-20154 Milan, Italy**

Tel: 39-02-290231   Fax: 39-02-290-3681

## LIFE TECHNOLOGIES INC.

9800 Medical Center Drive, Rockville, MD, 20850

Tel: (301) 840-8000     Fax: (301) 329-8635      www.lifetech.com

*Produces biotechnology research materials.*

**Life Technologies Italia SRL, Via Tolstoj 86 (I piano scala H), San Giuliano Milan (MI) 20098, Italy**

## ELI LILLY & COMPANY

Lilly Corporate Center, Indianapolis, IN, 46285

Tel: (317) 276-2000     Fax: (317) 277-6579      www.lilly.com

*Mfr. pharmaceuticals and animal health products.*

**Eli Lilly Italia SpA, Via Gramsci 731-733, Sesto Fiorentino, I-50019 Florence, Italy**

Tel: 39-055-42571   Fax: 39-055-4257-707

## LINCOLN ELECTRIC HOLDINGS

22801 St. Clair Ave., Cleveland, OH, 44117-1199

Tel: (216) 481-8100     Fax: (216) 486-8385      www.lincolnelectric.com

*Mfr. arc welding and welding related products, oxy-fuel and thermal cutting equipment and integral AC motors.*

**Lincoln Electric - EWS, Via Degh Artigram, I-17015 Celle Ligure Genoa, Italy**

Tel: 39-010-998981   Fax: 39-019-9910978    Contact: Giovanni Pedrazzo, Mng. Dir.

**Lincoln Electric - Sacit, Via Carlo Torre 23/27, I-20143 Milan, Italy**

Tel: 39-02-832-3741   Fax: 39-02-832-2688    Contact: Roberto Tavecchio, Mng. Dir.

**Lincoln Electric Italia SRL, Via Gelasio Adamoli 239 b/c, I-16141 Genoa, Italy**

Tel: 39-010-835-5507   Fax: 39-010-835-5050    Contact: Giovanni Pedrazzo, Mng. Dir.

## ARTHUR D. LITTLE, INC.

25 Acorn Park, Cambridge, MA, 02140-2390

Tel: (617) 498-5000     Fax: (617) 498-7200      www.adlittle.com

*Management, environmental, health and safety consulting; technical and product development.*

**Arthur D. Little International, Inc., Via Serbelloni 4, I-20122 Milan, Italy**

Tel: 39-02-7601-5046   Fax: 39-02-783-022

**Arthur D. Little International, Inc., Via Piave 7, I-00187 Rome, Italy**

Tel: 39-06-482-4606   Fax: 39-06-482-4623

## LITTON INDUSTRIES INC.

21240 Burbank Boulevard, Woodland Hills, CA, 91367

Tel: (818) 598-5000     Fax: (818) 598-3313      www.littoncorp.com

*Shipbuilding, electronics, and information technology.*

**Litton Italia S.p.A., Via Pontina km 27.800, 00040 Pomezia (Rome), Italy**

Tel: 39-06-911-921

**VEAM, Via Statuto 2, I-20020 Arese Milan, Italy**

## LOCKHEED MARTIN CORPORATION

6801 Rockledge Drive, Bethesda, MD, 20817

Tel: (301) 897-6000     Fax: (301) 897-6652      www.imco.com

*Design/mfr./management systems in fields of space, defense, energy, electronics and technical services.*

**CalComp S.p.A., Via del Tulipani 5, I-20090 Pieve Emanuele Milan, Italy**

Tel: 39-02-907-81519   Fax: 39-02-268-62616

**CalComp S.p.A., Via Thailandia, I-00144 Rome, Italy**

Tel: 39-06-591-4402    Fax: 39-06-591-2768

**CalComp S.p.A., Viale Masini 20, I-40126 Bologna, Italy**

Tel: 39-051-352-540    Fax: 39-051-369-711

**Lockheed Martin Intl., Via Fillungo 107, I-55100 Lucca, Italy**

## LOCTITE CORPORATION

1001 Trout Brook Crossing, Rocky Hill, CT, 06067-3910

Tel: (860) 571-5100        Fax: (860) 571-5465        www.loctite.com

*Mfr./sale industrial adhesives, sealants and coatings..*

**Loctite FAS SpA, Via Vigevano 27, I-28065 Cerano, Italy**

**Loctite Italia S.p.A., Via Talete 56, I-20047 Brugherio Milan, Italy**

Tel: 39-039-21251    Fax: 39-039-884672

## LORAL SPACE & COMMUNICATIONS LTD.

600 Third Ave., New York, NY, 10016

Tel: (212) 697-1105        Fax: (212) 338-5662        www.loral.com

*Marketing coordination: defense electronics, communications systems.*

**Loral CyberStar, Via Conservatorio 22, 20122 Milan, Italy**

Tel: 39-02-77-29293

## LOWE LINTAS & PARTNERS WORLDWIDE

One Dag Hammarskjold Plaza, New York, NY, 10017

Tel: (212) 605-8000        Fax: (212) 605-4705        www.interpublic.com

*Full-service, integrated marketing communications company/advertising agency.*

**Ammirati Puris Lintas Milan, Via Pantano 26, I-20122 Milan, Italy**

Tel: 39-01-85-721    Fax: 39-01--87-8778    Contact: Valeria Monti

## LSB INDUSTRIES INC.

16 S. Pennsylvania Ave., Oklahoma City, OK, 73107

Tel: (405) 235-4546        Fax: (405) 235-5067        www.lsbindustries.com

*Mfr. acids, agricultural and industrial chemicals.*

**LSB Europe Ltd., Via Vittor Pisani 14, I-20124 Milan, Italy**

Tel: 39-02-6698-4785    Fax: 39-02-6698-2082

## LSI LOGIC CORPORATION

1551 McCarthy Blvd, Milpitas, CA, 95035

Tel: (408) 433-8000        Fax: (408) 954-3220        www.lsilogic.com

*Develop/mfr. semiconductors.*

**LSI Logic S.p.A., Centro Direzionale Colleoni Palazzo Orione, Ingresso 1, I-20041 Agrate Brianza Milan, Italy**

Tel: 39-039-687371    Fax: 39-039-605-7867

## LTX CORPORATION

LTX Park, University Ave., Westwood, MA, 02090

Tel: (617) 461-1000        Fax: (617) 326-4883        www.ltx.com

*Design/mfr. computer-controlled semiconductor test systems.*

**LTX (Italia) SRL, Centro Colleoni, Palazzo Cassiopea-Scala 1, Italy**

Tel: 39-605-8080    Fax: 39-605-6416

## THE LUBRIZOL CORPORATION

29400 Lakeland Blvd., Wickliffe, OH, 44092-2298

Tel: (440) 943-4200    Fax: (440) 943-5337    www.lubrizol.com

*Mfr. chemicals additives for lubricants and fuels.*

**Lubrizol Italiana SpA, Milan, Italy**

Tel: 39-02-269761

## LUCENT TECHNOLOGIES, INC.

600 Mountain Ave., Murray Hill, NJ, 07974-0636

Tel: (908) 582-3000    Fax: (908) 582-2576    www.lucent.com

*Design/mfr. wide range of public and private networks, communication systems and software, data networking systems, business telephone systems and microelectronics components.*

**Lucent Technologies Italia S.p.A., 866 Via Aurelia, 00165 Rome, Italy**

Tel: 39-06-664961

**Lucent Technologies Italia S.p.A., 56 Via Tucidide - Torre 2, 20134 Milan, Italy**

Tel: 39-02-754-1161

**Lucent Technologies Italia S.p.A., Viale Fulvio Testi 117, 20092 Cinisell Balsamo, Italy**

Tel: 39-02-660-8131    Fax: 39-02-612-7005

**Lucent Technologies Italia S.p.A., 38 Via Nazario Sauro, 20099 Sesto S. Giovanno, Milan, Italy**

Tel: 39-02-262931

## LYONDELL

3801 West Chester Pike, Newtown Square, PA, 19073-2387

Tel: (610) 359-2000    Fax: (610) 359-2722    www.arcochem.com

*Mfr. propylene oxide, a chemical used for flexible foam products, coatings/paints and solvents/inks.*

**ARCO Chemical Europe Inc., Via Torino, 2, I-20123 Milan, Italy**

Tel: 39-02-7254-6611    Fax: 39-02-7254-6421

## M/A-COM INC.

1011 Pawtucket Boulevard, Lowell, MA, 01853-3295

Tel: (978) 442-5000    Fax: (978) 442-5354    www.macom.com

*Mfr. electronic components, semiconductor devices and communications equipment.*

**M/A-COM, Centro Direzionale Colleoni, Palazzo Taurus - Scala 2, Viale Colleoni N. 3, 20041 Agrate Brianza, Milan Italy**

Tel: 39-039-6091436    Fax: 39-039-6091502

**M/A-COM, Via Dei Luxardo 37, 00156 Rome, Italy**

Tel: 39-06-412-10242    Fax: 39-06-412-10227

## MacDERMID INC.

245 Freight Street, Waterbury, CT, 06702-0671

Tel: (203) 575-5700    Fax: (203) 575-7900    www.macdermid.com

*Chemicals processing for metal industrial, plastics, electronics cleaners, strippers.*

**MacDermid Italiana SRL, Via. A. Machieraldo 21, I-13042 Cavaglia Vercelli, Italy**

Tel: 39-01-61-966721    Fax: 39-0161-966740

## R.H. MACY & COMPANY INC.

151 West 34th Street, New York, NY, 10001

Tel: (212) 695-4400    Fax: (212) 643-1307    www.macys.com

*Department stores; importers.*

**R.H. Macy & Co. Intl., Piazza Independenza 21, I-50129 Florence, Italy**

## MAGNETEK

26 Century Blvd., Ste. 600, Nashville, TN, 37214
Tel: (615) 316-5100    Fax: (615) 316-5181    www.magnetek.com
*Mfr. fractional horsepower electric motors.*
**MagneTek Power, Valdarno, Italy**

## MAGNETROL INTERNATIONAL

5300 Belmont Road, Downers Grove, IL, 60515-4499
Tel: (630) 969-4000    Fax: (630) 969-9489    www.magnetrol.com
*Mfr. level and flow instrumentation.*
**Magnetrol International, Via Arese 12, I-20159 Milan, Italy**
Tel: 39-02-607-2298   Fax: 39-02-27001960   Contact: Carlo Mariani, Sales Mgr.

## MALLINCKRODT INC.

675 McDonnell Blvd., St. Louis, MO, 63134
Tel: (314) 654-2000    Fax: (314) 654-5380    www.mallinckrodt.com
*Distributes health care products and specialty pharmaceuticals.*
**Mallinckrodt Italia SRL, Via Edison 6, 20090 Assago, Milan Italy**
Tel: 39-02-4577161   Fax: 39-02-45706239
**Mallinckrodt Italia SRL, Via Galvani 22, 41037 Mirandola, Italy**
Tel: 39-05-35617711   Fax: 39-053526442

## MANPOWER INTERNATIONAL INC.

5301 N. Ironwood Rd., PO Box 2053, Milwaukee, WI, 53201-2053
Tel: (414) 961-1000    Fax: (414) 961-7081    www.manpower.com
*Temporary help, contract service, training and testing.*
**Manpower Italia SRL, Via Baracchini 9, I-20123 Milan, Italy**
Tel: 39-02-7200-1663   Fax: 39-02-7200-1666

## MARK IV INDUSTRIES INC.

501 John James Audubon Pkwy., PO Box 810, Amherst, NY, 14226-0810
Tel: (716) 689-4972    Fax: (716) 689-1529    www.mark-iv.com
*Mfr. of engineered systems and components utilizing mechanical and fluid power transmission, fluid transfer, and power systems and components.*
**Dayco Europe SpA, Strade Cebrosa 70, I-10036 Settimo Torinese, Italy**
Tel: 39-011-816-2311
**Dayco Europe SpA, Via Torino, 71, 1-10060 Airasca, Italy**
Tel: 39-011-986-861   Fax: 39-011-986-8723

## MARKEM CORPORATION

150 Congress Street, Keene, NH, 03431
Tel: (603) 352-1130    Fax: (603) 357-1835    www.markem.com.
*Mfr./sales of industrial marking, print machinery and hot stamping foils.*
**Markem SRL, Frazione, Venina 7, I-20090 Assago Milan, Italy**
Tel: 39-02-892-2041   Fax: 39-02-895-1159

## MARLEY COOLING TOWER COMPANY

7401 West 129th Street, Overland Park, KS, 66213
Tel: (913) 664-7400    Fax: (913) 664-7641    www.marleyct.com
*Cooling and heating towers and waste treatment systems.*
**SPIG International S.P.A., Piazza San Graziano 2, I-28041 Arona, Italy**
Tel: 39-0322-233456   Fax: 39-0322-233458

## MARSH & McLENNAN COS INC.

1166 Ave. of the Americas, New York, NY, 10036-2774

Tel: (212) 345-5000      Fax: (212) 345-4808      www.marshmac.com

*Insurance agents/brokers, pension and investment management consulting services.*

**J&H Marsh & McLennan Italia & Co. SpA, Viale della Liberazione 18, I-20124 Milan, Italy**

Tel: 39-02-669-9981  Fax: 39-02-669-6333   Contact: Irelio Offman

**J&H Marsh & McLennan Italia & Co. SpA, Via Del Porto 1, I-40122 Bologna, Italy**

Tel: 39-051-124-9900  Fax: 39-051-124-8657   Contact: Maurizio Vaghi

**J&H Marsh & McLennan Italia & Co. SpA, Piazza G. Marconi 25, I-00144 Rome, Italy**

Tel: 39-06-654-5161   Fax: 39-06-591-9718   Contact: Vincenzo Albini

**J&H Marsh & McLennan Italia & Co. SpA, Via Turazza 30, I-35128 Padova, Italy**

Tel: 39-049-828-5411  Fax: 39-049-828-5430   Contact: Loris Fasolato

**J&H Marsh & McLennan Italia & Co. SpA, Via Cavour1, I-10123 Torino, Italy**

Tel: 39-011-156-5471  Fax: 39-011-154-2215   Contact: Emanuele Cordero di Vonzo

## MASCO CORPORATION

21001 Van Born Road, Taylor, MI, 48180

Tel: (313) 274-7400      Fax: (313) 374-6666      www.masco.com

*Mfr. faucets, cabinets, locks and numerous home improvement, building and home furnishings products.*

**Keoma SRL, Z.I. Sant' Andrea, I-34170 Gorizia, Italy**

**Rubinetterie Mariani SpA, Via Berlino 2/4, I-24040 Zingonia Bergamo, Italy**

**S.T.S.R. (Studio Tecnico Sviluppoe Ricerche), Via Delli Artigianato N. 3, I-20084 Lacchiarella Milan, Italy**

Tel: 39-02-9007-6832

## MATTEL INC.

333 Continental Blvd., El Segundo, CA, 90245-5012

Tel: (310) 252-2000      Fax: (310) 252-2179      www.mattelmedia.com

*Mfr. toys, dolls, games, crafts and hobbies.*

**Fisher-Price SRL, Via Cassanese 224, I-20090 Segrate, Italy**

**Mattel Mfg. Europe SRL, Via Vittorio Veneto 119, I-28040 Oleggio Castello Piemonte, Italy**

## GEORGE S. MAY INTERNATIONAL COMPANY

303 S Northwest Hwy., Park Ridge, IL, 60068-4255

Tel: (847) 825-8806      Fax: (847) 825-7937      www.georgesmay.com

*Engaged in management consulting.*

**George S. May International, Centro Direzionale Colleoni, Palazzo Orio 1, I-20041 Agrate Brianza Milan, Italy**

Contact: Daniel Hostetler, Mng. Dir.

## McCANN-ERICKSON WORLDGROUP

750 Third Ave., New York, NY, 10017

Tel: (212) 984-3644      Fax: (212) 984-2629      www.mccann.com

*International advertising and marketing services.*

**McCann-Erickson Italiana SpA, La Ferratella, Via Elio Vittorini 129, I-00144 Rome, Italy**

**McCann-Erickson Italiana SpA, Via Meravegli 2, I-20123 Milan, Italy**

**Universal McCann SRL, Via Bassano Parrone 6, I-20123 Milan, Italy**

## McDONALD'S CORPORATION

McDonald's Plaza, Oak Brook, IL, 60523

Tel: (630) 623-3000      Fax: (630) 623-7409      www.mcdonalds.com

*Fast food chain stores.*

**McDonald's Corp., Milan, Italy**

## THE McGRAW-HILL COMPANIES

1221 Ave. of the Americas, New York, NY, 10020

Tel: (212) 512-2000     Fax: (212) 512-2703     www.mccgraw-hill.com

*Books, magazines, information systems, financial service, publishing and broadcast operations.*

**McGraw-Hill Libri Italia, s.r.l., Piazza Emila 5, 1-20129 Milan, Italy**

## McKINSEY & COMPANY

55 East 52nd Street, New York, NY, 10022

Tel: (212) 446-7000     Fax: (212) 446-8575     www.mckinsey.com

*Management and business consulting services.*

**McKinsey & Company, Piazza del Duomo 31, I-20122 Milan, Italy**
Tel: 39-02-724-061   Fax: 39-02-7200-1440

**McKinsey & Company, Viale Liegi 44, I-00198 Rome, Italy**
Tel: 39-06-85-7981   Fax: 39-06-841-5287

## MCS SOFTWARE CORPORATION

815 Colorado Blvd., Los Angeles, CA, 90041

Tel: (323) 258-9111     Fax: (323) 259-3838     www.macsch.com

*Develop finite element analysis software used in the field of computer-aided engineering.*

**MacNeal-Schwendler Co. (Italia) SRL, Via Confienza 15, I-10121 Turin, Italy**

**MacNeal-Schwendler Srl, Viale America 93, I-00144 Rome, Italy**

**PDA Engineering Srl, Via Confienza 15, I-10121 Turin, Italy**

## MEAD CORPORATION

Courthouse Plaza, NE, Dayton, OH, 45463

Tel: (937) 495-6323     Fax: (937) 461-2424     www.mead.com

*Mfr. paper, packaging, pulp, lumber and other wood products, school and office products; electronic publishing and distribution.*

**Avio Cart SpA, Via G. Galilei 91C, I-20090 Assago Milan, Italy**
Tel: 39-02-475-7171   Fax: 39-02-457-7222   Contact: E. de'Dorato, Gen. Mgr.

## MECHANICAL DYNAMICS, INC.

2301 Commonwealth Blvd., Ann Arbor, MI, 48105

Tel: (734) 994-3800     Fax: (734) 994-6418     www.adams.com

*Mfr. Adams prototyping software to automotive industry.*

**Mechanical Dynamics Italy Srl, 98 via Palladio, I-33010 Tavagnacco, Italy**
Tel: 390-432-573942

**Mechanical Dynamics Italy Srl, 25/4 via Onorato Vigliani, 10137 Torino, Italy**
Tel: 390-11-316-1412

## MEDICUS GROUP INTERNATIONAL

1675 Broadway, New York, NY, 10019

Tel: (212) 468-3100     Fax: (212) 468-3222     www.medicusgroup.com

*Healthcare communications company engaged in professional advertising, sales promotion, global branding and launch planning.*

**Medicus Intercon S.r.L., Via Correggio 18, 20149 Milan, Italy**
Tel: 39-02-480-611   Contact: Mario Ammirati

**Medicus Intercon S.r.L., Viale di Val Fiorita 88, 00144 Rome, Italy**
Tel: 39-02-480-611   Contact: Mario Ammirati

## MEDTRONIC INC.

7000 Central Ave., NE, Minneapolis, MN, 55432

Tel: (612) 574-4000     Fax: (612) 574-4879     www.medtronic.com

*Mfr./sale/service electrotherapeutic medical devices.*

**Medtronic Italia SpA, Piazza Duca d'Aosta 12, I-20124 Milan, Italy**

## MEMC ELECTRONIC MATERIALS, INC.

501 Pearl Drive, St. Peters, MO, 63376

Tel: (636) 474-5500     Fax: (636) 474-5161     www.memc.com

*Mfg. and distribution of silicon wafers.*

**MEMC Electronic Materials, SpA, Via Nazionale 59, I-39012 Merano Bolzano, Italy**

Tel: 39-0472-333-333   Fax: 39-0473-333-270

**MEMC Electronic Materials, SpA, Viale Gherzi 31, I-28100 Novara, Italy**

Tel: 39-0321-334-444   Fax: 39-0321-691-000

## MERCK & COMPANY, INC.

One Merck Drive, PO Box 100, Whitehouse Station, NJ, 08889-0100

Tel: (908) 423-1000     Fax: (908) 423-2592     www.merck.com

*Pharmaceuticals, chemicals and biologicals.*

**Merck, Sharp & Dohme Italia SpA, Via G. Fabbroni 6, I-00191 Rome, Italy**

## MERIDIAN DIAGNOSTICS INC.

3471 River Hills Drive, Cincinnati, OH, 45244

Tel: (513) 271-3700     Fax: (513) 271-3762     www.meridiandiagnostics.com

*Develops, manufactures and markets a broad range of disposable diagnostic test kits and related diagnostic products used for the rapid diagnosis of infectious diseases*

**Meridian Diagnostics Europe SRL, Milan, Italy**

Tel: 39-0331-433-636   Contact: Antonio Interno

## MERITOR AUTOMOTIVE, INC.

2135 West Maple Road, Troy, MI, 48084-7186

Tel: (248) 435-1000     Fax: (248) 435-1393     www.meritorauto.com

*Mfr./sales of light and heavy vehicle systems for trucks, cars and specialty vehicles.*

**Meritor Light Vehicle Systems, Avellino S.r.l., Avellino, Italy**

## MERRILL LYNCH & COMPANY, INC.

World Financial Center, 250 Vesey Street, New York, NY, 10281-1332

Tel: (212) 449-1000     Fax: (212) 449-2892     www.ml.com

*Security brokers and dealers, investment and business services.*

**Merrill Lynch International Bank, Lago Fontanella di Borghese 19, I-00186 Rome, Italy**

Tel: 39-06-683-931   Fax: 39-06-683-93231

**Merrill Lynch International Bank, Via Manzoni 31, I-20121 Milan, Italy**

Tel: 39-02-290-02663   Fax: 39-02-290-00384

## M-I

PO Box 48242, Houston, TX, 77242-2842

Tel: (713) 739-0222     Fax: (713) 308-9503     www.midf.com

*Drilling fluids.*

**M-I Italliana, S.p.A., Viale Famagosta 75, 20142 Milan, Italy**

Tel: 39-02-89515401   Fax: 39-02-89516993

## MICRO TOUCH SYSTEMS, INC.

300 Griffin Brook Park Drive, Methuen, MA, 01844

Tel: (978) 659-9000     Fax: (978) 659-9100     www.microtouch.com

*Mfr. clear coatings for computer monitors.*

**MicroTouch Systems Srl, C.so Milano 19, 20052 Monza (MI), Italy**

Tel: 39-39-230-2230

## MICROCHIP TECHNOLOGY INCORPORATED

2355 West Chandler Boulevard, Chandler, AZ, 85224

Tel: (602) 786-7200     Fax: (602) 899-9210     www.microchip.com

*Mfr. electronic subassemblies and components.*

**Arizona Microchip Technology SRL, Centro Direzionale Colleoni, Palazzo Tauru 1, I-20041 Agrate Brianza Milan, Italy**

Tel: 39-039-689-9939    Fax: 39-039-689-9883

## MICROMERITICS INSTRUMENT CORPORATION

One Micromeritics Drive, Norcross, GA, 30093-1877

Tel: (770) 662-3620     Fax: (770) 662-3696     www.micromeritics.com

*Mfr. analytical instruments.*

**Micromeritics SRL, Via W. Tibagi 26/7, I-20068 Peschiera Borromeo Milan, Italy**

Tel: 39-2-553-02833

## MICRON TECHNOLOGY, INC. (MTI)

8000 S. Federal Way, Boise, ID, 83707-0006

Tel: (208) 368-4000     Fax: (208) 368-4435     www.micron.com

*Mfr. random-access memory chips and semi-conductor memory components.*

**Micron Technology Italy, S.R.L., Via Antonia Pacinotti 5/7, Nuclco Industrial (AQ) Building #2, 67051 Avezzano (AQ), Italy**

Tel: 39-0863-4231

## MICROSOFT CORPORATION

One Microsoft Way, Redmond, WA, 98052-6399

Tel: (425) 882-8080     Fax: (425) 936-7329     www.microsoft.com

*Computer software, peripherals and services.*

**Microsoft Italy SpA, Centro Direzionale San Felice, Via Rivoltana 13m Palazzo A, I-20090 Segrate Milan, Italy**

Tel: 39-02-703921    Fax: 39-02-703-92020

## MILACRON INC.

2090 Florence Ave., Cincinnati, OH, 45206

Tel: (513) 487-5000     Fax: (513) 487-5057     www.milacron.com

*Metalworking and plastics technologies.*

**Gallazzi Macchine S.r.l., Via Tonso, 100I-15100 Alessandria, Italy**

Tel: 39-131-265433    Fax: 39-131-68101    Contact: Dr. Ricardo Gallazzi

## MILLER ELECTRIC MFG. COMPANY

PO Box 1079, 1636 W. Spencer, Appleton, WI, 54912-1079

Tel: (920) 734-9821     Fax: (920) 735-4125     www.millerwelds.com

*Mfr. arc welding machines.*

**ITW Welding Products, Via Prato 6, 24030 Caprino (BG), Italy**

Tel: 39-035-788-132    Fax: 39-035-788-082

## MILTON ROY COMPANY

201 Ivyland Road, Ivylan, PA, 18974

Tel: (215) 441-0800     Fax: (215) 293-0468     www.miltonroy.com

*Mfr. medical and industry equipment and process control instruments.*

**Milton Roy Italia, Via Paraceiso 16 Ing., 1 Palazzo Andromeda, 20041 Agrate Brianza Milan, Italy**

Tel: 39-39-60-56-891    Fax: 39-39-60-56-906    Contact: Enrico Andreoli

## MINE SAFETY APPLIANCES COMPANY

121 Gamma Drive, PO Box 426, Pittsburgh, PA, 15230

Tel: (412) 967-3000      Fax: (412) 967-3452      www.msa.net

*Safety equipment, industry filters.*

**MSA Italiana SpA, Caselle Postale 1719, I-20101 Milan, Italy**

## MINTEQ INTERNATIONAL INC.

405 Lexington Ave., 19th Fl., New York, NY, 10174-1901

Tel: (212) 878-1800      Fax: (212) 878-1952      www.mineralstech.com

*Mfr./market specialty refractory and metallurgical products and application systems.*

**MINTEQ Italiana S.p.A., Via Creta 8, I-25124 Brescia, Italy**

Tel: 39-030-24-566-1    Fax: 39-030-24-555-20    Contact: D. Rosenberg, Pres.,G. Felchilcher, Mgr.    Emp: 18

## MODINE MANUFACTURING COMPANY

1500 DeKoven Ave., Racine, WI, 53403

Tel: (262) 636-1200      Fax: (262) 636-1424      www.modine.com

*Mfr. heat-transfer products.*

**Modine Manufacturing Co., Milan, Italy**

## MOLEX INC.

2222 Wellington Court, Lisle, IL, 60532

Tel: (630) 969-4550      Fax: (630) 969-1352      www.molex.com

*Mfr. electronic, electrical and fiber optic interconnection products and systems, switches, application tooling.*

**Molex Inc., Centro Direzionale Lombardo, Palazzo CD1, Rome 108-20060 Italy**

## MONSANTO SEED CORP.

3100 Sycamore Road, DeKalb, IL, 60115-9600

Tel: (815) 758-3461      Fax: (815) 758-3711      www.dekalb.com

*Develop/produce hybrid corn, sorghum, sunflower seed, varietal soybeans, alfalfa.*

**DeKalb Italiana SpA, Corso del Popolo 58, I-30172 Venice, Italy**

**Deris SRL, Via Toscanini 40, I-30016 Jesolo, Italy**

## MOODY'S INVESTOR SERVICES, INC.

99 Church St., New York, NY, 10007

Tel: (212) 553-1658      Fax: (212) 553-0462      www.moodys.com

*Publishes credit ratings*

**Moody's Italia S.r.l., Via Monte di Pieta 21, 20121 Milan, Italy**

Tel: 39-02-86-337-470

## MOOG INC.

Jamison Road, East Aurora, NY, 14052-0018

Tel: (716) 652-2000      Fax: (716) 687-4471      www.moog.com

*Mfr. precision control components and systems.*

**Moog Italiana SRL, Via dei Tre Corsi, Zona Industriale Sud-D1, I-21046 Malnate, Italy**

**Moog Microset Srl, Via GB Cacciamali 71, 25125 Brescia, Italy**

## J. P. MORGAN CHASE & CO. INC.

World Headquarters, 270 Park Ave., New York, NY, 10017

Tel: (212) 270-6000      Fax: (212) 622-9030      www.jpmorganchase.com

*Provides integrated financial solutions for institutions and individuals worldwide, including asset management, investment banking and commercial banking.*

**J. P. Morgan Chase & Co., Via Catena 4, I-20121 Milan, Italy**

Tel: 39-02-8895-1    Fax: 39-02-8895-2218

**J. P. Morgan Chase & Co.,  Viale Bertoloni 26B, I-00197 Rome, Italy**
Tel: 39-06-808-5655   Fax: 39-06-808-8766

**J. P. Morgan Chase & Co.,  Piazzale Accursio 18, I-20156 Milan, Italy**

**J. P. Morgan Chase & Co.,  Piazza Meda 1, I-20121 Milan, Italy**

**J. P. Morgan Chase & Co.,  Via Catena 4, I-20121 Milan, Italy**

## MORGAN STANLEY DEAN WITTER & CO.

1585 Broadway, New York, NY, 10036
Tel:  (212) 761-4000      Fax:  (212) 761-0086      www.msdw.com
*Securities and commodities brokerage, investment banking, money management, personal trusts.*

**Banca Morgan Stanley S.p.A.,  Corso Venezia 16, I-20121 Milan, Italy**
Contact: Carlo Pagliani

## MOTION PICTURE ASSN. OF AMERICA

1600 Eye Street, NW, Washington, DC, 20006
Tel:  (202) 293-1966      Fax:  (202) 293-7674      www.mpaa.org
*Motion picture trade association.*

**Motion Picture Export Assn. of Rome,  Via del Tritone 61, Scala D Int. 12, I-00187 Rome, Italy**
Tel: 39-06-679-8842   Fax: 39-06-678-8834   Contact: Marc M. Spiegel

## MOTOROLA, INC.

1303 East Algonquin Road, Schaumburg, IL, 60196
Tel:  (847) 576-5000      Fax:  (847) 538-5191      www.motorola.com
*Mfr. communications equipment, semiconductors and cellular phones.*

**Motorola SpA,  Centro Milanofiori Stabile C-2, I-20090 Assago Milan, Italy**
Tel: 39-02-82-20-329   Fax: 39-02-82-20350

## MTS SYSTEMS CORPORATION

1400 Technology Drive, Eden Prairie, MN, 55344-2290
Tel:  (612) 937-4000      Fax:  (612) 937-4515      www.mts.com
*Develop/mfr. mechanical testing and simulation products and services, industry measure and automation instrumentation.*

**MTS Systems SRL,  Via Tirreno 151, I-10136 Turin, Italy**

## NALCO CHEMICAL COMPANY

One Nalco Center, Naperville, IL, 60563-1198
Tel:  (630) 305-1000      Fax:  (630) 305-2900      www.nalco.com
*Chemicals for water and waste water treatment, oil products and refining, industry processes; water and energy management service.*

**Nalco Diversified Technologies,  Via G. de Notaris 51.5, I-20128 Milan, Italy**
Tel: 39-01-158-0322   Fax: 39-01-158-0322

**Nalco Italiana SpA,  Viale dell Esperanto 71, I-00144 Rome, Italy**
Tel: 39-06-542-971   Fax: 39-06-542-97300

## NATIONAL GYPSUM COMPANY

2001 Rexford Road, Charlotte, NC, 28211
Tel:  (704) 365-7300      Fax:  (704) 365-7276      www.national-gypsum.com
*Mfr. building products and services.*

**Austin Italia SpA,  Milan, Italy**

## NATIONAL MACHINERY COMPANY

161 Greenfield St., Tiffin, OH, 44883-2471
Tel:  (419) 447-5211      Fax:  (419) 447-5299      www.nationalmachinery.com
*Mfr. high-speed metal parts forming machines.*

**National Machinery Company,  Bolzano, Italy**
Tel: 34-93-301-9510

## NATIONAL SERVICE INDUSTRIES INC.

1420 Peachtree Street NE, Atlanta, GA, 30309

Tel: (404) 853-1000        Fax: (404) 853-1211        www.nationalservice.com

*Mfr. lighting equipment, specialty chemicals; textile rental.*

**Zep Europe,  Rome, Italy**

## NATIONAL STARCH AND CHEMICAL COMPANY

10 Finderne Ave., Bridgewater, NJ, 08807-3300

Tel: (908) 685-5000        Fax: (908) 685-5005        www.nationalstarch.com

*Mfr. adhesives and sealants, resins and specialty chemicals, electronic materials and adhesives, food products, industry starch.*

**National Starch & Chemical SpA,  Via Roma 29, Mezzago Milan, Italy**

Tel: 39-039-60921    Fax: 39-039-3092201

## NCR (NATIONAL CASH REGISTER)

1700 South Patterson Blvd., Dayton, OH, 45479

Tel: (937) 445-5000        Fax: (937) 445-7042        www.ncr.com

*Mfr. automated teller machines and high-performance stationary bar code scanners.*

**NCR Milan,  Viale Cassala, 150/4, I-20153 Milan, Italy**

Tel: 39-01-479-04448    Fax: 39-01-479-04011    Contact: Carmelo Leornadis, VP

## NEAC COMPRESSOR SERVICE USA, INC.

191 Howard Street, Franklin, PA, 16323

Tel: (814) 437-3711        Fax: (814) 432-3334        www.neacusa.com

*Mfr. air tools and equipment.*

**Chicago Pneumatic Tool SpA,  Via Bisceglie 91/7, I-20152 Milan, Italy**

## NETMANAGE, INC.

10725 N. De Anza Blvd., Cupertino, CA, 95014

Tel: (408) 973-7171        Fax: (408) 257-6405        www.netmanage.com

*Develop/mfr. computer software applications and tools.*

**NetManage Italia,  Via Washington 88, I-20146 Milan, Italy**

Tel: 39-02-4771-9224    Fax: 39-02-4771-1363

## NETSCAPE COMMUNICATIONS

501 East Middlefield Road, Mountain View, CA, 94043

Tel: (650) 254-1900        Fax: (650) 528-4124        www.netscape.com

*Mfr./distribute Internet-based commercial and consumer software applications.*

**Netscape Communications Italia, SRL,  Corso Monforte 54, I-20122 Milan, Italy**

Tel: 39-02-77-39-95-16    Fax: 39-02-77-39-94-00

## NETWORK ASSOCIATES, INC.

3965 Freedom Circle, Santa Clara, CA, 95054

Tel: (408) 988-3832        Fax: (408) 970-9727        www.networkassociates.com

*Designs and produces network security and network management software and hardware.*

**Network Associates Italia S.r.l.,  Centro Direzionale Summit, Via Brescia 28 Palazzo D/1, Cernusco sul Naviglio Milan D-20063, Italy**

Tel: 39-02-926-501

## THE NEW YORK TIMES COMPANY

229 West 43rd Street, New York, NY, 10036-3959

Tel: (212) 556-1234        Fax: (212) 556-7389        www.nytimes.com

*Diversified media company including newspapers, magazines, television and radio stations, and electronic information and publishing.*

**International Herald Tribune (IHT),  Via Mecenate 91, Milan 20138, Italy**

Tel: 39-25095-6545

The New York Times Rome Bureau SRL, Corso Victorio Emanuel 2,154, I-00186 Rome, Italy

## NEWELL RUBBERMAID

29 East Stephenson Street, Freeport, IL, 61032-0943

Tel: (815) 235-4171     Fax: (815) 489-8212     www.newellco.com

*Mfr. hardware, housewares, and office products.*

**The Newell Company, Milan, Italy**

## NEWPORT CORPORATION

1791 Deere Ave., PO Box 19607, Irvine, CA, 92606

Tel: (949) 863-3144     Fax: (949) 253-1800     www.newport.com

*Mfr./distributor precision components and systems for laser/optical technology, vibration/motion measure and control.*

**Newport/Micro-Controle Italia, Via G. Pascoli 19, I-20063 Cernusco Sul Naviglio Milan, Italy**

Tel: 39-02-924-5518   Fax: 39-02-923-2448   Contact: Franco Pepe, Mgr.

## NICHOLSON FILE COMPANY

PO Box 728, Apex, NC, 27502

Tel: (919) 362-7500     Fax: (919) 362-1670     www.coopertool.com

*Mfr. files, rasps and saws.*

**Cooper Group SpA, Via Canova 19, I-20090 Trezzanosul Naviglio Milan, Italy**

## NICOLET INSTRUMENT CORPORATION

5225 Verona Road, Madison, WI, 53711-4495

Tel: (608) 276-6100     Fax: (608) 276-6222     www.nicolet.com

*Mfr. infrared spectrometers and oscilloscopes and medical electro-diagnostic equipment.*

**Thermo Optek Italia SpA, Via Fl lli Gracchi 27, Cinisello Balsamo, 20092 Milan, Italy**

Tel: 39-02-6601-6362   Fax: 39-02-6128429

## A .C. NIELSEN COMPANY

177 Broad Street, Stamford, CT, 06901

Tel: (203) 961-3000     Fax: (203) 961-3190     www.acnielsen.com

*Market and consumer research firm.*

**D&B Marketing Information Services SpA, Via G. DiVittorio 10, I-20094 Corsico Milan, Italy**

## NORDSON CORPORATION

28601 Clemens Road, Westlake, OH, 44145-4551

Tel: (440) 892-1580     Fax: (440) 892-9507     www.nordson.com

*Mfr. industry application equipment, sealants and packaging machinery.*

**Nordson Italia S.p.A., Via Dei Gigli 3/b, I-20090 Pieve Emanuele Milan, Italy**

Tel: 39-02-90-4691   Fax: 39-02-90782485

## NORGREN

5400 S. Delaware Street., Littleton, CO, 80120-1663

Tel: (303) 794-2611     Fax: (303) 795-9487     www.usa.norgren.com

*Mfr. pneumatic filters, regulators, lubricators, valves, automation systems, dryers, push-in fittings.*

**IMI Norgren S.p.A., Via Marzabotto 2, I-20059 Vimercate Milan, Italy**

Tel: 39-06-0631   Fax: 39-06-063-301

## NORTEK INC.

50 Kennedy Plaza, Providence, RI, 02903

Tel: (401) 751-1600     Fax: (401) 751-4610     www.nortek-inc.com

*Mfr. residential and commercial building products.*

**Best S.p.A, Fabriano, Italy**

**Elektromec S.p.A, Montefano, Italy**

## NORTON ABRASIVES COMPANY

1 New Bond Street, Worcester, MA, 01606

Tel: (508) 795-5000      Fax: (508) 795-5741      www.nortonabrasives.com

*Mfr. abrasives for industrial manufacturing.*

**Christensen Diamond Product Co. SpA, Via Flaminia 160, I-00196 Rome, Italy**

**Norton SpA, Via per Cesano Boscone 4, I-20094 Corsico Milan, Italy**

## NU SKIN ENTERPRISES, INC.

75 West Center St., Provo, UT, 84601

Tel: (801) 345-6100      Fax: (801) 345-5999      www.nuskin.com

*Develops and distributes premium-quality personal care and nutritional products.*

**NuSkin Italy, Via E. Fermi 44, 20090 Assago, Italy**

## NUS INFORMATION SERVICES, INC.

2650 McCormick Dr., Ste. 300, Clearwater, FL, 33759-1049

Tel: (727) 669-3000      Fax: (727) 669-3100      www.nus.com

*Provides case-based expert knowledge, bench-marking, trending, and operational services to the electric power and inventory industries.*

**NUS Italia SRL, Via Deruta 20, I-20132 Milan, Italy**

## OGILVY PUBLIC RELATIONS WORLDWIDE

909 Third Ave., New York, NY, 10022

Tel: (212) 880-5201      Fax: (212) 697-8250      www.ogilvypr.com

*Engaged in public relations and communications.*

**Ogilvy One Worldwide S.P.A., Via Lancetti 29, Milan 20158, Italy**

Tel: 39-02-60789   Contact: Nick May, Pres.

## OHAUS CORPORATION

29 Hanover Road, PO Box 900, Florham Park, NJ, 07932-0900

Tel: (973) 377-9000      Fax: (973) 593-0359      www.ohaus.com

*Mfr. balances and scales for laboratories, industry and education.*

**Ohaus Italian Representative Office, Via Vialba 42, I-20026 Novate Milanese Milan, Italy**

Tel: 39-02-33332297

## THE OILGEAR COMPANY

2300 S. 51st Street, Milwaukee, WI, 53219

Tel: (414) 327-1700      Fax: (414) 327-0532      www.oilgear.com

*Mfr. hydraulic power transmission machinery.*

**Oilgear Towler SRL, Via Artigianale 23, I-25010 Montirone Brescia, Italy**

## OPEN MARKET, INC.

1 Wayside Road, Burlington, MA, 01803

Tel: (781) 359-3000      Fax: (781) 359-8111      www.openmarket.com

*Mfr. catalog management software.*

**Open Market Italy Srl, Via Leonardo da Vinci 43, 20090 Trezzano sul Naviglio, Milan, Italy**

Tel: 39-0248409866

## ORACLE CORPORATION

500 Oracle Parkway, Redwood Shores, CA, 94065

Tel: (650) 506-7000      Fax: (650) 506-7200      www.oracle.com

*Develop/manufacture software.*

**Oracle Italia/Datamat SpA, Via Laurentina 756, I-00143 Rome, Italy**

## OSMONICS INC.

5951 Clearwater Drive, Minnetonka, MN, 55343-8995

Tel: (952) 933-2277    Fax: (952) 933-0141    www.osmonics.com

*Mfr. equipment, controls and components for the filtration and water-treatment industries.*

**Osmonics, Milan, Italy**

## OSRAM SYLVANIA CHEMICALS INC.

100 Endicott Street, Danvers, MA, 01923

Tel: (978) 777-1900    Fax: (978) 750-2152    www.osramsylvania.com

*Lighting applications.*

**Osram Sylvania Chemicals, Milan, Italy**

## OTIS ELEVATOR COMPANY

10 Farm Springs Road, Farmington, CT, 06032

Tel: (860) 676-6000    Fax: (860) 676-5111    www.otis.com

*Mfr. elevators and escalators.*

**Otis SpA, Via Firenze 11, I-20063 Cernusco sul Naviglio, Milan, Italy**

## OWENS-CORNING CORPORATION

One Owens Corning Pkwy., Toledo, OH, 43659

Tel: (419) 248-8000    Fax: (419) 248-8445    www.owenscorning.com

*Mfr. building materials systems and composites systems.*

**Owens-Corning Alcopor, Strada Settimo 399/11, 10156 Torino, Italy**

Tel: 39-011-223-4411

## OWENS-ILLINOIS, INC.

One SeaGate, PO Box 1035, Toledo, OH, 43666

Tel: (419) 247-5000    Fax: (419) 247-2839    www.o-i.com

*Largest mfr. of glass containers in the US; plastic containers, compression-molded closures and dispensing systems.*

**AVIR S.p.A., Bari, Italy**

**Owens-Illinois Inc., Via Montelungo 4, Casella Postale 243, I-56100 Pisa, Italy**

## PACIFIC ARCHITECTS & ENGINEERS INC.

888 South Figueroa Street, 17th Fl., Los Angeles, CA, 90017

Tel: (213) 481-2311    Fax: (213) 481-7189    www.pae.com

*Technical engineering services.*

**PAE Aviation Management, Sigonella Air Terminal Services Rome, PSC 812, Box 3450, FPO AE 09627**

Tel: 39-06-9500-2556  Fax: 39-06-6500-8203  Contact: Tim Travis, Proj. Mgr.

## PALL CORPORATION

2200 Northern Boulevard, East Hills, NY, 11548-1289

Tel: (516) 484-5400    Fax: (516) 484-5228    www.pall.com

*Specialty materials and engineering; filters and related fluid clarification equipment.*

**Pall Gelman Sciences, Via Gioacchino Murat 84, I-10159 Milan, Italy**

Tel: 39-01-690-06109  Fax: 39-02-69-006110

**Pall Italia s.r.l., Via G. Bruzzesi 38/40, I-20146 Milan, Italy**

Tel: 39-0247-7961  Fax: 39-02-412-2985

## PANAMETRICS

221 Crescent Street, Waltham, MA, 02154

Tel: (781) 899-2719  Fax: (781) 899-1552  www.panametrics.com

*Process/non-destructive test instrumentation.*

**Panametrics S.r.l., Via Feltre 19/A, I-20132 Milan, Italy**

Tel: 39-02-264-2131  Fax: 39-02-26414454  Contact: Emilio Elzi

## PANDUIT CORPORATION

17301 Ridgeland Ave., Tinley Park, IL, 60477-0981

Tel: (708) 532-1800  Fax: (708) 532-1811  www.panduit.com

*Mfr. electrical/electronic wiring components.*

**Panduit SAS, Via Como 10, I-20020 Lainate, Milan, Italy**

## PARAMETRIC TECHNOLOGY CORPORATION

128 Technology Drive, Waltham, MA, 02154

Tel: (781) 398-5000  Fax: (781) 398-5674  www.ptc.com

*Supplier of mechanical design automation and product data management software and services.*

**Parametric Technology Italy, S.r.l., Bat. C-445, Ave. Andre Ampere BP 267000, I-13797 Aix-en-Provence Cedex, Italy**

Tel: 39-04-42-970000  Fax: 39-04-42-970001

**Parametric Technology Italy, S.r.l., Centro Polifunzionale Lingotto, Via Nizza 262/42 Torre Sud, I-10126 Torino, Italy**

Tel: 39-011-6643211  Fax: 39-011-664-3258

**Parametric Technology Italy, S.r.l., Via Filippo Tommaso Marinetti 221, I-00143 Rome, Italy**

Tel: 39-06-5028-1229  Fax: 39-06-502-0016

**Parametric Technology Italy, S.r.l., Via Lisbona 7, I-35135 Padova, Italy**

Tel: 39-049-870-1481  Fax: 39-049-870-1479

**Parametric Technology Italy, S.r.l., Viale Della Costituzione, Isola E/1, I-80043 Napoli, Italy**

Tel: 39-08-15-628535  Fax: 39-08-15-628538

**Parametric Technology Italy, S.r.l., Viala Colleoni 5, Palazzo Taurus 3, I-20041 Agrate Brianza Milan, Italy**

Tel: 39-02-605-7942  Fax: 39-02-605-7931

**Parametric Technology Italy, S.r.l., Brixia Business Ctr. S.R.L., Via Cipro 1, I-25024 Brescia, Italy**

Tel: 39-030-295601  Fax: 39-030-295535

**Parametric Technology Italy, S.r.l., Via Aperanza N. 35/A, I-40068 S. Lazzaro di Savena Bologna, Italy**

Tel: 39-051-6279411  Fax: 39-051-453172

**Parametric Technology Italy, S.r.l., Via Grandi 46/C, I-60131 Ancona, Italy**

Tel: 39-07-12-901073  Fax: 39-07-12-901137

## PAREXEL INTERNATIONAL CORPORATION

195 West Street, Waltham, MA, 02154

Tel: (781) 487-9900  Fax: (781) 487-0525  www.parexel.com

*Provides contract medical, biotechnology, and pharmaceutical research and consulting services.*

**PAREXEL International s.r.l., Via Filippo Turati, 28, I-20121 Milan, Italy**

Tel: 39-02-624-1111  Fax: 39-02-624-11150

## PARKER HANNIFIN CORPORATION

6035 Parkland Blvd., Cleveland, OH, 44124-4141

Tel: (216) 896-3000  Fax: (216) 896-4000  www.parker.com

*Mfr. motion-control products.*

**Parker Hannifin SpA, Via Privata Archimede 1, I-20094 Corsico Milan, Italy**

**Parker Hannifin SpA, Viale Lombardia 87, I-25031 Capriolo, Italy**

Parker Hannifin SpA, Cylinder & Pneumatics, Via Carducci 11, I-21010 Arsago Seprio, Italy

Parker Hannifin SpA, Div. SCEM RCD, Via E. Fermi 5, I-20060 Gessate Milan, Italy

## PEOPLESOFT INC.

4460 Hacienda Drive, Pleasanton, CA, 94588-8618

Tel: (925) 225-3000      Fax: (925) 694-4444      www.peoplesoft.com

*Mfr. applications to manage business operations across computer networks.*

PeopleSoft S.r.L., Via Amonte de Pieta 21, 20121 Milan, Italy

Tel: 39-2-8633-7313

## PFIZER INC.

235 East 42nd Street, New York, NY, 10017-5755

Tel: (212) 573-2323      Fax: (212) 573-7851      www.pfizer.com

*Research-based, global health care company.*

Pfizer Italiana SpA, Via Valbondione 113, I-10018, Rome, Italy

Tel: 39-06-33-182

Roerig Farmaceutici Italiana SRL, Milan, Italy

SudFarma SRL, Milan, Italy

## PHARMACIA CORPORATION

100 Route 206 North, Peapack, NJ, 07977

Tel: (908) 901-8000      Fax: (908) 901-8379      www.pharmacia.com

*Mfr. pharmaceuticals, agricultural products, industry chemicals.*

Pharmacia & Upjohn, Via Robert Koch 1 2, I-20152 Milan, Italy

## PHARMACIA MONSANTO

800 N. Lindbergh Boulevard, St. Louis, MO, 63167

Tel: (314) 694-1000      Fax: (314) 694-7625      www.monsanto.com

*Life sciences company focusing on agriculture, nutrition, pharmaceuticals, health and wellness and sustainable development.*

Monsanto Co. Chemical Group, Via Walter Tobagi 8, 20068 Peschiera Borromeo, Milan, Italy

## PHELPS DODGE CORPORATION

2600 North Central Ave., Phoenix, AZ, 85004-3089

Tel: (602) 234-8100      Fax: (602) 234-8337      www.phelpsdodge.com

*Copper, minerals, metals and special engineered products for transportation and electrical markets.*

Columbia Carbon Europa, San Martino Di Trecate, Italy

Columbian Carbon Europe SRL, 10 Via P. Verri, I-20121 Milan, Italy

## PHH VEHICLE MANAGEMENT SERVICES

307 International Circle, Hunt Valley, MD, 21030

Tel: (410) 771-3600      Fax: (410) 771-2841      www.phh.com

*Provides vehicle fleet management, corporate relocation, and mortgage banking services.*

Arvil Service Lease Italia SpA, Milanfiori Strada 4, Palazzo A2, I-20090 Assago Milan, Italy

Tel: 39-02-892-2071

## PHILLIPS PETROLEUM COMPANY

Phillips Building, 411 S. Keeler Ave., Bartlesville, OK, 74004

Tel: (918) 661-6600      Fax: (918) 661-7636      www.phillips66.com

*Crude oil, natural gas, liquefied petroleum gas, gasoline and petro-chemicals.*

Phillips Petroleum Intl. SRL, Via Cavallotti 13, I-20122 Milan, Italy

## PICTURETEL CORPORATION

100 Minuteman Road, Andover, MA, 01810

Tel: (978) 292-5000     Fax: (978) 292-3300     www.picturetel.com

*Mfr. video conferencing systems, network bridging and multiplexing products, system peripherals.*

**PictureTel Italy,  Via Cavriana 3, I-20134 Milan, Italy**

Tel: 39-02-7391-214   Fax: 39-02-7391-410

## PINNACLE WORLDWIDE, INC.

1201 Marquette Ave., Ste. 300, Minneapolis, MN, 55403

Tel: (612) 338-2215     Fax: (612) 338-2572     www.pinnacleww.com

*International network of independent public relations firms.*

**Noesis S.R.L,  Via Savona 19/a, 20144 Milan, Italy**

Tel: 39-02-83-1051   Fax: 39-02-83-201161   Contact: Martin Slater, Pres.

## PIONEER HI-BRED INTERNATIONAL INC.

400 Locust Street, Ste. 800, Des Moines, IA, 50309

Tel: (515) 248-4800     Fax: (515) 248-4999     www.pioneer.com

*Agricultural chemicals, farm supplies, biological products, research.*

**Pioneer Hi-Bred Italia SpA,  Via Provinciale 42/44, I-43018 Sissa, Italy**

## PIONEER-STANDARD ELECTRONICS, INC.

6065 Parkland Blvd., Cleveland, OH, 44124

Tel: (440) 720-8500     Fax: (440) 720-8501     www.pios.com

*Mfr./distribution of electronic parts for computers and networking equipment.*

**Eurodis Fanton,  Via Melegnano 22, 200 19 Settimo M Milan, Italy**

## PITNEY BOWES INC.

1 Elmcroft Road, Stamford, CT, 06926-0700

Tel: (203) 356-5000     Fax: (203) 351-6835     www.pitneybowes.com

*Mfr. postage meters, mailroom equipment, copiers, bus supplies, bus services, facsimile systems and financial services.*

**Pitney Bowes Italia Srl.,  Via Martiri Della Liberta 46, I-20060 Liscate Milan, Italy**

Tel: 39-01-9535-1110   Fax: 39-02-9535-1210   Contact: Oscar Parigi, Mng. Dir.   Emp: 60

## PITTSTON BAX GROUP

16808 Armstrong Ave., PO Box 19571, Irvine, CA, 92623

Tel: (949) 752-4000     Fax: (949) 260-3182     www.baxworld.com

*Air freight forwarder.*

**BAX Global,  Blocco 2/3, I-40010 Interporto Bologna, Italy**

Tel: 39-051-665-1001   Fax: 39-051-665-0643

**BAX Global - Reg. Office,  Via Salomone 43, I-20138 Milan, Italy**

Tel: 39-02-506761   Fax: 39-02-5801-0619

**BAX Global - Rome,  Via Fulco Ruffo di Calabria 3/5 - 7/9, I-00054 Fiumicino Paese Rome, Italy**

Tel: 39-06-6504-7551   Fax: 39-06-650-5546

## PITTWAY CORPORATION

200 South Wacker Drive, Chicago, IL, 60606

Tel: (312) 831-1070     Fax: (312) 831-0808     www.pittway.com

*Mfr. alarm and other controls.*

**ADEMCO Italia SpA,  Via Cristoforo Colombo 1, 20094 Corsico, Italy**

Tel: 39-02-458-8861   Fax: 39-02-458-0762

## PLANET HOLLYWOOD INTERNATIONAL, INC.

8669 Commodity Circle, Orlando, FL, 32819

Tel: (407) 363-7827    Fax: (407) 363-4862    www.planethollywood.com

*Theme-dining restaurant chain and merchandise retail stores.*

**Planet Hollywood International, Inc., Rome, Italy**

## PLANTRONICS

345 Encinal Street, Santa Cruz, CA, 95060

Tel: (831) 426-5858    Fax: (831) 425-5198    www.plantronics.com

*Mfr. communications equipment, electrical and electronic appliances and apparatus.*

**Plantronics Acoustics Italia SRL, Centro Direzionale Lombardo, Via Rome; 108 Palazzo E/2, I-20060 Cassina De'Pecchi Milan, Italy**

Tel: 39-02-951-1900   Fax: 39-02-951-1903   Contact: Gian Carlo Degortes

## PLAYTEX APPAREL INC.

700 Fairfield Ave., Stamford, CT, 06904

Tel: (203) 356-8000    Fax: (203) 356-8448    www.playtexbras.com

*Mfr. intimate apparel.*

**Playtex Italia SpA, Piazza L. Sturzo 31, I-00144 Rome, Italy**

## POLAROID CORPORATION

784 Memorial Dr., Cambridge, MA, 02139

Tel: (781) 386-2000    Fax: (781) 386-3924    www.polaroid.com

*Photographic equipment and supplies, optical products.*

**Polaroid Corp., Casella Postale 13, I-06911 Brusino Ticino Arsizio, Italy**

## PPG INDUSTRIES

One PPG Place, Pittsburgh, PA, 15272

Tel: (412) 434-3131    Fax: (412) 434-2190    www.ppg.com

*Mfr. coatings, flat glass, fiber glass, chemicals, coatings.*

**Ampaspace SRL, Via Montello 40, I-26010 Casaletto Vaprio Cremona, Italy**

**PPG Industries Italia SRLe SpA, Via Sera 1, I-15028 Quattoraio , Italy**

## PRAXAIR, INC.

39 Old Ridgebury Road, Danbury, CT, 06810-5113

Tel: (203) 837-2000    Fax: (203) 837-2450    www.praxair.com

*Produces and distributes industrial and specialty gases.*

**Praxair S.p.A., Via Durini 7, I--20122 Milan, Italy**

Tel: 39-02-7600-9110

**Rivoira S.p.A., Via Durini 7, I-20122 Milan, Italy**

Tel: 39-02-771191   Fax: 39-02-77119600

**SAID S.p.A., Via S. Bernardino 92, I-24126 Bergamo, Italy**

Tel: 39-035-328-111   Fax: 39-035-315-486

## PRECISION VALVE & TRIM, INC.

PO Box 3091, 1923 Cloverland Avenue, Baton Rouge, LA, 70809

Tel: (225) 752-5600    Fax: (225) 752-5400    www.precisionvalve.com

*Mfr. aerosol valves.*

**Precision Valve Italia SpA, Via Ravello 1/3, I-20081 Vermezzo Milan, Italy**

## PREMARK INTERNATIONAL INC.

1717 Deerfield Road, Deerfield, IL, 60015

Tel: (847) 405-6000  Fax: (847) 405-6013  www.premarkintl.com

*Mfr. Hobart commercial food equipment, diversified consumer and commercial products, small appliances, and exercise equipment.*

**Premark Italia SpA, Via Mascagni 1, I-20129 Milan, Italy**

## PRICEWATERHOUSECOOPERS LLP

1301 Ave. of the Americas, New York, NY, 10019

Tel: (212) 596-7000  Fax: (212) 259-1301  www.pwcglobal.com

*Accounting and auditing, tax and management, and human resource consulting services.*

**PriceWaterhouseCoopers, Via Del Rione Sirignano 7, I-80121 Naples, Italy**
Tel: 39-08-17614100 Fax: 39-08-1667802

**PriceWaterhouseCoopers, Via Trieste 31/A, I-35121 Padova, Italy**
Tel: 39-049-655222 Fax: 39-049-657814

**PriceWaterhouseCoopers, Via Fieschi 3/14, I-16121 Genoa, Italy**
Tel: 39-010-530061 Fax: 39-010-593996

**PriceWaterhouseCoopers, Corso Italia 191, I-70123 Bari, Italy**
Tel: 39-080-5793139 Fax: 39-080-5797088

**PriceWaterhouseCoopers, Via Vallescura 2, I-40136 Bologna, Italy**
Tel: 39-051-334893 Fax: 39-051-330756

**PriceWaterhouseCoopers, Via Bonifacio Lupi 11, I-50129 Florence, Italy**
Tel: 39-055-471747 Fax: 39-055-470779

**PriceWaterhouseCoopers, Largo Augusto 1/3, I-20122 Milan, Italy**
Tel: 39-02-77851 Fax: 39-02-7785402

**PriceWaterhouseCoopers, Viale Tanara 20/A, I-43100 Parma, Italy**
Tel: 39-052-1242848 Fax: 39-052-1781844

**PriceWaterhouseCoopers, Corso Europa 2, I-20122 Milan, Italy**
Tel: 39-02-77851 Fax: 39-02-7785240

**PriceWaterhouseCoopers, Via Antonio Bosio 22, I-00161 Rome, Italy**
Tel: 39-06-44240373 Fax: 39-06-44242098

**PriceWaterhouseCoopers, Via Giovanni Battista de Rossi 32/B, I-00161 Rome, Italy**
Tel: 39-06-441921 Fax: 39-06-44244890

**PriceWaterhouseCoopers, Via Bogino 23, I-10123 Turin, Italy**
Tel: 39-011-88081 Fax: 39-011-8395613

**PriceWaterhouseCoopers, Via Corridoni 2, I-60123 Ancona, Italy**
Tel: 39-07-136881 Fax: 39-07-136623

## PRIMARK CORPORATION

100 Winter Street, Ste. 4300-N, Waltham, MA, 02451

Tel: (781) 466-6611  Fax: (781) 890-6187  www.primark.com

*Provides financial and business information.*

**Primark Italy Srl, Via San Clemente 1- 6/F, 20122 Milan, Italy**

## PROCTER & GAMBLE COMPANY

One Procter & Gamble Plaza, Cincinnati, OH, 45202

Tel: (513) 983-1100  Fax: (513) 562-4500  www.pg.com

*Personal care, food, laundry, cleaning and industry products.*

**Procter & Gamble Italia SpA, Via Cesare Pavese 385, I-00144 Rome, Italy**

### PRUDENTIAL INSURANCE COMPANY OF AMERICA
751 Broad Street, Newark, NJ, 07102-3777
Tel: (973) 802-6000    Fax: (973) 802-2804    www.prudential.com
*Sale of life insurance and provides financial services.*
**Pricoa Vita, Milan, Italy**

### PSDI MAXIMO
100 Crosby Drive, Bedford, MA, 01730
Tel: (781) 280-2000    Fax: (781) 280-0200    www.psdi.com
*Develops, markets and provides maintenance management software systems.*
**PSDI Italy, Via Doberdò 8, 10152 Torino, Italy**

### PSI NET (PERFORMANCE SYSTEMS INTERNATIONAL INC.)
510 Huntmar Park Drive, Herndon, VA, 22170
Tel: (703) 904-4100    Fax: (703) 904-4200    www.psinet.com
*Internet service provider.*
**PSINet Italy, S Giovanni Bosco 15/B, 25125 Brescia, Italy**

### PUBLIC SERVICE ENTERPRISE GROUP (PSEG)
80 Park Plaza, Newark, NJ, 07101
Tel: (973) 430-7000    Fax: (973) 623-5389    www.pseg.com
*Electric and gas utility.*
**PSEG Global, c/o Office Point Sr 1, via Guido D'Arezzo 4, 20145 Milan, Italy**
Tel: 39-02-4855-9415   Fax: 39-02-4855-9307

### THE QUAKER OATS COMPANY
Quaker Tower, 321 North Clark Street, Chicago, IL, 60610-4714
Tel: (312) 222-7111    Fax: (312) 222-8323    www.quakeroats.com
*Mfr. foods and beverages.*
**Chiari & Forti, Via Cendon 20, I-31057 Silea Treviso, Italy**
**Quaker Chiari & Forti SpA, Viale Monterosa 21, I-20149 Milan, Italy**

### QUINTILES TRANSNATIONAL CORPORATION
4709 Creekstone Dr., Durham, NC, 27703
Tel: (919) 998-2000    Fax: (919) 998-9113    www.quintiles.com
*Mfr. pharmaceuticals.*
**Innovex S.r.l., Centro Direzionale Colleoni, Palazzo Taurus Viale Colleoni 3, Agrate Brianza MI 20041, Italy**
**Quintiles S.r.l., Via Clemente Prudenzio 16, Milan 20138, Italy**

### R&B FALCON CORPORATION
901 Threadneedle, Ste. 200, Houston, TX, 77079
Tel: (281) 496-5000    Fax: (281) 496-4363    www.rbfalcon.com
*Offshore contract drilling.*
**R&B Falcon Drilling Co./Shore Services Inc., Via Magazzini Anteriori, Trav. Nord. 51, Ravenna 48100, Italy**

### RADISSON HOTELS INTERNATIONAL
Carlson Pkwy., PO Box 59159, Minneapolis, MN, 55459-8204
Tel: (612) 540-5526    Fax: (612) 449-3400    www.radisson.com
*Hotels and resorts.*
**Radisson SAS Hotels Italy, Milan, Italy**
Tel: 39-0371-410461   Fax: 39-0371-410464

## RALSTON PURINA COMPANY

Checkerboard Square, St. Louis, MO, 63164-0001

Tel: (314) 982-1000      Fax: (314) 982-1211      www.ralston.com

*Produces dog and cat food and animal feed.*

**Purina Italia SpA, Via e. mattei 120, I-30020, Summaga di Porto, Gruaro, Italy**

## RAMSEY TECHNOLOGY INC.

501 90th Ave. NW, Coon Rapids, MN, 55433

Tel: (763) 783-2500      Fax: (763) 780-2525

*Mfr. in-motion weighing, inspection, monitoring and control equipment for the process industry.*

**Ramsey Italia SRL, Via Perugino 44, I-20093 Cologno Monzese Milan, Italy**

## RANCO INC.

8115 US Route 42 North, Plain City, OH, 43064

Tel: (614) 873-9000      Fax: (614) 873-3819      www.rancocontrols.com

*Mfr. controls for appliance, automotive, comfort, commercial and consumer markets.*

**Ranco Italian Controls, Via del Seprio 42, I-22074 Lomazzo, Italy**

## RAY & BERNDTSON, INC.

301 Commerce, Ste. 2300, Fort Worth, TX, 76102

Tel: (817) 334-0500      Fax: (817) 334-0779      www.prb.com

*Executive search, management audit and management consulting firm.*

**Ray & Berndtson, Piazza Erculea 11, I-20122 Milan, Italy**

Tel: 39-02-72000404  Fax: 39-02-72000389   Contact: Catherine B. Nelson, Mng. Ptnr.

## RAYCHEM CORPORATION

300 Constitution Dr., Menlo Park, CA, 94025-1164

Tel: (650) 361-3333      Fax: (650) 361-5579      www.raychem.com

*Develop/mfr./market materials science products for electronics, telecommunications and industry.*

**Raychem SpA, Centro Direzionale Milanofiori, Palazzo E5, I-20090 Assago Milan, Italy**

## RAYMOND JAMES FINANCIAL, INC.

880 Carillon Parkway, St. Petersburg, FL, 33716

Tel: (813) 573-3800      Fax: (813) 573-8244      www.rjf.com

*Financial services; securities brokerage, asset management, and investment banking services.*

**Raymond James Milan, Via Cerva 25, 20122 Milan, Italy**

Tel: 39-02-76-00-22-31  Fax: 39-02-76-01-44-15   Contact: L. Biasi

## RAYTHEON COMPANY

141 Spring Street, Lexington, MA, 02173

Tel: (781) 862-6600      Fax: (781) 860-2172      www.raytheon.com

*Mfr. diversified electronics, appliances, aviation, energy and environmental products; publishing, industry and construction services.*

**Badger Italiana SRL, Via Vincenzo Monti 51, I-20123 Milan, Italy**

## READER'S DIGEST ASSOCIATION, INC.

Reader's Digest Rd., Pleasantville, NY, 10570

Tel: (914) 238-1000      Fax: (914) 238-4559      www.readersdigest.com

*Publisher of magazines and books and direct mail marketer.*

**Selezione dal Reader's Digest SpA, Via Alserio 10, I-20159 Milan, Italy**

## REEBOK INTERNATIONAL LTD.

100 Technology Center Drive, Stoughton, MA, 02072

Tel: (781) 401-5000      Fax: (781) 401-7402      www.reebok.com

*Mfr. athletic shoes including casual, dress golf and walking shoes.*

**Reebok Italia SRL, Viale Enrico Fermi 17, I-20052 Monza Milan, Italy**

## REED-HYCALOG INC.

6501 Navigation Blvd., PO Box 2119, Houston, TX, 77252

Tel: (713) 924-5200    Fax: (713) 924-5667    www.schlumberger.com

*Mfr. rock bits for oil and gas exploration.*

**Reed-Hycalog Tool Co.,  Via Raiale 187, I-65128 Pescara, Italy**

## REEVES BROTHERS, INC.

PO Box 1898, Hwy. 29 South, Spartanburg, SC, 29304

Tel: (864) 576-1210    Fax: (864) 595-2180    www.reevesbrothers.com

*Printing blanket and industrial coated fabrics.*

**Reeves Italia SpA,  I-20090 Lodivecchio Milan, Italy**

Tel: 39-0371-752643   Fax: 39-0371-752908   Contact: Daria Porta

## REFCO GROUP LTD.

111 West Jackson Blvd, Suite 1800, Chicago, IL, 60604

Tel: (312) 930-6500    Fax: (312) 930-6534    www.refco.com

*Commodity and security brokers engaged in the execution and clearing of futures and options and institutional asset management services.*

**Refco Futures Ltd.,  Rome, Italy**

## REFLEXITE TECHNOLOGY

120 Darling Drive, Avon, CT, 06001

Tel: (860) 676-7100    Fax: (860) 676-7199    www.reflexite.com

*Mfr. plastic film, sheet, materials and shapes, optical lenses.*

**Reflexite Italia,  Via Giovanni da Udine 34, l-20156 Milan, Italy**

Tel: 39-02380-93415   Fax: 39-02380-93418

## REGAL-BELOIT CORPORATION

200 State Street, Beloit, WI, 53512-0298

Tel: (608) 364-8800    Fax: (608) 364-8818    www.regal-beloit.com

*Mfr. power transmission equipment, perishable cutting tools.*

**Costruzioni Meccaniche Legnanesi SRL (CML),  Via Del Brugo 5, I-20025 Legnano Milan, Italy**

Tel: 39-331-548-847   Fax: 39-331-592-800

## REMEDY CORPORATION

1505 Salado Drive, Mountain View, CA, 94043-1110

Tel: (650) 903-5200    Fax: (650) 903-9001    www.remedy.com

*Developer and marketer of computer applications for the operations management market.*

**Remedy S.r.l.,  Eur Trade Center S.r.l., Via del Casale Solaro 119, 0143 Rome, Italy**

Tel: 39-06-515-731

## REMINGTON PRODUCTS COMPANY, L.L.C.

60 Main Street, Bridgeport, CT, 06604

Tel: (203) 367-4400    Fax: (203) 332-4848    www.remington-products.com

*Mfr. home appliances, electric shavers.*

**Remington Italia S.r.l.,  Largo Guido Novello - 1/F, 50126 Firenze, Italy**

Tel: 39-055-6800506

## REVLON INC.

625 Madison Ave., New York, NY, 10022

Tel: (212) 527-4000    Fax: (212) 527-4995    www.revlon.com

*Mfr. cosmetics, fragrances, toiletries and beauty care products.*

**Revlon SpA,  Casella Postale 4128, Via Appia Nuova Km. 17.850, I-00100 Rome, Italy**

Contact: Maria Rosario Montiroli, Gen. Mgr.

## REXNORD CORPORATION

4701 West Greenfield Ave., Milwaukee, WI, 53214

Tel: (414) 643-3000    Fax: (414) 643-3078    www.rexnord.com

*Mfr. power transmission products.*

**Rexnord Harbett, S.p.A., Via Della Costituzione, 45, I-42015 Correggio, Italy**

## RICHCO, INC.

5825 N. Tripp Ave., PO Box 804238, Chicago, IL, 60680

Tel: (773) 539-4060    Fax: (773) 539-6770    www.richco.com

*Mfr. plastic and metal parts for the electric, electronic, appliance, and fiber-optic industries.*

**Richco Italia SRL, Via G. Masserenti 1, Loc. 1 Maggio, 40013 Castelmaggiore Bologna, Italy**

Tel: 39-51-6325266

## RIDGE TOOL COMPANY

400 Clark Street, Elyria, OH, 44035

Tel: (440) 323-5581    Fax: (440) 329-4853    www.ridgid.com

*Mfr. hand and power tools for working pipe, drain cleaning equipment, etc.*

**Ridge Tool Div. Emerson Electric SRL, Milan, Italy**

## C. H. ROBINSON WORLDWIDE, INC. (CHR)

8100 Mitchell Road, Eden Prairie, MN, 55344

Tel: (612) 937-8500    Fax: (612) 937-6714    www.chrobinson.com

*Global door-to-door freight forwarding services, including flexible transportation solutions and global logistics.*

**C. H. Robinson (CHR), Milan, Italy**

Tel: 39-29-101-381

## THE ROCKPORT COMPANY

220 Donald J. Lynch Blvd., Marlboro, MA, 01752

Tel: (508) 485-2090    Fax: (508) 480-0012    www.rockport.com

*Mfr./import dress and casual footwear.*

**Rockport International Trading Co., Via Don Lorenzo Peroso 14, I-50018 Scandicci, Italy**

## ROCKWELL INTERNATIONAL CORPORATION

777 East Wisconsin Ave., Ste. 1400, Milwaukee, WI, 53202

Tel: (414) 212-5200    Fax: (414) 212-5201    www.rockwell.com

*Products and service for aerospace and defense, automotive, electronics, graphics and automation industry.*

**Breter S.r.l., Via Cardinale Riboldi 616, I-20037 Paderno Dugnana Milan, Italy**

Tel: 39-02-99061-1    Fax: 39-02-910-3516

**Rockwell Automation S.r.L., Viale de Gasperi 126, I-20017 Mazzo di Rho Milan, Italy**

Tel: 39-02-939721    Fax: 39-02-93972-201

**Rockwell Automation S.r.l., Via Persicetana 12, I-40012 Calderara di Reno BO, Italy**

Tel: 39-051-6464-111    Fax: 39-051-728-670

**Rockwell Collins, Via Monte Giberto 157, I-00138 Rome, Italy**

Tel: 39-06-8818-038    Fax: 39-06-8819-129

**Rockwell Semiconductor Systems, Via di Vittorio, 1 Milan, I-20017 Mazzo di Rho Milan, Italy**

Tel: 39-02-9317-9911    Fax: 39-02-9317-9913

## ROHM AND HAAS COMPANY

100 Independence Mall West, Philadelphia, PA, 19106

Tel: (215) 592-3000    Fax: (215) 592-3377    www.rohmhaas.com

*Mfr. industrial and agricultural chemicals, plastics.*

**Morton International, Via Brescia 13/15, 20020 Robecchetto, Italy**

**Morton International Spa, Via Trieste 25, 22076 Mozzate, Italy**

**Morton International Spa, Via Borgo S. Siro 63, 27026 Garlasco, Italy**

Morton International Spa, Strada Statale 11, Kilometro 190 200, 24050 Mozzanica, Italy

Poliolchimica/Morton, 7 Strada Marziana, 27020 arona Lomellina PV, Italy

Pulverlac S.p.A., 10 Via Monte Tomba, 36060 Romano d'Ezzelino, Italy

Rohm and Haas Italia S.R.L., Via della Filanda, I-20060 Gessate Milan, Italy
Tel: 39-02-952501

Shipley Italia S.R.L., Viale Delle Industrie 10/23, I-20020 Arese Milan, Italy
Tel: 39-02-935-83003

## ROSENBLUTH INTERNATIONAL

2401 Walnut Street, Philadelphia, PA, 19103-4390

Tel: (215) 977-4000      Fax: (215) 977-4028      www.rosenbluth.com

*Provides corporate business travel services.*

Rosenbluth International Alliance (RIA), Milan, Italy

## RUSSELL REYNOLDS ASSOCIATES INC.

200 Park Ave., New York, NY, 10166-0002

Tel: (212) 351-2000      Fax: (212) 370-0896      www.russreyn.com

*Executive recruiting services.*

Russell Reynolds Associates Inc., Via Andrea Appiani 7, I-20121 Milan, Italy
Tel: 39-02-6231-121   Fax: 39-02-6552-837   Contact: Alberto Gavazzi

## SAMSONITE CORPORATION

11200 East 45th Ave., Denver, CO, 80239-3018

Tel: (303) 373-2000      Fax: (303) 373-6300      www.samsonite.com

*Mfr. luggage and leather goods.*

Samsonite Italy, Via Enrico de Nicola 18, I-20090 Cesano Boscone, Italy

## SAPHIRE INTERNATIONAL LTD.

3060 Main Street, Ste. 202, Stratford, CT, 06614

Tel: (203) 375-8668      Fax: (203) 375-1965      www.dataease.com

*Mfr. applications development software.*

DataEase Italia, Italy

## SAPIENT CORPORATION

1 Memorial Drive, Cambridge, MA, 02142

Tel: (617) 621-0200      Fax: (617) 621-1300      www.sapient.com

*Engaged in information technology and consulting services.*

Sapient SpA, Via Crocefisso 19, 20122 Milan, Italy
Tel: 39-02-5821-71

## SARA LEE CORPORATION

3 First National Plaza, Chicago, IL, 60602-4260

Tel: (312) 726-2600      Fax: (312) 558-4995      www.saralee.com

*Mfr./distributor food and consumer packaged goods, intimate apparel and knitwear.*

Maglificio Bellia SpA, Via C. Bellia 34, I-13050 Pettinengo, Italy

## SAS INSTITUTE INC.

SAS Campus Drive, Cary, NC, 27513

Tel: (919) 677-8000      Fax: (919) 677-4444      www.sas.com

*Mfr./distributes decision support software.*

SAS Institute (Italia) SpA, Milan, Italy
Tel: 39-02-5830-1686   Fax: 39-02-5830-0602

## SCHENKER INTERNATIONAL FORWARDERS INC.

150 Albany Ave., Freeport, NY, 11520

Tel: (516) 377-3000    Fax: (516) 377-3005    www.schenkerusa.com

*Freight forwarders.*

**Schenker Italiana S.P.A., Via Don L. Sturzo 3, I-24020 Gorle Bergamo, Italy**

Tel: 39-035-299451   Fax: 39-035-296984

**Schenker Italiana S.P.A., Via S. Romano In Carfagnana 45, I-00148 Rome, Italy**

Tel: 39-06-657-0741   Fax: 39-06-653-2820

**Schenker Italiana S.P.A., Via Fratelli Bandiera 27, I-20068 Peschiera Borromeo Milan, Italy**

Tel: 39-01-51666-398   Fax: 39-01-51666-50`

## R. P. SCHERER CORPORATION

645 Martinsville Rd., Ste. 200, Baskin Ridge, NJ, 07920

Tel: (908) 580-1500    Fax: (908) 580-9220    www.rpscherer.com

*Mfr. pharmaceuticals; soft gelatin and two-piece hard shell capsules.*

**R.P. Scherer SpA, Via Nettunense, km 20 100, I-04011 Aprilia Latina, Italy**

Tel: 39-06-927141   Fax: 39-06-92727890   Contact: Dr, Giuliane Bider, Gen. Mgr.   Emp: 128

## SCHERING-PLOUGH CORPORATION

One Giralda Farms, Madison, NJ, 07940-1000

Tel: (973) 822-7000    Fax: (973) 822-7048    www.sch-plough.com

*Proprietary drug and cosmetic products.*

**Schering-Plough Animal Health, Centro Dir Milano Due, Palazzo Borromini, 20090 Segrate Milan, Italy**

Tel: 39-02-210-181

## SCHLEGEL SYSTEMS

1555 Jefferson Road, PO Box 23197, Rochester, NY, 14692-3197

Tel: (716) 427-7200    Fax: (716) 427-9993    www.schlegel.com

*Mfr. engineered perimeter sealing systems for residential and commercial construction; fibers; rubber product.*

**Schlegel SRL, Via Miglioli 9, I-20090 Segrate Milan, Italy**

## SCHLUMBERGER LIMITED

277 Park Avenue, New York, NY, 10021

Tel: (212) 350-9400    Fax: (212) 350-9564    www.schlumberger.com

*Engaged in oil and gas services, metering and payment systems, and produces semiconductor testing equipment and smart cards.*

**Schlumberger Industries Spa, 2 Via Enrico Schievano, 20143 Milan, Italy**

**Schlumberger Test & Transactions, Cards Div., Via Cornelio Celso 22/A, 00161 Rome, Italy**

## SCIENCE APPLICATIONS INTL. CORPORATION (SAIC)

10260 Campus Point Dr., San Diego, CA, 92121

Tel: (858) 826-6000    Fax: (858) 535-7589    www.saic.com

*Engaged in research and engineering.*

**US Naval Hospital, Via Eduardo Scarfogolio, Agano 80125, Italy**

Tel: 39-81-7243699   Fax: 39-81-7243665   Contact: Ronald Freeman

## SCIENTIFIC-ATLANTA, INC.

1 Technology Pkwy South, Norcross, GA, 30092-2967

Tel: (770) 903-5000    Fax: (770) 903-2967    www.sciatl.com

*A leading supplier of broadband communications systems, satellite-based video, voice and data communications networks and worldwide customer service and support.*

**Scientific-Atlanta Mediterranean, Inc., Via Fosso Centroni 4, I-00040 Morena Rome, Italy**

Tel: 39-06-7489-011   Fax: 39-06-7984-0034

## SCOTSMAN INDUSTRIES

775 Corporate Woods Pkwy., Vernon Hills, IL, 60061

Tel: (847) 215-4500    Fax: (847) 913-9844    www.scotsman-ice.com

*Mfr. ice machines and refrigerators, drink dispensers.*

**Scotsman Ice Systems Frimont S.p.A.,  Via Puccini 22, I-20010 Bettolino di Pogliano Milan, Italy**

Tel: 39-2-939601   Fax: 39-2-93550500   Contact: Emanuele Lanzani

## SEAGATE TECHNOLOGY, INC.

920 Disc Dr., Scotts Valley, CA, 95066

Tel: (408) 438-6550    Fax: (408) 438-7205    www.seagate.com

*Develop computer technology, software and hardware.*

**Seagate Technology SRL,  Via Litta Modignani 7, I-20161 Milan, Italy**

Tel: 39-02-662-01515   Fax: 39-02-662-02530   Contact: Walter Fontana   Emp: 1

## SEALED AIR CORPORATION

Park 80 East, Saddle Brook, NJ, 07663

Tel: (201) 791-7600    Fax: (201) 703-4205    www.sealedair.com

*Mfr. protective and specialty packaging solutions for industrial, food and consumer products.*

**Instapak Italia SpA,  Via Belvedere 18, I-20043 Arcore Milan, Italy**

**Sealed Air S.p.A.,  Via per Ornago, I-20040 Bellusco Milan, Italy**

Tel: 39-039-6835-1   Fax: 39-039-6835-350

## SEAQUIST PERFECT DISPENSING

1160 North Silver Lake Road, Cary, IL, 60013

Tel: (847) 639-2124    Fax: (847) 639-2142    www.seaquistperect.com

*Mfr. and sale of dispensing systems; lotion pumps and spray-through overcaps.*

**SAR S.p.A.,  Chieti, Italy**

## G.D. SEARLE & COMPANY

5200 Old Orchard Road, Skokie, IL, 60077

Tel: (847) 982-7000    Fax: (847) 470-1480    www.searlehealthnet.com

*Mfr. pharmaceuticals, health care, optical products and specialty chemicals.*

**Searle Framaceutici S.p.A.,  Via Walter Tobagi 8, I-20068 Peschiera Borromeo Milan, Italy**

Tel: 39-02-516-611   Fax: 39-02-516-61203

## SELAS CORPORATION OF AMERICA

2034 S. Limekiln Pike, Dresher, PA, 19025

Tel: (215) 646-6600    Fax: (215) 646-3536    www.selas.com

*Mfr. heat treating equipment for metal, glass, ceramic and chemical industry.*

**Selas Italiana SRL,  Via delle Tuberose 14, I-20146 Milan, Italy**

## SENSIENT TECHNOLOGIES CORPORATION

433 E. Michigan Street, Milwaukee, WI, 53202

Tel: (414) 271-6755    Fax: (414) 347-4783    www.sensient.com

*Mfr. food products and food ingredients.*

**Curt Georgi Imes SpA,  Milan, Italy**

## SENSORMATIC ELECTRONICS CORPORATION

951 Yamato Road, Boca Raton, FL, 33431-0700

Tel: (561) 989-7000    Fax: (561) 989-7774    www.sensormatic.com

*Electronic article surveillance equipment.*

**Sensormatic Italy,  Via Teocrito 54, 20128 Milan, Italy**

## SERVICE CORPORATION INTERNATIONAL

1929 Allen Parkway, Houston, TX, 77019

Tel: (713) 522-5141     Fax: (713) 525-5586     www.sci-corp.com

*Operates funeral homes, cemeteries and crematoriums and sells caskets, burial vaults and cremation receptacles.*

**Pompes Funereraves Geneacuterales (PFG),  Milan, Italy**

## SFX ENTERTAINMENT, INC.

650 Madison Ave., 16th Fl., New York, NY, 10022

Tel: (212) 838-3100     Fax: (212) 750-6682     www.sfx.com

*Sports marketing, management and consulting.*

**SFX Sports Group  Italy,  Milan, Italy**

## SHARED MEDICAL SYSTEMS CORPORATION

51 Valley Stream Pkwy, Malvern, PA, 19355

Tel: (610) 219-6300     Fax: (610) 219-3124     www.smed.com

*Computer-based information processing for healthcare industry.*

**SMS Italia S.r.l.,  Piazza Sante Bargellini 21, 00157 Rome, Italy**

Tel: 39-6-4393350

## SHIPLEY COMPANY, LLC

455 Forest Street, Marlborough, MA, 01752

Tel: (508) 481-7950     Fax: (508) 485-9113     www.shipley.com

*Supplier of materials and processes technology to the microelectronics and printed wiring board industries.*

**Shipley Italy,  Viale Lombardia 52, 21040 Castronno (Varese), Italy**

Tel: 39-033-289-6311    Fax: 39-033-289-6398

## SHOOK, HARDY & BACON L.L.P.

1200 Main Street, Ste. 3100, Kansas City, MO, 64105-2118

Tel: (816) 474-6550     Fax: (816) 421-5547     www.shb.com

*International law firm.*

**Shook, Hardy & Bacon Office,  Via Meravigli 3, I-20123 Milan, Italy**

## SILICON GRAPHICS INC.

2011 N. Shoreline Blvd., Mountain View, CA, 94043-1389

Tel: (650) 960-1980     Fax: (650) 961-0595     www.sgi.com

*Design/mfr. special-effects computer graphic systems and software.*

**Silicon Graphics,  Centro Dir. Piero della Francesca, Corso Svizzera 185, 10149 Torino, Italy**

**Silicon Graphics,  Centro Dir. Milanofiori, Strada 6 Palazzo N3, 20089 Rozzano MI Italy**

**Silicon Graphics,  Via Montecassiano 155, 01156 Rome, Italy**

## SMITH INTERNATIONAL, INC.

PO Box 60068, Houston, TX, 77205-0068

Tel: (713) 443-3370     Fax: (713) 233-5996     www.smith.com

*Mfr. drilling tools and equipment and provides related services for the drilling, completion and production sectors of the petroleum and mining industries.*

**Smith International Italia SpA,  Via Grandi 1, Castle Maggiore, I-40013 Bologna, Italy**

Tel: 39-051-713-401    Contact: Luciano Bernardini, Area Mgr.

## SMURFIT-STONE CONTAINER CORPORATION

150 N. Michigan Ave., Chicago, IL, 60601-7568

Tel: (312) 346-6600     Fax: (312) 580-3486     www.smurfit-stone.net

*Mfr. paper and paper packaging.*

**Smurfit-Stone Container Corporation,  Milan, Italy**

## SONESTA INTERNATIONAL HOTELS CORPORATION

200 Clarendon Street, Boston, MA, 02166

Tel: (617) 421-5400  Fax: (617) 421-5402  www.sonesta.com

*Own/manage hotels, resorts, and Nile cruises.*

**Sonesta Resort & Country Club, Tuscany, Italy**

## SONOCO PRODUCTS COMPANY

North Second Street, PO Box 160, Hartsville, SC, 29550

Tel: (843) 383-7000  Fax: (843) 383-7008  www.sonoco.com

*Mfr. packaging for consumer and industrial market and recycled paperboard.*

**Sonoco L.P.D. Italia, s.r.l., S.S. 87 Sannitica Km 21500, Via Delle Industrie, I-81020 S. Marco Evangelista Caserta, Italy**

Tel: 39-0823-424388

## SOTHEBY'S HOLDINGS, INC.

1334 York Avenue, New York, NY, 10021

Tel: (212) 606-7000  Fax: (212) 606-7027  www.sothebys.com

*Auction house specializing in fine art and jewelry.*

**Sotheby's Holdings, Inc., Palazzo Broggi, Via Broggi 19, 20129 Milan, Italy**

Tel: 39-02-295-001  Fax: 39-02-295-18595  Contact: Paul Mack

## SPALDING HOLDINGS CORPORATION

425 Meadow Street, Chicopee, MA, 01021

Tel: (413) 536-1200  Fax: (413) 536-1404  www.spalding.com

*Mfr. sports equipment and infant and juvenile furniture and accessories.*

**Spalding Sports, Milan, Italy**

## SPENCER STUART MANAGEMENT CONSULTANTS

401 North Michigan Ave., Ste. 3400, Chicago, IL, 60611

Tel: (312) 822-0080  Fax: (312) 822-0116  www.spencerstuart.com

*Executive recruitment firm.*

**Spencer Stuart & Associates Inc., 36 Corso Monforte, I-20122 Milan, Italy**

Tel: 39-02-771251  Fax: 39-02-782452  Contact: Luca Pacces

**Spencer Stuart & Associates Inc., 7 Via A. Kircher, I-00198 Rome, Italy**

Tel: 39-06-802071  Fax: 39-06-8020-7200  Contact: Luca Pacces

## SPHERION CORPORATION

2050 Spectrum Boulevard, Fort Lauderdale, FL, 33309

Tel: (954) 938-7600  Fax: (954) 938-7666  www.spherion.com

*Provides temporary personnel placement and staffing.*

**Michael Page Finance, Via Meravigli 3, I-20123 Milan, Italy**

Tel: 39-02-806-8001

## SPRINT INTERNATIONAL

World Headquarters, 2330 Shawnee Mission Parkway, Westwood, KS, 66205

Tel: (913) 624-3000  Fax: (913) 624-3281  www.sprint.com

*Telecommunications equipment and services.*

**Sprint International, Centro Direzionale Lombardo, Palazzo CD - Via Roma 108, I-20060 Cassina de'Pecchi Milan, Italy**

## SPS TECHNOLOGIES INC.

101 Greenwood Avenue, Ste. 470, Jenkintown, PA, 19046

Tel: (215) 517-2000  Fax: (215) 517-2032  www.spstech.com

*Mfr. aerospace and industry fasteners, tightening systems, magnetic materials, superalloys.*

**Asti Aircraft Services, Via Balme No. 5, 10143 Torino, Italy**

**Unbrako SRL,** Via XXV Aprile 19, I-20097 San Donato Milan, Italy

## SPX CORPORATION

700 Terrace Point Drive, PO Box 3301, Muskegon, MI, 49443-3301

Tel: (231) 724-5000    Fax: (231) 724-5720    www.spx.com

*Mfr. auto parts, special service tools, engine and drive-train parts.*

**Bear Italiana SRL,** Via dei Confini 201, I-50010 Capalle Florence, Italy

## SRI INTERNATIONAL

333 Ravenswood Ave., Menlo Park, CA, 94025-3493

Tel: (650) 859-2000    Fax: (650) 326-5512    www.sri.com

*Engaged in international consulting and research.*

**SRI Italy,** Via Lanzone 6, I-20123 Milan, Italy

## THE ST. PAUL COMPANIES, INC.

385 Washington Street, St. Paul, MN, 55102

Tel: (651) 310-7911    Fax: (651) 310-8294    www.stpaul.com

*Provides investment, insurance and reinsurance services.*

**Toro Assicuraziona S.A.,** Via Arcivescovado 16, I-10121 Turin, Italy

## STANDARD COMMERCIAL CORPORATION

2201 Miller Rd., PO Box 450, Wilson, NC, 27893

Tel: (919) 291-5507    Fax: (919) 237-1109    www.sccgroup.com

*Leaf tobacco dealers/processors and wool processors.*

**Transcatab, SpA,** Via Provinciale Appia, 81020 San Nicola La Strada, Caserta, Italy

## STANDEX INTERNATIONAL CORPORATION

6 Manor Parkway, Salem, NH, 03079

Tel: (603) 893-9701    Fax: (603) 893-7324    www.standex.com

*Mfr. diversified graphics, institutional, industry/electronic and consumer products.*

**Standex International S.R.L.,** Via 1 Maggio 20, I-20064 Gorgonzola Milan, Italy

Tel: 39-02-95-740-951    Fax: 39-02-95-740-713    Contact: Giorgio Mazza, Mgr.

## THE STANLEY WORKS

1000 Stanley Drive, PO Box 7000, New Britain, CT, 06053

Tel: (860) 225-5111    Fax: (860) 827-3987    www.stanleyworks.com

*Mfr. hand tools and hardware.*

**Stanley Mediterranea SpA,** Via Motolense Supino, Frosinone, Italy

**Stanley Tools SpA,** Via Trieste 1, I-22060 Figino Serenza Como, Italy

**Stanley Works (Italia) SRL,** Via Leopardi 9, I-22060 Figino Serenza Como, Italy

## STA-RITE INDUSTRIES INC.

293 Wright Street, Delavan, WI, 53115

Tel: (262) 728-5551    Fax: (262) 728-7323    www.sta-rite.com

*Mfr. water pumps, filters and systems.*

**Nocchi Pompe SPA,** Via Masaccio 13, I-56010 Lugnano Pisa, Italy

Tel: 39-050-71-6111    Fax: 39-050-70-3137    Contact: Georgio Nocchi    Emp: 228

## STARWOOD HOTELS & RESORTS WORLDWIDE

777 Westchester Avenue, White Plains, NY, 10604

Tel: (914) 640-8100    Fax: (914) 640-8316    www.starwoodhotels.com

*Hotel operations including Sheraton, Westin, St. Regis, Four Points and Caesars.*

**Sheraton Sales Center,** Via Vittor Pisani 7, I-20124 Milan, Italy

### STEINER CORPORATION

505 E. South Temple, Salt Lake City, UT, 84102

Tel: (801) 328-8831     Fax: (801) 363-5680

*Soap and towel dispensers.*

**L.S.I., Piazza de Angeli 9, I-20146 Milan, Italy**

### STIEFEL LABORATORIES INC.

255 Alhambra Circle, Ste. 1000, Coral Gables, FL, 33134

Tel: (305) 443-3807     Fax: (305) 443-3467     www.stiefel.com

*Mfr. pharmaceuticals, dermatological specialties.*

**Stiefel Laboratories SRL, Via Calabria 15, I-20090 Redecesio Di Segrate Milan, Italy**

### STORAGE TECHNOLOGY CORPORATION

One Storagetech Dr., Louisville, CO, 80028-4377

Tel: (303) 673-5151     Fax: (303) 673-5019     www.stortek.com

*Mfr./market/service information, storage and retrieval systems.*

**Storage Technology SpA, Via Cina 413, I-00144 Rome, Italy**

### STOWE WOODWARD MOUNT HOPE

333 Turnpike Rd., Southborough, MA, 01772

Tel: (508) 460-9600     Fax: (508) 481-5392     www.mounthope.com

*Mfr. roll covering and bowed roll technologies for the web handling industries.*

**Stowe Woodward IRGA Italy, Via A. Volta 73, 21010 Cardano al Campo, Italy**

Tel: 39-3-3126-1514

### STRUCTURAL DYNAMICS RESEARCH CORPORATION

2000 Eastman Dr., Milford, OH, 45150-2740

Tel: (513) 576-2400     Fax: (513) 576-2922     www.sdrc.com

*Developer of software used in Modeling testing, drafting and manufacturing.*

**SDRC Italia Srl., Via Piero Portaluppi 11/2, I-20138 Milan, Italy**

Tel: 39-02-58-011777   Fax: 39-02-58-011800

### SUDLER & HENNESSEY

1633 Broadway, 25th Fl., New York, NY, 10019

Tel: (212) 969-5800     Fax: (212) 969-5996     www.sudler-hennessey.com

*Engaged in healthcare products advertising.*

**G&R Pubblicita/Sudler & Hennessey, Via M.V. Traiano 7, I-20149 Milan, Italy**

Tel: 39-02-349-721   Fax: 39-01-349-1698   Contact: Massimo Vergnano

### SUN MICROSYSTEMS, INC.

901 San Antonio Road, Palo Alto, CA, 94303

Tel: (650) 960-1300     Fax: (650) 856-2114     www.sun.com

*Computer peripherals and programming services.*

**Sun Microsystems, Centro Direzionale Colleoni, Palazzo Andromeda 1 Via Paracelso 16, 20041 Agrate Brianza, Italy**

Tel: 39-0167-874-707

### SUNRISE MEDICAL INC.

2382 Faraday Ave., Ste. 200, Carlsbad, CA, 92008

Tel: (760) 930-1500     Fax: (760) 930-1580     www.sunrisemedical.com

*Designs, manufactures and markets rehabilitation products and assistive technology devices for people with disabilities, and patient care products used in nursing homes, hospitals and homecare settings.*

**Sunrise Medical Italy, Via Riva 20 - Montale, 29100 Piacenza (PC), Italy**

## SUPERIOR GRAPHITE COMPANY

10 South Riverside Plaza, Chicago, IL, 60606

Tel: (312) 559-2999     Fax: (312) 559-9064     www.graphitesgc.com

*Mfr. natural and synthetic graphites, electrodes, lubricants, suspensions, carbide and carbon.*

**Tesi S.p.A, Via Manzoni 20, Monza (MI) I-20052, Italy**

## SYBASE, INC.

6475 Christie Ave., Emeryville, CA, 94608

Tel: (510) 922-3500     Fax: (510) 922-3210     www.sybase.com

*Design/mfg/distribution of database management systems, software development tools, connectivity products, consulting and technical support services..*

**Sybase Italia, Via del Poggio Laurentino 118, I-00144 Rome, Italy**

Tel: 39-06-592-6324   Fax: 39-06-593-2924

**Sybase Italia, Via Anna Kuliscioff 35, I-20152 Milan, Italy**

Tel: 39-02-483-241   Fax: 39-02-483-0660

## SYBRON INTERNATIONAL CORPORATION

411 E. Wisconsin Ave., Milwaukee, WI, 53202

Tel: (414) 274-6600     Fax: (414) 274-6561     www.sybron.com

*Mfr. products for laboratories, professional orthodontic and dental markets.*

**Kerr Italia SpA, Via Passanti 332, Casella Postale 46, I-84018 Scafati Salerno, Italy**

## SYMANTEC CORPORATION

20330 Stevens Creek Blvd., Cupertino, CA, 95014-2132

Tel: (408) 253-9600     Fax: (408) 253-3968     www.symantec.com

*Designs and produces PC network security and network management software and hardware.*

**Symantec Srl, Voa Abbadesse 40, I-20124 Milan, Italy**

Tel: 39-02-695521   Fax: 39-02-5501-2270

## SYMBOL TECHNOLOGIES, INC.

One Symbol Plaza, Holtsville, NY, 11742-1300

Tel: (631) 738-2400     Fax: (631) 738-5990     www.symbol.com

*Mfr. Bar code-driven data management systems, wireless LAN's, and Portable Shopping System™.*

**Symbol Technologies Italy S.r.l., Via Cristoforo Colombo, 49, I-20090 Trezzano S/N Milan, Italy**

Tel: 39-02-44-84441   Fax: 39-02-44-54385

## SYNOPSYS, INC.

700 East Middlefield Road, Mountain View, CA, 94043

Tel: (650) 962-5000     Fax: (650) 965-8637     www.synopsys.com

*Mfr. electronic design automation software.*

**Synopsys Srl, Centro Direzionale Colleoni, Viale Colleoni 11 - Palazzo Sirio 3 , 20041 Agrate Brianza-Mi, Italy**

Tel: 39-039-657-981   Fax: 39-039-657-98300

## SYNTEGRA

4201 Lexington Ave., North Arden Hills, MN, 55126-6198

Tel: (651) 415-2999     Fax: (651) 415-4891     www.cdc.com

*Computer peripherals and hardware.*

**Syntegra Italy S.p.A., Palazzo Verrocchio, Centro Diezionale, Milan 2, I-20090 Segrate Milan, Italy**

Tel: 39-02-21741   Fax: 39-02-2641-4187

## SYSTEMAX INC.

22 Harbor Park Dr., Port Washington, NY, 11050

Tel: (516) 608-7000    Fax: (516) 608-7111    www.systemax.com

*Direct marketer of computers and related products to businesses.*

**Misco Italy Computer Supplies S.p.A., Il Girasole UDV 2.01, 20084 Lacchiarella, Milan, Italy**

Tel: 39-02-900-90977

## TBWA CHIAT/DAY

488 Madison Avenue, 6th Floor, New York, NY, 10022

Tel: (212) 804-1000    Fax: (212) 804-1200    www.tbwachiat.com

*International full service advertising agency.*

**TBWA Italia, Milan, Italy**

## TECHNITROL INC.

1210 Northbrook Drive, #385, Trevose, PA, 19053

Tel: (215) 355-2900    Fax: (215) 355-7397    www.technitrol.com

*Mfr. of electronic components, electrical contacts, and other parts/materials.*

**Mec Betras Italia s.r.l. Contatti Elettrici, Lentate Seveso, Italy**

## TECUMSEH PRODUCTS COMPANY

100 E. Patterson Street, Tecumseh, MI, 49286-1899

Tel: (517) 423-8411    Fax: (517) 423-8526    www.tecumseh.com

*Mfr. of hermetic compressors for air conditioning and refrigeration products, gasoline engines and power train components for lawn and garden applications, and pumps.*

**Tecnamotor SRL, Casella Postale 1221, I-10100 Torino, Italy**

## TEKELEC

26580 West Agoura Road, Calabasas, CA, 91302

Tel: (818) 880-5656    Fax: (818) 880-6993    www.tekelec.com

*Mfr. telecommunications testing equipment.*

**Tekelec Europe S.r.L, Via Zante 14, 20128 Milan, Italy**

Tel: 39-2-580-3951

## TEKTRONIX INC.

14200 SW Karl Braun Dr., PO Box 500, Beaverton, OR, 97077

Tel: (503) 627-7111    Fax: (503) 627-2406    www.tek.com

*Mfr. test and measure, visual systems/color printing and communications/video and networking products.*

**Tektronix SpA, Via XI Febbraio 99, I-20090 Vimodrome Milan, Italy**

Tel: 39-02-25086-501   Fax: 39-02-25086-500

## TELEFLEX INC.

630 W. Germantown Pike, Ste. 450, Plymouth Meeting, PA, 19462

Tel: (610) 834-6301    Fax: (610) 834-8307    www.teleflex.com

*Designs/mfr./market mechanical and electro-mechanical systems, measure systems.*

**Rüsch S.r.l., Varedo (MI) Italy**

**TFX Marine European Sales Office, Varedo (MI) Italy**

## TELLABS INC.

4951 Indiana Ave. 6303788800, Lisle, IL, 60532-1698

Tel: (630) 378-8800    Fax: (630) 679-3010    www.tellabs.com

*Design/mfr./service voice/data transport and network access systems.*

**Tellabs Italy, Palazzo Valadier, Piazza del Popolo 18, Rome 00187, Italy**

## TELXON CORPORATION

1000 Summitt Dr., Cincinnati, OH, 45150

Tel: (330) 664-1000    Fax: (330) 664-2220    www.telxon.com

*Develop/mfr. portable computer systems and related equipment.*

**Telxon Italia SRL, Palazzo Cimabue, Via Cassanese 224, I-20090 Segrate Milan, Italy**

## TENNECO AUTOMOTIVE INC.

500 North Field Drive, Lake Forest, IL, 60045

Tel: (847) 482-5241    Fax: (847) 482-5295    www.tenneco-automotive.com

*Mfr. automotive parts, exhaust systems and service equipment.*

**Monroe Italia SRL, Via Plinio 43, I-20129 Milan, Italy**

## TENNECO PACKAGING CORPORATION OF AMERICA

1900 West Field Court, Lake Forest, IL, 60045

Tel: (847) 482-2000    Fax: (847) 482-2181    www.agplus.net/tenneco

*Mfr. custom packaging, aluminum and plastic molded fibre, corrugated containers.*

**Tenneco Packaging, Ossago, Italy**

## TERADYNE INC.

321 Harrison Ave., Boston, MA, 02118

Tel: (617) 482-2700    Fax: (617) 422-2910    www.teradyne.com

*Mfr. electronic test equipment and blackplane connection systems.*

**Teradyne Italia SRL, Via Modigliani 27, I-20090 Segrate, Italy**

## TEXAS INSTRUMENTS INC.

8505 Forest Lane, Dallas, TX, 75243

Tel: (972) 995-3773    Fax: (972) 995-4360    www.ti.com

*Mfr. semiconductor devices, electronic electro-mechanical systems, instruments and controls.*

**Texas Instruments Italia SpA, Avezzano, Italy**

**Texas Instruments Italia SpA, Via John F. Kennedy 141, Aversa, Italy**

## TEXTRON INC.

40 Westminster Street, Providence, RI, 02903

Tel: (401) 421-2800    Fax: (401) 421-2878    www.textron.com

*Mfr. Aerospace (Bell Helicopter and Cessna Aircraft), industry and consumer products, fasteners and financial services.*

**Maag Italia S.p.A., Viale Romagna 7, I-20089 Rozzano, Italy**

Tel: 39-02-824-71310

**Textron Fastening Systems, Via D Manin 350/21, 20099 Sesto San Giovanni (MI), Italy**

Tel: 39-02-262-9171

## THERMADYNE HOLDINGS CORPORATION

101 South Hanley Road, Suite 300, St. Louis, MO, 63105

Tel: (314) 746-2197    Fax: (314) 746-2349    www.thermadyne.com

*Mfr. welding, cutting, and safety products.*

**Genset S.P.A., Pavia, Italy**

Tel: 39-0382-5091

**Thermadyne Italy, Milan, Italy**

Tel: 39-039-287-2113

## THERMON MANUFACTURING COMPANY

100 Thermon Drive, PO Box 609, San Marcos, TX, 78667-0609

Tel: (512) 396-5801    Fax: (512) 396-3627    www.thermon.com

*Mfr. steam and electric heat tracing systems, components and accessories.*

**Thermon Italia SpA, Viale Lomellina 12A (ang. Via Piemonte), I-20090 Buccinasco Milan, Italy**

## THETFORD CORPORATION

7101 Jackson Road, PO Box 1285, Ann Arbor, MI, 48106

Tel: (734) 769-6000     Fax: (734) 769-2023     www.thetford.com

*Mfr. sanitation products and chemicals.*

**Thetford Italia, Via 28 Luglio n.180, 47893 Borgo Maggiore, Italy**

Contact: Gianni Minzoni

## THOMAS & BETTS CORPORATION

8155 T&B Blvd., Memphis, TN, 38125

Tel: (901) 252-5000     Fax: (901) 685-1988     www.tnb.com

*Mfr. elect/electronic connectors and accessories.*

**Thomas & Betts SpA, Via Archimede Angola Piazzale Labriola, I-20092 Balsamo, Italy**

## TIDEWATER INC.

601 Poydras Street, Ste.1900, New Orleans, LA, 70130

Tel: (504) 568-1010     Fax: (504) 566-4582     www.tdw.com

*Marine service and equipment to companies engaged in exploration, development and production of oil, gas and minerals.*

**Tidewater Marine, Inc./o Petromed Ltd., Via Angelo Moro 119, 20097 San Donato, Milanese, Italy**

Tel: 39-02-516-4031   Fax: 39-02-5164-0343

## TIFFANY & COMPANY

727 Fifth Ave., New York, NY, 10022

Tel: (212) 755-8000     Fax: (212) 605-4465     www.tiffany.com

*Mfr./retail fine jewelry, silverware, china, crystal, leather goods, etc.*

**Tiffany & Co. Florence, At Faraone S.p.A., Via Tornabuoni 25/R, I-50123 Florence, Italy**

Tel: 39-055-215506

**Tiffany & Co. Milan, At Faraone S.p.A., Via Montenapoleone 7A, I-20121 Milan, Italy**

Tel: 39-02-7601-3656

## THE TIMBERLAND COMPANY

200 Domain Drive, Stratham, NH, 03885

Tel: (603) 772-9500     Fax: (603) 773-1640     www.timberland.com

*Design/mfr. footwear, apparel and accessories for men and women.*

**Timberland Europe Inc., Centro Direczionale Colleoni, Palazzo Orione, Viale Colleoni, I-20041 Agrate Brianza, Italy**

## TIMKEN SUPER PRECISION (MPB)

7 Optical Ave., Keene, NH, 03431-0547

Tel: (603) 352-0310     Fax: (603) 355-4553     www.timken.com

*Mfr./sales/distribution bearings, tape guides and systems for missiles, etc.*

**GIMAR di D.F. eM. Giordano, Via Busoni 7a, 20137 Milan, Italy**

Tel: 39-2-5516918

## TMP WORLDWIDE, INC.

622 Third Ave., New York, NY, 10017

Tel: (212) 351-7000     Fax: (212) 658-0540     www.tmpw.com

*#1 Yellow Pages agency and a leader in the recruitment and interactive advertising fields.*

**TMP Worldwide Executive Search, Via Agnello 18, Milan 20121, Italy**

**TMP Worldwide Executive Search, Via Emilia 65, Rome 00187, Italy**

**TMP Worldwide/SMET, Via P. Colletta, 59, I-20137 Milan, Italy**

Tel: 39-02-546-5168

## TOKHEIM CORPORATION

PO Box 360, 10501 Corporate Drive, Fort Wayne, IN, 46845

Tel: (219) 470-4600     Fax: (219) 482-2677     www.tokheim.com

*Engaged in design, manufacture and service of electronic and mechanical petroleum marketing systems.*

**Tokheim Sofitam, Quattordio KM 10800, S.P. 26, 14030 Scurzolengo (AT), Italy**

## TOPFLIGHT CORPORATION

277 Commerce Dr., Glen Rock, PA, 17327

Tel: (717) 227-5400     Fax: (717) 227-1415     www.topflight.com

*Commercial printing and service paper.*

**Topflight Italia, Vidigulfo, Italy**

## THE TOPPS COMPANY, INC.

1 Whitehall Street, New York, NY, 10004-2108

Tel: (212) 376-0300     Fax: (212) 376-0573     www.topps.com

*Mfr. entertainment products, principally collectible trading cards, confections, sticker collections, and comic books.*

**Topps Italia SRL, Via Villoresi 13, I-20143 Milan, Italy**

Tel: 39-02-58-100100   Fax: 39-02-58-101122

## TOWERS PERRIN

335 Madison Ave., New York, NY, 10017-4605

Tel: (212) 309-3400     Fax: (212) 309-0975     www.towers.com

*Management consulting services.*

**Tillinghast Towers Perrin, Via Pontaccio 10, I-20121 Milan, Italy**

Tel: 39-02-863-921   Fax: 39-02-809-753

## TOWNSEND ENGINEERING COMPANY, INC.

2425 Hubbell Ave., Des Moines, IA, 50317

Tel: (515) 265-8181     Fax: (515) 263-3355     www.townsendeng.com

*Mfr. machinery for food industry.*

**Townsend Engineering Company, S.S. 33 del Sempione no. 30, 20014 Nerviano (Milan), Italy**

Tel: 39-033-155-5846

## THE TRANE COMPANY

3600 Pammel Creek Road, La Crosse, WI, 54601

Tel: (608) 787-2000     Fax: (608) 787-4990     www.trane.com

*Mfr./distributor/service A/C systems and equipment.*

**Trane Italia SRL, Via Enrico Fermi 21/23, I-20090 Assago, Italy**

## TRANS WORLD AIRLINES INC.

515 North Sixth Street, St. Louis, MO, 63101

Tel: (314) 589-3000     Fax: (314) 589-3129     www.twa.com

*Air transport services.*

**Trans World Airlines Inc., Via Partemope 23, Naples, Italy**

**Trans World Airlines Inc., Via Barberini 59, I-00187 Rome, Italy**

Tel: 39-06-47211

**Trans World Airlines Inc., 5th Fl., Corsa Europa 11, I-20122 Milan, Italy**

Tel: 39-02-77961

**Trans World Airlines Inc., Via dei Vecchietti 4, I-50123 Florence, Italy**

Tel: 39-055-284691

**TRANTER PHE, INC.**

PO Box 2289, Wichita Falls, TX, 76306

Tel: (940) 723-7125     Fax: (706) 723-1131     www.tranter.com

*Mfr. heat exchangers.*

**SWEP Italia SRL,  Via E Toti 36/A, I-2002 Monza, Italy**

Tel: 39-02-612-3096   Fax: 39-02-660-49496

**TRIMBLE NAVIGATION LIMITED**

645 N. Mary Ave., Sunnyvale, CA, 94086

Tel: (408) 481-8000     Fax: (408) 481-2000     www.trimble.com

*Design/mfr. electronic geographic instrumentation.*

**Trimble Navigation Italia s.r.l.,  Largo T. Solera 7, Ed. 1 Sc.B, I-00199 Rome, Italy**

Tel: 39-06-8621-6070   Fax: 39-06-8621-7970

**TRUE NORTH COMMUNICATIONS INC.**

101 East Erie Street, Chicago, IL, 60611

Tel: (312) 425-6500     Fax: (312) 425-5010     www.truenorth.com

*Holding company, advertising agency.*

**Foote, Cone & Belding,  Corso Magenta 85, I-20123 Milan, Italy**

**TruServ CORPORATION**

8600 West Bryn Mawr, Chicago, IL, 60631-3505

Tel: (773) 695-5000     Fax: (773) 695-6541     www.truserv.com

*Dealer-owned, independent, hardware store cooperative.*

**TruServ Corporation,  Milan, Italy**

**TRW INC.**

1900 Richmond Road, Cleveland, OH, 44124-3760

Tel: (216) 291-7000     Fax: (216) 291-7932     www.trw.com

*Electric and energy-related products, automotive and aerospace products, tools and fasteners.*

**TRW Italia SpA,  Via Valtrompia 87, I-25063 Gardone Valtrompia Brescial, Italy**

**TWIN DISC INCORPORATED**

1328 Racine Street, Racine, WI, 53403-1758

Tel: (414) 638-4000     Fax: (414) 638-4482     www.twindisc.com

*Mfr. industry clutches, reduction gears and transmissions.*

**Twin Disc Italia SRL,  Via Coppino 425-427, I-55049 Viareggio, Italy**

Tel: 39-058-4387-797   Fax: 39-058-4387-798

**UNION CARBIDE CORPORATION**

39 Old Ridgebury Road, Danbury, CT, 06817

Tel: (203) 794-2000     Fax: (203) 794-6269     www.unioncarbide.com

*Mfr. industrial chemicals, plastics and resins.*

**Union Carbide Chemicals SpA,  Milan, Italy**

**UNISYS CORPORATION.**

PO Box 500, Union Meeting Road, Blue Bell, PA, 19424

Tel: (215) 986-4011     Fax: (215) 986-6850     www.unisys.com

*Mfr./marketing/servicing electronic information systems.*

**Unisys Italia SpA,  Via B. Crespi 57, I-20159 Milan, Italy**

**UNITED AIRLINES INC.**

1200 E. Algonquin Rd., Chicago, IL, 60007

Tel: (847) 700-4000     Fax: (847) 700-4081     www.ual.com

*Air transportation, passenger and freight services.*

**United Airlines,  Tokyo, Japan**

## UNITED PARCEL SERVICE, INC.

55 Glenlake Parkway, NE, Atlanta, GA, 30328

Tel: (404) 828-6000      Fax: (404) 828-6593      www.ups.com

*International package-delivery service.*

**UPS Italy s.r.l.,  Via G. Fantoli, 15/2, I-20138 Milan, Italy**

Tel: 39-02-167-822054   Fax: 39-02-554-00180

## UNITED STATES SURGICAL CORPORATION

150 Glover Ave., Norwalk, CT, 06856

Tel: (203) 845-1000      Fax: (203) 847-0635      www.ussurg.com

*Mfr./development/market surgical staplers, laparoscopic instruments and sutures.*

**Auto Suture Italia SpA,  Attn: Italy Office, U.S. Surgical, 150 Glover Avenue, Norwalk CT 06856**

## UNITED TECHNOLOGIES CORPORATION

One Financial Plaza, Hartford, CT, 06103

Tel: (860) 728-7000      Fax: (860) 728-7979      www.utc.com

*Mfr. aircraft engines, elevators, A/C, auto equipment, space and military electronic and rocket propulsion systems.  Products include Pratt and Whitney, Otis elevators, Carrier heating and air conditioning and Sikorsky helicopters.*

**Carnier Italia SpA,  Via Boccaccio 35, I-20090 Trezzano Sul Naviglio Milan, Italy**

**Marlo SpA,  Via Vincenzo Monti 23, I-20016 Pero Milan, Italy**

**S.P. Elettronica,  Via Carlo Pisacane 7, I-20016 Pero Milan, Italy**

## UNIVERSAL CORPORATION

1501 N. Hamilton Street, Richmond, VA, 23230

Tel: (804) 359-9311      Fax: (804) 254-3582      www.universalcorp.com

*Holding company for tobacco and commodities.*

**Deltafina SpA,  Via Donizetti 10, I-00198 Rome, Italy**

## UNIVERSAL INSTRUMENTS

90 Bevier Street, S. Dock, Binghamton, NY, 13904

Tel: (607) 779-7522      Fax: (607) 779-7971      www.uic.com

*Mfr./sales of instruments for electronic circuit assembly.*

**Laser Optronic SRL,  Milan, Italy**

Tel: 39-02-57-46-51   Fax: 39-01-57-4101-27

## UNIVERSAL WEATHER & AVIATION INC.

8787 Tallyho Road, Houston, TX, 77061

Tel: (713) 944-1622      Fax: (713) 943-4650      www.univ-wea.com

*Provides service management, and worldwide weather and communications to the corporate aviation community.*

**Universal Aviation Italy SRL,  Aereoporto Malpensa, I-21013 Gallarte, Italy**

## UOP LLC.

25 East Algonquin Road, Des Plaines, IL, 60017

Tel: (847) 391-2000      Fax: (847) 391-2253      www.uop.com

*Engaged in developing and commercializing technology for license to the oil refining, petrochemical and gas processing industries.*

**UOP M.S., S.p.A.,  Viale Milano Fiori, Strada 1, Palazzo E1 1-20090 ASSAGO MI Milan, Italy**

Tel: 39-02-57540-1   Fax: 39-02-5750-0145

## URS CORPORATION

100 California Street, Ste. 500, San Francisco, CA, 94111-4529

Tel: (415) 774-2700     Fax: (415) 398-1904     www.urscorp.com

*Provides planning, design and construction management services, pollution control and hazardous waste management.*

**URS (Dames & Moore),  Milan, Italy**

## UUNET

22001 Loudoun County Pkwy., Ashburn, VA, 20147

Tel: (703) 206-5600     Fax: (703) 206-5601     www.uu.net

*World's largest Internet service provider; World Wide Web hosting services, security products and consulting services to businesses, professionals, and on-line service providers.*

**UUNET Italy,  Via Vasto 1, 20121 Milan, Italy**

## VALENITE INC

31751 Research Park Dr., Madison Heights, MI, 48071-9636

Tel: (248) 589-1000     Fax: (248) 597-4820     www.valenite.com

*Cemented carbide, high speed steel, ceramic and diamond cutting tool products, etc.*

**Valenite-Modco SRL,  Direzione Commerciale, Via C. Battisti 3, I-20070 Vizzolo Predabissi Milan, Italy**

## VAPOR CORPORATION

6420 West Howard Street, Niles, IL, 60714-3395

Tel: (847) 967-8300     Fax: (847) 965-9874     www.vapordoors.com

*Mfr. bus and rail transit automatic door systems, railcar/locomotive relays and contractors, vehicle ID systems.*

**HP S.r.l.,  Viale Regina Pacis 298, I-41049 Sassuolo Modena, Italy**

Tel: 39-053-680-6441  Fax: 39-053-680-178   Contact: Luigi Camellini, Mng. Dir.

## VARIAN MEDICAL SYSTEMS, INC.

3050 Hansen Way, Palo Alto, CA, 94304-100

Tel: (650) 493-4000     Fax: (650) 424-5358     www.varian.com

*Mfr. microwave tubes and devices, analytical instruments, semiconductor process and medical equipment, vacuum systems.*

**Varian Medical System Italia SpA,  Via Brescia 28 D1, 20063 Cernusco Sul Naviglio, Milan, Italy**

**Varian Medical System Italia SpA,  Via Varian 54, I-10040 Lenini Turin, Italy**

## VARIAN, INC.

3050 Hansen Way, Palo Alto, CA, 94304

Tel: (650) 424-5352     Fax: (650) 213-8200     www.varianinc.com

*Mfr. scientific instruments and related equipment.*

**Varian, Inc.,  Via Flli Varian 54, 10040 Leini (Torino), Italy**

Tel: 39-011-997-9111

## VELCRO USA INC.

406 Brown Avenue, Manchester, NH, 03108

Tel: (603) 669-4892     Fax: (603) 669-9271     www.velcro.com

*Mfr./sales of velcro brand hook and loop fasteners, plastic buckles and metal hardware and cable control straps.*

**Velcro Italia, S.R.L.,  Via Nazario Sauro 12, I-20043 Arcore Milan, Italy**

Tel: 39-39-688-2004  Fax: 39-39-601-5518

## VERIZON

1095 Ave. of the Americas, New York, NY, 10036

Tel: (212) 395-2121      Fax: (212) 395-1285      www.verizon.com

*Telecommunications.*

**Omnitel Pronto Italia S.p.A., 15 Via Caboto, 20094 Corsico, Italy**

Tel: 39-02-41431   Fax: 39-02-4143-3610   Contact: Carlo Peretti, Chmn.

## VERIZON COMMUNICATIONS INC.

1255 Corporate Drive, Irving, TX, 75038

Tel: (972) 507-5000      Fax: (972) 507-5002      www.gte.com

*Engaged in wireline and wireless communications.*

**Omnitel Pronto Italia, Viale Europa 46, I-20093 Col. Monzesz, Milan, Italy**

Contact: Vittorio Colao

## VERNAY LABORATORIES INC.

120 East South College St., Box 310, Yellow Springs, OH, 45387

Tel: (937) 767-7261      Fax: (937) 767-1208      www.vernay.com

*Mfr. precision fluid handling products.*

**Vernay Italia SRL, Localita Rilate 21, I-14100 Asti Piemonte, Italy**

## VICOR CORPORATION

23 Frontage Road, Andover, MA, 01810

Tel: (978) 470-2900      Fax: (978) 749-3536      www.vicr.com

*Designs, manufactures, and markets modular power components and complete configurable and custom power systems.*

**Vicor Italy, Via Milanese 20, 20099 Sesto S. Giovanni, Milan, Italy**

## THE VIKING CORPORATION

210 N. Industrial Park Rd., Hastings, MI, 49058

Tel: (616) 945-9501      Fax: (616) 945-9599      www.vikingcorp.com

*Mfr. fire extinguishing equipment.*

**Viking Italia SRL, Via Leonardo da Vinci 46/B, I-20030 Senago (Milan), Italy**

## VIKING OFFICE PRODUCTS

950 West 190th Street, Torrance, CA, 90502

Tel: (310) 225-4500      Fax: (310) 324-2396      www.vikingop.com

*International direct marketer of office products, computer supplies, business furniture and stationery.*

**Viking Office Products S.R.L., Via Milanofiori, Palazzo "E, Scala 3/4, I-20092 Assago Milan, Italy**

Tel: 39-02-5750-4421   Fax: 39-02-5750-4425   Contact: Luca Borroni, Mgr.   Emp: 93

## VISHAY INTERTECHNOLOGY INC.

63 Lincoln Hwy., Malvern, PA, 19355

Tel: (610) 644-1300      Fax: (610) 296-0657      www.vishay.com

*Mfr. resistors, strain gages, capacitors, inductors, printed circuit boards.*

**Vishay S.r.l., Via Gadames 128, 20151 Milan, Italy**

Tel: 39-02-30011911   Fax: 39-02-30011999

## VITESSE SEMICONDUCTOR CORPORATION

741 Calle Plano, Camarillo, CA, 93012

Tel: (805) 388-3700      Fax: (805) 389-7188      www.vitesse.com

*Mfr. integrated circuits.*

**Vitesse Semiconductor S.r.L., Via F. Ferruccio 2, 20145 Milan, Italy**

Tel: 39-02-3453-8747   Fax: 39-02-3453-5611   Contact: Guido Carasso

## WALBRO CORPORATION, TI GROUP AUTOMOTIVE

6242 Garfield Ave., Cass City, MI, 48726-1325

Tel: (517) 872-2131     Fax: (517) 872-3090     www.walbro.com

*Mfr. motor vehicle accessories and parts, automotive fluid carrying systems.*

**TI Group Automotive Systems, Viale Arno 11, PO Box 248, 72100 Brindisi, Italy**

**TI Group Automotive Systems, Strada Farnese 9, 43100 Parma, Italy**

**TI Group Automotive Systems/Bundy Refrig, Via Giacomo Ponassi 11, Loc La Palazzina, PO Box 9, 15060 Borghetto Borbera (AL), Italy**

## WARNACO INC.

90 Park Ave., New York, NY, 10016

Tel: (212) 661-1300     Fax: (212) 687-0480     www.warnaco.com

*Mfr./sales intimate apparel and men's and women's sportswear.*

**Warnaco, Milan, Italy**

## WARNER BROS INTERNATIONAL TELEVISION

4000 Warner Boulevard, Bldg.170, 3rd Fl., Burbank, CA, 91522

Tel: (818) 954-6000     Fax: (818) 977-4040     www.wbitv.com

*Distributor TV programming and theatrical features.*

**Warner Bros. Italia S.R.L., Via Giuseppe Avezzana 51, I-00195 Rome, Italy**

Tel: 39-06-321-7779   Fax: 39-06-321-7278   Contact: Rosario Ponzio, Mng. Dir.

## WARNER ELECTRIC BRAKE & CLUTCH COMPANY

449 Gardner St., South Beloit, IL, 61080

Tel: (815) 389-3771     Fax: (815) 389-2582     www.warnernet.com

*Global supplier of Power Transmission and Motion Control Solution Systems; automotive, industry brakes, and clutches.*

**Dana Italia S.p.A., Via Bernardina Vero 90, 1-20141, Milan, Italy**

Tel: 39-02-582-1761   Fax: 39-02-5696318

## WASHINGTON GROUP INTERNATIONAL, INC.

720 Park Blvd., PO Box 73, Boise, ID, 83729

Tel: (208) 386-5000     Fax: (208) 386-7186     www.wgint.com

*Engaged in engineering and construction.*

**Washington Group International, Inc., Via C. Boncompagni 60, 20139 Milan, Italy**

Tel: 39-02-5220-2661   Fax: 39-02-5220-2665

## THE WASHINGTON POST COMPANY

1150 15th St. NW, Washington, DC, 20071

Tel: (202) 334-6000     Fax: (202) 334-4536     www.washpostco.com

*Engaged in magazine publishing, cable and television broadcasting, educational services and the Internet,*

**International Herald Tribune, Via Mecenate 91, Milan 20138, Italy**

Tel: 39-2-5095-6545

## WASTE MANAGEMENT, INC.

1001 Fannin Street, Ste. 4000, Houston, TX, 77002

Tel: (713) 512-6200     Fax: (713) 512-6299     www.wastemanagement.com

*Environmental services and disposal company; collection, processing, transfer and disposal facilities.*

**Waste Management Italia SRL, Via XXV Aprile 59, I-22070 Guanzate, Italy**

## WATERS CORPORATION

34 Maple Street, Milford, MA, 01757

Tel: (508) 478-2000     Fax: (508) 872-1990     www.waters.com

*Mfr./distribute liquid chromatographic instruments and test and measurement equipment.*

**Waters SpA, Via Cassanese 218, I-20090 Segrate Milan, Italy**

## WATLOW ELECTRIC MFG. COMPANY

12001 Lackland Rd., St. Louis, MO, 63146-4039

Tel: (314) 878-4600      Fax: (314) 434-1020      www.watlow.com

*Mfr. electrical heating units, electronic controls, thermocouple wire, metal-sheathed cable, infrared sensors.*

**Watlow Italy SRL,  Via Adige 13, I-20135 Milan, Italy**

Tel: 39-02-541-6941   Fax: 39-02-5519-1596

## WATSON WYATT & COMPANY HOLDINGS

6707 Democracy Blvd., Ste. 800, Bethesda, MD, 20817

Tel: (301) 581-4600      Fax: (301) 581-4937      www.watsonwyatt.com

*Creates compensation and benefits programs for major corporations.*

**Watson Wyatt S.r.l.,  Via Monti Parioli 49/A, I-00197 Rome, Italy**

Tel: 39-06-320-2026   Fax: 39-06-320-2028   Contact: Sandro Catani

## WATTS INDUSTRIES, INC.

815 Chestnut Street, North Andover, MA, 01845-6098

Tel: (978) 688-1811      Fax: (978) 688-5841      www.wattsind.com

*Designs/mfr./sales of industry valves and safety control products.*

**Intermes SpA,  Via Bellini 30, I-20095 Cusano Milanino Milan, Italy**

**Intermes SpA,  Zona Industriale, I-39052 Caldaro, Italy**

**ISI Industria Saracinesche Idrauliche SpA,  Zona Industriale, Localita Ischiello, I-38015 Lavis, Italy**

## WEATHERFORD INTERNATIONAL, INC.

5 Post Oak Blvd, Ste. 1760, Houston, TX, 77227-3415

Tel: (713) 287-8400      Fax: (713) 963-9785      www.weatherford.com

*Oilfield services, products and equipment; mfr. marine cranes for oil and gas industry.*

**Weatherford Intl. Inc.,  Via Stabbio 90, Bergamo 24044, Dalmine Italy**

Tel: 39-353-70573   Fax: 39-353-70584

**Weatherford Italiana SpA,  Via Pirano 19, I-48100 Ravenna, Italy**

Tel: 39-054-443-5911   Fax: 39-054-4436-519

## WELCH ALLYN DCD INC.

4341 State Street Road, Skaneateles Falls, NY, 13153

Tel: (315) 685-4100      Fax: (315) 685-4091      www.welchallyn.com

*Mfr. bar code data collection systems.*

**Welch Allyn Italy,  Napo Torriani 29, 20124 Milan, Italy**

Tel: 39-2-6738-0317

## WENDY'S INTERNATIONAL, INC.

428 West Dublin Granville Roads, Dublin, OH, 43017-0256

Tel: (614) 764-3100      Fax: (614) 764-3459      www.wendysintl.com

*Fast food restaurant chain.*

**Wendy's International,  Rome, Italy**

## WENNER MEDIA

1290 Ave. of the Americas, New York, NY, 10104

Tel: (212) 484-1616      Fax: (212) 484-1713      www.usmagazine.com

*Publishes entertainment magazines, including Rolling Stone, US Weekly and Men's Journal.*

**Rolling Stone Magazine,  Via G. Compagnoni 24, Milan 20129, Italy**

Tel: 39-02-7000-3528

## WEST PHARMACEUTICAL SERVICES

101 Gordon Drive, PO Box 645, Lionville, PA, 19341-0645

Tel: (610) 594-2900     Fax: (610) 594-3014     www.westpharma.com

*Mfr. products for filling, sealing, dispensing and delivering needs of health care and consumer products markets.*

**Pharma-Gummi Italia SRL, Milan, Italy**

Tel: 39-02-29-40-6007

## WEYERHAEUSER COMPANY

33663 Weyerhaeuser Way South, Federal Way, WA, 98003

Tel: (253) 924-2345     Fax: (253) 924-2685     www.weyerhaeuser.com

*Wood and wood fiber products.*

**Weyerhaeuser Italia SRL, Viale Tunisia 38, I-20124 Milan, Italy**

## WHIRLPOOL CORPORATION

2000 N. M-63, Benton Harbor, MI, 49022-2692

Tel: (616) 923-5000     Fax: (616) 923-5443     www.whirlpoolcorp.com

*Mfr./market home appliances: Whirlpool, Roper, KitchenAid, Estate, and Inglis.*

**Whirlpool Europe BV, Viale G. Borghi 27, I-21025 Comerio, Italy**

## WHITEHALL-ROBINS INC.

1407 Cummings Drive, PO Box 26609, Richmond, VA, 23261-6609

Tel: (804) 257-2000     Fax: (804) 257-2120     www.ahp.com

*Mfr. ethical pharmaceuticals and consumer healthcare products.*

**Eurand Intl. SpA, Milan, Italy**

## W. A. WHITNEY COMPANY

650 Race Street, PO Box 1206, Rockford, IL, 61105-1206

Tel: (815) 964-6771     Fax: (815) 964-3175     www.wawhitney.com

*Mfr. hydraulic punch/plasma cutting metal fabricating equipment.*

**W.A. Whitney Italia SpA, Strade del Francese 132/9, I-10156 Torino, Italy**

Tel: 39-011-470-2702

## WILLKIE FARR & GALLAGHER

787 Seventh Avenue, New York, NY, 10019-6099

Tel: (212) 821-8000     Fax: (212) 821-8111     www.willkie.com

*International law firm.*

**Willkie Farr & Gallagher, Via di Ripetta 142, 00186 Rome, Italy**

**Willkie Farr & Gallagher, Via Michele Barozzi 2, 20122 Milan, Italy**

## WIND RIVER SYSTEMS, INC.

500 Wind River Way, Alameda, CA, 94501

Tel: (510) 748-4100     Fax: (510) 749-2010     www.isi.com

*Develops and markets computer software products and services.*

**Wind River Systems Italia s.r.l., Piazza Don Enrico Mapelli 60, Sestet San Giovanni, Milan 20099, Italy**

**Wind River Systems Italia s.r.l., Centro Direzionale ``Piero della Francesca", Corso Svizzera 185, 10149 Torino Italy**

Tel: 39-011-750-1511

## WONDERWARE CORPORATION

100 Technology Dr., Irvine, CA, 92618

Tel: (949) 727-3200     Fax: (949) 727-3270     www.wonderware.com

*Mfr. industrial strength applications software and services.*

**Marcam Italy Srl, Milan, Italy**

Tel: 39-02-724491

**Wonderware Italia, SpA, Gallarate, Italy**
Tel: 39-0331-709411

## WOODHEAD INDUSTRIES INC.

Three Parkway North, Ste. 550, Deerfield, IL, 60015

Tel: (847) 236-9300     Fax: (847) 236-0503     www.woodhead.com

*Develop/mfr./sale/distributor elect/electronic, fiber optic and ergonomic special-function, non-commodity products.*

**mPm S.p.A., Via Zucchi, 39 int. G, I-20095 Cusano Milanino Milan, Italy**

## WORLD COURIER INC.

1313 Fourth Ave., New Hyde Park, NY, 11041

Tel: (516) 354-2600     Fax: (516) 354-2644     www.worldcourier.com

*International courier service.*

**World Courier Italia SRL, Via Mecenate 30/6, Milan, Italy**

## WORLD MINERALS INC.

130 Castilian Drive, Santa Barbara, CA, 93117

Tel: (805) 562-0200     Fax: (805) 562-0298     www.worldminerals.com

*Mfr. premium quality diatomite and perlite products.*

**World Minerals Italiana SRL, 6 Alzaia Trento, Corsico (MI) 20094, Italy**
Tel: 39-02-451-741    Fax: 39-02-440-9451

## WORLDCOM, INC.

500 Clinton Center Drive, Clinton, MS, 39060

Tel: (601) 360-8600     Fax: (601) 360-8616     www.wcom.com

*Telecommunications company serving local, long distance and Internet customers domestically and internationally.*

**WorldCom International, Via San Simpliciano 1, Corso Garibaldi 86, I-20121 Milano, Italy**

## WYETH-AYERST INTERNATIONAL INC.

150 Radnot-Chester Road, St. Davids, PA, 19087

Tel: (610) 902-4100     Fax: (610) 989-4586     www.ahp.com/wyeth

*Antibiotics and pharmaceutical products.*

**Wyeth-Lederle SpA, Via Franco Gorgone, Zone Industriale, 95030 Catania Italy**
Tel: 39-95-59-8111

**Wyeth-Lederle SpA, Via Nettunense 90, 04011 Aprilia (Latina), Italy**
Tel: 39-06-927-151

## XEROX CORPORATION

800 Long Ridge Road, PO Box 1600, Stamford, CT, 06904

Tel: (203) 968-3000     Fax: (203) 968-4312     www.xerox.com

*Mfr. document processing equipment, systems and supplies.*

**Xerox, S.p.A, Strada Padana Superiore 28, I-20063 Cernusco SN Milan, Italy**
Tel: 39-02-92-1881    Fax: 39-02-9236-8209

## XIRCOM, INC.

2300 Corporate Center Drive, Thousand Oaks, CA, 91320

Tel: (805) 376-9300     Fax: (805) 376-9311     www.xircom.com

*Mfr. PC card network adapters and modems.*

**Xircom France Srl, Via Giovanni da Udine 34, 20156 Milan, Italy**

## XTRA CORPORATION

1807 Park 270 Dr., Ste. 400, St. Louis, MO, 63146-4020

Tel: (314) 579-9320     Fax: (314) 579-0299     www.xtracorp.com

*Holding company: leasing.*

**XTRA International,  Milan, Italy**

## YAHOO! INC.

3420 Central Expressway, Santa Clara, CA, 95051

Tel: (408) 731-3300     Fax: (408) 731-3301     www.yahoo-inc.com

*Internet media company providing specialized content, free electronic mail and community offerings and commerce.*

**Yahoo! Inc.,  Regus Milan, Via Torino 2, I-20122 Milan, Italy**

Tel: 39-02-7254-6207    Fax: 39-02-7254-6400

## YORK INTERNATIONAL CORPORATION

631 South Richland Ave., York, PA, 17403

Tel: (717) 771-7890     Fax: (717) 771-6212     www.york.com

*Mfr. heating, ventilating, air conditioning and refrigeration equipment.*

**York International S.p.A, 29 Via XXV Aprile, 20030 Barlassina, Milan Italy**

Tel: 39-362-5381

## YOUNG & RUBICAM INC.

285 Madison Ave., New York, NY, 10017

Tel: (212) 210-3000     Fax: (212) 370-3796     www.yr.com

*Advertising, public relations, direct marketing and sales promotion, corporate and product ID management.*

**Young & Rubicam Italia SpA,  Piazza Eleonora Duse 2, I-20122 Milan, Italy**

## JOHN ZINK COMPANY

PO Box 21220, Tulsa, OK, 74121-1220

Tel: (918) 234-1800     Fax: (918) 234-2700     www.johnzink.com

*Mfr. flare systems, thermal oxidizers, vapor recovery systems, process heater burners.*

**John Zink Italy,  Milan, Italy**

Tel: 390-2-6698-1232    Contact: Daniel Civardi

# Ivory Coast

**AMERICAN INTERNATIONAL GROUP INC. (AIG)**

70 Pine Street, New York, NY, 10270

Tel: (212) 770-7000     Fax: (212) 509-9705     www.aig.com

*Worldwide insurance and financial services.*

**American Intl. Assurance Co. Ltd., 08 Boite Postale 873, Abidjan, Ivory Coast**

**LOUIS BERGER INTERNATIONAL INC.**

100 Halsted Street, East Orange, NJ, 07019

Tel: (201) 678-1960     Fax: (201) 672-4284     www.louisberger.com

*Consulting engineers, engaged in architecture, environmental and advisory services.*

**Louis Berger International Inc., Route de Facobly, Boite Postale 346, Man, Ivory Coast**

**Louis Berger International Inc., Residence Sainte Anne, 04 Boite Postale 295, Cocody Abidjan, Ivory Coast**

Tel: 225-210-079   Fax: 225-211-058

**CITIGROUP, INC.**

153 East 53rd Street, New York, NY, 10043

Tel: (212) 559-1000     Fax: (212) 559-3646     www.citigroup.com

*Provides insurance and financial services worldwide.*

**Citibank N.A., Immeuble Botreau-Roussel, 18 Ave. Delafosse, 01 Boite Postale 3698, Abidjan, Ivory Coast**

Contact: Mark H. Wiessing

**COLGATE-PALMOLIVE COMPANY**

300 Park Ave., New York, NY, 10022

Tel: (212) 310-2000     Fax: (212) 310-2919     www.colgate.com

*Mfr. pharmaceuticals, cosmetics, toiletries and detergents.*

**Colgate-Palmolive Cote d'Ivoire, Blvd. Giscard d'Estaing, 01 Boite Postale 1283, Abidjan, Ivory Coast**

**DELOITTE TOUCHE TOHMATSU INTERNATIONAL**

1633 Broadway, New York, NY, 10019

Tel: (212) 492-4000     Fax: (212) 392-4154     www.deloitte.com

*Accounting, audit, tax and management consulting services.*

**Deloitte & Touche, Immeuble Alpha 2000 14e Etage, rue Gourgas, Plateau,(B.P. 224) Abidjan 01, Ivory Coast**

**DHL WORLDWIDE EXPRESS**

50 California Avenue, San Francisco, CA, 94111

Tel: (415) 677-6100     Fax: (415) 824-9700     www.dhl.com

*Worldwide air express carrier.*

**DHL Worldwide Express, Ivory Coast**

Tel: 225-249999

**THE DOW CHEMICAL COMPANY**

2030 Dow Center, Midland, MI, 48674

Tel: (517) 636-1000     Fax: (517) 636-3228     www.dow.com

*Mfr. chemicals, plastics, pharmaceuticals, agricultural products, consumer products.*

**Dow Chemical Co., Boite Postale 1521, Abidjan, Ivory Coast**

### ERNST & YOUNG, LLP

787 Seventh Ave., New York, NY, 10019

Tel: (212) 773-3000      Fax: (212) 773-6350      www.eyi.com

*Accounting and audit, tax and management consulting services.*

**Ernst & Young, 5 Ave. Marchand, 01 Boite Postale 2715, Abidjan, Ivory Coast**

**FFA Ernst & Young, 5 Ave. Marchand, 01 Boite Postale 1222, Abidjan, Ivory Coast**

Tel: 225-21-11-15   Fax: 225-21-12-59   Contact: Leon Dakouri

### FMC CORPORATION

200 E. Randolph Drive, Chicago, IL, 60601

Tel: (312) 861-6000      Fax: (312) 861-6141      www.fmc.com

*Produces chemicals and precious metals, mfr. machinery, equipment and systems for industrial, agricultural and government use.*

**FMC Overseas Ltd., Ivory Coast**

### FRITZ COMPANIES, INC.

706 Mission Street, Ste. 900, San Francisco, CA, 94103

Tel: (415) 904-8360      Fax: (415) 904-8661      www.fritz.com

*Integrated transportation, sourcing, distribution and customs brokerage services.*

**Fritz Companies Inc., Ivory Coast**

### H.J. HEINZ COMPANY

600 Grant Street, Pittsburgh, PA, 15219

Tel: (412) 456-5700      Fax: (412) 456-6128      www.heinz.com

*Processed food products and nutritional services.*

**Star-Kist Foods Inc., Abidjan, Ivory Coast**

### S C JOHNSON & SON INC.

1525 Howe St., Racine, WI, 53403

Tel: (414) 260-2000      Fax: (414) 260-2133      www.scjohnsonwax.com

*Home, auto, commercial and personal care products and specialty chemicals.*

**S.C. Johnson & Son Inc., c/o CFCI Div. Technique, Boite Postale 1844, Abidjan, Ivory Coast**

### LEXMARK INTERNATIONAL

1 Lexmark Centre Dr., Lexington, KY, 40550

Tel: (606) 232-2000      Fax: (606) 232-1886      www.lexmark.com

*Develop, manufacture, supply of printing solutions and products, including laser, inkjet, and dot matrix printers.*

**Revendeur Lexmark, BP 2292, Abidjan 11, Ivory Coast**

### ELI LILLY & COMPANY

Lilly Corporate Center, Indianapolis, IN, 46285

Tel: (317) 276-2000      Fax: (317) 277-6579      www.lilly.com

*Mfr. pharmaceuticals and animal health products.*

**Eli Lilly - Bureau d'Informations, 01 Boite Postale 8615, Abidjan, Ivory Coast**

Tel: 225-22-36-18   Fax: 225-22-36-14

### LOWE LINTAS & PARTNERS WORLDWIDE

One Dag Hammarskjold Plaza, New York, NY, 10017

Tel: (212) 605-8000      Fax: (212) 605-4705      www.interpublic.com

*Full-service, integrated marketing communications company/advertising agency.*

**Ammirati Puris Lintas, 16 Boite Poste 1340, Abidjan, Ivory Coast**

Tel: 225-21-2549   Fax: 225-22-8182   Contact: Yannick Merand

## McCANN-ERICKSON WORLDGROUP

750 Third Ave., New York, NY, 10017

Tel: (212) 984-3644    Fax: (212) 984-2629    www.mccann.com

*International advertising and marketing services.*

**Nelson McCann-Ivory Coast, Ave. Giscard d'Estaing face a "La Galerie", 01 Boite Postale 3420, Abidjan, Ivory Coast**

## J. P. MORGAN CHASE & CO. INC.

World Headquarters, 270 Park Ave., New York, NY, 10017

Tel: (212) 270-6000    Fax: (212) 622-9030    www.jpmorganchase.com

*Provides integrated financial solutions for institutions and individuals worldwide, including asset management, investment banking and commercial banking.*

**J. P. Morgan Chase & Co., 01 Boite Postale 4107, Abidjan, Ivory Coast**

## PHILLIPS PETROLEUM COMPANY

Phillips Building, 411 S. Keeler Ave., Bartlesville, OK, 74004

Tel: (918) 661-6600    Fax: (918) 661-7636    www.phillips66.com

*Crude oil, natural gas, liquefied petroleum gas, gasoline and petro-chemicals.*

**Phillips Petroleum, Boite Postale 20947, Abidjan, Ivory Coast**

## PRICEWATERHOUSECOOPERS LLP

1301 Ave. of the Americas, New York, NY, 10019

Tel: (212) 596-7000    Fax: (212) 259-1301    www.pwcglobal.com

*Accounting and auditing, tax and management, and human resource consulting services.*

**PriceWaterhouseCoopers, Boite Postale 2921, Abidjan 01, Ivory Coast**

Tel: 225-22-22-89   Fax: 225-22-87-02

## R&B FALCON CORPORATION

901 Threadneedle, Ste. 200, Houston, TX, 77079

Tel: (281) 496-5000    Fax: (281) 496-4363    www.rbfalcon.com

*Offshore contract drilling.*

**R&B Falcon Exploration Co./c/o Ranger Oil Cote D'Ivoire Sarl, Avenue Houdaille, Imeuble Ranger Oil, 01 B.P. 8707 Abidjan, Ivory Coast**

## TEXACO INC.

2000 Westchester Ave., White Plains, NY, 10650

Tel: (914) 253-4000    Fax: (914) 253-7753    www.texaco.com

*Exploration/marketing crude oil, mfr. petro chemicals and products.*

**Texaco Cote d'Ivoire, Boite Postale 1782, Abidjan, Ivory Coast**

## TIDEWATER INC.

601 Poydras Street, Ste.1900, New Orleans, LA, 70130

Tel: (504) 568-1010    Fax: (504) 566-4582    www.tdw.com

*Marine service and equipment to companies engaged in exploration, development and production of oil, gas and minerals.*

**Tidewater Marine International, Inc., Apt. 38A 57/F, Immeuble Longchamp Plateau, Abidjan 01, Ivory Coast**

Tel: 225-22-69-58   Fax: 225-21-72-00

## UNITED PARCEL SERVICE, INC.

55 Glenlake Parkway, NE, Atlanta, GA, 30328

Tel: (404) 828-6000    Fax: (404) 828-6593    www.ups.com

*International package-delivery service.*

**UPS, Treichville Immeuble Nanan Yamousso, Esc I - Apt. 141-1 er étage, 05 Boite Postale 2877 Abidjan, Ivory Coast**

Tel: 225-25-97-40   Fax: 225-25-97-40

## WACKENHUT CORPORATION

4200 Wackenhut Dr., Ste. 100, Palm Beach Gardens, FL, 33410

Tel: (561) 622-5656      Fax: (561) 691-6736      www.wackenhut.com

*Security systems and services.*

**Wackenhut Seges, 2 Plateaux rue des Jardins, Boite Postale 2159, Abidjan, Ivory Coast**

Tel: 225-425926   Fax: 225-425141

## HARRY WINSTON INC.

718 Fifth Ave., New York, NY, 10019

Tel: (212) 245-2000      Fax:           www.harry-winston.com

*Diamonds and lapidary work.*

**Societe Wharton, Boite Postale 2816, Abidjan, Ivory Coast**

## XEROX CORPORATION

800 Long Ridge Road, PO Box 1600, Stamford, CT, 06904

Tel: (203) 968-3000      Fax: (203) 968-4312      www.xerox.com

*Mfr. document processing equipment, systems and supplies.*

**Ivoire Document Systems, Immeuble Carville Bd, Giscard d'Estaing, 01 Boite Postale 402, Abdijan, Ivory Coast**

Tel: 225-256-060   Fax: 225-255-950

## YORK INTERNATIONAL CORPORATION

631 South Richland Ave., York, PA, 17403

Tel: (717) 771-7890      Fax: (717) 771-6212      www.york.com

*Mfr. heating, ventilating, air conditioning and refrigeration equipment.*

**AFRIC Refrigeration, rue de Chimistes - Z,.I. Vridi, 15BP 1111, Abidjan 15-RCI Ivory Coast**

Tel: 225-27-3448

# Jamaica

**3M**

3M Center, St. Paul, MN, 55144-1000

Tel: (651) 733-1110    Fax: (651) 733-9973    www.mmm.com

*Mfr. diversified products for industry, health care, imaging, communications, transport, safety, consumer, etc.*

**3M Interamerica Inc. (Jamaica Div.), 218 Marcus Garvey Lane, Kingston 11, Jamaica**

Tel: 809-937-3859   Fax: 809-937-4369

## AIR EXPRESS INTERNATIONAL CORPORATION

120 Tokeneke Road, PO Box 1231, Darien, CT, 06820

Tel: (203) 655-7900    Fax: (203) 655-5779    www.aeilogistics.com

*International air freight forwarder.*

**Aeor International Shipping, 89 East St., Kingston, Jamaica**

Tel: 809-922-2537   Fax: 809-967-2773

## ALCOA INC.

Alcoa Center, 201 Isabella Street, Pittsburgh, PA, 15215-5858

Tel: (412) 553-4545    Fax: (412) 553-4498    www.alcoa.com

*World's leading producer of aluminum and alumina; mining, refining, smelting, fabricating and recycling.*

**Alcoa Minerals of Jamaica L.L.C., PO Box 241, Kingston 6, Jamaica**

## ALCOA FUJIKURA LTD.

105 Westpark Drive, Brentwood, TN, 37027

Tel: (615) 370-2100    Fax: (615) 370-2180    www.alcoa-fujikura.com

*Mfr. optical groundwire, tube cable, fiber optic connectors and automotive wiring harnesses.*

**Alcoa Minerals of Jamaica, L.L.C., Clarendon, Jamaica**

## AMERICAN AIRLINES INC.

4333 Amon Carter Boulevard, Ft. Worth, TX, 76155

Tel: (817) 963-1234    Fax: (817) 967-9641    www.amrcorp.com

*Air transport services.*

**American Airlines, PO Box 159, Windward Rd. Station, Kingston 2, Jamaica**

## AMERICAN INTERNATIONAL GROUP INC. (AIG)

70 Pine Street, New York, NY, 10270

Tel: (212) 770-7000    Fax: (212) 509-9705    www.aig.com

*Worldwide insurance and financial services.*

**American Intl. Underwriters (Jamaica) Ltd., 25 Dominica Drive, 5th Fl., Kingston, Jamaica**

## ANC RENTAL CORP.

110 Southeast Sixth St., Ft. Lauderdale, FL, 33301

Tel: (954) 769-7000    Fax: (954) 769-7000    www.ancrental.com

*Engaged in car rental services, including National Car Rental and Alamo Rent A Car.*

**National Car Rental, 16 Beechwood Ave., Kingston 5, Jamaica**

## AVIS GROUP HOLDINGS, INC.

900 Old Country Road., Garden City, NY, 11530

Tel: (516) 222-3000     Fax: (516) 222-4381     www.avis.com

*Car rental services.*

**Avis Group Holdings Ltd.., 3 Oxford Rd., New Kingston, Jamaica**

## D. D. BEAN & SONS COMPANY

Peterborough Road, PO Box 348, Jaffrey, NH, 03452

Tel: (603) 532-8311     Fax: (603) 532-7361     www.ddbean.com

*Mfr. paper book and wooden stick matches.*

**Jamaica Match Holdings Ltd., PO Box 370, Kingston 11, Jamaica**

## LOUIS BERGER INTERNATIONAL INC.

100 Halsted Street, East Orange, NJ, 07019

Tel: (201) 678-1960     Fax: (201) 672-4284     www.louisberger.com

*Consulting engineers, engaged in architecture, environmental and advisory services.*

**Louis Berger International Inc., Office Center UDC Building, 12 Ocean Boulevard 7th Floor, Kingston, Jamaica**

## SAMUEL BINGHAM COMPANY

127 East Lake Street, Ste. 300, Bloomingdale, IL, 60108

Tel: (630) 924-9250     Fax: (630) 924-0469     www.binghamrollers.com

*Print and industrial rollers and inks.*

**Coates Bros. (Jamaica) Ltd., PO Box 317, Kingston 11, Jamaica**

Tel: 876-923-6028

## BLUE CROSS AND BLUE SHIELD ASSOC.

225 N. Michigan Ave., Chicago, IL, 60601-7680

Tel: (312) 297-6000     Fax: (312) 297-6609     www.blueshield.com

*Provides health care coverage through indemnity insurance, HMO's and Medicare programs.*

**BlueCare Worldwide, Jamaica**

## BRISTOL-MYERS SQUIBB COMPANY

345 Park Ave., New York, NY, 10154-0037

Tel: (212) 546-4000     Fax: (212) 546-4020     www.bms.com

*Pharmaceutical and food preparations, medical and surgical instruments.*

**Mead Johnson Jamaica Ltd., 16 Half Way Tree Rd., Kingston 5, Jamaica**

**Mead Johnson Jamaica Ltd., 8 Carvalho Drive, Kingston 10, Jamaica**

**Media-Grace, 33 1/2 Eastwood Park Road, Kingston, Jamaica West Indies**

## BUSH BOAKE ALLEN INC.

7 Mercedes Drive, Montvale, NJ, 07645

Tel: (201) 391-9870     Fax: (201) 391-0860     www.bushboakeallen.com

*Mfr. aroma chemicals for fragrances and flavor products for seasonings.*

**Bush Boake Allen Ltd., 226 Spanish Town Road, Kingston 11, Jamaica**

Tel: 876-923-5111    Fax: 876-923-4323

## CARBOLINE COMPANY

350 Hanley Industrial Court, St. Louis, MO, 63144

Tel: (314) 644-1000     Fax: (314) 644-4617     www.carboline.com

*Mfr. coatings and sealants.*

**Berger Paints Jamaica Ltd., PO Box 8, 256 Spanish Town Rd., Kingston 11, Jamaica**

## CHOICE HOTELS INTERNATIONAL, INC.

10750 Columbia Pike, Silver Springs, MD, 20902

Tel: (301) 592-5000      Fax: (301) 592-6157      www.choicehotels.com

*Hotel franchises, including Comfort Inn, Econo Lodge, Roadway Inn and Quality.*

**Comfort Suites Crane Ridge,  17 La Costa Drive, Ocho Rios, Jamaica**

## CIGNA COMPANIES

One Liberty Place, Philadelphia, PA, 19192

Tel: (215) 761-1000      Fax: (215) 761-5511      www.cigna.com

*Insurance, invest, health care and other financial services.*

**Insurance Co. of North America,  21 Constant Spring Rd., Kingston, Jamaica**

## CITIGROUP, INC.

153 East 53rd Street, New York, NY, 10043

Tel: (212) 559-1000      Fax: (212) 559-3646      www.citigroup.com

*Provides insurance and financial services worldwide.*

**Citibank N.A.,  63-67 Knutsford Blvd., PO Box 286, Kingston 5, Jamaica**

Contact: Peter H. Moses

## COLGATE-PALMOLIVE COMPANY

300 Park Ave., New York, NY, 10022

Tel: (212) 310-2000      Fax: (212) 310-2919      www.colgate.com

*Mfr. pharmaceuticals, cosmetics, toiletries and detergents.*

**Colgate-Palmolive (Jamaica) Ltd.,  26 Marcus Garvey Dr., Kingston 11, Jamaica**

## CUNA MUTUAL BUSINESS SERVICES

5910 Mineral Point Rd., PO Box 391, Madison, WI, 53701

Tel: (608) 238-5851      Fax: (608) 238-0830      www.cunamutual.com

*Insurance services.*

**CUNA Mutual Insurance,  2A Manhattan Rd., PO Box 396, Kingston 5, Jamaica**

## DELOITTE TOUCHE TOHMATSU INTERNATIONAL

1633 Broadway, New York, NY, 10019

Tel: (212) 492-4000      Fax: (212) 392-4154      www.deloitte.com

*Accounting, audit, tax and management consulting services.*

**Deloitte & Touche,  7 West Ave., PO Box 13, Kingston Gardens Kingston 4, Jamaica**

**Deloitte & Touche,  42B & 42C Union St., PO Box 60, Montego Bay, Jamaica**

## DEVELOPMENT ASSOCIATES INC.

1730 North Lynn Street, Arlington, VA, 22209-2023

Tel: (703) 276-0677      Fax: (703) 276-0432      www.developmentassociates.com

*Management consulting services.*

**Development Associates, Inc.,  1 Holborn Rd., Kingston 10, Jamaica**

Tel: 876-929-3574    Fax: 876-926-1813

## DHL WORLDWIDE EXPRESS

50 California Avenue, San Francisco, CA, 94111

Tel: (415) 677-6100      Fax: (415) 824-9700      www.dhl.com

*Worldwide air express carrier.*

**DHL Worldwide Express,  54 Duke St., Kingston, Jamaica**

Tel: 876-922-7333

## DOVER CORPORATION

280 Park Ave., New York, NY, 10017-1292

Tel: (212) 922-1640      Fax: (212) 922-1656      www.dovercorporation.com

*Holding company for varied industries; assembly and testing equipment, oil-well gear and other industrial products.*

**Multi-Tec Engineering Services, Ltd., 4 Balmoral Ave., Kingston, Jamaica**

Tel: 876-926-4663    Fax: 876-929-9119

## EAGLE GLOBAL LOGISTICS (EGL)

15350 Vickery Drive, Houston, TX, 77032

Tel: (281) 618-3100      Fax: (281) 618-3100      www.eaglegl.com

*Ocean/air freight forwarding, customs brokerage, packing and wholesale, logistics management and insurance.*

**Inter Freight Agencies, Ltd., 105 Second St., Newport West, PO Box 113, Kingston 15 Jamaica**

Tel: 809-923-6562    Fax: 809-923-3139

## ECOLAB INC.

370 N. Wabasha Street, St. Paul, MN, 55102

Tel: (651) 293-2233      Fax: (651) 293-2379      www.ecolab.com

*Develop/mfr. premium cleaning, sanitizing and maintenance products and services for the hospitality, institutional, and residential markets.*

**Ecolab Ltd., Kingston, Jamaica**

Tel: 876-926-0750

## ENRON CORPORATION

1400 Smith Street, Houston, TX, 77002-7369

Tel: (713) 853-6161      Fax: (713) 853-3129      www.enron.com

*Exploration, production, transportation and distribution of integrated natural gas and electricity.*

**Industrial Gases Ltd., 595 Spanish Town Road, PO Box 224, Kingston Jamaica**

Tel: 809-923-8434   Fax: 809-923-4058

## ERNST & YOUNG, LLP

787 Seventh Ave., New York, NY, 10019

Tel: (212) 773-3000      Fax: (212) 773-6350      www.eyi.com

*Accounting and audit, tax and management consulting services.*

**Ernst & Young, 28 Beechwood Ave., PO Box 351, Kingston 5, Jamaica**

Tel: 809-929-1616   Fax: 809-926-7580   Contact: Vilma Wallen

## FRITZ COMPANIES, INC.

706 Mission Street, Ste. 900, San Francisco, CA, 94103

Tel: (415) 904-8360      Fax: (415) 904-8661      www.fritz.com

*Integrated transportation, sourcing, distribution and customs brokerage services.*

**Fritz Companies Inc., Kingston, Jamaica**

## THE GILLETTE COMPANY

Prudential Tower Building, Boston, MA, 02199

Tel: (617) 421-7000      Fax: (617) 421-7123      www.gillette.com

*Develop/mfr. personal care/use products: blades and razors, toiletries, cosmetics, stationery.*

**Gillette Caribbean Ltd., Kingston, Jamaica**

Contact: Práxedes M. Rivera-Ferrer, Gen. Mgr.

**Gillette Foreign Sales Corp. Ltd., Kingston, Jamaica**

Contact: Práxedes M. Rivera-Ferrer, Gen. Mgr.

## THE GOODYEAR TIRE & RUBBER COMPANY

1144 East Market Street, Akron, OH, 44316

Tel: (330) 796-2121    Fax: (330) 796-1817    www.goodyear.com

*Mfr. tires, automotive belts and hose, conveyor belts, chemicals; oil pipeline transmission.*

**Goodyear (Jamaica) Ltd., 29 Tobago Ave., Kingston 10, Jamaica**

## GREY GLOBAL GROUP

777 Third Ave., New York, NY, 10017

Tel: (212) 546-2000    Fax: (212) 546-1495    www.grey.com

*International advertising agency.*

**Grimax Advertising, Kingston, Jamaica**

## HOLIDAY INN (BASS RESORTS) WORLDWIDE, INC.

3 Ravinia Drive, Ste. 2900, Atlanta, GA, 30346-2149

Tel: (770) 604-2000    Fax: (770) 604-5403    www.holidayinn.com

*Hotels, restaurants and casinos.*

**Rose Hall, PO Box 480, Montego Bay, Jamaica**

## HORWATH INTERNATIONAL ASSOCIATION

415 Madison Ave., New York, NY, 10017

Tel: (212) 838-5566    Fax: (212) 838-3636    www.horwath.com

*Public accountants and auditors.*

**Horwath & Horwath (Jamaica), PO Box 26, 2 Ripon Road, Kingston 5, Jamaica**

## IBM CORPORATION

New Orchard Road, Armonk, NY, 10504

Tel: (914) 765-1900    Fax: (914) 765-7382    www.ibm.com

*Information products, technology and services.*

**IBM World Trade Corporation, 52-56 Knutsford Blvd., PO Box 391, New Kingston, Kingston 5 Jamaica**

Tel: 876-926-3200

## INTELLIGROUP, INC.

499 Thornall Street, Edison, NJ, 08837

Tel: (732) 590-1600    Fax: (732) 362-2100    www.intelligroup.com

*Provides systems integration, customer software and Internet application development.*

**Intelligroup Jamaica Ltd., 89 East Street Ste. 203, Kingston Jamaica BWI**

Tel: 876-7023557

## J. WALTER THOMPSON COMPANY

466 Lexington Ave., New York, NY, 10017

Tel: (212) 210-7000    Fax: (212) 210-6944    www.jwt.com

*International advertising and marketing services.*

**Dunlop Corbin Communications, Kingston, Jamaica**

## JOHNSON & JOHNSON

One Johnson & Johnson Plaza, New Brunswick, NJ, 08933

Tel: (732) 524-0400    Fax: (732) 214-0334    www.jnj.com

*Mfr./distributor/R&D pharmaceutical, health care and cosmetic products.*

**Johnson & Johnson Ltd., PO Box 8103, Kingston 11, Jamaica**

## KAISER ALUMINUM CORPORATION

5847 San Felipe, Ste. 2600, Houston, TX, 77057-3010

Tel: (713) 267-3777    Fax: (713) 267-3701    www.kaiseral.com

*Aluminum refining and manufacturing.*

**Alumina Partners of Jamaica (Alpart), Nain, Jamaica**

Kaiser Jamaica Bauxite Company (KJBC), Jamaica

## KOPPERS INDUSTRIES INC.

Koppers Bldg, 436 Seventh Ave., Pittsburgh, PA, 15219-1800

Tel: (412) 227-2000    Fax: (412) 227-2333    www.koppers.com

*Construction materials and services; chemicals and building products.*

**Wood Preservation Ltd., Kingston, Jamaica**

## KPMG INTERNATIONAL LLP

345 Park Avenue, New York, NY, 10022

Tel: (201) 307-7000    Fax: (201) 930-8617    www.kpmg.com

*Accounting and audit, tax and management consulting services.*

**KPMG Peat Marwick, The Victoria Mutual Bldg., 6 Duke St., Kingston, Jamaica**

Tel: 809-922-6640  Fax: 809-922-7198  Contact: Rolf Lanigan, Sr. Ptnr.

## LAND O' LAKES, INC.

4001 Lexington Ave. North, Arden Hills, MN, 55126

Tel: (612) 481-2222    Fax: (612) 481-2022    www.landolakes.com

*Produces butter, margarine, packaged milk, sour cream, snack dips and Alpine Lace cheeses and crop protection products.*

**Land O' Lakes, Inc., Jamaica**

## MAIDENFORM WORLDWIDE INC.

154 Avenue E, Bayonne, NJ, 07002

Tel: (201) 436-9200    Fax: (201) 436-9009    www.maidenform.com

*Mfr. intimate apparel.*

**Jamaica Needlecraft Ltd., PO Box 28, Kingston 15, Jamaica**

## MARSH & McLENNAN COS INC.

1166 Ave. of the Americas, New York, NY, 10036-2774

Tel: (212) 345-5000    Fax: (212) 345-4808    www.marshmac.com

*Insurance agents/brokers, pension and investment management consulting services.*

**Allied Insurance Brokers Ltd., 26 Belmont Rd., Kingston 5, Jamaica**

Tel: 876-926-6784   Fax: 876-929-9391   Contact: Paul A. Bitter

## MAXXAM INC.

5847 San Felipe, Ste. 2600, Houston, TX, 77057

Tel: (713) 975-7600    Fax: (713) 267-3701

*Holding company for aluminum and timber products and real estate industries.*

**MAXXAM Inc., Jamaica**

## McCANN-ERICKSON WORLDGROUP

750 Third Ave., New York, NY, 10017

Tel: (212) 984-3644    Fax: (212) 984-2629    www.mccann.com

*International advertising and marketing services.*

**McCann-Erickson (Jamaica) Ltd., 7 Knutsford Street, PO Box 168, Kingston 5, Jamaica**

## McDONALD'S CORPORATION

McDonald's Plaza, Oak Brook, IL, 60523

Tel: (630) 623-3000    Fax: (630) 623-7409    www.mcdonalds.com

*Fast food chain stores.*

**McDonald's Corp., Montego Bay, Jamaica**

## NABISCO HOLDINGS, CORP.

7 Campus Drive, Parsippany, NJ, 07054

Tel: (973) 682-5000     Fax: (973) 503-2153     www.nabisco.com

*Mfr. consumer packaged food products and tobacco products.*

**West Indies Yeast Co. Ltd., 38 Jobs Lane, Spanish Town, St. Catherine, Jamaica**

## NALCO CHEMICAL COMPANY

One Nalco Center, Naperville, IL, 60563-1198

Tel: (630) 305-1000     Fax: (630) 305-2900     www.nalco.com

*Chemicals for water and waste water treatment, oil products and refining, industry processes; water and energy management service.*

**Nalco Chemical Jamaica, Kingston, Jamaica**

Tel: 809-968-8165   Fax: 809-929-2848

## PIONEER HI-BRED INTERNATIONAL INC.

400 Locust Street, Ste. 800, Des Moines, IA, 50309

Tel: (515) 248-4800     Fax: (515) 248-4999     www.pioneer.com

*Agricultural chemicals, farm supplies, biological products, research.*

**Pioneer Hi-Bred/Tropical Research Station, PO Box 197, Kingston 11, Jamaica**

Tel: 876-984-3234

## PRICEWATERHOUSECOOPERS LLP

1301 Ave. of the Americas, New York, NY, 10019

Tel: (212) 596-7000     Fax: (212) 259-1301     www.pwcglobal.com

*Accounting and auditing, tax and management, and human resource consulting services.*

**PriceWaterhouseCoopers, Scotiabank Centre, Duke St., PO Box 372, Kingston Jamaica**

Tel: 809-922-6230   Fax: 809-922-7581

**PriceWaterhouseCoopers, 32 Market St., PO Box 180, Montego Bay, Jamaica**

Tel: 809-952-5065   Fax: 809-952-1273

## RADISSON HOTELS INTERNATIONAL

Carlson Pkwy., PO Box 59159, Minneapolis, MN, 55459-8204

Tel: (612) 540-5526     Fax: (612) 449-3400     www.radisson.com

*Hotels and resorts.*

**Ciboney, Ocho Rios, PO Box 728, Ocho Rios, Jamaica**

**Poinciana Beach Resort, Negril, Jamaica**

## RENAISSANCE HOTELS AND RESORTS

10400 Fernwood Road, Bethesda, MD, 20817

Tel: (301) 380-3000     Fax: (301) 380-5181     www.renaissancehotels.com

*Hotel and resort chain.*

**Renaissance Hotel, Ocho Rios, Jamaica**

Tel: 809-974-2201

## SHERWIN-WILLIAMS CO., INC.

101 Prospect Ave., N.W., Cleveland, OH, 44115-1075

Tel: (216) 566-2000     Fax: (216) 566-2947     www.sherwin-williams.com

*Mfr. paint, wallcoverings and related products.*

**Sherwin-Williams West Indies Ltd., PO Box 35, Spanish Town, St. Catherine, Jamaica**

### STANLEY CONSULTANTS, INC.

Stanley Building, 225 Iowa Ave., Muscatine, IA, 52761-3764

Tel: (319) 264-6600    Fax: (319) 264-6658    www.stanleygroup.com

*Engaged in engineering, architectural, planning and management services.*

**Stanley Consultants, Inc.,  Barnett & Harbour St., South Gully, Montego Bay, Jamaica**

Tel: 876-956-3698   Fax: 876-956-3641

**Stanley Consultants, Inc.,  3A Dumfries Road, Kingston 5, Jamaica BWI**

Tel: 876-926-4820

### TEXACO INC.

2000 Westchester Ave., White Plains, NY, 10650

Tel: (914) 253-4000    Fax: (914) 253-7753    www.texaco.com

*Exploration/marketing crude oil, mfr. petro chemicals and products.*

**Texaco Caribbean Inc.,  Mutual Life Centre, 2 Oxford St., Kingston 5, Jamaica**

### TRANS WORLD AIRLINES INC.

515 North Sixth Street, St. Louis, MO, 63101

Tel: (314) 589-3000    Fax: (314) 589-3129    www.twa.com

*Air transport services.*

**Trans World Airlines,  Montego Bay, Jamaica**

### TRUE NORTH COMMUNICATIONS INC.

101 East Erie Street, Chicago, IL, 60611

Tel: (312) 425-6500    Fax: (312) 425-5010    www.truenorth.com

*Holding company, advertising agency.*

**Lindo/FCB,  14 Ruthven Rd., Kingston 10, Jamaica**

### UNITED PARCEL SERVICE, INC.

55 Glenlake Parkway, NE, Atlanta, GA, 30328

Tel: (404) 828-6000    Fax: (404) 828-6593    www.ups.com

*International package-delivery service.*

**UPS / Airpak Express,  Tinson Pen Aerodrome, PO Box 50, Kingston 11, Jamaica**

Tel: 876-923-0371   Fax: 876-923-5089

### WATSON WYATT & COMPANY HOLDINGS

6707 Democracy Blvd., Ste. 800, Bethesda, MD, 20817

Tel: (301) 581-4600    Fax: (301) 581-4937    www.watsonwyatt.com

*Creates compensation and benefits programs for major corporations.*

**Watson Wyatt Kingston,  1 Holborn Rd., Kingston 10, Jamaica**

Tel: 809-926-1659   Fax: 809-926-1212   Contact: Astor Duggan

### WYNDHAM INTERNATIONAL, INC.

1950 Stemmons Fwy., Ste. 6001, Dallas, TX, 75207

Tel: (214) 863-1000    Fax: (214) 863-1527    www.wyndhamintl.com

*Hotel operator.*

**Wyndham Rose Hall Resort and Country Club,  PO Box 599, Mnontego Bay, Jamaica**

Tel: 876-953-2650   Fax: 876-953-2617

### XEROX CORPORATION

800 Long Ridge Road, PO Box 1600, Stamford, CT, 06904

Tel: (203) 968-3000    Fax: (203) 968-4312    www.xerox.com

*Mfr. document processing equipment, systems and supplies.*

**Xerox (Jamaica) Ltd.,  L.O.J. Centre Ground Fl., PO Box 226, Kingston 5, Jamaica**

Tel: 809-926-5630   Fax: 809-929-5372

# Japan

## 3COM CORPORATION
5400 Bayfront Plaza, Santa Clara, CA, 95052-8145
Tel: (408) 326-5000    Fax: (408) 326-5001    www.3com.com
*Develop/mfr. computer networking products and systems.*
**3Com (USR), B-6F Shuwa Shiba Park Bldg. 4-1, 2-chome Shibakoen, Minato-ku, Tokyo 105 Japan**
Tel: 81-3-5402-6182    Fax: 81-3-5402-6201
**3Com Japan, Shinjuku Sumitomo Bldg. 23F, 2-6-1 Nishi Shinjuku, Shinjuku-ku, Tokyo 163-02 Japan**
Tel: 81-3-3345-7251    Fax: 81-3-3345-7261
**3Com Japan - Osaka, Nishi Honmaci Mitsui Bldg. 3F, 1-3-15 Awaza, Nishi-ku, Oska-shi, Osaka 550 Japan**
Tel: 81-6-536-3303    Fax: 81-6-536-3304

## 3D LABS INC., LTD.
480 Potrero Avenue, Sunnyvale, CA, 94086
Tel: (408) 530-4700    Fax: (408) 530-4701    www.3dlabs.com
*Produces 3D graphics accelerators chips for the PC computer platform.*
**3D Labs K.K., Level 16 Shiroyama Hills, 4-3-1 Toranomon, Minato-ku Tokyo 105 Japan**
Tel: 81-3-5403-4653    Fax: 81-3-5403-4654

## 3M
3M Center, St. Paul, MN, 55144-1000
Tel: (651) 733-1110    Fax: (651) 733-9973    www.mmm.com
*Mfr. diversified products for industry, health care, imaging, communications, transport, safety, consumer, etc.*
**Sumitomo 3M Ltd., PO Box 43, 33-1 Tamagawa-dai 2-chome, Setagaya-ku, Tokyo 158 Japan**
Tel: 81-3-3709-8170    Fax: 81-3-3709-8751    Contact: William G. Allen

## AAF INTERNATIONAL (AMERICAN AIR FILTER)
215 Central Ave., PO Box 35690, Louisville, KY, 40232-5690
Tel: (502) 637-0011    Fax: (502) 637-0321    www.aafintl.com
*Mfr. air filtration/pollution control and noise control equipment.*
**Japan Air Filter Co. Ltd., 1-37 Kuryozutsumi, Hiratsuka, Kanagawa 254, Japan**
Tel: 81-463-231611    Fax: 81-463-234027

## ABBOTT LABORATORIES
One Abbott Park, Abbott Park, IL, 60064-3500
Tel: (847) 937-6100    Fax: (847) 937-1511    www.abbott.com
*Development/mfr./sale diversified health care products and services.*
**Abbott/Dainabot Co., Osaka Tokio Marine Bldg., 2-53 Shiromi 2- chome, Chuo-ku Osaka 540-001, Japan**

## ACADEMIC PRESS INC.
6277 Sea Harbor Drive, Orlando, FL, 32887
Tel: (407) 345-2000    Fax: (407) 345-8388    www.academicpress.com
*Publisher of educational and scientific books.*
**Harcourt Brace - Academic Press Japan, 22-1 Ichibancho, Chiyoda-ku, Tokyo 102 Japan**
Tel: 81-3-3234-3911    Fax: 81-3-3265-7186

## ACCLAIM ENTERTAINMENT, INC.

One Acclaim Plaza, Glen Cove, NY, 11542

Tel: (516) 656-5000    Fax: (516) 656-2040    www.acclaim.com

*Mfr. video games.*

**Acclaim Japan, Ltd., 210 Nomora Bldg. 6th Fl., 2-10-9 Shibuya, Shibuyaku Tokyo 150-0002, Japan**

## ACCO BRANDS, INC.

300 Tower Parkway, Lincoln, IL, 60069

Tel: (847) 541-9500    Fax: (847) 541-5750    www.acco.com

*Provides services in the office and computer markets and manufactures paper fasteners, clips, metal fasteners, binders and staplers.*

**ACCO Japan, Ste. 513, 2-1-15 Takanawa, Minato-ku, Tokyo 108, Japan**

## ACCURIDE INTERNATIONAL, INC.

12311 Shoemaker Ave., Santa Fe Springs, CA, 90670-4721

Tel: (562) 903-0200    Fax: (562) 903-0208    www.accuride.com

*Mfr. drawer slides.*

**Accuride, 2-5-13 Nihonbashi Muromachi, Chuo-ku, Tokyo 103, Japan**

## ACE CONTROLS INC.

23435 Industrial Park Drive, Farmington Hills, MI, 48024

Tel: (248) 476-0213    Fax: (248) 276-2470    www.acecontrols.com

*Industry hydraulic shock absorbers, cylinders, valves and automation controls.*

**ACE Controls Japan Ltd., 261-1-102 Tamasaki, Ichihara City - Chiba Pref., 290 Japan**
Tel: 81-436-246711  Fax: 81-436-246712

## ACHESON COLLOIDS COMPANY

PO Box 611747, Port Huron, MI, 48061-1747

Tel: (810) 984-5581    Fax: (810) 984-1446    www.achesoncolloids.com

*Chemicals, chemical preparations, paints and lubricating oils.*

**Acheson Japan Ltd., 6-B Kakogawa, Kogyo Danchi, Kakogawa 675-0011, Japan**
Tel: 81-79-426-2188  Fax: 81-79-421-8006

## ACTERNA CORPORATION

3 New England Executive Park, Burlington, MA, 01803

Tel: (781) 272-6100    Fax: (781) 272-2304    www.acterna.com

*Develop, manufacture and market communications test instruments, systems, software and services.*

**Acterna Corporation, Tokyo, Japan**

## ACTIVISION

3100 Ocean Park Boulevard, Santa Monica, CA, 90405

Tel: (310) 255-2000    Fax: (310) 255-2100    www.activision.com

*Development/mfr. entertainment software and video games.*

**Activision Japan, Aobadai Tower, Annex SF, 3-1-18, Aobadai, Meguro-ku, Tokyo 153, Japan**
Tel: 81-3-5458-6561  Fax: 81-3-5458-6562  Emp: 10

## ACTUATE CORPORATION

701 Gateway Boulevard South, San Francisco, CA, 94080

Tel: (650) 837-2000    Fax: (650) 827-1560    www.actuate.com

*Develops software.*

**Actuate Japan, 2-2-8 Roppongi, Minato-ku, Tokyo 106, Japan**
Tel: 81-03-3584-0970

## ADAPTEC INC.

691 South Milpitas Boulevard, Milpitas, CA, 95035

Tel: (408) 945-8600      Fax: (408) 262-2533      www.adaptec.com

*Design/mfr./marketing hardware and software solutions.*

**Adaptec Japan Ltd., Harmony Tower 3/F, 1-32-2 Honcho Nakano-ku, Tokyo 164 Japan**

Tel: 81-3-5365-6700   Fax: 81-3-5365-6950

## ADE CORPORATION

80 Wilson Way, Westwood, MA, 02090

Tel: (781) 467-3500      Fax: (781) 467-0500      www.ade.com

*Mfr. semiconductor wafers and computer disks.*

**Japan ADE Ltd., 16-1 Minami Kamata 2-Chome, Ohta-Ku, Tokyo 144, Japan**

Tel: 81-35703-5611   Fax: 81-35703-5600

## ADOBE SYSTEMS INCORPORATED

345 Park Avenue, San Jose, CA, 95110

Tel: (408) 536-6000      Fax: (408) 537-6000      www.adobe.com

*Engaged in print technology and distributor of Acrobat Reader.*

**Adobe Systems Co., Ltd., Gate City Osaki East Tower, 1-11-2 Osaki Shinagawa-ku, Tokyo 141-0032, Japan**

Tel: 81-3-5740-2400   Fax: 81-3-5423-8209

## ADVANCED MICRO DEVICES INC.

1 AMD Place, Sunnyvale, CA, 94086

Tel: (408) 732-2400      Fax: (408) 982-6164      www.amd.com

*Mfr. integrated circuits for communications and computation industry.*

**AMD/Sanyo Denki Co., Ltd., 1-15-1, Kita ootsuka, Toshimaku, Tokyo 170-8451 Japan**

## AEC INC.

801 AEC Drive, Wood Dale, IL, 60191

Tel: (630) 595-1060      Fax: (630) 595-8925      www.aecinternet.com

*Mfr./service auxiliary equipment for plastics industry.*

**The Sysko Corp., 8-9 Higeshiueno 4-chome, Taito-ku, Tokyo, Japan**

## THE AEROQUIP GROUP

3000 Strayer, PO Box 50, Maumee, OH, 43537

Tel: (419) 867-2200      Fax: (419) 867-2390      www.aeroquip.com

*Mfr. industrial, automotive, aerospace and defense products.*

**Aeroquip Automotive Japan, Inc., 13-1 Meieki-minami - 3/F, 2-chome Nakamuraku, Nagoya 450, Japan**

Tel: 81-52-561-8760   Fax: 81-52-561-8762

## AFLAC INCORPORATED

1932 Wynnton Rd., Columbus, GA, 31999

Tel: (706) 323-3431      Fax: (706) 324-6330      www.aflac.com

*Provides supplemental medical insurance policies for cancer care intensive care and nursing home care, accident and disability coverage.*

**AFLAC Japan, Tokyo, Japan**

**Dai-ichi Mutual Life Insurance Company, Tokyo, Japan**

## AIR EXPRESS INTERNATIONAL CORPORATION

120 Tokeneke Road, PO Box 1231, Darien, CT, 06820

Tel: (203) 655-7900      Fax: (203) 655-5779      www.aeilogistics.com

*International air freight forwarder.*

**AEI - Maruzen Ltd. - Reg. Hdqtrs., 3-6 Nohonbashi- Hamacho, 1-chome, Chuo-ku, Tokyo 103 Japan**

Tel: 81-3-5821-5851   Fax: 81-3-5821-5850

## AIR PRODUCTS AND CHEMICALS, INC.

7201 Hamilton Boulevard, Allentown, PA, 18195-1501

Tel: (610) 481-4911    Fax: (610) 481-5900    www.airproducts.com

*Mfr. industry gases and related equipment, specialty chemicals, environmental/energy systems.*

**Air Products Asia Inc., Shuwa 2, Kamiyacho Bldg., 3-18-19 Toranomon, Minato-ku, Tokyo 105, Japan**

Contact: Wayne A. Hinman, Pres.

## AJAX MAGNETHERMIC CORPORATION

1745 Overland Ave. NE, PO Box 991, Warren, OH, 44482

Tel: (330) 372-8511    Fax: (330) 372-8644    www.ajaxcan.com

*Mfr. induction heating and melting equipment.*

**Japan Ajax Magnethermic Co. Ltd., Kyodo Bldg. 6/F, 13-4 Kodenma-cho, Nihonbashi, Chuo-ku, Tokyo 103, Japan**

## ALBANY INTERNATIONAL CORPORATION

PO Box 1907, Albany, NY, 12201

Tel: (518) 445-2200    Fax: (518) 445-2265    www.albint.com

*Mfr. broadwoven and engineered fabrics, plastic products, filtration media.*

**Albany Intl. of Japan Ltd., 3/F Akasaka Sanno Bldg., 5-11 Akasaka 2-chome, Minato-ku, Tokyo 107, Japan**

## ALBEMARLE CORPORATION

PO Box 1335, 330 S. 4th Street, Richmond, VA, 23218-1335

Tel: (804) 788-6000    Fax: (804) 788-5688    www.albemarle.com

*Mfr. of specialty chemicals used in agriculture, photography, water treatment and petroleum products; mfr. phosphates used in beverages and detergents.*

**Albemarle Asano Corp., 2-2 Uchisaiwaicho-16/F., 2-Chome Chiyoda-ku, Tokyo 100 Japan**

Tel: 81-3-5251-0791   Fax: 81-3-3500-5623

## ALCOA INC.

Alcoa Center, 201 Isabella Street, Pittsburgh, PA, 15215-5858

Tel: (412) 553-4545    Fax: (412) 553-4498    www.alcoa.com

*World's leading producer of aluminum and alumina; mining, refining, smelting, fabricating and recycling.*

**Alcoa Fujikura Ltd., Tokyo, Japan**

Contact: Timothy J. Leveque, Pres.

**KSL Alcoa Aluminum Company, Ltd., Moka, Japan**

**Moralco Ltd., Iwakuni City, Japan**

## ALCOA FUJIKURA LTD.

105 Westpark Drive, Brentwood, TN, 37027

Tel: (615) 370-2100    Fax: (615) 370-2180    www.alcoa-fujikura.com

*Mfr. optical groundwire, tube cable, fiber optic connectors and automotive wiring harnesses.*

**Alcoa Fujikura Ltd., Shishiny Toho Bldg. (IOF), 3-17 Fukumachi, Naka-ku, Hiroshima City 730, Japan**

## ALLEGHENY LUDLUM CORPORATION

1000 Six PPG Place, Pittsburgh, PA, 15222

Tel: (412) 394-2805    Fax: (412) 394-2800    www.alleghenyludlum.com

*Mfr. steel and alloys.*

**Allegheny Ludlum, Tokyo, Japan**

Tel: 81-3-3239-9080   Fax: 813-3239-9021

## ALLEGHENY TECHNOLOGIES

1000 Six PPG Place, Pittsburgh, PA, 15222

Tel: (412) 394-2800     Fax: (412) 394-2805     www.alleghenytechnologies.com

*Diversified mfr. aviation and electronics, specialty metals, industrial and consumer products.*

**Allegheny Technologies, Nihon Seimei Akasaka Bldg. 3/F, 8-1-19 Akasaka, Minato-ku, Tokyo 107, Japan**

## ALLEN-BRADLEY COMPANY, INC.

1201 South Second Street, Milwaukee, WI, 53204

Tel: (414) 382-2000     Fax: (414) 382-4444     www.ab.com

*Mfr. electrical controls and information devices.*

**Allen-Bradley Japan Co. Ltd., Shinkawa Sanko Bldg., 3-17 Shinkawa 1-chome, Tokyo 104, Japan**

## ALLERGAN INC.

2525 Dupont Drive, PO Box 19534, Irvine, CA, 92713-9534

Tel: (714) 246-4500     Fax: (714) 246-6987     www.allergan.com

*Mfr. therapeutic eye care products, skin and neural care pharmaceuticals.*

**Allergan K.K., Toranomon 40 Mori Bldg., 13-1 Toranomon 5-Chome, Minato-ku, Tokyo 105 Japan**
Tel: 81-3-5402-8900  Fax: 81-3-5402-8970

## ALLIANCE CAPITAL MANAGEMENT HOLDING LP

1345 Ave. of the Americas, New York, NY, 10105

Tel: (212) 969-1000     Fax: (212) 969-2229     www.alliancecapital.com

*Engaged in fund management for large corporations.*

**Alliance Capital Management, Otemaci First Square West Tower 12/F, 1-5-1- Otemachi Chiyoda-ku, Tokyo 100-0004, Japan**
Tel: 81-3-3240-8410

## ALLIANCE SEMICONDUCTOR CORPORATION

2675 Augustine Drive, Santa Clara, CA, 95054

Tel: (408) 855-4900     Fax: (408) 855-4999     www.alsc.com

*Mfr. semi-conductors and related chips.*

**Alliance Semiconductor, Level 11 Park West Bldg., 6-12-1 Nishi Shinjuku Shinjuku-ku, Tokyo 160-0023, Japan**
Tel: 81-3-5325-3155

## ALTERA CORPORATION

101 Innovation Drive, San Jose, CA, 95134

Tel: (408) 544-7000     Fax: (408) 544-8303     www.altera.com

*Mfr. high-density programmable chips for semi-conductor industry.*

**Altera Japan, Ltd., Shinjukui i-Land Tower 32/F, 5-1 Nishi Shinjuku 6-Chome, Shinjuku-ku Tokyo 163-1332, Japan**
Tel: 81-3-3340-9480

## ALVEY INC.

9301 Olive Boulevard, St. Louis, MO, 63132

Tel: (314) 995-2446     Fax: (314) 995-2350     www.alvey.com

*Mfr./sales automatic case palletizers, package and pallet conveyor systems.*

**Tokyo Kanetsu KK, 19-20 Higashisuna 8-chome, Koto-ku, Tokyo 136, Japan**
Tel: 81-3-5690-7180  Fax: 81-3-5690-7770

## AMAZON.COM, INC.

1200 12th Ave. South, Ste. 1200, Seattle, WA, 98144-2734

Tel: (206) 266-1000     Fax: (206) 266-4206     www.amazon.com

*Computer site that offers books, CDs, DVDS, videos, toys, tools, and electronics.*

**Amazon.Com KK, Tokyo, Japan**

## AMERCORD

PO Box 458, Lumber City, GA, 31549

Tel: (912) 363-4371     Fax: (912) 363-4991     www.amercord.com

*Mfr. steel tire cord and bead wire for the automotive tire industry.*

**Amercord Far East Agencies Inc., Chiyoda House 2-A, 17-8 Nagata-cho 2-chome, Chiyoda-ku, Tokyo 100, Japan**

## AMEREX USA INC.

350 Fifth Avenue, Ste. 1401, New York, NY, 10118

Tel: (212) 967-3330     Fax: (212) 967-3352     www.amerexusa.com

*Mfr. outerwear for cold and wet seasons.*

**Amerex Intl. Corp., Amerex Bldg., 5-7 Azabudai 3-chome, Tokyo, Japan**

## AMERICAN AIRLINES INC.

4333 Amon Carter Boulevard, Ft. Worth, TX, 76155

Tel: (817) 963-1234     Fax: (817) 967-9641     www.amrcorp.com

*Air transport services.*

**American Airlines Inc., 231 Kokusai Bldg., 1-1 Marunouchi 3-chome, Chiyoda-ku, Tokyo 100, Japan**

**American Airlines Inc., KAL Bldg. 12-1 Honmachi 3-chome, Higashi-ku, Osaka 541, Japan**

## AMERICAN AMICABLE LIFE INSURANCE COMPANY

PO Box 2549, Waco, TX, 76703

Tel: (254) 297-2777     Fax: (254) 297-2733     www.americanamicable.com

*Life, accident and health insurance.*

**American Amicable Life Insurance Co., 607 Nikkatsu Apartment Bldg., 13-gochi, Shiba Koen, Minato-ku, Japan**

## AMERICAN APPRAISAL ASSOCIATES INC.

411 E. Wisconsin Ave., Milwaukee, WI, 53202

Tel: (414) 271-7240     Fax: (414) 271-1041     www.american-appraisal.com

*Valuation consulting services.*

**American Appraisal Japan Co. Ltd., Kabutocho Yachiyo Bldg., 20-5 Kabotocho, Nihonbashi, Chuo-ku, Tokyo 103, Japan**

## AMERICAN AXLE & MANUFACTURING HOLDINGS, INC.

1840 Holbrook Ave., Detroit, MI, 48212

Tel: (313) 974-2000     Fax: (313) 974-3090     www.aam.com

*Mfr. axles, propeller shafts and chassis components.*

**American Axle & Manufacturing, Minato Kirimura Bldg. 7/F, 3-6-1 Minato Chuo-Ku, Tokyo 104-0043, Japan**

Contact: James M. Uyeno, Dir.

## ABC, INC.

77 West 66th Street, New York, NY, 10023

Tel: (212) 456-7777     Fax: (212) 456-6384     www.abc.com

*Radio/TV production and broadcasting.*

**ABC News, Rokugo-ku Bldg., 6-5-9 Roppongi, Minato-ku, Tokyo 106, Japan**

## AMERICAN BUREAU OF SHIPPING

2 World Trade Center, 106th Fl., New York, NY, 10048

Tel: (212) 839-5000     Fax: (212) 839-5209     www.eagle.org

*Classification/certification of ships and offshore structures, development and technical assistance.*

**ABS Pacific, Kiyoken Bldg., 12-6 Takahima 2-chome, Nishi-ku, Yokohama 220, Japan**

## AMERICAN EXPRESS COMPANY

American Express Tower, World Financial Center, New York, NY, 10285-4765

Tel: (212) 640-2000    Fax: (212) 619-9802    www.americanexpress.com

*Travel, travelers cheques, charge card and financial services.*

**Amex Marketing Japan Ltd.,  Tokyo, Japan**

## AMERICAN FAMILY LIFE ASSURANCE COMPANY (AFLAC)

1932 Wynnton Road, Columbus, GA, 31999

Tel: (706) 323-3431    Fax: (706) 324-6330    www.aflac.com

*Insurance and TV broadcasting.*

**AFLAC - Japan,  Shinjuku Mitsui Bldg., 10F, 1-1 Nishishinjuku 2-chome, Shinjuku-ku, Tokyo 163, Japan**

## AMERICAN FINANCIAL GROUP

1 East Fourth St., Cincinnati, OH, 45202

Tel: (513) 579-2121    Fax: (513) 579-2113    www.amfnl.com

*Engaged in insurance services.*

**Mitsui Marine and Fire Insurance Ltd./Great American,  Tokyo, Japan**

Contact: Robert L. Hitch, Div. Pres.

## AMERICAN INTERNATIONAL GROUP INC. (AIG)

70 Pine Street, New York, NY, 10270

Tel: (212) 770-7000    Fax: (212) 509-9705    www.aig.com

*Worldwide insurance and financial services.*

**American Home Assurance Co.,  AIG Tower, 1-2-4 Kinshi, Surnida-Ku, Tokyo 130-8562 Japan**

## AMERICAN PRECISION INDUSTRIES INC.

2777 Walden Ave., Buffalo, NY, 14225

Tel: (716) 684-9700    Fax: (716) 684-2129    www.apicorporate.com

*Mfr. heat transfer equipment, motion control devices, coils, capacitors, electro-mechanical clutches and brakes.*

**API Motion AA,  7-10 Nihombashi-honcho 4 chome, Chuo-ku, Tokyo 103-0023 Japan**

Tel: 81-3-3241-0201   Fax: 81-3-3241-0221

## AMERICAN PRESIDENT LINES LTD.

1111 Broadway, Oakland, CA, 94607

Tel: (510) 272-8000    Fax: (510) 272-7941    www.apl.com

*Intermodal shipping services.*

**American President Lines Ltd.,  Shin Aoyama Bldg. East Wing 8th Fl., 1-1 Minami-Aoyama 1-chome, Minato-ku, Tokyo 107 Japan**

## AMGEN INC.

One Amgen Center Drive, Thousand Oaks, CA, 91320-1799

Tel: (805) 447-1000    Fax: (805) 499-2694    www.amgen.com

*Biotechnology research and pharmaceruticals.*

**Amgen Kabushiki Kaisha,  Hamacho Center Building 8F, 2-31-1 Nihonbashi Hamacho, Chuo-ku, Tokyo 103, Japan**

## AMKOR TECHNOLOGY, INC.

1345 Enterprise Dr., West Chester, PA, 19380

Tel: (610) 431-9600    Fax: (610) 431-1988    www.amkor.com

*Microchip technology engaged in semiconductor packaging and test services.*

**Amkor Technology Japan, KK,  Ebisu Prime Square Tower 4/F, 1-1-39 Hiroo, Shibuya-ku, Tokyo 150-0012, Japan**

Tel: 81-3-5469-6215

## AMPEX CORPORATION

500 Broadway, Redwood City, CA, 94063-3199

Tel: (650) 367-2011     Fax: (650) 367-4669     www.ampex.com

*Mfr. extremely high-performance digital data storage, data retrieval and image processing systems for a broad range of corporate scientific and government applications.*

**Ampex Japan Ltd.., PO Box 15, Tokyo Ryutsu Ctr., 6-1-1 Heiwajima, Ota-ku, Tokyo 143, Japan**

Tel: 81-3-3767-4521   Fax: 81-3-3767-8523   Contact: Hiroshi Okochi   Emp: 9

## AMPHENOL CORPORATION

358 Hall Ave., Wallingford, CT, 06492-7530

Tel: (203) 265-8900     Fax: (203) 265-8793     www.amphenol.com

*Mfr. electrictronic interconnect penetrate systems and assemblies.*

**Amphenol Japan K.K., 2-3-27 Kudan Minami, Chiyoda-Ku, Tokyo 102-0074 Japan**

Tel: 81-3-3263-5611   Fax: 81-3-5276-7059

## AMSTED INDUSTRIES INC.

205 North Michigan Ave., Chicago, IL, 60601

Tel: (312) 645-1700     Fax: (312) 819-8523     www.amsted.com

*Privately-held, diversified manufacturer of products for the construction and building markets, general industry and the railroads.*

**BAC-Japan Co., Ltd., 2-27-4 Shin-Machi, Setagaya-ku, Tokyo 154, Japan**

Tel: 81-3-5450-6161   Fax: 81-3-5450-6166   Contact: Tatsuro Nishimura, Pres.

## AMWAY CORPORATION

7575 Fulton Street East, Ada, MI, 49355-0001

Tel: (616) 787-6000     Fax: (616) 787-6177     www.amway.com

*Mfr./sale home care, personal care, nutrition and houseware products.*

**Amway (Japan) Ltd., Arco Tower, 1-8-1 Shimomeguro, Meguro-ku, Tokyo 153 Japan**

## ANALOG DEVICES INC.

1 Technology Way, Box 9106, Norwood, MA, 02062

Tel: (781) 329-4700     Fax: (781) 326-8703     www.analog.com

*Mfr. integrated circuits and related devices.*

**Analog Devices of Japan Inc., Jibiki Bldg., 7-8 Kojimachi 4-chome, Chiyoda-ku, Tokyo 102, Japan**

## ANDERSEN CONSULTING

100 S. Wacker Drive, Ste. 1059, Chicago, IL, 60606

Tel: (312) 693-0161     Fax: (312) 693-0507     www.ac.com

*Provides management and technology consulting services.*

**Andersen Consulting, Nihon Seimei Akasaka, Daini Bldg. 7-1-16, Akasaka, Minato-ku, Tokyo 107 Japan**

Tel: 81-3-3470-9241   Fax: 81-3-3423-2544

## ANDERSEN WORLDWIDE

33 West Monroe Street, Chicago, IL, 60603

Tel: (312) 580-0033     Fax: (312) 507-6748     www.arthurandersen.com

*Accounting and audit, tax and management consulting services.*

**Asahi & Co., Ohasi Bldg., 3-25-3 Meiki, Nakaamura-ku, Nagoya Aichi 450 Japan**

**Asahi & Co., Asahi Ctr. Bldg. 1-2, Tsukudo-cho, Shinjuku-ku, Tokyo 162 Japan**

Tel: 81-3-3266-7507

**Asahi & Co., Nissei Bldg., 1-18 Ageba-cho, Shinjuku-ku, Tokyo 162 Japan**

Tel: 81-52-571-5471

**Asahi & Co., Hankyu Grand Bldg. 18F, 8-47 Kakuta-cho, Kita-ku, Osaka 530 Japan**

Tel: 81-6-311-1425

**Uno Tax Accountant Office,** Chuo Bldg. 2-17, Kagurazaka, Shinjuku-ku, Tokyo 162 Japan
Tel: 81-3-5228-1600

## ANDREW CORPORATION

10500 West 153rd Street, Orland Park, IL, 60462

Tel: (708) 349-3300     Fax: (708) 349-5410     www.andrew.com

*Mfr. antenna systems, coaxial cable, electronic communications and network connectivity systems.*

**Andrew International Corp.,** Room 305 Nagatacho TBR Bldg., 2-10-1 Nagata-cho, Chiyoda-ku, Tokyo 100 Japan
Tel: 81-3-3581-0221    Fax: 81-3-3581-0222

## ANHEUSER-BUSCH INTERNATIONAL INC.

One Busch Place, St. Louis, MO, 63118-1852

Tel: (314) 577-2000     Fax: (314) 577-2900     www.anheuser-busch.com

*Malt production, aluminum beverage containers, rice milling, real estate development, metalized and paper label printing, railcar repair and theme-park facilities.*

**Anheuser-Busch Asia Inc.,** Akasalee Twin Tower, 17-22 Akasalee 2-chome, Minato-ku, Tokyo 107, Japan

## AOL TIME WARNER

75 Rockefeller Plaza, New York, NY, 10019

Tel: (212) 484-8000     Fax: (212) 275-3046     www.aoltimewarner.com

*Engaged in media and communications; provides internet services, communications, publishing and entertainment.*

**AOL Time Warner Asia,** Tokyo, Japan

**Time-Life International KK,** Tokyo, Japan

## AON CORPORATION

123 North Wacker Drive, Chicago, IL, 60606

Tel: (312) 701-3000     Fax: (312) 701-3100     www.aon.com

*Insurance brokers worldwide; underwrites accident and health insurance, specialty and professional insurance; and provides risk management consultation.*

**AON Risk Services Japan Ltd.,** Shirakiji Bldg. 10F, 2 - 33 Higashi Goana, 1-chome, Tokyo 141-0022 Japan
Tel: 81-3-3449-5503    Fax: 81-3-3449-9121    Contact: Michael Abbott

## API MOTION INC.

45 Hazelwood Dr., Amherst, NY, 14228

Tel: (716) 691-9100     Fax: (716) 691-9181     www.apimotion.com

*Engaged in motion control solutions using motors and drives, motor gearheads, resolver and encoder feedback devices.*

**API Motion Japan Ltd.,** 7-10 Nihombashi-Honcho 4-chome, Chuo-ku, Tokyo, Japan

## APPLE COMPUTER, INC.

One Infinite Loop, Cupertino, CA, 95014

Tel: (408) 996-1010     Fax: (408) 974-2113     www.apple.com

*Personal computers, peripherals and software.*

**Apple Computer Japan Inc.,** Akasaka Twin Tower, Main Bldg. 16/F, 217-22 Akasaka, Minato-ku Tokyo 107 Japan

## APPLERA CORPORATION

761 Main Avenue, Norwalk, CT, 06859-0001

Tel: (203) 762-1000     Fax: (203) 762-6000     www.applera.com

*Leading supplier of systems for life science research and related applications.*

**Applied Biosystems Japan KK,** 4-5-4 Hatchobori, Chuo-Ku, Tokyo 104-0032, Japan

## APPLIED MATERIALS, INC.

3050 Bowers Ave., Santa Clara, CA, 95054-3299

Tel: (408) 727-5555     Fax: (408) 727-9943     www.appliedmaterials.com

*Supplies manufacturing systems and services to the semiconductor industry.*

**Applied Materials Japan, Nogedaria Ind.Park,14-3 Shinizumi, Narita-shi, Chiba-ken 286-8516 Japan**
Tel: 81-476-362181  Fax: 81-476-361095

## APPLIED SCIENCE AND TECHNOLOGY, INC.

35 Cabot Road, Woburn, MA, 01801

Tel: (781) 933-5560     Fax: (781) 933-0750     www.astex.com

*Mfr. specialized components for semiconductor manufacturing systems.*

**AsTex Japan, 4/F Hisamatsu Building, 4-51 chome Saugaku-cho, Chiyoda-ku Tokyo 101, Japan**
Tel: 81-3-3233-4388  Fax: 81-3-3233-4373

## APW, INC.

PO Box 325, Milwaukee, WI, 53201-0325

Tel: (262) 523-7600     Fax: (262) 523-7624     www.apw1.com

*Mfr. hi-pressure tools, vibration control products, consumables, technical furniture and enclosures.*

**APW Japan Ltd., 10-17 Sasame Kita-cho, Toda-City, Saitama 335, Japan**

## AQUENT

711 Boylston Street, Boston, MA, 02116

Tel: (617) 535-5000     Fax: (617) 535-6001     www.aquent.com

*Engaged in temporary, specialized employment.*

**AQUENT, 1-3-3 Kyomachibori 4/F, Nishiku, Osaka-si 550-0003, Japan**
Tel: 81-6-6459-3303  Fax: 81-6-6459-3304

**AQUENT, 5-4 Kojimachi, Chiyoda-ku, Tokyo 102-0083, Japan**
Tel: 81-3-5214-3242

## ARAMARK CORPORATION

1101 Market Street, Philadelphia, PA, 19107-2988

Tel: (215) 238-3000     Fax: (215) 238-3333     www.aramark.com

*Provides managed services for food, work and safety clothing, education, recreation and facilities*

**AIM Services Co. Ltd., Bussam Bldg. Annex, 1-15 Nishi-Shinbashi 1-chome, Minato-ku, Tokyo Japan**
Tel: 81-3-3502-3721  Fax: 81-3-3502-6580   Contact: Hiromaso Tago, Dir.

## ARBOR ACRES FARM INC.

439 Marlborough Road, Glastonbury, CT, 06033

Tel: (860) 633-4681     Fax: (860) 633-2433

*Producers of male and female broiler breeders, commercial egg layers.*

**Arbor Acres Japan Co. Ltd., Kitamatsuno Sujikawa-cho, Ihara-gun, Shizwoka Pref., Japan**

## ARCHER-DANIELS-MIDLAND COMPANY

4666 Faries Parkway, Decatur, IL, 62526

Tel: (217) 424-5200     Fax: (217) 424-6196     www.admworld.com

*Grain processing: flours, grains, oils and flax fibre.*

**ADM Far East Ltd., Tokyo, Japan**

## ARDENT SOFTWARE, INC.

50 Washington Street, Westboro, MA, 01581-1021

Tel: (508) 366-3888     Fax: (508) 366-3669     www.ardentsoftware.com

*Publisher of database and file management software.*

**Ardent Software K.K., Tokyo, Japan**

## ARIBA, INC.

1565 Charleston Rd., Mountain View, CA, 94043

Tel: (650) 930-6200      Fax: (650) 930-6300      www.ariba.com

*Mfr. software.*

**Nihon Ariba KK, Shinjuku Park Tower 30/F, 3-7-1 Nishi-Shinjuku, Shinjuku-Ku Tokyo 163-1030, Japan**

Tel: 81-3-5326-3091

## ARMSTRONG HOLDINGS, INC.

2500 Columbia Avenue, Lancaster, PA, 17604-3001

Tel: (717) 397-0611      Fax: (717) 396-2787      www.armstrong.com

*Mfr. and marketing interior furnishings and specialty products for bldg, auto and textile industry.*

**Armstrong (Japan) KK, Onarimon Yusen Bldg.5 Nishi-Shinbashi, 3-Chome Minato-ku, Tokyo 105 Japan**

Tel: 813-343-344473

## ARROW ELECTRONICS INC.

25 Hub Drive, Melville, NY, 11747

Tel: (516) 391-1300      Fax: (516) 391-1640      www.arrow.com

*Distributor of electronic components.*

**Marubun Arrow Asia, Ltd., Marubun Daiya Bldg. 8-1, Nihonbashi Odenmacho, Chuo-ku Tokyo 103-8577 Japan**

## ARROW INTERNATIONAL, INC.

2400 Bernville Rd., Reading, PA, 19605

Tel: (610) 378-0131      Fax: (610) 374-5360      www.arrowintl.com

*Develop, manufacture, and marketing of medical devices.*

**Arrow Japan, Ltd., Nagaoka Bldg. 16-3, Kita-Otasuka 3-chome, Toshima-ku, Tokyo 170 Japan**

Contact: Kanji Kurisawa

**Arrow Japan, Ltd., 4F Shin Osaka Kita Bldg., 4-1-46 Miyahara 4-chome, Yodagawa-ku, Osaka 532 Japan**

Contact: Kanji Kurisawa

## ARVIN MERITOR INC

2135 W. Maple Rd., Troy, Mi, 48084-7186

Tel: (248) 435-1000      Fax: (248) 435-1393      www.arvinmeritor.com

*Mfr. of automotive exhaust systems and ride control products, axles and power-steering pumps.*

**ArvinMeritor International Inc., Halifax Bldg. 6F, 1-1 Asakusabashi 3-chome, Tailo-ku, Tokyo 111-0053 Japan**

Tel: 81-3-3862-4408    Fax: 81-3-3862-4498    Contact: Hiro Nakamura, Mng. Dir.    Emp: 5

**ArvinMeritor Intl. Inc., Kaneko Bldg., 3-25 Koraku 2-chome, Bunkyo-ku, Tokyo 112 Japan**

## ASHLAND OIL INC.

50 E. Rivercenter Blvd., Covington, KY, 41012-0391

Tel: (859) 815-3333      Fax: (859) 815-5053      www.ashland.com

*Petroleum exploration, refining and transportation; mfr. chemicals, oils and lubricants.*

**Hodogaya Ashland Co. Ltd., 4-2 Toranomon 1-chome, Minato-ku, Tokyo 105, Japan**

## ASPEN TECHNOLOGY, INC.

10 Canal Park, Cambridge, MA, 02141

Tel: (617) 949-1000      Fax: (617) 949-1030      www.aspentec.com

*Mfr. software for chemists and refineries.*

**AspenTech Japan Co. Ltd., Atlas Bldg.- 5 Ichibancho, Chiyoda-Ku, Tokyo 102, Japan**

Tel: 81-3-3262-1710    Fax: 81-3-3264-5425

## ASSOCIATED MERCHANDISING CORPORATION

500 Seventh Ave., 2nd Fl., New York, NY, 10018

Tel: (212) 819-6600      Fax: (212) 819-6701      www.theamc.com

*Retail service organization; apparel, shoes and accessories.*

**Associated Merchandising Corp., Nakanoshima Ctr. Bldg., 2-27 Nakanoshima 6-chome, Kita-ku, Osaka 530, Japan**

## ASSOCIATED METALS & MINERALS CORP. (ASOMA)

3 North Corporate Park Drive, White Plains, NY, 10604

Tel: (914) 872-2640      Fax: (914) 251-1073      www.macsteel.com

*Metals and ores.*

**Asoma Intl. KK,  World Trade Ctr., PO Box 22, Tokyo 105, Japan**

## ASSOCIATED PRESS INC.

50 Rockefeller Plaza, New York, NY, 10020-1605

Tel: (212) 621-1500      Fax: (212) 621-5447      www.ap.com

*News gathering agency.*

**The Associated Press,  CPO Box 607, Tokyo 100-91, Japan**
Tel: 81-3-3545-5902

## ASSOCIATES FIRST CAPITAL CORPORATION

250 E. Carpenter Freeway, Irving, TX, 75062-2729

Tel: (972) 652-4000      Fax: (972) 652-7420      www.theassociates.com

*Diversified consumer and commercial finance organization which provides finance, leasing and related services.*

**Associates First Capital Corporation,  Tokyo, Japan**

## ASYST TECHNOLOGIES, INC.

48761 Kato Road, Fremont, CA, 94538

Tel: (510) 661-5000      Fax: (510) 661-5166      www.asyst.com

*Produces wafer handling equipment.*

**Asyst Kabushiki Kaisha K.K.,  Kaneko Dai 2 Bldg. 7/F, 2-6-23 Shin-Yokohama, Kohoku-ku Yokohama-shi, Kanagawa-ken 222-0033, Japan**

## AT HOME CORPORATION

450 Broadway Street, Redwood City, CA, 94063

Tel: (650) 556-5000      Fax: (650) 556-5100      www.excite.com

*Online computer internet service provider.*

**Excite, Inc.,  Tokyo, Japan**

## AT&T BROADBAND, LLC

9197 South Peoria, Englewood, CO, 80112

Tel: (720) 875-5500      Fax: (720) 875-4984      www.broadband.att.com

*Provides broadband technology services; digital TV, digital telephone and high-speed cable internet services.*

**Chofu,  Tokyo, Japan**

**TITUS,  Tokyo, Japan**

## AT&T CORPORATION

32 Avenue of the Americas, New York, NY, 10013-2412

Tel: (212) 387-5400      Fax: (212) 387-5695      www.att.com

*Telecommunications.*

**AT&T Japan Ltd.,  25 Mori Bldg., 1-4-30 Roppongi, Minato-ku, Tokyo 106 Japan**

## ATMEL CORPORATION

2325 Orchard Pkwy., San Jose, CA, 95131

Tel: (408) 441-0311     Fax: (408) 436-4200      www.atmel.com

*Design, manufacture and marketing of advanced semiconductors.*

**Atmel Japan KK, Tonetsu Shinkawa Bldg. - 9/F, 1-24-8 Shinkawa, Chuo-ku Tokyo 104-0033, Japan**

Tel: 81-3-3523-3551   Fax: 81-3-3523-7581

## ATTACHMATE CORPORATION

3617 131st Ave. S.E., Bellevue, WA, 98006-1332

Tel: (425) 644-4010     Fax: (425) 747-9924      www.attachmate.com

*Mfr. connectivity software.*

**Attachmate Japan, Pier West Square, 1-11-8 Tsukuda Chuo-ku, Tokyo 104, Japan**

Tel: 81-3-5560-8970

## AUSPEX SYSTEMS, INC.

2800 Scott Blvd., Santa Clara, CA, 95050

Tel: (408) 566-2000     Fax: (408) 566-2020      www.auspex.com

*Mfr. data management and file sharing software.*

**Auspex KK, ATT Shinkan 6/F, 2-11-7 Akasaka Minato-ku, Tokyo 107-0052, Japan**

Tel: 81-3-3586-1751

## AUTODESK INC.

111 McInnis Parkway, San Rafael, CA, 94903

Tel: (415) 507-5000     Fax: (415) 507-6112      www.autodesk.com

*Develop/marketing/support computer-aided design, engineering, scientific and multimedia software products.*

**Autodesk Fukuoka Sales, Hakata Mitsui Bldg. No. 2 7F, 1-35 Tenyamachi, Hakata-ku, Fukuoka 812 Japan**

Tel: 81-92-282-0781   Fax: 81-92-282-0720

**Autodesk Ltd. Japan, Yebisu Garden Place Tower 24F, 4-20-3 Ebisu Shibuya-ku, Tokyo 150 Japan**

Tel: 81-33-473-9511   Fax: 81-33-473-9642

**Autodesk Nagoya Sales, 12/F Nishiki Park Bldg. 2-4-3, Nishiki, Naka-ku, Nagoya 460 Japan**

Tel: 81-52-232-7891   Fax: 81-52-232-7894

**Autodesk Osaka Sales, Shin Osaka Daini Mori Bldg. 14F, 3-5-36 Miyahara, Yodogawa-ku, Osaka 532 Japan**

Tel: 81-6-350-5221   Fax: 81-6-350-5222

## AUTOMATIC SWITCH CO. (ASCO)

50-60 Hanover Rd., Florham Park, NJ, 07932

Tel: (973) 966-2000     Fax: (973) 966-2628      www.asco.com

*Mfr. solenoid valves, emergency power controls, pressure and temp. switches.*

**Asco (Japan) Ltd., 1-20 Takahata-cho, Nishinomiya, Hyogo 663-8202, Japan**

Tel: 81-798-65-6361   Fax: 81-798-63-4443   Contact: M. Kato

## AUTOSPLICE INC.

10121 Barnes Canyon Road, San Diego, CA, 92121

Tel: (858) 535-0077     Fax: (858) 535-0130      www.autosplice.com

*Mfr. electronic components.*

**Autosplice Japan, 3-7-39 Minami-cho, Higashi Kurume-shi, Tokyo 203, Japan**

Tel: 81-424-62-8481   Fax: 81-424-62-8513   Contact: Koichi Itoh

## AVERSTAR

23 Fourth Ave., Burlington, MA, 01803-3303

Tel: (781) 221-6990    Fax: (781) 221-6991    www.averstar.com

*Software and systems engineering services.*

**Nihon Intermetrics KK, Fukozawa Bldg. 2/F, 36-3 Higashi Nakono 1-chome, Nakono-ka, Tokyo 164, Japan**

## AVERY DENNISON CORPORATION

150 N. Orange Grove Blvd., Pasadena, CA, 91103

Tel: (626) 304-2000    Fax: (626) 792-7312    www.averydennison.com

*Mfr. pressure-sensitive adhesives and materials, office products, labels, tags, retail systems, Carter's Ink and specialty chemicals.*

**Fasson-Avery Dennison/Sanyo, 3F Asahi Seimei Suginami Bldg., 2-3-9 Amanuma Suginami-ku, Tokyo 167-0032 Japan**

Tel: 813-5347-2720    Fax: 813-5347-2725

## AVID TECHNOLOGY, INC.

1 Park West, Tewksbury, MA, 01876

Tel: (978) 640-6789    Fax: (978) 640-1366    www.avid.com

*Mfr. animation design software and digital and audio systems.*

**Avid Japan KK, Sausuhoresuto Bldg., 1-14-19 Minamimorimachi, Kita-Ku Osaka 530-0054, Japan**
Tel: 81-6-6314-3132    Fax: 81-6-6314-2624

**Avid Japan KK, ATT New Tower 4/F, 2-11-7 Akasaka, Minato-Ku Tokyo 107-0052, Japan**
Tel: 81-3-3505-7937    Fax: 81-3-3505-7938

## AVON PRODUCTS INC.

1345 Avenue of the Americas, New York, NY, 10105-0196

Tel: (212) 282-5000    Fax: (212) 282-6049    www.avon.com

*Mfr./distributor beauty and related products, fashion jewelry, gifts and collectibles.*

**Avon Products Co. Ltd., Totate Int. Bldg., 12-19 Shibuya 2-chome, Shibuya-ku, Tokyo 150 Japan**
Tel: 81-3-3797-8224    Fax: 81-3-3400-6930    Contact: Wendy Allen, Sales Dir.

## BAIN & COMPANY, INC.

Two Copley Place, Boston, MA, 02116

Tel: (617) 572-2000    Fax: (617) 572-2427    www.bain.com

*Strategic management consulting services.*

**Bain & Company Japan Inc., Hibiya Kokusai Bldg. 14/F, 2-2-3 Uchisaiwai-cho, Chiyoda-ku, Tokyo 100, Japan**
Tel: 81-3-3502-6401    Fax: 81-3-3592-4960

## BAKER & McKENZIE

130 East Randolph Drive, Ste. 2500, Chicago, IL, 60601

Tel: (312) 861-8000    Fax: (312) 861-2899    www.bakerinfo.com

*International legal services.*

**Baker & McKenzie (Tokyo Aoyama Law Office), 2-3 Kita-Aoyama 1-chome, Minato-ku, Tokyo 107, Japan**
Tel: 81-3-3403-5281    Fax: 81-3-3470-3152

## BAKER & TAYLOR CORPORATION

2709 Water Ridge Pkwy., Charlotte, NC, 28217

Tel: (704) 357-3500    Fax: (704) 329-9105    www.btol.com

*Book wholesaler; supplies books and audio books, calendars and information services to public and university libraries.*

**Baker & Taylor Corporation, c/o Kinokuniya, 38-1 Sakuragaoka 5-chome, Setagaya-ku, Tokyo 156, Japan**

Tel: 81-3-3439-0115    Fax: 81-3-3439-0123

## BAKER PETROLITE CORPORATION

3900 Essex Lane, Houston, TX, 77027

Tel: (713) 599-7400    Fax: (713) 599-7592    www.bakerhughes.com/bapt/

*Mfr. specialty chemical treating programs, performance-enhancing additives and related equipment and services.*

**Tokyo-Petrolite Co., Toin Bldg., 12-15 Shinkawa 2-chome, Chuo-ku, Tokyo 104, Japan**

## BALDWIN TECHNOLOGY COMPANY, INC.

One Norwalk West, 40 Richards Ave., Norwalk, CT, 06854

Tel: (203) 838-7470    Fax: (203) 852-7040    www.baldwintech.com

*Mfr./services material handling, accessories, control and prepress equipment for print industry.*

**Baldwin Japan Ltd., 2-4-34 Toyo 2-chome, Kohtok-ku, Tokyo 135, Japan**

Tel: 81-3-5606-2771    Fax: 81-3-5606-2779    Contact: Y. Yano, Mng. Dir.

## BALTIMORE AIRCOIL CO., INC.

PO Box 7322, Baltimore, MD, 21227

Tel: (410) 799-6200    Fax: (410) 799-6416    www.baltimoreaircoil.com

*Mfr. evaporative heat transfer and ice thermal storage products.*

**BAC-Japan Co. Ltd., 2-27-4 Shin-Machi, Setagaya-Ku, Tokyo 154 Japan**

## BANK OF AMERICA CORPORATION

555 California Street, San Francisco, CA, 94104

Tel: (415) 622-3530    Fax: (415) 622-8467    www.bankofamerica.com

*Financial services.*

**Bank of America NT & SA, ARK Mori Bldg. 34/F, 1-12-32 Akasaka Minato-ku, PO Box 511, Tokyo 107 Japan**

Tel: 81-3-3587-3155    Fax: 81-3-3587-3460    Contact: Arun Duggal, SVP

## THE BANK OF NEW YORK

One Wall Street, New York, NY, 10286

Tel: (212) 495-1784    Fax: (212) 495-2546    www.bankofny.com

*Banking services.*

**The Bank of New York, Fukoku Seimei Bldg.-6th Fl., 2-2-2 Uchisaiwai-cho, Chiyoda-ku, Tokyo 100 Japan**

**The Bank of New York, Osaka Bldg.-8th Fl./8-15, Azuchimachi 1- chome Chuo-ku, Osaka 541 Japan**

## BANK ONE CORPORATION

One First National Plaza, Chicago, IL, 60670

Tel: (312) 732-4000    Fax: (312) 732-3366    www.fcnbd.com

*Provides financial products and services.*

**Bank One, NA, Hibiya Central Building 7F, 2-9 Hishi-Shimbashi, 1-chome Minato-ku, Tokyo 105 Japan**

Tel: 81-3-3596-8757    Fax: 81-3-3596-8745    Contact: Yoshio Kitazawa, Gen. Mgr.

## C. R. BARD, INC.

730 Central Ave., Murray Hill, NJ, 07974

Tel: (908) 277-8000     Fax: (908) 277-8078     www.crbard.com

*Mfr. health care products.*

**Medicon, Inc.,  Hiranomachi Century Building 8F, 2-5-8 Hiranomachi, Chou-ku Osaka 541-0046, Japan**

Tel: 81-66-203-6541    Fax: 81-66-203-1516

## BARRA, INC.

2100 Milvia Street, Berkeley, CA, 94704

Tel: (510) 548-5442        Fax: (510) 548-4374      www.barra.com

*Mfr. analytical software for private investors and portfolio managers.*

**BARRA International, Ltd.,  1-18-16 Hamamatsucho, Minato-ku, Sumitomo Hamamatsucho Bldg. 7/F, Tokyo 105-013, Japan**

Tel: 81-3-5402-4153    Fax: 81-3-5402-4154

## BATES WORLDWIDE INC.

405 Lexington Ave., New York, NY, 10174

Tel: (212) 297-7000        Fax: (212) 986-0270      www.batesww.com

*Advertising, marketing, public relations and media consulting.*

**Bates 141 Japan,  Shibaur Square Bldg. 3/F, 4-9-25 Shibaura, Minato-ku, Tokyo 108 Japan**

Tel: 81-3-3455-5181   Fax: 81-3-3455-6970   Contact: Naotaki Okuno, Dir.

**Saatchi & Saatchi Bates Yomiko,  Shibaura Square Bldg., 4-9-25 Shibaura, Minato-ku, Tokyo 108 Japan**

Tel: 81-3-3455-4123   Fax: 81-3-3455-4110   Contact: David Meredith, Pres.

## BAUSCH & LOMB INC.

One Bausch & Lomb Place, Rochester, NY, 14604-2701

Tel: (716) 338-6000        Fax: (716) 338-6007      www.bausch.com

*Mfr. vision care products and accessories.*

**B.L.J. Company Ltd.,  Tower B Omori Bellport 7/F, 6-26-2 Minami-Oi, Shinagawa-ku, Tokyo 140-0013 Japan**

**Charles River Japan, Inc.,  Locations in Atsugi, Hino, Tskuba, and Yokohama, Japan**

## BAXTER HEALTHCARE CORPORATION

One Baxter Parkway, Deerfield, IL, 60015

Tel: (847) 948-2000        Fax: (847) 948-3948      www.baxter.com

*Pharmaceutical preparations, surgical/medical instruments and cardiovascular products.*

**Baxter Ltd.,  4 Rokubancho, Chiyoda-ku, Tokyo 102, Japan**

## BDO SEIDMAN, LLP    BELGIUM

Two Prudential Plaza, 180 N. Stetson Ave., Ste. 2300, Chicago, IL, 60601

Tel: (312) 240-1236        Fax: (312) 240-3329      www.bdo.com

*International accounting and financial consulting firm.*

**BDO Binder & Company,  Nissei Bldg. 5F, 1-18 Ageba-cho, Shinjuku-ku, Tokyo 162 Japan**

Tel: 81-3-3266-7679   Fax: 81-3-3266-7699   Contact: Masayuki Takase

**BDO Sanyu & Company,  STEC 22F, 1-24-1 Nishi-Shinjuku, Shinjuku-ku, Tokyo 160 Japan**

Tel: 81-3-5322-3531   Fax: 81-3-5322-3593   Contact: Jum Sugita

## BEA SYSTEMS, INC.

2315 North First Street, St. Jose, CA, 95131

Tel: (408) 570-8000      Fax: (408) 570-8091      www.beasys.com

*Develops communications management software and provider of software consulting services.*

**BEA Systems Japan Ltd., Yokohama Landmark Tower 38F, 2-2-1 1 Minatomirai Nishiku, Yokohama, Kanagawa 220-8138 Japan**

Tel: 81-45-224-1250    Fax: 81-45-224-1251

## BEAR STEARNS & CO., INC.

245 Park Ave., New York, NY, 10167

Tel: (212) 272-2000      Fax: (212) 272-3092      www.bearstearns.com

*Investment banking, securities broker/dealer and investment advisory services.*

**Bear Stearns Japan Ltd., Shiroyama Hills, 3-1 Toranomon 4-chome, Minato-ku, Tokyo 105 Japan**

Tel: 81-3-3437-7800    Fax: 81-3-3437-7880

## BECHTEL GROUP INC.

50 Beale Street, PO Box 3965, San Francisco, CA, 94105-1895

Tel: (415) 768-1234      Fax: (415) 768-9038      www.bechtel.com

*General contractors in engineering and construction.*

**Bechtel International Corp., Fuji Bldg. Room 310-2-3, Marunouchi 3-chome, Chiyoda-ku, Tokyo 100 Japan**

Tel: 81-3-3214-4481    Fax: 81-3-3214-2596

## BECKMAN COULTER, INC.

4300 N. Harbor Boulevard, Fullerton, CA, 92834

Tel: (714) 871-4848      Fax: (714) 773-8898      www.beckmancoulter.com

*Develop/mfr./marketing automated systems and supplies for biological analysis.*

**Beckman Coulter KK, Toranomon 37 Mori Building, 3-5-1 Toranomon, Minato-ku Tokyo 105-0001, Japan**

Tel: 81-3-5404-8359    Fax: 81-3-5404-8436

## BECTON DICKINSON AND COMPANY

One Becton Drive, Franklin Lakes, NJ, 07417-1880

Tel: (201) 847-6800      Fax: (201) 847-6475      www.bd.com

*Mfr./sale medical supplies, devices and diagnostic systems.*

**Nippon Becton Dickinson, Shimato Bldg., 5-34 Akasaka 8-chome, Minato-ku, Tokyo 107 Japan**

## BELL & HOWELL COMPANY

5215 Old Orchard Road, Skokie, IL, 60077

Tel: (847) 470-7100      Fax: (847) 470-9625      www.bellhowell.com

*Diversified information products and services.*

**Bell & Howell Japan Ltd., Andoh Fukuyoshi Bldg., 11-28 Akasaka 1-chome, Minato-ku, Tokyo 107, Japan**

## BENTLY NEVADA CORPORATION

1617 Water Street, PO Box 157, Minden, NV, 89423

Tel: (775) 782-3611      Fax: (775) 782-9259      www.bently.com

*Provides hardware, software, and services for machinery information and management systems.*

**Rikei Corp., Nichimen Bldg. 4F, 2-2-3 Nakanoshima, Kita-ku, Osaka 530, Japan**

**Rikei Corp., Shinjuku Normura Bldg., 1-26-2 Nishi-Shinjuku, Shinjuku-ku, Tokyo 160, Japan**

## LOUIS BERGER INTERNATIONAL INC.

100 Halsted Street, East Orange, NJ, 07019

Tel: (201) 678-1960     Fax: (201) 672-4284     www.louisberger.com

*Consulting engineers, engaged in architecture, environmental and advisory services.*

**Louis Berger International Inc.,  Watase Building 2nd Floor, 5-8-3 Nishi-Shimbashi, Minato-ku Tokyo 105-0003, Japan**

Tel: 81-3-3437-1999   Fax: 81-3-3578-9581

## BERLITZ CROSS-CULTURAL TRAINING INC.

400 Alexander Park, Princeton, NJ, 08540

Tel: (609) 514-9650     Fax: (609) 514-9689     www.berlitz.com

*Consulting and management training services to bridge cultural gaps for international travelers as well as for business transferees and families.*

**Berlitz Japan, Inc.,  Mitsui Seimei Kitasenju Building 3/F, 41-1 Senju-Nakacho, Adachi-ku Tokyo 120-0036, Japan**

## BEST WESTERN INTERNATIONAL

6201 North 24th Place, Phoenix, AZ, 85106

Tel: (602) 957-4200     Fax: (602) 957-5740     www.bestwestern.com

*International hotel chain.*

**The Richmond Hotel,  3-5-14 Meijiro, Toshima-ku, Tokyo 171, Japan**

## BESTFOODS, INC.

700 Sylvan Ave., International Plaza, Englewood Cliffs, NJ, 07632-9976

Tel: (201) 894-4000     Fax: (201) 894-2186     www.bestfoods.com

*Consumer foods products; corn refining.*

**Best Foods (Japan) Ltd.,  2-12-1 Shimonoge, Takatsu-ku, Kawasaki-shi, 213-0006 Japan**

Tel: 81-44-811-3815   Fax: 81-44-850-3631   Contact: Jörg Aschwanden, Dir.

## BETZDEARBORN

4636 Somerton Road, PO Box 3002, Trevose, PA, 19053-6783

Tel: (215) 953-2568     Fax: (215) 953-5524     www.betzdearborn.com

*Mfr. water/wastewater and process system treatment chemicals and services.*

**Nippon BetzDearborn K.K.,  R Bldg.-7F, 8-12 Kita-Shinagawa 1-chome, Shinagawa-ku, Tokyo 140 Japan**

## BEVERLY ENTERPRISES INC.

1200 South Waldron Road, Ft. Smith, AR, 72903

Tel: (501) 452-6712     Fax: (501) 452-5131     www.beverlynet.com

*Nursing homes, retirement living centers, pharmacies.*

**Beverly Japan Corp. (JV),  Tohgeki Bldg., 1-1 Tsukiji 4-chome, Chuo-ku, Tokyo, Japan**

## BIO-RAD LABORATORIES INC.

1000 Alfred Nobel Drive, Hercules, CA, 94547

Tel: (510) 724-7000     Fax: (510) 724-3167     www.bio-rad.com

*Mfr. life science research products, clinical diagnostics, analytical instruments.*

**Nippon Bio-Rad Laboratories KK,  Fukuoka, Japan**

## BLACK & DECKER CORPORATION

701 E. Joppa Road, Towson, MD, 21286

Tel: (410) 716-3900     Fax: (410) 716-2933     www.blackanddecker.com

*Mfr. power tools and accessories, security hardware, small appliances, fasteners, information systems and services.*

**Black & Decker Japan,  Attn: Japan Office, 701 East Joppa Road, Towson MD 21286**

## BLACK & VEATCH LLP

8400 Ward Pkwy., PO Box 8405, Kansas City, MO, 64114

Tel: (913) 339-2000     Fax: (913) 339-2934     www.bv.com

*Engineering, architectural and construction services.*

**M&B Engineering Co. Ltd., 1-2 Uchikanda 2-chome, Chiyoda-ku, Tokyo 101, Japan**

## BLACK BOX CORPORATION

1000 Park Dr., Lawrence, PA, 15055

Tel: (724) 746-5500     Fax: (724) 746-0746     www.blackbox.com

*Direct marketer and technical service provider of communications, networking and related computer connectivity products.*

**Black Box Japan, Nec Eitai Bldg., 16-10 Fuyuki, Koto-ku, Tokyo 135, Japan**

Tel: 81-3-3820-5011   Fax: 81-3-3820-5036   Contact: Frances Wertheimber, Gen. Mgr.

## BLOOM ENGINEERING CO., INC.

5460 Horning Rd., Pittsburgh, PA, 15236

Tel: (412) 653-3500     Fax: (412) 653-2253     www.bloomeng.com

*Mfr. custom engineered burners and combustion systems.*

**Nippon Herr Company Ltd., Daiichi Choujiya Bldg., 1-2-13 Shibadaimon, Minato-Ku 105-0012 Tokyo, Japan**

Tel: 81-3-5425-6461   Fax: 81-3-5425-6433

## BLOOMBERG L.P.

499 Park Ave., New York, NY, 10022

Tel: (212) 318-2000     Fax: (212) 940-1954     www.bloomberg.com

*Publishes magazines and provides TV, radio and newspaper wire services.*

**Bloomberg L.P., Tokyo, Japan**

## BLOUNT INTERNATIONAL, INC

4520 Executive Park Dr., Montgomery, AL, 36116-1602

Tel: (334) 244-4000     Fax: (334) 271-8130     www.blount.com

*Mfr. cutting chain and equipment, timber harvest and handling equipment, sporting ammo, riding mowers.*

**Blount Japan Ltd., Toranomon Kotohira Kaikan, 2-8 Toranomon 1-chome, Minato-ku, Tokyo, Japan**

Tel: 81-3-3503-6716   Fax: 81-3-3504-1334   Contact: Toshio Suzuki, Mgr.

## BLUE CROSS AND BLUE SHIELD ASSOC.

225 N. Michigan Ave., Chicago, IL, 60601-7680

Tel: (312) 297-6000     Fax: (312) 297-6609     www.blueshield.com

*Provides health care coverage through indemnity insurance, HMO's and Medicare programs.*

**BlueCare Worldwide, Tokyo, Japan**

## BMC SOFTWARE, INC.

2101 City West Blvd., Houston, TX, 77042-2827

Tel: (713) 918-8800     Fax: (713) 918-8000     www.bmc.com

*Engaged in mainframe-related utilities software and services.*

**BMC Software, Nishi-Shinjuku Mitsui Bldg. 10F, 6-24-1 Nishi-Shinjuku, Shinjuku-ku Tokyo 160-0023, Japan**

## BOOZ-ALLEN & HAMILTON INC.

8283 Greensboro Drive, McLean, VA, 22102

Tel: (703) 902-5000     Fax: (703) 902-3333     www.bah.com

*International management and technology consultants.*

**Booz Allen & Hamilton (Japan) Inc., Shiroyama Hills 18F, 4-3-1 Toranoman, Minato-ku, Tokyo 105 Japan**

Tel: 81-3-3436-8600   Fax: 81-3-3436-8668

### BORG-WARNER AUTOMOTIVE INC.

200 S. Michigan Ave., Chicago, IL, 60604

Tel: (312) 322-8500     Fax: (312) 461-0507     www.bwauto.com

*Mfr. automotive components; provider of security services.*

**Borg-Warner Automotive KK, 1300-50 Yabata, Nabari City, Mie Prefecture 518-04, Japan**

**NSK-Warner KK, 2345 Aino, Fikuroi City, Shizuoka 437, Japan**

### BOSE CORPORATION

The Mountain, Framingham, MA, 01701-9168

Tel: (508) 879-7330     Fax: (508) 766-7543     www.bose.com

*Mfr. quality audio equipment/speakers.*

**BOSE KK, Shibuya YT Bldg., 28-3 Maruyamacho, Shibuya-ku, Tokyo, Japan**

### THE BOSTON CONSULTING GROUP

Exchange Place, 31st Fl., Boston, MA, 02109

Tel: (617) 973-1200     Fax: (617) 973-1339     www.bcg.com

*Management consulting company.*

**The Boston Consulting Group, The New Otani Garden Court, 4-1 Kioi-cho, Chiyoda-ku, Tokyo 102 Japan**

Tel: 81-3-5211-0300

### BOSTON SCIENTIFIC CORPORATION

One Scientific Place, Natick, MA, 01760-1537

Tel: (508) 650-8000     Fax: (508) 650-8923     www.bsci.com

*Mfr./distributes medical devices for use in minimally invasive surgeries.*

**Boston Scientific Japan, KK, STEC JYOHO Bldg. 23F, 1-24-1 Nishi-Shinjuku, Shinjuku, Tokyo 160, Japan**

Tel: 81-3-5322-3720   Fax: 81-3-5322-3700

### BOWNE & COMPANY, INC.

345 Hudson Street, New York, NY, 10014

Tel: (212) 924-5500     Fax: (212) 229-3420     www.bowne.com

*Financial printing and foreign language translation, localization (software), internet design and maintenance and facilities management.*

**Bowne International, Yokohama Landmark Tower 42F, 2-2-1-1 Minato-Mirai, Nishi-ku Yokohama 220-8142, Japan**

Tel: 81-45-640-4250   Fax: 81-45-6404206

**Bowne International, Tomoecho Annex No. 2 8/F, 3-8-27 Toranomon Minato-ku, Tokyo 105-0001, Japan**

Tel: 81-3-5425-6600   Fax: 81-3-5425-6605

### BOYDEN CONSULTING CORPORATION

364 Elwood Ave., Hawthorne, NY, 10502

Tel: (914) 747-0093     Fax: (914) 980-6147     www.boyden.com

*International executive search firm.*

**Boyden Assoc. (Japan) Ltd., #308 1-3-28 Motoazabu, Minato-ku, Tokyo 106, Japan**

Tel: 81-3-5232-1872

### BOZELL GROUP

40 West 23rd Street, New York, NY, 10010

Tel: (212) 727-5000     Fax: (212) 645-9173     www.bozell.com

*Advertising, marketing, public relations and media consulting.*

**Bozell Worldwide, Japan, Nisseki Shibuya Bldg. 3F, 2-16-1 Shibuya, Shibuya-ku, Tokyo 150 Japan**

Tel: 81-3-3797-6262   Fax: 81-3-3797-6261   Contact: Robert Jenkins, Pres.

## BRADY CORPORATION

6555 W. Good Hope Road, Milwaukee, WI, 53223

Tel: (414) 358-6600    Fax: (414) 358-6600    www.whbrady.com

*Mfr. industrial ID for wire marking, circuit boards; facility ID, signage, printing systems and software.*

**Nippon Brady KK, Sumitomo Fudosan Shin, Yokahama Building 8F, 2-5-5 Shin Yokahama Kohoku-ku, Yokohama Kanagawa 222 Japan**

Tel: 81-45-474-2800   Fax: 81-45-474-6701    Contact: Tsutomo Matsumoto, Mng. Dir.

## BRANSON ULTRASONICS CORPORATION

41 Eagle Road, Danbury, CT, 06813-1961

Tel: (203) 796-0400    Fax: (203) 796-2285    www.branson-plasticsjoin.com

*Mfr. plastics assembly equipment, ultrasonic cleaning equipment.*

**Branson Ultrasonics, 4-3-14 Okada, Atsugi-shi, Kanagawa 243, Japan**

Tel: 81-462-28-2881   Fax: 81-462-28-8992

## BRISTOL-MYERS SQUIBB COMPANY

345 Park Ave., New York, NY, 10154-0037

Tel: (212) 546-4000    Fax: (212) 546-4020    www.bms.com

*Pharmaceutical and food preparations, medical and surgical instruments.*

**Bristol-Myers Lion Ltd., Nihon Seimei Akasaka, 7-1-16 Akasaka Minato-ku, Japan**

**ConvaTec Japan, EBISU, MF Bldg. 6F, Tokyo 150, Japan**

**ConvaTec, Div. Bristol-Myers Squibb, 27/F Shinjuku I-Land Tower, 6-5-1 Nishi-Shinjuku 6-chome, Shinjuku-ku, Tokyo 163-13 Japan**

**Japan Toda Labs, 1-34-17 Naka-Cho, Toda City, Saitama Pref. 335, Japan**

**Zimmer, Japan K.K., Mita 43 Mori Bldg., Minato-ku, Tokyo, Japan**

**Zimmer, Japan K.K., 1656-1, Nakabata, Gotemba City 108, Japan**

## BROADCOM CORPORATION INTERNATIONAL

16215 Alton Parkway, PO Box 57013, Irvine, CA, 92618

Tel: (949) 450-8700    Fax: (949) 450-8710    www.broadcom.com

*Designs, develops and supplies integrated circuits and high density communication processors.*

**Broadcom Corporation, 4-35-14 Utsukushigaoka, Aoba-ku Yokohama, 225-0002, Japan**

Tel: 81-45-903-1116   Fax: 81-45-903-1412

## BROADVISION, INC.

585 Broadway, Redwood City, CA, 94063

Tel: (650) 261-5100    Fax: (650) 261-5900    www.broadvision.com

*Develops and delivers an integrated suite of packaged applications for personalized enterprise portals.*

**BroadVision Japan, Tennoz Parkside Bldg. 12/F, 2-5-8 Higashi-Shinagawa, Shinagawa-ku, Tokyo 140-0002, Japan**

Tel: 81-3-5461-8810   Fax: 81-3-5461-8833

## BROOKS AUTOMATION, INC.

15 Elizabeth Drive, Chelmsford, MA, 01824

Tel: (978) 262-2400    Fax: (978) 262-2500    www.brooks.com

*Mfr. tool automation products.*

**Brooks Automation Japan, K.K., 1500 Komakihara-Shinden, Komaki City - Aichi Pref 485-8653, Japan**

Tel: 81-568-74-1511   Fax: 81-568-74-1602

**Brooks Automation Japan, K.K., KSP R&D Business Park Bldg. 9/F, 3-2-1 Sakado Takatsu-ku, Kawasaki Kanagawa 213, Japan**

Tel: 81-44-850-2900   Fax: 81-44-850-2901

### BROWN & WOOD LLP

One World Trade Center, 59th Fl., New York, NY, 10048

Tel: (212) 839-5300     Fax: (212) 839-5599     www.brownwoodlaw.com

*International law firm.*

**Brown & Wood, Kioicho K Bldg. 6/F, 3-28 Kioicho, Chiyoda-ku, Tokyo 102, Japan**

Tel: 81-3-5276-0045   Fax: 81-3-5276-0049

### BROWN BROTHERS HARRIMAN & COMPANY

59 Wall Street, New York, NY, 10005

Tel: (212) 483-1818     Fax: (212) 493-8526     www.bbh.com

*Financial services.*

**Brown Brothers Harriman & Co., 8-14 Nihombashi 3-chome, Chuo-ku, Tokyo 103, Japan**

### BRUNSWICK CORPORATION

1 Northfield Court, Lake Forest, IL, 60045-4811

Tel: (847) 735-4700     Fax: (847) 735-4765     www.brunswickcorp.com

*Mfr. recreational boats, marine engines, bowling centers and equipment, fishing equipment, defense/aerospace.*

**Nippon Brunswick KK, Nippon Brunswick Bldg., 27-7 Sendagaya 5-chome, Skibuya-ku, Tokyo, Japan**

### BRUSH WELLMAN INC.

17876 St. Clair Ave., Cleveland, OH, 44110

Tel: (216) 486-4200     Fax: (216) 383-4091     www.brushwellman.com

*Mfr. beryllium, beryllium alloys and ceramics, specialty metal systems and precious metal products.*

**Brush Wellman (Japan) Ltd., Dai-Ichi Marusan Bldg, 9 Kanda Jimbocho 3-chome, Chiyoda-ku, Tokyo 101 Japan**

Tel: 81-3-3230-2961   Fax: 81-3-3230-2908

### BUDGET GROUP, INC.

125 Basin St., Ste. 210, Daytona Beach, FL, 32114

Tel: (904) 238-7035     Fax: (904) 238-7461     www.budgetrentacar.com

*Car and truck rental system.*

**Budget Rent A Car, 3-255 Kukomae, Hakata-ku 812, Tokyo, Japan**

Tel: 81-92-2810543

### BULAB HOLDINGS INC.

1256 N. McLean Blvd, Memphis, TN, 38108

Tel: (901) 278-0330     Fax: (901) 276-5343     www.buckman.com

*Biological products; chemicals and chemical preparations.*

**Buckman Laboratories KK, Kyodo Building 7F, 16-8 Nihonbashi Kodenmach, Chuo-ku, Tokyo 103-0001, Japan**

Tel: 81-3-3808-1199   Fax: 81-3-3808-1590

### LEO BURNETT, DIV. B-COM 3 GROUP

35 West Wacker Drive, Chicago, IL, 60601

Tel: (312) 220-5959     Fax: (312) 220-6533     www.bcom3group.com

*Engaged in advertising, marketing, media buying and planning, and public relations.*

**Leo Burnett-Kyodo Co. Ltd., 18F Akasaka Twin Tower, 17-22 Akasaka 2-chome, Minato-ku Tokyo 107, Japan**

## BURSON-MARSTELLER

230 Park Ave., New York, NY, 10003-1566

Tel: (212) 614-4000  Fax: (212) 614-4262  www.bm.com

*Public relations/public affairs consultants.*

**Dentsu Burson-Marsteller Co. Ltd., Sogo 3 Bldg., 6 Kojimachi 1-chome, Chiyoda-ku, Tokyo 102 Japan**

Tel: 81-3-3264-6701  Fax: 81-3-3234-9647

## BUSH BOAKE ALLEN INC.

7 Mercedes Drive, Montvale, NJ, 07645

Tel: (201) 391-9870  Fax: (201) 391-0860  www.bushboakeallen.com

*Mfr. aroma chemicals for fragrances and flavor products for seasonings.*

**Bush Boake Allen, Fujiko Bldg. 9-10/F, 21-46 Takanawa 2- Chome, Minato-Ku, Tokyo 108-0074, Japan**

Tel: 81-3-3449-3071

## CABOT CORPORATION

75 State Street, Boston, MA, 02109-1807

Tel: (617) 345-0100  Fax: (617) 342-6103  www.cabot-corp.com

*Mfr. carbon blacks, plastics; oil and gas, information systems.*

**Cabot Far East Inc., 8-15 Akasaka 4-chome, Minato-ku, Tokyo 107, Japan**

## CADENCE DESIGN SYSTEMS, INC.

2655 Seely Ave., Bldg. 5, San Jose, CA, 95134

Tel: (408) 943-1234  Fax: (408) 943-0513  www.cadence.com

*Mfr. electronic design automation software.*

**Cadence Design Systems KK, 3-17-6 Shin-Yokohama, Kohoku-ku, Yokohama Kanagawa 222-0033, Japan**

Tel: 81-45-475-2221

## CALGON CARBON CORPORATION

400 Calgon Carbon Drive, Pittsburgh, PA, 15230-0717

Tel: (412) 787-6700  Fax: (412) 787-4541  www.calgoncarbon.com

*Mfr. activated carbon, related systems and services.*

**Calgon Far East Co., Ltd., Tokyo, Japan**

## CALIFORNIA CEDAR PRODUCTS COMPANY

PO Box 528, 400 Fresno Ave., Stockton, CA, 95201

Tel: (209) 944-5800  Fax: (209) 944-9072  www.duraflame.com

*Mfr. Duraframe-brand matches and fireplace logs, and incense-cedar products.*

**California Cedar Products Co., Shuttle Bldg. Rm. 303, 1-17 3-chome, Ohji-Dai Sakura-Shi, Chiba-Ken Japan**

## CALLAWAY GOLF COMPANY

2285 Rutherford Road, Carlsbad, CA, 92008

Tel: (760) 931-1771  Fax: (760) 931-8013  www.callawaygolf.com

*Mfr./sales of golf clubs.*

**Callaway Golf KK Japan, Shin-Onarimon Bldg. 1F, 6-17-19 Shinbashi, Minato-Ku Tokyo 105-0004, Japan**

**Korea**

Tel: 81-3-5405-4500  Fax: 81-3-5472-0405

## CALTEX CORPORATION

125 East John Carpenter Fwy., Irving, TX, 75062-2794

Tel: (972) 830-1000     Fax: (972) 830-1081     www.caltex.com

*Petroleum products.*

**Caltex Oil Japan KK, Hisseki Honkan 9F, 3-12 Nishi Shinbashi 1-chome, Minato-ku, Tokyo 105 Japan**

**Caltraport (Far East) Co., 703 Uschisaiwaicho Osaka Bldg., 3-3 Uchisaiwai-cho 1-chome, Chiyoda-ku, Tokyo 100 Japan**

**Koa Oil Company, Tokyo, Japan**

## CALVIN KLEIN, INC.

205 West 39th Street, 4th Fl., New York, NY, 10018

Tel: (212) 719-2600     Fax: (212) 768-8922     www.calvinklein.com

*Mfr. of high quality clothing and accessories*

**Calvin Klein Ltd., Tokyo, Japan**

## CAMBRIDGE TECHNOLOGY PARTNERS, INC.

8 Cambridge Center, Cambridge, MA, 02142

Tel: (617) 374-9800     Fax: (617) 914-8300     www.ctp.com

*Engaged in e-commerce consultancy.*

**Cambridge Technology Partners KK, 7-1-1 Nishi-gotanda, Shinagawa-ku, Tokyo 141-0031, Japan**
Tel: 81-3-3492-9581   Fax: 81-3-3492-9582

## CAMPBELL SOUP COMPANY

Campbell Place, Camden, NJ, 08103-1799

Tel: (856) 342-4800     Fax: (856) 342-3878     www.campbellsoup.com

*Mfr. food products.*

**Campbell Japan Inc., Tokyo, Japan**

## CANBERRA-PACKARD INDUSTRIES

800 Research Parkway, Meriden, CT, 06450

Tel: (203) 238-2351     Fax: (203) 235-1347     www.canberra.com

*Mfr. instruments for nuclear research.*

**Packard Japan KK, Kansai Iwamotocho Bldg., 19-8 Iwamoto-cho 2-chome, Chiyoda-ku, Tokyo 101, Japan**

## CANDELA LASER CORPORATION

530 Boston Post Road, Wayland, MA, 01778

Tel: (508) 358-7400     Fax: (508) 358-5602     www.clzr.com

*Mfr./services medical laser systems.*

**Candela Japan, 3/F Tokyo Knit Bldg., 9-5 Ryogoku 2-chome, Sumida-ku, Tokyo 130, Japan**

## CANNONDALE CORPORATION

16 Trowbridge Drive, Bethel, CT, 06829

Tel: (203) 749-7000     Fax: (203) 748-4012     www.cannondale.com

*Mfr. bicycles.*

**Cannondale Japan KK, 12-5 Harayamadai, 5-Cho Sakai City, Osaka 590 132, Japan**
Tel: 81-722-99-9399

## THE CAPITAL GROUP COS INC.

333 South Hope Street, Los Angeles, CA, 90071

Tel: (213) 486-9200     Fax: (213) 486-9557     www.capgroup.com

*Investment management.*

**Capital Group Companies, Hibiya Kokusai Bldg. 19/F, 2-2-3 Uchisaiuaicho Chiyoda-ky, Tokyo 100-0011 Japan**
Tel: 81-3-3595-3362   Fax: 81-3-3595-1703

## CARBOLINE COMPANY

350 Hanley Industrial Court, St. Louis, MO, 63144

Tel: (314) 644-1000     Fax: (314) 644-4617     www.carboline.com

*Mfr. coatings and sealants.*

**Japan Carboline Co. Ltd., Wakura Bldg., 1-5 Fukagawa 1-chome, Koto-ku, Tokyo, Japan**

## CARGILL, INC.

15407 McGinty Road West, Minnetonka, MN, 55440-5625

Tel: (612) 742-7575     Fax: (612) 742-7393     www.cargill.com

*Food products, feeds, animal products.*

**Cargill Japan, Fugi Bldg., 3-2-3 Marunouchi, Chiyoda-ku, Tokyo 100, Japan**

## CARRIER CORPORATION

One Carrier Place, Farmington, CT, 06034-4015

Tel: (860) 674-3000     Fax: (860) 679-3010     www.carrier.com

*Mfr./distributor/services A/C, heating and refrigeration equipment.*

**Carrier Higashi-Chugoku Co. Ltd., Okayama, Japan**

**Carrier Nishi Chugoku Co. Ltd., Hiroshima, Japan**

**Carrier Transicold Japan Ltd., Yokohama, Japan**

**Ebara Carrier Co. Ltd., Tokyo, Japan**

**General Aircon Tecnica Inc., Tokyo, Japan**

**Keihin Sobi Co. Ltd., Tokyo, Japan**

**Nippon Building Systems Co. (NBS), Tokyo, Japan**

**NIT Intelligent Planning & Development Co. Ltd., Tokyo, Japan**

**Tokyo Carrier Engineering Co. Ltd., Mitsui Annex Bldg. #2, 4-4-20 Nihonbashi-Hongoku-cho, Chuo-ku, Tokyo 103 Japan**

Tel: 81-3-3270-9414    Fax: 81-3-3270-3779

**United Technologies Building Systems Co., Tokyo, Japan**

## J.C. CARTER COMPANY

671 W. 17th Street, Costa Mesa, CA, 92627

Tel: (949) 548-3421     Fax: (949) 752-2997     www.jccarter.com

*Mfr. aerospace valves and pumps, cryogenic pumps.*

**Nippon Carter, Rokko Atelier House, 1-15 Yamadacho 3-chome, Nada-ku, Kobe 657, Japan**

## CASCADE CORPORATION

2201 NE 201st Ave., Fairview, OR, 97024-9718

Tel: (503) 669-6300     Fax: (503) 669-6321     www.cascor.com

*Mfr. hydraulic forklift truck attachments.*

**Cascade (Japan) Ltd., 5-5-41, Torikai Kami Settsu, Osaka 566, Japan**

Tel: 81-726-53-3490    Fax: 81-726-53-3497

## CASE CORPORATION

700 State Street, Racine, WI, 53404

Tel: (414) 636-6011     Fax: (414) 636-0200     www.casecorp.com

*Mfr./sale agricultural and construction equipment.*

**New Holland Hft Japan Inc., No. 2-2-1-7 Nishi 25, Chrome Kita 7 Chuo-Ku, Sapporo 060 Japan**

Tel: 81-11-643-2151    Fax: 81-11-644-6173

## CATAPULT COMMUNICATIONS CORPORATION

160 South Whisman Road, Mountain View, CA, 94041

Tel: (650) 960-1025    Fax: (650) 960-1029    www.catapult.com

*Mfr. test systems for telecommunications service providers.*

**Catapult Communications Corp., Int's Nakano Bldg. 8/F, 3-33-3 Nakano Nakano-ku, Tokyo 164-0001, Japan**

Tel: 81-3-3384-7661

## CATERPILLAR INC.

100 NE Adams Street, Peoria, IL, 61629-6105

Tel: (309) 675-1000    Fax: (309) 675-1182    www.cat.com

*Mfr. earth/material-handling and construction machinery and equipment and engines.*

**Akashi GS Co., Ltd., Tokyo, Japan**

**Shin Caterpillar Mitsubishi Ltd., 3700 Tana, Sagamihara-shi, Kanagawaken 229, Japan**

## C.B. RICHARD ELLIS

533 South Fremont Ave., Los Angeles, CA, 90071-1712

Tel: (213) 613-3123    Fax: (213) 613-3535    www.cbrichardellis.com

*Commercial real estate services.*

**CB Richard Ellis KK, 4F Nishi Shimbashi JK Building, 3-15-12 Nishi Shimbashi, Minato-ku Tokyo 105-0013, Japan**

**Ikoma/CB Richard Ellis, 8/F Sumitomo Seimei Niigata Higashi-Odori Bldg., 2-5-1 Higashi-Odori, Niigata-shi 950-0087, Japan**

**Ikoma/CB Richard Ellis, 9/F Nakaya Mitsui Bldg., 2-17 Oyama-cho, Kanazawa-shi 920-0918, Japan**

**Ikoma/CB Richard Ellis, 5/F Asahi Seimei Sannomiya Bldg., 1-3-11 Sannomiya-cho Chuo-ku, Kobe-shi 650-0021 Japan**

**Ikoma/CB Richard Ellis, 2/F Kyoto Karasuma Dai-ichi Seimei Bldg.. 646 Nijohanjiki-cho, Bukkoji-agaru Karasuma-dori, Shimogyo-ku Kyoto-shi 600-8412 Japan**

**Ikoma/CB Richard Ellis, 2/F Meiji Seimei Matsuyama Ichibancho Bldg., 4-1-3 Ichibancho, Matsuyama-shi 790-0001, Japan**

**Ikoma/CB Richard Ellis, 11/F Fukuoka Center Bldg., 2-2-1 Hakata-ekimae, Hakata-ku, Fukuoka-shi 812-0011, Japan**

**Ikoma/CB Richard Ellis, 5/F Shizuoka Meiji Seimeikan Bldg., 1-4 Tokiwa-cho Shizuoka-shi 420-0034, Japan**

**Ikoma/CB Richard Ellis, 3-4/F Marunouchi ia Bldg., 3-17-29 Marunouchi Naka-ku Nagoya-shi 460-0002, Japan**

**Ikoma/CB Richard Ellis, 5/F Tachikawa Mitsubishi Bldg., 2-13-3 Akebonocho Tachikawa-shi, Tokyo 190-0012 Japan**

**Ikoma/CB Richard Ellis, 6/F Asahi Seimei Takamatsu Daini Bldg., 1-2-5 Kobobuki-cho Takamatsu-shi 760-0023, Japan**

**Ikoma/CB Richard Ellis, 4-5/F Dai-ichi Building, Shuwa Hamamatsucho 2-2-12 Hamamatsucho, Minato-ku Tokyo 105-0013, Japan**

**Ikoma/CB Richard Ellis, 7/F Nihon Dantai Seimei Kagoshima Bldg., Kagoshima-shi 892-0847, Japan**

**Ikoma/CB Richard Ellis, 2/F Mitsui Seimei Yokohama Bldg., 2-25-2 Tsuruyacho, Kanagawa-ku, Yokohama-shi 221-0835 Japan**

**Ikoma/CB Richard Ellis, 8/FYasuda Seimei Horishima Bldg., Naka-hu Hiroshima-shi 730-0035, Japan**

**Ikoma/CB Richard Ellis, 10/F Chiba TN Bldg., 3-13 Shinmachi Chuo-ku, Chiba-shi 260-0028, Japan**

**Ikoma/CB Richard Ellis, 2/F KE Bldg., 2-1-10,Shimoishii Okayama-shi 700-0907, Japan**

**Ikoma/CB Richard Ellis, 8/F Meiji Seimei Omiya Bldg., 3-1 Miyacho, Omiya-shi, Japan**

**Ikoma/CB Richard Ellis, 9/F Daini Yuraku Bldg., 4-1-7 Honcho Chuo-ku, Osaka 541-0053 Japan**

**Ikoma/CB Richard Ellis, 6/F Daiwa Bank Sapporo Bldg., 3-2 Nishi, Kita-ichijo Chuo-ku, Sapporo-shi 060-0001 Japan**

Ikoma/CB Richard Ellis, 8/F Nihon Seimei Shinjuku Bldg., 1-17-1 Nishi-Shinjuku, Shinjuku-ku Tokyo 160-0023, Japan

Ikoma/CB Richard Ellis, 9/F Tokyo Shintaku Bldg., 1-8-19 Chuo Aoba-ku, Sendai-shi 980-0021 Japan

## CCH INCORPORATED

2700 Lake Cook Road, Riverwoods, IL, 60015

Tel: (847) 267-7000     Fax: (800) 224-8299     www.cch.com

*Provides tax and business law information and software for accounting, legal, human resources, securities and health care professionals.*

**CCH Japan Ltd., Ginza TK Bldg. 3/F, 1-1-7 Shintomi, Chuo-ku, Tokyo 104, Japan**

## C-CUBE MICROSYSTEMS INC.

1778 McCarthy Blvd., Milpitas, CA, 95035

Tel: (408) 490-8000     Fax: (408) 490-8132     www.c-cube.com

*Designs video compression chips.*

**C-Cube Microsystems Inc., Paleana Building 4/F, 2-2-15 Shin-Yokohama Kohoku-ku, Yokohama Kanagawa 222-0033, Japan**

## CDM INTERNATIONAL INC.

50 Hampshire Street, Cambridge, MA, 02139

Tel: (617) 452-6000     Fax: (617) 452-8020     www.cdm.com

*Consulting engineers.*

**CDM Camp Dresser & McKee Internaitonal Inc., New Erimo Bldge 7/F, 2-2-1 Senba Nishi, Minoh Cit, Osaka 562-0036, Japan**
Tel: 81-727-27-3181

## CEILCOTE AIR POLLUTION CONTROL

14955 Sprague Road, Strongsville, OH, 44136

Tel: (440) 243-0700     Fax: (440) 234-3486     www.ceilcoteapc.com

*Mfr. corrosion-resistant material, air pollution control equipment, construction services.*

**Ceilcote Japan Ltd., Port PO Box 1, Yokohama 231-91, Japan**

## CENDANT CORPORATION

9 West 57th Street, New York, NY, 10019

Tel: (212) 413-1800     Fax: (212) 413-1918     www.cendant.com

*Membership-based, direct marketer offering shopping/travel/insurance and dining discount programs*

**Tax Free Shopping, Japan K.K., Uchida Bldg. 4F, 2-13-11 Shin Kawa, Tokyo 124-0033, Japan**
Tel: 81-3-5541-6718   Fax: 81-3-5541-6719

## CENTOCOR INC.

200 Great Valley Parkway, Malvern, PA, 19355-1307

Tel: (610) 651-6000     Fax: (610) 651-6100     www.centocor.com

*Develop/mfr./marketing diagnostic and therapeutic products for human health care.*

**Nippon Centocor KK, 2-8-3 Higashi-Nihonbashi Chuo-ku, Tokyo 103-0004, Japan**
Tel: 81-3-5823-6565

## CENTRAL NATIONAL-GOTTESMAN INC.

3 Manhattanville Road, Purchase, NY, 10577-2110

Tel: (914) 696-9000     Fax: (914) 696-1066

*Worldwide sales pulp and paper products.*

**Central National Pacific Ltd., Ginza Sunny Bldg., 4-16 Ginza 3-chome, Chuo-ku, Tokyo 104 Japan**
Tel: 81-3-3562-3701   Fax: 81-3-3562-3705   Contact: Taijiu Hatakeyama

## CENTURA SOFTWARE CORPORATION

975 Island Drive, Redwood Shores, CA, 94065

Tel: (650) 596-3400     Fax: (650) 596-4900      www.centurasoft.com

*Mfr. software and database management tools*

**Centura Embedded Systems KK, 5-11-12 Minamiazabu, Minato-ku, Tokyo 106-0047, Japan**

Tel: 81-3-5792-5367

## CENTURY 21 REAL ESTATE CORPORATION

6 Sylvan Way, Parsippany, NJ, 07054-3826

Tel: (973) 496-5722     Fax: (973) 496-5527      www.century21.com

*Engaged in real estate.*

**Century 21 Real Estate of Japan Ltd., Kita-Aoyama Yoshikawa Bldg. 7F, 2-12-16 Kita Aoyama, Minato-ku, Tokyo 107 Japan**

Tel: 81-3-3497-0021

## CH2M HILL INC.

6060 South Willow Drive, Greenwood Village, CO, 80111

Tel: (303) 771-0900     Fax: (303) 770-2616      www.ch2m.com

*Consulting engineers, planners, economists and scientists.*

**CH2M Hill, Chiyoda-ku, Tokyo, Japan**

Tel: 81-3-5259-1641

## CHADBOURNE & PARKE LLP

30 Rockefeller Plaza, New York, NY, 10112-0127

Tel: (212) 408-5100     Fax: (212) 541-5369      www.chadbourne.com

*International law firm.*

**Chadbourne & Parke Gaikokuho Jimu Bengoshi Jimusho, Aoyama Building No. 924, 1-2-3 Kita-Aoyama, Minato-Ku, Tokyo 107-0061, Japan**

Tel: 81-3-3478-6120

**Watanabe, Nakamori, Nishida & Sugiura, Aoyama Building No. 924, 1-2-3 Kita-Aoyama, Minato-Ku, Tokyo 107-0061, Japan**

Tel: 813-3470-0271    Contact: Yaeji Wantanabe

## CHAMPION INTERNATIONAL CORPORATION

One Champion Plaza, Stamford, CT, 06921

Tel: (203) 358-7000     Fax: (203) 358-2975      www.championinternational.com

*Manufacture/sales of pulp and paper.*

**Champion Intl. (Asia) Ltd., Izuya Bldg., 4-12 Nishi-Shimbashi 1-chome, Minato-ku, Tokyo 105, Japan**

## CHASE H&Q

One Bush Street, San Francisco, CA, 94104

Tel: (415) 439-3000     Fax: (415) 439-3638      www.jpmhq.com

*Investment banking and venture capital services.*

**Chase H&Q LLC, Kyodo Building (Chuo) Suite 552, 1-2-12 Kayaba-cho, Nihonbashi Chuo-ku, Tokyo 103 Japan**

Tel: 81-3-3249-0037

## CHECKPOINT SYSTEMS, INC.

101 Wolf Drive, Thorofare, NJ, 08086

Tel: (856) 848-1800     Fax: (856) 848-0937      www.checkpointsystems.com

*Mfr. test, measurement and closed-circuit television systems.*

**Checkpoint Systems Japan, 8F Marusho Bldg., 1-1-8, Asakusabashi, Taito-ku, Tokyo, Japan**

Tel: 81-3-3864-1774    Fax: 81-3-3864-4130    Contact: Katsutoshi Ono, Pres.

## CHEMFAB CORPORATION

701 Daniel Webster Hwy., PO Box 1137, Merrimack, NH, 03054

Tel: (603) 424-9000        Fax: (603) 424-9028        www.chemfab.com

*Mfr. advanced polymer materials.*

**Chemfab Japan KK, Sanko Bldg. No. 2 1/F, 2-23 Ichigaya-Tamachi Shinjuku-ku, Tokyo 162-0843, Japan**

Tel: 81-3-3235-7193    Fax: 81-3-3235-3737

## THE CHERRY CORPORATION

3600 Sunset Ave., PO Box 718, Waukegan, IL, 60087

Tel: (847) 662-9200        Fax: (847) 662-2990        www.cherrycorp.com

*Mfr. electrical switches, electronic keyboards, controls and displays.*

**Cherry Automotive-Japan, 20-20 Hiradai, Midori-ku, Yokohama-shi, Japan**

**Hirose Cherry Precision Co. Ltd., 8/F Kaneko No. 2 Building, No.2-6-23 Shin-Yokohama, Kohoku-Ku Yokohama, Kanagawa 222 Japan**

**Hirose Cherry Precision Co. Ltd., 5-30-11 Shukugawara, Tama-ku, Kawasaki, Kanagawa 214, Japan**

## CHESTERTON BINSWANGER INTERNATIONAL

Two Logan Square, 4th Floor, Philadelphia, PA, 19103-2759

Tel: (215) 448-6000        Fax: (215) 448-6238        www.cbbi.com

*Real estate and related services.*

**Sotsu Binswanger, 69 Waseda-machi, Shinjyuku-ku, Tokyo 162 Japan**

**Sotsu Binswanger, 1-3 Honcho, Naka-Ku, Yokohama-Shi Kanagawa 231, Japan**

**Sotsu Corp., 69 Waseda-Machi, Shinjuku-ku, Tokyo 162, Japan**

## CHEVRON CHEMICAL COMPANY

1301 McKinney Street, Houston, TX, 77010

Tel: (713) 754-2000        Fax: (713) 754-2016        www.chevron.com

*Mfr. petro chemicals.*

**Oronite Japan Ltd., Landmark Plaza 7/F, 1-6-7 Shiba-Koen, Minato-ku, Tokyo 105, Japan**

## CHICAGO BRIDGE & IRON COMPANY (CBI)

1501 North Division Street, Plainfield, IL, 60544

Tel: (815) 241-7546        Fax: (815) 439-6010        www.chicago-bridge.com

*Holding company: metal plate fabricating, construction, oil and gas drilling.*

**Chicago Bridge & Iron Company, Kamiyacho Square Building 5F, 1-7-3 Azabudai,Minato-ku, Tokyo 106 Japan**

Tel: 81-33-224-3981    Fax: 81-33-224-3986

## CHICAGO RAWHIDE INDUSTRIES (CRI)

735 Tollgate Road, Elgin, IL, 60123

Tel: (847) 742-7840        Fax: (847) 742-7845        www.chicago-rawhide.com

*Mfr. shaft and face seals.*

**Chicago Rawhide Asia-Pacific, 10/F - Meiji Seimei Bldg., 3-2 Shin Yokohama, Kouhoku-ku Yokohama, Kanagawa 222-0033 Japan**

**Koyo Chicago Rawhide Co. Ltd., Aizumi, Itanogun, Tokushima 771-12, Japan**

## CHIQUITA BRANDS INTERNATIONAL INC.

250 East Fifth Street, Cincinnati, OH, 45202

Tel: (513) 784-8000        Fax: (513) 784-8030        www.chiquita.com

*Sale and distribution of bananas, fresh fruits and processed foods.*

**United Brands Japan Ltd., Shichijo Bldg. 7/F, 2-20-10 Higashi Nihonbashi, Chuo-ku, Tokyo 103, Japan**

## THE CHRISTIAN SCIENCE PUBLISHING SOCIETY

1 Norway Street, Boston, MA, 02115

Tel: (617) 450-2000     Fax: (617) 450-7575     www.christianscience.com

*Publishing company.*

**The Christian Science Monitor, 6-14-18 Shimouma, Setagaya-ku, Tokyo 15Y, Japan**

Tel: 81-3-5722-4536    Emp: 2

## THE CHUBB CORPORATION

15 Mountain View Road, Warren, NJ, 07061-1615

Tel: (908) 580-2000     Fax: (908) 580-3606     www.chubb.com

*Holding company for property and casualty insurance.*

**Federal Insurance Co., 9F Sumitomo Ichigaya Bldg., 1-1 Ichigaya Honmura-cho, Shinjuku-ku, Tokyo 162 Japan**

Tel: 81-3-3266-1051    Fax: 81-3-3266-1060

## CIGNA COMPANIES

One Liberty Place, Philadelphia, PA, 19192

Tel: (215) 761-1000     Fax: (215) 761-5511     www.cigna.com

*Insurance, invest, health care and other financial services.*

**CIGNA Insurance Co., Akasaka Eight-One Bldg. 7F, 13-5 Mayata-cho 2-chome, Chiyoda-ku, Tokyo 100, Japan**

**CIGNA Intl. Investment Advisors KK, Tobaya Bldg., 9-22 Akasaka 4-chome, Minato-ku, Tokyo, Japan**

**Esis Intl. Inc., Akasaka 81 Bldg., 13-5 Nagata-Cho 2-chome, Chiyoda-ku, Tokyo 100, Japan**

**INA Himawari Life Insurance Company, Ltd., Shinjuku Mitsui Bldg. 35th Fl. 1-1 Nishi Shinjuku 2-Chome, Shinjuku-ku Tokyo 163-04 Japan**

Tel: 81-3-3344-7696   Fax: 81-3-3346-9415   Contact: Mike Clowes

**INA Life Insurance Co. Ltd., Shinjuku Ctr. Bldg. 48F, 1-25 Nishi-Shinjuku 1-chome, Shinjuku-ku, Tokyo 160, Japan**

**Yasuda Kasia CIGNA Securities, Shinjuku Center Building 50/F, 25-1 Nishi-shinjuku 1-chome, Shinjuku-ku, Tokyo 163-0650 Japan**

Tel: 81-3-5326-1407   Fax: 81-3-5326-1432   Contact: Akimasa Oshima

## CINCINNATI INCORPORATED

PO Box 11111, Cincinnati, OH, 45211

Tel: (513) 367-7100     Fax: (513) 367-7552     www.e-ci.com

*Mfr. metal fabricating equipment.*

**Cincinnati Japan Ltd., CPO Box 1643, Tokyo, Japan**

Tel: 81-33-861-2662   Fax: 81-22-861-2665   Contact: Matt Kubotera, Pres.

**Cincinnati Japan, Ltd., Central PO Box 1643, Tokyo, Japan**

Tel: 81-33-861-2262   Fax: 81-33-861-2665

## CINCINNATI MILACRON INC.

4701 Marburg Ave., Cincinnati, OH, 45209

Tel: (513) 841-8100     Fax: (513) 841-8919     www.cinbus.com

*Develop/mfr. technologies for metalworking and plastics processing industrial.*

**Cincinnati Milacron Inc., Tokyo, Japan**

## CINCOM SYSTEMS INC.

55 Merchant Street, Cincinnati, OH, 45446

Tel: (513) 612-2300     Fax: (513) 481-8332     www.cincom.com

*Develop/distributor computer software.*

**Cincom Systems Inc., Tokyo, Japan**

**Cincom Systems Inc., Osaka, Japan**

## CISCO SYSTEMS, INC.

170 West Tasman Drive, San Jose, CA, 95134-1706

Tel: (408) 526-4000     Fax: (408) 526-4100     www.cisco.com

*Develop/mfr./market computer hardware and software networking systems.*

**Cisco Nihon Systems K.K., Fuji Bldg., 3-2-3 Fl. 9 Marunouchi, Chiyoda-ku, Tokyo 100 Japan**

Tel: 81-3-5219-6370   Fax: 81-3-5219-6028

## CITIGROUP, INC.

153 East 53rd Street, New York, NY, 10043

Tel: (212) 559-1000     Fax: (212) 559-3646     www.citigroup.com

*Provides insurance and financial services worldwide.*

**Citibank N.A., Kanese Bldg. - 1F, 3-5-5 Honmachi Chuo-ku, Osaka 541-0053 Japan**

**Citibank N.A., Citicorp Centre 19F, 2-3-14 Higashi-Shinagawa, Shinagawa-ku, Tokyo 140 Japan**

Contact: Arthur M. de Graffenried III

## CLEARY GOTTLIEB STEEN & HAMILTON

One Liberty Plaza, New York, NY, 10006

Tel: (212) 225-2000     Fax: (212) 225-3999     www.cgsh.com

*International law firm.*

**Cleary, Gottlieb, Steen & Hamilton Gaikokuho Jimubengoshi, 20/F - 3-2 Kasumigaseki 3-chome, Chiyoda-ku, Tokyo 100, Japan**

## CNA FINANCIAL CORPORATION

CNA Plaza, Chicago, IL, 60685

Tel: (312) 822-5000     Fax: (312) 822-6419     www.cna.com

*Commercial property/casualty insurance policies.*

**CNA Insurance KK, Tokio Kaijo Bldg. 6F, 2-1 Marunouchi 1-chome, Chiyoda-ku, Tokyo 100, Japan**

## COACH LEATHERWEAR COMPANY

516 West 34 Street, New York, NY, 10001

Tel: (212) 594-1850     Fax: (212) 594-1682     www.coach.com

*Mfr. and sales of high-quality leather products, including handbags and wallets.*

**Coach Hibiya Shop, Toho Twin Tower Building 1F, 1-5-2 Yurakucho, Chiyoda-ku, Tokyo 100-0006 Japan**

## THE COCA-COLA COMPANY

PO Drawer 1734, Atlanta, GA, 30301

Tel: (404) 676-2121     Fax: (404) 676-6792     www.coca-cola.com

*Mfr./marketing/distributor soft drinks, syrups and concentrates, juice and juice-drink products.*

**Coca-Cola West Japan Co. Ltd., Shibuya PO Box 10, Tokyo 150, Japan**

Contact: Michael W. Hall

## COGNEX CORPORATION

1 Vision Drive, Natick, MA, 01760

Tel: (508) 650-3000     Fax: (508) 650-3333     www.cognex.com

*Mfr. machine vision systems.*

**Cognex KK, IT Meieki Building 4/F, 3-11-22 Meieki Nakamura-ku, Nagoya-shi Aichi-ken 451-0045, Japan**

Tel: 81-52-569-5900   Fax: 81-52-581-7760

**Cognex KK, 5th Hakata Kaisei Bldg. 5/F, 1-18-25 Hakataeki-Higashi, Hakata-ku Fukuoka-shi, Fukuoka-ken 812-0013, Japan**

Tel: 81-92-432-7741   Fax: 81-92-412-3590

**Cognex KK, Musashiya Bldg. 4/F, 3-1-4 Kokubun-cho, Aoba-ku Sendai-shi, Miyagi-ken 980-0803, Japan**

Tel: 81-22-222-6393   Fax: 81-22-723-2887

**Cognex KK, Central Shin-Osaka Building 302, 4-5-36 Miyahara Yodogawa-ku, Osaka-shi 532-0003, Japan**

Tel: 81-6-4807-8201    Fax: 81-6-4807-8202

**Cognex KK, Bunkyo Green Court 23/F, 2-28-8 Honkomagome, Bunkyo-ku, Tokyo 113-6591, Japan**

Tel: 81-3-5977-5400    Fax: 81-3-5977-5401

## COHERENT INC.

5100 Patrick Henry Drive, PO Box 54980, Santa Clara, CA, 95056

Tel: (408) 764-4000        Fax: (408) 764-4800        www.cohr.com

*Mfr. lasers for science, industrial and medical.*

**Coherent Japan Inc., 2 Asanuma Bldg. 6F, 21-10 Hongo 3-chome, Bunkyo-ku, Tokyo 113 Japan**

**lambda Physik Japan Co. Ltd., German Industry Ctr., 1-18-2 Hakusan, Midori-ku, Yokohama 226 Japan**

Tel: 81-45-939-7848

## COHU, INC.

5755 Kearny Vill Road, San Diego, CA, 92123

Tel: (858) 541-5194        Fax: (858) 277-0221        www.cohu.com

*Mfr. semiconductor test handling systems.*

**Kan Electronics Co., Ltd, Kirokoji, Bldg. 1/F, 1-17-6 Ueno Taito-Ku, Tokyo 110, Japan**

Tel: 81-33-836-2800    Fax: 81-33-836-2266

## THE COLEMAN COMPANY, INC.

2111 E. 37th St., North, Wichita, KS, 67219

Tel: (316) 832-2700        Fax: (316) 832-2794        www.colemanoutdoors.com

*Mfr./distributor/sales camping and outdoor recreation products.*

**Coleman Japan Ltd., JBP Hakozaki Bldg. 2/F, Nihonbashi Hakozakicho 5-14, Chuo-Ku Tokyo 103, Japan**

## COLGATE-PALMOLIVE COMPANY

300 Park Ave., New York, NY, 10022

Tel: (212) 310-2000        Fax: (212) 310-2919        www.colgate.com

*Mfr. pharmaceuticals, cosmetics, toiletries and detergents.*

**CKR (Japan) Co. Ltd., Kakihara Asahi Eitai Bldg. 7/F, 3-7-13 Toyo, Koto-ku, Tokyo 135 Japan**

## COMDISCO INC.

6111 N. River Road, Rosemont, IL, 60018

Tel: (847) 698-3000        Fax: (847) 518-5440        www.comdisco.com

*Hi-tech asset and facility management and equipment leasing.*

**Comdisco Japan Inc., 3-1-1 Marunouchi, Kokusai Bldg. 9/F, Chiyoda-Ku Tokyo 100-005 Japan**

## COMMERCIAL INTERTECH CORPORATION

1775 Logan Ave., PO Box 239, Youngstown, OH, 44501-0239

Tel: (330) 746-8011        Fax: (330) 746-1148

*Mfr. hydraulic components, pre-engineered buildings and stamped metal products.*

**The Oilgear Japan Co., 204 Nishikan, Daini Toyoda Bldg., 4-10-27 Meieki, Nakamura-ku, Nagoya 450, Japan**

## COMMERCIAL METALS COMPANY (CMC)

PO Box 1046, Dallas, TX, 75221

Tel: (214) 689-4300        Fax: (214) 689-4320        www.commercialmetals.com

*Metal collecting/processing, steel mills and metal trading.*

**Cometals Far East Inc., Daiichi Seimei Sogo-kan, 7-1 Kyobashi 3-chome, Chuo-ku, Tokyo 104, Japan**

## COMPAQ COMPUTER CORPORATION

20555 State Highway 249, PO Box 692000, Houston, TX, 77269-2000

Tel: (281) 370-0670      Fax: (281) 514-1740      www.compaq.com

*Develop/mfr. personal computers.*

**Compaq KK, Kamiya-cho Mori Bldg., 4-3-20 Toranomon, Minato-ku, Tokyo 105, Japan**

Tel: 81-3-5402-5700   Fax: 81-3-5402-5964

**Tandem, a Compaq Company, Japan Div. World Hdqtrs., Tennoz Central Tower 2-2-24, Higashi-Shinagawa, Shinagawa-ku, Tokyo 140, Japan**

Tel: 81-3-5463-6600

## COMPUTER ASSOCIATES INTERNATIONAL INC.

One Computer Associates Plaza, Islandia, NY, 11788

Tel: (516) 342-5224      Fax: (516) 342-5329      www.cai.com

*Integrated business software for enterprise computing and information management, application development, manufacturing, financial applications and professional services.*

**Computer Associates Japan Ltd., Shinjuku Mitsui Bldg., 2-1-1 Nishi-Shinjuku, Shinjuku, Tokyo 163-0439, Japan**

Tel: 81-3-5320-8080

## COMPUWARE CORPORATION

31440 Northwestern Hwy., Farmington Hills, MI, 48334-2564

Tel: (248) 737-7300      Fax: (248) 737-7108      www.compuware.com

*Develop and market software for enterprise and e-commerce solutions.*

**Compuware Japan Corporation, 2-4-7 Dojima - 13/F, Kita-Ku, Osaka 530-0003, Japan**

Tel: 81-6-6345-2816   Fax: 81-6-6345-2818

**MS Jyoho Systems Compuware Corp., Cho-Gin Jyoho Systems, LS Bldg. 1-1-17, Kamiohsaki 1-Chome, Shinagawa-Ku Tokyo 141, Japan**

## COMVERSE TECHNOLOGY, INC.

234 Crossways Park Drive, Woodbury, NY, 11797

Tel: (516) 677-7200      Fax: (516) 677-7355      www.comverse.com

*Mfr. telephone communication and recording systems.*

**Comverse Japan Limited, Meiho Bldg. 8/F, 1-21-1 Nishi-shinjuku, Shinjuku-ku Tokyo 160-0023, Japan**

Tel: 81-3-5324-9171   Fax: 81-3-5324-9121

## CONAGRA INC.

One ConAgra Drive, Omaha, NE, 68102-5001

Tel: (402) 595-4000      Fax: (402) 595-4707      www.conagra.com

*Prepared/frozen foods, grains, flour, animal feeds, agro chemicals, poultry, meat, dairy products, including Healthy Choice, Butterball and Hunt's.*

**ConAgra Inc., Tokyo, Japan**

## CONCURRENT COMPUTER CORPORATION

4375 River Green Pkwy., Duluth, GA, 30096

Tel: (678) 258-4000      Fax: (678) 258-4300      www.ccur.com

*Mfr. computer systems and software.*

**Concurrent Nippon Corporation, Shuwa Yanagibashi Bldg. 5F, 19-6 2-chome, Taito-ku, Tokyo 111, Japan**

Tel: 81-3-3864-5711   Fax: 81-3-3864-0898

## CONE MILLS CORPORATION

3101 N. Elm Street, PO Box 26540, Greensboro, NC, 27415-6540

Tel: (336) 379-6220     Fax: (336) 379-6287     www.cone.com

*Mfr. denims, flannels, chamois and other fabrics.*

**Sugi Enterprise, Tamaya Bldg. 5F, 2-chome 3-11, Minami Honmachi, Chuo-0ku, Osaka 541, Japan**

Tel: 81-6-262-5481   Fax: 81-6-262-5483   Contact: H. Sugiyama

## CONEXANT SYSTEMS, INC.

4311 Jamboree Road, PO Box C, Newport Beach, CA, 92658-8902

Tel: (949) 483-4600     Fax: (949) 483-4078     www.conexant.com

*Provides semiconductor products for communications electronics.*

**Conexant Systems Japan Company Limited, 1-46-3 Hatsudai, Shibuya-ku, Tokyo 151 Japan**

Tel: 81-3-5371-1520   Fax: 81-3-5371-1501

## CONOCO INC.

PO Box 2197, 600 N. Dairy Ashford, Houston, TX, 77252

Tel: (281) 293-1000     Fax: (281) 293-1440     www.conoco.com

*Oil, gas, coal, chemicals and minerals.*

**Conoco Chemical Far East Inc., PO Box 110, Kasumigaseki Bldg. 25F, Tokyo, Japan**

## COOPER STANDARD AUTOMOTIVE

2401 South Gulley Road, Dearborn, MI, 48124

Tel: (313) 561-1100     Fax: (313) 561-6526     www.cooperstandard.com

*Mfr. molded and extruded rubber and plastic products for automotive and appliance industry, retread tire industry.*

**Nishikawa Rubber Co., Ltd., 2-2-8 Misasa-cho, Nishi Ward, Hiroshima-shi 733, Japan**

Tel: 81-82-237-9372   Fax: 81-82-230-0403

## CORDANT TECHNOLOGIES INC.

15 W. South Temple, Ste. 1600, Salt Lake City, UT, 84101-1532

Tel: (801) 933-4000     Fax: (801) 933-4014     www.cordanttech.com

*Mfr. solid rocket boosters for space shuttles and fasteners, rivets, and lock bolts for the transportation and construction industries.*

**Huck Ltd. Osaka Hdqtrs., Toyosaki-Izumi-Building 8F, 2-7-9 Toyosaki, Kita-ku Osaka 531-0072, Japan**

Tel: 81-6-6372-1193   Fax: 81-6-6372-9346

## CORN PRODUCTS INTERNATIONAL, INC.

6500 South Archer Ave., Bedford Park, IL, 60501-1933

Tel: (708) 563-2400     Fax: (708) 563-6852     www.cornproducts.com

*Produces corn products for ingredients corn starch corn oil and corn syrups.*

**Corn Products Japan Ltd., 11 Kanda-Higashi-Matsushitacho, Chiyoda-ku, Tokyo 101-0042, Japan**

Tel: 81-03-5297-2717   Fax: 81-03-5297-2718

## CORNING INC.

One Riverfront Plaza, Corning, NY, 14831-0001

Tel: (607) 974-9000     Fax: (607) 974-8091     www.corning.com

*Mfr. glass and specialty materials, consumer products; communications, laboratory services.*

**Corning International K.K., No. 35 Kowa Bldg. 3F, 14-14 Akasaka 1-chome, Minato-Ku Tokyo 107-0052, Japan**

Tel: 81-3-3586-1052   Fax: 81-3-3587-0906

## COSMAIR INC.

575 Fifth Ave., New York, NY, 10017

Tel: (212) 818-1500      Fax: (212) 984-4776      www.cosmair.com

*Mfr. hair and skin care products.*

**Nihon Redken KK, Hirakawa-chuo Bldg., 2-4-16 Hirakawa-chuo, Chiyoda-ku, Tokyo, Japan**

## COSTCO WHOLESALE CORPORATION

999 Lake Dr., Issaquah, WA, 98027

Tel: (425) 313-8100      Fax: (425) 313-8103      www.costco.com

*Operates wholesale, membership warehouse stores.*

**Costco Wholesale Corp., Torium Value Centre, 1152-1 Aza Takayanagi, Oaza-Yamada, Hisayama-cho Kasuya-gun, Fukuoka Japan**

## COUDERT BROTHERS

1114 Ave. of the Americas, New York, NY, 10036-7794

Tel: (212) 626-4400      Fax: (212) 626-4120      www.coudert.com

*International law firm.*

**Coudert Brothers, Daini Okamotoya Bldg. 10F, 1-22-16 Toranomon, Minato-ku, Tokyo 105 Japan**

Tel: 81-3-3580-2290    Fax: 81-3-3580-2301

## COULTER PHARMACEUTICAL, INC.

600 Gateway Blvd., South San Francisco, CA, 94080

Tel: (650) 553-2000      Fax: (650) 553-2028      www.coulterpharm.com

*Mfr. blood analysis systems, flow cytometers, chemicals systems, scientific systems and reagents.*

**Japan Scientific Instrument Co. Ltd., 6-7-5 Higashi-Kasai, Edogawa-ku, Tokyo 134, Japan**

## SG COWEN SECURITIES

1221 Avenue of the America, New York, NY, 10020

Tel: (212) 495-6000      Fax: (212) 380-8212      www.cowen.com

*Securities research, trading, broker/dealer services; investment banking and asset management.*

**Cowen Securities, Toranomon Ctr. Bldg. 4F, 1-16-17, Toranomon, Minato-ku, Tokyo, 105 Japan**

Tel: 81-3-3503-0371    Fax: 81-3-3503-0375    Contact: Noryuki Onishi, Mgr.

## CRC PRESS LLC

2000 NW Corporate Blvd., Boca Raton, FL, 33431

Tel: (561) 994-0555      Fax: (561) 997-0949      www.crcpress.com

*Publishing: science, technical and medical books and journals.*

**CRC Press, Misuzu Bldg. 2/F, 2-42-14 Matsubara, Setagaya-ku, Tokyo 156, Japan**

## CRITICARE SYSTEMS INC.

20925 Crossroads Circle, Waukesha, WI, 53186

Tel: (262) 798-8282      Fax: (262) 798-8491      www.csiusa.com

*Develop/mfr. diagnostic and therapeutic products and patient monitoring systems..*

**Criticare Systems Inc. Japan, Maruki Bldg., 3-6-11 Hongo, Bunkyo-ku, Tokyo 113, Japan**

## A.T. CROSS COMPANY

One Albion Road, Lincoln, RI, 02865

Tel: (401) 333-1200      Fax: (401) 334-2861      www.cross.com

*Mfr. writing instruments, leads, erasers and ink refills.*

**Cross Company of Japan Ltd., Kando Grow Bldg. 6F, 1-34-4, Kando Sudacho, Chiyoda-ku, Tokyo 101, Japan**

Tel: 81-3-5294-1781

## CUMMINS ENGINE COMPANY, INC.

500 Jackson Street, PO Box 3005, Columbus, IN, 47202-3005

Tel: (812) 377-5000      Fax: (812) 377-4937      www.cummins.com

*Mfr. diesel engines.*

**Cummins Diesel Japan Ltd., Ark Mori Bldg. 17/F, PO Box 525 - 1232 Akasaka 1-chome, Minato-ku Tokyo 107 Japan**

**Cummins Diesel Sales Corp., 1-12-10 Shintomi, Chuo-ku, Tokyo 104, Japan**

## CYMER, INC.

16750 Via del Campo Court, San Diego, CA, 92127

Tel: (858) 385-7300      Fax: (858) 385-7100      www.cymer.com

*Mfr. excimer lasers.*

**Cymer Japan KK, Cosmos Motoyawata Building, 4-17-8 Minamiyawata, Ichikawa-shi, Chiba 272-0023 Japan**

Tel: 81-47-393-5668

## CYPRESS SEMICONDUCTOR CORPORATION

3901 N. First Street, San Jose, CA, 95134-1599

Tel: (408) 943-2600      Fax: (408) 943-2796      www.cypress.com

*Mfr. integrated circuits.*

**Cypress Japan K.K., Harmony Tower 17/F, 1-32-2 Hon-cho Nakano-ku, Tokyo 164-0012, Japan**

Tel: 81-3-5371-1921

## CYTEC INDUSTRIES, INC.

5 Garret Mountain Plaza, West Paterson, NJ, 07424

Tel: (973) 357-3100      Fax: (973) 357-3054      www.cytec.com

*Mfr. specialty chemicals and materials,*

**Mitsui Cytec Ltd., Torii Nihonbashi Bldg. 6/F, 3-4-1 Nihonbashi Honcho, Chou-Ku Tokyo 103, Japan**

Tel: 81-3-3231-6072

## DAMES & MOORE GROUP

911 Wilshire Boulevard, Ste. 700, Los Angeles, CA, 90017

Tel: (213) 996-2200      Fax: (213) 996-2290      www.dames.com

*Engineering, environmental and construction management services.*

**Dames & Moore Ltd., Asahi Bldg. 7F, 38-3 Kamata 5-chome, Ota-ku, Tokyo 144 Japan**

## DANA CORPORATION

4500 Dorr Street, Toledo, OH, 43615

Tel: (419) 535-4500      Fax: (419) 535-4643      www.dana.com

*Mfr./sales of automotive, heavy truck, off-highway, fluid and mechanical power components and engine parts, filters and gaskets.*

**Daido-Sprag Ltd., Central Bldg. 6, 19-10 Toranomon 1-chome, Minato-ku, Tokyo 105 Japan**

**Koshin-Racine, 1-12 Shin-Sayama 1 chome, Sayama-shi, Saitama-ken 350-115, Japan**

**Najico Spicer Co. Ltd., 1010 3-chrome Tsukiji, Chuo-Ku Tokyo 104-0045, Japan**

Tel: 81-03-5566-6781

## D'ARCY MASIUS BENTON & BOWLES INC. (DMB&B)

1675 Broadway, New York, NY, 10019

Tel: (212) 468-3622      Fax: (212) 468-2987      www.dmbb.com

*Full service international advertising and communications group.*

**DMB&B Asia Pacific, Akasaka Daiichi Bldg., 4-9-17 Akasaka, Minato-ku, Tokyo 107 Japan**

## DATA GENERAL CORPORATION

4400 Computer Drive, Westboro, MA, 01580

Tel: (508) 898-5000      Fax: (508) 366-1319      www.dg.com

*Design, mfr. general purpose computer systems and peripheral products and services.*

**Data General Japan, Fuerte Kojimachi Bldg., 1-7-25 Kojimachi Chiyoda-Ku, Tokyo 102-9983 Japan**

Tel: 81-2-5213-9171

## DATA I/O CORPORATION

PO Box 97046, 10525 Willows Road, NE, Redmond, WA, 98073-9746

Tel: (425) 881-6444      Fax: (425) 882-1043      www.dataio.com

*Mfr. computer testing devices.*

**Data I/O Japan, Sumitumoseimei Higashishinbashi Bldg. 8/F, 2-1-7 Higashi-Shinbashi, Minato-ku, Tokyo 105, Japan**

## DAVIS POLK & WARDWELL

450 Lexington Ave., New York, NY, 10017

Tel: (212) 450-4000      Fax: (212) 450-4800      www.dpw.com

*International law firm.*

**Davis Polk & Wardwell, Akasaka Twin Tower East 13F, 17-22 Akasaka 2-chome, Minato-ku, Tokyo 107, Japan**

Tel: 81-3-5561-4421   Fax: 81-3-5561-4425

## DAYTON PROGRESS CORPORATION

500 Progress Road, Dayton, OH, 45449

Tel: (937) 859-5111      Fax: (937) 859-5353      www.daytonprogress.com

*Punches, dies and guide bushings.*

**Dayton Progress Corporation of Japan, 2-7-35 Hashimotodai, Sagamihara-Shi Kanagawa-Ken, 229-1132 Japan**

## DDB NEEDHAM WORLDWIDE INC.

437 Madison Ave., New York, NY, 10022

Tel: (212) 415-2000      Fax: (212) 415-3417      www.ddbn.com

*Advertising agency.*

**DDB Needham Japan Inc., Hibiya Kokusai Bldg., 2-3 Uchisaiwai-cho 2-chome, Chiyoda-ku, Tokyo 100 Japan**

## DELL COMPUTER CORPORATION

One Dell Way, Round Rock, TX, 78682-2222

Tel: (512) 338-4400      Fax: (512) 728-3653      www.dell.com

*Direct marketer and supplier of computer systems.*

**Dell Computer K.K., Solid Square East Tower 20/21F, 580 Horikawa-cho, Saiwai-ku, Kawasaki Kanagawa 210 Japan**

Tel: 81-44-556-4300   Fax: 81-44-556-3205   Contact: Charles (Chip) H. Saunders, Mng. Dir.

## DELOITTE TOUCHE TOHMATSU INTERNATIONAL

1633 Broadway, New York, NY, 10019

Tel: (212) 492-4000      Fax: (212) 392-4154      www.deloitte.com

*Accounting, audit, tax and management consulting services.*

**Tohmatsu & Co., Sapporo Daiichikaikei Bldg.1-10, Kita Nijo, Nishi 13-chome Chuo-ku, Sapporo 060 Japan**

**Tohmatsu & Co., Nagoya Daiya Bldg. 2-Gukan, 15-1-Meieki 3-chome, Nakamura-ku, Nagoya 450 Japan**

**Tohmatsu & Co., M S Shibaur Bldg., 13-3 Shibaura 4-chome, Minato-ku, Tokyo 108 Japan**

**Tohmatsu & Co., Osaka Kokusai Bldg. 3-13, Azuchi-machi 2-chome, Chuo-ku, Osaka 541 Japan**

## DELTA AIR LINES INC.

PO Box 20706, Atlanta, GA, 30320-6001

Tel: (404) 715-2600     Fax: (404) 715-5494     www.delta-air.com

*Major worldwide airline; international air transport services.*

**Delta Air Lines Inc., Kioicho Bldg. 9/F, 3-12 Kioicho, Chiyoda-ku, Tokyo-Narita, Japan 102**

Tel: 81-3-5275-7510   Fax: 81-3-5275-7505

## DENTSPLY INTERNATIONAL

570 West College Ave., PO Box 872, York, PA, 17405-0872

Tel: (717) 845-7511     Fax: (717) 843-6357     www.dentsply.com

*Mfr. and distribution of dental supplies and equipment.*

**Dentsply Japan, Tsunashima No. 2 Bldg., 20-12 Yushima 3-chome, Bunkyo-ku Toyko 113, Japan**

Tel: 81-3-3836-9911

## THE DEXTER CORPORATION

1 Elm Street, Windsor Locks, CT, 06096

Tel: (860) 627-9051     Fax: (860) 627-7078     www.dexelec.com

*Mfr. polymer products, magnetic materials, biotechnology.*

**D & S Plastics Intl., 6 Kowa Bldg., 15-21 Nishi-azabu 4-chome, Minato-ku, Tokyo 106 Japan**

**Dexter Midland Co. Ltd., 37-2 Minamisuna 2-chome, Koto-ku, Tokyo 136, Japan**

**Dexter Pacific Inc., 6 Kowa Bldg., 15-21 Nishi-Azabu 4-chome, Minato-ku, Tokyo 106 Japan**

**Hysol Ltd., 2050 Kamiyabe-cho, Totsuka-ku, Yokohama-shi 245, Japan**

**Life Technologies Inc., Tejima Bldg. 3/F, 1-12-8 Toranomon, Minato-ku, Tokyo 105 Japan**

**Life Technologies Oriental Inc., Landic Nihonbashi 3 Bldg. 9/F, 14-4 Kodenmacha-cho, Nihonbashi Chuo-ku, Tokyo 103 Japan**

## DHL WORLDWIDE EXPRESS

50 California Avenue, San Francisco, CA, 94111

Tel: (415) 677-6100     Fax: (415) 824-9700     www.dhl.com

*Worldwide air express carrier.*

**DHL Worldwide Express, 37-8 Higashi-Shinagawa 1-chome, Shinagawa-ku, Tokyo 140-002, Japan**

Tel: 81-3-54792580

## DIGITAL ORIGIN, INC.

460 East Middlefield Road, Mountainview, CA, 94043

Tel: (650) 404-6300     Fax: (650) 404-6200     www.digitalorigin.com

*Mfr. Digital Video (DV) software products.*

**Media 100 KK, Yanaba Bldg. 5/F, 6-7-10 Roppongi, Minato-ku, Tokyo, Japan**

## DIONEX CORPORATION

1228 Titan Way, PO Box 3603, Sunnyvale, CA, 94086-3603

Tel: (408) 737-0700     Fax: (408) 730-9403     www.dionex.com

*Develop/mfr./market chromatography systems and related products.*

**Nippon Dionex KK, Shin-Osaka GH Bldg. #205, 9-20 Nishi-Nakajima 6-chome, Yodogawa-ku, Osaka 532, Japan**

## WALT DISNEY COMPANY

500 South Buena Vista Street, Burbank, CA, 91521

Tel: (818) 560-1000     Fax: (818) 560-1930     www.disney.com

*Film/TV production, theme parks, resorts, publishing, recording and retail stores.*

**Walt Disney Enterprises of Japan Ltd., Kanesaka Bldg., 5-4 Shimbashi 2-chome, Minato-ku, Tokyo 105, Japan**

## DME COMPANY
29111 Stephenson Highway, Madison Heights, MI, 48071

Tel: (248) 398-6000     Fax: (248) 544-5705     www.dmeco.com

*Basic tooling for plastic molding and die casting.*

**Japan DME Corp., Harumi Park Bldg. 3F, 2-22 Harumi 3-chome, Chuo-ku, Tokyo, Japan**

## DOCUMENTUM, INC.
6801 Koll Center Pkwy., Pleasanton, CA, 94566

Tel: (925) 600-6800     Fax: (925) 600-6850     www.documentum.com

*Mfr. content management software.*

**Nihon Documentum K.K., TE Building 3/F, 4-5-16 Yoga, Setagaya-Ku, Tokyo 158-0097, Japan**

## DONALDSON COMPANY, INC.
1400 West 94th Street, Minneapolis, MN, 55431

Tel: (612) 887-3131     Fax: (612) 887-3155     www.donaldson.com

*Mfr. filtration systems and replacement parts.*

**Nippon Donaldson, Ltd., 13-2 5-chome, Imadera, Ome City Tokyo 198, Japan**

Tel: 81-428-31-4111   Fax: 81-428-31-9074

## DONALDSON, LUFKIN & JENRETTE, INC.
277 Park Ave., New York, NY, 10172

Tel: (212) 892-3000     Fax: (212) 892-7272     www.dlj.com

*Investment banking, capital markets and financial services.*

**Donaldson, Lufkin & Jenrette, Inc., Fukoku Seimei Bldg., 2-2-2 Uchisaiwaicho, Chiyoda-ku Tokyo 100, Japan**

Tel: 81-3-3506-8222

## R.R. DONNELLEY & SONS COMPANY
77 West Wacker Drive, Chicago, IL, 60601-1696

Tel: (312) 326-8000     Fax: (312) 326-8543     www.rrdonnelley.com

*Commercial printing, allied communication services.*

**R. R. Donnelley Japan K.K., Donnelley Bldg., 2-28-7 Kami-Ochiai 4th Fl., 2-chome Shinjuku-ku, Tokyo 161, Japan**

Tel: 81-3-3227-5211

## DONNELLY CORPORATION
49 W. 3rd St., Holland, MI, 49423-2813

Tel: (616) 786-7000     Fax: (616) 786-6034     www.donnelly.com

*Mfr. fabricated, molded and coated glass products for the automotive and electronics industries.*

**Donnelly Corporation Sales Office, 10F - 101 Takanawa Empire Bldg., 3-24-18 Takanawa Minato-Ku, Tokyo 104-0074 Japan**

## DOUBLECLICK, INC.
450 West 33rd Street, New York, NY, 10001

Tel: (212) 683-0001     Fax: (212) 889-0062     www.doubleclick.net

*Engaged in online advertising.*

**Doubleclick, Ltd., Yotsubashi Park Building 1/F, 1-4-10 Itachibori Nishi-ku, Osaka-shi Osaka 550-0012, Japan**

**Doubleclick, Ltd., Step-Roppongi Bldg. West 1/F, 6-8-10 Roppongi Minato-ku, Tokyo 106-0032, Japan**

Tel: 81-3-5770-4109   Fax: 81-3-5770-4112

## THE DOW CHEMICAL COMPANY

2030 Dow Center, Midland, MI, 48674

Tel: (517) 636-1000     Fax: (517) 636-3228     www.dow.com

*Mfr. chemicals, plastics, pharmaceuticals, agricultural products, consumer products.*

**Dow Chemical Japan Ltd., Osaka, Japan**

**Dow Chemical Japan Ltd., Hibiya Chunichi Bldg. 6F, 2-1-4 Uchisaiwai-cho, Chiyoda-ku, Tokyo 100, Japan**

## DRAFT WORLDWIDE

633 North St. Clair Street, Chicago, IL, 60611-3211

Tel: (312) 944-3500     Fax: (312) 944-3566     www.draftworldwide.com

*Full service international advertising agency, engaged in brand building, direct and promotional marketing.*

**DraftWorldwide, Div. of Yomiko, 1-8-14 Ginza, 1-chome, Chuo-ku, Tokyo 104 Japan**

Tel: 81-3-3563-7889   Fax: 81-3-3562-2594

## DRAKE BEAM MORIN INC.

101 Huntington Ave., Boston, MA, 02199

Tel: (617) 375-9500     Fax: (617) 267-2011     www.dbm.com

*Human resource management consulting and training.*

**DBM Japan KK, MS Bldg. 9/F, 11-5 Shiba 4-chome, Minato-ku, Tokyo 108 Japan**

Tel: 81-3-3452-1461   Fax: 81-3-3452-4904

## DRESSER INSTRUMENT DIVISION

250 East Main Street, Stratford, CT, 06614-5145

Tel: (203) 378-8281     Fax: (203) 385-0357     www.dresserinstruments.com

*Mfr. pressure gauges and temperature instruments.*

**Dresser Japan Ltd., Room 818 Shin Tokyo Building, 3-3-1 Tokyo, Tokyo 100, Japan**

Tel: 81-3-3201-1501   Fax: 81-3-3213-6567

## DREVER COMPANY

PO Box 98, 380 Red Lion Road, Huntingdon, PA, 19006-0098

Tel: (215) 947-3400     Fax: (215) 947-7934     www.drever.com

*Mfr. industrial furnaces and heat processing equipment.*

**Drever Japan, 71-4, 3-chome Mutsukawa, Minami-ku Yokohama, 232-0066 Japan**

## E.I. DU PONT DE NEMOURS & COMPANY

1007 Market Street, Wilmington, DE, 19898

Tel: (302) 774-1000     Fax: (302) 774-7321     www.dupont.com

*Mfr./sale diversified chemicals, plastics, specialty products and fibers.*

**DuPont Far East Inc., Kowa Bldg., 11-39 Akasaka 1-chome, Minato-ku, Tokyo 107, Japan**

Contact: Masatoshi Yamamoto, Pres.

**Teijin DuPont, Tokyo, Japan**

## DUFF & PHELPS CREDIT RATING CO.

55 East Monroe Street, Chicago, IL, 60603

Tel: (312) 368-3100     Fax: (312) 442-4121     www.dcrco.com

*Engaged in rating stocks and bonds, municipal securities and insurance company claims paying capabilities.*

**Duff & Phelps Credit Rating Co., Kamiyacho Mori Bldg. 14/F, 4-3-20 Toranomon, Minato-ku, Tokyo 105-0001 Japan**

Tel: 81-3-5404-3542   Fax: 81-3-5404-3401

## DUNHILL INTERNATIONAL SEARCH

59 Elm Street, Ste. 520, New Haven, CT, 06510

Tel: (203) 562-0511      Fax: (203) 562-2637      www.internationalsearch.com

*International recruiting services: sales/marketing, accounting/finance, general managers.*

**Dunhill International Search, Tokyo, Japan**

## DURACELL INTERNATIONAL INC.

8 Research Drive, Bethel, CT, 06801

Tel: (203) 796-4000      Fax: (203) 796-4745      www.duracell.com

*Mfr. batteries.*

**Duracell Battery Japan Ltd., Masudaya Bldg. 8F, 2-6-4 Kuramae, Taito-ku, Tokyo 111, Japan**

## DURO-TEST CORPORATION

9 Law Drive, Fairfield, NJ, 07004

Tel: (973) 808-1800      Fax: (973) 808-7107      www.duro-test.com

*Mfr. fluorescent, incandescent and fluomeric lamps.*

**Duro-Test Japan Inc., Shinbashi Shinwa Bldg., 4-5-15 Shinbashi 8F, Minato-ku, Tokyo 105, Japan**

Tel: 81-3-3431-4495      Fax: 81-3-3431-7919

## EAGLE GLOBAL LOGISTICS (EGL)

15350 Vickery Drive, Houston, TX, 77032

Tel: (281) 618-3100      Fax: (281) 618-3100      www.eaglegl.com

*Ocean/air freight forwarding, customs brokerage, packing and wholesale, logistics management and insurance.*

**Circle Freight International Japan Incorporated, Air Import Gateway, Tokyo Aircargo City Terminal C-222, 2526 Baraki, Ichikawa-Shi, Chiba 272 Japan**

Tel: 81-473-282-685      Fax: 81-473-274-152

**Circle Freight International Japan Incorporated, Air Export Gateway, 4-10 Nihonbashi-Nakasu, Chuo-ku, Tokyo 103 Japan**

Tel: 81-3-324-90571      Fax: 81-3-324-9185-4

**Circle Freight International Japan Incorporated, New Tokyo International Airport, No.1 Cargo Bldg. Rm. 322, 154-4 Aza-Komamae Furugome Narita-Shi, Chiba Tokyo 282 Japan**

Tel: 81-476-328-201      Fax: 81-476-328-204

**Circle Freight International Japan, Inc., Araya Bldg., 9-13 Hatsudai 1-chome, Shibuya-ku, Tokyo 151 Japan**

Tel: 81-3-3337-30851      Fax: 81-3-337-30860

**Circle Freight International Japan, Inc., NACT Room No. 202, 11-43 Nanko-Higashi 4-chome, Suminoe-ku, Osaka-Shi 559 Japan**

Tel: 81-6-614-0820      Fax: 81-6-614-7176

**Circle Freight International Japan, Inc., 1 International Cargo Agent Bldg. Rm. 207, Sensyu Kuko Minami No.1, Sennan-Shi, Osaka 549 Japan**

Tel: 81-724-565-850      Fax: 81-724-565-851

## EASTMAN & BEAUDINE INC.

One Ravinia Drive, Ste. 1110, Atlanta, GA, 30346-2103

Tel: (770) 039-0080      Fax: (770) 390-0875      www.beaudine.com

*Investments.*

**Eastman & Beaudine Inc., 401 Akasaka Heights Bldg., 5-26 Akasaka 9-chome, Minato-ku, Tokyo 107, Japan**

## EASTMAN CHEMICAL

100 North Eastman Road, Kingsport, TN, 37660

Tel: (423) 229-2000    Fax: (423) 229-1351    www.eastman.com

*Mfr. plastics, chemicals, fibers.*

**Eastman Chemical Japan Ltd., Yebisu Garden Place Tower 32F, 4-20-3-Ebisu, Shibuya-ku, Tokyo 150 Japan**

Tel: 81-3-5424-1551   Fax: 81-3-5424-1590   Contact: Joe Imaizumi, Pres.

## EASTMAN KODAK COMPANY

343 State Street, Rochester, NY, 14650

Tel: (716) 724-4000    Fax: (716) 724-1089    www.kodak.com

*Develop/mfr. photo and chemicals products, information management/video/copier systems, fibers/plastics for various industry.*

**Eastman Kodak Asia-Pacific Ltd., Gotenyama Mori Bldg., 4-7-35 Kita-Shinagawa, Shinagawa-ku, Tokyo 140 Japan**

**Kodak Imagica KK, Gotenyama Mori Bldg., 4-7-35 Kita-Shinagawa, Shinagawa-ku, Tokyo 140 Japan**

**Kodak Japan Industries Ltd., 18-2 Hakusan 1-chome, Midori-ku, Kanagawa 226, Japan**

**Kodak Japan Ltd., Gotenyama Mori Bldg., 4-7-35 Kita-Shinagawa, Shinagawa-ku, Tokyo 140 Japan**

## EATON CORPORATION

Eaton Center, 1111 Superior Ave., Cleveland, OH, 44114-2584

Tel: (216) 523-5000    Fax: (216) 479-7068    www.eaton.com

*Advanced technical products for transportation and industrial markets.*

**Eaton Japan Co. Ltd., Ohno Bldg., 1-19-8 Kyobashi, Chuo-ku, Tokyo 104, Japan**

**Nitta-Moore Co. Ltd., Osaka, Japan**

## ECOLAB INC.

370 N. Wabasha Street, St. Paul, MN, 55102

Tel: (651) 293-2233    Fax: (651) 293-2379    www.ecolab.com

*Develop/mfr. premium cleaning, sanitizing and maintenance products and services for the hospitality, institutional, and residential markets.*

**Ecolab Ltd., Tokyo, Japan**

Tel: 81-3-5285-2653

## EDDIE BAUER INC.

PO Box 97000, Redmond, WA, 98073

Tel: (425) 882-6100    Fax: (425) 882-6383    www.eddiebauer.com

*Clothing retailer and mail order catalog company.*

**Eddie Bauer Inc., Tokyo, Japan**

## J.D. EDWARDS & COMPANY

One Technology Way, Denver, CO, 80237

Tel: (303) 334-4000    Fax: (303) 334-4970    www.jdedwards.com

*Computer software products.*

**IBM Japan General Business Solution Company, Minato-ku Tokyo 106, Japan**

Tel: 81-3-5563-5328   Fax: 81-3-5563-7755

**J. D. Edwards Tokyo, Sanbancho UF Building 3F, 6-3 Sanbancho, Chiyoda-ku Tokyo 102, Japan**

Tel: 81-3-3265-7141   Fax: 81-3-3265-7145

## EG&G INC.

900 Clopper Road, Ste. 200, Gaithersburg, MD, 20878

Tel: (301) 840-3000    Fax: (301) 590-0502    www.egginc.com

*Diversified R/D, mfr. and services.*

**Eagle EG&G Aerospace Co. Ltd., 1-12-15 Shiba-Daimon, Minato-ku, Tokyo 105, Japan**

**Eagle Industry Co. Ltd., 1-12-15 Shiba-Daimon, Minato-ku, Tokyo 105, Japan**

EG&G Japan, Shuwa Kioicho TBR #1223, 7 Kojimachi 5-chome, Chiyoda-ku, Tokyo 102, Japan

Nok EG&G Optoelectronics Corp., 4-3-1 Tsujido-Shinmachi, Fujisawa-shi, Kanagawa-ken 251, Japan

Seiko EG&G Co. Ltd., 31-1 Kameido 6-chome, Koto-ku, Tokyo 136, Japan

## ELANTEC SEMICONDUCTOR, INC.

675 Trade Zone Blvd., Milpitas, CA, 95035

Tel: (408) 945-1323      Fax: (408) 945-9305      www.elantec.com

*Mfr. of analog integrated circuits for electronic products.*

**Elantec Semiconductor, Inc., Queen's Tower A 8/F, 2-3-1 Minato Mirai Nishi-Ku, Yokohama Kanagawa, 220-6008 Japan**

Tel: 81-45-682-5820   Fax: 81-45-682-5821

## ELECTRO SCIENTIFIC INDUSTRIES, INC.

13900 NW Science Park Drive, Portland, OR, 97229

Tel: (503) 641-4141      Fax: (503) 643-4873      www.esi.com

*Mfg. production and testing equipment used in manufacture of electronic components in pagers and cellular communication devices.*

**Electro Scientific Industries Japan Co., Ltd.(KK), Denpa Bldg. 1-11-15, Higashi Gotanda, Shinagawa-ku, Tokyo 141 Japan**

Tel: 81-3-3440-5081   Fax: 81-3-3440-5029   Contact: Ted Hasegawa

## ELECTROGLAS INC.

6042 Silver Creek Valley Road, San Jose, CA, 95138

Tel: (408) 528-3000      Fax: (408) 528-3542      www.electroglas.com

*Mfr. semi-conductor test equipment, automatic wafer probers.*

**Electroglas KK, 8-3 Funado 1-chome, Itabashi-ku, Tokyo 174, Japan**

## ELECTRONIC DATA SYSTEMS CORPORATION (EDS)

5400 Legacy Dr., Plano, TX, 75024

Tel: (972) 605-6000      Fax: (972) 605-2643      www.eds.com

*Provides professional services; management consulting, e.solutions, business process management and information solutions.*

**EDS Japan, 4-2-12 Shibuya, Shibuya-ku, Tokyo 150-0002 Japan**

Tel: 81-3-3797-8811

## ELECTRONICS FOR IMAGING, INC.

303 Velocity Way, Foster City, CA, 94404

Tel: (650) 357-3500      Fax: (650) 357-3907      www.efi.com

*Design/mfr. computer software and hardware for color desktop publishing.*

**Electronics for Imaging KK, Shinjuku I-Land Wing 13/F, 3-1 Nishi-Shinjuku 6-chome, Shinjuku-ku, Tokyo 160-0023, Japan**

Tel: 81-3-3344 3123

## ELECTRO-SCIENCE LABORATORIES, INC.

416 East Church Road, King of Prussia, PA, 19406

Tel: (610) 272-8000      Fax: (610) 272-6759      www.electroscience.com

*Mfr. advanced thick film materials for hybrid microcircuits and other electronic packaging and component applications.*

**ESL-Nippon Company, Ltd., Sukegawa Building - 6/F, 3-4 Yanagibashi 1-chome Taito-ku, Tokyo 111-0052 Japan**

Tel: 81-3-3864-8521

## EMC CORPORATION

35 Parkwood Drive, Hopkinton, MA, 01748-9103

Tel: (508) 435-1000      Fax: (508) 435-8884      www.emc.com

*Designs/supplies intelligent enterprise storage and retrieval technology for open systems, mainframes and midrange environments.*

**EMC Japan KK, Shizuoka, Japan**

Tel: 81-54-203-2425

**EMC Japan KK, Kyushu, Japan**

Tel: 81-92-482-0081

**EMC Japan KK, Shinjuku-Miksui Bldg. 55F, 2-1 Nishi-Shinjuku 2-chome, Shinjuku-ku, Tokyo 163-0466 Japan**

Tel: 81-3-3345-3211

**EMC Japan KK, Kyoto-shi, Japan**

Tel: 81-75-352-0811

**EMC Japan KK, Nagoya Kokusai Ctr. Bldg. 18F, 47-1 Nagono 1-chome, Nakamura-ku, Nagoya 450-0001 Japan**

Tel: 81-52-562-0571

**EMC Japan KK (Osaka Branch), Umeda Ctr. Bldg. 6F, 4-12 Nakazaki-Nishi 2-chome, Kita-ku Osaka-shi, Osaka 530-0015 Japan**

Tel: 81-6-373-8300

## EMCO WHEATON DTM, INC.

2501 Constant Comment Place, Louisville, KY, 40299

Tel: (502) 266-6677      Fax: (502) 266-6689      www.emcowheaton.com

*Design, development and manufacture of environmentally safe vapor and fluid transfer products for petroleum, petrochemical, chemical and industrial applications.*

**Emco Wheaton (Japan) Ltd., 2-4 Tsunashima Higashi 4-chome, Kottoku-ku, Yokohama 223, Japan**

## EMERSON & CUMING SPECIALTY POLYMERS

46 Manning Road, Bellerica, MA, 01821

Tel: (978) 436-9700      Fax: (978) 436-9701      www.emersoncuming.com

*Mfr. high performance encapsulants, adhesives and coatings for the automotive, telecommunications and electronic industries.*

**Grace Specialty Polymers, Div. Emerson & Cuming, Grace Atsugi Ctr., 100 Kaneda, Atsugi-shi, Kanagawa-ken 243, Japan**

## EMERSON ELECTRIC COMPANY

8000 W. Florissant Ave., PO Box 4100, St. Louis, MO, 63136

Tel: (314) 553-2000      Fax: (314) 553-3527      www.emersonelectric.com

*Electrical and electronic products, industrial components and systems, consumer, government and defense products.*

**Emerson Japan Ltd., New Pier South Tower 7F, 1-16-1 Kaigan Minato-ku, Tokyo 105-0022 Japan**

Tel: 81-3-5403-2900

## EMERY WORLDWIDE

One Lagoon Drive, Ste. 400, Redwood City, CA, 94065

Tel: (650) 596-9600      Fax: (650) 596-7901      www.emeryworld.com

*Freight transport, global logistics and air cargo.*

**Emery Worldwide, No. 2 Shuwa Nihombashi, Honcho Bldg., 3-2 Nihombashi Ohdemmacho, Chuo-ku Tokyo 103 Japan**

Tel: 81-33-669-9088    Fax: 81-33-669-3462

## ENCYCLOPAEDIA BRITANNICA INC.

310 S. Michigan Ave., Chicago, IL, 60604

Tel: (312) 427-9700    Fax: (312) 294-2176    www.eb.com

*Publishing; books.*

**Encyclopaedia Britannica (Japan) Inc., Meiho Bldg., 1-21-1 Nishi Shinjuku, Shinjuku-ku, Tokyo 160, Japan**

**TBS-Britannica Ltd., Shuwa Sanbancho Bldg., 28-1 Sanbancho, Chiyoda-ku, Tokyo 102, Japan**

## ENERPAC

P.O. Box 3241, Milwaukee, WI, 53201-3241

Tel: (414) 781-6600    Fax: (414) 781-1049    www.enerpac.com

*Mfr. hydraulic cylinders, pumps, valves, presses, tools, accessories and system components.*

**Applied Power Japan Ltd., 10-17 Sasame Kita-Machi , Toda-Shi, Saitama 35 Japan**

Tel: 81-048-421-2311

## ENGELHARD CORPORATION

101 Wood Ave. S., CN 770, Iselin, NJ, 08830

Tel: (732) 205-5000    Fax: (732) 632-9253    www.engelhard.com

*Mfr. pigments, additives, catalysts, chemicals, engineered materials.*

**Engelhard Corporation, Masonic 39 Mori Bldg. 5/F, 245 Azabudai Minato-ku, Tokyo 1060041 Japan**

## EPSTEIN ISI COM CORP.

600 W. Fulton Street, Chicago, IL, 60606-1199

Tel: (312) 454-9100    Fax: (312) 559-1217    www.epstein-isi.com

*Engineering and construction.*

**A. Epstein and Sons Japan, Inc., Akasaka Tokyo Building 12/F, 2-14-3 Nagatacho Chiyoda-Ku, Tokyo 100-0014, Japan**

Tel: 81-3-3595-0363

## ERIEZ MAGNETICS

PO Box 10652, Erie, PA, 16514

Tel: (814) 835-6000    Fax: (814) 838-4960    www.eriez.com

*Mfr. magnets, vibratory feeders, metal detectors, screeners/sizers, mining equipment, current separators.*

**Eriez Magnetics Japan Co. Ltd., Shinkawa Ohara Bldg. 4F, 27-8 Chinkawa 1-chome, Chuo-ku, Tokyo 104, Japan**

Tel: 81-473-546381    Fax: 81-473-547643    Contact: T. Homma

## ERNST & YOUNG, LLP

787 Seventh Ave., New York, NY, 10019

Tel: (212) 773-3000    Fax: (212) 773-6350    www.eyi.com

*Accounting and audit, tax and management consulting services.*

**Sowa Ota / Ernst & Young Co., Ltd., Hitotsubashi Bldg., 2-6-3 Hitotsubashi, Chiyoda-ku, Tokyo 101 Japan**

Tel: 81-3-3288-2120    Fax: 3-3288-6389    Contact: Yoji Ishizaka

## ESTEE LAUDER INTERNATIONAL INC.

767 Fifth Ave., New York, NY, 10153

Tel: (212) 572-4200    Fax: (212) 572-3941    www.esteelauder.com

*Cosmetics, perfumes and Aveda hair care products.*

**Estee Lauder Cosmetics (Japan) Ltd., Nihon Seimei Akasaka Bldg., 1-19 Akasaka 8-chome, Minato-ku, Tokyo 107, Japan**

### ETEC SYSTEMS, INC.

26460 Corporate Ave., Hayward, CA, 94545

Tel: (510) 783-9210      Fax: (510) 887-2870      www.etec.com

*Mfr. of photolithography equipment used in semiconductor manufacturing.*

**Etec Systems Japan, Olympic Bldg. 3, 34-13 Akebonocho 2-chome, Tachikawa City, Tokyo 109, Japan**

Tel: 81-425-27-8381   Fax: 81-425-28-0197

### ETHAN ALLEN INTERIORS INC.

Ethan Allen Drive, Danbury, CT, 06811

Tel: (203) 743-8000      Fax: (203) 743-8298      www.ethanallen.com

*Mfr. and sale of premium-priced furniture and home furnishings.*

**Ethan Allen Home Interiors, IDC TFT Bldg. 4/F, 3-1 Ariake Koto-Ku, Tokyo, Japan**

Tel: 81-3-5530-5555   Fax: 81-3-5530-5556

**Ethan Allen Home Interiors, 1-17-28 Minami Horie, Nishi-Ku, Osaka Shi, Japan**

Tel: 61-6-539-4321   Fax: 61-6-539-4322

### ETHYL CORPORATION

330 South 4th Street, PO Box 2189, Richmond, VA, 23219

Tel: (804) 788-5000      Fax: (804) 788-5688      www.ethyl.com

*Provide additive chemistry solutions to enhance the performance of petroleum products.*

**Ethyl Japan, 19/F Shiroyama Hills 4-3-1, Toranomon Minato-ku, Tokyo 105-6019, Japan**

Tel: 81-3-5401-2901   Fax: 81-3-5401-3368

**Ethyl Japan Tsukuba Technical Center, 5-5 Toukoudai, Tsukuba Ibaraki 300-2635, Japan**

Tel: 81-298-47-1061   Fax: 81-298-47-1063

### EURO RSCG WORLDWIDE

350 Hudson Street, New York, NY, 10014

Tel: (212) 886-2000      Fax: (212) 886-2016      www.eurorscg.com

*International advertising agency group.*

**EURO RSCG Partnership, 2-3-11 Hirakawa-cho, Chiyoda-ku, Tokyo Japan**

### EXCELLON AUTOMATION

24751 Crenshaw Boulevard, Torrance, CA, 90505

Tel: (310) 534-6300      Fax: (310) 534-6777      www.excellon.com

*PCB drilling and routing machines; optical inspection equipment.*

**Excellon Japan, 2-15-22 Hirakawa-Cho, Chiyoda-Ku, Tokyo 102 Japan**

### EXCELON INC.

25 Mall Road, Burlington, MA, 01803

Tel: (781) 674-5000      Fax: (781) 674-5010      www.exceloncorp.com

*Developer of object-oriented database management systems software.*

**eXcelon Japan Co., Ltd., Kawakita Memorial Bldg., 18 Ichibancho, Chiyoda-ku, Tokyo 102-0082 Japan**

Tel: 81-33-556-7612   Fax: 81-33-556-7642

### EXE TECHNOLOGIES, INC.

8787 N. Stemmonds Fwy., Dallas, TX, 75247-3702

Tel: (214) 775-6000      Fax: (214) 775-0911      www.exe.com

*Provides a complete line of supply chain management execution software for WMS.*

**EXE Technologies, Inc. Japan, Akasaka Twin Tower, 2-17-22 Akasaka, Minato-ku, Tokyo 107 Japan**

Tel: 81-3-5562-3106   Fax: 81-3-5562-3146

## EXPEDITORS INTERNATIONAL OF WASHINGTON INC.

1015 Third Avenue, 12th Fl., Seattle, WA, 98104-1182

Tel: (206) 674-3400      Fax: (206) 682-9777      www.expd.com

*Air/ocean freight forwarding, customs brokerage, international logistics solutions.*

**Tokyo Expeditors (Japan) Ltd., 1-2-11 Minami-Shinagawa, Shinagawa-Ku Tokyo, 140-0004 Japan**

## EXXON MOBIL CORPORATION

5959 Las Colinas Blvd., Irving, TX, 75039-2298

Tel: (972) 444-1000      Fax: (972) 444-1882      www.exxon.com

*Petroleum exploration, production, refining; mfr. petroleum and chemicals products; coal and minerals.*

**Exxon Mobil KK, 34-1 Towada, Kamisu-Cho, Kashima-Gun, Ibaraki-Ken 314-02, Japan**

**Exxon Mobil KK, Kawasaki Chemical Plant, 7-1 Ukishima-Cho, Kawasaki-ku Kawasaki-Shi, Kanagawa-Ken 210 Japan**

**Exxon Mobil KK, TBS Kaikan Bldg., 3-3 Akasaka 5-chome, Minato-ku, Tokyo Japan**

**Exxon Mobil KK, Palace Side Bldg., 1-1 Hitotsubashi 1-chome, Chiyoda-ku, Tokyo 100 Japan**

**Exxon Mobil KK, New Pier Takeshiba, 16-1 Kaigan 1-Chome, Minato-ku, Tokyo 105-8572 Japan**

**Exxon Mobil KK, TBS Kaikan Bldg., 3-3 Akasaka 5-chome, Minato-ku, Tokyo 107 Japan**

## E-Z-EM INC.

717 Main Street, Westbury, NY, 11590

Tel: (516) 333-8230      Fax: (516) 333-8278      www.ezem.com

*World's leading supplier of barium contrast media for medical imaging and accessories.*

**Toho Kagaku Kenkyusho Co. Inc., 3-11-11 Tatekawa, Sumida-ku, Tokyo 130-0023, Japan**

Tel: 81-3-3634-0831   Fax: 81-3-3634-0955   Contact: Tohru Nagami, Pres   Emp: 35

## FACTSET RESEARCH SYSTEMS INC.

1 Greenwich Plaza, Greenwich, CT, 06830

Tel: (203) 863-1599      Fax: (203) 863-1501      www.factset.com

*Provides on-line financial information to financial professionals.*

**FactSet Limited, Daini Okamotoya Bldg. 8/F, 1-22-16 Toranomon.-ku, Minato-ku Tokyo 105-0001, Japan**

Tel: 81-3-5512-7700

## FAIR, ISAAC AND COMPANY, INC.

200 Smith Ranch Road, San Rafael, CA, 94903

Tel: (415) 472-2211      Fax: (415) 492-5691      www.fairisaac.com

*Mfr. automated systems for credit and loan approvals.*

**Fair, Isaac and Co., Kioi-cho TBR Bldg. #1200, 5-7 Kojimachi, Chiyoda-ku, Tokyo 102-0083, Japan**

Tel: 81-3-5213-3425

## FEDERAL-MOGUL CORPORATION

26555 Northwestern Highway, PO Box 1966, Southfield, MI, 48034

Tel: (248) 354-7700      Fax: (248) 354-8983      www.federal-mogul.com

*Mfr./distributor precision parts for automobiles, trucks, farm and construction vehicles.*

**Federal-Mogul Japan KK, Osaka, Japan**

## FEDEX CORPORATION

942 South Shady Grove Rd., Memphis, TN, 38120

Tel: (901) 369-3600      Fax: (901) 395-2000      www.fdxcorp.com

*Package express delivery service.*

**Federal Express (Japan) KK, Akaishi Bldg., 9-3 Higashi Azabu 1-chome, Minato-ku, Tokyo, Japan**

## FEI CORPORATION

7451 N.W. Evergreen Pkwy., Hillsboro, OR, 97124-5830

Tel: (503) 640-7500     Fax: (503) 640-7509     www.feicompany.com

*Design and mfr. of charged particle beam systems serving the research, development and production needs of customers in semiconductor, data storage, and industry/institute markets.*

**Micrion Japan K.K., 3F Shin Tachikawa Bldg., 3-1-5 Takamatsu-cho, Tachikawa, Tokyo T190 Japan**

Tel: 81-425-265455   Fax: 81-425-265457

## FERRO CORPORATION

1000 Lakeside Ave., Cleveland, OH, 44114-7000

Tel: (216) 641-8580     Fax: (216) 696-5784     www.ferro.com

*Mfr. Specialty chemicals, coatings, plastics, colors, refractories.*

**Ferro Enamels, Ltd. - Main Office, 1-27 Oyodo Kita 2-chome, Kita-ku, Osaka Japan**

Tel: 81-6-458-3551  Fax: 81-6-458-8911   Contact: Hirofumi Miki, Chmn,

**Ferro Enamels, Ltd. Agricultural R&D Center, 1152 Tsurumi Okuyamada, Beppu City, Oita Pref. Japan**

Tel: 81-977-67-7917

**Ferro Enamels, Ltd. Kyushu Plant, 997 Aza Gotanda, Oaza Kamisokoino, Nakama City Fukuoka Pref., Japan**

Tel: 81-93-245-3031

**Nissan Ferro Organic Chemical Co. Ltd., Nissan Edobashi Bldg., 10-5 Nihonbashi Honcho 1-chome, Chuo-ku, Tokyo 103 Japan**

Tel: 81-3-3245-0661   Fax: 81-3-3231-7810   Contact: H. Akabayashi, Pres.

## FERROFLUIDICS CORPORATION

40 Simon Street, Nashua, NH, 03061

Tel: (603) 883-9800     Fax: (603) 883-2308     www.ferrofluidics.com

*Mfr. rotary feedthrough designs, emission seals, automated crystal-growing systems, bearings, ferrofluids.*

**Ferrofluidics Japan Corp., 1001 Chisan Mansion, 24-8 Sakuragaoka-cho, Shibuya-ku, Tokyo 150, Japan**

## FIDUCIARY TRUST COMPANY OF NY

2 World Trade Center, 94th Fl., New York, NY, 10048

Tel: (212) 466-4100     Fax: (212) 313-2662     www.ftc.com

*Banking services.*

**Fiduciary Trust (Intl.) SA, Tokyo, Japan**

## FileNET CORPORATION

3565 Harbor Boulevard, Costa Mesa, CA, 92626

Tel: (714) 966-3400     Fax: (714) 966-3490     www.filenet.com

*Provides integrated document management (IDM) software and services for internet and client server-based imaging, workflow, cold and electronic document management solutions.*

**Nihon FileNET, Shiroyama-JT-Mori Bldg. 15F, 4-3-1 Toranomon, Minato-ku, Tokyo, 105 Japan**

Tel: 81-3-3436-8781   Fax: 81-3-3436-8793   Contact: Naoki Sudoh, Mng. Dir.

## FINANCIAL GUARANTY INSURANCE COMPANY

115 Broadway, New York, NY, 10006

Tel: (212) 312-3000     Fax: (212) 312-3093     www.fgic.com

*Engaged in insuring debt securities and investment, operation, and information services to state and local governments*

**Financial Guaranty Insurance Co. (Tokyo), Tokyo Sumitomo Twin Bldg., Sumitomo Marine Bldg.14/F, 27-2 Shinkawa #2-chome, Tokyo, Japan**

## FISHER SCIENTIFIC INC.

1 Liberty Lane, Hampton, NH, 03842

Tel: (603) 929-5911        Fax: (603) 929-0222        www.fisher1.com

*Mfr. science instruments and apparatus, chemicals, reagents.*

**Fisher Scientific Japan, Mita-Kokusai Bldg. Annex Room 111, 1-4-28 Mita, Minato-ku, Tokyo 108-0073, Japan**

Tel: 81-3-5484-4731   Fax: 81-3-5485-4736

## FISHER-ROSEMOUNT

8000 Maryland Ave., Ste. 500, Clayton, MO, 63105-4755

Tel: (314) 746-9900        Fax: (314) 746-9974        www.frco.com

*Mfr. industrial process control equipment.*

**Nippon Fisher Company Ltd., Empire Bldg. 10F, 23-1 Hatchobori 2-chome, Chuo-ku, Tokyo 104 Japan**

Tel: 81-3-3552-5751   Fax: 81-3-3555-0735

## FLEETBOSTON FINANCIAL CORPORATION

1 Federal Street, Boston, MA, 02110

Tel: (617) 346-4000        Fax: (617) 434-7547        www.fleet.com

*Banking and insurance services.*

**FleetBoston Financial, AIG Bldg. 7F, 1-3 Marunochi 1-chome, Chiyoda-ku, Tokyo 100 Japan**

Tel: 81-3-3211-2611   Fax: 81-3-3201-6879

## FLOW INTERNATIONAL CORPORATION

23500 64th Ave. S., PO Box 97040, Kent, WA, 98064-9740

Tel: (253) 872-4900        Fax: (253) 813-3285        www.flowcorp.com

*Mfr. high-pressure water jet cutting/cleaning equipment, powered scaffolding; concrete cleaning/removal.*

**Flow Japan, Tokyo, Japan**

## FLOWSERVE CORPORATION

222 W. Los Colinas Blvd., Irving, TX, 75039

Tel: (972) 443-6500        Fax: (972) 443-6858        www.flowserve.com

*Mfr. chemicals equipment, pumps, valves, filters, fans and heat exchangers.*

**Flowserve FCD Japan Business Development, Sandensha Building 5F, 2-7-15 Hamamatsu-cho, Minato-ku, Tokyo 105-0013 Japan**

## FLUKE CORPORATION

6920 Seaway Blvd. PO Box 9090, Everett, WA, 98203

Tel: (425) 347-6100        Fax: (425) 356-5116        www.fluke.com

*Mfr. handheld, electronic test tools for maintenance of electronic equipment.*

**Fluke Corporation, Sumitomo Higashi Shinbashi Bldg., 1-1-11 Hamamatsuco, Minato-ku, Tokyo 105 Japan**

Tel: 81-3-3434-0181   Fax: 81-3-3434-0170

## FLUOR CORPORATION

One Enterprise Drive, Aliso Viejo, CA, 92656-2606

Tel: (949) 349-2000        Fax: (949) 349-5271        www.flour.com

*Engineering and construction services.*

**Fluor Daniel Japan, Sanno Grand Building, 2-14-2 Nagata-cho, Chiyoda-ku, Tokyo 100 Japan**

## FMC CORPORATION

200 E. Randolph Drive, Chicago, IL, 60601

Tel: (312) 861-6000        Fax: (312) 861-6141        www.fmc.com

*Produces chemicals and precious metals, mfr. machinery, equipment and systems for industrial, agricultural and government use.*

**FMC Asia Pacific Inc., Sanbancho KS Bldg. 7/F, 2 Sanbancho, Chiyoda-ku, Tokyo 102, Japan**

FMC Smith Meter Inc./Tokyo Boecki Ltd., No. 13-8, 2-Chome, Hatchobori, Chuo-Ku Tokyo 104, Japan

L.H. Co. Ltd., Tokyo, Japan

## FMR (FIDELITY INVESTMENTS)

82 Devonshire Street, Boston, MA, 02109

Tel: (617) 563-7000     Fax: (617) 476-6105     www.fidelity.com

*Diversified financial services company offering investment management, retirement, brokerage, and shareholder services directly to individuals and institutions and through financial intermediaries.*

Fidelity Brokerage Services, Japan, LLC, Across Shinkawa Bldg. 4th Fl., 1-8-8 Shinkawa, Chuo-ku Tokyo 104-0333, Japan

Tel: 81-3-5543-8902   Fax: 81-3-5543-1041   Contact: Roger T. Servison, Pres.

## FOOT LOCKER USA

112 West 34th Street, New York, NY, 10020

Tel: (212) 720-3700     Fax: (212) 553-2042     www.venatorgroup.com

*Mfr./sales shoes and sneakers.*

Foot Locker International, Funabashi/Sogo 1-1, Hamamachi 2-chome Funabashi-Shi, Chiba, Japan

Tel: 81-4-7432-6750

Foot Locker International, Shin Yuri 1-1 Asi-ku, Kawasaki-Shi 1-2 Kanagawa, K, Japan

Foot Locker International, Parco Sr 6 15-1, Uchidagawa-Cho Shibya-ku Tokyo, Japan

## FORD MOTOR COMPANY

One American Road, Dearborn, MI, 48121

Tel: (313) 322-3000     Fax: (313) 322-9600     www.ford.com

*Mfr./sales motor vehicles.*

Ford Motor Co. (Japan) Ltd., Mori Bldg., 5-1 Toranomon 3-chome, Minato-ku, Tokyo 105, Japan

## FORTUNE BRANDS

200 Tower Parkway, Lincolnshire, IL, 60069

Tel: (847) 484-4400     Fax: (800) 310-5960     www.fortunebrands.com

*Mfr. diversified consumer products including Masterbrand, Acco office products, Jim Bean distillery products, Footjoy and Titleist golf products and Moen bath products.*

Fortune Brands International Corporation, Ichigaya K-T Bldg. #2 6/F, 7-16 Kudan Minami 4-chome, Ciyoda-ku Tokyo 102-0074 Japan

Tel: 8133-556-6263

## FOSTER WHEELER CORPORATION

Perryville Corporate Park, Clinton, NJ, 08809-4000

Tel: (908) 730-4000     Fax: (908) 730-4100     www.fwc.com

*Manufacturing, engineering and construction.*

Foster Wheeler K.K., 4-1 Hamamatsu-cho, 2-Chome Manato-ku, Tokyo 105-6137 Japan

Tel: 81-3-3434-8600

## FOUR WINDS INTERNATIONAL GROUP

1500 SW First Ave., Ste. 850, Portland, OR, 97201-2013

Tel: (503) 241-2732     Fax: (503) 241-1829     www.vanlines.com.au

*Transportation of household goods and general cargo and third party logistics.*

Four Winds Japan, 23 Mori Building 5/F, 23-7 Toranomon 1-chome, Minato-ku, Tokyo 105 Japan

Tel: 81-3-359-33191   Fax: 81-3-359-33195   Contact: Yutaka Morioka, Gen. Mgr.

## FRANK RUSSELL COMPANY

909 A Street, Tacoma, WA, 98402

Tel: (253) 572-9500 Fax: (253) 591-3495 www.russell.com

*Investment management and asset strategy consulting.*

**Frank Russell Japan, 49-13 Nishihara 3-chome, Shibuya-ku, Tokyo 151, Japan**

Tel: 81-3-3467-9800 Fax: 81-3-3467-9808 Contact: Masanori Tsuno, President Emp: 36

## FRANKLIN COVEY COMPANY

2200 W. Parkway Blvd., Salt Lake City, UT, 84119-2331

Tel: (801) 975-1776 Fax: (801) 977-1431 www.franklincovey.com

*Provides productivity and time management products and seminars.*

**Franklin Covey Japan, Marumasu Kojimachi Building 6 7F, 3-3 Kojimachi, Chiyoda-ku, Tokyo 102-0083 Japan**

Tel: 81-3-3237-7711 Fax: 81-3-3237-7722

## THE FRANKLIN MINT

US Route 1, Franklin Center, PA, 19091

Tel: (610) 459-6000 Fax: (610) 459-6880 www.franklinmint.com

*Design/marketing collectibles and luxury items.*

**Franklin Mint Co. Ltd., Recruit Kachidoki Bldg., 2-11-9 Kachidoki, Chuo-ku, Tokyo 104 Japan**

## FRANKLIN RESOURCES, INC.

777 Mariners Island Blvd., San Mateo, CA, 94404

Tel: (415) 312-2000 Fax: (415) 312-3655 www.frk.com

*Global and domestic investment advisory and portfolio management.*

**Templeton Investment Management Co., Ltd., Tokyo, Japan**

## FRITO-LAY COMPANY

7701 Legacy Drive, Plano, TX, 75024

Tel: (972) 334-7000 Fax: (972) 334-2019 www.firtolay.com

*Mfr. snack food products.*

**Japan Frito-Lay Ltd., Tokyo, Japan**

## FRITZ COMPANIES, INC.

706 Mission Street, Ste. 900, San Francisco, CA, 94103

Tel: (415) 904-8360 Fax: (415) 904-8661 www.fritz.com

*Integrated transportation, sourcing, distribution and customs brokerage services.*

**Suzuyo/Fritz Ltd., Suzuyo Tokyo Building 3/F, 1-2-12 Shibakoen, Minato-ku, Tokyo 105 Japan**

## FSI INTERNATIONAL INC.

322 Lake Hazeltine Drive, Chaska, MN, 55318

Tel: (612) 448-5440 Fax: (612) 448-2825 www.fsi-intl.com

*Manufacturing equipment for computer silicon wafers.*

**FSI Metron Japan, 24-6 Higashi Takasaki Tamano-shi, Okayama 706-01, Japan**

Tel: 81-863-71-3988 Fax: 81-863-71-3968

**FSI Metron Japan, Kyohan Kudan Bldg. 4F, 5-10 Iidabashi 1-chome, Chiyoda-ku, Tokyo 102 Japan**

Tel: 81-3-3265-9171 Fax: 81-3-3265-9179

## H.B. FULLER COMPANY

1200 Willow Lake Blvd., Vadnais Heights, MN, 55110

Tel: (651) 236-5900 Fax: (651) 236-5898 www.hbfuller.com

*Mfr./distributor adhesives, sealants, coatings, paints, waxes, sanitation chemicals.*

**H.B. Fuller Japan Co. Ltd., 700 Matsushimacho Hamamatsu City, Shizuoka 430-0834, Japan**

**H.B. Fuller Japan Co. Ltd., Kudan Nikkana Building, 3-9-12 Kudanminami, Chiyoda-ku Tokyo 102, Japan**

Tel: 81-3-5275-5831    Fax: 81-3-5275-2391

## GAF CORPORATION

1361 Alps Road, Wayne, NJ, 07470

Tel: (973) 628-3000        Fax: (973) 628-3326        www.gaf.com

*Mfr. roofing and building materials.*

**GAF Japan Ltd., Kogen Bldg., 17-2 Shinbashi 6-chome, Minato-ku, Tokyo, Japan**

## THE GAP

1 Harrison Street, San Francisco, CA, 94105

Tel: (650) 952-4400        Fax: (650) 952-5884        www.gap.com

*Clothing store chain.*

**The Gap, Tokyo, Japan**

## GARTNER GROUP, INC.

56 Top Gallant Road, Stamford, CT, 06904-2212

Tel: (203) 316-1111        Fax: (203) 316-1100        www.gartner.com

*Information technology and research.*

**Gartner Group Japan, Aobadai Hills 6F, 7-7 Aobadai 4-chome, Meguro-ku Tokyo 153-0042 Japan**

Tel: 81-3-3481-3670    Fax: 81-3-3481-3644

## GaSONICS INTERNATIONAL CORPORATION

404 East Plumeria Drive, San Jose, CA, 95134

Tel: (408) 570-7000        Fax: (408) 570-7612        www.gasonics.com

*Mfr. gas-based dry cleaning systems for semi-conductor production equipment.*

**GaSonics International/LCD Division, 686-1 Kami-echi, Atsugi, Kanagawa 243-0801, Japan**

Tel: 81-462-46-2171    Fax: 81-462-46-2181

**GaSonics International/Semiconductor Division, 2-7-2 Kuriki Asao-Ku, Kawasaki, Kanagawa 215-0033, Japan**

Tel: 81-44-986-6601    Fax: 81-44-986-6606

## THE GATES RUBBER COMPANY

990 S. Broadway, PO Box 5887, Denver, CO, 80217-5887

Tel: (303) 744-1911        Fax: (303) 744-4000        www.gatesrubber.com

*Mfr. automotive and industrial belts and hoses.*

**Gates Rubber Company Japan, Matsura Building 5/F, 1-9-6 Shiba, Minato-ku Sumida-ku, Tokyo 105-0014 Japan**

Tel: 81-3-5439-5188    Fax: 81-3-5439-5189    Contact: Tadashi Namiki

**GNAPCO Pte. Ltd., 4-26 Sakuragawa 4-Chome, Naniwa-Ku, Osaka 556 0022 Japan**

Tel: 81-6-6563-1266    Fax: 81-6-6563-1267

## GATX CAPITAL CORPORATION

Four Embarcadero Center, Ste. 2200, San Francisco, CA, 94111

Tel: (415) 955-3200        Fax: (415) 955-3449        www.gatxcapital.com

*Lease and loan financing, residual guarantees.*

**GATX Capital Corporation, Shiroyama Hills - Level 16, 4-3-1 Toranomon Minato-Ku, Tokyo 105 Japan**

Tel: 81-3-5403-4667    Fax: 81-3-5403-4646    Contact: Edward W. Cislo

## GE CAPITAL FLEET SERVICES

3 Capital Drive, Eden Prairie, MN, 55344

Tel: (612) 828-1000    Fax: (612) 828-2010    www.gefleet.com

*Corporate vehicle leasing and services.*

**Japan Leasing Auto./GE Capital Fleet, Tokyo, Japan**

Tel: 81-3-5442-6666

## GEMSTAR-TV GUIDE INTERNATIONAL, INC.

135 North Los Robles Avenue, Ste. 800, Pasadena, CA, 91101

Tel: (626) 792-5700    Fax: (626) 792-0257    www.gemstar.com

*Mfr. technology for VCR programming.*

**Gemstar Japan KK, 2-29-18 Nishi-Ikebukuro, Toshima-ku, Tokyo 171, Japan**

Tel: 81-3-5950-7777    Fax: 81-3-5950-7770

## GENERAL BINDING CORPORATION

One GBC Plaza, Northbrook, IL, 60062

Tel: (847) 272-3700    Fax: (847) 272-1369    www.gbc.com

*Engaged in the design, manufacture and distribution of branded office equipment, related supplies and thermal laminating films.*

**GBC Japan KK, Aya Kudan Bldg., 3-27 Kudan Minami 2-chome, Chiyoda-ku, Tokyo 102, Japan**

## GENERAL DYNAMICS CORPORATION

3190 Fairview Park Drive, Falls Church, VA, 22042-4523

Tel: (703) 876-3000    Fax: (703) 876-3125    www.gendyn.com

*Mfr. aerospace equipment, submarines, strategic systems, armored vehicles, defense support systems.*

**Bath Iron Works Corporation - Yokosuka Operations, Commander Logistic Group, Western Pacific USN, PSC 473, Box 82, FPO APO 96349-2907**

Tel: 81-311-743-8737    Fax: 81-311-743-8772    Contact: Mike Su, BIW Rep.

**General Dynamics Intl. Corp., 30 Mori Bldg., 2-2 Toranomon 3-chome, Minato-ku, Tokyo 105, Japan**

## GENERAL ELECTRIC CAPITAL CORPORATION

260 Long Ridge Road, Stamford, CT, 06927

Tel: (203) 357-4000    Fax: (203) 357-6489    www.gecapital.com

*Financial, property/casualty insurance, computer sales and trailer leasing services.*

**Employers Reinsurance Corp. (ERC), 14-14 Kowa 35 Bldg., Akasaka 1-chome, Minato-ku, Tokyo 107 Japan**

Tel: 81-3-3588-1821    Fax: 81-3-3588-1822

**GE Capital/Japan Leasing Corp., Tokyo, Japan**

**GE Edison Life Insurance, No. 35 Kowa Bldg., Minato-ku, Tokyo 107, Japan**

**Koei Credit/GE, Tokyo, Japan**

## GENERAL ELECTRIC COMPANY

3135 Easton Turnpike, Fairfield, CT, 06431

Tel: (203) 373-2211    Fax: (203) 373-3131    www.ge.com

*Diversified manufacturing, technology and services.*

**GE Aircraft Engines, 8-2 Haneda-kuko 1-choe, Tokyo 144, Japan**

Tel: 81-3-3747-8250

**GE Appliances, Bldg. 3-3 Kojamacki Chiyoda-ku, Tokyo 102, Japan**

Tel: 81-3-3264-1140

**GE Capital Services GENSTAR container, 7-F Tomoecho Annex II, Tokyo, Japan**

Tel: 81-3433-8661

**GE FANUC Automation, 589-12 Aza Ochiai, Motosoujamachi, Maebashi 371, Japan**

Tel: 81-2-7251-8431    Fax: 81-2-7251-8330

**GE Silicones Japan, Rm 1008 - Tower 1, Tokyo 106-8550, Japan**

**GE Toshiba Silicon, Roppongi 6-2-31 Mir Ku, Tokyo 106-8550 Japan**
Tel: 81-3-3479-3918

**General Electric Japan Ltd., No. 35 Kowa Bldg., Minato-ku, Tokyo 107, Japan**
Tel: 81-3-3588-5190   Fax: 81-3-3588-5288   Contact: Jay F. Lapin, Pres.

**GEPS Global Power Generation, No. 35 Kowa Bldg., Minato-ku, Tokyo 107, Japan**
Tel: 81-3-3588-5176   Fax: 81-3-3588-3372

**GETSCO, Honkan Ctr. Bldg. 3F, Fukui, Japan**
Tel: 81-7-7026-1376

## GENERAL INSTRUMENT CORPORATION

101 Tournament Road, Horsham, PA, 19044
Tel: (215) 674-4800      Fax: (215) 443-9554      www.gi.com

*Mfr. broadband communications and power rectifying components.*

**General Instrument Japan Ltd., 7/F Toranomon Daini Toyo Bldg., 1-12-15 Toranomon, Minato-ku Tokyo 105-0001, Japan**
Tel: 81-3-3502-1831   Fax: 81-3-3502-7832

## GENERAL MOTORS CORPORATION

300 Renaissance Center, Detroit, MI, 48285
Tel: (313) 556-5000      Fax: (313) 556-5108      www.gm.com

*Mfr. full line vehicles, automotive electronics, commercial technologies, telecommunications, space, finance.*

**Isuzu Motors Ltd., Tokyo, Japan**

**Suzuki Motor Co. Ltd., Hamamatsu, Japan**

## GENERAL REINSURANCE CORPORATION

695 E. Main Street, Stamford, CT, 06904-2350
Tel: (203) 328-5000      Fax: (203) 328-6423      www.genre.com

*Reinsurance services worldwide.*

**Cologne Reinsurance Company - Far East Liaison Office, TT-2 Bldg. 11F, 8-1 Nihonbashi Ningyocho, 3-chome Chuo-ku, Tokyo 103 Japan**
Tel: 81-3-3663-7447   Fax: 81-3-3663-7450   Contact: Rainer Schürmann, Gen. Mgr.

**General Re Financial Products (Japan) Inc. - Tokyo, Toranomon Waiko Bldg. 9F, 5-12-1 Toranomon, Minato-ku, Tokyo 105 Japan**
Tel: 81-3-5473-6655   Fax: 81-3-5473-6650

**General Reinsurance Corporation, TT-2 Bldg. 11F, 8-1 Nihonbashi Ningyocho, 3-chome Chuo-ku, Tokyo 103 Japan**
Tel: 81-3-3663-7449   Fax: 81-3-3663-7450   Contact: Elizabeth S. King

## GENERAL SEMICONDUCTOR, INC.

10 Melville Park Road., Melville, NY, 11747
Tel: (631) 847-3000      Fax: (631) 847-3236      www.gensemi.com

*Mfr. of low- and medium-current power rectifiers and transient voltage suppressors.*

**General Semiconductor Japan, Ltd., Silk Bldg. 5F, 3-31-11 Honcho, Nakano-ku, Tokyo 164-0012 Japan**
Tel: 81-3-5302-2565   Fax: 81-3-5302-2573   Contact: Makoto Haneishi

**General Semiconductor Japan, Ltd., Shin Osaka Nishiura Bldg 7F, 2-7-38 Nishi Miyahara, Yodogawa-ku Osaka-shi, Osaka 532 Japan**
Tel: 81-6-396-2102   Fax: 81-6-396-2107   Contact: Masakatsu Sakamoto

## GENETICS INSTITUTE INC.

150 Cambridge Park Drive, Cambridge, MA, 02140
Tel: (617) 876-1170      Fax: (617) 876-0388

*Develop/commercialize biopharmaceutical therapeutic products.*

**Genetics Institute Inc. of Japan, 1-10-13 Higashi Azabu, Minato-ku, Tokyo 106, Japan**

## GENUITY, INC.

150 Cambridge Park Drive, Cambridge, MA, 02140

Tel: (617) 873-2000    Fax: (617) 873-2857    www.genuity.com

*R/D computer, communications, acoustics technologies and internetworking services.*

**Genuity, Inc. Japan KK Shinjuku NS, Bldg. 22 Fl. 2-4-1 Nishishinjuku, Shinjuku-ku, Tokyo Japan**

Tel: 81-3-5339-6021

## GENZYME CORPORATION

1 Kendall Square, Cambridge, MA, 02139-1562

Tel: (617) 252-7500    Fax: (617) 252-7600    www.genzyme.com

*Mfr. healthcare products for enzyme deficient diseases.*

**Idenics, Div. Genzyme, Izumiyamabuki-Cho Bldg., 333 Yamabuki-Cho, Shinjuku-ku, Tokyo 162-0801, Japan**

Tel: 81-3-5228-6464    Fax: 81-3-5228-5933

## GEO LOGISTICS CORPORATION

1521 E. Dyer Rd., Santa Ana, CA, 92705

Tel: (714) 513-3000    Fax: (714) 513-3120    www.geo-logistics.com

*Freight forwarding, warehousing and distribution services, specializing in heavy cargo.*

**GeoLogistics Ltd., Kasen Building 5/F, 6-8 Kawara-machi 4-chome, Chuo-Ku, Osaka 541-0048 Japan**

Tel: 81-6-201-5461    Fax: 81-6-227-5230

## GEOWORKS CORPORATION

960 Atlantic Avenue, Alameda, CA, 94501

Tel: (510) 614-1660    Fax: (510) 614-4250    www.geoworks.com

*Mfr. operating system software.*

**Geoworks Corporation KK, Tokyo, Japan**

## GETZ BROS & COMPANY, INC.

150 Post Street, Ste. 500, San Francisco, CA, 94108-4750

Tel: (415) 772-5500    Fax: (415) 772-5659    www.getz.com

*Diversified manufacturing, marketing and distribution services and travel services.*

**Getz Bros. & Co. Ltd., Sumitomo Seimei Aoyama Bldg., 3-1-30 Minami-Aoyama, Minato-ku, Tokyo 107 Japan**

Tel: 81-3-3423-1302    Fax: 81-3-3402-5979    Contact: Paul Bond, Gen. Mgr.    Emp: 330

**Muller & Phipps (Japan) Ltd., Sumitomo Seimei Aoyama Bldg., 3-1-30 Minami-Aoyama, Minato-ku, Tokyo 107 Japan**

Tel: 81-3-3478-5611    Fax: 81-3-3478-5626    Contact: N. Andoli, Controller    Emp: 10

## THE GILLETTE COMPANY

Prudential Tower Building, Boston, MA, 02199

Tel: (617) 421-7000    Fax: (617) 421-7123    www.gillette.com

*Develop/mfr. personal care/use products: blades and razors, toiletries, cosmetics, stationery.*

**Braun Japan KK, Yokohama, Japan**

Contact: Hans Th. Pauli, Mgr.

**Gillette (Japan) Inc., Tokyo, Japan**

Contact: Richard L. Guilfoile, Mgr.

## GILSON INC.

3000 W. Beltline Hwy, PO Box 620027, Middleton, WI, 53562-0027

Tel: (608) 836-1551    Fax: (608) 831-4451    www.gilson.com

*Mfr. analytical/biomedical instruments.*

**M&S Instruments Trading Inc., 12-4 Mikuni-Hommachi 2-Chome, Yodogawa-ku, Osaka 532-0005, Japan**

**GLEASON CORPORATION**

1000 University Ave., Rochester, NY, 14692

Tel: (716) 473-1000     Fax: (716) 461-4348     www.gleasoncorp.com

*Mfr. gear making machine tools; tooling and services.*

**OGA Corporation, 8-3 Tsukishima 1-Chome, Chuo-Ku, Tokyo 104, Japan**

**GLENAYRE ELECTRONICS LTD.**

5935 Carnegie Blvd.., Ste. 300, Charlotte, NC, 28209

Tel: (704) 553-0038     Fax: (704) 553-7878     www.glenayre.com

*Mfr. infrastructure components and pagers.*

**Nihon Glenayre Electronics K.K., Akasaka 2-chome, 19-8 Annex Bldg. 4F, Minato-ku, Tokyo 107 Japan**

Tel: 81-3-5545-7811   Fax: 81-3-5545-7812

**GLOBAL SILVERHAWK**

2190 Meridian Park Blvd., Ste G, Concord, CA, 94520

Tel: (925) 681-2889     Fax: (925) 681-2755     www.globalsilverhawk.com

*International moving and forwarding.*

**Global Silverhawk, No. 2 AB Building 6F, 1-17 Roppongi 3-chome, Minato-ku, Tokyo 106 Japan**

Tel: 81-3-3589-6666   Contact: Lance Allen, Gen. Mgr.

**GODIVA CHOCOLATIER INC.**

355 Lexington Ave., New York, NY, 10017

Tel: (212) 984-5900     Fax: (212) 984-5901     www.godiva.com

*Mfr. chocolate candy, Biscotti dipping cookies and after-dinner coffees.*

**Godiva Chocolatier, Inc., Tokyo, Japan**

**THE GOLDMAN SACHS GROUP**

85 Broad Street, New York, NY, 10004

Tel: (212) 902-1000     Fax: (212) 902-3000     www.gs.com

*Investment bankers; securities broker dealers.*

**Goldman Sachs Group, K&K Shinsaibashi Building, 12-21 Nishi-Shinsaibashi 1-chome, Chuo-ku Osaka 542-0086, Japan**

Tel: 81-6-253-1333

**Goldman Sachs Group, ARK Mori Building, 12-32 Akasaka 1-chome, Minato-ku Tokyo 107-6005, Japan**

Tel: 81-3-3589-7000

**THE GOODYEAR TIRE & RUBBER COMPANY**

1144 East Market Street, Akron, OH, 44316

Tel: (330) 796-2121     Fax: (330) 796-1817     www.goodyear.com

*Mfr. tires, automotive belts and hose, conveyor belts, chemicals; oil pipeline transmission.*

**Nippon Goodyear KK, Sankaido Building, 9-13 Akasaka 1-chome, Minato-ku, Tokyo 107 Japan**

**GP STRATEGIES CORPORATION**

9 West 57th Street, New York, NY, 10019

Tel: (212) 230-9500     Fax: (212) 230-9545     www.genphysics.com

*Mfr./distributor medical, health care and specialty products.*

**Hydron Japan KK, 1-14-18 Shironganedai, Minato-ku, Tokyo 108, Japan**

**W. R. GRACE & COMPANY**

7500 Grace Drive, Columbia, MD, 21044

Tel: (410) 531-4000     Fax: (410) 531-4367     www.grace.com

*Mfr. specialty chemicals and materials: packaging, health care, catalysts, construction, water treatment/process.*

**Fuji-Davison Chemical Ltd., 1846 Kozoji-cho 2-chome, Kusagai-shi, Aichi-ken 487, Japan**

**Grace Japan KK, 100 Kaneda, Atsugi-shi 243, Japan**
Tel: 81-462-25-8800　Fax: 81-462-24-9254
**Grace Japan KK, Tomita Building 9F, 2-2 Ushijima-cho, Nishi-ku Nagoya 451, Japan**
Tel: 81-52-586-9630　Fax: 81-52-586-9616

## GRACO INC.
4050 Olson Memorial Hwy, PO Box 1441, Minneapolis, MN, 55440-1441
Tel: (612) 623-6000　　　Fax: (612) 623-6777　　　www.graco.com
*Mfr. systems and equipment to service fluid handling systems and automotive equipment.*
**Graco KK, 1-27-12 Hayabuchi, Tsuzuki-ku, Yokohama City, 224-0025, Japan**

## GRAHAM & JAMES LLP
One Maritime Plaza, Ste. 300, San Francisco, CA, 94111-3404
Tel: (415) 954-0200　　　Fax: (415) 391-2493　　　www.gj.com
*International law firm.*
**Graham & James LLP, Gaikokuho Jimu Bengoshi Jimusho, Akasaka Twin Towers Manin Tower 11th Fl.,17-22 Akasaka 2-chome Minato-ku, Tokyo 107 Japan**
Tel: 81-3-5570-5670　Fax: 81-3-5570-5455　Contact: Steven S. Doi

## GRANT THORNTON INTERNATIONAL
800 One Prudential Plaza, 130 E. Randolph Drive, Chicago, IL, 60601-6050
Tel: (312) 856-0001　　　Fax: (312) 616-7052　　　www.grantthornton.com
*Accounting, audit, tax and management consulting services.*
**Grant Thornton Shinko, Nikko Ichibancho Bldg. 7F, 13-3 Ichibancho, Chiyoda-ku, Tokyo 102 Japan**
Tel: 81-3-5210-9055　Fax: 81-3-5210-9050

## GRAYBAR ELECTRIC CO., INC.
PO Box 7231, Clayton, MO, 63177
Tel: (314) 512-9200　　　Fax: (314) 512-9453　　　www.graybar.com
*Electrical communications components distributor.*
**Konishi Electric Co., Ltd., 2-16-6 Minami Shinagawa, Shinagawa-Ku, Tokyo 140 Japan**
Tel: 81-35-479-5505　Fax: 81-35-479-5558　Contact: Jun Konishi, Pres.

## GREY GLOBAL GROUP
777 Third Ave., New York, NY, 10017
Tel: (212) 546-2000　　　Fax: (212) 546-1495　　　www.grey.com
*International advertising agency.*
**Grey-Daiko Advertising, Grey-Daiko Building, 2-3-20 Motoazabu, Minato-ku, Tokyo 106, Japan**

## GRIFFITH LABORATORIES INC.
One Griffith Center, Alsip, IL, 60658
Tel: (708) 371-0900　　　Fax: (708) 597-3294　　　www.griffithlabs.com
*Mfr. industrial food ingredients and equipment.*
**Griffith Laboratories Japan KK, Nissei Bldg., 13-31 Konan 2-chome, Minato-ku, Tokyo 108, Japan**
Tel: 81-3-3450-1231　Fax: 81-3-3450-2608

## GUARDIAN INDUSTRIES CORPORATION
2300 Harmon Road, Auburn Hills, MI, 48326-1714
Tel: (248) 340-1800　　　Fax: (248) 340-9988　　　www.guardian.com
*Mfr. and fabricate flat glass products and insulation materials.*
**Guardian Japan Ltd., Bridgestone Toranomon - Bldg. 802, 25-2 3-chome, Toranomon Minato-ku, Tokyo Japan**
Tel: 81-3-3436-5581　Fax: 81-3-3436-5583

## GUIDANT CORPORATION

111 Monument Circle, 29th Fl., Indianapolis, IN, 46204

Tel: (317) 971-2000    Fax: (317) 971-2040    www.guidant.com

*Mfr. cardiovascular therapeutic devices.*

**Guidant Japan KK,  Shin Aoyama Bldg East 4/F, 1-1 Minami-Aoyama, Minato-ku Tokyo 107, Japan**

## GUY CARPENTER & COMPANY, INC.

Two World Trade Center, New York, NY, 10048

Tel: (212) 323-1000    Fax: (212) 313-4970    www.guycarp.com

*Engaged in global reinsurance and risk management.*

**Guy Carpenter & Company, Inc. Rep Office,  3-20-2 Nishi-Shinjuku - 38/F, Shinjuku-Ku, Tokyo 163-1438 Japan**

Tel: 81-3-5353-0448   Fax: 81-3-3320-6131

## HAEMONETICS CORPORATION

400 Wood Road, Braintree, MA, 02184-9114

Tel: (781) 848-7100    Fax: (781) 848-5106    www.haemonetics.com

*Mfr. automated blood processing systems and blood products.*

**Haemonetics Japan Co., Ltd.,  Kyodo Building, 16 Ichiban-cho, Chiyoda-ku, Tokyo 102-0082, Japan**

Tel: 81-3-3237-7260   Fax: 81-3-3237-7330

## HAGGAR CORPORATION

6113 Lemmon Avenue, Dallas, TX, 75209

Tel: (214) 352-8481    Fax: (214) 956-4367    www.haggarcorp.com

*Mfr. apparel.*

**Haggar Japan Co. Ltd.,  11-6 Sarugaku-Cho, Sanroser Daikanyama 201, Shibuya-ku Tokyo 150-3300, Japan**

Tel: 81-3-5457-2093    Contact: Hirotoshi Tashiro

## HALLIBURTON COMPANY

500 North Akard Street, Ste. 3600, Dallas, TX, 75201-3391

Tel: (214) 978-2600    Fax: (214) 978-2685    www.halliburton.com

*Engaged in diversified energy services, engineering and construction.*

**Halliburton Ltd.,  2/F Tokyo Real Iwamotocho Bldg., 12-7 Iwamotocho 2-chome, Chiyoda-ku Tokyo 101, Japan**

Tel: 81-3-5821-2245   Fax: 81-3-5821-2248

## HALLMARK CARDS INC.

2501 McGee Street, Kansas City, MO, 64108

Tel: (816) 274-5100    Fax: (816) 274-5061    www.hallmark.com

*Mfr. greeting cards and related products.*

**Nihon Hallmark K.K.,  2-6-16 Komazawa, Setagaya-ku, Tokyo, Japan**

Tel: 81-3-348-77910

## HAMILTON SUNSTRAND

One Hamilton Rd., Windsor Locks, CT, 06096-1010

Tel: (860) 654-6000    Fax: (860) 654-3469    www.hamiltonsunstrandcorp.com

*Design/mfr. aerospace systems for commercial, regional, corporate and military aircraft.*

**Hamilton Sunstrand Corp.,  Reinazaka Annex 3F, 11-3 Akasaka 1-chome, Minato-ku, Tokyo 107 Japan**

## HANDY & HARMAN

555 Theodore Fremd Ave., Rye, NY, 10580

Tel: (914) 921-5200    Fax: (914) 925-4496    www.handyha

*Precious and specialty metals for industry, refining, scrap metal; diversified industrial mfr.*

**Mizuno Handy Harman Ltd.,  11-12 Kitaueno 2-chome, Taitoh-ku, Tokyo, Japan**

## HARCOURT GENERAL, INC.

27 Boylston St., Chestnut Hill, MA, 02467

Tel: (617) 232-8200     Fax: (617) 739-1395     www.harcourtgeneral.com

*Publisher of educational materials.*

**Harcourt General Japan, Inc., Ichibancho Central Building, 22-1 Ichibancho, Chiyoda-ku, Tokyo 102 Japan**

Tel: 81-3-3234-3911     Fax: 81-3-3265-7186

## HARLEY-DAVIDSON INTERNATIONAL

3700 West Juneau Ave., Milwaukee, WI, 53201

Tel: (414) 342-4680     Fax: (414) 343-4621     www.harleydavidson.com

*Mfr. motorcycles, recreational and commercial vehicles, parts and accessories.*

**Harley-Davidson Japan KK, PO Box 39, 718 Shin Nihon Kaikan Bldg., 7-18 Mita 3-chome, Minato-ku, Tokyo, Japan**

## HARMAN INTERNATIONAL INDUSTRIES, INC.

1101 Pennsylvania Ave. NW, Ste. 1010, Washington, DC, 20004

Tel: (202) 393-1101     Fax: (202) 393-3064     www.harman.com

*Mfr. audio and video equipment, loudspeakers and sound reinforcement equipment.*

**Harman Intl. Japan Co. Ltd., Hinoki Bldg. 3/F, 1-5 Azabudai 3-chome, Minato-ku, Tokyo 106, Japan**

## HARNISCHFEGER INDUSTRIES INC.

PO Box 554, Milwaukee, WI, 53201

Tel: (414) 797-6480     Fax: (414) 797-6573     www.harnischfeger.com

*Mfr. mining and material handling equipment, papermaking machinery and computer systems.*

**Beloit Nippon Ltd., 2-5-1 Marunouchi, Chiyoda-ku, Tokyo 100, Japan**

**Kobe Steel Ltd., 3-18 Wakinohama-cho 1-chome, Chuo-ku, Kobe 651, Japan**

## HARRIS CORPORATION

1025 West NASA Blvd., Melbourne, FL, 32919

Tel: (407) 727-9100     Fax: (407) 727-9344     www.harris.com

*Mfr. communications and information-handling equipment, including copying and fax systems.*

**Harris K.K., Kojimachi-Nakata Building 4F, 5-3-5 Kojimachi, Chiyoda-ku, Tokyo 102 Japan**

Tel: 81-3-3265-7571     Fax: 81-3-3265-7575

## HARTMARX CORPORATION

101 North Wacker Drive, Chicago, IL, 60606

Tel: (312) 372-6300     Fax: (312) 444-2710     www.hartmarx.com

*Mfr./licensing men's and women's apparel.*

**Hartmarx Japan, 4-2-1 Kyutaromachi, Chuo-ku, Osaka, Japan**

## HASBRO INDUSTRIES INC.

1027 Newport Ave., Pawtucket, RI, 02861

Tel: (401) 725-8697     Fax: (401) 727-5099     www.hasbro.com

*Mfr. toy products, including games and puzzles, dolls and plush products.*

**Hasbro Industries, Tokyo, Japan**

## HEIDRICK & STRUGGLES INTERNATIONAL, INC.

Sears Tower, 233 South Wacker Drive, Chicago, IL, 60606

Tel: (312) 496-1200     Fax: (312) 496-1290     www.heidrick.com

*Executive search firm.*

**Heidrick & Struggles Intl. Inc., Kasumigaseki Bldg. 31st Fl., 3-2-5 Kasumigaseki, Chiyoda-ku, Tokyo 100, Japan**

Tel: 81-3-3500-5310     Fax: 81-3-3500-5350

## H.J. HEINZ COMPANY

600 Grant Street, Pittsburgh, PA, 15219

Tel: (412) 456-5700     Fax: (412) 456-6128     www.heinz.com

*Processed food products and nutritional services.*

**Heinz Japan Ltd., Tokyo, Japan**

**Star-Kist Foods Inc., Tokyo, Japan**

## HERCULES INC.

Hercules Plaza, 1313 N. Market Street, Wilmington, DE, 19894-0001

Tel: (302) 594-5000     Fax: (302) 594-5400     www.herc.com

*Mfr. specialty chemicals, plastics, film and fibers, coatings, resins, food ingredients.*

**Hercules Japan Ltd., Seiwa Bldg. 9F, 3-4 Minami Aoyama 2-chome, Minato-ku, Tokyo 107, Japan**

## HERMAN MILLER INC.

855 East Main, Zeeland, MI, 49464

Tel: (616) 654-3000     Fax: (616) 654-5385     www.hermanmiller.com

*Mfr. office furnishings.*

**Herman Miller Japan, Tokyo Design Center 5F, 25-19 Higashi-Gotanda, Shinagawa-ku, Tokyo 141 Japan**

## HERSHEY FOODS CORPORATION

100 Crystal A Drive, Hershey, PA, 17033

Tel: (717) 534-6799     Fax: (717) 534-6760     www.hersheys.com

*Mfr. chocolate, food and confectionery products.*

**Fujiya Leaf Japan (JV), Tokyo, Japan**

**Hershey Japan, Keikyu Nakahara Bldg. 6/F, 30-6 Shinbashi 4-chome, Minato-ku, Tokyo 105, Japan**

## HEWITT ASSOCIATES LLC

100 Half Day Road, Lincolnshire, IL, 60069

Tel: (847) 295-5000     Fax: (847) 295-7634     www.hewitt.com

*Employee benefits consulting firm.*

**Hewitt Associates, Akasaka Twin Tower Main Tower 11F, 2-17-22 Akasaka, Minato-ku Tokyo 107-0052, Japan**

Tel: 81-3-5563-1261

## HEWLETT-PACKARD COMPANY

3000 Hanover Street, Palo Alto, CA, 94304-1185

Tel: (650) 857-1501     Fax: (650) 857-5518     www.hp.com

*Mfr. computing, communications and measurement products and services.*

**Hewlett-Packard Japan Ltd., 3-29-21 Takaido-Higashi, Suginami-ku, Tokyo 168, Japan**

## HEXCEL CORPORATION

281 Tresser Blvd., Stamford, CT, 06901

Tel: (203) 969-0666     Fax: (203) 358-3977     www.hexcel.com

*Honeycomb core materials, specialty chemicals, resins and epoxies.*

**Hexcel, 22-1 Ichiban-cho, Chiyoda-ku, Tokyo 102, Japan**

## HILLERICH & BRADSBY COMPANY INC

800 West Main St., PO Box 35700, Louisville, KY, 40202

Tel: (502) 585-5226     Fax: (502) 585-1179     www.slugger.com

*Golf, baseball and softball equipment.*

**Hillerich & Bradsby Co. Ltd., Takanawa Annex, 2-20-24 Takanawa, Minato-ku, Tokyo 108, Japan**

Tel: 81-3-3280-3911   Fax: 81-3-3280-3918

## HILTON HOTELS CORPORATION

9336 Civic Center Drive, Beverly Hills, CA, 90210

Tel: (310) 278-4321　　Fax: (310) 205-7880　　www.hiltonhotels.com

*International hotel chain: Hilton International, Vista Hotels and Hilton National Hotels.*

**Hilton International Company, 6F Shinjuku Kokusai Bldg., 6-2 Nishi-Shinjuku, 6-chome, Shinjuku-ku, Tokyo 160, Japan**

**Osaka Hilton, 8-8 Umeda 1-chome, Kita-ku, Osaka 530, Japan**

**Tokyo Bay Hilton, 1-8 Maihama, Urayasu-City, Chiba 279, Japan**

## HNC SOFTWARE INC.

5930 Cornerstone Court West, San Diego, CA, 92121

Tel: (858) 546-8877　　Fax: (858) 799-8006　　www.hnc.com

*Mfr. software to manage and detect fraud.*

**HNC Software KK, Shinjuku Nomura Bldg. 32/F, 1-26-2 Nishi-Shinjuku, Shinjuku-ku, Tokyo 163-05, Japan**

Tel: 81-3-5322-2800

## HOLIDAY INN (BASS RESORTS) WORLDWIDE, INC.

3 Ravinia Drive, Ste. 2900, Atlanta, GA, 30346-2149

Tel: (770) 604-2000　　Fax: (770) 604-5403　　www.holidayinn.com

*Hotels, restaurants and casinos.*

**Holiday Inn (Far East Ltd. Inc.), Kyoto, Japan**

**Holiday Inn(Far East Ltd. Inc.), Niben Bldg. 5F, 2-8 Muromachii, Nihonbashi, Chuo-ku, Tokyo 103, Japan**

## HOLLAND & KNIGHT

400 North Ashley Dr., Ste. 2300,, Tampa, FL, 33602

Tel: (813) 227-8500　　Fax: (813) 229-0134　　www.hklaw.com

*International law firm.*

**Holland & Knight, Tokyo, Japan**

## HOLLINGSWORTH & VOSE COMPANY

112 Washington Street, East Walpole, MA, 02032

Tel: (508) 668-0295　　Fax: (508) 668-3557　　www.hollingsworth-vose.com

*Mfr. technical and industrial papers and non-woven fabrics.*

**Hollingsworth & Vose, Japan, You Building 4F, 5-7 Nihonbashi-Horidome-Cho 1-Chome, Chuo-Ku Tokyo 103 Japan**

## HONEYWELL INTERNATIONAL INC.

101 Columbia Road, Morristown, NJ, 07962

Tel: (973) 455-2000　　Fax: (973) 455-4807　　www.honeywell.com

*Develop/mfr. controls for home and building, industry, space and aviation.*

**Honeywell Asia Pacific Inc., 1-14-6 Shibaura, Minato-ku, Tokyo 105-0023 Japan**

Tel: 81-3-5440-1395　Fax: 81-3-5440-1368

## HORWATH INTERNATIONAL ASSOCIATION

415 Madison Ave., New York, NY, 10017

Tel: (212) 838-5566　　Fax: (212) 838-3636　　www.horwath.com

*Public accountants and auditors.*

**Horwath & Showa Co. Ltd. Japan/Showa Audit Corp., Daiko Building, 3-2 Umeda 14-chome, Kita-ku, Osaka 530 Japan**

## HOUGHTON INTERNATIONAL INC.

PO Box 930, Madison & Van Buren Avenues, Valley Forge, PA, 19482-0930

Tel: (610) 666-4000 Fax: (610) 666-1376 www.houghtonintl.com

*Mfr. specialty chemicals, hydraulic fluids and lubricants.*

**Houghton Japan Co., Ltd., Matsuki Bldg. 1-3-8 Shibakoen, Minato-Ku, Tokyo 105 Japan**

Tel: 81-3-3434-4751

**Kyodo Yushi Co., Ltd., Dentsu-Kosan-Dai-3 Bldg., 2-16-7 Ginza Chuo-Ku, Tokyo, Japan**

Tel: 81-03-543-5813

## HOWMEDICA OSTEONICS, INC.

359 Veterans Blvd., Rutherford, NJ, 07070

Tel: (201) 507-7300 Fax: (201) 935-4873 www.howmedica.com

*Mfr. of maxillofacial products (orthopedic implants).*

**Howmedica Japan, Tokyo, Japan**

Tel: 81-3-3344-7523

## HOWMET CORPORATION

475 Steamboat Road, PO Box 1960, Greenwich, CT, 06836-1960

Tel: (203) 661-4600 Fax: (203) 661-1134 www.howmet.com

*Mfr. precision investment castings, alloys, engineering and refurbishment for jet aircraft and industrial gas turbine (IGT) engine components.*

**Komatsu-Howmet Ltd., 61-1 Acti-Nishi, Terai, Nomi Ishikawa 923-11, Japan**

Tel: 81-761-58-6667 Fax: 81-761-58-6668 Contact: Michio Ohta

## HQ GLOBAL WORKPLACES INC.

1155 Connecticut Ave. NW, Washington, DC, 20036

Tel: (202) 467-8500 Fax: (202) 467-8595 www.hq.com

*Provides office outsourcing, officing solutions, including internet access, telecommunications, meeting rooms, furnished offices and team rooms, state-of-the-art videoconferencing, and trained on-site administrative support teams -*

**HQ Global Workplaces, AIG Bldg. Level 9, 1-1-3 Marunouchi, Chiyoda-Ku, Tokyo 100-0005 Japan**

Tel: 81-3-5288-5100

## HUCK INTERNATIONAL INC.

3724 East Columbia Street, Tucson, AZ, 85714-3415

Tel: (520) 747-9898 Fax: (520) 750-7420 www.huck.com

*Designer and manufacturer of high-performance, proprietary fasteners and fastener installation systems.*

**Huck Ltd., Yodogawa-Gobankan 11/F, 2-1 Toyosaki 3-chome, Kita-ku, Osaka 531, Japan**

**Huck Ltd., Hosoda-Shoji-Building 6F, 1-10-19 Horidome-cho, Nihonbashi, Chuo-ku Tokyo 103-0012, Japan**

Tel: 81-33-665-1189 Fax: 81-33-665-0089 Contact: Hiroshi Kawai, Pres.

## HUGHES ELECTRONICS CORPORATION

200 N. Sepulveda Blvd., PO Box 956, El Segundo, CA, 90245-0956

Tel: (310) 662-9821 Fax: (310) 647-6213 www.hughes.com

*Provides digital television entertainment, satellite services, and satellite-based private business networks.*

**DirecTV Japan, Inc., 23F Yebisu Garden Place Tower, 4-20-3 Ebisu, Shibuya-ku, Tokyo, Japan**

Tel: 81-3-5424-1900 Fax: 81-3-5424-1901

**Hughes Japan, KK, 21F KDD Otemachi Blvd., 1-8-1 Otemachi, Chiyoda-ku, Tokyo 100-0004, Japan**

Tel: 81-3-3243-1093

## HUMPHREY PRODUCTS COMPANY

PO Box 2008, Kalamazoo, MI, 49003

Tel: (616) 381-5500    Fax: (616) 381-4113    www.humphreypc.com

*Mfr./sale/services pneumatic actuators and valves for factory automation, motion control, etc.*

**Koganei Corporation Partner, 3-2-3 Fuji Bldg., Marunouchi Chiyoda-ku, Tokyo 100, Japan**

## HUTCHINSON TECHNOLOGY INC.

40 West Highland Park, Hutchinson, MN, 55350-9784

Tel: (320) 587-1900    Fax: (320) 587-1892    www.htch.com

*Mfr. suspension assembly components for rigid disk drives.*

**Hutchinson Technology Incorporated, Level 32 Nomura Bldg., 1-26-2 Nishi-Shinjuku Shinjuku-ku, Tokyo 163-05, Japan**

Tel: 81-3-5322-1349

## HYATT CORPORATION

200 West Madison Street, Chicago, IL, 60606

Tel: (312) 750-1234    Fax: (312) 750-8578    www.hyatt.com

*International hotel management.*

**Grand Hyatt Fukuoka Hotel, 1-2-82 Sumiyoshi, Hakata-ku, Fukuoka 812, Japan**

Tel: 81-92-282-1234    Fax: 81-92282-2817

## HYPERION SOLUTIONS CORPORATION

1344 Crossman Avenue, Sunnyvale, CA, 94089

Tel: (408) 744-9500    Fax: (408) 744-0400    www.hyperion.com

*Mfr. data analysis software tools.*

**Hyperion KK, 10/F West Tower Shin-Nikko Bldg., 2-10-1 Toranomon Minato-ku, Tokyo 105-0001, Japan**

Tel: 81-3-5545-9300    Fax: 81-3-5545-9301

## i2 TECHNOLOGIES, INC.

11701 Luna Road, Dallas, TX, 75234

Tel: (214) 860-6106    Fax: (214) 860-6060    www.i2.com

*Mfr. business-to-business software.*

**i2 Technologies Japan, Shinagawa Intercity A-22/F, 2-15-1 Konan Minato-ku, Tokyo 108-6022, Japan**

Tel: 81-3-5783-1212

## IBM CORPORATION

New Orchard Road, Armonk, NY, 10504

Tel: (914) 765-1900    Fax: (914) 765-7382    www.ibm.com

*Information products, technology and services.*

**IBM Japan Ltd., 2-12 Roppongi 3-chome, Minato-ku, Tokyo, Japan**

Tel: 81-3-3586-111    Fax: 81-44-200-8600

## IBP INC.

PO Box 515, Dakota City, NE, 68731

Tel: (402) 494-2061    Fax: (402) 241-2068    www.ibpinc.com

*Produce beef and pork, hides and associated products, animal feeds, pharmaceuticals.*

**IBP Inc., Akasaka Daiichi Bldg. 10F, 9-17, Akasaka 4-chome, Minato-ku, Tokyo 107, Japan**

Tel: 81-33-746-1801    Fax: 81-33-746-1808    Contact: Takamichi Tawara, Mng. Dir.

## ICC INDUSTRIES INC.

460 Park Ave., New York, NY, 10022

Tel: (212) 521-1700     Fax: (212) 521-1794     www.iccchem.com

*Manufacturing and trading of chemicals, plastics and pharmaceuticals.*

**Fallek Chemical Japan K.K., 3/F - 11-4 Uchikanda 1 Chome, Chiyoda-Ku, Tokyo 101-0047, Japan**

Tel: 81-3-329-12017   Fax: 81-3-323-32978   Contact: Yoshihiro Tadono

## ICN PHARMACEUTICALS, INC.

3300 Hyland Ave., Costa Mesa, CA, 92626

Tel: (714) 545-0100     Fax: (714) 641-7268     www.icnpharm.com

*Mfr./distribute pharmaceuticals.*

**ICN Pharmaceuticals, Inc., c/o Kyowa Bldg., 1-32 Chome Kyobashi, Chuo-ku Tokyo 104, Japan**

## IDEC PHARMACEUTICALS CORPORATION

3030 Callan Road, San Diego, CA, 92121

Tel: (858) 431-8500     Fax: (858) 431-8750     www.idecpharm.com

*Engaged in development of pharmaceuticals for autoimmune diseases.*

**IDEC Seiyaku KK, 5/F Kyodo Bldg., Shin-Kyobashi, 4-2-2 Hacchobori Chuo-ku, Tokyo 104, Japan**

Tel: 81-3-3552-1721   Fax: 81-3-3552-1820   Contact: Michio Nishida

## IKOS SYSTEMS, INC.

19050 Pruneridge Avenue, Cupertino, CA, 95014

Tel: (408) 255-4567     Fax: (408) 366-8699     www.ikos.com

*Mfr. hardware and software.*

**IKOS KK, KSP R&D Business Park Bldg. D-337, 3-2-1 Sakado, Takatsu-ku, Kawasaki 213, Japan**

Tel: 81-44-850-1230   Fax: 81-44-850-1250

## ILLINOIS TOOL WORKS (ITW)

3600 West Lake Ave., Glenview, IL, 60025-5811

Tel: (847) 724-7500     Fax: (847) 657-4268     www.itw.com

*Mfr. gears, tools, fasteners, sealants, plastic and metal components for industrial, medical, etc.*

**Nifco Inc., Tokyo, Japan**

## IMG (INTERNATIONAL MANAGEMENT GROUP)

1360 East Ninth Street, Ste. 100, Cleveland, OH, 44114

Tel: (216) 522-1200     Fax: (216) 522-1145     www.imgworld.com

*Manages athletes, sports academies and real estate facilities worldwide.*

**IMG, Moto-Akasaka Kikutai Building 4/F, 1-7-18 Moto-Akasaka, Minato-ku, Tokyo 107-0051, Japan**

Tel: 81-3-3470-1331   Fax: 81-3-3470-6477

**Press Country Club, 4816 Banchi 1, Shimoakima Annaka-shi, Gunma Prefecture 379-01, Japan**

Tel: 81-27381-3727   Fax: 81-27392-2277

## IMO INDUSTRIES, DIV. COLFAX INC.

9211 Forest Hill Ave., Richmond, VA, 23235

Tel: (804) 560-4070     Fax: (804) 560-4076     www.imochain.com

*Mfr./support mechanical and electronic controls, chains and engineered power products.*

**NHK Morse Co. Ltd., 3-21-10 Shin-Yokohama, Kohoku-ku, Yokohama 222, Japan**

## IMPCO TECHNOLOGIES, INC.

16804 Gridley Place, Cerritos, CA, 90703

Tel: (562) 860-6666     Fax: (562) 809-1240     www.impco.ws

*Mfr. fuel control processors.*

**IMPCO Technologies Japan, 3-9 Morooka 4-Chome, Hakata-Ku, Fukuoka, 816-0094, Japan**

Tel: 81-9-2592-7270   Fax: 81-9-2592-7280

## INDUCTOTHERM CORPORATION

10 Indel Ave., PO Box 157, Rancocas, NJ, 08073-0157

Tel: (609) 267-9000     Fax: (609) 267-3537     www.inductotherm.com

*Mfr. induction melting furnaces, induction power supplies, charging and preheating systems, automatic pouring systems and computer control systems.*

**Inductotherm Japan Ltd., 3-10 Minamibefu 1-chome, Nishi-ku, Kobe 651-21, Japan**

Tel: 81-78-974-2552     Contact: Tada Yoshinori

## INFONET SERVICES CORPORATION

2100 East Grand Ave., El Segundo, CA, 90245-1022

Tel: (310) 335-2600     Fax: (310) 335-4507     www.infonet.com

*Provider of Internet services and electronic messaging services.*

**Infonet Services Corporation - Japan, KDD Building 30F, 2-3-2 Nishishinjuku, Shinjuku-ku Tolyo 163-03, Japan**

Tel: 81-3-3347-7663     Fax: 81-3-3342-5530

## INFORMATION RESOURCES, INC. (IRI)

150 N. Clinton St., Chicago, IL, 60661

Tel: (312) 726-1221     Fax: (312) 726-0360     www.infores.com

*Provides bar code scanner services for retail sales organizations; processes, analyzes and sells data from the huge database created from these services.*

**Information Resources Japan LTD., Iseki Bldg. 2F, 2-3-26 Kudan Minami, Chiyoda-ku, Tokyo 102 Japan**

Tel: 81-3-5276-5084     Fax: 81-3-5276-5082

## INFORMIX CORPORATION

4100 Bohannon Drive, Menlo Park, CA, 95025

Tel: (650) 926-6300     Fax: (650) 926-6593     www.informix.com

*Designs and produces database management software, connectivity interfaces and gateways, and other computer applications.*

**Informix K.K., ARK Mori Building 23F, 12-32 Akasaka, Minato-ku Tokyo 107, Japan**

Tel: 81-3-5562-4500

## INGERSOLL-RAND COMPANY

200 Chestnut Ridge Road, Woodcliff Lake, NJ, 07675

Tel: (201) 573-0123     Fax: (201) 573-3172     www.ingersoll-rand.com

*Mfr. compressors, rock drills, air tools, door hardware, ball bearings.*

**Ingersoll-Rand (Japan) Ltd., Kowa Bldg. #17, 1-2-7 Nishi-Azabu, Minato-ku, Tokyo 106, Japan**

## INGRAM MICRO INC.

PO Box 25125, 1600 E. St. Andrew Place, Santa Ana, CA, 92799

Tel: (714) 566-1000     Fax: (714) 566-7940     www.ingrammicro.com

*Engaged in wholesale distribution of microcomputer products.*

**Ingram Micro Japan Ltd., 24-1 Nihonbashi-Hakozakicho, Chuo-ku, Tokyo 103-8501, Japan**

Tel: 81-3-5642-8487     Fax: 81-3-5641-8311

## INKTOMI CORPORATION

4100 East Third Avenue, Foster City, CA, 94404

Tel: (650) 653-2800     Fax: (650) 653-2801     www.iktomi.com

*Mfr. software to boost speeds of computer networks.*

**Inktomi Corporation, Kamiyacho Mori Bldg. 16/F, 4-3-20 Toranomon Minato-ku, Tokyo 105-0001, Japan**

## INSTINET

875 Third Ave., New York, NY, 10022

Tel: (212) 310-9500    Fax: (212) 832-5183    www.instinet.com

*Online investment brokerage.*

**Instinet, Tokyo, Japan**

## INSTRON CORPORATION

100 Royal Street, Canton, MA, 02021-1089

Tel: (781) 575-5000    Fax: (781) 575-5751    www.instron.com

*Mfr. material testing instruments.*

**Instron Japan Co. Ltd., 1-30 Toyotsucho, Shuita-shi, Osaka 584 Japan**

**Instron Japan Co. Ltd., 2-9-30 Sakaa, Naka-ku, Nagoya 460, Japan**

**Instron Japan Co. Ltd., 1-8-9 Miyamaodaira, Miyamae-ku, Kawaskai-shi, Kanagawa-ken 216 Japan**

## INTEGRATED SILICON SOLUTION, INC.

2231 Lawson Lane, Santa Clara, CA, 95054-3311

Tel: (408) 588-0800    Fax: (408) 588-0805    www.issiusa.com

*Mfr. high-speed memory chips and SRAMs.*

**Integrated Silicon Solution, Inc., Tokyo Japan**

Tel: 81-3-3255-5351   Fax: 81-3-3255-3308

## INTEL CORPORATION

Robert Noyce Bldg., 2200 Mission College Blvd., Santa Clara, CA, 95052-8119

Tel: (408) 765-8080    Fax: (408) 765-1739    www.intel.com

*Mfr. semiconductor, microprocessor and micro-communications components and systems.*

**Intel (Japan) Kabushki Kaisha, PO Box 115 Tsukuba-gakuen, 5-6 Tokodai, Tsukuba-shi, Ibaraki-ken 305, Japan**

Tel: 81-298-47-8522

## INTELLIGROUP, INC.

499 Thornall Street, Edison, NJ, 08837

Tel: (732) 590-1600    Fax: (732) 362-2100    www.intelligroup.com

*Provides systems integration, customer software and Internet application development.*

**Intelligroup Japan Ltd., 5-1-1 Kiba Koto-Ku, Tokyo 135-0042, Japan**

Tel: 81-3-5620 0781   Contact: Sreenivas Unnamatla

## INTER-CONTINENTAL HOTELS

3 Ravina Drive, Suite 2900, Atlanta, GA, 30346-2149

Tel: (770) 604-2000    Fax: (770) 604-5403    www.interconti.com

*Worldwide hotel and resort accommodations.*

**Hotel Inter-Continental Tokyo, 2-1 Nishi-Shinjuku 2-chome, Shinjuku-ku Tokyo 160-8330, Japan**

Tel: 81-3-3344-0111   Fax: 81-3-3345-8269

**Inter-Continental Hotels, (9F) 1-16-2 Kaigan Minato-ku, Tokyo 105-8567, Japan**

Tel: 81-3-3578-7272   Fax: 81-3-3578-7273

## INTERGRAPH CORPORATION

One Madison Industrial Park, Huntsville, AL, 35894-0001

Tel: (256) 730-2000    Fax: (256) 730-7898    www.intergraph.com

*Develop/mfr. interactive computer graphic systems.*

**Intergraph Japan K.K., Shibuya Tohoseimei Bldg. 26F, 2-15-1 Shibuya, Shibuya-ku, Tokyo 150-0002, Japan**

Tel: 81-3-546-77360   Fax: 81-3-546-77061

**Intergraph Japan K.K. - Osaka, 12/F Shin-Osaka 2nd Mori-Bldg., 3-5-36 Miyahara, Yodogawa-ku, Osaka 532-0003, Japan**

Tel: 81-6-3947711   Fax: 81-6-3943733

## INTERMEC TECHNOLOGIES CORPORATION

6001 36th Ave. West, PO Box 4280, Everett, WA, 98203-9280

Tel: (425) 348-2600    Fax: (425) 355-9551    www.intermec.com

*Mfr./distributor automated data collection systems.*

**Intermec Corporation, Japan,  MKK Building,  5-7-2 Yashio Shinagawa-ku, Tokyo 140-0003, Japan**

Tel: 81-3-5492-7430   Fax: 81-3-3799-5595

## INTERNATIONAL COMPONENTS CORPORATION

420 N. May Street, Chicago, IL, 60622

Tel: (312) 829-2525    Fax: (312) 829-0213    www.icc-charge.com

*Mfr./sale/services portable DC battery chargers.*

**International Components Corp. (Japan) Ltd.,  Glory Bldg., 35-13 Nishikamata 6-chome, Ohta-ku, Tokyo 144, Japan**

## INTERNATIONAL FLAVORS & FRAGRANCES INC.

521 West 57th Street, New York, NY, 10019-2960

Tel: (212) 765-5500    Fax: (212) 708-7132    www.iff.com

*Design/mfr. flavors, fragrances and aroma chemicals.*

**International Flavors & Fragrances KK,  Gotemba, Japan**

**International Flavors & Fragrances Ltd.,  Green Fantasia Bldg., 11-11 Jingumae 1-chome, Shibuya-ku, Tokyo 150, Japan**

**International Flavors & Fragrances Ltd.,  Osaka, Japan**

## INTERNATIONAL GAME TECHNOLOGY INC.

9295 Prototype Drive, Reno, NV, 89511

Tel: (702) 448-0100    Fax: (702) 448-1488    www.igtonline.com

*Mfr. slot machines, video gaming machines and gaming terminals.*

**Japan K.K.,  Atago Toyo Bldg. 7F, 1-3-4 Atago, Minato-ku, Tokyo 105, Japan**

Tel: 81-3-5403-1760   Fax: 81-3-5403-1765

## INTERNATIONAL PAPER COMPANY

2 Manhattanville Road, Purchase, NY, 10577

Tel: (914) 397-1500    Fax: (914) 397-1596    www.ipaper.com

*Mfr./distributor container board, paper and wood products.*

**Ilford Anitec Ltd.,  4-7 Minamishinagawa 2-chome, Shinagawa-ku, Tokyo 140, Japan**

**International Paper (Asia) Ltd.,  14-11 Ginza 4-chome, Chuo-ku, Tokyo 10, Japan**

**IPI Corp.,  9-6 Nagata-cho 2-chome, Chiyoda-ku, Tokyo, Japan**

**Rengo Intl. Products Co.,  900-5 Kuboki, Soja City, Oklayama, Japan**

**Veratec Japan Ltd.,  14-11 Ginza 4-chome, Chuo-ku, Tokyo 104, Japan**

## INTERNATIONAL RECTIFIER CORPORATION

233 Kansas Street, El Segundo, CA, 90245

Tel: (310) 322-3331    Fax: (310) 322-3332    www.irf.com

*Mfr. power semiconductor components.*

**International Rectifier - Japan,  K & H Bldg. 2F, 30-4 Nishi-Ikebukuro, 3-chome, Toshima-ku, Tokyo 171-0021, Japan**

Tel: 81-33-983-0086   Fax: 81-33-983-0642

## INTERNATIONAL SPECIALTY PRODUCTS, INC.

1361 Alps Rd., Wayne, NJ, 07470

Tel: (877) 389-3083    Fax: (973) 628-4117    www.ispcorp.com

*Mfr. specialty chemical products.*

**ISP (Japan) Ltd.,  Annex 10F - 16-14 Shinkawa 1-chome, Chou-ku, Tokyo 104-0033 Japan**

Tel: 81-3-5566-8661   Fax: 81-3-5566-8682

ISP (Japan) Ltd., Shin-osaka Coper Bldg. 5F, 4-11-21 Nishinakajima, Yodogawa-ku Osaka-shi Osaka, 532-0011 Japan

Tel: 81-6-6838-5544   Fax: 81-6-838-5752

ISP (Japan) Ltd., Nihonbashi #2 Building 8F, 41-12 Hakozaki-Cho Nihonbashi, Chuo-ku Tokyo 103, Japan

Tel: 81-3-3667-0321   Fax: 81-3-3667-4538

## INTER-TEL INC.

7300 W. Boston Street, Chandler, AZ, 85226

Tel: (602) 961-9000   Fax: (602) 961-1370   www.inter-tel.com

*Design/mfr. business communications systems.*

Nihon Inter-Tel KK, 18-11 Uchikanda 1-chome, Chioyda-ku, Tokyo, Japan

## INTRALOX INC.

201 Laitram Lane, New Orleans, LA, 70123

Tel: (504) 733-0463   Fax: (504) 734-0063   www.intralox.com

*Mfr. plastic, modular conveyor belts and accessories.*

Intralox Japan Service Center, 37 Yamano-cho, Funabashi-city, Chiba 273 Japan

## INTUIT INC.

2535 Garcia Avenue, Mountain View, CA, 94043

Tel: (650) 944-6000   Fax: (650) 944-3699   www.intuit.com

*Mfr. personal finance software.*

Intuit KK, Seavans North Bldg., 1-2-1 Shibaura Minato-ku, Tokyo 105-6791, Japan

Tel: 81-3-5419-3001   Fax: 81-3-5419-3031

Intuit KK, WTC Bldg. 32/F, 1-14-16 Nanko-kita Suminoe-ku, Osaka 559-0034, Japan

Tel: 81-6-6613-7100   Fax: 81-6-6613-7105

## IONICS INC.

65 Grove Street, Watertown, MA, 02172

Tel: (617) 926-2500   Fax: (617) 926-4304   www.ionics.com

*Mfr. desalination equipment.*

Yuasa-Ionics Co. Ltd., Tokyo, Japan

## IRIDIUM LLC

1575 "I" Street, NW, Washington, DC, 20005

Tel: (202) 408-3800   Fax: (202) 408-3801   www.iridium.com

*Consortium of companies sharing the construction and implementation of a global satellite communications system.*

Nippon Iridium Corporation, Koji-machi Crystal City East Bldg. 8F, 408 Koji-machi, Chiyoda-ku Tokyo 102-0083, Japan

Tel: 81-3-3221-9577   Fax: 81-3-3221-9576   Contact: Yoshiharu Yasuda, Pres.

## ITW DEVCON PLEXUS

30 Endicott Street, Danvers, MA, 01923

Tel: (978) 777-1100   Fax: (978) 774-0516   www.devcon-equip.com

*Mfr. filled epoxies, urethanes, adhesives and metal treatment products.*

ITW Devcon, Tokyo, Japan

Tel: 81-66-330-7118

## ITW RANSBURG FINISHING SYSTEMS

320 Phillips Ave., Toledo, OH, 43612

Tel: (419) 470-2000    Fax: (419) 470-2112    www.itwransburg.com

*Mfr. liquid electrostatic paint application equipment.*

**Ransburg Industrial Finishing KK, 15-5 Fuku-Ura, 1 Chome Kanazawa-Ku, Yokohama 236-0004, Japan**

Tel: 81-45-785-6311

## J. WALTER THOMPSON COMPANY

466 Lexington Ave., New York, NY, 10017

Tel: (212) 210-7000    Fax: (212) 210-6944    www.jwt.com

*International advertising and marketing services.*

**J. Walter Thompson Japan, Tokyo, Japan**

## JAMESBURY CORPORATION

640 Lincoln Street, Box 15004, Worcester, MA, 01615-0004

Tel: (508) 852-0200    Fax: (508) 852-8172    www.jamesbury.com

*Mfr. valves and accessories.*

**Jamesbury Nippon Ltd., Shuwa Shibazonobashi Bldg., 1-20 Shiba 2-chome, Minato-ku, Tokyo 105, Japan**

## JDA SOFTWARE GROUP, INC.

14400 N. 87th St., Scottsdale, AZ, 85260-3649

Tel: (480) 308-3000    Fax: (480) 308-3001    www.jda.com

*Developer of information management software for retail, merchandising, distribution and store management.*

**JDA Software Japan Ltd., Units 35/36 - Kamiyacho Mori Bldg., 14/F - 4-3-20 Toranomon, Minato-ku Tokyo 105-0001, Japan**

Tel: 81-3-5404-3522    Fax: 81-35404-3578

**JDA Software Japan Ltd., Oxson Buildng 6/F - 1-2-13 Shintomi, Chuo-ku Tokyo 104-0041, Japan**

Tel: 81-3-3206-7201    Fax: 81-3-3206-7202

## JEFFERIES & COMPANY, INC.

11100 Santa Monica Boulevard, Los Angeles, CA, 90025

Tel: (310) 445-1199    Fax: (310) 914-1173

*Real estate and financial advisor.*

**Indosuez W.I. Carr Securities, 3-29-1 Kanda-Jimbochi Chi-yoda-ku, Tokyo, Japan**

## JOHNS MANVILLE CORPORATION

717 17th Street, Denver, CO, 80202

Tel: (303) 978-2000    Fax: (303) 978-2318    www.jm.com

*Mfr. fiberglass insulation, roofing products and systems, fiberglass material and reinforcements, filtration mats.*

**Johns Manville Japan, Neyasu #1 Bldg. 3/F, 1-21 Kanda Nishikicho, Chiyoda-ku, Tokyo 101, Japan**

## JOHNSON & JOHNSON

One Johnson & Johnson Plaza, New Brunswick, NJ, 08933

Tel: (732) 524-0400    Fax: (732) 214-0334    www.jnj.com

*Mfr./distributor/R&D pharmaceutical, health care and cosmetic products.*

**DePuy Japan, Inc., Tokyo, Japan**

**Ethicon Endo-Surgery, Tokyo, Japan**

**Janssen-Kyowa Co. Ltd., Tokyo, Japan**

**Johnson & Johnson KK, 3-2 Toya 6-chome, Koto-ku, Tokyo 135, Japan**

**Johnson & Johnson Medical KK, 3-2 Toyo 6-chome, Koto-ku, Tokyo 135, Japan**

**Ortho-Clinical Diagnostics KK, Tokyo, Japan**

Vistakon Japan,  Tokyo, Japan

## S C JOHNSON & SON INC.

1525 Howe St., Racine, WI, 53403

Tel: (414) 260-2000       Fax: (414) 260-2133       www.scjohnsonwax.com

*Home, auto, commercial and personal care products and specialty chemicals.*

**S.C. Johnson & Son Ltd.,  PO Box 237, Kanagawa-ken 259-01, Japan**

## JOHNSON CONTROLS INC.

5757 N. Green Bay Ave., PO Box 591, Milwaukee, WI, 53201-0591

Tel: (414) 228-1200       Fax: (414) 228-2077       www.johnsoncontrols.com

*Mfr. facility management and control systems and auto seating.*

**Johnson Controls SA/NV,  Shin-Hitokuchizaka Bldg., 3-9 Kudankita 3-chome, Chiyoda-ku Tokyo, Japan**

Tel: 81-3-3230-7222   Fax: 81-3-3230-7335   Contact: Marshall Grayson, Branch Mgr.

## THE JOHNSON CORPORATION

805 Wood Street, Three Rivers, MI, 49093

Tel:  (616) 278-1715       Fax: (616) 273-2230       www.joco.com

*Mfr. rotary joints and siphon systems.*

**The Nippon Joint Ltd.,  Kyoto, Japan**

## JOHNSON OUTDOORS, INC.

1326 Willow Road, Sturtevant, WI, 53177

Tel: (414) 884-1500       Fax: (414) 884-1600       www.jwa.com

*Mfr. diving, fishing, boating and camping sports equipment.*

**JWA Asia,  3-14-19 Arima Miyamae-ku, Kawasaki 216, Japan**

Tel: 81-44-854-1211   Fax: 81-44-877-1004

## JONES LANG LASALLE

101 East 52nd Street, New York, NY, 10022

Tel: (212) 688-8181       Fax: (212) 308-5199       www.jlw.com

*International marketing consultants, leasing agents and property management advisors.*

**Jones Lang Wootton,  Japan**

## JONES, DAY, REAVIS & POGUE

North Point, 901 Lakeside Ave., Cleveland, OH, 44114

Tel: (216) 586-3939       Fax: (216) 579-0212       www.jonesday.com

*International law firm.*

**Jones, Day, Reavis & Pogue Gaikokuho Jimu Bengoshi Jimusho,  Toranomon 45 Mori Bldg. 3/F, 1-5 Toranomon 5-chome, Minato-ku Tokyo 105-0001, Japan**

Tel: 81-3-3433-3939   Fax: 81-3-5401-2725   Contact: John C. Roebuck, Partner   Emp: 4

## JUKI UNION SPECIAL CORPORATION

5 Haul Road, Wayne, NJ, 07470

Tel: (973) 633-7200       Fax: (973) 633-9629       www.unionspecial.com

*Mfr. sewing machines.*

**Union Special Japan Ltd.,  1-5-17 Mikuni-Honmachi, Yodogawa-ku, Osaka 532, Japan**

**UNSP Japan Ltd.,  3-17-18 Tarumi-Cho, Suita-Shi, Osaka 564, Japan**

Tel: 81-6-339-2491   Fax: 81-6-339-2492

## JUPITER MEDIA METRIX INC.

21 Astor Place, New York, NY, 10003

Tel: (212) 780-6060 Fax: (212) 780-6075 www.jmm.com

*Engaged in research services to determine audience measurement.*

**Jupiter Media Metrix KK, 1-11-3 Akasaka, Reinanzaka Annex 4/F, Minato-ku Tokyo 107-0052, Japan**

Tel: 81-3-5549-2027

## K-2, INC.

4900 South Eastern Ave., Los Angeles, CA, 90040

Tel: (323) 724-2800 Fax: (323) 724-8174 www.k2sports.com

*Mfr. sporting goods, recreational and industrial products.*

**K2 Japan, A-4/F - Nishisando-Yamaki Bldg., 3-28-6 Yoyogi Shibuya-Ku, Tokyo 151-0053, Japan**

Tel: 81-3-3320-7822

## KATHABAR SYSTEMS INC.

370 Campus Drive, Somerset, NJ, 08873

Tel: (732) 356-6000 Fax: (732) 356-0643 www.kathabar.com

*Mfr./distribute dehumidification equipment.*

**Casco, 1-16-24 Nonaka Kita, Yodogawa-ku, Osaka 532, Japan**

Tel: 81-6-399-2671 Fax: 81-6-399-2672 Contact: Minoru Fukada

## KAYDON CORPORATION

315 E. Eisenhower Pkwy., Ste. 300, Ann Arbor, MI, 48108-3330

Tel: (734) 747-7025 Fax: (734) 747-6565 www.kaydon.com

*Design/mfr. custom engineered products: bearings, rings, seals, etc.*

**Kimura Corporation, Tokyo, Japan**

Tel: 81-3-3213-0255

## A.T. KEARNEY INC.

222 West Adams Street, Chicago, IL, 60606

Tel: (312) 648-0111 Fax: (312) 223-6200 www.atkearney.com

*Management consultants and executive search.*

**A. T. Kearney K. K., ARK Mori Bldg. 12-32, Akasaka 1-chome, Minato-ku, Tokyo 107 Japan**

Tel: 81-3-5561-9155

## KEITHLEY INSTRUMENTS INC.

28775 Aurora Road, Cleveland, OH, 44139

Tel: (440) 248-0400 Fax: (440) 248-6168 www.keithley.com

*Mfr. electronic test/measure instruments, PC-based data acquisition hardware/software.*

**Keithley Instruments/ NF Corporation, 3-20 Tsunashima-Higashi, 6-Chome Kohoku-Ku, Yokohama Japan**

**Keithley Instruments/Toyo Corporation, 1-6 Yaesu 1-chome, Chuo-ku Tokyo 103-8284, Japan**

Tel: 81-3-3279-0771

## KELLOGG BROWN & ROOT INC.

PO Box 3, Houston, TX, 77001

Tel: (713) 676-3011 Fax: (713) 676-8695 www.halliburton.com

*Engaged in technology-based engineering and construction.*

**Kellogg Brown & Root, Kamiyacho Mori Building 3/F, 3-20 Toranomon 4-Chome, Minato-ku Tokyo 105-0001, Japan**

**Kellogg Brown & Root Far East Inc., Kamiyacho Mori Bldg. 3/F, 3-20 Toranomon 4-Chome Minato-ku, Tokyo 105-0001, Japan**

Tel: 81-3-5776-2301 Contact: Peter Hedges, VP

**Kellogg Brown & Root KK,** Maruyama Bldg. 5F, 3-8 Azabudai 2-chome, Minato-ku, Tokyo 106 Japan

## KELLOGG COMPANY

One Kellogg Square, PO Box 3599, Battle Creek, MI, 49016-3599

Tel: (616) 961-2000      Fax: (616) 961-2871      www.kelloggs.com

*Mfr. ready-to-eat cereals and convenience foods.*

**Kellogg (Japan) KK,** Attn: Japanese Office, One Kellogg Square, PO Box 3599, Battle Creek MI 49016-3599

## THE KENDALL COMPANY (TYCO HEALTHCARE)

15 Hampshire Street, Mansfield, MA, 02048

Tel: (508) 261-8000      Fax: (508) 261-8542      www.kendalhq,com

*Mfr. medical disposable products, home health care products and specialty adhesive products.*

**Nihon Kendall K.K. (Kendall Japan Ltd.),** UK Hongo 4F, 3-44-2 Hongo Bunkyo-ku, Tokyo 113, Japan

Tel: 81-3-5684-0451    Fax: 81-3-5684-0450

## KENNAMETAL INC.

State Rte. 981, Latrobe, PA, 15650

Tel: (724) 539-5000      Fax: (724) 539-4710      www.kennametal.com

*Tools, hard carbide and tungsten alloys for metalworking industry.*

**Kennametal Hertel Japan Ltd. - Head Office,** Ma Bldg. 4F, 2-15-12 Kiba, Koto-ku, Tokyo 135 Japan

Tel: 81-3-3820-2888    Fax: 81-3-3820-2800

**Kennametal Hertel Japan Ltd. - Nagoya Office,** 2-177 Hongo, Meito-kul Nagoya 465, Japan

Tel: 81-52-776-6581    Fax: 81-52-776-6566

**Kennametal Hertel Japan Ltd. - Osaka Office,** Kanehira Bldg., 1-10-7 Itachbori, Nishi-ku, Osaka 550 Japan

Tel: 81-6-536-1314

## KENT-MOORE

28635 Mound Road, Ste. 335, Warren, MI, 48092-3499

Tel: (810) 578-7289      Fax: (810) 578-7375      www.spx.com

*Mfr. service equipment for auto, construction, recreational, military and agricultural vehicles.*

**Jatek,** Dai-Ni Maruzen Bldg. 8F, 9-2 Nihonbashi 3-chome, Chou-ku, Tokyo 103, Japan

## KEPNER-TREGOE INC.

PO Box 704, Princeton, NJ, 08542-0740

Tel: (609) 921-2806      Fax: (609) 497-0130      www.kepner-tregoe.com

*Management consulting; specializing in strategy formulation, problem solving, decision making, project management, and cost reduction.*

**Kepner-Tregoe (Japan) Inc.,** Moto-Akasaka Kikutei Bldg., 7-18 Moto-Akasaka 1-chome, Minato-ku, Tokyo 107, Japan

Tel: 81-3-3401-9521    Fax: 81-3-3479-0745

## KIDDE-FENWAL, INC.

400 Main Street, Ashland, MA, 01721

Tel: (508) 881-2000      Fax: (508) 881-6729      www.kidde-fenwal.com

*Temperature controls, ignition systems, fire/smoke detection and suppression systems.*

**Fenwal Controls of Japan Ltd.,** 3 Mori Bldg., 4-10 Nishi Shinbashi 1-chome, Minato-ku, Tokyo 105, Japan

## KIMBERLY-CLARK CORPORATION

351 Phelps Drive, Irving, TX, 75038

Tel: (972) 281-1200      Fax: (972) 281-1435      www.kimberly-clark.com

*Mfr./sales/distribution of consumer tissue, household and personal care products.*

**Kimberly-Clark Japan Ltd., Tokyo, Japan**

## KINKO'S, INC.

255 W. Stanley Ave., Ventura, CA, 93002-8000

Tel: (805) 652-4000      Fax: (805) 652-4347      www.kinkos.com

*Kinko's operates a 24-hour-a-day, global chain of photocopy stores.*

**Kinko's, 1-22-12, SVAX-TS Bldg., 1F, Toranomon, Minato-ku, Tokyo 105, Japan**
Tel: 81-3-3508-2644    Fax: 81-3-3508-2645

**Kinko's, 4-1-9 Minamisemba, Dai-Ichi, Toyo Bldg., Chuoh-ku, Osaka 542, Japan**
Tel: 81-6-245-1887    Fax: 81-6-258-0291

**Kinko's, 4-6 Chiyogaoka, Chikusa-ku, Nagoya 464, Japan**
Tel: 81-52-778-0871    Fax: 81-52-778-0778

**Kinko's, 2-5-58 Hakata Kaisei Bldg. 1F, Hakata Station Higashi, Hakata-ku, Fukuoka 100, Japan**
Tel: 81-92-414-3399    Fax: 81-92-414-3390

## KNOLL, INC.

1235 Water Street, East Greenville, PA, 18041

Tel: (215) 679-7991      Fax: (215) 679-3904      www.knoll.com

*Mfr. and sale of office furnishings.*

**Knoll Div./The Seibu Dept. Stores, Kokusai Bldg., 3-1-1 Marunouchi, Chiyoda-ku, Tokyo 100, Japan**
Tel: 81-3-3213-6767    Fax: 81-3-3213-1580

**Knoll International, Inc., 1-20 4-Chome Eda Nishi Aoba-Ku, Yokohama-Shi, Kanagawa-Ken, Japan**
Tel: 81-45-910-2403    Fax: 81-45-910-2404

## KNOWLES ELECTRONICS INC.

1151 Maplewood Drive, Itasca, IL, 60131

Tel: (630) 250-5100      Fax: (630) 250-0575      www.knowleselectronics.com

*Microphones and loudspeakers.*

**Knowles Electronics, Japan KK., Kyodo Bloom Building, 19-1 Miyasaka 2-chome, Setagaya-Ku, Tokyo 156 Japan**
Tel: 81-3-3439-1151    Fax: 81-3-3439-8822

## KOCH INDUSTRIES INC.

4111 East 37th Street North, Wichita, KS, 67220-3203

Tel: (316) 828-5500      Fax: (316) 828-5950      www.kochind.com

*Oil, financial services, agriculture and Purina Mills animal feed.*

**Koch International, Div. John Zink, KK, Recruit Shin-Otsuka Building 22-15, Minami-Otsuka 2 Chrome - Tochima-Ku, Tokyo 170 Japan**
Tel: 81-3-5978-5580    Fax: 81-3-3947-6551

## KOCH-GLITSCH, INC.

PO Box 8127, Wichita, KS, 67208

Tel: (316) 828-5110      Fax: (316) 828-5950      www.koch-ind.com

*Mfr./services mass transfer/chemicals separation equipment, process engineering.*

**Koch-Glitsch Japan, 3-1-4 Ikegamishincho, Kawasaki-ku, Kawasaki 210, Japan**
Tel: 81-44-287-1021    Fax: 81-44-287-1029    Contact: Akira Yanoma, Pres.

## THE KOHLER COMPANY

444 Highland Drive, Kohler, WI, 53044

Tel: (920) 457-4441     Fax: (920) 459-1274     www.kohlerco.com

*Plumbing products, ceramic tile and stone, cabinetry, furniture, engines, generators, switch gear and hospitality.*

**Kohler Engines, North Asia, Azanu Takahashi Bldg. 7F, 4-13-2 Minami-Aabu, Minato-ku, Tokyo, Japan 106**

Tel: 81-3-3440-4515   Fax: 81-3-3440-2727

**Kohler Japan KK, 4-13-2 Minami Azabu, Minato-ku, Tokyo 106, Japan**

Tel: 81-3-3440-4440   Fax: 81-3-3440-2727   Contact: Kakuo Hara, Sales Mgr.

**Kohler Power Systems International, Tokyo, Japan**

**Seidensha Electric Works Ltd., 1-2-23 Haramachida Machida-Shi, Tokyo 194, Japan**

Tel: 81-3-427-242471   Fax: 81-3-427-242478

## KOHN PEDERSEN FOX ASSOCIATES PC

111 West 57th Street, New York, NY, 10019

Tel: (212) 977-6500     Fax: (212) 956-2526     www.kpf.com

*Architectural design.*

**Kohn Pedersen Fox Associates KK, 2-17-42 Akasaka, Minato-ku, Tokyo 107, Japan**

## KORN/FERRY INTERNATIONAL

1800 Century Park East, Los Angeles, CA, 90067

Tel: (310) 843-4100     Fax: (310) 553-6452     www.kornferry.com

*Executive search; management consulting.*

**Korn/Ferry International Japan, AIG Bldg. 7/F, 1-3 Marunouchi 1-chome, Chiyoda-ku, Tokyo 100, Japan**

Tel: 81-3-3211-6851   Fax: 81-3-3216-1300

## KPMG INTERNATIONAL LLP

345 Park Avenue, New York, NY, 10022

Tel: (201) 307-7000     Fax: (201) 930-8617     www.kpmg.com

*Accounting and audit, tax and management consulting services.*

**Century Audit Corporation, Aqua Dojima East Tower 4-4, Dojimahama 1-chome, Osaka 530 Japan**

Tel: 81-6-346-7878   Fax: 81-6-346-7845   Contact: Yasushi Gorokawa, Ptnr.

**Century Audit Corporation, Kyoto, Japan**

**Century Audit Corporation, Nagoya, Japan**

**Century Audit Corporation, The Japan Red Cross Bldg. 1-3, Shiba Daimon 1-chome, Minato-ku, Tokyo 105 Japan**

Tel: 81-3-3578-1910   Fax: 81-3-3434-2122   Contact: Osamu Shigeta, Ptnr.

**Century Audit Corporation, Sapporo, Japan**

**Century Audit Corporation, Kobe, Japan**

**KPMG Peat Marwick International and Domestic Tax, SKF Bldg. 9-1, Shiba Daimon 1-chome, Minato-ku, Tokyo 105 Japan**

Tel: 81-3-5400-7300   Fax: 81-3-5400-7373   Contact: Takashi Kuboi, Ptnr.

**KPMG Peat Marwick Management Consulting & Corporate Finance, SKF Bldg. 9-1, Shiba Daimon 1-chome, Minato-ku, Tokyo 105 Japan**

Tel: 81-3-5400-7320   Fax: 81-2-5400-7330   Contact: Yoichi Kuze, Ptnr.

**KPMG Peat Marwick Project Japan, The Japan Red Cross Bldg., 1-3 Shiba Daimon 1-chome, Minato-ku, Tokyo 105 Japan**

## THE KROLL-O'GARA COMPANY

9113 Le Saint Drive, Fairfield, OH, 45014

Tel: (513) 874-2112 Fax: (513) 874-2558 www.kroll-ogara.com

*Security and consulting services and vehicles.*

**Kroll Associates (Asia) Ltd., AIG Bldg. 14F, 1-3 Marunouchi 1-chome, Choyoda-ku, Tokyo 100, Japan**

Tel: 81-3-3218-4558 Fax: 81-3-3218-7346

## K-SWISS INC.

31248 Oak Crest Dr., Westlake Village, CA, 91361

Tel: (818) 706-5100 Fax: (818) 706-5390 www.k-swiss.com

*Mfr. casual and athletic shoes, socks and leisure apparel.*

**K-Swiss Japan, Tokyo, Japan**

## KULICKE & SOFFA INDUSTRIES INC.

2101 Blair Mill Road, Willow Grove, PA, 19090

Tel: (215) 784-6000 Fax: (215) 659-7588 www.kns.com

*Semiconductor assembly systems and services.*

**Kulicke & Soffa (Japan) Ltd., 5 Koike Bldg. 3/F, 1-3-12 Kita-Shinagawa, Shinagawa-ku, Tokyo 140, Japan**

Tel: 81-3-5461-1520 Fax: 81-3-5461-1597 Contact: Terry Sawachi, Pres.

## KWIK LOK CORPORATION

PO Box 9548, Yakima, WA, 98909

Tel: (509) 248-4770 Fax: (509) 457-6531 www.kwiklok.com

*Mfr. bag closing machinery.*

**Kwik Lok Japan, 4-12 Motogo 2-Chome, Kawaguchi City, Saitama, Japan**

Tel: 81-48-224-1666 Fax: 81-48-225-3288

## LANDAUER INC.

2 Science Road, Glenwood, IL, 60425-1586

Tel: (708) 755-7000 Fax: (708) 755-7035 www.landauerinc.com

*Provider of radiation dosimetry services to hospitals, medical and dental offices, university and national laboratories, nuclear power plants and other industries.*

**Nagase Landauer Limited, 11-6 Hisamatsu-cho, Nihonbashi Chuo-ku, Tokyo 103-8487, Japan**

Tel: 81-3-3666-4300 Fax: 81-3-3662-9518 Contact: T. Iwai, Pres.

## LANDOR ASSOCIATES

Klamath House, 1001 Front Street, San Francisco, CA, 94111-1424

Tel: (415) 955-1400 Fax: (415) 365-3190 www.landor.com

*International marketing consulting firm, focused on developing and maintaining brand identity.*

**Landor Associates, Sogo Hirakawacho Bldg. 6F, 1-4-12 Hirakawacho, Chiyoda-ku, Tokyo 102 Japan**

Tel: 81-3-3263-2295 Fax: 81-3-3263-2291 Contact: Kazumoto Kawada, Mng. Dir.

## LANDS' END INC.

1 Lands' End Lane, Dodgeville, WI, 53595

Tel: (608) 935-9341 Fax: (608) 935-4260 www.landsend.com

*Clothing, home furnishings and mail order catalog company.*

**Lands' End Japan KK, Sun Hamada Bldg. 4F, 1-19-20 Shinyokohama, Tokyo 222 Japan**

Tel: 81-45-476-0830 Fax: 81-45-476-0836 Contact: John Butler, Pres. Emp: 250

## LATHAM & WATKINS

633 West 5th St., Ste. 4000,, Los Angeles, CA, 90071-2007

Tel: (213) 485-1234     Fax: (213) 891-8763     www.lw.com

*International law firm.*

**Latham & Watkins,  Infini Akasaka, 8-7-15 Akasaka, Minato-ku, Tokyo 107, Japan**

Tel: 81-3-3423-3981   Fax: 81-3-3423-3971

## LE TOURNEAU COMPANY

PO Box 2307, Longview, TX, 75606

Tel: (903) 237-7000     Fax: (903) 267-7032

*Mfr. heavy construction and mining machinery equipment.*

**C. Itoh & Co. Ltd.,  5-1 Kita-Aoyama 2-chome, Minato-ku, Tokyo, Japan**

## LEARNING TREE INTERNATIONAL, INC.

6053 West Century Blvd., Los Angeles, CA, 90045-0028

Tel: (310) 417-9700     Fax: (310) 417-8684     www.learningtree.com

*Information technology training services.*

**Learning Tree International KK (Japan),  Tohma Bldg. 6F, 2-1-2 Takadanobaba, Shinjuku-ku, Tokyo, Japan 169**

Tel: 81-3-5291-7391   Fax: 81-3-5291-7392   Contact: James Webb   Emp: 2

## LEARONAL INC.

272 Buffalo Ave., Freeport, NY, 11520

Tel: (516) 868-8800     Fax: (516) 868-8824     www.learonal.com

*Specialty chemicals for the printed circuit board, semiconductor, connector and metal finishing industries.*

**LeaRonal Japan,  14-5 Nihonbashi-Bakurocho 1-chome, Chuo-ku, Tokyo 103, Japan**

Tel: 81-33-639-2481   Fax: 82-33-639-2508   Contact: Tetsuya Kumita, Pres.

## LECROY CORPORATION

700 Chestnut Ridge Road, Chestnut Ridge, NY, 10977

Tel: (845) 425-2000     Fax: (845) 425-8967     www.lecroy.com

*Mfr. signal analyzers and electronic measurement systems.*

**LeCroy Japan Corporation,  Sasazuka Center Bldg. 6/F, 1-6 2 Chome, Sasazuka Shibuya-Ku, Tokyo, Japan**

Tel: 81-3--3376-9400

**LeCroy Japan Corporation,  Nakao Royal Bldg. 4/F, 14-10 2 Chome, Miyahara Yodogawa-Ku, Osaka City Osaka, Japan**

Tel: 81-6-6396-0961

## LEHMAN BROTHERS HOLDINGS INC.

Three World Financial Center, New York, NY, 10285

Tel: (212) 526-7000     Fax: (212) 526-3738     www.lehman.com

*Financial services, securities and merchant banking services.*

**Lehman Brothers - Asia-Pacific Hdqtrs.,  Ark Mori Building 36F, 12-32, Akasaka 1-Chrome, Minato-ku Tokyo 107, Japan**

Tel: 81-3-5571-7000   Fax: 81-3-5571-7900

## LEVI STRAUSS & COMPANY

1155 Battery St., San Francisco, CA, 94111-1230

Tel: (415) 544-6000     Fax: (415) 501-3939     www.levistrauss.com

*Mfr./distributor casual wearing apparel.*

**Levi Strauss Japan K.K.,  22F Yebisu Garden Place Tower, 20-3 Yebisu 4-chome, Shibuya-ku, Tokyo 150 Japan**

Tel: 81-3-5421-9200   Fax: 81-3-5421-9201

## LEXMARK INTERNATIONAL

1 Lexmark Centre Dr., Lexington, KY, 40550

Tel: (606) 232-2000     Fax: (606) 232-1886     www.lexmark.com

*Develop, manufacture, supply of printing solutions and products, including laser, inkjet, and dot matrix printers.*

**Lexmark International, Co, Ltd.,  Riverside Yomiuri Bldg., 36-2 Nihonbashi Hakozaki-cho Chuo-ku, Tokyo 103-0015 Japan**

Tel: 81-3-5649-0222   Fax: 81-3-5649-0230

## LIBERTY MUTUAL GROUP

175 Berkeley Street, Boston, MA, 02117

Tel: (617) 357-9500     Fax: (617) 350-7648     www.libertymutual. com

*Provides workers' compensation insurance and operates physical rehabilitation centers and provides risk prevention management.*

**Liberty International Japan,  Kamiyacho Mori Bldg. 5-F, 4-3-20 Toranomon, Minato-ku, Tokyo 105, Japan**

Tel: 81-3-3431-5575

## LIFE TECHNOLOGIES INC.

9800 Medical Center Drive, Rockville, MD, 20850

Tel: (301) 840-8000     Fax: (301) 329-8635     www.lifetech.com

*Produces biotechnology research materials.*

**Life Technologies Oriental KK (JV),  Nihonbashi Hama-Cho Park Bldg 4/F, 2-35-4 Hama-Cho Nihonbashi, Chuo-Ku, Tokyo 103-0007 Japan**

## ELI LILLY & COMPANY

Lilly Corporate Center, Indianapolis, IN, 46285

Tel: (317) 276-2000     Fax: (317) 277-6579     www.lilly.com

*Mfr. pharmaceuticals and animal health products.*

**Eli Lilly Japan KK,  Shin Aoyama Bldg. West 21F, 1-1 Minaniaoyama, 1-chome Minato-ku, Tokyo 107 Japan**

Tel: 81-3-3470-8230   Fax: 81-3-3470-8259

**Eli Lilly Japan KK,  Sannomiya Plaza Bldg., 7-1-5 Isogami-dori, Chuo-ku, Kobe 651 Japan**

Tel: 81-78-242-9000   Fax: 81-78-242-9502

## LINCOLN ELECTRIC HOLDINGS

22801 St. Clair Ave., Cleveland, OH, 44117-1199

Tel: (216) 481-8100     Fax: (216) 486-8385     www.lincolnelectric.com

*Mfr. arc welding and welding related products, oxy-fuel and thermal cutting equipment and integral AC motors.*

**Nippon Lincoln Electric K.K.,  6/F Kasuga Bldg., 4-24-5 Hongo Bunkyo, Tokyo 113, Japan**

Tel: 81-3-3813-6410   Fax: 81-3-3818-3208   Contact: Masaaki Suko, Mng. Dir.

**Nippon Lincoln Electric KK,  1-45 Aza-Nakamaru, Ohaza-Yamadaoka, Naraha-Machi Futaba-Gun, Fukushima-Ken 979-05 Japan**

## LINEAR TECHNOLOGY CORPORATION

1630 McCarthy Blvd., Milpitas, CA, 95035

Tel: (408) 432-1900     Fax: (408) 434-6441     www.linear-tech.com

*Mfr. linear integrated circuit chips.*

**Linear Technology KK,  5/F NAO Building, 1-14 Shin-Ogawa-Machi, Shinjuku-Ku, Tokyo 162-0814, Japan**

Tel: 81-3-3267-7891   Fax: 81-3-3267-8510

## ARTHUR D. LITTLE, INC.

25 Acorn Park, Cambridge, MA, 02140-2390

Tel: (617) 498-5000    Fax: (617) 498-7200    www.adlittle.com

*Management, environmental, health and safety consulting; technical and product development.*

**Arthur D. Little (Japan) Inc., Fukide Bldg., 4-1-13 Toranomon, Minato-ku, Tokyo 105, Japan**

Tel: 81-3-3436-2196   Fax: 81-3-3436-0092

## LITTON INDUSTRIES INC.

21240 Burbank Boulevard, Woodland Hills, CA, 91367

Tel: (818) 598-5000    Fax: (818) 598-3313    www.littoncorp.com

*Shipbuilding, electronics, and information technology.*

**Litton Industries Far East, 2-1-2 Marunouchi, Chiyoda-ku, Tokyo 100 Japan**

**Litton Marine Systems, Romco Building - 16-5 Misuji 1-chome, Taito-ku Tokyo, 111-0055 Japan**

Tel: 81-3-3863-7401

## LOCKHEED MARTIN CORPORATION

6801 Rockledge Drive, Bethesda, MD, 20817

Tel: (301) 897-6000    Fax: (301) 897-6652    www.imco.com

*Design/mfr./management systems in fields of space, defense, energy, electronics and technical services.*

**CalComp, Sumitomo Shoji Nagoya, Marunouchi Bldg., 3-5 1 Marunouchi Naka-ku, Nagoya 460 Japan**

Tel: 81-52-853-4011   Fax: 81-52-853-4031

**CalComp, Sumitomo Seimei Hakata Building, 3-2-8 Hakata-Ekimae Hakata-ku, Fukuoka 812, Japan**

Tel: 81-92-474-5761

**CalComp Japan Procurement Office, 3-6-3 Irifune, Chou-ku, Tokyo 104, Japan**

Tel: 81-3-3555-8917   Fax: 81-3-3555-8575

**Lockheed Fort Worth Intl. Corp., Misawa Air Base, Misawa City, Japan**

Tel: 81-3-3117-66-2917   Fax: 81-3117-62-7388   Contact: D. L. Berry, Mgr.

**Lockheed Martin Aero & Naval Systems Office, c/o Mitsubishi Heavy Industries Ltd., 101 Akunoura-Machi, Nagasaki 850-91 Japan**

Tel: 81-958-28-5753   Fax: 81-958-28-5721   Contact: B. Medina, Office Mgr.

**Lockheed Martin Global, Inc., Imperial Tower 9/F, 1-1-1- Uchisaiwaicho Chiyoda-ku, Tokyo 100-0011 Japan**

Tel: 81-3-3412-2210   Fax: 81-3-3419-8557   Contact: Arlo A. Brown VP

**Lockheed Martin Intl. Ltd., Akasaka Twin Tower 15F, 2-17-2 Akasaka Minato-ku, Tokyo 107, Japan**

Tel: 81-33-584-7011   Fax: 81-33-584-7083   Contact: M. Ikehata, Mgr.

**Lockheed Martin Intl. Ltd., Haneda Dai-Ichi Sogo Building 6-6, 1 Chome Haneda Kuko Ota-ku, Tokyo 144, Japan**

Tel: 81-33-747-5747   Fax: 81-33-747-1682   Contact: G. R. Racy, Mgr.

**Lockheed Martin Intl. Ltd., Kowa Building 5F, 1-14-14 Akasaka Minato-ku, Tokyo 107, Japan**

Tel: 81-3-3588-5232   Fax: 81-3-3588-5262   Contact: A. A. Brown, VP

**NS CalComp Corp., 2-3-1 Shintomi, Chuo Ku, Tokyo 104 Japan**

Tel: 81-3-3555-8911   Fax: 81-3-3555-8913

## LOCTITE CORPORATION

1001 Trout Brook Crossing, Rocky Hill, CT, 06067-3910

Tel: (860) 571-5100    Fax: (860) 571-5465    www.loctite.com

*Mfr./sale industrial adhesives, sealants and coatings..*

**Loctite (Japan) Corp., 15-13 Fukuura 1-chome, Kanazawa-ku, Yokohama 236, Japan**

Tel: 81-45-784-5883   Contact: Toru Yoden, Mgr.

## LORD CORPORATION

2000 West Grandview Blvd, Erie, PA, 16514

Tel: (814) 868-0924    Fax: (814) 486-4345    www.chemlok.com

*Adhesives, coatings, chemicals, film products.*

**Lord Far East Inc., 903 Kowa Bldg., 15-21 Nishi Azabu 4-chome, Minato-ku, Tokyo 106, Japan**

**Special Paint Co. Ltd., 4-15-1 Higashiogu, Arakawa-ku, Tokyo, Japan**

**Sunstar Chemical Inc., 7-1 Aketa-cho, Takatsuki, Osaka 569, Japan**

## LOWE LINTAS & PARTNERS WORLDWIDE

One Dag Hammarskjold Plaza, New York, NY, 10017

Tel: (212) 605-8000    Fax: (212) 605-4705    www.interpublic.com

*Full-service, integrated marketing communications company/advertising agency.*

**Hakuhodo Lintas Japan KK, Granpark Tower 4-1, Shibaura 3-chome, Minato-ku, Tokyo 108 Japan**

Tel: 81-3-5446-7640   Fax: 81-5446-7676   Contact: Richard Buddle

## LSI LOGIC CORPORATION

1551 McCarthy Blvd, Milpitas, CA, 95035

Tel: (408) 433-8000    Fax: (408) 954-3220    www.lsilogic.com

*Develop/mfr. semiconductors.*

**LSI Logic KK, Rivage-Shinagawa Building 14F, 4-1-8 Kounan Minato-ku, Tokyo 108, Japan**

Tel: 81-3-5463-7821   Fax: 81-3-5463-7820

**LSI Logic KK., 1-2-27 Shiromi, Chou-ku, Osaka 540, Japan**

Tel: 81-6-947-5281   Fax: 81-6-947-5287

## LTV CORPORATION

200 Public Square, Cleveland, OH, 44114-2308

Tel: (216) 622-5000    Fax: (216) 622-1066    www.ltvsteel.com

*Mfr. integrated and flat rolled steel.*

**LTV Steel Company, Tokyo, Japan**

## LTX CORPORATION

LTX Park, University Ave., Westwood, MA, 02090

Tel: (617) 461-1000    Fax: (617) 326-4883    www.ltx.com

*Design/mfr. computer-controlled semiconductor test systems.*

**LTX Asia International Inc., Kamata K-1 Building - 3/F, 5-8-7 Kamata Ota-ku, Tokyo 144-0052, Japan**

Tel: 81-3-3739-8011   Fax: 81-3-3739-8017

## THE LUBRIZOL CORPORATION

29400 Lakeland Blvd., Wickliffe, OH, 44092-2298

Tel: (440) 943-4200    Fax: (440) 943-5337    www.lubrizol.com

*Mfr. chemicals additives for lubricants and fuels.*

**Lubrizol Japan Ltd., Mori Bldg. 5F, 23-7 Toranomon 1-chome, Minato-ku, Tokyo 105, Japan**

Tel: 81-3- 5401-4170

## LUCENT NPS (NETWORK CARE PROFESSIONAL SERVICES)

1213 Innsbruck Dr., Sunnyvale, CA, 94089

Tel: (408) 542-0100    Fax: (408) 542-0101    www.ins.com

*Provides computer network support, designs networking systems, manages equipment purchase performance and software solutions.*

**Lucent NetworkCare, 19/F Shinjuku Daiichiseimei Bldg., 2-7-1 Nishi-Shinjuku, Shinjuku-ku, Tokyo 163-0719, Japan**

Tel: 813-5325-7591

## LUCENT TECHNOLOGIES, INC.

600 Mountain Ave., Murray Hill, NJ, 07974-0636

Tel: (908) 582-3000    Fax: (908) 582-2576    www.lucent.com

*Design/mfr. wide range of public and private networks, communication systems and software, data networking systems, business telephone systems and microelectronics components.*

**Lucent Technologies Japan Ltd., Mori Bldg. #25, 4-30 Roppongi 1-chome, Minatoku, Tokyo 106 Japan**

Tel: 81-3-5561-3000    Fax: 81-3-5561-3113    Contact: Teizo Hotto, PR Mgr.

## LYDALL INC.

1 Colonial Road, PO Box 151, Manchester, CT, 06040

Tel: (860) 646-1233    Fax: (860) 646-4917    www.lydall.com

*Mfr. converted paper products, paperboard, non-woven specialty media.*

**Lydall Intl. Inc., Rippongi SK Bldg., 3-15 Rippongi 3-chome, Minato-ku, Tokyo 106, Japan**

## LYONDELL

3801 West Chester Pike, Newtown Square, PA, 19073-2387

Tel: (610) 359-2000    Fax: (610) 359-2722    www.arcochem.com

*Mfr. propylene oxide, a chemical used for flexible foam products, coatings/paints and solvents/inks.*

**ARCO Chemical Japan, Inc., Kioicho Bldg. 4F, 3-12 Kioicho, Chiyoda-ku, Tokyo 102 Japan**

Tel: 81-3-3264-9010    Fax: 81-3-3264-9015

**Nihon Oxirane Company Ltd., No. 2 Yanagiya Bldg., 1-12-8 Nihonbashi, Chou-ku, Tokyo 103 Japan**

Tel: 81-3-3273-0401    Fax: 81-3-3271-6050

## LYONDELL CHEMICAL COMPANY

1221 McKinney St., Houston, TX, 77010

Tel: (713) 652-7200    Fax: (713) 309-2074    www.lyondell.com

*Mfr. polymers and petrochemicals.*

**Nihon Oxirane Company Limited, No. 2 Yanaglya Bldg., 1-12-8 Nihonbashi, Chou-ku Tokyo 103, Japan**

Tel: 81-3-3272-0401

## M/A-COM INC.

1011 Pawtucket Boulevard, Lowell, MA, 01853-3295

Tel: (978) 442-5000    Fax: (978) 442-5354    www.macom.com

*Mfr. electronic components, semiconductor devices and communications equipment.*

**AMP Japan, Ltd. M/A-COM, 5-8 Hisamoto 3 Chome, Takatsu-Ku, Kawasaki 213-8535 Japan**

Tel: 81-44-844-8296    Fax: 81-44-844-8298

**AMP Japan, Ltd. M/A-COM, 4-11 Minami Tsukaguchi Cho 2-Chome, Amagasaki City Hyogo-Ken 661-0012, Japan**

Tel: 81-6-6423-4351    Fax: 81-6-6423-2526

## MacDERMID INC.

245 Freight Street, Waterbury, CT, 06702-0671

Tel: (203) 575-5700    Fax: (203) 575-7900    www.macdermid.com

*Chemicals processing for metal industrial, plastics, electronics cleaners, strippers.*

**Nippon MacDermid Co. Ltd., 35-5 Sakuradai, Midori-ku, Yokohama-Shi, Kanagawa-Kan 227, Japan**

Tel: 81-45-984-2262    Fax: 81-45-984-1365

## R.H. MACY & COMPANY INC.

151 West 34th Street, New York, NY, 10001

Tel: (212) 695-4400    Fax: (212) 643-1307    www.macys.com

*Department stores; importers.*

**R.H. Macy & Co. Inc., Daiwa Bank Semba Bldg. 6/F, Minami-ku, Osaka 542, Japan**

## MALLINCKRODT INC.

675 McDonnell Blvd., St. Louis, MO, 63134

Tel: (314) 654-2000      Fax: (314) 654-5380      www.mallinckrodt.com

*Distributes health care products and specialty pharmaceuticals.*

**Mallinckrodt Japan Co., Ltd, 3-31 Ichigayanakano-cho, Shinjuku-ku, Tokyo 162-0064 Japan**

Tel: 81-3-5363-5700    Fax: 81-3-5379-5816

**Mallinckrodt Japan Co., Ltd, 236 Sanjyo-machi, Takamatsu City, Kagawa 761-8072 Japan**

Tel: 81-878-68-2201    Fax: 81-878-68-2205

**Mallinckrodt Japan Co., Ltd, 6-2-6 Ohdorinishi, Chuo-ku Sapporo City, Hokkaido 060-0042 Japan**

Tel: 81-11-210-7707    Fax: 81-11-241-8450

**Mallinckrodt Japan Co., Ltd, 8-23 Tsunaba-cho, Hakata-ku Fukuoka City, Fukuoka 812-0024 Japan**

Tel: 81-92-271-0408    Fax: 81-92-271-0277

**Mallinckrodt Japan Co., Ltd, 3-9-25 Danbara, Minami-ku Hiroshima City, Hiroshima 732-0811 Japan**

Tel: 81-82-262-7871    Fax: 81-82-262-9930

**Mallinckrodt Japan Co., Ltd, 1-5-1 Ohyodo-minami, Kita-ku Osaka City, Osaka Japan**

Tel: 81-6-6455-8900    Fax: 81-6-6455-8904

**Mallinckrodt Japan Co., Ltd, 11- 106-gaiku Sainen-machi Kanazawa City, Ishikawa 920-0026 Japan**

Tel: 81-762-32-4450    Fax: 81-762-32-4451

**Mallinckrodt Japan Co., Ltd, 10-20 Futsuka-machi, Aoba-ku Sendai City, Miyagi 980-0802 Japan**

Tel: 81-22-211-6422    Fax: 81-22-211-6425

**Mallinckrodt Japan Co., Ltd., 3-1203-2 Takahari, Meito-ku Nagoya City, Aichi 465-0061 Japan**

Tel: 81-52-709-3730    Fax: 81-52-709-3732

## MANPOWER INTERNATIONAL INC.

5301 N. Ironwood Rd., PO Box 2053, Milwaukee, WI, 53201-2053

Tel: (414) 961-1000      Fax: (414) 961-7081      www.manpower.com

*Temporary help, contract service, training and testing.*

**Manpower Japan Co. Ltd., CS Tower 3/F, 11-30 Akasaka 1-chome, Minato-ku, Tokyo 107, Japan**

Tel: 81-3-5570-5139    Fax: 81-3-5570-5148

## MARCONI DATA SYSTEMS, INC.

1500 Mittel Blvd., Wood Dale, IL, 60191

Tel: (630) 860-7300      Fax: (630) 616-3657      www.videojet.com

*Mfr. computer peripherals and hardware, state-of-the-art industrial ink jet marking and coding products.*

**Marconi Data Systems, Tetsuya Kawashima, Karasuma 2-JYO Agaru, Kakagyouko Kyoto 604, Japan**

Tel: 81-75-256-7288    Fax: 81-75-256-7288

## MARK IV INDUSTRIES INC.

501 John James Audubon Pkwy., PO Box 810, Amherst, NY, 14226-0810

Tel: (716) 689-4972      Fax: (716) 689-1529      www.mark-iv.com

*Mfr. of engineered systems and components utilizing mechanical and fluid power transmission, fluid transfer, and power systems and components.*

**Dayco Products, Inc., 502 Sannomiya First Bldg., 3-2-11 Isobe-dori, Chuo-ku, Kobe 651 Japan**

Tel: 81-78-251-0170    Fax: 81-78-221-2663

## MARKEM CORPORATION

150 Congress Street, Keene, NH, 03431

Tel: (603) 352-1130      Fax: (603) 357-1835      www.markem.com.

*Mfr./sales of industrial marking, print machinery and hot stamping foils.*

**Markem K.K., 2-19-7 Hatagaya, Shibuya-ku, Tokyo 151, Japan**

Tel: 81-3-5350-3051    Fax: 81-3-5350-3148

## MARLEY COOLING TOWER COMPANY

7401 West 129th Street, Overland Park, KS, 66213

Tel: (913) 664-7400     Fax: (913) 664-7641     www.marleyct.com

*Cooling and heating towers and waste treatment systems.*

**Marley Japan Kabushiki Kaisha (MJKK), Watanabe Building 3/F, 2-2 Miyamae-cho Kawasaki-ku, Kawasaki 210-0012, Japan**

Tel: 81-44-221-1018   Fax: 81-44-221-2019

## MARRIOTT INTERNATIONAL INC.

10400 Fernwood Rd., Bethesda, MD, 20817

Tel: (301) 380-3000     Fax: (301) 380-5181     www.marriott.com

*Hotel services.*

**Hotel New Otani Makuhari, Chiba, Japan**

Tel: 81-3-5405-1511

**Hotel New Otani Tokyo, Tokyo, Japan**

Tel: 81-3-5405-1511

## MARSH & McLENNAN COS INC.

1166 Ave. of the Americas, New York, NY, 10036-2774

Tel: (212) 345-5000     Fax: (212) 345-4808     www.marshmac.com

*Insurance agents/brokers, pension and investment management consulting services.*

**Marsh & McLennan Japan Ltd., Tokyo Opera City 38F, 3-20-2 Nishi-shinjuku, Shinjuku-ku, Tokyo 163-1438 Japan**

Tel: 81-35-334-8200   Fax: 81-35-371-4527   Contact: Phillip A. Grattan

**Marsh & McLennan Japan Ltd., Captain Bldg. 7F, 3-5-14 Kita-Kyuhoji-machi, Chou-ku, Osaka 541 Japan**

Tel: 81-6-243-4002   Fax: 81-6-243-4005   Contact: Phillip A, Grattan

## MASTERCARD INTERNATIONAL INC.

200 Purchase Street, Purchase, NY, 10577

Tel: (914) 249-2000     Fax: (914) 249-5475     www.mastercard.com

*Provides financial payment systems globally.*

**MasterCard International Inc., Dai-Tokyo Kasai Shinjuku Bldg. 16F, 25-3 Yoyogi 3-chome, Shibuya-ku, Tokyo 151 Japan**

## MAXTOR CORPORATION

510 Cottonwood Drive, Milpitas, CA, 95035-7403

Tel: (408) 432-1700     Fax: (408) 432-4510     www.maxtor.com

*Mfr. develops and markets hard disk drives for desktop computer systems.*

**Maxtor (Japan) Ltd., Shinjuku Monolith 21F, PO Box 7013, 3-1 Nishi-Shinjuku 2-chome Shinjuku-ku, Tokyo 163-09 Japan**

Tel: 81-3-3345-6990   Fax: 81-3-3345-6999

## MAYFRAN INTERNATIONAL, INC.

PO Box 43038, Cleveland, OH, 44143

Tel: (440) 461-4100     Fax: (440) 461-5565     www.mayfran.com

*Mfr. conveying systems, filtration equipment and separators that facilitate material handling and coolant recovery for automobile manufacturers and machine tool builders.*

**Mayfran Japan KK, 3-4 Kudankita 3-Chome, Chiyoda-ku, 102 Tokyo, Japan**

**Mayfran Japan KK, Ryokuchi-Eki Building, 4-1 Terauchi 2-chome, Toyonaka 560, Osaka Japan**

**Tsubakimoto Mayfran Inc., 5001 Ohno, Tsuchiyama-cho, Kouga-gun, Shiga 528-02, Japan**

Tel: 81-7-486-7-1001   Fax: 81-7-486-7-1097

## MBIA INC.

113 King Street, Armonk, NY, 10504

Tel: (914) 273-4545    Fax: (914) 765-3299    www.mbia.com

*Provides investment and treasury management services and insurance for municipal bonds.*

**MBIA-AMBAC International,  Shiroyama JT Mori Bldg. 16/F, 4-3-1 Toranomon Minato-ku, Tokyo 105, Japan**

Tel: 81-3-5403-4625    Contact: Steve Halpert

## McCANN-ERICKSON WORLDGROUP

750 Third Ave., New York, NY, 10017

Tel: (212) 984-3644    Fax: (212) 984-2629    www.mccann.com

*International advertising and marketing services.*

**McCann-Erickson Hakuhodo Inc.,  PO Box 90, Tokyo 107-91, Japan**

## McCORMICK & COMPANY, INC.

18 Loveton Circle, Sparks, MD, 21152-6000

Tel: (410) 771-7301    Fax: (410) 527-8289    www.mccormick.com

*Manufactures, markets and distributes spices, seasonings, flavours and other specialty food products.*

**McCormick-Lion Ltd. (JV),  1-3-7 Honjo, Sumida-ku, Tokyo 130, Japan**

Tel: 81-3-3621-6202    Fax: 81-3-3621-6669

**Stange (Japan) KK,  5-3 Kayabacho 3-chome, Nihonbashi, Chuo-ku, Tokyo 103, Japan**

## McDONALD'S CORPORATION

McDonald's Plaza, Oak Brook, IL, 60523

Tel: (630) 623-3000    Fax: (630) 623-7409    www.mcdonalds.com

*Fast food chain stores.*

**McDonald's Corp.,  Tokyo, Japan**

## THE McGRAW-HILL COMPANIES

1221 Ave. of the Americas, New York, NY, 10020

Tel: (212) 512-2000    Fax: (212) 512-2703    www.mccgraw-hill.com

*Books, magazines, information systems, financial service, publishing and broadcast operations.*

**McGraw-Hill Book Co., Japan,  20/F 1-1-7, Uchisaiwaicho Chiyoda-ku, Tokyo 100-0011, Japan**

Tel: 81-3-3593-8767

**McGraw-Hill Kogakusha Ltd.,  77 Bldg. 7/F, 14-11 Ginza 4-chome, Chuo-ku, Tokyo 104, Japan**

## McKINSEY & COMPANY

55 East 52nd Street, New York, NY, 10022

Tel: (212) 446-7000    Fax: (212) 446-8575    www.mckinsey.com

*Management and business consulting services.*

**McKinsey & Company,  Sakaisujihonmachi Ctr. Bldg., 1-6 Honmachi 2-chome, Chuo-ku, 541 Osaka, Japan**

Tel: 81-6-267-7400    Fax: 81-6-267-7423

**McKinsey & Company,  Roppongi First Bldg. 9F, 9-9 Roppongi 1-chome, Minato-ku, Tokyo 106, Japan**

Tel: 81-3-5562-2100    Fax: 81-3-5562-2200

## MCS SOFTWARE CORPORATION

815 Colorado Blvd., Los Angeles, CA, 90041

Tel: (323) 258-9111    Fax: (323) 259-3838    www.macsch.com

*Develop finite element analysis software used in the field of computer-aided engineering.*

**MSC Japan Ltd.,  Entsuji-Gadelius Bldg., 2-39 Akasaka 5-chome, Minato-ku, Tokyo 107, Japan**

**Nippon PDA Engineering KK,  Madre Matsuda Bldg. 4/F, 4-13 Kioi-cho, Chiyoda-ku, Tokyo 102, Japan**

## MEAD CORPORATION

Courthouse Plaza, NE, Dayton, OH, 45463

Tel: (937) 495-6323      Fax: (937) 461-2424      www.mead.com

*Mfr. paper, packaging, pulp, lumber and other wood products, school and office products; electronic publishing and distribution.*

**Mead KK, 2-10-12 Shibadaimon, Minato-ku, Tokyo 105, Japan**

Tel: 81-3-5401-5828   Fax: 81-3-5401-5831   Contact: Yutaka Suzuki, Rep. Dir.

## MECHANICAL DYNAMICS, INC.

2301 Commonwealth Blvd., Ann Arbor, MI, 48105

Tel: (734) 994-3800      Fax: (734) 994-6418      www.adams.com

*Mfr. Adams prototyping software to automotive industry.*

**Argo Graphics, Nihonbasi Chuou-Ku, Tokyo 10-0015, Japan**

Contact: Massayuki Fukunago

**Kozo Deikaku Engineering Inc., 4-5-3 Chuo, Kakano-Ku, Tokyo 164-0011 Japan**

**Mechanical Dynamics Japan, K.K., BABA Bldg. 6/F, 3-8-4 Nishi-Shinjuku, Sinjuku-ku Tokyo Japan**

Tel: 81-3-5354-7381

**Osaka Shipbuiding Co., Ltd., 3-1-202 Fukuzaki Minato-ku, Osaka 552, Japan**

## MEDICUS GROUP INTERNATIONAL

1675 Broadway, New York, NY, 10019

Tel: (212) 468-3100      Fax: (212) 468-3222      www.medicusgroup.com

*Healthcare communications company engaged in professional advertising, sales promotion, global branding and launch planning.*

**Medicus KK, Shinanomachi Rengakan 4/F, 35 Shinanomachi, Shinjuku-ku Tokyo 160-0016, Japan**

Tel: 81-3-5361-2750

**Medicus KK, Yasui Bldg. - 6/F, 6-8 Hiranomachi 1-chome, Chuo-ku Osaka 541-0046, Japan**

Tel: 81-66-208-0020

## MEDTRONIC INC.

7000 Central Ave., NE, Minneapolis, MN, 55432

Tel: (612) 574-4000      Fax: (612) 574-4879      www.medtronic.com

*Mfr./sale/service electrotherapeutic medical devices.*

**Medtronic Japan Co. Ltd., Shuwa Kioi-cho Park Bldg. 5/F, 3-6 Kioi-cho, Chiyoda-ku, Tokyo 102, Japan**

## MELLON FINANCIAL CORPORATION

One Mellon Bank Center, Pittsburgh, PA, 15258-0001

Tel: (412) 234-5000      Fax: (412) 236-1662      www.mellon.com

*Commercial and trade banking and foreign exchange.*

**Mellon Bank NA, New Yurakucho Bldg., 12-1 Yuraku-cho 1-chome, Chiyoda-ku, Tokyo 100, Japan**

Tel: 81-3-3216-5861

## MEMC ELECTRONIC MATERIALS, INC.

501 Pearl Drive, St. Peters, MO, 63376

Tel: (636) 474-5500      Fax: (636) 474-5161      www.memc.com

*Mfg. and distribution of silicon wafers.*

**MEMC Japan, Utsunomiya Plant, 11-2 Kiyohara Industrial Plant, Utsunomiya City Tochigi Pref., Japan**

Tel: 81-286-67-6333   Fax: 81-286-67-9000

**MEMC Japan Ltd., Tokyo Sales Office, 4F Bancho Fifth Building, 5-5 Nibancho Chiyoda-ku, Tokyo 102 Japan**

Tel: 81-3-3237-3221   Fax: 81-3-3237-3220

**MEMC Japan Ltd. - Osaka Sales Office,** 5th Floor Higashitenma Building, 1-7-17 Higashi Tenma, Kita-ku Osaka City, Osaka 530 Japan

Tel: 81-6-882-3831    Fax: 81-6-882-3805

## MEMOREX CORPORATION

10100 Pioneer Blvd., Ste. 110, Santa Fe Springs, CA, 90670

Tel: (562) 906-2800        Fax: (562) 906-2848        www.memorex.com

*Magnetic recording tapes, etc.*

**Memorex Japan Ltd.,** Yaesuguchi Kaikan 3F, 1-7-20 Yaesu, Chuo-ku, Tokyo, Japan

## THE MENTHOLATUM COMPANY, INC.

707 Sterling Drive, Orchard Park, NY, 14127-1587

Tel: (716) 677-2500        Fax: (716) 674-3696        www.mentholatum.com

*Mfr./distributor proprietary medicines, drugs, OTC's.*

**Rohto Pharmaceutical Co. Ltd. Intl Div.,** 1-8-1 Tatsumi-nishi, Sbuno-ku, Osaka 544, Japan

Tel: 81-6-758-9812    Fax: 81-6-758-9820

## MENTOR GRAPHICS/MICROTEC RESEARCH

8005 SW Boeckman Road, Wilsonville, OR, 97070-7777

Tel: (503) 685-7000        Fax: (503) 685-1202        www.mentorg.com

*Develop/mfr. software tools for embedded systems market.*

**Nihon Microtec Research KK,** Sanbancho MS Bldg., 20 Sanbancho, Chiyoda-ku, Tokyo 102, Japan

## MERCK & COMPANY, INC.

One Merck Drive, PO Box 100, Whitehouse Station, NJ, 08889-0100

Tel: (908) 423-1000        Fax: (908) 423-2592        www.merck.com

*Pharmaceuticals, chemicals and biologicals.*

**MSD (Japan) Co. Ltd.,** Kowa Bldg. 7F, 9-20 Akasaka 1-chome, Minato-ku, Tokyo 107 Japan

Tel: 81-3-3586-2711    Fax: 81-3-3587-1176

## MERCURY INTERACTIVE CORPORATION

1325 Borregas Ave., Sunnyvale, CA, 94089

Tel: (408) 822-5200        Fax: (408) 822-5300        www.merc-int.com

*Mfr. computer software to decipher and eliminate "bugs" from systems.*

**Mercury Interactive Japan K.K.,** 5F TG 115 Bldg., 1-15-7 Toranomon, Minato-ku, Tokyo 105, Japan

Tel: 81-3-3500-5161    Fax: 81-3-3500-5162

## MERITOR AUTOMOTIVE, INC.

2135 West Maple Road, Troy, MI, 48084-7186

Tel: (248) 435-1000        Fax: (248) 435-1393        www.meritorauto.com

*Mfr./sales of light and heavy vehicle systems for trucks, cars and specialty vehicles.*

**Nippon Bodei Sisutemuzu Meritor Audo Mapan K.K.,** Hiroshima, Japan

## MERRILL LYNCH & COMPANY, INC.

World Financial Center, 250 Vesey Street, New York, NY, 10281-1332

Tel: (212) 449-1000        Fax: (212) 449-2892        www.ml.com

*Security brokers and dealers, investment and business services.*

**Merrill Lynch Japan Incorporated,** Midosuji Diamodn Building 6F, 2-1-3 Nishi-Shinsaibashi, Chuo-ku, Osaka 542 Japan

Tel: 81-6-212-3850    Fax: 81-6-212-3874

**Merrill Lynch Japan Incorporated,** Ote Center Building 11F, 1-1-3 Otemachi, Chiyoda-ku, Tokyo 10 Japan

Tel: 81-3-3213-7000    Fax: 81-3-3213-7001

**Merrill Lynch Japan Incorporated,** Nagaya Mitsui Building 12F, 1-24-30 Meieki Minami, Nakamura-ku, Nagoya 450 Japan

Tel: 81-52-561-7940

Yamaichi Securities, Ote Center Building 11F, 1-1-3 Otemachi, Chiyoda-ku, Tokyo 10 Japan

## METALLURG INC.

6 East 43rd Street, New York, NY, 10017

Tel: (212) 687-9470     Fax: (212) 697-2874     www.mettalurg.com

*Mfr. ferrous and nonferrous alloys and metals.*

Metallurg (Far East) Ltd., PO Box 5221, Tokyo Intl. 100-31, Tokyo 105, Japan

## MICRO TOUCH SYSTEMS, INC.

300 Griffin Brook Park Drive, Methuen, MA, 01844

Tel: (978) 659-9000     Fax: (978) 659-9100     www.microtouch.com

*Mfr. clear coatings for computer monitors.*

MicroTouch Systems K.K., Bellevue Mizonokuchi Building 3/F, 3-2-3 Hisamoto, Takatsu-ku Kawasaki-shi, Kanagawa 213, Japan

Tel: 81-4-4811-1133

## MICROCHIP TECHNOLOGY INCORPORATED

2355 West Chandler Boulevard, Chandler, AZ, 85224

Tel: (602) 786-7200     Fax: (602) 899-9210     www.microchip.com

*Mfr. electronic subassemblies and components.*

Microchip Technology International, Inc., Benex S-1 6/F, 3-18-20 Shinyokohama, Kanagawa 222-0033, Japan

Tel: 81-45-471-6166   Fax: 81-45-471-6122

## MICRON TECHNOLOGY, INC. (MTI)

8000 S. Federal Way, Boise, ID, 83707-0006

Tel: (208) 368-4000     Fax: (208) 368-4435     www.micron.com

*Mfr. random-access memory chips and semi-conductor memory components.*

KMT (JV), 302-2 Hirano-Cho, Nishiwaki-City, Hyogo, Japan

Tel: 81-795-23-6611

Micron Technology Japan, K.K., 4-30 - 3 Chome Shiba Koen, #32 Mori Building 8/F, Minato Ku, Tokyo 105 Japan

Tel: 81-3-34365666   Fax: 81-3-34361444

## MICROSOFT CORPORATION

One Microsoft Way, Redmond, WA, 98052-6399

Tel: (425) 882-8080     Fax: (425) 936-7329     www.microsoft.com

*Computer software, peripherals and services.*

Microsoft Japan KK, Sasazuka NA Building, 50-1 Sasazuka 1-chome, Shibuyo-ku, Tokyo 151 Japan

Tel: 81-3-5454-8000   Fax: 81-3-5454-7970

## MIKASA, INC.

25 Enterprise Ave., Secaucus, NJ, 07094

Tel: (201) 867-9210     Fax: (201) 867-0457     www.mikasa.com

*Dinnerware, crystal and gifts.*

American Commercial Inc., 1-1 Shumoku-cho 3 chome, Higashi-ku, Nagoya, Japan

## MILACRON INC.

2090 Florence Ave., Cincinnati, OH, 45206

Tel: (513) 487-5000     Fax: (513) 487-5057     www.milacron.com

*Metalworking and plastics technologies.*

Cincinnati Milacron Japan, 726-4 Unane, Takatsu-ku Kawasaki-shi, Kangawa 213-0031, Japan

Tel: 81-44-811-5746   Fax: 81-44-822-0048

## MILBANK, TWEED, HADLEY & McCLOY LLP

1 Chase Manhattan Plaza, New York, NY, 10005-1413

Tel: (212) 530-5000     Fax: (212) 530-5219     www.milbank.com

*International law practice.*

**Milbank, Tweed, Hadley & McCloy, Nippon Press Ctr. Bldg., 2-1, Uchisaiwai-cho 2-chome, Chiyoda-ku, Tokyo 100, Japan**

Tel: 81-3-3504-1050   Fax: 81-3-3595-2790

## MILLENNIUM SPECIALTY CHEMICALS

PO Box 389, Jacksonville, FL, 32201-0389

Tel: (904) 768-5800     Fax: (904) 768-2200     www.aromachem.com

*Essential oils and extracts, perfumes and flavor material, aromatic chemicals.*

**Iwata Koryo Limited Company, 1230-3 Kuden-Cho, Sakae-ku, Yokohama Kanagawa, Japan**

Tel: 81-45-891-8418   Fax: 81-45-895-3063   Contact: Shoji Iwata

## MILLIPORE CORPORATION

80 Ashby Road, PO Box 9125, Bedford, MA, 01730

Tel: (781) 533-6000     Fax: (781) 533-3110     www.millipore.com

*Mfr. flow and pressure measurement and control components; precision filters, hi-performance liquid chromatography instruments.*

**Millipore Niho Ltd., Dai 5 Koike Bldg., 3-12 Kitashinagawa 1-chome, Shinagawa-ku, Tokyo 140 Japan**

## MILTON ROY COMPANY

201 Ivyland Road, Ivylan, PA, 18974

Tel: (215) 441-0800     Fax: (215) 293-0468     www.miltonroy.com

*Mfr. medical and industry equipment and process control instruments.*

**Milton Roy Co., Takanawa Daiichi Bldg. 9F, 1-41-2 Takanawa, Minato-ku, Tokyo 108 Japan**

## MINE SAFETY APPLIANCES COMPANY

121 Gamma Drive, PO Box 426, Pittsburgh, PA, 15230

Tel: (412) 967-3000     Fax: (412) 967-3452     www.msa.net

*Safety equipment, industry filters.*

**MSA Japan Ltd., Crest Bldg., 12-8 Roppongi 4-chome, Minatoku, Tokyo 106, Japan**

## MINOLTA QMS INC.

One Magnum Pass, Mobile, AL, 36618

Tel: (205) 633-4300     Fax: (205) 633-4866     www.qms.com

*Mfr. monochrome and color computer printers.*

**QMS Japan Inc., Shiba Dai-ichi Bldg., 5-3-2 Shiba Minato-ku, Tokyo 108, Japan**

## MINTEQ INTERNATIONAL INC.

405 Lexington Ave., 19th Fl., New York, NY, 10174-1901

Tel: (212) 878-1800     Fax: (212) 878-1952     www.mineralstech.com

*Mfr./market specialty refractory and metallurgical products and application systems.*

**MINTEQ Japan K.K., Higashi-Nihonbashi Sky Bldg. 6/F, 1-7 chome, Chuo-ku, Tokyo 103-0004 Japan**

Tel: 81-3-5821-5070   Fax: 81-3-5821-5066   Contact: I. Ohkuma, Mng. Dir.   Emp: 55

## MODEM MEDIA, INC.

230 East Avenue, Norwalk, CT, 06855

Tel: (203) 299-7000     Fax: (230) 299-7060     www.modemmedia.com

*Provides on-line marketing and consulting services.*

**Modem Media Tokyo, FIK Minami Aoyama Bldg, 5-13-3 Minami Aoyama Minato-Ku, Tokyo 107-0062, Japan**

Tel: 81-3-54640-0878   Contact: Susan C. MacDermid, Pres.

## MODINE MANUFACTURING COMPANY

1500 DeKoven Ave., Racine, WI, 53403

Tel: (262) 636-1200     Fax: (262) 636-1424     www.modine.com

*Mfr. heat-transfer products.*

**Modine Manufacturing Co., Yokohama, Japan**

## MOLEX INC.

2222 Wellington Court, Lisle, IL, 60532

Tel: (630) 969-4550     Fax: (630) 969-1352     www.molex.com

*Mfr. electronic, electrical and fiber optic interconnection products and systems, switches, application tooling.*

**Molex Inc., 4-21-1 Minami-Naruse, Machida, Tokyo 196 Japan**

**Molex Japan Co., Ltd., 1-5-4 Fukami Higashi, Yamato-City, Kanagawa 242-8585 Japan**

Tel: 81-462-61-4500   Fax: 81-462-65-2366

## MOODY'S INVESTOR SERVICES, INC.

99 Church St., New York, NY, 10007

Tel: (212) 553-1658     Fax: (212) 553-0462     www.moodys.com

*Publishes credit ratings*

**Moody's Japan K.K., Imperial Tower 13F, 1-1 Uchisaiwai-co 1-home, Chiyoda-ku, Tokyo 100 Japan**

Tel: 81-3-3593-0921

## MOOG INC.

Jamison Road, East Aurora, NY, 14052-0018

Tel: (716) 652-2000     Fax: (716) 687-4471     www.moog.com

*Mfr. precision control components and systems.*

**Moog Japan Ltd., 1532 Shindo, Hiratsuka, Kanagawa-ken 254, Japan**

## J. P. MORGAN CHASE & CO. INC.

World Headquarters, 270 Park Ave., New York, NY, 10017

Tel: (212) 270-6000     Fax: (212) 622-9030     www.jpmorganchase.com

*Provides integrated financial solutions for institutions and individuals worldwide, including asset management, investment banking and commercial banking.*

**J. P. Morgan Chase & Co., Nichimen Bldg. 8F, 2-2-2 Nakanoshima, Kita-ku, Osaka 530, Japan**

Tel: 81-6-229-8281   Fax: 81-6-229-8286

**J. P. Morgan Chase & Co., Akasaka Park Bldg. 11F, 5-2-20 Akasaka Minato-ku, Tokyo 107, Japan**

Tel: 81-3-5570-7600   Fax: 81-3-5570-1777

**J. P. Morgan Chase & Co., Akasaka Park Bldg. 12F, 5-2-20 Akasaka Minato-ku, Tokyo 107, Japan**

Tel: 81-3-5570-8200   Fax: 81-3-5570-7960

## MORGAN STANLEY DEAN WITTER & CO.

1585 Broadway, New York, NY, 10036

Tel: (212) 761-4000     Fax: (212) 761-0086     www.msdw.com

*Securities and commodities brokerage, investment banking, money management, personal trusts.*

**Morgan Stanley Japan Ltd., 2F Nishikawa Mitsui Bldg., 3-14 Kitahama 1-chome, Chuo-ku, Osaka 541, Japan**

**Morgan Stanley Japan Ltd., 20-3 Ebisu 4-chome, Shibuya-ku, Tokyo 150, Japan**

## MORGAN, LEWIS & BOCKIUS LLP

1701 Market St., Philadelphia, PA, 19103-6993

Tel: (215) 963-5000     Fax: (215) 963-5299     www.mlb.com

*International law firm.*

**Morgan, Lewis & Bockius LLP, Yurakucha Denki Building S-556, 7-1 Yurakucho 1-chome, Chiyoda-ku, Tokyo 100 Japan**

Tel: 81-3-3216-2500  Fax: 81-3-3216-2501   Contact: William R. Huss, Mng. Ptnr.   Emp: 8

## MORRISON & FOERSTER

425 Market Street, San Francisco, CA, 94105

Tel: (415) 268-7000     Fax: (415) 268-7522      www.mofo.com

*International law firm.*

**Morrison & Foerster, AIG Bldg. 7/F, 1-1-3 Marunouchi, Chiyoda-ku, Tokyo 100, Japan**

## MOTOROLA, INC.

1303 East Algonquin Road, Schaumburg, IL, 60196

Tel: (847) 576-5000     Fax: (847) 538-5191      www.motorola.com

*Mfr. communications equipment, semiconductors and cellular phones.*

**Nippon Motorola Ltd., Sumitomo Seimei, Shin-Isaka Bldg.-North 4F, 5-5-15 Nishinakajima, Yodogawa-ku Osaka 532 Japan**

Tel: 81-6-305-1801   Fax: 81-6-305-0369

**Nippon Motorola Ltd., Shiokawa-machi, Yama-gun, Fukushima, Ken 969-35 Japan**

Tel: 81-241-27-7511

**Nippon Motorola Ltd., 3-20-1 Minami-Azabu, Minato-ku, Tokyo 106, Japan**

Tel: 81-3-3440-3311   Fax: 81*3-3440-3505

**Tegal Intl., Tamahan Bldg., 1-1 Kugenuma-Higashi, Fujisawa-Shi, Kanagawa Prefecture 251 Japan**

## MPSI DATA METRIX INC.

4343 South 118 East Avenue, Tulsa, OK, 74146

Tel: (918) 877-6774     Fax: (918) 254-8764      www.mpsisys.com

*Computer software, information system services.*

**MPSI Systems K.K., No. 2 Shukaen Bldg. 6F, 11-3 Komazawa 2 Chome, Setagaya-Ku, Tokyo 154-0012 Japan**

Tel: 813-5481-8411   Fax: 813-5481-8412

## MTS SYSTEMS CORPORATION

1400 Technology Drive, Eden Prairie, MN, 55344-2290

Tel: (612) 937-4000     Fax: (612) 937-4515      www.mts.com

*Develop/mfr. mechanical testing and simulation products and services, industry measure and automation instrumentation.*

**MTS Japan Ltd., Izumikan Gobancho, 12-11 Gobancho, Chiyoda-ku, Tokyo 102 Japan**

## MULTI GRAPHICS

431 Lakeview Court, Mt. Prospect, IL, 60056

Tel: (847) 375-1700     Fax: (847) 375-1810      www.multigraphics.com

*Mfr./sale/service printing and print prod equipment, mailroom/bindery systems, services and supplies for graphics industry.*

**Multi Graphics Ltd., Yamato Bldg., 3-1 Kojimachie 5-chome, Chiyoda-ku, Tokyo 102, Japan**

## NABISCO HOLDINGS, CORP.

7 Campus Drive, Parsippany, NJ, 07054

Tel: (973) 682-5000     Fax: (973) 503-2153      www.nabisco.com

*Mfr. consumer packaged food products and tobacco products.*

**R.J. Reynolds/MC Tobacco Co. Ltd., 3-6 Minami-Aoyama 7-chome, Minato-ku, Tokyo 107, Japan**

## NACCO INDUSTRIES INC.

5875 Landerbrook Drive, Mayfield Heights, OH, 44124

Tel: (440) 449-9600     Fax: (440) 449-9607

*Mfr. fork lifts, trucks, trailers, towing winches, personnel lifts and compaction equipment and small appliances*

**NACCO Materials Handling Group, Obu, Japan**

## NANOMETRICS INC.

310 DeGuigne Drive, Sunnyvale, CA, 94086-3906

Tel: (408) 746-1600    Fax: (408) 720-0196    www.nanometrics.com

*Mfr. optical measurement and inspection systems for semiconductor industry.*

**Nanometrics Japan Ltd., Shin-isumi 34, Narita-shi, Chiba Ken T286, Japan**

Tel: 81-476-36-1831    Fax: 81-476-36-1866    Contact: Hiroshi Adachi    Emp: 40

## THE NASH ENGINEERING COMPANY

3 Trefoil Drive, Trumbull, CT, 06611

Tel: (203) 459-3900    Fax: (203) 459-3511    www.nasheng.com

*Mfr. air and gas compressors, vacuum pumps.*

**Nash International Company, Tokyo, Japan**

Tel: 81-33-449-0771

## NASHUA CORPORATION

11 Trafalgar Sq., 2nd Fl., Nashua, NH, 03061-2002

Tel: (603) 880-2323    Fax: (603) 880-5671    www.nashua.com

*Mfg. imaging supplies (printer cartridges, toners, developers), labels, and specialty coated papers.*

**Nashua Tokyo/High-C Inc., Onarimon Bldg., 3-23-11 Nishi-Shimbashi, Minato-ku, Tokyo 105, Japan**

## NATCO GROUP, INC.

2950 North Loop West, Houston, TX, 77092-8839

Tel: (713) 683-9292    Fax: (713) 683-6787    www.natcogroup.com

*Mfr./sale/service oil and gas products.*

**NATCO Japan Co. Ltd., 20 Kanda Nishikicho 3-chome, Chiyoda-ku, Tokyo 101, Japan**

## NATIONAL DATA CORPORATION

National Data Plaza, Atlanta, GA, 30329-2010

Tel: (404) 728-2000    Fax: (404) 728-2551    www.ndcorp.com

*Information systems and services for retail, healthcare, government and corporate markets.*

**National Data Corp., Uchisaiwaicho-Dai Bldg., 1-3-3 Uchisaiwaicho, Chiyoda-ku, Tokyo 100, Japan**

## NATIONAL GYPSUM COMPANY

2001 Rexford Road, Charlotte, NC, 28211

Tel: (704) 365-7300    Fax: (704) 365-7276    www.national-gypsum.com

*Mfr. building products and services.*

**The Austin Co., Tokyo, Japan**

## NATIONAL MACHINERY COMPANY

161 Greenfield St., Tiffin, OH, 44883-2471

Tel: (419) 447-5211    Fax: (419) 447-5299    www.nationalmachinery.com

*Mfr. high-speed metal parts forming machines.*

**National Machinery Asia Co., Ltd., No. 102 South Crest, 13-21 2-Chome, Minami-CHO Tanashi-City, Tokyo 188-0012 Japan**

Tel: 81-424-50-0571

**National Machinery Company, No. 18 Ocean Plaza, 61-6 1-Chome, Shirayama-CHO Kasugai-City, Aichi-Pref 487-0034 Japan**

## NATIONAL SEMICONDUCTOR CORPORATION

2900 Semiconductor Dr., PO Box 58090, Santa Clara, CA, 95052-8090

Tel: (408) 721-5000    Fax: (408) 739-9803    www.national.com

*Engaged in producing computer-on-a-chip solutions for the information highway.*

**National Semiconductor, URD Kiba Bldg., Kiba, Koto-du, Tokyo 135, Japan**

Contact: Tatsvo Ishihara, Pres.    Emp: 200

## NATIONAL STARCH AND CHEMICAL COMPANY

10 Finderne Ave., Bridgewater, NJ, 08807-3300

Tel: (908) 685-5000     Fax: (908) 685-5005     www.nationalstarch.com

*Mfr. adhesives and sealants, resins and specialty chemicals, electronic materials and adhesives, food products, industry starch.*

**Nippon National Starch & Chemical Co. Ltd., Ginza Wall Building 3F, 13-16 Ginza 6-chome, Chuo-ku, Tokyo 104 Japan**

Tel: 81-3-3542-7731   Fax: 81-3-3542-7794

## NATIONWIDE INSURANCE

One Nationwide Plaza, Columbus, OH, 43215-2220

Tel: (614) 249-7111     Fax: (614) 249-7705     www.nationwide.com

*Insurance services.*

**Gartmore Investment Management PLC, Tokyo, Japan**

## NCR (NATIONAL CASH REGISTER)

1700 South Patterson Blvd., Dayton, OH, 45479

Tel: (937) 445-5000     Fax: (937) 445-7042     www.ncr.com

*Mfr. automated teller machines and high-performance stationary bar code scanners.*

**NCR Japan, Ltd., 1-2-2 Akasaka, Minato-ku, Tokyo, Japan**

Tel: 81-2-5561-5484   Fax: 81-3-5561-8248   Contact: Kiichiro Tanaka, Pres.

## NETMANAGE, INC.

10725 N. De Anza Blvd., Cupertino, CA, 95014

Tel: (408) 973-7171     Fax: (408) 257-6405     www.netmanage.com

*Develop/mfr. computer software applications and tools.*

**NetManage Japan KK, Contact: NetManage Asia/Pacific, 10725 North De Anza Blvd., Cupertino, CA 95014 USA**

## NETSCAPE COMMUNICATIONS

501 East Middlefield Road, Mountain View, CA, 94043

Tel: (650) 254-1900     Fax: (650) 528-4124     www.netscape.com

*Mfr./distribute Internet-based commercial and consumer software applications.*

**Netscape Communications Japan Ltd., Tokyo Opera City Tower 29F, 3-20-2 Nishi Shinjuku, Shinjuku-ku, Tokyo 163-14 Japan**

Tel: 81-3-5354-1700   Fax: 81-2-5354-1770

## NETWORK ASSOCIATES, INC.

3965 Freedom Circle, Santa Clara, CA, 95054

Tel: (408) 988-3832     Fax: (408) 970-9727     www.networkassociates.com

*Designs and produces network security and network management software and hardware.*

**Network Associates, 5F Yaesu Hakata Bldg., 2-18-30 Hakata eki Higashi, Hakata-ku, Fukuoka 812-0013 Japan**

Tel: 81-92-452-3511   Fax: 81-92-452-3515

**Network Associates, Shibuya Mark City West 20/F, 1-12-1 Dougenzaka, Shibuya-ku, Tokyo 150-0043, Japan**

Tel: 81-3-5428-1100   Fax: 81-3-5428-1480

**Network Associates, 2-5-31 Kutarocho, Chuoku Osaka, Japan**

Tel: 81-6-6253-1031   Fax: 81-6-6253-1260

## NEW HAMPSHIRE BALL BEARINGS INC. (NHBB)

Route 202 South, Peterborough, NH, 03458-0805

Tel: (603) 924-3311     Fax: (603) 924-6632     www.nhbb.com

*Mfr. bearings and bearing assemblies.*

**Minebea Co., Ltd., Tokyo, Japan**

## THE NEW YORK TIMES COMPANY

229 West 43rd Street, New York, NY, 10036-3959

Tel: (212) 556-1234    Fax: (212) 556-7389    www.nytimes.com

*Diversified media company including newspapers, magazines, television and radio stations, and electronic information and publishing.*

**International Herald Tribute (IHT), 4 F Mainichi Newspapers, 1-1-1 Hitotsubashi Chiyoda-ku, Tokyo 100, Japan**

Tel: 81-3-3201-0210

## NEWELL RUBBERMAID

29 East Stephenson Street, Freeport, IL, 61032-0943

Tel: (815) 235-4171    Fax: (815) 489-8212    www.newellco.com

*Mfr. hardware, housewares, and office products.*

**Newell Office Products of Japan Inc., Tenkoh Bldg. 4/F, 220 Sakai, Atsugi City, Kanagawa, Japan**

## NEWPORT CORPORATION

1791 Deere Ave., PO Box 19607, Irvine, CA, 92606

Tel: (949) 863-3144    Fax: (949) 253-1800    www.newport.com

*Mfr./distributor precision components and systems for laser/optical technology, vibration/motion measure and control.*

**KK Newport/Hakato, 1-13 Shinjuku 1-chome, Shinjuku-ku, Tokyo 160, Japan**

Tel: 81-3-5379-0261   Fax: 81-3-3225-9012

## NEWSWEEK INTERNATIONAL INC.

251 West 57 Street, New York, NY, 10019

Tel: (212) 445-4000    Fax: (212) 445-4120    www.washpostco.com

*Engaged in magazine publishing.*

**Newsweek Japan Nihon Ban, Sumitomo Seimei Aoyama Bldg. 3F, 3-1-30 Minami-Aoyama, Minato-ku, Tokyo 107, Japan**

## NEXTEL COMMUNICATIONS

2001 Edmund Halley Dr., Reston, VA, 20191

Tel: (703) 433-4000    Fax: (703) 433-4343    www.nextel.com

*Engaged in wireless internet access.*

**J-COM Co., Ltd./Nextnet, Tokyo, Japan**

## NICOLET INSTRUMENT CORPORATION

5225 Verona Road, Madison, WI, 53711-4495

Tel: (608) 276-6100    Fax: (608) 276-6222    www.nicolet.com

*Mfr. infrared spectrometers and oscilloscopes and medical electro-diagnostic equipment.*

**Nicolet Japan Corp., Ryokuchi-Eki Bldg. 6F, 4-1 Terauchi 2-chome, Toyonaka, Osaka 560, Japan**

**Nicolet Japan Corp., 7-1 Hirakawa-cho 2-chome, Chiyoda-ku, Tokyo 102, Japan**

**Nicolet Japan Corp., 17-10 Uchiyama 3-chome, Chikusa-ku, Nagoya 464, Japan**

## A .C. NIELSEN COMPANY

177 Broad Street, Stamford, CT, 06901

Tel: (203) 961-3000    Fax: (203) 961-3190    www.acnielsen.com

*Market and consumer research firm.*

**A.C. Nielsen Co., Nielsen Bldg., 1-1-71 Nakameguro, Meguro-ku, Tokyo 153, Japan**

## NORDSON CORPORATION

28601 Clemens Road, Westlake, OH, 44145-4551

Tel: (440) 892-1580    Fax: (440) 892-9507    www.nordson.com

*Mfr. industry application equipment, sealants and packaging machinery.*

**Nordson K.K. Tokyo, 8F Toshin Bldg., 5-21 Katsushima 1-chome, Shinagawa-ku, Tokyo 140 Japan**

Tel: 81-3-5762-2700   Fax: 81-3-5762-2701   Contact: Shigeru Kobayashi

## NORGREN

5400 S. Delaware Street., Littleton, CO, 80120-1663

Tel: (303) 794-2611    Fax: (303) 795-9487    www.usa.norgren.com

*Mfr. pneumatic filters, regulators, lubricators, valves, automation systems, dryers, push-in fittings.*

**IMI Norgren K.K., 14-1 Aobaoka-Kita, Suita City, Osaka 565, Japan**

Tel: 81-6-876-8913    Fax: 81-6-876-8929

## NORTHWEST AIRLINES CORPORATION

5101 Northwest Dr., St. Paul, MN, 55121-3034

Tel: (612) 726-2111    Fax: (612) 727-7795    www.nwa.com

*Airline passenger and cargo carrier.*

**Northwest Airlines, Tokyo, Japan**

## NOVELLUS SYSTEMS INC.

4000 North First Street, San Jose, CA, 95134

Tel: (408) 943-9700    Fax: (408) 943-3422    www.novellus.com

*Mfr. chemical vapor deposition (CVD), physical vapor deposition (PVD) and copper electrofill systems.*

**Nippon Novellus Systems KK, KSP Building R&D C-10F, 3-2-1 Sakado Takatsu-ku Kawasaki-shi, Kanagawaken 213 Japan**

Tel: 81-44-850-1777    Fax: 81-44-850-1778    Contact: M. T. Matsumoto, Pres.

**Nippon Novellus Systems KK, Maruya Bldg. Annex 4/F, 1-21 Betsuin-cho, Ibanaki-shi, Osaka 567-0817 Japan**

Tel: 81-72-622-5558    Fax: 81-72-622-5715

**Nippon Novellus Systems KK, Hakkoh Ryutsu Center Building 7/F, 8-5-75 Yoshizuka, Hakata-Ku Fukuoka-shi, Fukuoka-ken 812-0041, Japan**

Tel: 81-92-629-1294    Fax: 81-92.611-2293

## NOVO SYSTEMS CORPORATION

4061 Clipper Court, Fremont, CA, 94538-6540

Tel: (510) 360-8100    Fax: (510) 623-4484    www.novosystems.com

*Design/development/mfr./market logic and fault simulation acceleration products; system engineering services.*

**Zycad Japan KK, Toshin 24, Shin-Yokohama Bldg. B-8F, 2-3-8 Shin-Yokohama, Kohoku-ku, Yokohama 222, Japan**

## NUS INFORMATION SERVICES, INC.

2650 McCormick Dr., Ste. 300, Clearwater, FL, 33759-1049

Tel: (727) 669-3000    Fax: (727) 669-3100    www.nus.com

*Provides case-based expert knowledge, bench-marking, trending, and operational services to the electric power and inventory industries.*

**Japan NUS Company Ltd., Tokyo, Japan**

## OCLI, INC. (OPTICAL COATING LABORATORY, INC.)

2789 Northpoint Pkwy., Santa Rosa, CA, 95407-7397

Tel: (707) 545-6440    Fax: (707) 525-7410    www.ocli.com

*Mfr. thin film precision coated optical devices.*

**OCLI Asia K.K., 1-1-16 Naka-machi, Machida Tokyo 194-0021, Japan**

Tel: 81-42-739-3561    Fax: 81-42-720-5211

**OCLI Asia K.K. Mfr., 3037-1 Liyama, Atsugi, Kanagawa-ken 243-0213, Japan**

## OFFICE DEPOT, INC.

2200 Old Germantown Road, Delray Beach, FL, 33445

Tel: (561) 278-4800     Fax: (561) 265-4406     www.officedepot.com

*Discount office product retailer with warehouse-style superstores.*

**Office Depot Japan, Ishizaki Bldg. 1F, 2-7-6 Otemachi, Naka-ku, Hiroshima 30-0051 Japan**
Tel: 81-82-240-9111   Fax: 81-82-240-9123

**Office Depot Japan, TOC Bldg. 3F, 7-22-17 Nishigotanda, Shinagawa-ku, Tokyo 141-0031 Japan**
Tel: 81-3-5487-1711   Fax: 81-3-5487-1712   Contact: Shigeru Manabe, Gen. Mgr.

## OFFICEMAX, INC.

3605 Warrensville Center Road, Shaker Heights, OH, 44122-5203

Tel: (216) 921-6900     Fax: (216) 491-4040     www.officemax.com

*Office furnishings, printing and copying services and super center office stores.*

**OfficeMax Japan Company, Ltd./JUSCO Company, Tokyo, Japan**

## OGDEN ENVIRONMENTAL & ENERGY SERVICES COMPANY

4455 Brookfield Corporate Dr., Suite 100, Chantilly, VA, 20151

Tel: (703) 488-3700     Fax: (703) 488-3701     www.ogden.com

*Environmental and energy consulting services for commercial clients and government agencies.*

**IEAL of Japan, 4 Sumitomo Higashi-Shimbashi Bldg., 9-6 Shimbashi 6-chome, Minato-ku, Tokyo 105, Japan**

## OHAUS CORPORATION

29 Hanover Road, PO Box 900, Florham Park, NJ, 07932-0900

Tel: (973) 377-9000     Fax: (973) 593-0359     www.ohaus.com

*Mfr. balances and scales for laboratories, industry and education.*

**Ohaus Far East Reg. Office, c/o Mettler-Toledo KK, Crystal Tower Bldg. DF, 1-2-27 Shiromi, Chuo-ku Osaka 540 Japan**
Tel: 81-66-949-5922

## THE OILGEAR COMPANY

2300 S. 51st Street, Milwaukee, WI, 53219

Tel: (414) 327-1700     Fax: (414) 327-0532     www.oilgear.com

*Mfr. hydraulic power transmission machinery.*

**The Oilgear Japan Co., 204 Nishikan, Daini Toyoda Bldg., 4-10-27 Meieki, Nakamara-ku, Nagoya 450 Japan**

## OLIN CORPORATION

501 Merritt Seven, Norwalk, CT, 06856-4500

Tel: (203) 750-3000     Fax: (203) 750-3292     www.olin.com

*Mfr. chemicals, metals, sporting ammunition and copper and copper alloy sheets.*

**Yamaha - Olin Metal Corp., 2360 Shingai, Iwata-shi, Shizuoka-Ken 438 Japan**
Tel: 81-5-383-7-5111   Fax: 81-5-383-7-0147

## OM GROUP, INC. (OMG)

3800 Terminal Tower, Cleveland, OH, 44113-2203

Tel: (216) 781-0083     Fax: (216) 781-0902     www.omgi.com

*Producer and marketer of metal-based specialty chemicals.*

**D & O, Inc. (JV with Dainippon Ink & Chemicals (DIC), Tokyo, Japan**

## ONAN CORPORATION

1400 73rd Ave. NE, Minneapolis, MN, 55432

Tel: (612) 574-5000     Fax: (612) 574-5298     www.onan.com

*Mfr. electric generators, controls and switchgears.*

**Onan International, 106 Sengokuyama Annex, 12-10 Shantome 1-chome, Chuo-ku, Tokyo 104, Japan**

## ONESOURCE INFORMATION SERVICES, INC.

300 Baker Avenue, Concord, MA, 01742

Tel: (978) 318-4300     Fax: (978) 318-4690     www.onesource.com

*Provides business information services on line.*

**One Source Information Services Japan KK,  9-1 Sakuragaoka-Cho, Shibuya-ku Bien Quad, Tokyo 150, Japan**

Tel: 81-3-3463-7181   Fax: 81-3-3770-1865

## ONTRACK DATA INTERNATIONAL, INC.

9023 Columbine Rd., Eden Prairie, MN, 55347

Tel: (612) 937-1107     Fax: (612) 937-5815     www.ontrack.com

*Computer data evidence services company, rescuing lost or corrupted data, and software sales.*

**Ontrack Data International, Inc.,  182 Shinkoh, Iruma, Saitama, 358-0055 Japan**

Tel: 81-42-932-6365   Fax: 81-42-932-6370

## OPEN MARKET, INC.

1 Wayside Road, Burlington, MA, 01803

Tel: (781) 359-3000     Fax: (781) 359-8111     www.openmarket.com

*Mfr. catalog management software.*

**Open Market Japan KK,  Nishino Kinryo Bldg. 6/F, 4-9-4 Hacchobori, Chuo-ku, Tokyo 104-0032, Japan**

Tel: 81-3-3537-6401   Fax: 81-3-3537-6420

## ORACLE CORPORATION

500 Oracle Parkway, Redwood Shores, CA, 94065

Tel: (650) 506-7000     Fax: (650) 506-7200     www.oracle.com

*Develop/manufacture software.*

**Oracle Japan,  Tokyo, Japan**

## OSCAR MAYER & COMPANY

PO Box 7188, Madison, WI, 53707

Tel: (608) 241-3311     Fax: (608) 242-6102     www.kraftfoods.com

*Meat and food products.*

**Oscar Mayer & Co. Inc.,  PO Box 55, Kasumigaseki Bldg., Tokyo 100, Japan**

## OSMONICS INC.

5951 Clearwater Drive, Minnetonka, MN, 55343-8995

Tel: (952) 933-2277     Fax: (952) 933-0141     www.osmonics.com

*Mfr. equipment, controls and components for the filtration and water-treatment industries.*

**Osmonics,  Tokyo, Japan**

## OTIS ELEVATOR COMPANY

10 Farm Springs Road, Farmington, CT, 06032

Tel: (860) 676-6000     Fax: (860) 676-5111     www.otis.com

*Mfr. elevators and escalators.*

**Nippon Otis Elevator Co.,  Shinjuku NS Bldg. 17/F, 4-1 Nishishinjuku 2-chome, Shinjuku-ku, Tokyo 163 Japan**

## OUTBACK STEAKHOUSE, INC.

2202 N. Westshore Blvd. 5th Fl., Tampa, FL, 33607

Tel: (813) 282-1225     Fax: (813) 282-1209     www.outback.com

*Chain of casual dining steak restaurants.*

**Outback Steakhouse, Inc.,  Minami Machida, Grandberry Mall F Tower 6-3, Tsuruma Machida-shi, Tokyo 194-8509, Japan**

Tel: 81-42-788-3662

## PACIFIC ARCHITECTS & ENGINEERS INC.

888 South Figueroa Street, 17th Fl., Los Angeles, CA, 90017

Tel: (213) 481-2311    Fax: (213) 481-7189    www.pae.com

*Technical engineering services.*

**K.K. Halifax Associates,  Halifax Builidng 8/F, 16-26 Roppongi 3-chome, Toyko 106-0032, Japan**

Tel: 81-3-3436-6381   Fax: 81-3-3436-4714   Contact: Richard van Rooij, Mng. Dir.

**PAE International,  Halifax Shiba Building 6/7F, 3-10 Shiba Park 1-chome, Minato-ku, Tokyo 105 Japan**

Tel: 81-3-3436-0591   Fax: 81-3-3436-0889   Contact: Mark Griffin, V.P. & Gen. Mgr.

## PACIFIC BELL

140 New Montgomery Street, San Francisco, CA, 94105

Tel: (415) 542-9000    Fax: (415) 543-7079    www.pacbell.com

*Telecommunications and information systems.*

**Pacific Bell Japan KK,  Toranomon Cntr. Bldg., 1-16-17 Toranomon, Minato-ku, Tokyo 105, Japan**

## PACIFIC CENTURY FINANCIAL CORPORATION

130 Merchant Street, Honolulu, HI, 96813

Tel: (808) 643-3888    Fax: (808) 537-8440    www.boh.com

*Engaged in commercial and consumer banking services.*

**Pacific Century Financial Corporation,  Akasaka Twin Tower 8/F, 17-22 Akasaka 2- Choma, Tokyo 107, Japan**

Tel: 81-33-588-1251

## PAINE WEBBER GROUP INC.

1285 Ave. of the Americas, New York, NY, 10019

Tel: (212) 713-2000    Fax: (212) 713-4889    www.painewebber.com

*Stock brokerage and investment services.*

**PaineWebber Intl.,  Asahi Seimei Hibiya, Bldg. 3F, 1-5-1 Yorako-cho, Chiyoda-ku, Tokyo 100, Japan**

Tel: 81-3-3593-5200

## PALL CORPORATION

2200 Northern Boulevard, East Hills, NY, 11548-1289

Tel: (516) 484-5400    Fax: (516) 484-5228    www.pall.com

*Specialty materials and engineering; filters and related fluid clarification equipment.*

**Nihon Pall Ltd.,  GotandaNomura Shoken Building,1-5-1 Nishi Gotanda, Shinagawa-ku, Tokyo 141 Japan**

Tel: 81-3-3495-8380   Fax: 81-3-3495-8369

**Pall Gelman Sciences,  1-9-12 Kita-Ueno, Taito-ku, Tokyo 110, Japan**

Tel: 81-3-3844-5411   Fax: 81-3-3844-5433

## PANAMETRICS

221 Crescent Street, Waltham, MA, 02154

Tel: (781) 899-2719    Fax: (781) 899-1552    www.panametrics.com

*Process/non-destructive test instrumentation.*

**Panametrics Japan Co., Ltd.,  5F Sumitomo Fudosan Bldg., 5-41-10 Koishikawa, Bunkyo-ku, Toyko 112 Japan**

Tel: 81-3-5802-8701   Fax: 81-3-5802-8706

## PANDUIT CORPORATION

17301 Ridgeland Ave., Tinley Park, IL, 60477-0981

Tel: (708) 532-1800    Fax: (708) 532-1811    www.panduit.com

*Mfr. electrical/electronic wiring components.*

**Panduit Corp. (Japan),  31-5 Omori Kita 6Cchome, Ota-ku, Tokyo 143-0016, Japan**

Tel: 81-3-3767-7011   Fax: 81-3-3767-7033

## PARADYNE NETWORKS, INC.

8545 126 Ave. North, Largo, FL, 33773

Tel: (727) 530-2000     Fax: (727) 530-2875     www.paradyne.com

*Engaged in data communications and high-speed network access solutions.*

**Paradyne Japan, Eitai Bldg. 7&8/F, 1-22-11 Shinkawa, Chuo-ku, Tokyo 104, Japan**

Tel: 81-3-5437-5388     Contact: Tsutomu Watabe

## PARAMETRIC TECHNOLOGY CORPORATION

128 Technology Drive, Waltham, MA, 02154

Tel: (781) 398-5000     Fax: (781) 398-5674     www.ptc.com

*Supplier of mechanical design automation and product data management software and services.*

**Nihon Parametric Technology K.K., 6/F Nagogya Hirokoji Building, 1-3-11 Kosakahonmachi, Toyoda-Shi, Aichi 471 Japan**

Tel: 81-92-441-2992   Fax: 81-52-223-3705

**Nihon Parametric Technology K.K., Shinjuku Monolith Building 20F, 2-3-1 Nishi Shin Juku, Tokyo 163-09 Japan**

Tel: 81-3-3346-8100   Fax: 81-3-3346-8290

**Nihon Parametric Technology K.K., Mihagino Center Building, 5-22 Tzutsujigaoka, Miyagino-ku Sendai-shi, Miyagi-ken 983 Japan**

Tel: 81-26-333-3951   Fax: 81-26-333-3915

**Nihon Parametric Technology K.K., Hiroden Mitsuikaijo Building, 9-9 Nishi Tohnkaichi-machi, Hiroshima-shi, Hiroshima-ken 730 Japan**

Tel: 81-53-451-0671   Fax: 81-53-451-0672

**Nihon Parametric Technology K.K., 1-4-4 Hakata-ekimae, Hakta-ku, Fukuoka-shi Fukuoka-pref, Fukuoka 812 Japan**

Tel: 81-92-441-2992   Fax: 81-92-441-2388

**Nihon Parametric Technology K.K., Hamamatsu Act Tower, 111-2 Itaya-cho, Hamamatsu-shi, Schizuoka-ken Japan**

Tel: 81-39-691-331-1333   Fax: 81-39-562-5232

**Nihon Parametric Technology K.K., Kenshin Tohon Seimei Building, 5-2 Fukashi 2-chome, Matsumoto-shi, Nagano 390 Japan**

Tel: 81-76-262-1561   Fax: 81-76-2962-1562

**Nihon Parametric Technology K.K., Green Tower Building, 14-1 Nishi Shinjuku 6-chome, Shinjuku-ku, Tokyo 163-09 Japan**

Tel: 81-2-2792-7301   Fax: 81-2-2792-7302

**Nihon Parametric Technology K.K., 4F Benes S-3, 3-20-8 Shin Yokohama, Kohonku-ku Yokohama, Kanagawa 222 Japan**

Tel: 81-3-3346-8981   Fax: 81-3-3346-8988

**Nihon Parametric Technology K.K., Crystal Tower 27F, 1-2-27 Shiromi, Chuo-ku Osaka-shi, Osaka 540 Japan**

Tel: 81-6-946-5071   Fax: 81-6-946-5070

**Nihon Parametric Technology K.K., Nagoya Hirokoji Bulding, 2-3-1 Sakae, Naka-ku, Nagoya 460 Japan**

Tel: 81-52-223-3701   Fax: 81-52-223-3705

**Nihon Parmaetric Technology K.K., Rifare, 5-2 Honmachi 1-chome, Kanazawa-shi, Ishikawa-ken Japan**

Tel: 81-82-219-8861   Fax: 81-82-291-8860

## PAREXEL INTERNATIONAL CORPORATION

195 West Street, Waltham, MA, 02154

Tel: (781) 487-9900     Fax: (781) 487-0525     www.parexel.com

*Provides contract medical, biotechnology, and pharmaceutical research and consulting services.*

**PAREXEL International Ltd., Urban Ace Sannomiya Bldg. 5F, 4-1-22 Onoe Dori, Chou-ku, Kobe 651, Japan**

Tel: 81-782-8026   Fax: 81-782-71-8027

**PAREXEL MIRAI, Toko Bldg. Room 102, -10-21 Takata, Toshima-ku, Tokyo 171, Japan**

Tel: 81-3-5287-7821   Fax: 81-3-5287-7822

## PARKER HANNIFIN CORPORATION

6035 Parkland Blvd., Cleveland, OH, 44124-4141

Tel: (216) 896-3000     Fax: (216) 896-4000     www.parker.com

*Mfr. motion-control products.*

**Parker Hannifin Japan Ltd., 626 Totsuka-cho, Totsuka-ku, Yokohama-shi 244, Japan**

Tel: 81-45-861-3811   Fax: 81-45-864-5305

## THE PARSONS CORPORATION

100 West Walnut Street, Pasadena, CA, 91124

Tel: (626) 440-2000     Fax: (626) 440-2630     www.parsons.com

*Engineering and construction.*

**Parsons Polytech Inc., Place Astre Bldg. 8/F, 2-3 Azabu Juban 1-chome, Minato-ku, Tokyo 106, Japan**

## PARSONS ENGINEERING SCIENCE INC.

100 West Walnut Street, Pasadena, CA, 91124

Tel: (626) 440-2000     Fax: (626) 440-4919     www.parsons.com

*Environmental engineering.*

**Parsons Engineering Science Inc., c/Parsons Polytech Inc., Kyobashi Maruki Bldg. 3/F, 17-9 Kyobashi 2-chome, Chuo-ku, Tokyo 104, Japan**

## PARTECH INTERNATIONAL

50 California Street, Ste. 3200, San Francisco, CA, 94111-4624

Tel: (415) 788-2929     Fax: (415) 788-6763     www.partechintl.com

*Invests in startup and growth companies in information technology, communications and healthcare.*

**Partech International Co. Ltd., SVAX TT Building, 3-11-15 Toranomon, Minato-Ku, Tokyo 105-0001, Japan**

## PATAGONIA INC.

259 West Santa Clara Street, Ventura, CA, 93001

Tel: (805) 643-8616     Fax: (805) 653-6355     www.patagonia.com

*Outdoor clothing retail stores and mail-order catalogue company.*

**Patagonia, Inc., Tokyo, Japan**

Contact: Bill Werlin

## PAUL, WEISS, RIFKIND, WHARTON & GARRISON

1285 Ave. of the Americas, New York, NY, 10019-6064

Tel: (212) 373-3000     Fax: (212) 373-2268     www.paulweiss.com

*Law firm engaged in American and international law practice.*

**Paul, Weiss, Rifkind, Wharton & Garrison, 2-2 Uchisaiwaicho 2-chome, Chiyoda-ku, Tokyo 100, Japan**

Tel: 81-3-3597-8101   Fax: 81-3-3597-8120

## J.C. PENNEY COMPANY, INC.

6501 Legacy Drive, Plano, TX, 75024-3698

Tel: (972) 431-1000      Fax: (972) 431-1977      www.jcpenney.com

*Markets family apparel, shoes, home furnishings, jewelry, and offers credit cards.*

**J. C. Penney Purchasing Corp., Shoho Bldg. 7F, 6-2 Bingo-Machi 3-chome, Chuo-ku, Osaka 541, Japan**

## PENNZOIL-QUAKER STATE COMPANY

PO Box 2967, Houston, TX, 77252-2967

Tel: (713) 546-4000      Fax: (713) 546-6589      www.pennzoil-quakerstate.com

*Produce/refine/market oil, natural gas, sulfur.*

**Pennzoil-Quaker State Japan, Kairaku Bldg., 6-5-12 Soto Kanda, Chiyoda-ku, Tokyo 101, Japan**

## PEOPLESOFT INC.

4460 Hacienda Drive, Pleasanton, CA, 94588-8618

Tel: (925) 225-3000      Fax: (925) 694-4444      www.peoplesoft.com

*Mfr. applications to manage business operations across computer networks.*

**PeopleSoft Japan, Carrot Tower 22/F, 4-4-1 Taishido - Setagaya-ku, Tokyo 154-0004 Japan**
Tel: 81-3-5432-7800   Fax: 81-3-5432-7855

## PEPSiCO INC.

700 Anderson Hill Road, Purchase, NY, 10577-1444

Tel: (914) 253-2000      Fax: (914) 253-2070      www.pepsico.com

*Beverages and snack foods.*

**Japan Frito-Lay Ltd., Tokyo, Japan**

## PERKIN ELMER, INC.

45 William Street, Wellesley, MA, 02481

Tel: (781) 237-5100      Fax: (781) 431-4255      www.perkinelmer.com

*Mfr. equipment and devices to detect explosives and bombs on airline carriers.*

**PerkinElmer Life Sciences, 18/F Parale - Mitsui Building 8, Higashida-Cho, Kawasaki-Ku Shi, Kanagawa-Ken 210-0005, Japan**
Tel: 81-44-200-9157   Fax: 81-44-200-9160

## PFIZER INC.

235 East 42nd Street, New York, NY, 10017-5755

Tel: (212) 573-2323      Fax: (212) 573-7851      www.pfizer.com

*Research-based, global health care company.*

**Pfizer KK, Tokyo, Japan**
**Pfizer Oral Care Inc., Tokyo, Japan**
**Pfizer Pharmaceuticals Inc., Tokyo, Japan**
**Pfizer Shoji Co. Ltd., Tokyo, Japan**
**Schneider Japan KK, Tokyo, Japan**

## PHARMACIA CORPORATION

100 Route 206 North, Peapack, NJ, 07977

Tel: (908) 901-8000      Fax: (908) 901-8379      www.pharmacia.com

*Mfr. pharmaceuticals, agricultural products, industry chemicals.*

**Pharmacia & Upjohn, Shuwa Kamiyacho Building, 3-13 Toranomon 4-chome, Minato-ku, Tokyo 105 Japan**

## PHARMACIA MONSANTO

800 N. Lindbergh Boulevard, St. Louis, MO, 63167

Tel: (314) 694-1000    Fax: (314) 694-7625    www.monsanto.com

*Life sciences company focusing on agriculture, nutrition, pharmaceuticals, health and wellness and sustainable development.*

**Monsanto Japan Ltd., Nihonbashi Daini (2nd) Building , 41-12 Nihonbashi Hakozaki-cho, Chuo-ku Tokyo 103-0015 Japan**

## PHELPS DODGE CORPORATION

2600 North Central Ave., Phoenix, AZ, 85004-3089

Tel: (602) 234-8100    Fax: (602) 234-8337    www.phelpsdodge.com

*Copper, minerals, metals and special engineered products for transportation and electrical markets.*

**Columbian Carbon Japan Ltd., 8-12 Nihonbashi Haridomecho 1-chome, Chuo-ku, Tokyo 103, Japan**

**Cyprus Amax Minerals Japan Corporation, Saisho Bldg. 2F, 8-1-14 Nishi Gotanda, Shinagawa-ku, Tokyo 141, Japan**

Tel: 81-3-3491-5651    Fax: 81-3-3491-5670

## PHILIP MORRIS COMPANIES, INC.

120 Park Ave., New York, NY, 10017--559

Tel: (917) 663-5000    Fax: (917) 663-2167    www.philipmorris.com

*Mfr. cigarettes, food products, beer.*

**Philip Morris Kabushiki Kaisha, Akasaka Twin Tower, Main Tower 13/14 Fl., 2-17-22, Akasaka, Minato-ku, Tokyo 107, Japan**

## PHILLIPS PETROLEUM COMPANY

Phillips Building, 411 S. Keeler Ave., Bartlesville, OK, 74004

Tel: (918) 661-6600    Fax: (918) 661-7636    www.phillips66.com

*Crude oil, natural gas, liquefied petroleum gas, gasoline and petro-chemicals.*

**Phillips Petroleum Intl. Ltd., 606 Shin Tokyo Bldg., 3-1 Marunouchi 3-chome, Chiyoda-ku, Tokyo 100, Japan**

## PICTURETEL CORPORATION

100 Minuteman Road, Andover, MA, 01810

Tel: (978) 292-5000    Fax: (978) 292-3300    www.picturetel.com

*Mfr. video conferencing systems, network bridging and multiplexing products, system peripherals.*

**PictureTel Japan Inc., URD Building 5/F, 3-19-6 Shirogane-dai, Minato-ku, Tokyo 108 Japan**

Tel: 81-3-5421-3636    Fax: 81-3-5421-3611

## PIER 1 IMPORTS, INC.

301 Commerce St., Ste. 600, Fort Worth, TX, 76102

Tel: (817) 878-8000    Fax: (817) 252-8801    www.pier1.com

*Specialty retailer of imported decorative home furnishings.*

**Pier 1 Imports, Inc., Kobe Fashion Plaza Rink 5/F, 2-9-1 Naka-Kouyou-cho, Higashinada-ku, Kobe-shi Hyouko 658, Japan**

Tel: 81-8846-2580    Contact: Takahiro Yoshida

## PIERCE & STEVENS CORPORATION

710 Ohio Street, Buffalo, NY, 14203

Tel: (716) 856-4910    Fax: (716) 856-0942    www.dualite-spheres.com

*Mfr. coatings, adhesives and specialty chemical for packaging and graphic arts..*

**Matsumoto Yushi-Seiyaku Co., Ltd., Shin-Edobashi Bldg., 4F 8-6 Kobuna-cho Nihonbashi, Chuo-ku Tokyo, Japan**

## PILLAR INDUSTRIES

21905 Gateway Road, Brookfield, WI, 53045

Tel: (262) 317-5300    Fax: (262) 317-5353    www.pillar.com

*Mfr. induction heating and melting equipment.*

**Pillar Orient Corp., 1-11-5 Hiroo 1308, Shibuya-ku, Tokyo 150, Japan**

## PILLSBURY MADISON & SUTRO LLP

50 Fremont Street, San Francisco, CA, 94105

Tel: (415) 983-1000    Fax: (415) 983-1200    www.pillsburylaw.com

*International law firm.*

**Pillsbury Madison & Sutro LLP, Toranomon Act Builidng 6F, 5-11-12 Toranomon 5-chome, Minato-ku, Tokyo 105 Japan**

Tel: 81-3-3354-3531   Fax: 81-3-3354-3534   Contact: Steven Nakasone, Sr. Counsel

## PIONEER HI-BRED INTERNATIONAL INC.

400 Locust Street, Ste. 800, Des Moines, IA, 50309

Tel: (515) 248-4800    Fax: (515) 248-4999    www.pioneer.com

*Agricultural chemicals, farm supplies, biological products, research.*

**Pioneer Hi-Bred Japan, Landic Toranomon Bldg. - 7/F, 3-7-10 Toranomon, Tokyo 105 Japan**

## PITNEY BOWES INC.

1 Elmcroft Road, Stamford, CT, 06926-0700

Tel: (203) 356-5000    Fax: (203) 351-6835    www.pitneybowes.com

*Mfr. postage meters, mailroom equipment, copiers, bus supplies, bus services, facsimile systems and financial services.*

**Pitney Bowes Japan, Togoshi Ni Bldg., No. 7-1 Togoshi 1-chome, Shinagawa-ku, Tokyo 142, Japan**

Tel: 81-3-5750-4111   Fax: 81-3-5750-4405   Contact: Glynn Brasington, VP Operations   Emp: 142

## PITTSTON BAX GROUP

16808 Armstrong Ave., PO Box 19571, Irvine, CA, 92623

Tel: (949) 752-4000    Fax: (949) 260-3182    www.baxworld.com

*Air freight forwarder.*

**BAX Global Japan K.K., G1 Higashi Nihonbashi Bldg., 9-7 Higashi Nihonbashi, 1-chome Chuo-ku, Tokyo 103-0004 Japan**

Tel: 81-3-5820-6851   Fax: 81-3-5820-6855

## PLAINS COTTON COOPERATIVE ASSOCIATES

3301 East 50th Street, Lubbock, TX, 79404

Tel: (806) 763-8011    Fax: (806) 762-7333    www.pcca.com

*Merchandisers of raw cotton to domestic and foreign textile mills.*

**Amcot, Tokyo, Japan**

## PNC FINANCIAL SERVICES GROUP

249 Fifth Ave., Pittsburgh, PA, 15222

Tel: (412) 762-2000    Fax: (412) 762-7829    www.pncbank.com

*Engaged in financial and asset management.*

**Nomura BlackRock Asset Management Co., Ltd., Div. PNC, Nihonbashi-Muromachi 2-1-1, Chuo-ku, Tokyo 10300022 Japan**

Tel: 81-3-3241-9980   Fax: 81-3-3241-9713

## POLAROID CORPORATION

784 Memorial Dr., Cambridge, MA, 02139

Tel: (781) 386-2000    Fax: (781) 386-3924    www.polaroid.com

*Photographic equipment and supplies, optical products.*

**Nippon Polaroid KK, 30 Mori Bldg., 2-2 Torinomon 3-chome, Minato-ku, Tokyo 105, Japan**

## POTTERS INDUSTRIES INC.

PO Box 840, Valley Forge, PA, 19482-0840

Tel: (610) 651-4700    Fax: (610) 408-9724    www.pottersbeads.com

*Mfr. glass spheres for road marking and industry applications.*

**Toshiba-Ballotini Co. Ltd.,  Meguro Suda Bldg. 6/F, 9-1 Meguro-ku, Tokyo 153, Japan**

## PPG INDUSTRIES

One PPG Place, Pittsburgh, PA, 15272

Tel: (412) 434-3131    Fax: (412) 434-2190    www.ppg.com

*Mfr. coatings, flat glass, fiber glass, chemicals, coatings.*

**Asahi-Penn Chemical Co. Ltd.,  Chiyoda-ku, Tokyo, Japan**

**PPG-CI Co. Ltd.,  KRT Aoyama Bldg., 12-5 Kita-Aoyama 2-chome, Minato-ku, Tokyo 107, Japan**

## PRAXAIR, INC.

39 Old Ridgebury Road, Danbury, CT, 06810-5113

Tel: (203) 837-2000    Fax: (203) 837-2450    www.praxair.com

*Produces and distributes industrial and specialty gases.*

**Iwatani Industrial Gases Corporation,  21-8 Nishi-Shimbasi 3-chome, Minato-ku, Tokyo, 105, Japan**
Tel: 81-3-3555-5920

**Praxair K. K.,  Minami Aoyama Watanabe Bldg., 1-4-2 Minami Aoyama, Minato-ku, Tokyo 107, Japan**
Tel: 81-3-3408-7341    Fax: 81-3-3408-7378

## PREMARK INTERNATIONAL INC.

1717 Deerfield Road, Deerfield, IL, 60015

Tel: (847) 405-6000    Fax: (847) 405-6013    www.premarkintl.com

*Mfr. Hobart commercial food equipment, diversified consumer and commercial products, small appliances, and exercise equipment.*

**Dart Industries Ltd.,  Bungei-Shunju Bldg., 3-23 Kioicho, Chiyoda-ku, Tokyo, Japan**

## PREMIX INC.

PO Box 281, Rt. 20, Harmon Road, North Kingsville, OH, 44068-0281

Tel: (440) 224-2181    Fax: (440) 224-2766    www.premix.com

*Mfr. molded fiber glass, reinforced thermoset molding compounds and plastic parts.*

**TyH Associates,  29-74, Chigusa-Dai, Aoba-ku, Yokohama, Kanagawa 227, Japan**
Tel: 81-45-973-5265   Fax: 81-45-973-5265   Contact: Takashi Hanajima   Emp: 1

## PRI AUTOMATION, INC.

805 Middlesex Turnpike, Billerica, MA, 01821-3986

Tel: (978) 663-8555    Fax: (978) 663-9755    www.pria.com

*Provides factory automation systems for silicon chip makers.*

**PRI Automation, OEM Systems Japan,  37 Hongo Kochino, Kounan Aichi, Nagoya 483-8273, Japan**
Tel: 81-587-56-6035   Fax: 81-587-56-6038

## PRICEWATERHOUSECOOPERS LLP

1301 Ave. of the Americas, New York, NY, 10019

Tel: (212) 596-7000    Fax: (212) 259-1301    www.pwcglobal.com

*Accounting and auditing, tax and management, and human resource consulting services.*

**PriceWaterhouseCoopers,  Osaka Centre Building 10F, 1-3 Kyutaro-machi 4-chome, Chuo-ku, Osaka 541 Japan**
Tel: 81-6-252-6791   Fax: 81-6-252-6798

**PriceWaterhouseCoopers,  Yebisu Garden Place Tower 14F, 20-3 Ebisu 4-chome Shibuya-ku, PO Box 5034, Tokyo 150 Japan**
Tel: 81-3-5424-8500   Fax: 81-3-5425-8423

PriceWaterhouseCoopers, **Sunmemoria Dai-ichi Seimei Bldg 6F, 1 Kita-Sanjo Nishi 1-chome Chuo-ku, Sapporo Hokkaido, Japan**

Tel: 81-11-232-7530    Fax: 81-11-232-7533

PriceWaterhouseCoopers, **Mainichi Building 5F, 7-35 Meieki 4-chome, Nakamura-ku, Nagoya 450 Japan**

Tel: 81-52-571-6271    Fax: 81-52-571-6273

PriceWaterhouseCoopers, **Asahi Seimei Yokohama Honcho Bldg., 36 Honcho 4-chome, Naka-ku, Yokohoma 231 Japan**

Tel: 81-45-212-4771    Fax: 81-45-212-4788

PriceWaterhouseCoopers, **Daiwa-Hiroshima Bldg. 6F, 2-27 Tatemachi, Naka-ku, Hiroshima 730 Japan**

Tel: 81-82-242-0102    Fax: 81-82-242-0166

## PRIMARK CORPORATION

100 Winter Street, Ste. 4300-N, Waltham, MA, 02451

Tel: (781) 466-6611        Fax: (781) 890-6187        www.primark.com

*Provides financial and business information.*

**Primark Japan KK, Nagai Building 5/F, 1-7-7 Hatchobori 1-Chome Chuo-Ku, Tokyo 104 0032, Japan**

## PROCTER & GAMBLE COMPANY

One Procter & Gamble Plaza, Cincinnati, OH, 45202

Tel: (513) 983-1100        Fax: (513) 562-4500        www.pg.com

*Personal care, food, laundry, cleaning and industry products.*

**Procter & Gamble Far East Inc., 1-17 Koyo-cho, Naka, Higashi-nada-ku, Kobe 658-0032 Japan**

Tel: 81-78-658-0032

## PRUDENTIAL INSURANCE COMPANY OF AMERICA

751 Broad Street, Newark, NJ, 07102-3777

Tel: (973) 802-6000        Fax: (973) 802-2804        www.prudential.com

*Sale of life insurance and provides financial services.*

**Sony Prudential Life Insurance Co. Ltd., 1-1 Minami Aoyama 1-chome, Minato-ku, Tokyo 107, Japan**

## PSI NET (PERFORMANCE SYSTEMS INTERNATIONAL INC.)

510 Huntmar Park Drive, Herndon, VA, 22170

Tel: (703) 904-4100        Fax: (703) 904-4200        www.psinet.com

*Internet service provider.*

**PSINet Japan Inc., Plaza Mikado Building 3F, 2-14-5 Akasaka, Minato-ku, Tokyo 107-0052 Japan**

Tel: 81-3-54-89-71-67    Fax: 81-3-55-74-71-73    Contact: Vincent Gebes, Dir.

**Rimnet Corporation, Nikko Nanpeidal Building, 2-17 Nanpeidal-cho Shibuya-ku, Tokyo, Japan**

Tel: 81-3-54-89-71-67    Fax: 81-3-54-89-56-40    Contact: Chi H. Kwan, SVP, Asia

**Tokyo Internet Corporation, Shinjuku Gyoen Building 5F, 2-3-10 Shinjuku Shinjuku-ku, Tokyo 160-0022, Japan**

Tel: 81-3-33-41-63-01    Fax: 81-3-33-41-28-81    Contact: Chi H. Kwan, SVP, Asia

**TWICS Company Ltd., 1-21 Yotsuya, Shinjuku-ku, Tokyo, Japan**

Tel: 81-3-33-51-59-77    Fax: 81-3-33-53-60-96    Contact: Chi H. Kwan, SVP, Asia

## PUTNAM INVESTMENTS

1 Post Office Square, Boston, MA, 02109

Tel: (617) 292-1000        Fax: (617) 292-1499        www.putnaminv.com

*Money management; mutual funds, annuities and retirement plans.*

**Putnam Advisory Co. Ltd., 18-19 Toranomon Main Bldg., 3-chome, Minato-ku, Tokyo 105, Japan**

## QUAKER CHEMICAL CORPORATION

Elm & Lee Streets, Conshohocken, PA, 19428-0809

Tel: (610) 832-4000    Fax: (610) 832-8682    www.quakerchem.com

*Mfr. developer, producer, and marketer of custom-formulated chemical specialty products.*

**Nippon Quaker Chemical Ltd. (JV), 1-3 2-chome, Shibukawa-cho, Yao City Osaka, Japan**

Tel: 81-729-92-1650    Contact: J. Aida, Pres.

## QUANTUM

500 McCarthy Blvd., Milpitas, CA, 95035

Tel: (408) 894-4000    Fax: (408) 894-3218    www.quantum.com

*Mfr. computer peripherals.*

**Quantum Japan Corporation, Shinjuku Square Tower 4/F, 6-22-1 Nishi-Shinjuku-Ku, Tokyo 163-11 Japan**

Tel: 81-3-5321-7901

## QUINTILES TRANSNATIONAL CORPORATION

4709 Creekstone Dr., Durham, NC, 27703

Tel: (919) 998-2000    Fax: (919) 998-9113    www.quintiles.com

*Mfr. pharmaceuticals.*

**Quintiles Transnational Japan K.K., Forefront Tower II - 3-13-1 Kachodoki, Chuo-Ku, Tokyo 104-0054, Japan**

## QWEST COMMUNICATIONS INTERNATIONAL INC.

1801 California Street, Ste. 5200, Denver, CO, 80202

Tel: (303) 896-2020    Fax: (303) 793-6654    www.uswest.com

*Tele-communications provider; integrated communications services.*

**Chofu Cable Television, Tokyo, Japan**

**TITUS Communications Corporation, Tokyo, Japan**

Tel: 81-3-3499-88-91    Fax: 81-3-3499-89-71    Contact: Rich Metoki, Mgr. Corp. Planning

## RADISSON HOTELS INTERNATIONAL

Carlson Pkwy., PO Box 59159, Minneapolis, MN, 55459-8204

Tel: (612) 540-5526    Fax: (612) 449-3400    www.radisson.com

*Hotels and resorts.*

**Radisson Miyako Hotel, 1-50 Shirokanedai 1-chome, Minato-ku-,Tokyo 108-8640, Japan**

Tel: 81-3-3447-3111    Fax: 81-3-3447-3133

## RAMBUS INC.

2465 Latham Street, Mountain View, CA, 94040

Tel: (650) 944-8000    Fax: (650) 944-8080    www.rambus.com

*Develops and licenses scalable bandwidth, chip connections technologies that enable semiconductor memory devices and ASICs to keep pace with faster generations of processors and controllers.*

**Rambus KK, 2-4-1, Hamamatsu-cho, Minato-ku, Tokyo 105, Japan**
**World Trade Center**
**Building 33F**

Tel: 81-3-5425-7321

## RANCO INC.

8115 US Route 42 North, Plain City, OH, 43064

Tel: (614) 873-9000    Fax: (614) 873-3819    www.rancocontrols.com

*Mfr. controls for appliance, automotive, comfort, commercial and consumer markets.*

**Ranco Japan Ltd., Shiozaki Bldg., 7-2-2 Hirakawa-cho, Chiyoda-ku, Tokyo 102, Japan**

## RAY & BERNDTSON, INC.

301 Commerce, Ste. 2300, Fort Worth, TX, 76102

Tel: (817) 334-0500     Fax: (817) 334-0779     www.prb.com

*Executive search, management audit and management consulting firm.*

**Ray & Berndtson, Sogo Hanzomon Bldg. 9, Fl-7 Kojimachi, Chiyoda-ku, Tokyo 102 Japan**

Tel: 81-3-5211-8411  Fax: 81-3-3264-0910   Contact: Roger J. Marshall, Mng. Ptnr.

## RAYCHEM CORPORATION

300 Constitution Dr., Menlo Park, CA, 94025-1164

Tel: (650) 361-3333     Fax: (650) 361-5579     www.raychem.com

*Develop/mfr./market materials science products for electronics, telecommunications and industry.*

**K.K. Raychem, Nagoya Chogin Bldg. 9/F, 1-17-19 Marunouchi, Naka-ku, Nagoya 460 Japan**

Tel: 81-52-204-1530  Fax: 81-52-204-1526

## RAYONIER INC.

50 N. Laura St., 18-19 Fls., Jacksonville, FL, 32202

Tel: (904) 357-9100     Fax: (904) 357-9155     www.rayonier.com

*Chemicals cellulose, paper pulps, logs and lumber.*

**Rayonier Japan, Tokyo, Japan**

## RAYTHEON COMPANY

141 Spring Street, Lexington, MA, 02173

Tel: (781) 862-6600     Fax: (781) 860-2172     www.raytheon.com

*Mfr. diversified electronics, appliances, aviation, energy and environmental products; publishing, industry and construction services.*

**New Japan Radio Co. Ltd., 5 Mitsuya-Toranomon Bldg., 22-14 Toranomon, Minato-ku, Tokyo 105, Japan**

**Raytheon International, Tokyo, Japan**

## RAZORFISH, INC.

107 Grand Street, 3rd Fl., New York, NY, 10013

Tel: (212) 966-5960     Fax: (212) 966-6915     www.razorfish.com

*Engaged in consulting and web services.*

**Razorfish Japan KK, Hiroo SK Bldg. 8/F, 2-36-13 Ebisu, Shibuya-ku Tokyo 1500013, Japan**

Tel: 81-3-5475-2011

## REEBOK INTERNATIONAL LTD.

100 Technology Center Drive, Stoughton, MA, 02072

Tel: (781) 401-5000     Fax: (781) 401-7402     www.reebok.com

*Mfr. athletic shoes including casual, dress golf and walking shoes.*

**Planet Reebok Japan, Tokyo, Japan**

## REFAC

115 River Rd., Edgewater, NJ, 07020-1099

Tel: (201) 943-4400     Fax: (201) 943-7400     www.refac.com

*Consults to international technology transfer, foreign trade and power supplies firms for brand and trademarking licensing services..*

**REFAC, 19 Mori Bldg., 2-20 Toranomon 1-chome, Tokyo 109, Japan**

## REFLEXITE TECHNOLOGY

120 Darling Drive, Avon, CT, 06001

Tel: (860) 676-7100     Fax: (860) 676-7199     www.reflexite.com

*Mfr. plastic film, sheet, materials and shapes, optical lenses.*

**Reflexite Japan KK, SS Bldg. 7/F - 3-4-2 Nishi-Shimbashi, Minato-ku, Tokyo 105-0003 Japan**

Tel: 81-3-3578-8201  Fax: 81-3-3578-8191

## REGAL WARE INC.

1675 Reigle Drive, PO Box 395, Kewaskum, WI, 53040-0395

Tel: (414) 626-2121    Fax: (414) 626-8565    www.regalware.com

*Mfr. cookware, small electrical appliances, water purification and filtration products for home.*

**Regal Japan Co. Ltd., Taishoseimei Nishiki Bldg., 18-24 Nishiki 1-chome, Naka-ku, Nagoya 460, Japan**

## REMEDY CORPORATION

1505 Salado Drive, Mountain View, CA, 94043-1110

Tel: (650) 903-5200    Fax: (650) 903-9001    www.remedy.com

*Developer and marketer of computer applications for the operations management market.*

**Remedy K.K., Izumi-Akasaka Bldg. 6/F, 2-22-24 Akasaka, Minato-ku, Tokyo 107-0052, Japan**
Tel: 81-3-3568-2500    Fax: 81-3-3568-2501

**Remedy K.K., Kasumigaseki Bldg. 35 F, 3-2-5, Kasumigaseki, Chiyoda-ku, Tokyo 100, Japan**
Tel: 81-3-5512-7487    Fax: 81-3-5512-7489

## RENAISSANCE HOTELS AND RESORTS

10400 Fernwood Road, Bethesda, MD, 20817

Tel: (301) 380-3000    Fax: (301) 380-5181    www.renaissancehotels.com

*Hotel and resort chain.*

**Renaissance Gifu Hotel, Tokyo, Japan**
Tel: 81-58-295-3100

**Renaissance Tokyo Hotel, Tokyo, Japan**
Tel: 81-3-3546-0111

## RENAISSANCE WORLDWIDE, INC.

52 Second Ave., Waltham, MA, 02451

Tel: (781) 290-3000    Fax: (781) 965-4807    www.rens.com

*Provides technology consulting, staffing services, corporate and systems strategies and software and hardware installation.*

**Renaissance Worldwide, Inc., Kaneyoshi Bldg. 4F, 11-8, Shibuya-Ku, Tokyo 150, Japan**
Tel: 81-3-3770-5350    Fax: 81-3-3770-1592

## REVLON INC.

625 Madison Ave., New York, NY, 10022

Tel: (212) 527-4000    Fax: (212) 527-4995    www.revlon.com

*Mfr. cosmetics, fragrances, toiletries and beauty care products.*

**Revlon KK, 2-3 Minami-Aoyama 2-chome, Minato-ku, Tokyo 107, Japan**
Contact: Thomas Seymour

## RHEOMETRIC SCIENTIFIC INC.

1 Possumtown Road, Piscataway, NJ, 08854

Tel: (732) 560-8550    Fax: (732) 560-7451    www.rheosci.com

*Design/mfr. rheological instruments and systems.*

**Rheometric Scientific F.E. Ltd., 19-6 Yanagibashi 2-chome, Taito-ku, Tokyo 111, Japan**

## RICH PRODUCTS CORPORATION

1150 Niagara St., Buffalo, NY, 14213

Tel: (716) 878-8000    Fax: (716) 878-8765    www.richs.com

*Mfr. non-dairy products.*

**Rich Products Corp., Ginza-Yamamato Bldg., 16-11 Ginza 6-chome, Chuo-ku, Tokyo 104 Japan**

## RICHCO, INC.

5825 N. Tripp Ave., PO Box 804238, Chicago, IL, 60680

Tel: (773) 539-4060    Fax: (773) 539-6770    www.richco.com

*Mfr. plastic and metal parts for the electric, electronic, appliance, and fiber-optic industries.*

**Richco Japan, 302 Yamadera Building, 12/19 Yutenji 2-Chome Meguro-ku, Tokyo 153, Japan**

Tel: 81-33791-1821

## RIDGE TOOL COMPANY

400 Clark Street, Elyria, OH, 44035

Tel: (440) 323-5581    Fax: (440) 329-4853    www.ridgid.com

*Mfr. hand and power tools for working pipe, drain cleaning equipment, etc.*

**Ridge Div. Emerson Japan Ltd., New Pier Takeshiba South Tower 7F, 1-16-1 Kaigan, Minato-ku, Tokyo 105, Japan**

Tel: 81-3-5403-8560   Fax: 81-3-5403-8569

## RIGHT MANAGEMENT CONSULTANTS, INC.

1818 Market Street, 14th Fl., Philadelphia, PA, 19103-3614

Tel: (215) 988-1588    Fax: (215) 988-9112    www.right.com

*Out placement and human resources consulting services.*

**Right Associates, 1-5 Hakozaki-cho Nihonbashi, Chuo-ku, Tokyo 103, Japan**

## THE RITZ-CARLTON HOTEL COMPANY, L.L.C.

3414 Peachtree Road NE, Ste. 300, Atlanta, GA, 30326

Tel: (404) 237-5500    Fax: (404) 365-9643    www.ritzcarlton.com

*5-star hotel and restaurant chain.*

**The Ritz-Carlton Hotel, 2-2-25 Umeda, Kita-ku, Osaka 530, Japan**

Tel: 81-6-347-4784   Fax: 81-6-343-1888

**The Ritz-Carlton Hotel Company, Homat Hanzomon 4F, 12-12 Kojimachi 1-chome, Chiyoda-ku, Tokyo 102 Japan**

Tel: 81-3-5210-7511   Fax: 81-3-5210-7524

## RMO INC.

650 West Colfax Ave., Denver, CO, 80204

Tel: (303) 534-8181    Fax: (303) 592-8209    www.rmotho.com

*Mfr. dental equipment and supplies.*

**Rocky Mountain Morita Corp. KK, Tokyo, Japan**

Tel: 81-3-3251-4631   Fax: 81-3-3255-4090

## ROCK OF AGES CORPORATION

369 N. State St., Concord, NH, 03301

Tel: (603) 225-8397    Fax: (603) 225-4801    www.rockofages.com

*Quarrier; dimension granite blocks, memorials, and precision industrial granite.*

**Rock of Ages Asia Corp., 3-8 Uchihonmachi 2-chome, Chuo-ku, Osaka 540, Japan**

Tel: 81-6-941-6511   Fax: 816-941-8526   Contact: Takashi Oshio   Emp: 3

## ROCKWELL INTERNATIONAL CORPORATION

777 East Wisconsin Ave., Ste. 1400, Milwaukee, WI, 53202

Tel: (414) 212-5200    Fax: (414) 212-5201    www.rockwell.com

*Products and service for aerospace and defense, automotive, electronics, graphics and automation industry.*

**Rockwell Automation Japan Co., Ltd., 8F/9F Shinkawa Sanko Bldg., 1-3-17 Shinkawa, Chuo-ku, Tokyo 104 Japan**

Tel: 81-3-3206-2783   Fax: 81-3-3206-2788

**Rockwell Automation Reliance Electric Ltd., Takeda Yakuhin Bldg. 5F, 1-25 Komachi Naka-ku, Hiroshima 730-0041 Japan**

Tel: 81-82-242-1201   Fax: 81-82-242-7001

**Rockwell Collins,** **8F/9F Shinkawa Sanko Bldg., 1-3-17 Shinkawa, Chuo-ku, Tokyo 104 Japan**
Tel: 81-3-5543-3535    Fax: 81-3-5543-3585

**Rockwell International Japan,** **Shimomoto Bldg., 1-46-3 Hatsudai, Shibuya-ku, Tokyo 151 Japan**
Tel: 81-3-5371-1791    Fax: 81-3-5371-1508

## ROGERS CORPORATION

One Technology Drive, PO Box 188, Rogers, CT, 06263-0188

Tel: (860) 774-9605       Fax: (860) 779-5509       www.rogers-corp.com

*Mfr. specialty materials including elastomers, circuit laminates and moldable composites.*

**Rogers Japan Inc.,** **7F St Bldg., 2-26-9, Nishi-nippori, Arakawa-ku, Tokyo 116-0013 Japan**
Tel: 81-33-807-6430    Fax: 81-33-807-6319    Contact: William Schunmann, VP

## ROHM AND HAAS COMPANY

100 Independence Mall West, Philadelphia, PA, 19106

Tel: (215) 592-3000       Fax: (215) 592-3377       www.rohmhaas.com

*Mfr. industrial and agricultural chemicals, plastics.*

**Japan Acrylic Chemical Co. Ltd.,** **Nagoya Plant, 1-64 Funami-cho, Minato-ku, Nagoya 455 Japan**
Tel: 81-52-611-0127

**Morton Electronic Materials,** **200-11 Oaza Motohara, Kamikawa-machi, Kodama-gun Saitama 36702, Japan**

**Nippon Bee Chemical,** **2-14-1 Shadai-Ohtani Hirakata, Osaka 573 Japan**

**Rodel-Nitta Company,** **8-3 Fujigaoka, Fujiwara-cho, Inabe-Gun, Mie, 511-05 Japan**

**Rohm and Haas Japan,** **2763 Happo Washinomiya-Machi, Kita-Katsushika-Gun, Saitama 340-020 Japan**

**Rohm and Haas Japan KK,** **The Vanguard Moto Azabu, 4-26 Moto Azabu 3-chome, Minato-ku, Tokyo 106-0046 Japan**
Tel: 81-3-5488-3100

**Shipley Far East Ltd.,** **Nishidai NC Bldg., 1-83-1 Takashimadaira, Itabashi-ku, Tokyo 175 Japan**
Tel: 81-3-5920-5300

**Shipley Far East, Ltd.,** **172 Ike Zawa-cho Yamato, Koriyame-shi 63911, Japan**

**Shipley Far East, Ltd.,** **2-3 Kouyo 1-Chome, Soma-shi, Fukushima 976-005, Japan**

## T. ROWE PRICE ASSOCIATES, INC.

100 East Pratt Street, Baltimore, MD, 21202

Tel: (410) 345-2000       Fax: (410) 345-2394       www.troweprice.com

*Investment and portfolio asset management.*

**Rowe Price-Fleming International,** **Tokyo, Japan**

## RUDER FINN INC.

301 East 57th Street, New York, NY, 10022

Tel: (212) 593-6400       Fax: (212) 593-6397       www.ruderfinn.com

*Engaged in public relations service and broadcast communications.*

**Ruder Finn Japan,** **Akasaka Q Bldg. 207, 9-5 Akasake 7-chome, Minato-ku, Tokyo 107, Japan**

## RUSSELL REYNOLDS ASSOCIATES INC.

200 Park Ave., New York, NY, 10166-0002

Tel: (212) 351-2000       Fax: (212) 370-0896       www.russreyn.com

*Executive recruiting services.*

**Russell Reynolds Associates Inc.,** **Taisho Seimei Hibiya Bldg. 5F 1-9-1, Yurakucho, Chiyoda-ku, Tokyo 100, Japan**
Tel: 81-3-3216-1911    Fax: 81-2-3216-5866    Contact: Hirohide Fujii

## SALOMON SMITH BARNEY HOLDINGS INC.

388 Greenwich Street, New York, NY, 10013

Tel: (212) 816-6000  Fax: (212) 816-8915  www.smithbarney.com

*Securities dealers and underwriters.*

**Nikko Securities Co., Tokyo, Japan**

**Salomon Smith Barney Holdings, Fukoku-Seimei Bldg., 2-2 Uchsaiwai-cho 2-chome, Chiyoda-ku, Tokyo, Japan**

## THE SANTA CRUZ OPERATION, INC.

400 Encinal Street, Santa Cruz, CA, 95060

Tel: (831) 425-7222  Fax: (831) 427-5448  www.sco.com

*Mfr. server software.*

**SCO Japan KK, Meguro-ku, Tokyo, Japan**

Tel: 81-3-5486-3905

## SAPIENT CORPORATION

1 Memorial Drive, Cambridge, MA, 02142

Tel: (617) 621-0200  Fax: (617) 621-1300  www.sapient.com

*Engaged in information technology and consulting services.*

**Sapient K.K., Toranomon 40 Mori Building, 5-13-1 Toranomon, Minato-ku, Tokyo 105-0001, Japan**

## SARA LEE CORPORATION

3 First National Plaza, Chicago, IL, 60602-4260

Tel: (312) 726-2600  Fax: (312) 558-4995  www.saralee.com

*Mfr./distributor food and consumer packaged goods, intimate apparel and knitwear.*

**HomCare Japan, Ltd., Tokyo, Japan**

## SAS INSTITUTE INC.

SAS Campus Drive, Cary, NC, 27513

Tel: (919) 677-8000  Fax: (919) 677-4444  www.sas.com

*Mfr./distributes decision support software.*

**SAS Institute (Japan) Ltd., Tokyo, Japan**

Tel: 81-3-3533-3760  Fax: 81-3-3533-6927

## W. B. SAUNDERS COMPANY

625 Walnut St., Ste. 300, Philadelphia, PA, 19106-3399

Tel: (215) 238-7800  Fax: (215) 238-7883  www.wbsaunders.com

*Develop medical educational software.*

**W.B. Saunders Co., Ichibancho Central Bldg., 22-1 Ichibancho, Chiyoda-ku, Tokyo 102, Japan**

## SCANSOFT, INC.

9 Centennial Dr., Peabody, MA, 01960

Tel: (978) 977-2000  Fax: (978) 977-2436  www.scansoft.com

*Mfr. digital imaging software.*

**Catena Corporation, 10-24 Shiomi 2-Chome Koto-Ku, Tokyo 135, Japan**

## SCHENECTADY INTERNATIONAL INC.

PO Box 1046, Schenectady, NY, 12301

Tel: (518) 370-4200  Fax: (518) 382-8129  www.siigroup.com

*Mfr. electrical insulating varnishes, enamels, phenolic resins, alkylphenols.*

**Nisshoku Schenectady Kagaku Inc., 5-8 Nishi Otabicho Suita, Osaka, 564-0034 Japan**

Tel: 81-6-6317-2826  Fax: 81-6-6317-2828  Contact: Hidemitsu Takizawa

## SCHENKER INTERNATIONAL FORWARDERS INC.

150 Albany Ave., Freeport, NY, 11520

Tel: (516) 377-3000    Fax: (516) 377-3005    www.schenkerusa.com

*Freight forwarders.*

**Japan Schenker Co., Taiyo Shoji Bldg 4F5, 11 Nakanoshima 3-chome, Kita-ku, Osaka 530 Japan**

Tel: 81-6-444-1191   Fax: 81-6-445-6987

**Japan Schenker Co., Kachidoki Sun Square 7-3, Kachidoki 1-chome, Chuo-ku, Tokyo Japan**

Tel: 81-3-5560-8600   Fax: 81-3-5560-8620

## R. P. SCHERER CORPORATION

645 Martinsville Rd., Ste. 200, Baskin Ridge, NJ, 07920

Tel: (908) 580-1500    Fax: (908) 580-9220    www.rpscherer.com

*Mfr. pharmaceuticals; soft gelatin and two-piece hard shell capsules.*

**P.R. Scherer KK, Shin Tokyo Akasaka Bldg., 4-9-25 Akasaka, Minato-ku, Tokyo 107-0052, Japan**

Tel: 81-3-3470-2311   Fax: 81-3-3408-5554   Contact: Shusuke Kato, President   Emp: 144

## SCHERING-PLOUGH CORPORATION

One Giralda Farms, Madison, NJ, 07940-1000

Tel: (973) 822-7000    Fax: (973) 822-7048    www.sch-plough.com

*Proprietary drug and cosmetic products.*

**Coppertone (Japan) Ltd., PO Box 36, Akasaka, Tokyo, Japan**

**Essex Nippon KK (Schering Corp.), CPO Box 1235, Osaka 530-91, Japan**

**Japan Schering-Plough K.K., Ichibancho 2/F, 10-2 Ichiban-cho Chiyoda-ku, Tokyo 102-0082 Japan**

## SCHLEGEL SYSTEMS

1555 Jefferson Road, PO Box 23197, Rochester, NY, 14692-3197

Tel: (716) 427-7200    Fax: (716) 427-9993    www.schlegel.com

*Mfr. engineered perimeter sealing systems for residential and commercial construction; fibers; rubber product.*

**Schlegel Engineering KK, 4/F Iwanami Shoten Annex, 3-1 Kanda Jinbocho 2-chome, Chiyoda-ku, Tokyo 101, Japan**

## SCHLUMBERGER LIMITED

277 Park Avenue, New York, NY, 10021

Tel: (212) 350-9400    Fax: (212) 350-9564    www.schlumberger.com

*Engaged in oil and gas services, metering and payment systems, and produces semiconductor testing equipment and smart cards.*

**Schlumberger K.K., Sumitomohamamatsucho Building 5F, 1-18-16, Hamamatsucho, Minato-ku, Tokyo 105-0013 Japan**

## THE CHARLES SCHWAB CORPORATION

101 Montgomery Street, San Francisco, CA, 94104

Tel: (415) 627-7000    Fax: (415) 627-8840    www.schawb.com

*Financial services; discount brokerage, retirement accounts.*

**Charles Schwab Tokio Marine Securities Co., Ltd., Tokyo, Japan**

## SCIENCE APPLICATIONS INTL. CORPORATION (SAIC)

10260 Campus Point Dr., San Diego, CA, 92121

Tel: (858) 826-6000    Fax: (858) 535-7589    www.saic.com

*Engaged in research and engineering.*

**SAIC Japan, Samon Eleven Building 4/F, 3-1 Samon-Cho Shinjuku-Ku, Tokyo 160, Japan**

Tel: 81-3-33578057   Fax: 81-3-3357-8176

## SCIENTIFIC-ATLANTA, INC.

1 Technology Pkwy South, Norcross, GA, 30092-2967

Tel: (770) 903-5000　　　Fax: (770) 903-2967　　　www.sciatl.com

*A leading supplier of broadband communications systems, satellite-based video, voice and data communications networks and worldwide customer service and support.*

**Scientific-Atlanta Japan, KK, Sat. 1 Bldg., 2204 Minami-Aoyama, Minatoku, Tokyo 107 Japan**

Tel: 81-3-3497-9715　Fax: 81-3-3497-0582

## SDI TECHNOLOGIES

1299 Main St., Rahway, NJ, 07065

Tel: (732) 574-9000　　　Fax: (732) 574-3797　　　www.sdidirect.com

*Mfr. clock radios and electronic products.*

**SDI Technologies, 9-14 Nihonbashi 2-chome, Chuo-ku, Tokyo, Japan**

## SEAGATE TECHNOLOGY, INC.

920 Disc Dr., Scotts Valley, CA, 95066

Tel: (408) 438-6550　　　Fax: (408) 438-7205　　　www.seagate.com

*Develop computer technology, software and hardware.*

**Nipon Seagate, Inc., Tennoz Parkside Bldg. 3F, 2-5-8 Higashi-Shinagawa, Shinagawa-ku Tokyo 140, Japan**

Tel: 81-3-5462-2901　Fax: 81-3-5462-2978　Contact: Tsuyoshi Kobayashi, Dir.　Emp: 50

## SEALED AIR CORPORATION

Park 80 East, Saddle Brook, NJ, 07663

Tel: (201) 791-7600　　　Fax: (201) 703-4205　　　www.sealedair.com

*Mfr. protective and specialty packaging solutions for industrial, food and consumer products.*

**Instapak Ltd., 3-20-5 Shiba, Minato-ku, Tokyo 105, Japan**

**Instapak Ltd., 2-53 Kamioka-cho, Meito-ku, Nagoya, Japan**

**Instapak Ltd., Kano Bldg., 2-5-14 Nanbanaka, Naniwa-ku, Osaka Japan**

**Sealed Air Japan Ltd., 1-14-2 Saga, Koto-ku, Tokyo 135, Japan**

Tel: 81-3-5245-1635　Fax: 81-3-5245-1636

## SEAQUIST PERFECT DISPENSING

1160 North Silver Lake Road, Cary, IL, 60013

Tel: (847) 639-2124　　　Fax: (847) 639-2142　　　www.seaquistperect.com

*Mfr. and sale of dispensing systems; lotion pumps and spray-through overcaps.*

**P&S Japan, Tokyo, Japan**

**Seaquist-Valois Japan Inc., Tokyo, Japan**

## G.D. SEARLE & COMPANY

5200 Old Orchard Road, Skokie, IL, 60077

Tel: (847) 982-7000　　　Fax: (847) 470-1480　　　www.searlehealthnet.com

*Mfr. pharmaceuticals, health care, optical products and specialty chemicals.*

**Searle, Division of Monsanto Japan Ltd., 730 Oaza-Noharu Yamaga-Cho, Hayami-Gun Oita-Ken 879-13, Japan**

Tel: 81-977-75-1311　Fax: 81-977-75-1576

## SECURE COMPUTING CORPORATION

One Almaden Blvd., Ste. 400, San Jose, CA, 95113

Tel: (408) 918-6100　　　Fax: (408) 918-6101　　　www.sctc.com

*Mfr. software.*

**Secure Computing Japan KK, Level 11 Aoyama Palacio Tower, 3-6-7 Kita Aoyama Minato-Ku, Tokyo 107-0061, Japan**

Tel: 813-5778-7687

## SELAS CORPORATION OF AMERICA

2034 S. Limekiln Pike, Dresher, PA, 19025

Tel: (215) 646-6600     Fax: (215) 646-3536     www.selas.com

*Mfr. heat treating equipment for metal, glass, ceramic and chemical industry.*

**Nippon Selas Co. Ltd.,  4-3 Arakawa 7-chome, Arakawa-ku, Tokyo 116, Japan**

## SEMTECH CORPORATION

652 Mitchell Road, PO Box 367, Newbury Park, CA, 91320

Tel: (805) 498-2111     Fax: (805) 498-3804     www.semtech.com

*Mfr. silicon rectifiers, rectifier assemblies, capacitors, switching regulators, AC/DC converters.*

**Semtech Ltd. Japan,  1-24-14-405 Kagahara, Tsuzuki-ku, Yokohama 224-0055, Japan**

Tel: 81-45-948-5925   Fax: 81-45-948-5930   Contact: Masa Sagano

## SENCO PRODUCTS INC.

8485 Broadwell Road, Cincinnati, OH, 45244

Tel: (513) 388-2000     Fax: (513) 388-2026     www.senco.com

*Mfr. industry nailers, staplers, fasteners and accessories.*

**Senco Products (Japan) Ltd.,  Wakasugi Grand Bldg. 11-D, 25-5 Tenjinbashi 2-chome, Kita-ku, Osaka 530, Japan**

## SENSIENT TECHNOLOGIES CORPORATION

433 E. Michigan Street, Milwaukee, WI, 53202

Tel: (414) 271-6755     Fax: (414) 347-4783     www.sensient.com

*Mfr. food products and food ingredients.*

**Sensient Asia Pacific,  Tokyo, Japan**

## THE SERVICEMASTER COMPANY

One ServiceMaster Way, Downers Grove, IL, 60515-1700

Tel: (630) 271-1300     Fax: (630) 271-2710     www.svm.com

*Management service to health care, school and industry facilities; diversified residential and commercial services.*

**ServiceMaster Japan Inc.,  PJ Bldg., 22 Kaikyo-cho, Shinjuku-ku, Tokyo 160, Japan**

## SHAKESPEARE FISHING TACKLE GROUP

3801 Westmore Drive, Columbia, SC, 29223

Tel: (803) 754-7000     Fax: (803) 754-7342     www.shakespeare-fishing.com

*Mfr. fishing tackle.*

**Shakespeare Japan Ltd.,  Nishiwaki Bldg., 1 Kohjimachi 4-chome, Chiyoda ku, Tokyo, Japan**

## THE SHARPER IMAGE CORPORATION

650 Davis Street, San Francisco, CA, 94111

Tel: (415) 445-6000     Fax: (415) 445-1588     www.sharperimage.com

*Specialty retailer of innovative products.*

**The Sharper Image,  Shinkobe Oriental City, 1 Kitano-cho, chul-ku, Kobe, Japan**

## SHEARMAN & STERLING

599 Lexington Ave., New York, NY, 10022-6069

Tel: (212) 848-4000     Fax: (212) 848-7179     www.shearman.com

*Law firm engaged in general American and international financial and commercial practice.*

**Shearman & Sterling,  Fukoku Seimei Bldg. 5/F, 2-2-2 Uchisaiwaicho, Chiyoda-ku, Tokyo 100 Japan**

Tel: 81-3-5251-1601   Fax: 81-3-5251-1602   Contact: William M. Burke, Mng. Ptnr.

## SHELDAHL, INC.

1150 Sheldahl Rd., Northfield, MN, 55057-9444

Tel:  (507) 663-8000        Fax:  (507) 663-8545        www.sheldahl.com

*Mfr. electrical and electronic components and laminated plastic products/adhesive-based tapes and materials and adhesiveless Novaclad®.*

**Shinko Electric Industrial Co., Ltd.,  Nagano, Japan**

## SHIPLEY COMPANY, LLC

455 Forest Street, Marlborough, MA, 01752

Tel:  (508) 481-7950        Fax:  (508) 485-9113        www.shipley.com

*Supplier of materials and processes technology to the microelectronics and printed wiring board industries.*

**Shipley Far East Ltd.,  Nishidai NC Bldg., 1-83-1 Takashimadaira, Itabashi-ku, Tokyo 175, Japan**

Tel: 81-35-920-5300   Fax: 81-35-920-5471   Contact: T. Suzuki, Pres.

## SIDLEY & AUSTIN

Bank One Plaza 10 S. Dearborn, Chicago, IL, 60603

Tel:  (312) 853-7000        Fax:  (312) 853-7036        www.sidley.com

*International law firm.*

**Sidley & Austin,  9-1 Yurakucho 1-chome, Chiyoda-ku, Tokyo 100, Japan**

Tel: 81-3-3218-5900   Fax: 81-3-3218-5922   Contact: Shuichi Suzuki, Ptnr.

## SIGNODE PACKAGING SYSTEMS

3610 West Lake Ave., Glenview, IL, 60025

Tel:  (847) 724-6100        Fax:  (847) 657-4392        www.signode.com

*Mfr. industrial tools and machinery for packaging and strapping.*

**Signode KK,  Sannomiya Intl. Bldg., 1-30 Hamabe-dori 2-chome, Chuo-ku, Kobe 651, Japan**

## SILICON GRAPHICS INC.

2011 N. Shoreline Blvd., Mountain View, CA, 94043-1389

Tel:  (650) 960-1980        Fax:  (650) 961-0595        www.sgi.com

*Design/mfr. special-effects computer graphic systems and software.*

**Silicon Graphics,  Japan**

## SILICON STORAGE TECHNOLOGY, INC.

1171 Sonora Court, Sunnyvale, CA, 94086

Tel:  (408) 735-9110        Fax:  (408) 735-9036        www.ssti.com

*Mfr./sale single power supply small ease-block flash memory components, and two-power supply MTP flash products.*

**Silicon Storage Technology Ltd.,  2-2-16 YK Bld., Sangenjaya, Setagaya-ku, Tokyo 154, Japan**

Tel: 81-3-3795-6461   Fax: 81-3-3795-2425

**Silicon Storage Technology Ltd.,  5F Kose #2, 1-14-20 Shin-Yokohama, Kohoku-ku, Yokohama 222-0033, Japan**

Tel: 81-45-471-1851   Fax: 81-45-471-3285   Contact: Masami Goto

## SIMON & SCHUSTER INC.

1230 Avenue of the Americas, New York, NY, 10020

Tel:  (212) 698-7000        Fax:  (212) 698-7007        www.simonandschuster.com

*Publishes and distributes hardcover and paperback books, audiobooks and software.*

**Prentice Hall of Japan Inc.,  Jochi Kojimachi Bldg. 3/F, 1-25 Kojimachi 6 chome, Chigoda-ku, Tokyo 102, Japan**

## SIMPLEX SOLUTIONS, INC.

521 Almanor Ave., Sunnyvale, CA, 94085

Tel: (408) 617-6100　　Fax: (408) 774-0285　　www.simplex.com

*Develops full-chip, multi-level IC extraction and analysis software.*

**Simplex K.K., Ebis-Five Bldg. 4/F, Ebisu Nishi 2-2-6, Shibuya-ku, Tokyo 150-0021 Japan**

Tel: 81-3-3780-7015　Fax: 81-3-3780-7016

**Simplex KK., Tokyo, Japan**

Contact: Jan L. Goodsell, Mgr.

## SIMPSON INVESTMENT COMPANY, INC.

1301 Fifth Ave., Ste. 2800, Seattle, WA, 98101

Tel: (206) 224-5000　　Fax: (206) 224-5060　　www.simpson.com

*Paper, pulp and saw mills, wood products.*

**Simpson Far East KK, 2 Onishi Bldg., 1-6 Toranomon 4-chome, Minato-ku, Tokyo 105, Japan**

## SIMPSON THACHER & BARTLETT

425 Lexington Ave., New York, NY, 10017

Tel: (212) 455-2000　　Fax: (212) 455-2502　　www.simpsonthacher.com

*International law Firm.*

**Simpson Thacher & Bartlett, Ark Mori Bldg., 30tj Fl., 12-32 Akasaka 1-chome, Minato-ku, Tokyo 107, Japan**

Tel: 81-3-5562-8601　Fax: 81-3-5562-8606　Contact: David A. Sneider, Ptnr.

## SKADDEN, ARPS, SLATE, MEAGHER & FLOM LLP

4 Times Square, New York, NY, 10036

Tel: (212) 735-3000　　Fax: (212) 735-2000　　www.sasmf.com

*American/International law practice.*

**Skadden, Arps, Slate, Meagher & Flom LLP, Shiroyama JT Mori Bldg.16/F 4-3-1 Toranomon, Minato-ku, Tokyo 105 Japan**

Tel: 81-3-5403-4730　Fax: 81-3-5403-4731　Contact: E. Anthony Zaloom, Partner

## SMURFIT-STONE CONTAINER CORPORATION

150 N. Michigan Ave., Chicago, IL, 60601-7568

Tel: (312) 346-6600　　Fax: (312) 580-3486　　www.smurfit-stone.net

*Mfr. paper and paper packaging.*

**Smurfit-Stone Container Corporation, Tokyo, Japan**

## SNAP-ON INCORPORATED

10801 Corporate Dr., Pleasant Prairie, WI, 53158-1603

Tel: (262) 656-5200　　Fax: (262) 656-5577　　www.snapon.com

*Mfr. auto maintenance, diagnostic and emission testing equipment, hand tools, hydraulic lifts and tire changers.*

**Snap-On Tools Japan KK (SOJ), 8-10 Shinkiba 1-chome, Kotoh-ku, Tokyo 136, Japan**

## SOLECTRON CORPORATION

777 Gibraltar Drive, Milpitas, CA, 95035

Tel: (408) 957-8500　　Fax: (408) 956-6075　　www.solectron.com

*Provides contract manufacturing services to equipment manufacturers.*

**Force Computers, Inc., Yurakucho Denki Building, South Tower 13F, 1-7-1 Yurakucho Chiyoda-ku, Tokyo 100-0006 Japan**

Tel: 81-3-3287-2031　Fax: 81-3-3287-2032

**Force Computers, Japan K.K., Shibadaimon MF Building, Shiba Daimon 2-1-16, Minato-ku, Tokyo 105 Japan**

Tel: 81-3-3437-3948　Fax: 81-3-3437-3968

## SOLUTIA INC.

575 Maryville Center Dr, St. Louis, MO, 63141

Tel: (314) 674-1000      Fax: (314) 694-8686      www.solutia.com

*Mfr. specialty chemical based products.*

**Solutia Japan Ltd., Shinkawa Sanko Building, 1-3-17 Shinkawa, Chuo-Ku, Tokyo 104-0033 Japan**
Tel: 81-3-56441638

## SONOCO PRODUCTS COMPANY

North Second Street, PO Box 160, Hartsville, SC, 29550

Tel: (843) 383-7000      Fax: (843) 383-7008      www.sonoco.com

*Mfr. packaging for consumer and industrial market and recycled paperboard.*

**Hiyoshimaru Shiko Co., Ltd., 10-2 Nanso-Cho, Higashi-Osaka 579, Japan**
Tel: 81-729-84-5231

**Showa Products Co. Ltd., 8 Fl.Nittochi Dojima Hama, 4-19 Dojima-Hama 1-chome, Kita-ku, Osaka 530 Japan**
Tel: 81-6-345-3751

**Showa Products Co., Ltd. (Tokyo Office), Sengoku Building 8F, 2-4-15 Nihinbashi-Muromachi, Chou-ku, Tokyo 103 Japan**
Tel: 81-3-3242-2751

## SOTHEBY'S HOLDINGS, INC.

1334 York Avenue, New York, NY, 10021

Tel: (212) 606-7000      Fax: (212) 606-7027      www.sothebys.com

*Auction house specializing in fine art and jewelry.*

**Sotheby's Holdings, Inc., Fuerte Kojimachi Bldge.3/F, 1-7 Kojimachi Chiyoda-ku, Tokyo 102, Japan**
Tel: 81-3-3230-2755

## SPALDING HOLDINGS CORPORATION

425 Meadow Street, Chicopee, MA, 01021

Tel: (413) 536-1200      Fax: (413) 536-1404      www.spalding.com

*Mfr. sports equipment and infant and juvenile furniture and accessories.*

**Spalding Sports, Tokyo, Japan**

## SPARTECH CORPORATION

120 S. Central, Ste. 1700, Clayton, MO, 63105-1705

Tel: (314) 721-4242      Fax: (314) 721-1447      www.spartech.com

*Mfr./sales of engineered thermoplastic materials and polymeric compounds.*

**Takiron Co. (JV), Osaka, Japan**

## SPENCER STUART MANAGEMENT CONSULTANTS

401 North Michigan Ave., Ste. 3400, Chicago, IL, 60611

Tel: (312) 822-0080      Fax: (312) 822-0116      www.spencerstuart.com

*Executive recruitment firm.*

**Spencer Stuart & Associates Inc., Kawakita Memorial Building 8F, 18 Ichibancho, Chiyoda-ku, Tokyo 102-0082 Japan**
Tel: 81-3-3238-8901   Fax: 81-3-3238-8902   Contact: Joji Hara

## SPRAYING SYSTEMS COMPANY

PO Box 7900, Wheaton, IL, 60189-7900

Tel: (630) 665-5000      Fax: (630) 260-0842      www.spray.com

*Designs and manufactures industrial spray nozzles.*

**Spraying Systems Co. Japan, 5-10-18 Higashi-Gotanda, Shinagawa-ku, Tokyo 141, Japan**

**Spraying Systems Japan, Park Side Bldg. 5/F 1-1, Sakae 5-chrome, Naka-ku Nagoya 460, Japan**

## SPRINT INTERNATIONAL

World Headquarters, 2330 Shawnee Mission Parkway, Westwood, KS, 66205

Tel: (913) 624-3000     Fax: (913) 624-3281     www.sprint.com

*Telecommunications equipment and services.*

**Sprint Japan Inc., 21-13 Himonya 4-chome, Meguro-ku, Tokyo 152, Japan**

## SPS TECHNOLOGIES INC.

101 Greenwood Avenue, Ste. 470, Jenkintown, PA, 19046

Tel: (215) 517-2000     Fax: (215) 517-2032     www.spstech.com

*Mfr. aerospace and industry fasteners, tightening systems, magnetic materials, superalloys.*

**SPS/Unbrako KK, Ogawa 2-25-5, Machida, Tokyo 194 Japan**

Tel: 81-427-99-5991   Fax: 81-427-99-5442   Contact: Kazutaka Mori, Pres.

## SPSS INC.

233 S. Wacker Dr., Chicago, IL, 60606

Tel: (312) 651-6000     Fax: (312) 329-3668     www.spss.com

*Mfr. statistical software.*

**SPSS Japan Inc., AY Bldg., 3-2-2 Kitaaoyama, Minato-ku, Tokyo 107, Japan**

## SPX CORPORATION

700 Terrace Point Drive, PO Box 3301, Muskegon, MI, 49443-3301

Tel: (231) 724-5000     Fax: (231) 724-5720     www.spx.com

*Mfr. auto parts, special service tools, engine and drive-train parts.*

**Kent-Moore Japan (JATEK), Dai-Ni Maruzen Building 8/F, 9-2 Nihonbashi 3-chome, Chuo-ku, Tokyo 103 Japan**

**Robinair Japan, c/o JATEK Ltd.,, Dai-Ni Maruzen Building, 9/2 Nihonbashi 3-chome, Chuo-ku Tokyo 103 Japan**

**RSV Corp., 4-38 Hokuto-cho, Kashiwazaki, Nigata 945, Japan**

## SRI INTERNATIONAL

333 Ravenswood Ave., Menlo Park, CA, 94025-3493

Tel: (650) 859-2000     Fax: (650) 326-5512     www.sri.com

*Engaged in international consulting and research.*

**SRI East Asia, Shin-Nikko Bldg., East Wing 15/F, 10-1 Toranoman 2-chome, Minato-ku, Tokyo 105, Japan**

**SRI International, Daito Building 2/F, 7-1 Kasumigaseki 3-chome Chiyoda-ku, Tokyo 100-0013 Japan**

Tel: 81-3-5251-1761   Fax: 81-3-5251-1766

## THE ST. PAUL COMPANIES, INC.

385 Washington Street, St. Paul, MN, 55102

Tel: (651) 310-7911     Fax: (651) 310-8294     www.stpaul.com

*Provides investment, insurance and reinsurance services.*

**Taisei Fire & Marine Insurance Company Ltd., 2-1 Kudan Kita 4-chome, Chiyoda-ku, Tokyo 102, Japan**

## STANDARD & POOR'S SECURITIES, INC.

25 Broadway, New York, NY, 10004

Tel: (212) 208-8000     Fax: (212) 410-0200     www.standardandpoors.com

*Investment, finance, economic, mutual funds data and marketing information.*

**Standard & Poor's Corp., Nihon Keisa Shambun, 5 Otemachi 1-chome, Chiyoda-ku, Tokyo, Japan**

## STAR TELECOMMUNICATIONS, INC.

223 East De La Guerra Street, Santa Barbara, CA, 93101

Tel: (805) 899-1962      Fax: (805) 899-2972      www.startel.com

*Provides long-distance telecommunications services.*

**Star Japan KK, Toushin Takanawa Bldg. 9/F, No. 11-3, 3-Chome Takanawa Minato-ku, Tokyo 108-0074, Japan**

Tel: 81-3-3448-0482   Fax: 81-3-3448-0490

## STARBUCKS COFFEE CORPORATION

PO Box 34067, Seattle, WA, 98124-1967

Tel: (206) 447-4127      Fax: (206) 682-7570      www.starbucks.com

*Coffee bean retail store and coffee bars.*

**Starbucks Coffee Japan, 4-22-5 Minomi-Aoyama, Minato-ku, Tokyo 107-0062, Japan**

Tel: 81-3-5412-7031   Fax: 81-3-5412-7564

## STARWOOD HOTELS & RESORTS WORLDWIDE

777 Westchester Avenue, White Plains, NY, 10604

Tel: (914) 640-8100      Fax: (914) 640-8316      www.starwoodhotels.com

*Hotel operations including Sheraton, Westin, St. Regis, Four Points and Caesars.*

**Sheraton Grande Tokyo Bay Hotel & Towers, 1-9 Maihama Uraysau, Chiba 279, Tokyo, Japan**

Tel: 81-473-55-5555   Fax: 81-473-55-5566

**Sheraton Intl. Sales & Reservations, Hotel New Otami, 4 Kioi-cho, Chiyoda-ku, Tokyo 102, Japan**

**Sheraton Intl. Sales & Reservations, Sumitomo Seimei Midosuji Bldg., 4-4-3 Nishi Tenma, Kita-ku, Osaka 530 Japan**

**Westin Tokyo, 1-4-1 Mita, Meguro-ku, Tokyo 153, Japan**

Tel: 81-3-5423-7000   Fax: 81-3-5423-7600

## STATE STREET BANK & TRUST COMPANY

225 Franklin Street, Boston, MA, 02101

Tel: (617) 786-3000      Fax: (617) 654-3386      www.statestreet.com

*Banking and financial services.*

**State Street Trust & Banking, Fuji Building - Ste. 227, 3-2-3 Marunouchi Chiyoda-ku, Tokyo 100-0005 Japan**

**State Street Trust & Banking, Shiroyama JT Mori Building 14/F, 4-3-1 Toranomon Minato-ku, Tokyo 105-6014 Japan**

## STEELCASE INC.

901 44th Street SE, Grand Rapids, MI, 49508

Tel: (616) 247-2710      Fax: (616) 248-7010      www.steelcase.com

*Mfr. office, computer-support and systems furniture.*

**Steelcase Japan Ltd., 32 Kowa Bldg., 5-2-32 Minami-Azabu, Minato-ku, Tokyo 106, Japan**

## STEINER CORPORATION

505 E. South Temple, Salt Lake City, UT, 84102

Tel: (801) 328-8831      Fax: (801) 363-5680

*Soap and towel dispensers.*

**Steiner Company, Tokyo, Japan**

## STEINWAY MUSICAL INSTRUMENTS, INC.

800 South St., Ste. 425, Waltham, MA, 02453

Tel: (718) 894-9770      Fax: (718) 894-9803      www.steinway.com

*Mfr./mktg. pianos.*

**Steinway & Sons Japan Ltd., Room 1305 Onarimon Yusen Bldg., No. 23-5 Nishi Shimbashi 3-chome, Minato-ku, Toyko 105 Japan**

Tel: 81-3-3432-1611   Fax: 81-3-3432-1640   Contact: Peter Suzuki, Pres.

## STERIS CORPORATION

5960 Heisley Road, Mentor, OH, 44060

Tel: (440) 354-2600     Fax: (440) 639-4459     www.steris.com

*Mfr. sterilization/infection control equipment, surgical tables, lighting systems for health, pharmaceutical and scientific industries.*

**Steris Corporation, Koji Kazuma, 6-11 Sakushindai 1-chome, Hanamigawa-ku, Chiba City 262, Japan**

## STIEFEL LABORATORIES INC.

255 Alhambra Circle, Ste. 1000, Coral Gables, FL, 33134

Tel: (305) 443-3807     Fax: (305) 443-3467     www.stiefel.com

*Mfr. pharmaceuticals, dermatological specialties.*

**Stiefel Laboratories Japan, 704 Ichibancho Central Bldg., 22-1 Ichiban-cho, Chiyoda-ku, Tokyo 102, Japan**

## STOKES VACUUM INC.

5500 Tabor Road, Philadelphia, PA, 19120

Tel: (215) 831-5400     Fax: (215) 831-5420     www.stokesvacuum.com

*Vacuum pumps and components, vacuum dryers, oil-upgrading equipment and metallizers.*

**Kyona Eng, 13-21 Tsumada Kitaz, Chome Atsugi City, Kanagawa, Japan**

Tel: 81-462-210160   Fax: 81-462-229065   Contact: Y. Tomita

## STORAGE TECHNOLOGY CORPORATION

One Storagetech Dr., Louisville, CO, 80028-4377

Tel: (303) 673-5151     Fax: (303) 673-5019     www.stortek.com

*Mfr./market/service information, storage and retrieval systems.*

**Storage Technology Ltd., 4-11 Jingumae 2-chome, Shibuya-ku, Tokyo 150-0001, Japan**

**StorageTek Ltd., Entsuji Gadelius Bldg., 5-2-39 Akasaka, Minato-ku, Tokyo 107, Japan**

## STREAM INTERNATIONAL

85 Dan Road, Canton, MA, 02021

Tel: (781) 575-6800     Fax: (781) 575-6999     www.stream.com

*Provider of outsourced technical support for major computer industry companies.*

**Corporate Software Ltd. K.K. (JV), Tennozu Parkside Building, Higashi Shinagawa 2-5-8, Shinagawa ku, Tokyo 140-0002 Japan**

Tel: 81-3-5462-2800   Fax: 81-3-5462-3830

## STRUCTURAL DYNAMICS RESEARCH CORPORATION

2000 Eastman Dr., Milford, OH, 45150-2740

Tel: (513) 576-2400     Fax: (513) 576-2922     www.sdrc.com

*Developer of software used in Modeling testing, drafting and manufacturing.*

**SDRC Japan K.K., Odakyu Southern Tower 9F, 2-2-1 Yoyogi Shibuya-ku, Tokyo 151-8583 Japan**

Tel: 81-3-5354-6700   Fax: 81-3-5354-6780

## STRYKER CORPORATION

2725 Fairfield Rd., Kalamazoo, MI, 49002

Tel: (616) 385-2600     Fax: (616) 385-1062     www.strykercorp.com

*Mfr. surgical instruments and medical equipment.*

**Stryker Japan, Tokyo, Japan**

Contact: Yoshiaki Nakazawa, Pres.

## SUDLER & HENNESSEY

1633 Broadway, 25th Fl., New York, NY, 10019

Tel: (212) 969-5800     Fax: (212) 969-5996     www.sudler-hennessey.com

*Engaged in healthcare products advertising.*

**Dentsu Sudler & Hennessey Havas KK, Tsukiji MK Bldg., 2-11-26 Tsukiji, Chuo-ku, Tokyo 104-0045, Japan**

Tel: 81-3-3546-0451   Fax: 81-3-3546-0455   Contact: Shinzo Ueno

## SUGHRUE, MION, ZINN, MACPEAK & SEAS PLLC

2100 Pennsylvania Ave., NW Ste. 800, Washington, DC, 20037-3202

Tel: (202) 293-7060     Fax: (202) 293-7860     www.sughrue.com

*International law firm.*

**Sughrue, Mion, Zinn, Macpeak & Seas, Toei Nishi Shimbashi Bldg. 4F, 13-5 Nishi Shinbashi 1-Chome, Minato-ku Tokyo 105, Japan**

Tel: 81-3-3503-3760   Fax: 81-3-3503-3756   Contact: John Inge & Abraham Rosner, Partners   Emp: 2

## SULLIVAN & CROMWELL

125 Broad Street, New York, NY, 10004-2498

Tel: (212) 558-4000     Fax: (212) 558-3588     www.sullcrom.com

*International law firm.*

**Sullivan & Cromwell, 2-1 Marunouchi 1-chome, Chiyoda-ku, Tokyo 100, Japan**

## SUMMIT INDUSTRIAL CORPORATION

600 Third Ave., New York, NY, 10016

Tel: (212) 490-1100     Fax: (212) 949-6328

*Pharmaceuticals, agricultural and chemical products.*

**Summit Co. Ltd., 4 Highashi Ginza 8-chome, Chuo-ku, Tokyo, Japan**

## SUNKIST GROWERS INC.

14130 Riverside Drive, Van Nuys, CA, 91423

Tel: (818) 986-4800     Fax: (818) 379-7405     www.sunkist.com

*Citrus marketing cooperative; fruits and vegetables.*

**Sunkist Pacific Ltd., 5-19 Akasaka 4-chome, Minato-ku, Tokyo, Japan**

## SUNRISE MEDICAL INC.

2382 Faraday Ave., Ste. 200, Carlsbad, CA, 92008

Tel: (760) 930-1500     Fax: (760) 930-1580     www.sunrisemedical.com

*Designs, manufactures and markets rehabilitation products and assistive technology devices for people with disabilities, and patient care products used in nursing homes, hospitals and homecare settings.*

**Sunrise Medical Japan, Higashi-Nakano Green 202, 32-8 Higashi-Nikano 1-chrome, Nakano-ku, Tokyo, Japan**

## SWECO INC.

7120 New Buffington Rd., PO Box 1509, Florence, KY, 41042-1509

Tel: (606) 727-5100     Fax: (606) 727-5106     www.sweco.com

*Mfr. vibratory process and solids control equipment.*

**Shinko Pantec Co. Ltd., 19 Niijima, Harima-Cyo, Kako-Gun, Hyougo-Ken T675-0, Japan**

## SYBASE, INC.

6475 Christie Ave., Emeryville, CA, 94608

Tel: (510) 922-3500     Fax: (510) 922-3210     www.sybase.com

*Design/mfg/distribution of database management systems, software development tools, connectivity products, consulting and technical support services..*

**Powersoft K.K., Chichibuya Building 6F, 3-7-4 Kojimachi, Chiyoda-ku, Tokyo 102 Japan**

Tel: 81-3-5214-0850   Fax: 81-3-5214-0888

**Sybase K.K.,** **Kioi-cho Building 12F, 3-12 Kioi-cho, Chiyoda-ku, Tokyo 102 Japan**
Tel: 81-3-5210-6000   Fax: 81-3-5210-6300

## SYBRON INTERNATIONAL CORPORATION

411 E. Wisconsin Ave., Milwaukee, WI, 53202

Tel: (414) 274-6600      Fax: (414) 274-6561      www.sybron.com

*Mfr. products for laboratories, professional orthodontic and dental markets.*

**Sybron Dental Specialties Japan Inc.,** **Onarimon #2 Bldg. 2/F, 16-12 Shimbashi 6-chome, Minato-ku, Tokyo 107, Japan**

## SYMANTEC CORPORATION

20330 Stevens Creek Blvd., Cupertino, CA, 95014-2132

Tel: (408) 253-9600      Fax: (408) 253-3968      www.symantec.com

*Designs and produces PC network security and network management software and hardware.*

**Symantec Japan Ltd.,** **Shibuya Infoss Tower 16F, 20-1 Sakuragaoka-cho, Shibuya-ku, Tokyo 150 Japan**
Tel: 81-3-5457-5300   Fax: 81-2-3498-0520

## SYMBOL TECHNOLOGIES, INC.

One Symbol Plaza, Holtsville, NY, 11742-1300

Tel: (631) 738-2400      Fax: (631) 738-5990      www.symbol.com

*Mfr. Bar code-driven data management systems, wireless LAN's, and Portable Shopping System™.*

**Olympus Symbol Inc.,** **San-Ei Bldg. 4F, 22-2 Nishi-Shinjuku, 1-chome Shinjuku-ku, Tokyo 160, Japan**
Tel: 81-3-3348-0212   Fax: 81-3-3348-0216

## SYNOPSYS, INC.

700 East Middlefield Road, Mountain View, CA, 94043

Tel: (650) 962-5000      Fax: (650) 965-8637      www.synopsys.com

*Mfr. electronic design automation software.*

**Nihon Synopsys Co. KK,** **19F/20F Shinjuku Mitsui Building, 2-1-1 Nishi Shinjuku Shinjuku-ku, Tokyo 163-0420, Japan**
Tel: 81-3-3346-7030   Fax: 81-3-3346-7050

**Nihon Synopsys Co. KK,** **3-19-3 Toyosaki, Kita-ku Osaka-shi, Osaka 531-0072, Japan**
Tel: 81-6-6359-8139   Fax: 81-6-6359-8149

## SYNTEGRA

4201 Lexington Ave., North Arden Hills, MN, 55126-6198

Tel: (651) 415-2999      Fax: (651) 415-4891      www.cdc.com

*Computer peripherals and hardware.*

**Syntegra Japan,** **Tokyo, Japan**

## TANDY CORPORATION

100 Throckmorton Street, Fort Worth, TX, 76102

Tel: (817) 390-3700      Fax: (817) 415-2647      www.tandy.com

*Mfr. electronic and acoustic equipment; Radio Shack retail stores.*

**A&A Japan Ltd.,** **1-21-1 Nishi-Shinjuku, Tokyo 160, Japan**

**Tandy Radio Shack Japan Ltd.,** **1-44-1 Tamagawa, Chofu City, Tokyo, Japan**

## THE TCW GROUP

865 S. Figueroa St., Ste. 1800, Los Angeles, CA, 90017

Tel: (213) 244-0000      Fax: (213) 244-0000      www.tcwgroup.com

*Engaged in managing pension and profit sharing funds, retirement/health and welfare funds, insurance company funds, endowments and foundations.*

**TCW Group (JV),** **Tokyo, Japan**

## TECH/OPS SEVCON INC.

40 North Ave., Burlington, MA, 01803

Tel: (718) 229-7896      Fax: (718) 229-8603      www.sevcon.com

*Design, manufacture, and marketing of microprocessor based control systems for battery powered vehicles.*

**Sevcon Japan., Room 1319, 1-24-7 Shinjuku, Tokyo 160 Japan**

## TEKELEC

26580 West Agoura Road, Calabasas, CA, 91302

Tel: (818) 880-5656      Fax: (818) 880-6993      www.tekelec.com

*Mfr. telecommunications testing equipment.*

**Tekelec Ltd., Daiichi Ogikubo Bldg., 27-8 Ogikubo 5-chome, Suginami-ku, Tokyo 167, Japan**

Contact: Akira Ohsone, Pres.   Emp: 34

## TEKTRONIX INC.

14200 SW Karl Braun Dr., PO Box 500, Beaverton, OR, 97077

Tel: (503) 627-7111      Fax: (503) 627-2406      www.tek.com

*Mfr. test and measure, visual systems/color printing and communications/video and  networking products.*

**Sony/Tektronix Corp. (JV), Tokyo International, 5-9-31 Kitashinagawa, Shinagawa-ku, Tokyo 141-0001 Japan**

Tel: 81-3-3448-3111    Fax: 81-3-3444-3663

## TELEFLEX INC.

630 W. Germantown Pike, Ste. 450, Plymouth Meeting, PA, 19462

Tel: (610) 834-6301      Fax: (610) 834-8307      www.teleflex.com

*Designs/mfr./market mechanical and electro-mechanical systems, measure systems.*

**Rüsch Asia Pacific Sdn. Bhd., Tokyo, Japan**

## TELEX COMMUNICATIONS INC.

12000 Portland Ave. South, Burnsville, MN, 55337

Tel: (952) 884-4051      Fax: (952) 884-0043      www.telexcommunications.com

*Mfr. communications, audio-visual and professional audio products.*

**EVI Audio Japan, Ltd., 3-29-10 1F Chiyoda, Naka-Ku Nagoya-shi, Aichi 460-001, Japan**

## TELLABS INC.

4951 Indiana Ave. 6303788800, Lisle, IL, 60532-1698

Tel: (630) 378-8800      Fax: (630) 679-3010      www.tellabs.com

*Design/mfr./service voice/data transport and network access systems.*

**Tellabs, Toranomon 40 - Mori Building 9/F, Toranomon 5-13-1, Minato-ku, Tokyo 105-0001, Japan**

## TELXON CORPORATION

1000 Summitt Dr., Cincinnati, OH, 45150

Tel: (330) 664-1000      Fax: (330) 664-2220      www.telxon.com

*Develop/mfr. portable computer systems and related equipment.*

**Telxon Japan, Oxson Bldg. 6/F, 102013 Shintomi, Chou-ku, Tokyo, Japan**

## TENNANT COMPANY

701 North Lilac Drive, Minneapolis, MN, 55440

Tel: (612) 540-1208      Fax: (612) 540-1437      www.tennantco.com

*Mfr. industry floor maintenance sweepers and scrubbers and floor coatings.*

**Tennant Japan, Sanka Bldg. 5/F, 2-9 Minami Saiwai-cho, Saiwai-ku, Kawasaki 210, Japan**

Tel: 81-44-556-1201   Fax: 81-44-556-1202   Contact: Sheila LeGeros, Mng. Dir.

## TENNECO AUTOMOTIVE INC.

500 North Field Drive, Lake Forest, IL, 60045

Tel: (847) 482-5241     Fax: (847) 482-5295     www.tenneco-automotive.com

*Mfr. automotive parts, exhaust systems and service equipment.*

**Tenneco Automotive Japan Ltd., 20-20 Hiradai, Tsuzuke-ku, Yokohama-shi, Kanagawa Prefecture 224, Japan**

Tel: 81-45-942-5211   Fax: 81-45-942-5228   Contact: Kan Shishikura, Mgr.   Emp: 23

## TENNECO PACKAGING CORPORATION OF AMERICA

1900 West Field Court, Lake Forest, IL, 60045

Tel: (847) 482-2000     Fax: (847) 482-2181     www.agplus.net/tenneco

*Mfr. custom packaging, aluminum and plastic molded fibre, corrugated containers.*

**Tenneco Packaging, Kyoto, Japan**

**Toyo Ekco Co. Ltd., Sumisei Shimojima Bldg., 3-8 Kitakyuhoji-machi 3-chome, Chuo-ku, Osaka 541 Japan**

## TERADYNE INC.

321 Harrison Ave., Boston, MA, 02118

Tel: (617) 482-2700     Fax: (617) 422-2910     www.teradyne.com

*Mfr. electronic test equipment and blackplane connection systems.*

**Teradyne K.K. - Far East Sales Office, Teradyne Bldg., Higashiyama 1-5-4, Meguro-ku, Tokyo, 153, Japan**

Tel: 81-3-3719-0180   Contact: Akira Kasai, Reg. Mgr.

## TEXACO INC.

2000 Westchester Ave., White Plains, NY, 10650

Tel: (914) 253-4000     Fax: (914) 253-7753     www.texaco.com

*Exploration/marketing crude oil, mfr. petro chemicals and products.*

**Texaco Japan Inc., c/o NOEC Producing Japan, 18-1 Shingashi 1-chome, Minato-ku, 1-chome, Tokyo 105, Japan**

## TEXAS INSTRUMENTS INC.

8505 Forest Lane, Dallas, TX, 75243

Tel: (972) 995-3773     Fax: (972) 995-4360     www.ti.com

*Mfr. semiconductor devices, electronic electro-mechanical systems, instruments and controls.*

**Texas Instruments Japan Ltd., 18-36 Minami 3-chome, Hatagoya City 334, Japan**

Tel: 81-48-282-2211

**Texas Instruments Japan Ltd., 305 Tangashira, Oyama-cho, Suntoh-gun, Shizuoka-ken, Oyama Plant 410-13, Japan**

Tel: 81-550-781211

**Texas Instruments Japan Ltd., 4260 Aza-Takao, Oaza-Kawasaki, Hayami-gun, Hiji-machi 879-15, Japan**

**Texas Instruments Japan Ltd., 2355 Kihara Miho-mura, Inashiki-gun, Ibaragi-ken, Miho Plant 300-04, Japan**

Tel: 81-298-40-4435

## THERMADYNE HOLDINGS CORPORATION

101 South Hanley Road, Suite 300, St. Louis, MO, 63105

Tel: (314) 746-2197     Fax: (314) 746-2349     www.thermadyne.com

*Mfr. welding, cutting, and safety products.*

**Thermadyne Japan, Osaka, Japan**

Tel: 81-726-303577

**Thermadyne Japan Ltd., Shiba White Bldg. 5F, 2-13-9 Shiba, Minato-ku, Tokyo 105, Japan**

## THERMO ELECTRIC COOLING AMERICA (TECA)

109 North Fifth Street, Saddle Brook, NJ, 07662

Tel: (201) 843-5800      Fax: (201) 843-7144      www.thermoelectric.com

*Mfr. solid state cooling products, including air-conditioners, cold plates and liquid chillers.*

**Tel-Thermco Engineering Co. Inc., 32-10 Kawajiri Shiroyama 1-chome, Tsukui, Kanakawa Pref. 220-01, Japan**

## THERMO ELECTRON CORPORATION

81 Wyman Street, Waltham, MA, 02454-9046

Tel: (781) 622-1000      Fax: (781) 622-1207      www.thermo.com

*Develop/mfr./sale of process equipment &instruments for energy intensive and healthcare industries.*

**Nicolet Biomedical Japan Inc., Nish-Shinjuku Forest Bldg. 3F, 32-12 4 chome, Nishi-Shinjuku-ku, Tokyo 160 Japan**

Tel: 81-3-332-0661

**Nicolet Biomedical Japan Inc., Ryokuci-eki Bldg. 6F, 4-1-2 chome Terauchi, Toyonaka City Osaka Pref. 560, Japan**

Tel: 81-6-866-3500

**Thermo Electron Nippon Co. Ltd., 3-5-11 Minami-Nakaburi, Hiakaba, Osaka, Japan**

## THERM-O-DISC, INC.

1320 S. Main Street, Mansfield, OH, 44907-0538

Tel: (419) 525-8500      Fax: (419) 525-8282      www.thermodisc.com

*Mfr. thermostats, controls, sensor and thermal cutoffs, switches.*

**Therm-O-Disc, 102 Takasago Bldg., 100 Edo-Machi, Chuo-ku, Kobe 650, Japan**

## THERMON MANUFACTURING COMPANY

100 Thermon Drive, PO Box 609, San Marcos, TX, 78667-0609

Tel: (512) 396-5801      Fax: (512) 396-3627      www.thermon.com

*Mfr. steam and electric heat tracing systems, components and accessories.*

**Thermon Far East, 3F Recruit Yokohama Building, 6-3 Kin Koa-Cho Kanagawa-ku, Yokohama 221 Japan**

## THOMAS & BETTS CORPORATION

8155 T&B Blvd., Memphis, TN, 38125

Tel: (901) 252-5000      Fax: (901) 685-1988      www.tnb.com

*Mfr. elect/electronic connectors and accessories.*

**Thomas & Betts Japan Ltd., 44 Kowa Bldg., 2-7 Higashiyama 1-chome, Meguru-ku, Tokyo 153, Japan**

## THOMAS PUBLISHING COMPANY

5 Penn Plaza, New York, NY, 10007

Tel: (212) 695-0500      Fax: (212) 290-7362      www.thomaspublishing.com

*Publishing magazines and directories.*

**Incom Co. Ltd., Plaza Edo Gawabashi, 1-23-6 Sekiguchi, Bunkyo-ku, Tokyo 112, Japan**

## TIFFANY & COMPANY

727 Fifth Ave., New York, NY, 10022

Tel: (212) 755-8000      Fax: (212) 605-4465      www.tiffany.com

*Mfr./retail fine jewelry, silverware, china, crystal, leather goods, etc.*

**Tiffany & Co. Japan, 6-16 Ginza 4-chome, Chuo-ku, Tokyo 104, Japan**

## TMP WORLDWIDE, INC.

622 Third Ave., New York, NY, 10017

Tel: (212) 351-7000     Fax: (212) 658-0540     www.tmpw.com

*#1 Yellow Pages agency and a leader in the recruitment and interactive advertising fields.*

**TMP Worldwide/JDAC,  #303 Yotsuya Mansion, 1-22 Arakicho, Shinjuki-ku, Tokyo 160, Japan**

Tel: 81-33-358-24-41

## TOMMY HILFIGER CORPORATION

25 West 39th St., New York, NY, 10018

Tel: (212) 840-8888     Fax: (212) 302-8718     www.tommy.com

*Clothing manufacturer and chain stores.  (JV with Tommy Hilfiger Corp., Hong Kong)*

**Tommy Hilfiger Sportswear, Inc.,  Tokyo, Japan**

## THE TORRINGTON COMPANY

59 Field St., PO Box 1008, Torrington, CT, 06790

Tel: (860) 626-2000     Fax: (860) 496-3625     www.torrington.com

*Mfr. precision bearings, motion control components and automotive steering assemblies.*

**NSK Torrington Company Ltd. (JV),  Tokyo, Japan**

## TOSCO CORPORATION

72 Cummings Point Rd., Stamford, CT, 06902

Tel: (203) 977-1000     Fax: (203) 964-3187     www.tosco.com

*Engaged in oil refining and marketing and operates service stations and convenience stores.*

**Circle K Ltd.,  26-8 3 Chome Meieki - 9/F, Nakamura-Ku, Nagoya 450 Japan**

Tel: 81-52-585-3911    Contact: Taizo Toyama, Pres.

## TOWERS PERRIN

335 Madison Ave., New York, NY, 10017-4605

Tel: (212) 309-3400     Fax: (212) 309-0975     www.towers.com

*Management consulting services.*

**Tillinghast Towers Perrin,  Imperial Tower, 1-1 Uchisaiwai-cho 1-chome, Chiyoda-ku, Tokyo 100, Japan**

Tel: 81-33-581-5731    Fax: 81-33-581-5719

## TOYS R US INC.

461 From Road, Paramus, NJ, 07652

Tel: (201) 262-7800     Fax: (201) 845-0973     www.toysrus.com

*Retail stores: toys and games, sporting goods, computer software, books, records.*

**Toys R Us Japan Ltd.,  3-1 Ekimae Honcho, Kawasaki, Kanagawa 0210, Japan**

## THE TRANE COMPANY

3600 Pammel Creek Road, La Crosse, WI, 54601

Tel: (608) 787-2000     Fax: (608) 787-4990     www.trane.com

*Mfr./distributor/service A/C systems and equipment.*

**Trane Japan,  Tokyodo Nishi-Cho Bldg. 5/F, 3-7-2 Kanda Nishi-cho, Chiyoda-ku, Tokyo Japan**

## TRANS WORLD AIRLINES INC.

515 North Sixth Street, St. Louis, MO, 63101

Tel: (314) 589-3000     Fax: (314) 589-3129     www.twa.com

*Air transport services.*

**Trans World Airlines,  Kokusai Bldg. 234, 3-1-1 Manunouchi, Chiyoda-ku, Tokyo 1-0005, Japan**

Tel: 81-3-3212-1477

## TRIMBLE NAVIGATION LIMITED

645 N. Mary Ave., Sunnyvale, CA, 94086

Tel: (408) 481-8000     Fax: (408) 481-2000     www.trimble.com

*Design/mfr. electronic geographic instrumentation.*

**Trimble Japan K.K., Sumitomo Hamamatsu-cho, Bldg. 10F, 1-18-16, Hamamatsu-cho, Minato-ku Tokyo 105, Japan**

Tel: 81-3-5472-0880   Fax: 81-2-5472-2326

## TROPICANA PRODUCTS, INC.

1001 13th Avenue East, Bradenton, FL, 34208

Tel: (941) 747-4461     Fax: (941) 665-5330     www.tropicana.com

*Marketer and producer of branded juices, including Tropicana, Dole, Looza and Copella.*

**Kirin-Tropicana, Inc., Kanda Izumicho Bldg. 11/F, 1 Kanda Izumicho, Chiyoda-ku Tokyo, Japan**

Tel: 81-3-5821-4080   Fax: 81-3-5821-4144

## TRUE NORTH COMMUNICATIONS INC.

101 East Erie Street, Chicago, IL, 60611

Tel: (312) 425-6500     Fax: (312) 425-5010     www.truenorth.com

*Holding company, advertising agency.*

**FCB Direct, Kanda System Bldg. 2F, 7 Kanda Konya-cho, Chiyoda-ku, Tokyo 101-8603 Japan**

## TRW INC.

1900 Richmond Road, Cleveland, OH, 44124-3760

Tel: (216) 291-7000     Fax: (216) 291-7932     www.trw.com

*Electric and energy-related products, automotive and aerospace products, tools and fasteners.*

**TRW Automotive-Electronics Asia Inc., Tameike Meisan Bldg. 8F, 1-12 Akasaka 1-chome, Minato-ku, Tokyo 107 Japan**

## TWIN DISC INCORPORATED

1328 Racine Street, Racine, WI, 53403-1758

Tel: (414) 638-4000     Fax: (414) 638-4482     www.twindisc.com

*Mfr. industry clutches, reduction gears and transmissions.*

**Nigata Converter Co. Ltd., 27-9 Sendagaya 5-chome, Shibuya-ku, Tokyo 151, Japan**

Tel: 81-3-3354-6931   Fax: 81-3-3341-5365

## TYSON FOODS INC.

2210 W. Oaklawn Dr., Springdale, AR, 72762-6999

Tel: (501) 290-4000     Fax: (501) 290-4061     www.tyson.com

*Production/mfr./distributor poultry, beef, pork and seafood products.*

**Tyson Japan, Market Makers, Seibunkin Bldg. 5F, 1-5-9 Iidabashi, Chiyoda-ku, Tokyo 102, Japan**

Tel: 81-3-3221-5852   Fax: 81-3-3221-5960   Contact: Jeff McNeill, Managing Director

## U.S. WHEAT ASSOCIATES

1620 I Street, NW, Washington, DC, 20006

Tel: (202) 463-0999     Fax: (202) 785-1052

*Market development for wheat products.*

**U.S. Wheat Associates Inc., 1-14 Akasaka 1-chome, Minato-ku, Tokyo 107, Japan**

## UNION CARBIDE CORPORATION

39 Old Ridgebury Road, Danbury, CT, 06817

Tel: (203) 794-2000     Fax: (203) 794-6269     www.unioncarbide.com

*Mfr. industrial chemicals, plastics and resins.*

**Nippon Uninar Co., Asahi Bldg. 16-17/F, 6-1 Ohtemachi 2-chome, Minato-ku, Tokyo 100 Japan**

## UNION PACIFIC CORPORATION

1416 Dodge St., Room 1230, Omaha, NE, 68179

Tel: (402) 271-5777     Fax: (402) 271-6408     www.up.com

*Holding company: railroad, crude oil, natural gas, petroleum refining, metal mining service, real estate.*

**Union Pacific Railroad, Satoh Bldg. 4F, 1-19-4 Hamamatsu-cho, Minato-ku, Tokyo 105, Japan**

## UNISYS CORPORATION.

PO Box 500, Union Meeting Road, Blue Bell, PA, 19424

Tel: (215) 986-4011     Fax: (215) 986-6850     www.unisys.com

*Mfr./marketing/servicing electronic information systems.*

**Nihon Unisys/Univac Ltd., 17-15 Akasaka 2-chome, Minato-ku, Tokyo 107, Japan**

**Unisys Japan Ltd., Mori Bldg. 31, Tokyo 102, Japan**

## UNITED AIRLINES INC.

1200 E. Algonquin Rd., Chicago, IL, 60007

Tel: (847) 700-4000     Fax: (847) 700-4081     www.ual.com

*Air transportation, passenger and freight services.*

**United Airlines, Honmachi Nomura Bldg., 3-4-10 Honmachi, Chuo-ku, Osaka 541, Japan**

## UNITED ASSET MANAGEMENT CORPORATION

One International Place, 44th Fl., Boston, MA, 02110

Tel: (617) 330-8900     Fax: (617) 330-1133     www.uam.com

*Investment management services.*

**United Asset Management, Sumitomo Toranomon Bldg. 8F, 1-6-12 Toranomon, Minato-ku, Tokyo 105, Japan**

Contact: Masaharu Izumi, Pres.

## UNITED PARCEL SERVICE, INC.

55 Glenlake Parkway, NE, Atlanta, GA, 30328

Tel: (404) 828-6000     Fax: (404) 828-6593     www.ups.com

*International package-delivery service.*

**UPS - Yamato Co. Ltd., 1-6 Ariake, Koto-ku, Tokyo 135-1163 Japan**

Tel: 81-3-3520-0090   Fax: 81-3-3520-0091

## UNITED TECHNOLOGIES CORPORATION

One Financial Plaza, Hartford, CT, 06103

Tel: (860) 728-7000     Fax: (860) 728-7979     www.utc.com

*Mfr. aircraft engines, elevators, A/C, auto equipment, space and military electronic and rocket propulsion systems. Products include Pratt and Whitney, Otis elevators, Carrier heating and air conditioning and Sikorsky helicopters.*

**United Technologies Intl. Operations Inc., Uchisaiwaicho Dai Building 7F, 3-3 Uchisaiwaicho 1-chome, Chiyoda-k, Tokyo 100 Japan**

Tel: 81-3-358-13221   Fax: 81-3-358-13226   Contact: Randall Green

## UNIVERSAL INSTRUMENTS

90 Bevier Street, S. Dock, Binghamton, NY, 13904

Tel: (607) 779-7522     Fax: (607) 779-7971     www.uic.com

*Mfr./sales of instruments for electronic circuit assembly.*

**Universal Instruments Japan Ltd., Tokyo, Japan**

Tel: 81-3-3861-9701   Fax: 81-3-3861-9500

## UNIVERSAL WEATHER & AVIATION INC.

8787 Tallyho Road, Houston, TX, 77061

Tel: (713) 944-1622     Fax: (713) 943-4650       www.univ-wea.com

*Provides service management, and worldwide weather and communications to the corporate aviation community.*

**Universal Weather & Aviation, Japan Airlines Bldg., Narita International Airport, Tokyo, Japan**

Tel: 81-476-34-3957   Fax: 81-476-34-6575   Contact: Hiroshi Higashiyama

## UNUMPROVIDENT

2211 Congress Street, Portland, ME, 04122

Tel: (207) 770-2211     Fax: (207) 770-4510       www.unum.com

*Disability and special risk insurance.*

**UNUM Japan Accident Insurance Co. Ltd., Sanbancho UF Building 2F, 6-3 Sanban-cho, Chiyada-ku, Tokyo 102-0075 Japan**

Tel: 81-3-5276-1391   Fax: 81-3-5276-0098   Contact: Kevin McCarthy, Pres.

## UOP LLC.

25 East Algonquin Road, Des Plaines, IL, 60017

Tel: (847) 391-2000     Fax: (847) 391-2253       www.uop.com

*Engaged in developing and commercializing technology for license to the oil refining, petrochemical and gas processing industries.*

**Nikki Universal Co., 2-4 Ohtemachi, Chiyoda-ku, Tokyo, Japan**

**Nikki-Universal Co. Ltd., Nissei Bldg. 6-3 Ohsaki 1-chome, Shinagawa-ku Tokyo 141, Japan**

Tel: 81-3-5436-8446   Fax: 81-3-5436-8388

**Union Showa K.K., Molecular Sieves, 27-17 Hamamatsu-cho 1-chome, Minato-ku, Tokyo 105, Japan**

**UOP KK, NK Bldg. Ohsaki City 6/F, 6-28 Kitashinagawa 5-chome, Shinagawa-ku Tokyo 141-001, Japan**

Tel: 81-3-5421-2560   Fax: 81-3-5421-2788

## URS CORPORATION

100 California Street, Ste. 500, San Francisco, CA, 94111-4529

Tel: (415) 774-2700     Fax: (415) 398-1904       www.urscorp.com

*Provides planning, design and construction management services, pollution control and hazardous waste management.*

**URS (Dames & Moore), Tokyo, Japan**

## URSCHEL LABORATORIES INC.

2503 Calumet Ave., PO Box 2200, Valparaiso, IN, 46384-2200

Tel: (219) 464-4811     Fax: (219) 462-3879       www.urschel.com

*Design/mfr. precision food processing equipment.*

**Urschel Japan, 2-18-9 Ningyocho, Nihonbashi, Chuo-ku, Tokyo, Japan**

## UUNET

22001 Loudoun County Pkwy., Ashburn, VA, 20147

Tel: (703) 206-5600     Fax: (703) 206-5601       www.uu.net

*World's largest Internet service provider; World Wide Web hosting services, security products and consulting services to businesses, professionals, and on-line service providers.*

**UUNET KK, Odakyu Southern Tower, 2-2-1 Yoyogi, Shibuya-ku, Tokyo 151-8583, Japan**

## VALENITE INC

31751 Research Park Dr., Madison Heights, MI, 48071-9636

Tel: (248) 589-1000     Fax: (248) 597-4820       www.valenite.com

*Cemented carbide, high speed steel, ceramic and diamond cutting tool products, etc.*

**Valenite-WIDIA Japan Inc., 21-10 Kita-Kohjiya 1-chome, Ohta-ku, Tokyo 144, Japan**

## VARIAN MEDICAL SYSTEMS, INC.

3050 Hansen Way, Palo Alto, CA, 94304-100

Tel: (650) 493-4000    Fax: (650) 424-5358    www.varian.com

*Mfr. microwave tubes and devices, analytical instruments, semiconductor process and medical equipment, vacuum systems.*

**Nippon Oncology Systems, Ltd. (JV),  Keio Chofu Kojimacho Building, 32-2 Kojimacho 1-Chome,Chofu-shi Tokyo 182 Japan**

**Nippon Oncology Systems, Ltd. (JV),  Sumitomo Shoji Yodogawa Building 11-16, Nishinakajima 1-Chome,Yodogawa-ku Osaka-shi, Osaka 532 Japan**

## VARIAN SEMICONDUCTOR EQUIPMENT ASSOCIATES, INC.

35 Dory Road, Gloucester, MA, 01930

Tel: (978) 281-2000    Fax: (978) 283-5391    www.vsea.com

*Mfr. ion implantation systems.*

**Varian Semiconductor Equipment Assocates,  4/F Nissou, 2-7-1 Shinyokohama Kouhoku-Ku, Yokohama-shi, Kanagawa 222-0033, Japan**

**Varian Semiconductor Equipment Assocates,  8/FYokohama Business Park West Tower, 134 Goudo-cho Hodogaya-ku, Yokohama-shi, Kanagawa 240-0005, Japan**

## VEECO INSTRUMENTS INC.

Terminal Drive, Plainview, NY, 11803

Tel: (516) 349-8300    Fax: (516) 349-9079    www.veeco.com

*Mfr. surface profiler, atomic force microscopes, leak and plating thickness detectors and semiconductor products.*

**Nihon Veeco K.K.,  Japan Headquarters, 13-7 Rokuban-cho, Chiyoda-ku, Tokyo 102, Japan**
Tel: 81-3-3262-6151   Fax: 81-3-3262-6155

## VELCRO USA INC.

406 Brown Avenue, Manchester, NH, 03108

Tel: (603) 669-4892    Fax: (603) 669-9271    www.velcro.com

*Mfr./sales of velcro brand hook and loop fasteners, plastic buckles and metal hardware and cable control straps.*

**Kuraray Co., Ltd.,  12-39 Umeda, 1 Chrome, Kita-Ku, Osaka 530, Japan**
Tel: 81-6-348-2111   Fax: 81-6-348-2106

## VENATOR GROUP INC.

112 West 34th St., New York, NY, 10279-0003

Tel: (212) 720-3700    Fax: (212) 553-2152    www.venatorgroup.com

*Operates retail specialty stores, including Foot Locker, Champs Sports and Eastbay Athletic apparel.*

**Foot Locker Japan,  Fujiya Bldg. 7/F, 3-1 Ginza 1-Chome, Chuo-ku Tokyo 104, Japan**

## VENTURE MEASUREMENT COMPANY

150 Venture Blvd., Spartanburg, SC, 29306

Tel: (864) 574-8960    Fax: (864) 578-7308    www.bindicator.com

*Mfr. level control instruments for measuring solids and liquids.*

**Kinsho - Mataichi (Bindicator),  1-24-1 Shinkawa Chuo-Ku, Toyko, Japan**
Tel: 81-33-2977111   Fax: 81-33-2977393

## VERIZON

1095 Ave. of the Americas, New York, NY, 10036

Tel: (212) 395-2121    Fax: (212) 395-1285    www.verizon.com

*Telecommunications.*

**TU-KA Cellular Tokyo Inc.,  1-10-11 Shiba Daimon, Minato-ku, Tokyo 105-8540 Japan**
Tel: 81-3-5400-6100   Fax: 81-3-5400-6150   Contact: Hajime Nakayama, Pres.

## VERIZON COMMUNICATIONS INC.

1255 Corporate Drive, Irving, TX, 75038

Tel: (972) 507-5000    Fax: (972) 507-5002    www.gte.com

*Engaged in wireline and wireless communications.*

**NEC Sylvania Corp., Minakuchi, Japan**

## VERNAY LABORATORIES INC.

120 East South College St., Box 310, Yellow Springs, OH, 45387

Tel: (937) 767-7261    Fax: (937) 767-1208    www.vernay.com

*Mfr. precision fluid handling products.*

**Vernay Japan, Shanshin Bldg., 1-14-15 Okubo 6/F, Shinjuku-ku, Tokyo 0169, Japan**

## VIACOM INC.

1515 Broadway, 28th Fl., New York, NY, 10036-5794

Tel: (212) 258-6000    Fax: (212) 258-6358    www.viacom.com

*Communications, publishing and entertainment.*

**Viacom Japan Inc., Mitsuwa Bldg., 7-2 Ginza 6-chome, Chuo-ku, Tokyo 104, Japan**

## THE VIKING CORPORATION

210 N. Industrial Park Rd., Hastings, MI, 49058

Tel: (616) 945-9501    Fax: (616) 945-9599    www.vikingcorp.com

*Mfr. fire extinguishing equipment.*

**The Viking Corporation (Japan), 507 AIOS Hiroo Building, 1-11-2 Hiroo Shibuya-Ku, Tokyo 150-0012, Japan**

Tel: 81-3-3440-8711

## VISHAY INTERTECHNOLOGY INC.

63 Lincoln Hwy., Malvern, PA, 19355

Tel: (610) 644-1300    Fax: (610) 296-0657    www.vishay.com

*Mfr. resistors, strain gages, capacitors, inductors, printed circuit boards.*

**Vishay Japan, K.K., Shibuya No. 2 Toho Seimei Bldg., 3-5-16 Shibuya, 150-0002 Shibuya-ku, Tokyo Japan**

Tel: 81-3-5464-6411    Fax: 81-3-5464-6433

## VITESSE SEMICONDUCTOR CORPORATION

741 Calle Plano, Camarillo, CA, 93012

Tel: (805) 388-3700    Fax: (805) 389-7188    www.vitesse.com

*Mfr. integrated circuits.*

**Vitesse Semiconductor Japan, 2-9-21-201 Honcho, Kokubunji, Tokyo 185-0012, Japan**

Tel: 81-42-326-6667    Fax: 81-42-320-5020

## VIVITAR CORPORATION

1280 Rancho Conejo Blvd, Newbury Park, CA, 91320

Tel: (805) 498-7008    Fax: (805) 498-5086    www.vivitar.com

*Mfr. photographic equipment, electronic supplies.*

**Vivitar Japan Ltd., Marusho Bldg. 6F, 12 Yotsuyu 3-chome, Shinyuku-ku, Tokyo 160, Japan**

## WACHOVIA CORPORATION

100 North Main Street, PO Box, Winston-Salem, NC, 27150

Tel: (336) 770-5000    Fax: (336) 770-5931    www.wachovia.com

*Engaged in commercial and retail banking services.*

**Wachovia Bank of North Carolina, Toranomon ACT Bldg., 21-1 Toranomon 5-chome, Minato-ku, Tokyo, Japan**

## WACKENHUT CORPORATION

4200 Wackenhut Dr., Ste. 100, Palm Beach Gardens, FL, 33410

Tel: (561) 622-5656    Fax: (561) 691-6736    www.wackenhut.com

*Security systems and services.*

**Wackenhut Keibi Co.,  Ginza-Matsuyoshi Bldg., 7-17-8 Ginza, Chuo-ku, Tokyo 104, Japan**

Tel: 81-3-3542-3213   Fax: 81-3-3542-3214

## WAHL CLIPPER CORPORATION

2902 N. Locust Street, Sterling, IL, 61081

Tel: (815) 625-6525    Fax: (815) 625-1193    www.wahlclipper.com

*Mfr. hair clippers, beard and mustache trimmers, shavers, pet clippers and soldering irons.*

**Nippon Wahl K.K.,  2-17-18, Shimo-yugi, Hachioji-shi, Tokyo 192-08, Japan**

## WALBRO CORPORATION, TI GROUP AUTOMOTIVE

6242 Garfield Ave., Cass City, MI, 48726-1325

Tel: (517) 872-2131    Fax: (517) 872-3090    www.walbro.com

*Mfr. motor vehicle accessories and parts, automotive fluid carrying systems.*

**TI Group Automotive Systems/Walbro,  23-1 Sanbyakukoku, Kunisada Azuma-mura, Sawa-gun, Gunma-ken 379-2221 Kiryu City, Japan**

**Walbro Engine Management,  Terada Building 4F, 2-3-3 Shiba Kouen, Minato-Ku Tokyo 105-0011, Japan**

Tel: 81-3-5401-4511

## WARNER BROS INTERNATIONAL TELEVISION

4000 Warner Boulevard, Bldg.170, 3rd Fl., Burbank, CA, 91522

Tel: (818) 954-6000    Fax: (818) 977-4040    www.wbitv.com

*Distributor TV programming and theatrical features.*

**Time Warner Entertainment Japan,  1-2-4 Hamamatsu-Cho, Minato-ku, Tokyo 105, Japan**

Tel: 81-3-5472-8341   Fax: 81-3-5472-6343   Contact: Teruji Mochimaru, Mng. Dir.

## THE WASHINGTON POST COMPANY

1150 15th St. NW, Washington, DC, 20071

Tel: (202) 334-6000    Fax: (202) 334-4536    www.washpostco.com

*Engaged in magazine publishing, cable and television broadcasting, educational services and the Internet,*

**Mainichi Newspapers,  1-1-1 Hitotsubashi - 4/F, Chiyoda-ku, Tokyo 100, Japan**

Tel: 81-3-3201-0210

## WASSERSTEIN PERELLA & CO., INC.

31 West 52nd Street, New York, NY, 10019

Tel: (212) 969-2700    Fax: (212) 969-7969    www.wassersteinperella.com

*Engaged in international investment banking and financial services.*

**Nomuro Wasserstein Perella Co., Ltd.,  Dai-Ichi Edobashi Bldg. 8F, 1-11-1 Nihonbashi, Chuo-ku, Tokyo 103, Japan**

Tel: 81-3-3281-2031   Fax: 81-3-3281-3304

## WATERS CORPORATION

34 Maple Street, Milford, MA, 01757

Tel: (508) 478-2000    Fax: (508) 872-1990    www.waters.com

*Mfr./distribute liquid chromatographic instruments and test and measurement equipment.*

**Nihon Waters Ltd.,  Shuwa Kioicho Park Bldg., 3 Kioi-cho, Chiyoda-ku, Tokyo 102, Japan**

## WATKINS-JOHNSON COMMUNICATIONS

401 River Oaks Pkwy., San Jose, CA, 95134

Tel: (408) 577-6200　　　Fax: (408) 577-6621　　　www.wj.com

*Mfr. innovative broadband communications products for current and next generation fiber optic, broadband cable and wireless communications networks.*

**W-J International - Japan, 1028 Kuriki Asao-ku, Kawasaki 215, Japan**

Tel: 81-44-989-7500　Fax: 81-44-988-9903

## WATSON WYATT & COMPANY HOLDINGS

6707 Democracy Blvd., Ste. 800, Bethesda, MD, 20817

Tel: (301) 581-4600　　　Fax: (301) 581-4937　　　www.watsonwyatt.com

*Creates compensation and benefits programs for major corporations.*

**Watson Wyatt & Co., Futaba Kudan Bldg., 4-5 Kudan Minami 3-chome, Chiyoda-ku, Tokyo 102 Japan**

## WEBER MARKING SYSTEMS INC.

711 West Algonquin Road, Arlington Heights, IL, 60005-4457

Tel: (847) 364-8500　　　Fax: (847) 364-8575　　　www.webermarking.com

*Mfr. label printing systems and custom labels.*

**Weber Marking Systems Far East Co. Ltd., 3-6 Tsukiji 1-chome, Chuo-ku, Tokyo 104, Japan**

## WELCH ALLYN DCD INC.

4341 State Street Road, Skaneateles Falls, NY, 13153

Tel: (315) 685-4100　　　Fax: (315) 685-4091　　　www.welchallyn.com

*Mfr. bar code data collection systems.*

**Hand Held Products Japan K.K., Bon Marrusan 8F, 3-5-1 Kanda Jinbo-cho, Chiyoda-ku Tokyo 101, Japan**

Tel: 81-5212-7391

## WENDY'S INTERNATIONAL, INC.

428 West Dublin Granville Roads, Dublin, OH, 43017-0256

Tel: (614) 764-3100　　　Fax: (614) 764-3459　　　www.wendysintl.com

*Fast food restaurant chain.*

**Wendy's International, Tokyo, Japan**

## WEST PHARMACEUTICAL SERVICES

101 Gordon Drive, PO Box 645, Lionville, PA, 19341-0645

Tel: (610) 594-2900　　　Fax: (610) 594-3014　　　www.westpharma.com

*Mfr. products for filling, sealing, dispensing and delivering needs of health care and consumer products markets.*

**Daikyo Seiko Ltd., Tokyo, Japan**

## WESTERN DIGITAL CORPORATION

8105 Irvine Center Drive, Irvine, CA, 92718

Tel: (949) 932-5000　　　Fax: (949) 932-6629　　　www.westerndigital.com

*Mfr. hard disk drives, video graphics boards, VLSI.*

**Western Digital Japan Ltd., 44 Kowa Bldg. 8/F, 1-2-7 Higashiyama, Megoro-ku, Tokyo, Japan**

## WESTVACO CORPORATION

299 Park Ave., New York, NY, 10171

Tel: (212) 688-5000　　　Fax: (212) 318-5055　　　www.westvaco.com

*Mfr. paper, packaging, chemicals.*

**Westvaco Asia KK, Shoyo Kaikan Bldg., 3-3-1 Kasumigaseki, Chiyoda-ku, Tokyo 100, Japan**

## WEYERHAEUSER COMPANY

33663 Weyerhaeuser Way South, Federal Way, WA, 98003

Tel: (253) 924-2345      Fax: (253) 924-2685      www.weyerhaeuser.com

*Wood and wood fiber products.*

**Weyerhaeuser Japan Ltd., PO Box 18, Tokyo 107, Japan**

## WHIRLPOOL CORPORATION

2000 N. M-63, Benton Harbor, MI, 49022-2692

Tel: (616) 923-5000      Fax: (616) 923-5443      www.whirlpoolcorp.com

*Mfr./market home appliances: Whirlpool, Roper, KitchenAid, Estate, and Inglis.*

**Whirlpool Corporation, Tokyo, Japan**

## WHITE & CASE LLP

1155 Ave. of the Americas, New York, NY, 10036-2767

Tel: (212) 819-8200      Fax: (212) 354-8113      www.whitecase.com

*International law firm.*

**White & Case LLP, Kandabashi Law Offices, Kandabashi Park Bldg., 19-1 Kanda-nishikicho 1-chome, Chiyoda-ku Tokyo 101-0054 Japan**

Tel: 81-3-3259-0200   Fax: 81-3-3259-0150   Contact: Christopher P. Wells

## WHITEHALL-ROBINS INC.

1407 Cummings Drive, PO Box 26609, Richmond, VA, 23261-6609

Tel: (804) 257-2000      Fax: (804) 257-2120      www.ahp.com

*Mfr. ethical pharmaceuticals and consumer healthcare products.*

**Whitehall-Robins Intl. Co., Dai 7 Chuo Bldg., 26-1 Hamamatsu-cho 1-chome, Minato-ku, Tokyo 105, Japan**

## WILBUR-ELLIS COMPANY

PO Box 7454, San Francisco, CA, 94120

Tel: (415) 772-4000      Fax: (415) 772-4011      www.wilburellis.com

*Marketing, distribution, formulation of agricultural products and industrial specialty chemicals and raw materials.*

**Connell Bros. Co. (Japan) Ltd., 2-12-18 Minato-machi, Naha, Okinawa 900, Japan**

**Wilbur-Ellis Co. (Japan) Ltd., Sanshin Building 4-1 Yurakucho 1-Chome, Chiyoda-Ku Tokyo 100-0006, Japan**

Tel: 813-3591-3221   Fax: 813-3591-3415

## WINCHESTER/RETCONN ELECTRONICS

400 Park Road, Watertown, CT, 06795-0500

Tel: (860) 945-5000      Fax: (860) 945-5191      www.litton-wed.com

*Mfr. electrical and electronic connectors, PCB assemblies and hardware.*

**Litton Winchester Electronics Japan, c/o Litton Westrex Co., Chiyoda Bldg., 2-1-2 Marunochi, Chiyoda-ku, Tokyo 100, Japan**

## WIND RIVER SYSTEMS, INC.

500 Wind River Way, Alameda, CA, 94501

Tel: (510) 748-4100      Fax: (510) 749-2010      www.isi.com

*Develops and markets computer software products and services.*

**Wind River Systems Japan/Asia-Pacific., Pola Ebisu Building 11/F, 3-9-19 Higashi, Shibuya-ku, Tokyo 150 Japan**

Tel: 81-03-5467-5900   Fax: 81-03-5467-5877

## HARRY WINSTON INC.

718 Fifth Ave., New York, NY, 10019

Tel: (212) 245-2000 Fax: www.harry-winston.com

*Diamonds and lapidary work.*

**Harry Winston Far East, 1-8-14 Ginza, Chuo-Ku Tokyo, Japan**

Tel: 81-3-3535-6441

**Harry Winston Far East, Yomiko Building 1/2F, 1-8-14 Ginza, Osaka, Japan**

Tel: 81-6-6448-3311

## WINTHROP, STIMSON, PUTNAM & ROBERTS

One Battery Park Plaza, 31st Fl., New York, NY, 10004-1490

Tel: (212) 858-1000 Fax: (212) 858-1500 www.winstim.com

*International law firm.*

**Winthrop, Stimson, Putnam & Roberts, 608 Atagoyama Bengoahi Bldg., 6-7 Atago 1-chome, Minato-ku, Tokyo 105 Japan**

Tel: 81-3-3437-9740 Fax: 81-3-3437-9261

## WIT SOUNDVIEW GROUP, INC.

826 Broadway, 6th Fl., New York, NY, 10003

Tel: (212) 253-4400 Fax: (212) 253-4428 www.witsoundview.com

*Internet-based investment bank.*

**Wit Soundview Group Japan, Shin Aoyama Bldg. 12/F, 1-1-1 Minami Aoyama, Minato-Ku Tokyo 1070062, Japan**

## WOMETCO ENTERPRISES INC.

3195 Ponce de Leon Blvd., Coral Gables, FL, 33134

Tel: (305) 529-1400 Fax: (305) 529-1499

*Television broadcasting, film distribution, bottling, vending machines.*

**Intl. Leisure Corp., Tokyo Tower Wax Museum, 20-1 Shiba Park, Minato-ku, Tokyo, Japan**

## WONDERWARE CORPORATION

100 Technology Dr., Irvine, CA, 92618

Tel: (949) 727-3200 Fax: (949) 727-3270 www.wonderware.com

*Mfr. industrial strength applications software and services.*

**CONTEC Co. Ltd., Koutou-ku, Tokyo, Japan**

Tel: 81-6-6472-7130

**NEC Corporation, Minato-Ku, Tokyo, Japan**

Tel: 81-3-3456-7503

## WOODHEAD INDUSTRIES INC.

Three Parkway North, Ste. 550, Deerfield, IL, 60015

Tel: (847) 236-9300 Fax: (847) 236-0503 www.woodhead.com

*Develop/mfr./sale/distributor elect/electronic, fiber optic and ergonomic special-function, non-commodity products.*

**Woodhead Japan Corporation, Unit 4309 Yokohama Landmark Tower, 2-2-1 Minato Mirai, Nishi-ku Yokohama-shi, Kanagawa-ken 220-8143, Japan**

Contact: Bela J. Horvath

## WOODWARD GOVERNOR COMPANY

5001 N. Second Street, PO Box 7001, Rockford, IL, 61125-7001

Tel: (815) 877-7441 Fax: (815) 639-6033 www.woodward.com

*Mfr./service speed control devices and systems for aircraft turbines, industrial engines and turbines.*

**Woodward Governor Japan Ltd., Tomisato, PO Box 1, 251-1 Nakazawa Tomisato-Machi Inba-Gun, Chiba-Ken 286--02 Japan**

Tel: 81-476-93-4661 Fax: 81-476-93-7939 Contact: John Sundstedt Emp: 150

**Woodward Governor Japan Ltd. (Kansai Branch), 105 Moritomo, Nishi-ku, Kobe-shi, Hyogoken 651-21 Japan**

Tel: 81-78-928-8500    Fax: 81-78-928-8322    Contact: Nikki Hayashi    Emp: 20

## WORLD COURIER INC.

1313 Fourth Ave., New Hyde Park, NY, 11041

Tel: (516) 354-2600        Fax: (516) 354-2644        www.worldcourier.com

*International courier service.*

**World Courier Japan, Ginza Chuo Bldg. 7/F, 3-10 Ginza 4-chome, Chuo-ku, Tokyo 104, Japan**

## WORLDCOM, INC.

500 Clinton Center Drive, Clinton, MS, 39060

Tel: (601) 360-8600        Fax: (601) 360-8616        www.wcom.com

*Telecommunications company serving local, long distance and Internet customers domestically and internationally.*

**WorldCom International, PO Box 17, 3-2 Nishi Shinjuku 2-chome, Shinjuku-ku, Tokyo 163-03 Japan**

## WORLDXCHANGE COMMUNICATIONS

9999 Willow Creek Road, San Diego, CA, 92131

Tel: (858) 547-4933        Fax: (800) 995-4502        www.worldxchange.com

*Provides international, long distance telecommunications services worldwide.*

**WorldxChange Communications S.A., Tokyo, Japan**

## WM WRIGLEY JR. COMPANY

410 N. Michigan Ave., Chicago, IL, 60611-4287

Tel: (312) 644-2121        Fax: (312) 644-0353        www.wrigley.com

*Mfr. chewing gum.*

**Wrigley & Company Ltd. Japan, Tokyo, Japan**

## WYETH-AYERST INTERNATIONAL INC.

150 Radnot-Chester Road, St. Davids, PA, 19087

Tel: (610) 902-4100        Fax: (610) 989-4586        www.ahp.com/wyeth

*Antibiotics and pharmaceutical products.*

**Lederle (Japan) Ltd., CPO Box 957, Tokyo 100-91, Japan**

**Lederle (Japan) Ltd., 1 Kyobashi 1-chome, Chuo-ku, Tokyo 104, Japan**

**Wyeth (Japan) Corporation, Kowa Building No. 6, 15-21 Nishi Azabu 4-Chome Minato-ku, Tokyo 106 Japan**

Tel: 81-3-5485-6043

**Wyeth-Lederle (Japan) Limited, Hattori Bldg. 5/F, 1-10-3 Kyobashi Chuo-Ku, Tokyo 104-0311 Japan**

Tel: 81-3-3561-8781

## XEROX CORPORATION

800 Long Ridge Road, PO Box 1600, Stamford, CT, 06904

Tel: (203) 968-3000        Fax: (203) 968-4312        www.xerox.com

*Mfr. document processing equipment, systems and supplies.*

**Akita Xerox Co., Ltd., 170-92 Aza Ookawa-bata, Kawajiri-machi, Akita-shi 010, Japan**

Tel: 81-188-23-4645    Fax: 81-188-23-7559

**Fuji Xerox Co. Ltd., 3-5 Akasaka 3-chome, Minato-ku, Tokyo 107, Japan**

**Hokkaido Xerox Co., Ltd., No. 3 Yuuraku-terashima Bldg. 7F, 4-133 Odori-Nishi 10-chome, Chuo-ku, Sapporo-shi 060 Japan**

Tel: 81-271-4533

**Xerox Co., Ltd., 17-48 Teppo-cho 1 chome, Yamagata-shi 990, Japan**

Tel: 81-2-3624-2468

## XILINX INC.

2100 Logic Drive, San Jose, CA, 95124-3400

Tel: (408) 559-7778     Fax: (408) 559-7114     www.xilinx.com

*Programmable logic and related development systems software.*

**Xilinx Japan KK, Shinjuku Square Tower 18F, 22-1 Nishi-Shinjuku 6 chome, Shinjuku-ku, Tokyo 163-1118 Japan**

Tel: 81-3-5321-7711     Contact: Hiroyuki Takasaki, Pres.

## XIRCOM, INC.

2300 Corporate Center Drive, Thousand Oaks, CA, 91320

Tel: (805) 376-9300     Fax: (805) 376-9311     www.xircom.com

*Mfr. PC card network adapters and modems.*

**Xircom Japan KK, 3-10-5 Shibuya, Shibuya-Ku, Tokyo 105-0002, Japan**

Tel: 81-3-3407-0056   Fax: 81-3-3407-0218

## XTRA CORPORATION

1807 Park 270 Dr., Ste. 400, St. Louis, MO, 63146-4020

Tel: (314) 579-9320     Fax: (314) 579-0299     www.xtracorp.com

*Holding company: leasing.*

**XTRA International, Tokyo, Japan**

## YAHOO! INC.

3420 Central Expressway, Santa Clara, CA, 95051

Tel: (408) 731-3300     Fax: (408) 731-3301     www.yahoo-inc.com

*Internet media company providing specialized content, free electronic mail and community offerings and commerce.*

**Yahoo! Inc., 24-1 Nihonbashi-Hakozaki Cho, Chuo-ku, Tokyo, Japan**

Tel: 81-3-5642-8028   Fax: 81-3-5641-3680

## YELLOW CORPORATION

10990 Roe Ave., PO Box 7270, Overland Park, KS, 66207

Tel: (913) 696-6100     Fax: (913) 696-6116     www.yellowcorp.com

*Commodity transportation.*

**Trans-Atlantic (Japan) Ltd., Osakan Sakuragaoka Bldg. 5/F, 31-14 Sakuragaoka-cho, Shibuya-ku Tokyo 150-0031 Japan**

## YORK INTERNATIONAL CORPORATION

631 South Richland Ave., York, PA, 17403

Tel: (717) 771-7890     Fax: (717) 771-6212     www.york.com

*Mfr. heating, ventilating, air conditioning and refrigeration equipment.*

**York International Corporation, 2-21-11 Ota-Ku Sanno, Tokyo 143, Japan**

Tel: 81-3-57009-1310

## YOUNG & RUBICAM INC.

285 Madison Ave., New York, NY, 10017

Tel: (212) 210-3000     Fax: (212) 370-3796     www.yr.com

*Advertising, public relations, direct marketing and sales promotion, corporate and product ID management.*

**Dentsu Young & Rubicam (Pvt.) Ltd., Kyobashi K-1 Bldg., 2-7-12 Yaesu, Chuo-ku, Tokyo 104-8477, Japan**

Tel: 81-3-3278-4811   Fax: 81-3-3278-4851

## YSI INC.

1725 Brannum Lane, PO Box 279, Yellow Springs, OH, 45387

Tel: (937) 767-7241     Fax: (937) 767-9353     www.ysi.com

*Mfr. analyzers, measure instruments and electrical components.*

**YSI Japan KK, 43-2 Ebisu 3-chome, Shibuya-ku, Tokyo, Japan**

## ZIEBART INTERNATIONAL CORPORATION

1290 East Maple Road, Troy, MI, 48083

Tel: (248) 588-4100     Fax: (248) 588-0718     www.ziebart.com

*Automotive aftermarket services.*

**Ziebart Japan Ltd., 5-1 Kita-Aoyama-a-chome, Minato-ku, Tokyo 107-77, Japan**

Tel: 81-3-3497-2554   Fax: 81-3-3497-4115

## ZIPPERTUBING COMPANY

13000 S. Broadway, PO Box 61129, Los Angeles, CA, 90061

Tel: (310) 527-0488     Fax: (310) 767-1714     www.zippertubing.com

*Mfr. zip-on plastic tubing, wire markers, pipe insulation, EMI shielding.*

**Zippertubing (Japan) Ltd., 3-2-56 Takatsukadai, Nishi-ku, Kobe 651-22, Japan**

## ZYGO CORPORATION

Laurel Brook Road, Middlefield, CT, 06455

Tel: (860) 347-8506     Fax: (860) 347-8372     www.zygo.com

*Mfr. high-precision, electro-optical measuring equipment.*

**Zygo KK, Ueno Sanwa Bldg., 1-14-4 Higashiueno, Taitou-Ku, Tokyo 110-0015, Japan**

Tel: 81-3-5812-6051   Fax: 81-3-5812-6055

# Jordan

## AIR EXPRESS INTERNATIONAL CORPORATION
120 Tokeneke Road, PO Box 1231, Darien, CT, 06820

Tel: (203) 655-7900    Fax: (203) 655-5779    www.aeilogistics.com

*International air freight forwarder.*

**AEI Amman Eastern Services, Peace Bldg. Jabal Lweidbeh, PO Box 815408, Amman 11180, Jordan**

Tel: 962-6-621-775   Fax: 962-6-656-270

## ANDERSEN WORLDWIDE
33 West Monroe Street, Chicago, IL, 60603

Tel: (312) 580-0033    Fax: (312) 507-6748    www.arthurandersen.com

*Accounting and audit, tax and management consulting services.*

**Allied Accountants/Shair, Dajani, Alaeddin & Co., Mecca St. - Wadi Saqra, Jabal Amman, PO Box 5552, Amman 11183 Jordan**

Tel: 962-6-686111

## BATES WORLDWIDE INC.
405 Lexington Ave., New York, NY, 10174

Tel: (212) 297-7000    Fax: (212) 986-0270    www.batesww.com

*Advertising, marketing, public relations and media consulting.*

**Bates Jordon, PO Box 3371, Amman 11181, Jordan**

Tel: 962-5-680-507   Fax: 962-5-687-451   Contact: R.G. Naljar, CEO

## BDO SEIDMAN, LLP    BELGIUM
Two Prudential Plaza, 180 N. Stetson Ave., Ste. 2300, Chicago, IL, 60601

Tel: (312) 240-1236    Fax: (312) 240-3329    www.bdo.com

*International accounting and financial consulting firm.*

**BDO National Brothers, Al-Youbeel Circle, Shukri Elaian Ctr., 3rd Fl. Office No 306, Amman, Jordan**

Tel: 962-6-5538-618   Fax: 962-6-5538-618   Contact: Mohammed Al-Nobani

## BECHTEL GROUP INC.
50 Beale Street, PO Box 3965, San Francisco, CA, 94105-1895

Tel: (415) 768-1234    Fax: (415) 768-9038    www.bechtel.com

*General contractors in engineering and construction.*

**Bechtel Corp., PO Box 5226, Amman, Jordan**

## BESTFOODS, INC.
700 Sylvan Ave., International Plaza, Englewood Cliffs, NJ, 07632-9976

Tel: (201) 894-4000    Fax: (201) 894-2186    www.bestfoods.com

*Consumer foods products; corn refining.*

**Best Foods Jordan, Jabal Amman-Absan St., PO Box 470, Amman 11118, Jordan**

Tel: 962-6-4624-290   Fax: 962-6-4625-701

## BRISTOL-MYERS SQUIBB COMPANY
345 Park Ave., New York, NY, 10154-0037

Tel: (212) 546-4000    Fax: (212) 546-4020    www.bms.com

*Pharmaceutical and food preparations, medical and surgical instruments.*

**Kawar Drug Stores, PO Box 922025, Amman, Jordan**

## CDM INTERNATIONAL INC.

50 Hampshire Street, Cambridge, MA, 02139

Tel: (617) 452-6000    Fax: (617) 452-8020    www.cdm.com

*Consulting engineers.*

**Camp Dresser & McKee Intl. Inc., 1 Queen Alia International Airport Road 4/F, PO Box 941895, Amman 11194, Jordan**

Tel: 9-6-585-5267

## CH2M HILL INC.

6060 South Willow Drive, Greenwood Village, CO, 80111

Tel: (303) 771-0900    Fax: (303) 770-2616    www.ch2m.com

*Consulting engineers, planners, economists and scientists.*

**CH2M Hill Inc., c/o Arabtech, PO Box 7323, Amman, Jordan**

## THE CHRISTIAN SCIENCE PUBLISHING SOCIETY

1 Norway Street, Boston, MA, 02115

Tel: (617) 450-2000    Fax: (617) 450-7575    www.christianscience.com

*Publishing company.*

**The Christian Science Monitor Publication, Box 2604, Amman, Jordan 11181**

Contact: Scott Peterson    Emp: 1

## CITIGROUP, INC.

153 East 53rd Street, New York, NY, 10043

Tel: (212) 559-1000    Fax: (212) 559-3646    www.citigroup.com

*Provides insurance and financial services worldwide.*

**Citibank N.A., Country Corporate Officer, PO Box 5055/11183, Amman, Jordan**

Contact: Suhair Al-Ali

## CUTLER-HAMMER, DIV. EATON CORP.

173 Heatherdown Drive, Westerville, OH, 43082

Tel: (614) 882-3282    Fax: (614) 895-7111    www.cutlerhammer.com

*Mfr. electrical control products and power distribution equipment.*

**Cutler-Hammer, Farraj Centre PO Box 510449, Amman 11151, Jordan**

## DELOITTE TOUCHE TOHMATSU INTERNATIONAL

1633 Broadway, New York, NY, 10019

Tel: (212) 492-4000    Fax: (212) 392-4154    www.deloitte.com

*Accounting, audit, tax and management consulting services.*

**Saba & Co., Jordan Ins. Co. Bldg., Third Circle, Jabal Amman, PO Box 248, Amman 11118, Jordan**

## DHL WORLDWIDE EXPRESS

50 California Avenue, San Francisco, CA, 94111

Tel: (415) 677-6100    Fax: (415) 824-9700    www.dhl.com

*Worldwide air express carrier.*

**DHL Worldwide Express, 7th Circle Jabal Amman, PO Box 927111, Amman, Jordan**

Tel: 962-6-858514

## EAGLE GLOBAL LOGISTICS (EGL)

15350 Vickery Drive, Houston, TX, 77032

Tel: (281) 618-3100    Fax: (281) 618-3100    www.eaglegl.com

*Ocean/air freight forwarding, customs brokerage, packing and wholesale, logistics management and insurance.*

**Jordan Express Co., PO Box 2143, Amman 11181, Jordan**

Tel: 962-6-662-722    Fax: 962-6-601-507

## ERNST & YOUNG, LLP

787 Seventh Ave., New York, NY, 10019

Tel: (212) 773-3000    Fax: (212) 773-6350    www.eyi.com

*Accounting and audit, tax and management consulting services.*

**Ernst & Young/Whinney, Murray & Company,  PO Box 1140 4F, Haddad Commercial Centre, Wasfi Al-Tai St. Gardens, Amman 11118 Jordan**

Tel: 962-6-681885   Fax: 962-6-681885   Contact: Mohamed A.K. Saadeh

## FRITZ COMPANIES, INC.

706 Mission Street, Ste. 900, San Francisco, CA, 94103

Tel: (415) 904-8360    Fax: (415) 904-8661    www.fritz.com

*Integrated transportation, sourcing, distribution and customs brokerage services.*

**Fritz Companies Inc.,  Amman, Jordan**

## GENZYME CORPORATION

1 Kendall Square, Cambridge, MA, 02139-1562

Tel: (617) 252-7500    Fax: (617) 252-7600    www.genzyme.com

*Mfr. healthcare products for enzyme deficient diseases.*

**Genzyme Jordan,  PO Box 911821 Amman 11191, Jordan**

Tel: 962-6-585-4444

## HOLIDAY INN (BASS RESORTS) WORLDWIDE, INC.

3 Ravinia Drive, Ste. 2900, Atlanta, GA, 30346-2149

Tel: (770) 604-2000    Fax: (770) 604-5403    www.holidayinn.com

*Hotels, restaurants and casinos.*

**Holiday Inn,  PO Box 6399, Amman, Jordan**

## HYATT CORPORATION

200 West Madison Street, Chicago, IL, 60606

Tel: (312) 750-1234    Fax: (312) 750-8578    www.hyatt.com

*International hotel management.*

**Grand Hyatt Amman,  Amman, Jordan**

## IBM CORPORATION

New Orchard Road, Armonk, NY, 10504

Tel: (914) 765-1900    Fax: (914) 765-7382    www.ibm.com

*Information products, technology and services.*

**IBM Jordan - United Business Machines,  Shmeisani, PO Box 6410, Amman 11118, Jordan**

Tel: 962-6-567-0171   Fax: 962-6-567-0173

## IDEX CORPORATION

630 Dundee Road, Ste. 400, Northbrook, IL, 60062

Tel: (847) 498-7070    Fax: (847) 498-3940    www.idexcorp.com

*Mfr. industrial pumps, lubrication systems, metal fabrication equipment, bending and clamping devices.*

**Viking Pump,  Shahatit Bureau Razan Hotel Building, Third Circle - PO Box 2674, Amman 11181, Jordan**

## INTER-CONTINENTAL HOTELS

3 Ravina Drive, Suite 2900, Atlanta, GA, 30346-2149

Tel: (770) 604-2000    Fax: (770) 604-5403    www.interconti.com

*Worldwide hotel and resort accommodations.*

**Petra Forum Hotel,  PO Box 30, Wadi Mousa, Jordan**

Tel: 962-3-215-6266   Fax: 962-3-215-6977

## IRRIDELCO INTERNATIONAL CORPORATION

440 Sylvan Ave., Englewood Cliffs, NJ, 07632

Tel: (201) 569-3030    Fax: (201) 569-9237    www.irridelco.com

*Mfr./distributor of the most comprehensive lines of mechanical and micro irrigation; pumps and irrigation systems.*

**IDC Jordan,  PO Box 5474, Amman, Jordan**

Tel: 962-6-832424   Fax: 962-6-832424   Contact: Marwan Hurani

## KPMG INTERNATIONAL LLP

345 Park Avenue, New York, NY, 10022

Tel: (201) 307-7000    Fax: (201) 930-8617    www.kpmg.com

*Accounting and audit, tax and management consulting services.*

**Khleif & Co.,  Amman Commercial Centre, Abdali 2F, Amman, Jordan**

Tel: 962-6-681798   Fax: 962-6-681798   Contact: Adnan Khleif, Sr. Ptnr.

## THE KULJIAN CORPORATION

3700 Science Center, Philadelphia, PA, 19104

Tel: (215) 243-1900    Fax: (215) 243-1909

*Studies, design, engineering, construction management and site supervision.*

**Kuljian Corp.,  PO Box 2749, Amman, Jordan**

## LOCKHEED MARTIN CORPORATION

6801 Rockledge Drive, Bethesda, MD, 20817

Tel: (301) 897-6000    Fax: (301) 897-6652    www.imco.com

*Design/mfr./management systems in fields of space, defense, energy, electronics and technical services.*

**Lockheed Aeronautical Systems,  Q.A.I. Airport, 41 Tabouk Street (Um Uthaina), Amman, Jordan**

Tel: 962-8-51821   Fax: 962-8-53337   Contact: N. D. Bowler, Mgr.

## MARRIOTT INTERNATIONAL INC.

10400 Fernwood Rd., Bethesda, MD, 20817

Tel: (301) 380-3000    Fax: (301) 380-5181    www.marriott.com

*Hotel services.*

**Amman Marriott Hotel,  Amman, Jordan**

Tel: 962-6-569-7756

## MERCK & COMPANY, INC.

One Merck Drive, PO Box 100, Whitehouse Station, NJ, 08889-0100

Tel: (908) 423-1000    Fax: (908) 423-2592    www.merck.com

*Pharmaceuticals, chemicals and biologicals.*

**Merck/Charles E. Frost & Co.,  PO Box 20604, Amman, Jordan**

## J. P. MORGAN CHASE & CO. INC.

World Headquarters, 270 Park Ave., New York, NY, 10017

Tel: (212) 270-6000    Fax: (212) 622-9030    www.jpmorganchase.com

*Provides integrated financial solutions for institutions and individuals worldwide, including asset management, investment banking and commercial banking.*

**J. P. Morgan Chase & Co.,  PO Box 20191, First Circle, Jebal Amman, Jordan**

## A .C. NIELSEN COMPANY

177 Broad Street, Stamford, CT, 06901

Tel: (203) 961-3000    Fax: (203) 961-3190    www.acnielsen.com

*Market and consumer research firm.*

**A. C. Nielsen,  Shmesani Suheib ben Sinan St., PO Box 5141, Amman 11183 Jordan**

## OTIS ELEVATOR COMPANY

10 Farm Springs Road, Farmington, CT, 06032

Tel: (860) 676-6000      Fax: (860) 676-5111         www.otis.com

*Mfr. elevators and escalators.*

**Otis/Jordan Elevator Overseas Ltd.,  PO Box 7490, Amman, Jordan**

## RAYTHEON COMPANY

141 Spring Street, Lexington, MA, 02173

Tel: (781) 862-6600      Fax: (781) 860-2172         www.raytheon.com

*Mfr. diversified electronics, appliances, aviation, energy and environmental products; publishing, industry and construction services.*

**Raytheon Technical Assistance Co.,  PO Box 3414, Jebal, Amman, Jordan**

## THE SERVICEMASTER COMPANY

One ServiceMaster Way, Downers Grove, IL, 60515-1700

Tel: (630) 271-1300      Fax: (630) 271-2710         www.svm.com

*Management service to health care, school and industry facilities; diversified residential and commercial services.*

**ServiceMaster,  Amman, Jordan**

## STANLEY CONSULTANTS, INC.

Stanley Building, 225 Iowa Ave., Muscatine, IA, 52761-3764

Tel: (319) 264-6600      Fax: (319) 264-6658         www.stanleygroup.com

*Engaged in engineering, architectural, planning and management services.*

**Stanley Consultants, Inc.,  PO Box 830746, Fourth Circle, 73 Almutanabi St., Amman 11183, Jordan**
Tel: 9626-4-612-377

## TRUE NORTH COMMUNICATIONS INC.

101 East Erie Street, Chicago, IL, 60611

Tel: (312) 425-6500      Fax: (312) 425-5010         www.truenorth.com

*Holding company, advertising agency.*

**Horizon Amman,  Al Aqad Bldg. Block B, Wasfi Al-Tal-St., Sports City Amman 11196, Jordan**

## UNION CARBIDE CORPORATION

39 Old Ridgebury Road, Danbury, CT, 06817

Tel: (203) 794-2000      Fax: (203) 794-6269         www.unioncarbide.com

*Mfr. industrial chemicals, plastics and resins.*

**Union Carbide Europe SA,  PO Box 927277, Amman, Jordan**

## WACKENHUT CORPORATION

4200 Wackenhut Dr., Ste. 100, Palm Beach Gardens, FL, 33410

Tel: (561) 622-5656      Fax: (561) 691-6736         www.wackenhut.com

*Security systems and services.*

**WII/Sound & Security Eng. Co.,  PO Box 9881, Amman, Jordan**
Tel: 962-6-642407   Fax: 962-6-656899

## WYETH-AYERST INTERNATIONAL INC.

150 Radnot-Chester Road, St. Davids, PA, 19087

Tel: (610) 902-4100      Fax: (610) 989-4586         www.ahp.com/wyeth

*Antibiotics and pharmaceutical products.*

**Wyeth-Ayerst International, Inc.,  Yousef Al Aseer St. No. 10, Rajab Commercial Bldg. 2/F, Amman Jordan**

## XEROX CORPORATION

800 Long Ridge Road, PO Box 1600, Stamford, CT, 06904

Tel: (203) 968-3000    Fax: (203) 968-4312    www.xerox.com

*Mfr. document processing equipment, systems and supplies.*

**Arabian Office Automation WLL, Amman Commercial Complex, Mezanin 1, Al-Abdaly-Amman, Jordan**

Tel: 962-6-698804    Fax: 962-6-698806

# Kazakhstan

**THE AES CORPORATION**

1001 North 19th Street, Arlington, VA, 22209

Tel: (703) 522-1315    Fax: (703) 528-4510    www.aesc.com

*Gas and electric utility.*

**AES Sogrinsk TETS, Almaty, Kazakhstan**

**AMERICAN INTERNATIONAL GROUP INC. (AIG)**

70 Pine Street, New York, NY, 10270

Tel: (212) 770-7000    Fax: (212) 509-9705    www.aig.com

*Worldwide insurance and financial services.*

**AIG Kaz. Ins. Co., 64 Almangeldy Street, Almtaz 480012, Kazakhstan**

**AMERICAN INTERNATIONAL PETROLEUM CORP.**

444 Madison Ave., New York, NY, 1002

Tel: (212) 688-3333    Fax: (212) 688-6657    www.aipcorp.com

*Engaged in oil and gas exploration.*

**American International Petroleum Kazakhstan (AIPK), Almaty, Kazakhstan**

**ANDERSEN WORLDWIDE**

33 West Monroe Street, Chicago, IL, 60603

Tel: (312) 580-0033    Fax: (312) 507-6748    www.arthurandersen.com

*Accounting and audit, tax and management consulting services.*

**Andersen Worldwide, 69 Tole Bi St., 480091 Almaty, Kazakhstan**

Tel: 7-327-269-1619

**AON CORPORATION**

123 North Wacker Drive, Chicago, IL, 60606

Tel: (312) 701-3000    Fax: (312) 701-3100    www.aon.com

*Insurance brokers worldwide; underwrites accident and health insurance, specialty and professional insurance; and provides risk management consultation.*

**Alexander Howden Group Kazakhstan Office Ltd., Ministry of Rd. 7th Fl., Construction UL Gogolya 86, Almaty, Kazakhstan**

Tel: 7-327-232-2549    Fax: 7-327-581-1475    Contact: Jack Murphy

**BAKER & McKENZIE**

130 East Randolph Drive, Ste. 2500, Chicago, IL, 60601

Tel: (312) 861-8000    Fax: (312) 861-2899    www.bakerinfo.com

*International legal services.*

**Baker & McKenzie - CIS Ltd., 155 Abai Ave. 29/30, 480009 Almaty, Kazakhstan**

Tel: 7-327-509945    Fax: 7-327-2509579

**LOUIS BERGER INTERNATIONAL INC.**

100 Halsted Street, East Orange, NJ, 07019

Tel: (201) 678-1960    Fax: (201) 672-4284    www.louisberger.com

*Consulting engineers, engaged in architecture, environmental and advisory services.*

**Louis Berger International Inc., c/o NIIAT(PK631), Prospekt ABAY 76/109, 480057 Almaty, Kazakhstan**

### BRISTOL-MYERS SQUIBB COMPANY

345 Park Ave., New York, NY, 10154-0037

Tel: (212) 546-4000     Fax: (212) 546-4020     www.bms.com

*Pharmaceutical and food preparations, medical and surgical instruments.*

**Bristol-Myer Squibb Company, 83 Ulitsa Zhectoksan, 480091 Almaty, Kazakhstan**

### LEO BURNETT, DIV. B-COM 3 GROUP

35 West Wacker Drive, Chicago, IL, 60601

Tel: (312) 220-5959     Fax: (312) 220-6533     www.bcom3group.com

*Engaged in advertising, marketing, media buying and planning, and public relations.*

**Styx & Leo Burnett, Almaty, Kazakhstan**

### CARANA CORPORATION

4350 N. Fairfax Drive, Ste. 500, Arlington, VA, 22203

Tel: (703) 243-1700     Fax: (703) 243-0471     www.carana.com

*Foreign trade consulting.*

**CARANA Corp., ul. Ablai-Khan 93/95 Ste. 528, Almaty, Kazakhstan**

### CATERPILLAR INC.

100 NE Adams Street, Peoria, IL, 61629-6105

Tel: (309) 675-1000     Fax: (309) 675-1182     www.cat.com

*Mfr. earth/material-handling and construction machinery and equipment and engines.*

**Caterpillar, Inc., Kazakhstan**

### CH2M HILL INC.

6060 South Willow Drive, Greenwood Village, CO, 80111

Tel: (303) 771-0900     Fax: (303) 770-2616     www.ch2m.com

*Consulting engineers, planners, economists and scientists.*

**CH2M Hill, Almaty, Kazakhstan**

### CHADBOURNE & PARKE LLP

30 Rockefeller Plaza, New York, NY, 10112-0127

Tel: (212) 408-5100     Fax: (212) 541-5369     www.chadbourne.com

*International law firm.*

**The Zanger Law Firm, 157 Abaya Street, Suite 26/27, Almaty 480124, Kazakhstan**

Tel: 7-327-250-9473   Contact: Maidan K. Suleimenov

### CHEVRON CORPORATION

575 Market Street, San Francisco, CA, 94105-2856

Tel: (415) 894-7700     Fax: (415) 894-2248     www.chevron.com

*Oil exploration, production and petroleum products.*

**Tengiz Chevroil TCO (JV), Tengiz, Kazakhstan**

### CITIGROUP, INC.

153 East 53rd Street, New York, NY, 10043

Tel: (212) 559-1000     Fax: (212) 559-3646     www.citigroup.com

*Provides insurance and financial services worldwide.*

**Citibank N.A., 155 Abai St. 11th Fl., 480009 Almaty, Kazakhstan**

Contact: Reza Ghaffari

### COUDERT BROTHERS

1114 Ave. of the Americas, New York, NY, 10036-7794

Tel: (212) 626-4400     Fax: (212) 626-4120     www.coudert.com

*International law firm.*

**Coudert Brothers, Samal -1. Bldg. 36 Third Fl., 480099 Almaty, Kazakhstan**

Tel: 7-327-253-3370   Fax: 7-327-253-3372

## DELOITTE TOUCHE TOHMATSU INTERNATIONAL

1633 Broadway, New York, NY, 10019

Tel: (212) 492-4000      Fax: (212) 392-4154      www.deloitte.com

*Accounting, audit, tax and management consulting services.*

**Deloitte & Touche CIS,  29 Kurmangazy St. Rooms 117-119, 480021 Almaty, Kazakhstan**

## DHL WORLDWIDE EXPRESS

50 California Avenue, San Francisco, CA, 94111

Tel: (415) 677-6100      Fax: (415) 824-9700      www.dhl.com

*Worldwide air express carrier.*

**DHL Worldwide Express,  Offices 1-4, 157 Abaya St., 480009 Almaty, Kazakhstan**

Tel: 7-327-250-9416

## ERNST & YOUNG, LLP

787 Seventh Ave., New York, NY, 10019

Tel: (212) 773-3000      Fax: (212) 773-6350      www.eyi.com

*Accounting and audit, tax and management consulting services.*

**Ernst & Young Kazakhstan,  Prospect Lenina 212a, 480051 Almaty, Kazakhstan**

Tel: 7-327-250-9423   Fax: 7-327-241-4800   Contact: Robert Langham

## EXXON MOBIL CORPORATION

5959 Las Colinas Blvd., Irving, TX, 75039-2298

Tel: (972) 444-1000      Fax: (972) 444-1882      www.exxon.com

*Petroleum exploration, production, refining; mfr. petroleum and chemicals products; coal and minerals.*

**Exxon Mobil, Inc.,  Almaty, Kazakhstan**

## FRITZ COMPANIES, INC.

706 Mission Street, Ste. 900, San Francisco, CA, 94103

Tel: (415) 904-8360      Fax: (415) 904-8661      www.fritz.com

*Integrated transportation, sourcing, distribution and customs brokerage services.*

**Kaz-Fritz Transportation (Ltd.),  127 Furmanov St., Almaty, Kazakhstan**

## GENERAL ELECTRIC COMPANY

3135 Easton Turnpike, Fairfield, CT, 06431

Tel: (203) 373-2211      Fax: (203) 373-3131      www.ge.com

*Diversified manufacturing, technology and services.*

**GE International,  153 Abai Avenue, Apt. 13-14, Almatzy, Kazakhstan**

Tel: 7-327-260-8528   Fax: 7-327-240-0558

## HONEYWELL INTERNATIONAL INC.

101 Columbia Road, Morristown, NJ, 07962

Tel: (973) 455-2000      Fax: (973) 455-4807      www.honeywell.com

*Develop/mfr. controls for home and building, industry, space and aviation.*

**Honeywell Automation Controls LLP,  Temirjazeva 42, Atakent Business Center 5/F, 480057 Almaty, Kazakhstan**

Tel: 7-327-2-447747   Fax: 7-327-2-473290

## HYATT CORPORATION

200 West Madison Street, Chicago, IL, 60606

Tel: (312) 750-1234      Fax: (312) 750-8578      www.hyatt.com

*International hotel management.*

**Hyatt Regency Almaty Hotel,  Akademik Satpaev Ave. 29/6, 480004 Almaty, Kazakhstan**

Tel: 7-327-581-1234   Fax: 7-327-581-1635

## INFORMIX CORPORATION

4100 Bohannon Drive, Menlo Park, CA, 95025

Tel: (650) 926-6300      Fax: (650) 926-6593      www.informix.com

*Designs and produces database management software, connectivity interfaces and gateways, and other computer applications.*

**Informix Ltd., ul. Tole Be str. 55/57 off 109, 480091 Almaty, Kazakhstan**

Tel: 7-327-262-9716

## KELLOGG BROWN & ROOT INC.

PO Box 3, Houston, TX, 77001

Tel: (713) 676-3011      Fax: (713) 676-8695      www.halliburton.com

*Engaged in technology-based engineering and construction.*

**Kellogg Brown & Root, #4 Mornyshully St., Atyrau 465002, Kazakhstan**

## KPMG INTERNATIONAL LLP

345 Park Avenue, New York, NY, 10022

Tel: (201) 307-7000      Fax: (201) 930-8617      www.kpmg.com

*Accounting and audit, tax and management consulting services.*

**KPMG Janat, 105 Ave. Abylai, Khan, 480091 Almaty, Kazakhstan**

Tel: 7-327-262-2694   Fax: 7-327-269-5927   Contact: Michael Roberts, Ptnr.

## LeBOEUF, LAMB, GREENE & MacRAE LLP

125 West 55th Street, 12th Fl., New York, NY, 10019

Tel: (212) 424-8000      Fax: (212) 424-8500      www.llgm.com

*International law firm.*

**LeBoeuf, Lamb, Greene & MacRae LLP, Prospect Seyfullina 531, 480083 Almaty, Kazakhstan**

Tel: 7-327-250-7575   Fax: 7-327-261-7576

## ELI LILLY & COMPANY

Lilly Corporate Center, Indianapolis, IN, 46285

Tel: (317) 276-2000      Fax: (317) 277-6579      www.lilly.com

*Mfr. pharmaceuticals and animal health products.*

**Eli Lilly (Suisse) S.A., c/o Republican Centre of Modern Medicine, Ul. Bazaikova 299, 480070 Almaty, Kazakhstan**

Tel: 7-327-244-2477   Fax: 7-327-250-9247

## MARSH & McLENNAN COS INC.

1166 Ave. of the Americas, New York, NY, 10036-2774

Tel: (212) 345-5000      Fax: (212) 345-4808      www.marshmac.com

*Insurance agents/brokers, pension and investment management consulting services.*

**J&H Unison, 5th Fl. 69 Tole Bi St., 480091 Almaty, Kazakhstan**

Tel: 7-327-269-4906   Fax: 7-327-269-4089   Contact: Laila Dosbaeva

## MAYER, BROWN & PLATT

190 S. LaSalle Street, Chicago, IL, 60603

Tel: (312) 782-0600      Fax: (312) 701-7711      www.mayerbrown.com

*International law firm.*

**Mayer, Brown & Platt, 162 Tulabaev St. # 32, Almaty, Kazakhstan**

Tel: 7-327-263-6388   Fax: 7-327-250-7828

## McCANN-ERICKSON WORLDGROUP

750 Third Ave., New York, NY, 10017

Tel: (212) 984-3644      Fax: (212) 984-2629      www.mccann.com

*International advertising and marketing services.*

**McCann-Erickson Kazakhstan, Almaty, Kazakhstan**

**McGUIRE, WOODS LLP**

One James Center, 901 E. Cary Street, Richmond, VA, 23219

Tel: (804) 775-1000     Fax: (804) 775-1061     www.mwbb.com

*International law firm.*

**McGuire, Woods, Battle & Boothe International LLC, Park Place, 41, Kazibek Bi St. 2nd Fl., 480100 Almaty, Kazakhstan**

Tel: 7-327-2608-3000   Fax: 7-327-260-8305

**MOTOROLA, INC.**

1303 East Algonquin Road, Schaumburg, IL, 60196

Tel: (847) 576-5000     Fax: (847) 538-5191     www.motorola.com

*Mfr. communications equipment, semiconductors and cellular phones.*

**Motorola Kazakhstan, Samal 1 Bldg. 36 Fl. 2, 48099 Almaty, Kazakhstan**

Tel: 7-327-581-1571   Fax: 7-327-581-1572

**A .C. NIELSEN COMPANY**

177 Broad Street, Stamford, CT, 06901

Tel: (203) 961-3000     Fax: (203) 961-3190     www.acnielsen.com

*Market and consumer research firm.*

**A. C. Nielsen, 65 Kazbek bi Street 705-706, 480091 Almaty Kazakstan**

**OUTOKUMPU TECHNOLOGY, INC. , CARPCO DIV.**

1310-1 Tradeport Drive, Jacksonville, FL, 32218

Tel: (904) 353-3681     Fax: (904) 353-8705     www.carpco.com

*Design/mfr. separation equipment for mining, recycling and research; testing and flowsheet design.*

**Outokumpu Technology, Ul. Bogembai Batyr, 188 kv 12, Almaty 480008, Kazakhstan**

Tel: 7-327-267-2715   Fax: 7-327-250-9942

**PALMS & COMPANY, INC. (U.S. FUR EXCHANGE)**

515 Lake Street South, Bldg. #103, Kirkland, WA, 98033

Tel: (425) 828-6774     Fax: (425) 827-5528     www.peterpalms.com

*Fur auctioning, distribution and sale; investment banking.*

**Palms & Co. Inc., Pr. Asddirova 46/2 Kv. 66, 470055 Karaganda, Kazakhstan**

Tel: 7-3212-580773   Contact: Sergei Voronov   Emp: 5

**PRICEWATERHOUSECOOPERS LLP**

1301 Ave. of the Americas, New York, NY, 10019

Tel: (212) 596-7000     Fax: (212) 259-1301     www.pwcglobal.com

*Accounting and auditing, tax and management, and human resource consulting services.*

**PriceWaterhouseCoopers, 105 Ablai Khan Prospect, 480091 Almaty, Kazakhstan**

Tel: 7-327-262-7635   Fax: 7-327-250-6102

**PROCTER & GAMBLE COMPANY**

One Procter & Gamble Plaza, Cincinnati, OH, 45202

Tel: (513) 983-1100     Fax: (513) 562-4500     www.pg.com

*Personal care, food, laundry, cleaning and industry products.*

**Procter & Gamble Almaty, 155 Abaya Ave., Apt 31/32 Alma-Ata, Almaty, Kazakhstan**

**SALANS HERTZFELD HEILBRONN CHRISTY & VIENER**

620 Fifth Avenue, New York, NY, 10020-2457

Tel: (212) 632-5500     Fax: (212) 632-5555     www.salans.com

*International law firm.*

**Salans Hertzfeld & Heilbronn, Ulitsa Gogolya 86, 480091 Almaty, Kazakhstan**

## SCHLUMBERGER LIMITED

277 Park Avenue, New York, NY, 10021

Tel: (212) 350-9400     Fax: (212) 350-9564     www.schlumberger.com

*Engaged in oil and gas services, metering and payment systems, and produces semiconductor testing equipment and smart cards.*

**Schlumberger, 86 Gogolya St., Almaty, 480091 Kazakhstan**

## SCIENTECH, INC.

1690 International Way, Idaho Falls, ID, 83402

Tel: (208) 525-3700     Fax: (208) 529-4721     www.scientech.com

*worldwide provider of expert services to the energy and telecommunication markets*

**Scientech, Inc., Almaty, Kazakhstan**

## SQUIRE, SANDERS & DEMPSEY

127 Public Square, Key Tower, Ste. 4900, Cleveland, OH, 44114-1304

Tel: (216) 479-8500     Fax: (216) 479-8780     www.ssd.com

*International law firm.*

**Squire, Sanders & Dempsey, 84 Gogol St. Ste. 213, 48091 Almaty, Kazakhstan**

Tel: 7-327-250-1125  Fax: 7-327-2322-539

## STA-RITE INDUSTRIES INC.

293 Wright Street, Delavan, WI, 53115

Tel: (262) 728-5551     Fax: (262) 728-7323     www.sta-rite.com

*Mfr. water pumps, filters and systems.*

**Nocchi Kazakhstan, 5a Jeltoksan Avenue, Almaty 480050, Kazakhstan**

## WESTERN GEOPHYSICAL, INC.

10205 Westheimer, Houston, TX, 77251-1407

Tel: (713) 972-4000     Fax: (713) 952-9837     www.bakerhughes.com

*Provides comprehensive seismic services for oil and gas exploration, field development, and reservoir monitoring.*

**Western Geophysical, 300/141 Prospect Dostyk, Almaty 480020, Kazakhstan**

Tel: 7-3272-506-320

## WHITE & CASE LLP

1155 Ave. of the Americas, New York, NY, 10036-2767

Tel: (212) 819-8200     Fax: (212) 354-8113     www.whitecase.com

*International law firm.*

**White & Case LLP, 64 Amangeldy St., 480012 Almaty, Kazakhstan**

Tel: 7-327-250-7491   Fax: 7-327-20-7493   Contact: Witold Danilowicz

# Kenya

## 3M

3M Center, St. Paul, MN, 55144-1000

Tel: (651) 733-1110     Fax: (651) 733-9973     www.mmm.com

*Mfr. diversified products for industry, health care, imaging, communications, transport, safety, consumer, etc.*

**3M Kenya Ltd., 3M House, Ngong Rd., PO Box 48567, Nairobi Kenya**

Tel: 254-2-560-100   Fax: 254-2-560-712

## AIR EXPRESS INTERNATIONAL CORPORATION

120 Tokeneke Road, PO Box 1231, Darien, CT, 06820

Tel: (203) 655-7900     Fax: (203) 655-5779     www.aeilogistics.com

*International air freight forwarder.*

**Air Express Intl. Kenya Ltd., Rahimtulla Trust Bldg., Moi Ave., PO Box 44469, Nairobi Kenya**

## AMERICAN INTERNATIONAL GROUP INC. (AIG)

70 Pine Street, New York, NY, 10270

Tel: (212) 770-7000     Fax: (212) 509-9705     www.aig.com

*Worldwide insurance and financial services.*

**Alico Kenya, PO Box 49460, Nairobi, Kenya**

## AON CORPORATION

123 North Wacker Drive, Chicago, IL, 60606

Tel: (312) 701-3000     Fax: (312) 701-3100     www.aon.com

*Insurance brokers worldwide; underwrites accident and health insurance, specialty and professional insurance; and provides risk management consultation.*

**AON Worldwide/ Bain Hogg Insurance Brokers Kenya Ltd., Chester House Koinange St., Nairobi, Kenya**

Tel: 254-2-335-766   Fax: 254-2-225476   Contact: Peter Hood

## ASSOCIATED PRESS INC.

50 Rockefeller Plaza, New York, NY, 10020-1605

Tel: (212) 621-1500     Fax: (212) 621-5447     www.ap.com

*News gathering agency.*

**The Associated Press (JV), PO Box 47590, Nairobi, Kenya**

Tel: 254-2-223-143

## LOUIS BERGER INTERNATIONAL INC.

100 Halsted Street, East Orange, NJ, 07019

Tel: (201) 678-1960     Fax: (201) 672-4284     www.louisberger.com

*Consulting engineers, engaged in architecture, environmental and advisory services.*

**Louis Berger International Inc., c/o USAID PO Box 30261, 10th Floor Union Towers, Nairobi, Kenya**

**Louis Berger International Inc., Esteer Wahome Bureau, Jubilee Insurance House, Wabera Street, Nairobi, Kenya**

Tel: 254-2-228178   Fax: 254-2-333448

**BESTFOODS, INC.**

700 Sylvan Ave., International Plaza, Englewood Cliffs, NJ, 07632-9976

Tel: (201) 894-4000    Fax: (201) 894-2186    www.bestfoods.com

*Consumer foods products; corn refining.*

**CPC Kenya Ltd.,  PO Box 41045, Nairobi, Kenya**

Tel: 254-2-802-633   Fax: 254-2-860-080

**SAMUEL BINGHAM COMPANY**

127 East Lake Street, Ste. 300, Bloomingdale, IL, 60108

Tel: (630) 924-9250    Fax: (630) 924-0469    www.binghamrollers.com

*Print and industrial rollers and inks.*

**Coates Bros. (East Africa) Ltd.,  PO Box 30607, Addis Ababa Rd., Industrial Area, Nairobi, Kenya**

**BUDGET GROUP, INC.**

125 Basin St., Ste. 210, Daytona Beach, FL, 32114

Tel: (904) 238-7035    Fax: (904) 238-7461    www.budgetrentacar.com

*Car and truck rental system.*

**Budget Rent A Car,  Saroya House, Moi Ave., Mombasa, Kenya**

Tel: 254-11-22629

**Budget Rent A Car,  Jomo Kenyatta Intl Airport, Arrivals Terminal, Nairobi, Kenya**

**Budget Rent A Car,  La Piazetta (Italian Complex), Lamu Rd., Malindi, Kenya**

Tel: 254-2-223-581

**BUSH BOAKE ALLEN INC.**

7 Mercedes Drive, Montvale, NJ, 07645

Tel: (201) 391-9870    Fax: (201) 391-0860    www.bushboakeallen.com

*Mfr. aroma chemicals for fragrances and flavor products for seasonings.*

**Bush Boake Allen,  PO Box 13526, Nairobi, Kenya**

Tel: 254-2-742-614   Fax: 254-2-742-642

**CALTEX  CORPORATION**

125 East John Carpenter Fwy., Irving, TX, 75062-2794

Tel: (972) 830-1000    Fax: (972) 830-1081    www.caltex.com

*Petroleum products.*

**Caltex Oil Kenya Ltd.,  Caltex House, Koinange St., Nairobi, Kenya**

**Kenya Petroleum Refinery, Ltd.,  Caltex House, Koinange St., Nairobi, Kenya**

**CITIGROUP, INC.**

153 East 53rd Street, New York, NY, 10043

Tel: (212) 559-1000    Fax: (212) 559-3646    www.citigroup.com

*Provides insurance and financial services worldwide.*

**Citibank N.A.,  PO Box 30711, Nairobi, Kenya**

Contact: Peter H. Harris

**THE COCA-COLA COMPANY**

PO Drawer 1734, Atlanta, GA, 30301

Tel: (404) 676-2121    Fax: (404) 676-6792    www.coca-cola.com

*Mfr./marketing/distributor soft drinks, syrups and concentrates, juice and juice-drink products.*

**The Coca-Cola Co. Kenya,  Nairobi, Kenya**

**COLGATE-PALMOLIVE COMPANY**

300 Park Ave., New York, NY, 10022

Tel: (212) 310-2000    Fax: (212) 310-2919    www.colgate.com

*Mfr. pharmaceuticals, cosmetics, toiletries and detergents.*

**Colgate-Palmolive (E.A.) Ltd.,  PO Box 30264, Nairobi, Kenya**

## CORN PRODUCTS INTERNATIONAL, INC.

6500 South Archer Ave., Bedford Park, IL, 60501-1933

Tel: (708) 563-2400      Fax: (708) 563-6852      www.cornproducts.com

*Produces corn products for ingredients corn starch corn oil and corn syrups.*

**Corn Products Kenya Ltd., Outer Ring Road, Ruaraka PO Box 11889, Nairobi Kenya**

Tel: 254-2-861537   Fax: 254-2-861754

## COULTER PHARMACEUTICAL, INC.

600 Gateway Blvd., South San Francisco, CA, 94080

Tel: (650) 553-2000      Fax: (650) 553-2028      www.coulterpharm.com

*Mfr. blood analysis systems, flow cytometers, chemicals systems, scientific systems and reagents.*

**Coulter Electronics Kenya Ltd., Valley Arcade Shopping Centre, Gitanga Rd., PO Box 25157, Lavington, Nairobi, Kenya**

## CROWN CORK & SEAL COMPANY, INC.

One Crown Way, Philadelphia, PA, 19154-4599

Tel: (215) 698-5100      Fax: (215) 698-5201      www.crowncork.com

*Mfr. metal and plastic packaging, including steel and aluminum cans for food, beverage and household products.*

**Crown Cork E.A. Ltd., PO Box 46408, Nairobi, Kenya**

## D'ARCY MASIUS BENTON & BOWLES INC. (DMB&B)

1675 Broadway, New York, NY, 10019

Tel: (212) 468-3622      Fax: (212) 468-2987      www.dmbb.com

*Full service international advertising and communications group.*

**DMB&B Mid East-Africa, Bishop's Garden Towers 6/F, PO Box 42379, Nairobi Kenya**

Tel: 254-2-71-9501

## DELOITTE TOUCHE TOHMATSU INTERNATIONAL

1633 Broadway, New York, NY, 10019

Tel: (212) 492-4000      Fax: (212) 392-4154      www.deloitte.com

*Accounting, audit, tax and management consulting services.*

**Deloitte & Touche, 8th Fl. Kenya Reinsurance Plaza, Moi Ave. (PO Box 84712), Mombasa, Kenya**

**Deloitte & Touche, "Kirungii" King Rd., Westlands, (PO Box 40092) Nairobi, Kenya**

## DELTA AIR LINES INC.

PO Box 20706, Atlanta, GA, 30320-6001

Tel: (404) 715-2600      Fax: (404) 715-5494      www.delta-air.com

*Major worldwide airline; international air transport services.*

**Delta Air Lines Inc., Nairobi, Kenya**

## DHL WORLDWIDE EXPRESS

50 California Avenue, San Francisco, CA, 94111

Tel: (415) 677-6100      Fax: (415) 824-9700      www.dhl.com

*Worldwide air express carrier.*

**DHL Worldwide Express, Longonot Place, Kijabe St., PO Box 67577, Nairobi Kenya**

Tel: 254-2-225063

## EAGLE GLOBAL LOGISTICS (EGL)

15350 Vickery Drive, Houston, TX, 77032

Tel: (281) 618-3100      Fax: (281) 618-3100      www.eaglegl.com

*Ocean/air freight forwarding, customs brokerage, packing and wholesale, logistics management and insurance.*

**Internet Express Cargo Ltd., Cannon Tower Bldg. 1st Fl., Moi Ave., PO Box 86466, Mombassa Kenya**

Tel: 254-11-227-338   Fax: 254-11-227-338

Internet Express Cargo Ltd., 4th Fl. St. Georges House, Parliament Rd., Nairobi Kenya
Tel: 254-2-217997   Fax: 254-2-218052

## EASTMAN KODAK COMPANY

343 State Street, Rochester, NY, 14650

Tel: (716) 724-4000       Fax: (716) 724-1089       www.kodak.com

*Develop/mfr. photo and chemicals products, information management/video/copier systems, fibers/plastics for various industry.*

**Kodak Kenya Ltd., PO Box 18210, Funzi Rd., Nairobi Kenya**

## ECOLAB INC.

370 N. Wabasha Street, St. Paul, MN, 55102

Tel: (651) 293-2233       Fax: (651) 293-2379       www.ecolab.com

*Develop/mfr. premium cleaning, sanitizing and maintenance products and services for the hospitality, institutional, and residential markets.*

**Ecolab Ltd., Nairobi, Kenya**
Tel: 254-2-860746

## ERNST & YOUNG, LLP

787 Seventh Ave., New York, NY, 10019

Tel: (212) 773-3000       Fax: (212) 773-6350       www.eyi.com

*Accounting and audit, tax and management consulting services.*

**Bellhouse Mwangi / Ernat & Young, PO Box 44286, Nairobi, Kenya**
Tel: 254-2-727640   Fax: 254-2-716271   Contact: Geoffrey Karuu

**Ernst & Young, PO Box 60, Nyeri, Kenya**

**Ernst & Young, PO Box 45 Nakuru, Kenya**

**Ernst & Young, PO Box 99361, Mombasa, Kenya**

**Ernst & Young, PO Box 43, Eldoret, Kenya**

## FMC CORPORATION

200 E. Randolph Drive, Chicago, IL, 60601

Tel: (312) 861-6000       Fax: (312) 861-6141       www.fmc.com

*Produces chemicals and precious metals, mfr. machinery, equipment and systems for industrial, agricultural and government use.*

**FMC Intl. AG, Nairobi, Kenya**

## FRITZ COMPANIES, INC.

706 Mission Street, Ste. 900, San Francisco, CA, 94103

Tel: (415) 904-8360       Fax: (415) 904-8661       www.fritz.com

*Integrated transportation, sourcing, distribution and customs brokerage services.*

**Fritz Companies Inc., Mombasa, Kenya**

## GENERAL MOTORS CORPORATION

300 Renaissance Center, Detroit, MI, 48285

Tel: (313) 556-5000       Fax: (313) 556-5108       www.gm.com

*Mfr. full line vehicles, automotive electronics, commercial technologies, telecommunications, space, finance.*

**General Motors Corp., PO Box 30527, Nairobi, Kenya**

## THE GILLETTE COMPANY

Prudential Tower Building, Boston, MA, 02199

Tel: (617) 421-7000       Fax: (617) 421-7123       www.gillette.com

*Develop/mfr. personal care/use products: blades and razors, toiletries, cosmetics, stationery.*

**Gillette Interproducts Ltd., Nairobi, Kenya**

## GREY GLOBAL GROUP

777 Third Ave., New York, NY, 10017

Tel: (212) 546-2000    Fax: (212) 546-1495    www.grey.com

*International advertising agency.*

**Century Advertising,  Nairobi, Kenya**

## HILTON HOTELS CORPORATION

9336 Civic Center Drive, Beverly Hills, CA, 90210

Tel: (310) 278-4321    Fax: (310) 205-7880    www.hiltonhotels.com

*International hotel chain: Hilton International, Vista Hotels and Hilton National Hotels.*

**Nairobi Hilton,  Mama Ngina St., PO Box 30624, Nairobi, Kenya**

## HORWATH INTERNATIONAL ASSOCIATION

415 Madison Ave., New York, NY, 10017

Tel: (212) 838-5566    Fax: (212) 838-3636    www.horwath.com

*Public accountants and auditors.*

**Muchekehu & Co.,  5th Floor Nationwide House, Koinange St., Nairobi, Kenya**

## IBM CORPORATION

New Orchard Road, Armonk, NY, 10504

Tel: (914) 765-1900    Fax: (914) 765-7382    www.ibm.com

*Information products, technology and services.*

**IBM East Africa Ltd.,  UNGA House Ltd., Westlands, PO Box 35475, Nairobi Kenya**

Tel: 254-2-446910   Fax: 254-2-447012

## INTER-CONTINENTAL HOTELS

3 Ravina Drive, Suite 2900, Atlanta, GA, 30346-2149

Tel: (770) 604-2000    Fax: (770) 604-5403    www.interconti.com

*Worldwide hotel and resort accommodations.*

**Hotel Inter-Continental Nairobi,  City Hall Way, PO Box 30353, Nairobi, Kenya**

Tel: 254-2-224302   Fax: 254-2-214617

## INTERNATIONAL FLAVORS & FRAGRANCES INC.

521 West 57th Street, New York, NY, 10019-2960

Tel: (212) 765-5500    Fax: (212) 708-7132    www.iff.com

*Design/mfr. flavors, fragrances and aroma chemicals.*

**International Flavors & Fragrances,  Nairobi, Kenya**

## JOHNSON & JOHNSON

One Johnson & Johnson Plaza, New Brunswick, NJ, 08933

Tel: (732) 524-0400    Fax: (732) 214-0334    www.jnj.com

*Mfr./distributor/R&D pharmaceutical, health care and cosmetic products.*

**Johnson & Johnson (Kenya) Ltd.,  PO Box 47591, Nairobi, Kenya**

## S C JOHNSON & SON INC.

1525 Howe St., Racine, WI, 53403

Tel: (414) 260-2000    Fax: (414) 260-2133    www.scjohnsonwax.com

*Home, auto, commercial and personal care products and specialty chemicals.*

**S.C. Johnson & Son Ltd.,  Lunga Rd., PO Box 18373, Nairobi, Kenya**

## KPMG INTERNATIONAL LLP

345 Park Avenue, New York, NY, 10022

Tel: (201) 307-7000    Fax: (201) 930-8617    www.kpmg.com

*Accounting and audit, tax and management consulting services.*

**Peat Marwick,  Jubilee Insurance Exchange, Mama Ngina St., Nairobi, Kenya**

Tel: 254-2-222862   Fax: 254-2-215695   Contact: Robin D. Cahill, Sr. Ptnr.

## THE KULJIAN CORPORATION

3700 Science Center, Philadelphia, PA, 19104

Tel: (215) 243-1900 Fax: (215) 243-1909

*Studies, design, engineering, construction management and site supervision.*

**Kuljian Corp., PO Box 53295, Nairobi, Kenya**

## ELI LILLY & COMPANY

Lilly Corporate Center, Indianapolis, IN, 46285

Tel: (317) 276-2000 Fax: (317) 277-6579 www.lilly.com

*Mfr. pharmaceuticals and animal health products.*

**Eli Lilly (Suisse) S.A., Chiromo Court 2nd Fl., Chiromo Rd., Westlands, Nairobi Kenya**

Tel: 254-2-74-7054 Fax: 254-2-74-7070

## LOWE LINTAS & PARTNERS WORLDWIDE

One Dag Hammarskjold Plaza, New York, NY, 10017

Tel: (212) 605-8000 Fax: (212) 605-4705 www.interpublic.com

*Full-service, integrated marketing communications company/advertising agency.*

**Scanad Kenya, 5th Fl. The Chancery, Valley Rd., PO Box 34537, Nairobi Kenya**

Tel: 254-2-710-021 Fax: 254-2-718-772 Contact: Bharat Thakrar

## MARSH & McLENNAN COS INC.

1166 Ave. of the Americas, New York, NY, 10036-2774

Tel: (212) 345-5000 Fax: (212) 345-4808 www.marshmac.com

*Insurance agents/brokers, pension and investment management consulting services.*

**Bain Hogg Insurance Brokers Kenya Ltd., Chester House, Koinange St., Nairobi, Kenya**

Tel: 254-233-5766 Fax: 254-222-5476 Contact: Peter Hood

## McCANN-ERICKSON WORLDGROUP

750 Third Ave., New York, NY, 10017

Tel: (212) 984-3644 Fax: (212) 984-2629 www.mccann.com

*International advertising and marketing services.*

**McCann-Erickson (Kenya) Ltd., PO Box 48541, Nairobi, Kenya**

## MERCK & COMPANY, INC.

One Merck Drive, PO Box 100, Whitehouse Station, NJ, 08889-0100

Tel: (908) 423-1000 Fax: (908) 423-2592 www.merck.com

*Pharmaceuticals, chemicals and biologicals.*

**Merck, Sharp & Dohme Intl., PO Box 30676, Arwings-Kodhek Road, Nairobi, Kenya**

## J. P. MORGAN CHASE & CO. INC.

World Headquarters, 270 Park Ave., New York, NY, 10017

Tel: (212) 270-6000 Fax: (212) 622-9030 www.jpmorganchase.com

*Provides integrated financial solutions for institutions and individuals worldwide, including asset management, investment banking and commercial banking.*

**J. P. Morgan Chase & Co., Kencom House 7th Fl., PO Box 57051, Nairobi, Kenya**

**J. P. Morgan Chase & Co., International House 13/F, Mama Ngina St., Nairobi, Kenya**

## A .C. NIELSEN COMPANY

177 Broad Street, Stamford, CT, 06901

Tel: (203) 961-3000 Fax: (203) 961-3190 www.acnielsen.com

*Market and consumer research firm.*

**A. C. Nielsen, PO Box 60680, Nairobi, Kenya**

## OGILVY PUBLIC RELATIONS WORLDWIDE

909 Third Ave., New York, NY, 10022

Tel: (212) 880-5201        Fax: (212) 697-8250        www.ogilvypr.com

*Engaged in public relations and communications.*

**Ogilvy Public Relations Worldwide,  Nairobi, Kenya**

## OTIS ELEVATOR COMPANY

10 Farm Springs Road, Farmington, CT, 06032

Tel: (860) 676-6000        Fax: (860) 676-5111        www.otis.com

*Mfr. elevators and escalators.*

**East African Elevator Co. Ltd.,  Finance House 9th Fl. Bondo Rd., Industrial Area, PO Box 20014, Nairobi Kenya**

## PARKER DRILLING COMPANY

8 East Third Street, Tulsa, OK, 74103-3637

Tel: (918) 585-8221        Fax: (918) 585-1058        www.parkerdrilling.com

*Provides land contract drilling services to firms in the oil and gas industry.*

**Parker Drilling Co.,  PO Box 45075, Nairobi, Kenya**

## PFIZER INC.

235 East 42nd Street, New York, NY, 10017-5755

Tel: (212) 573-2323        Fax: (212) 573-7851        www.pfizer.com

*Research-based, global health care company.*

**Pfizer Laboratories Ltd.,  Nairobi, Kenya**

## PIONEER HI-BRED INTERNATIONAL INC.

400 Locust Street, Ste. 800, Des Moines, IA, 50309

Tel: (515) 248-4800        Fax: (515) 248-4999        www.pioneer.com

*Agricultural chemicals, farm supplies, biological products, research.*

**Freshco International Ltd.,  PO Box 65082, Nairobi, Kenya**

## PRICEWATERHOUSECOOPERS LLP

1301 Ave. of the Americas, New York, NY, 10019

Tel: (212) 596-7000        Fax: (212) 259-1301        www.pwcglobal.com

*Accounting and auditing, tax and management, and human resource consulting services.*

**PriceWaterhouseCoopers,  Ralli House, Nyerere Avenue, PO Box 81824 Mombasa, Kenya**
Tel: 254-11-312394

**PriceWaterhouseCoopers,  Rattansi Educational Trust Building, Koinange Street, (PO Box 41968) Nairobi, Kenya**
Tel: 254-2-221244    Fax: 254-2-335937

## PROCTER & GAMBLE COMPANY

One Procter & Gamble Plaza, Cincinnati, OH, 45202

Tel: (513) 983-1100        Fax: (513) 562-4500        www.pg.com

*Personal care, food, laundry, cleaning and industry products.*

**Procter & Gamble,  PO BOX 30453, Nairobi, Kenya**
Tel: 254-2-540650

## ROCKWELL INTERNATIONAL CORPORATION

777 East Wisconsin Ave., Ste. 1400, Milwaukee, WI, 53202

Tel: (414) 212-5200        Fax: (414) 212-5201        www.rockwell.com

*Products and service for aerospace and defense, automotive, electronics, graphics and automation industry.*

**Rockwell Automation (Proprietary) Ltd.,  Lonrho House 6th Fl., Standard St., Nairobi, Kenya**
Tel: 254-2-223-961    Fax: 254-2-230-331

## SCHENKER INTERNATIONAL FORWARDERS INC.

150 Albany Ave., Freeport, NY, 11520

Tel: (516) 377-3000    Fax: (516) 377-3005    www.schenkerusa.com

*Freight forwarders.*

**Schenker & Co Ltd.,  Schenker House Cargo, Kenyatta Intl Airport, PO Box 46757, Nairobi Kenya**

Tel: 254-2-822-828   Fax: 254-2-823-269

**Schenker & Co. Ltd.,  Freed House, Kwashibu Rd., PO Box 84361, Mombasa Kenya**

Tel: 254-11-311-620   Fax: 254-11-314-083

## SCHERING-PLOUGH CORPORATION

One Giralda Farms, Madison, NJ, 07940-1000

Tel: (973) 822-7000    Fax: (973) 822-7048    www.sch-plough.com

*Proprietary drug and cosmetic products.*

**Essex East Africa Ltd.,  PO Box 30409, Nairobi, Kenya**

## SIGNODE PACKAGING SYSTEMS

3610 West Lake Ave., Glenview, IL, 60025

Tel: (847) 724-6100    Fax: (847) 657-4392    www.signode.com

*Mfr. industrial tools and machinery for packaging and strapping.*

**Signode Packaging Systems Ltd.,  Mombasa Rd., PO Box 78160, Nairobi, Kenya**

## THE ST. PAUL COMPANIES, INC.

385 Washington Street, St. Paul, MN, 55102

Tel: (651) 310-7911    Fax: (651) 310-8294    www.stpaul.com

*Provides investment, insurance and reinsurance services.*

**Insurance Company of East Africa Ltd.,  ICEA Building, Kenyatta Ave., PO Box 46142 Nairobi, Kenya**

## TRUE NORTH COMMUNICATIONS INC.

101 East Erie Street, Chicago, IL, 60611

Tel: (312) 425-6500    Fax: (312) 425-5010    www.truenorth.com

*Holding company, advertising agency.*

**TAC, The Advertising Company Ltd.,  Bruce House Standard St., PO Box 34782, Nairobi Kenya**

## UNITED PARCEL SERVICE, INC.

55 Glenlake Parkway, NE, Atlanta, GA, 30328

Tel: (404) 828-6000    Fax: (404) 828-6593    www.ups.com

*International package-delivery service.*

**UPS Kenya,  PO Box 46586, Nairobi, Kenya**

Tel: 254-2-820-804   Fax: 254-2-823-124

## VERIZON COMMUNICATIONS INC.

1255 Corporate Drive, Irving, TX, 75038

Tel: (972) 507-5000    Fax: (972) 507-5002    www.gte.com

*Engaged in wireline and wireless communications.*

**Eastern Telecommunications,  Nairobi, Kenya**

## WM WRIGLEY JR. COMPANY

410 N. Michigan Ave., Chicago, IL, 60611-4287

Tel: (312) 644-2121    Fax: (312) 644-0353    www.wrigley.com

*Mfr. chewing gum.*

**Wrigley Company Ltd.,  PO Box 30767, Nairobi, Kenya**

**WYETH-AYERST INTERNATIONAL INC.**

150 Radnot-Chester Road, St. Davids, PA, 19087

Tel: (610) 902-4100     Fax: (610) 989-4586     www.ahp.com/wyeth

*Antibiotics and pharmaceutical products.*

**Lederle Labs., Div. American Cyanamid,  PO Box 47341, Nairobi, Kenya**

**XEROX CORPORATION**

800 Long Ridge Road, PO Box 1600, Stamford, CT, 06904

Tel: (203) 968-3000     Fax: (203) 968-4312     www.xerox.com

*Mfr. document processing equipment, systems and supplies.*

**Rank Xerox Kenya Ltd.,  PO Box 20410, Parklands Rd., Westlands Nairobi, Kenya**

**YOUNG & RUBICAM INC.**

285 Madison Ave., New York, NY, 10017

Tel: (212) 210-3000     Fax: (212) 370-3796     www.yr.com

*Advertising, public relations, direct marketing and sales promotion, corporate and product ID management.*

**Ayton Young & Rubicam,  Nairobi, Kenya**

# Kirghizia

**LeBOEUF, LAMB, GREENE & MacRAE LLP**

125 West 55th Street, 12th Fl., New York, NY, 10019

Tel: (212) 424-8000    Fax: (212) 424-8500    www.llgm.com

*International law firm.*

**LeBoeuf, Lamb, Greene & MacRae LLP,  Ul. Panfilova 205, Bishkek, Kirghizia**

Tel: 7-3312-22-2994   Fax: 7-3312-62-0393

**MAYER, BROWN & PLATT**

190 S. LaSalle Street, Chicago, IL, 60603

Tel: (312) 782-0600    Fax: (312) 701-7711    www.mayerbrown.com

*International law firm.*

**Mayer, Brown & Platt,  66 Kalykh Akieva St., Bishkek 72000, Kirghizia**

Tel: 996-3312-620980   Fax: 996-3312-620980

# Kuwait

## AIR EXPRESS INTERNATIONAL CORPORATION

120 Tokeneke Road, PO Box 1231, Darien, CT, 06820

Tel: (203) 655-7900     Fax: (203) 655-5779     www.aeilogistics.com

*International air freight forwarder.*

**Kuwait Maritime & Mercantile Co. KSC, PO Box 78, Safat 13001, Kuwait City Kuwait**

Tel: 965-243-4752   Fax: 965-243-7956

## ANC RENTAL CORP.

110 Southeast Sixth St., Ft. Lauderdale, FL, 33301

Tel: (954) 769-7000     Fax: (954) 769-7000     www.ancrental.com

*Engaged in car rental services, including National Car Rental and Alamo Rent A Car.*

**National Car Rental, PO Box 81, Safat, Kuwait**

## ANDERSEN WORLDWIDE

33 West Monroe Street, Chicago, IL, 60603

Tel: (312) 580-0033     Fax: (312) 507-6748     www.arthurandersen.com

*Accounting and audit, tax and management consulting services.*

**Arthur Andersen/Al-Bazie & Co., Kuwait Airways Bldg. - 7th Fl., Shuhada St., PO Box 2115, Safat 13022 Kuwait**

Tel: 965-241-0010

## AON CORPORATION

123 North Wacker Drive, Chicago, IL, 60606

Tel: (312) 701-3000     Fax: (312) 701-3100     www.aon.com

*Insurance brokers worldwide; underwrites accident and health insurance, specialty and professional insurance; and provides risk management consultation.*

**AON Worldwide/ Insurance Management Bureau, PO Box 25483, Safat 13115, Kuwait City, Kuwait**

Tel: 965-241-4124   Fax: 965-245-7976   Contact: Sami Bekhazi

## BBDO WORLDWIDE

1285 Ave. of the Americas, New York, NY, 10019

Tel: (212) 459-5000     Fax: (212) 459-6645     www.bbdo.com

*Multinational group of advertising agencies.*

**Impact & Echo Advertising, Kuwait City, Kuwait**

## BDO SEIDMAN, LLP   BELGIUM

Two Prudential Plaza, 180 N. Stetson Ave., Ste. 2300, Chicago, IL, 60601

Tel: (312) 240-1236     Fax: (312) 240-3329     www.bdo.com

*International accounting and financial consulting firm.*

**BDO Burgan Auditing Office, Dasman Complex, Block 1 4th Fl., Ahmad Al Jaber St., Sharq Kuwait City Kuwait**

Tel: 965-242-6862   Fax: 965-241-4956   Contact: Hokmat Mukhaimer

**BECHTEL GROUP INC.**

50 Beale Street, PO Box 3965, San Francisco, CA, 94105-1895

Tel: (415) 768-1234     Fax: (415) 768-9038     www.bechtel.com

*General contractors in engineering and construction.*

**Eastern Bechtel Corp., PO Box 29396, Salhia Commercial Complex, Gate #1 First Fl., Safat 13020 Kuwait**

Tel: 965-244-4300   Fax: 965-245-5301

**BENTLY NEVADA CORPORATION**

1617 Water Street, PO Box 157, Minden, NV, 89423

Tel: (775) 782-3611     Fax: (775) 782-9259     www.bently.com

*Provides hardware, software, and services for machinery information and management systems.*

**A.Z. Trading Co. WWL, PO Box 25752, Safat, Kuwait**

**BLACK & VEATCH LLP**

8400 Ward Pkwy., PO Box 8405, Kansas City, MO, 64114

Tel: (913) 339-2000     Fax: (913) 339-2934     www.bv.com

*Engineering, architectural and construction services.*

**Black & Veatch International, Plot 110, Block 6, East Ahmadi, Kuwait**

Tel: 965-398-1765   Fax: 965-398-6297

**BOZELL GROUP**

40 West 23rd Street, New York, NY, 10010

Tel: (212) 727-5000     Fax: (212) 645-9173     www.bozell.com

*Advertising, marketing, public relations and media consulting.*

**Bozell Prime New Media, PO Box 17958, Khaldia 72460, Kuwait**

Tel: 965-533-0046   Fax: 965-533-0048   Contact: Bader Al Duwaisan, Chmn.

**BRISTOL-MYERS SQUIBB COMPANY**

345 Park Ave., New York, NY, 10154-0037

Tel: (212) 546-4000     Fax: (212) 546-4020     www.bms.com

*Pharmaceutical and food preparations, medical and surgical instruments.*

**Yusuf Ibrahim Al Ghanim & Sons, PO Box 435, 13005 Safat, Kuwait**

**LEO BURNETT, DIV. B-COM 3 GROUP**

35 West Wacker Drive, Chicago, IL, 60601

Tel: (312) 220-5959     Fax: (312) 220-6533     www.bcom3group.com

*Engaged in advertising, marketing, media buying and planning, and public relations.*

**Radius/Leo Burnett Advertising, Al Khalcejia Bldg., PO Box 26100, Safat 13121, Kuwait**

**CARRIER CORPORATION**

One Carrier Place, Farmington, CT, 06034-4015

Tel: (860) 674-3000     Fax: (860) 679-3010     www.carrier.com

*Mfr./distributor/services A/C, heating and refrigeration equipment.*

**Kuwait American Airconditioning Co., PO Box 146, 13002 Safat, Kuwait**

Tel: 965-481-9733   Fax: 98-65-483-3882

**COMPUWARE CORPORATION**

31440 Northwestern Hwy., Farmington Hills, MI, 48334-2564

Tel: (248) 737-7300     Fax: (248) 737-7108     www.compuware.com

*Develop and market software for enterprise and e-commerce solutions.*

**Bobyan & Al-Falak Compuware Corporation, New Khaleejia Building 14/F, PO Box 27598, Safat 13136, Kuwait**

## DANIEL MANN JOHNSON & MENDENHALL

3250 Wilshire Blvd., Los Angeles, CA, 90010

Tel: (213) 381-3663     Fax: (213) 383-3656     www.dmjm.com

*Architects and engineers.*

**DMJM Intl., PO Box 23406, 13095 Safat, Kuwait**

## D'ARCY MASIUS BENTON & BOWLES INC. (DMB&B)

1675 Broadway, New York, NY, 10019

Tel: (212) 468-3622     Fax: (212) 468-2987     www.dmbb.com

*Full service international advertising and communications group.*

**DMB&B Mid East-Africa, Kuwait City, Kuwait**

## DELOITTE TOUCHE TOHMATSU INTERNATIONAL

1633 Broadway, New York, NY, 10019

Tel: (212) 492-4000     Fax: (212) 392-4154     www.deloitte.com

*Accounting, audit, tax and management consulting services.*

**Al-Fahad Al-Marzook Deloitte & Touche, Fahad Al-Salem St., Salhia Complex E-2 4th Fl., (PO Box 23049 Safat 13091), Kuwait City, Kuwait**

## DHL WORLDWIDE EXPRESS

50 California Avenue, San Francisco, CA, 94111

Tel: (415) 677-6100     Fax: (415) 824-9700     www.dhl.com

*Worldwide air express carrier.*

**DHL Worldwide Express, Old TV Centre, Arabian Gulf St., Dasman. PO Box 26523, Safat 13126 Kuwait**

Tel: 965-244-2375

## DIONEX CORPORATION

1228 Titan Way, PO Box 3603, Sunnyvale, CA, 94086-3603

Tel: (408) 737-0700     Fax: (408) 730-9403     www.dionex.com

*Develop/mfr./market chromatography systems and related products.*

**Tareq Company, PO Box 20506 Safat, 13066 Safat Area 1, Block #103, Ardiya Kuwait**

Tel: 965-4313729 2063

## EAGLE GLOBAL LOGISTICS (EGL)

15350 Vickery Drive, Houston, TX, 77032

Tel: (281) 618-3100     Fax: (281) 618-3100     www.eaglegl.com

*Ocean/air freight forwarding, customs brokerage, packing and wholesale, logistics management and insurance.*

**Kuwait New York Transportation Group, PO Box 42491, Pin 70655, Kuwait City, Kuwait**

Tel: 965-473-8323     Fax: 965-473-5558

## EMERY WORLDWIDE

One Lagoon Drive, Ste. 400, Redwood City, CA, 94065

Tel: (650) 596-9600     Fax: (650) 596-7901     www.emeryworld.com

*Freight transport, global logistics and air cargo.*

**Namias/Emery Air Freight, PO Box 5133, Sufat 13052, Kuwait**

## ERNST & YOUNG, LLP

787 Seventh Ave., New York, NY, 10019

Tel: (212) 773-3000     Fax: (212) 773-6350     www.eyi.com

*Accounting and audit, tax and management consulting services.*

**Ernst & Young (Al Aiban, Al Osaimi & Partners), PO Box 72 Safat, Souk Al Maseel 4th Fl., Abdullah Mubarak St., 13001 Safat Kuwait City Kuwait**

Tel: 965-245-2880     Fax: 965-245-6419     Contact: Michael L. Hunter

### ETHAN ALLEN INTERIORS INC.

Ethan Allen Drive, Danbury, CT, 06811

Tel: (203) 743-8000   Fax: (203) 743-8298   www.ethanallen.com

*Mfr. and sale of premium-priced furniture and home furnishings.*

**Ethan Allen Home Interiors,  Hassawi Street, Al Rai, Kuwait City, Kuwait**

Tel: 965-471-0020

### EXPEDITORS INTERNATIONAL OF WASHINGTON INC.

1015 Third Avenue, 12th Fl., Seattle, WA, 98104-1182

Tel: (206) 674-3400   Fax: (206) 682-9777   www.expd.com

*Air/ocean freight forwarding, customs brokerage, international logistics solutions.*

**Expeditors International,  PO Box 27063, Block 125 J Shuwaikh, Safat 13131, Kuwait**

Tel: 965-482-2805   Fax: 965-482-2802

### FRITZ COMPANIES, INC.

706 Mission Street, Ste. 900, San Francisco, CA, 94103

Tel: (415) 904-8360   Fax: (415) 904-8661   www.fritz.com

*Integrated transportation, sourcing, distribution and customs brokerage services.*

**Fritz Companies Inc.,  Safat, Kuwait**

### GLOBAL SILVERHAWK

2190 Meridian Park Blvd., Ste G, Concord, CA, 94520

Tel: (925) 681-2889   Fax: (925) 681-2755   www.globalsilverhawk.com

*International moving and forwarding.*

**Global Silverhawk,  PO Box 42065, 70651 Shuwaikh, Kuwait**

Tel: 965-245-7406

### GRAHAM & JAMES LLP

One Maritime Plaza,  Ste. 300, San Francisco, CA, 94111-3404

Tel: (415) 954-0200   Fax: (415) 391-2493   www.gj.com

*International law firm.*

**Graham & James/Mishare M. Al-Ghazali & Partners,  Alia Ctr. 7th Fl., PO Box 4970, Safat 13050 Kuwait City, Kuwait**

Tel: 965-243-9690   Fax: 965-242-2895   Contact: Mishare Al-Ghazali

### GRANT THORNTON INTERNATIONAL

800 One Prudential Plaza, 130 E. Randolph Drive, Chicago, IL, 60601-6050

Tel: (312) 856-0001   Fax: (312) 616-7052   www.grantthornton.com

*Accounting, audit, tax and management consulting services.*

**Grant Thornton Anwar Al-Qatami & Co.,  Souq Al-Kabeer Bldg., Block A - 9/F, Kuwait City 13030, Kuwait**

Contact: Anwar Al-Qatami

### GREY GLOBAL GROUP

777 Third Ave., New York, NY, 10017

Tel: (212) 546-2000   Fax: (212) 546-1495   www.grey.com

*International advertising agency.*

**CSS & Grey,  Fisheries Building 4/F, Al Hilali Street, Safat 13103, Kuwait**

### HALLIBURTON COMPANY

500 North Akard Street, Ste. 3600, Dallas, TX, 75201-3391

Tel: (214) 978-2600   Fax: (214) 978-2685   www.halliburton.com

*Engaged in diversified energy services, engineering and construction.*

**Halliburton Ltd.,  PO Box 9022, 61001 Ahmadi, Kuwait**

Tel: 965-398-4801   Fax: 965-398-9145

## HONEYWELL INTERNATIONAL INC.

101 Columbia Road, Morristown, NJ, 07962

Tel: (973) 455-2000    Fax: (973) 455-4807    www.honeywell.com

*Develop/mfr. controls for home and building, industry, space and aviation.*

**Honeywell Kuwait KSC, PO Box 20825, Safat 13069, Kuwait**

Tel: 965-242-1327   Fax: 965-242-8315

## IBM CORPORATION

New Orchard Road, Armonk, NY, 10504

Tel: (914) 765-1900    Fax: (914) 765-7382    www.ibm.com

*Information products, technology and services.*

**IBM Kuwait - Khorafi Business Machines, PO Box 4175, Safat, Kuwait**

Tel: 965-243-9900   Fax: 965-242-4577

## IDEX CORPORATION

630 Dundee Road, Ste. 400, Northbrook, IL, 60062

Tel: (847) 498-7070    Fax: (847) 498-3940    www.idexcorp.com

*Mfr. industrial pumps, lubrication systems, metal fabrication equipment, bending and clamping devices.*

**Al Sultan & Khalaf Trading Co., Shuwaikh-Al-Mouasalet St., PO Box 42130, Shuwaikh, Kuwait**

## INTERGRAPH CORPORATION

One Madison Industrial Park, Huntsville, AL, 35894-0001

Tel: (256) 730-2000    Fax: (256) 730-7898    www.intergraph.com

*Develop/mfr. interactive computer graphic systems.*

**Intergraph Technical Services Middle East Ltd., c/o M.A.. Kharafi, PO Box 886, Safat, Kuwait 13009**

Tel: 965-5623571   Fax: 965-5623496

## KPMG INTERNATIONAL LLP

345 Park Avenue, New York, NY, 10022

Tel: (201) 307-7000    Fax: (201) 930-8617    www.kpmg.com

*Accounting and audit, tax and management consulting services.*

**KPMG Masoud & Co., Sahab Tower 6th Fl., Mohammed Thunian al Ghanim St., Al Salhia Area, Kuwait**

Tel: 965-240-0121   Fax: 965-240-0120   Contact: Masoud Sorkhou, Sr. Ptnr.

## LOCKHEED MARTIN CORPORATION

6801 Rockledge Drive, Bethesda, MD, 20817

Tel: (301) 897-6000    Fax: (301) 897-6652    www.imco.com

*Design/mfr./management systems in fields of space, defense, energy, electronics and technical services.*

**Lockheed Aeronautical Systems Support Company, Lockheed Rep., Mangaf Complex, Kuwait**

Tel: 965-431-1588   Fax: 965-372-4910   Contact: E. J. Wisner, Mgr.

## M-I

PO Box 48242, Houston, TX, 77242-2842

Tel: (713) 739-0222    Fax: (713) 308-9503    www.midf.com

*Drilling fluids.*

**Kuwait Drilling, Shuaiba Industrial Area, 13046 Kuwait**

Tel: 965-326-2455   Fax: 965-326-2269

## MOTOROLA, INC.

1303 East Algonquin Road, Schaumburg, IL, 60196

Tel: (847) 576-5000    Fax: (847) 538-5191    www.motorola.com

*Mfr. communications equipment, semiconductors and cellular phones.*

**Motorola S.A., PO Box 3301, Salmiya 22004, Kuwait**

Tel: 965-534-2365   Fax: 965-534-2361

**NEWSWEEK INTERNATIONAL INC.**

251 West 57 Street, New York, NY, 10019

Tel: (212) 445-4000    Fax: (212) 445-4120    www.washpostco.com

*Engaged in magazine publishing.*

**Dar Al-Watan Publishing Group (Newsweek Bil-Logha Al-Arabia), Kuwait**

**A .C. NIELSEN COMPANY**

177 Broad Street, Stamford, CT, 06901

Tel: (203) 961-3000    Fax: (203) 961-3190    www.acnielsen.com

*Market and consumer research firm.*

**A. C. Nielsen, PO Box 11743A1, Dasmah-Code 35158, Kuwait**

**OTIS ELEVATOR COMPANY**

10 Farm Springs Road, Farmington, CT, 06032

Tel: (860) 676-6000    Fax: (860) 676-5111    www.otis.com

*Mfr. elevators and escalators.*

**Otis Elevator Co. (Kuwait), PO Box 11169, Dasma 35152, Kuwait**

**PANAMETRICS**

221 Crescent Street, Waltham, MA, 02154

Tel: (781) 899-2719    Fax: (781) 899-1552    www.panametrics.com

*Process/non-destructive test instrumentation.*

**Al Siyahead Mechanical Contracting Est., PO Box 12309, 71654 Shamiya, Kuwait**

Tel: 965-240-1188    Fax: 965-240-1088

**PARKER DRILLING COMPANY**

8 East Third Street, Tulsa, OK, 74103-3637

Tel: (918) 585-8221    Fax: (918) 585-1058    www.parkerdrilling.com

*Provides land contract drilling services to firms in the oil and gas industry.*

**Parker Drilling Co., PO Box 9277, Ahmadi, Kuwait**

**THE PARSONS CORPORATION**

100 West Walnut Street, Pasadena, CA, 91124

Tel: (626) 440-2000    Fax: (626) 440-2630    www.parsons.com

*Engineering and construction.*

**Parsons Engineering Ltd., PO Box 9912, Ahmadi 61008, Kuwait**

**PARSONS ENGINEERING SCIENCE INC.**

100 West Walnut Street, Pasadena, CA, 91124

Tel: (626) 440-2000    Fax: (626) 440-4919    www.parsons.com

*Environmental engineering.*

**Parsons Engineering Science Inc., c/o Gulf Consult, PO Box 22412, Safat 13085, Kuwait**

**PARSONS TRANSPORTATION GROUP**

1133 15th Street NW, 9th Fl., Washington, DC, 20005

Tel: (202) 775-3300    Fax: (202) 775-3422    www.parsons.com

*Consulting engineers.*

**De Leuw Cather Intl. Ltd., PO Box 25582, Safat, Kuwait**

**POLARIS INDUSTRIES INC.**

2100 Highway 55, Medina, MN, 55440

Tel: (612) 542-0500    Fax: (612) 542-0599    www.polarisindustries.com

*Mfr. snowmobiles and all-terrain recreational and utility vehicles.*

**Amiry International Marine, PO Box 110, Safat l3002, Kuwait**

Tel: 965-484-5346

## RAYTHEON COMPANY

141 Spring Street, Lexington, MA, 02173

Tel: (781) 862-6600     Fax: (781) 860-2172     www.raytheon.com

*Mfr. diversified electronics, appliances, aviation, energy and environmental products; publishing, industry and construction services.*

**Raytheon Gulf Systems Co., PO Box 33147, Rawda, Kuwait**

## THE RENDON GROUP INC.

1875 Connecticut Ave., N.E., Washington, DC, 20009

Tel: (202) 745-4900     Fax: (202) 745-0215     www.rendon.com

*Public relations, print and video production, strategic communications.*

**The Rendon Group Inc., Flat 802 Tower 8 Floor 3, Bneid Al Ghar, Kuwait City, Kuwait**

## STARWOOD HOTELS & RESORTS WORLDWIDE

777 Westchester Avenue, White Plains, NY, 10604

Tel: (914) 640-8100     Fax: (914) 640-8316     www.starwoodhotels.com

*Hotel operations including Sheraton, Westin, St. Regis, Four Points and Caesars.*

**Kuwait Sheraton Hotel, PO Box 5902, Fahd al Salem St., Kuwait**

## TRUE NORTH COMMUNICATIONS INC.

101 East Erie Street, Chicago, IL, 60611

Tel: (312) 425-6500     Fax: (312) 425-5010     www.truenorth.com

*Holding company, advertising agency.*

**Horizon Kuwait, Aliaa Ctr. 9th Fl., Al Shuhadaa St. (Ex Hillali), Kuwait City 13062, Kuwait**

## THE TURNER CORPORATION

901 Main St., Ste. 4900, Dallas, TX, 75202

Tel: (214) 915-9600     Fax: (214) 915-9700     www.turnerconstruction.com

*Engaged in general construction and construction management.*

**Turner Steiner International SA, Kuwait City, Kuwait**

## UNION CARBIDE CORPORATION

39 Old Ridgebury Road, Danbury, CT, 06817

Tel: (203) 794-2000     Fax: (203) 794-6269     www.unioncarbide.com

*Mfr. industrial chemicals, plastics and resins.*

**Union Carbide (JV), Al-Shuaiba, Kuwait**

## UNITED PARCEL SERVICE, INC.

55 Glenlake Parkway, NE, Atlanta, GA, 30328

Tel: (404) 828-6000     Fax: (404) 828-6593     www.ups.com

*International package-delivery service.*

**UPS Kuwait, PO Box 20637, Safat 13067, Kuwait**
Tel: 965-434-4822     Fax: 965-434-4622

## WEATHERFORD INTERNATIONAL, INC.

5 Post Oak Blvd, Ste. 1760, Houston, TX, 77227-3415

Tel: (713) 287-8400     Fax: (713) 963-9785     www.weatherford.com

*Oilfield services, products and equipment; mfr. marine cranes for oil and gas industry.*

**Weatherford Intl. Inc., c/o Ajal Contracting & General Trading Co., PO Box 26256, Safat, Kuwait**
Tel: 965-242-7773     Fax: 965-240-5124

## WENDY'S INTERNATIONAL, INC.

428 West Dublin Granville Roads, Dublin, OH, 43017-0256

Tel: (614) 764-3100     Fax: (614) 764-3459     www.wendysintl.com

*Fast food restaurant chain.*

**Wendy's International, Kuwait**

## WESTERN GEOPHYSICAL, INC.

10205 Westheimer, Houston, TX, 77251-1407

Tel: (713) 972-4000     Fax: (713) 952-9837     www.bakerhughes.com

*Provides comprehensive seismic services for oil and gas exploration, field development, and reservoir monitoring.*

**Western Geophysical, c/o Exim Trading Company, PO Box 25371, Safat 13113 Kuwait**

Tel: 965-398-0759   Fax: 965-398-6066   Contact: V.W. Vagt, Res. Mgr.

## XEROX CORPORATION

800 Long Ridge Road, PO Box 1600, Stamford, CT, 06904

Tel: (203) 968-3000     Fax: (203) 968-4312     www.xerox.com

*Mfr. document processing equipment, systems and supplies.*

**Alamana Industries Co., SAK, POBox 20244, Safat 13063, Kuwait**

Tel: 965-242 4950   Fax: 965-243 6134

## YORK INTERNATIONAL CORPORATION

631 South Richland Ave., York, PA, 17403

Tel: (717) 771-7890     Fax: (717) 771-6212     www.york.com

*Mfr. heating, ventilating, air conditioning and refrigeration equipment.*

**York Air Conditioning & Refrigeration, Inc., PO Box 29034 Safat, Gate No. 1 Mez. 2, Salhia Complex, Kuwait City Kuwait**

Tel: 965-245-1599

# Laos

**BATES WORLDWIDE INC.**

405 Lexington Ave., New York, NY, 10174

Tel: (212) 297-7000      Fax: (212) 986-0270      www.batesww.com

*Advertising, marketing, public relations and media consulting.*

**Bates Laos, c/o Adena Mahavong, PO Box 1421, Vientiane Laos**

Tel: 856-21-313-868-069   Fax: 856-21-313-868   Contact: Herve Deville, CEO Indochine

**DHL WORLDWIDE EXPRESS**

50 California Avenue, San Francisco, CA, 94111

Tel: (415) 677-6100      Fax: (415) 824-9700      www.dhl.com

*Worldwide air express carrier.*

**DHL Worldwide Express, 27 Nongno St., Ban Wattay Noy Thong, PO Box 7083, Vientiane Laos**

Tel: 856-21-216830

**McCANN-ERICKSON WORLDGROUP**

750 Third Ave., New York, NY, 10017

Tel: (212) 984-3644      Fax: (212) 984-2629      www.mccann.com

*International advertising and marketing services.*

**Exprim McCann-Erickson (Laos), Vientiane, Laos**

# Latvia

## AMERICAN INTERNATIONAL GROUP INC. (AIG)

70 Pine Street, New York, NY, 10270

Tel:  (212) 770-7000       Fax:  (212) 509-9705       www.aig.com

*Worldwide insurance and financial services.*

**Seesan Latvia Ins. Co.,  Jekaba Kaz. Toma 4, 18-201 Regia, 1050 Latvia**

## ANDERSEN WORLDWIDE

33 West Monroe Street, Chicago, IL, 60603

Tel:  (312) 580-0033       Fax:  (312) 507-6748       www.arthurandersen.com

*Accounting and audit, tax and management consulting services.*

**Andersen Worldwide,  Pulkveza Brieza iela 15, LV-1010 Riga, Latvia**

Tel: 371-732-1140

## APPLERA CORPORATION

761 Main Avenue, Norwalk, CT, 06859-0001

Tel:  (203) 762-1000       Fax:  (203) 762-6000       www.applera.com

*Leading supplier of systems for life science research and related applications.*

**Ameto Ltd.,  Struktoru 14/A 312, LV-1039 Riga, Latvia**

## BATES WORLDWIDE INC.

405 Lexington Ave., New York, NY, 10174

Tel:  (212) 297-7000       Fax:  (212) 986-0270       www.batesww.com

*Advertising, marketing, public relations and media consulting.*

**Bates Latvia,  9/11 Perses St., LV1010 Riga, Latvia**

Tel: 371-7-770-585    Fax: 371-1-770-588    Contact: R. Plakajia, Dir.

## DDB NEEDHAM WORLDWIDE INC.

437 Madison Ave., New York, NY, 10022

Tel:  (212) 415-2000       Fax:  (212) 415-3417       www.ddbn.com

*Advertising agency.*

**Brand Sellers DDB Baltics,  Riga, Latvia**

## DELOITTE TOUCHE TOHMATSU INTERNATIONAL

1633 Broadway, New York, NY, 10019

Tel:  (212) 492-4000       Fax:  (212) 392-4154       www.deloitte.com

*Accounting, audit, tax and management consulting services.*

**Deloitte & Touche,  Kr. Barona 64-3, Riga LV-1001, Latvia**

## DHL WORLDWIDE EXPRESS

50 California Avenue, San Francisco, CA, 94111

Tel:  (415) 677-6100       Fax:  (415) 824-9700       www.dhl.com

*Worldwide air express carrier.*

**DHL Worldwide Express,  Dzintaru 22, Ventsplis 3602, Latvia**

Tel: 371-701-3292

## DIAGNOSTIC PRODUCTS CORPORATION

5700 West 96th Street, Los Angeles, CA, 90045

Tel: (310) 645-8200     Fax: (310) 645-9999     www.dpcweb.com

*Mfr. diagnostic products.*

**DPC Baltic SIÀ, Brivibas iela 226/2, LV-1039 Riga, Latvia**

Tel: 371-780-1187    Fax: 371-754-1477

## J.D. EDWARDS & COMPANY

One Technology Way, Denver, CO, 80237

Tel: (303) 334-4000     Fax: (303) 334-4970     www.jdedwards.com

*Computer software products.*

**Robertson & Blums - Riga CIBS, 12 Miesnieku iela, LV 1050 Riga, Latvia**

Tel: 371-721-1101    Fax: 371-782-0379

## ERNST & YOUNG, LLP

787 Seventh Ave., New York, NY, 10019

Tel: (212) 773-3000     Fax: (212) 773-6350     www.eyi.com

*Accounting and audit, tax and management consulting services.*

**Ernst & Young Latvia, Kalku St. 11, LV-1050 Riga, Latvia**

Tel: 371-2-225700    Fax: 371-2-227753    Contact: Monty Akesson

## FRITZ COMPANIES, INC.

706 Mission Street, Ste. 900, San Francisco, CA, 94103

Tel: (415) 904-8360     Fax: (415) 904-8661     www.fritz.com

*Integrated transportation, sourcing, distribution and customs brokerage services.*

**Fritz Companies Inc., Riga, Latvia**

## GENERAL REINSURANCE CORPORATION

695 E. Main Street, Stamford, CT, 06904-2350

Tel: (203) 328-5000     Fax: (203) 328-6423     www.genre.com

*Reinsurance services worldwide.*

**Die Kölnische Rück Riga GmbH, Elizabetes iela 11-1, LV - 1010 Riga, Latvia**

Tel: 371-783-0107    Fax: 371-783-0127    Contact: Michail Kuharenok

## GETZ BROS & COMPANY, INC.

150 Post Street, Ste. 500, San Francisco, CA, 94108-4750

Tel: (415) 772-5500     Fax: (415) 772-5659     www.getz.com

*Diversified manufacturing, marketing and distribution services and travel services.*

**Getz Bros. & Co. (Latvia) SIA, 11 Kugu Strasse 3rd Floor, Riga LV-108, Latvia**

Tel: 371-2-612345    Fax: 371-7-222356    Contact: Simons Kozlinskis, Gen. Mgr.    Emp: 12

## GREY GLOBAL GROUP

777 Third Ave., New York, NY, 10017

Tel: (212) 546-2000     Fax: (212) 546-1495     www.grey.com

*International advertising agency.*

**Grey Advertising, Riga, Latvia**

## IBM CORPORATION

New Orchard Road, Armonk, NY, 10504

Tel: (914) 765-1900     Fax: (914) 765-7382     www.ibm.com

*Information products, technology and services.*

**IBM Latvia, Elizabetes Str. 65, LV-1050 Riga, Latvia**

Tel: 371-724-2330    Fax: 371-782-8111

## KELLOGG COMPANY

One Kellogg Square, PO Box 3599, Battle Creek, MI, 49016-3599

Tel: (616) 961-2000    Fax: (616) 961-2871    www.kelloggs.com

*Mfr. ready-to-eat cereals and convenience foods.*

**Kellogg Latvia Inc., Attn: Latvian Office, One Kellogg Square, PO Box 3599, Battle Creek MI 49016-3599**

## KPMG INTERNATIONAL LLP

345 Park Avenue, New York, NY, 10022

Tel: (201) 307-7000    Fax: (201) 930-8617    www.kpmg.com

*Accounting and audit, tax and management consulting services.*

**KPMG Latvia, Kr. Valdemara Iela 33-4, Riga LV-1010, Latvia**

Tel: 371-733-3023   Fax: 371-733-3023   Contact: Daina Eiche, Sr. Ptnr.

## ELI LILLY & COMPANY

Lilly Corporate Center, Indianapolis, IN, 46285

Tel: (317) 276-2000    Fax: (317) 277-6579    www.lilly.com

*Mfr. pharmaceuticals and animal health products.*

**Eli Lilly (Suisse) S.A., Rep Office, Elizabetes 85a, LV-1011 Riga, Latvia**

Tel: 371-7-282-001   Fax: 371-7-288-078

## McCANN-ERICKSON WORLDGROUP

750 Third Ave., New York, NY, 10017

Tel: (212) 984-3644    Fax: (212) 984-2629    www.mccann.com

*International advertising and marketing services.*

**Division McCann-Erickson Latvia, Riga, Latvia**

## McDONALD'S CORPORATION

McDonald's Plaza, Oak Brook, IL, 60523

Tel: (630) 623-3000    Fax: (630) 623-7409    www.mcdonalds.com

*Fast food chain stores.*

**McDonald's Corp., Latvia**

## MOTOROLA, INC.

1303 East Algonquin Road, Schaumburg, IL, 60196

Tel: (847) 576-5000    Fax: (847) 538-5191    www.motorola.com

*Mfr. communications equipment, semiconductors and cellular phones.*

**Motorola Latvia, 15 Kalku Iela, 1050 Riga, Latvia**

Tel: 371-2-722-7285   Fax: 371-2-782-0322

## PROCTER & GAMBLE COMPANY

One Procter & Gamble Plaza, Cincinnati, OH, 45202

Tel: (513) 983-1100    Fax: (513) 562-4500    www.pg.com

*Personal care, food, laundry, cleaning and industry products.*

**Procter & Gamble, Vilandes 6, LV-1010 Riga, Latvia**

Tel: 371-800-3000

## THE ST. PAUL COMPANIES, INC.

385 Washington Street, St. Paul, MN, 55102

Tel: (651) 310-7911    Fax: (651) 310-8294    www.stpaul.com

*Provides investment, insurance and reinsurance services.*

**Balva Joint Stock Insurance Company, 36 Kr Valdemara, LV-1010 Riga, Latvia**

## UNITED PARCEL SERVICE, INC.

55 Glenlake Parkway, NE, Atlanta, GA, 30328

Tel: (404) 828-6000     Fax: (404) 828-6593     www.ups.com

*International package-delivery service.*

**UPS Latvia, 33 13th January Str., 1050 Riga, Latvia**

Tel: 371-7222247   Fax: 371-7211509

## XEROX CORPORATION

800 Long Ridge Road, PO Box 1600, Stamford, CT, 06904

Tel: (203) 968-3000     Fax: (203) 968-4312     www.xerox.com

*Mfr. document processing equipment, systems and supplies.*

**Xerox Corp., Riga, Latvia**

## YORK INTERNATIONAL CORPORATION

631 South Richland Ave., York, PA, 17403

Tel: (717) 771-7890     Fax: (717) 771-6212     www.york.com

*Mfr. heating, ventilating, air conditioning and refrigeration equipment.*

**York International, Krustpils iela 1, Riga LV-1073, Latvia**

Tel: 371-711-3068

# Lebanon

**AFRIDI & ANGELL**

230 Park Ave., Ste. 646, New York, NY, 10169

Tel: (212) 697-0300    Fax: (212) 697-0385    www.afridi.com

*International law firm.*

**Afridi & Angell, c/o Law Offices of A. Abboud & Associates, Beirut, Lebanon**

**AIR EXPRESS INTERNATIONAL CORPORATION**

120 Tokeneke Road, PO Box 1231, Darien, CT, 06820

Tel: (203) 655-7900    Fax: (203) 655-5779    www.aeilogistics.com

*International air freight forwarder.*

**AEI Lebanon S.A.L.,  PO Box 175772, Pasteur St. - Zoughbi Ctr. - 1st Fl., Achrafich Beirut, Lebanon**

Tel: 961-1-564-78992   Fax: 961-1-564-793

**ABC, INC.**

77 West 66th Street, New York, NY, 10023

Tel: (212) 456-7777    Fax: (212) 456-6384    www.abc.com

*Radio/TV production and broadcasting.*

**American Broadcasting Co.,  Gefinar Ctr., Block B, Rm. 1602, Beirut, Lebanon**

**ANC RENTAL CORP.**

110 Southeast Sixth St., Ft. Lauderdale, FL, 33301

Tel: (954) 769-7000    Fax: (954) 769-7000    www.ancrental.com

*Engaged in car rental services, including National Car Rental and Alamo Rent A Car.*

**National Car Rental,  PO Box 5965, Ain-Al-Mraisse St., Nsouli Bldg., Beirut, Lebanon**

**ANDERSEN WORLDWIDE**

33 West Monroe Street, Chicago, IL, 60603

Tel: (312) 580-0033    Fax: (312) 507-6748    www.arthurandersen.com

*Accounting and audit, tax and management consulting services.*

**Andersen Worldwide,  Ashrafieh - Sassin Square, Asco Centre - 10th Fl., PO Box 113-5309, Beirut Lebanon**

Tel: 961-1-602602

**AON CORPORATION**

123 North Wacker Drive, Chicago, IL, 60606

Tel: (312) 701-3000    Fax: (312) 701-3100    www.aon.com

*Insurance brokers worldwide; underwrites accident and health insurance, specialty and professional insurance; and provides risk management consultation.*

**AON Worldwide / Care Middle East S.A.L., c/o Santa Maria Bldg., PO Box 2119, Jounieh, Lebanon**

Tel: 961-9-912344   Fax: 961-9-936491   Contact: Antoine Khoury

**Care Middle East S.A.L.,  8th Fl. - Mardini Centre Mirna Chalouhi, Highway Sin-el-Fil, Beirut, Lebanon**

Tel: 961-1-480320   Fax: 961-1-502279   Contact: Antoine Khoury

## ASSOCIATED PRESS INC.

50 Rockefeller Plaza, New York, NY, 10020-1605

Tel: (212) 621-1500     Fax: (212) 621-5447     www.ap.com

*News gathering agency.*

**The Associated Press,  121 rue Clemenceau, PO Box 3780, Beirut Lebanon**

Tel: 961-1-602146

## THE BANK OF NEW YORK

One Wall Street, New York, NY, 10286

Tel: (212) 495-1784     Fax: (212) 495-2546     www.bankofny.com

*Banking services.*

**The Bank of New York,  Avco Center 2nd Fl, Autostrade Jdeideh, Beirut, Lebanon**

Tel: 961-1-898026

## BATES WORLDWIDE INC.

405 Lexington Ave., New York, NY, 10174

Tel: (212) 297-7000     Fax: (212) 986-0270     www.batesww.com

*Advertising, marketing, public relations and media consulting.*

**Bates Lebanon,  Asco Centre, Achralish, Beirut Lebanon**

Tel: 961-1-602-613   Fax: 961-1-602-612   Contact: R. Najjar, CEO

## BBDO WORLDWIDE

1285 Ave. of the Americas, New York, NY, 10019

Tel: (212) 459-5000     Fax: (212) 459-6645     www.bbdo.com

*Multinational group of advertising agencies.*

**Impact/BBDO Sal,  Beirut, Lebanon**

**Strategies Sal,  Beirut, Lebanon**

## BDO SEIDMAN, LLP    BELGIUM

Two Prudential Plaza, 180 N. Stetson Ave., Ste. 2300, Chicago, IL, 60601

Tel: (312) 240-1236     Fax: (312) 240-3329     www.bdo.com

*International accounting and financial consulting firm.*

**Fiduciaire de Moyen Orient SARL,  Geahchan Bldg. 2nd Fl., blvd Fouad Chehab, Sin El Fil-Mekalles, Beirut Lebanon**

Tel: 961-1-480-917   Fax: 961-1-496-682   Contact: Gérard Zovighoan

## LOUIS BERGER INTERNATIONAL INC.

100 Halsted Street, East Orange, NJ, 07019

Tel: (201) 678-1960     Fax: (201) 672-4284     www.louisberger.com

*Consulting engineers, engaged in architecture, environmental and advisory services.*

**Louis Berger International Inc.,  PO Box 11-8484, Weavers Center 5th Floor, Clemenceau Street, Beirut Lebanon**

Tel: 961-1-379-067   Fax: 961-1-379-065

## BRISTOL-MYERS SQUIBB COMPANY

345 Park Ave., New York, NY, 10154-0037

Tel: (212) 546-4000     Fax: (212) 546-4020     www.bms.com

*Pharmaceutical and food preparations, medical and surgical instruments.*

**Khalil Fattal & Fills SAL,  PO Box 773, Sin El Fil Jisr El Wati, Beirut, Lebanon**

## LEO BURNETT, DIV. B-COM 3 GROUP

35 West Wacker Drive, Chicago, IL, 60601

Tel: (312) 220-5959     Fax: (312) 220-6533     www.bcom3group.com

*Engaged in advertising, marketing, media buying and planning, and public relations.*

**H&C Leo Burnett,  Sofil Center, PO Box 55369, Beirut, Lebanon**

## CARLISLE SYNTEC SYSTEMS

PO Box 7000, Carlisle, PA, 17013

Tel: (717) 245-7000     Fax: (717) 245-9107     www.carlislesyntec.com

*Mfr. elastomeric roofing and waterproofing systems.*

**BMC Lebanon,  Sabbah Building 4/F, Memari Street, Hamra Beirut, Lebanon**

Tel: 961-1-353-171   Fax: 961-1-738-731

## CIGNA COMPANIES

One Liberty Place, Philadelphia, PA, 19192

Tel: (215) 761-1000     Fax: (215) 761-5511     www.cigna.com

*Insurance, invest, health care and other financial services.*

**Insurance Co. of North America,  c/o Joseph E. Zakhour & Co. SARL, Ashrafieh, Rmeil/Liberty Bldg., Beirut, Lebanon**

## CISCO SYSTEMS, INC.

170 West Tasman Drive, San Jose, CA, 95134-1706

Tel: (408) 526-4000     Fax: (408) 526-4100     www.cisco.com

*Develop/mfr./market computer hardware and software networking systems.*

**Cisco Systems Lebanon,  PO Box 16-5480, Sodeco Square Block C/11th Fl., Beirut**

Tel: 961-1-611-081   Fax: 961-1-611-083

## CITIGROUP, INC.

153 East 53rd Street, New York, NY, 10043

Tel: (212) 559-1000     Fax: (212) 559-3646     www.citigroup.com

*Provides insurance and financial services worldwide.*

**Citibank N.A.,  Beirut, Lebanon**

Contact: Elia S. Smaha

## DAMES & MOORE GROUP

911 Wilshire Boulevard, Ste. 700, Los Angeles, CA, 90017

Tel: (213) 996-2200     Fax: (213) 996-2290     www.dames.com

*Engineering, environmental and construction management services.*

**Dames & Moore,  PO Box 116-5249 Museum, Achrafieh-Beirut, Lebanon**

## D'ARCY MASIUS BENTON & BOWLES INC. (DMB&B)

1675 Broadway, New York, NY, 10019

Tel: (212) 468-3622     Fax: (212) 468-2987     www.dmbb.com

*Full service international advertising and communications group.*

**DMB&B Mid East-Africa,  Palm Center Rond Point Chev., Damascus Road, Beirut Lebanon**

## DDB NEEDHAM WORLDWIDE INC.

437 Madison Ave., New York, NY, 10022

Tel: (212) 415-2000     Fax: (212) 415-3417     www.ddbn.com

*Advertising agency.*

**Idees & Communications DDB,  Beirut, Lebanon**

## DELOITTE TOUCHE TOHMATSU INTERNATIONAL

1633 Broadway, New York, NY, 10019

Tel: (212) 492-4000     Fax: (212) 392-4154     www.deloitte.com

*Accounting, audit, tax and management consulting services.*

**Deloitte & Touche/Saba & Co.,  Arabia House, 131 Phoenicia St., (PO Box 961), Beirut Lebanon**

## DHL WORLDWIDE EXPRESS

50 California Avenue, San Francisco, CA, 94111

Tel: (415) 677-6100     Fax: (415) 824-9700     www.dhl.com

*Worldwide air express carrier.*

**SNAS DHL Worldwide, Park Bldg. Ground Fl., Sami El Solh Ave., PO Box 166/439, Beirut Lebanon**

Tel: 961-1-390900

## EAGLE GLOBAL LOGISTICS (EGL)

15350 Vickery Drive, Houston, TX, 77032

Tel: (281) 618-3100     Fax: (281) 618-3100     www.eaglegl.com

*Ocean/air freight forwarding, customs brokerage, packing and wholesale, logistics management and insurance.*

**Beirut (BEY), Beirut Cargo Ctr. Sarl - Charles Helou Ave., Sehnaoui Bldg. Fourth Fl. Ste. 41, PO Box 17-5040, Beirut Lebanon**

Tel: 961-1-585-164   Fax: 961-1-585-580

## EASTMAN KODAK COMPANY

343 State Street, Rochester, NY, 14650

Tel: (716) 724-4000     Fax: (716) 724-1089     www.kodak.com

*Develop/mfr. photo and chemicals products, information management/video/copier systems, fibers/plastics for various industry.*

**Kodak (Near East) Inc., Beirut, Lebanon, c/o Kodak (Near East) Inc., PO Box 11460, Dubai, UAE**

## ERNST & YOUNG, LLP

787 Seventh Ave., New York, NY, 10019

Tel: (212) 773-3000     Fax: (212) 773-6350     www.eyi.com

*Accounting and audit, tax and management consulting services.*

**Ernst & Young S.A.R.L., PO Box 11-1639, Sabbagh Ctr., Hamra St., Beirut Lebanon**

Tel: 961-1-353420   Fax: 961-1-346203   Contact: Yacoub Khoury

## ESCO ENGINEERING INC.

40 Robbie Road, Avon Industrial Park, Avon, MA, 02322

Tel: (508) 588-1500     Fax: (508) 588-0135     www.escogroup.com

*Water purification and sewage treatment.*

**Esco Group, PO Box 113-5993, Beirut, Lebanon**

## EXPEDITORS INTERNATIONAL OF WASHINGTON INC.

1015 Third Avenue, 12th Fl., Seattle, WA, 98104-1182

Tel: (206) 674-3400     Fax: (206) 682-9777     www.expd.com

*Air/ocean freight forwarding, customs brokerage, international logistics solutions.*

**Expeditors International Service Center, PO Box 50252, Furn El Chebback, Lebanon**

## JOHN FABICK TRACTOR COMPANY

1 Fabick Drive, Fenton, MO, 63026

Tel: (314) 343-5900     Fax: (314) 343-4910     www.johnfabick.com

*Wheel tractors, excavating and road building equipment.*

**A.K. Zarby & Associates, Ardeti Bldg., Bliss St., Manara, Beirut, Lebanon**

## FRITZ COMPANIES, INC.

706 Mission Street, Ste. 900, San Francisco, CA, 94103

Tel: (415) 904-8360     Fax: (415) 904-8661     www.fritz.com

*Integrated transportation, sourcing, distribution and customs brokerage services.*

**Fritz Companies Inc., Beirut, Lebanon**

## GENERAL ELECTRIC CAPITAL CORPORATION

260 Long Ridge Road, Stamford, CT, 06927

Tel: (203) 357-4000     Fax: (203) 357-6489     www.gecapital.com

*Financial, property/casualty insurance, computer sales and trailer leasing services.*

**Employers Reinsurance Corp. (ERC), SNA Bldg. 4th Fl., Tabais Square, Beirut, Lebanon**

Tel: 961-1-333-199   Fax: 961-1-329-812

## GENERAL REINSURANCE CORPORATION

695 E. Main Street, Stamford, CT, 06904-2350

Tel: (203) 328-5000     Fax: (203) 328-6423     www.genre.com

*Reinsurance services worldwide.*

**Cologne Re of Beirut S.A.L., Sami Solh St., Badaro Trade Centre 7th Fl., PO Box 116-5096, Museum Beirut Lebanon**

Tel: 961-1-399-000   Fax: 961-1-399-009   Contact: Nouhad Taleb, SVP

## GRACO INC.

4050 Olson Memorial Hwy, PO Box 1441, Minneapolis, MN, 55440-1441

Tel: (612) 623-6000     Fax: (612) 623-6777     www.graco.com

*Mfr. systems and equipment to service fluid handling systems and automotive equipment.*

**Duratrade Ltd., Kfan Rbab, Ghazir, Green Zone, V7 St., Bldg., 1774, Jounieh, Lebanon**

Tel: 961-991-8582   Fax: 961-140-2237   Contact: Samir Dibeh

## GRANT THORNTON INTERNATIONAL

800 One Prudential Plaza, 130 E. Randolph Drive, Chicago, IL, 60601-6050

Tel: (312) 856-0001     Fax: (312) 616-7052     www.grantthornton.com

*Accounting, audit, tax and management consulting services.*

**Grant Thornton Yafi & Co., PO Box 11, 35 Beirut, Lebanon**

Contact: Mowafak El Yafi

## GREY GLOBAL GROUP

777 Third Ave., New York, NY, 10017

Tel: (212) 546-2000     Fax: (212) 546-1495     www.grey.com

*International advertising agency.*

**CSS & Grey, Beitmery Roundabout, Beitmery, Beirut, Lebanon**

## HORWATH INTERNATIONAL ASSOCIATION

415 Madison Ave., New York, NY, 10017

Tel: (212) 838-5566     Fax: (212) 838-3636     www.horwath.com

*Public accountants and auditors.*

**Horwath Abou Chakra Co., Minkara Bldg., Clemenceau St., Beirut, Lebanon**

Contact: Wael Abou Chakra

## IDEX CORPORATION

630 Dundee Road, Ste. 400, Northbrook, IL, 60062

Tel: (847) 498-7070     Fax: (847) 498-3940     www.idexcorp.com

*Mfr. industrial pumps, lubrication systems, metal fabrication equipment, bending and clamping devices.*

**Bardawil & Co. S.A.R.L., PO Box 110967 Dora Blvd., Beirut, Lebanon**

## INTERGRAPH CORPORATION

One Madison Industrial Park, Huntsville, AL, 35894-0001

Tel: (256) 730-2000     Fax: (256) 730-7898     www.intergraph.com

*Develop/mfr. interactive computer graphic systems.*

**Integraph Middle East LLC, Dora Highway, Cite Dora 3 Bldg. 10th Fl., PO Box 90-710 Beirut, Lebanon**

Tel: 961-1-881-322   Fax: 961-1-915-575

## INTRACO CORPORATION

530 Stephenson Hwy., Troy, MI, 48083

Tel: (248) 585-6900      Fax: (248) 585-6920

*Export management and marketing consultants.*

**Intraco Corp., PO Box 135714 Shouran, Beirut, Lebanon**

## KPMG INTERNATIONAL LLP

345 Park Avenue, New York, NY, 10022

Tel: (201) 307-7000      Fax: (201) 930-8617      www.kpmg.com

*Accounting and audit, tax and management consulting services.*

**KPMG, Hamra Square Bldg., KPMG Level, Hamra St., Beirut Ras Lebanon**

Tel: 961-1-350518    Fax: 961-1-350238    Contact: Riad A. Mansour, Sr. Ptnr.

## ELI LILLY & COMPANY

Lilly Corporate Center, Indianapolis, IN, 46285

Tel: (317) 276-2000      Fax: (317) 277-6579      www.lilly.com

*Mfr. pharmaceuticals and animal health products.*

**Eli Lilly S.A., Spinnes Area, Yousif Hitti St., Kassar Bldg. 1st Fl., Beirut Lebanon**

Tel: 961-1-825-931    Fax: 961-1-823-570

## LOWE LINTAS & PARTNERS WORLDWIDE

One Dag Hammarskjold Plaza, New York, NY, 10017

Tel: (212) 605-8000      Fax: (212) 605-4705      www.interpublic.com

*Full-service, integrated marketing communications company/advertising agency.*

**Pimo Group, PO Box 11-5381, Beirut, Lebanon**

Tel: 961-1-202-323    Fax: 961-1-200-322    Contact: Alex Slim

## MARRIOTT INTERNATIONAL INC.

10400 Fernwood Rd., Bethesda, MD, 20817

Tel: (301) 380-3000      Fax: (301) 380-5181      www.marriott.com

*Hotel services.*

**Beirut Mrriott Hotel, Beirut, Lebanon**

## MERCK & COMPANY, INC.

One Merck Drive, PO Box 100, Whitehouse Station, NJ, 08889-0100

Tel: (908) 423-1000      Fax: (908) 423-2592      www.merck.com

*Pharmaceuticals, chemicals and biologicals.*

**Merck, Sharp & Dohme Intl. Middle East, Naji Itani Bldg., Jeanne d'Arc St., Ras Beirut, Lebanon**

## MERRILL LYNCH & COMPANY, INC.

World Financial Center, 250 Vesey Street, New York, NY, 10281-1332

Tel: (212) 449-1000      Fax: (212) 449-2892      www.ml.com

*Security brokers and dealers, investment and business services.*

**Merrill Lynch Pierce Fenner & Smith Middle East S.A.L., Sabbagh Center 15th Floor, Hamra Street, PO Box 11--5316, Beirut Lebanon**

Tel: 961-1-602120    Fax: 961-1-602123

## J. P. MORGAN CHASE & CO. INC.

World Headquarters, 270 Park Ave., New York, NY, 10017

Tel: (212) 270-6000      Fax: (212) 622-9030      www.jpmorganchase.com

*Provides integrated financial solutions for institutions and individuals worldwide, including asset management, investment banking and commercial banking.*

**J. P. Morgan Chase & Co., Gefinor Center, Block C - Clemenceau St. - 2nd. Fl., Beirut, Lebanon**

Tel: 961-1-351065    Fax: 961-1-739581

## A .C. NIELSEN COMPANY
177 Broad Street, Stamford, CT, 06901

Tel: (203) 961-3000     Fax: (203) 961-3190     www.acnielsen.com

*Market and consumer research firm.*

**A. C. Nielsen,  Geoco Center 3 (GGF) Bloc C 2/F, Sin El Fil Horch Tabet, Beirut Lebanon**

## OMNICOM GROUP
437 Madison Ave., New York, NY, 10022

Tel: (212) 415-3600     Fax: (212) 415-3530     www.omnicomgroup.com

*International network of advertising, marketing, direct mail, public relations and consulting services.*

**Intermarkets Advertising,  Chalouhi Canter, PO Box 55434, Sin El Fil, Beirut Lebanon**

Tel: 961-1-480477   Fax: 961-1-502121   Contact: Erwin Guerrovich, CEO   Emp: 287

## OTIS ELEVATOR COMPANY
10 Farm Springs Road, Farmington, CT, 06032

Tel: (860) 676-6000     Fax: (860) 676-5111     www.otis.com

*Mfr. elevators and escalators.*

**Otis Elevator Co. SAL,  Drab Bldg.- Mekalles, PO Box 11-7968, Beirut, Lebanon**

## PHILLIPS PETROLEUM COMPANY
Phillips Building, 411 S. Keeler Ave., Bartlesville, OK, 74004

Tel: (918) 661-6600     Fax: (918) 661-7636     www.phillips66.com

*Crude oil, natural gas, liquefied petroleum gas, gasoline and petro-chemicals.*

**Phillips Petroleum Intl. Corp.,  Shell Bldg., 14th Fl., 8 Raouche, PO Box 6106, Beirut, Lebanon**

## POLARIS INDUSTRIES INC.
2100 Highway 55, Medina, MN, 55440

Tel: (612) 542-0500     Fax: (612) 542-0599     www.polarisindustries.com

*Mfr. snowmobiles and all-terrain recreational and utility vehicles.*

**Empty Helmets S.A.R.L.,  PO Box 255 Zouk Mikael, Elias Nakhoul Bldg. St. Charbel Street, Sarba Jounich, Lebanon**

Tel: 961-963-6046

## PROCTER & GAMBLE COMPANY
One Procter & Gamble Plaza, Cincinnati, OH, 45202

Tel: (513) 983-1100     Fax: (513) 562-4500     www.pg.com

*Personal care, food, laundry, cleaning and industry products.*

**Procter & Gamble Mfg. Co. of Lebanon SAL,  PO Box 4992, Beirut, Lebanon**

## THE SERVICEMASTER COMPANY
One ServiceMaster Way, Downers Grove, IL, 60515-1700

Tel: (630) 271-1300     Fax: (630) 271-2710     www.svm.com

*Management service to health care, school and industry facilities; diversified residential and commercial services.*

**ServiceMaster,  Beirut, Lebanon**

## TELLABS INC.
4951 Indiana Ave. 6303788800, Lisle, IL, 60532-1698

Tel: (630) 378-8800     Fax: (630) 679-3010     www.tellabs.com

*Design/mfr./service voice/data transport and network access systems.*

**Tellabs,  Dbayeh Highway, Victoria Center 5/F, Dbayeh, Lebanon**

## TRUE NORTH COMMUNICATIONS INC.

101 East Erie Street, Chicago, IL, 60611

Tel: (312) 425-6500      Fax: (312) 425-5010      www.truenorth.com

*Holding company, advertising agency.*

**Horizon Beirut, Kallout Bldg., Chouran-Arslan St., Beirut Lebanon**

## UNITED PARCEL SERVICE, INC.

55 Glenlake Parkway, NE, Atlanta, GA, 30328

Tel: (404) 828-6000      Fax: (404) 828-6593      www.ups.com

*International package-delivery service.*

**UPS Lebanon, Achrafieh, Sassine Square, Le Doyen Bldg., Beirut Lebanon**

Tel: 961-1-218575

## URS CORPORATION

100 California Street, Ste. 500, San Francisco, CA, 94111-4529

Tel: (415) 774-2700      Fax: (415) 398-1904      www.urscorp.com

*Provides planning, design and construction management services, pollution control and hazardous waste management.*

**URS (Dames & Moore), Beirut, Lebanon**

## VERIZON COMMUNICATIONS INC.

1255 Corporate Drive, Irving, TX, 75038

Tel: (972) 507-5000      Fax: (972) 507-5002      www.gte.com

*Engaged in wireline and wireless communications.*

**GTE Sylvania SA, Dessouki Building 6th Floor, Patriarch Hoyek St., PO Box 3455, Beirut Lebanon**

## XEROX CORPORATION

800 Long Ridge Road, PO Box 1600, Stamford, CT, 06904

Tel: (203) 968-3000      Fax: (203) 968-4312      www.xerox.com

*Mfr. document processing equipment, systems and supplies.*

**Te Vega (Xerox), Sin El Fil, PO Box 110-773, Immeuble Fattal, Beirut, Lebanon**

Tel: 961-1-425 450    Fax: 961-1-494 820

## YOUNG & RUBICAM INC.

285 Madison Ave., New York, NY, 10017

Tel: (212) 210-3000      Fax: (212) 370-3796      www.yr.com

*Advertising, public relations, direct marketing and sales promotion, corporate and product ID management.*

**TEAM/Y&R Beirut, Beirut, Lebanon**

# Lesotho

**AON CORPORATION**

123 North Wacker Drive, Chicago, IL, 60606

Tel: (312) 701-3000       Fax: (312) 701-3100       www.aon.com

*Insurance brokers worldwide; underwrites accident and health insurance, specialty and professional insurance; and provides risk management consultation.*

**AON Worldwide/ Minet Kingsway (Lesotho) (Pty.) Ltd., 1/FCarlton Centre, Kingsway, Maseru, Lesotho**

Tel: 266-313540   Fax: 266-310033   Contact: Bonang Malebo

**DHL WORLDWIDE EXPRESS**

50 California Avenue, San Francisco, CA, 94111

Tel: (415) 677-6100       Fax: (415) 824-9700       www.dhl.com

*Worldwide air express carrier.*

**DHL Worldwide Express, Options Bldg. 1st Fl., Pioneer Road, Maseru, Lesotho**

Tel: 266-311082

**ERNST & YOUNG, LLP**

787 Seventh Ave., New York, NY, 10019

Tel: (212) 773-3000       Fax: (212) 773-6350       www.eyi.com

*Accounting and audit, tax and management consulting services.*

**Ernst & Young, Private Bag A169, LNDC 2ND Fl., Maseru, Lesotho**

**THE ST. PAUL COMPANIES, INC.**

385 Washington Street, St. Paul, MN, 55102

Tel: (651) 310-7911       Fax: (651) 310-8294       www.stpaul.com

*Provides investment, insurance and reinsurance services.*

**Lesotho National Insurnace Group, LNIC House, Constitution Roa, Private Bag A65, Maseru 100 Lesotho**

Tel: 266-313-031   Fax: 266-310-007

**XEROX CORPORATION**

800 Long Ridge Road, PO Box 1600, Stamford, CT, 06904

Tel: (203) 968-3000       Fax: (203) 968-4312       www.xerox.com

*Mfr. document processing equipment, systems and supplies.*

**Maseru Business Machines, BNP Centre Parliament Road, Pvt Bag 80, Maseru, Lesotho**

Tel: 266-324427   Fax: 266-310119

# Liberia

## AIR EXPRESS INTERNATIONAL CORPORATION
120 Tokeneke Road, PO Box 1231, Darien, CT, 06820

Tel: (203) 655-7900     Fax: (203) 655-5779     www.aeilogistics.com

*International air freight forwarder.*

**Air Express Intl., Scanship Inc.,  PO Box 209, Monrovia, Liberia**

## CIGNA COMPANIES
One Liberty Place, Philadelphia, PA, 19192

Tel: (215) 761-1000     Fax: (215) 761-5511     www.cigna.com

*Insurance, invest, health care and other financial services.*

**CIGNA Worldwide Insurance Co.,  c/o Lone Star Insurances Inc., 51 Broad St., PO Box 1142, Monrovia, Liberia**

## DHL WORLDWIDE EXPRESS
50 California Avenue, San Francisco, CA, 94111

Tel: (415) 677-6100     Fax: (415) 824-9700     www.dhl.com

*Worldwide air express carrier.*

**DHL Worldwide Express,  58 Broad St., Monrovia, Liberia**
Tel: 231-226986

## THE DOW CHEMICAL COMPANY
2030 Dow Center, Midland, MI, 48674

Tel: (517) 636-1000     Fax: (517) 636-3228     www.dow.com

*Mfr. chemicals, plastics, pharmaceuticals, agricultural products, consumer products.*

**Chief Shipping Co.,  Liberia**

## E.I. DU PONT DE NEMOURS & COMPANY
1007 Market Street, Wilmington, DE, 19898

Tel: (302) 774-1000     Fax: (302) 774-7321     www.dupont.com

*Mfr./sale diversified chemicals, plastics, specialty products and fibers.*

**World Wide Transport Inc.,  Monrovia, Liberia**

## IBM CORPORATION
New Orchard Road, Armonk, NY, 10504

Tel: (914) 765-1900     Fax: (914) 765-7382     www.ibm.com

*Information products, technology and services.*

**IBM Liberia,  c/o Liberia Business Machines, Mid Town Plaza, Carey St. - PO Box 1536, Monrovia Liberia**

## J. P. MORGAN CHASE & CO. INC.
World Headquarters, 270 Park Ave., New York, NY, 10017

Tel: (212) 270-6000     Fax: (212) 622-9030     www.jpmorganchase.com

*Provides integrated financial solutions for institutions and individuals worldwide, including asset management, investment banking and commercial banking.*

**J. P. Morgan Chase & Co.,  PO Box 46, Harbel, Monrovia, Liberia**

**J. P. Morgan Chase & Co.,  PO Box 181, Ashmun & Randall Sts., Monrovia, Liberia**

# Libya

**DHL WORLDWIDE EXPRESS**

50 California Avenue, San Francisco, CA, 94111

Tel:  (415) 677-6100        Fax:  (415) 824-9700        www.dhl.com

*Worldwide air express carrier.*

**DHL Worldwide Express,  Ahmed Swaihly St., Mahri House, PO Box 12499, Tripoli Libya**

Tel: 218-21-444-3782

**ERNST & YOUNG, LLP**

787 Seventh Ave., New York, NY, 10019

Tel:  (212) 773-3000        Fax:  (212) 773-6350        www.eyi.com

*Accounting and audit, tax and management consulting services.*

**Ernst & Young,  PO Box 91873, That El Emad Towers, Tripoli, Libya**

Tel: 218-21-75889   Fax: 218-21-360-0046   Contact: John Kirkpatrick

**KPMG INTERNATIONAL LLP**

345 Park Avenue, New York, NY, 10022

Tel:  (201) 307-7000        Fax:  (201) 930-8617        www.kpmg.com

*Accounting and audit, tax and management consulting services.*

**Ibrahim Al-Baruni & Company,  11 Omar Abdel Aziz, Tripoli, Libya**

Tel: 218-21-333-2225   Fax: 218-21-333-2225   Contact: Ibrahim Al-Baruni, Sr. Ptnr.

# Liechtenstein

## BLACK & DECKER CORPORATION

701 E. Joppa Road, Towson, MD, 21286

Tel: (410) 716-3900     Fax: (410) 716-2933     www.blackanddecker.com

*Mfr. power tools and accessories, security hardware, small appliances, fasteners, information systems and services.*

**Black & Decker Lichtenstein,  Liechtenstein Office, 701 East Joppa Road, Towson MD 21286**

## CARRIER CORPORATION

One Carrier Place, Farmington, CT, 06034-4015

Tel: (860) 674-3000     Fax: (860) 679-3010     www.carrier.com

*Mfr./distributor/services A/C, heating and refrigeration equipment.*

**Clymalynx AG,  Vaduz, Liechtenstein**

## DHL WORLDWIDE EXPRESS

50 California Avenue, San Francisco, CA, 94111

Tel: (415) 677-6100     Fax: (415) 824-9700     www.dhl.com

*Worldwide air express carrier.*

**DHL Worldwide Express,  Liechtenstein**
Tel: 41-1-734-5757

## ERNST & YOUNG, LLP

787 Seventh Ave., New York, NY, 10019

Tel: (212) 773-3000     Fax: (212) 773-6350     www.eyi.com

*Accounting and audit, tax and management consulting services.*

**Revikon, Revisions & Beratungs AG,  Aeulstresse 60, PO Box 651, FL-9490 Vaduz, Liechtenstein**
Tel: 41-756-70-70   Fax: 41-756-16-32   Contact: Dr. M. Oertli

# Lithuania

**AMERICAN INTERNATIONAL GROUP INC. (AIG)**
70 Pine Street, New York, NY, 10270
Tel: (212) 770-7000       Fax: (212) 509-9705       www.aig.com
*Worldwide insurance and financial services.*
**Seesam Ins. Co. Ltd.,  Sermukaniu 1/13-24, LT-2001 Vilnius, Lithuania**

**ANDERSEN WORLDWIDE**
33 West Monroe Street, Chicago, IL, 60603
Tel: (312) 580-0033       Fax: (312) 507-6748       www.arthurandersen.com
*Accounting and audit, tax and management consulting services.*
**Andersen Worldwide,  PO Box 2849, Aludariu 2, LT-2000 Vilnius, Lithuania**
Tel: 370-2-624-281

**APPLERA CORPORATION**
761 Main Avenue, Norwalk, CT, 06859-0001
Tel: (203) 762-1000       Fax: (203) 762-6000       www.applera.com
*Leading supplier of systems for life science research and related applications.*
**Applied Biosystems,  Linea Libera, Mokslininku 12A, 2021 Vilnius, Lithuania**

**BATES WORLDWIDE INC.**
405 Lexington Ave., New York, NY, 10174
Tel: (212) 297-7000       Fax: (212) 986-0270       www.batesww.com
*Advertising, marketing, public relations and media consulting.*
**Bates Adell Saatchi & Saatchi,  Trak g. 3/2, LT-2001 Vilnius, Lithuania**
Tel: 370-2-615-114   Fax: 370-2-626-048   Contact: V. Varlavicluz

**LEO BURNETT, DIV. B-COM 3 GROUP**
35 West Wacker Drive, Chicago, IL, 60601
Tel: (312) 220-5959       Fax: (312) 220-6533       www.bcom3group.com
*Engaged in advertising, marketing, media buying and planning, and public relations.*
**Dvyniu Ratas & Leo Burnett,  Vilnius, Lithuania**

**CHECKPOINT SYSTEMS, INC.**
101 Wolf Drive, Thorofare, NJ, 08086
Tel: (856) 848-1800       Fax: (856) 848-0937       www.checkpointsystems.com
*Mfr. test, measurement and closed-circuit television systems.*
**Checkpoint Systems Vilnius,  Rudninku 8-3, LT-2024 Vilnius, Lithuania**
Tel: 370-2-314-020   Fax: 370-2-22-7087   Contact: Andrius Vidas Gen. Mgr.

**DELOITTE TOUCHE TOHMATSU INTERNATIONAL**
1633 Broadway, New York, NY, 10019
Tel: (212) 492-4000       Fax: (212) 392-4154       www.deloitte.com
*Accounting, audit, tax and management consulting services.*
**Deloitte & Touche,  Didziojii 25-6, (PO Box 1024), LT-2001 Vilnius, Lithuania**

## DEVELOPMENT ASSOCIATES INC.

1730 North Lynn Street, Arlington, VA, 22209-2023

Tel: (703) 276-0677     Fax: (703) 276-0432     www.developmentassociates.com

*Management consulting services.*

**Development Associates, Inc., Municipality of Kaunas, Laisves a.96, LT-3000 Kaunas, Lithuania**

Tel: 370-7-206-733    Fax: 370-7-200-443

## DHL WORLDWIDE EXPRESS

50 California Avenue, San Francisco, CA, 94111

Tel: (415) 677-6100     Fax: (415) 824-9700     www.dhl.com

*Worldwide air express carrier.*

**DHL Worldwide Express, Dariaus Ir Gireno Str. 42, LT-2600 Vilnius, Lithuania**

Tel: 370-2-267-722

## GREY GLOBAL GROUP

777 Third Ave., New York, NY, 10017

Tel: (212) 546-2000     Fax: (212) 546-1495     www.grey.com

*International advertising agency.*

**Grey Advertising, Vilnius, Lithuania**

## KPMG INTERNATIONAL LLP

345 Park Avenue, New York, NY, 10022

Tel: (201) 307-7000     Fax: (201) 930-8617     www.kpmg.com

*Accounting and audit, tax and management consulting services.*

**KPMG Lietuva, Stulginskio 4 - 4/F, LT-2600 Vilnius, Lithuania**

Tel: 370-2-611-803    Fax: 370-2-620-851    Contact: Leif René Hansen, Sr. Ptnr.

## ELI LILLY & COMPANY

Lilly Corporate Center, Indianapolis, IN, 46285

Tel: (317) 276-2000     Fax: (317) 277-6579     www.lilly.com

*Mfr. pharmaceuticals and animal health products.*

**Eli Lilly (Suisse) S.A., Rep. Office, Rudninku 18/2-8, LT-2001 Vilnius, Lithuania**

Tel: 370-2-220-265    Fax: 370-2-220-235

## LUCENT TECHNOLOGIES, INC.

600 Mountain Ave., Murray Hill, NJ, 07974-0636

Tel: (908) 582-3000     Fax: (908) 582-2576     www.lucent.com

*Design/mfr. wide range of public and private networks, communication systems and software, data networking systems, business telephone systems and microelectronics components.*

**Lucent Technologies, Gedimino pr. 64-61, LT-2001 Vilnius Lithuania**

## McCANN-ERICKSON WORLDGROUP

750 Third Ave., New York, NY, 10017

Tel: (212) 984-3644     Fax: (212) 984-2629     www.mccann.com

*International advertising and marketing services.*

**Asta Dizainas McCann-Erickson, Vilnius, Lithuania**

## McDERMOTT WILL & EMERY

227 W. Monroe Street, Chicago, IL, 60606-5096

Tel: (312) 372-2000     Fax: (312) 984-7700     www.mwe.com

*International law firm.*

**UAB McDermott, Will & Emery, A. Smetones 6-6, LT-2600 Vilnius, Lithuania**

Tel: 370-2-791-000    Fax: 370-2-227-955    Contact: Vaiva Dumciute    Emp: 19

**McDONALD'S CORPORATION**

McDonald's Plaza, Oak Brook, IL, 60523

Tel: (630) 623-3000        Fax: (630) 623-7409        www.mcdonalds.com

*Fast food chain stores.*

**McDonald's Corp., Vilnius, Lithuania**

**MECHANICAL DYNAMICS, INC.**

2301 Commonwealth Blvd., Ann Arbor, MI, 48105

Tel: (734) 994-3800        Fax: (734) 994-6418        www.adams.com

*Mfr. Adams prototyping software to automotive industry.*

**IN RE Ltd., Gostauto 8 216, LT-2600 Vilnius, Lithuania**

Tel: 370-2-224-660   Fax: 370-2-22-4660

**A .C. NIELSEN COMPANY**

177 Broad Street, Stamford, CT, 06901

Tel: (203) 961-3000        Fax: (203) 961-3190        www.acnielsen.com

*Market and consumer research firm.*

**A. C. Nielsen, A. Juozapaviciaus Street, 6/2 LT-2600 Vilnius, Lithuania**

**PALMS & COMPANY, INC. (U.S. FUR EXCHANGE)**

515 Lake Street South, Bldg. #103, Kirkland, WA, 98033

Tel: (425) 828-6774        Fax: (425) 827-5528        www.peterpalms.com

*Fur auctioning, distribution and sale; investment banking.*

**Palms & Co. (Latvia) Inc., Verkiu str. 32/70, LT-3035 Kaunas, Lithuania**

Tel: 370-7-742-385   Fax: 370-7-799-786   Contact: Arunas Sialuys

**Palms & Co. Inc., Zirmunu 58-41, Vilnius, Lithuania**

Tel: 370-2-525-440   Fax: 370-2-721-134   Contact: Grigorij Kolesnikov   Emp: 2

**PAREXEL INTERNATIONAL CORPORATION**

195 West Street, Waltham, MA, 02154

Tel: (781) 487-9900        Fax: (781) 487-0525        www.parexel.com

*Provides contract medical, biotechnology, and pharmaceutical research and consulting services.*

**PAREXEL MEDSTAT, Kalinausko 10-11, LT-2009 Vilnius, Lithuania**

Tel: 370-2-313-725   Fax: 370-2-623-603

**PRICEWATERHOUSECOOPERS LLP**

1301 Ave. of the Americas, New York, NY, 10019

Tel: (212) 596-7000        Fax: (212) 259-1301        www.pwcglobal.com

*Accounting and auditing, tax and management, and human resource consulting services.*

**PriceWaterhouseCoopers, Seimynskiu 16, LT-2005 Vilnius, Lithuania**

Tel: 370-2-726-902   Fax: 370-2-726-903

**PROCTER & GAMBLE COMPANY**

One Procter & Gamble Plaza, Cincinnati, OH, 45202

Tel: (513) 983-1100        Fax: (513) 562-4500        www.pg.com

*Personal care, food, laundry, cleaning and industry products.*

**Sanitex (JV), P.d. Nr. 705, LT-3035 Kaunas, Lithuania**

Tel: 370-7-800-300

**SCIENTECH, INC.**

1690 International Way, Idaho Falls, ID, 83402

Tel: (208) 525-3700        Fax: (208) 529-4721        www.scientech.com

*worldwide provider of expert services to the energy and telecommunication markets*

**UAB Scientech Baltic, Kalvariju g. 126-629, LT-2600 Vilnius, Lithuania**

**UNITED PARCEL SERVICE, INC.**

55 Glenlake Parkway, NE, Atlanta, GA, 30328

Tel: (404) 828-6000        Fax: (404) 828-6593        www.ups.com

*International package-delivery service.*

**UPS Lithuania,  Laisvëa al. 99-3, LT-3000 Kaunas, Lithuania**

Tel: 370-7-209-194    Fax: 370-7-201-994

**YORK INTERNATIONAL CORPORATION**

631 South Richland Ave., York, PA, 17403

Tel:  (717) 771-7890        Fax:  (717) 771-6212        www.york.com

*Mfr. heating, ventilating, air conditioning and refrigeration equipment.*

**York International GmbH,  Verkiu 37 Rm. 210-212, LT-2600 Vilnius, Lithuania**

Tel: 370-2-724-758

# Luxembourg

### AETNA INC.
151 Farmington Avenue, Hartford, CT, 06156

Tel: (860) 273-0123    Fax: (860) 275-2677    www.aetna.com

*Managed health care, annuities, individual retirement and group pension services, and asset management products worldwide.*

**Aetna International Funds, Luxembourg**

### AIR EXPRESS INTERNATIONAL CORPORATION
120 Tokeneke Road, PO Box 1231, Darien, CT, 06820

Tel: (203) 655-7900    Fax: (203) 655-5779    www.aeilogistics.com

*International air freight forwarder.*

**AEI (Luxembourg), Room F2036-2038, New Cargocenter, L-1360 Luxembourg Airport, Luxembourg**
Tel: 352-34-640-9450    Fax: 352-34-640-9457

### ALLIANCE CAPITAL MANAGEMENT HOLDING LP
1345 Ave. of the Americas, New York, NY, 10105

Tel: (212) 969-1000    Fax: (212) 969-2229    www.alliancecapital.com

*Engaged in fund management for large corporations.*

**Acm Global Investor Services, 35 Blvd. Prince Henri L-1724, Luxembourg**
Tel: 352-22-6693

### AMERICAN INTERNATIONAL GROUP INC. (AIG)
70 Pine Street, New York, NY, 10270

Tel: (212) 770-7000    Fax: (212) 509-9705    www.aig.com

*Worldwide insurance and financial services.*

**AIG Europe S.A., 11 Avenue Guillaume, L-1651 Luxembourg**

### AMPACET CORPORATION
660 White Plains Road, Tarrytown, NY, 10591-5130

Tel: (914) 631-6600    Fax: (914) 631-7197    www.ampacet.com

*Mfr. color and additive concentrates for the plastics industry.*

**Ampacet Luxembourg S.A., Rue des Scillas 45, L-2529 Howald, Luxembourg**
Tel: 352-2920-991    Fax: 352-2920-99594

### ANC RENTAL CORP.
110 Southeast Sixth St., Ft. Lauderdale, FL, 33301

Tel: (954) 769-7000    Fax: (954) 769-7000    www.ancrental.com

*Engaged in car rental services, including National Car Rental and Alamo Rent A Car.*

**National Car Rental, 33 blvd Prince Henri, Luxembourg City, Luxembourg**

### ANDERSEN CONSULTING
100 S. Wacker Drive, Ste. 1059, Chicago, IL, 60606

Tel: (312) 693-0161    Fax: (312) 693-0507    www.ac.com

*Provides management and technology consulting services.*

**Andersen Consulting, 6 rue Jean Monnet, L-2180, Luxembourg**
Tel: 352-43-27-171    Fax: 352-43-27-233

## ANDERSEN WORLDWIDE

33 West Monroe Street, Chicago, IL, 60603

Tel: (312) 580-0033  Fax: (312) 507-6748  www.arthurandersen.com

*Accounting and audit, tax and management consulting services.*

**Andersen Worldwide, 6 rue Jean Monnet, PO Box 2381, L-2180 Luxembourg**

Tel: 352-42-22-331

## AON CORPORATION

123 North Wacker Drive, Chicago, IL, 60606

Tel: (312) 701-3000  Fax: (312) 701-3100  www.aon.com

*Insurance brokers worldwide; underwrites accident and health insurance, specialty and professional insurance; and provides risk management consultation.*

**AON Risk Services Europe SA, 283 Route d'Arion, L-8011 Strassen, Luxembourg**

Tel: 352-317-171  Fax: 352-317-174  Contact: Ronald Daene

## AVERY DENNISON CORPORATION

150 N. Orange Grove Blvd., Pasadena, CA, 91103

Tel: (626) 304-2000  Fax: (626) 792-7312  www.averydennison.com

*Mfr. pressure-sensitive adhesives and materials, office products, labels, tags, retail systems, Carter's Ink and specialty chemicals.*

**Fasson Roll Europe, Zone Industrielle PED, BP 38,L-4801 Rodange, Luxembourg**

Tel: 352-50-46-501  Fax: 352-50-46-50277

## THE BANK OF NEW YORK

One Wall Street, New York, NY, 10286

Tel: (212) 495-1784  Fax: (212) 495-2546  www.bankofny.com

*Banking services.*

**Bank of New York Luxembourg, S.A., 13 rue Beaumont, 4th Fl., L-1219 Luxembourg**

## BDO SEIDMAN, LLP  BELGIUM

Two Prudential Plaza, 180 N. Stetson Ave., Ste. 2300, Chicago, IL, 60601

Tel: (312) 240-1236  Fax: (312) 240-3329  www.bdo.com

*International accounting and financial consulting firm.*

**BDO Binder (Luxembourg) s.a.r.l., 17 rue des Pommiers, L-2343, Luxembourg**

Tel: 352-42-3042  Fax: 352-42-3040  Contact: Georg Peter Rockel

## BROWN BROTHERS HARRIMAN & COMPANY

59 Wall Street, New York, NY, 10005

Tel: (212) 483-1818  Fax: (212) 493-8526  www.bbh.com

*Financial services.*

**Brown Brothers Harriman (Luxembourg) SA, 23 rue Beaumont, BP 403, L-2014 Luxembourg**

## THE CHERRY CORPORATION

3600 Sunset Ave., PO Box 718, Waukegan, IL, 60087

Tel: (847) 662-9200  Fax: (847) 662-2990  www.cherrycorp.com

*Mfr. electrical switches, electronic keyboards, controls and displays.*

**Multiprox NV, Lion d'Orweg 12, B-009300 Aalst, Luxembourg**

Tel: 352-53-766566  Fax: 352-53-783977

## CISCO SYSTEMS, INC.

170 West Tasman Drive, San Jose, CA, 95134-1706

Tel: (408) 526-4000  Fax: (408) 526-4100  www.cisco.com

*Develop/mfr./market computer hardware and software networking systems.*

**Cisco Systems Luxembourg, Bd Royal 26/6th Fl., L-2449 Luxembourg**

Tel: 352-22-9999-5262  Fax: 352-22-9999-5499

## CITIGROUP, INC.

153 East 53rd Street, New York, NY, 10043

Tel: (212) 559-1000     Fax: (212) 559-3646     www.citigroup.com

*Provides insurance and financial services worldwide.*

**Citibank N.A., Luxembourg**

Contact: William M. O'Dea

## CLUBCORP, INC.

3030 LBJ Freeway, Ste. 700, Dallas, TX, 75234

Tel: (972) 243-6191     Fax: (972) 888-7700     www.clubcorp.com

*Operates golf courses and resorts.*

**Club Monet, Luxembourg**

## COMMERCIAL INTERTECH CORPORATION

1775 Logan Ave., PO Box 239, Youngstown, OH, 44501-0239

Tel: (330) 746-8011     Fax: (330) 746-1148

*Mfr. hydraulic components, pre-engineered buildings and stamped metal products.*

**Commercial Intertech SA, PO Box 152, Route d'Ettelbruck, L-9202 Diekirch, Luxembourg**

## CROMPTON CORPORATION

Benson Road, Middlebury, CT, 06749

Tel: (203) 573-2000     Fax: (203) 573-3077     www.uniroyalchemical.com

*Tires, tubes and other rubber products, chemicals, plastics and textiles.*

**Uniroyal Luxembourg SA, Steinfort, Luxembourg**

## DELOITTE TOUCHE TOHMATSU INTERNATIONAL

1633 Broadway, New York, NY, 10019

Tel: (212) 492-4000     Fax: (212) 392-4154     www.deloitte.com

*Accounting, audit, tax and management consulting services.*

**Fiduciaire Generale de Luxembourg, 3 Route d'Arlon, L-8009 Strassen, Luxembourg**

## DELTA AIR LINES INC.

PO Box 20706, Atlanta, GA, 30320-6001

Tel: (404) 715-2600     Fax: (404) 715-5494     www.delta-air.com

*Major worldwide airline; international air transport services.*

**Delta Air Lines Inc., Luxembourg City, Luxembourg**

## DHL WORLDWIDE EXPRESS

50 California Avenue, San Francisco, CA, 94111

Tel: (415) 677-6100     Fax: (415) 824-9700     www.dhl.com

*Worldwide air express carrier.*

**DHL Worldwide Express, 7 Ruede Bitbourg, Zone Industrielle Hamm, L-1273 Luxembourg**

Tel: 352-422542

## R.R. DONNELLEY & SONS COMPANY

77 West Wacker Drive, Chicago, IL, 60601-1696

Tel: (312) 326-8000     Fax: (312) 326-8543     www.rrdonnelley.com

*Commercial printing, allied communication services.*

**R. R. Donnelley Financial, European Bank & Business Centre 6D, Route de Treves, L-2633 Senningerberg, Luxembourg**

Tel: 352-34-14341

## THE DOW CHEMICAL COMPANY

2030 Dow Center, Midland, MI, 48674

Tel: (517) 636-1000     Fax: (517) 636-3228     www.dow.com

*Mfr. chemicals, plastics, pharmaceuticals, agricultural products, consumer products.*

**Administration de Participations Etrangeres SA, 13 blvd Royal, L-2449 Luxembourg City, Luxembourg**

## ELECTRONIC DATA SYSTEMS CORPORATION (EDS)

5400 Legacy Dr., Plano, TX, 75024

Tel: (972) 605-6000     Fax: (972) 605-2643     www.eds.com

*Provides professional services; management consulting, e.solutions, business process management and information solutions.*

**EDS Luxembourg S.A., Hamm Office Park, 13 a Rue du Bitbourg, Luxembourg L-1273 Luxembourg**
Contact: Jean Diederich

## ERNST & YOUNG, LLP

787 Seventh Ave., New York, NY, 10019

Tel: (212) 773-3000     Fax: (212) 773-6350     www.eyi.com

*Accounting and audit, tax and management consulting services.*

**Campagnie Fiduciare, 5 blvd de la Foire, PO Box 351, L-2013 Luxembourg City, Luxembourg**
Tel: 352-45-123-224   Fax: 352-45-123-204   Contact: Armand Haas

## FMR (FIDELITY INVESTMENTS)

82 Devonshire Street, Boston, MA, 02109

Tel: (617) 563-7000     Fax: (617) 476-6105     www.fidelity.com

*Diversified financial services company offering investment management, retirement, brokerage, and shareholder services directly to individuals and institutions and through financial intermediaries.*

**Fidelity Investments Luxembourg SA, Kanasallis House, Place de l'Etolie, BP 2174, L-1021 Luxembourg, Luxembourg**
Tel: 352-250340

## FOOT LOCKER USA

112 West 34th Street, New York, NY, 10020

Tel: (212) 720-3700     Fax: (212) 553-2042     www.venatorgroup.com

*Mfr./sales shoes and sneakers.*

**Foot Locker International, 43 Ave. De La Gare, L1611, Luxembourg**
Tel: 352-491214

**Foot Locker International, 18, rue De L'Alzette, Esch-Zur-Alzette, L-4010, Luxembourg**
Tel: 352-542825

## FRANKLIN RESOURCES, INC.

777 Mariners Island Blvd., San Mateo, CA, 94404

Tel: (415) 312-2000     Fax: (415) 312-3655     www.frk.com

*Global and domestic investment advisory and portfolio management.*

**Templeton Global Strategic Services, S.A., 26 Boulevard Royal, L-2449, Luxembourg**
Tel: 352-46-66-67-212   Fax: 352-46-66-76

## GENERAL ELECTRIC CAPITAL CORPORATION

260 Long Ridge Road, Stamford, CT, 06927

Tel: (203) 357-4000     Fax: (203) 357-6489     www.gecapital.com

*Financial, property/casualty insurance, computer sales and trailer leasing services.*

**Employers Reinsurance Corp. (ERC), 4 rue de l'Eau, L-1449, Luxembourg**
Tel: 352-467-250   Fax: 352-467-230

### GENERAL ELECTRIC COMPANY

3135 Easton Turnpike, Fairfield, CT, 06431

Tel: (203) 373-2211    Fax: (203) 373-3131    www.ge.com

*Diversified manufacturing, technology and services.*

**GE FANUC Automation, Zone Industrielle, L-6468 Echternach, Luxembourg**

Tel: 352-72797-9324   Fax: 352-72797-9351

### GENERAL MOTORS CORPORATION

300 Renaissance Center, Detroit, MI, 48285

Tel: (313) 556-5000    Fax: (313) 556-5108    www.gm.com

*Mfr. full line vehicles, automotive electronics, commercial technologies, telecommunications, space, finance.*

**General Motors Luxembourg Operations SA, Route de Luxembourg, BP 29, L-4901 Bascharage, Luxembourg**

### THE GOODYEAR TIRE & RUBBER COMPANY

1144 East Market Street, Akron, OH, 44316

Tel: (330) 796-2121    Fax: (330) 796-1817    www.goodyear.com

*Mfr. tires, automotive belts and hose, conveyor belts, chemicals; oil pipeline transmission.*

**Goodyear SA, Ave. Gordon Smith, L-7750 Colmar-Berg, Luxembourg**

### GRANT THORNTON INTERNATIONAL

800 One Prudential Plaza, 130 E. Randolph Drive, Chicago, IL, 60601-6050

Tel: (312) 856-0001    Fax: (312) 616-7052    www.grantthornton.com

*Accounting, audit, tax and management consulting services.*

**Grant Thornton Revision et Conseils S.A., 2 Bld Grande Duchesse Charlotte, L-1330, Luxembourg**

Tel: 352-459164   Fax: 352-452203    Contact: Jeffrey Davies

**Grant Thornton Revision et Conseils SA, 2 Blvd. Grande Duchesse, Charlotte L-1330, Luxembourg**

### GUARDIAN INDUSTRIES CORPORATION

2300 Harmon Road, Auburn Hills, MI, 48326-1714

Tel: (248) 340-1800    Fax: (248) 340-9988    www.guardian.com

*Mfr. and fabricate flat glass products and insulation materials.*

**Guardian Luxguard I S.A., Route de Luxembourg, L-4940 Bascharage, Luxembourg City, Luxembourg**

Tel: 352-50-301

### THE HARTFORD INTERNATIONAL FINANCIAL SERVICES GROUP, INC.

200 Hopmeadow St., Simsbury, CT, 06089

Tel: (860) 843-8370    Fax: (860) 843-8400    www.itthartford.com

*Provides property, casual and life insurance services.*

**ZA Lux S.A., 39, Val St. André, L-1128 Luxembourg Ville, Luxembourg**

Tel: 352-44-6774   Fax: 352-44-6933

### HOLIDAY INN (BASS RESORTS) WORLDWIDE, INC.

3 Ravinia Drive, Ste. 2900, Atlanta, GA, 30346-2149

Tel: (770) 604-2000    Fax: (770) 604-5403    www.holidayinn.com

*Hotels, restaurants and casinos.*

**Holiday Inn, BP 512, Luxembourg City, Luxembourg**

### HORWATH INTERNATIONAL ASSOCIATION

415 Madison Ave., New York, NY, 10017

Tel: (212) 838-5566    Fax: (212) 838-3636    www.horwath.com

*Public accountants and auditors.*

**Hoogewerf & Co., 19 rue Aldringen, L-1118 Luxembourg City, Luxembourg**

## IBM CORPORATION

New Orchard Road, Armonk, NY, 10504

Tel: (914) 765-1900     Fax: (914) 765-7382     www.ibm.com

*Information products, technology and services.*

**IBM World Trade Corporation, Ceinture "Um Schlass" 1, L-5880 Hesperange, Luxembourg**

## INFONET SERVICES CORPORATION

2100 East Grand Ave., El Segundo, CA, 90245-1022

Tel: (310) 335-2600     Fax: (310) 335-4507     www.infonet.com

*Provider of Internet services and electronic messaging services.*

**Infonet Luxembourg, 55 rue des Bruyeres, L-1274 Howald, Luxembourg**

Tel: 352-405-6371   Fax: 352-405-639

## JONES LANG LASALLE

101 East 52nd Street, New York, NY, 10022

Tel: (212) 688-8181     Fax: (212) 308-5199     www.jlw.com

*International marketing consultants, leasing agents and property management advisors.*

**Jones Lang Wootton, Luxembourg**

## KELLY SERVICES, INC.

999 W. Big Beaver Road, Troy, MI, 48084

Tel: (248) 362-4444     Fax: (248) 244-4154     www.kellyservices.com

*Temporary help placement.*

**Kelly Services Luxembourg S.A.R.L., 19-25 rue des Capucins, L-1313, Luxembourg**

Tel: 352-466266   Fax: 352-466267

## KOCH INDUSTRIES INC.

4111 East 37th Street North, Wichita, KS, 67220-3203

Tel: (316) 828-5500     Fax: (316) 828-5950     www.kochind.com

*Oil, financial services, agriculture and Purina Mills animal feed.*

**Koch Membrane Systems, Inc., PO Box 83, L-3400 Dudelange, Luxembourg**

## KORN/FERRY INTERNATIONAL

1800 Century Park East, Los Angeles, CA, 90067

Tel: (310) 843-4100     Fax: (310) 553-6452     www.kornferry.com

*Executive search; management consulting.*

**Korn/Ferry International, 19 Cote d'Eich, L-1450, Luxembourg**

Tel: 352-4643-421   Fax: 352-4643-45/60

## KPMG INTERNATIONAL LLP

345 Park Avenue, New York, NY, 10022

Tel: (201) 307-7000     Fax: (201) 930-8617     www.kpmg.com

*Accounting and audit, tax and management consulting services.*

**KPMG Audit, 31, Allée Scheffer, L-2520 Luxembourg, Luxembourg**

Tel: 352-2251511   Fax: 352-225171   Contact: Dennis Robertson, Ptnr.

**KPMG Financial Engineering, 121 Ave. de la Faïencerie, L-1511, Luxembourg**

Tel: 352-47-68-471   Fax: 352-47-0761   Contact: Bob Bernard, Sr. Ptnr.

## MANPOWER INTERNATIONAL INC.

5301 N. Ironwood Rd., PO Box 2053, Milwaukee, WI, 53201-2053

Tel: (414) 961-1000     Fax: (414) 961-7081     www.manpower.com

*Temporary help, contract service, training and testing.*

**Manpower SARL, 19 rue Glesener, Luxembourg City, Luxembourg**

Tel: 352-482-323

## MARSH & McLENNAN COS INC.

1166 Ave. of the Americas, New York, NY, 10036-2774

Tel: (212) 345-5000      Fax: (212) 345-4808      www.marshmac.com

*Insurance agents/brokers, pension and investment management consulting services.*

**J&H Marsh & McLennan Management Services S.A., 65 Ave. de la Gare, L-1611, Luxembourg**

Tel: 352-49-6951   Fax: 352-49-6936   Contact: Claude Weber

## MASS MUTUAL LIFE INSURANCE COMPANY

1295 State St., Springfield, MA, 01111

Tel: (413) 788-8411      Fax: (413) 744-6005      www.massmutual.com

*Individual insurance, personal accident insurance, credit and group life insurance.*

**MassMutual Luxembourg, Luxembourg**

## MERRILL LYNCH & COMPANY, INC.

World Financial Center, 250 Vesey Street, New York, NY, 10281-1332

Tel: (212) 449-1000      Fax: (212) 449-2892      www.ml.com

*Security brokers and dealers, investment and business services.*

**Merrill Lynch International Bank, 68-70 blvd de la Petrusse, L-2320, Luxembourg**

Tel: 352-49-5156-1   Fax: 352-48-1271

## MINERAIS U S INC.

105 Raider Boulevard, Ste. 104, Belle Mead, NJ, 08502

Tel: (908) 874-7666      Fax: (908) 874-7725

*Marketing/distributor ferro alloys, ores and minerals.*

**S.A. des Minerais, 13 rue Robert Stumper, BP 5, L-2010 Luxembourg City, Luxembourg**

## MOOG INC.

Jamison Road, East Aurora, NY, 14052-0018

Tel: (716) 652-2000      Fax: (716) 687-4471      www.moog.com

*Mfr. precision control components and systems.*

**Moog Hydrolux Luxembourg Sarl, PO Box 1963, 1 rue de l'Aciérie, L-1019 Luxembourg**

## J. P. MORGAN CHASE & CO. INC.

World Headquarters, 270 Park Ave., New York, NY, 10017

Tel: (212) 270-6000      Fax: (212) 622-9030      www.jpmorganchase.com

*Provides integrated financial solutions for institutions and individuals worldwide, including asset management, investment banking and commercial banking.*

**J. P. Morgan Chase & Co., 5 rue Plaetis, BP 240, L-2012 Luxembourg**

Tel: 352-46-26-851   Fax: 352-46-224590

**J. P. Morgan Chase & Co., 37 rue Notre Dame, Luxembourg City, Luxembourg**

## MORGAN STANLEY DEAN WITTER & CO.

1585 Broadway, New York, NY, 10036

Tel: (212) 761-4000      Fax: (212) 761-0086      www.msdw.com

*Securities and commodities brokerage, investment banking, money management, personal trusts.*

**Morgan Stanley Bank Luxembourg S.A., 6C Route de Treves, L-2633 Senningerberg, Luxembourg**

## NATIONWIDE INSURANCE

One Nationwide Plaza, Columbus, OH, 43215-2220

Tel: (614) 249-7111      Fax: (614) 249-7705      www.nationwide.com

*Insurance services.*

**PanEuroLife, 291 route d'Arlon, B.P.2408 L- 1024, Luxembourg**

## NORTON ABRASIVES COMPANY

1 New Bond Street, Worcester, MA, 01606

Tel: (508) 795-5000    Fax: (508) 795-5741    www.nortonabrasives.com

*Mfr. abrasives for industrial manufacturing.*

**Norton SA, Chemin Rouge Belvaux, Luxembourg City, Luxembourg**

## OTIS ELEVATOR COMPANY

10 Farm Springs Road, Farmington, CT, 06032

Tel: (860) 676-6000    Fax: (860) 676-5111    www.otis.com

*Mfr. elevators and escalators.*

**General Technic-Otis SARL, 44 rue des Bruyeres, BP 1056, L-1274 Howald, Luxembourg**

## PHOENIX HOME LIFE MUTUAL INSURANCE COMPANY

1 American Row, Hartford, CT, 06102-5056

Tel: (860) 403-5000    Fax: (860) 403-5855    www.phoenixwm.com

*Engaged in sales of individual and group insurance and annuities and mutual funds.*

**Lombard International Assurance S.A. (JV), Luxembourg**

## PRICEWATERHOUSECOOPERS LLP

1301 Ave. of the Americas, New York, NY, 10019

Tel: (212) 596-7000    Fax: (212) 259-1301    www.pwcglobal.com

*Accounting and auditing, tax and management, and human resource consulting services.*

**PriceWaterhouseCoopers, 24-26 Ave. de la Liberte, (PO Box 1443) L-1014 Luxembourg City, Luxembourg**

Tel: 352-402455-1   Fax: 352-402455-600

## PRIMARK CORPORATION

100 Winter Street, Ste. 4300-N, Waltham, MA, 02451

Tel: (781) 466-6611    Fax: (781) 890-6187    www.primark.com

*Provides financial and business information.*

**Primark Luxembourg SA, 24 rue Beaumont, L-1219 Luxembourg**

Tel: 352-26-20-1069

## RAYMOND JAMES FINANCIAL, INC.

880 Carillon Parkway, St. Petersburg, FL, 33716

Tel: (813) 573-3800    Fax: (813) 573-8244    www.rjf.com

*Financial services; securities brokerage, asset management, and investment banking services.*

**Raymond James Benelux, 25 rue Notre Dame, L-2240, Luxembourg**

Tel: 352-229-666   Fax: 352-221-044

## RPM INC.

PO Box 777, 2628 Pearl Road, Medina, OH, 44258

Tel: (330) 273-5090    Fax: (330) 225-8743    www.rpminc.com

*Mfr. protective coatings and paints.*

**Akron SARL, 3 rue de la Sapiniere, Bridel, Luxembourg**

## SILICON GRAPHICS INC.

2011 N. Shoreline Blvd., Mountain View, CA, 94043-1389

Tel: (650) 960-1980    Fax: (650) 961-0595    www.sgi.com

*Design/mfr. special-effects computer graphic systems and software.*

**Silicon Graphics, Luxembourg**

## SOTHEBY'S HOLDINGS, INC.

1334 York Avenue, New York, NY, 10021

Tel: (212) 606-7000     Fax: (212) 606-7027     www.sothebys.com

*Auction house specializing in fine art and jewelry.*

**Sotheby's Holdings, Inc., 156A Route de Luxembourg, L-7374 Bofferdange, Luxembourg**

Tel: 352-33-9747    Contact: Nadia Meyer-Quiring

## THE ST. PAUL COMPANIES, INC.

385 Washington Street, St. Paul, MN, 55102

Tel: (651) 310-7911     Fax: (651) 310-8294     www.stpaul.com

*Provides investment, insurance and reinsurance services.*

**Fortis Luxembourg Assurances, 74 Grand'rue, L-1660, Luxembourg**

## STARWOOD HOTELS & RESORTS WORLDWIDE

777 Westchester Avenue, White Plains, NY, 10604

Tel: (914) 640-8100     Fax: (914) 640-8316     www.starwoodhotels.com

*Hotel operations including Sheraton, Westin, St. Regis, Four Points and Caesars.*

**Aerogulf Sheraton Hotel, BP 1793, Luxembourg City, Luxembourg**

## STATE STREET BANK & TRUST COMPANY

225 Franklin Street, Boston, MA, 02101

Tel: (617) 786-3000     Fax: (617) 654-3386     www.statestreet.com

*Banking and financial services.*

**State Street Bank SA, 47 Blvd. Royal, L-2449, Luxembourg**

## TEXAS REFINERY CORPORATION

840 North Main Street, Fort Worth, TX, 76101

Tel: (817) 332-1161     Fax: (817) 332-2340     www.texasrefinery.com

*Mfr. lubricants and specialty coatings.*

**Texas Refinery Corp. Inter-Continental SA, BP 4, Zone Industrielle Echternach, L-6401 Echternach, Luxembourg**

## THOMAS & BETTS CORPORATION

8155 T&B Blvd., Memphis, TN, 38125

Tel: (901) 252-5000     Fax: (901) 685-1988     www.tnb.com

*Mfr. elect/electronic connectors and accessories.*

**Thomas & Betts (Luxembourg) SA, Zone Industrielle, rue de l'Industrie, L-2895 Fuetz, Luxembourg**

## UUNET

22001 Loudoun County Pkwy., Ashburn, VA, 20147

Tel: (703) 206-5600     Fax: (703) 206-5601     www.uu.net

*World's largest Internet service provider; World Wide Web hosting services, security products and consulting services to businesses, professionals, and on-line service providers.*

**UUNET Luxembourg, 39 Ual Saint André, L-1128, Luxembourg**

Tel: 352-44-0291   Fax: 352-25-4404   Contact: Luc Dierckx

## THE VIKING CORPORATION

210 N. Industrial Park Rd., Hastings, MI, 49058

Tel: (616) 945-9501     Fax: (616) 945-9599     www.vikingcorp.com

*Mfr. fire extinguishing equipment.*

**Viking SA, Zone Industrielle Haneboesch, L-4562 Differdange Niedercorn, Luxembourg**

**JOHN ZINK COMPANY**

PO Box 21220, Tulsa, OK, 74121-1220

Tel: (918) 234-1800      Fax: (918) 234-2700      www.johnzink.com

*Mfr. flare systems, thermal oxidizers, vapor recovery systems, process heater burners.*

**John Zink Luxembourg,  Luxembourg**

Tel: 352-51899206    Contact: Manuel Martinez

# Macau

## AMERICAN INTERNATIONAL GROUP INC. (AIG)

70 Pine Street, New York, NY, 10270

Tel: (212) 770-7000     Fax: (212) 509-9705     www.aig.com

*Worldwide insurance and financial services.*

**American Home Assurance Co., #61 Av da Almeida, Central Plaza, Blk G15, Macau**

## AMWAY CORPORATION

7575 Fulton Street East, Ada, MI, 49355-0001

Tel: (616) 787-6000     Fax: (616) 787-6177     www.amway.com

*Mfr./sale home care, personal care, nutrition and houseware products.*

**Amway Macau Lda., Rua de Pedro Coutinbo, Np. 52 Edif. Hio Fai, Bloco D R/C, Macau**

## BANK OF AMERICA CORPORATION

555 California Street, San Francisco, CA, 94104

Tel: (415) 622-3530     Fax: (415) 622-8467     www.bankofamerica.com

*Financial services.*

**Bank of America NT & SA, 2F-G Av. de Almeida, Ribeiro, Macau**

Tel: 853-568821    Fax: 853-570386

## BEL FUSE INC.

198 Van Vorst Street, Jersey City, NJ, 07302

Tel: (201) 432-0463     Fax: (201) 432-9542     www.belfuse.com

*Mfr. electronic components for networking, fuses, delay lines, hybrids and magnetic products.*

**Bel Fuse Macau Lda., 218 Largo do Pac On, Taipa, Macau**

## CITIGROUP, INC.

153 East 53rd Street, New York, NY, 10043

Tel: (212) 559-1000     Fax: (212) 559-3646     www.citigroup.com

*Provides insurance and financial services worldwide.*

**Citibank N.A., Macau**

Contact: Stephen H. Long

## DELOITTE TOUCHE TOHMATSU INTERNATIONAL

1633 Broadway, New York, NY, 10019

Tel: (212) 492-4000     Fax: (212) 392-4154     www.deloitte.com

*Accounting, audit, tax and management consulting services.*

**Deloitte Touche Tohmatsu, 223-225 Av Dr. Rodrigo Rodrigues, 14/F Nam Kwong Bldg. Apt.1, (PO Box 746), Macau**

## DHL WORLDWIDE EXPRESS

50 California Avenue, San Francisco, CA, 94111

Tel: (415) 677-6100     Fax: (415) 824-9700     www.dhl.com

*Worldwide air express carrier.*

**DHL Worldwide Express, 14-16 Beco do Praia Grande, Edidicio Hoi Tin R/C, Macau**

Tel: 853-372828

## IBM CORPORATION

New Orchard Road, Armonk, NY, 10504

Tel: (914) 765-1900     Fax: (914) 765-7382     www.ibm.com

*Information products, technology and services.*

**IBM World Trade Corporation, Av. Dr. Mario Soraes, Edif. Banco da China, Macau**

Tel: 853-786687   Fax: 853-782136

## INTERNATIONAL GAME TECHNOLOGY INC.

9295 Prototype Drive, Reno, NV, 89511

Tel: (702) 448-0100     Fax: (702) 448-1488     www.igtonline.com

*Mfr. slot machines, video gaming machines and gaming terminals.*

**IGT Macau, Box 1024, Macau, Macau**

Tel: 853-375111   Fax: 853-510239

## KPMG INTERNATIONAL LLP

345 Park Avenue, New York, NY, 10022

Tel: (201) 307-7000     Fax: (201) 930-8617     www.kpmg.com

*Accounting and audit, tax and management consulting services.*

**KPMG Peat Marwick e Associados, Bank of China Bldg., Av. Doutor Mario Soares, Macau**

## PRICEWATERHOUSECOOPERS LLP

1301 Ave. of the Americas, New York, NY, 10019

Tel: (212) 596-7000     Fax: (212) 259-1301     www.pwcglobal.com

*Accounting and auditing, tax and management, and human resource consulting services.*

**PriceWaterhouseCoopers, Edif. Banco Luso Internacional, rua Dr. Pedro Jose Lobo Nos 1-3 andar 27th, Macau**

Tel: 853-589589   Fax: 853-558861

## SCHENKER INTERNATIONAL FORWARDERS INC.

150 Albany Ave., Freeport, NY, 11520

Tel: (516) 377-3000     Fax: (516) 377-3005     www.schenkerusa.com

*Freight forwarders.*

**Schenker (H. K.) Ltd., Praia Grande Commercial Ctr. Rm. 1206429, Av. De Praia, Macau**

Tel: 853-712687   Fax: 853-712676

## STARWOOD HOTELS & RESORTS WORLDWIDE

777 Westchester Avenue, White Plains, NY, 10604

Tel: (914) 640-8100     Fax: (914) 640-8316     www.starwoodhotels.com

*Hotel operations including Sheraton, Westin, St. Regis, Four Points and Caesars.*

**Westin Resort, Estrada de Hac Sa, Ilha de Coloane, Coloane, Macau**

Tel: 853-871-111   Fax: 853-871-122

# Macedonia

## APPLERA CORPORATION

761 Main Avenue, Norwalk, CT, 06859-0001

Tel: (203) 762-1000     Fax: (203) 762-6000     www.applera.com

*Leading supplier of systems for life science research and related applications.*

**Interlab d.o.o., Leninova 16A, 91001 Skopje, Macedonia**

## BATES WORLDWIDE INC.

405 Lexington Ave., New York, NY, 10174

Tel: (212) 297-7000     Fax: (212) 986-0270     www.batesww.com

*Advertising, marketing, public relations and media consulting.*

**S Team Bates Saatchi & Saatchi Advertising Balkans, 52 Archleplakop Angelari St., 91000 Skopje, Macedonia**

Tel: 389-91-224131   Fax: 389-91-132505   Contact: Dragan Sakan, Chmn.

## BRISTOL-MYERS SQUIBB COMPANY

345 Park Ave., New York, NY, 10154-0037

Tel: (212) 546-4000     Fax: (212) 546-4020     www.bms.com

*Pharmaceutical and food preparations, medical and surgical instruments.*

**TP Panovski, Div. Bristol-Myers Squibb, 67 Leninova Street, 91000 Skopje, Macedonia**

## D'ARCY MASIUS BENTON & BOWLES INC. (DMB&B)

1675 Broadway, New York, NY, 10019

Tel: (212) 468-3622     Fax: (212) 468-2987     www.dmbb.com

*Full service international advertising and communications group.*

**DMB&B, 1 Prolet Street 3/F, 91000 Skopje, Macedonia**

## DDB NEEDHAM WORLDWIDE INC.

437 Madison Ave., New York, NY, 10022

Tel: (212) 415-2000     Fax: (212) 415-3417     www.ddbn.com

*Advertising agency.*

**Idea Plus DDB Skopje, 91000 Skopje, Macedonia**

## DELOITTE TOUCHE TOHMATSU INTERNATIONAL

1633 Broadway, New York, NY, 10019

Tel: (212) 492-4000     Fax: (212) 392-4154     www.deloitte.com

*Accounting, audit, tax and management consulting services.*

**Deloitte & Touche, Dame Gruev 16/7, 91000 Skopje, Macedonia**

## DHL WORLDWIDE EXPRESS

50 California Avenue, San Francisco, CA, 94111

Tel: (415) 677-6100     Fax: (415) 824-9700     www.dhl.com

*Worldwide air express carrier.*

**DHL Worldwide Express, Skopski Saem, Belasica B.B., 91000 Skopje, Macedonia**

Tel: 389-91-121111

## DIMON INCORPORATED

512 Bridge Street, PO Box 681, Danville, VA, 24543-0681

Tel: (804) 792-7511     Fax: (804) 791-0377     www.dimon.com

*One of world's largest importer and exporters of leaf tobacco.*

**AD DIMON Gorica, Industrika bb, Vinica F.Y.R.O., Skopje, Macedonia**

Tel: 389-93-76208

## DRAFT WORLDWIDE

633 North St. Clair Street, Chicago, IL, 60611-3211

Tel: (312) 944-3500     Fax: (312) 944-3566     www.draftworldwide.com

*Full service international advertising agency, engaged in brand building, direct and promotional marketing.*

**DraftWorldwide Hellas, V. Glavinov St., Business Ctr., Paloma Bianca 3/9, Skopje Macedonia**

Tel: 389-91-231251   Fax: 389-91-231251   Contact: Chris Gaitanaris, CEO

## GREY GLOBAL GROUP

777 Third Ave., New York, NY, 10017

Tel: (212) 546-2000     Fax: (212) 546-1495     www.grey.com

*International advertising agency.*

**Grey Advertising, 91000 Skopje, Macedonia**

## IBM CORPORATION

New Orchard Road, Armonk, NY, 10504

Tel: (914) 765-1900     Fax: (914) 765-7382     www.ibm.com

*Information products, technology and services.*

**IBM Macedonian Business Machines, Dame Gruev 28/IV, 91000 Skopje, Macedonia**

Tel: 389-91-113144   Fax: 389-91-113144

## ICN PHARMACEUTICALS, INC.

3300 Hyland Ave., Costa Mesa, CA, 92626

Tel: (714) 545-0100     Fax: (714) 641-7268     www.icnpharm.com

*Mfr./distribute pharmaceuticals.*

**ICN Pharmaceuticals, Inc., Bul. Koco Racin br. 14, 91000 Skopje, Macedonia**

## McCANN-ERICKSON WORLDGROUP

750 Third Ave., New York, NY, 10017

Tel: (212) 984-3644     Fax: (212) 984-2629     www.mccann.com

*International advertising and marketing services.*

**I & G Group/McCann Macedonia, 91000 Skopje, Macedonia**

# Madagascar

## LOUIS BERGER INTERNATIONAL INC.

100 Halsted Street, East Orange, NJ, 07019

Tel: (201) 678-1960      Fax: (201) 672-4284      www.louisberger.com

*Consulting engineers, engaged in architecture, environmental and advisory services.*

**Louis Berger International Inc.,  PO Box 4200, Antananarivo 101, Madagascar**

## DELOITTE TOUCHE TOHMATSU INTERNATIONAL

1633 Broadway, New York, NY, 10019

Tel: (212) 492-4000      Fax: (212) 392-4154      www.deloitte.com

*Accounting, audit, tax and management consulting services.*

**Delta Audit Associes,  PO Box 241, Antananarivo 101, Madagascar**

## DHL WORLDWIDE EXPRESS

50 California Avenue, San Francisco, CA, 94111

Tel: (415) 677-6100      Fax: (415) 824-9700      www.dhl.com

*Worldwide air express carrier.*

**DHL Worldwide Express,  Lott II J 181 F Bis, Ivandry, Antananarivo 101, Madagascar**

Tel: 261-2-42839

## HILTON HOTELS CORPORATION

9336 Civic Center Drive, Beverly Hills, CA, 90210

Tel: (310) 278-4321      Fax: (310) 205-7880      www.hiltonhotels.com

*International hotel chain: Hilton International, Vista Hotels and Hilton National Hotels.*

**Madagascar Hilton,  rue Pierre Stibbe - Anosy,  PO Box 959, Antananarivo, Madagascar**

## XEROX CORPORATION

800 Long Ridge Road, PO Box 1600, Stamford, CT, 06904

Tel: (203) 968-3000      Fax: (203) 968-4312      www.xerox.com

*Mfr. document processing equipment, systems and supplies.*

**APMA Xerox,  BP 4452 Angle rue Radama ler et, P Lumumba, Tsaralalana Antananarivo, Madagascar**

# Malawi

## AIR EXPRESS INTERNATIONAL CORPORATION

120 Tokeneke Road, PO Box 1231, Darien, CT, 06820

Tel: (203) 655-7900       Fax: (203) 655-5779       www.aeilogistics.com

*International air freight forwarder.*

**Air Express Intl.,  PO Box 30471, Chichiri Blantyre 3, Malawi**

## CALTEX CORPORATION

125 East John Carpenter Fwy., Irving, TX, 75062-2794

Tel: (972) 830-1000       Fax: (972) 830-1081       www.caltex.com

*Petroleum products.*

**Caltex Oil (Malawi) Ltd.,  Old Sites, Mission Rd., Blantyre, Malawi**

## DELOITTE TOUCHE TOHMATSU INTERNATIONAL

1633 Broadway, New York, NY, 10019

Tel: (212) 492-4000       Fax: (212) 392-4154       www.deloitte.com

*Accounting, audit, tax and management consulting services.*

**Deloitte & Touche,  Old Mutual House, (PO Box 30364), Capital City, Lilongwe 3, Malawi**

**Deloitte & Touche,  Hardelec House, Victoria Ave., (PO Box 187), Blantyre Malawi**

## DHL WORLDWIDE EXPRESS

50 California Avenue, San Francisco, CA, 94111

Tel: (415) 677-6100       Fax: (415) 824-9700       www.dhl.com

*Worldwide air express carrier.*

**DHL Worldwide Express,  Corner Haile Sellaise Rd. & St. David Str., Blantyre, Malawi**

Tel: 265-620688

## DIMON INCORPORATED

512 Bridge Street, PO Box 681, Danville, VA, 24543-0681

Tel: (804) 792-7511       Fax: (804) 791-0377       www.dimon.com

*One of world's largest importer and exporters of leaf tobacco.*

**DIMON (Malawi) Limited,  PO Box 30522, Lilongwe 3, Malawi**

## EAGLE GLOBAL LOGISTICS (EGL)

15350 Vickery Drive, Houston, TX, 77032

Tel: (281) 618-3100       Fax: (281) 618-3100       www.eaglegl.com

*Ocean/air freight forwarding, customs brokerage, packing and wholesale, logistics management and insurance.*

**A.M.I. (Malawi) Ltd.,  PO Box 838, Blantyre, Malawi**

Tel: 265-671-220   Fax: 265-670-240

**A.M.I. (Malawi) Ltd.,  PO Box 648, Lilongwe International Airport, Lilongwe, Malawi**

Tel: 265-765-233   Fax: 265-765-449

## ERNST & YOUNG, LLP

787 Seventh Ave., New York, NY, 10019

Tel: (212) 773-3000       Fax: (212) 773-6350       www.eyi.com

*Accounting and audit, tax and management consulting services.*

**Ernst & Young/W.B. Mwenelupembe & Co.,  1st Fl. Aquarius House, PO Box 366, Lilongwe, Malawi**

## FRITZ COMPANIES, INC.

706 Mission Street, Ste. 900, San Francisco, CA, 94103

Tel: (415) 904-8360     Fax: (415) 904-8661     www.fritz.com

*Integrated transportation, sourcing, distribution and customs brokerage services.*

**Fritz Companies Inc., Lilongwe, Malawi**

## IBM CORPORATION

New Orchard Road, Armonk, NY, 10504

Tel: (914) 765-1900     Fax: (914) 765-7382     www.ibm.com

*Information products, technology and services.*

**IBM Malawi, c/o Computer Sales & Services Ltd., Kamuzu Highway Ginnery Corner, PO Box 1445, Blantyre, Malawi**

Tel: 265-671-755   Fax: 265-671-809

## KPMG INTERNATIONAL LLP

345 Park Avenue, New York, NY, 10022

Tel: (201) 307-7000     Fax: (201) 930-8617     www.kpmg.com

*Accounting and audit, tax and management consulting services.*

**KPMG Peat Marwick, Aquarius House, New Capital City Centre, Lilongwe, Malawi**

**KPMG Peat Marwick, Able House, Hanover Ave., Blantyre, Malawi**

Tel: 265-620744   Fax: 265-620575   Contact: Farouk Sacranie, Sr. Ptnr.

## McCANN-ERICKSON WORLDGROUP

750 Third Ave., New York, NY, 10017

Tel: (212) 984-3644     Fax: (212) 984-2629     www.mccann.com

*International advertising and marketing services.*

**Graphic McCann, Blantyre, Malawi**

## PARSONS TRANSPORTATION GROUP

1133 15th Street NW, 9th Fl., Washington, DC, 20005

Tel: (202) 775-3300     Fax: (202) 775-3422     www.parsons.com

*Consulting engineers.*

**De Leuw Cather Intl. Ltd., PO Box 30394, Area 9164, Ulongwe, Malawi**

## PITTSTON BAX GROUP

16808 Armstrong Ave., PO Box 19571, Irvine, CA, 92623

Tel: (949) 752-4000     Fax: (949) 260-3182     www.baxworld.com

*Air freight forwarder.*

**BAX Global, PO Box 40132, Kaneneo, Lilongwe, Malawi**

## PRICEWATERHOUSECOOPERS LLP

1301 Ave. of the Americas, New York, NY, 10019

Tel: (212) 596-7000     Fax: (212) 259-1301     www.pwcglobal.com

*Accounting and auditing, tax and management, and human resource consulting services.*

**PriceWaterhouseCoopers, Plantation House 4th Fl., Victoria Ave., (PO Box 1147/1064) Blantyre, Malawi**

Tel: 265-620322   Fax: 265-621215

**PriceWaterhouseCoopers, KIA House 3rd Floor, Capital City, (PO Box 30379) Lilongwe 3, Malawi**

Tel: 265-783799   Fax: 265-782573

## STANDARD COMMERCIAL CORPORATION

2201 Miller Rd., PO Box 450, Wilson, NC, 27893

Tel: (919) 291-5507     Fax: (919) 237-1109     www.sccgroup.com

*Leaf tobacco dealers/processors and wool processors.*

**Stancom Tobacco Packers, PO Box 30224, Capital City, Lilongwe, Malawi**

**TRUE NORTH COMMUNICATIONS INC.**
101 East Erie Street, Chicago, IL, 60611
Tel: (312) 425-6500      Fax: (312) 425-5010      www.truenorth.com
*Holding company, advertising agency.*
**Top Advertising, Private Bag 63, Limbe, Malawi**

# Malaysia

## 3COM CORPORATION

5400 Bayfront Plaza, Santa Clara, CA, 95052-8145

Tel: (408) 326-5000     Fax: (408) 326-5001     www.3com.com

*Develop/mfr. computer networking products and systems.*

**3Com Asia Ltd. - Malaysia, 303 Level 3 - Uptown 2 - 2, Jalan SS 21/27, Damansara Uptown, 47400 Petaling Jaya Malaysia**

Tel: 60-3-715-1333   Fax: 60-3-715-2333

**3Com Asia Ltd. - Penang, Ste. 5A - Lower Level 5, Hotel Equatorial Penang, 1 Jalan Bukit Jambul, 11900 Penang Malaysia**

Tel: 60-4-644-1208   Fax: 60-4-64-1198

## 3M

3M Center, St. Paul, MN, 55144-1000

Tel: (651) 733-1110     Fax: (651) 733-9973     www.mmm.com

*Mfr. diversified products for industry, health care, imaging, communications, transport, safety, consumer, etc.*

**3M Malaysia Sdn. Bhd., PO Box 1115, Jalan Semangat, 46870 Petaling Jaya, Selangor Darul Ehsan Malaysia**

Tel: 60-3-775-7555   Fax: 60-3-775-7269

## ABBOTT LABORATORIES

One Abbott Park, Abbott Park, IL, 60064-3500

Tel: (847) 937-6100     Fax: (847) 937-1511     www.abbott.com

*Development/mfr./sale diversified health care products and services.*

**Abbott Laboratories, No. 22 U1/15 Seksyen U1, HICOM-Glenmarie Industrial Park, 40150 Shah Alam, Selangor Darul Ehsan, Malaysia**

## ACXIOM CORPORATION

301 Industrial Boulevard, Conway, AR, 72033-2000

Tel: (501) 336-1000     Fax: (501) 336-3919     www.acxiom.com

*Data warehouser, database manager, and other marketing information services.*

**Acxiom Asia, Ltd., Ste. 8.3 Menara Cold Storage, Jalan Semangat Section 14, 461000 Petaling Jaya, Malaysia**

Tel: 60-3-755-0458   Fax: 60-3-757-1293

## ADVANCED MICRO DEVICES INC.

1 AMD Place, Sunnyvale, CA, 94086

Tel: (408) 732-2400     Fax: (408) 982-6164     www.amd.com

*Mfr. integrated circuits for communications and computation industry.*

**Advanced Micro Devices Sdn. Ghd., Bayan Lepas Free Trade Zone, Phase II, Pulau Pinang, Malaysia**

## AETNA INC.

151 Farmington Avenue, Hartford, CT, 06156

Tel: (860) 273-0123     Fax: (860) 275-2677     www.aetna.com

*Managed health care, annuities, individual retirement and group pension services, and asset management products worldwide.*

**Aetna Universal Insurance, Kuala Lumpur, Malaysia**

## AIR EXPRESS INTERNATIONAL CORPORATION

120 Tokeneke Road, PO Box 1231, Darien, CT, 06820

Tel: (203) 655-7900     Fax: (203) 655-5779     www.aeilogistics.com

*International air freight forwarder.*

**AEI (Malaysia) Sdn. Bhd., Lot A9-14 Kompleks Kargo Udara, Sultan Abdul Aziz Shah International, 47200 Subang Selangor, Kuala Lumpur Malaysia**

Tel: 60-3-746-4411  Fax: 60-3-746-3972

## AIR PRODUCTS AND CHEMICALS, INC.

7201 Hamilton Boulevard, Allentown, PA, 18195-1501

Tel: (610) 481-4911     Fax: (610) 481-5900     www.airproducts.com

*Mfr. industry gases and related equipment, specialty chemicals, environmental/energy systems.*

**Sitt Tatt Industrial Gases Sdn. Bhd., Lot 54, Jalan Jitra 26/7, Sec. 26 (Hicom Sector B), 4000 Shah Alam, Selangor, Malaysia**

## ALCOA INC.

Alcoa Center, 201 Isabella Street, Pittsburgh, PA, 15215-5858

Tel: (412) 553-4545     Fax: (412) 553-4498     www.alcoa.com

*World's leading producer of aluminum and alumina; mining, refining, smelting, fabricating and recycling.*

**Unified Accord Sdn. Bhd., Kuala Lumpur, Malaysia**

## ALLEGHENY TECHNOLOGIES

1000 Six PPG Place, Pittsburgh, PA, 15222

Tel: (412) 394-2800     Fax: (412) 394-2805     www.alleghenytechnologies.com

*Diversified mfr. aviation and electronics, specialty metals, industrial and consumer products.*

**Allegheny Technologies, Wisma Consplant 4/F, 2 Jalan SS16/4, Sugang Jaya, 47500 Petaling Jaya, Selangor, Malaysia**

## ALLERGAN INC.

2525 Dupont Drive, PO Box 19534, Irvine, CA, 92713-9534

Tel: (714) 246-4500     Fax: (714) 246-6987     www.allergan.com

*Mfr. therapeutic eye care products, skin and neural care pharmaceuticals.*

**Allergan Pte., Ltd., No. 261 Jln Perkasa Satu, Taman Maturi, 55100 Kuala Lumpur, Malaysia**

Tel: 60-3-985-6708  Fax: 60-3-982-4160

## AMERICAN & EFIRD, INC.

PO Box 507, Mt. Holly, NC, 28120

Tel: (704) 827-4311     Fax: (704) 822-6054     www.amefird.com

*Mfr. industrial sewing thread for worldwide industrial and consumer markets.*

**American & Efird (Malaysia) Sdn. Bhd., 5 Jalan Tembaga, Desa Perindustrian Kulai Julai 81000, Johor Malaysia**

## AMERICAN EXPRESS COMPANY

American Express Tower, World Financial Center, New York, NY, 10285-4765

Tel: (212) 640-2000     Fax: (212) 619-9802     www.americanexpress.com

*Travel, travelers cheques, charge card and financial services.*

**American Express (Malaysia) Sdn. Bhd., Kuala Lumpur, Malaysia**

## AMERON INTERNATIONAL CORPORATION

245 South Los Robles Ave., Pasadena, CA, 91109-7007

Tel: (626) 683-4000     Fax: (626) 683-4060     www.ameron.com

*Mfr. steel pipe systems, concrete products, traffic and lighting poles, protective coatings.*

**Ameron Malaysia, Kuala Lumpur, Malaysia**

## AMWAY CORPORATION

7575 Fulton Street East, Ada, MI, 49355-0001

Tel: (616) 787-6000     Fax: (616) 787-6177     www.amway.com

*Mfr./sale home care, personal care, nutrition and houseware products.*

**Amway Malaysia Sdn. Bhd., No. 34 Jalan 223, 46100 Petaling Jaya, Selangor, Malaysia**

## ANC RENTAL CORP.

110 Southeast Sixth St., Ft. Lauderdale, FL, 33301

Tel: (954) 769-7000     Fax: (954) 769-7000     www.ancrental.com

*Engaged in car rental services, including National Car Rental and Alamo Rent A Car.*

**Natlional Car Rental, G10 Ground Fl., Wisma Stephens, 88 Jalan Raja Chula, Kuala Lumpur, Malaysia**

## ANDERSEN CONSULTING

100 S. Wacker Drive, Ste. 1059, Chicago, IL, 60606

Tel: (312) 693-0161     Fax: (312) 693-0507     www.ac.com

*Provides management and technology consulting services.*

**Andersen Consulting, 17th Fl. AMCORP Trade Ctr., 18 Persiaran Barat -Off Jalan Timur, 46200 Petaling Jaya, Selangor Durul Ehsan Malaysia**

Tel: 60-3-756-5133   Fax: 60-3-758-2210

## ANDERSEN WORLDWIDE

33 West Monroe Street, Chicago, IL, 60603

Tel: (312) 580-0033     Fax: (312) 507-6748     www.arthurandersen.com

*Accounting and audit, tax and management consulting services.*

**A. Andersen & Co./Hanafiah, Raslan & Mohamad, Level 1 Block C So., Pusat Bandar Damansara, POB 11040, 50734 Kuala Lumpur Malaysia**

Tel: 60-3-255-7000

**A. Andersen &Co./Hanafiah, Raslan & Mohamad, 3/F Asia Life Bdg. 45, Jalan Tun Sambanthan, 30000 Ipoh Perak Darul Ridzuan, Malaysia**

**A. Andersen &Co./Hanafiah, Raslan & Mohamad, Ste. 11.2A Level 11 Menara Pelangi, 2 Jalan Kuning Taman Pelangi, 80400 Johor Bahru Malaysia**

Tel: 60-7-334-1740

**Andersen Worldwide, Penthouse 11th Fl., Kompleks Mutiara, Jalan Anson, PO Box 308, 10730 Penang Malaysia**

Tel: 60-4-226-5603

**Andersen Worldwide, 7/F -Wisma PKNK, Jalan Sultan Badlishah, PO Box 49, 05700 Alor Setar Kedah Darulaman Malaysia**

Tel: 60-4-731-0711

**Andersen Worldwide, 3/4/F Wisma Budaya, Jalan Tuanku Abdul Rahman, Locked Bag 88, 88998 Kota Kinabalu Sabah Malaysia**

Tel: 60-9-748-5406

**Arthur Andersen/Lau Chua Kong & Co., Unit 5D Level 5 Main Office Tower, Financial Park Lubuan Complex Jalan Merdeka, POBox 82178, 98031 WP Labuan Malaysia**

Tel: 60-87-412-194

**Hanafiah Rasaln & Mohamad/A. Andersen, Taman Sri Sarawak Mall, Jalan Tunku Abdul Rahman, PO Box 2383, 93748 Kuching Sarawak Malaysia**

## ANDREW CORPORATION

10500 West 153rd Street, Orland Park, IL, 60462

Tel: (708) 349-3300    Fax: (708) 349-5410    www.andrew.com

*Mfr. antenna systems, coaxial cable, electronic communications and network connectivity systems.*

**Andrew Corporation, Level 12-03B Plaza Masalam, 2 Jalan Tengku Ampuan Zabedah E9/9, 40100 Shah Alam Selangor, Malaysia**

Tel: 60-3-552-6370   Fax: 60-3-552-7324

## AON CORPORATION

123 North Wacker Drive, Chicago, IL, 60606

Tel: (312) 701-3000    Fax: (312) 701-3100    www.aon.com

*Insurance brokers worldwide; underwrites accident and health insurance, specialty and professional insurance; and provides risk management consultation.*

**Alexander & Alexander (M) Sdn Bhd, Ste. 13.05 - 13.08 13th Fl., Bangunan AMDB No.1, Kuala Lumpur, Malaysia**

Tel: 60-3-443-8463   Fax: 60-3-443-8460   Contact: Mak Chee Keong

**AON Natural Resources Asia Ltd., 1st Fl., No.2, Kuala Lumpur, Malaysia**

Tel: 60-3-445-7309   Fax: 60-3-445-7313   Contact: Nick Becker

**Inchape Insurance Brokers (M) Sdn Bhd, Ste. 6.3 Menara Cold Storage, Selangor Darul Rhsan, Malaysia**

Tel: 60-3-754-1285   Fax: 60-3-754-0572   Contact: Peter Jackson

## APPLERA CORPORATION

761 Main Avenue, Norwalk, CT, 06859-0001

Tel: (203) 762-1000    Fax: (203) 762-6000    www.applera.com

*Leading supplier of systems for life science research and related applications.*

**Applied Biosystems, #HG08 Ground Level, Wisma Academy, Lot 4A Jalan 19/1, 46300 Petaling Jaya, Malaysia**

## ARDENT SOFTWARE, INC.

50 Washington Street, Westboro, MA, 01581-1021

Tel: (508) 366-3888    Fax: (508) 366-3669    www.ardentsoftware.com

*Publisher of database and file management software.*

**Ardent Software, Kuala Lumpur, Malaysia**

## ARROW ELECTRONICS INC.

25 Hub Drive, Melville, NY, 11747

Tel: (516) 391-1300    Fax: (516) 391-1640    www.arrow.com

*Distributor of electronic components.*

**Arrow Components Sdn Bhd., No. 105/106 Block A, 97 Jalan SS 7/2 Kelana Jaya, 47301 Petaling Jaya, Selangor Malaysia**

**Microtronica Sdn., 105/106 Blk. A Kelana Centre, 97 Jalan SS 7/2 Kelana Jaya, 47301 Petaling Selangor, Malaysia**

Tel: 60-3-704-6213

## ASSOCIATED PRESS INC.

50 Rockefeller Plaza, New York, NY, 10020-1605

Tel: (212) 621-1500    Fax: (212) 621-5447    www.ap.com

*News gathering agency.*

**The Associated Press, China Insurance Bldg., 174 Jalan Tuanku Abdul Rahman, Kuala Lumpur, Malaysia**

Tel: 60-3-292-6155

## AT&T BROADBAND, LLC

9197 South Peoria, Englewood, CO, 80112

Tel: (720) 875-5500     Fax: (720) 875-4984     www.broadband.att.com

*Provides broadband technology services; digital TV, digital telephone and high-speed cable internet services.*

**Binariang, Kuala Lumpur, Malaysia**

## ATTACHMATE CORPORATION

3617 131st Ave. S.E., Bellevue, WA, 98006-1332

Tel: (425) 644-4010     Fax: (425) 747-9924     www.attachmate.com

*Mfr. connectivity software.*

**Attachmate Malaysia Sdn. Bhd., Unit 23-02, Level 23 Plaza 138, 138 Jalan Ampang, 50450 Kuala Lumpur Malaysia**

Tel: 60-3-245-5660

## ATWOOD OCEANICS, INC.

15835 Park Ten Place Drive, Houston, TX, 77084

Tel: (281) 492-2929     Fax: (281) 492-0345     www.atwd.com

*Offshore drilling for gas and oil.*

**Clearways Drilling (M) Sdn. Bhd., 332A-11A 11/F, Ampang City, Jalan Ampeng, 50450 Kuala Lumpur Malaysia**

Tel: 60-3-456-9714   Fax: 60-3-456-8623   Contact: Jamaluddin Manso, Dir.   Emp: 100

## AUTODESK INC.

111 McInnis Parkway, San Rafael, CA, 94903

Tel: (415) 507-5000     Fax: (415) 507-6112     www.autodesk.com

*Develop/marketing/support computer-aided design, engineering, scientific and multimedia software products.*

**Autodesk Asia Ptd. Ltd., Ste. 6.04 Bangunan 3M No. 6A, Persiaran Tropicana 47410, Petaling jaya Selangor Darul Ehsan, Malaysia**

Tel: 60-3-704-5776   Fax: 60-3-704-5754

## AUTOMATIC SWITCH CO. (ASCO)

50-60 Hanover Rd., Florham Park, NJ, 07932

Tel: (973) 966-2000     Fax: (973) 966-2628     www.asco.com

*Mfr. solenoid valves, emergency power controls, pressure and temp. switches.*

**Asco Asia, Malaysia, c/o Emerson Electric Malaysia, 7th Fl. Blk. B Menara PKNS-PJ, Jalan Yong Shook Lin, 46050 Petaling Jaya Malaysia**

Tel: 60-3-754-6811   Fax: 60-3-469-8122   Contact: Yow Huat Chin

## AUTOTOTE CORPORATION

750 Lexington Avenue, 25th Fl., New York, Ny, 1022

Tel: (212) 754-2233     Fax: (212) 754-2372     www.autotote.com

*Mfr. video gaming machines and computerized pari-mutuel wagering systems used at racetracks.*

**Scientific Games International, Div. Auto tote, C504 Wisma Consplant, 2 Jalan SS16/4 Subang Jaya, 47500 Petaling Jaya Selangor, Malaysia**

Tel: 60-3-530-0060   Fax: 60-3-732-7611

## AVERY DENNISON CORPORATION

150 N. Orange Grove Blvd., Pasadena, CA, 91103

Tel: (626) 304-2000     Fax: (626) 792-7312     www.averydennison.com

*Mfr. pressure-sensitive adhesives and materials, office products, labels, tags, retail systems, Carter's Ink and specialty chemicals.*

**Avery Dennison Asia Pacific Group, 34M Jalan SS21/39, Damansarar Utama, 47400 Petaling Jaya, Malaysia**

Tel: 60-3-715-5010   Fax: 60-3-715-5020

## AVIS GROUP HOLDINGS, INC.

900 Old Country Road., Garden City, NY, 11530

Tel: (516) 222-3000    Fax: (516) 222-4381    www.avis.com

*Car rental services.*

**Avis Group Holdings Ltd.., 40 Jalan Suttan, Ismail, 50250 Kuala Lumpur, Malaysia**

## AVON PRODUCTS INC.

1345 Avenue of the Americas, New York, NY, 10105-0196

Tel: (212) 282-5000    Fax: (212) 282-6049    www.avon.com

*Mfr./distributor beauty and related products, fashion jewelry, gifts and collectibles.*

**Avon Cosmetics (Malaysia) Sdn. Bhd., Lot 13-A Jalan 219, Section 51A, 46100 Petaling Jaya, Malaysia**

Tel: 60-3-757-3848  Fax: 60-3-757-4828  Contact: Nur Azreen Yau Abdullah, Sales Dir.

## BAKER HUGHES INCORPORATED

3900 Essex Lane, Ste. 1200, Houston, TX, 77027

Tel: (713) 439-8600    Fax: (713) 439-8699    www.bakerhughes.com

*Develop and apply technology to drill, complete and produce oil and natural gas wells; provide separation systems to petroleum, municipal, continuous process and mining industries.*

**Baker (M) SDN Bhd., Warehouse No.11, Kemaman Supply Base, Kemaman, Terengganu Darul Iman 240 Malaysia**

Tel: 60-9-863-1224  Fax: 60-9-863-1287

**Baker (M) SDN Bhd., 10A 10th Fl. Plaza Ampang City 332-A, Jalan Ampang, 50450 Kuala Lumpur, Malaysia**

Tel: 60-3-457-6777  Fax: 60-3-457-8688

**Baker Hughes INTEQ, Warehouse No. 7 Asian Supply Base, PO Box 82014, 87030 Lubuan, Malaysia**

Tel: 60-87-412350  Fax: 60-87-412530

**Baker Oil Tools, Lot 2065 Jalan Bultan, Piasau Industrial Estate, 98001 Miri Sarawak, Malaysia**

Tel: 60-85-657086  Fax: 60-85-650428

## BAKER PETROLITE CORPORATION

3900 Essex Lane, Houston, TX, 77027

Tel: (713) 599-7400    Fax: (713) 599-7592    www.bakerhughes.com/bapt/

*Mfr. specialty chemical treating programs, performance-enhancing additives and related equipment and services.*

**Petrolite (Malaysia) Sdn. Bhd., 2.12 Angkasa Raya Bldg. 2nd Fl., Jalan Ampang, 50450 Kuala Lumpur, Malaysia**

## BALTIMORE AIRCOIL CO., INC.

PO Box 7322, Baltimore, MD, 21227

Tel: (410) 799-6200    Fax: (410) 799-6416    www.baltimoreaircoil.com

*Mfr. evaporative heat transfer and ice thermal storage products.*

**BAC Cooling Tower Sdn. Bhd., 20-A Jalan Perusahaan, Prai Industrial Complex, 13600 Prai Malaysia**

## BANDAG INCORPORATED

2905 North Highway 61, Muscatine, IA, 52761

Tel: (319) 262-1400    Fax: (319) 262-1252    www.bandag.com

*Mfr./sale retread tires.*

**Bandag (Malaysia) Sdn. Bhd., Kuala Lumpur, Malaysia**

## BANK OF AMERICA CORPORATION

555 California Street, San Francisco, CA, 94104

Tel: (415) 622-3530     Fax: (415) 622-8467     www.bankofamerica.com

*Financial services.*

**Bank of America Malaysia Bhd., Wisma Goldhill 18th Fl., Jalan Raja Chulan, PO Box 10950, 50730 Kuala Lumpur, Malaysia**

Tel: 60-3-209-4201   Fax: 60-3-201-9087   Contact: Frederick Chin, SVP

## BARRINGER TECHNOLOGIES INC.

30 Technology Drive, Warren, NJ, 07059

Tel: (908) 222-9100     Fax: (908) 222-1557     www.barringer.com

*Provides advanced technology for security, law enforcement, including drug and explosive detectors.*

**Barringer Instruments Asia-Pacific, No. 34, Jalan Tun Mohd Fuad 2, Taman Tun Drive Ismail 60000 Kuala Lumpur, Malaysia**

Tel: 60-3-982-5623   Fax: 60-3-982-5653

## BATES WORLDWIDE INC.

405 Lexington Ave., New York, NY, 10174

Tel: (212) 297-7000     Fax: (212) 986-0270     www.batesww.com

*Advertising, marketing, public relations and media consulting.*

**Bates Malaysia, 11th Flr. Pernas International, Jalan Sultan Ismali, 50250 Kuala Lumpur, Malaysia**

Tel: 60-3-261-0290   Fax: 60-3-261-0327   Contact: Tony Taylor, Pres.

## BAUSCH & LOMB INC.

One Bausch & Lomb Place, Rochester, NY, 14604-2701

Tel: (716) 338-6000     Fax: (716) 338-6007     www.bausch.com

*Mfr. vision care products and accessories.*

**Bausch & Lomb Malaysia Syd. Bhd., 3/F Delteq Tech Lot 2A Jalan 243, Section 51A, 46100 Petaling Jaya Selangor, Malaysia**

## BAXTER HEALTHCARE CORPORATION

One Baxter Parkway, Deerfield, IL, 60015

Tel: (847) 948-2000     Fax: (847) 948-3948     www.baxter.com

*Pharmaceutical preparations, surgical/medical instruments and cardiovascular products.*

**Baxter Healthcare SA, PO Box 515, 10760 Penang, Malaysia**

## BDO SEIDMAN, LLP   BELGIUM

Two Prudential Plaza, 180 N. Stetson Ave., Ste. 2300, Chicago, IL, 60601

Tel: (312) 240-1236     Fax: (312) 240-3329     www.bdo.com

*International accounting and financial consulting firm.*

**BDO Binder, 15th Fl. Wisma Hamzah Kwong Hing, No.1 Leboh Ampang, 50100 Kuala Lumpur, Malaysia**

Tel: 60-3-232-3875   Fax: 60-3-201-9742   Contact: Tam Kim Leong

## BECHTEL GROUP INC.

50 Beale Street, PO Box 3965, San Francisco, CA, 94105-1895

Tel: (415) 768-1234     Fax: (415) 768-9038     www.bechtel.com

*General contractors in engineering and construction.*

**Bechtel International Corp., The Weld Tower 76, Jalan Raja Chulan, 50200 Kuala Lumpur, Malaysia**

## BELDEN, INC.

7701 Forsyth Blvd., Ste. 800, St. Louis, MO, 63015

Tel: (314) 854-8000     Fax: (314) 854-8001     www.belden.com

*Mfr. electronic wire and cable products.*

**Belden International Inc., 31A Jalan SS 2/64, 47300 Petaling Jaya, Selangor Darul Ehsan Malaysia**

## BENTLY NEVADA CORPORATION

1617 Water Street, PO Box 157, Minden, NV, 89423

Tel: (775) 782-3611    Fax: (775) 782-9259    www.bently.com

*Provides hardware, software, and services for machinery information and management systems.*

**Satupadu Sdn. Bhd., 210-1 Jln Ipoh, Kuala Lumpur, Malaysia**

## LOUIS BERGER INTERNATIONAL INC.

100 Halsted Street, East Orange, NJ, 07019

Tel: (201) 678-1960    Fax: (201) 672-4284    www.louisberger.com

*Consulting engineers, engaged in architecture, environmental and advisory services.*

**Louis Berger International Inc., PO Box 10, 50450 Kuala Lumpur, Malaysia**

## BEST WESTERN INTERNATIONAL

6201 North 24th Place, Phoenix, AZ, 85106

Tel: (602) 957-4200    Fax: (602) 957-5740    www.bestwestern.com

*International hotel chain.*

**Berjaya Redang Beach Resort, PO Box 126, 20928 Redan Island, Malaysia**

## BESTFOODS, INC.

700 Sylvan Ave., International Plaza, Englewood Cliffs, NJ, 07632-9976

Tel: (201) 894-4000    Fax: (201) 894-2186    www.bestfoods.com

*Consumer foods products; corn refining.*

**CPC/AJI (Malaysia) Sdn. Bhd., PO Box 56, 46700 Petaling Jaya, Selangor, Malaysia**

**Stamford Food Industries Sdn. Bhd., PO Box 531, 46760 Petaling Jaya, Selangor, Malaysia**

## BETZDEARBORN

4636 Somerton Road, PO Box 3002, Trevose, PA, 19053-6783

Tel: (215) 953-2568    Fax: (215) 953-5524    www.betzdearborn.com

*Mfr. water/wastewater and process system treatment chemicals and services.*

**Betz (Malaysia) Sdn. BHD, No. 10 Jln ss25/3 Taman, Mayang, Industrial Park, 47301 Petaling Jaya Malaysia**

## BICC GENERAL

4 Tesseneer Drive, Highland Heights, KY, 41076

Tel: (606) 572-8000    Fax: (606) 572-8444    www.generalcable.com

*Mfr., marketing and distribution of copper, aluminum and fiber optic wire and cable products for the communications, energy and electrical markets.*

**BICC General, Lot 2 Jalan Kawat 15/18, PO Box 7065, 40702 Shah Alam - Selangor Darul Ehsan, Malaysia**

## BLACK & VEATCH LLP

8400 Ward Pkwy., PO Box 8405, Kansas City, MO, 64114

Tel: (913) 339-2000    Fax: (913) 339-2934    www.bv.com

*Engineering, architectural and construction services.*

**TBV Engineers Sdn. Bhd., Projek Penghantaran dan Pembahagian Aras 1, Banunan Penghantaran TNB Ibupejabat, 129 Jl. Bangsar Peti surat 11003, 50732 Kuala Lumpur Malaysia**

Tel: 60-3-285-5156   Fax: 60-3-287-1615   Contact: Jeff Jenson

**TBV Power (Malaysia) Sdn. Bhd., Beg Berkunci No. 225, 42209 Kapar Selangor, Malaysia**

Tel: 60-3-350-9800   Fax: 60-3-350-8202   Contact: R.C. Kohlleppel

## BMC SOFTWARE, INC.

2101 City West Blvd., Houston, TX, 77042-2827

Tel: (713) 918-8800    Fax: (713) 918-8000    www.bmc.com

*Engaged in mainframe-related utilities software and services.*

**BMC Software, Level 33 Menara Maxis, Kuala Lumpur City Centre, 50088 Kuala Lumpur, Malaysia**

Tel: 603-380-8999   Fax: 603-380-8080

## BORDEN INC.

180 East Broad Street, Columbus, OH, 43215-3799

Tel: (614) 225-4000     Fax: (614) 220-6453     www.bordenfamily.com

*Mfr. packaged foods, consumer adhesives, housewares and industrial chemicals.*

**Borden Chemical (M) Sdn. Bhd., Tingkat 27, Menara Tun Razak, Jalan Raja Laut, 50350 Kuala Lumpur, Malaysia**

Tel: 60-3-293-4749   Fax: 60-3-293-8107

## THE BOSTON CONSULTING GROUP

Exchange Place, 31st Fl., Boston, MA, 02109

Tel: (617) 973-1200     Fax: (617) 973-1339     www.bcg.com

*Management consulting company.*

**The Boston Consulting Group, Letter Box No. 6 Level 17 Menara IMC, No. 8 Jalan Sultan Ismail, 50250 Kuala Lumpur West Malaysia, Malaysia**

Tel: 60-3-238-5770

## BOYDEN CONSULTING CORPORATION

364 Elwood Ave., Hawthorne, NY, 10502

Tel: (914) 747-0093     Fax: (914) 980-6147     www.boyden.com

*International executive search firm.*

**Boyden Associates Sdn. Bhd., Ste. 16-02 16th Fl. Menara Keck, 203 Jalan Bukit Bintang, 55100 Kuala Lumpur, Malaysia**

Tel: 60-3-244-1327

## BOZELL GROUP

40 West 23rd Street, New York, NY, 10010

Tel: (212) 727-5000     Fax: (212) 645-9173     www.bozell.com

*Advertising, marketing, public relations and media consulting.*

**Bozell Worldwide Sdn. Bhd., 18 Jalan ss 22/25, Damansara Jaya, 47400 Petaling Jaya Selangor, Malaysia**

Tel: 60-3-719-2332   Fax: 60-3-717-1841   Contact: Bob Seymour, CEO

## BRADY CORPORATION

6555 W. Good Hope Road, Milwaukee, WI, 53223

Tel: (414) 358-6600     Fax: (414) 358-6600     www.whbrady.com

*Mfr. industrial ID for wire marking, circuit boards; facility ID, signage, printing systems and software.*

**W.H. Brady Asia - Pacific Pte., Ltd., 15 1st Fl. Lorong Mayang Pasir 5, Bayan Baru, 11950 Penang, Malaysia**

Tel: 60-4-6440-233   Fax: 60-4-6447960

## BRANSON ULTRASONICS CORPORATION

41 Eagle Road, Danbury, CT, 06813-1961

Tel: (203) 796-0400     Fax: (203) 796-2285     www.branson-plasticsjoin.com

*Mfr. plastics assembly equipment, ultrasonic cleaning equipment.*

**Branson Ultrasonics (Malaysia) Sdn. Bhd., Lot 46 Jalan PJS 11/20, Bandar Sunway, 46150 Petaling Jaya Selangor, Malaysia**

## BRISTOL-MYERS SQUIBB COMPANY

345 Park Ave., New York, NY, 10154-0037

Tel: (212) 546-4000     Fax: (212) 546-4020     www.bms.com

*Pharmaceutical and food preparations, medical and surgical instruments.*

**Bristol-Myers (Malaysia) Sdn. Bhd., PO Box 1044, Jalan Semangat, 46860 Petaling Jaya Selango, Malaysia**

**Bristol-Myers Squibb Malaysia/Singapore, Lot 1839, Jalan Gergaji 15/14, 40000 Shah Alam, Malaysia**

## BROOKS AUTOMATION, INC.

15 Elizabeth Drive, Chelmsford, MA, 01824

Tel: (978) 262-2400    Fax: (978) 262-2500    www.brooks.com

*Mfr. tool automation products.*

**Brooks Automation Sdn., Unit 1 Lower Level 5, Hotel Equatorial - 1 Jalan Bukit Jambul, Bayan Lepas 11900 Penang, Malaysia**

Tel: 60-4-645-2485   Fax: 60-4-644-9277

## BRY-AIR INC.

10793 Street, Rt. 37 West, Sunbury, OH, 43074

Tel: (740) 965-2974    Fax: (740) 965-5470    www.bry-air.thomasregister.com

*Mfr. industrial dehumidifiers/auxiliary equipment for plastics industrial.*

**Bry-Air Malaysia, Lot 11 Jalan P/7 Bangi Industrial Estate, 43650 Bandar Baru Bangi, Selangor, Malaysia**

Tel: 60-3-825-6622   Fax: 60-3-825-9957

## BUDGET GROUP, INC.

125 Basin St., Ste. 210, Daytona Beach, FL, 32114

Tel: (904) 238-7035    Fax: (904) 238-7461    www.budgetrentacar.com

*Car and truck rental system.*

**Budget Rent A Car, 32 Jalan Imgi Ground Fl., Wisma Sps, 50450 Kuala Lumpur, Malaysia**

## LEO BURNETT, DIV. B-COM 3 GROUP

35 West Wacker Drive, Chicago, IL, 60601

Tel: (312) 220-5959    Fax: (312) 220-6533    www.bcom3group.com

*Engaged in advertising, marketing, media buying and planning, and public relations.*

**Leo Burnett Sdn. Bhd., 8th Fl. Wisma Damansara, Damansara Heights, Jalan Semantan, 50490 Kuala Lumpur Malaysia**

## BURSON-MARSTELLER

230 Park Ave., New York, NY, 10003-1566

Tel: (212) 614-4000    Fax: (212) 614-4262    www.bm.com

*Public relations/public affairs consultants.*

**Burson-Marsteller (Malaysia) Sdn. Bhd., 11th Fl. Bangunan Getah Asli, 148 Jalan Ampang, 50450 Kuala Lumpur, Malaysia**

Tel: 60-3-261-7900   Fax: 60-3-261-3828   Emp: 25

## BUSH BOAKE ALLEN INC.

7 Mercedes Drive, Montvale, NJ, 07645

Tel: (201) 391-9870    Fax: (201) 391-0860    www.bushboakeallen.com

*Mfr. aroma chemicals for fragrances and flavor products for seasonings.*

**Bush Boake Allen, No. 59 Jalan PJS 11/9, Bandar Sunway, 46150 Petaling Jaya Selangor, Darul Ehsan Malaysia**

Tel: 60-3-733-5297

## C&D TECHNOLOGIES

1400 Union Meeting Road, Blue Bell, PA, 19422

Tel: (215) 619-2700    Fax: (215) 619-7840    www.cdtechno.com

*Mfr./produce electrical power storage and conversion products and industrial batteries.*

**C&D Technologies, Kuala Lumpur, Malaysia**

## CABOT CORPORATION

75 State Street, Boston, MA, 02109-1807

Tel: (617) 345-0100    Fax: (617) 342-6103    www.cabot-corp.com

*Mfr. carbon blacks, plastics; oil and gas, information systems.*

**Malaysia Carbon Sdn. Bhd., Affiliates Div., PO Box 30, Port Dickson, Negeri Sembilan, Malaysia**

## CALTEX CORPORATION

125 East John Carpenter Fwy., Irving, TX, 75062-2794

Tel: (972) 830-1000      Fax: (972) 830-1081      www.caltex.com

*Petroleum products.*

**Caltex Oil Malaysia Ltd., Wisma Mirama, Jalan Wisma Putra, 50460 Kuala Lumpur, Malaysia**

## CARRIER CORPORATION

One Carrier Place, Farmington, CT, 06034-4015

Tel: (860) 674-3000      Fax: (860) 679-3010      www.carrier.com

*Mfr./distributor/services A/C, heating and refrigeration equipment.*

**Carrier (Malaysia) Sdn. Bhd., Petaling Jaya, Malaysia**

Tel: 60-3-777-2377   Fax: 60-3-777-5377

**Carrier Experts Service (Central Malaysia) Sdn. Bhd., Kuala Lumpur, Malaysia**

**Carrier Intl. Sdn. Bhd., Lot 4 Jln P/6, Bandhar Baru Bangi, 43650 Bangi Selangor, Malaysia**

## CATERPILLAR INC.

100 NE Adams Street, Peoria, IL, 61629-6105

Tel: (309) 675-1000      Fax: (309) 675-1182      www.cat.com

*Mfr. earth/material-handling and construction machinery and equipment and engines.*

**Turboservices SDN BHD, Kuala Lumpur, Malaysia**

## CCH INCORPORATED

2700 Lake Cook Road, Riverwoods, IL, 60015

Tel: (847) 267-7000      Fax: (800) 224-8299      www.cch.com

*Provides tax and business law information and software for accounting, legal, human resources, securities and health care professionals.*

**Commerce Clearing House (Malaysia) Sdn Bhd, 9/F Menara Weld, 76 Jalan Raja Chulan, 50200 Kuala Lumpur, Malaysia**

## CELLSTAR CORPORATION

1730 Briercroft Ct., Carrollton, TX, 75006

Tel: (972) 466-5000      Fax: (972) 466-0288      www.cellstar.com

*Provides wireless communications products.*

**CellStar AmTel Sdn. Bhd., No. 5 Jalan, PJS 7/19 Bader Sunway 46150, Petaling Jaya Selgangor, Earul Ehsan Malaysia**

## CENDANT CORPORATION

9 West 57th Street, New York, NY, 10019

Tel: (212) 413-1800      Fax: (212) 413-1918      www.cendant.com

*Membership-based, direct marketer offering shopping/travel/insurance and dining discount programs*

**Pacific Leisure Group, 2.5 and 2.6 Angkusu Roya Bldg., Jolan Ampang, 50450 Kuala Lumpur, Malaysia**

## CENTRAL NATIONAL-GOTTESMAN INC.

3 Manhattanville Road, Purchase, NY, 10577-2110

Tel: (914) 696-9000      Fax: (914) 696-1066

*Worldwide sales pulp and paper products.*

**CNG (M) SDN BHD., 15-2B Jalan Perdana 4/1, Pandan Perdana, 55300 Kuala Lumpur, Malaysia**

Tel: 60-3-981-0615   Fax: 60-3-981-0623   Contact: Karen Wong

## CH2M HILL INC.

6060 South Willow Drive, Greenwood Village, CO, 80111

Tel: (303) 771-0900      Fax: (303) 770-2616      www.ch2m.com

*Consulting engineers, planners, economists and scientists.*

**CH2M Hill, Kuala Lumpur, Malaysia**

Tel: 60-3-925-5288

## THE CHERRY CORPORATION

3600 Sunset Ave., PO Box 718, Waukegan, IL, 60087

Tel: (847) 662-9200      Fax: (847) 662-2990      www.cherrycorp.com

*Mfr. electrical switches, electronic keyboards, controls and displays.*

**Ken Top Sdn. Bhd., Suite 11.3 Menara Aik Hua, Changkat Raja Chulan, MAL-50200 Kuala Lumpur, Malaysia**

Tel: 60-3-2327285    Fax: 60-3-2327301

## CHESTERTON BINSWANGER INTERNATIONAL

Two Logan Square, 4th Floor, Philadelphia, PA, 19103-2759

Tel: (215) 448-6000      Fax: (215) 448-6238      www.cbbi.com

*Real estate and related services.*

**Chesterton Intl. (Malaysia) Sdn. Bhd., Plaza See Hoy Chan - Ste. 1804, Jalan Raja Chulan, 50200 Kuala Lumpur, Malaysia**

## CIGNA COMPANIES

One Liberty Place, Philadelphia, PA, 19192

Tel: (215) 761-1000      Fax: (215) 761-5511      www.cigna.com

*Insurance, invest, health care and other financial services.*

**Insurance Co. of North America, Apera-ULG Centre 8/F, Jalan Raja Chulan, Kuala Lumpur, Malaysia**

## CISCO SYSTEMS, INC.

170 West Tasman Drive, San Jose, CA, 95134-1706

Tel: (408) 526-4000      Fax: (408) 526-4100      www.cisco.com

*Develop/mfr./market computer hardware and software networking systems.*

**Cisco Systems (Malaysia) Sdn. Bhd., 14.05 Menara Multi-Purpose 14/F, Capital Sq., 8 Jalan Munshi, 50100 Abdullah Kuala Lumpur Malaysia**

Tel: 60-3-292-8398    Fax: 60-3-292-8389

## THE CIT GROUP

1211 Avenue of the Americas, New York, NY, 10036

Tel: (212) 536-1390      Fax: (212) 536-1912      www.citgroup.com

*Engaged in commercial finance.*

**Capital Corp Sdn. Bhd., Ste. 3 Level 18 Central Plaza, 34 Jalah Sultan Ismail 50250, Kuala Lumpur Malaysia**

Tel: 60-3-2474-593    Fax: 60-3-2474-590

## CITIGROUP, INC.

153 East 53rd Street, New York, NY, 10043

Tel: (212) 559-1000      Fax: (212) 559-3646      www.citigroup.com

*Provides insurance and financial services worldwide.*

**Citibank Berhad, 28 Medan Pasar, 50050 Kuala Lumpur, Malaysia**

Contact: Robert D. Matthews Jr.

## THE CLOROX COMPANY

1221 Broadway, PO Box 24305, Oakland, CA, 94623-1305

Tel: (510) 271-7000      Fax: (510) 832-1463      www.clorox.com

*Mfr. soap and detergents, and domestic consumer packaged products.*

**Clorox (Malaysia) Industries Sdn. Bhd, Kuala Lumpur, Malaysia**

**Clorox (Malaysia) Sdn. Bhd., Kuala Lumpur, Malaysia**

### THE COCA-COLA COMPANY

PO Drawer 1734, Atlanta, GA, 30301

Tel: (404) 676-2121     Fax: (404) 676-6792     www.coca-cola.com

*Mfr./marketing/distributor soft drinks, syrups and concentrates, juice and juice-drink products.*

**Coca-Cola Malaysia, Kuala Lumpur, Malaysia**

### COHU, INC.

5755 Kearny Vill Road, San Diego, CA, 92123

Tel: (858) 541-5194     Fax: (858) 277-0221     www.cohu.com

*Mfr. semiconductor test handling systems.*

**Delta Design, Hotel Equatorial Penang Office Suite No.1, Lower Level 2, 1 Jalan Bukit Jambul Bayan Lepas, 11900 Penang, Malaysia**

Tel: 60-4-646-8342   Fax: 60-4-646-8348

### COLGATE-PALMOLIVE COMPANY

300 Park Ave., New York, NY, 10022

Tel: (212) 310-2000     Fax: (212) 310-2919     www.colgate.com

*Mfr. pharmaceuticals, cosmetics, toiletries and detergents.*

**Colgate-Palmolive (Malaysia) Sdn. Bhd., Jalan Semangat/Bersatu, Section 13, Petaling Jaya, Selangor Malaysia**

### COMPAQ COMPUTER CORPORATION

20555 State Highway 249, PO Box 692000, Houston, TX, 77269-2000

Tel: (281) 370-0670     Fax: (281) 514-1740     www.compaq.com

*Develop/mfr. personal computers.*

**Compaq Computer (Malaysia) Sdn.Bhd., 5th Fl. Nestle House, 4 Lorong Persiaran Barat, 46200 Petaling Jaya Selangor, Malaysia**

Tel: 60-3-754-1122   Fax: 60-3-754-8600

### COMPUTER ASSOCIATES INTERNATIONAL INC.

One Computer Associates Plaza, Islandia, NY, 11788

Tel: (516) 342-5224     Fax: (516) 342-5329     www.cai.com

*Integrated business software for enterprise computing and information management, application development, manufacturing, financial applications and professional services.*

**Computer Associates (Malaysia) Sdn. Bhd., 32.03 Level 32 Menar Lion, 165 Jalan Ampang, 50450 Kuala Lumpur, Malaysia**

Tel: 60-3-261-1818

### CONAGRA INC.

One ConAgra Drive, Omaha, NE, 68102-5001

Tel: (402) 595-4000     Fax: (402) 595-4707     www.conagra.com

*Prepared/frozen foods, grains, flour, animal feeds, agro chemicals, poultry, meat, dairy products, including Healthy Choice, Butterball and Hunt's.*

**ConAgra Inc., Kuala Lumpur, Malaysia**

### CONOCO INC.

PO Box 2197, 600 N. Dairy Ashford, Houston, TX, 77252

Tel: (281) 293-1000     Fax: (281) 293-1440     www.conoco.com

*Oil, gas, coal, chemicals and minerals.*

**Petronas (JV) Conoco, Melaka, Malaysia**

## COOPER CAMERON CORPORATION

515 Post Oak Blvd., Ste.1200, Houston, TX, 77027

Tel: (713) 513-3300     Fax: (713) 513-3355     www.coopercameron.com

*Mfr. oil and gas industry equipment.*

**Cooper Cameron (Malaysia) Sdn. Bhd., Lot 1431 - Piasau Jaya Industrial Estate, 98000 Miri, Sarawak, Malaysia**

**Cooper Cameron (Malaysia) Sdn. Bhd., Jalan Utas 15/7, Kawasan Perusahaan Section 15, 40200 Shah Alam, Selangor Malaysia**

## COOPER INDUSTRIES INC.

6600 Travis Street, Ste. 5800, Houston, TX, 77002

Tel: (713) 209-8400     Fax: (713) 209-8995     www.cooperindustries.com

*Mfr./distributor electrical products, tools, hardware and automotive products, fuses and accessories for electronic applications and circuit boards.*

**Cooper Hand Tools, Penang, Malaysia**

## CORE LABORATORIES

6315 Windfern, Houston, TX, 77040

Tel: (713) 328-2673     Fax: (713) 328-2150     www.corelab.com

*Petroleum testing/analysis, analytical chemicals, laboratory and octane analysis instrumentation.*

**Core Laboratories (Malaysia) Sdn. Bhd., Lot 10B Jalan 51A/223, 46100 Petaling Jaya Selangor, Malaysia**

## CORN PRODUCTS INTERNATIONAL, INC.

6500 South Archer Ave., Bedford Park, IL, 60501-1933

Tel: (708) 563-2400     Fax: (708) 563-6852     www.cornproducts.com

*Produces corn products for ingredients corn starch corn oil and corn syrups.*

**Stamford Food Industries, 112 Jalan Semangat, 46100 Petaling Jaya, Selangor Darul Ehsan, Malaysia**
Tel: 60-3-7566988   Fax: 60-3-7573968

## CORNING INC.

One Riverfront Plaza, Corning, NY, 14831-0001

Tel: (607) 974-9000     Fax: (607) 974-8091     www.corning.com

*Mfr. glass and specialty materials, consumer products; communications, laboratory services.*

**Iwaki-Corning Malaysia Ltd., Jahore Baru, Malaysia**

## CROWN CORK & SEAL COMPANY, INC.

One Crown Way, Philadelphia, PA, 19154-4599

Tel: (215) 698-5100     Fax: (215) 698-5201     www.crowncork.com

*Mfr. metal and plastic packaging, including steel and aluminum cans for food, beverage and household products.*

**Crown Corks of Malaysia Sdn. Bhd., Jalan Tampoi, PO Box 252, Johor Bahru, Johor, Malaysia**

## CUTLER-HAMMER, DIV. EATON CORP.

173 Heatherdown Drive, Westerville, OH, 43082

Tel: (614) 882-3282     Fax: (614) 895-7111     www.cutlerhammer.com

*Mfr. electrical control products and power distribution equipment.*

**Tamco Cutler-Hammer Sdn. Bhd., PO Box 156, 46710 Petaling Jaya, Selangor, Malaysia**

## DAMES & MOORE GROUP

911 Wilshire Boulevard, Ste. 700, Los Angeles, CA, 90017

Tel: (213) 996-2200     Fax: (213) 996-2290     www.dames.com

*Engineering, environmental and construction management services.*

**Dames & Moore Malaysia Sdn. Bhd., 7/F Wisma Budiman, Jalan Raja Chulan, 50200 Kuala Lumpur, Malaysia**

## D'ARCY MASIUS BENTON & BOWLES INC. (DMB&B)

1675 Broadway, New York, NY, 10019

Tel: (212) 468-3622     Fax: (212) 468-2987     www.dmbb.com

*Full service international advertising and communications group.*

**DMB&B Asia Pacific,  6 Jalan Wan Kadir, Taman Tun Dr. Ismail, Kuala Lumpur, Malaysia**

## DATA GENERAL CORPORATION

4400 Computer Drive, Westboro, MA, 01580

Tel: (508) 898-5000     Fax: (508) 366-1319     www.dg.com

*Design, mfr. general purpose computer systems and peripheral products and services.*

**Data General Computers Sdn. Bhd.,  11 Jalan Pinang, 50450 Kuala Lumpur, Malaysia**

Tel: 60-3-269-6518

## DDB NEEDHAM WORLDWIDE INC.

437 Madison Ave., New York, NY, 10022

Tel: (212) 415-2000     Fax: (212) 415-3417     www.ddbn.com

*Advertising agency.*

**Naga DDB Needham DIK Sdn. Bhd.,  Jalan SS 6/8-#8, Kelana Jaya, 47301 Petaling Jaya, Selangor Malaysia**

## DELL COMPUTER CORPORATION

One Dell Way, Round Rock, TX, 78682-2222

Tel: (512) 338-4400     Fax: (512) 728-3653     www.dell.com

*Direct marketer and supplier of computer systems.*

**Dell Asia Pacific Sdn.,  805 - 8th Fl. Wisma HLA, Jalan Raja Chulan, 50200 Kuala Lumpur, Malaysia**

Tel: 60-3-201-8481   Fax: 60-3-201-8482   Contact: Albert Loo, Country Mgr.

## DELOITTE TOUCHE TOHMATSU INTERNATIONAL

1633 Broadway, New York, NY, 10019

Tel: (212) 492-4000     Fax: (212) 392-4154     www.deloitte.com

*Accounting, audit, tax and management consulting services.*

**Deloitte Touche Tohmatsu,  3 Changkat Raja Chulan, (PO Box 10093), 50200 Kuala Lumpur, Malaysia**

## THE DEXTER CORPORATION

1 Elm Street, Windsor Locks, CT, 06096

Tel: (860) 627-9051     Fax: (860) 627-7078     www.dexelec.com

*Mfr. polymer products, magnetic materials, biotechnology.*

**Dexter Electronic Materials,  BHD A506 - 5/F West Wing, Wisma Tractors 7 Jalan SS 16/1, 47500 Petaling Jaya Selangor, Malaysia**

## DHL WORLDWIDE EXPRESS

50 California Avenue, San Francisco, CA, 94111

Tel: (415) 677-6100     Fax: (415) 824-9700     www.dhl.com

*Worldwide air express carrier.*

**DHL Worldwide Express,  Lot 14 Jalan 51A/223, 46100 Petaling Jaya, Malaysia**

Tel: 60-3-757-1188

## DIMON INCORPORATED

512 Bridge Street, PO Box 681, Danville, VA, 24543-0681

Tel: (804) 792-7511     Fax: (804) 791-0377     www.dimon.com

*One of world's largest importer and exporters of leaf tobacco.*

**DIMON International, Tabak, B.V.,  902 Level 9 Uptown 2, 2 Jalan SS21/37, 47400 Petaling Jaya, Selangor Darul Ehsan Malaysia**

## DIONEX CORPORATION

1228 Titan Way, PO Box 3603, Sunnyvale, CA, 94086-3603

Tel: (408) 737-0700    Fax: (408) 730-9403    www.dionex.com

*Develop/mfr./market chromatography systems and related products.*

**Omega Malaysia, No. 36B Jalan Kuning,Taman Pelangi, 80400 Johor Bahru, Malaysia**

## DMC STRATEX NETWORKS, INC.

170 Rose Orchard Way, San Jose, CA, 95134

Tel: (408) 943-0777    Fax: (408) 944-1648    www.dmcstratexnetworks.com

*Designs, manufactures, and markets advanced wireless solutions for wireless broadband access.*

**DMC Stratex Networks, Unit 630 Block A, Kelana Centre Point, No. 3 Jalan SS 7/19, Kelana Jaya 47301 Petaling Jaya, Selangor Malaysia**

Tel: 60-3-703-43-42   Fax: 60-3-703-06-42

## DME COMPANY

29111 Stephenson Highway, Madison Heights, MI, 48071

Tel: (248) 398-6000    Fax: (248) 544-5705    www.dmeco.com

*Basic tooling for plastic molding and die casting.*

**Leong Bee & Soo Bee Sdn. Bhd., 1-3 Mac Callum St., PO Box 23, Pulau Pinang, Malaysia**

## DONNELLY CORPORATION

49 W. 3rd St., Holland, MI, 49423-2813

Tel: (616) 786-7000    Fax: (616) 786-6034    www.donnelly.com

*Mfr. fabricated, molded and coated glass products for the automotive and electronics industries.*

**Varitronix Sdn. Bhd. (JV), Plot No. 40 Phase 4, Bayan Lepas Free Industrial Zone, 11900 Penang Malaysia**

## DOUBLECLICK, INC.

450 West 33rd Street, New York, NY, 10001

Tel: (212) 683-0001    Fax: (212) 889-0062    www.doubleclick.net

*Engaged in online advertising.*

**Double-click, Ltd., C8-1 Megan Phileo Promenade, 189 Jalan Tun Razak 50400 Kuala Lumpur, Malaysia**

Tel: 60-3-460-5817

## DOVER CORPORATION

280 Park Ave., New York, NY, 10017-1292

Tel: (212) 922-1640    Fax: (212) 922-1656    www.dovercorporation.com

*Holding company for varied industries; assembly and testing equipment, oil-well gear and other industrial products.*

**Intermet Engineering Sdn. Bhd., Room A 14A Jalan Utara, 55100 Kuala Lumpur, Malaysia**

Tel: 60-3-984-8028   Fax: 60-3-984-2663

## THE DOW CHEMICAL COMPANY

2030 Dow Center, Midland, MI, 48674

Tel: (517) 636-1000    Fax: (517) 636-3228    www.dow.com

*Mfr. chemicals, plastics, pharmaceuticals, agricultural products, consumer products.*

**Dow Chemical Pacific Ltd., PO Box 714, Kuala Lumpur, Malaysia**

## DRAFT WORLDWIDE

633 North St. Clair Street, Chicago, IL, 60611-3211

Tel: (312) 944-3500    Fax: (312) 944-3566    www.draftworldwide.com

*Full service international advertising agency, engaged in brand building, direct and promotional marketing.*

**DraftWorldwide Sdn. Bhd., 15B Jalan SS22/23 Damansara Jaya, 47400 Petaling Jaya, Selangor Darul Ehsan, Kuala Lumpur Malaysia**

**DRAKE BEAM MORIN INC.**

101 Huntington Ave., Boston, MA, 02199

Tel: (617) 375-9500        Fax: (617) 267-2011        www.dbm.com

*Human resource management consulting and training.*

**DBM (Malaysia) Sdn. Bhd., 11.02 Level 11 Amoda Bldg., 22 Jalan Imbi, 55100 Kuala Lumpur, Malaysia**

**DUNHAM-BUSH INC.**

175 South Street, West Hartford, CT, 06110

Tel: (860) 548-3780        Fax: (860) 548-1703        www.dunham-bush.com

*Provides innovative solutions for the heating, air conditioning and refrigeration segments.*

**Kawasan Perusahaan Bangi, Kuala Lumpur, Malaysia**

**EAGLE GLOBAL LOGISTICS (EGL)**

15350 Vickery Drive, Houston, TX, 77032

Tel: (281) 618-3100        Fax: (281) 618-3100        www.eaglegl.com

*Ocean/air freight forwarding, customs brokerage, packing and wholesale, logistics management and insurance.*

**Circle Freight (Malaysia ) Sdn. Bhd., Plot 29, Bayan Lepas Free Industrial Zone, Phase 4, 11900 Penang Malaysia**

Tel: 60-4-643-8927    Fax: 60-4-643-6282

**Circle Freight (Malaysia ) Sdn. Bhd., 49B - 2nd Fl. Lorong Cunggah, 42000 Port Klang, Selangor, Malaysia**

Tel: 60-3-734-0070    Fax: 60-3-368-6712

**Circle Freight (Malaysia) Sdn. Bhd., Lot 14 Block C Cargo Forwarders Bldg., MAS Cargo Complex, Subang International Airport, Subang Selangor 47200 Malaysia**

Tel: 60-3-746-8770    Fax: 60-3-746-8767

**Circle Freight (Malaysia) Sdn. Bhd., 29 Jalan Permatang 12, Taman Desa Jaya, Johor Bahru 81100 Malaysia**

Tel: 60-7-353-5654    Fax: 60-7-353-5655

**EASTMAN CHEMICAL**

100 North Eastman Road, Kingsport, TN, 37660

Tel: (423) 229-2000        Fax: (423) 229-1351        www.eastman.com

*Mfr. plastics, chemicals, fibers.*

**Eastman Chemical Sdn., Lot 118/119 Gebeng Industrial Estate, PO Box 12, 26080 Balok Kuantn, Pahang Darul Makmur, Malaysia**

Tel: 60-9-583-8600    Fax: 60-9-583-9696    Contact: David C. Brubaker

**EASTMAN KODAK COMPANY**

343 State Street, Rochester, NY, 14650

Tel: (716) 724-4000        Fax: (716) 724-1089        www.kodak.com

*Develop/mfr. photo and chemicals products, information management/video/copier systems, fibers/plastics for various industry.*

**Kodak Malaysia Sdn. Bhd., Jalan Semangat, 46860 Petaling Jaya, Selangor Darul Ehsan Malaysia**

**EATON CORPORATION**

Eaton Center, 1111 Superior Ave., Cleveland, OH, 44114-2584

Tel: (216) 523-5000        Fax: (216) 479-7068        www.eaton.com

*Advanced technical products for transportation and industrial markets.*

**Tamco Cutler-Hammer Snd. Bhd., Lot 9D Jalan, Kemajuan 12/18, PO Box 156, Petaling Jaya Selangor, Malaysia**

## ECOLAB INC.

370 N. Wabasha Street, St. Paul, MN, 55102

Tel: (651) 293-2233     Fax: (651) 293-2379     www.ecolab.com

*Develop/mfr. premium cleaning, sanitizing and maintenance products and services for the hospitality, institutional, and residential markets.*

**Ecolab Ltd., Kuala Lumpur, Malaysia**

Tel: 60-3-983-2145

## EDELMAN PUBLIC RELATIONS WORLDWIDE

200 East Randolph Drive, 62nd Fl., Chicago, IL, 60601

Tel: (312) 240-3000     Fax: (312) 240-0596     www.edelman.com

*International independent public relations firm.*

**Edelman PR Worldwide, Wisma Damansara 2nd Fl., Jalan Semantan, Damansara Heights, 50490 Kuala Lumpur, Malaysia**

Tel: 60-3-255-2277    Fax: 60-3-255-0234    Contact: Indira Nair, Mng. Dir.

## J.D. EDWARDS & COMPANY

One Technology Way, Denver, CO, 80237

Tel: (303) 334-4000     Fax: (303) 334-4970     www.jdedwards.com

*Computer software products.*

**Sunway Computer Services, Jalan Lagun Timur, Bandar Sunway, 46150 Petaling Haya Selangor, Malaysia**

Tel: 60-3-735-9996    Fax: 60-3-735-7656

## ELECTRONIC DATA SYSTEMS CORPORATION (EDS)

5400 Legacy Dr., Plano, TX, 75024

Tel: (972) 605-6000     Fax: (972) 605-2643     www.eds.com

*Provides professional services; management consulting, e.solutions, business process management and information solutions.*

**Electronic Data Systems IT Services (M) Sdn. Bhd., Petronas Twin Towers - Tower 2 Level 63, Kuala Lumpur City Centre, 50088 Kuala Lumpur Malaysia**

## EMC CORPORATION

35 Parkwood Drive, Hopkinton, MA, 01748-9103

Tel: (508) 435-1000     Fax: (508) 435-8884     www.emc.com

*Designs/supplies intelligent enterprise storage and retrieval technology for open systems, mainframes and midrange environments.*

**EMC Computer Systems (FE) Ltd., Ste. 19.03 Level 19 Wisma Goldhill 67, Jalan Raja Chulan, 50200 Kuala Lumpur, Malaysia**

Tel: 60-3-469-9488

## EMERSON ELECTRIC COMPANY

8000 W. Florissant Ave., PO Box 4100, St. Louis, MO, 63136

Tel: (314) 553-2000     Fax: (314) 553-3527     www.emersonelectric.com

*Electrical and electronic products, industrial components and systems, consumer, government and defense products.*

**Emerson Electric Sdn. Bhd., 7/F/Blk.B - Menara PKNS-PJ, Jalan Yong Shook Lin, 46050 Petaling Jaya, Selangor Malaysia**

Tel: 60-3-754-6811

## EMERY WORLDWIDE

One Lagoon Drive, Ste. 400, Redwood City, CA, 94065

Tel: (650) 596-9600     Fax: (650) 596-7901     www.emeryworld.com

*Freight transport, global logistics and air cargo.*

**Emery Worldwide (M) Sdn Bhd, 21 Jalan Mokek 2/5 Taman Mokek, 81100 Johor Bahru, Mohore Darul Takzim, Malaysia**

## ERNST & YOUNG, LLP

787 Seventh Ave., New York, NY, 10019

Tel: (212) 773-3000    Fax: (212) 773-6350    www.eyi.com

*Accounting and audit, tax and management consulting services.*

**Ernst & Young, PO Box 10068, Kuala Lumpur, Malaysia**

Tel: 60-3-2423884   Fax: 3-2443492   Contact: Lee Hock Khoon

## EURO RSCG WORLDWIDE

350 Hudson Street, New York, NY, 10014

Tel: (212) 886-2000    Fax: (212) 886-2016    www.eurorscg.com

*International advertising agency group.*

**EURO RSCG Partnership, 801C Lvl 8 Tower C, No.5 Jln., SS21/39 Damansara Uptown, Petaling Jaya Selangor, Malaysia**

## EXE TECHNOLOGIES, INC.

8787 N. Stemmonds Fwy., Dallas, TX, 75247-3702

Tel: (214) 775-6000    Fax: (214) 775-0911    www.exe.com

*Provides a complete line of supply chain management execution software for WMS.*

**EXE Technologies, Inc. Malaysia Sdn. Bhd., 55-2 Jalan USJ 9/5S, Subang Business Centre, UEP Subang Jaya, Selangor Malaysia**

Tel: 60-3-724-2385   Fax: 60-3-724-2384

## EXPEDITORS INTERNATIONAL OF WASHINGTON INC.

1015 Third Avenue, 12th Fl., Seattle, WA, 98104-1182

Tel: (206) 674-3400    Fax: (206) 682-9777    www.expd.com

*Air/ocean freight forwarding, customs brokerage, international logistics solutions.*

**EI Freight Sdn. Bhd., Unit 4 Block B MAS Cargo Comples, Jalan Garuda Bayan Lepas, 11900 Penang, Malaysia**

Tel: 60-3-703-6370   Fax: 60-3-703-5890

## EXXON MOBIL CORPORATION

5959 Las Colinas Blvd., Irving, TX, 75039-2298

Tel: (972) 444-1000    Fax: (972) 444-1882    www.exxon.com

*Petroleum exploration, production, refining; mfr. petroleum and chemicals products; coal and minerals.*

**Exxon Mobil, Inc., Kompleks Antarabangs, Jalan Sultan Ismail, 50250 Kuala Lumpur, Malaysia**

**Exxon Mobil, Inc., Rexplas Sdn. Bhd., 1 1/2 Mile Batu Pahat, PO Box 508, 86009 Kluang Johur Malaysia**

**Exxon Mobil, Inc., 9/F Menara Esso, Kuala Lumpur City Centre, 50088 Kuala Lumpur Malaysia**

## FAIR, ISAAC AND COMPANY, INC.

200 Smith Ranch Road, San Rafael, CA, 94903

Tel: (415) 472-2211    Fax: (415) 492-5691    www.fairisaac.com

*Mfr. automated systems for credit and loan approvals.*

**Software Alliance, Plaza Damansara, Block B 4/F, Kuala Lumpur 50490, Malaysia**

Tel: 60-3-461-6432

## FARR COMPANY

2201 Park Place, El Segundo, CA, 90245

Tel: (310) 727-6300    Fax: (310) 643-9086    www.farrco.com

*Mfr. air and liquid filtration equipment.*

**QF Filter Sdn. Bhd. (JV), Block C Lot 1560, Kampung Jaya, Batu 12 1/2 Sungai Buloh, 47000 Selangor Darul Ehsan, Malaysia**

### FEDERAL-MOGUL CORPORATION

26555 Northwestern Highway, PO Box 1966, Southfield, MI, 48034

Tel: (248) 354-7700     Fax: (248) 354-8983     www.federal-mogul.com

*Mfr./distributor precision parts for automobiles, trucks, farm and construction vehicles.*

**Federal-Mogul World Trade Sdn. Bhd., Brunei, Malaysia**

### FERRO CORPORATION

1000 Lakeside Ave., Cleveland, OH, 44114-7000

Tel: (216) 641-8580     Fax: (216) 696-5784     www.ferro.com

*Mfr. Specialty chemicals, coatings, plastics, colors, refractories.*

**Ferro Far East Company, 303B Jalan Mahkota, Taman Maluri, Cheras, 55100 Kuala Lumpur Malaysia**

Tel: 60-3-985-8969   Fax: 60-3-985-9826   Contact: S.M. Kok, Mgr.

### FISHER SCIENTIFIC INC.

1 Liberty Lane, Hampton, NH, 03842

Tel: (603) 929-5911     Fax: (603) 929-0222     www.fisher1.com

*Mfr. science instruments and apparatus, chemicals, reagents.*

**Fisher General Scientific (M) Sdn. Bhd., No. 7 Jalan 222, Section 51A, Petaling Jaya, 46100 Selangor Darul Ehsan, Malaysia**

Tel: 60-3-757-5433   Fax: 60-3-757-1768

### FISHER-ROSEMOUNT

8000 Maryland Ave., Ste. 500, Clayton, MO, 63105-4755

Tel: (314) 746-9900     Fax: (314) 746-9974     www.frco.com

*Mfr. industrial process control equipment.*

**Transwater Tenaga Sdn. Bhd., No. 81- 83 & 85 Jalan SS 25/2, Taman Bukit Emas, 47301 Petaling Jaya, Selangor Darul Ehsan Malaysia**

Tel: 60-3-703-3131   Fax: 60-3-703-7575

### FLEXTRONICS INC. INTERNATIONAL

2241 Lundy Ave., San Jose, CA, 95131-1822

Tel: (408) 428-1300     Fax: (408) 428-0420     www.flextronics.com

*Contract manufacturer for electronics industry.*

**Flextronics International, Lot Plot 37, Kawason Perindustrian Senai, 81400 Senai Johore Malaysia**

Tel: 60-7-599-1968

**Flextronics International, No. 8688 (Lot 19/20) Kawasen MIEL, Batu Berendam FTZ Phase III, 7530 Melaka, Malaysia**

### FLUKE CORPORATION

6920 Seaway Blvd. PO Box 9090, Everett, WA, 98203

Tel: (425) 347-6100     Fax: (425) 356-5116     www.fluke.com

*Mfr. handheld, electronic test tools for maintenance of electronic equipment.*

**Fluke Corporation, Wisma Mah Sing Suite 6 (2nd Fl.), 163 Jalan Sungai Besi, 57100 Kuala Lumpur, Malaysia**

Tel: 60-3-233-1215   Fax: 60-3-223-1218

### FLUOR CORPORATION

One Enterprise Drive, Aliso Viejo, CA, 92656-2606

Tel: (949) 349-2000     Fax: (949) 349-5271     www.flour.com

*Engineering and construction services.*

**Fluor Daniel Malaysia Sdn. Bhd., 30 Menara Olympia, 8 Jalan Raja Chulan, 50200 Kuala Lumpur, Malaysia**

Tel: 60-3-232-9460   Fax: 60-3-232-9450

## FMC CORPORATION

200 E. Randolph Drive, Chicago, IL, 60601

Tel: (312) 861-6000     Fax: (312) 861-6141     www.fmc.com

*Produces chemicals and precious metals, mfr. machinery, equipment and systems for industrial, agricultural and government use.*

**FMC Petroleum Equipment (Malaysia) Sdn. Bhd., Kuala Lumpur, Malaysia**

**SOFEC, Inc., Menara IMC, No. 8 Jalan Sultan Ismail, 50250 Kuala Lumpur, Malaysia**

## FORD MOTOR COMPANY

One American Road, Dearborn, MI, 48121

Tel: (313) 322-3000     Fax: (313) 322-9600     www.ford.com

*Mfr./sales motor vehicles.*

**AMIM Holdings Sdn. Bhd., GPO Box 12612, 50784 Kuala Lumpur, Malaysia**

## FOSTER WHEELER CORPORATION

Perryville Corporate Park, Clinton, NJ, 08809-4000

Tel: (908) 730-4000     Fax: (908) 730-4100     www.fwc.com

*Manufacturing, engineering and construction.*

**Foster Wheeler Malaysia Sdn. Bhd., Box No. 28 - Wisma Selangor Dridging, 142A Jalan Ampang, 50450 Kuala Lumpur, Malaysia**

Tel: 60-3-263-3108

## FOUR WINDS INTERNATIONAL GROUP

1500 SW First Ave., Ste. 850, Portland, OR, 97201-2013

Tel: (503) 241-2732     Fax: (503) 241-1829     www.vanlines.com.au

*Transportation of household goods and general cargo and third party logistics.*

**Four Winds Malaysia, 656 (2/F) 4th Mile, Jalan Ipoh Rd., 51200 Kuala Lumpur, Malaysia**

Tel: 60-3-621-7175   Fax: 60-3-621-4258   Contact: Edgar S. Pereira, Gen. Mgr.

## FRANKLIN COVEY COMPANY

2200 W. Parkway Blvd., Salt Lake City, UT, 84119-2331

Tel: (801) 975-1776     Fax: (801) 977-1431     www.franklincovey.com

*Provides productivity and time management products and seminars.*

**Franklin Covey Malaysia, J-4 Bangunan Khas, Lorong 8 1E, 46050 Petaling Jaya Selangor, Malaysia**

Tel: 60-3-758-6418   Fax: 60-3-755-2589

**Leadership Resources Malaysia Pte., G-2 - Bangunan Khas, Lorong 8/1E, 46050 Petaling Jaya Selangor, Malaysia**

## THE FRANKLIN MINT

US Route 1, Franklin Center, PA, 19091

Tel: (610) 459-6000     Fax: (610) 459-6880     www.franklinmint.com

*Design/marketing collectibles and luxury items.*

**Franklin Porcelain Sdn. Bhd., Kulim Industrial Estate, 09000 Kulim Kedah, Malaysia**

## FRITZ COMPANIES, INC.

706 Mission Street, Ste. 900, San Francisco, CA, 94103

Tel: (415) 904-8360     Fax: (415) 904-8661     www.fritz.com

*Integrated transportation, sourcing, distribution and customs brokerage services.*

**Fritz Air Freight (Malaysia) Sdn. Bhd., Lot 1 & 2 Cargo Agent Bonded Complex, Subang International Airport, 47200 Kuala Lumpur, Malaysia**

**FTI-Fritz Transportation (Malaysia) Sdn. Bhd., Level 50 Unit 12, Komtar Tower, 10000 Penang, Malaysia**

## H.B. FULLER COMPANY

1200 Willow Lake Blvd., Vadnais Heights, MN, 55110

Tel: (651) 236-5900    Fax: (651) 236-5898    www.hbfuller.com

*Mfr./distributor adhesives, sealants, coatings, paints, waxes, sanitation chemicals.*

**H.B. F. Adhesives (Malaysia) Sdn. Bhd., Suite E407 4th Floor, East Tower Wisma Consplant, No. 2 Jalan SS 16/4, 47500 Petaling Jaya, Malaysia**

Tel: 60-3-731-8790    Fax: 60-3-731-8835

## GENERAL ELECTRIC CAPITAL CORPORATION

260 Long Ridge Road, Stamford, CT, 06927

Tel: (203) 357-4000    Fax: (203) 357-6489    www.gecapital.com

*Financial, property/casualty insurance, computer sales and trailer leasing services.*

**Employers Reinsurance Corp. (ERC), Ste. 10.01-10.02 - 10th Fl. Wisma PJD, 80 Jalan Raja Chulan, 52100 Kuala Lumpur, Malaysia**

Tel: 60-3-206-8098    Fax: 60-3-206-6990

## GENERAL ELECTRIC COMPANY

3135 Easton Turnpike, Fairfield, CT, 06431

Tel: (203) 373-2211    Fax: (203) 373-3131    www.ge.com

*Diversified manufacturing, technology and services.*

**GE FANUC Automation, 803C Block B Kelana Business, 47301 Petaling Jaya Selangor, Malaysia**

Tel: 60-3-582-2566    Fax: 60-3-582-0803

**General Electric Co., Attn: Malyasia Office, 3135 Easton Turnpike, Fairfield CT 06431**

Tel: 518-438-6500

**GETSCO, 25th Fl. UBN Tower, 50250 Kuala Lumpur, Malaysia**

Tel: 60-3-238-2344    Fax: 60-3-202-1129

## GEO LOGISTICS CORPORATION

1521 E. Dyer Rd., Santa Ana, CA, 92705

Tel: (714) 513-3000    Fax: (714) 513-3120    www.geo-logistics.com

*Freight forwarding, warehousing and distribution services, specializing in heavy cargo.*

**GeoLogistics (Malaysia) Sdn Bhd., 17 Jalan PJS 11/8, Bandar Sunway, 46150 Petaling Jaya, Selangor Darul Ehsan Malaysia**

Tel: 60-3-732-9355    Fax: 60-3-732-9330

**GeoLogistics (Malaysia) Sdn Bhd., 2A Persiaran Silibin Utara, Jalan Jelapang 30020 Ipoh, Perak Darul Ridzuan, West Malaysia Malaysia**

Tel: 60-5-527-9435    Fax: 60-5-527-9129

## GETZ BROS & COMPANY, INC.

150 Post Street, Ste. 500, San Francisco, CA, 94108-4750

Tel: (415) 772-5500    Fax: (415) 772-5659    www.getz.com

*Diversified manufacturing, marketing and distribution services and travel services.*

**Getz Bros. & Co. Malaysia, No. 1 Jalan PJS 11/16, Sunway Industrial Park, 46150 Petaling Jaya, Selangor Malaysia**

Tel: 60-3-738-3221    Fax: 60-3-738-3220    Contact: Tony Pritzker, VP    Emp: 7

## THE GILLETTE COMPANY

Prudential Tower Building, Boston, MA, 02199

Tel: (617) 421-7000    Fax: (617) 421-7123    www.gillette.com

*Develop/mfr. personal care/use products: blades and razors, toiletries, cosmetics, stationery.*

**Gilco (Malaysia) Sdn. Bhd., Selangor, Malaysia**

**Gillette (Malaysia) Sdn. Bhd., Selangor, Malaysia**

**Interpena Sdn. Bhd., Selangor, Malaysia**

**Jafra Cosmeticos (Malaysia) Sdn. Bhd., Selangor, Malaysia**

Moorgate Industries Sdn. Bhd., Selangor, Malaysia

## GILSON INC.

3000 W. Beltline Hwy, PO Box 620027, Middleton, WI, 53562-0027

Tel: (608) 836-1551          Fax: (608) 831-4451          www.gilson.com

*Mfr. analytical/biomedical instruments.*

Chemopharm Sdn. Bdh., No. 20 - Jalan SS 2/66, 47300 Petaling Jaya Selangor, Malaysia

## GLOBAL SILVERHAWK

2190 Meridian Park Blvd., Ste G, Concord, CA, 94520

Tel: (925) 681-2889          Fax: (925) 681-2755          www.globalsilverhawk.com

*International moving and forwarding.*

Global Silverhawk, No.1 Jalan Penghulu Ul/73, Batu Tiga Industrial Park, 40150 Shah Alam, Selangor Malaysia

Tel: 60-3-705-4322    Contact: Kamar Wahab, Gen. Mgr.

## THE GOODYEAR TIRE & RUBBER COMPANY

1144 East Market Street, Akron, OH, 44316

Tel: (330) 796-2121          Fax: (330) 796-1817          www.goodyear.com

*Mfr. tires, automotive belts and hose, conveyor belts, chemicals; oil pipeline transmission.*

Goodyear Malaysia Bhd., PO Box 7049, 40914 Shah Alam, Selangor Darul Ehsan, Malaysia

## W. R. GRACE & COMPANY

7500 Grace Drive, Columbia, MD, 21044

Tel: (410) 531-4000          Fax: (410) 531-4367          www.grace.com

*Mfr. specialty chemicals and materials: packaging, health care, catalysts, construction, water treatment/process.*

W.R. Grace (Malaysia) Sdn. Bhd., 7 Lorong 1, Off Jalan Balakong, 43200 Cheras Jaya, Selangor Darul Ehsan Malaysia

Tel: 60-3-904-6133   Fax: 60-3-904-7322

W.R. Grace Specialty Chemicals (Malaysia) Sdn. Bhd., Lot 114&115 Gebeng Industrial Estate, 26080 Kuantan Pahang Darul Makmur, Malaysia

Tel: 60-9-583-6225   Fax: 60-9-583-6642

## GREY GLOBAL GROUP

777 Third Ave., New York, NY, 10017

Tel: (212) 546-2000          Fax: (212) 546-1495          www.grey.com

*International advertising agency.*

Grey Malaysia, Empire Tower 37/F, 182 Jalan Tun Razak, 50400 Kuala Lumpur, Malaysia

## HALLIBURTON COMPANY

500 North Akard Street, Ste. 3600, Dallas, TX, 75201-3391

Tel: (214) 978-2600          Fax: (214) 978-2685          www.halliburton.com

*Engaged in diversified energy services, engineering and construction.*

Halliburton Ltd., 12/F Menara Tan & Tan, 207 Jalan Tun Razak, 50400 Kuala Lumpur, Malaysia

Tel: 60-3-263-4567   Fax: 60-3-263-7128

## HARCOURT GENERAL, INC.

27 Boylston St., Chestnut Hill, MA, 02467

Tel: (617) 232-8200          Fax: (617) 739-1395          www.harcourtgeneral.com

*Publisher of educational materials.*

Harcourt General Asia Pte.Ltd., 28A Jalan USJ 10/1B, 47620 Subang Jaya, Selangor Darul Ehsan, Malaysia

Tel: 60-3-37-731-1537   Fax: 60-3-731-5446   Contact: Wee Sang Jong, Mgr.

## HARRIS CORPORATION

1025 West NASA Blvd., Melbourne, FL, 32919

Tel: (407) 727-9100     Fax: (407) 727-9344     www.harris.com

*Mfr. communications and information-handling equipment, including copying and fax systems.*

**BBS Electronics (M) Sdn Bhd., Lot 2-01 Wisma Denka, 41 Lorong Adu Siti, 10400 Penang Malaysia**

Tel: 60-4-228-0433   Fax: 60-4-228-1710

## HARSCO CORPORATION

PO Box 8888, 350 Poplar Church Rd., Camp Hill, PA, 17001-8888

Tel: (717) 763-7064     Fax: (717) 763-6424     www.harsco.com

*Metal reclamation and mill services, infrastructure and construction and process industry products.*

**Taylor-Wharton Asis (M) Sdn. Bhd., PO Box 7193, 40706 Shah Alam, Selangor Darul Ehsan, Malaysia**

## HELLER FINANCIAL INC.

500 West Monroe Street, Chicago, IL, 60661

Tel: (312) 441-7000     Fax: (312) 441-7367     www.hellerfin.com

*Financial services.*

**Heller Factoring (M), Kuala Lumpur, Malaysia**

## HEWITT ASSOCIATES LLC

100 Half Day Road, Lincolnshire, IL, 60069

Tel: (847) 295-5000     Fax: (847) 295-7634     www.hewitt.com

*Employee benefits consulting firm.*

**Hewitt Associates Sdn. Bhd., Ste. 2.01 Wisma E&C, No. 2, Lorong Dungun Kiri -Damansara Heights, 50490 Kuala Lumpur**
**Malaysia**

Tel: 60-3-254-4088

## HEWLETT-PACKARD COMPANY

3000 Hanover Street, Palo Alto, CA, 94304-1185

Tel: (650) 857-1501     Fax: (650) 857-5518     www.hp.com

*Mfr. computing, communications and measurement products and services.*

**Hewlett-Packard Sales (Malaysia) Sdn. Bhd., Wisma Cyclecarri, 288 Jalan Raja Laut, 50350 Kuala Lumpur, Malaysia**

## HILTON HOTELS CORPORATION

9336 Civic Center Drive, Beverly Hills, CA, 90210

Tel: (310) 278-4321     Fax: (310) 205-7880     www.hiltonhotels.com

*International hotel chain: Hilton International, Vista Hotels and Hilton National Hotels.*

**Hilton International Company, PO Box 10577, Jalan Sultan Ismail, 50718 Kuala Lumpur, Malaysia**

## HOLIDAY INN (BASS RESORTS) WORLDWIDE, INC.

3 Ravinia Drive, Ste. 2900, Atlanta, GA, 30346-2149

Tel: (770) 604-2000     Fax: (770) 604-5403     www.holidayinn.com

*Hotels, restaurants and casinos.*

**Holiday Inn, 23111 Jalan Tunku Abdul Rahman, Kuching, Sarawak, Malaysia**

## HONEYWELL INTERNATIONAL INC.

101 Columbia Road, Morristown, NJ, 07962

Tel: (973) 455-2000     Fax: (973) 455-4807     www.honeywell.com

*Develop/mfr. controls for home and building, industry, space and aviation.*

**Honeywell Engineering Sdn. Bhd., Wisma CSA - 2/F, No. 4 Jalan Bersatu 13/4, 46200 Petaling Jaya, Selangor Malaysia**

Tel: 60-3-758-4988   Fax: 60-3-758-8722

## HORWATH INTERNATIONAL ASSOCIATION

415 Madison Ave., New York, NY, 10017

Tel: (212) 838-5566     Fax: (212) 838-3636     www.horwath.com

*Public accountants and auditors.*

**Horwath & Hals & Oh, 17th Fl. UMBC Annexe Bldg., Jalan Sulaiman, 50000 Kuala Lumpur, Malaysia**

## HOWMEDICA OSTEONICS, INC.

359 Veterans Blvd., Rutherford, NJ, 07070

Tel: (201) 507-7300     Fax: (201) 935-4873     www.howmedica.com

*Mfr. of maxillofacial products (orthopedic implants).*

**Howmedica - Medimax, Kuala Lumpur, Malaysia**

Tel: 60-3-793-8389

## HUBBELL INCORPORATED

584 Derby Milford Road, Orange, CT, 06477

Tel: (203) 799-4100     Fax: (203) 799-4208     www.hubbell.com

*Electrical wiring components.*

**Harvey Hubbell Sdn. Bhd., 14A Jalan SS 4C/5, Taman Rasa Sayang, 47301 Petaling Jaya Selangor, Malaysia**

## HUNTSMAN CORPORATION

500 Huntsman Way, Salt Lake City, UT, 84108

Tel: (801) 532-5200     Fax: (801) 536-1581     www.huntsman.com

*Mfr./sales specialty chemicals, industrial chemicals and petrochemicals.*

**Huntsman Tioxide, 5/F Wisma Avon, 13A Jalan 219, 46100 Petaling Jaya, Selangor Darul Ehsan, Malaysia**

## HYATT CORPORATION

200 West Madison Street, Chicago, IL, 60606

Tel: (312) 750-1234     Fax: (312) 750-8578     www.hyatt.com

*International hotel management.*

**Hyatt Regency Johor Bahru Hotel, Jalan Sungai Chat, PO Box 222, 80720 Johor Bahru, Johor Darul Taksim, Malaysia**

Tel: 60-7-22-1234   Fax: 60-6-223-2718

## IBM CORPORATION

New Orchard Road, Armonk, NY, 10504

Tel: (914) 765-1900     Fax: (914) 765-7382     www.ibm.com

*Information products, technology and services.*

**IBM World Trade Corp., Plaza IBM, No. 1 Jalan Tun Mohd Fuad, Taman Tun DR. Ismail, 60000 Kuala Lumpur, Malaysia**

Tel: 60-3-7177788   Fax: 60-37172188

## ICO, INC.

11490 Westheimer, Ste. 1000, Houston, TX, 77077

Tel: (281) 721-4200     Fax: (281) 721-4203     www.icoinc.com

*Engaged in processing petrochemicals and reconditioning oil well drilling equipment.*

**ICO Sanko Manufacturer (M) Sdn Bhd, Batu Pahat, Malaysia**

## IMG (INTERNATIONAL MANAGEMENT GROUP)

1360 East Ninth Street, Ste. 100, Cleveland, OH, 44114

Tel: (216) 522-1200      Fax: (216) 522-1145      www.imgworld.com

*Manages athletes, sports academies and real estate facilities worldwide.*

**IMG Artists Asia, Petronas Twin Towers #2 - Level 61, Kuala Lumpur City Centre, Kuala Lumpur 50088, Malaysia**

Tel: 60-3-2166-2166   Fax: 60-3-2162-6634

## INDEL-DAVIS INC.

4401 S. Jackson Ave., Tulsa, OK, 74107

Tel: (918) 587-2151      Fax: (918) 446-1583      www.indel-davis.com

*Mfr. exploration supplies to seismic industrial.*

**Indel-Davis Malaysia, Kuala Lumpur, Malaysia**

## INFONET SERVICES CORPORATION

2100 East Grand Ave., El Segundo, CA, 90245-1022

Tel: (310) 335-2600      Fax: (310) 335-4507      www.infonet.com

*Provider of Internet services and electronic messaging services.*

**Infonet Malaysia, 3rd Fl. Block A Wisma Semantan, Jalan Gelenggang, Damansara Heights, 50490 Kuala Lumpur Malaysia**

Tel: 60-3-208-8576   Fax: 60-3-254-0675

## INFORMIX CORPORATION

4100 Bohannon Drive, Menlo Park, CA, 95025

Tel: (650) 926-6300      Fax: (650) 926-6593      www.informix.com

*Designs and produces database management software, connectivity interfaces and gateways, and other computer applications.*

**Informix Sdn Bhd, MCB Plaza Ground Fl., No. 6 Cangkat Raja, Chulan, 50200 Kuala Lumpur Malaysia**

Tel: 60-3-238-5292

## INGRAM MICRO INC.

PO Box 25125, 1600 E. St. Andrew Place, Santa Ana, CA, 92799

Tel: (714) 566-1000      Fax: (714) 566-7940      www.ingrammicro.com

*Engaged in wholesale distribution of microcomputer products.*

**Ingram Micro Malaysia, 15-15C - Lorong Bukit Kecil, Taman Sri Nibong 11900 Penang, Malaysia**

**Ingram Micro Malaysia, 29 Jalan Dedap 7, Taman Johor Jaya, 81100 Johor Bahru Malaysia**

**Ingram Micro Malaysia, 56 and 56A Jalan Kota Laksamana 1/1, Taman Kota Laksamana, 75200 Malacca Malaysia**

**Ingram Micro Malaysia Sdn. Bhd., Lot 116 Jalan Semangat, 46200 Petaling Jaya Selango, Darul Ehsan Malaysia**

## INTER-CONTINENTAL HOTELS

3 Ravina Drive, Suite 2900, Atlanta, GA, 30346-2149

Tel: (770) 604-2000      Fax: (770) 604-5403      www.interconti.com

*Worldwide hotel and resort accommodations.*

**Forum Fairland Kuala Lumpur, Jalan Walter Grenier, 55100 Kuala Lumpur, Malaysia**

Tel: 60-3-248-6888   Fax: 60-3-242-4881

## INTERGRAPH CORPORATION

One Madison Industrial Park, Huntsville, AL, 35894-0001

Tel: (256) 730-2000    Fax: (256) 730-7898    www.intergraph.com

*Develop/mfr. interactive computer graphic systems.*

**Intergraph Systems (Malaysia) Sdn. Bhd., 46-1 Jalan Telawi, Bangsar Baru, 59100 Kuala Lumpur, Malaysia**

Tel: 60-3-28-33504    Fax: 60-3-28-33512

## INTERNATIONAL SPECIALTY PRODUCTS, INC.

1361 Alps Rd., Wayne, NJ, 07470

Tel: (877) 389-3083    Fax: (973) 628-4117    www.ispcorp.com

*Mfr. specialty chemical products.*

**ISP (Singapore) Pte. Ltd., Worldwide Business Centre, 3A 1st Floor Block 1 Sec 13 Jalan 13/50, 40100 Shah Alam Selangor, Malaysia**

Tel: 60-3-553-1448    Fax: 60-3-552-8311

## INTRUSION.COM, INC.

1101 East Arapaho Road, Richardson, TX, 75081

Tel: (972) 234-6400    Fax: (972) 234-1467    www.intrusion.com

*Mfr. security software.*

**Intrusion.Com, Malaysia, The Weld Tower Ste. 76-7-3, 76 Jalan Raja Chulan, 50200 Kuala Lumpur, Malaysia**

## IONICS INC.

65 Grove Street, Watertown, MA, 02172

Tel: (617) 926-2500    Fax: (617) 926-4304    www.ionics.com

*Mfr. desalination equipment.*

**Ionics Enersave Engineering Sdn. Bhd., Selangor, Malaysia**

## J. WALTER THOMPSON COMPANY

466 Lexington Ave., New York, NY, 10017

Tel: (212) 210-7000    Fax: (212) 210-6944    www.jwt.com

*International advertising and marketing services.*

**JWT-Kuala Lumpur, Kuala Lumpur, Malaysia**

## JABIL CIRCUIT, INC.

10560 Ninth St. North, St. Petersburg, FL, 33716

Tel: (727) 557-9749    Fax: (727) 579-8529    www.jabil.com

*Mfr. printed circuit boards, electronic components and systems.*

**Jabil Circuit Malaysia, 56 Hilir Sungai Keluang 1, Bayan Lepas Ind. Park - Phase 4, 11900 Penang, Malaysia**

Tel: 60-4-642-7975

## JDA SOFTWARE GROUP, INC.

14400 N. 87th St., Scottsdale, AZ, 85260-3649

Tel: (480) 308-3000    Fax: (480) 308-3001    www.jda.com

*Developer of information management software for retail, merchandising, distribution and store management.*

**JDA Software Malaysia, 68 Jalan SS 2/24, 7300 Petaling Jaya, Selangor Malaysia**

Tel: 60-3-7873-9473    Fax: 60-3-7875-3292

## JOHN HANCOCK FINANCIAL SERVICES, INC.

John Hancock Place, Boston, MA, 02117

Tel: (617) 572-6000    Fax: (617) 572-9799    www.johnhancock.com

*Life insurance services.*

**John Hancock Malaysia, Kuala Lumpur, Malaysia**

## JOHNSON & JOHNSON

One Johnson & Johnson Plaza, New Brunswick, NJ, 08933

Tel: (732) 524-0400        Fax: (732) 214-0334        www.jnj.com

*Mfr./distributor/R&D pharmaceutical, health care and cosmetic products.*

**Johnson & Johnson Medical Mfg., Snd. Bhd., PO Box 7188, 40706 Selangor Darul Ehsan, Malaysia**

**Johnson & Johnson Sdn. Bhd., PO Box 8017, Petaling Jaya, Selangor Darul Ehsan, Malaysia**

## S C JOHNSON & SON INC.

1525 Howe St., Racine, WI, 53403

Tel: (414) 260-2000        Fax: (414) 260-2133        www.scjohnsonwax.com

*Home, auto, commercial and personal care products and specialty chemicals.*

**S.C. Johnson & Pte. Ltd., PO Box 1079, Jalan Semangat, Petaling Jaya, Selangor Malaysia**

## JOHNSON CONTROLS INC.

5757 N. Green Bay Ave., PO Box 591, Milwaukee, WI, 53201-0591

Tel: (414) 228-1200        Fax: (414) 228-2077        www.johnsoncontrols.com

*Mfr. facility management and control systems and auto seating.*

**Johnson Controls (m) Sdn. Bhd., Ste. 2.2 (2/F) No. 2A Jalan 243, Section 51A, 46100 Petaling Jaya, Selanger Darul Ehsan Malaysia**

Tel: 60-3-774-8040    Fax: 60-3-744-1180    Contact: Francis Liew, Branch Mgr.

## JONES LANG LASALLE

101 East 52nd Street, New York, NY, 10022

Tel: (212) 688-8181        Fax: (212) 308-5199        www.jlw.com

*International marketing consultants, leasing agents and property management advisors.*

**Jones Lang Wootton, Kuala Lumpur, Malaysia**

## A.T. KEARNEY INC.

222 West Adams Street, Chicago, IL, 60606

Tel: (312) 648-0111        Fax: (312) 223-6200        www.atkearney.com

*Management consultants and executive search.*

**A. T. Kearney, Inc., Level & Wisma Hong Leong, 18 Jalan Perak, 5045 Kuala Lumpur Malaysia**

Tel: 60-3-263-3388

## KELLOGG BROWN & ROOT INC.

PO Box 3, Houston, TX, 77001

Tel: (713) 676-3011        Fax: (713) 676-8695        www.halliburton.com

*Engaged in technology-based engineering and construction.*

**Kellogg Brown & Root (Malaysia) Sdn. Bhd., MRR Project Eng Office Level 52 Twr 2, Petronas Twin Towers, Kuala Lumpur City Centre, Kuala Lumpur, 50088 Malaysia**

## KELLOGG COMPANY

One Kellogg Square, PO Box 3599, Battle Creek, MI, 49016-3599

Tel: (616) 961-2000        Fax: (616) 961-2871        www.kelloggs.com

*Mfr. ready-to-eat cereals and convenience foods.*

**Kellogg Malaysia, Attn: Malaysian Office, One Kellogg Square, PO Box 3599, Battle Creek MI 49016-3599**

## THE KENDALL COMPANY (TYCO HEALTHCARE)

15 Hampshire Street, Mansfield, MA, 02048

Tel: (508) 261-8000        Fax: (508) 261-8542        www.kendalhq,com

*Mfr. medical disposable products, home health care products and specialty adhesive products.*

**Lovytex Sdn. Bhd., Lot 8 Jalan Suasa, 42500 Telok Panglima Garang, Selangor Darul Ehsan, Malaysia**

**Mediquip Sdn. Bhd., Padang Lati - Mukim Paya, PO Box 25, 01700 Kangar Perlis, Malaysia**

## KENNAMETAL INC.

State Rte. 981, Latrobe, PA, 15650

Tel: (724) 539-5000     Fax: (724) 539-4710     www.kennametal.com

*Tools, hard carbide and tungsten alloys for metalworking industry.*

**Kennametal Hertel Singapore Pte. Ltd. - Malaysian Office, 29 G Jalan PJS 11/2 Subang Indah, 46000 Petaling Jaya Selangor, Malaysia**

Tel: 60-3-732-8806   Fax: 60-3-732-5080

## KEPNER-TREGOE INC.

PO Box 704, Princeton, NJ, 08542-0740

Tel: (609) 921-2806     Fax: (609) 497-0130     www.kepner-tregoe.com

*Management consulting; specializing in strategy formulation, problem solving, decision making, project management, and cost reduction.*

**Kepner-Tregoe (m) Sdn. Bhd., Unit 607 Block D, Phileo Damansara 1 No. 9 16/11, 46350 Petaling Jaya, Malaysia**

Tel: 60-3-460-9128   Fax: 60-3-460-9138

## KIMBERLY-CLARK CORPORATION

351 Phelps Drive, Irving, TX, 75038

Tel: (972) 281-1200     Fax: (972) 281-1435     www.kimberly-clark.com

*Mfr./sales/distribution of consumer tissue, household and personal care products.*

**Kimberly-Clark Malaysia Sdn. Bhd., Petaling Jaya, Selangor, Malaysia**

## KNOWLES ELECTRONICS INC.

1151 Maplewood Drive, Itasca, IL, 60131

Tel: (630) 250-5100     Fax: (630) 250-0575     www.knowleselectronics.com

*Microphones and loudspeakers.*

**Knowles Electronics, Sdn. Bhd., Plot 104 Leduhraya Kg. Jawa , Beyan Lepas Industrial Estate, 11900 Penang Malaysia**

Tel: 60-4-837-466   Fax: 60-4-837-446

## KORN/FERRY INTERNATIONAL

1800 Century Park East, Los Angeles, CA, 90067

Tel: (310) 843-4100     Fax: (310) 553-6452     www.kornferry.com

*Executive search; management consulting.*

**Korn/Ferry International Sdn. Bhd., UBN Tower 6/F, Letter Box 33, 10 Jalan P. Ramlee, 50250 Kuala Lumpur, Malaysia**

Tel: 60-3-238-1655   Fax: 60-3-238-8276

## KPMG INTERNATIONAL LLP

345 Park Avenue, New York, NY, 10022

Tel: (201) 307-7000     Fax: (201) 930-8617     www.kpmg.com

*Accounting and audit, tax and management consulting services.*

**KPMG Management Consulting Sdn Bhd, Semantan, 12 Jalan Gelenggang, Damansara Heights, 50490 Kuala Lumpur Malaysia**

**KPMG Peat Marwick/KPMG - Desa Megat & Co., Lai Piang Kee Bldg., Jalan Pryer, Sandakan, 90000 Sabah, Malaysia**

**KPMG Peat Marwick/KPMG - Desa Megat & Co., Ste. 1.01 1st Fl. Wisma MBF, 37C Jalan Melarum, 80000 Johore Bahru, Malaysia**

**KPMG Peat Marwick/KPMG - Desa Megat & Co., Wisma Perdana, Jalan Dungun, Damansara Heights, 50490 Kuala Lumpur, Malaysia**

Tel: 60-3-255-3388   Fax: 60-3-255-0971   Contact: Abdul Jabbar Majid, Sr. Ptnr.

**KPMG Peat Marwick/KPMG - Desa Megat & Co., 64-66 Jolan Yang, Kalsom, 30250 Ipoh Perak, Malaysia**

## LEARONAL INC.

272 Buffalo Ave., Freeport, NY, 11520

Tel: (516) 868-8800    Fax: (516) 868-8824    www.learonal.com

*Specialty chemicals for the printed circuit board, semiconductor, connector and metal finishing industries.*

**LeaRonal (SE Asia)Ltd., 56 1/F Jalan Mahsuri, 11900 Bayan Baru Penang, Malaysia**

Tel: 60-4-642-3937   Fax: 60-4-642-3940   Contact: K.G. Ng, Branch Mgr.

## LEVI STRAUSS & COMPANY

1155 Battery St., San Francisco, CA, 94111-1230

Tel: (415) 544-6000    Fax: (415) 501-3939    www.levistrauss.com

*Mfr./distributor casual wearing apparel.*

**Levi Strauss (Malaysia) Sdn. Bhd., Lot 3.20 3/F Wisma SPS, 32 Jalan Lmbi, 55100 Kuala Lumpur, Malaysia**

Tel: 60-3-241-6296   Fax: 60-3-248-0113

## LEXMARK INTERNATIONAL

1 Lexmark Centre Dr., Lexington, KY, 40550

Tel: (606) 232-2000    Fax: (606) 232-1886    www.lexmark.com

*Develop, manufacture, supply of printing solutions and products, including laser, inkjet, and dot matrix printers.*

**Lexmark Asia Pacific Corporation Inc., 208 Level 2 Block A, Kelana Business Centre 97, Jalan SS7/2, Kelana Jaya 47301 Petaling Jaya, Malaysia**

Tel: 60-3-7492-0862   Fax: 60-3-7492-0863

## LHS GROUP INC.

6 Concourse Pkwy., Ste. 2700, Atlanta, GA, 30328

Tel: (770) 280-3000    Fax: (770) 280-3099    www.lhsgroup.com

*Provides multilingual software for telecommunications carriers.*

**LHS Asia Pacific Sdn. Bhd., Level 3 CGC Bldg., 97 Jalan SS 7/2, 47301 Petaling Jaya Selangor, Malaysia**

Tel: 60-3-704-9100   Fax: 60-3-704-1779

## LIBERTY MUTUAL GROUP

175 Berkeley Street, Boston, MA, 02117

Tel: (617) 357-9500    Fax: (617) 350-7648    www.libertymutual. com

*Provides workers' compensation insurance and operates physical rehabilitation centers and provides risk prevention management.*

**Liberty Mutual Group, Kuala Lumpur, Malaysia**

## LIGHTBRIDGE, INC.

67 South Bedfore Street, Burlington, MA, 01803

Tel: (781) 359-4000    Fax: (781) 359-4500    www.lightbridge.com

*Engaged in consulting for telecom companies.*

**Lightbridge Asia/Pacific, Inc., Suite 530 - Wisma Goldhill, 67 Jalan Raja Chulan, 50200 Kuala Lumpur, Malaysia**

Tel: 60-3-236-5166   Fax: 60-3-236-51

## ELI LILLY & COMPANY

Lilly Corporate Center, Indianapolis, IN, 46285

Tel: (317) 276-2000    Fax: (317) 277-6579    www.lilly.com

*Mfr. pharmaceuticals and animal health products.*

**Eli Lilly Malaysia Sdn. Bhd., Menara Cold Storage #7-4, Letter Box 21 Section 14, Jl. Semangat, 46100 Petaling Jaya Selangor Malaysia**

Tel: 60-3-755-1268   Fax: 60-3-757-9144

## LILLY INDUSTRIES

200 W. 103rd St., Indianapolis, IN, 46290

Tel: (317) 814-8700     Fax: (317) 814-8880     www.lillyindustries.com

*Mfr. industrial coatings and specialty chemicals.*

**Lilly Industries Malaysia,  Lot No. 756 Jalan Haji Sitar, Off Jalan Kapar, 42100 Klang Selangor Darul Ehsan, Malaysia**

Tel: 60-3-344-1331   Fax: 60-3-344-0033

## ARTHUR D. LITTLE, INC.

25 Acorn Park, Cambridge, MA, 02140-2390

Tel: (617) 498-5000     Fax: (617) 498-7200     www.adlittle.com

*Management, environmental, health and safety consulting; technical and product development.*

**Arthur D. Little (Malaysia) Sdn. Bhd.,  Office Ste. 19-16-3A, UOA Centre, 19 Jalan Pinang, 50450 Kuala Lumpur, Malaysia**

## LOCKHEED MARTIN CORPORATION

6801 Rockledge Drive, Bethesda, MD, 20817

Tel: (301) 897-6000     Fax: (301) 897-6652     www.imco.com

*Design/mfr./management systems in fields of space, defense, energy, electronics and technical services.*

**Lockheed Martin Global, Inc., Ste. 520 Level 5 Wisma Goldhill, 67 Jalan Raja Chulan, 50200 Kuala Lumpur Malaysia**

**Lockheed Martin Intl. Ltd.,  UBN Tower 10th Floor Letter Box 123, 10 Jalan P. Ramlee, 50250 Kuala Lumpur, Malaysia**

Tel: 60-3-202-2363   Fax: 60-3-202-2361

## LOCTITE CORPORATION

1001 Trout Brook Crossing, Rocky Hill, CT, 06067-3910

Tel: (860) 571-5100     Fax: (860) 571-5465     www.loctite.com

*Mfr./sale industrial adhesives, sealants and coatings..*

**Loctite (Malaysia) Sdn. Bhd.,  5 Jalan 2/118B, Desa Tun Razak Industrial Park, 56000 Cheras Kuala Lumpur, Malaysia**

## LOWE LINTAS & PARTNERS WORLDWIDE

One Dag Hammarskjold Plaza, New York, NY, 10017

Tel: (212) 605-8000     Fax: (212) 605-4705     www.interpublic.com

*Full-service, integrated marketing communications company/advertising agency.*

**Ammirati Puris Lintas Malaysia,  Wisma Perdana Jalan Dungun, Damansara Heights, 50490 Kuala Lumpur, Malaysia**

Tel: 60-3-254-5122   Fax: 60-3-255-9985   Contact: Kharudin Rahim

## LTX CORPORATION

LTX Park, University Ave., Westwood, MA, 02090

Tel: (617) 461-1000     Fax: (617) 326-4883     www.ltx.com

*Design/mfr. computer-controlled semiconductor test systems.*

**LTX Malaysia,  Kuala Lumpur, Malaysia**

## LUCENT NPS (NETWORK CARE PROFESSIONAL SERVICES)

1213 Innsbruck Dr., Sunnyvale, CA, 94089

Tel: (408) 542-0100     Fax: (408) 542-0101     www.ins.com

*Provides computer network support, designs networking systems, manages equipment purchase performance and software solutions.*

**Lucent NetworkCare,  31/F Tower 2 Petronas Twin Towers, Kuala Lumpur City Centre, 50088 Kuala Lumpur, Malaysia**

## LUCENT TECHNOLOGIES, INC.

600 Mountain Ave., Murray Hill, NJ, 07974-0636

Tel: (908) 582-3000     Fax: (908) 582-2576     www.lucent.com

*Design/mfr. wide range of public and private networks, communication systems and software, data networking systems, business telephone systems and microelectronics components.*

**Lucent Technologies Malaysia, Level 5 Amoda, 22 Jalan Imbi, 55100 Kuala Lumpur, Malaysia**

Tel: 60-3-247-2233   Fax: 60-3-241-5145   Contact: Eu Meng Khng, PR Mgr.

## MALLINCKRODT INC.

675 McDonnell Blvd., St. Louis, MO, 63134

Tel: (314) 654-2000     Fax: (314) 654-5380     www.mallinckrodt.com

*Distributes health care products and specialty pharmaceuticals.*

**Mallinckrodt Malaysia, 14 Jalan PJS 11/22, 46150 Bandar Sunway, Selangor DE Malaysia**

Tel: 60-3-731-4323   Fax: 60-3-731-4304

## MARKEM CORPORATION

150 Congress Street, Keene, NH, 03431

Tel: (603) 352-1130     Fax: (603) 357-1835     www.markem.com.

*Mfr./sales of industrial marking, print machinery and hot stamping foils.*

**Markem Pte.Ltd., Unit P2-06 Building Information Centre, Lot 2 Jalan 243/51A, 46100 Petaling Jaya Selagor Malaysia**

Tel: 60-3-773-8533   Fax: 60-3-773-8530

## MARLEY COOLING TOWER COMPANY

7401 West 129th Street, Overland Park, KS, 66213

Tel: (913) 664-7400     Fax: (913) 664-7641     www.marleyct.com

*Cooling and heating towers and waste treatment systems.*

**Marley Cooling Tower Asia Pacific Sdn Bhd, Suite 904 Block B Kelana Business Centre, No. 97 Jalan SS 7/2, Kelana Jaya, 47301 Petaling Jaya, Selangor Malaysia**

Tel: 60-3-582-1333   Fax: 60-3-582-1322

## MARRIOTT INTERNATIONAL INC.

10400 Fernwood Rd., Bethesda, MD, 20817

Tel: (301) 380-3000     Fax: (301) 380-5181     www.marriott.com

*Hotel services.*

**JW Marriott Hotel, Kuala Lumpur, Malaysia**

Tel: 60-3-291-8584

## MARSH & McLENNAN COS INC.

1166 Ave. of the Americas, New York, NY, 10036-2774

Tel: (212) 345-5000     Fax: (212) 345-4808     www.marshmac.com

*Insurance agents/brokers, pension and investment management consulting services.*

**J&H Marsh & McLennan Insurance Brokers (M) SDN BHD, 2.07 2 Fl. Wisma Denko, 41 Aboo Sittee Lane, 10400 Penang Malaysia**

Tel: 60-4-229-7547   Fax: 60-4-228-8493

**J&H Marsh & McLennan Insurance Brokers (M) SDN BHD, 19/F West Block, Wisma Selagor Dredging, 142-C Jalan Ampang, 50450 Kuala Lumpur Malaysia**

Tel: 60-3-261-3455   Fax: 60-3-261-2230   Contact: Razak Shakor

## MATTEL INC.

333 Continental Blvd., El Segundo, CA, 90245-5012

Tel: (310) 252-2000     Fax: (310) 252-2179     www.mattelmedia.com

*Mfr. toys, dolls, games, crafts and hobbies.*

**Mattel, Kuala Lumpar, Malaysia**

## McCANN-ERICKSON WORLDGROUP

750 Third Ave., New York, NY, 10017

Tel: (212) 984-3644     Fax: (212) 984-2629     www.mccann.com

*International advertising and marketing services.*

**McCann-Erickson (Malaysia) Sdn. Bhd.,  Menara Aik Hua, Jalan Hicks, 50200 Kuala Lumpur, Malaysia**

## McDONALD'S CORPORATION

McDonald's Plaza, Oak Brook, IL, 60523

Tel: (630) 623-3000     Fax: (630) 623-7409     www.mcdonalds.com

*Fast food chain stores.*

**McDonald's Corp.,  Kuala Lumpur, Malaysia**

## THE McGRAW-HILL COMPANIES

1221 Ave. of the Americas, New York, NY, 10020

Tel: (212) 512-2000     Fax: (212) 512-2703     www.mccgraw-hill.com

*Books, magazines, information systems, financial service, publishing and broadcast operations.*

**McGraw-Hill Malaysia Sdn. Bhd.,  3 Jalan PJS 11/14 Bandar Sunway, 46150 Petaling Jaya, Selangor Malaysia**

Tel: 60-3-731-6933   Fax: 60-3-731-3308

## McKINSEY & COMPANY

55 East 52nd Street, New York, NY, 10022

Tel: (212) 446-7000     Fax: (212) 446-8575     www.mckinsey.com

*Management and business consulting services.*

**McKinsey & Company,  Ste. 2212 Renaissance Hotel, Corner of Jalan Sultan Ismail & Jalan Ampang, 50450 Kuala Lumpur, Malaysia**

Tel: 60-3-262-9595   Fax: 60-3-262-9585

## MECHANICAL DYNAMICS, INC.

2301 Commonwealth Blvd., Ann Arbor, MI, 48105

Tel: (734) 994-3800     Fax: (734) 994-6418     www.adams.com

*Mfr. Adams prototyping software to automotive industry.*

**CAD-IT Consultants (M) Sdn. Bhd.,  Kelena Centre Point 607 Block A, No. 3 Jalan SS 7/19 Kelena Jaya, 47301 Petaling Jaya Selangor, Malaysia**

## MECHANICAL SYSTEMS INC.

4110 Romaine, Greensboro, NC, 27407

Tel: (336) 292-4956     Fax: (336) 294-7182

*Mechanical and electrical contractors.*

**Mechanical Systems (Malaysia) Sdn. Bhd.,  Paramount Gardens, Petaling Jaya, Kuala Lumpur, Malaysia**

## MEMC ELECTRONIC MATERIALS, INC.

501 Pearl Drive, St. Peters, MO, 63376

Tel: (636) 474-5500     Fax: (636) 474-5161     www.memc.com

*Mfg. and distribution of silicon wafers.*

**MEMC Electronic Materials Sdn. Bhd.,  No.1 Jalan 8/2 Sungeway Subang, 47300 Petaling Jaya, Selangor Daral Ehsan, Malaysia**

Tel: 60-3-777-3277   Fax: 60-3-774-5246

## THE MENTHOLATUM COMPANY, INC.

707 Sterling Drive, Orchard Park, NY, 14127-1587

Tel: (716) 677-2500      Fax: (716) 674-3696      www.mentholatum.com

*Mfr./distributor proprietary medicines, drugs, OTC's.*

**Rohto-Mentholatum (Malaysia) Sdn. Bhd., 818 Block A Kelana Business Centre, 97 Jalan SS 7/2, 47301 Kelana Jaya, Malaysia**

Tel: 60-3-582-1388    Fax: 60-3-582-1688

## M-I

PO Box 48242, Houston, TX, 77242-2842

Tel: (713) 739-0222      Fax: (713) 308-9503      www.midf.com

*Drilling fluids.*

**M-I Drilling Fluids, 13 & 13A Plaza Ampang City, Jalan Ampang, 50450 Kuala Lumpur, Malaysia**

Tel: 60-3-4579649

## MICRO AGE, INC.

2400 South MicroAge Way, Tempe, AZ, 85282-1896

Tel: (480) 366-2000      Fax: (480) 966-7339      www.microage.com

*Computer systems integrator, software products and telecommunications equipment.*

**Fullmark Micro Pte. Ltd., Kuala Lumpur, Malaysia**

## MICROSOFT CORPORATION

One Microsoft Way, Redmond, WA, 98052-6399

Tel: (425) 882-8080      Fax: (425) 936-7329      www.microsoft.com

*Computer software, peripherals and services.*

**Microsoft (Malaysia) Sdn. Bhd., Level 15 Menara Amcorp, 18 Persiaran Barat, 46050 Petaling Jaya Selangor Darul Ehsan, Malaysia**

Tel: 60-3-757-2266    Fax: 60-3-757-2265

## MOLEX INC.

2222 Wellington Court, Lisle, IL, 60532

Tel: (630) 969-4550      Fax: (630) 969-1352      www.molex.com

*Mfr. electronic, electrical and fiber optic interconnection products and systems, switches, application tooling.*

**Molex Malaysia Sdn. Bhd. (KL),, 8A Jalan Dedap 17, Taman Johor Jaya, 81100 Johor Bahru Johor, Malaysia**

## J. P. MORGAN CHASE & CO. INC.

World Headquarters, 270 Park Ave., New York, NY, 10017

Tel: (212) 270-6000      Fax: (212) 622-9030      www.jpmorganchase.com

*Provides integrated financial solutions for institutions and individuals worldwide, including asset management, investment banking and commercial banking.*

**J. P. Morgan Chase & Co., 26th & 27th Fl. Menara Dion, Jalan Sultan Ismail, 50250 Kuala Lumpur, Malaysia**

Tel: 60-3-270-4101    Fax: 60-3-270-4105

**J. P. Morgan Chase & Co., 5/F Main Office Tower, Financial Park Labuan Complex, Jalan Merdeka, 87000 Labuan Malaysia**

Tel: 60-87-424384    Fax: 60-87-424390

## MOTOROLA, INC.

1303 East Algonquin Road, Schaumburg, IL, 60196

Tel: (847) 576-5000      Fax: (847) 538-5191      www.motorola.com

*Mfr. communications equipment, semiconductors and cellular phones.*

**Motorola International Inc., 2nd Fl. Wisma Damansara, Jalan Semantan, 50490 Kuala Lumpur, Malaysia**

Tel: 60-3-255-7746    Fax: 60-3-255-0219

Motorola Malaysia Sdn. Bhd., No. 2 Jalan SS 8/2, 47300 Petaling Jaya, Selangor, Malaysia

Tel: 60-3-773-1133 Fax: 60-3-773-1355

Motorola Military & Aerospace Electronics Inc., Sungei Way Free Trade Zone, Singei Way, 47300 Subang Selangor, Malaysia

Tel: 60-3-773-1133 Fax: 60-3-773-1075

Motorola Semiconductor Sdn. Bhd., Lot 122 Senawang Ind. Estate, Seremban, Negeri Sembilan, Malaysia

Tel: 60-6-677-3088 Fax: 60-6-677-4062

## NABISCO HOLDINGS, CORP.

7 Campus Drive, Parsippany, NJ, 07054

Tel: (973) 682-5000 Fax: (973) 503-2153 www.nabisco.com

*Mfr. consumer packaged food products and tobacco products.*

R.J. Reynolds Tobacco Sdr. Bhd., Jalan Perbadanan 3/5, Kelangor, Malaysia

## NATIONAL SEMICONDUCTOR CORPORATION

2900 Semiconductor Dr., PO Box 58090, Santa Clara, CA, 95052-8090

Tel: (408) 721-5000 Fax: (408) 739-9803 www.national.com

*Engaged in producing computer-on-a-chip solutions for the information highway.*

National Semiconductor, Batu Berendan Free Trade Zone, 75350 Melaka, Malaysia

Tel: 60-6-32-5644 Fax: 60-6-32-5650 Contact: C. S. Liu Emp: 2500

## NATIONAL STARCH AND CHEMICAL COMPANY

10 Finderne Ave., Bridgewater, NJ, 08807-3300

Tel: (908) 685-5000 Fax: (908) 685-5005 www.nationalstarch.com

*Mfr. adhesives and sealants, resins and specialty chemicals, electronic materials and adhesives, food products, industry starch.*

National Starch & Chemical (M) Sdn. Bhd., Lot 8 & 10 Jalan Tukul 16/5, PO Box 7019, 40904 Shah Alam, Selangor Darul Ehsan Malaysia

Tel: 60-3-559-1104 Fax: 60-3-550-9718

## NORDSON CORPORATION

28601 Clemens Road, Westlake, OH, 44145-4551

Tel: (440) 892-1580 Fax: (440) 892-9507 www.nordson.com

*Mfr. industry application equipment, sealants and packaging machinery.*

Nordson (Mayalsia) Sdn. Bhd., 3 Jalan SS-13/6C, Subang Jaya Industrial Estate, Subang Jaya, 47500 Selangor Darul Ehsan Malaysia

Tel: 60-3-734-6281 Fax: 60-3-735-2977

## NORGREN

5400 S. Delaware Street., Littleton, CO, 80120-1663

Tel: (303) 794-2611 Fax: (303) 795-9487 www.usa.norgren.com

*Mfr. pneumatic filters, regulators, lubricators, valves, automation systems, dryers, push-in fittings.*

IMI Norgren Sdn Bhd, No. 16 Jalan Jimat 25-87, Taman Sri Muda, 4000 Shah Alam, Selangor Darul Ehsan, Malaysia

Tel: 60-3-5219-255 Fax: 60-3-5212-889

## NOVELLUS SYSTEMS INC.

4000 North First Street, San Jose, CA, 95134

Tel: (408) 943-9700 Fax: (408) 943-3422 www.novellus.com

*Mfr. chemical vapor deposition (CVD), physical vapor deposition (PVD) and copper electrofill systems.*

Novellus Systems Malaysia, Suite B3-1 Ground Floor, Kumlin Hi-Tech Park, 09000 Kulim Kedah Darul Amam, Malaysia

## OCCIDENTAL PETROLEUM CORPORATION

10889 Wilshire Blvd., Los Angeles, CA, 90024

Tel: (310) 208-8800    Fax: (310) 443-6690    www.oxy.com

*Petroleum and petroleum products, chemicals, plastics.*

**Occidental of Malaysia Inc, Kuala Lumpur, Malaysia**

## OCEANEERING INTERNATIONAL INC.

11911 FM 529, Houston, TX, 77041

Tel: (713) 329-4500    Fax: (713) 329-4951    www.oceaneering.com

*Transportation equipment, underwater service to offshore oil and gas industry.*

**Solus Oceaneering Sdn. Bhd., Lot 1353 1/F Lorong 3, Jalan Jee Foh, Krokop 98000 Miri, Sarawak Malaysia**

**Solus Oceaneering Sdn. Bhd., Unit No.19A-12-3A Level 12, UOA Centre No.19 Jalan Pinang, 50450 Kuala Lumpur, Malaysia**

**Solus Oceaneering Sdn. Bhd., Box 43 Warehouse 12 Door No.14/15, Kemaman Supply Base, 24000 Terengganu Malaysia**

## ONYX SOFTWARE CORPORATION

3180 139th Avenue, SE, Bellevue, WA, 98005

Tel: (425) 451-8060    Fax: (425) 451-8277    www.onyx.com

*Mfr. customer relationship management software.*

**Onyx Software Malaysia, Ste. 3 Level 10 Block B, hileo Damansara 1, 9 Jalan 16/11, Petaling Jaya 46350 Selangor, Malaysia**

Tel: 603-461-3311

## OTIS ELEVATOR COMPANY

10 Farm Springs Road, Farmington, CT, 06032

Tel: (860) 676-6000    Fax: (860) 676-5111    www.otis.com

*Mfr. elevators and escalators.*

**Pernas Otis Elevator Co. Sdn. Bhd., PO Box 11242, 50740 Kuala Lumpur, Malaysia**

## PACIFIC ARCHITECTS & ENGINEERS INC.

888 South Figueroa Street, 17th Fl., Los Angeles, CA, 90017

Tel: (213) 481-2311    Fax: (213) 481-7189    www.pae.com

*Technical engineering services.*

**PAE Services Sendirian Berhad, Suite 7.07 (7th Fl.) Pudu Plaza, Jalan Landak, 55100 Kuala Lumpur, Malaysia**

Tel: 60-3-248-0520    Fax: 60-3-248-0186    Contact: Alfred Ow, Office Mgr.

**PAE Services Sendirian Berhad, Block A No. 68 Level 4, Taman Sri Sarawak Mall, Lalan Tengku Abdul Rahman, 3100 Kuching Sarawak Malaysia**

Tel: 60-82-238-653    Fax: 60-82-238-654    Contact: Edmund ak Nyanggar, Office Supervisor

## PACIFIC BELL

140 New Montgomery Street, San Francisco, CA, 94105

Tel: (415) 542-9000    Fax: (415) 543-7079    www.pacbell.com

*Telecommunications and information systems.*

**Pacific Bell (Malaysia) Sdn. Bhd., Lot 420 Kompleks Antarabangsa, Jalan Sultan Ismail, 50250 Kuala Lumpur, Malaysia**

## PANAMETRICS

221 Crescent Street, Waltham, MA, 02154

Tel: (781) 899-2719    Fax: (781) 899-1552    www.panametrics.com

*Process/non-destructive test instrumentation.*

**Altec Ind. & Eng. Supply SND BHD, No. 11 Block B Lot 756, Off Persiaran Subang, 47500 Subang Jaya Malaysia**

Tel: 60-3-734-9239    Fax: 60-3-734-7313

**PANDUIT CORPORATION**

17301 Ridgeland Ave., Tinley Park, IL, 60477-0981

Tel: (708) 532-1800      Fax: (708) 532-1811      www.panduit.com

*Mfr. electrical/electronic wiring components.*

**Panduit Malaysia,  Suite 505 - Wisma Goldhill, 67 Jalan Raja Chulan, Kuala Lumpur 50200, Malaysia**

**PARAMETRIC TECHNOLOGY CORPORATION**

128 Technology Drive, Waltham, MA, 02154

Tel: (781) 398-5000      Fax: (781) 398-5674      www.ptc.com

*Supplier of mechanical design automation and product data management software and services.*

**Parametric Technology Singapore Co. Ltd.,  4/F Block B Menara PKNS-PJ, 17 Jalan Yong Shook Lin, 4050 Petaling Jaya Selangor, Malaysia**

Tel: 60-3-754-8198   Fax: 60-3-754-8197

**PARKER HANNIFIN CORPORATION**

6035 Parkland Blvd., Cleveland, OH, 44124-4141

Tel: (216) 896-3000      Fax: (216) 896-4000      www.parker.com

*Mfr. motion-control products.*

**Parker Hannifin Singapore Pte. Ltd.,  2nd. Fl. Wisma C.S.A., No.4 Jin Bersaru 1314, 46200 Petaling Jaya, Selangor Malaysia**

Tel: 60-3-758-4988   Fax: 60-3-759-8922

**PEOPLESOFT INC.**

4460 Hacienda Drive, Pleasanton, CA, 94588-8618

Tel: (925) 225-3000      Fax: (925) 694-4444      www.peoplesoft.com

*Mfr. applications to manage business operations across computer networks.*

**PeopleSoft Malaysia,  Level 36 Menara Lion, 165 Jalan Ampang, Kuala Lumpur 50450, Malaysia**

**PERFECSEAL COMPANY**

9800 Bustleton Ave., Philadelphia, PA, 19115

Tel: (215) 673-4500      Fax: (215) 676-1311      www.perfecseal.com

*Mfr. packaging materials and converted products for medical and pharmaceutical products.*

**Perfecseal (Asia Pacific) Sdn. Bhd.,  No. 8 Jalan TP 5, 47600 Subang Java, Selangor, Malaysia**

Tel: 60-3-724-4215

**PFIZER INC.**

235 East 42nd Street, New York, NY, 10017-5755

Tel: (212) 573-2323      Fax: (212) 573-7851      www.pfizer.com

*Research-based, global health care company.*

**Pfizer (Malaysia) Sdn. Bhd.,  Kuala Lumpur, Malaysia**

**PHARMACIA CORPORATION**

100 Route 206 North, Peapack, NJ, 07977

Tel: (908) 901-8000      Fax: (908) 901-8379      www.pharmacia.com

*Mfr. pharmaceuticals, agricultural products, industry chemicals.*

**Pharmacia & Upjohn Asia Ltd.,  c/o CCM Chemicals Sdn. Bhd., 9th Fl. Wisma Sime Darby, 14 Jalan Raja Laut, 50350 Kuala Lumpur Malaysia**

**PHARMACIA MONSANTO**

800 N. Lindbergh Boulevard, St. Louis, MO, 63167

Tel: (314) 694-1000      Fax: (314) 694-7625      www.monsanto.com

*Life sciences company focusing on agriculture, nutrition, pharmaceuticals, health and wellness and sustainable development.*

**Monsanto (Malaysia) Sdn. Bhd.,  Kompleks Pejabat Damansara, Jalan Dungun Damansara Heights, 50490 Kuala Lumpur, Malaysia**

Tel: 60-3-254-3355

## PICTURETEL CORPORATION

100 Minuteman Road, Andover, MA, 01810

Tel: (978) 292-5000      Fax: (978) 292-3300      www.picturetel.com

*Mfr. video conferencing systems, network bridging and multiplexing products, system peripherals.*

**PictureTel Videoconferencing Systems Corporation, Suite 25 Level 28 Central Plaza, 34 Jalan Sultan Ismail, 50250 Kuala Lumpur, Malaysia**

Tel: 60-3-247-4579   Fax: 60-3-247-4580

## PILLAR INDUSTRIES

21905 Gateway Road, Brookfield, WI, 53045

Tel: (262) 317-5300      Fax: (262) 317-5353      www.pillar.com

*Mfr. induction heating and melting equipment.*

**Pillar Industries Malaysia, Kuala Lumpur, Malaysia**

## PIONEER-STANDARD ELECTRONICS, INC.

6065 Parkland Blvd., Cleveland, OH, 44124

Tel: (440) 720-8500      Fax: (440) 720-8501      www.pios.com

*Mfr./distribution of electronic parts for computers and networking equipment.*

**WPI Components Sdn. Bhd., Wisma Tractors, 7 Jalan SS 16/1, 47500 Subang Jaya, Malaysia**

## PITTSTON BAX GROUP

16808 Armstrong Ave., PO Box 19571, Irvine, CA, 92623

Tel: (949) 752-4000      Fax: (949) 260-3182      www.baxworld.com

*Air freight forwarder.*

**BAX Global Malaysia Sdn, 1 Jalan SS 15/8B, Subang Jaya, 47500 Petaling Jaya, Selangor Malaysia**

Tel: 60-3-746-3119   Fax: 60-3-746-3436

**BAX Global Malaysia Sdn, Wisma Apex 2/F, 2A Jalan TP5, SIME UEP Industrial Park, Subang Jaya Selangor Malaysia**

Tel: 60-3-724-2008   Fax: 60-3-724-1968

## POWER TECHNOLOGIES INC. (PTI)

1482 Erie Blvd., PO Box 1058, Schenectady, NY, 12301

Tel: (518) 395-5000      Fax: (518) 346-2777      www.pti-us.com

*Power systems engineering, consulting, services and related control software; power quality hardware.*

**PTI Asia, 17-B PJS 10/32, Bandar SRI Subang, 46000 Petaling Jaya Selangor, Malaysia**

## PRICEWATERHOUSECOOPERS LLP

1301 Ave. of the Americas, New York, NY, 10019

Tel: (212) 596-7000      Fax: (212) 259-1301      www.pwcglobal.com

*Accounting and auditing, tax and management, and human resource consulting services.*

**PriceWaterhouseCoopers, Standard Chartered Bank Chambers 2/Fl, 21-27 Jalan Dato' Maharajalela, 30000 Ipoh Perak Malaysia**

Tel: 60-5-254-9427   Fax: 60-5-253-3206

**PriceWaterhouseCoopers, Wisma Oceanic Lot B/11, Jalan OKK Awang Besar - WDT 102, 87009 Wilayah Persekutuan Labuan, Malaysia**

Tel: 60-87-422088   Fax: 60-87-422198

**PriceWaterhouseCoopers, Bangunan Tabung Haji Lot 9 2nd Floor, Jalan Banda Kaba, POBox 140, 75720 Melaka Malaysia**

Tel: 60-6-23-6169   Fax: 60-6-24-4368

**PriceWaterhouseCoopers, Bangunan UMBC 5th Fl., Lebuh Pantai, POBox 331, 10740 Pulau Pinang Malaysia**

Tel: 60-4-262-1700   Fax: 60-4-262-8402

**PriceWaterhouseCoopers, Wisma Sime Darby 11th Floor, Jalan Raja Laut, PO Box 10192, 50706 Kuala Lumpur Malaysia**

Tel: 60-3-239-1077   Fax: 60-3-293-0997

## PROCTER & GAMBLE COMPANY

One Procter & Gamble Plaza, Cincinnati, OH, 45202

Tel: (513) 983-1100     Fax: (513) 562-4500     www.pg.com

*Personal care, food, laundry, cleaning and industry products.*

**Procter & Gamble, Wisma Consplant 9/F, No.2 Jalan SS16/4, 46500 Subang Jaya Selangor, Kulaa Lumpur Malaysia**

## PSDI MAXIMO

100 Crosby Drive, Bedford, MA, 01730

Tel: (781) 280-2000     Fax: (781) 280-0200     www.psdi.com

*Develops, markets and provides maintenance management software systems.*

**PSDI Malaysia, MN1 Twin Tower 2, JLN Pinang, Kuala Lumpur Malaysia**

Tel: 60-3-269-6598   Fax: 60-3-269-6506

## THE QUAKER OATS COMPANY

Quaker Tower, 321 North Clark Street, Chicago, IL, 60610-4714

Tel: (312) 222-7111     Fax: (312) 222-8323     www.quakeroats.com

*Mfr. foods and beverages.*

**Quaker Products (Malaysia) Sdn. Bhd., 7 Jalan SS 16/1 12/F Wisma Tractors, Subang Jaya, 47500 Petaling Jaya, Selangor Malaysia**

## QWEST COMMUNICATIONS INTERNATIONAL INC.

1801 California Street, Ste. 5200, Denver, CO, 80202

Tel: (303) 896-2020     Fax: (303) 793-6654     www.uswest.com

*Tele-communications provider; integrated communications services.*

**Binariang - Malaysia, Kuala Lumpur, Malaysia**

## R&B FALCON CORPORATION

901 Threadneedle, Ste. 200, Houston, TX, 77079

Tel: (281) 496-5000     Fax: (281) 496-4363     www.rbfalcon.com

*Offshore contract drilling.*

**R&B Falcon (M) Sdn. Bhd., PO Box 2156, Lot 2066 Block 4 MCLD, Jl. Bulatan Piasau Ind. Area, 98000 Miri Sarawak Malaysia**

## RADISSON HOTELS INTERNATIONAL

Carlson Pkwy., PO Box 59159, Minneapolis, MN, 55459-8204

Tel: (612) 540-5526     Fax: (612) 449-3400     www.radisson.com

*Hotels and resorts.*

**Radisson Hotel and Convention Centre (Kuala Lumpur), Persiaran Perbandaran Seksyen 14, 40000 Shah Alam, Selangor Darul Ehsan, Malaysia**

Tel: 60-3-531-3388   Fax: 60-3-531-2288

## RAYCHEM CORPORATION

300 Constitution Dr., Menlo Park, CA, 94025-1164

Tel: (650) 361-3333     Fax: (650) 361-5579     www.raychem.com

*Develop/mfr./market materials science products for electronics, telecommunications and industry.*

**Raychem Sdn. Bhd., Wisma Ali Bawal - 3/F, Lot 11 Jalan Tandang, 46050 Petaling Jaya, Selangor Malaysia**

## RAYTHEON COMPANY

141 Spring Street, Lexington, MA, 02173

Tel: (781) 862-6600     Fax: (781) 860-2172     www.raytheon.com

*Mfr. diversified electronics, appliances, aviation, energy and environmental products; publishing, industry and construction services.*

**Raytheon International, Kuala Lumpur, Malaysia**

## REFLEXITE TECHNOLOGY

120 Darling Drive, Avon, CT, 06001

Tel: (860) 676-7100     Fax: (860) 676-7199     www.reflexite.com

*Mfr. plastic film, sheet, materials and shapes, optical lenses.*

**Reflexite Malaysia, 13A Jalan Sulaiman 3, Taman Putra Ampang Selangor 68000, Malaysia**

Tel: 60-3-456-6588    Fax: 60-3-457-1598    Contact: Andrew Lee, Mgr.

## RENA WARE DISTRIBUTORS INC.

PO Box 97050, Redmond, WA, 98073-9750

Tel: (425) 881-6171     Fax: (425) 882-7500     www.renaware.com

*Mfr. stainless steel cookware and water filtration products.*

**Rena Ware Snd Bhd., Company No. 260561-M - 3/F, Wisma TCL 470, 3rd Mile Jalan Ipoh, 51200 Kuala Lumpur, Malaysia**

## RENAISSANCE HOTELS AND RESORTS

10400 Fernwood Road, Bethesda, MD, 20817

Tel: (301) 380-3000     Fax: (301) 380-5181     www.renaissancehotels.com

*Hotel and resort chain.*

**Renaissance Kota Kinabalu Hotel, Kota Kinabalu, Malaysia**

Tel: 60-88-252-233

**Renaissance Kuala Lumpur Hotel, Kuala Lumpur, Malaysia**

Tel: 60-3-262-2233

**Renaissance Melaka Hotel, Melaka, Malaysia**

Tel: 60-6-284-8888

**Renaissance Palm Garden, Kuala Lumpur, Malaysia**

Tel: 60-3-943-2233

**Renaissance Sandakan Hotel, Sandakan, Malaysia**

Tel: 60-89-213299

## RESMED INC.

1440 Danielson Street, Poway, CA, 92064

Tel: (858) 746-2400     Fax: (858) 880-1618     www.resmed.com

*Mfr. sleep apnea aids, including nasal masks and accessories.*

**ResMed Malaysia Sdn. Bhd., Unit 4 - 04 Wisma BICMA, Lot 2 Jalan 243/51A, 46100 Petaling Jaya, Selangor D.E. Malaysia**

Tel: 60-3-7877-1068    Fax: 60-3-7877-6099

## RICHCO, INC.

5825 N. Tripp Ave., PO Box 804238, Chicago, IL, 60680

Tel: (773) 539-4060     Fax: (773) 539-6770     www.richco.com

*Mfr. plastic and metal parts for the electric, electronic, appliance, and fiber-optic industries.*

**Richco Asia, Pte. Ltd., 458 Jalan SS 15/48, Subang Jaya, 47500 Pedaling Jaya, Selangor Darul Ehsan, Malaysia**

Tel: 60-37-37-0566

## THE RITZ-CARLTON HOTEL COMPANY, L.L.C.

3414 Peachtree Road NE, Ste. 300, Atlanta, GA, 30326

Tel: (404) 237-5500     Fax: (404) 365-9643     www.ritzcarlton.com

*5-star hotel and restaurant chain.*

**The Ritz-Carlton Hotel, 20th Fl. Menara Keck Seng, 203 Jalan Bukit Bintang, 55100 Kuala Lumpur, Malaysia**

Tel: 60-3-243-0400

## ROCKWELL INTERNATIONAL CORPORATION

777 East Wisconsin Ave., Ste. 1400, Milwaukee, WI, 53202

Tel: (414) 212-5200      Fax: (414) 212-5201      www.rockwell.com

*Products and service for aerospace and defense, automotive, electronics, graphics and automation industry.*

**Rockwell Automation (Malaysia) Sdn. Bhd., Menara Luxor Level 12 Ste. 12-01, No. 6B Persiaran Tropicana, 47410 Petaling Jaya, Selangor Malaysia**

Tel: 60-3-706-3000   Fax: 60-3-706-3300

**Rockwell-Collins International, Inc., Ste. 14.01 Wisma Cosway, 88 Jalan Raja Chulan, 50200 Kuala Lumpur, Malaysia**

Tel: 60-3-248-2812   Fax: 60-3-242-5463

## ROHM AND HAAS COMPANY

100 Independence Mall West, Philadelphia, PA, 19106

Tel: (215) 592-3000      Fax: (215) 592-3377      www.rohmhaas.com

*Mfr. industrial and agricultural chemicals, plastics.*

**Rohm and Haas Asia Inc., Ste. A301 & 302 (3rd Fl.) West Wing, Wisma Tractros No. 7, JLN SS 16/1 Subang Jaya, 47500 Petaling Jaya Malaysia**

Tel: 60-3-731-1267

## SAS INSTITUTE INC.

SAS Campus Drive, Cary, NC, 27513

Tel: (919) 677-8000      Fax: (919) 677-4444      www.sas.com

*Mfr./distributes decision support software.*

**SAS Institute (Malaysia) Ltd., Kuala Lumpur, Malaysia**

Tel: 60-3-982-6785   Fax: 60-3-982-6785

## SBC COMMUNICATIONS INC.

175 East Houston, San Antonio, TX, 78205

Tel: (210) 821-4105      Fax: (210) 351-5034      www.sbc.com

*Engaged in telecommunications.*

**Telkom Malaysia Berhad, Kuala Lumpur, Malaysia**

## SCHENKER INTERNATIONAL FORWARDERS INC.

150 Albany Ave., Freeport, NY, 11520

Tel: (516) 377-3000      Fax: (516) 377-3005      www.schenkerusa.com

*Freight forwarders.*

**Schenker Malaysia Sdn. Bhd., PO Box 632, 46770 Subang Jaya, Malaysia**

Tel: 60-3-737-5962   Fax: 60-3-734-6964

## SCHERING-PLOUGH CORPORATION

One Giralda Farms, Madison, NJ, 07940-1000

Tel: (973) 822-7000      Fax: (973) 822-7048      www.sch-plough.com

*Proprietary drug and cosmetic products.*

**Schering-Ploug Malaysia, Lorong 51A/227B, 461000 Petating jaya, Selangor Darul Ehsan, Malaysia**

## SCHLUMBERGER LIMITED

277 Park Avenue, New York, NY, 10021

Tel: (212) 350-9400      Fax: (212) 350-9564      www.schlumberger.com

*Engaged in oil and gas services, metering and payment systems, and produces semiconductor testing equipment and smart cards.*

**Mertertek Schlumberger Sdn Bhd., No. 4 Jalan Sejahtera 25/124, Section 25, 40400 Sha Alam Selangor Darul Ehsan, Malaysia**

## SCI SYSTEMS INC.

2101 W. Clinton Avenue, Huntsville, AL, 35807

Tel: (256) 882-4800     Fax: (256) 882-4804     www.sci.com

*R/D and mfr. electronics systems for commerce, industry, aerospace, etc.*

**SCI Systems Malaysia, 202 Lorong Perusahaan Maju 9, Bukit Tengah Industrial Park, 13600 Perai, Penang Malaysia**

## SEAGATE TECHNOLOGY, INC.

920 Disc Dr., Scotts Valley, CA, 95066

Tel: (408) 438-6550     Fax: (408) 438-7205     www.seagate.com

*Develop computer technology, software and hardware.*

**Senai Seagate Industries (M) Sdn. Bhd., PLO 171 Jalan Perindustrian 7, Kawasan Perindustrian Senai III, 81400 Senai Johor Darul, Malaysia**

Tel: 60-7-598-2888   Fax: 60-7-598-2007   Contact: Jeremy Lee, Dir.   Emp: 800

## SEALED AIR CORPORATION

Park 80 East, Saddle Brook, NJ, 07663

Tel: (201) 791-7600     Fax: (201) 703-4205     www.sealedair.com

*Mfr. protective and specialty packaging solutions for industrial, food and consumer products.*

**Sealed Air Malaysia Sdn Bhd., Bandar Pinggiran Subang, Section 1, 40150 Shah Alam Selangor, Malaysia**

Tel: 60-3-747-6998   Fax: 60-3-747-6689

## G.D. SEARLE & COMPANY

5200 Old Orchard Road, Skokie, IL, 60077

Tel: (847) 982-7000     Fax: (847) 470-1480     www.searlehealthnet.com

*Mfr. pharmaceuticals, health care, optical products and specialty chemicals.*

**Searle Malaysia Sdn. Bhd., No. 74 Jalan University, 46700 Petaling Jaya Selangor, West Malaysia**

Tel: 60-3-755-2322   Fax: 60-3-757-3199

## THE SERVICEMASTER COMPANY

One ServiceMaster Way, Downers Grove, IL, 60515-1700

Tel: (630) 271-1300     Fax: (630) 271-2710     www.svm.com

*Management service to health care, school and industry facilities; diversified residential and commercial services.*

**ServiceMaster, Kuala Lumpur, Malaysia**

## SHEAFFER PEN, INC.

301 Ave. H, Fort Madison, IA, 52627

Tel: (319) 372-3300     Fax: (319) 372-1263     www.sheaffer.com

*Mfr. writing instruments.*

**BIC Asia, 6/F-UOA Building, Jalan Dungun, Damansara Heights, 50490 Kuala Lumpur, Malaysia**

Tel: 60-3-2530033   Fax: 60-3-2530622

## SHIPLEY COMPANY, LLC

455 Forest Street, Marlborough, MA, 01752

Tel: (508) 481-7950     Fax: (508) 485-9113     www.shipley.com

*Supplier of materials and processes technology to the microelectronics and printed wiring board industries.*

**Shipley Asia, Ltd., 56 1/F Jalan, Mahsuri , 11900 Bayan Baru, Penang Malaysia**

Tel: 60-4-642-3937   Fax: 60-4-642-3940

## SIKORSKY AIRCRAFT CORPORATION

6900 Main Street,  PO Box 9729, Stratford, CT, 06615-9129

Tel:  (203) 386-4000        Fax:  (203) 386-4000        www.sikorsky.com

*Design and manufacture of advanced helicopters for commercial, industrial and military uses.*

**SIKORSKY EXPORT CORP. (SEC),  Suite 21-1, Plaza 138, Jalanampang 50450, Kuala Lumpur, Malaysia**

## SILICON GRAPHICS INC.

2011 N. Shoreline Blvd., Mountain View, CA, 94043-1389

Tel:  (650) 960-1980        Fax:  (650) 961-0595        www.sgi.com

*Design/mfr. special-effects computer graphic systems and software.*

**Silicon Graphics Sdn. Bhd.,  Ste. 9.01 Menara Keck Seng, 203 Jalan Bukit Bintang, 55100 Juala Lumpur, Malaysia**

Tel: 60-3-243-2848    Fax: 60-3-243-2699

**Wisma Sime Darby Silicon Graphics,  17th Fl. East Wing, Jalan Raja Laut, 50350 Kuala Lumpur, Malaysia**

Tel: 60-3-293-9322    Fax: 60-3-293-9376    Contact: Wahab Yusoff, Mgr.

## SIMPLEX TIME RECORDER COMPANY

100 Simplex Dr., Westminster, MA, 01441

Tel:  (978) 731-2500        Fax:  (978) 731-7052        www.simplexnet.com

*Provides safety, fire detection, integrated security, communications, time and attendance and workforce management systems.*

**Simplex Malaysia Fire and Security Sdn. Bhd.,  Lot 5.02 - 5/F Wisma Ali Bawal 2 No. 11, Jalan Tandang , 46050 Petaling Jaya, Selangor Darul Ehsan, Malaysia**

## SKYTEL COMMUNICATIONS, INC.

PO Box 2469, Jackson, MS, 39225

Tel:  (601) 944-1300        Fax:  (601) 944-3900        www.skytel.com

*Provides wireless messaging services, radio paging services and systems implementation.*

**SkyTel Systems Malaysia,  Kuala Lumpur, Malaysia**

**SkyTel Systems Malaysia Sdn Bhd (JV),  Kuala Lumpur, Malaysia**

## SOLECTRON CORPORATION

777 Gibraltar Drive, Milpitas, CA, 95035

Tel:  (408) 957-8500        Fax:  (408) 956-6075        www.solectron.com

*Provides contract manufacturing services to equipment manufacturers.*

**Solectron Corporation,  Plot 12 Phase IV Prai Industrial Estate, 13600 Prai Penang, Malaysia**

Tel: 60-4-507-5600    Fax: 60-4-507-8728

**Solectron Corporation,  Lot 7963 Jalan Air Hitam, Batu 11, 81000 Kulai Johor, Malaysia**

Tel: 60-7-662-6500    Fax: 60-7-662-4129

## SOLUTIA INC.

575 Maryville Center Dr, St. Louis, MO, 63141

Tel:  (314) 674-1000        Fax:  (314) 694-8686        www.solutia.com

*Mfr. specialty chemical based products.*

**Solutia Hong Kong Limited,  12/F 1309-B - Kelana Parkview Tower, No. 1 Jalan SS 6/2 Kelana Jaya, 47301 Petaling Jaya Selangor, Malaysia**

## SONOCO PRODUCTS COMPANY

North Second Street, PO Box 160, Hartsville, SC, 29550

Tel: (843) 383-7000     Fax: (843) 383-7008     www.sonoco.com

*Mfr. packaging for consumer and industrial market and recycled paperboard.*

**Sonoco (Malaysia) Sdn Bhd, Lots A43-A44 Lorang Kuang Bulan, Kepong Garden Ind. Estate, Kepong Kuala Lumpur, Malaysia 52100**

Tel: 60-3-636-7969

## SOTHEBY'S HOLDINGS, INC.

1334 York Avenue, New York, NY, 10021

Tel: (212) 606-7000     Fax: (212) 606-7027     www.sothebys.com

*Auction house specializing in fine art and jewelry.*

**Sotheby's Holdings, Inc., 25 Jalan Pudu Lama, 50200 Kuala Lumpur, Malaysia**

Tel: 60-3-230-0319

## SPERRY-SUN DRILLING

3000 North Sam Houston Pkwy. East, Houston, TX, 77032

Tel: (281) 871-5100     Fax: (281) 871-5742     www.sperry-sun.com

*Provides drilling services to the oil and gas drilling industry.*

**Antah Sperry-Sun Sdn. Bhd., Lot 2100 - Miri Concession Land District, Jalan Daluk Edward Jeli, PO Box 60 98107 Lutong, Sarawak, Malaysia**

**Antah Sperry-Sun Sdn. Bhd., Kemaman Supply Base Bldg. B 2/F, 24007 Kemaman, Terengganu Malaysia**

## SPRAYING SYSTEMS COMPANY

PO Box 7900, Wheaton, IL, 60189-7900

Tel: (630) 665-5000     Fax: (630) 260-0842     www.spray.com

*Designs and manufactures industrial spray nozzles.*

**Spraying Systems (S) Pte Ltd., 128-A Jalan Burhanuddin Helmi, Taman Tun Drive, Ismail 6000 Kuala Lumpur, Malaysia**

## THE ST. PAUL COMPANIES, INC.

385 Washington Street, St. Paul, MN, 55102

Tel: (651) 310-7911     Fax: (651) 310-8294     www.stpaul.com

*Provides investment, insurance and reinsurance services.*

**Hong Leong Asurance Bhd., Tingkat 18 Wisma HLA, Jalan Raja Chulan, 50200 Kuala Lumpur, Malaysia**

**QBE Insurance Malaysia Snd Bhd., Jalan Sultan Ismail 15th Fl., Bangunan MAS, 50250 Kuala Lumpur, Malaysia**

## STARWOOD HOTELS & RESORTS WORLDWIDE

777 Westchester Avenue, White Plains, NY, 10604

Tel: (914) 640-8100     Fax: (914) 640-8316     www.starwoodhotels.com

*Hotel operations including Sheraton, Westin, St. Regis, Four Points and Caesars.*

**Sheraton Imperial Kuala Lumpur, Kuala Lumpur, Malaysia**

## STEPAN COMPANY

22 West Frontage Road, Northfield, IL, 60093

Tel: (847) 446-7500     Fax: (847) 501-2443     www.stepan.com

*Mfr. basic intermediate chemicals.*

**Stepan Asia, 35A Jalan SS 18/6, Subang Jaya, 47500 Petaling Jaya, Selangor, Malaysia**

## STONE & WEBSTER ENGINEERING CORPORATION

8545 United Plaza Blvd., Baton Rouge, LA, 02210-2288

Tel: (617) 589-5111     Fax: (617) 589-2156     www.shawgroup.com

*Engineering, construction, environmental and management services.*

**Stone & Webster Services Sdn. Bhd., Ste. 25A-B Empire Tower 25/F, City Square Center, 182 Jalan Tun Razak, 50400 Kuala Lumpur Malaysia**

## STORAGE TECHNOLOGY CORPORATION

One Storagetech Dr., Louisville, CO, 80028-4377

Tel: (303) 673-5151     Fax: (303) 673-5019     www.stortek.com

*Mfr./market/service information, storage and retrieval systems.*

**StorageTek Malaysia, 301 Level 3 Uptown 2, 2 Jalan SS21/37, 47400 Petaling Jaya, Selangor, Malaysia**

## SULLAIR CORPORATION

3700 E. Michigan Blvd., Bldg. 1-2, Michigan City, IN, 46360

Tel: (219) 879-5451     Fax: (219) 874-1273     www.sullair.com

*Mfr. high efficiency tandem compressors, vacuum systems, encapsulated compressors and air tools.*

**Sullair Malaysia Ltd., 17 Jalan 4906 off Jalan SS 13/3 Subang, Jaya Industrial Estate, Subang Jaya Selangor Malaysia**

## SUMMIT INDUSTRIAL CORPORATION

600 Third Ave., New York, NY, 10016

Tel: (212) 490-1100     Fax: (212) 949-6328

*Pharmaceuticals, agricultural and chemical products.*

**Summit Co. (Malaysia) Sdn. Bhd., PO Box 1088, Jalan Semangat, Petaling Jaya Selangor, Malaysia**

## SYBASE, INC.

6475 Christie Ave., Emeryville, CA, 94608

Tel: (510) 922-3500     Fax: (510) 922-3210     www.sybase.com

*Design/mfg/distribution of database management systems, software development tools, connectivity products, consulting and technical support services..*

**Sybase Software (Malaysia) Sdn Bhd, Level 7 Menara Genesis, Number 3 Jalan Sultan Ismail, 50250 Kuala Lumpur, Malaysia**

Tel: 60-3-242-4218   Fax: 60-3-243-4318

## SYMANTEC CORPORATION

20330 Stevens Creek Blvd., Cupertino, CA, 95014-2132

Tel: (408) 253-9600     Fax: (408) 253-3968     www.symantec.com

*Designs and produces PC network security and network management software and hardware.*

**Symantec Malaysia Ltd., Block 3A-7-3 Pantal Panorama, Jalan 112H Off Kg. Kerinchi, 52900 Kuala Lumpur, Malaysia**

Tel: 60-3-756-7662   Fax: 60-3-756-4226

## SYNTEGRA

4201 Lexington Ave., North Arden Hills, MN, 55126-6198

Tel: (651) 415-2999     Fax: (651) 415-4891     www.cdc.com

*Computer peripherals and hardware.*

**Syntegra Malaysia, Kuala Lumpur, Malaysia**

## TECHNITROL INC.

1210 Northbrook Drive, #385, Trevose, PA, 19053

Tel: (215) 355-2900     Fax: (215) 355-7397     www.technitrol.com

*Mfr. of electronic components, electrical contacts, and other parts/materials.*

**Pulse Engineering - Electronic Components, Sungei Petani, Malaysia**

## TEKNIS CORPORATION

PO Box 3189, North Attleboro, MA, 02761

Tel: (508) 695-3591      Fax: (508) 699-6059      www.teknis.com

*Sale advanced technical products, fiber optics, materials for semiconductor mfr., security holographics*

**Teknis Malaysia, Kuala Lumpur, Malaysia**

## TEKTRONIX INC.

14200 SW Karl Braun Dr., PO Box 500, Beaverton, OR, 97077

Tel: (503) 627-7111      Fax: (503) 627-2406      www.tek.com

*Mfr. test and measure, visual systems/color printing and communications/video and networking products.*

**TekMark Sdn. Bhd., No. 2 Jalan Radin Anum 2, Sri Petailing, Kuala Lumpur, Malaysia**

Tel: 60-3-957-8999    Fax: 60-3-957-3999

## TELEFLEX INC.

630 W. Germantown Pike, Ste. 450, Plymouth Meeting, PA, 19462

Tel: (610) 834-6301      Fax: (610) 834-8307      www.teleflex.com

*Designs/mfr./market mechanical and electro-mechanical systems, measure systems.*

**Rüsch Sdn. Bhd., Perak, West Malaysia**

## TEXAS INSTRUMENTS INC.

8505 Forest Lane, Dallas, TX, 75243

Tel: (972) 995-3773      Fax: (972) 995-4360      www.ti.com

*Mfr. semiconductor devices, electronic electro-mechanical systems, instruments and controls.*

**Texas Instruments Sdn. Bhd., 1 Lorong Enggang 33, Ampang/Ulu, Keland, Kuala Lumpur Malaysia**

Tel: 60-3-456-7077

## THERMADYNE HOLDINGS CORPORATION

101 South Hanley Road, Suite 300, St. Louis, MO, 63105

Tel: (314) 746-2197      Fax: (314) 746-2349      www.thermadyne.com

*Mfr. welding, cutting, and safety products.*

**Thermadyne Asia SDN BHD, Kuala Lumpur, Malaysia**

Tel: 60-3-791-0086    Fax: 60-3-791-0129

## TIDEWATER INC.

601 Poydras Street, Ste.1900, New Orleans, LA, 70130

Tel: (504) 568-1010      Fax: (504) 566-4582      www.tdw.com

*Marine service and equipment to companies engaged in exploration, development and production of oil, gas and minerals.*

**Asie Zapata Marine Service Sdn. Bhd., 28-2 Jalan 1/76 C, Desa Pandan, 55100 Kuala Lumpur, Malaysia**

Tel: 60-3-98-18917    Fax: 60-3-98-18922

## TOWERS PERRIN

335 Madison Ave., New York, NY, 10017-4605

Tel: (212) 309-3400      Fax: (212) 309-0975      www.towers.com

*Management consulting services.*

**Tillinghast Towers Perrin, Level 28 Menara Haw Par, Jalan Sultan Ismail, 50250 Kuala Lumpur, Malaysia**

Tel: 60-3-233-6236    Fax: 60-3-233-6133

## THE TRANE COMPANY

3600 Pammel Creek Road, La Crosse, WI, 54601

Tel: (608) 787-2000      Fax: (608) 787-4990      www.trane.com

*Mfr./distributor/service A/C systems and equipment.*

**TM Sales & Services Sdn. Bhd., Lot 3 & 5 Jalan PJS 11/1, Bandar Sunway, 46150 Petaling Jaya Selangor, Darul Ehsan W. Malaysia**

## TRANSOCEAN SEDCO FOREX INC.

PO Box 2765, Houston, TX, 77252-2765

Tel: (713) 871-7500     Fax: (713) 850-3834     www.deepwater.com

*Engaged in oil and gas offshore drilling.*

**Asie Sonat Offshore Sdn. Bhd., 10/F Menara Apera, 84 Jalan Raja Chulan, 50200 Kuala Lumpur, Malaysia**

## TRUE NORTH COMMUNICATIONS INC.

101 East Erie Street, Chicago, IL, 60611

Tel: (312) 425-6500     Fax: (312) 425-5010     www.truenorth.com

*Holding company, advertising agency.*

**FCB Malaysia, 21st & 22nd Fl. Menara MPPJ Jalan Tengah, PO Box 102, 46710 Petaling Jaya, Selangor Darul Ehsan Malaysia**

## U.S. SUMMIT CORPORATION

600 Third Ave., New York, NY, 10016

Tel: (212) 490-1100     Fax: (212) 557-3875

*Marketing/distribution pharmaceuticals, chemicals.*

**Summit Co. (Malaysia) Sdn. Bhd., PO Box 1088, Jalan Semangat, Petaling Jaya, Selangor Malaysia**

## UNION CARBIDE CORPORATION

39 Old Ridgebury Road, Danbury, CT, 06817

Tel: (203) 794-2000     Fax: (203) 794-6269     www.unioncarbide.com

*Mfr. industrial chemicals, plastics and resins.*

**UC Chemicals (Malaysia) Sdn. Bhd., Suite 3 Level 28 Fujitsu Plaza, 1A Jalan Tangdang 204, 46050 Petaling Selangor, Malaysia**

## UNISYS CORPORATION.

PO Box 500, Union Meeting Road, Blue Bell, PA, 19424

Tel: (215) 986-4011     Fax: (215) 986-6850     www.unisys.com

*Mfr./marketing/servicing electronic information systems.*

**Unisys (Malaysia) Sdn. Bhd., 10 Jalan P. Ramlee, UBN Tower, 50250 Kuala Lumpur, Malaysia**

## UNITED PARCEL SERVICE, INC.

55 Glenlake Parkway, NE, Atlanta, GA, 30328

Tel: (404) 828-6000     Fax: (404) 828-6593     www.ups.com

*International package-delivery service.*

**UPS (M) Sdn Bhd, No. 11 Jalan Tandang, Wisma Ali Bawal, 46050 Petaling Jaya, Selangor Darul Ehsan Malaysia**

Tel: 60-3-794-1233     Fax: 60-3-794-2372

## UNIVERSAL INSTRUMENTS

90 Bevier Street, S. Dock, Binghamton, NY, 13904

Tel: (607) 779-7522     Fax: (607) 779-7971     www.uic.com

*Mfr./sales of instruments for electronic circuit assembly.*

**Universal Instruments (M) Sdn. Bhd., Penang, Malaysia**

Tel: 60-4-644-7067     Fax: 60-4-644-7068

## UPRIGHT INC.

1775 Park Street, Selma, CA, 93662

Tel: (209) 891-5200     Fax: (209) 896-9012     www.upright.com

*Mfr. aerial work platforms and telescopic handlers.*

**UpRight (Far East) Inc., 22 King St., 10200 Penang, Malaysia**

## URS CORPORATION

100 California Street, Ste. 500, San Francisco, CA, 94111-4529

Tel: (415) 774-2700      Fax: (415) 398-1904      www.urscorp.com

*Provides planning, design and construction management services, pollution control and hazardous waste management.*

**URS (Dames & Moore), Kuala Lumpur, Malaysia**

## USG CORPORATION

125 South Franklin Street, Chicago, IL, 60606-4678

Tel: (312) 606-4000      Fax: (312) 606-4093      www.usg.com

*Holding company for the building products industry.*

**USG Interiors (Far East) Sdn. Bhd., Kuala Lumpur, Malaysia**

## VERITAS DGC INC.

3701 Kirby Drive, Houston, TX, 77096

Tel: (713) 512-8300      Fax: (713) 512-8701      www.veritasdgc.com

*Geophysical services.*

**Veritas DGC (M) Sdn. Bhd., Level 56 Tower 2, Petronas Twin Towers, KLCC Kuala Lumpur 50888, Malaysia**

Tel: 60-3--382-1100    Contact: K. T. Tong

## VERIZON COMMUNICATIONS INC.

1255 Corporate Drive, Irving, TX, 75038

Tel: (972) 507-5000      Fax: (972) 507-5002      www.gte.com

*Engaged in wireline and wireless communications.*

**GTE Intl Inc., 112 Jalan Pudu, Kuala Lumpur, Malaysia**

## VITAL SIGNS, INC.

20 Campus Road, Totowa, NJ, 07512

Tel: (973) 790-1330      Fax: (973) 790-3307      www.vital-signs.com

*Mfr. disposable medical products for critical care procedures.*

**Vital Signs Malaysia, Kuala Lumpur, Malaysia**

## VTEL (VIDEOTELECOM CORPORATION )

108 Wild Basin Road, Austin, TX, 78746

Tel: (512) 314-2700      Fax: (512) 314-2792      www.vtel.com

*Design/mfr. long-distance interactive video communications products.*

**VTEL Malaysia, Menara IMC - 26/F, #8 Jalan Sultan Ismail, 50250 Kuala Lumpur, Malaysia**

Tel: 60-3-209-4788

## WATERS CORPORATION

34 Maple Street, Milford, MA, 01757

Tel: (508) 478-2000      Fax: (508) 872-1990      www.waters.com

*Mfr./distribute liquid chromatographic instruments and test and measurement equipment.*

**Waters Associates, Kuala Lumpur, Malaysia**

## WATSON WYATT & COMPANY HOLDINGS

6707 Democracy Blvd., Ste. 800, Bethesda, MD, 20817

Tel: (301) 581-4600      Fax: (301) 581-4937      www.watsonwyatt.com

*Creates compensation and benefits programs for major corporations.*

**Watson Wyatt & Co., Chung Khiaw Bank Building Level 11, Letter Box 8.3, Jalan Raja Laut, 50350 Kuala Lumpur Malaysia**

Tel: 60-3-293-3466    Fax: 60-3-291-3967    Contact: Florence Iles

## WD-40 COMPANY

1061 Cudahy Place, San Diego, CA, 92110-3998

Tel: (619) 275-1400    Fax: (619) 275-5823    www.wd40.com

*Mfr. branded multiple-purpose lubrication, protection and general maintenance products.*

**WD-40 Company (Malaysia), Ste. 1302 West Tower, Wisma Consplant #2, Jalan SS 16/4, Subang Jaya 47500 Selangor Malaysia**

## WEATHERFORD INTERNATIONAL, INC.

5 Post Oak Blvd, Ste. 1760, Houston, TX, 77227-3415

Tel: (713) 287-8400    Fax: (713) 963-9785    www.weatherford.com

*Oilfield services, products and equipment; mfr. marine cranes for oil and gas industry.*

**Weatherford Intl., 10F Wisma On Tai, 161-8 Jalan Ampang, 50450 Kuala Lumpur, Malaysia**
Tel: 60-3-452-9060   Fax: 60-3-452-9058

**Weatherford Malaysia, 332A-12 Plaza Ampang City, Kuala Lumpur 50450, Malaysia**
Tel: 60-34-52-9060   Fax: 60-34-52-9146

## WESTERN GEOPHYSICAL, INC.

10205 Westheimer, Houston, TX, 77251-1407

Tel: (713) 972-4000    Fax: (713) 952-9837    www.bakerhughes.com

*Provides comprehensive seismic services for oil and gas exploration, field development, and reservoir monitoring.*

**Western Geophysical, Lot 35 Block 4, SEDC Piasau Industrial Estate, 98000 Miri, Sarawak Malaysia**
Tel: 60-3-230-0997   Fax: 60-3-230-1137

## WILBUR-ELLIS COMPANY

PO Box 7454, San Francisco, CA, 94120

Tel: (415) 772-4000    Fax: (415) 772-4011    www.wilburellis.com

*Marketing, distribution, formulation of agricultural products and industrial specialty chemicals and raw materials.*

**Connell Bros. Co. Ltd., A606 6/F West Wisma Tractors, 7 Jalan SS16/1 Subang Jaya, 47500 Petaling Jaya Selangor, Malaysia**

## WM WRIGLEY JR. COMPANY

410 N. Michigan Ave., Chicago, IL, 60611-4287

Tel: (312) 644-2121    Fax: (312) 644-0353    www.wrigley.com

*Mfr. chewing gum.*

**The Wrigley Co. (Malaysia) Sdn. Bhd., Kuala Lumpur, Malaysia**

## WYETH-AYERST INTERNATIONAL INC.

150 Radnot-Chester Road, St. Davids, PA, 19087

Tel: (610) 902-4100    Fax: (610) 989-4586    www.ahp.com/wyeth

*Antibiotics and pharmaceutical products.*

**Wyeth Malaysia Sdn./Bhd., 701/702 Block C Kelana Bus. Center, No. 97 Jalan SS 7/2 Kelana Jaya, 47301 Petaling Jaya Selangor Malaysia**
Tel: 60-3-582-3111

## XEROX CORPORATION

800 Long Ridge Road, PO Box 1600, Stamford, CT, 06904

Tel: (203) 968-3000    Fax: (203) 968-4312    www.xerox.com

*Mfr. document processing equipment, systems and supplies.*

**Fuji Xerox Malaysia, 1A Jalan Bersatu, Section 13/4, 46100 Petaling-Jaya Selangor, Malaysia**
Tel: 60-3-757-9988   Fax: 603755-0319

## YORK INTERNATIONAL CORPORATION

631 South Richland Ave., York, PA, 17403

Tel: (717) 771-7890        Fax: (717) 771-6212        www.york.com

*Mfr. heating, ventilating, air conditioning and refrigeration equipment.*

**Oyl-Condair Industries Sdn. Bhd.,  Post Box 7196 - 40706 Shah Alam, Selangor Darl Ehsan, Malaysia**
Tel: 60-3-559-2293

**York (Malaysia) Service Sdn. Bhd.,  51B SS21/Al Damansara Utama, 47400 Petaling Jaya, Selangor, Malaysia**

## YOUNG & RUBICAM INC.

285 Madison Ave., New York, NY, 10017

Tel: (212) 210-3000        Fax: (212) 370-3796        www.yr.com

*Advertising, public relations, direct marketing and sales promotion, corporate and product ID management.*

**Dentsu Young & Rubicam Pte. Ltd.,  Kuala Lumpur, Malaysia**

# Mali

## LOUIS BERGER INTERNATIONAL INC.

100 Halsted Street, East Orange, NJ, 07019

Tel: (201) 678-1960    Fax: (201) 672-4284    www.louisberger.com

*Consulting engineers, engaged in architecture, environmental and advisory services.*

**Louis Berger International Inc.,  BP 1901, Bamako, Mali**

Tel: 223-233083   Fax: 223-233084

**Louis Berger S.A.,  425 Segou, Mali**

Tel: 223-237856   Fax: 223-237856

## DHL WORLDWIDE EXPRESS

50 California Avenue, San Francisco, CA, 94111

Tel: (415) 677-6100    Fax: (415) 824-9700    www.dhl.com

*Worldwide air express carrier.*

**DHL Worldwide Express,  Quartier de Fleuve Rez de Chaussee, rue No.146, Bamako, Mali**

Tel: 223-226376

## LEXMARK INTERNATIONAL

1 Lexmark Centre Dr., Lexington, KY, 40550

Tel: (606) 232-2000    Fax: (606) 232-1886    www.lexmark.com

*Develop, manufacture, supply of printing solutions and products, including laser, inkjet, and dot matrix printers.*

**Revendeur Lexmark,  Avenue Moussa Travel, BP 5053, Bamako, Mali**

# Malta

## AIR EXPRESS INTERNATIONAL CORPORATION

120 Tokeneke Road, PO Box 1231, Darien, CT, 06820

Tel: (203) 655-7900    Fax: (203) 655-5779    www.aeilogistics.com

*International air freight forwarder.*

**B.A.S. Ltd.,  Air Cargo House, Luqa-By-Pass, Luqa, OQA 05, Malta**

Tel: 356-678-000   Fax: 356-677-102

## ALAMO RENT A CAR

110 Southeast 6th Street, Fort Lauderdale, FL, 33301

Tel: (954) 522-0000    Fax: (954) 220-0120    www.alamo.com

*Car rentals.*

**Alamo Rent A Car,  Malta International Airport, Luga Airport, Malta**

## ALLEGIANCE HEALTHCARE CORPORATION

1430 Waukegan Road, McGaw Park, IL, 60085

Tel: (847) 689-8410    Fax: (847) 578-4437    www.allegiance.net

*Manufactures and distributes medical, surgical,  respiratory therapy and laboratory products.*

**Allegiance Ltd. Manufacturing,  A47 Industrial Estate, Marsa, Malta**

Tel: 356-231-894   Fax: 356-238-875

## AON CORPORATION

123 North Wacker Drive, Chicago, IL, 60606

Tel: (312) 701-3000    Fax: (312) 701-3100    www.aon.com

*Insurance brokers worldwide; underwrites accident and health insurance, specialty and professional insurance; and provides risk management consultation.*

**AON Worldwide / Bain Hogg Malta Ltd.,  Mediterranean Bldg. Abate Rigord St., Ta 'Xbiex MSD 12, Malta**

Tel: 356-340-530  Fax: 356-341-599   Contact: Joseph Cutajar

## BAXTER HEALTHCARE CORPORATION

One Baxter Parkway, Deerfield, IL, 60015

Tel: (847) 948-2000    Fax: (847) 948-3948    www.baxter.com

*Pharmaceutical preparations, surgical/medical instruments and cardiovascular products.*

**Baxter Ltd.,  A47 Industrial Estate, Marsa, Malta**

## BDO SEIDMAN, LLP    BELGIUM

Two Prudential Plaza, 180 N. Stetson Ave., Ste. 2300, Chicago, IL, 60601

Tel: (312) 240-1236    Fax: (312) 240-3329    www.bdo.com

*International accounting and financial consulting firm.*

**BDO Attard Buttigeg Psaila & Company,  136 St. Christopher St., Valletta VLT 05, Malta**

Tel: 356-221-242   Fax: 356-243-219   Contact: Lino Butigeg

## BESTFOODS, INC.

700 Sylvan Ave., International Plaza, Englewood Cliffs, NJ, 07632-9976

Tel: (201) 894-4000    Fax: (201) 894-2186    www.bestfoods.com

*Consumer foods products; corn refining.*

**Vadala Food Processing Co. Ltd.,  16, Triq IL-Kummerc, Qormi QRM 05, Malta**

Tel: 356-44-95-92  Fax: 356-44-96-97   Contact: Thomas Agius-Vadala, Mgr.

## BRISTOL-MYERS SQUIBB COMPANY

345 Park Ave., New York, NY, 10154-0037

Tel: (212) 546-4000     Fax: (212) 546-4020     www.bms.com

*Pharmaceutical and food preparations, medical and surgical instruments.*

**ConvaTec Malta,  Tiber Onorato Bres Street, Ta'xoieux MSD II, Malta**

## BUDGET GROUP, INC.

125 Basin St., Ste. 210, Daytona Beach, FL, 32114

Tel: (904) 238-7035     Fax: (904) 238-7461     www.budgetrentacar.com

*Car and truck rental system.*

**Budget Rent A Car,  Malta Intl Airport Luqa, Arrivals Hall, Malta**

Tel: 356-244023

**Budget Rent A Car,  Palmex Station, 261 Tower Rd., Sliema, Malta**

## D'ARCY MASIUS BENTON & BOWLES INC. (DMB&B)

1675 Broadway, New York, NY, 10019

Tel: (212) 468-3622     Fax: (212) 468-2987     www.dmbb.com

*Full service international advertising and communications group.*

**DMB&B Mid East-Africa,  Valetta, Malta**

## DELOITTE TOUCHE TOHMATSU INTERNATIONAL

1633 Broadway, New York, NY, 10019

Tel: (212) 492-4000     Fax: (212) 392-4154     www.deloitte.com

*Accounting, audit, tax and management consulting services.*

**Deloitte & Touche,  1 Col. Savona St., Sliema SLM 07, Malta**

## DETROIT DIESEL CORPORATION

13400 Outer Drive West, Detroit, MI, 48239

Tel: (313) 592-5000     Fax: (313) 592-5058     www.detroitdiesel.com

*Mfr. diesel and aircraft engines, heavy-duty transmissions.*

**Power Diesel Products Ltd.,  193 Industrial Estate, Luqa LQA 05, Malta**

Tel: 356-248-157   Fax: 356-248-143

## DHL WORLDWIDE EXPRESS

50 California Avenue, San Francisco, CA, 94111

Tel: (415) 677-6100     Fax: (415) 824-9700     www.dhl.com

*Worldwide air express carrier.*

**DHL Worldwide Express,  DHL Bldg., Triq G. Vassalio, Luqa Lqa 02, Malta**

Tel: 356-800148

## EMERY WORLDWIDE

One Lagoon Drive, Ste. 400, Redwood City, CA, 94065

Tel: (650) 596-9600     Fax: (650) 596-7901     www.emeryworld.com

*Freight transport, global logistics and air cargo.*

**M.A.L./Emery Services, Ltd.,  14 Zurrieq Rd., Luqa Lqa 04, Malta**

## ERNST & YOUNG, LLP

787 Seventh Ave., New York, NY, 10019

Tel: (212) 773-3000     Fax: (212) 773-6350     www.eyi.com

*Accounting and audit, tax and management consulting services.*

**Ernst & Young,  54 St. Dominic St., Valletta VLT 03, Malta**

Tel: 356-233188   Fax: 356-234647   Contact: Andre Zarb

## FRITZ COMPANIES, INC.

706 Mission Street, Ste. 900, San Francisco, CA, 94103

Tel: (415) 904-8360      Fax: (415) 904-8661      www.fritz.com

*Integrated transportation, sourcing, distribution and customs brokerage services.*

**Fritz Companies Inc.,  Gozo, Malta**

## GILSON INC.

3000 W. Beltline Hwy, PO Box 620027, Middleton, WI, 53562-0027

Tel: (608) 836-1551      Fax: (608) 831-4451      www.gilson.com

*Mfr. analytical/biomedical instruments.*

**Technoline Ltd.,  Regional House  - Edgar Bernard Street, GZR 06 Gzira, Malta**

## GRANT THORNTON INTERNATIONAL

800 One Prudential Plaza, 130 E. Randolph Drive, Chicago, IL, 60601-6050

Tel: (312) 856-0001      Fax: (312) 616-7052      www.grantthornton.com

*Accounting, audit, tax and management consulting services.*

**Grant Thornton,  Grant Thornton House, Princess Elizabeth St., Ta'Xbiex MSD II, Malta**

Tel: 356-344751   Fax: 356-331161   Contact: Martin E. Bonello-Cole

**Grant Thornton International,  Grant Thornton House, Princess Elizabeth Street, Ta'Xbiex MSD 11, Malta**

## HORWATH INTERNATIONAL ASSOCIATION

415 Madison Ave., New York, NY, 10017

Tel: (212) 838-5566      Fax: (212) 838-3636      www.horwath.com

*Public accountants and auditors.*

**Diamantino, Mizzi & Co.,  Valletta Bldgs, South St., Valletta, Malta**

## IBM CORPORATION

New Orchard Road, Armonk, NY, 10504

Tel: (914) 765-1900      Fax: (914) 765-7382      www.ibm.com

*Information products, technology and services.*

**IBM - Computer Solutions Ltd.,  141 Old Bakery St., PO Box 336, Valletta, Malta**

## INTER-CONTINENTAL HOTELS

3 Ravina Drive, Suite 2900, Atlanta, GA, 30346-2149

Tel: (770) 604-2000      Fax: (770) 604-5403      www.interconti.com

*Worldwide hotel and resort accommodations.*

**Forum Hotel Malta,  St. Andrews Rd., St. Andrews, Malta**

Tel: 356-374729   Fax: 356-370324

## KPMG INTERNATIONAL LLP

345 Park Avenue, New York, NY, 10022

Tel: (201) 307-7000      Fax: (201) 930-8617      www.kpmg.com

*Accounting and audit, tax and management consulting services.*

**Joseph Tabone & Co.,  3 V. Dimech St., Floriana VLT 16, Malta**

Tel: 356-233-188   Fax: 356-234-647   Contact: Edward Cachia Caruana, Sr. Ptnr.

## PHARMACIA CORPORATION

100 Route 206 North, Peapack, NJ, 07977

Tel: (908) 901-8000      Fax: (908) 901-8379      www.pharmacia.com

*Mfr. pharmaceuticals, agricultural products, industry chemicals.*

**Pharmacia & Upjohn,  Pharlap, Bergamott St., Mosta Mst 07, Malta**

## PRICEWATERHOUSECOOPERS LLP

1301 Ave. of the Americas, New York, NY, 10019

Tel: (212) 596-7000    Fax: (212) 259-1301    www.pwcglobal.com

*Accounting and auditing, tax and management, and human resource consulting services.*

**PriceWaterhouseCoopers, Villa Mauramy, Mgr. A Mifsud St., Ta'Xbiex MSD 11, Malta**

Tel: 356-344360    Fax: 356-343958

## RADISSON HOTELS INTERNATIONAL

Carlson Pkwy., PO Box 59159, Minneapolis, MN, 55459-8204

Tel: (612) 540-5526    Fax: (612) 449-3400    www.radisson.com

*Hotels and resorts.*

**Radisson SAS Bay Point Resort, St. George's Bay, St. Julian's STJ02, Malta**

Tel: 356-374-894    Fax: 356-374-895

## SCHENKER INTERNATIONAL FORWARDERS INC.

150 Albany Ave., Freeport, NY, 11520

Tel: (516) 377-3000    Fax: (516) 377-3005    www.schenkerusa.com

*Freight forwarders.*

**M.A.L. Services Ltd., Airways House, High St., Sliema City, Malta**

Tel: 356-334-051    Fax: 356-334414

## TEKTRONIX INC.

14200 SW Karl Braun Dr., PO Box 500, Beaverton, OR, 97077

Tel: (503) 627-7111    Fax: (503) 627-2406    www.tek.com

*Mfr. test and measure, visual systems/color printing and communications/video and networking products.*

**ITEC - International Technology Ltd., B 'Kara Road, San Gwan, SGN 08 Malta**

Tel: 356-37-43-00

## UNITED PARCEL SERVICE, INC.

55 Glenlake Parkway, NE, Atlanta, GA, 30328

Tel: (404) 828-6000    Fax: (404) 828-6593    www.ups.com

*International package-delivery service.*

**UPS Malta, 14 Zurrieq Rd., Luqa LQA 04, Malta**

Tel: 356-803670    Fax: 356-809282

## XEROX CORPORATION

800 Long Ridge Road, PO Box 1600, Stamford, CT, 06904

Tel: (203) 968-3000    Fax: (203) 968-4312    www.xerox.com

*Mfr. document processing equipment, systems and supplies.*

**Image Systems Ltd., 11/11 Vincenti Bldg.s, Strait St., Valetta, Malta**

Tel: 356-236 550    Fax: 356-237 907

# Mauritius

**AMERICAN & EFIRD, INC.**

PO Box 507, Mt. Holly, NC, 28120

Tel: (704) 827-4311 Fax: (704) 822-6054 www.amefird.com

*Mfr. industrial sewing thread for worldwide industrial and consumer markets.*

**A&W Wong & Company, La Tour Koenig Ind. Estate, Pointe Aux Sables, Mauritius, PO Box 604, Bell Village Mauritius**

**BDO SEIDMAN, LLP BELGIUM**

Two Prudential Plaza, 180 N. Stetson Ave., Ste. 2300, Chicago, IL, 60601

Tel: (312) 240-1236 Fax: (312) 240-3329 www.bdo.com

*International accounting and financial consulting firm.*

**BDO Fideco, 44 St.George St., Port Louis, Mauritius**

Tel: 230-210-1867 Fax: 230-210-3386 Contact: A. Kader Mungly

**BEST WESTERN INTERNATIONAL**

6201 North 24th Place, Phoenix, AZ, 85106

Tel: (602) 957-4200 Fax: (602) 957-5740 www.bestwestern.com

*International hotel chain.*

**Berjaya Le Moren Beach Resort & Casino, Case Noyale, Mauritius**

**BUCYRUS INTERNATIONAL, INC.**

1100 Milwaukee Ave., PO Box 500, South Milwaukee, WI, 53172

Tel: (414) 768-4000 Fax: (414) 768-4474 www.bucyrus.com

*Mfr. of surface mining equipment, primarily walking draglines, electric mining shovels and blast hole drills.*

**Bucyrus (Mauritius) Ltd., Port Louis, Mauritius**

**COMPUWARE CORPORATION**

31440 Northwestern Hwy., Farmington Hills, MI, 48334-2564

Tel: (248) 737-7300 Fax: (248) 737-7108 www.compuware.com

*Develop and market software for enterprise and e-commerce solutions.*

**Currimjee Jeewanjee & Co., 38 Royal Street, Port Louis, Mauritius**

Tel: 230-242-6011

**DHL WORLDWIDE EXPRESS**

50 California Avenue, San Francisco, CA, 94111

Tel: (415) 677-6100 Fax: (415) 824-9700 www.dhl.com

*Worldwide air express carrier.*

**DHL Worldwide Express, 7 MGR Gonin St., Port Louis, Mauritius**

Tel: 230-208-9261

**EAGLE GLOBAL LOGISTICS (EGL)**

15350 Vickery Drive, Houston, TX, 77032

Tel: (281) 618-3100 Fax: (281) 618-3100 www.eaglegl.com

*Ocean/air freight forwarding, customs brokerage, packing and wholesale, logistics management and insurance.*

**Trans World Cargo Ltd., Labourdonnais Court 3rd Floor, St. George St., Port Louis, Mauritius**

Tel: 230-211-2815 Fax: 230-211-2852

**Trans World Cargo Ltd., Freight Forwarders Centre 1st Floor, Plaino Magnien, Mauritius**

Tel: 230-637-3230 Fax: 230-637-3262

**Trans World Cargo Ltd., Riche Terre Freight Centre, Rogers Industrial Zone No. 2, Riche Terre, Mauritius**

Tel: 230-248-1819   Fax: 230-248-0038

## ERNST & YOUNG, LLP

787 Seventh Ave., New York, NY, 10019

Tel: (212) 773-3000       Fax: (212) 773-6350       www.eyi.com

*Accounting and audit, tax and management consulting services.*

**Ernst & Young, Louis Leconte St., Curepipe, Mauritius**

Tel: 230-675-4777   Fax: 230-676-3921   Contact: Beryl Seeyave-Papas

## FRITZ COMPANIES, INC.

706 Mission Street, Ste. 900, San Francisco, CA, 94103

Tel: (415) 904-8360       Fax: (415) 904-8661       www.fritz.com

*Integrated transportation, sourcing, distribution and customs brokerage services.*

**Fritz Companies Inc., Port Louis, Mauritius**

## GRANT THORNTON INTERNATIONAL

800 One Prudential Plaza, 130 E. Randolph Drive, Chicago, IL, 60601-6050

Tel: (312) 856-0001       Fax: (312) 616-7052       www.grantthornton.com

*Accounting, audit, tax and management consulting services.*

**Grant Thornton International, 5/F Orchid Tower, 20 Sir William Newton Street, Port Louis Mauritius**

## GREY GLOBAL GROUP

777 Third Ave., New York, NY, 10017

Tel: (212) 546-2000       Fax: (212) 546-1495       www.grey.com

*International advertising agency.*

**Grey Mauritius, Port-Louis, Mauritius**

## KPMG INTERNATIONAL LLP

345 Park Avenue, New York, NY, 10022

Tel: (201) 307-7000       Fax: (201) 930-8617       www.kpmg.com

*Accounting and audit, tax and management consulting services.*

**KPMG Peat Marwick, 12 Remy Ollier Street 3rd Floor, Port Louis, Mauritius**

Tel: 230-208-8000   Fax: 230-208-3026   Contact: W. Koon Kam King, Sr. Ptnr.

## PRICEWATERHOUSECOOPERS LLP

1301 Ave. of the Americas, New York, NY, 10019

Tel: (212) 596-7000       Fax: (212) 259-1301       www.pwcglobal.com

*Accounting and auditing, tax and management, and human resource consulting services.*

**PriceWaterhouseCoopers, Cerne House 6th Floor, Chaussee, Port Louis, Mauritius**

Tel: 230-208-8036   Fax: 230-208-8037

**PriceWaterhouseCoopers, Training Centre, Champ de Mars, Port Louis, Mauritius**

Tel: 230-212-9308   Fax: 230-212-9405

## ROCKWELL INTERNATIONAL CORPORATION

777 East Wisconsin Ave., Ste. 1400, Milwaukee, WI, 53202

Tel: (414) 212-5200       Fax: (414) 212-5201       www.rockwell.com

*Products and service for aerospace and defense, automotive, electronics, graphics and automation industry.*

**Rockwell Automation (Proprietary) Ltd., c/o Rey & Lenferna, Royal Road, Bell Village, Mauritius**

Tel: 230-208-9872   Fax: 230-208-9876

**SCHENKER INTERNATIONAL FORWARDERS INC.**

150 Albany Ave., Freeport, NY, 11520

Tel: (516) 377-3000      Fax: (516) 377-3005      www.schenkerusa.com

*Freight forwarders.*

**Emcar Ltd., Harel Mallac Bldg., 18 Edith Cavell St., PO Box 222, Port Louis Mauritius**

Tel: 230-208-0891   Fax: 230-208-8191

**SUN INTERNATIONAL, INC.**

1415 East Sunrise Blvd., Fort Lauderdale, FL, 33304

Tel: (954) 713-2500      Fax: (954) 713-2019      www.sunint.com

*Ownership, development and operation of resort complexes.*

**Sun International Ltd., Port Louis, Mauritius**

**TRUE NORTH COMMUNICATIONS INC.**

101 East Erie Street, Chicago, IL, 60611

Tel: (312) 425-6500      Fax: (312) 425-5010      www.truenorth.com

*Holding company, advertising agency.*

**Cre-Ad Advertising, Corner Lord Kitchener & De Conti, Port Louis, Mauritius**

**XEROX CORPORATION**

800 Long Ridge Road, PO Box 1600, Stamford, CT, 06904

Tel: (203) 968-3000      Fax: (203) 968-4312      www.xerox.com

*Mfr. document processing equipment, systems and supplies.*

**Harel Mallac & Co., Ltd., 18 Edith Cavell St., PO Box 36, Port Louis, Mauritius**

Tel: 230-208-4802   Fax: 230-208-1674

VOLUME 2

---

# PUBLISHER'S NOTES

## *Related publications*

# 10th Edition
# DIRECTORY OF FOREIGN FIRMS OPERATING IN THE UNITED STATES

## EDITED & PUBLISHED BY
## UNIWORLD BUSINESS PUBLICATIONS, INC.
Published January 2000

**ONE VOLUME • 1216 PAGES • PRICE: $225.00 • ISBN: 0-8360-0044-7**

---

## PREHENSIVE LISTINGS

00 Foreign Firms
00 U.S. Affiliates
Countries

## AND FLEXIBLE ACCESS

(s) you are looking for can
d:
*ntry* — (Part I)
*e* — the name of the parent
y (Part II)
*iate* — the name of the
an based affiliate (Part III)

---

## KEY CONTACT AND LOCATION INFORMATION

**Italy**

• **FILA HOLDINGS S.p.A.**
26 Viale Cesare Battisti, 13051 Biella, Italy
CEO: Dr. Enrico Frachey, Chmn.
Bus: *Sales/distribution of sports footwear and clothing*
Tel: 39-015-350-6246
Fax: 39-015-350-6347
www.fila.com
Sales (mil): $1.2
Emp: 3,125

**FILA SPORTS DIVISION**
40 East 34 Street, New York, NY 10016
CEO: Rosa Lorenzo, Mgr.
Bus: *Sales/distribution of sports footwear & clothing*
Tel: (212) 726-5800
Fax: (212) 679-7450
%FO: 100
Emp: 50

**FILA U.S.A., INC.**
14114 York Road, Sparks, MD 21152
CEO: Jon Epstein, Pres. & CEO
Bus: *Mfr./sales sports footwear & clothing*
Tel: (410) 773-3000
Fax: (410) 773-4967
%FO: 100
Emp: 200

---

## TIAL BUYERS LIST

d Library
University Office of Career Services
erhouse
ational Trade Commission

& Struggles
Embassy

iversity Career Services

Executive Office of the President
US Chamber of Commerce
Rochester Public Library
LA Chamber of Commerce
Merrill Lynch
Hitachi Foundation
Johns Hopkins Hospital
Columbia University
CBS

IBM
New York Public Library
University of Texas
Sprint International
Notre Dame University
Stentor International
The Washington Opera
Zagat
Liberty Mutual

# Country, Regiona
# State Editions &
# Mailing Lists

16<sup>th</sup> Edition of *Directory of American Firms Operating in Foreign Countries and the*
10<sup>th</sup> Edition of the *Directory of Foreign Firms Operating in The United States*
in **Country**, **Regional** or **State** editions with all the same information that is in the library s

- ## Country and Regional Editions
  ~ list the companies alphabetically within each country.

- ## State Editions
  ~ *Directory of American Firms Operating in Foreign Countri*
  lists by State the American firms (alphabetically), at the
  headquarters location within the state.

  ~ *Directory of Foreign Firms Operating in The United State*
  lists by State the Foreign Firms (alphabetically), at each Ame·
  Affiliate headquarters location within the state.

- ## Mail Lists-Labels
  ~ available for all directories, **Country**, **Regional** or the com·
  **World List:** *Name and American Address of the Parent Co*
  with a corporate officer: *CEO, International Operations Off*
  *Human Resources Director* (where available), with telemark
  list.

- ## Custom Order
  ~ Create your own regions or country groupings to suit your
  needs.

  To place an order, please call (212) 496-2448 or send the attach
  **Form** by FAX (212) 769-0413. Orders for Country, Regional,
  editions and Mailing lists require pre-payment by credit card, c
  money order in U.S. dollars, drawn on a U.S. Bank. **All sales**

  Please see reverse side for title and pricing information.

Uniworld Business Publications, Inc.
257 Central Park West, Suite 10A
New York, New York 10024
Tel: (212) 496-2448
Fax: (212) 769-0413
E-mail: uniworldbp@aol.com
Website: http://uniworldbp.com

Prices subject to change without notice

01/15/01

## Operating in Foreign Countries

**AFRICA** $79.00
Algeria, Angola, Benin, Botswana, Burkina Faso, Burundi, Cameroon, Cent. African Rep., Chad, Congo, Dem. Rep. of Congo, Djibouti, Egypt, Ethiopia, Gabon, Ghana, Guinea, Ivory Coast, Kenya, Lesotho, Liberia, Libya, Madagascar, Malawi, Mali, Mauritius, Morocco, Mozambique, Namibia, Niger, Nigeria, Reunion, Senegal, Seychelles, Sierra Leone, South Africa, Sudan, Swaziland, Tanzania, Tunisia, Uganda, Zambia, Zimbabwe

**ASIA** $169.00
Bangladesh, Brunei, Cambodia, China, Hong Kong, India, Indonesia, Japan, Kazakhstan, Kirgnizia, Laos, Macau, Malaysia, Mongolia, Myanmar, Nepal, North Korea, Pakistan, Philippines, Singapore, South Korea, Sri Lanka, Taiwan, Tajikistan, Thailand, Uzbekistan, Vietnam

**South Asia** $49.00
Bangladesh, India, Myanmar, Pakistan, Sri Lanka

**South East Asia** $99.00
Brunei, Cambodia, Indonesia, Laos, Malaysia, Philippines, Singapore, Thailand, Vietnam

**Japan & Korea** $79.00

**China Group** $109.00
China, Hong Kong, Macau, Singapore, Taiwan

**NEAR & MIDDLE EAST** $69.00
Bahrain, Cyprus, Iran, Israel, Jordan, Kuwait, Lebanon, Oman, Palestine, Qatar, Saudi Arabia, Syria, Turkey, United Arab Emirates, Yemen

**The Arabic Countries** $69.00
Algeria, Bahrain, Egypt, Iran, Jordan, Kuwait, Lebanon, Libya, Morocco, Oman, Palestine, Qatar, Saudi Arabia, Sudan, Syria, Tunisia, United Arab Emirates, Yemen

**NORTH AMERICA** $109.00
Canada, Greenland, Mexico
Canada $89.00
Mexico $59.00

## Countries Combined

**AUSTRALIA GROUP** $79.00
Australia, New Zealand, Fiji, French Polynesia, Guam, New Caledonia No. Mariana Isl., Palau, Papua New Guinea, Polynesia, Solomon Isl., Vanuatu

**EUROPE** $189.00
Austria, Belgium, Channel Isl., Denmark, England, Finland, France, Germany, Gibraltar, Greece, Iceland, Ireland, Isle of Man, Italy, Liechtenstein, Luxembourg, Madeira, Malta, Monaco, Netherlands, No. Ireland, Norway, Portugal, San Marino, Scotland, Spain, Sweden, Switzerland, Wales

**British Isles** $109.00
Channel Is., England, Gibraltar, Ireland, Isle of Man, No. Ireland, Scotland, Wales

**EUROPE West. excl. British Is** $169.00
Belgium $49.00
France $69.00
Germany $79.00
Italy $59.00
Netherlands $59.00
Spain $49.00
Sweden $49.00
Switzerland $39.00
Scandinavia (Denmark, Finland, $79.00
Iceland, Norway, Sweden)

**EUROPE Eastern** $109.00
Albania, Armenia, Azerbaijan, Belarus, Bosnia-Herzegovina, Bulgaria, Croatia, Czech Rep., Estonia, Georgia, Hungary, Kazakhstan, Kirgnizia, Latvia, Lithuania, Macedonia, Poland, Romania, Russia, Slovakia, Slovenia, Tajikistan, Turkmenistan, Ukraine, Uzbekistan, Yugoslavia

**NORTH AMERICA** $109.00
Canada, Greenland, Mexico
Canada $89.00
Mexico $59.00

**CENTRAL AMERICA** $49.00
Belize, Costa Rica, El Salvador, Guatemala, Honduras, Nicaragua, Panama

**Caribbean Islands** $49.00
Anguilla, Antigua, Aruba, Bahamas, Barbados, Bermuda, British Virgin Is., Cayman Isl., Dominican Rep., French Antilles, Grenada, Haiti, Jamaica, Neth. Antilles, Trinidad & Tobago, Turks & Caicos

**SOUTH AMERICA** $109.00
Argentina, Bolivia, Brazil, Chile, Colombia, Ecuador, French Guiana, Guyana, Paraguay, Peru, Surinam, Uruguay, Venezuela
Argentina $39.00
Brazil $59.00
Argentina, Brazil, Chile $79.00
Venezuela $39.00

---

## 10th Edition Directory of Foreign Firms Operating in The United States

**AFRICA** $29.00
Egypt, Ivory Coast, Nigeria, South Africa

**ASIA** $89.00
China, Hong Kong, India, Indonesia, Japan, Malaysia, Pakistan, Philippines, Singapore, South Korea, Taiwan, Thailand

**Japan & Korea** $79.00

**China Group** $39.00
China, Hong Kong, Singapore, Taiwan

**NEAR & MIDDLE EAST** $39.00
Bahrain, Cyprus, Egypt, Iran, Israel, Jordan, Kuwait, Lebanon, Saudi Arabia, Turkey, United Arab Emirates

**AUSTRALIA GROUP** $29.00
Australia, New Zealand

**NORTH AMERICA** $49.00
Canada, Mexico

**LATIN AMERICA** $39.00
**South/Central America & Caribbean Islands**
Argentina, Bahamas, Bermuda, Bolivia, Brazil, Cayman Isl., Chile, Colombia, Costa Rica, Dominican Rep., El Salvador, Guatemala, Guyana, Mexico, Panama, Peru, Uruguay, Venezuela

**EUROPE** $139.00
Austria, Belgium, Czech Rep., Denmark, England, Finland, France, Germany, Greece, Hungary, Iceland, Ireland, Italy, Luxembourg, Monaco, Netherlands, Norway, Poland, Portugal, Romania, Russia, Scotland, Slovenia, Spain, Sweden, Switzerland

**British Isles** $59.00
England, Ireland, Scotland

**Europe - excluding the British Isles** $119.00
France $49.00
Germany $59.00
Italy $29.00
Netherlands $39.00
Scandinavia $59.00
Sweden $39.00
Switzerland $49.00

**EUROPE Eastern** $29.00
Czech Rep., Hungary, Poland, Russian, Slovenia